The Norton Anthology of English Literature

FOURTH EDITION

VOLUME 1

VOLUME 1

The Middle Ages • Donaldson

The Sixteenth Century • Smith

The Seventeenth Century • Adams

The Restoration and the Eighteenth Century • Monk / Lipking

VOLUME 2

The Romantic Period • Abrams

The Victorian Age • Ford

The Twentieth Century • Daiches

The Norton Anthology of English Literature

FOURTH EDITION

M. H. Abrams, *General Editor*

E. Talbot Donaldson

Hallett Smith

Robert M. Adams

Samuel Holt Monk

Lawrence Lipking

George H. Ford

David Daiches

VOLUME 1

W · W · NORTON & COMPANY · NEW YORK · LONDON

END PAPER MAP BY A. KARL/H. GEORGE

W. W. Norton & Company, Inc. 500 Fifth Avenue, New York, N.Y. 10110

BOOK DESIGN BY JOHN WOODLOCK

The page that follows constitutes an extention of the copyright page.

Library of Congress Cataloging in Publication Data
Abrams, Meyer Howard, ed.
The Norton anthology of English literature.
Bibliography: p.
Includes index.
1. English literature. I. Title.
PR1109.A2 1979 820'.8 78-27117

9 0

ISBN 0-393-95039-5 CL

ISBN 0-393-95048-4 PBK

Beowulf, A New Prose Translation by E. Talbot Donaldson. Reprinted with the permission of W. W. Norton & Company, Inc. and Longmans Green Ltd. Copyright © 1966 by W. W. Norton & Company, Inc.

From *The New English Bible*. © The Delegates of the Oxford University Press and The Syndics of the Cambridge University Press 1961, 1970. Reprinted by permission.

James Boswell: *From Boswell on the Grand Tour: Germany and Switzerland, 1764*, edited by Frederick A. Pottle. Copyright © 1928, 1953 by Yale University. Reprinted by permission of McGraw-Hill Book Company, Inc. and William Heinemann Ltd.

Geoffrey Chaucer: From *Chaucer's Poetry: An Anthology for the Modern Reader*, Selected and Edited by E. T. Donaldson. Copyright © 1958 by The Ronald Press Company, New York. Reprinted by permission of John Wiley Sons.

Thomas Gray: Manuscript of "Elegy Written in a Country Churchyard" transcribed by permission of The Provost and the Fellows of Eton College.

Samuel Johnson: Manuscript of *The Vanity of Human Wishes* transcribed by permission of the Hyde Collection, Somerville, New Jersey.

John Milton: Manuscripts of *Lycidas* transcribed by permission of The Master and Fellows of Trinity College, Cambridge.

Lady Mary Wortley Montagu: From *Essays and Poems by Lady Mary Wortley Montagu*, edited by Robert Halsband and Isobel Grundy; © Isobel Grundy 1977. Reprinted by permission of Oxford University Press.

Sir Thomas More: Selection reprinted from *Utopia*, by Sir Thomas More, A Norton Critical Edition, Translated and Edited by Robert M. Adams, with the permission of W. W. Norton & Company, Inc. Copyright © 1975 by W. W. Norton & Company, Inc.

Pearl, A New Verse Translation by Marie Borroff. Reprinted with the permission of W. W. Norton & Company, Inc. Copyright © 1977 by W. W. Norton & Company, Inc.

Samuel Pepys: From *The Diary of Samuel Pepys*, transcribed and edited by Robert Latham and William Matthews. Originally published by the University of California Press; reprinted by permission of The Regents of the University of California and Bell & Hyman, Ltd.

Alexander Pope: Manuscripts of *The Essay on Man* transcribed by permission of The Houghton Library and The Pierpont Morgan Library.

Sir Gawain and the Green Knight, A New Verse Translation by Marie Borroff. Reprinted by permission of W. W. Norton & Company, Inc. Copyright © 1967 by W. W. Norton & Company, Inc.

Sir Philip Sidney: From *The Poems of Sir Philip Sidney*, edited by William A. Ringler Jr.; © Oxford University Press 1962. Reprinted by permission of Oxford University Press.

Christopher Smart: "My Cat Jeoffry" from *Jubilate Agno*, reprinted by permission of Granada Publishing Ltd.

Thomas Traherne: From Thomas Traherne's *Centuries, Poems, and Thanksgivings*, edited by H. M. Margoliouth; © Oxford University Press 1958. Reprinted by permission of Oxford University Press.

Contents

Preface to the Fourth Edition

The intention of *The Norton Anthology of English Literature* from the beginning has been to maintain continuity, yet to allow for change. Its continuing aim is to provide, for the indispensable courses which introduce students to the greatness and variety of English literature, the major works in verse and prose from *Beowulf* to the present day, ordered chronologically, and presented in accurate and readable texts. A vital literary culture, however, is always on the move. The interests of readers change; new texts are discovered; old texts are better edited; new scholarly information and critical viewpoints become available; teachers and students want fresh materials that invite experimentation in the way literature is to be presented and studied. The policy, accordingly, has been to issue periodic revisions which, without violating the principle that only major writings be represented, are designed to keep the anthology in the mainstream of contemporary literary, cultural, and intellectual knowledge and concerns.

The strength of this collection is that its contents and editorial matter are grounded, not on theoretical views of what might be taught in an introduction to English literature, but on long experience in actually teaching such a course. The first edition in 1962 was the product of a decade of experimentation by several of its editors, and some of them (including the general editor) have proceeded to test each new edition by using it in the classroom. And ever since 1962 we have received a steady flow of voluntary suggestions from hundreds of users, students as well as teachers, who view the anthology with a loyal but critical eye. For this edition, we have also solicited detailed judgments about the utility of materials in the last version, together with recommendations for new materials, from almost one hundred critics—some of them experts in individual periods, but most of them instructors who use the book in a course. With each new edition, *The Norton Anthology* thus becomes more and more the product of a sustained collaboration between editors, teachers, and students.

The criteria for the choice, editing, and printing of texts remain what they were for the original edition: (1) that the selection make possible a study in depth of the major English writers in prose and verse, in the context of the chief literary modes and traditions of each age; (2) that the works selected be so far as feasible complete, and copious enough to allow instructors to select from the total those that they prefer to teach; (3) that the student be provided the most accurate texts available, edited so as to make them immediately accessible, and printed in a format that is easy to the hand and inviting to the eye; (4) that introductions and glosses be adequate to make an understanding of the texts independent of a reference library, so that the anthology may be read anywhere—in the student's room, in a coffee lounge, or under a tree; and (5) that the book, in size and weight, be comfortably portable, for if students won't carry the anthology to class, lectures are lamed and discussions rendered profitless.

Some earlier selections, which our canvass of teachers showed to have been assigned infrequently or not at all, have been dropped from this edition. Only three of these omissions are prominent ones. (1) In the third edition, we undertook to represent Victorian fiction by long excerpts from the novels of Dickens and from George Eliot's *Mill on the Floss*. This was, we believe, a worthwhile experiment; but in the almost unanimous judgment of teachers, the experiment failed, and the selections languished unassigned. (2) The "Topics," designed to exhibit the social and intellectual ambiance of each period, had begun to outlive their usefulness, and have in this edition been deleted. There are two exceptions. Since it is impossible to understand the greater part of Victorian literature outside the context of its dominant social, scientific, and religious concerns, the "Topics" of "Evolution" and "Industrialism" have been retained under the more accurate heading "Victorian Issues" and have been supplemented by a third issue, "The Woman Question." Also, the attested and varied usefulness of "Romantic Poems in Process" has been enhanced, by extending it to include authors from the 17th century to the present, and by including a section of pertinent "Poems in Process" in each of the two volumes. (3) In the preceding editions, the examples of 16th- and 17th-century prose were selected mainly to illustrate prominent subjects of discussion and debate, such as "The Dispute over Natural Law." In the present edition, we simply represent, chronologically, the best writers of each period, chosen also to represent the diversity of the prose styles current at that time.

The various deletions have provided the space for a number of additions to the anthology, and for completing items hitherto represented by excerpts. Almost all of the additions are in response to many requests; a few of them, as veteran users of the anthology will recognize, are selections which had been dropped from the first or second editions but are reintroduced by widespread demand. An overview here of the more important changes may help the teacher to appraise the teaching opportunities that this new edition provides.

Medieval selections now include the complete *Pearl* (in a new translation by Marie Borroff); a retranslation of *Piers Plowman,* with two passages on the Deadly Sins replacing "The Harrowing of Hell"; and new translations of three Old English poems. Among the added materials in the 16th century is the text of *Hero and Leander* as, according to the scholar, Louis L. Martz, it was originally written in a complete form, by Christopher Marlowe, with Chapman's unwarranted division into "Sestiads" deleted. The *Mutabilitie Cantos* of Spenser's *Faerie Queene* are now printed in their entirety, thereby providing a possible alternative to assigning the complete Book I, which is retained in this edition. The sections of More's *Utopia* are presented in Robert M. Adams's cogent new translation. There are new prose selections from Thomas Nashe's *Pierce Penniless* and from Hoby's influential translation of Castiglione's *The Courtier*. There are also additions to the lyrics by various poets and, in response to insistent demands, a number of changes in our representation of Shakespeare's sonnets. In a major innovation, Ben Jonson's *Volpone* has been added to the four Elizabethan and Jacobean plays in the previous edition, thereby creating a mini-anthology of the golden age of English dramatic literature. Other new items in the 17th century are Donne's complete *Anatomy of the World;* a number of songs from the plays of Beaumont and Fletcher; poems by Donne, Jonson, various Cavalier lyrists, Traherne, and Cowley; five poems by Herbert (attesting to the great current interest in that craftsman in verse); as well as a number of poems by Andrew Marvell (several on a single, related subject). The writings in prose now include Bacon's essay on *Masques and Triumphs,* and, to demonstrate the development of a prose adapted to practical and scientific exposition, selections from Sprat's *History of the Royal Society* and Isaac Newton's letter to the Society announcing his "New Theory about Light and Colors." The selections from *Paradise Lost* (already including four complete Books) have also been augmented so as to clarify the evolving relations between Adam and Eve, by Book V, lines 377–505 (before the Fall) and the concluding section of Book X (after the Fall).

In accord with many recommendations, Congreve's *The Way of The World* has been replaced by his more simply and coherently plotted *Love for Love*. Two poems by Lady Wortley Montagu, hitherto known mainly through footnotes to the writings of Alexander Pope, show her to have been a trenchant exponent of what women are, as against what male poets suppose them to be. There is an added poem by Jonathan Swift (*Stella's Birthday, 1721*), and Pope's *Essay on Criticism* is now printed in its entirety. Additional essays are included from the *Tatler* and the *Spectator*, while Dr. Johnson's writings have been supplemented by his *Brief to Free a Slave* and by materials from his great achievement, *A Dictionary of the English Language*—important sections of the Preface, as well as some of the more notable definitions. The selections from Thomson's *Seasons* and Cowper's *Task* have been improved. We have also added the "Peter Grimes" story from Crabbe's *The Borough*, as well as new odes by Thomson, Gray, and Collins.

To the Romantic section have been added two writers: Mary Wollstonecraft (the central sections from her pioneering treatise, *A Vindication of the Rights of Woman*, together with selections from her *Letters Written in Sweden*) and Mary Shelley (her remarkable Introduction to *Frankenstein* and a Gothic tale of the supernatural, *Transformation*). Two additional long works are Byron's complete *Manfred* and Shelley's urbane dialogue with Byron in his poem *Julian and Maddalo*. In response to numerous suggestions, we have added Burns's poem of homely realism, *To a Louse*, as well as several early Romantic poems written in the deliberately simple style—two more of Blake's *Songs of Innocence* and another of Wordsworth's lyrical ballads, *Simon Lee*, in the version of 1798. We have also included three short items by Blake on natural religion and deism, added a third letter, and replaced the excerpts from *Jerusalem* by a complete and more readily intelligible instance of Blake's prophetic mode, *America: A Prophecy*. Wordsworth's *Prelude* is still represented (though in newly edited texts) by its first and last versions of 1799 (complete) and 1850; but the latter has been supplemented by some 300 lines, so as to reveal the complex internal design of that poem. Two new poems by Wordsworth exemplify moments of vision: *The Two April Mornings* and *Nutting*. The selections from Coleridge include an added section of *Biographia Literaria* on "rustic" language, and two excerpts from *The Statesman's Manual* on "Symbol and Allegory" and the "Satanic Hero." Shelley's *Prometheus Unbound* has been supplemented by a passage on Prometheus's temptation by the Furies (Act I); Byron's *Childe Harold* has been expanded; and in his *Don Juan*, while Canto XVI (infrequently assigned) has been deleted, other Cantos have been supplemented: Canto II, for example, now includes Byron's description of cannibalism at sea. In the writings by Lamb, Hazlitt, and De Quincey, furthermore, some essays have been replaced by others which, on the testimony of instructors, will be of greater use and interest to students.

The most conspicuous addition in the Victorian period is a complete play, Oscar Wilde's *The Importance of Being Earnest*, but there are numerous other innovations. Among the prose writings, we now have selections from Carlyle's *French Revolution,* an added passage from Ruskin's *Modern Painters,* and Pater's *The Child in the House,* which serves as a revealing introduction to that writer's characteristic concerns and literary artistry. *St. Agnes' Eve* has been added to Tennyson's poems; in response to persistent demand, there are also five new passages from *Maud,* and six additional sections from *In Memoriam* (6, 8, 12, 29, 105, 113) which clarify the structure, and bring the total selections to more than two-thirds of the entire poem. Other poets whose works are more fully represented are Elizabeth Barrett Browning, George Meredith (six additional sonnets from *Modern Love*), Dante and Christina Rossetti, and William Morris. W. S. Gilbert has been added to the group now entitled "Light Verse." In a major reorganization, the section on "The Nineties" has been transferred from "The Twentieth Century" to the end of the Victorian section (where it belongs); it is strengthened not only by adding to the poems of Wilde and Dowson, but also by representing more fully the "hearty" writers of that decade—Rudyard Kipling and a new writer, William Ernest Henley.

The writers in "The Twentieth Century," like those in "The Victorian Age," have been reordered so as to make them more readily locatable. Conrad's long (and, to most students, too familiar) *Heart of Darkness* has been replaced by two short stories and a passage of critical comment on fiction; similarly, D.H. Lawrence's *The Fox* has been replaced by a new story, *The Princess,* a selection from the travel book *Mornings in Mexico,* and several often-demanded poems. As befits a major writer, the representation of Virginia Woolf has been signally increased; to *The Mark on the Wall* we add the title sketch from the one volume of short fiction she herself published, *Monday or Tuesday,* as well as *An Unwritten Novel* and several pieces of social and literary criticism, including an excerpt from *A Room of One's Own.* For the earlier selections from Yeats's autobiographic writings, we have substituted others which are more central to his life and work, and have replaced Joyce's short story, *Clay,* by his more lucid *Counterparts.* In line with a strong current interest, there is a substantial new section of "Poetry of World War I" which, in addition to poets in the previous edition (Brooke, Edward Thomas, Owen, Jones), now includes Siegfried Sassoon, Ivor Gurney, and Isaac Rosenberg. Other writers of verse and prose added in the present edition are Edith Sitwell, Katherine Mansfield, F. R. Leavis (a complete essay), Stevie Smith, and George Orwell. Shaw's *Major Barbara* has been replaced by the more teachable (and in its vigorous feminism, a very topical) play, *Mrs. Warren's Profession.* Samuel Beckett is now represented by a most characteristic short story, *The End;* and we have added to our long array of dramas Harold Pinter's very "modern" play,

The Dumb Waiter. The selections from Robert Graves and Hugh MacDiarmid have been altered. Finally, the passage of time and an emerging critical consensus have provided greater assurance in the choice of writers and writings for "Poetry after Mid-Century." The reconstituted section now includes two new poets, Molly Holden and Elaine Feinstein, as well as more recent selections by Donald Davie, Philip Larkin, Thom Gunn, Ted Hughes, Jon Silkin, Geoffrey Hill, and Seamus Heaney.

It should be noted that the number and variety of the works included in the anthology make possible not only a chronological approach to major writers, but also generic or topical ways of organizing a course, or parts of a course. English poetry, in all its species and magnitudes, is of course represented fully, and now supplemented by the diversely useful sections on "Poems in Process." The broad spectrum of plays, augmented by four new titles, constitutes an overview of English drama in its various modes, starting with *The Second Shepherds' Play and Everyman,* ranging through Marlowe, Shakespeare (a history play and a tragedy), Jonson, Webster, two masques (Jonson's *Pleasure Reconciled to Virtue* and Dryden's *Secular Masque*), a Restoration comedy of manners, two Romantic closet dramas (*Manfred,* complete, and *Prometheus Unbound*), Wilde's great farce, and Shaw's satiric social drama, and ending with a contemporary play by Harold Pinter. It is also possible to study the evolution of shorter forms of prose fiction, from *Pilgrim's Progress* through the narrative papers in the *Tatler* and *Spectator,* Defoe's *Mrs. Veal,* Swift's *Gulliver's Travels,* Johnson's *Rasselas,* and a great variety of short stories, including a Gothic tale by Mary Shelley and the diverse stories by Conrad, Forster, Woolf, Joyce, Mansfield, Beckett, and Lessing.

The third edition of the anthology undertook to redress the neglect of women in traditional literary study; the present edition has enlarged the representation of these authors, as well as of writings that deal with women in western culture. Literature centrally concerned with the social and sexual roles of women may be studied in a range from "the marriage group" in the *Canterbury Tales,* through many intervening works (e.g., *Paradise Lost, The Rape of the Lock, Rasselas*), to a number of poems and stories in our own age. Social and literary criticism specifically addressed to the situation of women is represented by selections from two classic works, Mary Wollstonecraft's *A Vindication of the Rights of Woman* and J. S. Mill's *The Subjection of Women;* by documents by George Eliot, Florence Nightingale, and other Victorians in the new section "The Woman Question," and by selections from Virginia Woolf. And the earlier list of women poets and writers of fiction has been enlarged by the inclusion of Lady Mary Wortley Montagu, Mary Shelley, Molly Holden, and Elaine Feinstein.

Many other topics can be profitably studied from materials in the present anthology, including such matters of current interest as (1) the imaginative response of writers to the changing aspects of war, from *Beowulf* and *The Battle of Maldon*, to the many poems in "Poetry of World War I"; (2) the visionary mode in literature, as exemplified by Spenser's *Mutabilitie Cantos*, several 17th-century visionary poets, Christopher Smart, William Blake, a number of Romantic and Victorian representations, in verse and prose, of visions and dreams, and the poems and autobiographic writings of Yeats; (3) the persistent but ever-altering form of spiritual autobiography, crisis, and the quest for identity, as represented in Bunyan's *Grace Abounding*, Wordsworth's *Prelude*, De Quincey's *Confessions*, Carlyle's *Sartor Resartus*, Mill's *Autobiography*, Pater's *Child in the House*, Tennyson's *In Memoriam*, Joyce's *Portrait of the Artist*, and Eliot's *Little Gidding*.

The organization of the contents in each period of English literature has been simplified by putting in chronological order the authors, whether they wrote in verse or prose, as well as the titles written by each author; there are a few exceptions to this principle, most of them instances when it has seemed helpful to group short, related items under such headings as "Sixteenth-Century Lyrics," Victorian "Light Verse," or "Poetry of World War I."

In accord with our policy to adopt improved texts as they become available, we now print Jonathan Wordsworth's revised versions of *The Prelude* of 1799 and 1850 (from *Wordsworth's Prelude, 1799, 1805, 1850*: A Norton Critical Edition, edited by Wordsworth, M. H. Abrams, and Stephen Gill, 1979); Jack Stillinger's new edition of Keats's *Poems* (Harvard University Press, 1978); the poems of Gerard Manley Hopkins as edited by W. H. Gardner and N. H. MacKenzie (Oxford University Press, 4th edition, 1970); and the stories from Joyce's *Dubliners* in the definitive edition by Robert Scholes (1968). To make texts as accessible as possible to student readers, we have normalized spelling and capitalization (and, very sparingly, punctuation) according to modern American usage. There are two kinds of exceptions to this procedure. (1) We have left unaltered texts in which modernization would change semantic, phonological, or metric qualities, or would affect distinctive features of the original publications. Thus the verse of Spenser, Burns, Hopkins, MacDiarmid, and David Jones, as well as the prose of Dorothy Wordsworth's *Journals* and of the writings of Carlyle, Joyce, and Shaw have been reproduced exactly. Only minor changes required for ready intelligibility (mainly in punctuation) have been made in the poems etched by William Blake. The works of Chaucer and other writers in Middle English that are not too difficult for the novice have also been left in the original language; each word, however, is consistently spelled in that variant of its scribal forms which is closest to modern English. (2) We have also left unaltered certain texts for which we use specially edited versions (identified in a headnote or footnote): Wollstonecraft's *Vindication* and *Letters from Sweden*, the two versions of Wordsworth's *Prelude*, all the verse and prose of Shelley and Keats, and the selections from Mary Shelley.

Each editor has reconsidered and rewritten (in some instances, radically) his introductory essays and headnotes and has revised his footnotes, both to take advantage of recent scholarship and in a continuing effort to make them as informative and clear as possible. In selected instances editorial headnotes or footnotes briefly indicate interpretations of a difficult work or passage. The reason for this procedure is a practical one. The anthology includes some of the most complex and difficult writings in the language, and the normal procedure is to assign some texts which there is not time to discuss adequately—or sometimes, to discuss at all—in the classroom. We therefore undertake to give an essential modicum of guidance to the student, but to present it in such a way as to open out possibilities for independent judgment and to provide, not definitive readings, but points of departure for dialogue in the classroom.

We continue other editorial procedures which have proved their usefulness in earlier editions. The historical and biographical introductions, although succinct, are informative enough to eliminate the need for supplementary books on the lives of authors and on the literary, social, and cultural history of England. In most introductions we identify at the beginning a few dates which are important for orienting the student. After each work we cite (when known) the date of composition on the left and the date of first publication on the right; in some instances the latter is followed by the date of a revised reprinting. Texts which include a large proportion of unfamiliar words are glossed in the margin, so that readers may assimilate the translation without interrupting the flow of their reading. In the limited instances when part of a work has been omitted, that fact is indicated by the word *From* before the title, and the place of the omission in the text is indicated by three asterisks.

The selected bibliographical guides at the end of each volume are designed to encourage students to read further on their own, and also to serve as points of departure in assigned essays. In this edition all the bibliographies have been brought up to date, and the authors and subgroups within each period have been put in alphabetic order. In both volumes a brief glossary of terms is provided under the title "Poetic Forms and Literary Terminology."

We have also added, in Volume 1, illustrations of two subjects in which graphic representations are of special value: a schematic drawing of the universe according to Ptolemy, and exterior and interior views of a London playhouse of Shakespeare's time (drawn especially for us by C. Walter Hodges, author of *The Globe Restored*).

To the hundreds of teachers throughout the United States and Canada who have helped us to design and improve these volumes, the editors express their deep gratitude; we cannot name every one of them here, but all will recognize the changes that they have suggested. A separate list of "Acknowledgments" names advisors who provided detailed critiques of the anthology as a whole or of particular periods, or were especially helpful in the preparation of texts and editorial matter. We wish to mention here the assistance of Jennifer Sutherland, Valerie Eads, John W. N. Francis, and of Diane O'Connor, Marjorie Flock, Nelda Freeman, Marian Johnson, Tam Putnam, Josepha Gutelius, Roy Tedoff, Hugh O'Neill, and James Mairs of Norton's production department; we also owe thanks to Norman McAfee; to Julie Aidelberg of Cornell University; to Susan Metzger of the Harvard University Press; to Barbara Zimmerman; and to Barbara and Paul Bodin. Our greatest debt is to George P. Brockway and John Benedict of W. W. Norton and Company, Inc., who have helped mitigate the chronic dilemmas in the continuing process of representing, justly, accurately, and in accord with changing interests and advancing knowledge, the immense scope of English literature within a single book.

M. H. Abrams

Acknowledgments

Among our many critics, advisors, and friends, the following were of especial help in providing critiques of particular periods or of the anthology as a whole, or assisted in preparing texts and editorial matter: Barry B. Adams (Cornell University); Paul Alpers (University of California, Berkeley); Judith H. Anderson (Indiana University); Colin B. Atkinson; Paula Backscheider (University of Rochester); Sheridan Baker (University of Michigan); Jerome Beaty (Emory University); Miriam J. Benkovitz (Skidmore College); Marie Borroff (Yale University); A. T. J. Cairns (University of Calgary); Jenni Calder (Edinburgh University); Angus Calder (The Open University); Tom J. Collins (University of Arizona); Rebecca Crump (Louisiana State University); Stuart Curran (University of Washington); Beth Darlington (Vassar College); Roman R. Dubinski (University of Waterloo); Dwight Eddins (University of Alabama); Scott Elledge (Cornell University); Hubert M. English, Jr. (University of Michigan); John P. Farrell (University of Texas at Austin); Barbara Charlesworth Gelpi (Stanford University); Marilyn Gaull (Temple University); Stephen Gill (Lincoln College, Oxford); Homer B. Goldberg (State University of New York at Stony Brook); Nancy M. Goslee (University of Tennessee); Donald J. Gray (Indiana University); David V. Harrington (Gustavus Adolphus College); Carolyn G. Heilbrun (Columbia University); Richard Helgerson (University of California, Santa Barbara); Robert D. Hume (Cornell University); J. Paul Hunter (Emory University); Joel Hurstfield (University of London); Robert Kiely (Harvard University); Ruth P. M. Lehmann (University of Texas at Austin); William T. Liston (Ball State University); James R. McAdams (Pennsylvania State University); N. H. MacKenzie (Queen's University); Hugh Maclean (State University of New York at Albany); Leslie H. Martin (University of Notre Dame); Dorothy Mermin (Cornell University); Helene Moglen (State University of New York College at Purchase); David Novarr (Cornell University); Robert O'Clair (Manhattanville College); William Park (Sarah Lawrence College); Reeve Parker (Cornell University); Carol H. Poston (University of Illinois at Chicago Circle); Jon A. Quitslund (George Washington University; Donald H. Reiman (The Carl H. Pforzheimer Library); M. L. Rosenthal (New York University); H. Grant Sampson (Queen's University); Ronald A. Sharp (Kenyon College); David Shore (University of Ottawa); Sally K. Slocum (University of Akron); Jon Stallworthy (Cornell University); Jack Stillinger (University of Illinois at Urbana-Champaign); E. E. Stokes, Jr. (Texas A&M University); Roger G. Swearingen (University of North Carolina at Chapel Hill); Nina L. Thiess (Santa Monica College); Charles H. Vivian (Bentley College); Jonathan Wordsworth (Exeter College, Oxford).

The Norton Anthology of English Literature

FOURTH EDITION

VOLUME 1

The Middle Ages

(to 1485)

ca. 450:	Anglo-Saxon Conquest.
597:	St. Augustine arrives in Kent; beginning of Anglo-Saxon conversion to Christianity.
871–899:	Reign of King Alfred.
1066:	Norman Conquest.
ca. 1200:	Beginnings of Middle English literature.
1360–1400:	The summit of Middle English literature: Geoffrey Chaucer; *Piers Plowman; Sir Gawain and the Green Knight.*
1485:	William Caxton's printing of Sir Thomas Malory's *Morte Darthur*, one of the first books printed in England.

The medieval period in English literature extends for more than 800 years, from Cædmon's *Hymn* at the end of the 7th century to *Everyman* at the end of the 15th. Historians used to divide this period into two parts, calling the earlier centuries the Dark Ages in order to distinguish their quality from that of the later centuries, when European culture attained one of the summits of its history. Though this distinction is misleading—for the Dark Ages were only relatively dark—it is nevertheless true that the English Middle Ages embraced two quite different periods of literary history, the Old English (or Anglo-Saxon) and the Middle English, sharply divided from each other by the Norman duke William's conquest of the island in 1066. Both English culture and the English language changed radically in the years following this event, and English literature was given a new spirit.

Because it is impossible to read the Old English language without a great deal of study, Old English texts printed in this book are given in translation. Middle English texts such as Chaucer's, written in a dialect which is the ancestor of Modern Standard English, appear in the original, but have been spelled in a way that it is hoped will aid the reader. Middle English texts written in the more difficult regional dialects are given in translation. Analyses of the sounds and grammar of Middle English, and of Old and Middle English prosody, appear at the end of this introduction.

THE ANGLO-SAXONS AND THE HEROIC IDEAL

The Anglo-Saxon invasion of the island of Britain which began in the first half of the 5th century was a phase of a great folk migration that had started some centuries earlier and was to continue for several more—the movement of the Germanic tribes from the northeast of Europe into the areas of the Roman Empire to the west, south, and southeast. The so-called Anglo-Saxon invaders of Britain actually consisted of three tribes, the Angles, the Saxons, and the Jutes. Although each was independent, through their common Germanic heritage these tribes were closely allied with one another and with the many other tribes that already had or would in the future overrun much of the old Roman Empire. They shared the same prehistoric ancestors: even in historical times their individual tongues amounted to little other than variant dialects of a common language, while the customs of one tribe differed little from those of another.

In its earliest period Germanic society had been organized by families: the head of the family was the chief of his close kinsmen, and the family formed an independent political entity. With the passing of time, the unit of society tended to grow larger as a number of families united under a single superior chieftain or "king," to use the word derived from the Old Germanic name for chief. But the unit grew to be very large only rarely, when some particularly successful king attracted others to him in order to perform some specific exploit; and such larger unions rarely endured long after the completion of the venture for which they had been formed. The normal order of society was made up of a number of small bands, which, while they did not always live at peace with one another, still shared a sense of community and kinship, especially in the face of a common enemy such as the people whose lands they were invading; but when they had conquered, their natural political divisiveness reasserted itself. Thus long after the Anglo-Saxons had become settled in Britain, the island was still broken up into a bewildering number of kingdoms, some of them very short-lived, and a coherent union of all Englishmen was not achieved until after the Norman conquest.

The same general organization of many kings coexisting within a common culture had been characteristic of that other migratory people, the Greeks (or, more accurately, Achaeans), who centuries earlier had overrun the region of the eastern Mediterranean. And both to the Achaeans and to the Germanic peoples the ideal of kingly behavior was enormously important—indeed, it was perhaps the chief spiritual force behind the civilizations they both developed, the creative power that, in their earliest periods, shaped their history and their literature. It is generally called the heroic ideal; and put most simply, the heroic ideal was excellence. The hero-king strove to do better than anyone else the things that an essentially migratory life demanded: to sail a ship through a storm, to swim a river or a bay, to tame a horse, to choose a campsite and set firm defenses, in times of peace even to plow a field or build a hall, but always and above all, to fight. Skill and courage were the primary qualities of a king who should successfully lead his people in battle and sustain them during peace.

In its oldest form, the ideal was appropriate only to kings, but because society was so closely knit, all the more important male members of the tribe tended to imitate it. (Germanic society was wholly dominated by males: women are rarely mentioned in the surviving records of it, and only if they are the wives or daughters of kings.) In general, of course, the heroic ideal of conduct was aristocratic, restricted to the king and his immediate retainers, though without that quality of unreality and remoteness from daily life that we associate with later medieval aristocracy. The king was the active leader of a small number of fellow warriors who, as members of his household, beheld all that he did. A successful king won from his retainers complete loyalty. It was their duty to defend him in battle, to give up their own lives while defending or avenging his. In return the king gave his retainers gifts from the spoil that had been accumulated in warfare. Royal generosity was one of the most important aspects of heroic behavior, for it symbolized the excellence of the king's rule, implying on the one hand that the retainers deserved what they were given because of their loyalty to him, and, on the other, showing that he himself was worthy of such loyalty. The heroic ideal had a very practical bearing on the life of the people whom the king ruled.

While the heroic ideal would win practical success for a king, it had also another, perhaps more important end—enduring fame. In cultures whose religion, unlike Christianity, offers no promise of an afterlife, a name that will live on after one's death serves as the closest substitute for immortality. From this arises the heroic paradox, still latent in our own civilization, that by dying gloriously one may achieve immortality. The poet who could sing the story of his heroic life was, of course, the agent upon whom the hero depended for his fame, and a good poet—or bard, to use the customary term for the poet of heroic life—was a valued member of a primitive court. Alexander is said to have expressed envy of Achilles because he had had a Homer to celebrate his deeds. The poetic form which primitive bards evolved for their heroic narratives is called "epic"; it is characterized by a solemn dignity of tone and elevation of style. Their poems were not written down, but recited aloud from memory, and hence most of them have been lost: in Greek there have survived Homer's two epics, the *Iliad* and the *Odyssey*, while from Germanic culture the chief survivor is the Old English *Beowulf*. But enough has been preserved to show the enduring popularity of heroic stories throughout the migratory phase of the two peoples, who never tired of hearing the deeds of their folk heroes. Thus the immortality that the old heroes had sought was achieved through poetry, and poetry in turn gave inspiration to later men in leading their own lives.

CHRISTIANITY AND OLD ENGLISH CULTURE

Whatever literary materials the Anglo-Saxons brought with them when they came to Britain existed only in their memories, for the making of written records was something they learned only when they were converted to Christianity. The Celtic inhabitants whose land they were seizing were Christians, as had been the Romans whose forces had occupied the island since the 1st century and whose withdrawal at the beginning of the 5th had opened the way to the Anglo-Saxons; but for 150 years after the beginning of the invasion Christianity was maintained only in the remoter regions where the Anglo-Saxons failed to penetrate. In the year 597, however, St. Augustine was sent by Pope Gregory as a missionary to King Ethelbert of Kent, one of the most southerly of the kingdoms into which England was divided, and about the same time missionaries from Ireland began to preach

Christianity in the north. Within 75 years the island was once more predominantly Christian. Ethelbert himself was one of the first Englishmen to be converted, and it is indicative of the relationship between Christianity and writing that the first written specimen of the Old English (Anglo-Saxon) language is a code of laws promulgated by the first English Christian king.

In the centuries that followed up till the Norman Conquest England produced a large number of distinguished, highly literate churchmen. One of the earliest of these was Bede, whose *Ecclesiastical History of the English People*, written in Latin, was completed in 731; this remains our most important source of knowledge about the Anglo-Saxon period. In the next generation Alcuin, a man of wide culture, became the friend and advisor of the Frankish Emperor Charlemagne, whom he assisted in making the Frankish court a great center of learning: thus by the year 800 English culture had developed so richly that it overflowed its insular boundaries. But the greatest impetus on English culture came from a man who was not of the clergy: Alfred, king of the West Saxons from 871 to 899, who for a time united all the kingdoms of southern England and beat off those new Germanic invaders, the Vikings. This most active king was an enthusiastic patron of literature. He himself translated various works from Latin, the most important of which was Boethius' *Consolation of Philosophy*, the early 6th-century Roman work whose heroic stoicism has proved continuingly congenial to the English temperament. Apparently under Alfred's direction Bede's *History* was also translated into Old English, and the *Anglo-Saxon Chronicle* was begun: this year-by-year record of important events in England was maintained until the middle of the 12th century. Furthermore, the preservation of many of the surviving earlier English works, including *Beowulf*, is due to the fact that copies of them were made in the West Saxon dialect because, in large part, of the impetus Alfred gave to literary studies. Though the political stability that Alfred achieved was not long-lived, the culture he nourished so lovingly was maintained at a high level until the very end of the Old English period.

OLD ENGLISH POETRY

The genius for heroic poetry the Anglo-Saxons brought with them when they came to Britain, as they probably also brought with them the alliterative form (see the section on "Old and Middle English Prosody") in which all the Old English poetry that has survived was composed. Since they wrote nothing down until they had become Christianized, and since in many respects Christian ideals and heroic ideals are antipathetic, it is natural that very little poetry has survived that is surely pre-Christian in composition. But much of *Beowulf*, the greatest of Germanic epics, is evidently pre-Christian, even though the author of the particular form of the poem that has come down to us was a Christian who refers to events of the Old (but not of the New) Testament. Several other short pieces or fragments also seem to reflect the pagan period without Christian coloring. Yet the vast bulk of Old English poetry is specifically Christian, devoted to religious subjects. Interestingly enough, however, it is almost all in the heroic mode: while the Anglo-Saxons adapted themselves readily to the ideals of Christianity, they did not do so without adapting Christianity to their own heroic ideal. In order to make the alien world of the Bible intelligible to their hearers, Old English poets (almost all of whom are nameless) infused it with many of the values that they had inherited from their own history. Thus Moses and St. Andrew, Christ and God the Father share the attributes of a *Beowulf*, are represented as heroes who performed famous deeds. In the *Dream of the Rood*, the Cross speaks of Christ as "the young hero, . . . strong and stouthearted," whose crucifixion is less a passion than an heroic action. In *Cædmon's Hymn* the creation of heaven and earth is seen as a mighty deed, an "establishment of wonders" not altogether unlike Hrothgar's building of the hall Heorot in *Beowulf*. The sad consciousness of the transience of all earthly good combined with the compulsion to go on striving—so characteristic of the heroic spirit—appears most poignantly in two Christian laments, the *Wanderer* and the *Seafarer*. That the heroic ideal held its value down to the end of the Old English period is shown by the *Battle of Maldon*, in which the defeat of English defenders by a band of marauding Vikings is described in the highest tradition of Germanic heroism. Against doom, there is only courage.

The world of Old English poetry is a dark one, and to a modern reader it may also seem a narrow one with narrow laws that exclude all but sardonic laughter. Men in the mead-hall are said to be cheerful, but even there they think of struggle in war, of possible triumph but more possible failure. Romantic love—one of the principal topics of later literature—appears hardly at all. Men seem seldom to relax: clothed in their armor, they are always preparing to test their courage against fate. (They are, indeed, so habitually seen as warriors that in the earlier poetry the words for "man" and "warrior" are often interchangeable.) Depressing as this world may seem, it is recreated in Old English poetry with extraordinary intensity, with high spiritual excitement. This excitement is achieved in part by the frequent use of ironic understatement. Actions and things are spoken of as less than they really are because, apparently, the speaker wishes to suggest that they are more—or perhaps other—than they are. "They cared not for battle," says the author of the *Battle of Maldon* about those cowardly Englishmen who fled the fight. Even the "kenning," that highly formalized compound metaphor common to Old Germanic poetry, often seems to suggest potentials ironically—"whale's road" or "swan's path" for a sea so perilous for men lacking the physical equipment of whales and swans. The dignity the Anglo-Saxons assigned to poetry—which was the repository of the ancient traditions by which they lived—apparently prevented the humor latent in ironic understatement from reaching any expression more overt than a grim smile. Yet despite its somberness, Old English poetry goes about its business of depicting harsh reality with an extraordinary subtlety and intensity.

THE NORMAN CONQUEST AND ITS EFFECTS

In the year 1066 England was once more invaded and conquered by a Germanic people, though one whose culture was widely different from the Anglo-Saxons. The Normans—the name is actually a form of "Norsemen" —were the descendants of Scandinavian adventurers who at the beginning of the 10th century had seized a wide part of northern France. A highly adaptable nation, they had adopted the language of the land they had settled in and had set up a powerful state; while its ruler was technically a duke subject to the king of France, Normandy was actually an independent political entity. The invasion of England was led by the energetic Duke William. The English were divided and irresolute; at the decisive Battle of Hastings they were defeated by the Normans and their leader Harold was killed. Thereafter William's forces overran much of England, and the Norman duke became its king and insured the succession to his descendants. But, kings of England though they were, he and his followers were not as much interested in the country he had won (though they were constantly fighting the Welsh, the Scots, and their own barons for control of parts or the whole of it) as they were in their continental possessions. The first seven English kings were mostly absentee rulers—and their presence within the kingdom was seldom less troublesome for it than their absence from it. It was not, indeed, until the 13th century, with the reign of Henry III (1216–72) that England became the principal concern of its kings. And it was not until the very end of the Middle Ages that English monarchs finally gave up trying to make good their continental claims and became, perforce, purely English.

The immediate effect of the Norman Conquest upon English literature was to remove it from the care of the aristocracy—the spiritual if not actual descendants of the Anglo-Saxon kings and their retainers—and to deprive it of that cohesive spirit that it had previously possessed. The great aristocratic households, which were the centers of pre-Conquest cultural activity, were broken up or parceled out to the Conqueror's Norman barons, and the English aristocracy was either displaced or forced into service with the invaders. For a considerable time, even the English language seems to have fallen into disuse as a vehicle for written literature, for very little survives of English between the Conquest and the year 1200. Initially, men of education who continued to produce literary works wrote either in Latin or in Anglo-Norman, the dialect of French that was spoken by the new rulers of England. But since the practical Normans were less preoccupied with culture than the English, the literature in Anglo-Norman was not very distinguished and was not very long-enduring, hardly surviving the reign of Edward I (1272–1307). Latin, which had always been and continued to be the language of the international church, produced a fairly rich literature in England during this period—especially in the 12th century. But throughout the Middle Ages, Latin literature remained essentially conservative and remote, not much dealing with the subjects that are of importance in the development of vernacular literature. Thus for more than a century the twin snobberies—social on the part of Anglo-Norman, intellectual on the part of Latin—probably pre-empted the energies of educated men who might at an earlier or a later time have written in English.

But even if the educated were writing literature in other languages, the uneducated were undoubtedly continuing to compose—if not to write—in English. When written English literature begins to reappear at the end of the 12th century, the larger part of it carries the stamp of popular or at least semi-popular origin; indeed, considered in its bulk, Middle English literature is a popular literature. Its origin in the orders of society below the top provides its most striking contrast with Old English literature: most of the latter seems to be uttered by a single aristocratic voice, grave, decorous, responsible, speaking in terms of high communal aspirations. Middle English literature, on the other hand, is uttered by a medley of different voices, dealing with a wide range of topics in a great diversity of styles and tones and genres. Originality of thought, to be sure, is a rare feature of this literature, for no matter how diverse the voices may be, they often seem to be saying precisely the same things as each other. Yet Middle English literature has virtues not found in Old English. Because its writers addressed themselves to a popular audience, they achieved a greater immediacy, a greater recognizability; a modern reader experiences little difficulty in understanding the world they are talking about. The change is perhaps most obvious in the narrative of adventure, where the idealized hero of Old English yields place to the more sympathetic if less admirable man who not only fights and fights again, but also laughs and cries, plays games, and, above all, falls in and out of love—the non-aristocratic man was the readier to supplant the epic hero because a mature Christianity places as much value on a plain man's soul as it does on an epic hero's. In dealing with this new kind of hero the writer's imaginative perspective was broadened as much, perhaps, as his ability to see deeply was decreased. And the perspective now included women, who became, finally, recognized as half of the human race. True, they appear ordinarily as stereotypes, whether in romance and love lyric or in anti-feminist satire—that enormous body of literature that had its foundation in the monastic culture that dominated so much of European thought in the Middle Ages. But woman's place in society was, in any case, recognized in literature, and this recognition undoubtedly reflects a changing attitude in history itself. There are no arch-feminists in literature before Chaucer's Wife of Bath, but she could never have been invented, even by a Chaucer, unless she had had recognizable forebears, with independent minds and incomes, in Bath and elsewhere before Chaucer's time.

While the portrayal of life in Middle English literature is often shallow, it is nevertheless a life in which we find much that evokes our sympathy. Sometimes, when it is portrayed as lively and gay, colorful, full of surprise, its attractiveness earns our active appreciation, and even when some austere moralist reduces human experience to mere wretchedness we may experience amid the overlying gloom the sudden charm of poignancy. Lack of profound vision does not prevent an accurate presentation of the details of life from being pleasing and sometimes moving. And humor—the chief virtue of Middle English literature—is apt to flash anywhere, even in the most solemn and foreboding of moralizations.

The lack of originality in Middle English literature is partly due to the attempt by many writers, both religious and secular, to make their works reflect the unchanging principles of medieval Christian doctrine. Until almost the end of the 14th century Christian teaching was primarily concerned with the issue of personal salvation, putting more emphasis on the moral and spiritual responsibilities of the individual than it did on his ethical or social responsibilites. Medieval religious idealism characteristically looked to the world to come for the only answer to men's troubles and considered the reformation of this world neither possible nor especially desirable. So constant is the attitude that life in this world is only a waiting period before we enter something better (or worse) that the modern reader is apt to get the impression that the Middle Ages was a period of intellectual and social stasis, a period in which time was standing still. And the fact is that not only in specifically moral and doctrinal literature, whose premises are timeless, but also in ephemeral literature designed merely to provide entertainment one senses this unchangingness: a romance written at the beginning of the 13th century differs little from one written in the 15th (with which it shares its plot), and at the very end of the period Malory is still peopling with his knights a never-never land of chivalry that had its origin in 12th-century France.

It is clear enough that between 1066 and 1485 England underwent large political and social changes—in the developments in feudalism, the gradual evolution of Parliament, the growth of cities and of the middle class along with the increase in foreign trade, and in many other similar phenomena. But apparently the changes occurred too slowly to produce much intellectual awareness of them on the part of writers. The great exception—to this and to all other generalizations—is Chaucer, whose pages are informed, especially in his handling of the bourgeois, by an excited sense of the novelty of social life in his own times. Langland's *Piers Plowman* also possesses something of this quality—though without Chaucer's tone of approval. But in an age where most people were born in the same village where their grandparents had been born and lived virtually the same lives, doing the same work with the same tools, enjoying the same sports and the same festivals, large slow-moving change is probably bound to be imperceptible to all but the most acute observers—imperceptible and, if perceived, disapproved.

But if in a broad historical sense change was imperceptible, in the daily lives of medieval men it was all too visible. Indeed, the inevitability of change—for the worse, even in the lives of people already apparently wholly wretched—is one of the most insistently repetitive themes of Middle English literature. Nor is this theme to be thought of merely as another expression of the world-hating doctrine. Rather, the theme and the world-hating doctrine itself are both results of the violence of life in the Middle Ages, a violence not matched again in western history until our own times. Famine, war, pestilence, and death—these are the riders who passed through the streets of medieval cities and villages by night and by day. The fact that eight of the eighteen kings who ruled England between 1066 and 1485 died deaths of violence or deaths resulting from violent activity is characteristic of the times. Men hardly less august were also constantly meeting death in battles, or by murder, or by accident, or, not infrequently, on the scaffold before a fascinated populace. The chroniclers who record these events say little of the lower orders of society, but constant warfare against enemies at home and abroad, the depredations of the powerful in supplying themselves from the fruits of the toil of the poor, the fearful severity of the laws combined with the failure to enforce them against the strong, and, especially after the middle of the 14th century, recurrent pestilence compounded by famine—all these explain why change for the worse seems to have been the unchanging expectation of medieval people. And, even in the temporary absence of these events, the coldness and darkness of an English winter for people living in badly insulated dwellings with only minimal heat and light might well seem to make life a bleak perpetual twilight.

In view of the violence prevalent during most of the period, it is perhaps extraordinary that so much literature was produced. But even in the worst of times things are not always and everywhere at their worst; spring does come, and some people get through life almost untouched by disasters that seem historically to be omnipresent. And the fact is that, except in its most ruthlessly world-hating forms, Middle English literature is often permeated by a curious normality, and is, indeed, less preoccupied with its age's violence than we are with ours, probably because people then never conceived of a time when violence was not a fact of life. Despite being constantly warned to expect change for the worse, people in the Middle Ages seem, in their daily lives, to have pursued the same pleasures that we pursue today —pursued them with rather more relish because they were rarer: this is clear from the accounts both of those who approved of the pursuit and of those who did not. As the general atmosphere of violence suggests, medieval society was in some ways more primitive than our own—or more frankly primitive—and may thus seem to us more childlike. People took tremendous pleasure in color, in dress, in ritual, in parades, in spectacles, in elaborate food and drink (when they could get them), in all those aspects of life that children especially love, and most adults do not scorn. Like children, medieval people were subject to emotional extremes—they wept more quickly than we do, went more quickly from weeping to laughter and back again, were headstrong and hasty, quick to sin zestily and to repent heartily and then to sin and repent again. Yet is is a mistake to overemphasize this childishness: their life was physically more limited than ours, without our comforts, our mobility, our communications; it was even more precarious, more uncertain; but as it is reflected in the best writers, they lived their life very richly and perhaps with greater awareness and greater savor than we do ours.

MIDDLE ENGLISH LITERATURE

It has been said earlier that from the century and a half after the Conquest very little English literature has survived, and it is probable that in that period very little was written. But that literature was still being composed, if not written down, during the period is suggested by the first considerable Middle English poem to have come down to us: this is Layamon's *Brut,* written about 1205 in an alliterative prosody that is clearly directly descended from the Old English poetic measure, though the subleties of the older measure have disappeared. Apparently, at least for oral purposes, alliterative poetry never ceased to be composed, as is further suggested by its reappearance later in written form in the so-called "alliterative revival" of the 14th century, which culminated in *Piers Plowman* and *Sir Gawain and the Green Knight*. Layamon's *Brut* is also interesting because it contains the first treatment in English of the Arthurian legend, the story that was to catch the imagination of so many English writers of later times. Layamon's source was a Norman work by the poet Wace, which was in turn based on the Englishman Geoffrey of Monmouth's Latin *History of the Kings of Britain*. According to the old tradition, England had been founded by one Brutus who was a descendant of the Trojan Aeneas, the founder of Rome, and after whom *Brit*ain was named (hence the title *Brut*). Of Brutus' descendants the most distinguished was Arthur, who according to the legend freed Britain from the Roman yoke and successfully defended it from the Anglo-Saxon invaders. It is a double curiosity about the Arthurian legend that not only did the British (Celtic) Arthur become in later centuries the great legendary hero of Englishmen—whose ancestors he was presumably successful in beating off the island—but also that the Arthurian legend itself reached its fullest development in France, whither it may have been brought by Celts crossing the channel to Brittany—some of them perhaps fleeing from the Anglo-Saxons. In any case, after Geoffrey and Layamon, England produced no original writers on Arthur—as opposed to translators from the French—until the poet of *Gawain* (whom some critics suspect of translating) and Malory—also a translator, but on so grand a scale as to rank as truly original.

Both Layamon and the poet of *Beowulf* dealt with legendary materials which they thought of as history. Layamon's treatment, however, is different from (and far less impressive than) the epic mode of *Beowulf*: it moves toward the genre, so characteristic of the later Middle Ages, known as "romance." The romance has certain typical features: it generally concerns knights and involves a large amount of fighting as well as a number of miscellaneous adventures; it makes liberal use of the improbable, often of the supernatural; it is often—though not always—involved with romantic love; characterization is standardized, so that heroes, heroines, and wicked stewards could easily move from one romance to another without causing any disturbance in the narrative; the plots generally consist of a great number of events, and the same event is apt to occur several times within the same romance; and the style is apt to be easy and colloquial—not infrequently loose and repetitious.

Although it was enormously popular in medieval England—it makes up a large fraction of the total of preserved Middle English literature—Middle English romance is apt to disappoint the modern reader. Unfortunately, very few accomplished poets—the *Gawain*-poet and Chaucer are two of the principal exceptions—turned their hand to romance; it was apparently left largely to minstrels and other uncultivated versifiers addressing a semi-literate audience, often in dog-trot verse full of windy clichés. The great age of medieval romance had been the 12th and early 13th centuries, and its chief breeding ground had been aristocratic society in France, where such poets as Chrétien de Troyes spun their marvelously sophisticated tales. The Middle English purveyors of romance, functioning before non-aristocratic audiences in the second half of the 13th and in the 14th century, introduced the French romances into English (the majority of the surviving English romances are either proved or suspected adaptations from the French). The result of the lag in time and change in audience is artistically unfortunate, though often unintentionally amusing. Aristocratic ideals of behavior of a different era and an alien society were replaced by patterns of behavior that could be easily comprehended by bourgeois and lower-class Englishmen. Heroes who have all the accouterments of the most chivalrous of knights are apt to behave in the crudest fashion, whether they are fighting, eating, or making love: they act as a petty bourgeois might if suddenly given an opportunity to enjoy the high scale of living of chivalric aristocracy with no education in how such a life should be conducted. Nevertheless, it is often agreeable to watch the blunt Englishman who replaced the aristocratic hero react with practical common sense to the extravagant situations in which the poem has placed him. And there is one very charming exception to the rule that translation brings deterioration: *Sir Orfeo*, apparently based on a lost French poem recasting the classical legend of Orpheus and Eurydice, transmits much of that delicacy and magic which the reader who first approaches medieval romance expects to find in it.

By far the larger proportion of surviving Middle English literature is religious, though it is not necessarily true that an equal proportion of the literature actually composed in Middle English was religious. The church had a virtual monopoly on literacy during much of the Middle Ages, for the average person who had learned to read and write probably had done so because he had signified his intention (not always fulfilled) of becoming a cleric—that is, an ecclesiast, performing one of the many functions of the church: otherwise, he would probably not have received any but the most elementary kind of education. Furthermore, the church not only had this direct claim upon the services of the majority of literate men but also was itself a large producer of books in the physical sense (books were actually handwritten manuscripts) as well as a maintainer (especially in monasteries) of libraries. Therefore it is quite natural that religious literature should bulk large. But the literature that has been lost probably contained a very large number of secular items. Professional storytellers such as minstrels committed to memory tales that they had heard others recite or had composed themselves and did not trouble to write down—if, indeed, they could write. Their stories depended for survival on some literate hearer who thought them worth recording—and perhaps few clerics would take the trouble. And even secular literature that had been recorded might sometimes be lost because of the low esteem in which it was held by austere churchmen who would enforce St. Paul's precept that everything that is written ought to express specific Christian doctrine: when library shelves became crowded, it was probably the secular works that were removed to make room for books more beneficial to the spirit.

Unfortunately, good doctrine is not necessarily good literature, and the larger part of Middle English religious writing is literature at all only in the broadest sense of that word: sermons, homilies, saints' lives, penitential tracts, manuals for priests, mystical writings, lyric poems, moral allegories, stories of miracles—all the possible genres of religious writing are represented profusely, though not, in quality, richly. An occasional individual work distinguishes itself strikingly from the surrounding drabness—for instance, the very early *Ancrene Riwle*, or "Rule for Anchoresses" (female religious recluses), or a late lyric like *I Sing of a Maiden*. But the brilliant exceptions are few and far between: few minds were able to sustain originality amid the oppressive conventionality of doctrine and response to doctrine. And few educated people before the time of Chaucer seem to have had the temerity to venture into the secular. We are fortunate that the work of one such person, the author of the early *Owl and the Nightingale*, has survived, for this humorous debate between birds is the most original and Chaucer-like poem before Chaucer himself.

During the last quarter of the 14th century Middle English literature flowered suddenly and inexplicably in three great poets, writing at almost the same time and giving supreme artistic expression to almost all the characteristic genres of Middle English. The author of *Sir Gawain and the Green Knight* not only produced the best romance of the entire period, but also wrote some of its best religious poetry; his Biblical narrative in alliterative verse, *Patience*, the story of Jonah, is rivaled only by certain Old English poems. In the *Pearl* he combined elegy with theology to produce the most moving religious poem—and the most finely wrought poem—of the

English later Middle Ages. William Langland's achievement in *Piers Plowman* is important both in literature and in history, since he faced squarely the great religious and social issues of his day—and these became the great issues of the following century and a half: imitations of *Piers Plowman* which borrow both Piers himself and Langland's anti-ecclesiastical satire played an important part in bringing on the reformation of the church which Langland prophesied but would have deplored. Needless to say, no imitator approaches Langland in the extraordinary originality of his weaving together of all sorts of genres of religious literature, from the most menacing sermon to the most dazzling lyric. Geoffrey Chaucer's achievement was greatest of all. The new perspective which English literature after the Conquest had attained had revealed broader horizons, but they were too broad and too clouded with distractions to enable the average writer to bring everything into clear focus. It takes a powerfully disciplined mind to comprehend infinite variety in a single artistic vision. Such a mind was Chaucer's. While he was entirely rooted in the soil of the Middle Ages and tried his hand at a large number of medieval genres, his art is so fully realized as to carry him out of the Middle Ages and make him one of the two or three greatest poets in English.

This sudden florescence in the *Gawain*-poet, Langland, and Chaucer may have been partly due to patronage of literature by the well-to-do. Chaucer was a "court" poet who seems to have been encouraged not only by John of Gaunt but perhaps also by Gaunt's father, Edward III (died 1377), as well as by his nephew Richard II (deposed 1399), and, in the last year of the poet's life, by Gaunt's son, Henry IV. The *Gawain*-poet probably wrote for a provincial aristocratic court, remote from London but no less interested in literary art. Even William Langland seems to have enjoyed patronage, but from what source it is hard to be sure; it is probable that at one time or another he was sheltered by monasteries, and it is not unlikely that he ended his life in one. In any case English literature is fortunate that these three great contemporary poets all found encouragement from one source or another.

But patronage does not assure great poetry. Chaucer's friend, the poet John Gower, also enjoyed royal patronage, but he has not proved much of a threat to Chaucer's reputation. He seems a far more typically medieval writer than Chaucer: he wrote three works which, linguistically at least, summarized the English Middle Ages: one in Latin, one in Norman French, and one, *Confessio Amantis* ("The Lover's Confession"), in English. Were it not for its proximity to Chaucer, this last would probably be rated somewhat higher than it has been, for it is a work of considerable skill and interest. And it is certainly infinitely superior to anything produced by the English poets of the next century, some of whom enjoyed patronage but all of whom seem, after Chaucer, to represent regression into the worst vices of medieval literature. The most Chaucerian of Chaucer's followers are, indeed, Scotsmen, and the best of them, Robert Henryson and William Dunbar, who often reflect Chaucer's satirical spirit and his liveliness, belong not to the medieval period but to the Renaissance.

Yet if the 15th century in England lacks great names (Thomas Malory alone enjoys a high reputation as a literary artist), it is nevertheless a period in which popular literature flourished. Some of the best lyrics, religious and secular, date from this time; and this was also the century in which many of the ballads were composed. It was also the period of much activity in drama. The mystery plays, which had probably become established in the previous century, continued to be performed widely, and the cycles of these religious dramas that have been preserved from York, Chester, and Wakefield date from the 15th century. The same century saw the development of the morality play, culminating in *Everyman*. The authors of the plays, ballads, and lyrics of the century are nameless; aside from the plays, manuscripts of which were kept only by the towns in which the performances were given, these anonymous works were probably transmitted orally and only haphazardly written down. Fortunately for the future history of English literature, Malory's *Morte Darthur,* written during its author's long sojourn in prison, did not have to depend on the chance survival of a manuscript; it was printed in 1485 by William Caxton, who had introduced printing by movable type to England less than ten years earlier. Malory's is the last great medieval work of literature. Using mostly French sources, Malory put together a history of King Arthur and his knights which, while wholly fictional, has received much the same honor from later Englishmen that earlier Englishmen accorded *Beowulf*.

MEDIEVAL ENGLISH

The medieval works in this book were composed in two different states of our language: Old English, the language which took shape among the Germanic settlers of England and preserved its integrity until the Norman Conquest radically altered English civilization; and Middle English, the earliest records of which date from the early 12th century and which gave way to Modern English shortly after the introduction of printing at the end of the 15th century. Old English is a very heavily inflected language (that is, the words change form to indicate changes in usage, such as person, number, tense, case, mood, etc. Most languages have some inflection—for example, the personal pronouns in Modern English have different forms when used as objects—but a "heavily inflected" language is one in which almost all classes of words undergo elaborate patterns of change). Its vocabulary is almost entirely Germanic. In Middle English, the inflectional system was weakened; and a large number of words were introduced into it from France, so that many of the older native words disappeared. Because of the difficulty of Old English, all selections from it in this book have been given in translation. In order that the reader may see an example of the language, *Cædmon's Hymn* has been printed in the original, together with an interlinear translation. The present discussion, then, is concerned only with Middle English.

The chief difficulty with Middle English for the modern reader is caused not by its inflections so much as by its spelling, which may be described as a rough-and-ready phonetic system, and by the fact that it is not a single standardized language, but consists of a number of regional dialects each with its own peculiarities of sound and its own systems for representing sounds in writing. The Midland dialect—the dialect of London and of Chaucer, and the ancestor of our own standard speech—differs greatly from the dialect spoken in the west of England (the original dialect of *Piers Plowman*), and from that of the northwest (*Sir Gawain and the Green Knight*), and from that of the north (*The Second Shepherds' Play*), and these dialects differ from one another. In this book, the long texts composed in the more difficult dialects have been translated or modernized; and those which, like Chaucer, *Everyman*, the lyrics, and the ballads, appear in the original, have been respelled in a way that it is hoped will aid the reader. The remarks which follow apply chiefly to Chaucer's Midland English, though certain non-Midland dialectal variations are noted if they occur in some of the other selections.

I. THE SOUNDS OF MIDDLE ENGLISH: GENERAL RULES

The following general analysis of the sounds of Middle English will enable the reader who has not time for detailed study to read Middle English aloud so as to preserve some of its most essential characteristics, without, however, giving heed to many important details. Section II, Detailed Analysis, is designed for the reader who wishes to go more deeply into the pronunciation of Middle English.

Middle English differs from Modern English in three principal respects: 1. the pronunciation of the long vowels *a, e, i* (or *y*), *o*, and *u* (spelled *ou, ow*); 2. the fact that Middle English final *e* is often sounded; 3. the fact that all Middle English consonants are sounded.

1. *Long Vowels*

Middle English vowels are long when they are doubled (*aa, ee, oo*) or when they are terminal (*he, to, holy*); *a, e,* and *o* are long when followed by a single consonant plus a vowel (*name, mete, note*). Middle English vowels are short when they are followed by two consonants.

Long *a* is sounded like the *a* in Modern English "father": *maken, maad.*

Long *e* may be sounded like the *a* in Modern English "name" (ignoring the distinction between the close and open vowel): *be, sweete.*

Long *i* (or *y*) is sounded like the *i* in Modern English "machine": *lif, whit; myn, holy.*

Long *o* may be sounded like the *o* in Modern English "note" (again ignoring the distinction between the close and open vowel): *do, soone.*

Long *u* (spelled *ou, ow*) is sounded like the *oo* in Modern English "goose": *hous, flowr.*

Note that in general Middle English long vowels are pronounced like long vowels in modern languages other than English. Short vowels and diphthongs, however, may be pronounced as in Modern English.

2. *Final* e

In Middle English syllabic verse, final *e* is sounded like the *a* in "sofa" to provide a needed unstressed syllable: *Another Nonnë with hire haddë she.* But (cf. *hire* in the example) final *e* is suppressed when not needed for the meter. It is commonly silent before words beginning with a vowel or *h*.

3. *Consonants*

Middle English consonants are pronounced separately in all combinations—*gnat: g-nat; knave: k-nave; write: w-rite; folk: fol-k.* In a simplified system of pronunciation the combination *gh* as in *night* or *thought* may be treated as if it were silent.

II. THE SOUNDS OF MIDDLE ENGLISH: DETAILED ANALYSIS

1. *Simple Vowels*

Sound	Pronunciation	Example
long *a* (spelled *a, aa*)	*a* in "father"	*maken, maad*
short *a*	o in "hot"	*cappe*
long *e* close (spelled *e, ee*)	*a* in "name"	*be, sweete*
long *e* open (spelled *e, ee*)	*e* in "there"	*mete, heeth*
short *e*	*e* in "set"	*setten*
final *e*	*a* in "sofa"	*large*
long *i* (spelled *i, y*)	*i* in "machine"	*lif, myn*
short *i*	*i* in "wit"	*wit*
long *o* close (spelled *o, oo*)	o in "note"	*do, soone*
long *o* open (spelled *o, oo*)	*oa* in "broad"	*go, goon*
short *o*	o in "oft"	*pot*
long *u* when spelled *ou, ow*	*oo* in "goose"	*hous, flowr*
long *u* when spelled *u*	*u* in "pure"	*vertu*
short *u* (spelled *u, o*)	*u* in "full"	*ful, love*

Doubled vowels and terminal vowels are always long, while single vowels before two consonants other than *th, ch* are always short. The vowels *a, e*, and *o* are long before a single consonant followed by a vowel: *nāmë, sēkë* (sick), *hōly*. In general, words that have descended into Modern English reflect their original Middle English quantity: *lĭven* (to live), but *līf* (life).

The close and open sounds of long *e* and long *o* may often be identified by the Modern English spellings of the words in which they appear. Original long close *e* is generally represented in Modern English by *ee*: "sweet," "knee," "teeth," "see" have close *e* in Middle English, but so does "be"; original long open *e* is generally represented in Modern English by *ea*: "meat," "heath," "sea," "great," "breath" have open *e* in Middle English. Similarly, original long close *o* is now generally represented by *oo*: "soon," "food," "good," but also "do," "to"; original long open *o* is represented either by *oa* or by *o*: "coat," "boat," "moan," but also "go," "bone," "foe," "home." Notice that original close *o* is now almost always pronounced like the *oo* in "goose," but that original open *o* is almost never so pronounced; thus it is often possible to identify the Middle English vowels through Modern English sounds.

The nonphonetic Middle English spelling of *o* for short *u* has been preserved in a number of Modern English words ("love," "son," "come"), but in others *u* has been restored: "sun" (*sonne*), "run" (*ronne*).

For the treatment of final *e*, see above, General Rules, section 2.

2. *Diphthongs*

Sound	Pronunciation	Example
ai, ay, ei, ay	between *ai* in "aisle" and *ay* in "day"	*saide, day, veine, preye*
au, aw	*ou* in "out"	*chaunge, bawdy*
eu, ew	*ew* in "few"	*newe*

oi, oy	*oy* in "joy"	*joye, point*
ou, ow	*ou* in "thought"	*thought, lowe*

Note that in words with *ou, ow* which in Modern English are sounded with the *ou* of "about," the combination indicates not the diphthong but the simple vowel long *u* (see above, Simple Vowels).

3. *Consonants*

In general, all consonants except *h* were always sounded in Middle English, including consonants that have become silent in Modern English, such as the *g* in *gnaw*, the *k* in *knight*, the *l* in *folk*, and the *w* in *write*. In noninitial *gn*, however, the g was silent as in Modern English "sign." Initial *h* was silent in short common English words and in words borrowed from French, and may have been almost silent in all words. The combination *gh* as in *night* or *thought* was sounded like the *ch* of German *ich* or *nach*. Note that Middle English *gg* represents both the hard sound of "dagger" and the soft sound of "bridge."

III. PARTS OF SPEECH AND GRAMMAR

1. *Nouns*

The plural and possessive of nouns end in *es*, formed by adding *s* or *es* to the singular: *knight, knightes; roote, rootes;* a final consonant is frequently doubled before *es: bed, beddes*. A common irregular plural is *yën*, from *yë*, eye.

2. *Pronouns*

The chief differences from Modern English are as follows:

Modern English	Middle English
I	*I, ich* (*ik* is a northern form)
you (singular)	*thou* (subjective); *thee* (objective)
her	*hir*(*e*), *her*(*e*)
its	*his*
you (plural)	*ye* (subjective); *you* (objective)
their	*hir*
them	*hem*

In formal speech, the second person plural is often used for the singular. The possessive adjectives *my, thy* take *n* before a word beginning with a vowel or *h: thyn yë, myn host*.

3. *Adjectives*

Adjectives ending in a consonant add final *e* when they stand before the noun they modify and after another modifying word such as *the, this, that*, or nouns or pronouns in the possessive: *a good hors*, but *the* (*this, my, the kinges*) *goode hors*. They also generally add *e* when standing before and modifying a plural noun, a noun in the vocative, or any proper noun: *goode men, oh goode man, faire Venus*.

Adjectives are compared by adding *er*(*e*) for the comparative, *est*(*e*) for the superlative. Sometimes the stem vowel is shortened or altered in the process: *sweete, swettere, swettest; long, lenger, lengest.*

4. *Adverbs*

Adverbs are formed from adjectives by adding *e, ly*, or *liche;* the adjective *fair* thus yields *faire, fairly, fairliche.*

5. *Verbs*

Middle English verbs, like Modern English verbs, are either "weak" or "strong." Weak verbs form their preterites and past participles with a *t* or *d* suffix and preserve the same stem vowel throughout their systems, though it is sometimes shortened in the preterite and past participle: *love, loved; bend, bent; hear, heard; meet, met.* Strong verbs do not use the *t* or *d* suffix, but vary their stem vowel in the preterite and past participle: *take, took, taken; begin, began, begun; find, found, found.*

The inflectional endings are the same for Middle English strong verbs and weak verbs except in the preterite singular and the imperative singular. In the following paradigms, the weak verbs *loven* (to love) and *heeren* (to hear), and the strong verbs *taken* (to take) and *ginnen* (to begin) serve as models.

	Present Indicative	Preterite Indicative
I	*love, heere*	*loved(e), herde*
	take, ginne	*took, gan*
thou	*lovest, heerest*	*lovedest, herdest*
	takest, ginnest	*tooke, gonne*
he, she, it	*loveth, heereth*	*loved(e), herde*
	taketh, ginneth	*took, gan*
we, ye, they	*love(n) (th), heere(n) (th)*	*loved(e) (en), herde(n)*
	take(n) (th), ginne(n) (th)	*tooke(n), gonne(n)*

The present plural ending *eth* is southern, while the *e(n)* ending is Midland and characteristic of Chaucer. In the north, *s* may appear as the ending of all persons of the present. In the weak preterite, when the ending *e* gave a verb three or more syllables, it was frequently dropped. Note that in certain strong verbs like *ginnen* there are two distinct stem vowels in the preterite: even in Chaucer's time, however, one of these had begun to replace the other, and Chaucer occasionally writes *gan* for all persons of the preterite.

	Present Subjunctive	Preterite Subjunctive
Singular	*love, heere*	*lovede, herde*
	take, ginne	*tooke, gonne*
Plural	*love(n), heere(n)*	*lovede(n), herde(n)*
	take(n), ginne(n)	*tooke(n), gonne(n)*

In verbs like *ginnen,* which have two stem vowels in the indicative preterite, it is the vowel of the plural and of the second person singular that is used for the preterite subjunctive.

The imperative singular of most weak verbs is *e: (thou) love,* but of some weak verbs and all strong verbs, the imperative singular is without termination: *(thou) heer, taak, gin.* The imperative plural of all verbs is either *e* or *eth: (ye) love(th), heere(th), take(th), ginne(th).*

The infinitive of verbs is *e* or *en: love(n), heere(n), take(n), ginne(n).*

The past participle of weak verbs is the same as the preterite without inflectional ending: *loved, herd.* In strong verbs the ending is either *e* or *en: take(n), gonne(n).* The prefix *y* often appears on past participles: *yloved, yherd, ytake(n).*

OLD AND MIDDLE ENGLISH PROSODY

All the poetry of Old English is in the same verse form. The verse unit is the single line, since rhyme was not used to link one line to another, except very occasionally in late Old English. The organizing device of the line is alliteration, the beginning of several words with the same sound ("Foemen fled"). The Old English alliterative line contains four principal stresses, and is divided into two half-lines of two stresses each by a strong medial caesura, or pause. These two half-lines are linked to each other by the alliteration: at least one of the two stressed words in the first half-line, and often both of them, begin with the same sound as the first stressed word of the second half-line (the second stressed word is generally non-alliterative). The fourth line of *Beowulf* is an example:

Oft Scyld Scefing   sceaþena þreatum.

For further examples, see *Cædmon's Hymn*, printed below. It will be noticed that any vowel alliterates with any other vowel. In addition to the alliteration, the length of the unstressed syllables and their number and pattern is governed by a highly complex set of rules. When sung or intoned—as it was—to the rhythmic strumming of a harp, Old English poetry must have been wonderfully impressive in the dignified, highly formalized way which aptly fits both its subject matter and tone.

The majority of Middle English verse is either in alternately stressed rhyming verse, adapted from French after the Conquest, or in alliterative verse that is descended from Old English. The latter preserves the caesura of Old English and in its purest form the same alliterative system, the two stressed words of the first half-line (or at least one of them) alliterating with the first stressed word in the second half-line. But most of the alliterative poets allowed themselves a number of deviations from the norm. All four stressed words may alliterate, as in the first line of *Piers Plowman:*

In a *s*ummer *s*eason   when *s*oft was the *s*un.

Or the line may contain five, six, or even more stressed words, of which all or only the basic minimum may alliterate:

A *f*air *f*ield *f*ull of *f*olk   *f*ound I therebetween.

There is no rule determining the number of unstressed syllables, and at times some poets are apt to ignore alliteration entirely. As in Old English, any vowel may alliterate with any other vowel; furthermore, since initial *h* was silent or lightly pronounced in Middle English, words beginning with *h* are treated as though they began with the following vowel.

There are two general types of stressed verse with rhyme. In the more common, stressed and unstressed syllables alternate regularly: x X x X x X; or, with two unstressed syllables intervening: x x X x x X x x X; or a combination of the two: x x X x X x x X (of the reverse patterns, only X x X x X x is common in English). There is also a line which can only be defined as containing a predetermined number of stressed syllables but an irregular number and pattern of unstressed syllables. Much Middle English verse has to be read without expectation of regularity: some of this was evidently composed in the irregular meter, but some was probably originally composed according to a strict metrical system which has been obliterated by scribes careless of fine points. One receives the impression that many of the lyrics—as well as the *Second Shepherd's Play*—were at least composed with regular syllabic alternation. In the ballads, on the other hand, and in the play *Everyman*, only the number of stresses is predetermined (and perhaps not even this in *Everyman*), but not the number or placement of unstressed syllables.

In pre-Chaucerian verse the number of stresses, whether regularly or irregularly alternated, was most often four, though sometimes the number was three, and rose in some poems to seven. Rhyme in Middle English as in Modern English may be either between adjacent or alternate lines, or may occur in more complex patterns. The *Canterbury Tales* are in rhymed couplets, the line containing five stresses with regular alternation —technically known as iambic pentameter, the standard English poetic line, perhaps introduced into English by Chaucer. In reading Chaucer and much pre-Chaucerian verse one must remember that the final *e*, which is silent in Modern English, was pronounced at any time in order to provide a needed unstressed syllable. Evidence seems to indicate that it was also pronounced at the end of the line, even though it thus produced a line with eleven syllables. Although he was a very regular metricist, Chaucer used various conventional devices which are apt to make the reader stumble until he understands them. Final *e* is often not pronounced before a word beginning with a vowel or *h*, and may be suppressed whenever metrically convenient. The same medial and terminal syllables that are slurred in Modern English are apt to be suppressed in Chaucer's English: *Canterb'ry* for *Canterbury; ev'r* (perhaps *e'er*) for *evere*. The plural in *es* may either be syllabic or reduced to *s* as in Modern English. Despite these seeming irregularities, Chaucer's verse is not difficult to read if one constantly bears in mind the basic pattern of the iambic pentameter line.

Old English Poetry

CÆDMON'S HYMN

Cædmon's *Hymn* is one of the oldest of preserved English poems, having been written between 658 and 680. Bede, the great cleric of Old English times, tells the story of its composition in his *Ecclesiastical History of the English People* (completed in 731). Cædmon, a Northumbrian layman, had all his life felt himself incompetent in the art of verse, and when, according to the custom that was used at feasts, the harp was passed around the table so that each guest might entertain the others with a song, Cædmon always found a pretext to take himself from the table before the harp reached him. One night when he had thus avoided singing, he fell asleep in the stable where he had gone to tend the animals. He dreamed that someone came to him and said, "Cædmon, sing me something," and when Cædmon excused himself, the other insisted that he sing, directing him to celebrate the beginning of created things. Cædmon at once sang the *Hymn*. On waking, he remembered his verses; and thereafter, Bede tells us, he was able to express any given sacred topic in excellent poetry after only a few hours of work. He became a monk and devoted his life to the composition of Christian verse, but none of the religious poetry in Old English that has been preserved may surely be ascribed to him except his first short work.

The poem is given here in a West Saxon form with a literal interlinear translation. In Old English spelling, æ (as in Cædmon's name and line 3) is a vowel symbol that has not survived; it represented both a short *a* sound and a long open *e* sound. þ (line 2) and ð both represented the sound *th*. The large space in the middle of the line indicates the caesura.

Cædmon's Hymn

Nu sculon herigean   heofonrices Weard
Now we must praise   heaven-kingdom's Guardian,

Meotodes meahte   and his modgeþanc
the Creator's might   and his mind-plans,

weorc Wuldor-Fæder   swa he wundra gehwæs
the work of the Glory-Father,   when he of wonders of every one,

ece Drihten eternal Lord.	or onstealde the beginning established.[1]
He ærest sceop He first created	ielda[2] bearnum for men's sons
heofon to hrofe heaven as a roof,	halig Scyppend holy Creator;
ða middangeard then middle-earth	moncynnes Weard mankind's Guardian,
ece Drihten eternal Lord,	æfter teode afterwards made—
firum foldan for men earth,	Frea aelmihtig Master almighty.

1. I.e., "established the beginning of every one of wonders."
2. The later manuscript copies read *eorþan*, "earth," for *ælda* (West Saxon *ielda*), "men's."

THE DREAM OF THE ROOD

The *Dream of the Rood* (i.e., of the Cross) is the finest of a rather large number of religious poems in Old English. Neither its author nor its date of composition is known. It appears in a late 10th-century manuscript located in Vercelli in northern Italy, a manuscript made up of Old English religious poems and sermons. The poet Cynewulf, about whom nothing is surely known except that he wrote four Old English homiletic poems (two of them found in the Vercelli manuscript), has sometimes been credited with the *Dream*, but on no very convincing evidence. The poem may antedate its manuscript by almost three centuries, for some passages from the Rood's speech were carved, with some variations, in runes on a stone cross early in the 8th century: this is the famous Ruthwell Cross, which is preserved near Dumfries in southern Scotland. The precise relation of the poem to this cross is, however, uncertain.

The homiletic tone of the Dreamer's meditation may seem anticlimactic after the intensity, so terse and exciting, of the Rood's address to him, but the former is nevertheless an admirable frame for the latter. The experience of the Cross—its humiliation at the hands of those who changed it from tree to instrument of punishment for criminals, its humility when the young hero Christ mounts upon it, and its pride as the restored "tree of glory"—has a suggestive relevance to the condition of the sad, lonely, sin-stained Dreamer. In the Cross's experience, hope has replaced torment; when, at the end of the poem, the Dreamer describes Christ's triumphant progress from hell to heaven, the verse recaptures some of the excitement of the Cross's address, reflecting the Dreamer's response to the hope that has been brought him.

The Dream of the Rood[1]

Listen, I will speak of the best of dreams, of what I dreamed at midnight when men and their voices were at rest. It seemed to me that I saw a most rare tree reach high aloft, wound in light, brightest of beams. All that beacon[2] was covered with gold; gems stood fair where it met the ground, five were above about the crosspiece. Many hosts of angels gazed on it, fair in the form created for them. This was surely no felon's gallows, but holy spirits beheld it there, men upon earth, and all this glorious creation. Wonderful was the triumph-tree, and I stained with sins, wounded with wrongdoings. I saw the tree of glory shine splendidly, adorned with garments, decked with gold: jewels had worthily covered the Lord's tree. Yet through that gold I might perceive ancient agony of wretches, for now it began to bleed on the right side.[3] I was all afflicted with sorrows, I was afraid for that fair sight. I saw that bright beacon change in clothing and color: now it was wet with moisture, drenched with flowing of blood, now adorned with treasure. Yet I, lying there a long while troubled, beheld the Saviour's tree until I heard it give voice: the best of trees began to speak words.

"It was long ago—I remember it still—that I was hewn down at the wood's edge, taken from my stump. Strong foes seized me there, hewed me to the shape they wished to see, commanded me to lift their criminals. Men carried me on their shoulders, then set me on a hill; foes enough fastened me there. Then I saw the Lord of mankind hasten with stout heart, for he would climb upon me. I dared not bow or break against God's word when I saw earth's surface tremble. I might have felled all foes, but I stood fast. Then the young Hero stripped himself—that was God Almighty—strong and stouthearted. He climbed on the high gallows, bold in the sight of many, when he would free mankind. I trembled when the Warrior embraced me, yet I dared not bow to earth, fall to the ground's surface; but I must stand fast. I was raised up, a cross; I lifted up the Mighty King, Lord of the Heavens: I dared not bend. They pierced me with dark nails: the wounds are seen on me, open gashes of hatred. Nor did I dare harm any of them. They mocked us both together. I was all wet with blood, drenched from the side of that Man after he had sent forth his spirit. I had endured many bitter happenings on that hill. I saw the God of Hosts cruelly racked. The shades of night had covered the Ruler's body with their mists, the

1. This new prose translation, by the present editor, has been based in general on the edition of the poem by John C. Pope, *Seven Old English Poems* (1966).
2. The Old English word *beacen* means also "token" or "sign" and "battle standard."
3. The wound Christ received on the Cross was supposed to have been on the right side.

bright splendor. Shadow came forth, dark beneath the clouds. All creation wept, bewailed the King's fall; Christ was on Cross.

"Yet from afar some came hastening to the Lord.[4] All that I beheld. I was sore afflicted with griefs, yet I bowed to the men's hands, meekly, eagerly. Then they took Almighty God, lifted him up from his heavy torment. The warriors left me standing, covered with blood. I was all wounded with arrows. They laid him down weary of limb, stood at the body's head, looked there upon Heaven's Lord; and he rested there a while, tired after the great struggle. Then warriors began to build him an earth-house in the sight of his slayer,[5] carved it out of bright stone; they set there the Wielder of Triumphs. Then they began to sing him a song of sorrow, desolate in the evening. Then they wished to turn back, weary, from the great Prince; he remained with small company.[6] Yet we[7] stood in our places a good while, weeping. The voice of the warriors departed. The body grew cold, fair house of the spirit. Then some began to fell us to earth—that was a fearful fate! Some buried us in a deep pit. Yet thanes[8] of the Lord, friends, learned of me there. . . . decked me in gold and silver.[9]

"Now you might understand, my beloved man, that I had endured the work of evildoers, grievous sorrows. Now the time has come that men far and wide upon earth honor me—and all this glorious creation—and pray to this beacon. On me God's Son suffered a while; therefore I tower now glorious under the heavens, and I may heal every one of those who hold me in awe. Of old I became the hardest of torments, most loathed of men, before I opened the right road of life to those who have voices. Behold, the Lord of Glory honored me over all the trees of the wood, the Ruler of Heaven, just as also he honored his mother Mary, Almighty God for all men's sake, over all woman's kind.

"Now I command you, my beloved man, that you tell men of this vision. Disclose with your words that it is of the tree of glory on which Almighty God suffered for mankind's many sins and the deeds Adam did of old. He tasted death there; yet the Lord arose again to help mankind in his great might. Then he climbed to the heavens. He will come again hither on this earth to seek mankind on Doomsday, the Lord himself, Almighty God, and his angels with him, for then he will judge, he who has power to judge, each one just as in this brief life he has deserved. Nor may any one be unafraid of the word the Ruler will speak. Before his host he will ask

4. According to John xix. 38–39, it was Joseph of Arimathea and Nicodemus who received Christ's body from the Cross.
5. I.e., the Cross.
6. I.e., alone (an understatement).
7. I.e., Christ's Cross and those on which the two thieves were crucified.
8. Members of the king's body of warriors.
9. A number of lines describing the finding of the Cross have apparently been lost here.

where the man is who in the name of the Lord would taste bitter death as he did on the Cross. But then they will be afraid, and will think of little to begin to say to Christ. There need none be afraid who bears on his breast the best of tokens, but through the Cross shall the kingdom be sought by each soul on this earthly journey that thinks to dwell with the Lord."

Then I prayed to the tree, blithe-hearted, confident, there where I was alone with small company. My heart's thoughts were urged on the way hence. I endured many times of longing. Now is there hope of life for me, that I am permitted to seek the tree of triumph, more often than other men honor it well, alone. For it my heart's desire is great, and my hope of protection is directed to the Cross. I do not possess many powerful friends on earth, but they have gone hence from the delights of the world, sought for themselves the King of Glory. They live now in the heavens with the High Father, dwell in glory. And every day I look forward to when the Lord's Cross that I beheld here on earth will fetch me from this short life and bring me then where joy is great, delight in the heavens, where the Lord's folk are seated at the feast, where bliss is eternal. And then may it place me where thenceforth I may dwell in glory, fully enjoy bliss with the saints. May the Lord be my friend, who once here on earth suffered on the gallows-tree for man's sins: he freed us and granted us life, a heavenly home. Hope was renewed, with joys and with bliss, to those who endured fire.[1] The Son was victorious in that foray, mighty and successful. Then he came with his multitude, a host of spirits, into God's kingdom, the Almighty Ruler; and the angels and all the saints who dwelt then in glory rejoiced when their Ruler, Almighty God, came where his home was.

1. This and the following sentences refer to the Harrowing (i.e., pillaging) of Hell: after His death upon the Cross, Christ descended into hell, from which He released the souls of certain of the patriarchs and prophets, conducting them triumphantly to heaven.

BEOWULF

Beowulf, the oldest of the great long poems written in English, was probably composed more than twelve hundred years ago, in the first half of the eighth century. Its author may have been a native of what was then West Mercia, the West Midlands of England today, though the late tenth-century manuscript, which alone preserves the poem, originated in the south in the kingdom of the West Saxons. In 1731, before any modern transcription of the text had been made, the manuscript was seriously damaged in the fire that destroyed the building in London which housed the extraordinary collection of medieval English manuscripts made by Sir Robert Bruce Cotton (1571–1631). As a result of the fire and of subsequent deterioration of the manuscript, a number of lines and words have been lost from the poem, but even if the manuscript had not been damaged, the poem would still have been difficult, because the poetic Old English (or Anglo-Saxon) in which it was written is itself hard, the style is allusive, the ideas often seem remote and strange to modern perceptions, and because the text was inevitably corrupted during the many transcriptions which must have intervened in the two and a half centuries between the poem's composition and the copying of the extant manuscript. Yet despite its difficulty, the somber grandeur of *Beowulf* is still capable of stirring the hearts of readers, and because of its excellence as well as its antiquity, the poem merits the high position that it is generally assigned in the study of English poetry.

While the poem itself is English in language and origin, it deals not with native Englishmen, but with their Germanic forebears, especially with two south Scandinavian tribes, the Danes and the Geats, who lived on the Danish island of Zealand and in southern Sweden, respectively. Thus, the historical period it concerns—insofar as it may be said to refer to history at all—is some two centuries before the poem was written; that is, it concerns a time following the initial invasion of England by Germanic tribes in 449, but before the Anglo-Saxon migration was completed, and perhaps before the arrival of the ancestors of the audience to whom the poem was sung: this audience may have considered itself to be of the same Geatish stock as the hero, Beowulf. The one datable fact of history mentioned in the poem is a raid on the Franks made by Hygelac, the king of the Geats at the time Beowulf was a young man, and this raid occurred in the year 520. Yet despite their antiquity, the poet's materials must have been very much alive to his audience, for the elliptical way in which he alludes to events not directly concerned with his plot demands of the listener a wide knowledge of traditional Germanic history. This knowledge was probably kept alive by other heroic poetry, of which little has been preserved in English, though much must once have existed. As it stands, *Beowulf* is not only unique as an example of the Old English epic, but is also the greatest of the surviving epics composed by the Germanic peoples.

It is generally agreed that the poet who put the old materials into their present form was a Christian, and that his poem reflects a Christian tradition: the conversion of the Cermanic settlers in England had largely been completed during the century preceding the one in which the poet wrote. But there is little general agreement as to how clearly *Beowulf* reflects a Christian tradition or, conversely, the actual nature of the Christian tradition that it is held to reflect. Many specifically Christian references occur, especially to the Old Testament: God is said to be the Creator of all things and His will seems recognized (sporadically if not systematically) as being identical with Fate (*wyrd*); Grendel is described as a descendant of Cain, and the sword that Beowulf finds in Grendel's mother's lair has engraved on it the story of the race of giants and their destruction by flood; the dead await God's judgment, and Hell and the Devil are ready to receive the souls of Grendel and his mother, while believers will find the Father's embrace; Hrothgar's speech of advice to Beowulf (section XXV) seems to reflect patristic doctrine in its emphasis on conscience and the Devil's lying in wait for the unwary. Yet there is no reference to the New Testament—to Christ and His Sacrifice which are the real bases of Christianity in any intelligible sense of the term. Furthermore, readers may well feel that the poem achieves rather little of its emotional power through invocation of Christian values or of values that are consonant with Christian doctrine as we know it. Perhaps the sense of tragic waste which pervades the Finnsburg episode (section XVI) springs from a Christian perception of the insane futility of the primitive Germanic thirst for vengeance; and the facts that Beowulf's chief adversaries are not men but monsters and that before his death he is able to boast that as king of the Geats he did not seek wars with neighboring tribes may reflect a Christian's appreciation for peace among men. But while admitting such values, the poet also invokes many others of a very different order, values that seem to belong to an ancient, pagan, warrior society of the kind described by the Roman historian Tacitus at the end of the first century. It should be noted that even Hrothgar's speech about conscience is directed more toward making Beowulf a good Germanic leader of men than a good Christian. One must, indeed, draw the conclusion from the poem itself that while Christian is a correct term for the religion of the poet and of his audience, it was a Christianity that had not yet by any means succeeded in obliterating an older pagan tradition, which still called forth powerful responses from men's hearts, despite the fact that many aspects of this tradition must be abhorrent to a sophisticated Christian. In this connection it is well to recall that the missionaries from Rome who initiated the conversion of the English proceeded in a conciliatory manner, not so much uprooting paganism in order to plant Christianity as planting Christianity in the faith that it would ultimately choke out the weeds of paganism. And the English clung long to some of their ancient traditions: for instance, the legal principle of the payment of *wergild* (defined below) remained in force until the Norman Conquest, four centuries after the conversion of the English.

In the warrior society whose values the poem constantly invokes, the most important of human relationships was that which existed between the warrior—the thane—and his lord, a relationship based less on subordination of one man's will to another's than on mutual trust and respect. When a warrior vowed loyalty to his lord, he became not so much his servant as his voluntary companion, one who would take pride in defending him and fighting in his wars. In return, the lord was expected to take affectionate care of his thanes and to reward them richly for their valor: a good king, one like Hrothgar or Beowulf, is referred to by such poetic epithets as "protector of warriors" and "dispenser of treasure" or "ring-giver," and the failure of bad kings is ascribed to their ill-temper and avarice, both of which alienate them from their retainers. The material benefit of this arrangement between lord and thane is obvious, yet under a good king the relationship seems to have had a significance more spiritual than material. Thus the treasure that an ideal Germanic king seizes from his enemies and rewards his retainers with is regarded as something more than mere wealth that will serve the well-being of its possessor; rather, it is a kind of visible proof that all parties are realizing themselves to the full in a spiritual sense—that the men of this band are congenially and successfully united with one another. The symbolic importance of treasure is illustrated by the poet's remark that the gift Beowulf gave the Danish coast-guard brought the latter honor among his companions, and even more by the fact that although Beowulf dies while obtaining a great treasure for his people, such objects as are removed from the dragon's hoard are actually buried with him as a fitting sign of his ultimate achievement.

The relationship between kinsmen was also of deep significance to this society and provides another emotional value for Old English heroic poetry. If one of his kinsmen had been slain, a man had the special duty of either killing the slayer or exacting from him the payment of *wergild* ("man-price"): each rank of society was evaluated at a definite price, which had to be paid to the dead man's kinsmen by the killer who wished to avoid their vengeance—even if the killing had been accidental. Again, the money itself had less significance as wealth than as a proof that the kinsmen had done what was right. Relatives who failed either to exact *wergild* or to take vengeance could never be happy, having found no practical way of satisfying their grief for their kinsmen's death. "It is better for a man to avenge his friend than much mourn," Beowulf says to the old Hrothgar, who is bewailing Aeschere's killing by Grendel's mother. And one of the most poignant passages in the poem describes the sorrow of King Hrethel after one of his sons had accidentally killed another: by the code of kinship Hrethel was forbidden to kill or to exact compensation from a kinsman, yet by the same code he was required to do one or the other in order to avenge the dead. Caught in this curious dilemma, Hrethel became so disconsolate that he could no longer face life.

It is evident that the need to take vengeance would create never-ending feuds, which the practice of marrying royal princesses to the kings or princes of hostile tribes did little to mitigate, though the purpose of such marriages was to replace hostility by alliance. Hrothgar wishes to make peace with the Heatho-Bards by marrying his daughter to their king, Ingeld, whose father was killed by the Danes; but as Beowulf predicts, sooner or later the Heatho-Bards' desire for vengeance on the Danes will erupt, and there will be more bloodshed. And the Danish princess Hildeburh, married to Finn of the Jutes, will see her son and her brother both killed while fighting on opposite sides in a battle at her own home, and ultimately will see her husband killed by the Danes in revenge for her brother's death. Beowulf himself is, for a Germanic hero, curiously free of involvement in feuds of this sort, though he does boast that he avenged the death of his king, Heardred, on his slayer Onela. Yet the potentiality—or inevitability—of sudden attack, sudden change, swift death is omnipresent in *Beowulf:* men seem to be caught in a vast web of reprisals and counterreprisals from which there is little hope of escape. This is the aspect of the poem which is apt to make the most powerful impression on the reader—its strong sense of doom.

Beowulf himself is chiefly concerned not with tribal feuds but with fatal evil both less and more complex. Grendel and the dragon are threats to the security of the lands they infest just as human enemies would be, but they are not part of the social order and presumably have no one to avenge their deaths (that Grendel's mother appeared as an avenger seems to have been a surprise both to Beowulf and to the Danes). On the other hand, because they are outside the normal order of things, they require of their conqueror something greater than normal warfare requires. In each case, it is the clear duty of the king and his companions to put down the evil. But the Danish Hrothgar is old and his companions unenterprising, and excellent though Hrothgar has been in the kingship, he nevertheless lacks the quality that later impels the old Beowulf to fight the dragon that threatens his people. The poem makes no criticism of Hrothgar for this lack; he merely seems not to be the kind of man—one might almost say he was not fated—to develop his human potential to the fullest extent that Fate would permit: that is

Beowulf's role. In undertaking to slay Grendel, and later Grendel's mother, Beowulf is testing his relationship with unknowable destiny. At any time, as he is fully aware, his luck may abandon him and he may be killed, as, indeed, he is in the otherwise successful encounter with the dragon. But whether he lives or dies, he will have done all that any man could do to develop his character heroically. It is this consciousness of testing Fate that probably explains the boasting that modern readers of heroic poetry often find offensive. When he boasts, Beowulf is not only demonstrating that he has chosen the heroic way of life, but is also choosing it, for when he invokes his former courage as pledge of his future courage, his boast becomes a vow; the hero has put himself in a position from which he cannot withdraw.

Courage is the instrument by which the hero realizes himself. "Fate often saves an undoomed man when his courage is good," says Beowulf in his account of his swimming match: that is, if Fate has not entirely doomed a man in advance, courage is the quality that can perhaps influence Fate against its natural tendency to doom him now. It is this complex statement (in which it is hard to read the will of God for Fate) that Beowulf's life explores: he will use his great strength in the most courageous way by going alone, even unarmed, against monsters. Doom, of course, ultimately claims him, but not until he has fulfilled to its limits the pagan ideal of a heroic life. And despite the desire he often shows to Christianize pagan virtues, the Christian poet remains true to the older tradition when, at the end of his poem, he leaves us with the impression that Beowulf's chief reward is pagan immortality: the memory in the minds of later men of a hero's heroic actions. The poem itself is, indeed, a noble expression of that immortality

TRIBES AND GENEALOGIES

I. The Danes (Bright-, Half-, Ring-, Spear-, North-, East-, South-, West-Danes; Scyldings, Honor-, Victor-, War-Scyldings; Ing's friends).

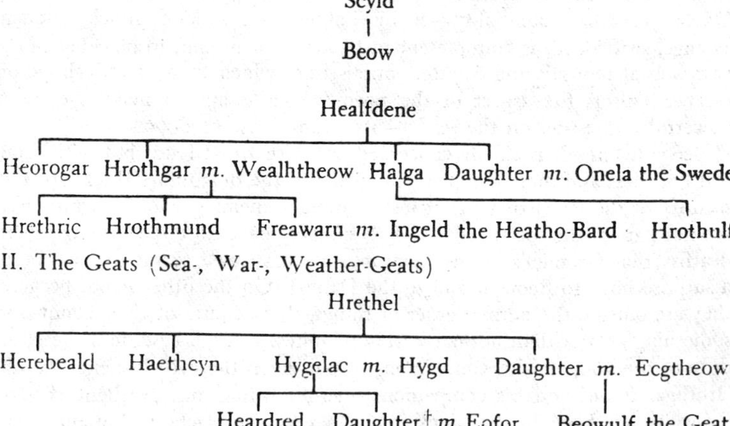

† The daughter of Hygelac who was given to Eofor may have been born to him by a former wife, older than Hygd.

III. The Swedes.

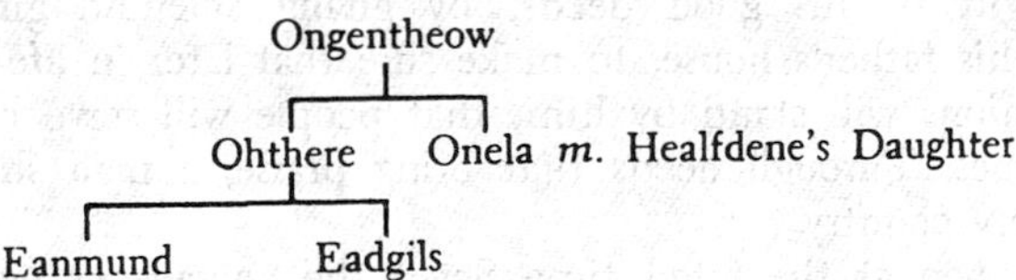

IV. Miscellaneous.

A. The Half-Danes (also called Scyldings) involved in the fight at Finnsburg may represent a different tribe from the Danes of paragraph I, above. Their king Hoc had a son, Hnaef, who succeeded him, and a daughter Hildeburh, who married Finn, king of the Jutes.

B. The Jutes or Frisians are represented as enemies of the Danes in the fight at Finnsburg and as allies of the Franks or Hugas at the time Hygelac the Geat made the attack in which he lost his life and from which Beowulf swam home. Also allied with the Franks at this time were the Hetware.

C. The Heatho-Bards (i.e., "Battle-Bards") are represented as inveterate enemies of the Danes. Their king Froda had been killed in an attack on the Danes, and Hrothgar's attempt to make peace with them by marrying his daughter Freawaru to Froda's son Ingeld failed when the latter attacked Heorot. The attack was repulsed, though Heorot was burned.

Beowulf[1]

[*Prologue: The Earlier History of the Danes*]

Yes, we have heard of the glory of the Spear-Danes' kings in the old days—how the princes of that people did brave deeds.

Often Scyld Scefing[2] took mead-benches away from enemy bands, from many tribes, terrified their nobles—after the time that he was first found helpless.[3] He lived to find comfort for that, became great under the skies, prospered in honors until every one of those who lived about him, across the whale-road, had to obey him, pay him tribute. That was a good king.

Afterwards a son was born to him, a young boy in his house, whom God sent to comfort the people: He had seen the sore need they had suffered during the long time they lacked a king. Therefore the Lord of Life, the Ruler of Heaven, gave him honor in the world: Beow[4] was famous, the glory of the son of

1. The translation into modern English, by the editor (1966), is based on F. Klaeber's third edition of the poem (1950); in general, the emendations suggested by J. C. Pope, *The Rhythm of Beowulf*, second edition (1966), have been adopted. The division into sections headed by roman numerals is that of the manuscript, which makes, however, no provision for Section XXX.

2. The meaning is probably "son of Sceaf," although Scyld's origins are mysterious.

3. As is made clear shortly below, Scyld arrived in Denmark as a child alone in a ship loaded with treasures.

4. Although the manuscript reads "Beowulf," most scholars now agree that it should read "Beow." Beow was the grandfather of the Danish king Hrothgar.

Scyld spread widely in the Northlands. In this way a young man ought by his good deeds, by giving splendid gifts while still in his father's house, to make sure that later in life beloved companions will stand by him, that people will serve him when war comes. Through deeds that bring praise, a man shall prosper in every country.

Then at the fated time Scyld the courageous went away into the protection of the Lord. His dear companions carried him down to the sea-currents, just as he himself had bidden them do when, as protector of the Scyldings,[5] he had ruled them with his words —long had the beloved prince governed the land. There in the harbor stood the ring-prowed ship, ice-covered and ready to sail, a prince's vessel. Then they laid down the ruler they had loved, the ring-giver, in the hollow of the ship, the glorious man beside the mast. There was brought great store of treasure, wealth from lands far away. I have not heard of a ship more splendidly furnished with war-weapons and battle-dress, swords and mail-shirts. On his breast lay a great many treasures that should voyage with him far out into the sea's possession. They provided him with no lesser gifts, treasure of the people, than those had done who at his beginning first sent him forth on the waves, a child alone. Then also they set a golden standard high over his head, let the water take him, gave him to the sea. Sad was their spirit, mournful their mind. Men cannot truthfully say who received that cargo, neither counsellors in the hall nor warriors under the skies.

(I) Then in the cities was Beow of the Scyldings beloved king of the people, long famous among nations (his father had gone elsewhere, the king from his land), until later great Healfdene was born to him. As long as he lived, old and fierce in battle, he upheld the glorious Scyldings. To him all told were four children born into the world, to the leader of the armies: Heorogar and Hrothgar and the good Halga. I have heard tell that [. . . was On]ela's queen,[6] beloved bed-companion of the Battle-Scylfing.

[*Beowulf and Grendel*]

[THE HALL HEOROT IS ATTACKED BY GRENDEL]

Then Hrothgar was given success in warfare, glory in battle, so that his retainers gladly obeyed him and their company grew into a great band of warriors. It came to his mind that he would command men to construct a hall, a mead-building large[r]

5. I.e., the Danes ("descendants of Scyld").

6. The text is faulty, so that the name of Healfdene's daughter has been lost; her husband Onela was a Swedish (Scylfing) king.

than the children of men had ever heard of, and therein he would give to young and old all that God had given him, except for common land and men's bodies.[7] Then I have heard that the work was laid upon many nations, wide through this middle-earth, that they should adorn the folk-hall. In time it came to pass—quickly, as men count it—that it was finished, the largest of hall-dwellings. He gave it the name of Heorot,[8] he who ruled wide with his words. He did not forget his promise: at the feast he gave out rings, treasure. The hall stood tall, high and wide-gabled: it would wait for the fierce flames of vengeful fire;[9] the time was not yet at hand for sword-hate between son-in-law and father-in-law to awaken after murderous rage.

Then the fierce spirit[1] painfully endured hardship for a time, he who dwelt in the darkness, for every day he heard loud mirth in the hall; there was the sound of the harp, the clear song of the scop.[2] There he spoke who could relate the beginning of men far back in time, said that the Almighty made earth, a bright field fair in the water that surrounds it, set up in triumph the lights of the sun and the moon to lighten land-dwellers, and adorned the surfaces of the earth with branches and leaves, created also life for each of the kinds that move and breathe.—Thus these warriors lived in joy, blessed, until one began to do evil deeds, a hellish enemy. The grim spirit was called Grendel, known as a rover of the borders, one who held the moors, fen and fastness. Unhappy creature, he lived for a time in the home of the monsters' race, after God had condemned them as kin of Cain. The Eternal Lord avenged the murder in which he slew Abel. Cain had no pleasure in that feud, but He banished him far from mankind, the Ruler, for that misdeed. From him sprang all bad breeds, trolls and elves and monsters—likewise the giants who for a long time strove with God: He paid them their reward for that.

(II.) Then, after night came, Grendel went to survey the tall house—how, after their beer-drinking, the Ring-Danes had disposed themselves in it. Then he found therein a band of nobles asleep after the feast: they felt no sorrow, no misery of men. The creature of evil, grim and fierce, was quickly ready, savage and cruel, and seized from their rest thirty thanes. From there he turned to go back to his home, proud of his plunder, sought his dwelling with that store of slaughter.

7. Or "men's lives." Apparently slaves, along with public land, were not in the king's power to give away.
8. I.e., "Hart."
9. The destruction by fire of Heorot occurred at a later time than that of the poem's action, probably during the otherwise unsuccessful attack of the Heatho-Bard Ingeld on his father-in-law Hrothgar, mentioned in the next clause.
1. I.e., Grendel.
2. The "scop" was the Anglo-Saxon minstrel, who recited poetic stories to the accompaniment of a harp.

Then in the first light of dawning day Grendel's war-strength was revealed to men: then after the feast weeping arose, great cry in the morning. The famous king, hero of old days, sat joyless; the mighty one suffered, felt sorrow for his thanes, when they saw the track of the foe, of the cursed spirit: that hardship was too strong, too loathsome and long-lasting. Nor was there a longer interval, but after one night Grendel again did greater slaughter—and had no remorse for it—vengeful acts and wicked: he was too intent on them. Thereafter it was easy to find the man who sought rest for himself elsewhere, farther away, a bed among the outlying buildings—after it was made clear to him, told by clear proof, the hatred of him who now controlled the hall.[3] Whoever escaped the foe held himself afterwards farther off and more safely. Thus Grendel held sway and fought against right, one against all, until the best of houses stood empty. It was a long time, the length of twelve winters, that the lord of the Scyldings suffered grief, all woes, great sorrows. Therefore, sadly in songs, it became well-known to the children of men that Grendel had fought a long time with Hrothgar, for many half-years maintained mortal spite, feud, and enmity—constant war. He wanted no peace with any of the men of the Danish host, would not withdraw his deadly rancor, or pay compensation: no counselor there had any reason to expect splendid repayment at the hands of the slayer.[4] For the monster was relentless, the dark death-shadow, against warriors old and young, lay in wait and ambushed them. In the perpetual darkness he held to the misty moors: men do not know where hell-demons direct their footsteps.

Thus many crimes the enemy of mankind committed, the terrible walker-alone, cruel injuries one after another. In the dark nights he dwelt in Heorot, the richly adorned hall. He might not approach the throne, [receive] treasure, because of the Lord; He had no love for him.[5]

This was great misery to the lord of the Scyldings, a breaking of spirit. Many a noble sat often in council, sought a plan, what would be best for strong-hearted men to do against the awful attacks. At times they vowed sacrifices at heathen temples, with their words prayed that the soul-slayer[6] would give help for the distress of the people. Such was their custom, the hope of heathens;

3. I.e., Grendel.
4. According to old Germanic law, a slayer could achieve peace with his victim's kinsmen only by paying them *wergild*, i.e., compensation for the life of the slain man.
5. Behind this obscure passage seems to lie the idea that Grendel, unlike Hrothgar's thanes, could not approach the throne to receive gifts from the king, having been condemned by God as an outlaw.
6. I.e., the Devil. Despite this assertion that the Danes were heathen, their king, Hrothgar, speaks consistently as a Christian.

in their spirits they thought of Hell, they knew not the Ruler, the Judge of Deeds, they recognized not the Lord God, nor indeed did they know how to praise the Protector of Heaven, the glorious King. Woe is him who in terrible trouble must thrust his soul into the fire's embrace, hope for no comfort, not expect change. Well is the man who after his death-day may seek the Lord and find peace in the embrace of the Father.

[THE COMING OF BEOWULF TO HEOROT]

(III.) So in the cares of his times the son of Healfdene constantly brooded, nor might the wise warrior set aside his woe. Too harsh, hateful and long-lasting was the hardship that had come upon the people, distress dire and inexorable, worst of night-horrors.

A thane of Hygelac,[7] a good man among the Geats, heard in his homeland of Grendel's deeds: of mankind he was the strongest of might in the time of this life, noble and great. He bade that a good ship be made ready for him, said he would seek the war-king over the swan's road, the famous prince, since he had need of men. Very little did wise men blame him for that adventure, though he was dear to them; they urged the brave one on, examined the omens. From the folk of the Geats the good man had chosen warriors of the bravest that he could find; one of fifteen he led the way, the warrior sought the wooden ship, the sea-skilled one the land's edge. The time had come: the ship was on the waves, the boat under the cliff. The warriors eagerly climbed on the prow—the sea-currents eddied, sea against sand; men bore bright weapons into the ship's bosom, splendid armor. Men pushed the well-braced ship from shore, warriors on a well-wished voyage. Then over the sea-waves, blown by the wind, the foam-necked boat traveled, most like a bird, until at good time on the second day the curved prow had come to where the seafarers could see land, the sea-cliffs shine, towering hills, great headlands. Then was the sea crossed, the journey at end. Then quickly the men of the Geats climbed upon the shore, moored the wooden ship; mail-shirts rattled, dress for battle. They thanked God that the wave-way had been easy for them.

Then from the wall the Scyldings' guard who should watch over the sea-cliffs saw bright shields borne over the gangway, armor ready for battle; strong desire stirred him in mind to learn what the men were. He went riding on his horse to the shore, thane of Hrothgar, forcefully brandished a great spear in his hands, with formal words questioned them:

7. I.e., Beowulf the Geat, whose king was Hygelac.

"What are you, bearers of armor, dressed in mail-coats, who thus have come bringing a tall ship over the sea-road, over the water to this place? Lo, for a long time I have been guard of the coast, held watch by the sea so that no foe with a force of ships might work harm on the Danes' land: never have shield-bearers more openly undertaken to come ashore here; nor did you know for sure of a word of leave from our warriors, consent from my kinsmen. I have never seen a mightier warrior on earth than is one of you, a man in battle-dress. That is no retainer made to seem good by his weapons—unless his appearance belies him, his unequalled form. Now I must learn your lineage before you go any farther from here, spies on the Danes' land. Now you far-dwellers, sea-voyagers, hear what I think: you must straightway say where you have come from."

(IV.) To him replied the leader, the chief of the band unlocked his word-hoard: "We are men of the Geatish nation and Hygelac's hearth-companions. My father was well-known among the tribes, a noble leader named Ecgtheow. He lived many winters before he went on his way, an old man, from men's dwellings. Every wise man wide over the earth readily remembers him. Through friendly heart we have come to seek your lord, the son of Healfdene, protector of the people. Be good to us and tell us what to do: we have a great errand to the famous one, the king of the Danes. And I too do not think that anything ought to be kept secret: you know whether it is so, as we have indeed heard, that among the Scyldings I know not what foe, what dark doer of hateful deeds in the black nights, shows in terrible manner strange malice, injury and slaughter. In openness of heart I may teach Hrothgar remedy for that, how he, wise and good, shall overpower the foe—if change is ever to come to him, relief from evil's distress—and how his surging cares may be made to cool. Or else ever after he will suffer tribulations, constraint, while the best of houses remains there on its high place."

The guard spoke from where he sat on his horse, brave officer: "A sharp-witted shield-warrior who thinks well must be able to judge each of the two things, words and works. I understand this: that here is a troop friendly to the Scyldings' king. Go forward, bearing weapons and war-gear. I will show you the way; I shall also bid my fellow-thanes honorably to hold your boat against all enemies, your new-tarred ship on the sand, until again over the sea-streams it bears its beloved men to the Geatish shore, the wooden vessel with curved prow. May it be granted by fate that one who behaves so bravely pass whole through the battle-storm."

Then they set off. The boat lay fixed, rested on the rope, the deep-bosomed ship, fast at anchor. Boar-images [8] shone over cheek-guards gold-adorned, gleaming and fire-hardened—the war-minded boar held guard over fierce men. The warriors hastened, marched together until they might see the timbered hall, stately and shining with gold; for earth-dwellers under the skies that was the most famous of buildings in which the mighty one waited—its light gleamed over many lands. The battle-brave guide pointed out to them the shining house of the brave ones so that they might go straight to it. Warrior-like he turned his horse, then spoke words: "It is time for me to go back. The All-Wielding Father in His grace keep you safe in your undertakings. I shall go back to the sea to keep watch against hostile hosts."

(V.) The road was stone-paved, the path showed the way to the men in ranks. War-corselet shone, hard and hand-wrought, bright iron rings sang on their armor when they first came walking to the hall in their grim gear. Sea-weary they set down their broad shields, marvelously strong protections, against the wall of the building. Then they sat down on the bench—mail-shirts, warrior's clothing, rang out. Spears stood together, sea-men's weapons, ash steel-gray at the top. The armed band was worthy of its weapons.

Then a proud-spirited man [9] asked the warriors there about their lineage: "Where do you bring those gold-covered shields from, gray mail-shirts and visored helmets, this multitude of battle-shafts? I am Hrothgar's herald and officer. I have not seen strangers—so many men—more bold. I think that it is for daring—not for refuge, but for greatness of heart—that you have sought Hrothgar." The man known for his courage replied to him; the proud man of the Geats, hardy under helmet, spoke words in return: "We are Hygelac's table-companions. Beowulf is my name. I will tell my errand to Healfdene's son, the great prince your lord, if, good as he is, he will grant that we might address him." Wulfgar spoke—he was a man of the Wendels, his bold spirit known to many, his valor and wisdom: "I will ask the lord of the Danes about this, the Scyldings' king, the ring-giver, just as you request—will ask the glorious ruler about your voyage, and will quickly make known to you the answer the good man thinks best to give me."

He returned at once to where Hrothgar sat, old and hoary, with his company of earls. The man known for his valor went forward till he stood squarely before the Danes' king: he knew the custom of tried retainers. Wulfgar spoke to his lord and

8. Carved images of boars (sometimes represented as clothed like human warriors) were placed on helmets in the belief that they would protect the wearer in battle.

9. Identified below as Wulfgar.

friend: "Here have journeyed men of the Geats, come far over the sea's expanse. The warriors call their chief Beowulf. They ask that they, my prince, might exchange words with you. Do not refuse them your answer, gracious Hrothgar. From their war-gear they seem worthy of earls' esteem. Strong indeed is the chief who has led the warriors here."

(VI.) Hrothgar spoke, protector of the Scyldings: "I knew him when he was a boy. His father was called Ecgtheow: Hrethel of the Geats [1] gave him his only daughter for his home. Now has his hardy offspring come here, sought a fast friend. Then, too, seafarers who took gifts there to please the Geats used to say that he has in his handgrip the strength of thirty men, a man famous in battle. Holy God of His grace has sent him to us West-Danes, as I hope, against the terror of Grendel. I shall offer the good man treasures for his daring. Now make haste, bid them come in together to see my company of kinsmen. In your speech say to them also that they are welcome to the Danish people."

Then Wulfgar went to the hall's door, gave the message from within: "The lord of the East-Danes, my victorious prince, has bidden me say to you that he knows your noble ancestry, and that you brave-hearted men are welcome to him over the sea-swells. Now you may come in your war-dress, under your battle helmets, to see Hrothgar. Let your war-shields, your wooden spears, await here the outcome of the talk."

Then the mighty one rose, many a warrior about him, a company of strong thanes. Some waited there, kept watch over the weapons as the brave one bade them. Together they hastened, as the warrior directed them, under Heorot's roof. The war-leader, hardy under helmet, advanced till he stood on the hearth. Beowulf spoke, his mail-shirt glistened, armor-net woven by the blacksmith's skill: "Hail, Hrothgar! I am kinsman and thane of Hygelac. In my youth I have set about many brave deeds. The affair of Grendel was made known to me on my native soil: sea-travelers say that this hall, best of buildings, stands empty and useless to all warriors after the evening-light becomes hidden beneath the cover of the sky. Therefore my people, the best wise earls, advised me thus, lord Hrothgar, that I should seek you because they know what my strength can accomplish. They themselves looked on when, bloody from my foes, I came from the fight where I had bound five, destroyed a family of giants, and at night in the waves slain water-monsters, suffered great pain, avenged an affliction of the Weather-Geats on those who had asked for trouble—ground enemies to bits. And now alone I shall settle affairs with Grendel, the monster, the demon. Therefore, lord of the Bright-Danes, protector of the

1 Hrethel was the father of Hygelac and Beowulf's grandfather and guardian.

Scyldings, I will make a request of you, refuge of warriors, fair friend of nations, that you refuse me not, now that I have come so far, that alone with my company of earls, this band of hardy men, I may cleanse Heorot. I have also heard say that the monster in his recklessness cares not for weapons. Therefore, so that my liege lord Hygelac may be glad of me in his heart, I scorn to bear sword or broad shield, yellow wood, to the battle, but with my grasp I shall grapple with the enemy and fight for life, foe against foe. The one whom death takes can trust the Lord's judgment. I think that if he may accomplish it, unafraid he will feed on the folk of the Geats in the war-hall as he has often done on the flower of men. You will not need to hide my head [2] if death takes me, for he will have me blood-smeared; he will bear away my bloody flesh meaning to savor it, he will eat ruthlessly, the walker alone, will stain his retreat in the moor; no longer will you need trouble yourself to take care of my body. If battle takes me, send to Hygelac the best of war-clothes that protects my breast, finest of mail-shirts. It is a legacy of Hrethel, the work of Weland.[3] Fate always goes as it must."

(VII.) Hrothgar spoke, protector of the Scyldings: "For deeds done, my friend Beowulf, and for past favors you have sought us. A fight of your father's brought on the greatest of feuds. With his own hands he became the slayer of Heatholaf among the Wylfings. After that the country of the Weather-Geats might not keep him, for fear of war. From there he sought the folk of the South-Danes, the Honor-Scyldings, over the sea-swell. At that time I was first ruling the Danish people and, still in my youth, held the wide kingdom, hoard-city of heroes. Heorogar had died then, gone from life, my older brother, son of Healfdene—he was better than I. Afterwards I paid blood-money to end the feud; over the sea's back I sent to the Wylfings old treasures; he [4] swore oaths to me.

"It is a sorrow to me in spirit to say to any man what Grendel has brought me with his hatred—humiliation in Heorot, terrible violence. My hall-troop, warrior-band, has shrunk; fate has swept them away into Grendel's horror. (God may easily put an end to the wild ravager's deeds!) Full often over the ale-cups warriors made bold with beer have boasted that they would await with grim swords Grendel's attack in the beer-hall. Then in the morning this mead-hall was a hall shining with blood, when the day lightened, all the bench-floor blood-wet, a gore-hall. I had fewer faithful men, beloved retainers, for death had destroyed them. Now sit down to the feast and unbind your thoughts, your famous victories, as heart inclines."

2. I.e., "bury my body."
3. The blacksmith of the Norse gods.
4. Ecgtheow, whose feud with the Wylfings Hrothgar had settled.

[THE FEAST AT HEOROT]

Then was a bench cleared in the beer-hall for the men of the Geats all together. Then the stout-hearted ones went to sit down, proud in their might. A thane did his work who bore in his hands an embellished ale-cup, poured the bright drink. At times a scop sang, clear-voiced in Heorot. There was joy of brave men, no little company of Danes and Weather-Geats.

(VIII.) Unferth spoke, son of Ecglaf, who sat at the feet of the king of the Scyldings, unbound words of contention—to him was Beowulf's undertaking, the brave seafarer, a great vexation, for he would not allow that any other man of middle-earth should ever achieve more glory under the heavens than himself: "Are you that Beowulf who contended with Breca, competed in swimming on the broad sea, where for pride you explored the water, and for foolish boast ventured your lives in the deep? Nor might any man, friend nor enemy, keep you from the perilous venture of swimming in the sea. There you embraced the sea-streams with your arms, measured the sea-ways, flung forward your hands, glided over the ocean; the sea boiled with waves, with winter's swell. Seven nights you toiled in the water's power. He overcame you at swimming, had more strength. Then in the morning the sea bore him up among the Heathoraemas; from there he sought his own home, dear to his people, the land of the Brondings, the fair stronghold, where he had folk, castle, and treasures. All his boast against you the son of Beanstan carried out in deed. Therefore I expect the worse results for you—though you have prevailed everywhere in battles, in grim war—if you dare wait near Grendel a night-long space."

Beowulf spoke, the son of Ecgtheow: "Well, my friend Unferth, drunk with beer you have spoken a great many things about Breca—told about his adventures. I maintain the truth that I had more strength in the sea, hardship on the waves, than any other man. Like boys we agreed together and boasted—we were both in our first youth—that we would risk our lives in the salt sea, and that we did even so. We had naked swords, strong in our hands, when we went swimming; we thought to guard ourselves against whale-fishes. He could not swim at all far from me in the flood-waves, be quicker in the water, nor would I move away from him. Thus we were together on the sea for the time of five nights until the flood drove us apart, the swelling sea, coldest of weathers, darkening night, and the north wind battle-grim turned against us: rough were the waves. The anger of the sea-fishes was roused. Then my body-mail, hard and hand-linked, gave me help against my foes; the woven war-garment, gold-adorned, covered my breast. A fierce cruel attacker dragged me to the bottom, held me grim in his grasp, but it was granted me to reach the monster with my sword-point, my battle-blade. The war-stroke destroyed the mighty sea-beast—through my hand.

(IX.) "Thus often loathsome assailants pressed me hard. I served them with my good sword, as the right was. They had no joy at all of the feast, the malice-workers, that they should eat me, sit around a banquet near the sea-bottom. But in the morning, sword-wounded they lay on the shore, left behind by the waves, put to sleep by the blade, so that thereafter they would never hinder the passage of sea-voyagers over the deep water. Light came from the east, bright signal of God, the sea became still so that I might see the headlands, the windy walls of the sea. Fate often saves an undoomed man when his courage is good. In any case it befell me that I slew with my sword nine sea-monsters. I have not heard tell of a harder fight by night under heaven's arch, nor of a man more hard-pressed in the sea-streams. Yet I came out of the enemies' grasp alive, weary of my adventure. Then the sea bore me onto the lands of the Finns, the flood with its current, the surging waters.

"I have not heard say of you any such hard matching of might, such sword-terror. Breca never yet in the games of war—neither he nor you—achieved so bold a deed with bright swords (I do not much boast of it), though you became your brothers' slayer, your close kin; for that you will suffer punishment in hell, even though your wit is keen. I tell you truly, son of Ecglaf, that Grendel, awful monster, would never have performed so many terrible deeds against your chief, humiliation in Heorot, if your spirit, your heart, were so fierce in fight as you claim. But he has noticed that he need not much fear the hostility, not much dread the terrible sword-storm of your people, the Victory-Scyldings. He exacts forced levy, shows mercy to none of the Danish people; but he is glad, kills, carves for feasting, expects no fight from the Spear-Danes. But I shall show him soon now the strength and courage of the Geats, their warfare. Afterwards he will walk who may, glad to the mead, when the morning light of another day, the bright-clothed sun, shines from the south on the children of men."

Then was the giver of treasure in gladness, gray-haired and battle-brave. The lord of the Bright-Danes could count on help. The folk's guardian had heard from Beowulf a fast-resolved thought.

There was laughter of warriors, voices rang pleasant, words were cheerful. Wealhtheow came forth, Hrothgar's queen, mindful of customs, gold-adorned, greeted the men in the hall; and the noble woman offered the cup first to the keeper of the land of the East-Danes, bade him be glad at the beer-drinking, beloved of the people. In joy he partook of feast and hall-cup, king famous for victories. Then the woman of the Helmings went about to each one of the retainers, young and old, offered them the costly cup, until the time came that she brought the mead-bowl to Beowulf, the ring-adorned queen, mature of mind. Sure of speech she greeted the man of the Geats, thanked God that her wish was fulfilled, that she might trust in some man for help against deadly deeds. He took the cup, the warrior fierce in battle, from Wealhtheow, and then spoke, one ready for fight—Beowulf spoke, the son of Ecgtheow: "I resolved, when I set out on the sea, sat down in the sea-boat with my band of men, that I should altogether fulfill the will of your people or else fall in slaughter, fast in the foe's grasp. I shall achieve a deed of manly courage or else have lived to see in this mead-hall my ending day." These words were well-pleasing to the woman, the boast of the Geat. Gold-adorned, the noble folk-queen went to sit by her lord.

Then there were again as at first strong words spoken in the hall, the people in gladness, the sound of a victorious folk, until, in a little while, the son of Healfdene wished to seek his evening rest. He knew of the battle in the high hall that had been plotted by the monster, plotted from the time that they might see the light of the sun until the night, growing dark over all things, the shadowy shapes of darkness, should come gliding, black under the clouds. The company all arose. Then they saluted each other, Hrothgar and Beowulf, and Hrothgar wished him good luck, control of the wine-hall, and spoke these words: "Never before, since I could raise hand and shield, have I entrusted to any man the great hall of the Danes, except now to you. Hold now and guard the best of houses: remember your fame, show your great courage, keep watch against the fierce foe. You will not lack what you wish if you survive that deed of valor."

[THE FIGHT WITH GRENDEL]

(X.) Then Hrothgar went out of the hall with his company of warriors, the protector of the Scyldings. The war-chief would seek the bed of Wealhtheow the queen. The King of Glory—as men had learned—had appointed a hall-guard against Grendel; he had a special mission to the prince of the Danes: he kept watch against monsters.

And the man of the Geats had sure trust in his great might, the favor of the Ruler. Then he took off his shirt of armor, the helmet from his head, handed his embellished sword, best of irons, to an attendant, bade him keep guard over his war-gear. Then the good warrior spoke some boast-words before he went to his bed, Beowulf of the Geats: "I claim myself no poorer in war-strength, war works, than Grendel claims himself. Therefore I will not put him to sleep with a sword, so take away his life, though surely I might. He knows no good tools with which he might strike against me, cut my shield in pieces, though he is strong in fight. But we shall forgo the sword in the night—if he dare seek war without weapon—and then may wise God, Holy Lord, assign glory on whichever hand seems good to Him."

The battle-brave one laid himself down, the pillow received the earl's head, and about him many a brave seaman lay down to hall-rest. None of them thought that he would ever again seek from there his dear home, people or town where he had been brought up; for they knew that bloody death had carried off far too many men in the wine-hall, folk of the Danes. But the Lord granted to weave for them good fortune in war, for the folk of the Weather-Geats, comfort and help that they should quite overcome their foe through the might of one man, through his sole strength: the truth has been made known that mighty God has always ruled mankind.

There came gliding in the black night the walker in darkness. The warriors slept who should hold the horned house—all but one. It was known to men that when the Ruler did not wish it the hostile creature might not drag them away beneath the shadows. But he, lying awake for the fierce foe, with heart swollen in anger awaited the outcome of the fight.

(XI.) Then from the moor under the mist-hills Grendel came walking, wearing God's anger. The foul ravager thought to catch some one of mankind there in the high hall. Under the clouds he moved until he could see most clearly the wine-hall, treasure-house of men, shining with gold. That was not the first time that he had sought Hrothgar's home. Never before or since in his life-days did he find harder luck, hardier hall-thanes. The creature deprived of joy came walking to the hall. Quickly the door gave way, fastened with fire-forged bands, when he touched it with his hands. Driven by evil desire, swollen with rage, he tore it open, the hall's mouth. After that the foe at once stepped onto the shining floor, advanced angrily. From his eyes came a light not fair, most like a flame. He saw many men in the hall, a band of kinsmen all asleep together, a company of war-men. Then his heart laughed: dreadful monster, he thought that before the day came he would divide the life from the body of every one of them, for there had come to him a hope of full-feasting. It was not his fate that when that night was over he should feast on more of mankind.

The kinsman of Hygelac, mighty man, watched how the evil-doer would make his quick onslaught. Nor did the monster mean to delay it, but, starting his work, he suddenly seized a sleeping man, tore at him ravenously, bit into his bone-locks, drank the blood from his veins, swallowed huge morsels; quickly he had eaten all of the lifeless one, feet and hands. He stepped closer, then felt with his arm for the brave-hearted man on the bed, reached out towards him, the foe with his hand; at once in fierce response Beowulf seized it and sat up, leaning on his own arm. Straightway the fosterer of crimes knew that he had not encountered on middle-earth, anywhere in this world, a harder hand-grip from another man. In mind he became frightened, in his spirit: not for that might he escape the sooner. His heart was eager to get away, he would flee to his hiding-place, seek his rabble of devils. What he met there was not such as he had ever before met in the days of his life. Then the kinsman of Hygelac, the good man, thought of his evening's speech, stood upright and laid firm hold on him: his fingers cracked. The giant was pulling away, the earl stepped forward. The notorious one thought to move farther away, wherever he could, and flee his way from there to his fen-retreat; he knew his fingers' power to be in a hateful grip. That was a painful journey that the loathsome despoiler had made to Heorot. The retainers' hall rang with the noise—terrible drink [5] for all the Danes, the house-dwellers, every brave man, the earls. Both were enraged, fury-filled, the two who meant to control the hall. The building resounded. Then was it much wonder that the wine-hall withstood them joined in fierce fight, that it did not fall to the ground, the fair earth-dwelling; but it was so firmly made fast with iron bands, both inside and outside, joined by skillful smith-craft. There started from the floor—as I have heard say—many a mead-bench, gold-adorned, when the furious ones fought. No wise men of the Scyldings ever before thought that any men in any manner might break it down, splendid with bright horns, have skill to destroy it, unless flame should embrace it, swallow it in fire. Noise rose up, sound strange enough. Horrible fear came upon the North-Danes, upon every one of those who heard the weeping from the wall, God's enemy sing his terrible song, song without triumph—the hell-slave bewail his pain. There held him fast he who of men was strongest of might in the days of this life.

(XII.) Not for anything would the protector of warriors let the murderous guest go off alive: he did not consider his life-days of use to any of the nations. There more than enough of Beowulf's earls drew swords, old heirlooms, wished to protect

5. The metaphor reflects the idea that the chief purpose of a hall such as Heorot was as a place for men to feast in.

the life of their dear lord, famous prince, however they might. They did not know when they entered the fight, hardy-spirited warriors, and when they thought to hew him on every side, to seek his soul, that not any of the best of irons on earth, no war-sword, would touch the evil-doer: for with a charm he had made victory-weapons useless, every sword-edge. His departure to death from the time of this life was to be wretched; and the alien spirit was to travel far off into the power of fiends. Then he who before had brought trouble of heart to mankind, committed many crimes—he was at war with God—found that his body would do him no good, for the great-hearted kinsman of Hygelac had him by the hand. Each was hateful to the other alive. The awful monster had lived to feel pain in his body, a huge wound in his shoulder was exposed, his sinews sprang apart, his bone-locks broke. Glory in battle was given to Beowulf. Grendel must flee from there, mortally sick, seek his joyless home in the fen-slopes. He knew the more surely that his life's end had come, the full number of his days. For all the Danes was their wish fulfilled after the bloody fight. Thus he who had lately come from far off, wise and stout-hearted, had purged Heorot, saved Hrothgar's house from affliction. He rejoiced in his night's work, a deed to make famous his courage. The man of the Geats had fulfilled his boast to the East-Danes; so too he had remedied all the grief, the malice-caused sorrow that they had endured before, and had had to suffer from harsh necessity, no small distress. That was clearly proved when the battle-brave man set the hand up under the curved roof—the arm and the shoulder: there all together was Grendel's grasp.

[CELEBRATION AT HEOROT]

(XIII.) Then in the morning, as I have heard, there was many a warrior about the gift-hall. Folk-chiefs came from far and near over the wide-stretching ways to look on the wonder, the foot-prints of the foe. Nor did his going from life seem sad to any of the men who saw the tracks of the one without glory—how, weary-hearted, overcome with injuries, he moved on his way from there to the mere[6] of the water-monsters with life-failing footsteps, death-doomed and in flight. There the water was boiling with blood, the horrid surge of waves swirling, all mixed with hot gore, sword-blood. Doomed to die he had hidden, then, bereft of joys, had laid down his life in his fen-refuge, his heathen soul: there hell took him.

From there old retainers—and many a young man, too—turned back in their glad journey to ride from the mere, high-

6. Lake.

spirited on horseback, warriors on steeds. There was Beowulf's fame spoken of; many a man said—and not only once—that, south nor north, between the seas, over the wide earth, no other man under the sky's expanse was better of those who bear shields, more worthy of ruling. Yet they found no fault with their own dear lord, gracious Hrothgar, for he was a good king. At times battle-famed men let their brown horses gallop, let them race where the paths seemed fair, known for their excellence. At times a thane of the king, a man skilled at telling adventures, songs stored in his memory, who could recall many of the stories of the old days, wrought a new tale in well-joined words; this man undertook with his art to recite in turn Beowulf's exploit, and skillfully to tell an apt tale, to lend words to it.

He spoke everything that he had heard tell of Sigemund's valorous deeds, many a strange thing, the strife of Waels's son,[7] his far journeys, feuds and crimes, of which the children of men knew nothing—except for Fitela with him, to whom he would tell everything, the uncle to his nephew, for they were always friends in need in every fight. Many were the tribes of giants that they had laid low with their swords. For Sigemund there sprang up after his death-day no little glory—after he, hardy in war, had killed the dragon, keeper of the treasure-hoard: under the hoary stone the prince's son had ventured alone, a daring deed, nor was Fitela with him. Yet it turned out well for him, so that his sword went through the gleaming worm and stood fixed in the wall, splendid weapon: the dragon lay dead of the murdering stroke. Through his courage the great warrior had brought it about that he might at his own wish enjoy the ring-hoard. He loaded the sea-boat, bore into the ship's bosom the bright treasure, offspring of Waels. The hot dragon melted.

He was adventurer most famous, far and wide through the nations, for deeds of courage—he had prospered from that before, the protector of warriors—after the war-making of Heremod had come to an end, his strength and his courage.[8] Among the Jutes Heremod came into the power of his enemies, was betrayed, quickly dispatched. Surging sorrows had oppressed him too long: he had become a great care to his people, to all his princes; for many a wise man in former times had bewailed the journey of the fierce-hearted one—people who had counted on him as a relief from affliction—that that king's son should prosper, take the rank of his father, keep guard over the folk, the treasure and stronghold, the kindgom of heroes, the home of the Scyldings. The kinsman of Hygelac became dearer to his friends, to all man-

7. Waels was Sigemund's father.

8. Heremod was an unsuccessful king of the Danes, one who began brilliantly but became cruel and avaricious, ultimately having to take refuge among the Jutes, who put him to death. His reputation was thus overshadowed by that of Sigemund.

kind: crime took possession of Heremod.

Sometimes racing their horses they passed over the sand-covered ways. By then the morning light was far advanced, hastening on. Many a stout-hearted warrior went to the high hall to see the strange wonder. The king himself walked forth from the women's apartment, the guardian of the ring-hoards, secure in his fame, known for his excellence, with much company; and his queen with him passed over the path to the mead-hall with a troop of attendant women.

(XIV.) Hrothgar spoke—he had gone to the hall, taken his stand on the steps, looked at the high roof shining with gold, and at Grendel's hand: "For this sight may thanks be made quickly to the Almighty: I endured much from the foe, many griefs from Grendel: God may always work wonder upon wonder, the Guardian of Heaven. It was not long ago that I did not expect ever to live to see relief from any of my woes—when the best of houses stood shining with blood, stained with slaughter, a far-reaching woe for each of my counselors, for every one, since none thought he could ever defend the people's stronghold from its enemies, from demons and evil spirits. Now through the Lord's might a warrior has accomplished the deed that all of us with our skill could not perform. Yes, she may say, whatever woman brought forth this son among mankind—if she still lives—that the God of Old was kind to her in her child-bearing. Now, Beowulf, best of men, in my heart I will love you as a son: keep well this new kinship. To you will there be no lack of the good things of the world that I have in my possession. Full often I have made reward for less, done honor with gifts to a lesser warrior, weaker in fighting. With your deeds you yourself have made sure that your glory will be ever alive. May the Almighty reward you with good—as just now he has done."

Beowulf spoke, the son of Ecgtheow: "With much good will we have achieved this work of courage, that fight, have ventured boldly against the strength of the unknown one. I should have wished rather that you might have seen him, your enemy brought low among your furnishings. I thought quickly to bind him on his deathbed with hard grasp, so that because of my hand-grip he should lie struggling for life—unless his body should escape. I could not stop his going, since the Lord did not wish it, nor did I hold him firmly enough for that, my life-enemy: he was too strong, the foe in his going. Yet to save his life he has left his hand behind to show that he was here—his arm and shoulder; nor by that has the wretched creature bought any comfort; none the longer will the loathsome ravager live, hard-pressed by his crimes, for a wound has clutched him hard in its strong grip, in deadly bonds. There, like a man outlawed for guilt, he shall await the great judgment, how the bright Lord will decree for him."

Then was the warrior more silent in boasting speech of warlike deeds, the son of Ecglaf,[9] after the nobles had looked at the hand, now high on the roof through the strength of a man, the foe's fingers. The end of each one, each of the nail-places, was most like steel; the hand-spurs of the heathen warrior were monstrous spikes. Everyone said that no hard thing would hurt him, no iron good from old times would harm the bloody battle-hand of the monster.

(XV.) Then was it ordered that Heorot be within quickly adorned by hands. Many there were, both men and women, who made ready the wine-hall, the guest-building. The hangings on the walls shone with gold, many a wondrous sight for each man who looks on such things. That bright building was much damaged, though made fast within by iron bonds, and its door-hinges sprung; the roof alone came through unharmed when the monster, outlawed for his crimes, turned in flight, in despair of his life. That is not easy to flee from—let him try it who will—but driven by need one must seek the place prepared for earth-dwellers, soul-bearers, the sons of men, the place where, after its feasting, one's body will sleep fast in its death-bed.

Then had the proper time come that Healfdene's son should go to the hall; the king himself would share in the feast. I have never heard that a people in a larger company bore themselves better about their treasure-giver. Men who were known for courage sat at the benches, rejoiced in the feast. Their kinsmen, stout-hearted Hrothgar and Hrothulf, partook fairly of many a mead-cup in the high hall. Heorot within was filled with friends: the Scylding-people had not then known treason's web.[1]

Then the son of Healfdene gave Beowulf a golden standard to reward his victory—a decorated battle-banner—a helmet and mail-shirt: many saw the glorious, costly sword borne before the warrior. Beowulf drank of the cup in the mead-hall. He had no need to be ashamed before fighting men of those rich gifts. I have not heard of many men who gave four precious, gold-adorned things to another on the ale-bench in a more friendly way. The rim around the helmet's crown had a head-protection, wound of wire, so that no battle-hard sharp sword might badly hurt him when the shield-warrior should go against his foe. Then the people's protector commanded eight horses with golden bridles to be led into the hall, within the walls. The saddle of one of them stood shining with hand-ornaments, adorned with jewels: that had been

9. I.e., Unferth, who had taunted Beowulf the night before.

1. A reference to the later history of the Danes, when, after Hrothgar's death, his nephew Hrothulf apparently drove his son and successor Hrethric from the throne.

the war-seat of the high king when the son of Healfdene would join sword-play: never did the warfare of the wide-known one fail when men died in battle. And then the prince of Ing's friends[2] yielded possession of both, horses and weapons, to Beowulf: he bade him use them well. So generously the famous prince, guardian of the hoard, repaid the warrior's battle-deeds with horses and treasure that no man will ever find fault with them—not he that will speak truth according to what is right.

(XVI.) Then further the lord gave treasure to each of the men on the mead-bench who had made the sea-voyage with Beowulf, gave heirlooms; and he commanded that gold be paid for the one whom in his malice Grendel had killed—as he would have killed more if wise God and the man's courage had not forestalled that fate. The Lord guided all the race of men then, as he does now. Yet is discernment everywhere best, forethought of mind. Many a thing dear and loath he shall live to see who here in the days of trouble long makes use of the world.

There was song and music together before Healfdene's battle-leader, the wooden harp touched, tale oft told, when Hrothgar's scop should speak hall-pastime among the mead-benches . . . [of] Finn's retainers when the sudden disaster fell upon them. . . .[3]

The hero of the Half-Danes, Hnaef of the Scyldings, was fated to fall on Frisian battlefield. And no need had Hildeburh[4] to praise the good faith of the Jutes: blameless she was deprived of her dear ones at the shield-play, of son and brother; wounded by spears they fell to their fate. That was a mournful woman. Not without cause did Hoc's daughter lament the decree of destiny when morning came and she might see, under the sky, the slaughter of kinsmen—where before she had the greatest of world's joy. The fight took away all Finn's thanes except for only a few, so that he could in no way continue the battle on the field against Hengest, nor protect the survivors by fighting against the prince's thane. But they offered them peace-terms,[5] that they should clear

2. Ing was a legendary Danish king, and his "friends" are the Danes.

3. The lines introducing the scop's song seem faulty. The story itself is recounted in a highly allusive way, and many of its details are obscure, though some help is offered by an independent version of the story given in a fragmentary Old English lay called *The Fight at Finnsburg*.

4. Hildeburh, daughter of the former Danish king Hoc and sister of the ruling Danish king Hnaef, was married to Finn, king of the Jutes (Frisians). Hnaef with a party of Danes made what was presumably a friendly visit to Hildeburh and Finn at their home Finnsburg, but during a feast a quarrel broke out between the Jutes and the Danes (since the scop's sympathies are with the Danes, he ascribes the cause to the bad faith of the Jutes), and in the ensuing fight Hnaef and his nephew, the son of Finn and Hildeburh, were killed, along with many other Danes and Jutes.

5. It is not clear who proposed the peace terms, but in view of the teller's Danish sympathies, it was probably the Jutes that sought the uneasy truce from Hengest, who became the Danes' leader after Hnaef's death. The truce imposed upon Hengest and the Danes the intolerable condition of having to dwell in peace with the Jutish king who was responsible for the death of their own king.

another building for them, hall and high seat, that they might have control of half of it with the sons of the Jutes; and at givings of treasure the son of Folcwalda[6] should honor the Danes each day, should give Hengest's company rings, such gold-plated treasure as that with which he would cheer the Frisians' kin in the high hall. Then on both sides they confirmed the fast peace-compact. Finn declared to Hengest, with oaths deep-sworn, unfeigned, that he would hold those who were left from the battle in honor in accordance with the judgment of his counselors, so that by words or by works no man should break the treaty nor because of malice should ever mention that, princeless, the Danes followed the slayer of their own ring-giver, since necessity forced them. If with rash speech any of the Frisians should insist upon calling to mind the cause of murderous hate, then the sword's edge should settle it.

The funeral pyre was made ready and gold brought up from the hoard. The best of the warriors of the War-Scyldings[7] was ready on the pyre. At the fire it was easy to see many a blood-stained battle-shirt, boar-image all golden—iron-hard swine—many a noble destroyed by wounds: more than one had died in battle. Then Hildeburh bade give her own son to the flames on Hnaef's pyre, burn his blood vessels, put him in the fire at the shoulder of his uncle. The woman mourned, sang her lament. The warrior took his place.[8] The greatest of death-fires wound to the skies, roared before the barrow. Heads melted as blood sprang out—wounds opened wide, hate-bites of the body. Fire swallowed them—greediest of spirits—all of those whom war had taken away from both peoples: their strength had departed.

(XVII.) Then warriors went to seek their dwellings, bereft of friends, to behold Friesland, their homes and high city.[9] Yet Hengest stayed on with Finn for a winter darkened with the thought of slaughter, all desolate. He thought of his land, though he might not drive his ring-prowed ship over the water—the sea boiled with storms, strove with the wind, winter locked the waves in ice-bonds—until another year came to men's dwellings, just as it does still, glorious bright weather always watching for its time. Then winter was gone, earth's lap fair, the exile was eager to go, the guest from the dwelling: [yet] more he thought of revenge for his wrongs than of the sea-journey—if he might bring about a fight where he could take account of the sons of the Jutes with his iron. So he made no refusal of the world's

6. I.e., Finn.
7. I.e., Hnaef.
8. The line is obscure, but it perhaps means that the body of Hildeburh's son was placed on the pyre.
9. This seems to refer to the few survivors on the Jutish side.

custom when the son of Hunlaf[1] placed on his lap Battle-Bright, best of swords: its edges were known to the Jutes. Thus also to war-minded Finn in his turn cruel sword-evil came in his own home, after Guthlaf and Oslaf complained of the grim attack, the injury after the sea-journey, assigned blame for their lot of woes: breast might not contain the restless heart. Then was the hall reddened from foes' bodies, and thus Finn slain, the king in his company, and the queen taken. The warriors of the Scyldings bore to ship all the hall-furnishings of the land's king, whatever of necklaces, skillfully wrought treasures, they might find at Finn's home. They brought the noble woman on the sea-journey to the Danes, led her to her people.

The lay was sung to the end, the song of the scop. Joy mounted again, bench-noise brightened, cup-bearers poured wine from wonderful vessels. Then Wealhtheow came forth to walk under gold crown to where the good men sat, nephew and uncle: their friendship was then still unbroken, each true to the other.[2] There too Unferth the spokesman sat at the feet of the prince of the Scyldings: each of them trusted his spirit, that he had much courage, though he was not honorable to his kinsmen at sword-play. Then the woman of the Scyldings spoke:

"Take this cup my noble lord, giver of treasure. Be glad, gold-friend of warriors, and speak to the Geats with mild words, as a man ought to do. Be gracious to the Geats, mindful of gifts [which] [3] you now have from near and far. They have told me that you would have the warrior for your son. Heorot is purged, the bright ring-hall. Enjoy while you may many rewards, and leave to your kinsmen folk and kingdom when you must go forth to look on the Ruler's decree. I know my gracious Hrothulf, that he will hold the young warriors in honor if you, friend of the Scyldings, leave the world before him. I think he will repay our sons with good if he remembers all the favors we did to his pleasure and honor when he was a child."

Then she turned to the bench where her sons were, Hrethric and Hrothmund, and the sons of the warriors, young men together. There sat the good man Beowulf of the Geats beside the two brothers.

(XVIII.) The cup was borne to him and welcome offered

1. The text is open to various interpretations. The one adopted here assumes that the Dane Hunlaf, brother of Guthlaf and Oslaf, had been killed in the fight, and that ultimately Hunlaf's son demanded vengeance by the symbolical act of placing his father's sword in Hengest's lap, while at the same time Guthlaf and Oslaf reminded Hengest of the Jutes' treachery. It is not clear whether the subsequent fight in which Finn was killed was waged by the Danish survivors alone, or whether the party first went back to Denmark and then returned to Finnsburg with reinforcements.

2. See section XV, note 1, above.

3. The text seems corrupt.

in friendly words to him, and twisted gold courteously bestowed on him, two arm-ornaments, a mail-shirt and rings, the largest of necklaces of those that I have heard spoken of on earth. I have heard of no better hoard-treasure under the heavens since Hama carried away to his bright city the necklace of the Brosings,[4] chain and rich setting: he fled the treacherous hatred of Eormenric, got eternal favor. This ring Hygelac of the Geats,[5] grandson of Swerting, had on his last venture, when beneath his battle-banner he defended his treasure, protected the spoils of war: fate took him when for pride he sought trouble, feud with the Frisians. Over the cup of the waves the mighty prince wore that treasure, precious stone. He fell beneath his shield; the body of the king came into the grasp of the Franks, his breast-armor and the neck-ring together. Lesser warriors plundered the fallen after the war-harvest: people of the Geats held the place of corpses.

The hall was filled with noise. Wealhtheow spoke, before the company she said to him: "Wear this ring, beloved Beowulf, young man, with good luck, and make use of this mail-shirt from the people's treasure, and prosper well; make yourself known with your might, and be kind of counsel to these boys: I shall remember to reward you for that. You have brought it about that, far and near, for a long time all men shall praise you, as wide as the sea surrounds the shores, home of the winds. While you live, prince, be prosperous. I wish you well of your treasure. Much favored one, be kind of deeds to my son. Here is each earl true to other, mild of heart, loyal to his lord; the thanes are at one, the people obedient, the retainers cheered with drink do as I bid."

Then she walked to her seat. There was the best of feasts, men drank wine. They did not know the fate, the grim decree made long before, as it came to pass to many of the earls after evening had come and Hrothgar had gone to his chambers, the noble one to his rest. A great number of men remained in the hall, just as they had often done before. They cleared the benches from the floor. It was spread over with beds and pillows. One of the beer-drinkers, ripe and fated to die, lay down to his hall-rest. They set at their heads their battle-shields, bright wood; there on the bench it was easy to see above each man his helmet that towered in battle, his ringed mail-shirt, his great spear-wood. It was their custom to be always ready for war whether at home or in the

4. The Brisings' (Brosings') necklace had been worn by the goddess Freya. Nothing more is known of this story of Hama, who seems to have stolen the necklace from the famous Gothic king Eormenric.

5. Beowulf is later said to have presented the necklace to Hygelac's queen, Hygd, though here Hygelac is said to have been wearing it on his ill-fated expedition against the Franks and Frisians, into whose hands it fell at his death.

field, in any case at any time that need should befall their liege lord: that was a good nation.

[GRENDEL'S MOTHER'S ATTACK]

(XIX.) Then they sank to sleep. One paid sorely for his evening rest, just as had often befallen them when Grendel guarded the gold-hall, wrought wrong until the end came, death after misdeeds. It came to be seen, wide-known to men, that after the bitter battle an avenger still lived for an evil space: Grendel's mother, woman, monster-wife, was mindful of her misery, she who had to dwell in the terrible water, the cold currents, after Cain became sword-slayer of his only brother, his own father's son. Then Cain went as an outlaw to flee the cheerful life of men, marked for his murder, held to the wasteland. From him sprang many a devil sent by fate. Grendel was one of them, hateful outcast who at Heorot found a waking man waiting his warfare. There the monster had laid hold upon him, but he was mindful of the great strength, the large gift God had given him, and relied on the Almighty for favor, comfort and help. By that he overcame the foe, subdued the hell-spirit. Then he went off wretched, bereft of joy, to seek his dying-place, enemy of mankind. And his mother, still greedy and gallows-grim, would go on a sorrowful venture, avenge her son's death.

Then she came to Heorot where the Ring-Danes slept throughout the hall. Then change came quickly to the earls there, when Grendel's mother made her way in. The attack was the less terrible by just so much as is the strength of women, the war-terror of a wife, less than an armed man's when a hard blade, forge-hammered, a sword shining with blood, good of its edges, cuts the stout boar on a helmet opposite. Then in the hall was hard-edged sword raised from the seat, many a broad shield lifted firmly in hand: none thought of helmet, of wide mail-shirt, when the terror seized him. She was in haste, would be gone out from there, protect her life after she was discovered. Swiftly she had taken fast hold on one of the nobles, then she went to the fen. He was one of the men between the seas most beloved of Hrothgar in the rank of retainer, a noble shield-warrior whom she destroyed at his rest, a man of great repute. Beowulf was not there, for earlier, after the treasure-giving, another lodging had been appointed for the renowned Geat. Outcry arose in Heorot: she had taken, in its gore, the famed hand. Care was renewed, come again on the dwelling. That was not a good bargain, that on both sides they had to pay with the lives of friends.

Then was the old king, the hoary warrior, of bitter mind when he learned that his chief thane was lifeless, his dearest man dead. Quickly Beowulf was fetched to the bed-chamber, man happy in victory. At daybreak together with his earls he went, the noble champion himself with his retainers, to where the wise one was, waiting to know whether after tidings of woe the All-Wielder would ever bring about change for him. The worthy warrior walked over the floor with his retainers—hall-wood resounded —that he might address words to the wise prince of Ing's friends, asked if the night had been pleasant according to his desires.

(XX.) Hrothgar spoke, protector of the Scyldings: "Ask not about pleasure. Sorrow is renewed to the people of the Danes: Aeschere is dead, Yrmenlaf's elder brother, my speaker of wisdom and my bearer of counsel, my shoulder-companion when we used to defend our heads in battle, when troops clashed, beat on boar-images. Whatever an earl should be, a man good from old times, such was Aeschere. Now a wandering murderous spirit has slain him with its hands in Heorot. I do not know by what way the awful creature, glorying in its prey, has made its retreat, gladdened by its feast. She has avenged the feud—that last night you killed Grendel with hard hand-grips, savagely, because too long he had diminished and destroyed my people. He fell in the fight, his life forfeited, and now the other has come, a mighty worker of wrong, would avenge her kinsman, and has carried far her revenge—as many a thane may think who weeps in his spirit for his treasure-giver, bitter sorrow in heart. Now the hand lies lifeless that was strong in support of all your desires.

"I have heard landsmen, my people, hall-counselors, say this, that they have seen two such huge walkers in the wasteland holding to the moors, alien spirits. One of them, so far as they could clearly discern, was the likeness of a woman. The other wretched shape trod the tracks of exile in the form of a man, except that he was bigger than any other man. Land-dwellers in the old days named him Grendel. They know of no father, whether in earlier times any was begotten for them among the dark spirits. They hold to the secret land, the wolf-slopes, the windy headlands, the dangerous fen-paths where the mountain stream goes down under the darkness of the hills, the flood under the earth. It is not far from here, measured in miles, that the mere stands; over it hang frost-covered woods, trees fast of root close over the water. There each night may be seen fire on the flood, a fearful wonder. Of the sons of men there lives none, old of wisdom, who knows the bottom. Though the heath-stalker, the strong-horned hart, harassed by hounds makes for the forest after long flight, rather will he give his life, his being, on the bank than save his head by entering. That is no pleasant place. From it the surging waves rise up black to the heavens when the wind stirs up awful storms, until the air becomes gloomy, the skies weep. Now once again is the cure in you alone. You do not yet know the land, the perilous place, where you might find the seldom-seen creature: seek if you dare. I will give you wealth for the feud, old treasure, as I did before, twisted gold—if you come away."

(XXI.) Beowulf spoke, the son of Ecgtheow: "Sorrow not, wise warrior. It is better for a man to avenge his friend than much mourn. Each of us must await his end of the world's life. Let him who may get glory before death: that is best for the warrior after he has gone from life. Arise, guardian of the kingdom, let us go at once to look on the track of Grendel's kin. I promise you this: she will not be lost under cover, not in the earth's bosom nor in the mountain woods nor at the bottom of the sea, go where she will. This day have patience in every woe—as I expect you to."

Then the old man leapt up, thanked God, the mighty Lord, that the man had so spoken. Then was a horse bridled for Hrothgar, a curly-maned mount. The wise king moved in state; the band of shield-bearers marched on foot. The tracks were seen wide over the wood-paths where she had gone on the ground, made her way forward over the dark moor, borne lifeless the best of retainers of those who watched over their home with Hrothgar. The son of noble forebears[6] moved over the steep rocky slopes, narrow paths where only one could go at a time, an unfamiliar trail, steep hills many a lair of water-monsters. He went before with a few wise men to spy out the country, until suddenly he found mountain trees leaning out over hoary stone, a joyless wood: water lay beneath, bloody and troubled. It was pain of heart for all the Danes to suffer, for the friends of the Scyldings, for many a thane, grief to each earl when on the cliff over the water they came upon Aeschere's head. The flood boiled with blood—the men looked upon it—with hot gore. Again and again the horn sang its urgent war-song. The whole troop sat down to rest. Then they saw on the water many a snake-shape, strong sea-serpents exploring the mere, and water-monsters lying on the slopes of the shore such as those that in the morning often attend a perilous journey on the paths of the sea, serpents and wild beasts.

These fell away from the shore, fierce and rage-swollen: they had heard the bright sound, the war-horn sing. One of them a man of the Geats with his bow cut off from his life, his water-warring, after the hard war-arrow stuck in his heart: he was weaker in swimming the lake when death took him. Straightway he was hard beset on the waves with barbed boar-spears, strongly surrounded, pulled up on the shore, strange spawn of the waves. The men looked on the terrible alien thing.

6. I.e., Hrothgar.

Beowulf put on his warrior's dress, had no fear for his life. His war-shirt, hand-fashioned, broad and well-worked, was to explore the mere: it knew how to cover his body-cave so that foe's grip might not harm his heart, or grasp of angry enemy his life. But the bright helmet guarded his head, one which was to stir up the lake-bottom, seek out the troubled water—made rich with gold, surrounded with splendid bands, as the weapon-smith had made it in far-off days, fashioned it wonderfully, set it about with boar-images so that thereafter no sword or battle-blade might bite into it. And of his strong supports that was not the least which Hrothgar's spokesman[7] lent to his need: Hrunting was the name of the hilted sword; it was one of the oldest of ancient treasures; its edge was iron, decorated with poison-stripes, hardened with battle-sweat. Never had it failed in war any man of those who grasped it in their hands, who dared enter on dangerous enterprises, onto the common meeting place of foes: this was not the first time that it should do work of courage. Surely the son of Ecglaf, great of strength, did not have in mind what, drunk with wine, he had spoken, when he lent that weapon to a better sword-fighter. He did not himself dare to risk his life under the warring waves, to engage his courage: there he lost his glory, his name for valor. It was not so with the other when he had armed himself for battle.

[BEOWULF ATTACKS GRENDEL'S MOTHER]

(XXII.) Beowulf spoke, the son of Ecgtheow: "Think now, renowned son of Healfdene, wise king, now that I am ready for the venture, gold-friend of warriors, of what we said before, that, if at your need I should go from life, you would always be in a father's place for me when I am gone: be guardian of my young retainers, my companions, if battle should take me. The treasure you gave me, beloved Hrothgar, send to Hygelac. The lord of the Geats may know from the gold, the son of Hrethel may see when he looks on that wealth, that I found a ring-giver good in his gifts, enjoyed him while I might. And let Unferth have the old heirloom, the wide-known man my splendid-waved sword, hard-edged: with Hrunting I shall get glory, or death will take me."

After these words the man of the Weather-Geats turned away boldly, would wait for no answer: the surging water took the warrior. Then was it a part of a day before he might see the bottom's floor. Straightway that which had held the flood's tract a hundred half-years, ravenous for prey, grim and greedy, saw that some man from above was exploring the dwelling of monsters. Then she groped toward him, took the warrior in her awful

7. I.e., Unferth.

grip. Yet not the more for that did she hurt his hale body within: his ring-armor shielded him about on the outside so that she could not pierce the war-dress, the linked body-mail, with hateful fingers. Then as she came to the bottom the sea-wolf bore the ring-prince to her house so that—no matter how brave he was—he might not wield weapons; but many monsters attacked him in the water, many a sea-beast tore at his mail-shirt with war-tusks, strange creatures afflicted him. Then the earl saw that he was in some hostile hall where no water harmed him at all, and the flood's onrush might not touch him because of the hall-roof. He saw firelight, a clear blaze shine bright.

Then the good man saw the accursed dweller in the deep, the mighty mere-woman. He gave a great thrust to his sword—his hand did not withhold the stroke—so that the etched blade sang at her head a fierce war-song. Then the stranger found that the battle-lightning would not bite, harm her life, but the edge failed the prince in his need: many a hand-battle had it endured before, often sheared helmet, war-coat of man fated to die: this was the first time for the rare treasure that its glory had failed.

But still he was resolute, not slow of his courage, mindful of fame, the kinsman of Hygelac. Then, angry warrior, he threw away the sword, wavy-patterned, bound with ornaments, so that it lay on the ground, hard and steel-edged: he trusted in his strength, his mighty hand-grip. So ought a man to do when he thinks to get long-lasting praise in battle: he cares not for his life. Then he seized by the hair Grendel's mother—the man of the War-Geats did not shrink from the fight. Battle-hardened, now swollen with rage, he pulled his deadly foe so that she fell to the floor. Quickly in her turn she repaid him his gift with her grim claws and clutched at him: then weary-hearted, the strongest of warriors, of foot-soldiers, stumbled so that he fell. Then she sat upon the hall-guest and drew her knife, broad and bright-edged. She would avenge her child, her only son. The woven breast-armor lay on his shoulder: that protected his life, withstood entry of point or of edge. Then the son of Ecgtheow would have fared amiss under the wide ground, the champion of the Geats, if the battle-shirt had not brought help, the hard war-net—and holy God brought about victory in war; the wise Lord, Ruler of the Heavens, decided it with right, easily, when Beowulf had stood up again.

XXIII. Then he saw among the armor a victory-blessed blade, an old sword made by the giants, strong of its edges, glory of warriors: it was the best of weapons, except that it was larger than any other man might bear to war-sport, good and adorned, the work of giants. He seized the linked hilt, he who fought for the Scyldings, savage and slaughter-bent, drew the patterned-blade; desperate of life, he struck angrily so that it bit her hard on the neck, broke the bone-rings. The blade went through all the doomed body. She fell to the floor, the sword was sweating, the man rejoiced in his work.

The blaze brightened, light shone within, just as from the sky heaven's candle shines clear. He looked about the building; then he moved along the wall, raised his weapon hard by the hilt, Hygelac's thane, angry and resolute: the edge was not useless to the warrior, for he would quickly repay Grendel for the many attacks he had made on the West-Danes—many more than the one time when he slew in their sleep fifteen hearth-companions of Hrothgar, devoured men of the Danish people while they slept, and another such number bore away, a hateful prey. He had paid him his reward for that, the fierce champion, for there he saw Grendel, weary of war, lying at rest, lifeless with the wounds he had got in the fight at Heorot. The body bounded wide when it suffered the blow after death, the hard sword-swing; and thus he cut off his head.

At once the wise men who were watching the water with Hrothgar saw that the surging waves were troubled, the lake stained with blood. Gray-haired, old, they spoke together of the good warrior, that they did not again expect of the chief that he would come victorious to seek their great king; for many agreed on it, that the sea-wolf had destroyed him.

Then came the ninth hour of the day. The brave Scyldings left the hill. The gold-friend of warriors went back to his home. The strangers sat sick at heart and stared at the mere. They wished—and did not expect—that they would see their beloved lord himself.

Then the blade began to waste away from the battle-sweat, the war-sword into battle-icicles. That was a wondrous thing, that it should all melt, most like the ice when the Father loosens the frost's fetters, undoes the water-bonds—He Who has power over seasons and times: He is the true Ruler. Beowulf did not take from the dwelling, the man of the Weather-Geats, more treasures—though he saw many there—but only the head and the hilt, bright with jewels. The sword itself had already melted, its patterned blade burned away: the blood was too hot for it, the spirit that had died there too poisonous. Quickly he was swimming, he who had lived to see the fall of his foes; he plunged up through the water. The currents were all cleansed, the great tracts of the water, when the dire spirit left her life-days and this loaned world.

Then the protector of seafarers came toward the land, swimming stout-hearted; he had joy of his sea-booty, the great burden he had with him. They went to meet him, thanked God, the strong band of thanes, rejoiced in their chief that they might see him again sound. Then the helmet and war-shirt of the mighty one were quickly loosened. The lake drowsed, the water beneath the skies, stained with blood. They went forth on the foot-tracks, glad in their hearts, measured the path back, the known ways, men bold as kings. They bore the head from the mere's cliff, toilsomely for each of the great-hearted ones: four of them had trouble in carrying Grendel's head on spear-shafts to the gold-hall —until at last they came striding to the hall, fourteen bold warriors of the Geats; their lord, high-spirited, walked in their company over the fields to the mead-hall.

Then the chief of the thanes, man daring in deeds, enriched by new glory, warrior dear to battle, came in to greet Hrothgar. Then Grendel's head was dragged by the hair over the floor to where men drank, a terrible thing to the earls and the woman with them, an awful sight: the men looked upon it.

[FURTHER CELEBRATION AT HEOROT]

(XXIV.) Beowulf spoke, the son of Ecgtheow: "Yes, we have brought you this sea-booty, son of Healfdene, man of the Scyldings, gladly, as evidence of glory—what you look on here. Not easily did I come through it with my life, the war under water, not without trouble carried out the task. The fight would have been ended straightway if God had not guarded me. With Hrunting I might not do anything in the fight, though that is a good weapon. But the Wielder of Men granted me that I should see hanging on the wall a fair, ancient great-sword—most often He has guided the man without friends—that I should wield the weapon. Then in the fight when the time became right for me I hewed the house-guardians. Then that war-sword, wavy-patterned, burnt away as their blood sprang forth, hottest of battle-sweats. I have brought the hilt away from the foes. I have avenged the evil deeds, the slaughter of Danes, as it was right to do. I promise you that you may sleep in Heorot without care with your band of retainers, and that for none of the thanes of your people, old or young, need you have fear, prince of the Scyldings—for no life-injury to your men on that account, as you did before."

Then the golden hilt was given into the hand of the old man, the hoary war-chief—the ancient work of giants. There came into the possession of the prince of the Danes, after the fall of devils, the work of wonder-smiths. And when the hostile-hearted creature, God's enemy, guilty of murder, gave up this world, and his mother too, it passed into the control of the best of worldly kings between the seas, of those who gave treasure in the Northlands.

Hrothgar spoke—he looked on the hilt, the old heirloom, on

which was written the origin of ancient strife, when the flood, rushing water, slew the race of giants—they suffered terribly: that was a people alien to the Everlasting Lord. The Ruler made them a last payment through water's welling. On the sword-guard of bright gold there was also rightly marked through rune-staves, set down and told, for whom that sword, best of irons, had first been made, its hilt twisted and ornamented with snakes. Then the wise man spoke, the son of Healfdene—all were silent: "Lo, this may one say who works truth and right for the folk, recalls all things far distant, an old guardian of the land: that this earl was born the better man. Glory is raised up over the far ways—your glory over every people, Beowulf my friend. All of it, all your strength, you govern steadily in the wisdom of your heart. I shall fulfill my friendship to you, just as we spoke before. You shall become a comfort, whole and long-lasting, to your people, a help to warriors.

"So was not Heremod to the sons of Ecgwela, the Honor-Scyldings. He grew great not for their joy, but for their slaughter, for the destruction of Danish people. With swollen heart he killed his table-companions, shoulder-comrades, until he turned away from the joys of men, alone, notorious king, although mighty God had raised him in power, in the joys of strength, had set him up over all men. Yet in his breast his heart's thought grew blood-thirsty: no rings did he give to the Danes for glory. He lived joyless to suffer the pain of that strife, the long-lasting harm of the people. Teach yourself by him, be mindful of munificence. Old of winters, I tell this tale for you.

"It is a wonder to say how in His great spirit mighty God gives wisdom to mankind, land and earlship—He possesses power over all things. At times He lets the thought of a man of high lineage move in delight, gives him joy of earth in his homeland, a stronghold of men to rule over, makes regions of the world so subject to him, wide kingdoms, that in his unwisdom he may not himself have mind of his end. He lives in plenty; illness and age in no way grieve him, neither does dread care darken his heart, nor does enmity bare sword-hate, for the whole world turns to his will—he knows nothing worse—(XXV.) until his portion of pride increases and flourishes within him; then the watcher sleeps, the soul's guardian; that sleep is too sound, bound in its own cares, and the slayer most near whose bow shoots treacherously. Then is he hit in the heart, beneath his armor, with the bitter arrow—he cannot protect himself—with the crooked dark commands of the accursed spirit. What he has long held seems to him too little, angry-hearted he covets, no plated rings does he give in men's honor, and then he forgets and regards not his destiny because of what God, Wielder of Heaven, has given him before, his portion of glories. In the end it happens in turn that the loaned body weakens, falls doomed; another takes the earl's ancient treasure, one who recklessly gives precious gifts, does not fearfully guard them.

"Keep yourself against that wickedness, beloved Beowulf, best of men, and choose better—eternal gains. Have no care for pride, great warrior. Now for a time there is glory in your might: yet soon it shall be that sickness or sword will diminish your strength, or fire's fangs, or flood's surge, or sword's swing, or spear's flight, or appalling age; brightness of eyes will fail and grow dark; then it shall bc that death will overcome you, warrior.

"Thus I ruled the Ring-Danes for a hundred half-years under the skies, and protected them in war with spear and sword against many nations over middle-earth, so that I counted no one as my adversary underneath the sky's expanse. Well, disproof of that came to me in my own land, grief after my joys, when Grendel, ancient adversary, camc to invade my home. Great sorrow of heart I have always suffered for his persecution. Thanks be to the Ruler, the Eternal Lord, that after old strife I have come to see in my lifetime, with my own eyes, his blood-stained head. Go now to your seat, have joy of the glad feast, made famous in battle. Many of our treasures will be shared when morning comes."

The Geat was glad at heart, went at once to seek his seat as the wise one bade. Then was a feast fairly served again, for a second time, just as before, for those famed for courage, sitting about the hall.

Night's cover lowered, dark over the warriors. The retainers all arose. The gray-haired one would seek his bed, the old Scylding. It pleased the Geat, the brave shield-warrior, immensely that he should have rest. Straightway a hall-thane led the way on for the weary one, come from far country, and showed every courtesy to the thane's need, such as in those days seafarers might expect as their due.

Then the great-hearted one rested; the hall stood high, vaulted and gold-adorned; the guest slept within until the black raven, blithe-hearted, announced heaven's joy. Then the bright light came passing over the shadows. The warriors hastened, the nobles were eager to set out again for their people. Bold of spirit, the visitor would seek his ship far thence.

Then the hardy one bade that Hrunting be brought to the son of Ecglaf,[8] that he take back his sword, precious iron. He spoke thanks for that loan, said that he accounted it a good war-friend,

8. I.e., Unferth.

strong in battle; in his words he found no fault at all with the sword's edge. he was a thoughtful man. And then they were eager to depart, the warriors ready in their armor. The prince who had earned honor of the Danes went to the high seat where the other was: the man dear to war greeted Hrothgar.

[*Beowulf Returns Home*]

(XXVI.) Beowulf spoke, the son of Ecgtheow: "Now we sea-travelers come from afar wish to say that we desire to seek Hygelac. Here we have been entertained splendidly according to our desire: you have dealt well with us. If on earth I might in any way earn more of your heart's love, prince of warriors, than I have done before with warlike deeds, I should be ready at once. If beyond the sea's expanse I hear that men dwelling near threaten you with terrors, as those who hated you did before, I shall bring you a thousand thanes, warriors to your aid. I know of Hygelac, lord of the Geats, though he is young as a guardian of the people, that he will further me with words and works so that I may do you honor and bring spears to help you, strong support where you have need of men. If Hrethric, king's son, decides to come to the court of the Geats, he can find many friends there; far countries are well sought by him who is himself strong."

Hrothgar spoke to him in answer: "The All-Knowing Lord sent those words into your mind: I have not heard a man of so young age speak more wisely. You are great of strength, mature of mind, wise of words. I think it likely if the spear, sword-grim war, takes the son of Hrethel, sickness or weapon your prince, the people's ruler, and you have your life, that the Sea-Geats will not have a better to choose as their king, as guardian of their treasure, if you wish to hold the kingdom of your kinsmen. So well your heart's temper has long pleased me, beloved Beowulf. You have brought it about that peace shall be shared by the peoples, the folk of the Geats and the Spear-Danes, and enmity shall sleep, acts of malice which they practiced before; and there shall be, as long as I rule the wide kingdom, sharing of treasures, many a man shall greet his fellow with good gifts over the sea-bird's baths; the ring-prowed ship will bring gifts and tokens of friendship over the sea. I know your people, blameless in every respect, set firm after the old way both as to foe and to friend."

Then the protector of earls, the kinsman of Healfdene, gave him there in the hall twelve precious things; he bade him with these gifts seek his own dear people in safety, quickly come back. Then the king noble of race, the prince of the Scyldings, kissed the best of thanes and took him by his ncek: tears fell from the gray-haired one. He had two thoughts of the future, the old and wise man, one more strongly than the other—that they would not see each other again, bold men at council. The man was so dear to him that he might not restrain his breast's welling, for fixed in his heartstrings a deep-felt longing for the beloved man burned in his blood. Away from him Beowulf, warrior glorious with gold, walked over the grassy ground, proud of his treasure. The sea-goer awaited its owner, riding at anchor. Then on the journey the gift of Hrothgar was oft-praised: that was a king blameless in all things until age took from him the joys of his strength—old age that has often harmed many.

(XXVII.) There came to the flood the band of brave-hearted ones, of young men. They wore mail-coats, locked limb-shirts. The guard of the coast saw the coming of the earls, just as he had done before. He did not greet the guests with taunts from the cliff's top, but rode to meet them, said that the return of the warriors in bright armor in their ship would be welcome to the people of the Weather-Geats. There on the sand the broad sea-boat was loaded with armor, the ring-prowed ship with horses and rich things. The mast stood high over Hrothgar's hoard-gifts. He gave the boat-guard a sword wound with gold, so that thereafter on the mead-bench he was held the worthier for the treasure, the heirloom. The boat moved out to furrow the deep water, left the land of the Danes. Then on the mast a sea-cloth, a sail, was made fast by a rope. The boat's beams creaked: wind did not keep the sea-floater from its way over the waves. The sea-goer moved, foamy-necked floated forth over the swell, the ship with bound prow over the sea-currents until they might see the cliffs of the Geats, the well-known headlands. The ship pressed ahead, borne by the wind, stood still at the land. Quickly the harbor-guard was at the sea-side, he who had gazed for a long time far out over the currents, eager to see the beloved men. He [9] moored the deep ship in the sand, fast by its anchor ropes, lest the force of the waves should drive away the fair wooden vessel. Then he bade that the prince's wealth be borne ashore, armor and plated gold. It was not far for them to seek the giver of treasure, Hygelac son of Hrethel, where he dwelt at home near the sea-wall, himself with his retainers.

The building was splendid, its king most valiant, set high in the hall, Hygd [1] most youthful, wise and well-taught, though she had lived within the castle walls few winters, daughter of Haereth. For she was not niggardly, nor too sparing of gifts to the men of the Geats, of treasures. Modthryth,[2] good folk-queen, did

9. Beowulf.

1. Hygd is Hygelac's young queen. The suddenness of her introduction here is perhaps due to a faulty text.

2. A transitional passage introducing the contrast between Hygd's good behavior and Modthryth's bad behavior as young women of royal blood seems to have been lost. Modthryth's practice of having those who looked into her face put to death may reflect the folk-motif of the princess whose unsuccessful suitors are executed, though the text does not say that Modthryth's victims were suitors. Modthryth's "great lord" was probably her father.

dreadful deeds [in her youth]: no bold one among her retainers dared venture—except her great lord—to set his eyes on her in daylight, but [if he did] he should reckon deadly bonds prepared for him, arresting hands: that straightway after his seizure the sword awaited him, that the patterned blade must settle it, make known its death-evil. Such is no queenly custom for a woman to practice, though she is peerless—that one who weaves peace [3] should take away the life of a beloved man after pretended injury. However the kinsman of Hemming stopped that: [4] ale-drinkers gave another account, said that she did less harm to the people, fewer injuries, after she was given, gold-adorned, to the young warrior, the beloved noble, when by her father's teaching she sought Offa's hall in a voyage over the pale sea. There on the throne she was afterwards famous for generosity, while living made use of her life, held high love toward the lord of warriors, [who was] of all mankind the best, as I have heard, between the seas of the races of men. Since Offa was a man brave of wars and gifts, wide-honored, he held his native land in wisdom. From him sprang Eomer to the help of warriors, kinsman of Hemming, grandson of Garmund, strong in battle.[5]

(XXVIII.) Then the hardy one came walking with his troop over the sand on the sea-plain, the wide shores. The world-candle shone, the sun moved quickly from the south. They made their way, strode swiftly to where they heard that the protector of earls, the slayer of Ongentheow,[6] the good young war-king, was dispensing rings in the stronghold. The coming of Beowulf was straightway made known to Hygelac, that there in his home the defender of warriors, his comrade in battle, came walking alive to the court, sound from the battle-play. Quickly the way within was made clear for the foot-guests, as the mighty one bade.

Then he sat down with him, he who had come safe through the fight, kinsman with kinsman, after he had greeted his liege lord with formal speech, loyal, with vigorous words. Haereth's daughter moved through the hall-building with mead-cups, cared lovingly for the people, bore the cup of strong drink to the hands of the warriors. Hygelac began fairly to question his companion in the high hall, curiosity pressed him, what the adventures of the

3. Daughters of kings were frequently given in marriage to the king of a hostile nation in order to bring about peace; hence Modthryth may be called "one who weaves peace."

4. Offa, an Angle king who according to legend ruled Mercia in England; who Hemming was—besides being Offa's forebear—is not known.

5. Offa, the only person that may be identified as English in this English poem, receives high praise; apparently the names of his father Garmund and son Eomer would strike a responsive chord in the poet's audience.

6. Ongentheow was a Scylfing (Swedish) king, whose story is fully told below, sections XL and XLI. In fact Hygelac was not his slayer, but is called so because he led the attack on the Scylfings in which Ongentheow was killed.

Sea-Geats had been. "How did you fare on your journey, beloved Beowulf, when you suddenly resolved to seek distant combat over the salt water, battle in Heorot? Did you at all help the wide-known woes of Hrothgar, the famous prince? Because of you I burned with seething sorrows, care of heart—had no trust in the venture of my beloved man. I entreated you long that you should in no way approach the murderous spirit, should let the South-Danes themselves settle the war with Grendel. I say thanks to God that I may see you sound."

Beowulf spoke, the son of Ecgtheow: "To many among men it is not hidden, lord Hygelac, the great encounter—what a fight we had, Grendel and I, in the place where he made many sorrows for the Victory-Scyldings, constant misery. All that I avenged, so that none of Grendel's kin over the earth need boast of that clash at night—whoever lives longest of the loathsome kind, wrapped in malice. There I went forth to the ring-hall to greet Hrothgar. At once the famous son of Healfdene, when he knew my purpose, gave me a seat with his own sons. The company was in joy: I have not seen in the time of my life under heaven's arch more mead-mirth of hall-sitters. At times the famous queen, peace-pledge of the people, went through all the hall, cheered the young men; often she would give a man a ring-band before she went to her seat. At times Hrothgar's daughter bore the ale-cup to the retainers, to the earls throughout the hall. I heard hall-sitters name her Freawaru when she offered the studded cup to warriors. Young and gold-adorned, she is promised to the fair son of Froda.[7] That has seemed good to the lord of the Scyldings, the guardian of the kingdom, and he believes of this plan that he may, with this woman, settle their portion of deadly feuds, of quarrels.[8] Yet most often after the fall of a prince in any nation the deadly spear rests but a little while, even though the bride is good.

"It may displease the lord of the Heatho-Bards and each thane of that people when he goes in the hall with the woman, [that while] the noble sons of the Danes, her retainers, [are] feasted,[9] the heirlooms of their ancestors will be shining on them [1]—the hard and wave-adorned treasure of the Heatho-Bards, [which was theirs] so long as they might wield those weapons, (XXIX.) until they led to the shield-play, to destruction, their dear companions and their own lives. Then at the beer he[2] who sees

7. I.e., Ingeld, who succeeded his father a king of the Heatho-Bards.

8. I.e., the feud between the Danes and Heatho-Bards.

9. The text is faulty here.

1. I.e., the weapons and armor which had once belonged to the Heatho-Bards and were captured by the Danes will be worn by the Danish attendants of Hrothgar's daughter Freawaru when she goes to the Heatho-Bards to marry king Ingeld.

2. I.e., some old Heatho-Bard warrior.

the treasure, an old ash-warrior who remembers it all, the spear-death of warriors—grim is his heart—begins, sad of mind, to tempt a young fighter in the thoughts of his spirit, to awaken war-evil, and speaks this word:

"'Can you, my friend, recognize that sword, the rare iron-blade, that your father, beloved man, bore to battle his last time in armor, where the Danes slew him, the fierce Scyldings, got possession of the battle-field, when Withergeld[3] lay dead, after the fall of warriors? Now here some son of his murderers walks in the hall, proud of the weapon, boasts of the murder, and wears the treasure that you should rightly possess.' So he will provoke and remind at every chance with wounding words until that moment comes that the woman's thane,[4] forfeiting life, shall lie dead, blood-smeared from the sword-bite, for his father's deeds. The other escapes with his life, knows the land well. Then on both sides the oath of the earls will be broken; then deadly hate will well up in Ingeld, and his wife-love after the surging of sorrows will become cooler. Therefore I do not think the loyalty of the Heatho-Bards, their part in the alliance with the Danes, to be without deceit—do not think their friendship fast.

"I shall speak still more of Grendel, that you may readily know, giver of treasure, what the hand-fight of warriors came to in the end. After heaven's jewel had glided over the earth, the angry spirit came, awful in the evening, to visit us where, unharmed, we watched over the hall. There the fight was fatal to Hondscioh, deadly to one who was doomed. He was dead first of all, armed warrior. Grendel came to devour him, good young retainer, swallowed all the body of the beloved men. Yet not for this would the bloody-toothed slayer, bent on destruction, go from the gold-hall empty-handed; but, strong of might, he made trial of me, grasped me with eager hand. His glove[5] hung huge and wonderful, made fast with cunning clasps: it had been made all with craft, with devil's devices and dragon's skins. The fell doer of evils would put me therein, guiltless, one of many. He might not do so after I had stood up in anger. It is too long to tell how I repaid the people's foe his due for every crime. My prince, there with my deeds I did honor to your people. He slipped away, for a little while had use of life's joy. Yet his right hand remained as his spoor in Heorot, and he went from there abject, mournful of heart sank to the mere's bottom.

"The lord of the Scyldings repaid me for that bloody combat

3. Apparently a leader of the Heatho-Bards in their unsuccessful war with the Danes.

4. I.e., the Danish attendant of Freawaru who is wearing the sword of his Heatho-Bard attacker's father.

5. Apparently a large glove that could be used as a pouch.

with much plated gold, many treasures, after morning came and we sat down to the feast. There was song and mirth. The old Scylding, who has learned many things, spoke of times far-off. At times a brave one in battle touched the glad wood, the harp's joy; at times he told tales, true and sad; at times he related strange stories according to right custom; at times, again, the great-hearted king, bound with age, the old warrior, would begin to speak of his youth, his battle-strength. His heart welled within when, old and wise, he thought of his many winters. Thus we took pleasure there the livelong day until another night came to men.

"Then in her turn Grendel's mother swiftly made ready to take revenge for his injuries, made a sorrowful journey. Death had taken her son, war-hate of the Weather-Geats. The direful woman avenged her son, fiercely killed a warrior: there the life of Aeschere departed, a wise old counselor. And when morning came the folk of the Danes might not burn him, death-weary, in the fire, nor place him on the pyre, beloved man: she had borne his body away in fiend's embrace beneath the mountain stream. That was the bitterest of Hrothgar's sorrows, of those that had long come upon the people's prince. Then the king, sore-hearted, implored me by your life[6] that I should do a man's work in the tumult of the waters, venture my life, finish a glorious deed. He promised me reward. Then I found the guardian of the deep pool, the grim horror, as is now known wide. For a time there we were locked hand in hand. Then the flood boiled with blood, and in the war-hall I cut off the head of Grendel's mother with a mighty sword. Not without trouble I came from there with my life. I was not fated to die then, but the protector of earls again gave me many treasures, the son of Healfdene.

(XXXI.) "Thus the king of that people lived with good customs. I had lost none of the rewards, the meed of my might, but he gave me treasures, the son of Healfdene, at my own choice. I will bring these to you, great king, show my good will. On your kindnesses all still depends: I have few close kinsmen besides you, Hygelac."

Then he bade bring in the boar-banner—the head-sign—the helmet towering in battle, the gray battle-shirt, the splendid sword —afterwards spoke words: "Hrothgar, wise king, gave me this armor; in his words he bade that I should first tell you about his gift: he said that king Heorogar,[7] lord of the Scyldings, had had it for a long time; not for that would he give it, the breast-armor, to his son, bold Heoroweard, though he was loyal to him. Use it all well!"

6. I.e., "in your name."
7. Hrothgar's elder brother, whom Hrothgar succeeded as king.

I have heard that four horses, swift and alike, followed that treasure, fallow as apples. He gave him the gift of both horses and treasure. So ought kinsmen do, not weave malice-nets for each other with secret craft, prepare death for comrades. To Hygelac his nephew was most true in hard fights, and each one mindful of helping the other. I have heard that he gave Hygd the neck-ring, the wonderfully wrought treasure, that Wealhtheow had given him—gave to the king's daughter as well three horses, supple and saddle-bright. After the gift of the necklace, her breast was adorned with it.

Thus Beowulf showed himself brave, a man known in battles, of good deeds, bore himself according to discretion. Drunk, he slew no hearth-companions. His heart was not savage, but he held the great gift that God had given him, the most strength of all mankind, like one brave in battle. He had long been despised,[8] so that the sons of the Geats did not reckon him brave, nor would the lord of the Weather-Geats do him much gift-honor on the mead-bench. They strongly suspected that he was slack, a young man unbold. Change came to the famous man for each of his troubles.

Then the protector of earls bade fetch in the heirloom of Hrethel,[9] king famed in battle, adorned with gold. There was not then among the Geats a better treasure in sword's kind. He laid that in Beowulf's lap, and gave him seven thousand [hides of land], a hall and a throne. To both of them alike land had been left in the nation, home and native soil: to the other more especially wide was the realm, to him who was higher in rank.

[*Beowulf and the Dragon*]

Afterwards it happened, in later days, in the crashes of battle, when Hygelac lay dead and war-swords came to slay Heardred[1] behind the shield-cover, when the Battle-Scylfings, hard fighters, sought him among his victorious nation, attacked bitterly the nephew of Hereric—then the broad kingdom came into Beowulf's hand. He held it well fifty winters—he was a wise king, an old guardian of the land—until in the dark nights a certain one, a dragon, began to hold sway, which on the high heath kept watch over a hoard, a steep stone-barrow. Beneath lay a path unknown to men. By this there went inside a certain man [who made his way near to the heathen hoard; his hand took a cup, large, a shining treasure. The dragon did not afterwards conceal it though in his sleep he was tricked by the craft of the thief. That the

8. Beowulf's poor reputation as a young man is mentioned only here.
9. Hygelac's father.
1. Hygelac's son Heardred, who succeeded Hygelac as king, was killed by the Swedes (Battle-Scylfings) in his own land, as is explained more fully below, section XXXIII. His uncle Hereric was perhaps Hygd's brother.

people discovered, the neighboring folk—that he was swollen with rage].[2]

(XXXII.) Not of his own accord did he who had sorely harmed him [3] break into the worm's hoard, not by his own desire, but for hard constraint; the slave of some son of men fled hostile blows, lacking a shelter, and came there, a man guilty of wrong-doing. As soon as he saw him,[4] great horror arose in the stranger; [yet the wretched fugitive escaped the terrible worm . . . When the sudden shock came upon him, he carried off a precious cup.][5] There were many such ancient treasures in the earth-house, as in the old days some one of mankind had prudently hidden there the huge legacy of a noble race, rare treasures. Death had taken them all in earlier times, and the only one of the nation of people who still survived, who walked there longest, a guardian mourning his friends, supposed the same of himself as of them—that he might little while enjoy the long-got treasure. A barrow stood all ready on the shore near the sea-waves, newly placed on the headland, made fast by having its entrances skillfully hidden. The keeper of the rings carried in the part of his riches worthy of hoarding, plated gold; he spoke few words:

"Hold now, you earth, now that men may not, the possession of earls. What, from you good men got it first! War-death has taken each man of my people, evil dreadful and deadly, each of those who has given up this life, the hall-joys of men. I have none who wears sword or cleans the plated cup, rich drinking vessel. The company of retainers has gone elsewhere. The hard helmet must be stripped of its fair-wrought gold, of its plating. The polishers are asleep who should make the war-mask shine. And even so the coat of mail, which withstood the bite of swords after the crashing of the shields, decays like its warrior. Nor may the ring-mail travel wide on the war-chief beside his warriors. There is no harp-delight, no mirth of the singing wood, no good hawk flies through the hall, no swift horse stamps in the castle court. Baleful death has sent away many races of men."

So, sad of mind, he spoke his sorrow, alone of them all, moved joyless through day and night until death's flood reached his heart. The ancient night-ravager found the hoard-joy standing open, he who burning seeks barrows, the smooth hateful dragon who flies at night wrapped in flame. Earth-dwellers much dread him. He it is who must seek a hoard in the earth where he will guard heathen gold, wise for his winters: he is none the better for it.

2. This part of the manuscript is badly damaged, and the text within brackets is highly conjectural.
3. The dragon.
4. The dragon.
5. Several lines of the text have been lost.

So for three hundred winters the harmer of folk held in the earth one of its treasure-houses, huge and mighty, until one man angered his heart. He bore to his master a plated cup, asked his lord for a compact of peace: thus was the hoard searched, the store of treasures diminished. His requests were granted the wretched man: the lord for the first time looked on the ancient work of men. Then the worm woke; cause of strife was renewed: for then he moved over the stones, hard-hearted beheld his foe's footprints—with secret stealth he had stepped forth too near the dragon's head. (So may an undoomed man who holds favor from the Ruler easily come through his woes and misery.) The hoard-guard sought him eagerly over the ground, would find the man who had done him injury while he slept. Hot and fierce-hearted, often he moved all about the outside of the barrow. No man at all was in the emptiness. Yet he took joy in the thought of war, in the work of fighting. At times he turned back into the barrow, sought his rich cup. Straightway he found that some man had tampered with his gold, his splendid treasure. The hoard-guard waited restless until evening came; then the barrow-keeper was in rage: he would requite that precious drinking cup with vengeful fire. Then the day was gone—to the joy of the worm. He would not wait long on the sea-wall, but set out with fire, ready with flame. The beginning was terrible to the folk on the land, as the ending was soon to be sore to their giver of treasure.

(XXXIII.) Then the evil spirit began to vomit flames, burn bright dwellings; blaze of fire rose, to the horror of men; there the deadly flying thing would leave nothing alive. The worm's warfare was wide-seen, his cruel malice, near and far—how the destroyer hated and hurt the people of the Geats. He winged back to the hoard, his hidden hall, before the time of day. He had circled the land-dwellers with flame, with fire and burning. He had trust in his barrow, in his war and his wall: his expectation deceived him.

Then the terror was made known to Beowulf, quickly in its truth, that his own home, best of buildings, had melted in surging flames, the throne-seat of the Geats. That was anguish of spirit to the good man, the greatest of heart-sorrows. The wise one supposed that he had bitterly offended the Ruler, the Eternal Lord, against old law. His breast within boiled with dark thoughts—as was not for him customary. The fiery dragon with his flames had destroyed the people's stronghold, the land along the sea, the heart of the country. Because of that the war-king, the lord of the Weather-Geats, devised punishment for him. The protector of fighting men, lord of earls, commanded that a wonderful battle-shield be made all of iron. Well he knew that the wood of the forest might not help him—linden against flame. The prince good from old times was to come to the end of the days that had been lent him, life in the world, and the worm with him, though he had long held the hoarded wealth. Then the ring-prince scorned to seek the far-flier with a troop, a large army. He had no fear for himself of the combat, nor did he think the worm's war-power anything great, his strength and his courage, because he himself had come through many battles before, dared perilous straits, clashes of war, after he had purged Hrothgar's hall, victorious warrior, and in combat crushed to death Grendel's kin, loathsome race.

Nor was that the least of his hand-combats where Hygelac was slain, when the king of the Geats, the noble lord of the people, the son of Hrethel, died of sword-strokes in the war-storm among the Frisians, laid low by the blade. From there Beowulf came away by means of his own strength, performed a feat of swimming; he had on his arm the armor of thirty earls when he turned back to the sea. There was no need for the Hetware [6] to exult in the foot-battle when they bore their shields against him: few came again from that warrior to seek their homes. Then the son of Ecgtheow swam over the water's expanse, forlorn and alone, back to his people. There Hygd offered him hoard and kingdom, rings and a prince's throne. She had no trust in her son, that he could hold his native throne against foreigners now that Hygelac was dead. By no means the sooner might the lordless ones get consent from the noble that he would become lord of Heardred or that he would accept royal power.[7] Yet he held him up among the people by friendly counsel, kindly with honor, until he became older,[8] ruled the Weather-Geats.

Outcasts from over the sea sought him, sons of Ohthere.[9] They had rebelled against the protector of the Scylfings, the best of the sea-kings of those who gave treasure in Sweden, a famous lord. For Heardred that became his life's limit: because of his hospitality there the son of Hygelac got his life's wound from the strokes of a sword. And the son of Ongentheow went back to seek his home after Heardred lay dead, let Beowulf hold the royal throne, rule the Geats: that was a good king.

(XXXIV.) In later days he was mindful of repaying the prince's fall, became the friend of the destitute Eadgils; [1] with folk he

6. I.e., a tribe, with whom the Frisians were allied.

7. I.e., Beowulf refused to take the throne from the rightful heir Heardred.

8. I.e., Beowulf supported the young Heardred.

9. Ohthere succeeded his father Ongentheow as king of the Scylfings (Swedes), but after his death his brother Onela seized the throne, driving out Ohthere's sons Eanmund and Eadgils. They were given refuge at the Geatish court by Heardred, whom Onela attacked for this act of hospitality. In the fight Eanmund and Heardred were killed, and Onela left the kingdom in Beowulf's charge.

1. The surviving son of Ohthere was befriended by Beowulf, who supported him in his successful attempt to gain the Swedish throne and who killed the usurper Onela.

supported the son of Ohthere over the wide sea, with warriors and weapons. Afterwards he got vengeance by forays that brought with them cold care: he took the king's life.

Thus he had survived every combat, every dangerous battle, every deed of courage, the son of Ecgtheow, until that one day when he should fight with the worm. Then, one of twelve, the lord of the Geats, swollen with anger, went to look on the dragon. He had learned then from what the feud arose, the fierce malice to men: the glorious cup had come to his possession from the hand of the finder: he was the thirteenth of that company, the man who had brought on the beginning of the war, the sad-hearted slave—wretched, he must direct them to the place. Against his will he went to where he knew of an earth-hall, a barrow beneath the ground close to the sea-surge, to the struggling waves: within, it was full of ornaments and gold chains. The terrible guardian, ready for combat, held the gold treasure, old under the earth. It was no easy bargain for any man to obtain. Then the king, hardy in fight, sat down on the headland; there he saluted his hearth-companions, gold-friend of the Geats. His mind was mournful, restless and ripe for death: very close was the fate which should come to the old man, seek his soul's hoard, divide life from his body; not for long then was the life of the noble one wound in his flesh.

Beowulf spoke, the son of Ecgtheow: "In youth I lived through many battle-storms, times of war. I remember all that. I was seven winters old when the lord of treasure, the beloved king of the folk, received me from my father: King Hrethel had me and kept me, gave me treasure and feast, mindful of kinship. During his life I was no more hated by him as a man in his castle than any of his own sons, Herebeald and Haethcyn, or my own Hygelac. For the eldest a murder-bed was wrongfully spread through the deed of a kinsman, when Haethcyn struck him down with an arrow from his horned bow—his friend and his lord—missed the mark and shot his kinsman dead, one brother the other, with the bloody arrowhead. That was a fatal fight, without hope of recompense, a deed wrongly done, baffling to the heart; yet it had happened that a prince had to lose life unavenged.

"So it is sad for an old man to endure that his son should ride young on the gallows. Then he may speak a story, a sorrowful song, when his son hangs for the joy of the raven, and, old in years and knowing, he can find no help for him. Always with every morning he is reminded of his son's journey elsewhere. He cares not to wait for another heir in his hall, when the first through death's force has come to the end of his deeds. Sorrowful he sees in his son's dwelling the empty wine-hall, the windy resting place without joy—the riders sleep, the warriors in the grave. There is no sound of the harp, no joy in the dwelling, as there was of old. (XXXV.) Then he goes to his couch, sings a song of sorrow, one alone for one gone. To him all too wide has seemed the land and the dwelling.

"So the protector of the Weather-Geats bore in his heart swelling sorrow for Herebeald. In no way could he settle his feud with the life-slayer; not the sooner could he wound the warrior with deeds of hatred, though he was not dear to him. Then for the sorrow that had too bitterly befallen him he gave up the joys of men, chose God's light. To his sons he left—as a happy man does—his land and his town when he went from life.

"Then there was battle and strife of Swedes and Geats, over the wide water a quarrel shared, hatred between hardy ones, after Hrethel died. And the sons of Ongentheow [2] were bold and active in war, wanted to have no peace over the seas, but about Hreosnabeorh often devised awful slaughter. That my friends and kinsmen avenged, both the feud and the crime, as is well-known, though one of them bought it with his life, a hard bargain: the war was mortal to Haethcyn, lord of the Geats.[3] Then in the morning, I have heard, one kinsman avenged the other on his slayer with the sword's edge, when Ongentheow attacked Eofor: the war-helm split, the old Scylfing fell mortally wounded: his hand remembered feuds enough, did not withstand the life-blow.

"I repaid in war the treasures that he [4] gave me—with my bright sword, as was granted me by fate: he had given me land, a pleasant dwelling. There was not any need for him, any reason, that he should have to seek among the Gifthas or the Spear-Danes or in Sweden in order to buy with treasure a worse warrior. I would always go before him in the troop, alone in the front. And so all my life I shall wage battle while this sword endures that has served me early and late ever since I became Daeghrefn's slayer in the press—the warrior of the Hugas.[5] He could not bring armor to the king of the Frisians, breast ornament, but fell in the fight, keeper of the standard, a noble man. Nor was my sword's edge his slayer, but my warlike grip broke open his heart-streams, his bone-house. Now shall the sword's edge, the hand and hard blade, fight for the hoard."

2. I.e., the Swedes Onela and Ohthere: the reference is, of course, to a time earlier than that referred to in section XXXIII, note 9.

3. Haethcyn had succeeded his father Hrethel as king of the Geats after his accidental killing of his brother Herebeald. When Haethcyn was killed while attacking the Swedes, he was succeeded by Hygelac, who, as the next sentence relates, avenged Haethcyn's death on Ongentheow. The death of Ongentheow is described below, sections XL and XLI.

4. Hygelac.

5. I.e., the Franks.

[BEOWULF ATTACKS THE DRAGON]

Beowulf spoke, for the last time spoke words in boast: "In my youth I engaged in many wars. Old guardian of the people, I shall still seek battle, perform a deed of fame, if the evil-doer will come to me out of the earth-hall."

Then he saluted each of the warriors, the bold helmet-bearers, for the last time—his own dear companions. "I would not bear sword, weapon, to the worm, if I knew how else according to my boast I might grapple with the monster, as I did of old with Grendel. But I expect here hot battle-fire, steam and poison. Therefore I have on me shield and mail-shirt. I will not flee a foot-step from the barrow-ward, but it shall be with us at the wall as fate allots, the ruler of every man. I am confident in heart, so I forgo help against the war-flier. Wait on the barrow, safe in your mail-shirts, men in armor—which of us two may better bear wounds after our bloody meeting. This is not your venture, nor is it right for any man except me alone that he should spend his strength against the monster, do this man's deed. By my courage I shall get gold, or war will take your king, dire life-evil."

Then the brave warrior arose by his shield; hardy under helmet he went in his mail-shirt beneath the stone-cliffs, had trust in his strength—that of one man: such is not the way of the cowardly. Then he saw by the wall—he who had come through many wars, good in his great-heartedness, many clashes in battle when troops meet together—a stone arch standing, through it a stream bursting out of the barrow: there was welling of a current hot with killing fires, and he might not endure any while unburnt by the dragon's flame the hollow near the hoard. Then the man of the Weather-Geats, enraged as he was, let a word break from his breast. Stout-hearted he shouted; his voice went roaring, clear in battle, in under the gray stone. Hate was stirred up, the hoard's guard knew the voice of a man. No more time was there to ask for peace. First the monster's breath came out of the stone, the hot war-steam. The earth resounded. The man below the barrow, the lord of the Geats, swung his shield against the dreadful visitor. Then the heart of the coiled thing was aroused to seek combat. The good war-king had drawn his sword, the old heirloom, not blunt of edge. To each of them as they threatened destruction there was terror of the other. Firm-hearted he stood with his shield high, the lord of friends, while quickly the worm coiled itself; he waited in his armor. Then, coiling in flames, he came gliding on, hastening to his fate. The good shield protected the life and body of the famous prince, but for a shorter while than his wish was. There for the first time, the first day in his life, he might not prevail, since fate did not assign him such glory in battle. The lord of the Geats raised his hand, struck the shining horror so with his forged blade that the edge failed, bright on the bone, bit less surely than its folk-king had need, hard-pressed in perils. Then because of the battle-stroke the barrow-ward's heart was savage, he exhaled death-fire—the war-flames sprang wide. The gold-friend of the Geats boasted of no great victories: the war blade had failed, naked at need, as it ought not to have done, iron good from old times. That was no pleasant journey, not one on which the famous son of Ecgtheow would wish to leave his land; against his will he must take up a dwelling-place elsewhere—as every man must give up the days that are lent him.

It was not long until they came together again, dreadful foes. The hoard-guard took heart, once more his breast swelled with his breathing. Encircled with flames, he who before had ruled a folk felt harsh pain. Nor did his companions, sons of nobles, take up their stand in a troop about him with the courage of fighting men, but they crept to the wood, protected their lives. In only one of them the heart surged with sorrows: nothing can ever set aside kinship in him who means well.

(XXXVI.) He was called Wiglaf, son of Weohstan, a rare shield-warrior, a man of the Scylfings,[6] kinsman of Aelfhere. He saw his liege lord under his war-mask suffer the heat. Then he was mindful of the honors he had given him before, the rich dwelling-place of the Waegmundings, every folk-right such as his father possessed. He might not then hold back, his hand seized his shield, the yellow linden-wood; he drew his ancient sword. Among men it was the heirloom of Eanmund, the son of Ohthere:[7] Weohstan had become his slayer in battle with sword's edge—an exile without friends; and he bore off to his kin the bright-shining helmet, the ringed mail-armor, the old sword made by giants that Onela had given him,[8] his kinsman's war-armor, ready battle-gear: he did not speak of the feud, though he had

6. Though in the next sentence Wiglaf is said to belong to the family of the Waegmundings, the Geatish family to which Beowulf belonged, he is here called a Scylfing (Swede), and immediately below his father Weohstan is represented as having fought for the Swede Onela in his attack on the Geats. But for a man to change his nation was not unusual, and Weohstan, who may have had both Swedish and Geatish blood, had evidently become a Geat long enough before to have brought up his son Wiglaf as one. The identity of Aelfhere is not known.

7. See above, section XXXIII, note 9. Not only did Weohstan support Onela's attack on the Geat king Heardred, but actually killed Eanmund whom Heardred was supporting, and it is Eanmund's sword that Wiglaf is now wielding.

8. The spoils of war belonged to the victorious king, who apportioned them among his fighters: thus Onela gave Weohstan the armor of Eanmund, whom Weohstan had killed.

killed his brother's son.[9] He [1] held the armor many half-years, the blade and the battle-dress, until his son might do manly deeds like his old father. Then he gave him among the Geats war-armor of every kind, numberless, when, old, he went forth on the way from life. For the young warrior this was the first time that he should enter the war-storm with his dear lord. His heart's courage did not slacken, nor did the heirloom of his kinsman fail in the battle. That the worm found when they had come together.

Wiglaf spoke, said many fit words to his companions—his mind was mournful: "I remember that time we drank mead, when we promised our lord in the beer-hall—him who gave us these rings—that we would repay him for the war-arms if a need like this befell him—the helmets and the hard swords. Of his own will he chose us among the host for this venture, thought us worthy of fame—and gave me these treasures—because he counted us good war-makers, brave helm-bearers, though our lord intended to do this work of courage alone, as keeper of the folk, because among men he had performed the greatest deeds of glory, daring actions. Now the day has come that our liege lord has need of the strength of good fighters. Let us go to him, help our war-chief while the grim terrible fire persists. God knows of me that I should rather that the flame enfold my body with my gold-giver. It does not seem right to me for us to bear our shields home again unless we can first fell the foe, defend the life of the prince of the Weather-Geats. I know well that it would be no recompense for past deeds that he alone of the company of the Geats should suffer pain, fall in the fight. For us both shall there be a part in the work of sword and helmet, of battle-shirt and war-clothing."

Then he waded through the deadly smoke, bore his war-helmet to the aid of his king, spoke in few words: "Beloved Beowulf, do all well, for, long since in your youth, you said that you would not let your glory fail while you lived. Now, great-spirited noble, brave of deeds, you must protect your life with all your might. I shall help you."

After these words, the worm came on, angry, the terrible malice-filled foe, shining with surging flames, to seek for the second time his enemies, hated men. Fire advanced in waves; shield burned to the boss; mail-shirt might give no help to the young spear-warrior; but the young man went quickly under his kinsman's shield when

9. This ironic remark points out that Onela did not claim *wergild* or seek vengeance from Weohstan, as in other circumstances he ought to have done inasmuch as Weohstan had killed Onela's close kinsman, his nephew Eanmund: but Onela was himself trying to kill Eanmund.

1. Weohstan.

his own was consumed with flames. Then the war-king was again mindful of fame, struck with his war-sword with great strength so that it stuck in the head-bone, driven with force: Naegling broke, the sword of Beowulf failed in the fight, old and steel-gray. It was not ordained for him that iron edges might help in the combat. Too strong was the hand that I have heard strained every sword with its stroke, when he bore wound-hardened weapon to battle: he was none the better for it.

Then for the third time the folk-harmer, the fearful fire-dragon, was mindful of feuds, set upon the brave one when the chance came, hot and battle-grim seized all his neck with his sharp fangs: he was smeared with life-blood, gore welled out in waves.

(XXXVII.) Then, I have heard, at the need of the folk-king the earl at his side made his courage known, his might and his keenness—as was natural to him. He took no heed for that head,[2] but the hand of the brave man was burned as he helped his kinsman, as the man in armor struck the hateful foe a little lower down, so that the sword sank in, shining and engraved; and then the fire began to subside. The king himself then still controlled his senses, drew the battle-knife, biting and war-sharp, that he wore on his mail-shirt: the protector of the Weather-Geats cut the worm through the middle. They felled the foe, courage drove his life out, and they had destroyed him together, the two noble kinsmen. So ought a man be, a thane at need. To the prince that was the last moment of victory for his own deeds, of work in the world.

Then the wound that the earth-dragon had caused began to burn and to swell; at once he felt dire evil boil in his breast, poison within him. Then the prince, wise of thought, went to where he might sit on a seat near the wall. He looked on the work of giants, how the timeless earth-hall held within it stone-arches fast on pillars. Then with his hands the thane, good without limit, washed him with water, blood-besmeared, the famous prince, his beloved lord, sated with battle; and he unfastened his helmet.

Beowulf spoke—despite his wounds spoke, his mortal hurts. He knew well he had lived out his days' time, joy on earth; all passed was the number of his days, death very near. "Now I would wish to give my son my war-clothing, if any heir after me, part of my flesh, were granted. I held this people fifty winters. There was no folk-king of those dwelling about who dared approach me with swords, threaten me with fears. In my

2. I.e., the dragon's flame-breathing head.

land I awaited what fate brought me, held my own well, sought no treacherous quarrels, nor did I swear many oaths unrightfully. Sick with life-wounds, I may have joy of all this, for the Ruler of Men need not blame me for the slaughter of kinsmen when life goes from my body. Now quickly go to look at the hoard under the gray stone, beloved Wiglaf, now that the worm lies sleeping from sore wounds, bereft of his treasure. Be quick now, so that I may see the ancient wealth, the golden things, may clearly look on the bright curious gems, so that for that, because of the treasure's richness, I may the more easily leave life and nation I have long held."

(XXXVIII.) Then I have heard that the son of Weohstan straightway obeyed his lord, sick with battle-wounds, according to the words he had spoken, went wearing his ring-armor, woven battle-shirt, under the barrow's roof. Then he saw, as he went by the seat, the brave young retainer, triumphant in heart, many precious jewels, glittering gold lying on the ground, wonders on the wall, and the worm's lair, the old night-flier's—cups standing there, vessels of men of old, with none to polish them, stripped of their ornaments. There was many a helmet old and rusty, many an arm-ring skillfully twisted. (Easily may treasure, gold in the ground, betray each one of the race of men, hide it who will.) Also he saw a standard all gold hang high over the hoard, the greatest of hand-wonders, linked with fingers' skill. From it came a light so that he might see the ground, look on the works of craft. There was no trace of the worm, for the blade had taken him. Then I have heard that one man in the mound pillaged the hoard, the old work of giants, loaded in his bosom cups and plates at his own desire. He took also the standard, brightest of banners. The sword of the old lord—its edge was iron—had already wounded the one who for a long time had been guardian of the treasure, waged his fire-terror, hot for the hoard, rising up fiercely at midnight, till he died in the slaughter.

The messenger was in haste, eager to return, urged on by the treasures. Curiosity tormented him, whether eagerly seeking he should find the lord of the Weather-Geats, strength gone, alive in the place where he had left him before. Then with the treasures he found the great prince, his lord, bleeding, at the end of his life. Again he began to sprinkle him with water until this word's point broke through his breast-hoard—he spoke, the king, old man in sorrow, looked on the gold: "I speak with my words thanks to the Lord of All for these treasures, to the King of Glory, Eternal Prince, for what I gaze on here, that I might get such for my people before my death-day. Now that I have bought the hoard of treasures with my old life, you attend to the people's needs hereafter: I can be here no longer. Bid the battle-renowned make a mound, bright after the funeral fire, on the sea's cape. It shall stand high on Hronesness as a reminder to my people, so that sea-travelers later will call it Beowulf's barrow, when they drive their ships far over the darkness of the seas."

He took off his neck the golden necklace, bold-hearted prince, gave it to the thane, to the young spear-warrior—gold-gleaming helmet, ring, and mail-shirt, bade him use them well. "You are the last left of our race, of the Waegmundings. Fate has swept away all my kinsmen, earls in their strength, to destined death. I have to go after." That was the last word of the old man, of the thoughts of his heart, before he should taste the funeral pyre, hot hostile flames. The soul went from his breast to seek the doom of those fast in truth.

[*Beowulf's Funeral*]

(XXXIX.) Then sorrow came to the young man that he saw him whom he most loved on the earth, at the end of his life, suffering piteously. His slayer likewise lay dead, the awful earth-dragon bereft of life, overtaken by evil. No longer should the coiled worm rule the ring-hoard, for iron edges had taken him, hard and battle-sharp work of the hammers, so that the wide-flier, stilled by wounds, had fallen on the earth near the treasure-house. He did not go flying through the air at midnight, proud of his property, showing his aspect, but he fell to earth through the work of the chief's hands. Yet I have heard of no man of might on land, though he was bold of every deed, whom it should prosper to rush against the breath of the venomous foe or disturb with hands the ring-hall, if he found the guard awake who lived in the barrow. The share of the rich treasures became Beowulf's, paid for by death: each of the two had journeyed to the end of life's loan.

Then it was not long before the battle-slack ones left the woods, ten weak troth-breakers together, who had not dared fight with their spears in their liege lord's great need. But they bore their shields, ashamed, their war-clothes, to where the old man lay, looked on Wiglaf. He sat wearied, the foot-soldier near the shoulders of his lord, would waken him with water: it gained him nothing. He might not, though he much wished it, hold life in his chieftain on earth nor change anything of the Ruler's: the judgment of God would control the deeds of every man, just as it still does now. Then it was easy to get from the young man a grim answer to him who before had lost courage. Wiglaf spoke, the son of Weohstān, a man sad at heart, looked on the unloved ones:

"Yes, he who will speak truth may say that the liege lord who gave you treasure, the war-gear that you stand in there, when he used often to hand out to hall-sitters on the ale-benches, a prince to his thanes, helmets and war-shirts such as he could find mightiest anywhere, both far and near—that he quite threw away the war-gear, to his distress when war came upon him. The folk-king had no need to boast of his war-comrades. Yet God, Ruler of Victories, granted him that he might avenge himself, alone with his sword, when there was need for his courage. I was able to give him little life-protection in the fight, and yet beyond my power I did begin to help my kinsman. The deadly foe was ever the weaker after I struck him with my sword, fire poured less strongly from his head. Too few defenders thronged about the prince when the hard time came upon him. Now there shall cease for your race the receiving of treasure and the giving of swords, all enjoyment of pleasant homes, comfort. Each man of your kindred must go deprived of his land-right when nobles from afar learn of your flight, your inglorious deed. Death is better for any earl than a life of blame."

(XL.) Then he bade that the battle-deed be announced in the city, up over the cliff-edge, where the band of warriors sat the whole morning of the day, sad-hearted, shield-bearers in doubt whether it was the beloved man's last day or whether he would come again. Little did he fail to speak of new tidings, he who rode up the hill, but spoke to them all truthfully: "Now the joy-giver of the people of the Weathers, the lord of the Geats, is fast on his death-bed, lies on his slaughter-couch through deeds of the worm. Beside him lies his life-enemy, struck down with dagger-wounds—with his sword he might not work wounds of any kind on the monster. Wiglaf son of Weohstan sits over Beowulf, one earl by the lifeless other, in weariness of heart holds death-watch over the loved and the hated.

"Now may the people expect a time of war, when the king's fall becomes wide-known to the Franks and the Frisians. A harsh quarrel was begun with the Hugas when Hygelac came traveling with his sea-army to the land of the Frisians, where the Hetware assailed him in battle, quickly, with stronger forces, made the mailed warrior bow; he fell in the ranks: that chief gave no treasure to his retainers. Ever since then the good will of the Merewioing king has been denied us.

"Nor do I expect any peace or trust from the Swedish people, for it is wide-known that Ongentheow took the life of Haethcyn,

Hrethel's son, near Ravenswood when in their over-pride the people of the Geats first went against the War-Scylfings. Straightway the wary father of Ohthere,[3] old and terrible, gave a blow in return, cut down the sea-king,[4] rescued his wife, old woman of times past, bereft of her gold, mother of Onela and Ohthere, and then he followed his life-foes until they escaped, lordless, painfully, to Ravenswood. Then with a great army he besieged those whom the sword had left, weary with wounds, often vowed woes to the wretched band the livelong night, said that in the morning he would cut them apart with sword-blades, [hang] some on gallows-trees as sport for birds. Relief came in turn to the sorry-hearted together with dawn when they heard Hygelac's horn and trumpet, his sound as the good man came on their track with a body of retainers. (XLI.) Wide-seen was the bloody track of Swedes and Geats, the slaughter-strife of men, how the peoples stirred up the feud between them. Then the good man went with his kinsmen, old and much-mourning, to seek his stronghold: the earl Ongentheow moved further away. He had heard of the warring of Hygelac, of the war-power of the proud one. He did not trust in resistance, that he might fight off the sea-men, defend his hoard against the war-sailors, his children and wife. Instead he drew back, the old man behind his earth-wall.

"Then pursuit was offered to the people of the Swedes, the standards of Hygelac overran the stronghold as Hrethel's people pressed forward to the citadel. There Ongentheow the gray-haired was brought to bay by sword-blades, and the people's king had to submit to the judgment of Eofor alone. Wulf[5] son of Wonred had struck him angrily with his weapon so that for the blow the blood sprang forth in streams beneath his hair. Yet not for that was he afraid, the old Scylfing, but he quickly repaid the assault with worse exchange, the folk-king, when he turned toward him. The strong son of Wonred could not give the old man a return blow, for Ongentheow had first cut through the helmet of his head so that he had to sink down, smeared with blood—fell on the earth: he was not yet doomed, for he recovered, though the wound hurt him. The hardy thane of Hygelac,[6] when his brother lay low, let his broad sword, old blade made by giants, break the great helmet across the shield-wall; then the king bowed, the keeper of the folk was hit to the quick.

3. I.e., Ongentheow.

4. I.e., Haethcyn, king of the Geats. Haethcyn's brother Hygelac, who succeeded him, was not present at this battle, but arrived after the death of Haethcyn with reinforcements to relieve the survivors and to pursue Ongentheow in his retreat to his city.

5. The two sons of Wonred, Wulf and Eofor, attacked Ongentheow in turn. Wulf was struck down but not killed by the old Swedish king, who was then slain by Eofor.

6. I.e., Eofor.

"Then there were many who bound up the brother, quickly raised him up after it was granted them to control the battle-field. Then one warrior stripped the other, took from Ongentheow his iron-mail, hard-hilted sword, and his helmet, too; he bore the arms of the hoary one to Hygelac. He accepted that treasure and fairly promised him rewards among the people, and he stood by it thus: the lord of the Geats, the son of Hrethel, when he came home, repaid Wulf and Eofor for their battle-assault with much treasure, gave each of them a hundred thousand [units] of land and linked rings: there was no need for any man on middle-earth to blame him for the rewards, since they had performed great deeds. And then he gave Eofor his only daughter as a pledge of friendship—a fair thing for his home.

"That is the feud and the enmity, the death-hatred of men, for which I expect that the people of the Swedes, bold shield-warriors after the fall of princes, will set upon us after they learn that our prince has gone from life, he who before held hoard and kingdom against our enemies, did good to the people, and further still, did what a man should. Now haste is best, that we look on the people's king there and bring him who gave us rings on his way to the funeral pyre. Nor shall only a small share melt with the great-hearted one, but there is a hoard of treasure, gold uncounted, grimly purchased, and rings bought at the last now with his own life. These shall the fire devour, flames enfold—no earl to wear ornament in remembrance, nor any bright maiden add to her beauty with neck-ring; but mournful-hearted, stripped of gold, they shall walk, often, not once, in strange countries—now that the army-leader has laid aside laughter, his game and his mirth. Therefore many a spear, cold in the morning, shall be grasped with fingers, raised by hands; no sound of harp shall waken the warriers, but the dark raven, low over the doomed, shall tell many tales, say to the eagle how he fared at the feast when with the wolf he spoiled the slain bodies."

Thus the bold man was a speaker of hateful news, nor did he much lie in his words or his prophecies. The company all arose. Without joy they went below Earnaness[7] to look on the wonder with welling tears. Then they found on the sand, soulless, keeping his bed of rest, him who in former times had given them rings. Then the last day of the good man had come, when the war-king, prince of the Weather-Geats, died a wonderful death. First they saw the stranger creature, the worm lying loathsome, opposite him in the place. The fire-dragon was grimly terrible with his many colors, burned by the flames; he was fifty feet

7. The headland near where Beowulf had fought the dragon.

long in the place where he lay. Once he had joy of the air at night, came back down to seek his den. Then he was made fast by death, had made use of the last of his earth-caves. Beside him stood cups and pitchers, plates and rich swords lay eaten through by rust, just as they had been there in the bosom of the earth for a thousand winters. Then that huge heritage, gold of men of old, was wound in a spell, so that no one of men must touch the ring-hall unless God himself, the True King of Victories—He is men's protection—should grant to whom He wished to open the hoard—whatever man seemed fit to Him.

(XLII.) Then it was seen that the act did not profit him who wrongly kept hidden the handiworks under the wall. The keeper had first slain a man like few others, then the feud had been fiercely avenged. It is a wonder where an earl famed for courage may reach the end of his allotted life—then may dwell no longer in the mead-hall, man with his kin. So it was with Beowulf when he sought quarrels, the barrow's ward: he himself did not then know in what way his parting with the world should come. The great princes who had put it[8] there had laid on it so deep a curse until doomsday that the man who should plunder the place should be guilty of sins, imprisoned in idol-shrines, fixed with hell-bonds, punished with evils—unless the Possessor's favor were first shown the more clearly to him who desired the gold.

Wiglaf spoke, the son of Weohstan: "Often many a man must suffer distress for the will of one man, as has happened to us. We might by no counsel persuade our dear prince, keeper of the kingdom, not to approach the gold-guardian, let him lie where he long was, live in his dwelling to the world's end. He held to his high destiny. The hoard has been made visible, grimly got. What drove the folk-king thither was too powerfully fated. I have been therein and looked at it all, the rare things of the chamber, when it was granted me—not at all friendly was the journey that I was permitted beneath the earth-wall. In haste I seized with my hands a huge burden of hoard-treasures, of great size, bore it out here to my king. He was then still alive, sound-minded and aware. He spoke many things, old man in sorrow, and bade greet you, commanded that for your lord's deeds you make a high barrow in the place of his pyre, large and conspicuous, since he was of men the worthiest warrior through the wide earth, while he might enjoy wealth in his castle.

"Let us now hasten to see and visit for the second time the heap of precious jewels, the wonder under the walls. I shall direct you so that you may look on enough of them from near

8. The treasure.

at hand—rings and broad gold. Let the bier be made ready, speedily prepared, when we come out, and then let us carry our prince, beloved man, where he shall long dwell in the Ruler's protection."

Then the son of Weohstan, man brave in battle, bade command many warriors, men who owned houses, leaders of the people, that they carry wood from afar for the pyre for the good man. "Now shall flame eat the chief of warriors—the fire shall grow dark—who often survived the iron-shower when the storm of arrows driven from bow-strings passed over the shield-wall—the shaft did its task, made eager by feather-gear served the arrowhead."

And then the wise son of Weohstan summoned from the host thanes of the king, seven together, the best; one of eight warriors, he went beneath the evil roof. One who walked before bore a torch in his hands. Then there was no lot to decide who should plunder that hoard, since the men could see that every part of it rested in the hall without guardian, lay wasting. Little did any man mourn that hastily they should bear out the rare treasure. Also they pushed the dragon, the worm, over the cliff-wall, let the wave take him, the flood enfold the keeper of the treasure. Then twisted gold was loaded on a wagon, an uncounted number of things, and the prince, hoary warrior, borne to Hronesness.

(XLIII.) Then the people of the Geats made ready for him a funeral pyre on the earth, no small one, hung with helmets, battle-shields, bright mail-shirts, just as he had asked. Then in the midst they laid the great prince, lamenting their hero, their beloved lord. Then warriors began to awaken on the barrow the greatest of funeral-fires; the wood-smoke climbed, black over the fire; the roaring flame mixed with weeping—the wind-surge died down—until it had broken the bone-house, hot at its heart. Sad in spirit they lamented their heart-care, the death of their liege lord. [And the Geatish woman, wavy-haired, sang a sorrowful song about Beowulf, said] [9] again and again that she sorely feared for herself invasions of armies, many slaughters, terror of troops, humiliation, and captivity. Heaven swallowed the smoke.

Then the people of the Weather-Geats built a mound on the promontory, one that was high and broad, wide-seen by seafarers, and in ten days completed a monument for the bold in battle, surrounded the remains of the fire with a wall, the most splendid that men most skilled might devise. In the barrow they placed rings and jewels, all such ornaments as troubled men had earlier taken from the hoard. They let the earth hold the wealth of

9. The manuscript is badly damaged and the interpretation conjectural.

earls, gold in the ground, where now it still dwells, as useless to men as it was before. Then the brave in battle rode round the mound, children of nobles, twelve in all, would bewail their sorrow and mourn their king, recite dirges and speak of the man. They praised his great deeds and his acts of courage, judged well of his prowess. So it is fitting that man honor his liege lord with words, love him in heart when he must be led forth from the body. Thus the people of the Geats, his hearth-companions, lamented the death of their lord. They said that he was of world-kings the mildest of men and the gentlest, kindest to his people, and most eager for fame.

THE WANDERER

The lament of *The Wanderer* is an excellent example of the elegiac mood so common in Old English poetry. The loss of a lord, of companions in arms, of a mead-hall (in which Anglo-Saxon life realized itself to the full) are themes that enhance the melancholy tone of *Beowulf* as they are the emotional basis for such a poem as the present one. But nowhere more poignantly expressed than in *The Wanderer* is the loneliness of the exile in search of a new lord and hall: this is what Beowulf's father, Ecgtheow, would have suffered, had it not been for Hrothgar's hospitality. To the wretched seeker all weather is wintry, for nature seems to conspire to match a man's mood as he moves over the water from one land to another, yearning for a home and kin to replace those vanished ones that still fill his thoughts.

As is true of most Old English elegiac laments, both the language and the structure of *The Wanderer* are difficult. At the beginning the speaker (whom the poet identifies as an "earth-walker") voices hope of finding comfort after his many tribulations. After the poet's interruption, the wanderer continues to speak—to himself—of his long search for a new home, describing how he must keep his thoughts locked within him while he makes his search. But these thoughts form the most vivid and moving part of his soliloquy—how, floating upon the sea, dazed with sorrow and fatigue, he imagines that he sees his old companions, and how, as he wakens to reality, they vanish over the water like sea-birds. The second part of the poem, beginning with the seventh paragraph ("Therefore I cannot think why * * * "), expands the theme from one man to all men in a world wasted by war and time, and the speaker draws philosophical implications from his harsh experiences (presumably now in the past). He derives such cold comfort as he can from asking the old question, *Ubi sunt?*—where are they who were once so glad to be alive? And he concludes with the thought that "all this earthly habitation shall be emptied" of mankind. The narrator, "wise in heart," sits apart at the council, apparently as an indication of his detachment from life. The poem concludes with a characteristic Old English injunction to practice restraint on earth, place hope only in heaven.

The Wanderer is preserved only in the Exeter Book, a manuscript copied about 975, which contains the largest surviving collection of Old English poetry.

The Wanderer[1]

"He who is alone often lives to find favor, mildness of the Lord, even though he has long had to stir with his arms the frost-cold sea, troubled in heart over the water-way had to tread the tracks of exile. Fully-fixed is his fate."

So spoke the earth-walker, remembering hardships, fierce war-slaughters—the fall of dear kinsmen.

"Often before the day dawned I have had to speak of my cares, alone: there is now none among the living to whom I dare clearly express the thought of my heart. I know indeed that it is a fine custom for a man to lock tight his heart's coffer, keep closed the hoard-case of his mind, whatever his thoughts may be. Words of a weary heart may not withstand fate, nor those of an angry spirit bring help. Therefore men eager for fame shut sorrowful thought up fast in their breast's coffer.

"Thus I, wretched with care, removed from my homeland, far from dear kinsmen, have had to fasten with fetters the thoughts of my heart—ever since the time, many years ago, that I covered my gold-friend in the darkness of the earth; and from there I crossed the woven waves, winter-sad, downcast for want of a hall, sought a giver of treasure—a place, far or near, where I might find one in a mead-hall who should know of my people, or would comfort me friendless, receive me with gladness. He who has experienced it knows how cruel a companion sorrow is to the man who has no beloved protectors. Exile's path awaits him, not twisted gold—frozen thoughts in his heart-case, no joy of earth. He recalls the hall-warriors and the taking of treasure, how in youth his gold-friend made him accustomed to feasting. All delight has gone.

"He who has had long to forgo the counsel of a beloved lord knows indeed how, when sorrow and sleep together bind the poor dweller-alone, it will seem to him in his mind that he is embracing and kissing his liege lord and laying his hands and his head on his knee, as it some times was in the old days when he took part in the gift-giving. Then he wakens again, the man with no lord, sees the yellow waves before him, the sea-birds bathe, spread their feathers, frost and snow fall, mingled with hail.

"Then the wounds are deeper in his heart, sore for want of his dear one. His sorrow renews as the memory of his kinsmen moves

1. This new translation by the editor is based on the text as edited by John C. Pope in *Seven Old English Poems* (1966).

through his mind: he greets them with glad words, eagerly looks at them, a company of warriors. Again they fade, moving off over the water; the spirit of these fleeting ones brings to him no familiar voices. Care renews in him who must again and again send his weary heart out over the woven waves.

"Therefore I cannot think why the thoughts of my heart should not grow dark when I consider all the life of men through this world—with what terrible swiftness they forgo the hall-floor, bold young retainers. So this middle-earth each day fails and falls. No man may indeed become wise before he has had his share of winters in this world's kingdom. The wise man must be patient, must never bc too hot-hearted, nor too hasty of speech, nor too fearful, nor too glad, nor too greedy for wealth, nor ever too eager to boast before he has thought clearly. A man must wait, when he speaks in boast, until he knows clearly, sure-minded, where the thoughts of his heart may turn.

"The wise warrior must consider how ghostly it will be when all the wealth of world stands waste, just as now here and there through this middle-earth wind-blown walls stand covered with frost-fall, storm-beaten dwellings. Wine-halls totter, the lord lies bereft of joy, all the company has fallen, bold men beside the wall. War took away some, bore them forth on their way; a bird carried one away over the deep sea; a wolf shared one with Death; another a man sad of face hid in an earth-pit.

"So the Maker of mankind laid waste this dwelling-place until the old works of giants stood idle, devoid of the noise of the stronghold's keepers. Therefore the man wise in his heart considers carefully this wall-place and this dark life, remembers the multitude of deadly combats long ago, and speaks these words: 'Where has the horse gone? Where the young warrior? Where is the giver of treasure? What has become of the feasting seats? Where are the joys of the hall? Alas, the bright cup! Alas, the mailed warrior! Alas, the prince's glory! How that time has gone, vanished beneath night's cover, just as if it never had been! The wall, wondrous high, decorated with snake-likenesses, stands now over traces of the beloved company. The ash-spears' might has borne the earls away—weapons greedy for slaughter, Fate the mighty; and storms beat on the stone walls, snow, the herald of winter, falling thick binds the earth when darkness comes and the night-shadow falls, sends harsh hailstones from the north in hatred of men. All earth's kingdom is wretched, the world beneath the skies is changed by the work of the fates. Here wealth is fleeting, here friend is fleeting, here man is fleeting, here woman is fleeting—all this earthly habitation shall be emptied.' "

So spoke the man wise in heart, sat apart at the council. He is good who keeps his word; a man must never utter too quickly his breast's passion, unless he knows first how to achieve remedy, as a leader with his courage. It will be well with him who seeks favor, comfort from the Father in heaven, where for us all stability resides.

THE BATTLE OF MALDON

The *Battle of Maldon* celebrates an event of the year 991, when a large party of Scandinavian raiders met the English defense forces on the estuary of the Blackwater River (the Pant of the poem), near Maldon in Essex. The Vikings had made a number of successful raids on seaports in the vicinity, after which they had encamped on an island near the mouth of the river. The island, since it was accessible from the mainland by a causeway that might be used only at low tide, provided a natural base from which the Vikings could continue their hit-and-run depredations on the countryside. Birhtnoth, the Earl of Essex, who was leader of the English militia, took up his position at the end of the causeway and from there was able to prevent the enemy from crossing to the mainland. As the poem relates, however, in his "overconfidence" he allowed them free passage so that a battle might take place. As a result, he was himself killed, and many of the defenders took to their heels; but the earl's retinue —his close associates and retainers—continued to fight bravely until they were overwhelmed. In the incomplete form in which the poem has come down to us we do not hear of the ultimate defeat of the English, though the grim tone and in particular the famous speech of Birhtwold prepare us for the disaster.

The unknown poet of late Anglo-Saxon times was apparently well versed in heroic English poetry of the type of *Beowulf*, and he does a brilliant job of adapting traditional epic mannerisms to his description of a local battle of no particular historical importance, which involved people with whom he was acquainted. The defense forces were actually no more than a home guard: inexperienced farmers and laborers conscripted for the local defense, together with a small group of aristocrats who were acquainted with heroic martial tradition but had not before had the opportunity to behave heroically. Since the defeat of the Scandinavians at Brunanburg in 937, the kingdom had enjoyed a long, peaceful respite from attack; the present Viking raid was, indeed, the beginning of a new and bloody era during which the realm that Alfred had consolidated weakened badly under Ethelred "the Unready." Godric and his brothers, who, according to the poem, fled from the battle, are representative of those Englishmen who preferred to pay tribute rather than to fight. But Birhtnoth and his retinue are of the traditional tough fiber, and it is especially in their speeches and single combats that the poet uses the epic style, contenting himself elsewhere with a forceful but generally realistic narrative of what occurred. Birhtnoth's decision to let the Vikings cross the river is treated in the epic manner as an instance of heroic overconfidence, like Beowulf's refusal to use his sword against the unarmed Grendel

—but in this case it is a gesture that leads to tragic doom. Probably Birhtnoth had a practical motive for his rashness: if the Vikings were prevented from raiding here, they would simply sail along the coast to a less well-defended spot in order to continue their depredations. Only their destruction would insure general peace; but from the local point of view, Birhtnoth's permitting the enemy to come where he could fight with them might well appear as the rashly noble act of a traditional hero.

The poem was written down in a manuscript that was reduced to charred fragments in the same fire that damaged the *Beowulf* manuscript. Fortunately, a transcript had been made of it before the fire, and on this modern editions depend. Even before the manuscript was burned the poem must have lacked a number of lines at its beginning and end, though most scholars feel that nothing very substantial has been lost.

The Battle of Maldon[1]

Then he[2] commanded each of his warriors to leave his horse, drive it far away, and walk forward, trusting in his hands and in his good courage. When Offa's kinsman[3] understood that the earl would not put up with cowardice, he let his beloved hawk fly from his hand toward the woods and advanced to the battle: by this men might know that the youth would not weaken in the fight once he had taken up his weapons. Eadric wished also to serve his lord the earl in the battle; he carried his spear forward to the conflict. He was of good heart as long as he might hold shield and broad-sword in his hands; he carried out the vow that he had made, now that he was to fight before his lord.

Then Birhtnoth began to place his men at their stations; he rode about and advised them, taught the troops how they should stand and hold the place and bade them grasp their shields aright, firm in their hands, and have no fear. When he had arranged his folk properly, he alighted among them where it seemed best to him, where he knew his retainers to be most loyal.

Then the Vikings' herald stood on the river bank, cried out loudly, spoke words, boastfully proclaimed the seafarers' message to the earl where he stood on the shore: "Bold seamen have sent me to you, have commanded me to say to you that you must quickly send treasure in order to protect yourself; and it is better for you to buy off this spear-assault with tribute than to have us give you harsh war. There is no need for us to destroy one another, if you are rich

1. In this prose translation by the present editor, a few liberties have been taken with the text in order to make clear the references of some of the loosely used Old English terms for "warrior." The translation is in general based on the text in J. C. Pope's *Seven Old English Poems* (1966).

2. Earl Birhtnoth, commander of the English defense forces.

3. Offa is mentioned later in the poem as one of Birhtnoth's principal retainers; his young kinsman is not otherwise identified.

enough to pay. With the gold we will confirm truce. If you that are highest here decide upon this, that you will ransom your people, and in return for peace give the seamen money in the amount they request, and receive peace from us, we will go to ship with the tribute, set sail on the sea, and keep peace with you."

Birhtnoth spoke, raised his shield, his slender ash-spear, uttered words, angry and resolute gave him answer: "Do you hear, seafarer, what this folk says? They will give you spears for tribute, poisoned point and old sword, heriot[4] that avails you not in battle. Sea-wanderers' herald, take back our answer, speak to your people a message far more hateful, that here stands with his host an undisgraced earl who will defend this country, my lord Æthelred's[5] homeland, folk and land. Heathen shall fall in the battle. It seems to me too shameful that you should go unfought to ship with our tribute, now that you have come thus far into our land. Not so easily shall you get treasure: point and edge shall first reconcile us, grim battle-play, before we give tribute."

Then he ordered the men to bear their shields, go forward so that they all stood on the river bank. Because of the water neither band could come to the other: after the ebb, the floodtide came flowing in; currents met and crossed. It seemed to them too long a time before they might bear their spears together. On the river Pant they stood in proud array, the battle-line of the East Saxons and the men from the ash-ships. Nor might any of them injure another, unless one should receive death from the flight of an arrow.

The tide went out. The seamen stood ready, many Vikings eager for war. The earl, protector of men, bade a war-hard warrior—he was named Wulfstan, of bold lineage—to hold the bridge:[6] he was Ceola's son, who with his spear pierced the first man bold enough to step upon the bridge. There stood with Wulfstan fearless fighters, Ælfhere and Maccus, bold men both who would not take flight from the ford, but defended themselves stoutly against the enemy as long as they might wield weapons.

When the loathed strangers saw that, and understood clearly that they would face bitter bridge-defenders there, they began to prefer words to deeds,[7] prayed that they might have access to the bank, pass over the ford and lead their forces across. Then in his overconfidence the earl began to yield ground—too much ground—to the hateful people: Birhthelm's son began to call over the cold water while warriors listened: "Now the way is laid open for you.

4. The weapons a tenant received from his lord; they were returned to the lord upon the tenant's death.

5. King Ethelred "the Unready," who reigned from 978 to 1016.

6. Not a bridge in the modern sense, but probably a stone causeway, under water even at low tide; immediately below, it is called a ford.

7. Literally, "to practice deception"—an overstatement due to the poet's scorn for fighters who refused to do things the hard heroic way.

Come straightway to us, as men to battle. God alone knows which of us may be master of the field."

The slaughter-wolves advanced, minded not the water, a host of Vikings westward over the Pant, over the bright water bore their shields: sailors to land brought shields of linden. Opposite stood Birhtnoth with his warriors, ready for the fierce invaders. He ordered his men to form a war-hedge[8] with their shields and to hold the formation fast against the enemy. Now was combat near, glory in battle. The time had come when doomed men should fall. Shouts were raised; ravens circled, the eagle eager for food. On earth there was uproar.

They let the file-hard spears fly from their hands, grim-ground javelins. Bows were busy, shield felt point. Bitter was the battle-rush. On either side warriors fell, young men lay dead. Wulfmær was wounded, chose the slaughter-bed: kinsman of Birhtnoth—his sister's son—he was cruelly hewn down with swords. Then requital was made to the Vikings: I have heard that Eadweard struck one fiercely with his sword, withheld not the stroke, so that the warrior fell doomed at his feet; for this his lord gave the chamberlain[9] thanks when he had opportunity. Thus men stood firm in the battle, stern of purpose. Eagerly all these armed fighters contended with one another to see who could be the first with his weapon's point to take life from doomed man. The slain fell, carrion, to the earth. The defenders stood fast; Birhtnoth urged them on, bade each man who would win glory from the Danes to give his whole heart to the battle.

A war-hard Viking advanced, raised up his weapon, his shield to defend himself, moved against Birhtnoth. As resolute as the churl,[1] the earl advanced toward him. Each of them meant harm to the other. Then the seaman threw his southern-made[2] spear so that the fighters' chief was wounded. But he thrust the spear with his shield so that the shaft split and the spearhead broke off and sprang away.[3] The war-chief was maddened; with his spear he stabbed the proud Viking that had given him the wound. Wise in war was the host's leader: he let his spear go through the man's neck, guided his hand so that he mortally wounded the raider. Then he quickly stabbed another, breaking through the mail-shirt: in the breast, quite through the corselet, was this one wounded; at his heart stood the poisoned point. The earl was the blither; the bold man laughed, gave thanks to God that the Lord had given him this day's work.

8. A wall of shields (a common defensive formation).

9. I.e., Eadweard.

1. Here "churl" means something like "villain."

2. Apparently the Vikings preferred weapons made in England or France—the "south."

3. The maneuver described frees the spear from the wounded man's body and enables him to take retaliatory action.

One of the Vikings loosed a javelin from his hand, let it fly from his fist, and it sped its way through Æthelred's noble thane. By the earl's side stood a lad not yet grown, a boy in the battle, son of Wulfstan, Wulfmær the young, who plucked full boldly the bloody spear from the warrior. He sent the hard spear flying back again: its point went in, and on the earth lay the man who had sorely wounded his lord. Then an armed Viking stepped toward the earl. He wished to seize the earl's war-gear, make booty of rings and ornamented sword. Then Birhtnoth took his sword from its sheath, broad and bright-edged, and struck at his assailant's coat of mail. Too soon one of the seafarers hindered him, wounded the earl in his arm. Then the gold-hilted sword fell to the earth: he might not hold the hard blade, wield his weapon. Yet he spoke words, the hoar battle-leader, encouraged his men, bade them go forward stoutly together. He might no longer stand firm on his feet. He looked toward Heaven and spoke: "I thank thee, Ruler of Nations, for all the joys that I have had in the world. Now, gentle Lord, I have most need that thou grant my spirit grace, that my soul may travel to thee—under thy protection, Prince of Angels, depart in peace. I beseech thee that fiends of hell harm it not." Then the heathen warriors slew him and both the men who stood by him; Ælfnoth and Wulfmær both were laid low; close by their lord they gave up their lives.

Then there retired from the battle those who did not wish to be there. The son of Odda was the first to flee: Godric went from the fight and left the good man that had given him many a steed. He leaped upon the horse that his lord had owned, upon trappings that he had no right to, and both his brothers galloped with him, Godwine and Godwig cared not for battle, but went from the war and sought the wood, fled to its fastness and saved their lives—and more men than was in any way right, if they remembered all the favors he had done for their benefit. So Offa had said to him that day at the meeting he had held in the place, that many there spoke boldly who would not remain firm at need.

The folk's leader had fallen, Æthelred's earl: all his hearth-companions saw that their lord lay dead. Then the proud thanes advanced; men without fear pressed eagerly on. They all desired either of two things, to leave life or avenge the man they loved. Thus Ælfric's son urged them on; the warrior young of winters spoke words; Ælfwine it was who spoke, and spoke boldly: "Remember the speeches we have spoken so often over our mead,[4] when we raised boast on the bench, heroes in the hall, about hard fighting. Now may the man who is bold prove that he is. I will make my

4. Boasting of prowess while drinking is a common element in Old English poetry.

noble birth known to all, that I was of great kin in Mercia. My grandfather was named Ealhelm, a wise earl, worldly-prosperous. Thanes among that people shall not have reason to reproach me that I would go from this band of defenders, seek my home, now that my lord lies hewn down in battle. To me that is greatest of griefs: he was both my kinsman and my lord." Then he went forward, bent on revenge, and with the point of his spear pierced one of the pirate band, so that he lay on the earth, destroyed by the weapon. Then Ælfwine began to encourage his comrades, friends and companions, to go forward.

Offa spoke, shook his ash-spear: "Lo, you, Ælfwine, have encouraged us all, thanes in need. Now that our lord the earl lies on the earth, there is need for us all that each one of us encourage the other, warriors to battle, as long as he may have and hold weapon, hard sword, spear and good blade. The coward son of Odda, Godric, has betrayed us all; when he rode off on that horse, on that proud steed, many a man thought that he was our lord. Therefore here on the field folk were dispersed, the shield-wall broken. Curses on his action, by which he caused so many men here to flee."

Leofsunu spoke, raised the linden buckler, his shield to defend himself; he answered the warrior: "I promise that I will not flee a footstep hence, but I will go forward, avenge my dear lord in the fight. Steadfast warriors about Sturmer[5] need not reproach me with their words that now that my patron is dead I would go lordless home, abandon the battle. But weapon, point and iron, shall take me." Full wrathful he went forward, fought fiercely; flight he despised.

Then Dunnere spoke, shook his spear; humble churl,[6] he cried over all, bade each warrior avenge Birhtnoth: "He who intends to avenge his lord on the folk may not hesitate nor care for life." Then they advanced: they cared not for life. The retainers began to fight hardily, fierce spear-bearers, and prayed God that they might avenge their patron and bring destruction to their enemies.

The hostage[7] began to help them eagerly. He was of bold kin among the Northumbrians, the son of Ecglaf: his name was Æscferth. He did not flinch at the war-play, but threw spears without pause. Now he hit shield, now he pierced man: each moment he caused some wound, as long as he might wield weapons.

Eadweard the Long still stood in the line, ready and eager, spoke boasting words, how he would not flee a footstep nor turn back, now that his chief lay dead. He broke the shield-wall and fought against

5. The Essex village where the speaker lived.
6. I.e., freeman of the lowest rank.
7. Among Germanic peoples, hostages of high rank generally fought on the side of the warriors who held them in hostage.

the foe until he had worthily avenged his treasure-giver on the seamen—before he himself lay on the slaughter-bed.

So also did Æthelric, noble companion, eager and impetuous; he fought most resolutely, this brother of Sibirht, as did many another: they split the hollow shield and defended themselves boldly [8]. . . The shield's rim broke and the mail-shirt sang one of horror's songs. Then in the battle Offa struck the seafarer so that he fell on the earth, and there Gadd's kinsman himself sought the ground: Offa was quickly hewn down in the fight. He had, however, performed what he had promised his lord, what he had vowed before to his ring-giver, that they should either both ride to the town, hale to their home, or fall among the host, die of wounds in the slaughter-place. He lay as a thane should, near his lord.

Then there was a crash of shields. The seamen advanced, enraged by the fight. Spear oft pierced life-house of doomed man. Then Wistan advanced: Thurstan's son fought against the men. He was the slayer of three of them in the throng before the son of Wigelm [9] lay dead in the carnage. There was stubborn conflict. Warriors stood fast in the fight. Fighting men fell, worn out with wounds: slain fell among slain.

All the while Oswold and Eadwold, brothers both, encouraged the men, with their words bade their dear kinsmen that they should stand firm at need, wield their weapons without weakness.

Birhtwold spoke, raised his shield—he was an old retainer—shook his ash-spear; full boldly he exhorted the men: "Purpose shall be the firmer, heart the keener, courage shall be the more, as our might lessens.[1] Here lies our lord all hewn down, good man on ground. Ever may he lament who now thinks to turn from war-play. I am old of life; from here I will not turn, but by my lord's side, by the man I loved, I intend to lie."

So also the son of Æthelgar encouraged them all to the battle: this Godric oft let spear go, slaughter-shaft fly on the Vikings; thus he advanced foremost among the folk, hewed and laid low until he died in the fighting: he was not that Godric who fled the battle.

8. Apparently a description of a Viking's attack on Offa has been lost.

9. Identification uncertain: perhaps Offa was the son of Wigelm.

1. These famous lines appear thus in the original: "Hige sceal Þe heardra, heorte Þe cenre, / mod sceal Þe mare, Þe ure mægen lytlaÞ."

GEOFFREY CHAUCER

(ca. 1343–1400)

1370: The *Book of the Duchess* (first important extant poem).
1372: First Italian journey: contact with Italian literature.
1385: *Troilus and Criseide*.
1386: *Canterbury Tales* begun.

Social thought in the Middle Ages lagged far behind social realities. Medieval England did not recognize the existence of any class between the aristocracy, a relatively small group that attained its position by birth alone, and the commons, which included everyone not of high birth. There was, theoretically, no way by which one might advance from the commons to the aristocracy. But in actual fact there existed a large and increasingly important middle class that was constantly infiltrating the aristocracy, and it was into this middle class that Chaucer was born. He was the son of a well-to-do wine merchant, and probably spent his boyhood in the down-to-earth atmosphere of London's Vintry, the wine-merchandising area; here, despite the privileges, especially in the way of education, that his father's wealth secured for him, he must have mixed daily with other commoners of all sorts. He might well have passed his whole life there, counting casks and money; but in his early teens he was sent to serve as a page in one of the great aristocratic households of England, that of Lionel of Antwerp, a son of the reigning monarch, Edward III. The rest of his life Chaucer spent in close association with the ruling nobility of the kingdom, not only with Lionel, but with his more powerful brother John of Gaunt; with their father King Edward; with their nephew Richard II, who succeeded to the throne in 1377; and finally with John's son Henry IV, who desposed his cousin and became king in 1399. Chaucer's wife Philippa was a member of the households of Edward's queen and of John of Gaunt's second wife, Constance of Castile, and she was doubtless of higher birth than the poet. A Thomas Chaucer, who was probably their son, was an eminent man in the next generation, and an Alice Chaucer, quite possibly Chaucer's granddaughter, was sufficiently important in her day to have been married successively to the Earl of Salisbury and the Duke of Norfolk. The theoretically unbridgeable gap between the commons and the aristocracy was thus ably bridged by the poet.

In order to accomplish this, Chaucer must have been able in other ways than as a poet, though doubtless his extraordinary poetic ability was of great service to his advancement. Yet if one were to rely merely on the preserved historical records, one would have little reason to suspect that the Geoffrey Chaucer they keep mentioning ever wrote a line of verse. We catch glimpses of him serving as a page in Lionel's household (1357); as a soldier getting himself captured by the French in one of Edward III's many sallies to the continent (1359); of his being the well-beloved *vallectus* of Edward III (1367)—despite the term, which means "valet," Chaucer's duties were hardly menial—and the well-beloved servant of John of Gaunt (1374), and of receiving substantial rewards for his services; of his being sent to Italy to assist in arranging a trade agreement with the Genoese (1372), and to France, perhaps to assist in getting a royal bride for young Prince Richard (1377); of his receiving a rent-free house on the city wall of London (1374); of his keeping, "in his own hand," the accounts for which he was responsible as Controller of the Customs and Subsidies on Wool for the port of London (1374–86)—and the wool trade was England's largest trade; of other trips abroad on official business; of his becoming Justice of the Peace and Knight of the Shire (Member of Parliament) for the county of Kent (1385–86); of his erecting grandstands, inventorying pots and pans, and getting himself robbed as Clerk of the King's Works (1389–91); of his being appointed deputy forester of one of the royal preserves in Somerset (1391); and—throughout his life—of his receiving grants and annuities, or having them confirmed by royal act when a new king took the throne, or asking that butts of wine given him by the crown be transformed into cash, or merely asking for money or more money. We last glimpse him, in the final months of his life, renting a house in the garden of Westminster Abbey, within a stone's throw of Westminster Hall, the ancient seat of English government.

CHAUCER'S LITERARY CAREER

It might seem that a man so busy would have had little time to write poetry, but Chaucer seems to have been an assiduous versifier all his adult life. Unfortunately, few of his poems can be precisely dated, and some have not been preserved. Probably among his earliest works was a translation of the *Roman de la Rose,* a 13th-century French poem that exercised a profound influence on Chaucer's work. The first part of the *Roman* is an allegory, written by Guillaume de Lorris, which tells, in the form of a dream, the progress of a youthful love affair. Guillaume left the poem unfinished, but an enormous sequel was added to it after Guillaume's death by Jean de Meun: in this sequel the young courtier finally wins his lady (the rose), but not until Jean has discussed at great length many of the issues considered important by medieval intellectuals. The poem is a mixture of highly diverse elements, and it is characteristic of Chaucer's love of variety that he was able to assimilate into his own work both the courtly emotionalism of Guillaume and the philosophical, often satiric, detachment of Jean. Of a 14th-century English translation of the French poem only a fragment has come down to us, and that without any mention of the translator's name; scholars are generally agreed that the first 1700 lines of this fragment are Chaucer's.

Chaucer's work on the *Roman* is thought to have been done during the 60's. During this decade he probably made other translations from the French, and kept on sharpening his rhetorical tools. At the end of the decade he produced his first major work (and the only one of his poems that can be accurately dated): the *Book of the Duchess,* probably completed in early 1369, an elegy for John of Gaunt's first wife, the lovely Blanche of Lancaster, who died in 1368. This is at once one of Chaucer's most derivative and most original poems: many of its octosyllabic lines are translated directly from various works by Jean Froissart, a French poet contemporary with Chaucer, and from his countryman Guillaume de Machaut as well as from other Frenchmen; yet the plan of the work is imaginative and daring, and as a whole the elegy is on a level of excellence never attained by the poets from whom Chaucer is borrowing. It is also interesting to observe how that tact which was later to earn Chaucer his status as a minor diplomat controls the direction of the poem and gives it artistic form.

In the first period of his literary activity Chaucer's specific poetic models were French, but a knowledge of writings in Latin lies behind virtually everything he wrote—although the Latin writers Chaucer read were not the same as those which we should study today. He probably had a more than adequate knowledge of the *Aeneid* and of Ovid in the original, but it is likely that he knew the other classical authors mostly through French translations and paraphrases. He was directly familiar with a number of (to us) cumbersome medieval Latin poems. Certainly his favorite Latin writer was Boethius, the 6th-century Roman whose *Consolation of Philosophy,* written while its author was in prison awaiting his execution, became one of the most valued of books for the whole Middle Ages, which never failed to find inspiration and comfort in its nobly stoic doctrine. Chaucer's own philosophical attitude, that of living wholeheartedly in the world while remaining spiritually detached from it, is at least partially a legacy from Boethius. His wooden but painstaking prose translation of the *Consolation,* probably made during the 70's, is only one of innumerable indications of Chaucer's reverence for the Roman writer.

The journey that Chaucer made to Italy in 1372 was in all likelihood a milestone in his literary development. Hitherto the influences upon him had been largely French and Latin, and while he may have read Italian before, it is likely that it was his Italian journey that immersed him in the works of Dante, Petrarch, and Boccaccio—the last two still alive at the time of Chaucer's visit, though he probably did not meet them. Between Chaucer and the greatest of the Italian writers, Dante, there was a large dissimilarity of temperament; yet if Chaucer could not assimilate *The Divine Comedy,* he nevertheless appreciated its austere moral grandeur, and his work shows its influences in subtle, oblique ways. Moreover, one of his funniest poems, the *House of Fame,* written sometime while he was in the customs (1374–86), may be read as a lighthearted imitation of the *Comedy,* though not a wholly successful one. From the works of Petrarch, also a writer of alien temperament, Chaucer obtained less, though he accords him respect on the several occasions when he mentions him. It was Boccaccio, whose cast of mind was far more congenial to Chaucer than the more sober Dante and Petrarch, who was to provide the source for some of Chaucer's finest poems—though his name is never mentioned in Chaucer's works. Many of the *Canterbury Tales* are indebted to one or another of Boccaccio's works, as is his lovely, cryptic love vision, the *Parliament of Fowls* (between 1375 and 1385). And his longest poem, *Troilus and Criseide,* probably completed about 1385, is an adaptation of Boccaccio's *Il Filostrato* ("The

Love-Stricken"). The Italian work is one of considerable stature, which Chaucer reworked into one of the greatest love poems in any language. Even if he had never written the *Canterbury Tales, Troilus* would have secured Chaucer a place among the great English poets.

Chaucer probably began work on the *Canterbury Tales* in 1386, and this was his chief literary interest until his death. The old tripartite division of Chaucer's literary career which assigns him a French period (to 1372), and an Italian period (1372–85), calls this last period of his life "English." But it was not English in the same sense as the earlier periods were French and Italian (i.e., dominated by French and Italian models), for the fact is that Chaucer from the beginning to the end stands apart from the mainstream of English literature. In the Rhyme of Sir Thopas, which he assigns himself in the *Canterbury Tales,* the wonderful fun he makes of popular Middle English romances shows his intimate knowledge of them; and undoubtedly he had read much English writing of all kinds. Yet his notion of literary art seems to have excluded many of the common characteristics—and the characteristic vices—of what had been and was being written in English, so that it is difficult to relate his work to that of his fellow English writers. His friend John Gower is a case in point: like Chaucer, he wrote a collection of English narrative poems in his *Confessio Amantis* ("The Lover's Confession"), and Chaucer tells some of the same stories in the *Canterbury Tales* and in the *Legend of Good Women*. The last, which may have interrupted Chaucer's work on the *Canterbury Tales* in the late 80's, was apparently assigned him by some eminent person; in order to make amends for his portrait of the unfaithful Criseide, he had to write a series of short poems celebrating famous faithful women. To make each story prove exactly the same point and nothing more is something that the conventional Gower had no trouble in doing. Yet Chaucer was able to complete the tales of only nine solemnly steadfast ladies before giving up in something like despair, and the most amusing thing about his narratives is his evident exasperation with having to make everything accord to a single formula. He could not bring himself to use the simple moralistic technique of conventional English poetry, and what Gower treats seriously appears in Chaucer often to be bordering on burlesque. Every comparison between Chaucer and run-of-the-mill English poetry either so exalts him as to make the act of comparison ludicrous or else, when Chaucer is trying to behave conventionally, shows him writing with his left hand. Chaucer had no really "English" period; English poetry had little to teach the first great English poet.

CHAUCER'S ART

The extraordinary variety of the *Canterbury Tales* as well as their number might well have demanded their author's full energy and attention during the last fourteen years of his life, but while he was at work on them he continued, almost to the end, to perform what seem to have been full-time jobs having nothing to do with literaure. Doubtless this practical business prevented him from achieving more than the 22 tales he finished; and it probably made him search his old papers for tales that he could work in without substantial revision. Yet if it reduced his literary output—which, even so, is enormous—this lifelong involvement with the practical is one of the chief reasons for his greatness as a poet. From his birth to his death he dealt continually with all sorts of people, the highest and the lowest, and his wonderfully observant mind made the most of this ever-present opportunity. His wide reading gave him plots and ideas, but his experience gave him people. As a commoner himself he had a sympathy with and understanding of the lower classes that few men who attained his ultimate station might boast of—and the lower classes must have accepted him. Similarly, he seems to have won full acceptance from the proud and important personages with whom he associated at court, and this he could not have won if he had not understood them perfectly. He understands both the high and the low, but he remains curiously detached from both, and it is detachment, perfectly balanced in his poetry by sympathy, which distinguishes Chaucer's art. Although he was born a commoner, he did not live as a commoner; and although he was accepted by the aristocracy, he must always have been conscious of the fact that he did not really belong to that society of which birth alone could make one a true member. Medieval aristocratic society arrogated to itself all idealism, and Chaucer characteristically regards life in terms of aristocratic ideals; but he never lost the ability, which for the poorer class was also a positive necessity, of regarding life as a purely practical matter. The art of being at once involved in and detached from a given situation is peculiarly Chaucer's.

In the physical realm, double vision results in a blurred image, but not so in Chaucer's poetic world, where images have often an extraordinary clarity, as if reality itself were made more real. His Prioress in the *Canterbury Tales* is an example of the basic human paradox which places what people are in opposition to what they think they are or pretend to be: Chaucer shows us clearly her inability to be what she professes to be, a nun; shows also the inadequacy of what she thinks a nun ought to be, a lady; and shows the great human charm of what she is, a woman. The elements of the portrait are divided between the critical and the admiring: a heavily satiric poet might well enhance the critical comment, so that our ultimate impression would be of the Prioress' weakness, while a sentimental one might enhance her amiable side so as to make that the aspect which we should remember. But in Chaucer's handling the reality comprehends both sides of the Prioress, expresses the paradox without attempting to resolve it. He appears to have been a man who had no illusions about the world or its inhabitants, but was nevertheless deeply fond of them both, and thought it worth while to keep the world spinning as well as possible, either by telling stories of high artistic truth or by counting pots and pans.

The text given here is from the present editor's *Chaucer's Poetry: An Anthology for the Modern Reader* (1958, 1975). For the *Canterbury Tales* the Hengwrt Manuscript has provided the textual basis. The spelling has been altered to improve consistency, and has been modernized in so far as is possible without distorting the phonological values of the Middle English. Discussions of Middle English pronunciation, grammar, and prosody will be found in the introduction to the period.

The Canterbury Tales Chaucer's original plan for the *Canterbury Tales* projected about 120 stories, two for each pilgrim to tell on the way to Canterbury and two more on the way back. Chaucer actually completed only 22, though two more exist in fragments; a modification of the original plan is seen in the assignment of one of the completed tales to a pilgrim who was not a member of the group that assembled at Southwark. The work was probably first conceived in 1386, when Chaucer was living in Greenwich, some miles east of London. From his house he might have been able to see the pilgrim road that led toward the shrine of the famous English saint, Thomas à Becket, the Archbishop of Canterbury who was murdered in his cathedral in 1170. Medieval pilgrims were notorious tale-tellers (liars, according to the austere Langland), and the sight and sound of the bands riding toward Canterbury may well have suggested to Chaucer the idea of using a fictitious pilgrimage as a "framing" device for a number of stories. Collections of stories linked by such a device were common in the later Middle Ages. Chaucer's contemporary John Gower had used one in his *Confessio Amantis;* earlier in the century Boccaccio had placed the hundred tales of his *Decameron* in the mouths of ten characters, each of whom told a tale a day for ten days; and another Italian, Giovanni Sercambi, had placed a series of stories in the mouth of the leader of a group of persons journeying on horseback. Even if, as seems likely, Chaucer was unaware of the Italian precedents, the device of the framing fiction was in the air.

Chaucer's artistic exploitation of the device is, however, altogether his own. In Gower and Sercambi, one speaker relates all the stories; and in Boccaccio, the relationship between any one of the ten speakers and the story he tells is haphazard, so that reassignment of all the stories to different speakers would not materially change the effect. But in the best of the *Canterbury Tales* there is a fascinating accord between the narrator and his story, so that the story takes on rich overtones from what we have learned of its teller in the General Prologue and elsewhere, and the character himself grows and is revealed by his story. Chaucer conducts two fictions simultaneously—that of the individual tale and that of the pilgrim to whom he has assigned it. He develops the second fiction not only through the General Prologue but also through the "links," the interchanges among the pilgrims between stories. These interchanges sometimes lead to animosities. Thus the Miller's Tale offends the Reeve, who, formerly a carpenter, sees himself slandered in the figure of the Miller's silly, cuckolded carpenter; and the Reeve replies with a story that scores a miller who seems very like the pilgrim Miller. Similarly the Friar and the Summoner quarrel at the end of the Wife of Bath's Prologue, so that when the Friar is called upon he tells a tale most offensive to the Summoner, who in turn retaliates with an even more offensive story about a friar. The effect of each of these tales is enhanced by the animus of its teller, while the description of the animus in the links is exciting in itself: we are given at once a story and a drama. Furthermore, the Wife of Bath's monstrous feminism sets up resonances that are felt through all the succeeding tales. Indeed, so powerful are these resonances that some see in them a thematic unifying device: the question of marriage that the Wife introduces is further treated from two opposing points of view by the Clerk and the Merchant, and is finally settled by the common sense of the Franklin. In addition to such artistic stratagems as these, the personality and mind of the reporter—a half-burlesque version of Chaucer himself—permeate the poem and enrich its meaning.

The composition of none of the tales can be accurately dated; most of them were written during the last fourteen years of Chaucer's life, though some which fail to fit their tellers may be much earlier. The popularity of the poem in late medieval England is attested by the number of surviving manuscripts: more than 80, mostly from the 15th century. It was also twice printed by Caxton, and often reprinted by Caxton's early successors. The manuscripts reflect the unfinished state of the poem—the fact that when he died Chaucer had not made up his mind about a number of details, and hence left many inconsistencies. The poem appears in the manuscripts as nine or ten "fragments" or blocks of tales; the order of the poems within each fragment is generally the same, but the order of the fragments themselves varies widely. The fragment containing the General Prologue, the Knight's, Miller's and Reeve's Tales, and the Cook's unfinished tale, always comes first, and the fragment consisting of the Parson's Tale and the Retraction always comes last; but the others, such as that containing the Wife of Bath, the Friar, and the Summoner, or that consisting of the Physician and Pardoner, or the longest fragment consisting of six tales concluding with the Nun's Priest's, are by no means stable in relation to one another. The order followed here is one of the two that seems most nearly satisfactory.

THE GENERAL PROLOGUE

Chaucer did not need to make a pilgrimage himself in order to meet the types of people that his fictitious pilgrimage includes, for most of them had long inhabited literature as well as life: the ideal Knight, who had fought against the pagans in all the great battles of the last half-century; his son the Squire, a lover out of any love poem; the Prioress without a vocation but with the dogs and jewelry that satirical literature was always condemning nuns for; the hunting Monk and flattering Friar, chief butts of medieval satirists; the too-busy and too-rich lawyer; the prosperous Franklin; the fraudulent Doctor; the Wife—or Archwife—of Bath; the austere Parson; and so on down through the lower orders to that flamboyant hypocrite, the Pardoner, a living vice. One meets all these types in medieval literature, and, since literature imitates life, one might have met them also in medieval society, as Chaucer, with his wide experience, undoubtedly did. Indeed, it has been argued that in some of his portraits he is drawing real people; but the appearance of doing so is actually a function of his art, which is able to endow types with a reality we generally associate only with people we know. Chaucer achieves this effect largely by persuading us that his own interest lies only in the visible, in what actually met his eye on the pilgrimage. He pretends to let the salient features of each pilgrim leap out directly at the reader, and does not seem to mind if some of his descriptions are from top to toe, others all toe and no top. This imitation of the way our minds actually perceive reality may make us fail to notice the care with which Chaucer has selected his details in order to give an integrated sketch of the person being described. While they are generally not full-blown literary symbols, most of these details give something more than mere verisimilitude to the description; actually, they mediate between the world of types and the world of real people. Independent bourgeois women of the time were often makers of cloth, so that the Wife of Bath's proficiency at the trade is, in one way, merely part of her historical reality; yet the first weaver of cloth was the unparadised Eve, and her descendant is an unregenerate member of the distaff side. The Franklin's red face and white beard are in the same way merely individualizing factors in the portrait; yet the red face and white beard seem always to associate themselves with a man of good will who likes good living, and since Chaucer's time they have become the distinguishing marks of a kind of mythic Franklin, Santa Claus.

The rich suggestiveness of the details is what makes the portraits worth reading again and again. One may begin by enjoying the bright if flat photographic image of reality that the reporter creates, but one will find that the initial appearance of flatness is deceptive, and that the more one rereads the more complex and significant the portraits become. Here, as elsewhere in his work, Chaucer shows himself to be a rival to Shakespeare in the art of providing entertainment on the most primitive level, and at the same time, of significantly increasing the reader's ability to comprehend reality.

From The Canterbury Tales

The General Prologue

Whan that April with his° showres soote° *its / sweet*
The droughte of March hath perced to the roote,
And bathed every veine[1] in swich° licour,° *such / liquid*
Of which vertu[2] engendred is the flowr;
Whan Zephyrus[3] eek° with his sweete breeth *also*
Inspired hath in every holt° and heeth° *grove / field*
The tendre croppes,° and the yonge sonne[4] *shoots*
Hath in the Ram his halve cours yronne,
And smale fowles maken melodye
That sleepen al the night with open yë°— *eye*
So priketh hem° Nature in hir corages[5]— *them*
Thanne longen folk to goon° on pilgrimages, *go*
And palmeres[6] for to seeken straunge strondes

1. I.e., in plants.
2. By the power of which.
3. The west wind.
4. The sun is young because it has run only halfway through its course in Aries, the Ram—the first sign of the zodiac in the solar year.
5. Their hearts.
6. Palmers, wide-ranging pilgrims—especially those who sought out the "straunge strondes" (foreign shores) of the Holy Land. "Ferne halwes": far-off shrines.

To ferne halwes, couthe° in sondry londes; *known*
And specially from every shires ende
Of Engelond to Canterbury they wende,
The holy blisful martyr[7] for to seeke
That hem hath holpen° whan that they were seke.° *helped / sick*
  Bifel that in that seson on a day,
In Southwerk[8] at the Tabard as I lay,
Redy to wenden on my pilgrimage
To Canterbury with ful° devout corage, *very*
At night was come into that hostelrye
Wel nine and twenty in a compaignye
Of sondry folk, by aventure° yfalle *chance*
In felaweshipe, and pilgrimes were they alle
That toward Canterbury wolden° ride. *would*
The chambres and the stables weren wide,
And wel we weren esed° at the beste.[9] *accommodated*
And shortly, whan the sonne was to reste,[1]
So hadde I spoken with hem everichoon° *every one*
That I was of hir felaweshipe anoon,° *at once*
And made forward[2] erly for to rise,
To take oure way ther as[3] I you devise.° *describe*
  But nathelees,° whil I have time and space,[4] *nevertheless*
Er° that I ferther in this tale pace,° *before / pass*
Me thinketh it accordant to resoun[5]
To telle you al the condicioun
Of eech of hem, so as it seemed me,
And whiche they were, and of what degree,
And eek in what array that they were inne:
And at a knight thanne° wol I first biginne. *then*
  A Knight ther was, and that a worthy man,
That fro the time that he first bigan
To riden out, he loved chivalrye,
Trouthe[6] and honour, freedom and curteisye.
Ful worthy was he in his lordes werre,° *war*
And therto hadde he riden, no man ferre,° *further*
As wel in Cristendom as hethenesse,° *heathen lands*
And[7] evere honoured for his worthinesse.
  At Alisandre[8] he was whan it was wonne;
Ful ofte time he hadde the boord bigonne[9]

7. St. Thomas à Becket, murdered in Canterbury Cathedral in 1170.
8. Southwark, site of the Tabard Inn, was then a suburb of London, south of the Thames River.
9. In the best possible way.
1. Had set.
2. I.e., (we) made an agreement.
3. "Ther as": where.
4. I.e., opportunity.
5. It seems to me according to reason.
6. Integrity. "Freedom" is here generosity of spirit, while "curteisye" is courtesy.
7. I.e., and he was.
8. The Knight has taken part in campaigns fought against all three groups of pagans who threatened Europe during the 14th century: the Moslems in the Near East, from whom Alexandria was seized after a famous siege; the northern barbarians in Prussia, Lithuania, and Russia; and the Moors in North Africa. The place names in the following lines refer to battlegrounds in these continuing wars.
9. Sat in the seat of honor at military feasts.

Aboven alle nacions in Pruce;
In Lettou had he reised,° and in Ruce, *campaigned*
No Cristen man so ofte of his degree;
In Gernade at the sege eek hadde he be
Of Algezir, and riden in Belmarye;
At Lyeis was he, and at Satalye,
Whan they were wonne; and in the Grete See[1]
At many a noble arivee° hadde he be. *military landing*
  At mortal batailes[2] hadde he been fifteene,
And foughten for oure faith at Tramissene
In listes[3] thries,° and ay° slain his fo. *thrice / always*
  This ilke° worthy Knight hadde been also *same*
Somtime with the lord of Palatye[4]
Again° another hethen in Turkye; *against*
And everemore he hadde a soverein pris.° *reputation*
And though that he were worthy,[5] he was wis,
And of his port° as meeke as is a maide. *demeanor*
He nevere yit no vilainye° ne saide *rudeness*
In al his lif unto no manere wight:[6]
He was a verray,° parfit,° gentil knight. *true / perfect*
But for to tellen you of his array,
His hors° were goode, but he was nat gay. *horses*
Of fustian° he wered° a gipoun[7] *thick cloth / wore*
Al bismotered with his haubergeoun,[8]
For he was late come from his viage,° *expedition*
And wente for to doon his pilgrimage.
  With him ther was his sone, a yong Squier,[9]
A lovere and a lusty bacheler,
With lokkes crulle° as they were laid in presse. *curly*
Of twenty yeer of age he was, I gesse.
Of his stature he was of evene° lengthe, *moderate*
And wonderly delivere,° and of greet° strengthe. *agile / great*
And he hadde been som time in chivachye[1]
In Flandres, in Artois, and Picardye,
And born him wel as of so litel space,[2]
In hope to stonden in his lady° grace. *lady's*
  Embrouded° was he as it were a mede,[3] *embroidered*
Al ful of fresshe flowres, white and rede;° *red*
Singing he was, or floiting,° al the day: *whistling*

1. The Mediterranean.
2. Tournaments fought to the death.
3. Lists, tournament grounds.
4. "The lord of Palatye" was a pagan: alliances of convenience were often made during the Crusades between Christians and pagans.
5. I.e., a valiant knight.
6. "No manere wight": any sort of person. In Middle English, negatives are multiplied for emphasis, as in these two lines: "nevere," "no," "ne," "no."
7. Tunic worn underneath the coat of mail.
8. All rust-stained from his hauberk (coat of mail).
9. The vague term "Squier" (Squire) here seems to be the equivalent of "bacheler," a young knight still in the service of an older one.
1. On cavalry expeditions. The places in the next line are sites of skirmishes in the constant warfare between the English and the French.
2. I.e., considering the little time he had been in service.
3. Mead, meadow.

He was as fressh as is the month of May.
Short was his gowne, with sleeves longe and wide.
Wel coude he sitte on hors, and faire ride;
He coude songes make, and wel endite,° *compose verse*
Juste[4] and eek daunce, and wel portraye° and write. *sketch*
So hote° he loved that by nightertale[5] *hotly*
He slepte namore than dooth a nightingale.
Curteis he was, lowely,° and servisable, *humble*
And carf biforn his fader at the table.[6]
A Yeman[7] hadde he and servants namo° *no more*
At that time, for him liste[8] ride so;
And he[9] was clad in cote and hood of greene.
A sheef of pecok arwes,° bright and keene, *arrows*
Under his belt he bar° ful thriftily;° *bore / properly*
Wel coude he dresse° his takel° yemanly:[1] *tend to / gear*
His arwes drouped nought with fetheres lowe.
And in his hand he bar a mighty bowe.
A not-heed° hadde he with a brown visage. *close-cut head*
Of wodecraft wel coude° he al the usage. *knew*
Upon his arm he bar a gay bracer,[2]
And by his side a swerd° and a bokeler,[3] *sword*
And on that other side a gay daggere,
Harneised° wel and sharp as point of spere; *mounted*
A Cristophre[4] on his brest of silver sheene;° *bright*
An horn he bar, the baudrik[5] was of greene.
A forster° was he soothly,° as I gesse. *forester / truly*
Ther was also a Nonne, a Prioresse,[6]
That of hir smiling was ful simple and coy.
Hir gretteste ooth was but by sainte Loy!° *Eloi*
And she was cleped° Madame Eglantine. *named*
Ful wel she soong° the service divine, *sang*
Entuned° in hir nose ful semely;[7] *chanted*
And Frenssh she spak ful faire and fetisly,° *elegantly*
After the scole° of Stratford at the Bowe[8]— *school*
For Frenssh of Paris was to hire unknowe.
At mete° wel ytaught was she withalle:° *meals / besides*
She leet° no morsel from hir lippes falle, *let*
Ne wette hir fingres in hir sauce deepe;
Wel coude she carye a morsel, and wel keepe° *take care*
That no drope ne fille° upon hir brest. *should fall*

4. Joust, fight in a tournament.
5. At night.
6. It was a squire's duty to carve his lord's meat.
7. The "Yeman" (Yeoman) is an independent commoner who acts as the Knight's military servant; "he" is the Knight.
8. "Him liste": it pleased him to.
9. I.e., the Yeoman.
1. In a workmanlike way.
2. Wristguard for archers.
3. Buckler (a small shield).
4. St. Christopher medal.
5. Baldric (a supporting strap).
6. The Prioress is the mother superior of her nunnery. "Simple and coy": sincere and mild.
7. In a seemly manner.
8. The French learned in a convent school in Stratford-at-the-Bow, a suburb of London, was evidently not up to the Parisian standard.

In curteisye was set ful muchel hir lest.[9]
Hir over-lippe wiped she so clene
That in hir coppe° ther was no ferthing° seene *cup / bit*
Of grece,° whan she dronken hadde hir draughte; *grease*
Ful semely after hir mete she raughte.° *reached*
And sikerly° she was of greet disport,[1] *certainly*
And ful plesant, and amiable of port,° *mien*
And pained hire to countrefete cheere[2]
Of court, and to been statlich° of manere, *dignified*
And to been holden digne[3] of reverence.
But, for to speken of hir conscience,
She was so charitable and so pitous° *merciful*
She wolde weepe if that she saw a mous
Caught in a trappe, if it were deed° or bledde. *dead*
Of[4] smale houndes hadde she that she fedde
With rosted flessh, or milk and wastelbreed;° *fine white bread*
But sore wepte she if oon of hem were deed,
Or if men smoot it with a yerde smerte;[5]
And al was conscience and tendre herte.
Ful semely hir wimpel° pinched° was, *headdress / pleated*
Hir nose tretis,° hir yën° greye as glas, *well-formed / eyes*
Hir mouth ful smal, and therto° softe and reed,° *moreover / red*
But sikerly° she hadde a fair forheed: *certainly*
It was almost a spanne brood,[6] I trowe,° *believe*
For hardily,° she was nat undergrowe. *assuredly*
Ful fetis° was hir cloke, as I was war;° *becoming / aware*
Of smal° coral aboute hir arm she bar *dainty*
A paire[7] of bedes, gauded al with greene,
And theron heeng° a brooch of gold ful sheene,° *hung / bright*
On which ther was first writen a crowned A,[8]
And after, *Amor vincit omnia*.[9]
Another Nonne with hire hadde she
That was hir chapelaine,° and preestes three.[1] *secretary*
A Monk ther was, a fair for the maistrye,[2]
An outridere[3] that loved venerye,° *hunting*
A manly man, to been an abbot able.° *worthy*
Ful many a daintee° hors hadde he in stable, *fine*
And whan he rood,° men mighte his bridel heere *rode*
Ginglen° in a whistling wind as clere *jingle*
And eek as loude as dooth the chapel belle

9. I.e., her chief delight lay in good manners.
1. Of great good cheer.
2. And took pains to imitate the behavior.
3. And to be considered worthy.
4. I.e., some.
5. If someone struck it with a rod sharply.
6. A handsbreadth wide.
7. String (i.e., a rosary); "gauded al with greene": provided with green beads to mark certain prayers.
8. An *A* with an ornamental crown on it.
9. A Latin motto meaning "Love conquers all."
1. Although he here awards this charming lady three priests, Chaucer later reduces the number to one.
2. I.e., a superlatively fine one.
3. A monk charged with supervising property distant from the monastery.

Ther as this lord was kepere of the celle.[4]
The rule of Saint Maure or of Saint Beneit,[5]
By cause that it was old and somdeel strait—
This ilke Monk leet olde thinges pace,° *pass away*
And heeld° after the newe world the space.[6] *held*
He yaf nought of that text a pulled hen[7]
That saith that hunteres been° nought holy men, *are*
Ne that a monk, whan he is recchelees,[8]
Is likned til° a fissh that is waterlees— *to*
This is to sayn, a monk out of his cloistre;
But thilke° text heeld he nat worth an oystre. *that same*
And I saide his opinion was good:
What° sholde he studye and make himselven wood° *why / crazy*
Upon a book in cloistre alway to poure,
Or swinke° with his handes and laboure, *work*
As Austin bit?[9] How shal the world be served?
Lat Austin have his swink to him reserved!
Therfore he was a prikasour° aright. *hard rider*
Grehoundes he hadde as swift as fowl in flight.
Of priking° and of hunting for the hare *riding*
Was al his lust,° for no cost wolde he spare. *pleasure*
I sawgh his sleeves purfiled° at the hand *fur-lined*
With gris,° and that the fineste of a land; *gray fur*
And for to festne his hood under his chin
He hadde of gold wrought a ful curious[1] pin:
A love-knotte in the grettere° ende ther was. *greater*
His heed was balled,° that shoon as any glas, *bald*
And eek his face, as he hadde been anoint:
He was a lord ful fat and in good point;[2]
His yën steepe,° and rolling in his heed, *protruding*
That stemed as a furnais of a leed,[3]
His bootes souple,° his hors in greet estat°— *supple / condition*
Now certainly he was a fair prelat.[4]
He was nat pale as a forpined° gost: *wasted away*
A fat swan loved he best of any rost.
His palfrey° was as brown as is a berye. *saddle horse*
  A Frere[5] ther was, a wantoune and a merye,
A limitour, a ful solempne° man. *pompous*
In alle the ordres foure is noon that can° *knows*
So muche of daliaunce° and fair langage: *flirtation*

4. Keeper of an outlying cell (branch) of the monastery.
5. St. Maurus and St. Benedict, authors of monastic rules. "Somdeel strait": somewhat strict.
6. I.e., in his own lifetime (?).
7. He didn't give a plucked hen for that text.
8. Reckless, careless of rule.
9. I.e., as St. Augustine bids. St. Augustine had written that monks should perform manual labor.

1. Of careful workmanship.
2. In good shape, plump.
3. That glowed like a furnace with a pot in it.
4. Prelate (an important churchman).
5. The "Frere" (Friar) is a member of one of the four religious orders whose members live by begging; as a "limitour" (line 209) he has been granted by his order exclusive begging rights within a certain limited area.

He hadde maad ful many a mariage
Of yonge wommen at his owene cost;
Unto his ordre he was a noble post.[6]
Ful wel biloved and familier was he
With frankelains over al[7] in his contree,
And with worthy wommen of the town—
For he hadde power of confessioun,
As saide himself, more than a curat,° *parish priest*
For of° his ordre he was licenciat.[8] *by*
Ful swetely herde he confessioun,
And plesant was his absolucioun.
He was an esy man to yive penaunce
Ther as he wiste to have[9] a good pitaunce;° *donation*
For unto a poore ordre for to yive
Is signe that a man is wel yshrive;[1]
For if he yaf, he dorste make avaunt° *boast*
He wiste that a man was repentaunt;
For many a man so hard is of his herte
He may nat weepe though him sore smerte:[2]
Therfore, in stede of weeping and prayeres,
Men mote° yive silver to the poore freres.[3] *may*
His tipet° was ay farsed° ful of knives *scarf / packed*
And pinnes, for to yiven faire wives;
And certainly he hadde a merye note;
Wel coude he singe and playen on a rote;° *fiddle*
Of yeddinges he bar outrely the pris.[4]
His nekke whit was as the flowr-de-lis;° *lily*
Therto he strong was as a champioun.
He knew the tavernes wel in every town,
And every hostiler° and tappestere,° *innkeeper / barmaid*
Bet° than a lazar[5] or a beggestere. *better*
For unto swich a worthy man as he
Accorded nat, as by his facultee,[6]
To have with sike° lazars aquaintaunce: *sick*
It is nat honeste,° it may nought avaunce,° *dignified / profit*
For to delen with no swich poraile,[7]
But al with riche, and selleres of vitaile;° *foodstuffs*
And over al ther as profit sholde arise,
Curteis he was, and lowely of servise.
Ther was no man nowher so vertuous:° *efficient*
He was the beste beggere in his hous.° *friary*

6. I.e., pillar.
7. I.e., with franklins everywhere. Franklins were well-to-do country men.
8. I.e., licensed to hear confessions.
9. Where he knew he would have.
1. Shriven, absolved.
2. Though he is sorely grieved.
3. Before granting absolution, the confessor must be sure the sinner is contrite; moreover, the absolution is contingent upon the sinner's performance of an act of satisfaction. In the case of Chaucer's Friar, a liberal contribution served both as proof of contrition and as satisfaction.
4. He absolutely took the prize for ballads.
5. Leper; "beggestere": female beggar.
6. It was not suitable because of his position.
7. I.e., poor people. The oldest order of friars had been founded by St. Francis to administer to the spiritual needs of precisely those classes the Friar avoids.

And yaf a certain ferme for the graunt:[8]
Noon of his bretheren cam ther in his haunt.[9]
For though a widwe° hadde nought a sho,° *widow / shoe*
So plesant was his *In principio*[1]
Yit wolde he have a ferthing° er he wente; *small coin*
His purchas was wel bettre than his rente.[2]
And rage he coude as it were right a whelpe;[3]
In love-dayes[4] ther coude he muchel° helpe, *much*
For ther he was nat lik a cloisterer,
With a thredbare cope, as is a poore scoler,
But he was lik a maister[5] or a pope.
Of double worstede was his semicope,° *short robe*
And rounded as a belle out of the presse.° *bell-mold*
Somwhat he lipsed° for his wantounesse° *lisped / affectation*
To make his Englissh sweete upon his tonge;
And in his harping, whan he hadde songe,° *sung*
His yën twinkled in his heed aright
As doon the sterres° in the frosty night. *stars*
This worthy limitour was cleped Huberd.
A Marchant was ther with a forked beerd,
In motelee,[6] and hye on hors he sat,
Upon his heed a Flandrissh° bevere hat, *Flemish*
His bootes clasped faire and fetisly.° *elegantly*
His resons° he spak ful solempnely, *opinions*
Souning° alway th'encrees of his winning. *sounding*
He wolde the see were kept for any thing[7]
Bitwixen Middelburgh and Orewelle.
Wel coude he in eschaunge sheeldes[8] selle.
This worthy man ful wel his wit bisette:° *employed*
Ther wiste° no wight that he was in dette, *knew*
So statly° was he of his governaunce,[9] *dignified*
With his bargaines,[1] and with his chevissaunce.
Forsoothe he was a worthy man withalle;
But, sooth to sayn, I noot° how men him calle. *don't know*
A Clerk[2] ther was of Oxenforde also
That unto logik hadde longe ygo.[3]
As lene was his hors as is a rake,

8. And he paid a certain rent for the privilege of begging.
9. Assigned territory.
1. A friar's usual salutation (John i.1): "In the beginning (was the Word)."
2. I.e., the money he got through such activity was more than his regular income.
3. And he could flirt wantonly, as if he were a puppy.
4. Days appointed for the settlement of lawsuits out of court.
5. A man of recognized learning.
6. Motley, a cloth of mixed color.
7. I.e., he wished the sea to be guarded at all costs. The sea route between Middelburgh (in the Netherlands) and Orwell (in Suffolk) was vital to the Merchant's export and import of wool—the basis of England's chief trade at the time.
8. Shields, *ecus* (French coins): he could speculate profitably (if illegally) in foreign exchange.
9. The management of his affairs.
1. Bargainings; "chevissaunce": borrowing.
2. The Clerk is a student at Oxford; in order to become a student, he would have had to signify his intention of becoming a cleric, but he was not bound to proceed to a position of responsibility in the church.
3. Who had long since matriculated in philosophy.

And he was nought right fat, I undertake,
But looked holwe,° and therto sobrely. *hollow*
Ful thredbare was his overeste courtepy,[4]
For he hadde geten him yit no benefice,
Ne was so worldly for to have office.° *secular employment*
For him was levere[5] have at his beddes heed
Twenty bookes, clad in blak or reed,
Of Aristotle and his philosophye,
Than robes riche, or fithele,° or gay sautrye.[6] *fiddle*
But al be that he was a philosophre[7]
Yit hadde he but litel gold in cofre;° *coffer*
But al that he mighte of his freendes hente,° *take*
On bookes and on lerning he it spente,
And bisily gan for the soules praye
Of hem that yaf him wherwith to scoleye.° *study*
Of studye took he most cure° and most heede. *care*
Nought oo° word spak he more than was neede, *one*
And that was said in forme[8] and reverence,
And short and quik,° and ful of heigh sentence:[9] *lively*
Souning° in moral vertu was his speeche, *resounding*
And gladly wolde he lerne, and gladly teche.
  A Sergeant of the Lawe,[1] war and wis,
That often hadde been at the Parvis[2]
Ther was also, ful riche of excellence.
Discreet he was, and of greet reverence—
He seemed swich, his wordes weren so wise.
Justice he was ful often in assise° *circuit courts*
By patente[3] and by plein° commissioun. *full*
For his science° and for his heigh renown *knowledge*
Of fees and robes hadde he many oon.
So greet a purchasour° was nowher noon; *speculator in land*
Al was fee simple[4] to him in effect—
His purchasing mighte nat been infect.[5]
Nowher so bisy a man as he ther nas;° *was not*
And yit he seemed bisier than he was.
In termes[6] hadde he caas and doomes alle
That from the time of King William[7] were falle.
Therto he coude endite and make a thing,[8]
Ther coude no wight pinchen° at his writing; *cavil*
And every statut coude° he plein° by rote.[9] *knew / entire*
He rood but hoomly ° in a medlee cote,[1] *unpretentiously*

4. Outer cloak. "Benefice": ecclesiastical living.
5. He would rather.
6. Psaltery (a kind of harp).
7. The word may also mean "alchemist."
8. With decorum.
9. Elevated thought.
1. The Sergeant is not only a practicing lawyer, but one of the high justices of the nation. "War and wis": wary and wise.
2. The "Paradise," a meeting place for lawyers and their clients.
3. Royal warrant.
4. "Fee simple": owned outright without legal impediments.
5. Invalidated on a legal technicality.
6. I.e., by heart. "Caas and doomes": lawcases and decisions.
7. I.e., the Conqueror (reigned 1066–87).
8. Compose and draw up a deed.
9. By heart.
1. A coat of mixed color. "Ceint": belt; "barres": transverse stripes.

Girt with a ceint of silk, with barres smale.
Of his array telle I no lenger tale.
A Frankelain[2] was in his compaignye:
Whit was his beerd as is the dayesye;° *daisy*
Of his complexion he was sanguin.[3]
Wel loved he by the morwe a sop in win.[4]
To liven in delit° was evere his wone,° *sensual delight / wont*
For he was Epicurus[5] owene sone,
That heeld opinion that plein° delit *full*
Was verray felicitee parfit.
An housholdere and that a greet was he:
Saint Julian[6] he was in his contree.
His breed, his ale, was always after oon;[7]
A bettre envined° man was nevere noon. *wine-stocked*
Withouten bake mete was nevere his hous,
Of fissh and flessh, and that so plentevous° *plenteous*
It snewed° in his hous of mete and drinke, *snowed*
Of alle daintees that men coude thinke.
After° the sondry sesons of the yeer *according to*
So chaunged he his mete[8] and his soper.
Ful many a fat partrich hadde he in mewe,° *cage*
And many a breem,° and many a luce° in stewe.[9] *carp / pike*
Wo was his cook but if his sauce were
Poinant° and sharp, and redy all his gere. *pungent*
His table dormant in his halle alway
Stood redy covered all the longe day.[1]
At sessions[2] ther was he lord and sire.
Ful ofte time he was Knight of the Shire.
An anlaas° and a gipser° al of silk *dagger / purse*
Heeng at his girdel,[3] whit as morne° milk. *morning*
A shirreve° hadde he been, and countour.[4] *sheriff*
Was nowher swich a worthy vavasour.[5]
An Haberdasshere and a Carpenter,
A Webbe,° a Dyere, and a Tapicer°— *weaver / tapestry-maker*
And they were clothed alle in oo liveree[6]
Of a solempne and greet fraternitee.
Ful fresshe and newe hir gere apiked° was; *polished*
Hir knives were chaped° nought with bras, *mounted*

2. The "Frankelain" (Franklin) is a prosperous country man, whose lower-class ancestry is no impediment to the importance he has attained in his county.
3. A reference to the fact that the Franklin's temperament is dominated by blood as well as to his red face.
4. I.e., in the morning he was very fond of a piece of bread soaked in wine.
5. The Greek philosopher whose teaching is popularly believed to make pleasure the chief goal of life.
6. The patron saint of hospitality.
7. Always of the same high quality.
8. Dinner; "soper": supper.
9. Fishpond.
1. Tables were usually dismounted when not in use, but the Franklin kept his mounted and set ("covered"), hence "dormant."
2. I.e., sessions of the justices of the peace. "Knight of the Shire": county representative in Parliament.
3. Hung at his belt.
4. Auditor of county finances.
5. Member of an upper, but not an aristocratic, feudal class.
6. In one livery, i.e., the uniform of their "fraternitee" or guild, a partly religious, partly social organization.

But al with silver; wrought ful clene and weel
Hir girdles and hir pouches everydeel.° *altogether*
Wel seemed eech of hem a fair burgeis° *burgher*
To sitten in a yeldehalle° on a dais. *guildhall*
Everich, for the wisdom that he can,[7]
Was shaply° for to been an alderman. *suitable*
For catel° hadde they ynough and rente,° *property / income*
And eek hir wives wolde it wel assente—
And elles certain were they to blame:
It is ful fair to been ycleped "Madame,"
And goon to vigilies[8] all bifore,
And have a mantel royalliche ybore.[9]
  A Cook they hadde with hem for the nones,[1]
To boile the chiknes with the marybones,° *marrowbones*
And powdre-marchant tart and galingale.[2]
Wel coude he knowe° a draughte of London ale. *recognize*
He coude roste, and seethe,° and broile, and frye, *boil*
Maken mortreux,° and wel bake a pie. *stews*
But greet harm was it, as it thoughte° me, *seemed to*
That on his shine a mormal° hadde he. *ulcer*
For blankmanger,[3] that made he with the beste.
  A Shipman was ther, woning° fer by weste— *dwelling*
For ought I woot,° he was of Dertemouthe.[4] *know*
He rood upon a rouncy° as he couthe,[5] *large nag*
In a gowne of falding° to the knee. *heavy wool*
A daggere hanging on a laas° hadde he *strap*
Aboute his nekke, under his arm adown.
The hote somer hadde maad his hewe° al brown; *color*
And certainly he was a good felawe.
Ful many a draughte of win hadde he drawe[6]
Fro Burdeuxward,[7] whil that the chapman sleep:
Of nice° conscience took he no keep;° *fastidious / heed*
If that he faught and hadde the hyer hand,
By water he sente hem hoom to every land.
But of his craft, to rekene wel his tides,
His stremes° and his daungers° him bisides,[8] *currents / hazards*
His herberwe° and his moone, his lodemenage,[9] *anchorage*
There was noon swich from Hulle to Cartage.[1]
Hardy he was and wis to undertake;
With many a tempest hadde his beerd been shake;
He knew alle the havenes° as they were *harbors*

7. Was capable of.
8. Feasts held on the eve of saints' days. "Al bifore": i.e., at the head of the procession.
9. Royally carried.
1. For the occasion.
2. "Powdre-marchant" and "galingale" are flavoring materials.
3. An elaborate stew.
4. Dartmouth, a port in the southwest of England.
5. As best he could.
6. Drawn, i.e., stolen.
7. From Bordeaux; i.e., while carrying wine from Bordeaux (the wine center of France). "Chapman sleep": merchant slept.
8. Around him.
9. Pilotage.
1. From Hull (in northern England) to Cartagena (in Spain).

Fro Gotlond to the Cape of Finistere,[2]
And every crike° in Britaine° and in Spaine. *inlet / Brittany*
His barge ycleped was the Maudelaine.° *Magdalene*
  With us ther was a Doctour of Physik:° *medicine*
In al this world ne was ther noon him lik
To speken of physik and of surgerye.
For° he was grounded in astronomye,° *because / astrology*
He kepte° his pacient a ful greet deel[3] *tended to*
In houres[4] by his magik naturel.
Wel coude he fortunen the ascendent
Of his images[5] for his pacient.
He knew the cause of every maladye,
Were it of hoot or cold or moiste or drye,
And where engendred and of what humour:[6]
He was a verray parfit praktisour.[7]
The cause yknowe,° and of his harm the roote, *known*
Anoon he yaf the sike man his boote.° *remedy*
  Ful redy hadde he his apothecaries
To senden him drogges° and his letuaries,° *drugs / medicines*
For eech of hem made other for to winne:
Hir frendshipe was nought newe to biginne.
Wel knew he the olde Esculapius,[8]
And Deiscorides and eek Rufus,
Olde Ipocras, Hali, and Galien,
Serapion, Razis, and Avicen,
Averrois, Damascien, and Constantin,
Bernard, and Gatesden, and Gilbertin.
Of his diete mesurable° was he, *moderate*
For it was of no superfluitee,
But of greet norissing° and digestible. *nourishment*
His studye was but litel on the Bible.
In sanguin° and in pers° he clad was al, *blood-red / blue*
Lined with taffata and with sendal;° *silk*

2. From Gotland (an island in the Baltic) to Finisterre (the westernmost point in Spain).
3. Closely.
4. I.e., the astrologically important hours (when conjunctions of the planets might help his recovery). "Magik naturel": natural—as opposed to black—magic.
5. Assign the propitious time, according to the position of stars, for using talismanic images. Such images, representing either the patient himself or points in the zodiac, were thought to be influential on the course of the disease.
6. Diseases were thought to be caused by a disturbance of one or another of the four bodily "humors," each of which, like the four elements, was a compound of two of the elementary qualities mentioned in line 422: the melancholy humor, seated in the black bile was cold and dry (like earth); the sanguine, seated in the blood, hot and moist (like air); the choleric, seated in the yellow bile, hot and dry (like fire); the phlegmatic, seated in the phlegm, cold and moist (like water).
7. True perfect practitioner.
8. The Doctor is familiar with the treatises that the Middle Ages attributed to the "great names" of medical history, whom Chaucer names in lines 431–36: the purely legendary Greek demigod Aesculapius; the Greeks Dioscorides, Rufus, Hippocrates, Galen, and Serapion; the Persians Hali and Rhazes; the Arabians Avicenna and Averroës; the early Christians John (?) of Damascus and Constantine Afer; the Scotsman Bernard Gordon; the Englishmen John of Gatesden and Gilbert, the former an early contemporary of Chaucer.

And yit he was but esy of dispence;° *expenditure*
He kepte that he wan in pestilence.[9]
For° gold in physik is a cordial,[1] *because*
Therfore he loved gold in special.
  A good Wif was ther of biside Bathe,
But she was somdeel deef, and that was scathe.° *a pity*
Of cloth-making she hadde swich an haunt,° *practice*
She passed° hem of Ypres and of Gaunt.[2] *surpassed*
In al the parissh wif ne was ther noon
That to the offring[3] bifore hire sholde goon,
And if ther dide, certain so wroth° was she *angry*
That she was out of alle charitee.
Hir coverchiefs ful fine were of ground°— *texture*
I dorste° swere they weyeden° ten pound *dare / weighed*
That on a Sonday weren° upon hir heed. *were*
Hir hosen weren of fin scarlet reed,° *red*
Ful straite yteyd,[4] and shoes ful moiste° and newe. *unworn*
Bold was hir face and fair and reed of hewe.
She was a worthy womman al hir live:
Housbondes at chirche dore[5] she hadde five,
Withouten other compaignye in youthe—
But therof needeth nought to speke as nouthe.° *now*
And thries hadde she been at Jerusalem;
She hadde passed many a straunge° streem; *foreign*
At Rome she hadde been, and at Boloigne,
In Galice at Saint Jame, and at Coloigne:[6]
She coude° muchel of wandring by the waye. *knew*
Gat-toothed° was she, soothly for to saye. *gap-toothed*
Upon an amblere[7] esily she sat,
Ywimpled° wel, and on hir heed an hat *veiled*
As brood as is a bokeler or a targe,[8]
A foot-mantel° aboute hir hipes large, *riding skirt*
And on hir feet a paire of spores° sharpe. *spurs*
In felaweshipe wel coude she laughe and carpe:° *talk*
Of remedies of love she knew parchaunce,° *as it happened*
For she coude of that art the olde daunce.[9]
  A good man was ther of religioun,
And was a poore Person° of a town, *parson*
But riche he was of holy thought and werk.
He was also a lerned man, a clerk,
That Cristes gospel trewely° wolde preche; *faithfully*

9. He saved the money he made during the plague time.
1. A stimulant. Gold was thought to have some medicinal properties.
2. Ypres and Ghent ("Gaunt") were Flemish cloth-making centers.
3. The offering in church, when the congregation brought its gifts forward.
4. Tightly laced.
5. In medieval times, weddings were performed at the church door.
6. Rome; Boulogne (in France); St. James (of Compostella) in Galicia (Spain); Cologne (in Germany): all sites of shrines much visited by pilgrims.
7. Horse with an easy gait.
8. "Bokeler" and "targe": small shields.
9. I.e., she knew all the tricks of that trade.

His parisshens° devoutly wolde he teche. *parishioners*
Benigne he was, and wonder° diligent, *wonderfully*
And in adversitee ful pacient,
And swich he was preved° ofte sithes.° *proved / times*
Ful loth were him to cursen for his tithes,[1]
But rather wolde he yiven, out of doute,[2]
Unto his poore parisshens aboute
Of his offring[3] and eek of his substaunce:° *property*
He coude in litel thing have suffisaunce.° *sufficiency*
Wid was his parissh, and houses fer asonder,
But he ne lafte° nought for rain ne thonder, *neglected*
In siknesse nor in meschief,° to visite *misfortune*
The ferreste° in his parissh, muche and lite,[4] *farthest*
Upon his feet, and in his hand a staf.
This noble ensample° to his sheep he yaf *example*
That first he wroughte,[5] and afterward he taughte.
Out of the Gospel he tho° wordes caughte,° *those / took*
And this figure he added eek therto:
That if gold ruste, what shal iren do?
For if a preest be foul, on whom we truste,
No wonder is a lewed° man to ruste. *uneducated*
And shame it is, if a preest take keep,° *heed*
A shiten° shepherde and a clene sheep. *befouled*
Wel oughte a preest ensample for to yive
By his clennesse how that his sheep sholde live.
He sette nought his benefice[6] to hire
And leet his sheep encombred in the mire
And ran to London, unto Sainte Poules,[7]
To seeken him a chaunterye[8] for soules,
Or with a bretherhede to been withholde,[9]
But dwelte at hoom and kepte wel his folde,
So that the wolf ne made it nought miscarye:
He was a shepherde and nought a mercenarye.
And though he holy were and vertuous,
He was to sinful men nought despitous,° *scornful*
Ne of his speeche daungerous° ne digne,° *disdainful / haughty*
But in his teching discreet and benigne,
To drawen folk to hevene by fairnesse
By good ensample—this was his bisinesse.
But it° were any persone obstinat, *if there*
What so he were, of heigh or lowe estat,

1. He would be most reluctant to invoke excommunication in order to collect his tithes.
2. Without doubt.
3. The offering made by the congregation of his church was at the Parson's disposal.
4. Great and small.
5. I.e., he practiced what he preached.
6. I.e., his parish. A priest might rent his parish to another and take a more profitable position. "Leet": i.e., he did not leave.
7. St. Paul's Cathedral.
8. Chantry, i.e., a foundation that employed priests for the sole duty of saying masses for the souls of certain persons. St. Paul's had many of them.
9. Or to be employed by a brotherhood; i.e., to take a lucrative and fairly easy position as chaplain with a parish guild.

Him wolde he snibben° sharply for the nones:[1] *scold*
A bettre preest I trowe° ther nowher noon is. *believe*
He waited after[2] no pompe and reverence,
Ne maked him a spiced conscience,[3]
But Cristes lore° and his Apostles twelve *teaching*
He taughte, but first he folwed it himselve.
With him ther was a Plowman, was his brother,
That hadde ylad° of dong° ful many a fother.[4] *carried / dung*
A trewe swinkere° and a good was he, *worker*
Living in pees° and parfit charitee. *peace*
God loved he best with al his hoole° herte *whole*
At alle times, though him gamed or smerte,[5]
And thanne his neighebor right as himselve.
He wolde thresshe, and therto dike° and delve, *dig ditches*
For Cristes sake, for every poore wight,
Withouten hire, if it laye in his might.
His tithes payed he ful faire and wel,
Bothe of his propre swink[6] and his catel.° *property*
In a tabard° he rood upon a mere.° *short coat / mare*
Ther was also a Reeve° and a Millere, *estate manager*
A Somnour, and a Pardoner[7] also,
A Manciple,° and myself—ther were namo. *steward*
The Millere was a stout carl° for the nones. *fellow*
Ful big he was of brawn° and eek of bones— *muscle*
That preved[8] wel, for overal ther he cam
At wrastling he wolde have alway the ram.[9]
He was short-shuldred, brood,° a thikke knarre.° *broad / bully*
Ther was no dore that he nolde heve of harre,[1]
Or breke it at a renning° with his heed.° *running / head*
His beerd as any sowe or fox was reed,° *red*
And therto brood, as though it were a spade;
Upon the cop° right of his nose he hade *ridge*
A werte,° and theron stood a tuft of heres, *wart*
Rede as the bristles of a sowes eres;
His nosethirles° blake were and wide. *nostrils*
A swerd and a bokeler° bar° he by his side. *shield / bore*
His mouth as greet was as a greet furnais.° *furnace*
He was a janglere° and a Goliardais,[2] *chatterer*
And that was most of sinne and harlotries.° *obscenities*
Wel coude he stelen corn and tollen thries[3]—

1. On any occasion.
2. I.e., expected.
3. Nor did he assume an overfastidious conscience.
4. Load.
5. Whether he was pleased or grieved.
6. His own work.
7. "Somnour" (Summoner): server of summonses to the ecclesiastical court; Pardoner: dispenser of papal pardons. See lines 625 and 671, and notes, below.
8. Proved, i.e., was evident.
9. A ram was frequently offered as the prize in wrestling.
1. He would not heave off (its) hinge.
2. Goliard, teller of ribald stories.
3. Take toll thrice—i.e., deduct from the grain far more than the lawful percentage.

And yit he hadde a thombe[4] of gold, pardee.° *by heaven*
A whit cote and a blew hood wered° he. *wore*
A baggepipe wel coude he blowe and soune,° *sound*
And therwithal° he broughte us out of towne. *therewith*
  A gentil Manciple[5] was ther of a temple,
Of which achatours° mighte take exemple *buyers of food*
For to been wise in bying of vitaile;° *victuals*
For wheither that he paide or took by taile,[6]
Algate he waited so in his achat[7]
That he was ay biforn[8] and in good stat.
  Now is nat that of God a ful fair grace
That swich a lewed° mannes wit shal pace° *ignorant / surpass*
The wisdom of an heep of lerned men?
Of maistres° hadde he mo than thries ten *masters*
That weren of lawe expert and curious,° *cunning*
Of whiche ther were a dozeine in that hous
Worthy to been stiwardes of rente° and lond *income*
Of any lord that is in Engelond,
To make him live by his propre good[9]
In honour dettelees but if[1] he were wood,° *insane*
Or live as scarsly° as him list° desire, *sparely / it pleases*
And able for to helpen al a shire
In any caas° that mighte falle° or happe, *event / befall*
And yit this Manciple sette hir aller cappe![2]
  The Reeve[3] was a sclendre° colerik man; *slender*
His beerd was shave as neigh° as evere he can; *close*
His heer was by his eres ful round yshorn;
His top was dokked[4] lik a preest biforn;
Ful longe were his legges and ful lene,
Ylik a staf, ther was no calf yseene.° *visible*
Wel coude he keepe° a gerner° and a binne— *guard / granary*
Ther was noon auditour coude on him winne.[5]
Wel wiste° he by the droughte and by the rain *knew*
The yeelding of his seed and of his grain.
His lordes sheep, his neet,° his dayerye, *cattle*
His swin, his hors, his stoor,° and his pultrye *stock*
Was hoolly° in this Reeves governinge, *wholly*
And by his covenant yaf[6] the rekeninge,
Sin° that his lord was twenty-yeer of age. *since*

4. Thumb. The narrator seems to be questioning the validity of the adage that (only) an honest miller has a golden thumb.
5. The Manciple is the steward of a community of lawyers in London (a "temple").
6. By talley, i.e., on credit.
7. Always he was on the watch in his purchasing.
8. I.e., ahead of the game. "Stat": financial condition.
9. His own money.

1. Out of debt unless.
2. This Manciple made fools of them all.
3. The Reeve is the superintendent of a large farming estate; "colerik" (choleric) describes a man whose dominant humor is yellow bile (choler)—i.e., a hot-tempered man.
4. Cut short: the clergy wore the head partially shaved.
5. I.e., find him in default.
6. And according to his contract he gave.

There coude no man bringe him in arrerage.[7]
Ther nas baillif, hierde, nor other hine,
That he ne knew his sleighte and his covine[8]—
They were adrad° of him as of the deeth.° *afraid / plague*
His woning° was ful faire upon an heeth;° *dwelling / meadow*
With greene trees shadwed was his place.
He coude bettre than his lord purchace.° *acquire goods*
Ful riche he was astored° prively.° *stocked / secretly*
His lord wel coude he plesen subtilly,
To yive and lene° him of his owene good,° *lend / property*
And have a thank, and yit a cote and hood.
In youthe he hadde lerned a good mister:° *occupation*
He was a wel good wrighte, a carpenter.
This Reeve sat upon a ful good stot° *stallion*
That was a pomely° grey and highte° Scot. *dapple / was named*
A long surcote° of pers° upon he hade,[9] *overcoat / blue*
And by his side he bar° a rusty blade. *bore*
Of Northfolk was this Reeve of which I telle,
Biside a town men clepen Baldeswelle.° *Bawdswell*
Tukked[1] he was as is a frere aboute,
And evere he rood the hindreste of oure route.[2]
  A Somnour[3] was ther with us in that place
That hadde a fir-reed° cherubinnes[4] face, *fire-red*
For saucefleem° he was, with yën narwe, *pimply*
And hoot° he was, and lecherous as a sparwe,° *hot / sparrow*
With scaled° browes blake and piled[5] beerd: *scabby*
Of his visage children were aferd.° *afraid*
Ther nas quiksilver, litarge, ne brimstoon,
Boras, ceruce, ne oile of tartre noon,[6]
Ne oinement that wolde clense and bite,
That him mighte helpen of his whelkes° white, *blotches*
Nor of the knobbes° sitting on his cheekes. *lumps*
Wel loved he garlek, oinons, and eek leekes,
And for to drinke strong win reed as blood.
Thanne wolde he speke and crye as he were wood;° *mad*
And whan that he wel dronken hadde the win,
Thanne wolde he speke no word but Latin:
A fewe termes hadde he, two or three,
That he hadde lerned out of som decree;
No wonder is—he herde it al the day,

7. Convict him of being in arrears financially.
8. There was no bailiff (i.e., foreman), shepherd, nor other farm laborer whose craftiness and plots he didn't know.
9. "Upon he hade": he had on.
1. With clothing tucked up.
2. Hindmost of our group.
3. The "Somnour" (Summoner) is an employee of the ecclesiastical court, whose defined duty is to bring to court persons whom the archdeacon—the justice of the court—suspects of offenses against canon law. By this time, however, summoners had generally transformed themselves into corrupt detectives who spied out offenders and blackmailed them by threats of summonses.
4. Cherub's, often depicted in art with a red face.
5. Uneven, partly hairless.
6. These are all ointments for diseases affecting the skin, probably diseases of venereal origin.

And eek ye knowe wel how that a jay° *parrot*
Can clepen "Watte"[7] as wel as can the Pope—
But whoso coude in other thing him grope,° *examine*
Thanne hadde he spent all his philosophye;[8]
Ay *Questio quid juris*[9] wolde he crye.
  He was a gentil harlot° and a kinde; *rascal*
A bettre felawe sholde men nought finde:
He wolde suffre,° for a quart of win, *permit*
A good felawe to have his concubin
A twelfmonth, and excusen him at the fulle;[1]
Ful prively a finch eek coude he pulle.[2]
And if he foond° owher° a good felawe *found / anywhere*
He wolde techen him to have noon awe
In swich caas of the Ercedekenes curs,[3]
But if[4] a mannes soule were in his purs,
For in his purs he sholde ypunisshed be.
"Purs is the Ercedekenes helle," saide he.
  But wel I woot he lied right in deede:
Of cursing° oughte eech gilty man drede, *excommunication*
For curs wol slee° right as assoiling° savith— *slay / absolution*
And also war him of a *significavit*.[5]
  In daunger[6] hadde he at his owene gise° *disposal*
The yonge girles of the diocise,
And knew hir conseil,° and was al hir reed.[7] *secrets*
A gerland hadde he set upon his heed
As greet as it were for an ale-stake;[8]
A bokeler hadde he maad him of a cake.
  With him ther rood a gentil Pardoner[9]
Of Rouncival, his freend and his compeer,° *comrade*
That straight was comen fro the Court of Rome.
Ful loude he soong,° "Com hider, love, to me." *sang*
This Somnour bar to him a stif burdoun:[1]
Was nevere trompe° of half so greet a soun. *trumpet*
  This Pardoner hadde heer as yelow as wex,
But smoothe it heeng° as dooth a strike° of
    flex;° *hung / hank / flax*
By ounces[2] heenge his lokkes that he hadde,

7. Call out: "Walter"—like modern parrots' "Polly."
8. I.e., learning.
9. "What point of law does this investigation involve?": a phrase frequently used in ecclesiastical courts.
1. "At the fulle": fully. Ecclesiastical courts had jurisdiction over many offenses which today would come under civil law, including sexual offenses.
2. "To pull a finch" is to have carnal dealings with a woman.
3. Archdeacon's sentence of excommunication.
4. "But if": unless.
5. And also one should be careful of a *significavit* (the writ which transferred the guilty offender from the ecclesiastical to the civil arm for punishment).
6. Under his domination.
7. Was their chief source of advice.
8. A tavern was signalized by a pole ("ale-stake"), rather like a modern flagpole, projecting from its front wall; on this hung a garland, or "bush."
9. A Pardoner dispensed papal pardon for sins to those who contributed to the charitable institution that he was licensed to represent; this Pardoner purported to be collecting for the hospital of Roncesvalles ("Rouncival") in Spain, which had a London branch.
1. I.e., provided him with a strong vocal accompaniment.
2. I.e., thin strands.

And therwith he his shuldres overspradde,° *overspread*
But thinne it lay, by colpons,° oon by oon; *strands*
But hood for jolitee° wered° he noon, *nonchalance / wore*
For it was trussed up in his walet:° *pack*
Him thoughte he rood al of the newe jet.° *fashion*
Dischevelee° save his cappe he rood al bare. *with hair down*
Swiche glaring yën hadde he as an hare.
A vernicle[3] hadde he sowed upon his cappe,
His walet biforn him in his lappe,
Bretful° of pardon, comen from Rome al hoot.° *brimful / hot*
A vois he hadde as smal° as hath a goot;° *fine / goat*
No beerd hadde he, ne nevere sholde have;
As smoothe it was as it were late yshave:
I trowe° he were a gelding or a mare. *believe*
But of his craft, fro Berwik into Ware,[4]
Ne was ther swich another pardoner;
For in his male° he hadde a pilwe-beer° *bag / pillowcase*
Which that he saide was Oure Lady veil;
He saide he hadde a gobet° of the sail *piece*
That Sainte Peter hadde whan that he wente
Upon the see, til Jesu Crist him hente.° *seized*
He hadde a crois° of laton,° ful of stones, *cross / brassy metal*
And in a glas he hadde pigges bones,
But with thise relikes[5] whan that he foond° *found*
A poore person° dwelling upon lond,[6] *parson*
Upon° a day he gat° him more moneye *in / got*
Than that the person gat in monthes twaye;
And thus with feined° flaterye and japes° *false / tricks*
He made the person and the peple his apes.° *dupes*
But trewely to tellen at the laste,
He was in chirche a noble ecclesiaste;
Wel coude he rede a lesson and a storye,° *liturgical narrative*
But alderbest° he soong an offertorye, *best of all*
For wel he wiste° whan that song was songe, *knew*
He moste° preche and wel affile° his tonge *must / sharpen*
To winne silver, as he ful wel coude—
Therfore he soong the merierly° and loude. *more merrily*
  Now have I told you soothly in a clause[7]
Th'estaat, th'array, the nombre, and eek the cause
Why that assembled was this compaignye
In Southwerk at this gentil hostelrye
That highte the Tabard, faste° by the Belle;[8] *close*
But now is time to you for to telle
How that we baren us[9] that ilke° night *same*

3. Portrait of Christ's face as it was said to have been impressed on St. Veronica's handkerchief.
4. Probably towns south and north of London.
5. Relics—i.e., the pigs' bones which the Pardoner represented as saints' bones.
6. "Upon lond": upcountry.
7. I.e., in a short space.
8. Another tavern in Southwark.
9. Bore ourselves.

Whan we were in that hostelrye alight;
And after wol I telle of oure viage,° *trip*
And al the remenant of oure pilgrimage.
But first I praye you of youre curteisye
That ye n'arette it nought my vilainye[1]
Though that I plainly speke in this matere
To telle you hir wordes and hir cheere,° *behavior*
Ne though I speke hir wordes proprely;° *accurately*
For this ye knowen also wel as I:
Who so shal telle a tale after a man
He moot° reherce,° as neigh as evere he can, *must / repeat*
Everich a word, if it be in his charge,° *responsibility*
Al speke he[2] nevere so rudeliche and large,° *broadly*
Or elles he moot telle his tale untrewe,
Or feine° thing, or finde° wordes newe; *falsify / devise*
He may nought spare[3] although he were his brother:
He moot as wel saye oo word as another.
Crist spak himself ful brode° in Holy Writ, *broadly*
And wel ye woot no vilainye is it;
Eek Plato saith, who so can him rede,
The wordes mote be cosin to the deede.
Also I praye you to foryive it me
Al° have I nat set folk in hir degree *although*
Here in this tale as that they sholde stonde:
My wit is short, ye may wel understonde.
Greet cheere made oure Host[4] us everichoon,
And to the soper sette he us anoon.° *at once*
He served us with vitaile° at the beste. *food*
Strong was the win, and wel to drinke us leste.° *it pleased*
A semely man oure Hoste was withalle
For to been a marchal[5] in an halle;
A large man he was, with yën steepe,° *prominent*
A fairer burgeis° was ther noon in Chepe[6]— *burgher*
Bold of his speeche, and wis, and wel ytaught,
And of manhood him lakkede right naught.
Eek therto he was right a merye man,
And after soper playen he bigan,
And spak of mirthe amonges othere thinges—
Whan that we hadde maad oure rekeninges[7]—
And saide thus, "Now, lordinges, trewely,
Ye been to me right welcome, hertely.° *heartily*
For by my trouthe, if that I shal nat lie,
I sawgh nat this yeer so merye a compaignye
At ones in this herberwe° as is now. *inn*

1. That you do not charge it to my lack of decorum.
2. Although he speak.
3. I.e., spare anyone.
4. The Host is the landlord of the Tabard Inn.
5. Marshal, one who was in charge of feasts.
6. Cheapside, bourgeois center of London.
7. Had paid our bills.

Fain° wolde I doon you mirthe, wiste I[8] how. *gladly*
And of a mirthe I am right now bithought,
To doon you ese, and it shal coste nought.
"Ye goon to Canterbury—God you speede;
The blisful martyr quite you youre meede.[9]
And wel I woot as ye goon by the waye
Ye shapen you[1] to talen° and to playe, *converse*
For trewely, confort ne mirthe is noon
To ride by the waye domb as stoon;° *stone*
And therfore wol I maken you disport
As I saide erst,° and doon you som confort; *before*
And if you liketh alle, by oon assent,
For to stonden at[2] my juggement,
And for to werken as I shal you saye,
Tomorwe whan ye riden by the waye—
Now by my fader° soule that is deed, *father's*
But° ye be merye I wol yive you myn heed!° *unless / head*
Holde up youre handes withouten more speeche."
Oure counseil was nat longe for to seeche;° *seek*
Us thoughte it was nat worth to make it wis,[3]
And graunted him withouten more avis,° *deliberation*
And bade him saye his voirdit° as him leste.[4] *verdict*
"Lordinges," quod he, "now herkneth for the beste;
But taketh it nought, I praye you, in desdain.
This is the point, to speken short and plain,
That eech of you, to shorte with oure waye
In this viage, shal tellen tales twaye°— *two*
To Canterburyward, I mene it so,
And hoomward he shal tellen othere two,
Of aventures that whilom° have bifalle; *once upon a time*
And which of you that bereth him best of alle—
That is to sayn, that telleth in this cas
Tales of best sentence° and most solas°— *purport / delight*
Shal have a soper at oure aller cost,[5]
Here in this place, sitting by this post,
Whan that we come again fro Canterbury.
And for to make you the more mury° *merry*
I wol myself goodly° with you ride— *kindly*
Right at myn owene cost—and be youre gide.
And who so wol my juggement withsaye° *contradict*
Shal paye al that we spende by the waye.
And if ye vouche sauf that it be so,
Telle me anoon, withouten wordes mo,° *more*
And I wol erly shape me[6] therfore."
This thing was graunted and oure othes swore
With ful glad herte, and prayden[7] him also

8. If I knew.
9. Pay you your reward.
1. "Shapen you": intend.
2. Abide by.
3. We didn't think it worthwhile to make an issue of it.
4. It pleased.
5. At the cost of us all.
6. Prepare myself.
7. I.e., we prayed.

That he wolde vouche sauf for to do so,
And that he wolde been oure governour,
And of oure tales juge and reportour,° *accountant*
And sette a soper at a certain pris,° *price*
And we wol ruled been at his devis,° *disposal*
In heigh and lowe; and thus by oon assent
We been accorded to his juggement.
And therupon the win was fet° anoon; *fetched*
We dronken and to reste wente eechoon
Withouten any lenger° taryinge. *longer*
Amorwe° whan that day bigan to springe *in the morning*
Up roos oure Host and was oure aller cok,[8]
And gadred us togidres in a flok,
And forth we riden, a litel more than pas,° *a step*
Unto the watering of Saint Thomas;[9]
And ther oure Host bigan his hors arreste,° *halt*
And saide, "Lordes, herkneth if you leste:° *it please*
Ye woot youre forward° and it you recorde:[1] *agreement*
If evensong and morwesong° accorde,° *morningsong / agree*
Lat see now who shal telle the firste tale.
As evere mote I drinken win or ale,
Who so be rebel to my juggement
Shal paye for al that by the way is spent.
Now draweth cut[2] er that we ferrer twinne:
He which that hath the shorteste shal biginne.
"Sire Knight," quod he, "my maister and my lord,
Now draweth cut, for that is myn accord.° *will*
Cometh neer," quod he, "my lady Prioresse,
And ye, sire Clerk, lat be youre shamefastnesse°— *modesty*
Ne studieth nought. Lay hand to, every man!"
Anoon to drawen every wight bigan,
And shortly for to tellen as it was,
Were it by aventure, or sort, or cas,[3]
The soothe° is this, the cut fil° to the Knight; *truth / fell*
Of which ful blithe and glad was every wight,
And telle he moste° his tale, as was resoun, *must*
By forward and by composicioun,[4]
As ye han herd. What needeth wordes mo?
And whan this goode man sawgh that it was so,
As he that wis was and obedient
To keepe his forward by his free assent,
He saide, "Sin I shal biginne the game,
What, welcome be the cut, in Goddes name!
Now lat us ride, and herkneth what I saye."
And with that word we riden forth oure waye,
And he bigan with right a merye cheere° *countenance*
His tale anoon, and saide as ye may heere.

8. Was rooster for us all.
9. A watering place near Southwark.
1. You recall it.
2. I.e., draw lots; "ferrer twinne": go farther.
3. Whether it was luck, fate, or chance.
4. By agreement and compact.

The Miller's Tale[1]

The Introduction

Whan that the Knight hadde thus his tale ytold,[2]
In al the route° nas ther yong ne old — *group*
That he ne saide it was a noble storye,
And worthy for to drawen° to memorye, — *recall*
And namely° the gentils everichoon. — *especially*
Oure Hoste lough° and swoor, "So mote I goon,[3] — *laughed*
This gooth aright: unbokeled is the male.° — *pouch*
Lat see now who shal telle another tale.
For trewely the game is wel bigonne.
Now telleth ye, sire Monk, if that ye conne,° — *can*
Somwhat to quite° with the Knightes tale." — *repay*
The Millere, that for dronken[4] was al pale,
So that unnethe° upon his hors he sat, — *with difficulty*
He nolde avalen° neither hood ne hat, — *doff*
Ne abiden no man for his curteisye,
But in Pilates vois[5] he gan to crye,
And swoor, "By armes[6] and by blood and bones,
I can° a noble tale for the nones, — *know*
With which I wol now quite the Knightes tale."
Oure Hoste sawgh that he was dronke of ale,
And saide, "Abide, Robin, leve° brother, — *dear*
Som bettre man shal telle us first another.
Abide, and lat us werken thriftily."° — *with propriety*
"By Goddes soule," quod he, "that wol nat I,
For I wol speke or elles go my way."
Oure Host answerde, "Tel on, a devele way![7]
Thou art a fool; thy wit is overcome."
"Now herkneth," quod the Millere, "alle and some.[8]

1. The Miller's Tale belongs to the literary genre known as the "fabliau," a short story in verse that generally involves bourgeois or lower-class characters in an outrageous, often obscene plot, which is, however, realistically handled by the narrator. The fabliau is peculiarly French, and aside from the three or four examples in Chaucer there are few representatives of it in English. Yet Chaucer was supreme in this kind of tale as in many others, and the Miller's Tale is generally considered the best-told fabliau in any language.

Two originally separate plots are the basis of the Miller's Tale, both of them probably already old in Chaucer's time. In the first, a student—students are often the heroes of fabliaux and were probably often their authors—creates an opportunity to sleep with a woman by persuading her husband that Noah's flood is about to be repeated; and in the second, a lover who has been tricked into a humiliatingly misdirected kiss takes a dreadful vengeance on his tormentor. Whether or not Chaucer first united these traditional plots is not clear, but in any case their union, culminating in the scorched student's cry of "Water!" is a brilliant stroke, and brilliantly handled by Chaucer.

2. The Knight's Tale is actually the first one told on the Canterbury pilgrimage, immediately following the General Prologue.

3. So might I walk.

4. I.e., drunkenness.

5. The harsh voice usually associated with the character of Pontius Pilate in the mystery plays.

6. I.e., by God's arms.

7. I.e., in the devil's name.

8. Each and every one.

But first I make a protestacioun°   *public affirmation*
That I am dronke: I knowe it by my soun.°   *tone of voice*
And therfore if that I mis° speke or saye,   *amiss*
Wite it[9] the ale of Southwerk, I you praye;
For I wol telle a legende and a lif
Bothe of a carpenter and of his wif,
How that a clerk hath set the wrightes cappe."[1]
  The Reeve answerde and saide, "Stint thy clappe![2]
Lat be thy lewed° dronken harlotrye.°   *ignorant / obscenity*
It is a sinne and eek° a greet folye   *also*
To apairen° any man or him defame,   *injure*
And eek to bringen wives in swich fame.°   *report*
Thou maist ynough of othere thinges sayn."
  This dronken Millere spak ful soone again,
And saide, "Leve° brother Osewold,   *dear*
Who hath no wif, he is no cokewold.°   *cuckold*
But I saye nat therfore that thou art oon.
Ther ben ful goode wives many oon,°   *a one*
And evere a thousand goode ayains oon badde.
That knowestou wel thyself but if thou madde.°   *rave*
Why artou angry with my tale now?
I have a wif, pardee, as wel as thou,
Yit nolde° I, for the oxen in my plough,   *would not*
Take upon me more than ynough
As deemen of myself that I were oon:
I wol bileve wel that I am noon.
An housbonde shal nought been inquisitif
Of Goddes privetee,° nor of his wif.   *secrets*
So[3] he may finde Goddes foison° there,   *plenty*
Of the remenant° needeth nought enquere."°   *rest / inquire*
  What sholde I more sayn but this Millere
He nolde his wordes for no man forbere,
But tolde his cherles tale in his manere.
M'athinketh° that I shal reherce° it here,   *I regret / repeat*
And therfore every gentil wight I praye,
Deemeth nought, for Goddes love, that I saye
Of yvel entente, but for° I moot reherse   *because*
Hir tales alle, be they bet° or werse,   *better*
Or elles falsen° som of my matere.   *falsify*
And therfore, whoso list it nought yheere
Turne over the leef, and chese° another tale,   *choose*
For he shal finde ynowe,° grete and smale,   *enough*
Of storial[4] thing that toucheth gentilesse,°   *gentility*
And eek moralitee and holinesse:
Blameth nought me if that ye chese amis.
The Millere is a cherl, ye knowe wel this,
So was the Reeve eek, and othere mo,

9. Blame it on.
1. I.e., how a clerk made a fool of a carpenter.
2. Stop your chatter.
3. Provided that.
4. Historical, i.e., true.

And harlotrye° they tolden bothe two. *ribaldry*
Aviseth you,[5] and putte me out of blame:
And eek men shal nought maken ernest of game.

The Tale

Whilom° ther was dwelling at Oxenforde *once upon a time*
A riche gnof° that gestes heeld to boorde,[6] *boor*
And of his craft he was a carpenter.
With him ther was dwelling a poore scoler,
Hadde lerned art,[7] but al his fantasye° *interest*
Was turned for to lere° astrologye, *learn*
And coude a certain of conclusiouns,
To deemen by interrogaciouns,[8]
If that men axed° him in certain houres *asked*
Whan that men sholde have droughte or elles showres,
Or if men axed him what shal bifalle
Of every thing—I may nat rekene hem alle.
This clerk was cleped° hende[9] Nicholas. *called*
Of derne love he coude, and of solas,[1]
And therto he was sly and ful privee,° *secretive*
And lik a maide meeke for to see.
A chambre hadde he in that hostelrye
Allone, withouten any compaignye,
Ful fetisly ydight[2] with herbes swoote,° *sweet*
And he himself as sweete as is the roote
Of licoris or any setewale.[3]
His *Almageste*[4] and bookes grete and smale,
His astrelabye,[5] longing for his art,
His augrim stones,[6] layen faire apart
On shelves couched° at his beddes heed; *set*
His presse° ycovered with a falding reed;[7] *storage chest*
And al above ther lay a gay sautrye,° *psaltery*
On which he made a-nightes melodye
So swetely that al the chambre roong,° *rang*
And *Angelus ad Virginem*[8] he soong,
And after that he soong the *Kinges Note:*
Ful often blessed was his merye throte.
And thus this sweete clerk his time spente
After his freendes finding and his rente.[9]
This carpenter hadde wedded newe° a wif *lately*

5. Take heed.
6. I.e., took in boarders.
7. Who had completed the first stage of university education (the trivium).
8. I.e., and he knew a number of propositions on which to base astrological analyses (which would reveal the matters in ll. 87–90).
9. Handy, sly, attractive.
1. I.e., he knew about secret love and pleasurable practices.
2. Elegantly furnished.
3. Setwall, a spice.
4. 2nd-century treatise by Ptolemy, still the standard astronomy textbook.
5. Astrolabe, an astronomical instrument. "Longing for": belonging to.
6. Counters used in arithmetic.
7. Red coarse wool.
8. "The Angel's Address to the Virgin," a hymn; *"Kinges Note":* probably a popular song of the time.
9. In accordance with his friends' provision and his own income.

Which that he loved more than his lif.
Of eighteteene yeer she was of age;
Jalous he was, and heeld hire narwe in cage,
For she was wilde and yong, and he was old,
And deemed himself been lik a cokewold.[1]
He knew nat Caton,[2] for his wit was rude,
That bad men sholde wedde his similitude:[3]
Men sholde wedden after hir estat,[4]
For youthe and elde° is often at debat. *age*
But sith that he was fallen in the snare,
He moste endure, as other folk, his care.
 Fair was this yonge wif, and therwithal
As any wesele° hir body gent and smal.[5] *weasel*
A ceint she wered, barred[6] al of silk;
A barmcloth° as whit as morne milk *apron*
Upon hir lendes,° ful of many a gore;° *loins / strip of cloth*
Whit was hir smok,° and broiden[7] al bifore *undergarment*
And eek bihinde, on hir coler° aboute, *collar*
Of° col-blak silk, withinne and eek withoute; *with*
The tapes° of hir white voluper° *ribbons / cap*
Were of the same suite of[8] hir coler;
Hir filet° brood° of silk and set ful hye; *headband / broad*
And sikerly° she hadde a likerous° yë; *certainly / wanton*
Ful smale ypulled[9] were hir browes two,
And tho were bent,° and blake as any slo.° *arching / sloeberry*
She was ful more blisful on to see
Than is the newe perejonette° tree, *pear*
And softer than the wolle° is of a wether;° *wool / ram*
And by hir girdel° heeng° a purs of lether, *belt / hung*
Tasseled with silk and perled with latoun.[1]
In al this world, to seeken up and down,
Ther nis no man so wis that coude thenche° *imagine*
So gay a popelote° or swich° a wenche. *doll / such*
Ful brighter was the shining of hir hewe
Than in the Towr[2] the noble° yforged newe. *gold coin*
But of hir song, it was as loud and yerne° *lively*
As any swalwe sitting on a berne.° *barn*
Therto she coude skippe and make game[3]
As any kide or calf folwing his dame.° *mother*
Hir mouth was sweete as bragot or the meeth,[4]
Or hoord of apples laid in hay or heeth.° *heather*

1. I.e., suspected of himself that he was like a cuckold.
2. Dionysius Cato, the supposed author of a book of maxims used in elementary education.
3. Commanded that one should wed his equal.
4. Men should marry according to their condition.
5. Slender and delicate.
6. A belt she wore, with transverse stripes.
7. Embroidered.
8. I.e., the same pattern as.
9. Delicately plucked.
1. I.e., with brassy spangles on it.
2. The Tower of London.
3. Play.
4. "Bragot" and "meeth" are honey drinks.

Winsing° she was as is a joly° colt, *skittish / high-spirited*
Long as a mast, and upright° as a bolt.° *straight / arrow*
A brooch she bar upon hir lowe coler
As brood as is the boos° of a bokeler;° *boss / shield*
Hir shoes were laced on hir legges hye.
She was a primerole,° a piggesnye,° *cowslip / pig's eye*
For any lord to leggen° in his bedde, *lay*
Or yit for any good yeman to wedde.
  Now sire, and eft° sire, so bifel the cas *again*
That on a day this hende Nicholas
Fil° with this yonge wif to rage° and playe, *happened / flirt*
Whil that hir housbonde was at Oseneye[5]
(As clerkes been ful subtil and ful quainte),° *clever*
And prively he caughte hire by the queinte,° *pudendum*
And saide, "Ywis, but if ich° have my wille, *I*
For derne° love of thee, lemman, I spille,"° *secret / die*
And heeld hire harde by the haunche-bones,
And saide, "Lemman,° love me al atones,[6] *mistress*
Or I wol dien, also° God me save." *so*
And she sproong° as a colt dooth in a trave,[7] *sprang*
And with hir heed she wried° faste away; *twisted*
She saide, "I wol nat kisse thee, by my fay.° *faith*
Why, lat be," quod she, "lat be, Nicholas!
Or I wol crye 'Out, harrow,° and allas!' *help*
Do way youre handes, for your curteisye!"
  This Nicholas gan mercy for to crye,
And spak so faire, and profred him so faste,[8]
That she hir love him graunted atte laste,
And swoor hir ooth by Saint Thomas of Kent[9]
That she wolde been at his comandement,
Whan that she may hir leiser[1] wel espye.
"Myn housbonde is so ful of jalousye
That but ye waite° wel and been privee, *be on guard*
I woot right wel I nam but deed," quod she.
"Ye moste been ful derne as in this cas."
  "Nay, therof care thee nought," quod Nicholas.
"A clerk hadde litherly biset his while,[2]
But if he coude a carpenter bigile."
And thus they been accorded and ysworn
To waite° a time, as I have told biforn. *watch for*
Whan Nicholas hadde doon this everydeel,
And thakked° hire upon the lendes° weel, *patted / loins*
He kiste hire sweete, and taketh his sautrye,
And playeth faste, and maketh melodye.
  Thanne fil° it thus, that to the parissh chirche, *befell*

5. A town near Oxford.
6. Right now.
7. Frame for a restive horse.
8. I.e., pushed himself so vigorously.
9. Thomas à Becket.
1. I.e., opportunity.
2. Poorly employed his time.

Cristes owene werkes for to wirche,° *perform*
This goode wif wente on an haliday:° *holy day*
Hir forheed shoon as bright as any day,
So was it wasshen whan she leet° hir werk. *left*
 Now was ther of that chirche a parissh clerk,
The which that was ycleped° Absolon: *called*
Crul° was his heer, and as the gold it shoon, *curly*
And strouted° as a fanne[3] large and brode; *spread out*
Ful straight and evene lay his joly shode.[4]
His rode° was reed, his yën greye as goos.° *complexion / goose*
With Poules window corven[5] on his shoos,
In hoses° rede he wente fetisly.° *stockings / elegantly*
Yclad he was ful smale° and proprely, *finely*
Al in a kirtel° of a light waget°— *tunic / blue*
Ful faire and thikke been the pointes[6] set—
And therupon he hadde a gay surplis,° *surplice*
As whit as is the blosme upon the ris.° *bough*
A merye child° he was, so God me save. *lad*
Wel coude he laten° blood, and clippe, and shave, *let*
And maken a chartre of land, or acquitaunce;[7]
In twenty manere° coude he trippe and daunce *ways*
After the scole of Oxenforde tho,
And with his legges casten° to and fro, *prance*
And playen songes on a smal rubible;° *fiddle*
Therto he soong somtime a loud quinible,[8]
And as wel coude he playe on a giterne:° *guitar*
In al the town nas brewhous ne taverne
That he ne visited with his solas,° *entertainment*
Ther any gailard tappestere[9] was.
But sooth to sayn, he was somdeel squaimous° *squeamish*
Of farting, and of speeche daungerous.° *fastidious*
 This Absolon, that joly° was and gay, *pretty, amorous*
Gooth with a cencer° on the haliday, *incense-burner*
Cencing the wives of the parissh faste,
And many a lovely look on hem he caste,
And namely° on this carpenteres wif: *especially*
To looke on hire him thoughte a merye lif.
She was so propre° and sweete and likerous,[1] *neat*
I dar wel sayn, if she hadde been a mous,
And he a cat, he wolde hire hente° anoon. *pounce on*
This parissh clerk, this joly Absolon,
Hath in his herte swich a love-longinge° *lovesickness*
That of no wif ne took he noon offringe—
For curteisye he saide he wolde noon.

3. Wide-mouthed basket for separating grain from chaff.
4. Parting of the hair.
5. Carved with intricate designs, like the tracery in the windows of St. Paul's.
6. Laces for fastening the tunic and holding up the hose.
7. Legal release.
8. Part requiring a very high voice.
9. Gay barmaid.
1. Wanton, appetizing.

The moone, whan it was night, ful brighte shoon,° *shone*
And Absolon his giterne° hath ytake— *guitar*
For paramours° he thoughte for to wake— *love*
And forth he gooth, jolif° and amorous, *pretty*
Til he cam to the carpenteres hous,
A litel after cokkes hadde ycrowe,
And dressed him up by a shot-windowe[2]
That was upon the carpenteres wal.
He singeth in his vois gentil and smal,° *dainty*
"Now dere lady, if thy wille be,
I praye you that ye wol rewe° on me," *have pity*
Ful wel accordant to his giterninge.[3]
This carpenter awook and herde him singe,
And spak unto his wif, and saide anoon,
"What, Alison, heerestou nought Absolon
That chaunteth thus under oure bowres° wal?" *bedroom's*
And she answerde hir housbonde therwithal,
"Yis, God woot, John, I heere it everydeel."
    This passeth forth. What wol ye bet than weel?[4]
Fro day to day this joly Absolon
So woweth° hire that him is wo-bigoon: *woos*
He waketh° al the night and al the day; *stays awake*
He kembed° his lokkes brode[5] and made him gay; *combed*
He woweth hire by menes and brocage,[6]
And swoor he wolde been hir owene page;° *personal servant*
He singeth, brokking° as a nightingale; *trilling*
He sente hire piment,[7] meeth, and spiced ale,
And wafres° piping hoot out of the gleede;° *pastries / coals*
And for she was of towne,[8] he profred meede°— *bribe*
For som folk wol be wonnen for richesse,
And som for strokes,° and som for gentilesse. *blows*
Somtime to shewe his lightnesse and maistrye,[9]
He playeth Herodes[1] upon a scaffold° hye. *platform, stage*
But what availeth him as in this cas?
She loveth so this hende Nicholas
That Absolon may blowe the bukkes horn;[2]
He ne hadde for his labour but a scorn.
And thus she maketh Absolon hir ape,[3]
And al his ernest turneth til a jape.° *joke*
Ful sooth is this proverbe, it is no lie;
Men saith right thus: "Alway the nye slye
Maketh the ferre leve to be loth."[4]

2. Took his position by a hinged window.
3. In harmony with his guitar-playing.
4. Better than well.
5. I.e., wide-spreading.
6. By intermediaries and mediation.
7. Spiced wine; "meeth": mead.
8. Since she was a town woman.
9. Facility and virtuosity.
1. Herod, a role traditionally played as a bully in the mystery plays.
2. Blow the buck's horn, i.e., go without reward.
3. I.e., thus she makes a fool of Absolon.
4. Always the sly man at hand makes the distant dear one hated.

For though that Absolon be wood° or wroth, *furious*
By cause that he fer was from hir sighte,
This nye° Nicholas stood in his lighte. *nearby*
Now beer° thee wel, thou hende Nicholas, *bear*
For Absolon may waile and singe allas.
And so bifel it on a Saterday
This carpenter was goon til Oseney,
And hende Nicholas and Alisoun
Accorded been to this conclusioun,
That Nicholas shal shapen° hem a wile° *arrange / trick*
This sely[5] jalous housbonde to bigile,
And if so be this game wente aright,
She sholden sleepen in his arm al night—
For this was his desir and hire° also. *hers*
And right anoon, withouten wordes mo,
This Nicholas no lenger wolde tarye,
But dooth ful softe unto his chambre carye
Bothe mete and drinke for a day or twaye,
And to hir housbonde bad hire for to saye,
If that he axed after Nicholas,
She sholde saye she niste° wher he was— *didn't know*
Of al that day she sawgh him nought with yë:
She trowed° that he was in maladye, *believed*
For for no cry hir maide coude him calle,
He nolde answere for no thing that mighte falle.° *happen*
This passeth forth al thilke° Saterday *this*
That Nicholas stille in his chambre lay,
And eet,° and sleep,° or dide what him leste,[6] *ate / slept*
Til Sonday that the sonne gooth to reste.
This sely carpenter hath greet mervaile
Of Nicholas, or what thing mighte him aile,
And saide, "I am adrad,° by Saint Thomas, *afraid*
It stondeth nat aright with Nicholas.
God shilde° that he deide sodeinly! *forbid*
This world is now ful tikel,° sikerly: *changeable*
I sawgh today a corps yborn to chirche
That now a° Monday last I sawgh him wirche.° *on / work*
Go up," quod he unto his knave° anoon, *manservant*
"Clepe° at his dore or knokke with a stoon.° *call / stone*
Looke how it is and tel me boldely."
This knave gooth him up ful sturdily,
And at the chambre dore whil that he stood
He cride and knokked as that he were wood,° *mad*
"What? How? What do ye, maister Nicholay?
How may ye sleepen al the longe day?"
But al for nought: he herde nat a word.
An hole he foond ful lowe upon a boord,
Ther as the cat was wont in for to creepe,

5. "Poor innocent."

6. He wanted.

And at that hole he looked in ful deepe,
And atte laste he hadde of him a sighte.
  This Nicholas sat evere caping° uprighte *gaping*
As he hadde kiked° on the newe moone. *gazed*
Adown he gooth and tolde his maister soone
In what array° he saw this ilke° man. *condition / same*
  This carpenter to blessen him[7] bigan,
And saide, "Help us, Sainte Frideswide!
A man woot litel what him shal bitide.
This man is falle, with his astromye,[8]
In som woodnesse° or in som agonye. *madness*
I thoughte ay° wel how that it sholde be: *always*
Men sholde nought knowe of Goddes privetee.
Ye, blessed be alway a lewed° man *ignorant*
That nought but only his bileve° can.° *creed / knows*
So ferde° another clerk with astromye: *fared*
He walked in the feeldes for to prye
Upon the sterres,° what ther sholde bifalle, *stars*
Til he was in a marle-pit[9] yfalle—
He saw nat that. But yit, by Saint Thomas,
Me reweth sore[1] for hende Nicholas.
He shal be rated of[2] his studying,
If that I may, by Jesus, hevene king!
Get me a staf that I may underspore,° *pry up*
Whil that thou, Robin, hevest° up the dore. *heave*
He shal[3] out of his studying, as I gesse."
And to the chambre dore he gan him dresse.[4]
His knave was a strong carl° for the nones,° *fellow / purpose*
And by the haspe he haaf° it up atones: *heaved*
Into° the floor the dore fil° anoon. *on / fell*
This Nicholas sat ay as stille as stoon,
And evere caped up into the air.
This carpenter wende° he were in despair, *thought*
And hente° him by the shuldres mightily, *seized*
And shook him harde, and cride spitously,° *roughly*
"What, Nicholay, what, how! What! Looke adown!
Awaak and thenk on Cristes passioun![5]
I crouche[6] thee from elves and fro wightes."
Therwith the nightspel saide he anoonrightes[7]
On foure halves° of the hous aboute, *sides*
And on the thresshfold° on the dore withoute: *threshold*
"Jesu Crist and Sainte Benedight,° *Benedict*
Blesse this hous from every wikked wight!
For nightes nerye the White Pater Noster.[8]

7. Cross himself.
8. Illiterate form of "astronomye."
9. Pit from which a fertilizing clay is dug.
1. I sorely pity.
2. Scolded for.
3. I.e., shall come.
4. Took his stand.
5. I.e., the Crucifixion.
6. Make the sign of the cross on; "wightes": wicked creatures.
7. The night-charm he said right away.
8. I.e., the White Lord's Prayer defend (us). This personification was considered a powerful beneficent spirit.

Where wentestou, thou Sainte Petres soster?"° *sister*
And at the laste this hende Nicholas
Gan for to sike° sore, and saide, "Allas, *sigh*
Shal al the world be lost eftsoones° now?" *again*
  This carpenter answerde, "What saistou?
What, thenk on God as we doon, men that swinke."[9]
  This Nicholas answerde, "Fecche me drinke,
And after wol I speke in privetee
Of certain thing that toucheth me and thee.
I wol telle it noon other man, certain."
  This carpenter gooth down and comth again,
And broughte of mighty ale a large quart,
And when that eech of hem hadde dronke his part,
This Nicholas his dore faste shette,° *shut*
And down the carpenter by him he sette,
And saide, "John, myn hoste lief° and dere, *beloved*
Thou shalt upon thy trouthe° swere me here *word of honor*
That to no wight thou shalt this conseil° wraye;° *secret / disclose*
For it is Cristes conseil that I saye,
And if thou telle it man,[1] thou art forlore,° *lost*
For this vengeance thou shalt have therfore,
That if thou wraye me, thou shalt be wood." [2]
  "Nay, Crist forbede it, for his holy blood,"
Quod tho this sely° man. "I nam no labbe,[3] *innocent*
And though I saye, I nam nat lief to gabbe.[4]
Say what thou wilt, I shal it nevere telle
To child ne wif, by him that harwed helle."[5]
  "Now John," quod Nicholas, "I wol nought lie.
I have yfounde in myn astrologye,
As I have looked in the moone bright,
That now a Monday next, at quarter night,[6]
Shal falle a rain, and that so wilde and wood,° *furious*
That half so greet was nevere Noees° flood. *Noah's*
This world," he saide, "in lasse° than an hour *less*
Shal al be dreint,° so hidous is the showr. *drowned*
Thus shal mankinde drenche° and lese° hir lif." *drown / lose*
  This carpenter answerde, "Allas, my wif!
And shal she drenche? Allas, myn Alisoun!"
For sorwe of this he fil almost[7] adown,
And saide, "Is there no remedye in this cas?"
  "Why yis, for[8] Gode," quod hende Nicholas,
"If thou wolt werken after lore and reed[9]—
Thou maist nought werken after thyn owene heed;° *head*
For thus saith Salomon that was ful trewe,
'Werk al by conseil and thou shalt nought rewe.'° *be sorry*

9. Work.
1. To anyone.
2. Go mad.
3. Blabbermouth.
4. And though I say it myself, I don't like to gossip.
5. By Him that despoiled hell—i.e., Christ.
6. I.e., shortly before dawn.
7. Almost fell.
8. I.e., by.
9. Act according to learning and advice.

And if thou werken wolt by good conseil,
I undertake, withouten mast or sail,
Yit shal I save hire and thee and me.
Hastou nat herd how saved was Noee
Whan that oure Lord hadde warned him biforn
That al the world with water sholde be lorn?"° *lost*
"Yis," quod this carpenter, "ful yore ago."
"Hastou nat herd," quod Nicholas, "also
The sorwe of Noee with his felaweshipe?
Er that he mighte gete his wif to shipe,
Him hadde levere,[1] I dar wel undertake,
At thilke time than alle his wetheres blake
That she hadde had a ship hirself allone.[2]
And therfore woostou° what is best to doone? *do you know*
This axeth° haste, and of an hastif° thing *requires / urgent*
Men may nought preche or maken tarying.
Anoon go gete us faste into this in° *lodging*
A kneeding trough or elles a kimelin° *brewing tub*
For eech of us, but looke that they be large,° *wide*
In whiche we mowen swimme as in a barge,[3]
And han therinne vitaile suffisaunt[4]
But for a day—fy° on the remenaunt! *fie*
The water shal aslake° and goon away *diminish*
Aboute prime[5] upon the nexte day.
But Robin may nat wite° of this, thy knave, *know*
Ne eek thy maide Gille I may nat save.
Axe nought why, for though thou axe me,
I wol nought tellen Goddes privetee.° *secrets*
Suffiseth thee, but if thy wittes madde,° *go mad*
To han° as greet a grace as Noee hadde. *have*
Thy wif shal I wel saven, out of doute.
Go now thy way, and speed thee heraboute.
But whan thou hast for hire° and thee and me *her*
Ygeten us thise kneeding-tubbes three,
Thanne shaltou hangen hem in the roof ful hye,
That no man of oure purveyance° espye. *foresight*
And whan thou thus hast doon as I have said,
And hast oure vitaile faire in hem ylaid,
And eek an ax to smite the corde atwo,
Whan that the water comth that we may go,
And broke an hole an heigh[6] upon the gable
Unto the gardinward,[7] over the stable,
That we may freely passen forth oure way,
Whan that the grete showr is goon away,

1. He had rather. "Wetheres": rams. I.e., he'd have given all the rams he had.
2. The reluctance of Noah's wife to board the ark is a traditional comic theme in the mystery plays.
3. In which we can float as in a vessel.
4. Sufficient food.
5. 9 A.M.
6. On high.
7. Toward the garden.

Thanne shaltou swimme as merye, I undertake,
As dooth the white doke° after hir drake. *duck*
Thanne wol I clepe,° 'How, Alison? How, John? *call*
Be merye, for the flood wol passe anoon.'
And thou wolt sayn, 'Hail, maister Nicholay!
Good morwe, I see thee wel, for it is day!'
And thanne shal we be lordes al oure lif
Of al the world, as Noee and his wif.
But of oo thing I warne thee ful right:
Be wel avised on that ilke night
That we been entred into shippes boord
That noon of us ne speke nought a word,
Ne clepe, ne crye, but been in his prayere,
For it is Goddes owene heeste dere.[8]
Thy wif and thou mote hange fer atwinne,[9]
For that bitwixe you shal be no sinne—
Namore in looking than ther shal in deede.
This ordinance is said: go, God thee speede.
Tomorwe at night whan men been alle asleepe,
Into oure kneeding-tubbes wol we creepe,
And sitten there, abiding Goddes grace.
Go now thy way, I have no lenger space° *time*
To make of this no lenger sermoning.
Men sayn thus: 'Send the wise and say no thing.'
Thou art so wis it needeth thee nat teche:
Go save oure lif, and that I thee biseeche."
  This sely carpenter gooth forth his way:
Ful ofte he saide allas and wailaway,
And to his wif he tolde his privetee,
And she was war,° and knew it bet° than he, *aware / better*
What al this quainte cast° was for to saye.° *trick / mean*
But nathelees she ferde° as she wolde deye, *acted*
And saide, "Allas, go forth thy way anoon.
Help us to scape,° or we been dede eechoon. *escape*
I am thy trewe verray wedded wif:
Go, dere spouse, and help to save oure lif."
  Lo, which a greet thing is affeccioun!° *emotion*
Men may dien of imaginacioun,
So deepe° may impression be take. *deeply*
This sely carpenter biginneth quake;
Him thinketh verrailiche° that he may see *truly*
Noees flood come walwing° as the see *rolling*
To drenchen° Alison, his hony dere. *drown*
He weepeth, waileth, maketh sory cheere;
He siketh° with ful many a sory swough,° *sighs / breath*
And gooth and geteth him a kneeding-trough,
And after a tubbe and a kimelin,
And prively he sente hem to his in,° *dwelling*

8. Precious commandment.
9. Far apart.

And heeng° hem in the roof in privetee; *hung*
His owene hand he made laddres three,
To climben by the ronges° and the stalkes° *rungs / uprights*
Unto the tubbes hanging in the balkes,° *rafters*
And hem vitailed,° bothe trough and tubbe, *victualed*
With breed and cheese and good ale in a jubbe,° *jug*
Suffising right ynough as for a day.
But er that he hadde maad al this array,
He sente his knave, and eek his wenche also,
Upon his neede[1] to London for to go.
And on the Monday whan it drow to[2] nighte,
He shette° his dore withouten candel-lighte, *shut*
And dressed° alle thing as it sholde be, *arranged*
And shortly up they clomben° alle three. *climbed*
They seten° stille wel a furlong way.[3] *sat*
"Now, Pater Noster, clum,"[4] saide Nicholay,
And "Clum" quod John, and "Clum" saide Alisoun.
This carpenter saide his devocioun,
And stille he sit° and biddeth his prayere, *sits*
Awaiting on the rain, if he it heere.° *might hear*
The dede sleep, for wery bisinesse,
Fil° on this carpenter right as I gesse *fell*
Aboute corfew time,[5] or litel more.
For travailing of his gost[6] he groneth sore,
And eft° he routeth,° for his heed mislay.[7] *then / snores*
Down of the laddre stalketh Nicholay,
And Alison ful softe adown she spedde:
Withouten wordes mo they goon to bedde
Ther as the carpenter is wont to lie.
Ther was the revel and the melodye,
And thus lith° Alison and Nicholas *lies*
In bisinesse of mirthe and of solas,° *pleasure*
Til that the belle of Laudes[8] gan to ringe,
And freres in the chauncel° gonne singe. *chancel*
This parissh clerk, this amorous Absolon,
That is for love alway so wo-bigoon,
Upon the Monday was at Oseneye,
With compaignye him to disporte and playe,
And axed upon caas[9] a cloisterer
Ful prively after John the carpenter;
And he drow him apart out of the chirche,
And saide, "I noot:[1] I sawgh him here nought wirche
Sith Saterday. I trowe that he be went
For timber ther oure abbot hath him sent.

1. On an errand for him.
2. Drew toward.
3. The time it takes to go a furlong (i.e., a few minutes).
4. Hush (?).
5. Probably about 8 P.M.
6. Affliction of his spirit.
7. Lay in the wrong position.
8. The first church service of the day.
9. By chance; "cloisterer": here, a member of the religious order of Osney Abbey.
1. Don't know; "wirche": work.

For he is wont for timber for to go,
And dwellen atte grange[2] a day or two.
Or elles he is at his hous, certain.
Where that he be I can nought soothly sayn."
  This Absolon ful jolif was and light,[3]
And thoughte, "Now is time to wake al night,
For sikerly,° I sawgh him nought stiringe — *certainly*
Aboute his dore sin day bigan to springe.
So mote° I thrive, I shal at cokkes crowe — *may*
Ful prively knokken at his windowe
That stant° ful lowe upon his bowres[4] wal. — *stands*
To Alison now wol I tellen al
My love-longing,° for yet I shal nat misse — *lovesickness*
That at the leeste way[5] I shal hire kisse.
Som manere confort shal I have, parfay.° — *in faith*
My mouth hath icched al this longe day:
That is a signe of kissing at the leeste.
Al night me mette[6] eek I was at a feeste.
Therfore I wol go sleepe an hour or twaye,
And al the night thanne wol I wake and playe."
  Whan that the firste cok hath crowe, anoon
Up rist° this joly lovere Absolon, — *rises*
And him arrayeth gay at point devis.[7]
But first he cheweth grain[8] and licoris,
To smellen sweete, er he hadde kembd° his heer. — *combed*
Under his tonge a trewe-love[9] he beer,° — *bore*
For therby wende° he to be gracious.° — *supposed / pleasing*
He rometh° to the carpenteres hous, — *strolls*
And stille he stant° under the shot-windowe— — *stands*
Unto his brest it raughte,° it was so lowe— — *reached*
And ofte he cougheth with a semisoun.° — *small sound*
"What do ye, hony-comb, sweete Alisoun,
My faire brid,[1] my sweete cinamome?
Awaketh, lemman° myn, and speketh to me. — *mistress*
Wel litel thinken ye upon my wo
That for your love I swete° ther I go. — *sweat*
No wonder is though that I swelte° and swete: — *melt*
I moorne as doth a lamb after the tete.° — *tit*
Ywis, lemman, I have swich love-longinge,
That lik a turtle° trewe is my moorninge: — *dove*
I may nat ete namore than a maide."
  "Go fro the windowe, Jakke fool," she saide.
"As help me God, it wol nat be com-pa-me.° — *come-kiss-me*
I love another, and elles I were to blame,
Wel bet° than thee, by Jesu, Absolon. — *better*

2. The outlying farm belonging to the abbey.
3. Was very amorous and gay.
4. Bower's, bedroom's.
5. I.e., at least.
6. I dreamed.
7. To perfection.
8. Grain of paradise (a spice).
9. Sprig of a clover-like plant.
1. Bird or bride.

Go forth thy way or I wol caste a stoon,
And lat me sleepe, a twenty devele way."[2]
"Allas," quod Absolon, "and wailaway,
That trewe love was evere so yvele biset.[3]
Thanne kis me, sin that it may be no bet,
For Jesus love and for the love of me."
"Woltou thanne go thy way therwith?" quod she.
"Ye, certes, lemman," quod this Absolon.
"Thanne maak thee redy," quod she. "I come anoon."
And unto Nicholas she saide stille,° *quietly*
"Now hust,° and thou shalt laughen al thy fille." *hush*
This Absolon down sette him on his knees,
And said, "I am a lord at alle degrees,[4]
For after this I hope ther cometh more.
Lemman, thy grace, and sweete brid, thyn ore!"° *mercy*
The windowe she undooth, and that in haste.
"Have do," quod she, "come of and speed thee faste,
Lest that oure neighebores thee espye."
This Absolon gan wipe his mouth ful drye:
Derk was the night as pich or as the cole,
And at the windowe out she putte hir hole,
And Absolon, him fil no bet ne wers,[5]
But with his mouth he kiste hir naked ers,
Ful savourly,° er he were war of this. *with relish*
Abak he sterte,° and thoughte it was amis, *started*
For wel he wiste a womman hath no beerd.
He felte a thing al rough and longe yherd,° *haired*
And saide, "Fy, allas, what have I do?"
"Teehee," quod she, and clapte the windowe to.
And Absolon gooth forth a sory pas.[6]
"A beerd, a beerd!" quod hende Nicholas,
"By Goddes corpus,° this gooth faire and weel." *body*
This sely Absolon herde everydeel,
And on his lippe he gan for anger bite,
And to himself he saide, "I shal thee quite."° *repay*
Who rubbeth now, who froteth° now his lippes *wipes*
With dust, with sond,[7] with straw, with cloth, with chippes,
But Absolon, that saith ful ofte allas?
"My soule bitake° I unto Satanas,° *commit / Satan*
But me were levere[8] than all this town," quod he,
"Of this despit° awroken° for to be. *insult / avenged*
Allas," quod he, "allas I ne hadde ybleint!"° *turned aside*
His hote love was cold and al yqueint,° *quenched*
For fro that time that he hadde kist hir ers
Of paramours he sette nought a kers,[9]

2. In the name of twenty devils.
3. Ill-used.
4. In every way.
5. It befell him neither better nor worse.
6. I.e., walking sadly.
7. Sand.
8. I had rather.
9. He didn't care a piece of cress for woman's love.

For he was heled° of his maladye. *cured*
Ful ofte paramours he gan defye,° *renounce*
And weep° as dooth a child that is ybete. *wept*
A softe paas[1] he wente over the streete
Until° a smith men clepen daun Gervais,[2] *to*
That in his forge smithed plough harneis:° *equipment*
He sharpeth shaar and cultour[3] bisily.
This Absolon knokketh al esily,° *quietly*
And saide, "Undo, Gervais, and that anoon."° *at once*
"What, who artou?" "It am I, Absolon."
"What, Absolon? What, Cristes sweete tree!
Why rise ye so rathe?° Ey, benedicite,° *early / bless me*
What aileth you? Som gay girl, God it woot,
Hath brought you thus upon the viritoot.[4]
By Sainte Note, ye woot wel what I mene."
This Absolon ne roughte nat a bene[5]
Of al his play. No word again he yaf:
He hadde more tow on his distaf[6]
Than Gervais knew, and saide, "Freend so dere,
This hote cultour in the chimenee° here, *fireplace*
As lene[7] it me: I have therwith to doone.
I wol bringe it thee again ful soone."
Gervais answerde, "Certes, were it gold,
Or in a poke nobles alle untold,[8]
Thou sholdest have, as I am trewe smith.
Ey, Cristes fo,[9] what wol ye do therwith?"
"Therof," quod Absolon, "be as be may.
I shal wel telle it thee another day,"
And caughte the cultour by the colde stele.° *handle*
Ful softe out at the dore he gan to stele,
And wente unto the carpenteres wal:
He cougheth first and knokketh therwithal
Upon the windowe, right as he dide er.° *before*
This Alison answerde, "Who is ther
That knokketh so? I warante[1] it a thief."
"Why, nay," quod he, "God woot, my sweete lief,° *dear*
I am thyn Absolon, my dereling.
Of gold," quod he, "I have thee brought a ring—
My moder yaf it me, so God me save;
Ful fin it is and therto wel ygrave:° *engraved*
This wol I yiven thee if thou me kisse."
This Nicholas was risen for to pisse,
And thoughte he wolde amenden[2] al the jape:° *joke*
He sholde kisse his ers er that he scape.

1. I.e., quiet walk.
2. Master Gervais.
3. He sharpens plowshare and coulter (the turf-cutter on a plow).
4. I.e., on the prowl.
5. Didn't care a bean.
6. I.e., more on his mind.
7. I.e., please lend.
8. Or gold coins all uncounted in a bag.
9. Foe, i.e., Satan.
1. I.e., wager.
2. Improve on.

And up the windowe dide he hastily,
And out his ers he putteth prively,
Over the buttok to the haunche-boon.
  And therwith spak this clerk, this Absolon,
"Speek, sweete brid, I noot nought wher thou art."
This Nicholas anoon leet flee[3] a fart
As greet as it hadde been a thonder-dent° *thunderbolt*
That with the strook he was almost yblent,° *blinded*
And he was redy with his iren hoot,° *hot*
And Nicholas amidde the ers he smoot:° *smote*
Of gooth the skin an hande-brede° aboute; *handsbreadth*
The hote cultour brende so his toute° *buttocks*
That for the smert he wende for to[4] die;
As he were wood° for wo he gan to crye, *crazy*
"Help! Water! Water! Help, for Goddes herte!"
  This carpenter out of his slomber sterte,
And herde oon cryen "Water!" as he were wood,
And thoughte, "Allas, now cometh Noweles[5] flood!"
He sette him up withoute wordes mo,
And with his ax he smoot the corde atwo,
And down gooth al: he foond neither to selle
Ne breed ne ale til he cam to the celle,[6]
Upon the floor, and ther aswoune° he lay. *in a faint*
  Up sterte hire[7] Alison and Nicholay,
And criden "Out" and "Harrow" in the streete.
The neighebores, bothe smale and grete,
In ronnen for to gauren° on this man *gape*
That aswoune lay bothe pale and wan,
For with the fal he brosten° hadde his arm; *broken*
But stonde he moste° unto his owene harm, *must*
For whan he spak he was anoon bore down[8]
With° hende Nicholas and Alisoun: *by*
They tolden every man that he was wood—
He was agast so of Noweles flood,
Thurgh fantasye, that of his vanitee° *folly*
He hadde ybought him kneeding-tubbes three,
And hadde hem hanged in the roof above,
And that he prayed hem, for Goddes love,
To sitten in the roof, *par compaignye*.[9]
  The folk gan laughen at his fantasye.
Into the roof they kiken° and they cape,° *peer / gape*
And turned al his harm unto a jape,° *joke*
For what so that this carpenter answerde,
It was for nought: no man his reson° herde; *argument*
With othes grete he was so sworn adown,
That he was holden° wood in al the town, *considered*

3. Let fly.
4. Thought he would.
5. The carpenter is confusing Noah and Noel (Christmas).
6. He found time to sell neither bread nor ale until he arrived at the foundation.
7. Started.
8. Refuted.
9. For company's sake.

For every clerk anoonright heeld with other:
They saide, "The man was wood, my leve brother,"
And every wight gan laughen at this strif.° *fuss*
Thus swived° was the carpenteres wif *slept with*
For al his keeping° and his jalousye, *guarding*
And Absolon hath kist hir nether° yë, *lower*
And Nicholas is scalded in the toute:
This tale is doon, and God save al the route!° *company*

The Wife of Bath's Prologue and Tale

The Prologue [1]

Experience, though noon auctoritee
Were in this world, is right ynough for me
To speke of wo that is in mariage:
For lordinges,° sith I twelf yeer was of age— *gentlemen*
Thanked be God that is eterne on live—
Housbondes at chirche dore[2] I have had five
(If I so ofte mighte han wedded be),
And alle were worthy men in hir degree.
But me was told, certain, nat longe agoon is,
That sith that Crist ne wente nevere but ones

1. The Wife of Bath is the remarkable culmination of many centuries of an antifeminism that was particularly nurtured by the medieval church. In their eagerness to exalt the spiritual ideal of chastity, certain theologians developed an idea of womankind that was nothing less than monstrous. According to these, insatiable lecherousness and indomitable shrewishness (plus a host of attendant vices) were characteristic of women. This notion was given most eloquent expression by St. Jerome in his attack (written about A.D. 400) on the monk Jovinian, who had uttered some good words for matrimony, and it is Jerome that the Wife of Bath comes forward not, curiously enough, to refute, but to confirm. The first part of her Prologue is a mass of quotations from that part of Jerome's tract where he is appealing to St. Paul's Epistle (I Corinthians vii) for antimatrimonial authority. On the narrow issue of her right to remarry, to be sure, the Wife finds fault—rather mildly—with Jerome, but on the more central issue of why she wishes to marry and remarry she expresses no disagreement with him. Yet in the failure to defend herself and refute the saint, she somehow manages to make the latter's point of view look a good deal sillier than she looks herself; and instead of embodying the satire on womanhood that one would expect because of her origins in antifeminist literature, she becomes instead a satirist of the grotesquely woman-hating men who had first defined her personality.

More important, because of the extraordinary vitality that Chaucer has imparted to her, the Wife of Bath by the end of her Prologue comes to bear a less significant relation to satire than she does to reality itself. Making the best of the world in which they have arbitrarily been placed is the occupation of both the Wife of Bath and the reader, and it is in doing this that the Wife ceases to be a monstrosity of fiction and becomes alive—wonderfully alive, both to the potentialities of which she and her world are capable and to the limitations that even in her world time and age place upon her. It is especially in the attitude with which she regards these limitations that her fiction becomes most true to life, since they are also the limitations imposed by the real world. Despite the loss of youth and beauty, her best weapons, she faces her future not only with a woman's ability to endure and enjoy what she cannot reshape, but also with a zest for life on its own terms that is almost more than human.

2. The actual wedding ceremony was celebrated at the church door, not in the chancel.

To wedding in the Cane[3] of Galilee,
That by the same ensample° taughte he me — *example*
That I ne sholde wedded be but ones.
Herke eek,° lo, which° a sharp word for the nones,[4] — *also / what*
Biside a welle, Jesus, God and man,
Spak in repreve° of the Samaritan: — *reproof*
"Thou hast yhad five housbondes," quod he,
"And that ilke° man that now hath thee — *same*
Is nat thyn housbonde." Thus saide he certain.
What that he mente therby I can nat sayn,
But that I axe° why the fifthe man — *ask*
Was noon housbonde to the Samaritan?[5]
How manye mighte she han in mariage?
Yit herde I nevere tellen in myn age
Upon this nombre diffinicioun.° — *definition*
Men may divine° and glosen° up and down, — *guess / interpret*
But wel I woot,° expres,° withouten lie, — *know / expressly*
God bad us for to wexe[6] and multiplye:
That gentil text can I wel understonde.
  Eek wel I woot° he saide that myn housbonde — *know*
Sholde lete° fader and moder and take to me,[7] — *leave*
But of no nombre mencion made he—
Of bigamye or of octogamye:[8]
Why sholde men thanne speke of it vilainye?
  Lo, here the wise king daun° Salomon: — *master*
I trowe° he hadde wives many oon,[9] — *believe*
As wolde God it leveful° were to me — *permissible*
To be refresshed half so ofte as he.
Which yifte[1] of God hadde he for alle his wives!
No man hath swich that in this world alive is.
God woot this noble king, as to my wit,° — *knowledge*
The firste night hadde many a merye fit° — *bout*
With eech of hem, so wel was him on live.[2]
Blessed be God that I have wedded five,
Of whiche I have piked out the beste,[3]
Bothe of hir nether° purs and of hir cheste.° — *lower / moneybox*
Diverse scoles maken parfit° clerkes, — *perfect*
And diverse practikes[4] in sondry werkes
Maken the werkman parfit sikerly:° — *certainly*
Of five housbondes scoleying° am I. — *schooling*
Welcome the sixte whan that evere he shal![5]

3. Cana (see John ii.1).
4. To the purpose.
5. Christ was actually referring to a sixth man who was not married to the Samaritan woman (cf. John iv.6 ff.).
6. I.e., increase. See Genesis i.28.
7. See Matthew xix.5.
8. I.e., of two or even eight marriages. The Wife is referring to successive, rather than simultaneous marriages.
9. Solomon had 700 wives and 300 concubines (I Kings xi.3).
1. What a gift.
2. I.e., so pleasant a life he had.
3. Whom I have cleaned out of everything worthwhile.
4. Practical experiences.
5. I.e., shall come along.

For sith I wol nat kepe me chast in al,
Whan my housbonde is fro the world agoon,
Som Cristen man shal wedde me anoon.° *right away*
For thanne th'Apostle[6] saith that I am free
To wedde, a Goddes half,[7] where it liketh me.
He said that to be wedded is no sinne:
Bet° is to be wedded than to brinne.° *better / burn*
What rekketh me[8] though folk saye vilainye
Of shrewed° Lamech[9] and his bigamye? *cursed*
I woot wel Abraham was an holy man,
And Jacob eek, as fer as evere I can,° *know*
And eech of hem hadde wives mo than two,
And many another holy man also.
Where can ye saye in any manere age
That hye God defended° mariage *prohibited*
By expres word? I praye you, telleth me.
Or where comanded he virginitee?
I woot as wel as ye, it is no drede,° *doubt*
Th'Apostle, whan he speketh of maidenhede,° *maidenhood*
He saide that precept therof hadde he noon:
Men may conseile a womman to be oon,° *single*
But conseiling nis no comandement.
He putte it in oure owene juggement.
For hadde God comanded maidenhede,
Thanne hadde he dampned° wedding with the deede;[1] *condomned*
And certes, if there were no seed ysowe,
Virginitee, thanne wherof sholde it growe?
Paul dorste nat comanden at the leeste
A thing of which his maister yaf° no heeste.° *gave / command*
The dart[2] is set up for virginitee:
Cacche whoso may, who renneth° best lat see. *runs*
But this word is nought take of[3] every wight,
But ther as[4] God list° yive it of his might. *it pleases*
I woot wel that th'Apostle was a maide,° *virgin*
But nathelees, though that he wroot and saide
He wolde that every wight were swich° as he, *such*
Al nis but conseil to virginitee;
And for to been a wif he yaf me leve
Of indulgence; so nis it no repreve° *disgrace*
To wedde me[5] if that my make° die, *mate*
Withouten excepcion of bigamye[6]—

6. St. Paul.
7. On God's behalf; "it liketh me": I please.
8. What do I care.
9. The first man whom the Bible mentions as having two wives (Genesis iv.19–24).

1. I.e., at the same time.
2. I.e., prize in a race.
3. Understood for, i.e., applicable to.
4. Where.
5. For me to marry.
6. I.e., without there being any legal objection on the score of remarriage.

Al° were it good no womman for to touche — *although*
(He mente as in his bed or in his couche,
For peril is bothe fir° and tow° t'assemble— — *fire / flax*
Ye knowe what this ensample may resemble).[7]
This al and som,[8] he heeld virginitee
More parfit than wedding in freletee.° — *frailty*
(Freletee clepe I but if[9] that he and she
Wolde leden al hir lif in chastitee.)
I graunte it wel, I have noon envye
Though maidenhede preferre° bigamye:° — *excel / remarriage*
It liketh hem to be clene in body and gost.° — *spirit*
Of myn estaat ne wol I make no boost;
For wel ye knowe, a lord in his houshold
Ne hath nat every vessel al of gold:
Some been of tree,° and doon hir lord servise. — *wood*
God clepeth folk to him in sondry wise,
And everich hath of God a propre[1] yifte,
Som this, som that, as him liketh shifte.° — *ordain*
Virginitee is greet perfeccioun,
And continence eek with devocioun,
But Crist, that of perfeccion is welle,° — *source*
Bad nat every wight he sholde go selle
Al that he hadde and yive it to the poore,
And in swich wise folwe him and his fore:[2]
He spak to hem that wolde live parfitly°— — *perfectly*
And lordinges, by youre leve, that am nat I.
I wol bistowe the flour of al myn age
In th'actes and in fruit of mariage.

Telle me also, to what conclusioun° — *end*
Were membres maad of generacioun
And of so parfit wis a wrighte ywrought?[3]
Trusteth right wel, they were nat maad for nought.
Glose° whoso wol, and saye bothe up and down — *interpret*
That they were maked for purgacioun
Of urine, and oure bothe thinges smale
Was eek to knowe a femele from a male,
And for noon other cause—saye ye no?
Th'experience woot it is nought so.
So that the clerkes be nat with me wrothe,
I saye this, that they been maad for bothe—
That is to sayn, for office° and for ese — *excretion*
Of engendrure, ther we nat God displese.
Why sholde men elles in hir bookes sette
That man shal yeelde[4] to his wif hir dette?

7. I.e., what this metaphor may apply to.
8. This is all there is to it.
9. Frailty I call it unless.
1. I.e., his own.
2. Matthew xix.21. "Fore": footsteps.
3. And wrought by so perfectly wise a maker.
4. I.e., pay.

Now wherwith sholde he make his payement
If he ne used his sely° instrument? *innocent*
Thanne were they maad upon a creature
To purge urine, and eek for engendrure.
But I saye nought that every wight is holde,° *bound*
That hath swich harneis° as I to you tolde, *equipment*
To goon and usen hem in engendrure:
Thanne sholde men take of chastitee no cure.° *heed*
Crist was a maide° and shapen as a man, *virgin*
And many a saint sith that the world bigan,
Yit lived they evere in parfit chastitee.
I nil envye no virginitee:
Lat hem be breed° of pured° whete seed, *bread / refined*
And lat us wives hote° barly breed— *be called*
And yit with barly breed, Mark telle can,
Oure Lord Jesu refresshed many a man.[5]
In swich estaat as God hath cleped us
I wol persevere: I nam nat precious.° *fastidious*
In wifhood wol I use myn instrument
As freely° as my Makere hath it sent. *generously*
If I be daungerous,° God yive me sorwe: *stand-offish*
Myn housbonde shal it han both eve and morwe,° *morning*
Whan that him list[6] come forth and paye his dette.
An housbonde wol I have, I wol nat lette,[7]
Which shal be bothe my dettour° and my thral,° *debtor / slave*
And have his tribulacion withal
Upon his flessh whil that I am his wif.
I have the power during al my lif
Upon his propre° body, and nat he: *own*
Right thus th'Apostle tolde it unto me,
And bad oure housbondes for to love us weel.
Al this sentence° me liketh everydeel.° *purport / entirely*

[AN INTERLUDE]

Up sterte° the Pardoner and that anoon: *started*
"Now dame," quod he, "by God and by Saint John,
Ye been a noble prechour in this cas.
I was aboute to wedde a wif: allas,
What° sholde I bye° it on my flessh so dere? *why / purchase*
Yit hadde I levere wedde no wif toyere."° *this year*
"Abid," quod she, "my tale is nat bigonne.
Nay, thou shalt drinken of another tonne,° *tun*
Er that I go, shal savoure wors than ale.
And whan that I have told thee forth my tale
Of tribulacion in mariage,
Of which I am expert in al myn age—

5. In the descriptions of the miracle of the loaves and fishes, it is actually John, not Mark, who mentions barley bread (vi.9).
6. When he wishes to.
7. I will make no difficulty.

This is to saye, myself hath been the whippe—
Thanne maistou chese° wheither thou wolt sippe *choose*
Of thilke° tonne that I shal abroche:° *this same / broach*
Be war of it, er thou too neigh approche,
For I shal telle ensamples mo than ten.
'Whoso that nile° be war by othere men, *would not*
By him shal othere men corrected be.'
Thise same wordes writeth Ptolomee:
Rede in his *Almageste* and take it there."[8]
"Dame, I wolde praye you if youre wil it were,"
Saide this Pardoner, "as ye bigan,
Telle forth youre tale; spareth for no man,
And teche us yonge men of youre practike."° *mode of operation*
"Gladly," quod she, "sith it may you like;° *please*
But that I praye to al this compaignye,
If that I speke after my fantasye,[9]
As taketh nat agrief° of that I saye, *amiss*
For myn entente nis but for to playe."

[THE WIFE CONTINUES]

Now sire, thanne wol I telle you forth my tale.
As evere mote I drinke win or ale,
I shal saye sooth: tho° housbondes that I hadde, *those*
As three of hem were goode, and two were badde.
The three men were goode, and riche, and olde;
Unnethe° mighte they the statut holde *with difficulty*
In which they were bounden unto me—
Ye woot wel what I mene of this, pardee.
As help me God, I laughe whan I thinke
How pitously anight I made hem swinke;° *work*
And by my fay,° I tolde of it no stoor:[1] *faith*
They hadde me yiven hir land and hir tresor;
Me needed nat do lenger diligence
To winne hir love or doon hem reverence.
They loved me so wel, by God above,
That I ne tolde no daintee of[2] hir love.
A wis womman wol bisye hire evere in oon[3]
To gete hire love, ye, ther as she hath noon.
But sith I hadde hem hoolly in myn hand,
And sith that they hadde yiven me al hir land,
What° sholde I take keep° hem for to plese, *why / care*
But it were for my profit and myn ese?
I sette hem so awerke,° by my fay,° *awork / faith*
That many a night they songen° wailaway. *sang*

8. The *Almagest*, an astronomical work by the Greek astronomer and mathematician Ptolemy (second century A.D.), contains no such aphorism. The aphorism does, however, appear in a collection ascribed to him.
9. If I speak according to my whim.
1. I set no store by it.
2. Set no value on.
3. Busy herself constantly.

The bacon was nat fet° for hem, I trowe, *brought back*
That some men han in Essexe at Dunmowe.[4]
I governed hem so wel after° my lawe *according to*
That eech of hem ful blisful was and fawe° *glad*
To bringe me gaye thinges fro the faire;
They were ful glade whan I spak hem faire,
For God it woot, I chidde° hem spitously.° *chided / cruelly*
Now herkneth how I bar me[5] proprely:
Ye wise wives, that conne understonde,
Thus sholde ye speke and bere him wrong on honde[6]—
For half so boldely can ther no man
Swere and lie as a woman can.
I saye nat this by wives that been wise,
But if it be whan they hem misavise.[7]
A wis wif, if that she can hir good,[8]
Shal bere him on hande the cow is wood,[9]
And take witnesse of hir owene maide
Of hir assent.[1] But herkneth how I saide:
"Sire olde cainard,° is this thyn array?[2] *sluggard*
Why is my neighebores wif so gay?
She is honoured overal ther she gooth:
I sitte at hoom; I have no thrifty° cloth. *decent*
What doostou at my neighebores hous?
Is she so fair? Artou so amorous?
What roune° ye with oure maide, benedicite?[3] *whisper*
Sire olde lechour, lat thy japes° be. *tricks, intrigues*
And if I have a gossib° or a freend, *confidant*
Withouten gilt ye chiden as a feend,
If that I walke or playe unto his hous.
Thou comest hoom as dronken as a mous,
And prechest on thy bench, with yvel preef.[4]
Thou saist to me, it is a greet meschief° *misfortune*
To wedde a poore womman for costage.[5]
And if that she be riche, of heigh parage,° *descent*
Thanne saistou that it is a tormentrye
To suffre hir pride and hir malencolye.
And if that she be fair, thou verray knave,
Thou saist that every holour° wol hire have: *whoremonger*
She may no while in chastitee abide
That is assailed upon eech a side.
"Thou saist som folk desiren us for richesse,

4. The Dunmow flitch was awarded to the couple who after a year of marriage could claim no quarrels, no regrets, and the desire, if freed, to remarry one another.
5. Bore myself, behaved.
6. Accuse him falsely.
7. When they make a mistake.
8. If she knows what's good for her.
9. Shall persuade him the chough has gone crazy. The chough, or jackdaw, was popularly supposed to tell husbands of their wives' infidelity.
1. And call as a witness her maid, who is on her side.
2. I.e., is this how you behave?
3. Bless me.
4. I.e., (may you have) bad luck.
5. Because of the expense.

Som[6] for oure shap, and som for oure fairnesse,
And som for she can outher° singe or daunce, *either*
And som for gentilesse and daliaunce,° *flirtatiousness*
Som for hir handes and hir armes smale°— *slender*
Thus gooth al to the devel by thy tale![7]
Thou saist men may nat keepe[8] a castel wal,
It may so longe assailed been overal.° *everywhere*
And if that she be foul, thou saist that she
Coveiteth° every man that she may see; *desires*
For as a spaniel she wol on him lepe,
Til that she finde som man hire to chepe.° *buy*
Ne noon so grey goos gooth ther in the lake,
As, saistou, wol be withoute make;° *mate*
And saist it is an hard thing for to weelde° *possess*
A thing that no man wol, his thankes, heelde.[9]
Thus saistou, lorel,° whan thou goost to bedde, *loafer*
And that no wis man needeth for to wedde,
Ne no man that entendeth° unto hevene— *aims*
With wilde thonder-dint[1] and firy levene
Mote thy welked nekke be tobroke![2]
Thou saist that dropping° houses and eek smoke *leaking*
And chiding wives maken men to flee
Out of hir owene hous: a, benedicite,
What aileth swich an old man for to chide?
Thou saist we wives wil oure vices hide
Til we be fast,[3] and thanne we wol hem shewe—
Wel may that be a proverbe of a shrewe!° *villain*
Thou saist that oxen, asses, hors,° and houndes, *horses*
They been assayed at diverse stoundes;° *times*
Bacins, lavours,° er that men hem bye, *washbowls*
Spoones, stooles, and al swich housbondrye,° *household goods*
And so be° pottes, clothes, and array°— *are / clothing*
But folk of wives maken noon assay
Til they be wedded—olde dotard shrewe!
And thanne, saistou, we wil oure vices shewe.
Thou saist also that it displeseth me
But if that thou wolt praise my beautee,
And but thou poure alway upon my face,
And clepe me 'Faire Dame' in every place,
And but thou make a feeste on thilke day
That I was born, and make me fressh and gay,
And but thou do to my norice° honour, *nurse*
And to my chamberere within my bowr,[4]
And to my fadres folk, and his allies[5]—

6. "Som," in this and the following lines, means "one."
7. I.e., according to your story.
8. I.e., keep safe.
9. No man would willingly hold.
1. Thunderbolt; "levene": lightning.
2. May thy withered neck be broken!
3. I.e., married.
4. And to my chambermaid within my bedroom.
5. Relatives by marriage.

Thus saistou, olde barel-ful of lies.
And yit of our apprentice Janekin,
For his crispe° heer, shining as gold so fin, *curly*
And for he squiereth me bothe up and down,
Yit hastou caught a fals suspecioun;
I wil° him nat though thou were deed° tomorwe. *want / dead*
"But tel me this, why hidestou with sorwe[6]
The keyes of thy cheste away fro me?
It is my good° as wel as thyn, pardee. *property*
What, weenestou° make an idiot of oure dame? *do you think to*
Now by that lord that called is Saint Jame,
Thou shalt nought bothe, though thou were wood,° *furious*
Be maister of my body and of my good:
That oon thou shalt forgo, maugree thine yën.[7]
"What helpeth it of me enquere° and spyen? *inquire*
I trowe thou woldest loke° me in thy cheste. *lock*
Thou sholdest saye, 'Wif, go wher thee leste.° *it may please*
Taak youre disport. I nil leve° no tales: *believe*
I knowe you for a trewe wif, dame Alis.'
We love no man that taketh keep or charge[8]
Wher that we goon: we wol been at oure large.[9]
Of alle men yblessed mote he be
The wise astrologen° daun Ptolomee, *astronomer*
That saith this proverbe in his *Almageste*:
'Of alle men his wisdom is the hyeste
That rekketh° nat who hath the world in honde.' *cares*
By this proverbe thou shalt understonde,
Have thou[1] ynough, what thar° thee rekke or care *need*
How merily that othere folkes fare?
For certes, olde dotard, by youre leve,
Ye shal han queinte° right ynough at eve: *pudendum*
He is too greet a nigard that wil werne° *refuse*
A man to lighte a candle at his lanterne;
He shal han nevere the lasse° lighte, pardee. *less*
Have thou ynough, thee thar nat plaine thee.[2]
"Thou saist also that if we make us gay
With clothing and with precious array,
That it is peril of oure chastitee,
And yit with sorwe thou moste enforce thee,[3]
And saye thise wordes in th'Apostles name:
'In habit° maad with chastitee and shame *clothing*
Ye wommen shal apparaile you,' quod he,
'And nat in tressed heer[4] and gay perree,° *jewelry*
As perles ne with gold ne clothes riche.'[5]

6. I.e., with sorrow to you.
7. Despite your eyes—i.e., despite anything you can do about it.
8. Notice or interest.
9. I.e., liberty.
1. If you have.
2. I.e., you need not complain.
3. Strengthen your position.
4. I.e., elaborate hairdo.
5. See I Timothy ii.9.

After thy text, ne after thy rubriche,[6]
I wol nat werke as muchel as a gnat.
Thou saidest this, that I was lik a cat:
For whoso wolde senge° a cattes skin, *singe*
Thanne wolde the cat wel dwellen in his in;° *lodging*
And if the cattes skin be slik° and gay, *sleek*
She wol nat dwelle in house half a day,
But forth she wol, er any day be dawed,[7]
To shewe her skin and goon a-caterwawed.° *caterwauling*
This is to saye, if I be gay, sire shrewe,
I wol renne° out, my borel° for to shewe. *run / clothing*
Sire olde fool, what helpeth[8] thee t'espyen?
Though thou praye Argus with his hundred yën
To be my wardecors,° as he can best, *bodyguard*
In faith, he shal nat keepe° me but me lest:[9] *guard*
Yit coude I make his beerd,[1] so mote I thee.° *thrive*
"Thou saidest eek that ther been thinges three,
The whiche thinges troublen al this erthe,
And that no wight may endure the ferthe.° *fourth*
O leve° sire shrewe, Jesu shorte° thy lif! *dear / shorten*
Yit prechestou and saist an hateful wif
Yrekened is for oon of thise meschaunces.
Been ther nat none othere resemblaunces
That ye may likne youre parables to,[2]
But if[3] a sely° wif be oon of tho? *innocent*
"Thou liknest eek wommanes love to helle,
To bareine° land ther water may nat dwelle; *barren*
Thou liknest it also to wilde fir—
The more it brenneth,° the more it hath desir *burns*
To consumen every thing that brent° wol be; *burned*
Thou saist right° as wormes shende° a tree, *just / destroy*
Right so a wif destroyeth hir housbonde—
This knowen they that been to wives bonde."° *bound*
Lordinges, right thus, as ye han understonde,
Bar I stifly mine olde housbondes on honde[4]
That thus they saiden in hir dronkenesse—
And al was fals, but that I took witnesse
On Janekin and on my nece also.
O Lord, the paine I dide hem and the wo,
Ful giltelees, by Goddes sweete pine!° *suffering*
For as an hors I coude bite and whine;° *whinny*
I coude plaine° and° I was in the gilt, *complain / if*
Or elles often time I hadde been spilt.° *ruined*
Whoso that first to mille comth first grint.° *grinds*

6. Rubric, i.e., direction.
7. Has dawned.
8. What does it help.
9. Unless I please.
1. I.e., deceive him.
2. Isn't there something else appropriate that you can apply your metaphors to?
3. Unless.
4. I rigorously accused my old husbands.

I plained first: so was oure werre stint.[5]
They were ful glade to excusen hem ful blive° *quickly*
Of thing of which they nevere agilte hir live.[6]
Of wenches wolde I beren hem on honde,
Whan that for sik[7] they mighte unnethe° stonde, *scarcely*
Yit tikled I his herte for that he
Wende° I hadde had of him so greet cheertee.[8] *thought*
I swoor that al my walking out by nighte
Was for to espye wenches that he dighte.[9]
Under that colour[1] hadde I many a mirthe.
For al swich wit is yiven us in oure birthe:
Deceite, weeping, spinning God hath yive
To wommen kindely° whil they may live. *naturally*
And thus of oo thing I avaunte me:[2]
At ende I hadde the bet° in eech degree, *better*
By sleighte or force, or by som manere thing,
As by continuel murmur° or grucching;° *complaint / grumbling*
Namely° abedde hadden they meschaunce: *especially*
Ther wolde I chide and do hem no plesaunce;[3]
I wolde no lenger in the bed abide
If that I felte his arm over my side,
Til he hadde maad his raunson° unto me; *ransom*
Thanne wolde I suffre him do his nicetee.° *lust*
And therfore every man this tale I telle:
Winne whoso may, for al is for to selle;
With empty hand men may no hawkes lure.
For winning° wolde I al his lust endure, *profit*
And make me a feined appetit—
And yit in bacon[4] hadde I nevere delit.
That made me that evere I wolde hem chide;
For though the Pope hadde seten° hem biside, *sat*
I wolde nought spare hem at hir owene boord.
For by my trouthe, I quitte° hem word for word. *repaid*
As help me verray God omnipotent,
Though I right now sholde make my testament,
I ne owe hem nat a word that it nis quit.
I broughte it so aboute by my wit
That they moste yive it up as for the beste,
Or elles hadde we nevere been in reste;
For though he looked as a wood° leoun, *furious*
Yit sholde he faile of his conclusioun.° *object*
Thanne wolde I saye, "Goodelief, taak keep,[5]
How mekely looketh Wilekin, oure sheep!

5. Our war brought to an end.
6. Of a thing in which they never offended in their lives.
7. I.e., sickness.
8. Affection.
9. Had intercourse with.
1. I.e., excuse.
2. Boast.
3. Show them no affection.
4. I.e., old meat.
5. Good friend, take notice.

Com neer my spouse, lat me ba° thy cheeke— *kiss*
Ye sholden be al pacient and meeke,
And han a sweete-spiced[6] conscience,
Sith ye so preche of Jobes pacience;
Suffreth alway, sin ye so wel can preche;
And but ye do, certain, we shal you teche
That it is fair to han a wif in pees.
Oon of us two moste bowen, doutelees,
And sith a man is more resonable
Than womman is, ye mosten been suffrable.° *patient*
What aileth you to grucche° thus and grone? *grumble*
Is it for ye wolde have my queinte° allone? *pudendum*
Why, taak it al—lo, have it everydeel.° *altogether*
Peter, I shrewe° you but ye love it weel. *curse*
For if I wolde selle my bele chose,[7]
I coude walke as fressh as is a rose;
But I wol keepe it for youre owene tooth.° *taste*
Ye be to blame. By God, I saye you sooth!"
Swiche manere° wordes hadde we on honde. *kind of*
Now wol I speke of my ferthe° housbonde. *fourth*
  My ferthe housbonde was a revelour—
This is to sayn, he hadde a paramour°— *mistress*
And I was yong and ful of ragerye,° *wantonness*
Stibourne° and strong and joly as a pie:° *untamable / magpie*
How coude I daunce to an harpe smale,° *gracefully*
And singe, ywis,° as any nightingale, *indeed*
Whan I hadde dronke a draughte of sweete win.
Metellius, the foule cherl, the swin,
That with a staf birafte° his wif hir lif *deprived*
For° she drank win, though I hadde been his wif, *because*
Ne sholde nat han daunted me fro drinke;
And after win on Venus moste° I thinke, *must*
For also siker° as cold engendreth hail, *sure*
A likerous° mouth moste han a likerous° tail: *greedy / lecherous*
In womman vinolent° is no defence— *bibulous*
This knowen lechours by experience.
  But Lord Crist, whan that it remembreth me[8]
Upon my youthe and on my jolitee,
It tikleth me aboute myn herte roote—
Unto this day it dooth myn herte boote° *good*
That I have had my world as in my time.
But age, allas, that al wol envenime,° *poison*
Hath me biraft[9] my beautee and my pith—
Lat go, farewel, the devel go therwith!
The flour is goon, ther is namore to telle:
The bren° as I best can now moste I selle; *bran*
But yit to be right merye wol I fonde.° *strive*

6. I.e., delicate.
7. Fair thing.
8. When I look back.
9. Has taken away from me.

Now wol I tellen of my ferthe housbonde.
    I saye I hadde in herte greet despit
That he of any other hadde delit,
But he was quit,° by God and by Saint Joce: *paid back*
I made him of the same wode a croce[1]—
Nat of my body in no foul manere—
But, certainly, I made folk swich cheere
That in his owene grece I made him frye,
For angre and for verray jalousye.
By God, in erthe I was his purgatorye,
For which I hope his soule be in glorye.
For God it woot, he sat ful ofte and soong° *sang*
Whan that his sho ful bitterly him wroong.° *pinched*
Ther was no wight save God and he that wiste° *knew*
In many wise how sore I him twiste.
He deide whan I cam fro Jerusalem,
And lith ygrave under the roode-beem,[2]
Al° is his tombe nought so curious[3] *although*
As was the sepulcre of him Darius,
Which that Apelles wroughte subtilly:[4]
It nis but wast to burye him preciously.° *expensively*
Lat him fare wel, God yive his soule reste;
He is now in his grave and in his cheste.
    Now of my fifthe housbonde wol I telle—
God lete his soule nevere come in helle
And yit he was to me the moste shrewe:[5]
That feele I on my ribbes al by rewe,[6]
And evere shal unto myn ending day.
But in oure bed he was so fressh and gay,
And therwithal so wel coulde he me glose° *wheedle*
Whan that he wolde han my bele chose,
That though he hadde me bet° on every boon,° *beaten / bone*
He coude winne again my love anoon.° *immediately*
I trowe I loved him best for that he
Was of his love daungerous[7] to me.
We wommen han, if that I shal nat lie,
In this matere a quainte fantasye:
Waite what[8] thing we may nat lightly° have, *easily*
Therafter wol we crye al day and crave;
Forbede us thing, and that desiren we;
Preesse on us faste, and thanne wol we flee.
With daunger oute we al oure chaffare:[9]
Greet prees° at market maketh dere° ware, *crowd / expensive*

1. I made him a cross of the same wood. The proverb has much the same sense as the one quoted in line 493.
2. And lies buried under the rood beam (the crucifix beam running between nave and chancel).
3. Carefully wrought.
4. According to medieval legend, the artist Apelles decorated the tomb of Darius, king of the Persians.
5. Worst rascal.
6. In a row.
7. I.e., he played hard to get.
8. "Waite what": whatever.
9. With coyness, we spread out our merchandise.

And too greet chepe is holden at litel pris.[1]
This knoweth every womman that is wis.
My fifthe housbonde—God his soule blesse!—
Which that I took for love and no richesse,
He somtime was a clerk at Oxenforde,
And hadde laft° scole and wente at hoom to boorde *left*
With my gossib,° dwelling in oure town— *confidante*
God have hir soule!—hir name was Alisoun;
She knew myn herte and eek my privetee° *secrets*
Bet° than oure parissh preest, as mote I thee.° *better / thrive*
To hire biwrayed° I my conseil° al, *disclosed / secrets*
For hadde myn housbonde pissed on a wal,
Or doon a thing that sholde han cost his lif,
To hire,° and to another worthy wif, *her*
And to my nece which I loved weel,
I wolde han told his conseil everydeel;° *entirely*
And so I dide ful often, God it woot,
That made his face often reed° and hoot° *red / hot*
For verray shame, and blamed himself for he
Hadde told to me so greet a privetee.
And so bifel that ones in a Lente—
So often times I to my gossib wente,
For evere yit I loved to be gay,
And for to walke in March, Averil, and May,
From hous to hous, to heere sondry tales—
That Janekin clerk and my gossib dame Alis
And I myself into the feeldes wente.
Myn housbonde was at London al that Lente:
I hadde the better leiser for to playe,
And for to see, and eek for to be seye° *seen*
Of lusty folk—what wiste I wher my grace° *luck*
Was shapen° for to be, or in what place? *destined*
Therfore I made my visitaciouns
To vigilies[2] and to processiouns,
To preching eek, and to thise pilgrimages,
To playes of miracles and to mariages,
And wered upon[3] my gaye scarlet gites°— *dress*
Thise wormes ne thise motthes ne thise mites,
Upon my peril, frete° hem neveradeel: *ate*
And woostou why? For they were used weel.
Now wol I tellen forth what happed me.
I saye that in the feeldes walked we,
Til trewely we hadde swich daliaunce,° *flirtation*
This clerk and I, that of my purveyaunce° *foresight*
I spak to him and saide him how that he,
If I were widwe, sholde wedde me.

1. Too good a bargain is held at little value.
2. Feasts preceding a saint's day.
3. Wore.

For certainly, I saye for no bobaunce,° *boast*
Yit was I nevere withouten purveyaunce
Of mariage n'of othere thinges eek:
I holde a mouses herte nought worth a leek
That hath but oon hole for to sterte° to, *run*
And if that faile thanne is al ydo.[4]
I bar him on hand[5] he hadde enchaunted me
(My dame taughte me that subtiltee);
And eek I saide I mette° of him al night: *dreamed*
He wolde han slain me as I lay upright,° *supine*
And al my bed was ful of verray blood—
"But yit I hope that ye shul do me good;
For blood bitokeneth gold, as me was taught."
And al was fals, I dremed of it right naught,
But as I folwed ay my dames° lore° *mother's / teaching*
As wel of that as othere thinges more.
But now sire—lat me see, what shal I sayn?
Aha, by God, I have my tale again.
 Whan that my ferthe housbonde was on beere,° *bier*
I weep° algate,° and made sory cheere, *wept / anyhow*
As wives moten,° for it is usage,° *must / custom*
And with my coverchief covered my visage;
But for I was purveyed° of a make.° *provided / mate*
I wepte but smale, and that I undertake.° *guarantee*
 To chirche was myn housbonde born amorwe[6]
With neighebores that for him maden sorwe,
And Janekin oure clerk was oon of tho.
As help me God, whan that I saw him go
After the beere, me thoughte he hadde a paire
Of legges and of feet so clene[7] and faire,
That al myn herte I yaf unto his hold.° *possession*
He was, I trowe,° twenty winter old, *believe*
And I was fourty, if I shal saye sooth—
But yit I hadde alway a coltes tooth:[8]
Gat-toothed° was I, and that bicam me weel; *gap-toothed*
I hadde the prente[9] of Sainte Venus seel.
As help me God, I was a lusty oon,
And fair and riche and yong and wel-bigoon,° *well-situated*
And trewely, as mine housbondes tolde me,
I hadde the beste quoniam° mighte be. *pudendum*
For certes I am al Venerien[1]
In feeling, and myn herte is Marcien:
Venus me yaf my lust, my likerousnesse,° *lecherousness*
And Mars yaf me my sturdy hardinesse.

4. I.e., the game is up.
5. I pretended to him.
6. In the morning.
7. I.e., neat.
8. I.e., youthful appetites.
9. Print, i.e., a birthmark; "seel": seal.
1. Astrologically influenced by Venus; "Marcien": influenced by Mars.

Myn ascendent was Taur[2] and Mars therinne—
Allas, allas, that evere love was sinne!
I folwed ay° my inclinacioun *ever*
By vertu of my constellacioun;[3]
That made me I coude nought withdrawe
My chambre of Venus from a good felawe.
Yit have I Martes° merk upon my face, *Mars'*
And also in another privee place.
For God so wis° be my savacioun,° *surely / salvation*
I loved nevere by no discrecioun,
But evere folwede myn appetit,
Al were he short or long or blak or whit;
I took no keep,° so that he liked° me, *heed / pleased*
How poore he was, ne eek of what degree.
What sholde I saye but at the monthes ende
This joly clerk Janekin that was so hende° *nice*
Hath wedded me with greet solempnitee,° *splendor*
And to him yaf I al the land and fee° *property*
That evere was me yiven therbifore—
But afterward repented me ful sore:
He nolde suffre no thing of my list.° *pleasure*
By God, he smoot° me ones on the list° *struck / ear*
For that I rente° out of his book a leef, *tore*
That of the strook° myn ere weex° al deef. *blow / grew*
Stibourne° I was as is a leonesse, *stubborn*
And of my tonge a verray jangleresse,° *blabbermouth*
And walke I wolde, as I hadde doon biforn,
From hous to hous, although he hadde it[4] sworn;
For which he often times wolde preche,
And me of olde Romain geestes° teche, *stories*
How he Simplicius Gallus lafte° his wif, *left*
And hire forsook for terme of al his lif,
Nought but for open-heveded he hire sey[5]
Looking out at his dore upon a day.
Another Romain tolde he me by name
That, for his wif was at a someres° game *summer's*
Withouten his witing,° he forsook hire eke; *knowledge*
And thanne wolde he upon his Bible seeke
That ilke proverbe of Ecclesiaste[6]
Where he comandeth and forbedeth faste° *strictly*
Man shal nat suffre his wif go roule° aboute; *roam*
Thanne wolde he saye right thus withouten doute:
"Whoso that buildeth his hous al of salwes,° *willow sticks*
And priketh° his blinde hors over the falwes,[7] *rides*

2. My birth sign was the constellation Taurus.
3. I.e., horoscope.
4. I.e., the contrary.
5. Just because he saw her bareheaded.
6. Ecclesiasticus (xxv.25).
7. Plowed land.

And suffreth his wif to go seeken halwes,° *shrines*
Is worthy to be hanged on the galwes."° *gallows*
But al for nought—I sette nought an hawe[8]
Of his proverbes n'of his olde sawe;
N'I wolde nat of him corrected be:
I hate him that my vices telleth me,
And so doon mo, God woot, of us than I.
This made him with me wood al outrely:[9]
I nolde nought forbere° him in no cas. *submit to*
Now wol I saye you sooth, by Saint Thomas,
Why that I rente° out of his book a leef, *tore*
For which he smoot me so that I was deef.
He hadde a book that gladly night and day
For his disport he wolde rede alway.
He cleped it *Valerie*[1] *and Theofraste*,
At which book he lough° alway ful faste; *laughed*
And eek ther was somtime a clerk at Rome,
A cardinal, that highte Saint Jerome,
That made a book[2] again Jovinian;
In which book eek ther was Tertulan,[3]
Crysippus, Trotula, and Helouis,
That was abbesse nat fer fro Paris;
And eek the Parables of Salomon,[4]
Ovides *Art*, and bookes many oon—
And alle thise were bounden in oo volume.
And every night and day was his custume,
Whan he hadde leiser and vacacioun
From other worldly occupacioun,
To reden in this book of wikked wives.
He knew of hem mo legendes and lives
Than been of goode wives in the Bible.
For trusteth wel, it is an impossible° *impossibility*
That any clerk wol speke good of wives,
But if it be of holy saintes lives,
N'of noon other womman nevere the mo—
Who painted the leon, tel me who?[5]
By God, if wommen hadden writen stories,
As clerkes han within hir oratories,

8. I did not rate at the value of a hawthorn berry.
9. Entirely.
1. I.e., the *Letter of Valerius Concerning Not Marrying*, by Walter Map; "*Theofraste*": Theophrastus' *Book Concerning Marriage*. Medieval manuscripts often contained a number of different works, sometimes, as here, dealing with the same subject.
2. St. Jerome's antifeminist *Reply to Jovinian;* "again": against.
3. Tertullian, author of treatises on sexual modesty. Crysippus (or Chrysippus), in the next line, is mentioned by Jerome as an antifeminist; Trotula was a female doctor whose presence here is unexplained; "Helouis" is Eloise, whose love affair with the great scholar Abelard was a medieval scandal.
4. The Biblical Book of Proverbs; "Ovides *Art*": Ovid's *Art of Love*.
5. In one of Aesop's fables, the lion, shown a picture of a man killing a lion, asked who painted the picture. Had a lion been the artist, of course, the roles would have been reversed.

They wolde han writen of men more wikkednesse
Than al the merk[6] of Adam may redresse.
The children of Mercurye and Venus[7]
Been in hir werking° ful contrarious:° *operation / opposed*
Mercurye loveth wisdom and science,
And Venus loveth riot° and dispence;° *parties / expenditures*
And for hir diverse disposicioun
Each falleth in otheres exaltacioun,[8]
And thus, God woot, Mercurye is desolat
In Pisces wher Venus is exaltat,[9]
And Venus falleth ther Mercurye is raised:
Therfore no womman of no clerk is praised.
The clerk, whan he is old and may nought do
Of Venus werkes worth his olde sho,° *shoe*
Thanne sit° he down and writ° in his dotage *sits / writes*
That wommen can nat keepe hir mariage.
  But now to purpose why I tolde thee
That I was beten for a book, pardee:
Upon a night Janekin, that was oure sire,[1]
Redde on his book as he sat by the fire
Of Eva first, that for hir wikkednesse
Was al mankinde brought to wrecchednesse,
For which that Jesu Crist himself was slain
That boughte° us with his herte blood again— *redeemed*
Lo, heer expres of wommen may ye finde
That womman was the los° of al mankinde.[2] *ruin*
  Tho° redde he me how Sampson loste his heres: *then*
Sleeping his lemman° kitte° it with hir sheres, *mistress / cut*
Thurgh which treson loste he both his yën.
  Tho redde he me, if that I shal nat lien,
Of Ercules and of his Dianire,[3]
That caused him to sette himself afire.
  No thing forgat he the sorwe and wo
That Socrates hadde with his wives two—
How Xantippa caste pisse upon his heed:
This sely° man sat stille as he were deed; *silly*
He wiped his heed, namore dorste he sayn
But "Er that thonder stinte,° comth a rain." *stops*
  Of Pasipha[4] that was the queene of Crete—
For shrewednesse° him thoughte the tale sweete— *malice*

6. Mark, sex.
7. I.e., clerks and women, astrologically ruled by Mercury and Venus respectively.
8. Because of their contrary positions (as planets), each one descends (in the belt of the zodiac) as the other rises; hence one loses its power as the other becomes dominant.
9. I.e., Mercury is deprived of power in Pisces (the sign of the Fish), where Venus is most powerful.
1. My husband.
2. The stories of wicked women Chaucer drew mainly from St. Jerome and Walter Map.
3. Dejanira unwittingly gave Hercules a poisoned shirt, which hurt him so much that he committed suicide by fire.
4. Pasiphaë, who fell in love with a bull.

Fy, speek namore, it is a grisly thing
Of hir horrible lust and hir liking.° *pleasure*
Of Clytermistra[5] for hir lecherye
That falsly made hir housbonde for to die,
He redde it with ful good devocioun.
He tolde me eek for what occasioun
Amphiorax[6] at Thebes loste his lif:
Myn housbonde hadde a legende of his wif
Eriphylem, that for an ouche° of gold *trinket*
Hath prively unto the Greekes told
Wher that hir housbonde hidde him in a place,
For which he hadde at Thebes sory grace.
Of Livia[7] tolde he me and of Lucie:
They bothe made hir housbondes for to die,
That oon for love, that other was for hate;
Livia hir housbonde on an even late
Empoisoned hath for that she was his fo;
Lucia likerous° loved hir housbonde so *lecherous*
That for° he sholde alway upon hire thinke, *in order that*
She yaf him swich a manere love-drinke
That he was deed er it were by the morwe.[8]
And thus algates° housbondes han sorwe. *constantly*
Thanne tolde he me how oon Latumius
Complained unto his felawe Arrius
That in his gardin growed swich a tree,
On which he saide how that his wives three
Hanged hemself for herte despitous.[9]
"O leve° brother," quod this Arrius, *dear*
"Yif me a plante of thilke blessed tree,
And in my gardin planted shal it be."
Of latter date of wives hath he red
That some han slain hir housbondes in hir bed
And lete hir lechour dighte[1] hire al the night,
Whan that the cors° lay in the floor upright;° *corpse / supine*
And some han driven nailes in hir brain
Whil that they sleepe, and thus they han hem slain;
Some han hem yiven poison in hir drinke.
He spak more harm than herte may bithinke,° *imagine*
And therwithal he knew of mo proverbes
Than in this world ther growen gras or herbes:
"Bet is," quod he, "thyn habitacioun
Be with a leon or a foul dragoun

5. Clytemnestra, who, with her lover Aegisthus, slew her husband Agamemnon.
6. Amphiaraus, betrayed by his wife Eriphyle and forced to go to the war against Thebes.
7. Livia murdered her husband in behalf of her lover Sejanus. "Lucie": Lucilla, who was said to have poisoned her husband, the poet Lucretius, with a potion designed to keep him faithful.
8. He was dead before it was near morning.
9. For malice of heart.
1. Have intercourse with.

Than with a womman using° for to chide." *accustomed*
"Bet is," quod he, "hye in the roof abide
Than with an angry wif down in the hous:
They been so wikked° and contrarious, *perverse*
They haten that hir housbondes loveth ay."
He saide, "A womman cast° hir shame away *casts*
Whan she cast of° hir smok,"[2] and ferthermo, *off*
"A fair womman, but she be chast also,
Is like a gold ring in a sowes nose."
Who wolde weene,° or who wolde suppose *think*
The wo that in myn herte was and pine?° *suffering*
And whan I sawgh he wolde nevere fine° *end*
To reden on this cursed book al night,
Al sodeinly three leves have I plight° *snatched*
Out of his book right as he redde, and eke
I with my fist so took[3] him on the cheeke
That in oure fir he fil° bakward adown. *fell*
And up he sterte as dooth a wood° leoun, *raging*
And with his fist he smoot me on the heed° *head*
That in the floor I lay as I were deed.
And whan he sawgh how stille that I lay,
He was agast, and wolde have fled his way,
Til atte laste out of my swough° I braide:° *swoon / started*
"O hastou slain me, false thief?" I saide,
"And for my land thus hastou mordred° me? *murdered*
Er I be deed° yit wol I kisse thee." *dead*
And neer he cam and kneeled faire adown,
And saide, "Dere suster Alisoun,
As help me God, I shal thee nevere smite.
That I have doon, it is thyself to wite.° *blame*
Foryif it me, and that I thee biseeke."
And yit eftsoones° I hitte him on the cheeke, *again*
And saide, "Thief, thus muchel am I wreke.° *avenged*
Now wol I die: I may no lenger speke."
But at the laste with muchel care and wo
We fille[4] accorded by us selven two.
He yaf me al the bridel° in myn hand, *bridle*
To han the governance of hous and land,
And of his tonge and his hand also;
And made[5] him brenne° his book anoonright tho. *burn*
And whan that I hadde geten unto me
By maistrye° al the sovereinetee,° *skill / dominion*
And that he saide, "Myn owene trewe wif,
Do as thee lust° the terme of al thy lif; *it pleases*
Keep thyn honour, and keep eek myn estat,"
After that day we hadde nevere debat.

2. Undergarment.
3. I.e., hit.
4. I.e., became.
5. I.e., I made.

God help me so, I was to him as kinde
As any wif from Denmark unto Inde,
And also trewe, and so was he to me.
I praye to God that sit° in majestee, *sits*
So blesse his soule for his mercy dere.
Now wol I saye my tale if ye wol heere.

[ANOTHER INTERRUPTION]

The Frere lough° whan he hadde herd al this: *laughed*
"Now dame," quod he, "so have I joye or blis,
This is a long preamble of a tale."
And whan the Somnour herde the Frere gale,° *exclaim*
"Lo," quod the Somnour, "Goddes armes two,
A frere wol entremette him[6] everemo!
Lo, goode men, a flye and eek a frere
Wol falle in every dissh and eek matere.
What spekestou of preambulacioun?
What, amble or trotte or pisse or go sitte down!
Thou lettest° oure disport in this manere." *hinder*
"Ye, woltou so, sire Somnour?" quod the Frere.
"Now by my faith, I shal er that I go
Telle of a somnour swich a tale or two
That al the folk shal laughen in this place."
"Now elles, Frere, I wol bishrewe° thy face," *curse*
Quod this Somnour, "and I bishrewe me,
But if I telle tales two or three
Of freres, er I come to Sidingborne,[7]
That I shal make thyn herte for to moorne—
For wel I woot thy pacience is goon."
Oure Hoste cride, "Pees, and that anoon!"
And saide, "Lat the womman telle hir tale:
Ye fare as folk that dronken been of ale.
Do, dame, tel forth youre tale, and that is best."
"Al redy, sire," quod she, "right as you lest°— *it pleases*
If I have licence of this worthy Frere."
"Yis, dame," quod he, "tel forth and I wol heere."

6. Intrude himself.
7. Sittingbourne (a town forty miles from London).

The Tale[1]

In th'olde dayes of the King Arthour,
Of which that Britouns° speken greet honour, *Bretons*
Al was this land fulfild of faïrye:[2]
The elf-queene with hir joly compaignye
Daunced ful ofte in many a greene mede°— *meadow*
This was the olde opinion as I rede;
I speke of many hundred yeres ago.
But now can no man see none elves mo,
For now the grete charitee and prayeres
Of limitours,[3] and othere holy freres,
That serchen every land and every streem,
As thikke as motes in the sonne-beem,
Blessing halles, chambres, kichenes, bowres,
Citees, burghes,° castels, hye towres, *townships*
Thropes, bernes, shipnes,[4] dayeries—
This maketh that ther been no faïries.
For ther as wont to walken was an elf
Ther walketh now the limitour himself,
In undermeles° and in morweninges,° *afternoons / mornings*
And saith his Matins and his holy thinges,
As he gooth in his limitacioun.[5]
Wommen may go saufly° up and down: *safely*
In every bussh or under every tree
Ther is noon other incubus[6] but he,
And he ne wol doon hem but dishonour.
And so bifel it that this King Arthour
Hadde in his hous a lusty bacheler,
That on a day cam riding fro river,[7]
And happed° that, allone as he was born, *it happened*

1. The story of the knight who fully realizes what women most desire only after having been told it in a number of ways was popular in Chaucer's time and a natural one for him to assign to the Wife of Bath, whose well-loved fifth husband had also been slow to learn. But Chaucer reshaped the tale in such a way as to make it fit the Wife and her thesis even more closely. In the other medieval versions of the story the knight is guiltless of any offense to womanhood, and in several of them he is Sir Gawain, traditional model of chivalric courtesy, who weds the hideous hag to save not his own life but that of his lord, King Arthur. Chaucer has made the knight a most ill-behaved and ill-mannered man who needs to learn what women most desire as much in order to redeem his disagreeably virile character as to save his neck. Because within her story he is the sole male in a world of women, Dame Alice is able not only to prove conclusively the value of woman's sovereignty, but also to pay her respects to a world of men that had preached antifeminism, a world here represented by a single rapist.
The story is suited to the Wife's own character psychologically as well as dramatically, for she, like the old hag, had wedded a young man—though unlike the hag she could not restore her former beauty. But if there is a touch of melancholy in the incompleteness of this similarity, it is sharply dispelled by the Wife's final comments, which reassert the sturdy fighting spirit that permeates her Prologue.
2. I.e., filled full of supernatural creatures.
3. Friars licenced to beg in a certain territory.
4. Thorps (villages), barns, stables.
5. I.e., the friar's assigned area. His "holy thinges" are prayers.
6. A spirit that lies with mortal women. "Ne * * * but" in the next line means "only."
7. Hawking, usually carried out on the banks of a stream.

He sawgh a maide walking him biforn;
Of which maide anoon, maugree hir heed,[8]
By verray force he rafte° hir maidenheed; *deprived her of*
For which oppression° was swich clamour, *rape*
And swich pursuite° unto the King Arthour, *petitioning*
That dampned was this knight for to be deed[9]
By cours of lawe, and sholde han lost his heed—
Paraventure° swich was the statut tho— *perhaps*
But that the queene and othere ladies mo
So longe prayeden the king of grace,
Til he his lif him graunted in the place,
And yaf him to the queene, al at hir wille,
To chese° wheither she wolde him save or spille.[1] *choose*
The queene thanked the king with al hir might,
And after this thus spak she to the knight,
Whan that she saw hir time upon a day:
"Thou standest yit," quod she, "in swich array° *condition*
That of thy lif yit hastou no suretee.° *guarantee*
I graunte thee lif if thou canst tellen me
What thing it is that wommen most desiren:
Be war and keep thy nekke boon° from iren. *bone*
And if thou canst nat tellen me anoon,
Yit wol I yive thee leve for to goon
A twelfmonth and a day to seeche° and lere° *search / learn*
An answere suffisant° in this matere, *satisfactory*
And suretee wol I han er that thou pace,° *pass*
Thy body for to yeelden in this place."
  Wo was this knight, and sorwefully he siketh.° *sighs*
But what, he may nat doon al as him liketh,
And atte laste he chees° him for to wende, *chose*
And come again right at the yeres ende,
With swich answere as God wolde him purveye,° *provide*
And taketh his leve and wendeth forth his waye.
He seeketh every hous and every place
Wher as he hopeth for to finde grace,
To lerne what thing wommen love most.
But he ne coude arriven in no coost[2]
Wher as he mighte finde in this matere
Two creatures according in fere.[3]
  Some saiden wommen loven best richesse;
Some saide honour, some saide jolinesse;° *wantonness*
Some riche array, some saiden lust° abedde, *pleasure*
And ofte time to be widwe and wedde.
Some saide that oure herte is most esed
Whan that we been yflatered and yplesed—
He gooth ful neigh the soothe, I wol nat lie:
A man shal winne us best with flaterye,

8. Despite her head, i.e., despite anything she could do.
9. This knight was condemned to death.
1. Put to death.
2. I.e., country.
3. Agreeing together.

And with attendance and with bisinesse° *assiduousness*
Been we ylimed,° bothe more and lesse. *ensnared*
And some sayen that we loven best
For to be free, and do right as us lest,° *it pleases*
And that no man repreve° us of oure vice, *reprove*
But saye that we be wise and no thing nice.° *foolish*
For trewely, ther is noon of us alle,
If any wight wol clawe us on the galle,° *sore spot*
That we nil kike° for° he saith us sooth: *kick / because*
Assaye and he shal finde it that so dooth.
For be we nevere so vicious withinne,
We wol be holden° wise and clene of sinne. *considered*
And some sayn that greet delit han we
For to be holden stable and eek secree,[4]
And in oo purpos stedefastly to dwelle,
And nat biwraye° thing that men us telle— *disclose*
But that tale is nat worth a rake-stele.° *rake handle*
Pardee, we wommen conne no thing hele:° *conceal*
Witnesse on Mida.° Wol ye heere the tale? *Midas*
Ovide, amonges othere thinges smale,
Saide Mida hadde under his longe heres,
Growing upon his heed, two asses eres,
The whiche vice° he hidde as he best mighte *defect*
Ful subtilly from every mannes sighte,
That save his wif ther wiste° of it namo. *knew*
He loved hire most and trusted hire also.
He prayed hire that to no creature
She sholde tellen of his disfigure.° *deformity*
She swoor him nay, for al this world to winne,
She nolde do that vilainye or sinne
To make hir housbonde han so foul a name:
She nolde nat telle it for hir owene shame.
But nathelees, hir thoughte that she dyde° *would die*
That she so longe sholde a conseil° hide; *secret*
Hire thoughte it swal° so sore aboute hir herte *swelled*
That nedely som word hire moste asterte,[5]
And sith she dorste nat telle it to no man,
Down to a mareis° faste° by she ran— *marsh / close*
Til she cam there hir herte was afire—
And as a bitore[6] bombleth in the mire,
She laide hir mouth unto the water down:
"Biwray° me nat, thou water, with thy soun,"° *betray / sound*
Quod she. "To thee I telle it and namo:° *to no one else*
Myn housbonde hath longe asses eres two.
Now is myn herte al hool,[7] now is it oute.
I mighte no lenger keepe it, out of doute."
Here may ye see, though we a time abide,

4. Reliable and also close-mouthed.
5. Of necessity some word must escape her.
6. Bittern, a heron. "Bombleth": makes a booming noise.
7. I.e., sound.

Yit oute it moot:° we can no conseil hide. *must*
The remenant of the tale if ye wol heere,
Redeth Ovide, and ther ye may it lere.[8]
This knight of which my tale is specially,
Whan that he sawgh he mighte nat come therby—
This is to saye what wommen loven most—
Within his brest ful sorweful was his gost,° *spirit*
But hoom he gooth, he mighte nat sojurne:° *delay*
The day was come that hoomward moste° he turne. *must*
And in his way it happed him to ride
In al this care under a forest side,
Wher as he sawgh upon a daunce go
Of ladies foure and twenty and yit mo;
Toward the whiche daunce he drow ful yerne,[9]
In hope that som wisdom sholde he lerne.
But certainly, er he cam fully there,
Vanisshed was this daunce, he niste° where. *knew not*
No creature sawgh he that bar° lif, *bore*
Save on the greene he sawgh sitting a wif—
A fouler wight ther may no man devise.° *imagine*
Again[1] the knight this olde wif gan rise,
And saide, "Sire knight, heer forth lith° no way.° *lies / road*
Telle me what ye seeken, by youre fay.° *faith*
Paraventure it may the better be:
Thise olde folk conne° muchel thing," quod she. *know*
"My leve moder,"° quod this knight, "certain, *mother*
I nam but deed but if that I can sayn
What thing it is that wommen most desire.
Coude ye me wisse,° I wolde wel quite youre hire."[2] *teach*
"Plight me thy trouthe here in myn hand," quod she,
"The nexte thing that I requere° thee, *require of*
Thou shalt it do, if it lie in thy might,
And I wol telle it you er it be night."
"Have heer my trouthe," quod the knight. "I graunte."
"Thanne," quod she, "I dar me wel avaunte° *boast*
Thy lif is sauf,° for I wol stande therby. *safe*
Upon my lif the queene wol saye as I.
Lat see which is the pruddeste° of hem alle *proudest*
That wereth on[3] a coverchief or a calle° *headdress*
That dar saye nay of that I shal thee teche.
Lat us go forth withouten lenger speeche."
Tho rouned° she a pistel° in his ere, *whispered / sentence*
And bad him to be glad and have no fere.
Whan they be comen to the court, this knight
Saide he hadde holde his day as he hadde hight,° *promised*
And redy was his answere, as he saide.
Ful many a noble wif, and many a maide,

8. Learn. The reeds disclosed the secret by whispering *"aures aselli"* (asses' ears).
9. Drew very quickly.
1. I.e., to meet.
2. Repay your trouble.
3. That wears.

And many a widwe—for that they been wise—
The queene hirself sitting as justise,
Assembled been this answere for to heere,
And afterward this knight was bode° appere. *bidden to*
To every wight comanded was silence,
And that the knight sholde telle in audience° *open hearing*
What thing that worldly wommen loven best.
This knight ne stood nat stille as dooth a best,° *beast*
But to his question anoon answerde
With manly vois that al the court it herde.
"My lige° lady, generally," quod he, *liege*
"Wommen desire to have sovereinetee° *dominion*
As wel over hir housbonde as hir love,
And for to been in maistrye him above.
This is youre moste desir though ye me kille.
Dooth as you list:° I am here at youre wille." *please*
In al the court ne was ther wif ne maide
Ne widwe that contraried° that he saide, *contradicted*
But saiden he was worthy han° his lif. *to have*
And with that word up sterte° that olde wif, *started*
Which that the knight sawgh sitting on the greene;
"Mercy," quod she, "my soverein lady queene,
Er that youre court departe, do me right.
I taughte this answere unto the knight,
For which he plighte me his trouthe there
The firste thing I wolde him requere° *require*
He wolde it do, if it laye in his might.
Bifore the court thanne praye I thee, sire knight,"
Quod she, "that thou me take unto thy wif,
For wel thou woost that I have kept° thy lif. *saved*
If I saye fals, say nay, upon thy fay."
This knight answerde, "Allas and wailaway,
I woot right wel that swich was my biheeste.° *promise*
For Goddes love, as chees° a newe requeste: *choose*
Taak al my good and lat my body go."
"Nay thanne," quod she, "I shrewe° us bothe two. *curse*
For though that I be foul and old and poore,
I nolde for al the metal ne for ore
That under erthe is grave° or lith° above, *buried / lies*
But if thy wif I were and eek thy love."
"My love," quod he. "Nay, my dampnacioun!° *damnation*
Allas, that any of my nacioun[4]
Sholde evere so foule disparaged° be." *disgraced*
But al for nought, th'ende is this, that he
Constrained was: he needes moste hire wedde,
And taketh his olde wif and gooth to bedde.
Now wolden some men saye, paraventure,
That for my necligence I do no cure[5]
To tellen you the joy and al th'array

4. I.e., family.

5. I do not take the trouble.

That at the feeste was that ilke day.
To which thing shortly answere I shal:
I saye ther nas no joye ne feeste at al;
Ther nas but hevinesse and muche sorwe.
For prively he wedded hire on morwe,[6]
And al day after hidde him as an owle,
So wo was him, his wif looked so foule.
   Greet was the wo the knight hadde in his thought:
Whan he was with his wif abedde brought,
He walweth° and he turneth to and fro. *tosses*
His olde wif lay smiling everemo,
And saide, "O dere housbonde, benedicite,° *bless me*
Fareth° every knight thus with his wif as ye? *behaves*
Is this the lawe of King Arthures hous?
Is every knight of his thus daungerous?° *stand-offish*
I am youre owene love and youre wif;
I am she which that saved hath youre lif;
And certes yit ne dide I you nevere unright.
Why fare ye thus with me this firste night?
Ye faren like a man hadde lost his wit.
What is my gilt? For Goddes love, telle it,
And it shal been amended if I may."
   "Amended!" quod this knight. "Allas, nay, nay,
It wol nat been amended neveremo.
Thou art so lothly° and so old also, *loathsome*
And therto comen of so lowe a kinde,° *race*
That litel wonder is though I walwe and winde.° *turn*
So wolde God myn herte wolde breste!"° *break*
   "Is this," quod she, "the cause of youre unreste?"
   "Ye, certainly," quod he. "No wonder is."
   "Now sire," quod she, "I coude amende al this,
If that me liste, er it were dayes three,
So° wel ye mighte bere you[7] unto me. *provided that*
   "But for ye speken of swich gentilesse
As is descended out of old richesse—
That therfore sholden ye be gentilmen—
Swich arrogance is nat worth an hen.
Looke who that is most vertuous alway,
Privee and apert,[8] and most entendeth ay
To do the gentil deedes that he can,
Taak him for the gretteste° gentilman. *greatest*
Crist wol° we claime of him oure gentilesse, *desires that*
Nat of oure eldres for hir 'old richesse.'[9]
For though they yive us al hir heritage,
For which we claime to been of heigh parage,° *descent*
Yit may they nat biquethe for no thing
To noon of us hir vertuous living,
That made hem gentilmen ycalled be,

6. In the morning.
7. Behave.
8. Privately and publicly.
9. See Chaucer's *Gentilesse*, line 16.

And bad[1] us folwen hem in swich degree.
"Wel can the wise poete of Florence,
That highte Dant,[2] speken in this sentence;° *topic*
Lo, in swich manere rym is Dantes tale:
'Ful selde° up riseth by his braunches[3] smale *seldom*
Prowesse° of man, for God of his prowesse *excellence*
Wol that of him we claime oure gentilesse.'
For of oure eldres may we no thing claime
But temporel thing that man may hurte and maime.
Eek every wight woot this as wel as I,
If gentilesse were planted natureelly
Unto a certain linage down the line,
Privee and apert, thanne wolde they nevere fine° *cease*
To doon of gentilesse the faire office°— *function*
They mighte do no vilainye or vice.
"Taak fir and beer° it in the derkeste hous *bear*
Bitwixe this and the Mount of Caucasus,
And lat men shette° the dores and go thenne,° *shut / thence*
Yit wol the fir as faire lie[4] and brenne° *burn*
As twenty thousand men mighte it biholde:
His° office natureel ay wol it holde, *its*
Up° peril of my lif, til that it die. *upon*
Heer may ye see wel how that genterye° *gentility*
Is nat annexed° to possessioun,[5] *related*
Sith folk ne doon hir operacioun
Alway, as dooth the fir, lo, in his kinde.° *nature*
For God it woot, men may wel often finde
A lordes sone do shame and vilainye;
And he that wol han pris of his gentrye,[6]
For he was boren° of a gentil hous, *born*
And hadde his eldres noble and vertuous,
And nil himselven do no gentil deedes,
Ne folwen his gentil auncestre that deed° is, *dead*
He nis nat gentil, be he duc or erl—
For vilaines sinful deedes maken a cherl.
Thy gentilesse[7] nis but renomee° *renown*
Of thine auncestres for hir heigh bountee,° *magnanimity*
Which is a straunge° thing for thy persone. *alien*
For gentilesse[8] cometh fro God allone.
Thanne comth oure verray gentilesse of grace:
It was no thing biquethe us with oure place.
Thenketh how noble, as saith Valerius,[9]
Was thilke Tullius Hostilius
That out of poverte° roos to heigh noblesse. *poverty*
Redeth Senek,° and redeth eek Boece:° *Seneca / Boethius*
Ther shul ye seen expres that no drede° is *doubt*

1. I.e., they bade.
2. Dante; see his *Convivio*.
3. I.e., by its own efforts.
4. I.e., remain.
5. I.e., inheritable property.
6. Have credit for his noble birth.
7. I.e., the gentility you claim.
8. I.e., true gentility.
9. A Roman historian.

That he is gentil that dooth gentil deedes.
And therfore, leve housbonde, I thus conclude:
Al were it that mine auncestres weren rude,[1]
Yit may the hye God—and so hope I—
Graunte me grace to liven vertuously.
Thanne am I gentil whan that I biginne
To liven vertuously and waive° sinne. *avoid*
"And ther as ye of poverte me repreve,° *reprove*
The hye God, on whom that we bileve,
In wilful° poverte chees° to live his lif; *voluntary / chose*
And certes every man, maiden, or wif
May understonde that Jesus, hevene king,
Ne wolde nat chese° a vicious living. *choose*
Glad poverte is an honeste° thing, certain; *honorable*
This wol Senek and othere clerkes sayn.
Whoso that halt him paid of[2] his poverte,
I holde him riche al hadde he nat a sherte.° *shirt*
He that coveiteth[3] is a poore wight,
For he wolde han that is nat in his might;
But he that nought hath, ne coveiteth° have, *desires to*
Is riche, although we holde him but a knave.
Verray poverte it singeth proprely.° *appropriately*
Juvenal saith of poverte, 'Merily
The poore man, whan he gooth by the waye,
Biforn the theves he may singe and playe.'
Poverte is hateful good, and as I gesse,
A ful greet bringere out of bisinesse;[4]
A greet amendere eek of sapience
To him that taketh it in pacience;
Poverte is thing, although it seeme elenge,° *wretched*
Possession that no wight wol chalenge;[5]
Poverte ful often, whan a man is lowe,
Maketh[6] his God and eek himself to knowe;
Poverte a spectacle° is, as thinketh me, *pair of spectacles*
Thurgh which he may his verray freendes see.
And therfore, sire, sin that I nought you greve,
Of my poverte namore ye me repreve.° *reproach*
"Now sire, of elde° ye repreve me: *old age*
And certes sire, though noon auctoritee
Were in no book, ye gentils of honour
Sayn that men sholde an old wight doon favour,
And clepe him fader for youre gentilesse—
And auctours[7] shal I finden, as I gesse.
"Now ther ye saye that I am foul and old:
Thanne drede you nought to been a cokewold,° *cuckold*
For filthe and elde, also mote I thee,[8]
Been grete wardeins° upon chastitee. *guardians*

1. I.e., low born.
2. Considers himself satisfied with.
3. I.e., suffers desires.
4. I.e., cares.
5. Claim as his property.
6. I.e., makes him.
7. I.e., authorities.
8. So may I thrive.

But nathelees, sin I knowe your delit,
I shal fulfille youre worldly appetit.
"Chees now," quod she, "oon of thise thinges twaye:
To han me foul and old til that I deye
And be to you a trewe humble wif,
And nevere you displese in al my lif,
Or elles ye wol han me yong and fair,
And take youre aventure° of the repair[9] — *chance*
That shal be to youre hous by cause of me—
Or in som other place, wel may be.
Now chees youreselven wheither° that you liketh." — *whichever*
This knight aviseth him[1] and sore siketh;° — *sighs*
But atte laste he saide in this manere:
"My lady and my love, and wif so dere,
I putte me in youre wise governaunce:
Cheseth° youreself which may be most plesaunce[2] — *choose*
And most honour to you and me also.
I do no fors the wheither[3] of the two,
For as you liketh it suffiseth° me." — *satisfies*
"Thanne have I gete° of you maistrye," quod she, — *got*
"Sin I may chese and governe as me lest?"° — *it pleases*
"Ye, certes, wif," quod he. "I holde it best."
"Kisse me," quod she. "We be no lenger wrothe.
For by my trouthe, I wol be to you bothe—
This is to sayn, ye, bothe fair and good.
I praye to God that I mote sterven wood,[4]
But° I to you be al so good and trewe — *unless*
As evere was wif sin that the world was newe.
And but I be tomorn° as fair to seene — *tomorrow morning*
As any lady, emperisse, or queene,
That is bitwixe the eest and eek the west,
Do with my lif and deeth right as you lest:
Caste up the curtin, looke how that it is."
And whan the knight sawgh verraily al this,
That she so fair was and so yong therto,
For joye he hente° hire in his armes two; — *took*
His herte bathed in a bath of blisse;
A thousand time arewe° he gan hire kisse, — *in a row*
And she obeyed him in every thing
That mighte do him plesance or liking.° — *pleasure*
And thus they live unto hir lives ende
In parfit° joye. And Jesu Crist us sende — *perfect*
Housbondes meeke, yonge, and fresshe abedde—
And grace t'overbide° hem that we wedde. — *outlive*
And eek I praye Jesu shorte° hir lives — *shorten*
That nought wol be governed by hir wives,
And olde and angry nigardes of dispence°— — *expenditure*
God sende hem soone a verray° pestilence! — *veritable*

9. I.e., visits.
1. Considers.
2. Pleasure.
3. I do not care whichever.
4. Die mad.

The Franklin's Tale[1]

The Introduction[2]

"In faith, Squier, thou hast thee wel yquit° *acquitted*
And gentilly. I praise wel thy wit,"
Quod the Frankelain. "Considering thy youthe,
So feelingly thou spekest, sire, I allowe° thee: *praise*
As to my doom° ther is noon that is heer *judgment*
Of eloquence that shal be thy peer,
If that thou live. God yive thee good chaunce,
And in vertu sende thee continuaunce,
For of thy speeche I have greet daintee.° *delight*
I have a sone, and by the Trinitee,
I hadde levere than twenty pound worth land,
Though it right now were fallen[3] in myn hand,
He were a man of swich discrecioun
As that ye been. Fy on possessioun
But if[4] a man be vertuous withal!
I have my sone snibbed° and yit shal *scolded*
For he to vertu listeth nat entende,° *attend*
But for to playe at dees° and to dispende,[5] *dice*
And lese° al that he hath is his usage. *lose*
And he hath levere talken with a page

1. The Franklin says that his tale is a Breton lay, a sub-genre of romance of which *Sir Orfeo* is the best English representative. Indeed, the Franklin's definition of the Breton lay resembles the definition at the beginning of *Sir Orfeo* so closely that it has led to suspicions that the latter was not only the Franklin's source but the chief source of Chaucer's own knowledge of the genre. The source of the Franklin's Tale itself is probably not a lost Breton lay but an old story told by, among others, Boccaccio. But in any case, features found in Breton lays also occur in the Franklin's Tale: a rash promise that must be kept; a supernatural intervention in a plot containing a love situation; stylistic simplicity; and a generally optimistic spirit.

The Franklin is a fine type of the man of humble origins who has risen to the middle class and has adopted the aspirations of the aristocracy while accumulating wealth. His tale shows a nice blend of unselfconscious interest in the value of money and a self-conscious one in *gentilesse*, the gentle behavior which should distinguish not only the nobly born but (as the Wife of Bath's old hag tells her husband) any free-born man. In this tale *gentilesse* embraces the virtues of patience (which Dorigen has to learn the hard way) and, more significantly, of *trouthe* and *freedom*, "integrity" and "generosity." Though the Franklin shows no awareness of the Biblical text, "Ye shall know the truth and the truth shall make you free" (John viii.32), his tale exemplifies it almost in the manner of a parable. The characters concerned resolve to maintain their *trouthe*—their pledged word—and this sets up a chain reaction of *freedom* which releases them from the dire consequences that keeping their word would entail: when the old law of the covenant is honored, it brings into being the new law of forgiveness. The word *franklin* means "freeman," a meaning Chaucer seems to be playing on when in the last lines of the tale he has the Franklin ask about the three men in the story, "Which was the most free?"

2. The Squire has been speaking for more than 650 lines but has not made much narrative progress in his enormously over-plotted Oriental tale of Cambyuskan and his three children when the Franklin speaks, apparently interrupting the story. It is uncertain, however, whether the Franklin's words represent an intentional interruption or whether they were written to be spoken at the end of the Squire's Tale, which Chaucer intended sometime to complete.

3. I.e., delivered.

4. Unless.

5. Spend money.

Than to commune with any gentil wight,
Where he mighte lerne gentilesse° aright." *gentility*
"Straw for thy gentilesse!" Quod oure Host.
"What, Frankelain, pardee sire, wel thou woost° *know*
That eech of you moot° tellen atte leeste *must*
A tale or two, or breken his biheeste."° *promise*
"That knowe I wel, sire," quod the Frankelain.
"I praye you, haveth me nat in desdain,
Though to this man I speke a word or two."
"Tel on thy tale withouten wordes mo."
"Gladly, sire Host," quod he, "I wol obeye
Unto youre wil. Now herkneth what I saye.
I wol you nat contrarien[6] in no wise
As fer as that my wittes wol suffise.
I praye to God that it may plesen you:
Thanne woot I wel that it is good ynow."° *enough*

The Prologue

Thise olde gentil Britons° in hir dayes *Bretons*
Of diverse adventures maden layes,
Rymeyed[7] in hir firste Briton tonge;
Whiche layes with hir instruments they songe,° *sung*
Or elles redden° hem for hir plesaunce; *read*
And oon of hem have I in remembraunce,
Which I shal sayn with good wil as I can.
But sires, by cause I am a burel° man, *ignorant*
At my biginning first I you biseeche
Have me excused of my rude speeche.
I lerned nevere retorike,° certain: *rhetoric*
Thing that I speke it moot° be bare and plain; *must*
I sleep° nevere in the Mount of Parnaso,[8] *slept*
Ne lerned Marcus Tullius Scithero;° *Cicero*
Colours[9] ne knowe I noon, withouten drede,° *doubt*
But swiche colours as growen in the mede,° *meadow*
Or elles swiche as men dye or painte;
Colours of retorike been too quainte:° *unfamiliar*
My spirit feeleth nat of swich matere.
But if you list, my tale shul ye heere.

The Tale

In Armorik,° that called is Britaine,° *Armorica / Brittany*
Ther was a knight that loved and dide his paine[1]
To serve a lady in his beste wise;
And many a labour, many a greet emprise° *enterprise*

6. Act contrary to.
7. Composed in rhyme.
8. Parnassus, home of the Muses.
9. I.e., rhetorical figures.
1. I.e., made every effort.

He for his lady wroughte er she were wonne,
For she was oon[2] the faireste under sonne,
And eek therto come of so heigh kinrede° *kindred*
That wel unnethes[3] dorste this knight for drede
Telle hire his wo, his paine, and his distresse.
But atte laste she for his worthinesse,
And namely° for his meeke obeisaunce,° *especially / obedience*
Hath swich a pitee caught of his penaunce° *suffering*
That prively she fil of[4] his accord
To taken him for hir housbonde and hir lord,
Of swich lordshipe as men han over hir wives.
And for to lede the more in blisse hir lives,
Of his free wil he swoor hire as a knight
That nevere in al his lif he day ne night
Ne sholde upon him take no maistrye° *dominion*
Again hir wil, ne kithe° hire jalousye, *show*
But hire obeye and folwe hir wil in al,
As any lovere to his lady shal°— *ought*
Save that the name of sovereinete,° *sovereignty*
That wolde he have, for shame of[5] his degree.
  She thanked him, and with ful greet humblesse
She saide, "Sire, sith of youre gentilesse
Ye profre me to have so large[6] a reine.
Ne wolde nevere God bitwixe us twaine,
As in[7] my gilt, were outher° werre° or strif. *either / war*
Sire, I wol be your humble, trewe wif—
Have heer my trouthe[8]—til that myn herte breste."° *break*
Thus been they bothe in quiete and in reste.
  For oo thing, sires, saufly° dar I saye: *safely*
That freendes° everich° other moot° obeye, *lovers / each / must*
If they wol longe holden compaignye.
Love wol nat be constrained by maistrye:° *force*
Whan maistrye comth, the God of Love anoon
Beteth his winges and farewel, he is goon!
Love is a thing as any spirit free;
Wommen of kinde[9] desiren libertee,
And nat to been constrained as a thral°— *slave*
And so doon men, if I sooth sayen shal.
Looke who that is most pacient in love,
He is at his avantage al above.
Pacience is an heigh vertu, certain,
For it venquissheth,° as thise clerkes sayn, *vanquishes*
Thinges that rigour sholde nevere attaine.[1]
For° every word men may nat chide or plaine:° *at / complain*
Lerneth to suffre, or elles, so mote I goon,[2]

2. I.e., one of.
3. With difficulty.
4. I.e., fell in.
5. Out of respect for.
6. I.e., free.
7. As a result of.
8. Troth, word of honor.
9. By nature.
1. I.e., overcome.
2. So may I walk.

Ye shul it lerne, wherso° ye wol or noon. *whether*
For in this world, certain, ther no wight is
That he ne dooth or saith somtime amis:
Ire, siknesse, or constellacioun,[3]
Win, wo, or chaunging of complexioun[4]
Causeth ful ofte to doon amis or speken.
On every wrong a man may nat be wreken:° *avenged*
After the time moste° be temperaunce *must*
To every wight that can on governaunce.[5]
And therfore hath this wise worthy knight
To live in ese suffrance° hire bihight,° *toleration / promised*
And she to him ful wisly° gan to swere *surely*
That nevere sholde ther be defaute° in here. *defect*
Here may men seen an humble wis accord:
Thus hath she take hir servant and hir lord—
Servant in love and lord in marriage.
Thanne was he bothe in lordshipe and servage.[6]
Servage? Nay, but in lordshipe above,
Sith° he hath bothe his lady and his love; *since*
His lady, certes, and his wif also,
The which that[7] lawe of love accordeth to.
And whan he was in this prosperitee,
Hoom with his wif he gooth to his contree,
Nat fer fro Pedmark[8] ther his dwelling was,
Wher as he liveth in blisse and in solas.° *delight*
Who coude telle but he hadde wedded be
The joye, the ese, and the prosperitee
That is bitwixe an housbonde and his wif?
A yeer and more lasted this blisful lif,
Til that the knight of which I speke of thus,
That of Kairrud[9] was cleped° Arveragus, *called*
Shoop him[1] to goon and dwelle a yeer or twaine
In Engelond, that cleped was eek° Britaine, *also*
To seeke in armes worshipe and honour—
For al his lust° he sette in swich labour— *pleasure*
And dwelled ther two yeer, the book saith thus.
Now wol I stinte° of this Arveragus, *cease*
And speke I wol of Dorigen his wif,
That loveth hir housbonde as hir hertes lif.
For his absence weepeth she and siketh,° *sighs*
As doon thise noble wives whan hem liketh.[2]
She moorneth, waketh, waileth, fasteth, plaineth;° *complains*
Desir of his presence hire so distraineth° *afflicts*
That al this wide world she sette[3] at nought.
Hir freendes, whiche that knewe hir hevy thought,

3. I.e., planetary influences.
4. The balance of humors in the body.
5. Is capable of self-control.
6. Position of a servant.
7. As.
8. Penmarch, in Brittany.
9. Kerru, a town in Brittany.
1. Prepared.
2. It pleases.
3. I.e., valued.

Conforten hire in al that evere they may:
They prechen hire, they telle hire night and day
That causelees she sleeth° hirself, allas; *slays*
And every confort possible in this cas
They doon to hire with al hir bisinesse,° *assiduousness*
Al for to make hire leve° hir hevinesse. *abandon*
By proces,[4] as ye knowen everichoon,
Men may so longe graven° in a stoon *engrave*
Til som figure therinne emprinted be:
So longe han they conforted hire til she
Received hath, by hope and by resoun,
The emprinting of hir consolacioun,
Thurgh which hir grete sorwe gan assuage:
She may nat alway duren° in swich rage.° *remain / passion*
And eek Arveragus in al this care
Hath sent hir lettres hoom of his welfare,
And that he wol come hastily again—
Or elles hadde this sorwe hir herte slain.
Hir freendes sawe hir sorwe gan to slake,° *diminish*
And prayed hire on knees, for Goddes sake,
To come and romen hire in compaignye,
Away to drive hir derke fantasye,
And finally she graunted that requeste:
For wel she saw that it was for the beste.
Now stood hir castel faste by the see,
And often with hir freendes walketh she,
Hire to disporte upon the bank an heigh,
Wher as she many a ship and barge° seigh,° *vessel / saw*
Sailing hir cours wher as hem liste go—
But thanne was that a parcel° of hir wo, *component*
For of hirself ful ofte, "Allas!" saith she,
"Is ther no ship of so manye as I see
Wol bringen hoom my lord? Thanne were myn herte
Al warisshed° of his bittre paines smerte." *recovered*
Another time ther wolde she sitte and thinke,
And caste hir yën downward fro the brinke;
But whan she sawgh the grisly rokkes blake,
For verray° fere so wolde hir herte quake *real*
That on hir feet she mighte hire nat sustene:° *sustain*
Thanne wolde she sitte adown upon the greene
And pitously into the see biholde,
And sayn right thus, with sorweful sikes° colde:[5] *sighs*
"Eterne God that thurgh thy purveyaunce° *providence*
Ledest the world by certain governaunce,
In idel,[6] as men sayn, ye nothing make:
But Lord, thise grisly feendly° rokkes blake, *hostile*
That seemen rather a foul confusioun

4. Course of time.
5. I.e., grievous.
6. I.e., without purpose.

Of werk, than any fair creacioun
Of swich a parfit° wis God and a stable, *perfect*
Why han ye wrought this werk unresonable?
For by this werk south, north, ne west ne eest,
Ther nis yfostred man ne brid[7] ne beest:
It dooth no good, to my wit, but anoyeth.
See ye nat, Lord, how mankinde it destroyeth?
An hundred thousand bodies of mankinde
Han rokkes slain, al° be they nat in minde: *although*
Which mankinde is so fair part of thy werk
That thou it madest lik to thyn owene merk:[8]
Thanne seemed it ye hadde a greet cheertee° *affection*
Toward mankinde. But how thanne may it be
That ye swiche menes° make it to destroyen?— *means*
Whiche menes do no good, but evere anoyen.
I woot wel clerkes wol sayn as hem leste,[9]
By arguments, that al is for the beste,
Though I ne can the causes nat yknowe.
But thilke° God that made wind to blowe, *that*
As keepe my lord! This[1] my conclusioun.
To clerkes lete° I al disputisoun,° *leave / disputation*
But wolde God that alle thise rokkes blake
Were sonken° into helle for his sake! *sunken*
Thise rokkes slain myn herte for the fere."
Thus wolde she sayn with many a pitous tere.
  Hir freendes sawe that it was no disport
To romen by the see, but disconfort,
And shopen° for to playen somwher elles: *arranged*
They leden hire by rivers and by welles,° *springs*
And eek in othere places delitables;° *delightful*
They dauncen and they playen at ches and tables.° *backgammon*
  So on a day, right in the morwetide,° *morning*
Unto a gardin that was ther biside,
In which that they hadde maad hir ordinaunce° *arrangements*
Of vitaile° and of other purveyaunce,° *food / provisions*
They goon and playe hem al the longe day.
And this was on the sixte morwe° of May, *morning*
Which May had painted with his softe showres
This gardin ful of leves and of flowres;
And craft of mannes hand so curiously° *skillfully*
Arrayed hadde this gardin trewely
That nevere was ther gardin of swich pris,° *excellence*
But if[2] it were the verray Paradis.
The odour of flowres and the fresshe sighte
Wolde han maked any herte lighte
That evere was born, but if too greet siknesse,

7. Bird; "yfostred": fed.
8. Mark, i.e., image.
9. May please.
1. I.e., this is.
2. Unless.

Or too greet sorwe heeld it in distresse,
So ful it was of beautee with plesaunce.
At after-diner gonne they to daunce,
And singe also, save Dorigen allone,
Which made alway hir complainte and hir mone,° *moan*
For she ne sawgh him on the daunce go
That was hir housbonde and hir love also.
But nathelees she moste° a time abide, *must*
And with good hope lete° hir sorwe slide. *make*
  Upon this daunce, amonges othere men,
Daunced a squier bifore Dorigen
That fressher was and jolier° of array, *gayer*
As to my doom,° than is the month of May. *judgment*
He singeth, daunceth, passing° any man *surpassing*
That is or was sith° that the world bigan. *since*
Therwith he was, if men him sholde descrive,° *describe*
Oon of the beste-faring° man on live: *handsomest*
Yong, strong, right vertuous, and riche and wis,
And wel-biloved, and holden in greet pris.° *repute*
And shortly, if the soothe I tellen shal,
Unwiting of[3] this Dorigen at al,
This lusty squier, servant to Venus,
Which that ycleped° was Aurelius, *called*
Hadde loved hire best of any creature
Two yeer and more, as was his aventure.
But nevere dorste he tellen hire his grevaunce:
Withouten coppe° he drank al his penaunce.[4] *cup*
He was despaired, no thing dorste he saye—
Save in his songes somwhat wolde he wraye° *disclose*
His wo, as in a general complaining:
He saide he loved and was biloved no thing;[5]
Of which matere made he manye layes,
Songes, complaintes, roundels, virelayes,[6]
How that he dorste nat his sorwe telle,
But languissheth as a furye dooth in helle;
And die he moste,° he saide, as dide Ekko *must*
For Narcisus that dorste nat telle hir wo.[7]
In other manere than ye heere me saye
Ne dorste he nat to hire his wo biwraye,° *disclose*
Save that paraventure° som time at daunces, *perchance*
Ther yonge folk keepen hir observaunces,[8]
It may wel be he looked on hir face
In swich a wise as man that asketh grace;
But no thing wiste° she of his entente. *knew*

3. Unknown to.
4. Suffering; i.e., he suffered in silence.
5. Not at all.
6. The lover unable to declare his love conventionally expressed his frustration by writing verse: Aurelius produced five kinds of verse, but only rondels and virelays are strictly defined forms.
7. Echo was unable to communicate her love for Narcissus and eventually died in despair.
8. Carry on their rituals.

Nathelees° it happed, er they thennes°
wente, *nevertheless / thence*
By cause that he was hir neighebour,
And was a man of worshipe and honour,
And hadde[9] yknowen him of time yore,[1]
They fille° in speeche, and forth more and more *fell*
Unto his purpos drow° Aurelius, *drew*
And whan he sawgh his time, he saide thus:
"Madame," quod he, "by God that this world made,
So that I wiste° it mighte youre herte glade,° *knew / gladden*
I wolde that day that youre Arveragus
Wente over the see that I, Aurelius,
Hadde went ther nevere I sholde have come again.
For wel I woot my service is in vain:
My gerdon° is but bresting° of myn herte. *reward / breaking*
Madame, reweth[2] upon my paines smerte,
For with a word ye may me slee° or save. *slay*
Here at youre feet God wolde that I were grave!° *buried*
I ne have as now no leiser more to saye:
Have mercy, sweete, or ye wol do° me deye." *make*
She gan to looke upon Aurelius:
"Is this youre wil?" quod she, "and saye ye thus?
Nevere erst,"° quod she, "ne wiste I what ye mente. *before*
But now, Aurelie, I knowe youre entente,
By thilke° God that yaf me soule and lif, *that*
Ne shal I nevere been untrewe wif,
In word ne werk, as fer as I have wit.
I wol be his to whom that I am knit:° *joined*
Take this for final answere as of me."
But after that in play thus saide she:
"Aurelie," quod she, "by hye God above,
Yit wolde I graunte you to been youre love,
Sin° I you see so pitously complaine, *since*
Looke what day that endelong° Britaine *along*
Ye remeve° alle the rokkes, stoon by stoon, *remove*
That they ne lette° ship ne boot° to goon. *hinder / boat*
I saye, whan ye han maad the coost° so clene *coast*
Of rokkes that there nis no stoon yseene,
Thanne wol I love you best of any man—
Have heer my trouthe°—in al that evere I can. *word*
For wel I woot that it shal nevere bitide.
Lat swiche folies out of youre herte slide!
What daintee° sholde a man han by his lif *delight*
For to love another mannes wif,
That hath hir body whan so that him liketh?"[3]
Aurelius ful ofte sore siketh:° *sighs*

9. I.e., she had.
1. Long past.
2. Have pity on.
3. It pleases.

"Is ther noon other grace in you?" quod he.
"No, by that Lord," quod she, "that maked me."
Wo was Aurelie whan that he this herde,
And with a sorweful herte he thus answerde.
"Madame," quod he, "this were an impossible.
Thanne moot° I die of sodein deeth horrible." *must*
And with that word he turned him anoon.
Tho° come hir othere freendes many oon, *then*
And in the aleyes° romeden up and down, *paths*
And no thing wiste of this conclusioun,
But sodeinly bigonne revel newe,
Til that the brighte sonne loste his hewe,
For th' orisonte° hath reft[4] the sonne his light— *horizon*
This is as muche to saye as it was night.
And hoom they goon in joye and in solas,° *delight*
Save only wrecche° Aurelius, allas. *wretched*
He to his hous is goon with sorweful herte;
He seeth he may nat from his deeth asterte;° *escape*
Him seemed that he felte his herte colde;
Up to the hevene his handes he gan holde,
And on his knees bare he sette him down,
And in his raving saide his orisoun.
For verray wo out of his wit he braide;° *went*
He niste[5] what he spak, but thus he saide;
With pitous herte his plainte° hath he bigonne *lamont*
Unto the goddes, and first unto the sonne:
He saide, "Appollo, god and governour
Of every plaunte, herbe, tree and flowr,
That yivest after thy declinacioun[6]
To eech of hem his time and his sesoun,
As thyn herberwe[7] chaungeth, lowe or hye;
Lord Phebus, cast thy merciable° yë *merciful*
On wrecche Aurelie which that am but lorn.° *lost*
Lo, lord, my lady hath my deeth ysworn
Withouten gilt, but° thy benignitee *unless*
Upon my deedly herte have som pitee;
For wel I woot, lord Phebus, if you lest,[8]
Ye may me helpen, save my lady, best.[9]
Now voucheth sauf that I may you devise° *describe*
How that I may been holpe,° and in what wise: *helped*
Youre blisful suster, Lucina[1] the sheene,° *bright*
That of the see is chief goddesse and queene—
Though Neptunus have deitee in the see,
Yit emperisse° aboven him is she— *empress*
Ye knowen wel, lord, that right as hir desir

4. Deprived of.
5. Knew not.
6. Who give, according to your position in the sky.
7. Lodging, i.e., one of the astrological houses in which the planets reside in alternation.
8. It pleases.
9. Except for my lady, you may help me best.
1. I.,e., Diana, the Moon.

Is to be quiked° and lighted of youre fir, *quickened*
For which she folweth you ful bisily,° *constantly*
Right so the see desireth naturelly
To folwen hire, as she that is goddesse
Bothe in the see and rivers more and lesse;
Wherfore, lord Phebus, this is my requeste:
Do this miracle—or do° myn herte breste°— *make / break*
That now next at this opposicioun,[2]
Which in the signe shal be of the Leoun,
As prayeth hire so greet a flood to bringe.
That five fadme° at the leeste it overspringe° *fathoms / overrun*
The hyeste rok in Armorik Britaine;
And lat this flood endure yeres twaine:
Thanne certes to my lady may I saye,
'Holdeth youre heeste,° the rokkes been awaye.' *promise*
  Lord Phebus, dooth this miracle for me!
Praye hire she go no faster cours than ye—
I saye this, prayeth youre suster that she go
No faster cours than ye thise yeres two:
Thanne shal she been evene at the fulle alway,
And spring-flood lasten bothe night and day.
And but° she vouche sauf in swich manere *unless*
To graunte me my soverein lady dere,
Praye hire[3] to sinken every rok adown
Into hir owene derke regioun
Under the ground ther Pluto dwelleth inne,
Or nevere mo° shal I my lady winne. *more*
Thy temple in Delphos° wol I barefoot seeke. *Delphi*
Lord Phebus, see the teres on my cheeke,
And of my paine have som compassioun."
And with that word in swoune° he fil° adown, *swoon / fell*
And longe time he lay forth in a traunce.
  His brother, which that knew of his penaunce,° *pain*
Up caughte him, and to bedde he hath him brought.
Despaired in this torment and this thought
Lete° I this woful creature lie— *leave*
Chese[4] he for me wher° he wol live or die. *whether*
  Arveragus with hele° and greet honour, *prosperity*
As he that was of chivalrye the flowr,
Is comen hoom, and othere worthy men:
O, blisful artou now, thou Dorigen,
That hast thy lusty housbonde in thine armes,
The fresshe knight, the worthy man of armes,
That loveth thee as his owene hertes lif.
No thing list[5] him to been imaginatif
If any wight hadde spoke whil he was oute

2. The position of the sun and moon when they are at a 180-degree angle from one another as seen from the earth.

3. I.e., Diana in her capacity as goddess of the underworld.

4. Let him choose.

5. It pleases.

To hire of love; he ne hadde of it no doute:
He nought entendeth[6] to swich matere,
But daunceth, justeth,° maketh hire good cheere. *jousts*
And thus in joye and blisse I lete hem dwelle,
And of the sike Aurelius wol I telle.
  In langour and in torment furious
Two yeer and more lay wrecche Aurelius,
Er any foot he mighte on erthe goon,
Ne confort in this hadde he noon,
Save of his brother, which that was a clerk:
He knew of al this wo and al this werk,
For to noon other creature, certain,
Of this matere he dorste no word sayn.
Under his brest he bar it more secree° *secret*
Than evere dide Pamphilus for Galathee.[7]
His brest was hool° withoute° for to seene, *whole / outwardly*
But in his herte ay° was the arwe keene; *ever*
And wel ye knowe that of a sursanure[8]
In surgerye is perilous the cure,
But° men mighte touche the arwe or come therby. *unless*
His brother weep° and wailed prively, *wept*
Til at the laste him fil in remembrance[9]
That whiles he was at Orliens° in France, *Orleans*
As yonge clerkes that been likerous° *desirous*
To reden artes[1] that been curious,° *occult*
Seeken in every halke and every herne[2]
Particuler[3] sciences for to lerne,
He him remembred that, upon a day,
At Orliens in studye a book he sey° *saw*
Of magik naturel,[4] which his felawe,
That was that time a bacheler of lawe—
Al were he[5] ther to lerne another craft—
Hadde prively upon his desk ylaft:° *left*
Which book spak muchel of the operaciouns
Touching the eighte and twenty mansiouns[6]
That longen° to the moone—and swich folye *belong*
As in oure dayes is nat worth a flye,
For holy chirches faith in oure bileve° *creed*
Ne suffreth noon illusion us to greve.
And whan this book was in his remembraunce,
Anoon for joye his herte gan to daunce,
And to himself he saide prively,
"My brother shal be warisshed° hastily, *cured*
For I am siker° that ther be sciences *sure*

6. Pays attention.
7. Pamphilus and Galataea are the lovers in the medieval Latin *Pamphilus de Amore*.
8. Superficially healed wound.
9. I.e., he happened to remember.
1. Study subjects.
2. Every nook and cranny.
3. Out of the way.
4. Natural magic employs astrological knowledge rather than spirits.
5. Although he was.
6. I.e., daily positions.

By whiche men make diverse apparences,° *apparitions*
Swiche as thise subtile tregettoures° playe; *magicians*
For ofte at feestes have I wel herd saye
That tregettours withinne an halle large
Have maad come in a water and a barge,° *ship*
And in the halle rowen up and down;
Som time hath seemed come a grim leoun;
Som time flowres springe° as in a mede; *grow*
Som time a vine and grapes white and rede;
Som time a castel al of lim° and stoon— *lime*
And whan hem liked voided[7] it anoon:
Thus seemed it to every mannes sighte.
Now thanne conclude I thus: that if I mighte
At Orliens som old felawe yfinde
That hadde thise moones mansions in minde,
Or other magik naturel above,
He sholde wel make my brother han his love.
For with an apparence a clerk may make
To mannes sighte that alle the rokkes blake
Of Britaine were yvoided everichoon,
And shippes by the brinke comen and goon,
And in swich forme enduren a day or two:
Thanne were my brother warisshed° of his wo; *cured*
Thanne moste° she needes holden hir biheeste,° *must / promise*
Or elles he shal shame hire at the leeste."
What sholde I make a lenger° tale of this? *longer*
Unto his brothers bed he comen is,
And swich confort he yaf him for to goon
To Orliens, that up he sterte° anoon, *started*
And on his way forthward thanne is he fare,
In hope for to been lissed° of his care. *assuaged*
Whan they were come almost to that citee,
But if it were a two furlong or three,
A yong clerk roming by himself they mette,
Which that in Latin thriftily° hem grette,° *properly / greeted*
And after that he saide a wonder thing:
"I knowe," quod he, "the cause of your coming."
And er they ferther any foote wente,
He tolde hem al that was in hir entente.
This Briton clerk him axed° of felawes, *asked*
The whiche that he hadde knowe in olde dawes,° *days*
And he answerde him that they dede° were; *dead*
For which he weep° ful ofte many a tere. *wept*
Down of his hors Aurelius lighte anoon,
And with this magicien forth is he goon
Hoom to his hous, and maden hem wel at ese:
Hem lakked no vitaile that mighte hem plese;
So wel arrayed hous as ther was oon
Aurelius in his lif saw nevere noon.

7. Caused to disappear.

He shewed him er he wente to soper° *supper*
Forestes, parkes ful of wilde deer:
Ther saw he hertes° with hir hornes hye, *harts*
The gretteste° that evere were seen with yë; *greatest*
He sawgh of hem an hundred slain with houndes,
And some with arwes bledde of bittre woundes.
He saw, when voided[8] were thise wilde deer,
Thise fauconers° upon a fair river, *falconers*
That with hir hawkes han the heron slain.
Tho sawgh he knightes justing° in a plain. *jousting*
And after this he dide him this plesaunce,
That he him shewed his lady on a daunce—
On which himself he daunced, as him thoughte.
And whan this maister that this magik wroughte
Sawgh it was time, he clapte his handes two,
And farewel, al oure revel was ago.
And yit remeved° they nevere out of the hous *moved*
Whil they sawe al this sighte merveilous,
But in his studye, ther as his bookes be,
They sitten stille, and no wight but they three.
To him this maister called his squier
And saide him thus, "Is redy oure soper?
Almost an houre it is, I undertake,
Sith I you bad oure soper for to make,
Whan that thise worthy men wenten with me
Into my studye, ther as my bookes be."
"Sire," quod this squier, "whan it liketh you,
It is al redy, though ye wol right now."
"Go we thanne soupe," quod he, "as for the beste:
This amorous folk som time mote° han hir reste." *must*
At after-soper fille° they in tretee° *fell / negotiation*
What somme° sholde this maistres gerdon° be *sum / reward*
To remeven° alle the rokkes of Britaine, *remove*
And eek from Gerounde[9] to the mouth of Seine:
He made it straunge,[1] and swoor, so God him save,
Lasse° than a thousand pound he wolde nat have, *less*
Ne gladly for that somme he wolde nat goon.
Aurelius with blisful herte anoon
Answerde thus, "Fy on a thousand pound!
This wide world, which that men saye is round,
I wolde it yive, if I were lord of it.
This bargain is ful drive, for we been knit.[2]
Ye shal be payed trewely, by my trouthe.
But looketh now, for no necligence or slouthe,° *sloth*
Ye tarye us heer no lenger than tomorwe."
"Nay," quod this clerk, "have heer my faith to borwe."[3]
To bedde is goon Aurelius whan him leste,° *pleased*

8. Made to disappear.
9. The Gironde river.
1. I.e., difficulties.
2. I.e., this bargain is fully made, for we are in accord.
3. As a pledge.

And wel neigh al that night he hadde his reste:
What for his labour and his hope of blisse,
His woful herte of penance° hadde a lisse.° *suffering / alleviation*
Upon the morwe, whan that it was day,
To Britaine tooke they the righte° way, *direct*
Aurelius and this magicien biside,
And been descended ther they wolde abide;
And this was, as thise bookes me remembre,[4]
The colde frosty seson of Decembre.
Phebus wax° old, and hewed° lik latoun,° *grew / colored / brass*
That in his hote declinacioun[5]
Shoon as the burned° gold with stremes° brighte; *burnished / beams*
But now in Capricorn[6] adown he lighte,
Wher as he shoon ful pale, I dar wel sayn:
The bittre frostes with the sleet and rain
Destroyed hath the greene in every yeerd.° *yard*
Janus[7] sit° by the fir with double beerd, *sits*
And drinketh of his bugle horn[8] the win;
Biforn him stant° brawn° of the tusked swin, *stands / flesh*
And "Nowel!" crieth every lusty man.
Aurelius in al that evere he can
Dooth to this maister cheere and reverence,
And prayeth him to doon his diligence
To bringen him out of his paines smerte,
Or with a swerd that he wolde slitte his herte.[9]
This subtil clerk swich routhe° hadde of this man *pity*
That night and day he spedde him[1] that he can
To waiten a time of his conclusioun[2]—
This is to sayn, to make illusioun
By swich an apparence° or jogelrye[3] *apparition*
(I ne can° no termes of astrologye) *know*
That she and every wight sholde weene° and saye *think*
That of Britaine the rokkes were awaye,
Or elles they were sonken° under grounde. *sunk*
So at the laste he hath his time yfounde
To maken his japes° and his wrecchednesse[4] *tricks*
Of swich a supersticious cursednesse.° *wickedness*
His tables tolletanes[5] forth hath he brought,
Ful wel corrected; ne ther lakked nought,
Neither his collect ne his expans yeres,[6]

4. Recall to me.
5. I.e., celestial position.
6. The House of the Goat.
7. The god with two faces who knew both past and future, perpetuated in the name "January."
8. Wild ox horn.
9. I.e., stab his own heart.
1. Hurried.
2. To watch for a time for his astrological operation.
3. Optical illusion.
4. Miserable performance.
5. Astronomical tables based on the latitude of Toledo, in Spain.
6. Neither his table of collect years nor his table of expanse years: the former recorded planetary movements for long periods such as twenty years, the latter for short periods of a year.

Ne his rootes,[7] ne his othere geres,° *paraphernalia*
As been his centres and his arguments,[8]
And his proporcionels convenients,[9]
For his equacions in every thing;
And by his eighte spere[1] in his werking° *operation*
He knew ful wel how fer Alnath was shove[2]
Fro the heed of thilke fixe Aries above
That in the ninte spere considered is:[3]
Ful subtilly he calculed° al this. *calculated*
When he hadde founde his firste mansioun,[4]
He knew the remenant by proporcioun,[5]
And knew the arising of his moone weel,
And in whos face and terme[6] and every deel,° *part*
And knew ful wel the moones mansioun
Accordant[7] to his operacioun,
And knew also his othere observaunces° *rules*
For swiche illusions and swiche meschaunces
As hethen folk useden in thilke° dayes; *those*
For which no lenger maked he delayes,
But, thurgh his magik, for a wike° or twaye *week*
It seemed that alle the rokkes were awaye.
Aurelius, which that yit despaired is
Wher° he shall han his love or fare amis, *whether*
Awaiteth night and day on this miracle;
And whan he knew that there was noon obstacle,
That voided were thise rokkes everichoon,
Down to his maistres feet he fil° anoon, *fell*
And saide, "I, woful wrecche Aurelius,
Thanke you, lord, and lady myn Venus,
That me han holpen° fro my cares colde." *helped*
And to the temple his way forth hath he holde,
Wher as he knew he sholde his lady see.
And whan he saw his time, anoon right he,
With dredful° herte and with ful humble cheere, *fear-struck*
Salued° hath his soverein lady dere. *greeted*
"My right[8] lady," quod this woful man,
"Whom I most drede and love as best I can,
And lothest were of al this world displese,
Nere it[9] that I for you have swich disese
That I moste° dien heer at youre foot anoon, *must*

7. Tables for making astrological propositions concerning planetary position, degrees of influence, etc.
8. Centers and arguments are astronomical instruments for determining the positions of planets in relation to fixed stars.
9. Fitting proportionals, i.e., special tables for scaling down more general planetary motions to the most particular.
1. Sphere: i.e., the sphere of the fixed stars.
2. He knew full well how far Alnath (the star Aries) had moved.
3. From the head of that fixed star Aries which is considered to be above, in the ninth sphere.
4. I.e., the first position of the moon.
5. He knew the remnant (rest of the positions) by the use of proportion.
6. Face and term are sectors of the signs of the zodiac.
7. I.e., to be comfortable.
8. Own true.
9. Were it not.

Nought wolde I telle how me is wo-bigoon.
But certes, outher° moste I die or plaine:° *either / complain*
Ye sleen° me giltelees for verray paine; *slay*
But of my deeth though that ye have no routhe,° *pity*
Aviseth you[1] er that ye breke youre trouthe.
Repenteth you, for thilke God above,
Er ye me sleen° by cause that I you love. *slay*
For Madame, wel ye woot what ye han hight°— *promised*
Not that I chalenge any thing of right
Of you, my soverein lady, but youre grace:
But in a gardin yond at swich a place,
Ye woot right wel what ye bihighten° me, *promised*
And in myn hand youre trouthe plighten ye
To love me best. God woot ye saiden so,
Al° be that I unworthy am therto. *although*
Madame, I speke it for the honour of you
More than to save myn hertes lif right now.
I have do so as ye comanded me,
And if ye vouche sauf, ye may go see.
Dooth as you list, have youre biheeste° in minde, *promise*
For quik° or deed° right ther ye shal me finde. *living / dead*
In you lith° al to do° me live or deye: *lies / cause*
But wel I woot the rokkes been awaye."
He taketh his leve and she astoned° stood: *astonished*
In al hir face nas a drope of blood;
She wende° nevere have come in swich a trappe. *thought*
"Allas," quod she, "that evere this sholde happe!
For wende I nevere by possibilitee
That swich a monstre° or merveile mighte be; *wonder*
It is agains the proces[2] of nature."
And hoom she gooth a sorweful creature.
For verray fere unnethe° may she go.° *scarcely / walk*
She weepeth, waileth al a day or two,
And swouneth° that it routhe° was to see. *swoons / pity*
But why it was to no wight tolde she,
For out of town was goon Arveragus.
But to hirself she spak and saide thus,
With face pale and with ful sorweful cheere,° *countenance*
In hir complainte, as ye shal after heere:
"Allas," quod she, "on thee, Fortune, I plaine,° *complain*
That unwar° wrapped hast me in thy chaine, *unawares*
For which t' escape woot I no socour°— *help*
Save only deeth or dishonour:
Oon of thise two bihoveth me to chese.° *choose*
But nathelees yit have I levere to lese° *lose*
My lif, than of my body to have a shame,
Or knowen myselven fals or lese my name,

1. Consider.
2. Due course.

And with my deeth I may be quit,[3] ywis.
Hath ther nat many a noble wif er this,
And many a maide, yslain hirself, allas,
Rather than with hir body doon trespas?° *sin*
Yis, certes, lo, thise stories beren witnesse:
Whan thritty tyrants ful of cursednesse° *wickedness*
Hadde slain Phidon[4] in Atthenes atte feeste,
They comanded his doughtren for t'arreste,
And bringen hem biforn hem in despit° *scorn*
Al naked, to fulfille hir foule delit,
And in hir fadres blood they made hem daunce
Upon the pavement—God yive hem meschaunce!
For which thise woful maidens, ful of drede,
Rather than they wolde lese° hir maidenhede, *lose*
They prively been stert[5] into a welle,
And dreinte° hemselven, as the bookes telle. *drowned*
They of Messene lete enquere and seeke[6]
Of Lacedomye° fifty maidens eke, *Lacedaemonia*
On whiche they wolden doon hir lecherye;
But ther was noon of al that compaignye
That she nas slain, and with a good entente
Chees° rather for to die than assente *chose*
To been oppressed° of hir maidenhede: *ravished*
Why sholde I thanne to die been in drede?
Lo, eek, the tyrant Aristoclides
That loved a maiden highte Stymphalides,° *Stymphalis*
Whan that hir fader slain was on a night,
Unto Dianes temple gooth she aright,
And hente° the image in hir handes two; *seized*
Fro which image wolde she nevere go:
No wight ne mighte hir handes of it arace,° *tear*
Til she was slain right in the selve° place. *same*
Now sith° that maidens hadden swich despit° *since / indignation*
To been defouled with mannes foul delit,
Wel ought a wif rather hirselven slee° *slay*
Than be defouled, as it thinketh me.
What shal I sayn of Hasdrubales wif
That at Cartage birafte[7] hirself hir lif?
For whan she saw that Romains wan° the town, *won*
She took hir children alle and skipte adown
Into the fir, and chees rather to die
Than any Romain dide hire vilainye.
Hath nat Lucrece yslain hirself, allas,

3. Freed from dilemma.
4. The story of Phidon's daughters and the thirty tyrants, as well as all the following stories about virtuous women, are from St. Jerome's tract against Jovinian.
5. Have jumped.
6. Had inquiries and searches made.
7. Deprived; Hasdrubal was King of Carthage when it was destroyed by the Romans.

At Rome whan that she oppressed° was — *raped*
Of° Tarquin, for hire thoughte it was a shame — *by*
To liven whan that she hadde lost hir name?
The sevene maidens of Milesie° also — *Miletus*
Han slain hemself for verray drede and wo
Rather than folk of Gaule hem sholde oppresse:
Mo° than a thousand stories, as I gesse, — *more*
Coude I now telle as touching this matere.
Whan Habradate° was slain, his wif so dere — *Abradates*
Hirselven slow,° and leet hir blood to glide — *slew*
In Habradates woundes deepe and wide,
And saide, 'My body at the leeste way
Ther shal no wight defoulen, if I may.'[8]
What sholde I mo ensamples° herof sayn? — *examples*
Sith° that so manye han hemselven slain — *since*
Wel rather than they wolde defouled be,
I wol conclude that it is bet° for me — *better*
To sleen° myself than been defouled thus: — *slay*
I wol be trewe unto Arveragus,
Or rather slee myself in som manere—
As dide Demociones° doughter dere, — *Demotion's*
By cause that she wolde nat defouled be.
O Cedasus,° it is ful greet pitee — *Scedasus*
To reden how thy doughtren deide, allas,
That slowe hemself for[9] swich manere cas.
As greet a pitee was it, or wel moor,
The Theban maiden that for Nichanor° — *Nicanor*
Hirselven slow right for swich manere wo.
Another Theban maiden dide right so:
For oon of Macedonie hadde hire oppressed,
She with hir deeth hir maidenhede redressed.[1]
What shal I sayn of Nicerates wif
That for swich caas birafte hirself hir lif?
How trewe eek was to Alcebiades[2]
His love, that rather for to dien chees° — *chose*
Than for to suffre his body unburied be.
Lo, which a wif was Alceste,"[3] quod she.
"What saith Omer[4] of goode Penolopee?
Al Greece knoweth of hir chastitee.
Pardee, of Laodomia[5] is writen thus,
That whan at Troye was slain Protheselaus,

8. If I can help it.
9. I.e., for fear of.
1. Made amends for.
2. Alcibiades' mistress risked death by burying his body after he had been decapitated by the Spartan Lysander; she did not, however, lose her life as a result.
3. Alcestis, the proposed heroine of Chaucer's *Legend of Good Women,* died in her husband's place.
4. Homer relates Odysseus' return from Troy to his faithful wife Penelope.
5. Lacodamia followed her dead husband Proteslaus to the underworld.

No lenger wolde she live after his day.
  The same of noble Porcia[6] telle I may:
Withoute Brutus coude she nat live,
To whom she hadde al hool° hir herte yive. *whole*
  The parfit wifhood of Arthemesie[7]
Honoured is thurgh al the Barbarye.
  O Teuta[8] queen, thy wifly chastitee
To alle wives may a mirour be!
  The same thing I saye of Biliea,
Of Rodogone, and eek Valeria."[9]
Thus plained° Dorigen a day or twaye, *lamented*
Purposing evere that she wolde deye.
  But nathelees upon the thridde night
Hoom cam Arveragus, this worthy knight,
And axed° hire why that she weep° so sore, *asked / wept*
And she gan weepen evere lenger the more.[1]
  "Allas," quod she, "that evere I was born:
Thus have I said," quod she; "thus have I sworn—"
And tolle him al as ye han herd bifore:
It needeth nat reherce it you namore.
  This housbonde with glad cheer° in freendly wise *manner*
Answerde and saide as I shal you devise:
  "Is there ought elles, Dorigen, but this?"
  "Nay, nay," quod she, "God help me so as wis,° *surely*
This is too muche, and° it were Goddes wille." *if*
  "Ye, wif," quod he, "lat sleepen that° is stille. *what*
It may be wel paraunter° yit today. *perhaps*
Ye shul youre trouthe[2] holden, by my fay,° *faith*
For God so wisly° have mercy upon me, *surely*
I hadde wel levere ystiked° for to be, *stabbed*
For verray love which that I to you have,
But if[3] ye sholde youre trouthe keepe and save:
Trouthe is the hyeste thing[4] that man may keepe."
But with that word he brast° anoon to weepe, *burst*
And saide, "I you forbede, up° paine of deeth, *upon*
That nevere whil thee lasteth lif ne breeth,
To no wight tel thou of this aventure.
As I may best I wol my wo endure,
Ne make no countenance° of hevinesse, *appearance*
That folk of you may deemen° harm or gesse." *suspect*

6. Portia swallowed burning coals on learning of Brutus' death at the battle of Philippi.
7. Artemesia built for her husband King Mausolus the famed tomb called the Mausoleum.
8. Teuta, Queen of Illyria, was unmarried: Dorigen seems to be stretching a point.
9. Bilia's prowess seems to have consisted in enduring her husband's bad breath in uncomplaining silence; Rhodogune slew her nurse, who suggested that she remarry; Valeria refused to marry again.
1. Always more and more.
2. Pledged word.
3. Unless.
4. Legal bond.

And forth he cleped° a squier and a maide: *called*
"Go forth anoon with Dorigen," he saide,
"And bringeth hire to swich a place anoon."
They tooke hir leve and on hir way they goon,
But they ne wiste° why they thider wente: *knew*
He nolde no wight tellen his entente.
Paraventure an heep of you, ywis,° *indeed*
Wol holden him a lewed° man in this, *stupid*
That he wol putte his wif in jupartye.° *jeopardy*
Herkneth the tale er ye upon hire crye:
She may have better fortune than you seemeth,[5]
And whan that ye han herd the tale, deemeth.° *judge*
This squier which that highte Aurelius,
On Dorigen that was so amorous,
Of aventure[6] happed° hire to meete *happened*
Amidde the town, right in the quikkest° streete, *busiest*
As she was boun° to goon the way forth right° *prepared / direct*
Toward the gardin ther as she hadde hight;° *promised*
And he was to the gardinward also,
For wel he spied whan she wolde go
Out of hir hous to any manere place.
But thus they meete of aventure or grace,
And he salueth° hire with glad entente, *greets*
And axed° of hire whiderward she wente. *asked*
And she answerde half as she were mad,
"Unto the gardin as myn housbonde bad,° *bade*
My trouthe for to holde, allas, allas!"
Aurelius gan wondren on this cas,
And in his herte hadde greet compassioun
Of hire and of hir lamentacioun,
And of Arveragus, the worthy knight,
That bad hire holden al that she hadde hight,
So loth him was his wif sholde breke hir trouthe;
And in his herte he caughte of this greet routhe,° *pity*
Considering the beste on every side
That fro his lust° yit were him levere abide[7] *pleasure*
Than doon so heigh a cherlissh wrecchednesse[8]
Agains franchise° and alle gentilesse; *generosity*
For which in fewe wordes saide he thus:
"Madame, sayeth to youre lord Arveragus
That sith° I see his grete gentilesse *since*
To you, and eek I see wel youre distresse,
That him were levere han shame—and that were routhe—
Than ye to me sholde breke thus youre trouthe,
I have wel levere[9] evere to suffre wo

5. It seems.
6. By chance.
7. I.e., abstain.
8. I.e., low-born, miserable act.
9. Had much rather.

Than I departe° the love bitwixe you two. *divide*
I you releesse, Madame, into youre hond,
Quit every serement° and every bond *oath*
That ye han maad to me as herbiforn,
Sith° thilke time which that ye were born. *since*
My trouthe I plighte, I shal you nevere repreve° *reproach*
Of no biheeste.° And here I take my leve, *promise*
As of the treweste and the beste wif
That evere yit I knew in al my lif.
But every wif be war of hir biheeste:
On Dorigen remembreth at the leeste.
Thus can a squier doon a gentil deede
As wel as can a knight, withouten drede."° *doubt*
She thanketh him upon hir knees al bare,
And hoom unto hir housbonde is she fare,
And tolde him al as ye han herd me said.
And be ye siker,° he was so wel apaid° *sure / pleased*
That it were impossible me to write.
What sholde I lenger of this caas endite?
  Arveragus and Dorigen his wif
In soverein blisse leden forth hir lif.
Never eft° ne was ther angre hem bitweene: *again*
He cherisseth hire as though she were a queene,
And she was to him trewe of everemore.
Of thise two folk ye gete of me namore.
  Aurelius, that his cost hath al forlorn,° *lost*
Curseth the time that evere he was born.
"Allas," quod he, "allas that I bihighte° *promised*
Of pured° gold a thousand pound of wighte° *refined / weight*
Unto this philosophre. How shall I do?
I see namore but that I am fordo.° *ruined*
Myn heritage moot° I needes selle *must*
And been a beggere. Here may I nat dwelle,
And shamen al my kinrede° in this place, *kindred*
But° I of him may gete bettre grace. *unless*
But nathelees I wol of him assaye
At certain dayes yeer by yere to paye,
And thanke him of his grete curteisye:
My trouthe wol I keepe, I nil nat lie."
  With herte soor he gooth unto his cofre,
And broughte gold unto this philosophre
The value of five hundred pound, I gesse,
And him biseecheth of his gentilesse
To graunten him dayes[1] of the remenaunt,° *remainder*
And saide, "Maister, I dar wel make avaunt° *boast*
I failed nevere of my trouthe as yit,
For sikerly° my dette shal be quit *surely*

1. I.e., extended terms.

Towardes you, how evere that I fare,
To goon abegged° in my kirtel° bare. *abegging / undergarment*
But wolde ye vouche sauf upon suretee° *security*
Two yeer or three for to respiten[2] me,
Thanne were I wel, for elles moot° I selle *must*
Myn heritage: ther is namore to telle."
This philosophre sobrely answerde,
And saide thus, whan he thise wordes herde,
"Have I nat holden covenant unto thee?"
"Yis, certes, wel and trewely," quod he.
"Hastou nat had thy lady as thee liketh?"[3]
"No, no," quod he and sorwefully he siketh.° *sighs*
"What was the cause? Tel me if thou can."
Aurelius his tale anoon bigan,
And tolde him al as ye han herd bifore:
It needeth nat to you reherce it more.
He saide, "Arveragus, of gentilesse,
Hadde levere die in sorwe and in distresse
Than that his wif were on hir trouthe fals."
The sorwe of Dorigen he tolde him als,° *also*
How loth hire was to been a wikked wif,
And that she levere hadde lost that day hir lif,
And that hir trouthe she swoor thurgh innocence:
She nevere erst° hadde herd speke of apparence.° *before / illusion*
"That made me han of hire so greet pitee;
And right as freely° as he sente hire me, *generously*
As freely sente I hire to him again:
This al and som,[4] ther is namore to sayn."
This philosophre answerde, "Leve° brother, *dear*
Everich of you dide gentilly to other.
Thou art a squier, and he is a knight:
But God forbede, for his blisful might,
But if a clerk coude doon a gentil deede
As wel as any of you, it is no drede.° *doubt*
Sire, I releesse thee thy thousand pound,
As thou right now were cropen out of the ground,[5]
Ne nevere er° now ne haddest knowen me. *before*
For sire, I wol nat take a peny of thee,
For al my craft° ne nought for my travaile.° *art / labor*
Thou hast ypayed wel for my vitaile:° *food*
It is ynough. And farewel, have good day."
And took his hors and forth he gooth his way.
Lordinges, this question thanne wol I axe now:
Which was the moste free,° as thinketh you? *generous*
Now telleth me, er that ye ferther wende.
I can namore: my tale is at an ende.

2. Give respite.
3. It pleases.
4. This is all there is to it.
5. Had crept.

The Pardoner's Prologue and Tale[1]

The Introduction

Oure Hoste gan to swere as he were wood;° *insane*
"Harrow,"° quod he, "by nailes[2] and by blood, *help*

1. The Pardoner is the chief actor in a grim comedy which shows how a clever hypocrite exploits Christian principles in order to enrich himself—and which, in the Epilogue, suggests that the exploiter of Christian principles is not immune to their operation. The medieval pardoner's function was to collect money for charitable enterprises supported by branches of the church and to act as the Pope's agent in rewarding donors with some temporal remission of their sins. According to theological doctrine, St. Peter—and through him his papal successors—received from Christ the power to make a gift of mercy from God's infinite treasury to those of the faithful that had earned special favor, such as contributors to charity. The charitable enterprises themselves—generally hospitals—hired pardoners to raise money, but the pardoners had also to be licensed by the Pope to pass on to contributors the papal indulgence. By canon law pardoners were permitted to work only in a prescribed area; within that area they might visit churches during Sunday service, briefly explain their mission, receive contributions, and, in the Pope's name, issue indulgence, which was considered not a sale, but a free gift made in return for a free gift. In actual fact pardoners seem seldom to have behaved as the law required them. Since a parish priest was forbidden to exclude properly licensed pardoners, they made their way into churches at will, and once there did not confine themselves to a mere statement of their business, but rather, in order to make the congregation free of its gifts, preached highly emotive sermons and boasted of the extraordinary efficacy of their own particular pardon, claiming for it powers that not even the Pope could have invested it with. An honest pardoner, if such existed, was entitled to a percentage of his collections; dishonest pardoners took more than their share, and some took everything; indeed, some were complete frauds, bearing forged credentials which, in an age when even clerical illiteracy was common, were no less impressive than if they had been real.

While Chaucer's Pardoner belongs, as he boastfully tells us, to the most dishonest class of fund-gatherers, he is an extremely able one. His text is always the same: *Radix malorum est cupiditas*, "The love of money is the root of all evil," and he uses it most effectively in order to frighten his hearers into a generosity that will fulfill his own cupidity. The Pardoner's audacious description of his behavior in a parish church is followed by a sample sermon on his invariable text. Aware that his audience is more interested in narrative than in the moralization one expects of a sermon he first introduces the three dissolute young men of his *exemplum*, that is, of the story which is to illustrate concretely the sermon's point. Having titillated his hearers with the promise of a lurid story, he proceeds to the moralization; curiously enough, this does not concern the sin of avarice, but drunkenness, gluttony, lechery, gambling, and cursing. Yet the apparent lack of logic serves the Pardoner's deeper purpose, for these are the sins people find it exciting to hear about. When his audience has thus been emotionally prepared by a discussion of the debauchees' more flamboyant sins, the Pardoner tells his *exemplum* of the destructiveness of avarice, shutting it off at the moment of highest interest, and concluding with a demand to the congregation for money in return for his pardon.

The story of the young men who seek Death only to find him in a treasure that had made them forget him is a masterpiece of irony, and indeed the Pardoner is in all ways a master ironist. So highly developed is his own sense of irony that it enables him to feel superior not only to other men but to God, for he dares to exempt himself from the effect of his Christian text. Yet the brief Epilogue seems to show that God's irony, like His other attributes, is supreme. The one fact that the Pardoner's candid confession has concealed—that it was perhaps spoken in order to conceal—is that he is a eunuch. When in the Epilogue his proud avarice leads him to see if he can get money from the pilgrims to whom he has revealed his hypocrisy, the Pardoner's secret is revealed by the Host's coarse response, and the verbal facility by which he maintains his superiority fails him.

2. I.e., God's nails.

This was a fals cherl and a fals justise.[3]
As shameful deeth as herte may devise
Come to thise juges and hir advocats.
Algate° this sely° maide is slain, allas! *at any rate / innocent*
Allas, too dere boughte she beautee!
Wherfore I saye alday° that men may see *always*
The yiftes of Fortune and of Nature
Been cause of deeth to many a creature.
As bothe yiftes that I speke of now,
Men han ful ofte more for harm than prow.° *benefit*
"But trewely, myn owene maister dere,
This is a pitous tale for to heere.
But natheless, passe over, is no fors:[4]
I praye to God so save thy gentil cors,° *body*
And eek thine urinals and thy jurdones,[5]
Thyn ipocras[6] and eek thy galiones,
And every boiste° ful of thy letuarye°— *box / medicine*
God blesse hem, and oure lady Sainte Marye.
So mote I theen,[7] thou art a propre man,
And lik a prelat, by Saint Ronian![8]
Saide I nat wel? I can nat speke in terme.[9]
But wel I woot, thou doost° myn herte to erme° *make / grieve*
That I almost have caught a cardinacle.[1]
By corpus bones,[2] but if I have triacle,° *medicine*
Or elles a draughte of moiste° and corny° ale, *fresh / malty*
Or but I heere anoon° a merye tale, *at once*
Myn herte is lost for pitee of this maide.
"Thou bel ami,[3] thou Pardoner," he saide,
"Tel us som mirthe or japes° right anoon." *joke*
"It shal be doon," quod he, "by Saint Ronion.
But first," quod he, "here at this ale-stake[4]
I wol bothe drinke and eten of a cake."
And right anoon thise gentils gan to crye,
"Nay, lat him telle us of no ribaudye.° *ribaldry*
Tel us som moral thing that we may lere,° *learn*
Som wit,[5] and thanne wol we gladly heere."
"I graunte, ywis," quod he, "but I moot thinke
Upon som honeste° thing whil that I drinke." *decent*

3. The Host has been affected by the Physician's sad tale of the Roman maiden Virginia, whose great beauty caused a judge to attempt to obtain her person by means of a trumped-up lawsuit in which he connived with a "churl" who claimed her as his slave; in order to preserve her chastity, her father killed her.
4. I.e., never mind.
5. Jordans (chamber pots): the Host is somewhat confused in his endeavor to use technical medical terms.
6. A medicinal drink named after Hippocrates; "galiones": a medicine, probably invented on the spot by the Host, named after Galen.
7. So might I thrive.
8. St. Ronan or St. Ninian, with a possible play on "runnion" (sexual organ).
9. Speak in technical idiom.
1. Apparently a cardiac condition, confused in the Host's mind with a cardinal.
2. An illiterate oath, mixing "God's bones" with *corpus dei*. "But if": unless.
3. Fair friend.
4. Sign of a tavern.
5. I.e., something with significance.

The Prologue

Lordinges—quod he—in chirches whan I preche,
I paine me[6] to han an hautein° speeche, *loud*
And ringe it out as round as gooth a belle,
For I can al by rote[7] that I telle.
My theme is alway oon,[8] and evere was:
Radix malorum est cupiditas.[9]
First I pronounce whennes° that I come, *whence*
And thanne my bulles[1] shewe I alle and some:
Oure lige lordes seel on my patente,[2]
That shewe I first, my body to warente,° *keep safe*
That no man be so bold, ne preest ne clerk,
Me to destourbe of Cristes holy werk.
And after that thanne telle I forth my tales[3]—
Bulles of popes and of cardinales,
Of patriarkes and bisshopes I shewe,
And in Latin I speke a wordes fewe,
To saffron with[4] my predicacioun,° *preaching*
And for to stire hem to devocioun.
Thanne shewe I forth my longe crystal stones,° *jars*
Ycrammed ful of cloutes° and of bones— *rags*
Relikes been they, as weenen° they eechoon. *suppose*
Thanne have I in laton° a shulder-boon *zinc*
Which that was of an holy Jewes sheep.
"Goode men," I saye, "take of my wordes keep:° *notice*
If that this boon be wasshe in any welle,
If cow, or calf, or sheep, or oxe swelle,
That any worm hath ete or worm ystonge,[5]
Take water of that welle and wassh his tonge,
And it is hool[6] anoon. And ferthermoor,
Of pokkes° and of scabbe and every soor° *pox / sore*
Shal every sheep be hool that of this welle
Drinketh a draughte. Take keep eek° that I telle: *also*
If that the goode man that the beestes oweth° *owns*
Wol every wike,° er that the cok him croweth, *week*
Fasting drinken of this welle a draughte—
As thilke° holy Jew oure eldres taughte— *that same*
His beestes and his stoor° shal multiplye. *stock*
"And sire, also it heleth jalousye:
For though a man be falle in jalous rage,
Lat maken with this water his potage,° *soup*
And nevere shal he more his wif mistriste,° *mistrust*

6. Take pains.
7. I know all by heart.
8. I.e., the same.
9. Avarice is the root of evil (I Timothy vi.10).
1. Episcopal mandates; "alle and some": each and every one.
2. I.e., the Pope's seal on my papal license.
3. I go on with my yarn.
4. To add spice to.
5. That has eaten or been bitten by any worm.
6. I.e., sound.

Though he the soothe of hir defaute wiste,[7]
Al hadde she[8] taken preestes two or three.
"Here is a mitein° eek that ye may see: *mitten*
He that his hand wol putte in this mitein
He shal have multiplying of his grain,
Whan he hath sowen, be it whete or otes—
So that he offre pens or elles grotes.[9]
"Goode men and wommen, oo thing warne I you:
If any wight be in this chirche now
That hath doon sinne horrible, that he
Dar nat for shame of it yshriven° be, *absolved*
Or any womman, be she yong or old,
That hath ymaked hir housbonde cokewold,° *cuckold*
Swich folk shal have no power ne no grace
To offren to[1] my relikes in this place;
And whoso findeth him out of swich blame,
He wol come up and offre in Goddes name,
And I assoile° him by the auctoritee *absolve*
Which that by bulle ygraunted was to me."
By this gaude° have I wonne, yeer by yeer, *trick*
An hundred mark[2] sith° I was pardoner. *since*
I stonde lik a clerk in my pulpet,
And whan the lewed° peple is down yset, *ignorant*
I preche so as ye han herd bifore,
And telle an hundred false japes° more. *tricks*
Thanne paine I me[3] to strecche forth the nekke,
And eest and west upon the peple I bekke[4]
As dooth a douve,° sitting on a berne;° *dove / barn*
Mine handes and my tonge goon so yerne° *fast*
That it is joye to see my bisinesse.
Of avarice and of swich cursednesse° *sin*
Is al my preching, for to make hem free° *generous*
To yiven hir pens, and namely° unto me, *especially*
For myn entente is nat but for to winne,[5]
And no thing for correccion of sinne:
I rekke° nevere whan that they been beried° *care / buried*
Though that hir soules goon a-blakeberied.[6]
For certes, many a predicacioun° *sermon*
Comth ofte time of yvel entencioun:
Som for plesance of folk and flaterye,
To been avaunced° by ypocrisye, *promoted*
And som for vaine glorye, and som for hate;
For whan I dar noon otherways debate,° *fight*
Thanne wol I stinge him with my tonge smerte
In preching, so that he shal nat asterte° *escape*
To been defamed falsly, if that he

7. Knew the truth of her infidelity.
8. Even if she had.
9. Pennies, groats, coins.
1. To make gifts in reverence of.
2. Marks (pecuniary units).
3. I take pains.
4. I.e., I shake my head.
5. Only to gain.
6. Go blackberrying, i.e., go to hell.

Hath trespassed to[7] my bretheren or to me.
For though I telle nought his propre name,
Men shal wel knowe that it is the same
By signes and by othere circumstaunces.
Thus quite° I folk that doon us displesaunces;[8] *pay back*
Thus spete° I out my venim under hewe° *spit / color*
Of holinesse, to seeme holy and trewe.
But shortly myn entente I wol devise:° *describe*
I preche of no thing but for coveitise;
Therfore my theme is yit and evere was
Radix malorum est cupiditas.
　Thus can I preche again that same vice
Which that I use, and that is avarice.
But though myself be gilty in that sinne,
Yit can I make other folk to twinne° *separate*
From avarice, and sore to repente—
But that is nat my principal entente:
I preche no thing but for coveitise.
Of this matere it oughte ynough suffise.
　Thanne telle I hem ensamples[9] many oon
Of olde stories longe time agoon,
For lewed° peple loven tales olde— *ignorant*
Swiche thinges can they wel reporte and holde.[1]
What, trowe° ye that whiles I may preche, *believe*
And winne gold and silver for° I teche, *because*
That I wol live in poverte wilfully?
Nay, nay, I thoughte° it nevere, trewely, *intended*
For I wol preche and begge in sondry landes;
I wol nat do no labour with mine handes,
Ne make baskettes and live therby,
By cause I wol nat beggen idelly.[2]
I wol none of the Apostles countrefete:° *imitate*
I wol have moneye, wolle,° cheese, and whete, *wool*
Al were it[3] yiven of the pooreste page,
Or of the pooreste widwe in a village—
Al sholde hir children sterve[4] for famine.
Nay, I wol drinke licour of the vine
And have a joly wenche in every town.
But herkneth, lordinges, in conclusioun,
Youre liking° is that I shal telle a tale: *pleasure*
Now have I dronke a draughte of corny ale,
By God, I hope I shal you telle a thing
That shal by reson been at youre liking;
For though myself be a ful vicious man,
A moral tale yit I you telle can,
Which I am wont to preche for to winne.
Now holde youre pees, my tale I wol biginne.

7. Injured.
8. Do us discourtesies.
9. *Exempla* (stories illustrating moral principles).
1. Repeat and remember.
2. I.e., without profit.
3. Even though it were.
4. Even though her children should die.

The Tale

In Flandres whilom° was a compaignye *once*
Of yonge folk that haunteden° folye— *practiced*
As riot, hasard, stewes,[5] and tavernes,
Wher as with harpes, lutes, and gifternes° *guitars*
They daunce and playen at dees° bothe day and night, *dice*
And ete also and drinke over hir might,[6]
Thurgh which they doon the devel sacrifise
Within that develes temple in cursed wise
By superfluitee° abhominable. *overindulgence*
Hir othes been so grete and so dampnable
That it is grisly for to heere hem swere:
Oure blessed Lordes body they totere[7]—
Hem thoughte that Jewes rente° him nought ynough. *tore*
And eech of hem at otheres sinne lough.° *laughed*
And right anoon thanne comen tombesteres,° *dancing girls*
Fetis° and smale,° and yonge frutesteres,[8] *shapely / neat*
Singeres with harpes, bawdes,° wafereres[9]— *pimps*
Whiche been the verray develes officeres,
To kindle and blowe the fir of lecherye
That is annexed unto glotonye:[1]
The Holy Writ take I to my witnesse
That luxure° is in win and dronkenesse. *lechery*
Lo, how that dronken Lot[2] unkindely° *unnaturally*
Lay by his doughtres two unwitingly:
So dronke he was he niste° what he wroughte. *didn't know*
Herodes, who so wel the stories soughte,[3]
Whan he of win was repleet at his feeste,
Right at his owene table he yaf his heeste° *command*
To sleen° the Baptist John, ful giltelees. *slay*
Senek[4] saith a good word doutelees:
He saith he can no difference finde
Bitwixe a man that is out of his minde
And a man which that is dronkelewe,° *drunken*
But that woodnesse, yfallen in a shrewe,[5]
Persevereth lenger than dooth dronkenesse.
O glotonye, ful of cursednesse!° *wickedness*
O cause first of oure confusioun!° *downfall*
O original of oure dampnacioun,° *damnation*
Til Crist hadde bought° us with his blood again! *redeemed*
Lo, how dere, shortly for to sayn,
Abought° was thilke° cursed vilainye; *paid for / that same*
Corrupt was al this world for glotonye:

5. Wild parties, gambling, brothels.
6. Beyond their capacity.
7. Tear apart (a reference to oaths sworn by parts of His body, such as "God's bones!" or "God's teeth!").
8. Fruit-selling girls.
9. Girl cake-vendors.
1. I.e., closely related to gluttony.
2. For Lot, see Genesis xix.30–36.
3. For the story of Herod and St. John the Baptist, see Mark vi.17–29. "Who so * * * soughte": i.e., whoever looked it up in the Gospel would find.
4. Seneca, the Roman Stoic philosopher.
5. But that madness, occurring in a wicked man.

Adam oure fader and his wif also
Fro Paradis to labour and to wo
Were driven for that vice, it is no drede.° *doubt*
For whil that Adam fasted, as I rede,
He was in Paradis; and whan that he
Eet° of the fruit defended° on a tree, *ate / forbidden*
Anoon he was out cast to wo and paine.
O glotonye, on thee wel oughte us plaine!° *complain*
O, wiste a man[6] how manye maladies
Folwen of excesse and of glotonies,
He wolde been the more mesurable° *moderate*
Of his diete, sitting at his table.
Allas, the shorte throte, the tendre mouth,
Maketh that eest and west and north and south,
In erthe, in air, in water, men to swinke,° *work*
To gete a gloton daintee mete and drinke.
Of this matere, O Paul, wel canstou trete:
"Mete unto wombe,° and wombe eek unto mete, *belly*
Shal God destroyen bothe," as Paulus saith.[7]
Allas, a foul thing is it, by my faith,
To saye this word, and fouler is the deede
Whan man so drinketh of the white and rede[8]
That of his throte he maketh his privee° *privy*
Thurgh thilke cursed superfluitee.° *overindulgence*
The Apostle[9] weeping saith ful pitously,
"Ther walken manye of which you told have I—
I saye it now weeping with pitous vois—
They been enemies of Cristes crois,° *cross*
Of whiche the ende is deeth—wombe is hir god!"[1]
O wombe, O bely, O stinking cod,° *bag*
Fulfilled° of dong° and of corrupcioun! *filled full / dung*
At either ende of thee foul is the soun.° *sound*
How greet labour and cost is thee to finde!° *provide for*
Thise cookes, how they stampe[2] and straine and grinde,
And turnen substance into accident[3]
To fulfillen al thy likerous° talent!° *dainty / appetite*
Out of the harde bones knokke they
The mary,° for they caste nought away *marrow*
That may go thurgh the golet[4] softe and soote.° *sweetly*
Of spicerye° of leef and bark and roote *spices*
Shal been his sauce ymaked by delit,
To make him yit a newer appetit.
But certes, he that haunteth swiche delices° *pleasures*
Is deed° whil that he liveth in tho° vices. *dead / those*
A lecherous thing is win, and dronkenesse

6. If a man knew.
7. See I Corinthians vi.13.
8. I.e., white and red wines.
9. I.e., St. Paul.
1. See Philippians iii.18.
2. Pound.
3. A philosophic joke, depending on the distinction between inner reality (substance) and outward appearance (accident).
4. Through the gullet.

Is ful of striving° and of wrecchednesse. *quarreling*
O dronke man, disfigured is thy face!
Sour is thy breeth, foul artou to embrace!
And thurgh thy dronke nose seemeth the soun
As though thou saidest ay,° "Sampsoun, Sampsoun." *always*
And yit, God woot,° Sampson drank nevere win.[5] *knows*
Thou fallest as it were a stiked swin;[6]
Thy tonge is lost, and al thyn honeste cure,
For dronkenesse is verray sepulture° *burial*
Of mannes wit° and his discrecioun. *intelligence*
In whom that drinke hath dominacioun
He can no conseil° keepe, it is no drede.° *secrets / doubt*
Now keepe you fro the white and fro the rede—
And namely° fro the white win of Lepe[7] *particularly*
That is to selle in Fisshstreete or in Chepe:[8]
The win of Spaine creepeth subtilly
In othere wines growing faste° by, *close*
Of which ther riseth swich fumositee° *heady fumes*
That whan a man hath dronken draughtes three
And weeneth° that he be at hoom in Chepe, *supposes*
He is in Spaine, right at the town of Lepe,
Nat at The Rochele ne at Burdeux town;[9]
And thanne wol he sayn, "Sampsoun, Sampsoun."
  But herkneth, lordinges, oo° word I you praye, *one*
That alle the sovereín actes,[1] dar I saye,
Of victories in the Olde Testament,
Thurgh verray God that is omnipotent,
Were doon in abstinence and in prayere:
Looketh° the Bible and ther ye may it lere.° *behold / learn*
  Looke Attila, the grete conquerour,[2]
Deide° in his sleep with shame and dishonour, *died*
Bleeding at his nose in dronkenesse:
A capitain sholde live in sobrenesse.
  And overal this, aviseth you[3] right wel
What was comanded unto Lamuel[4]—
Nat Samuel, but Lamuel, saye I—
Redeth the Bible and finde it expresly,
Of win-yiving° to hem that han[5] justise: *wine-serving*
Namore of this, for it may wel suffise.
  And now that I have spoken of glotonye,
Now wol I you defende° hasardrye:° *prohibit / gambling*
Hasard is verray moder° of lesinges,° *mother / lies*

5. Before Samson's birth an angel told his mother that he would be a Nazarite throughout his life; members of this sect took no strong drink.
6. Stuck pig. "Honeste cure": care for self-respect.
7. A town in Spain.
8. Fishstreet and Cheapside in the London market district.
9. The Pardoner is joking about the illegal custom of adulterating fine wines of Bordeaux and La Rochelle with strong Spanish wine.
1. Distinguished deeds.
2. Attila was the leader of the Huns who captured Rome in the 5th century.
3. Consider.
4. Lemuel's mother told him that kings should not drink (Proverbs xxxi.4–5).
5. I.e., administer.

And of deceite and cursed forsweringes,
Blaspheme of Crist, manslaughtre, and wast° also — *waste*
Of catel° and of time; and ferthermo, — *property*
It is repreve° and contrarye of honour — *disgrace*
For to been holden a commune hasardour,° — *gambler*
And evere the hyer he is of estat
The more is he holden desolat.[6]
If that a prince useth hasardrye,
In alle governance and policye
He is, as by commune opinioun,
Yholde the lasse° in reputacioun. — *less*
  Stilbon, that was a wis embassadour,
Was sent to Corinthe in ful greet honour
Fro Lacedomye° to make hir alliaunce, — *Sparta*
And whan he cam him happede° parchaunce — *it happened*
That alle the gretteste° that were of that lond — *greatest*
Playing at the hasard he hem foond, — *found*
For which as soone as it mighte be
He stal him[7] hoom again to his contree,
And saide, "Ther wol I nat lese° my name, — *lose*
N'I wol nat take on me so greet defame° — *dishonor*
You to allye unto none hasardours:
Sendeth othere wise embassadours,
For by my trouthe, me were levere[8] die
Than I you sholde to hasardours allye.
For ye that been so glorious in honours
Shal nat allye you with hasardours
As by my wil, ne as by my tretee."° — *treaty*
This wise philosophre, thus saide he.
  Looke eek that to the king Demetrius
The King of Parthes,° as the book[9] saith us, — *Parthians*
Sente him a paire of dees° of gold in scorn, — *dice*
For he hadde used hasard therbiforn,
For which he heeld his glorye or his renown
At no value or reputacioun.
Lordes may finden other manere play
Honeste° ynough to drive the day away. — *honorable*
  Now wol I speke of othes false and grete
A word or two, as olde bookes trete:
  Greet swering is a thing abhominable,
And fals swering is yit more reprevable.° — *reprehensible*
The hye God forbad swering at al—
Witnesse on Mathew.[1] But in special
Of swering saith the holy Jeremie,[2]
"Thou shalt swere sooth thine othes and nat lie,

6. I.e., dissolute.
7. He stole away.
8. I had rather.
9. The book that relates this and the previous incident is the *Policraticus* of the 12th-century Latin writer, John of Salisbury.
1. "But I say unto you, Swear not at all" (Matthew v.34).
2. Jeremiah (iv.2).

And swere in doom[3] and eek in rightwisnesse,
But idel swering is a cursednesse."° *wickedness*
  Biholde and see that in the firste Table[4]
Of hye Goddes heestes° honorable *commandments*
How that the seconde heeste of him is this:
"Take nat my name in idel or amis."
Lo, rather° he forbedeth swich swering *sooner*
Than homicide, or many a cursed thing.
I saye that as by ordre thus it stondeth—
This knoweth that[5] his heestes understondeth
How that the seconde heeste of God is that.
And fertherover,° I wol thee telle al plat° *moreover / flat*
That vengeance shal nat parten° from his hous *depart*
That of his othes is too outrageous.
"By Goddes precious herte!" and "By his nailes!"° *fingernails*
And "By the blood of Crist that is in Hailes,[6]
Sevene is my chaunce, and thyn is cink and traye!"[7]
"By Goddes armes, if thou falsly playe
This daggere shal thurghout thyn herte go!"
This fruit cometh of the bicche bones[8] two—
Forswering, ire, falsnesse, homicide.
Now for the love of Crist that for us dyde,
Lete° youre othes bothe grete and smale. *leave*
But sires, now wol I telle forth my tale.
  Thise riotoures° three of whiche I telle, *revelers*
Longe erst er prime[9] ronge of any belle,
Were set hem in a taverne to drinke,
And as they sat they herde a belle clinke
Biforn a cors° was caried to his grave. *corpse*
That oon of hem gan callen to his knave:° *servant*
"Go bet,"[1] quod he, "and axe° redily° *ask / promptly*
What cors is this that passeth heer forby,
And looke° that thou reporte his name weel."° *be sure / well*
  "Sire," quod this boy, "it needeth neveradeel:[2]
It was me told er ye cam heer two houres.
He was, pardee, an old felawe of youres,
And sodeinly he was yslain tonight,° *last night*
Fordronke° as he sat on his bench upright; *very drunk*
Ther cam a privee° thief men clepeth° Deeth, *stealthy / call*
That in this contree al the peple sleeth,° *slays*
And with his spere he smoot his herte atwo,
And wente his way withouten wordes mo.
He hath a thousand slain this° pestilence. *during this*
And maister, er ye come in his presence,

3. Equity; "rightwisnesse": righteousness.
4. I.e., the first four of the Ten Commandments.
5. I.e., he that.
6. An abbey in Gloucestershire supposed to possess some of Christ's blood.
7. Five and three.
8. I.e., damned dice.
9. Long before 9 A.M.
1. Better, i.e., quick.
2. It isn't a bit necessary.

Me thinketh that it were necessarye
For to be war of swich an adversarye;
Beeth redy for to meete him evermore:
Thus taughte me my dame.° I saye namore." *mother*
"By Sainte Marye," saide this taverner,
"The child saith sooth, for he hath slain this yeer,
Henne° over a mile, within a greet village, *hence*
Bothe man and womman, child and hine[3] and page.
I trowe° his habitacion be there. *believe*
To been avised° greet wisdom it were *wary*
Er that he dide a man a dishonour."
"Ye, Goddes armes," quod this riotour,
"Is it swich peril with him for to meete?
I shal him seeke by way and eek by streete,[4]
I make avow to Goddes digne° bones. *worthy*
Herkneth, felawes, we three been alle ones:° *of one mind*
Lat eech of us holde up his hand to other
And eech of us bicome otheres brother,
And we wol sleen this false traitour Deeth.
He shal be slain, he that so manye sleeth,
By Goddes dignitee, er it be night."
Togidres han thise three hir trouthes plight[5]
To live and dien eech of hem with other,
As though he were his owene ybore° brother. *born*
And up they sterte,° al dronken in this rage, *started*
And forth they goon towardes that village
Of which the taverner hadde spoke biforn.
And many a grisly ooth thanne han they sworn,
And Cristes blessed body they torente:° *tore apart*
Deeth shal be deed° if that they may him hente.° *dead / catch*
Whan they han goon nat fully half a mile,
Right as they wolde han treden° over a stile, *stepped*
An old man and a poore with hem mette;
This olde man ful mekely hem grette,° *greeted*
And saide thus, "Now lordes, God you see."[6]
The pruddeste° of thise riotoures three *proudest*
Answerde again, "What, carl° with sory grace, *churl*
Why artou al forwrapped save thy face?
Why livestou so longe in so greet age?"
This olde man gan looke in his visage,
And saide thus, "For° I ne can nat finde *because*
A man, though that I walked into Inde,
Neither in citee ne in no village,
That wolde chaunge his youthe for myn age;
And therfore moot I han myn age stille,
As longe time as it is Goddes wille.
"Ne Deeth, allas, ne wol nat have my lif.
Thus walke I lik a restelees caitif,° *captive*

3. Farm laborer.
4. By highway and byway.
5. Pledged their words of honor.
6. May God protect you.

And on the ground which is my modres° gate *mother's*
I knokke with my staf bothe erly and late,
And saye, 'Leve° moder, leet me in: *dear*
Lo, how I vanisshe, flessh and blood and skin.
Allas, whan shal my bones been at reste?
Moder, with you wolde I chaunge° my cheste[7] *exchange*
That in my chambre longe time hath be,
Ye, for an haire-clout[8] to wrappe me.'
But yit to me she wol nat do that grace,
For which ful pale and welked° is my face. *withered*
But sires, to you it is no curteisye
To speken to an old man vilainye,° *rudeness*
But° he trespasse° in word or elles in deede. *unless / offend*
In Holy Writ ye may yourself wel rede,
'Agains[9] an old man, hoor° upon his heed, *hoar*
Ye shal arise.'[1] Wherfore I yive you reed,° *advice*
Ne dooth unto an old man noon harm now,
Namore than that ye wolde men dide to you
In age, if that ye so longe abide.
And God be with you wher ye go° or ride: *walk*
I moot go thider as I have to go."
"Nay, olde cherl, by God thou shalt nat so,"
Saide this other hasardour anoon.
"Thou partest nat so lightly,° by Saint John! *easily*
Thou speke° right now of thilke traitour Deeth, *spoke*
That in this contree alle oure freendes sleeth:
Have here my trouthe, as thou art his espye,
Tel wher he is, or thou shalt it abye,° *pay for*
By God and by the holy sacrament!
For soothly thou art oon of his assent[2]
To sleen us yonge folk, thou false thief."
"Now sires," quod he, "if that ye be so lief° *anxious*
To finde Deeth, turne up this crooked way,
For in that grove I lafte° him, by my fay,° *left / faith*
Under a tree, and ther he wol abide:
Nat for youre boost° he wol him no thing hide. *boast*
See ye that ook?° Right ther ye shal him finde. *oak*
God save you, that boughte again[3] mankinde,
And you amende." Thus saide this olde man.
And everich of thise riotoures ran
Til he cam to that tree, and ther they founde
Of florins° fine of gold ycoined rounde *coins*
Wel neigh an eighte busshels as hem thoughte—
Ne lenger thanne after Deeth they soughte,
But eech of hem so glad was of the sighte,
For that the florins been so faire and brighte,

7. Chest for one's belongings, used here as the symbol for life—or perhaps a coffin.
8. Haircloth, for a winding sheet.
9. In the presence of.
1. Cf. Leviticus xix.32.
2. I.e., one of his party.
3. Redeemed.

That down they sette hem by this precious hoord.
The worste of hem he spak the firste word:
"Bretheren," quod he, "take keep° what that I saye: *heed*
My wit is greet though that I bourde° and playe. *joke*
This tresor hath Fortune unto us yiven
In mirthe and jolitee oure lif to liven,
And lightly° as it cometh so wol we spende. *easily*
Ey, Goddes precious dignitee, who wende[4]
Today that we sholde han so fair a grace?
But mighte this gold be caried fro this place
Hoom to myn hous—or elles unto youres—
For wel ye woot that al this gold is oures—
Thanne were we in heigh felicitee.
But trewely, by daye it mighte nat be:
Men wolde sayn that we were theves stronge,° *flagrant*
And for oure owene tresor doon us honge.[5]
This tresor moste ycaried be by nighte,
As wisely and as slyly as it mighte.
Therfore I rede° that cut° amonges us alle *advise / lots*
Be drawe, and lat see wher the cut wol falle;
And he that hath the cut with herte blithe
Shal renne° to the town, and that ful swithe,° *run / quickly*
And bringe us breed and win ful prively;
And two of us shal keepen° subtilly *guard*
This tresor wel, and if he wol nat tarye,
Whan it is night we wol this tresor carye
By oon assent wher as us thinketh best."
That oon of hem the cut broughte in his fest° *fist*
And bad hem drawe and looke wher it wol falle;
And it fil° on the yongeste of hem alle, *fell*
And forth toward the town he wente anoon.
And also° soone as that he was agoon,° *as / gone away*
That oon of hem spak thus unto that other:
"Thou knowest wel thou art my sworen brother;
Thy profit wol I telle thee anoon:
Thou woost wel that oure felawe is agoon,
And here is gold, and that ful greet plentee,
That shal departed° been among us three. *divided*
But nathelees, if I can shape° it so *arrange*
That it departed were among us two,
Hadde I nat doon a freendes turn to thee?"
That other answerde, "I noot[6] how that may be:
He woot that the gold is with us twaye.
What shal we doon? What shal we to him saye?"
"Shal it be conseil?"[7] saide the firste shrewe.° *villain*
"And I shal telle in a wordes fewe
What we shul doon, and bringe it wel aboute."
"I graunte," quod that other, "out of doute,

4. Who would have supposed.
5. Have us hanged.
6. Don't know.
7. A secret.

That by my trouthe I wol thee nat biwraye."° *expose*
"Now," quod the firste, "thou woost wel we be twaye,
And two of us shal strenger° be than oon: *stronger*
Looke whan that he is set that right anoon
Aris as though thou woldest with him playe,
And I shal rive° him thurgh the sides twaye, *pierce*
Whil that thou strugelest with him as in game,
And with thy daggere looke thou do the same;
And thanne shal al this gold departed be,
My dere freend, bitwixe thee and me.
Thanne we may bothe oure lustes° al fulfille, *desires*
And playe at dees° right at oure owene wille." *dice*
And thus accorded been thise shrewes twaye
To sleen the thridde, as ye han herd me saye.
This yongeste, which that wente to the town,
Ful ofte in herte he rolleth up and down
The beautee of thise florins newe and brighte.
"O Lord," quod he, "if so were that I mighte
Have al this tresor to myself allone,
Ther is no man that liveth under the trone° *throne*
Of God that sholde live so merye as I."
And at the laste the feend oure enemy
Putte in his thought that he sholde poison beye,° *buy*
With which he mighte sleen his felawes twaye—
Forwhy° the feend foond him in swich livinge *because*
That he hadde leve° him to sorwe bringe:[8] *permission*
For this was outrely° his fulle entente, *plainly*
To sleen hem bothe, and nevere to repente.
And forth he gooth—no lenger wolde he tarye—
Into the town unto a pothecarye,° *apothecary*
And prayed him that he him wolde selle
Som poison that he mighte his rattes quelle,° *kill*
And eek ther was a polcat[9] in his hawe° *yard*
That, as he saide, his capons hadde yslawe,° *slain*
And fain he wolde wreke him[1] if he mighte
On vermin that destroyed him[2] by nighte.
The pothecarye answerde, "And thou shalt have
A thing that, also° God my soule save, *as*
In al this world there is no creature
That ete or dronke hath of this confiture°— *mixture*
Nat but the mountance° of a corn° of whete— *amount / grain*
That he ne shal his lif anoon forlete.° *lose*
Ye, sterve° he shal, and that in lasse° while *die / less*
Than thou wolt goon a paas[3] nat but a mile,
The poison is so strong and violent."
This cursed man hath in his hand yhent° *taken*

8. Christian doctrine teaches that the devil may not tempt men except with God's permission.
9. A weasel-like animal.
1. He would gladly avenge himself.
2. I.e., were ruining his farming.
3. Take a walk.

This poison in a box and sith° he ran — *then*
Into the nexte streete unto a man
And borwed of him large botels three,
And in the two his poison poured he—
The thridde he kepte clene for his drinke,
For al the night he shoop him[4] for to swinke° — *work*
In carying of the gold out of that place.
And whan this riotour with sory grace
Hadde filled with win his grete botels three,
To his felawes again repaireth he.

What needeth it to sermone of it more?
For right as they had cast° his deeth bifore, — *plotted*
Right so they han him slain, and that anoon.
And whan that this was doon, thus spak that oon:
"Now lat us sitte and drinke and make us merye,
And afterward we wol his body berye."° — *bury*
And with that word it happed him par cas[5]
To take the botel ther the poison was,
And drank, and yaf his felawe drinke also,
For which anoon they storven° bothe two. — *died*

But certes I suppose that Avicen
Wroot nevere in no canon ne in no *fen*[6]
Mo wonder signes[7] of empoisoning
Than hadde thise wrecches two er hir ending:
Thus ended been thise homicides two,
And eek the false empoisonere also.

O cursed sinne of alle cursednesse!
O traitours homicide, O wikkednesse!
O glotonye, luxure,° and hasardrye! — *lechery*
Thou blasphemour of Crist with vilainye
And othes grete of usage° and of pride! — *habit*
Allas, mankinde, how may it bitide
That to thy Creatour which that thee wroughte,
And with his precious herte blood thee boughte,° — *redeemed*
Thou art so fals and so unkinde,° allas? — *unnatural*

Now goode men, God foryive you youre trespas,
And ware° you fro the sinne of avarice: — *guard*
Myn holy pardon may you alle warice°— — *save*
So that ye offre nobles or sterlinges,[8]
Or elles silver brooches, spoones, ringes.
Boweth your heed under this holy bulle!
Cometh up, ye wives, offreth of youre wolle!° — *wool*
Youre name I entre here in my rolle: anoon
Into the blisse of hevene shul ye goon.
I you assoile° by myn heigh power— — *absolve*
Ye that wol offre—as clene and eek as cleer

4. He was preparing.
5. By chance.
6. The *Canon of Medicine*, by Avicenna, an 11th-century Arabic philosopher, was divided into sections called "*fens*."
7. More wonderful symptoms.
8. "Nobles" and "sterlinges" were valuable coins.

As ye were born.—And lo, sires, thus I preche.
And Jesu Crist that is oure soules leeche° *physician*
So graunte you his pardon to receive,
For that is best—I wol you nat deceive.

The Epilogue

"But sires, oo word forgat I in my tale:
I have relikes and pardon in my male° *bag*
As faire as any man in Engelond,
Whiche were me yiven by the Popes hond.
If any of you wol of devocioun
Offren and han myn absolucioun,
Come forth anoon, and kneeleth here adown,
And mekely receiveth my pardoun,
Or elles taketh pardon as ye wende,
Al newe and fressh at every miles ende—
So that ye offre alway newe and newe[9]
Nobles or pens whiche that be goode and trewe.
It is an honour to everich that is heer
That ye have a suffisant° pardoner *competent*
T'assoile you in contrees as ye ride,
For aventures whiche that may bitide:
Paraventure ther may falle oon or two
Down of his hors and breke his nekke atwo;
Looke which a suretee° is it to you alle *safeguard*
That I am in youre felaweship yfalle
That may assoile you, bothe more and lasse,[1]
Whan that the soule shal fro the body passe.
I rede° that oure Hoste shal biginne, *advise*
For he is most envoluped° in sinne. *involved*
Com forth, sire Host, and offre first anoon,
And thou shalt kisse the relikes everichoon,° *each one*
Ye, for a grote: unbokele° anoon thy purs." *unbuckle*
"Nay, nay," quod he, "thanne have I Cristes curs!
Lat be," quod he, "it shal nat be, so theech!° *may I thrive*
Thou woldest make me kisse thyn olde breech° *breeches*
And swere it were a relik of a saint,
Though it were with thy fundament depeint.° *stained*
But, by the crois which that Sainte Elaine foond,[2]
I wolde I hadde thy coilons° in myn hond, *testicles*
In stede of relikes or of saintuarye.° *relic-box*
Lat cutte hem of: I wol thee helpe hem carve.
They shal be shrined in an hogges tord."° *turd*
This Pardoner answerde nat a word:
So wroth he was no word ne wolde he saye.
"Now," quod oure Host, "I wol no lenger playe
With thee, ne with noon other angry man."

9. Over and over.
1. Both high and low (i.e., everybody).
2. I.e., by the cross that St. Helena found. Helena, mother of Constantine the Great, was reputed to have found the True Cross.

But right anoon the worthy Knight bigan,
Whan that he sawgh that al the peple lough,° *laughed*
"Namore of this, for it is right ynough.
Sire Pardoner, be glad and merye of cheere,
And ye, sire Host that been to me so dere,
I praye you that ye kisse the Pardoner,
And Pardoner, I praye thee, draw thee neer,
And as we diden lat us laughe and playe."
Anoon they kiste and riden forth hir waye.

The Nun's Priest's Tale[1]

A poore widwe somdeel stape° in age *advanced*
Was whilom° dwelling in a narwe[2] cotage, *once upon a time*
Biside a grove, stonding in a dale:
This widwe of which I telle you my tale,
Sin thilke° day that she was last a wif, *that same*
In pacience ladde° a ful simple lif. *led*
For litel was hir catel° and hir rente,° *property / income*
By housbondrye° of swich as God hire sente *economy*
She foond° hirself and eek hir doughtren two. *provided for*
Three large sowes hadde she and namo,
Three kin,° and eek a sheep that highte Malle. *cows*
Ful sooty was hir bowr° and eek hir halle. *bedroom*
In which she eet ful many a sclendre° meel; *scanty*
Of poinant° sauce hire needed neveradeel: *pungent*
No daintee morsel passed thurgh hir throte—

1. The Nun's Priest's Tale is an example of the literary genre known as the "beast fable," in which animals behave like human beings. The beast fable is inevitably injurious to man's dignity, since to pretend that animals behave like men is to suggest that men behave like animals, for a pig cannot look like a man unless a man in some way looks like a pig. In the Nun's Priest's Tale, as in its French source, the history of Reynard the Fox, the beast fable is combined with the mock heroic, and the result is doubly injurious to man's dignity. The elevated language of true heroic poetry means to enhance the splendid deeds of men of great stature, while the elevated language of mock heroic, by treating the trivial as if it were sublime, reveals man's lack of dignity in the awful gulf that separates the idealized language from the petty action it describes; and when the petty action is carried on not even by men, but by animals masquerading as men (that is, by men reduced to the status of animals), the loss of human dignity is even greater.

The nominal hero of the Tale is Chauntecleer, a fowl of courtly bearing, profound learning, and superior crowing. This rooster is, like Achilles or Aeneas, made the center of a "great" action—which, however, takes up a relatively small portion of the total number of lines in the poem. The hero of the larger portion, and the real hero of the poem, is rhetoric, which is responsible for all Chauntecleer's importance, though it almost drowns his story in its vast tumid flow. Rhetoric as employed by the Nun's Priest includes not only elevated speech, but proverbs, saws, conventional similes—all the clichés of formal language and thought. Epic mannerisms abound; proverbs fly thick and fast and contradict one another with impunity; sententious generalizations about the tragic inevitability of certain events, the bad counsel given by women, and the folly of heeding flattery are successively used to account for Chauntecleer's near-fall; and throughout the tale learned pedantry invokes rhetorical tradition to footnote the least original of ideas. All rhetoric's ordering devices achieve a fine disorder.

2. I.e., small.

Hir diete was accordant to hir cote.° *cottage*
Repleccioun° ne made hire nevere sik: *overeating*
Attempre° diete was al hir physik,° *moderate / medicine*
And exercise and hertes suffisaunce.° *contentment*
The goute lette hire nothing for to daunce,[3]
N'apoplexye shente° nat hir heed.° *hurt / head*
No win ne drank she, neither whit ne reed:° *red*
Hir boord° was served most with whit and blak,[4] *table*
Milk and brown breed, in which she foond no lak;[5]
Seind bacon, and somtime an ey° or twaye, *egg*
For she was as it were a manere daye.[6]
A yeerd° she hadde, enclosed al withoute *yard*
With stikkes, and a drye dich aboute,
In which she hadde a cok heet° Chauntecleer: *named*
In al the land of crowing nas° his peer. *was not*
His vois was merier than the merye orgon
On massedayes that in the chirche goon;[7]
Wel sikerer[8] was his crowing in his logge° *dwelling*
Than is a clok or an abbeye orlogge;° *timepiece*
By nature he knew eech ascensioun
Of th'equinoxial[9] in thilke town:
For whan degrees fifteene were ascended,
Thanne crew[1] he that it mighte nat been amended.
His comb was redder than the fin coral,
And batailed° as it were a castel wal; *battlemented*
His bile° was blak, and as the jeet° it shoon; *bill / jet*
Like asure[2] were his legges and his toon;° *toes*
His nailes whitter° than the lilye flowr, *whiter*
And lik the burned° gold was his colour. *burnished*
This gentil cok hadde in his governaunce
Sevene hennes for to doon al his plesaunce,° *pleasure*
Whiche were his sustres and his paramours,[3]
And wonder like to him as of colours;
Of whiche the faireste hewed° on hir throte *colored*
Was cleped faire damoisele Pertelote:
Curteis she was, discreet, and debonaire,° *meek*
And compaignable,[4] and bar° hirself so faire, *bore*
Sin thilke day that she was seven night old,
That trewely she hath the herte in hold
Of Chauntecleer, loken° in every lith.° *locked / limb*
He loved hire so that wel was him therwith.[5]

3. The gout didn't hinder her at all from dancing.
4. I.e., milk and bread.
5. Found no fault. "Seind": scorched (i.e., broiled).
6. I.e., a kind of dairymaid.
7. I.e., is played.
8. More reliable.
9. I.e., he knew by instinct each step in the progression of the celestial equator. The celestial equator was thought to make a 360-degree rotation around the earth every 24 hours; therefore a progression of 15 degrees would be equal to the passage of an hour (line 37).
1. Crowed; "amended": improved.
2. Lapis lazuli.
3. His sisters and his mistresses.
4. Companionable.
5. That he was well contented.

But swich a joye was it to heere hem singe,
Whan that the brighte sonne gan to springe,
In sweete accord *My Lief is Faren in Londe*[6]—
For thilke time, as I have understonde,
Beestes and briddes couden speke and singe.
  And so bifel that in a daweninge,
As Chauntecleer among his wives alle
Sat on his perche that was in the halle,
And next him sat this faire Pertelote,
This Chauntecleer gan gronen in his throte,
As man that in his dreem is drecched° sore. *troubled*
  And whan that Pertelote thus herde him rore,
She was agast, and saide, "Herte dere,
What aileth you to grone in this manere?
Ye been a verray slepere,[7] fy, for shame!"
  And he answerde and saide thus, "Madame,
I praye you that ye take it nat agrief.° *amiss*
By God, me mette I was in swich meschief[8]
Right now, that yit myn herte is sore afright.
Now God," quod he, "my swevene recche aright,[9]
And keepe my body out of foul prisoun!
Me mette how that I romed up and down
Within oure yeerd, wher as I sawgh a beest,
Was lik an hound and wolde han maad arrest[1]
Upon my body, and han had me deed.[2]
His colour was bitwixe yelow and reed,
And tipped was his tail and bothe his eres
With blak, unlik the remenant° of his heres;° *rest / hairs*
His snoute smal, with glowing yën twaye.
Yit of his look for fere almost I deye:° *die*
This caused me my groning, doutelees."
  "Avoi,"° quod she, "fy on you, hertelees!° *fie / coward*
Allas," quod she, "for by that God above,
Now han ye lost myn herte and al my love!
I can nat love a coward, by my faith.
For certes, what so any womman saith,
We alle desiren, if it mighte be,
To han housbondes hardy, wise, and free,° *generous*
And secree,° and no nigard, ne no fool, *discreet*
Ne him that is agast of every tool,° *weapon*
Ne noon avauntour.° By that God above, *boaster*
How dorste ye sayn for shame unto youre love
That any thing mighte make you aferd?
Have ye no mannes herte and han a beerd?
Allas, and conne° ye been agast of swevenes?° *can / dreams*
No thing, God woot, but vanitee[3] in swevene is!

6. A popular song of the time.
7. Sound sleeper.
8. I dreamed that I was in such misfortune.
9. Interpret my dream correctly (i.e., in an auspicious manner).
1. Would have laid hold.
2. I.e., killed me.
3. I.e., empty illusion.

Swevenes engendren of replexiouns,[4]
And ofte of fume° and of complexiouns,° *gas / bodily humors*
Whan humours been too habundant in a wight.[5]
Certes, this dreem which ye han met° tonight *dreamed*
Comth of the grete superfluitee
Of youre rede colera,[6] pardee,
Which causeth folk to dreden° in hir dremes *fear*
Of arwes,° and of fir with rede lemes,° *arrows / flames*
Of rede beestes, that they wol hem bite,
Of contek,° and of whelpes grete and lite[7]— *strife*
Right° as the humour of malencolye[8] *just*
Causeth ful many a man in sleep to crye
For fere of blake beres° or boles° blake, *bears / bulls*
Or elles blake develes wol hem take.
Of othere humours coude I tell also
That werken many a man in sleep ful wo,
But I wol passe as lightly° as I can. *quickly*
Lo, Caton,[9] which that was so wis a man,
Saide he nat thus? 'Ne do no fors of[1] dremes.'
Now, sire," quod she, "whan we flee fro the bemes,[2]
For Goddes love, as take som laxatif.
Up° peril of my soule and of my lif, *upon*
I conseile you the beste, I wol nat lie,
That bothe of colere and of malencolye
Ye purge you; and for° ye shal nat tarye, *in order that*
Though in this town is noon apothecarye,
I shal myself to herbes techen you,
That shal been for youre hele[3] and for youre prow,
And in oure yeerd tho herbes shal I finde,
The whiche han of hir propretee by kinde° *nature*
To purge you binethe and eek above.
Foryet° nat this, for Goddes owene love. *forget*
Ye been ful colerik° of complexioun; *bilious*
Ware° the sonne in his ascencioun *beware that*
Ne finde you nat repleet° of humours hote;° *filled / hot*
And if it do, I dar wel laye° a grote *bet*
That ye shul have a fevere terciane,[4]
Or an agu that may be youre bane.° *death*
A day or two ye shul han digestives
Of wormes, er ye take youre laxatives
Of lauriol, centaure, and fumetere,[5]

4. Dreams have their origin in overeating.
5. I.e., when humors are too abundant in a person. Pertelote's diagnosis is based on the familiar concept that an overabundance of one of the bodily humors in a person affected his temperament.
6. Red bile.
7. And of big and little dogs.
8. I.e., black bile.
9. Dionysius Cato, supposed author of a book of maxims used in elementary education.
1. Pay no attention to.
2. Fly down from the rafters.
3. Health; "prow": benefit.
4. Tertian (recurring every other day).
5. Of laureole, centaury, and fumitory. These, and the herbs mentioned in the next lines, were all common medieval medicines used as cathartics.

Or elles of ellebor° that groweth there, *hellebore*
Of catapuce, or of gaitres beries,[6]
Of herbe-ive° growing in oure yeerd ther merye is.[7] *herb ivy*
Pekke hem right up as they growe and ete hem in.
Be merye, housbonde, for youre fader kin!
Dredeth no dreem: I can saye you namore."
"Madame," quod he, "graunt mercy of youre lore.[8]
But nathelees, as touching daun° Catoun, *master*
That hath of wisdom swich a greet renown,
Though that he bad no dremes for to drede,
By God, men may in olde bookes rede
Of many a man more of auctoritee° *authority*
Than evere Caton was, so mote I thee,° *thrive*
That al the revers sayn of his sentence,° *opinion*
And han wel founden by experience
That dremes been significaciouns
As wel of joye as tribulaciouns
That folk enduren in this lif present.
Ther needeth make of this noon argument:
The verray preve[9] sheweth it in deede.
"Oon of the gretteste auctour[1] that men rede
Saith thus, that whilom two felawes wente
On pilgrimage in a ful good entente,
And happed so they comen in a town,
Wher as ther was swich congregacioun
Of peple, and eek so strait of herbergage,[2]
That they ne founde as muche as oo cotage
In which they bothe mighte ylogged° be; *lodged*
Wherfore they mosten° of necessitee *must*
As for that night departe° compaignye. *part*
And eech of hem gooth to his hostelrye,
And took his logging as it wolde falle.° *befall*
That oon of hem was logged in a stalle,
Fer° in a yeerd, with oxen of the plough; *far away*
That other man was logged wel ynough,
As was his aventure° or his fortune, *lot*
That us governeth alle as in commune.
And so bifel that longe er it were day,
This man mette° in his bed, ther as he lay, *dreamed*
How that his felawe gan upon him calle,
And saide, 'Allas, for in an oxes stalle
This night I shal be mordred° ther I lie! *murdered*
Now help me, dere brother, or I die!
In alle haste com to me,' he saide.
"This man out of his sleep for fere abraide,° *started up*
But whan that he was wakened of his sleep,

6. Of caper berry or of gaiter berry.
7. Where it is pleasant.
8. Many thanks for your instruction.
9. Actual experience.
1. I.e., one of the greatest authors (perhaps Cicero).
2. And also such a shortage of lodging.

He turned him and took of this no keep:° *heed*
Him thoughte his dreem nas but a vanitee.
Thus twies in his sleeping dremed he,
And atte thridde time yit his felawe
Cam, as him thoughte, and saide, 'I am now slawe:° *slain*
Bihold my bloody woundes deepe and wide.
Aris up erly in the morwe tide[3]
And atte west gate of the town,' quod he,
'A carte ful of dong° ther shaltou see, *dung*
In which my body is hid ful prively:
Do thilke carte arresten boldely.[4]
My gold caused my mordre, sooth to sayn'—
And tolde him every point how he was slain,
With a ful pitous face, pale of hewe.
And truste wel, his dreem he foond° ful trewe, *found*
For on the morwe° as soone as it was day, *morning*
To his felawes in° he took the way, *lodging*
And whan that he cam to this oxes stalle,
After his felawe he bigan to calle.
"The hostiler° answerde him anoon, *innkeeper*
And saide, 'Sire, youre felawe is agoon:° *gone away*
As soone as day he wente out of the town.'
"This man gan fallen in suspecioun,
Remembring on his dremes that he mette;° *dreamed*
And forth he gooth, no lenger wolde he lette,° *tarry*
Unto the west gate of the town, and foond
A dong carte, wente as it were to donge° lond, *put manure on*
That was arrayed in that same wise
As ye han herd the dede° man devise; *dead*
And with an hardy herte he gan to crye,
'Vengeance and justice of this felonye!
My felawe mordred is this same night,
And in this carte he lith° gaping upright!° *lies / supine*
I crye out on the ministres,' quod he,
'That sholde keepe and rulen this citee.
Harrow,° allas, here lith my felawe slain!' *help*
What sholde I more unto this tale sayn?
The peple up sterte° and caste the carte to grounde, *started*
And in the middel of the dong they founde
The dede man that mordred was al newe,[5]
"O blisful God that art so just and trewe,
Lo, how that thou biwrayest° mordre alway! *disclose*
Mordre wol out, that see we day by day:
Mordre is so wlatsom° and abhominable *loathsome*
To God that is so just and resonable,
That he ne wol nat suffre it heled° be, *concealed*
Though it abide a yeer or two or three.
Mordre wol out: this my conclusioun.

3. In the morning.
4. Boldly have this same cart stopped.
5. Recently.

And right anoon ministres of that town
Han hent° the cartere and so sore him pined,[6] *seized*
And eek the hostiler so sore engined,° *racked*
That they biknewe° hir wikkednesse anoon, *confessed*
And were anhanged° by the nekke boon. *hanged*
Here may men seen that dremes been to drede.[7]
"And certes, in the same book I rede—
Right in the nexte chapitre after this—
I gabbe° nat, so have I joye or blis— *lie*
Two men that wolde han passed over see
For certain cause into a fer contree,
If that the wind ne hadde been contrarye
That made hem in a citee for to tarye,
That stood ful merye upon an haven° side— *harbor's*
But on a day again° the even tide *toward*
The wind gan chaunge, and blewe right as hem leste:[8]
Jolif° and glad they wenten unto reste, *merry*
And casten hem[9] ful erly for to saile.
"But to that oo man fil° a greet mervaile; *befell*
That oon of hem, in sleeping as he lay,
Him mette[1] a wonder dreem again the day:
Him thoughte a man stood by his beddes side,
And him comanded that he sholde abide,
And saide him thus, 'If thou tomorwe wende,
Thou shalt be dreint:° my tale is at an ende.' *drowned*
"He wook and tolde his felawe what he mette,
And prayed him his viage° to lette;° *voyage / delay*
As for that day he prayed him to bide.
"His felawe that lay by his beddes side
Gan for to laughe, and scorned him ful faste.° *hard*
'No dreem,' quod he, 'may so myn herte agaste° *terrify*
That I wol lette° for to do my thinges.° *delay / business*
I sette nat a straw by thy dreminges,[2]
For swevenes been but vanitees and japes:[3]
Men dreme alday° of owles or of apes,[4] *constantly*
And of many a maze° therwithal— *delusion*
Men dreme of thing that nevere was ne shal.[5]
But sith I see that thou wolt here abide,
And thus forsleuthen° wilfully thy tide,° *waste / time*
Good woot, it reweth me;[6] and have good day.'
And thus he took his leve and wente his way.
But er that he hadde half his cours ysailed—
Noot I nat why ne what meschaunce it ailed—
But casuelly the shippes botme rente,[7]

6. Tortured.
7. Worthy of being feared.
8. Just as they wished.
9. Determined.
1. He dreamed.
2. I don't care a straw for your dreamings.
3. Dreams are but illusions and frauds.
4. I.e., of absurdities.
5. I.e., shall be.
6. I'm sorry.
7. I don't know why nor what was the trouble with it—but accidentally the ship's bottom split.

And ship and man under the water wente,
In sighte of othere shippes it biside,
That with hem sailed at the same tide.
And therfore, faire Pertelote so dere,
By swiche ensamples olde maistou lere° *learn*
That no man sholde been too recchelees° *careless*
Of dremes, for I saye thee doutelees
That many a dreem ful sore is for to drede.
"Lo, in the lif of Saint Kenelm[8] I rede—
That was Kenulphus sone, the noble king
Of Mercenrike°—how Kenelm mette a thing *Mercia*
A lite° er he was mordred on a day. *little*
His mordre in his avision° he sey.° *dream / saw*
His norice° him expounded everydeel° *nurse / entirely*
His swevene, and bad him for to keepe him[9] weel
For traison, but he nas but seven yeer old,
And therfore litel tale hath he told
Of any dreem,[1] so holy was his herte.
By God, I hadde levere than my sherte[2]
That ye hadde rad° his legende as have I. *read*
"Dame Pertelote, I saye you trewely,
Macrobeus,[3] that writ the *Avisioun*
In Affrike of the worthy Scipioun,
Affermeth° dremes, and saith that they been *confirms*
Warning of thinges that men after seen.
"And ferthermore, I praye you looketh wel
In the Olde Testament of Daniel,
If he heeld° dremes any vanitee.[4] *considered*
"Rede eek of Joseph[5] and ther shul ye see
Wher° dremes be somtime—I saye nat alle— *whether*
Warning of thinges that shul after falle.
"Looke of Egypte the king daun Pharao,
His bakere and his botelere° also, *butler*
Wher they ne felte noon effect in dremes.[6]
Whoso wol seeke actes of sondry remes° *realms*
May rede of dremes many a wonder thing.
"Lo Cresus, which that was of Lyde° king, *Lydia*
Mette° he nat that he sat upon a tree, *dreamed*
Which signified he sholde anhanged° be? *hanged*
"Lo here Andromacha, Ectores° wif, *Hector's*
That day that Ector sholde lese° his lif, *lose*
She dremed on the same night biforn
How that the lif of Ector sholde be lorn,° *lost*
If thilke° day he wente into bataile; *that same*

8. Kenelm succeeded his father as king of Mercia at the age of 7, but was slain by his aunt (in 821).
9. Guard himself.
1. Therefore he has set little store by any dream.
2. I.e., I'd give my shirt.
3. Macrobius wrote a famous commentary on Cicero's account in *De Republica* of the dream of Scipio Africanus Minor; the commentary came to be regarded as a standard authority on dream lore.
4. See Daniel vii.
5. See Genesis xxxvii.
6. See Genesis xxxix–xli.

She warned him, but it mighte nat availe:° *do any good*
He wente for to fighte nathelees,
But he was slain anoon° of Achilles. *right away*
But thilke tale is al too long to telle,
And eek it is neigh day, I may nat dwelle.
Shortly I saye, as for conclusioun,
That I shal han of this avisioun[7]
Adversitee, and I saye ferthermoor
That I ne telle of[8] laxatives no stoor,
For they been venimes,° I woot it weel: *poisons*
I hem defye, I love hem neveradeel.° *not a bit*
"Now lat us speke of mirthe and stinte° al this. *stop*
Madame Pertelote, so have I blis,
Of oo thing God hath sente me large grace:
For whan I see the beautee of youre face—
Ye been so scarlet reed° aboute youre yën— *red*
It maketh al my drede for to dien.
For also siker° as *In principio*,[9] *certain*
Mulier est hominis confusio.[1]
Madame, the sentence° of this Latin is, *meaning*
'Womman is mannes joye and al his blis.'
For whan I feele anight youre softe side—
Al be it that I may nat on you ride,
For that oure perche is maad so narwe, allas—
I am so ful of joye and of solas° *delight*
That I defye bothe swevene and dreem."
And with that word he fleigh° down fro the beem, *flew*
For it was day, and eek his hennes alle,
And with a "chuk" he gan hem for to calle,
For he hadde founde a corn lay in the yeerd.
Real° he was, he was namore aferd:° *regal / afraid*
He fethered[2] Pertelote twenty time,
And trad[3] hire as ofte er it was prime.
He looketh as it were a grim leoun,
And on his toes he rometh up and down:
Him deined[4] nat to sette his foot to grounde.
He chukketh whan he hath a corn yfounde,
And to him rennen° thanne his wives alle. *run*
Thus royal, as a prince is in his halle,
Leve I this Chauntecleer in his pasture,
And after wol I telle his aventure.
Whan that the month in which the world bigan,
That highte March, whan God first maked man,
Was compleet, and passed were also,

7. Divinely inspired dream (as opposed to the more ordinary "swevene" or "dreem").
8. Set by.
9. A tag from the Gospel of St. John which gives the essential premises of Christianity: "In the beginning was the Word."
1. Woman is man's ruination.
2. I.e., embraced.
3. Trod, copulated with; "prime": 9 A.M.
4. He deigned.

Sin March bigan, thritty days and two,[5]
Bifel that Chauntecleer in al his pride,
His sevene wives walking him biside,
Caste up his yën to the brighte sonne,
That in the signe of Taurus hadde yronne
Twenty degrees and oon and somwhat more,
And knew by kinde,° and by noon other lore, *nature*
That it was prime, and crew with blisful stevene.° *voice*
"The sonne," he saide, "is clomben[6] up on hevene
Fourty degrees and oon and more, ywis.
Madame Pertelote, my worldes blis,
Herkneth thise blisful briddes° how they singe, *birds*
And see the fresshe flowres how they springe:
Ful is myn herte of revel and solas."
But sodeinly him fil° a sorweful cas,° *befell / chance*
For evere the latter ende of joye is wo—
God woot that worldly joye is soone ago,
And if a rethor° coude faire endite, *rhetorician*
He in a cronicle saufly° mighte it write, *safely*
As for a soverein notabilitee.[7]
Now every wis man lat him herkne me:
This storye is also° trewe, I undertake, *as*
As is the book of *Launcelot de Lake*,[8]
That wommen holde in ful greet reverence.
Now wol I turne again to my sentence.° *main point*
  A colfox[9] ful of sly iniquitee,
That in the grove hadde woned° yeres three, *dwelled*
By heigh imaginacion forncast,[1]
The same night thurghout the hegges° brast° *hedges / burst*
Into the yeerd ther Chauntecleer the faire
Was wont, and eek his wives, to repaire;
And in a bed of wortes° stille he lay *cabbages*
Til it was passed undren° of the day, *midmorning*
Waiting his time on Chauntecleer to falle,
As gladly doon thise homicides alle,
That in await liggen to mordre[2] men.
O false mordrour, lurking in thy den!
O newe Scariot![3] Newe Geniloun!
False dissimilour!° O Greek Sinoun,[4] *dissembler*
That broughtest Troye al outrely° to sorwe! *utterly*
O Chauntecleer, accursed be that morwe° *morning*

5. The rhetorical time-telling is perhaps burlesque; it can be read as yielding the date April 3, though May 3 seems intended from lines 374–75: on May 3 the sun would have passed some twenty degrees through Taurus (the Bull), the second sign of the zodiac; the sun would be forty degrees from the horizon at 9 o'clock in the morning.
6. Has climbed.
7. Indisputable fact.
8. Romances of the courteous knight Lancelot of the Lake were very popular.
9. Fox with black markings.
1. Predestined by divine planning.
2. That lie in ambush to murder.
3. Judas Iscariot. "Geniloun" is Ganelon, who betrayed Roland to the Saracens (in the medieval French epic *The Song of Roland*).
4. Sinon, who persuaded the Trojans to take the Greeks' wooden horse into their city—with, of course, the result that the city was destroyed.

That thou into the yeerd flaugh° fro the bemes! *flew*
Thou were ful wel ywarned by thy dremes
That thilke day was perilous to thee;
But what that God forwoot° moot° needes be, *foreknows / must*
After° the opinion of certain clerkes: *according to*
Witnesse on him that any parfit° clerk is *perfect*
That in scole is greet altercacioun
In this matere, and greet disputisoun,° *disputation*
And hath been of an hundred thousand men.
But I ne can nat bulte° it to the bren,° *sift / husks*
As can the holy doctour Augustin,
Or Boece, or the bisshop Bradwardin[5]—
Wheither that Goddes worthy forwiting° *foreknowledge*
Straineth me nedely[6] for to doon a thing
("Nedely" clepe I simple necessitee),
Or elles if free chois be graunted me
To do that same thing or do it nought,
Though God forwoot° it er that I was wrought; *foreknew*
Or if his witing° straineth neveradeel, *knowledge*
But by necessitee condicionel[7]—
I wol nat han to do of swich matere:
My tale is of a cok, as ye may heere,
That took his conseil of his wif with sorwe,
To walken in the yeerd upon that morwe
That he hadde met° the dreem that I you tolde. *dreamed*
Wommenes conseils been ful ofte colde,[8]
Wommanes conseil broughte us first to wo,
And made Adam fro Paradis to go,
Ther as he was ful merye and wel at ese.
But for I noot° to whom it mighte displese *don't know*
If I conseil of wommen wolde blame,
Passe over, for I saide it in my game°— *sport*
Rede auctours where they trete of swich matere,
And what they sayn of wommen ye may heere—
Thise been the cokkes wordes and nat mine:
I can noon harm of no womman divine.° *guess*
Faire in the sond° to bathe hire merily *sand*
Lith° Pertelote, and alle hir sustres by, *lies*
Again° the sonne, and Chauntecleer so free° *in / noble*
Soong° merier than the mermaide in the see— *sang*
For Physiologus[9] saith sikerly
How that they singen wel and merily.
And so bifel that as he caste his yë
Among the wortes on a boterflye,° *butterfly*

5. St. Augustine, Boethius (6th-century Roman philosopher, whose *Consolation of Philosophy* was translated by Chaucer), and Thomas Bradwardine (Archbishop of Canterbury, d. 1349) were all concerned with the interrelationship between man's free will and God's foreknowledge.

6. Constrains me necessarily.

7. Boethius' "conditional necessity" permitted a large measure of free will.

8. I.e., baneful.

9. Supposed author of a bestiary, a book of moralized zoology describing both natural and supernatural animals (including mermaids).

He was war of this fox that lay ful lowe.
No thing ne liste him[1] thanne for to crowe,
But cride anoon "Cok cok!" and up he sterte,° *started*
As man that[2] was affrayed in his herte—
For naturelly a beest desireth flee
Fro his contrarye[3] if he may it see,
Though he nevere erst° hadde seen it with his yë. *before*
This Chauntecleer, whan he gan him espye,
He wolde han fled, but that the fox anoon
Saide, "Gentil sire, allas, wher wol ye goon?
Be ye afraid of me that am youre freend?
Now certes, I were worse than a feend
If I to you wolde° harm or vilainye. *meant*
I am nat come youre conseil° for t'espye, *secrets*
But trewely the cause of my cominge
Was only for to herkne how that ye singe:
For trewely, ye han as merye a stevene° *voice*
As any angel hath that is in hevene.
Therwith ye han in musik more feelinge
Than hadde Boece,[4] or any that can singe.
My lord your fader—God his soule blesse!—
And eek youre moder, of hir gentilesse,° *gentility*
Han in myn hous ybeen, to my grete ese.
And certes sire, ful fain° wolde I you plese. *gladly*
"But for men speke of singing, I wol saye,
So mote I brouke[5] wel mine yën twaye,
Save ye, I herde nevere man so singe
As dide youre fader in the morweninge.
Certes, it was of herte[6] al that he soong.° *sang*
And for to make his vois the more strong,
He wolde so paine him[7] that with bothe his yën
He moste winke,[8] so loude wolde he cryen;
And stonden on his tiptoon therwithal,
And strecche forth his nekke long and smal;
And eek he was of swich discrecioun
That ther nas no man in no regioun
That him in song or wisdom mighte passe.
I have wel rad° in *Daun Burnel the Asse*[9] *read*
Among his vers how that ther was a cok,
For a preestes sone yaf him a knok[1]
Upon his leg whil he was yong and nice,° *foolish*
He made him for to lese° his benefice.[2] *lose*

1. He wished.
2. Like one who.
3. I.e., his natural enemy.
4. Boethius also wrote a treatise on music.
5. So might I enjoy the use of.
6. Heartfelt.
7. Take pains.
8. He had to shut his eyes.
9. Master Brunellus, a discontented donkey, was the hero of a 12th-century satirical poem by Nigel Wireker.
1. Because a priest's son gave him a knock.
2. The offended cock neglected to crow so that his master, now grown to manhood, overslept, missing his ordination and losing his benefice.

But certain, ther nis no comparisoun
Bitwixe the wisdom and discrecioun
Of youre fader and of his subtiltee.
Now singeth, sire, for sainte° charitee! *holy*
Lat see, conne° ye youre fader countrefete?"° *can / imitate*
This Chauntecleer his winges gan to bete,
As man that coude his traison nat espye,
So was he ravissshed with his flaterye.
Allas, ye lordes, many a fals flatour° *flatterer*
Is in youre court, and many a losengeour,° *deceiver*
That plesen you wel more, by my faith,
Than he that soothfastnesse° unto you saith! *truth*
Redeth Ecclesiaste[3] of flaterye.
Beeth war, ye lordes, of hir trecherye.
This Chauntecleer stood hye upon his toos,
Strecching his nekke, and heeld his yën cloos,
And gan to crowe loude for the nones;° *occasion*
And daun Russel the fox sterte° up atones, *jumped*
And by the gargat° hente° Chauntecleer, *throat / seized*
And on his bak toward the wode him beer,° *bore*
For yit ne was ther no man that him sued.° *followed*
O destinee that maist nat been eschued!° *eschewed*
Allas that Chauntecleer fleigh° fro the bemes! *flew*
Allas his wif ne roughte nat of[4] dremes!
And on a Friday fil° al this meschaunce! *befell*
O Venus that art goddesse of plesaunce,
Sin that thy servant was this Chauntecleer,
And in thy service dide al his power—
More for delit than world[5] to multiplye—
Why woldestou suffre him on thy day[6] to die?
O Gaufred,[7] dere maister soverein,
That, whan thy worthy king Richard was slain
With shot,[8] complainedest his deeth so sore,
Why ne hadde I now thy sentence and thy lore,[9]
The Friday for to chide as diden ye?
For on a Friday soothly slain was he.
Thanne wolde I shewe you how that I coude plaine[1]
For Chaunteclercs drede and for his paine.
Certes, swich cry ne lamentacioun
Was nevere of ladies maad whan Ilioun° *Ilium, Troy*
Was wonne, and Pyrrus[2] with his straite swerd,
Whan he hadde hent° King Priam by the beerd *seized*
And slain him, as saith us *Eneidos*,[3]

3. The Book of Ecclesiasticus, in the Apocrypha.
4. Didn't care for.
5. I.e., population.
6. Friday is Venus' day.
7. Geoffrey of Vinsauf, a famous medieval rhetorician, who wrote a lament on the death of Richard I in which he scolded Friday, the day on which the king died.
8. I.e., a missile.
9. Thy wisdom and thy learning.
1. Lament.
2. Pyrrhus was the Greek who slew Priam, king of Troy. "Straite": rigorous, unsparing.
3. As the *Aeneid* tells us.

As maden alle the hennes in the cloos,° *yard*
Whan they hadde seen of Chauntecleer the sighte.
But sovereinly[4] Dame Pertelote shrighte° *shrieked*
Ful louder than dide Hasdrubales[5] wif
Whan that hir housbonde hadde lost his lif,
And that the Romains hadden brend° Cartage: *burned*
She was so ful of torment and of rage° *madness*
That wilfully unto the fir she sterte,° *jumped*
And brende hirselven with a stedefast herte.
  O woful hennes, right so criden ye
As, whan that Nero brende the citee
Of Rome, criden senatoures wives
For that hir housbondes losten alle hir lives:[6]
Withouten gilt this Nero hath hem slain.
Now wol I turne to my tale again.
  The sely° widwe and eek hir doughtres two *innocent*
Herden thise hennes crye and maken wo,
And out at dores sterten° they anoon, *leaped*
And sien° the fox toward the grove goon, *saw*
And bar upon his bak the cok away,
And criden, "Out, harrow,° and wailaway, *help*
Ha, ha, the fox," and after him they ran,
And eek with staves many another man;
Ran Colle oure dogge, and Talbot and Gerland,[7]
And Malkin with a distaf in hir hand,
Ran cow and calf, and eek the verray hogges,
Sore aferd° for berking of the dogges *frightened*
And shouting of the men and wommen eke.
They ronne° so hem thoughte hir herte breke;[8] *ran*
They yelleden as feendes doon in helle;
The dokes° criden as men wolde hem quelle;° *ducks / kill*
The gees for fere flowen° over the trees; *flew*
Out of the hive cam the swarm of bees;
So hidous was the noise, a, benedicite,° *bless me*
Certes, he Jakke Straw[9] and his meinee° *company*
Ne made nevere shoutes half so shrille
Whan that they wolden any Fleming kille,
As thilke day was maad upon the fox:
Of bras they broughten bemes° and of box,° *trumpets / boxwood*
Of horn, of boon,° in whiche they blewe and pouped,[1] *bone*
And therwithal they skriked[2] and they houped—
It semed as that hevene sholde falle.
  Now goode men, I praye you herkneth alle:
Lo, how Fortune turneth° sodeinly *reverses, overturns*

4. Splendidly.
5. Hasdrubal was king of Carthage when it was destroyed by the Romans.
6. According to the legend, Nero not only set fire to Rome (in A.D. 64) but also put many senators to death.
7. Two other dogs.
8. Would break.
9. One of the leaders of the Peasant's Revolt in 1381, which was partially directed against the Flemings living in London.
1. Tooted.
2. Shrieked; "houped": whooped.

The hope and pride eek of hir enemy.
This cok that lay upon the foxes bak,
In al his drede unto the fox he spak,
And saide, "Sire, if that I were as ye,
Yit sholde I sayn, as wis° God helpe me, *surely*
'Turneth ayain, ye proude cherles alle!
A verray pestilence upon you falle!
Now am I come unto this wodes side,
Maugree your heed,[3] the cok shal here abide.
I wol him ete, in faith, and that anoon.' "
  The fox answerde, "In faith, it shal be doon."
And as he spak that word, al sodeinly
The cok brak from his mouth deliverly,° *nimbly*
And hye upon a tree he fleigh° anoon. *flew*
  And whan the fox sawgh that he was agoon,
"Allas," quod he, "O Chauntecleer, allas!
I have to you," quod he, "ydoon trespas,
In as muche as I maked you aferd
Whan I you hente° and broughte out of the yeerd. *seized*
But sire, I dide it in no wikke° entente: *wicked*
Come down, and I shal telle you what I mente.
I shal saye sooth to you, God help me so."
  "Nay thanne," quod he, "I shrewe° us bothe two: *curse*
But first I shrewe myself, bothe blood and bones,
If thou bigile me ofter than ones;
Thou shalt namore thurgh thy flaterye
Do° me to singe and winken with myn yë. *cause*
For he that winketh whan he sholde see,
Al wilfully, God lat him nevere thee."° *thrive*
  "Nay," quod the fox, "but God yive him meschaunce
That is so undiscreet of governaunce° *self-control*
That jangleth° whan he sholde holde his pees." *chatters*
  Lo, swich it is for to be recchelees° *careless*
And necligent and truste on flaterye.
But ye that holden this tale a folye
As of a fox, or of a cok and hen,
Taketh the moralitee, goode men.
For Saint Paul saith that al that writen is
To oure doctrine it is ywrit, ywis:[4]
Taketh the fruit, and lat the chaf be stille.
Now goode God, if that it be thy wille,
As saith my lord, so make us alle goode men,
And bringe us to his hye blisse. Amen.

3. Despite your head—i.e., despite anything you can do.

4. See Romans xv.4.

From The Parson's Tale[1]

The Introduction

By that[2] the Manciple hadde his tale al ended,
The sonne fro the south line[3] was decended
So lowe, that he nas nat to my sighte
Degrees nine and twenty as in highte.
Four of the clokke it was, so as I gesse,
For elevene foot, or litel more or lesse,
My shadwe was at thilke time as there,
Of swich feet as° my lengthe parted° were *as if / divided*
In sixe feet equal of proporcioun.[4]
Therwith the moones exaltacioun[5]—
I mene Libra—alway gan ascende,
As we were entring at a thropes° ende. *village's*
For which oure Host, as he was wont to gie° *lead*
As in this caas oure joly compaignye,
Saide in this wise, "Lordinges everichoon,
Now lakketh us no tales mo than oon:
Fulfild is my sentence° and my decree; *purpose*
I trowe° that we han herd of eech degree; *believe*
Almost fulfild is al myn ordinaunce.
I praye to God, so yive him right good chaunce

1. Among the moral writers of the later Middle Ages the pilgrimage was so commonly treated as an allegory of man's life that Chaucer's audience must have been surprised to find the *Canterbury Tales* so little allegorical. At the end of his life, however, and at the end of his work, Chaucer seems to have been caught up in the venerable allegory. Some ten months before his death he rented a house in the garden of Westminster Abbey, and it is possible that during these months—perhaps when he felt his death approaching—he fell under the influence of the monks of Westminster. In any case, in the Parson's Tale, and in its short Introduction and in the Retraction that follows it, Chaucer seems to be making an end for two pilgrimages that had become one, that of his fiction and that of his life.

In the Introduction to the tale we find the 29 pilgrims moving through a nameless little village as the sun sinks to within 29 degrees of the horizon. The atmosphere contains something of both the chill and the urgency of a late autumn afternoon, and we are surprised to find that the pilgrimage is almost over, that there is need for haste in order to make that "good end" that every medieval Christian hoped for. This delicately suggestive passage, rich with allegorical overtones, introduces an extremely long sermon on penitence and the seven deadly sins, probably translated by Chaucer from French or Latin some years earlier, before he had begun the *Canterbury Tales*.

The sermon is at times not without animation, but in general Chaucer provides no exception to the statement that Middle English prose is inferior to Middle English verse. But then the intent of the sermon is didactic, not artistic, and according to the more rigorous theologians of the time, didactic intent is infinitely more important than artistic expression.

It is to this doctrine that Chaucer yielded at the end of his life. The Retraction which follows and concludes the Parson's Tale offers Chaucer's apology for having written all the works on which his reputation as a great poet depends, not only such stories as the Miller's Tale, but also his loveliest and seemingly most harmless poems. Yet a readiness to deny his own reality before the reality of his God is implicit in many of Chaucer's works, and the placement of the Retraction within the artistic structure of the *Canterbury Tales* suggests that while Chaucer denied his art, he seems to have recognized that he and it were inseparable.

2. By the time that.

3. I.e., the line that runs some 28 degrees to the south of the celestial equator and parallel to it.

4. This detailed analysis merely says that the shadows are lengthening.

5. I.e., the astrological sign in which the moon's influence was dominant. "Libra": the constellation of the Scales.

That telleth this tale to us lustily.
Sire preest," quod he, "artou a vicary,° *vicar*
Or arte a Person? Say sooth, by thy fay.° *faith*
Be what thou be, ne breek° thou nat oure play, *break*
For every man save thou hath told his tale.
Unbokele and shew us what is in thy male!° *bag*
For trewely, me thinketh by thy cheere° *expression*
Thou sholdest knitte up wel a greet matere.
Tel us a fable anoon, for cokkes bones!"
This Person answerde al atones,[6]
"Thou getest fable noon ytold for me,
For Paul, that writeth unto Timothee,
Repreveth° hem that waiven soothfastnesse,[7] *reproves*
And tellen fables and swich wrecchednesse.
Why sholde I sowen draf° out of my fest,° *chaff / fist*
Whan I may sowen whete if that me lest?[8]
For which I saye that if you list to heere
Moralitee and vertuous matere,
And thanne that ye wol yive me audience,
I wol ful fain,° at Cristes reverence, *gladly*
Do you plesance leveful° as I can. *lawful*
But trusteth wel, I am a southren man:
I can nat geeste Rum-Ram-Ruf by lettre[9]—
Ne, God woot, rym holde° I but litel bettre. *consider*
And therfore, if you list, I wol nat glose;[1]
I wol you telle a merye tale in prose,
To knitte up al this feeste and make an ende.
And Jesu for his grace wit me sende
To shewe you the way in this viage° *journey*
Of thilke parfit glorious pilgrimage
That highte Jerusalem celestial.
And if ye vouche sauf, anoon I shal
Biginne upon my tale, for which I praye
Telle youre avis:° I can no bettre saye. *opinion*
But nathelees, this meditacioun
I putte it ay under correccioun
Of clerkes, for I am nat textuel:[2]
I take but the sentence,° trusteth wel. *meaning*
Therfore I make protestacioun° *public acknowledgment*
That I wol stonde to correccioun."
Upon this word we han assented soone,
For, as it seemed, it was for to doone
To enden in som vertuous sentence,° *doctrine*
And for to yive him space and audience;
And bede[3] oure Host he sholde to him saye
That alle we to telle his tale him praye.

6. Immediately.
7. Depart from truth. See I Timothy i.4.
8. It pleases me.
9. I.e., I cannot tell stories in the alliterative measure (without rhyme): this form of poetry was not common in southeastern England.
1. I.e., speak in order to please.
2. Literal, faithful to the letter.
3. I.e., we bade.

Oure Hoste hadde the wordes for us alle:
"Sire preest," quod he, "now faire you bifalle:
Telleth," quod he, "youre meditacioun.
But hasteth you; the sonne wol adown.
Beeth fructuous,° and that in litel space,° *fruitful / time*
And to do wel God sende you his grace.
Saye what you list, and we wol gladly heere."
And with that word he saide in this manere.

Chaucer's Retraction

Now praye I to hem alle that herkne this litel tretis[8] or rede, that if ther be any thing in it that liketh[9] hem, that therof they thanken oure Lord Jesu Crist, of whom proceedeth al wit[1] and al goodnesse. And if ther be any thing that displese him, I praye hem also that they arrette it to the defaute of myn unconning,[2] and nat to my wil, that wolde ful fain have said bettre if I hadde had conning. For oure book saith, "Al that is writen is writen for oure doctrine,"[3] and that is myn entente. Wherfore I biseeke[4] you mekely, for the mercy of God, that ye praye for me that Crist have mercy on me and foryive me my giltes, and namely[5] of my translacions and enditinges of worldly vanitees, the whiche I revoke in my retraccions: as is the *Book of Troilus*; the Book also of *Fame*; the *Book of the Five and Twenty Ladies;*[6] the *Book of the Duchesse;* the *Book of Saint Valentines Day of the Parlement of Briddes*; the *Tales of Canterbury*, thilke that sounen into[7] sinne; the *Book of the Leon;*[8] and many another book, if they were in my remembrance, and many a song and many a leccherous lay: that Crist for his grete mercy foryive me the sinne. But of the translacion of Boece[9] *De Consolatione*, and othere bookes of legendes of saintes, and omelies,[1] and moralitee, and devocion, that thanke I oure Lord Jesu Crist and his blisful Moder and alle the saintes of hevene, biseeking hem that they from hennes[2] forth unto my lives ende sende me grace to biwaile my giltes and to studye to the salvacion of my soule, and graunte me grace of verray penitence, confession, and satisfaccion to doon in this present lif, thurgh the benigne grace of him that is king of kinges and preest over alle preestes, that boughte[3] us with the precious blood of his herte, so that I may been oon of hem at the day of doom that shulle be saved. *Qui cum patre et Spiritu Sancto vivis et regnas Deus per omnia saecula.*[4] *Amen.*

1386–1400

8. Hear this little treatise.
9. Pleases.
1. Understanding.
2. Ascribe it to the defect of my lack of skill.
3. Romans xv.4.
4. Beseech.
5. Especially. "Enditinges": compositions.
6. I.e., the *Legend of Good Women.*
7. Those that tend toward.
8. The *Book of the Lion* has not been preserved.
9. Boethius.
1. Homilies.
2. Hence.
3. Redeemed.
4. Who with the Father and the Holy Spirit livest and reignest God forever.

Lyrics and Occasional Verse[1]

To Rosamond[2]

Madame, ye been of alle beautee shrine
As fer as cercled is the mapemounde:[3]
For as the crystal glorious ye shine,
And like ruby been youre cheekes rounde.
Therwith ye been so merye and so jocounde
That at a revel whan that I see you daunce
It is an oinement unto my wounde,
Though ye to me ne do no daliaunce.[4]

For though I weepe of teres ful a tine,° *tub*
Yit may that wo myn herte nat confounde;
Youre semy° vois, that ye so smale outtwine,[5] *small*
Maketh my thought in joye and blis habounde:° *abound*
So curteisly I go with love bounde
That to myself I saye in my penaunce,[6]
"Suffiseth me to love you, Rosemounde,
Though ye to me ne do no daliaunce."

Was nevere pik walwed in galauntine[7]
As I in love am walwed and ywounde,
For which ful ofte I of myself divine
That I am trewe Tristam[8] the secounde;
My love may not refreide nor affounde;[9]
I brenne° ay in amorous plesaunce: *burn*
Do what you list, I wol youre thral° be founde, *slave*
Though ye to me ne do no daliaunce.

1. As a man of accomplishments who was often at court, Chaucer must, like other courtiers, have been called upon to write both occasional verses and lyrics. Of the handful of these shorter poems that have survived, several of the best are included here: they reveal the ways in which Chaucer handled some of the poetic modes and attitudes of his time. These modes—particularly the lyric strain, which seeks expression in a brief form—seem to have been uncongenial to his temperament. Some, in fact, might well be termed "anti-lyrics"; these are the poems where the extreme conventions of the courtly-love lyric become a framework in which Chaucer's irony and indirection may be brought into immediate play. Chaucer's best work, however, is in his longer poems, for irony and indirection are qualities which can be given proper development only if the poet has ample room to work in.

2. This lyric extends the extravagant images of the stylized courtly-love lyric to outrageous lengths: a lover might well weep a flood of tears but would hardly measure them by the tubful (line 9), and he might be overwhelmed with love—but not like a fish buried in sauce (line 17). The general imperturbability of tone contrasts ironically with the grotesque metaphors.

3. I.e., to the farthest circumference of the map of the world.

4. I.e., show me no encouragement.

5. That you so delicately spin out.

6. I.e., pangs of unrequited love.

7. Pike rolled in galantine sauce.

8. The famous lover of Isolt (Iseult, Isolde) in medieval legend, renowned for his constancy.

9. Cool nor chill.

To His Scribe Adam[1]

Adam scrivain,° if evere it thee bifalle — *scribe*
Boece[2] or *Troilus* for to writen newe,
Under thy longe lokkes thou moste[3] have the scalle,° — *scurf*
But after my making thou write more trewe,[4]
So ofte a day I moot° thy werk renewe, — *must*
It to correcte, and eek to rubbe and scrape:
And al is thurgh thy necligence and rape.° — *haste*

Complaint to His Purse[5]

To you. my purs, and to noon other wight,
Complaine I, for ye be my lady dere.
I am so sory, now that ye be light,
For certes, but if[6] ye make me hevy cheere,
Me were as lief[7] be laid upon my beere;° — *bier*
For which unto youre mercy thus I crye:
Beeth hevy again, or elles moot° I die. — *must*

Now voucheth sauf this day er it be night
That I of you the blisful soun may heere,
Or see youre colour, lik the sonne bright,
That of yelownesse hadde nevere peere.
Ye be my life, ye be myn hertes steere,° — *rudder, guide*
Queene of confort and of good compaignye:
Beeth hevy again, or elles moot I die.

Ye purs, that been to me my lives light
And saviour, as in this world down here,
Out of this tonne[8] helpe me thurgh your might,
Sith that ye wol nat be my tresorere;° — *disburser*
For I am shave as neigh° as any frere.° — *close / friar*
But yit I praye unto youre curteisye:
Beeth hevy again, or elles moot I die.

1. This *jeu d'esprit*, called forth by the inefficiency of his amanuensis, is written in the verse form of Chaucer's great poem *Troilus and Criseide*.
2. I.e., Chaucer's translation of Boethius' *De Consolatione*. "*Troilus*": *Troilus and Criseide*.
3. I.e., may you.
4. Unless you write more accurately what I've composed.
5. In this variation on the courtly-love lyric the conventional language of love is both used and misused to express love of cash. Ladies, like coins, should be golden, and like purses they should not be "light" (i.e., fickle). On the other hand, they should not be heavy, as purses should be. The poem is in the characteristic three-stanza *ballade* form, with the usual "envoy" addressed to a noble patron. In this case the patron apparently heard the complaint, for, three days after his accession (in 1399), King Henry IV renewed and increased the pension Chaucer had received from Richard II.
6. Unless.
7. I'd just as soon.
8. Tun, meaning "predicament."

Envoy to Henry IV

O conquerour of Brutus Albioun,[9]
Which that by line and free eleccioun
Been verray king, this song to you I sende:
And ye, that mowen° alle oure harmes amende, *may*
Have minde upon my supplicacioun.

Merciless Beauty[1]

1

Youre yën two wol slee° me sodeinly: *slay*
I may the beautee of hem nat sustene,° *withstand*
So woundeth it thurghout myn herte keene.° *keenly*

And but° youre word wol helen hastily *unless*
Myn hertes wounde, whil that it is greene,[2]
  Youre yën two wol slee me sodeinly:
  I may the beautee of hem nat sustene.

Upon my trouthe, I saye you faithfully
That ye been of my lif and deeth the queene,
For with my deeth the trouthe shal be seene.
  Youre yën two wol slee me sodeinly:
  I may the beautee of hem nat sustene,
  So woundeth it thurghout myn herte keene.

2

So hath youre beautee fro youre herte chaced
Pitee, that me ne availeth nought to plaine:° *complain*
For Daunger halt[3] youre mercy in his chaine.

Giltelees my deeth thus han ye me purchaced;° *procured*
I saye you sooth, me needeth nought to feine:° *dissemble*
  So hath youre beautee fro youre herte chaced
  Pitee, that me ne availeth nought to plaine.

Allas, that nature hath in you compaced° *enclosed*
So greet beautee that no man may attaine
To mercy, though he sterve° for the paine. *die*
  So hath youre beautee fro youre herte chaced

9. Britain (Albion) was supposed to have been founded by Brutus, the grandson of Aeneas, the founder of Rome.

1. The first two sections of this poem employ the typical imagery and extravagant emotion of courtly-love lyrics—the power of the lady's eyes to slay the lover, for instance, and the struggle between her native pity and her "daunger" (haughtiness). But it ends where a real lyric could never end: the poet's self-congratulation, at the failure of his affair, on his unimpaired health.

2. I.e., fresh.

3. Haughtiness holds.

Pitee, that me ne availeth nought to plaine:
For Daunger halt youre mercy in his chaine.

3

Sin I fro Love escaped am so fat,
I nevere thenke° to been in his prison lene: *intend*
Sin I am free, I counte him nat a bene.[4]

He may answere and saye right this and that;
I do no fors,[5] I speke right as I mene:
Sin I fro Love escaped am so fat,
I nevere thenke to been in his prison lene.

Love hath my name ystrike° out of his sclat,° *struck / slate*
And he is strike out of my bookes clene
For everemo; ther is noon other mene.° *solution*
Sin I fro Love escaped am so fat,
I nevere thenke to been in his prison lene:
Sin I am free, I counte him nat a bene.

Gentilesse[6]

The firste fader and findere° of gentilesse, *founder*
What° man desireth gentil for to be *whatever*
Moste folwe his traas,° and alle his wittes dresse[7] *path*
Vertu to sue,° and vices for to flee: *follow*
For unto vertu longeth° dignitee, *belongs*
And nought the revers, saufly° dar I deeme, *safely*
Al were he[8] mitre, crowne, or diademe.

This firste stok was ground of rightwisnesse,° *righteousness*
Trewe of his word, sobre, pietous,[9] and free,
Clene of his gost,° and loved bisinesse *spirit*
Against the vice of slouthe,° in honestee; *sloth*
And but his heir love vertu as dide he,
He is nat gentil, though he riche° seeme, *noble*
Al were he mitre, crowne, or diademe.

Vice may wel be heir to old richesse,
But ther may no man, as ye may wel see,
Biquethe his heir his vertuous noblesse:
That is appropred° unto no degree *exclusively assigned*

4. I don't consider him worth a bean.
5. I don't care.
6. The virtue of "gentilesse" combined a courtesy of manner with a courtesy of mind. That it is not the inevitable adjunct of aristocratic birth (though most appropriate to it) was a medieval commonplace, to which Chaucer here gives succinct—if conventional—expression. It is important to observe, however, that the moral democracy implied by this doctrine was never transferred by the Middle Ages to the political or even the social realm.
7. I.e., must follow his (the first father's) path and dispose all his (own) wits.
8. Even if he wear.
9. Merciful; "free": generous.

But to the firste fader in majestee,
That maketh his heir him that wol him queme,° — *please*
Al were he mitre, crowne, or diademe.

Truth[1]

Flee fro the prees° and dwelle with soothfastnesse; — *crowd*
Suffise unto° thy thing, though it be smal; — *be content with*
For hoord hath[2] hate, and climbing tikelnesse;° — *insecurity*
Prees hath envye, and wele° blent° overal. — *prosperity / blinds*
Savoure° no more than thee bihoove shal; — *relish*
Rule wel thyself that other folk canst rede:° — *advise*
And Trouthe shal delivere,[3] it is no drede.° — *doubt*

Tempest thee nought al crooked to redresse[4]
In trust of hire[5] that turneth as a bal;
Muche wele stant in litel bisinesse;[6]
Be war therfore to spurne ayains an al.[7]
Strive nat as dooth the crokke° with the wal. — *pot*
Daunte° thyself that dauntest otheres deede: — *master*
And Trouthe shal delivere, it is no drede.

That thee is sent, receive in buxomnesse;° — *obedience*
The wrastling for the world axeth° a fal; — *asks for*
Here is noon hoom, here nis but wildernesse:
Forth, pilgrim, forth! Forth, beest, out of thy stal!
Know thy countree, looke up, thank God of al.
Hold the heigh way and lat thy gost° thee lede: — *spirit*
And Trouthe shal delivere, it is no drede.

Therfore, thou Vache,[8] leve thyn olde wrecchednesse
Unto the world; leve[9] now to be thral.
Crye him mercy that of his heigh goodnesse
Made thee of nought, and in especial
Draw unto him, and pray in general,
For thee and eek for othere, hevenelich meede:° — *reward*
And Trouthe shal delivere, it is no drede.

1. Taking as his theme Christ's words to his disciples (in John viii.32), "And ye shall know the truth, and the truth shall make you free," Chaucer plays upon the triple meaning that the Middle English word "trouthe" seems to have had for him: the religious truth of Christianity, the moral virtue of integrity, and the philosophical idea of reality. By maintaining one's faith and one's integrity, one rises superior to the vicissitudes of this world and comes eventually to know reality—which is not, however, of this world.
2. Hoarding causes.
3. I.e., truth shall make you free.
4. Do not disturb yourself to straighten all that's crooked.
5. Fortune, who turns like a ball in that she is always presenting a different aspect to men.
6. Peace of mind stands in little anxiety.
7. I.e. to kick against the pricks.
8. Probably Sir Philip de la Vache, with a pun on the French for "cow."
9. I.e. cease.

SIR ORFEO

(ca. 1300)

Sir Orfeo is a reworking of the classical myth of the great musician Orpheus and his wife Eurydice. According to Ovid's *Metamorphoses*, Eurydice died of a snake-bite at her wedding and went to Hades, the place of the dead. Orpheus undertook to follow her there, and having come before Pluto and Proserpina, the king and queen of Hades, he so pleased them with his music that they granted Eurydice's release—on the condition, however, that she should follow behind Orpheus as they left Hades and that he should not look back at her. But Orpheus did look back, and Eurydice disappeared into Hades. Ovid's stories were told and retold during the Middle Ages, and frequently the teller altered the plot to suit his own purposes—in her tale the Wife of Bath (lines 958ff.) substitutes Midas' wife for his barber as the discoverer of his asses' ears. The poet of *Sir Orfeo* has given the story a happy ending and has replaced its alien classical elements with familiar elements of medieval folklore. Hades has become the land of *Fairye*, the medieval otherworld, inhabited by supernatural creatures who seem human in most respects but who exist under laws incomprehensible to ordinary human beings. There is no rational explanation of why the king of Fairye should seize Dame Heurodis (Eurydice), except that by going to sleep under an *impe-tree* (a grafted fruit-tree), she unwittingly violated a taboo and put herself in his power. In folklore trees are, of course, often given sinister properties: in lines 885 ff. of her tale the Wife of Bath comments that incubi once resided under trees, and in *The Faerie Queene* I.ii.30 the Redcross Knight has a frightening experience with a tree he is sitting under. In the Otherworld Dame Heurodis continues to sleep under a tree—apparently a replica of the one in her own garden.

That the poem was the product of a minstrel seems certain because of the emphasis laid upon the value of music. Orfeo is an excellent harper who welcomes all good harpers to his court. When he becomes a hermit, he keeps his harp near him and plays on it to solace himself. The animals and birds crowd around him in delight—as they did with Orpheus—and like the original Orpheus he frees his wife by his music. When he returns to his own kingdom it is by his harp and his harping that he is identified. Even Orfeo's steward appreciates music: in most medieval romances stewards are pictured as wicked, for they were the court officers responsible for offering or withholding hospitality for minstrels, and apparently they often withheld it. With unusual tact, the poet depicts a good steward who, partly because of his courtesy to harpers, becomes king after Orfeo's death.

The poem was probably translated from a French romance of the kind called a Breton lay. As the name implies, this genre of romance had its origin in Brittany, a place noted for its minstrelsy. Other surviving lays share with *Sir Orfeo* a plot involving the supernatural, wedded or romantic love, and a rash promise; they also share the poem's stylistic simplicity, brevity, and a generally optimistic spirit. Chaucer's Franklin's Tale imitates the form, and it is probable that his model was *Sir Orfeo*, whose opening lines the Franklin seems to be echoing in his own story. The English translation was probably made before 1300, but it has survived in only three manuscripts of later date. Some scholars believe that the best of these, the Auchinleck manuscript, may once have been read by Chaucer. Only the Auchinleck manuscript makes the interesting identification of *Traciens* (Thrace) with Winchester: some English minstrel poet obviously adapted the poem to a performance at Winchester, which had, indeed, in Old English times been the seat of a kingdom. (It was probably the same poet who, fractionally learned, names King Pluto and King Juno among Orfeo's ancestors.)

The text presented here is based on the Auchinleck manuscript, though the spelling has been normalized and readings from the other manuscripts adopted where they seem better than Auchinleck's. In view of the large amount of evident corruption in all three manuscripts, the editor has made a number of conjectural emendations. The original metrical form was probably octosyllabic couplets with alternating stress, but what has come down to us are loose four-stressed couplets. As in Chaucer, there are many "headless" lines, where the stress falls on the first syllable of the line, even though the syllable is not a rhetorically important one; and also as in Chaucer, while final *e* is frequently used to achieve an unstressed syllable, it is equally often ignored.

Sir Orfeo

We reden ofte and finden ywrite—
As thise clerkes doon° us wite°— *cause / to learn*
The layes that been of harping[1]
Been yfounde° of freely° thing. *composed / pleasant*
Some been of werre° and some of wo, *war*
And some of joye and mirthe also,
And some of trecherye and of gile;
And some of happes° that fellen° while,° *events / occurred / once*
And some of bourdes° and ribaudye,° *jokes / ribaldry*
And manye been of faïrye.[2]
Of alle thing that men may see,
Most of love forsoothe they be.
In Britain° thise layes been wrought, *Brittany*
First yfounde° and forth ybrought. *composed*
Of aventures that felle° by dayes[3] *occurred*
The Britons° therof maden layes: *Bretons*
Whan they mighte owher° yheere° *anywhere / hear*
Of any merveiles that ther were,
They tooken hem hir harpes with game,° *pleasure*
Maden layes and yaf° hem name. *gave*
Of aventures that han bifalle
I can some telle, but nought alle.
Herkneth, lordinges° that been trewe, *gentlemen*
I wol you telle of Sir Orfewe.
Orfeo was a riche° king, *noble*

1. I.e., composed to be sung to the harp.
2. Fairyland, and, more commonly, the other-world and its supernatural inhabitants.
3. Once.

In Engelond an heigh lording,
A stalworth° man and hardy bo,° *valiant / both*
Large° and curteis° he was also. *generous / courteous*
His fader was come of King Pluto,
And his moder of King Juno,
That somtime were as goddes yholde° *considered*
For aventures that they dide and tolde.
This king sojourned in Traciens° *Thrace*
That is a citee of noble defens° *fortification*
(For Winchester was cleped° tho° *called / then*
Traciens withouten no°). *denial*
Orfeo most of any thing
Loved the glee° of harping: *music*
Siker° was every good harpour *certain*
Of him to have muche honour.
Himself he lerned for to harpe,
And laide° theron his wittes sharpe;° *applied / keenly*
He lerned so ther nothing was
A bettre harpour in no plas.° *place*
In al the world was no man bore° *born*
That ones° Orfeo sat bifore, *once*
And° he mighte of his harping heere, *if*
But he sholde thinke that he were
In oon of the joyes of Paradis,
Swich melodye in his harping is.
Orfeo hadde a queene of pris° *excellence*
That was ycleped° Dame Heurodis, *named*
The fairest lady for the° nones° *that / matter*
That mighte goon° on body and bones, *walk*
Ful of love and of goodnesse—
But no man may telle hir fairnesse.
Bifel so, the comsing° of May, *beginning*
When merye and hot is the day,
And away been winter showres,
And every feeld is ful of flowres,
And blosme breme° on every bough *glorious*
Overal° wexeth° merye ynough, *everywhere / grows*
This eeche° queene Dame Heurodis *same*
Took with hire two maides of pris° *excellence*
And wente in the undertide° *forenoon*
To playe in an orchard-side,
To see the flowres sprede° and springe *open*
And to heere the fowles singe.
They setten hem down alle three
Faire° under an impe-tree;° *fairly / grafted fruit tree*
And wel soone this faire queene
Fel on sleepe upon the greene.
The maidens durste hire not awake,
But lete hire lie and reste take.
So she slepte til afternoon
That undertide was al ydoon.° *passed*

But as soone as she gan wake
She cried and loothly bere° gan make: *outcry*
She frotte° hir hondes and hir feet *tore at*
And cracched° hir visage—it bledde weet;° *scratched / wet*
Hir riche robe she al torit,° *tears apart*
And was ravised° out of her wit. *ravished*
The two maidenes hire biside
Ne durste with hire no leng° abide, *longer*
But runne to the palais right
And tolde bothe squier and knight
That hir queene awede° wolde, *go mad*
And bad hem go and hire atholde.° *restrain*
Knightes runne and ladies also,
Damiseles sixty and mo,° *more*
In th' orchard to the queene they come,
And hire up in armes nome,° *took*
And broughte hire to bed at laste,
And heelde hire there fine° faste. *very*
But evere she heeld° in oo° cry, *continued / one*
And wolde uppe° and awy.° *get up / go away*
   Whan the king herde that tiding
Nevere him nas worse for no thing:
Orfeo cam with knightes tene° *ten*
To chambre right bifore the queene,
And looked and saide with greet° pitee, *great*
"O leve° lif, what aileth thee?— *dear*
That evere yit hast been so stille,
And now thou gredest° wonder shille.° *cry out / shrilly*
Thy body that was so whit ycore° *excellent*
With thine nailes is all totore.° *torn*
Allas, thy rode° that was so reed° *complexion / red*
Is as wan as thou were deed.° *dead*
And also thy fingres smale
Been al bloody and al pale.
Allas, thy lovesome yën two
Looketh so° man dooth on his fo. *as*
A, dame, ich° biseeche mercy— *I*
Lete been al this reweful° cry, *pitiful*
And tel me what° thee is and how, *what the matter with*
And what thing may thee helpe now."
   Tho° lay she stille at the laste, *then*
And gan to weepe swithe° faste,° *very / hard*
And saide thus the king unto:
"Allas, my lord Sir Orfeo,
Sitthen° we first togider were *since*
Ones wrothe° nevere we nere, *angry*
But evere ich have yloved thee
As my lif, and so thou me.
But now we mote° deele° atwo— *must / separate*
Do thy best, for I moot° go." *must*
   "Allas," quath he, "forlorn ich am!

Whider wilt thou go and to wham?° *whom*
Whider thou goost ich wil with thee,
And whider I go thou shalt with me."
"Nay, nay, sire, that nought nis.[4]
Ich wil thee telle al how it is:
As ich lay this undertide° *forenoon*
And slepte under oure orchard-side,
Ther come to me two faire knightes,
Wel y-armed al to rightes,
And bad me comen on hying° *in haste*
And speke with hir lord the king;
And ich answerede at° wordes bolde *in*
That I ne durste nought ne I nolde.° *would not*
They prikked again as they mighte drive.[5]
Tho° cam hir king also blive° *then / straightway*
With an hundred knightes and mo,
And damiseles an hundred also,
Alle on snow-white steedes;
As white as milk were hir weedes:° *clothes*
I ne seigh° nevere yit bifore *saw*
So faire creatures ycore.° *splendid*
The king hadde a crown on his heed:° *head*
It nas of silver n'of gold reed,° *red*
But it was of a precious stoon;
As brighte as the sonne it shoon.
And as soone as he to me cam,
Wolde ich, nolde ich, he me nam° *took*
And made me with him to ride
Upon a palfrey him biside,
And broughte me to his palais
Wel attired° in eech a ways,° *equipped / way*
And shewed me castels and towrs,
Riveres, foreestes, frith° with flowres, *meadow*
And his riche steedes eechoon,
And sitthen° broughte me again hoom *afterwards*
Into oure owene orche-yard,° *orchard*
And saide to me thus afterward,
'Looke tomorwe that thou be
Right here under this impe-tree,
And thanne thou shalt with us go,
And live with us everemo.° *evermore*
And if thou makest us ylet,° *resistance*
Where° thou be, thou worst° yfet.° *wherever / shall be / fetched*
And al totore° thy limes al *torn apart*
That no thing thee helpe shal.
And though thou beest so totorn,
Yit thou worst° with us yborn.' "° *shall be / carried off*

4. I.e., that's no use.

5. I.e., they rode as fast as they could.

When king Orfeo herde this cas,° *circumstance*
"O, wee!"° quath he, "allas, allas! *woe*
Lever me were to lete° my lif *leave*
Than thus to lese° the queene my wif." *lose*
He asked conseil at° eech a man, *from*
But no man him helpe can.
Amorwe° the undertide is come, *next day*
And Orfeo hath his armes ynome,° *taken*
And wel ten hundred knightes with him,
Eech y-armed, stout and grim.
And with the queene wenten he° *they*
Right unto that impe-tree.
They made sheltrom° in eech a side, *military formation*
And saide they wolde ther abide
And die there everichoon,
Er the queene sholde from hem goon.
And yit amiddes hem ful right
The queene was away ytwight,° *snatched*
With° faïrye forth ynome:° *by / taken*
Men wiste nevere wher she was bicome.[6]
Tho° was ther crying, weep and wo; *then*
The king into his chambre is go
And ofte swooned upon the stoon,° *floor*
And made swich dool and swich moon[7]
That nye° his lif was yspent°— *nearly / finished*
Ther was noon amendement.° *remedy*
He clepte° togider his barouns, *called*
Eerles, lordes of renouns,° *great names*
And whan they alle ycomen were,
"Lordinges," he saide, "bifor you here
Ich ordaine myn heigh steward
To wite° my kingdom afterward; *keep*
In my stede been he shal
To keepe my londes overal.° *everywhere*
For now I have my queene ylore,° *lost*
The faireste lady that evere was bore,° *born*
Nevere eft° I nil° no womman see; *again / will not*
In wildernesse now wil ich tee° *go*
And live ther for everemore,
With wilde beestes in holtes° hore.° *woods / gray*
And whan ye wite° that I be spent,° *learn / dead*
Make you than a parlement
And chese° you° a newe king: *choose / for yourselves*
Now dooth youre best with al my thing."
Tho° was ther weeping in the halle, *then*
And greet° cry among hem alle; *great*
Unnethe° mighte olde or yong *scarcely*

6. No one knew what had become of her.
7. And made such lamentation and such complaint.

For weeping speke a word with tonge.
They kneeled alle adown in fere°   *together*
And prayede him if his wille were,
That he ne sholde from hem go.
"Do way," quath he, "it shal be so."
  Al his kingdom he forsook;
But° a sclavin° on him he took: *only / pilgrim's cloak*
He hadde no kirtel° ne noon hood,   *short coat*
Shert ne yit noon other good.
But his harp he took algate,°   *at any rate*
And dide him barefoot out at yate:°   *gate*
No man moste° with him go.   *must*
  O way,° what° ther was weep and wo,   *alas / how*
Whan he that hadde been king with crown
Wente so poorelich out of town.
Thrugh the wode° and over heeth   *wood*
Into the wildernesse he geeth.°   *goes*
Nothing he fint° that him is aise,°   *finds / easy*
But evere he liveth in greet malaise.
He that hadde wered° the fowe and gris,[8]   *worn*
And on bed the purper° bis,°   *purple / linen*
Now on harde heeth he lith,°   *lies*
With leves and grasse he him writh.°   *covers*
He that hadde had castels and towres,
Rivere, foreest, frith° with flowres,   *meadow*
Now though it ginne snowe and freese,
This king moot° make his bed in meese.°   *must / moss*
He that hadde had knightes of pris,°   *renown*
Bifore him kneeling and ladis,
Now seeth he nothing that him liketh,°   *pleases*
But wilde wormes° by him striketh.°   *snakes / glide*
He that hadde yhad plentee
Of mete and drinke, of eech daintee,
Now may he alday° digge and wrote°   *constantly / scrounge*
Er he finde his fille of roote.
In somer he liveth by wilde fruit
And berien° but goode lite;[9]   *berries*
In winter may he nothing finde
But roote, grasses, and the rinde.°   *bark*
Al his body away was dwined°   *wasted*
For misaise, and al tochined.°   *scarred*
Lord, who may telle of the sore
This king suffered ten yeer and more?
His heer of his beerd, blak and rowe,°   *rugged*
To his girdel-stede° was growe.   *waist*
His harp wheron was al his glee
He hidde in an holwe tree,
And whan the weder was cleer and bright,

8. White and gray fur; i.e., royal ermine. 9. Little good.

He took his harp to him wel right,
And harped at his owene wille:° *pleasure*
In al the woode the soun gan shille,° *resound*
That wilde beestes that ther beeth
For joy abouten him they teeth;° *draw*
And alle the fowles that ther were
Come and sete on eech a brere° *briar*
To here his harping afine,° *to the end*
So muche melodye was therine.
When he his harping lete° wolde, *leave off*
No beest by him abide nolde.
  Ofte he mighte see him bisides
In the hote undertides° *mornings*
The king of fairy with his route° *company*
Come to hunte him al aboute
With dinne, cry, and with blowing,
And houndes also with him berking.
But no beeste they ne nome° *took*
Ne nevere he niste wher they bicome.[1]
And otherwhile he mighte see,
As a greet oost° by him tee,° *host / passed*
Wel atourned° ten hundred knightes, *equipped*
Eech y-armed to his rightes,° *fittingly*
Of countenance stout and fiers,° *fierce*
With manye displayed° baners, *unfurled*
And eech his swerd ydrawe holde,
But nevere he niste° wher they wolde, *knew not*
And somwhile he seigh° other thing: *saw*
Knightes and ladies come dauncing,
In quainte° atir, degisely,° *elegant / wonderfully*
Quainte pas° and softely. *step*
Tabours° and trumpes yede° him by, *drums / went*
And al manere minstracy.° *minstrelsy*
  And on a day he seigh° biside *saw*
Sixty ladies on horse ride,
Gentil and jolif° as brid° on ris°— *pretty / bird / bough*
Nought oo man amonges hem nis.
And eech a faucon on hond beer,° *bore*
And riden on hawking by river.
Of game they founde wel good haunt,° *plenty*
Maulardes,° hairoun,° and cormeraunt. *mallards / herons*
The fowles of° the water ariseth; *from*
The faucons hem wel deviseth:° *descry*
Eech faucon his preye slough.° *slew*
That seigh° Orfeo and lough:° *saw / laughed*
"Parfay!"° quath he, "ther is fair game! *by faith*
Thider ich wil,° by Goddes name. *will go*
Ich was ywon° swich° werk to see." *accustomed / such*

1. Nor did he ever learn what happened to them.

He aroos and thider gan tee.° *draw*
To a lady he was ycome,
Biheeld, and hath wel undernome,° *understood*
And seeth by al thing that it is
His owene queene Dame Heurodis,
Yerne° biheeld hire and she him eke,° *eagerly / also*
But neither to other a word ne speke.
For misaise that she on him seigh° *saw*
That hadde been so riche and heigh,
The teres felle out of hir yë.
The othere ladies this ysye° *saw*
And maked hire away to ride:
She moste° with him no lenger° abide. *must / longer*
  "Allas," quath he, "now me is wo.
Why nil° deeth now me nought slo?° *will not / slay*
Allas, wrecche,° that I ne mighte *wretched one*
Die now after this sighte.
Allas, too longe last° my lif *lasts*
Whan I ne dar nought to my wif—
Ne she to me—oo word ne speke.
Allas, why nil myn herte breke?
Parfay,"° quath he, "tide what bitide, *by faith*
Whider so thise ladies ride
The selve° waye ich wil strecche:° *same / go*
Of lif ne deeth me nothing recche."° *care*
  His sclavin° he dide on also spak° *cloak / at once*
And heeng° his harp upon his bak, *hung*
And hadde wel good wil to goon:
He ne spared neither stub ne stoon.[2]
In at a roche° the ladies rideth *rock, cave*
And he after and nought abideth.
  Whan he was in the roche ago
Wel three mile other° mo, *or*
He cam into a fair countrey,
As bright so° sonne on somers day, *as*
Smoothe and plain° and alle greene: *flat*
Hil ne dale nas ther noon seene.
Amidde the lond a castel he seigh,° *saw*
Riche and real° and wonder heigh. *royal*
Al the utemoste° wal *outmost*
Was cleer° and shined as crystal. *bright*
An hundred towres ther were aboute,
Degiseliche,° and batailed[3] stoute. *wonderful*
The butres° cam out of the diche *buttress*
Of reed gold y-arched riche.[4]
The vousour° was anourned° al *vaulting / adorned*

2. I.e., neither stump nor stone prevented him.
3. I.e., furnished with battlements.
4. I.e., made of red gold that arched splendidly: gold was commonly described as red in Middle English.

Of eech manere divers aumal.° *enamel*
Within ther were wide wones,° *halls*
And alle were fulle of precious stones.
The worste pilar on to biholde
Al it was of burnist golde.
Al that lond was evere light,
For when it sholde be therk° and night *dark*
The riche stones lighte gonne[5]
As brighte as dooth at noon the sonne.
No man may telle ne thinke in thought
The riche werk that ther was wrought.
By alle thing him thinkth it is
The proude court of Paradis.
In this castel the ladies alighte:
He wolde in after, if he mighte.
Orfeo knokketh at the yate:° *gate*
The porter was redy therate
And asked what he wolde have ydo.° *done*
"Parfay,° ich am a minstrel, lo, *by faith*
To solace° thy lord with my glee *delight*
If[6] his sweete wille be."
The porter undide the gate anoon
And lete him into the castel goon.
Than he gan looke aboute al
And seigh,° lying within the wal, *saw*
Of folk that ther were thider ybrought,
And thoughte° dede,° and nere nought:[7] *seemed / dead*
Some stoode withouten hade,° *head*
And some none armes hade,
And some thurgh the body hadde wounde,
And some laye woode° ybounde; *mad*
And some armed on horse sete,
And some astrangled as they ete,
And some were in watre adreint,° *drowned*
And some with fire al forshreint,° *shriveled*
Wives ther laye on child-bedde,
Some dede and some awedde.° *driven mad*
And wonder fele° ther laye bisides *many*
Right as they slepte hir undertides.° *forenoons*
Each was thus in this world ynome,° *taken*
With° faïrye thider ycome. *by force of*
Ther he seigh his owene wif,
Dame Heurodis, his leve° lif, *dear*
Sleepe under an impe-tree:
By hir clothes he knew it was she.
Whan he hadde seen thise mervailes alle
He wente into the kinges halle.

5. Did light it.
6. If it.
7. Were not.
8. I.e., an alcove.

Than seigh he ther a seemly sighte:
A tabernacle[8] wel ydight°— *arrayed*
Hir maister king therinne sete,
And hir queene fair and sweete.
Hir crownes, hir clothes shoon so brighte
That unnethe° he biholde hem mighte. *with difficulty*
  Whan he hadde seen al this thing,
He kneeled adoun bifor the king:
"O lord," he saide, "if thy wil were,
My minstracye thou sholdest yheere."° *hear*
The king answerede, "What man art thou
That art hider ycomen now?
Ich, ne noon that is with me,
Ne sente never after thee.
Sith° that ich here regne° gan *since / reign*
I ne foond° nevere so hardy man *found*
That hider to us durste wende
But° that ich him wolde ofsende."° *unless / send for*
"Lord," quath he, "ye trowe° wel *may believe*
I nam but a poore minstrel,
And, sire, it is the maner of us
To seeche many a lordes hous.
And theigh° we not welcome be, *though*
Yit we mote° profere forth oure glee."° *must / music*
  Bifor the king he sat adown
And took his harp so merye of soun,
And tempreth° it as he wel can. *tunes*
And blisful notes he ther gan
That alle that in the palais were
Come to him for to heere,
And lieth adown to his feete,
Hem thinkth his melodye so sweete.
The king herkneth and sit° ful stille: *sits*
To heere his glee he hath good wille.
Good bourde° he hadde of his glee: *entertainment*
The riche queene also hadde she.
  Whan he hadde stint° of his harping, *ceased*
Then saide to him the riche king,
"Minstrel, me liketh wel thy glee.
Now aske of me what it may be—
Largeliche° ich wil thee paye. *generously*
Now speke and thou might it assaye."
"Sire," he saide, "ich praye thee
That thou woldest yive me
The eeche° lady, bright on blee,° *very / of hue*
That sleepeth under the impe-tree."
"Nay," quath the king, "that nought nere:[9]
A sory couple of you it were;

9. I.e., that wouldn't do.

For thou art lene,° rowe,° and blak, *lean / rough*
And she is lovesom, withoute lak.° *blemish*
A loothly thing it were forthy° *therefore*
To seen hire in thy compaigny."
"O sire," he saide, "gentil king,
Yit were it a wel fouler thing
To heere a lesing° of thy mouthe. *lie*
So, sire, as ye saide nouthe° *now*
What ich wolde aske, have I wolde,
A kinges word moot° needes be holde." *must*
"Thou sayest sooth," the king saide than,
"And sith° I am a trewe man, *since*
I wol wel that it be so:
Taak hire by the hond and go.
Of hire ich wol that thou be blithe."
He kneeled adown and thanked him swithe;° *quickly*
His wif he took by the hond
And dide him swithe out of that lond,
And wente° him out of that thede:° *turned / country*
Right as he cam the way he yede.° *went*
So longe he hath the way ynome° *taken*
To Winchester he is ycome,
That somtime was his owene citee,
But no man knew that it was he.
No forther than the townes ende
For knoweleche[1] he durste wende.
But in a beggeres bild° ful narwe° *house / small*
Ther he hath take his herbarwe° *lodging*
(To him and to his owene wife),
As a minstrel of poore lif,
And asked tidinges of that lond,
And who the kingdom heeld in hond.
The poore begger in his cote° *hovel*
Tolde him everich° a grote°— *every / bit*
How hir queene was stole awy,° *away*
Ten yeer goon, with° faïry. *by*
And how hir king in exile yede° *went*
But no man wiste° in which thede;° *knew / country*
And how the steward the lond gan holde,
And othere many thinges him tolde.
Amorwe ayain the noon-tide[2]
He maked his wif ther abide,
And beggeres clothes he borwed anoon,° *straightaway*
And heeng° his harp his rigge° upon, *hung / back*
And wente him into that citee,
That men mighte him biholde and see.
Bothe eerles and barouns bolde,
Burgeis° and ladies him gan biholde: *burgesses*

1. I.e., for fear of being recognized.
2. In the morning towards noontime.

"Lord," they saide, "swich° a man! *such*
How longe the heer° him hangeth upon! *hair*
Lo, how his beerd hangeth to his knee!
He is yclungen° also° a tree!" *withered / as*
And as he yede° in the streete, *walked*
With his steward he gan meete.
And loude he sette him on a cry,
"Sir steward," he saide, "grant mercy!
Ich am an harpour of hethenesse:° *heathen country*
Help me now in this distresse."
The steward saide, "Com with me, com:
Of that I have thou shalt have som.
Eech harpour is welcome me to
For my lordes love, Sir Orfeo."
Anoon they wente into the halle,
The steward and the lordes alle.
The steward wessh° and wente to mete, *washed*
And manye lordes by him sete.
Ther were trumpours° and tabourers,° *trumpeters / drummers*
Harpours fele,° and crouders:° *many / fiddlers*
Muche melodye they maked alle.
And Orfeo sat stille in halle.
And herkneth; whan they been al stille,
He took his harp and tempered° shille°— *played / loudly*
The blisfullest notes he harped there
That evere man yherde with ere.
Eech man liked wel his glee.
The steward looked and gan ysee,
And the harp knew also blive.° *right away*
"Minstrel," he saide, "so mote° thou thrive, *may*
Where haddest thou this harp and how?
I praye that thou me telle now."
"Lord," quath he, "in uncouthe° thede,° *strange / country*
Thurgh a foreest as I yede,° *walked*
I foond° lying in a dale *found*
A man with° lions totorn° smale, *by / torn to bits*
And wolves him frette° with teeth so sharp. *bit*
By him I foond this eeche° harp *very*
Wel ten yeer it is ago."
"O," quath the steward, "now me is wo!
That was my lord Sir Orfeo.
Allas, wrecche, what shal I do
That have swich° a lord ylore?° *such / lost*
A, way,° that evere ich was ybore° *woe / born*
That him was so harde grace y-yarked,° *ordained*
And so vile deeth ymarked."° *appointed*
Adown he fel aswoone to grounde.
His barouns him tooke up that stounde° *time*
And telleth him how that it geeth:° *goes*

It is no boote° of mannes deeth. *remedy*
King Orfeo knew wel by than° *that*
His steward was a trewe man
And loved him as him oughte to do,
And stondeth up and saith thus, "Lo,
Steward, herkne now this thing:
If ich were Orfeo the king
And hadde ysuffered ful yore° *long*
In wildernesse muche sore,
And hadde ywonne my queene awy° *away*
Out of the lond of faïry,
And hadde ybrought the lady hende° *gracious*
Right here to the townes ende,
And with a begger hir in°ynome,° *lodging / taken*
And were myselve hider ycome
Poorelich to thee thus stille,° *secretly*
For to assaye° thy goode wille, *test*
And° ich founde thee thus trewe, *if*
Thou ne sholdest it nevere rewe:° *regret*
Sikerliche,° for love or ay,° *surely / dread*
Thou sholdest be king after my day.
If thou of my deeth haddest been blithe,
Thou sholdest have voided° also swithe." *been dismissed*
Tho° alle tho° that therinne sete *then / those*
That is was Orfeo underyete,° *understood*
And the steward wel him knew:
Over and over the boord° he threw *table*
And fel adown to his feete.
So dide eech lord that ther sete,
And alle they saide at oo° crying, *one*
"Ye beeth oure lord, sire, and oure king."
Glade they were of his live:
To chambre they ladde him as blive,° *at once*
And bathed him and shaved his beard,
And tired° him as a king apert.° *dressed / openly*
And sith° with greet processioun *after*
They broughte the queene into the town,
With alle manere minstracye.
Lord, ther was greet melodye:
For joye they wepte with hir yë
That hem so sound° ycomen sye.° *healthy / saw*
Now Orfeo newe corouned° is, *crowned*
And his queene Dame Heurodis,
And lived longe afterward,
And sitthen° king was the steward. *afterward*
Harpours in Britain after than° *that*
Herde how this merveile bigan
And made a lay of good liking,° *well-pleasing*
And nempned° it after the king. *named*

That lay is "Orfeo" yhote:° *called*
Good is the lay, sweete is the note.
  Thus cam Sir Orfeo out of his care:
God grante us alle wel to fare.

SIR GAWAIN AND THE GREEN KNIGHT
(ca. 1375–1400)

Nothing is known about the author of *Sir Gawain and the Green Knight* except that he probably wrote the three religious poems—*Pearl* (see below), *Patience*, and *Purity*—that are preserved in the same manuscript as *Sir Gawain* (no other copies of any of the poems have come to light); and he may also have written a fifth poem, which, like the others, is alliterative, but is preserved in a different manuscript—a charming legend of St. Erkenwald. The dialect of *Sir Gawain* points to an origin in provincial England, about 150 miles northwest of the capital: thus of the three great poets of late medieval England, two, the authors of *Sir Gawain* and *Piers Plowman*, were representatives of cultural centers remote from the royal court at London where Chaucer spent his life. We know almost nothing about these provincial centers, but the works that emanated from them demonstrate a high level of culture. The poet of *Sir Gawain*, indeed, was a most sophisticated and urbane writer, and even though his language (a dialect most difficult for us today and probably difficult for London men in his own time) and his alliterative measure would have been considered barbaric by Chaucer's London audience, the subtlety of his perceptions and the delicacy with which he handles his narrative is not unworthy of Chaucer himself. And although it is impossible to date the poem with any accuracy, its author must have been an almost exact contemporary of Chaucer.

It is possible that the plot of *Sir Gawain* came ready-made to the poet, who may have found it in some lost French poem or have heard it recited in English—perhaps even in Welsh—in his own country. The motif of the green man's decapitation originates in very ancient folklore, probably in a vegetation myth in which the beheading would have been a ritual death that insured the return of spring to the earth and the regrowth of the crops. But this primitive theme has been entirely rationalized by the late medieval poet, who sees in his inherited plot an opportunity to study how successfully Gawain, as a man wholly dedicated to Christian ideals, maintains those ideals when he is subjected to unusual pressures. The poem is a rare combination: at once a comedy—even a satire—of manners and a profoundly Christian view of man's character and his destiny. The court of King Arthur is presented, in the most grandiose and laudatory of language, as the place where the ideal of chivalry has reached its zenith, where all is courtesy and martial prowess in defense of the right. The praise bestowed by the poet upon this court may seem excessive, and indeed the sequel suggests that the author made it so intentionally. For when the court is invaded by the Green Knight, arrogant, monstrous, and yet exasperatingly reasonable, it suddenly seems to become slightly unreal, as if, the Green Knight insultingly implies, its reputation were founded more on fiction than on fact—as if the poets that celebrated it had been working harder to enhance its glory than the knights themselves. In any case, the court is to receive a testing, which is naturally entrusted to the most courteous and valiant knight of the Round Table (in this most English of Arthurian romances Gawain has not been replaced as the best of knights by the continental-born Lancelot).

Once Gawain has set out to keep his promise to the Green Knight, his humiliation—and by inference that of the court—begins: in describing Gawain's adventures the poet, for all his epic enhancement and overt praise for the hero, actually tells a tale of his increasing helplessness. First of all Gawain's courtesy fails him—not, to be sure, in the sense that he relinquishes it, but in the sense that it involves him in a profoundly embarrassing and dangerous situation with the lady: it results in trouble instead of the serenity that courtesy, as the diplomat's virtue, is supposed to procure. Then the second of his great virtues, his martial prowess, is denied to him by the promise he has made not to defend himself against the Green Knight's return stroke. Thus betrayed by or cut off from the two qualities that he supposes to have made him the splendid knight people think him to be, he also, with very human lack of logic, momentarily cuts himself off from the power that has actually permitted those qualities to flourish in him. For when the pressures increase, St. Mary's knight, no longer able to rely on himself, relies not on St. Mary but on a belt of supposed magical powers, which he must accept from the lady with ignominy and hide from her lord with dishonesty. When the Green Knight spares his life there is revealed to Gawain his own real impoverishment, the complete incapacity of the greatest of Arthur's knights to help himself. He has found that without God's grace the virtues which he has made particularly his own are of no use to him—that, indeed, he no longer possesses them. The poem ends happily; but the baldric that the courtiers wear in honor of Gawain's adventure is a reminder that what God asks of men is not primarily courtly or martial prowess, but a humble and a contrite heart.

This didactic point is made with a most Chaucer-like indirection, a fine irony that strips Gawain of his pretensions but leaves him his charm and shows him sympathy for the really quite unfair nature of his predicament—and which also enjoys, and makes the reader enjoy, the embarrassment the hero is made to suffer. *Sir Gawain* is one of the latest and certainly the best of the Middle English romances; yet its greatness lies in the fact that, without ever ceasing to be a romance, a fiction full of the most exquisite comic touches, it is something much larger, one of the really significant literary achievements of the Middle Ages.

Sir Gawain and the Green Knight[1]

Part I

Since the siege and the assault was ceased at Troy,
The walls breached and burnt down to brands and ashes,
The knight that had knotted the nets of deceit
Was impeached for his perfidy, proven most true,[2]
It was high-born Aeneas and his haughty race
That since prevailed over provinces, and proudly reigned
Over well-nigh all the wealth of the West Isles.[3]
Great Romulus[4] to Rome repairs in haste;
With boast and with bravery builds he that city
And names it with his own name, that it now bears.
Ticius[5] to Tuscany, and towers raises,
Langobard in Lombardy lays out homes,
And far over the French Sea, Felix Brutus[6]
On many broad hills and high Britain he sets,
most fair.
Where war and wrack and wonder
By shifts have sojourned there,
And bliss by turns with blunder
In that land's lot had share.

And since this Britain was built by this baron great,
Bold boys bred there, in broils delighting,
That did in their day many a deed most dire.
More marvels have happened in this merry land
Than in any other I know, since that olden time,
But of those that here built, of British kings,
King Arthur was counted most courteous of all,
Wherefore an adventure I aim to unfold,
That a marvel of might some men think it,
And one unmatched among Arthur's wonders.
If you will listen to my lay but a little while,
As I heard it in hall, I shall hasten to tell
anew.
As it was fashioned featly
In tale of derring-do,
And linked in measures meetly
By letters tried and true.

1. The Modern English translation is by Marie Borroff (1967), who has reproduced the alliterative meter of the original as well as the "bob and wheel," the five-line rhyming group that concludes each of the long irregular stanzas.
2. The treacherous knight is either Aeneas himself or Antenor, both of whom were, according to medieval tradition, traitors to their city Troy; but Aeneas was actually tried ("impeached") by the Greeks for his refusal to hand over to them his sister Polyxena.
3. Perhaps western Europe.
4. The legendary founder of Rome is here given Trojan ancestry, like Aeneas.
5. Not otherwise known. "Langobard" was the reputed founder of Lombardy.
6. Great-grandson of Aeneas and legendary founder of Britain; not elsewhere given the name Felix (Latin "happy").

This king lay at Camelot[7] at Christmastide;
Many good knights and gay his guests were there,
Arrayed of the Round Table[8] rightful brothers,
With feasting and fellowship and carefree mirth.
There true men contended in tournaments many,
Joined there in jousting these gentle knights,
Then came to the court for carol-dancing,
For the feast was in force full fifteen days,
With all the meat and the mirth that men could devise,
Such gaiety and glee, glorious to hear,
Brave din by day, dancing by night.
High were their hearts in halls and chambers,
These lords and these ladies, for life was sweet.
In peerless pleasures passed they their days,
The most noble knights known under Christ,
And the loveliest ladies that lived on earth ever,
And he the comeliest king, that that court holds,
For all this fair folk in their first age
were still.
Happiest of mortal kind,
King noblest famed of will;
You would now go far to find
So hardy a host on hill.

While the New Year was new, but yesternight come,
This fair folk at feast two-fold was served,
When the king and his company were come in together,
The chanting in chapel achieved and ended.
Clerics and all the court acclaimed the glad season,
Cried Noel anew, good news to men;
Then gallants gather gaily, hand-gifts to make,
Called them out clearly, claimed them by hand,
Bickered long and busily about those gifts.
Ladies laughed aloud, though losers they were,
And he that won was not angered, as well you will know.[9]
All this mirth they made until meat was served;
When they had washed them worthily, they went to their seats,
The best seated above, as best it beseemed,
Guenevere the goodly queen gay in the midst
On a dais well-decked and duly arrayed
With costly silk curtains, a canopy over,
Of Toulouse and Turkestan tapestries rich,
All broidered and bordered with the best gems
Ever brought into Britain, with bright pennies
to pay.

7. Capital of Arthur's kingdom, presumably located in southwest England or southern Wales.

8. According to legend, Merlin made the Round Table after a dispute broke out among Arthur's knights about precedence: it seated 100 knights. The table described in the poem is not round.

9. The dispensing of New Year's gifts seems to have involved kissing.

Fair queen, without a flaw,
She glanced with eyes of grey.
A seemlier that once he saw,
In truth, no man could say.

But Arthur would not eat till all were served;
So light was his lordly heart, and a little boyish;
His life he liked lively—the less he cared
To be lying for long, or long to sit,
So busy his young blood, his brain so wild.
And also a point of pride pricked him in heart,
For he nobly had willed, he would never eat
On so high a holiday, till he had heard first
Of some fair feat or fray some far-borne tale,
Of some marvel of might, that he might trust,
By champions of chivalry achieved in arms,
Or some suppliant came seeking some single knight
To join with him in jousting, in jeopardy each
To lay life for life, and leave it to fortune
To afford him on field fair hap or other.
Such is the king's custom, when his court he holds
At each far-famed feast amid his fair host
so dear.
The stout king stands in state
Till a wonder shall appear;
He leads, with heart elate,
High mirth in the New Year.

So he stands there in state, the stout young king,
Talking before the high table [1] of trifles fair.
There Gawain the good knight by Guenevere sits,
With Agravain à la dure main on her other side,
Both knights of renown, and nephews of the king.
Bishop Baldwin above begins the table,
And Yvain, son of Urien, ate with him there.
These few with the fair queen were fittingly served;
At the side-tables sat many stalwart knights.
Then the first course comes, with clamor of trumpets
That were bravely bedecked with bannerets bright,
With noise of new drums and the noble pipes.
Wild were the warbles that wakened that day
In strains that stirred many strong men's hearts.
There dainties were dealt out, dishes rare,
Choice fare to choose, on chargers so many
That scarce was there space to set before the people
The service of silver, with sundry meats,
on cloth.
Each fair guest freely there
Partakes, and nothing loth;

1. The high table is on a dais; the side tables (line 115) are on the main floor and run along the walls at a right angle with the high table.

Twelve dishes before each pair;
Good beer and bright wine both.

Of the service itself I need say no more,
For well you will know no tittle was wanting.
Another noise and a new was well-nigh at hand,
That the lord might have leave his life to nourish;
For scarce were the sweet strains still in the hall,
And the first course come to that company fair,
There hurtles in at the hall-door an unknown rider,
One the greatest on ground in growth of his frame:
From broad neck to buttocks so bulky and thick,
And his loins and his legs so long and so great,
Half a giant on earth I hold him to be,
But believe him no less than the largest of men,
And that the seemliest in his stature to see, as he rides,
For in back and in breast though his body was grim,
His waist in its width was worthily small,
And formed with every feature in fair accord
was he.
Great wonder grew in hall
At his hue most strange to see,
For man and gear and all
Were green as green could be.

And in guise all of green, the gear and the man:
A coat cut close, that clung to his sides,
And a mantle to match, made with a lining
Of furs cut and fitted—the fabric was noble,
Embellished all with ermine, and his hood beside,
That was loosed from his locks, and laid on his shoulders.
With trim hose and tight, the same tint of green,
His great calves were girt, and gold spurs under
He bore on silk bands that embellished his heels,
And footgear well-fashioned, for riding most fit.
And all his vesture verily was verdant green;
Both the bosses on his belt and other bright gems
That were richly ranged on his raiment noble
About himself and his saddle, set upon silk,
That to tell half the trifles would tax my wits,
The butterflies and birds embroidered thereon
In green of the gayest, with many a gold thread.
The pendants of the breast-band, the princely crupper,
And the bars of the bit were brightly enameled;
The stout stirrups were green, that steadied his feet,
And the bows of the saddle and the side-panels both,
That gleamed all and glinted with green gems about.
The steed he bestrides of that same green
so bright.
A green horse great and thick;
A headstrong steed of might;

In broidered bridle quick,
Mount matched man aright.

Gay was this goodly man in guise all of green,
And the hair of his head to his horse suited;
Fair flowing tresses enfold his shoulders;
A beard big as a bush on his breast hangs,
That with his heavy hair, that from his head falls,
Was evened all about above both his elbows,
That half his arms thereunder were hid in the fashion
Of a king's cap-à-dos,[2] that covers his throat.
The mane of that mighty horse much to it like,
Well curled and becombed, and cunningly knotted
With filaments of fine gold amid the fair green,
Here a strand of the hair, here one of gold;
His tail and his foretop twin in their hue,
And bound both with a band of a bright green
That was decked adown the dock with dazzling stones
And tied tight at the top with a triple knot
Where many bells well burnished rang bright and clear.
Such a mount in his might, nor man on him riding,
None had seen, I dare swear, with sight in that hall
so grand.
As lightning quick and light
He looked to all at hand;
It seemed that no man might
His deadly dints withstand.

Yet had he no helm, nor hauberk neither,
Nor plate, nor appurtenance appending to arms,
Nor shaft pointed sharp, nor shield for defense,
But in his one hand he had a holly bob
That is goodliest in green when groves are bare,
And an ax in his other, a huge and immense,
A wicked piece of work in words to expound:
The head on its haft was an ell long;
The spike of green steel, resplendent with gold;
The blade burnished bright, with a broad edge,
As well shaped to shear as a sharp razor;
Stout was the stave in the strong man's gripe,
That was wound all with iron to the weapon's end,
With engravings in green of goodliest work.
A lace lightly about, that led to a knot,
Was looped in by lengths along the fair haft,
And tassels thereto attached in a row,
With buttons of bright green, brave to behold.
This horseman hurtles in, and the hall enters;

2. The word *capados* occurs in this form in Middle English only in *Gawain*, here and in line 572. The translator has interpreted it, as the poet apparently did also, as *cap-à-dos*—i.e., a garment covering its wearer "from head to back," on the model of *cap-à-pie,* "from head to foot," referring to armor.

Riding to the high dais, recked he no danger;
Not a greeting he gave as the guests he o'erlooked,
Nor wasted his words, but "Where is," he said,
"The captain of this crowd? Keenly I wish
To see that sire with sight, and to himself say
my say."
He swaggered all about
To scan the host so gay;
He halted, as if in doubt
Who in that hall held sway.

There were stares on all sides as the stranger spoke,
For much did they marvel what it might mean
That a horseman and a horse should have such a hue,
Grow green as the grass, and greener, it seemed,
Than green fused on gold more glorious by far.
All the onlookers eyed him, and edged nearer,
And awaited in wonder what he would do,
For many sights had they seen, but such a one never,
So that phantom and faerie the folk there deemed it,
Therefore chary of answer was many a champion bold,
And stunned at his strong words stone-still they sat
In a swooning silence in the stately hall.
As all were slipped into sleep, so slackened their speech
apace.
Not all, I think, for dread,
But some of courteous grace
Let him who was their head
Be spokesman in that place.

Then Arthur before the high dais that entrance beholds,
And hailed him, as behooved, for he had no fear,
And said "Fellow, in faith you have found fair welcome;
The head of this hostelry Arthur am I;
Leap lightly down, and linger, I pray,
And the tale of your intent you shall tell us after."
"Nay, so help me," said the other, "He that on high sits,
To tarry here any time, 'twas not mine errand;
But as the praise of you, prince, is puffed up so high,
And your court and your company are counted the best,
Stoutest under steel-gear on steeds to ride,
Worthiest of their works the wide world over,
And peerless to prove in passages of arms,
And courtesy here is carried to its height,
And so at this season I have sought you out.
You may be certain by the branch that I bear in hand
That I pass here in peace, and would part friends,
For had I come to this court on combat bent,
I have a hauberk at home, and a helm beside,
A shield and a sharp spear, shining bright,

And other weapons to wield, I ween well, to boot,
But as I willed no war, I wore no metal.
But if you be so bold as all men believe,
You will graciously grant the game that I ask
by right."
Arthur answer gave
And said, "Sir courteous knight,
If contest here you crave,
You shall not fail to fight."

"Nay, to fight, in good faith, is far from my thought;
There are about on these benches but beardless children,
Were I here in full arms on a haughty steed,
For measured against mine, their might is puny.
And so I call in this court for a Christmas game,
For 'tis Yule and New Year, and many young bloods about;
If any in this house such hardihood claims,
Be so bold in his blood, his brain so wild,
As stoutly to strike one stroke for another,
I shall give him as my gift this gisarme noble,
This ax, that is heavy enough, to handle as he likes,
And I shall bide the first blow, as bare as I sit.
If there be one so wilful my words to assay,
Let him leap hither lightly, lay hold of this weapon;
I quitclaim it forever, keep it as his own,
And I shall stand him a stroke, steady on this floor,
So you grant me the guerdon to give him another,
sans blame.
In a twelvemonth and a day
He shall have of me the same;
Now be it seen straightway
Who dares take up the game."

If he astonished them at first, stiller were then
All that household in hall, the high and the low;
The stranger on his green steed stirred in the saddle,
And roisterously his red eyes he rolled all about,
Bent his bristling brows, that were bright green,
Wagged his beard as he watched who would arise.
When the court kept its counsel he coughed aloud,
And cleared his throat coolly, the clearer to speak:
"What, is this Arthur's house," said that horseman then,
"Whose fame is so fair in far realms and wide?
Where is now your arrogance and your awesome deeds,
Your valor and your victories and your vaunting words?
Now are the revel and renown of the Round Table
Overwhelmed with a word of one man's speech,
For all cower and quake, and no cut felt!"
With this he laughs so loud that the lord grieved;
The blood for sheer shame shot to his face,
and pride.

With rage his face flushed red,
And so did all beside.
Then the king as bold man bred
Toward the stranger took a stride.

And said "Sir, now we see you will say but folly,
Which whoso has sought, it suits that he find.
No guest here is aghast of your great words.
Give to me your gisarme, in God's own name,
And the boon you have begged shall straight be granted."
He leaps to him lightly, lays hold of his weapon;
The green fellow on foot fiercely alights.
Now has Arthur his ax, and the haft grips,
And sternly stirs it about, on striking bent.
The stranger before him stood there erect,
Higher than any in the house by a head and more;
With stern look as he stood, he stroked his beard,
And with undaunted countenance drew down his coat,
No more moved nor dismayed for his mighty dints
Than any bold man on bench had brought him a drink
of wine.
Gawain by Guenevere
Toward the king doth now incline:
"I beseech, before all here,
That this melee may be mine."

"Would you grant me the grace," said Gawain to the king,
"To be gone from this bench and stand by you there,
If I without discourtesy might quit this board,
And if my liege lady misliked it not,
I would come to your counsel before your court noble.
For I find it not fit, as in faith it is known,
When such a boon is begged before all these knights,
Though you be tempted thereto, to take it on yourself
While so bold men about upon benches sit,
That no host under heaven is hardier of will,
Nor better brothers-in-arms where battle is joined;
I am the weakest, well I know, and of wit feeblest;
And the loss of my life would be least of any;
That I have you for uncle is my only praise;
My body, but for your blood, is barren of worth;
And for that this folly befits not a king,
And 'tis I that have asked it, it ought to be mine,
And if my claim be not comely let all this court judge,
in sight."
The court assays the claim,
And in counsel all unite
To give Gawain the game
And release the king outright.

Then the king called the knight to come to his side,

And he rose up readily, and reached him with speed,
Bows low to his lord, lays hold of the weapon,
And he releases it lightly, and lifts up his hand,
And gives him God's blessing, and graciously prays
That his heart and his hand may be hardy both.
"Keep, cousin," said the king, "what you cut with this day,
And if you rule it aright, then readily, I know,
You shall stand the stroke it will strike after."
Gawain goes to the guest with gisarme in hand,
And boldly he bides there, abashed not a whit.
Then hails he Sir Gawain, the horseman in green:
"Recount we our contract, ere you come further.
First I ask and adjure you, how you are called
That you tell me true, so that trust it I may."
"In good faith," said the good knight, "Gawain am I
Whose buffet befalls you, whate'er betide after,
And at this time twelvemonth take from you another
With what weapon you will, and with no man else
alive."
The other nods assent:
"Sir Gawain, as I may thrive,
I am wondrous well content
That you this dint shall drive."

"Sir Gawain," said the Green Knight, "By God, I rejoice
That your fist shall fetch this favor I seek,
And you have readily rehearsed, and in right terms,
Each clause of my covenant with the king your lord,
Save that you shall assure me, sir, upon oath,
That you shall seek me yourself, wheresoever you deem
My lodgings may lie, and look for such wages
As you have offered me here before all this host."
"What is the way there?" said Gawain, "Where do you dwell?
I heard never of your house, by Him that made me,
Nor I know you not, knight, your name nor your court.
But tell me truly thereof, and teach me your name,
And I shall fare forth to find you, so far as I may,
And this I say in good certain, and swear upon oath."
"That is enough in New Year, you need say no more,"
Said the knight in the green to Gawain the noble,
"If I tell you true, when I have taken your knock,
And if you handily have hit, you shall hear straightway
Of my house and my home and my own name;
Then follow in my footsteps by faithful accord.
And if I spend no speech, you shall speed the better:
You can feast with your friends, nor further trace
my tracks.
Now hold your grim tool steady
And show us how it hacks."
"Gladly, sir; all ready,"
Says Gawain; he strokes the ax.

The Green Knight upon ground girds him with care:
Bows a bit with his head, and bares his flesh:
His long lovely locks he laid over his crown,
Let the naked nape for the need be shown.
Gawain grips to his ax and gathers it aloft—
The left foot on the floor before him he set—
Brought it down deftly upon the bare neck,
That the shock of the sharp blow shivered the bones
And cut the flesh cleanly and clove it in twain,
That the blade of bright steel bit into the ground.
The head was hewn off and fell to the floor;
Many found it at their feet, as forth it rolled;
The blood gushed from the body, bright on the green,
Yet fell not the fellow, nor faltered a whit,
But stoutly he starts forth upon stiff shanks,
And as all stood staring he stretched forth his hand,
Laid hold of his head and heaved it aloft,
Then goes to the green steed, grasps the bridle,
Steps into the stirrup, bestrides his mount,
And his head by the hair in his hand holds,
And as steady he sits in the stately saddle
As he had met with no mishap, nor missing were
his head.
His bulk about he haled,
That fearsome body that bled;
There were many in the court that quailed
Before all his say was said.

For the head in his hand he holds right up;
Toward the first on the dais directs he the face,
And it lifted up its lids, and looked with wide eyes,
And said as much with its mouth as now you may hear:
"Sir Gawain, forget not to go as agreed,
And cease not to seek till me, sir, you find,
As you promised in the presence of these proud knights.
To the Green Chapel come, I charge you, to take
Such a dint as you have dealt—you have well deserved
That your neck should have a knock on New Year's morn.
The Knight of the Green Chapel I am well-known to many,
Wherefore you cannot fail to find me at last;
Therefore come, or be counted a recreant knight."
With a roisterous rush he flings round the reins,
Hurtles out at the hall-door, his head in his hand,
That the flint-fire flew from the flashing hooves.
Which way he went, not one of them knew
Nor whence he was come in the wide world
so fair.
The king and Gawain gay
Make game of the Green Knight there,
Yet all who saw it say
'Twas a wonder past compare.

Though high-born Arthur at heart had wonder,
He let no sign be seen, but said aloud
To the comely queen, with courteous speech,
"Dear dame, on this day dismay you no whit;
Such crafts are becoming at Christmastide,
Laughing at interludes, light songs and mirth,
Amid dancing of damsels with doughty knights.
Nevertheless of my meat now let me partake,
For I have met with a marvel, I may not deny."
He glanced at Sir Gawain, and gaily he said,
"Now, sir, hang up your ax, that has hewn enough,"
And over the high dais it was hung on the wall
That men in amazement might on it look,
And tell in true terms the tale of the wonder.
Then they turned toward the table, these two together,
The good king and Gawain, and made great feast,
With all dainties double, dishes rare,
With all manner of meat and minstrelsy both,
Such happiness wholly had they that day
in hold.
Now take care, Sir Gawain,
That your courage wax not cold
When you must turn again
To your enterprise foretold.

Part II

This adventure had Arthur of handsels first
When young was the year, for he yearned to hear tales;
Though they wanted for words when they went to sup,
Now are fierce deeds to follow, their fists stuffed full.
Gawain was glad to begin those games in hall,
But if the end be harsher, hold it no wonder,
For though men are merry in mind after much drink,
A year passes apace, and proves ever new:
First things and final conform but seldom.
And so this Yule to the young year yielded place,
And each season ensued at its set time;
After Christmas there came the cold cheer of Lent,
When with fish and plainer fare our flesh we reprove;
But then the world's weather with winter contends:
The keen cold lessens, the low clouds lift;
Fresh falls the rain in fostering showers
On the face of the fields; flowers appear.
The ground and the groves wear gowns of green;
Birds build their nests, and blithely sing
That solace of all sorrow with summer comes
ere long.
And blossoms day by day

Bloom rich and rife in throng;
Then every grove so gay
Of the greenwood rings with song.

And then the season of summer with the soft winds,
When Zephyr sighs low over seeds and shoots;
Glad is the green plant growing abroad,
When the dew at dawn drops from the leaves,
To get a gracious glance from the golden sun.
But harvest with harsher winds follows hard after,
Warns him to ripen well ere winter comes;
Drives forth the dust in the droughty season,
From the face of the fields to fly high in air.
Wroth winds in the welkin wrestle with the sun,
The leaves launch from the linden and light on the ground,
And the grass turns to gray, that once grew green.
Then all ripens and rots that rose up at first,
And so the year moves on in yesterdays many,
And winter once more, by the world's law,
draws nigh.
At Michaelmas[3] the moon
Hangs wintry pale in sky;
Sir Gawain girds him soon
For travails yet to try.

Till All-Hallows' Day[4] with Arthur he dwells,
And he held a high feast to honor that knight
With great revels and rich, of the Round Table.
Then ladies lovely and lords debonair
With sorrow for Sir Gawain were sore at heart;
Yet they covered their care with countenance glad:
Many a mournful man made mirth for his sake.
So after supper soberly he speaks to his uncle
Of the hard hour at hand, and openly says,
"Now, liege lord of my life, my leave I take;
The terms of this task too well you know—
To count the cost over concerns me nothing.
But I am bound forth betimes to bear a stroke
From the grim man in green, as God may direct."
Then the first and foremost came forth in throng:
Yvain and Eric and others of note,
Sir Dodinal le Sauvage, the Duke of Clarence,
Lionel and Lancelot and Lucan the good,
Sir Bors and Sir Bedivere, big men both,
And many manly knights more, with Mador de la Porte.
All this courtly company comes to the king
To counsel their comrade, with care in their hearts;
There was much secret sorrow suffered that day
That one so good as Gawain must go in such wise

3. September 29.

4. All Saints' Day, November 1.

To bear a bitter blow, and his bright sword
lay by.
He said, "Why should I tarry?"
And smiled with tranquil eye;
"In destinies sad or merry,
True men can but try."

He dwelt there all that day, and dressed in the morning;
Asked early for his arms, and all were brought.
First a carpet of rare cost was cast on the floor
Where much goodly gear gleamed golden bright;
He takes his place promptly and picks up the steel,
Attired in a tight coat of Turkestan silk
And a kingly cap-à-dos, closed at the throat,
That was lavishly lined with a lustrous fur.
Then they set the steel shoes on his sturdy feet
And clad his calves about with comely greaves,
And plate well-polished protected his knees,
Affixed with fastenings of the finest gold.
Fair cuisses enclosed, that were cunningly wrought,
His thick-thewed thighs, with thongs bound fast,
And massy chain-mail of many a steel ring
He bore on his body, above the best cloth,
With brace burnished bright upon both his arms,
Good couters and gay, and gloves of plate,
And all the goodly gear to grace him well
that tide.
His surcoat blazoned bold;
Sharp spurs to prick with pride;
And a brave silk band to hold
The broadsword at his side.

When he had on his arms, his harness was rich,
The least latchet or loop laden with gold;
So armored as he was, he heard a mass,
Honored God humbly at the high altar.
Then he comes to the king and his comrades-in-arms,
Takes his leave at last of lords and ladies,
And they clasped and kissed him, commending him to Christ.
By then Gringolet was girt with a great saddle
That was gaily agleam with fine gilt fringe,
New-furbished for the need with nail-heads bright;
The bridle and the bars bedecked all with gold;
The breast-plate, the saddlebow, the side-panels both,
The caparison and the crupper accorded in hue,
And all ranged on the red the resplendent studs
That glittered and glowed like the glorious sun.
His helm now he holds up and hastily kisses,
Well-closed with iron clinches, and cushioned within;

It was high on his head, with a hasp behind,
And a covering of cloth to encase the visor,
All bound and embroidered with the best gems
On broad bands of silk, and bordered with birds,
Parrots and popinjays preening their wings,
Lovebirds and love-knots as lavishly wrought
As many women had worked seven winters thereon,
entire.
The diadem costlier yet
That crowned that comely sire,
With diamonds richly set,
That flashed as if on fire.

Then they showed forth the shield, that shone all red,
With the pentangle[5] portrayed in purest gold.
About his broad neck by the baldric he casts it,
That was meet for the man, and matched him well.
And why the pentangle is proper to that peerless prince
I intend now to tell, though detain me it must.
It is a sign by Solomon sagely devised
To be a token of truth, by its title of old,
For it is a figure formed of five points,
And each line is linked and locked with the next
For ever and ever, and hence it is called
In all England, as I hear, the endless knot.
And well may he wear it on his worthy arms,
For ever faithful five-fold in five-fold fashion
Was Gawain in good works, as gold unalloyed,
Devoid of all villainy, with virtues adorned
in sight.
On shield and coat in view
He bore that emblem bright,
As to his word most true
And in speech most courteous knight.

And first, he was faultless in his five senses,
Nor found ever to fail in his five fingers,
And all his fealty was fixed upon the five wounds
That Christ got on the cross, as the creed tells;
And wherever this man in melee took part,
His one thought was of this, past all things else,
That all his force was founded on the five joys[6]
That the high Queen of heaven had in her child.
And therefore, as I find, he fittingly had
On the inner part of his shield her image portrayed,
That when his look on it lighted, he never lost heart.
The fifth of the five fives followed by this knight

5. A five-pointed star, formed by five lines which are drawn without lifting the pencil from the paper, supposed to have mystical significance; as Solomon's sign (line 625) it was enclosed in a circle.

6. The Annunciation, Nativity, Resurrection, Ascension, and Assumption.

Were beneficence boundless and brotherly love
And pure mind and manners, that none might impeach,
And compassion most precious—these peerless five
Were forged and made fast in him, foremost of men.
Now all these five fives were confirmed in this knight,
And each linked in other, that end there was none,
And fixed to five points, whose force never failed,
Nor assembled all on a side, nor asunder either,
Nor anywhere at an end, but whole and entire
However the pattern proceeded or played out its course.
And so on his shining shield shaped was the knot
Royally in red gold against red gules,
That is the peerless pentangle, prized of old
in lore.
Now armed is Gawain gay,
And bears his lance before,
And soberly said good day,
He thought forevermore.

He struck his steed with the spurs and sped on his way
So fast that the flint-fire flashed from the stones.
When they saw him set forth they were sore aggrieved,
And all sighed softly, and said to each other,
Fearing for their fellow, "Ill fortune it is
That you, man, must be marred, that most are worthy!
His equal on this earth can hardly be found;
To have dealt more discreetly had done less harm,
And have dubbed him a duke, with all due honor.
A great leader of lords he was like to become,
And better so to have been than battered to bits,
Beheaded by an elf-man,[7] for empty pride!
Who would credit that a king could be counseled so,
And caught in a cavil in a Christmas game?"
Many were the warm tears they wept from their eyes
When goodly Sir Gawain was gone from the court
that day.
No longer he abode,
But speedily went his way
Over many a wandering road,
As I heard my author say.

Now he rides in his array through the realm of Logres,[8]
Sir Gawain, God knows, though it gave him small joy!
All alone must he lodge through many a long night
Where the food that he fancied was far from his plate;
He had no mate but his mount, over mountain and plain,
Nor man to say his mind to but almighty God,
Till he had wandered well-nigh into North Wales.
All the islands of Anglesey he holds on his left,

7. Supernatural being.
8. One of the names for Arthur's kingdom.

And follows, as he fares, the fords by the coast,
Comes over at Holy Head, and enters next
The Wilderness of Wirral [9]—few were within
That had great good will toward God or man.
And earnestly he asked of each mortal he met
If he had ever heard aught of a knight all green,
Or of a Green Chapel, on ground thereabouts,
And all said the same, and solemnly swore
They saw no such knight all solely green
in hue.
Over country wild and strange
The knight sets off anew;
Often his course must change
Ere the Chapel comes in view.

Many a cliff must he climb in country wild;
Far off from all his friends, forlorn must he ride;
At each strand or stream where the stalwart passed
'Twere a marvel if he met not some monstrous foe,
And that so fierce and forbidding that fight he must.
So many were the wonders he wandered among
That to tell but the tenth part would tax my wits.
Now with serpents he wars, now with savage wolves,
Now with wild men of the woods, that watched from the rocks,
Both with bulls and with bears, and with boars besides,
And giants that came gibbering from the jagged steeps.
Had he not borne himself bravely, and been on God's side,
He had met with many mishaps and mortal harms.
And if the wars were unwelcome, the winter was worse,
When the cold clear rains rushed from the clouds
And froze before they could fall to the frosty earth.
Near slain by the sleet he sleeps in his irons
More nights than enough, among naked rocks,
Where clattering from the crest the cold stream ran
And hung in hard icicles high overhead.
Thus in peril and pain and predicaments dire
He rides across country till Christmas Eve,
our knight.
And at that holy tide
He prays with all his might
That Mary may be his guide
Till a dwelling comes in sight.

By a mountain next morning he makes his way
Into a forest fastness, fearsome and wild;
High hills on either hand, with hoar woods below,
Oaks old and huge by the hundred together.
The hazel and the hawthorn were all intertwined

9. Gawain went from Camelot north to the northern coast of Wales, opposite the islands of Anglesey; there he turned east across the Dee to the forest of Wirral in Cheshire.

With rough raveled moss, that raggedly hung,
With many birds unblithe upon bare twigs
That peeped most piteously for pain of the cold.
The good knight on Gringolet glides thereunder
Through many a marsh and mire, a man all alone;
He feared for his default, should he fail to see
The service of that Sire that on that same night
Was born of a bright maid, to bring us His peace.
And therefore sighing he said, "I beseech of Thee, Lord,
And Mary, thou mildest mother so dear,
Some harborage where haply I might hear mass
And Thy matins tomorrow—meekly I ask it,
And thereto proffer and pray my pater and ave
and creed."
He said his prayer with sighs,
Lamenting his misdeed;
He crosses himself, and cries
On Christ in his great need.

No sooner had Sir Gawain signed himself thrice
Than he was ware, in the wood, of a wondrous dwelling,
Within a moat, on a mound, bright amid boughs
Of many a tree great of girth that grew by the water—
A castle as comely as a knight could own,
On grounds fair and green, in a goodly park
With a palisade of palings planted about
For two miles and more, round many a fair tree.
The stout knight stared at that stronghold great
As it shimmered and shone amid shining leaves,
Then with helmet in hand he offers his thanks
To Jesus and Saint Julian,[1] that are gentle both,
That in courteous accord had inclined to his prayer;
"Now fair harbor," said he, "I humbly beseech!"
Then he pricks his proud steed with the plated spurs,
And by chance he has chosen the chief path
That brought the bold knight to the bridge's end
in haste.
The bridge hung high in air;
The gates were bolted fast;
The walls well-framed to bear
The fury of the blast.

The man on his mount remained on the bank
Of the deep double moat that defended the place.
The wall went in the water wondrous deep,
And a long way aloft it loomed overhead.
It was built of stone blocks to the battlements' height,
With corbels under cornices in comeliest style;
Watch-towers trusty protected the gate,

1. Patron saint of hospitality.

With many a lean loophole, to look from within:
A better-made barbican the knight beheld never.
And behind it there hoved a great hall and fair:
Turrets rising in tiers, with tines [2] at their tops,
Spires set beside them, splendidly long,
With finials [3] well-fashioned, as filigree fine.
Chalk-white chimneys over chambers high
Gleamed in gay array upon gables and roofs;
The pinnacles in panoply, pointing in air,
So vied there for his view that verily it seemed
A castle cut of paper for a king's feast.
The good knight on Gringolet thought it great luck
If he could but contrive to come there within
To keep the Christmas feast in that castle fair
and bright.
There answered to his call
A porter most polite;
From his station on the wall
He greets the errant knight.

"Good sir," said Gawain, "Wouldst go to inquire
If your lord would allow me to lodge here a space?"
"Peter!" said the porter, "For my part, I think
So noble a knight will not want for a welcome!"
Then he bustles off briskly, and comes back straight,
And many servants beside, to receive him the better.
They let down the drawbridge and duly went forth
And kneeled down on their knees on the naked earth
To welcome this warrior as best they were able.
They proffered him passage—the portals stood wide—
And he beckoned them to rise, and rode over the bridge.
Men steadied his saddle as he stepped to the ground,
And there stabled his steed many stalwart folk.
Now come the knights and the noble squires
To bring him with bliss into the bright hall.
When his high helm was off, there hied forth a throng
Of attendants to take it, and see to its care;
They bore away his brand and his blazoned shield;
Then graciously he greeted those gallants each one,
And many a noble drew near, to do the knight honor.
All in his armor into hall he was led,
Where fire on a fair hearth fiercely blazed.
And soon the lord himself descends from his chamber
To meet with good manners the man on his floor.
He said, "To this house you are heartily welcome:
What is here is wholly yours, to have in your power
and sway."
"Many thanks," said Sir Gawain;
"May Christ your pains repay!"

2. Spikes.

3. Gable ornaments.

The two embrace amain
As men well met that day.

Gawain gazed on the host that greeted him there,
And a lusty fellow he looked, the lord of that place:
A man of massive mold, and of middle age;
Broad, bright was his beard, of a beaver's hue,
Strong, steady his stance, upon stalwart shanks,
His face fierce as fire, fair-spoken withal,
And well-suited he seemed in Sir Gawain's sight
To be a master of men in a mighty keep.
They pass into a parlor, where promptly the host
Has a servant assigned him to see to his needs,
And there came upon his call many courteous folk
That brought him to a bower where bedding was noble,
With heavy silk hangings hemmed all in gold,
Coverlets and counterpanes curiously wrought,
A canopy over the couch, clad all with fur,
Curtains running on cords, caught to gold rings,
Woven rugs on the walls of eastern work,
And the floor, under foot, well-furnished with the same.
With light talk and laughter they loosed from him then
His war-dress of weight and his worthy clothes.
Robes richly wrought they brought him right soon,
To change there in chamber and choose what he would.
When he had found one he fancied, and flung it about,
Well-fashioned for his frame, with flowing skirts,
His face fair and fresh as the flowers of spring,
All the good folk agreed, that gazed on him then,
His limbs arrayed royally in radiant hues,
That so comely a mortal never Christ made
as he.
Whatever his place of birth,
It seemed he well might be
Without a peer on earth
In martial rivalry.

A couch before the fire, where fresh coals burned,
They spread for Sir Gawain splendidly now
With quilts quaintly stitched, and cushions beside,
And then a costly cloak they cast on his shoulders
Of bright silk, embroidered on borders and hems,
With furs of the finest well-furnished within,
And bound about with ermine, both mantle and hood;
And he sat at that fireside in sumptuous estate
And warmed himself well, and soon he waxed merry.
Then attendants set a table upon trestles broad,
And lustrous white linen they laid thereupon,
A saltcellar of silver, spoons of the same.
He washed himself well and went to his place,
Men set his fare before him in fashion most fit.

There were soups of all sorts, seasoned with skill,
Double-sized servings, and sundry fish,
Some baked, some breaded, some broiled on the coals,
Some simmered, some in stews, steaming with spice,
And with sauces to sup that suited his taste.
He confesses it a feast with free words and fair;
They requite him as kindly with courteous jests,
well-sped.
"Tonight you fast [4] and pray;
Tomorrow we'll see you fed."
The knight grows wondrous gay
As the wine goes to his head.

Then at times and by turns, as at table he sat,
They questioned him quietly, with queries discreet,
And he courteously confessed that he comes from the court,
And owns him of the brotherhood of high-famed Arthur,
The right royal ruler of the Round Table,
And the guest by their fireside is Gawain himself,
Who has happened on their house at that holy feast.
When the name of the knight was made known to the lord,
Then loudly he laughed, so elated he was,
And the men in that household made haste with joy
To appear in his presence promptly that day,
That of courage ever-constant, and customs pure,
Is pattern and paragon, and praised without end:
Of all knights on earth most honored is he.
Each said solemnly aside to his brother,
"Now displays of deportment shall dazzle our eyes
And the polished pearls of impeccable speech;
The high art of eloquence is ours to pursue
Since the father of fine manners is found in our midst.
Great is God's grace, and goodly indeed,
That a guest such as Gawain he guides to us here
When men sit and sing of their Savior's birth
in view.
With command of manners pure
He shall each heart imbue;
Who shares his converse, sure,
Shall learn love's language true."

When the knight had done dining and duly arose,
The dark was drawing on; the day nigh ended.
Chaplains in chapels and churches about
Rang the bells aright, reminding all men
Of the holy evensong of the high feast.
The lord attends alone; his fair lady sits
In a comely closet, secluded from sight.
Gawain in gay attire goes thither soon;

4. Gawain is said to be "fasting" because the meal, though elaborate, consisted only of fish dishes, appropriate to a fasting day.

The lord catches his coat, and calls him by name,
And has him sit beside him, and says in good faith
No guest on God's earth would he gladlier greet.
For that Gawain thanked him; the two then embraced
And sat together soberly the service through.
Then the lady, that longed to look on the knight,
Came forth from her closet with her comely maids.
The fair hues of her flesh, her face and her hair
And her body and her bearing were beyond praise,
And excelled the queen herself, as Sir Gawain thought.
He goes forth to greet her with gracious intent;
Another lady led her by the left hand
That was older than she—an ancient, it seemed,
And held in high honor by all men about.
But unlike to look upon, those ladies were,
For if the one was fresh, the other was faded:
Bedecked in bright red was the body of one;
Flesh hung in folds on the face of the other;
On one a high headdress, hung all with pearls;
Her bright throat and bosom fair to behold,
Fresh as the first snow fallen upon hills;
A wimple the other one wore round her throat;
Her swart chin well swaddled, swathed all in white;
Her forehead enfolded in flounces of silk
That framed a fair fillet, of fashion ornate,
And nothing bare beneath save the black brows,
The two eyes and the nose, the naked lips,
And they unsightly to see, and sorrily bleared.
A beldame, by God, she may well be deemed,
of pride!
She was short and thick of waist,
Her buttocks round and wide;
More toothsome, to his taste,
Was the beauty by her side.

When Gawain had gazed on that gay lady,
With leave of her lord, he politely approached;
To the elder in homage he humbly bows;
The lovelier he salutes with a light embrace.
He claims a comely kiss, and courteously he speaks;
They welcome him warmly, and straightway he asks
To be received as their servant, if they so desire.
They take him between them; with talking they bring him
Beside a bright fire; bade then that spices
Be freely fetched forth, to refresh them the better,
And the good wine therewith, to warm their hearts.
The lord leaps about in light-hearted mood;
Contrives entertainments and timely sports;
Takes his hood from his head and hangs it on a spear,
And offers him openly the honor thereof
Who should promote the most mirth at that Christmas feast;

"And I shall try for it, trust me—contend with the best,
Ere I go without my headgear by grace of my friends!"
Thus with light talk and laughter the lord makes merry
To gladden the guest he had greeted in hall
that day.
At the last he called for light
The company to convey;
Gawain says goodnight
And retires to bed straightway.

On the morn when each man is mindful in heart
That God's son was sent down to suffer our death,
No household but is blithe for His blessed sake;
So was it there on that day, with many delights.
Both at larger meals and less they were lavishly served
By doughty lads on dais, with delicate fare;
The old ancient lady, highest she sits;
The lord at her left hand leaned, as I hear;
Sir Gawain in the center, beside the gay lady,
Where the food was brought first to that festive board,
And thence throughout the hall, as they held most fit,
To each man was offered in order of rank.
There was meat, there was mirth, there was much joy,
That to tell all the tale would tax my wits,
Though I pained me, perchance, to paint it with care;
But yet I know that our knight and the noble lady
Were accorded so closely in company there,
With the seemly solace of their secret words,
With speeches well-sped, spotless and pure,
That each prince's pastime their pleasures far
outshone.
Sweet pipes beguile their cares,
And the trumpet of martial tone;
Each tends his affairs
And those two tend their own.

That day and all the next, their disport was noble,
And the third day, I think, pleased them no less;
The joys of St. John's Day [5] were justly praised,
And were the last of their like for those lords and ladies;
Then guests were to go in the gray morning,
Wherefore they whiled the night away with wine and
with mirth,
Moved to the measures of many a blithe carol;
At last, when it was late, took leave of each other,
Each one of those worthies, to wend his way.
Gawain bids goodbye to his goodly host
Who brings him to his chamber, the chimney beside,
And detains him in talk, and tenders his thanks
And holds it an honor to him and his people

5. December 27.

That he has harbored in his house at that holy time
And embellished his abode with his inborn grace.
"As long as I may live, my luck is the better
That Gawain was my guest at God's own feast!"
"Noble sir," said the knight, "I cannot but think
All the honor is your own—may heaven requite it!
And your man to command I account myself here
As I am bound and beholden, and shall be, come
what may."
The lord with all his might
Entreats his guest to stay;
Brief answer makes the knight:
Next morning he must away.

Then the lord of that land politely inquired
What dire affair had forced him, at that festive time,
So far from the king's court to fare forth alone
Ere the holidays wholly had ended in hall.
"In good faith," said Gawain, "you have guessed the truth:
On a high errand and urgent I hastened away,
For I am summoned by myself to seek for a place—
I would I knew whither, or where it might be!
Far rather would I find it before the New Year
Than own the land of Logres, so help me our Lord!
Wherefore, sir, in friendship this favor I ask,
That you say in sober earnest, if something you know
Of the Green Chapel, on ground far or near,
Or the lone knight that lives there, of like hue of green.
A certain day was set by assent of us both
To meet at that landmark, if I might last,
And from now to the New Year is nothing too long,
And I would greet the Green Knight there, would God but allow,
More gladly, by God's Son, than gain the world's wealth!
And I must set forth to search, as soon as I may;
To be about the business I have but three days
And would as soon sink down dead as desist from my errand."
Then smiling said the lord, "Your search, sir, is done,
For we shall see you to that site by the set time.
Let Gawain grieve no more over the Green Chapel;
You shall be in your own bed, in blissful ease,
All the forenoon, and fare forth the first of the year,
And make the goal by midmorn, to mind your affairs,
no fear!
Tarry till the fourth day
And ride on the first of the year.
We shall set you on your way;
It is not two miles from here."

Then Gawain was glad, and gleefully he laughed:

"Now I thank you for this, past all things else!
Now my goal is here at hand! With a glad heart I shall
Both tarry, and undertake any task you devise."
Then the host seized his arm and seated him there;
Let the ladies be brought, to delight them the better,
And in fellowship fair by the fireside they sit;
So gay waxed the good host, so giddy his words,
All waited in wonder what next he would say.
Then he stares on the stout knight, and sternly he speaks:
"You have bound yourself boldly my bidding to do—
Will you stand by that boast, and obey me this once?"
"I shall do so indeed," said the doughty knight;
"While I lie in your lodging, your laws will I follow."
"As you have had," said the host, "many hardships abroad
And little sleep of late, you are lacking, I judge,
Both in nourishment needful and nightly rest;
You shall lie abed late in your lofty chamber
Tomorrow until mass, and meet then to dine
When you will, with my wife, who will sit by your side
And talk with you at table, the better to cheer
our guest.
A-hunting I will go
While you lie late and rest."
The knight, inclining low,
Assents to each behest.

"And Gawain," said the good host, "agree now to this:
Whatever I win in the woods I will give you at eve,
And all you have earned you must offer to me;
Swear now, sweet friend, to swap as I say,
Whether hands, in the end, be empty or better."
"By God," said Sir Gawain, "I grant it forthwith!
If you find the game good, I shall gladly take part."
"Let the bright wine be brought, and our bargain is done,"
Said the lord of that land—the two laughed together.
Then they drank and they dallied and doffed all constraint,
These lords and these ladies, as late as they chose,
And then with gaiety and gallantries and graceful adieux
They talked in low tones, and tarried at parting.
With compliments comely they kiss at the last;
There were brisk lads about with blazing torches
To see them safe to bed, for soft repose
long due.
Their covenants, yet awhile,
They repeat, and pledge anew;
That lord could well beguile
Men's hearts, with mirth in view.

Part III

Long before daylight they left their beds;
Guests that wished to go gave word to their grooms,
And they set about briskly to bind on saddles,
Tend to their tackle, tie up trunks.
The proud lords appear, appareled to ride,
Leap lightly astride, lay hold of their bridles,
Each one on his way to his worthy house.
The liege lord of the land was not the last
Arrayed there to ride, with retainers many;
He had a bite to eat when he had heard mass;
With horn to the hills he hastens amain.
By the dawn of that day over the dim earth,
Master and men were mounted and ready.
Then they harnessed in couples the keen-scented hounds,
Cast wide the kennel-door and called them forth,
Blew upon their bugles bold blasts three;
The dogs began to bay with a deafening din,
And they quieted them quickly and called them to heel,
A hundred brave huntsmen, as I have heard tell,
together.
Men at stations meet;
From the hounds they slip the tether;
The echoing horns repeat,
Clear in the merry weather.

At the clamor of the quest, the quarry trembled;
Deer dashed through the dale, dazed with dread;
Hastened to the high ground, only to be
Turned back by the beaters, who boldly shouted.
They harmed not the harts, with their high heads,
Let the bucks go by, with their broad antlers,
For it was counted a crime, in the close season,
If a man of that demesne should molest the male deer.
The hinds were headed up, with "Hey!" and "Ware!"
The does with great din were driven to the valleys.
Then you were ware, as they went, of the whistling of arrows;
At each bend under boughs the bright shafts flew
That tore the tawny hide with their tapered heads.
Ah! they bray and they bleed, on banks they die,
And ever the pack pell-mell comes panting behind;
Hunters with shrill horns hot on their heels—
Like the cracking of cliffs their cries resounded.
What game got away from the gallant archers
Was promptly picked off at the posts below
When they were harried on the heights and herded to the streams:
The watchers were so wary at the waiting-stations,
And the greyhounds so huge, that eagerly snatched,
And finished them off as fast as folk could see
with sight.
The lord, now here, now there,

Spurs forth in sheer delight.
And drives, with pleasures rare,
The day to the dark night.

So the lord in the linden-wood leads the hunt
And Gawain the good knight in gay bed lies,
Lingered late alone, till daylight gleamed,
Under coverlet costly, curtained about.
And as he slips into slumber, slyly there comes
A little din at his door, and the latch lifted,
And he holds up his heavy head out of the clothes;
A corner of the curtain he caught back a little
And waited there warily, to see what befell.
Lo! it was the lady, loveliest to behold,
That drew the door behind her deftly and still
And was bound for his bed—abashed was the knight,
And laid his head low again in likeness of sleep;
And she stepped stealthily, and stole to his bed,
Cast aside the curtain and came within,
And set herself softly on the bedside there,
And lingered at her leisure, to look on his waking.
The fair knight lay feigning for a long while,
Conning in his conscience what his case might
Mean or amount to—a marvel he thought it.
But yet he said within himself, "More seemly it were
To try her intent by talking a little."
So he started and stretched, as startled from sleep,
Lifts wide his lids in likeness of wonder,
And signs himself swiftly, as safer to be,
with art.
Sweetly does she speak
And kindling glances dart,
Blent white and red on cheek
And laughing lips apart.

"Good morning, Sir Gawain," said that gay lady,
"A slack sleeper you are, to let one slip in!
Now you are taken in a trice—a truce we must make,
Or I shall bind you in your bed, of that be assured."
Thus laughing lightly that lady jested.
"Good morning, good lady," said Gawain the blithe,
"Be it with me as you will; I am well content!
For I surrender myself, and sue for your grace,
And that is best, I believe, and behooves me now."
Thus jested in answer that gentle knight.
"But if, lovely lady, you misliked it not,
And were pleased to permit your prisoner to rise,
I should quit this couch and accoutre me better,
And be clad in more comfort for converse here."
"Nay, not so, sweet sir," said the smiling lady;
"You shall not rise from your bed; I direct you better:
I shall hem and hold you on either hand,

And keep company awhile with my captive knight.
For as certain as I sit here, Sir Gawain you are,
Whom all the world worships, whereso you ride;
Your honor, your courtesy are highest acclaimed
By lords and by ladies, by all living men;
And lo! we are alone here, and left to ourselves:
My lord and his liegemen are long departed,
The household asleep, my handmaids too,
The door drawn, and held by a well-driven bolt,
And since I have in this house him whom all love,
I shall while the time away with mirthful speech
at will.
My body is here at hand,
Your each wish to fulfill;
Your servant to command
I am, and shall be still."

"In good faith," said Gawain, "my gain is the greater,
Though I am not he of whom you have heard;
To arrive at such reverence as you recount here
I am one all unworthy, and well do I know it.
By heaven, I would hold me the happiest of men
If by word or by work I once might aspire
To the prize of your praise—'twere a pure joy!"
"In good faith, Sir Gawain," said that gay lady,
"The well-proven prowess that pleases all others,
Did I scant or scout it, 'twere scarce becoming.
But there are ladies, believe me, that had liefer far
Have thee here in their hold, as I have today,
To pass an hour in pastime with pleasant words,
Assuage all their sorrows and solace their hearts,
Than much of the goodly gems and gold they possess.
But laud be to the Lord of the lofty skies,
For here in my hands all hearts' desire
doth lie."
Great welcome got he there
From the lady who sat him by;
With fitting speech and fair
The good knight makes reply.

"Madame," said the merry man, "Mary reward you!
For in good faith, I find your beneficence noble.
And the fame of fair deeds runs far and wide,
But the praise you report pertains not to me,
But comes of your courtesy and kindness of heart."
"By the high Queen of heaven" (said she) "I count it not so,
For were I worth all the women in this world alive,
And all wealth and all worship were in my hands,
And I should hunt high and low, a husband to take,
For the nurture I have noted in thee, knight, here,
The comeliness and courtesies and courtly mirth—
And so I had ever heard, and now hold it true—

No other on this earth should have me for wife."
"You are bound to a better man," the bold knight said,
"Yet I prize the praise you have proffered me here,
And soberly your servant, my sovereign I hold you,
And acknowledge me your knight, in the name of Christ."
So they talked of this and that until 'twas nigh noon,
And ever the lady languishing in likeness of love.
With feat words and fair he framed his defense,
For were she never so winsome, the warrior had
The less will to woo, for the wound that his bane
must be.
He must bear the blinding blow,
For such is fate's decree;
The lady asks leave to go;
He grants it full and free.

Then she gaily said goodbye, and glanced at him, laughing,
And as she stood, she astonished him with a stern speech:
"Now may the Giver of all good words these glad hours repay!
But our guest is not Gawain—forgot is that thought."
"How so?" said the other, and asks in some haste,
For he feared he had been at fault in the forms of his speech.
But she held up her hand, and made answer thus:
"So good a knight as Gawain is given out to be,
And the model of fair demeanor and manners pure,
Had he lain so long at a lady's side,
Would have claimed a kiss, by his courtesy,
Through some touch or trick of phrase at some tale's end."
Said Gawain, "Good lady, I grant it at once!
I shall kiss at your command, as becomes a knight,
And more, lest you mislike, so let be, I pray."
With that she turns toward him, takes him in her arms,
Leans down her lovely head, and lo! he is kissed.
They commend each other to Christ with comely words,
He sees her forth safely, in silence they part,
And then he lies no later in his lofty bed,
But calls to his chamberlain, chooses his clothes,
Goes in those garments gladly to mass,
Then takes his way to table, where attendants wait,
And made merry all day, till the moon rose
in view
Was never knight beset
'Twixt worthier ladies two:
The crone and the coquette;
Fair pastimes they pursue.

And the lord of the land rides late and long,
Hunting the barren hind over the broad heath.
He had slain such a sum, when the sun sank low,
Of does and other deer, as would dizzy one's wits.
Then they trooped in together in triumph at last,
And the count of the quarry quickly they take.

The lords lent a hand with their liegemen many,
Picked out the plumpest and put them together
And duly dressed the deer, as the deed requires.
Some were assigned the assay of the fat:
Two fingers'-width fully they found on the leanest.
Then they slit the slot open and searched out the paunch,
Trimmed it with trencher-knives and tied it up tight.
They flayed the fair hide from the legs and trunk,
Then broke open the belly and laid bare the bowels,
Deftly detaching and drawing them forth.
And next at the neck they neatly parted
The weasand [6] from the windpipe, and cast away the guts.
At the shoulders with sharp blades they showed their skill,
Boning them from beneath, lest the sides be marred;
They breached the broad breast and broke it in twain,
And again at the gullet they begin with their knives,
Cleave down the carcass clear to the breach;
Two tender morsels they take from the throat,
Then round the inner ribs they rid off a layer
And carve out the kidney-fat, close to the spine,
Hewing down to the haunch, that all hung together,
And held it up whole, and hacked it free,
And this they named the numbles,[7] that knew such terms
of art.
They divide the crotch in two,
And straightway then they start
To cut the backbone through
And cleave the trunk apart.

With hard strokes they hewed off the head and the neck,
Then swiftly from the sides they severed the chine,
And the corbie's bone [8] they cast on a branch.
Then they pierced the plump sides, impaled either one
With the hock of the hind foot, and hung it aloft,
To each person his portion most proper and fit.
On a hide of a hind the hounds they fed
With the liver and the lights,[9] the leathery paunches,
And bread soaked in blood well blended therewith.
High horns and shrill set hounds a-baying,
Then merrily with their meat they make their way home,
Blowing on their bugles many a brave blast.
Ere dark had descended, that doughty band
Was come within the walls where Gawain waits
at leisure.
Bliss and hearth-fire bright
Await the master's pleasure;
When the two men met that night,
Joy surpassed all measure.

6. Esophagus.
7. The other internal organs.
8. A bit of gristle assigned to the ravens ("corbies").
9. Lungs.

Then the host in the hall his household assembles,
With the dames of high degree and their damsels fair.
In the presence of the people, a party he sends
To convey him his venison in view of the knight.
And in high good-humor he hails him then,
Counts over the kill, the cuts on the tallies,
Holds high the hewn ribs, heavy with fat.
"What think you, sir, of this? Have I thriven well?
Have I won with my woodcraft a worthy prize?"
"In good earnest," said Gawain, "this game is the finest
I have seen in seven years in the season of winter."
"And I give it to you, Gawain," said the goodly host,
"For according to our covenant, you claim it as your own."
"That is so," said Sir Gawain, "the same say I:
What I worthily have won within these fair walls,
Herewith I as willingly award it to you."
He embraces his broad neck with both his arms,
And confers on him a kiss in the comeliest style.
"Have here my profit, it proved no better;
Ungrudging do I grant it, were it greater far."
"Such a gift," said the good host, "I gladly accept—
Yet it might be all the better, would you but say
Where you won this same award, by your wits alone."
"That was no part of the pact; press me no further,
For you have had what behooves; all other claims
forbear."
With jest and compliment
They conversed, and cast off care;
To the table soon they went;
Fresh dainties wait them there.

And then by the chimney-side they chat at their ease;
The best wine was brought them, and bounteously served;
And after in their jesting they jointly accord
To do on the second day the deeds of the first:
That the two men should trade, betide as it may,
What each had taken in, at eve when they met.
They seal the pact solemnly in sight of the court;
Their cups were filled afresh to confirm the jest;
Then at last they took their leave, for late was the hour,
Each to his own bed hastening away.
Before the barnyard cock had crowed but thrice
The lord had leapt from his rest, his liegemen as well.
Both of mass and their meal they made short work:
By the dim light of dawn they were deep in the woods
away.
With huntsmen and with horns
Over plains they pass that day;
They release, amid the thorns,
Swift hounds that run and bay.

Soon some were on a scent by the side of a marsh;
When the hounds opened cry, the head of the hunt
Rallied them with rough words, raised a great noise.
The hounds that had heard it came hurrying straight
And followed along with their fellows, forty together.
Then such a clamor and cry of coursing hounds
Arose, that the rocks resounded again.
Hunters exhorted them with horn and with voice;
Then all in a body bore off together
Between a mere in the marsh and a menacing crag,
To a rise where the rock stood rugged and steep,
And boulders lay about, that blocked their approach.
Then the company in consort closed on their prey:
They surrounded the rise and the rocks both,
For well they were aware that it waited within,
The beast that the bloodhounds boldly proclaimed.
Then they beat on the bushes and bade him appear,
And he made a murderous rush in the midst of them all;
The best of all boars broke from his cover,
That had ranged long unrivaled, a renegade old,
For of tough-brawned boars he was biggest far,
Most grim when he grunted—then grieved were many,
For three at the first thrust he threw to the earth,
And dashed away at once without more damage.
With "Hi!" "Hi!" and "Hey!" "Hey!" the others followed,
Had horns at their lips, blew high and clear.
Merry was the music of men and of hounds
That were bound after this boar, his bloodthirsty heart
to quell.
Often he stands at bay,
Then scatters the pack pell-mell;
He hurts the hounds, and they
Most dolefully yowl and yell.

Men then with mighty bows moved in to shoot,
Aimed at him with their arrows and often hit,
But the points had no power to pierce through his hide,
And the barbs were brushed aside by his bristly brow;
Though the shank of the shaft shivered in pieces,
The head hopped away, wheresoever it struck.
But when their stubborn strokes had stung him at last,
Then, foaming in his frenzy, fiercely he charges,
Hies at them headlong that hindered his flight,
And many feared for their lives, and fell back a little.
But the lord on a lively horse leads the chase;
As a high-mettled huntsman his horn he blows;
He sounds the assembly and sweeps through the brush,
Pursuing this wild swine till the sunlight slanted.
All day with this deed they drive forth the time
While our lone knight so lovesome lies in his bed,

Sir Gawain safe at home, in silken bower
so gay.
The lady, with guile in heart,
Came early where he lay;
She was at him with all her art
To turn his mind her way.

She comes to the curtain and coyly peeps in;
Gawain thought it good to greet her at once,
And she richly repays him with her ready words,
Settles softly at his side, and suddenly she laughs,
And with a gracious glance, she begins on him thus:
"Sir, if you be Gawain, it seems a great wonder—
A man so well-meaning, and mannerly disposed,
And cannot act in company as courtesy bids,
And if one takes the trouble to teach him, 'tis all in vain.
That lesson learned lately is lightly forgot,
Though I painted it as plain as my poor wit allowed."
"What lesson, dear lady?" he asked all alarmed;
"I have been much to blame, if your story be true."
"Yet my counsel was of kissing," came her answer then,
"Where favor has been found, freely to claim
As accords with the conduct of courteous knights."
"My dear," said the doughty man, "dismiss that thought;
Such freedom, I fear, might offend you much;
It were rude to request if the right were denied."
"But none can deny you," said the noble dame,
"You are stout enough to constrain with strength, if you choose,
Were any so ungracious as to grudge you aught."
"By heaven," said he, "you have answered well,
But threats never throve among those of my land,
Nor any gift not freely given, good though it be.
I am yours to command, to kiss when you please;
You may lay on as you like, and leave off at will."
With this,
The lady lightly bends
And graciously gives him a kiss;
The two converse as friends
Of true love's trials and bliss.

"I should like, by your leave," said the lovely lady,
"If it did not annoy you, to know for what cause
So brisk and so bold a young blood as you,
And acclaimed for all courtesies becoming a knight—
And name what knight you will, they are noblest esteemed
For loyal faith in love, in life as in story;
For to tell the tribulations of these true hearts,
Why, 'tis the very title and text of their deeds,
How bold knights for beauty have braved many a foe,
Suffered heavy sorrows out of secret love,
And then valorously avenged them on villainous churls

And made happy ever after the hearts of their ladies.
And you are the noblest knight known in your time;
No household under heaven but has heard of your fame,
And here by your side I have sat for two days
Yet never has a fair phrase fallen from your lips
Of the language of love, not one little word!
And you, that with sweet vows sway women's hearts,
Should show your winsome ways, and woo a young thing,
And teach by some tokens the craft of true love.
How! are you artless, whom all men praise?
Or do you deem me so dull, or deaf to such words?
Fie! Fie!
In hope of pastimes new
I have come where none can spy;
Instruct me a little, do,
While my husband is not nearby."

"God love you, gracious lady!" said Gawain then;
"It is a pleasure surpassing, and a peerless joy,
That one so worthy as you would willingly come
And take the time and trouble to talk with your knight
And content you with his company—it comforts my heart.
But to take to myself the task of telling of love,
And touch upon its texts, and treat of its themes
To one that, I know well, wields more power
In that art, by a half, than a hundred such
As I am where I live, or am like to become,
It were folly, fair dame, in the first degree!
In all that I am able, my aim is to please,
As in honor behooves me, and am evermore
Your servant heart and soul, so save me our Lord!"
Thus she tested his temper and tried many a time,
Whatever her true intent, to entice him to sin,
But so fair was his defense that no fault appeared,
Nor evil on either hand, but only bliss
they knew.
They linger and laugh awhile;
She kisses the knight so true,
Takes leave in comeliest style
And departs without more ado.

Then he rose from his rest and made ready for mass,
And then a meal was set and served, in sumptuous style;
He dallied at home all day with the dear ladies,
But the lord lingered late at his lusty sport;
Pursued his sorry swine, that swerved as he fled,
And bit asunder the backs of the best of his hounds
When they brought him to bay, till the bowmen appeared
And soon forced him forth, though he fought for dear life,
So sharp were the shafts they shot at him there.
But yet the boldest drew back from his battering head,

Till at last he was so tired he could travel no more,
But in as much haste as he might, he makes his retreat
To a rise on rocky ground, by a rushing stream.
With the bank at his back he scrapes the bare earth,
The froth foams at his jaws, frightful to see.
He whets his white tusks—then weary were all
Those hunters so hardy that hoved round about
Of aiming from afar, but ever they mistrust
his mood.
He had hurt so many by then
That none had hardihood
To be torn by his tusks again,
That was brainsick, and out for blood.

Till the lord came at last on his lofty steed,
Beheld him there at bay before all his folk;
Lightly he leaps down, leaves his courser,
Bares his bright sword, and boldly advances;
Straight into the stream he strides towards his foe.
The wild thing was wary of weapon and man;
His hackles rose high; so hotly he snorts
That many watched with alarm, lest the worst befall.
The boar makes for the man with a mighty bound
So that he and his hunter came headlong together
Where the water ran wildest—the worse for the beast,
For the man, when they first met, marked him with care,
Sights well the slot, slips in the blade,
Shoves it home to the hilt, and the heart shattered,
And he falls in his fury and floats down the water,
ill-sped.
Hounds hasten by the score
To maul him, hide and head;
Men drag him in to shore
And dogs pronounce him dead.

With many a brave blast they boast of their prize,
All hallooed in high glee, that had their wind;
The hounds bayed their best, as the bold men bade
That were charged with chief rank in that chase of renown.
Then one wise in woodcraft, and worthily skilled,
Began to dress the boar in becoming style:
He severs the savage head and sets it aloft,
Then rends the body roughly right down the spine;
Takes the bowels from the belly, broils them on coals,
Blends them well with bread to bestow on the hounds.
Then he breaks out the brawn in fair broad flitches,
And the innards to be eaten in order he takes.
The two sides, attached to each other all whole,
He suspended from a spar that was springy and tough;
And so with this swine they set out for home;
The boar's head was borne before the same man

That had stabbed him in the stream with his strong arm,
right through.
He thought it long indeed
Till he had the knight in view;
At his call, he comes with speed
To claim his payment due.

The lord laughed aloud, with many a light word,
When he greeted Sir Gawain—with good cheer he speaks.
They fetch the fair dames and the folk of the house;
He brings forth the brawn, and begins the tale
Of the great length and girth, the grim rage as well,
Of the battle of the boar they beset in the wood.
The other man meetly commended his deeds
And praised well the prize of his princely sport,
For the brawn of that boar, the bold knight said,
And the sides of that swine surpassed all others.
Then they handled the huge head; he owns it a wonder,
And eyes it with abhorrence, to heighten his praise.
"Now, Gawain," said the good man, "this game becomes yours
By those fair terms we fixed, as you know full well."
"That is true," returned the knight, "and trust me, fair friend,
All my gains, as agreed, I shall give you forthwith."
He clasps him and kisses him in courteous style,
Then serves him with the same fare a second time.
"Now we are even," said he, "at this evening feast,
And clear is every claim incurred here to date,
and debt."
"By Saint Giles!" the host replies,
"You're the best I ever met!
If your profits are all this size,
We'll see you wealthy yet!"

Then attendants set tables on trestles about,
And laid them with linen; light shone forth,
Wakened along the walls in waxen torches.
The service was set and the supper brought;
Royal were the revels that rose then in hall
At that feast by the fire, with many fair sports:
Amid the meal and after, melody sweet,
Carol-dances comely and Christmas songs,
With all the mannerly mirth my tongue may describe.
And ever our gallant knight beside the gay lady;
So uncommonly kind and complaisant was she,
With sweet stolen glances, that stirred his stout heart,
That he was at his wits' end, and wondrous vexed;
But he could not in conscience her courtship repay,
Yet took pains to please her, though the plan might
go wrong.
When they to heart's delight
Had reveled there in throng,

To his chamber he calls the knight,
And thither they go along.

And there they dallied and drank, and deemed it good sport
To enact their play anew on New Year's Eve,
But Gawain asked again to go on the morrow,
For the time until his tryst was not two days.
The host hindered that, and urged him to stay,
And said, "On my honor, my oath here I take
That you shall get to the Green Chapel to begin your chores
By dawn on New Year's Day, if you so desire.
Wherefore lie at your leisure in your lofty bed,
And I shall hunt hereabouts, and hold to our terms,
And we shall trade winnings when once more we meet,
For I have tested you twice, and true have I found you;
Now think this tomorrow: the third pays for all;
Be we merry while we may, and mindful of joy,
For heaviness of heart can be had for the asking."
This is gravely agreed on and Gawain will stay.
They drink a last draught and with torches depart
to rest.
To bed Sir Gawain went;
His sleep was of the best;
The lord, on his craft intent,
Was early up and dressed.

After mass, with his men, a morsel he takes;
Clear and crisp the morning; he calls for his mount;
The folk that were to follow him afield that day
Were high astride their horses before the hall gates.
Wondrous fair were the fields, for the frost was light;
The sun rises red amid radiant clouds,
Sails into the sky, and sends forth his beams.
They let loose the hounds by a leafy wood;
The rocks all around re-echo to their horns;
Soon some have set off in pursuit of the fox,
Cast about with craft for a clearer scent;
A young dog yaps, and is yelled at in turn;
His fellows fall to sniffing, and follow his lead,
Running in a rabble on the right track,
And he scampers all before; they discover him soon,
And when they see him with sight they pursue him the faster,
Railing at him rudely with a wrathful din.
Often he reverses over rough terrain,
Or loops back to listen in the lee of a hedge;
At last, by a little ditch, he leaps over the brush,
Comes into a clearing at a cautious pace,
Then he thought through his wiles to have thrown off the hounds
Till he was ware, as he went, of a waiting-station
Where three athwart his path threatened him at once,
all gray.

Quick as a flash he wheels
And darts off in dismay;
With hard luck at his heels
He is off to the wood away.

Then it was heaven on earth to hark to the hounds
When they had come on their quarry, coursing together!
Such harsh cries and howls they hurled at his head
As all the cliffs with a crash had come down at once.
Here he was hailed, when huntsmen met him;
Yonder they yelled at him, yapping and snarling;
There they cried "Thief!" and threatened his life,
And ever the harriers at his heels, that he had no rest.
Often he was menaced when he made for the open,
And often rushed in again, for Reynard was wily;
And so he leads them a merry chase, the lord and his men,
In this manner on the mountains, till midday or near,
While our hero lies at home in wholesome sleep
Within the comely curtains on the cold morning.
But the lady, as love would allow her no rest,
And pursuing ever the purpose that pricked her heart,
Was awake with the dawn, and went to his chamber
In a fair flowing mantle that fell to the earth,
All edged and embellished with ermines fine;
No hood on her head, but heavy with gems
Were her fillet and the fret [1] that confined her tresses;
Her face and her fair throat freely displayed;
Her bosom all but bare, and her back as well.
She comes in at the chamber-door, and closes it with care,
Throws wide a window—then waits no longer,
But hails him thus airily with her artful words,
with cheer:
"Ah, man, how can you sleep?
The morning is so clear!"
Though dreams have drowned him deep,
He cannot choose but hear.

Deep in his dreams he darkly mutters
As a man may that mourns, with many grim thoughts
Of that day when destiny shall deal him his doom
When he greets his grim host at the Green Chapel
And must bow to his buffet, bating all strife.
But when he sees her at his side he summons his wits,
Breaks from the black dreams, and blithely answers.
That lovely lady comes laughing sweet,
Sinks down at his side, and salutes him with a kiss.
He accords her fair welcome in courtliest style;
He sees her so glorious, so gaily attired,
So faultless her features, so fair and so bright,

1. Ornamental net.

His heart swelled swiftly with surging joys.
They melt into mirth with many a fond smile,
And there was bliss beyond telling between those two,
at height.
Good were their words of greeting;
Each joyed in other's sight;
Great peril attends that meeting
Should Mary forget her knight.

For that high-born beauty so hemmed him about,
Made so plain her meaning, the man must needs
Either take her tendered love or distastefully refuse.
His courtesy concerned him, lest crass he appear,
But more his soul's mischief, should he commit sin
And belie his loyal oath to the lord of that house.
"God forbid!" said the bold knight, "That shall not befall!"
With a little fond laughter he lightly let pass
All the words of special weight that were sped his way;
"I find you much at fault," the fair one said,
"Who can be cold toward a creature so close by your side,
Of all women in this world most wounded in heart,
Unless you have a sweetheart, one you hold dearer,
And allegiance to that lady so loyally knit
That you will never love another, as now I believe.
And, sir, if it be so, then say it, I beg you;
By all your heart holds dear, hide it no longer
with guile."
"Lady, by Saint John,"
He answers with a smile,
"Lover have I none,
Nor will have, yet awhile."

"Those words," said the woman, "are the worst of all,
But I have had my answer, and hard do I find it!
Kiss me now kindly: I can but go hence
To lament my life long like a maid lovelorn."
She inclines her head quickly and kisses the knight,
Then straightens with a sigh, and says as she stands,
"Now, dear, ere I depart, do me this pleasure:
Give me some little gift, your glove or the like,
That I may think on you, man, and mourn the less."
"Now by heaven," said he, "I wish I had here
My most precious possession, to put it in your hands,
For your deeds, beyond doubt, have often deserved
A repayment far passing my power to bestow.
But a love-token, lady, were of little avail;
It is not to your honor to have at this time
A glove as a guerdon from Gawain's hand,
And I am here on an errand in unknown realms
And have no bearers with baggage with becoming gifts,
Which distresses me, madame, for your dear sake.

A man must keep within his compass: account it neither grief
nor slight."
"Nay, noblest knight alive,"
Said that beauty of body white,
"Though you be loath to give,
Yet you shall take, by right."

She reached out a rich ring, wrought all of gold,
With a splendid stone displayed on the band
That flashed before his eyes like a fiery sun;
It was worth a king's wealth, you may well believe.
But he waved it away with these ready words:
"Before God, good lady, I forego all gifts;
None have I to offer, nor any will I take."
And she urged it on him eagerly, and ever he refused,
And vowed in very earnest, prevail she would not.
And she sad to find it so, and said to him then,
"If my ring is refused for its rich cost—
You would not be my debtor for so dear a thing—
I shall give you my girdle; you gain less thereby."
She released a knot lightly, and loosened a belt
That was caught about her kirtle, the bright cloak beneath,
Of a gay green silk, with gold overwrought,
And the borders all bound with embroidery fine,
And this she presses upon him, and pleads with a smile,
Unworthy though it were, that it would not be scorned.
But the man still maintains that he means to accept
Neither gold nor any gift, till by God's grace
The fate that lay before him was fully achieved.
"And be not offended, fair lady, I beg,
And give over your offer, for ever I must
decline.
I am grateful for favor shown
Past all deserts of mine,
And ever shall be your own
True servant, rain or shine."

"Now does my present displease you," she promptly inquired,
"Because it seems in your sight so simple a thing?
And belike, as it is little, it is less to praise,
But if the virtue that invests it were verily known,
It would be held, I hope, in higher esteem.
For the man that possesses this piece of silk,
If he bore it on his body, belted about,
There is no hand under heaven that could hew him down,
For he could not be killed by any craft on earth."
Then the man began to muse, and mainly he thought
It was a pearl for his plight, the peril to come
When he gains the Green Chapel to get his reward:
Could he escape unscathed, the scheme were noble!
Then he bore with her words and withstood them no more,

And she repeated her petition and pleaded anew,
And he granted it, and gladly she gave him the belt,
And besought him for her sake to conceal it well,
Lest the noble lord should know—and the knight agrees
That not a soul save themselves shall see it thenceforth
with sight.
He thanked her with fervent heart,
As often as ever he might;
Three times, before they part,
She has kissed the stalwart knight.

Then the lady took her leave, and left him there,
For more mirth with that man she might not have.
When she was gone, Sir Gawain got from his bed,
Arose and arrayed him in his rich attire;
Tucked away the token the temptress had left,
Laid it reliably where he looked for it after.
And then with good cheer to the chapel he goes,
Approached a priest in private, and prayed to be taught
To lead a better life and lift up his mind,
Lest he be among the lost when he must leave this world.
And shamefaced at shrift he showed his misdeeds
From the largest to the least, and asked the Lord's mercy,
And called on his confessor to cleanse his soul,
And he absolved him of his sins as safe and as clean
As if the dread Day of Judgment should dawn on the morrow.
And then he made merry amid the fine ladies
With deft-footed dances and dalliance light,
As never until now, while the afternoon wore
away.
He delighted all around him,
And all agreed, that day,
They never before had found him
So gracious and so gay.

Now peaceful be his pasture, and love play him fair!
The host is on horseback, hunting afield;
He has finished off this fox that he followed so long:
As he leapt a low hedge to look for the villain
Where he heard all the hounds in hot pursuit,
Reynard comes racing out of a rough thicket,
And all the rabble in a rush, right at his heels.
The man beholds the beast, and bides his time,
And bares his bright sword, and brings it down hard,
And he blenches from the blade, and backward he starts;
A hound hurries up and hinders that move,
And before the horse's feet they fell on him at once
And ripped the rascal's throat with a wrathful din.
The lord soon alighted and lifted him free,
Swiftly snatched him up from the snapping jaws,
Holds him over his head, halloos with a will,

And the dogs bayed the dirge, that had done him to death.
Hunters hastened thither with horns at their lips,
Sounding the assembly till they saw him at last.
When that comely company was come in together,
All that bore bugles blew them at once,
And the others all hallooed, that had no horns.
It was the merriest medley that ever a man heard,
The racket that they raised for Sir Reynard's soul
that died.
Their hounds they praised and fed,
Fondling their heads with pride,
And they took Reynard the Red
And stripped away his hide.

And then they headed homeward, for evening had come,
Blowing many a blast on their bugles bright.
The lord at long last alights at his house,
Finds fire on the hearth where the fair knight waits,
Sir Gawain the good, that was glad in heart.
With the ladies, that loved him, he lingered at ease;
He wore a rich robe of blue, that reached to the earth
And a surcoat lined softly with sumptuous furs;
A hood of the same hue hung on his shoulders;
With bands of bright ermine embellished were both.
He comes to meet the man amid all the folk,
And greets him good-humoredly, and gaily he says,
"I shall follow forthwith the form of our pledge
That we framed to good effect amid fresh-filled cups."
He clasps him accordingly and kisses him thrice,
As amiably and as earnestly as ever he could.
"By heaven," said the host, "you have had some luck
Since you took up this trade, if the terms were good."
"Never trouble about the terms," he returned at once,
"Since all that I owe here is openly paid."
"Marry!" said the other man, "mine is much less,
For I have hunted all day, and nought have I got
But this foul fox pelt, the fiend take the goods!
Which but poorly repays those precious things
That you have cordially conferred, those kisses three
so good."
"Enough!" said Sir Gawain;
"I thank you, by the rood!"
And how the fox was slain
He told him, as they stood.

With minstrelsy and mirth, with all manner of meats,
They made as much merriment as any men might
(Amid laughing of ladies and light hearted girls,
So gay grew Sir Gawain and the goodly host)
Unless they had been besotted, or brainless fools.
The knight joined in jesting with that joyous folk,

Until at last it was late; ere long they must part,
And be off to their beds, as behooved them each one.
Then politely his leave of the lord of the house
Our noble knight takes, and renews his thanks:
"The courtesies countless accorded me here,
Your kindness at this Christmas, may heaven's King repay!
Henceforth, if you will have me, I hold you my liege,
And so, as I have said, I must set forth tomorrow,
If I may take some trusty man to teach, as you promised,
The way to the Green Chapel, that as God allows
I shall see my fate fulfilled on the first of the year."
"In good faith," said the good man, "with a good will
Every promise on my part shall be fully performed."
He assigns him a servant to set him on the path,
To see him safe and sound over the snowy hills,
To follow the fastest way through forest green
and grove.
Gawain thanks him again,
So kind his favors prove,
And of the ladies then
He takes his leave, with love.

Courteously he kissed them, with care in his heart,
And often wished them well, with warmest thanks,
Which they for their part were prompt to repay.
They commend him to Christ with disconsolate sighs;
And then in that hall with the household he parts—
Each man that he met, he remembered to thank
For his deeds of devotion and diligent pains,
And the trouble he had taken to tend to his needs;
And each one as woeful, that watched him depart,
As he had lived with him loyally all his life long.
By lads bearing lights he was led to his chamber
And blithely brought to his bed, to be at his rest.
How soundly he slept, I presume not to say,
For there were matters of moment his thoughts might well
pursue.
Let him lie and wait;
He has little more to do,
Then listen, while I relate
How they kept their rendezvous.

Part IV

Now the New Year draws near, and the night passes,
The day dispels the dark, by the Lord's decree;
But wild weather awoke in the world without:
The clouds in the cold sky cast down their snow
With great gusts from the north, grievous to bear.
Sleet showered aslant upon shivering beasts;

The wind warbled wild as it whipped from aloft,
And drove the drifts deep in the dales below.
Long and well he listens, that lies in his bed;
Though he lifts not his eyelids, little he sleeps;
Each crow of the cock he counts without fail.
Readily from his rest he rose before dawn,
For a lamp had been left him, that lighted his chamber.
He called to his chamberlain, who quickly appeared,
And bade him get him his gear, and gird his good steed,
And he sets about briskly to bring in his arms,
And makes ready his master in manner most fit.
First he clad him in his clothes, to keep out the cold,
And then his other harness, made handsome anew,
His plate-armor of proof, polished with pains,
The rings of his rich mail rid of their rust,
And all was fresh as at first, and for this he gave thanks
indeed.
With pride he wears each piece,
New-furbished for his need:
No gayer from here to Greece;
He bids them bring his steed.

In his richest raiment he robed himself then:
His crested coat-armor, close-stitched with craft,
With stones of strange virtue on silk velvet set;
All bound with embroidery on borders and seams
And lined warmly and well with furs of the best.
Yet he left not his love-gift, the lady's girdle;
Gawain, for his own good, forgot not that:
When the bright sword was belted and bound on his haunches,
Then twice with that token he twined him about.
Sweetly did he swathe him in that swatch of silk,
That girdle of green so goodly to see,
That against the gay red showed gorgeous bright.
Yet he wore not for its wealth that wondrous girdle,
Nor pride in its pendants, though polished they were,
Though glittering gold gleamed at the tips,
But to keep himself safe when consent he must
To endure a deadly dint, and all defense
denied.
And now the bold knight came
Into the courtyard wide;
That folk of worthy fame
He thanks on every side.

Then was Gringolet girt, that was great and huge,
And had sojourned safe and sound, and savored his fare;
He pawed the earth in his pride, that princely steed.
The good knight draws near him and notes well his look,
And says sagely to himself, and soberly swears,
"Here is a household in hall that upholds the right!

The man that maintains it, may happiness be his!
Likewise the dear lady, may love betide her!
If thus they in charity cherish a guest
That are honored here on earth, may they have His reward
That reigns high in heaven—and also you all;
And were I to live in this land but a little while,
I should willingly reward you, and well, if I might."
Then he steps into the stirrup and bestrides his mount;
His shield is shown forth; on his shoulder he casts it;
Strikes the side of his steed with his steel spurs,
And he starts across the stones, nor stands any longer
to prance.
On horseback was the swain
That bore his spear and lance;
"May Christ this house maintain
And guard it from mischance!"

The bridge was brought down, and the broad gates
Unbarred and carried back upon both sides;
He commended him to Christ, and crossed over the planks;
Praised the noble porter, who prayed on his knees
That God save Sir Gawain, and bade him good day,
And went on his way alone with the man
That was to lead him ere long to that luckless place
Where the dolorous dint must be dealt him at last.
Under bare boughs they ride, where steep banks rise,
Over high cliffs they climb, where cold snow clings;
The heavens held aloof, but heavy thereunder
Mist mantled the moors, moved on the slopes.
Each hill had a hat, a huge cape of cloud;
Brooks bubbled and broke over broken rocks,
Flashing in freshets that waterfalls fed.
Roundabout was the road that ran through the wood
Till the sun at that season was soon to rise,
that day.
They were on a hilltop high;
The white snow round them lay;
The man that rode nearby
Now bade his master stay.

"For I have seen you here safe at the set time,
And now you are not far from that notable place
That you have sought for so long with such special pains.
But this I say for certain, since I know you, sir knight,
And have your good at heart, and hold you dear—
Would you heed well my words, it were worth your while—
You are rushing into risks that you reck not of:
There is a villain in yon valley, the veriest on earth,
For he is rugged and rude, and ready with his fists,
And most immense in his mold of mortals alive,
And his body bigger than the best four

That are in Arthur's house, Hector [2] or any.
He gets his grim way at the Green Chapel;
None passes by that place so proud in his arms
That he does not dash him down with his deadly blows,
For he is heartless wholly, and heedless of right,
For be it chaplain or churl that by the Chapel rides,
Monk or mass-priest or any man else,
He would as soon strike him dead as stand on two feet.
Wherefore I say, just as certain as you sit there astride,
You cannot but be killed, if his counsel holds,
For he would trounce you in a trice, had you twenty lives
for sale.
He has lived long in this land
And dealt out deadly bale;
Against his heavy hand
Your power cannot prevail.

"And so, good Sir Gawain, let the grim man be;
Go off by some other road, in God's own name!
Leave by some other land, for the love of Christ,
And I shall get me home again, and give you my word
That I shall swear by God's self and the saints above,
By heaven and by my halidom [3] and other oaths more,
To conceal this day's deed, nor say to a soul
That ever you fled for fear from any that I knew."
"Many thanks!" said the other man—and demurring he speaks—
"Fair fortune befall you for your friendly words!
And conceal this day's deed I doubt not you would,
But though you never told the tale, if I turned back now,
Forsook this place for fear, and fled, as you say,
I were a caitiff coward; I could not be excused.
But I must to the Chapel to chance my luck
And say to that same man such words as I please,
Befall what may befall through Fortune's will
or whim.
Though he be a quarrelsome knave
With a cudgel great and grim,
The Lord is strong to save:
His servants trust in Him."

"Marry," said the man, "since you tell me so much,
And I see you are set to seek your own harm,
If you crave a quick death, let me keep you no longer!
Put your helm on your head, your hand on your lance,
And ride the narrow road down yon rocky slope
Till it brings you to the bottom of the broad valley.
Then look a little ahead, on your left hand,
And you will soon see before you that self-same Chapel,
And the man of great might that is master there.

2. Either the Trojan hero or one of Arthur's knights.

3. Holiness or, more likely, patron saints.

Now goodbye in God's name, Gawain the noble!
For all the world's wealth I would not stay here,
Or go with you in this wood one footstep further!"
He tarried no more to talk, but turned his bridle,
Hit his horse with his heels as hard as he might,
Leaves the knight alone, and off like the wind
goes leaping.
"By God," said Gawain then,
"I shall not give way to weeping;
God's will be done, amen!
I commend me to His keeping."

He puts his heels to his horse, and picks up the path;
Goes in beside a grove where the ground is steep,
Rides down the rough slope right to the valley;
And then he looked a little about him—the landscape was wild,
And not a soul to be seen, nor sign of a dwelling,
But high banks on either hand hemmed it about,
With many a ragged rock and rough-hewn crag;
The skies seemed scored by the scowling peaks.
Then he halted his horse, and hoved there a space,
And sought on every side for a sight of the Chapel,
But no such place appeared, which puzzled him sore,
Yet he saw some way off what seemed like a mound,
A hillock high and broad, hard by the water,
Where the stream fell in foam down the face of the steep
And bubbled as if it boiled on its bed below.
The knight urges his horse, and heads for the knoll;
Leaps lightly to earth; loops well the rein
Of his steed to a stout branch, and stations him there.
He strides straight to the mound, and strolls all about,
Much wondering what it was, but no whit the wiser;
It had a hole at one end, and on either side,
And was covered with coarse grass in clumps all without,
And hollow all within, like some old cave,
Or a crevice of an old crag—he could not discern
aright.
"Can this be the Chapel Green?
Alack!" said the man, "Here might
The devil himself be seen
Saying matins at black midnight!"

"Now by heaven," said he, "it is bleak hereabouts;
This prayer-house is hideous, half-covered with grass!
Well may the grim man mantled in green
Hold here his orisons, in hell's own style!
Now I feel it is the Fiend, in my five wits,
That has tempted me to this tryst, to take my life;
This is a Chapel of mischance, may the mischief take it!
As accursed a country church as I came upon ever!"

With his helm on his head, his lance in his hand,
He stalks toward the steep wall of that strange house.
Then he heard, on the hill, behind a hard rock,
Beyond the brook, from the bank, a most barbarous din:
Lord! it clattered in the cliff fit to cleave it in two,
As one upon a grindstone ground a great scythe!
Lord! it whirred like a mill-wheel whirling about!
Lord! it echoed loud and long, lamentable to hear!
Then "By heaven," said the bold knight, "That business up there
Is arranged for my arrival, or else I am much misled.
Let God work! Ah me!
All hope of help has fled!
Forfeit my life may be
But noise I do not dread."

Then he listened no longer, but loudly he called,
"Who has power in this place, high parley to hold?
For none greets Sir Gawain, or gives him good day;
If any would a word with him, let him walk forth
And speak now or never, to speed his affairs."
"Abide," said one on the bank above over his head,
"And what I promised you once shall straightway be given."
Yet he stayed not his grindstone, nor stinted its noise,
But worked awhile at his whetting before he would rest,
And then he comes around a crag, from a cave in the rocks,
Hurtling out of hiding with a hateful weapon,
A Danish[4] ax devised for that day's deed,
With a broad blade and bright, bent in a curve,
Filed to a fine edge—four feet it measured
By the length of the lace that was looped round the haft.
And in form as at first, the fellow all green,
His lordly face and his legs, his locks and his beard,
Save that firm upon two feet forward he strides,
Sets a hand on the ax-head, the haft to the earth;
When he came to the cold stream, and cared not to wade,
He vaults over on his ax, and advances amain
On a broad bank of snow, overbearing and brisk of mood.
Little did the knight incline
When face to face they stood;
Said the other man, "Friend mine,
It seems your word holds good!"

"God love you, Sir Gawain!" said the Green Knight then,
"And well met this morning, man, at my place!
And you have followed me faithfully and found me betimes,
And on the business between us we both are agreed:

4. I.e., long-bladed.

Twelve months ago today you took what was yours,
And you at this New Year must yield me the same.
And we have met in these mountains, remote from all eyes:
There is none here to halt us or hinder our sport;
Unhasp your high helm, and have here your wages;
Make no more demur than I did myself
When you hacked off my head with one hard blow."
"No, by God," said Sir Gawain, "that granted me life,
I shall grudge not the guerdon, grim though it prove;
Bestow but one stroke, and I shall stand still,
And you may lay on as you like till the last of my part
be paid."
He proffered, with good grace,
His bare neck to the blade,
And feigned a cheerful face:
He scorned to seem afraid.

Then the grim man in green gathers his strength,
Heaves high the heavy ax to hit him the blow.
With all the force in his frame he fetches it aloft,
With a grimace as grim as he would grind him to bits;
Had the blow he bestowed been as big as he threatened,
A good knight and gallant had gone to his grave.
But Gawain at the great ax glanced up aside
As down it descended with death-dealing force,
And his shoulders shrank a little from the sharp iron.
Abruptly the brawny man breaks off the stroke,
And then reproved with proud words that prince among knights.
"You are not Gawain the glorious," the green man said,
"That never fell back on field in the face of the foe,
And now you flee for fear, and have felt no harm:
Such news of that knight I never heard yet!
I moved not a muscle when you made to strike,
Nor caviled at the cut in King Arthur's house;
My head fell to my feet, yet steadfast I stood,
And you, all unharmed, are wholly dismayed—
Wherefore the better man I, by all odds,
must be."
Said Gawain, "Strike once more;
I shall neither flinch nor flee;
But if my head falls to the floor
There is no mending me!"

"But go on, man, in God's name, and get to the point!
Deliver me my destiny, and do it out of hand,
For I shall stand to the stroke and stir not an inch
Till your ax has hit home—on my honor I swear it!"
"Have at thee then!" said the other, and heaves it aloft,
And glares down as grimly as he had gone mad.
He made a mighty feint, but marred not his hide;

Withdrew the ax adroitly before it did damage.
Gawain gave no ground, nor glanced up aside,
But stood still as a stone, or else a stout stump
That is held in hard earth by a hundred roots.
Then merrily does he mock him, the man all in green:
"So now you have your nerve again, I needs must strike;
Uphold the high knighthood that Arthur bestowed,
And keep your neck-bone clear, if this cut allows!"
Then was Gawain gripped with rage, and grimly he said,
"Why, thrash away, tyrant, I tire of your threats;
You make such a scene, you must frighten yourself."
Said the green fellow, "In faith, so fiercely you speak
That I shall finish this affair, nor further grace
allow."
He stands prepared to strike
And scowls with both lip and brow;
No marvel if the man mislike
Who can hope no rescue now.

He gathered up the grim ax and guided it well:
Let the barb at the blade's end brush the bare throat;
He hammered down hard, yet harmed him no whit
Save a scratch on one side, that severed the skin;
The end of the hooked edge entered the flesh,
And a little blood lightly leapt to the earth.
And when the man beheld his own blood bright on the snow,
He sprang a spear's length with feet spread wide,
Seized his high helm, and set it on his head,
Shoved before his shoulders the shield at his back,
Bares his trusty blade, and boldly he speaks—
Not since he was a babe born of his mother
Was he once in this world one-half so blithe—
"Have done with your hacking—harry me no more!
I have borne, as behooved, one blow in this place;
If you make another move I shall meet it midway
And promptly, I promise you, pay back each blow
with brand.
One stroke acquits me here;
So did our covenant stand
In Arthur's court last year—
Wherefore, sir, hold your hand!"

He lowers the long ax and leans on it there,
Sets his arms on the head, the haft on the earth,
And beholds the bold knight that bides there afoot,
How he faces him fearless, fierce in full arms,
And plies him with proud words—it pleases him well.
Then once again gaily to Gawain he calls,
And in a loud voice and lusty, delivers these words:
"Bold fellow, on this field your anger forbear!

No man has made demands here in manner uncouth,
Nor done, save as duly determined at court.
I owed you a hit and you have it; be happy therewith!
The rest of my rights here I freely resign.
Had I been a bit busier, a buffet, perhaps,
I could have dealt more directly, and done you some harm.
First I flourished with a feint, in frolicsome mood,
And left your hide unhurt—and here I did well
By the fair terms we fixed on the first night;
And fully and faithfully you followed accord:
Gave over all your gains as a good man should.
A second feint, sir, I assigned for the morning
You kissed my comely wife—each kiss you restored.
For both of these there behooved but two feigned blows
by right.
True men pay what they owe;
No danger then in sight.
You failed at the third throw,
So take my tap, sir knight.

"For that is my belt about you, that same braided girdle,
My wife it was that wore it; I know well the tale,
And the count of your kisses and your conduct too,
And the wooing of my wife—it was all my scheme!
She made trial of a man most faultless by far
Of all that ever walked over the wide earth;
As pearls to white peas, more precious and prized,
So is Gawain, in good faith, to other gay knights.
Yet you lacked, sir, a little in loyalty there,
But the cause was not cunning, nor courtship either,
But that you loved your own life; the less, then, to blame."
The other stout knight in a study stood a long while,
So gripped with grim rage that his great heart shook.
All the blood of his body burned in his face
As he shrank back in shame from the man's sharp speech.
The first words that fell from the fair knight's lips:
"Accursed be a cowardly and covetous heart!
In you is villainy and vice, and virtue laid low!"
Then he grasps the green girdle and lets go the knot,
Hands it over in haste, and hotly he says:
"Behold there my falsehood, ill hap betide it!
Your cut taught me cowardice, care for my life,
And coveting came after, contrary both
To largesse and loyalty belonging to knights.
Now am I faulty and false, that fearful was ever
Of disloyalty and lies, bad luck to them both!
and greed.
I confess, knight, in this place,
Most dire is my misdeed;
Let me gain back your good grace,
And thereafter I shall take heed."

Then the other laughed aloud, and lightly he said,
"Such harm as I have had, I hold it quite healed.
You are so fully confessed, your failings made known,
And bear the plain penance of the point of my blade,
I hold you polished as a pearl, as pure and as bright
As you had lived free of fault since first you were born.
And I give you, sir, this girdle that is gold-hemmed
And green as my garments, that, Gawain, you may
Be mindful of this meeting when you mingle in throng
With nobles of renown—and known by this token
How it chanced at the Green Chapel, to chivalrous knights.
And you shall in this New Year come yet again
And we shall finish out our feast in my fair hall,
with cheer."
He urged the knight to stay,
And said, "With my wife so dear
We shall see you friends this day,
Whose enmity touched you near."

"Indeed," said the doughty knight, and doffed his high helm,
And held it in his hands as he offered his thanks,
"I have lingered long enough—may good luck be yours,
And He reward you well that all worship bestows!
And commend me to that comely one, your courteous wife,
Both herself and that other, my honoured ladies,
That have trapped their true knight in their trammels so quaint.
But if a dullard should dote, deem it no wonder,
And through the wiles of a woman be wooed into sorrow,
For so was Adam by one, when the world began,
And Solomon by many more, and Samson the mighty—
Delilah was his doom, and David thereafter
Was beguiled by Bathsheba, and bore much distress;
Now these were vexed by their devices—'twere a very joy
Could one but learn to love, and believe them not.
For these were proud princes, most prosperous of old,
Past all lovers lucky, that languished under heaven,
bemused.
And one and all fell prey
To women that they had used;
If I be led astray,
Methinks I may be excused.

"But your girdle, God love you! I gladly shall take
And be pleased to possess, not for the pure gold,
Nor the bright belt itself, nor the beauteous pendants,
Nor for wealth, nor worldly state, nor workmanship fine,
But a sign of excess it shall seem oftentimes
When I ride in renown, and remember with shame
The faults and the frailty of the flesh perverse,
How its tenderness entices the foul taint of sin;
And so when praise and high prowess have pleased my heart,
A look at this love-lace will lower my pride.

But one thing would I learn, if you were not loath,
Since you are lord of yonder land where I have long sojourned
With honor in your house—may you have His reward
That upholds all the heavens, highest on throne!
How runs your right name?—and let the rest go."
"That shall I give you gladly," said the Green Knight then;
"Bercilak de Hautdesert this barony I hold,
Through the might of Morgan le Faye,[5] that lodges at my house,
By subtleties of science and sorcerers' arts,
The mistress of Merlin,[6] she has caught many a man,
For sweet love in secret she shared sometime
With that wizard, that knows well each one of your knights
and you.
Morgan the Goddess, she,
So styled by title true;
None holds so high degree
That her arts cannot subdue.

"She guided me in this guise to your glorious hall,
To assay, if such it were, the surfeit of pride
That is rumored of the retinue of the Round Table.
She put this shape upon me to puzzle your wits,
To afflict the fair queen, and frighten her to death
With awe of that elvish man that eerily spoke
With his head in his hand before the high table.
She was with my wife at home, that old withered lady,
Your own aunt [7] is she, Arthur's half-sister,
The Duchess' daughter of Tintagel, that dear King Uther
Got Arthur on after, that honored is now.
And therefore, good friend, come feast with your aunt;
Make merry in my house; my men hold you dear,
And I wish you as well, sir, with all my heart,
As any mortal man, for your matchless faith."
But the knight said him nay, that he might by no means.
They clasped then and kissed, and commended each other
To the Prince of Paradise, and parted with one
assent.
Gawain sets out anew;
Toward the court his course is bent;
And the knight all green in hue,
Wheresoever he wished, he went.

Wild ways in the world our worthy knight rides
On Gringolet, that by grace had been granted his life.
He harbored often in houses, and often abroad,
And with many valiant adventures verily he met
That I shall not take time to tell in this story.

5. Arthur's half-sister, an enchantress who sometimes abetted him, sometimes made trouble for him.
6. The wise magician who had helped Arthur become king.
7. Morgan was the daughter of Igraine, Duchess of Tintagel, and her husband the Duke; Igraine conceived Arthur when his father Uther lay with her through one of Merlin's trickeries.

The hurt was whole that he had had in his neck,
And the bright green belt on his body he bore,
Oblique, like a baldric, bound at his side,
Below his left shoulder, laced in a knot,
In betokening of the blame he had borne for his fault;
And so to court in due course he comes safe and sound.
Bliss abounded in hall when the high-born heard
That good Gawain was come; glad tidings they thought it.
The king kisses the knight, and the queen as well,
And many a comrade came to clasp him in arms,
And eagerly they asked, and awesomely he told,
Confessed all his cares and discomfitures many,
How it chanced at the Chapel, what cheer made the knight,
The love of the lady, the green lace at last.
The nick on his neck he naked displayed
That he got in his disgrace at the Green Knight's hands,
alone.
With rage in heart he speaks,
And grieves with many a groan;
The blood burns in his cheeks
For shame at what must be shown.

"Behold, sir," said he, and handles the belt,
"This is the blazon of the blemish that I bear on my neck;
This is the sign of sore loss that I have suffered there
For the cowardice and coveting that I came to there;
This is the badge of false faith that I was found in there,
And I must bear it on my body till I breathe my last.
For one may keep a deed dark, but undo it no whit,
For where a fault is made fast, it is fixed evermore."
The king comforts the knight, and the court all together
Agree with gay laughter and gracious intent
That the lords and the ladies belonging to the Table,
Each brother of that band, a baldric should have,
A belt borne oblique, of a bright green,
To be worn with one accord for that worthy's sake.
So that was taken as a token by the Table Round,
And he honored that had it, evermore after,
As the best book of knighthood bids it be known.
In the old days of Arthur this happening befell;
The books of Brutus' deeds bear witness thereto
Since Brutus, the bold knight, embarked for this land
After the siege ceased at Troy and the city fared
amiss.
Many such, ere we were born,
Have befallen here, ere this.
May He that was crowned with thorn
Bring all men to His bliss! Amen.

Hony Soyt Qui Mal Pense [8]

8. "Shame be to the man who has evil in his mind." This is the motto of the Order of the Garter, founded ca. 1350: apparently a copyist of the poem associated this order with the one founded to honor Gawain.

PEARL
(ca. 1375–1400)

Pearl is preserved in the same manuscript as *Sir Gawain and the Green Knight* and is generally believed to have been written by the same poet. Like *Piers Plowman,* it is a dream vision concerning love and, again like *Piers Plowman,* it purports to be written by a Dreamer who needs to learn in his heart Christian truths that he already knows in his head. In *Pearl* the narrator's grief for the loss of a jewel is so extravagant as to suggest that the pearl he speaks of must stand for something more irreplaceable than a mere ornament. Yet it is only gradually that we come to realize that the pearl-bedecked maiden he meets in his dream is the thing he has lost, and that on earth she was his infant daughter—the adult form in which he sees her is of course "spiritual." It is her mission to explain to him that his grief for her death is not only extravagant but according to Christian principles wrong, for she has become a Bride of the Lamb of God in a heaven whose physical characteristics are those of the New Jerusalem described by St. John in the Book of Revelation. She resolves the Dreamer's doubts about infant salvation—whether those who die in infancy can attain heaven—which apparently increased his grief for her death. But it is not without a struggle—and some impatience—that she manages to do this, for the Dreamer remains stubbornly earth-bound: he cannot easily accept the fact that his daughter has become so exalted in heaven, and fears that she has misbehaved, pushing herself forward too aggressively. He has trouble comprehending the paradox that in heaven varying degrees of honor and total equality exist simultaneously, and one feels that even after his dream he will find it hard to accept in his heart Pearl's doctrine that the pearl he ought to seek is not herself but the one the merchant in Matthew gave all his wealth for—the kingdom of heaven. The vision he is granted at the end of the poem is broken off when he tries to cross the stream that separates him from the Heavenly City because he is eager to rejoin his Pearl, whom he sees among the 144,000 virgins (as described by St. John) before the throne of the Lamb. He awakens from his dream a chastened and perhaps more patient man, who, like Langland's Will, has been taught that he must apprehend more profoundly what he already knew.

Technically the poem imitates a perfectly rounded gem. It consists of twenty sections, all but one of which contain five twelve-line stanzas with the inordinately difficult rhyme scheme *ababababbcbc,* not unexampled in Middle English poetry but never elsewhere attempted in so long a poem. Within the sections, the last word of each stanza is the same (in form if not in meaning) and is repeated in the first line of the following stanza, and this word also appears in the first line of the succeeding section. The chain thus formed is made whole by the fact that the last lines of the poem echo, with expanded meaning, the first. Perfection of form is broken only by Section XV, which contains six instead of five stanzas, so that the poem is not of the round number of 1,200 lines, but of 1,212. Perhaps the poet intentionally broke the pattern because he felt that any jewel of man's making must be imperfect; or perhaps he was responding to the fact that the multiple $12 \times 12 = 144$, and that 144 is a reflection of the 144,000 virgins in the Book of Revelation that provides much of the imaginative stimulus for the poem.

Pearl[1]

I

1

Pearl, that a prince is well content
To give a circle of gold to wear,
Boldly I say, all orient
Brought forth none precious like to her;
So comely in every ornament,
So slender her sides, so smooth they were,
Ever my mind was bound and bent
To set her apart without a peer.
In a garden of herbs I lost my dear;
Through grass to ground away it shot;
Now, lovesick, the heavy loss I bear
Of that secret pearl without a spot.

2

Since in that spot it sped from me so,
Often I watched and wished for that grace
That once was wont to banish woe
And bless with brightness all my days;
That clutches my heart in cruel throe
And causes my blood to rage and race,
Yet sweeter songs could no man know
Than silence taught my ear to trace;
And many there came, to think of her face
With cover of clay so coldly fraught:
O earth, you mar a gem past praise,
My secret pearl without a spot.

3

That spot with spice must spring and spread
Where riches rotted in narrow room;
Blossoms white and blue and red
Lift now alight in blaze of noon;
Flower and fruit could never fade
Where pearl plunged deep in earthen tomb,
For the seed must die to bear the blade
That the wheat may be brought to harvest home.[2]

1. The verse translation, which follows the intricate pattern of the original, is by Marie Borroff (1976).
2. John xii.24.

Good out of good to all and some:
Such a seed could never have come to naught
Nor spice in splendor spare to bloom
From that precious pearl without a spot.

4

To that especial spot I hied
And entered that same garden green
In August at a festive tide
When corn is cut with scythe-edge keen.
On the mound where pearl went tumbling wide,
Leaf vied with leaf in shade and sheen:
Gillyflower and ginger on every side
And peonies peerless blooming between.
But fairer yet, and all unseen,
Was the fragrance that my senses sought;
There, I know, is the dear demesne
Of my precious pearl without a spot.

5

Before that spot with head inclined
I stretched my hand in stark despair;
My heart lamented, deaf and blind,
Though reason reconciled my care.
I mourned my pearl so close confined
With thoughts in throng contending there;
Comfort of Christ might come to mind
But wretched will would not forbear.
I fell upon that flower-bed fair;
Such odor seized my brain distraught
I slipped into slumber unaware,
On that precious pearl without a spot.

II

1

My soul forsook that spot in space
And left my body on earth to bide.
My spirit sped, by God's good grace,
On a quest where marvels multiplied.
I knew not where in the world it was,
But I saw I was set where cliffs divide;
A forest flourished in that place
Where many rich rocks might be descried.
The glory that flashed there far and wide
Eye could not credit, nor mind invent;
Pure cloth-of-gold were pale beside
Such rich and rare embellishment.

2

Embellished were those hills in view
With crystal cliffs as clear as day
And groves of trees with boles as blue

As indigo silks of rich assay;
The leaves, like silver burnished new,
Slide rustling rife on every spray;
As shifts of cloud let sunshine through,
They shot forth light in shimmering play.
The gravelstones that strewed the way
Were precious pearls of orient;
The beams of the sun but blind and gray
Beside such bright embellishment.

3

Amid those hills embellished bright
My sorrows fled in full retreat;
Fragrance of fruits with great delight
Filled me like food that mortals eat.
Birds of all colors fanned in flight
Their iridescent pinions fleet,
But lute or lyre, by craft or sleight,
Could not make music half so sweet,
For while in time their wings they beat
In glad accord their voices blent;
With more of mirth might no man meet
Than hear each brave embellishment.

4

So all embellished was the land
Where Fortune bears me on my way;
No tongue is worthy to command
Fit words those splendors to display.
I walked along with bliss at hand;
No slope so steep to make me stay;
The further, the fairer the pear trees stand,
The spice-plants spread, the blossoms sway,
And hedgerows run by banks as gay
As glittering golden filament;
I came to the shore of a waterway:
Dear God, what brave embellishment!

5

Embellishing those waters deep,
Banks of pure beryl greet my gaze;
Sweetly the eddies swirl and sweep
With a rest and a rush in murmuring phrase;
Stones in the stream their colors steep,
Gleaming like glass where sunbeam strays,
As stars, while men of the marshlands sleep,
Flash in winter from frosty space;
For every one was a gem to praise,
A sapphire or emerald opulent,
That seemed to set the pool ablaze,
So brilliant their embellishment.

III

1

Embellished with such wondrous grace
Were wood and water and shining plain,
My pleasures multiplied apace,
Conquered my cares, dispelled my pain.
By the brink of a river that runs a race
Blissful I walked with busy brain;
The more I explored that plashy place
The greater strength did gladness gain.
As proof of Fortune's purpose plain
Makes a man's heart to sink or soar,
He whom she plies with bliss or bane
Of what he draws is dealt still more.

2

More of bliss was there to prize
Than ever my tongue could testify,
For earthly heart could not suffice
To sustain one tenth of that pure joy.
It could not be but Paradise
Lay beyond those noble banks, thought I,
And the stream itself seemed a device,
A mark to know a boundary by.
Those peerless precincts to espy
I need but gain the further shore;
But I dared not wade, for the water ran high,
And longing mastered me more and more.

3

More than ever and ever the more
To cross that river was all my care,
For lovely though this landscape were,
What lay beyond was past compare.
I stared about, scanning the shore
For a ford to afford me thoroughfare,
But dangers direr than before
Appeared, the more I wandered there.
And still it seemed I should not forbear
For dangers, with delights in store;
But now was broached a new affair
My mind was moved by, more and more.

4

More marvels now amazed me quite:
Beyond that stream, strange to behold,
There rose a cliff of crystal bright
With resplendent rays all aureoled.
At the foot was seated in plain sight
A maiden child of mortal mold,

A gracious lady gowned in white;
I knew her well, I had seen her of old.
As fine-spun floss of burnished gold,
So shone she, peerless, as of yore;
I gazed on her with joy untold,
The longer, I knew her more and more.

5

The more I mused on that fair face,
The person of that most precious one,
Such gladness grew in my heart by grace
As little before had been, or none.
I longed to call across that space
But found my power of speech had flown;
To meet her in so strange a place—
Such a sight, in truth, might shock or stun!
Then raised she up her brow, that shone
All ivory pale on that far shore,
That stabbed my heart to look upon
And ever the longer, more and more.

IV

1

More dread diminished my delight;
I stood stock-still and dared not call.
With eyes wide open and mouth shut tight
I hoved there tame as hawk in hall.
Unearthly, I knew, must be that plight;
I dreaded much what might befall,
Lest she I viewed should vanish quite
And leave me there to stare and stall.
That slender one, so smooth, so small,
Unblemished, void of every vice,
Rose up in robes imperial,
A precious pearl in pearls of price.

2

Pearls of price in ample store
Were there to see by grace divine
As she, approaching, shone on shore
Like fleurs-de-lys[3] to kings condign.
Her surcoat of white linen pure[4]
Had open sides of fair design,
And filigree on bands it bore
Where lavish pearls their luster join,
And lappets large, with double line
Of pearls set round in that same guise;
Her gown of that same linen fine,
And all bedecked with pearls of price.

3. Flower of the iris.

4. See Revelation xix.7–8 (cf. VII., 5.5-6). "Surcoat": outer coat.

3

Her priceless crown with pearls alone
Was set, in fashion fit and fair;
High pinnacles upon it shone,
And florets carved with craft and care.
Other headdress had she none
To frame her ivory forehead bare;
As earl or duke by royal throne,
So sage she seemed, so grave her air.
About her shoulders fell her hair
Like gold spun fine by artifice,
Whose deepest hue yet had a share
Of pallor pure of pearls of price.

4

Pearls of price in rows ornate
On hem, on side, on wristband rest;
No other gem could suit her state
Who was in white so richly dressed.
But one pure pearl, a wonder great,
Was set secure upon her breast;
A man might ponder long and late
Ere its full worth were well assessed.
I think no tongue could ever attest
A discourteous thought of that device,
So white it was, so wholly blessed,
And proudest placed of pearls of price.

5

In pearls of price she moved at ease
Toward the rim of the river that flowed so free;
No gladder man from here to Greece
Than I, that blesséd sight to see.
She was nearer my heart than aunt or niece:
So much the more my joy must be;
She proffered parley in sign of peace,
Bowed womanlike with bended knee,
Took off her crown of high degree
And bade me welcome with courteous voice;
That I was born O well for me
To greet that girl in pearls of price.

V

1

"O pearl," said I, "in pearls of price,
Are you my pearl come back again,
Lost and lamented with desolate sighs
In darkest night, alone and in vain?
Since you slipped to ground where grasses rise
I wander pensive, oppressed with pain,
And you in the bliss of Paradise,
Beyond all passion and strife and strain.

What fate removed you from earth's domain
And left me hapless and heartsick there?
Since parting was set between us twain
I have been a joyless jeweler."

2

That jewel then with fair gems fraught
Lifted her face with eyes of gray,
Set on her crown and stood in thought,
And soberly then I heard her say,
"Sir, your tale is told for naught,
To say your pearl has gone away
That is closed in a coffer so cunningly wrought
As this same garden green and gay,
And here forever in joy to stay
Where lack nor loss can never come near;
Here were a casket fit to display
A prize for a proper jeweler.

3

"But, jeweler, if your mind is bound
To mourn for a gem in solitude,
Your care has set you a course unsound,
And a cause of a moment maddens your mood;
You lost a rose that grew in the ground:
A flower that fails and is not renewed,
But such is the coffer closing it round,
With the worth of a pearl it is now imbued.
And fate, you say, has robbed you of good,
That rendered you profit free and clear;
You blame a blessing misunderstood:
You are no proper jeweler."

4

A jewel to me then was this guest
And jewels her gentle sayings were.
"O blissful one," I said, "and best,
You have healed me wholly of heartache here!
To be excused I make request:
My pearl was away, I knew not where;
Now I have found it, now I shall rest,
And live with it ever, and make good cheer,
And love the Lord and his laws revere
That brought me the blissful sight of her.
Let me once cross and behold you near,
And I am a joyful jeweler!"

5

"Jeweler," said that gem at this,
"Such mockery comes of mortal pride!
Most ill-advised your answer is
And errors grave your thoughts misguide.
Three statements you have made amiss;

Your words from your wit have wandered wide;
You think me set in this vale of bliss
For so you see me, the brook beside;
The second, you say you shall abide
With me in this far country here;
The third, to cross this deep divide,
Behooves no joyful jeweler.

VI

1

"I hold that jeweler little to praise
Who believes no more than meets the eye,
And little courtesy he displays
Who doubts the word of the Lord on high
That faithfully pledged your flesh to raise
Though Fortune made it fail and die;
They twist the sense of his words and ways
Who believe what they see, and else deny;
And that is pride and obstinacy
And ill accords with honest intent,
To think each tale must be a lie
Except his reason give assent.

2

"Say, do you not, dissenting, strive
Against God's will that all should uphold?
Here in this land you mean to live—
You might ask leave to make so bold!
Nor can you with such ease contrive
To cross this water deep and cold;
Your body fair, with senses five,
Must first sink down in mire and mold,
For in Eden garden, in days of old,
Our fathers' father his life misspent;
Each man must suffer a death foretold
Ere God to this crossing give consent."

3

"Consent," said I, "to that hard fate
And you have cleft my heart in twain.
That which I lost I found but late—
And must I now forgo it again?
Why must I meet it and miss it straight?
My precious pearl has doubled my pain.
What use is treasure in worldly state
If a man must lose it and mourn in vain?
Now little I reck what trials remain,
What bitter exile and banishment,
For Fortune is bound to be my bane
And suffer I must by her consent."

4

"Such dire presentiments of distress,"
Said she, "I cannot comprehend;
But grief for a loss that matters less
Makes many miss what might amend.
Better to cross yourself, and bless
The name of the Lord, whatever he send;
No good can come of your willfulness;
Who bears bad luck must learn to bend.
Though like a stricken doe, my friend,
You plunge and bray, with loud lament,
This way and that, yet in the end
As he decrees, you must consent.

5

"Dissent, indict him through the years,
His step stirs not one inch astray.
No tittle is gained for all your tears,
Though you should grieve and never be gay.
Abate your bluster, be not so fierce,
And seek his grace as soon as you may,
For prayer has power to bite and pierce
And call compassion into play.
His mercy can wipe your tears away,
Redeem your loss, restore content,
But, grudge or be glad, agree or gainsay,
All lies with him to give consent."

VII

1

Then I assented, answering in dread,
"Let not my Lord be wrathful here
Though blindly I rave, with speech ill-sped;
Mourning had made me mad, or near.
As water flows from a fountainhead
I cast myself in his mercy clear;
Heap no reproaches on my head
Though I should stray, my dearest dear,
But speak in charity and good cheer;
Be merciful, remembering this:
You gave me a heavy grief to bear,
Who once were ground of all my bliss.

2

"My bliss you have been and bitterest woe;
The grief was the greater as time ran on;
Since last I looked for you high and low
I could not tell where my pearl had gone.
I rejoice in it now as long ago,
And when we parted we were as one;
God forbid I should vex you so—

We meet so seldom at any milestone.
Your courtesy is second to none;
I am of earth, and speak amiss,
But the mercy of Christ and Mary and John,[5]
These are the ground of all my bliss.

3

"I see you set in bliss profound,
And I afflicted, felled by fate;
And little you care though I am bound
To suffer harm and hardship great;
But since we are met upon this ground
I would beseech, without debate,
That in sober speech you would expound
The life you lead both early and late.
Indeed, I am glad that your estate
Is raised to such honor and worthiness;
It is my joy to contemplate
And royal road of all my bliss."

4

"Now bliss befall you!" she replied
In form and feature that had no peer,
"And welcome here to walk and bide;
Such words are grateful to my ear.
Headstrong hearts and arrogant pride,
I tell you, are wholly detested here;
My Lord the Lamb is loath to chide,
For all are meek who behold him near.
And when in his house you shall appear,
Be wholly devout in humbleness,
For that delights my Lord so dear
That is the ground of all my bliss.

5

"A blissful life I lead, you say;
You ask in what station I reside;
You know when pearl first slipped away
I was tender of age, by time untried.
But my Lord the Lamb whom all obey,
He took me to him to be his bride,
Crowned me queen in bliss to stay,
Forever and ever glorified.
And seized of his heritage far and wide
Am I, his love, being wholly his;
His royal rank, his praise, his pride
Are root and ground of all my bliss."

5. St. John the apostle, generally identified in the Middle Ages with the author of the Book of Revelation.

VIII

1

"Oh, blissful one, can this be right?"
Said I, "Forgive me if I should err;
Are you the queen of heaven's height
Whom we in this world must all revere?
We believe in Mary, a virgin bright,
Who bore to man God's Son so dear;
Now who could assume her crown, by right,
But she in some feature fairer were?
Yet as none is lovely like unto her,
We call her Phoenix of Araby,[6]
Sent flawless from the artificer
As was our Queen of courtesy."

2

"Courteous Queen!" that blithe one said
Kneeling to ground with upturned face,
"Matchless Mother, most lovely Maid,
Blesséd beginner of every grace!"
Then rose she up, and silent stayed,
And spoke to me across that space:
"Sir, gifts are gained here, and prizes paid,
But none on another presumes or preys.
Empress peerless ever to praise
Of heaven and earth and hell is she,
Yet puts no man from his rightful place,
For she is Queen of courtesy.

3

"The court of the kingdom whose crown I bear
Has a property by nature and name:
Each who gains admittance there
Is king of that realm, or queen of the same,
And none would lessen the others' share
But each one, glad of the others' fame,
Would wish their crowns five times as fair,
Had they the power of amending them;
But she who bore Jesu in Bethlehem
Over all of us here has sovereignty,
And none of our number carps at that claim,
For she is Queen of courtesy.

4

"By courtesy, so says St. Paul,[7]
We are members of Christ in joy profound,
As head, arms, legs, and navel and all
Are parts of one person hale and sound;

6. A mythical Arabian bird of which there was said to be only one, which burned itself alive every five or six centuries and then rose rejuvenated from its ashes.

7. I Corinthians xii.12–21, 26–27.

Likewise each Christian soul I call
A loyal limb of the Lord renowned;
Now what dispute could ever befall
Between two limbs in a body bound?
Though hand or wrist bear a golden round,
Your head will never the sorrier be:
Just so in love is each of us crowned
A king or queen by courtesy."

5

"Courtesy, no doubt, there is,
And charity rife your ranks among;
Yet truly—take it not amiss—
[I cannot but think your words are wrong.][8]
You set yourself too high in this,
To be crowned a queen, that was so young;
Why, what more honor might be his
That had lived in hardship late and long
And suffered pains and penance strong
To purchase bliss in heaven on high?
How might he more have thriven in throng
Than be crowned a king by courtesy?

IX

1

"That courtesy too free appears
If all be true as you portray;
You lived in our country not two years—
You could not please the Lord, or pray,
Or say 'Our Father,' or Creed rehearse—
And crowned a queen the very first day!
I cannot well believe my ears,
That God could go so far astray.
The style of countess, so I would say,
Were fair enough to attain unto,
Or a lesser rank in heaven's array,
But a queen! It is beyond your due."

2

"Beyond all due his bounty flows,"
So answered she in words benign;
"For all is justice that he does,
And truth is in his each design.
As the tale in the Gospel of Matthew goes
In the mass that blesses the bread and wine,
In parable his words propose
A likeness to the realm divine.[9]
A man possessed a vineyard fine—
So runs the tale in sermon true—

8. This line, omitted from the manuscript, is supplied by conjecture.

9. Matthew xx.1–16.

The time was come to tend the vine
By tasks assigned in order due.

3

"The laborers duly gathered round;
The lord rose up by daybreak bright,
Sought at the marketplace, and found
Some who would serve his turn aright.
By the same bargain each was bound:
Let a penny a day his pains requite;
Then forth they go into his ground
And prune and bind and put things right.
He went back late by morning light,
Found idle fellows not a few;
'Why stand you idle here in sight?
Has not this day its service due?'

4

" 'Duly we came ere break of day,'
So answered they in unison;
'The sun has risen and here we stay
And look for labor and yet find none.'
'Go to the vine; do what you may,'
So said the lord, 'till day is done;
Promptly at nightfall I shall pay
Such hire as each by right has won.'
So at the vine they labored on,
And still the lord, the long day through,
Brought in new workmen one by one
Till dusk approached at season due.

5

"When time was due of evensong,
The sunset but one hour away,
He saw there idle men in throng
And had these sober words to say:
'Why stand you idle all day long?'
None had required their help, said they.
'Go to the vine, young men and strong,
And do as much there as you may.'
Soon the earth grew dim and gray;
The sun long since had sunk from view;
He summoned them to take their pay;
The day had passed its limit due.

X

1

"Duly the lord, at day's decline,
Said to the steward, 'Sir, proceed;
Pay what I owe this folk of mine;
And lest men chide me here, take heed:

Set them all in a single line,
Give each a penny as agreed;
Start with the last that came to the vine,
And let the first the last succeed.'
And then the first began to plead;
Long had they toiled, they said and swore;
'These in an hour had done their deed;
It seems to us we should have more.

2

" 'More have we served, who suffered through
The heat of the day till evening came,
Than these who stayed but an hour or two,
Yet you allow them equal claim.'
Then said the lord to one of that crew,
'Friend, I will not change the game;
Take your wage and away with you!
I offered a penny, to all the same;
Why begin to bicker and blame?
Was not our covenant set of yore?
Higher than covenant none should aim;
Why should you then ask for more?

3

" 'More, am I not at liberty
To give my own as I wish to do?
Or have you lifted an evil eye,
As I am good, to none untrue?'
'Thus,' says Christ, 'shall I shift it awry:
The last shall be the first in the queue,
And the first the last, were he never so spry,
For many are called, but friends are few.'
So poor men take their portion too,
Though late they came and puny they were,
And though they make but little ado,
The mercy of God is much the more.

4

"More of ladyship here is mine,
Of life in flower and never to fade,
Than any man in the world could win
By right and right alone," she said.
"Although but late I began in the vine—
I came at evening, as Fortune bade—
The lord allowed me first in the line
And then and there I was fully paid.
There were others came early and later stayed,
Who labored long and sweated sore,
And still their payment is delayed,
Shall be, perhaps, for many years more."

5

Then with more discourse I demurred:
"There seems small reason in this narration:
God's justice carries across the board
Or Holy Writ is prevarication!
In the psalter of David there stands a word
Admits no cavil or disputation:[1]
'You render to each his just reward,
O ruler of every dispensation!'
Now he who all day kept his station,
If you to payment come in before,
Then the less, the more remuneration,
And ever alike, the less, the more."

XI

1

"Of more and less," she answered straight,
"In the Kingdom of God, no risk obtains,
For each is paid at the selfsame rate
No matter how little or great his gains.
No niggard is our chief of state,
Be it soft or harsh his will ordains;
His gifts gush forth like a spring in spate
Or a stream in a gulley that runs in rains.
His portion is large whose prayers and pains
Please him who rescues when sinners call.
No bliss in heaven but he attains:
The grace of God is enough for all.

2

"Yet for all that, you stubbornly strive
To prove I have taken too great a fee;
You say I, the last to arrive,
Am not worthy so high degree.
When was there ever a man alive,
Were none so pious and pure as he,
Who by some transgression did not contrive
To forfeit the bliss of eternity?
And the older, the oftener the case must be
That he lapsed into sins both great and small.
Then mercy and grace must second his plea:
The grace of God is enough for all.

3

"But grace enough have the innocent:
When first they see the light of day
To the water of baptism they are sent
And brought to the vine without delay.
At once the light, its splendor spent,

1. Psalms lxii (lxi).12.

Bows down to darkness and decay;
They had done no harm ere home they went;
From the Master's hands they take their pay.
Why should he not acknowledge them, pray?
They were there with the rest, they came at his call—
Yes, and give them their hire straightway:
The grace of God is enough for all.

4

"It is known well enough, the human race
Was formed to live in pure delight.
Our first forefather altered that case
By an apple of which he took a bite.
We all were damned by that disgrace
To die in sorrow and desperate plight
And then in hell to take our place
And dwell there lost in eternal night.[2]
But then there came a remedy right:
Rich blood ran down rood-tree[3] tall
And with it flowed forth water bright:
The grace of God was enough for all.[4]

5

"Enough for all flowed from that well,
Blood and water plain to behold:
By the blood our souls were saved from hell
And the second death decreed of old.[5]
The water is baptism, truth to tell,
That followed the spearhead keen and cold,[6]
Old Adam's deadly guilt to dispel
That swamped us in sins a thousandfold.
Now all is withdrawn that ever could hold
Mankind from bliss, since Adam's fall,
And that was redeemed at a time foretold
And the grace of God is enough for all.

XII

1

"Grace enough that man can have
Who is penitent, having sinned anew,
If with sorrow at heart he cry and crave
And perform the penance that must ensue.
But by right reason, that cannot rave,
The innocent ever receives his due:
To punish the guiltless with the knave
Is a plan God never was party to.
The guilty, by contrition true,

2. Genesis iii.17–19; Matthew xiii.41–42; Romans v.12.
3. I.e., the Cross.
4. John xix.34; Ephesians i.3–7.
5. Revelation xx.14.
6. I.e., the spear with which Christ was pierced on the Cross (see John xix.34).

Can attain to mercy requisite,
But he that never had guile in view,
The innocent is safe and right.

2

"I know right reason in this case
And thereto cite authority:
The righteous man shall see his face
And the innocent bear him company.
So in a verse the psalter says,[7]
'Lord, who shall climb your hill on high
Or rest within your holy place?'
And readily then he makes reply:
'Hands that did no injury,
Heart that was always pure and light:
There shall his steps be stayed in joy';
The innocent is safe by right.

3

"The righteous also in due time,
He shall approach that noble tor,
Who cozens his neighbor with no crime
Nor wastes his life in sin impure.
King Solomon tells in text sublime
Of Wisdom and her honored lore;[8]
By narrow ways she guided him
And lo! God's kingdom lay before.
As who should say, 'Yon distant shore—
Win it you may ere fall of night
If you make haste'; but evermore
The innocent is safe by right.

4

"Of the righteous man I find report
In the psalter of David, if ever you spied it:[9]
'Call not your servant, Lord, to court,
For judgment is grim if justice guide it.'
And when to that seat you must resort
Where each man's case shall be decided,
Claim the right, you may be caught short
By this same proof I have provided.
But he who, scourged and sore derided,
Bled on the cross through mortal spite,
Grant that your sentence be decided
By innocence and not by right.

5

"Who reads the Book of rightful fame
May learn of it infallibly
How good folk with their children came

7. Psalms xxiv (xxiii).3–4.
8. Wisdom (Apocrypha) x.9–10.
9. Psalms cxliii (cxlii).2.

To Jesus walking in Galilee.[1]
The touch of his hand they sought for them
For the goodness in him plain to see;
The disciples banned that deed with blame
And bade the children let him be.
But Jesus gathered them round his knee
And of that reprimand made light;
'Of such is the kingdom of heaven,' said he;
The innocent is safe by right.

XIII

1

"Jesus on his faithful smiled
And said, 'God's kingdom shall be won
By him who seeks it as a child,
For other entry-right is none.'
Harmless, steadfast, undefiled,
Unsullied bright to gaze upon,
When such stand knocking, meek and mild,
Straightway the gate shall be undone.
There is the endless bliss begun
That the jeweler sought in earthly estate
And sold all his goods, both woven and spun,
To purchase a pearl immaculate.'[2]

2

"This immaculate pearl I tell you of,
The jeweler gave his wealth to gain,
Is like the realm of heaven above;
The Father of all things said it plain.
No spot it bears, nor blemish rough,
But blithe in rondure ever to reign,
And of righteousness it is prize and proof:
Lo, here on my breast it long has lain;
Bestowed by the Lamb so cruelly slain,
His peace to betoken and designate;
I bid you turn from the world insane
And purchase your pearl immaculate."

3

"Immaculate pearl whom white pearls crown,
Who bear," said I, "the pearl of price,
Who fashioned your form? Who made your gown?
Oh, he that wrought it was most wise!
Such beauty in nature never was known;
Pygmalion[3] never painted your eyes,
Nor Aristotle,[4] of long renown,

1. Mark x.13–16; Luke xviii.15–17.
2. Matthew xiii.45–46.
3. A legendary Greek sculptor (statues in the Middle Ages were usually painted)
4. The Greek philosopher, referred to here because of his work on natural history.

Discoursed of these wondrous properties;
Your gracious aspect, your angel guise,
More white than the lily, and delicate:
What duties high, what dignities
Are marked by the pearl immaculate?"

4

"My immaculate Lamb, my destiny sweet,"
Said she, "who can all harm repair,
He made me his mate in marriage meet,
Though once such a match unfitting were.
When I left your world of rain and sleet
He called me in joy to join him there:
'Come hither, my dove without deceit,
For you are spotless, past compare.'[5]
He gave me strength, he made me fair,
He crowned me a virgin consecrate,
And washed in his blood these robes I wear,[6]
And clad me in pearls immaculate."

5

"Immaculate being, bright as flame,
In royalties set and sanctified,
Tell me now, what is that Lamb
That sought you out to become his bride?
Over all others you pressed your claim
To live in honor with him allied,
Yet many a noble and worthy dame
For Christ's dear sake has suffered and died;
And you have thrust those others aside
And reserved for yourself that nuptial state,
Yourself all alone, so big with pride,
A matchless maid and immaculate?"

XIV

1

"Immaculate," came her answer clear,
"Unblemished am I, my peers among;
So much I claim with honor here,
But matchless—there you have it wrong.
We all are brides of the Lamb so dear,
One hundred and forty-four thousand strong,
In Apocalypse the words appear
As John beheld it and told with tongue.[7]
Thousands on thousands, virgins young,
He saw on Mount Sion in sacred dream,
Arrayed for the wedding in comely throng
In the city called New Jerusalem.

5. Song of Solomon iv.7, v.2.
6. Revelation vii.13–14.
7. Revelation xiv.1.

2

"Of Jerusalem I speak perforce,
To tell his nature and degree,
My jewel dear, my joy's sole source,
My Lamb, my lord, my love, all three.
In the prophet Isaiah we find discourse
Of him and his humility,[8]
Condemned and martyred without remorse
And on false charges of felony,
As a sheep to the slaughter led was he,
As a lamb to the shearers meek and tame;
His lips were sealed to all inquiry
When Jews were his judge in Jerusalem.

3

"In Jerusalem my true love died,
Rent by rude hands with pain and woe;
Freely he perished for our pride,
And suffered our doom in mortal throe.[9]
His blesséd face, or ever he died,
Was made to bleed by many a blow;[1]
For sin he set his power aside
Though never he sinned who suffered so.
For us he was beaten and bowed low
And racked on the rood-tree rough and grim,
And meek as the lamb with fleece of snow
He breathed his last in Jerusalem.

4

"In Jerusalem, Jordan, and Galilee,
When John the Baptist preached abroad,
The words with Isaiah well agree
That he said when Jesus before him stood;[2]
He made of him this prophecy:
'Steadfast as stone, O Lamb of God,
Who takes away the iniquity
That all this world has wrought in blood';
And he was guiltless and ever good,
Yet bore our sins and atoned for them;
O who can reckon his parenthood
Who perished for us in Jerusalem?

5

"In Jerusalem my lover true
Appeared as a lamb of purest white
In the eyes of the prophets old and new
For his meek mien and piteous plight.
The third fits well with the other two,
In Revelation written aright;[3]

8. Isaiah liii.7, 9.
9. Isaiah liii.4–5.
1. Matthew xxvi.67.
2. John i.29.
3. Revelation v.1, 6–7.

Where the saints sat round in retinue
The Apostle saw him throned in light,
Bearing the book with pages bright
And the seven seals set round the rim,
And all hosts trembled at that sight,
In hell, in earth, and Jerusalem.

XV

1

"This Jerusalem Lamb in his array
Was whiter far than tongue could tell;
No spot or speck might on him stay,
His fair rich fleece did so excel.
And so each sinless soul, I say,
Is a worthy wife with the Lamb to dwell,
And though he fetch a score each day
No strife is stirred in our citadel,
But would each brought four others as well—
The more the merrier in blessedness!
Our love is increased as our numbers swell,
And honor more and never the less.

2

"Less of bliss none brings us here
Who bear the pearl upon our breast;
No mark of strife could ever appear
Where the precious pearl is worn for crest.
Our bodies lie on earthen bier,
And you go grieving, sore distressed,
But we, with knowledge full and clear,
See in one death all wrong redressed.
The Lamb has laid our cares to rest;
We partake of his table in joyfulness;
Each one's share of bliss is best.
Nor ever in honor any the less.

3

"Lest less you believe, incline your ear
To the Book of Revelation true: [4]
'I saw,' says John, 'the Lamb appear
On the Mount of Sion, all white of hue,
With a hundred thousand maidens dear
And forty-four thousand more in view;
On all their foreheads written were
The name of the Lamb, of his Father too.
But then in heaven a clamor grew,
Like waters running in rapid race;
As thunder crashes in storm-cloud blue,
Such was that sound, and nothing less.

4. Revelation xiv.1–5.

4

" 'Nevertheless, though it shouted shrill
And made the heavens resound again,
I heard them sing upon that hill
A new song, a most noble strain;
As harpers touch their harps with skill
Their voices lifted, full and plain;
And well they followed with a will
The phrases of that fair refrain.
Before his throne who ever shall reign
And the four beasts ranged about the dais[5]
And the solemn elders of that domain,
Great was their song, and grew no less.

5

" 'Nevertheless, there was none had might
Or for all his art might ever aspire
To sing that song, save those in white
Who follow the Lamb their lord and sire;
For they are redeemed from earth's dark night
As first fruits given to God entire,
And joined with the Lamb on Sion's height,
As like himself in speech and attire,
For never, in deed or heart's desire,
Their tongues were touched with untruthfulness;
And none can sever that sinless choir
From that master immaculate, nevertheless.' "

6

"Never less welcome let me find,"
Said I, "for the queries I propose;
I should not tempt your noble mind
Whom Christ the Lord to his chamber chose.
I am of mire and mere mankind,
And you so rich and rare a rose,
And here to eternal bliss assigned
Where joy fails not, but forever grows.
Now, dame, whom simplicity's self endows,
I would beseech a favor express,
And though I am rough and rude, God knows,
Let it be granted nevertheless.

XVI

1

"Nevertheless, if you can see
In my request a reason sound,
Deny not my dejected plea,
But where grace is, let grace abound.
Have you no hall, no hostelry,

5. Revelation iv.6–9.

To dwell in and meet in daily round?
You tell of Jerusalem rich and free
Where reigned King David the renowned,
But that cannot be near this ground
But lies in Judea, by reckoning right;
As you under moon are flawless found,
Your lodgings should be wholly bright.

2

"These holy virgins in radiant guise,
By thousands thronged in processional—
That city must be of uncommon size
That keeps you together, one and all.
It were not fit such jewels of price
Should lie unsheltered by roof or wall,
Yet where these river-banks arise
I see no building large or small.
Beside this stream celestial
You linger alone, none else in sight;
If you have another house or hall,
Show me that dwelling wholly bright."

3

That wholly blissful, that spice heaven-sent,
Declared, "In Judea's fair demesne
The city lies, where the Lamb once went
To suffer for man death's anguish keen.
The old Jerusalem by that is meant,
For there the old guilt was canceled clean,
But the new, in vision prescient,
John saw sent down from God pristine.[6]
The spotless Lamb of gracious mien
Has carried us all to that fair site,
And as in his flock no fleck is seen,
His hallowed halls are wholly bright.

4

"Two holy cities I figure forth;
One name suits well with both of these,
Which in the language of your birth
Is 'City of God,' or 'Sight of Peace.'[7]
In the one the Lamb brought peace on earth
Who suffered for our iniquities;
In the other is peace with heavenly mirth,
And ever to last, and never to cease.
And to that city in glad release
From fleshly decay our souls take flight;
There glory and bliss shall ever increase
In the household that is wholly bright."

6. Revelation xxi.2.

7. Revelation iii.12; Ezekiel xiii.16.

5

"Holy maid compassionate,"
Said I to that fresh flower and gay,
"Let me approach those ramparts great
And see the chamber where you stay."
"The Lord forbids," she answered straight,
"That a stranger in his streets should stray,
But through the Lamb enthroned in state
I have won you a sight of it this day.
Behold it from far off you may,
But no man's foot may there alight;
You have no power to walk that way
Save as a spirit wholly bright.

XVII

1

"This holy city that I may show,
Walk upwards toward the river's head,
And here against you I shall go
Until to a hill your path has led."
Then to stir I was not slow,
But under leafy boughs I sped
Until from a hill I looked below
And saw the city, as she had said,
Beyond the stream in splendor spread,
That brighter than shafts of sunlight shone.
In Apocalypse it may all be read
As he set it forth, the apostle John.[8]

2

As John the apostle saw it of old
I saw the city beyond the stream,
Jerusalem the new and fair to behold,
Sent down from heaven by power supreme.
The streets were paved with precious gold,
As flawless pure as glass agleam,
Based on bright gems of worth untold,
Foundation-stones twelvefold in team;
And set in series without a seam,
Each level was a single stone,
As he beheld it in sacred dream
In Apocalypse, the apostle John.

3

As John had named them in writ divine
Each stone in order by name I knew;
Jasper was the first in line;
At the lowest level it came in view;
Green ingrained I saw it shine.

8. Revelation xxi.10–27; xxii.1–2.

The second was the sapphire blue;
The clear chalcedony, rare and fine,
Was third in degree in order due.
The fourth the emerald green of hue;
Sardonyx fifth was set thereon;
The sixth the ruby he saw ensue
In Apocalypse, the apostle John.

4

To these John joined the chrysolite,
The seventh in that foundation's face;
The eighth the beryl clear and white,
The twin-hued topaz ninth to trace;
The chrysoprase tenth in order right;
Jacinth held the eleventh place;
The twelfth, the amethyst most of might,
Blent blue and purple in royal blaze.
The jasper walls above that base
Like lustrous glass to gaze upon;
I knew them all by his every phrase
In Apocalypse, the apostle John.

5

As John had written, so I was ware
How broad and steep was each great tier;
As long as broad as high foursquare
The city towered on twelvefold pier.
The streets like glass in brilliance bare,
The walls like sheen on parchment sheer;
The dwellings all with gemstones rare
Arrayed in radiance far and near.
The sides of that perimeter
Twelve thousand furlongs spanned, each one;
Length, breadth, and height were measured there
Before his eyes, the apostle John.

XVIII

1

Yet more, John saw on every side
Three gateways set commensurate,
So twelve I counted in compass wide,
The portals rich with precious plate.
Each gate a pearl of princely pride,
Unfading, past all earthly fate,
On which a name was signified
Of Israel's sons, in order of date,
That is, by birthright ranked in state,
The eldest ever the foremost one.
The streets were alight both early and late;
They needed neither sun nor moon.

2

Sun and moon were far surpassed;
The Lord was their lamp eternally,
The Lamb their lantern ever to last
Made bright that seat of sovereignty.
Through roof and wall my looking passed,
Pure substance hindered not to see;
There I beheld the throne steadfast
With the emblems that about it be,
As John in text gave testimony;
Upon it sat the Lord triune;[9]
A river therefrom ran fresh and free,
More bright by far than sun or moon.

3

Sun nor moon shone never so fair
As that flood of plenteous waters pure;
Full it flowed in each thoroughfare;
No filth or taint its brightness bore.
Church they had none, nor chapel there,
House of worship, nor need therefor;
The Almighty was their place of prayer,
The Lamb the sacrifice all to restore.
No lock was set on gate or door
But evermore open both night and noon;
None may take refuge on that floor
Who bears any spot beneath the moon.

4

The moon has in that reign no right;
Too spotty she is, of body austere;
And they who dwell there know no night—
Of what avail her varying sphere?
And set beside that wondrous light
That shines upon the waters clear
The planets would lose their luster quite,
And the sun itself would pale appear.
Beside the river are trees that bear
Twelve fruits of life their boughs upon;
Twelve times a year they burgeon there
And renew themselves with every moon.

5

Beneath the moon so much amazed
No fleshly heart could bear to be
As by that city on which I gazed,
Its form so wondrous was to see.
As a quail that couches, dumb and dazed,
I stared on that great symmetry;

9. I.e., three in one: the Trinity.

Nor rest nor travail my soul could taste,
Pure radiance so had ravished me.
For this I say with certainty:
Had a man in the body borne that boon,
No doctor's art, for fame or fee,
Had saved his life beneath the moon.

XIX

1

As the great moon begins to shine
While lingers still the light of day,
So in those ramparts crystalline
I saw a procession wend its way.
Without a summons, without a sign,
The city was full in vast array
Of maidens in such raiment fine
As my blissful one had worn that day.
As she was crowned, so crowned were they;
Adorned with pearls, in garments white;
And in like fashion, gleaming gay,
They bore the pearl of great delight.

2

With great delight, serene and slow,
They moved through every golden street;
Thousands on thousands, row on row,
All in one raiment shining sweet.
Who gladdest looked, was hard to know;
The Lamb led on at station meet,
Seven horns of gold upon his brow,[1]
His robe like pearls with rays replete.
Soon they approached God's mighty seat;
Though thick in throng, unhurried quite;
As maidens at communion meet
They moved along with great delight.

3

Delight that at his coming grew
Was greater than my tongue can tell;
The elders when he came in view
Prostrate as one before him fell;
Hosts of angels in retinue
Cast incense forth of sweetest smell;
Then all in concert praised anew
That jewel with whom in joy they dwell.[2]
The sound could pierce through the earth to hell
When the powers of heaven in song unite;
To share his praises in citadel
My heart indeed had great delight.

1. Revelation v.6.

2. Revelation v.8, 11–14.

4

Delight and wonder filled me in flood
To hear all heaven the Lamb acclaim;
Gladdest he was, most kind and good
Of any that ever was known to fame.
His dress so white, so mild his mood,
His looks so gracious, himself the same;
But a wound there was, and wide it stood,
Thrust near his heart with deadly aim.
Down his white side the red blood came;
"O God," thought I, "who had such spite?
A breast should consume with sorrow and shame
Ere in such deeds it took delight."

5

The Lamb's delight was clearly seen,
Though a bitter wound he had to bear;
So glorious was his gaze serene,
It gladdened all who beheld him there.
I looked where that host had been,
How charged with life, how changed they were,
And then I saw my little queen
That I thought but now I had stood so near.
Lord! how she laughed and made good cheer
Among her friends, who was so white!
To rush in the river then and there
I longed with love and great delight.

XX

1

Moved by delight of sight and sound,
My maddened mind all fate defied.
I would follow her there, my newly found,
Beyond the river though she must bide.
I thought that nothing could turn me round,
Forestall me, or stop me in mid-stride,
And wade I would from the nearer ground
And breast the stream, though I sank and died.
But soon those thoughts were thrust aside;
As I made for the river incontinent
I was summoned away and my wish denied:
My Prince therewith was not content.

2

It contented him not that I, distraught,
Should dare the river that rimmed the glade;
Though reckless I was, and overwrought,
In a moment's space my steps were stayed.
For just as I started from the spot
I was reft of my dream and left dismayed;
I waked in that same garden-plot,

On that same mound my head was laid.
I stretched my hand where Pearl had strayed;
Great fear befell me, and wonderment;
And, sighing, to myself I said,
"Let all things be to his content."

3

I was ill content to be dispossessed
Of the sight of her that had no peer
Amid those scenes so bright and blessed;
Such longing seized me, I swooned, or near;
Then sorrow broke from my burning breast;
"O honored Pearl," I said, "how dear
Was your every word and wise behest
In this true vision vouchsafed me here.
If you in a garland never sere
Are set by that Prince all-provident,
Then happy am I in dungeon drear
That he with you is well content."

4

Had I but sought to content my Lord
And taken his gifts without regret,
And held my place and heeded the word
Of the noble Pearl so strangely met,
Drawn heavenward by divine accord
I had seen and heard more mysteries yet;
But always men would have and hoard
And gain the more, the more they get.
So banished I was, by cares beset,
From realms eternal untimely sent;
How madly, Lord, they strive and fret
Whose acts accord not with your content!

5

To content that Prince and well agree,
Good Christians can with ease incline,
For day and night he has proved to be
A Lord, a God, a friend benign.
These words came over the mound to me
As I mourned my Pearl so flawless fine,
And to God committed her full and free,
With Christ's dear blessing bestowing mine,
As in the form of bread and wine
Is shown us daily in sacrament;
O may we serve him well, and shine
As precious pearls to his content.

Amen.

PIERS PLOWMAN
(ca 1372–1389)

The large number of manuscripts in which the *Vision of Piers Plowman* has been preserved indicates its wide popularity from the end of the 14th century up to the reign of Elizabeth I. Yet celebrated as the poem was, we know little about its origin. It exists in three versions, which scholars refer to as the A, B, and C Texts. The first, about 2,400 lines long, stops at a rather inconclusive point in the action; the second (generally agreed to be the best form of the poem) is a revision of the first plus an extension of more than 4,000 lines; and the third is a revision of the second. The name frequently associated with the poem is William Langland, but who he was and whether he wrote all three versions is not known. The little that can be inferred about him suggests that he came from the west of England and was probably a native of the Malvern Hills area in which the poem is set and where many of the surviving manuscripts were copied. If he wrote all three versions, then his interests and opinions must have changed while he was at work, for the versions differ from one another in many respects; but if more than one poet was involved, then it is extraordinary that all three versions share the same highly individual style and reflect the same curious and interesting poetic personality. Whatever its origin, the poem was avidly read and studied by a great many people. Within four years of the writing of the second version—which scholars have good evidence to date 1377, the year of Edward III's death and Richard II's accession to the throne—it had become so well known that the leaders of the Peasants' Revolt of 1381 used phrases borrowed from it as part of the rhetoric of the rebellion. The poem must therefore have managed to catch the imagination of a number of readers.

Piers Plowman has the form of a dream vision, a common medieval type in which the author presents his story under the guise of having dreamed it. Most dream visions concern romantic love; *Piers Plowman* also concerns love, but in this instance the love is theological. The dream vision generally involves allegory, not only because one expects from a dream the unrealistic, the fanciful, but also because people have always suspected that dreams relate the truth in a disguised form—that they are natural allegories. *Piers Plowman* is perhaps the greatest of English allegories, though the reader who expects to find in it the kind of definite and clear statement that allegory makes in the morality *Everyman* will be disappointed; allegory here is used not so much in order to define the known, as the character "Good Deeds" does in that play, as to explore the unknown, in particular the great spiritual mysteries of Christianity. When handling these the poet's imagination (for convenience let us assume a single poet, Langland) is apt to soar into a mode of expression that stimulates and excites readers' imaginations while, perhaps, bewildering their intellects. Langland's theme is nothing less than the history of Christianity as it unfolds both in the world of the Old and New Testaments and in the life and heart of an individual 14th-century Christian—two seemingly distinct realms between which the poet's allegory moves with dizzying rapidity.

Expanding the genre of dream-vision, *Piers Plowman* takes the form of a whole series of visions, separated by brief intervals when the narrator is awake. The first passage chosen for translation—the Prologue to the poem —introduces the famous first vision of the Field of Folk. The poet thought of Christianity as properly informing—and reforming—society, and he describes 14th-century English society in terms of its failure to represent an ideal society living in accord with Christian principles: hence the satirical poetry for which Langland is generally noted. Society's failure, of course, is attributable in part to the corruption of the church and churchmen, and whenever he considers clerical and ecclesiastical corruption, he pours out savagely indignant satire. But he is equally angry with the failure of the wealthy laity—untaught by the church to practice charity—to alleviate the sufferings of the poor, and it was probably his preoccupation with the poor that made his poem popular with the rebels of 1381; these, though confused in their motives, were eager to obtain correction of certain social abuses that Langland touches upon. This use of his poem must have horrified him, for despite his interest in social reform, he remains a fundamentally conservative and orthodox thinker: yet his passionate sympathy for the common man—idealized in his titular hero Piers the Plowman—made him seem a radical who felt that true religion was best represented not by the church but by the humblest orders of society. Many persons reading his poem more than a century and a half after it was written (it was first printed in 1550) saw in its Prologue strong historical reasons for the reformation of the church that had been carried out in the intervening years.

After his vision of the Field of Folk in the Prologue, Will the Dreamer is in Passus I ("Passus" is Latin for step, and the word the poet uses for the sections of his poem) approached by Lady Holy Church, who explains to him the fundamental principles of Christianity—with which, presumably, he has been familiar since childhood. But mere knowledge is not enough for him: he must learn by experience and feel in his heart what he learns. Now that he has seen truth in the person of Lady Holy Church, he asks to be shown the false, and Holy Church leaves him to witness the marriage of a suddenly personified False to Lady Meed. Meed, portrayed as an alluring wealthy woman, is an ambiguous allegorical figure: her many rascally followers recognize her as bribery, but Theology considers her the reward God has promised to give to true men, and objects to her proposed marriage to False. As a result of this objection, Meed and False, accompanied by a vast train of dishonest members of society, proceed to London to get legal opinion on the validity of their marriage. The king is warned of their coming and sends officers to arrest Meed: all the remainder of the company runs away. Though under arrest, Meed is warmly welcomed in the royal court, whose functionaries she at once starts to corrupt with money and promises of influence. The king proposes that she marry one of his knights named Conscience, to which she gladly assents; but when Conscience appears, he refuses to marry her, and she and he have a long debate about the true meaning of her name Meed. She tries to describe herself as merely payment for services rendered or things purchased, but Conscience will allow her no licit role in society. He declines to obey the king's command to become reconciled with her, unless Reason advises him to do so. Reason is summoned and, aided by Meed's flagrant attempts to corrupt the king's justice, succeeds in persuading the king and his subjects that Meed must be condemned.

Here the Dreamer awakes for the first time, but after a very short interval he falls asleep again and dreams that Reason preaches a sermon to the entire kingdom. At the end of this, the people confess their sins, an action which Langland describes by personifying the seven deadly sins; each one then relates (to a personified figure Repentance) how he behaves in society. These confessions, constituting much of Passus V of the B text of the poem, display most clearly Langland's social realism.

From The Vision of Piers Plowman[1]

From *The Prologue* [*The Field of Folk*]

In a summer season when the sun was mild
I got myself up in garb as though I'd grown into a sheep;
In the habit of a hermit, unholy of works,[2]
I went wide in the world, watching for wonders.
And on a May morning on Malvern Hills
A marvel befell me—magic it seemed.
I was wearied from wandering and went to rest
At the bottom of a broad bank by a brook's side,
And as I lay lazily looking in the water
I slid into a slumber, it sounded so soothing.
Then there came to me reclining there a most curious dream,
That I was in a wilderness—where, I'd no idea.
But as I looked into the east, up high toward the sun,
I saw a tower on a hill-top, trimly constructed,
A deep dale beneath, a dungeon-tower in it,
With deep dark ditches, dreadful to see.
A fair field full of folk I found between the towers,
Of people of all positions, the poor and the rich,
Working and wandering as the world requires.
Some applied themselves to plowing, played full seldom,
Sowing seeds and setting plants worked full hard;
Won what wasters destroy with their gluttony.
And some applied themselves to pride, wore proud garments,
Came all costumed in costly clothes.
To prayers and to penance many put themselves,
All for love of our Lord lived hard lives
In hope to have afterwards heaven's bliss—
Such as anchorites and hermits that hold to their cells
And don't care to go cantering about the countryside,
With some lush livelihood delighting their bodies.

1. The translations by the editor of the beginning and end of the Prologue and of two excerpts from Passus V of the B text are based on *Piers Plowman: The B Version*, edited by George Kane and E. T. Donaldson (1975).

2. For Langland's opinion of hermits see lines 28–30 immediately below.

And some made themselves merchants—they managed better,
As it seems to our sight that such men prosper.
And some make mirths as minstrels can,
And get gold with their glee,[3] guiltless, I think.
But word-jugglers and jokers, Judas' children,[4]
Invent fantasies to speak of and make fools of themselves,
Yet they have whatever wit they need to work if they wanted.
What Paul preaches of them I don't dare repeat it here:
Qui loquitur turpiloquim[5] is Lucifer's servant.
Beggars and beadsmen[6] went about fast
Till both their bellies and their bags were crammed to the brim;
Staged flytings[7] for their food, fought over ale.
In gluttony, God knows, they go to bed
And rise up with ribaldry, those Robert's boys;[8]
Sleep and sloth always pursue them.
Pilgrims and palmers[9] made pacts with each other
To seek Saint James[1] and saints at Rome.
They went along the way with many wise tales,
And had leave to tell lies all their lives after.
I saw some that said they'd sought after saints:
In every tale they told their tongues tended to lie
More than to tell the truth, their talk was such.
A heap of hermits carrying hooked staffs
Went off to Walsingham,[2] with their wenches behind.
Great long lubbers that don't like to work
Clothed themselves in copes[3] to keep distinct from other men,
And behaved like hermits to have their ease.
Friars I found there, all the four orders,[4]
Preaching to the populace for their own paunches' profit,
Explaining Holy Scripture as seemed best for themselves,
In hope to acquire copes[5] construed it as they pleased.
Many of these Masters[6] may clothe themselves gaily
For their money and their merchandise march hand in hand.[7]
Since Charity[8] has proved a peddler and principally shrives lords
Many marvels have been meted out within a few years.

3. I.e., music.
4. Minstrels who entertain with jokes and fantastic stories are regarded as descendants of Christ's betrayer, Judas.
5. "Who speaks slander": the text is not St. Paul's but expresses the poet's reason for not quoting St. Paul in such a way as to speak maliciously about the minstrels under discussion.
6. Prayer-sayers, i.e., people who offered to pray for the souls of those who gave them alms.
7. Contests in which the participants took turns insulting each other, preferably in verse.
8. I.e., robbers.
9. Virtually professional pilgrims, who took advantage of the hospitality offered pilgrims in order to go on traveling year after year.
1. I.e., his shrine at Compostella, Spain.
2. English town, site of a famous shrine to the Virgin Mary.
3. Monks', friars', and hermits' capes.
4. In Langlands' day there were four orders of friars in England: Franciscans, Dominicans, Carmelites, and Augustinians.
5. I.e., new garments.
6. I.e., Masters of Divinity.
7. The "merchandise" sold by the friars for money is shrift, which by canon law may not be sold.
8. The ideal of the friars, as stated by St. Francis, founder of the Franciscans, was simply love.

Unless Holy Church and friars' orders hold together better
The worst trouble in the world will well up soon.
A pardoner[9] preached there as if he'd a priest's rights,
Brought out a bull with bishop's seals,
And said he himself could absolve them all
Of failure to fast, of vows they'd broken.
Unlearnéd men believed him and liked his words,
Came crowding up on knees to kiss his bulls.
He banged them with his brevet[1] and bleared their eyes,
And raked in with his parchment-roll rings and brooches.
Thus you give your gold for gluttons' profit,
And squander it on scoundrels who're schooled as lechers.
If the bishop were blessed and worth both his ears
His seal should not be sent out to deceive the people.
It's not by the bishop's leave that the blackguard preaches;
What's more, the parish priest and the pardoner split the money
That the poor people of the parish should otherwise have.
Parsons and parish priests complained to the bishop
That their parishes were poor since the pestilence-time,[2]
Asked for licence and leave to live in London,
And sing masses there for simony, for silver is sweet.[3]

* * *

Yet there stood scores of men in scarves of silk,[4]
Law-sergeants[5] they seemed to be who served at the bar,
Pleaded cases for pennies[6] and impounded the law,
And for love of our Lord not once unloosed their lips:
You might better measure mist on Malvern Hills
Than get a "mum" from their mouths till money is produced.
Barons and burgesses and bondmen also
I saw in this assemblage, as you shall hear later;
Bakers and brewers and butchers aplenty.
Woolen-weavers and weavers of linen.
Tailors, tinkers, tax-collectors in markets,
Masons, miners, many other craftsmen.
Of all kinds of living laborers there leapt forth some,
Such as diggers of ditches that do their jobs badly
And dawdle away the long day with "*Dieu save dame Emma.*"[7]

9. An official empowered to pass on from the pope temporal indulgence for the sins of people who contributed to charitable enterprises—a function frequently abused (see Chaucer's Pardoner, General Prologue to the *Canterbury Tales,* lines 671 ff.). "Bull": papal license.
1. Pardoner's license.
2. Since 1349, England had suffered a number of epidemics of the plague, which had caused famine and depopulated the countryside.
3. Wealthy persons, especially in London, set up foundations to pay priests to sing masses for their souls and those of their relatives. "Simony": abuse of ecclesiastical office; a priest who had charge of a parish was forbidden to exercise any other salaried function in the church.
4. A silk scarf was a lawyer's badge of office.
5. Important lawyers (see the General Prologue to the *Canterbury Tales,* lines 311 ff.).
6. Pennies were fairly valuable coins in medieval England; "impounded": detained in legal custody.
7. "God save Dame Emma": apparently a popular song.

Cooks and their kitchen-boys cried, "Hot pies, hot!
Good goose and pork! Let's go and dine!"
Taverners told the same tale to them:
"White wine of Alsace and wine of Gascony,
Of the Rhine and of La Rochelle, to wash the roast down."
All this I saw sleeping and seven times more.

From *Passus V*

[THE CONFESSION OF ENVY]

Envy with heavy heart asked for shrift
And, grieving for his guilt, began his confession.
He was pale as a sheep's pelt, appeared to have the palsy;
He was clothed in a coarse cloth—I couldn't describe it—
A tabard[1] and a tunic, a knife attached to his side,
Like those of a friar's frock were the foresleeves.
Like a leek that had lain long in the sun
So he looked with lean cheeks, louring foully.
His body was so blown up for wrath that he bit his lips
And shook his fist fiercely—he wanted to avenge himself
With deeds or with words when he saw his chance.
Every syllable he spat out was of a serpent's tongue;
From chiding and bringing charges was his chief livelihood,
With backbiting and bitter scorn and bearing false witness.
This was all his courtesy wherever he showed himself.
"I'd like to be shriven," said this scoundrel, "if shame
would let me.
By God, I'd be gladder that Gib had bad luck
Than if I'd won this week a wey[2] of Essex cheese.
I have a near neighbor, I've nettled him often
And blamed him behind his back to blacken his name:
I've done my best to damage him day after day,
And lied to lords about him to make him lose money,
And turned his friends into his foes with my false tongue.
His good luck and glad lot grieve me greatly.
Between one household and another I often start disputes
So that both life and limb are lost for my speech.
When I met in the market the man I most hated
I fondled him affectionately as if I was a friend of his:
He's stronger than I am—I don't dare harm him.
But if I had might and mastery I'd murder him once for all.
When I come to kirk[3] and kneel before Christ's cross
And ought to pray for the people as the priest teaches,
For pilgrims, for palmers, for all the people after,
Then crouching there I call on Christ to give him sorrow
That took away my tankard and my torn sheet.[4]

1. A loose sleeveless jacket, worn over the tunic.
2. A very large measure.
3. Church.
4. The loss of Envy's tankard and torn sheet, and his fury at it, have not been explained.

Away from the altar I turn my eyes
And see how Heinie has a new coat;
Then I wish it were mine, and all the web[5] it came from.
And when he loses I laugh—that lightens my heart;
But when he wins I weep and wail the time.
I condemn men when they do evil, yet I do much worse:
Whoever upbraids me for that, I hate him deadly after.
I wish that everyone were my servant,
And if any man has more than I, that angers my heart.
So I live loveless like a loathsome dog
So that all my breast is blown up for bitterness of spirit.
For many years I might not eat as a man ought,
For envy and ill will are hard to digest.
Is there any sugar or sweet thing to assuage my swelling,
Or any *diapenidion*[6] that will drive it from my heart,
Or any shrift or shame, unless I have my stomach scraped?"
"Yes, readily," said Repentance, directing him to live better;
"Sorrow for sins is salvation for souls."
"I am sorry," said Envy. "I'm seldom otherwise,
And that makes me so miserable, since I may not avenge myself.
I've been among burgesses[7] buying at London
And made Backbiting a broker to blame men's wares.
When he sold and I didn't, then I was ready
To lie and to lour at my neighbor and belittle his merchandise.
I will amend this if I may, by might of God almighty.

[THE CONFESSION OF GLUTTONY]

Now Glutton begins to go to shrift
And takes his way toward the church to tell his sins.
But Betty the brewer bade him good morning
And she asked him where he was going.
"To Holy Church," he said, "to hear mass,
And then I shall be shriven and sin no more."
"I've good ale, good friend," said she. "Glutton, will you try it?"
"Have you," he asked, "any hot spices?"
"I have pepper and peony[8] and a pound of garlic,
A farthing-worth of fennel seed[9] for fasting days."
Then Glutton goes in, and great oaths after.
Cissy the seamstress was sitting on the bench,
Wat the warren-keeper and his wife both,
Tim the tinker and two of his servants,
Hick the hackneyman and Hugh the needle-seller,
Clarice of Cock's Lane[1] and the clerk of the church,
Sir Piers of Pridie and Parnel of Flanders,
Dave the ditch-digger and a dozen others,

5. I.e., bolt.
6. A twist of medicinal sugar.
7. City people.
8. In the Middle Ages, a spice.
9. This herb was apparently considered salubrious to one drinking on an empty stomach.
1. Clarice (and Parnel of the next line) are prostitutes.

A rebeck-player,[2] a rat-catcher, a street-raker of Cheapside,
A rope-maker, a redingking, and Rose the dish-vendor,
Godfrey of Garlickhithe and Griffin the Welshman,
A heap of old clothesmen early in the morning
Gladly treated Glutton to drinks of good ale.
Clement the cobbler took the coat off his back
And put it up as a prize for whoever would play "New Fair."[3]
Then Hick the ostler[4] took off his hood
And bade Bette the butcher to be on his side.
Then peddlers were appointed to appraise the goods:
Clement for his coat should get the hood plus compensation.
They went to work quickly and whispered together
And appraised these prizes apart by themselves.
There were heaps of oaths for anyone to hear.
They couldn't in conscience come to an agreement
Till Robin the roper was requested to arise
And named as an umpire so no quarrel should break out.
Then Hick the ostler had the cloak
In covenant that Clement should have his cup filled
And have Hick the ostler's hood, and call it a deal;
The first to regret the agreement should get up at once
And greet Sir Glutton with a gallon of ale.
There was laughing and louring and "Let go the cup!"
They began to make bets and bought more rounds,
And sat so till evensong and sang sometimes,
Till Glutton had gulped down a gallon and a gill.[5]
His guts began to grumble like two greedy sows;
He pissed four pints in a Paternoster's length,[6]
And on the bugle of his backside he blew a fanfare
So that all that heard that horn held their noses after
And wished it had been waxed[7] with a wisp of gorse.
He had no strength to stand before he had his staff in hand,
And then he made off, moving like a minstrel's bitch,[8]
Sometimes sidewards and sometimes backwards,
Like some one laying lines to lime[9] birds with.
But as he started stepping to the door his sight grew dim;

2. Fiddle-player: "street-raker": a scavenger—hence street-cleaner—of Cheapside, a section of London. What a "redingking" was is not known.

3. "New Fair" was a game in which two participants exchanged items in their possession which were not of equal value and hence involved a cash payment by the player who put up the least valuable object. Clement puts up his cloak, Hick his hood; each chooses an agent to represent him in the evaluation of the objects, which is carried on by peddlers. Hick is represented by Bette, but since the evaluators are unable to agree, Robin is named as an umpire. It is decided that Hick should have Clement's cloak and Clement Hick's hood, but that Clement should receive a cup of ale as well, or perhaps the money for a cup of ale which he would then share with all the participants. A fine of further ale would be placed on either of the men who grumbled at the exchange.

4. I.e., a stableman.

5. I.e., a quarter-pint.

6. I.e., the time it takes to say the Lord's Prayer.

7. I.e., sealed; "gorse" is a spiny shrub.

8. I.e., a trained dog.

9. Birds were caught by smearing a sticky substance ("lime") on strings laid out on the ground.

He felt for the threshold and fell on the ground.
Clement the cobbler caught him by the waist
To lift him aloft, and laid him on his knees.
But Glutton was a large lout and a load to lift.
And he coughed up a custard in Clement's lap.
There's no hound so hungry in Hertfordshire
That would dare lap up that leaving, so unlovely the taste.
With all the woe of this world his wife and his maid
Brought him to his bed and bundled him in it,
And after all this excess he had a fit of sloth
So that he slept Saturday and Sunday till the sun set.
When he was awake and had wiped his eyes,
The first word he spoke was, "Where is the bowl?"
His spouse scolded him for his sin and wickedness,
And right so Repentance rebuked him at that time.
"As with words and with deeds you've worked evil in your life
Shrive yourself and be ashamed, and show it with your mouth."
"I, Glutton," he began, "admit I'm guilty of this:
That I've trespassed with my tongue, I can't tell how often;
Sworn by God's soul and his sides and 'so God help me!'
When there was no need for it, nine hundred times;
And overstuffed myself at supper and sometimes at midday
So that I, Glutton, got rid of it before I'd gone a mile;
And swilled what might have been saved and dispensed
 to the hungry;
Overindulgently on feast days I've drunk and eaten both;
And sometimes sat so long there that I slept and ate at once;
To hear tales in taverns I've taken more drink;
Fed myself before noon on fasting days."
"This full confession," said Repentance, "will procure favor for
 you."
Then Glutton began to groan and to make great woe
For his life that he had lived in so loathsome a way,
And vowed he would fast, what for hunger or for thirst:
"Never shall fish on Friday be fed to my belly
Till Abstinence my aunt has given me leave,
And yet I have hated her all my lifetime."

MIDDLE ENGLISH LYRICS

The best of the Middle English lyrics, both religious and secular, seem remarkably fresh despite the fact that in both theme and form they are extremely conventional—at times almost stylized. The song of spring (the French *reverdie*), the love lyric and love complaint, the celebration of the Virgin Mary, the witty satire of women, the meditation upon Calvary—even the rollicking verse in praise of good food, good drink, and good living—are members of ancient genres, most of which had developed in France (some of the poems here printed closely parallel French lyrics). The poet's love in *Alison* is conventional even in her name, which is that of the Wife of Bath and of the heroine of the Miller's Tale, and the poet could have written her praise without ever having loved anything more feminine than books, which contained hundreds of ladies with Alison's charms. The fact that most of them would have been blue-eyed blondes might make love for a black-eyed brunette seem daringly realistic, but conventions set up anti-conventions which become as rigid as their older antitheses. Yet those who feel that such a lyric as *Alison* is the genuine complaint of a 13th-century English lad are right in their reactions as readers if wrong in fact, for the poem re-creates excellently the excitement of young love—and the time must have been full of young men yearning for black-eyed Alisons.

It is the same with the spring songs. Spring returns in much the same literary terms in poem after poem, year after year, century after century, but the best medieval spring songs also vigorously reproduce the actual excitement of its natural return every March and April. For while every good poet brings something of his own observing to the tradition he is following, the writers of medieval lyrics are especially distinguished for their unself-consciousness and immediacy. Just as there was no consciousness on the part of the medieval man of anachronism—historical differences in time or place—there seems to have been no self-consciousness about his attempts to express himself in poetic terms: convention apparently liberated him, instead of oppressing him in the way it is often supposed to do. It is with perfect naturalness that the poet of *Sunset on Calvary* relives the scene, standing with the mother Mary beside the cross on which her Son hangs; or the poet of *I Sing of a Maiden* visualizes the mystery of the Virgin Birth in terms of the most natural of mysteries, the falling dew; or the poet of *Adam Lay Bound* cheerfully regards Adam's sin and its dire consequences as a kind of childish naughtiness and punishment that had the tremendous effect of bringing Christ to earth. The very simplicity of the poet's attitude achieves the most striking artistic results.

Several of the poems printed here depend on traditions that are no longer alive. The *Corpus Christi Carol* relies upon the ancient fertility myth of the Fisher King which had been caught up and Christianized in Arthurian legend. *I Have a Young Sister* is a riddling poem that is reminiscent of the Old English riddles, though its clues, highly suggestive sexual symbols, are of a fully developed sophistication.

It is impossible to date the individual lyrics with any certainty. Perhaps the oldest is the *Cuckoo Song*, which is probably of the 12th century, and one may guess that the other spring songs are of the late 13th or early 14th; but some of the best of the lyrics (*I Sing of a Maiden, Adam Lay Bound*) may be of the 15th century. In general, we know only that the poems must be earlier than the manuscripts in which they appear, but because of the fact that an early lyric might have been reworded by a late scribe in such a way as to make it appear late, we can rarely tell by how many years any given lyric preceded the manuscript that records it. The sources of the texts printed here are too diverse to be listed. Spelling has been normalized as in the selections from Chaucer.

Fowls in the Frith

Fowles° in the frith,° *birds / woods*
The fisshes in the flood,
And I mon waxe wood:[1]
Much sorwe° I walke with *sorrow*
For beste[2] of boon° and blood. *bone*

Alison

Bitweene° Merch and Averil, *in the seasons of*
When spray biginneth to springe,
The litel fowl hath hire wil° *pleasure*
On hire leod[3] to singe.
Ich° libbe° in love-longinge *I / live*
For semlokest° of alle thinge. *seemliest, fairest*
Heo° may me blisse bringe: *she*
  Ich am in hire baundoun.° *power*
  An hendy hap ich habbe yhent,[4]
  Ichoot° from hevene it is me sent: *I know*
  From alle[5] wommen my love is lent,° *removed*
  And light° on Alisoun. *alights*

On hew° hire heer° is fair ynough, *hue / hair*
Hire browe browne, hire yë° blake; *eye*
With lossum cheere heo on me lough;[6]
With middel smal and wel ymake.
But° heo me wolle to hire take *Unless*
For to been hire owen make,° *mate*
Longe to liven ichulle° forsake, *I will*
  And feye° fallen adown. *dead*
  An hendy hap, etc.

Nightes when I wende° and wake, *turn*
Forthy° mine wonges° waxeth wan: *therefore / cheeks*
Levedy,° al for thine sake *lady*
Longinge is ylent me on.[7]
In world nis noon so witer° man *clever*
That al hire bountee° telle can; *excellence*
Hire swire° is whittere° than the swan, *neck / whiter*
  And fairest may° in town. *maid*
  An hendy, etc.

Ich am for wowing° al forwake,° *wooing / worn out from waking*
Wery so water in wore.[8]
Lest any reve me[9] my make
Ich habbe y-yerned yore.[1]

1. Must go mad.
2. Probably "the best," i.e., his lady. The meaning "beast" is, however, not impossible.
3. In her language.
4. A gracious chance I have received.
5. I.e., all other.
6. With lovely face she on me smiled.
7. Longing has come upon me.
8. Perhaps "millpond."
9. Deprive me.
1. I have been worrying long since.

Bettere is tholien° while° sore — *endure / for a time*
Than mournen evermore.
Geinest under gore,[2]
  Herkne to my roun:° — *song*
  An hendy, etc.

My Lief Is Faren in Londe

My lief is faren in londe[3]—
Allas, why is she so?
And I am so sore bonde° — *bound*
I may nat come her to.
She hath myn herte in holde
Wherever she ride or go°— — *walk*
With trewe love a thousand folde.

Western Wind

Westron wind, when will thou blow?
The small rain down can rain.
Christ, that my love were in my arms,
And I in my bed again.

I Have a Young Sister

I have a yong suster
  Fer° biyonde the see; — *far*
Manye be the druries° — *gifts*
  That she sente me.

She sente me the cherye
  Withouten any stoon,° — *stone*
And so she dide the dove
  Withouten any boon.° — *bone*

She sente me the brere° — *briar*
  Withouten any rinde;° — *bark*
She bad me love my lemman° — *mistress*
  Withoute longinge.

How sholde any cherye
  Be withoute stoon?
And how sholde any dove
  Be withoute boon?

How sholde any brere
  Be withoute rinde?
How sholde I love my lemman
  Withoute longinge?

2. Fairest beneath clothing.

3. My beloved has gone away.

Whan the cherye was a flowr,
  Thanne hadde it no stoon;
Whan the dove was an ey,° *egg*
  Thanne hadde it no boon.

Whan the brere was unbred,° *ungrown*
  Thanne hadde it no rinde;
Whan the maiden hath that° she loveth, *what*
  She is withoute longinge.

A Bitter Lullaby

Lullay, lullay, litel child, why weepestou so sore?
Needes most° thou weepe, it was y-yarked° thee yore[4] *must / destined*
Evere to live in sorwe, and siken° everemore, *sigh*
As thine eldren dide er this, whil they alives° wore.° *alive / were*
  Lullay, lullay, litel child, child, lullay, lullow,
  Into uncouth° world ycomen so art thou. *strange*

Beestes and thise fowles, the fisshes in the flood,
And eech sheef° alives, ymaked of boon and blood, *creature*
Whan they cometh to the world they dooth hemself som good—
Al but the wrecche° brol° that is of Adames blood. *wretched / brat*
  Lullay, lullay, litel child, to care art thou bimet:° *destined*
  Thou noost nat this worldes wilde bifore thee is yset.[5]

Child, if it bitideth that thou shalt thrive and thee,° *prosper*
Thenk° thou were yfostered up thy moder° knee; *remember / mother's*
Evere have minde° in thyn herte of thise thinges three: *thought*
Whennes thou comest, what thou art, and what shal come of thee.
  Lullay, lullay, litel child, child, lullay, lullay:
  With sorwe thou come into this world, with sorwe thou shalt away.

Ne tristou[6] to this world, it is thy fulle° fo: *entire*
The riche it maketh poore, the poore riche also;
It turneth wo to wele° and eek wele to wo: *well-being*
Ne triste° no man to this world whil it turneth so. *trust*
  Lullay, lullay, litel child, the foot is in the wheele:[7]
  Thou noost[8] whether it wol turne to wo other to wele.
Child, thou art a pilgrim in wikkednesse ybore;° *born*
Thou wandrest in this false world—thou looke thee bifore:

4. Long since.
5. You don't know that the wild beasts of this world are set before you (i.e., preferred to you).
6. Don't trust.
7. I.e., Fortune's foot is turning the wheel on which all people must ride.
8. Don't know.

Deeth shal come with a blast out of a wel dim bore° *cranny*
Adames kinne down to caste—himself hath do bifore.[9]
Lullay, lullay, litel child, so wo thee warp° Adam *wove*
In the land of Paradis through wikkenesse° of
Satan. *wickedness*

Child, thou nart[1] a pilgrim, but an uncouth° gest: *unknown*
Thy dayes beeth ytold,° thy journeys
beeth ycest° *numbered / determined*
Whider thou shalt wenden, north other° est,° *or / east*
Deeth thee shal bitide with bitter bale° in brest. *pain*
Lullay, lullay, litel child, this wo Adam thee wroughte
Whan he the apple eet, and Eve it him bitoughte.[2]

The Cuckoo Song

Sumer is ycomen in,
Loude sing cuckou!
Groweth seed and bloweth meed,[3]
And springth the wode° now. *wood*
Sing cuckou!

Ewe bleteth after lamb,
Loweth after calve cow,
Bulloc sterteth,° bucke verteth,° *leaps / breaks wind*
Merye sing cuckou!
Cuckou, cuckou,
Wel singest thou cuckou:
Ne swik° thou never now! *cease*

Tell Me, Wight in the Broom

"Say me, wight in the broom,° *shrub*
What is me for to doon?
Ich° have the werste bonde° *I / husband*
That is in any londe."

"If thy bonde is ille,° *bad*
Hold thy tonge stille."

I Am of Ireland

Ich am of Irlonde,
And of the holy londe
Of Irlonde.
Goode sire, praye ich thee,

9. ? To cast down Adam's kin as Adam himself has previously caused that it should be cast down.

1. Are not.
2. Gave it to him.
3. The meadow blossoms.

For of° sainte charitee, *sake of*
Com and dance with me
In Irlonde.

Sunset on Calvary

Now gooth sunne under wode:[4]
Me reweth,[5] Marye, thy faire rode.° *face*
Now gooth sunne under tree:
Me reweth, Marye, thy sone and thee.

I Sing of a Maiden

I sing of a maiden
That is makelees:° *matchless*
King of alle kinges
To° her sone she chees.° *as / chose*

He cam also° stille *as*
Ther° his moder° was *where / mother*
As dewe in Aprille
That falleth on the gras.

He cam also stille
To his modres bowr
As dewe in Aprille
That falleth on the flowr.

He cam also stille
Ther his moder lay
As dewe in Aprille
That falleth on the spray.

Moder and maiden
Was nevere noon but she:
Wel may swich° a lady *such*
Godes moder be.

Adam Lay Bound

Adam lay ybounden, bounden in a bond,
Four thousand winter thoughte he not too long;
And al was for an apple, an apple that he took,
As clerkes finden writen, writen in hire book.
Ne hadde[6] the apple taken been, the apple taken been,
Ne hadde nevere Oure Lady ybeen hevene Queen.
Blessed be the time that apple taken was:
Therfore we mown° singen *Deo Gratias*.[7] *may*

4. Wood, i.e., the Cross.
5. I pity.
6. Had not.
7. Thanks be to God.

The Corpus Christi Carol

Lully, lullay, lully, lullay,
The faucon° hath borne my make° away. *falcon / mate*

He bare him up, he bare him down,
He bare him into an orchard brown.

In that orchard ther was an hall
That was hanged with purple and pall.° *black velvet*

And in that hall ther was a bed:
It was hanged with gold so red.

And in that bed ther lith° a knight, *lies*
His woundes bleeding by day and night.

By that beddes side ther kneeleth a may,° *maid*
And she weepeth both night and day.

And by that beddes side ther standeth a stoon:° *stone*
Corpus Christi[8] writen theron.

8. Body of Christ.

THE SECOND SHEPHERDS' PLAY
(ca. 1425)

The *Second Shepherds' Play* is the finest example in English of a medieval mystery play. The word "mystery" in this context refers to the spiritual mystery of Christ's redemption of mankind, and mystery plays are dramatizations of incidents of the Old Testament, which foretells that redemption, and of the New, which recounts it. In England the mysteries were generally composed in cycles containing as many as 48 individual plays; a typical cycle would begin with the Creation, continue with the Fall of Man, and proceed through the most significant events of the Old Testament, such as the Flood, to the New Testament, which provided plays on the Nativity, the chief events of Christ's life, the Crucifixion, the Harrowing of Hell (based on sources now deemed apocryphal), and the Last Judgment. This kind of drama had its origin within the very walls of the medieval church, in the liturgical dialogue that had long been a characteristic feature of formal Christian worship. The exchanges between priest and congregation in the celebration of the Mass are essentially dramatic, as are also the exchanges between several sections of the choir in the singing of an anthem. By a natural elaboration of these dialogues, the texts of which are based on Biblical or Apocryphal sources, a church drama came into being—indeed, it ultimately developed so fully that there was no longer room for it within the liturgy; it then had to be presented separately. In England it was given a home in the churchyard, but as it became increasingly secularized and increasingly pervaded by the rough popular humor of medieval minstrelsy, it lost its place even in the churchyard. By the time of their fullest development, the mysteries were acted in the streets of the town.

Despite secularization and separation from the church proper, mystery plays never lost their religious impulse. They were generally performed at the time of one of two great church festivals—Whitsuntide, the week following the seventh Sunday after Easter, or Corpus Christi, a week later—and their performance was one of the important ways in which the unlearned layman of the Middle Ages participated directly in the celebration of his religion. Every trade in urban society had its guild, an organization combining the functions of a modern club, trade union, and religious society, and each of these guilds had its traditional play to perform on the days when the cycles were presented. In certain of the towns each company had a wagon which served as a stage. The wagon would proceed from one strategic point in the town to another, and the play would be performed a number of times on the same day: the spectators gathered at any one strategic point would never be without a play before them, and might see the whole cycle without moving. In other towns, however, the plays were probably acted out in sequence at a single place—an innyard or some other such natural theater.

The *Second Shepherds' Play*, which was probably played at Wakefield in Yorkshire, is a member of one of the four great cycles of English mysteries that have been preserved in their entirety; from what must have originally been a great number of other cycles we possess only a few individual pieces. The Wakefield cycle has two plays for shepherds; it is the second which is reprinted below. The artistic level of most of the Middle English mysteries is not high: a kind of rough piety, at times mixed with a crude humor, is characteristic of most of them, though there are happy exceptions. The happiest of these are certain of the Wakefield plays, which display a sophisticated artistic intelligence at work beneath the apparent naïveté. This intelligence belonged undoubtedly to one individual, who probably revised traditional plays. His identity is not known, but because of his achievement scholars refer to him as the Wakefield Master. He was probably a highly educated cleric stationed in the vicinity of Wakefield, perhaps a friar of a nearby priory. He appreciated the rough humor and rough piety of the traditional plays, but he also knew how to refine both qualities without appearing to do so, and, more important, he knew how to combine the humorous and the religious so that the former serves the latter rather than detracting from it. In the *Second Shepherds' Play*, by linking the comic subplot of Mak and Gill with the solemn story of Christ's nativity, the Wakefield Master has produced a dramatic parable of what the Nativity means in Christian history and in Christian hearts. No one will fail to observe the parallelism between the stolen sheep, ludicrously disguised as Mak's latest heir, lying in the cradle, and the real Lamb of God, born in the stable among beasts. A complex of relationships based upon this relationship suggests itself. But perhaps the most important point is that the charity twice shown by the shepherds—in the first instance to the supposed son of Mak and in the second instance to Mak and Gill when they decide to let them off with only the mildest of punishments—is rewarded when they are invited to visit the Christ Child, the embodiment of charity. The bleak beginning of the play, with its series of individual complaints, is ultimately balanced by the optimistic ending, which sees the shepherds once again singing together in harmony.

Characterization in the mystery plays is usually rather slight, except in the case of stereotypes like Noah's stubborn wife or the ranting Herod (both mentioned in Chaucer's Miller's Tale). Mak therefore stands high above the generality and is perhaps the best humorous character outside of Chaucer's works in this period. A braggart of the worst kind, he has something of Falstaff's charm; and he resembles Falstaff also in his grotesque attempts to maintain the last shreds of his dignity when he is caught in a lie. Most readers will be glad that the shepherds do not carry out their threat to have the death penalty invoked for his crime.

The Second Shepherds' Play[1]

Dramatis Personae

COLL	GILL
GIB	ANGEL
DAW	MARY
MAK	

[*A moor.*]

[*Enter* COLL.]

COLL. Lord, what[2] these weathers are cold, and I am ill happed;
I am nearhand dold,° so long have I napped; *numb*
My legs they fold,° my fingers are chapped. *give way*
It is not as I would, for I am all lapped° *wrapped*
In sorrow:
In storms and tempest,
Now in the east, now in the west,
Woe is him has never rest
Midday nor morrow.

But we silly° husbands° that walks on the moor, *poor / farmers*
In faith we are nearhands out of the door.[3]
No wonder, as it stands, if we be poor,
For the tilth° of our lands lies fallow as the floor, *arable part*
As ye ken.° *know*
We are so hammed,
Fortaxed, and rammed,
We are made hand-tamed
With these gentlery-men.[4]

Thus they reave us[5] our rest—Our Lady them wary!° *curse*
These men that are lord-fest,[6] they cause the plow tarry.

1. The text is based on that given by A. W. Pollard in *The Towneley Plays* (1897), but has been freely edited. Spelling has been normalized except where rhyme makes changes impossible. Since the original text has no indications of scenes and only four stage directions, written in Latin, appropriate scenes of action and additional stage directions have been added; the four original stage directions are identified in the footnotes.
2. How; "ill happed": badly covered.
3. I.e., homeless.
4. We are so hamstrung, overtaxed, and beaten down (that) we are made slaves by these highborn men. Coll is complaining of the peasant's hard lot, at the mercy of the agents of the Crown and of the wealthy landholders.
5. Deprive us of.
6. Attached to lords.

That men say is for the best, we find it contrary.
Thus are husbands oppressed in point to miscarry.[7]
On live
Thus hold they us under,
Thus they bring us in blunder,° *trouble*
It were a great wonder
And° ever should we thrive. *if*

There shall come a swain as proud as a po:° *peacock*
He must borrow my wain,° my plow also; *wagon*
Then I am full fain° to grant ere he go. *glad*
Thus live we in pain, anger, and woe,
By night and by day.
He must have if he lang° it, *wants*
If I should forgang it:[8]
I were better be hanged
Than once say him nay.[9]

For may he get a paint-sleeve[1] or a brooch nowadays,
Woe is him that him grieve or once again-says.° *gainsays*
Dare no man him reprieve, what mastery he maes.[2]
And yet may no man lieve° one word that he says, *believe*
No letter.
He can make purveyance[3]
With boast and bragance,° *bragging*
And all is through maintenance° *protection*
Of men that are greater.

It does me good, as I walk thus by mine one,° *self*
Of this world for to talk in manner of moan.
To my sheep will I stalk, and hearken anon,
There abide on a balk,° or sit on a stone, *grassy mound*
Full soon;
For I trow,° pardie,° *think / by God*
True men if they be,
We get more company
Ere it be noon.

[*Enter* GIB, *who at first does not see* COLL.]

GIB. Benste and Dominus,[4] what may this bemean?° *mean*
Why fares this world thus? Such have we not seen.
Lord, these winds are spiteous° and the weathers full keen *cruel*
And the frosts so hideous they water mine een,° *eyes*
No lie.
Now in dry, now in wet,

7. To the point of ruin. "On live": in life.
8. Even if I have to do without it.
9. In the manuscript, this stanza follows the next.
1. Embroidered sleeve (i.e., sign of authority).
2. No one dares to reprove him, no matter what force he uses.
3. Requisition (of private property).
4. Bless us and Lord.

Now in snow, now in sleet,
When my shoon° freeze to my feet *shoes*
It is not all easy.

But as far as I ken,° or yet as I go,° *see / walk*
We silly wedmen dree mickle woe;[5]
We have sorrow then and then[6]—it falls oft so.
Silly Capple,[7] our hen, both to and fro
She cackles;
But begin she to croak,
To groan or to cluck,
Woe is him our cock,
For he is in the shackles.

These men that are wed have not all their will:
When they are full hard stead[8] they sigh full still;
God wot° they are led full hard and full ill; *knows*
In bower nor in bed they say nought theretill.° *thereagainst*
This tide° *time*
My part have I fun;° *found, learned*
I know my lesson:
Woe is him that is bun,° *bound*
For he must abide.

But now late in our lives—a marvel to me,
That I think my heart rives° such wonders to see; *splits*
What that destiny drives it should so be[9]—
Some men will have two wives, and some men three
In store.
Some are woe[1] that has any,
But so far can° I, *know*
Woe is him that has many,
For he feels sore.

But young men a-wooing, for God that you
bought,° *redeemed*
Be well ware of wedding and think in your thought:
"Had I wist"° is a thing, it serves of nought. *known*
Mickle° still° mourning has wedding home
brought, *much / continual*
And griefs
With many a sharp shower,° *fight*
For thou may catch in an hour
That° shall savor° full sour *what / taste*
As long as thou lives.

For as ever read I 'pistle,° I have one to my fere[2] *Epistle*
As sharp as a thistle, as rough as a brere;° *briar*

5. We poor married men suffer much woe.
6. Constantly.
7. I.e., one's wife.
8. Beset; "still": constantly.
9. What destiny causes must occur.
1. I.e., wretched.
2. As my mate.

She is browed like a bristle, with a sour-loten cheer;[3]
Had she once wet her whistle she could sing full clear
Her Pater Noster.
She is great as a whale;
She has a gallon of gall:
By Him that died for us all,
I would I had run to° I had lost her. *until*

COLL. Gib, look over the raw!° Full deafly ye stand! *hedge*
GIB. Yea, the devil in thy maw, so tariand![4]
Saw thou awhere° of Daw? *anywhere*
COLL. Yea, on a
lea-land° *pasture land*
Heard I him blaw.[5] He comes here at hand,
Not far.
Stand still.
GIB. Why?
COLL. For he comes, hope° I. *think*
GIB. He will make us both a lie
But if[6] we be ware.

[*Enter* DAW, *who does not see the others.*]

DAW. Christ's cross me speed, and Saint Nicholas!
Thereof had I need: it is worse than it was.
Whoso could take heed and let the world pass,
It is ever in dread° and brickle° as glass, *doubt / brittle*
And slithes.° *slips away*
This world foor° never so, *behaved*
With marvels mo° and mo, *more*
Now in weal, now in woe,
And all thing writhes.° *changes*

Was never sin° Noah's flood such floods seen, *since*
Winds and rains so rude and storms so keen:
Some stammered, some stood in doubt,[7] as I
ween.° *suppose*
Now God turn all to good! I say as I mean.
For ponder:
These floods so they drown
Both in fields and in town,
And bears all down,
And that is a wonder.

We that walk on the nights, our cattle to keep,
We see sudden° sights when other men sleep. *unexpected*
Yet methink my heart lights: I see shrews peep.[8]

3. She has brows like pig's bristles and a sour-looking face.
4. Yes, the devil take thy guts for being so late.
5. Blow (his horn).
6. Unless.
7. The line apparently refers to men's behavior at the time of Noah's flood.
8. I see rascals are watching.

[*He sees the others, but does not hail them.*]
Ye are two tall wights.° I will give my sheep *creatures*
A turn.
But full ill have I meant:[9]
As I walk on this bent° *field*
I may lightly° repent, *quickly*
My toes if I spurn.° *stub*

Ah, sir, God you save, and master mine!
A drink fain would I have, and somewhat to dine.
COLL. Christ's curse, my knave, thou art a lither hine![1]
GIB. What, the boy list° rave! Abide unto sine.[2] *wants to*
We have made it.[3]
Ill thrift on thy pate!
Though the shrew° came late *rascal*
Yet is he in state
To dine, if he had it.

DAW. Such servants as I, that sweats and swinks,° *toil*
Eats our bread full dry, and that me forthinks.° *angers*
We are oft wet and weary when master-men winks,° *sleep*
Yet comes full lately° both dinners and drinks. *tardily*
But nately° *profitably*
Both our dame and our sire,
When we have run in the mire,
They can nip at our hire,[4]
And pay us full lately.

But here my troth, master, for the fare° that ye
make° *food / provide*
I shall do thereafter: work as I take.[5]
I shall do a little, sir, and among° ever
lake,° *meanwhile / play*
For yet lay my supper never on my stomach
In fields.
Whereto should I threap?° *haggle*
With my staff can I leap,[6]
And men say, "Light cheap
Litherly foryields."[7]

COLL. Thou were an ill lad to ride a-wooing
With a man that had but little of spending.[8]
GIB. Peace, boy, I bade—no more jangling,
Or I shall make thee full rad,° by the heaven's
King, *frightened*
With thy gauds.° *tricks*

9. But that is a poor idea.
1. Thou art a worthless servant.
2. Wait till later.
3. I.e., had dinner.
4. They can deduct from our wages.
5. I.e., work in the same way as I am paid.
6. I.e., run away.
7. A cheap bargain repays badly (a proverb).
8. You would be a bad servant for a poor man to take wooing with him.

Where are our sheep, boy? We scorn.[9]
DAW. Sir, this same day at morn
I them left in the corn
When they rang Lauds.[1]

They have pasture good, they cannot go wrong.
COLL. That is right. By the rood,° these nights are long! *cross*
Yet I would, ere we yode,° one gave us a song. *went*
GIB. So I thought as I stood, to mirth° us
among.° *cheer / meanwhile*
DAW. I grant.
COLL. Let me sing the tenory.° *tenor*
GIB. And I the treble so hee.° *high*
DAW. Then the mean° falls to me. *middle part*
Let see how you chant.

[*They sing.—Enter* MAK *with a cloak over his clothes.*[2]]
MAK. Now, Lord, for thy names seven, that made both moon
and starns[3]
Well mo than I can neven, thy will, Lord, of me tharns.[4]
I am all uneven°—that moves oft my harns.[5] *at odds*
Now would God I were in heaven, for there weep no
barns° *children*
So still.° *continually*
COLL. Who is that pipes so poor?
MAK. [*aside*] Would God ye wist° how I foor!° *knew / fared*
[*aloud*] Lo, a man that walks on the moor
And has not all his will.

GIB. Mak, where has thou gane?° Tell us tiding. *gone*
DAW. Is he come? Then ilkane[6] take heed to his thing.
[*Snatches a cloak from him.*]
MAK. What! Ich[7] be a yeoman, I tell you, of the king,
The self and the same, sond° from a great
lording *messenger*
And sich.° *suchlike*
Fie on you! Goth hence
Out of my presence:
I must have reverence.
Why, who be ich?

COLL. Why make ye it so quaint? Mak, ye do wrang.[8]
GIB. But, Mak, list ye saint? I trow that ye lang.[9]

9. I.e., waste time.
1. Rang the bells for the church service held at dawn.
2. Mak's entrance is a stage direction in the original MS.
3. Stars.
4. Well more than I can name, thy will, Lord, falls short in regard to me.
5. That often disturbs my brains.
6. Each one; "thing": possessions. The stage direction here is in the MS.
7. I (the southern form): Mak is pretending to be an important person from the south.
8. Why do you behave in such an unfriendly manner? Mak, you do wrong.
9. But, Mak, do you want to act as if you were a saint? I guess you do.

DAW. I trow the shrew can paint[1]—the devil might him hang!
MAK. Ich shall make complaint and make you all to
thwang° *be flogged*
At a word,
And tell even° how ye doth. *exactly*
COLL. But Mak, is that sooth?
Now take out that southern tooth,[2]
And set in a turd!

GIB. Mak, the devil in your ee![3] A stroke would I lean you!
DAW. Mak, know ye not me? By God, I could teen° you. *vex*
MAK. God look° you all three: Methought I had seen you. *guard*
Ye are a fair company.
COLL. Can ye now mean you?[4]
GIB. Shrew, peep![5]
Thus late as thou goes,
What will men suppose?
Thou has an ill nose[6]
Of stealing of sheep.

MAK. And I am true as steel, all men wate.° *know*
But a sickness I feel that holds me full hate:° *hot, feverish*
My belly fares not weel, it is out of estate.
DAW. Seldom lies the devil dead by the gate.[7]
MAK. Therefore
Full sore am I and ill
If I stand stone-still:
I eat not a needill[8]
This month and more.

COLL. How fares thy wife? By my hood, how fares sho?° *she*
MAK. Lies waltering,° by the rood, by the fire, lo! *lounging*
And a house full of brood.° She drinks well, too: *children*
Ill speed other good that she will do![9]
But sho
Eats as fast as she can;
And ilk° year that comes to man *every*
She brings forth a lakan,° *baby*
And some years two.

But were I now more gracious° and richer by
far, *prosperous*
I were eaten out of house and of harbar.° *home*
Yet is she a foul douce,° if ye come nar:[1] *sweetheart*
There is none that trows° nor knows a
war° *imagines / worse*

1. I think the shrew can play tricks.
2. Now stop speaking like a southerner.
3. Eye; "lean": lend.
4. Remember.
5. Rascal, watch out.
6. Noise, i.e., reputation.
7. Road (i.e., the devil is always on the move).
8. Needle, i.e., a little bit.
9. I.e., that's the only good thing she does.
1. I.e., near the truth.

Than ken° I. *know*
Now will ye see what I proffer:
To give all in my coffer
Tomorn at next[2] to offer
Her head-masspenny.[3]

GIB. I wot° so forwaked° is none in this shire. *know / sleepless*
I would sleep if° I taked less to my hire. *even if*
DAW. I am cold and naked and would have a fire.
I am weary forraked° and run in the mire. *from walking*
Wake thou.[4]
GIB. Nay, I will lie down by,
For I must sleep, truly.
DAW. As good a man's son was I
As any of you.

But Mak, come hither, between shall thou lie down.
MAK. Then might I let you bedeen of that ye would rown,[5]
No dread.° *doubt*
From my top to my toe,
[*Saying his prayers.*]
Manus tuas commendo
Pontio Pilato.[6]
Christ's cross me speed!

[*He gets up as the others sleep and speaks.*][7]
Now were time for a man that lacks what he would
To stalk privily than° unto a fold, *then*
And nimbly to work than, and be not too bold,
For he might abuy° the bargain if it were told *pay for*
At the ending.
Now were time for to reel:° *move spryly*
But he needs good counseel
That fain would fare weel° *well*
And has but little spending.

[*He casts a spell.*]
But about you a circill,° as round as a moon, *circle*
To° I have done that° I will, till that it be
noon, *until / what*
That ye lie stone-still to that I have done;
And I shall say theretill° of good words a
foon:° *moreover / few*
"On height,
Over your heads my hand I lift.
Out go your eyes! Fordo your sight!"[8]

2. "Tomorn at next": tomorrow.
3. The penny paid for a mass for her departed spirit.
4. You stay awake.
5. Then I might hinder you if you wanted to whisper together.
6. Mak's prayer means, "Thy hands I commend to Pontius Pilate."
7. One of the original stage directions.
8. May your sight be rendered powerless.

But yet I must make better shift
And it be right.[9]

Lord, what° they sleep hard—that may ye all hear. *how*
Was I never a shephard, but now will I lear.° *learn*
If the flock be scar'd, yet shall I nip near.
How! Draws hitherward! Now mends our cheer
From sorrow.
A fat sheep, I dare say!
A good fleece, dare I lay!° *bet*
Eft-quit° when I may, *repay*
But this will I borrow.
[*Exit with sheep.*]

[MAK'S *house.* MAK *speaks outside the door.*]

MAK. How, Gill, art thou in? Get us some light.
GILL. [*within*] Who makes such a din this time of the night?
I am set for to spin; I hope not I might[1]
Rise a penny to win—I shrew° them on height! *curse*
So fares
A housewife that has been
To be raised thus between:[2]
Here may no note° be seen *completed work*
For such small chares.° *chores*

MAK. Good wife, open the heck!° Sees thou not what I bring? *door*
GILL. I may thole thee draw the sneck.[3] Ah, come in, my sweeting.
MAK. Yea, thou thar not reck of[4] my long standing.
[*She opens the door.*]
GILL. By the naked neck art thou like for to hing.° *hang*
MAK. Do way!
I am worthy° my meat, *worthy of*
For in a strait° can I get *pinch*
More than they that swink° and sweat *work*
All the long day.

Thus it fell to my lot, Gill, I had such grace.
GILL. It were a foul blot to be hanged for the case.
MAK. I have 'scaped,° Jelot,[5] oft as hard a glase.° *escaped / blow*
GILL. But "So long goes the pot to the water," men says,
"At last
Comes it home broken."
MAK. Well know I the token,
But let it never be spoken!
But come and help fast.

9. If it is to be all right.
1. I don't think I could.
2. This is what happens to anyone who's been a housewife—to be got up all the time.
3. I may let you draw the latch.
4. You need not care about.
5. I.e., Gill.

I would he were flain,° I list° well eat: *skinned / wish*
This twelvemonth was I not so fain of one sheep-meat.
GILL. Come they ere he be slain, and hear the sheep bleat—
MAK. Then might I be taen°—that were a cold sweat! *taken*
Go spar° *fasten*
The gate° door. *street*
GILL. Yes, Mak,
For and° they come at thy back— *if*
MAK. Then might I buy,° for all the pack, *have to pay*
The devil of the war.° *worse*

GILL. A good bourd have I spied, sin thou can none:[6]
Here shall we him hide, to° they be gone, *until*
In my cradle. Abide, let me alone,
And I shall lie beside in childbed and groan.
MAK. Thou red,° *get ready*
And I shall say thou was light° *delivered*
Of a knave-child° this night. *boy child*
GILL. Now well is me day bright
That ever was I bred.[7]

This is a good guise° and a fair cast:° *method / trick*
Yet a woman's advise helps at the last.
I wot° never who spies: again go thou fast. *know*
MAK. But° I come ere they rise, else blows a cold blast. *unless*
I will go sleep.
Yet sleeps all this meny,° *company*
And I shall go stalk privily,
As it had never been I
That carried their sheep.

[*The moor. The shepherds are waking.*]

COLL. *Resurrex a mortruus!*[8] Have hold my hand!
Judas carnas dominus![9] I may not well stand.
My foot sleeps, by Jesus, and I walter°
fastand.° *lie / fasting*
I thought that we laid us full near England.
GIB. Ah, yea?
Lord, what° I have slept weel!° *how / well*
As fresh as an eel,
As light I me feel
As leaf on a tree.

DAW. Benste° be herein! So my body quakes, *blessing*
My heart is out of skin, what-so° it
makes.° *whatever / causes*

6. A good trick have I found, since you know none.
7. Now it was a good day that I was born.
8. An illiterate oath referring, apparently, to Christ's Resurrection from the dead.
9. Judas, (in?)carnate lord.

Who makes all this din? So my brows blakes,[1]
To the door will I win. Hark, fellows, wakes!
We were four:
See ye awhere of Mak now?
COLL. We were up ere thou.
GIB. Man, I give God avow
Yet yede he naw're.[2]

DAW. Methought he was lapped° in a wolfskin. *covered*
COLL. So are many happed° now, namely°
within. *clad / especially*
DAW. When we had long napped, methought with a gin° *snare*
A fat sheep he trapped, but he made no din.
GIB. Be still:
Thy dream makes thee wood.° *mad*
It is but phantom, by the rood.° *cross*
COLL. Now God turn all to good,
If it be his will.

GIB. Rise, Mak, for shame! Thou lies right lang.° *long*
MAK. Now Christ's holy name be us amang!° *among*
What is this? For Saint Jame, I may not well gang.° *walk*
I trow° I be the same. Ah, my neck has lain
wrang.° *think / wrong*
[*One of them twists his neck.*]
Enough!
Mickle thank! Sin yestereven
Now, by Saint Strephen,[3]
I was flayed with a sweven[4]—
My heart out of slough.° *skin*

I thought Gill began to croak and travail full sad,° *hard*
Well-near at the first cock, of a young lad,
For to mend° our flock—then be I never glad: *increase*
I have tow on my rock[5] more than ever I had.
Ah, my head!
A house full of young tharms!° *guts*
The devil knock out their harns!° *brains*
Woe is him has many barns,° *children*
And thereto little bread.

I must go home, by your leave, to Gill, as I thought.
I pray you look° my sleeve, that I steal nought. *examine*
I am loath you to grieve or from you take aught.
DAW. Go forth! Ill might thou chieve!° Now would I we
sought[6] *prosper*
This morn

1. The meaning is probably "my eyes are dim." Daw's head may be under a blanket.
2. He's gone nowhere yet.
3. Probably St. Stephen.
4. I was terrified by a dream.
5. Flax on my distaff (i.e., trouble).
6. I want us to seek.

That we had all our store.
COLL. But I will go before.
Let us meet.
GIB. Whore?° *where*
DAW. At the crooked thorn.

[MAK'S *house.* MAK *at the door.*]

MAK. Undo this door! Who is here? How long shall I stand?
GILL. Who makes such a bere?° Now walk in the weniand![7] *clamor*
MAK. Ah, Gill, what cheer? It is I, Mak, your husband.
GILL. Then may we see here the devil in a band,[8]
Sir Guile!
Lo, he comes with a lote° *noise*
As he were holden in the throat:
I may not sit at my note° *work*
A hand-long° while. *short*

MAK. Will ye here what fare[9] she makes to get her a glose?
And does nought but lakes° and claws her toes? *plays*
GILL. Why, who wanders? Who wakes? Who comes? Who goes?
Who brews? Who bakes? What makes me thus hose?° *hoarse*
And than° *then*
It is ruth° to behold, *pity*
Now in hot, now in cold,
Full woeful is the household
That wants° a woman. *lacks*

But what end has thou made with the herds,° Mak? *shepherds*
MAK. The last word that they said when I turned my back,
They would look that they had their sheep all the pack.
I hope[1] they will not be well paid when they their sheep lack.
Pardie!° *by God*
But how-so the game goes,
To me they will suppose,° *suspect*
And make a foul nose,° *noise*
And cry out upon me.

But thou must do as thou hight.° *promised*
GILL. I accord me theretill.[2]
I shall swaddle him right in my cradill.
If it were a greater sleight, yet could I help till.[3]

7. Waning of the moon (an unlucky time).
8. On a leash.
9. Fuss; "glose": excuse.
1. Expect; "paid": pleased.
2. I agree to it.
3. I.e., with it.

I will lie down straight.° Come, hap°
me. *straightway / cover*
MAK. I will.
GILL. Behind
Come Coll and his marrow;° *mate*
They will nip us full narrow.
MAK. But I may cry "Out, harrow,"° *help*
The sheep if they find.

GILL. Hearken ay when they call—they will come anon.
Come and make ready all, and sing by thine one.° *self*
Sing "lullay"° thou shall, for I must groan, *lullaby*
And cry out by the wall on Mary and John
For sore.° *pain*
Sing "lullay" on fast
When thou hears at the last,
And but I play a false cast,[4]
Trust me no more.

[*The moor.*]

DAW. Ah, Coll, good morn. Why sleeps thou not?
COLL. Alas that ever I was born! We have a foul blot:
A fat wether° have we lorn.° *ram / lost*
DAW. Marry, God's forbot![5]
GIB. Who should do us that scorn? That were a foul spot!
COLL. Some shrew.° *rascal*
I have sought with my dogs
All Horbury shrogs,° *thickets*
And of fifteen hogs
Found I but one ewe.[6]

DAW. Now trow me,° if ye will, by Saint Thomas of
Kent, *believe*
Either Mak or Gill was at that assent.° *conspiracy*
COLL. Peace, man, be still! I saw when he went.
Thou slanders him ill, thou ought to repent
Good speed.
GIB. Now as ever might I thee,° *thrive*
If I should even here dee,° *die*
I would say it were he
That did that same deed.

DAW. Go we thither, I read,° and run on our feet. *advise*
Shall I never eat bread the sooth to I weet.[7]
COLL. Nor drink in my head, with him till I meet.

4. Unless I play a false trick.
5. God forbid.
6. And with fifteen young sheep I found only a ewe (i.e., the wether was missing).
7. Until I know the truth.

GIB. I will rest in no stead° till that I him greet, *place*
My brother.
One I will hight:[8]
Till I see him in sight
Shall I never sleep one night
There° I do another. *where*

[MAK's *house.* MAK *and* GILL *within, she in bed groaning, he singing a lullaby; the shepherds enter outside the door.*]

DAW. Will ye hear how they hack?[9] Our sire list croon.
COLL. Heard I never none crack° so clear out of tune. *song*
Call on him.
GIB. Mak, undo your door soon!° *at once*
MAK. Who is that spake, as° it were noon, *as if*
On loft?[1]
Who is that, I say?
DAW. Good fellows, were it day.[2]
MAK. As far as ye may,
[*opening*] Good,° speaks soft *good men*

Over a sick woman's head, that is at malease.[3]
I had liefer° be dead ere she had any
disease.° *rather / distress*
GILL. Go to another stead, I may not well wheeze:° *breathe*
Each foot that ye tread goes through my nese.° *nose*
So, hee!° *scat*
COLL. Tell us, Mak, if you may,
How fare ye, I say?
MAK. But are ye in this town today?
Now how fare ye?

Ye have run in the mire and are wet yit.
I shall make you a fire if you will sit.
A nurse would I hire—Think ye one[4] yit?
Well quit is my hire—my dream, this is it
A season.[5]
I have barns,° if ye knew, *children*
Well mo° than enew:° *more / enough*
But we must drink as we brew,
And that is but reason.

I would ye dined ere ye yode.° Methink that ye
sweat. *went*
GIB. Nay, neither mends our mood[6] drink nor meat.
MAK. Why, sir, ails you aught but good?[7]

8. One thing will I promise.
9. Bellow. "List": wants to.
1. Loudly.
2. Good companions, if it were daytime.
3. That feels badly.
4. Can you think of one?
5. Right on time.
6. Appeases our anger.
7. Is there anything wrong with you? "Get": tend.

DAW. Yea, our sheep that we get
Are stolen as they yode:° our loss is great. *walked*
MAK. Sirs, drinks!
Had I been thore° *there*
Some should have bought° it full sore. *paid for*
COLL. Marry, some men trows° that ye wore,° *think / were*
And that us forthinks.° *disturbs*

GIB. Mak, some men trows that it should be ye.
DAW. Either ye or your spouse, so say we.
MAK. Now if you have suspouse° to Gill or to me, *suspicion*
Come and ripe° the house, and then may ye see *search*
Who had her[8]—
If I any sheep fot,° *fetched*
Either cow or stot[9]—
And Gill my wife rose not
Here sin she laid her.

As I am true and leal,° to God here I pray *just*
That this be the first meal that I shall eat this day.
COLL. Mak, as I have sele,[1] advise thee, I say:
[*They begin the search.*]
He learned timely to steal that could not say nay.
GILL. I swelt!° *die*
Out, thieves, from my wones!° *dwelling*
Ye come to rob us for the nones.[2]
MAK. Hear ye not how she groans?
Your hearts should melt.

GILL. Out, thieves, from my barn!° Nigh him not thore![3] *child*
MAK. Wist ye how she had farn,[4] your hearts would be sore.
You do wrong, I you warn, that thus comes before
To a womman that has farn°—but I say no
more. *been in labor*
GILL. Ah, my middill!
I pray to God so mild,
If ever I you beguiled,
That I eat this child
That lies in this cradill.

MAK. Peace, woman, for God's pain, and cry not so!
Thou spills° thy brain and makes me full woe. *spoil*
GIB. I trow our sheep be slain. What find ye two?
DAW. All work we in vain; as well may we go.
But hatters,[5]
I can find no flesh,

8. I.e., the sheep.
9. Either female or male.
1. Happiness; "advise thee": take thought.
2. You come for the purpose of robbing us.
3. Approach him not there.
4. If you knew how she had fared.
5. Except for clothing.

Hard nor nesh,° *soft*
Salt nor fresh,
But two tome° platters. *empty*

Quick cattle[6] but this, tame nor wild,
None, as have I bliss, as loud as he smiled.[7]
[*Approaches the cradle.*]
GILL. No, so God me bliss,° and give me joy of my child! *bless*
COLL. We have marked° amiss—I hold us beguiled. *aimed*
GIB. Sir, don!° *thoroughly*
Sir—Our Lady him save—
Is your child a knave?[8]
MAK. Any lord might him have,
This child, to his son.

When he wakens he kips,° that joy is to see. *kicks*
DAW. In good time to his hips, and in sely.[9]
But who were his gossips,° so soon ready? *godparents*
MAK. So fair fall their lips—
COLL. Hark, now, a lee.° *lie*
MAK. So God them thank,
Perkin, and Gibbon Waller, I say,
And gentle John Horne, in good fay°— *faith*
He made all the garray
With the great shank.[1]

GIB. Mak, friends will we be, for we are all one.° *in accord*
MAK. We? Now I hold for me, for mends get I none.[2]
Farewell all three, all glad[3] were ye gone.
DAW. Fair words may there be, but love is there none
This year.
[*They go out the door.*]
COLL. Gave ye the child anything?
GIB. I trow not one farthing.
DAW. Fast again will I fling.° *dash*
Abide ye me there.

Mak, take it to no grief if I come to thy barn.° *child*
MAK. Nay, thou does me great reprief,[4] and foul has thou farn.
DAW. Thy child it will not grief, that little day-starn° *day star*
Mak, with your leaf,° let me give your barn *leave*
But sixpence.
MAK. Nay, do way, he sleeps.
DAW. Methinks he peeps.° *opens his eyes*
MAK. When he wakens he weeps.
I pray you go hence.

6. Livestock.
7. Smelled as badly as he (the baby).
8. Boy (although Mak takes the word in its alternate meaning of "rascal").
9. Perhaps "that's the best thing for him."
1. He made all the trouble with his long legs (the reference is obscure).
2. Now I'll remain apart, for I get no apology.
3. I.e., I would be glad.
4. Shame; "farn": behaved.

DAW. Give me leave him to kiss, and lift up the clout.[5]
[*Lifts the cover.*]
What the devil is this? He has a long snout.
[*The others re-enter.*]
COLL. He is marked[6] amiss. We wot ill about.
GIB. Ill-spun weft, ywis, ay comes foul out.[7]
Aye, so!
He is like to our sheep.
DAW. How, Gib, may I peep?
COLL. I trow kind will creep
Where it may not go.[8]

GIB. This was quaint gaud and a fair cast.[9]
It was a high fraud.
DAW. Yea, sirs, was't.
Let burn this bawd and bind her fast.
A false scaud° hang at the last: *scold*
So shall thou.
Will you see how they swaddle
His four feet in the middle?
Saw I never in cradle
A horned lad ere now.

MAK. Peace bid I! What, let be your fare!° *fuss*
I am he that him gat,° and yond woman him bare. *begot*
COLL. What devil shall he hat?° Mak? Lo, Gib, Mak's
heir! *be named*
GIB. Let be all that: now God give him care°— *sorrow*
I sawgh.[1]
GILL. A pretty child is he
As sits on a woman's knee,
A dillydown, pardie,
To gar° a man laugh. *make*

DAW. I know him by the earmark—that is a good token.
MAK. I tell you, sirs, hark, his nose was broken.
Sithen° told me a clark that he was
forspoken.° *later / bewitched*
COLL. This is a false wark.° I would fain be
wroken.° *work / avenged*
Get wapen.° *weapon*
GILL. He was taken with° an elf— *by*
I saw it myself—
When the clock struck twelf
He was forshapen.° *transformed*

5. Cover.
6. Fashioned. "We wot ill about": we know mischief has been at work.
7. An ill-spun web, indeed, always comes out badly.
8. I think kinship will creep where it can't walk (i.e., only a parent could love this child).
9. This was a strange trick and a fine dodge.
1. Probably "I saw it."

GIB. Ye two are well feft sam in a stead.[2]
DAW. Sin[3] they maintain their theft, let do them to dead.
MAK. If I trespass eft,° gird° off my head. *again / cut*
With you will I be left.[4]
COLL. Sirs, do my read:° *advice*
For this trespass
We will neither ban° ne flite,° *curse / wrangle*
Fight nor chite,° *chide*
But have done as tite,° *quickly*
And cast him in canvas.
[*They toss* MAK *in a blanket.*]

[*The moor.*]

COLL. Lord, what° I am sore, in point for to brist!° *how / burst*
In faith, I may no more—therefore will I rist.° *rest*
GIB. As a sheep of seven score[5] he weighed in my fist:
For to sleep aywhore° methink that I list.° *anywhere / want*
DAW. Now I pray you
Lie down on this green.
COLL. On these thieves yit I mean.° *think*
DAW. Whereto should ye teen?° *worry*
Do as I say you.

[*An* ANGEL *sings* Gloria in Excelsis *and then speaks.*][6]
ANGEL. Rise, herdmen hend,° for now is he born *gentle*
That shall take fro the fiend that Adam had lorn;[7]
That warlock° to shend,° this night is he
born. *devil / confound*
God is made your friend now at this morn
He behests.° *promises*
At Bedlem° go see: *Bethlehem*
There lies that free,° *noble one*
In a crib full poorly,
Betwixt two beasts.
[*Exit.*]

COLL. This was a quaint steven[8] that ever yet I hard.° *heard*
It is a marvel to neven° thus to be scar'd.° *tell of / scared*
GIB. Of God's Son of heaven he spake upward.° *on high*
All the wood on a leven methought that he gard
Appear.[9]
DAW. He spake of a barn° *child*
In Bedlem, I you warn.
COLL. That betokens yond starn.[1]
Let us seek him there.

2. I.e., you two birds of a feather properly flock together.
3. Since; "dead": death.
4. I put myself in your mercy.
5. 140 pounds.
6. One of the original stage directions.
7. What Adam had brought to ruin.
8. Fine voice.
9. I thought he made the whole wood seem full of light.
1. That's what yonder star means.

GIB. Say, what was his song? Heard ye not how he cracked it,[2]
Three breves[3] to a long?
DAW. Yea, marry, he hacked it.
Was no crochet° wrong, nor nothing that lacked it.[4] *note*
COLL. For to sing us among, right as he knacked° it, *trilled*
I can.° *know how*
GIB. Let see how ye croon!
Can ye bark at the moon?
DAW. Hold your tongues! Have done!
COLL. Hark after, than!

GIB. To Bedlem he bade that we should gang:° *go*
I am full rad° that we tarry too lang.° *afraid / long*
DAW. Be merry and not sad; of mirth is our sang:
Everlasting glad to meed may we fang.[5]
COLL. Without nose° *noise*
Hie we thither forthy° *therefore*
To that child and that lady;
If° we be wet and weary, *though*
We have it not to lose.[6]

GIB. We find by the prophecy—let be your din!—
Of David and Isay, and mo than I min,[7]
That prophesied by clergy° that in a virgin *learning*
Should he light° and lie, to sloken° our sin *alight / quench*
And slake° it, *relieve*
Our kind,[8] from woe,
For Isay said so:
Ecce virgo
Concipiet[9] a child that is naked.

DAW. Full glad may we be and° we abide that day *if*
That lovely to see, that all mights may.[1]
Lord, well were me for once and for ay
Might I kneel on my knee, some word for to say
To that child.
But the angel said
In a crib was he laid,
He was poorly arrayed,
Both mean° and mild. *lowly*

COLL. Patriarchs that has been, and prophets beforn,
That desired to have seen this child that is born,
They are gone full clean—that have they lorn.[2]
We shall see him, I ween,° ere it be morn, *think*

2. Sang it out.
3. Short notes; "hacked": sang loud.
4. It lacked.
5. Eternal joy as our reward may we receive.
6. We must not neglect it.
7. Of David and Isaiah and more than I remember.
8. I.e., mankind.
9. Behold, a virgin shall conceive (Isaiah vii.14).
1. I.e., when we see that lovely one who is all-powerful.
2. That (sight) have they lost.

To token.[3]
When I see him and feel,
Then wot I full weel[4]
It is true as steel
That prophets have spoken:

To so poor as we are that he would appear,
First find, and declare by his messenger.
GIB. Go we now, let us fare, the place is us near.
DAW. I am ready and yare,° go we in fere[5] *prepared*
To that bright.° *glorious one*
Lord, if thy wills be—
We are lewd° all three— *ignorant*
Thou grant us some kins glee[6]
To comfort thy wight.° *creature*

[A *stable in Bethlehem.*]

COLL. Hail, comely and clean! Hail, young child!
Hail Maker, as I mean, of° a maiden so mild! *born of*
Thou has waried,° I ween, the warlock° so
wild. *put a curse on / devil*
The false guiler of teen,[7] now goes he beguiled.
Lo, he merries!
Lo, he laughs, my sweeting!
A well fair meeting!
I have holden my heting:° *promise*
Have a bob° of cherries. *bunch*

GIB. Hail, sovereign Saviour, for thou has us sought!
Hail freely food[8] and flower, that all thing has wrought!
Hail, full of favor, that made all of nought!
Hail! I kneel and I cower.° A bird have I brought *crouch*
To my barn.° *child*
Hail, little tiny mop!° *baby*
Of our creed thou art crop.° *head*
I would drink on thy cup,
Little day-starn.

DAW. Hail, darling dear, full of Godhead!
I pray thee be near when that I have need.
Hail, sweet is thy cheer°—my heart would bleed *face*
To see thee sit here in so poor weed,° *clothing*
With no pennies.
Hail! Put forth thy dall!° *hand*
I bring thee but a ball:
Have and play thee withal,
And go to the tennis.

3. As a sign.
4. Then know I full well.
5. Together.
6. Some kind of cheer.
7. The false grievous deceiver.
8. Noble child.

MARY. The Father of heaven, God omnipotent,
That set all on seven,[9] his Son has he sent.
My name could he neven, and light ere he went.[1]
I conceived him full even through might as he meant.[2]
And now is he born.
He[3] keep you from woe!
I shall pray him so.
Tell forth as ye go,
And min on[4] this morn.

COLL. Farewell, lady, so fair to behold,
With thy child on thy knee.
GIB. But he lies full cold.
Lord, well is me. Now we go, thou behold.
DAW. Forsooth, already it seems to be told
Full oft.
COLL. What grace we have fun!° *received*
GIB. Come forth, now are we won!° *redeemed*
DAW. To sing are we bun:° *bound*
Let take on loft.[5]
[*They sing.*]

9. Who created everything perfectly.
1. My name did he name, and alighted ere he went.
2. I conceived him through his power, just as he intended.
3. May he.
4. Remember.
5. Let's raise our voices.

EVERYMAN
(after 1485)

Everyman is the best surviving example of that kind of medieval drama which is known as the morality play. Moralities apparently evolved side by side with the mysteries and in England were, like them, acted by trade guilds, though they were composed individually and not in cycles. They too have a primarily religious purpose, though their method of attaining it is different. The mysteries endeavored to make the Christian religion more real to the unlearned by dramatizing significant events in Biblical history and by showing what these events meant in terms of human experience. The moralities, on the other hand, employed allegory to dramatize the moral struggle that Christianity envisions as present in every man: the actors are every man and the qualities within him, good or bad, and the plot consists of his various reactions to these qualities as they push and pull him one way or another—that is, in Christian terms, toward heaven or toward hell. The intent of the morality is more overtly didactic than the mystery, but most of the moralities share with the mysteries a good deal of rough humor. This is perhaps more evident in other plays of the genre than in *Everyman*, where the chief humor lies in the undue haste with which the hero's friends abandon him when he calls on them for help.

Everyman inculcates its austere lesson by the simplicity and directness of its language and of its approach. A fine sense of inevitability is built up as Everyman is stripped, one by one, of those apparent goods on which he had relied. First he is deserted by his patently false friends: his casual companions, his kinsmen, and his wealth. Receiving some comfort from his enfeebled good deeds, he falls back on them and on his other resources—his strength, his beauty, his intelligence, and his knowledge—qualities which, when properly used, help to make an integrated man. These assist him through the crisis in which he must make up his book of accounts, but at the end, when he must go to the grave, all desert him save his good deeds alone. While the play contains rather too much direct sermonizing, it makes most effectively its grim point that man can take with him from this world nothing that he has received, only what he has given.

In *Everyman* allegory appears in its most meticulously worked-out form. Each actor has his allegorical significance defined by his name and behaves entirely within the limits of that definition. The onlooker takes a good deal of intellectual satisfaction in watching the nice operation of the allegorical equations. On the other hand, one might object that allegory, when so neatly handled, sacrifices for a kind of mathematical regularity the suggestiveness that inheres in the far looser allegory of such a work as *Piers Plowman,* which stimulates the imagination more than it satisfies the intellect. Nevertheless, when it is well staged and well acted, *Everyman,* despite its uncompromising didacticism, is a powerful drama.

The play was written near the end of the 15th century. It is probably a translation of a Flemish play, though it is not impossible that the Flemish play is the translation and the English *Everyman* the original.

Everyman[1]

Dramatis Personae

MESSENGER	KNOWLEDGE
GOD	CONFESSION
DEATH	BEAUTY
EVERYMAN	STRENGTH
FELLOWSHIP	DISCRETION
KINDRED	FIVE-WITS
COUSIN	ANGEL
GOODS	DOCTOR
GOOD DEEDS	

HERE BEGINNETH A TREATISE HOW THE HIGH FATHER OF HEAVEN SENDETH DEATH TO SUMMON EVERY CREATURE

1. The text is based upon the earliest printing of the play (no manuscript is known) by John Skot about 1530, as reproduced by W. W. Greg (Louvain, 1904). The spelling has been modernized except where modernization would spoil the rhyme, and modern punctuation has been added. The stage directions have been amplified.

TO COME AND GIVE ACCOUNT OF THEIR LIVES IN THIS WORLD, AND IS IN MANNER OF A MORAL PLAY

[*Enter* MESSENGER.]

MESSENGER. I pray you all give your audience,
And hear this matter with reverence,
By figure[2] a moral play,
The Summoning of Everyman called it is,
That of our lives and ending shows
How transitory we be all day.[3]
The matter is wonder precious,
But the intent of it is more gracious
And sweet to bear away.
The story saith: Man, in the beginning
Look well, and take good heed to the ending,
Be you never so gay.
You think sin in the beginning full sweet,
Which in the end causeth the soul to weep,
When the body lieth in clay.
Here shall you see how fellowship and jollity,
Both stréngth, pleasure, and beauty,
Will fade from thee as flower in May.
For ye shall hear how our Heaven-King
Calleth Everyman to a general reckoning.
Give audience and hear what he doth say.

[*Exit* MESSENGER.—*Enter* GOD.]

GOD. I perceive, here in my majesty,
How that all creatures be to me unkind,° *thoughtless*
Living without dread in worldly prosperity.
Of ghostly° sight the people be so blind, *spiritual*
Drowned in sin, they know me not for their God.
In worldly riches is all their mind:
They fear not of my righteousness the sharp rod;
My law that I showed when I for them died
They forget clean, and shedding of my blood red.
I hanged between two,[4] it cannot be denied:
To get them life I suffered to be dead.
I healed their feet, with thorns hurt was my head.
I could do no more than I did, truly—
And now I see the people do clean forsake me.
They use the seven deadly sins damnable,
As pride, coveitise,° wrath, and lechery[5] *avarice*
Now in the world be made commendable.
And thus they leave of angels the heavenly company.
Every man liveth so after his own pleasure,
And yet of their life they be nothing sure.
I see the more that I them forbear,
The worse they be from year to year:
All that liveth appaireth° fast. *degenerates*

2. In form.
3. Always.
4. I.e., the two thieves between whom Christ was crucified.
5. The other three deadly sins are envy, gluttony, and sloth.

Therefore I will, in all the haste,
Have a reckoning of every man's person.
For, and° I leave the people thus alone *it*
In their life and wicked tempests,
Verily they will become much worse than beasts;
For now one would by envy another up eat.
Charity do they all clean forgeet.
I hoped well that every man
In my glory should make his mansion,
And thereto I had them all elect.° *chosen*
But now I see, like traitors deject,° *abased*
They thank me not for the pleasure that I to° them meant, *for*
Nor yet for their being that I them have lent.
I proffered the people great multitude of mercy,
And few there be that asketh it heartily.° *sincerely*
They be so cumbered° with worldly riches *encumbered*
That needs on them I must do justice—
On every man living without fear.
Where art thou, Death, thou mighty messenger?
[*Enter* DEATH.]

DEATH. Almighty God, I am here at your will,
Your commandment to fulfill.

GOD. Go thou to Everyman,
And show him, in my name,
A pilgrimage he must on him take,
Which he in no wise may escape;
And that he bring with him a sure reckoning
Without delay or any tarrying.

DEATH. Lord, I will in the world go run over all,[6]
And cruelly out-search both great and small.
[*Exit* GOD.]
Everyman will I beset that liveth beastly
Out of God's laws, and dreadeth not folly.
He that loveth riches I will strike with my dart,
His sight to blind, and from heaven to depart°— *separate*
Except that Almsdeeds be his good friend—
In hell for to dwell, world without end
Lo, yonder I see Everyman walking:
Full little he thinketh on my coming;
His mind is on fleshly lusts and his treasure,
And great pain it shall cause him to endure
Before the Lord, Heaven-King.
[*Enter* EVERYMAN.]
Everyman, stand still! Whither art thou going
Thus gaily? Hast thou thy Maker forgeet?° *forgotten*

EVERYMAN. Why askest thou?
Why wouldest thou weet?° *know*

DEATH. Yea, sir, I will show you:
In great haste I am sent to thee

6. Everywhere.

From God out of his majesty.
EVERYMAN. What! sent to me?
DEATH. Yea, certainly.
Though thou have forgot him here,
He thinketh on thee in the heavenly sphere,
As, ere we depart, thou shalt know.
EVERYMAN. What desireth God of me?
DEATH. That shall I show thee:
A reckoning he will needs have
Without any longer respite.
EVERYMAN. To give a reckoning longer leisure I crave.
This blind° matter troubleth my wit. *unexpected*
DEATH. On thee thou must take a long journay:
Therefore thy book of count° with thee thou bring, *accounts*
For turn again thou cannot by no way.
And look thou be sure of thy reckoning,
For before God thou shalt answer and shew
Thy many bad deeds and good but a few—
How thou hast spent thy life and in what wise,
Before the Chief Lord of Paradise.
Have ado that we were in that way,[7]
For weet thou well thou shalt make none attornay.[8]
EVERYMAN. Full unready I am such reckoning to give.
I know thee not. What messenger art thou?
DEATH. I am Death that no man dreadeth,[9]
For every man I 'rest,° and no man spareth; *arrest*
For it is God's commandment
That all to me should be obedient.
EVERYMAN. O Death, thou comest when I had thee least in mind.
In thy power it lieth me to save:
Yet of my good° will I give thee, if thou will be kind, *goods*
Yea, a thousand pound shalt thou have—
And defer this matter till another day.
DEATH. Everyman, it may not be, by no way.
I set nought by[1] gold, silver, nor riches,
Nor by pope, emperor, king, duke, nor princes,
For, and° I would receive gifts great, *if*
All the world I might get.
But my custom is clean contrary:
I give thee no respite. Come hence and not tarry!
EVERYMAN. Alas, shall I have no longer respite?
I may say Death giveth no warning.
To think on thee it maketh my heart sick,
For all unready is my book of reckoning.
But twelve year and I might have a biding,[2]
My counting-book I would make so clear
That my reckoning I should not need to fear.

7. I.e., let's get started at once.
8. I.e., none to appear in your stead.
9. That fears nobody.
1. I care nothing for.
2. If I might have a delay for just twelve years.

Wherefore, Death, I pray thee, for God's mercy,
Spare me till I be provided of remedy.
DEATH. Thee availeth not to cry, weep, and pray;
But haste thee lightly° that thou were gone that
journay, *quickly*
And prove° thy friends, if thou can. *test*
For weet° thou well the tide° abideth no man, *know / time*
And in the world each living creature
For Adam's sin must die of nature.[3]
EVERYMAN. Death, if I should this pilgrimage take
And my reckoning surely make,
Show me, for saint° charity, *holy*
Should I not come again shortly?
DEATH. No, Everyman. And thou be once there,
Thou mayst never more come here,
Trust me verily.
EVERYMAN. O gracious God in the high seat celestial,
Have mercy on me in this most need!
Shall I have no company from this vale terrestrial
Of mine acquaintance that way me to lead?
DEATH. Yea, if any be so hardy
That would go with thee and bear thee company.
Hie° thee that thou were gone to God's magnificence, *hasten*
Thy reckoning to give before his presence.
What, weenest° thou thy life is given thee, *suppose*
And thy worldly goods also?
EVERYMAN. I had weened so, verily.
DEATH. Nay, nay, it was but lent thee.
For as soon as thou art go,
Another a while shall have it and then go therefro,
Even as thou hast done.
Everyman, thou art mad! Thou hast thy wits° five, *senses*
And here on earth will not amend thy live![4]
For suddenly I do come.
EVERYMAN. O wretched caitiff! Whither shall I flee
That I might 'scape this endless sorrow?
Now, gentle Death, spare me till tomorrow,
That I may amend me
With good advisement.° *preparation*
DEATH. Nay, thereto I will not consent,
Nor no man will I respite,
But to the heart suddenly I shall smite,
Without any advisement.
And now out of thy sight I will me hie:
See thou make thee ready shortly,
For thou mayst say this is the day
That no man living may 'scape away.
[*Exit* DEATH.]

3. Naturally.

4. In thy life.

EVERYMAN. Alas, I may well weep with sighs deep:
Now have I no manner of company
To help me in my journey and me to keep.° *guard*
And also my writing[5] is full unready—
How shall I do now for to excuse me?
I would to God I had never be geet![6]
To my soul a full great profit it had be.
For now I fear pains huge and great.
The time passeth: Lord, help, that all wrought!
For though I mourn, it availeth nought.
The day passeth and is almost ago:° *gone by*
I wot° not well what for to do. *know*
To whom were I best my complaint to make?
What and I to Fellowship thereof spake,
And showed him of this sudden chance?
For in him is all mine affiance,° *trust*
We have in the world so many a day
Be good friends in sport and play.
I see him yonder, certainly.
I trust that he will bear me company.
Therefore to him will I speak to ease my sorrow.
[*Enter* FELLOWSHIP.]
Well met, good Fellowship, and good morrow!
FELLOWSHIP. Everyman, good morrow, by this day!
Sir, why lookest thou so piteously?
If anything be amiss, I pray thee me say,
That I may help to remedy.
EVERYMAN. Yea, good Fellowship, yea:
I am in great jeopardy.
FELLOWSHIP. My true friend, show to me your mind.
I will not forsake thee to my life's end
In the way of good company.
EVERYMAN. That was well spoken, and lovingly!
FELLOWSHIP. Sir, I must needs know your heaviness.° *sorrow*
I have pity to see you in any distress.
If any have you wronged, ye shall revenged be,
Though I on the ground be slain for thee,
Though that I know before that I should die.
EVERYMAN. Verily, Fellowship, gramercy.° *many thanks*
FELLOWSHIP. Tush! by thy thanks I set not a stree.° *straw*
Show me your grief and say no more.
EVERYMAN. If I my heart should to you break,° *disclose*
And then you to turn your mind fro me,
And would not me comfort when ye hear me speak,
Then should I ten times sorrier be.
FELLOWSHIP. Sir, I say as I will do, indeed.
EVERYMAN. Then be you a good friend at need.
I have found you true herebefore.

5. I.e., ledger.

6. Been begotten.

FELLOWSHIP. And so ye shall evermore.
For, in faith, and thou go to hell,
I will not forsake thee by the way.
EVERYMAN. Ye speak like a good friend. I believe you well.
I shall deserve° it, and° I may. *repay / if*
FELLOWSHIP. I speak of no deserving, by this day!
For he that will say and nothing do
Is not worthy with good company to go.
Therefore show me the grief of your mind,
As to your friend most loving and kind.
EVERYMAN. I shall show you how it is:
Commanded I am to go a journay,
A long way, hard and dangerous,
And give a strait° count,° without delay, *strict / accounting*
Before the high judge Adonai.[7]
Wherefore I pray you bear me company,
As ye have promised, in this journay.
FELLOWSHIP. This is matter indeed! Promise is duty—
But, and I should take such a voyage on me,
I know it well, it should be to my pain.
Also it maketh me afeard, certain.
But let us take counsel here, as well as we can—
For your words would fear° a strong man. *frighten*
EVERYMAN. Why, ye said if I had need,
Ye would me never forsake, quick ne dead,
Though it were to hell, truly.
FELLOWSHIP. So I said, certainly.
But such pleasures° be set aside, the sooth to say. *jokes*
And also, if we took such a journay,
When should we again come?
EVERYMAN. Nay, never again, till the day of doom.
FELLOWSHIP. In faith, then will not I come there!
Who hath you these tidings brought?
EVERYMAN. Indeed, Death was with me here.
FELLOWSHIP. Now by God that all hath bought,° *redeemed*
If Death were the messenger,
For no man that is living today
I will not go that loath° journay— *loathsome*
Not for the father that begat me!
EVERYMAN. Ye promised otherwise, pardie.° *by God*
FELLOWSHIP. I wot well I said so, truly.
And yet, if thou wilt eat and drink and make good cheer,
Or haunt to women the lusty company,[8]
I would not forsake you while the day is clear,
Trust me verily!
EVERYMAN. Yea, thereto ye would be ready—
To go to mirth, solace,° and play: *pleasure*

7. I.e., God.
8. Or frequent the lusty company of women.

Your mind to folly will sooner apply° *attend*
Than to bear me company in my long journay.
FELLOWSHIP. Now in good faith, I will not that way.
But, and thou will murder or any man kill,
In that I will help thee with a good will.
EVERYMAN. O that is simple° advice, indeed! *foolish*
Gentle fellow, help me in my necessity:
We have loved long, and now I need—
And now, gentle Fellowship, remember me!
FELLOWSHIP. Whether ye have loved me or no,
By Saint John, I will not with thee go!
EVERYMAN. Yet I pray thee take the labor and do so much for me,
To bring me forward,[9] for saint charity,
And comfort me till I come without the town.
FELLOWSHIP. Nay, and thou would give me a new gown,
I will not a foot with thee go.
But, and thou had tarried, I would not have left thee so.
And as now, God speed thee in thy journay!
For from thee I will depart as fast as I may.
EVERYMAN. Whither away, Fellowship? Will thou forsake me?
FELLOWSHIP. Yea, by my fay!° To God I betake° thee. *faith / commend*
EVERYMAN. Farewell, good Fellowship! For thee my heart is sore.
Adieu forever—I shall see thee no more.
FELLOWSHIP. In faith, Everyman, farewell now at the ending:
For you I will remember that parting is mourning.
[*Exit* FELLOWSHIP.]
EVERYMAN. Alack, shall we thus depart° indeed— *part*
Ah, Lady, help!—without any more comfort?
Lo, Fellowship forsaketh me in my most need!
For help in this world whither shall I resort?
Fellowship herebefore with me would merry make,
And now little sorrow for me doth he take.
It is said, "In prosperity men friends may find
Which in adversity be full unkind."
Now whither for succor shall I flee,
Sith° that Fellowship hath forsaken me? *since*
To my kinsmen I will, truly,
Praying them to help me in my necessity.
I believe that they will do so,
For kind will creep where it may not go.[1]
I will go 'say°—for yonder I see them— *assay*
Where° be ye now my friends and kinsmen. *whether*
[*Enter* KINDRED *and* COUSIN.]
KINDRED. Here be we now at your commandment:

9. Escort me.
1. For kinship will creep where it cannot walk (i.e., kinsmen will suffer hardship for one another).

Cousin, I pray you show us your intent
In any wise, and not spare.
COUSIN. Yea, Everyman, and to us declare
If ye be disposed to go anywhither.
For, weet° you well, we will live and die togither. *know*
KINDRED. In wealth and woe we will with you hold,
For over his kin a man may be bold.[2]
EVERYMAN. Gramercy,° my friends and kinsmen
kind. *much thanks*
Now shall I show you the grief of my mind.
I was commanded by a messenger
That is a high king's chief officer:
He bade me go a pilgrimage, to my pain—
And I know well I shall never come again.
Also I must give a reckoning strait,° *strict*
For I have a great enemy that hath me in wait,[3]
Which intendeth me to hinder.
KINDRED. What account is that which ye must render?
That would I know.
EVERYMAN. Of all my works I must show
How I have lived and my days spent;
Also of ill deeds that I have used
In my time sith life was me lent,
And of all virtues that I have refused.
Therefore I pray you go thither with me
To help me make mine account, for saint charity.
COUSIN. What, to go thither? Is that the matter?
Nay, Everyman, I had liefer fast[4] bread and water
All this five year and more!
EVERYMAN. Alas, that ever I was bore!° *born*
For now shall I never be merry
If that you forsake me.
KINDRED. Ah, sir, what? Ye be a merry man:
Take good heart to you and make no moan.
But one thing I warn you, by Saint Anne,
As for me, ye shall go alone.
EVERYMAN. My Cousin, will you not with me go?
COUSIN. No, by Our Lady! I have the cramp in my toe:
Trust not to me. For, so God me speed,
I will deceive you in your most need.
KINDRED. It availeth you not us to 'tice.° *entice*
Ye shall have my maid with all my heart:
She loveth to go to feasts, there to be nice,° *wanton*
And to dance, and abroad to start.[5]
I will give her leave to help you in that journey,
If that you and she may agree.

2. I.e., for a man may make demands of his kinsmen.
3. I.e., Satan lies in ambush for me.
4. I.e., rather fast on.
5. To go gadding about.

EVERYMAN. Now show me the very effect° of your mind: *bent*
Will you go with me or abide behind?
KINDRED. Abide behind? Yea, that will I and I may!
Therefore farewell till another day.
[*Exit* KINDRED.]
EVERYMAN. How should I be merry or glad?
For fair promises men to me make,
But when I have most need they me forsake.
I am deceived. That maketh me sad.
COUSIN. Cousin Everyman, farewell now,
For verily I will not go with you;
Also of mine own an unready reckoning
I have to account—therefore I make tarrying.
Now God keep thee, for now I go.
[*Exit* COUSIN.]
EVERYMAN. Ah, Jesus, is all come hereto?° *to this*
Lo, fair words maketh fools fain:° *glad*
They promise and nothing will do, certain.
My kinsmen promised me faithfully
For to abide with me steadfastly,
And now fast away do they flee.
Even so Fellowship promised me.
What friend were best me of to provide?
I lose my time here longer to abide.
Yet in my mind a thing there is:
All my life I have loved riches;
If that my Good° now help me might, *Goods*
He would make my heart full light.
I will speak to him in this distress.
Where art thou, my Goods and riches?
GOODS. [*within*] Who calleth me? Everyman? What, hast thou haste?
I lie here in corners, trussed and piled so high,
And in chests I am locked so fast—
Also sacked in bags—thou mayst see with thine eye
I cannot stir, in packs low where I lie.
What would ye have? Lightly° me say. *quickly*
EVERYMAN. Come hither, Good, in all the haste thou may,
For of counsel I must desire thee.
[*Enter* GOODS.]
GOODS. Sir, and° ye in the world have sorrow or adversity, *if*
That can I help you to remedy shortly.
EVERYMAN. It is another disease° that grieveth me: *distress*
In this world it is not, I tell thee so.
I am sent for another way to go,
To give a strait count general
Before the highest Jupiter[6] of all.
And all my life I have had joy and pleasure in thee:

6. I.e., God.

Therefore I pray thee go with me,
For, peradventure, thou mayst before God Almighty
My reckoning help to clean and purify.
For it is said ever among[7]
That money maketh all right that is wrong.
GOODS. Nay, Everyman, I sing another song:
I follow no man in such voyages.
For, and I went with thee,
Thou shouldest fare much the worse for me;
For because on me thou did set thy mind,
Thy reckoning I have made blotted and blind,° *illegible*
That thine account thou cannot make truly—
And that hast thou for the love of me.
EVERYMAN. That would grieve me full sore,
When I should come to that fearful answer.
Up, let us go thither together.
GOODS. Nay, not so, I am too brittle, I may not endure.
I will follow no man one foot, be ye sure.
EVERYMAN. Alas, I have thee loved and had great pleasure
All my life-days on good and treasure.
GOODS. That is to thy damnation, without leasing,° *lie*
For my love is contrary to the love everlasting.
But if thou had me loved moderately during,° *in the meanwhile*
As to the poor to give part of me,
Then shouldest thou not in this dolor be,
Nor in this great sorrow and care.
EVERYMAN. Lo, now was I deceived ere I was ware,
And all I may wite° misspending of time. *blame on*
GOODS. What, weenest° thou that I am thine? *suppose*
EVERYMAN. I had weened so.
GOODS. Nay, Everyman, I say no.
As for a while I was lent thee;
A season thou hast had me in prosperity.
My condition° is man's soul to kill; *disposition*
If I save one, a thousand I do spill.° *ruin*
Weenest thou that I will follow thee?
Nay, from this world, not verily.
EVERYMAN. I had weened otherwise.
GOODS. Therefore to thy soul Good is a thief;
For when thou art dead, this is my guise°— *custom*
Another to deceive in the same wise
As I have done thee, and all to his soul's repreef.° *shame*
EVERYMAN. O false Good, cursed thou be,
Thou traitor to God, that hast deceived me
And caught me in thy snare!
GOODS. Marry, thou brought thyself in care,° *sorrow*
Whereof I am glad:

7. Now and then.

I must needs laugh, I cannot be sad.
EVERYMAN. Ah, Good, thou hast had long my heartly° love; *sincere*
I gave thee that which should be the Lord's above.
But wilt thou not go with me, indeed?
I pray thee truth to say.
GOODS. No, so God me speed!
Therefore farewell and have good day.
[*Exit* GOODS.]
EVERYMAN. Oh, to whom shall I make my moan
For to go with me in that heavy° journay? *sorrowful*
First Fellowship said he would with me gone:° *go*
His words were very pleasant and gay,
But afterward he left me alone.
Then spake I to my kinsmen, all in despair,
And also they gave me words fair—
They lacked no fair speaking,
But all forsake me in the ending.
Then went I to my Goods that I loved best,
In hope to have comfort; but there had I least,
For my Goods sharply did me tell
That he bringeth many into hell.
Then of myself I was ashamed,
And so I am worthy to be blamed:
Thus may I well myself hate.
Of whom shall I now counsel take?
I think that I shall never speed
Till that I go to my Good Deed.
But alas, she is so weak
That she can neither go° nor speak. *walk*
Yet will I venture° on her now. *gamble*
My Good Deeds, where be you?
GOOD DEEDS. [*speaking from the ground*] Here I lie, cold in the ground:
Thy sins hath me sore bound
That I cannot stear.° *stir*
EVERYMAN. O Good Deeds, I stand in fear:
I must you pray of counsel,
For help now should come right well.
GOOD DEEDS. Everyman, I have understanding
That ye be summoned, account to make,
Before Messiah of Jer'salem King.
And you do by me,[8] that journey with you will I take.
EVERYMAN. Therefore I come to you my moan to make.
I pray you that ye will go with me.
GOOD DEEDS. I would full fain, but I cannot stand, verily.
EVERYMAN. Why, is there anything on you fall?° *fallen*
GOOD DEEDS. Yea, sir, I may thank you of all:

8. I.e., if you do what I say.

If ye had perfectly cheered me,
Your book of count full ready had be.
[GOOD DEEDS *shows him the account book.*]
Look, the books of your works and deeds eke,° *also*
As how they lie under the feet,
To your soul's heaviness.° *distress*
EVERYMAN. Our Lord Jesus help me!
For one letter here I cannot see.
GOOD DEEDS. There is a blind° reckoning in time of distress! *illegible*
EVERYMAN. Good Deeds, I pray you help me in this need,
Or else I am forever damned indeed.
Therefore help me to make reckoning
Before the Redeemer of all thing
That King is and was and ever shall.
GOOD DEEDS. Everyman, I am sorry of° your fall *for*
And fain would help you and I were able.
EVERYMAN. Good Deeds, your counsel I pray you give me.
GOOD DEEDS. That shall I do verily,
Though that on my feet I may not go;
I have a sister that shall with you also,
Called Knowledge, which shall with you abide
To help you to make that dreadful reckoning.
[*Enter* KNOWLEDGE.]
KNOWLEDGE. Everyman, I will go with thee and be thy guide,
In thy most need to go by thy side.
EVERYMAN. In good condition I am now in everything,
And am whole content with this good thing,
Thanked be God my Creator.
GOOD DEEDS. And when she hath brought you there
Where thou shalt heal thee of thy smart,° *pain*
Then go you with your reckoning and your Good Deeds together
For to make you joyful at heart
Before the blessed Trinity.
EVERYMAN. My Good Deeds, gramercy!
I am well content, certainly,
With your words sweet.
KNOWLEDGE. Now go we together lovingly
To Confession, that cleansing river.
EVERYMAN. For joy I weep—I would we were there!
But I pray you give me cognition,° *knowledge*
Where dwelleth that holy man Confession?
KNOWLEDGE. In the House of Salvation:
We shall find him in that place
That shall us comfort, by God's grace.
[KNOWLEDGE *leads* EVERYMAN *to* CONFESSION.]
Lo, this is Confession: kneel down and ask mercy,
For he is in good conceit° with God Almighty. *esteem*

EVERYMAN. [*kneeling*] O glorious fountain that all uncleanness
doth clarify,[9]
Wash from me the spots of vice unclean,
That on me no sin may be seen.
I come with Knowledge for my redemption,
Redempt° with heart and full contrition, *redeemed*
For I am commanded a pilgrimage to take
And great accounts before God to make.
Now I pray you, Shrift, mother of Salvation,
Help my Good Deeds for my piteous exclamation.
CONFESSION. I know your sorrow well, Everyman:
Because with Knowledge ye come to me,
I will you comfort as well as I can,
And a precious jewel I will give thee,
Called Penance, voider° of adversity. *expeller*
Therewith shall your body chastised be—
With abstinence and perseverance in God's service.
Here shall you receive that scourge of me,
Which is penance strong° that ye must endure, *harsh*
To remember thy Saviour was scourged for thee
With sharp scourges, and suffered it patiently.
So must thou ere thou 'scape that painful pilgrimage.
Knowledge, keep° him in this voyage, *guard*
And by that time Good Deeds will be with thee.
But in any wise be secure° of mercy— *certain*
For your time draweth fast—and ye will saved be.
Ask God mercy and he will grant, truly.
When with the scourge of penance man doth him°
bind, *himself*
The oil of forgiveness then shall he find.
EVERYMAN. Thanked be God for his gracious work,
For now I will my penance begin.
This hath rejoiced and lighted my heart,
Though the knots[1] be painful and hard within.
KNOWLEDGE. Everyman, look your penance that ye fulfill,
What pain that ever it to you be;
And Knowledge shall give you counsel at will
How your account ye shall make clearly.
EVERYMAN. O eternal God, O heavenly figure,
O way of righteousness, O goodly vision,
Which descended down in a virgin pure
Because he would every man redeem,
Which Adam forfeited by his disobedience;
O blessed Godhead, elect and high Divine,° *divinity*
Forgive my grievous offense!
Here I cry thee mercy in this presence:
O ghostly Treasure, O Ransomer and Redeemer,

9. Purify.
1. I.e., the knots on the scourge (whip) of penance. "Within": i.e., to my senses.

Of all the world Hope and Conduiter,° *guide*
Mirror of joy, Foundator° of mercy, *Founder*
Which enlumineth° heaven and earth thereby, *lights up*
Hear my clamorous complaint, though it late be;
Receive my prayers, of thy benignity.
Though I be a sinner most abominable,
Yet let my name be written in Moses' table.[2]
O Mary, pray to the Maker of all thing
Me for to help at my ending,
And save me from the power of my enemy,
For Death assaileth me strongly.
And Lady, that I may by mean of thy prayer
Of your Son's glory to be partner—
By the means of his passion I it crave.
I beseech you help my soul to save.
Knowledge, give me the scourge of penance:
My flesh therewith shall give acquittance.° *satisfaction for sins*
I will now begin, if God give me grace.

KNOWLEDGE. Everyman, God give you time and
space!° *opportunity*
Thus I bequeath you in the hands of our Saviour:
Now may you make your reckoning sure.

EVERYMAN. In the name of the Holy Trinity
My body sore punished shall be:
Take this, body, for the sin of the flesh!
Also° thou delightest to go gay and fresh, *as*
And in the way of damnation thou did me bring,
Therefore suffer now strokes of punishing!
Now of penance I will wade the water clear,
To save me from purgatory, that sharp fire.

GOOD DEEDS. I thank God, now can I walk and go,
And am delivered of my sickness and woe.
Therefore with Everyman I will go, and not spare:
His good works I will help him to declare.

KNOWLEDGE. Now, Everyman, be merry and glad:
Your Good Deeds cometh now, ye may not be sad.
Now is your Good Deeds whole and sound,
Going° upright upon the ground. *walking*

EVERYMAN. My heart is light, and shall be evermore.
Now will I smite faster than I did before.

GOOD DEEDS. Everyman, pilgrim, my special friend,
Blessed be thou without end!
For thee is preparate° the eternal glory. *prepared*
Ye have me made whole and sound·
Therefore I will bide by thee in every stound.° *trial*

EVERYMAN. Welcome, my Good Deeds! Now I hear thy voice,
I weep for very sweetness of love.

2. "Moses' table" is here the tablet on which are recorded those who have been baptized and have done penance.

KNOWLEDGE. Be no more sad, but ever rejoice:
God seeth thy living in his throne above.
Put on this garment to thy behove,° *advantage*
Which is wet with your tears—
Or else before God you may it miss
When ye to your journey's end come shall.
EVERYMAN. Gentle Knowledge, what do ye it call?
KNOWLEDGE. It is a garment of sorrow;
From pain it will you borrow:° *redeem*
Contrition it is
That getteth forgiveness;
It pleaseth God passing° well. *surpassingly*
GOOD DEEDS. Everyman, will you wear it for your heal?° *welfare*
EVERYMAN. Now blessed be Jesu, Mary's son,
For now have I on true contrition.
And let us go now without tarrying.
Good Deeds, have we clear our reckoning?
GOOD DEEDS. Yea, indeed, I have it here.
EVERYMAN. Then I trust we need not fear.
Now friends, let us not part in twain.
KNOWLEDGE. Nay, Everyman, that will we not, certain.
GOOD DEEDS. Yet must thou lead with thee
Three persons of great might.
EVERYMAN. Who should they be?
GOOD DEEDS. Discretion and Strength they hight,° *are called*
And thy Beauty may not abide behind.
KNOWLEDGE. Also ye must call to mind
Your Five-Wits° as for your counselors. *senses*
GOOD DEEDS. You must have them ready at all hours.
EVERYMAN. How shall I get them hither?
KNOWLEDGE. You must call them all togither,
And they will be here incontinent.° *at once*
EVERYMAN. My friends, come hither and be present,
Discretion, Strength, my Five-Wits, and Beauty!
[*They enter.*]
BEAUTY. Here at your will we be all ready.
What will ye that we should do?
GOOD DEEDS. That ye would with Everyman go
And help him in his pilgrimage.
Advise you:[3] will ye with him or not in that voyage?
STRENGTH. We will bring him all thither,
To his help and comfort, ye may believe me.
DISCRETION. So will we go with him all togither.
EVERYMAN. Almighty God, loved° might thou be! *praised*
I give thee laud that I have hither brought
Strength, Discretion, Beauty, and Five-Wits—lack I nought—
And my Good Deeds, with Knowledge clear,

3. Take thought.

All be in my company at my will here:
I desire no more to my business.

STRENGTH. And I, Strength, will by you stand in distress,
Though thou would in battle fight on the ground.

FIVE-WITS. And though it were through the world round,
We will not depart for sweet ne sour.

BEAUTY. No more will I, until death's hour,
Whatsoever thereof befall.

DISCRETION. Everyman, advise you first of all:
Go with a good advisement° and deliberation. *preparation*
We all give you virtuous° monition° *confident / prediction*
That all shall be well.

EVERYMAN. My friends, hearken what I will tell;
I pray God reward you in his heaven-sphere;
Now hearken all that be here,
For I will make my testament,
Here before you all present:
In alms half my good° I will give with my hands twain, *goods*
In the way of charity with good intent;
And the other half, still[4] shall remain,
I 'queath° to be returned there it ought to be. *bequeath*
This I do in despite of the fiend of hell,
To go quit out of his perel,[5]
Ever after and this day.

KNOWLEDGE. Everyman, hearken what I say:
Go to Priesthood, I you advise,
And receive of him, in any wise,[6]
The holy sacrament and ointment° togither; *extreme unction*
Then shortly see ye turn again hither:
We will all abide you here.

FIVE-WITS. Yea, Everyman, hie you that ye ready were.
There is no emperor, king, duke, ne baron,
That of God hath commission
As hath the least priest in the world being:
For of the blessed sacraments pure and bening° *benign*
He beareth the keys, and thereof hath the cure° *care*
For man's redemption—it is ever sure—
Which God for our souls' medicine
Gave us out of his heart with great pine,° *torment*
Here in this transitory life for thee and me.
The blessed sacraments seven there be:
Baptism, confirmation, with priesthood° good, *ordination*
And the sacrament of God's precious flesh and blood,
Marriage, the holy extreme unction, and penance:
These seven be good to have in remembrance,
Gracious sacraments of high divinity.

EVERYMAN. Fain° would I receive that holy body, *gladly*

4. I.e., which still.
5. In order to go free of danger from him.
6. At all costs.

And meekly to my ghostly° father I will go. *spiritual*
FIVE-WITS. Everyman, that is the best that ye can do:
God will you to salvation bring.
For priesthood exceedeth all other thing:
To us Holy Scripture they do teach,
And converteth man from sin, heaven to reach;
God hath to them more power given
Than to any angel that is in heaven.
With five words[7] he may consecrate
God's body in flesh and blood to make,
And handleth his Maker between his hands.
The priest bindeth and unbindeth all bands,[8]
Both in earth and in heaven.
Thou ministers° all the sacraments seven; *administer*
Though we kiss thy feet, thou were worthy;
Thou art surgeon that cureth sin deadly;
No remedy we find under God
But all only priesthood.[9]
Everyman, God gave priests that dignity
And setteth them in his stead among us to be.
Thus be they above angels in degree.
[*Exit* EVERYMAN.]
KNOWLEDGE. If priests be good, it is so, surely.
But when Jesu hanged on the cross with great smart,° *pain*
There he gave out of his blessed heart
The same sacrament in great torment,
He sold them not to us, that Lord omnipotent:
Therefore Saint Peter the Apostle doth say
That Jesu's curse hath all they
Which God their Saviour do buy or sell,[1]
Or they for any money do take or tell.[2]
Sinful priests giveth the sinners example bad:
Their children sitteth by other men's fires, I have heard;
And some haunteth women's company
With unclean life, as lusts of lechery.
These be with sin made blind.
FIVE-WITS. I trust to God no such may we find.
Therefore let us priesthood honor,
And follow their doctrine for our souls' succor.
We be their sheep and they shepherds be
By whom we all be kept in surety.
Peace, for yonder I see Everyman come,
Which hath made true satisfaction.

7. The five words ("For this is my body") spoken by the priest when he offers the wafer at communion.
8. A reference to the power of the keys, inherited by the priesthood from St. Peter, who received it from Christ (Matthew xvi.19) with the promise that whatever St. Peter bound or loosed on earth would be bound or loosed in heaven.
9. Except from priesthood alone.
1. To give or receive money for the sacraments is simony, named after Simon, who wished to buy the gift of the Holy Ghost and was cursed by St. Peter.
2. Or who, for any sacrament, take or count out money.

GOOD DEEDS. Methink it is he indeed.
[*Re-enter* EVERYMAN.]
EVERYMAN. Now Jesu be your alder speed![3]
I have received the sacrament for my redemption,
And then mine extreme unction.
Blessed be all they that counseled me to take it!
And now, friends, let us go without longer respite.
I thank God that ye have tarried so long.
Now set each of you on this rood° your hond — *cross*
And shortly follow me:
I go before there° I would be. God be our guide! — *where*
STRENGTH. Everyman, we will not from you go
Till ye have done this voyage long.
DISCRETION. I, Discretion, will bide by you also.
KNOWLEDGE. And though this pilgrimage be never so strong,° — *harsh*
I will never part you fro.
STRENGTH. Everyman, I will be as sure by thee
As ever I did by Judas Maccabee.[4]
EVERYMAN. Alas, I am so faint I may not stand—
My limbs under me doth fold!
Friends, let us not turn again to this land,
Not for all the world's gold.
For into this cave must I creep
And turn to earth, and there to sleep.
BEAUTY. What, into this grave, alas?
EVERYMAN. Yea, there shall ye consume,° more and lass.[5] — *decay*
BEAUTY. And what, should I smother here?
EVERYMAN. Yea, by my faith, and nevermore appear.
In this world live no more we shall,
But in heaven before the highest Lord of all.
BEAUTY. I cross out all this! Adieu, by Saint John—
I take my tape in my lap and am gone.[6]
EVERYMAN. What, Beauty, whither will ye?
BEAUTY. Peace, I am deaf—I look not behind me,
Not and thou wouldest give me all the gold in thy chest.
[*Exit* BEAUTY.]
EVERYMAN. Alas, whereto may I trust?
Beauty goeth fast away fro me—
She promised with me to live and die!
STRENGTH. Everyman, I will thee also forsake and deny.
Thy game liketh° me not at all. — *pleases*
EVERYMAN. Why then, ye will forsake me all?
Sweet Strength, tarry a little space.
STRENGTH. Nay, sir, by the rood of grace,
I will hie me from thee fast,

3. The prosperer of you all.
4. Judas Maccabaeus was an enormously powerful warrior in the defense of Israel against the Syrians in late Old Testament times.
5. More and less (i.e., all of you).
6. I tuck my skirts in my belt and am off.

Though thou weep till thy heart tobrast.° *break*
EVERYMAN. Ye would ever bide by me, ye said.
STRENGTH. Yea, I have you far enough conveyed!° *escorted*
Ye be old enough, I understand,
Your pilgrimage to take on hand:
I repent me that I hither came.
EVERYMAN. Strength, you to displease I am to blame,[7]
Yet promise is debt, this ye well wot.° *know*
STRENGTH. In faith, I care not:
Thou art but a fool to complain;
You spend your speech and waste your brain.
Go, thrust thee into the ground.
[*Exit* STRENGTH.]
EVERYMAN. I had weened° surer I should you have found. *supposed*
He that trusteth in his Strength
She him deceiveth at the length.
Both Strength and Beauty forsaketh me—
Yet they promised me fair and lovingly.
DISCRETION. Everyman, I will after Strength be gone:
As for me, I will leave you alone.
EVERYMAN. Why Discretion, will ye forsake me?
DISCRETION. Yea, in faith, I will go from thee.
For when Strength goeth before,
I follow after evermore.
EVERYMAN. Yet I pray thee, for the love of the Trinity,
Look in my grave once piteously.
DISCRETION. Nay, so nigh will I not come.
Farewell everyone!
[*Exit* DISCRETION.]
EVERYMAN. O all thing faileth save God alone—
Beauty, Strength, and Discretion.
For when Death bloweth his blast
They all run fro me full fast.
FIVE-WITS. Everyman, my leave now of thee I take.
I will follow the other, for here I thee forsake.
EVERYMAN. Alas, then may I wail and weep,
For I took you for my best friend.
FIVE-WITS. I will no longer thee keep.° *watch over*
Now farewell, and there an end!
[*Exit* FIVE-WITS.]
EVERYMAN. O Jesu, help, all hath forsaken me!
GOOD DEEDS. Nay, Everyman, I will bide with thee:
I will not forsake thee indeed;
Thou shalt find me a good friend at need.
EVERYMAN. Gramercy, Good Deeds! Now may I true friends see.
They have forsaken me every one—

7. I'm to blame for displeasing you.

I loved them better than my Good Deeds alone.
Knowledge, will ye forsake me also?
KNOWLEDGE. Yea, Everyman, when ye to Death shall go,
But not yet, for no manner of danger.
EVERYMAN. Gramercy, Knowledge, with all my heart!
KNOWLEDGE. Nay, yet will I not from hence depart
Till I see where ye shall become.[8]
EVERYMAN. Methink, alas, that I must be gone
To make my reckoning and my debts pay,
For I see my time is nigh spent away.
Take example, all ye that this do hear or see,
How they that I best loved do forsake me,
Except my Good Deeds that bideth truly.
GOOD DEEDS. All earthly things is but vanity.
Beauty, Strength, and Discretion do man forsake,
Foolish friends and kinsmen that fair spake—
All fleeth save Good Deeds, and that am I.
EVERYMAN. Have mercy on me, God most mighty,
And stand by me, thou mother and maid, holy Mary!
GOOD DEEDS. Fear not: I will speak for thee.
EVERYMAN. Here I cry God mercy!
GOOD DEEDS. Short our end, and 'minish our pain.[9]
Let us go, and never come again.
EVERYMAN. Into thy hands, Lord, my soul I commend:
Receive it, Lord, that it be not lost.
As thou me boughtest,° so me defend, *redeemed*
And save me from the fiend's boast,
That I may appear with that blessed host
That shall be saved at the day of doom.
In manus tuas, of mights most,
Forever *commendo spiritum meum.*[1]
[EVERYMAN *and* GOOD DEEDS *descend into the grave.*]
KNOWLEDGE. Now hath he suffered that we all shall endure,
The Good Deeds shall make all sure.
Now hath he made ending,
Methinketh that I hear angels sing
And make great joy and melody
Where Everyman's soul received shall be.
ANGEL. [*within*] Come, excellent elect° spouse to Jesu![2] *chosen*
Here above thou shalt go
Because of thy singular virtue.
Now the soul is taken the body fro,
Thy reckoning is crystal clear:
Now shalt thou into the heavenly sphere—
Unto the which all ye shall come
That liveth well before the day of doom.

8. Till I see what shall become of you.
9. I.e., make our dying quick and diminish our pain.
1. "Into thy hands, O greatest of powers, I commend my spirit forever."
2. Man's soul is often referred to as the bride of Jesus.

[*Enter* DOCTOR.[3]]

DOCTOR. This memorial° men may have in mind: *reminder*
Ye hearers, take it of worth,[4] old and young,
And forsake Pride, for he deceiveth you in the end.
And remember Beauty, Five-Wits, Strength, and Discretion,
They all at the last do Everyman forsake,
Save his Good Deeds there doth he take—
But beware, for and they be small,
Before God he hath no help at all—
None excuse may be there for Everyman.
Alas, how shall he do than?° *then*
For after death amends may no man make,
For then mercy and pity doth him forsake.
If his reckoning be not clear when he doth come,
God will say, "*Ite, maledicti, in ignem eternum!*"[5]
And he that hath his account whole and sound,
High in heaven he shall be crowned,
Unto which place God bring us all thither,
That we may live body and soul togither.
Thereto help, the Trinity!
Amen say ye, for saint charity.

3. The Doctor is the learned theologian who explains the meaning of the play.

4. Prize it.

5. "Depart, ye cursed, into everlasting fire."

POPULAR BALLADS

Ballads are anonymous narrative songs that have been preserved by oral transmission. Although any stage of a given culture may produce ballads, they are most characteristic of primitive societies such as that of the American frontier in the 18th and 19th centuries or that of the English-Scottish border region in the later Middle Ages. These northern English songs, even divorced from the tunes to which they were once sung, are narrative poems of great literary interest.

The origins of the popular (or folk) ballad are much disputed. The theory that they were first composed by communal effort, taking shape as the songs with which primitive people accompanied ritual dances, no longer seems plausible. On the other hand, the forms in which the ballads have come down to us show that they have been subjected to a continuing process of revision, both conscious and unconscious, by those through whose lips and memories they passed. Though the English ballads were probably composed during the 500 year period from 1200 to 1700, few of them were printed before the 18th century and some not until the 19th. Bishop Thomas Percy (1729–1811) was among the first to take a literary interest in ballads, stimulated by his chance discovery of a 17th-century manuscript in which a number of them had been copied down among a great welter of Middle English verse. Percy's publication of this material in his *Reliques of Ancient English Poetry* inspired others, notably

Sir Walter Scott, to go to the living source of the ballads and to set them down on paper at the dictation of the border people among whom the old songs were still being sung. These collectors often found that one ballad was remembered differently by different people: for instance, when one speaks of *Sir Patrick Spens* one is actually speaking of a number of poems that tell the same story in slightly or widely different words. If a single original form by a single author lies behind this diversity, it is too far back in the mists of time to be recovered.

A work that is the product of a consciously artistic mind will not ordinarily be improved by the revision that most ballads have been subjected to, but some of the ballads are probably better in their revised form than they were in their original form. The distinctive quality that popular ballads share is spareness: they are apt to deal only with the culminating incident or climax of a plot, to describe that event with intense compression, to put the burden of narration on allusive monologue or dialogue, and to avoid editorial comment. This concentration upon the bare essential is precisely that quality that the fallible human memory is likely not only to preserve but also to enhance, for the effort of remembering causes a sloughing-off of what is not strictly relevant. Some of the best of the ballads may have thus been refined in their transmission through men's minds, gaining rather than losing artistic stature.

The fact that ballads were originally songs is important to their development. The simplicity of the tunes to which they were sung not only influenced the distinctive verse form—normally a quatrain with four stresses per line—but also encouraged a corresponding simplicity in the narrative itself, and made individualizing flourishes impossible. Furthermore, the choral practice of using refrains and other kinds of repetitions probably lent the ballad one of its most impressive qualities, for while the actual narratives are tightly compressed, ballads rarely develop in an unbroken line. The reader originally, the hearer—is constantly made to pause by a repeated phrase, or even by nonsense syllables, which provide suspense in a very primitive and effective form. The progress to a foreknown, foredoomed conclusion is paradoxically made to seem more inevitable, more urgent, by such relaxations of narrative tension. The use of repetition and refrain also imparts to the ballads something of the quality of incantation, of ritual, of liturgy—all of which are, of course, themselves closely allied with music.

Most of the best ballads have as their subject a tragic incident, often a murder or accidental death, generally involving supernatural elements. These motifs are a part of the common legacy of European folklore, and many of the English ballads have counterparts in other languages. To this class belong, among the selections chosen for inclusion here, *Lord Randall*, *Edward*, *Barbara Allan*, the *Wife of Usher's Well*, the *Three Ravens*, and—though not in its present form—*Sir Patrick Spens*. Not all the ballads with folklore motifs are tragic, however, for *Thomas Rhymer* has a happy ending. This ballad has gone through an added stage of evolution, for it is a shortening—a reduction to ballad form—of a romance which is preserved in a longer and more sophisticated form; but the romance itself had its origin in some ancient folk tale, and there may have been an earlier ballad on the same theme, with, perhaps, a less happy conclusion.

Some ballads have as their subject actual historical incidents. Two late songs, the *Bonny Earl of Murray* and *Bonny George Campbell*, lament the political murders of two popular 16th-century Scots nobles. The presumably much older ballad *Sir Patrick Spens* may be based on a historical incident of the end of the 13th century. Yet all three of these achieve that mood of sadness that is characteristic of the best of the tragic stories derived from ancient folklore. The quasi-historical Robin Hood ballads, which form a large class by themselves, are less impressive. Most of them seem to have been composed relatively late and hence not to have gone through many stages of oral transmission; they lack the better ballads' intensity, often exhibiting an expansive development that is not free from chattiness. They are probably the work of minstrels who exploited the old folklore figure of Robin Hood by making him a symbol of that rebellion against authority that their own hearers perhaps longed for but did not dare to undertake. In the ballads Robin Hood is placed in a kind of never-never land of English history, where he can strike down tyrants with impunity, but often with far too much gloating: the attractive folklore figure of a natural, freedom-loving man has been burdened with too many political and social implications.

St. Steven and King Herod is hardly a ballad in the same sense as the other poems discussed here. It was probably not transmitted orally, for it contains Latin, and it shows none of the characteristic signs of having passed through more than a single stage of composition. Its author was probably a learned cleric who was exploiting the ballad form for religious purposes—an exploitation so successful as to earn the poem classification as a true ballad despite its evident artificiality.

The great collection of English ballads is that of F. J. Child, *The English and Scottish Popular Ballads*, first published in 1882. The numbers under which Child lists the various versions of each of the ballads printed here are given in footnotes to the individual titles. The versions chosen for this anthology are those which the editor considers the most effective as poetry. Spelling has been modernized; the majority of the northernisms in the originals have been retained.

Lord Randall[1]

"Oh where ha'e ye been, Lord Randall my son?
O where ha'e ye been, my handsome young man?"
"I ha'e been to the wild wood: mother, make my bed soon,
For I'm weary wi' hunting, and fain° wald° lie
down." *gladly / would*

"Where gat ye your dinner, Lord Randall my son?
Where gat ye your dinner, my handsome young man?"
"I dined wi' my true love; mother, make my bed soon,
For I'm weary wi' hunting, and fain wald lie down."

1. Child, No. 12.

"What gat ye to your dinner, Lord Randall my son?
What gat ye to your dinner, my handsome young man?"
"I gat eels boiled in broo:° mother, make my bed
soon, *broth*
For I'm weary wi' hunting and fain wald lie down."

"What became of your bloodhounds, Lord Randall my son?
What became of your bloodhounds, my handsome young man?"
"O they swelled and they died: mother, make my bed soon,
For I'm weary wi' hunting and fain wald lie down."

"O I fear ye are poisoned, Lord Randall my son!
O I fear ye are poisoned, my handsome young man!"
"O yes, I am poisoned: mother, make my bed soon,
For I'm sick at the heart, and I fain wald lie down."

Edward[2]

"Why does your brand sae drap wi' bluid,[3]
Edward, Edward?
Why does your brand sae drap wi' bluid,
And why sae sad gang° ye, O?" *go*
"O I ha'e killed my hawk sae guid,
Mither, mither,
O I ha'e killed my hawk sae guid,
And I had nae mair° but he, O." *more*

"Your hawkes bluid was never sae reid,° *red*
Edward, Edward.
Your hawkes bluid was never sae reid,
My dear son I tell thee, O."
"O I ha'e killed my reid-roan° steed, *chestnut*
Mither, mither,
O I ha'e killed my reid-roan steed,
That erst° was sae fair and free, O." *before*

"Your steed was auld° and ye ha'e gat mair, *old*
Edward, Edward.
Your steed was auld and ye ha'e gat mair:
Som other dule° ye dree,° O." *grief / suffer*
"O I ha'e killed my fader dear,
Mither, mither,
O I ha'e killed my fader dear,
Alas and wae° is me, O!" *woe*

"And whatten° penance wul ye dree for that, *what sort of*
Edward, Edward?
And whatten penance wul ye dree for that,
My dear son, now tell me, O?"

2. Child, No. 13.

3. I.e., why does your sword so drip with blood?

"I'll set my feet in yonder boat,
Mither, mither,
I'll set my feet in yonder boat,
And I'll fare over the sea, O."

"And what wul ye do wi' your towers and your ha',
Edward, Edward?
And what wul ye do wi' your towers and your ha',
That were sae fair to see, O?"
"I'll let thame stand til they down fa',
Mither, mither,
I'll let thame stand til they down fa',
For here never mair maun° I be, O." *must*

"And what wul ye leave to your bairns° and your wife, *children*
Edward, Edward,
And what wul ye leave to your bairns and your wife,
Whan ye gang over the sea, O?"
"The warldes room[4] late° them beg thrae° life, *let / through*
Mither, mither,
The warldes room late them beg thrae life,
For thame never mair wul I see, O."

"And what wul ye leave to your ain° mither dear, *own*
Edward, Edward?
And what wul ye leave to your ain mither dear,
My dear son, now tell me, O?"
"The curse of hell frae° me sal° ye bear, *from / shall*
Mither, mither,
The curse of hell frae me sal ye bear,
Sic° counseils ye gave to me, O." *such*

Barbara Allan[1]

It was in and about the Martinmas[2] time,
When the green leaves were a-fallin',
That Sir John Graeme in the West Country
Fell in love with Barbara Allan.

He sent his man down through the town
To the place where she was dwellin':
"O haste and come to my master dear,
Gin° ye be Barbara Allan." *if*

O slowly, slowly rase° she up, *rose*
To the place where he was lyin',
And when she drew the curtain by:
"Young man, I think you're dyin'."

4. The world's space.
1. Child, No. 84.
2. November 11.

"O it's I'm sick, and very, very sick,
And 'tis a' for Barbara Allan."
"O the better for me ye sal° never be, *shall*
Though your heart's blood were a-spillin'.

"O dinna ye mind,[3] young man," said she,
"When ye the cups were fillin',
That ye made the healths gae° round and round, *go*
And slighted Barbara Allan?"

He turned his face unto the wall,
And death with him was dealin':
"Adieu, adieu, my dear friends all,
And be kind to Barbara Allan."

And slowly, slowly, rase she up,
And slowly, slowly left him;
And sighing said she could not stay,
Since death of life had reft° him. *deprived*

She had not gane° a mile but twa,° *gone / two*
When she heard the dead-bell knellin',
And every jow° that the dead-bell ga'ed[4] *stroke*
It cried, "Woe to Barbara Allan!"

"O mother, mother, make my bed,
O make it soft and narrow:
Since my love died for me today,
I'll die for him tomorrow."

The Wife of Usher's Well[1]

There lived a wife at Usher's Well,
And a wealthy wife was she;
She had three stout and stalwart sons,
And sent them o'er the sea.

They hadna' been a week from her,
A week but barely ane,° *one*
When word came to the carlin° wife *old*
That her three sons were gane.° *gone*

They hadna' been a week from her,
A week but barely three,
When word came to the carlin wife
That her sons she'd never see.

"I wish the wind may never cease,
Nor fashes° in the flood, *disturbances*

3. Don't you remember.
4. I.e., made.

1. Child, No. 79.

Till my three sons come hame° to me, *home*
  In earthly flesh and blood."

It fell about the Martinmas,[2]
  When nights are lang and mirk,° *dark*
The carlin wife's three sons came hame,
  And their hats were o' the birk.[3]

It neither grew in sike° nor ditch, *field*
  Nor yet in ony sheugh,° *furrow*
But at the gates o' Paradise
  That birk grew fair eneugh.

"Blow up the fire, my maidens,
  Bring water from the well:
For a' my house shall feast this night,
  Since my three sons are well."

And she has made to them a bed,
  She's made it large and wide,
And she's ta'en her mantle her about,
  Sat down at the bedside.

Up then crew the red, red cock,
  And up and crew the gray.
The eldest to the youngest said,
  " 'Tis time we were away."[4]

The cock he hadna' crawed but once,
  And clapped his wings at a',
When the youngest to the eldest said,
  "Brother, we must awa'.° *away*

"The cock doth craw, the day doth daw,° *dawn*
  The channerin'° worm doth chide: *fretting*
Gin° we be missed out o' our place, *if*
  A sair pain we maun bide.[5]

"Fare ye weel,° my mother dear, *well*
  Fareweel to barn and byre.° *cow house*
And fare ye weel, the bonny lass
  That kindles my mother's fire."

The Three Ravens[1]

There were three ravens sat on a tree,
  Down a down, hay down, hay down,
There were three ravens sat on a tree,
  With a down,

2. November 11.
3. Birch: those returning from the dead were thought to wear vegetation on their heads.
4. Dead men must return to their graves at cockcrow.
5. A sore pain we must abide.
1. Child, No. 26.

There were three ravens sat on a tree,
They were as black as they might be,
With a down, derry, derry, derry, down, down.

The one of them said to his mate,
"Where shall we our breakfast take?

"Down in yonder green field
There lies a knight slain under his shield.

"His hounds they lie down at his feet,
So well they can their master keep.

"His hawks they fly so eagerly,° *fiercely*
There's no fowl° dare him come nigh." *bird*

Down there comes a fallow° doe, *red-brown*
As great with young as she might go.° *walk*

She lifted up his bloody head,
And kissed his wounds that were so red.

She got him up upon her back,
And carried him to earthen lake.° *pit*

She buried him before the prime;[2]
She was dead herself ere evensong time.
God send every gentleman
Such hawks, such hounds, and such a lemman.° *mistress*

Bonny George Campbell[3]

High upon Highlands
  And low upon Tay,
Bonny George Campbell
  Rade° out on a day. *rode*

Saddled and bridled
  And gallant rade he:
Hame° cam his guid horse, *home*
  But never cam he.

Out cam his auld mither,
  Greeting fu' sair,[4]
And out cam his bonny bride,
  Riving° her hair. *tearing*

Saddled and bridled
  And booted rade he:
Toom° hame cam the saddle, *empty*
  But never cam he.

2. The first hour of the morning.
3. Child, No. 210. The form printed here is a composite, made up from several variant versions by the ballad-collector Motherwell.
4. Weeping full sore.

"My meadow lies green,
And my corn is unshorn,
My barn is to build,
And my babe is unborn."

Saddled and bridled
And booted rade he;
Toom hame cam the saddle,
But never cam he.

Sir Patrick Spens[1]

The king sits in Dumferline town,
Drinking the blude-reid° wine: *blood-red*
"O whar will I get a guid sailor
To sail this ship of mine?"

Up and spak an eldern° knicht, *ancient*
Sat at the king's richt knee:
"Sir Patrick Spens is the best sailor
That sails upon the sea."

The king has written a braid° letter *broad*
And signed it wi' his hand,
And sent it to Sir Patrick Spens,
Was walking on the sand.

The first line that Sir Patrick read,
A loud lauch° lauched he; *laugh*
The next line that Sir Patrick read,
The tear blinded his ee.° *eye*

"O wha° is this has done this deed, *who*
This ill deed done to me,
To send me out this time o' the year,
To sail upon the sea?

"Make haste, make haste, my mirry men all,
Our guid ship sails the morn."
"O say na° sae,° my master dear, *not / so*
For I fear a deadly storm.

"Late late yestre'en I saw the new moon
Wi' the auld° moon in her arm, *old*
And I fear, I fear, my dear master,
That we will come to harm."

O our Scots nobles were richt laith° *loath*
To weet° their cork-heeled shoon,° *wet / shoes*
But lang owre° a' the play were played *ere*
Their hats they swam aboon.° *above*

1. Child, No. 58.

O lang, lang may their ladies sit,
Wi' their fans into their hand,
Or e'er they see Sir Patrick Spens
Come sailing to the land.

O lang, lang may the ladies stand,
Wi' their gold kembs° in their hair, *combs*
Waiting for their ain° dear lords, *own*
For they'll see thame na mair.° *more*

Half o'er,[2] half o'er to Aberdour
It's fifty fadom° deep, *fathoms*
And there lies guid Sir Patrick Spens,
Wi' the Scots lords at his feet.

The Bonny Earl of Murray[1]

Ye Highlands and ye Lawlands,° *Lowlands*
O where have you been?
They have slain the Earl of Murray,
And they laid him on the green.

"Now wae° be to thee, Huntly,[2] *woe*
And wherefore did you sae?° *so*
I bade you bring him wi' you,
But forbade you him to slay."

He was a braw° gallant, *brave*
And he rid[3] at the ring;
And the bonny Earl of Murray,
O he might have been a king.

He was a braw gallant,
And he played at the ba';° *ball*
And the bonny Earl of Murray
Was the flower amang them a'.

He was a braw gallant,
And he played at the glove;[4]
And the bonny Earl of Murray,
O he was the queen's love.

O lang will his lady
Look o'er the Castle Down,
Ere she see the Earl of Murray
Come sounding[5] through the town.

2. Halfway over.

1. Child, No. 181.

2. Huntly, who slew Murray in 1592, had been ordered by King James VI of Scotland (the speaker of this stanza) to arrest the earl.

3. Rode. "The ring" was a hanging ring which mounted knights tried to impale on their spears.

4. Either the goal in a race or else a lady's favor.

5. Blowing horns.

Thomas Rhymer[1]

True Thomas lay on Huntly bank;
A ferly° he spied wi' his ee;° *wonder / eye*
And there he saw a lady bright
Come riding down by the Eildon Tree.[2]

Her shirt was o' the grass-green silk,
Her mantle o' the velvet fine;
At ilka° tett° of her horse's mane *every / braid*
Hung fifty sil'er bells and nine.

True Thomas he pulled off his cap
And louted° low down to his knee: *bowed*
"All hail, thou mighty Queen of Heaven!
For thy peer on earth I never did see."

"O no, O no, Thomas," she said,
"That name does not belang to me;
I am but the Queen of fair Elfland,
That am hither come to visit thee.

"Harp° and carp,° Thomas," she said, *play / speak*
"Harp and carp along wi' me;
And if ye dare to kiss my lips,
Sure of your body I will be."

"Betide me weal, betide me woe,
That weird° shall never daunten me." *fate*
Sine° he has kissed her rosy lips, *then*
All underneath the Eildon Tree.

"Now ye maun° go wi' me," she said, *must*
"True Thomas, ye maun go wi' me;
And ye maun serve me seven years
Through weal or woe, as may chance to be."

She mounted on her milk-white steed;
She's ta'en True Thomas up behind;
And ay whene'er her bridle rung,
The steed flew swifter than the wind.

O they rade° on and farther on; *rode*
The steed gaed° swifter than the wind, *went*
Until they reached a desert wide,
And living land was left behind.

"Light down, light down now, True Thomas,
And lean your head upon my knee.

1. I.e., Thomas the Minstrel. Child, No. 37.

2. Trees in folklore are often frequented by supernatural beings.

Abide and rest a little space,
And I will show you ferlies three.

"O see ye not yon narrow road,
So thick beset with thorns and briars?
That is the path of righteousness,
Though after it but few inquires.

"And see ye not that braid,° braid road — *broad*
That lies across that lily leven?[3]
That is the path of wickedness,
Though some call it the road to heaven.

"And see not ye that bonny road
That winds about the ferny brae?° — *hillside*
That is the road to fair Elfland,
Where thou and I this night maun gae.° — *go*

"But Thomas, ye maun hold your tongue,
Whatever ye may hear or see;
For if you speak word in Elfenland,
Ye'll ne'er get back to your ain° country." — *own*

O they rade on and farther on,
And they waded through rivers aboon° the knee, — *above*
And they saw neither sun nor moon,
But they heard the roaring of the sea.

It was mirk,° mirk night, and there was nae stern-light,[4] — *dark*
And they waded through red blude to the knee,
For a' the blude that's shed on earth
Rins° through the springs o' that country. — *runs*

Sine they came onto a garden green,
And she pulled an apple frae° a tree. — *from*
"Take this for thy wages, True Thomas,
It will give thee the tongue that never can lee."° — *lie*

"My tongue is mine ain," True Thomas said;
"A gudely° gift ye wad° gi'e to me! — *goodly / would*
I neither dought° to buy nor sell — *feared*
At fair or tryst° where I may be. — *meeting place*

"I dought neither speak to prince or peer,
Nor ask of grace frae fair lady."
"Now hold thy peace," the lady said,
"For as I say, so must it be."

He has gotten a coat of the even° cloth, — *smooth*
And a pair of shoes of velvet green;
And till seven years were gane and past,
True Thomas on earth was never seen.

3. Probably "lawn."

4. No starlight.

Robin Hood and the Three Squires[1]

There are twelve months in all the year,
As I hear many men say,
But the merriest month in all the year
Is the merry month of May.

Now Robin Hood is to Nottingham gone,
With a link-a-down and a-day,
And there he met a silly° old woman, *poor, innocent*
Was weeping on the way.

"What news? what news, thou silly old woman?
What news hast thou for me?"
Said she, "There's three squires in Nottingham town,
Today is condemned to dee."° *die*

"O have they parishes burnt?" he said,
"Or have they ministers slain?
Or have they robbed any virgin,
Or with other men's wives have lain?"

"They have no parishes burnt, good sir,
Nor yet have ministers slain,
Nor have they robbed any virgin,
Nor with other men's wives have lain."

"O what have they done?" said bold Robin Hood,
"I pray thee tell to me."
"It's for slaying of the king's fallow° deer, *brown-red*
Bearing their longbows with thee."

"Dost thou not mind,° old woman," he said, *remember*
"Since thou made me sup and dine?
By the truth of my body," quoth bold Robin Hood,
"You could not tell it in better time."

Now Robin Hood is to Nottingham gone,
With a link-a-down and a-day,
And there he met with a silly old palmer,[2]
Was walking along the highway.

"What news? what news, thou silly old man?
What news, I do thee pray?"
Said he, "Three squires in Nottingham town
Are condemned to die this day."

"Come change thine apparel with me, old man,
Come change thine apparel for mine.

1. Child, No. 140.
2. A poor old palmer: a palmer was one who had made the pilgrimage to the Holy Land.

Here is forty shillings in good silver,
Go drink it in beer or wine."

"O thine apparel is good," he said,
"And mine is ragged and torn.
Wherever you go, wherever you ride,
Laugh ne'er an old man to scorn."

"Come change thine apparel with me, old churl,
Come change thine apparel with mine:
Here are twenty pieces of good broad gold,
Go feast thy brethren with wine."

Then he put on the old man's hat,
It stood full high on the crown:
"The first bold bargain that I come at,
It shall make thee come down."

Then he put on the old man's cloak,
Was patched black, blue, and red:
He thought it no shame all the day long
To wear the bags of bread.

Then he put on the old man's breeks,° *underbreeches*
Was patched from ballup[3] to side:
"By the truth of my body," bold Robin can° say, *did*
"This man loved little pride."

Then he put on the old man's hose,° *tights*
Were patched from knee to wrist:
"By the truth of my body," said bold Robin Hood,
"I'd laugh if I had any list."° *desire*

Then he put on the old man's shoes,
Were patched both beneath and aboon:° *above*
Then Robin Hood swore a solemn oath,
"It's good habit° that makes a man." *clothing*

Now Robin Hood is to Nottingham gone,
With a link-a-down and a-down,
And there he met with the proud sheriff,
Was walking along the town.

"O Christ you save, O sheriff," he said,
"O Christ you save and see:
And what will you give to a silly old man
Today will your hangman be?"

"Some suits, some suits," the sheriff he said,
"Some suits I'll give to thee;
Some suits, some suits, and pence thirteen,
Today's a hangman's fee."

3. I.e., center.

Then Robin he turns him round about,
And jumps from stock° to stone: *stump*
"By the truth of my body," the sheriff he said,
"That's well jumped, thou nimble old man."

"I was ne'er a hangman in all my life,
Nor yet intends to trade.
But cursed be he," said bold Robin,
"That first a hangman was made.

"I've a bag for meal, and a bag for malt,
And a bag for barley and corn,
A bag for bread, and a bag for beef,
And a bag for my little small horn.

"I have a horn in my pocket:
I got it from Robin Hood;
And still when I set it to my mouth,
For thee it blows little good."

"O wind° thy horn, thou proud fellow: *blow*
Of thee I have no doubt:° *fear*
I wish that thou give such a blast
Till both thy eyes fall out."

The first loud blast that he did blow,
He blew both loud and shrill,
A hundred and fifty of Robin Hood's men
Came riding over the hill.

The next loud blast that he did give,
He blew both loud and amain,
And quickly sixty of Robin Hood's men
Came shining[4] over the plain.

"O who are those," the sheriff he said,
"Come tripping over the lea?"° *meadow*
"They're my attendants," brave Robin did say,
"They'll pay a visit to thee."
They took the gallows from the slack,° *hollow*
They set it in the glen;
They hanged the proud sheriff on that,
Released their own three men.

St. Steven and King Herod[1]

Saint Steven was a clerk
In King Herodes hall,
And served him of bread and cloth
As every king befall.[2]

4. I.e., making a brave show.
1. Child, No. 22.
2. As is appropriate to every king.

Steven out of kitchen came
With boar's head on hand;
He saw a star was fair and bright
Over Bedlem° stand. *Bethlehem*

He cast adown the boar's head
And went into the hall:
"I forsake thee, King Herodes,
And thy works all.

"I forsake thee, King Herodes,
And thy works all:
There is a child in Bedlem born
Is better than we all."

"What aileth thee, Steven?
What is thee befall?
Lacketh thee either meat or drink
In King Herodes hall?"

"Lacketh me neither meat ne drink
In King Herodes hall:
There is a child in Bedlem born
Is better than we all."

"What aileth thee, Steven?
Art thou wood, or ginnest weede?[3]
Lacketh thee either gold or fee° *property*
Or any rich weed?"° *clothing*

"Lacketh me neither gold ne fee
Ne none rich weed:
There is a child in Bedlem born
Shall help us at our need."

"That is also° sooth,° Steven, *as / true*
Also sooth, ywis,° *indeed*
As this capon crow shal
That lith° here in my dish." *lies*

That word was not so soon said,
That word in that hall,
The capon crew *Christus natus est*[4]
Among the lords all.

"Riseth up, my tormentors,
By two and all by one,
And leadeth Steven out of this town,
And stoneth him with stone."

Tooken they Steven,
And stoned him in the way;
And therefore is his even[5]
Christ's own day.

3. Art thou insane or beginning to go mad?

4. Christ is born.

5. Eve: the day before his feast day.

SIR THOMAS MALORY
(ca. 1405–1471)

1451: First of a long series of arrests and imprisonments.
ca. 1469–70: *Morte Darthur* completed in prison.
1485: *Morte Darthur* printed by William Caxton.

The little that we know of Malory (and that the Malory discussed here was indeed the Malory who wrote the *Morte Darthur* is an assumption that has recently been challenged severely though by no means fatally) suggests a man of violent temperament much given to lawless action. He seems to have been a respectable enough person in his youth, but in 1451 he got into difficulties with the law that lasted the rest of his life. In that year he was arrested in order to prevent his doing injury—presumably further injury—to a priory in Lincolnshire, and shortly thereafter he was accused of a number of criminal acts. These included escaping from prison after his first arrest, twice breaking into and plundering the Abbey of Coombe, extorting money from various persons, and committing rape. Malory pleaded innocent of all charges, and it is indeed possible that he was less guilty of (or had more provocation for) the crimes than the records make it appear. The years of the Wars of the Roses were violent ones, when a supporter of the party out of power was apt to be subjected to much persecution by the ruling group; such a man might at times feel himself justified in taking the law into his own hands in order to recover what had wrongfully been taken from him. But one suspects that Malory took the law into his own hands with unnecessary enthusiasm.

How much time Malory passed in prison is not known, but he was surely a prisoner in 1468 after he had supported an unsuccessful Lancastrian revolt against the Yorkist king, Edward IV, who specifically excluded Malory from two amnesties granted to the Lancastrians. It was probably in prison that he became engaged on the *Morte Darthur;* he was still in prison when he completed it, and may have died there. The book was printed (and edited) in 1485 by William Caxton, the first English printer. A manuscript of it that has recently come to light helps us to a better text than Caxton's.

Arthurian romance, of which Malory's book is a compilation, is a body of highly diverse narrative materials which originated at various times among various peoples and which only gradually became associated with the name of Arthur. Arthur himself was probably a British or Roman-British king who resisted the Anglo-Saxon invasions of England in the 6th century, but his historical reality is less important than the legendary role he played as the great figure around whom the medieval ideal of chivalry flourished. At its simplest, chivalry is the code that governs the actions of the knight-adventurer who rides out in search of wrongs that he may right—typically in search of ladies whom he may rescue from monsters, churls, and wicked (non-Arthurian) knights. The ideal was invented and given a local habitation in the brilliantly imaginative and idealistic 12th century. History had, of course, never witnessed such knights, such ladies, nor such a landscape as that on which their adventures took place, and when chivalry was first invented it was already placed in the past. Man's urge to devise an idealized past seems to be recurrent, for the Camelot of Arthur has its counterpart in the Sherwood Forest of Robin Hood and in the American West. All three of these fictions have the same ideal: that of maintaining order in an essentially lawless land by the efforts of the individual, who fights for the right against seemingly overwhelming odds. Naïve as the practice of this ideal may seem in the Arthurian fiction, the ideal itself has made an important contribution to civilization—though if one imitates literally the Arthurian practice of enforcing the right by violence, as Malory's life suggests that he did, one will find oneself not maintaining order, but disrupting it.

The Arthurian milieu attracted to itself all sorts of diverse motifs, such as the remnants of primitive pagan religious rites, heavily moralized Christianity, an elaborate and in general flagrantly immoral code of romantic love, and others equally miscellaneous. In 13th-century France the amorphous Arthurian material was given a kind of order in a series of prose narratives. Long and often rather vaguely told, these formed the chief material which Malory further edited and ordered while translating it into English.

His book is attractive, however, not only because it is the best and most complete treatment of the story of Arthur and his knights, but also because it is one of the greatest pieces of prose in English. Malory was the first English writer to make prose as sensitive an instrument of narrative as English poetry had always been. One has only to turn from a page of Chaucer's prose to a page of Malory's to be struck by the naturalness and lack of self-consciousness of the later writer. Indeed, Malory achieves in his prose that wonderful impression of simplicity that Chaucer achieves only in his poetry. No matter how extravagant the adventure Malory is recounting, he always manages to give it a hard base of realism. He is in particular a master of naturalistic dialogue, with which he keeps his narrative close to earth. And both he and the majority of his characters are masters of understatement who express themselves, in moments of great emotional tension, with a bare minimum of words. The result is highly provocative to the reader's imagination, which is made, in a sense, to do the writer's work for him. This appeal to the reader's creative imagination probably explains why the *Morte Darthur* brings forth such widely differing responses from its readers, who agree, perhaps, only in their affection for the work.

"The Death of Arthur"—the incident that gives the book its title, though the book itself concerns the whole life of Arthur—is one of Malory's finest passages, and the one on which Tennyson based a famous *Idyll.* Largely at the insistence of his nephew Gawain, Arthur has been in France, futilely besieging his friend Lancelot in a halfhearted attempt to punish him for having been Queen Guinevere's lover. Word comes to the King that his bastard son Mordred has seized the kingdom, and Arthur leads his forces back to England. Mordred attacks them upon their landing, and Gawain is mortally wounded and dies, though not before he has repented for having insisted that Arthur fight Lancelot and has written Lancelot to come to the aid of his former lord.

From Morte Darthur[1]

[*The Death of Arthur*]

So upon Trinity Sunday at night King Arthur dreamed a wonderful dream, and in his dream him seemed[2] that he saw upon a chafflet a chair, and the chair was fast to a wheel, and thereupon sat King Arthur in the richest cloth of gold that might be made. And the King thought there was under him, far from him, an hideous deep black water, and therein was all manner of serpents, and worms, and wild beasts, foul and horrible. And suddenly the King thought that the wheel turned upside down, and he fell among the serpents, and every beast took him by a limb. And then the King cried as he lay in his bed, "Help, help!"

And then knights, squires, and yeomen awaked the king, and then he was so amazed that he wist[3] not where he was. And then so he awaked[4] until it was nigh day, and then he fell on slumbering again, not sleeping nor thoroughly waking. So the King seemed[5] verily that there came Sir Gawain unto him with a number of fair ladies with him. So when King Arthur saw him, he said, "Welcome, my sister's son. I weened ye had been dead. And now I see thee on-live, much am I beholden unto Almighty Jesu. Ah, fair nephew and my sister's son, what been these ladies that hither be come with you?"

"Sir," said Sir Gawain, "all these be ladies for whom I have foughten for when I was man living. And all these are tho[6] that I did battle for in righteous quarrels, and God hath given them that grace, at their great prayer, because I did battle for them for their right, that they should bring me hither unto you. Thus much hath given me leave God, for to warn you of your death. For and ye fight as tomorn[7] with Sir Mordred, as ye both have assigned,[8] doubt ye not ye must be slain, and the most party of your people on both parties. And for the great grace and goodness that Almighty Jesu hath unto you, and for pity of you and many mo[9] other good men there shall be slain, God hath sent me to you of his special grace to give you warning that in no wise ye do battle as tomorn, but that ye take a treatise[1] for a month-day. And proffer you largely,[2] so that tomorn

1. The selection here given is from the section of the book that Caxton called Book XXI, Chaps. 3–7, with omissions. The text has been based on the Winchester MS., with some readings introduced from the Caxton edition; spelling has been modernized and modern punctuation added.
2. It seemed to him. "Chafflet": scaffold.
3. Knew.
4. Lay awake.
5. It seemed to the King.
6. Those.
7. If you fight tomorrow.
8. Decided.
9. More. "There": i.e., who there.
1. Treaty, truce. "For a month-day": for a month from today.
2. Make generous offers.

ye put in a delay. For within a month shall come Sir Lancelot with all his noble knights and rescue you worshipfully and slay Sir Mordred and all that ever will hold with him."

Then Sir Gawain and all the ladies vanished. And anon the King called upon his knights, squires, and yeomen, and charged them wightly[3] to fetch his noble lords and wise bishops unto him. And when they were come the King told them of his avision,[4] that Sir Gawain had told him and warned him that, and he fought on the morn, he should be slain. Then the King commanded Sir Lucan the Butler[5] and his brother Sir Bedivere the Bold, with two bishops with them, and charged them in any wise to take a treatise for a month-day with Sir Mordred. "And spare not: proffer him lands and goods as much as ye think reasonable."

So then they departed and came to Sir Mordred where he had a grim host of an hundred thousand, and there they entreated[6] Sir Mordred long time. And at the last Sir Mordred was agreed for to have Cornwall and Kent by King Arthur's days,[7] and after that, all England, after the days of King Arthur.

Then were they condescended[8] that King Arthur and Sir Mordred should meet betwixt both their hosts, and everich[9] of them should bring fourteen persons. And so they came with this word unto Arthur. Then said he, "I am glad that this is done," and so he went into the field.

And when King Arthur should depart, he warned all his host that, and they see any sword drawn, "Look ye come on fiercely and slay that traitor Sir Mordred, for I in no wise trust him." In like wise Sir Mordred warned his host that "And ye see any manner of sword drawn, look that ye come on fiercely, and so slay all that ever before you standeth, for in no wise I will not trust for this treatise." And in the same wise said Sir Mordred unto his host, "For I know well my father will be avenged upon me."

And so they met as their pointment[1] was and were agreed and accorded thoroughly. And wine was fetched and they drank together. Right so came an adder out of a little heath-bush, and it stung a knight in the foot. And so when the knight felt him so stung, he looked down and saw the adder. And anon he drew his sword to slay the adder, and thought[2] none other harm. And when the host on both parties saw that sword drawn, then they blew beams,[3] trumpets, and horns, and shouted grimly. And so both hosts dressed them[4] together. And King Arthur took his horse and

3. Quickly.
4. Dream.
5. "Butler" here is probably only a title of high rank, although it was originally used to designate the officer who had charge of wine for the king's table.
6. Dealt with.
7. During King Arthur's lifetime.
8. Agreed.
9. Each.
1. Arrangement.
2. Meant.
3. Trumpets.
4. Prepared to come.

said, "Alas, this unhappy day!" and so rode to his party, and Sir Mordred in like wise.

And never since was there never seen a more dolefuller battle in no Christian land, for there was but rushing and riding, foining[5] and striking; and many a grim word was there spoken of either to other, and many a deadly stroke. But ever King Arthur rode throughout the battle[6] of Sir Mordred many times and did full nobly, as a noble king should do, and at all times he fainted never. And Sir Mordred did his devoir[7] that day and put himself in great peril.

And thus they fought all the long day, and never stinted[8] till the noble knights were laid to the cold earth. And ever they fought still till it was near night, and by then was there an hundred thousand laid dead upon the down. Then was King Arthur wood-wroth[9] out of measure when he saw his people so slain from him. And so he looked about him and could see no mo[1] of all his host, and good knights left no mo on-live, but two knights: the t'one[2] was Sir Lucan the Butler and [the other] his brother Sir Bedivere. And yet they were full sore wounded.

"Jesu, mercy," said the King, "where are all my noble knights become?[3] Alas that ever I should see this doleful day! For now," said King Arthur, "I am come to mine end. But would to God," said he, "that I wist[4] now where were that traitor Sir Mordred that has caused all this mischief."

Then King Arthur looked about and was ware where stood Sir Mordred leaning upon his sword among a great heap of dead men.

"Now give me my spear," said King Arthur unto Sir Lucan, "for yonder I have espied the traitor that all this woe hath wrought."

"Sir, let him be," said Sir Lucan, "for he is unhappy.[5] And if ye pass this unhappy day ye shall be right well revenged upon him. And, good lord, remember ye of your night's dream, and what the spirit of Sir Gawain told you tonight, and yet God of his great goodness hath preserved you hitherto. And for God's sake, my lord, leave off by this,[6] for, blessed be God, ye have won the field: for yet we been here three on-live, and with Sir Mordred is not one on-live. And therefore if ye leave off now, this wicked day of destiny is past."

"Now, tide[7] me death, tide me life," said the King, "now I see him yonder alone, he shall never escape mine hands. For at a better avail[8] shall I never have him."

"God speed you well!" said Sir Bedivere.

5. Lunging.
6. Battalion.
7. Knightly duty.
8. Stopped.
9. Mad with rage.
1. Others.
2. That one, i.e., the first.
3. What has become of all my noble knights?
4. Knew.
5. I.e., unlucky for you.
6. I.e., with this much accomplished.
7. Betide.
8. Advantage.

Then the King got his spear in both his hands and ran toward Sir Mordred, crying and saying, "Traitor, now is thy deathday come!"

And when Sir Mordred saw King Arthur he ran until him with his sword drawn in his hand, and there King Arthur smote Sir Mordred under the shield, with a foin[9] of his spear, throughout the body more than a fathom.[1] And when Sir Mordred felt that he had his death's wound, he thrust himself with the might that he had up to the burr[2] of King Arthur's spear, and right so he smote his father King Arthur with his sword holden in both his hands, upon the side of the head, that the sword pierced the helmet and the tay[3] of the brain. And therewith Sir Mordred dashed down stark dead to the earth.

And noble King Arthur fell in a swough[4] to the earth, and there he swooned oftentimes, and Sir Lucan and Sir Bedivere ofttimes heaved him up. And so, weakly betwixt them, they led him to a little chapel not far from the seaside, and when the King was there, him thought him reasonably eased. Then heard they people cry in the field. "Now go thou, Sir Lucan," said the King, "and do me to wit[5] what betokens that noise in the field."

So Sir Lucan departed, for he was grievously wounded in many places. And so as he yede[6] he saw and harkened by the moonlight how that pillers[7] and robbers were come into the field to pill and to rob many a full noble knight of brooches and bees[8] and of many a good ring and many a rich jewel. And who that were not dead all out[9] there they slew them for their harness and their riches. When Sir Lucan understood this work, he came to the King as soon as he might and told him all what he had heard and seen. "Therefore by my read,"[1] said Sir Lucan, "it is best that we bring you to some town."

"I would it were so," said the King, "but I may not stand, my head works[2] so. Ah, Sir Lancelot," said King Arthur, "this day have I sore missed thee. And alas that ever I was against thee, for now have I my death, whereof Sir Gawain me warned in my dream."

Then Sir Lucan took up the King the t'one party[3] and Sir Bedivere the other party; and in the lifting up the King swooned and in the lifting Sir Lucan fell in a swoon that part of his guts fell out of his body, and therewith the noble knight's heart burst. And when the King awoke he beheld Sir Lucan how he lay foaming at the mouth and part of his guts lay at his feet.

9. Thrust.
1. Six feet.
2. Hand guard.
3. Edge.
4. Swoon.
5. Let me know.
6. Walked.
7. Plunderers.
8. Bracelets.
9. Entirely. "Harness": armor.
1. Advice.
2. Aches.
3. On one side.

"Alas," said the King, "this is to me a full heavy[4] sight to see this noble duke so die for my sake, for he would have holpen[5] me that had more need of help than I. Alas that he would not complain him for[6] his heart was so set to help me. Now Jesu have mercy upon his soul."

Then Sir Bedivere wept for the death of his brother.

"Now leave this mourning and weeping, gentle knight," said the King, "for all this will not avail me. For wit thou well, and[7] I might live myself, the death of Sir Lucan would grieve me evermore. But my time passeth on fast," said the King. "Therefore," said King Arthur unto Sir Bedivere, "take thou here Excalibur[8] my good sword and go with it to yonder water's side; and when thou comest there I charge thee throw my sword in that water and come again and tell me what thou sawest there."

"My lord," said Sir Bedivere, "your commandment shall be done, and [I shall] lightly[9] bring you word again."

So Sir Bedivere departed. And by the way he beheld that noble sword, that the pommel[1] and the haft was all precious stones. And then he said to himself, "If I throw this rich sword in the water, thereof shall never come good, but harm and loss." And then Sir Bedivere hid Excalibur under a tree. And so, as soon as he might, he came again unto the King and said he had been at the water and had thrown the sword into the water.

"What saw thou there?" said the King.

"Sir," he said, "I saw nothing but waves and winds."

"That is untruly said of thee," said the King. "And therefore go thou lightly again and do my commandment; as thou art to me lief[2] and dear, spare not, but throw it in."

Then Sir Bedivere returned again and took the sword in his hand. And yet him thought[3] sin and shame to throw away that noble sword. And so eft[4] he hid the sword and returned again and told the King that he had been at the water and done his commandment.

"What sawest thou there?" said the King.

"Sir," he said, "I saw nothing but waters wap and waves wan."[5]

"Ah, traitor unto me and untrue," said King Arthur, "now hast thou betrayed me twice. Who would have weened that thou that hast been to me so lief and dear, and thou art named a noble knight, and would betray me for the riches of this sword. But now go again

4. Sorrowful.
5. Helped.
6. Because.
7. If.
8. The sword which Arthur had received as a young man from the Lady of the Lake; it is presumably she who catches it when Bedivere finally throws it into the water.
9. Quickly.
1. Rounded knob on the hilt; "haft": handle.
2. Beloved.
3. It seemed to him.
4. Again.
5. The phrase seems to mean "waters wash the shore and waves grow dark."

lightly, for thy long tarrying putteth me in great jeopardy of my life, for I have taken cold. And but if thou do now as I bid thee, if ever I may see thee I shall slay thee mine[6] own hands, for thou wouldest for my rich sword see me dead."

Then Sir Bedivere departed and went to the sword and lightly took it up, and so he went to the water's side; and there he bound the girdle[7] about the hilts, and threw the sword as far into the water as he might. And there came an arm and an hand above the water and took it and clutched it, and shook it thrice and brandished; and then vanished away the hand with the sword into the water. So Sir Bedivere came again to the King and told him what he saw.

"Alas," said the King, "help me hence, for I dread me I have tarried overlong."

Then Sir Bedivere took the King upon his back and so went with him to that water's side. And when they were at the water's side, even fast[8] by the bank hoved[9] a little barge with many fair ladies in it; and among them all was a queen; and all they had black hoods, and all they wept and shrieked when they saw King Arthur.

"Now put me into that barge," said the King; and so he did softly. And there received him three ladies with great mourning, and so they set them[1] down. And in one of their laps King Arthur laid his head, and then the queen said, "Ah, my dear brother, why have ye tarried so long from me? Alas, this wound on your head hath caught overmuch cold." And anon they rowed fromward the land, and Sir Bedivere beheld all tho ladies go froward him.

Then Sir Bedivere cried and said, "Ah, my lord Arthur, what shall become of me, now ye go from me and leave me here alone among mine enemies?"

"Comfort thyself," said the King, "and do as well as thou mayest, for in me is no trust for to trust in. For I must into the vale of Avilion[2] to heal me of my grievous wound. And if thou hear nevermore of me, pray for my soul."

But ever the queen and ladies wept and shrieked that it was pity to hear. And as soon as Sir Bedivere had lost the sight of the barge he wept and wailed and so took[3] the forest, and went all that night. And in the morning he was ware betwixt two holts hoar[4] of a chapel and an hermitage.[5] * * *

6. I.e., with mine.
7. Sword belt.
8. Close.
9. Waited.
1. I.e., they sat.
2. A legendary island, sometimes identified with the earthly paradise.
3. Took to. "Went": walked.
4. Ancient copses.
5. In the passage here omitted, Sir Bedivere meets the former Bishop of Canterbury, now a hermit, who describes how on the previous night a company of ladies had brought to the chapel a dead body, asking that it be buried. Sir Bedivere exclaims that the dead man must have been King Arthur, and vows to spend the rest of his life there in the chapel as a hermit.

Thus of Arthur I find no more written in books that been authorized,[6] neither more of the very certainty of his death heard I never read,[7] but thus was he led away in a ship wherein were three queens: that one was King Arthur's sister, Queen Morgan la Fée, the t'other[8] was the Queen of North Wales, and the third was the Queen of the Waste Lands. * * *

Now more of the death of King Arthur could I never find but that these ladies brought him to his burials,[9] and such one was buried there that the hermit bore witness that sometime was Bishop of Canterbury.[1] But yet the hermit knew not in certain that he was verily the body of King Arthur, for this tale Sir Bedivere, a Knight of the Table Round, made it to be written. Yet some men say in many parts of England that King Arthur is not dead, but had by the will of our Lord Jesu into another place. And men say that he shall come again and he shall win the Holy Cross. Yet I will not say that it shall be so, but rather I will say, Here in this world he changed his life. And many men say that there is written upon his tomb this verse: *Hic iacet Arthurus, rex quondam, rexque futurus.*[2]

1469–70 1485

6. That have authority.
7. Tell.
8. The second.
9. Grave.
1. Of whom the hermit, who was formerly Bishop of Canterbury, bore witness.
2. "Here lies Arthur, who was once king and king will be again."

WILLIAM CAXTON

(ca. 1422–1491)

In his early years Caxton was a prosperous merchant who traded mostly in the low countries. In 1470, at the command of his patroness, Margaret of Burgundy, he completed a translation into English of the French *Recueil des Histoires de Troie* (i.e., collection of the stories of Troy), which he had begun earlier in his leisure time. This work, circulated in manuscript, became so popular that the demand for it exceeded the number of copies that could be readily produced by scribes. Caxton thereupon went to Cologne, where he studied the newly developed art of printing, and subsequently set up a press at Bruges in Belgium. In 1475 he printed his translation of the Troy book (the first book printed in English), and in the next year returned to England, where he established England's first printing press, in London. Among his first publications were Chaucer's *Canterbury Tales* (1478; second edition about 1484). In 1485 he printed Malory's work, with the Preface reproduced here.

A shrewd publisher and practiced writer, as well as a pioneer printer,

Caxton gives a most astute and inviting account of Malory's work and the personage after whom it was named. Caxton himself evidently put small credence in the historicity of Arthur, but by appearing—in all modesty—to have been overwhelmed by the faith that eminent people had in Arthur's existence, as well as by the survival of certain relics that seemed to support such faith, he encourages the reader to lay aside his own skepticism (although the warning remains: "ye are at your liberty" to accept or reject the truth of Malory's narrative). In describing the work itself, Caxton is careful to emphasize its exemplary qualities, "the noble acts of chivalry" that knights performed in the old days, from which one may learn virtuous conduct; but he is also careful not to suppress the fact—though he presents it in tantalizing subordination—that the book contains much that is exemplary only in the negative sense: "cowardice, murder, hate, * * * and sin," which for some might, perhaps, enhance the book's appeal.

Preface to *Morte Darthur*

After that I had accomplished and finished divers histories as well of contemplation as of other historial and worldly acts of great conquerors and princes, and also certain books of ensamples [1] and doctrine, many noble and divers gentlemen of this royalme of England camen and demanded me many and ofttimes wherefore that I have not do [2] made and imprint the noble history of the Saint Grail and of the most renommed [3] Christian king, first and chief of the three best Christian, and worthy,[4] king Arthur, which ought most to be remembered among us Englishmen tofore all other Christian kings.

For it is notoirly [5] known through the universal world that there been nine worthy and the best that ever were, that is to wit, three Paynims,[6] three Jews, and three Christian men. As for the Paynims, they were tofore the Incarnation of Christ, which were named, the first Hector of Troy, of whom th'istory is common both in ballad and in prose, the second Alexander the Great, and the third Julius Caesar, Emperor of Rome, of whom th'istories been well known and had.[7] And as for the three which also were tofore th'Incarnation of our Lord, of whom the first was Duke Joshua which brought the children of Israel into the land of behest,[8] the second David, king of Jerusalem, and the third Judas Maccabeus, of these three the Bible rehearseth all their noble histories and acts. And sith [9] the said Incarnation have been three noble Christian men stalled [1] and admitted through the universal world into the number of the nine best and worthy, of whom was first the noble Arthur, whose noble acts I

1. Exemplary stories.
2. Caused to be.
3. Renowned.
4. I.e., one of the Nine Worthies
5. Notoriously.
6. Pagans.
7. Available.
8. Promised Land.
9. Since.
1. Assigned.

purpose to write in this present book here following. The second was Charlemagne, or Charles the Great, of whom th'istory is had in many places, both in French and English; and the third and last was Godefroy of Bouillon, of whose acts and life I made a book unto th'excellent prince and king of noble memory, King Edward the Fourth.

The said noble gentlemen instantly required[2] me t'imprint th'istory of the said noble king and conqueror king Arthur and of his knights, with th'istory of the Saint Grail and of the death and ending of the said Arthur, affirming that I ought rather t'imprint his acts and noble feats than of Godefroy of Bouillon or any of the other eight, considering that he was a man born within this royalme and king and emperor of the same, and that there been in French divers and many noble volumes of his acts, and also of his knights.

To whom I answered that divers men hold opinion that there was no such Arthur and that all such books as been made of him been but feigned and fables, because that some chronicles make of him no mention ne remember him nothing, ne of his knights.

Whereto they answered, and one in special said, that in him that should say or think that there was never such a king called Arthur might well be aretted[3] great folly and blindness, for he said that there were many evidences of the contrary. First, ye may see his sepulture[4] in the monastery of Glastonbury; and also in *Polychronicon*,[5] in the fifth book, the sixth chapter, and in the seventh book, the twenty-third chapter, where his body was buried, and after founden and translated[6] into the said monastery. Ye shall see also in th'istory of Bochas,[7] in his book *De Casu Principum*, part of his noble acts, and also of his fall. Also Galfridus, in his British book,[8] recounteth his life. And in divers places of England many remembrances been yet of him and shall remain perpetually, and also of his knights: first, in the abbey of Westminster, at Saint Edward's shrine, remaineth the print of his seal in red wax, closed in beryl, in which is written PATRICIUS ARTHURUS BRITANNIE GALLIE GERMANIE DACIE IMPERATOR;[9] item, in the castle of Dover ye may see Gawain's skull and Cradok's mantle; at Winchester, the Round Table; in other places Lancelot's sword and many other things.

Then, all these things considered, there can no man reasonably

2. Urgently requested.
3. Imputed.
4. Burial place.
5. A Latin history by Ranulph Higden (d. 1364), an English translation of which was printed by Caxton in 1482.
6. Carried
7. The Italian Giovanni Boccaccio (d. 1375), whose book *Concerning the Falls of Illustrious Men* ("Concerning the Fall of Princes," according to Caxton) was a favorite of the later Middle Ages.
8. Geoffrey of Monmouth, whose *History of the Kings of Britain* (ca. 1136), begins with the story of the founding of Britain by Brutus, Aeneas' great-grandson, who was believed to have given his name to Britain: hence Caxton's "Brutish."
9. The Noble Arthur, Emperor of Britain, Gaul, Germany, and Dacia.

gainsay but there was a king of this land named Arthur. For in all places, Christian and heathen, he is reputed and taken for one of the nine worthy, and the first of the three Christian men. And also he is more spoken of beyond the sea, mo [1] books made of his noble acts, than there be in England; as well in Dutch, Italian, Spanish, and Greekish, as in French. And yet of record remain in witness of him in Wales, in the town of Camelot, the great stones and marvelous works of iron lying under the ground, and royal vaults, which divers now living hath seen. Wherefore it is a marvel why he is no more renommed in his own country, save only it accordeth to the word of God, which saith that no man is accept for a prophet in his own country.

Then, all these things foresaid alleged,[2] I could not well deny but that there was such a noble king named Arthur, and reputed one of the nine worthy, and first and chief of the Christian men. And many noble volumes be made of him and of his noble knights in French, which I have seen and read beyond the sea, which been not had in our maternal tongue. But in Welsh been many, and also in French, and some in English, but nowhere nigh all. Wherefore, such as have late been drawn out briefly into English, I have, after the simple cunning that God hath sent to me, under the favor and correction of all noble lords and gentlemen, emprised [3] to imprint a book of the noble histories of the said king Arthur and of certain of his knights, after a copy unto me delivered, which copy sir Thomas Malory did take out of certain books of French and reduced it into English.

And I, according to my copy, have done set it [4] in imprint to the intent that noble men may see and learn the noble acts of chivalry, the gentle and virtuous deeds that some knights used in tho [5] days, by which they came to honor, and how they that were vicious were punished and oft put to shame and rebuke; humbly beseeching all noble lords and ladies with all other estates, of what estate or degree they been of, that shall see and read in this said book and work, that they take the good and honest acts in their remembrance, and to follow the same; wherein they shall find many joyous and pleasant histories and noble and renommed acts of humanity, gentleness, and chivalries. For herein may be seen noble chivalry, courtesy, humanity, friendliness, hardiness, love, friendship, cowardice, murder, hate, virtue, and sin. Do after the good and leave the evil, and it shall bring you to good fame and renommee.[6]

And for to pass the time this book shall be pleasant to read in, but for to give faith and belief that all is true that is contained herein, ye be at your liberty. But all is written for our doctrine, and for to

1. More.
2. Having been cited.
3. Undertaken.
4. Have caused it to be set.
5. Those.
6. Renown.

beware that we fall not to vice ne sin, but t'exercise and follow virtue, by which we may come and attain to good fame and renommee in this life, and after this short and transitory life to come unto everlasting bliss in heaven; the which He grant us that reigneth in heaven, the Blessed Trinity. AMEN.

Then, to proceed forth in this said book, which I direct unto all noble princes, lords and ladies, gentlemen or gentlewomen, that desire to read or hear read of the noble and joyous history of the great conqueror and excellent king, king Arthur, sometime king of this noble royalme then called Britain, I, William Caxton, simple person, present this book following which I have emprised t'imprint: and treateth of the noble acts, feats of arms of chivalry, prowess, hardiness, humanity, love, courtesy, and very[7] gentleness, with many wonderful histories and adventures.

1485

7. True.

The Sixteenth Century

(1485-1603)

1485: Accession of Henry VII inaugurates age of the Tudor sovereigns.
1509: Accession of Henry VIII.
1517: Martin Luther's Wittenberg Theses; beginning of the Reformation.
1534: Henry VIII acknowledged "Supreme Head on Earth" of the English church.
1557: Publication of *Tottel's Miscellany,* containing poems by Sir Thomas Wyatt, Henry Howard Earl of Surrey, and others.
1558: Accession of Queen Elizabeth I.
1576: The Theatre, the first permanent structure in England for the presentation of plays, is built.
1588: Defeat of the Spanish Armada.
1603: Death of Elizabeth I; accession of James I, first of the Stuart line.

ENGLAND UNDER HENRY VII

The 16th century in England is the age of the Tudor sovereigns. There were three generations of them; they ruled England from 1485 to 1603. Before the first Tudor, the Earl of Richmond who became Henry VII, won his crown by defeating Richard III at Bosworth field, the country had for more than thirty years been torn by a dynastic strife between the houses of York and Lancaster. Henry VII was Lancastrian, but he married Elizabeth of the house of York, sister of Edward V and niece of the Yorkist king he defeated, Richard III. The barons, impoverished and divided by the dynastic wars, could not effectively oppose the power of the crown, and the church, the other great force in society, was closer to alliance with royal power than to opposition. So Tudor government meant, in comparison with what had gone before and with other conceivable alternatives, a government of strong central authority, of order, and of practical solutions to problems.

About a decade before Henry VII won his throne, the art of printing from movable type, a German invention, had been introduced into England by William Caxton (ca. 1422–91), who had learned and practiced it in the Low Countries. Literacy had been increasing during the 15th century, so that many more people could read than in Chaucer's time. It is estimated that some 30 per cent of the people could read English in the early 15th century and some 60 per cent by 1530. Printing of course made books cheaper and more plentiful, and accordingly there were more opportunities to read and more incentive to learn to read.

Seven years after Henry VII became king, Columbus discovered America, and a few years later Vasco da Gama reached the Orient by sailing around the Cape of Good Hope. The English were not pioneers in the discovery and exploration of the western hemisphere, but the consequences of new discoveries were to affect their place in the world profoundly, for in the next century they became great colonizers and merchant-adventurers.

Significant changes in trade and in the arts of war also marked the early years of the Tudor regime. Henry VII made commercial treaties with European countries; England, which had always been a sheep-raising country, was by now manufacturing and exporting significant amounts of cloth. As lands were enclosed to permit grazing on a larger scale, people were driven off the land to the cities, and London grew into a metropolitan market, with more sophisticated commercial institutions. At the same time the feudal order continued its decline, partly because the introduction of firearms had made obsolete the old armored knight on horseback, as well as the English bowman who had won such famous victories in France under King Henry V. The "new men" who supported the Tudors and profited from their favor could adapt themselves more easily to a changed society than could the survivors of the great families of the feudal 15th century.

Yet it would be a mistake to visualize these changes as sudden and dramatic. Although Caxton introduced printed books, and was an author and translator as well as a printer, his publications consisted of long prose romances translated from the French, collections of moral sayings, and other works—such as Malory's *Morte Darthur*—that were medieval rather than modern. And even though the armored knight was obsolete, for a century jousts and tournaments took place at court and the approved code of behavior was the traditional code of chivalry. As often in an age of spectacular novelty, full of significance for the future, men's minds looked back instead of forward. Confronted with innovation, they dreamed of an idealized past instead of looking forward to an uncertain future. The best writers of the time of Henry VII were imitators of Chaucer, who had died about a century before. They were Scottish rather than English: William Dunbar (ca. 1460–ca. 1520), Gavin Douglas (1475–1522), and Sir David Lindsay (1485–1555). Even the English writers looked back; a typical one is Stephen Hawes (1474–1523), who imitated not Chaucer but John Lydgate, monk of Bury.

HUMANISM

During the 15th century a few English clerics and government officials had journeyed to Italy and had seen something of the extraordinary cultural and intellectual movement flourishing in the city-states there. But it was only near the end of the century that Italian influence came to be important, and it was not until the accession of Henry VIII to the throne in 1509 that a notable renaissance took place in England.

A great leader of the intellectual movement known as humanism was

Sir Thomas More, Henry's Lord Chancellor, who gave up his life rather than bow to Henry as head of the English church. More's masterpiece, *Utopia*, was written in Latin, and was an appeal to all of Europe to reconsider social institutions in the light of reason and to achieve economic equality and peace. His English writings were largely on controversial subjects; his most ambitious one was a history of Richard III. More's friend Erasmus of Rotterdam spent some time in England, and his influence was strong, especially in the field of education. In the humanists' view, education was based upon the classics and the Bible, was to be liberal in the modern sense, yet extremely practical. It was designed to prepare able people for the duties of government. Queen Elizabeth herself, with her command of languages and her practical sense of the problems of diplomacy, was a fine example of the humanistically educated ruler.

Elizabethan education was based upon the medieval *trivium* (grammar, logic, and rhetoric) and *quadrivium* (arithmetic, geometry, astronomy, and music). Grammar was of course Latin grammar, and the rhetoric that went with it was a rigorous discipline in all the stylistic devices used by classical authors. The purpose was a utilitarian one—to train the student to speak and write good Latin, the language of diplomacy, of the professions, and of all higher learning. But the books read and studied rhetorically were not considered mere exhibitions of literary style; from the *Sententiae Pueriles* for beginners, on up through Terence, Virgil, Horace, and Cicero's *De Officiis*, the works were studied for the moral, political, and philosophical content they offered. Elizabethan schoolmasters might use the system of double translation, from English into Latin and then from Latin back into English, to develop facility and rhetorical elegance, but they well knew that the rapid development from child into man (so much more rapid than we consider either feasible or desirable) required moral instruction, and this was to be found in the Latin classics. It was a mission of the English humanists like Colet, Elyot, and Ascham to persuade the English gentry that their sons should be bred to this kind of learning as the most suitable preparation for public service.

Although Sir Thomas More had turned naturally to Latin in writing his *Utopia*, the choice was not as easy for succeeding generations. In fact, the question of whether to write in English or in Latin became a question of great seriousness. The vernaculars seemed relatively new and unstable to learned men, and with their great desire for eternal fame it was natural that they should concern themselves about the durability of their medium. Furthermore, the age of the humanists had emphasized the value of the classical languages; Cicero and the other masters of rhetoric were imitated in their own tongues. But in Italy, France, and England alike, there came to be a revolt against this sterile and slavish imitation of the classics. It is the contention of Joachim Du Bellay's *Défense et Illustration de la Langue Française* (1549) that the value of a language is not inherent in the language itself, but depends upon what great and fine works are written in that language; furthermore, and this is even more important, the feeling of nationality itself dictates that the vernacular should be used. If the tongue of the people is not so refined and polished as the Greek or Latin, all the more reason why men of learning should improve it by studying it and writing their most ambitious works in it. Roger Ascham (1515–

68), tutor to Princess Elizabeth, included in his book on archery called *Toxophilus* (1545) a defense of writing in English, though he said it would be easier for him to write in Latin or Greek. He dedicated the book to King Henry, and his patriotic motives are expressed in verses addressed to England:

> Stick to the truth, and evermore thou shall
> Through Christ, King Henry, the book and the bow,
> All manner of enemies quite overthrow.

Richard Mulcaster (ca. 1530–1611), principal of the Merchant Taylors' School and teacher of Edmund Spenser, said:

> I do write in my natural English tongue, because though I make the learned my judges, which understand Latin, yet I mean good to the unlearned, which understand but English. * * * For is it not indeed a marvelous bondage, to become servants to one tongue for learning's sake the most of our time, with loss of most time, whereas we may have the very same treasure in our own tongue, with the gain of most time? our own bearing the joyful title of our liberty and freedom, the Latin tongue remembering us of our thralldom and bondage? I love Rome, but London better; I favor Italy, but England more; I honor the Latin, but I worship the English.

THE REFORMATION—HENRY VIII, EDWARD VI, AND MARY

Humanists like Erasmus advocated and practiced a scholarly and critical study of the Scriptures; humanists like More were opposed to corrupt and ignorant clergy and such abuses as the sale of papal indulgences and pardons. But when, after Martin Luther nailed his famous Theses to the church door in Wittenberg in 1517, the Reformation itself gathered force, Erasmus and More drew back. Humanism and Reformation for a while seemed to be hostile forces.

What was the Reformation? From the point of view of those who supported it, it was a return to pure Christianity—cleansing the church of all the filth and idolatry that had accumulated over the centuries. From a less partisan point of view it was the break-up of western Christendom, the secularization of society, the establishment of princely ascendancy over the church, and consequently the identification of religious feelings with patriotic, nationalistic ones. From the point of view of the Catholic Church it was, of course, damnable heresy.

In England, one cannot say that the Reformation had an ideological basis. In the time of Chaucer there had been John Wycliffe and the Lollard movement, a grass-roots challenge to the practices and doctrines of the church, and some elements lasted on into the 16th century. But the split with the Church of Rome was caused by a man who considered himself a Catholic champion against Luther and his opinions: Henry VIII, who for writing a book against Luther had been give the title "Defender of the Faith" by Pope Leo X. Henry's motives were dynastic, not religious; he needed a legitimate son and he could not get one without the divorce which Rome refused him. He insisted upon being Supreme Head of the English church and requiring oaths of allegiance to him in that role; Sir Thomas More, his Lord Chancellor, resigned and finally gave up his life rather than sign such an oath. Thomas Cromwell, the powerful secretary of state, dissolved the monasteries and distributed the property to a group of people who thereafter would not side with Rome. And though under Henry the great English translator of the Bible, William Tyndale, was persecuted, driven out of England, and finally martyred in 1536, it was also in Henry's reign that the Scriptures in English were made available in The Great Bible of 1538 to anyone who could read.

Under Henry's son, the child king Edward VI (b. 1537; reigned 1547–53), the English Reformation, which had taken place for political reasons, acquired a strong religious and spiritual force. Protestant theologians from the Continent swarmed to England, the Book of Common Prayer was published in 1549 and 1552, and by 1553, the year of the boy king's death, the 42 Articles which officially defined the beliefs of the English church were thoroughly Protestant.

The successor to the young Protestant king was his older sister Mary, half-Spanish and devoutly Catholic, who married her cousin, Philip II of Spain. The leading Protestants either fled to the Continent or were burned at the stake as heretics; ideologically the Reformation could be reversed, but some of its practical consequences, like the distribution of monastery lands, could not. A Spaniard on the throne of England was not popular, and Mary, whose accession had been opposed by the Council which had proclaimed Lady Jane Grey queen, and whose throne was challenged by a rebellion led by Sir Thomas Wyatt the Younger, son of the poet, dared not press her people too far. She could maintain her Roman allegiance but she could not undo the work of her father and brother. The most necessary thing to do was something she could not do—produce an heir. (Had she done so, England and the United States would probably be Catholic countries today.) Her reign was short, and the Protestant exiles swarmed back at her death to be a potent force in English society during the long reign of Mary's half sister, Elizabeth.

NATIONALISM—ELIZABETH I

Elizabeth Tudor, who ascended the throne in 1558 and ruled until 1603, was one of the most remarkable political geniuses ever produced by a people which has not been barren of political geniuses. Vain, difficult, and headstrong, she nevertheless had a very shrewd instinct about her country's strengths and weaknesses, and she identified herself with her country as no previous ruler had done. Although she was susceptible to the flattery of her courtiers and favorites, she nevertheless entrusted power to such solid men as William Cecil and Francis Walsingham. Cecil (1520–98) was her chief and most trusted Secretary. He devoted his great talents with unswerving loyalty to the service of the queen in domestic affairs as well as in the complex relations with the governments of Europe. He sought also, with limited success, to raise money from Parliament to pay for the increasing cost of government. Walsingham (ca. 1530–90) was a radical Protestant, who tried to introduce a more ideologically committed foreign policy than the queen and Cecil were prepared to support.

England's strength lay in its middle position in the balance of power in Europe—it could throw its weight either way in the power contest between Spain and France; it could support or fail to support the Protestant uprising in the Low Countries. Moreover the queen was unmarried, and the general assumption was that of course she would marry, since as her father had undoubtedly taught her, one of a monarch's major duties is to provide an unquestioned, strong, legitimate heir to the throne. As long as she was capable of bearing children, Elizabeth's possible marriage was an important factor in European diplomacy. By the time it was too late to marry, England was strong and united, capable of shaking off (in 1588) the attempt of the Spanish king, Philip II, to invade the country. What unified England more than anything else was the papal bull of 1570, excommunicating Elizabeth and relieving her subjects of their loyalty to her. This bull, had it taken effect, would have brought to the throne Mary Queen of Scots, Catholic by faith and French by culture—an insupportable thought; Englishmen rallied to their queen and she became a symbol of Englishness and nationalism. The adulation of her, in the face of trouble on the Scottish border, near-chaos in Ireland, and varying threats from the Continent, grew to almost religious heights; her beauty (which was exaggerated), her wisdom (which generally did not need exaggeration), and her divine mission to guide England became articles of faith. In 1588 the defeat of the great Spanish Armada, the mightiest invasion fleet ever mounted against England, seemed to justify that faith.

England's weakness was its politico-religious division. The Catholics, who had never been reformed and who adhered to the pro-Spanish faction of the previous reign, and the Protestant exiles, whose sojourn on the Continent had only sharpened their zeal for the eradication of papistry everywhere in Europe, were the extremes. Between them were the majority of Englishmen whose main desire was for order (remembering the civil conflicts of the previous century), and for these Englishmen Elizabeth, in her person and her policy, became the symbol and the cause.

In matters of religion Elizabeth chose a middle way which satisfied neither the Catholics nor the Puritans. She imposed a form of service, compelled her subjects to attend it, and left their consciences to themselves. The effect was again nationalistic; in the settled and established Elizabethan church, Christians looked toward neither Rome nor Geneva as the prime source of authority, but to the throne of their own sovereign.

The desire for commercial profit also strengthened nationalistic feelings. In 1493 the Pope had divided the new world between the Spanish and the Portuguese by drawing a line from pole to pole (hence Brazil speaks Portuguese today and the rest of Latin America speaks Spanish): the English were not in the picture. But by the end of Edward VI's reign the Company of Merchant Adventurers was founded and Englishmen had become interested in Asia and North America. In order to maintain a vigorous shipping fleet, Cecil introduced "fish days" on Wednesdays and Fridays (popularly known as "Cecil's fast"), and there is reason to believe that shipping was at least maintained at its old level, in the days when Catholic rules against eating meat were an encouragement to fishermen. Some seagoing men, however, found a more profitable crop than fish and turned to piracy, preying on Spanish ships which were returning laden with wealth from the New World. This business soon became a private undeclared war, with the queen and her courtiers investing in these raids privately but accepting no responsibility for them. The greatest of many dazzling exploits was the voyage of Francis Drake in 1577–80: he sailed through the Straits of Magellan, pillaged Spanish towns on the Pacific, reached as far north as San

Francisco, crossed to the Philippines and returned around the Cape of Good Hope; he came back with £1,000,000 in treasure, and his investors earned a dividend of 5,000 per cent. Queen Elizabeth knighted him on the deck of his ship, *The Golden Hind*.

More than anything else, the mere survival of Elizabeth for so long provided the opportunity for nationalistic consciousness and feeling to become established. When she came to the throne in 1558 she was 25 years old; her sister had reigned only five years and her brother only six, but she would remain queen for almost 45 years. The second half of the 16th century is very appropriately called the Elizabethan age.

DRAMATIC LITERATURE

If the morality play *Everyman* at the end of the 15th century marks the end of the Middle Ages, we must look for the beginnings of modern drama to the household of John Morton, Archbishop of Canterbury and Chancellor of England under Henry VII, where young Thomas More served as a page. There at Christmastime plays or revels were put on, and the story goes that young More would sometimes improvise a part and step in with the players. Cardinal Morton even maintained a chaplain on his staff, Henry Medwall, to write plays for his princely entertainment; two of them have survived, called *Nature* and *Fulgens and Lucrece*. These plays were short, given in the great hall at Lambeth Palace, and were called "interludes." Some of these interludes, especially those by John Heywood, are heavily dependent upon French farce.

Interludes and morality plays continued to be popular down to Shakespeare's lifetime, but the development of the drama into a sophisticated art form required another influence—the classics. In the middle of the century we find a schoolmaster, Nicholas Udall, writing a classical comedy in English, based upon the Latin comedies his students had been reading. He called it *Ralph Roister Doister*. About the same time another comedy, classical in form but English in content, was amusing the students at Cambridge. It was called *Gammar Gurton's Needle*. Lively, vivid, native English material put into the regular form of the Latin comedies of Plautus and Terence: this is the fortunate combination that looked forward to the comedies of Shakespeare. *Ralph Roister Doister* contains a classical *miles gloriosus* (cowardly braggart soldier) who is the remote ancestor of Shakespeare's Sir John Falstaff in *I Henry IV*.

The Latin tragedies of Seneca had a similar influence. They were constructed in five acts and had violent and bloody plots, resounding rhetorical speeches, and ghosts among the cast of characters. Moreover Seneca is full of references to Fortune, a Roman goddess who turned her wheel and brought those who had reached the top down to the bottom. The precarious position of men in high estate formed a basis for Elizabethan tragedy, as it had for medieval. The mid-16th century contribution to the type of literature represented by Boccaccio's *Falls of Illustrious Men*, Chaucer's *Monk's Tale*, and Lydgate's *Falls of Princes* was a collection of verse complaints called *The Mirror for Magistrates*. A "mirror" in the old sense was a warning, and a "magistrate" was anyone in a position of power or authority. The first regular English tragedy was called *Gorboduc or Ferrex and Porrex*; it was written by two lawyers, Thomas Sackville and

Thomas Norton. It was first produced at the Inner Temple (a law school) in 1561 and later acted before the queen. The play is set in the legendary very early period of English history shared by Shakespeare's *King Lear*, and, like Lear, its hero divides his kingdom among his children with disastrous results. It is important also that *Gorboduc* is in blank verse rather than in one of the awkward verse forms characteristic of much midcentury writing.

The fusion of classical form with English content brought about the possibility of a mature and artistic drama. But such drama must have an audience, a theater, and professional actors. The earliest English drama had been acted by members of the clergy in the church; medieval miracle and mystery plays had been acted by amateurs—members of the local trade guilds—ordinarily on wagons in the streets of the towns. Moralities and interludes were produced by semi-amateur groups who traveled about, or by the servants of a lord in the hall of his castle. Much dramatic activity took place at winter and midsummer festivals, and it should be remembered that before the Reformation there were many more holidays than there were later. The drama of the Elizabethan age retained much of the festive atmosphere of its infancy.

The actors who traveled about giving their performances wherever they could were not men of respectable status; they tended to be classified with jugglers, acrobats, mountebanks, and other persons of dubious character. In 1545 they were classified by statute as idle rogues and vagabonds; as such, they were subject to arrest. Some noblemen maintained a company of actors as their personal servants, wearing livery and the badge of their masters. They could travel and practice their craft when not needed by their lords, and they were of course exempt from the statute. So it came about that the professional acting companies of Shakespeare's time, including Shakespeare's own, attached themselves to a nobleman and were technically his servants, even though virtually all of their time was devoted to, and their income came from, the public. The rise in social status of actors during Shakespeare's lifetime is illustrated by the fact that he and his fellows were made officers of the royal household when James came to the throne and were sworn as Grooms of the Chamber in ordinary without fee.

The earliest successful acting companies, if success is measured by acceptance at court, were companies of boys. Richard Edwards, Master of the Children of the Chapel Royal in the 1560's, wrote plays for them, and for almost twenty years the rival company, the Children of Paul's (the choir school of St. Paul's cathedral) regularly presented plays at court.

The adult actors played in various places—great houses, the hall of an Inn of Court, on makeshift stages, or in London inn-yards. In 1576 James Burbage, one of the Earl of Leicester's players, built a structure to house their performances and called it The Theatre. It was in Shoreditch, outside the limits of the City of London and accordingly beyond the jurisdiction of the city authorities, who were generally hostile to dramatic spectacles. Other public theaters were erected, and before long enclosed private theaters were secured, under conditions which would allow them freedom from municipal control.

The public theaters were usually oval in shape, with an unroofed yard in the center where the groundlings stood, covered seats in three rising tiers around the yard, and a platform stage jutting out into the yard and surrounded on three sides by spectators. Plays were given in the afternoon and of course were dependent on fair weather. The private theaters were indoors, artificially lighted, and patronized by a more select audience. After 1608 Shakespeare's company had its regular public theater, the Globe, and a private theater, the Blackfriars.

The companies were what would now be called "repertory companies"—that is, they filled the roles of each play from members of their own group, not employing outsiders, and they performed a number of different plays on consecutive days, not continuing a single play for a "run." The principal actors were shareholders in the profits of the company. Boys were apprenticed to actors just as they had been apprenticed to master craftsmen in the guilds; they took the women's parts in plays until their voices changed. The plays might be bought for the company from hack writers; or, as in Shakespeare's company, the group might include an actor-playwright who could supply it with some (but by no means all) of its plays. The text remained the property of the company, but a popular play was eagerly sought by the printers, and the company sometimes had trouble achieving effective control over its rights to the play. The editors of the first collected edition of Shakespeare's plays, the First Folio (1623) said that up until then the readers had been "abused with divers stolen and surreptitious copies, maimed and deformed by the frauds and stealths of injurious impostors." This is true of the so-called "bad quartos," such as the first quarto of *Hamlet* (1603) but the second quarto of that play (1604) was probably printed from Shakespeare's manuscript.

POET, PATRON, AND PUBLISHER

In the court the greatest opportunities existed, but there also were the greatest disappointments to be found. "It was overrun with place-seekers," writes M. St. Clare Byrne in *Elizabethan Life in Town and Country*, "but it was also undeniably the focus of the national life. It drew to it the clever mountebanks, but also the real vigor and talent. It captured and stimulated men's imaginations, even if eventually it disheartened and disgusted them." Men like Sir Christopher Hatton and Sir Walter Ralegh leaped from obscurity to great power and prominence as a result of their success as courtiers, but it must not be forgotten that they had other abilities than the gallantry and dancing which have made them famous in anecdote. The security of the courtier was always precarious, and there was scarcely one of Queen Elizabeth's courtiers who did not know, at some time or other, the harshness of the sovereign's disapproval. The great guide and conduct book for the courtier was Castiglione's *Il Cortegiano* (1528, translated into English by Sir Thomas Hoby in 1561), and according to its theses the function of the courtier was to give good and honest advice to the prince. But, as Sir Philip Sidney found out when he tried to advise the queen against a French marriage, advice is not always relished by a monarch whose powers over any individual subject are almost absolute. As a result there was a long tradition of literature against court life, comparing it unfavorably to the country life of the retired and obscure man. Sir Thomas Wyatt's verse epistles to Sir Francis Bryan and John Poins are early examples of this attitude, and it runs all through the period. Of course the fact that there was a "tradition" means that everything unfavorable said about the court should not be taken at its face value. But enough evidence exists to show that there was a definite feeling that court life was too precarious, too superficial, too corrupt, too hypocritical. From the time of Wyatt to the time of Ralegh the bitter tone is consistent.

For literary men like Edmund Spenser and Lyly, men who by birth were not in a position to be real courtiers, the court offered a faint hope of livelihood, notice, and encouragement. But for these two, at any rate, it was a source of bitter disappointment. Lyly's long wait for the office of the Revels and Spenser's disillusionment after hoping for court favor (reflected in *Mother Hubberds Tale* and *Colin Clouts Come Home Againe*) tell the story. Much of the satire of the period is directed against the superficiality and treachery of the court atmosphere. "A thousand hopes, but all nothing," wailed Lyly, "a hundred promises, but yet nothing."

Although most of the literature which is still considered worth reading shows the predominant influences of the court, it would be a mistake to underestimate the influence of the City of London on the literary taste and production of the period. London had grown tremendously since the time of Chaucer. Instead of a population of about 50,000 it had 93,276 in 1563 and 224,275 in 1605. It was by far the most important city in the realm, and the political history of the 17th century is understandable only if one recognizes the great power the City had, even as against the Crown. The printing presses were located in London, the publishers were located in London, and the mass of the middle-class population which set the style for literature written for the ordinary man lived in London. The middle class found among the university men some writers who catered to them: Thomas Heywood is a good example. And although Thomas Nashe scornfully rejects the claim of the bourgeois to have any literary taste at all or to have any ability at producing literature, still the class had its own writers, like Thomas Deloney, and it knew what it liked—books of instruction, romances, religious tracts, and sensational ballads. Whether the aristocrats admitted it or not, the standards and tastes of the middle class affected all writing, all publishing, and all literary success. For finally the writer saw his work exhibited on the stalls of St. Paul's churchyard, and the customers who frequented that center of the book trade were more often members of the middle class than of the court circle. Louis B. Wright has shown (in his *Middle-Class Culture in Elizabethan England*) how extensive and profound was the influence of the citizenry upon the writing and publication of books, and how bourgeois standards of edification and utility dictated to most of the authors of the time.

Next to the Court and the City, the most important sources of literature were of course the two universities. Before Elizabeth's time the universities were mainly devoted to educating the clergy, and of course that remained an important part of their function. But in the second half of the century the sons of the gentry and the aristocracy were going in increasing numbers to the universities and the Inns of Court (where law was studied), though often they did not take degrees or get called to the bar. Their residence in these places was simply an educational preparation for public service or managing their estates. The career of a professional man of letters as such did not exist: literature was regarded as an adjunct, not a primary occupation.

The university graduate who came to London to make a literary career for himself faced a very difficult situation. It is best pictured, perhaps, in the Cambridge trilogy of *Parnassus* plays, performed at the end of the century but fairly faithfully reflecting conditions which held good during the whole period. It was the university wits, to be sure, who gave to the drama some of the classical form it needed, and who inaugurated the great literary vogue of the 90's. But the lives of Nashe and Marlowe, of Robert Greene and George Peele, do not suggest that the path was easy. The diary of Philip Henslowe, a leading theatrical manager, has entry after entry showing university graduates in prison or in debt or even at best miserably eking out an existence patching plays.

Financial rewards for writing and publishing prose or poetry came mostly in the form of gifts from patrons—in reality the old system of master and servant which had come down from the Middle Ages and had not changed much with the invention of printing. The writer by a dedication hoped for a suitable reward, and in an age when honor and vanity were motives much more sharply defined or observed than they are today, this procedure sometimes worked. Yet the patron whose vanity was amply satisfied by his own conceit and would not reward an author for a dedication remained a constant irritation to the writers of the time, and we hear many complaints that the age is degenerate because patrons are not more munificent. There were some generous and literary-minded patrons, notably Sir Philip Sidney and his sister Mary, the Countess of Pembroke. Shakespeare's relations with his patron, the Earl of Southampton, little as we know about them, were apparently satisfactory, as the dedication to *The Rape of Lucrece* (1594) is much warmer and more personal than the earlier one, to *Venus and Adonis* (1593). But the experience of Robert Greene is perhaps more typical than that of Shakespeare in this respect. He had sixteen different patrons for seventeen books; this suggests that he was not fortunate in finding favor or support from any one. A fraudulent practice grew up of printing the book and then printing off separate dedications, so that an impecunious author could deceive several patrons each into thinking that he was the one to be honored by the volume. Two or three pounds seems to have been the usual reward for the dedication of a pamphlet or small volume of verse. Ben Jonson, who fared much better than most of his contemporaries, sums up the matter, for poets at least, when he says: "Poetry in this latter age hath proved but a mean mistress to such as have wholly addicted themselves to her, or given their names up to her family. Those who have but saluted her on the way, and now and then tendered their visits, she hath done much for, and advanced in the way of their own professions (both the law and the gospel) beyond all they could have hoped or done for themselves without her favor."

The other possible source of reward, besides the patron, was the publisher. And rewards from the publisher in the 16th century were nothing at all like the rewards from that source now. In the first place there was no such thing as copyright, and no such thing, in the ordinary way, as royalties paid according to the sale of the book. An author sold his manuscript to the publisher outright, for what seems now like a ridiculously low price—for a pamphlet or small book of poetry, usually forty shillings.

The writer's troubles were not over when he had written his book, gone through the difficulty of finding a publisher, and finally come to terms with him for the sale of it. He still had to face the many and stringent regulations of the press by political and ecclesiastical authorities, and the fact that he had sold the manuscript did not exempt him from responsibility for what was in it. The authorities were, first, the Privy Council, the highest political authority in the realm below the queen; then the Court of Star Chamber, which punished breaches of censorship; then the Court of High Commission, the supreme ecclesiastical authority, which sometimes supervised matters which had only the slightest connection with religion; then the Stationers' Company, with whom a book had to be registered but who supervised and protected the publisher and printer rather than the author.

The principal rules governing the publication of books were that the number of printers (not publishers) was strictly limited; that nothing could be printed except in the City of London and the Universities of Oxford and Cambridge; that everything printed must receive the imprimatur of the Archbishop of Canterbury and the Bishop of London or their representatives; and that everything published in London must be entered in the registers of the Stationers' Company, if any kind of property protection were desired for it. An example of the regulation which reached back of the publisher to the author himself can be seen in the history of John Stubbs, who protested against Elizabeth's projected French marriage in a pamphlet called *The Discovery of a Gaping Gulf* (1579). For writing this pamphlet, Stubbs was condemned to have his right hand cut off with one stroke of a butcher's cleaver. When the execution had taken place, Stubbs took off his hat with his left hand and cried "God save the queen!"

Almost every writer of the period got into some sort of trouble for publishing a book. It might be prison, it might be merely a reprimand, it might be an investigation by the Star Chamber. It was dangerous to put pen to paper, and it was so unprofitable that it is a wonder that any original writing was published at all. Yet the Elizabethan age is an extremely prolific one in writing and publishing. The *Short Title Catalogue* of the Bibliographical Society, which lists works and editions published between 1475 and 1640, includes over 26,000 items, and it does not include all that were published.

To suppose that poetry, or even prose, circulated only in printed form would be a mistake. The 16th century was the first century of the printed book, and the older way, of circulating in manuscript, lingered on into the 17th century. This was particularly true of poets of gentle or noble rank. Sidney is the most prominent example. Sir John Harington, in his translation of Ariosto's *Orlando Furioso* in 1591, mentions a sonnet of Sidney's "which many I am sure have read"; that particular sonnet was not published until seven years later. Many people kept commonplace books in which they would copy down poems from borrowed manuscript copies. Professional scribes made a living by copying manuscripts, for authors or for readers. There are even complaints by printers of the hoarding of literary manuscripts by "their grand possessors." There is a difference, which has not always been appreciated, between the poetry of the professional poets who wrote for print and the gentle or noble poets who wrote for circulation in manuscript among their cultivated friends.

ART, NATURE, AND POETRY

Elizabethan taste had some very definite and particular characteristics of its own, and the student who wishes to read Elizabethan literature in the spirit of its own time must adjust his mind to the differences between the aesthetic principles of the 16th century and those of our own day. In the 16th century there still remained much of the medieval awareness of the arts as *crafts*, and every writer of the period shows an amazing knowledge of the techniques of many crafts or "mysteries" now unfamiliar. Shakespeare is not an isolated example, and it has been often noticed that his works show an intimate knowledge of such matters as gardening, hawking, dressmaking, archery, building, and so on. Managing the great horse in the tournament was an art. Sailing was an art. Planting a kitchen garden was an art. What they had in common was that they all used the materials of nature but exploited the ingenuity of man's mind. The same fundamental characteristic was thought to apply to the art or craft of writing.

We have been taught by the Romantic movement to glorify nature and to regard the works of art as attempts, usually unsuccessful, to emulate nature. This conception would have seemed strange indeed to the Elizabethans. They recognized, of course, that nature was the cause and basis of all; but that seemed to them no reason why the ingenuity of man should not be used in enabling nature to outdo herself. In *The Winter's Tale* Polixenes is amused at the naïveté of Perdita, who protests that she will have no streaked carnations or gillyflowers in her garden because

> I have heard it said
> There is an art which in their piedness shares
> With great creating nature.

"Say there be," replies Polixenes,

> Yet nature is made better by no mean
> But nature makes that mean. So, over that art
> Which you say adds to nature, is an art
> That nature makes. You see, sweet maid, we marry
> A gentler scion to the wildest stock
> And make conceive a bark of baser kind
> By bud of nobler race. This is an art
> Which does mend nature—change it rather; but
> The art itself is nature.

There was no uneasiness in the Elizabethan mind about a possible conflict between art and nature, for the reason that Polixenes gives. And the improvement by device, by arrangement, by art, of something naturally beautiful extended to all aspects of life, so that there was felt to be no great gulf between literature and the sports of the field or the arts of the kitchen.

The Elizabethan garden was designed as a square, filled with elaborate and intricate, but perfectly regular, design. Francis Bacon protests at gardens which include plots of different colored earths, so arranged as to form a design even without the flowers planted in them; he says he sees enough of this kind of thing in confections and tarts. Yet the very protest shows that his taste was perhaps not typical, and a contemporary might well have asked him why a garden should not look like a confection from the baker's—they were both samples of the art of design. Some Elizabethans had their houses built in the shape of an E, out of honor to the queen, and one man, John Thorpe, designed his house in the form of his own initials. These instances were extreme, of course, but they show the tendency.

Contrapuntal music (composed of several independent melodies joined together), which was sung by the Elizabethans in an accomplished amateur manner, was an intricate kind of music, with elaborate patterns and complex harmonies. The composer Thomas Morley (ca. 1557–1603) says of the madrigal:

> As for the music, it is, next unto the motet, the most artificial and to men of understanding most delightful. If therefore you will compose in this kind you must possess yourself with an amorous humor * * * so that you must in your music be wavering like the wind, sometime wanton, sometime grave and staid, otherwise effeminate; you may maintain points and revert them, use triplaes and show the very uttermost of your variety, and the more variety you show the better shall you please.

But a rigid form was to control all of this extravagance, just as the square border of a garden and the regularity of the pattern controlled the exuberance of the curves in the "knot" or design.

The verse forms used by the Elizabethans range from the extremely simple four-line ballad stanza through the rather complicated form of the sonnet to the elaborate and beautiful 18-line stanza of Spenser's *Epithalamion*. A stanza such as

> The man of life upright
> Whose guileless heart is free
> From all dishonest deeds
> Or thought of vanity

might have been written by any one of many poets at almost any time in the 16th century; it happened to have been written by a fine craftsman, Thomas Campion, near the end of it. Henry Howard, Earl of Surrey, who introduced blank verse into English and helped introduce the sonnet in the reign of Henry VIII, was also a practitioner of a form of iambic couplet in which the first line had twelve syllables and the second fourteen:

> The young man eke that feels his bones with pains oppressed,
> How he would be a rich old man, to live and lie at rest.

This verse form, called "poulter's measure" (because a poulter's dozen was supposed to be sometimes twelve and sometimes fourteen), was the most common verse form in the 60's and 70's. Its dreary monotony in long stretches is matched only by the "fourteener" couplet of fourteen syllables in a line. We still have examples of these forms in our hymnbooks; when each line of poulter's measure is printed as two lines, the hymnbooks call it "short meter"; when they so divide fourteeners they call it "common meter."

Sonnets, which the Elizabethans often called "quatorzains," using the term "sonnet" loosely for any short poem, are fourteen-line poems in iambic pentameter with elaborate rhyme schemes. The most common Italian form, which Wyatt, Sidney, and others imitated, was divided structurally into the octave (first eight lines) and the sestet (last six). A typical rhyme scheme was *abba abba cddc ee*. The so-called English sonnet, introduced by Surrey and practiced by Shakespeare, is structurally three quatrains and a couplet: *abab cdcd efef gg*. Spenser, the most experimental and the most gifted prosodist of the century, preferred a form that is harder to write and richer in rhymes: *abab bcbc cdcd ee*.

The six-line and the seven-line rhyme royal stanza, both practiced by Chaucer, survived into the 16th century. Shakespeare used the former in *Venus and Adonis* and the latter in *The Rape of Lucrece*; the popular collection of historical poems, *The Mirror for Magistrates*, features rhyme royal.

An innovation was Spenser's nine-line stanza, called after him the "Spenserian stanza," which added to the eight-line stanza of iambic pentameter (rhyming *ababbcbc*) an additional line of twelve syllables, an Alexandrine, rhyming with the preceding line. This is the stanza form which serves so well the large descriptive and narrative requirements of *The Faerie Queene*. The elaborate scheme of the stanza Spenser devised for his *Epithalamion* perhaps illustrates the height of Elizabethan craftsmanship in verse. Its eighteen lines rhyme *ababcc*, then various combinations in the second six, and finally three couplets. Lines 6, 11, and 16 are short, having only six syllables contrasted to the pentameter's ten, and the last line is an Alexandrine, as in the Spenserian stanza.

GENRES AND CONVENTIONS IN POETRY

A literary convention is a pattern that has become habitual and arouses certain expectations in the reader. For the Elizabethan poet available conventions enabled him to assume particular responses from his audience and to show his learning by his exploitation of these well-known patterns and his virtuosity by his ingenious elaborations of them. It must not be supposed that these conventions were lifeless forms, so stale with use that they no longer carried meaning or conviction. They were charged with values, with associations. They related writer and reader to other times, other languages, other cultures.

The pastoral convention presented a simple and idealized world, inhabited by shepherds and shepherdesses, concerned not at all with war or politics or commerce. Its business consisted of tending the flocks, friendly poetic contests among shepherds, love, and the pursuit of contentment rather than fame or fortune.

Pastoral lyrics expressed the joys of pastoral life or disappointment in love. Pastoral eclogues were dialogues between shepherds in which a poetic contest was staged, or there was serious, satirical comment on abuses in the great world concealed in the disguise of the homely local concerns of country folk. There were also, of course, pastoral dramas and pastoral romances (prose fiction) which embodied the same values of *otium* (leisure), freedom from pride and ambition, and the pursuit of humble contentment.

Another popular convention was that of the mythological-erotic poem, derived from Ovid mainly but influenced by Italian imitations of him. In the middle ages Ovid's poetry had been allegorized and interpreted morally —the same process that has overtaken the love songs in the Song of Solomon in the Old Testament. This process continued on into the 17th century, but a newer treatment of the convention returned to the frank sensuality of the Latin amatory poets and allowed for elaborate mythological decoration of the narrative without worrying about moral propriety or allegorical interpretation. Such poems appealed to a courtly taste; they validated the senses and they asserted the primacy of physical beauty and the imagination. Shakespeare in *Venus and Adonis* and Marlowe in *Hero and Leander* were among the poets who practiced in this convention.

Sometimes related to the Ovidian tradition but separate from it in origin was the convention of the complaint poem. This goes back to a medieval genre represented by works of the Italian Boccaccio and his English imitators, Lydgate and the authors of *The Mirror for Magistrates.* The complaint poem is essentially tragic and moral. In it the ghost of someone who fell from high place bemoans his fate and warns others. If the ghost is a woman, like Daniel's Rosamund, her fall was caused by the frailty of her sex and the poem may be related to the Ovidian tradition. Another kind of poem, which came both from Ovid and the *Mirror for Magistrates* tradition, was the heroical epistle, practised notably by Drayton.

The Elizabethan sonnet, which reached the height of its vogue in the last decade of the 16th century, depended upon a convention established by Petrarch and followed by his many imitators in Italy and France. In this tradition the poet complains of his lady's coldness; he describes the contrary states of feeling the lover experiences; and he writes sonnets on the conventional themes of sleep, absence, originality, renunciation, and others. The purposes of the love sonneteers differed, of course, but what they had in common might be described as an ambition to give dignity and power to the theme of love by the elaborate rhetorical and stylistic devices available in the Petrarchan tradition. Lesser poets often produced nothing but standard conceits served up in fourteen-line helpings, but major poets such as Sidney, Spenser, and Shakespeare wrote sonnets of power and originality that stand out as major poetic products of the Elizabethan Age.

The conventional forms for satire were less well fixed in the 16th century than in some later periods, though there is a good deal of Elizabethan satirical verse. Some examples belong to a medieval tradition coming down from *Piers Plowman,* which was believed to be the only English masterpiece in satire until satires by the "university wits" in the tradition of the Latin satirists Persius and Juvenal began to appear, and some were written by young John Donne and circulated only in manuscript until after the poet's death in 1631. The epigram was a form that flourished, both in the classical tradition of Martial and in the lyric form of words for a madrigal; the famous *The Silver Swan* is an example.

Poetry for music also followed some conventions: the dance song of course had its definite rhythms and refrains, and many well-known tunes provided the formula by which poet after poet composed new words. In the polyphonic madrigal, the same phrases tend to be repeated again and again, while the words often get lost in the music because various voices sing different words at the same time. As a result, the poem written as a madrigal is usually short and simple both in language and ideas. The "ayre," however, is a song written for a single voice to a lute accompaniment and is usually sung straight through. Since the words are much more intelligible, the thought can be more complex. While the poem is often a good deal longer than the madrigal (since the same melody is repeated over and over), the poem is divided into repetitive stanzas.

There were conventions as well for the heroic poem, of which Spenser's *Faerie Queene* is the prime example. The classical epics of Homer and Virgil had their influence, but so did the romantic Italian epics of Ariosto and Tasso. Chapman's Homer and Harington's Ariosto were regarded by contemporaries as something more than translation, having much of the interest and significance of original poems.

The major conventions in poetry did not stifle originality; they served as both an ordering device and a challenge that stimulated the poet to something fresh and new. When these conventions were alive for writers and readers, they had significance in themselves, which was an essential part of the total significance of the poem. Knowledge of the more important Elizabethan conventions is not simply of scholarly interest; it is essential to the experience of the poem as a poem.

ELIZABETHAN MOODS AND ATTITUDES

The English Renaissance was no sharp break with the past. Attitudes and feelings which had been characteristic of the 15th or 14th centuries persisted well down into the era of humanism and Reformation. George Gascoigne, the leading writer of the 1570's, has in many ways a medieval point of view, and the popular collection of verse tales of the fall of princes called *The Mirror for Magistrates* (first published in 1559, and reprinted with additions in 1563, 1587, and 1610) derives from Lydgate and Boccaccio. Even a lyric by that flamboyant and "modern" Elizabethan, Sir Walter Ralegh, may embody a sentiment of the vanity and transitoriness of all earthly ambitions and achievements. The Dance of Death and related images were still living symbols to the Elizabethan imagination; witness Shakespeare's *Richard II* (III.ii.152–70):

> And nothing can we call our own but death
> And that small model of the barren earth
> Which serves as paste and cover to our bones.
> For God's sake let us sit upon the ground
> And tell sad stories of the death of kings!
> How some have been deposed; some slain in war;
> Some haunted by the ghosts they have deposed;
> Some poisoned by their wives; some sleeping killed—
> All murthered; for within the hollow crown
> That rounds the mortal temples of a king
> Keeps Death his court, and there the antic sits,
> Scoffing his state and grinning at his pomp;
> Allowing him a breath, a little scene,
> To monarchize, be feared, and kill with looks;
> Infusing him with self and vain conceit,
> As if this flesh which walls about our life
> Were brass impregnable: and humored thus,
> Comes at the last, and with a little pin
> Bores through the castle wall, and farewell king!

Yet there was at the same time a spirit of joy and gaiety, of innocence and lightheartedness, that future ages were to look back on as "merry England." This spirit is popular, it comes from the folk and from the persistent love of Englishmen for their countryside; it is spontaneous, yet it seems somehow stable and permanent. Perhaps its best expression is in the songs of Shakespeare's plays:

> When daffodils begin to peer,
> With heigh! the doxy over the dale,
> Why, then comes in the sweet o' the year;
> For the red blood reigns in the winter's pale.

or

> When daisies pied and violets blue
> And ladysmocks all silver-white
> And cuckoobuds of yellow hue
> Do paint the meadows with delight.

The mood of pastoral, as we have already seen in our notice of that convention, is generally one of quiet contentment, of reflective leisure, of the enjoyment of a simple, idealized world. Marlowe's *Passionate Shepherd to His Love* beautifully invokes this world.

There was of course also among the Elizabethans the opposite mood: the burning desire for conquest, for achievement, for surmounting all obstacles. The Elizabethans called it "the aspiring mind." The great projector of this mood is Christopher Marlowe, who has his heroes fling themselves into the pursuit of power—

> Is it not passing brave to be a king
> And ride in triumph through Persepolis?—

or into the lust for gold—

> Infinite riches in a little room—

or into the search for knowledge—

> All things that move between the quiet poles
> Shall be at my command; emperors and kings
> Are but obeyed in their several provinces,
> Nor can they raise the wind or rend the clouds;
> But his dominion that excels in this
> Stretcheth as far as doth the mind of man.

Marlowe's heroes are defeated finally, all of them, but their fiery spirit in assaulting the limits of the possible echoes after they are gone.

The Elizabethan spirit has been described as "sensuous, comprehensive, extravagant, disorderly, thirsty for beauty, abounding in the zest for life." This is part of the truth, but not all of it. Fundamentally, the thought and feeling of Shakespeare's contemporaries was far more deeply affected by Christian humanism than by the extravagances of Marlowe. We need to remember Ben Jonson, with his classical principles of structure and decorum and his ideal of the balanced man. Jonson was in every respect more typical of his age than Shakespeare. His emphasis upon learning, his reconciliation of ancient models and English content, and his critical responsibility truly represent the ideal English poet of his time, as Sidney would have visualized him. Because his major work was done after 1603, he is represented in the 17th-century section of this anthology.

The second generation of English humanists—men like Roger Ascham (1515–68, tutor to Queen Elizabeth), Sir John Cheke (1514–57, professor of Greek at Cambridge), and Thomas Wilson (1525–81, rhetorician and translator)—combined an earnest Protestant Christianity with their classical learning, and Ascham vigorously opposed the more secular, pagan humanism that was coming out of Italy. These men shaped the University of Cambridge, which in turn shaped many men. It was an Oxford man, however—Richard Hooker—who provided in his great work, *The Laws of Ecclesiastical Polity* (1593 and later), the supreme masterpiece of English Christian humanism. In so far as his doctrine is concerned, Spenser is a Christian humanist, and the label can justly be applied to John Milton, both in content and in form.

If the beginning of the Tudor era showed more links with the past than with the future, it is equally true that the end of Elizabeth's reign prefigured some of the conflict and uncertainty of the time to come. "The disenchantment of the Elizabethans" is a phrase that has been used to describe it. In 1599, the year of Spenser's death, the headstrong Earl of Essex returned from Ireland, inaugurating a course of events that would lead to his rebellion and execution in 1601. Elizabeth was old, a peaceful succession was by no means assured, and the rifts in society which were to mean civil war in the midcentury were already present. An outbreak of satire and epigrams had to be stopped by the authorities. Some of the cynical undercurrent in Shakespeare's *Hamlet* and *Troilus and Cressida* reflects the spirit of the time. John Donne was already writing his poems, and a very different age, the 17th century, was in the offing. In 1603 Elizabeth, the last of the Tudors, died, and to the immense relief of anxious Englishmen, the succession took place peacefully. The new monarch was the Protestant James VI of Scotland, who became James I of England.

SIR THOMAS MORE
(1478–1535)

1514–16: Writing *Utopia*.
1532: Resigns as Lord Chancellor after refusing to take oath to support Act of Succession and Supremacy.

More's famous philosophical romance *Utopia* (the name means "nowhere") is the father of a whole class of writings, from Bacon's *New Atlantis* (1626), through Swift's *Gulliver's Travels* (1726), Butler's *Erewhon* (1872), and Bellamy's *Looking Backward* (1888), to the "science fiction" stories of the present. But More's book has its own ancestry. It derives in part from Plato's *Republic* (and hence is philosophical) and in part from the accounts of travelers like Amerigo Vespucci (1507) and hence is romantic. It is a major monument of the great Christian humanist awakening of which Pico della Mirandola (1463–94), Desiderius Erasmus (ca. 1466–1536), and More himself were the most brilliant figures. Since the first of these was Italian, the second Dutch, and the third English, the movement was obviously international; *Utopia* was written in Latin, the international language.

Utopia represents itself as a traveler's tale, told by a veteran mariner (who is also a philosopher) to a group of somewhat skeptical companions as they sit in a garden one afternoon in Antwerp, in Holland. It is divided into two books. In the first, written in dialogue form, the corruption of European civil life is criticized. In the second, the traveler Raphael Hythloday describes the institutions of Utopia, with many ironic references to the real world with which the listeners are familiar.

Utopia is thus not presented as a mere dream or impractical fancy, as the modern use of the word "utopian" sometimes suggests. It is the fruit of More's serious thought—though he was never wholly serious—on the great social problems of his time. More felt, very strongly, the value of the ideals embodied in the rules of the monastic orders. Yet he was himself a man of the world, a lawyer and negotiator; he saw how far from realization in practice were the social ideals he admired. Central to his thought is the idea of community of property, for which he had a precedent in Plato as well as in the rules of the monastic orders; no fundamental reform in society is possible until private property is abolished. Yet it is typical of More's carefully balanced method that a standard defense of private property is put into the mouth of More as a character in the dialogue, against the position of the main speaker, Hythloday.

More's life was even more remarkable than his writings. He was born in London, the son of a prominent lawyer; as a boy he served in Archbishop Morton's household, then proceeded to Oxford and the Inns of Court. He became a friend of Erasmus, the great humanist, scholar, and editor of the New Testament; it was to More that Erasmus dedicated his satire *The Praise of Folly*. Soon after he wrote *Utopia* More rose to positions of great responsibility under King Henry VIII: Master of Requests, Privy Councillor, Speaker of the House of Commons, and finally Lord Chancellor. In 1532, after the king's marriage to Anne Boleyn, More refused to take the oath for the Act of Succession and Supremacy. Although he had compromised before, as any successful administrator must, his conscience would not permit him to assert that any temporal lord, even Henry, could or ought to be head of that spiritual body, the church. From the point of view of the government, his refusal was treason, and he was condemned to death; efforts, including those of his wife, to reconcile him with Henry failed, and in 1535 he was executed. No death in English history is more famous: as he mounted the shaky steps to the scaffold, he said to the sheriff's officer, "I pray you, Master Lieutenant, see me safe up, and for my coming down let me shift for myself"; as he put his head on the block he moved his beard aside, remarking that his beard had done the king no offense. He was of course certain that he was not dying for treason, but in and for the faith of the Catholic Church. Four hundred years later he was canonized by the church as St. Thomas More.

From Utopia[1]

From *Book I*

[MORE MEETS A RETURNED TRAVELER]

The most invincible King of England, Henry the Eighth of that name, a prince adorned with the royal virtues beyond any other, had recently some differences of no slight import with Charles, the most serene Prince of Castille,[2] and sent me into Flanders as his spokesman to discuss and settle them. I was companion and associate to that incomparable man Cuthbert Tunstall,[3] whom the King has recently created Master of the Rolls, to everyone's great satisfaction. I will say nothing in praise of this man, not because I fear the judgment of a friend might be questioned, but because his learning and integrity are greater than I can describe and too well-known everywhere to need my commendation—unless I would, according to the proverb, "Show the sun with a lantern."

Those appointed by the prince to deal with us, all excellent men, met us at Bruges by prearrangement. Their head man and leader was the Margrave, so called, of Bruges, a most distinguished person. But their main speaker and guiding spirit was Georges de Themsecke, the Provost of Cassel, a man eloquent by nature as well as by training, very learned in the law, and most skillful in diplomatic affairs through his ability and long practice. After we had met several times, certain points remained on which we could not come to agreement; so they adjourned the meetings and went to Brussels for some days to consult their prince in person.

Meanwhile, since my business permitted it, I went to Antwerp. Of those who visited me while I was there, Peter Giles[4] was more

1. The translation from which these selections are taken is by Robert M. Adams (1975).
2. Later Charles V (1500–58), King of Spain and Holy Roman Emperor. The differences had to do with the wool trade.
3. Later Bishop of London and of Durham, one of More's closest friends (1474–1599).
4. Peter Giles (Petrus Aegidius), pupil and friend of Erasmus, town clerk of Antwerp. He arranged for the first printing, in Latin, of *Utopia* (1516).

welcome to me than any of the others. He was a native of Antwerp, a man of high reputation, already appointed to a good position and worthy of the very best: a young man distinguished equally by learning and character. Apart from being cultured, virtuous, and courteous to all, with his intimates he is so open, trustworthy, loyal, and affectionate that it would be hard to find another friend like him anywhere. No man is more modest or more frank; none better combines simplicity with wisdom. His conversation is so merry, and so witty without malice, that the ardent desire I felt to see my native country, my wife and my children (from whom I had been separated more than four months) was much eased by his agreeable company and pleasant talk.

One day after I had heard mass at Nôtre Dame, the most beautiful and most popular church in Antwerp, I was about to return to my quarters when I happened to see him talking with a stranger, a man of quite advanced years. The stranger had a sunburned face, a long beard, and a cloak hanging loosely from his shoulders; from his appearance and dress, I took him to be a ship's captain. When Peter saw me, he approached and greeted me. As I was about to return his greeting, he drew me aside, and, indicating the stranger, said, "Do you see that man? I was just on the point of bringing him to you."

"He would have been very welcome on your behalf," I answered.

"And on his own too, if you knew him," said Peter, "for there is no man alive today can tell you so much about unknown peoples and lands; and I know that you're always greedy for such information."

"In that case," said I, "my guess wasn't a bad one, for at first glance I supposed he was a skipper."

"Then you're not quite right," he replied, "for his sailing has not been like that of Palinurus, but more that of Ulysses, or rather of Plato.[5] This man, who is named Raphael—his family name is Hythloday—knows a good deal of Latin, and is particularly learned in Greek. He studied Greek more than Latin because his main interest is philosophy, and in that field he found that the Romans have left us nothing very valuable except certain works of Seneca and Cicero. Being eager to see the world, he left his patrimony to his brothers (he is Portuguese by birth) and took service with Amerigo Vespucci.[6] He accompanied Vespucci on the last three of his four voyages, accounts of which are now common read-

5. Palinurus, Aeneas's pilot, fell asleep, fell overboard and drowned. Ulysses, by contrast, was a wily, alert traveler. Plato is cited as the profound philosopher; his *Republic* strongly influenced *Utopia*. Raphael Hythloday is an invented character. His last name is coined from Greek words meaning "a skilled conveyor of nonsense."

6. Vespucci's last two voyages were made for the King of Portugal (hence Hythloday's birthplace). His account of his voyages, published in 1507, made him more famous than Columbus.

ing everywhere; but on the last voyage, he did not return home with the commander. After much persuasion and expostulation he got Amerigo's permission to be one of the twenty-four men who were left in a fort at the farthest point of the last voyage. Being marooned in this way was altogether agreeable to him, as he was more anxious to pursue his travels than afraid of death. He would often say, "The man who has no grave is covered by the sky,' and 'The road to heaven is equally short from all places.' Yet this frame of mind would have cost him dear, if God had not been gracious to him. After Vespucci's departure, he traveled through many countries with five companions from the fort. At last, by strange good fortune, he got, via Ceylon, to Calcutta, where by good luck he found some Portuguese ships; and so, beyond anyone's expectation, he returned to his own own country."

When Peter had told me this, I thanked him for his kindness in wishing to introduce me to a man whose conversation he hoped I would enjoy, and then I turned toward Raphael. After greeting one another and exchanging the usual civilities of strangers upon their first meeting, we all went to my house. There in the garden we sat down on a bench covered with turf to talk together.

He told us that when Vespucci sailed away, he and his companion who had stayed behind in the fort often met with the people of the countryside, and by ingratiating speeches gradually won their friendship. Before long they came to dwell with them safely and even affectionately. The prince also gave them his favor (I have forgotten his name and that of his country), furnishing Raphael and his five companions not only with ample provisions, but with means for traveling—rafts when they went by water, wagons when they went by land. In addition, he sent with them a most trusty guide who was to introduce and recommend them to such other princes as they desired to visit. After many days' journey, he said, they came to towns and cities, and to commonwealths that were both populous and not badly governed.

To be sure, under the equator and as far on both sides of the line as the sun moves, there lie vast empty deserts, scorched with the perpetual heat. The whole region is desolate and squalid, grim and uncultivated, inhabited by wild beasts, serpents, and also by men no less wild and dangerous than the beasts themselves. But as they went on, conditions gradually grew milder. The heat was less fierce, the earth greener, men and even beasts less savage. At last they reached people, cities, and towns which not only traded among themselves and with their neighbors, but even carried on commerce by sea and land with remote countries. After that, he said, they were able to visit different lands in every direction, for he and his companions were welcome as passengers aboard any ship about to make a journey.

The first vessels that they saw were flat-bottomed, with sails made of papyrus-reeds and wicker, or occasionally of leather. Farther on, they found ships with pointed keels and canvas sails, very much like our own. The seamen were skilled in managing wind and water; but they were most grateful to him, Raphael said, for showing them the use of the compass, of which they had been ignorant. For that reason, they had formerly sailed with great timidity, and only in summer. Now they have such trust in the compass that they no longer fear winter at all, and tend to be overconfident rather than secure. There is some danger that through their imprudence, this discovery, which they thought would be so advantageous to them, may become the cause of much mischief.

It would take too long to repeat all that Raphael told us he had observed, nor would it make altogether for our present purpose. Perhaps in another place we shall tell more about the things that are most profitable, especially the wise and sensible institutions that he observed among the civilized nations. We asked him many questions about such things, and he answered us willingly enough. We made no inquiries, however, about monsters, which are the routine of travelers' tales. Scyllas, ravenous Celaenos, man-eating Lestrygonians[7] and that sort of monstrosity you can hardly avoid, but it is not so easy to find good citizens and wise governments. While he told us of many ill-considered usages in these new-found nations, he also described quite a few other customs from which our own cities, nations, races, and kingdoms might take example in order to correct their errors. These I shall discuss in another place, as I said. Now I intend to relate only what he told us about the manners and laws of Utopians, first explaining the occasion that led him to speak of that commonwealth. Raphael had been talking very wisely about the many errors and also the wise institutions found both in that hemisphere and this (as many of both sorts in one place as in the other), speaking as shrewdly about the manners and governments of each place he had visited briefly as though he had lived there all his life. Peter was amazed.

"My dear Raphael," he said, "I'm surprised that you don't enter some king's service; for I don't know of a single prince who wouldn't be eager to have you. Your learning, and your knowledge of various countries and men would entertain him while your advice and your supply of examples would be very helpful. Thus you might advance your own interest and be useful at the same time to all your relatives and friends."

"I am not much concerned about my relatives and friends," he replied, "because I consider that I have already done my duty by

7. "Scyllas" were fabulous monsters, like the one who lived in a cave in the rock Scylla in the *Odyssey;* Celaeno was leader of the harpies in the *Aeneid,* large birds with the faces of women, pale with hunger, and provided with long, sharp talons. Lestrygonians were cannibals in the *Odyssey*.

them. While still young and healthy, I distributed among my relatives and friends the possessions that most men do not part with till they are old and sick (and then only reluctantly, because they can no longer keep them). I think they should be content with this gift of mine, and not expect that for their sake I should enslave myself to any king whatever."

"Well said," Peter replied; "but I do not mean that you should be in servitude to any king, only in his service."

"The difference is only a matter of one syllable," Raphael replied.[8]

"All right," said Peter, "but whatever you call it, I do not see any other way in which you can be so useful to your friends or to the general public, apart from making yourself happier."

"Happier indeed!" exclaimed Raphael. "Would a way of life so absolutely repellent to my spirit make my life happier? As it is now, I live as I please, and I fancy very few courtiers, however splendid, can say that. As a matter of fact, there are so many men soliciting favors from the great that it will be no great loss if they have to do without me and a couple of others like me."

Then I said, "It is clear, my dear Raphael, that you want neither wealth nor power, and indeed I value and revere a man of such a disposition as much as I do the greatest men in the world. Yet I think if you would devote your time and energy to public affairs, you would do a thing worthy of a generous and philosophical nature, even if you did not much like it. You could best perform such a service by joining the council of some great prince, whom you would incite to noble and just actions. I am sure you would do this if you held such an office, and your influence would be felt, because a people's welfare or misery flows in a stream from their prince, as from a never-failing spring. Your learning is so full, even if it weren't combined with experience, and your experience is so great, even if you didn't have any learning, that you would be an extraordinary councillor to any king in the world."

"You are twice mistaken, my dear More," he replied, "first in me and then in the situation itself. I don't have the capacity you ascribe to me, and if I had it in the highest degree, the public would not be any better off through the destruction of my peace. In the first place, most princes apply themselves to the arts of war, in which I have neither ability nor interest, instead of to the good arts of peace. They are generally more set on acquiring new kingdoms by hook or by crook than on governing well those that they already have. Moreover, the councillors of kings are all so wise that they need no other knowledge (or at least that's the way they see it). At the same time, they accept and even flatter the most absurd statements of favorites through whose influence they seek to stand

8. The play on words here depends on the Latin original: *servias* and *inservias*.

well with the prince. It is only natural, of course, that each man should think his own opinions best: the old crow loves his fledglings, and the ape his cubs. Now in a court composed of people who envy everyone else and admire only themselves, if a man should suggest something he had read of in other ages or seen in other places, the other councillors would think their reputation for wisdom was endangered, and they would look like simpletons, unless they could find fault with his proposal. If all else failed, they would take refuge in some remark like this: 'The way we're doing it is the way we've always done it, this custom was good enough for our fathers, and I only hope we're as wise as they were.' And with this deep thought they would take their seats, as though they had said the last word on the subject—implying, forsooth, that it would be a very dangerous matter if a man were found to be wiser in any point than his forefathers were. As a matter of fact, we quietly neglect the best examples they have left us; but if something better is proposed, we seize the excuse of reverence for times past and cling to it desperately. Such proud, obstinate, ridiculous judgments I have encountered many times, and once even in England."

* * *

From *Book II*

THE GEOGRAPHY OF UTOPIA

The island of the Utopians is two hundred miles across in the middle part where it is widest, and is nowhere much narrower than this except toward the two ends. These ends, drawn toward one another in a five-hundred-mile circle, make the island crescent-shaped like a new moon. Between the horns of the crescent, which are about eleven miles apart, the sea enters and spreads into a broad bay. Being sheltered from the wind by the surrounding land, the bay is never rough, but quiet and smooth instead, like a big lake. Thus, nearly the whole inner coast is one great harbor, across which ships pass in every direction, to the great advantage of the people. What with shallows on one side, and rocks on the other, the entrance into the bay is very dangerous. Near the middle of the channel, there is one rock that rises above the water, and so presents no dangers in itself; on top of it a tower has been built, and there a garrison is kept. Since the other rocks lie under water, they are very dangerous to navigation. The channels are known only to the Utopians, so hardly any strangers enter the bay without one of their pilots; and even they themselves could not enter safely if they did not direct themselves by some landmarks on the coast. If they should shift these landmarks about, they could lure to destruction an enemy fleet coming against them, however big it was.

On the outer side of the island there are likewise occasional harbors; but the coast is rugged by nature, and so well fortified that a few defenders could beat off the attack of a strong force. They say (and the appearance of the place confirms this) that their land was not always an island. But Utopus, who conquered the country and gave it his name (it had previously been called Abraxa),[9] brought its rude and uncouth inhabitants to such a high level of culture and humanity that they now excel in that regard almost every other people. After subduing them at his first landing, he cut a channel fifteen miles wide where their land joined the continent, and caused the sea to flow around the country. He put not only the natives to work at this task, but all his own soldiers too, so that the vanquished would not think the labor a disgrace. With the work divided among so many hands, the project was finished quickly, and the neighboring peoples, who at first had laughed at his folly, were struck with wonder and terror at his success.

There are fifty-four cities on the island, all spacious and magnificent, identical in language, customs, institutions, and laws. So far as the location permits, all of them are built on the same plan, and have the same appearance. The nearest are at least twenty-four miles apart, and the farthest are not so remote that a man cannot go on foot from one to the other in a day.

Once a year each city sends three of its old and experienced citizens to Amaurot[1] to consider affairs of common interest to the island. Amaurot is the chief city, lies near the omphalos[2] of the land, so to speak, and convenient to every other district, so it acts as a capital. Every city has enough ground assigned to it so that at least ten miles of farm land are available in every direction, though where the cities are farther apart, they have much more land. No city wants to enlarge its boundaries, for the inhabitants consider themselves good tenants rather than landlords. At proper intervals all over the countryside they have built houses and furnished them with farm equipment. These houses are inhabited by citizens who come to the country by turns to occupy them. No rural house has fewer than forty men and women in it, besides two slaves.[3] A master and mistress, serious and mature persons, are in charge of each household. Over every thirty households is placed a single phylarch.[4] Each year twenty persons from each rural household move back to the city, after completing a two-year stint in the country. In their place, twenty others are sent out from town, to learn farm work from those who have already been in the country for a year, and who are better skilled in farming. They, in turn, will teach

9. From Greek, "not small" or "insignificant."

1. Coined from a Greek adjective meaning "dark, obscure"—a suitable name for the capital of a country whose name means "Nowhere."

2. Navel, umbilicus—the spiritual as well as physical center of a nation.

3. More provides for a few bondmen or slaves in Utopia, to perform tasks unfit for citizens, such as slaughtering.

4. From Greek words meaning "head of a tribe."

those who come the following year. If all were equally ignorant of farm work, and new to it, they might harm the crops out of ignorance. This custom of alternating farm workers is solemnly established so that no one will have to do such hard work against his will for more than two years; but many of them who take a natural pleasure in farm life ask to stay longer.

The farm workers till the soil, raise cattle, hew wood, and take it to the city by land or water, as is most convenient. They breed an enormous number of chickens by a marvelous method. Men, not hens, hatch the eggs by keeping them in a warm place at an even temperature. As soon as they come out of the shell, the chicks recognize the men, follow them around, and are devoted to them instead of to their real mothers.

They raise very few horses, and these full of mettle, which they keep only to exercise the young men in the art of horsemanship. For the heavy work of plowing and hauling they use oxen, which they agree are inferior to horses over the short haul, but which can hold out longer under heavy burdens, are less subject to disease (as they suppose), and so can be kept with less cost and trouble. Moreover, when oxen are too old for work, they can be used for meat.

Grain they use only to make bread. They drink wine, apple or pear cider, or simple water, which they sometimes mix with honey or licorice, of which they have an abundance. Although they know very well, down to the last detail, how much grain each city and its surrounding district will consume, they produce much more grain and cattle than they need for themselves, and share the surplus with their neighbors. Whatever goods the folk in the country need which cannot be produced there, they request of the town magistrates, and since there is nothing to be paid or exchanged, they get what they want at once, without any haggling. They generally go to town once a month in any case, to observe the holy days. When harvest time approaches, the phylarchs in the country notify the town-magistrates how many hands will be needed. Crews of harvesters come just when they're wanted, and in one day of good weather they can usually get in the whole crop.

THEIR GOLD AND SILVER

For these reasons,[5] therefore, they have accumulated a vast treasure, but they do not keep it like a treasure. I'm really quite ashamed to tell you how they do keep it, because you probably won't believe me. I would not have believed it myself if someone had just told me about it; but I was there, and saw it with my own eyes. It is a general rule that the more different anything is from what people

5. More has explained, in a section here omitted, that the Utopians hire mercenary soldiers in time of war and pay them very highly; enemy soldiers often desert to them.

are used to, the harder it is to accept. But, considering that all their other customs are so unlike ours, a sensible man will not be surprised that they use gold and silver quite differently than we do. After all, they never do use money among themselves, but keep it only for a contingency which may or may not actually arise. So in the meanwhile they take care that no one shall overvalue gold and silver, of which money is made, beyond what the metals themselves deserve. Anyone can see, for example, that iron is far superior to either; men could not live without iron, by heaven, any more than without fire or water. But gold and silver have, by nature, no function that we cannot easily dispense with. Human folly has made them precious because they are rare. Like a most wise and generous mother, nature has placed the best things everywhere and in the open, like air, water, and the earth itself; but she has hidden away in remote places all vain and unprofitable things.

If in Utopia gold and silver were kept locked up in some tower, foolish heads among the common people might well concoct a story that the prince and the senate[6] were out to cheat ordinary folk and get some advantage for themselves. They might indeed put the gold and silver into beautiful plate-ware and rich handiwork, but then in case of necessity the people would not want to give up such articles, on which they had begun to fix their hearts, only to melt them down for soldiers' pay. To avoid all these inconveniences, they thought of a plan which conforms with their institutions as clearly as it contrasts with our own. Unless we've actually seen it working, their plan may seem ridiculous to us, because we prize gold so highly and are so careful about protecting it. With them it's just the other way. While they eat from pottery dishes and drink from glass cups, well made but inexpensive, their chamber pots and stools —all their humblest vessels, for use in the common halls and private homes—are made of gold and silver. The chains and heavy fetters of slaves are also made of these metals. Finally, criminals who are to bear through life the mark of some disgraceful act are forced to wear golden rings on their ears, golden bands on their fingers, golden chains around their necks, and even golden crowns on their heads. Thus they hold gold and silver up to scorn in every conceivable way. As a result, when they have to part with these metals, which other nations give up with as much agony as if they were being disemboweled, the Utopians feel it no more than the loss of a penny.

They find pearls by the seashore, diamonds and rubies in certain cliffs, but never go out of set purpose to look for them. If they

6. The prince, as More has earlier explained, is chosen for life by the senate, whose members are selected by an assembly, whose members in turn are selected from households.

happen to find some, they polish them, and give them to the children who, when they are small, feel proud and pleased with such gaudy decorations. But after, when they grow a bit older, and notice that only babies like such toys, they lay them aside. Their parents don't have to say anything, they simply put these trifles away out of a shamefaced sense that they're no longer suitable, just as our children when they grow up put away their rattles, marbles, and dolls.

Different customs, different feelings: I never saw the adage better illustrated than in the case of the Anemolian[7] ambassadors, who came to Amaurot while I was there. Because they came to discuss important business, the senate had assembled ahead of time, three citizens from each city. But the ambassadors from nearby nations, who had visited Utopia before and knew something of their customs, realized that fine clothing was not much respected in that land, silk was despised, and gold was a badge of contempt; and therefore they came in the very plainest of their clothes. But the Anemolians, who lived farther off and had had fewer dealings with the Utopians, had heard only that they all dressed alike, and very simply; so they took for granted that their hosts had nothing to wear that they didn't put on. Being themselves rather more proud than wise, they decided to dress as resplendently as the very gods and dazzle the eyes of the poor Utopians by the splendor of their garb.

Consequently the three ambassadors made a grand entry with a suite of a hundred attendants, all in clothing of many colors, and most in silk. Being noblemen at home, the ambassadors were arrayed in cloth of gold, with heavy gold chains on their necks, gold rings on their ears and fingers, and sparkling strings of pearls and gems on their caps. In fact, they were decked out in all the articles which in Utopia are used to punish slaves, shame wrongdoers, or pacify infants. It was a sight to see how they strutted when they compared their finery with the dress of the Utopians who had poured out into the street to see them pass. But it was just as funny to see how wide they fell of the mark, and how far they were from getting the consideration they wanted and expected. Except for a very few Utopians who for some special reason had visited foreign countries, all the onlookers considered this pomp and splendor a mark of disgrace. They therefore bowed to the humblest servants as lords, and took the ambassadors to be slaves because they were wearing golden chains, passing them by without any reverence at all. You might have seen children, who had themselves thrown away their pearls and gems, nudge their mothers when they saw the ambassadors' jeweled caps, and say:

7. From Greek, "windy people."

"Look at that big lummox, mother, who's still wearing pearls and jewels as if he were a little kid!"

But the mother, in all seriousness, would answer:

"Hush, my boy, I think he is one of the ambassadors' fools."

Others found fault with the golden chains as useless, because they were so flimsy any slave could break them, and so loose that he could easily shake them off and run away whenever he wanted. But after the ambassadors had spent a couple of days among the Utopians, they learned of the immense amounts of gold which were as thoroughly despised there as they were prized at home. They saw too that more gold and silver went into making the chains and fetters of a single runaway slave than into costuming all three of them. Somewhat crestfallen, then, they put away all the finery in which they had strutted so arrogantly; but they saw the wisdom of doing so after they had talked with the Utopians enough to learn their customs and opinions.

MARRIAGE CUSTOMS

Women do not marry till they are eighteen, nor men till they are twenty-two. Premarital intercourse by either men or women, if discovered and proved, is severely punished, and the guilty parties are forbidden to marry during their whole lives, unless the prince, by his pardon, alleviates the sentence. In addition both the father and mother of the household where the offense occurred suffer public disgrace for having been remiss in their duty. The reason they punish this offense so severely is that they suppose few people would join in married love— with confinement to a single partner, and all the petty annoyances that married life involves—unless they were strictly restrained from a life of promiscuity.

In choosing marriage partners, they solemnly and seriously follow a custom which seemed to us foolish and absurd in the extreme. Whether she is a widow or a virgin, the bride-to-be is shown naked to the groom by a responsible and respectable matron; and, similarly, some respectable man presents the groom naked to his future bride. We laughed at this custom and called it absurd; but they were just as amazed at the folly of all other nations. When men go to buy a colt, where they are risking only a little money, they are so suspicious that though he is almost bare they won't close the deal until the saddle and blanket have been taken off, lest there be a hidden sore underneath. Yet in the choice of a mate, which may cause either delight or disgust for the rest of their lives, people are completely careless. They leave all the rest of her body covered up with clothes and estimate the attractiveness of a woman from a mere handsbreadth of her person, the face, which is all they can see. And so they marry, running great risk of hating one another for the rest of their lives, if something in either's person should offend the other. Not all people are so wise as to concern themselves solely with character; even the wise appreciate physical beauty, as a supplement to a good disposition. There's no question but that deformity may lurk under clothing, serious enough to make a man hate his wife when it's too late to be separated from her. When deformities are discovered after marriage, each person must bear his own fate, so the Utopians think everyone should be protected by law beforehand.

There is extra reason for them to be careful, because in that part of the world, they are the only people who practice monogamy. Their marriages are seldom terminated except by death, though they do allow divorce for adultery or for intolerably difficult behavior. A husband or wife who is an aggrieved party to such a divorce is granted permission by the senate to remarry, but the guilty party is considered disreputable and permanently forbidden to take another mate. They absolutely forbid a husband to put away his wife against her will because of some bodily misfortune; they think it cruel that a person should be abandoned when most in need of comfort; and they add that old age, since it not only entails disease but is actually a disease itself, needs more than a precarious fidelity.

It happens occasionally that a married couple cannot get along, and have both found other persons with whom they hope to live more harmoniously. After getting the approval of the senate, they may then separate by mutual consent and contract new marriages. But such divorces are allowed only after the senators and their wives have carefully investigated the case. They allow divorce only very reluctantly because they know that husbands and wives will find it hard to settle down together if each has in mind that another new relation is easily available.

They punish adulterers with the strictest form of slavery. If both parties were married, they are both divorced, and the injured parties may marry one another, if they want, or someone else. But if one of the injured parties continues to love such an undeserving spouse, the marriage may go on, providing the innocent person chooses to share in the labor to which every slave is condemned. And sometimes it happens that the repentance of the guilty, and the devotion of the innocent party, move the prince to pity, so that he restores both to freedom. But a second conviction of adultery is punished by death.

RELIGIONS

There are different forms of religion throughout the island, and in each particular city as well. Some worship as a god the sun, others the moon, and still others one of the planets. There are some who worship a man of past ages who was conspicuous either for virtue or glory; they consider him not only a god but the supreme god. Most of the Utopians, however, and among these all the wisest, believe nothing of the sort: they believe in a single power, unknown, eternal, infinite, inexplicable, far beyond the grasp of the human mind, and diffused throughout the universe, not physically, but in influence. Him they call father, and to him alone they attribute the origin, increase, progress, change, and end of all visible things; they do not offer divine honors to any other.

Though the other sects of the Utopians differ from this main group in various particular doctrines, they all agree in this main head, that there is one supreme power, the maker and ruler of the universe, whom they all call in their native language Mithra.[8] Different people define him differently, and each supposes the object of his worship is the special vessel of that great force which all people agree in worshiping. But gradually they are coming to forsake this mixture of superstitions, and to unite in that one religion which seems more reasonable than any of the others. And there is no doubt that the other religions would have disappeared long ago, except for various unlucky accidents which befell certain Utopians who were thinking about changing their religion. All the others immediately construed these events as a sign of heavenly anger, not chance, as if the deity who was being abandoned were avenging an insult against himself.

But after they had heard from us the name of Christ, and learned of his teachings, his life, his miracles, and the no less marvelous devotion of the many martyrs who shed their blood to draw nations far and near into the Christian fellowship, you would not believe how they were impressed. Either through the mysterious inspiration of God, or because Christianity is very like the religion already prevailing among them, they were well disposed toward it from the start. But I think they were also much influenced by the fact that Christ had encouraged his disciples to practice community of goods, and that among the truest groups of Christians, the practice still prevails.[9] Whatever the reason, no small number of them chose to join our communion, and received the holy water of baptism. By that time, two of our group had died, and among us four survivors there was, I am sorry to say, no priest; so, though they received instruction in other matters, they still lack those sacraments which in our religion can be administered only by priests. They do, however, understand what they are and earnestly desire them. In fact, they dispute vigorously among themselves whether a

8. The spirit of light in ancient Persian religion, which More could have learned about from reading Pico della Mirandola.

9. Many monastic orders of More's time abolished private property for their members.

man chosen from among themselves could be considered a priest, even if not ordained by a Christian bishop. Though they seemed on the point of selecting such a person, they had not yet done so when I left.

Those who have not accepted Christianity make no effort to restrain others from it, nor do they criticize new converts to it. While I was there, only one of the Christians got into trouble with the law. As soon as he was baptized, he took on himself to preach the Christian religion publicly, with more zeal than discretion. We warned him not to do so, but he soon worked himself up to a pitch where he not only preferred our religion, but condemned all others as profane in themselves, leading their impious and sacrilegious followers to the hell-flames they richly deserved. After he had been going on in this style for a long time, they arrested him. He was tried, not on a charge of despising their religion, but of creating a public disorder, convicted and sentenced to exile. For it is one of their oldest institutions that no man's religion, as such, shall be held against him.

Even before he came to the island, King Utopus had heard that the inhabitants were continually quarreling over religious matters. In fact, he found it was easy to conquer the country because the different sects were too busy fighting one another to oppose him. As soon as he had gained the victory, therefore, he decreed that every man might cultivate the religion of his choice, and might proselytize for it, provided he did so quietly, modestly, rationally, and without bitterness toward others. If persuasions failed, no man was allowed to resort to abuse or violence, under penalty of exile or enslavement.

Utopus laid down these rules, not simply for the sake of peace, which he saw was in danger of being destroyed by constant quarrels and implacable hatred; but also for the sake of religion itself. In matters of religion, he was not at all quick to dogmatize, because he suspected that God perhaps likes various forms of worship and has therefore deliberately inspired different people with different views. On the other hand, he was quite sure that it was arrogant folly for anyone to enforce conformity with his own beliefs by means of threats or violence. He supposed that if one religion is really true and the rest false, that true one will prevail by its own natural strength, provided only that men consider the matter reasonably and moderately. But if they try to decide these matters by fighting and rioting, since the worst men are always the most headstrong, the best and holiest religion in the world will be crowded out by blind superstitions, like grain choked out of a field by thorns and briars. So he left the whole matter open, allowing each individual man to choose what he would believe. The only exception he made was a positive and strict law against any person who should sink so far below the dignity of human nature as to think that the soul perishes with the body, or that the universe is ruled by mere chance, rather than divine providence.

Thus the Utopians all believe that after this life vices are to be punished and virtue rewarded; and they consider that anyone who opposes this proposition is hardly a man, since he has degraded the sublimity of his own soul to the base level of a beast's wretched body. They will not even count him as one of their citizens, since he would undoubtedly betray all the laws and customs of society, if not prevented by fear. Who can doubt that a man who has nothing to fear but the law, and no hope of life beyond the grave, will do anything he can to evade his country's laws by craft or break them by violence, in order to gratify his own private greed? Therefore a man who holds such views is offered no honors, entrusted with no offices, and given no public responsibility; he is universally regarded as a low and sordid fellow. Yet they do not afflict him with punishments, because they are persuaded that no man can choose to believe by a mere act of the will. They do not compel him by threats to dissemble his views, nor do they tolerate in the matter any deceit or lying, which they detest as next door to deliberate malice. The man may not argue in the presence of the common people in behalf of his opinion; but in the presence of the priests and other important persons, they not only permit but encourage it. For they are confident that in the end his madness will yield to reason.

There are some others, in fact no small number of them, who err in the opposite direction, in supposing that animals too have immortal souls, though not comparable to ours in excellence, nor destined to equal felicity. These men are not thought to be evil, their opinion is not thought to be wholly unreasonable, and so they are not interfered with.

Almost all the Utopians are absolutely convinced that man's bliss after death will be enormous and eternal; thus they lament every man's sickness, but mourn over a death only if the man was torn from life anxiously and against his will. Such behavior they take to be a very bad sign, as if the soul, being in despair and conscious of guilt, dreaded death through a secret premonition of punishments to come. Besides, they suppose God can hardly be well pleased with the coming of one who, when he is summoned, does not come gladly, but is dragged off reluctantly and against his will. Such a death fills the onlookers with horror, and they carry away the corpse to the cemetery in melancholy silence. There, after begging God to have mercy on his spirit, and pardon his infirmities, they bury the unhappy man. But when a man dies blithely and full of good hope, they do not mourn for him, but carry the body cheerfully away, singing and commending the dead man's soul to God. They cremate him in a spirit more of reverence than of grief, and erect a tombstone on which the dead man's honors are inscribed. As they go home, they talk of his character and deeds, and no part of his life is mentioned more frequently or more gladly than his joyful death.

They think that recollecting the good qualities of a man helps the living to behave virtuously and is also the most acceptable form of honor to the dead. For they think that dead persons are actually present among us, and hear what we say about them, though through the dullness of human sight they are invisible to our eyes. Given their state of bliss, the dead must be able to travel freely where they please, and they are bound to want to revisit their friends, whom they loved and honored during their lives. Like all other good things, they think that after death freedom of motion is increased rather than decreased in all good men; and thus they believe the dead come frequently among the living, to observe their words and actions. Hence they go about their business the more confidently because of their trust in such protectors; and the belief that their forefathers are physically present keeps men from any secret dishonorable deed.

Fortune-telling and other vain forms of superstitious divination, such as other people take very seriously, they consider ridiculous and contemptible. But they venerate miracles which occur without the help of nature, considering them direct and visible manifestations of the divine power. Indeed, they report that miracles have frequently occurred in their country. Sometimes in great and dangerous crises they pray publicly for a miracle, which they then anticipate with great confidence, and obtain.

They think that the careful investigation of nature, and the sense of reverence arising from it, are acts of worship to God.

* * *

[CONCLUSION]

Now I have described to you as accurately as I could the structure of that commonwealth which I consider not only the best but the only one that can rightfully claim that name. In other places men talk very liberally of the common wealth, but what they mean is simply their own wealth; in Utopia, where there is no private business, every man zealously pursues the public business. And in both places, men are right to act as they do. For among us, even though the state may flourish, each man knows that unless he makes separate provision for himself, he may perfectly well die of hunger. Bitter necessity, then, forces men to look out for themselves rather than for others, that is, for the people. But in Utopia, where everything belongs to everybody, no man need fear that, so long as the public warehouses are filled, he will ever lack for anything he needs. Distribution is simply not one of their problems; in Utopia no men are poor, no men are beggars. Though no man owns anything, everyone is rich.

For what can be greater riches than for a man to live joyfully and peacefully, free from all anxieties, and without worries about making a living? No man is bothered by his wife's querulous complaints about money, no man fears poverty for his son, or struggles to scrape up a dowry for his daughter. Each man can feel secure of his own livelihood and happiness and of his whole family's as well: wife, sons, grandsons, great-grandsons, great-great-grandsons, and that whole long line of descendants that gentlefolk are so fond of contemplating. Indeed, even those who once worked but can do so no longer are cared for just as well as if they were still productive.

Let me now make bold to compare this justice of the Utopians with the so-called justice that prevails among other nations—among whom let me perish if I can discover the slightest scrap of justice or fairness. What kind of justice is it when a nobleman or a goldsmith[1] or a moneylender, or someone else who makes his living by doing either nothing at all or something completely useless to the public, gets to live a life of luxury and grandeur? In the meantime, a laborer, a carter, a carpenter, or a farmer works so hard and so constantly that even a beast of burden would perish under the load; and this work of theirs is so necessary that no commonwealth could survive a year without it. Yet they earn so meager a living and lead such miserable lives that a beast of burden would really be better off. Beasts do not have to work every minute, and their food is not much worse; in fact they like it better. And, besides, they do not have to worry about their future. But workingmen not only have to sweat and suffer without present reward, but agonize over the prospect of a penniless old age. Their daily wage is inadequate even for their present needs, so there is no possible chance of their saving toward the future.

Now isn't this an unjust and ungrateful commonwealth? It lavishes rich rewards on so-called gentry, bankers and goldsmiths and the rest of that crew, who don't work at all, are mere parasites, or purveyors of empty pleasures. And yet it makes no provision whatever for the welfare of farmers and colliers, laborers, carters, and carpenters, without whom the commonwealth would simply cease to exist. After the state has taken the labor of their best years, when they are worn out by age and sickness and utter destitution, then the thankless state, forgetting all their pains and services, throws

1. Banker.

them out to die a miserable death. What is worse, the rich constantly try to grind out of the poor part of their meager wages, not only by private swindling, but by public tax-laws. It is basically unjust that people who deserve most from the commonwealth should receive least. But now they have distorted and debased the right even further by giving their extortion the color of law; and thus they have palmed injustice off as "legal." When I run over in my mind the various commonwealths flourishing today, so help me God, I can see nothing in them but a conspiracy of the rich, who are fattening up their own interests under the name and title of the commonwealth. They invent ways and means to hang onto whatever they have acquired by sharp practice, and then they scheme to oppress the poor by buying up their toil and labor as cheaply as possible. These devices become law as soon as the rich, speaking through the commonwealth—which, of course, includes the poor as well—say they must be observed.

And yet, when these insatiably greedy and evil men have divided among themselves goods which would have sufficed for the entire people, how far they remain from the happiness of the Utopians, who have abolished not only money but with it greed! What a mass of trouble was uprooted by that one step! What a multitude of crimes was pulled up by the roots! Everyone knows that if money were abolished, fraud, theft, robbery, quarrels, brawls, seditions, murders, treasons, poisonings, and a whole set of crimes which are avenged but not prevented by the hangman would at once die out. If money disappeared, so would fear, anxiety, worry, toil, and sleepless nights. Even poverty, which seems to need money more than anything else for its relief, would vanish if money were entirely done away with.

Consider if you will this example. Take a barren year of failed harvests, when many thousands of men have been carried off by hunger. If at the end of the famine the barns of the rich were searched, I dare say positively enough grain would be found in them to save the lives of all those who died from starvation and disease, if it had been divided equally among them. Nobody really need have suffered from a bad harvest at all. So easily might men get the necessities of life if that cursed money, which is supposed to provide access to them, were not in fact the chief barrier to our getting what we need to live. Even the rich, I'm sure, understand this. They must know that it's better to have enough of what we really need than an abundance of superfluities, much better to escape from our many present troubles than to be burdened with great masses of wealth. And in fact I have no doubt that every man's perception of where his true interest lies, along with the authority of Christ our Saviour (whose wisdom could not fail to recognize the best, and whose goodness would not fail to counsel it), would long ago have brought the whole world to adopt Utopian laws, if it were not for one single monster, the prime plague and begetter of all others—I mean Pride.

Pride measures her advantages not by what she has but by what other people lack. Pride would not condescend even to be made a goddess, if there were no wretches for her to sneer at and domineer over. Her good fortune is dazzling only by contrast with the miseries of others, her riches are valuable only as they torment and tantalize the poverty of others. Pride is a serpent from hell which twines itself around the hearts of men; and it acts like the suckfish[2] in holding them back from choosing a better way of life.

Pride is too deeply fixed in the hearts of men to be easily plucked out. So I am glad that the Utopians at least have been lucky enough to achieve this commonwealth, which I wish all mankind would imitate. The institutions they have adopted have made their community most happy, and as far as anyone can tell, capable of lasting forever. Now that they have rooted up the seeds of ambition and faction at home, along with most other vices, they are in no danger from internal strife, which at home has been the ruin of many other states that seemed secure. As long as they preserve harmony at home, and keep their institutions healthy, the Utopians can never be overcome or even shaken by their envious neighbors, who have often attempted their ruin, but always in vain.

When Raphael had finished his story, it seemed to me that not a few of the customs and laws he had described as existing among the Utopians were quite absurd. Their methods of waging war, their religious ceremonies, and their social customs were some of these, but my chief objection was to the basis of their whole system, that is, their communal living and their moneyless economy. This one thing alone takes away all the nobility, magnificence, splendor, and majesty which (in the popular view) are considered the true ornaments of any nation. But I saw Raphael was tired with talking, and I was not sure he could take contradiction in these matters, particularly when I remembered what he had said about certain councillors who were afraid they might not appear wise unless they found out something to criticize in other men's ideas.

So with praise for the Utopian way of life and his account of it, I took him by the hand and led him in to supper. But first I said that we would find some other time for thinking of these matters more deeply, and for talking them over in more detail. And I still hope such an opportunity will present itself some day.

2. The remora, which attaches itself by a suction cup to larger fish or ships. It was fabled to be strong enough to hold back a ship under sail.

Meanwhile, though he is a man of unquestioned learning, and highly experienced in the ways of the world, I cannot agree with everything he said. Yet I confess there are many things in the Commonwealth of Utopia which I wish our own country would imitate—though I don't really expect it will.

1514–16 1516

JOHN SKELTON
(ca. 1460–1529)

According to one of the jest-book tales, John Skelton suddenly interrupted one of his sermons to ask the members of his congregation why they had complained that he kept a fair wench in the rectory. To be sure, he said, he did keep a fair wench; she was fairer than his parishioners' wives and had given him a son. Holding the child up naked before the congregation, he exclaimed, "How say you, neighbors all? Is not this child as fair as is the best of all yours? It hath nose, eyes, hands, and feet, as well as any of yours. It is not like a pig, nor a calf, nor like no foul nor no monstrous beast. If I had brought forth this child without arms or legs, or that it were deformed being a monstrous thing, I would never have blamed you to have complained to the Bishop of me, but to complain without a cause! I say as I said before, in my antetheme, *vos estis*, you be, and have been, and will and shall be knaves to complain of me without a cause reasonable."

Many and colorful were the stories circulated about the mad wag Skelton—who was also the major poet of the first quarter of the century, with the title of Poet Laureate from both Oxford and Cambridge. He was famous as a rhetorician and a translator, and he was also, for a time, tutor to the young Henry VIII. He took orders and, after writing *The Bowge of Court* (1498), a satire on courtiers and court life, retired about 1503, became rector of the parish church at Diss, in Norfolk. By 1512 he had returned to the court, appointed King's Orator. He moved to a house in the sanctuary of Westminster in 1518, and shortly thereafter began his vituperous attacks upon Cardinal Wolsey, the great prelate-statesman, including *Speak, Parrot, Colin Clout,* and *Why Come Ye Not To Court?* (1521–22). Wolsey had him imprisoned for a time but later released him.

While in retirement at Diss, he began to write poetry in a "plain style" that rejected ornate rhetorical devices and aureate language. His satires gain some of their most startling effects by mixing high and low styles. These "open satires," as they are called, are written in short rhymed lines that to the modern ear resemble doggerel, although something like this form was probably familiar enough to readers of medieval satire. A Skeltonic line may have from two to five beats, and the lines can keep on rhyming until the resources of the language give out. To many of his poems, particularly the satires, this strange meter is singularly appropriate. *The Tunning of Elinour Rumming* is, for example, a wonderfully disordered, clattering portrait of an alewife that reminds one of Brueghel's paintings in its realism, and the Skeltonics do much to contribute to the effect of disorder. The lines give the voice of the narrator of the satires a breathless urgency much admired by Robert Graves and W. H. Auden, among other modern poets. Skelton's satires draw upon a long tradition of medieval anti-clerical satire, but he brings a fresh voice to the genre.

Skelton's lyrics also partake of traditional medieval modes which the poet makes his own. To the three-part song *Mannerly Margery*, a traditional ballad of the clerk and the serving-maid, he gives an ironic ending. His rather salacious *Lullay, Lullay* is a parody on traditional lullabies in which the Virgin Mary rocks the Christ child in her lap. In an entirely different mood is the pleasant lyric in praise of Mistress Margaret Hussey. It is one of several which Skelton published in 1523 in *The Garland of Laurel;* in that work the poet is crowned with a laurel wreath by the Countess of Surrey and her ladies, and in gratitude he writes a poem to each of them. In his lyrics as well as his satires we hear a genuine music and find, as always, the impress of the distinctive character of their author.

From Colin Clout[1]

And if ye stand in doubt
Who brought this rhyme about,
My name is Colin Clout.
I purpose to shake out
All my conning° bag, *learning*
Like a clerkly hag.[2]
For though my rhyme be ragged,
Tattered and jagged,
Rudely rain-beaten,
Rusty and moth-eaten,
If ye take well therewith,
It hath in it some pith.
For, as far as I can see,
It is wrong with each degree.
For the temporality° *laymen*
Accuseth the spirituality;
The spirituality again
Doth grudge and complain
Upon the temporal men;
Thus, each of other blother° *babble*
The one against the other.
Alas, they make me shudder!
For in hugger-mugger° *haste*
The Church is put in fault;
The prelates been so haut,° *haughty*
They say, and look so high
As though they wouldé fly
Above the starry sky.

1519

1. These are lines 47–74, comprising part of the introductory matter. Colin Clout, the narrator, here introduces the theme of the whole long poem, in the characteristically jagged Skeltonic line.
2. Old scholar.

Upon a Dead Man's Head

That was sent to him from an honorable gentlewoman for a token, Skelton, Laureate, devised this ghostly[3] meditation in English covenable,[4] in sentence, commendable, lamentable, lacrimable, profitable for the soul.

Your ugly token
My mind hath broken
From worldly lust;
For I have discussed,
We are but dust
And die we must.

It is general
To be mortal;
I have well espied
No man may him hide
From Death hollow-eyed
With sinews wyderéd° *withered*
With bones shyderéd,° *shattered*
With his worm-eaten maw
And his ghastly jaw
Gaping aside,
Naked of hide,
Neither flesh nor fell.° *skin*

Then, by my counsel
Look that ye spell° *study*
Well this gospel,
For whereso we dwell
Death will us quell
And with us mell.° *mix*

For all our pampered paunches
There may no fraunchis° *franchise*
Nor worldly bliss
Redeem us from this:
Our days be dated
To be checkmated
With draughtes of death
Stopping our breath;
Our eyen° sinking, *eyes*
Our bodies stinking,
Our gummes grinning,
Our soules brinning.° *burning*

3. Spiritual.

4. Suitable; "in sentence": in meaning.

To whom, then, shall we sue
For to have rescue
But to sweet Jesu
On us then for to rue?
O goodly child
Of Mary mild
Then be our shield,
That we be not exiled
To the dyne° dale *dark*
Of bootless bale[5]
Nor to the lake
Of fiendes° black. *devils*

But grant us grace
To see thy face
And to purchase
Thine heavenly place
And thy palace
Full of solace
Above the sky
That is so high,
Eternally
To behold and see
The Trinity.

Amen.

Myrres vous y.[6]

ca. 1498

Mannerly Margery Milk and Ale[7]

Aye, beshrew you, by my fay,[8]
These wanton clerks be nice° alway, *foolish*
Avaunt, avaunt, my popinjay!
"What, will you do nothing but play?"
Tilly vally straw, let be I say!
Gup,[9] Christian Clout, gup, Jack of the Vale!
With Mannerly Margery milk and ale.

"By God, ye be a pretty pode,° *toad*
And I love you an whole cartload."
Straw, James Foder, ye play the fode,° *deceiver, seducer*
I am no hackney for your rod:° *riding*
Go watch a bull, your back is broad!
Gup, Christian Clout, gup, Jack of the Vale!
With Mannerly Margery milk and ale.

5. Irremediable sorrow.
6. See yourself in it.
7. The clerk's lines are in quotation marks; Margery sings the rest, except the chorus lines, which are sung by a bass.
8. "Beshrew": curse (not used seriously); "fay": faith.
9. Contracted from "go up."

Ywis° ye deal uncourteously; *certainly*
What, would ye frumple° me? now fie! *rumple, tumble*
"What, and ye shall not be my pigsny?"° *darling*
By Christ, ye shall not, no hardily:
I will not be japped° bodily! *tricked, deceived*
Gup, Christian Clout, gup, Jack of the Vale!
With Mannerly Margery milk and ale.

"Walk forth your way, ye cost me naught;
Now have I found that I have sought:
The best cheap flesh that ever I bought."
Yet, for his love that hath all wrought,
Wed me, or else I die for thought.
Gup, Christian Clout, your breath is stale!
Go, Mannerly Margery milk and ale!
Gup, Christian Clout, gup, Jack of the Vale!
With Mannerly Margery milk and ale.

ca. 1510 1523

Lullay, Lullay, Like a Child

With lullay, lullay, like a child,
Thou sleepest too long, thou art beguiled.° *deceived*

"My darling dear, my daisy flower,
Let me," quod° he, "lie in your lap." *quoth*
"Lie still," quod she, "my paramour,
Lie still, hardily,° and take a nap." *confidently*
His head was heavy, such was his hap,
All drowsy dreaming, drowned in sleep,
That of his love he took no keep.
With hey, lullay, lullay, like a child,
Thou sleepest too long, thou art beguiled.

With ba, ba, ba![1] and bas, bas, bas!
She cherished him, both cheek and chin,
That he wist never where he was,
He had forgotten all deadly sin.
He wanted wit her love to win,
He trusted her payment and lost all his pay;
She left him sleeping and stale° away, *stole*
With hey, lullay, lullay, like a child,
Thou sleepest too long, thou art beguiled.

The rivers rough, the waters wan,
She sparéd not to wet her feet;
She waded over, she found a man
That halséd° her heartily and kissed her sweet— *embraced*
Thus after her cold she caught a heat.

1. The "by" of *lullaby;* "bas, bas, bas": kiss, kiss, kiss.

"My lief," she said, "routeth[2] in his bed;
Ywis° he hath an heavy head." *certainly*
With hey, lullay, lullay, like a child,
Thou sleepest too long, thou are beguiled.

What dreamest thou, drunkard, drowsy pate?
Thy lust and liking is from thee gone.
Thou blinkard blowboll,[3] thou wakest too late.
Behold thou liest, luggard,° alone! *sluggard*
Well may thou sigh, well may thou groan,
To deal with her so cowardly.
Ywis, pole-hatchet,° she bleared thine eye. *barfly*

1490–1503

To Mistress Margaret Hussey

Merry Margaret,
As midsummer flower,
Gentle as falcon
Or hawk of the tower;[1]
With solace and gladness,
Much mirth and no madness,
All good and no badness;
So joyously,
So maidenly,
So womanly
Her demeaning
In every thing,
Far, far passing
That I can endite,[2]
Or suffice to write
Of merry Margaret
As midsummer flower,
Gentle as falcon
Or hawk of the tower.
As patient and as still
And as full of good will
As fair Isaphill;[3]
Colyander,
Sweet pomander,[4]
Good Cassander;[5]

2. My lover snores.
3. Blink-eyed drunkard.
1. "Falcon-gentle" was the term applied to the female and young of the goshawk; a "hawk of the tower" was one that towered aloft, sailing high in the air before swooping on its prey.
2. I.e., surpassing anything that I can compose.
3. Hypsipyle, Queen of Lemnos, famous for her devotion to her father and to her children.
4. Colyander or coriander was an herb supposed to soothe pain; like sweet pomander, it had a pleasant odor.
5. The beautiful daughter of Priam of Troy; she could prophesy accurately but no one believed her prophecies. This did not discourage her; she is preeminently "steadfast of thought" (line 26).

Steadfast of thought,
Well made, well wrought,
Far may be sought
Ere that ye can find
So courteous, so kind
As merry Margaret,
This midsummer flower,
Gentle as falcon
Or hawk of the tower.

1523

SIR THOMAS WYATT THE ELDER

(1503–1542)

Wyatt was born at Allington Castle in Kent, and educated at St. John's College, Cambridge. He spent most of his life as a courtier and diplomat, serving King Henry VIII as Clerk of the King's Jewels and as ambassador to Spain and to the Emperor Charles V. He was also a member of various missions to France and Italy. He spent much of his adult life abroad; his interest in foreign literature, especially Italian, is evident from his translations and imitations of poems by the Italian sonneteers Petrarch, Sannazaro, Alamanni, and others. The life of a courtier under Henry VIII was not a calm life: Wyatt was twice arrested and imprisoned, once in 1536, after a quarrel with the Duke of Suffolk, and again in 1541, when he was charged with treason, lodged in the Tower of London, and stripped of all his property. On both occasions he was fortunate enough to regain the king's favor and receive a pardon. His praise of quiet retired life in the country and the cynical comments about foreign courts in his verse epistle to John Poins derive from his own experience.

For all his travel abroad, Wyatt remained essentially an Englishman. His poetry includes not only the sonnets, based upon Italian models, but also many delightful lyrics with short stanzas and refrains in the manner of the native English "ballet" (pronounced to rhyme with *mallet*) or dance-song. Wyatt's own temperament and disposition show more clearly in these English poems than in the sonnets. The lover in the Petrarchan sonnet is usually in a mood of doleful despair; the typical poem is essentially a complaint, though the interest lies in following the elaborately worked out "conceits" or comparisons. The lover is abject, he is the lady's slave; her coldness is a perpetual torture to him. In the ballets, however, a rather gay, manly independence is the characteristic note.

The sonnet, a 14-line poem with a complicated rhyme scheme, was introduced into English by Wyatt. He took his subject matter from Petrarch's sonnets, for the most part, but his rhyme schemes came from other Italian models. The most common rhyme scheme in Wyatt's sonnets is *abba abba cddc ee;* the usual Italian structure of an octave (first eight lines) followed after a turn in the sense by a sestet (last six lines) was already beginning to break down into the "English" structure for the sonnet, three quatrains and a couplet.

Although Wyatt intended to publish a collection of his poems, he never did so. In fact, very little of his verse was published until after his death. In aristocratic circles poems circulated in manuscript and were copied by hand; the general public usually saw courtiers' poems only when some enterprising publisher acquired manuscripts, perhaps already formed into a collection, and printed them as a miscellany. An early volume of this sort, called *The Court of Venus*, published a few Wyatt poems before 1540. A dozen such collections were published during the second half of the 16th century, with titles like *A Paradise of Dainty Devices, A Handful of Pleasant Delights*, and *A Gorgeous Gallery of Gallant Inventions*. By far the most important of these miscellanies was issued by the printer Richard Tottel in 1557 (15 years after Wyatt's death) with the title *Songs and Sonnets written by the Right Honorable Lord Henry Howard late Earl of Surrey and other*. Until modern times it was always called simply *Songs and Sonnets* (Shakespeare has his Master Slender in *The Merry Wives of Windsor* say "I had rather than forty shillings I had my book of Songs and Sonnets here"); but now it is always referred to as *Tottel's Miscellany*. The printer, Richard Tottel, addressed the reader in an interesting epistle:

> That to have well written in verse, yea and in small parcels, deserveth great praise, the works of divers Latins, Italians and other do prove sufficiently. That our tongue is able in that kind to do as praiseworthy as the rest, the honorable style of the noble Earl of Surrey and the weightiness of the deep-witted Sir Thomas Wyatt the Elder's verse, with several graces in sundry good English writers, do show abundantly. It resteth now, gentle reader, that thou think it not ill done to publish, to the honor of the English tongue, and for profit of the studious of English eloquence, those works which the ungentle hoarders up of such treasure have heretofore envied thee. And for this point, good reader, thine own profit and pleasure in these presently, and moe hereafter, shall answer for my defence. If perhaps some mislike the stateliness of style, removed from the rude skill of common ears, I ask help of the learned to defend their learned friends, the authors of this work. And I exhort the unlearned, by reading to be more skilfull, and to purge that swinelike grossness that maketh the sweet marjoram not to smell to their delight.

The anthology includes 271 poems—97 attributed to Wyatt, 40 to Surrey, 40 to Nicholas Grimald, and 94 to "Uncertain Authors." It is surely one of the most important books in the history of English literature, for it was the channel through which the main currents of European Renaissance poetry flowed into the British Isles. In it the sonnet, blank verse, *terza rima*, ottava rima, rondeau, and other forms were naturalized into English, and suddenly the ragged, undisciplined, pedestrian verse of the first part of the century became antiquated. When Wyatt was a boy it was possible for Alexander Barclay, an ambitious and by no means uneducated poet, to write verse like this:

> The famous poets with the muses nine
> With wit inspired, fresh, pregnant and divine,
> Say boldly endite in style substantial;
> Some in poems high and historical,
> Some them delight in heavy tragedies
> And some in wanton or merry comedies.

Wyatt was not primarily concerned with regularity of accent and smoothness of rhythm. By the time *Tottel's Miscellany* was published, Wyatt's rather rough and vigorous metrical practice was felt to be crude, and Tottel's editor smoothed out the versification. We reprint *They Flee from Me* in the versions of the Egerton manuscript and of Tottel. The Egerton manuscript (E. MS.) contains poems in Wyatt's own hand and corrections in his hand of scribal texts. The Devonshire manuscript (D. MS.) was not apparently in the poet's possession, but some of its texts seem earlier than Egerton's and it furnishes additional poems.

The Long Love That in My Thought Doth Harbor[1]

The long love that in my thought doth harbor,
And in my heart doth keep his residence,
Into my face presseth with bold pretense
And therein campeth, spreading his banner.[2]
She that me learneth to love and suffer
And wills that my trust and lust's negligence[3]
Be reined by reason, shame, and reverence
With his hardiness taketh displeasure.
Wherewithal unto the heart's forest he fleeth,
Leaving his enterprise with pain and cry,
And there him hideth, and not appeareth.
What may I do, when my master feareth,
But in the field with him to live and die?
For good is the life ending faithfully.

E. MS.

Farewell, Love

Farewell, Love, and all thy laws forever,
Thy baited hooks shall tangle me no more;
Senec and Plato call me from thy lore,
To perfect wealth my wit for to endeavor.[4]
In blind error when I did persever,
Thy sharp repulse, that pricketh aye so sore,
Hath taught me to set in trifles no store

1. Wyatt's version of Petrarch's *Sonnetto in Vita* 91; his younger friend, the Earl of Surrey, also translated it (see *Love, That Doth Reign and Live Within My Thought*).
2. I.e., the poet's blush. The first four lines of this sonnet contain the "conceit" (or elaborately sustained metaphor) of love as a kind of warrior who "harbors" in the speaker's thought, lives in his heart, and occasionally invades his face "with bold pretense" (i.e., making bold claim). He flaunts his warlike presence by means of the "banner." Elaborate metaphors of this kind are found often in Elizabethan love poetry; sometimes an entire sonnet will turn on one conceit. "Learns": teaches.
3. I.e., my open and careless revelation of my love. "Shame": modesty, shamefastness.
4. I.e., "Senec" (Seneca, the Roman moral philosopher and tragedian) and Plato call him to educate his mind to perfect well-being ("wealth").

And 'scape forth since liberty is lever.[5]
Therefore farewell, go trouble younger hearts,
And in me claim no more authority;
With idle youth go use thy property,
And thereon spend thy many brittle darts.
For hitherto though I have lost all my time,
Me lusteth[6] no longer rotten boughs to climb.

E. MS.

My Galley[7]

My galley chargéd with forgetfulness
Thorough[8] sharp seas, in winter nights doth pass
'Tween rock and rock; and eke[9] mine enemy, alas,
That is my lord, steereth with cruelness,
And every oar a thought in readiness,
As though that death were light in such a case.[1]
An endless wind doth tear the sail apace
Of forcéd sighs and trusty fearfulness.[2]
A rain of tears, a cloud of dark disdain,
Hath done the wearied cords great hinderance;
Wreathéd with error and eke with ignorance.
The stars be hid that led me to this pain.
Drownéd is reason that should me consort,[3]
And I remain despairing of the port.

E. MS.

Madam, Withouten Many Words

Madam, withouten many words,
Once[4] I am sure ye will or no,
And if ye will, then leave your bordes,[5]
And use your wit and show it so.

And with a beck ye shall me call,
And if of one that burneth alway
Ye have any pity at all,
Answer him fair with yea or nay.

If it be yea I shall be fain,
If it be nay, friends as before;
Ye shall another man obtain
And I mine own and yours no more.

E. MS.

5. More pleasing, dearer.
6. I care.
7. Translated from Petrarch, *Sonnetto in Vita* 137.
8. Through.
9. Also.
1. As though my destruction wouldn't matter much.
2. Fear to trust.
3. Accompany.
4. Sometime.
5. Jests.

Whoso List to Hunt[1]

Whoso list[2] to hunt, I know where is an hind,
But as for me, alas, I may no more.
The vain travail hath wearied me so sore
I am of them that farthest cometh behind.
Yet may I, by no means, my wearied mind
Draw from the deer, but as she fleeth afore,
Fainting I follow. I leave off therefore,
Since in a net I seek to hold the wind.
Who list her hunt, I put him out of doubt,
As well as I, may spend his time in vain.
And graven with diamonds in letters plain
There is written, her fair neck round about,
"*Noli me tangere,* for Caesar's I am,
And wild for to hold, though I seem tame."

E. MS.

My Lute, Awake!

My lute, awake! Perform the last
Labor that thou and I shall waste,
And end that I have now begun;
For when this song is sung and past,
My lute, be still, for I have done.

As to be heard where ear is none,
As lead to grave in marble stone[3]
My song may pierce her heart as soon.
Should we then sigh or sing or moan?
No, no, my lute, for I have done.

The rocks do not so cruelly
Repulse the waves continually
As she my suit and affection.
So that I am past remedy,
Whereby my lute and I have done.

Proud of the spoil that thou hast got
Of simple hearts, thorough love's shot;
By whom, unkind, thou hast them won,
Think not he hath his bow forgot,
Although my lute and I have done.

1. An adaptation of Petrarch, *Rime* 190, perhaps influenced by commentators on Petrarch, who said that *Noli me tangere quia Caesaris sum* ("Touch me not, for I am Caesar's") was inscribed on the collars of Caesar's hinds which were then set free and were presumably safe from hunters. Wyatt's sonnet is usually supposed to refer to Anne Boleyn, in whom Henry VIII became interested in 1526.
2. Cares.
3. I.e., when sound may be heard with no ear to hear it, or when soft lead is able to carve ("grave") hard marble.

Vengeance shall fall on thy disdain
That makest but game on earnest pain.
Think not alone under the sun
Unquit[4] to cause thy lovers plain,
Although my lute and I have done.

Perchance thee lie withered and old
The winter nights that are so cold,
Plaining in vain unto the moon.
Thy wishes then dare not be told.
Care then who list,[5] for I have done.

And then may chance thee to repent
The time that thou hast lost and spent
To cause thy lovers sigh and swoon.
Then shalt thou know beauty but lent,
And wish and want as I have done.

Now cease, my lute. This is the last
Labor that thou and I shall waste,
And ended is that we begun.
Now is this song both sung and past;
My lute, be still, for I have done.

E. MS.

They Flee from Me

They flee from me, that sometime did me seek,
With naked foot stalking in my chamber.
I have seen them, gentle, tame, and meek,
That now are wild, and do not remember
That sometime they put themselves in danger
To take bread at my hand; and now they range,
Busily seeking with a continual change.

Thankéd be fortune it hath been otherwise,
Twenty times better; but once in special,
In thin array, after a pleasant guise,
When her loose gown from her shoulders did fall,
And she me caught in her arms long and small,[1]
Therewithall sweetly did me kiss
And softly said, "Dear heart, how like you this?"

It was no dream, I lay broad waking.
But all is turned, thorough my gentleness,
Into a strange fashion of forsaking;
And I have leave to go, of her goodness,

4. Unrevenged. "Plain": to complain.
5. Likes.

1. Slender.

And she also to use newfangleness.[2]
But since that I so kindely[3] am servéd,
I fain would know what she hath deservéd.

E. MS.

The Lover Showeth How He Is Forsaken of Such as He Sometime Enjoyed

They flee from me, that sometime did me seek
With naked foot stalking within my chamber.
Once have I seen them gentle, tame, and meek
That now are wild, and do not once remember
That sometime they have put themselves in danger
To take bread at my hand, and now they range,
Busily seeking in continual change.

Thankéd be fortune, it hath been otherwise,
Twenty times better; but once especial,
In thin array, after a pleasant guise,
When her loose gown did from her shoulders fall,
And she me caught in her arms long and small,
And therewithal, so sweetly did me kiss
And softly said, "Dear heart, how like you this?"

It was no dream, for I lay broad awaking.
But all is turned now, through my gentleness,
Into a bitter fashion of forsaking.
And I have leave to go, of her goodness,
And she also to use newfangleness.
But since that I unkindly so am servéd,
How like you this, what hath she now deservéd?

Tottel, 1557

Divers Doth Use

Divers doth use, as I have heard and know,
When that to change their ladies do begin,
To mourne and wail, and never for to lin,[4]
Hoping thereby to pease[5] their painful woe.
And some there be, that when it chanceth so
That women change and hate where love hath been,
They call them false and think with words to win
The hearts of them which otherwhere doth grow.
But as for me, though that by chance indeed
Change hath outworn the favor that I had,
I will not wail, lament, nor yet be sad,

2. Fickleness.
3. Naturally, but with an ironic suggestion of the modern meaning of "kindly."
4. Cease.
5. Appease, relieve.

Nor call her false that falsely did me feed,
But let it pass, and think it is of kind [6]
That often change doth please a woman's mind.

D. MS.

Tangled I Was in Love's Snare

Tangled I was in love's snare,
Oppressed with pain, torment with care,
Of grief right sure, of joy full bare,
Clean in despair by cruelty—
But ha! ha! ha! full well is me,
For I am now at liberty.

The woeful day so full of pain,
The weary night all spent in vain,
The labor lost for so small gain,
To write them all it will not be.
But ha! ha! ha! full well is me,
For I am now at liberty.

Everything that fair doth show,
When proof is made it proveth not so,
But turneth mirth to bitter woe;
Which in this case full well I see.
But ha! ha! ha! full well is me,
For I am now at liberty.

Too great desire was my guide
And wanton will went by my side;
Hope rulèd still, and made me bide
Of love's craft th' extremity.
But ha! ha! ha! full well is me,
For I am now at liberty.

With feignèd words which were but wind
To long delays I was assigned;
Her wily looks my wits did blind;
Thus as she would I did agree.
But ha! ha! ha! full well is me,
For I am now at liberty.

Was never bird tangled in lime [7]
That brake away in better time
Than I, that rotten boughs did climb,
And had no hurt, but 'scapèd free.
Now ha! ha! ha! full well is me,
For I am now at liberty.

1557

6. Nature.
7. A sticky substance made from holly bark, used to catch small birds.

In Spain

Tagus,[8] Farewell, that westward with thy streams
Turns up the grains of gold already tried;
With spur and sail for I go seek the Thames,
Gainward[9] the sun, that showeth her wealthy pride;
And to the town which Brutus[1] sought by dreams,
Like bended moon[2] doth lend her lusty side,
My king, my country, alone for whom I live—
Of mighty Love the wings for this me give!

E. MS.

Mine Own John Poins[1]

Mine own John Poins, since ye delight to know
The cause why that homeward I me draw,
And flee the press of courts, whereso they go,
Rather than to live thrall, under the awe
Of lordly looks, wrapped within my cloak,
To will and lust[2] learning to set a law;
It is not for because I scorn and mock
The power of them to whom Fortune hath lent
Charge over us, of right to strike the stroke.[3]
But true it is that I have always meant
Less to esteem them than the common sort,
Of outward things that judge in their intent
Without regard what doth inward resort.
I grant sometime that of glory the fire
Doth touch my heart; me list not to report
Blame by honor, and honor to desire.[4]
But how may I this honor now attain
That cannot dye the color black a liar?
My Poins, I cannot frame me tune to feign,
To cloak the truth, for praise without desert,
Of them that list all vice for to retain.
I cannot honor them that sets their part

8. The Tagus River flows through Spain and Portugal. The poem was written at the poet's departure from Spain in 1539.
9. Toward.
1. The legendary founder of London, after whom Britain was supposedly named.
2. Crescent moon.
1. A friend of Wyatt's. This verse epistle of informal satire is based upon the tenth satire of the Italian Luigi Alamanni, but personalized and Anglicized in detail by Wyatt. It was apparently written during Wyatt's banishment from court in 1536. Lines 1–51 of the poem are from the Devonshire manuscript, lines 52–103 from the Egerton manuscript.
2. Pleasure.
3. I.e., my retirement from court is not because I scorn great and powerful princes. But (lines 10–13) I esteem them less than do the "common sort" of people, who judge by externals only.
4. I.e., I do not wish to attack honor, nor to call dishonorable desire honorable.

With Venus and Bacchus all their life long;[5]
Nor hold my peace of them, although I smart.
I cannot crouch nor kneel to do so great a wrong,
To worship them like God on earth alone,
That are as wolves these sely[6] lambs among.
I cannot with my words complain and moan
Nor suffer naught, nor smart without complaint,
Nor turn the word that from my mouth is gone;
I cannot speak and look like a saint,
Use wiles for wit, or make deceit a pleasure;
And call craft counsel, for profit still to paint;
I cannot wrest the law to fill the coffer,
With innocent blood to feed myself fat,
And do most hurt where most help I offer.
I am not he that can allow the state
Of high Caesar, and damn Cato[7] to die,
That with his death did 'scape out of the gate
From Caesar's hands, if Livy[8] do not lie,
And would not live where liberty was lost,
So did his heart the common weal[9] apply.
I am not he, such eloquence to boast
To make the crow in singing as the swan,
Nor call the lion of coward beasts the most,
That cannot take a mouse as the cat can;
And he that dieth of hunger of the gold,
Call him Alexander,[1] and say that Pan
Passeth Apollo in music manifold;[2]
Praise Sir Thopas for a noble tale,
And scorn the story that the Knight told;[3]
Praise him for counsel that is drunk of ale;
Grin when he laugheth that beareth all the sway,
Frown when he frowneth, and groan when he is pale;
On others' lust to hang both night and day—
None of these points would ever frame in me;
My wit is naught: I cannot learn the way;
And much the less of things that greater be
That asken help of colors of device[4]
To join the mean with each extremity.
With nearest virtue to cloak alway the vice,
And as to purpose, likewise it shall fall

5. I.e., I cannot honor those who devote themselves to Venus (goddess of love-making) and Bacchus (god of drinking).
6. Innocent.
7. Cato the Younger, the famous Roman patriot who committed suicide rather than submit to Caesar.
8. Titus Livius (59 B.C.–A.D. 17), the great Roman historian.
9. The common good, or the state.

1. Alexander yearned for more worlds to conquer.
2. Pan's music was simple and rustic, played on "Pan's pipes."
3. The silly tale of Sir Thopas, in Chaucer's *Canterbury Tales*, is told by Chaucer himself, until the Host forces him to stop. The Knight's Tale is the most courtly and dignified of the tales.
4. Tricks of rhetoric.

To press the virtue that it may not rise;
As drunkenness, good fellowship to call;
The friendly foe, with his double face,
Say he is gentle and courteous therewithal;
And say that favel[5] hath a goodly grace
In eloquence; and cruelty to name
Zeal of justice, and change in time and place;
And he that suff'reth offense without blame,
Call him pitiful, and him true and plain
That raileth reckless to every man's shame,
Say he is rude that cannot lie and feign,
The lecher a lover, and tyranny
To be the right of a prince's reign.
I cannot, I: no, no, it will not be.
This is the cause that I could never yet
Hang on their sleeves, that weigh, as thou mayst see,
A chip of chance more than a pound of wit.
This maketh me at home to hunt and hawk,
And in foul weather at my book to sit,
In frost and snow then with my bow to stalk.
No man doth mark whereso I ride or go.
In lusty leas[6] at liberty I walk,
And of these news I feel nor weal nor woe,
Save that a clog doth hang yet at my heel.[7]
No force for that, for it is ordered so
That I may leap both hedge and dike full well;
I am not now in France, to judge the wine,
With sav'ry sauce those delicates[8] to feel;
Nor yet in Spain, where one must him incline,
Rather than to be, outwardly to seem.
I meddle not with wits that be so fine;
Nor Flanders' cheer[9] letteth not my sight to deem
Of black and white, nor taketh my wit away
With beastliness, they beasts do so esteem.
Nor am I not where Christ is given in prey
For money, poison, and treason—at Rome[1]
A common practice, uséd night and day.
But here I am in Kent and Christendom,
Among the Muses, where I read and rhyme;
Where, if thou list, my Poins, for to come,
Thou shalt be judge how I do spend my time.

E. MS.

5. Flattery.

6. Pleasant fields.

7. "I feel neither happiness nor unhappiness about current political affairs, except that a 'clog' (i.e., his confinement on parole to his estate) keeps me from traveling far." Note that "news" is a plural in Elizabethan English. "No force": no matter.

8. Delicacies.

9. I.e., the drinking for which Flemings were notorious in the 16th century; "letteth": hinders, prevents.

1. In *Tottel's Miscellany,* published in the reign of the Catholic Queen Mary, these lines were altered as follows: "where *truth* is given in prey / For money, poison and treason; *of some.*"

HENRY HOWARD, EARL OF SURREY
(1517–1547)

Surrey was the eldest son of the Duke of Norfolk, who was the premier English nobleman and the chief bulwark of the old aristocracy against the rising tide of "new men" and the Reformed religion. Surrey was descended from kings on both sides of his family; he was brought up with Henry VIII's illegitimate son, the Duke of Richmond, who married Surrey's sister. Some stories indicate that Surrey was a proud, high-spirited youth, not above wandering about the streets at night, in the company of Sir Thomas Wyatt's son, using stone-bows to break the windows of sober sleeping citizens. Surrey, like his father and grandfather, was an able soldier, and the Howards were called upon whenever military brilliance was needed. But their fortunes at court depended upon Henry's queens; the Howards were in high favor when Surrey's cousin, Catherine Howard, was queen, but they were low on Fortune's wheel when the queen was Jane Seymour, the mother of the future king.

Surrey's importance and interest as a poet depend upon his continuing the practice of the sonnet in English as instituted by Wyatt and establishing a form for it which was used by Shakespeare and has become known as the "English" sonnet form: three quatrains and a couplet, rhyming *abab cdcd efef gg*. Even more significantly, he was the first English poet to publish in blank verse—unrhymed iambic pentameter—a verse form that has so flourished in the succeeding four centuries that it seems almost indigenous to the language. The work in which he used this "strange meter," as the publisher called it, was a translation of part of Virgil's *Aeneid*. Book IV was published in 1554 and Book II in 1557. A brief sample from Book II introduces Aeneas about to tell Dido and her court the story of the fall of Troy:

> They whisted [quieted down] all, with fixéd face attent,
> When Prince Aeneas from the royal seat
> Thus gan to speak: "O Queen, it is thy will
> I should renew a woe cannot be told,
> How that the Greeks did spoil and overthrow
> The Phrygian wealth and wailful realm of Troy,
> Those ruthful [pitiful] things that I myself beheld,
> And whereof no small part fell to my share,
> Which to express, who could refrain from tears?"

Surrey was a courtier poet, interested in circulating his poems in manuscript in aristocratic court circles. His friends would have read with interest his poem about being imprisoned in Windsor Castle, where he had spent his boyhood under happier circumstances. He did publish his *Epitaph on Wyatt*, but the bulk of his poetry first appeared in *Tottel's Miscellany*, ten years after his death.

Surrey shows a more regular maintenance of normal accent than Wyatt, and he is often more fluent and musical. His poetic diction is clear and consistent, and in many ways Surrey indicates the direction in which the main stream of English verse will flow. Yet he often seems less vivid and vigorous than Wyatt, and he perhaps takes the figurative language he uses less seriously.

Love, That Doth Reign and Live Within My Thought[1]

Love, that doth reign and live within my thought,
And built his seat within my captive breast,
Clad in the arms wherein with me he fought,
Oft in my face he doth his banner rest.
But she that taught me love and suffer pain,
My doubtful hope and eke[2] my hot desire
With shamefast look to shadow and refrain,
Her smiling grace converteth straight to ire.
And coward Love, then, to the heart apace
Taketh his flight, where he doth lurk and plain,[3]
His purpose lost, and dare not show his face.
For my lord's guilt thus faultless bide I pain,
Yet from my lord shall not my foot remove:
Sweet is the death that taketh end by love.

1557

The Soote Season[4]

The soote season, that bud and bloom forth brings,
With green hath clad the hill and eke the vale;
The nightingale with feathers new she sings;
The turtle to her make[5] hath told her tale.
Summer is come, for every spray now springs;
The hart hath hung his old head on the pale;
The buck in brake his winter coat he flings,
The fishes float with new repairéd scale;
The adder all her slough away she slings,
The swift swallow pursueth the fliés small;
The busy bee her honey now she mings.[6]
Winter is worn, that was the flowers' bale.[7]
And thus I see among these pleasant things,
Each care decays, and yet my sorrow springs.

1557

1. Compare this version of Petrarch's *Sonnetto in Vita* 91 with Wyatt's translation of the same original (*The Long Love That in My Thought Doth Harbor*, printed earlier in this anthology).
2. Also; "shamefast": modest.
3. Complain.
4. In this adaptation from Petrarch's *Sonnetto in Morte* 42, Surrey has changed the details of nature from Italian to English. Note that the sonnet has only two rhymes. "Soote": sweet, fragrant.
5. Turtledove to her mate.
6. Mingles.
7. Harm.

Alas! So All Things Now Do Hold Their Peace[7a]

Alas! so all things now do hold their peace,
Heaven and earth disturbéd in no thing;
The beasts, the air, the birds their song do cease,
The nightés chare[8] the stars about doth bring.
Calm is the sea, the waves work less and less;
So am not I, whom love, alas, doth wring,
Bringing before my face the great increase
Of my desires, whereat I weep and sing,
In joy and woe, as in a doubtful ease.
For my sweet thoughts sometime do pleasure bring,
But by and by the cause of my disease[9]
Gives me a pang that inwardly doth sting,
When that I think what grief it is again
To live and lack the thing should rid my pain.

1557

Give Place, Ye Lovers, Here Before

Give place, ye lovers, here before
That spent your boasts and brags in vain;
My lady's beauty passeth more
The best of yours, I dare well sayn[1]
Than doth the sun the candlelight,
Or brightest day the darkest night,

And thereto hath a troth as just[2]
As had Penelope the fair,
For what she saith, ye may it trust
As it by writing sealéd were,
And virtues hath she many moe
Than I with pen have skill to show.

I could rehearse, if that I wold,[3]
The whole effect of Nature's plaint,
When she had lost the perfect mold
The like to whom she could not paint;
With wringing hands how she did cry
And what she said, I know it, I.

I know she swore, with raging mind,
Her kingdom only set apart,

7a. Translated from Petrarch's *Sonnetto in Vita* 113.
8. From Italian *carro* (the Great Bear).
9. Dis-ease, i.e., discomfort.

1. Say.
2. Constancy as firm.
3. Would.

There was no loss, by law of kind,[4]
That could have gone so near her heart;
And this was chiefly all her pain:
She could not make the like again.

Sith [5] nature thus gave her the praise
To be the chiefest work she wrought,
In faith, methinks some better ways
On your behalf might well be sought
Than to compare, as ye have done,
To match the candle with the sun.

1557

My Friend, the Things That Do Attain[6]

My friend, the things that do attain
The happy life be these, I find:
The riches left, not got with pain;
The fruitful ground; the quiet mind;

The equal friend; no grudge, no strife;
No charge of rule, nor governance;
Without disease, the healthy life;
The household of continuance;

The mean diet, no dainty fare;
Wisdom joined with simpleness;
The night dischargéd of all care,
Where wine the wit may not oppress:

The faithful wife, without debate;
Such sleeps as may beguile the night;
Content thyself with thine estate,
Neither wish death, nor fear his might.

1547

Epitaph on Sir Thomas Wyatt

Wyatt resteth here, that quick[1] could never rest,
Whose heavenly gifts, increaséd by disdain[2]
And virtue, sank the deeper in his breast:
Such profit he of envy could obtain.

4. Nature.
5. Since.
6. A translation of an epigram by the Latin poet Martial (X.47). The theme, a glorification of "the mean estate," is very common in Elizabethan literature.
1. Alive.
2. Hostility (equivalent to "envy" in line 4). I.e., he could turn hostility toward him to his advantage.

A head where wisdom mysteries[3] did frame,
Whose hammers beat still in that lively brain
As on a stithy,[4] where some work of fame
Was daily wrought to turn to Britain's gain.

A visage stern and mild, where both did grow
Vice to condemn, in virtues to rejoice;
Amid great storms whom grace assuréd so
To live upright and smile at fortune's choice.

A hand that taught what may be said in rhyme,
That reft[5] Chaucer the glory of his wit—
A mark the which, unperfected for time,
Some may approach but never none shall hit.

A tongue that served in foreign realms his king,
Whose courteous talk to virtue did inflame
Each noble heart: a worthy guide to bring
Our English youth by travail unto fame.

An eye whose judgment no affect[6] could blind,
Friends to allure and foes to reconcile,
Whose piercing look did represent a mind
With virtue fraught, reposéd, void of guile.

A heart where dread yet never so impressed
To hide the thought that might the truth advance;
In neither fortune lift[7] nor yet repressed
To swell in wealth or yield unto mischance.

A valiant corpse[8] where force and beauty met,
Happy—alas, too happy, but for foes,
Lived and ran the race that Nature set,
Of manhood's shape, where she the mold did lose.[9]

But to the heavens that simple[1] soul is fled,
Which left with such as covet Christ to know
Witness of faith[2] that never shall be dead,
Sent for our health, but not receivéd so.

Thus, for our guilt, this jewel have we lost;
The earth his bones, the heaven possess his ghost.[3]
AMEN.

1542

3. Subtle meanings.
4. Forge or anvil (a conventional image from Horace; see Ben Jonson's poem on Shakespeare, lines 58–64).
5. Bereft, robbed.
6. Passion or prejudice.
7. Elevated.
8. Body (not, as now, a dead body).
9. Another conventional idea, that Nature, in creating someone, made a masterpiece and lost the pattern.
1. Innocent. The soul is referred to as "simple" by Plato and Dante.
2. I.e., which left with Christians ("such as covet Christ to know") a testimony.
3. Spirit.

Prisoned in Windsor, He Recounteth His Pleasure There Passed[1]

So cruel prison how could betide,[2] alas,
As proud Windsor, where I in lust[3] and joy,
With a king's son, my childish[4] years did pass
In greater feast than Priam's sons of Troy?[5]

Where each sweet place returns a taste full sour:
The large green courts, where we were wont to hove,[6]
With eyes cast up unto the Maidens' Tower,
And easy sighs, such as folk draw in love.

The stately seats, the ladies bright of hue;
The dances short, long tales of great delight,
With words and looks that tigers could but rue,[7]
Where each of us did plead the other's right.

The palm play[8] where, dispoiléd for the game,
With dazed eyes oft we by gleams of love
Have missed the ball and got sight of our dame
To bait[9] her eyes, which kept the leads above.

The gravel ground, with sleeves tied on the helm,
On foaming horse, with swords and friendly hearts,
With cheer[1] as though one should another whelm,
Where we have fought and chaséd oft with darts.

With silver drops the mead[2] yet spread for ruth,
In active games of nimbleness and strength,
Where we did strain, trainéd with[3] swarms of youth,
Our tender limbs that yet shot up in length.

The secret groves, which oft we made resound
Of pleasant plaint and of our ladies' praise,
Recording oft what grace each one had found,
What hope of speed, what dread of long delays.

The wild forest, the clothéd holts[4] with green,
With reins availed[5] and swift ybreathed horse,
With cry of hounds and merry blasts between,
Where we did chase the fearful hart of force.[6]

1. In the summer of 1537 Surrey was imprisoned at Windsor Castle for striking a courtier. In the poem he recalls his boyhood stay there (1530–32) with Henry Fitzroy, illegitimate son of Henry VIII.
2. I.e., how could there happen to be.
3. Pleasure.
4. Youthful.
5. Priam, ancient King of Troy, had fifty sons whom he feasted, according to Homer.
6. Linger.
7. Sympathize with, despite tigers' legendary fierceness.
8. Handball.
9. Attract, as in fishing.
1. Appearance.
2. The dewy meadow.
3. Accompanied by.
4. I.e, wooded hills.
5. Slackened.
6. Perforce.

The wide vales eke that harbored us each night
Wherewith, alas, reviveth in my breast
The sweet accord; such sleeps as yet delight,
The pleasant dreams, the quiet bed of rest.

The secret thoughts imparted with such trust;
The wanton talk, the divers change of play;
The friendship sworn, each promise kept so just,
Wherewith we pass the winter nights away.

And with this thought, the blood forsakes my face,
The tears berain my cheeks of deadly hue,
The which, as soon as sobbing sighs, alas,
Upsuppéd have, thus I my plaint renew:

"Oh place of bliss, renewer of my woes,
Give me accompt, where is my noble fere,[7]
Whom in thy walls thou didst each night enclose,
To other lief,[8] but unto me most dear."

Each stone, alas, that doth my sorrow rue,
Returns thereto a hollow sound of plaint.
Thus I alone, where all my freedom grew,
In prison pine with bondage and restraint.

And with remembrance of the greater grief
To banish the less I find my chief relief.

1557

7. Companion. The reference is to Henry Fitzroy, who had died the year before, aged 17; he was married to Surrey's sister.

8. Dear.

SIR PHILIP SIDNEY

(1554–1586)

Sir Philip Sidney—courtier, soldier, scholar, poet, friend, and patron—seemed to the Elizabethans to embody all the traits of character and personality they admired: he was Castiglione's *Il Cortegiano* come to life. When he was killed in battle in the Low Countries at the age of 32, all England mourned.

He was the son of Sir Henry Sidney, thrice Lord Deputy of Ireland, and of a sister of Robert Dudley, Earl of Leicester, the most spectacular and powerful of all the queen's subjects. He entered Shrewsbury School in 1564, at the age of 10, on the same day as Fulke Greville, who became his lifelong friend and biographer. Greville said of Sidney, "though I lived with him and knew him from a child, yet I never knew him other than a man—with such staidness of mind, lovely and familiar gravity, as carried grace and reverence above greater years." Although he attended Oxford, he left without taking a degree. His education was completed by extended travels on the Continent, where he had opportunities to meet the most important men of the time and to be witness to such crucial events as the Massacre of St. Bartholomew's Day, August 23, 1572. Sidney's family background and education were Protestant, but this slaughter of the French Huguenots undoubtedly strengthened his Protestant sympathies. Another important influence was his friendship with the scholar-diplomat Hubert Languet.

On his return to England he lived the life of a prominent courtier, serving occasionally on diplomatic missions and actively encouraging literary men such as Edward Dyer, Fulke Greville, and, most importantly, the young Edmund Spenser, who dedicated *The Shepheardes Calender* to him as "the president of noblesse and of chevalree." So strong were Sidney's Protestant convictions that he incurred the queen's displeasure by opposing her projected marriage to the Duke of Anjou; this led to his dismissal from court for a time. He retired to Wilton, the estate of his beloved sister Mary, Countess of Pembroke, and there he wrote, at her request and for her entertainment, a pastoral romance called *Arcadia*.

Sidney's romance exists in two forms, called the "Old Arcadia" and the "New Arcadia." The "New Arcadia" was published in fragmentary form, almost three books, in 1590. In 1593 the Countess of Pembroke republished it with slight changes and added the last three books of the "Old Arcadia," but the first three books of the earlier version remained in manuscript until the 20th century. As William Ringler says, "The *Arcadia*, in both its old and new forms, is the most important original work of English prose fiction produced before the 18th century." The romance's complicated plot is full of oracles, disguisings, mistaken identity, melodramatic incidents and tangled love situations. Some episodes are of political interest, and Sidney clearly put more of his serious thought on statecraft into it than he pretends when he describes the book as mere entertainment. The *Arcadia* also contains many poems—eclogues and songs which are interspersed throughout the narrative; they represent Sidney's experimental and exploratory ventures into verse. A good example is the double sestina, *Ye Goatherd Gods*.

In 1579, the same year in which he dedicated *The Shepheardes Calender* to Sidney, Spenser wrote to his friend Gabriel Harvey, "New books I hear of none but only of one that writing a certain book called *The School of Abuse*, and dedicating it to Master Sidney, was for his labor scorned, if at least it be in the goodness of that nature to scorn." The book referred to was by Stephen Gosson; it was an attack upon poets and players from a narrowly Puritan point of view. Sidney did not specifically answer Gosson's attack, but he must have had it in mind when he composed, at some uncertain date, a major piece of critical prose which was published after his death under the titles *The Defense of Poesy* and *An Apology for Poetry*. In this long essay Sidney systematically defends poetry (indeed all imaginative literature) against its attackers. He points out the antiquity of poetry, and its prestige in the ancient world. He establishes its universality. He cites the names given to poets by the Romans (*vates* or prophet) and the Greeks (*poietes* or maker) to indicate their ancient dignity. But, he says, the real defense of the poet depends not upon what he has been but upon what he does. All arts depend upon works of nature, but the poet, supreme among artists, can make another nature, new and more beautiful.

"Nature never set forth the earth in so rich tapestry as divers poets have done, neither with pleasant rivers, fruitful trees, sweet-smelling flowers, nor whatsoever else may make the too much loved earth more lovely." Moreover, the poet presents virtues and vices in a more lively and telling way than nature does; his function is to teach and delight at the same time. He is superior to the philosopher and the historian, because he is more concrete than the one and more universal than the other. Sidney shows himself to be a thorough student of Aristotle when he explains poetry as an art of imitation in which the artist imitates not merely what is, but also what might be. He refutes the charge that poets are liars by stating that "the poet nothing affirmeth," and he maintains that poetry does not abuse man's wits by arousing base desires but that man's wits abuse poetry. Then Sidney surveys the English literary scene as it looked to him. He found little to praise: Surrey's lyrics, the *Mirror for Magistrates*, Spenser's *Shepheardes Calender* (though he disliked Spenser's use of antique language). The drama was generally bad (he was writing before the great achievements of the Elizabethans), and its failure to observe the classical unities of time and place was, for Sidney, a particular weakness. He concludes by a general defense of English as a language suitable for poetry and a humorous defiance of those who will not be converted by his defense. Despite the seriousness and logical rigor of Sidney's essay, it has many delightful personal touches. His manner is graceful and easy; it exhibits that *sprezzatura*, or casualness in doing something difficult perfectly, which Castiglione had held up as an ideal in *The Courtier*.

Sidney's *Astrophel and Stella* ("Starlover and Star") is the first of the great Elizabethan sonnet cycles. These collections, imitative of Petrarch or of his French imitators, were based upon a well-understood convention. The poet undertook to display all the contrary feelings of a lover—hope and despair, tenderness and bitterness, exultation and modesty, by the use of "conceits" or ingenious comparisons. Many of these became traditional, and eventually, stale: the poet who complained that in love he both burned and froze, or that his sighs were the winds driving his ship on a tossing sea, was echoing many an earlier poet. So Sidney protests, in the role of Astrophel, that he uses no standard conventional phrases; his verse is original and comes from the heart. (This pretense is also conventional.) But what gives Sidney's sonnets their extraordinary vigor and freshness is Sidney's ability to dramatize. He uses dialogue, is often colloquial, and he heightens the situation as much as he can within the fourteen lines.

The sonnet cycle has a framework of plot, but it does not tell a story. Yet there is a rather mysterious story hinted at in Sidney's cycle, and some of these hints point to what may be an actual episode in the poet's life. Penelope Devereux, Lady Rich, is supposed to be the original of Stella, and some of the sonnets contain puns on the name "Rich." On the other hand, Stella is virtuous in the sonnets, and refuses Astrophel anything more than a kiss, whereas the historical Penelope Devereux was apparently a different kind of woman. But there is little profit in speculating on the events behind an Elizabethan sonnet cycle; as Sidney said in his *Apology*, "the poet nothing affirmeth."

Sidney called poetry his "unelected vocation," and he did not publish it himself. His view of himself was probably more that of patron than of artist. Yet his achievement as the author of the most important work of prose fiction in his age, the most important piece of literary criticism, and the most important sonnet cycle surely qualify him as a major author.

Ye Goatherd Gods[1]

STREPHON. Ye goatherd gods, that love the grassy mountains,
Ye nymphs which haunt the springs in pleasant valleys,
Ye satyrs joyed with free and quiet forests,
Vouchsafe your silent ears to plaining music,
Which to my woes gives still an early morning,
And draws the dolor on till weary evening.

KLAIUS. O Mercury,[2] foregoer to the evening,
O heavenly huntress of the savage mountains,
O lovely star, entitled of the morning,
While that my voice doth fill these woeful valleys,
Vouchsafe your silent ears to plaining music,
Which oft hath Echo tired in secret forests.

STREPHON. I, that was once free burgess[3] of the forests,
Where shade from sun, and sport I sought in evening,
I, that was once esteemed for pleasant music,
Am banished now among the monstrous mountains
Of huge despair, and foul affliction's valleys,
Am grown a screech owl to myself each morning.

KLAIUS. I, that was once delighted every morning,
Hunting the wild inhabiters of forests,
I, that was once the music of these valleys,
So darkened am that all my day is evening,
Heartbroken so that molehills seem high mountains
And fill the vales with cries instead of music.

STREPHON. Long since, alas, my deadly swannish[4] music
Hath made itself a crier of the morning,
And hath with wailing strength climbed highest moun-
tains;

1. From Sidney's pastoral-heroic romance, the *Arcadia*. The poem is a dialogue between two shepherds, Strephon and Klaius, both of whom are in love with the absent Urania. Sidney, of course, knew no shepherds like this: the figures and the landscape in the poem belong to the pastoral tradition of an elegant idealized country life—usually Greek.

The form of the poem is basically that of the sestina, which has six-line stanzas and a final triplet of three lines; the terminal words of each stanza are the same, but rearranged according to a definite pattern, and all six terminal words must appear in the final triplet. Sestinas usually have six stanzas, but Sidney has here created a double sestina, of twelve stanzas. The *Arcadia* has about eighty interpolated poems, some of them ingenious metrical experiments like this one.

2. The evening star. The "huntress" is Diana, the moon; the "lovely star" is Lucifer, the morning star.

3. Citizen.

4. Doleful, like the song supposedly sung by the swan just before its death.

Long since my thoughts more desert be than forests,
Long since I see my joys come to their evening,
And state[5] thrown down to overtrodden valleys.

KLAIUS. Long since the happy dwellers of these valleys
Have prayed me leave my strange exclaiming music
Which troubles their day's work and joys of evening;
Long since I hate the night, more hate the morning;
Long since my thoughts chase me like beasts in forests
And make me wish myself laid under mountains.

STREPHON. Meseems I see the high and stately mountains
Transform themselves to low dejected valleys;
Meseems I hear in these ill-changéd forests
The nightingales do learn of owls their music;
Meseems I feel the comfort of the morning
Turned to the mortal serene[6] of an evening.

KLAIUS. Meseems I see a filthy cloudy evening
As soon as sun begins to climb the mountains;
Meseems I feel a noisome[7] scent, the morning
When I do smell the flowers of these valleys;
Meseems I hear, when I do hear sweet music,
The dreadful cries of murdered men in forests.

STREPHON. I wish to fire the trees of all those forests;
I give the sun a last farewell each evening;
I curse the fiddling finders-out of music;
With envy I do hate the lofty mountains
And with despite despise the humble valleys;
I do detest night, evening, day, and morning.

KLAIUS. Curse to myself my prayer is, the morning;
My fire is more than can be made with forests,
My state more base than are the basest valleys.
I wish no evenings more to see, each evening;
Shaméd, I hate myself in sight of mountains
And stop mine ears, lest I grow mad with music.

STREPHON. For she whose parts maintained a perfect music,
Whose beauties shined more than the blushing morning,
Who much did pass[8] in state the stately mountains,
In straightness passed the cedars of the forests,
Hath cast me, wretch, into eternal evening
By taking her two suns from these dark valleys.

KLAIUS. For she, to whom compared, the Alps are valleys,
She, whose least word brings from the spheres their music,

5. High position.
6. Deadly dew.
7. Stinking. "The morning": i.e., in the morning.
8. Surpass.

At whose approach the sun rose in the evening,
Who where she went bare[9] in her forehead morning,
Is gone, is gone, from these our spoilėd forests,
Turning to deserts our best pastured mountains.

STREPHON. These mountains witness shall, so shall these valleys.
KLAIUS. These forests eke, made wretched by our music,
Our morning hymn is this, and song at evening.

1577–1580 1593

Thou Blind Man's Mark

Thou blind man's mark,[1] thou fool's self-chosen snare,
Fond fancy's scum, and dregs of scattered thought;
Band [2] of all evils, cradle of causeless care;
Thou web of will, whose end is never wrought;
Desire, desire! I have too dearly bought,
With price of mangled mind, thy worthless ware;
Too long, too long, asleep thou hast me brought,
Who should my mind to higher things prepare.
But yet in vain thou hast my ruin sought;
In vain thou madest me to vain things aspire;
In vain thou kindlest all thy smoky fire;
For virtue hath this better lesson taught—
Within myself to seek my only hire,
Desiring naught but how to kill desire.

1581 1598

Leave Me, O Love

Leave me, O love which reachest but to dust;
And thou, my mind, aspire to higher things;
Grow rich in that which never taketh rust,
Whatever fades but fading pleasure brings.
Draw in thy beams, and humble all thy might
To that sweet yoke where lasting freedoms be;
Which breaks the clouds and opens forth the light,
That doth both shine and give us sight to see.
O take fast hold; let that light be thy guide
In this small course which birth draws out to death,
And think how evil becometh him to slide,
Who seeketh heav'n, and comes of heav'nly breath.[3]

9. Bore.
1. Target.
2. Swaddling band.
3. I.e., and think how evil it is for one who is seeking heaven and has a divine spirit or soul in him to descend to earthly things.

Then farewell, world; thy uttermost I see;
Eternal Love, maintain thy life in me.

1581 1598

The Nightingale

The nightingale, as soon as April bringeth[1]
Unto her rested sense a perfect waking
(While late bare earth, proud of new clothing, springeth),
Sings out her woes, a thorn her song-book making,
And mournfully bewailing,
Her throat in tunes expresseth
What grief her breast oppresseth
For Tereus' force on her chaste will prevailing.
O Philomela fair, O take some gladness,
That here is juster cause of plaintful sadness:
Thine earth now springs, mine fadeth;
Thy thorn without, my thorn my heart invadeth.

Alas, she hath no other cause of anguish
But Tereus' love, on her by strong hand wroken,[2]
Wherein she suffering, all her spirits languish;
Full womanlike complains her will was broken.
But I, who daily craving,
Cannot have to content me,
Have more cause to lament me,
Since wanting is more woe than too much having.
O Philomela fair, O take some gladness,
That here is juster cause of plaintful sadness:
Thine earth now springs, mine fadeth;
Thy thorn without, my thorn my heart invadeth.

1581 1598

From Astrophel and Stella[1]

1

Loving in truth, and fain [2] in verse my love to show,
That the dear she might take some pleasure of my pain,
Pleasure might cause her read, reading might make her know,
Knowledge might pity win, and pity grace obtain,
I sought fit words to paint the blackest face of woe:
Studying inventions fine, her wits to entertain,

1. The nightingale sings in England for only a few weeks after its return from winter quarters in the south. Mythology has it that while singing "she" presses her breast against a thorn, to remind her of the bitter pain suffered when, as Philomela, she was raped by her brother-in-law King Tereus, and had her tongue torn out.

2. Inflicted.

1. The first sonnet is one of six in the cycle that are written in hexameters.

2. Desirous.

Oft turning others' leaves, to see if thence would flow
Some fresh and fruitful showers upon my sunburnt brain.
But words came halting[3] forth, wanting Invention's stay;
Invention, Nature's child, fled stepdame Study's blows;
And others' feet still seemed but strangers in my way.
Thus, great with child to speak, and helpless in my throes,
Biting my truant pen, beating myself for spite:
"Fool," said my Muse to me, "look in thy heart, and write!"

5

It is most true that eyes are formed to serve
The inward light,[4] and that the heavenly part
Ought to be king, from whose rules who do swerve,
Rebels to nature, strive for their own smart.
It is most true, what we call Cupid's dart
An image is, which for ourelves we carve,
And, fools, adore in temple of our heart,
Till that good god make church and churchman starve.
True, that true beauty virtue is indeed,
Whereof this beauty can be but a shade,
Which elements with mortal mixture breed.[5]
True, that on earth we are but pilgrims made,
And should in soul up to our country move.
True, and yet true that I must Stella love.

6

Some lovers speak, when they their Muses entertain,
Of hopes begot by fear, of wot[6] not what desires,
Of force of heavenly beams infusing hellish pain,
Of living deaths, dear wounds, fair storms, and freezing fires;
Someone his song in Jove and Jove's strange tales attires,
Bordered with bulls and swans, powdered with golden rain;[7]
Another humbler wit to shepherd's pipe[8] retires,
Yet hiding royal blood full oft in rural vein.
To some a sweetest plaint a sweetest style affords,
While tears pour out his ink, and sighs breathe out his words,
His paper pale despair, and pain his pen doth move.
I can speak what I feel, and feel as much as they,[9]
But think that all the map of my state I display
When trembling voice brings forth, that I do Stella love.

3. Limping. "Stay": crutch, support.
4. I.e., the soul. The concessions made in the argument of this sonnet are to Platonic and Christian doctrines as opposed to romantic love.
5. This beauty is a mixture of the four elements (earth, air, water, fire) and as such is mortal. According to Platonic doctrine the only true beauty (identical with virtue) is a divine idea or essence and is immortal.
6. Know.
7. In classical mythology Jove courted Europa in the shape of a bull, Leda as a swan, and Danaë as a golden shower.
8. In the pastoral convention the poet pretends to be a shepherd and his poems are the songs he plays on his oaten or reed pipe.
9. I.e., the Petrarchan sonneteers in Italy and France, whose literary conventions he had been describing. As a matter of fact, he utilizes some of these conventions himself and is not so direct and simple as he would have us believe here and in sonnets 1 and 74.

15

You that do search for every purling[1] spring
Which from the ribs of old Parnassus[2] flows,
And every flower, not sweet, perhaps, which grows
Near thereabout, into your poesy wring;
You that do dictionary's method bring
Into your rhymes, running in rattling rows;
You that poor Petrarch's long-deceaséd woes
With newborn sighs and denizened wit[3] do sing;
You take wrong ways: those far-fet[4] helps be such
As do beweray[5] a want of inward touch.
And sure, at length stolen goods do come to light.
But if, both for your love and skill, your name
You seek to nurse at fullest breast of Fame,
Stella behold, and then begin to endite.[6]

18

With what sharp checks I in myself am shent,[7]
When into Reason's audit I do go,
And by just counts myself a banckrout[8] know
Of all those goods, which heaven to me hath lent;
Unable quite to pay even Nature's rent,
Which unto it by birthright I do owe;
And which is worse, no good excuse can show,
But that my wealth I have most idly spent.
My youth doth waste, my knowledge brings forth toys,[9]
My wit doth strive those passions to defend,
Which for reward spoil it with vain annoys.
I see my course to lose myself doth bend:
I see and yet no greater sorrow take,
Then that I lose no more for Stella's sake.

21

Your words, my friend, right healthful caustics, blame
My young mind marred, whom Love doth windlass[1] so,
That mine own writings like bad servants show
My wits, quick in vain thoughts, in virtue lame;
That Plato I read for nought, but if he tame
Such coltish gyres,[2] that to my birth I owe
Nobler desires, lest else that friendly foe,
Great expectation, wear a train of shame.
For since mad March great promise made of me,
If now the May of my years much decline,

1. Gently murmuring.
2. The mountain above Delphi, sacred to the Muses; hence, poetic inspiration.
3. Ingenuity ("wit") imported from abroad ("denizened"), here Italy.
4. Farfetched.
5. Reveal.
6. Compose, write.
7. Disgraced; "checks": reproofs.
8. Bankrupt.
9. Trifles, i.e. these poems.
1. Ambush, ensnare.
2. Youthful gyrations.

What can be hoped my harvest time will be?
Sure you say well; your wisdom's golden mine
Dig deep with learning's spade; now tell me this,
Hath this world ought so fair as Stella is?

31

With how sad steps, Oh Moon, thou climb'st the skies!
How silently, and with how wan a face!
What, may it be that even in heavenly place
That busy archer [3] his sharp arrows tries?
Sure, if that long-with-love-acquainted eyes
Can judge of love, thou feel'st a lover's case,
I read it in thy looks; thy languished grace,
To me, that feel the like, thy state descries.
Then, even of fellowship, Oh Moon, tell me,
Is constant love deemed there but want of wit?
Are beauties there as proud as here they be?
Do they above love to be loved, and yet
Those lovers scorn whom that love doth possess?
Do they call virtue there ungratefulness? [4]

39

Come sleep! Oh sleep, the certain knot of peace,
The baiting place [1] of wit, the balm of woe,
The poor man's wealth, the prisoner's release,
The indifferent judge between the high and low;
With shield of proof [2] shield me from out the prease
Of those fierce darts Despair at me doth throw;
Oh make in me those civil wars to cease;
I will good tribute pay, if thou do so.
Take thou of me smooth pillows, sweetest bed,
A chamber deaf to noise and blind to light,
A rosy garland and a weary head;
And if these things, as being thine by right,
Move not thy heavy grace, thou shalt in me,
Livelier than elsewhere, Stella's image see.

41

Having this day my horse, my hand, my lance
Guided so well that I obtained the prize,[3]
Both by the judgment of the English eyes
And of some sent from that sweet enemy, France,
Horsemen my skill in horsemanship advance,
Town-folks my strength; a daintier judge applies
His praise to sleight which from good use [4] doth rise;

3. Cupid.
4. I.e., do they call ungratefulness virtue there (as they do here)?
1. A place for refreshment on a journey.
2. Proven strength. "Prease": press, crowd.
3. At an actual tournament in the summer of 1581.
4. Cleverness which from experience.

Some lucky wits impute it but to chance;
Others, because of both sides I do take
My blood from them who did excel in this,[5]
Think nature me a man-at-arms did make.
How far they shoot awry! The true cause is,
Stella looked on, and from her heavenly face
Sent forth the beams which made so fair my race.

45

Stella oft sees the very face of woe
Painted in my beclouded, stormy face,
But cannot skill[6] to pity my disgrace,
Not though thereof the cause herself she know;[7]
Yet, hearing late a fable which did show,
Of lovers never known, a grievous case,
Pity thereof got in her breast such place
That, from that sea derived, tears' springs did flow.
Alas! If fancy,[8] drawn by imaged things,
Though false, yet with free scope more grace doth breed
Than servant's wrack, where new doubts honor brings,[9]
Then think, my dear, that you in me do read
Of lover's ruin some sad tragedy.
I am not I; pity the tale of me.

64

No more, my dear, no more these counsels try;
Oh, give my passions leave to run their race;
Let Fortune lay on me her worst disgrace;
Let folk o'ercharged with brain against me cry;
Let clouds bedim my face, break in mine eye;
Let me no steps but of lost labor trace;
Let all the earth with scorn recount my case;
But do not will me from my Love to flie.
I do not envy Aristotle's wit,[1]
Nor do aspire to Caesar's bleeding fame,
Nor ought do care, though some above me sit,
Nor hope nor wish another course to frame,
But that which once may win thy cruel heart:
Thou art my wit, and thou my virtue art.

71

Who will in fairest book of Nature know,
How Virtue may best lodged in beauty be,
Let him but learn of Love to read in thee,
Stella, those fair lines, which true goodness show.

5. I.e., because my ancestors on both sides were distinguished in the tournament.

6. Is unable. "Disgrace": i.e., her lack of favor.

7. I.e., even though she knows herself to be the cause of it.

8. Imagination, but often involving love.

9. I.e., than the despair of a lover ("servant"), caused by her new scruples ("doubts") based on her honor.

1. Wisdom.

There shall he find all vices' overthrow,
Not by rude force, but sweetest sovereignty
Of reason, from whose light those night birds[2] fly;
That inward sun in thine eyes shineth so.
And not content to be Perfection's heir
Thyself, dost strive all minds that way to move,
Who mark in thee what is in thee most fair.
So while thy beauty draws the heart to love,
As fast thy Virtue bends that love to good:
"But ah," desire still cries, "give me some food."

74

I never drank of Aganippe well,
Nor ever did in shade of Tempe sit,[3]
And Muses scorn with vulgar brains to dwell;
Poor layman I, for sacred rites unfit.
Some do I hear of poets' fury tell,
But, God wot, wot not what they mean by it;
And this I swear by blackest brook of hell,[4]
I am no pick-purse of another's wit.
How falls it then that with so smooth an ease
My thoughts I speak; and what I speak doth flow
In verse, and that my verse best wits doth please?
Guess we the cause. What, is it thus? Fie, no.
Or so? Much less. How then? Sure thus it is:
My lips are sweet, inspired with Stella's kiss.

1582 1591

Fourth Song[1]

Only joy, now here you are,
Fit to hear and ease my care;
Let my whispering voice obtain
Sweet reward for sharpest pain;
Take me to thee, and thee to me.
"No, no, no, no, my dear, let be."

Night hath closed all in her cloak,
Twinkling stars love-thoughts provoke,
Danger hence good care doth keep,
Jealousy itself doth sleep;
Take me to thee, and thee to me.
"No, no, no, no, my dear, let be."

2. Night birds, like owls, conventionally symbolized vices.

3. Aganippe: a well at the foot of Mt. Helicon in Greece, sacred to the Muses; Tempe: a valley beside Mt. Olympus, sacred to Apollo, the god of song.

4. The river Styx.

1. One of a number of songs that appear among *Astrophel and Stella* sonnets in the Folio edition of 1598; this one comes between Sonnets 85 and 86.

Better place no wit can find,
Cupid's yoke to loose or bind;
These sweet flowers on fine bed too,
Us in their best language woo;
Take me to thee, and thee to me.
"No, no, no, no, my dear, let be."

This small light the moon bestows
Serves thy beams but to disclose;
So to raise my hap more high,
Fear not else, none can us spy;
Take me to thee, and thee to me.
"No, no, no, no, my dear, let be."

That you heard was but a mouse,
Dumb sleep holdeth all the house;
Yet asleep, methinks they say,
Young folks, take time while you
    may;
Take me to thee, and thee to me.
"No, no, no, no, my dear, let be."

Niggard time threats, if we miss
This large offer of our bliss,
Long stay ere he grant the same;
Sweet, then, while each thing doth
    frame,
Take me to thee, and thee to me.
"No, no, no, no, my dear, let be."

Your fair mother is abed,
Candles out and curtains spread;
She thinks you do letters write;
Write, but let me first endite;
Take me to thee, and thee to me.
"No, no, no, no, my dear, let be."

Sweet, alas, why strive you thus?
Concord better fitteth us;
Leave to Mars the force of hands,
Your power in your beauty stands;
Take me to thee, and thee to me.
"No, no, no, no, my dear, let be."

Woe to me, and do you swear
Me to hate? but I forbear;
Cursed be my destines all,
That brought me so high to fall;
Soon with my death I will please
    thee.
"No, no, no, no, my dear, let be."

1591, 1598

From An Apology for Poetry

* * * There is no art delivered to mankind that hath not the works of nature for his principal object, without which they could not consist, and on which they so depend, as they become actors and players, as it were, of what nature will have set forth. So doth the astronomer look upon the stars, and, by that he seeth, setteth down what order nature hath taken therein.[1] So do the geometrician and arithmetician in their diverse sorts of quantities. So doth the musician in times tell you which by nature agree,[2] which not. The natural philosopher thereon[3] hath his name, and the moral philosopher standeth upon the natural virtues, vices, and passions of man; and "follow nature," saith he, "therein, and thou shalt not err." The lawyer saith what men have determined; the historian what men have done. The grammarian speaketh only of the rules of speech; and the rhetorician and logician, considering what in nature will soonest prove and persuade, thereon give artificial rules, which still are compassed within the circle of a question according to the proposed matter.[4] The physician weigheth the nature of a man's body, and the nature of things helpful or hurtful unto it. And the metaphysic, though it be in the second and abstract notions, and therefore be counted supernatural, yet doth he indeed build upon the depth of nature. Only the poet, disdaining to be tied to any such subjection, lifted up with the vigor of his own invention, doth grow in effect another nature, in making things either better than nature bringeth forth, or, quite anew, forms such as never were in nature, as the Heroes,[5] Demigods, Cyclops, Chimeras, Furies, and such like: so as he goeth hand in hand with nature, not enclosed within the narrow warrant of her gifts, but freely ranging only within the zodiac of his own wit.

Nature never set forth the earth in so rich tapestry as divers poets have done—neither with pleasant rivers, fruitful trees, sweet-smelling flowers, nor whatsoever else may make the too much loved earth more lovely. Her[6] world is brazen, the poets only deliver a golden. But let those things alone, and go to man—for whom as the other things are, so it seemeth in him her uttermost cunning

1. I.e., according to that which he sees, he sets down what arrangements nature has made.

2. Which musical measures fit together naturally.

3. I.e., from studying nature; the "natural philosopher" is what we would call a scientist. "Standeth upon": takes as his subject matter.

4. I.e., which apply only to the particular situation for which the rule was devised. "Weigheth": studies, considers.

5. Sidney uses the word in its Greek sense, meaning a deified man; "Cyclops": one-eyed giants in Homer's *Odyssey;* "Chimeras": fire-breathing monsters, with lion's head, goat's body, and serpent's tail.

6. I.e., nature's. "Brazen": a reference to the traditional idea that the first age of man was the Golden Age, and that deterioration then followed through the Silver Age and the Brazen Age down to the present Iron Age.

is employed—and know whether she have brought forth so true a lover as Theagenes, so constant a friend as Pylades, so valiant a man as Orlando, so right a prince as Xenophon's Cyrus,[7] so excellent a man every way as Virgil's Aeneas. Neither let this be jestingly conceived, because the works of the one be essential, the other in imitation or fiction; for any understanding knoweth the skill of the artificer standeth in that idea or foreconceit of the work, and not in the work itself. And that the poet hath that idea is manifest, by delivering them forth in such excellency as he hath imagined them. Which delivering forth also is not wholly imaginative, as we are wont to say by them that build castles in the air: but so far substantially it worketh, not only to make a Cyrus, which had been but a particular excellency, as nature might have done, but to bestow a Cyrus upon the world, to make many Cyruses, if they will learn aright why and how that maker made him.

Neither let it be deemed too saucy a comparison to balance the highest point of man's wit with the efficacy of nature; but rather give right honor to the heavenly Maker of that maker,[8] who, having made man to his own likeness, set him beyond and over all the works of that second nature: which in nothing he showeth so much as in poetry, when with the force of a divine breath he bringeth things forth far surpassing her doings, with no small argument to the incredulous of that first accursed fall of Adam, since our erected wit[9] maketh us know what perfection is, and yet our infected will keepeth us from reaching unto it.[1] But these arguments will by few be understood, and by fewer granted. Thus much (I hope) will be given me, that the Greeks with some probability of reason gave him the name above all names of learning. Now let us go to a more ordinary opening[2] of him, that the truth may be more palpable: and so I hope, though we get not so unmatched a praise as the etymology of his names will grant, yet his very description, which no man will deny, shall not justly be barred from a principal commendation.

Poesy therefore is an art of imitation, for so Aristotle termeth it[3] in his word *mimesis*, that is to say, a representing, counter-

7. Theagenes: hero of Heliodorus' Greek romance *Aethiopica;* Pylades was the constant friend of the Greek hero Orestes; Orlando: hero of Ariosto's *Orlando Furioso;* Cyrus: hero of Xenophon's *Cyropaedia*.

8. Sidney had earlier explained that the word "poet" comes from the Greek word for "maker." The "maker" is then in a role like that of God, but on a lower level—an anticipation of the idea of the poet as creator.

9. I.e., our elevated, undebased intelligence.

1. The "will" is "infected" because corrupted and weakened by original sin in the Fall.

2. Analysis or explanation. Sidney goes on to explain poetry as an art of imitation, following Aristotle. There are three kinds: divine poetry, which imitates the excellencies of God; philosophical poetry, which imitates learning; and a third kind, which we generally call simple "poetry," and which imitates life as it might be and should be, for the purpose of conveying instruction and delight.

3. In the *Poetics* 1.2, but Sidney is probably drawing here on Scaliger's *Poetice* 1.i.

feiting, or figuring forth—to speak metaphorically, a speaking picture; with this end, to teach and delight. Of this have been three several kinds.

The chief, both in antiquity and excellency, were they that did imitate the inconceivable excellencies of God. Such were David in his Psalms; Solomon in his Song of Songs, in his Ecclesiastes, and Proverbs; Moses and Deborah in their Hymns; and the writer of Job, which, beside other, the learned Emanuel Tremellius and Franciscus Junius[4] do entitle the poetical part of the Scripture. Against these none will speak that hath the Holy Ghost in due holy reverence. In this kind, though in a full wrong divinity, were Orpheus, Amphion, Homer in his Hymns, and many other, both Greeks and Romans, and this poesy must be used by whosoever will follow St. James's counsel in singing psalms when they are merry, and I know is used with the fruit of comfort by some, when, in sorrowful pangs of their death-bringing sins, they find the consolation of the never-leaving goodness.

The second kind is of them that deal with matters philosophical: either moral, as Tyrtaeus, Phocylides, and Cato;[5] or natural, as Lucretius and Virgil's *Georgics;* or astronomical, as Manilius and Pontanus; or historical, as Lucan; which who mislike, the fault is in their judgments quite out of taste, and not in the sweet food of sweetly uttered knowledge.

But because this second sort is wrapped within the fold of the proposed subject, and takes not the course of his own invention, whether they properly be poets or no let grammarians dispute; and go to the third, indeed right[6] poets, of whom chiefly this question ariseth, betwixt whom and these second is such a kind of difference as betwixt the meaner sort of painters, who counterfeit only such faces as are set before them, and the more excellent, who, having no law but wit, bestow that in colors upon you which is fittest for the eye to see, as the constant though lamenting look of Lucretia, when she punished in herself another's fault[7] (wherein he painteth not Lucretia whom he never saw, but painteth the outward beauty of such a virtue). For these third be they which most properly do imitate to teach and delight, and to imitate borrow nothing of what is, hath been, or shall be; but range, only reined with learned discretion, into the divine consideration of what may be, and should be. These be they that, as the first and most noble sort may justly be termed *vates,*[8] so these are waited on in the excellentest languages and best understandings, with the

4. Two 16th-century Protestant scholars who published a Latin translation of the Bible in 1575–80.

5. Dionysius Cato was the reputed author of *Disticha de moribus,* four books of epigrammatic moral precepts in Latin hexameters used as a textbook in Elizabethan schools.

6. Real.

7. Lucretia was the wife of L. Tarquinius Colatinus, outraged by Sextus, son of Tarquinius Superbus. See Shakespeare *The Rape of Lucrece.*

8. A *vates* was originally a prophet or oracle; later the term was used for a poet.

foredescribed name of poets; for these indeed do merely make to imitate, and imitate both to delight and teach, and delight to move men to take that goodness in hand, which without delight they would fly as from a stranger, and teach, to make them know that goodness whereunto they are moved: which being the noblest scope to which ever any learning was directed, yet want there not idle tongues to bark at them.

These be subdivided into sundry more special denominations. The most notable be the heroic, lyric, tragic, comic, satiric, iambic, elegiac, pastoral, and certain others, some of these being termed according to the matter they deal with, some by the sorts of verses they liked best to write in; for indeed the greatest part of poets have appareled their poetical inventions in that numbrous[9] kind of writing which is called verse—indeed but appareled, verse being but an ornament and no cause to poetry, since there have been many most excellent poets that never versified, and now swarm many versifiers that need never answer to the name of poets. For Xenophon,[1] who did imitate so excellently as to give us *effigiem iusti imperii*, "the portraiture of a just Empire," under name of Cyrus (as Cicero saith of him), made therein an absolute heroical poem. So did Heliodorus in his sugared invention of that picture of love in Theagenes and Chariclea;[2] and yet both these writ in prose: which I speak to show that it is not rhyming and versing that maketh a poet—no more than a long gown maketh an advocate, who though he pleaded in armor should be an advocate and no soldier. But it is that feigning notable images of virtues, vices, or what else, with that delightful teaching, which must be the right describing note to know a poet by, although indeed the Senate of Poets hath chosen verse as their fittest raiment, meaning, as in matter they passed all in all, so in manner to go beyond them—not speaking (table-talk fashion or like men in a dream) words as they chanceably fall from the mouth, but peizing[3] each syllable of each word by just proportion according to the dignity of the subject.

Now therefore it shall not be amiss first to weigh this latter sort of poetry by his works, and then by his parts, and, if in neither of these anatomies[4] he be condemnable, I hope we shall obtain a more favorable sentence. This purifying of wit, this enriching of memory, enabling of judgment, and enlarging of conceit, which commonly we call learning, under what name soever it come forth, or to what immediate end soever it be directed, the final end is to lead and draw us to as high a perfection as our degenerate souls, made worse by their clayey lodgings, can be capable of. This, ac-

9. Not "numerous," but in "numbers" or metrical lines.
1. Xenophon's *Cyropaedia* is an idealized and romanticized biography, in prose, of Cyrus the Great.
2. Heliodorus's popular Greek romance. written in the 4th century A.D., but not known in western Europe until the 16th century.
3. Weighing.
4. Analyses.

cording to the inclination of the man, bred many formed impressions. For some that thought this felicity principally to be gotten by knowledge and no knowledge to be so high and heavenly as acquaintance with the stars, gave themselves to astronomy; others, persuading themselves to be demigods if they knew the causes of things, became natural and supernatural philosophers; some an admirable delight drew to music; and some the certainty of demonstration to the mathematics. But all, one and other, having this scope—to know, and by knowledge to lift up the mind from the dungeon of the body to the enjoying his own divine essence. But when by the balance of experience it was found that the astronomer looking to the stars might fall into a ditch, that the inquiring philosopher might be blind in himself, and the mathematician might draw forth a straight line with a crooked heart, then, lo, did proof, the overruler of opinions, make manifest that all these are but serving sciences, which, as they have each a private end in themselves, so yet are they all directed to the highest end of the mistress-knowledge, by the Greeks called *architectonike,* which stands (as I think) in the knowledge of a man's self, in the ethic and politic consideration, with the end of well doing and not of well knowing only:—even as the saddler's next end is to make a good saddle, but his farther end to serve a nobler faculty, which is horsemanship; so the horseman's to soldiery, and the soldier not only to have the skill, but to perform the practice of a soldier. So that, the ending end of all earthly learning being virtuous action, those skills, that most serve to bring forth that, have a most just title to be princes over all the rest. Wherein if we can show the poet's nobleness by setting him before his other competitors, among whom as principal challengers step forth the moral philosophers, whom, me thinketh, I see coming towards me with a sullen gravity, as though they could not abide vice by daylight, rudely clothed for to witness outwardly their contempt of outward things, with books in their hands against glory, whereto they set their names, sophistically[5] speaking against subtlety and angry with any man in whom they see the foul fault of anger. These men, casting largess[6] as they go of definitions, divisions, and distinctions, with a scornful interrogative do soberly ask whether it be possible to find any path so ready to lead a man to Virtue as that which teacheth what Virtue is. And teacheth it not only by delivering forth his very being, his causes and effects, but also by making known his enemy Vice, which must be destroyed, and his cumbersome servant Passion, which must be mastered; by showing the generalities that containeth it and the specialities that are derived from it; lastly, by plain setting down how it extendeth itself out of the limits of a man's own little world to the govern-

5. With deceptive subtlety.

6. Bountiful gifts.

ment of families and maintaining of public societies.

The historian scarcely giveth leisure to the moralist to say so much but that he, laden with old mouse-eaten records, authorizing himself,[7] for the most part, upon other histories, whose greatest authorities are built upon the notable foundation of hearsay; having much ado to accord differing writers and to pick truth out of partiality,[8] better acquainted with a thousand years ago than with the present age, and yet better knowing how this world goeth than how his own wit runneth, curious for antiquities and inquisitive[9] of novelties, a wonder to young folks and a tyrant in table talk, denieth, in a great chafe, that any man teaching of virtue and virtuous actions, is comparable to him. "I am *Lux vitae, temporum magistra, nuncia vetustatis*, etc."[1] * * *

But since I have run so long a career in this matter, methinks, before I give my pen a full stop, it shall be but a little more lost time to inquire why England (the mother of excellent minds) should be grown so hard a stepmother to poets, who certainly in wit ought to pass all other, since all only proceedeth from their wit, being indeed makers of themselves, not takers of others. How can I but exclaim,

Musa, mihi causas memora, quo numine laeso![2]

Sweet poesy, that hath anciently had kings, emperors, senators, great captains, such as, besides a thousand others, David, Adrian, Sophocles, Germanicus,[3] not only to favor poets, but to be poets; and of our nearer times can present for her patrons a Robert, King of Sicily, the great King Francis of France, King James of Scotland;[1] such cardinals as Bembus and Bibiena; such famous preachers and teachers as Beza and Melancthon; so learned philosophers as Fracastorius and Scaliger; so great orators as Pontanus and Muretus; so piercing wits as George Buchanan;[2] so grave counselors as, be-

7. Basing his authority.
8. Prejudice.
9. Impertinently curious, prying.
1. "The light of life, mistress of the times, interpreter of the past" (paraphrased from Cicero, *De Oratore* II.36). In the omitted portion, Sidney defends the various kinds of literature and refutes the traditional complaints that poets tell lies, that poetry is effeminate, that poetry abuses man's wit, and that Plato banished poets from his commonwealth. He calls for laurels for poets instead of abuse of their art.
2. "O Muse, call to mind the causes: what divinity was injured?" (*Aeneid* I.8).
3. Adrian is the Emperor Hadrian; Sophocles, the great Greek dramatist, was also a general; Germanicus, 1st-century Roman emperor, translated poetry.
1. Robert d'Anjou, King of Naples, friend of Petrarch and Boccaccio; Francis I of France was a great patron of arts and letters; King James I of Scotland was author of the *King's Quair*.
2. Pietro Cardinal Bembo, a stylist and man of letters (he also appears in Castiglione's *Courtier*); Bernardo da Bibbiena, a writer of comedy and private secretary to Lorenzo de Medici. Theodore Beza and Philip Melancthon were prominent European Protestant theologians. Fracastorius and Julius Caesar Scaliger were famous Italian scholars. John Jovius Pontanus was an Italian medieval poet; Muretus was the Latinized name of Marc Antoine Muret, French scholar and writer. George Buchanan was the foremost Scottish writer of the 16th century.

sides many, but before all, that Hospital of France,[3] than whom (I think) that realm never brought forth a more accomplished judgment, more firmly builded upon virtue—I say these, with numbers of others, not only to read others' poesies, but to poetize for others' reading—that poesy, thus embraced in all other places, should only find in our time a hard welcome in England, I think the very earth lamenteth it. and therefore decketh our soil with fewer laurels than it was accustomed. For heretofore poets have in England also flourished, and, which is to be noted, even in those times when the trumpet of Mars did sound loudest. And now that an overfaint quietness should seem to strew the house for poets,[4] they are almost in as good reputation as the mountebanks at Venice. Truly even that, as of the one side it giveth great praise to poesy, which like Venus (but to better purpose) hath rather be troubled in the net with Mars than enjoy the homely quiet of Vulcan;[5] so serves it for a piece of a reason why they are less grateful to idle England, which now can scarce endure the pain of a pen. Upon this necessarily followeth, that base men with servile wits undertake it, who think it enough if they can be rewarded of the printer. And so as Epaminondas is said, with the honor of his virtue, to have made an office, by his exercising it, which before was contemptible, to become highly respected,[6] so these, no more but setting their names to it, by their own disgracefulness disgrace the most graceful poesy. For now, as if all the Muses were got with child, to bring forth bastard poets, without any commission they do post over the banks of Helicon, till they make the readers more weary than posthorses, while, in the meantime, they,

Queis meliore luto finxit praecordia Titan,[7]

are better content to suppress the outflowing of their wit than, by publishing them, to be accounted knights of the same order. But I that, before ever I durst aspire unto the dignity, am admitted into the company of the paper-blurrers, do find the very true cause of our wanting estimation is want of desert, taking upon us to be poets in despite of Pallas. Now, wherein we want desert were a thankworthy labor to express: but if I knew, I should have mended myself. But I, as I never desired the title, so have I neglected the means to come by it. Only, overmastered by some thoughts, I yielded an inky tribute unto them. Marry, they that delight in poesy itself should seek to know what they do, and how they do, and, especially,

3. Michel de l'Hospital, Chancellor of France and defender of the Huguenots.
4. I.e., now that peace has strewn rushes on the floor to make poets comfortable. "Mountebanks": vendors of quack medicines.
5. Vulcan discovered his wife Venus in bed with Mars; he entrapped them in a net and called the other gods to see them, expecting the lovers to suffer ridicule and shame, but he was the victim of their laughter himself.
6. He was sewer commissioner in Thebes.
7. "Whose hearts Titan [Prometheus] had formed of better clay" (Juvenal, *Satires* XIV.34–35).

look themselves in an unflattering glass of reason, if they be inclinable unto it. For poesy must not be drawn by the ears; it must be gently led, or rather it must lead; which was partly the cause that made the ancient-learned affirm it was a divine gift, and no human skill: since all other knowledges lie ready for any that hath strength of wit; a poet no industry can make, if his own genius be not carried unto it; and therefore is it an old proverb, *Orator fit, Poeta nascitur.*[8] Yet confess I always that as the fertilest ground must be manured, so must the highest-flying wit have a Daedalus[9] to guide him. That Daedalus, they say, both in this and in other, hath three wings to bear itself up into the air of due commendation: that is, Art, Imitation, and Exercise. But these, neither artificial rules nor imitative patterns, we much cumber ourselves withal. Exercise indeed we do, but that very fore-backwardly: for where we should exercise to know, we exercise as having known: and so is our brain delivered of much matter which never was begotten by knowledge. For, there being two principal parts—matter to be expressed by words and words to express the matter—in neither we use Art or Imitation rightly. Our matter is *Quodlibet*[1] indeed, though wrongly performing Ovid's verse,

Quicquid conabar dicere, versus erit:

never marshaling it into an assured rank, that almost the readers cannot tell where to find themselves.

Chaucer, undoubtedly, did excellently in his *Troilus and Cressida;* of whom, truly, I know not whether to marvel more, either that he in that misty time could see so clearly, or that we in this clear age walk so stumblingly after him. Yet had he great wants, fit to be forgiven in so reverent antiquity. I account the *Mirror of Magistrates*[2] meetly furnished of beautiful parts, and in the Earl of Surrey's *Lyrics* many things tasting of a noble birth, and worthy of a noble mind. The *Shepherd's Calendar* hath much poetry in his Eclogues, indeed worthy the reading, if I be not deceived. That same framing of his style to an old rustic language I dare not allow, since neither Theocritus in Greek, Virgil in Latin, nor Sannazaro in Italian[3] did affect it. Besides these, do I not remember to have seen but few (to speak boldly) printed, that have poetical sinews in them: for proof whereof, let but most of the verses be put in prose, and then ask the meaning; and it will be found that one verse did but beget another, without ordering at the first what should be at the last; which becomes a confused mass of words,

8. "An orator is made, but a poet must be born one."

9. The legendary craftsman who invented wings for himself and his son Icarus. Icarus did not follow his father's instructions and fell into the sea.

1. "Anything you please." The phrase following may be translated, "Whatever I try to write will become verse."

2. A large collection of Elizabethan poems on the downfall of princes and men of power. The "beautiful parts" were probably in Sackville's Induction to it.

3. Three models for pastoral poetry.

with a tingling sound of rhyme, barely accompanied with reason.

Our tragedies and comedies (not without cause cried out against), observing rules neither of honest civility nor of skillful poetry, excepting *Gorboduc*[4] (again, I say, of those that I have seen), which notwithstanding, as it is full of stately speeches and well-sounding phrases, climbing to the height of Seneca's style, and as full of notable morality, which it doth most delightfully teach, and so obtain the very end of poesy, yet in truth it is very defectious in the circumstances, which grieveth me, because it might not remain as an exact model of all tragedies. For it is faulty both in place and time, the two necessary companions of all corporal actions. For where the stage should always represent but one place, and the uttermost time presupposed in it should be, both by Aristotle's precept and common reason, but one day, there is both many days, and many places, inartificially imagined. But if it be so in *Gorboduc*, how much more in all the rest, where you shall have Asia of the one side, and Afric of the other, and so many other under-kingdoms, that the player, when he cometh in, must ever begin with telling where he is, or else the tale will not be conceived? Now ye shall have three ladies walk to gather flowers, and then we must believe the stage to be a garden. By and by we hear news of shipwreck in the same place, and then we are to blame if we accept it not for a rock. Upon the back of that comes out a hideous monster, with fire and smoke, and then the miserable beholders are bound to take it for a cave. While in the meantime two armies fly in, represented with four swords and bucklers,[5] and then what hard heart will not receive it for a pitched field? Now, of time they are much more liberal, for ordinary it is that two young princes fall in love. After many traverses,[6] she is got with child, delivered of a fair boy; he is lost, groweth a man, falls in love, and is ready to get another child; and all this in two hours' space: which, how absurd it is in sense, even sense may imagine, and art hath taught, and all ancient examples justified, and, at this day, the ordinary players in Italy will not err in. Yet will some bring in an example of *Eunuchus* in Terence,[7] that containeth matter of two days, yet far short of twenty years. True it is, and so was it to be played in two days, and so fitted to the time it set forth. And though Plautus hath in one place done amiss, let us hit with him, and not miss with him. But they will say, How then shall we set forth a story, which containeth both many places and many times? And do they not know that a tragedy is tied to the laws of poesy, and not of history; not bound to follow the story, but, having liberty, either to feign a quite new

4. A Senecan play by Thomas Sackville and Thomas Norton, published in 1565 and called the first regular English tragedy. The tragedies of the Roman dramatist Seneca (5 B.C.–A.D. 65) are written in a highly rhetorical, declamatory style.
5. Shields.
6. Difficulties, mishaps.
7. Terence (195–159 B.C.) and Plautus (251–184 B.C.) were the chief Latin writers of comedy.

matter, or to frame the history to the most tragical conveniency? Again, many things may be told which cannot be showed, if they know the difference betwixt reporting and representing. As, for example, I may speak (though I am here) of Peru, and in speech digress from that to the description of Calicut; but in action I cannot represent it without Pacolet's horse.[8] And so was the manner the ancients took, by some Nuncius[9] to recount things done in former time or other place. Lastly, if they will represent an history, they must not (as Horace saith) begin *ab ovo*,[1] but they must come to the principal point of that one action which they will represent. By example this will be best expressed. I have a story of young Polydorus,[2] delivered for safety's sake, with great riches, by his father Priam to Polymnestor, king of Thrace, in the Trojan war time. He, after some years, hearing the overthrow of Priam, for to make the treasure his own, murdereth the child. The body of the child is taken up by Hecuba. She, the same day, findeth a sleight to be revenged most cruelly of the tyrant. Where now would one of our tragedy writers begin, but with the delivery of the child? Then should he sail over into Thrace, and so spend I know not how many years, and travel numbers of places. But where doth Euripides? Even with the finding of the body, leaving the rest to be told by the spirit of Polydorus. This need no further to be enlarged; the dullest wit may conceive it.

But besides these gross absurdities, how all their plays be neither right tragedies, nor right comedies, mingling kings and clowns, not because the matter so carrieth it, but thrust in clowns by head and shoulders, to play a part in majestical matters, with neither decency nor discretion,[3] so as neither the admiration and commiseration, nor the right sportfulness, is by their mongrel tragicomedy obtained. I know Apuleius[4] did somewhat so, but that is a thing recounted with space of time, not represented in one moment: and I know the ancients have one or two examples of tragicomedies, as Plautus hath *Amphitruo*.[5] But, if we mark them well, we shall find, that they never, or very daintily, match hornpipes[6] and funerals. So falleth it out that, having indeed no right comedy, in that comical part of our tragedy we have nothing but scurrility, unworthy of any chaste ears, or some extreme show of doltishness, indeed fit to lift up a loud laughter, and nothing else: where the whole tract of a comedy should be full of delight, as the tragedy should be still maintained in a well-raised admiration. But our comedians

8. A magic horse in the French romance *Valentine and Orson*. "Calicut": Calcutta.
9. Messenger.
1. From the beginning (literally, "from the egg").
2. In Euripides' *Hecuba*.
3. Mingling of social levels (kings and clowns) was thought to be a violation of the principle of decorum.
4. Not a dramatist, but the 2nd-century Roman author of the popular satirical novel, *The Golden Ass*.
5. *Amphitruo* is tragicomic only in that it contains gods and heroes; otherwise it is pure comedy.
6. Merry tunes for country dances.

think there is no delight without laughter; which is very wrong, for though laughter may come with delight, yet cometh it not of delight, as though delight should be the cause of laughter; but well may one thing breed both together. Nay, rather in themselves they have, as it were, a kind of contrariety: for delight we scarcely do but in things that have a conveniency to ourselves or to the general nature: laughter almost ever cometh of things most disproportioned to ourselves and nature. Delight hath a joy in it, either permanent or present. Laughter hath only a scornful tickling. For example, we are ravished with delight to see a fair woman, and yet are far from being moved to laughter. We laugh at deformed creatures, wherein certainly we cannot delight. We delight in good chances, we laugh at mischances; we delight to hear the happiness of our friends, or country, at which he were worthy to be laughed at that would laugh. We shall, contrarily, laugh sometimes to find a matter quite mistaken and go down the hill against the bias, in the mouth of some such men, as for the respect of them one shall be heartily sorry, yet he cannot choose but laugh; and so is rather pained than delighted with laughter. Yet deny I not but that they may go well together. For as in Alexander's picture well set out we delight without laughter, and in twenty mad antics we laugh without delight, so in Hercules, painted with his great beard and furious countenance, in woman's attire, spinning at Omphale's commandment,[7] it breedeth both delight and laughter. For the representing of so strange a power in love procureth delight: and the scornfulness of the action stirreth laughter. But I speak to this purpose, that all the end of the comical part be not upon such scornful matters as stirreth laughter only, but, mixed with it, that delightful teaching which is the end of poesy. And the great fault even in that point of laughter, and forbidden plainly by Aristotle, is that they stir laughter in sinful things, which are rather execrable than ridiculous; or in miserable, which are rather to be pitied than scorned. For what is it to make folks gape at a wretched beggar, or a beggarly clown; or, against law of hospitality, to jest at strangers, because they speak not English so well as we do? What do we learn? Since it is certain

Nil habet infelix paupertas durius in se,
Quam quod ridiculos homines facit.[8]

But rather a busy loving courtier, a heartless threatening Thraso, a self-wise-seeming schoolmaster, an awry-transformed traveler—these if we saw walk in stage names, which we play naturally, therein were delightful laughter, and teaching delightfulness: as in the

7. Hercules was so infatuated with Omphale, queen of Lydia, that he submitted to being dressed as a female slave and forced to spin wool.

8. "Unfortunate poverty has in itself nothing harder to bear than that it makes men ridiculous" (Juvenal, *Satires* III.152–53).

other, the tragedies of Buchanan do justly bring forth a divine admiration. But I have lavished out too many words of this play matter. I do it because, as they are excelling parts of poesy, so is there none so much used in England, and none can be more pitifully abused; which, like an unmannerly daughter showing a bad education, causeth her mother Poesy's honesty to be called in question.

Other sorts of poetry almost have we none, but that lyrical kind of songs and sonnets: which, Lord, if He gave us so good minds, how well it might be employed, and with how heavenly fruit, both private and public, in singing the praises of the immortal beauty, the immortal goodness of that God who giveth us hands to write and wits to conceive; of which we might well want words, but never matter; of which we could turn our eyes to nothing, but we should ever have new budding occasions. But truly many of such writings as come under the banner of unresistible love, if I were a mistress, would never persuade me they were in love; so coldly they apply fiery speeches, as men that had rather read lovers' writings, and so caught up certain swelling phrases (which hang together like a man which once told me the wind was at northwest, and by south, because he would be sure to name winds enough), than that in truth they feel those passions, which easily (as I think) may be betrayed by that same forcibleness, or *energia* (as the Greeks call it) of the writer. But let this be a sufficient though short note, that we miss the right use of the material point of poesy.

Now, for the outside of it, which is words, or (as I may term it) diction, it is even well worse. So is that honey-flowing matron Eloquence appareled, or rather disguised, in a courtesan-like painted affectation: one time with so farfetched words, they may seem monsters, but must seem strangers, to any poor Englishman; another time, with coursing of a letter,[9] as if they were bound to follow the method of a dictionary; another time, with figures and flowers,[1] extremely winter-starved. But I would this fault were only peculiar to versifiers, and had not as large possession among prose-printers, and (which is to be marveled) among many scholars, and (which is to be pitied) among some preachers. Truly I could wish, if at least I might be so bold to wish in a thing beyond the reach of my capacity, the diligent imitators of Tully[2] and Demosthenes (most worthy to be imitated) did not so much keep Nizolian paperbooks[3] of their figures and phrases, as by attentive translation (as it were) devour them whole, and make them wholly theirs. For now

9. Alliteration.
1. Of rhetoric.
2. Cicero.
3. Marius Nizolius or Nizzoli (1498?–1576), Italian rhetorician and lexicographer, published a collection of Ciceronian phrases in 1535. Ascham mentions the keeping of similar books in *The Scholemaster*.

they cast sugar and spice upon every dish that is served to the table, like those Indians, not content to wear earrings at the fit and natural place of the ears, but they will thrust jewels through their nose and lips, because they will be sure to be fine. Tully, when he was to drive out Catiline, as it were with a thunderbolt of eloquence, often used that figure of repetition, *Vivit. Vivit? Immo in Senatum venit,*[4] etc. Indeed, inflamed with a well-grounded rage, he would have his words (as it were) double out of his mouth, and so do that artificially which we see men do in choler naturally. And we, having noted the grace of those words, hale them in sometime to a familiar epistle, when it were too much choler to be choleric.

Now for similitudes in certain printed discourses, I think all Herbarists,[5] all stories of beasts, fowls, and fishes are rifled up, that they come in multitudes to wait upon any of our conceits; which certainly is as absurd a surfeit to the ears as is possible: for the force of a similitude not being to prove anything to a contrary disputer, but only to explain to a willing hearer; when that is done, the rest is a most tedious prattling, rather over-swaying the memory from the purpose whereto they were applied, than any whit informing the judgment, already either satisfied, or by similitudes not to be satisfied. For my part, I do not doubt, when Antonius and Crassus, the great forefathers of Cicero in eloquence, the one (as Cicero testifieth of them) pretended not to know art, the other not to set by it, because with a plain sensibleness they might win credit of popular ears; which credit is the nearest step to persuasion; which persuasion is the chief mark of oratory—I do not doubt (I say) but that they used these knacks very sparingly; which, who doth generally use, any man may see doth dance to his own music; and so be noted by the audience more careful to speak curiously than to speak truly.

Undoubtedly (at least to my opinion undoubtedly) I have found in divers small-learned courtiers a more sound style than in some professors of learning: of which I can guess no other cause, but that the courtier, following that which by practice he findeth fittest to nature, therein (though he know it not) doth according to art, though not by art: where the other, using art to show art, and not to hide art (as in these cases he should do), flieth from nature, and indeed abuseth art.

But what? Methinks I deserve to be pounded for straying from poetry to oratory: but both have such an affinity in this wordish consideration, that I think this digression will make my meaning receive the fuller understanding—which is not to take upon me to teach poets how they should do, but only, finding myself sick among the rest, to show some one or two spots of the common in-

4. Sidney quotes rather freely from memory a line from Cicero (*Catiline*, 1, 2): "He lives, nay more, he comes into the Senate."

5. Writers who, like Lyly, introduce botanical and zoological analogies into their writing.

fection grown among the most part of writers: that, acknowledging ourselves somewhat awry, we may bend to the right use both of matter and manner; whereto our language giveth us great occasion, being indeed capable of any excellent exercising of it. I know some will say it is a mingled language. And why not so much the better, taking the best of both the other? Another will say it wanteth grammar. Nay truly, it hath that praise, that it wanteth not grammar: for grammar it might have, but it needs it not; being so easy of itself, and so void of those cumbersome differences of cases, genders, moods, and tenses, which I think was a piece of the Tower of Babylon's curse, that a man should be put to school to learn his mother tongue. But for the uttering sweetly and properly the conceits of the mind, which is the end of speech, that hath it equally with any other tongue in the world: and is particularly happy in compositions of two or three words together, near the Greek, far beyond the Latin: which is one of the greatest beauties can be in a language.

Now, of versifying there are two sorts, the one ancient, the other modern: the ancient marked the quantity of each syllable, and according to that framed his verse; the modern observing only number[6] (with some regard of the accent), the chief life of it standeth in that like sounding of the words, which we call rhyme. Whether of these be the most excellent, would bear many speeches. The ancient, no doubt, more fit for music, both words and tune observing quantity, and more fit lively to express divers passions, by the low and lofty sound of the well-weighed syllable. The latter likewise, with his rhyme, striketh a certain music to the ear: and, in fine, since it doth delight, though by another way, it obtains the same purpose: there being in either sweetness, and wanting in neither majesty. Truly the English, before any other vulgar language I know, is fit for both sorts: for, for the ancient, the Italian is so full of vowels that it must ever be cumbered with elisions; the Dutch so, of the other side, with consonants, that they cannot yield the sweet sliding fit for a verse; the French, in his whole language, hath not one word that hath his accent in the last syllable saving two, called *antepenultima;* and little more hath the Spanish: and, therefore, very gracelessly may they use dactyls. The English is subject to none of these defects.

Now, for the rhythm, though we do not observe quantity, yet we observe the accent very precisely: which other languages either cannot do, or will not do so absolutely. That *caesura,* or breathing place in the midst of the verse, neither Italian nor Spanish have, the French, and we, never almost fail of. Lastly, even the very

6. "Quantity" meant length or duration of a syllable; by "number" Sidney means merely counting the syllables.

rhyme itself the Italian cannot put in the last syllable, by the French named the "masculine rhyme," but still in the next to the last, which the French call the "female," or the next before that, which the Italians term *sdrucciola*. The example of the former is *buono: suono*, of the *sdrucciola, femina: semina*. The French, of the other side, hath both the male, as *bon: son*, and the female, as *plaise: taise*, but the *sdrucciola* he hath not: where the English hath all three, as *due: true; father: rather; motion: potion;*[1] with much more which might be said, but that I find already the triflingness of this discourse is much too much enlarged.

So that since the ever-praiseworthy poesy is full of virtue-breeding delightfulness, and void of no gift that ought to be in the noble name of learning; since the blames laid against it are either false or feeble; since the cause why it is not esteemed in England is the fault of poet-apes, not poets; since, lastly, our tongue is most fit to honor poesy, and to be honored by poesy; I conjure you all that have had the evil luck to read this ink-wasting toy of mine, even in the name of the Nine Muses, no more to scorn the sacred mysteries of poesy, no more to laugh at the name of "poets," as though they were next inheritors to fools, no more to jest at the reverent title of a "rhymer"; but to believe, with Aristotle, that they were the ancient treasurers of the Grecians' divinity; to believe, with Bembus, that they were first bringers-in of all civility; to believe, with Scaliger, that no philosopher's precepts can sooner make you an honest man than the reading of Virgil; to believe, with Clauserus,[2] the translator of Cornutus, that it pleased the heavenly Deity, by Hesiod and Homer, under the veil of fables, to give us all knowledge, logic, rhetoric, philosophy, natural and moral, and *Quid non?*;[3] to believe, with me, that there are many mysteries contained in poetry, which of purpose were written darkly, lest by profane wits it should be abused; to believe, with Landin,[4] that they are so beloved of the gods that whatsoever they write proceeds of a divine fury; lastly, to believe themselves, when they tell you they will make you immortal by their verses.

Thus doing, your name shall flourish in the printers' shops; thus doing, you shall be of kin to many a poetical preface; thus doing, you shall be most fair, most rich, most wise, most all; you shall dwell upon superlatives. Thus doing, though you be *libertino patre natus*,[5] you shall suddenly grow *Herculea proles*,[6]

1. These were three-syllable words in Elizabethan pronunciation.
2. Conrad Clauser (ca. 1520–1611), a German scholar; he translated a Greek treatise by Cornutus, who was a contemporary of Nero's.
3. What not.
4. Cristofero Landino, 15th-century Italian scholar and onetime tutor to Lorenzo de Medici.
5. "Born of a freed slave father."
6. I.e., a descendent of Hercules. The next phrase means "if my songs are of any avail" (*Aeneid* IX.446).

Si quid mea carmina possunt.

Thus doing, your soul shall be placed with Dante's Beatrix, or Virgil's Anchises. But if (fie of such a but) you be born so near the dull-making cataract of Nilus[7] that you cannot hear the planet-like music of poetry, if you have so earth-creeping a mind that it cannot lift itself up to look to the sky of poetry, or rather, by a certain rustical disdain, will become such a mome[8] as to be a Momus of poetry; then, though I will not wish unto you the ass's ears of Midas,[9] nor to be driven by a poet's verses (as Bubonax[1] was) to hang himself, nor to be rhymed to death, as is said to be done in Ireland;[2] yet thus much curse I must send you, in the behalf of all poets, that while you live, you live in love, and never get favor for lacking skill of a sonnet, and, when you die, your memory die from the earth for want of an epitaph.

1595

7. According to Cicero, people living near the cataracts of the Nile became deaf from the noise. "Planet-like music": the music of the spheres was supposed to be the most beautiful of all music.
8. A stupid person; "Momus": a critic.
9. He was given ass's ears because he preferred Pan's playing to Apollo's.
1. Bupalus, a sculptor, was so ashamed when his works were satirized by the poet Hipponax that he hanged himself. Sidney fuses the two names.
2. There was a popular tradition that Irish bards could cause death by their incantations.

EDMUND SPENSER

(1552–1599)

1579: Publication of *The Shepheardes Calender*.
1580: In Ireland, where he remains for the rest of his life.
1590: First three books of *The Faerie Queene* published.

The greatest nondramatic poet of the English Renaissance, Edmund Spenser, was born in London, probably in 1552, and attended the Merchant Taylors' School under its famous headmaster Richard Mulcaster. In 1569 he went to Cambridge as a "sizar" or poor scholar. His Cambridge experience strongly colored the rest of his life; it was at the university that Spenser began as a poet by translating some poems for a volume of anti-Catholic propaganda. His work, then and later, reflects the strong Puritanical environment of Cambridge where the popular preacher Thomas Cartwright was beginning to make the authorities uneasy. Spenser's friendship with Gabriel Harvey, a Cambridge don, humanist, pamphleteer, and eccentric, also began at the university. Some correspondence between Harvey and Spenser, published in 1580, shows that they were interested in theories of poetry and in experiments in quantitative versification in English; it also shows that Spenser had ambitious plans as a poet.

He proceeded through the university, receiving the degree of B.A. in 1573 and M.A. in 1576. He then entered upon a series of positions in the retinues of prominent men, including Dr. John Young, Bishop of Rochester; the Earl of Leicester, the queen's favorite; and finally, Lord Grey of Wilton, Lord Deputy of Ireland. During his employment in Leicester's household he came to know Sir Philip Sidney and his friend Sir Edward Dyer, courtiers who were interested in promoting a new English poetry. Spenser's own contribution to the movement is *The Shepheardes Calender*, published in 1579 and dedicated to Sidney in the verses:

To His Booke

Goe little booke: thy selfe present,
As child whose parent is unkent,
To him that is the president
Of noblesse and of chevalree.
And if that Envie barke at thee,
As sure it will, for succoure flee
Under the shadow of his wing
And, asked who thee forth did bring,
A shepheardes swaine saye did thee sing,
All as his straying flocke he fedde;
And when his honor has thee redde,
Crave pardon for my hardy hedde.
But if that any aske thy name,
Say thou wert base begot with blame,
For thy thereof thou takest shame.
And when thou art past jeopardee,
Come tell me what was said of mee
And I will send more after thee.

Immerito [Unworthy].

The *Calender* consists of twelve pastoral eclogues, one for each month of the year. Each is prefaced by an illustrative woodcut representing the characters or theme of the poem and picturing the appropriate sign of the zodiac for that month in the clouds above. The eclogue was a classical form, practiced by Virgil and others; it presents, usually in dialogue between shepherds, the moods and feelings and attitudes of the simple life. But often the pastoral eclogue criticizes the world as it is by reflection from the world as it might be, and in Spenser, as in other Renaissance poets, the eclogue at times becomes didactic or satirical. Though it pretends to represent simple shepherds, it is really commenting on contemporary affairs. The eclogues of the *Calender* are divided by its commentator, "E. K.," into three groups—plaintive, recreative, and moral. Of the moral eclogues, the final and climactic one is *October*, which deals with the problem of poetry in modern life and the responsibility of the poet in time—in an important way, the theme of the whole *Calender*. It looks forward to related themes in Milton's *Lycidas*.

Spenser used a deliberately archaic language, partly out of homage to Chaucer, whom he refers to as Tityrus, the god of shepherds, "who taught me, homely as I can, to make." But Spenser also used this language to get a rustic effect. The patron to whom the *Calender* is dedicated did not approve; Sidney wrote in his *Apology for Poetry*, "*The Shepheardes Calender* hath much poetry in his Eclogues, indeed worthy the reading, if I be not deceived. That same framing of his style to an old rustic language I dare not allow, since neither Theocritus in Greek, Virgil in Latin, nor Sannazaro in Italian did affect it." Another classical purist, Ben Jonson, growled that Spenser "writ no language," but that he would have him read for his matter. It would be a pity to follow Jonson's advice too literally, for Spenser's skillful use of many verse forms and his extraordinary musical effects indicate that here indeed is a poet to inaugurate the "new poetry" of the Elizabethan age.

There are thirteen different meters in *The Shepheardes Calender:* three kinds of couplet; three kinds of four-line stanza; three kinds of six-line stanza; stanzas of eight, nine, and ten lines; and a sestina. Some of these Spenser invented, some he adapted, but most of them were novel: only three or four were at all common in 1579. Spenser was a prolific experimenter: of the thirteen different meters in the *Calender* he used only three in his later poems. He went on to make further innovations—the special rhyme scheme of the Spenserian sonnet, richer than any other; the remarkably beautiful adaptation of Italian *canzone* forms for the *Epithalamion* and *Prothalamion*, and the nine-line stanza of *The Faerie Queene*, with its extraordinary six-foot line at the end, are only the most famous. Spenser is sometimes called the "poet's poet" because so many later English poets have learned the art of versification from him. In the 19th century alone his influence may be seen in Shelley's *Revolt of Islam*, Byron's *Childe Harold's Pilgrimage*, Keats's *Eve of St. Agnes*, and Tennyson's *The Lotos Eaters*.

The year after the publication of *The Shepheardes Calender* Spenser went to Ireland to serve Lord Grey; he spent the rest of his life there, except for two visits to England. He was at work on his great romantic epic, *The Faerie Queene*, when Sir Walter Ralegh visited him at Kilcolman Castle; the result was a trip to England and the publication, in 1590, of the first three books of *The Faerie Queene*. After that there was no question that Edmund Spenser was "the prince of poets in his time." He published a volume of poems called *Complaints*; a pastoral sequel to some of the eclogues in *The Shepheardes Calender* called *Colin Clouts Come Home Againe* (1595), which gave his views of the English court on his visit there in 1590; a sonnet cycle, *Amoretti*, and two marriage poems, *Epithalamion* and *Prothalamion*, but he completed only six of his projected twelve books of *The Faerie Queene*: in 1596 the first three books appeared again, with alterations, together with Books IV, V, and VI; the so-called "Mutability Cantos" first appeared in the edition of 1609.

In the second half of the decade, Ireland was torn by revolt and civil war; Spenser's castle was destroyed, and the poet was sent to England with messages from the besieged garrison in Ireland. He died in Westminster on January 13, 1599, and was buried near his beloved Chaucer in what is now called the Poets' Corner of Westminster Abbey.

Spenser is a complex genius who cannot be put into neatly labeled categories. He is, for instance, strongly influenced by Renaissance Neoplatonism, but remains always firmly grounded in earthiness and practicality. In *The Faerie Queene* he reaches toward the highest ideals of the Renaissance but knows, at the same time, what it is to want to remain an animal. He is a lover and celebrator of physical beauty, and he is sternly moral. His "morality" is, however, not of the repressive sort; it arises from his understanding of right action and of the temptations that entrap men as they try to achieve such action. Spenser was strongly influenced by Puritanism in his early days; he always remained a thoroughgoing Protestant; the Roman Catholic Church is made a villain in *The Faerie Queene*—and yet his understanding of faith and of sin has its roots in the great Catholic thinkers. He is profoundly English and patriotic; in him nationality and religion were inextricably joined. In the Proem to Book V of *The Faerie Queene* he characteristically looks back to the antique world and compares his own time with it most unfavorably. Yet his strongest links are not with the past, despite his love of Chaucer and his deliberately antique language: his closest affinity is with Milton, who was born nine years after Spenser's death. Milton called Spenser a better teacher than Scotus or Aquinas. He recognized Spenser, his great predecessor, as, like himself, a Christian humanist and British poet-prophet.

Spenser's poetry is always printed in the original spelling and punctuation (although a few of the most confusing punctuation marks have been altered in the present text), since it was a deliberate choice on Spenser's part that his language should seem antique. (A modern reader who read Shakespeare or the King James version of the Bible in the original spelling would not find as much difference in Spenser, but he would find some.) Furthermore, Spenser uses his spelling to suggest rhymes to the eye, sometimes to suggest etymologies, often incorrectly. The fact that Spenser's spelling is inconsistent is simply typical of his time; in the 16th century a man varied the spelling of even his name to suit convenience or a whim.

From THE SHEPHEARDES CALENDER[1]

October

Argument

In Cuddie[2] is set out the perfecte paterne of a Poete, whiche finding no maintenaunce of his state and studies, complayneth of the contempte of Poetrie, and the causes thereof: Specially having

1. When *The Shepheardes Calender* was published in 1579, each of the twelve eclogues was followed by a "Glosse," which contained explications of difficult or archaic words, together with learned discussions of—and disagreements with—Spenser's ideas, imagery, and poetics. The Glosses are by one "E. K.," whose identity has never been satisfactorily ascertained. Although certain scholars have suggested that E. K. was Spenser himself, it is equally possible that he was a friend.

E. K.'s editorial apparatus is usually printed along with the poems from the *Calender*. In the text that follows, the present editor has incorporated the glosses into the footnotes, abridging only some of E. K.'s longer exegeses, anecdotes, and tags from classical and contemporary authors; the original spelling has also been retained. E. K. first discusses the poem's sources: "This Aeglogue is made in imitation of Theocritus his xvi. Idilion, wherein hee reproved the Tyranne Hiero of Syracuse for his nigardise towarde Poetes, in whome is the power to make men immortal for theyr good dedes, or shameful for their naughty lyfe. And the lyke also is in Mantuane. The style hereof as also that in Theocritus, is more loftye then the rest, and applyed to the heighte of Poeticall witte." Actually Spenser's eclogue owes very little to Theocritus, but it does draw heavily upon the fifth eclogue of Baptista Spagnuoli, called Mantuan.

2. "I doubte whether by Cuddie be specified the authour selfe, or some

bene in all ages, and even amongst the most barbarous alwayes of singular accounpt[3] and honor, and being indede so worthy and commendable an arte: or rather no arte, but a divine gift and heavenly instinct not to bee gotten by laboure and learning, but adorned with both: and poured into the witte by a certaine ἐνθουσιασμὸς[4] and celestiall inspiration, as the Author hereof els where at large discourseth, in his booke called the *English Poete*, which booke being lately come to my hands, I mynde also by Gods grace upon further advisement to publish.

PIERS

Cuddie, for shame hold up thy heavye head,
And let us cast with what delight to chace,
And weary thys long lingring Phoebus race.[5]
Whilome° thou wont the shepheards laddes to leade, *formerly*
In rymes, in ridles, and in bydding base:[6]
Now they in thee, and thou in sleepe art dead.

CUDDIE

Piers, I have pyped erst° so long with payne, *up to now*
That all mine Oten reedes[7] bene rent and wore:
And my poore Muse hath spent her sparéd store,
Yet little good hath got, and much lesse gayne.
Such pleasaunce makes the Grashopper so poore,
And ligge so layd,[8] when Winter doth her straine:

The dapper[9] ditties, that I wont devise,
To feede youthes fancie, and the flocking fry,
Delighten much: what I the bett forthy?
They han the pleasure, I a sclender prise.
I beate the bush, the byrds to them doe flye:
What good thereof to Cuddie can arise?

PIERS

Cuddie, the prayse is better, then the price,
The glory eke much greater then the gayne:
O what an honor is it, to restraine
The lust of lawlesse youth with good advice:[1]

---

other. For in the eyght Aeglogue the same person was brought in, singing a Cantion of Colins making, as he sayth. So that some doubt, that the persons be different" [E. K.'s Glosse].

3. Account, reputation.

4. The Greek word from which "enthusiasm" comes; its original meaning was "possessed by a god." The "*English Poete*" is a lost work by Spenser, apparently never published.

5. I.e., let us see how we may pass the day pleasantly.

6. A popular game, here probably a poetry contest.

7. "Avena" [E. K.'s Glosse]. Avena means "stalks" and was used by Virgil (*Eclogues* I.2) to signify the shepherd's pipe. E. K. thinks Spenser's "oten reeds" translates Avena.

8. "Lye so faynt and unlustie" [E. K.'s Glosse]. The reference is to the fable of the industrious ant and the carefree grasshopper.

9. "Pretye" [E. K.'s Glosse]. "Frye is a bold Metaphore, forced from the spawning fishes. For the multitude of young fish be called the frye" [E. K.'s Glosse]. In the next line, "what * * * for thy?" means, "what better am I for this reason?"

1. "This place seemeth to conspyre with Plato, who in his first booke *de Legibus* sayth, that the first invention of Poetry was of very vertuous intent * * * " [E. K.'s Glosse].

Or pricke° them forth with pleasaunce of thy vaine,[2] *stimulate*
Whereto thou list their traynéd° willes entice. *ensnared*

Soone as thou gynst to sette thy notes in frame,
O how the rurall routes° to thee doe cleave: *crowds*
Seemeth thou dost their soule of sence bereave,[3]
All as the shepheard, that did fetch his dame
From Plutoes balefull bowre withouten leave:
His musicks might the hellish hound did tame.

CUDDIE

So praysen babes the Peacoks spotted traine,
And wondren at bright Argus blazing eye:[4]
But who rewards him ere the more forthy?
Or feedes him once the fuller by a graine?
Sike° prayse is smoke, that sheddeth in the skye, *such*
Sike words bene wynd, and wasten soone in vayne.

PIERS

Abandon then the base and viler clowne,° *rustic*
Lyft up thy selfe out of the lowly dust:
And sing of bloody Mars, of wars, of giusts,° *jousts*
Turne thee to those, that weld° the awful crowne. *wield*
To doubted[5] Knights, whose woundlesse armour rusts,
And helmes unbruzéd wexen dayly browne.

There may thy Muse display her fluttryng wing,[6]
And stretch herselfe at large from East to West:
Whither thou list in fayre Elisa rest,
Or if thee please in bigger notes to sing,
Advaunce the worthy whome shee loveth best,
That first the white beare to the stake did bring.[7]

2. I.e., pleasure in your distinctive style.

3. "What the secrete working of Musick is in the myndes of men, as well appeareth, hereby, that some of the auncient Philosophers, and those the moste wise, as Plato and Pythagoras held for opinion, that the mynd was made of a certaine harmonie and musicall nombers, for the great compassion and likenes of affection in thone and in the other * * * So that it is not incredible which the Poete here sayth, that Musick can bereave the soule of sence" [E. K.'s Glosse]. The "shepheard" in the next line is "Orpheus: of whom is sayd, that by his excellent skil in Musick and Poetry, he recovered his wife Eurydice from hell" [E. K.'s Glosse].

4. "Of Argus is before said, that Juno to him committed hir husband Jupiter his Paragon Iô, bicause he had an hundred eyes: but afterwarde Mercury wyth hys Musick lulling Argus aslepe, slew him and brought Iô away, whose eyes it is sayd that Juno for his eternall memory placed in her byrd the Peacocks tayle. For those coloured spots indeede resemble eyes" [E. K.'s Glosse].

5. Redoubted, dreaded. The knights' "armour" is "woundlesse" because "unwounded in warre, [they] doe rust through long peace" [E. K.'s Glosse].

6. "A poeticall metaphore: whereof the meaning is, that if the Poet list showe his skill in matter of more dignitie, then is the homely Aeglogue, good occasion is him offered of higher veyne and more Heroicall argument, in the person of our most gratious soveraign, whom (as before) he calleth Elisa. Or if mater of knighthoode and chevalrie please him better, that there be many Noble and valiaunt men, that are both worthy of his payne in theyr deserved prayses, and also favourers of hys skil and faculty" [E. K.'s Glosse].

7. "He meaneth (as I guesse) the most honorable and renowmed the Erle of Leycester * * * " [E. K.'s Glosse]. Leicester's device was the bear and ragged staff.

And when the stubborne stroke of stronger stounds,° *efforts*
Has somewhat slackt the tenor of thy string:[8]
Of love and lustihead° tho mayst thou sing, *pleasure*
And carrol lowde, and leade the Myllers rownde,[9]
All° were Elisa one of thilke same ring. *although*
So mought our Cuddies name to Heaven sownde.

CUDDIE

Indeede the Romish Tityrus,[1] I heare,
Through his Mecaenas left his Oaten reede,
Whereon he earst° had taught his flocks to feede, *before*
And laboured lands to yield the timely eare,
And eft did sing of warres and deadly drede,[2]
So as the Heavens did quake his verse to here.

But ah Mecaenas is yclad in claye,
And great Augustus long ygoe is dead:
And all the worthies liggen wrapt in leade,
That matter made for Poets on to play:
For ever, who in derring doe[3] were dreade,
The loftie verse of hem was lovéd aye.[4]

But after vertue gan for age to stoupe,
And mighty manhode brought a bedde of ease:[5]
The vaunting Poets found nought worth a pease,
To put in preace[6] emong the learned troupe.
Tho gan the streames of flowing wittes to cease,
And sonnebright honour pend in shamefull coupe.[7]

And if that any buddes of Poesie,
Yet of the old stocke gan to shoote agayne:

8. "That is when thou chaungest thy verse from stately discourse, to matter of more pleasaunce and delight" [E. K.'s Glosse].
9. "A kind of daunce" [E. K.'s Glosse]. "Ring," in the next line, E. K. explains as a "company of dauncers."
1. "Well knowen to be Virgile, who by Mecaenas means was brought into the favour of the Emperor Augustus, and by him moved to write in loftier kinde, then he erst had doen" [E. K.'s Glosse].
2. "In these three verses are the three severall workes of Virgile intended. For in teaching his flocks to feede, is meant his Aeglogues. In labouring of lands, is hys Bucoliques. In singing of wars and deadly dreade, is his divine Aeneis figured" [E. K.'s Glosse].
3. "In manhoode and chevalrie" [E. K.'s Glosse].
4. "He sheweth the cause, why Poetes were wont be had in such honor of noble men; that is, that by them their worthines and valor shold through theyr famous Posies be commended to al posterities. Wherefore it is sayd, that Achilles had never bene so famous, as he is, but for Homeres immortal verses. Which is the only advantage, which he had of Hector. * * * As also that Alexander destroying Thebes, when he was enformed that the famous Lyrick Poet Pindarus was borne in that citie, not onely commaunded streightly, that no man should upon payne of death do any violence to that house by fire or otherwise: but also specially spared most, and some highly rewarded, that were of hys kinne. * * * Such honor have Poetes alwayes found in the sight of princes and noble men. Which this author here very well sheweth, as els where more notably" [E. K.'s Glosse].
5. "He sheweth the cause of contempt of Poetry to be idlenesse and basenesse of mynd" [E. K.'s Glosse].
6. Put in press, crowd in among.
7. Coop. E. K. explains the phrase as "shut up in slouth, as in a coope or cage."

Or° it mens follies mote be frost to fayne, *either*
And rolle with rest in rymes of rybaudrye:
Or as it sprong, it wither must agayne:
Tom Piper makes us better melodie.[8]

PIERS

O pierlesse Poesye, where is then thy place?
If nor in Princes pallace thou doe sitt:
(And yet is Princes pallace the most fitt)
Ne brest of baser birth[9] doth thee embrace.
Then make thee winges of thine aspyring wit,
And, whence thou camst, flye backe to heaven apace.

CUDDIE

Ah Percy it is all to weake and wanne,
So high to sore, and make so large a flight:
Her peecéd pyneons[1] bene not so in plight,
For Colin fittes such famous flight to scanne:
He, were he not with love so ill bedight,° *furnished*
Would mount as high, and sing as soote as Swanne.[2]

PIERS

Ah fon,° for love does teach him climbe so hie, *fool*
And lyftes him up out of the loathsome myre:
Such immortall mirrhor,[3] as he doth admire,
Would rayse ones mynd above the starry skie.
And cause a caytive corage[4] to aspire,
For lofty love doth loath a lowly eye.

CUDDIE

All otherwise the state of Poet stands,
For lordly love is such a Tyranne fell:
That where he rules, all power he doth expell.
The vaunted verse a vacant head demaundes,
Ne wont with crabbéd care the Muses dwell.
Unwisely weaves, that takes two webbes in hand.

Who ever casts° to compasse weightye prise, *tries*
And thinks to throwe out thondring words of threate:
Let powre in lavish cups and thriftie bitts of meate,[5]
For Bacchus fruite is frend to Phoebus wise.

8. "An Ironicall Sarcasmus, spoken in derision of these rude wits, whych make more account of a ryming rybaud, then of skill grounded upon learning and judgment" [E. K.'s Glosse].
9. "The meaner sort of men" [E. K.'s Glosse].
1. Patched-up wings. "Unperfect skil. Spoken wyth humble modestie" [E. K.'s Glosse]. "Colin fittes": it is appropriate for Colin (Spenser).
2. "The comparison seemeth to be strange: for the swanne hath ever wonne small commendation for her swete singing: but it is sayd of the learned that the swan a little before hir death, singeth most pleasantly, as prophecying by a secrete instinct her neere destinie * * * " [E. K.'s Glosse].
3. "Beauty, which is an excellent object of Poeticall spirites * * * " [E. K.'s Glosse].
4. "A base and abject minde" [E. K.'s Glosse].
5. I.e., let him pour lavish drink and nourishing ("thrifty") food.

And when with Wine the braine begins to sweate,
The nombers flowe as fast as spring doth ryse.

Thou kenst not Percie howe the ryme should rage.
O if my temples were distaind° with wine,[6] *distended*
And girt in girlonds of wild Yvie twine,
How I could reare the Muse on stately stage,
And teache her tread aloft in bus-kin[7] fine,
With queint Bellona[8] in her equipage.

But ah my corage cooles ere it be warme,
For thy, content us in thys humble shade:
Where no such troublous tydes° han us assayde, *seasons*
Here we our slender pipes may safely charme.[9]

PIERS

And when my Gates shall han their bellies layd:[1]
Cuddie shall have a Kidde to store his farme.

Cuddies Embleme.[2]
Agitante calescimus illo &c.

1579

6. "He seemeth here to be ravished with a Poetical furie. For (if one rightly mark) the numbers rise so ful, and the verse groweth so big, that it seemeth he hath forgot the meanenesse of shepheards state and stile" [E. K.'s Glosse]. E. K. adds an explanation of "wild Yvie" in the next line: "For it is dedicated to Bacchus and therefore it is sayd that the Maenades (that is Bacchus franticke priestes) used in theyr sacrifice to carry *Thyrsos,* which were pointed staves or Javelins, wrapped about with yvie."

7. "It was the maner of Poetes and plaiers in tragedies to were buskins, as also in Comedies to use stockes and light shoes. So that the buskin in Poetry is used for tragical matter * * * " [E. K.'s Glosse].

8. "Strange Bellona; the goddesse of battaile, that is Pallas, which may therefore wel be called queint for that (as Lucian saith) when Jupiter hir father was in traveile of her, he caused his sonne Vulcane with his axe to hew his head. Out of which leaped forth lustely a valiant damsell armed at all poyntes, whom seeing Vulcane so faire and comely, lightly leaping to her, proferred her some cortesie, which the Lady disdeigning, shaked her speare at him, and threatned his saucinesse. Therefore such straungenesse is well applyed to her" [E. K.'s Glosse]. E. K. also glosses "equipage": order.

9. "Temper and order. For Charmes were wont to be made by verses as Ovid sayth, *Aut si carminibus*" [E. K.'s Glosse]. E. K. had a slip of memory: the fragment is not in Ovid.

1. I.e., when my goats bear their young.

2. An "embleme" is a motto or relevant quotation. The Latin line, of which Spenser gives the first three words here, is from Ovid, *Fasti* vi.5: "There is a god within us; it is from his stirring that we feel warm." E. K. comments on the quotation: "Hereby is meant, as also in the whole course of this Aeglogue, that Poetry is a divine instinct and unnatural rage passing the reache of comen reason. Whom Piers answereth *Epiphonematicos* [by way of summary] as admiring the excellencye of the skyll whereof in Cuddie hee hadde alreadye hadde a taste."

The Faerie Queene

Spenser's masterpiece is a poem peculiarly characteristic of its age. It is a "courtesy book," like Castiglione's *Courtier,* intended to "fashion a gentleman or noble person" by exhibiting the traits such a person should have. Only six of the twelve projected books were finished. These exhibit the virtues of Holiness, Temperance, Chastity, Friendship, Justice, and Courtesy. A fragment of another book, the cantos on Mutability, also survives. But whereas the ordinary courtesy book was a piece of explanation and exhortation, *The Faerie Queene* is also a poem, and, as Elizabethans all believed, a poem teaches by delighting. Spenser's great work is full of adventures and marvels, dragons, witches, enchanted trees, giants, jousting knights, and castles; a romantic epic, like Ariosto's *Orlando Furioso* (1516). But it is also an allegory, like Tasso's *Gerusalemme Liberata* (1575); the heroes of the several books represent the virtues portrayed in those books. The Redcrosse Knight in Book I is of course St. George, the patron saint of England, but he also represents Holiness, as Sir Guyon in Book II represents Temperance (not simply abstinence in drinking but self-control under all the temptations of the senses). The heroes do not have the virtues they represent at the beginning of their adventures—they acquire them in the course of the book. Spenser explains his allegorical method in a preliminary letter to Sir Walter Ralegh; however he does not explain what would be obvious to every contemporary reader, the many conventional symbols and attributes which would identify his characters. For example, when a woman appears who has a miter, wears scarlet clothes, and comes from the river Tiber, the reader is supposed to know immediately that she stands for the Roman Catholic Church, which had been so often identified by Protestant preachers with the Whore of Babylon in the Book of Revelation.

Book I of *The Faerie Queene* is in a way an epitome of the whole poem, or the part of it Spenser completed. It is almost entirely self-contained; it has been called a miniature epic in itself. It consists of twelve cantos, as Virgil's *Aeneid* consists of twelve books. The introductory lines are intended to remind the reader of Virgil, who began with pastoral poetry and moved on to the epic, as Spenser is now doing.

The theme is not arms and the man, however, but something more romantic—"Fierce warres and faithfull loves." The scenery, too, is not classical but romantic. There are plains and forests and caves and castles and magical trees and springs; one meets dwarfs and giants and lions and pilgrims and magicians and Saracens or "paynims" (with French names). An accurate map of Faerie Land is impossible but unnecessary; if you are going somewhere you just start out and, after many adventures, get there. A clear, pleasant stream may be dangerous to drink because it produces loss of strength. Any stranger you meet is more than likely to be a villain and to be in disguise.

The good people are subject to the Faerie Queene and are called Faeries or Elves. They are human beings, though not much individualized. They undergo the trials and tribulations men undergo in the ordinary world, but these events are told in a romantic, fantastic way in order to arouse wonder. The bad creatures, people and monsters, are various vices, evils, and temptations, often revealed to the reader by their names or by the short verse summaries at the beginning of each canto but not revealed to the hero until he has conquered them. Houses, castles, and animals also stand for abstract virtues or vices. The world of Faerie Land is a visual world in which the meaning of something is made fully evident by its appearance when stripped of all disguise.

Read as romantic narrative, the plot of Book I is a series of chivalric adventures undertaken by the Redcrosse Knight culminating in his killing the dragon, rescuing Una's parents, and winning her as his bride. Read as spiritual allegory, the book tells the story of the Christian's struggle for salvation—his wandering between the evil extremes of pride and despair, his encounter with the seven deadly sins, his separation from and reunion with the one true faith, the purgation of his sinfulness, and his final salvation by divine grace added to heroic effort.

The poem can be enjoyed on many levels, and it may, in fact, work on several of these levels at a time. In addition to being—most especially—a heroic poem and a spiritual allegory, it also embodies many religious and political aspects of Spenser's own England; a "political allegory" runs all through Book I. This is a romantic, "medieval," heroic, religious, political, magical world, and the reader entering it must be prepared to move as the story moves, taking the meanings on whatever level seems most viable at the moment. Spenser is not a great explainer; more usually, he gives the reader a scene or a surface, and lets the full allegorical import work its way out.

Moreover, that scene or surface may draw on the riches of literary and pictorial traditions. Entire episodes may be adopted from the Italian romantic epics of Ariosto and Tasso and, either through them or independently, from Homer, Virgil, or Ovid (this was an age when borrowing and reworking earlier materials was praiseworthy in a poet). Places, such as Lucifera's castle; individual attributes, such as Una's lamb or Speranza's anchor; even names or colors came to Spenser from the classics, from theologians, from liturgical tradition, from the village pulpit, from folk tales and pageants, from tapestries, paintings, and emblem books. In our notes we have attempted to show what some of the sources were—but more important is the understanding that these traditions had a life for Spenser and his readers; they could flow together, separate, recombine.

The strangeness of *The Faerie Queene* becomes, on closer acquaintance, a source of delight. No work of the English Renaissance is more exuberant, more fertile, more full.

From The Faerie Queene

A Letter of the Authors

EXPOUNDING HIS WHOLE INTENTION IN THE COURSE OF THIS WORKE: WHICH FOR THAT IT GIVETH GREAT LIGHT TO THE READER, FOR THE BETTER UNDERSTANDING IS HEREUNTO ANNEXED

To the Right noble, and Valorous, Sir Walter Raleigh knight, Lo. Wardein of the Stanneryes, and her Majesties liefetenaunt of the County of Cornewayll

Sir knowing how doubtfully all Allegories may be construed, and this booke of mine, which I have entituled the *Faery Queene*, being a continued Allegory, or darke conceit, I have thought good as well for avoyding of gealous opinions and misconstructions, as also for your better light in reading thereof, (being so by you commanded,) to discover unto you the general intention and meaning, which in the whole course thereof I have fashioned, without expressing of any particular purposes or by-accidents [1] therein occasioned. The generall end therefore of all the booke is to fashion [2] a gentleman or noble person in vertuous and gentle discipline: Which for that I conceived shoulde be most plausible and pleasing, being coloured with an historicall fiction, the which the most part of men delight to read, rather for variety of matter, then for profite of the ensample: I chose the historye of King Arthure, as most fitte for the excellency of his person, being made famous by many mens former workes, and also furthest from the daunger of envy, and suspition of present time.[3] In which I have followed all the antique Poets historicall, first Homere, who in the Persons of Agamemnon and Ulysses hath ensampled a good governour and a vertuous man, the one in his *Ilias*, the other in his *Odysseis:* then Virgil, whose like intention was to doe in the person of Aeneas: after him Ariosto comprised them both in his Orlando: and lately Tasso dissevered them againe, and formed both parts in two persons, namely that part which they in Philosophy call Ethice, or vertues of a private man, coloured in his Rinaldo: The other named Politice in his Godfredo.[4] By ensample of which excellente Poets, I labour to pourtraict in Arthure, before he was king, the image of a brave knight, perfected in the twelve private morall vertues, as Aristotle

1. Secondary matters.
2. I.e., to represent (secondarily, to educate).
3. I.e., free from current political controversy.
4. Lodovico Ariosto (1474–1533) was author of the epic-romance *Orlando Furioso,* first published in complete form in 1532; Torquato Tasso (1544–95) published his chivalric romance *Rinaldo* in 1562 and the epic *Gerusalemme Liberata* (centered on the heroic figure of Count Godfredo) in 1581.

hath devised,[5] the which is the purpose of these first twelve bookes: which if I finde to be well accepted, I may be perhaps encouraged, to frame the other part of polliticke vertues in his person, after that hee came to be king. To some I know this Methode will seeme displeasaunt, which had rather have good discipline delivered plainly in way of precepts, or sermoned at large, as they use, then thus clowdily enwrapped in Allegoricall devises. But such, me seeme, should be satisfide with the use of these dayes, seeing all things accounted by their showes, and nothing esteemed of, that is not delightfull and pleasing to commune sence. For this cause is Xenophon preferred before Plato, for that the one in the exquisite depth of his judgment, formed a Commune welth[6] such as it should be, but the other in the person of Cyrus and the Persians fashioned a governement such as might best be: So much more profitable and gratious is doctrine by ensample, then by rule. So have I laboured to doe in the person of Arthure: whome I conceive after his long education by Timon, to whom he was by Merlin delivered to be brought up, so soone as he was borne of the Lady Igrayne, to have seene in a dream or vision the Faery Queen, with whose excellent beauty ravished, he awaking resolved to seeke her out, and so being by Merlin armed, and by Timon throughly instructed, he went to seeke her forth in Faerye land. In that Faery Queene I meane glory in my generall intention, but in my particular I conceive the most excellent and glorious person of our soveraine the Queene, and her kingdome in Faery land. And yet in some places els, I doe otherwise shadow[7] her. For considering she beareth two persons, the one of a most royall Queene or Empresse, the other of a most vertuous and beautifull Lady, this latter part in some places I doe express in Belphoebe, fashioning her name according to your owne excellent conceipt of Cynthia,[8] (Phoebe and Cynthia being both names of Diana.) So in the person of Prince Arthure I sette forth magnificence in particular, which vertue for that (according to Aristotle and the rest) it is the perfection of all the rest, and conteineth in it them all, therefore in the whole course I mention the deedes of Arthure applyable to that vertue, which I write of in that booke. But of the xii. other vertues, I make xii. other knights the patrones, for the more variety of the history. Of which these three bookes contayn three, The first of the knight of the Redcrosse, in whome I expresse Holynes: The seconde of Sir Guyon, in whome I sette forth Temperaunce: The third of Brito-

5. Aristotle did not devise twelve private moral virtues: Spenser was in fact relying upon more modern philosophers—his friend Lodowick Bryskett and the Italian Piccolomini. That Spenser actually planned a poem four times as long as the six books we now have rather staggers the imagination, but his language is plain.

6. The allusion is to Plato's *Republic* and Xenophon's *Cyropaedia*.

7. Picture, portray.

8. Ralegh's poem *Cynthia* praised Queen Elizabeth.

martis a Lady knight, in whome I picture Chastity. But because the beginning of the whole worke seemeth abrupte and as depending upon other antecedents, it needs that ye know the occasion of these three knights severall adventures. For the Methode of a Poet historical is not such, as of an Historiographer. For an Historiographer discourseth of affayres orderly as they were donne, accounting as well the times as the actions; but a Poet thrusteth into the middest, even where it most concerneth him, and there recoursing to the thinges forepaste, and divining of thinges to come, maketh a pleasing Analysis of all. The beginning therefore of my history, if it were to be told by an Historiographer, should be the twelfth booke, which is the last, where I devise that the Faery Queene kept her Annuall feaste xii. dayes, uppon which xii. severall dayes, the occasions of the xii. severall adventures hapned, which being undertaken by xii. severall knights, are in these xii books severally handled and discoursed. The first was this. In the beginning of the feaste, there presented him selfe a tall clownishe[9] younge man, who falling before the Queen of Faeries desired a boone (as the manner then was) which during that feast she might not refuse: which was that hee might have the atchievement of any adventure, which during that feaste should happen, that being graunted, he rested him on the floore, unfitte through his rusticity for a better place. Soone after entred a faire Ladye in mourning weedes, riding on a white Asse, with a dwarfe behind her leading a warlike steed, that bore the Armes of a knight, and his speare in the dwarfes hand. Shee falling before the Queene of Faeries, complayned that her father and mother an ancient King and Queene, had bene by an huge dragon many years shut up in a brasen Castle, who thence suffred them not to yssew: and therefore besought the Faery Queene to assygne her some one of her knights to take on him that exployt. Presently that clownish person upstarting, desired that adventure: whereat the Queene much wondering, and the Lady much gainesaying, yet he earnestly importuned his desire. In the end the Lady told him that unlesse that armour which she brought, would serve him (that is the armour of a Christian man specified by Saint Paul v. Ephes.) that he could not succeed in that enterprise, which being forthwith put upon him with dewe furnitures[1] thereunto, he seemed the goodliest man in al that company, and was well liked of the Lady. And eftesoones taking on him knighthood, and mounting on that straunge Courser, he went forth with her on that adventure: where beginneth the first booke, vz.

A gentle knight was pricking on the playne. &c.

The second day ther came in a Palmer bearing an Infant with

9. Rustic-looking.

1. Suitable equipment.

bloody hands, whose Parents he complained to have bene slayn by an Enchaunteresse called Acrasia: and therfore craved of the Faery Queene, to appoint him some knight, to performe that adventure, which being assigned to Sir Guyon, he presently went forth with that same Palmer: which is the beginning of the second booke and the whole subject thereof. The third day there came in, a Groome who complained before the Faery Queene, that a vile Enchaunter called Busirane had in hand a most faire Lady called Amoretta, whom he kept in most grievous torment, because she would not yield him the pleasure of her body. Whereupon Sir Scudamour the lover of that Lady presently tooke on him that adventure. But being unable to performe it by reason of the hard Enchauntments, after long sorrow, in the end met with Britomartis, who succoured him, and reskewed his love.

But by occasion hereof, many other adventures are intermedled, but rather as Accidents, then intendments.[2] As the love of Britomart, the overthrow of Marinell, the misery of Florimell, the vertuousnes of Belphoebe, the lasciviousnes of Hellenora, and many the like.

Thus much Sir, I have briefly overronne to direct your understanding to the wel-head of the History, that from thence gathering the whole intention of the conceit, ye may as in a handfull gripe al the discourse, which otherwise may happily[3] seeme tedious and confused. So humbly craving the continuaunce of your honorable favour towards me, and th'eternall establishment of your happines, I humbly take leave.

23. January, 1589
Yours most humbly affectionate.
ED. SPENSER.

The First Booke of the Faerie Queene

CONTAYNING
The Legende of the
Knight of the Red Crosse,
OR
OF HOLINESSE

1

Lo I the man, whose Muse whilome did maske,
As time her taught, in lowly Shepheards weeds,[4]

2. That is, there are episodes that are merely romantic and not specifically allegorical. Characters are often types, not symbols.
3. By chance.
4. I.e., behold me, the poet who appropriately appeared before ("whilome") as a writer of humble pastoral (i.e., *The Shepheardes Calender*). These lines are imitated from the verses prefixed to Virgil's *Aeneid*.

Am now enforst a far unfitter taske,
For trumpets sterne to chaunge mine Oaten reeds,[5]
And sing of Knights and Ladies gentle deeds;
Whose prayses having slept in silence long,[6]
Me, all too meane, the sacred Muse areeds ° *appoints*
To blazon broad emongst her learned throng:
Fierce warres and faithfull loves shall moralize my song.

2

Helpe then, O holy Virgin chiefe of nine,[7]
Thy weaker Novice to performe thy will,
Lay forth out of thine everlasting scryne [8]
The antique rolles, which there lye hidden still,
Of Faerie knights and fairest Tanaquill,[9]
Whom that most noble Briton Prince [1] so long
Sought through the world, and suffered so much ill,
That I must rue his undeservéd wrong:
O helpe thou my weake wit, and sharpen my dull tong.

3

And thou most dreaded impe [2] of highest Jove,
Faire Venus sonne, that with thy cruell dart
At that good knight so cunningly didst rove,° *shoot*
That glorious fire it kindled in his hart,
Lay now thy deadly Heben ° bow apart, *ebony*
And with thy mother milde come to mine ayde:
Come both, and with you bring triumphant Mart,[3]
In loves and gentle jollities arrayd,
After his murdrous spoiles and bloudy rage allayd.

4

And with them eke,° O Goddesse heavenly bright, *also*
Mirrour of grace and Majestie divine,
Great Lady of the greatest Isle, whose light
Like Phoebus lampe throughout the world doth shine,
Shed thy faire beames into my feeble eyne,
And raise my thoughts too humble and too vile,° *lowly*
To thinke of that true glorious type ° of thine, *pattern*
The argument of mine afflicted stile:
The which to heare, vouchsafe, O dearest dred [4] a-while.

Canto I

The Patron of true Holinesse,
Foule Errour doth defeate:
Hypocrisie him to entrappe,
Doth to his home entreate.

5. To write heroic poetry, of which the trumpet is a symbol, instead of pastoral poetry like *The Shepheardes Calender*, symbolized by the humble shepherd's pipe ("Oaten reeds").
6. Lines 5 and 6 are imitated from the opening lines of Ariosto's *Orlando Furioso*.
7. Clio, the Muse of history; "weaker": too weak.
8. A chest for papers.
9. I.e., Gloriana.
1. I.e., Arthur.
2. Child, i.e., Cupid.
3. Mars, god of war and lover of Venus.
4. Object of awe.

1

A Gentle Knight was pricking ° on the plaine, *cantering*
Ycladd in mightie armes and silver shielde,
Wherein old dints of deepe wounds did remaine,
The cruell markes of many a bloudy fielde;
Yet armes till that time did he never wield:[5]
His angry steede did chide his foming bitt,
As much disdayning to the curbe to yield:
Full jolly ° knight he seemd, and faire did sitt, *courageous*
As one for knightly giusts ° and fierce encounters fitt. *tourneys, jousts*

2

But on his brest a bloudie Crosse he bore,
The deare remembrance of his dying Lord,
For whose sweete sake that glorious badge he wore,
And dead as living ever him adored:
Upon his shield the like was also scored,
For soveraine[6] hope, which in his helpe he had:
Right faithfull true he was in deede and word,
But of his cheere[7] did seeme too solemne sad; ° *serious*
Yet nothing did he dread, but ever was ydrad.° *dreaded, feared*

3

Upon a great adventure he was bond,
That greatest Gloriana to him gave,
That greatest Glorious Queene of Faerie Lond,
To winne him worship,° and her grace to have, *honor*
Which of all earthly things he most did crave;
And ever as he rode, his hart did earne ° *yearn*
To prove his puissance in battell brave
Upon his foe, and his new force to learne;
Upon his foe, a Dragon horrible and stearne.

4

A lovely Ladie rode him faire beside,
Upon a lowly Asse more white then snow,
Yet she much whiter, but the same did hide
Under a vele, that wimpled ° was full low, *folded*
And over all a blacke stole she did throw,
As one that inly mournd: so was she sad,
And heavie sat upon her palfrey slow:
Seeméd in heart some hidden care she had,
And by her in a line a milke white lambe she lad.

5

So pure an innocent, as that same lambe,
She was in life and every vertuous lore,
And by descent from Royall lynage came

5. Redcrosse wears the armor of the Christian man, as Spenser explained in the letter to Ralegh: "put on the whole armor of God, that ye may be able to stand against the wiles of the devil" (Ephesians vi.10–22). The armor bears the dents of every Christian's fight against evil; Redcrosse himself is as yet untried.

6. Having greatest power (often applied to medical remedies).

7. Facial expression.

Of ancient Kings and Queenes, that had of yore
Their scepters stretcht from East to Westerne shore,
And all the world in their subjection held;
Till that infernall feend with foule uprore
Forwasted all their land, and them expeld:
Whom to avenge, she had this Knight from far compeld.° *summoned*

6

Behind her farre away a Dwarfe did lag,
That lasie seemd in being ever last,
Or wearied with bearing of her bag
Of needments at his backe. Thus as they past,
The day with cloudes was suddeine overcast,
And angry Jove an hideous storme of raine
Did poure into his Lemans[8] lap so fast,
That every wight° to shrowd° it did constrain, *creature/cover*
And this faire couple eke ° to shroud themselves were fain. *also*

7

Enforst to seeke some covert nigh at hand,
A shadie grove not far away they spide,
That promist ayde the tempest to withstand:
Whose loftie trees yclad with sommers pride,
Did spred so broad, that heavens light did hide,
Not perceable with power of any starre:
And all within were pathes and alleies wide,
With footing worne, and leading inward farre:
Faire harbour that them seemes; so in they entred arre.

8

And foorth they passe, with pleasure forward led,
Joying to heare the birdes sweete harmony,
Which therein shrouded from the tempest dred,
Seemd in their song to scorne the cruell sky.
Much can° they prayse the trees, so straight and hy, *did*
The sayling Pine, the Cedar proud and tall,
The vine-prop Elme, the Poplar never dry,
The builder Oake, sole king of forrests all,
The Aspine good for staves, the Cypresse funerall.

9

The Laurell, meed° of mightie Conquerours *reward*
And Poets sage, the Firre that weepeth still,
The Willow worne of forlorne Paramours,
The Eugh° obedient to the benders will, *yew*
The Birch for shaftes, the Sallow° for the mill, *willow*
The Mirrhe sweete bleeding in the bitter wound,
The warlike Beech, the Ash for nothing ill,
The fruitfull Olive, and the Platane° round, *plane-tree*
The carver Holme,° the Maple seeldom inward sound.[9] *holly*

8. His lover, i.e., the earth.

9. In these lines, Spenser has been imitating Chaucer's catalogue of trees in the *Parliament of Fowls;* the convention goes back to Ovid.

10

Led with delight, they thus beguile the way,
Untill the blustring storme is overblowne;
When weening° to returne, whence they did stray, *supposing*
They cannot finde that path, which first was showne,
But wander too and fro in wayes unknowne,
Furthest from end then, when they neerest weene,
That makes them doubt, their wits be not their owne:
So many pathes, so many turnings seene,
That which of them to take, in diverse doubt they been.

11

At last resolving forward still to fare,
Till that some end they finde or° in or out, *either*
That path they take, that beaten seemd most bare,
Which when by tract[1] they hunted had throughout,
And like to lead the labyrinth about;° *out of*
At length it brought them to a hollow cave,
Amid the thickest woods. The Champion stout
Eftsoones° dismounted from his courser brave, *forthwith*
And to the Dwarfe a while his needlesse spere he gave.

12

"Be well aware," quoth then that Ladie milde,
"Least suddaine mischiefe ye too rash provoke:
The danger hid, the place unknowne and wilde,
Breedes dreadfull doubts: Oft fire is without smoke,
And perill without show: therefore your stroke
Sir knight with-hold, till further triall made."
"Ah Ladie," said he, "shame were to revoke
The forward footing for° an hidden shade: *because of*
Vertue gives her selfe light, through darkenesse for to wade."

13

"Yea but," quoth she, "the perill of this place
I better wot then[2] you, though now too late
To wish you backe returne with foule disgrace,
Yet wisedome warnes, whilest foot is in the gate,
To stay the steepe, ere forcéd to retrate.
This is the wandring wood, this Errours den,
A monster vile, whom God and man does hate:
Therefore I read° beware." "Fly fly," quoth then *advise*
The fearefull Dwarfe: "this is no place for living men."

14

But full of fire and greedy hardiment,° *boldness*
The youthfull knight could not for ought be staide,
But forth unto the darksome hole he went,
And lookéd in: his glistring armor made
A litle glooming light, much like a shade,
By which he saw the ugly monster plaine,

1. By following the track.
2. Know than.

Halfe like a serpent horribly displaide,[3]
But th' other halfe did womans shape retaine,
Most lothsom, filthie, foule, and full of vile disdaine.

15

And as she lay upon the durtie ground,
Her huge long taile her den all overspred,
Yet was in knots and many boughtes° upwound, *coils*
Pointed with mortall sting. Of her there bred
A thousand yong ones, which she dayly fed,
Sucking upon her poisonous dugs, eachone
Of sundry shapes, yet all ill favoréd:
Soone as that uncouth° light upon them shone, *unfamiliar*
Into her mouth they crept, and suddain all were gone.

16

Their dam upstart, out of her den effraide,
And rushéd forth, hurling her hideous taile
About her curséd head, whose folds displaid
Were stretcht now forth at length without
entraile.° *winding, coiling*
She lookt about, and seeing one in mayle
Arméd to point,[4] sought backe to turne againe;
For light she hated as the deadly bale,° *evil*
Ay wont in desert darknesse to remaine,
Where plaine none might her see, nor she see any plaine.

17

Which when the valiant Elfe[5] pereived, he lept
As Lyon fierce upon the flying pray,
And with his trenchand° blade her boldly kept *cutting*
From turning backe, and forcéd her to stay:
Therewith enraged she loudly gan to bray,
And turning fierce, her speckled taile advaunst,
Threatning her angry sting, him to dismay:
Who nough aghast, his mightie hand enhaunst:° *lifted up*
The stroke down from her head unto her shoulder glaunst.

18

Much daunted with that dint, her sence was dazd,
Yet kindling rage, her selfe she gathered round,
And all attonce her beastly body raizd
With doubled forces high above the ground:
Tho° wrapping up her wrethéd sterne arownd, *then*
Lept fierce upon his shield, and her huge traine° *tail*
All suddenly about his body wound,
That hand or foot to stirre he strove in vaine:
God helpe the man so wrapt in Errours endlesse traine.

3. That Errour (or theological, doctrinal heresy) is half serpent reminds us of the primal error in Eden, which the serpent instigated. "Errour," at first glance, may not seem an important demon; here Lewis is helpful in reminding us that "Spenser is writing in an age of religious doubt and controversy when the avoidance of error is a problem as pressing as, and in a sense prior to, the conquest of sin" (*Allegory of Love,* p. 334). The description echoes both classical and Biblical monsters (cf. Revelation ix.7–10).

4. I.e., completely.

5. Knight of Faerie Land.

19

His Lady sad to see his sore constraint,
Cride out, "Now now Sir knight, shew what ye bee,
Add faith unto your force, and be not faint:
Strangle her, else she sure will strangle thee."
That when he heard, in great perplexitie,
His gall did grate for griefe° and high disdaine, *wrath*
And knitting all his force got one hand free,
Wherewith he grypt her gorge° with so great paine, *neck*
That soone to loose her wicked bands did her constraine.

20

Therewith she spewd out of her filthy maw
A floud of poyson horrible and blacke,
Full of great lumpes of flesh and gobbets raw,
Which stunck so vildly, that it forst him slacke
His grasping hold, and from her turne him backe:
Her vomit full of bookes and papers[6] was,
With loathly frogs and toades, which eyes did lacke,
And creeping sought way in the weedy gras:
Her filthy parbreake° all the place defiléd has.[7] *vomit*

21

As when old father Nilus gins to swell
With timely° pride above the Aegyptian vale, *in season*
His fattie° waves do fertile slime outwell, *rich*
And overflow each plaine and lowly dale:
But when his later spring gins to avale,° *subside*
Huge heapes of mudd he leaves, wherein there breed
Ten thousand kindes of creatures, partly male
And partly female of his fruitfull seed;
Such ugly monstrous shapes elswhere may no man reed.° *see*

22

The same so sore annoyéd has the knight,
That welnigh chokéd with the deadly stinke,
His forces faile, ne can no longer fight.
Whose corage when the feend perceived to shrinke,
She pouréd forth out of her hellish sinke
Her fruitfull curséd spawne of serpents small,
Deforméd monsters, fowle, and blacke as inke,
Which swarming all about his legs did crall,
And him encombred sore, but could not hurt at all.

23

As gentle Shepheard in sweete even-tide,
When ruddy Phoebus gins to welke° in west, *sink*
High on an hill, his flocke to vewen wide,
Markes which do byte their hasty supper best;

6. The reference is to books and pamphlets of Catholic propaganda, particularly attacks on Queen Elizabeth in 1588—and, indeed, to violent religious controversy of any kind.

7. Revelation xvi.13: "And I saw three unclean spirits like frogs come out of the mouth of the dragon, and out of the mouth of the beast, and out of the mouth of the false prophet."

A cloud of combrous gnattes do him molest,
All striving to infixe their feeble stings,
That from their noyance he no where can rest,
But with his clownish° hands their tender wings *rustic*
He brusheth oft, and oft doth mar their murmurings.

24

Thus ill bestedd,° and fearfull more of shame, *situated*
Then of the certaine perill he stood in,
Halfe furious unto his foe he came,
Resolved in minde all suddenly to win,
Or soone to lose, before he once would lin;° *cease, stop*
And strooke at her with more then manly force,
That from her body full of filthie sin
He raft° her hatefull head without remorse; *cut away*
A streame of cole black bloud forth gushéd from her corse.

25

Her scattred brood, soone as their Parent deare
They saw so rudely° falling to the ground, *with great force*
Groning full deadly, all with troublous feare,
Gathred themselves about her body round,
Weening their wonted entrance to have found
At her wide mouth: but being there withstood
They flockéd all about her bleeding wound,
And suckéd up their dying mothers blood,
Making her death their life, and eke her hurt their good. *also*

26

That detestable sight him much amazde,
To see th' unkindly Impes of heaven accurst,
Devoure their dam; on whom while so he gazd,
Having all satisfide their bloudy thurst,
Their bellies swolne he saw with fulnesse burst,
And bowels gushing forth: well worthy end
Of such as drunke her life, the which them nurst;
Now needeth him no lenger labour spend,
His foes have slaine themselves, with whom he should contend.

27

His Ladie seeing all, that chaunst, from farre
Approcht in hast to greet his victorie,
And said, "Faire knight, borne under happy starre,
Who see your vanquisht foes before you lye;
Well worthy be you of that Armorie,[8]
Wherein ye have great glory wonne this day,
And prooved your strength on a strong enimie,
Your first adventure: many such I pray,
And henceforth ever wish, that like succeed it may."

28

Then mounted he upon his Steede againe,
And with the Lady backward sought to wend;° *go*

8. I.e., Christian armor.

That path he kept, which beaten was most plaine,
Ne ever would to any by-way bend,
But still did follow one unto the end,
The which at last out of the wood them brought.
So forward on his way (with God to frend[9])
He passéd forth, and new adventure sought;
Long way he travelléd, before he heard of ought.

29

At length they chaunst to meet upon the way
An aged Sire, in long blacke weedes yclad,[1]
His feete all bare, his beard all hoarie gray,
And by his belt his booke he hanging had;
Sober he seemde, and very sagely sad,° *pensive*
And to the ground his eyes were lowly bent,
Simple in shew, and voyde of malice bad,
And all the way he prayéd, as he went,
And often knockt his brest, as one that did repent.

30

He faire the knight saluted, louting° low, *bowing*
Who faire him quited,° as that courteous was: *answered*
And after askéd him, if he did know
Of straunge adventures, which abroad did pas.
"Ah my deare Sonne," quoth he, "how should, alas,
Silly° old man, that lives in hidden cell, *innocent*
Bidding° his beades all day for his trespas, *telling*
Tydings of warre and worldly trouble tell?
With holy father sits not with such things to mell.° *meddle*

31

"But if of daunger which hereby doth dwell,
And homebred evill ye desire to heare,
Of a straunge man I can you tidings tell,
That wasteth all this countrey farre and neare."
"Of such," said he, "I chiefly do inquere,
And shall you well reward to shew the place,
In which that wicked wight his dayes doth weare.° *spend*
For to all knighthood it is foule disgrace,
That such a cursed creature lives so long a space."

32

"Far hence," quoth he, "in wastfull° wildernesse *desolate*
His dwelling is, by which no living wight
May ever passe, but thorough great distresse."
"Now," sayd the Lady, "draweth toward night,
And well I wote, that of your later° fight *recent*
Ye all forwearied be: for what so strong,
But wanting rest will also want of might?
The Sunne that measures heaven all day long,
At night doth baite° his steedes the Ocean waves emong. *feed, refresh*

9. With God as friend.

1. Dressed in long black garments.

33

"Then with the Sunne take Sir, your timely rest,
And with new day new worke at once begin:
Untroubled night they say gives counsell best."
"Right well Sir knight ye have advisèd bin,"
Quoth then that aged man; "the way to win
Is wisely to advise: now day is spent;
Therefore with me ye may take up your In° *lodging*
For this same night." The knight was well content:
So with that godly father to his home they went.

34

A little lowly Hermitage it was,
Downe in a dale, hard by a forests side,
Far from resort of people, that did pas
In travell to and froe: a little wyde° *apart*
There was an holy Chappell edifyde,° *built*
Wherein the Hermite dewly wont° to say *was wont*
His holy things each morne and eventyde:
Thereby a Christall streame did gently play,
Which from a sacred fountaine wellèd forth alway.

35

Arrivèd there, the little house they fill,
Ne looke for entertainement, where none was:
Rest is their feast, and all things at their will;
The noblest mind the best contentment has.
With faire discourse the evening so they pas:
For that old man of pleasing wordes had store,
And well could file his tongue as smooth as glas;
He told of Saintes and Popes, and evermore
He strowd an *Ave-Mary* after and before.

36

The drouping Night thus creepeth on them fast,
And the sad humour[2] loading their eye liddes,
As messenger of Morpheus[3] on them cast
Sweet slombring deaw, the which to sleepe them biddes.
Unto their lodgings then his guestes he riddes:° *leads*
Where when all drownd in deadly sleepe he findes,
He to his study goes, and there amiddes
His Magick bookes and artes of sundry kindes,
He seekes out mighty charmes, to trouble sleepy mindes.

37

Then choosing out few wordes most horrible
(Let none them read), thereof did verses frame,
With which and other spelles like terrible,
He bade awake blacke Plutoes griesly Dame,[4]
And cursèd heaven, and spake reprochfull shame
Of highest God, the Lord of life and light;

2. Heavy moisture.
3. The god of sleep.
4. I.e., Proserpine.

A bold bad man, that dared to call by name
Great Gorgon, Prince of darknesse and dead night,
At which Cocytus quakes, and Styx[5] is put to flight.

38

And forth he cald out of deepe darknesse dred
Legions of Sprights, the which like little flyes
Fluttring about his ever damnéd hed,
A-waite whereto their service he applyes,
To aide his friends, or fray° his enimies: *frighten*
Of those he chose out two, the falsest twoo,
And fittest for to forge true-seeming lyes;
The one of them he gave a message too,
The other by him selfe staide other worke to doo.

39

He making speedy way through sperséd° ayre, *dispersed*
And through the world of waters wide and deepe,
To Morpheus house doth hastily repaire.
Amid the bowels of the earth full steepe,
And low, where dawning day doth never peepe,
His dwelling is; there Tethys[6] his wet bed
Doth ever wash, and Cynthia[7] still doth steepe
In silver deaw his ever-drouping hed,
Whiles sad Night over him her mantle black doth spred.

40

Whose double gates he findeth lockéd fast,
The one faire framed of burnisht Yvory,
The other all with silver overcast;
And wakefull dogges before them farre do lye,
Watching to banish Care their enimy,
Who oft is wont to trouble gentle Sleepe.
By them the Sprite doth passe in quietly,
And unto Morpheus comes, whom drownéd deepe
In drowsie fit he findes: of nothing he takes keepe.° *notice*

41

And more, to lulle him in his slumber soft,
A trickling streame from high rocke tumbling downe
And ever-drizling raine upon the loft,
Mixt with a murmuring winde, much like the sowne° *sound*
Of swarming Bees, did cast him in a swowne:° *faint*
No other noyse, nor peoples troublous cryes,
As still° are wont t'annoy the walléd towne, *always*
Might there be heard: but carelesse Quiet lyes,
Wrapt in eternall silence farre from enemyes.[8]

42

The messenger approching to him spake,
But his wast° wordes returnd to him in vaine: *wasted*

5. Rivers of hell.
6. The wife of Ocean.
7. I.e., Diana, the goddess of the moon.
8. Spenser is imitating descriptions of the house of Morpheus in Chaucer, Ovid, and other ancient writers, but he achieves originality, particularly by means of the sound effects in stanza 41.

So sound he slept, that nought mought him awake.
Then rudely he him thrust, and pusht with paine,
Whereat he gan to stretch: but he againe
Shooke him so hard, that forced him to speake.
As one then in a dreame, whose dryer braine[9]
Is tost with troubled sights and fancies weake,
He mumbled soft, but would not all his silence breake.

43

The Sprite then gan more boldly him to wake,
And threatned unto him the dreaded name
Of Hecate:[1] whereat he gan to quake,
And lifting up his lumpish head, with blame
Halfe angry askéd him, for what he came.
"Hither," quoth he, "me Archimago[2] sent,
He that the stubborne Sprites can wisely tame,
He bids thee to him send for his intent
A fit false dreame, that can delude the sleepers sent."° *senses*

44

The God obayde, and calling forth straight way
A diverse° dreame out of his prison darke, *misleading*
Delivered it to him, and downe did lay
His heavie head, devoide of carefull carke,[3]
Whose sences all were straight benumbd and starke.
He backe returning by the Yvorie dore,[4]
Remounted up as light as chearefull Larke,
And on his litle winges the dreame he bore
In hast unto his Lord, where he him left afore.

45

Who all this while with charmes and hidden artes,
Had made a Lady of that other Spright,
And framed of liquid ayre her tender partes
So lively,° and so like in all mens sight, *lifelike*
That weaker° sence it could have ravisht quight *too weak*
The maker selfe for all his wondrous witt,
Was nigh beguiléd with so goodly sight:
Her all in white he clad, and over it
Cast a blacke stole, most like to seeme for Una[5] fit.

46

Now when that ydle dreame was to him brought
Unto that Elfin knight he bad him fly,
Where he slept soundly void of evill thought
And with false shewes abuse his fantasy,° *imagination*
In sort as[6] he him schooléd privily:

9. According to the old physiology, old people and other light sleepers had too little moisture in the brain.
1. Queen of Hades.
2. Archmagician or chief deceiver.
3. Anxious concerns.
4. False dreams came through the ivory door, true dreams through the gate of horn (Homer, *Odyssey* XIX.562–67; Virgil, *Aeneid* VI.893–96).
5. Her name means "one, unity." Elizabethan readers would know the Latin *Una Vera Fides* (one true faith); the idea was that there can be only one true faith, though many erroneous or false ones.
6. In the way.

And that new creature borne without her dew[7]
Full of the makers guile, with usage sly
He taught to imitate that Lady trew,
Whose semblance she did carrie under feignéd hew.° *form*

47

Thus well instructed, to their worke they hast
And comming where the knight in slomber lay
The one upon his hardy head him plast,
And made him dreame of loves and lustfull play
That nigh his manly hart did melt away,
Bathéd in wanton blis and wicked joy:
Then seeméd him his Lady by him lay,
And to him playnd,° how that false wingéd boy *complained*
Her chast hart had subdewd, to learne Dame pleasures toy.

48

And she her selfe of beautie soveraigne Queene
Faire Venus seemde unto his bed to bring
Her, whom he waking evermore did weene
To be the chastest flowre, that ay° did spring *ever*
On earthly braunch, the daughter of a king,
Now a loose Leman° to vile service bound: *paramour*
And eke the Graces seeméd all to sing,
Hymen iô Hymen, dauncing all around,
Whilst freshest Flora her with Yvie girlond crownd.[8]

49

In this great passion of unwonted° lust, *unaccustomed*
Or wonted feare of doing ought amis,
He started up, as seeming to mistrust
Some secret ill, or hidden foe of his:
Lo there before his face his Lady is,
Under blake stole hyding her bayted hooke,
And as halfe blushing offred him to kis,
With gentle blandishment and lovely looke,
Most like that virgin true, which for her knight him took.

50

All cleane dismayd to see so uncouth° sight, *unseemly*
And halfe enragéd at her shamelesse guise,
He thought have slaine her in his fierce despight:° *indignation*
But hasty heat tempring with sufferance wise,
He stayde his hand, and gan himselfe advise
To prove his sense, and tempt her faignéd truth.
Wringing her hands in wemens pitteous wise,
Tho can she[9] weepe, to stirre up gentle ruth,° *pity*
Both for her noble bloud, and for her tender youth.

51

And said, "Ah Sir, my liege Lord and my love,
Shall I accuse the hidden cruell fate,

7. Unnaturally.
8. The three graces of classical mythology were personifications of grace and beauty, yet here they sing a call to the pleasures of the marriage bed (Hymen was god of marriage). On Flora, cf. E.K.'s Glosse to the March eclogue: "the Goddesse of flowres, but indede (as saith Tacitus) a famous harlot."
9. Then she began to.

And mightie causes wrought in heaven above,
Or the blind God, that doth me thus amate,° *dismay*
For° hopéd love to winne me certaine hate? *instead of*
Yet thus perforce he bids me do, or die.
Die is my dew: yet rew my wretched state
You, whom my hard avenging destinie
Hath made judge of my life or death indifferently.

52

"Your owne deare sake forst me at first to leave
My Fathers kingdome," There she stopt with teares;
Her swollen hart her speach seemd to bereave,
And then againe begun, "My weaker yeares
Captived to fortune and frayle worldly feares,
Fly to your faith for succour and sure ayde:
Let me not dye in languor and long teares.
"Why Dame," quoth he, "what hath ye thus dismayd?
What frayes ye, that were wont to comfort me affrayd?"

53

"Love of your selfe," she said, "and deare° constraint *dire*
Lets me not sleepe, but wast the wearie night
In secret anguish and unpittied plaint,
Whiles you in carelesse sleepe are drownéd quight."
Her doubtfull° words made that redoubted knight *questionable*
Suspect her truth: yet since no untruth he knew,
Her fawning love with foule disdainefull spight
He would not shend,° but said, "Deare dame I rew, *reject*
That for my sake unknowne such griefe unto you grew.

54

"Assure your selfe, it fell not all to ground;
For all so deare as life is to my hart,
I deeme your love, and hold me to you bound;
Ne let vaine feares procure your needlesse smart,
Where cause is none, but to your rest depart."
Not all content, yet seemd she to appease° *cease*
Her mournefull plaintes, beguiléd of her art,
And fed with words, that could not chuse but please,
So slyding softly forth, she turnd as to her ease.

55

Long after lay he musing at her mood,
Much grieved to thinke that gentle Dame so light,
For whose defence he was to shed his blood.
At last dull wearinesse of former fight
Having yrockt a sleepe his irkesome spright,° *spirit*
That troublous dreame gan freshly tosse his braine,
With bowres, and beds, and Ladies deare delight:
But when he[1] saw his labour all was vaine,
With that misforméd spright he backe returnd againe.

1. I.e., Archimago.

Canto II

The guilefull great Enchaunter parts
The Redcrosse Knight from Truth:
Into whose stead faire falshood steps,
And workes him wofull ruth.

1

By this the Northerne wagoner had set
His seven fold teame behind the stedfast starre,[2]
That was in Ocean waves yet never wet,
But firme is fixt, and sendeth light from farre
To all, that in the wide deepe wandring arre.
And chearefull Chaunticlere with his note shrill
Had warnéd once, that Phoebus fiery carre[3]
In hast was climbing up the Easterne hill,
Full envious that night so long his roome did fill.

2

When those accurséd messengers of hell,
That feigning dreame, and that faire-forgéd Spright
Came to their wicked maister, and gan tell
Their bootelesse° paines, and ill succeeding night: *useless*
Who all in rage to see his skilfull might
Deluded so, gan threaten hellish paine
And sad Prosérpines wrath, them to affright.
But when he saw his threatning was but vaine,
He cast about, and searcht his balefull° bookes againe. *deadly*

3

Eftsoones he tooke that miscreated faire,
And that false other Spright, on whom he spred
A seeming body of the subtile aire,
Like a young Squire, in loves and lusty-hed
His wanton dayes that ever loosely led,
Without regard of armes and dreaded fight:
Those two he tooke, and in a secret bed,
Covered with darknesse and misdeeming° night, *misleading*
Them both together laid, to joy in vaine delight.

4

Forthwith he runnes with feignéd faithfull hast
Unto his guest, who after troublous sights
And dreames, gan now to take more sound repast,° *rest*
Whom suddenly he wakes with fearefull frights,
As one aghast with feends or damnéd sprights,
And to him cals, "Rise rise unhappy Swaine,
That here wex°old in sleepe, whiles wicked wights *grows*
Have knit themselves in Venus shamefull chaine;
Come see, where your false Lady doth her honour staine."

2. I.e., by this time the Big Dipper had set behind the North Star.

3. The chariot of the sun.

5

All in amaze he suddenly up start
With sword in hand, and with the old man went;
Who soone him brought into a secret part,
Where that false couple were full closely ment° *mingled*
In wanton lust and lewd embracément:
Which when he saw, he burnt with gealous fire,
The eye of reason was with rage yblent,° *blinded*
And would have slaine them in his furious ire,
But hardly° was restreinéd of that aged sire. *with difficulty*

6

Returning to his bed in torment great,
And bitter anguish of his guiltie sight,
He could not rest, but did his stout heart eat,
And wast his inward gall with deepe despight,
Yrkesome° of life, and too long lingring night. *tired*
At last faire Hesperus[4] in highest skie
Had spent his lampe, and brought forth dawning light
Then up he rose, and clad him hastily;
The Dwarfe him brought his steed: so both away do fly.[5]

7

Now when the rosy-fingred Morning faire,
Weary of aged Tithones[6] saffron bed,
Had spred her purple robe through deawy aire,
And the high hils Titan° discoveréd, *the sun*
The royall virgin shooke off drowsy-hed,
And rising forth out of her baser° bowre, *humbler*
Lookt for her knight, who far away was fled,
And for her Dwarfe, that wont to wait each houre;
Then gan she waile and weepe, to see that woefull stowre.° *affliction*

8

And after him she rode with so much speede
As her slow beast could make; but all in vaine:
For him so far had borne his light-foot steede,
Prickéd with wrath and fiery fierce disdaine,
That him to follow was but fruitlesse paine;
Yet she her weary limbes would never rest,
But every hill and dale, each wood and plaine
Did search, sore grievéd in her gentle brest,
He so ungently left her, whom she lovéd best.

9

But subtill Archimago, when his guests
He saw divided into double parts,
And Una wandring in woods and forrests,
Th' end of his drift,° he praisd his divelish arts *plot*
That had such might over true meaning harts;
Yet rests not so, but other meanes doth make,

4. The evening star.
5. Reason and discrimination are defeated, and so "Holiness" is separated from the one true faith.
6. The husband of Aurora, goddess of the dawn.

How he may worke unto her further smarts:
For her he hated as the hissing snake,
And in her many troubles did most pleasure take.

10

He then devisde himselfe how to disguise;
For by his mightie science° he could take *knowledge*
As many formes and shapes in seeming wise,° *in appearance*
As ever Proteus to himselfe could make:
Sometime a fowle, sometime a fish in lake,
Now like a foxe, now like a dragon fell,° *fierce*
That of himselfe he oft for feare would quake,
And oft would flie away. O who can tell
The hidden power of herbes, and might of Magicke spell?

11

But now seemde best, the person to put on
Of that good knight, his late beguiléd guest:
In mighty armes he was yclad anon,
And silver shield: upon his coward brest
A bloudy crosse, and on his craven crest
A bounch of haires discolourd diversly:° *variously colored*
Full jolly knight he seemde, and well addrest,
And when he sate upon his courser free,
Saint George himself ye would have deeméd him to be.

12

But he the knight, whose semblaunt° he did beare, *likeness*
The true Saint George was wandred far away,
Still flying from° his thoughts and gealous feare; *because of*
Will was his guide,[7] and griefe led him astray.
At last him chaunst to meete upon the way
A faithlesse Sarazin° all armed to point, *Saracen*
In whose great shield was writ with letters gay
Sans foy: full large of limbe and every joint
He was, and caréd not for God or man a point.[8]

13

He had a faire companion of his way,
A goodly Lady clad in scarlot red,
Purfled° with gold and pearle of rich assay, *decorated*
And like a Persian mitre on her hed
She wore, with crownes and owches° garnishéd, *brooches*
The which her lavish lovers to her gave;
Her wanton palfrey all was overspred
With tinsell trappings, woven like a wave,
Whose bridle rung with golden bels and bosses brave.[1]

7. Will was his guide; but will, of all the human faculties, is least fitted to be one's guide; it should itself be under the guidance of intelligence or truth. Redcrosse's victory over the monster Errour did not give him the discrimination to pierce the deceptions of either Archimago or the false Una.

8. At all.

1. Handsome metal knobs.

14

With faire disport° and courting dalliaunce *diversion*
She intertainde her lover all the way:
But when she saw the knight his speare advaunce,
She soone left off her mirth and wanton play,
And bad her knight addresse him to the fray:
His foe was nigh at hand. He prickt° with pride *pranced*
And hope to winne his Ladies heart that day,
Forth spurréd fast: adowne his coursers side
The red bloud trickling staind the way, as he did ride.

15

The knight of the Redcrosse when him he spide,
Spurring so hote with rage dispiteous,
Gan fairely couch° his speare, and towards ride: *lower*
Soone meete they both, both fell and furious,
That daunted with their forces hideous,
Their steeds do stagger, and amazéd stand,
And eke themselves too rudely rigorous,
Astonied° with the stroke of their owne hand, *stunned*
Do backe rebut,° and each to other yeeldeth land. *recoil*

16

As when two rams stird with ambitious pride,
Fight for the rule of the rich fleecéd flocke,
Their hornéd fronts so fierce on either side
Do meete, that with the terrour of the shocke
Astonied both, stand sencelesse as a blocke,° *inanimate object*
Forgetfull of the hanging victory:
So stood these twaine, unmovéd as a rocke,
Both staring fierce, and holding idely
The broken reliques of their former cruelty.

17

The Sarazin sore daunted with the buffe
Snatcheth his sword, and fiercely to him flies;
Who well it wards, and quyteth° cuff with cuff: *requites*
Each others equall puissaunce envies,
And through their iron sides with cruell spies° *looks*
Does seeke to perce: repining courage yields
No foote to foe. The flashing fier flies
As from a forge out of their burning shields,
And streames of purple bloud new dies the verdant fields.

18

"Curse on that Crosse," quoth then the Sarazin,
"That keepes thy body from the bitter fit;° *stroke*
Dead long ygoe I wote thou haddest bin,
Had not that charme from thee forwarnéd° it: *guarded*
But yet I warne thee now assuréd sitt,
And hide thy head." Therewith upon his crest
With rigour so outrageous he smitt,
That a large share it hewd out of the rest,
And glauncing downe his shield, from blame him fairely blest.[1]

1. Preserved him from harm.

19

Who thereat wondrous wroth, the sleeping spark
Of native vertue° gan eftsoones revive, *strength*
And at his haughtie helmet making mark,
So hugely stroke, that it the steele did rive,
And cleft his head. He tumbling downe alive,
With bloudy mouth his mother earth did kis
Greeting his grave: his grudging° ghost did strive *complaining*
With the fraile flesh; at last it flitted is,
Whither the soules do fly of men, that live amis.

20

The Lady when she saw her champion fall,
Like the old ruines of a broken towre,
Staid not to waile his woefull funerall,
But from him fled away with all her powre;
Who after her as hastily gan scowre,° *scurry*
Bidding the Dwarfe with him to bring away
The Sarazins shield, signe of the conqueroure.
Her soone he overtooke, and bad to stay,
For present cause was none of dread her to dismay.

21

She turning backe with ruefull countenaunce,
Cride, "Mercy mercy Sir vouchsafe to show
On silly° Dame, subject to hard mischaunce, *innocent*
And to your mighty will." Her humblesse low
In so ritch weedes and seeming glorious show,
Did much emmove his stout heroicke heart,
And said, "Deare dame, your suddein overthrow
Much rueth° me; but now put feare apart, *grieves*
And tell, both who ye be, and who that tooke your part."

22

Melting in teares, then gan she thus lament;
"The wretched woman, whom unhappy howre
Hath now made thrall to your commandément,
Before that angry heavens list to lowre,° *frown*
And fortune false betraide me to your powre
Was (O what now availeth that I was!)
Borne the sole daughter of an Emperour,
He that the wide West under his rule has,
And high hath set his throne, where Tiberis doth pas.[2]

2. The Tiber River runs through Rome. The lady's admission that she is the daughter of Rome (and hence the Roman Catholic Church) is an immediate clue to the fact that she is evil. Her appearance, as described in stanza 13, was, however, also full of clues. She resembles the Whore of Babylon (Revelation xvii.3–4): "and I saw a woman sit upon a scarlet coloured beast, full of names of blasphemy, having seven heads and ten horns. And the woman was arrayed in purple and scarlet colour, and decked with gold and precious stones and pearls, having a golden cup in her hand full of abominations and filthiness of her fornication." Her father, she says, is ruler of the West—but Una's father had the rule of both East *and* West (I.i.5): on the historical plane, the true church once embraced east and west whereas the false rules only the west; truth is universal and comprehends falsehood, which is partial. As the false church, she wears the pope's miter.

23

"He in the first flowre of my freshest age,
Betrothéd me unto the onely haire° *heir*
Of a most mighty king, most rich and sage;
Was never Prince so faithfull and so faire,
Was never Prince so meeke and debonaire;° *gracious*
But ere my hopéd day of spousall shone,
My dearest Lord fell from high honours staire,
Into the hands of his accursed fone,° *foes*
And cruelly was slaine, that shall I ever mone.

24

"His blessed body spoild of lively breath,
Was afterward, I know not how, convaid
And fro me hid: of whose most innocent death
When tidings came to me unhappy maid,
O how great sorrow my sad soule assaid.° *afflicted*
Then forth I went his woefull corse to find,
And many yeares throughout the world I straid,
A virgin widow, whose deepe wounded mind
With love, long time did languish as the striken hind.

25

"At last it chauncéd this proud Sarazin
To meete me wandring, who perforce me led
With him away, but yet could never win
The fort, that Ladies hold in soveraigne dread.
There lies he now with foule dishonour dead,
Who whiles he livde, was calléd proud Sans foy,
The eldest of three brethren, all three bred
Of one bad sire, whose youngest is Sans joy,
And twixt them both was borne the bloudy bold Sans loy.[3]

26

"In this sad plight, friendlesse, unfortunate,
Now miserable I Fidessa dwell,
Craving of you in pitty of my state,
To do none° ill, if please ye not do well." *no*
He in great passion all this while did dwell,
More busying his quicke eyes, her face to view,
Then his dull eares, to heare what she did tell;
And said, "Faire Lady hart of flint would rew
The undeservéd woes and sorrowes, which ye shew.

27

"Henceforth in safe assuraunce may ye rest,
Having both found a new friend you to aid,
And lost an old foe, that did you molest:
Better new friend than an old foe is[4] said."
With chaunge of cheare the seeming simple maid

3. Literally, "without law." Sans foy means "without faith"; Sans joy, "without joy." *The Faerie Queene* is full of characters who come in sets—opposing principles or double and triple incarnations of the same principle. Una and this lady (falsely named Fidessa, or "faith"), for example, are in opposition; the three Saracens form a triad of degenerative qualities that Holiness must defeat. For Holiness, even untried, to defeat atheism ("without faith") was comparatively easy.

4. I.e., it is.

Let fall her eyen, as shamefast to the earth,
And yeelding soft, in that she nought gain-said,
So forth they rode, he feining seemely merth,
And she coy lookes: so dainty they say maketh derth.[5]

28

Long time they thus together traveiléd,
Till weary of their way, they came at last,
Where grew two goodly trees, that faire did spred
Their armes abroad, with gray mosse overcast,
And their greene leaves trembling with every blast,° *breeze*
Made a calme shadow far in compasse round:
The fearefull Shepheard often there aghast
Under them never sat, ne wont[6] there sound
His mery oaten pipe, but shund th' unlucky ground.

29

But this good knight soone as he them can° spie, *did*
For the coole shade him thither hastly got:
For golden Phoebus now ymounted hie,
From fiery wheeles of his faire chariot
Hurléd his beame so scorching cruell hot,
That living creature mote it not abide;
And his new Lady it enduréd not.
There they alight, in hope themselves to hide
From the fierce heat, and rest their weary limbs a tide.° *time*

30

Faire seemely pleasaunce° each to other makes, *courtesy*
With goodly purposes there as they sit:
And in his falséd fancy he her takes
To be the fairest wight that livéd yit;
Which to expresse, he bends his gentle wit,
And thinking of those braunches greene to frame
A girlond for her dainty forehead fit,
He pluckt a bough; out of whose rift there came
Small drops of gory bloud, that trickled downe the same.

31

Therewith a piteous yelling voyce was heard,
Crying, "O spare with guilty hands to teare
My tender sides in this rough rynd embard,° *imprisoned*
But fly, ah fly far hence away, for feare
Least to you hap, that happened to me heare,
And to this wretched Lady, my deare love,
O too deare love, love bought with death too deare."
Astond he stood, and up his haire did hove° *heave, raise*
And with that suddein horror could no member move.

32

At last whenas the dreadfull passion
Was overpast, and manhood well awake,
Yet musing at the straunge occasion,
And doubting much his sence, he thus bespake;

5. Proverbial: "what's dear is rare." Here, "coyness creates unsatisfied desire."

6. Nor was accustomed to.

"What voyce of damnéd Ghost from Limbo[7] lake,
Or guilefull spright wandring in empty aire,
Both which fraile men do oftentimes mistake,° *mislead*
Sends to my doubtfull eares these speaches rare,
And ruefull plaints, me bidding guiltlesse bloud to spare?"

33

Then groning deepe, "Nor damned Ghost," quoth he,
"Nor guilefull sprite to thee these wordes doth speake,
But once a man Fradubio,° now a tree, *Doubt*
Wretched man, wretched tree; whose nature weake,
A cruell witch her curséd will to wreake,
Hath thus transformed, and plast in open plaines,
Where Boreas° doth blow full bitter bleake, *the North Wind*
And scorching Sunne does dry my secret vaines:
For though a tree I seeme, yet cold and heat me paines."

34

"Say on Fradubio then, or° man, or tree," *whether*
Quoth then the knight, "by whose mischievous arts
Art thou misshapéd thus, as now I see?
He oft finds med'cine, who his griefe imparts;
But double griefs afflict concealing harts,
As raging flames who striveth to suppresse."
"The author then," said he, "of all my smarts,
Is one Duessa[8] a false sorceresse,
That many errant° knights hath brought to wretchednesse. *wandering*

35

"In prime of youthly yeares, when corage hot
The fire of love and joy of chevalree
First kindled in my brest, it was my lot
To love this gentle Lady, whom ye see,
Now not a Lady, but a seeming tree;
With whom as once I rode accompanyde,
Me chauncéd of a knight encountred bee,
That had a like faire Lady by his syde,
Like a faire Lady, but did fowle Duessa hyde.

36

"Whose forgéd beauty he did take in hand,[9]
All other Dames to have exceeded farre;
I in defence of mine did likewise stand,
Mine, that did then shine as the Morning starre:
So both to battell fierce arraungéd arre,
In which his harder fortune was to fall
Under my speare: such is the dye° of warre: *hazard*
His Lady left as a prise martiall,[10]
Did yield her comely person, to be at my call.

37

"So doubly loved of Ladies unlike faire,
Th' one seeming such, the other such indeede,

7. The abode of lost spirits.
8. Duessa means "double being, duplicity, deception."
9. He maintained.
10. Spoil of battle.

One day in doubt I cast for to compare,
Whether° in beauties glorie did exceede; *which one (of two)*
A Rosy girlond was the victors meede:° *reward*
Both seemde to win, and both seemde won to bee,
So hard the discord was to be agreede.
Fraelissa° was as faire, as faire mote bee, *Frailty*
And ever false Duessa seemde as faire as shee.

38

"The wicked witch now seeing all this while
The doubtfull ballaunce equally to sway,
What not by right, she cast to win by guile,
And by her hellish science raisd streight way
A foggy mist, that overcast the day,
And a dull blast, that breathing on her face,
Dimmed her former beauties shining ray,
And with foule ugly forme did her disgrace:
Then was she faire alone, when none was faire in place.[1]

39

"Then cride she out, 'Fye, fye, deforméd wight,
Whose borrowed beautie now appeareth plaine
To have before bewitchéd all mens sight;
O leave her soone, or let her soone be slaine.'
Her lothly visage viewing with disdaine,
Eftsoones I thought her such, as she me told,
And would have kild her; but with faignéd paine,
The false witch did my wrathfull hand withhold;
So left her, where she now is turnd to trëen mould.[2]

40

"Thens forth I tooke Duessa for my Dame,
And in the witch unweeting° joyd long time, *unknowingly*
Ne ever wist, but that she was the same,
Till on a day (that day is every Prime,[3]
When Witches wont do penance for their crime)
I chaunst to see her in her proper hew,
Bathing her selfe in origane and thyme:[4]
A filthy foule old woman I did vew,
That ever to have toucht her, I did deadly rew.

41

"Her neather partes misshapen, monstruous,
Were hidd in water, that I could not see,
But they did seeme more foule and hideous,
Then womans shape man would beleeve to bee.
Thens forth from her most beastly companie
I gan refraine, in minde to slip away,
Soone as appeard safe opportunitie:
For danger great, if not assured decay° *destruction*
I saw before mine eyes, if I were knowne to stray.

1. Perhaps, "when nobody else was fair."
2. The form of a tree.
3. The first appearance of the new moon.
4. Two kinds of herbs; they were associated, in classical tradition, with witches like Scylla, Circe, and Medea.

42

"The divelish hag by chaunges of my cheare° *countenance*
Perceived my thought, and drownd in sleepie night,
With wicked herbes and ointments did besmeare
My bodie all, through charmes and magicke might,
That all my senses were bereavéd quight:
Then brought she me into this desert waste,
And by my wretched lovers side me pight,° *pitched*
Where now enclosd in wooden wals full faste,
Banisht from living wights, our wearie dayes we waste."

43

"But how long time," said then the Elfin knight,
"Are you in this misforméd house to dwell?"
"We may not chaunge," quoth he, "this evil plight,
Till we be bathéd in a living well;
That is the terme prescribéd by the spell."
"O how," said he, "mote I that well out find,
That may restore you to your wonted well?"° *well-being*
"Time and suffiséd fates to former kynd
Shall us restore, none else from hence may us unbynd."[5]

44

The false Duessa, now Fidessa hight,° *called*
Heard how in vaine Fradubio did lament,
And knew well all was true. But the good knight
Full of sad feare and ghastly dreriment,° *gloom*
When all this speech the living tree had spent,
The bleeding bough did thrust into the ground,
That from the bloud he might be innocent,
And with fresh clay did close the wooden wound:
Then turning to his Lady, dead with feare her found.

45

Her seeming dead he found with feignéd feare,
As all unweeting of that well she knew,[6]
And paynd himselfe with busie care to reare
Her out of carelesse° swowne. Her eylids blew *unconscious*
And dimméd sight with pale and deadly hew
At last she up gan lift: with trembling cheare° *demeanor*
Her up he tooke, too simple and too trew,
And oft her kist. At length all passéd feare,[7]
He set her on her steede, and forward forth did beare.

Canto III

Forsaken Truth long seekes her love,
And makes the Lyon mylde,

5. The tale of a man imprisoned in a tree is paralleled by Virgil's *Aeneid* III. 27–42 and Ariosto's *Orlando Furioso* VI.26–53. His hesitation between Fraelissa and Duessa parallels Redcrosse's own spiritual state between Una and Duessa (the real name of "Fidessa," as line 388 casually informs us). The very name "Duessa" (two) reveals her falsity next to Una ("one"). Note that Fradubio ("brother doubt") cannot warn Redcrosse against Duessa, who is present at the whole recital: doubt is not, perhaps, a trustworthy help to Holiness. Doubt and frailty can only be helped by baptism (lines 381–82).

6. I.e., pretending ignorance of what she knew well.

7. I.e., having passed all fear.

Marres° blind Devotions mart,° and fals — *spoils / business*
In hand of leachour vylde.

1

Nought is there under heav'ns wide hollownesse,° — *concavity*
That moves more deare compassion of mind,
Then beautie brought t'unworthy° wretchednesse — *undeserved*
Through envies snares or fortunes freakes° unkind: — *sudden changes*
I, whether lately through her brightnesse blind,
Or through alleageance and fast fealtie,
Which I do owe unto all woman kind,
Feele my heart perst° with so great agonie, — *pierced*
When such I see, that all for pittie I could die.

2

And now it is empassionéd so deepe,
For fairest Unas sake, of whom I sing,
That my fraile eyes these lines with teares do steepe,
To thinke how she through guilefull handeling,° — *treatment*
Though true as touch,° though daughter of a king, — *touchstone*
Though faire as ever living wight was faire,
Though nor in word nor deede ill meriting,
Is from her knight divorcéd in despaire
And her due loves derived° to that vile witches share. — *diverted*

3

Yet she most faithfull Ladie all this while
Forsaken, wofull, solitarie mayd
Farre from all peoples prease,° as in exile, — *press, crowd*
In wildernesse and wastfull deserts strayd,
To seeke her knight; who subtilly betrayd
Through that late vision, which th' Enchaunter wrought,
Had her abandond. She of nought affrayd,
Through woods and wastnesse wide him daily sought;
Yet wishéd tydings none of him unto her brought.

4

One day nigh wearie of the yrkesome way,
From her unhastie beast she did alight,
And on the grasse her daintie limbes did lay
In secret shadow,° farre from all mens sight: — *shade*
From her faire head her fillet she undight,[8]
And laid her stole aside. Her angels face
As the great eye of heaven shynéd bright,
And made a sunshine in the shadie place;
Did never mortall eye behold such heavenly grace.

5

It fortunéd out of the thickest wood
A ramping° Lyon rushéd suddainly, — *raging*
Hunting full greedie after salvage blood;[9]
Soone as the royall virgin he did spy,
With gaping mouth at her ran greedily,
To have attonce devoured her tender corse;° — *body*

8. She took off her headband.

9. Wild game.

But to the pray when as he drew more ny,
His bloudie rage asswagéd with remorse,
And with the sight amazd, forgat his furious forse.

6

In stead thereof he kist her wearie feet,
And lickt her lilly hands with fawning tong,
As[1] he her wrongéd innocence did weet.° *understand*
O how can beautie maister the most strong,
And simple truth subdue avenging wrong?
Whose yeelded pride and proud submission,
Still dreading death, when she had markéd long,
Her hart gan melt in great compassion,
And drizling teares did shed for pure affection.

7

"The Lyon Lord of everie beast in field,"
Quoth she, "his princely puissance° doth abate *power*
And mightie proud to humble weake does yield,
Forgetfull of the hungry rage, which late
Him prickt, in pittie of my sad estate:° *condition*
But he my Lyon, and my noble Lord,
How does he find in cruell hart to hate
Her that him loved, and ever most adord,
As the God of my life? why hath he me abhord?"

8

Redounding° teares did choke th'end of her plaint, *overflowing*
Which softly ecchoed from the neighbour wood;
And sad to see her sorrowfull constraint° *affliction*
The kingly beast upon her gazing stood;
With pittie calmd, downe fell his angry mood.
At last in close hart shutting up her paine,
Arose the virgin borne of heavenly brood,° *parentage*
And to her snowy Palfrey got againe,
To seeke her strayéd Champion, if she might attaine.° *overtake*

9

The Lyon would not leave her desolate,
But with her went along, as a strong gard
Of her chast person, and a faithfull mate
Of her sad troubles and misfortunes hard:
Still when she slept, he kept both watch and ward,
And when she wakt, he waited diligent,
With humble service to her will prepard:
From her faire eyes he tooke commaundement,
And ever by her lookes conceivéd her intent.[2]

1. As though.

2. Whereas Redcrosse, the man, has confusedly abandoned truth, the lion, king of beasts, an animal under nature's law, follows truth instinctively. Lions revere the heroine in the romance *Sir Bevis of Hamptoun* and accompany the heroes of other medieval romances; they have long been associated with the British crown.

10

Long she thus traveiléd through deserts wyde,
By which she thought her wandring knight shold pas,
Yet never shew of living wight espyde;
Till that at length she found the troden gras,
In which the tract° of peoples footing was, *track*
Under the steepe foot of a mountaine hore;° *gray*
The same she followes, till at last she has
A damzell spyde slow footing her before,
That on her shoulders sad° a pot of water bore. *heavy*

11

To whom approching she to her gan call,
To weet, if dwelling place were nigh at hand;
But the rude° wench her answered nought at all, *ignorant*
She could not heare, nor speake, nor understand;
Till seeing by her side the Lyon stand,
With suddaine feare her pitcher downe she threw,
And fled away: for never in that land
Face of faire Ladie she before did vew,
And that dread Lyons looke her cast in deadly° hew. *deathlike*

12

Full fast she fled, ne ever lookt behynd,
As if her life upon the wager lay,
And home she came, whereas her mother blynd
Sate in eternall night: nought could she say,
But suddaine catching hold, did her dismay
With quaking hands, and other signes of feare:
Who full of ghastly fright and cold affray,° *terror*
Gan shut the dore. By this arrivéd there
Dame Una, wearie Dame, and entrance did requere.° *request*

13

Which when none yeelded, her unruly Page
With his rude clawes the wicket° open rent, *door*
And let her in; where of his cruell rage
Nigh dead with feare, and faint astonishment,
She found them both in darkesome corner pent;° *huddled*
Where that old woman day and night did pray
Upon her beades devoutly penitent;
Nine hundred *Pater nosters* every day,
And thrise nine hundred *Aves* she was wont to say.

14

And to augment her painefull pennance more,
Thrise every weeke in ashes she did sit,
And next her wrinkled skin rough sackcloth wore,
And thrise three times did fast from any bit:° *food*
But now for feare her beads she did forget.
Whose needlesse dread for to remove away,
Faire Una framéd words and count'nance fit:
Which hardly° doen, at length she gan them pray, *with difficulty*
That in their cotage small, that night she rest her may.

15

The day is spent, and commeth drowsie night,
When every creature shrowded is in sleepe;
Sad Una downe her laies in wearie plight,
And at her feet the Lyon watch doth keepe:
In stead of rest, she does lament, and weepe
For the late losse of her deare lovéd knight,
And sighes, and grones, and evermore does steepe
Her tender brest in bitter teares all night,
All night she thinks too long, and often lookes for light.

16

Now when Aldeboran was mounted hie
Above the shynie Cassiopeias chaire,[3]
And all in deadly sleepe did drownéd lie,
One knockéd at the dore, and in would fare;
He knockéd fast,° and often curst, and sware, *insistently*
That readie entrance was not at his call:
For on his backe a heavy load he bare
Of nightly stelths and pillage severall,
Which he had got abroad by purchase° criminall. *acquisition*

17

He was to weete[4] a stout and sturdie thiefe,
Wont to robbe Churches of their ornaments,
And poore mens boxes[5] of their due reliefe,
Which given was to them for good intents;
The holy Saints of their rich vestiments
He did disrobe, when all men carelesse slept,
And spoild the Priests of their habiliments,° *vestments*
Whiles none the holy things in safety kept;
Then he by cunning sleights in at the window crept.

18

And all that he by right or wrong could find,
Unto this house he brought, and did bestow
Upon the daughter of this woman blind,
Abessa daughter of Corceca[6] slow,
With whom he whoredome usd, that few did know,
And fed her fat with feast of offerings,
And plentie, which in all the land did grow;
Ne sparéd he to give her gold and rings:
And now he to her brought part of his stolen things.

19

Thus long the dore with rage and threats he bet,° *beat*
Yet of those fearefull women none durst rize,
The Lyon frayéd° them, him in to let: *terrify*

3. Aldebaran, in the constellation Taurus, mounts over the constellation Cassiopeia.
4. In fact.
5. A box for alms for the poor, especially one placed near the door of a church.
6. Corceca means "blind heart"; her daughter Abessa's name comes from "abbess."

He would no longer stay him to advize,° *consider*
But open breakes the dore in furious wize,
And entring is; when that disdainfull beast
Encountring fierce, him suddaine doth surprize,
And seizing° cruell clawes on trembling brest, *fastening*
Under his Lordly foot him proudly hath supprest.

20

Him booteth not resist,[7] nor succour call,
His bleeding hart is in the vengers hand,
Who streight him rent in thousand peeces small,
And quite dismembred hath: the thirstie land
Drunke up his life; his corse left on the strand.° *ground*
His fearefull friends weare out the wofull night,
Ne dare to weepe, nor seeme to understand
The heavie hap,° which on them is alight,° *lot / fallen*
Affraid, least to themselves the like mishappen might.

21

Now when broad day the world discovered° has, *revealed*
Up Una rose, up rose the Lyon eke,
And on their former journey forward pas,
In wayes unknowne, her wandring knight to seeke,
With paines farre passing that long wandring Greeke,
That for his love refuséd deitie;[8]
Such were the labours of this Lady meeke,
Still seeking him, that from her still did flie,
Then furthest from her hope, when most she weenéd nie.[1]

22

Soone as she parted thence, the fearefull twaine,
That blind old woman and her daughter deare
Came forth, and finding Kirkrapine° there slaine, *church robber*
For anguish great they gan to rend their heare,
And beat their brests, and naked flesh to teare.
And when they both had wept and wayld their fill,
Then forth they ranne like two amazéd deare,
Halfe mad through malice, and revenging will,[2]
To follow her, that was the causer of their ill.

23

Whom overtaking, they gan loudly bray,
With hollow howling, and lamenting cry,
Shamefully at her rayling all the way,
And her accusing of dishonesty,° *unchastity*
That was the flowre of faith and chastity;
And still amidst her rayling, she[3] did pray,
That plagues, and mischiefs, and long misery

7. It does no good to resist.
8. Odysseus, who renounced immortality and the love of the nymph Calypso for his wife Penelope.
1. Believed near.
2. Desire of revenge.
3. I.e., Corceca.

Might fall on her, and follow all the way,
And that in endlesse error° she might ever stray. *wandering*

24

But when she saw her prayers nought prevaile,
She backe returnéd with some labour lost;
And in the way as she did weepe and waile,
A knight her met in mighty armes embost,° *encased*
Yet knight was not for all his bragging bost,° *boast*
But subtill Archimag, that Una sought
By traynes° into new troubles to have tost: *tricks*
Of that old woman tydings he besought,
If that of such a Ladie she could tellen ought.

25

Therewith she gan her passion to renew,
And cry, and curse, and raile, and rend her heare,
Saying, that harlot she too lately knew,
That causd her shed so many a bitter teare,
And so forth told the story of her feare:
Much seeméd he to mone her haplesse chaunce,
And after for that Ladie did inquere;
Which being taught, he forward gan advaunce
His fair enchaunted steed, and eke his charméd launce.

26

Ere long he came, where Una traveild slow,
And that wilde Champion wayting° her besyde: *attending*
Whom seeing such, for dread he durst not show
Himselfe too nigh at hand, but turnéd wyde
Unto an hill; from whence when she him spyde,
By his like seeming shield, her knight by name
She weend it was, and towards him gan ryde:
Approching nigh, she wist° it was the same, *believed*
And with faire fearefull humblesse° towards him shee came. *humility*

27

And weeping said, "Ah my long lackéd Lord,
Where have ye bene thus long out of my sight?
Much fearéd I to have bene quite abhord,
Or ought° have done, that ye displeasen might, *aught*
That should as death unto my deare hart light:[4]
For since mine eye your joyous sight did mis,
My chearefull day is turnd to chearelesse night,
And eke my night of death the shadow is;
But welcome now my light, and shining lampe of blis."

28

He thereto meeting[5] said, "My dearest Dame,
Farre be it from your thought, and fro my will,
To thinke that knighthood I so much should shame,
As you to leave, that have me lovéd still,
And chose in Faery court of meere° goodwill, *pure*
Where noblest knights were to be found on earth:

4. I.e., be as a death-blow to my sad heart.

5. Answering in like manner.

The earth shall sooner leave her kindly° skill *natural*
To bring forth fruit, and make eternall derth,° *desert*
Then I leave you, my liefe, yborne of heavenly berth.

29

"And sooth to say, why I left you so long,
Was for to seeke adventure in strange place,
Where Archimago said a felon strong
To many knights did daily worke disgrace;
But knight he now shall never more deface:
Good cause of mine excuse; that mote° ye please *may*
Well to accept, and evermore embrace
My faithfull service, that by land and seas
Have vowd you to defend, now then your plaint appease."

30

His lovely° words her seemd due recompence *loving*
Of all her passéd paines: one loving howre
For many yeares of sorrow can dispence:° *make amends*
A dram of sweet is worth a pound of sowre:
She has forgot, how many a wofull stowre° *trouble*
For him she late endured; she speakes no more
Of past: true is, that true love hath no powre
To looken backe; his eyes be fixt before.
Before her stands her knight, for whom she toyld so sore.

31

Much like, as when the beaten marinere,
That long hath wandred in the Ocean wide,
Oft soust° in swelling Tethys[6] saltish teare, *soaked*
And long time having tand his tawney hide
With blustring breath of heaven, that none can bide,
And scorching flames of fierce Orions hound,[7]
Soone as the port from farre he has espide,
His chearefull whistle merrily doth sound,
And Nereus crownes with cups;[8] his mates him pledg° around. *toast*

32

Such joy made Una, when her knight she found;
And eke th'enchaunter joyous seemd no lesse,
Then the glad marchant, that does vew from ground.
His ship farre come from watrie wildernesse,
He hurles out vowes, and Neptune oft doth blesse:
So forth they past, and all the way they spent
Discoursing of her dreadfull late distresse,
In which he askt her, what the Lyon ment:
Who told her all that fell° in journey as she went. *befell*

33

They had not ridden farre, when they might see
One pricking towards them with hastie heat,

6. The wife of Ocean; here, Ocean.
7. Sirius, the dog star, symbolizing hot weather (the "dog days").
8. Nereus is god of the Mediterranean, to whom the mariner in gratitude makes libations.

Full strongly armd, and on a courser free,
That through his fiercenesse fomed all with sweat,
And the sharpe yron° did for anger eat, *bit*
When his hot ryder spurd his chaufféd° side; *heated*
His looke was sterne, and seeméd still to threat
Cruell revenge, which he in hart did hyde,
And on his shield Sans loy[1] in bloudie lines was dyde.

34

When nigh he drew unto this gentle payre
And saw the Red-crosse, which the knight did beare,
He burnt in fire, and gan eftsoones prepare
Himselfe to battell with his couchéd speare.
Loth was that other, and did faint through feare,
To taste th'untryed dint of deadly steele;
But yet his Lady did so well him cheare,
That hope of new good hap he gan to feele;
So bent° his speare, and spurnd his horse with yron heele. *lowered*

35

But that proud Paynim° forward came so fierce, *pagan*
And full of wrath, that with his sharp-head speare
Through vainely crosséd shield[2] he quite did pierce,
And had his staggering steede not shrunke for feare,
Through shield and bodie eke he should him beare:° *thrust*
Yet so great was the puissance of his push,
That from his saddle quite he did him beare:
He tombling rudely downe to ground did rush,
And from his goréd wound a well of bloud did gush.

36

Dismounting lightly from his loftie steed,
He to him lept, in mind to reave° his life, *take*
And proudly said, "Lo there the worthie meed
Of him, that slew Sans foy with bloudie knife;
Henceforth his ghost freed from repining strife,
In peace may passen over Lethe[3] lake,
When mourning altars purgd° with enemies life, *cleansed*
The blacke infernall Furies[4] doen aslake:° *appease*
Life from Sans foy thou tookst, Sans loy shall from thee take."

37

Therewith in haste his helmet gan unlace,
Till Una cride, "O hold that heavie hand,
Deare Sir, what ever that thou be in place:[5]
Enough is, that thy foe doth vanquisht stand
Now at thy mercy: Mercie not withstand:
For he is one the truest knight alive,

1. The name means "without law." Law here is not, of course, merely state law, but the law of the cosmos, of nature, of civil government, and of man—the law that holds all life, both above the earth and on it, together. Hence "Sans loy" stands for the loss of all order, or chaos.

2. The cross on Archimago's shield was false and did not give him the protection the Redcrosse knight received in his fight with Sans foy; see I.ii.18.

3. A river in Hades.

4. Spirits of discord and revenge.

5. Whoever you are.

Though conquered now he lie on lowly land,
And whilest him fortune favourd, faire did thrive
In bloudie field: therefore of life him not deprive."

38

Her piteous words might not abate his rage,
But rudely rending up his helmet, would
Have slaine him straight: but when he sees his age,
And hoarie head of Archimago old,
His hastie hand he doth amazéd hold,
And halfe ashaméd, wondred at the sight:
For the old man well knew he, though untold,
In charmes and magicke to have wondrous might,
Ne ever wont in field, ne in round lists[6] to fight.

39

And said, "Why Archimago, lucklesse syre,
What doe I see? what hard mishap is this,
That hath thee hither brought to taste mine yre?
Or thine the fault, or mine the error is,
In stead of foe to wound my friend amis?"
He answered nought, but in a traunce still lay,
And on those guilefull dazéd eyes of his
The cloud of death did sit. Which doen away,[7]
He left him lying so, ne would no lenger stay.

40

But to the virgin comes, who all this while
Amaséd stands, her selfe so mockt° to see *deceived*
By him, who has the guerdon° of his guile, *reward*
For so misfeigning her true knight to bee:
Yet is she now in more perplexitie,
Left in the hand of that same Paynim bold,
From whom her booteth not at all to flie;
Who by her cleanly garment catching hold,
Her from her Palfrey pluckt, her visage to behold.

41

But her fierce servant full of kingly awe
And high disdaine, whenas his soveraine Dame
So rudely handled by her foe he sawe,
With gaping jawes full greedy at him came,
And ramping on his shield, did weene° the same *intend*
Have reft away with his sharpe rending clawes
But he was stout, and lust did now inflame
His corage more, that from his griping pawes
He hath his shield redeemed,° and foorth his swerd he drawes. *recovered*

42

O then too weake and feeble was the forse
Of salvage beast, his puissance to withstand:
For he was strong, and of so mightie corse,

6. Enclosures for fighting tournaments.
7. When he recovered from the swoon.

As ever wielded speare in warlike hand,
And feates of armes did wisely° understand. *skilfully*
Eftsoones he perced through his chaufed chest
With thrilling° point of deadly yron brand,° *penetrating / sword*
And launcht° his Lordly hart: with death opprest *pierced*
He roared aloud, whiles life forsooke his stubborne brest.

43

Who now is left to keepe the forlorne maid
From raging spoile of lawlesse victors will?
Her faithfull gard removed, her hope dismaid,
Her selfe a yeelded pray to save or spill.° *destroy*
He now Lord of the field, his pride to fill,
With foule reproches, and disdainfull spight
Her vildly entertaines,° and will or nill, *deals with*
Beares her away upon his courser light:
Her prayers nought prevaile; his rage is more of might.

44

And all the way, with great lamenting paine,
And piteous plaints she filleth his dull° eares, *deaf*
That stony hart could riven have in twaine,
And all the way she wets with flowing teares:
But he enraged with rancor, nothing heares.
Her servile beast yet would not leave her so,
But followes her farre off, ne ought he feares,
To be partaker of her wandring woe,
More mild in beastly kind,° then that her beastly foe. *nature*

Canto IV

To sinfull house of Pride, Duessa
guides the faithfull knight,
Where brothers death to wreak° Sansjoy *avenge*
doth chalenge him to fight.

1

Young knight, what ever that dost armes professe,
And through long labours huntest after fame,
Beware of fraud, beware of ficklenesse,
In choice, and change of thy deare lovéd Dame,
Least thou of her beleeve too lightly blame,
And rash misweening doe thy hart remove:
For unto knight there is no greater shame,
Then lightnesse and inconstancie in love;
That doth this Redcrosse knights ensample° plainly prove. *example*

2

Who after that he had faire Una lorne,° *lost*
Through light misdeeming° of her loialtie, *misjudging*
And false Duessa in her sted had borne,
Called Fidess', and so supposd to bee;
Long with her traveild, till at last they see

A goodly building, bravely garnishéd,° *adorned*
The house of mightie Prince it seemd to bee:
And towards it a broad high way[1] that led,
All bare through peoples feet, which thither traveiléd.

3

Great troupes of people traveild thitherward
Both day and night, of each degree and place,° *rank*
But few returnéd, having scapéd hard,° *with difficulty*
With balefull beggerie, or foule disgrace,
Which ever after in most wretched case,
Like loathsome lazars,° by the hedges lay. *lepers*
Thither Duessa bad him bend his pace:
For she is wearie of the toilesome way,
And also nigh consuméd is the lingring day.

4

A stately Pallace built of squaréd bricke,
Which cunningly was without morter laid,
Whose wals were high, but nothing strong, nor thick,
And golden foile° all over them displaid, *thin layer*
That purest skye with brightnesse they dismaid°: *outdid*
High lifted up were many loftie towres,
And goodly galleries farre over laid,[2]
Full of faire windowes, and delightfull bowres;
And on the top a Diall told the timely howres.

5

It was a goodly heape° for to behould, *building*
And spake the praises of the workmans wit;° *skill*
But full great pittie, that so faire a mould° *structure*
Did on so weake foundation ever sit:
For on a sandie hill, that still did flit,° *give way*
And fall away, it mounted was full hie,
That every breath of heaven shakéd it:
And all the hinder parts, that few could spie,
Were ruinous and old, but painted cunningly.

6

Arrivéd there they passéd in forth right;
For still to all the gates stood open wide,
Yet charge of them was to a Porter hight° *committed*
Cald Malvenù,[3] who entrance none denide:
Thence to the hall, which was on every side
With rich array and costly arras dight:[4]
Infinite sorts of people did abide
There waiting long, to win the wishéd sight
Of her, that was the Lady of that Pallace bright.

1. "Broad is the way that leadeth to destruction" (Matthew vii.13).
2. Placed above.
3. The name means "unwelcome." In courtly-love allegories, the porter is often called "Bienvenu" or "Bel-accueil" ("welcome").
4. Decorated with costly wall hangings.

7

By them they passe, all gazing on them round,
And to the Presence° mount; whose glorious vew *reception hall*
Their frayle amazéd senses did confound:
In living Princes court none ever knew
Such endlesse richesse, and so sumptuous shew;
Ne Persia selfe, the nourse of pompous pride
Like ever saw. And there a noble crew
Of Lordes and Ladies stood on every side,
Which with their presence faire, the place much beautifide.

8

High above all a cloth of State[5] was spred,
And a rich throne, as bright as sunny day,
On which there sate most brave embellishéd[6]
With royall robes and gorgeous array,
A mayden Queene, that shone as Titans° ray, *the sun's*
In glistring gold, and peerelesse pretious stone:
Yet her bright blazing beautie did assay° *attempt*
To dim the brightnesse of her glorious throne,
As envying her selfe, that too exceeding shone.

9

Exceeding shone, like Phoebus fairest childe,
That did presume his fathers firie wayne,° *chariot*
And flaming mouthes of steedes unwonted° wilde *unusually*
Through highest heaven with weaker° hand to rayne; *too weak*
Proud of such glory and advancement vaine,
While flashing beames do daze his feeble eyen,
He leaves the welkin° way most beaten plaine, *skyey*
And rapt° with whirling wheeles, inflames the skyen, *carried away*
With fire not made to burne, but fairely for to shyne.[7]

10

So proud she shynéd in her Princely state,° *throne*
Looking to heaven; for earth she did disdayne,
And sitting high; for lowly° she did hate: *lowliness*
Lo underneath her scornefull feete, was layne
A dreadfull Dragon with an hideous trayne,° *tail*
And in her hand she held a mirrhour bright,[8]
Wherein her face she often vewéd fayne,° *with pleasure*
And in her selfe-loved semblance tooke delight;
For she was wondrous faire, as any living wight.

11

Of griesly Pluto she the daughter was,
And sad Proserpina the Queene of hell;

5. Canopy.
6. Handsomely clad.
7. Phaëthon tried to drive the chariot of Phoebus, his father, but set the skies on fire and fell.
8. Pride, and figures associated with her in Renaissance literature and art, often hold a mirror, emblematic of self-love.

Yet did she thinke her pearelesse worth to pas
That parentage, with pride so did she swell,
And thundring Jove, that high in heaven doth dwell,
And wield° the world, she claymèd for her syre, *govern*
Or if that any else did Jove excell:
For to the highest she did still aspyre,
Or if ought higher were then that, did it desyre.

12

And proud Lucifera men did her call,
That made her selfe a Queene, and crownd to be,
Yet rightfull kingdome she had none at all,
Ne heritage of native soveraintie,
But did usurpe with wrong and tyrannie
Upon the scepter, which she now did hold:
Ne ruld her Realmes with lawes, but pollicie,° *conspiracy*
And strong advizement of six wisards old,
That with their counsels bad her kingdome did uphold.

13

Soone as the Elfin knight in presence came,
And false Duessa seeming Lady faire,
A gentle Husher,° Vanitie by name *usher*
Made rowme, and passage for them did prepaire:
So goodly brought them to the lowest staire
Of her high throne, where they on humble knee
Making obeyssance, did the cause declare,
Why they were come, her royall state to see,
To prove° the wide report of her great Majestee. *verify*

14

With loftie eyes, halfe loth to looke so low,
She thankèd them in her disdainefull wise,
Ne other grace vouchsafèd them to show
Of Princesse worthy, scarse them bad arise.
Her Lordes and Ladies all this while devise
Themselves to setten forth to straungers sight:
Some frounce° their curlèd haire in courtly guise, *frizzle*
Some prancke° their ruffes, and others trimly dight° *display/adjust*
Their gay attire: each others greater pride does spight.

15

Goodly they all that knight do entertaine,
Right glad with him to have increast their crew:
But to Duess' each one himselfe did paine
All kindnesse and faire courtesie to shew;
For in that court whylome° her well they knew: *formerly*
Yet the stout Faerie mongst the middest° crowd *thickest*
Thought all their glorie vaine in knightly vew,
And that great Princesse too exceeding prowd,
That to strange knight no better countenance allowd.

16

Suddein upriseth from her stately place
The royall Dame, and for her coche doth call:

All hurtlen° forth, and she with Princely pace, (*rush*)
As faire Aurora in her purple pall,° (*robe*)
Out of the East the dawning day doth call:
So forth she comes: her brightnesse brode° doth blaze; (*abroad*)
The heapes of people thronging in the hall,
Do ride° each other, upon her to gaze: (*climb up*)
Her glorious glitterand° light doth all mens eyes amaze. (*glittering*)

17

So forth she comes, and to her coche does clyme,
Adornéd all with gold, and girlonds gay,
That seemd as fresh as Flora in her prime,
And strove to match, in royall rich array,
Great Junos golden chaire,° the which they say (*chariot*)
The Gods stand gazing on, when she does ride
To Joves high house through heavens bras-pavéd way
Drawne of faire Pecocks, that excell in pride,
And full of Argus eyes their tailes dispredden wide.[1]

18

But this was drawne of six unequall beasts,
On which her six sage Counsellours did ryde,
Taught to obay their bestiall beheasts,
With like conditions to their kinds applyde:[2]
Of which the first, that all the rest did guyde,
Was sluggish Idlenesse the nourse of sin;
Upon a slouthfull Asse he chose to ryde,
Arayd in habit blacke, and amis° thin, (*hood, cape*)
Like to an holy Monck, the service to begin.

19

And in his hand his Portesse° still he bare, (*breviary*)
That much was worne, but therein little red,
For of devotion he had little care,
Still drownd in sleepe, and most of his dayes ded;
Scarse could he once uphold his heavie hed,
To looken, whether it were night or day:
May seeme the wayne° was very evill led, (*chariot*)
When such an one had guiding of the way,
That knew not, whether right he went, or else astray.

20

From worldly cares himselfe he did esloyne,° (*withdraw*)
And greatly shunnéd manly exercise,
From every worke he chalengéd essoyne,° (*excuse*)
For contemplation sake: yet otherwise,
His life he led in lawlesse riotise;
By which he grew to grievous malady;

1. The many-eyed monster Argus was set by Juno to watch Jupiter's love Io. When Mercury killed Argus, his eyes were put in the peacock's tail feathers.

2. The "sage Counsellours" do not guide their beasts, but are guided by them (i.e., by their bestial "kinds," or natures). This procession of the seven deadly sins—of which Pride is the queen, the chief sin—had a long tradition in medieval art and literature. And see Marlowe's *Dr. Faustus* (II.ii.111–64).

For in his lustlesse° limbs through evill guise° *feeble/living*
A shaking fever raignd continually:
Such one was Idlenesse, first of this company.

21

And by his side rode loathsome Gluttony,
Deforméd creature, on a filthie swyne,
His belly was up-blowne with luxury.° *indulgence in rich food*
And eke with fatnesse swollen were his eyne,
And like a Crane his necke was long and fyne,° *thin*
With which he swallowd up excessive feast,
For want whereof poore people oft did pyne;° *starve*
And all the way, most like a brutish beast,
He spuéd up his gorge, that all did him deteast.

22

In greene vine leaves he was right fitly clad;
For other clothes he could not weare for heat,
And on his head an yvie girland had,
From under which fast trickled downe the sweat:
Still as he rode, he somewhat° still did eat, *something*
And in his hand did beare a bouzing can,
Of which he supt so oft, that on his seat
His dronken corse he scarse upholden can,
In shape and life more like a monster, then a man.

23

Unfit he was for any worldly thing,
And eke unhable once° to stirre or go,° *at all/walk*
Not meet to be of counsell to a king,
Whose mind in meat and drinke was drownéd so,
That from his friend he seldome knew his fo:
Full of diseases was his carcas blew,° *livid*
And a dry dropsie through his flesh did flow:
Which by misdiet daily greater grew:
Such one was Gluttony, the second of that crew.

24

And next to him rode lustfull Lechery,
Upon a bearded Goat, whose rugged haire,
And whally° eyes (the signe of gelosy,) *greenish*
Was like the person selfe, whom he did beare:
Who rough, and blacke, and filthy did appeare,
Unseemely man to please faire Ladies eye;
Yet he of Ladies oft was lovéd deare,
When fairer faces were bid standen by:° *away*
O who does know the bent of womens fantasy?

25

In a greene gowne he clothéd was full faire,
Which underneath did hide his filthinesse,
And in his hand a burning hart he bare,
Full of vaine follies, and new fanglenesse:° *fickleness*
For he was false, and fraught with ficklenesse,

And learnéd had to love with secret lookes,
And well could daunce, and sing with ruefulnesse,° *pity*
And fortunes tell, and read in loving° bookes, *erotic*
And thousand other wayes, to bait his fleshly hookes.

26

Inconstant man, that lovéd all he saw,
And lusted after all, that he did love,
Ne would his looser life be tide to law,
But joyd weake wemens hearts to tempt and prove° *try*
If from their loyall loves he might them move;
Which lewdnesse fild him with reprochfull paine
Of that fowle evill,[3] which all men reprove,
That rots the marrow, and consumes the braine:
Such one was Lecherie, the third of all this traine.

27

And greedy Avarice by him did ride,
Upon a Camell loaden all with gold;
Two iron coffers hong on either side,
With precious mettall full, as they might hold,
And in his lap an heape of coine he told;° *counted*
For of his wicked pelfe his God he made,
And unto hell him selfe for money sold;
Accurséd usurie was all his trade,
And right and wrong ylike in equall ballaunce waide.[4]

28

His life was nigh unto deaths doore yplast,
And thread-bare cote, and cobled shoes he ware,
Ne scarse good morsell all his life did tast,
But both from backe and belly still did spare,
To fill his bags, and richesse to compare;° *acquire*
Yet chylde ne kinsman living had he none
To leave them to; but thorough daily care
To get, and nightly feare to lose his owne,
He led a wretched life unto him selfe unknowne.

29

Most wretched wight, whom nothing might suffise,
Whose greedy lust did lacke in greatest store,° *plenty*
Whose need had end, but no end covetise,
Whose wealth was want, whose plenty made him pore,
Who had enough, yet wishéd ever more;
A vile disease, and eke in foote and hand
A grievous gout tormented him full sore,
That well he could not touch, not go,° nor stand: *walk*
Such one was Avarice, the fourth of this faire band.

30

And next to him malicious Envie rode,
Upon a ravenous wolfe, and still did chaw

3. I.e., syphilis.

4. I.e., made no distinction between right and wrong.

Betweene his cankred teeth a venemous tode,
That all the poison ran about his chaw;° *jaw*
But inwardly he chawéd his owne maw° *entrails*
At neighbours wealth, that made him ever sad;
For death it was, when any good he saw,
And wept, that cause of weeping none he had,
But when he heard of harme, he wexéd wondrous glad.

31

All in a kirtle of discolourd say[5]
He clothéd was, ypainted full of eyes;
And in his bosome secretly there lay
An hatefull Snake, the which his taile uptyes
In many folds, and mortall sting implyes.° *enfolds*
Still as he rode, he gnasht his teeth, to see
Those heapes of gold with griple° Covetyse, *grasping*
And grudgéd at the great felicitie
Of proud Lucifera, and his owne companie.

32

He hated all good workes and vertuous deeds,
And him no lesse, that any like did use,
And who with gracious bread the hungry feeds,
His almes for want of faith he doth accuse;
So every good to bad he doth abuse:° *twist*
And eke the verse of famous Poets witt
He does backebite, and spightfull poison spues
From leprous mouth on all, that ever writt:
Such one vile Envie was, that fifte in row did sitt.

33

And him beside rides fierce revenging Wrath,
Upon a Lion, loth for to be led;
And in his hand a burning brond° he hath, *sword*
The which he brandisheth about his hed;
His eyes did hurle forth sparkles fiery red,
And staréd sterne on all, that him beheld,
As ashes pale of hew and seeming ded;
And on his dagger still his hand he held,
Trembling through hasty rage, when choler° in him sweld. *anger*

34

His ruffin° raiment all was staind with blood, *disarranged*
Which he had spilt, and all to rags yrent,° *torn*
Through unadviséd rashnesse woxen wood,[6]
For of his hands he had no governement,° *control*
Ne cared for bloud in his avengement:
But when the furious fit was overpast,
His cruell facts° he often would repent; *actions*
Yet wilfull man he never would forecast,
How many mischieves should ensue his heedlesse hast.

5. Jacket of many-colored wool.

6. Grown insane.

35

Full many mischiefes follow cruell Wrath;
Abhorréd bloudshed, and tumultuous strife,
Unmanly° murder, and unthrifty scath,° *inhuman/damage*
Bitter despight, with rancours rusty knife,
And fretting griefe the enemy of life;
All these, and many evils moe° haunt ire,° *more/anger*
The swelling Splene,° and Frenzy raging rife, *malice*
The shaking Palsey, and Saint Fraunces fire:[7]
Such one was Wrath, the last of this ungodly tire.° *train*

36

And after all, upon the wagon beame
Rode Sathan, with a smarting whip in hand,
With which he forward lasht the laesie teme,
So oft as Slowth still in the mire did stand.
Huge routs of people did about them band,
Showting for joy, and still before their way
A foggy mist had covered all the land;
And underneath their feet, all scattered lay
Dead sculs and bones of men, whose life had gone astray.

37

So forth they marchen in this goodly sort,
To take the solace° of the open aire, *recreation*
And in fresh flowring fields themselves to sport;
Emongst the rest rode that false Lady faire,
The fowle Duessa, next unto the chaire
Of proud Lucifera, as one of the traine:
But that good knight would not so nigh repaire,° *approach*
Him selfe estraunging from their joyaunce vaine,
Whose fellowship seemd far unfit for warlike swaine.

38

So having solacéd themselves a space
With pleasaunce of the breathing° fields yfed, *fragrant*
They backe returnéd to the Princely Place;
Whereas an errant knight in armes ycled,° *clad*
And heathnish shield, wherein with letters red
Was writ Sans joy, they new arrivéd find:
Enflamed with fury and fiers hardy-hed,° *audacity*
He seemd in hart to harbour thoughts unkind,
And nourish bloudy vengeaunce in his bitter mind.[8]

39

Who when the shaméd shield[9] of slaine Sans foy
He spied with that same Faery champions page,
Bewraying° him, that did of late destroy *revealing*

7. St. Anthony's fire, erysipelas, or the flaming itch; appropriate to Wrath.

8. Sans joy ("without joy") stands, not simply for gloom or "no fun," but for *accidie*, loss of heart. Redcrosse's high-minded rejection of the seven deadly sins (lines 331–33) does not protect him from this darkness of the spirit.

9. With the arms reversed. See below, line 369.

His eldest brother, burning all with rage
He to him leapt, and that same envious gage[1]
Of victors glory from him snatcht away:
But th'Elfin knight, which ought° that warlike wage,° *owned/trophy*
Disdaind to loose the meed he wonne in fray,
And him rencountring fierce, reskewd the noble pray.

40

Therewith they gan to hurtlen° greedily, *skirmish*
Redoubted battaile ready to darrayne,° *contest*
And clash their shields, and shake their swords on hy,
That with their sturre they troubled all the traine;
Till that great Queene upon eternall paine
Of high displeasure, that ensewen might,
Commaunded them their fury to refraine,
And if that either to that shield had right,
In equall lists they should the morrow next it fight.

41

"Ah dearest Dame," quoth then the Paynim bold,
"Pardon the errour of enragéd wight,
Whom great griefe made forget the raines to hold
Of reasons rule, to see this recreant knight,
No knight, but treachour full of false despight
And shamefull treason, who through guile hath slayn
The prowest° knight, that ever field did fight, *bravest*
Even stout Sans foy (O who can then refrayn?)
Whose shield he beares renverst, the more to heape disdayn.

42

"And to augment the glorie of his guile,
His dearest love[2] the faire Fidessa loe
Is there possessed of° the traytour vile, *by*
Who reapes the harvest sowen by his foe,
Sowen in bloudy field, and bought with woe:
That brothers hand shall dearely well requight
So be, O Queene, you equall favour showe."
Him litle answerd th'angry Elfin knight:
He never meant with words, but swords to plead his right.

43

But threw his gauntlet as a sacred pledge,
His cause in combat the next day to try:
So been they parted both, with harts on edge,
To be avenged each on his enimy.
That night they pas in joy and jollity,
Feasting and courting both in bowre and hall;
For Steward was excessive Gluttonie,
That of his plenty pouréd forth to all;
Which doen,° the Chamberlain Slowth did to rest them call. *done*

1. Envied prize.
2. I.e. Sans foy's.

44

Now whenas darkesome night had all displayd
Her coleblacke curtein over brightest skye,
The warlike youthes on dayntie couches layd,
Did chace away sweet sleepe from sluggish eye,
To muse on meanes of hopéd victory.
But whenas Morpheus[3] had with leaden mace
Arrested all that courtly company,
Up-rose Duessa from her resting place,
And to the Paynims lodging comes with silent pace.

45

Whom broad awake she finds, in troublous fit,° *mood*
Forecasting, how his foe he might annoy,
And him amoves with speaches seeming fit:
"Ah deare Sans joy, next dearest to Sans foy,
Cause of my new griefe, cause of my new joy,
Joyous, to see his ymage in mine eye,
And greeved, to thinke how foe did him destroy,
That was the flowre of grace and chevalrye;
Lo his Fidessa to thy secret faith I flye."

46

With gentle wordes he can° her fairely greet, *did*
And bad say on the secret of her hart.
Then sighing soft, "I learne that litle sweet
Oft tempred is," quoth she, "with muchell smart:
For since my brest was launcht° with lovely dart *pierced*
Of deare Sans foy, I never joyéd howre,
But in eternall woes my weaker hart
Have wasted, loving him with all my powre,
And for his sake have felt full many an heavie stowre.° *grief*

47

"At last when perils all I weenéd past,
And hoped to reape the crop of all my care,
Into new woes unweeting° I was cast, *unknowing*
By this false faytor,° who unworthy ware *deceiver*
His worthy shield, whom he with guilefull snare
Entrappéd slew, and brought to shamefull grave.
Me silly° maid away with him he bare, *innocent*
And ever since hath kept in darksome cave,
For that I would not yeeld, that° to Sans foy I gave. *what*

48

"But since faire Sunne hath sperst° that lowring clowd, *dispersed*
And to my loathéd life now shewes some light,
Under your beames I will me safely shrowd,
From dreaded storme of his disdainfull spight:
To you th'inheritance belongs by right
Of brothers prayse, to you eke longs° his love. *belongs*
Let not his love, let not his restlesse spright° *ghost*
Be unrevenged, that calles to you above
From wandring Stygian[4] shores, where it doth endlesse move."

3. The god of sleep.

4. Of the river Styx, in the underworld.

49

Thereto said he, "Faire Dame be nought dismaid
For sorrowes past; their griefe is with them gone:
Ne yet of present perill be affraid;
For needlesse feare did never vantage° none, *aid*
And helplesse hap it booteth not to mone.
Dead is Sans-foy, his vitall paines are past,
Though greevéd ghost for vengeance deepe do grone:
He lives, that shall him pay his dewties° last, *rites*
And guiltie Elfin bloud shall sacrifice in hast."

50

"O but I feare the fickle freakes,"[5] quoth shee,
"Of fortune false, and oddes of armes in field."
"Why dame," quoth he, "what oddes can ever bee,
Where both do fight alike, to win or yield?"
"Yea but," quoth she, "he beares a charméd shield,
And eke enchaunted armes, that none can perce,
Ne none can wound the man, that does them wield."
"Charmd or enchaunted," answerd he then ferce,° *fiercely*
"I no whit reck, ne you the like need to reherce.° *recount*

51

"But faire Fidessa, sithens° fortunes guile, *since*
Or enimies powre hath now captivéd you,
Returne from whence ye came, and rest a while
Till morrow next, that I the Elfe subdew,
And with Sans foyes dead dowry you endew."[6]
"Ay me, that is a double death," she said,
"With proud foes sight my sorrow to renew:
Where ever yet I be, my secrete aid
Shall follow you." So passing forth she him obaid.

Canto V

The faithfull knight in equall field
subdewes his faithlesse foe,
Whom false Duessa saves, and for
his cure to hell does goe.

1

The noble hart, that harbours vertuous thought,
And is with child of glorious great intent,
Can never rest, untill it forth have brought
Th'eternall brood of glorie excellent:[7]
Such restlesse passion did all night torment
The flaming corage of that Faery knight,
Devizing, how that doughtie turnament
With greatest honour he atchieven might;
Still did he wake, and still did watch for dawning light.

5. Unpredictable tricks.

6. I.e., endow you with the dowry of the dead Sans foy.

7. That good is manifested only in action, not in mere intent, is an important commonplace of Renaissance thinking.

2

At last the golden Orientall gate
Of greatest heaven gan to open faire,
And Phoebus fresh, as bridegrome to his mate,
Came dauncing forth, shaking his deawie haire:
And hurld his glistring beames through gloomy aire.
Which when the wakeful Elfe perceived, streight way
He started up, and did him selfe prepaire,
In sun-bright armes, and battailous array:
For with that Pagan proud he combat will that day.

3

And forth he comes into the commune hall,
Where earely waite him many a gazing eye,
To weet what end to straunger knights may fall.
There many Minstrales maken melody,
To drive away the dull melancholy,
And many Bardes, that to the trembling chord
Can tune their timely° voyces cunningly, *measured*
And many Chroniclers, that can record
Old loves, and warres for ladies doen by many a Lord.

4

Soone after comes the cruell Sarazin,
In woven maile all arméd warily,
And sternly lookes at him, who not a pin
Does care for looke of living creatures eye.
They bring them wines of Greece and Araby,
And daintie spices fetcht from furthest Ynd,° *India*
To kindle heat of courage privily:° *within*
And in the wine a solemne oth they bynd
T'observe the sacred lawes of armes, that are assynd.

5

At last forth comes that far renowméd Queene,
With royall pomp and Princely majestie;
She is ybrought unto a paléd° greene, *fenced*
And placéd under stately canapee,° *canopy*
The warlike feates of both those knights to see.
On th'other side in all mens open vew
Duessa placéd is, and on a tree
Sans-foy his shield is hangd with bloudy hew:
Both those the lawrell girlonds to the victor dew.

6

A shrilling trompet sownded from on hye,
And unto battaill bad them selves addresse:
Their shining shieldes about their wrestes° they tye, *wrists*
And burning blades about their heads do blesse,° *brandish*
The instruments of wrath and heavinesse:
With greedy force each other doth assayle,
And strike so fiercely, that they do impresse

Deepe dinted furrowes in the battred mayle;
The yron walles to ward their blowes are weake and fraile.

7

The Sarazin was stout, and wondrous strong,
And heapéd blowes like yron hammers great:
For after bloud and vengeance he did long.
The knight was fiers, and full of youthly heat:
And doubled strokes, like dreaded thunders threat:
For all for prayse and honour he did fight.
Both stricken strike, and beaten both do beat,
That from their shields forth flyeth firie light,
And helmets hewen deepe, shew marks of eithers might.

8

So th'one for wrong, the other strives for right:
As when a Gryfon[8] seizéd of his pray,
A Dragon fiers encountreth in his flight,
Through widest ayre making his ydle° way, *empty*
That would his rightfull ravine° rend away: *prey*
With hideous horrour both together smight,
And souce° so sore, that they the heavens affray: *strike*
The wise Southsayer° seeing so sad sight, *soothsayer*
Th'amazéd vulgar tels of warres and mortall fight.

9

So th'one for wrong, the other strives for right,
And each to deadly shame would drive his foe:
The cruell steele so greedily doth bight
In tender flesh, that streames of bloud down flow,
With which the armes, that earst so bright did show,
Into a pure vermillion now are dyde:
Great ruth in all the gazers harts did grow,
Seeing the goréd woundes to gape so wyde,
That victory they dare not wish to either side.

10

At last the Paynim chaunst to cast his eye,
His suddein° eye, flaming with wrathfull fyre, *darting*
Upon his brothers shield, which hong thereby:
Therewith redoubled was his raging yre,
And said, "Ah wretched sonne of wofull syre,
Doest thou sit wayling by black Stygian lake,
Whilest here thy shield is hangd for victors hyre,° *reward*
And sluggish german[1] doest thy forces slake,
To after-send his foe, that him may overtake?

11

"Goe caytive° Elfe, him quickly overtake, *wretched*
And soone redeeme from his long wandring woe;
Goe guiltie ghost, to him my message make,
That I his shield have quit° from dying foe." *rescued*

8. A legendary monster, half eagle, half lion.

1. I.e., his brother.

Therewith upon his crest he stroke him so,
That twise he reeléd, readie twise to fall;
End of the doubtfull battell deeméd tho° *then*
The lookers on, and lowd to him gan call
The false Duessa, "Thine the shield, and I, and all."[2]

12

Soone as the Faerie heard his Ladie speake,
Out of his swowning dreame he gan awake,
And quickning° faith, that earst was woxen weake, *vitalizing*
The creeping deadly cold away did shake:
Tho moved with wrath, and shame, and Ladies sake,
Of all attonce he cast° avengd to bee, *determined*
And with so'exceeding furie at him strake,
That forcéd him to stoupe upon his knee;
Had he not stoupéd so, he should have cloven bee,

13

And to him said, "Goe now proud Miscreant,
Thy selfe thy message doe° to german deare, *give*
Alone he wandring thee too long doth want:
Goe say, his foe thy shield with his doth beare."
Therewith his heavie hand he high gan reare,
Him to have slaine; when loe a darkesome clowd
Upon him fell: he no where doth appeare,
But vanisht is. The Elfe him cals alowd,
But answer none receives: the darknes him does shrowd.[3]

14

In haste Duessa from her place arose,
And to him running said, "O prowest° knight, *bravest*
That ever Ladie to her love did chose,
Let now abate the terror of your might,
And quench the flame of furious despight,
And bloudie vengeance; lo th'infernall powres
Covering your foe with cloud of deadly night,
Have borne him hence to Plutoes balefull bowres.
The conquest yours, I yours, the shield, and glory yours."

15

Not all so satisfide, with greedie eye
He sought all round about, his thirstie blade
To bath in bloud of faithlesse enemy;
Who all that while lay hid in secret shade:
He standes amazéd, how he thence should fade.
At last the trumpets Triumph sound on hie,
And running Heralds humble homage made,
Greeting him goodly with new victorie,
And to him brought the shield, the cause of enmitie.

2. Duessa is, of course, calling to Sans joy, but Redcrosse (lines 100 ff.) hears her as "Fidessa."

3. This inconclusive ending to the fight is a traditional epic device. Cf., in *Iliad* III, the battle between Menelaus and Paris and *Paradise Lost* IV. In Tasso's *Gerusalemme Liberata* (VII.44–45) the enchantress Armida protects Rambaldo in like manner.

16

Wherewith he goeth to that soveraine Queene,
And falling her before on lowly knee,
To her makes present of his service seene;° *proved*
Which she accepts, with thankes, and goodly gree,° *favor*
Greatly advauncing° his gay chevalree. *extolling*
So marcheth home, and by her takes the knight,
Whom all the people follow with great glee,
Shouting, and clapping all their hands on hight,
That all the aire it fils, and flyes to heaven bright.

17

Home is he brought, and laid in sumptuous bed:
Where many skilfull leaches° him abide,° *doctors/attend*
To salve his hurts, that yet still freshly bled.
In wine and oyle they wash his woundes wide,
And softly can embalme° on every side. *anoint*
And all the while, most heavenly melody
About the bed sweet musicke did divide,[4]
Him to beguile of griefe and agony:
And all the while Duessa wept full bitterly.

18

As when a wearie traveller that strayes
By muddy shore of broad seven-mouthéd Nile,
Unweeting of the perillous wandring wayes,
Doth meet a cruell craftie Crocodile,
Which in false griefe hyding his harmefull guile,
Doth weepe full sore, and sheddeth tender teares:
The foolish man, that pitties all this while
His mournefull plight, is swallowed up unwares,
Forgetfull of his owne, that mindes anothers cares.

19

So wept Duessa untill eventide,
That° shyning lampes in Joves high house were light: *when*
Then forth she rose, ne lenger would abide,
But comes unto the place, where th'Hethen knight
In slombring swownd nigh voyd of vitall spright,
Lay covered with inchaunted cloud all day:
Whom when she found, as she him left in plight,
To wayle his woefull case she would not stay,
But to the easterne coast of heaven makes speedy way.

20

Where griesly° Night, with visage deadly sad, *grim, horrible*
That Phoebus chearefull face durst never vew,
And in a foule blacke pitchie mantle clad,
She findes forth comming from her darkesome mew,° *den*
Where she all day did hide her hated hew.
Before the dore her yron charet stood,

4. Played variations.

Alreadie harnesséd for journey new;
And cole blacke steedes yborne of hellish brood,
That on their rustie bits did champ, as they were wood.[5]

21

Who when she saw Duessa sunny bright,
Adornd with gold and jewels shining cleare,
She greatly grew amazéd at the sight,
And th'unacquainted light began to feare:
For never did such brightnesse there appeare,
And would have backe retyred to her cave,
Untill the witches speech she gan to heare,
Saying, "Yet O thou dreaded Dame, I crave
Abide, till I have told the message, which I have."

22

She stayd, and foorth Duessa gan proceede,
"O thou most auncient Grandmother of all,
More old then Jove, whom thou at first didst breede,
Or that great house of Gods caelestiall,
Which wast begot in Daemogorgons hall,[6]
And sawst the secrets of the world unmade,[7]
Why suffredst thou thy Nephewes° deare to fall *grandsons*
With Elfin sword, most shamefully betrade?
Lo where the stout Sans joy doth sleepe in deadly shade.

23

"And him before, I saw with bitter eyes
The bold Sans foy shrinke underneath his speare;
And now the pray of fowles in field he lyes,
Nor wayld of friends, nor laid on groning beare,° *bier*
That whylome was to me too dearely deare.
O what of Gods then boots it to be borne,
If old Aveugles sonnes so evill heare?[8]
Or who shall not great Nightes children scorne,
When two of three her Nephews are so fowle forlorne.

24

"Up then, up dreary Dame, of darknesse Queene,
Go gather up the reliques of thy race,
Or else goe them avenge, and let be seene,
That dreaded Night in brightest day hath place,
And can the children of faire light deface."° *destroy*
Her feeling speeches some compassion moved
In hart, and chaunge in that great mothers face:
Yet pittie in her hart was never proved
Till then: for evermore she hated, never loved.

25

And said, "Deare daughter rightly may I rew
The fall of famous children borne of mee,

5. Mad. The description of night echoes not only descriptions in classical poetry but also the world of popular superstition in the English countryside.
6. I.e., in Chaos.
7. Before it was made.
8. I.e., are so badly thought of. "Aveugle" means "blind"; he is son of Night and father of Sans foy, Sans joy, and Sans loy.

And good successes, which their foes ensew:° *attend*
But who can turne the streame of destinee,
Or breake the chayne of strong necessitee,
Which fast is tyde to Joves eternall seat?[9]
The sonnes of Day he favoureth, I see,
And by my ruines thinkes to make them great:
To make one great by others losse, is bad excheat.° *profit*

26

"Yet shall they not escape so freely all;
For some shall pay the price of others guilt:
And he the man that made Sans foy to fall,
Shall with his owne bloud price that[1] he hath spilt.
But what art thou, that telst of Nephews kilt?"
"I that do seeme not I, Duessa am,"
Quoth she, "how ever now in garments gilt,
And gorgeous gold arayd I to thee came;
Duessa I, the daughter of Deceipt and Shame."

27

Then bowing downe her agéd backe, she kist
The wicked witch, saying; "In that faire face
The false resemblance of Deceipt, I wist° *knew*
Did closely lurke; yet so true-seeming grace
It carried, that I scarse in darkesome place
Could it discerne, though I the mother bee
Of falshood, and root of Duessaes race.
O welcome child, whom I have longd to see,
And now have seene unwares. Lo now I go with thee."

28

Then to her yron wagon she betakes,
And with her beares the fowle welfavourd witch:
Through mirkesome aire her readie way she makes.
Her twyfold° Teme, of which two blacke as pitch, *twofold*
And two were browne, yet each to each unlich,° *unlike*
Did softly swim away, ne ever stampe,
Unlesse she chaunst their stubborne mouths to twitch;
Then forming tarre,[2] their bridles they would champe,
And trampling the fine element,[3] would fiercely rampe.° *rear*

29

So well they sped, that they be come at length
Unto the place, whereas the Paynim lay,
Devoid of outward sense, and native strength,
Coverd with charméd cloud from vew of day,
And sight of men, since his late luckelesse fray.
His cruell wounds with cruddy° bloud congealed, *clotted*
They binden up so wisely, as they may,

9. The golden chain of concord or design that binds the entire universe; the image goes back as far as Homer (*Iliad* VIII.18–27) and was given classic statement by Boethius (*Consolation of Philosophy* II.8). Cf. ix.1.

1. I.e., pay for what.

2. Black froth.

3. The air.

And handle softly, till they can be healed:
So lay him in her charet, close in night concealed.

30

And all the while she stood upon the ground,
The wakefull dogs did never cease to bay,
As giving warning of th'unwonted sound,
With which her yron wheeles did them affray,
And her darke griesly looke them much dismay;
The messenger of death, the ghastly Owle
With drearie shriekes did also her bewray;° *reveal*
And hungry Wolves continually did howle,
At her abhorréd face, so filthy and so fowle.

31

Thence turning backe in silence soft they stole,
And brought the heavie corse with easie pace
To yawning gulfe of deepe Avernus hole.[4]
By that same hole an entrance darke and bace
With smoake and sulphure hiding all the place,
Descends to hell: there creature never past,
That backe returnéd without heavenly grace;
But dreadfull Furies, which their chaines have brast,° *burst*
And damnéd sprights sent forth to make ill° men aghast. *evil*

32

By that same way the direfull dames doe drive
Their mournefull charet, fild with rusty blood,
And downe to Plutoes house are come bilive:° *quickly*
Which passing through, on every side them stood
The trembling ghosts with sad amazéd mood,
Chattring their yron teeth, and staring wide
With stonie eyes; and all the hellish brood
Of feends infernall flockt on every side,
To gaze on earthly wight, that with the Night durst ride.

33

They pas the bitter waves of Acheron,
Where many soules sit wailing woefully,
And come to fiery flood of Phlegeton,
Whereas the damnéd ghosts in torments fry,
And with sharpe shrilling shriekes doe bootlesse cry,
Cursing high Jove, the which them thither sent.
The house of endlesse paine is built thereby,
In which ten thousand sorts of punishment
The curséd creatures doe eternally torment.

34

Before the threshold dreadfull Cerberus
His three deforméd heads did lay along,° *down*

4. In classical mythology, Avernus is Hell, where Pluto reigns (line 282). Acheron (line 289) and Phlegeton (line 291) are rivers in Hell. Cerberus (line 298), the three-headed dog, is guardian there. Stanzas 31–35 recall much of Aeneas's descent into Hell (Virgil, *Aeneid* VI.200, 239–40).

Curled with thousands adders venemous,
And lilléd° forth his bloudie flaming tong: *lolled*
At them he gan to reare his bristles strong,
And felly gnarre,[5] untill dayes enemy
Did him appease; then downe his taile he hong
And suffered them to passen quietly:
For she in hell and heaven had power equally.

35

There was Ixion turnéd on a wheele,
For daring tempt the Queene of heaven to sin;
And Sisyphus an huge round stone did reele° *roll*
Against an hill, ne might from labour lin;° *cease*
There thirstie Tantalus hong by the chin;
And Tityus fed a vulture on his maw;° *liver*
Typhoeus joynts were stretchéd on a gin,° *rack*
Theseus condemned to endlesse slouth° by law, *sloth*
And fifty sisters water in leake° vessels draw.[6] *leaky*

36

They all beholding worldly wights in place,
Leave off their worke, unmindfull of their smart,
To gaze on them; who forth by them doe pace,
Till they be come unto the furthest part:
Where was a Cave ywrought by wondrous art,
Deepe, darke, uneasie, dolefull, comfortlesse,
In which sad Aesculapius farre a part
Emprisond was in chaines remedilesse,
For that Hippolytus rent corse he did redresse.[7]

37

Hippolytus a jolly° huntsman was, *fine*
That wont in charet chace the foming Bore;
He all his Peeres in beautie did surpas,
But Ladies love as losse of time forbore:
His wanton stepdame[8] lovéd him the more,
But when she saw her offred sweets refused
Her love she turnd to hate, and him before
His father fierce of treason false accused,
And with her gealous termes his open eares abused.

38

Who all in rage his Sea-god syre[9] besought,
Some curséd vengeance on his sonne to cast:

5. Savagely growl.
6. Ixion was being punished for attempting to seduce Juno; Sisyphus for refusing to pray to the gods; Tantalus for stealing the gods' nectar; Tityus for having tried to seduce Apollo's mother; the monster Typhoeus for creating unfavorable winds; Theseus for stealing Persephone from Hades; and the daughters of King Danaus for having killed their husbands on the wedding night. Ovid, Virgil, and Homer are Spenser's sources here.
7. Aesculapius was god of medicine. Spenser draws most closely for the story of Hippolytus upon Boccaccio's *De Genealogia Deorum* (X.50), although Ovid, Virgil, and Seneca also tell the story.
8. Phaedra, the wife of his father, Theseus.
9. Poseidon (Neptune).

From surging gulf two monsters straight were brought,
With dread whereof his chasing steedes aghast,
Both charet swift and huntsman overcast.
His goodly corps on ragged cliffs yrent,
Was quite dismembred, and his members chast
Scattered on every mountaine, as he went,
That of Hippolytus was left no moniment.[1]

39

His cruell stepdame seeing what was donne,
Her wicked dayes with wretched knife did end,
In death avowing th'innocence of her sonne.
Which hearing his rash Syre, began to rend
His haire, and hastie tongue, that did offend:
Tho gathering up the relicks of his smart[2]
By Dianes meanes, who was Hippolyts frend,
Them brought to Aesculape, that by his art
Did heale them all againe, and joynéd every part.

40

Such wondrous science in mans wit to raine
When Jove avizd,° that could the dead revive, *discovered*
And fates expiréd could renew againe,
Of endlesse life he might him not deprive,
But unto hell did thrust him downe alive,
With flashing thunderbolt ywounded sore:
Where long remaining, he did alwaies strive
Himselfe with salves to health for to restore,
And slake the heavenly fire, that raged evermore.

41

There auncient Night arriving, did alight
From her nigh wearie waine, and in her armes
To Aesculapius brought the wounded knight:
Whom having softly disarayd of armes,
Tho gan to him discover all his harmes,
Beseeching him with prayer, and with praise,
If either salves, or oyles, or herbes, or charmes
A fordonne° wight from dore of death mote raise, *undone*
He would at her request prolong her nephews daies.

42

"Ah Dame," quoth he, "thou temptest me in vaine,
To dare the thing, which daily yet I rew,
And the old cause of my continued paine
With like attempt to like end to renew.
Is not enough, that thrust from heaven dew° *fitting*
Here endlesse penance for one fault I pay,
But that redoubled crime with vengeance new
Thou biddest me to eeke?° Can Night defray° *increase/appease*
The wrath of thundring Jove, that rules both night and day?"

1. I.e., no trace of identity.

2. I.e., his remains.

43

"Not so," quoth she; "but sith that heavens king
From hope of heaven hath thee excluded quight,
Why fearest thou, that canst not hope for thing,
And fearest not, that more thee hurten might,
Now in the powre of everlasting Night?
Goe to then, O thou farre renowmèd sonne
Of great Apollo, shew thy famous might
In medicine, that else° hath to thee wonne — *already*
Great paines, and greater praise, both never to be donne."° — *ended*

44

Her words prevaild: And then the learnèd leach° — *doctor*
His cunning hand gan to his wounds to lay,
And all things else, the which his art did teach:
Which having seene, from thence arose away
The mother of dread darknesse, and let stay
Aveugles sonne there in the leaches cure,
And backe returning tooke her wonted way,
To runne her timely race,[3] whilst Phoebus pure
In westerne waves his wearie wagon did recure.° — *refresh*

45

The false Duessa leaving noyous° Night, — *harmful*
Returnd to stately pallace of dame Pride;
Where when she came, she found the Faery knight
Departed thence, albe° his woundes wide — *although*
Not throughly heald, unreadiè were to ride.
Good cause he had to hasten thence away;
For on a day his wary Dwarfe had spide,
Where in a dongeon deepe huge numbers lay
Of caytive° wretched thrals,° that waylèd night and day. — *captive/slaves*

46

A ruefull sight, as could be seene with eie;
Of whom he learnèd had in secret wise
The hidden cause of their captivitie,
How mortgaging their lives to Covetise,
Through wastfull Pride, and wanton Riotise,
They were by law of that proud Tyrannesse[4]
Provokt with Wrath, and Envies false surmise,
Condemnèd to that Dongeon mercilesse,
Where they should live in woe, and die in wretchednesse.

47

There was that great proud king of Babylon,[5]
That would compell all nations to adore,
And him as onely God to call upon,
Till through celestiall doome° throwne out of dore, — *judgment*
Into an Oxe he was transformed of yore:
There also was king Croesus,[6] that enhaunst° — *exalted*

3. Her measured (nightly) journey.
4. I.e., Lucifera, whose "law" is that of destruction by sin. The noble sinners named in stanzas 47–50 exemplify a theme common to Renaissance morality, the fall of princes.
5. Nebuchadnezzar (Daniel iii–iv).
6. King of Lydia, famous for his riches.

His heart too high through his great riches store;
And proud Antiochus,[7] the which advaunst
His curséd hand gainst God, and on his altars daunst.

48

And them long time before, great Nimrod[8] was,
That first the world with sword and fire warrayd;° *ravaged*
And after him old Ninus farre did pas° *surpass*
In princely pompe, of all the world obayd;
There also was that mightie Monarch layd
Low under all, yet above all in pride,
That name of native° syre did fowle upbrayd, *natural*
And would as Ammons sonne[9] be magnifide,
Till scornd of God and man a shamefull death he dide.

49

All these together in one heape were throwne,
Like carkases of beasts in butchers stall.
And in another corner wide were strowne
The antique ruines of the Romaines fall:[1]
Great Romulus the Grandsyre of them all,
Proud Tarquin, and too lordly Lentulus,
Stout Scipio, and stubborne Hanniball,
Ambitious Sylla, and sterne Marius,
High Caesar, great Pompey, and fierce Antonius.

50

Amongst these mighty men were wemen mixt,
Proud wemen, vaine, forgetfull of their yoke:
The bold Semiramis,[2] whose sides transfixt
With sonnes owne blade, her fowle reproches spoke;
Faire Sthenoboea,[3] that her selfe did choke
With wilfull cord, for wanting° of her will; *lacking*
High minded Cleopatra, that with stroke
Of Aspes sting her selfe did stoutly kill:
And thousands moe the like, that did that dongeon fill.

51

Besides the endlesse routs of wretched thralles,
Which thither were assembled day by day,
From all the world after their wofull falles,
Through wicked pride, and wasted wealthes decay.
But most of all, which in that Dongeon lay
Fell from high Princes courts, or Ladies bowres,
Where they in idle pompe, or wanton play,

7. King of Syria, who tried to stamp out the Jewish religion (I Maccabees i.20–24).

8. A mighty hunter, associated with the Tower of Babel (Genesis x.9). "Ninus": founder of Nineveh.

9. Alexander the Great, occasionally worshiped as the son of Jupiter Ammon.

1. Romulus, founder of Rome; Tarquin, Roman tyrant; Lentulus, a conspirator with Catiline; Scipio, Roman general, conqueror of Carthage; Hannibal, Carthaginian general; Sulla, Roman civil war general; Marius, Sulla's rival; Julius Caesar; Pompey the Great; and Mark Anthony. All are memorialized in Plutarch's *Lives*.

2. Wife of Ninus.

3. Queen of King Proetus of Argos, who fell vainly in love with Bellerophon.

Consuméd had their goods, and thriftlesse howres,
And lastly throwne themselves into these heavy stowres.° *disasters*

52

Whose case whenas the carefull Dwarfe had tould,
And made ensample of their mournefull sight
Unto his maister, he no lenger would
There dwell in perill of like painefull plight,
But early rose, and ere that dawning light
Discovered had the world to heaven wyde,
He by a privie Posterne° tooke his flight, *gate*
That of no envious eyes he mote be spyde:
For doubtlesse death ensewd, if any him descryde.

53

Scarse could he footing find in that fowle way,
For many corses, like a great Lay-stall° *rubbish heap*
Of murdred men which therein strowéd lay,
Without remorse, or decent funerall:
Which all through that great Princesse pride did fall
And came to shamefull end. And them beside
Forth ryding underneath the castell wall,
A donghill of dead carkases he spide,
The dreadfull spectacle° of that sad house of Pride. *example*

Canto VI

From lawlesse lust by wondrous grace
fayre Una is releast:
Whom salvage nation does adore,
and learnes her wise beheast.° *bidding*

1

As when a ship, that flyes faire under saile,
An hidden rocke escapéd hath unwares,
That lay in waite her wrack for to bewaile,
The Marriner yet halfe amazéd stares
At perill past, and yet in doubt ne dares
To joy at his foole-happie oversight:
So doubly is distrest twixt joy and cares
The dreadlesse courage° of this Elfin knight, *heart*
Having escapt so sad ensamples in his sight.

2

Yet sad he was that his too hastie speed
The faire Duess' had forst him leave behind;
And yet more sad,. that Una his deare dreed° *object of reverence*
Her truth had staind with treason so unkind;° *unnatural*
Yet crime in her could never creature find,
But for his love, and for her owne selfe sake,
She wandred had° from one to other Ynd, *would have*
Him for to seeke, ne ever would forsake,
Till her unwares the fierce Sansloy did overtake.

3

Who after Archimagoes fowle defeat,
  Led her away into a forrest wilde,
  And turning wrathfull fire to lustfull heat,
  With beastly sin thought her to have defilde,
  And made the vassall of his pleasures vilde.° *vile*
  Yet first he cast by treatie,° and by traynes,° *persuasion/tricks*
  Her to perswade, that stubborne fort to yilde:
  For greater conquest of hard love he gaynes,
That workes it to his will, then he that it constraines.° *forces*

4

With fawning wordes he courted her a while,
  And looking lovely,° and oft sighing sore, *lovingly*
  Her constant hart did tempt with diverse guile:
  But wordes, and lookes, and sighes she did abhore,
  As rocke of Diamond stedfast evermore.[4]
  Yet for to feed his fyrie lustfull eye,
  He snatcht the vele, that hong her face before;
  Then gan her beautie shine, as brightest skye,
And burnt his beastly hart t'efforce° her chastitye. *violate*

5

So when he saw his flatt'ring arts to fayle,
  And subtile engines bet° from batteree, *beaten*
  With greedy force he gan the fort assayle,
  Whereof he weend possesséd soone to bee,
  And win rich spoile of ransackt chastetee.
  Ah heavens, that do this hideous act behold,
  And heavenly virgin thus outragéd see,
  How can ye vengeance just so long withhold,
And hurle not flashing flames upon that Paynim bold?

6

The pitteous maden carefull° comfortlesse, *full of cares*
  Does throw out thrilling shriekes, and shrieking cryes,
  The last vaine helpe of womens great distresse,
  And with loud plaints importuneth the skyes,
  That molten starres do drop like weeping eyes;
  And Phoebus flying so most shamefull sight,
  His blushing face in foggy cloud implyes,° *buries*
  And hides for shame. What wit of mortall wight
Can now devise to quit a thrall[5] from such a plight?

7

Eternall providence exceeding thought,
  Where none appeares can make her selfe a way:
  A wondrous way it for this Lady wrought,
  From Lyons clawes to pluck the gripéd pray.
  Her shrill outcryes and shriekes so loud did bray,
  That all the woodes and forestes did resownd;

4. The diamond, because of its hardness, was traditionally considered the perfect material.
5. Release a victim.

A troupe of Faunes and Satyres far away
Within the wood were dauncing in a rownd,
Whiles old Sylvanus slept in shady arber sownd.[6]

8

Who when they heard that pitteous strainéd voice,
In hast forsooke their rurall meriment,
And ran towards the far rebownded noyce,
To weet, what wight so loudly did lament.
Unto the place they come incontinent:° *immediately*
Whom when the raging Sarazin espide,
A rude, misshapen, monstrous rablement,
Whose like he never saw, he durst not bide,
But got his ready steed, and fast away gan ride.[7]

9

The wyld woodgods arrivéd in the place,
There find the virgin dolefull desolate,
With ruffled rayments, and faire blubbred face,
As her outrageous foe had left her late,
And trembling yet through feare of former hate;
All stand amazéd at so uncouth° sight, *strange*
And gin to pittie her unhappie state,
All stand astonied at her beautie bright,
In their rude eyes unworthie° of so wofull plight. *undeserving*

10

She more amazed, in double dread doth dwell;
And every tender part for feare does shake:
As when a greedie Wolfe through hunger fell
A seely° Lambe farre from the flocke does take, *innocent*
Of whom he meanes his bloudie feast to make,
A Lyon spyes fast running towards him,
The innocent pray in hast he does forsake,
Which quit from death yet quakes in every lim
With chaunge of feare, to see the Lyon looke so grim.

11

Such fearefull fit assaid° her trembling hart, *afflicted*
Ne word to speake, ne joynt to move she had:
The salvage nation feele her secret smart,
And read her sorrow in her count'nance sad;
Their frowning forheads with rough hornes yclad,
And rusticke horror[8] all a side doe lay,
And gently grenning, shew a semblance glad
To comfort her, and feare to put away,
Their backward bent knees teach[9] her humbly to obay.

6. Fauns and satyrs, creatures with men's bodies above the waist and goats' bodies below, noted in classical mythology for their sensuality, engage here in "rurall meriment"; Sylvanus, Román god of the woods, is traditionally associated with fauns.
7. The "woodgods," like the Lyon of Canto iii, bear some natural goodness—unlike Sans loy, who is alien to nature.
8. Rough manner.
9. I.e., teach their knees to obey her.

12

The doubtfull Damzell dare not yet commit
  Her single° person to their barbarous truth,° *solitary/honesty*
  But still twixt feare and hope amazd does sit,
  Late learnd what harme to hastie trust ensu'th,
  They in compassion of her tender youth,
  And wonder of her beautie soveraine,
  Are wonne with pitty and unwonted ruth,
  And all prostrate upon the lowly plaine,
Do kisse her feete, and fawne on her with count'nance faine.° *pleasant*

13

Their harts she ghesseth by their humble guise,
  And yieldes her to extremitie of time;[1]
  So from the ground she fearelesse doth arise,
  And walketh forth without suspect of crime:
  They all as glad, as birdes of joyous Prime,° *springtime*
  Thence lead her forth, about her dauncing round,
  Shouting, and singing all a shepheards ryme,
  And with greene braunches strowing all the ground,
Do worship her, as Queene, with olive girlond cround.

14

And all the way their merry pipes they sound,
  That all the woods with doubled Eccho ring,
  And with their hornéd feet do weare the ground,
  Leaping like wanton kids in pleasant Spring.
  So towards old Sylvanus they her bring;
  Who with the noyse awakéd, commeth out,
  To weet the cause, his weake steps governing
  And agéd limbs on Cypresse stadle° stout, *staff*
And with an yvie twyne his wast is girt about.

15

Far off he wonders, what them makes so glad,
  Or° Bacchus merry fruit[2] they did invent,° *whether/find*
  Or Cybeles franticke rites[3] have made them mad;
  They drawing nigh, unto their God present
  That flowre of faith and beautie excellent.
  The God himselfe vewing that mirrhour rare,
  Stood long amazd, and burnt in his intent;[4]
  His owne faire Dryope now he thinkes not faire,
And Pholoe fowle, when her to this he doth compaire.[5]

16

The woodborne people fall before her flat,
  And worship her as Goddesse of the wood;
  And old Sylvanus selfe bethinkes not, what
  To thinke of wight so faire, but gazing stood,

1. I.e., necessity of the time.
2. Wine grapes.
3. Orgiastic dances in worship of Cybele, goddess of the powers of Nature.
4. Glowed with intense concentration. Una is a "mirrhour rare" in that she reflects heavenly beauty.
5. Dryope and Pholoe were nymphs loved by Faunus and Pan; for Spenser, the names "Faunus," "Pan," and "Sylvanus" were apparently interchangeable.

In doubt to deeme her borne of earthly brood;
Sometimes Dame Venus selfe he seemes to see,
But Venus never had so sober° mood; *calm, temperate*
Sometimes Diana he her takes to bee,
But misseth bow, and shaftes, and buskins° to her knee. *soft boots*

17

By vew of her he ginneth to revive
His ancient love, and dearest Cyparisse,[6]
And calles to mind his pourtraiture alive,[7]
How faire he was, and yet not faire to this,
And how he slew with glauncing dart amisse
A gentle Hynd, the which the lovely boy
Did love as life, above all worldly blisse;
For griefe whereof the lad n'ould° after joy, *would not*
But pynd away in anguish and selfe-wild annoy.° *suffering*

18

The wooddy Nymphes, faire Hamadryades[8]
Her to behold do thither runne apace,
And all the troupe of light-foot Naiades,[9]
Flocke all about to see her lovely face:
But when they vewéd have her heavenly grace,
They envie her in their malitious mind,
And fly away for feare of fowle disgrace:
But all the Satyres scorne their woody kind,
And henceforth nothing faire, but her on earth they find.

19

Glad of such lucke, the luckelesse lucky maid,
Did her content to please their feeble eyes,
And long time with that salvage people staid,
To gather breath in many miseries.
During which time her gentle wit she plyes,
To teach them truth, which worshipt her in vaine,
And made her th'Image of Idolatryes;
But when their bootlesse zeale she did restraine
From her own worship, they her Asse would worship fayn.[1]

20

It fortunéd a noble warlike knight
By just occasion to that forrest came,
To seeke his kindred, and the lignage right,° *true*
From whence he tooke his well deservéd name:
He had in armes abroad wonne muchell fame,
And fild far landes with glorie of his might,
Plaine, faithfull, true, and enimy of shame,
And ever loved to fight for Ladies right,
But in vaine glorious frayes he litle did delight.

6. A fair youth, beloved of Sylvanus, turned into a cypress tree.
7. I.e., his appearance when alive.
8. Nymphs whose lives depended upon the trees with which they were associated.
9. Water nymphs.
1. I.e., willingly. Natural goodness can give some recognition, albeit only externally, to Una. Though Una does her best to teach the satyrs true religion, they are idolaters even in the truth.

21

A Satyres sonne yborne in forrest wyld,
By straunge adventure as it did betyde,° *happen*
And there begotten of a Lady myld,
Faire Thyamis the daughter of Labryde,
That was in sacred bands of wedlocke tyde
To Therion, a loose unruly swayne;[2]
Who had more joy to raunge the forrest wyde,
And chase the salvage beast with busie payne,[3]
Then serve his Ladies love, and wast° in pleasures vayne. *live idly*

22

The forlorne mayd did with loves longing burne,
And could not lacke° her lovers company, *be without*
But to the wood she goes, to serve her turne,
And seeke her spouse, that from her still does fly,
And followes other game and venery:[4]
A Satyre chaunst her wandring for to find,
And kindling coles of lust in brutish eye,
The loyall links of wedlocke did unbind,
And made her person thrall unto his beastly kind.

23

So long in secret cabin there he held
Her captive to his sensuall desire,
Till that with timely fruit her belly sweld,
And bore a boy unto that salvage sire:
Then home he suffred her for to retire,
For ransome leaving him the late borne childe;
Whom till to ryper yeares he gan aspire,° *grow up*
He noursled up in life and manners wilde,
Emongst wild beasts and woods, from lawes of men exilde.

24

For all he taught the tender ymp,° was but *child*
To banish cowardize and bastard° feare; *base*
His trembling hand he would him force to put
Upon the Lyon and the rugged Beare,
And from the she Beares teats her whelps to teare;
And eke wyld roring Buls he would him make
To tame, and ryde their backes not made to beare;
And the Robuckes in flight to overtake,
That every beast for feare of him did fly and quake.

25

Thereby so fearelesse, and so fell° he grew, *fierce*
That his owne sire and maister of his guise[5]

2. "Thyamis" means "passion," "Therion," "wild beast." Their child Satyrane (he is named in line 249) ought to be a savage creature, but instead his natural goodness welcomes and reveres truth and grace in Una with a higher understanding than the lion or the woodgods can give.

3. Painstaking care.

4. The word means both "hunting" and "sexual play."

5. Teacher of his manners.

Did often tremble at his horrid° vew, *rough*
And oft for dread of hurt would him advise,
The angry beasts not rashly to despise,
Nor too much to provoke; for he would learne° *teach*
The Lyon stoup to him in lowly wise,
(A lesson hard) and make the Libbard° sterne *leopard*
Leave roaring, when in rage he for revenge did earne.° *yearn*

26

And for to make his powre approvéd° more, *extended*
Wyld beasts in yron yokes he would compell;
The spotted Panther, and the tuskéd Bore,
The Pardale° swift, and the Tigre cruell; *panther*
The Antelope, and Wolfe both fierce and fell;
And them constraine in equall teme to draw.
Such joy he had, their stubborne harts to quell,
And sturdie courage tame with dreadfull aw,
That his beheast they fearéd, as a tyrans law.

27

His loving mother came upon a day
Unto the woods, to see her little sonne;
And chaunst unwares to meet him in the way,
After his sportes, and cruell pastime donne,
When after him a Lyonesse did runne,
That roaring all with rage, did lowd requere° *demand*
Her children deare, whom he away had wonne:
The Lyon whelpes she saw how he did beare,
And lull in rugged armes, withouten childish feare.

28

The fearefull Dame all quakéd at the sight,
And turning backe, gan fast to fly away,
Untill with love revokt° from vaine affright, *restrained*
She hardly yet perswaded was to stay,
And then to him these womanish words gan say;
"Ah Satyrane, my dearling, and my joy,
For love of me leave off this dreadfull play;
To dally thus with death, is no fit toy,
Go find some other play-fellowes, mine own sweet boy."

29

In these and like delights of bloudy game
He traynéd was, till ryper yeares he raught,° *reached*
And there abode, whilst any beast of name
Walkt in that forest, whom he had not taught
To feare his force: and then his courage haught° *high*
Desird of forreine foemen to be knowne,
And far abroad for straunge adventures sought:
In which his might was never overthrowne,
But through all Faery lond his famous worth was blown.

30

Yet evermore it was his manner faire,
  After long labours and adventures spent,
  Unto those native woods for to repaire,
  To see his sire and ofspring° auncient. *origin*
  And now he thither came for like intent;
  Where he unwares the fairest Una found,
  Straunge Lady, in so straunge habiliment,
  Teaching the Satyres, which her sat around,
Trew sacred lore, which from her sweet lips did redound.° *flow*

31

He wondred at her wisedome heavenly rare,
  Whose like in womens wit he never knew;
  And when her curteous deeds he did compare,
  Gan her admire, and her sad sorrowes rew,
  Blaming of Fortune, which such troubles threw,
  And joyd to make proofe of her crueltie
  On gentle Dame, so hurtlesse,° and so trew: *harmless*
  Thenceforth he kept her goodly company,
And learnd her discipline of faith and veritie.

32

But she all vowd unto the Redcrosse knight,
  His wandring perill closely° did lament, *secretly*
  Ne in this new acquaintaunce could delight,
  But her deare heart with anguish did torment,
  And all her wit in secret counsels spent,
  How to escape. At last in privie wise[6]
  To Satyrane she shewéd her intent;
  Who glad to gain such favour, gan devise,
How with that pensive Maid he best might thence arise.° *depart*

33

So on a day when Satyres all were gone,
  To do their service to Sylvanus old,
  The gentle virgin left behind alone
  He led away with courage stout and bold.
  Too late it was, to Satyres to be told,
  Or ever hope recover her againe:
  In vaine he seekes that having cannot hold.
  So fast he carried her with carefull paine,[7]
That they the woods are past, and come now to the plaine.

34

The better part now of the lingring day,
  They traveild had, when as they farre espide
  A wearie wight forwandring° by the way, *wandering along*
  And towards him they gan in hast to ride,
  To weet of newes, that did abroad betide,
  Or tydings of her knight of the Redcrosse.
  But he them spying, gan to turne aside,

6. Privately.

7. Painstaking care.

For feare as seemid, or for some fieignéd losse;° *harm*
More greedy they of newes, fast towards him do crosse.

35

A silly° man, in simple weedes forworne,° *simple/worn out*
And soild with dust of the long dried way;
His sandales were with toilesome travell torne,
And face all tand with scorching sunny ray,
As he had traveild many a sommers day,
Through boyling sands of Arabie and Ynde;
And in his hand a Jacobs staffe,[8] to stay
His wearie limbes upon: and eke behind,
His scrip° did hang, in which his needments he did bind. *bag*

36

The knight approching nigh, of him inquerd
Tydings of warre, and of adventures new;
But warres, nor new adventures none he herd.
Then Una gan to aske, if ought he knew,
Or heard abroad of that her champion trew,
That in his armour bare a croslet° red. *small cross*
"Aye me, Deare dame," quoth he, "well may I rew
To tell the sad sight, which mine eies have red:° *beheld*
These eyes did see that knight both living and eke ded."

37

That cruell word her tender hart so thrild,° *pierced*
That suddein cold did runne through every vaine,
And stony horrour all her sences fild
With dying fit, that downe she fell for paine.
The knight her lightly rearéd up againe,
And comforted with curteous kind reliefe:
Then wonne from death, she bad him tellen plaine
The further processe° of her hidden griefe; *account*
The lesser pangs can beare, who hath endured the chiefe.

38

Then gan the Pilgrim thus, "I chaunst this day,
This fatall day, that shall I ever rew,
To see two knights in travell on my way
(A sory sight) arraunged in battell new,
Both breathing vengeaunce, both of wrathfull hew:
My fearefull flesh did tremble at their strife,
To see their blades so greedily imbrew,° *thrust*
That drunke with bloud, yet thristed after life:
What more? the Redcrosse knight was slaine with Paynim knife."

39

"Ah dearest Lord," quoth she, "how might that bee,
And he the stoutest knight, that ever wonne?"° *fought*
"Ah dearest dame," quoth he, "how might I see
The thing, that might not be, and yet was donne?"
"Where is," said Satyrane, "that Paynims sonne,
That him of life, and us of joy hath reft?"

8. I.e., pilgrim's staff.

"Not far away," quoth he, "he hence doth wonne° *stay*
Foreby a fountaine, where I late him left
Washing his bloudy wounds, that through° the steele were cleft." *by*

40

Therewith the knight thence marchéd forth in hast,
Whiles Una with huge heavinesse° opprest, *grief*
Could not for sorrow follow him so fast;
And soone he came, as he the place had ghest,
Whereas that Pagan proud him selfe did rest,
In secret shadow by a fountaine side:
Even he it was, that earst would have supprest° *violated*
Faire Una: whom when Satyrane espide,
With fowle reprochfull words he boldly him defide.

41

And said, "Arise thou curséd Miscreaunt,
That hast with knightlesse guile and trecherous train° *deceit*
Faire knighthood fowly shamed, and doest vaunt
That good knight of the Redcrosse to have slain:
Arise, and with like treason now maintain
Thy guilty wrong, or else thee guilty yield."
The Sarazin this hearing, rose amain,° *at once*
And catching up in hast his three square[9] shield,
And shining helmet, soone him buckled to the field.

42

And drawing nigh him said, "Ah misborne° Elfe, *base-born*
In evill houre thy foes thee hither sent,
Anothers wrongs to wreake upon thy selfe:
Yet ill thou blamest me, for having blent° *stained*
My name with guile and traiterous intent;
That Redcrosse knight, perdie, I never slew,
But had he beene, where earst his armes were lent,
Th' enchaunter vaine his errour should not rew:
But thou his errour shalt, I hope now proven trew."[10]

43

Therewith they gan, both furious and fell,
To thunder blowes, and fiersly to assaile
Each other bent° his enimy to quell,° *determined/kill*
That with their force they perst both plate and maile,
And made wide furrowes in their fleshes fraile,
That it would pitty° any living eie. *bring pity to*
Large floods of bloud adowne their sides did raile:° *flow*
But floods of bloud could not them satisfie:
Both hungred after death: both chose to win, or die.

9. Triangular.

10. I.e., had Redcrosse been where his arms were, the enchanter Archimago would not have to regret his error in fighting me. But you will now repeat his error in fighting me and demonstrate what an error it is.

44

So long they fight, and fell revenge pursue,
That fainting each, themselves to breathen let,
And oft refreshéd, battell oft renue:
As when two Bores with rancling malice met,
Their gory sides fresh bleeding fiercely fret,° *tear*
Til breathlesse both them selves aside retire,
Where foming wrath, their cruell tuskes they whet,
And trample th'earth, the whiles they may respire
Then backe to fight againe, new breathéd and entire.° *refreshed*

45

So fiersly, when these knights had breathéd once,
They gan to fight returne, increasing more
Their puissant force, and cruell rage attonce,
With heapéd strokes more hugely, then before,
That with their drerie° wounds and bloudy gore *dreadful*
They both deforméd, scarsely could be known.
By this sad Una fraught with anguish sore,
Led with their noise, which through the aire was thrown,
Arrived, where they in erth their fruitles bloud had sown.

46

Whom all so soone as that proud Sarazin
Espide, he gan revive the memory
Of his lewd lusts, and late attempted sin,
And left the doubtfull° battell hastily, *undecided*
To catch her, newly offred to his eie:
But Satyrane with strokes him turning, staid,
And sternely bad him other businesse plie,
Then hunt the steps of pure unspotted Maid:
Wherewith he all enraged, these bitter speaches said.

47

"O foolish faeries sonne, what furie mad
Hath thee incenst, to hast thy dolefull fate?
Were it not better, I that Lady had,
Then that thou hadst repented it too late?
Most sencelesse man he, that himselfe doth hate,
To love another. Lo then for thine ayd
Here take thy lovers token on thy pate."
So they to fight; the whiles the royall Mayd
Fled farre away, of that proud Paynim sore afrayd.

48

But that false Pilgrim, which that leasing° told, *falsehood*
Being in deed old Archimage, did stay
In secret shadow, all this to behold,
And much rejoycéd in their bloudy fray:
But when he saw the Damsell passe away
He left his stond,° and her pursewd apace, *place*

In hope to bring her to her last decay.° *destruction*
But for to tell her lamentable cace,
And eke this battels end, will need another place.

Canto VII

The Redcrosse knight is captive made
By Gyaunt proud opprest,
Prince Arthur meets with Una great-
ly with those newes distrest.

1

What man so wise, what earthly wit so ware,° *wary*
As to descry° the crafty cunning traine, *perceive*
By which deceipt doth maske in visour faire,
And cast her colours dyéd deepe in graine,
To seeme like Truth, whose shape she well can faine,
And fitting gestures to her purpose frame,
The guiltlesse man with guile to entertaine?° *receive*
Great maistresse of her art was that false Dame,
The false Duessa, clokéd with Fidessaes name.

2

Who when returning from the drery Night,
She fownd not in that perilous house of Pryde,
Where she had left, the noble Redcrosse knight,
Her hopéd pray, she would no lenger bide,
But forth she went, to seeke him far and wide.
Ere long she fownd, whereas° he wearie sate, *where*
To rest him selfe, foreby° a fountaine side, *beside*
Disarméd all of yron-coted Plate,
And by his side his steed the grassy forage ate.

3

He feedes upon the cooling shade, and bayes° *bathes*
His sweatie forehead in the breathing wind,
Which through the trembling leaves full gently playes
Wherein the cherefull birds of sundry kind
Do chaunt sweet musick, to delight his mind:
The Witch approaching gan him fairely greet,
And with reproch of carelesnesse unkind
Upbrayd, for leaving her in place unmeet,° *unfitting*
With fowle words tempring faire, soure gall with hony sweet.

4

Unkindnesse past, they gan of solace treat,° *speak*
And bathe in pleasaunce of the joyous shade,
Which shielded them against the boyling heat,
And with greene boughes decking a gloomy glade,
About the fountaine like a girlond made;
Whose bubbling wave did ever freshly well,
Ne ever would through fervent° sommer fade: *hot*
The sacred Nymph, which therein wont to dwell,
Was out of Dianes favour, as it then befell.

5

The cause was this: one day when Phoebe[1] fayre
With all her band was following the chace,
This Nymph, quite tyred with heat of scorching ayre
Sat downe to rest in middest of the race:
The goddesse wroth gan fowly her disgrace,° *scold*
And bad the waters, which from her did flow,
Be such as she her selfe was then in place.[2]
Thenceforth her waters waxéd dull and slow,
And all that drunke thereof, did faint and feeble grow.

6

Hereof this gentle knight unweeting was,
And lying downe upon the sandie graile,° *gravel*
Drunke of the streame, as cleare as cristall glas;
Eftsoones his manly forces gan to faile,
And mightie strong was turnd to feeble fraile.
His chaunged powres at first themselves not felt,
Till crudled° cold his corage° gan assaile, *congealing/vigor*
And chearefull bloud in faintnesse chill did melt,
Which like a fever fit through all his body swelt.° *raged*

7

Yet goodly court he made still to his Dame,
Pourd out in loosnesse on the grassy grownd,
Both carelesse of his health, and of his fame:
Till at the last he heard a dreadfull sownd,
Which through the wood loud bellowing, did rebownd,
That all the earth for terrour seemed to shake,
And trees did tremble. Th'Elfe therewith astownd,° *amazed*
Upstarted lightly from his looser make,° *companion*
And his unready weapons gan in hand to take.[3]

8

But ere he could his armour on him dight,
Or get his shield, his monstrous enimy
With sturdie steps came stalking in his sight,
An hideous Geant horrible and hye,
That with his talnesse seemd to threat the skye,
The ground eke groned under him for dreed;
His living like saw never living eye,
Ne durst behold: his stature did exceed
The hight of three the tallest sonnes of mortall seed.

9

The greatest Earth his uncouth mother was,
And blustring Aeolus his boasted sire,[4]
Who with his breath, which through the world doth pas,
Her hollow womb did secretly inspire,° *breathe into*

1. I.e., Diana, goddess of the moon.
2. At that time.
3. Redcrosse is weakened by his encounter with the despair of Sans joy; he has been seduced by falsehood, Duessa; he has drunk of the waters of spiritual sloth: he is thus, now, an easy victim.
4. Aeolus was keeper of the winds.

And fild her hidden caves with stormie yre,
That she conceived; and trebling the dew time,
In which the wombes of women do expire,° *bring forth*
Brought forth this monstrous masse of earthly slime,
Puft up with emptie wind, and fild with sinfull crime.

10

So growen great through arrogant delight
Of th'high descent, whereof he was yborne,
And through presumption of his matchlesse might,
All other powres and knighthood he did scorne.
Such now he marcheth to this man forlorne,
And left to losse:° his stalking steps are stayde *destruction*
Upon a snaggy Oke, which he had torne
Out of his mothers bowelles, and it made
His mortall mace, wherewith his foemen he dismayde.

11

That when the knight he spide, he gan advance
With huge force and insupportable mayne,[5]
And towardes him with dreadfull fury praunce;
Who haplesse, and eke hopelesse, all in vaine
Did to him pace, sad battaile to darrayne,° *undertake*
Disarmd, disgrast, and inwardly dismayde,[6]
And eke so faint in every joynt and vaine,
Through that fraile° fountaine, which him feeble made, *enfeebling*
That scarsely could he weeld his bootlesse° single blade. *futile*

12

The Geaunt strooke so maynly° mercilesse, *mightily*
That could have overthrowne a stony towre,
And were not heavenly grace, that him did blesse,
He had beene pouldred° all, as thin as flowre: *powdered*
But he was wary of that deadly stowre,° *peril*
And lightly lept from underneath the blow:
Yet so exceeding was the villeins powre,
That with the wind it did him overthrow,
And all his sences stound,° that still he lay full low. *stunned*

13

As when that divelish yron Engin[7] wrought
In deepest Hell, and framd by Furies skill,
With windy Nitre and quick° Sulphur fraught,° *explosive/filled*
And ramd with bullet round, ordaind to kill,
Conceiveth fire, the heavens it doth fill
With thundring noyse, and all the ayre doth choke,
That none can breath, nor see, nor heare at will,
Through smouldry cloud of duskish stincking smoke,
That th'onely breath[8] him daunts, who hath escapt the stroke.

5. Irresistible power.
6. Dis-made, dissolved.
7. I.e., cannon.
8. I.e., the blast alone.

14

So daunted when the Geaunt saw the knight,
His heavie hand he heavéd up on hye,
And him to dust thought to have battred quight,
Untill Duessa loud to him gan crye;
"O great Orgoglio,[9] greatest under skye,
O hold thy mortall hand for Ladies sake,
Hold for my sake, and do him not to dye,
But vanquisht thine eternall bondslave make,
And me thy worthy meed unto thy Leman take."[10]

15

He hearkned, and did stay from further harmes,
To gayne so goodly guerdon,° as she spake: *reward*
So willingly she came into his armes,
Who her as willingly to grace° did take, *favor*
And was possesséd of his new found make.° *mate*
Then up he tooke the slombred sencelesse corse,
And ere he could out of his swowne awake,
Him to his castle brought with hastie forse,
And in a Dongeon deepe him threw without remorse.

16

From that day forth Duessa was his deare,
And highly honourd in his haughtie eye,
He gave her gold and purple pall° to weare, *robe*
And triple crowne set on her head full hye,[1]
And her endowd with royall majestye:
Then for to make her dreaded more of men,
And peoples harts with awfull terrour tye,
A monstrous beast ybred in filthy fen
He chose, which he had kept long time in darksome den.

17

Such one it was, as that renowméd Snake
Which great Alcides in Stremona slew,
Long fostred in the filth of Lerna lake,
Whose many heads out budding ever new,
Did breed him endlesse labour to subdew:[2]
But this same Monster much more ugly was;
For seven great heads out of his body grew,
An yron brest, and backe of scaly bras,
And all embrewd° in bloud, his eyes did shine as glas. *stained*

9. *Orgoglio* is Italian for "pride." That this sin, pride of the flesh, un-Christian and unreasonable, should be the son of the gross earth and the "blustring" wind seems appropriate.

10. I.e., take me, your worthy reward, as your mistress.

1. Duessa is attired like the Whore of Babylon in Revelation xvii.3–4; the triple crown is that of the papacy. See i.13, also i.22 and note.

2. The nine-headed Lernean hydra slain by Hercules (Alcides). The seven-headed monster is the red dragon of Revelation: "behold a great red dragon, having seven heads and ten horns, and seven crowns upon his heads * * * [whose] tail drew the third part of the stars of heaven, and did cast them to the earth * * * [he is] that old serpent, called the Devil, and Satan, which deceiveith the whole world" (xii.3–4,9). Pictures of the Beast of the Apocalypse illustrate medieval literature on the vices. On the historical plane, Spenser associates it with the Roman church.

18

His tayle was stretchéd out in wondrous length,
That to the house of heavenly gods it raught,° *reached*
And with extorted powre, and borrowed strength,
The ever-burning lamps from thence it brought,
And prowdly threw to ground, as things of nought;
And underneath his filthy feet did tread
The sacred things, and holy heasts° foretaught. *commandments*
Upon this dreadfull Beast with sevenfold head
He set the false Duessa, for more aw and dread.

19

The wofull Dwarfe, which saw his maisters fall,
Whiles he had keeping of his grasing steed,
And valiant knight become a caytive° thrall, *captive*
When all was past, tooke up his forlorne weed,[3]
His mightie armour, missing most at need;
His silver shield, now idle maisterlesse;
His poynant° speare, that many made to bleed, *piercing*
The ruefull moniments° of heavinesse, *memorials*
And with them all departes, to tell his great distresse.

20

He had not travaild long, when on the way
He wofull Ladie, wofull Una met,[4]
Fast flying from the Paynims greedy pray,° *clutch*
Whilest Satyrane him from pursuit did let:° *prevent*
Who when her eyes she on the Dwarfe had set,
And saw the signes, that deadly tydings spake,
She fell to ground for sorrowfull regret,
And lively breath her sad brest did forsake,
Yet might her pitteous hart be seene to pant and quake.

21

The messenger of so unhappie newes
Would faine have dyde: dead was his hart within,
Yet outwardly some little comfort shewes:
At last recovering hart, he does begin
To rub her temples, and to chaufe her chin,
And every tender part does tosse and turne:
So hardly he the flitted life does win,° *prevail upon*
Unto her native prison[5] to retourne:
Then gins her grievéd ghost° thus to lament and mourne. *spirit*

22

"Ye dreary instruments of dolefull sight,
That doe this deadly spectacle behold,
Why do ye lenger feed on loathéd light,
Or liking find to gaze on earthly mould,° *form*
Sith cruell fates the carefull° threeds unfould, *anguished*
The which my life and love together tyde?

3. Abandoned garment.
4. Only in Faerie Land could the Dwarfe find Una so soon after Redcrosse's fortunes are at their lowest.
5. I.e., the body.

Now let the stony dart of senselesse cold
Perce to my hart, and pas through every side,
And let eternall night so sad sight fro me hide.

23

"O lightsome day, the lampe of highest Jove,
First made by him, mens wandring wayes to guyde,
When darknesse he in deepest dongeon drove,
Henceforth thy hated face for ever hyde,
And shut up heavens windowes shyning wyde:
For earthly sight can nought but sorrow breed,
And late repentance, which shall long abyde.
Mine eyes no more on vanitie shall feed,
But seeléd up with death, shall have their deadly meed."[6]

24

Then downe againe she fell unto the ground;
But he her quickly rearéd up againe:
Thrise did she sinke adowne in deadly swownd,
And thrise he her revived with busie paine:
At last when life recovered had the raine,° *rein*
And over-wrestled his strong enemie,
With foltring tong, and trembling every vaine,
"Tell on," quoth she, "the wofull Tragedie,
The which these reliques sad present unto mine eie.

25

"Tempestuous fortune hath spent all her spight,
And thrilling sorrow throwne his utmost dart;
Thy sad tongue cannot tell more heavy plight,
Then that I feele, and harbour in mine hart:
Who hath endured the whole, can beare each part.
If death it be, it is not the first wound,
That launchéd° hath my brest with bleeding smart. *pierced*
Begin, and end the bitter balefull stound;° *disaster*
If lesse, then that I feare, more favour I have found."

26

Then gan the Dwarfe the whole discourse declare,
The subtill traines of Archimago old;
The wanton loves of false Fidessa faire,
Bought with the bloud of vanquisht Paynim bold:
The wretched payre transformed to treen mould;[7]
The house of Pride, and perils round about;
The combat, which he with Sans joy did hould;
The lucklesse conflict with the Gyant stout,
Wherein captived, of life or death he stood in doubt.

27

She heard with patience all unto the end,
And strove to maister sorrowfull assay,[8]
Which greater grew, the more she did contend,
And almost rent her tender hart in tway;

6. Reward of death.
7. Shape of a tree.
8. I.e., attack of sorrow.

And love fresh coles unto her fire did lay:
For greater love, the greater is the losse.
Was never Ladie lovéd dearer° day, *more dearly*
Then she did love the knight of the Redcrosse;
For whose deare sake so many troubles her did tosse.

28

At last when fervent sorrow slakéd was,
She up arose, resolving him to find
Alive or dead: and forward forth doth pas,
All as the Dwarfe the way to her assynd:° *showed*
And evermore in constant carefull mind
She fed her wound with fresh renewéd bale;° *anguish*
Long tost with stormes, and bet° with bitter wind, *beat*
High over hils, and low adowne the dale,
She wandred many a wood, and measurd many a vale.

29

At last she chauncéd by good hap to meet
A goodly knight,[9] faire marching by the way
Together with his Squire, arayéd meet:° *properly*
His glitterand° armour shinéd farre away, *glittering*
Like glauncing light of Phoebus brightest ray;
From top to toe no place appearéd bare,
That deadly dint of steele endanger may:
Athwart his brest a bauldrick° brave he ware, *sash*
That shynd, like twinkling stars, with stons most pretious rare.

30

And in the midst thereof one pretious stone
Of wondrous worth, and eke of wondrous mights,
Shapt like a Ladies head,[1] exceeding shone,
Like Hesperus° emongst the lesser lights, *evening star*
And strove for to amaze the weaker sights;
Thereby his mortall blade full comely hong
In yvory sheath, ycarved with curious slights;° *patterns*
Whose hilts were burnisht gold, and handle strong
Of mother pearle, and buckled with a golden tong.° *pin*

31

His haughtie helmet, horrid° all with gold, *bristling*
Both glorious brightnesse, and great terrour bred;
For all the crest a Dragon did enfold
With greedie pawes, and over all did spred

9. Prince Arthur, the supreme hero of the entire *Faerie Queene*. As Spenser explained to Ralegh, "So in the person of Prince Arthure I sette forth magnificence in particular, which vertue for that (according to Aristotle and the rest) it is the perfection of all the rest, and conteineth in it them all." Since, he says, "I mention [in each book] the deedes of Arthur applyable to that vertue which I write of in that booke," and since the "virtue" in Book I is Holiness, Arthur will be not unlike Christ, or the power of Christian grace, in the ensuing episodes.

1. I.e., that of the Faerie Queene, Gloriana.

His golden wings: his dreadfull hideous hed
Close couchéd on the bever,° seemed to throw *visor*
From flaming mouth bright sparkles fierie red,
That suddeine horror to faint harts did show;
And scaly tayle was stretcht adowne his backe full low.

32

Upon the top of all his loftie crest,
A bunch of haires discolourd° diversly, *dyed*
With sprincled pearle, and gold full richly drest,
Did shake, and seemed to daunce for jollity,
Like to an Almond tree ymounted hye
On top of greene Selinis all alone,
With blossomes brave bedeckéd daintily;
Whose tender locks do tremble every one
At every little breath, that under heaven is blowne.

33

His warlike shield all closely covered was,
Ne might of mortall eye be ever seene;
Not made of steele, nor of enduring bras,
Such earthly mettals soone consuméd bene:
But all of Diamond perfect pure and cleene° *clear*
It framéd was, one massie entire mould,
Hewen out of Adamant rocke with engines keene,
That point of speare it never percen could,
Ne dint of direfull sword divide the substance would.[2]

34

The same to wight he never wont disclose,
But° when as monsters huge he would dismay, *except*
Or daunt unequall armies of his foes,
Or when the flying heavens he would affray;° *frighten*
For so exceeding shone his glistring ray,
That Phoebus golden face it did attaint,° *dim*
As when a cloud his beames doth over-lay;
And silver Cynthia° wexéd pale and faint, *the moon*
As when her face is staynd with magicke arts constraint.° *force*

35

No magicke arts hereof had any might,
Nor bloudie wordes of bold Enchaunters call,
But all that was not such, as seemd in sight,
Before that shield did fade, and suddeine fall:
And when him list the raskall routes[3] appall,
Men into stones therewith he could transmew,° *change*
And stones to dust, and dust to nought at all;
And when him list the prouder lookes subdew,
He would them gazing blind, or turne to other hew.° *form*

2. The diamond—unflawed, unpierceable, translucent—is emblematic of the perfect faith which is Arthur's shield. Cf. Ephesians vi.16: "Above all, taking the shield of faith, wherewith ye shall be able to quench all the fiery darts of the wicked."

3. Unruly mobs.

36

Ne let it seeme, that credence this exceedes,
For he that made the same, was knowne right well
To have done much more admirable deedes.
It Merlin was, which whylome° did excell *formerly*
All living wightes in might of magicke spell:
Both shield, and sword, and armour all he wrought
For this young Prince, when first to armes he fell;° *came*
But when he dyde, the Faerie Queene it brought
To Faerie lond, where yet it may be seene, if sought.[4]

37

A gentle youth, his dearely lovéd Squire
His speare of heben° wood behind him bare, *ebony*
Whose harmefull head, thrice heated in the fire,
Had riven many a brest with pikehead square;
A goodly person, and could menage° faire *control*
His stubborne steed with curbéd canon bit,[5]
Who under him did trample as the aire,
And chauft,° that any on his backe should sit; *fretted*
The yron rowels into frothy fome he bit.

38

When as this knight nigh to the Ladie drew,
With lovely court he gan her entertaine;
But when he heard her answers loth, he knew
Some secret sorrow did her heart distraine:° *oppress*
Which to allay, and calme her storming paine,
Faire feeling words he wisely gan display,
And for her humour fitting purpose faine,[6]
To tempt the cause it selfe for to bewray;
Wherewith emmoved, these bleeding words she gan to say.

39

"What worlds delight, or joy of living speach
Can heart, so plunged in sea of sorrowes deepe,
And heapéd with so huge misfortunes, reach?
The carefull° cold beginneth for to creepe, *afflicting*
And in my heart his yron arrow steepe,
Soone as I thinke upon my bitter bale:° *grief*
Such helplesse harmes yts better hidden keepe,
Then rip up griefe, where it may not availe,
My last left comfort is, my woes to weepe and waile."

40

"Ah Ladie deare," quoth then the gentle knight,
"Well may I weene, your griefe is wondrous great;
For wondrous great griefe groneth in my spright,° *spirit*
Whiles thus I heare you of your sorrowes treat.
But wofull Ladie let me you intrete,
For to unfold the anguish of your hart:
Mishaps are maistred by advice discrete,

4. I.e., Arthur's virtues may be seen still in Queen Elizabeth's England.

5. Cannon-bit; a smooth, round bit.

6. I.e., suited his manner to her mood.

And counsell mittigates the greatest smart;
Found never helpe, who never would his hurts impart."

41

"O but," quoth she, "great griefe will not be tould,
And can more easily be thought, then said."
"Right so"; quoth he, "but he, that never would,
Could never: will to might gives greatest aid."
"But grief," quoth she, "does greater grow displaid,
If then it find not helpe, and breedes despaire."
"Despaire breedes not," quoth he, "where faith is staid."° *firm*
"No faith so fast," quoth she, "but flesh does paire."° *impair*
"Flesh may empaire," quoth he, "but reason can repaire."

42

His goodly reason, and well guided speach
So deepe did settle in her gratious thought,
That her perswaded to disclose the breach,
Which love and fortune in her heart had wrought,
And said; "Faire Sir, I hope good hap hath brought
You to inquire the secrets of my griefe,
Or that your wisedome will direct my thought,
Or that your prowesse can me yield reliefe:
Then heare the storie sad, which I shall tell you briefe.

43

"The forlorne Maiden, whom your eyes have seene
The laughing stocke of fortunes mockeries,
Am th'only daughter of a King and Queene,
Whose parents deare, whilest equall destinies
Did runne about,[7] and their felicities
The favourable heavens did not envy,
Did spread their rule through all the territories,
Which Phison and Euphrates floweth by,
And Gehons golden waves doe wash continually.[8]

44

"Till that their cruell curséd enemy,
An huge great Dragon horrible in sight,
Bred in the loathly lakes of Tartary,° *Tartarus (Hell)*
With murdrous ravine,° and devouring might *destruction*
Their kingdome spoild, and countrey wasted quight:
Themselves, for feare into his jawes to fall,
He forst to castle strong to take their flight,
Where fast embard in mightie brasen wall,
He has them now foure yeres besiegd to make them thrall.

45

"Full many knights adventurous and stout
Have enterprizd that Monster to subdew;
From every coast that heaven walks about,
Have thither come the noble Martiall crew,
That famous hard atchievements still pursew,

7. I.e., while impartial destinies surrounded them.

8. These three rivers flow in the Garden of Eden (Genesis ii.11–14).

Yet never any could that girlond win,
But all still shronke,° and still he greater grew: *quailed*
All they for want of faith, or guilt of sin,
The pitteous pray of his fierce crueltie have bin.

46

"At last yledd° with farre reported praise, *led*
Which flying fame throughout the world had spread,
Of doughtie knights, whom Faery land did raise,
That noble order hight° of Maidenhed,[9] *called*
Forthwith to court of Gloriane I sped,
Of Gloriane great Queene of glory bright,
Whose kingdomes seat Cleopolis is red,[1]
There to obtaine some such redoubted knight,
That Parents deare from tyrants powre deliver might.

47

"It was my chance (my chance was faire and good)
There for to find a fresh unprovéd knight,
Whose manly hands imbrewed° in guiltie blood *stained*
Had never bene, ne ever by his might
Had throwne to ground the unregarded° right: *unrespected*
Yet of his prowesse proofe he since hath made
(I witnesse am) in many a cruell fight;
The groning ghosts of many one dismaide
Have felt the bitter dint of his avenging blade.

48

"And ye the forlorne reliques of his powre,
His byting sword, and his devouring speare,
Which have enduréd many a dreadfull stowre,° *conflict*
Can speake his prowesse, that did earst you beare,
And well could rule: now he hath left you heare,
To be the record of his ruefull losse,
And of my dolefull disaventurous deare:[2]
O heavie record of the good Redcrosse,
Where have you left your Lord, that could so well you tosse?

49

"Well hopéd I, and faire beginnings had,
That he my captive langour should redeeme,[3]
Till all unweeting, an Enchaunter bad
His sence abusd, and made him to misdeeme
My loyalty, not such as it did seeme;
That° rather death desire, then such despight. *I, who*
Be judge ye heavens, that all things right esteeme,
How I him loved, and love with all my might,
So thought I eke of him, and thinke I thought aright.

9. Historically, the Order of the Garter. Its emblem shows St. George killing the dragon.
1. Named. "Cleopolis" means "famous city." In the historical allegory, it is London, as Gloriana is Elizabeth. In other contexts, however, it may be Camelot or the earthly counterpart of the New Jerusalem.
2. Unfortunate lover.
3. I.e., relieve my state, captive to sadness.

50

"Thenceforth me desolate he quite forsooke,
To wander, where wilde fortune would me lead,
And other bywaies he himselfe betooke,
Where never foot of living wight did tread,
That brought not backe the balefull body dead;[4]
In which him chauncéd false Duessa meete,
Mine onely foe, mine onely deadly dread,
Who with her witchcraft and misseeming° sweete, *deception*
Inveigled him to follow her desires unmeete.° *improper*

51

"At last by subtill sleights she him betraid
Unto his foe, a Gyant huge and tall,
Who him disarméd, dissolute,° dismaid, *enfeebled*
Unwares surpriséd, and with mightie mall° *club*
The monster mercilesse him made to fall,
Whose fall did never foe before behold;
And now in darkesome dungeon, wretched thrall,
Remedilesse, for aie° he doth him hold; *ever*
This is my cause of griefe, more great, then may be told."

52

Ere she had ended all, she gan to faint:
But he her comforted and faire bespake,
"Certes, Madame, ye have great cause of plaint,
That stoutest heart, I weene, could cause to quake.
But be of cheare, and comfort to you take:
For till I have acquit° your captive knight, *freed*
Assure your selfe, I will you not forsake."
His chearefull words revived her chearelesse spright,
So forth they went, the Dwarfe them guiding ever right.

Canto VIII

Faire virgin to redeeme her deare
brings Arthur to the fight:
Who slayes the Gyant, wounds the beast,
and strips Duessa quight.

1

Ay me, how many perils doe enfold
The righteous man, to make him daily fall?
Were not, that heavenly grace doth him uphold,
And stedfast truth acquite him out of all.
Her love is firme, her care continuall,
So oft as he through his owne foolish pride,
Or weaknesse is to sinfull bands° made thrall: *bonds*
Else should this Redcrosse knight in bands have dyde,
For whose deliverance she this Prince doth thither guide.

4. I.e., who returned alive.

2

They sadly traveild thus, untill they came
Nigh to a castle builded strong and hie:
Then cryde the Dwarfe, "lo yonder is the same,
In which my Lord my liege doth lucklesse lie,
Thrall to that Gyants hatefull tyrannie:
Therefore, deare Sir, your mightie powres assay."
The noble knight alighted by and by[5]
From loftie steede, and bad the Ladie stay,
To see what end of fight should him befall that day.

3

So with the Squire, th'admirer of his might,
He marchéd forth towards that castle wall;
Whose gates he found fast shut, ne living wight
To ward° the same, nor answere commers call. *guard*
Then tooke that Squire an horne of bugle small,[6]
Which hong adowne his side in twisted gold,
And tassels gay. Wyde wonders over all
Of that same hornes great vertues weren told,
Which had approvéd° bene in uses manifold. *demonstrated*

4

Was never wight, that heard that shrilling sound,
But trembling feare did feele in every vaine;
Three miles it might be easie heard around,
And Ecchoes three answered it selfe againe:
No false enchauntment, nor deceiptfull traine° *snare*
Might once abide the terror of that blast,
But presently was voide and wholly vaine:
No gate so strong, no locke so firme and fast,
But with that percing noise flew open quite, or brast.° *burst*

5

The same before the Geants gate he blew,
That all the castle quakéd from the ground,
And every dore of freewill open flew.
The Gyant selfe dismaiéd with that sownd,
Where he with his Duessa dalliance° fownd, *amorous play*
In hast came rushing forth from inner bowre,
With staring countenance sterne, as one astownd,
And staggering steps, to weet, what suddein stowre° *disturbance*
Had wrought that horror strange, and dared his dreaded powre.

6

And after him the proud Duessa came,
High mounted on her manyheaded beast,
And every head with fyrie tongue did flame,
And every head was crownéd on his creast,
And bloudie mouthéd with late cruell feast.
That when the knight beheld, his mightie shild

5. Immediately.
6. A "bugle" is a wild ox; the "wide wonders" (marvelous tales) told of the horn connect it with the horn of Roland and the ram's horn of Joshua, with which he razed the walls of Jericho (Joshua vi.5).

Upon his manly arme he soone addrest,° *adjusted*
And at him fiercely flew, with courage fild,
And eger greedinesse° through every member thrild. *desire*

7

Therewith the Gyant buckled him to fight,
Inflamed with scornefull wrath and high disdaine,
And lifting up his dreadfull club on hight,
All armed with ragged snubbes° and knottie graine, *snags*
Him thought at first encounter to have slaine.
But wise and warie was that noble Pere,° *peer*
And lightly leaping from so monstrous maine,° *force*
Did faire avoide the violence him nere;
It booted nought, to thinke, such thunderbolts to beare.[7]

8

Ne shame he thought to shunne so hideous might:
The idle° stroke, enforcing furious way, *inaccurate*
Missing the marke of his misaymèd sight
Did fall to ground, and with his° heavie sway° *its/force*
So deepely dinted in the driven clay,
That three yardes deepe a furrow up did throw:
The sad earth wounded with so sore assay,° *assault*
Did grone full grievous underneath the blow,
And trembling with strange feare, did like an earthquake show.

9

As when almightie Jove in wrathfull mood,
To wreake° the guilt of mortall sins is bent, *punish*
Hurles forth his thundring dart with deadly food,[8]
Enrold in flames, and smouldring dreriment,
Through riven cloudes and molten firmament;
The fierce threeforkèd engin° making way, *weapon*
Both loftie towres and highest trees hath rent,
And all that might his angrie passage stay,
And shooting in the earth, casts up a mount of clay.

10

His boystrous° club, so buried in the ground, *huge*
He could not rearen up againe so light,° *easily*
But that the knight him at avantage found,
And whiles he strove his combred clubbe to quight° *release*
Out of the earth, with blade all burning bright
He smote off his left arme, which like a blocke
Did fall to ground, deprived of native might;
Large streames of bloud out of the trunckèd stocke
Forth gushèd, like fresh water streame from riven rocke.[1]

11

Dismaièd with so desperate deadly wound,
And eke impatient of[2] unwonted paine,
He loudly brayd with beastly yelling sound,
That all the fields rebellowèd againe;

7. The ensuing battle may be taken as the struggle of the Protestant against the Roman church—or that of Christian grace against evil, the Antichrist.

8. Hatred (feud).

1. Cf. Exodus xvii.6, where Moses smites the rock and water flows forth.

2. Agonized by.

As great a noyse, as when in Cymbrian plaine
An heard of Bulles, whom kindly° rage doth sting, *natural*
Do for the milkie mothers want complaine,[3]
And fill the fields with troublous bellowing,
The neighbour woods around with hollow murmur ring.

12

That when his deare Duessa heard, and saw
The evill stownd,° that daungerd her estate, *blow*
Unto his aide she hastily did draw
Her dreadfull beast, who swolne with bloud of late
Came ramping forth with proud presumpteous gate,
And threatned all his heads like flaming brands.° *torches*
But him the Squire made quickly to retrate,
Encountring fierce with single° sword in hand, *only*
And twixt him and his Lord did like a bulwarke stand,

13

The proud Duessa full of wrathfull spight,
And fierce disdaine, to be affronted so,
Enforst her purple beast with all her might
That stop° out of the way to overthroe, *obstacle*
Scorning the let° of so unequall foe: *obstruction*
But nathemore° would that courageous swayne *never the more*
To her yeeld passage, gainst his Lord to goe,
But with outrageous strokes did him restraine,
And with his bodie bard the way atwixt them twaine.

14

Then tooke the angrie witch her golden cup,
Which still she bore, replete with magick artes;[4]
Death and despeyre did many thereof sup,
And secret poyson through their inner parts,
Th' eternall bale of heavie wounded harts;
Which after charmes and some enchauntments said,
She lightly sprinkled on his weaker° parts; *too weak*
Therewith his sturdie courage soone was quayd,° *quelled*
And all his senses were with suddeine dread dismayd.

15

So downe he fell before the cruell beast,
Who on his necke his bloudie clawes did seize,
That life nigh crusht out of his panting brest:
No powre he had to stirre, nor will to rize.
That when the carefull° knight gan well avise, *watchful*
He lightly left the foe, with whom he fought,
And to the beast gan turne his enterprise;
For wondrous anguish in his hart it wrought,
To see his lovéd Squire into such thraldome brought.

16

And high advauncing his bloud-thirstie blade,

3. I.e., mourn the cows' absence.
4. Cf. the golden cup of the woman in Revelation, which is "full of abominations" (xvii.4), the chalice of the Roman church, and the cup of Circe (in *Odyssey* X).

Stroke one of those deforméd heads so sore,[5]
That of his puissance proud ensample made;
His monstrous scalpe° downe to his teeth it tore *skull*
And that misforméd shape mis-shapéd more:
A sea of bloud gusht from the gaping wound,
That her gay garments staynd with filthy gore,
And overflowéd all the field around;
That over shoes in bloud he waded on the ground.

17

Thereat he roaréd for exceeding paine,
That to have heard, great horror would have bred,
And scourging th' emptie ayre with his long traine,
Through great impatience° of his grievéd hed *agony*
His gorgeous ryder from her loftie sted
Would have cast downe, and trod in durtie myre,
Had not the Gyant soone her succouréd;
Who all enraged with smart and franticke yre,
Came hurtling in full fierce, and forst the knight retyre.

18

The force, which wont in two to be disperst,
In one alone left hand he now unites,
Which is through rage more strong then both were erst;
With which his hideous club aloft he dites,° *raises*
And at his foe with furious rigour smites,
That strongest Oake might seeme to overthrow:
The stroke upon his shield so heavie lites,
That to the ground it doubleth him full low:
What mortall wight could ever beare so monstrous blow?

19

And in his fall his shield, that covered was,
Did loose his vele° by chaunce, and open flew: *its veil*
The light whereof, that heavens light did pas,° *surpass*
Such blazing brightnesse through the aier threw,
That eye mote not the same endure to vew.
Which when the Gyaunt spyde with staring° eye, *awed*
He downe let fall his arme, and soft withdrew
His weapon huge, that heavéd was on hye
For to have slaine the man, that on the ground did lye.

20

And eke the fruitfull-headed° beast, amazed *many-headed*
At flashing beames of that sunshiny shield,
Became starke blind, and all his senses dazed,
That downe he tumbled on the durtie field,
And seemed himselfe as conqueréd to yield.
Whom when his maistresse proud perceived to fall,
Whiles yet his feeble feet for faintnesse reeld,
Unto the Gyant loudly she gan call,
"O helpe Orgoglio, helpe, or else we perish all."

5. "I saw one of [the beast's] heads as it were wounded to death" (Revelation xiii.3).

21

At her so pitteous cry was much amooved
  Her champion stout, and for to ayde his frend,
  Againe his wonted angry weapon prooved:° *tried*
  But all in vaine: for he has read his end
  In that bright shield, and all their forces spend
  Themselves in vaine: for since that glauncing° sight, *flashing*
  He hath no powre to hurt, nor to defend;
  As where th' Almighties lightning brond does light,
It dimmes the dazéd eyen, and daunts the senses quight.

22

Whom when the Prince, to battell new addrest,
  And threatning high his dreadfull stroke did see,
  His sparkling blade about his head he blest,° *waved*
  And smote off quite his right leg by the knee,
  That downe he tombled; as an aged tree,
  High growing on the top of rocky clift,
  Whose hartstrings with keene steele nigh hewen be,
  The mightie trunck halfe rent, with ragged rift
Doth roll adowne the rocks, and fall with fearefull drift.° *impact*

23

Or as a Castle rearéd high and round,
  By subtile engins and malitious slight° *trickery*
  Is underminéd from the lowest ground,
  And her foundation forst,° and feebled quight, *shattered*
  At last downe falles, and with her heapéd hight
  Her hastie ruine does more heavie make,
  And yields it selfe unto the victours might;
  Such was this Gyaunts fall, that seemed to shake
The stedfast globe of earth, as it for feare did quake.

24

The knight then lightly leaping to the pray,
  With mortall steele him smot againe so sore,
  That headlesse his unweldy bodie lay,
  All wallowd in his owne fowle bloudy gore,
  Which flowéd from his wounds in wondrous store.
  But soone as breath out of his breast did pas,
  That huge great body, which the Gyaunt bore,
  Was vanisht quite, and of that monstrous mas
Was nothing left, but like an emptie bladder was.

25

Whose grievous fall, when false Duessa spide,
  Her golden cup she cast unto the ground,
  And crownéd mitre rudely threw aside;
  Such percing griefe her stubborne hart did wound,
  That she could not endure that dolefull stound,° *sorrow*
  But leaving all behind her, fled away:
  The light-foot Squire her quickly turned around,
  And by hard meanes enforcing her to stay,
So brought unto his Lord, as his deservéd pray.

26

The royall Virgin, which beheld from farre,

In pensive plight, and sad perplexitie,
The whole atchievement° of this doubtfull warre, — *course*
Came running fast to greet his victorie,
With sober gladnesse, and myld modestie,
And with sweet joyous cheare him thus bespake;
"Faire braunch of noblesse, flowre of chevalrie,
That with your worth the world amazéd make,
How shall I quite° the paines, ye suffer for my sake? — *requite*

27

"And you [6] fresh bud of vertue springing fast,
Whom these sad eyes saw nigh unto deaths dore,
What hath poore Virgin for such perill past,
Wherewith you to reward? Accept therefore
My simple selfe, and service evermore;
And he that high does sit, and all things see
With equall° eyes, their merites to restore,° — *impartial/reward*
Behold what ye this day have done for mee,
And what I cannot quite, requite with usuree.° — *interest*

28

"But sith the heavens, and your faire handeling° — *conduct*
Have made you maister of the field this day,
Your fortune maister eke with governing,[7]
And well begun end all so well, I pray,
Ne let that wicked woman scape away;
For she it is, that did my Lord bethrall,
My dearest Lord, and deepe in dongeon lay,
Where he his better dayes hath wasted all.
O heare, how piteous he to you for ayd does call."

29

Forthwith he gave in charge unto his Squire,
That scarlot whore to keepen carefully;
Whiles he himselfe with greedie° great desire — *eager*
Into the Castle entred forcibly,
Where living creature none he did espye;
Then gan he lowdly through the house to call:
But no man cared to answere to his crye.
There raignd a solemne silence over all,
Nor voice was heard, nor wight was seene in bowre or hall.

30

At last with creeping crooked pace forth came
An old old man, with beard as white as snow,
That on a staffe his feeble steps did frame,° — *support*
And guide his wearie gate both too and fro:
For his eye sight him failéd long ygo,
And on his arme a bounch of keyes he bore,
The which unuséd rust did overgrow:
Those were the keyes of every inner dore,
But he could not them use, but kept them still in store.

6. I.e., the Squire. Una's reward to the Squire who has done such faithful service in the war against Pride is itself an exemplary act of humility.

7. Secure your good fortune also by prudent management.

31

But very uncouth sight was to behold,
How he did fashion his untoward° pace, *awkward*
For as he forward mooved his footing old,
So backward still was turned his wrincled face,
Unlike to men, who ever as they trace,° *walk*
Both feet and face one way are wont to lead.
This was the auncient keeper of that place,
And foster father of the Gyant dead;
His name Ignaro did his nature right aread.[8]

32

His reverend haires and holy gravitie
The knight much honord, as beseeméd well,[1]
And gently askt, where all the people bee,
Which in that stately building wont to dwell.
Who answerd him full soft, he could not tell.
Againe he askt, where that same knight was layd,
Whom great Orgoglio with his puissaunce fell
Had made his caytive thrall; againe he sayde,
He could not tell: ne ever other answere made.

33

Then askéd he, which way he in might pas:
He could not tell, againe he answeréd.
Thereat the curteous knight displeaséd was,
And said, "Old sire, it seemes thou hast not red ° *recognized*
How ill it sits with [2] that same silver hed
In vaine to mocke, or mockt in vaine to bee:
But if thou be, as thou art pourtrahéd
With natures pen, in ages grave degree,[3]
Aread° in graver wise, what I demaund of thee." *answer*

34

His answere likewise was, he could not tell.
Whose sencelesse speach, and doted ignorance
When as the noble Prince had markéd well,
He ghest his nature by his countenance,
And calmd his wrath with goodly temperance.
Then to him stepping, from his arme did reach
Those keyes, and made himselfe free enterance.
Each dore he openéd without any breach;° *forcing*
There was no barre to stop, nor foe him to empeach.° *hinder*

35

There all within full rich arayd he found,
With royal arras° and resplendent gold. *tapestry*
And did with store of every thing abound,
That greatest Princes presence° might behold. *person*
But all the floore (too filthy to be told)
With bloud of guiltlesse babes, and innocents trew,
Which there were slaine, as sheepe out of the fold,

8. Make known. Doting ignorance ("Ignaro") is a fit servant for pride and the false church; he has his counterparts in Abessa and Corceca.

1. Seemed proper.

2. I.e., suits.

3. I.e., dignity.

Defiléd was, that dreadfull was to vew,
And sacred° ashes over it was strowéd new. *accursed*

36

And there beside of marble stone was built
An Altare, carved with cunning imagery,
On which true Christians bloud was often spilt,
And holy Martyrs often doen to dye,[4]
With cruell malice and strong tyranny:
Whose blessed sprites from underneath the stone
To God for vengeance cryde continually,[5]
And with great griefe were often heard to grone,
That hardest heart would bleede, to heare their piteous mone.

37

Through every rowme he sought, and every bowr,
But no where could he find that wofull thrall:
At last he came unto an yron doore,
That fast was lockt, but key found not at all
Emongst that bounch, to open it withall;
But in the same a little grate was pight,° *placed*
Through which he sent his voyce, and lowd did call
With all his powre, to weet, if living wight
Were houséd therewithin, whom he enlargen° might. *release*

38

Therewith an hollow, dreary, murmuring voyce
These piteous plaints and dolours did resound;
"O who is that, which brings me happy choyce° *chance*
Of death, that here lye dying every stound,° *moment*
Yet live perforce in balefull darkenesse bound?
For now three Moones have changéd thrice their hew,° *shape*
And have beene thrice hid underneath the ground,
Since I the heavens chearefull face did vew,
O welcome thou, that doest of death bring tydings trew."

39

Which when that Champion heard, with percing point
Of pitty deare° his hart was thrilléd sore, *extreme*
And trembling horrour ran through every joynt,
For ruth of gentle knight so fowle forlore:[6]
Which shaking off, he rent that yron dore,
With furious force, and indignation fell;° *fierce*
Where entred in, his foot could find no flore,
But all a deepe descent, as darke as hell,
That breathéd ever forth a filthie banefull smell.

40

But neither darkenesse fowle, nor filthy bands,
Nor noyous° smell his purpose could withhold, *noxious, harmful*
(Entire affection hateth nicer° hands) *too fastidious*

4. Put to death.
5. "And when he had opened the fifth seal, I saw under the altar the souls of them that were slain for the word of God, and for the testimony which they held: And they cried with a loud voice, saying, How long, O Lord, holy and true, dost thou not judge and avenge our blood on them that dwell on the earth?" (Revelation vi.9–10).
6. Foully deserted.

But that with constant zeale, and courage bold,
After long paines and labours manifold,
He found the meanes that Prisoner up to reare;
Whose feeble thighes, unhable to uphold
His pinéd° corse, him scarse to light could beare, *wasted*
A ruefull spectacle of deathe and ghastly drere.° *wretchedness*

41

His sad dull eyes deepe sunck in hollow pits,
Could not endure th' unwonted sunne to view;
His bare thin cheekes for want of better bits,° *food*
And empty sides deceivéd° of their dew, *cheated*
Could make a stony hart his hap to rew;
His rawbone armes, whose mighty brawnéd bowrs° *muscles*
Were wont to rive steele plates, and helmets hew,
Were cleane consumed, and all his vitall powres
Decayd, and all his flesh shronk up like withered flowres.

42

Whom when his Lady saw, to him she ran
With hasty joy: to see him made her glad,
And sad to view his visage pale and wan,
Who earst in flowres of freshest youth was clad.
Tho° when her well of teares she wasted had, *then*
She said, "Ah dearest Lord, what evill starre
On you hath fround, and pourd his influence bad,
That of your selfe ye thus berobbéd arre,
And this misseeming hew[7] your manly looks doth marre?

43

"But welcome now my Lord, in wele or woe,
Whose presence I have lackt to long a day;
And fie on Fortune mine avowéd foe,
Whose wrathfull wreakes° them selves do now alay. *punishments*
And for these wrongs shall treble penaunce pay
Of treble good: good growes of evils priefe."[8]
The chearelesse man, whom sorrow did dismay,° *unnerve*
Had no delight to treaten° of his griefe; *speak*
His long enduréd famine needed more reliefe.

44

"Faire Lady," then said that victorious knight,[9]
"The things, that grievous were to do, or beare,
Them to renew,° I wote, breeds no delight; *recall*
Best musicke breeds delight in loathing eare:
But th'onely good, that growes of passéd feare,
Is to be wise, and ware° of like agein. *wary*
This dayes ensample hath this lesson deare
Deepe written in my heart with yron pen,
That blisse may not abide in state of mortall men.

45

"Henceforth sir knight, take to you wonted strength,
And maister these mishaps with patient might;

7. Unseemly shape.
8. Endurance of evil.
9. I.e., Arthur.

Loe where your foe lyes stretcht in monstrous length,
And loe that wicked woman in your sight,[10]
The roote of all your care, and wretched plight,
Now in your powre, to let her live, or dye."
"To do her dye," quoth Una, "were despight,° *spiteful*
And shame t'avenge so weake an enimy;
But spoile her of her scarlot robe, and let her fly."

46

So as she bad, that witch they disaraid,
And robd of royall robes, and purple pall,
And ornaments that richly were displaid;
Ne sparéd they to strip her naked all.
Then when they had despoild her tire° and call,° *robe/headdress*
Such as she was, their eyes might her behold,
That her misshapéd parts did them appall,
A loathly, wrinckled hag, ill favoured, old,
Whose secret filth good manners biddeth not be told.

47

Her craftie head was altogether bald,
And as in hate of honorable eld,° *age*
Was overgrowne with scurfe and filthy scald;° *scabs*
Her teeth out of her rotten gummes were feld,° *fallen*
And her sowre breath abhominably smeld;
Her dried dugs, like bladders lacking wind,
Hong downe, and filthy matter from them weld;
Her wrizled skin as rough, as maple rind,
So scabby was, that would have loathd all womankind.

48

Her neather parts, the shame of all her kind,[1]
My chaster Muse for shame doth blush to write;
But at her rompe she growing had behind
A foxes taile, with dong all fowly dight;° *covered*
And eke her feete most monstrous were in sight;
For one of them was like an Eagles claw,
With griping talaunts armd to greedy fight,
The other like a Beares uneven° paw: *rough*
More ugly shape yet never living creature saw.[2]

49

Which when the knights beheld, amazd they were,
And wondred at so fowle deforméd wight.
"Such then," said Una, "as she seemeth here,
Such is the face of falshood, such the sight
Of fowle Duessa, when her borrowed light
Is laid away, and counterfesaunce° knowne." *disguise*
Thus when they had the witch disrobéd quight,
And all her filthy feature° open showne, *form*
They let her goe at will, and wander wayes unknowne.

10. Over there.
1. I.e., womankind.
2. Cf. Duessa with the House of Pride: fair above, foul below. Her filthiness is like that of Alcina in Ariosto's *Orlando Furioso,* VII.71–73. Cf. also Revelation xvii.16: "these shall hate the whore, and shall make her desolate and naked." Foxes (cf. line 427) were noted for cunning; eagles and bears (lines 429, 431) for rapacity, cruelty, and brutality.

50

She flying fast from heavens hated face,
  And from the world that her discovered wide,
  Fled to the wastfull wildernesse apace,
  From living eyes her open shame to hide,
  And lurkt in rocks and caves long unespide.
  But that faire crew of knights, and Una faire
  Did in that castle afterwards abide,
  To rest them selves, and weary powres repaire,
Where store they found of all, that dainty was and rare.

Canto IX

His loves and lignage Arthur tells:
The knights knit friendly bands:
Sir Trevisan flies from Despayre,
Whom Redcrosse knight withstands.

1

O goodly golden chaine,[3] wherewith yfere° *together*
  The vertues linkéd are in lovely wize:
  And noble minds of yore allyéd were,
  In brave poursuit of chevalrous emprize,° *adventure*
  That none did others safety despize,
  Nor aid envy° to him, in need that stands, *begrudge*
  But friendly each did others prayse devize
  How to advaunce with favourable hands,
As this good Prince redeemd the Redcrosse knight from bands.° *bonds*

2

Who when their powres, empaird through labour long,
  With dew repast they had recuréd° well, *restored*
  And that weake captive wight now wexéd strong,
  Them list no lenger there at leasure dwell,
  But forward fare, as their adventures fell,
  But ere they parted, Una faire besought
  That straunger knight his name and nation tell;
  Least so great good, as he for her had wrought,
Should die unknown, and buried be in thanklesse thought.

3

"Faire virgin," said the Prince, "ye me require
  A thing without the compas[4] of my wit:
  For both the lignage and the certain Sire,
  From which I sprong, from me are hidden yit.
  For all so soone as life did me admit
  Into this world, and shewéd heavens light,
  From mothers pap I taken was unfit:° *unsuitably*
  And streight delivered to a Faery knight,
To be upbrought in gentle thewes° and martiall might. *manners*

3. Stanza 1 opens with an invocation of the golden chain of love or concord which binds the world and the human race together (cf. v.25 and note). It will be reaffirmed in stanza 19 when the two knights exchange symbolic gifts and shake hands in token of fellowship.

4. I.e., beyond the reach of.

4

"Unto old Timon[5] he me brought bylive,° *immediately*
Old Timon, who in youthly yeares hath beene
In warlike feates th'expertest man alive,
And is the wisest now on earth I weene;
His dwelling is low in a valley greene,
Under the foot of Rauran mossy hore,° *gray*
From whence the river Dee as silver cleene° *pure*
His tombling billowes rolls with gentle rore:[6]
There all my dayes he traind me up in vertuous lore.

5

"Thither the great Magicien Merlin came,
As was his use, ofttimes to visit me:
For he had charge my discipline to frame,
And Tutours nouriture° to oversee. *training*
Him oft and oft I askt in privitie,
Of what loines and what lignage I did spring:
Whose aunswere bad me still assuréd bee,
That I was sonne and heire unto a king,
As time in her just terme[7] the truth to light should bring."

6

"Well worthy impe,"° said then the Lady gent,° *offspring/gentle*
"And Pupill fit for such a Tutours hand.
But what adventure, or what high intent
Hath brought you hither into Faery land,
Aread° Prince Arthur, crowne of Martiall band?" *declare*
"Full hard it is," quoth he, "to read° aright *discern*
The course of heavenly cause, or understand
The secret meaning of th'eternall might,
That rules mens wayes, and rules the thoughts of living wight.

7

"For whither he through fatall° deepe foresight *prophetic*
Me hither sent, for cause to me unghest,
Or that fresh bleeding wound, which day and night
Whilome° doth rancle in my riven brest, *incessantly*
With forcéd fury following his° behest, *its*
Me hither brought by wayes yet never found,
You to have helpt I hold my selfe yet blest."
"Ah curteous knight," quoth she, "what secret wound
Could ever find,° to grieve the gentlest hart on ground?" *succeed*

8

"Deare Dame," quoth he, "you sleeping sparkes awake,
Which trubled once, into huge flames will grow,
Ne ever will their fervent fury slake
Till living moysture into smoke do flow,
And wasted° life do lye in ashes low. *consumed*
Yet sithens° silence lesseneth not my fire, *since*

5. The name means "Honor."
6. The hill Rauran is in Wales; the river Dee also flows in, and forms part of the boundary of Wales. The Tudors (Queen Elizabeth's family) were originally Welsh, and the legends of Arthur had their beginnings in the Celtic mythology of early Wales.
7. Due course.

But told it flames, and hidden it does glow,
I will revele, what ye so much desire:
Ah Love, lay downe thy bow, the whiles I may respire.° *breathe*

9

"It was in freshest flowre of youthly yeares,
When courage first does creepe in manly chest,
Then first the coale of kindly° heat appeares *of nature*
To kindle love in every living brest;
But me had warnd old Timons wise behest,
Those creeping flames by reason to subdew,
Before their rage grew to so great unrest,
As miserable lovers use to rew,
Which still wex old in woe, whiles woe still wexeth new.

10

"That idle name of love, and lovers life,
As losse of time, and vertues enimy
I ever scornd, and joyd to stirre up strife,
In middest of their mournfull Tragedy,
Ay wont to laugh, when them I heard to cry,
And blow the fire, which them to ashes brent:° *burned*
Their God himselfe, grieved at my libertie,
Shot many a dart at me with fiers intent,
But I them warded all with wary government.[8]

11

"But all in vaine: no fort can be so strong,
Ne fleshly brest can armèd be so sound,
But will at last be wonne with battrie° long, *siege*
Or unawares at disavantage found;
Nothing is sure, that growes on earthly ground:
And who most trustes in arme of fleshly might,
And boasts, in beauties chaine not to be bound,
Doth soonest fall in disaventrous° fight. *disastrous*
And yeeldes his caytive neck to victours most° despight. *greatest*

12

"Ensample make of him your haplesse joy,
And of my selfe now mated,° as ye see; *overcome*
Whose prouder° vaunt that proud avenging boy *too proud*
Did soone pluck downe, and curbd my libertie.
For on a day prickt° forth with jollitie *rode*
Of looser life, and heat of hardiment,° *boldness*
Raunging the forest wide on courser free,
The fields, the floods, the heavens with one consent
Did seeme to laugh° on me, and favour mine intent. *smile*

13

"For-wearied with my sports, I did alight
From loftie steed, and downe to sleepe me layd;
The verdant gras my couch did goodly dight,° *make*
And pillow was my helmet faire displayd:

8. I.e., self-control. The descriptions here of Cupid's archery and of the siege of the castle of chastity (in the next stanza) have many echoes from the courtly-love traditions.

Whiles every sence the humour sweet embayd,° *pervaded*
And slombring soft my hart did steale away,
Me seeméd, by my side a royall Mayd
Her daintie limbes full softly down did lay:
So faire a creature yet saw never sunny day.

14

"Most goodly glee° and lovely blandishment° *pleasure/compliment*
She to me made, and bad me love here deare,
For dearely sure her love was to me bent,
As when just time expiréd[9] should appeare.
But whether dreames delude, or true it were,
Was never hart so ravisht with delight,
Ne living man like words did ever heare,
As she to me delivered all that night;
And at her parting said, She Queene of Faeries hight.[1]

15

"When I awoke, and found her place devoyd,° *empty*
And nought but presséd gras, where she had lyen,
I sorrowed all so much, as earst I joyd,
And washéd all her place with watry eyen.
From that day forth I loved that face divine;
From that day forth I cast in carefull mind,
To seeke her out with labour, and long tyne,° *hardship*
And never vow to rest, till her I find,
Nine monethes I seeke in vaine yet ni'll° that vow unbind." *will not*

16

Thus as he spake, his visage wexéd pale,
And chaunge of hew great passion did bewray;° *reveal*
Yet still he strove to cloke his inward bale,° *grief*
And hide the smoke, that did his fire display,
Till gentle Una thus to him gan say;
"Oh happy Queene of Faeries, that hast found
Mongst many, one that with his prowesse may
Defend thine honour, and thy foes confound:
True Loves are often sown, but seldom grow on ground."

17

"Thine, O then," said the gentle Redcrosse knight,
"Next to that Ladies love, shalbe the place,
O fairest virgin, full of heavenly light,
Whose wondrous faith, exceeding earthly race,
Was firmest fixt in mine extremest case.
And you, my Lord, the Patrone° of my life, *protector*
Of that great Queene may well gaine worthy grace:
For onely worthy you through prowes priefe[2]
Yf living man mote worthy be, to be her liefe."° *love*

9. A fitting length of time having passed.
1. Was called. Gloriana is also, in the two principal allegories, Queen Elizabeth and Heavenly Grace. This is one of the passages where the "faery" nature of *The Faerie Queene* makes itself strongly felt. In the background are many folk-tales and ballads of a hero bewitched by the Queen of Faery. Note further the complex layering, by which Arthur, who is a character in Faery, has entered this world through a vision in a dream.
2. Demonstration of prowess.

18

So diversly discoursing of their loves,
The golden Sunne his glistring head gan shew,
And sad remembraunce now the Prince amoves,
With fresh desire his voyage to pursew:
Als° Una earnd° her traveill to renew. *so/yearned*
Then those two knights, fast friendship for to bynd,
And love establish each to other trew,
Gave goodly gifts, the signes of gratefull mynd,
And eke as pledges firme, right hands together joynd.

19

Prince Arthur gave a boxe of Diamond sure,° *flawless*
Embowd° with gold and gorgeous ornament, *bound*
Wherein were closd few drops of liquor pure,
Of wondrous worth, and vertue excellent,
That any wound could heale incontinent:° *immediately*
Which to requite, the Redcrosse knight him gave
A booke, wherein his Saveours testament
Was writ with golden letters rich and brave;
A worke of wondrous grace, and able soules to save.[3]

20

Thus beene they parted, Arthur on his way
To seeke his love, and th'other for to fight
With Unas foe, that all her realme did pray.° *prey upon*
But she now weighing the decayéd plight,
And shrunken synewes of her chosen knight,
Would not a while her forward course pursew,
Ne bring him forth in face of dreadfull fight,
Till he recovered had his former hew:
For him to be yet weake and wearie well she knew.

21

So as they traveild, lo they gan espy
An arméd knight towards them gallop fast,
That seeméd from some fearéd foe to fly,
Or other griesly thing, that him agast.° *scared*
Still as he fled, his eye was backward cast,
As if his feare still followed him behind;
Als flew his steed, as he his bands had brast,
And with his wingéd heeles did tread the wind,
As he had beene a fole of Pegasus his kind.[4]

22

Nigh as he drew, they might perceive his head
To be unarmd, and curld uncombéd heares
Upstaring° stiffe, dismayd with uncouth dread; *bristling*
Nor drop of bloud in all his face appeares
Nor life in limbe: and to increase his feares,
In fowle reproch° of knighthoods faire degree,° *disgrace/position*
About his neck an hempen rope he weares,

3. Medieval romances mention such healing balms, but here the "drops of liquor pure" probably represent the Eucharist; Redcrosse gives Arthur the New Testament.

4. I.e., like Pegasus (a flying horse).

That with his glistring armes does ill agree;[5]
But he of rope or armes has now no memoree.

23

The Redcrosse knight toward him crosséd fast,
To weet, what mister° wight was so dismayd: *kind of*
There him he finds all sencelesse and aghast,
That of him selfe he seemd to be afrayd;
Whom hardly he from flying forward stayd,
Till he these wordes to him deliver might;
"Sir knight, aread who hath ye thus arayd,
And eke from whom make ye this hasty flight:
For never knight I saw in such misseeming° plight." *unseemly*

24

He answerd nought at all, but adding new
Feare to his first amazment, staring wide
With stony eyes, and hartlesse hollow hew,
Astonisht stood, as one that had aspide
Infernall furies, with their chaines untide.
Him yet againe, and yet againe bespake
The gentle knight; who nought to him replide,
But trembling every joynt did inly quake,
And foltring tongue at last these words seemd forth to shake.

25

"For Gods deare love, Sir knight, do me not stay;
For loe he comes, he comes fast after mee."
Eft° looking backe would faine have runne away; *again*
But he him forst to stay, and tellen free
The secret cause of his perplexitie:
Yet nathemore° by his bold hartie speach, *not at all*
Could his bloud-frosen hart emboldned bee,
But through his boldnesse rather feare did reach,
Yet forst, at last he made through silence suddein breach.

26

"And am I now in safetie sure," quoth he,
"From him, that would have forcéd me to dye?
And is the point of death now turnd fro mee,
That I may tell this haplesse history?"
"Feare nought:" quoth he, "no daunger now is nye."
"Then shall I you recount a ruefull cace,"
Said he, "the which with this unlucky eye
I late beheld, and had not greater grace
Me reft from it, had bene partaker of the place.[6]

27

"I lately chaunst (Would I had never chaunst)
With a faire knight to keepen companee,
Sir Terwin hight, that well himselfe advaunst
In all affaires, and was both bold and free,
But not so happie as mote happie bee:
He loved, as was his lot, a Ladie gent,° *noble*

5. The rope around his neck suggests attempts (past and future) at suicide—the reason for which becomes clear a few stanzas later.

6. I.e., shared the same fate.

That him againe° loved in the least degree: *in return*
For she was proud, and of too high intent,° *ambition*
And joyd to see her lover languish and lament.

28

"From whom returning sad and comfortlesse,
As on the way together we did fare,
We met that villen (God from him me blesse°) *defend*
That curséd wight, from whom I scapt why leare,° *recently*
A man of hell, that cals himselfe Despaire;[1]
Who first us greets, and after faire areedes° *tells*
Of tydings strange, and of adventures rare:
So creeping close, as Snake in hidden weedes,
Inquireth of our states, and of our knightly deedes.

29

"Which when he knew, and felt our feeble harts
Embost° with bale,° and bitter byting griefe, *exhausted/sorrow*
Which love had launchéd with his deadly darts,
With wounding words and termes of foule repriefe° *insult*
He pluckt from us all hope of due reliefe,
That earst us held in love of lingring life;
Then hopelesse hartlesse, gan the cunning thiefe
Perswade us die, to stint° all further strife: *end*
To me he lent this rope, to him a rustie knife.

30

"With which sad instrument of hastie death,
That wofull lover, loathing lenger° light, *longer*
A wide way made to let forth living breath.
But I more fearefull, or more luckie wight,
Dismayd with that deforméd dismall sight,
Fled fast away, halfe dead with dying feare:[2]
Ne yet assured of life by you, Sir knight,
Whose like infirmitie like chaunce may beare:
But God you never let his charméd speeches heare."

31

"How may a man," said he, "with idle speach
Be wonne, to spoyle° the Castle of his health?" *destroy*
"I wote," quoth he, "whom triall° late did teach, *experience*
That like would not[3] for all this worldes wealth:
His subtill tongue, like dropping honny, mealt'th° *melts*
Into the hart, and searcheth every vaine,
That ere one be aware, by secret stealth
His powre is reft, and weaknesse doth remaine.
O never Sir desire to try° his guilefull traine." *test*

32

"Certes,"° said he, "hence shall I never rest, *surely*

1. Redcrosse has hitherto been the victim of pride and rashness; here, another spiritual vice, directly contrary, is met—the temptation to the ultimate Christian sin, the despair of God's grace. Such despair was a concern to Renaissance writers of religious and medical works. Robert Burton, in his *Anatomy of Melancholy* (1621), wrote that the despair "which concerns God * * * [is] opposite to hope, and a most pernicious sin * * * The part affected is the whole soul" ("Religious Melancholy," II.i.2).

2. Fear of death.

3. I.e., would not do the like again.

Till I that treachours art have heard and tride;
And you Sir knight, whose name mote° I request, *might*
Of grace do me unto his cabin guide."
"I that hight Trevisan," quoth he, "will ride
Against my liking backe, to doe you grace:
But nor for gold nor glee° will I abide *glitter*
By you, when ye arrive in that same place;
For lever° had I die, then see his deadly face." *rather*

33

Ere long they come, where that same wicked wight
His dwelling has, low in an hollow cave,
Farre underneath a craggie clift ypight,° *placed*
Darke, dolefull, drearie, like a greedie grave,
That still for carrion carcases doth crave:
On top whereof aye dwelt the ghastly Owle,
Shrieking his balefull note, which ever drave
Farre from that haunt all other chearefull fowle;
And all about it wandring ghostes did waile and howle.

34

And all about old stockes and stubs of trees,
Whereon nor fruit, nor leafe was ever seene,
Did hang upon the ragged rocky knees;° *crags*
On which had many wretches hangéd beene,
Whose carcases were scattered on the greene,
And throwne about the cliffs. Arrivéd there,
That bare-head knight for dread and dolefull teene,° *grief*
Would faine have fled, ne durst approachen neare,
But th'other forst him stay, and comforted in feare.

35

That darkesome cave they enter, where they find
That curséd man, low sitting on the ground,
Musing full sadly in his sullein mind;
His griesie° lockes, long growen, and unbound, *gray*
Disordred hong about his shoulders round,
And hid his face; through which his hollow eyne
Lookt deadly dull, and staréd as astound;
His raw-bone cheekes through penurie and pine,° *starvation*
Were shronke into his jawes, as° he did never dine. *as if*

36

His garment nought but many ragged clouts,° *cloths*
With thornes together pind and patchéd was,
The which his naked sides he wrapt abouts;
And him beside there lay upon the gras
A drearie corse, whose life away did pas,
All wallowd in his owne yet luke-warme blood,
That from his wound yet welléd fresh alas;
In which a rustie knife fast fixéd stood,
And made an open passage for the gushing flood.

37

Which piteous spectacle, approving° trew *confirming*
The wofull tale that Trevisan had told,

When as the gentle Redcrosse knight did vew,
With firie zeale he burnt in courage bold,
Him to avenge, before his bloud were cold,
And to the villein said, "Thou damnéd wight,
The author of this fact,° we here behold, *deed*
What justice can but judge against thee right,
With thine owne bloud to price° his bloud, here shed in sight?" *pay for*

38

"What franticke fit," quoth he,[4] "hath thus distraught
Thee, foolish man, so rash a doome° to give? *judgment*
What justice ever other judgement taught,
But he should die, who merites not to live?
None else to death this man despayring drive,° *drove*
But his owne guiltie mind deserving death.
Is then unjust to each his due to give?
Or let him die, that loatheth living breath?
Or let him die at ease, that liveth here uneath°? *uneasily*

39

"Who travels by the wearie wandring way,
To come unto his wishéd home in haste,
And meetes a flood, that doth his passage stay,
Is not great grace to helpe him over past,
Or free his feet, that in the myre sticke fast?
Most envious man, that grieves at neighbours good,
And fond,° that joyest in the woe thou hast, *foolish*
Why wilt not let him passe, that long hath stood
Upon the banke, yet wilt thy selfe not passe the flood?

40

"He there does now enjoy eternall rest
And happie ease, which thou doest want and crave,
And further from it daily wanderest:
What if some litle paine the passage have,
That makes fraile flesh to feare the bitter wave?
Is not short paine well borne, that brings long ease,
And layes the soule to sleepe in quiet grave?
Sleepe after toyle, port after stormie seas,
Ease after warre, death after life does greatly please."[1]

41

The knight much wondred at his suddeine° wit, *quick*
And said, "The terme of life is limited,
Ne may a man prolong, nor shorten it;
The souldier may not move from watchfull sted,° *position*
Nor leave his stand, untill his Captaine bed."° *commands*
"Who life did limit by almightie doome,"
Quoth he,[2] "knowes best the termes establishéd;
And he, that points the Centonell his roome,° *station*
Doth license him depart at sound of morning droome.

4. I.e., Despaire.

1. Despaire's arguments on behalf of suicide as against a painful life are derived, like those of Hamlet in his third soliloquy (*Hamlet* III.i.56–88), principally from Seneca, Marcus Aurelius, and the ancient stoics, and from Old Testament utterings on divine justice.

2. I.e., Despaire.

42

"Is not his deed, what ever thing is donne,
In heaven and earth? did not he all create
To die againe? all ends that was begonne.
Their times in his eternall booke of fate
Are written sure, and have their certaine date.
Who then can strive with strong necessitie,
That holds the world in his° still chaunging state, *its*
Or shunne the death ordaynd by destinie?
When houre of death is come, let none aske whence, nor why.

43

"The lenger life, I wote° the greater sin, *know*
The greater sin, the greater punishment:
All those great battels, which thou boasts to win,
Through strife, and bloud-shed, and avengement,
Now praysd, hereafter deare° thou shalt repent: *bitterly*
For life must life, and bloud must bloud repay.
Is not enough thy evill life forespent?
For he, that once hath misséd the right way,
The further he doth goe, the further he doth stray.

44

"Then do no further goe, no further stray,
But here lie downe, and to thy rest betake,
Th'ill to prevent, that life ensewen may.[3]
For what hath life, that may it lovéd make,
And gives not rather cause it to forsake?
Feare, sicknesse, age, losse, labour, sorrow, strife,
Paine, hunger, cold, that makes the hart to quake;
And ever fickle fortune rageth rife,
All which, and thousands mo° do make a loathsome life. *more*

45

"Thou wretched man, of death hast greatest need,
If in true ballance thou wilt weigh thy state:
For never knight, that daréd warlike deede,
More lucklesse disaventures did amate:° *appall*
Witnesse the dongeon deepe, wherein of late
Thy life shut up, for death so oft did call;
And though good lucke prolongéd hath thy date,° *span of life*
Yet death then, would the like mishaps forestall,
Into the which hereafter thou maiest happen fall.

46

"Why then doest thou, O man of sin, desire
To draw thy dayes forth to their last degree?
Is not the measure of thy sinfull hire[4]
High heapéd up with huge iniquitie,
Against the day of wrath,[5] to burden thee?
Is not enough that to this Ladie milde
Thou falséd hast thy faith with perjurie,
And sold thy selfe to serve Duessa vilde,° *vile*
With whom in all abuse thou hast thy selfe defilde?

3. I.e., to prevent the evil that will ensue in the rest of your life.
4. Service to sin.
5. Judgment Day.

47

"Is not he just, that all this doth behold
From highest heaven, and beares an equall° eye? *impartial*
Shall he thy sins up in his knowledge fold,
And guiltie be of thine impietie?
Is not his law, Let every sinner die:
Die shall all flesh? what then must needs be donne,
Is it not better to doe willinglie,
Then linger, till the glasse be all out ronne?
Death is the end of woes: die soone, O faeries sonne."

48

The knight was much enmovéd with his speach,
That as a swords point through his hart did perse,
And in his conscience made a secret breach,
Well knowing true all, that he did reherse° *recount*
And to his fresh remembrance did reverse° *bring back*
The ugly vew of his deforméd crimes,
That all his manly powres it did disperse,
As he were charméd with inchaunted rimes,
That oftentimes he quakt, and fainted oftentimes.

49

In which amazement, when the Miscreant
Perceivéd him to waver weake and fraile,
Whiles trembling horror did his conscience dant,° *daunt*
And hellish anguish did his soule assaile,
To drive him to despaire, and quite to quaile,° *be dismayed*
He shewed him painted in a table° plaine, *picture*
The damnéd ghosts, that doe in torments waile,
And thousand feends that doe them endlesse paine
With fire and brimstone, which for ever shall remaine.

50

The sight whereof so throughly him dismaid,
That nought but death before his eyes he saw,
And ever burning wrath before him laid,
By righteous sentence of th'Almighties law:
Then gan the villein him to overcraw,° *exult over*
And brought unto him swords, ropes, poison, fire,
And all that might him to perdition draw;
And bad him choose, what death he would desire:
For death was due to him, that had provokt Gods ire.

51

But when as none of them he saw him take,
He to him raught° a dagger sharpe and keene, *reached*
And gave it him in hand: his hand did quake,
And tremble like a leafe of Aspin greene,
And troubled bloud through his pale face was seene
To come, and goe with tydings from the hart,
As it a running messenger had beene.
At last resolved to worke his finall smart,
He lifted up his hand, that backe againe did start.

52

Which when as Una saw, through every vaine
  The crudled° cold ran to her well of life,° *congealing/heart*
  As in a swowne: but soone relived° againe, *revived*
  Out of his hand she snatcht the curséd knife,
  And threw it to the ground, enragéd rife,° *deeply*
  And to him said, "Fie, fie, faint harted knight,
  What meanest thou by this reprochfull strife?
  Is this the battell, which thou vauntst to fight
With the fire-mouthéd Dragon, horrible and bright?

53

"Come, come away, fraile, feeble, fleshly wight,
  Ne let vaine words bewitch thy manly hart,
  Ne divelish thoughts dismay thy constant spright.
  In heavenly mercies hast thou not a part?
  Why shouldst thou then despeire, that chosen art?
  Where justice growes, there grows eke greater grace,
  The which doth quench the brond of hellish smart,
  And that accurst hand-writing doth deface.° *blot out*
Arise, Sir knight arise, and leave this curséd place."[6]

54

So up he rose, and thence amounted streight.
  Which when the carle° beheld, and saw his guest *churl*
  Would safe depart, for all his subtill sleight,
  He chose an halter from among the rest,
  And with it hung himselfe, unbid° unblest. *unprayed for*
  But death he could not worke himselfe thereby;
  For thousand times he so himselfe had drest,° *made ready*
  Yet nathelesse it could not doe him die,
Till he should die his last, that is eternally.

Canto X

Her faithfull knight faire Una brings
  to house of Holinesse,
Where he is taught repentance, and
  the way to heavenly blesse.° *bliss*

1

What man is he, that boasts of fleshly might,
  And vaine assurance of mortality,° *mortal life*
  Which all so soone, as it doth come to fight,
  Against spirituall foes, yeelds by and by,[1]
  Or from the field most cowardly doth fly?
  Ne let the man ascribe it to his skill,
  That thorough grace hath gainéd victory.
  If any strength we have, it is to ill,

6. Una reminds Redcrosse of God's mercy, the "greater grace" conspicuously missing from Despaire's eloquent speeches.

1. Immediately.

But all the good is Gods, both power and eke will.[2]

2

By that, which lately hapned, Una saw,
That this her knight was feeble, and too faint;
And all his sinews woxen weake and raw,° *unready*
Through long enprisonment, and hard constraint,
Which he enduréd in his late restraint,
That yet he was unfit for bloudie fight:
Therefore to cherish him with diets daint,° *dainty*
She cast to bring him, where he chearen° might, *be cheered*
Till he recovered had his[3] late decayéd plight.

3

There was an auntient house not farre away,
Renowmd throughout the world for sacred lore,
And pure unspotted life: so well they say
It governd was, and guided evermore,
Through wisedome of a matrone grave and hore;° *gray-haired*
Whose onely joy was to relieve the needes
Of wretched soules, and helpe the helpelesse pore:
All night she spent in bidding of her bedes,[4]
And all the day in doing good and godly deedes.

4

Dame Caelia[5] men did her call, as thought
From heaven to come, or thither to arise,
The mother of three daughters, well upbrought
In goodly thewes,° and godly exercise: *habits*
The eldest two most sober, chast, and wise,
Fidelia and Speranza virgins were,
Though spousd,° yet wanting wedlocks solemnize; *bethrothed*
But faire Charissa to a lovely fere° *mate*
Was linckéd, and by him had many pledges dere.[6]

5

Arrivéd there, the dore they find fast lockt;
For it was warely watchéd night and day,
For feare of many foes: but when they knockt,
The Porter opened unto them streight way:
He was an agéd syre, all hory gray,
With lookes full lowly cast, and gate full slow,
Wont on a staffe his feeble steps to stay,
Hight Humilta.° They passe in stouping low; *humility*
For streight and narrow was the way, which he did show.[7]

2. "For by grace are ye saved through faith; and that not of yourselves: it is the gift of God: Not of works, lest any men should boast" (Ephesians ii.8–9).

3. I.e., from his.

4. Saying prayers.

5. The name means "heavenly."

6. I.e., many children. The daughters' names mean "faith," "hope," and "charity." Cf. with them the three Saracens, Sans foy, Sans joy, and Sans loy: "faith" is the answer to atheism; "hope," the answer to empty despair; and "charity" (the highest law that embraces all other laws) the answer to chaos. "And now abideth faith, hope, charity, these three; but the greatest of these is charity" (I Corinthians xiii.13). Canto x, in which Spenser's didactic purpose is expressed with particular directness, is especially rich in scriptural references and echoes. Many aspects of the House of Holiness oppose their counterparts in the House of Pride (Canto iv).

7. "Strait is the gate, and narrow is the way, which leadeth unto life, and few there be that find it" (Matthew vii.14).

6

Each goodly thing is hardest to begin,
But entred in a spacious court they see,
Both plaine, and pleasant to be walkéd in,
Where them does meete a francklin° faire and free, *freeholder*
And entertaines with comely courteous glee,
His name was Zele, that him right well became,
For in his speeches and behaviour hee
Did labour lively to expresse the same,
And gladly did them guide, till to the Hall they came.

7

There fairely them receives a gentle Squire,
Of milde demeanure, and rare courtesie,
Right cleanly clad in comely sad° attire; *sober*
In word and deede that shewed great modestie,
And knew his good° to all of each degree, *proper respect*
Hight Reverence. He them with speeches meet
Does faire entreat; no courting nicetie,° *affectation*
But simple true, and eke unfainéd sweet,
As might become a Squire so great persons to greet.

8

And afterwards them to his Dame he leades,
That agéd Dame, the Ladie of the place:
Who all this while was busie at her beades:
Which doen, she up arose with seemely grace,
And toward them full matronely did pace.
Where when that fairest Una she beheld,
Whom well she knew to spring from heavenly race,
Her hart with joy unwonted inly sweld,
As feeling wondrous comfort in her weaker eld.° *older age*

9

And her embracing said, "O happie earth,
Whereon thy innocent feet doe ever tread,
Most vertuous virgin borne of heavenly berth,
That to redeeme thy woefull parents head,
From tyrans rage, and ever-dying dread,[8]
Hast wandred through the world now long a day;
Yet ceasest not thy wearie soles to lead,
What grace hath thee now hither brought this way?
Or doen thy feeble feet unweeting hither stray?

10

"Strange thing it is an errant° knight to see *wandering*
Here in this place, or any other wight,
That hither turnes his steps. So few there bee,
That chose the narrow path, or seeke the right:
All keepe the broad high way, and take delight
With many rather for to go astray,
And be partakers of their evill plight,
Then with a few to walke the rightest way;
O foolish men, why haste ye to your owne decay?"

8. Continuing fear of death.

11

"Thy selfe to see, and tyred limbs to rest,
O matrone sage," quoth she, "I hither came,
And this good knight his way with me addrest,
Led with thy prayses and broad-blazéd fame,
That up to heaven is blowne." The auncient Dame
Him goodly greeted in her modest guise,
And entertaynd them both, as best became,
With all the court'sies, that she could devise,
Ne wanted ought, to shew her bounteous or wise.

12

Thus as they gan of sundry things devise,° *talk*
Loe two most goodly virgins came in place,
Ylinkéd arme in arme in lovely° wise, *loving*
With countenance demure, and modest grace,
They numbred even steps and equall pace:
Of which the eldest, that Fidelia hight,
Like sunny beames threw from her Christall face,
That could have dazd the rash beholders sight,
And round about her head did shine like heavens light.

13

She was araiéd all in lilly white,
And in her right hand bore a cup of gold,
With wine and water fild up to the hight,
In which a Serpent did himselfe enfold,
That horrour made to all, that did behold;
But she no whit did chaunge her constant mood:[1]
And in her other hand she fast did hold
A booke, that was both signd and seald with blood,
Wherein darke things were writ, hard to be understood.[2]

14

Her younger sister, that Speranza hight,
Was clad in blew, that her beseemed well;
Not all so chearefull seeméd she of sight,[3]
As was her sister; whether dread did dwell,
Or anguish in her hart, is hard to tell:
Upon her arme a silver anchor[4] lay,
Whereon she leanéd ever, as befell:
And ever up to heaven, as she did pray,
Her stedfast eyes were bent, ne swarvéd other way.

15

They seeing Una, towards her gan wend,

1. Expression. The serpent in the cup is a symbol of St. John the Evangelist, whose faith was so great he could drink venom without harm. The symbolic details in these portraits appear also in the allegorical figures in other works of Renaissance literature and art—particularly the emblem books.
2. The New Testament. See II Peter iii.16: "in which are some things hard to be understood, which they that are unlearned and unstable wrest, as they do also the other scriptures, unto their own destruction." Peter says this of St. Paul's writings, but it could also be said of many other parts of the New Testament—which is "signed and sealed with [the] blood" of Christ and the martyrs.
3. In appearance.
4. The iconographic symbol of hope.

Who them encounters with like courtesie;
Many kind speeches they betwene them spend,
And greatly joy each other well to see:
Then to the knight with shamefast° modestie *humble*
They turne themselves, at Unas meeke request,
And him salute with well beseeming glee;
Who faire them quites,° as him beseeméd best, *returns the salute*
And goodly gan discourse of many a noble gest.° *achievement*

16

Then Una thus; "But she your sister deare;
The deare Charissa where is she become?
Or wants she health, or busie is elsewhere?"
"Ah no," said they, "but forth she may not come:
For she of late is lightned of her wombe,
And hath encreast the world with one sonne more,[5]
That her to see should be but troublesome."
"Indeede," quoth she, "that should her trouble sore,
But thankt be God, that her encrease so evermore."[5a]

17

Then said the aged Caelia, "Deare dame,
And you good Sir, I wote that of your toyle,
And labours long, through which ye hither came,
Ye both forwearied° be: therefore a whyle *tired out*
I read° you rest, and to your bowres recoyle."[6] *suggest*
Then calléd she a Groome, that forth him led
Into a goodly lodge, and gan despoile° *disrobe*
Of puissant armes, and laid in easie bed;
His name was meeke Obedience rightfully aréd.° *understood*

18

Now when their wearie limbes with kindly° rest, *natural*
And bodies were refresht with due repast,
Faire Una gan Fidelia faire request,
To have her knight into her schoolehouse plaste,
That of her heavenly learning he might taste,
And heare the wisedome of her words divine.
She graunted, and that knight so much agraste,° *favored*
That she him taught celestiall discipline,
And opened his dull eyes, that light mote in them shine.

19

And that her sacred Booke, with bloud[7] ywrit,
That none could read, except she did them teach,
She unto him discloséd every whit,
And heavenly documents° thereout did preach, *doctrines*
That weaker wit of man could never reach,
Of God, of grace, of justice, of free will,
That wonder was to heare her goodly speach:
For she was able, with her words to kill,
And raise againe to life the hart, that she did thrill.° *pierce*

5. Charity, the fruitful virtue, is often depicted pictorially as a mother with children.

5a. And may he keep on encreasing her in this way.

6. Retire to your rooms.

7. I.e., the blood of Christ.

20

And when she list poure out her larger spright,[8]
She would commaund the hastie Sunne to stay,
Or backward turne his course from heavens hight;
Sometimes great hostes of men she could dismay,
Dry-shod to passe, she parts the flouds in tway;
And eke huge mountaines from their native seat
She would commaund, themselves to beare away,
And throw in raging sea with roaring threat.
Almightie God her gave such powre, and puissance great.[9]

21

The faithfull knight now grew in litle space,
By hearing her, and by her sisters lore,
To such perfection of all heavenly grace,
That wretched world he gan for to abhore,
And mortall life gan loath, as thing forelore,° *abandoned*
Greeved with remembrance of his wicked wayes,
And prickt with anguish of his sinnes so sore,
That he desirde to end his wretched dayes:
So much the dart of sinfull guilt the soule dismayes.

22

But wise Speranza gave him comfort sweet,
And taught him how to take assuréd hold
Upon her silver anchor, as was meet;
Else had his sinnes so great, and manifold
Made him forget all that Fidelia told.
In this distresséd doubtfull agonie,
When him his dearest Una did behold,
Disdeining life, desiring leave to die,
She found her selfe assayld with great perplexitie.

23

And came to Caelia to declare her smart,
Who well acquainted with that commune plight,
Which sinfull horror[1] workes in wounded hart,
Her wisely comforted all that she might,
With goodly counsell and advisement right;
And streightway sent with carefull diligence,
To fetch a Leach,° the which had great insight *doctor*
In that disease of grievéd conscience,
And well could cure the same; His name was Patience.

24

Who comming to that soule-diseaséd knight,
Could hardly him intreat, to tell his griefe:
Which knowne, and all that noyd° his heavie spright *troubled*
Well searcht, eftsoones he gan apply reliefe
Of salves and med'cines, which had passing priefe,[2]

8. Full spiritual power.

9. Joshua made the sun stand still (Joshua x.12); Hezekiah made it turn backwards (II Kings xx.10); Gideon was victorious over the Midianites (Judges vii.7); Moses led the Israelites through the parted waters of the Red Sea (Exodus xiv.21–31); faith, said Christ, can move mountains (Matthew xxi.21). All these are miracles of faith.

1. Horror of sin.

2. Which had extraordinary power.

And thereto added words of wondrous might:[3]
By which to ease he him recuréd briefe,° *speedily*
And much asswaged the passion° of his plight, *suffering*
That he his paine endured, as seeming now more light.

25

But yet the cause and root of all his ill,
Inward corruption, and infected sin,
Not purged nor heald, behind remainéd still,
And festring sore did rankle yet within,
Close° creeping twixt the marrow and the skin. *secretly*
Which to extirpe,° he laid him privily *extirpate*
Downe in a darkesome lowly place farre in,
Whereas he meant his corrosives to apply,
And with streight° diet tame his stubborne malady. *strict*

26

In ashes and sackcloth he did array
His daintie corse, proud humors[4] to abate,
And dieted with fasting every day,
The swelling of his wounds to mitigate,
And made him pray both earely and eke late:
And ever as superfluous flesh did rot
Amendment readie still at hand did wayt,
To pluck it out with pincers firie whot,° *hot*
That soone in him was left no one corrupted jot.

27

And bitter Penance with an yron whip,
Was wont him once to disple° every day: *discipline*
And sharpe Remorse his hart did pricke and nip,
That drops of bloud thence like a well did play;
And sad Repentance used to embay° *bathe*
His bodie in salt water smarting sore,
The filthy blots of sinne to wash away.[5]
So in short space they did to health restore
The man that would not live, but earst° lay at deathes dore. *formerly*

28

In which his torment often was so great,
That like a Lyon he would cry and rore,
And rend his flesh, and his owne synewes eat.
His own deare Una hearing evermore
His ruefull shriekes and gronings, often tore
Her guiltlesse garments, and her golden heare,
For pitty of his paine and anguish sore;
Yet all with patience wisely she did beare;
For well she wist, his crime could else be never cleare.° *cleansed*

29

Whom thus recovered by wise Patience,
And trew Repentance they to Una brought:
Who joyous of his curéd conscience,
Him dearely kist, and fairely eke besought

3. I.e., absolution, or spiritual counseling generally.
4. Passions—i.e., pride.
5. "Wash me throughly from mine iniquity, and cleanse me from my sin" (Psalms li.2).

Himselfe to chearish,° and consuming thought *cheer*
To put away out of his carefull brest.
By this Charissa, late in child-bed brought,
Was woxen strong, and left her fruitfull nest;
To her faire Una brought this unacquainted guest.

30

She was a woman in her freshest age,
Of wondrous beauty, and of bountie° rare, *virtue*
With goodly grace and comely personage,
That was on earth not easie to compare;
Full of great love, but Cupids wanton snare
As hell she hated, chast in worke and will;
Her necke and breasts were ever open bare,
That ay thereof her babes might sucke their fill;
The rest was all in yellow robes arayéd still.[6]

31

A multitude of babes about her hong,
Playing their sports, that joyd her to behold,
Whom still she fed, whiles they were weake and young,
But thrust them forth still, as they wexéd old:
And on her head she wore a tyre° of gold, *headdress*
Adornd with gemmes and owches° wondrous faire, *jewels*
Whose passing° price uneath° was to be told; *surpassing/scarcely*
And by her side there sate a gentle paire
Of turtle doves, she sitting in an yvorie chaire.

32

The knight and Una entring, faire her greet,
And bid her joy of that her happie brood;
Who them requites with court'sies seeming meet,° *appropriate*
And entertaines with friendly chearefull mood.
Then Una her besought, to be so good,
As in her vertuous rules to schoole her knight,
Now after all his torment well withstood,
In that sad° house of Penaunce, where his spright *solemn*
Had past the paines of hell, and long enduring night.

33

She was right joyous of her just request,
And taking by the hand that Faeries sonne,
Gan him instruct in every good behest,
Of love, and righteousness, and well to donne,[7]
And wrath, and hatred warely to shonne,
That drew on men Gods hatred, and his wrath,
And many soules in dolours° had fordonne:° *misery/destroyed*
In which when him she well instructed hath,
From thence to heaven she teacheth him the ready path.

34

Wherein his weaker° wandring steps to guide, *too weak*
An auncient matrone she to her does call,

6. Her yellow (saffron) robe is the emblem of fruitfulness. That she is "chast in work and will" and hates "Cupids wanton snare" does not contradict her "multitude of babes"; Spenser is distinguishing between *eros* and *agape*, sexual love and Christian love.

7. I.e., right action.

Whose sober lookes her wisedome well descride:° *made known*
Her name was Mercie, well knowne over all,
To be both gratious, and eke liberall:
To whom the carefull charge of him she gave,
To lead aright, that he should never fall
In all his wayes through this wide worldés wave,° *expanse*
That Mercy in the end his righteous soule might save.

35

The godly Matrone by the hand him beares
Forth from her presence, by a narrow way,
Scattred with bushy thornes, and ragged breares,° *briers*
Which still before him she removed away,
That nothing might his ready passage stay:
And ever when his feet encombred were,
Or gan to shrinke, or from the right to stray,
She held him fast, and firmely did upbeare,
As carefull Nourse her child from falling oft does reare.

36

Eftsoones unto an holy Hospitall,° *retreat*
That was fore°by the way, she did him bring, *close*
In which seven Bead-men[8] that had vowéd all
Their life to service of high heavens king
Did spend their dayes in doing godly thing:
Their gates to all were open evermore,
That by the wearie way were traveiling,
And one sate wayting ever them before,
To call in commers-by, that needy were and pore.

37

The first of them that eldest was, and best,° *chief*
Of all the house had charge and governement,
As Guardian and Steward of the rest:
His office was to give entertainement
And lodging, unto all that came, and went:
Not unto such, as could him feast againe,
And double quite,° for that he on them spent, *repay*
But such, as want of harbour° did constraine: *shelter*
Those for Gods sake his dewty was to entertaine.

38

The second was as Almner° of the place, *almoner*
His office was, the hungry for to feed,
And thristy give to drinke, a worke of grace:
He feard not once him selfe to be in need,
Ne cared to hoord for those, whom he did breede:[9]
The grace of God he layd up still in store,
Which as a stocke° he left unto his seede; *resource*
He had enough, what need him care for more?
And had he lesse, yet some he would give to the pore.

39

The third had of their wardrobe custodie,
In which were not rich tyres,° nor garments gay, *robes*

8. Men of prayer.

9. I.e., his children.

The plumes of pride, and wings of vanitie,
But clothes meet to keepe keene could° away, *cold*
And naked nature seemely to aray;
With which bare wretched wights he dayly clad,
The images of God in earthly clay;
And if that no spare clothes to give he had,
His owne coate he would cut, and it distribute glad.

40

The fourth appointed by his office was,
Poore prisoners to relieve with gratious ayd,
And captives to redeeme with price of bras,° *money*
From Turkes and Sarazins, which them had stayd;° *held captive*
And though they faultie were, yet well he wayd,
That God to us forgiveth every howre
Much more then that, why° they in bands were layd, *for which*
And he that harrowd hell[1] with heavie stowre,° *encounter*
The faultie soules from thence brought to his heavenly bowre.

41

The fift had charge sicke persons to attend,
And comfort those, in point of death which lay;
For them most needeth comfort in the end,
When sin, and hell, and death do most dismay
The feeble soule departing hence away.
All is but lost, that living we bestow,° *store up*
If not well ended at our dying day.
O man have mind of that last bitter throw;° *throe*
For as the tree does fall, so lyes it ever low.

42

The sixt had charge of them now being dead,
In seemely sort their courses to engrave,° *bodies to bury*
And deck with dainty flowres their bridall bed,
That to their heavenly spouse both sweet and brave° *fair*
They might appeare, when he their soules shall save.
The wondrous workemanship of Gods owne mould,° *image*
Whose face he made, all beasts to feare, and gave
All in his hand, even dead we honour should.
Ah dearest God me graunt, I dead be not defould.° *abused*

43

The seventh now after death and buriall done,
Had charge the tender Orphans of the dead
And widowes ayd, least they should be undone:
In face of judgement[2] he their right would plead,
Ne ought the powre of mighty men did dread
In their defence, nor would for gold or fee
Be wonne their rightfull causes downe to tread:
And when they stood in most necessitee,
He did supply their want, and gave them ever free.[3] *freely*

1. I.e., Christ, who journeyed to hell to deliver those good people who lived before his time, according to a popular story in the Middle Ages. It originated in the apocryphal gospel of Nicodemus.
2. I.e., in court.
3. Always freely. The seven Bead-men here correspond to, and perform, the seven works of charity, or corporal mercy: lodging the homeless, feeding the hungry, clothing the naked, redeeming the captive, comforting the sick, honoring the dead, and succoring the orphan.

44

There when the Elfin knight arrivéd was,
The first and chiefest of the seven, whose care
Was guests to welcome, towardes him did pas:
Where seeing Mercie, that his steps up bare,° *supported*
And alwayes led, to her with reverence rare
He humbly louted° in meeke lowlinesse, *bowed*
And seemely welcome for her did prepare:
For of their order she was Patronesse,
Albe° Charissa were their chiefest founderesse. *although*

45

There she awhile him stayes, him selfe to rest,
That to the rest more able he might bee:
During which time, in every good behest
And godly worke of Almes and charitee
She him instructed with great industree;
Shortly therein so perfect he became,
That from the first unto the last degree,
His mortall life he learnéd had to frame
In holy righteousnesse, without rebuke or blame.

46

Thence forward by that painfull way they pas,
Forth to an hill, that was both steepe and hy;
On top whereof a sacred chappell was,
And eke a litle Hermitage thereby,
Wherein an agéd holy man did lye,° *live*
That day and night said his devotion,
Ne other worldly busines did apply;
His name was heavenly Contemplation;
Of God and goodnesse was his meditation.

47

Great grace that old man to him given had;
For God he often saw from heavens hight,
All° were his earthly eyen both blunt° and bad, *although/dim*
And through great age had lost their kindly° sight, *natural*
Yet wondrous quick and persant° was his spright, *piercing*
As Eagles eye, that can behold the Sunne:
That hill they scale with all their powre and might,
That his frayle thighes nigh wearie and fordonne° *exhausted*
Gan faile, but by her helpe the top at last he wonne.

48

There they do finde that godly agéd Sire,
With snowy lockes adowne his shoulders shed,
As hoarie frost with spangles doth attire
The mossy braunches of an Oke halfe ded.
Each bone might through his body well be red,° *observed*
And every sinew seene through° his long fast: *because of*
For nought he cared his carcas long unfed;
His mind was full of spirituall repast,
And pyned° his flesh, to keepe his body low° and chast. *starved/thin*

49

Who when these two approching he aspide,
At their first presence grew agrievéd sore,

That forst him lay his heavenly thoughts aside;
And had he not that Dame respected more,° *greatly*
Whom highly he did reverence and adore,
He would not once have movéd for the knight.
They him saluted standing far afore;° *away*
Who well them greeting, humbly did requight,
And asked, to what end they clomb° that tedious height. *had climbed*

50

"What end," quoth she, "should cause us take such paine,
But that same end, which every living wight
Should make his marke, high heaven to attaine?
Is not from hence the way, that leadeth right
To that most glorious house, that glistreth bright
With burning starres, and everliving fire,
Whereof the keyes are to thy hand behight° *entrusted*
By wise Fidelia? she doth thee require,
To shew it to this knight, according his desire."

51

"Thrise happy man," said then the father grave,
"Whose staggering steps thy steady hand doth lead,
And shewes the way, his sinfull soule to save.
Who better can the way to heaven aread° *direct*
Then thou thy selfe, that was both borne and bred
In heavenly throne, where thousand Angels shine?
Thou doest the prayers of the righteous sead° *offspring*
Present before the majestie divine,
And his avenging wrath to clemencie incline.

52

"Yet since thou bidst, thy pleasure shalbe donne.
Then come thou man of earth, and see the way,
That never yet was seene of Faeries sonne,
That never leads the traveiler astray,
But after labours long, and sad delay,
Brings them to joyous rest and endlesse blis.
But first thou must a season fast and pray,
Till from her bands the spright assoiléd° is, *released*
And have her strength recured° from fraile infirmitis." *recovered*

53

That done, he leads him to the highest Mount;
Such one, as that same mighty man of God,
That bloud-red billowes like a walléd front
On either side disparted with his rod,
Till that his army dry-foot through them yod,° *went*
Dwelt fortie dayes upon; where writ in stone
With bloudy letters by the hand of God,
The bitter doome° of death and balefull mone *judgment*
He did receive, whiles flashing fire about him shone.

54

Or like that sacred hill, whose head full hie,
Adornd with fruitfull Olives all arownd,

Is, as it were for endlesse memory
Of that deare Lord, who oft thereon was fownd,
For ever with a flowring girlond crownd:
Or like that pleasaunt Mount, that is for ay
Through famous Poets verse each where° renownd, *everywhere*
On which the thrise three learned Ladies play
Their heavenly notes, and make full many a lovely lay.[4]

55

From thence, far off he unto him did shew
A litle path, that was both steepe and long,
Which to a goodly Citie led his vew;
Whose wals and towres were builded high and strong
Of perle and precious stone, that earthly tong
Cannot describe, nor wit of man can tell;
Too high a ditty° for my simple song; *subject*
The Citie of the great king hight it well,
Wherein eternall peace and happinesse doth dwell.

56

As he thereon stood gazing, he might see
The blessed Angels to and fro descend
From highest heaven, in gladsome companee,
And with great joy into that Citie wend,
As commonly° as friend does with his frend.[5] *generally*
Whereat he wondred much, and gan enquere,
What stately building durst so high extend
Her loftie towres unto the starry sphere,
And what unknowen nation there empeopled were.

57

"Faire knight," quoth he, "Hierusalem that is,
The new Hierusalem, that God has built
For those to dwell in, that are chosen his,
His chosen people purged from sinfull guilt,
With pretious bloud, which cruelly was spilt
On curséd tree, of that unspotted lam,
That for the sinnes of all the world was kilt:
Now are they Saints all in that Citie sam,° *together*
More deare unto their God, then younglings to their dam."[6]

58

"Till now," said then the knight, "I weenéd well,
That great Cleopolis,[7] where I have beene,

4. The mountain is successively compared to Mount Sinai (lines 469–77), where Moses, after parting the "bloud-red billowes" of the Red Sea, received the tablets of the laws of Judaism; to the Mount of Olives (lines 478–82), associated with Christ; and to Mount Parnassus (lines 483–86), where dwelled the nine muses of art and poetry. This last has the effect of equating poetry with the profoundest religious experience —a tradition that Sidney's *Apology* also incorporates.

5. Cf. Jacob's ladder: "And he dreamed, and behold a ladder set up on the earth, and the top of it reached to heaven; and behold the angels of God ascending and descending on it" (Genesis xxviii.12).

6. The New Jerusalem is described in Revelation xxi-xxii; "the nations of them which are saved shall walk in the light of it" (xxi.24).

7. London, Camelot—and here, the earthly counterpart of the Heavenly Kingdom.

In which that fairest Faerie Queene doth dwell,
The fairest Citie was, that might be seene;
And that bright towre all built of christall cleene,° *clear*
Panthea,[8] seemd the brightest thing, that was:
But now by proofe all otherwise I weene;
For this great Citie that does far surpas,
And this bright Angels towre quite dims that towre of glas."

59

"Most trew," then said the holy aged man;
"Yet is Cleopolis for earthly frame,° *structure*
The fairest peece, that eye beholden can:
And well beseemes all knights of noble name,
That covet in th'immortall booke of fame
To be eternizéd, that same to haunt,° *frequent*
And doen their service to that soveraigne Dame,
That glorie does to them for guerdon° graunt: *reward*
For she is heavenly borne, and heaven may justly vaunt.° *claim*

60

"And thou faire ymp, sprong out from English race,
How ever now accompted° Elfins sonne, *accounted*
Well worthy doest thy service for her grace,° *favor*
To aide a virgin desolate foredonne.
But when thou famous victorie hast wonne,
And high emongst all knights has hong thy shield,
Thenceforth the suit° of earthly conquest shonne, *pursuit*
And wash thy hands from guilt of bloudy field:
For bloud can nought but sin, and wars but sorrowes yield.

61

"Then seeke this path, that I to thee presage,° *point out*
Which after all to heaven shall thee send;
Then peaceably thy painefull pilgrimage
To yonder same Hierusalem do bend,
Where is for thee ordaind a blessed end:
For thou emongst those Saints, whom thou doest see,
Shalt be a Saint, and thine owne nations frend
And Patrone: thou Saint George shalt calléd bee,
Saint George of mery England, the signe of victoree."[9]

62

"Unworthy wretch," quoth he, "of so great grace,
How dare I thinke such glory to attaine?"
"These that have it attaind, were in like cace,"
Quoth he, "as wretched, and lived in like paine."
"But deeds of armes must I at last be faine,
And Ladies love to leave so dearely bought?"
"What need of armes, where peace doth ay remaine,"
Said he, "and battailes none are to be fought?
As for loose loves are[10] vaine, and vanish into nought."

8. Reminiscent of the temple of glass in Chaucer's *Hous of Fame;* perhaps intended to represent Richmond Palace or Westminster Abbey.

9. Spenser's conception of St. George, patron saint of England, draws on the *Legenda Aurea* (translated by Caxton in 1487); on pictures, tapestries, and pageants; and on folklore.

10. I.e., they are.

63

"O let me not," quoth he, "then turne againe
Backe to the world, whose joyes so fruitlesse are;
But let me here for aye in peace remaine,
Or streight way on that last long voyage fare,
That nothing may my present hope empare."° *impair*
"That may not be," said he, "ne maist thou yit
Forgo that royall maides bequeathéd care,° *charge*
Who did her cause into thy hand commit,
Till from her curséd foe thou have her freely quit."° *released*

64

"Then shall I soone," quoth he, "so God me grace,
Abet° that virgins cause disconsolate, *support*
And shortly backe returne unto this place
To walke this way in Pilgrims poore estate.
But now aread, old father, why of late
Didst thou behight° me borne of English blood, *call*
Whom all a Faeries sonne doen nominate?"° *name*
"That word shall I," said he, "avouchen° good, *prove*
Sith to thee is unknowne the cradle of thy brood.

65

"For well I wote,° thou springst from ancient race *know*
Of Saxon kings, that have with mightie hand
And many bloudie battailes fought in place° *there*
High reard their royall throne in Britane land,
And vanquisht them, unable to withstand:
From thence a Faerie thee unweeting reft,[1]
There as thou slepst in tender swadling band,
And her base Elfin brood there for thee left.
Such men do Chaungelings call, so chaungd by Faeries theft.

66

"Thence she thee brought into this Faerie lond,
And in an heapéd furrow did thee hyde,
Where thee a Ploughman all unweeting fond,
As he his toylesome teme that way did guyde,
And brought thee up in ploughmans state to byde,
Whereof Georgos he thee gave to name;[2]
Till prickt with courage, and thy forces pryde,
To Faery court thou cam'st to seeke for fame,
And prove thy puissaunt armes, as seemes thee best became."° *suited*

67

"O holy Sire," quoth he, "how shall I quight° *repay*
The many favours I with thee have found,
That has my name and nation red aright,
And taught the way that does to heaven bound?"° *go*
This said, adowne he lookéd to the ground,
To have returnd, but dazéd were his eyne,
Through passing° brightnesse, which did quite confound *surpassing*
His feeble sence, and too exceeding shyne.
So darke are earthly things compard to things divine.

1. Secretly stole.
2. *Georgos* is Greek for "farmer" (cf. Virgil's *Georgics*, on farming).

68

At last whenas himselfe he gan to find,° *recover*
To Una back he cast him to retire;
Who him awaited still with pensive mind.
Great thankes and goodly meed° to that good syre, *gift*
He thence departing gave for his paines hyre.° *reward*
So came to Una, who him joyd to see,
And after litle rest, gan him desire,
Of her adventure mindfull for to bee.
So leave they take of Caelia, and her daughters three.

Canto XI

The knight with that old Dragon fights
two dayes incessantly:
The third him overthrowes, and gayns
most glorious victory.

1

High time now gan it wex° for Una faire, *develop*
To thinke of those her captive Parents deare,
And their forwasted kingdome to repaire:[3]
Whereto whenas they now approachéd neare,
With hartie words her knight she gan to cheare,
And in her modest manner thus bespake;
"Deare knight, as deare, as ever knight was deare,
That all these sorrowes suffer for my sake,
High heaven behold the tedious toyle, ye for me take.

2

"Now are we come unto my native soyle,
And to the place, where all our perils dwell;
Here haunts that feend, and does his dayly spoyle,
Therefore henceforth be at your keeping well,[4]
And ever ready for your foeman fell.
The sparke of noble courage now awake,
And strive your excellent selfe to excell;
That shall ye evermore renowméd make,
Above all knights on earth, that batteill undertake."

3

And pointing forth, "lo yonder is," said she,
"The brasen towre in which my parents deare
For dread of that huge feend emprisond be,
Whom I from far see on the walles appeare,
Whose sight my feeble° soule doth greatly cheare: *melancholy*
And on the top of all I do espye
The watchman wayting tydings glad to heare,
That O my parents might I happily
Unto you bring, to ease you of your misery."

4

With that they heard a roaring hideous sound,

3. I.e., to restore their kingdom, laid waste (by the dragon), to health.

4. I.e., be alert to your responsibilities.

That all the ayre with terrour filléd wide,
And seemd uneath° to shake the stedfast ground. *almost*
Eftsoones that dreadfull Dragon they espide,
Where stretcht he lay upon the sunny side
Of a great hill, himselfe like a great hill.
But all so soone, as he from far descride
Those glistring armes, that heaven with light did fill,
He rousd himselfe full blith,° and hastned them untill.° *eagerly/toward*

5

Then bad the knight his Lady yede° aloofe, *step*
And to an hill her selfe withdraw aside,
From whence she might behold that battailles proof° *outcome*
And eke be safe from daunger far descryde:
She him obayd, and turnd a little wyde.° *aside*
Now O thou sacred Muse,[5] most learned Dame,
Faire ympe° of Phoebus, and his aged bride,[6] *child*
The Nourse of time, and everlasting fame,
That warlike hands ennoblest with immortall name;

6

O gently come into my feeble brest,
Come gently, but not with that mighty rage,
Wherewith the martiall troupes thou doest infest,° *arouse*
And harts of great Heroës doest enrage,
That nought their kindled courage may aswage,
Soone as thy dreadfull trompe begins to sownd;
The God of warre with his fiers equipage
Thou doest awake, sleepe never he so sownd,
And scaréd nations doest with horrour sterne astown.° *appall*

7

Faire Goddesse lay that furious fit° aside, *mood*
Till I of warres and bloudy Mars do sing[7]
And Briton fields with Sarazin bloud bedyde,
Twixt that great faery Queene and Paynim king,
That with their horrour heaven and earth did ring,
A worke of labour long, and endlesse prayse:
But now a while let downe that haughtie string,
And to my tunes thy second tenor rayse,[8]
That I this man of God his godly armes may blaze.° *describe*

8

By this the dreadfull Beast drew nigh to hand,
Halfe flying, and halfe footing in his hast,
That with his largenesse measuréd much land,
And made wide shadow under his huge wast;° *girth*
As mountaine doth the valley overcast.
Approching nigh, he rearéd high afore
His body monstrous, horrible, and vast,
Which to increase his wondrous greatnesse more,
Was swolne with wrath, and poyson, and with bloudy gore.

5. Calliope, muse of epic poetry, or Clio, muse of history.
6. I.e., Mnemosyne (memory).
7. Spenser refers to a projected book of *The Faerie Queene* which he never wrote.
8. The "haughtie" (high-pitched) mode would be appropriate to a large-scale epic war; the "second tenor" (lower in pitch) to this present battle.

9

And over, all with brasen scales was armd,
Like plated coate of steele, so couchéd neare,[9]
That nought mote perce, ne might his corse be harmd
With dint of sword, nor push of pointed speare;
Which as an Eagle, seeing pray appeare,
His aery Plumes doth rouze,° full rudely dight,° *shake/arrayed*
So shakéd he, that horrour was to heare,
For as the clashing of an Armour bright,
Such noyse his rouzéd scales did send unto the knight.

10

His flaggy° wings when forth he did display, *drooping*
Were like two sayles, in which the hollow wynd
Is gathered full, and worketh speedy way:
And eke the pennes,° that did his pineons bynd, *quills*
Were like mayne-yards, with flying canvas lynd,
With which whenas him list the ayre to beat,
And there by force unwonted passage find,
The cloudes before him fled for terrour great,
And all the heavens stood still amazéd with his threat.

11

His huge long tayle wound up in hundred foldes,
Does overspred his long bras-scaly backe,
Whose wreathéd boughts° when ever he unfoldes, *coils*
And thicke entangled knots adown does slacke,
Bespotted as with shields of red and blacke,
It sweepeth all the land behind him farre,
And of three furlongs does but litle lacke;
And at the point two stings in-fixéd arre,
Both deadly sharpe, that sharpest steele exceeden farre.

12

But stings and sharpest steele did far exceed[1]
The sharpnesse of his cruell rending clawes;
Dead was it sure, as sure as death in deed,
What ever thing does touch his ravenous pawes,
Or what within his reach he ever drawes.
But his most hideous head my toung to tell
Does tremble: for his deepe devouring jawes
Wide gapéd, like the griesly mouth of hell,
Through which into his darke abisse all ravin° fell.[2] *prey, booty*

13

And that° more wondrous was, in either jaw *what*
Three ranckes of yron teeth enraungéd were,
In which yet trickling bloud and gobbets raw
Of late devouréd bodies did appeare,
That sight thereof bred cold congealéd feare:
Which to increase, and all at once to kill,
A cloud of smoothering smoke and sulphur seare° *burning*

9. Closely overlaid.
1. I.e., were far exceeded by.
2. In emphasizing the deathly, hellish aspects of the dragon, this stanza reveals the stakes of the battle: holiness v. sin, the Protestant v. the Catholic churches, life v. death.

Out of his stinking gorge° forth steeméd still, *maw*
That all the ayre about with smoke and stench did fill.

14

His blazing eyes, like two bright shining shields,
Did burne with wrath, and sparkled living fyre;
As two broad Beacons, set in open fields,
Send forth their flames farre off to every shyre,
And warning give, that enemies conspyre,
With fire and sword the region to invade;
So flamed his eyne with rage and rancorous yre:
But farre within, as in a hollow glade,
Those glaring lampes were set, that made a dreadfull shade.[3]

15

So dreadfully he towards him did pas,
Forelifting up aloft his speckled brest,
And often bounding on the bruséd gras,
As for great joyance of his newcome guest.
Eftsoones he gan advance his haughtie crest,
As chaufféd° Bore his bristles doth upreare, *vexed*
And shoke his scales to battell readie drest;
That made the Redcrosse knight nigh quake for feare,
As bidding bold defiance to his foeman neare.

16

The knight gan fairely couch° his steadie speare, *rest, aim*
And fiercely ran at him with rigorous might:
The pointed steele arriving rudely theare,
His harder hide would neither perce, nor bight,
But glauncing by forth passéd forward right;
Yet sore amovéd with so puissant push,
The wrathfull beast about him turnéd light,° *quickly*
And him so rudely passing by, did brush
With his long tayle, that horse and man to ground did rush.

17

Both horse and man up lightly rose againe,
And fresh encounter towards him addrest:
But th' idle stroke yet backe recoyld in vaine,
And found no place his° deadly point to rest. *its*
Exceeding rage enflamed the furious beast,
To be avengéd of so great despight;° *outrage*
For never felt his imperceable brest
So wondrous force, from hand of living wight;
Yet had he proved° the powre of many a puissant knight. *tested*

18

Then with his waving wings displayéd wyde,
Himselfe up high he lifted from the ground,
And with strong flight did forcibly divide
The yielding aire, which nigh too feeble found
Her flitting partes, and element unsound,° *weak*

3. Cf. among other echoes, the great beast of Revelation (xiii.2): "And the beast which I saw was like unto a leopard, and his feet were as the feet of a bear, and his mouth as the mouth of a lion: and the dragon gave him his power, and his seat, and great authority."

To beare so great a weight: he cutting way
With his broad sayles, about him soaréd round:
At last low stouping with unweldie sway,[4]
Snatcht up both horse and man, to beare them quite away.

19

Long he them bore above the subject plaine,[5]
So farre as Ewghen[6] bow a shaft may send,
Till struggling strong did him at last constraine,
To let them downe before his flightés end:
As hagard° hauke presuming to contend *untrained*
With hardie fowle, above his hable might,[7]
His wearie pounces° all in vaine doth spend, *claws*
To trusse° the pray too heavie for his flight; *seize*
Which comming downe to ground, does free it selfe by fight.

20

He so disseizéd of his gryping grosse,[8]
The knight his thrillant° speare againe assayd *piercing*
In his bras-plated body to embosse,° *plunge*
And three mens strength unto the stroke he layd;
Wherewith the stiffe beame quakéd, as affrayd,
And glauncing from his scaly necke, did glyde
Close under his left wing, then broad displayd.
The percing steele there wrought a wound full wyde,
That with the uncouth° smart the Monster lowdly cryde. *unusual*

21

He cryde, as raging seas are wont to rore,
When wintry storme his wrathfull wreck does threat,
The rolling billowes beat the ragged shore,
As they the earth would shoulder from her seat,
And greedie gulfe does gape, as he would eat
His neighbour element[9] in his revenge:
Then gin the blustring brethren[1] boldly threat,
To move the world from off his stedfast henge,° *axis*
And boystrous battell make, each other to avenge.

22

The steely head stucke fast still in his flesh,
Till with his cruell clawes he snatcht the wood,
And quite a sunder broke. Forth flowéd fresh
A gushing river of blacke goarie blood,
That drownéd all the land, whereon he stood;
The stream thereof would drive a water-mill.
Trebly augmented was his furious mood
With bitter sense of his deepe rooted ill,
That flames of fire he threw forth from his large noséthrill.

23

His hideous tayle then hurléd he about,
And therewith all enwrapt the nimble thyes

4. Ponderous force.
5. I.e., the ground below.
6. Yewen, of yew.
7. Able power.
8. Freed from his formidable grip.
9. I.e., earth.
1. I.e., the winds.

Of his froth-fomy steed, whose courage stout
Striving to loose the knot, that fast him tyes,
Himselfe in streighter bandes too rash implyes,[2]
That to the ground he is perforce constraynd
To throw his rider: who can° quickly ryse — *began to*
From off the earth, with durty bloud distaynd,
For that reprochfull fall right fowly he disdaynd.

24

And fiercely tooke his trenchand° blade in hand, — *sharp*
With which he stroke so furious and so fell,
That nothing seemd the puissance could withstand:
Upon his crest the hardned yron fell,
But his more hardned crest was armd so well,
That deeper dint therein it would not make;
Yet so extremely did the buffe him quell,° — *dismay*
That from thenceforth he shund the like to take,
But when he saw them come, he did them still forsake.° — *avoid*

25

The knight was wrath to see his stroke beguyld,
And smote againe with more outrageous might;
But backe againe the sparckling steele recoyld,
And left not any marke, where it did light;
As if in Adamant rocke it had bene pight.° — *struck against*
The beast impatient of his smarting wound,
And of so fierce and forcible despight,° — *injury*
Thought with his wings to stye° above the ground; — *mount*
But his late wounded wing unserviceable found.

26

Then full of griefe and anguish vehement,
He lowdly brayd, that like was never heard,
And from his wide devouring oven sent
A flake° of fire, that flashing in his beard, — *flash*
Him all amazd, and almost made affeard;
The scorching flame sore swingéd° all his face, — *singed*
And through his armour all his bodie seard,
That he could not endure so cruell cace,
But thought his armes to leave, and helmet to unlace.

27

Not that great Champion of the antique world,
Whom famous Poetes verse so much doth vaunt,
And hath for twelve huge labours high extold,
So many furies and sharpe fits did haunt,
When him the poysoned garment did enchaunt
With Centaures bloud, and bloudie verses charmed,
As did this knight twelve thousand dolours° daunt, — *sufferings*
Whom fyrie steele now burnt, that earst° him armed, — *formerly*
That erst him goodly armed, now most of all him harmed.[3]

2. I.e., too suddenly entangles.
3. Redcrosse's fire-baptism is compared to the burning shirt of Nessus, which killed Hercules, "that great Champion of the antique world" (line 235).

28

Faint, wearie, sore, emboylèd, grievèd, brent° *burned*
With heat, toyle, wounds, armes, smart, and inward fire
That never man such mischiefes did torment;
Death better were, death did he oft desire,
But death will never come, when needes require.
Whom so dismayd when that his foe beheld,
He cast to suffer him no more respire,° *rest*
But gan his sturdie sterne° about to weld,° *tail/lash*
And him so strongly stroke, that to the ground him feld.

29

It fortunèd (as faire it then befell)
Behind his backe unweeting,° where he stood, *unnoticed*
Of auncient time there was a springing well,
From which fast trickled forth a silver flood,
Full of great vertues, and for med'cine good.
Whylome,° before that cursèd Dragon got *formerly*
That happie land, and all with innocent blood
Defyld those sacred waves, it rightly hot° *was called*
The Well of Life, ne yet his° vertues had forgot. *its*

30

For unto life the dead it could restore,
And guilt of sinfull crimes cleane wash away,
Those that with sicknesse were infected sore,
It could recure, and aged long decay
Renew, as one were borne that very day.
Both Silo this, and Jordan did excell,
And th' English Bath, and eke the german Spau,
Ne can Cephise, nor Hebrus match this well:
Into the same the knight backe overthrowen, fell.[4]

31

Now gan the golden Phoebus for to steepe
His fierie face in billowes of the west,
And his faint steedes watred in Ocean deepe,
Whiles from their journall° labours they did rest, *daily*
When that infernall Monster, having kest° *cast*
His wearie foe into that living well,
Can° high advaunce his broad discoloured brest, *did*
Above his wonted pitch,° with countenance fell,° *height/sinister*
And clapt his yron wings, as victor he did dwell.° *remain*

32

Which when his pensive Ladie saw from farre,
Great woe and sorrow did her soule assay,° *attack*
As weening that the sad end of the warre,
And gan to highest God entirely° pray, *earnestly*
That fearèd chaunce° from her to turne away; *fate*

4. In the old English metrical romance *Sir Bevis of Hampton*, the hero is saved in his fight with a dragon by a healing well; "a pure river of water of life" is also described in Revelation xxii.1–2. The Well of Life, with its baptismal powers of renewal, is successively compared to waters of the Bible, of England and Europe, and of classical antiquity. In Siloam (Silo) a blind man was cured by Christ (John ix.7); the crossing of the river Jordan saved the Jews (Deuteronomy xxvii.2–9), and Christ was baptized therein (Matthew iii.16); "Bath" and "Spau" (Spa) were famed for their medicinal waters; "Cephise" and "Hebrus" in Greece were noted for their clear streams.

With folded hands and knees full lowly bent
All night she watcht, ne once adowne would lay
Her daintie limbs in her sad dreriment,
But praying still did wake, and waking did lament.

33

The morrow next gan early to appeare,
That Titan[5] rose to runne his daily race;
But early ere the morrow next gan reare
Out of the sea faire Titans deawy face,
Up rose the gentle virgin from her place,
And lookéd all about, if she might spy
Her loved knight to move his manly pace:
For she had great doubt of his safety,
Since late she saw him fall before his enemy.

34

At last she saw, where he upstarted brave
Out of the well, wherein he drenchéd lay;
As Eagle fresh out of the Ocean wave,
Where he hath left his plumes all hoary gray,
And deckt himselfe with feathers youthly gay,
Like Eyas° hauke up mounts unto the skies, *young*
His newly budded pineons to assay,
And marveiles at himselfe, still as he flies:
So new this new-borne knight to battell new did rise.[1]

35

Whom when the damnéd feend so fresh did spy,
No wonder if he wondred at the sight,
And doubted, whether his late enemy
It were, or other new suppliéd knight.
He, now to prove his late renewéd might,
High brandishing his bright deaw-burning blade,
Upon his crested scalpe so sore did smite,
That to the scull a yawning wound it made:
The deadly dint his dulléd senses all dismaid.

36

I wote not, whether the revenging steele
Were hardnéd with that holy water dew,
Wherein he fell, or sharper edge did feele,
Or his baptizéd hands now greater° grew; *stronger*
Or other secret vertue did ensew;
Else never could the force of fleshly arme,
Ne molten mettall in his bloud embrew:° *plunge*
For till that stownd° could never wight him harme, *stunning blow*
By subtilty, nor slight,° nor might, nor mighty charme. *trickery*

37

The cruell wound enragéd him so sore,
That loud he yelléd for exceeding paine;
As hundred ramping Lyons seemed to rore,
Whom ravenous hunger did there to constraine:
Then gan he tosse aloft his stretchéd traine,
And therewith scourge the buxome° aire so sore, *yielding*

5. **When the sun.**
1. The ancient notion that the eagle could renew its youth by bathing in a spring is embodied in Psalm ciii.5.

That to his force to yeelden it was faine;
Ne ought° his sturdie strokes might stand afore, *anything*
That high trees overthrew, and rocks in peeces tore.

38

The same advauncing high above his head,
With sharpe intended° sting so rude him smot, *shot out*
That to the earth him drove, as stricken dead,
Ne living wight would have him life behot:° *granted*
The mortall sting his angry needle shot
Quite through his shield, and in his shoulder seasd,
Where fast it stucke, ne would there out be got:
The griefe thereof him wondrous sore diseasd,° *afflicted*
Ne might his ranckling paine with patience be appeasd.

39

But yet more mindfull of his honour deare,
Then of the grievous smart, which him did wring,° *torment*
From loathéd soile he can° him lightly reare, *began to*
And strove to loose the farre infixéd sting:
Which when in vaine he tryde with struggeling,
Inflamed with wrath, his raging blade he heft,
And strooke so strongly, that the knotty string
Of his huge taile he quite a sunder cleft,
Five joynts thereof he hewd, and but the stump him left.

40

Hart cannot thinke, what outrage, and what cryes,
With foule enfouldred[2] smoake and flashing fire,
The hell-bred beast threw forth unto the skyes,
That all was coveréd with darknesse dire:
Then fraught with rancour, and engorgéd° ire, *choking*
He cast at once him to avenge for all,
And gathering up himselfe out of the mire,
With his uneven wings did fiercely fall
Upon his sunne-bright shield, and gript it fast withall.

41

Much was the man encombred with his hold,
In feare to lose his weapon in his paw,
Ne wist yet, how his talents° to unfold; *talons*
Nor harder was from Cerberus greedie jaw
To plucke a bone, then from his cruell claw
To reave° by strength the gripéd gage° away: *seize/prize*
Thrise he assayd it from his foot to draw,
And thrise in vaine to draw it did assay,
It booted nought to thinke, to robbe him of his pray.

42

Tho° when he saw no power might prevaile, *then*
His trustie sword he cald to his last aid,
Wherewith he fiercely did his foe assaile,
And double blowes about him stoutly laid,
That glauncing fire out of the yron plaid;
As sparckles from the Andvile use to fly,

2. Hurled out like thunder.

When heavie hammers on the wedge are swaid;° *struck*
Therewith at last he forst him to unty° *loosen*
One of his grasping feete, him to defend thereby.

43

The other foot, fast fixéd on his shield,
Whenas no strength, nor stroks mote him constraine
To loose, ne yet the warlike pledge to yield,
He smot thereat with all his might and maine,
That nought so wondrous puissance might sustaine;
Upon the joynt the lucky steele did light,
And made such way, that hewd it quite in twaine;
The paw yet misséd not his minisht° might, *lessened*
But hong still on the shield, as it at first was pight.° *placed*

44

For griefe thereof, and divelish despight,
From his infernall fournace forth he threw
Huge flames, that dimméd all the heavens light,
Enrold in duskish smoke and brimstone blew;
As burning Aetna from his boyling stew° *cauldron*
Doth belch out flames, and rockes in peeces broke,
And ragged ribs of mountaines molten new
Enwrapt in coleblacke clouds and filthy smoke,
That all the land with stench, and heaven with horror choke.

45

The heate whereof, and harmefull pestilence
So sore him noyd,° that forst him to retire *troubled*
A little backward for his best defence,
To save his bodie from the scorching fire,
Which he from hellish entrailes did expire.° *breathe out*
It chaunst (eternall God that chaunce did guide)
As he recoyléd backward, in the mire
His nigh forwearied feeble feet did slide,
And downe he fell, with dread of shame sore terrifide.

46

There grew a goodly tree him faire beside,
Loaden with fruit and apples rosie red,
As they in pure vermilion had beene dide,
Whereof great vertues over all were red:° *declared*
For happie life to all, which thereon fed,
And life eke everlasting did befall:
Great God it planted in that blessed sted° *place*
With his almightie hand, and did it call
The Tree of Life, the crime of our first fathers fall.[3]

47

In all the world like was not to be found,
Save in that soile, where all good things did grow,
And freely sprong out of the fruitfull ground,
As incorrupted Nature did them sow,

3. In Genesis ii.9 appears the Tree of Life which God planted in the Garden of Eden. The "crime of our first fathers fall" is that Adam, in being banished from Eden, separated himself—and us—from the tree. The tree appears again in the New Jerusalem (Revelation xxii.2).

Till that dread Dragon all did overthrow.
Another like faire tree eke grew thereby,
Whereof who so did eat, eftsoones did know
Both good and ill: O mornefull memory:
That tree through one mans fault hath doen us all to dy.[4]

48

From that first tree forth flowd, as from a well,
A trickling streame of Balme, most soveraine
And daintie deare,[5] which on the ground still fell,
And overflowéd all the fertill plaine,
As it had deawéd bene with timely° raine: *seasonable*
Life and long health that gratious° ointment gave, *full of grace*
And deadly woundes could heale, and reare againe
The senselesse corse appointed° for the grave. *made ready*
Into that same he fell: which did from death him save.[1]

49

For nigh thereto the ever damnéd beast
Durst not approch, for he was deadly made,[2]
And all that life preservéd, did detest:
Yet he it oft adventured to invade.
By this the drouping day-light gan to fade,
And yeeld his roome to sad succeeding night,
Who with her sable mantle gan to shade
The face of earth, and wayes of living wight,
And high her burning torch set up in heaven bright.

50

When gentle Una saw the second fall
Of her deare knight, who wearie of long fight,
And faint through losse of bloud, moved not at all,
But lay as in a dreame of deepe delight,
Besmeard with pretious Balme, whose vertuous might
Did heale his wounds, and scorching heat alay,
Againe she stricken was with sore affright,
And for his safetie gan devoutly pray;
And watch the noyous° night, and wait for joyous day. *afflicting*

51

The joyous day gan early to appeare,
And faire Aurora from the deawy bed
Of aged Tithone gan her selfe to reare,[3]
With rosie cheekes, for shame as blushing red;
Her golden lockes for haste were loosely shed
About her eares, when Una her did marke
Clymbe to her charet, all with flowers spred,
From heaven high to chase the chearelesse darke;
With merry note her loud salutes the mounting larke.

4. I.e., killed us. The tree described here is the Tree of Knowledge of Good and Evil in the Garden of Eden.

5. Precious.

1. A healing balm flowing from the tree of mercy is used by Seth to anoint Adam in the apocryphal Gospel of Nicodemus. This same balm is used later by Christ and is understood to be His blood. Christ's blood was shed to redeem mankind from eternal damnation.

2. I.e., a child of death.

3. Aurora is goddess of the dawn, Tithonus her husband ("aged" because he was granted everlasting life without everlasting youth).

52

Then freshly up arose the doughtie knight,
All healéd of his hurts and woundés wide,
And did himselfe to battell readie dight;
Whose early foe awaiting him beside
To have devourd, so soone as day he spyde,
When now he saw himselfe so freshly reare,
As if late fight had nought him damnifyde,° *injured*
He woxe dismayd, and gan his fate to feare;
Nathlesse° with wonted rage he him advauncéd neare. *nevertheless*

53

And in his first encounter, gaping wide,
He thought attonce him to have swallowed quight,
And rusht upon him with outragious pride;
Who him r'encountring fierce, as hauke in flight,
Perforce rebutted° backe. The weapon bright *drove*
Taking advantage of his open jaw,
Ran through his mouth with so importune° might, *violent*
That deepe emperst his darksome hollow maw,
And back retyrd,° his life bloud forth with all did draw. *withdrawn*

54

So downe he fell, and forth his life did breath,
That vanisht into smoke and cloudés swift;
So downe he fell, that th' earth him underneath
Did grone, as feeble so great load to lift;
So downe he fell, as an huge rockie clift,
Whose false° foundation waves have washt away, *insecure*
With dreadfull poyse° is from the mayneland rift, *falling weight*
And rolling downe, great Neptune doth dismay;
So downe he fell, and like an heapéd mountaine lay.

55

The knight himselfe even trembled at his fall,
So huge and horrible a masse it seemed;
And his deare Ladie, that beheld it all,
Durst not approch for dread, which she misdeemed,° *misjudged*
But yet at last, when as the direfull feend
She saw not stirre, off-shaking vaine affright,
She nigher drew, and saw that joyous end:
Then God she praysd, and thankt her faithfull knight,
That had atchieved so great a conquest by his might.

Canto XII

Faire Una to the Redcrosse knight
betrouthéd is with joy:
Though false Duessa it to barre
her false sleights doe imploy.

1

Behold I see the haven nigh at hand,
To which I meane my wearie course to bend;

Vere the maine shete, and beare up with the land,[4]
The which afore is fairely to be kend,° *recognized*
And seemeth safe from stormes, that may offend;
There this faire virgin wearie of her way
Must landed be, now at her journeyes end:
There eke my feeble barke° a while may stay, *ship*
Till merry wind and weather call her thence away.

2

Scarsely had Phoebus in the glooming East
Yet harnesséd his firie-footed teeme,
Ne reard above the earth his flaming creast,
When the last deadly smoke aloft did steeme,
That signe of last outbreathéd life did seeme
Unto the watchman on the castle wall;
Who thereby dead that balefull Beast did deeme,
And to his Lord and Ladie lowd gan call,
To tell, how he had seene the Dragons fatall fall.

3

Uprose with hastie joy, and feeble speed
That aged Sire, the Lord of all that land,
And lookéd forth, to weet, if true indeede
Those tydings were, as he did understand,
Which whenas true by tryall he out fond,
He bad to open wyde his brazen gate,
Which long time had bene shut, and out of hond[5]
Proclaymed joy and peace through all his state;
For dead now was their foe, which them forrayéd late.[6]

4

Then gan triumphant Trompets sound on hie,
That sent to heaven the ecchoéd report
Of their new joy, and happie victorie
Gainst him, that had them long opprest with tort,° *wrong*
And fast imprisonéd in siegéd fort.
Then all the people, as in solemne feast,
To him assembled with one full consort,[7]
Rejoycing at the fall of that great beast,
From whose eternall bondage now they were releast.

5

Forth came that auncient Lord and aged Queene,
Arayd in antique robes downe to the ground,
And sad° habiliments right well beseene;° *dignified/proper*
A noble crew about them waited round
Of sage and sober Peres, all gravely gownd;
Whom farre before did march a goodly band
Of tall young men, all hable armes to sownd,[8]
But now they laurell braunches bore in hand;
Glad signe of victorie and peace in all their land.

4. Release the mainsail line and sail toward the land. The metaphor in this stanza echoes many classical authors and Chaucer's *Troilus and Criseyde* (II.1–7).
5. Straightway.
6. Had recently ravaged.
7. All together.
8. Able to fight with weapons.

6

Unto that doughtie Conquerour they came,
And him before themselves prostrating low,
Their Lord and Patrone loud did him proclame,
And at his feet their laurell boughes did throw.
Soone after them all dauncing on a row
The comely virgins came, with girlands dight,
As fresh as flowres in medow greene do grow,
When morning deaw upon their leaves doth light:
And in their hands sweet Timbrels° all upheld on hight. *tambourines*

7

And them before, the fry° of children young *crowd*
Their wanton° sports and childish mirth did play, *playful*
And to the Maydens sounding tymbrels sung
In well attunéd notes, a joyous lay,
And made delightfull musicke all the way,
Untill they came, where that faire virgin stood;
As faire Diana in fresh sommers day
Beholds her Nymphes, enraunged in shadie wood,
Some wrestle, some do run, some bathe in christall flood.

8

So she beheld those maydens meriment
With chearefull vew; who when to her they came,
Themselves to ground with gratious humblesse bent,
And her adored by honorable name,
Lifting to heaven her everlasting fame:
Then on her head they set a girland greene,
And crownéd her twixt earnest and twixt game; [9]
Who in her selfe-resemblance well beseene,[1]
Did seeme such, as she was, a goodly maiden Queene.

9

And after all, the raskall many° ran, *mob*
Heapéd together in rude rablement,° *confusion*
To see the face of that victorious man:
Whom all admired, as from heaven sent,
And gazd upon with gaping wonderment.
But when they came, where that dead Dragon lay,
Stretcht on the ground in monstrous large extent,
The sight with idle° feare did them dismay, *baseless*
Ne durst approch him nigh, to touch, or once assay.

10

Some feard, and fled; some feard and well it faynd;° *concealed*
One that would wiser seeme, then all the rest,
Warnd him not touch, for yet perhaps remaynd
Some lingring life within his hollow brest,
Or in his wombe might lurke some hidden nest
Of many Dragonets, his fruitfull seed;
Another said, that in his eyes did rest
Yet sparckling fire, and bad thereof take heed;
Another said, he saw him move his eyes indeed.

9. I.e., half in fun.

1. I.e., looking appropriately like herself.

11

One mother, when as her foolehardie chyld
Did come too neare, and with his talants play,
Halfe dead through feare, her litle babe revyld,° *scolded*
And to her gossips° gan in counsell say; *women friends*
"How can I tell, but that his talants may
Yet scratch my sonne, or rend his tender hand?"
So diversly themselves in vaine they fray;° *scare*
Whiles some more bold, to measure him nigh stand,
To prove° how many acres he did spread of land. *determine*

12

Thus flockéd all the folke him round about,
The whiles that hoarie° king, with all his traine, *gray-haired*
Being arrivéd, where that champion stout
After his foes defeasance° did remaine, *defeat*
Him goodly greetes, and faire does entertaine,
With princely gifts of yvorie and gold,
And thousand thankes him yeelds for all his paine.
Then when his daughter deare he does behold,
Her dearely doth imbrace, and kisseth manifold.° *many times*

13

And after to his Pallace he them brings,
With shaumes,[2] and trompets, and with Clarions sweet;
And all the way the joyous people sings,
And with their garments strowes the pavéd street:
Whence mounting up, they find purveyance° meet *provisions*
Of all, that royall Princes court became,° *suited*
And all the floore was underneath their feet
Bespred with costly scarlot of great name,[3]
On which they lowly sit, and fitting purpose frame.

14

What needs me tell their feast and goodly guize,° *mode of life*
In which was nothing riotous nor vaine?
What needs of daintie dishes to devize,° *talk*
Of comely services, or courtly trayne?
My narrow leaves cannot in them containe
The large discourse[4] of royall Princes state.
Yet was their manner then but bare and plaine:
For th' antique world excesse and pride did hate;[5]
Such proud luxurious pompe is swollen up but late.

15

Then when with meates and drinkes of every kinde
Their fervent appetites they quenchéd had,
That auncient Lord gan fit occasion finde,
Of straunge adventures, and of perils sad,
Which in his travell him befallen had,
For to demaund of his renowméd guest:
Who then with utt'rance grave, and count'nance sad,
From point to point, as is before exprest,
Discourst his voyage long, according his request.

2. Ancient wind instrument like an oboe.
3. I.e., famous scarlet cloth.
4. I.e., full description.
5. The question of "excesse" will be paramount in Book II, "The Legend of Sir Guyon, or of Temperance."

16

Great pleasure mixt with pittifull° regard, *sympathetic*
That godly King and Queene did passionate,[6]
Whiles they his pittifull adventures heard,
That oft they did lament his lucklesse state,
And often blame the too importune° fate, *severe*
That heapd on him so many wrathfull wreakes:° *injuries*
For never gentle knight, as he of late,
So tosséd was in fortunes cruell freakes;° *whims*
And all the while salt teares bedeawd the hearers cheaks.

17

Then said that royall Pere in sober wise:
"Deare Sonne, great beene the evils, which ye bore
From first to last in your late enterprise,
That I note,° whether prayse, or pitty more: *know not*
For never living man, I weene, so sore
In sea of deadly daungers was distrest;
But since now safe ye seiséd° have the shore, *reached*
And well arrivéd are (high God be blest),
Let us devize of ease and everlasting rest."

18

"Ah dearest Lord," said then that doughty knight,
"Of ease or rest I may not yet devize;
For by the faith, which I to armes have plight,
I bounden am streight after this emprize,° *enterprise*
As that your daughter can ye well advize,
Backe to returne to that great Faerie Queene,
And her to serve six yeares in warlike wize,
Gainst that proud Paynim king, that workes her teene:° *sorrow*
Therefore I ought crave pardon, till I there have beene."[7]

19

"Unhappie falles that hard necessitie,"
Quoth he, "the troubler of my happie peace,
And vowéd foe of my felicitie;
Ne I against the same can justly preace:° *press*
But since that band° ye cannot now release, *obligation*
Nor doen undo (for vowes may not be vaine),
Soone as the terme of those six yeares shall cease,
Ye then shall hither backe returne againe,
The marriage to accomplish vowd betwixt you twain.

20

"Which for my part I covet to performe,
In sort as through the world I did proclame,
That who so kild that monster most deforme,
And him in hardy battaile overcame,
Should have mine onely daughter to his Dame,° *wife*

6. I.e., did feel and express.

7. That the marriage of Redcrosse and Una cannot be made final here and now signifies primarily that the final Christian triumph, the marriage of Christ and the true church will be achieved only at the end of time, the Day of Judgment. Meanwhile, the struggle against evil (and the Roman Church) continues.

And of my kingdome heire apparaunt bee:
Therefore since now to thee perteines° the same, *belongs*
By dew desert of noble chevalree,
Both daughter and eke kingdome, lo I yield to thee."

21

Then forth he callèd that his daughter faire,
The fairest Un' his onely daughter deare,
His onely daughter, and his onely heyre;
Who forth proceeding with sad° sober cheare,° *grave/countenance*
As bright as doth the morning starre appeare
Out of the East, with flaming lockes bedight,° *bedecked*
To tell that dawning day is drawing neare,
And to the world does bring long wishèd light;
So faire and fresh that Lady shewd her selfe in sight.

22

So faire and fresh, as freshest flowre in May;
For she had layd her mournefull stole aside,
And widow-like sad wimple° throwne away, *veil*
Wherewith her heavenly beautie she did hide,
Whiles on her wearie journey she did ride;
And on her now a garment she did weare,
All lilly white, withoutten spot, or pride,° *ornament*
That seemed like silke and silver woven neare,° *tightly*
But neither silke nor silver therein did appeare.[8]

23

The blazing brightnesse of her beauties beame,
And glorious light of her sunshyny face[9]
To tell, were as to strive against the streame.
My ragged rimes are all too rude and bace,
Her heavenly lineaments for to enchace.° *adorn*
Ne wonder; for her owne deare lovèd knight,
All° were she dayly with himselfe in place, *although*
Did wonder much at her celestiall sight:
Oft had he seene her faire, but never so faire dight.

24

So fairely dight, when she in presence came,
She to her Sire made humble reverence,
And bowèd low, that her right well became,
And added grace unto her excellence:
Who with great wisdome, and grave eloquence
Thus gan to say. But eare° he thus had said, *ere*
With flying speede, and seeming great pretence,° *importance*
Came running in, much like a man dismaid,
A Messenger with letters, which his message said.

8. "The marriage of the Lamb is come, and his wife hath made herself ready. And to her was granted that she should be arrayed in fine linen, clean and white: for the fine linen is the righteousness of saints" (Revelation xix.7–8).

9. Revelation xxi.9, 11 describes the New Jerusalem as "the bride, the Lamb's wife * * * her light was like unto a store most precious." Contemplation showed Redcrosse the "real New Jerusalem" (xi.505–13); by these allusions, Spenser associates it with Una and her father's kingdom, Eden (now restored).

25

All in the open hall amazéd stood,
At suddeinnesse of that unwarie° sight, *unexpected*
And wondred at his breathlesse hastie mood.
But he for nought would stay his passage right° *direct*
Till fast° before the king he did alight; *close*
Where falling flat, great humblesse he did make,
And kist the ground, whereon his foot was pight;° *placed*
Then to his hands that writ° he did betake, *document*
Which he disclosing, red thus, as the paper spake.

26

"To thee, most mighty king of Eden faire,
Her greeting sends in these sad lines addrest,
The wofull daughter, and forsaken heire
Of that great Emperour of all the West;
And bids thee be advizéd for the best,
Ere thou thy daughter linck in holy band
Of wedlocke to that new unknowen guest:
For he already plighted his right hand
Unto another love, and to another land.

27

"To me sad mayd, or rather widow sad,
He was affiauncéd long time before,
And sacred pledges he both gave, and had,
False erraunt knight, infamous, and forswore:
Witnesse the burning Altars, which° he swore, *by which*
And guiltie heavens of[1] his bold perjury,
Which though he hath polluted oft of yore,
Yet I to them for judgement just do fly,
And them conjure t' avenge this shamefull injury.

28

"Therefore since mine he is, or° free or bond, *whether*
Or false or trew, or living or else dead,
Withhold, O soveraine Prince, your hasty hond
From knitting league with him, I you aread;° *advise*
Ne wene° my right with strength adowne to tread, *think*
Through weakenesse of my widowhed, or woe:
For truth is strong, her rightfull cause to plead,
And shall find friends, if need requireth soe,
So bids thee well to fare, Thy neither friend, nor foe, Fidessa."

29

When he these bitter byting words had red,
The tydings straunge did him abashéd make,
That still he sate long time astonishéd
As in great muse, ne word to creature spake.
At last his solemne silence thus he brake,
With doubtfull eyes fast fixéd on his guest:
"Redoubted knight, that for mine onely sake
Thy life and honour late adventurest,
Let nought be hid from me, that ought to be exprest.

1. I.e., and heavens polluted by.

30

"What meane these bloudy vowes, and idle threats,
Throwne out from womanish impatient mind?
What heavens? what altars? what enragéd heates
Here heapéd up with termes of love unkind,° *unnatural*
My conscience cleare with guilty bands[2] would bind?
High God be witnesse, that I guiltlesse ame.
But if your selfe, Sir knight, ye faultie find,
Or wrappéd be in loves of former Dame,
With crime do not it cover, but disclose the same."

31

To whom the Redcrosse knight this answere sent,
"My Lord, my King, be nought hereat dismayd,
Till well ye wote by grave intendiment,[3]
What woman, and wherefore doth me upbrayd
With breach of love, and loyalty betrayd.
It was in my mishaps, as hitherward
I lately traveild, that unwares I strayd
Out of my way, through perils straunge and hard;
That day should faile me, ere I had them all declard.

32

"There did I find, or rather I was found
Of this false woman, that Fidessa hight,
Fidessa hight the falsest Dame on ground,
Most false Duessa, royall richly dight,
That easie was t' invegle° weaker sight: *deceive*
Who by her wicked arts, and wylie skill,
Too false and strong for earthly skill or might,
Unwares me wrought unto her wicked will,
And to my foe betrayd, when least I fearéd ill."

33

Then steppéd forth the goodly royall Mayd,
And on the ground her selfe prostrating low,
With sober countenaunce thus to him sayd:
"O pardon me, my soveraigne Lord, to show
The secret treasons, which of late I know
To have bene wroght by that false sorceresse.
She onely she it is, that earst did throw
This gentle knight into so great distresse,
That death him did awaite in dayly wretchednesse.

34

"And now it seemes, that she subornéd hath
This craftie messenger with letters vaine,
To worke new woe and improvided scath,[4]
By breaking of the band betwixt us twaine;
Wherein she uséd hath the practicke paine[5]
Of this false footman, clokt with simplenesse,
Whom if ye please for to discover plaine,
Ye shall him Archimago find, I ghesse,
The falsest man alive; who tries shall find no lesse."

2. I.e., bonds of guilt.
3. I.e., serious investigation.
4. Unexpected harm.
5. Treacherous skill.

35

The king was greatly movéd at her speach,
And all with suddein indignation fraight,° *filled*
Bad° on that Messenger rude hands to reach. *bade*
Eftsoones the Gard, which on his state did wait,
Attacht that faitor° false, and bound him strait: *impostor*
Who seeming sorely chauffèd° at his band, *angered*
As chainéd Beare, whom cruell dogs do bait,
With idle force did faine them to withstand,
And often semblaunce made to scape out of their hand.

36

But they him layd full low in dungeon deepe,
And bound him hand and foote with yron chains.
And with continaull watch did warely keepe;
Who then would thinke, that by his subtile trains
He could escape fowle death or deadly paines?[6]
Thus when that Princes wrath was pacifide,
He gan renew the late forbidden banes,[7]
And to the knight his daughter deare he tyde,
With sacred rites and vowes for ever to abyde.

37

His owne two hands the holy knots did knit,
That none but death for ever can devide;
His owne two hands, for such a turne most fit,
The housling° fire did kindle and provide, *sacramental*
And holy water thereon sprinckled wide;[8]
At which the bushy Teade° a groome did light, *marriage torch*
And sacred lampe in secret chamber hide,
Where it should not be quenchéd day nor night,
For feare of evill fates, but burnen ever bright.

38

Then gan they sprinckle all the posts with wine,
And made great feast to solemnize that day;
They all perfumde with frankensense divine,
And precious odours fetcht from far away,
That all the house did sweat with great aray:
And all the while sweete Musicke did apply
Her curious° skill, the warbling notes to play, *intricate*
To drive away the dull Melancholy;
The whiles one sung a song of love and jollity.

39

During the which there was an heavenly noise
Heard sound through all the Pallace pleasantly,

6. "And he laid hold on the dragon, that old serpent, which is the Devil, and Satan, and bound him a thousand years, And cast him into the bottomless pit, and shut him up, and set a seal upon him, that he should deceive the nations no more, till the thousand years should be fulfilled: and after that he must be loosed a little season" (Revelation xx.2–3).

7. Banns, i.e., announcements of marriage.

8. So marriages in ancient times were solemnized with sacramental fire and water. Plutarch (*Roman Questions* 1) explains the practice on four counts, of which two may especially have interested Spenser: (a) fire is masculine and active, water feminine and relatively passive; (b) as fire and water are most usefully productive in combination, so the joining of male and female in marriage appropriately completes society.

Like as it had bene many an Angels voice,
Singing before th' eternall majesty,
In their trinall triplicities[9] on hye;
Yet wist no creature, whence that heavenly sweet° *delight*
Proceeded, yet each one felt secretly° *inwardly*
Himselfe thereby reft of his sences meet,° *proper*
And ravishéd with rare impression in his sprite.[10]

40

Great joy was made that day of young and old,
And solemne feast proclaimd throughout the land,
That their exceeding merth may not be told:
Suffice it heare by signes to understand
The usuall joyes at knitting of loves band.
Thrise happy man the knight himselfe did hold,
Possesséd of his Ladies hart and hand,
And ever, when his eye did her behold,
His heart did seeme to melt in pleasures manifold.

41

Her joyous presence and sweet company
In full content he there did long enjoy,
Ne wicked envie, ne vile gealosy
His deare delights were able to annoy:
Yet swimming in that sea of blisfull joy,
He nought forgot, how he whilome had sworne,
In case he could that monstrous beast destroy,
Unto his Faerie Queene backe to returne:
The which he shortly did, and Una left to mourne.

42

Now strike your sailes ye jolly Mariners,
For we be come unto a quiet rode,° *harbor*
Where we must land some of our passengers,
And light this wearie vessell of her lode.
Here she a while may make her safe abode,
Till she repairéd have her tackles spent,° *worn out*
And wants supplide. And then againe abroad
On the long voyage whereto she is bent:
Well may she speede and fairely finish her intent.

9. The "trinall triplicities" are the nine angelic orders, divided, according to the pseudo-Areopagite, into three groups of three, the whole hierarchy corresponding to the nine spheres of the universe; what is heard in this stanza is, therefore, the music of the spheres.

10. Spirit. "Let us be glad and rejoice, and give honor to him: for the marriage of the Lamb is come" (Revelation xix.6). In Revelation, the marriage of Christ and the New Jerusalem signalizes the general redemption.

From The Second Booke of the Faerie Queene[1]

CONTAYNING

The Legend of Sir Guyon,
OR
OF TEMPERAUNCE

1

Right well I wote° most mighty Soveraine, — *know*
  That all this famous antique history,
  Of some th'aboundance of an idle braine
  Will judgéd be, and painted forgery,
  Rather then matter of just° memory, — *well-founded*
  Sith none, that breatheth living aire, does know,
  Where is that happy land of Faéry,
  Which I so much do vaunt, yet no where show,
But vouch° antiquities, which no body can know. — *assert*

2

But let that man with better sence advize,° — *consider*
  That of the world least part to us is red:° — *read, revealed*
  And dayly how through hardy enterprize,
  Many great Regions are discoveréd,
  Which to late age[2] were never mentionéd.
  Who ever heard of th' Indian *Peru*?
  Or who in venturous vessell measuréd

1. Book II is the story of Guyon, who represents and becomes the virtue of Temperance (or moderation, self-control) as Redcross represented, and became, Holiness. Guyon's companion is a "palmer," a "sage and sober" pilgrim, who represents Reason, and accordingly is left behind on some adventures which lead Guyon into sensuality. For example, though Guyon can overcome enemies which represent anger, fury, wrath, he is more vulnerable to the seductions of Acrasia's servant Phaedria, "immodest Merth," who conducts him across her Idle Lake. He doesn't stay, but in this adventure he loses the help of the Palmer, Reason. There are not as many battles and jousts in Book II as in Book I, because Temperance is a virtue which consists mainly of *not* doing things. The trials are appeals to the senses, so the eminent qualities of Book II are descriptive rather than narrative. Canto vii, the Cave of Mammon, corresponds roughly to the encounters with Orgoglio and Despair in Book I, but it is much more elaborately worked out and the atmosphere is especially notable. Guyon is not really tempted by Mammon's blandishments: there are some similarities here to the temptation of Christ by Satan. As Graham Hough says, (*A Preface to "The Faerie Queene,"* p. 157) "Guyon never seems to be in danger from Mammon, and if he faints at the end it is not that his virtue has been shaken but that he is exhausted by long dwelling in a life-destroying atmosphere. The strength of the Mammon scenes partly depends on this; they depart from the conventional pattern of temptations presented and overcome to the subtler horror of a poisoned atmosphere, an air that suffocates while it repels." The Mammon episode gave Spenser the opportunity to present a trip to the underworld, conventional in the epic, and in typical Renaissance fashion he mixes classical and Christian motifs: among those seen in Hell are Tantalus and Pontius Pilate. Sir Guyon stays below three days, as Jonah had spent three days in the whale's belly and Jesus three days in the tomb. There is much of the old folklore element in the Cave of Mammon episode, also: Guyon must not eat anything while he is there, for fear an "ugly feend" who follows in his footsteps will tear him into a thousand pieces (stanzas 27 and 64). So Proserpina in the classical myth had to spend time in Hell because she ate something there, and in the ancient Eleusinian mystery rites initiates were followed by "furies" to make sure they followed the ritual exactly.

2. To recent times.

The Amazons huge river now found trew?
Or fruitfullest Virginia who did ever vew?[3]

3

Yet all these were, when no man did them know;
Yet have from wisest ages hidden beene:
And later times things more unknowne shall show.
Why then should witless man so much misweene° *think wrongly*
That nothing is, but that which he hath seene?
What if within the Moones faire shining spheare?
What if in every other starre unseene
Of other worldes he happily° should heare? *by chance*
He wonder would much more: yet such to some appeare.

4

Of Faerie lond yet if he more inquire,
By certaine signes here set in sundry place
He may it find; ne let him then admire,° *wonder*
But yield his sence to be too blunt and bace,
That n'ote° without an hound fine footing trace. *cannot*
And thou, O fairest Princesse under sky,
In this faire mirrhour maist behold thy face,
And thine owne realmes in lond of Faéry,
And in this antique Image[4] thy great auncestry.

5

The which O pardon me thus to enfold
In covert vele,[5] and wrap in shadowes light,
That feeble eyes your glory may behold,
Which else could not endure those beamés bright;
But would be dazled with exceeding light.
O pardon, and vouchsafe with patient eare
The brave adventures of this Faery knight
The good Sir Guyon gratiously to heare,
In whom great rule of Temp'raunce goodly doth appeare.

Canto VII. [The Cave of Mammon]

Guyon findes Mammon in a delve,° pit, den
Sunning his threasure hore:° ancient
Is by him tempted, and led downe,
To see his secret store.

1

As Pilot well expert in perilous wave,
That to a stedfast starre his course hath bent,
When foggy mistes, or cloudy tempests have

3. In 1584 Sir Walter Ralegh laid at the feet of the Virgin Queen his claim to newly discovered lands in North America; she named the country "Virginia." In the second edition of *The Faerie Queene* the dedication calls Elizabeth "Queene of England, Fraunce and Ireland, *and of Virginia.*"

4. I.e., the poem.

5. Concealing veil.

The faithfull light of that faire lampe yblent,° *blinded*
And cover'd heaven with hideous dreriment,
Upon his card° and compas firmes his eye, *chart, map*
The maisters of his long experiment,° *experience*
And to them does the steddy helme apply,
Bidding his wingéd vessell fairely forward fly.

2

So Guyon having lost his trusty guide,[6]
Late left beyond that Ydle lake, proceedes
Yet on his way, of none accompanide;
And evermore himselfe with comfort feedes,
Of his owne vertues, and prayse-worthy deedes.
Long so he yode,° yet no adventure found, *went*
Which fame of her shrill trompet worthy reedes:° *considers*
For still he traveild through wide wastfull ground,
That nought but desert wildernesse shew'd all around.

3

At last he came unto a gloomy glade,
Cover'd with boughes and shrubs from heavens light,
Whereas he sitting found in secret shade
An uncouth, salvage,° and uncivile° wight, *savage / wild*
Of griesly hew, and fowle ill favour'd sight;
His face with smoke was tand, and eyes were bleard,
His head and beard with sout° were ill bedight,° *soot / covered*
His cole-blacke hands did seeme to have been seard
In smithes fire-spitting forge, and nayles like clawes appeard.

4

His yron coate all overgrowne with rust,
Was underneath envelopéd with gold,
Whose glistring glosse darkned with filthy dust,
Well it appeared, to have beene of old
A worke of rich entayle,° and curious mould,[7] *carving*
Woven with antickes° and wild Imagery: *fantastic figures*
And in his lap a masse of coyne he told,° *counted*
And turned upsidowne, to feed his eye
And covetous desire with his huge threasury.

5

And round about him lay on every side
Great heapes of gold, that never could be spent:
Of which some were rude owre,° not purifide *ore*
Of Mulcibers devouring element;[8]
Some others were new driven,° and distent° *beaten / drawn out*
Into great Ingoes,° and to wedges square; *ingots*
Some in round plates withouten moniment;° *impression*
But most were stampt, and in their metall bare
The antique shapes of kings and kesars° straunge and rare. *caesars*

6. Guyon's guide, the Palmer, was left behind when Phaedria ferried Guyon over the Idle Lake in Canto vi.

7. Intricate design.

8. Mulciber, also known as Hephaestos and Vulcan, was the classical god of fire.

6

Soone as he Guyon saw, in great affright
And hast he rose, for to remove aside
Those pretious hils from straungers envious sight,
And downe them pouréd through an hole full wide,
Into the hollow earth, them there to hide.
But Guyon lightly to him leaping, stayd
His hand, that trembled, as one terrifyde;
And though him selfe were at the sight dismayd,
Yet him perforce restrayed, and to him doubtfull sayd.

7

What art thou man, (if man at all thou art)
That here in desert hast thin habitaunce,
And these rich heapes of wealth doest hide apart
From the worldes eye, and from her right usaunce?° *usage*
Thereat with staring eyes fixéd askaunce° *as if*
In great disdaine, he answered, "Hardy Elfe,
That darest vew my direfull countenaunce,
I read° thee rash, and heedlesse of thy selfe, *consider*
To trouble my still seate,° and heapes of pretious pelfe.° *residence / plunder*

8

"God of the world and worldlings I me call,
Great Mammon, greatest god below the skye,
That of my plenty poure out unto all,
And unto none my graces do envye:° *begrudge*
Riches, renowme, and principality,
Honour, estate, and all this worldés good,
For which men swinck° and sweat incessantly, *labor*
Fro me do flow into an ample flood,
And in the hollow earth have their eternall brood.° *breeding place*

9

Wherefore if me thou deigne to serve and sew,° *follow*
At thy commaund lo all these mountaines bee;
Or if to thy great mind, or greedy vew
All these may not suffise, there shall to thee
Ten times so much be numbred francke and free."
"Mammon," said he, "thy godheades vaunt° is vaine, *boast*
And idle offers of thy golden fee;° *reward*
To them, that covet such eye-glutting gaine,
Proffer thy giftes, and fitter servaunts entertaine.

10

"Me ill besits, that in der-doing° armes, *courageous*
And honours suit° my vowed dayes do spend, *pursuit*
Unto thy bounteous baytes, and pleasing charmes,
With which weake men thou witchest,° to attend: *bewitchest*
Regard of worldly mucke doth fowly blend,° *defile*
And low abase the high heroicke spright,° *spirit*

That joyes for crownes and kingdomes to contend;
Faire shields, gay steedes, bright armes be my delight:
Those be the riches fit for an advent'rous knight."

11

"Vaine glorious Elfe," said he, "doest not thou weet,° *know*
That money can thy wantes at will supply?
Sheilds, steeds, and armes, and all things for thee meet
It can purvay in twinckling of an eye;
And crownes and kingdomes to thee multiply.
Do not I kings create, and throw the crowne
Sometimes to him, that low in dust doth ly?
And him that raignd, into his rowme° thrust downe, *place*
And whom I lust,° do heape with glory and renowne? *please*

12

"All otherwise," said he, "I riches read,° *interpret*
And deeme them roote of all disquietnesse;
First got with guile, and then preserv'd with dread,
And after spent with pride and lavishnesse,
Leaving behind them griefe and heavinesse.
Infinite mischiefes of them do arize,
Strife, and debate, bloudshed, and bitternesse,
Outrageous wrong, and hellish covetize,° *covetousness*
That noble heart as great dishonour doth despize.

13

"Ne thine be kingdomes, ne the scepters thine;
But realmes and rulers thou doest both confound,
And loyall truth to treason doest incline;
Witnesse the guiltlesse bloud pourd oft on ground,
The crownéd often slaine, the slayer cround,
The sacred Diademe in peeces rent,
And purple robe goréd with many a wound;
Castles surprizd, great cities sackt and brent:° *burned*
So mak'st thou kings, and gaynest wrongfull governement.

14

"Long were to tell the troublous stormes, that tosse
The private state,° and make the life unsweet: *condition*
Who° swelling sayles in Caspian sea doth crosse, *he who with*
And in frayle wood on Adrian° gulfe doth fleet,° *Adriatic / float*
Doth not, I weene, so many evils meet."
Then Mammon wexing wroth, "And why then," said.
Are mortall men so fond° and undiscreet, *foolish*
So evill thing to seeke unto their ayd,
And having not complaine, and having it upbraid?

15

"Indeede," quote he, "through fowle intemperaunce.
Frayle men are oft capitiv'd to covetise:
But would they thinke, with how small allowaunce
Untroubled Nature doth her selfe suffise,

Such superfluities they would despise,
Which with sad cares empeach° our native joyes: *impair*
At the well head the purest streames arise:
But mucky filth his braunching armes annoyes,
And with uncomely weedes the gentle wave accloyes°. *clogs*

16

"The antique° world, in his first flowring youth,[9] *ancient*
Found no defect in his Creatours grace,
But with glad thankes, and ureprovéd truth,
The gifts of soveraigne bountie did embrace:
Like Angels life was then mens happy cace;
But later ages pride, like corn-fed steed,
Abusd her plenty, and fat swolne encreace
To all licentious lust, and gan exceed
The measure of her meane,[1] and naturall first need.

17

"Then gan a curséd hand the quiet wombe
Of his great Grandmother with steele to wound,
And the hid treasures in her sacred tombe,
With Sacriledge to dig. Therein he found
Fountaines of gold and silver to abound,
Of which the matter of his huge desire
And pompous pride eftsoones° he did compound; *presently*
Then avarice gan through his veines inspire° *breathe*
His greedy flames, and kindled life-devouring fire."

18

"Sonne," said he then, "let by thy bitter scorne.
And leave the rudenesse of that antique age
To them, that liv'd therein in state forlorne;
Thou that doest live in later times, must wage° *barter*
Thy workes for wealth, and life for gold engage.° *hire out*
If then thee list my offred grace to use,
Take what thou please of all this surplusage;
If thee list not, leave have thou to refuse:
But thing refused, do not afterward accuse."

19

"Me list not," said the Elfin knight, "receave
Thing offred, till I know it well be got,
Ne wote° I, but thou didst these goods bereave° *know / remove*
From rightfull owner by unrighteous lot,[2]
Or that bloud guiltinesse or guile them blot.
"Perdy,"° quoth he. "yet never eye did vew, *truly*
Ne toung did tell,° ne hand these handled not, *count*
But safe I have them kept in secret mew,° *cave*
From heavens sight, and powre of all which them pursew."

9. Stanzas 16 and 17 present a traditional picture of the Golden Age, before technology, pride, and avarice had turned man into what he now is. The next ages, Silver, Brazen, and Iron (the present) showed gradual deterioration.

1. Limit of moderation.

2. Partition of plunder.

20

"What secret place," quoth he,[20] "can safely hold
So huge a masse, and hide from heavens eye?
Or where hast thou thy wonne,° that so much gold *home*
Thou canst preserve from wrong and robbery?
"Come thou," quoth he. "and see." So by and by
Through that thicke covert he him led, and found
A darkesome way, which no man could descry,° *discover*
That deepe descended through the hollow ground,
And was with dread and horrour compasséd around.

21

At length they came into a larger space,
That stretcht it selfe into an ample plaine,
Through which a beaten broad high way did trace,
That streight did lead to Plutoes griesly raine:[3]
By that wayes side, there sate infernall Payne,
And fast beside him sat tumultuous Strife:
The one in hand an yron whip did straine,° *grip*
The other brandishéd a bloudy knife,
And both did gnash their teeth, and both did threaten life.

22

On thother side in one consort° there sate, *group*
Cruell Revenge, and rancorous Despight,
Disloyall Treason, and hart-burning Hate,
But gnawing Gealosie out of their sight
Sitting alone, his bitter lips did bight,
And trembling Feare still to and fro did fly,
And found no place, where safe he shroud° him might, *hide*
Lamenting Sorrow did in darknesse lye.
And Shame his ugly face did hide from living eye.

23

And over them sad Horrour with grim hew,° *aspect*
Did alwayes sore, beating his yron wings;
And after him Owles and Night-ravens flew,
The hatefull messengers of heavy° things, *doleful*
Of death and dolour telling sad tidings;
Whiles sad Celeno,[4] sitting on a clift,
A song of bale° and bitter sorrow sings, *misfortune*
That hart of flint a sunder could have rift:° *torn*
Which having ended, after him she flyeth swift.

24

All these before the gates of Pluto lay,
By whom the passing, spake unto them nought.
But th' Elfin knight with wonder all the way

3. I.e., Pluto's horrible kingdom. Mammon was associated in Christian thought with wealth. According to the Sermon on the Mount, "where your treasure is, there will your heart be also. Ye cannot serve God and Mammon." The classical Plutus, god of wealth, and Pluto, god of the underworld, were often confused.

4. Celeno was a harpy in Virgil's *Aeneid* III.245–46. Harpies had the faces and breasts of women, but the wings and talons of birds. They were monsters of ill omen.

Did feed his eyes, and fild his inner thought.
At last him to a litle dore he brought,
That to the gate of Hell, which gaped wide,
Was next adjoyning, ne them parted ought:[5]
Betwixt them both was but a litle stride,
That did the house of Richesse from hell-mouth divide.

25

Before the dore sat selfe-consuming Care,
Day and night keeping wary watch and ward,
For feare least Force or Fraud should unaware
Breake in, and spoile° the treasure there in gard: *steal*
Ne would he suffer Sleepe once thither-ward
Approch, albe° his drowsie den were next; *although*
For next to death is Sleepe to be compard:
Therefore his house is unto his annext;
Here Sleep, there Richesse, and Hel-gate them both betwext.

26

So soone as Mammon there arriv'd, the dore
To him did open, and affoorded way;
Him followed eke Sir Guyon evermore,
Ne darkenesse him, ne daunger might dismay.
Soone as he entred was, the dore streight way
Did shut, and from behind it forth there lept
An ugly feend, more fowle then dismall day,[6]
The which with monstrous stalke behind him stept,
And ever as he went, dew° watch upon him kept. *due, proper*

27

Well hopéd he, ere long that hardy guest,
If ever covetous hand, or lustfull eye,
Or lips he layd on thing, that likt° him best, *pleased*
Or ever sleepe his eye-strings did untye,
Should be his pray. And therefore still° on hye *always*
He over him did hold his cruell clawes,
Threatning with greedy gripe to do him dye
And rend in peeces with his ravenous pawes,
If ever he transgrest the fatall Stygian lawes.[7]

28

That houses forme within was rude and strong
Like an huge cave, hewne out of rocky clift,
From whose rough vaut the ragged breaches° hong, *stalactites*
Embost with massy gold of glorious gift,° *quality*
And with rich metall loaded every rift,
That heavy ruine they did seeme to threat;
And over them Arachne[8] high did lift
Her cunning web, and spred her subtile net,
Enwrappéd in fowle smoke and clouds more blacke then jet.

5. Nothing separated them.
6. Latin *dies mali,* "evil days." There were two in each month, the first and the seventh from last.
7. Laws of the underworld, so called from Styx, its boundary.
8. For her arrogance and excessive pride in her weaving, she was turned into a spider by Athena (Ovid, *Metamorphoses*).

29

Both roofe, and floore, and wals were all of gold,
But overgrowne with dust and old decay,
And hid in darkenesse, that none could behold
The hew thereof: for vew of chearefull day
Did never in that house it selfe display,
But a faint shadow of uncertain light;
Such as a lamp, whose life does fade away:
Or as the Moone cloathed with clowdy night,
Does shew to him, that walkes in feare and sad affright.

30

In all that rowme was nothing to be seene,
But huge great yron chests and coffers strong,
All bard with double bends,° that none could weene° *bands/ think*
Them to efforce° by violence or wrong; *force open*
On every side they placéd were along.
But all the ground with sculs was scatteréd,
And dead mens bones, which round about were flong,
Whose lives, it seeméd, whilome° there were shed, *in the past*
And their vile carcases now left unburiéd.

31

They forward passe, ne Guyon yet spoke word,
Till that they came unto an yron dore,
Which to them opened of his owne accord,
And shewd of richesse such exceeding store,
As eye of man did never see before;
Ne ever could within one place be found,
Though all the wealth, which is, or was of yore,
Could gathered be through all the world around,
And that above were added to that under ground.

32

The charge thereof unto a covetous Spright
Commaunded was, who thereby did attend,
And warily awaited day and night,
From other covetous feends it to defend,
Who it to rob and ransacke did intend.
Then Mammon turning to that warriour, said;
"Loe here° the worldés blis, loe here the end, *behold*
To which all men do ayme, rich to be made:
Such grace now to be happy, is before thee laid."

33

"Certes," said he, "I n'ill° thine offred grace, *will not accept*
Ne to be made so° happy do intend: *thus*
Another blis before mine eyes I place,
Another happinesse, another end.
To them, that list, these base regardes° I lend:° *aims / relinquish*
But I in armes, and in atchievements brave,
Do rather choose my flitting houres to spend,
And to be Lord of those that riches have,
Then them to have my selfe, and be their servile sclave."

34

Thereat the feend his gnashing teeth did grate,
And griev'd, so long to lacke his greedy pray;[9]
For well he weenéd,° that so glorious bayte *supposed*
Would tempt his guest, to take thereof assay:° *trial*
Had he so doen, he had him snatcht away,
More light then Culver° in the Faulcons fist. *dove*
Eternall God thee save from such decay.° *ruin*
But whenas Mammon saw his purpose mist,
Him to entrap unwares another way he wist.° *thought of*

35

Thence forward he him led, and shortly brought
Unto another rowme, whose dore forthright,
To him did open, as it had beene taught:
Therein an hundred raunges weren pight,° *placed*
And hundred fornaces all burning bright;
By every fornace many feends did bide,
Deforméd creatures, horrible in sight,
And every feend his busie paines applide,
To melt the golden metall, ready to be tride.° *refined*

36

One with great bellowes gathered filling aire,
And with forst wind the fewell did inflame;
Another did the dying bronds° repaire *burning logs*
With yron toungs, and sprinckled oft the same
With liquid waves, fiers Vulcans rage to tame,
Who maistring them, renewd his former heat;
Some scumd the drosse, that from the metall came;
Some stird the molten owre with ladles great;
And every one did swincke,° and every one did sweat. *work*

37

But when as earthly wight they present saw,
Glistring in armes and battailous° aray, *warlike*
From their whot worke they did themselves withdraw
To wonder at the sight: for till that day,
They never creature saw, that came that way.
Their staring eyes sparckling with fervent fire,
And ugly shapes did nigh the man dismay,
That were it not for shame, he would retire,
Till that him thus bespake their soveraigne Lord and sire.

38

Behold, thou Faeries sonne, with mortall eye,
That° living eye before did never see: *what*
The thing, that thou didst crave so earnestly,
To weet, whence all the wealth late shewd by mee,
Proceeded, lo now is reveald to thee.
Here is the fountaine of the worldés good:

9. To be denied for so long the prey he desired.

Now therefore, if thou wilt enrichéd bee,
Avise thee° well, and chaunge thy wilfull mood, *consider*
Least thou perhaps hereafter wish, and be withstood."

39

"Suffise it then, thou Money God," quoth hee,
"That all thine idle offers I refuse.
All that I need I have; what needeth mee
To covet more, then I have cause to use?
With such vaine shewes thy worldlings vile abuse:° *delude*
But give me leave to follow mine emprise.°" *enterprise*
Mammon was much displeased, yet no'te° he chuse, *might not*
But beare the rigour of his bold mesprise,° *contempt*
And thence him forward led, him further to entise.

40

He brought him through a darksome narrow strait,
To a broad gate, all built of beaten gold:
The gate was open, but therein did wait
A sturdy villein, striding stiffe and bold,
As if that highest God defie he would;
In his right hand an yron club he held,
But he himselfe was all of golden mould,
Yet had both life and sence, and well could weld° *wield*
That curséd weapon, when his cruell foes he queld.° *killed*

41

Disdayne he calléd was, and did disdaine
To be so cald, and who so did him call:
Sterne was his looke, and full of stomacke° vaine, *arrogance*
His portaunce° terrible, and stature tall, *bearing*
Far passing th' hight of men terrestriall;
Like an huge Gyant of the Titans race,
That made him scorne all creatures great and small,
And with his pride all others powre deface:° *destroy*
More fit amongst blacke fiendes, then men to have his place.

42

Soone as those glitterand° armes he did espye, *glittering*
That with their brightnesse made that darknesse light,
His harmefull club he gan to hurtle° hye, *brandish*
And threaten batteill to the Faery knight;
Who likewise gan himselfe to batteill dight,° *prepare*
Till Mammon did his hasty hand withhold,
And counseld him abstaine from perilous fight:
For nothing might abash the villein bold,
Ne mortall steele emperce his miscreated mould.

43

So having him with reason pacifide,
And the fiers Carle° commaunding to forbeare, *churl*
He brought him in. The rowme was large and wide,
As it some Gyeld° or solemne Temple weare: *guild, guild-hall*

Many great golden pillours did upbeare
The massy roofe, and riches huge sustayne,
And every pillour deckéd was full deare° *richly*
With crownes and Diademes, and titles vaine,
Which mortall Princes wore, whiles they on earth did rayne.

44

A route° of people there assembled were, *crowd*
Of every sort and nation under skye,
Which with great uprore preacéd° to draw nere *pressed*
To th' upper part, where was advancéd hye
A stately siege° of soveraigne majestye; *seat*
And thereon sat a woman gorgeous gay,
And richly clad in robes of royaltye,
That never earthly Prince in such aray
His glory did enhaunce, and pompous pride display.

45

Her face right wondrous faire did seeme to bee,
That her broad beauties beam great brightness threw
Through the dim shade, that all men might it see:
Yet was not that same her owne native hew,
But wrought by art and counterfetted shew,
Thereby more lovers unto her to call;
Nath'lesse most heavenly faire in deed and vew
She by creation was, till she did fall;
Thenceforth she sought for helps, to cloke her crime withall.

46

There, as in glistring glory she did sit,
She held a great gold chaine ylincked well,[1]
Whose upper end to highest heaven was knit,
And lower part did reach to lowest Hell;
And all that preace° did round about her swell, *crowd*
To catchen hold of that long chaine, thereby
To clime aloft, and others to excell:
That was Ambition, rash desire to sty,° *rise*
And every lincke thereof a step of dignity.

47

Some thought to raise themselves to high degree,
By riches and unrighteous reward,
Some by close shouldring,[2] some by flatteree;
Others through friends, others for base regard;° *bribes*
And all by wrong wayes for themselves prepard.
Those that were up themselves, kept others low,
Those that were low themselves, held others hard,
Ne suffred them to rise or greater grow,
But every one did strive his fellow downe to throw.

48

Which whenas Guyon saw, he gan inquire,
What meant that preace about that Ladies throne,

1. The golden chain reaching to heaven appears in the *Iliad* VIII.19–22. Renaissance mythographers such as Natalis Comes took it to represent ambition.

2. Thrusting aside.

And what she was that did so high aspire.
Him Mammon answeréd: "That goodly one,
Whom all that folke with such contention,
Do flocke about, my deare, my daughter is;
Honour and dignitie from her alone,
Derivéd are, and all this worldés blis
For which ye men do strive: few get, but many mis.

49

"And faire Philotimé[3] she rightly hight,° *is called*
The fairest wight that wonneth° under skye, *lives*
But that this darksome neather world her light
Doth dim with horrour and deformitie,
Worthy of heaven and hye felicitie,
From whence the gods have her for envy thrust:
But sith thou hast found favour in mine eye,
Thy spouse I will her make, if that thou lust,° *wish*
That she may thee advance for workes and merites just."

50

"Gramercy° Mammon," said the gentle knight, *Thanks*
"For so great grace and offred high estate;
But I, that am fraile flesh and earthly wight,
Unworthy match for such immortall mate
My selfe well wote, and mine unequall fate;
And were I not, yet is my trouth yplight,
And love avowed to other Lady late,° *recently*
That to remove the same I have no might:
To chaunge love causelesse is reproch to warlike knight."

51

Mammon emmovéd was with inward wrath;
Yet forcing it to faine,[4] him forth thence led
Through griesly shadowes by a beaten path,
Into a gardin goodly garnishéd
With hearbs and fruits, whose kinds mote not be red:° *told*
Not such, as earth out of her fruitfull woomb
Throwes forth to men, sweet and well savouréd,
But direfull deadly blacke both leafe and bloom,
Fit to adorne the dead, and decke the drery toombe.

52

There mournful Cypresse grew in greatest store,
And trees of bitter Gall, and Heben sad,
Dead sleeping Poppy, and blacke Hellebore,
Cold Coloquintida, and Tetra mad,
Mortall Samnitis, and Cicuta bad,[5]
With which th' unjust Atheniens made to dy
Wise Socrates, who thereof quaffing glad
Pourd out his life, and last Philosophy
To the faire Critias his dearest Belamy.° *good friend*

3. The name, in Greek, means love of distinction or ambition.
4. Hiding his anger.
5. Cicuta is hemlock. The other plants mentioned are poisonous or associated with death.

53

The Gardin of Proserpina this hight;° *is called*
And in the midst thereof a silver seat,[6]
With a thicke Arber goodly over dight,° *spread*
In which she often vsd from open heat
Her selfe to shroud, and pleasures to entreat.° *enjoy*
Next thereunto did grow a goodly tree,
With braunches broad dispred° and body great, *spread out*
Clothed with leaves, that none the wood mote see
And loaden all with fruit as thicke as it might bee.

54

Their fruit were golden apples glistring bright,
That goodly was their glory to behold,
On earth like never grew, ne living wight
Like ever saw, but° they from hence were sold;° *unless / brought*
For those, which Hercules with conquest bold
Got from great Atlas daughters, hence began,
And planted there, did bring forth fruit of gold:
And those with which th' Eubaean young man wan° *won*
Swift Atalanta, when through craft he her out ran.[7]

55

Here also sprong that goodly golden fruit,
With which Acontius got his lover trew,
Whom he had long time sought with fruitlesse suit:
Here eke that famous golden Apple grew,
The which emongst the gods false Ate threw;
For which th' Idaean Ladies disagreed,
Till partiall° Paris dempt° it Venus dew, *prejudiced / judged*
And had of her, faire Helen for his meed,° *reward*
That many noble Greekes and Trojans made to bleed.

56

The warlike elfe, much wondred at this tree,
So faire and great, that shadowed all the ground,
And his broad braunches, laden with rich fee,° *bounty*
Did stretch themselves without the utmost bound
Of this great gardin, compast° with a mound, *surrounded*
Which over-hanging, they themselves did steepe,
In a blacke flood which flow'd about it round;
That is the river of Cocytus deepe,[8]
In which full many soules do endlesse waile and weepe.

57

Which to behold, he clomb up to the banke,
And looking downe, saw many damned wights,

6. The seat (mentioned again in Stanza 63) on which Theseus was condemned to sit in endless sloth. See Book I, Canto v, Stanza 35.

7. The famous golden apples from classical legend mentioned in these two stanzas are the apples of the Hesperides which Hercules had to steal as his eleventh labor; the apples tossed to the ground by Melanion of Euboea, causing the swift Atalanta to stop and pick them up, thereby losing the race to him; and finally, the apple which Ate, goddess of discord, tossed into a feast of the gods. It was marked "For the Fairest," and a contest arose among Venus, Juno, and Minerva, here called "*Idaean* Ladies" because the decision in favor of Venus was made on Mt. Ida by the prejudiced ("partiall") shepherd Paris.

8. A river of hell. The name means "lamentation" in Greek.

In those sad waves, which direfull deadly stanke,
Plongéd continually of° cruell Sprights, *by*
That with their pitteous cryes, and yelling shrights,° *shrieks*
They made the further shore resounden wide:
Emongst the rest of those same ruefull sights,
One cursed creature, he by chaunce espide,
That drenchéd lay full deepe, under the Garden side.

58

Deepe was he drenchéd to the upmost chin,
Yet gaped still, as coveting to drinke
Of the cold liquor, which he waded in,
And stretching forth his hand, did often thinke
To reach the fruit, which grew upon the brincke:
But both the fruit from hand, and floud from mouth
Did flie abacke, and made him vainely swinke:° *labor*
Thc whiles he sterv'd° with hunger and with drouth° *starved / thirst*
He daily dyde, yet never throughly° dyen couth.° *thoroughly / could*

59

The knight him seeing labour so in vaine,
Askt who he was, and what he ment thereby:
Who groning deepe, thus answerd him againe;
"Most curséd of all creatures under skye,
Lo Tantalus, I here tormented lye:
Of whom high Jove wont whylome feasted bee,[9]
Lo here I now for want of food doe dye:
But if that thou be such, as I thee see,
Of grace I pray thee, give to eat and drinke to mee."

60

"Nay, nay, thou greedie Tantalus," quoth he,
"Abide the fortune of thy present fate,
And unto all that live in high degree,° *rank*
Ensample be of mind intemperate,
To teach them how to use their present state."
Then gan the cursed wretch aloud to cry,
Accusing highest Jove and gods ingrate,
And eke blaspheming heaven bitterly,
As authour of unjustice, there to let him dye.

61

He lookt a little further, and espyde
Another wretch, whose carkasse deepe was drent° *submerged*
Within the river, which the same did hyde:
But both his hands most filthy feculent,° *feces-laden*
Above the water were on high extent,° *extended*
And faynd° to wash themselves incessantly; *tried*
Yet nothing cleaner were for such intent,
But rather fowler seemed to the eye;
So lost his labour vaine and idle° industry. *futile*

9. By whom Jove was formerly feasted. According to the Renaissance mythographer Natalis Comes, Tantalus was condemned to perpetual thirst because avaricious people can never get enough no matter how much wealth they have.

62

The knight him calling, askéd who he was,
Who lifting up his head, him answered thus:
I Pilate am the falsest Judge, alas,
And most unjust, that by unrightéous
And wicked doome,° to Jewes despiteous° *verdict / cruel*
Delivered up the Lord of life to die,
And did acquite a murdrer felonous;
The whiles my hands I washt in puritie,[10]
The whiles my soule was soyld with foule iniquitie."

63

Infinite moe,° tormented in like paine *more*
He there beheld, too long here to be told:
Ne Mammon would there let him long remaine,
For terrour of the tortures manifold,
In which the damnéd soules he did behold,
But roughly him bespake. "Thou fearefull foole,
Why takest not of that same fruit of gold,
Ne sittest downe on that same silver stoole,
To rest thy wearie person, in the shadow coole?"

64

All which he did, to doe him deadly fall
In frayle intemperance through sinfull bayt;
To which if he inclinéd had at all,
That dreadfull feend, which did behind him wayt,
Would him have rent in thousand peeces strayt:° *straightaway*
But he was warie wise in all his way,
And well perceivéd his deceiptfull sleight,° *trick*
Ne suffred lust° his safetie to betray; *greed*
So goodly did beguile the Guyler° of the pray. *deceiver*

65

And now he has so long remainéd there,
That vitall powres gan wexe both weake and wan,° *faint*
For want of food, and sleepe, which two upbeare,
Like mightie pillours, this fraile life of man,
That none without the same enduren can.
For now three dayes of men were full outwrought,° *completed*
Since he this hardie enterprize began:
For thy° great Mammon fairely he besought, *therefore*
Into the world to guide him backe, as he him brought.

66

The God, though loth, yet was constraind t' obay,
For lenger time, then that, no living wight
Below the earth, might suffred° be to stay: *allowed*
So backe againe, him brought to living light.
But all so soone as his enfeebled spright° *spirit*
Gan sucke this vitall aire into his brest,
As overcome with too exceeding might,
The life did flit away out of her nest,
And all his senses were with deadly fit opprest.

10. In token of purity. See Matthew xxvii.24.

From *Canto XII.* [*The Bower of Bliss*][1]

42

Thence passing forth, they shortly do arrive,
Whereas the Bowre of Blisse was situate;
A place pickt out by choice of best alive,[2]
That natures worke by art can imitate:
In which what ever in this worldly state
Is sweet, and pleasing unto living sense,
Or that may dayntiest fantasie aggrate,° — *please, satisfy*
Was pouréd forth with plentifull dispence,° — *liberality*
And made there to abound with lavish affluence.

43

Goodly it was encloséd round about,
Aswell their entred guestes to keepe within,
As those unruly beasts to hold without;
Yet was the fence thereof but weake and thin;
Nought feard their force, that fortilage° to win, — *fortalice, fort*
But wisedomes powre, and temperaunces might,[3]
By which the mightiest things efforcéd bin:° — *were*
And eke the gate was wrought of substaunce light,
Rather for pleasure, then for battery or fight.

44

Yt framéd was of precious yvory,
That seemd a worke of admirable wit;
And therein all the famous history
Of Jason and Medaea was ywrit;
Her mighty charmes, her furious loving fit,

1. In the present selection from the last Canto, Sir Guyon and the Palmer visit and destroy the Bower of Bliss. The Bower functions, much as Lucifera's palace or Orgoglio's dungeon did in Book I, as an allegorical locale where a symbolic action takes place. Spenser had first shown his readers the Bower in Canto v; there Cymochles is found reclining "amidst a flock of Damzelles"; they are half-naked, wantonly flirtatious, while he,"like an Adder lurking in the weedes, / His wandring thought in deep desire does steepe." That was, however, only a preliminary glimpse.

The "Bower of Bliss," perhaps the most famous of Spenser's "set pieces," has been variously interpreted. In *The Allegory of Love*, C. S. Lewis argues convincingly that the Bower "is not a picture of lawless, that is, unwedded love as opposed to lawful love. It is a picture, one of the most powerful ever painted, of the whole sexual nature in disease. There is not a kiss or an embrace in the island: only male prurience and female provocation" (p. 332). This is especially true of Acrasia, the mistress of the Bower, whose name means both "excess" and "impotence"; she is seen (stanzas 77–79) statically posed, doing nothing, only *appearing* as the archetypal seductress. The Bower is certainly a place where sexuality is sterile. Some readers may find, however, that imagery partly overflows moral intention. For example, the two girls bathing in a pool (stanzas 63–68) are assuredly pin-ups out of a man's magazine of the mid-20th century—and yet Spenser compares them to the morning star and to the Venus of Cyprus (lines 577–80).

2. I.e., the best living artists. The imitating of nature by art had been foreshadowed in Canto v, where "art, striving to compare / with nature, did an Arber greene dispred" (II.v.272–73). Nature is important to Sir Guyon, as it was not to Redcrosse, because temperance is attainable by unaided nature, whereas holiness requires the help of grace.

3. The fear is not of the physical force of Guyon and the Palmer but of the virtuous power of their temperance and wisdom.

His goodly conquest of the golden fleece,
His falséd faith, and love too lightly flit,
The wondred° Argo, which in venturous peece — *admired*
First through the Euxine seas bore all the flowr of Greece.

45

Ye might have seene the frothy billowes fry° — *foam*
Under the ship, as thorough them she went,
That seemd the waves were into yvory,
Or yvory into the waves were sent;
And other where the snowy substaunce sprent° — *sprinkled*
With vermell,° like the boyes bloud therein shed, — *vermilion*
A piteous spectacle did represent,
And otherwhiles° with gold besprinkeléd; — *elsewhere*
Yt seemd th' enchaunted flame, which did Creüsa wed.[4]

46

All this, and more might in that goodly gate
Be red; that ever open stood to all,[5]
Which thither came: but in the Porch there sate
A comely personage of stature tall,
And semblaunce° pleasing, more than naturall, — *appearance*
That travellers to him seemd to entize;
His looser° garment to the ground did fall, — *too loose*
And flew about his heeles in wanton wize,
Not fit for speedy pace, or manly exercize.

47

They in that place him Genius° did call: — *guiding spirit*
Not that celestiall powre, to whom the care
Of life, and generation of all
That lives, pertaines in charge particulare,
Who wondrous things concerning our welfare,
And straunge phantomes doth let us oft forsee,
And oft of secret ill bids us beware:
That is our Selfe, whom though we do not see,
Yet each doth in him selfe it well perceive to bee.

48

Therefore a God him sage Antiquity
Did wisely make, and good Agdistes call:
But this same was to that quite contrary,
The foe of life, that good envyes° to all, — *grudges*
That secretly doth us procure to fall,
Through guilefull semblaunts,° which he makes us see. — *illusions*

4. Jason, in his ship the *Argo*, sought the Golden Fleece of the king of Colchis; the witch Medea, the king's daughter, fell in love with him and used "her mighty charmes" to help him obtain it (lines 392–93). The "boyes bloud" (line 402) refers to Absyrtus, Medea's younger brother, whose body she cut into pieces and scattered, to delay her father's pursuit by making him stop to collect the fragments. Later, Jason deserted Medea for Creüsa; in revenge, Medea gave the girl a dress which burst into fire when she put it on; the flame consumed and thus "wed" her (line 405). This tale of unnatural "furious loving," with all its attendant violence, is appropriate to the Bower.

5. "Wide is the gate, and broad is the way, that leadeth to destruction, and many there be which go in thereat" (Matthew vii.13).

He of this Gardin had the governall,
And Pleasures porter was devizd° to bee, *considered*
Holding a staffe in hand for more formalitee.

49

With diverse flowres he daintily was deckt,
And strowéd round about, and by his side
A mighty mazer° bowle of wine was set, *drinking*
As if it had to him bene sacrifide;
Wherewith all new-come guests he gratifide:
So did he eke Sir Guyon passing by:
But he his idle curtesie defide,
And overthrew his bowle disdainfully;
And broke his staffe, with which he charméd semblants sly.[6]

50

Thus being entred, they behold around
A large and spacious plaine, on every side
Strowed with pleasauns,° whose faire grassy ground *gardens*
Mantled with greene, and goodly beautifide
With all the ornaments of Floraes pride,
Wherewith her mother Art, as halfe in scorne
Of niggard Nature, like a pompous bride
Did decke her, and too lavishly adorne,
When forth from virgin bowre she comes in th' early morne.[7]

51

Thereto the Heavens alwayes Joviall,° *propitious*
Lookt on them lovely,° still in stedfast state, *lovingly*
Ne suffred storme nor frost on them to fall,
Their tender buds or leaves to violate,
Nor scorching heat, nor cold intemperate
T' afflict the creatures, which therein did dwell,
But the milde aire with season moderate
Gently attempred, and disposd so well,
That still it breathéd forth sweet spirit and holesome smell.

52

More sweet and holesome, then the pleasaunt hill
Of Rhodope, on which the Nimphe, that bore
A gyaunt babe, her selfe for griefe did kill;
Or the Thessalian Tempe, where of yore
Faire Daphne Phoebus hart with love did gore;
Or Ida, where the Gods loved to repaire,
When ever they their heavenly bowres forlore;[8]

6. I.e., raised deceitful apparitions. The rod and bowl are traditional emblems of enchantment (cf. for example, Duessa's cup, in I.viii.14).

7. Art no longer merely imitates nature but undertakes to supplant it, by excess.

8. Deserted. The nymph Rhodope, who had a "gyaunt babe," Athos, by Neptune (lines 460–62), was turned into a mountain; Daphne, another nymph, charmed Apollo so that he pursued her until she prayed for aid and was turned into a laurel tree; Mount Ida was the scene of the rape of Ganymede and the judgment of Paris, and the gods watched the Trojan War from its heights. These are all allusions to violent and unhappy passion—and yet the Bower is also compared to Mt. Parnassus, home of the Muses, and to the Garden of Eden.

Or sweet Parnasse, the haunt of Muses faire;
Or Eden selfe, if ought with Eden mote compaire.

53

Much wondred Guyon at the faire aspect
Of that sweet place, yet suffred no delight
To sincke into his sence, nor mind affect,
But passéd forth, and lookt still forward right,° *straight ahead*
Bridling his will, and maistering his might:
Till that he came unto another gate;
No gate, but like one, being goodly dight
With boughes and braunches, which did broad dilate° *spread out*
Their clasping armes, in wanton wreathings intricate.

54

So fashionéd a Porch with rare device,
Archt over head with an embracing vine,
Whose bounches hanging downe, seemed to entice
All passers by, to tast their lushious wine
And did themselves into their hands incline,
As freely offering to be gatheréd:
Some deepe empurpled as the Hyacint,° *jacinth*
Some as the Rubine,° laughing sweetly red, *ruby*
Some like faire Emeraudes, not yet well ripenéd.

55

And them amongst, some were of burnisht gold,
So made by art, to beautifie the rest,
Which did themselves emongst the leaves enfold,
As lurking from the vew of covetous guest,
That the weake bowes, with so rich load opprest,
Did bowe adowne, as over-burdenéd.
Under that Porch a comely dame did rest,
Clad in faire weedes,° but fowle disorderéd, *garments*
And garments loose, that seemd unmeet for womanhed.° *womanhood*

56

In her left hand a Cup of gold she held,
And with her right the riper° fruit did reach, *overripe*
Whose sappy liquor, that with fulnesse sweld,
Into her cup she scruzd,° with daintie breach *crushed*
Of her fine fingers, without fowle empeach,° *hindrance*
That so faire wine-presse made the wine more sweet:
Thereof she usd to give to drinke to each,
Whom passing by she happenéd to meet:
It was her guise,° all Straungers goodly so to greet. *custom*

57

So she to Guyon offred it to tast;
Who taking it out of her tender hond,
The cup to ground did violently cast,
That all in peeces it was broken fond,° *found*
And with the liquor stainéd all the lond.° *land*
Whereat Excesse exceedingly was wroth,
Yet no'te° the same amend, ne yet withstond, *knew not how to*

But suffered him to passe, all° were she loth; *although*
Who nought regarding her displeasure forward goth.

58

There the most daintie Paradise on ground,
It selfe doth offer to his sober eye,
In which all pleasures plenteously abound,
And none does others happinesse envye:
The painted[9] flowres, the trees upshooting hye,
The dales for shade, the hilles for breathing space,
The trembling groves, the Christall running by;
And that, which all faire workes doth most aggrace,° *add grace to*
The art, which all that wrought, appearéd in no place.

59

One would have thought (so cunningly, the rude,
And scornéd parts were mingled with the fine)
That nature had for wantonesse ensude° *imitated*
Art, and that Art at nature did repine;° *complain*
So striving each th' other to undermine,
Each did the others worke more beautifie;
So diff'ring both in willes, agreed in fine:[1]
So all agreed through sweete diversitie,
This Gardin to adorne with all varietie.

60

And in the midst of all, a fountaine stood,
Of richest substaunce, that on earth might bee,
So pure and shiny, that the silver flood
Through every channell running one might see;
Most goodly it with curious imageree
Was over-wrought, and shapes of naked boyes,
Of which some seemd with lively jollitee,
To fly about, playing their wanton toyes,° *sports*
Whilest others did them selves embay° in liquid joyes. *drench*

61

And over all, of purest gold was spred,
A trayle of yvie in his native hew:
For the rich metall was so colouréd,
That wight, who did not well avised it vew,
Would surely deeme it to be yvie trew:[2]
Low his lascivious armes adown did creepe,
That themselves dipping in the silver dew,
Their fleecy flowres they tenderly did steepe,
Which° drops of Christall seemd for wantones° to weepe. *on which/wantonness*

62

Infinit streames continually did well
Out of this fountaine, sweet and faire to see,

9. I.e., in bright colors (figurative).

1. I.e., at the end. Art and nature harmonize with each other in effect, although antagonistic in intention.

2. The golden ivy has attracted much critical comment as an image of artifice with a touch of the repellent about it.

The which into an ample laver° fell, *basin*
And shortly grew to so great quantitie,
That like a little lake it seemd to bee;
Whose depth exceeded not three cubits hight,
That through the waves one might the bottom see,
All pavéd beneath with Jasper shining bright,
That seemd the fountaine in that sea did sayle upright.

63

And all the margent round about was set,
With shady Laurell trees, thence to defend° *ward off*
The sunny beames, which on the billowes bet,
And those which therein bathéd, mote offend.
As Guyon hapned by the same to wend,
Two naked Damzelles he therein espyde,
Which therein bathing, seeméd to contend,
And wrestle wantonly, ne cared to hyde,
Their dainty parts from vew of any, which them eyde.

64

Sometimes the one would lift the other quight
Above the waters, and then downe againe
Her plong, as over maisteréd by might,
Where both awhile would coveréd remaine,
And each the other from to rise restraine;
The whiles their snowy limbes, as through a vele,
So through the Christall waves appearéd plaine:
Then suddeinly both would themselves unhele,° *uncover*
And th' amarous sweet spoiles to greedy eyes revele.

65

As that faire Starre, the messenger of morne,
His deawy face out of the sea doth reare:
Or as the Cyprian goddesse,[3] newly borne
Of th' Oceans fruitfull froth, did first appeare:
Such seeméd they, and so their yellow heare
Christalline humour[4] droppéd downe apace.
Whom such when Guyon saw, he drew him neare,
And somewhat gan relent his earnest pace,
His stubborne brest gan secret pleasaunce to embrace.

66

The wanton Maidens him espying, stood
Gazing a while at his unwonted guise;° *manner*
Then th' one her selfe low duckéd in the flood,
Abasht, that her a straunger did avise:° *see*
But th' other rather higher did arise,
And her two lilly paps aloft displayd,
And all, that might his melting hart entise
To her delights, she unto him bewrayed:° *revealed*
The rest hid underneath, him more desirous made.

3. Venus (one of whose principal shrines was on the island of Cyprus).

4. Clear liquid.

67

With that, the other likewise up arose,
And her faire lockes, which formerly were bownd
Up in one knot, she low adowne did lose:° — *loosen*
Which flowing long and thick, her clothed arownd,
And th' yvorie in golden mantle gownd:
So that faire spectacle from him was reft,
Yet that, which reft it, no lesse faire was fownd:
So hid in lockes and waves from lookers theft,
Nought but her lovely face she for his looking left.

68

Withall she laughéd, and she blusht withall,
That blushing to her laughter gave more grace,
And laughter to her blushing, as did fall:
Now when they spide the knight to slacke his pace,
Them to behold, and in his sparkling face
The secret signes of kindled lust appeare,
Their wanton meriments they did encreace,
And to him beckned, to approach more neare,
And shewd him many sights, that courage cold could reare.[5]

69

On which when gazing him the Palmer saw,
He much rebukt those wandring eyes of his,
And counseld well, him forward thence did draw.
Now are they come nigh tc the Bowre of blis
Of her fond favorites so named amis:
When thus the Palmer: "Now Sir, well avise;° — *take care*
For here the end of all our travell is:
Here wonnes° Acrasia, whom we must surprise, — *dwells*
Else she will slip away, and all our drift° despise." — *plan, effort*

70

Eftsoones they heard a most melodious sound,
Of all that mote delight a daintie eare,
Such as attonce might not on living ground,
Save in this Paradise, be heard elswhere:
Right hard it was, for wight, which did it heare,
To read, what manner musicke that mote bee:
For all that pleasing is to living eare,
Was there consorted in one harmonee,
Birdes, voyces, instruments, windes, waters, all agree.

71

The joyous birdes shrouded in chearefull shade,
Their notes unto the voyce attempred° sweet; — *attuned*
Th' Angelicall soft trembling voyces made
To th' instruments divine respondence meet:° — *fitting*
The silver sounding instruments did meet° — *join*
With the base murmure of the waters fall:
The waters fall with difference discreet,° — *suitable*

5. That could arouse a cold spirit.

Now soft, now loud, unto the wind did call:
The gentle warbling wind low answered to all.[6]

72

There, whence that Musick seeméd heard to bee,
Was the faire Witch her selfe now solacing,
With a new Lover, whom through sorceree
And witchcraft, she from farre did thither bring:
There she had him now layd a slombering,
In secret shade, after long wanton joyes:
Whilst round about them pleasauntly did sing
Many faire Ladies, and lascivious boyes,
That ever mixt their song with light licentious toyes.° *games*

73

And all that while, right over him she hong,
With her false° eyes fast fixéd in his sight, *deceitful*
As seeking medicine, whence she was stong,
Or greedily depasturing° delight: *feeding on*
And oft inclining downe with kisses light,
For feare of waking him, his lips bedewd,
And through his humid eyes did sucke his spright,
Quite molten into lust and pleasure lewd;
Wherewith she sighéd soft, as if his case she rewd.° *pitied*

74

The whiles some one did chaunt this lovely lay:
"Ah see, who so faire thing doest faine° to see *delight*
In springing flowre the image of thy day;
Ah see the Virgin Rose, how sweetly shee
Doth first peepe forth with bashfull modestee
That fairer seemes, the lesse ye see her may;
Lo see soone after, how more bold and free
Her baréd bosome she doth broad display;
Loe see soone after, how she fades, and falles away.

75

"So passeth, in the passing of a day,
Of mortall life the leafe, the bud, the flowre,
Ne more doth flourish after first decay,
That earst was sought to decke both bed and bowre,
Of many a Ladie, and many a Paramowre: ° *lover*
Gather therefore the Rose, whilest yet is prime
For soone comes age, that will her pride deflowre:
Gather the Rose of love, whilest yet is time,
Whilest loving thou mayst lovéd be with equal crime."° *sin*

6. Taste, sight, smell, and sound are all titillated here; little is said, however, of touching. Acrasia, whom we are about to see, bears many resemblances to Circe (not only the cool figure of *Odyssey* X, but the much more witchlike and seductive creature painted by Ovid) and to the enchantresses of Italian romance who derive from Circe, such as Acratia in Trissino's *L'Italia Liberata* and Armida in Tasso's *Gerusalemme Liberata* In fact, much of the description in Canto xii is imitated from Armida's garden in that poem, and the rose song of stanzas 74 and 75 (a classic statement of the *carpe-diem* theme) is a direct translation.

76

He ceast, and then gan all the quire of birdes
  Their diverse notes t' attune unto his lay,
  As in approvance of his pleasing words.
  The constant paire heard all, that he did say,
  Yet swarved not, but kept their forward way,
  Through many covert groves, and thickets close,
  In which they creeping did at last display° *discover*
  That wanton Ladie, with her lover lose,° *wanton*
Whose sleepie head she in her lap did soft dispose.

77

Upon a bed of Roses she was layd,
  As faint through heat, or dight to pleasant sin,
  And was arayd, or rather disarayd,
  All in a vele of silke and silver thin,
  That hid no whit her alablaster skin,
  But rather shewd more white, if more might bee:
  More subtile web Arachne° cannot spin, *the spider*
  Nor the fine nets, which oft we woven see
Of scorched deaw, do not in th' aire more lightly flee.° *float*

78

Her snowy brest was bare to readie spoyle
  Of hungry eies, which n'ote° therewith be fild, *could not*
  And yet through languor of her late sweet toyle,
  Few drops, more cleare than Nectar, forth distild,
  That like pure Orient perles adowne it trild,° *trickled*
  And her faire eyes sweet smyling in delight,
  Moystened their fierie beames, with which she thrild
  Fraile harts, yet quenchéd not; like starry light
Which sparckling on the silent waves, does seeme more bright.

79

The young man sleeping by her, seemd to bee
  Some goodly swayne of honorable place,° *rank*
  That certés it great pittie was to see
  Him his nobilitie so foule deface;° *disgrace*
  A sweet regard, and amiable grace,
  Mixed with manly sternnesse did appeare
  Yet sleeping, in his well proportioned face,
  And on his tender lips the downy heare
Did now but freshly spring, and silken blossomes beare.

80

His warlike armes, the idle instruments
  Of sleeping praise,° were hong upon a tree, *worthiness*
  And his brave shield, full of old moniments,° *marks of honor*
  Was fowly ra'st,[7] that none the signes might see;
  Ne for them, ne for honour caréd hee,
  Ne ought, that did to his advauncement tend,

7. Erased. The removal of the emblems from his shield was the last disgrace of a knight.

But in lewd loves, and wastfull luxuree,
His dayes, his goods, his bodie he did spend:
O horrible enchantment, that him so did blend.° *blind*

81

The noble Elfe,[8] and carefull Palmer drew
So nigh them, minding nought, but lustfull game,
That suddein forth they on them rusht, and threw
A subtile net, which onely for the same
The skilfull Palmer formally° did frame. *scientifically*
So held them under fast, the whiles the rest
Fled all away for feare of fowler shame.
The faire Enchauntresse, so unwares opprest,° *surprised*
Tryde all her arts, and all her sleights, thence out to wrest.

82

And eke her lover strove: but all in vaine;
For that same net so cunningly was wound,
That neither guile, nor force might it distraine.° *tear*
They tooke them both, and both them strongly bound
In captive bandes, which there they readie found:
But her in chaines of adamant he tyde;
For nothing else might keepe her safe and sound;
But Verdant[9] (so he hight) he soone untyde,
And counsell sage in steed thereof to him applyde.

83

But all those pleasant bowres and Pallace brave,° *splendid*
Guyon broke downe, with rigour pittilesse;
Ne ought their goodly workmanship might save
Them from the tempest of his wrathfulnesse,
But that their blisse he turned to balefulnesse:
Their groves he feld, their gardins did deface,
Their arbers spoyle, their Cabinets° suppresse, *summerhouses*
Their banket houses burne, their buildings race,° *raze*
And of the fairest late, now made the fowlest place.

84

Then led they her away, and eke that knight
They with them led, both sorrowfull and sad:
The way they came, the same retourned they right,
Till they arrivéd, where they lately had
Charmed those wild-beasts, that raged with furie mad.
Which now awaking, fierce at them gan fly,
As in their mistresse reskew, whom they lad;° *lead*
But them the Palmer soone did pacify.
Then Guyon askt, what meant those beastes, which there did ly.

85

Said he, "These seeming beasts are men indeed,
Whom this Enchauntresse hath transforméd thus,
Whylome her lovers, which her lusts did feed,
Now turned into figures hideous,

8. Knight of fairyland.
9. The name means "green" and may refer, therefore, to a young man in the springtime of his sensuality.

According to their mindes like monstruous."[10]
"Sad end," quoth he, "of life intemperate,
And mournefull meed of joyes delicious:
But Palmer, if it mote thee so aggrate,° *please*
Let them returnéd be unto their former state."

86

Streight way he with his vertuous staffe them strooke,
And streight of beasts they comely men became;
Yet being men they did unmanly looke,
And staréd ghastly, some for inward shame,
And some for wrath, to see their captive Dame:
But one above the rest in speciall,
That had an hog beene late, hight Grille by name,
Repinéd greatly, and did him miscall,° *abuse*
That had from hoggish forme him brought to naturall.

87

Said Guyon, "See the mind of beastly man,
That hath so soone forgot the excellence
Of his creation, when he life began,
That now he chooseth, with vile difference,° *change*
To be a beast, and lacke intelligence."
To whom the Palmer thus, "The donghill kind
Delights in filth and foule incontinence:
Let Grill be Grill, and have his hoggish mind,
But let us hence depart, whilest wether serves and wind."

Book VII. Two Cantos of Mutabilitie[1]

Canto VI

Proud Change (not pleasd, in mortall things,
beneath the Moon, to raigne)
Pretends,° as well of Gods, as Men, *attempts*
To be the Soveraine.

1

What man that sees the ever-whirling wheele
Of Change, the which all mortall things doth sway,° *rule*
But that thereby doth find, and plainly feele,
How MUTABILITY in them doth play

10. Circe had changed Odysseus' companions into swine, but Odysseus was empowered to release them. Cf. also the animals upon which the sins rode in I.v.

1. Two cantos and two stanzas of another, called "the Mutability Cantos," were first published in 1609, ten years after Spenser's death. According to the title page, they "appear to be parcel of some following book of *The Faerie Queene*, under the legend of Constancie." If so, they are a longer digression from the story than any now in the poem. These cantos give Spenser's reflections, influenced perhaps by Lucretius, on change and permanence in the world—a subject which fascinated the Elizabethan imagination.

Her cruell sports, to many mens decay?° *destruction*
Which that to all may better yet appeare,
I will rehearse that whylome° I heard say, *formerly*
How she at first her selfe began to reare,
Gainst all the Gods, and th' empire sought from them to beare.

2

But first, here falleth fittest to unfold
Her antique race and linage ancient,
As I have found it registred of old,
In Faery Land mongst records permanent:
She was, to weet,° a daughter by descent *wit*
Of those old Titans,[2] that did whylome strive
With Saturnes sonne for heavens regiment.° *rule*
Whom though high Jove of kingdome did deprive,
Yet many of their stemme long after did survive.

3

And many of them, afterwards obtained
Great power of Jove, and high authority;
As Hecaté,[3] in whose almighty hand,
He plac't all rule and principality,
To be by her disposéd diversly,
To Gods, and men, as she them list° divide: *wished to*
And drad Bellona,[4] that doth sound on hie
Warres and allarums unto Nations wide,
That makes both heaven and earth to tremble at her pride.

4

So likewise did this Titanesse aspire,
Rule and dominion to her selfe to gaine;
That as a Goddesse, men might her admire,° *wonder at*
And heavenly honours yield, as to them twaine.
At first, on earth she sought it to obtaine;
Where she such proofe and sad examples shewed
Of her great power, to many ones great paine,
That not men onely (whom she soone subdewed)
But eke all other creatures, her bad dooings rewed.

5

For she the face of earthly things so changed,
That all which Nature had establisht first
In good estate, and in meet° order ranged, *fitting*
She did pervert, and all their statutes burst:
And all the worlds faire frame (which none yet durst
Of Gods or men to alter or misguide)
She altered quite, and made them all accurst
That God had blest; and did at first provide
In that still happy state for ever to abide.

2. The Titans were the sons and daughters of sky and earth; their king was Cronus (time). Jove, Cronus' son, dethroned him and established the rule of the gods. But some descendants of the original Titans, such as Prometheus, Hecate, and others, survived. Spenser invents another, a Titaness called Mutability.

3. A triple goddess, in heaven known as Luna, on earth Diana, in hell Hecate.

4. Patroness of war and conflict.

6

Ne shee the lawes of Nature onely brake,
But eke of Justice, and of Policie;° *prudent rule*
And wrong of right, and bad of good did make,
And death for life exchangéd foolishlie;
Since which, all living wights have learned to die,
And all this world is woxen° daily worse. *grown*
O pittious worke of MUTABILITIE!
By which, we all are subject to that curse,
And death in stead of life have suckéd from our Nurse.

7

And now, when all the earth she thus had brought
To her behest,° and thralléd to her might, *bidding*
She gan to cast° in her ambitious thought, *resolve*
T' attempt the empire of the heavens hight,
And Jove himself to shoulder from his right.
And first, she past the region of the ayre,
And of the fire, whose substance thin and slight,
Made no resistance, ne could her contraire,° *oppose*
But ready passage to her pleasure did prepaire.

8

Thence, to the Circle of the Moone she clambe,° *climbed*
Where Cynthia raignes in everlasting glory,[5]
To whose bright shining palace straight she came,
All fairely deckt with heavens goodly story;[6]
Whose silver gates (by which there sate an hory
Old aged Sire, with hower-glasse in hand,
Hight Tyme) she entred, were he liefe or sory;[7]
Ne staide till she the highest stage° had scand,° *level / reached*
Where Cynthia did sit, that never still did stand.

9

Her sitting on an Ivory throne shee found,
Drawne of two steeds, th' one black, the other white,
Environd with tenne thousand starres around,
That duly her attended day and night;
And by her side, there ran her Page, that hight
Vesper, whom we the Evening-starre intend:° *call*
That with his Torche, still twinkling like twylight,
Her lightened all the way where she should wend,
And joy to weary wandring travailers did lend:

10

That when the hardy Titanesse beheld
The goodly building of her Palace bright,
Made of the heavens substance, and up-held
With thousand Crystall pillors of huge hight,
Shee gan to burne in her ambitious spright,° *spirit*

5. Cynthia, Diana, or Phoebe, the moon goddess, often associated with Queen Elizabeth in poetry.

6. I.e., rows of stars.

7. I.e., whether he liked it or not.

And t' envie her that in such glorie raigned.
Eftsoones she cast by force and tortious° might, *wrongful*
Her to displace; and to her self to have gained
The kingdome of the Night, and waters by her wained.° *moved*

11

Boldly she bid the Goddesse downe descend,
And let her selfe into that Ivory throne;
For, shee her selfe more worthy thereof wend,° *thought*
And better able it to guide alone:
Whether to men, whose fall she did bemone,
Or unto Gods, whose state she did maligne,° *envy*
Or to th' infernall powers, her need give lone° *loan*
Of her faire light, and bounty most benigne,
Her selfe of all that rule shee deeméd most condigne.° *worthy*

12

But shee that had to her that soveraigne seat
By highest Jove assigned, therein to beare
Nights burning lamp, regarded not her threat,
Ne yielded ought for favour or for feare;
But with sterne countenaunce and disdainfull cheare,° *expression*
Bending her hornéd browes, did put her back:
And boldly blaming her for comming there,
Bade her attonce from heavens coast to pack,
Or at her peril bide the wrathfull Thunders wrack.° *destruction*

13

Yet nathemore° the Giantesse forbare: *not at all*
But boldly preacing-on, raught° forth her hand *reached*
To pluck her downe perforce° from off her chaire *by force*
And there-with lifting up her golden wand,
Threatened to strike her if she did with-stand.
Where-at the starres, which round about her blazed,
And eke° the Moones bright wagon, still did stand, *also*
All beeing with so bold attempt amazed.
And on her uncouth° habit and sterne looke still gazed. *strange*

14

Meane-while, the lower World, which nothing knew
Of all that chauncéd here, was darkned quite;
And eke the heavens, and all the heavenly crew
Of happy wights,° now unpurvaide° of light, *beings/deprived*
Were much afraid, and wondred at that sight;
Fearing least° Chaos broken had his chaine, *lest*
And brought againe on them eternall night:
But chiefely Mercury, that next doth raigne,[8]
Ran forth in haste, unto the king of Gods to plaine.° *complain*

15

All ran together with a great out-cry,
To Joves faire Palace, fixt in heavens hight;

8. In the Ptolemaic system, the sphere of Mercury was next beyond that of the moon; in mythology, Mercury was the messenger of the gods. His Greek name was Hermes.

And beating at his gates full earnestly,
Gan call to him aloud with all their might,
To know what meant that suddaine lack of light.
The father of the Gods when this he heard,
Was troubled much at their so strange affright,
Doubting least Typhon[9] were againe upreared,
Or, other his old foes, that once him sorely feared.° *frightened*

16

Eftsoones the sonne of Maia[1] forth he sent
Downe to the Circle of the Moone, to knowe
The cause of this so strange astonishment,
And why shee did her wonted course forslowe,° *delay*
And if that any were on earth belowe
That did with charmes or Magick her molest,
Him to attache,° and downe to hell to throwe: *seize*
But, if from heaven it were, then to arrest
The Author, and him bring before his presence prest.° *immediately*

17

The wingd-foot God, so fast his plumes did beat,
That soone he came where-as the Titanesse
Was striving with fair Cynthia for her seat:
At whose strange sight, and haughty hardinesse,° *boldness*
He wondred much, and fearéd her no lesse.
Yet laying feare aside to doe his charge,° *assignment*
At last, he bade her, with bold stedfastnesse,
Cease to molest the Moone to walke at large,[2]
Or come before high Jove, her dooings to discharge.° *justify*

18

And there-with-all, he on her shoulder laid
His snaky-wreathéd Mace,[3] whose awfull power
Doth make both Gods and hellish fiends affraid;
Where-at the Titanesse did sternely lower,° *scowl*
And stoutly answered, that in evill hower
He from his Jove such message to her brought,
To bid her leave faire Cynthias silver bower;
Sith shee his Jove and him esteeméd nought,
No more than Cynthia's selfe; but all their kingdoms sought.

19

The Heavens Herald staid not to reply,
But past away, his doings to relate
Unto his Lord; who now in th' highest sky,
Was placéd in his principall Estate,
With all the Gods about him congregate:
To whom when Hermes had his message told,
It did them all exceedingly amate,° *dismay*
Save Jove; who, changing nought his count'nance bold,
Did unto them at length these speeches wise unfold:

9. A giant who had rebelled against Jove.
1. I.e., Mercury.
2. I.e., stop interfering with the moon's free movement.
3. I.e., the caduceus, Mercury's rod which could bring spirits from the underworld.

20

"Harken to mee awhile yee heavenly Powers;
Ye may remember since° th' Earth's curséd seed *before this*
Sought to assaile the heavens eternall towers,
And to us all exceeding feare did breed:
But how we then defeated all their deed,
Yee all doe knowe, and them destroiéd quite;
Yet not so quite, but that there did succeed
An off-spring of their bloud, which did alite
Upon the fruitfull earth, which doth us yet despite.° *treat with contempt*

21

"Of that bad seed is this bold woman bred,
That now with bold presumption doth aspire
To thrust faire Phoebe from her silver bed,
And eke ourselves from heavens high Empire,
If that her might were match to her desire:
Wherefore, it now behoves us to advise° *consider*
What way is best to drive her to retire;
Whether by open force, or counsell wise,
Areed° ye sonnes of God, as best ye can devise." *advise*

22

So having said, he ceast; and with his brow,
His black eye-brow, whose doomefull dreaded beck[4]
Is wont to wield the world unto his vow,° *will*
And even the highest Powers of heaven to check,
Made signe to them in their degrees to speake:
Who straight gan cast their counsell grave and wise.
Meane-while, th' Earths daughter,[5] thogh she nought did reck
Of Hermes message, yet gan now advise
What course were best to take in this hot bold emprize.° *undertaking*

23

Eftsoones she thus resolved; that whilst the Gods,
After return of Hermes Embassie,
Were troubled, and amongst themselves at ods,
Before they could new counsels re-allie,° *reorganize*
To set upon them in that extasie;° *disorder*
And take what fortune time and place would lend:
So, forth she rose, and through the purest sky
To Joves high Palace straight cast° to ascend *resolved*
To prosecute her plot: Good on-set boads good end.

24

Shee there arriving, boldly in did pass;
Where all the Gods she found in counsell close,° *secluded*
All quite unarmed, as then their manner was.
At sight of her they suddaine all arose,
In great amaze, ne wist what way to chose.

4. I.e., his awesome nod of judgment. 5. I.e., Mutability.

But Jove, all fearlesse, forced them to aby;° *remain*
And in his soveraine throne, gan straight dispose
Himselfe more full of grace and Majestie,
That mote° encheare° his friends, and foes mote terrifie. *might/encourage*

25

That, when the haughty Titanesse beheld
All° were she fraught with pride and impudence, *although*
Yet with the sight thereof was almost queld;° *killed*
And inly quaking, seemed as reft of sense,
And void of speech in that drad° audience; *dread*
Untill that Jove himself, herself bespake:
"Speake thou fraile woman, speake with confidence,
Whence art thou, and what doost thou here now make?° *do*
What idle errand hast thou, earth's mansion to forsake?"

26

Shee, halfe confuséd with his great commaund,
Yet gathering spirit of her natures pride,
Him boldly answered thus to his demaund:
"I am a daughter, by the mothers side
Of her that is Grand-mother magnifide° *glorified*
Of all the Gods, great Earth, great Chaos child.[6]
But by the fathers (be it not envíde)
I greater am in bloud, whereon I build,° *argue*
Then all the Gods, though wrongfully from heaven exiled.

27

"For Titan, as ye all acknowledge must,
Was Saturnes elder brother by birth-right,
Both sonnes of Uranus: but by unjust
And guilefull meanes, through Corybantes slight,° *trickery*
The younger thrust the elder from his right:[7]
Since which, thou Jove, injuriously hast held
The Heavens rule from Titans sonnes by might;
And them to hellish dungeons downe hast feld:° *thrown*
Witnesse ye Heavens the truth of all that I have teld."

28

Whilst she thus spake, the Gods that gave good eare
To her bold words, and markéd well her grace,
Beeing of stature tall as any there
Of all the Gods, and beautifull of face,
As any of the Goddesses in place,
Stood all astonied, like a sort° of Steeres *herd*
Mongst whom, some beast of strange and forraine race,
Unwares is chaunc't, far straying from his peeres:
So did their ghastly gaze bewray° their hidden feares. *reveal*

6. Earth is the offspring of Chaos in Hesiod and later mythologies.

7. Titan, eldest son of Uranus, abdicated in favor of his younger brother Saturn on condition that Saturn would eat all his own children. When Jove was born to Rhea, Saturn's wife, she gave Saturn a stone to swallow instead of the baby, and her attendants, the Corybantes, beat on their shields to drown out the baby's cries. Eventually Jove deposed his father.

29

Till having pauzed awhile, Jove thus bespake;
"Will never mortall thoughts ceasse to aspire,
In this bold sort, to Heaven claime to make,
And touch celestiall seates with earthly mire?
I would have thought, that bold Procrustes hire,° *reward*
Or Typhons fall, or proud Ixions paine,
Or great Prometheus,[8] tasting of our ire,
Would have suffized, the rest for to restraine;
And warned all men by their example to refraine;

30

"But now, this off-scum of that curséd fry,° *progeny*
Dare to renew the like bold enterprize,
And chalenge th' heritage of this our skie;
Whom what should hinder, but that we likewise
Should handle as the rest of her allies,
And thunder-drive to hell?" With that, he shooke
His Nectar-deawéd[9] locks, with which the skyes
And all the world beneath for terror quooke,° *quaked*
And eft° his burning levin-brond° in hand he tooke. *then/lightning-bolt*

31

But when he lookéd on her lovely face,
In which, faire beames of beauty did appeare,
That could the greatest wrath soone turne to grace
(Such sway doth beauty even in Heaven beare)
He staide his hand; and having changed his cheare,° *mood*
He thus againe in milder wise began;
"But ah! if Gods should strive with flesh yfere,° *together*
Then shortly should the progeny of Man
Be rooted out, if Jove should doe still° what he can. *always*

32

"But thee faire Titans child, I rather weene,° *suppose*
Through some vaine errour or inducement light,
To see that° mortall eyes have never seene; *that which*
Or through ensample of thy sisters might,
Bellona;[1] whose great glory thou dost spight,° *envy*
Since thou hast seene her dreadfull power belowe,
Mongst wretched men, dismaide with her affright,
To bandie Crownes, and Kingdomes to bestowe;
And sure thy worth, no less then hers doth seem to showe.

33

"But wote° thou this, thou hardy Titanesse, *know*
That not the worth of any living wight

8. Procrustes was a robber who waylaid strangers and made them fit his bed by cutting or stretching them (Spenser includes him among those punished by Jove). Ixion tried to seduce Jove's wife and was punished by being bound to a wheel of fire in hell. Prometheus stole fire from heaven and gave it to man, for which Jove punished him by chaining him to a cliff where an eagle consumed his liver, which grew back every night. Typhon was a giant who had rebelled against Jove.

9. I.e., sprinkled with a fragrant balm; "nectar" more often referred to the drink of the gods.

1. Goddess of war, not a Titan in classical literature.

May challenge ought in Heavens interesse;[2]
Much lesse the Title of old Titans Right:
For we by Conquest of our soveraine might,
And by eternail doome of Fates decree,
Have wonne the Empire of the Heavens bright;
Which to our selves we hold, and to whom wee
Shall worthy deeme partakers of our blisse to bee.

34

"Then cease thy idle claime thou foolish gerle,
And seeke by grace and goodnesse to obtaine
That place from which by folly Titan fell;
There-to thou maist perhaps, if so thou faine° *wish*
Have Jove thy gratious Lord and Soveraigne."
So, having said, she thus to him replide,
"Ceasse Saturnes sonne, to seeke by proffers vaine
Of idle hopes t' allure me to thy side,
For° to betray my Right, before I have it tride. *in order*

35

"But thee, O Jove, no equall° Judge I deeme *impartial*
Of my desert, or of my dewfull° Right; *due*
That in thine owne behalfe maist partiall seeme:
But to the highest him, that is behight
Father of Gods and men by equall might;[3]
To weet,° the God of Nature, I appeale." *wit*
There-at Jove wexéd wroth, and in his spright
Did inly grudge, yet did it well conceale;
And bade Dan Phoebus Scribe[4] her Appellation° seale. *appeal*

36

Eftsoones the time and place appointed were,
Where all, both heavenly Powers, and earthly wights,
Before great Natures presence should appeare,
For triall of their Titles and best Rights:
That was, to weet, upon the highest hights
Of Arlo-hill[5] (Who knowes not Arlo-hill?)
That is the highest head, in all mens sights,
Of my old father Mole, whom Shepheards quill
Renowméd hath with hymnes fit for a rurall skill.

37

And, were it not ill fitting for this file,° *narrative*
To sing of hilles and woods, mongst warres and Knights,
I would abate the sternenesse of my stile,
Mongst these sterne stounds° to mingle soft delights; *clashes*
And tell how Arlo through Dianaes spights
(Being of old the best and fairest Hill

2. I.e., no living person, however worthy, can claim any title to power or authority in heaven.

3. I.e., who is called father of gods and men, with equal authority over both.

4. Phoebus (Apollo) is called "scribe" or secretary of the gods because he is the god of poetry.

5. I.e., Galtymore, a peak in the mountain range Spenser calls "my old father Mole," near Kilcolman Castle where he lived in Ireland. The last two lines of the stanza refer to Spenser's praise of Mole in his pastoral eclogue, *Colin Clouts Come Home Againe*.

That was in all this holy-Islands[6] hights)
Was made the most unpleasant, and most ill.
Meane while, O Clio, lend Calliope[7] thy quill.

38

Whylome,° when Ireland florishéd in fame *formerly*
Of wealths and goodnesse, far above the rest
Of all that beare the British Islands name,
The Gods then used, for pleasure and for rest,
Oft to resort there-to, when seemed them best:
But none of all there-in more pleasure found,
Then Cynthia;[8] that is soveraine Queene profest° *acknowledged*
Of woods and forrests, which therein abound,
Sprinkled with wholsom waters, more then most on ground.° *earth*

39

But mongst them all, as fittest for her game,° *recreation*
Either for chace of beasts with hound or boawe,
Or for to shroude in shade from Phoebus flame,
Or bathe in fountaines that doe freshly flowe,
Or from high hilles, or from the dales belowe,
She chose this Arlo; where she did resort
With all her Nymphes enrangéd on a rowe,
With whom the woody Gods did oft consort:
For with the Nymphes, the Satyres love to play and sport.[9]

40

Amongst the which, there was a Nymph that hight
Molanna;[1] daughter of old father Mole,
And sister unto Mulla, faire and bright:
Unto whose bed false Bregog whylome stole,
That Shepheard Colin dearely° did condole,° *earnestly/lament*
And made her lucklesse loves well knowne to be.
But this Molanna, were she not so shole,° *shallow*
Were no lesse faire and beautifull then shee:
Yet as she is, a fairer flood may no man see.

41

For, first, she springs out of two marble Rocks,
On which, a grove of Oakes high mounted growes,
That as a girlond seemes to deck the locks
Of som faire Bride, brought forth with pompous° showes *with pomp*
Out of her bowre, that many flowers strowes:
So, through the flowry Dales she tumbling downe,

6. Ireland is called the "holy-Island" because according to legend, Christianity first found a foothold there and thence spread to the other British isles.
7. Clio was the muse of history, Calliope of epic poetry.
8. I.e., Diana, goddess of the forest, fond of hunting.
9. Nymphs in Greek mythology were minor female deities of streams, springs, trees, and other parts of nature. Satyrs were minor male gods of the woods, given to drinking and sensual pleasure. The Romans identified them with their goat-footed *fauni*; hence "Faunus" (line 376) and "Faune" (line 411).
1. The shallow, rocky river Behanna; Mulla is the river Awbeg, whose joining with the river Bregog is told in *Colin Clouts Come Home Againe*.

Through many woods, and shady coverts flowes,
That on each side her silver channell crowne,
Till to the Plaine she come, whose Valleyes shee
doth drowne.

42

In her sweet streames, Diana uséd oft,
After her sweatie chace and toilsome play,
To bathe her selfe; and after, on the soft
And downy grasse, her dainty limbes to lay
In covert shade, where none behold her may:
For much she hated sight of living eye.
Foolish God Faunus, though full many a day
He saw her clad, yet longéd foolishly
To see her naked mongst her Nymphes in privity.[2]

43

No way he found to compasse° his desire, *accomplish*
But to corrupt Molanna, this her maid,
Her to discover for some secret hire:° *bribe*
So, her with flattering words he first assaid;
And after, pleasing gifts for her purvaid,
Queene-apples,[3] and red Cherries from the tree,
With which he her alluréd and betraid
To tell what time he might her Lady see
When she her selfe did bathe, that he might secret° bee. *hidden*

44

There-to hee promist, if shee would him pleasure
With this small boone, to quit° her with a better; *repay*
To weet, that where-as shee had out of measure
Long loved the Fanchin, who by nought did set her,[4]
That he would undertake, for this to get her
To be his Love, and of him likéd well:
Besides all which, he vowed to be her debter
For many moe good turnes then he would tell:
The least of which, this little pleasure should excell.

45

The simple maid did yield to him anone;
And eft him placed where he close° might view *secretly*
That° never any saw, save onely one; *that which*
Who, for his hire to so foole-hardy dew,
Was of his hounds devoured in Hunters hew.[5]
Tho° as her manner was on sunny day, *then*
Diana, with her Nymphes about her, drew
To this sweet spring; where, doffing her array,
She bathed her lovely limbes, for Jove a likely pray.° *prey*

2. Spenser here adapts the classical story of Actaeon with local Irish geographical references. Actaeon while hunting happened to see Diana bathing; he was turned into a stag and pursued and killed by his own hounds.

3. Probably quinces.

4. I.e., who cared nothing for her. Fanchin is the river Funsheon.

5. I.e., as a deserved punishment for his foolhardiness was devoured by his hunting dogs.

46

There Faunus saw that pleaséd much his eye,
And made his hart to tickle in his brest,
That for great joy of some-what° he did spy, *something*
He could him not contain in silent rest,
But breaking forth in laughter, loud profest
His foolish thought. A foolish Faune indeed,
That couldst not hold thy selfe so° hidden blest, *thus*
But wouldest needs thine own conceit areed.° *declare*
Babblers unworthy been of so divine a meed.° *reward*

47

The Goddesse, all abashéd with that noise,
In haste forth started from the guilty brooke;
And running straight where-as she heard his voice,
Enclosed the bush about, and there him tooke,
Like darréd° Larke; not daring up to looke *cowering*
On her whose sight before so much he sought.
Thence, forth they drew him by the hornes, and shooke
Nigh all to peeces, that they left him nought;
And then into the open light they forth him brought.

48

Like as an huswife, that with busie care
Thinks of her Dairie to make wondrous gaine,
Finding where-as some wicked beast unware° *unobserved*
That breakes into her Dayr'house, there doth draine
Her creaming pannes, and frustrate all her paine;
Hath in some snare or gin° set close behind, *trap*
Entrappéd him, and caught into her traine,° *snare*
Then thinkes what punishment were best assigned,
And thousand deathes deviseth in her vengefull mind:

49

So did Diana and her maydens all
Use silly Faunus, now within their baile;° *custody*
They mocke and scorne him, and him foule miscall;° *revile*
Some by the nose him pluckt, some by the taile,
And by his goatish beard some did him haile:° *pull*
Yet he, poore soule, with patience all did beare;
For, nought against their wils might countervaile:
Ne ought he said, what ever he did heare;
But hanging downe his head, did like a Mome° appeare. *fool*

50

At length, when they had flouted him their fill,
They gan to cast what penaunce him to give.
Some would have gelt° him, but that same would spill°
gelded/destroy
The Wood-gods breed, which must for ever live:
Others would through the river him have drive,
And duckéd deepe; but that seemed penaunce light;
But most agreed and did this sentence give,

Him in Deares skin to clad; and in that plight,
To hunt him with their hounds, him selfe save how hee might.

51

But Cynthia's selfe, more angry then the rest,
Thought not enough, to punish him in sport,
And of her shame to make a gamesome jest;
But gan examine him in straighter° sort, *stricter*
Which of her Nymphes, or other close consort,° *companion*
Him thither brought, and her to him betraid?
He, much affeard, to her confesséd short,
That 'twas Molanna which her so bewraid,
Then all attonce their hands upon Molanna laid.

52

But him, according as they had decreed,
With a Deeres-skin they covered, and then chast
With all their hounds that after him did speed;
But he more speedy, from them fled more fast
Then any Deere: so sore him dread aghast.
They after followed all with shrill outcry,
Shouting as they the heavens would have brast: *burst*
That all the woods and dales where he did flie,
Did ring againe, and loud reeccho to the skie.

53

So they him followed till they weary were,
When, back returning to Molann' againe,
They, by commaundment of Diana, there
Her whelmed with stones.[6] Yet Faunus, for her pain,° *trouble*
Of her beloved Fanchin did obtaine,
That her he would receive unto his bed.
So now her waves passe through a pleasant Plaine,
Till with the Fanchin she her selfe doe wed,
And, both combined, themselves in one faire river spred.

54

Nath'lesse, Diana, full of indignation,
Thence-forth abandoned her delicious brooke;
In whose sweet streame, before that bad occasion,
So much delight to bathe her limbes she tooke:
Ne onely her, but also quite forsooke
All those faire forrests about Arlo hid,
And all that Mountaine, which doth over-looke
The richest champian° that may else be rid,° *country/seen*
And the faire Shure,[7] in which are thousand Salmons bred.

55

Them all, and all that she so deare did way,° *esteem*
Thence-forth she left; and parting from the place,
There-on an heavy haplesse curse did lay,

6. I.e., filled with stones (an allusion to the shallowness of the river, mentioned in line 358).

7. The river Suir.

To weet, that Wolves, where she was wont to space,° *roam*
Should harboured be, and all those Woods deface,
And Thieves should rob and spoile that Coast° around. *territory*
Since which, those Woods, and all that goodly Chase,° *hunting-ground*
Doth to this day with Wolves and Thieves abound:
Which too-too true that lands in-dwellers since have found.

Canto VII

Pealing, from Jove, to Natur's Bar,
bold Alteration[1] *pleades*
Large Evidence: but Nature soone
her righteous Doome areads.[2]

1

Ah! whither doost thou now thou greater Muse[3]
Me from these woods and pleasing forrests bring?
And my fraile spirit (that dooth oft refuse
This too high flight, unfit for her weake wing)
Lift up aloft, to tell of heavens King
(Thy soveraine Sire)[4] his fortunate successe,
And victory, in bigger noates to sing,
Which he obtained against that Titanesse,
That him of heavens Empire sought to dispossesse.

2

Yet sith I needs must follow thy behest,
Doe thou my weaker wit with skill inspire,
Fit for this turne,° and in my feeble brest *verse of praise*
Kindle fresh sparks of that immortall fire,
Which learned minds inflameth with desire
Of heavenly things: for, who but thou alone,
That art yborne of heaven and heavenly Sire,
Can tell things doen in heaven so long ygone;
So farre past memory of man that may be knowne.

3

Now, at the time that was before agreed,
The Gods assembled all on Arlo hill;[5]
As well those that are sprung of heavenly seed,
As those that all the other world[6] doe fill,
And rule both sea and land unto their will:
Onely th' infernall Powers might not appeare;
Aswell for horror of their count'naunce ill,
As for th' unruly fiends which they did feare;
Yet Pluto and Proserpina were present there.

1. I.e., Mutabilitie.
2. Proclaims judgment.
3. I.e., Clio, muse of history.
4. Jove, father of Apollo, hence grandfather of the Muses.
5. Galtymore in southern Ireland, near Spenser's home, Kilcolman Castle.
6. I.e., the Earth.

4

And thither also came all other creatures,
What-ever life or motion doe retaine,
According to their sundry kinds of features;
That Arlo scarsly could them all containe;
So full they filléd every hill and Plaine:
And had not Natures Sergeant (that is Order)
Them well disposéd by his busie paine,
And raungéd farre abroad in every border,
They would have causéd much confusion and disorder.

5

Then forth issewed (great goddesse) great dame Nature,
With goodly port and gracious Majesty:
Being far greater and more tall of stature
Then any of the gods or Powers on hie:
Yet certes by her face and physnomy,° *countenance*
Whether she man or woman inly were,
That could not any creature well descry:
For, with a veile that wimpled° every where, *lay in folds*
Her head and face was hid, that mote to none appeare.

6

That some doe say was so by skill devized,
To hide the terror of her uncouth hew,[7]
From mortall eyes that should be sore agrized ° *horrified*
For that her face did like a Lion shew,
That eye of wight would not indure to view:
But others tell that it so beautious was,
And round about such beames of splendor threw,
That it the Sunne a thousand times did pass,° *surpass*
Ne could be seene, but like an image in a glass.

7

That well may seemen true: for, well I weene
That this same day, when she on Arlo sat,[8]
Her garment was so bright and wondrous sheene,° *beautiful*
That my fraile wit cannot devize to what
It to compare, nor finde like stuffe to that,
As those three sacred Saints, though else most wise,
Yet on mount Thabor quite their wits forgat,
When they their glorious Lord in strange disguise
Transfigured sawe; his garments so did daze their eyes.[9]

8

In a fayre Plaine upon an equal° Hill, *symmetrical*
She placéd was in a pavilion;
Not such as Crafts-men by their idle° skill *vain*
Are wont for Princes states° to fashion: *thrones*
But th' earth her self of her owne motion,
Out of her fruitfull bosome made to growe

7. Strange appearance.
8. I.e., sat in judgment.
9. Peter, James, and John saw Jesus transfigured on a mountain. See Matthew xvii.1–8.

Most dainty trees; that, shooting up anon,
Did seeme to bow their bloosming heads full lowe,
For homage unto her, and like a throne did shew.

9

So hard it is for any living wight,
All her array and vestiments to tell,
That old Dan° Geffrey (in whose gentle spright° — *Sir / spirit*
The pure well head of Poesie did dwell)
In his *Foules parley* durst not with it mel,° — *meddle*
But it transferd to Alane, who he thought
Had in his *Plaint of kindes* described it well:[1]
Which who will read set forth so as it ought,
Go seek he out that Alane where he may be sought.

10

And all the earth far underneath her feete
Was dight° with flowres, that voluntary grew — *decked out*
Out of the ground, and sent forth odours sweet;
Tenne thousand mores° of sundry sent and hew, — *plants*
That might delight the smell, or please the view:
The which, the Nymphes, from all the brooks thereby
Had gatheréd, which they at her foot-stoole threw;
That richer seemed then any tapestry,
That Princes bowres adorne with painted imagery.

11

And Mole[2] himselfe, to honour her the more,
Did deck himself in freshest faire attire,
And his high head, that seemeth alwaies hore
With hardned frosts of former winters ire,
He with an Oaken girlond now did tire,° — *adorn his head*
As if the love of some new Nymph late seene,
Had in him kindled youthfull fresh desire,
And made him change his gray attire to greene;
Ah gentle Mole! such joyance hath thee well beseene.° — *beautified*

12

Was never so great joyance since the day,
That all the gods whylome assembled were,
On Haemus hill in their divine array,
To celebrate the solemne bridall cheare,
Twixt Peleus, and dame Thetis pointed° there:[3] — *appointed*
Where Phoebus self, that god of Poets hight,
They say did sing the spousall hymne full cleere,
That all the gods were ravisht with delight
Of his celestiall song, and Musicks wondrous might.

13

This great Grandmother of all creatures bred
Great Nature, ever young yet full of eld,° — *age*

1. Chaucer, in his *Parliament of Fowls*, lines 316–18, refers to Alanus de Insulis' *De Planctu Naturae* as Aleyn's *Pleynt of Kind* ("Complaint of Nature").

2. The mountain range of which Arlo is the highest peak.

3. Mortal king and sea goddess, the parents of Achilles. "Pointed": appointed.

Still mooving, yet unmovéd from her sted;° *place*
Unseene of any, yet of all beheld;
Thus sitting in her throne as I have teld,
Before her came dame Mutabilitie;
And being lowe before her presence feld,° *prostrated*
With meek obaysance and humilitie,
Thus gan her plaintif Plea, with words to amplifie:

14

"To thee O greatest goddesse, onely° great, *uniquely*
An humble suppliant loe, I lowely fly
Seeking for Right, which I of thee entreat;
Who Right to all dost deal indifferently,° *impartially*
Damning all Wrong and tortious° Injurie, *wrongful*
Which any of thy creatures doe to other
(Oppressing them with power, unequally)
Sith of them all thou art the equall mother,
And knittest each to each, as brother unto brother.

15

"To thee therefore of this same Jove I plaine,
And of his fellow gods that faine° to be, *pretend*
That challenge° to themselves the whole worlds raign: *claim*
Of which, the greatest part is due to me,
And heaven it selfe by heritage in Fee:[4]
For, heaven and earth I both alike do deeme,
Sith heaven and earth are both alike to thee;
And, gods no more than men thou doest esteeme:
For, even the gods to thee, as men to gods do seeme.

16

"Then weigh, O soveraigne goddesse, by what right
These gods do claime the worlds whole soverainty;
And that° is onely dew unto thy might *that which*
Arrogate to themselves ambitiously:
As for the gods owne principality,
Which Jove usurpes unjustly; that to be
My heritage, Jove's self cannot deny,
From my great Grandsire Titan, unto mee,
Derived by dew descent; as is well knowen to thee.

17

"Yet mauger° Jove, and all his gods beside, *despite*
I doe possesse the worlds most regiment,° *control*
As, if ye please it into parts divide,
And every parts inholders° to convent,° *occupants / assemble*
Shall to your eyes appeare incontinent.° *immediately*
And first, the Earth (great mother of us all)
That only seems unmoved and permanent,
And unto Mutability not thrall;
Yet is she changed in part, and eeke in generall.

4. Legally.

18

"For, all that from her springs, and is ybredde,
How-ever fayre it flourish for a time,
Yet see we soone decay; and, being dead,
To turne again unto their earthly slime:
Yet, out of their decay and mortall crime,° *corruption*
We daily see new creatures to arize;
And of their Winter spring another Prime,° *springtime*
Unlike in forme, and changed by strange disguise:
So turne they still about, and change in restlesse wise.

19

"As for her tenants; that is, man and beasts,
The beasts we daily see massácred dy,
As thralls and vassalls unto mens beheasts:
And men themselves doe change continually
From youth to eld, from wealth to poverty,
From good to bad, from bad to worst of all.
Ne doe their bodies only flit and fly:
But eeke their minds (which they immortall call)
Still change and vary thoughts, as new occasions fall.

20

"Ne is the water in more constant case;
Whether those same on high,[5] or these belowe.
For, th' Ocean moveth stil, from place to place;
And every River still° doth ebbe and flowe: *continually*
Ne any Lake, that seems most still and slowe,
Ne Poole so small, that can his smoothnesse holde,
When any winde doth under heaven blowe;
With which, the clouds are also tost and rolled;
Now like great Hills; and, streight,° like sluces, them unfold. *suddenly*

21

"So likewise are all watry living wights
Still tost, and turnéd, with continuall change,
Never abyding in their stedfast plights.
The fish, still floting, doe at randon range,
And never rest; but evermore exchange
Their dwelling places, as the streames them carrie:
Ne have the watry foules a certaine grange,° *dwelling place*
Wherein to rest, ne in one stead° do tarry; *place*
But flitting still doe flie, and still their places vary.

22

"Next is the Ayre: which who feeles not by sense
(For, of all sense it is the middle meane[6])
To flit still? and, with subtill influence
Of his thin spirit,° all creatures to maintaine, *essence*
In state of life? O weake life! that does leane
On thing so tickle° as th' unsteady ayre; *uncertain*
Which every howre is changed, and altred cleane

5. I.e., the clouds.

6. The conductor or medium.

With every blast that bloweth fowle or faire:
The faire doth it prolong; the fowle doth it impaire.

23

"Therein the changes infinite beholde,
Which to her creatures every minute chaunce;
Now, boyling hot: streight, friezing deadly cold:
Now, faire sun-shine, that makes all skip and daunce:
Streight, bitter storms and balefull countenance,
That makes them all to shiver and to shake:
Rayne, hayle, and snowe do pay them sad penance,
And dreadful thunder-claps (that make them quake)
With flames and flashing lights that thousand changes make.

24

"Last is the fire: which, though it live for ever,
Ne can be quenchéd quite; yet, every day,
Wee see his parts, so soone as they do sever,
To lose their heat, and shortly to decay;
So, makes himself his owne consuming pray.
Ne any living creatures doth he breed:
But all, that are of others bredd, doth slay;
And, with their death, his cruell life dooth feed;
Nought leaving but their barren ashes, without seede.

25

"Thus, all these fower° (the which the ground-work bee *four*
Of all the world, and of all living wights)
To thousand sorts of Change we subject see.
Yet are they changed (by other wondrous slights°) *tricks*
Into themselves, and lose their native mights;
The Fire to Aire, and th' Ayre to Water sheere,° *clear*
And Water into Earth: yet Water fights
With Fire, and Aire with Earth approaching neere:
Yet all are in one body, and as one appeare.

26

"So, in them all raignes Mutabilitie;
How-ever these, that Gods themselves do call,
Of them doe claime the rule and soverainty:
As, Vesta, of the fire aethereall;
Vulcan, of this, with us so usuall;[7]
Ops, of the earth; and Juno of the Ayre;
Neptune, of Seas; and Nymphes, of Rivers all.
For, all those Rivers to me subject are:
And all the rest, which they usurp, be all my share.

27

"Which to approven° true, as I have told, *prove*
Vouchsafe, O goddesse, to thy presence call
The rest which doe the world in being hold:° *maintain*

7. Vesta, Roman goddess of the hearth, is assigned by Spenser to rule over the fire that is above the air, as Vulcan rules over earthly fire ("this, with us so usuall"). Ops, Roman goddess of plenty and fertility, rules the earth.

As, times and seasons of the yeare that fall:
Of all the which, demand in generall,
Or judge thy selfe, by verdit of thine eye,
Whether to me they are not subject all."
Nature did yeeld thereto; and by-and-by,
Bade Order call them all, before her Majesty.

28

So, forth issewed the Seasons of the yeare;
First, lusty Spring, all dight in leaves of flowres
That freshly budded and new bloosmes did beare
(In which a thousand birds had built their bowres
That sweetly sung, to call forth Paramours):
And in his hand a javelin he did beare,
And on his head (as fit for warlike stoures°) *combats*
A guilt engraven morion° he did weare; *helmet*
That as some did him love, so others did him feare.

29

Then came the jolly Sommer, being dight
In a thin silken cassock coloured greene,
That was unlynéd all, to be more light:
And on his head a girlond well beseene
He wore, from which as he had chaufféd° been *heated*
The sweat did drop; and in his hand he bore
A boawe and shaftes, as he in forrest greene
Had hunted late the Libbard° or the Bore, *leopard*
And now would bathe his limbes, with labor heated sore.

30

Then came the Autumne all in yellow clad,
As though he joyéd in his plentious store,
Laden with fruits that made him laugh, full glad
That he had banisht hunger, which to-fore
Had by the belly oft him pinchéd sore.
Upon his head a wreath that was enrold
With eares of corne, of every sort he bore:
And in his hand a sickle he did holde,
To reape the ripened fruits the which the earth had yold.° *yielded*

31

Lastly, came Winter cloathéd all in frize,[8]
Chattering his teeth for cold that did him chill,
Whil'st on his hoary beard his breath did freese;
And the dull drops that from his purpled bill° *nose*
As from a limbeck did adown distill.
In his right hand a tippéd staffe he held,
With which his feeble steps he stayéd still:
For, he was faint with cold, and weak with eld;
That scarse his looséd° limbes he hable was to weld.° *feeble/control*

32

These, marching softly,° thus in order went, *slowly*
And after them, the Monthes all riding came;

8. A coarse woolen cloth.

First, sturdy March[9] with brows full sternly bent,
And arméd strongly, rode upon a Ram,
The same which over Hellespontus swam:[1]
Yet in his hand a spade he also hent,° *held*
And in a bag all sorts of seeds ysame,° *together*
Which on the earth he strowéd as he went,
And fild her womb with fruitfull hope of nourishment.

33

Next came fresh Aprill full of lustyhed,° *vigor*
And wanton as a Kid whose horne new buds:
Upon a Bull he rode, the same which led
Europa floting through th' Argolick fluds:[2]
His hornes were gilden all with golden studs
And garnishéd with garlonds goodly dight
Of all the fairest flowres and freshest buds
Which th' earth brings forth, and wet he seemed in sight
With waves, through which he waded for his loves[3] delight.

34

Then came faire May, the fayrest mayd on ground,
Deckt all with dainties of her seasons pryde,
And throwing flowres out of her lap around:
Upon two brethrens shoulders she did ride,
The twinnes of Leda;[4] which on eyther side
Supported her like to their soveraine Queene.
Lord! how all creatures laught, when her they spide,
And leapt and daunc't as they had ravisht° beene! *entranced*
And Cupid selfe about her fluttred all in greene.

35

And after her, came jolly June, arrayd
All in greene leaves, as he a Player were;
Yet in his time, he wrought as well as playd,
That by his plough-yrons mote right well appeare:
Upon a Crab he rode, that him did beare
With crooked crawling steps an uncouth pase,
And backward yode,° as Bargemen wont to fare *went*
Bending their force contrary to their face,
Like that ungracious crew which faines demurest grace.

36

Then came hot July boyling like to fire,
That all his garments he had cast away:
Upon a Lyon raging yet with ire
He boldly rode and made him to obay:
It was the beast that whylome did forray
The Nemaean forrest, till th' Amphytrionide[5]
Him slew, and with his hide did him array;

9. In the old calendar, the year began in March.

1. The ram with the golden fleece, on which Helle and her brother Phrixus flew through the air to escape an evil stepmother. Helle fell off into a body of water that was named after her: the Hellespont.

2. The bull was Jupiter in disguise. He swam with Europa to Crete. "Argolick": Greek.

3. I.e., Europa's.

4. Castor and Pollux (the zodiacal sign of Gemini). Each month brings its zodiacal sign to the conference.

5. I.e., Hercules.

Behinde his back a sithe, and by his side
Under his belt he bore a sickle circling wide.

37

The sixt was August, being rich arrayd
In garment all of gold downe to the ground
Yet rode he not, but led a lovely Mayd
Forth by the lilly hand, the which was cround
With eares of corne, and full her hand was found;
That was the righteous Virgin,[6] which of old
Lived here on earth, and plenty made abound;
But, after Wrong was loved and Justice solde,
She left th' unrighteous world and was to heaven extold.° *raised*

38

Next him, September marchéd eeke on foote;
Yet was he heavy laden with the spoyle
Of harvests riches, which he made his boot,° *booty*
And him enricht with bounty of the soyle:
In his one hand, as fit for harvests toyle,
He held a knife-hook; and in th' other hand
A paire of waights, with which he did assoyle° *weigh*
Both more and lesse, where it in doubt did stand,
And equall gave to each as Justice duly scanned.

39

Then came October full of merry glee:
For, yet his noule was totty of the must,[7]
Which he was treading in the wine-fats see,
And of the joyous oyle, whose gentle gust° *taste*
Made him so frollick and so full of lust:° *pleasure*
Upon a dreadfull Scorpion he did ride,
The same which by Dianaes doom unjust
Slew great Orion:[8] and eeke by his side
He had his ploughing share, and coulter[9] ready tyde.

40

Next was November, he full grosse and fat,
As fed with lard, and that right well might seeme;
For, he had been a fatting hogs of late,
That yet his browes with sweat, did reek and steem,
And yet the season was full sharp and breem;° *bitter*
In planting eeke he took no small delight:
Whereon he rode, not easie was to deeme;
For it a dreadfull Centaure was in sight,
The seed of Saturne and faire Naïs, Chiron hight.

41

And after him, came next the chill December:
Yet he through merry feasting which he made,
And great bonfires, did not the cold remember;

6. Astraea, who symbolized Justice.
7. I.e., his head was unsteady from the wine-mash. "Wine-fats see": wine vats' sea.
8. According to one legend, Orion boasted that he could kill anything that came from the earth. Indignant at his arrogance, Diana sent a scorpion which stung and killed him.
9. Cutting edge of a plow.

His Saviours birth his mind so much did glad:
Upon a shaggy-bearded Goat he rode,
The same wherewith Dan Jove in tender yeares,
They say, was nourisht by th' Idaean mayd;[1]
And in his hand a broad deepe boawle he beares;
Of which, he freely drinks an health to all his peeres.

42

Then came old January, wrappéd well
In many weeds to keep the cold away;
Yet did he quake and quiver like to quell,° *curdle*
And blowe his nayles to warme them if he may:
For, they were numbd with holding all the day
An hatchet keene, with which he felléd wood,
And from the trees did lop the needlesse spray:
Upon an huge great Earth-pot steane[2] he stood;
From whose wide mouth, there flowéd forth the Romane floud.[3]

43

And lastly, came cold February, sitting
In an old wagon, for he could not ride;
Drawne of two fishes for the season fitting,
Which through the flood before did softly slyde
And swim away: yet had he by his side
His plough and harnesse fit to till the ground,
And tooles to prune the trees, before the pride
Of hasting Prime did make them burgein° round: *bud*
So past the twelve Months forth, and their dew places found.

44

And after these, there came the Day, and Night,
Riding together both with equall pase,
Th' one on a Palfrey blacke, the other white;
But Night had covered her uncomely face
With a black veile, and held in hand a mace,
On top whereof the moon and stars were pight,° *placed*
And sleep and darknesse round about did trace:
But Day did beare, upon his scepters hight,
The goodly Sun, encompast all with beamés bright.

45

Then came the Howres, faire daughters of high Jove,
And timely° Night, the which were all endewed *passing*
With wondrous beauty fit to kindle love;
But they were Virgins all, and love eschewed,
That might forslack° the charge to them foreshewed *cause neglect of*
By mighty Jove; who did them Porters make
Of heavens gate (whence all the gods issued)
Which they did dayly watch, and nightly wake
By even turnes, ne ever did their charge forsake.

1. Jove was saved by his mother Rhea from being eaten by Cronus, his father. He was brought up in Crete and suckled by a goat. The "Idaean mayd" is the nymph of a Mt. Ida in Crete.

2. Jar (here standing for the constellation Aquarius).

3. I.e., the Tiber River.

46

And after all came Life, and lastly Death;
Death with most grim and griesly visage seene,
Yet is he nought but parting of the breath;
Ne ought to see, but like a shade to weene,° *be imagined*
Unbodiéd, unsouled, unheard, unseene.
But Life was like a faire young lusty boy,
Such as they faine Dan Cupid to have beene,
Full of delightfull health and lively joy,
Deckt all with flowres, and wings of gold fit to employ.

47

When these were past, thus gan the Titanesse:
"Lo, mighty mother, now be judge and say,
Whether in all thy creatures more or lesse
CHANGE doth not raign and beare the greatest sway:
For, who sees not, that Time on all doth pray?
But Times do change and move continually.
So nothing here long standeth in one stay:
Wherefore, this lower world who can deny
But to be subject still to Mutabilitie?"

48

Then thus gan Jove: "Right true it is, that these
And all things else that under heaven dwell
Are chaunged of Time, who doth them all disseise° *deprive*
Of being: But, who is it (to me tell)
That Time himselfe doth move and still compell
To keepe his course? Is not that namely° wee *only*
Which poure that vertue° from our heavenly cell, *power*
That moves them all, and makes them changéd be?
So them we gods doe rule, and in them also thee."

49

To whom, thus Mutability: "The things
Which we see not how they are moved and swayd,
Ye may attribute to your selves as Kings,
And say they by your secret powre are made:
But what we see not, who shall us perswade?
But were they so, as ye them faine to be,
Moved by your might, and ordred by your ayde;
Yet what if I can prove, that even yee
Your selves are likewise changed, and subject unto mee?

50

"And first, concerning her that is the first,[4]
Even you faire Cynthia, whom so much ye make
Joves dearest darling, she was bred and nurst
On Cynthus hill, whence she her name did take:
Then is she mortall borne, how-so ye crake;° *boast*
Besides, her face and countenance every day
We changéd see, and sundry forms partake,

4. The moon is first because its orbit is closest to the earth.

Now hornd, now round, now bright, now brown and gray:
So that *as changefull as the Moone* men use to say.

51

"Next, Mercury, who though he lesse appeare
To change his hew, and alwayes seeme as one;
Yet, he his course doth altar every yeare,
And is of late far out of order gone:
So Venus eeke, that goodly Paragone,
Though faire all night, yet is she darke all day;
And Phoebus self, who lightsome is alone,[5]
Yet is he oft eclipséd by the way,[6]
And fills the darkned world with terror and dismay.

52

"Now Mars that valiant man is changéd most:
For, he some times so far runs out of square,
That he his way doth seem quite to have lost,
And cleane without his usuall sphere to fare;
That even these Star-gazers stonisht are
At sight thereof, and damne their lying bookes:
So likewise, grim Sir Saturne oft doth spare
His sterne aspect, and calme his crabbéd lookes:
So many turning cranks° these have, so many crookes.° *twists/bends*

53

"But you Dan Jove, that only constant are,
And King of all the rest, as ye do clame,
Are you not subject eeke to this misfare?° *mishap*
Then let me aske you this withouten blame,
Where were ye borne? some say in Crete by name,
Others in Thebes, and others other-where;
But wheresoever they comméntº the same, *invent*
They all consent that ye begotten were,
And borne here in this world, ne other can appeare.

54

"Then are ye mortall borne, and thrall to me,
Unlesse the kingdome of the sky yee make
Immortall, and unchangeable to bee;
Besides, that power and vertue which ye spake,
That ye here worke, doth many changes take,
And your owne natures change: for, each of you
That vertue have, or this, or that to make,
Is checkt and changéd from his nature trew,
By others opposition or obliquid view.[7]

55

"Besides, the sundry motions of your Spheares,
So sundry waies and fashions as clerkes° faine, *learned men*
Some in short space, and some in longer yeares;

5. Alone is radiant.
6. In his course.
7. A reference to the central idea of astrology—that each planet has a "virtue" that it sheds on earth; the effect is dependent upon its position and the position of other planets.

What is the same but alteration plaine?
Onely the starrie skie doth still remaine:
Yet do the Starres and Signes therein still move,
And even it self is moved, as wizards saine.[8]
But all that moveth, doth mutation love:
Therefore both you and them to me I subject prove.

56

"Then since within this wide great Universe
Nothing doth firme and permanent appeare,
But all things tost and turnéd by transverse:[9]
What then should let,° but I aloft should reare *hinder*
My Trophee, and from all, the triumph beare?
Now judge then (O thou greatest goddesse trew!)
According as thy selfe doest see and heare,
And unto me addoom° that is my dew; *decree, award*
That is the rule of all, all being ruled by you."

57

So having ended, silence long ensewed,
Ne Nature to or fro spake for a space,
But with firme eyes affixt, the ground still viewed.
Meane while, all creatures, looking in her face,
Expecting th' end of this so doubtfull case,
Did hang in long suspence what would ensew,
To whether° side should fall the soveraigne place: *which*
At length, she looking up with chearefull view,
The silence brake, and gave her doome° in speeches few. *judgment*

58

"I well consider all that ye have sayd,
And find that all things stedfastnes doe hate
And changéd be: yet being rightly wayd° *weighed*
They are not changéd from their first estate;
But by their change their being doe dilate:° *develop*
And turning to themselves at length againe,
Doe worke their owne perfection so by fate:
Then over them Change doth not rule and raigne;
But they raigne over change, and doe their states maintaine.

59

"Cease therefore daughter further to aspire,
And thee content thus to be ruled by me:
For thy decay thou seekst by thy desire;
But time shall come that all shall changéd bee,
And from thenceforth, none no more change shall see."
So was the Titaness put downe and whist,° *silenced*
And Jove confirmed in his imperiall see.° *throne*
Then was that whole assembly quite dismist,
And Natur's selfe did vanish, wither no man wist.° *knew*

8. As scientists say.

9. Haphazardly.

The VIII Canto, Unperfite

1

When I bethinke me on that speech whyleare,° *recent*
Of Mutability, and well it way:
Me seemes, that though she all unworthy were
Of the Heav'ns Rule; yet very sooth to say,
In all things else she beares the greatest sway.
Which makes me loath this state of life so tickle,° *precarious*
And love of things so vaine to cast away;
Whose flowring pride, so fading and so fickle,
Short° Time shall soon cut down with his consuming sickle. *fleeting*

2

Then gin I thinke on that which Nature sayd,
Of that same time when no more Change shall be,
But stedfast rest of all things firmely stayd
Upon the pillours of Eternity,
That is contrayr to Mutabilitie:
For, all that moveth, doth in Change delight:
But thence-forth all shall rest eternally
With Him that is the God of Sabbaoth hight:
O that great Sabbaoth God, graunt me that Saboaths[10] sight.

1590, 1596, 1609

From Amoretti[1]

Sonnet 1

Happy ye leaves when as those lilly hands,
Which hold my life in their dead doing[2] might,
Shall handle you and hold in loves soft bands,
Lyke captives trembling at the victors sight.
And happy lines, on which with starry light,
Those lamping° eyes will deigne sometimes to look *flashing*
And reade the sorrowes of my dying spright,° *spirit*
Written with teares in harts close° bleeding book. *secret*
And happy rymes bathed in the sacred brooke,
Of Helicon[3] whence she derivéd is,

10. Spenser here confuses, perhaps intentionally, the Hebrew words for "armies, hosts" and for "rest."

1. I.e., "little loves" or "little love poems." They are sonnets to a woman named Elizabeth—probably Elizabeth Boyle, who became Spenser's second wife. The sequence, or cycle, tells of a courtship (*Epithalamion*, with which they were published, is a song for a wedding). The *Amoretti* draws, like other sonnet cycles, upon characteristic and conventional themes and conceits; what is characteristically Spenserian about them is his understanding, and yoking, of the spirit and the flesh; see, for example, lines 9–12 of Sonnet 1. The rhyme scheme is *abab bcbc cdcd ee*, a difficult pattern requiring four words for two of the rhymes.

2. I.e., killing.

3. The "sacred brooke" is the Hippocrene, which flows from Mount Helicon, the mountain sacred to the Muses. It not only inspires the poet but here represents heaven, where his beloved originated.

When ye behold that Angels blessed looke,
My soules long lackéd foode, my heavens blis.
Leaves, lines, and rymes, seeke her to please alone,
Whom if ye please, I care for other none.

Sonnet 15

Ye tradefull merchants, that with weary toyle
Do seeke most pretious things to make your gain,
And both the Indias[4] of their treasures spoile,
What needeth you to seeke so farre in vaine?
For loe my love doth in her selfe containe
All this world's riches that may farre° be found. *anywhere*
If saphyres, loe her eyes be saphyres plaine;
If rubies, loe her lips be rubies sound;
If pearls, her teeth be pearls both pure and round;
If yvorie, her forhead yvory weene;° *suppose*
If gold, her locks are finest gold on ground;° *earth*
If silver, her faire hands are silver sheene.
But that which fairest is, but few behold:
Her mind, adornd with vertues manifold.

Sonnet 34

Lyke as a ship that through the ocean wyde,
By conduct of some star doth make her way,
Whenas a storme hath dimd her trusty guyde,
Out of her course doth wander far astray.
So I whose star, that wont with her bright ray,
Me to direct, with cloudes is overcast,
Doe wander now in darknesse and dismay,
Through hidden perils round about me plast.° *placed*
Yet hope I well, that when this storme is past
My Helice[5] the lodestar of my lyfe
Will shine again, and looke on me at last,
With lovely light to cleare my cloudy grief.
Till then I wander carefull° comfortlesse, *full of cares*
In secret sorow and sad pensivenesse.

Sonnet 37

What guyle is this, that those her golden tresses,
She doth attyre under a net of gold:
And with sly° skill so cunningly them dresses, *clever*
That which is gold or heare, may scarse be told?
Is it that mens frayle eyes, which gaze too bold,
She may entangle in that golden snare:
And being caught may craftily enfold,
Theyr weaker harts, which are not wel aware?
Take heed therefore, myne eyes, how ye doe stare
Henceforth too rashly on that guilefull net,
In which if ever ye entrappéd are,
Out of her bands ye by no means shall get.

4. I.e., India and the West Indies.

5. The Big Dipper or North Star.

Fondnesse° it were for any being free, *foolishness*
To covet fetters, though they golden bee.

Sonnet 54

Of this worlds theatre in which we stay,
My love like the spectator ydly sits
Beholding me that all the pageants° play, *roles*
Disguysing diversly my troubled wits.
Sometimes I joy when glad occasion fits,
And mask in myrth lyke to a comedy:
Soone after when my joy to sorrow flits,
I waile and make my woes a tragedy.
Yet she, beholding me with constant eye,
Delights not in my merth nor rues my smart:
But when I laugh she mocks, and when I cry
She laughs and hardens evermore her heart.
What then can move her? if nor merth nor mone,° *moan*
She is no woman, but a sencelesse stone.

Sonnet 64[6]

Comming to kisse her lyps (such grace I found)
Me seemd I smelt a gardin of sweet flowres
That dainty odours from them threw around
For damzels fit to decke their lovers bowres.
Her lips did smell lyke unto gillyflowers,° *carnations*
Her ruddy cheeks like unto roses red;
Her snowy browes lyke budded bellamoures,° *bellflowers*
Her lovely eyes like pincks but newly spred,
Her goodly bosome lyke a strawberry bed,
Her neck lyke to a bounch of cullambynes;
Her brest lyke lillyes ere theyr leaves be shed,
Her nipples lyke yong blossomd jessemynes.° *jasmines*
Such fragrant flowres doe give most odorous smell,
But her sweet odour did them all excell.

Sonnet 68

Most glorious Lord of lyfe, that on this day,[7]
Didst make thy triumph over death and sin:
And having harrowed hell,[1] didst bring away
Captivity thence captive us to win:
This joyous day, deare Lord, with joy begin,
And grant that we for whom thou diddest dye
Being with thy deare blood clene washt from sin,
May live for ever in felicity.
And that thy love we weighing worthily,
May likewise love thee for the same againe:

6. Much of the imagery of this sonnet is imitated from the Song of Solomon iv.10–16.

7. Easter Day.

1. In the apocryphal gospels, Christ descended into hell and led out those who had lived before his time that deserved to be saved. "Captivity thence captive" is a Biblical phrase, as in Judges v.12 and Ephesians iv.8.

And for thy sake that all lyke deare didst buy,
With love may one another entertayne.
So let us love, deare love, lyke as we ought,
Love is the lesson which the Lord us taught.[2]

Sonnet 70

Fresh spring the herald of loves mighty king,
In whose cote armour[3] richly are displayd
All sorts of flowers the which on earth do spring
In goodly colours gloriously arrayd.
Goe to my love, where she is carelesse layd,
Yet in her winters bowre not well awake:
Tell her the joyous time wil not be staid
Unlesse she doe him by the forelock take.
Bid her therefore her selfe soone ready make,
To wayt on love amongst his lovely crew:
Where every one that misseth then her make,° *mate, lover*
Shall be by him amearest with penance dew.[4]
Make hast therefore sweet love, whilest it is prime,° *early morning*
For none can call againe the passéd time.

Sonnet 74

Most happy letters fram'd by skilfull trade,° *practice*
With which that happy name was first desynd:
The which three times thrise happy hath me made,
With guifts of body, fortune and of mind.
The first my being to me gave by kind,° *nature*
From mothers womb deriv'd by dew descent,
The second is my sovereigne Queene most kind,
That honour and large richesse to me lent.
The third my love, my lives last ornament,
By whom my spirit out of dust was raysed:
To speake her prayse and glory excellent,
Of all alive most worthy to be praysed.
Ye three Elizabeths for ever live,
That three such graces did unto me give.

Sonnet 75[5]

One day I wrote her name upon the strand,° *beach*
But came the waves and washéd it away:
Agayne I wrote it with a second hand,
But came the tyde, and made my paynes his pray.° *prey*
"Vayne man," sayd she, "that doest in vaine assay,
A mortall thing so to immortalize,
For I my selve shall lyke to this decay,
And eek my name bee wypéd out lykewize."

2. Cf. John xv.12: "This is my commandment, That ye love one another, as I have loved you."
3. Coat of arms.
4. I.e., have suitable penance imposed upon him.
5. The theme here expressed is an ancient and traditional one. Cf. Shakespeare's Sonnet 55, "Not marble, nor the gilded monuments."

"Not so," quod° I, "let baser things devize,° *quoth/contrive*
To dy in dust, but you shall live by fame:
My verse your vertues rare shall eternize,
And in the heavens wryte your glorious name.
Where whenas death shall all the world subdew,
Our love shall live, and later life renew."

Sonnet 79

Men call you fayre, and you doe credit° it, *believe*
For that your selfe ye dayly such doe see:
But the trew fayre,° that is the gentle wit, *beauty*
And vertuous mind, is much more praysd of me.
For all the rest, how ever fayre it be,
Shall turne to nought and loose that glorious hew:° *form*
But onely that is permanent and free
From frayle corruption, that doth flesh ensew.° *outlast*
That is true beautie: that doth argue you
To be divine and borne of heavenly seed:
Derived from that fayre Spirit,[6] from whom al true
And perfect beauty did at first proceed.
He onely fayre, and what he fayre hath made:
All other fayre, lyke flowres, untymely fade.

1595

Epithalamion[1]

Ye learned sisters which have oftentimes
Beene to me ayding, others to adorne:[2]

6. I.e., the Holy Spirit.

1. An epithalamion is a wedding song or poem; its Greek name conveys that it was sung on the threshold of the bridal chamber. The genre was widely practiced by the Latin poets, particularly Catullus. Catullus wrote two kinds of epithalamion: one in an elevated ceremonial style, the other in a more private, lyric style; it is the latter style that Spenser follows. Common elements are the invocation to the Muses, the bringing home of the bride, the singing and dancing at the wedding party, and the preparations for the wedding night. The reader should be aware that the poem's merit is not in its "originality" but in its evocative, many-layered commingling of the conventions. Spenser blends with these conventional elements his own Irish setting and native folklore.

In addition, the *Epithalamion* is highly structured. First there is an introductory stanza, then two 10-stanza sections on each side of the two central stanzas about the church ceremony itself. Each of the 10-stanza sections is divided into units of 3-4-3. As A. Kent Hieatt has pointed out in his book, *Short Time's Endless Monument* (1960), the poem also has a surprising and complex numerical structure that reinforces the motif of the passage of time. For example, the poem has exactly 365 long lines (composed of five or more metrical feet) matching the number of days in the year. There are 24 stanzas, counting the envoy, matching the hours of one day and night. Of these stanzas, the first 16 describe the course of the day, in which the woods echo the various sounds; the last 8 describe the night, a time of silence in which the woods no longer echo. At the summer solstice (cf. line 266 and note) in the latitude of Ireland, night in fact falls after 16 hours of daylight.

To point to these elements of high artistry is not, of course, to explain why the *Epithalamion* is one of the great poems of the language. The subtle time structure serves to reinforce the idea implicit throughout the poem that this marriage has reference to all marriages; it emphasizes the endless cycle of time, measured by the passing of the hours and the years—as against which marriage, as a Christian sacrament, stands firm, "eterne in mutabilitie."

2. I.e., to write poems in praise of others (e.g., Queen Elizabeth in *The Faerie Queene*). The "learned sisters" are the Muses.

Whom ye thought worthy of your gracefull rymes,
That even the greatest did not greatly scorne
To heare theyr names sung in your simple layes,
But joyéd in theyr prayse.
And when ye list your owne mishaps to mourne,
Which death, or love, or fortunes wreck did rayse,
Your string could soone to sadder tenor° turne, *mood*
And teach the woods and waters to lament
Your dolefull dreriment.° *sorrow*
Now lay those sorrowfull complaints aside,
And having all your heads with girland crownd,
Helpe me mine owne loves prayses to resound,
Ne let the same of° any be envide: *by*
So Orpheus did for his owne bride,[3]
So I unto my selfe alone will sing,
The woods shall to me answer and my Eccho ring.

Early before the worlds light giving lampe,
His golden beame upon the hils doth spred,
Having disperst the nights unchearefull dampe,
Doe ye awake, and with fresh lustyhed° *vigor*
Go to the bowre° of my belovéd love, *bedchamber*
My truest turtle dove,
Bid her awake; for Hymen[4] is awake,
And long since ready forth his maske to move,
With his bright Tead[5] that flames with many a flake,° *spark*
And many a bachelor to waite on him,
In theyr fresh garments trim.
Bid her awake therefore and soone her dight,° *dress*
For lo the wishéd day is come at last,
That shall for al the paynes and sorrowes past,
Pay to her usury° of long delight: *interest*
And whylest she doth her dight,
Doe ye to her of joy and solace sing,
That all the woods may answer and your eccho ring.

Bring with you all the Nymphes that you can heare[6]
Both of the rivers and the forrests greene:
And of the sea that neighbours to her neare,
Al with gay girlands goodly wel beseene.[7]
And let them also with them bring in hand,
Another gay girland
For my fayre love of lillyes and of roses,
Bound truelove wize[8] with a blew silke riband.
And let them make great store of bridale poses,° *posies*
And let them eeke bring store of other flowers

3. Orpheus, the most famous musician of classical antiquity, was equally famous for his love for his wife Eurydice.
4. The god of marriage, who leads a "maske" or procession at weddings.
5. A ceremonial torch, associated with marriages since classical times.
6. I.e., that can hear you.
7. I.e., beautified.
8. I.e., in a love knot.

To deck the bridale bowers.
And let the ground whereas her foot shall tread,
For feare the stones her tender foot should wrong
Be strewed with fragrant flowers all along,
And diapred lyke the discolored mead. [9]
Which done, doe at her chamber dore awayt,
For she will waken strayt, ° *straightway*
The whiles doe ye this song unto her sing,
The woods shall to you answer and your Eccho ring.

Ye Nymphes of Mulla[1] which with careful heed,
The silver scaly trouts doe tend full well,
And greedy pikes which use therein to feed,
(Those trouts and pikes all others doo excell)
And ye likewise, which keepe the rushy lake,
Where none doo fishes take,
Bynd up the locks the which hang scatterd light,
And in his waters which your mirror make,
Behold your faces as the christall bright,
That when you come whereas my love doth lie,
No blemish she may spie.
And eke ye lightfoot mayds which keepe the deere,[2]
That on the hoary mountayne use to towre,
And the wylde wolves which seeke them to devoure,
With your steele darts doo chace from comming neer
Be also present heere,
To helpe to decke her and to help to sing,
That all the woods may answer and your eccho ring.

Wake, now my love, awake; for it is time,
The Rosy Morne long since left Tithones bed,
All ready to her silver coche to clyme,
And Phoebus gins to shew his glorious hed.
Hark how the cheerefull birds do chaunt theyr laies
And carroll of loves praise.
The merry Larke hir mattins° sing aloft, *morning prayers*
The thrush replyes, the Mavis descant[3] playes,
The Ouzell shrills, the Ruddock warbles soft,
So goodly all agree with sweet consent,
To this dayes merriment.
Ah my deere love why doe ye sleepe thus long,
When meeter° were that ye should now awake, *more fitting*
T' awayt the comming of your joyous make,° *mate*
And hearken to the birds lovelearnéd song,
The deawy leaves among.

9. I.e., ornamented like the many-colored meadow.
1. The vale of Mulla, near Spenser's home in Ireland.
2. I.e., all wild animals, kept by the forest nymphs. To "towre" (a falconry term) is to occupy heights.
3. A melody or counterpoint written above a musical theme—a soprano obbligato. The "Mavis" is the thrush. The "Ouzell" is the blackbird (which sings in England); the "Ruddock," the European robin. The birds' concert is a convention of medieval love poetry.

For they of joy and pleasance to you sing,
That all the woods them answer and theyr eccho ring.

My love is now awake out of her dreame,
And her fayre eyes like stars that dimméd were
With darksome cloud, now shew theyr goodly beams
More bright then Hesperus° his head doth rere. *evening star*
Come now ye damzels, daughters of delight,
Helpe quickly her to dight,° *adorn*
But first come ye fayre houres which were begot
In Joves sweet paradice, of Day and Night,
Which doe the seasons of the yeare allot,
And al that ever in this world is fayre
Doe make and still repayre.[4]
And ye three handmayds of the Cyprian Queene,[5]
The which doe still adorne her beauties pride,
Helpe to addorne my beautifullest bride:
And as ye her array, still throw betweene° *now and then*
Some graces to be seene,
And as ye use to Venus, to her sing,
The whiles the woods shal answer and your eccho ring.

Now is my love all ready forth to come,
Let all the virgins therefore well awayt,
And ye fresh boyes that tend upon her groome
Prepare your selves; for he is comming strayt.
Set all your things in seemely good aray° *order*
Fit for so joyfull day,
The joyfulst day that ever sunne did see.
Faire Sun, shew forth thy favourable ray,
And let thy lifull° heat not fervent be *lifegiving*
For feare of burning her sunshyny face,
Her beauty to disgrace.
O fayrest Phoebus, father of the Muse,
If ever I did honour thee aright,
Or sing the thing, that mote° thy mind delight, *might*
Doe not thy servants simple boone° refuse, *request*
But let this day let this one day be myne,
Let all the rest be thine.
Then I thy soverayne prayses loud wil sing,
That all the woods shal answer and theyr eccho ring.

Harke how the Minstrels gin to shrill aloud
Their merry Musick that resounds from far,
The pipe, the tabor, and the trembling Croud,[6]
That well agree withouten breach or jar.° *discord*
But most of all the Damzels doe delite,

4. In the passage of the hours, all things on earth change. "Still": continuously.
5. The Graces attending on Venus ("Cyprian Queene"), representing brightness, joy, and bloom.
6. Primitive fiddle; the "tabor" is a small drum. Spenser here designates Irish, not classical, instruments and music for the classical masque or ballet.

When they their tymbrels° smyte, *tambourines*
And thereunto doe daunce and carrol sweet,
That all the sences they doe ravish quite,
The whyles the boyes run up and downe the street,
Crying aloud with strong confuséd noyce,
As if it were one voyce.
Hymen iô Hymen, Hymen[7] they do shout,
That even to the heavens theyr shouting shrill
Doth reach, and all the firmament doth fill,
To which the people standing all about,
As in approvance doe thereto applaud
And loud advaunce her laud,° *praise*
And evermore they *Hymen Hymen* sing,
That al the woods them answer and theyr eccho ring.

Loe where she comes along with portly° pace *stately*
Lyke Phoebe from her chamber of the East,
Arysing forth to run her mighty race,[8]
Clad all in white, that seemes° a virgin best. *suits*
So well it her beseems that ye would weene
Some angell she had beene.
Her long loose yellow locks lyke golden wyre,
Sprinckled with perle, and perling° flowres a tweene, *winding*
Doe lyke a golden mantle her attyre,
And being crownéd with a girland greene,
Seeme lyke some mayden Queene.
Her modest eyes abashéd to behold
So many gazers, as on her do stare,
Upon the lowly ground affixéd are.
Ne dare lift up her countenance too bold,
But blush to heare her prayses sung so loud,
So farre from being proud.
Nathlesse doe ye still loud her prayses sing.
That all the woods may answer and your eccho ring.

Tell me ye merchants daughters did ye see
So fayre a creature in your towne before,
So sweet, so lovely, and so mild as she,
Adornd with beautyes grace and vertues store,
Her goodly eyes lyke Saphyres shining bright,
Her forehead yvory white,
Her cheekes lyke apples which the sun hath rudded,° *made red*
Her lips lyke cherryes charming men to byte,
Her brest like to a bowle of creame uncrudded,° *uncurdled*
Her paps lyke lyllies budded,
Her snowie necke lyke to a marble towre,
And all her body like a pallace fayre,
Ascending uppe with many a stately stayre,

7. The name of the god of marriage, used as a conventional exclamation at weddings.

8. Phoebe is the moon, a virgin like the bride; the reference to her anticipates the night.

To honors seat and chastities sweet bowre.[9]
Why stand ye still ye virgins in amaze,
Upon her so to gaze,
Whiles ye forget your former lay to sing,
To which the woods did answer and your eccho ring.

But if ye saw that which no eyes can see,
The inward beauty of her lively spright,° *soul*
Garnisht with heavenly guifts of high degree,
Much more then would ye wonder at that sight,
And stand astonisht lyke to those which red° *saw*
Medusaes mazeful hed.[1]
There dwels sweet love and constant chastity,
Unspotted fayth and comely womanhood,
Regard of honour and mild modesty,
There vertue raynes as Queene in royal throne,
And giveth lawes alone.
The which the base° affections doe obay, *lower*
And yeeld theyr services unto her will,
Ne thought of thing uncomely ever may
Thereto approch to tempt her mind to ill.
Had ye once seene these her celestial threasures,
And unrevealéd pleasures,
Then would ye wonder and her prayses sing,
That al the woods should answer and your echo ring.

Open the temple gates unto my love,
Open them wide that she may enter in,
And all the postes adorne as doth behove,[2]
And all the pillours deck with girlands trim,
For to recyve this Saynt with honour dew,
That commeth in to you.
With trembling steps and humble reverence,
She commeth in, before th' almighties vew,
Of her ye virgins learne obedience,
When so ye come into those holy places,
To humble your proud faces:
Bring her up to th' high altar, that she may
The sacred ceremonies there partake,
The which do endless matrimony make,
And let the roring Organs loudly play
The praises of the Lord in lively notes,
The whiles with hollow throates
The Choristers the joyous Antheme sing,
That al the woods may answere and their eccho ring.

9. The head, where the higher faculties are. The catalogue of qualities is a convention in love poetry. Cf. also The Song of Solomon iv–viii.

1. Medusa, one of the Gorgons, had serpents instead of hair (hence a "mazeful hed"): the effect on a beholder was to turn him to stone.

2. As is proper. The doorposts were trimmed for weddings in classical times, and the custom was often referred to in classical and medieval love poetry.

Behold whiles she before the altar stands
Hearing the holy priest that to her speakes
And blesseth her with his two happy hands,
How the red roses flush up in her cheekes,
And the pure snow with goodly vermill° stayne, *vermilion*
Like crimsin dyde in grayne,° *fast color*
That even th' Angels which continually,
About the sacred Altare doe remaine,
Forget their service and about her fly,
Ofte peeping in her face that seemes more fayre,
The more they on it stare.
But her sad° eyes still fastened on the ground, *modest*
Are governéd with goodly modesty,
That suffers not one looke to glaunce awry,
Which may let in a little thought unsownd.
Why blush ye love to give to me your hand,
The pledge of all our band?° *bond, tie*
Sing ye sweet Angels, Alleluya sing,
That all the woods may answere and your eccho ring.

Now al is done; bring home the bride againe,
Bring home the triumph of our victory,
Bring home with you the glory of her gaine,[3]
With joyance bring her and with jollity.
Never had man more joyfull day then this,
Whom heaven would heape with blis.
Make feast therefore now all this live long day,
This day for ever to me holy is,
Poure out the wine without restraint or stay,
Poure not by cups, but by the belly full,
Poure out to all that wull,° *want it*
And sprinkle all the postes and wals with wine,
That they may sweat, and drunken be withall.
Crowne ye God Bacchus with a coronall,° *flower garland*
And Hymen also crowne with wreathes of vine,
And let the Graces daunce unto the rest;
For they can doo it best:
The whiles the maydens doe theyr carroll sing,
To which the woods shal answer and theyr eccho ring.

Ring ye the bels, ye young men of the towne,
And leave your wonted° labors for this day: *usual*
This day is holy; doe ye write it downe,
That ye for ever it remember may.
This day the sunne is in his chiefest hight,
With Barnaby the bright,[4]
From whence declining daily by degrees,
He somewhat loseth of his heat and light,

3. I.e., the glory of gaining her.
4. St. Barnabas' Day, at the time of the summer solstice.

When once the Crab[5] behind his back he sees.
But for this time it ill ordainéd was,
To chose the longest day in all the yeare,
And shortest night, when longest fitter weare:
Yet never day so long, but late° would passe. *at last*
Ring ye the bels, to make it weare away,
And bonefiers make all day,
And daunce about them, and about them sing:
That all the woods may answer, and your eccho ring.

Ah when will this long weary day have end,
And lende me leave to come unto my love?
How slowly do the houres theyr numbers spend?
How slowly does sad Time his feathers move?
Hast thee O fayrest Planet to thy home
Within the Westerne fome:
Thy tyred steedes long since have need of rest.
Long though it be, at last I see it gloome,
And the bright evening star with golden creast
Appeare out of the East.
Fayre childe of beauty, glorious lampe of love
That all the host of heaven in rankes doost lead,
And guydest lovers through the nightés dread,
How chearefully thou lookest from above,
And seemst to laugh atweene thy twinkling light
As joying in the sight
Of these glad many which for joy doe sing,
That all the woods them answer and their echo ring.

Now ceasse ye damsels your delights forepast;
Enough is it, that all the day was youres:
Now day is doen, and night is nighing fast:
Now bring the Bryde into the brydall boures.
Now night is come, now soone her disaray,
And in her bed her lay;
Lay her in lillies and in violets,
And silken courteins over her display,° *spread*
And odourd sheetes, and Arras° coverlets. *tapestry*
Behold how goodly my faire love does ly
In proud humility;
Like unto Maia,[6] when as Jove her tooke,
In Tempe, lying on the flowry gras,
Twixt sleepe and wake, after she weary was,
With bathing in the Acidalian brooke.
Now it is night, ye damsels may be gon,
And leave my love alone,
And leave likewise your former lay to sing:
The woods no more shal answere, nor your echo ring.

5. The constellation Cancer between Gemini and Leo. The sun, passing through the zodiac, leaves the Crab behind toward the end of July.

6. The eldest and most beautiful of the Pleiades.

Now welcome night, thou night so long expected,
That long daies labour doest at last defray,° *pay*
And all my cares, which cruell love collected,
Hast sumd in one, and cancellèd for aye:
Spread thy broad wing over my love and me,
That no man may us see,
And in thy sable mantle us enwrap,
From feare of perrill and foule horror free.
Let no false treason seeke us to entrap,
Nor any dread disquiet once annoy
The safety of our joy:
But let the night be calme and quietsome,
Without tempestuous storms or sad afray:
Lyke as when Jove with fayre Alcmena[7] lay,
When he begot the great Tirynthian groome:
Or lyke as when he with thy selfe[8] did lie,
And begot Majesty.
And let the mayds and yongmen cease to sing:
Ne let the woods them answer, nor theyr eccho ring.

Let no lamenting cryes, nor dolefull teares,
Be heard all night within nor yet without.
Ne let false whispers, breeding hidden feares,
Breake gentle sleepe with misconceivèd dout.° *fear*
Let no deluding dreames, nor dreadful sights
Make sudden sad affrights;
Ne let housefyres, nor lightnings helpelesse harmes,
Ne let the Pouke,[9] nor other evill sprights,
Ne let mischivous witches with theyr charmes,
Ne let hob Goblins, names whose sence we see not,
Fray° us with things that be not. *terrify*
Let not the shriech Oule, nor the Storke be heard:
Nor the night Raven that still° deadly yels,[1] *continuously*
Nor damnèd ghosts cald up with mighty spels,
Nor griesly vultures make us once affeard:
Ne let th'unpleasant Quyre of Frogs still croking
Make us to wish theyr choking.
Let none of these theyr drery accents sing;
Ne let the woods them answer, nor theyr eccho ring.

But let stil Silence trew night watches keepe,
That sacred peace may in assurance rayne,
And tymely sleep, when it is tyme to sleepe,
May poure his limbs forth on your[2] pleasant playne,
The whiles an hundred little wingèd loves,[3]

7. The mother of Hercules ("the great Tirynthian groome").
8. I.e., night.
9. Puck, Robin Goodfellow—here more powerful and evil than Shakespeare made him.
1. The owl and the night raven were birds of ill omen; the stork, in Chaucer's *Parliament of Fowls*, is called an avenger of adultery. "Still": always.
2. I.e., Night's.
3. Cupids (or amoretti).

Like divers fethered doves,
Shall fly and flutter round about your bed,
And in the secret darke, that none reproves,
Their prety stealthes shal worke, and snares shal spread
To filch away sweet snatches of delight,
Conceald through covert night.
Ye sonnes of Venus, play your sports at will,
For greedy pleasure, carelesse of your toyes,° *frivolities*
Thinks more upon her paradise of joyes,
Then what ye do, albe it good or ill.
All night therefore attend your merry play,
For it will soone be day:
Now none doth hinder you, that say or sing,
Ne will the woods now answer, nor your Eccho ring.

Who is the same, which at my window peepes?
Or whose is that faire face, that shines so bright,
Is it not Cinthia,[4] she that never sleepes,
But walkes about high heaven al the night?
O fayrest goddesse, do thou not envy
My love with me to spy:
For thou likewise didst love, though now unthought,° *unsuspected*
And for a fleece of woll,° which privily, *wool*
The Latmian shephard[5] once unto thee brought,
His pleasures with thee wrought,
Therefore to us be favorable now;
And sith of wemens labours thou hast charge,[6]
And generation goodly dost enlarge,
Encline thy will t' effect our wishfull vow,
And the chast wombe informe° with timely seed, *give life to*
That may our comfort breed:
Till which we cease our hopefull hap to sing,
Ne let the woods us answere, nor our Eccho ring.

And thou great Juno, which with awful might
The lawes of wedlock still dost patronize,
And the religion of the faith first plight
With sacred rites hast taught to solemnize:
And eeke for comfort often calléd art
Of women in their smart,° *labor*
Eternally bind thou this lovely band,
And all thy blessings unto us impart.
And thou glad Genius,[7] in whose gentle hand,
The bridale bowre and geniall bed remaine,
Without blemish or staine,
And the sweet pleasures of theyr loves delight
With secret ayde doest succour and supply,

4. I.e., the moon.
5. Endymion, beloved by the moon. The "fleece of woll," however, comes from another story—that of Pan's enticement of the moon.
6. Diana (the moon, "Cinthia") is, as Lucina, patroness of births; the "labours" are, of course, those of childbirth.
7. Patron of sex, pregnancy, reproduction.

Till they bring forth the fruitfull progeny,
Send us the timely fruit of this same night.
And thou fayre Hebe,[8] and thou Hymen free,
Grant that it may so be.
Til which we cease your further prayse to sing,
Ne any woods shal answer, nor your Eccho ring.

And ye high heavens, the temple of the gods,
In which a thousand torches flaming bright
Doe burne, that to us wretched earthly clods,
In dreadful darknesse lend desiréd light;
And all ye powers which in the same remayne,
More than we men can fayne,
Poure out your blessing on us plentiously,
And happy influence upon us raine,
That we may raise a large posterity,
Which from the earth, which they may long possesse,
With lasting happinesse,
Up to your haughty pallaces may mount,
And for the guerdon of theyr glorious merit
May heavenly tabernacles there inherit,
Of blessed Saints for to increase the count.
So let us rest, sweet love, in hope of this,
And cease till then our tymely joyes to sing,
The woods no more us answer, nor our eccho ring.

Song made in lieu of many ornaments,
With which my love should duly have bene dect,° *adorned*
Which cutting off through hasty accidents,
Ye would not stay your dew time to expect,° *await*
But promist both to recompens,
Be unto her a goodly ornament,
And for short time an endlesse moniment.[9]

1595

8. Patron of youth and freedom.
9. The envoy is traditionally apologetic in tone: the poem is offered as a substitute for wedding presents ("ornaments") that did not arrive in time for the wedding. But this elaborate poem is itself a "goodly ornament," for (in a final reference to the theme of time and eternity) it stands as a timeless monument of art to the passing day which it celebrates.

CHRISTOPHER MARLOWE
(1564–1593)

ca. 1587: *Tamburlaine* produced, introducing blank verse, "Marlowe's mighty line," to the stage.
ca. 1592–93: *Dr. Faustus, Hero and Leander.*

Christopher Marlowe was born two months before William Shakespeare. He was the son of a Canterbury shoemaker; in 1580 he went to Corpus

Christi College, Cambridge, on a scholarship which was ordinarily awarded to students preparing for the ministry. He held the scholarship for the maximum time, six years, but did not take holy orders. Instead, he began to write plays. When he came to supplicate for his Master of Arts degree in 1587, the university was about to deny it to him on the grounds that he intended to go abroad to Reims, the center of Catholic intrigue and propaganda against Elizabeth, and remain there. But the Privy Council intervened and requested that, since Marlowe had done the queen good service, he be granted his degree at the next commencement "because it is not Her Majesty's pleasure that anyone employed as he had been in matters touching the benefit of his country should be defamed by those that are ignorant in the affairs he went about." Although much sensational information about Marlowe has been discovered in modern times, we are still "ignorant in the affairs he went about."

Before he left Cambridge, he had certainly written his tremendously successful play *Tamburlaine* and perhaps also, in collaboration with his younger Cambridge contemporary, Thomas Nashe, the tragedy of *Dido, Queen of Carthage*. *Tamburlaine*, which soon was followed by a sequel (*Tamburlaine*, Part II), dramatizes the exploits of a 14th-century Scythian shepherd who conquered much of the known world, as Alexander had before him. In some 16th-century narratives Tamburlaine is represented as the type of modern (i.e., Renaissance) man, and in others he is portrayed as God's Scourge. In Marlowe's play he is the vehicle for the expression of boundless energy and ambition, the impulse to strive constantly upward to absolute power. When one of his victims accuses him of bloody cruelty, Tamburlaine answers that ambition to rule is embedded in the laws of nature and in basic human psychology:

Nature, that framed us of four elements
Warring within our breasts for regiment,
Doth teach us all to have aspiring minds;
Our souls, whose faculties can comprehend
The wondrous architecture of the world
And measure every planet's wandering course,
Still climbing after knowledge infinite,
And always moving as the restless spheres,
Wills us to wear ourselves and never rest
Until we reach the ripest fruit of all,
That perfect bliss and sole felicity,
The sweet fruition of an earthly crown.

The English theater had heard nothing like this before. Here is a resonant, rhetorical blank verse, eminently suited to projection from the stage, and appropriate also, as it turned out, for the robust talents of the actor Edward Alleyn who happily appeared in time to portray Marlowe's heroes.

From the time of his first great success, when he was 23, Marlowe had only six years to live. They were not calm years. In 1589 he was involved in a brawl with one William Bradley, in which the poet Thomas Watson intervened and killed Bradley. Both poets were jailed, but Watson got off on a plea of self-defense and Marlowe was released. In 1591 Marlowe was living in London with the playwright Thomas Kyd, who later gave information to the Privy Council accusing Marlowe of atheism and treason. On

May 30, 1593, at the inn of the Widow Bull in Deptford, Marlowe was killed by a dagger thrust in an argument over the bill. In these six violent years, Marlowe composed five more plays: his sequel to *Tamburlaine; The Massacre at Paris;* two major tragedies, *The Jew of Malta* and *Dr. Faustus;* and a chronicle history play, *Edward II.*

Hero and Leander[1]

On Hellespont, guilty of true-loves'[2] blood,
In view and opposite, two cities stood,
Sea-borderers, disjoined by Neptune's might;
The one Abydos, the other Sestos hight.[3]
At Sestos Hero dwelt; Hero the fair,
Whom young Apollo courted for her hair,
And offered as a dower his burning throne,
Where she should sit for men to gaze upon.
The outside of her garments were of lawn,[4]
The lining purple silk, with gilt stars drawn;
Her wide sleeves green, and bordered with a grove
Where Venus in her naked glory strove

1. Marlow's mythological-erotic poem, *Hero and Leander*, cannot be dated precisely. It was entered in the Stationers' Register on September 28, 1593, just four months after the poet's death, but the earliest known edition was not published until 1598. The poem has something in common with Marlowe's translation of Ovid's *Elegies*, generally thought to be early work, possibly done while he was still at Cambridge. The same verse form, the closed couplet, is used in both, though the versification is much more expert in *Hero and Leander*. Not much can be inferred about the interrelationship of Marlowe's poem with Shakespeare's *Venus and Adonis*, probably composed in late 1592. They are different in verse form (Shakespeare used a six-line stanza) and somewhat different in tone, though they belong to the same genre of erotic narrative, along with about a dozen other Elizabethan poems.

Hero and Leander is a free and original treatment of a classic tale of two tragic lovers. The story had been told by the 5th-century Alexandrian poet Musaeus. Marlowe's poem, however, is in the manner of Ovid, who had told the story in two epistles of his *Heroides* and who refers to it in one of his *Elegies* that Marlowe translated.

George Chapman, the playwright and translator of Homer, undertook to complete Marlowe's poem. His continuation, with his division of the poem into "Sestiads" (named after Sestos, where Hero lived) and verse summaries preceding each, was published shortly after the first surviving edition of Marlowe's poem. For a long time Chapman's altered version remained the standard form of the poem. Thanks to Louis L. Martz, however, Marlowe's poem has recently been freed of its accretions and can now be read as a single unified work. As Martz points out, the poem has a three-part structure: the meeting of the lovers at the Feast of Adonis; the inserted tale of Mercury and the Fates; and the concluding narrative of the consummation.

The narrative serves mainly as a framework on which to hang the poetry, and the characters are not intended to be consistent or psychologically credible, they inhabit a world of fancy and delight, of strange contrasts between innocence and the wild riot of amorous intrigues among the gods which is Ovid's subject matter. Hero is paradoxically a nun vowed to chastity and a devotee of Venus, the love goddess; Leander is both a sharp, sophisticated seducer and an incredibly innocent novice in sex. The gravely spoken asides, sometimes platitudes and sometimes cynical remarks about women, in the manner of Ovid, give a distance or disengagement to the experience of reading about the ill-fated lovers. The poem is rich in many ways: it is comic, erotic, decorative, now swiftly narrative, now deliberate and, in a light way, philosophical.

2. Sweethearts'.

3. Called.

4. A kind of fine linen or thin cambric.

To please the careless and disdainful eyes
Of proud Adonis, that before her lies;[5]
Her kirtle blue, whereon was many a stain,
Made with the blood of wretched lovers slain.[6]
Upon her head she ware a myrtle wreath,
From whence her veil reached to the ground beneath.
Her veil was artificial flowers and leaves,
Whose workmanship both man and beast deceives;
Many would praise the sweet smell as she passed,
When 'twas the odor which her breath forth cast;
And there for honey, bees have sought in vain,
And, beat from thence, have lighted there again.
About her neck hung chains of pebble-stone,
Which, lightened[7] by her neck, like diamonds shone.
She ware no gloves, for neither sun nor wind
Would burn or parch her hands, but to her mind[8]
Or warm or cool them, for they took delight
To play upon those hands, they were so white.
Buskins[9] of shells all silvered, uséd she,
And branched with blushing coral to the knee,
Where sparrows perched, of hollow pearl and gold,
Such as the world would wonder to behold;
Those with sweet water oft her handmaid fills,
Which, as she went, would chirrup through the bills.
Some say, for her the fairest Cupid pined,
And looking in her face, was strooken blind.
But this is true: so like was one the other,
As he imagined Hero was his mother;[1]
And oftentimes into her bosom flew,
About her naked neck his bare arms threw,
And laid his childish head upon her breast,
And with still[2] panting rocked, there took his rest.
So lovely fair was Hero, Venus' nun,[3]
As Nature wept, thinking she was undone,
Because she took more from her than she left
And of such wondrous beauty her bereft;
Therefore, in sign her treasure suffered wrack,
Since Hero's time hath half the world been black.
Amorous Leander, beautiful and young,
(Whose tragedy divine Musaeus[4] sung)
Dwelt at Abydos; since him dwelt there none

5. Venus's love for the young hunter, Adonis, and his death in the boar hunt are told by Ovid and by Shakespeare in *Venus and Adonis*. "Kirtle": skirt.
6. The extravagant claim is made that many "wretched lovers" had committed suicide at her feet because Hero would not have them.
7. Illuminated.
8. As she wished.
9. High shoes or boots.
1. I.e., Venus.
2. Continual.
3. The connotations of these two words are contradictory; Marlowe gets a similar effect elsewhere in the poem. Hero is a maiden in attendance at the temple of Venus, who is, of course, the goddess of love.
4. I.e., the author of the Greek poem upon which *Hero and Leander* is remotely based. He was sometimes confused with a legendary early Musaeus, supposed son of Orpheus—hence Marlowe calls him "divine."

For whom succeeding times make greater moan.
His dangling tresses that were never shorn,
Had they been cut and unto Colchos[5] borne,
Would have allured the vent'rous youth of Greece
To hazard more than for the Golden Fleece.
Fair Cynthia[6] wished his arms might be her sphere;
Grief makes her pale, because she moves not there.
His body was as straight as Circe's wand;[7]
Jove might have sipped out nectar from his hand.
Even as delicious meat is to the taste,
So was his neck in touching, and surpassed
The white of Pelops' shoulder.[8] I could tell ye
How smooth his breast was, and how white his belly,
And whose immortal fingers did imprint
That heavenly path, with many a curious[9] dint,
That runs along his back; but my rude pen
Can hardly blazon forth the loves of men,
Much less of powerful gods; let it suffice
That my slack[1] muse sings of Leander's eyes,
Those orient cheeks and lips, exceeding his
That leapt into the water for a kiss
Of his own shadow, and despising many,
Died ere he could enjoy the love of any.[2]
Had wild Hippolytus[3] Leander seen,
Enamored of his beauty had he been;
His presence made the rudest peasant melt,
That in the vast uplandish country dwelt;
The barbarous Thracian soldier, moved with naught,
Was moved with him, and for his favor sought.
Some swore he was a maid in man's attire,
For in his looks were all that men desire:
A pleasant smiling cheek, a speaking[4] eye,
A brow for love to banquet royally;
And such as knew he was a man, would say,
"Leander, thou art made for amorous play;
Why art thou not in love, and loved of all?
Though thou be fair, yet be not thine own thrall."
  The men of wealthy Sestos every year,
For his sake whom their goddess held so dear,
Rose-cheeked Adonis, kept a solemn feast.
Thither resorted many a wandering guest
To meet their loves; such as had none at all
Came lovers home from this great festival;
For every street, like to a firmament,

5. A country in Asia where the Argonauts ("the ven'trous youth of Greece") found the Golden Fleece.
6. The moon; "sphere": orbit.
7. The wand with which Circe, in the *Odyssey*, turned men into beasts.
8. Pelops, according to Ovid, had a shoulder of ivory.
9. Exquisite.
1. Dull. "Orient": shining.
2. An allusion to Narcissus.
3. Like Adonis, he preferred hunting to love.
4. Expressive.

Glistered with breathing stars, who, where they went,
Frighted the melancholy earth, which deemed
Eternal heaven to burn, for so it seemed
As if another Phaëton[5] had got
The guidance of the sun's rich chariot.
But, far above the loveliest, Hero shined,
And stole away th' enchanted gazer's mind;
For like sea nymphs' inveigling harmony,
So was her beauty to the standers by.
Nor that night-wandering pale and watery star[6]
(When yawning dragons draw her thirling[7] car
From Latmus' mount up to the gloomy sky,
Where, crowned with blazing light and majesty,
She proudly sits) more over-rules[8] the flood
Than she the hearts of those that near her stood.
Even as when gaudy nymphs pursue the chase,
Wretched Ixion's shaggy-footed race,[9]
Incensed with savage heat, gallop amain
From steep pine-bearing mountains to the plain,
So ran the people forth to gaze upon her,
And all that viewed her were enamored on her.
And as in fury of a dreadful fight,
Their fellows being slain or put to flight,
Poor soldiers stand with fear of death dead-strooken,
So at her presence all, surprised and tooken,
Await the sentence of her scornful eyes;
He whom she favors lives, the other dies.
There might you see one sigh, another rage,
And some, their violent passions to assuage,
Compile sharp satires; but alas, too late,
For faithful love will never turn to hate.
And many, seeing great princes were denied,
Pined as they went, and thinking on her, died.
On this feast day, oh, cursėd day and hour!
Went Hero thorough[1] Sestos, from her tower
To Venus' temple, where unhappily,
As after chanced, they did each other spy.
So fair a church as this had Venus none;
The walls were of discolored[2] jasper stone,
Wherein was Proteus carvėd, and o'erhead
A lively[3] vine of green sea-agate spread,
Where, by one hand, light-headed Bacchus hung,
And with the other, wine from grapes out-wrung.

5. A son of the sun god, he drove his father's chariot across the sky and almost burned up the world.
6. The moon.
7. Flying like a spear. Latmus was the mountain where the moon visited her lover, Endymion.
8. Rules over.
9. I.e., the centaurs, fathered by Ixion upon a cloud. For his presumption in loving Juno, Ixion was chained to a wheel—hence "wretched."
1. Through.
2. Of various colors.
3. Lifelike.

Of crystal shining fair the pavement was;
The town of Sestos called it Venus' glass;
There might you see the gods in sundry shapes,
Committing heady[4] riots, incest, rapes;
For know that underneath this radiant floor
Was Danaë's statue in a brazen tower;[5]
Jove slyly stealing from his sister's bed
To dally with Idalian Ganymed,[6]
And for his love Europa bellowing loud,
And tumbling with the rainbow in a cloud;
Blood-quaffing Mars heaving the iron net
Which limping Vulcan and his Cyclops set;[7]
Love kindling fire to burn such towns as Troy;
Silvanus weeping for the lovely boy[8]
That now is turned into a cypress tree,
Under whose shade the wood-gods love to be.
And in the midst a silver altar stood;
There Hero sacrificing turtles'[9] blood,
Veiled to the ground, veiling her eyelids close,
And modestly they opened as she rose;
Thence flew love's arrow with the golden head,[1]
And thus Leander was enamoréd.
Stone still he stood, and evermore he gazed,
Till with the fire that from his countenance blazed,
Relenting Hero's gentle heart was strook;
Such force and virtue hath an amorous look.
  It lies not in our power to love or hate,
For will in us is overruled by fate.
When two are stripped, long ere the course[2] begin
We wish that one should lose, the other win;
And one especially do we affect[3]
Of two gold ingots, like in each respect.
The reason no man knows, let it suffice,
What we behold is censured[4] by our eyes.
Where both deliberate, the love is slight;
Who ever loved, that loved not at first sight?[5]
  He kneeled, but unto her devoutly prayed.
Chaste Hero to herself thus softly said,
"Were I the saint he worships, I would hear him,"
And as she spake those words, came somewhat near him.

4. Passionate, violent. In the next lines, specific examples of the "riots, incest, rapes" are given.
5. Danaë, imprisoned in a tower, was visited by Jove in the form of a shower of gold. "His sister's": i.e., Juno's; she was also Jove's wife.
6. A beautiful youth whom Jove kidnaped from Mt. Ida (hence "Idalian"). In order to seduce Europa, Jove took the form of a "bellowing" bull.
7. Vulcan used a net to trap Venus, his wife, and Mars, "blood-quaffing" god of war, in the act of love.
8. I.e., Cyparissus, beloved of the wood god Sylvanus.
9. Turtledoves, symbolic of constancy in love.
1. The "golden head" of some of Cupid's arrows produced love; he had others, of lead, that produced dislike.
2. Race.
3. Have affection for.
4. Judged.
5. Shakespeare quotes this line in *As You Like It* (III.v.82).

He started up; she blushed as one ashamed,
Wherewith Leander much more was inflamed.
He touched her hand; in touching it she trembled:
Love deeply grounded hardly[6] is dissembled.
These lovers parlèd[7] by the touch of hands;
True love is mute, and oft amazèd stands.
Thus, while dumb signs their yielding hearts entangled,
The air with sparks of living fire was spangled,
And Night, deep drenched in misty Acheron,[8]
Heaved up her head, and half the world upon
Breathed darkness forth. (Dark night is Cupid's day.)
And now begins Leander to display
Love's holy fire, with words, with sighs and tears,
Which like sweet music entered Hero's ears,
And yet at every word she turned aside
And always cut him off as he replied.
At last, like to a bold sharp sophister,[9]
With cheerful hope thus he accosted her:
"Fair creature, let me speak without offense;
I would my rude words had the influence
To lead my thoughts, as thy fair looks do mine,
Then shouldst thou be his prisoner who is thine.
Be not unkind and fair—misshapen stuff[1]
Are of behavior boisterous and rough.
O shun me not, but hear me ere you go;
God knows I cannot force[2] love, as you do.
My words shall be as spotless as my youth,
Full of simplicity and naked truth.
This sacrifice, whose sweet perfume descending
From Venus' altar to your footsteps bending,[3]
Doth testify that you exceed her far
To whom you offer and whose nun you are.
Why should you worship her? Her you surpass
As much as sparkling diamonds flaring[4] glass.
A diamond set in lead his worth retains;
A heavenly nymph, beloved of human swains,
Receives no blemish but ofttimes more grace;
Which makes me hope, although I am but base—
Base in respect of thee, divine and pure,
Dutiful service may thy love procure,
And I in duty will excel all other,
As thou in beauty dost exceed Love's mother.
Nor heaven, nor thou, were made to gaze upon;
As heaven preserves all things, so save thou one.
A stately builded ship, well rigged and tall,
The ocean maketh more majestical.

6. With difficulty.
7. Parleyed, spoke.
8. One of the rivers of Hades.
9. A second- or third-year Cambridge student, trained in logic and argument. "Accosted": wooed.
1. Persons.
2. Compel.
3. Turning.
4. Gaudy.

Why vowest thou then to live in Sestos here,
Who on Love's seas more glorious wouldst appear?
Like untuned golden strings all women are,
Which long time lie untouched, will harshly jar.[5]
Vessels of brass, oft handled, brightly shine.
What difference betwixt the richest mine[6]
And basest mold, but use, for both not used
Are of like worth. Then treasure is abused
When misers keep it; being put to loan,
In time it will return us two for one.
Rich robes themselves and others do adorn;
Neither themselves nor others, if not worn.
Who builds a palace and rams up the gate
Shall see it ruinous and desolate.
Ah, simple Hero, learn thyself to cherish;
Lone women, like to empty houses, perish.
Less sins the poor rich man that starves himself
In heaping up a mass of drossy pelf,
Than such as you: his golden earth remains,
Which after his decease some other gains.
But this fair gem, sweet in the loss alone,
When you fleet hence can be bequeathed to none.
Or if it could, down from th' enameled[7] sky
All heaven would come to claim this legacy,
And with intestine[8] broils the world destroy
And quite confound Nature's sweet harmony.
Well therefore by the gods decreed it is,
We human creatures should enjoy that bliss.
One is no number;[9] maids are nothing then
Without the sweet society of men.
Wilt thou live single still? One shalt thou be,
Though never-singling[1] Hymen couple thee.
Wild savages, that drink of running springs,
Think water far excels all earthly things;
But they that daily taste neat[2] wine despise it.
Virginity, albeit some highly prize it,
Compared with marriage, had you tried them both,
Differs as much as wine and water doth.
Base bullion for the stamp's sake[3] we allow:
Even so for men's impression do we you;
By which alone, our reverend fathers[4] say,
Women receive perfection every way.
This idol which you term Virginity,
Is neither essence,[5] subject to the eye—

5. I.e., instruments not played upon will be out of tune and harsh.
6. Ore; "mold": earth.
7. Beautiful, many-colored.
8. Internal, civil.
9. A traditional concept, going back to Aristotle.
1. I.e., who never separates, but always joins. Hymen was the god of marriage.
2. Undiluted.
3. For the impression which makes metal ("bullion") into a coin.
4. Ancient philosophers, like Aristotle.
5. Something that exists, is real.

No, nor to any one exterior sense,
Nor hath it any place of residence,
Nor is 't of earth or mold[6] celestial,
Or capable of any form at all.
Of that which hath no being do not boast:
Things that are not at all are never lost.
Men foolishly do call it virtuous:
What virtue is it that is born with us?[7]
Much less can honor be ascribed thereto:
Honor is purchased by the deeds we do.
Believe me, Hero, honor is not won
Until some honorable deed be done.
Seek you for chastity, immortal fame,
And know that some have wronged Diana's name?[8]
Whose name is it, if she be false or not,
So she be fair, but some vile tongues will blot?
But you are fair, aye me! so wondrous fair,
So young, so gentle, and so debonair,[9]
As Greece will think, if thus you live alone,
Some one or other keeps you as his own.
Then, Hero, hate me not, nor from me fly
To follow swiftly-blasting infamy.
Perhaps thy sacred priesthood makes thee loath.
Tell me, to whom madest thou that heedless oath?"
"To Venus," answered she, and as she spake,
Forth from those two tralucent cisterns[1] brake
A stream of liquid pearl, which down her face
Made milk-white paths whereon the gods might trace[2]
To Jove's high court. He thus replied: "The rites
In which Love's beauteous empress most delights
Are banquets, Doric music,[3] midnight revel,
Plays, masques, and all that stern age counteth evil.
Thee as a holy idiot doth she scorn;
For thou, in vowing chastity, hast sworn
To rob her name and honor, and thereby
Commit'st a sin far worse than perjury—
Even sacrilege against her Deity,
Through regular and formal purity.
To expiate which sin, kiss and shake hands;
Such sacrifice as this Venus demands."
Thereat she smiled and did deny him so
As, put[4] thereby, yet might he hope for mo.
Which makes him quickly reinforce his speech

6. Form.
7. I.e., a virtue is not a virtue unless it is acquired.
8. I.e., no fame for chastity is secure. Even Diana, goddess of chastity, has been slandered.
9. Affable, agreeable.
1. Translucent eyes; "stream": i.e., of tears.
2. Go.
3. A solemn, military mode. Marlowe presumably meant "Lydian" (as in Milton's *L'Allegro*, line 136); Lydian music was soft and sensual.
4. Put off; "mo": more.

And her in humble manner thus beseech:
"Though neither gods nor men may thee deserve,
Yet for her sake whom you have vowed to serve,
Abandon fruitless, cold Virginity,
The gentle Queen of Love's sole enemy.
Then shall you most resemble Venus' nun,
When Venus' sweet rites are performed and done.
Flint-breasted Pallas[5] joys in single life,
But Pallas and your mistress are at strife.
Love, Hero, then, and be not tyrannous,
But heal the heart that thou hast wounded thus,
Nor stain thy youthful years with avarice;
Fair fools delight to be accounted nice.[6]
The richest corn dies, if it be not reaped;
Beauty alone is lost, too warily kept."
These arguments he used, and many more,
Wherewith she yielded, that was won before.
Hero's looks yielded, but her words made war:
Women are won when they begin to jar.[7]
Thus, having swallowed Cupid's golden hook,
The more she strived, the deeper was she strook.
Yet, evilly feigning anger, strove she still
And would be thought to grant against her will.
So having paused a while, at last she said:
"Who taught thee rhetoric to deceive a maid?
Aye me, such words as these should I abhor,
And yet I like them for the orator."
With that, Leander stooped to have embraced her,
But from his spreading arms away she cast her,[8]
And thus bespake him: "Gentle youth, forbear
To touch the sacred garments which I wear.
"Upon a rock, and underneath a hill,
Far from the town, where all is whist[9] and still,
Save that the sea, playing on yellow sand,
Sends forth a rattling murmur to the land,
Whose sound allures the golden Morpheus[1]
In silence of the night to visit us,
My turret stands, and there, God knows, I play
With Venus' swans and sparrows[2] all the day.
A dwarfish beldame[3] bears me company,
That hops about the chamber where I lie
And spends the night, that might be better spent,
In vain discourse and apish[4] merriment.
Come thither." As she spake this, her tongue tripped,

5. Athena, a rival goddess, usually portrayed in armor.
6. Shy, reluctant.
7. Dispute.
8. Withdrew.
9. Silent.
1. God of sleep; "golden slumbers" was a common expression.
2. Venus was often portrayed in a chariot drawn by swans, and sparrows were associated with her because of their traditional lechery.
3. Old hag.
4. Silly.

For unawares "Come thither" from her slipped;
And suddenly her former color changed
And here and there her eyes through anger ranged.
And like a planet, moving several ways,[5]
At one self instant, she, poor soul, assays[6]
Loving, not to love at all, and every part
Strove to resist the motions of her heart;
And hands so pure, so innocent, nay, such
As might have made heaven stoop to have a touch,
Did she uphold to Venus, and again
Vowed spotless chastity, but all in vain.
Cupid beat down her prayers with his wings;
Her vows above the empty air he flings.
All deep enraged, his sinewy[7] bow he bent,
And shot a shaft that burning from him went,
Wherewith she, strooken, looked so dolefully
As made Love sigh to see his tyranny.
And as she wept, her tears to pearl he turned,
And wound them on his arm, and for her mourned.
Then towards the palace of the Destinies,[8]
Laden with languishment and grief, he flies,
And to those stern nymphs humbly made request
Both might enjoy each other and be blessed.
But with a ghastly dreadful countenance,
Threatening a thousand deaths at every glance,
They answered Love, nor would vouchsafe so much
As one poor word, their hate to him was such.
Harken a while, and I will tell you why:
Heaven's wingéd herald, Jove-born Mercury,
The selfsame day that he asleep had laid
Enchanted Argus,[9] spied a country maid
Whose careless hair, instead of pearl t' adorn it,
Glistered with dew, as one that seemed to scorn it,[1]
Her breath as fragrant as the morning rose,
Her mind pure, and her tongue untaught to glose.[2]
Yet proud she was, for lofty pride that dwells
In towered courts is oft in shepherds' cells,[3]
And too-too well the fair vermilion knew
And silver tincture of her cheeks, that drew
The love of every swain. On her, this god
Enamored was, and with his snaky rod[4]
Did charm her nimble feet and made her stay;
The while upon a hillock down he lay,

5. In Ptolemaic astronomy each planet moved in its own orbit or sphere, but was also carried in other directions by a surrounding sphere.
6. Attempts.
7. Strong.
8. The Fates.
9. Mercury, or Hermes, the messenger god with winged feet, put to sleep Argus, the hundred-eyed monster whom Juno had placed as a guard over Io, with whom her husband Jupiter was in love.
1. I.e., pearl or other jewelry.
2. Speak insincerely.
3. Huts.
4. Caduceus (now the symbol of medicine).

And sweetly on his pipe began to play,
And with smooth speech, her fancy to assay,
Till in his twining arms he locked her fast,
And then he wooed with kisses, and at last,
As shepherds do, her on the ground he laid,
And tumbling in the grass, he often strayed
Beyond the bounds of shame, in being bold
To eye those parts which no eye should behold;
And, like an insolent commanding lover,
Boasting his parentage, would needs discover
The way to new Elysium; but she,
Whose only dower was her chastity,
Having striven in vain, was now about to cry
And crave the help of shepherds that were nigh.
Herewith he stayed his fury,[5] and began
To give her leave to rise. Away she ran;
After went Mercury, who used such cunning
As she, to hear his tale, left off her running.
Maids are not won by brutish force and might
But speeches full of pleasure and delight.
And knowing Hermes courted her, was glad
That she such loveliness and beauty had
As could provoke his liking, yet was mute,
And neither would deny nor grant his suit.
Still vowed he love; she, wanting no excuse
To feed him with delays, as women use,[6]
Or thirsting after immortality
(All women are ambitious naturally),
Imposed upon her lover such a a task
As he ought not perform, nor yet she ask.
A draft of flowing nectar she requested
Wherewith the king of gods and men is feasted.
He, ready to accomplish what she willed,
Stole some from Hebe (Hebe Jove's cup filled),
And gave it to his simple rustic love,
Which being known (as what is hid from Jove?)
He inly stormed and waxed more furious
Than for the fire filched by Prometheus
And thrusts him down from heaven. He, wandering here,
In mournful terms,[7] with sad and heavy cheer
Complained to Cupid. Cupid for his sake,
To be revenged on Jove did undertake;
And those on whom heaven, earth, and hell relies
(I mean the adamantine[8] Destinies)
He wounds with love and forced them equally
To dote upon deceitful Mercury.
They offered him the deadly fatal knife

5. Passion.
6. Practice.
7. Condition; "cheer": countenance.
8. Of extreme hardness (so called because the Destinies' decrees were irrevocable).

That shears the slender threads of human life;[9]
At his fair feathered feet the engines laid
Which th' earth from ugly Chaos' den upweighed.[1]
These he regarded not, but did entreat
That Jove, usurper of his father's seat,
Might presently be banished into hell
And agéd Saturn in Olympus dwell.
They granted what he craved, and once again
Saturn and Ops began their golden reign.
Murder, rape, war, lust, and treachery
Were with Jove closed in Stygian empery.
But long this blesséd time continued not;
As soon as he his wishéd purpose got,
He, reckless of his promise, did despise
The love of th' everlasting Destinies.
They seeing it, both Love and him abhorred
And Jupiter unto his place restored.[2]
And but that Learning, in despite of Fate,
Will mount aloft and enter heaven gate,
And to the seat of Jove itself advance,
Hermes had slept in hell with Ignorance.
Yet as a punishment they added this,
That he and Poverty should always kiss.[3]
And to this day is every scholar poor;
Gross gold from them runs headlong to the boor.
Likewise the angry sisters, thus deluded,
To venge themselves on Hermes, have concluded
That Midas' brood[4] shall sit in Honor's chair,
To which the Muses' sons are only heir.
And fruitful wits that inaspiring[5] are
Shall discontent run into regions far;
And few great lords in virtuous deeds shall joy,
But be surprised with every garish toy,
And still enrich the lofty servile clown[6]
Who, with encroaching guile, keeps learning down.

9. According to classical mythology, the Fates spun and cut the threads that measure each human life.

1. The Fates also controlled the supports ("beams") that had supported ("upweighed") the earth since it arose out of Chaos, the yawning abyss from which all things came.

2. The story in lines 451–64 may be summarized as follows: Mercury scorns the gifts offered by the Fates but asks instead that Jove be dethroned (Jove had overthrown his father Saturn, who ruled heaven during the Golden Age). Mercury persuades the Fates to reverse this revolution, so Saturn and his wife Ops return to Olympus and Jove is thrust down into "Stygian empery" (line 458) or Hades. During the Golden Age there was no murder, rape, war, lust, or treachery; these came in with Jove, so when he is sent to Hades these crimes go with him. But this second Golden Age did not last long, because once he got what he wanted, Mercury (Hermes) forgot the Destinies and they restored Jove.

3. Marlowe invents the mythology that Mercury, the god of learning, would have slept in hell with Ignorance, but Learning is so divine that it always mounts up, even to heaven, the "seat of Jove." But it was not beyond the Fates' power to make learning and poverty go together, which they decreed in revenge for Mercury's neglect.

4. The rich, since everything Midas touched turned to gold.

5. Not ambitious for riches or power.

6. Ignorant person.

Then muse not[7] Cupid's suit no better sped,
Seeing in their loves the Fates were injurèd.
By this, sad Hero, with love unacquainted,
Viewing Leander's face, fell down and fainted.
He kissed her and breathed life into her lips,
Wherewith, as one displeased, away she trips.
Yet as she went, full often looked behind,
And many poor excuses did she find
To linger by the way, and once she stayed
And would have turned again, but was afraid
In offering parley to be counted light.
So on she goes, and in her idle flight
Her painted fan of curlèd plumes let fall,
Thinking to train[8] Leander therewithal.
He, being a novice, knew not what she meant
But stayed, and after her a letter sent,
Which joyful Hero answered in such sort
As he had hope to scale the beauteous fort
Wherein the liberal Graces[9] locked their wealth,
And therefore to her tower he got by stealth.
Wide open stood the door; he need not climb,
And she herself before the pointed[1] time
Had spread the board,[2] with roses strewed the room,
And oft looked out, and mused he did not come.
At last he came; O who can tell the greeting
These greedy lovers had at their first meeting?
He asked, she gave, and nothing was denied;
Both to each other quickly were affied.[3]
Look how their hands, so were their hearts united,
And what he did, she willingly requited.
(Sweet are the kisses, the embracements sweet,
When like desires and affections meet,
For from the earth to heaven is Cupid raised
Where fancy is in equal balance peised.)[4]
Yet she this rashness suddenly repented
And turned aside and to herself lamented,
As if her name and honor had been wronged
By being possessed of him for whom she longed.
Ay, and she wished, albeit not from her heart,
That he would leave her turret and depart.
The mirthful god of amorous pleasure smiled
To see how he this captive nymph beguiled,
For hitherto he did but fan the fire
And kept it down that it might mount the higher.
Now waxed she jealous[5] lest his love abated,

7. I.e., don't be surprised.
8. Entice.
9. Three goddesses associated with everything beautiful.
1. Appointed.
2. Set the table.
3. Affianced, engaged. "Look how": just as.
4. Weighed.
5. Fearful.

Fearing her own thoughts made her to be hated.
Therefore unto him hastily she goes
And, like light Salmacis,[6] her body throws
Upon his bosom where, with yielding eyes,
She offers up herself a sacrifice
To slake his anger; if he were displeased,
O what god would not therewith be appeased?
Like Aesop's cock,[7] this jewel he enjoyed,
And as a brother with his sister toyed,
Supposing nothing else was to be done
Now he her favor and good will had won.
But know you not that creatures wanting sense[8]
By nature have a mutual appetence,[9]
And wanting organs to advance a step,
Moved by love's force, unto each other leap?
Much more in subjects having intellect,
Some hidden influence breeds like effect.
Albeit Leander, rude in[1] love and raw,
Long dallying with Hero, nothing saw
That might delight him more, yet he suspected
Some amorous rites or other were neglected.
Therefore unto his body, hers he clung;
She, fearing on the rushes[2] to be flung,
Strived with redoubled strength. The more she strived,
The more a gentle, pleasing heat revived,
Which taught him all that elder lovers know.
And now the same gan so to scorch and glow,
As, in plain terms, yet cunningly,[3] he craved it.
(Love always makes those eloquent that have it.)
She, with a kind of granting, put him by it
And, ever as he thought himself most nigh it,
Like to the tree of Tantalus,[4] she fled
And, seeming lavish, saved her maindenhead.
Ne'er king more sought to keep his diadem
Than Hero this inestimable gem.
Above our life we love a steadfast friend;
Yet, when a token of great worth we send,
We often kiss it, often look thereon,
And stay the messenger that would be gone.
No marvel then, though Hero would not yield
So soon to part from that she dearly held.
Jewels being lost are found again, this never;
'Tis lost but once and once lost, lost forever.
　　Now had the Morn espied her lover's steeds,[5]

6. An amorous nymph in Ovid's *Metamorphoses*.
7. In the Aesopic fable a cock, scratching in the barnyard, uncovers a jewel, but prefers a barley corn to it.
8. Intelligence.
9. Attraction, as iron to a magnet.
1. Untutored.
2. Reeds used as carpeting in Elizabethan homes.
3. Skillfully.
4. Tantalus was punished in Hades by constantly reaching for fruit from a tree that eluded him.
5. The chariot of the sun.

Whereat she starts, puts on her purple weeds,[6]
And, red for anger that he stayed so long,
All headlong throws herself the clouds among.
And now Leander, fearing to be missed,
Embraced her suddenly, took leave, and kissed;
Long was he taking leave, and loath to go,
And kissed again, as lovers use to do.
Sad Hero wrung him by the hand and wept,
Saying, "Let your vows and promises be kept."
Then, standing at the door, she turned about,
As loath to see Leander going out.
And now the sun that through th' horizon peeps,
As pitying these lovers, downward creeps,
So that in silence of the cloudy night,
Though it was morning, did he take his flight.
But what the secret trusty night concealed,
Leander's amorous habit[7] soon revealed.
With Cupid's myrtle[8] was his bonnet crowned;
About his arms the purple riband[9] wound
Wherewith she wreathed her largely spreading hair;
Nor could the youth abstain but he must wear
The sacred ring wherewith she was endowed
When first religious chastity she vowed;
Which made his love through Sestos to be known,
And thence unto Abydos sooner blown
Than he could sail, for incorporeal Fame,
Whose weight consists in nothing but her name,
Is swifter than the wind, whose tardy plumes
Are reeking water and dull earthly fumes.[1]
Home when he came, he seemed not to be there,
But like exilèd air thrust from his sphere,
Set in a foreign place, and straight from thence,
Alcides-like,[2] by mighty violence
He would have chased away the swelling main
That him from her unjustly did detain.
Like as the sun in a diameter[3]
Fires and inflames objects removèd far,
And heateth kindly, shining lat'rally;
So beauty sweetly quickens when 'tis nigh.
But being separated and removed,
Burns where it cherished, murders where it loved.[4]
Therefore, even as an index to a book,
So to his mind was young Leander's look.
O none but gods have power their love to hide:
Affection by the count'nance is descried.
The light of hidden fire itself discovers,

6. Clothes.
7. Dress.
8. A flower sacred to Venus or Cupid, symbolic of love. "Bonnet": hat.
9. Ribbon.
1. I.e., fame is as incorporeal as mist or smoke.
2. Like Hercules, with brute force.
3. I.e., shining straight down.
4. I.e., inaccessible beauty can burn and murder.

And love that is concealed betrays[5] poor lovers.
His secret flame apparently[6] was seen;
Leander's father knew where he had been
And for the same mildly rebuked his son,
Thinking to quench the sparkles new begun.
But love resisted, once[7] grows passionate
And nothing more than counsel, lovers hate.
For as a hot, proud horse highly disdains
To have his head controlled, but breaks the reins,
Spits forth the ringled[8] bit, and with his hooves
Checks[9] the submissive ground; so he that loves,
The more he is restrained, the worse he fares.
What is it now but mad Leander dares?[1]
"O Hero, Hero!" thus he cried full oft,
And then he got him to a rock aloft,
Where, having spied her tower, long stared he on 't
And prayed the narrow toiling Hellespont
To part in twain, that he might come and go,
But still the rising billows answered no.
With that he stripped him to the ivory skin
And crying, "Love, I come!" leapt lively in.
Whereat the sapphire-visaged god[2] grew proud
And made his capering Triton[3] sound aloud;
Imagining that Ganimed,[4] displeased,
Had left the heavens, therefore on him seized.
Leander strived; the waves about him wound
And pulled him to the bottom, where the ground
Was strewed with pearl, and in low coral groves
Sweet singing mermaids sported with their loves
On heaps of heavy gold and took great pleasure
To spurn in careless sort[5] the shipwrack treasure;
For here the stately azure palace stood
Where kingly Neptune and his train abode.
The lusty god embraced him, called him love,
And swore he never should return to Jove.
But when he knew it was not Ganimed,
For under water he was almost dead,
He heaved him up, and looking on his face,
Beat down the bold waves with his triple mace,[6]
Which mounted up, intending to have kissed him,
And fell in drops like tears because they missed him.
Leander being up, began to swim
And, looking back, saw Neptune follow him.
Whereat aghast, the poor soul gan to cry,

5. Gives away.
6. Openly.
7. At once.
8. With rings at the ends.
9. Stamps.
1. I.e., what is there now Leander dares not do?
2. Neptune, god of the sea.
3. A subordinate sea god who blew on a conch shell.
4. A beautiful boy, taken by Jove to be his cupbearer.
5. Manner.
6. The three-pronged fork carried by Neptune.

"O let me visit Hero ere I die!"
The god put Helle's bracelet[7] on his arm
And swore the sea should never do him harm.
He clapped his plump cheeks, with his tresses played
And, smiling wantonly, his love bewrayed.[8]
He watched his arms, and as they opened wide,
At every stroke betwixt them he would slide
And steal a kiss, and then run out and dance
And, as he turned, cast many a lustful glance
And throw him gaudy toys to please his eye,
And dive into the water and there pry
Upon his breast, his thighs, and every limb,
And up again and close beside him swim
And talk of love. Leander made reply,
"You are deceived; I am no woman, I."
Thereat smiled Neptune and then told a tale
How that a shepherd, sitting in a vale,
Played with a boy so fair and so kind
As, for his love, both earth and heaven pined;
That of the cooling river durst not drink
Lest water nymphs should pull him from the brink.
And when he sported in the fragrant lawns,
Goat-footed satyrs and up-staring fawns[9]
Would steal him thence. Ere half this tale was done
"Ay me!" Leander cried, "th' enamored sun
That now should shine on Thetis' glassy bower[1]
Descends upon my radiant Hero's tower.
O that these tardy arms of mine were wings!"
And as he spake, upon the waves he springs.
Neptune was angry that he gave no ear,
And in his heart revenging malice bare.
He flung at him his mace, but as it went
He called it in, for love made him repent.
The mace returning back, his own hand hit,
As meaning to be venged for darting it.
When this fresh bleeding wound Leander viewed,
His color went and came, as if he rued
The grief[2] which Neptune felt. In gentle breasts
Relenting thoughts, remorse, and pity rests;
And who have hard hearts and obdurate minds
But vicious, harebrained, and illit'rate hinds?[3]
The god, seeing him with pity to be moved,
Thereon concluded that he was beloved.
(Love is too full of faith, too credulous,

7. Helle was the daughter of King Athamas of Thebes. To escape a cruel stepmother, she fled on a winged, golden-fleeced ram but fell off into the Hellespont, which was named for her. Marlowe apparently invents the detail of the bracelet.

8. Revealed.

9. *Fauni*, woodland spirits, who prophesied by looking up to the heavens.

1. I.e., the sea; Thetis was a sea nymph, mother of the hero Achilles.

2. Pain.

3. Rustics, boors.

With folly and false hope deluding us.)
Wherefore Leander's fancy to surprise,[4]
To the rich ocean for gifts he flies.
'Tis wisdom to give much; a gift prevails
When deep persuading oratory fails.
By this[5] Leander, being near the land,
Cast down his weary feet and felt the sand.
Breathless albeit he were, he rested not
Till to the solitary tower he got.
And knocked and called; at which celestial noise,
The longing heart of Hero much more joys
Than nymphs and shepherds when the timbrel rings,
Or crooked dolphin[6] when the sailor sings.
She stayed not for her robes, but straight arose
And, drunk with gladness, to the door she goes;
Where, seeing a naked man, she screeched for fear
(Such sights as this to tender maids are rare),
And ran into the dark herself to hide.
Rich jewels in the dark are soonest spied.
Unto her was he led, or rather drawn
By those white limbs which sparkled through the lawn.[7]
The nearer that he came, the more she fled
And, seeking refuge, slipped into her bed.
Whereon Leander sitting, thus began,
Through numbing cold, all feeble, faint, and wan:
"If not for love, yet, love, for pity's sake
Me in thy bed and maiden bosom take;
At least vouchsafe these arms some little room
Who, hoping to embrace thee, cheerly[8] swum.
This head was beat with many a churlish billow,
And therefore let it rest upon thy pillow."
Herewith affrighted Hero shrunk away
And in her lukewarm place Leander lay;
Whose lively heat, like fire from heaven fet,[9]
Would animate gross clay, and higher set
The drooping thoughts of base declining souls
Than dreary Mars[1] carousing nectar bowls.
His hands he cast upon her like a snare;
She, overcome with shame and sallow[2] fear,
Like chaste Diana when Actaeon spied her,[3]
Being suddenly betrayed, dived down to hide her,
And as her silver body downward went,
With both her hands she made the bed a tent,
And in her own mind thought herself secure,

4. Love to capure.
5. At this time.
6. "Crooked" because of the undulating path of the dolphin in the water. The musician Arion was saved from drowning by a dolphin charmed by his music. "Timbrel": tambourine.
7. Fine linen or cambric.
8. Gladly.
9. Fetched.
1. God of war; "dreary": bloody.
2. Pale, yellowish.
3. Actaeon, a hunter came upon Diana bathing; she turned him into a stag, and he was killed by his own hounds.

O'ercast with dim and darksome coverture.
And now she lets him whisper in her ear,
Flatter, entreat, promise, protest, and swear;
Yet ever as he greedily assayed
To touch those dainties, she the Harpy[4] played,
And every limb did, as a soldier stout,
Defend the fort and keep the foeman out.
For though the rising ivory mount he scaled,
Which is with azure circling lines empaled,[5]
Much like a globe (a globe may I term this
By which love sails to regions full of bliss),
Yet there with Sisyphus[6] he toiled in vain
Till gentle parley did the truce obtain.
Wherein Leander on her quivering breast,
Breathless spoke something and sighed out the rest;
Which so prevailed, as he, with small ado,
Enclosed her in his arms and kissed her, too.
And every kiss to her was as a charm
And to Leander as a fresh alarm.[7]
So that the truce was broke, and she, alas,
Poor silly[8] maiden, at his mercy was.
Love is not full of pity, as men say,
But deaf and cruel, where he means to prey.
Even as a bird which in our hands we wring[9]
Forth plungeth and oft flutters with her wing,
She trembling strove; this strife of hers, like that
Which made the world,[1] another world begat
Of unknown joy. Treason was in her thought,
And cunningly to yield herself she sought.
Seeming not won, yet won she was, at length.
(In such wars women use but half their strength.)
Leander now, like Theban Hercules,
Entered the orchard of th' Hesperides,
Whose fruit none rightly can describe but he
That pulls or shakes it from the golden tree.[2]
And now she wished this night were never done,
And sighed to think upon th' approaching sun,
For much it grieved her that the bright daylight
Should know the pleasure of this blesséd night,
And them like Mars and Erycine[3] displayed,
Both in each other's arms chained as they laid.
Again she knew not how to frame her look
Or speak to him who in a moment took

4. A monster, half bird, half woman, who snatches away banquets in Virgil's *Aeneid* and Shakespeare's *Tempest*.
5. Surrounded.
6. Condemned in Hades to endlessly roll a stone uphill.
7. Call to battle.
8. Innocent.
9. Hold firmly.
1. The Greek philosopher Empedocles held that creation was the result of love and strife.
2. One of Hercules's labors was to get the golden apples of the Hesperides, guarded by a dragon. Hercules was born in Thebes.
3. A name for Venus, who was caught in bed with Mars by her husband Vulcan, who cast a fine chain net over them.

That which so long so charily she kept;
And fain by stealth away she would have crept
And to some corner secretly have gone,
Leaving Leander in the bed alone.
But as her naked feet were whipping out,
He on the sudden clinged her so about
That mermaidlike unto the floor she slid:
One half appeared, the other half was hid.
Thus near the bed she blushing stood upright;
And from her countenance behold ye might
A kind of twilight break, which through the hair,
As from an orient[4] cloud, glims here and there,
And round about the chamber this false morn
Brought forth the day before the day was born.
So Hero's ruddy cheek Hero betrayed,
And her all naked to his sight displayed,
Whence his admiring eyes more pleasure took
Than Dis,[5] on heaps of gold fixing his look.
By this Apollo's golden harp began
To sound forth music to the Ocean,
Which watchful Hesperus[6] no sooner heard
But he the day's bright-bearing car prepared,
And ran before, as harbinger of light,
And with his flaring beams mocked ugly Night,
Till she, o'ercome with anguish, shame and rage,
Danged[7] down to hell her loathsome carriage.

1598

The Passionate Shepherd to His Love[1]

Come live with me and be my love,
And we will all the pleasures prove[2]
That valleys, groves, hills, and fields,
Woods, or steepy mountain yields.

And we will sit upon the rocks,
Seeing the shepherds feed their flocks,
By shallow rivers to whose falls
Melodious birds sing madrigals.

And I will make thee beds of roses
And a thousand fragrant posies,

4. Bright, shining; "glims": gleams.
5. Pluto, god of the underworld and of wealth.
6. The evening star; apparently Marlowe's error for Lucifer, the morning star.
7. Hurled.
1. This pastoral lyric of invitation is one of the most famous of Elizabethan songs, and a few lines from it are sung in Shakespeare's *Merry Wives of Windsor*. Many poets have written replies to it, the finest of which is by that other great Elizabethan romantic, Sir Walter Ralegh.
2. Test, experience.

A cap of flowers, and a kirtle
Embroidered all with leaves of myrtle;

A gown made of the finest wool
Which from our pretty lambs we pull;
Fair lined slippers for the cold,
With buckles of the purest gold;

A belt of straw and ivy buds,
With coral clasps and amber studs:
And if these pleasures may thee move,
Come live with me, and be my love.

The shepherds' swains shall dance and sing
For thy delight each May morning:
If these delights thy mind may move,
Then live with me and be my love.

1599, 1600

Dr. Faustus Marlowe's major tragedies, *Tamburlaine, The Jew of Malta,* and *Dr. Faustus,* all portray a hero who passionately seeks power—the power of rule, the power of money, and the power of knowledge, respectively. Each of the heroes is an "overreacher," striving beyond the bounds of human capacity, or at least the limits imposed upon human achievement.

Unlike Tamburlaine, whose aim and goal is "the sweet fruition of an earthly crown," and Barabas, the Jew of Malta, who lusts for "infinite riches in a little room," Faustus seeks the power that comes from knowledge, no matter at what cost that knowledge is acquired. To get this power Faustus must make (or chooses to make) a bargain with the devil. Such a situation is an old folklore motif, but it would have been taken seriously in a time when everyone believed in the reality of devils. Faustus on his part is in search of the power that comes from black magic, but the devil on his side exacts a fearful price in exchange—the eternal damnation of Faustus's soul. This, like the reality of devils, would have been taken literally by an Elizabethan audience. Faustus aspires to be more than a man—a demigod, a deity. His fall is caused by the same pride and ambition that caused the fall of the angels in heaven, and of humanity in the Garden of Eden. So to aspire is to incur inevitable defeat, but it is characteristic of Marlowe that he makes those aspirations nonetheless magnificent.

The immediate source of the play is a German narrative called, in its English translation, *The History of the Damnable Life and Deserved Death of Doctor John Faustus.* It contains those scenes of horseplay and low practical joking which, in the drama, contrast so markedly with the passages of grand aspiration. It is quite possible that these low scenes are the work of a collaborator, and the early records from the theater and the early editions of the play (1604 and 1616, both long after Marlowe's death) show that the true text of the play is difficult to establish. What does seem clear is that no other Elizabethan could have written the first scene (which projects the insatiable aspiring mind of the hero), the famous address to Helen of Troy, or the final scene of Faustus's last hour.

The Tragical History of the Life and Death of Doctor Faustus

Dramatis Personae

CHORUS
DR. JOHN FAUSTUS, *of the University of Wittenberg*
WAGNER, *his servant*
GOOD ANGEL *and* BAD ANGEL
VALDES and CORNELIUS, *magicians and friends of* FAUSTUS
THREE SCHOLARS, *students at the university*
LUCIFER, MEPHISTOPHILIS, *and* BELZEBUB, *devils*
ROBIN *and* DICK, *rustic clowns*
THE SEVEN DEADLY SINS
POPE ADRIAN
RAYMOND, *King of Hungary*
BRUNO, *a rival Pope, appointed by the* EMPEROR
CARDINALS OF FRANCE *and* PADUA
ARCHBISHOP OF RHEIMS
MARTINO, FREDERICK, *and* BENVOLIO, *gentlemen at the* EMPEROR'S *court*
CAROLUS (CHARLES) THE FIFTH, EMPEROR
DUKE OF SAXONY
DUKE *and* DUCHESS OF VANHOLT
HORSE-COURSER
CARTER
HOSTESS *of a tavern*
OLD MAN
SPIRITS *of* DARIUS, ALEXANDER *and his* PARAMOUR, *and* HELEN OF TROY
ATTENDANTS, MONKS *and* FRIARS, SOLDIERS, PIPER, *two* CUPIDS

Act I

[*Enter* CHORUS.[1]]

CHO. Not marching in the fields of Trasimene[2]
Where Mars did mate the warlike Carthagens,
Nor sporting in the dalliance of love
In courts of kings where state[3] is overturned,
Nor in the pomp of proud audacious deeds
Intends our Muse to vaunt his heavenly verse:
Only this, gentles, we must now perform
The form of Faustus' fortunes good or bad.
And so to patient judgments we appeal
And speak for Faustus in his infancy.
Now is he born, his parents base of stock,
In Germany within a town called Rhode;[4]

1. A single actor who recited a prologue to an act or a whole play, and occasionally delivered an epilogue.
2. The battle of Lake Trasimene (217 B.C.) was one of the Carthaginian leader Hannibal's great victories. "Mate": join with.
3. Political power.
4. Roda. Wittenberg, in the next line, was the famous university where Martin Luther studied, as did Shakespeare's Hamlet and Horatio; "whereas": where.

At riper years to Wittenberg he went
Whereas his kinsmen chiefly brought him up;
So much he profits in divinity,
The fruitful plot of scholarism graced,[5]
That shortly he was graced with Doctor's name,
Excelling all whose sweet delight disputes[6]
In th' heavenly matters of theology,
Till, swollen with cunning,[7] of a self-conceit,
His waxen wings did mount above his reach
And melting, heavens conspired his overthrow.[8]
For, falling to a devilish exercise
And glutted more with learning's golden gifts,
He surfeits upon curséd necromancy;[9]
Nothing so sweet as magic is to him,
Which he prefers before his chiefest bliss[1]—
And this the man that in his study sits.
[*Draws the curtain*[2] *and exit.*]

SCENE 1

[FAUSTUS *in his study.*]

FAUST. Settle thy studies, Faustus, and begin
To sound the depth of that thou wilt profess.
Having commenced, be a divine in show,
Yet level[3] at the end of every art
And live and die in Aristotle's works:
Sweet Analytics,[4] 'tis thou hast ravished me! [*Reads.*]
Bene disserere est finis logicis—
Is to dispute well logic's chiefest end?
Affords this art no greater miracle?
Then read no more; thou hast attained the end.
A greater subject fitteth Faustus' wit:
Bid ὀν χαὶ μὴ ὀν[5] farewell, Galen come,
Seeing *ubi desinit philosophus, ibi incipit medicus;*[6]
Be a physician, Faustus, heap up gold
And be eternized for some wondrous cure. [*Reads.*]
Summum bonum medicinae sanitas[7]—
The end of physic is our bodies' health:
Why, Faustus, hast thou not attained that end?
Is not thy common talk sound aphorisms?[8]

5. Grazed. In line 17 "graced" refers to the Cambridge word for permission to proceed to a degree.
6. The usual academic exercises were disputations, which took the place of examinations.
7. Learning.
8. The reference is to the Greek myth of Icarus, who flew too near the sun on wings of feathers and wax made by his father Daedalus. The wax melted and he fell into the sea and was drowned.
9. Black magic.
1. The salvation of his soul.
2. A curtain to the enclosed space at the rear of the stage.

3. "Commenced": graduated, i.e., received the doctor's degree; "in show": in external appearance; "level": aim.
4. The title of a treatise on logic by Aristotle. The Latin means, "To carry on a disputation well is the end or purpose of logic."
5. "Being and not being," i.e., philosophy. Galen: the ancient authority on medicine (2nd century A.D.).
6. "Where the philosopher leaves off the physician begins."
7. "Good health is the object of medicine" (or "physic").
8. I.e., reliable medical pronouncements. "Bills": prescriptions.

Are not thy bills hung up as monuments
Whereby whole cities have escaped the plague
And thousand desperate maladies been cured?
Yet art thou still but Faustus, and a man.
Couldst thou make men to live eternally
Or, being dead, raise them to life again,
Then this profession were to be esteemed.
Physic, farewell. Where is Justinian?[9] [*Reads.*]
Si una eademque res legatur duobus,
Alter rem, alter valorem rei, etc.[1]—
A pretty case of paltry legacies!
Exhaereditare filium non potest pater nisi—
Such is the subject of the Institute
And universal body of the law.
This study fits a mercenary drudge
Who aims at nothing but external trash,
Too servile and illiberal for me.
When all is done, divinity is best.
Jerome's Bible,[2] Faustus, view it well: [*Reads.*]
Stipendium peccati mors est—Ha! *Stipendium, etc.*
The reward of sin is death? That's hard.
Si pecasse negamus, fallimur, et nulla est in nobis veritas[3]—
If we say that we have no sin
We deceive ourselves, and there's no truth in us.
Why then belike
We must sin and so consequently die,
Aye, we must die an everlasting death.
What doctrine call you this, *Che sera, sera:*[4]
What will be, shall be? Divinity, adieu!
These metaphysics[5] of magicians
And necromantic books are heavenly:
Lines, circles, signs, letters, and characters—
Aye, these are those that Faustus most desires.
O what a world of profit and delight,
Of power, of honor, of omnipotence,
Is promised to the studious artisan![6]
All things that move between the quiet[7] poles
Shall be at my command. Emperors and kings
Are but obeyed in their several provinces,
Nor can they raise the wind or rend the clouds;
But his dominion that exceeds in this
Stretcheth as far as doth the mind of man.
A sound magician is a demigod:

9. Roman emperor and authority on law (483–565), author of the *Institutes*.
1. "If something is bequeathed to two persons, one shall have the thing itself, the other something of equal value." The next Latin phrase means: "A father cannot disinherit his son unless."
2. The Latin translation, or "Vulgate," of St. Jerome (ca. 340–420). The Latin (Romans vi.23) is translated in line 40.
3. I John i.8, translated in the next two lines.
4. Translated in the first half of the next line.
5. Basic principles.
6. I.e., a master of the occult arts, such as necromancy.
7. Unmoving.

Here tire my brains to gain a deity!
Wagner!
[*Enter* WAGNER.]
Commend me to my dearest friends,
The German Valdes and Cornelius;
Request them earnestly to visit me.
WAG. I will, sir. [*Exit*.]
FAUST. Their conference will be a greater help to me
Than all my labors, plod I ne'er so fast.
[*Enter the* GOOD ANGEL *and the* BAD ANGEL.]
G. ANG. O Faustus, lay that damnéd book aside
And gaze not on it, lest it tempt thy soul
And heap God's heavy wrath upon thy head.
Read, read the Scriptures! That is blasphemy.
B. ANG. Go forward, Faustus, in that famous art
Wherein all nature's treasury is contained:
Be thou on earth, as Jove[8] is in the sky,
Lord and commander of these elements.
[*Exeunt* ANGELS.]
FAUST. How am I glutted with conceit[9] of this!
Shall I make spirits fetch me what I please,
Resolve me of all ambiguities,
Perform what desperate enterprise I will?
I'll have them fly to India[1] for gold,
Ransack the ocean for orient pearl,
And search all corners of the new-found world[2]
For pleasant fruits and princely delicates;
I'll have them read me strange philosophy
And tell the secrets of all foreign kings;
I'll have them wall all Germany with brass
And make swift Rhine circle fair Wittenberg;
I'll have them fill the public schools[3] with silk
Wherewith the students shall be bravely clad;
I'll levy soldiers with the coin they bring,
And chase the Prince of Parma[4] from our land
And reign sole king of all our provinces;
Yea, stranger engines for the brunt of war
Than was the fiery keel[5] at Antwerp's bridge
I'll make my servile spirits to invent!
[*Enter* VALDES *and* CORNELIUS.]
Come, German Valdes and Cornelius,
And make me blest with your sage conference.
Valdes, sweet Valdes and Cornelius,
Know that your words have won me at the last
To practice magic and concealéd arts;

8. God (a common substitution in Elizabethan drama).
9. Filled with the idea.
1. "India" could mean the West Indies, America, or Ophir (in the east).
2. The western hemisphere.
3. The university lecture rooms.
4. The Duke of Parma was the Spanish governor general of the Low Countries from 1579 to 1592.
5. A reference to the burning ship sent by the Netherlanders in 1585 against the barrier on the river Scheldt which Parma had built as a part of the blockade of Antwerp.

Yet not your words only, but mine own fantasy
That will receive no object,[6] for my head
But ruminates on necromantic skill.
Philosophy is odious and obscure,
Both law and physic are for petty wits,
Divinity is basest of the three,
Unpleasant, harsh, contemptible, and vile;
'Tis magic, magic, that hath ravished me!
Then, gentle friends, aid me in this attempt,
And I, that have with concise syllogisms
Graveled[7] the pastors of the German church,
And made the flowering pride of Wittenberg
Swarm to my problems[8] as the infernal spirits
On sweet Musaeus when he came to hell,
Will be as cunning as Agrippa[9] was
Whose shadows made all Europe honor him.

VALD. Faustus, these books, thy wit, and our experience
Shall make all nations to canonize us.
As Indian Moors[1] obey their Spanish lords
So shall the spirits of every element
Be always serviceable to us three:
Like lions shall they guard us when we please,
Like Almain rutters[2] with their horsemen's staves,
Or Lapland giants trotting by our sides;
Sometimes like women, or unwedded maids,
Shadowing [3] more beauty in their airy brows
Than in the white breasts of the queen of love;
From Venice shall they drag huge argosies
And from America the golden fleece
That yearly stuffs old Philip's[4] treasury,
If learned Faustus will be resolute.

FAUST. Valdes, as resolute am I in this
As thou to live; therefore object it not.[5]

CORN. The miracles that magic will perform
Will make thee vow to study nothing else.
He that is grounded in astrology,
Enriched with tongues, well seen[6] in minerals,
Hath all the principles magic doth require.
Then doubt not, Faustus, but to be renowned
And more frequented for this mystery[7]
Than heretofore the Delphian oracle.
The spirits tell me they can dry the sea
And fetch the treasure of all foreign wrecks—

6. That will pay no attention to physical reality.
7. Confounded.
8. Lectures in logic and mathematics. Musaeus was a mythical singer, son of Orpheus; it was, however, the latter who charmed the denizens of hell with his music.
9. Cornelius Agrippa, German author of *The Vanity and Uncertainty of Arts and Sciences,* popularly supposed to have the power of calling up shades ("shadows") of the dead.

1. I.e., dark-skinned American Indians.
2. German horsemen.
3. Harboring.
4. Philip II, king of Spain.
5. I.e., don't make it a condition.
6. Expert.
7. Craft. The "Delphian oracle" was the oracle of Apollo at Delphi, much frequented in antiquity.

Aye, all the wealth that our forefathers hid
Within the massy[8] entrails of the earth.
Then tell me, Faustus, what shall we three want?

FAUST. Nothing, Cornelius. O this cheers my soul!
Come, show me some demonstrations magical
That I may conjure in some lusty[9] grove
And have these joys in full possession.

VALD. Then haste thee to some solitary grove
And bear wise Bacon's[10] and Abanus' works,
The Hebrew Psalter and New Testament;
And whatsoever else is requisite
We will inform thee ere our conference cease.

CORN. Valdes, first let him know the words of art,
And then, all other ceremonies learned,
Faustus may try his cunning by himself.

VALD. First I'll instruct thee in the rudiments,
And then wilt thou be perfecter than I.

FAUST. Then come and dine with me, and after meat
We'll canvass every quiddity[1] thereof;
For ere I sleep I'll try what I can do:
This night I'll conjure[2] though I die therefore. [*Exeunt.*]

SCENE 2

[*Enter two* SCHOLARS.]

1 SCH. I wonder what's become of Faustus, that was wont to make our schools ring with *sic probo*.[3]

2 SCH. That shall we presently know; here comes his boy.[4]

[*Enter* WAGNER *carrying wine.*]

1 SCH. How now, sirrah; where's thy master?

WAG. God in heaven knows.

2 SCH. Why, dost not thou know then?

WAG. Yes, I know; but that follows not.

1 SCH. Go to, sirrah; leave your jesting and tell us where he is.

WAG. That follows not by force of argument, which you, being licentiate,[5] should stand upon; therefore acknowledge your error and be attentive.

2 SCH. Then you will not tell us?

WAG. You are deceived, for I will tell you. Yet if you were not dunces you would never ask me such a question, for is he not *corpus naturale*, and is not that *mobile?*[6] Then wherefore should you ask me such a question? But that I am by nature phlegmatic,[7] slow to wrath and prone to lechery (to love, I would say), it were not for you to come within forty foot of

8. Massive.
9. Flourishing, beautiful.
10. Roger Bacon, the medieval friar and scientist, popularly thought a magician. "Abanus" is Pietro d'Abano, 13th-century alchemist.
1. Essential feature.
2. Call up spirits.
3. "Thus I prove," a phrase in scholastic disputation.
4. Poor student earning his keep.
5. I.e., graduate students.
6. *Corpus naturale et mobile* (natural, movable matter) was a scholastic definition of the subject matter of physics. Wagner is here parodying the language of learning he hears around the university.
7. Dominated by the phlegm, one of the four humors of medieval medicine and psychology.

the place of execution,[8] although I do not doubt to see you both hanged the next sessions. Thus having triumphed over you, I will set my countenance like a precisian,[9] and begin to speak thus: Truly, my dear brethren, my master is within at dinner with Valdes and Cornelius, as this wine, if it could speak, would inform your worships; and so the Lord bless you, preserve you, and keep you, my dear brethren.
[*Exit.*]

1 SCH. O Faustus, then I fear that which I have long suspected,
That thou art fallen into that damnéd art
For which they two are infamous through the world.
2 SCH. Were he a stranger, not allied to me,
The danger of his soul would make me mourn.
But come, let us go and inform the Rector,[1]
It may be his grave counsel may reclaim him.
1 SCH. I fear me nothing will reclaim him now.
2 SCH. Yet let us see what we can do. [*Exeunt.*]

SCENE 3

[*Enter* FAUSTUS *to conjure.*]

FAUST. Now that the gloomy shadow of the night,
Longing to view Orion's drizzling look,[2]
Leaps from the antarctic world unto the sky
And dims the welkin[3] with her pitchy breath,
Faustus, begin thine incantations
And try if devils will obey thy hest,
Seeing thou hast prayed and sacrificed to them.
Within this circle is Jehovah's name
[*He draws the circle*[4] *on the ground.*]
Forward and backward anagrammatized,
The breviated names of holy saints,
Figures of every adjunct[5] to the heavens
And characters of signs and erring stars,
By which the spirits are enforced to rise.
Then fear not, Faustus, but be resolute
And try the uttermost magic can perform. [*Thunder.*]
Sint mihi dei Acherontis propitii! Valeat numen triplex Iehovae! Ignei aerii aquatici terreni spiritus, salvete! Orientis princeps Lucifer Belzebub, inferni ardentis monarcha, et Demogorgon, propitiamus vos, ut appareat et surgat Mephistophilis![6]
[FAUSTUS *pauses. Thunder still.*]

8. I.e., the dining room.
9. A Puritan. The rest of his speech is in the style of the Puritans.
1. The head of a German university.
2. Orion appears at the beginning of winter. The phrase is a reminiscence of Virgil.
3. Sky.
4. I.e., the magic circle on the ground within which the spirits rise.
5. Heavenly body, thought to be joined to the solid firmament. "Characters of signs" are signs of the zodiac and the planets; "erring": wandering.
6. This first part of the incantation means: "May the gods of the lower regions favor me! Goodbye to the Trinity! Hail, spirits of fire, air, water, and earth! Prince of the East, Belzebub, monarch of burning hell, and Demogorgon, we pray to you that Mephistophilis may appear and rise."

Quid tu moraris?[7] *Per Iehovam, Gehennam et consecratam aquam quam nunc spargo, signumque crucis quod nunc facio, et per vota nostra, ipse nunc surgat nobis dicatus Mephistophilis!*

[MEPHISTOPHILIS *in the shape of a dragon rises from the earth outside the circle.*]

I charge thee to return and change thy shape;
Thou art too ugly to attend on me.
Go, and return an old Franciscan friar;
That holy shape becomes a devil best. [*Exit* MEPH.]
I see there's virtue in my heavenly words:
Who would not be proficient in this art?
How pliant is this Mephistophilis,
Full of obedience and humility!
Such is the force of magic and my spells.
Now, Faustus, thou art conjurer laureate
That canst command great Mephistophilis:
Quin redis, Mephistophilis, fratris imagine![8]

[*Re-enter* MEPHISTOPHILIS *like a Friar.*]

MEPH. Now, Faustus, what wouldst thou have me do?
FAUST. I charge thee wait upon me whilst I live
To do whatever Faustus shall command,
Be it be make the moon drop from her sphere
Or the ocean to overwhelm the world.
MEPH. I am a servant to great Lucifer
And may not follow thee without his leave:
No more than he commands must we perform.
FAUST. Did not he charge thee to appear to me?
MEPH. No, I came now hither of my own accord.
FAUST. Did not my conjuring speeches raise thee?
Speak!
MEPH. That was the cause, but yet *per accidens*,[9]
For when we hear one rack[1] the name of God,
Abjure the Scriptures and his Saviour Christ,
We fly in hope to get his glorious soul;
Nor will we come unless he use such means
Whereby he is in danger to be damned;
Therefore the shortest cut for conjuring
Is stoutly to abjure the Trinity
And pray devoutly to the prince of hell.
FAUST. So I have done, and hold this principle,
There is no chief but only Belzebub
To whom Faustus doth dedicate himself.
This word "damnation" terrifies not me
For I confound hell in Elysium;

7. Nothing has happened, so Faustus asks, "What are you waiting for?" and continues to conjure: "By Jehovah, Gehenna, and the holy water which I now sprinkle, and the sign of the cross which I now make, and by our vows, may Mephistophilis himself now rise to serve us."

8. "Return, Mephistophilis, in the shape of a friar."

9. By the immediate, not ultimate, cause.

1. Torture (by anagrammatizing).

My ghost be with the old philosophers![2]
But leaving these vain trifles of men's souls—
Tell me, what is that Lucifer thy lord?
MEPH. Arch-regent and commander of all spirits.
FAUST. Was not that Lucifer an angel once?
MEPH. Yes, Faustus, and most dearly loved of God.
FAUST. How comes it, then, that he is prince of devils?
MEPH. O, by aspiring pride and insolence,
For which God threw him from the face of heaven.
FAUST. And what are you that live with Lucifer?
MEPH. Unhappy spirits that fell with Lucifer,
Conspired against our God with Lucifer,
And are forever damned with Lucifer.
FAUST. Where are you damned?
MEPH. In hell.
FAUST. How comes it, then, that thou art out of hell?
MEPH. Why, this is hell, nor am I out of it:
Thinkst thou that I who saw the face of God
And tasted the eternal joys of heaven
Am not tormented with ten thousand hells
In being deprived of everlasting bliss?[3]
O Faustus, leave these frivolous demands
Which strike a terror to my fainting soul!
FAUST. What, is great Mephistophilis so passionate
For being deprivéd of the joys of heaven?
Learn thou of Faustus manly fortitude
And scorn those joys thou never shalt possess.
Go, bear these tidings to great Lucifer:
Seeing Faustus hath incurred eternal death
By desperate thoughts against Jove's deity,
Say he surrenders up to him his soul
So he will spare him four and twenty years,
Letting him live in all voluptuousness,
Having thee ever to attend on me:
To give me whatsoever I shall ask,
To tell me whatsoever I demand,
To slay mine enemies and aid my friends,
And always be obedient to my will.
Go, and return to mighty Lucifer,
And meet me in my study at midnight
And then resolve me of thy master's mind.[4]
MEPH. I will, Faustus. [*Exit.*]
FAUST. Had I as many souls as there be stars
I'd give them all for Mephistophilis!
By him I'll be great emperor of the world,
And make a bridge thorough the moving air
To pass the ocean with a band of men;
I'll join the hills that bind the Afric shore

2. I.e., I consider the true hell to be the classical Elysium, where philosophy is discussed, not the Christian place of punishment for sinners.

3. This is the *poena damni*, or punishment of loss, supposed to constitute the greatest spiritual suffering.

4. Give me his decision.

And make that country continent to Spain,
And both contributory to my crown;
The Emperor[5] shall not live but by my leave,
Nor any potentate of Germany.
Now that I have obtained what I desire
I'll live in speculation[6] of this art
Till Mephistophilis return again. [*Exit.*]

SCENE 4

[*Enter* WAGNER *and the* CLOWN ⟨ROBIN.⟩[7]]

WAG. Come hither, sirrah boy.

CLOWN. Boy! O disgrace to my person! Zounds, boy in your face! You have seen many boys with such pickadevaunts, I am sure.[8]

WAG. Sirrah, hast thou no comings in?[9]

CLOWN. Yes, and goings out too; you may see, sir.

WAG. Alas, poor slave. See how poverty jests in his nakedness: the villain's out of service, and so hungry that I know he would give his soul to the devil for a shoulder of mutton, though it were blood-raw.

CLOWN. Not so, neither; I had need to have it well-roasted, and good sauce to it, if I pay so dear, I can tell you.

WAG. Sirrah, wilt thou be my man and wait on me? And I will make thee go like *Qui mihi discipulus*.[1]

CLOWN. What, in verse?

WAG. No, slave, in beaten silk and staves-acre.[2]

CLOWN. Staves-acre! that's good to kill vermin. Then, belike, if I serve you I shall be lousy.

WAG. Why, so thou shalt be, whether thou dost it or no; for, sirrah, if thou dost not presently bind thyself to me for seven years, I'll turn all the lice about thee into familiars[3] and make them tear thee in pieces.

CLOWN. Nay, sir, you may save yourself a labor, for they are as familiar with me as if they paid for their meat and drink, I can tell you.

WAG. Well, sirrah, leave your jesting and take these guilders.[4]

CLOWN. Yes, marry, sir, and I thank you, too.

WAG. So, now thou art to be at an hour's warning whenever and wheresoever the devil shall fetch thee.

CLOWN. Here, take your guilders again, I'll none of 'em.

WAG. Not I, thou art pressed;[5] prepare thyself, for I will presently raise up two devils to carry thee away. Banio! Belcher!

5. The Holy Roman Emperor.
6. Contemplation.
7. Not a court jester (as in some of Shakespeare's plays), but the older-fashioned stock character, a rustic buffoon. The name "Robin" has been interpolated by later editors of the text; all such interpolations, introduced for clarity of understanding, are indicated by the special brackets used here.
8. The point of the Clown's retort is that he is a man and wears a beard ("pickadevaunt"). "Zounds": an oath ("God's wounds").
9. Income, but the Clown then puns on the literal meaning.
1. "You who are my pupil" (the opening phrase of a poem on how students should behave, from Lily's *Latin Grammar*). Wagner means, "like a proper servant of a learned man."
2. A kind of delphinium used for killing vermin.
3. Familiar spirits, demons.
4. Money.
5. Impressed, i.e., hired.

CLOWN. Belcher? And Belcher come here I'll belch him. I am not afraid of a devil.

[*Enter two* DEVILS, *and the* CLOWN *runs up and down crying.*]

WAG. How now, sir! Will you serve me now?

CLOWN. Aye, good Wagner, take away the devil then.

WAG. Spirits, away! [DEVILS *exeunt.*]
Now, sirrah, follow me.

CLOWN. I will, sir. But hark you, master, will you teach me this conjuring occupation?

WAG. Aye, sirrah, I'll teach thee to turn thyself to a dog, or a cat, or a mouse, or a rat, or anything.

CLOWN. A dog, or a cat, or a mouse, or a rat! O brave[6] Wagner!

WAG. Villain, call me Master Wagner; and see that you walk attentively, and let your right eye be always diametrally[7] fixed upon my left heel, that thou mayst *quasi vestigiis nostris insistere.*[8]

CLOWN. Well, sir, I warrant you. [*Exeunt.*]

Act II

SCENE 1

[*Enter* FAUSTUS *in his study.*]

FAUST. Now, Faustus, must thou needs be damned,
And canst not be saved.
What boots[9] it, then, to think of God or heaven?
Away with such vain fancies, and despair—
Despair in God and trust in Belzebub.
Now go not backward, no, be resolute!
Why waverest thou? O something soundeth in mine ears:
"Abjure this magic, turn to God again!"
Aye, and Faustus will turn to God again.
To God? He loves thee not;
The God thou servest is thine own appetite,
Wherein is fixed the love of Belzebub.
To him I'll build an altar and a church
And offer lukewarm blood of newborn babes.

[*Enter* GOOD ANGEL *and* BAD ANGEL.]

G. ANG. Sweet Faustus, leave that execrable art.

B. ANG. Go forward, Faustus, in that famous art.

FAUST. Contrition, prayer, repentance—what of them?

G. ANG. O they are means to bring thee unto heaven!

B. ANG. Rather illusions, fruits of lunacy,
That makes men foolish that do use them most.

G. ANG. Sweet Faustus, think of heaven and heavenly things.

B. ANG. No, Faustus, think of honor and of wealth.

[⟨*Exeunt* ANGELS.⟩]

FAUST. Of wealth!
Why, the signiory of Emden[1] shall be mine.
When Mephistophilis shall stand by me

6. Marvelous, wonderful.
7. Diametrically.
8. A pedantic way of saying "follow my footsteps."
9. Avails.
1. A wealthy German trade center.

What power can hurt me? Faustus, thou art safe;
Cast no more doubts. Come, Mephistophilis,
And bring glad tidings from great Lucifer.
Is't not midnight? Come, Mephistophilis!
Veni, veni, Mephistophile![2]
[*Enter* MEPHISTOPHILIS.]
Now tell me what saith Lucifer, thy lord?
MEPH. That I shall wait on Faustus whilst I live,
So he will buy my service with his soul.
FAUST. Already Faustus hath hazarded that for thee.
MEPH. But, Faustus, thou must bequeath it solemnly
And write a deed of gift with thine own blood,
For that security craves Lucifer.
If thou deny it, I must back to hell.
FAUST. Stay, Mephistophilis, and tell me what good
Will my soul do thy lord?
MEPH. Enlarge his kingdom.
FAUST. Is that the reason why he tempts us thus?
MEPH. *Solamen miseris socios habuisse doloris.*[3]
FAUST. Why, have you any pain that tortures others?
MEPH. As great as have the human souls of men.
But tell me, Faustus, shall I have thy soul?
And I will be thy slave, and wait on thee,
And give thee more than thou hast wit to ask.
FAUST. Aye, Mephistophilis, I'll give it him.
MEPH. Then, Faustus, stab thine arm courageously,
And bind thy soul that at some certain day
Great Lucifer may claim it as his own,
And then be thou as great as Lucifer.
FAUST. Lo, Mephistophilis, for love of thee
[*Stabbing his arm.*]
Faustus hath cut his arm, and with his proper[4] blood
Assures his soul to be great Lucifer's:
Chief lord and regent of perpetual night,
View here the blood that trickles from mine arm
And let it be propitious for my wish!
MEPH. But, Faustus,
Write it in manner of a deed of gift.
FAUST. Aye, so I do. [*Writes.*] But, Mephistophilis,
My blood congeals and I can write no more.
MEPH. I'll fetch thee fire to dissolve it straight. [*Exit.*]
FAUST. What might the staying of my blood portend?
Is it unwilling I should write this bill?[5]
Why streams it not, that I may write afresh?
"Faustus gives to thee his soul"—ah, there it stayed.
Why shouldst thou not? Is not thy soul thine own?
Then write again: "Faustus gives to thee his soul."
[*Enter* MEPHISTOPHILIS *with a chafer*[6] *of fire.*]

2. "Come, come, Mephistophilis!"
3. "Misery loves company."
4. Own.
5. Contract.
6. A portable grate.

MEPH. See, Faustus, here is fire; set it on.
FAUST. So: now the blood begins to clear again;
Now will I make an end immediately. [⟨*Writes*.⟩]
MEPH. [*aside*] What will not I do to obtain his soul!
FAUST. *Consummatum est*[7]—this bill is ended;
And Faustus hath bequeathed his soul to Lucifer.
But what is this inscription on mine arm?
"*Homo, fuge!*"[8] Whither should I fly?
If unto God, he'll throw me down to hell.
My senses are deceived; here's nothing writ.
O yes, I see it plain: even here is writ
"*Homo, fuge!*" Yet shall not Faustus fly.
MEPH. I'll fetch him somewhat to delight his mind. [*Exit*.]
[*Re-enter* MEPHISTOPHILIS *with* DEVILS, *giving crowns and rich apparel to* FAUSTUS, *and dance, and then depart*.]
FAUST. What means this show?
Speak, Mephistophilis.
MEPH. Nothing, Faustus, but to delight thy mind
And let thee see what magic can perform.
FAUST. But may I raise such spirits when I please?
MEPH. Aye, Faustus, and do greater things than these.
FAUST. Then, Mephistophilis, receive this scroll,
A deed of gift of body and of soul;
But yet conditionally that thou perform
All covenant-articles between us both.
MEPH. Faustus, I swear by hell and Lucifer
To effect all promises between us made.
FAUST. Then hear me read it, Mephistophilis. [⟨*Reads*.⟩]
"On these conditions following:
First, that Faustus may be a spirit in form and substance.
Secondly, that Mephistophilis shall be his servant and at his command.
Thirdly, that Mephistophilis shall do for him, and bring him whatsoever.
Fourthly, that he shall be in his chamber or house invisible.
Lastly, that he shall appear to the said John Faustus at all times, in what form or shape soever he please.
I, John Faustus of Wittenberg, Doctor, by these presents do give both body and soul to Lucifer, Prince of the East, and his minister Mephistophilis, and furthermore grant unto them, that four and twenty years being expired, the articles above written inviolate, full power to fetch or carry the said John Faustus, body and soul, flesh, blood, or goods, into their habitation wheresoever.
By me John Faustus."
MEPH. Speak, Faustus, do you deliver this as your deed?
FAUST. Aye, take it, and the devil give thee good of it.
MEPH. Now, Faustus, ask what thou wilt.
FAUST. First will I question with thee about hell.

7. "It is finished." A blasphemy, as these are the words of Christ on the Cross (see John xix.30).

8. "O man, flee!"

Tell me, where is the place that men call hell?
MEPH. Under the heavens.
FAUST. Aye, but whereabout?
MEPH. Within the bowels of these elements,
Where we are tortured and remain forever.
Hell hath no limits, nor is circumscribed
In one self place, for where we are is hell,
And where hell is there must we ever be;
And, to be short, when all the world dissolves
And every creature shall be purified,
All places shall be hell that is not heaven.
FAUST. I think hell's a fable.
MEPH. Aye, think so still, till experience change thy mind.
FAUST. Why, thinkst thou that Faustus shall be damned?
MEPH. Aye, of necessity, for here's the scroll
In which thou hast given thy soul to Lucifer.
FAUST. Aye, and body too; but what of that?
Thinkst thou that Faustus is so fond[9] to imagine
That after this life there is any pain?
No, these are trifles and mere old wives' tales.
MEPH. But I am an instance to prove the contrary,
For I tell thee I am damned and now in hell.
FAUST. Nay, and this be hell I'll willingly be damned.
What, sleeping, eating, walking, and disputing?
But leaving off this, let me have a wife,
The fairest maid in Germany,
For I am wanton and lascivious
And cannot live without a wife.
MEPH. I prithee, Faustus, talk not of a wife.[1]
FAUST. Nay, sweet Mephistophilis, fetch me one, for I will have one.
MEPH. Well, thou shalt have a wife. Sit there till I come. [⟨*Exit.*⟩]
[*Re-enter* MEPHISTOPHILIS *with a* DEVIL *dressed like a woman, with fireworks.*]
FAUST. What sight is this?
MEPH. Now Faustus, how dost thou like thy wife?
FAUST. Here's a hot whore indeed! No, I'll no wife.
MEPH. Marriage is but a ceremonial toy,
And if thou lovest me, think no more of it.
I'll cull thee out the fairest courtesans
And bring them every morning to thy bed;
She whom thine eye shall like thy heart shall have,
Were she as chaste as was Penelope,[2]
As wise as Saba, or as beautiful
As was bright Lucifer before his fall.
Hold, take this book: peruse it thoroughly.
The iterating[3] of these lines brings gold,

9. Foolish.
1. Mephistophilis cannot produce a wife for Faustus because marriage is a sacrament.
2. The wife of Ulysses, famed for chastity and fidelity. "Saba": the Queen of Sheba.
3. Repeating.

The framing[4] of this circle on the ground
Brings whirlwinds, tempests, thunder, and lightning;
Pronounce this thrice devoutly to thyself
And men in harness[5] shall appear to thee,
Ready to execute what thou desirest.

FAUST. Thanks, Mephistophilis, yet fain would I have a book wherein I might behold all spells and incantations, that I might raise up spirits when I please.

MEPH. Here they are in this book. [*There turn to them.*]

FAUST. Now would I have a book where I might see all characters and planets of the heavens, that I might know their motions and dispositions.

MEPH. Here they are too. [*Turn to them.*]

FAUST. Nay, let me have one book more, and then I have done, wherein I might see all plants, herbs, and trees that grow upon the earth.

MEPH. Here they be.

FAUST. O thou art deceived!

MEPH. Tut, I warrant thee. [*Turn to them.*]
[⟨*Exeunt.*⟩][6]

SCENE 2

[*Enter* FAUSTUS *in his study and* MEPHISTOPHILIS.]

FAUST. When I behold the heavens then I repent
And curse thee, wicked Mephistophilis,
Because thou hast deprived me of those joys.

MEPH. 'Twas thine own seeking, Faustus, thank thyself.
But thinkest thou heaven is such a glorious thing?
I tell thee, Faustus, it is not half so fair
As thou or any man that breathes on earth.

FAUST. How provest thou that?

MEPH. 'Twas made for man; then he's more excellent.

FAUST. If heaven was made for man 'twas made for me.
I will renounce this magic and repent.

[*Enter* GOOD ANGEL *and* BAD ANGEL.]

G. ANG. Faustus, repent; yet God will pity thee.

B. ANG. Thou art a spirit; God cannot pity thee.

FAUST. Who buzzeth in mine ears I am a spirit?[7]
Be I a devil, yet God may pity me.
Yea, God will pity me, if I repent.

B. ANG. Aye, but Faustus never shall repent.

[*Exeunt* ANGELS.]

FAUST. My heart is hardened; I cannot repent.
Scarce can I name salvation, faith, or heaven,
But fearful echoes thunder in mine ears:
"Faustus, thou are damned!" Then guns and knives,

4. Drawing.
5. Armor.
6. After this a comic scene has been lost from the text. In it, apparently the Clown, Robin, stole one of Faustus' conjuring books and left Wagner's service. He then became an hostler at an inn.
7. Evil spirit, devil.

Swords, poison, halters, and envenomed steel
Are laid before me to dispatch myself,
And long ere this I should have done the deed
Had not sweet pleasure conquered deep despair.
Have I not made blind Homer sing to me
Of Alexander's love and Oenon's death,[8]
And hath not he that built the walls of Thebes
With ravishing sound of his melodious harp[9]
Made music with my Mephistophilis?
Why should I die, then, or basely despair?
I am resolved Faustus shall not repent.
Come, Mephistophilis, let us dispute again
And reason of divine astrology.
Speak, are there many spheres above the moon?
Are all celestial bodies but one globe
As is the substance of this centric earth?[1]

MEPH. As are the elements, such are the heavens,
Even from the moon unto the empyreal orb,
Mutually folded in each other's spheres,
And jointly move upon one axletree
Whose termine[2] is termed the world's wide pole;
Nor are the names of Saturn, Mars, or Jupiter
Feigned, but are erring stars.

FAUST. But tell me, have they all one motion, both *situ et tempore?*[3]

MEPH. All move from east to west in four and twenty hours upon the poles of the world, but differ in their motions upon the poles of the zodiac.[4]

FAUST. These slender questions Wagner can decide.
Hath Mephistophilis no greater skill?
Who knows not the double motion of the planets?
That the first is finished in a natural day;
The second thus, Saturn in thirty years, Jupiter in twelve, Mars in four, the Sun, Venus, and Mercury in a year, the Moon in twenty-eight days. These are freshmen's suppositions. But tell me, hath every sphere a dominion or *intelligentia?*[5]

MEPH. Aye.

FAUST. How many heavens or spheres are there?

MEPH. Nine: the seven planets, the firmament, and the empyreal heaven.

8. Alexander is another name for Paris, the lover of Oenone; later he deserted her and abducted Helen, causing the Trojan War. Oenone refused to heal the wounds Paris received in battle, and when he died of them she killed herself in remorse.

9. I.e., the legendary musician Amphion.

1. "Faustus asks whether all the apparently different heavenly bodies form really one globe, like the earth. Mephistophilis answers that like the elements, which are separate but combined, the heavenly bodies are separate, though their spheres are infolded, and they move on one axletree. Hence we are not in error in giving individual names to Saturn, Mars, or Jupiter; they are separate planets" (F. S. Boas). The "empyreal orb," or outermost sphere, was also called the empyrean.

2. End.

3. In position and time.

4. I.e., the common axletree on which all the spheres revolve.

5. I.e., an angel or intelligence (thought to be the source of motion in each sphere).

FAUST. But is there not *coelum igneum, et crystallinum?*[6]
MEPH. No, Faustus, they be but fables.
FAUST. Resolve me then in this one question: why are not conjunctions, oppositions, aspects, eclipses, all at one time, but in some years we have more, in some less?
MEPH. *Per inequalem motum respectu totius.*[7]
FAUST. Well, I am answered. Tell me, who made the world?
MEPH. I will not.
FAUST. Sweet Mephistophilis, tell me.
MEPH. Move[8] me not, Faustus.
FAUST. Villain, have I not bound thee to tell me anything?
MEPH. Aye, that is not against our kingdom; this is.
Thou art damned; think thou of hell.
FAUST. Think, Faustus, upon God that made the world!
MEPH. Remember this! [*Exit.*]
FAUST. Aye, go, accurséd spirit, to ugly hell;
'Tis thou has damned distressed Faustus' soul.
Is 't too late?
[*Enter* GOOD ANGEL *and* BAD ANGEL.]
B. ANG. Too late.
G. ANG. Never too late, if Faustus will repent.
B. ANG. If thou repent, devils will tear thee in pieces.
G. ANG. Repent, and they shall never raze[9] thy skin.
[*Exeunt* ANGELS.]
FAUST. O Christ, my Saviour! my Saviour!
Help to save distresséd Faustus' soul.
[*Enter* LUCIFER, BELZEBUB, *and* MEPHISTOPHILIS.]
LUC. Christ cannot save thy soul, for he is just;
There's none but I have interest in the same.
FAUST. O what art thou that lookst so terrible?
LUC. I am Lucifer,
And this is my companion prince in hell.
FAUST. O Faustus, they are come to fetch thy soul!
BEL. We are come to tell thee thou dost injure us.
LUC. Thou call'st on Christ, contrary to thy promise.
BEL. Thou shouldst not think on God.
LUC. Think on the devil.
BEL. And his dam too.[10]
FAUST. Nor will I henceforth. Pardon me in this,
And Faustus vows never to look to heaven,
Never to name God or pray to him,
To burn his Scriptures, slay his ministers,
And make my spirits pull his churches down.
LUC. So shalt thou show thyself an obedient servant, and we will highly gratify thee for it.
BEL. Faustus, we are come from hell in person to show thee some

6. The "heaven of fire" and the "crystalline sphere," introduced by some of the old authorities to explain the precession of the equinoxes.
7. "Because of their unequal velocities within the system."
8. Anger.
9. Scratch.
10. "The devil and his dam" was a common colloquial expression.

pastime. Sit down, and thou shalt behold the Seven Deadly Sins appear to thee in their own proper shapes and likeness.

FAUST. That sight will be as pleasant to me as Paradise was to Adam, the first day of his creation.

LUC. Talk not of Paradise or Creation, but mark the show. Go, Mephistophilis, fetch them in.

[*Enter the* SEVEN DEADLY SINS,[11] *led by a piper.*]

Now, Faustus, question them of their names and dispositions.

FAUST. That shall I soon. What art thou, the first?

PRIDE. I am Pride. I disdain to have any parents. I am like to Ovid's flea:[1] I can creep into every corner of a wench; sometimes like a periwig I sit upon her brow; next like a necklace I hang about her neck; then like a fan of feathers I kiss her lips; and then turning myself to a wrought smock[2] do what I list. But fie, what a smell is here! I'll not speak another word except the ground be perfumed and covered with cloth of arras.[3]

FAUST. Thou art a proud knave indeed. What art thou, the second?

COVET. I am Covetousness, begotten of an old churl in a leather bag; and, might I now obtain my wish, this house, you and all, should turn to gold, that I might lock you safe into my chest. O my sweet gold!

FAUST. And what art thou, the third?

ENVY. I am Envy, begotten of a chimney-sweeper and an oyster-wife. I cannot read, and therefore wish all books were burned. I am lean with seeing others eat. O that there would come a famine over all the world, that all might die, and I live alone; then thou shouldst see how fat I'd be! But must thou sit and I stand? Come down, with a vengeance!

FAUST. Out, envious wretch! But what art thou, the fourth?

WRATH. I am Wrath. I had neither father nor mother; I leapt out of a lion's mouth when I was scarce an hour old, and ever since have run up and down the world with these case of rapiers, wounding myself when I could get none to fight withal. I was born in hell; and look to it, for some of you shall be my father.

FAUST. And what art thou, the fifth?

GLUT. I am Gluttony. My parents are all dead, and the devil a penny they have left me but a small pension, and that buys me thirty meals a day and ten bevers[4]—a small trifle to suffice nature. I come of a royal pedigree: my father was a gammon[5] of bacon, and my mother was a hogshead of claret wine. My

11. The Seven Deadly Sins are pride, avarice, gluttony, lust, sloth, envy, and anger. (They are deadly because other sins grow out of them.) They were frequently represented in medieval plays, sometimes in the rather grimly comic tone used here; in the old morality plays all the characters, not merely the sins, were abstractions.

1. A salacious medieval poem *Carmen de Pulice* ("The Flea") was attributed to Ovid.

2. A decorated or ornamented petticoat.

3. Arras in Flanders exported fine cloth used for tapestry hangings.

4. Snacks.

5. The lower side of pork, including the leg.

godfathers were these: Peter Pickle-herring and Martin Martlemas-beef. But my godmother, O, she was a jolly gentlewoman, and well beloved in every good town and city: her name was mistress Margery March-beer. Now, Faustus, thou hast heard all my progeny;[6] wilt thou bid me to supper?

FAUST. Not I. Thou wilt eat up all my victuals.

GLUT. Then the devil choke thee!

FAUST. Choke thyself, glutton. What art thou, the sixth?

SLOTH. Heigh ho! I am Sloth. I was begotten on a sunny bank, where I have lain ever since, and you have done me great injury to bring me from thence; let me be carried thither again by Gluttony and Lechery. Heigh ho! I'll not speak word more for a king's ransom.

FAUST. And what are you, mistress minx, the seventh and last?

LECHERY. Who, I, sir? I am one that loves an inch of raw mutton[7] better than an ell of fried stockfish, and the first letter of my name begins with Lechery.

LUC. Away, to hell, away! On, piper![8]

[*Exeunt the* SINS.]

FAUST. O how this sight doth delight my soul!

LUC. Tut, Faustus, in hell is all manner of delight.

FAUST. O might I see hell and return again safe, how happy were I then!

LUC. Faustus, thou shalt. At midnight I will send for thee. In meantime peruse this book, and view it throughly, and thou shalt turn thyself into what shape thou wilt.

FAUST. Thanks, mighty Lucifer; this will I keep as chary[9] as my life.

LUC. Now Faustus, farewell.

FAUST. Farewell, great Lucifer. Come, Mephistophilis.

[*Exeunt* OMNES.]

SCENE 3

[*Enter the* CLOWN ⟨ROBIN⟩.]

ROBIN. What, Dick, look to the horses there till I come again. I have gotten one of Dr. Faustus' conjuring books, and now we'll have such knavery as 't passes.

[*Enter* DICK.]

DICK. What, Robin, you must come away and walk the horses.

ROBIN. I walk the horses! I scorn 't, faith: I have other matters in hand; let the horses walk themselves and they will. "A *per se*[1] a; t, h, e, the; o *per se* o; deny orgon, gorgon." Keep further from me, O thou illiterate and unlearned hostler.

6. Ancestry, lineage.
7. Frequently a word of indecent meaning in Elizabethan English; here it means the penis. "Ell": 45 inches; "stockfish": dried cod.
8. The command to the piper who led the procession of the Deadly Sins onto the stage to strike up a tune for their exit.
9. Carefully.
1. "A by itself," a method of reading the letters of the alphabet taught to children. Robin's semi-literacy is being satirized. "Deny orgon, gorgon" is a parody of Faustus' invocation of Demogorgon in I.iii.

DICK. 'Snails,[2] what has thou got there? a book? Why, thou canst not tell ne'er a word on 't.

ROBIN. That thou shalt see presently. Keep out of the circle, I say, lest I send you into the ostry[3] with a vengeance.

DICK. That's like, faith! You had best leave your foolery, for an my master come, he'll conjure you, faith.

ROBIN. My master conjure me! I'll tell thee what; an my master come here, I'll clap as fair a pair of horns on 's head as e'er thou sawest in thy life.[4]

DICK. Thou needst not do that, for my mistress hath done it.

ROBIN. Aye, there be of us here have waded as deep into matters as other men, if they were disposed to talk.

DICK. A plague take you! I thought you did not sneak up and down after her for nothing. But I prithee tell me in good sadness, Robin, is that a conjuring book?

ROBIN. Do but speak what thou 't have me do, and I'll do 't. If thou 't dance naked, put off thy clothes, and I'll conjure thee about presently. Or if thou 't but to the tavern with me, I'll give thee white wine, red wine, claret wine, sack, muscadine, malmesey, and whippincrust,[5] hold-belly-hold, and we'll not pay one penny for it.

DICK. O brave! Prithee let's to it presently, for I am as dry as a dog.

ROBIN. Come then, let's away. [*Exeunt.*]

Act III

[*Enter* CHORUS.]

CHO. Learned Faustus,
To find the secrets of astronomy
Graven in the book of Jove's high firmament,
Did mount himself to scale Olympus' top.
Where sitting in a chariot burning bright
Drawn by the strength of yokéd dragons' necks,
He views the clouds, the planets, and the stars,
The tropics, zones, and quarters of the sky
From the bright circle of the hornéd moon
Even to the height of *Primum Mobile*;[6]
And whirling round with this circumference
Within the concave compass of the pole,
From east to west his dragons swiftly glide
And in eight days did bring him home again.
Not long he stayed within his quiet house
To rest his bones after his weary toil
But new exploits do hale him out again;
And mounted then upon a dragon's back
That with his wings did part the subtle air,
He now is gone to prove cosmography[7]

2. I.e., God's nails (on the Cross).
3. Hostelry, inn.
4. A wife's infidelity was supposed in legend, and in the standard Elizabethan joke, to cause her husband to grow horns.
5. Robin's pronunciation of "hippocras," a spiced wine; "hold-belly-hold": as much as we can drink.
6. The outermost sphere, the empyrean.
7. I.e., to test the accuracy of maps.

That measures coasts and kingdoms of the earth:
And, as I guess, will first arrive at Rome
To see the Pope and manner of his court
And take some part of holy Peter's feast,
The which this day is highly solemnized.
[*Exit.*]

SCENE 1

[*Enter* FAUSTUS *and* MEPHISTOPHILIS.]

FAUST. Having now, my good Mephistophilis,
Passed with delight the stately town of Trier[8]
Environed round with airy mountain tops,
With walls of flint and deep-entrenchéd lakes,[9]
Not to be won by any conquering prince;
From Paris next coasting the realm of France,
We saw the river Maine fall into Rhine,
Whose banks are set with groves of fruitful vines;
Then up to Naples, rich Campania,
With buildings fair and gorgeous to the eye,
Whose streets straight forth and paved with finest brick
Quarter the town in four equivalents.
There saw we learned Maro's[1] golden tomb,
The way he cut, an English mile in length,
Thorough a rock of stone in one night's space.
From thence to Venice, Padua, and the rest,
In midst of which a sumptuous temple[2] stands
That threats the stars with her aspiring top,
Whose frame is paved with sundry colored stones
And roofed aloft with curious work in gold.
Thus hitherto hath Faustus spent his time.
But tell me now, what resting place is this?
Hast thou, as erst I did command,
Conducted me within the walls of Rome?

MEPH. I have, my Faustus, and for proof thereof
This is the goodly palace of the Pope,
And 'cause we are no common guests
I choose his privy chamber for our use.

FAUST. I hope his Holiness will bid us welcome.

MEPH. All's one, for we'll be bold with his venison.
But now, my Faustus, that thou mayst perceive
What Rome contains for to delight thine eyes,
Know that this city stands upon seven hills
That underprop the groundwork of the same;
Just through the midst runs flowing Tiber's stream,
With winding banks that cut it in two parts
Over the which four stately bridges lean

8. Treves (in Prussia).
9. Moats.
1. Virgil's. In medieval legend the Roman poet Virgil was considered a magician, and a tunnel ("way") on the promontory of Posilippo at Naples, near his tomb, was accredited to his magical powers.
2. I.e., St. Mark's in Venice.

That make safe passage to each part of Rome.
Upon the bridge called Ponte Angelo
Erected is a castle passing strong,
Where thou shalt see such store of ordnance
As that the double cannons forged of brass
Do match the number of the days contained
Within the compass of one complete year;
Besides the gates and high pyramides[3]
That Julius Caesar brought from Africa.

FAUST. Now by the kingdoms of infernal rule,
Of Styx, Acheron, and the fiery lake
Of ever-burning Phlegethon,[4] I swear
That I do long to see the monuments
And situation of bright-splendent Rome.
Come, therefore, let's away.

MEPH. Nay, stay, my Faustus; I know you'd see the Pope
And take some part of holy Peter's feast,
The which in state and high solemnity
This day is held through Rome and Italy
In honor of the Pope's triumphant victory.

FAUST. Sweet Mephistophilis, thou pleasest me;
Whilst I am here on earth let me be cloyed
With all things that delight the heart of man.
My four and twenty years of liberty
I'll spend in pleasure and in dalliance,
That Faustus' name, whilst this bright frame doth stand,
May be admiréd through the furthest land.

MEPH. 'Tis well said, Faustus; come then, stand by me
And thou shalt see them come immediately.

FAUST. Nay, stay, my gentle Mephistophilis,
And grant me my request, and then I go.
Thou knowst, within the compass of eight days
We viewed the face of heaven, of earth, of hell;
So high our dragons soared into the air
That, looking down, the earth appeared to me
No bigger than my hand in quantity.
There did we view the kingdoms of the world,
And what might please mine eye I there beheld.
Then in this show let me an actor be,
That this proud Pope may Faustus' cunning see.

MEPH. Let it be so, my Faustus, but first stay
And view their triumphs[5] as they pass this way,
And then devise what best contents thy mind,
By cunning of thine art to cross the Pope
Or dash the pride of this solemnity,
To make his monks and abbots stand like apes
And point like antics[6] at his triple crown,

3. *Py-rám-i-des,* a singular noun, meaning an obelisk.

4. Classical names for rivers of the underworld; symbolic of hell, they are appropriate as oaths for Faustus.

5. Parades.

6. Grotesque figures.

To beat the beads about the friars' pates
Or clap huge horns upon the cardinals' heads,
Or any villainy thou canst devise,
And I'll perform it, Faustus. Hark, they come!
This day shall make thee be admired in Rome.

[*Enter the* CARDINALS *and* BISHOPS, *some bearing crosiers, some the pillars;* MONKS *and* FRIARS *singing their procession; then the* POPE *and* RAYMOND, *King of Hungary, with* BRUNO *led in chains.*][7]

POPE. Cast down our footstool.
RAY. Saxon Bruno, stoop,
Whilst on thy back his Holiness ascends
St. Peter's chair and state pontifical.
BRUNO. Proud Lucifer, that state belongs to me;
But thus I fall, to Peter, not to thee.
POPE. To me and Peter shalt thou groveling lie
And crouch before the papal dignity.
Sound trumpets, then, for thus St. Peter's heir
From Bruno's back ascends St. Peter's chair.

[*A flourish while he ascends.*]

Thus as the gods creep on with feet of wool
Long ere with iron hands they punish men,
So shall our sleeping vengeance now arise
And smite with death thy hated enterprise.
Lord Cardinals of France and Padua,
Go forthwith to our holy consistory
And read among the statutes decretal
What, by the holy council held at Trent,[8]
The sacred synod hath decreed for him
That doth assume the papal government
Without election and a true consent.
Away and bring us word with speed.
1 CARD. We go, my lord. [*Exeunt* CARDINALS.]
POPE. Lord Raymond—
FAUST. Go, haste thee, gentle Mephistophilis,
Follow the cardinals to the consistory,
And as they turn their superstitious books,
Strike them with sloth and drowsy idleness
And make them sleep so sound that in their shapes
Thyself and I may parley with this Pope,
This proud confronter of the Emperor,[9]
And in despite of all his holiness
Restore this Bruno to his liberty

7. "Crosiers": crosses borne before prelates; "the pillars" (of silver), however, are known to have been used by only two English cardinals, Wolsey and De la Pole. "Raymond, King of Hungary" is unknown to history. "Bruno" is likewise fictitious; he is the German pretender to the papal throne over whom the Pope has just triumphed (line 57).

8. The famous council of the Catholic Church which lasted from 1545 to 1563.

9. Holy Roman Emperor. Faustus refers to the conflict between the Pope and the Emperor; the former was victorious and captured the Emperor's choice for Pope, "Saxon Bruno."

And bear him to the states of Germany.
MEPH. Faustus, I go.
FAUST. Dispatch it soon.
The Pope shall curse that Faustus came to Rome.
[*Exeunt* FAUSTUS *and* MEPHISTOPHILIS.]
BRUNO. Pope Adrian, let me have some right of law;
I was elected by the Emperor.
POPE. We will depose the Emperor for that deed
And curse the people that submit to him;
Both he and thou shalt stand excommunicate
And interdict from church's privilege
And all society of holy men.
He grows too proud in his authority,
Lifting his lofty head above the clouds,
And like a steeple overpeers the church,
But we'll pull down his haughty insolence.
And as Pope Alexander,[1] our progenitor,
Trod on the neck of German Frederick,
Adding this golden sentence to our praise,
That Peter's heirs should tread on emperors
And walk upon the dreadful adder's back,
Treading the lion and the dragon down,
And fearless spurn the killing basilisk;[2]
So will we quell that haughty schismatic,
And by authority apostolical
Depose him from his regal government.
BRUNO. Pope Julius swore to princely Sigismond,
For him and the succeeding popes of Rome,
To hold the emperors their lawful lords.
POPE. Pope Julius did abuse the church's rights,
And therefore none of his decrees can stand.
Is not all power on earth bestowed on us?
And therefore though we would we cannot err.
Behold this silver belt, whereto is fixed
Seven golden keys fast sealed with seven seals
In token of our sevenfold power from heaven,
To bind or loose, lock fast, condemn, or judge,
Resign or seal, or whatso pleaseth us.
Then he and thou and all the world shall stoop,
Or be assuréd of our dreadful curse
To light as heavy as the pains of hell.
[*Enter* FAUSTUS *and* MEPHISTOPHILIS *like cardinals*.]
MEPH. Now tell me, Faustus, are we not fitted well?
FAUST. Yes, Mephistophilis, and two such cardinals
Ne'er served a holy pope as we shall do.
But whilst they sleep within the consistory
Let us salute his reverend Fatherhood.
RAY. Behold, my lord, the cardinals are returned.

1. Pope Alexander III (1159–81) compelled the Emperor Frederick Barbarossa to submit to him.

2. A mythical monster capable of killing by a look.

POPE. Welcome, grave fathers, answer presently;[3]
What have our holy council there decreed
Concerning Bruno and the Emperor
In quittance of their late conspiracy
Against our state and papal dignity?
FAUST. Most sacred patron of the church of Rome,
By full consent of all the synod
Of priests and prelates it is thus decreed:
That Bruno and the German Emperor
Be held as lollards[4] and bold schismatics
And proud disturbers of the church's peace.
And if that Bruno by his own assent,
Without enforcement of the German peers,
Did seek to wear the triple diadem
And by your death to climb St. Peter's chair,
The statutes decretal have thus decreed:
He shall be straight condemned of heresy
And on a pile of fagots burned to death.
POPE. It is enough. Here, take him to your charge
And bear him straight to Ponte Angelo,
And in the strongest tower enclose him fast.
Tomorrow, sitting in our consistory
With all our college of grave cardinals,
We will determine of his life or death.
Here, take his triple crown along with you
And leave it in the church's treasury.
Make haste again, my good lord cardinals,
And take our blessing apostolical.
MEPH. So, so. Was never devil thus blessed before!
FAUST. Away, sweet Mephistophilis, be gone;
The cardinals will be plagued for this anon.
[*Exeunt* FAUSTUS *and* MEPHISTOPHILIS *with* BRUNO.]
POPE. Go presently and bring a banquet forth,
That we may solemnize St. Peter's feast
And with Lord Raymond, King of Hungary,
Drink to our late and happy victory. [*Exeunt.*]

SCENE 2

[*The banquet is brought in, and then enter* FAUSTUS *and* MEPHISTOPHILIS *in their own shapes.*]

MEPH. Now Faustus, come prepare thyself for mirth;
The sleepy cardinals are hard at hand
To censure Bruno, that is posted hence
And on a proud-paced steed as swift as thought
Flies o'er the Alps to fruitful Germany,
There to salute the woeful Emperor.
FAUST. The Pope will curse them for their sloth today
That slept both Bruno and his crown away.

3. Immediately.
4. Protestants, usually English followers of Wycliffe, the 14th-century religious reformer.

But now, that Faustus may delight his mind
And by their folly make some merriment,
Sweet Mephistophilis, so charm me here
That I may walk invisible to all
And do whate'er I please unseen of any.
MEPH. Faustus, thou shalt; then kneel down presently,
Whilst on thy head I lay my hand
And charm thee with this magic wand.
First wear this girdle, then appear
Invisible to all are here.
The planets seven, the gloomy air,
Hell, and the Furies' forkéd hair,
Pluto's blue fire and Hecate's[5] tree
With magic spells so compass thee
That no eye may thy body see.
So, Faustus, now, for all their holiness,
Do what thou wilt thou shalt not be discerned.
FAUST. Thanks, Mephistophilis. Now friars, take heed
Lest Faustus make your shaven crowns to bleed.
MEPH. Faustus, no more; see where the cardinals come.
[*Enter* POPE *and all the lords, with* KING RAYMOND *and the* ARCHBISHOP OF RHEIMS. *Enter the two* CARDINALS *with a book.*]
POPE. Welcome, lord cardinals; come, sit down.
Lord Raymond, take your seat. Friars, attend,
And see that all things be in readiness
As best beseems this solemn festival.
1 CARD. First may it please your sacred holiness
To view the sentence of the reverend synod
Concerning Bruno and the Emperor.
POPE. What needs this question? Did I not tell you
Tomorrow we would sit i' th' consistory
And there determine of his punishment?
You brought us word, even now, it was decreed
That Bruno and the curséd Emperor
Were by the holy council both condemned
For loathéd lollards and base schismatics;
Then wherefore would you have me view that book?
1 CARD. Your Grace mistakes; you gave us no such charge.
RAY. Deny it not; we all are witnesses
That Bruno here was late delivered you,
With his rich triple crown to be reserved
And put into the church's treasury
BOTH CARD. By holy Paul we saw them not.
POPE. By Peter, you shall die
Unless you bring them forth immediately.

5. The goddess of magic and witchcraft, whose name the Elizabethans pronounced *Héc-at*. She is not known to have any special "tree"; the word may be a mistake for "three," since she was often represented as a triple goddess—of heaven, earth, and hell.

Hale them to prison! Lade their limbs with gyves![6]
False prelates, for this hateful treachery,
Cursed be your souls to hellish misery. [*Exeunt* CARDINALS.]

FAUST. So they are safe. Now, Faustus, to the feast;
The Pope had never such a frolic guest.

POPE. Lord Archbishop of Rheims, sit down with us.

ARCH. I thank your Holiness.

FAUST. Fall to! The devil choke you an you spare!

POPE. Who's that spoke? Friars, look about.
Lord Raymond, pray fall to. I am beholden
To the Bishop of Milan for this so rare a present.

FAUST. I thank you, sir.

[FAUSTUS *snatches the meat from the* POPE.]

POPE. How now! Who snatched the meat from me? Villains, why speak you not?

FRIAR. Here's nobody, if it like your Holiness.

POPE. My good Lord Archbishop, here's a most dainty dish
Was sent me from a cardinal in France.

FAUST. I'll have that, too.

[FAUSTUS *snatches the dish from the* POPE.]

POPE. What lollards do attend our Holiness
That we receive such great indignity?
Fetch me some wine.

FAUST. Aye, pray do, for Faustus is adry.

POPE. Lord Raymond, I drink unto your Grace.

FAUST. I pledge your Grace.

[FAUSTUS *snatches the cup from the* POPE.]

POPE. My wine gone, too? Ye lubbers, look about
And find the man that doth this villainy,
Or by my sanctitude you all shall die.
I pray, my lords, have patience at this troublesome banquet.

ARCH. Please your Holiness, I think it be some ghost crept out of purgatory and now is come unto your Holiness for his pardon.

POPE. It may be so;
Go then, command our priests to sing a dirge
To lay the fury of this same troublesome ghost.
Once again, my lord, fall to.

[*The* POPE *crosses himself.*]

FAUST. How now!
Must every bit be spicéd with a cross?
Well, use that trick no more, I would advise you.

[*The* POPE *crosses himself.*]

Well, there's the second time; aware the third;
I give you fair warning.

[*The* POPE *crosses himself again.*]

Nay then, take that!

[FAUSTUS *hits the* POPE *a box on the ear.*]

POPE. O, I am slain! Help me, my lords!
O come and help to bear my body hence!

6. I.e., load their limbs with prisoners' shackles.

Damned be his soul forever for this deed.

[*Exeunt the* POPE *and his train.*]

MEPH. Now Faustus, what will you do now? For I can tell you you'll be cursed with bell, book, and candle.[7]

FAUST. Bell, book, and candle; candle, book, and bell
Forward and backward, to curse Faustus to hell!

[*Enter all the* FRIARS *with bell, book, and candle to sing the dirge.*]

FRIAR. Come, brethren, let's about our business with good devotion.

[ALL *sing this:*]

Curséd be he that stole away his Holiness' meat from the table—*maledicat dominus!*[8]

Curséd be he that struck his Holiness a blow on the face—*maledicat dominus!*

Curséd be he that took Friar Sandelo a blow on the face—*maledicat dominus!*

Curséd be he that disturbeth our holy dirge—*maledicat dominus!*

Curséd be he that took away his Holiness' wine—*maledicat dominus! Et omnes sancti!*[9] *Amen.*

[FAUSTUS *and* MEPHISTOPHILIS *beat the* FRIARS, *and fling fireworks among them, and so exeunt.*]

SCENE 3

[*Enter* CLOWN ⟨ROBIN⟩ *and* DICK *with a cup.*]

DICK. Sirrah Robin, we were best look that your devil can answer the stealing of this same cup, for the vintner's boy follows us at the hard heels.

ROBIN. 'Tis no matter, let him come! An he follow us I'll so conjure him as he was never conjured in his life, I warrant him. Let me see the cup.

[*Enter* VINTNER.]

DICK. Here 'tis. Yonder he comes. Now, Robin, now or never show thy cunning.

VINT. O, are you here? I am glad I have found you. You are a couple of fine companions! Pray, where's the cup you stole from the tavern?

ROBIN. How, how? We steal a cup? Take heed what you say! We look not like cup-stealers, I can tell you.

VINT. Never deny it, for I know you have it, and I'll search you.

ROBIN. Search me? Aye, and spare not. Hold the cup, Dick! Come, come; search me, search me.

VINT. Come on, sirrah, let me search you now.

DICK. Aye, aye, do; do. Hold the cup, Robin. I fear not your searching. We scorn to steal your cups, I can tell you.

VINT. Never outface me for the matter, for sure the cup is between you two.

7. The traditional paraphernalia for cursing and excommunication.

8. "May the Lord curse him!"

9. And all saints (also curse him).

ROBIN. Nay, there you lie. 'Tis beyond us both.

VINT. A plague take you! I thought 'twas your knavery to take it away. Come, give it me again.

ROBIN. Aye, much! When, can you tell?[1] Dick, make me a circle, and stand close at my back and stir not for thy life. Vintner, you shall have your cup anon. Say nothing, Dick. O *per se* O; Demogorgon, Belcher and Mephistophilis!

[*Enter* MEPHISTOPHILIS.]

MEPH. Monarch of hell, under whose black survey
Great potentates do kneel with awful fear,
Upon whose altars thousand souls do lie,
How am I vexéd with these villains' charms!
From Constantinople am I hither brought
Only for pleasure of these damnéd slaves. [*Exit* VINTNER.]

ROBIN. By Lady, sir, you have had a shrewd journey of it; will it please you to take a shoulder of mutton to supper and a tester[2] in your purse, and go back again?

DICK. Aye, I pray you heartily, sir; for we called you but in jest, I promise you.

MEPH. To purge the rashness of this curséd deed,
First be thou turnéd to this ugly shape:
For apish deeds transforméd to an ape.

ROBIN. O brave! an ape! I pray, sir, let me have the carrying of him about to show some tricks.

MEPH. And so thou shalt. Be thou transformed to a dog and carry him upon thy back. Away! Be gone!

ROBIN. A dog! That's excellent! Let the maids look well to their porridge pots, for I'll into the kitchen presently. Come, Dick, come.

[*Exit* ROBIN *and* DICK.]

MEPH. Now with the flames of ever-burning fire
I'll wing myself and forthwith fly amain
Unto my Faustus, to the Great Turk's court. [*Exit.*]

Act IV

[*Enter* CHORUS.]

CHO. When Faustus had with pleasure ta'en the view
Of rarest things and royal courts of kings,
He stayed his course and so returnéd home,
Where such as bear his absence but with grief,
I mean his friends and nearest companións,
Did gratulate his safety with kind words,
And in their conference of what befell
Touching his journey through the world and air,
They put forth questions of astrology
Which Faustus answered with such learned skill
As they admired and wondered at his wit.
Now is his fame spread forth in every land:

1. A common Elizabethan scornful retort.

2. Sixpence.

Amongst the rest the Emperor is one,
Carolus the Fifth,[3] at whose palace now
Faustus is feasted 'mongst his noblemen.
What there he did in trial of his art
I leave untold, your eyes shall see performed. [*Exit.*]

SCENE 1

[*Enter* MARTINO *and* FREDERICK *at several doors.*[4]]

MART. What ho! Officers, gentlemen!
Hie to the presence to attend the Emperor.
Good Frederick, see the rooms be voided straight;
His Majesty is coming to the hall.
Go back, and see the state in readiness.
FRED. But where is Bruno, our elected Pope,
That on a fury's back came post from Rome?
Will not his Grace consort[5] the Emperor?
MART. O yes, and with him comes the German conjurer,
The learned Faustus, fame of Wittenberg,
The wonder of the world for magic art;
And he intends to show great Carolus
The race of all his stout progenitors
And bring in presence of his majesty
The royal shapes and warlike semblances
Of Alexander and his beauteous paramour.[6]
FRED. Where is Benvolio?
MART. Fast asleep, I warrant you;
He took his rouse with stoups[7] of Rhenish wine
So kindly yesternight to Bruno's health
That all this day the sluggard keeps his bed.
FRED. See, see; his window's ope; we'll call to him.
MART. What ho, Benvolio!

[*Enter* BENVOLIO *above at a window, in his nightcap, buttoning.*]

BENV. What a devil ail you two?
MART. Speak softly, sir, lest the devil hear you;
For Faustus at the court is late arrived
And at his heels a thousand furies wait
To accomplish whatsoever the Doctor please.
BENV. What of this?
MART. Come, leave thy chamber first and thou shalt see
This conjurer perform such rare exploits
Before the Pope[8] and royal Emperor
As never yet was seen in Germany.
BENV. Has not the Pope enough of conjuring yet?
He was upon the devil's back late enough,
And if he be so far in love with him
I would he would post home to Rome with him again.

3. I.e., Emperor Charles V (1519–56).
4. I.e., at different entrances.
5. Accompany.
6. Alexander the Great and his mistress Thaïs.
7. Drank many full glasses.
8. Bruno.

FRED. Speak, wilt thou come and see this sport?
BENV. Not I.
MART. Wilt thou stand in thy window and see it, then?
BENV. Aye, and I fall not asleep i' th' meantime.
MART. The Emperor is at hand, who comes to see
What wonders by black spells may compassed be.
BENV. Well, go you attend the Emperor. I am content for this once to thrust my head out a window, for they say if a man be drunk overnight the devil cannot hurt him in the morning. If that be true, I have a charm in my head shall control him as well as the conjurer, I warrant you.

[*Exit* MARTINO *and* FREDERICK.]

SCENE 2

[*A sennet.*[9] *Enter* CHARLES THE GERMAN EMPEROR, BRUNO, *the* DUKE OF SAXONY, FAUSTUS, MEPHISTOPHILIS, FREDERICK, MARTINO *and* ATTENDANTS. BENVOLIO *remains at his window.*]

EMP. Wonder of men, renowned magician,
Thrice-learned Faustus, welcome to our court.
This deed of thine, in setting Bruno free
From his and our professéd enemy,
Shall add more excellence unto thine art
Than if by powerful necromantic spells
Thou couldst command the world's obedience.
Forever be beloved of Carolus;
And if this Bruno thou hast late redeemed
In peace possess the triple diadem
And sit in Peter's chair despite of chance,
Thou shalt be famous through all Italy
And honored of the German Emperor.
FAUST. These gracious words, most royal Carolus,
Shall make poor Faustus to his utmost power
Both love and serve the German Emperor
And lay his life at holy Bruno's feet.
For proof whereof, if so your Grace be pleased,
The Doctor stands prepared by power of art
To cast his magic charms that shall pierce through
The ebon gates of ever-burning hell
And hale the stubborn furies from their caves
To compass whatsoe'er your Grace commands.
BENV. [*aside*] Blood! He speaks terribly, but for all that I do not greatly believe him. He looks as like a conjurer as the Pope to a costermonger.[1]
EMP. Then Faustus, as thou late didst promise us,
We would behold that famous conqueror,
Great Alexander and his paramour,
In their true shapes and state majestical,
That we may wonder at their excellence.

9. A trumpet signal. 1. Fruitseller.

FAUST. Your Majesty shall see them presently.
Mephistophilis, away!
And with a solemn noise of trumpets' sound
Present before this royal Emperor
Great Alexander and his beauteous paramour.

MEPH. Faustus, I will. [*Exit.*]

BENV. [*aside*] Well, master Doctor, an your devils come not away quickly, you shall have me asleep presently. Zounds, I could eat myself for anger to think I have been such an ass all this while to stand gaping after the devil's governor, and can see nothing.

FAUST. [*aside*] I'll make you feel something anon if my art fail me not.—
My lord, I must forewarn your Majesty
That when my spirits present the royal shapes
Of Alexander and his paramour,
Your Grace demand no questions of the King,
But in dumb silence let them come and go.

EMP. Be it as Faustus please; we are content.

BENV. [*aside*] Aye, Aye, and I am content, too. And thou bring Alexander and his paramour before the Emperor, I'll be Actaeon[2] and turn myself into a stag.

FAUST. [*aside*] And I'll play Diana and send you the horns presently.

[*Sennet. Enter at one door the emperor* ALEXANDER, *at the other* DARIUS. *They meet;* DARIUS *is thrown down;* ALEXANDER *kills him, takes off his crown and, offering to go out, his* PARAMOUR *meets him; he embraceth her and sets* DARIUS' *crown upon her head and, coming back, both salute the* EMPEROR, *who, leaving his state,*[3] *offers to embrace them, which* FAUSTUS *seeing, suddenly stays him. Then trumpets cease and music sounds.*]

FAUST. My gracious lord, you do forget yourself;
These are but shadows, not substantial.

EMP. O pardon me; my thoughts are ravished so
With sight of this renownéd Emperor
That in mine arms I would have compassed him.
But Faustus, since I may not speak to them
To satisfy my longing thoughts at full,
Let me this tell thee: I have heard it said
That this fair lady, whilst she lived on earth,
Had on her neck a little wart or mole.
How may I prove that saying to be true?

FAUST. Your Majesty may boldly go and see.

EMP. Faustus, I see it plain;
And in this sight thou better pleasest me
Than if I gained another monarchy.

FAUST. Away, be gone! [*Exit* SHOW.]
See, see, my gracious lord, what strange beast is yon, that

2. The hunter of classical legend who happened to see the goddess Diana bathing. In punishment he was changed into a stag and pursued by his own hounds.
3. Throne.

thrusts its head out at the window!

EMP. O wondrous sight! See, Duke of Saxony, two spreading horns most strangely fastened upon the head of young Benvolio.

SAX. What, is he asleep, or dead?

FAUST. He sleeps, my lord, but dreams not of his horns.

EMP. This sport is excellent. We'll call and wake him. What ho! Benvolio!

BENV. A plague upon you! Let me sleep a while.

EMP. I blame thee not to sleep, much, having such a head of thine own.

SAX. Look up, Benvolio. 'Tis the Emperor calls.

BENV. The Emperor! Where? O zounds, my head!

EMP. Nay, and thy horns hold 'tis no matter for thy head, for that's armed sufficiently.

FAUST. Why, how now, sir knight! What, hanged by the horns? This is most horrible. Fie, fie! Pull in your head, for shame! Let not all the world wonder at you.

BENV. Zounds, Doctor, is this your villainy?

FAUST. O, say not so, sir. The Doctor has no skill,
No art, no cunning to present these lords
Or bring before this royal Emperor
The mighty monarch, warlike Alexander?
If Faustus do it, you are straight resolved
In bold Actaeon's shape to turn a stag?
And therefore, my lord, so please your Majesty,
I'll raise a kennel of hounds shall hunt him so
As all his footmanship shall scarce prevail
To keep his carcass from their bloody fangs.
Ho, Belimote, Argiron, Asterote!

BENV. Hold, hold! Zounds, he'll raise up a kennel of devils, I think, anon. Good my lord, entreat for me. 'Sblood, I am never able to endure these torments.

EMP. Then good master Doctor,
Let me entreat you to remove his horns;
He has done penance now sufficiently.

FAUST. My gracious lord, not so much for injury done to me, as to delight your Majesty with some mirth, hath Faustus justly requited this injurious knight; which, being all I desire, I am content to remove his horns.—Mephistophilis, transform him. —And hereafter, sir, look you speak well of scholars.

BENV. [*aside*] Speak well of ye! 'Sblood, and scholars be such cuckoldmakers to clap horns of honest men's heads o' this order, I'll ne'er trust smooth faces and small ruffs[4] more. But an I be not revenged for this, would I might be turned to a gaping oyster and drink nothing but salt water!

EMP. Come, Faustus. While the Emperor lives,
In recompense of this thy high desert,

4. I.e., scholars, who were often smooth-shaven and did not wear the large "ruffs" (collars) of courtiers. But Faustus has a beard; see the next scene.

Thou shalt command the state of Germany
And live beloved of mighty Carolus. [*Exeunt* OMNES.]

SCENE 3

[*Enter* BENVOLIO, MARTINO, FREDERICK, *and* SOLDIERS.]

MART. Nay, sweet Benvolio, let us sway thy thoughts
From this attempt against the conjurer.

BENV. Away! You love me not to urge me thus.
Shall I let slip so great an injury
When every servile groom jests at my wrongs
And in their rustic gambols proudly say,
"Benvolio's head was graced with horns today"?
O, may these eyelids never close again
Till with my sword I have that conjurer slain.
If you will aid me in this enterprise,
Then draw your weapons and be resolute;
If not, depart. Here will Benvolio die,
But Faustus' death shall quit[5] my infamy.

FRED. Nay, we will stay with thee, betide what may,
And kill that Doctor if he come this way.

BENV. Then gentle Frederick, hie thee to the grove
And place our servants and our followers
Close in an ambush there behind the trees.
By this I know the conjurer is near;
I saw him kneel and kiss the Emperor's hand
And take his leave laden with rich rewards.
Then, soldiers, boldly fight. If Faustus die,
Take you the wealth, leave us the victory.

FRED. Come, soldiers, follow me unto the grove;
Who kills him shall have gold and endless love.

[*Exit* FREDERICK *with the* SOLDIERS.]

BENV. My head is lighter than it was by th' horns,
But yet my heart's more ponderous than my head
And pants until I see that conjurer dead.

MART. Where shall we place ourselves, Benvolio?

BENV. Here will we stay to bide the first assault.
O, were that damnéd hell-hound but in place
Thou soon shouldst see me quit my foul disgrace.

[*Enter* FREDERICK.]

FRED. Close, close! The hated conjurer is at hand
And all alone comes walking in his gown;
Be ready then and strike the peasant down.

BENV. Mine be that honor then. Now, sword, strike home!
For horns he gave I'll have his head anon.

[*Enter* FAUSTUS *wearing a false head.*]

MART. See, see, he comes.

BENV. No words; this blow ends all;
Hell take his soul, his body thus must fall.

FAUST. O!

5. Avenge.

FRED. Groan you, master Doctor?
BENV. Break may his heart with groans. Dear Frederick, see
Thus will I end his griefs immediately.
[*Cuts off the false head.*]
MART. Strike with a willing hand! His head is off.
BENV. The devil's dead; the furies now may laugh.
FRED. Was this that stern aspect, that awful frown,
Made the grim monarch of infernal spirits
Tremble and quake at his commanding charms?
MART. Was this that damnéd head whose art conspired
Benvolio's shame before the Emperor?
BENV. Aye, that's the head, and here the body lies
Justly rewarded for his villainies.
FRED. Come, let's devise how we may add more shame
To the black scandal of his hated name.
BENV. First, on his head, in quittance of my wrongs,
I'll nail huge forkéd horns and let them hang
Within the window where he yoked me first,
That all the world may see my just revenge.
MART. What use shall we put his beard to?
BENV. We'll sell it to a chimney-sweeper; it will wear out ten birchen brooms, I warrant you.
FRED. What shall his eyes do?
BENV. We'll pull out his eyes, and they shall serve for buttons to his lips to keep his tongue from catching cold.
MART. An excellent policy. And now, sirs, having divided him, what shall the body do?
[FAUSTUS *rises.*]
BENV. Zounds, the devil's alive again!
FRED. Give him his head, for God's sake!
FAUST. Nay, keep it. Faustus will have heads and hands,
Aye, all your hearts, to recompense this deed.
Knew you not, traitors, I was limited
For four and twenty years to breathe on earth?
And had you cut my body with your swords
Or hewed this flesh and bones as small as sand,
Yet in a minute had my spirit returned
And I had breathed a man made free from harm.
But wherefore do I dally my revenge?
Asteroth, Belimoth, Mephistophilis!
[*Enter* MEPHISTOPHILIS *and other* DEVILS.]
Go, horse these traitors on your fiery backs
And mount aloft with them as high as heaven,
Then pitch them headlong to the lowest hell.
Yet stay, the world shall see their misery,
And hell shall after plague their treachery.
Go, Belimoth, and take this caitiff[6] hence
And hurl him in some lake of mud and dirt;
Take thou this other, drag him through the woods

6. Wretch.

Amongst the pricking thorns and sharpest briars,
Whilst with my gentle Mephistophilis
This traitor flies unto some steepy rock
That rolling down may break the villain's bones
As he intended to dismember me.
Fly hence, dispatch my charge immediately.

FRED. Pity us, gentle Faustus; save our lives!

FAUST. Away!

FRED. He must needs go that the devil drives.

[*Exeunt* SPIRITS *with the* KNIGHTS.]

[*Enter the ambushed* SOLDIERS.]

1 SOLD. Come, sirs, prepare yourselves in readiness;
Make haste to help these noble gentlemen;
I heard them parley with the conjurer.

2 SOLD. See where he comes; dispatch, and kill the slave!

FAUST. What's here? An ambush to betray my life?
Then, Faustus, try thy skill. Base peasants, stand!
For lo, these trees remove at my command
And stand as bulwarks 'twixt yourselves and me
To shield me from your hated treachery;
Yet to encounter this, your weak attempt,
Behold an army comes incontinent.[7]

[FAUSTUS *strikes the door, and enter a* DEVIL *playing on a drum; after him another bearing an ensign, and divers with weapons;* MEPHISTOPHILIS *with fireworks. They set upon the* SOLDIERS *and drive them out. Exeunt.*]

SCENE 4

[*Enter at several doors* BENVOLIO, FREDERICK, *and* MARTINO, *their heads and faces bloody and besmeared with mud and dirt, all having horns on their heads.*]

MART. What ho, Benvolio!

BENV. Here! What, Frederick, ho!

FRED. O help me, gentle friend. Where is Martino?

MART. Dear Frederick, here—
Half smothered in a lake of mud and dirt
Through which the furies dragged me by the heels.

FRED. Martino, see! Benvolio's horns again.

MART. O misery! How now, Benvolio!

BENV. Defend me, heaven! Shall I be haunted still?

MART. Nay, fear not, man; we have no power to kill.

BENV. My friends transformèd thus! O hellish spite!
Your heads are all set with horns.

FRED. You hit it right;
It is your own you mean; feel on your head.

BENV. Zounds, horns again!

MART. Nay, chafe not, man; we are all sped.[8]

BENV. What devil attends this damned magician
That spite of spite our wrongs are doublèd?

7. Immediately.

8. Don't fret, man, we are all done for.

FRED. What may we do that we may hide our shames?
BENV. If we should follow him to work revenge,
He'd join long asses' ears to those huge horns
And make us laughingstocks to all the world.
MART. What shall we then do, dear Benvolio?
BENV. I have a castle joining near these woods,
And thither we'll repair and live obscure
Till time shall alter this our brutish shapes.
Sith black disgrace hath thus eclipsed our fame,
We'll rather die with grief than live with shame.
[*Exeunt* OMNES.]

SCENE 5

[*Enter* FAUSTUS *and the* HORSE-COURSER.[9]]

HOR. I beseech your Worship, accept of these forty dollars.[1]

FAUST. Friend, thou canst not buy so good a horse for so small a price. I have no great need to sell him, but if thou likest him for ten dollars more, take him, because I see thou hast a good mind to him.

HOR. I beseech you, sir, accept of this; I am a very poor man and have lost very much of late by horseflesh, and this bargain will set me up again.

FAUST. Well, I will not stand with thee; give me the money. Now, sirrah, I must tell you that you may ride him o'er hedge and ditch and spare him not; but—do you hear?—in any case ride him not into the water.

HOR. How, sir, not into the water? Why, will he not drink of all waters?

FAUST. Yes, he will drink of all waters, but ride him not into the water; o'er hedge and ditch or where thou wilt, but not into the water. Go bid the hostler deliver him unto you, and remember what I say.

HOR. I warrant you, sir. O joyful day! Now am I a made man forever.

[*Exit.*]

FAUST. What art thou, Faustus, but a man condemned to die?
Thy fatal time draws to a final end;
Despair doth drive distrust into my thoughts.
Confound these passions with a quiet sleep.
Tush, Christ did call the thief upon the cross;[2]
Then rest thee, Faustus, quiet in conceit.
[*He sits to sleep in his chair.*]

[*Enter the* HORSE-COURSER *wet.*]

HOR. O, what a cozening Doctor was this! I riding my horse into the water, thinking some hidden mystery had been in the horse, I had nothing under me but a little straw, and had much ado to escape drowning. Well, I'll go rouse him and make him give

9. Horse-trader, traditionally a sharp bargainer or cheat.
1. Common German coins; the word originally comes from the German *Joachimsthaler*.
2. In Luke xxiii.39–43 one of the two thieves crucified with Jesus is promised Paradise. "In conceit": in mind.

me my forty dollars again. Ho! sirrah Doctor, you cozening scab! Master Doctor, awake and arise, and give me my money again, for your horse is turned to a bottle[3] of hay. Master Doctor—

[*He pulls off his leg.*]

Alas, I am undone! What shall I do? I have pulled off his leg.

FAUST. O help! Help! The villain hath murdered me!

HOR. Murder or not murder, now he has but one leg I'll outrun him and cast this leg into some ditch or other.

[*Exit.*]

FAUST. Stop him, stop him, stop him! Ha ha ha! Faustus hath his leg again, and the horse-courser a bundle of hay for his forty dollars.

[*Enter* WAGNER.]

FAUST. How now, Wagner! What news with thee?

WAG. If it please you, the Duke of Vanholt doth earnestly entreat your company and hath sent some of his men to attend you with provision fit for your journey.

FAUST. The Duke of Vanholt's an honorable gentleman, and one to whom I must be no niggard of my cunning. Come, away!

[*Exeunt* OMNES.]

SCENE 6

[*Enter* ROBIN, DICK, HORSE-COURSER, *and a* CARTER.]

CART. Come, my masters, I'll bring you to the best beer in Europe— What ho, Hostess!—Where be these whores?[4]

[*Enter* HOSTESS.]

HOST. How now! What lack you? What, my old guests, welcome.

ROBIN. Sirrah Dick, dost thou know why I stand so mute?

DICK. No, Robin, why is 't?

ROBIN. I am eighteen pence on the score,[5] but say nothing; see if she have forgotten me.

HOST. Who's this that stands so solemnly by himself? What, my old guest!

ROBIN. O, hostess, how do you do? I hope my score stands still.

HOST. Aye, there's no doubt of that, for methinks you make no haste to wipe it out.

DICK. Why, hostess, I say, fetch us some beer.

HOST. You shall presently; look up into th' hall. There, ho!

[*Exit.*]

DICK. Come, sirs; what shall we do now till mine hostess comes?

CART. Marry, sir, I'll tell you the bravest tale how a conjurer served me. You know Dr. Faustus?

HOR. Aye, a plague take him! Here's some on 's have cause to know him. Did he conjure thee too?

CART. I'll tell you how he served me. As I was going to Wittenberg t' other day, he met me and asked me what he should give me for as much hay as he could eat. Now, sir, I, thinking that a little would serve his turn, bade him take as much as he

3. Bundle.

4. I.e., the hostess and maids of the inn.

5. Charged, not paid for.

would for three farthings. So he presently gave me my money and fell to eating; and, as I am a cursen[6] man, he never left eating till he had eat up all my load of hay.

ALL. O monstrous; eat a whole load of hay!

ROBIN. Yes, yes; that may be, for I have heard of one that has eat a load of logs.[7]

HOR. Now, sirs, you shall hear how villainously he served me. I went to him yesterday to buy a horse of him, and he would by no means sell him under forty dollars. So, sir, because I knew him to be such a horse as would run over hedge and ditch and never tire, I gave him his money. So, when I had my horse, Dr. Faustus bade me ride him night and day and spare him no time; "But," quoth he, "in any case ride him not into the water." Now sir, I thinking the horse had had some quality that he would not have me know of, what did I but ride him into a great river, and when I came just in the midst my horse vanished away and I sat straddling upon a bottle of hay.

ALL. O brave Doctor!

HOR. But you shall hear how bravely I served him for it. I went me home to his house, and there I found him asleep; I kept a hallowing and whooping in his ears, but all could not wake him. I seeing that, took him by the leg and never rested pulling till I had pulled me his leg quite off, and now 'tis at home in mine hostry.

DICK. And has the Doctor but one leg then? That's excellent, for one of his devils turned me into the likeness of an ape's face.

CART. Some more drink, hostess!

ROBIN. Hark you, we'll into another room and drink awhile, and then we'll go seek out the Doctor.

[*Exeunt* OMNES.]

SCENE 7

[*Enter the* DUKE OF VANHOLT, *his* DUCHESS, FAUSTUS, *and* MEPHISTOPHILIS.]

DUKE. Thanks, master Doctor, for these pleasant sights; nor know I how sufficiently to recompense your great deserts in erecting that enchanted castle in the air, the sight whereof so delighted me as nothing in the world could please me more.

FAUST. I do think myself, my good lord, highly recompensed that it pleaseth your Grace to think but well of that which Faustus hath performed. But gracious lady, it may be that you have taken no pleasure in those sights; therefore I pray you tell me what is the thing you most desire to have; be it in the world it shall be yours. I have heard that great-bellied women do long for things that are rare and dainty.

DUCH. True, master Doctor, and since I find you so kind, I will make known unto you what my heart desires to have; and were it now summer, as it is January, a dead time of winter, I would

6. Mispronunciation of "Christian."
7. Comic expression for being drunk—to carry a jag (or load) of logs.

request no better meat than a dish of ripe grapes.

FAUST. This is but a small matter.—Go, Mephistophilis, away!—

[*Exit* MEPHISTOPHILIS.]

Madam, I will do more than this for your content.

[*Enter* MEPHISTOPHILIS *again with the grapes.*]

Here, now taste ye these; they should be good, for they come from a far country, I can tell you.

DUKE. This makes me wonder more than all the rest, that at this time of year, when every tree is barren of his fruit, from whence you had these ripe grapes.

FAUST. Please it your Grace, the year is divided into two circles over the whole world, so that when it is winter with us, in the contrary circle it is likewise summer with them, as in India, Saba,[8] and such countries that lie far east, where they have fruit twice a year. From whence, by means of a swift spirit that I have, I had these grapes brought as you see.

DUCH. And trust me they are the sweetest grapes that e'er I tasted.

[*The* CLOWNS *bounce*[9] *at the gate within.*]

DUKE. What rude disturbers have we at the gate?
Go pacify their fury, set it ope,
And then demand of them what they would have.

[*They knock again and call out to talk with* FAUSTUS.]

A SERVANT. Why, how now, masters, what a coil[1] is there!
What is the reason you disturb the Duke?

DICK. We have no reason for it, therefore a fig[2] for him!

SERV. Why, saucy varlets! Dare you be so bold?

HOR. I hope, sir, we have wit enough to be more bold than welcome.

SERV. It appears so; Pray be bold elsewhere
And trouble not the Duke.

DUKE. What would they have?

SERV. They all cry out to speak with Dr. Faustus.

CART. Aye, and we will speak with him.

DUKE. Will you, sir? Commit[3] the rascals!

DICK. Commit with us? He were as good commit with his father as commit with us.

FAUST. I do beseech your Grace, let them come in;
They are good subject for a merriment.

DUKE. Do as thou wilt, Faustus; I give thee leave.

FAUST. I thank your Grace.

[*Enter* ROBIN, DICK, CARTER, *and* HORSE-COURSER.]

Why, how now, my good friends?
'Faith you are too outrageous; but come near,
I have procured your pardons. Welcome all!

ROBIN. Nay, sir, we will be welcome for our money, and we will pay for what we take. What ho! Give 's half a dozen of beer here, and be hanged.

8. Sheba.
9. Bang.
1. Disturbance.
2. An obscene gesture, implying contempt.
3. Put in jail. Dick puns on its other meaning ("commit adultery"), from the Ten Commandments.

FAUST. Nay, hark you, can you tell me where you are?[4]

CART. Aye, marry, can I; we are under heaven.

SERV. Aye, but, sir saucebox, know you in what place?

HOR. Aye, aye, the house is good enough to drink in. Zounds, fill us some beer, or we'll break all the barrels in the house and dash out all your brains with your bottles.

FAUST. Be not so furious; come, you shall have beer.
My lord, beseech you give me leave awhile;
I'll gage my credit 'twill content your Grace.

DUKE. With all my heart, kind Doctor, please thyself;
Our servants and our court's at thy command.

FAUST. I humbly thank your Grace. Then fetch some beer.

HOR. Aye, marry, there spake a doctor indeed; and, faith, I'll drink a health to thy wooden leg for that word.

FAUST. My wooden leg! What dost thou mean by that?

CART. Ha ha ha, dost hear him, Dick? He has forgot his leg.

HOR. Aye, he does not stand much upon that.

FAUST. No, faith, not much upon a wooden leg.

CART. Good lord, that flesh and blood should be so frail with your worship! Do you not remember a horse-courser you sold a horse to?

FAUST. Yes, I remember I sold one a horse.

CART. And do you remember you bid he should not ride him into the water?

FAUST. Yes, I do very well remember that.

CART. And do you remember nothing of your leg?

FAUST. No, in good sooth.

CART. Then I pray remember your courtesy.

FAUST. I thank you, sir.

CART. 'Tis not so much worth. I pray you tell me one thing.

FAUST. What's that?

CART. Be both of your legs bedfellows every night together?

FAUST. Wouldst thou make a colossus[5] of me, that thou askest me such questions?

CART. No, truly, sir, I would make nothing of you, but I would fain know that.

[*Enter* HOSTESS *with drink.*]

FAUST. Then I assure thee certainly they are.

CART. I thank you; I am fully satisfied.

FAUST. But wherefore dost thou ask?

CART. For nothing, sir; but methinks you should have a wooden bedfellow to one of 'em.

HOR. Why, do you hear, sir, did not I pull off one of your legs when you were asleep?

FAUST. But I have it again now I am awake; look you here, sir.

ALL. O horrible! Had the doctor three legs?

CART. Do you remember, sir, how you cozened me and eat up my load of——

4. At the end of IV.6, the clowns thought they were stepping into another room, but Faustus has had them transported to the court of the Duke of Vanholt.

5. The huge statue which stood at the entrance to the harbor at Rhodes; boats sailed between its legs, and Dr. Faustus is suggesting that the clowns are making his legs as important.

[FAUSTUS *charms him dumb.*]

DICK. Do you remember how you made me wear an ape's——

HOR. You whoreson conjuring scab, do you remember how you cozened me of a ho——

ROBIN. Ha' you forgotten me? You think to carry it away with your hey-pass and your re-pass;[6] do you remember the dog's fa——

[*Exeunt* CLOWNS.]

HOST. Who pays for the ale? Hear you, master Doctor, now you have sent away my guests, I pray who shall pay me for my a——

[*Exit* HOSTESS.]

DUCH. My lord,
We are much beholding to this learned man.

DUKE. So are we, madam, which we will recompense
With all the love and kindness that we may;
His artful sport drives all sad thoughts away. [*Exeunt.*]

Act V

SCENE 1

[*Thunder and lightning. Enter* DEVILS *with covered dishes;* MEPHISTOPHILIS *leads them into* FAUSTUS' *study. Then enter* WAGNER.]

WAG. I think my master means to die shortly;
He has made his will and given me his wealth,
His house, his goods, and store of golden plate,
Besides two thousand ducats ready coined.
And yet I wonder, for if death were nigh
He would not banquet and carouse and swill
Amongst the students as even now he doth,
Who are at supper with such belly-cheer
As Wagner ne'er beheld in all his life.
See where they come; belike the feast is ended. [*Exit.*]

[*Enter* FAUSTUS *and* MEPHISTOPHILIS *with two or three* SCHOLARS.]

1 SCH. Master Doctor Faustus, since our conference about fair ladies, which was the beautifullest in all the world, we have determined with ourselves that Helen of Greece was the admirablest lady that ever lived. Therefore, master Doctor, if you will do us that favor as to let us see that peerless dame of Greece whom all the world admires for majesty, we should think ourselves much beholding unto you.

FAUST. Gentlemen,
For that I know your friendship is unfeigned,
And Faustus' custom is not to deny
The just requests of those that wish him well,
You shall behold that peerless dame of Greece,
No otherways for pomp and majesty

6. Traditional exclamations of a conjurer.

Than when Sir Paris crossed the seas with her
And brought the spoils to rich Dardania.[7]
Be silent, then, for danger is in words.

[*Music sounds.* MEPHISTOPHILIS *brings in* HELEN; *she passeth over the stage.*]

2 SCH. Too simple is my wit to tell her praise
Whom all the world admires for majesty.

3 SCH. No marvel though the angry Greeks pursued
With ten years' war the rape of such a queen
Whose heavenly beauty passeth all compare.

1 SCH. Since we have seen the pride of Nature's works
And only paragon of excellence,
Let us depart, and for this glorious deed
Happy and blest be Faustus evermore.

FAUST. Gentlemen, farewell; the same I wish to you.

[*Exeunt* SCHOLARS.]

[*Enter an* OLD MAN.]

OLD MAN. O gentle Faustus, leave this damnéd art,
This magic, that will charm thy soul to hell
And quite bereave[8] thee of salvation.
Though thou hast now offended like a man,
Do not persévér in it like a devil.
Yet, yet, thou hast an amiable soul
If sin by custom grow not into nature;
Then, Faustus, will repentance come too late;
Then thou art banished from the sight of heaven.
No mortal can express the pains of hell.
It may be this my exhortation
Seems harsh and all unpleasant; let it not;
For, gentle son, I speak it not in wrath
Or envy of thee, but in tender love
And pity of thy future misery,
And so have hope that this my kind rebuke,
Checking thy body, may amend thy soul.

FAUST. Where art thou, Faustus? Wretch, what hast thou done?
Damned art thou, Faustus, damned! Despair and die.

[MEPHISTOPHILIS *gives him a dagger.*]

Hell claims his right, and with a roaring voice
Says, "Faustus, come; thine hour is almost come!"
And Faustus now will come to do thee right.

OLD MAN. O stay, good Faustus, stay thy desperate steps!
I see an angel hovers o'er thy head
And with a vial full of precious grace
Offers to pour the same into thy soul:
Then call for mercy and avoid despair.

FAUST. Ah my sweet friend, I feel thy words
To comfort my distresséd soul.
Leave me awhile to ponder on my sins.

OLD MAN. Faustus, I leave thee, but with grief of heart,
Fearing the ruin of thy hapless soul. [*Exit.*]

7. Troy.

8. Deprive.

FAUST. Accurséd Faustus, where is mercy now?
I do repent and yet I do despair:
Hell strives with grace for conquest in my breast.
What shall I do to shun the snares of death?
MEPH. Thou traitor, Faustus, I arrest thy soul
For disobedience to my sovereign lord.
Revolt, or I'll in piecemeal tear thy flesh.
FAUST. I do repent I e'er offended him.
Sweet Mephistophilis, entreat thy lord
To pardon my unjust presumption,
And with my blood again I will confirm
The former vow I made to Lucifer.
MEPH. Do it then, Faustus, with unfeignéd heart
Lest greater danger do attend thy drift.
FAUST. Torment, sweet friend, that base and aged man
That durst dissuade me from thy Lucifer,
With greatest torments that our hell affords.
MEPH. His faith is great; I cannot touch his soul;
But what I may afflict his body with
I will attempt, which is but little worth.
FAUST. One thing, good servant, let me crave of thee
To glut the longing of my heart's desire:
That I might have unto my paramour
That heavenly Helen which I saw of late,
Whose sweet embracings may extinguish clear
These thoughts that do dissuade me from my vow,
And keep mine oath I made to Lucifer.
MEPH. This, or what else my Faustus shall desire
Shall be performed in twinkling of an eye.
[*Enter* HELEN *again, passing over between two* CUPIDS.]
FAUST. Was this the face that launched a thousand ships
And burnt the topless[9] towers of Ilium?
Sweet Helen, make me immortal with a kiss.
Her lips suck forth my soul—see where it flies!
Come, Helen, come, give me my soul again.
Here will I dwell, for heaven is in these lips
And all is dross that is not Helena.
[*Enter* OLD MAN *and stands watching* FAUSTUS.]
I will be Paris, and for love of thee
Instead of Troy shall Wittenberg be sacked,
And I will combat with weak Menelaus
And wear thy colors on my plumèd crest;
Yea, I will wound Achilles in the heel
And then return to Helen for a kiss.
O thou art fairer than the evening air
Clad in the beauty of a thousand stars!
Brighter art thou than flaming Jupiter
When he appeared to hapless Semele,[10]

9. So high they seemed to have no tops.

10. A Theban girl, loved by Jupiter and destroyed by the fire of his lightning when he appeared to her in his full splendor.

More lovely than the monarch of the sky
In wanton Arethusa's azured arms,[1]
And none but thou shalt be my paramour!

[*Exeunt* ALL *except the* OLD MAN.]

OLD MAN. Accurséd Faustus, miserable man,
That from thy soul exclud'st the grace of heaven
And fliest the throne of his tribunal seat.

[*Enter the* DEVILS *to torment him.*]

Satan begins to sift me with his pride.[2]
As in this furnace God shall try my faith,
My faith, vile hell, shall triumph over thee!
Ambitious fiends, see how the heavens smiles
At your repulse, and laughs your state to scorn.
Hence, hell! for hence I fly unto my God. [*Exeunt.*]

SCENE 2

[*Thunder. Enter* LUCIFER, BELZEBUB, *and* MEPHISTOPHILIS.]

LUC. Thus from infernal Dis[3] do we ascend
To view the subjects of our monarchy,
Those souls which sin seals the black sons of hell.
'Mong which as chief, Faustus, we come to thee,
Bringing with us lasting damnation
To wait upon thy soul; the time is come
Which makes it forfeit.

MEPH. And this gloomy night
Here in this room will wretched Faustus be.

BEL. And here we'll stay
To mark him how he doth demean himself.

MEPH. How should he but with desperate lunacy?
Fond worldling, now his heart-blood dries with grief,
His conscience kills it, and his laboring brain
Begets a world of idle fantasies
To overreach the devil, but all in vain.
His store of pleasure must be sauced with pain.
He and his servant Wagner are at hand;
Both come from drawing Faustus' latest will.
See where they come!

[*Enter* FAUSTUS *and* WAGNER.]

FAUST. Say, Wagner, thou has perused my will;
How dost thou like it?

WAG. Sir, so wondrous well
As in all humble duty I do yield
My life and lasting service for your love.

[*Enter the* SCHOLARS.]

FAUST. Gramercies, Wagner.—Welcome, gentlemen.

1 SCH. Now, worthy Faustus, methinks your looks are changed.

1. Arethusa was the nymph of a fountain, as well as the fountain itself; no classical myth, however, records her love affair with Jupiter, the "monarch of the sky."

2. I.e., to test me with his strength.

3. The underworld.

FAUST. Ah, gentlemen!

2 SCH. What ails Faustus?

FAUST. Ah, my sweet chamber-fellow, had I lived with thee, then had I lived still, but now must die eternally. Look, sirs! Comes he not? Comes he not?

1 SCH. O my dear Faustus, what imports this fear?

2 SCH. Is all our pleasure turned to melancholy?

3 SCH. He is not well with being over-solitary.

2 SCH. If it be so, we'll have physicians, and Faustus shall be cured.

3 SCH. 'Tis but a surfeit,[4] sir; fear nothing.

FAUST. A surfeit of deadly sin that hath damned both body and soul.

2 SCH. Yet, Faustus, look up to heaven: remember God's mercies are infinite.

FAUST. But Faustus' offense can ne'er be pardoned; the Serpent that tempted Eve may be saved, but not Faustus. Ah, gentlemen, hear me with patience, and tremble not at my speeches. Though my heart pants and quivers to remember that I have been a student here these thirty years, O would I had never seen Wittenberg, never read book! And what wonders I have done all Germany can witness, yea all the world, for which Faustus hath lost both Germany and the world, yea heaven itself—heaven the seat of God, the throne of the blessed, the kingdom of joy, and must remain in hell forever, hell, ah hell, forever! Sweet friends, what shall become of Faustus, being in hell forever?

3 SCH. Yet, Faustus, call on God.

FAUST. On God, whom Faustus hath abjured? on God, whom Faustus hath blasphemed? Ah, my God, I would weep, but the devil draws in my tears! Gush forth, blood, instead of tears, yea life and soul! O he stays my tongue; I would lift up my hands but, see, they hold 'em, they hold 'em!

ALL. Who, Faustus?

FAUST. Why, Lucifer and Mephistophilis.
Ah, gentlemen, I gave them my soul for my cunning.

ALL. God forbid!

FAUST. God forbade it indeed, but Faustus hath done it: for vain pleasure of four and twenty years hath Faustus lost eternal joy and felicity. I writ them a bill with mine own blood; the date is expired, this is the time, and he will fetch me.

1 SCH. Why did not Faustus tell us of this before, that divines might have prayed for thee?

FAUST. Oft have I thought to have done so, but the devil threatened to tear me in pieces if I named God, to fetch both body and soul if I once gave ear to divinity; and now 'tis too late. Gentlemen, away, lest you perish with me!

2 SCH. O what may we do to save Faustus?

FAUST. Talk not of me, but save yourselves and depart.

4. Indigestion; the effects of overindulgence.

3 SCH. God will strengthen me: I will stay with Faustus.

1 SCH. Tempt not God, sweet friend, but let us into the next room, and there pray for him.

FAUST. Aye, pray for me, pray for me! And what noise soever ye hear, come not unto me, for nothing can rescue me.

2 SCH. Pray thou, and we will pray that God may have mercy upon thee.

FAUST. Gentlemen, farewell. If I live till morning I'll visit you; if not, Faustus is gone to hell.

ALL. Faustus, farewell. [*Exeunt* SCHOLARS.]

MEPH. Aye, Faustus, now thou hast no hope of heaven;
Therefore despair, think only upon hell,
For that must be thy mansion, there to dwell.

FAUST. O thou bewitching fiend, 'twas thy temptation
Hath robbed me of eternal happiness.

MEPH. I do confess it, Faustus, and rejoice.
'Twas I, that when thou wert i' the way to heaven
Damned up thy passage; when thou tookest the book
To view the scriptures, then I turned the leaves
And led thine eye.
What, weepst thou? 'tis too late. Despair, farewell!
Fools that will laugh on earth must weep in hell. [*Exit.*]

[*Enter the* GOOD ANGEL *and the* BAD ANGEL *at several doors.*]

G. ANG. Ah Faustus, if thou hadst given ear to me,
Innumerable joys had followed thee,
But thou didst love the world.

B. ANG. Gave ear to me
And now must taste hell's pains perpetually.

G. ANG. O what will all thy riches, pleasures, pomps
Avail thee now?

B. ANG. Nothing but vex thee more,
To want in hell, that had on earth such store.

[*Music while the throne descends.*[5]]

G. ANG. O, thou hast lost celestial happiness,
Pleasures unspeakable, bliss without end.
Hadst thou affected sweet divinity
Hell or the devil had had no power on thee.
Hadst thou kept on that way, Faustus, behold
In what resplendent glory thou hadst sit
In yonder throne, like those bright shining saints,
And triumphed over hell; that hast thou lost.
And now, poor soul, must thy good angel leave thee;
The jaws of hell are open to receive thee.

[*Exit. Hell is discovered.*]

B. ANG. Now Faustus, let thine eyes with horror stare
Into that vast perpetual torture-house.
There are the furies, tossing damnéd souls

5. A throne suspended by ropes descended to the stage near the end of many Elizabethan plays and was an expected theatrical display. Here the throne clearly symbolizes heaven, as the next speech shows.

On burning forks; their bodies boil in lead.
There are live quarters[6] broiling on the coals
That ne'er can die; this ever-burning chair
Is for o'ertortured souls to rest them in;
These that are fed with sops of flaming fire
Were gluttons and loved only delicates
And laughed to see the poor starve at their gates.
But yet all these are nothing; thou shalt see
Ten thousand tortures that more horrid be.

FAUST. O, I have seen enough to torture me.

B. ANG. Nay, thou must feel them, taste the smart of all;
He that loves pleasure must for pleasure fall.
And so I leave thee, Faustus, till anon;
Then wilt thou tumble in confusión.[7]
[*Exit. The clock strikes eleven.*]

FAUST. Ah, Faustus,
Now hast thou but one bare hour to live
And then thou must be damned perpetually!
Stand still, you ever-moving spheres of heaven,
That time may cease and midnight never come;
Fair Nature's eye, rise, rise again, and make
Perpetual day; or let this hour be but
A year, a month, a week, a natural day,
That Faustus may repent and save his soul!
O lente lente currite noctis equi.[8]
The stars move still, time runs, the clock will strike,
The devil will come, and Faustus must be damned.
O, I'll leap up to my God! Who pulls me down?
See, see, where Christ's blood streams in the firmament!—
One drop would save my soul—half a drop! ah, my Christ!
Rend not my heart for naming of my Christ;
Yet will I call on him—O, spare me, Lucifer!
Where is it now? 'Tis gone; and see where God
Stretcheth out his arm and bends his ireful brows.
Mountains and hills, come, come and fall on me
And hide me from the heavy wrath of God,
No, no?
Then will I headlong run into the earth:
Earth, gape! O no, it will not harbor me.
You stars that reigned at my nativity,
Whose influence hath allotted death and hell,
Now draw up Faustus like a foggy mist
Into the entails of yon laboring cloud
That when you vomit forth into the air,
My limbs may issue from your smoky mouths,
So that my soul may but ascend to heaven.[9]
[*The watch strikes.*]
Ah, half the hour is past; 'twill all be past anon.

6. Bodies.
7. Destruction, perdition.
8. "Slowly, slowly run, O horses of the night," adapted from a line in Ovid's *Amores*.
9. Faustus begs his natal stars to draw him up into the cloud, where his body may be compacted into a thunderstone and fall to earth, so that his soul, thus purified, may ascend to heaven.

O God,
If thou wilt not have mercy on my soul,
Yet for Christ's sake whose blood hath ransomed me
Impose some end to my incessant pain:
Let Faustus live in hell a thousand years,
A hundred thousand, and at last be saved!
O, no end is limited to damnéd souls!
Why wert thou not a creature wanting soul?
Or why is this immortal that thou hast?
Ah, Pythagoras' *metempsychosis*[10]—were that true,
This soul should fly from me, and I be changed
Unto some brutish beast. All beasts are happy,
For when they die
Their souls are soon dissolved in elements,
But mine must live still[1] to be plagued in hell.
Cursed be the parents that engendered me!
No, Faustus, curse thyself, curse Lucifer
That hath deprived thee of the joys of heaven.
[*The clock strikes twelve.*]
It strikes, it strikes! Now, body, turn to air
Or Lucifer will bear thee quick[2] to hell!
[*Thunder and lightning.*]
O soul, be changed to little water drops
And fall into the ocean, ne'er be found.
My God, my God, look not so fierce on me!
[*Enter* DEVILS.]
Adders and serpents, let me breathe awhile!
Ugly hell, gape not—come not, Lucifer—
I'll burn my books—ah, Mephistophilis!
[*Exeunt* DEVILS *with* FAUSTUS.]

SCENE 3

[*Enter the* SCHOLARS.]

1 SCH. Come, gentlemen, let us go visit Faustus,
For such a dreadful night was never seen
Since first the world's creation did begin,
Such fearful shrieks and cries were never heard.
Pray heaven the Doctor have escaped the danger.
2 SCH. O, help us heaven! See, here are Faustus' limbs
All torn asunder by the hand of death.
3 SCH. The devils whom Faustus served have torn him thus;
For 'twixt the hours of twelve and one, methought
I heard him shriek and call aloud for help.
At which self[3] time the house seemed all on fire
With dreadful horror of these damnéd fiends.
2 SCH. Well, gentlemen, though Faustus' end be such
As every Christian heart laments to think on,
Yet for he was a scholar once admired

10. Pythagoras' doctrine of the transmigration of souls.
1. Always.
2. Alive.
3. Same, exact.

For wondrous knowledge in our German schools,
We'll give his mangled limbs due burial;
And all the students, clothed in mourning black,
Shall wait upon his heavy[4] funeral. [*Exeunt.*]
[*Enter* CHORUS.]
CHO. Cut is the branch that might have grown full straight,
And burnèd is Apollo's laurel bough[5]
That sometime grew within this learnèd man.
Faustus is gone: regard his hellish fall,
Whose fiendful fortune may exhort the wise
Only to wonder at[6] unlawful things
Whose deepness doth entice such forward wits
To practice more than heavenly power permits. [*Exit.*]

1604, 1616

4. Tragic, sorrowful.
5. Laurel is a symbol of wisdom and learning; Apollo was the god of divination, one of whose shrines was the oracle at Delphi. The image, though it sounds classical, is really Marlowe's.
6. I.e., to be content with observing with awe. "Fiendful fortune": devilish fate.

WILLIAM SHAKESPEARE
(1564–1616)

ca. 1588–92: In London as actor and playwright.
ca. 1592–98: Devotes himself mainly to chronicle histories and comedies.
ca. 1601–9: Period of the great tragedies and romantic comedies.
ca. 1610: Retires to Stratford

William Shakespeare was born in Stratford-on-Avon in April (probably April 23), 1564. His father was a citizen of some prominence who became an alderman and bailiff, but who later suffered financial reverses. Shakespeare presumably attended the Stratford grammar school, where he could have acquired a respectable knowledge of Latin, but he did not proceed to Oxford or Cambridge. There are legends about Shakespeare's youth but no documented facts. The first record we have of his life after his christening is that of his marriage in 1582 to Anne Hathaway. A daughter was born to the young Shakespeares in 1583 and twins, a boy and a girl, in 1585. We possess no information about his activities for the next seven years, but by 1592 he was in London as an actor and apparently well-known as a playwright, for Robert Greene refers to him resentfully in *A Groatsworth of Wit* as "an upstart crow, beautified with our feathers," who, "being an absolute *Johannes Factotum*, is in his own conceit the only Shake-scene in a country."

At this time, there were several companies of actors in London and in the provinces. What connection Shakespeare had with one or more of them before 1592 is conjectural, but we do know of his long and fruitful connection with the most successful troupe, the Lord Chamberlain's Men, who later, when James I came to the throne, became the King's Men. Shakespeare not only acted with this company, but eventually became a leading shareholder and the principal playwright. The company included some of the most famous actors of the day, such as Richard Burbage, who no doubt created the roles of Hamlet, Lear, and Othello, and Will Kempe and Robert Armin, who acted Shakespeare's clowns and fools. In 1599 the Chamberlain's Men built and occupied that best known of Elizabethan theaters, the Globe.

Shakespeare did not, in his early years, confine himself to the theater. In 1593 he published a mythological-erotic poem, *Venus and Adonis*, dedicated to the Earl of Southampton; in the next year he dedicated a "graver labor," *The Rape of Lucrece*, to the same noble patron. By 1597 Shakespeare had so prospered that he was able to purchase New Place, a handsome house in Stratford; he could now call himself a gentleman, as his father had been granted a coat of arms in the previous year.

Our first record of the playwright's actual work occurs in Francis Meres' *Palladis Tamia: Wit's Treasury* (1598), in which Meres compared English poets with the ancients; of Shakespeare he says, "As Plautus and Seneca are accounted the best for Comedy and Tragedy among the Latins, so Shakespeare among the English is the most excellent in both kinds for the stage." He goes on to list *Richard II*, *Richard III*, *Henry IV*, *King John*, *Titus Andronicus*, and *Romeo and Juliet* for tragedy and *Two Gentlemen of Verona*, *The Comedy of Errors*, *A Midsummer Night's Dream*, *The Merchant of Venice*, *Love's Labor's Lost*, and the unknown (or perhaps retitled) *Love's Labor's Won* as comedy. All of the plays Meres lists as tragedy (except for *Romeo and Juliet* and the very early *Titus Andronicus*) we would call chronicle history plays, a popular kind of drama based upon history books like Raphael Holinshed's *Chronicle* and presenting dramatically the events in the reigns of various English kings. About the turn of the century Shakespeare wrote his great romantic comedies, *As You Like It*, *Twelfth Night*, and *Much Ado About Nothing*, and his concluding history play in the Prince Hal series, *Henry V*. The next decade was the period of the great tragedies: *Hamlet*, *Macbeth*, *Othello*, *King Lear*, and *Antony and Cleopatra*.

About 1610 Shakespeare apparently retired to Stratford, though he continued to write, both by himself (*The Tempest*) and in collaboration (*Henry VIII*). This is the period of the "romances" or "tragicomedies," which include, besides *The Tempest*, *Cymbeline* and *The Winter's Tale*. Aside from his two early nondramatic poems, Shakespeare devoted his genius primarily to the stage. Meres mentioned in 1598, however, that he was known for "his sugared sonnets among his private friends"; the sonnets were published in 1609, apparently without his authorization. He contributed the strange and beautiful poem, *The Phoenix and the Turtle*, to an anthology in 1601.

The plays contain some of the finest songs ever written. They are of various types: the aubade, or morning song, the gay pastoral invitation, love songs of various kinds, the ballad sung by wandering minstrels, and the funeral dirge. They illustrate many sides of Shakespeare's genius—his incomparable lyric gift, his ready humor, and his marvelous sensitivity to the sights and sounds of English life, especially the life of the country.

The sonnets are Shakespeare's contribution to a popular vogue, but his cycle is quite unlike the other sonnet sequences of his day. Shakespeare's cycle suggests a story, though the details are vague, and there is doubt even whether the sonnets as published in 1609 are in the correct order. Certain motifs are clear: a series celebrating the beauty of a young man and urging him to marry; some sonnets to a lady; some sonnets (like 144) about a strange triangle of love involving two men and a woman; sonnets on the destructive power of time and the permanence of poetry; sonnets about a rival poet; and incidental sonnets of moral insight, like 129 and 146. The biographical background of the sonnets has aroused much speculation, but very little of it is convincing. The poems themselves are what is important. Though the vocabulary is often simple, the metaphorical style of the sonnets is rich. "Shall I compare thee to a summer's day" is a question which might lead to a very ordinary conceit; instead it introduces a profound meditation on time, change, and beauty.

The structure of the sonnet frequently reinforces the power of the metaphors; each quatrain in 73 develops an image of lateness, of approaching extinction—of a season, of a day, and of a fire, but they also apply to a life. The three quatrains may be equally and successively at work preparing for the conclusion in the couplet, or the first eight lines may contain a catalogue and the last six turn in quite a different direction, as in sonnet 29. The rhetorical strategy of the sonnets is also worth careful attention. Some begin with a purported reminiscence; some are imperative; others make an almost proverbial statement, then elaborate it. The imagery comes from a wide variety of sources: gardening, navigation, law, farming, business, pictorial art, astrology, domestic affairs. The moods are also not confined to what the Renaissance thought were those of the despairing Petrarchan lover; they include delight, pride, melancholy, shame, disgust, fear. It is evident that the poet of the sonnets is also the author of the great plays.

When Shakespeare died, in Stratford in 1616, no collected edition of his plays had been published. Some of them had been printed in separate editions ("quartos") without his editorial supervision, sometimes from his manuscripts, sometimes from playhouse prompt books, sometimes from pirated texts secured by shorthand reports of a performance or from reconstruction from memory by an actor or spectator.

In 1623, two members of Shakespeare's company, John Heminges and Henry Condell, published the great collection of all the plays they considered authentic; it is called the First Folio. They printed the best texts they had, according to their lights. The Folio contains an epistle "to the great variety of readers" which urges us to read Shakespeare again and again; if we do not like him, say Heminges and Condell, it is evident that we do not understand him. Another preliminary document in the First Folio is a poem by Shakespeare's great rival, critic, and opposite, Ben Jonson. In it he asserts the superiority of Shakespeare not only to other English playwrights but to the Greek and Latin masters. Jonson first states what has come to be a universal opinion:

> Triumph, my Britain, thou hast one to show
> To whom all scenes of Europe homage owe.
> He was not of an age, but for all time!

Songs from the Plays

When Daisies Pied[1]

SPRING

When daisies pied and violets blue
  And ladysmocks all silver-white
And cuckoobuds of yellow hue
  Do paint the meadows with delight,
The cuckoo then, on every tree,
Mocks married men; [2] for thus sings he,
                Cuckoo;
Cuckoo, cuckoo: Oh word of fear,
Unpleasing to a married ear!

When shepherds pipe on oaten straws,[3]
  And merry larks are plowmen's clocks,
When turtles tread,[4] and rooks, and daws,
  And maidens bleach their summer smocks,
The cuckoo then, on every tree,
Mocks married men; for thus sings he,
                Cuckoo;
Cuckoo, cuckoo: Oh word of fear,
Unpleasing to a married ear!

WINTER

When icicles hang by the wall
  And Dick the shepherd blows his nail [5]
And Tom bears logs into the hall,
  And milk comes frozen home in pail,
When blood is nipped and ways be foul,
Then nightly sings the staring owl,
                Tu-who;
Tu-whit, tu-who: a merry note,
While greasy Joan doth keel[6] the pot.

When all aloud the wind doth blow,
  And coughing drowns the parson's saw,[7]
And birds sit brooding in the snow,
  And Marian's nose looks red and raw,
When roasted crabs[8] hiss in the bowl,
Then nightly sings the staring owl,
                Tu-who;
Tu-whit, tu-who: a merry note
While greasy Joan doth keel the pot.

1. This song concludes *Love's Labour's Lost* (1594–95), one of Shakespeare's earliest comedies. Announced as a "Dialogue * * * in praise of the Owl and the Cuckoo," it provides a lyric commentary on the bittersweet mood that dominates the play's last scene. "Pied": variegated.
2. The cuckoo's song—"Cuckoo!"—is taken to mean "Cuckold!"
3. The reed pipes played by shepherds.
4. Turtledoves mate. The "larks" are "plowmen's clocks" because they sing at sunrise.
5. Warms his fingers by blowing on them.
6. Stir, to prevent boiling over.
7. Wise saying.
8. Crabapples.

Tell Me Where Is Fancy Bred[9]

Tell me where is fancy bred,
Or in the heart or in the head?
How begot, how nourishéd?
Reply, reply.
It is engendered in the eyes,
With gazing fed; and fancy dies
In the cradle where it lies.
Let us all ring fancy's knell:
I'll begin it—Ding, dong, bell.
Ding, dong, bell.

Sigh No More, Ladies[1]

Sigh no more, ladies, sigh no more,
Men were deceivers ever;
One foot in sea, and one on shore,
To one thing constant never.
Then sigh not so,
But let them go,
And be you blithe and bonny,
Converting all your sounds of woe
Into Hey nonny, nonny.

Sing no more ditties, sing no mo
Of dumps [2] so dull and heavy;
The fraud of men was ever so,
Since summer first was leavy.
Then sigh not so,
But let them go,
And be you blithe and bonny,
Converting all your sounds of woe
Into Hey nonny, nonny.

Under the Greenwood Tree[3]

Under the greenwood tree
Who loves to lie with me,

9. *The Merchant of Venice* (1596–97) III.ii.63 ff.; sung while Bassanio is trying to choose between the caskets of gold, silver, and lead—one of which contains the token that will enable him to gain Portia as his wife. The song is perhaps intended to help Bassanio's choice: notice the number of words that rhyme with "lead." "Fancy" is a superficial love or liking for something attractive.

1. *Much Ado About Nothing* (1598–99) II.iii.64 ff.

2. Sad songs.

3. *As You Like It* (1599–1600) II.v.1 ff.; this song provides a comment on the happy existence of the banished Duke and his followers in the Forest of Arden, where life is "more sweet / Than that of painted pomp."

And turn his merry note
Unto the sweet bird's throat,[4]
Come hither, come hither, come hither:
Here shall he see
No enemy
But winter and rough weather.

Who doth ambition shun
And loves to live i' the sun,
Seeking the food he eats,
And pleased with what he gets,
Come hither, come hither, come hither:
Here shall he see
No enemy
But winter and rough weather.

Blow, Blow, Thou Winter Wind[5]

Blow, blow, thou winter wind,
Thou art not so unkind
As man's ingratitude;
Thy tooth is not so keen,
Because thou art not seen,
Although thy breath be rude.
Heigh-ho! sing, heigh-ho! unto the green holly:
Most friendship is feigning, most loving mere folly:
Then, heigh-ho, the holly!
This life is most jolly.

Freeze, freeze, thou bitter sky,
That dost not bite so nigh
As benefits forgot:
Though thou the waters warp,[6]
Thy sting is not so sharp
As friend remembered not.
Heigh-ho! sing, etc.

Oh Mistress Mine[7]

Oh mistress mine! where are you roaming?
Oh! stay and hear; your true love's coming,
That can sing both high and low.
Trip no further, pretty sweeting;
Journeys end in lovers meeting,
Every wise man's son doth know.

What is love? 'tis not hereafter;
Present mirth hath present laughter;
What's to come is still unsure:

4. I.e., improvise his song in harmony with the bird's.
5. Also from *As You Like It* II.vii. 174 ff. The contrast here between nature and man's willful behavior is one of the continuing themes of the play.
6. I.e., roughen by freezing.
7. *Twelfth Night* (1601–2) II.iii.40 ff.

In delay there lies no plenty;
Then come kiss me, sweet and twenty,
Youth's a stuff will not endure.

Take, Oh, Take Those Lips Away[8]

Take, Oh, take those lips away,
That so sweetly were forsworn;
And those eyes, the break of day, -
Lights that do mislead the morn:
But my kisses bring again, bring again;
Seals of love, but sealed in vain, sealed in vain.

Fear No More the Heat o' the Sun[9]

Fear no more the heat o' the sun,
Nor the furious winter's rages;
Thou thy worldly task hast done,
Home art gone, and ta'en thy wages:
Golden lads and girls all must,
As [1] chimney-sweepers, come to dust.

Fear no more the frown o' the great;
Thou art past the tyrant's stroke;
Care no more to clothe and eat;
To thee the reed is as the oak:
The scepter, learning, physic, must
All follow this, and come to dust.

Fear no more the lightning flash,
Nor the all-dreaded thunder stone;[2]
Fear not slander, censure rash;
Thou hast finished joy and moan:
All lovers young, all lovers must
Consign to thee, and come to dust.

No exorciser harm thee!
Nor no witchcraft charm thee!
Ghost unlaid forbear thee!
Nothing ill come near thee!
Quiet consummation have;
And renownéd be thy grave!

When Daffodils Begin to Peer[3]

When daffodils begin to peer,
With heigh! the doxy[4] over the dale,

8. *Measure for Measure* (1604) IV.i. 1 ff.; Mariana's desolation at being jilted by her lover Angelo is poignantly conveyed in this song, which is sung at her first entrance.
9. A lament for the supposedly dead Imogen, sung in *Cymbeline* IV.ii.258 ff.
1. Like.
2. The sound of thunder was commonly thought to be caused by the falling of stones or meteorites.
3. *The Winter's Tale* (1610–11) IV. iii.1 ff. Autolycus, ballad-singer, peddler, and rogue, makes his entrance singing this song, which not only effectively establishes his character but also helps to move the play from the wintry mood of the earlier scenes to the spring mood of the later scenes.
4. Girl or mistress (thieves' slang).

Why, then comes in the sweet o' the year;
For the red blood reigns in the winter's pale.[5]

The white sheet bleaching on the hedge,[6]
With heigh! the sweet birds, Oh, how they sing!
Doth set my pugging[7] tooth on edge;
For a quart of ale is a dish for a king.

The lark, that tirra-lirra chants,
With heigh! with heigh! the thrush and the jay,
Are summer songs for me and my aunts,[8]
While we lie tumbling in the hay.

Full Fathom Five[9]

Full fathom five thy father lies;
Of his bones are coral made;
Those are pearls that were his eyes:
Nothing of him that doth fade,
But doth suffer a sea change
Into something rich and strange.
Sea nymphs hourly ring his knell:
Ding-dong.
Hark! now I hear them—Ding-dong, bell.

Where the Bee Sucks, There Suck I[10]

Where the bee sucks, there suck I:
In a cowslip's bell I lie;
There I couch when owls do cry.
On the bat's back I do fly
After summer merrily.
Merrily, merrily shall I live now
Under the blossom that hangs on the bough.

Sonnets

3

Look in thy glass, and tell the face thou viewest
Now is the time that face should form another,
Whose fresh repair if now thou not renewest,

5. A pun on (1) a territory over which one has jurisdiction (2) lacking in color.
6. Laundry, dried or bleached on hedges, was sometimes stolen by passing vagabonds like Autolycus.
7. Thieving.
8. Girls or mistresses.
9. *The Tempest* (1611–12) I.ii.396 ff. Ariel, the airy spirit of the enchanted isle, sings this song to Ferdinand, prince of Naples. Ferdinand wonders at it: "The ditty does remember my drowned father. / This is no mortal business, nor no sound/ That the earth owes [owns]."
10. Also from *The Tempest* V.i.88 ff.: Ariel is happily anticipating the freedom of his future life.

Thou dost beguile the world, unbless some mother.
For where is she so fair whose uneared[1] womb
Disdains the tillage of thy husbandry?
Or who is he so fond[2] will be the tomb
Of his self-love, to stop posterity?
Thou art thy mother's glass,[3] and she in thee
Calls back the lovely April of her prime;
So thou through windows of thine age shalt see,
Despite of wrinkles, this thy golden time.
But if thou live rememb'red not to be,
Die single, and thine image dies with thee.

1609

12

When I do count the clock that tells the time
And see the brave[4] day sunk in hideous night,
When I behold the violet past prime
And sable curls all silver'd o'er with white,
When lofty trees I see barren of leaves,
Which erst[5] from heat did canopy the herd,
And summer's green all girded up in sheaves
Borne on the bier with white and bristly beard—
Then of thy beauty do I question make
That thou among the wastes of time must go,
Since sweets and beauties do themselves forsake
And die as fast as they see others grow,
And nothing 'gainst Time's scythe can make defense
Save breed,[6] to brave him when he takes thee hence.

1609

15

When I consider every thing that grows
Holds[1] in perfection but a little moment;
That this huge stage presenteth naught but shows
Whereon the stars in secret influence comment;[2]
When I perceive that men as plants increase,
Cheeréd and checked[3] even by the selfsame sky,
Vaunt[4] in their youthful sap, at height decrease,
And wear their brave state out of memory;[5]
Then the conceit[6] of this inconstant stay
Sets you most rich in youth before my sight,
Where wasteful Time debateth[7] with Decay
To change your day of youth to sullied[8] night,

1. Unplowed.
2. Foolish.
3. Mirror.
4. Splendid.
5. Formerly.
6. Offspring; "to brave": to defy.

1. Remains.
2. The stars in an occult way affect human actions; "shows": (1) appearances (2) performances.
3. Encouraged and reproached or stopped.
4. Exult, display themselves.
5. Wear their showy splendor out and are forgotten.
6. Conception.
7. Discusses.
8. Soiled, blackened.

And all in war with Time for love of you,
As he takes from you, I ingraft[9] you new.

1609

18

Shall I compare thee to a summer's day?
Thou art more lovely and more temperate:
Rough winds do shake the darling buds of May,
And summer's lease hath all too short a date:
Sometime too hot the eye of heaven shines
And often is his gold complexion dimmed;
And every fair from fair sometimes declines,
By chance or nature's changing course untrimmed;[1]
But thy eternal summer shall not fade,
Nor lose possession of that fair thou ow'st;[2]
Nor shall death brag thou wander'st in his shade,
When in eternal lines to time thou grow'st:[3]
So long as men can breathe, or eyes can see,
So long lives this, and this gives life to thee.[4]

1609

29

When, in disgrace[1] with fortune and men's eyes,
I all alone beweep my outcast state,
And trouble deaf heaven with my bootless[2] cries,
And look upon myself, and curse my fate,
Wishing me like to one more rich in hope,
Featured like him, like him with friends possessed,
Desiring this man's art and that man's scope,
With what I most enjoy contented least;
Yet in these thoughts myself almost despising,
Haply I think on thee—and then my state,[3]
Like to the lark at break of day arising
From sullen earth, sings hymns at heaven's gate;
For thy sweet love rememb'red such wealth brings
That then I scorn to change my state with kings.[4]

1609

30

When to the sessions[5] of sweet silent thought
I summon up remembrance of things past,
I sigh the lack of many a thing I sought,
And with old woes new wail[6] my dear time's waste:

9. Renew by grafting, implant beauty again (by my verse).
1. Stripped of gay apparel.
2. Ownest.
3. When in [this] immortal poetry you become even with time.
4. The boast of immortality for one's verse was a Renaissance convention and goes back to the classics. It implies, not egotism on the part of the poet, but a faith in the permanence of poetry.

1. Out of favor.
2. Futile.
3. Condition, state of mind; but in line 14 there is a pun on "state" meaning chair of state, throne.
4. This sonnet and the next are companion pieces, one dealing with present troubles, the other with those past.
5. Sittings of court; "summon up" (line 2) continues the metaphor.
6. Bewail anew.

Then can I drown an eye, unused to flow,
For precious friends hid in death's dateless[7] night,
And weep afresh love's long since canceled woe,
And moan the expense [8] of many a vanished sight:
Then can I grieve at grievances foregone,[9]
And heavily from woe to woe tell o'er
The sad account of fore-bemoanéd moan,
Which I new pay as if not paid before.
But if the while I think on thee, dear friend,
All losses are restored and sorrows end.

1609

55

Not marble, nor the gilded monuments
Of princes, shall outlive this powerful rhyme;
But you shall shine more bright in these contents
Than unswept stone, besmeared with sluttish time.[1]
When wasteful war shall statues overturn,
And broils root out the work of masonry,
Nor Mars his[2] sword nor war's quick fire shall burn
The living record of your memory.
'Gainst death and all-oblivious enmity[3]
Shall you pace forth; your praise shall still find room
Even in the eyes of all posterity
That wear this world out to the ending doom.[4]
So, till the judgment that yourself arise,
You live in this, and dwell in lovers' eyes.

1609

60

Like as the waves make towards the pebbled shore,
So do our minutes hasten to their end;
Each changing place with that which goes before,
In sequent toil all forwards do contend.[1]
Nativity, once in the main[2] of light,
Crawls to maturity, wherewith being crowned,
Crooked eclipses 'gainst his glory fight,
And time that gave doth now his gift confound.
Time doth transfix the flourish [3] set on youth
And delves the parallels in beauty's brow,
Feeds on the rarities of nature's truth,
And nothing stands but for his scythe to mow.
And yet to times in hope[4] my verse shall stand,
Praising thy worth, despite his cruel hand.

1609

7. Endless.
8. Loss.
9. Old subjects for grief. "Tell": count.
1. I.e., than in a stone tomb or effigy which time wears away and covers with dust.
2. Mars's.
3. The enmity of oblivion, of being forgotten.
4. Judgment Day. The next line is paraphrased, "Until you rise from the dead on Judgment Day."
1. Toiling and following each other, the waves struggle to press forward.
2. Broad expanse.
3. Remove the embellishment. "Delves the parallels": digs the parallel furrows (wrinkles). To "flourish" is also to blossom.
4. Future times.

71

No longer mourn for me when I am dead
Than you shall hear the surly sullen bell[5]
Give warning to the world that I am fled
From this vile world, with vilest worms to dwell:
Nay, if you read this line, remember not
The hand that writ it; for I love you so,
That I in your sweet thoughts would be forgot,
If thinking on me then should make you woe.
Oh, if, I say, you look upon this verse
When I perhaps compounded am with clay,
Do not so much as my poor name rehearse,
But let your love even with my life decay;
Lest the wise world should look into your moan,
And mock you with me after I am gone.

1609

73

That time of year thou mayst in me behold
When yellow leaves, or none, or few, do hang
Upon those boughs which shake against the cold,
Bare ruined choirs, where late the sweet birds sang.
In me thou see'st the twilight of such day
As after sunset fadeth in the west;
Which by and by black night doth take away,
Death's second self that seals up all in rest.
In me thou see'st the glowing of such fire,
That on the ashes of his youth doth lie,
As the deathbed whereon it must expire,
Consumed with that which it was nourished by.[6]
This thou perceiv'st, which makes thy love more strong,
To love that well which thou must leave ere long.

1609

74

But be contented; when that fell[7] arrest
Without all bail shall carry me away,
My life hath in this line[8] some interest,
Which for memorial still[9] with thee shall stay.
When thou reviewest this, thou dost review
The very part was[1] consecrate to thee.
The earth can have but earth, which is his due;
My spirit is thine, the better part of me.
So then thou hast but lost the dregs of life,
The prey of worms, my body being dead,
The coward conquest of a wretch's knife,[2]

5. The bell was tolled to announce the death of a member of the parish—one stroke for each year of his life.
6. Choked by the ashes of that which once nourished its flame.
7. Cruel. Hamlet says, "this fell sergeant Death is strict in his arrest" (V.ii.337–38).
8. I.e., poetry; "interest": share, participation.
9. Always.
1. I.e., which was.
2. Death's weapon (like Time's scythe).

Too base of thee to be rememberéd.
The worth of that is that which it contains.[3]
And that is this, and this with thee remains.

1609

87

Farewell: thou art too dear[4] for my possessing,
And like enough thou know'st thy estimate.[5]
The charter[6] of thy worth gives thee releasing;
My bonds in thee are all determinate.[7]
For how do I hold thee but by thy granting,
And for that riches where is my deserving?
The cause of this fair gift in me is wanting,
And so my patent [8] back again is swerving.
Thy self thou gav'st, thy own worth then not knowing,
Or me, to whom thou gav'st it, else mistaking;
So thy great gift, upon misprision[9] growing,
Comes home again, on better judgment making.
Thus have I had thee as a dream doth flatter,
In sleep a king, but waking no such matter.

1609

94

They that have power to hurt and will do none,
That do not do the thing they most do show,[1]
Who, moving others, are themselves as stone,
Unmovéd, cold, and to temptation slow;
They rightly do inherit heaven's graces
And husband nature's riches from expense; [2]
They are the lords and owners of their faces,
Others but stewards of their excellence.
The summer's flower is to the summer sweet,
Though to itself it only live and die,
But if that flower with base infection meet,
The basest weed outbraves [3] his dignity:
For sweetest things turn sourest by their deeds;
Lilies that fester smell far worse than weeds.[4]

1609

97

How like a winter hath my absence been
From thee, the pleasure of the fleeting year!
What freezings have I felt, what dark days seen!
What old December's bareness everywhere!
And yet this time removed was summer's time,
The teeming autumn big with rich increase,

3. I.e., the only value of the body is that it contains the spirit.
4. Expensive, beloved.
5. Value.
6. Deed, contract for property.
7. Expired.
8. Title.
9. Mistake, oversight.
1. Seem to do.
2. I.e., they do not squander nature's gifts.
3. Surpasses. Gerard's *Herbal* (1597) says "the lilies of the field outbraved him."
4. This line appears in *Edward III* (II. i.451), an apocryphal Shakespearean play licensed December 1, 1595.

Bearing the wanton burthen of the prime,[5]
Like widowed wombs after their lords' decease;
Yet this abundant issue seemed to me
But hope of orphans and unfathered fruit;
For summer and his pleasures wait on thee,
And, thou away, the very birds are mute;
Or, if they sing, 'tis with so dull a cheer[6]
That leaves look pale, dreading the winter's near.

1609

98

From you have I been absent in the spring,
When proud-pied[7] April, dressed in all his trim,
Hath put a spirit of youth in everything,
That heavy Saturn[8] laughed and leaped with him.
Yet nor the lays of birds, nor the sweet smell
Of different flowers in odor and in hue,
Could make me any summer's story tell,
Or from their proud lap pluck them where they grew;
Nor did I wonder at[9] the lily's white,
Nor praise the deep vermilion in the rose;
They were but sweet, but figures of delight,
Drawn after you, you pattern of all those.
Yet seemed it winter still, and, you away,
As with your shadow I with these did play.

1609

106

When in the chronicle of wasted[1] time
I see descriptions of the fairest wights,[2]
And beauty making beautiful old rhyme
In praise of ladies dead and lovely knights,
Then, in the blazon[3] of sweet beauty's best,
Of hand, of foot, of lip, of eye, of brow,
I see their antique pen would have expressed
Even such a beauty as you master now.
So all their praises are but prophecies
Of this our time, all you prefiguring;
And, for they looked but with divining eyes,[4]
They had not skill enough your worth to sing:
For we, which now behold these present days,
Have eyes to wonder, but lack tongues to praise.

1609

107

Not mine own fears, nor the prophetic soul
Of the wide world dreaming on things to come,[5]

5. Spring, which has engendered the lavish crop ("wanton burthen") that autumn is now left to bear.
6. Disposition.
7. Magnificent in many colors.
8. God of melancholy.
9. Admire.
1. Past.
2. Persons.
3. Display.
4. Because ("for") they were able *only* ("but") to foresee prophetically.
5. This sonnet refers to contemporary events and the prophecies, common in Elizabethan almanacs, of disaster.

Can yet the lease of my true love control,
Supposed as forfeit to a confinéd doom.[6]
The mortal moon hath her eclipse endured,
And the sad augurs mock their own presage;[7]
Incertainties now crown themselves assured,
And peace[8] proclaims olives of endless age.
Now with the drops of this most balmy time
My love looks fresh, and death to me subscribes,[9]
Since, spite of him, I'll live in this poor rhyme,
While he insults o'er dull and speechless tribes:
And thou in this shalt find thy monument,
When tyrants' crests and tombs of brass are spent.[1]

1609

116

Let me not to the marriage of true minds
Admit impediments.[2] Love is not love
Which alters when it alteration finds,
Or bends with the remover to remove:
Oh, no! it is an ever-fixéd mark,[3]
That looks on tempests and is never shaken;
It is the star to every wandering bark,
Whose worth's unknown, although his height[4] be taken.
Love's not Time's fool,[5] though rosy lips and cheeks
Within his[6] bending sickle's compass come;
Love alters not with his brief hours and weeks,
But bears it out even to the edge of doom.[7]
If this be error and upon me proved,
I never writ, nor no man ever loved.

1609

124

If my dear love were but the child of state,[1]
It might for Fortune's bastard be unfathered,[2]
As subject to Time's love, or to Time's hate:
Weeds among weeds, or flowers with flowers gathered.[3]
No, it was builded far from accident;[4]
It suffers not in smiling pomp, nor falls

6. I.e., can yet put an end to my love, which I thought doomed to early forfeiture.
7. The "mortal moon" is Queen Elizabeth; her "eclipse" is probably her climacteric year, her 63rd (thought significant because the product of two "significant" numbers, 7 and 9), which ended in September, 1596. The sober astrologers ("sad augurs") now ridicule their own predictions ("presage") of catastrophe, since they turned out to be false.
8. Probably an agreement between Henry IV of France and Elizabeth.
9. Submits.
1. Wasted away.
2. From the Marriage Service: "If any of you know cause or just impediment why these persons should not be joined together * * *"
3. Sea-mark (cf. "landmark").
4. The star's value is not known, though the star's "height" (altitude) may be known and used for practical investigation.
5. I.e., slave or victim.
6. I.e., Time's (as also in line 11).
7. Brink of the Last Judgment.
1. I.e., if my intense love were based merely upon (1) circumstance (2) high rank.
2. I.e., have no parent but Fortune (hence be subject to chance and time).
3. I.e., worthless or precious as chance dictates.
4. I.e., far away from chance events.

Under the blow of thrallèd discontent
Whereto th' inviting time our fashion calls;[5]
It fears not Policy,[6] that heretic,
Which works on leases of short-numb'red hours,
But all alone stands hugely politic,[7]
That it nor grows with heat nor drowns with show'rs.[8]
To this I witness call the fools of Time,[9]
Which die for goodness who have lived for crime.[1]

1609

128

How oft when thou, my music, music play'st
Upon that blessèd wood[2] whose motion sounds
With thy sweet fingers when thou gently sway'st[3]
The wiry concord that mine ear confounds,[4]
Do I envy those jacks[5] that nimble leap
To kiss the tender inward of thy hand,
Whilst my poor lips, which should that harvest reap,
At the wood's boldness by thee blushing stand.
To be so tickled they would change their state
And situation[6] with those dancing chips,
O'er whom thy fingers walk with gentle gait,
Making dead wood more blessed than living lips.
Since saucy jacks[7] so happy are in this,
Give them thy fingers, me thy lips to kiss.

1609

129

Th' expense of spirit in a waste of shame
Is lust in action;[1] and till action, lust
Is perjured, murderous, bloody, full of blame,
Savage, extreme, rude, cruel, not to trust;
Enjoyed no sooner but despisèd straight:
Past reason hunted; and no sooner had,
Past reason hated, as a swallowed bait,
On purpose laid to make the taker mad:
Mad in pursuit, and in possession so;
Had, having, and in quest to have, extreme;
A bliss in proof[2] and proved, a very woe;

5. I.e., the blows of fortune which make one a slave to grief, a melancholy mood now very much the fashion.
6. Expediency or material self-interest.
7. Spectacularly prudent.
8. I.e., so that it is not affected by changing climate. "Show'rs": downpours.
9. Victims or playthings of Time. Cf. Sonnet 116, line 9, and *1 Henry IV* V.v.81.
1. I.e., who are so inconstant that they undergo a deathbed conversion (calling them as witnesses is ironic).
2. Keys of the spinet or virginal.
3. Governest.
4. The harmony from the strings which overcomes my ear with delight.
5. I.e., keys (actually, "jacks" are the plectra which pluck the strings when activated by the keys).
6. Physical location; "state": place in the order of things.
7. With a quibble on the sense "impertinent fellows."
1. The word order here is inverted and slightly obscures the meaning. Lust, when put into action, expends "spirit" (life, vitality) in a "waste" (desert, with a possible pun on "waist," also) of shame.
2. A bliss during the experience.

Before, a joy proposed; behind, a dream.
All this the world well knows; yet none knows well
To shun the heaven that leads men to this hell.

1609

130

My mistress' eyes are nothing like the sun;[3]
Coral is far more red than her lips' red;
If snow be white, why then her breasts are dun;
If hairs be wires, black wires grow on her head.
I have seen roses damasked,[4] red and white,
But no such roses see I in her cheeks;
And in some perfumes is there more delight
Than in the breath that from my mistress reeks.
I love to hear her speak, yet well I know
That music hath a far more pleasing sound;
I grant I never saw a goddess go;[5]
My mistress, when she walks, treads on the ground.
And yet, by heaven, I think my love as rare[6]
As any she belied[7] with false compare.

1609

135

Whoever hath her wish, thou hast thy Will,[1]
And Will to boot, and Will in overplus;
More than enough am I that vex thee still,
To thy sweet will making addition thus.
Wilt thou, whose will is large and spacious,
Not once vouchsafe to hide my will in thine?
Shall will in others seem right gracious,
And in my will no fair acceptance shine?
The sea, all water, yet receives rain still,
And in abundance addeth to his store,[2]
So thou being rich in Will add to thy Will
One will of mine to make thy large Will more.
Let no unkind, no fair beseechers kill;[3]
Think all but one, and me in that one Will.

1609

138

When my love swears that she is made of truth,
I do believe her, though I know she lies,
That she might think me some untutored youth,
Unlearned in the world's false subtleties.
Thus vainly thinking that she thinks me young,

3. An anti-Petrarchan sonnet. All of the details commonly attributed by other Elizabethan sonneteers to their ladies are here denied to the poet's mistress.
4. Variegated. The damask rose (supposedly from Damascus, originally) is pink.
5. Walk.
6. Admirable, extraordinary.
7. Misrepresented.

1. (1) wishes (2) carnal desire (3) the male and female sexual organs (4) one or more persons named Will. This is one of three, possibly four, sonnets punning on the word.
2. Plenty.
3. I.e., do not kill with unkindness any of your wooers.

Although she knows my days are past the best,[1]
Simply I credit her false-speaking tongue:
On both sides thus is simple truth suppressed.
But wherefore says she not she is unjust?[2]
And wherefore say not I that I am old?
Oh, love's best habit[3] is in seeming trust,
And age in love loves not to have years told.
Therefore I lie with her and she with me,
And in our faults by lies we flattered be.

1599

144

Two loves I have of comfort and despair,
Which like two spirits do suggest me still:[1]
The better angel is a man right fair,
The worser spirit a woman, colored ill.[2]
To win me soon to hell, my female evil
Tempteth my better angel from my side,
And would corrupt my saint to be a devil,
Wooing his purity with her foul pride.
And whether that my angel be turned fiend
Suspect I may, yet not directly tell;
But being both from[3] me, both to each friend,
I guess one angel in another's hell.
Yet this shall I ne'er know, but live in doubt,
Till my bad angel fire[4] my good one out.

1599

146

Poor soul, the center of my sinful earth,
Lord of[5] these rebel powers that thee array,[6]
Why dost thou pine within and suffer dearth,
Painting thy outward walls so costly gay?
Why so large cost, having so short a lease,
Dost thou upon thy fading mansion spend?
Shall worms, inheritors of this excess,
Eat up thy charge? Is this thy body's end?
Then, soul, live thou upon thy servant's loss,
And let that pine to aggravate thy store;[7]
Buy terms[8] divine in selling hours of dross;

. Shakespeare was 35 or younger when he wrote this sonnet (it first appeared in *The Passionate Pilgrim,* 1599). "Simply": like a simpleton.
2. Unfaithful.
3. Appearance, deportment.
1. Tempt me constantly.
2. Dark.
3. Away from; "each": each other.
4. Drive out by fire.
5. An emendation. The Quarto repeats the last three words of line 1. Other suggestions are "Thrall to," "Starv'd by," "Press'd by," and leaving the repetition but dropping "that thee" in line 2
6. Dress out, often used in a military sense.
7. Let "that" (i.e., the body) deteriorate to increase ("aggravate") the soul's riches ("thy store").
8. Long periods; "dross": refuse, rubbish.

Within be fed, without be rich no more.
So shalt thou feed on death, that feeds on men,
And death once dead, there's no more dying then.

1609

147

My love is as a fever, longing still[1]
For that which longer nurseth[2] the disease,
Feeding on that which doth preserve the ill,[3]
Th' uncertain sickly appetite[4] to please.
My reason, the physician to my love,
Angry that his prescriptions are not kept,
Hath left me, and I desperate now approve
Desire is death, which physic did except.[5]
Past cure I am, now reason is past care,[6]
And frantic mad with evermore unrest;
My thoughts and my discourse as madmen's are,
At random from the truth vainly expressed;[7]
For I have sworn thee fair, and thought thee bright,
Who art as black as hell, as dark as night.

1609

The Phoenix and the Turtle[1]

Let the bird of loudest lay,[2]
On the sole Arabian tree,
Herald sad and trumpet be,
To whose sound chaste wings obey.

But thou shrieking harbinger,
Foul precurrer of the fiend,[3]

1. Continually.
2. (1) Nourishes (2) takes care of.
3. Maintain the illness.
4. (1) Desire for food (2) lust.
5. I.e., learn by experience, that desire, which medicine forbade, is death.
6. I.e., medical care (of me). The line is a version of the proverb "past cure, past care."
7. Wide of the mark and senselessly uttered.

1. First published in Robert Chester's *Love's Martyr, or Rosalin's Complaint* (1601). It is part of an appendix containing "divers poetical essays" by other poets, all supposedly dealing with the same subject. This subject has something to do with a Welsh knight, Sir John Salusbury, and his lady. But Shakespeare's poem is not consistent with the other poems in the volume, for some of them celebrate the birth of offspring to the phoenix and the turtle, whereas Shakespeare says the birds died leaving no posterity. The phoenix is a legendary bird of Arabia: it perishes in flames and a new one arises from the ashes; only one is alive at a time. Queen Elizabeth, the Virgin Queen, was sometimes symbolized by the unique and virginal phoenix. The "turtle" (turtledove) is common in Elizabethan imagery as the most loving of birds. Bird poems were traditionally allegorical, from Chaucer's time on down, but the key to this allegory (if it is one) has been lost.
2. Cry or song. This stanza might be paraphrased, "Let the bird with the loudest voice proclaim from the perch of the phoenix ('Arabian tree'); all gentle birds ('chaste wings') will respond to the summons."
3. Forerunner of the devil. "Harbinger": precursor. The screech owl is probably meant.

Augur of the fever's end,
To this troop come thou not near!

From this session interdict
Every fowl of tyrant wing,
Save the eagle, feathered king:
Keep the obsequy so strict.

Let the priest in surplice white,
That defunctive music can,[4]
Be the death-divining swan,
Lest the requiem lack his right.

And thou treble-dated[5] crow,
That thy sable gender mak'st
With the breath thou giv'st and tak'st,[6]
'Mongst our mourners shalt thou go.

Here the anthem doth commence:
Love and constancy is dead,
Phoenix and the turtle fled
In a mutual flame from hence.

So they loved as love in twain
Had the essence but in one;[7]
Two distincts, division none:
Number there in love was slain.

Hearts remote, yet not asunder;
Distance, and no space was seen
'Twixt this turtle and his queen;
But in them[8] it were a wonder.

So between them love did shine
That the turtle saw his right[9]
Flaming in the phoenix' sight:
Either was the other's mine.[1]

Property[2] was thus appalled,
That the self was not the same;
Single nature's double name
Neither two nor one was called.

4. I.e., skilled in funeral ("defunctive") music. The swan was supposed to sing only once, just before its death.
5. Living three lifetimes.
6. "Sable gender": black offspring. The crow was supposed to conceive and lay its eggs through the bill.
7. They were originally two, but by love were united into one. Since one is singular, and not a number, "Number there in love was slain."
8. In any other case than theirs.
9. What was due him, love returned.
1. Rich source of wealth or treasure.
2. Peculiar or essential quality. "Property" is "appalled" to find that personality ("self") is obliterated in the union of the two. Accordingly it is impossible to say whether they were two or one.

Reason, in itself confounded,
Saw division grow together,[3]
To themselves yet either neither,
Simple were so well compounded;

That it cried, "How true a twain
Seemeth this concordant one!
Love hath reason, reason none,
If what parts can so remain."[4]

Whereupon it made this threne[5]
To the phoenix and the dove,
Co-supremes and stars of love,
As chorus to their tragic scene.

Threnos

Beauty, truth, and rarity,
Grace in all simplicity,
Here enclosed in cinders lie.

Death is now the phoenix' nest;
And the turtle's loyal breast
To eternity doth rest,

Leaving no posterity:
'Twas not their infirmity,
It was married chastity.

Truth may seem, but cannot be;
Beauty brag, but 'tis not she:[6]
Truth and Beauty buried be.

To this urn let those repair
That are either true or fair;
For these dead birds sigh a prayer.

1601

3. Reason, which discriminates parts of a thing, is here confounded because the two parts are merged. Each element lost its identity in being fused with the other.
4. Love is more reasonable than reason, because it has proved that the separateness of entities (one of reason's laws) does not always hold true.
5. Threnody, funeral song.
6. Whatever may appear hereafter as truth or beauty will be only illusion. Real truth and beauty lie buried here.

1 Henry IV

The title page of the first quarto edition of Shakespeare's 1 *Henry IV*, published in 1598, reads:"THE HISTORY OF HENRIE THE FOURTH; With the the battell at Shrewsburie, *betweene the King and Lord* Henry Percy, surnamed Henrie Hotspur of the North. *With the humorous conceits of Sir* John Falstalffe." It had been performed on the stage and at court before publication, and from that time to this it has remained one of Shakespeare's most popular plays.

Shakespeare had already inaugurated a new dramatic type by writing four plays dealing with fairly recent English history, and had then gone back to a period two centuries earlier to portray, in *Richard II*, the downfall of the weak, effeminate and poetic young King Richard ("that sweet lovely rose," as he is called in this play) at the hands of the hard, efficient Bolingbroke, who came to the throne as Henry IV. Before this seizure of the crown there had been a prophecy, put by Shakespeare into the mouth of the Bishop of Carlisle in *Richard II* (IV.i.136–44), of the dire consequences to follow:

> And if you crown him, let me prophesy,
> The blood of English shall manure the ground
> And future ages groan for this foul act;
> Peace shall go sleep with Turks and infidels,
> And in this seat of peace tumultuous wars
> Shall kin with kin and kind with kind confound;
> Disorder, horror, fear, and mutiny
> Shall here inhabit, and this land be called
> The field of Golgotha and dead men's skulls.

Shakespeare drew his historical material from the prose chronicle histories, specifically Raphael Holinshed's *Chronicles of England, Scotland, and Ireland*, Samuel Daniel's historical poem *Civil Wars*, and an earlier play, either the popular farcical piece called *The Famous Victories of Henry V* or a lost play which was its source. His sources gave him the portrait of a madcap and reckless Prince of Wales and his roistering companions. Chief of these was a fat knight, Sir John Oldcastle; Shakespeare at first used this name, but later, because of protests from the descendants of that Protestant martyr, changed the name to Sir John Falstaff. This character, whose "humorous conceits" are advertised on the title page, is one of the greatest comic creations in all literature. Shakespeare continued to exploit his inexhaustible exuberance through a sequel, *The Second Part of Henry IV*, and a comedy of middle-class life, supposed to have been written at Queen Elizabeth's command, *The Merry Wives of Windsor*.

The ominous wars of Carlisle's prophecy could thus be mixed with hilarious fooling, but *1 Henry IV* succeeds, not only as a comedy, but as a serious play about character and history. The real hero is not King Henry IV, nor the fat Falstaff, but Prince Hal, the handsome playboy who in time of crisis reforms and saves his father's throne. He is the prince who later became Henry V, the English national hero who reconquered France.

Shakespeare's theme in all his history plays is the importance of order and degree, of the disruptive effects of civil strife and rebellion. But as he matured as a dramatist (and *1 Henry IV* stands at the beginning of his great period of maturity), he found character to be more interesting than the philosophy or events of history. How to demonstrate the kind of character that would make the English national hero was his problem, and he solved it by a method of comparison and contrast, utilizing four men of different types. At one extreme is Falstaff, who loves to eat, drink, joke, and dramatize himself, and to whom anything as intangible as honor is a mere word, a breath of air. Opposite in every way is Hotspur, fiery and impatient, completely ambitious for honor and fame, scornful of the soft, civilized arts of poetry and music, a hardheaded fanatic. A third type is the wild Welshman Glendower, a believer in magic and a practitioner of it, an accomplished poet yet a valiant, if superstitious, warrior, and an egotist like his ally Hotspur. Finally there is Prince Hal, whose sense of humor rivals Falstaff's, but who turns out to be the match for Hotspur in valor and his superior in knightly courtesy. It is worth noting that Shakespeare changed history in order to make this dramatic contrast: in Holinshed's *Chronicle* Hotspur is older than Prince Hal's father, but Shakespeare makes them contemporaries. It is in the excesses of the other three that we see the merits of the Prince's character illuminated. The four characters represent not only men but ways of life. And these ways of life are all relevant to fundamental questions about social and political responsibility, honor, and loyalty to a cause.

Some background in 15th-century English history, as Shakespeare understood it, is needed if we are to respond readily to the play. Henry Hereford, called Bolingbroke, was in exile in France when his father, John of Gaunt, died. He returned to England to claim his inheritance, and profited from the aid of the Percy family, powerful nobles in the north. The two brothers, Henry Percy, Earl of Northumberland, and Thomas Percy, Earl of Worcester, together with Northumberland's son Henry (called Hotspur) received Bolingbroke's oath at Doncaster (see V.i.32–58) to seize only his inheritance. But King Richard II was in Ireland fighting, having named Edmund Mortimer, Earl of March, his successor if he did not return. In the confused situation in England, Bolingbroke was able to collect enough power so that on Richard's return he could force him to abdicate and then have him killed in prison. Various troubles on the borders made the throne of the new king (Henry IV) insecure. Hotspur managed to defeat the Scots under Douglas at Holmedon (see I.i.62–75) and took many important prisoners. But Mortimer, in fighting against Glendower in Wales, was taken captive and married Glendower's daughter. Henry IV refused to ransom Mortimer, and the indignation of Mortimer's brother-in-law, Hotspur, led him to refuse to turn over his prisoners to the king. So came the conspiracy into being—and such a formidable opposition as that of the Percies, Douglas, Glendower, and certain disaffected churchmen like the Archbishop of York meant a critical danger to Henry's throne. The Battle of Shrewsbury, the climax of this play, decides the conflict.

Much critical comment has been devoted to the character of Falstaff. He has certain resemblances to the traditional *miles gloriosus* (braggart soldier) of Latin comedy, but he far transcends the type; he sometimes resembles the Vice, a comic character in the old morality plays, who is usually an allegorical personification of extreme self-indulgence or of a particular sin; and he often uses, or parodies, the language of the Puritans. Critics differ on whether Falstaff is really a coward or not, and on the question of how much he expects his lies to be believed. But everyone agrees about his inexhaustible vitality and resiliency. It is not surprising that he, like other immortal characters in literature, remains something of a mystery.

The First Part of King Henry the Fourth

Dramatis Personae

KING HENRY THE FOURTH
HENRY, *Prince of Wales* } *Sons to the* KING
PRINCE JOHN OF LANCASTER } *Sons to the* KING
EARL OF WESTMORELAND
SIR WALTER BLUNT
THOMAS PERCY, *Earl of Worcester*
HENRY PERCY, *Earl of Northumberland*
HENRY PERCY, *surnamed* HOTSPUR, *his son*
EDMUND MORTIMER, *Earl of March*
RICHARD SCROOP, *Archbishop of York*
ARCHIBALD, *Earl of Douglas*
OWEN GLENDOWER
SIR RICHARD VERNON
SIR MICHAEL, *a friend to the* ARCHBISHOP OF YORK
SIR JOHN FALSTAFF
POINS
GADSHILL
PETO
BARDOLPH
LADY PERCY, *wife to* HOTSPUR, *and sister to* MORTIMER
LADY MORTIMER, *daughter to* GLENDOWER, *and wife to* MORTIMER
MISTRESS QUICKLY, *hostess of a tavern in Eastcheap*
LORDS, OFFICERS, SHERIFF, VINTNER, CHAMBERLAIN, DRAWERS, *two* CARRIERS, TRAVELERS, *and* ATTENDANTS

Act I

SCENE 1

[*Enter the* KING, PRINCE JOHN OF LANCASTER, THE EARL OF WESTMORELAND, SIR WALTER BLUNT, *with others.*]

KING. So shaken as we are, so wan with care,
Find we a time for frighted peace to pant,[1]
And breathe short-winded accents of new broils[2]
To be commenced in stronds afar remote.
No more the thirsty entrance[3] of this soil
Shall daub her lips with her own children's blood;
No more shall trenching war channel her fields,
Nor bruise her flowerets with the armèd hoofs
Of hostile paces:[4] those opposèd eyes,
Which, like the meteors of a troubled heaven,
All of one nature, of one substance bred,
Did lately meet in the intestine shock[5]
And furious close of civil butchery,
Shall now, in mutual well-beseeming ranks,

1. I.e., let us allow peace to catch her breath.
2. I.e., news of new wars; "stronds": strands, regions.
3. Surface.
4. The tread of war horses.
5. Internal violence; "close": encounter.

March all one way and be no more opposed
Against acquaintance, kindred, and allies.
The edge of war, like an ill-sheathéd knife,
No more shall cut his master: therefore, friends,
As far as to the sepulcher of Christ,
Whose soldier now, under whose blessed cross
We are impresséd and engaged to fight,
Forthwith a power[6] of English shall we levy,
Whose arms were molded in their mother's womb
To chase these pagans in those holy fields
Over whose acres walked those blessed feet
Which fourteen hundred years ago were nailed
For our advantage on the bitter cross.
But this our purpose now is twelve month old,
And bootless[7] 'tis to tell you we will go.
Therefore we meet not now:[8] then let me hear
Of you, my gentle cousin Westmoreland,
What yesternight our council did decree
In forwarding this dear expedience.[9]

WEST. My liege, this haste was hot in questión,[1]
And many limits of the charge set down
But yesternight, when all athwart[2] there came
A post from Wales loaden with heavy news,
Whose worst was that the noble Mortimer,
Leading the men of Herefordshire to fight
Against the irregular[3] and wild Glendower,
Was by the rude hands of that Welshman taken,
A thousand of his people butcheréd,
Upon whose dead corpse[4] there was such misuse,
Such beastly shameless transformatión,
By those Welshwomen done as may not be
Without much shame retold or spoken of.

KING. It seems then that the tidings of this broil
Brake off our business for the Holy Land.

WEST. This matched with other did, my gracious lord,
For more uneven and unwelcome news
Came from the north, and thus it did import:
On Holyrood Day[5] the gallant Hotspur there,
Young Harry Percy, and brave Archibald,
That ever-valiant and approvéd Scot,
At Holmedon met,
Where they did spend a sad and bloody hour;
As by discharge of their artillery,
And shape of likelihood,[6] the news was told;
For he that brought them[7] in the very heat

6. Army. He is planning a crusade, in expiation of his guilt for the death of Richard II.
7. Useless.
8. I.e., that is not the reason for our present meeting. "Cousin": kinsman.
9. Important, urgent matter.
1. Actively discussed. "Limits of the charge": assignment of commands.
2. Interrupting, crossing our purpose. "Post": messenger.
3. Guerilla.
4. Bodies.
5. Holy Cross Day (Sept. 14).
6. Probable inference. "As": since.
7. I.e., the news (usually a plural in Shakespeare). "Pride": height; literally, the top of a falcon's flight.

And pride of their contention did take horse,
Uncertain of the issue any way.

KING. Here is a dear, a true industrious friend,
Sir Walter Blunt, new lighted from his horse,
Stained with the variation of each soil
Betwixt that Holmedon and this seat of ours;
And he hath brought us smooth and welcome news.
The Earl of Douglas is discomfited;
Ten thousand bold Scots, two and twenty knights
Balked[8] in their own blood did Sir Walter see
On Holmedon's plains. Of prisoners Hotspur took
Mordake Earl of Fife, and eldest son
To beaten Douglas, and the Earl of Athol,
Of Murray, Angus, and Menteith;
And is not this an honorable spoil,
A gallant prize? ha, cousin, is it not?

WEST. In faith,
It is a conquest for a prince to boast of.

KING. Yea, there thou mak'st me sad and mak'st me sin
In envy that my Lord Northumberland
Should be the father to so blest a son,
A son who is the theme of honor's tongue,
Amongst a grove the very straightest plant,
Who is sweet Fortune's minion[9] and her pride;
Whilst I, by looking on the praise of him,
See riot and dishonor stain the brow
Of my young Harry. O that it could be proved
That some night-tripping fairy had exchanged
In cradle-clothes our children where they lay,
And called mine Percy, his Plantagenet!
Then would I have his Harry, and he mine.
But let him from my thoughts. What think you, coz,
Of this young Percy's pride? The prisoners
Which he in this adventure hath surprised
To his own use he keeps, and sends me word
I shall have none but Mordake Earl of Fife.

WEST. This is his uncle's teaching, this is Worcester,
Malevolent to you in all aspects,[1]
Which makes him prune himself,[2] and bristle up
The crest of youth against your dignity.

KING. But I have sent for him to answer this;
And for this cause awhile we must neglect
Our holy purpose to Jerusalem.
Cousin, on Wednesday next our council we
Will hold at Windsor, so inform the lords;
But come yourself with speed to us again,
For more is to be said and to be done
Than out of anger can be uttered.

WEST. I will, my liege. [*Exeunt.*]

8. Heaped.
9. Favorite.
1. Hostile in every way. The figure is from astrology.
2. Plume himself. "Bristle up" and "crest" continue the image, which is that of a fighting cock.

SCENE 2

[*Enter* HENRY, PRINCE OF WALES, *and* SIR JOHN FALSTAFF.]

FAL. Now Hal, what time of day is it, lad?

PRINCE. Thou art so fat-witted with drinking of old sack,[3] and unbuttoning thee after supper, and sleeping upon benches after noon, that thou hast forgotten to demand that truly which thou wouldst truly know. What a devil hast thou to do with the time of the day? Unless hours were cups of sack, and minutes capons, and clocks the tongues of bawds, and dials the signs of leaping-houses,[4] and the blessed sun himself a fair hot wench in flame-colored taffeta, I see no reason why thou shouldst be so superfluous to demand the time of the day.

FAL. Indeed you come near me now, Hal, for we that take purses go by the moon and the seven stars, and not by Phoebus,[5] he, "that wandering knight so fair." And I prithee, sweet wag, when thou art king, as, God save thy grace—majesty I should say, for grace[6] thou wilt have none—

PRINCE. What, none?

FAL. No, by my troth, not so much as will serve to be prologue to an egg and butter.

PRINCE. Well, how then? come, roundly, roundly.[7]

FAL. Marry then, sweet wag, when thou art king, let not us that are squires of the night's body[8] be called thieves of the day's beauty; let us be Diana's foresters, gentlemen of the shade, minions of the moon; and let men say we be men of good government, being governed as the sea is, by our noble and chaste mistress the moon, under whose countenance we steal.

PRINCE. Thou sayest well, and it holds well too, for the fortune of us that are the moon's men doth ebb and flow like the sea, being governed as the sea is by the moon. As for proof now: a purse of gold most resolutely snatched on Monday night and most dissolutely spent on Tuesday morning, got with swearing "Lay by" and spent with crying "Bring in," now in as low an ebb as the foot of the ladder and by and by in as high a flow as the ridge of the gallows.[9]

FAL. By the Lord thou sayest true, lad. And is not my hostess of the tavern a most sweet wench?

PRINCE. As the honey of Hybla,[1] my old lad of the castle. And is not a buff jerkin a most sweet robe of durance?[2]

3. Sherry.
4. Whorehouses.
5. The sun. Falstaff then quotes from a popular ballad.
6. A triple pun: (1) "your Grace," the correct manner of addressing a prince or duke; (2) the divine influence which produces sanctity; and (3) a short prayer before a meal—hence Falstaff's allusion to "egg and butter," a common hasty breakfast.
7. Plainly.
8. Two puns are involved: a "squire of the body" was an attendant on a knight, and "body" would be pronounced *bawdy*. "Beauty" also puns with "booty" (which thieves take); Diana is, of course, the moon goddess.
9. "Lay by": i.e., hand over (a robber's command to his victim); "bring in": a customer's command for more drink at a tavern. The "foot of the ladder" is at the bottom of the gallows (robbery was a hanging offense); the "ridge" is the crosspiece at the top.
1. A town in Sicily, famous for honey; "old lad of the castle" is a reference to Falstaff's original name, Oldcastle.
2. A "buff jerkin" was the leather jacket worn by a sheriff's sergeant; "durance" is a pun: (1) lasting quality and (2) imprisonment.

FAL. How now, how now, mad wag! what, in thy quips and thy quiddities?[3] what a plague have I to do with a buff jerkin?

PRINCE. Why, what a pox have I to do with my hostess of the tavern?

FAL. Well, thou hast called her to a reckoning many a time and oft.

PRINCE. Did I ever call for thee to pay thy part?

FAL. No, I'll give thee thy due, thou hast paid all there.

PRINCE. Yea, and elsewhere, so far as my coin would stretch, and where it would not I have used my credit.

FAL. Yea, and so used it that were it not here apparent that thou art heir apparent[4]—but I prithee, sweet wag, shall there be gallows standing in England when thou art king? and resolution thus fobbed as it is with the rusty curb of old father antic the law?[5] Do not thou, when thou art king, hang a thief.

PRINCE. No, thou shalt.

FAL. Shall I? O rare! By the Lord, I'll be a brave judge.

PRINCE. Thou judgest false already; I mean thou shalt have the hanging of the thieves and so become a rare hangman.

FAL. Well, Hal, well; and in some sort it jumps with my humor[6] as well as waiting in the court, I can tell you.

PRINCE. For obtaining of suits?[7]

FAL. Yea, for obtaining of suits, whereof the hangman hath no lean wardrobe. 'Sblood,[8] I am as melancholy as a gib cat or a lugged bear.

PRINCE. Or an old lion, or a lover's lute.

FAL. Yea, or the drone of a Lincolnshire bagpipe.

PRINCE. What sayest thou to a hare, or the melancholy of Moorditch?[9]

FAL. Thou hast the most unsavory similes and art indeed the most comparative,[1] rascalliest, sweet young prince. But Hal, I prithee, trouble me no more with vanity. I would to God thou and I knew where a commodity of good names were to be bought. An old lord of the council rated[2] me the other day in the street about you, sir, but I marked him not; and yet he talked very wisely, but I regarded him not; and yet he talked wisely, and in the street too.

PRINCE. Thou didst well, for wisdom cries out in the streets and no man regards it.[3]

FAL. O, thou hast damnable iteration[4] and art indeed able to corrupt a saint. Thou hast done much harm upon me, Hal, God forgive thee for it! Before I knew thee, Hal, I knew noth-

3. Quibbles.
4. "Here" and "heir" would pun in Elizabethan pronunciation.
5. "Resolution": bravery; "fobbed": cheated; "antic": a clown.
6. I.e., agrees with my disposition.
7. Special favors, but "clothing" in the next line. The hangman was given the clothes of his victims.
8. God's blood, a common oath. "Gib cat": tomcat; "lugged": baited (in the bear-baiting pits a bear was attacked by dogs as a public amusement).
9. The "hare" was traditionally associated with melancholy; Moorditch was a foul-smelling ditch on the outskirts of London.
1. Affecting wit, dealing in comparisons.
2. Scolded, berated.
3. Prince Hal is quoting Proverbs i. 20 and 24.
4. Repetition, especially of sacred texts.

ing, and now am I, if a man should speak truly, little better than one of the wicked. I must give over this life, and I will give it over; by the Lord, an[5] I do not, I am a villain; I'll be damned for never a king's son in Christendom.

PRINCE. Where shall we take a purse tomorrow, Jack?

FAL. Zounds, where thou wilt, lad; I'll make one; an I do not, call me villain and baffle[6] me.

PRINCE. I see a good amendment of life in thee—from praying to purse-taking.

FAL. Why, Hal, 'tis my vocation,[7] Hal; 'tis no sin for a man to labor in his vocation.

[*Enter* POINS.]

Poins! Now shall we know if Gadshill[8] have set a match. O, if men were to be saved by merit, what hole in hell were hot enough for him? This is the most omnipotent villain that ever cried "stand" to a true man.

PRINCE. Good morrow, Ned.

POINS. Good morrow, sweet Hal. What says Monsieur Remorse? what says Sir John Sack and Sugar? Jack! how agrees the devil and thee about thy soul, that thou soldest him on Good Friday last for a cup of Madeira and a cold capon's leg?

PRINCE. Sir John stands to his word; the devil shall have his bargain, for he was never yet a breaker of proverbs; he will give the devil his due.

POINS. Then art thou damned for keeping thy word with the devil.

PRINCE. Else he had been damned for cozening[9] the devil.

POINS. But my lads, my lads, tomorrow morning by four o'clock, early at Gadshill, there are pilgrims going to Canterbury with rich offerings, and traders riding to London with fat purses. I have vizards[1] for you all, you have horses for yourselves; Gadshill lies tonight in Rochester; I have bespoke supper tomorrow night in Eastcheap; we may do it as secure as sleep. If you will go, I will stuff your purses full of crowns; if you will not, tarry at home and be hanged.

FAL. Hear ye, Yedward, if I tarry at home and go not, I'll hang you for going.

POINS. You will, chops?[2]

FAL. Hal, wilt thou make one?

PRINCE. Who, I rob? I a thief? not I, by my faith.

FAL. There's neither honesty, manhood, nor good fellowship in thee, nor thou camest not of the blood royal,[3] if thou darest

5. If.
6. A knight in the days of chivalry was "baffled" or disgraced by having his shield hung upside down. Falstaff may mean "hang me up by the heels." "Zounds": a common oath, a contraction of "by God's wounds" (i.e., Jesus' wounds on the Cross).
7. Falstaff is here making fun of the Puritan doctrine of "calling" or vocation, based on the parable of the talents (see Matthew xxv.25 ff.).
8. Gadshill is both a man and a place: the place is a hill 27 miles from London on the road to Rochester; it was notorious for robberies. The man, so called from the place, is the thieves' "setter," who arranges when and where the robbery will occur.
9. Cheating.
1. Masks.
2. Fat face.
3. A pun: the coin called a "royal" was worth ten shillings. "Stand for" also puns: it means both "represent" and "fight for."

not stand for ten shillings.

PRINCE. Well then, once in my days I'll be a madcap.

FAL. Why, that's well said.

PRINCE. Well, come what will, I'll tarry at home.

FAL. By the Lord, I'll be a traitor then, when thou art king.

PRINCE. I care not.

POINS. Sir John, I prithee leave the prince and me alone; I will lay him down such reasons for this adventure that he shall go.

FAL. Well, God give thee the spirit of persuasion and him the ears of profiting, that what thou speakest may move and what he hears may be believed, that the true prince may, for recreation sake, prove a false thief; for the poor abuses of the time want countenance.[4] Farewell; you shall find me in Eastcheap.

PRINCE. Farewell, thou latter spring, farewell, Allhallown summer![5]

[⟨*Exit* FALSTAFF.⟩][6]

POINS. Now, my good sweet honey lord, ride with us tomorrow; I have a jest to execute that I cannot manage alone. Falstaff, Bardolph, Peto, and Gadshill shall rob those men that we have already waylaid;[7] yourself and I will not be there, and when they have the booty, if you and I do not rob them, cut this head off from my shoulders.

PRINCE. How shall we part with them in setting forth?

POINS. Why, we will set forth before or after them, and appoint them a place of meeting, wherein it is at our pleasure to fail, and then will they adventure upon the exploit themselves, which they shall have no sooner achieved but we'll set upon them.

PRINCE. Yea, but 'tis like that they will know us by our horses, by our habits,[8] and by every other appointment to be ourselves.

POINS. Tut, our horses they shall not see—I'll tie them in the wood; our vizards we will change after we leave them: and, sirrah, I have cases of buckram for the nonce,[9] to immask our noted outward garments.

PRINCE. Yea, but I doubt they will be too hard for us.

POINS. Well, for two of them, I know them to be as true-bred cowards as ever turned back; and for the third, if he fight longer than he sees reason, I'll forswear arms. The virtue of this jest will be the incomprehensible lies that this same fat rogue will tell us when we meet at supper: how thirty at least he fought with; what wards,[10] what blows, what extremities he endured; and in the reproof[11] of this lies the jest.

4. A satirical reference to the common complaint that the nobility did not properly give "countenance" to (i.e., encourage) good causes, and to the Puritan habit of attacking the "abuses of the time." This entire speech parodies the language of the Puritans.

5. I.e., Indian summer. The two epithets are intended to suggest how unseasonable it is for Falstaff, an old man, to be engaged in youthful, hoodlum exploits.

6. This stage direction, like some others in the play, does not appear in the earliest editions; it was added by a later editor. All such interpolated directions are indicated in our text by the special brackets used here.

7. Set an ambush for.

8. Clothes.

9. I.e., outer clothes (of a coarse, stiff cloth) for the occasion.

10. Guards in fencing.

11. Disproof.

use of "yet"). "But": except. "straight": immediately.

PRINCE. Well, I'll go with thee. Provide us all things necessary and meet me tomorrow night[1] in Eastcheap; there I'll sup. Farewell.

POINS. Farewell, my lord. [*Exit* POINS.]

PRINCE. I know you all, and will awhile uphold
The unyoked humor[2] of your idleness;
Yet herein will I imitate the sun,
Who doth permit the base contagious clouds
To smother up his beauty from the world,
That, when he please again to be himself,
Being wanted, he may be more wondered at
By breaking through the foul and ugly mists
Of vapors that did seem to strangle him.
If all the year were playing holidays,
To sport would be as tedious as to work;
But when they seldom come, they wished for come,
And nothing pleaseth but rare accidents.
So, when this loose behavior I throw off
And pay the debt I never promiséd,
By how much better than my word I am,
By so much shall I falsify men's hopes,
And like bright metal on a sullen ground,[3]
My reformation, glittering o'er my fault,
Shall show more goodly and attract more eyes
Than that which hath no foil[4] to set it off.
I'll so offend to make offense a skill,[5]
Redeeming time when men think least I will. [*Exit.*]

SCENE 3

[*Enter the* KING, NORTHUMBERLAND, WORCESTER, HOTSPUR, SIR WALTER BLUNT, *with others.*]

KING. My blood hath been too cold and temperate,
Unapt to stir at these indignities,
And you have found me,[6] for accordingly
You tread upon my patience; but be sure
I will from henceforth rather be myself,
Mighty and to be feared, than my condition,[7]
Which hath been smooth as oil, soft as young down,
And therefore lost that title of respect
Which the proud soul ne'er pays but to the proud.

WOR. Our house, my sovereign liege, little deserves
The scourge of greatness to be used on it,

1. Either the text should read "tonight" (before the robbery) or else Shakespeare intends to show Prince Hal's mind intent, not on the robbery, but on its aftermath. The soliloquy of the Prince that follows has provoked much critical discussion. Read psychologically, it makes Hal seem like a prig and a self-conscious schemer, but this surely was not Shakespeare's intention. Rather, the speech belongs to the old dramatic convention in which the speaker steps out of character for a moment to deliver a message from the playwright to the audience.
2. Undisciplined whim.
3. Dull background.
4. I.e., contrast.
5. Piece of good policy. "Redeeming time": making good use of time, following the advice given to Christians in a non-Christian world. See Ephesians v.16.
6. Discovered this to be true.
7. Disposition.

And that same greatness too which our own hands
Have holp[8] to make so portly.

NORTH. My lord—

KING. Worcester, get thee gone, for I do see
Danger and disobedience in thine eye;
O, sir, your presence is too bold and peremptory,
And majesty might never yet endure
The moody frontier of a servant brow.[9]
You have good leave to leave us; when we need
Your use and counsel we shall send for you. [*Exit* WOR.]
You were about to speak. [⟨*to* NORTH.⟩]

NORTH. Yea, my good lord.
Those prisoners in your highness' name demanded,
Which Harry Percy here at Holmedon took,
Were, as he says, not with such strength denied
As is delivered to your majesty.
Either envy therefore or misprisión[1]
Is guilty of this fault, and not my son.

HOT. My liege, I did deny no prisoners.
But I remember, when the fight was done,
When I was dry with rage and extreme toil,
Breathless and faint, leaning upon my sword,
Came there a certain lord, neat and trimly dressed,
Fresh as a bridegroom, and his chin new reaped
Showed like a stubble-land at harvest-home;
He was perfumèd like a milliner,[2]
And 'twixt his finger and his thumb he held
A pouncet box,[3] which ever and anon
He gave his nose and took 't away again;
Who therewith angry, when it next came there,
Took it in snuff;[4] and still he smiled and talked,
And as the soldiers bore dead bodies by,
He called them untaught knaves, unmannerly,
To bring a slovenly[5] unhandsome corse
Betwixt the wind and his nobility.
With many holiday and lady terms[6]
He questioned me; amongst the rest, demanded
My prisoners in your majesty's behalf.
I then, all smarting with my wounds being cold,
To be so pestered with a popinjay,[7]
Out of my grief and my impatience
Answered neglectingly I know not what,
He should, or he should not; for he made me mad
To see him shine so brisk and smell so sweet
And talk so like a waiting-gentlewoman

8. Helped; "portly": stately.
9. I.e., a servant's brow showing defiance, like a fortification ("frontier").
1. "Envy": malice; "misprision": mistake.
2. Not a maker of hats, but a dealer in perfumes, women's gloves, etc.
3. Perfume box.
4. I.e., was annoyed at it, with a pun on "snuffing it up."
5. Nasty, disgusting; "corse": corpse, body.
6. Affected and effeminate language (not "everyday" English).
7. Parrot.

Of guns and drums and wounds—God save the mark!—
And telling me the sovereign'st thing on earth
Was parmaceti[8] for an inward bruise,
And that it was great pity, so it was,
This villanous saltpeter[9] should be digged
Out of the bowels of the harmless earth,
Which many a good tall[1] fellow had destroyed
So cowardly, and but for these vile guns
He would himself have been a soldier.
This bald[2] unjointed chat of his, my lord,
I answered indirectly as I said,
And I beseech you, let not his report
Come current[3] for an accusation
Betwixt my love and your high majesty.

BLUNT. The circumstance considered, good my lord,
Whate'er Lord Harry Percy then had said
To such a person and in such a place,
At such a time, with all the rest retold,
May reasonably die and never rise
To do him wrong or any way impeach
What then he said, so he unsay it now.

KING. Why, yet[4] he doth deny his prisoners,
But with proviso and exceptión,
That we at our own charge shall ransom straight
His brother-in-law, the foolish Mortimer,
Who, on my soul, hath willfully betrayed
The lives of those that he did lead to fight
Against that great magician, damned Glendower,
Whose daughter, as we hear, the Earl of March
Hath lately married. Shall our coffers then
Be emptied to redeem a traitor home?
Shall we buy treason? and indent with fears,[5]
When they have lost and forfeited themselves?
No, on the barren mountains let him starve;
For I shall never hold that man my friend
Whose tongue shall ask me for one penny cost
To ransom home revolted Mortimer.

HOT. Revolted Mortimer!
He never did fall off, my sovereign liege,
But by the chance of war. To prove that true
Needs no more but one tongue for all those wounds,
Those mouthéd wounds[6] which valiantly he took
When on the gentle Severn's sedgy bank
In single opposition, hand to hand,

8. Spermaceti, whale oil used as an ointment.
9. Used in gunpowder.
1. Brave.
2. Trivial. "Indirectly": negligently.
3. Be considered valid.
4. I.e., even after all this (the strong use of "yet"). "But": except. "Straight": immediately.
5. Enter into a contract with cowards.
6. Wounds are often likened to mouths in Shakespeare. The image may derive from their appearance and from the idea that they could speak as witnesses to what caused them. Cf. *Julius Caesar* III.ii.229–31 and *Richard III* I.ii. 55–56.

He did confound the best part of an hour
In changing hardiment[7] with great Glendower;
Three times they breathed[8] and three times did they drink
Upon agreement of swift Severn's flood,
Who then, affrighted with their bloody looks,
Ran fearfully among the trembling reeds,
And hid his crisp[9] head in the hollow bank
Bloodstainéd with these valiant combatants.
Never did bare and rotten policy[1]
Color her working with such deadly wounds,
Nor never could the noble Mortimer
Receive so many, and all willingly;
Then let not him be slandered with revolt.

KING. Thou dost belie him, Percy, thou dost belie him;
He never did encounter with Glendower.
I tell thee,
He durst as well have met the devil alone
As Owen Glendower for an enemy.
Art thou not ashamed? But, sirrah,[2] henceforth
Let me not hear you speak of Mortimer;
Send me your prisoners with the speediest means,
Or you shall hear in such a kind from me
As will displease you. My Lord Northumberland,
We license your departure with your son.
Send us your prisoners, or you will hear of it.
[*Exeunt* KING, ⟨BLUNT, *and train.*⟩]

HOT. An if the devil come and roar for them
I will not send them; I will after straight
And tell him so, for I will ease my heart
Albeit I make a hazard of my head.

NORTH. What, drunk with choler?[3] stay and pause awhile.
Here comes your uncle.
[*Enter* WORCESTER.]

HOT. Speak of Mortimer!
Zounds, I will speak of him, and let my soul
Want mercy if I do not join with him;
Yea, on his part[4] I'll empty all these veins,
And shed my dear blood drop by drop in the dust,
But I will lift the downtrod Mortimer
As high in the air as this unthankful king,
As this ingrate and cankered[5] Bolingbroke.

NORTH. Brother, the king hath made your nephew mad.

WOR. Who struck this heat up after I was gone?

HOT. He will, forsooth, have all my prisoners;
And when I urged the ransom once again
Of my wife's brother, then his cheek looked pale,
And on my face he turned an eye of death,

7. Testing prowess and exchanging blows. "Confound": spend.
8. Paused for breath.
9. I.e., curly (because of the waves).
1. Craftiness or conspiracy; "color": disguise.
2. A form of "Sir," but used familiarly, and sometimes, as here, with a tone of contempt. "Speak of": i.e., even mention (an emphatic sense of "speak").
3. Anger.
4. Behalf.
5. Ungrateful and malignant.

Trembling even at the name of Mortimer.
WOR. I cannot blame him; was not he proclaimed
By Richard, that dead is, the next of blood?
NORTH. He was—I heard the proclamatión;
And then it was when the unhappy king
(Whose wrongs in us God pardon![6]) did set forth
Upon his Irish expeditión;
From whence he intercepted did return
To be deposed and shortly murderéd.
WOR. And for whose death we in the world's wide mouth
Live scandalized and foully spoken of.
HOT. But soft, I pray you; did King Richard then
Proclaim my brother[7] Edmund Mortimer
Heir to the crown?
NORTH. He did; myself did hear it.
HOT. Nay, then I cannot blame his cousin king
That wished him on the barren mountains starve.
But shall it be that you, that set the crown
Upon the head of this forgetful man
And for his sake wear the detested blot
Of murderous subornation[8]—shall it be
That you a world of curses undergo,
Being the agents, or base second means,[9]
The cords, the ladder, or the hangman rather?
O pardon me that I descend so low
To show the line and the predicament
Wherein you range[1] under this subtle king!
Shall it for shame be spoken in these days,
Or fill up chronicles in time to come,
That men of your nobility and power
Did gage[2] them both in an unjust behalf,
As both of you—God pardon it!—have done,
To put down Richard, that sweet lovely rose,
And plant this thorn, this canker,[3] Bolingbroke?
And shall it in more shame be further spoken,
That you are fooled, discarded, and shook off
By him for whom these shames ye underwent?
No; yet time serves wherein you may redeem
Your banished honors and restore yourselves
Into the good thoughts of the world again,
Revenge the jeering and disdained[4] contempt
Of this proud king, who studies day and night
To answer all the debt he owes to you
Even with the bloody payment of your deaths:
Therefore, I say—
WOR. Peace, cousin, say no more;
And now I will unclasp a secret book,

6. I.e., God pardon in us the wrongs we did to him.
7. Brother-in-law.
8. I.e., the stain of aiding and abetting murder.
9. Tools, helpers.
1. I.e., to show the position and the category (or class) in which you are placed.
2. Pledge; "behalf": cause.
3. "Canker" meant not only a wild rose but also a diseased spot (a cancer).
4. Disdainful.

And to your quick-conceiving discontents
I'll read you matter deep and dangerous,
As full of peril and adventurous spirit
As to o'er-walk a current roaring loud
On the unsteadfast footing of a spear.[5]

HOT. If he fall in, good night, or sink or swim;
Send danger from the east unto the west,
So[6] honor cross it from the north to south,
And let them grapple; O, the blood more stirs
To rouse a lion than to start[7] a hare!

NORTH. Imagination of some great exploit
Drives him beyond the bounds of patience.

HOT. By heaven, methinks it were an easy leap
To pluck bright honor from the pale-faced moon,
Or dive into the bottom of the deep,
Where fathom line could never touch the ground,
And pluck up drownéd honor by the locks,
So he that doth redeem her thence might wear
Without corrival[8] all her dignities;
But out upon this half-faced fellowship![9]

WOR. He apprehends a world of figures[10] here,
But not the form of what he should attend.
Good cousin, give me audience for a while.

HOT. I cry you mercy.[11]

WOR. Those same noble Scots
That are your prisoners—

HOT. I'll keep them all;
By God, he shall not have a Scot of them;
No, if a Scot would save his soul he shall not.
I'll keep them, by this hand.

WOR. You start away
And lend no ear unto my purposes.
Those prisoners you shall keep.

HOT. Nay, I will; that's flat.
He said he would not ransom Mortimer,
Forbade my tongue to speak of Mortimer,
But I will find him when he lies asleep,
And in his ear I'll holla "Mortimer!"
Nay,
I'll have a starling shall be taught to speak[1]
Nothing but "Mortimer," and give it him
To keep his anger still in motion.

WOR. Hear you, cousin, a word.

HOT. All studies here I solemnly defy,
Save how to gall[2] and pinch this Bolingbroke;
And that same sword-and-buckler[3] Prince of Wales,
But that I think his father loves him not

5. A spear laid down as a foot-bridge.
6. Provided that.
7. Arouse, in hunting.
8. Rival.
9. Miserable sharing (of honor) with someone else.
10. Rhetorical figures of speech.
11. Beg your pardon.
1. Starlings used to be taught to speak, as parrots are now.
2. Irritate.
3. Weapons used not by gentlemen but by servants or rustic clowns.

And would be glad he met with some mischance,
I would have him poisoned with a pot of ale.[4]
WOR. Farewell, kinsman; I'll talk to you
When you are better tempered to attend.
NORTH. Why, what a wasp-stung and impatient fool
Art thou to break into this woman's mood,
Tying thine ear to no tongue but thine own!
HOT. Why, look you, I am whipped and scourged with rods,
Nettled and stung with pismires,[5] when I hear
Of this vile politician Bolingbroke.
In Richard's time—what do you call the place?—
A plague upon it, it is in Gloucestershire—
'Twas where the madcap duke his uncle kept,[6]
His uncle York, where I first bowed my knee
Unto this king of smiles, this Bolingbroke—
'Sblood!—
When you and he came back from Ravenspurgh.
NORTH. At Berkeley castle.
HOT. You say true.
Why, what a candy deal of courtesy
This fawning greyhound[7] then did proffer me!
"Look when his infant fortune came to age,"
And "gentle Harry Percy," and "kind cousin";
O, the devil take such cozeners![8] God forgive me!
Good uncle, tell your tale; I have done.
WOR. Nay, if you have not, to it again;
We will stay your leisure.
HOT. I have done, i' faith.
WOR. Then once more to your Scottish prisoners.
Deliver them up without their ransom straight,
And make the Douglas' son your only mean
For powers in Scotland, which, for divers reasons
Which I shall send you written, be assured
Will easily be granted. You, my lord, [⟨*to* NORTHUMBERLAND⟩]
Your son in Scotland being thus employed,
Shall secretly into the bosom creep
Of that same noble prelate well beloved,
The archbishop.
HOT. Of York, is it not?
WOR. True; who bears hard
His brother's death at Bristol, the Lord Scroop.
I speak not this in estimation,[9]
As what I think might be, but what I know
Is ruminated, plotted, and set down,
And only stays but to behold the face
Of that occasion that shall bring it on.

4. The drink of the lower classes.
5. Ants.
6. Lived.
7. A complex image which occurs in Shakespeare several times (cf. *Hamlet* III.ii.65–67 and *Antony and Cleopatra* IV.xii.20–23). The idea of fawning or flattery called up to Shakespeare's mind the image of a dog begging for sweetmeats ("candy").
8. Cheaters, with of course a pun on the word "cousin."
9. I.e., guessing.

HOT. I smell it; upon my life, it will do well.
NORTH. Before the game is afoot, thou still let'st slip.[1]
HOT. Why, it cannot choose but be a noble plot;
And then the power of Scotland and of York
To join with Mortimer, ha?
WOR. And so they shall.
HOT. In faith, it is exceedingly well aimed.
WOR. And 'tis no little reason bids us speed,
To save our heads by raising of a head;[2]
For, bear ourselves as even as we can,
The king will always think him in our debt,
And think we think ourselves unsatisfied,
Till he hath found a time to pay us home;
And see already how he doth begin
To make us strangers to his looks of love.
HOT. He does, he does; we'll be revenged on him.
WOR. Cousin, farewell. No further go in this
Than I by letters shall direct your course.
When time is ripe, which will be suddenly,
I'll steal to Glendower and Lord Mortimer,
Where you and Douglas and our powers at once,
As I will fashion it, shall happily meet,
To bear our fortunes in our own strong arms,
Which now we hold at much uncertainty.
NORTH. Farewell, good brother; we shall thrive, I trust.
HOT. Uncle, adieu; O, let the hours be short
Till fields and blows and groans applaud our sport! [*Exeunt.*]

Act II

SCENE 1

[*Enter a* CARRIER *with a lantern in his hand.*]

FIRST CAR. Heigh-ho! an it be not four by the day, I'll be hanged; Charles' wain[3] is over the new chimney, and yet our horse not packed. What, ostler!

OST. [*within*] Anon, anon.

FIRST CAR. I prithee, Tom, beat Cut's saddle,[4] put a few flocks in the point; poor jade, is wrung in the withers out of all cess.[5]

[*Enter another* CARRIER.]

SEC. CAR. Peas and beans are as dank here as a dog, and that is the next way to give poor jades the bots;[6] this house is turned upside down since Robin Ostler died.

FIRST CAR. Poor fellow, never joyed since the price of oats rose; it was the death of him.

SEC. CAR. I think this be the most villainous house in all London

1. An image from hunting. The meaning is: "You always ('still') release the dogs before we are ready to pursue the game."
2. Raising an army.
3. The constellation of the Great Bear or Big Dipper.
4. The saddle was beaten to make it soft; "Cut" is a name for a horse with a docked tail. "Flocks in the point": pieces of wool under the point of the saddle.
5. I.e., is sore in the shoulders excessively.
6. I.e., that is the easiest way to give poor nags worms in the stomach.

road for fleas; I am stung like a tench.[7]

FIRST CAR. Like a tench! by the mass, there is ne'er a king christen[8] could be better bit than I have been since the first cock.

SEC. CAR. Why, they will allow us ne'er a jordan, and then we leak in your chimney, and your chamber-lye breeds fleas like a loach.[9]

FIRST CAR. What, ostler! come away and be hanged, come away!

SEC. CAR. I have a gammon[1] of bacon and two razes of ginger, to be delivered as far as Charing Cross.

FIRST CAR. God's body! the turkeys in my pannier[2] are quite starved. What, ostler! A plague on thee, hast thou never an eye in thy head? canst not hear? An 'twere not as good deed as drink to break the pate on thee, I am a very villain. Come and be hanged! hast no faith in thee?

[*Enter* GADSHILL.]

GADS. Good morrow, carriers. What's o'clock?

FIRST CAR. I think it be two o'clock.

GADS. I prithee lend me thy lantern to see my gelding in the stable.

FIRST CAR. Nay, by God, soft; I know a trick worth two of that, i' faith.

GADS. I pray thee lend me thine.

SEC. CAR. Aye, when? canst tell?[3] Lend me thy lantern, quoth he? marry, I'll see thee hanged first.

GADS. Sirrah carrier, what time do you mean to come to London?

SEC. CAR. Time enough to go to bed with a candle, I warrant thee. Come, neighbor Mugs, we'll call up the gentlemen; they will along with company, for they have great charge.[4]

[*Exeunt* ⟨CARRIERS.⟩]

GADS. What ho! chamberlain!

CHAM. [*within*] At hand, quoth pickpurse.

GADS. That's even as fair as At hand, quoth the chamberlain, for thou variest no more from picking of purses than giving direction[5] doth from laboring; thou layest the plot how.

[*Enter* CHAMBERLAIN.]

CHAM. Good morrow, Master Gadshill. It holds current[6] that I told you yesternight; there's a franklin[7] in the weald of Kent hath brought three hundred marks with him in gold—I heard him tell it to one of his company last night at supper—a kind of auditor,[8] one that hath abundance of charge too, God knows what. They are up already and call for eggs and butter;

7. A fish covered with red spots, like fleabites.
8. Christian king.
9. "Jordan": chamber pot; "chamber-lye": urine. The "loach" is a fish which breeds prolifically.
1. Haunch; "razes": roots.
2. Basket.
3. A colloquial expression of contemptuous refusal.
4. Valuable cargo.
5. A pun: "giving direction" means supervising, as contrasted with "laboring," but it was also the name for informing thieves about the journeys of prospective victims (laying "the plot how").
6. Remains true.
7. A freeholder, just below a gentleman in rank. "Weald of Kent": a section of that county, formerly wooded.
8. Revenue officer; "abundance of charge": considerable property.

they will away presently.[9]

GADS. Sirrah, if they meet not with Saint Nicholas' clerks,[1] I'll give thee this neck.

CHAM. No, I'll none of it; I pray thee, keep that for the hangman, for I know thou worshipest Saint Nicholas as truly as a man of falsehood may.

GADS. What talkest thou to me of the hangman? if I hang, I'll make a fat pair of gallows; for if I hang, old Sir John hangs with me, and thou knowest he is no starveling. Tut! there are other Trojans[2] that thou dreamest not of, the which for sport sake are content to do the profession some grace, that would, if matters should be looked into, for their own credit sake make all whole. I am joined with no foot land-rakers,[3] no long-staff sixpenny strikers, none of these mad mustachio purple-hued maltworms,[4] but with nobility and tranquility, burgomasters and great oneyers, such as can hold in, such as will strike sooner than speak, and speak sooner than drink, and drink sooner than pray; and yet, zounds, I lie, for they pray continually to their saint, the commonwealth, or rather, not pray to her but prey on her, for they ride up and down on her and make her their boots.[5]

CHAM. What, the commonwealth their boots? will she hold out water in foul way?

GADS. She will, she will; justice hath liquored her. We steal as in a castle, cocksure; we have the receipt of fern seed,[6] we walk invisible.

CHAM. Nay, by my faith, I think you are more beholding to the night than to fern seed for your walking invisible.

GADS. Give me thy hand; thou shalt have a share in our purchase,[7] as I am a true man.

CHAM. Nay, rather let me have it, as you are a false thief.

GADS. Go to; *homo* is a common name to all men. Bid the ostler bring my gelding out of the stable. Farewell, you muddy[8] knave. [*Exeunt.*]

SCENE 2

[*Enter* PRINCE *and* POINS.]

POINS. Come shelter, shelter; I have removed Falstaff's horse, and he frets like a gummed velvet.[9]

PRINCE. Stand close.

[*Enter* FALSTAFF.]

FAL. Poins! Poins, and be hanged! Poins!

PRINCE. Peace, ye fat-kidneyed rascal! what a brawling dost thou keep!

FAL. Where's Poins, Hal?

PRINCE. He is walked up to the top of the hill; I'll go seek him.

9. At once.
1. Highwaymen.
2. Roisterers, good fellows.
3. Footpads; "sixpenny strikers": small-time thieves.
4. Flushed, swaggering barflies. "Oneyers": dignitaries; "hold in": keep secret.
5. Booty.
6. I.e., we have the recipe for fern seed (supposed to make one invisible). "Liquored": greased.
7. Takings.
8. Muddle-headed.
9. Cheap velvet was treated with gum to make the pile stiff; as a result it soon fretted or wore away. "Stand close": hide.

[⟨*He pretends to go, but hides onstage with* POINS.⟩]

FAL. I am accursed to rob in that thief's company; the rascal hath removed my horse, and tied him I know not where. If I travel but four foot by the squier[1] further afoot, I shall break my wind. Well, I doubt not but to die a fair death for all this, if I 'scape hanging for killing that rogue. I have forsworn his company hourly any time this two and twenty years, and yet I am bewitched with the rogue's company. If the rascal have not given me medicines to make me love him, I'll be hanged; it could not be else; I have drunk medicines. Poins! Hal! a plague upon you both! Bardolph! Peto! I'll starve ere I'll rob a foot further. An 'twere not as good a deed as drink to turn true man and to leave these rogues, I am the veriest varlet that ever chewed with a tooth. Eight yards of uneven ground is threescore and ten miles afoot with me, and the stony-hearted villains know it well enough; a plague upon it when thieves cannot be true one to another! [*They whistle.*] Whew! A plague upon you all! Give me my horse, you rogues; give me my horse, and be hanged!

PRINCE. Peace, ye fat-guts! lie down; lay thine ear close to the ground and list if thou canst hear the tread of travelers.

FAL. Have you any levers to lift me up again, being down? 'Sblood, I'll not bear my own flesh so far afoot again for all the coin in thy father's exchequer. What a plague mean ye to colt[2] me thus?

PRINCE. Thou liest; thou art not colted, thou art uncolted.

FAL. I prithee, good Prince, Hal, help me to my horse, good king's son.

PRINCE. Out, ye rogue! shall I be your ostler?

FAL. Go hang thyself in thine own heir-apparent garters![3] If I be ta'en, I'll peach for this. An I have not ballads made on you all and sung to filthy tunes, let a cup of sack be my poison; when a jest is so forward, and afoot too! I hate it.

[*Enter* GADSHILL, ⟨BARDOLPH *and* PETO *with him.*⟩]

GADS. Stand.

FAL. So I do, against my will.

POINS. O, 'tis our setter; I know his voice. Bardolph, what news?

BARD. Case[4] ye, case ye, on with your vizards; there's money of the king's coming down the hill; 'tis going to the king's exchequer.

FAL. You lie, you rogue; 'tis going to the king's tavern.

GADS. There's enough to make us all.

FAL. To be hanged.

PRINCE. Sirs, you four shall front them in the narrow lane; Ned Poins and I will walk lower; if they 'scape from your encounter, then they light on us.

PETO. How many be there of them?

GADS. Some eight or ten.

FAL. Zounds, will they not rob us?

1. Ruler, yardstick.
2. Trick.
3. As heir apparent to the throne, Hal would of course be a knight of the Order of the Garter.
4. Mask.

PRINCE. What, a coward, Sir John Paunch?

FAL. Indeed, I am not John of Gaunt your grandfather, but yet no coward, Hal.

PRINCE. Well, we leave that to the proof.

POINS. Sirrah Jack, thy horse stands behind the hedge; when thou needest him, there thou shalt find him. Farewell, and stand fast.

FAL. Now cannot I strike him, if I should be hanged.

PRINCE. [⟨*aside to* POINS⟩] Ned, where are our disguises?

POINS. [⟨*aside*⟩] Here, hard by; stand close.

[⟨*Exeunt* PRINCE *and* POINS.⟩]

FAL. Now, my masters, happy man be his dole,[5] say I; every man to his business.

[*Enter the* TRAVELERS.]

FIRST TRAV. Come, neighbor, the boy shall lead our horses down the hill; we'll walk afoot awhile, and ease our legs.

THIEVES. Stand!

TRAVELERS. Jesus bless us!

FAL. Strike; down with them; cut the villains' throats. Ah, whoreson caterpillars,[6] bacon-fed knaves, they hate us youth! Down with them, fleece them.

TRAVELERS. O, we are undone, both we and ours forever!

FAL. Hang ye, gorbellied[7] knaves, are ye undone? No, ye fat chuffs, I would your store were here! On, bacons, on! What, ye knaves, young men must live! You are grand jurors, are ye? we'll jure ye, faith.

[*Here they rob them and bind them. Exeunt.*]

[*Enter the* PRINCE *and* POINS.]

PRINCE. The thieves have bound the true men. Now could thou and I rob the thieves and go merrily to London; it would be argument[8] for a week, laughter for a month, and a good jest forever.

POINS. Stand close; I hear them coming.

[*Enter the* THIEVES *again.*]

FAL. Come, my masters, let us share, and then to horse before day. An the Prince and Poins be not two arrant cowards, there's no equity stirring;[9] there's no more valor in that Poins than in a wild duck.

PRINCE. Your money!

POINS. Villains!

[*As they are sharing, the* PRINCE *and* POINS *set upon them; they all run away; and* FALSTAFF, *after a blow or two, runs away too, leaving the booty behind them.*]

PRINCE. Got with much ease. Now merrily to horse;
The thieves are all scattered and possessed with fear
So strongly that they dare not meet each other;
Each takes his fellow for an officer.
Away, good Ned. Falstaff sweats to death,

5. I.e., good luck!
6. "Caterpillars of the commonwealth" was a common phrase, referring to rogues. Falstaff here applies ridiculously inappropriate terms to the travelers and to himself (e.g., "youth").
7. Fat; "chuffs": misers.
8. Subject of stories.
9. There's no justice.

And lards the lean earth as he walks along;
Were 't not for laughing, I should pity him.

POINS. How the fat rogue roared! [*Exeunt.*]

SCENE 3

[*Enter* HOTSPUR, *alone, reading a letter.*]

HOT. "But for mine own part, my lord, I could be well contented to be there, in respect of the love I bear your house." "He could be contented"; why is he not, then? "In respect of the love he bears our house," he shows in this, he loves his own barn better than he loves our house. Let me see some more. "The purpose you undertake is dangerous." Why, that's certain. 'Tis dangerous to take a cold, to sleep, to drink; but I tell you, my lord fool, out of this nettle, danger, we pluck this flower, safety.[1] "The purpose you undertake is dangerous, the friends you have named uncertain, the time itself unsorted,[2] and your whole plot too light for the counterpoise of so great an opposition." Say you so, say you so? I say unto you again, you are a shallow cowardly hind,[3] and you lie. What a lack-brain is this! By the Lord, our plot is a good plot as ever was laid, our friends true and constant; a good plot, good friends, and full of expectation; an excellent plot, very good friends. What a frosty-spirited rogue is this! Why, my lord of York[4] commends the plot and the general course of the action. Zounds, an I were now by this rascal I could brain him with his lady's fan. Is there not my father, my uncle, and myself? Lord Edmund Mortimer, my lord of York, and Owen Glendower? is there not besides the Douglas? have I not all their letters to meet me in arms by the ninth of the next month, and are they not some of them set forward already? What a pagan rascal is this, an infidel! Ha! you shall see now in very sincerity of fear and cold heart, will he to the king and lay open all our proceedings. O, I could divide myself and go to buffets,[5] for moving such a dish of skim milk with so honorable an action! Hang him! let him tell the king. We are prepared; I will set forward tonight.

[*Enter his* LADY.]

How now, Kate! I must leave you within these two hours.

LADY. O, my good lord, why are you thus alone?
For what offense have I this fortnight been
A banished woman from my Harry's bed?
Tell me, sweet lord, what is 't that takes from thee
Thy stomach,[6] pleasure, and thy golden sleep?
Why dost thou bend thine eyes upon the earth,
And start so often when thou sit'st alone?
Why hast thou lost the fresh blood in thy cheeks,
And given my treasures and my rights of thee
To thick-eyed musing and cursed melancholy?
In thy faint slumbers I by thee have watched
And heard thee murmur tales of iron wars,

1. The nettle if touched tenderly will sting; if grasped firmly, will not.
2. Unsuitable.
3. Peasant.
4. The Archbishop of York.
5. Split myself in two and let the parts fight each other; "moving": urging.
6. Appetite.

Speak terms of manage[7] to thy bounding steed,
Cry "Courage! to the field!" And thou hast talked
Of sallies and retires, of trenches, tents,
Of palisadoes, frontiers, parapets,
Of basilisks, of cannon, culverin,[8]
Of prisoners' ransom and of soldiers slain,
And all the currents of a heady fight.
Thy spirit within thee hath been so at war
And thus hath so bestirred thee in thy sleep
That beads of sweat have stood upon thy brow
Like bubbles in a late-disturbèd stream,
And in thy face strange motions have appeared
Such as we see when men restrain their breath
On some great sudden hest.[9] O, what portents are these?
Some heavy business hath my lord in hand
And I must know it, else he loves me not.

HOT. What, ho!
[⟨*Enter* SERVANT.⟩]
Is Gilliams with the packet gone?

SERV. He is, my lord, an hour ago.

HOT. Hath Butler brought those horses from the sheriff?

SERV. One horse, my lord, he brought even now.

HOT. What horse? a roan, a crop-ear, is it not?

SERV. It is, my lord.

HOT. That roan shall be my throne.
Well, I will back[1] him straight; O Esperance![2]
Bid Butler lead him forth into the park. [⟨*Exit* SERVANT.⟩]

LADY. But hear you, my lord.

HOT. What say'st thou, my lady?

LADY. What is it carries you away?

HOT. Why, my horse, my love, my horse.

LADY. Out, you mad-headed ape!
A weasel hath not such a deal of spleen[3]
As you are tossed with. In faith
I'll know your business, Harry, that I will.
I fear my brother Mortimer doth stir
About his title, and hath sent for you
To line his enterprise; but if you go[4]—

HOT. So far afoot, I shall be weary, love.

LADY. Come, come, you paraquito, answer me
Directly unto this question that I ask;
In faith, I'll break thy little finger, Harry,
An if thou wilt not tell me all things true.

HOT. Away,
Away, you trifler! Love! I love thee not,

7. Horsemanship.
8. Three kinds of artillery (named here in decreasing order of weight).
9. Command.
1. Mount.
2. The battle cry of the Percies: "Hope!"
3. The spleen was supposed to be the source of sudden and violent emotions; the weasel was considered a very impetuous animal.
4. Besides its ordinary sense, which Lady Percy uses, "go" also meant "walk," the sense in which Hotspur takes it. "Line": support.

I care not for thee, Kate; this is no world
To play with mammets and to tilt with lips;
We must have bloody noses and cracked crowns,[5]
And pass them current too. God's me, my horse!
What say'st thou, Kate? what wouldst thou have with me?

LADY. Do you not love me? do you not, indeed?
Well, do not then, for since you love me not
I will not love myself. Do you not love me?
Nay, tell me if you speak in jest or no.

HOT. Come, wilt thou see me ride?
And when I am o' horseback, I will swear
I love thee infinitely. But hark you, Kate,
I must not have you henceforth question me
Whither I go, nor reason whereabout;
Whither I must, I must; and, to conclude,
This evening must I leave you, gentle Kate.
I know you wise, but yet no farther wise
Than Harry Percy's wife; constant you are,
But yet a woman, and for secrecy
No lady closer; for I well believe
Thou wilt not utter what thou dost not know,
And so far will I trust thee, gentle Kate.

LADY. How! so far?

HOT. Not an inch further. But hark you, Kate,
Whither I go, thither shall you go too;
Today will I set forth, tomorrow you.
Will this content you, Kate?

LADY. It must of force.[6] *[Exeunt.]*

SCENE 4

[Enter the PRINCE *and* POINS.*]*

PRINCE. Ned, prithee come out of that fat[7] room, and lend me thy hand to laugh a little.

POINS. Where hast been, Hal?

PRINCE. With three or four loggerheads[8] amongst three or fourscore hogsheads. I have sounded the very bass string of humility. Sirrah, I am sworn brother to a leash of drawers,[9] and can call them all by their christen names, as Tom, Dick, and Francis. They take it already upon their salvation, that though I be but Prince of Wales, yet I am the king of courtesy, and tell me flatly I am no proud Jack, like Falstaff, but a Corinthian,[10] a lad of mettle, a good boy—by the Lord, so they call me—and when I am king of England I shall command all the good lads in Eastcheap. They call drinking deep, dyeing scarlet, and when you breathe in your watering[1] they cry "hem!" and bid you play it off. To conclude, I am so good a proficient in one quarter of an hour that I can drink with any tinker in his own lan-

5. Broken heads, with a pun on "crowns" as coins. "Mammets": dolls.
6. Of necessity.
7. Vat. This establishes that the scene is a tavern.
8. Blockheads.
9. Group of tapsters, waiters.
10. Good fellow.
1. Drinking.

guage during my life. I tell thee, Ned, thou hast lost much honor, that thou wert not with me in this action. But, sweet Ned—to sweeten which name of Ned, I give thee this pennyworth of sugar, clapped even now into my hand by an under-skinker,[2] one that never spake other English in his life than "Eight shillings and sixpence," and "You are welcome," with this shrill addition, "Anon, anon, sir! Score a pint of bastard in the Half-Moon,"[3] or so. But, Ned, to drive away the time till Falstaff come, I prithee do thou stand in some by-room, while I question my puny drawer to what end he gave me the sugar, and do thou never leave calling "Francis," that his tale to me may be nothing but "Anon." Step aside, and I'll show thee a precedent.

POINS. Francis!

PRINCE. Thou art perfect.

POINS. Francis! [⟨*Exit* POINS.⟩]

[*Enter* DRAWER.]

FRAN. Anon, anon, sir. Look down into the Pomgarnet,[4] Ralph.

PRINCE. Come hither, Francis.

FRAN. My lord?

PRINCE. How long hast thou to serve,[5] Francis?

FRAN. Forsooth, five years, and as much as to—

POINS. [*within*] Francis!

FRAN. Anon, anon, sir.

PRINCE. Five year! by'r Lady, a long lease for the clinking of pewter. But, Francis, darest thou be so valiant as to play the coward with thy indenture and show it a fair pair of heels and run from it?

FRAN. O Lord, sir, I'll be sworn upon all the books[6] in England, I could find in my heart—

POINS. [*within*] Francis!

FRAN. Anon, sir.

PRINCE. How old art thou, Francis?

FRAN. Let me see—about Michaelmas[7] next I shall be—

POINS. [*within*] Francis!

FRAN. Anon, sir. Pray stay a little, my lord.

PRINCE. Nay, but hark you, Francis: for the sugar thou gavest me, 'twas a pennyworth, was't not?

FRAN. O Lord, I would it had been two!

PRINCE. I will give thee for it a thousand pound; ask me when thou wilt, and thou shalt have it.

POINS. [*within*] Francis!

FRAN. Anon, anon.

PRINCE. Anon, Francis? No, Francis, but tomorrow, Francis; or Francis, o' Thursday, or indeed, Francis, when thou wilt. But,

2. Assistant waiter.
3. I.e., charge a pint of "bastard" (a sweet Spanish wine) to a customer in the room called "Half-Moon." "Anon": immediately (the reply of a servant when called, equivalent to "Coming!").
4. Pomegranate (another room in the tavern).
5. I.e., to finish out his apprenticeship, usually a seven-year period under an "indenture" or agreement.
6. I.e., Bibles.
7. September 29.

Francis!

FRAN. My lord?

PRINCE. Wilt thou rob this leathern-jerkin,[8] crystal-button, not-pated, agate-ring, puke-stocking, caddis-garter, smooth-tongue, Spanish-pouch—

FRAN. O Lord, sir, who do you mean?

PRINCE. Why, then, your brown bastard is your only drink, for look you, Francis, your white canvas doublet will sully. In Barbary, sir, it cannot come to so much.[9]

FRAN. What, sir?

POINS. [*within*] Francis!

PRINCE. Away, you rogue, dost thou not hear them call?

[*Here they both call him; the drawer stands amazed, not knowing which way to go.*]

[*Enter* VINTNER.]

VINT. What, stand'st thou still, and hear'st such a calling? Look to the guests within. [*Exit* FRANCIS.] My lord, old Sir John with half-a-dozen more are at the door; shall I let them in?

PRINCE. Let them alone awhile, and then open the door. [*Exit* VINTNER.] Poins!

[*Enter* POINS.]

POINS. Anon, anon, sir.

PRINCE. Sirrah, Falstaff and the rest of the thieves are at the door; shall we be merry?

POINS. As merry as crickets, my lad. But hark ye, what cunning match have you made with this jest of the drawer? come, what's the issue?

PRINCE. I am now of all humors[1] that have showed themselves humors since the old days of goodman Adam to the pupil[2] age of this present twelve o'clock at midnight.

[⟨*Enter* FRANCIS.⟩]

What's o'clock, Francis?

FRAN. Anon, anon, sir. [⟨*Exit.*⟩]

PRINCE. That ever this fellow should have fewer words than a parrot, and yet the son of a woman! His industry is upstairs and downstairs, his eloquence the parcel[3] of a reckoning. I am not yet of Percy's mind, the Hotspur of the north, he that kills me some six or seven dozen of Scots at a breakfast, washes his hands, and says to his wife "Fie upon this quiet life! I want work." "O my sweet Harry," says she, "how many hast thou killed today?" "Give my roan horse a drench," says he, and answers "Some fourteen," an hour after, "a trifle, a trifle." I prithee, call in Falstaff; I'll play Percy, and that damned brawn shall play Dame Mortimer his wife. "Rivo!"[4] says the drunkard. Call in ribs, call in tallow.

[*Enter* FALSTAFF, ⟨GADSHILL, BARDOLPH, *and* PETO, FRAN-

8. Leather-jacketed; "not-pated": with short hair; "puke": dark gray; "caddis": worsted tape.

9. Deliberate nonsense to confuse Francis, and one of the first instances of doubletalk in English literature.

1. Temperaments, dispositions.

2. Youthful.

3. Item.

4. Drink up!

CIS *following with wine.*〉]

POINS. Welcome, Jack; where hast thou been?

FAL. A plague of all cowards, I say, and a vengeance too, marry and amen! Give me a cup of sack, boy. Ere I lead this life long, I'll sew nether stocks[5] and mend them and foot them too. A plague of all cowards! Give me a cup of sack, rogue. Is there no virtue extant? [*He drinks.*]

PRINCE. Didst thou ever see Titan[6] kiss a dish of butter, pitiful-hearted butter that melted at the sweet tale of the sun's? If thou didst, then behold that compound.

FAL. You rogue, here's lime in this sack too;[7] there is nothing but roguery to be found in villainous man, yet a coward is worse than a cup of sack with lime in it. A villainous coward! Go thy ways, old Jack, die when thou wilt; if manhood, good manhood, be not forgot upon the face of the earth, then am I a shotten herring.[8] There lives not three good men unhanged in England, and one of them is fat and grows old. God help the while; a bad world, I say. I would I were a weaver; I could sing psalms[9] or anything. A plague of all cowards, I say still.

PRINCE. How now, woolsack, what mutter you?

FAL. A king's son![1] If I do not beat thee out of thy kingdom with a dagger of lath, and drive all thy subjects afore thee like a flock of wild geese, I'll never wear hair on my face more. You Prince of Wales!

PRINCE. Why, you whoreson round man, what's the matter?

FAL. Are not you a coward? answer me to that; and Poins there?

POINS. Zounds, ye fat paunch, an ye call me coward, by the Lord I'll stab thee.

FAL. I call thee coward! I'll see thee damned ere I call thee coward; but I would give a thousand pound I could run as fast as thou canst. You are straight enough in the shoulders, you care not who sees your back; call you that backing of your friends? A plague upon such backing! give me them that will face me. Give me a cup of sack; I am a rogue if I drunk today.

PRINCE. O villain! thy lips are scarce wiped since thou drunkest last.

FAL. All's one for that. [*He drinks.*] A plague of all cowards, still say I.

PRINCE. What's the matter?

FAL. What's the matter! there be four of us here have ta'en a thousand pound this day morning.

PRINCE. Where is it, Jack? where is it?

FAL. Where is it? taken from us it is—a hundred upon poor four of us.

PRINCE. What, a hundred, man?

FAL. I am a rogue if I were not at half-sword[2] with a dozen of them two hours together. I have 'scaped by miracle. I am

5. Stockings.
6. The sun.
7. Lime was used to make wine sparkle.
8. A herring that has cast its spawn and is lean.
9. Protestant weavers from Flanders were notorious for singing psalms.
1. A stick used by the Vice in the old morality plays.
2. At half a sword's length.

eight times thrust through the doublet, four through the hose;[3] my buckler cut through and through, my sword hacked like a handsaw—*ecce signum!*[4] I never dealt better since I was a man; all would not do. A plague of all cowards! Let them speak; if they speak more or less than truth, they are villains and the sons of darkness.

PRINCE. Speak, sirs; how was it?

GADS. We four set upon some dozen—

FAL. Sixteen at least, my lord.

GADS. And bound them.

PETO. No, no, they were not bound.

FAL. You rogue, they were bound, every man of them, or I am a Jew else, an Ebrew Jew.

GADS. As we were sharing, some six or seven fresh men set upon us—

FAL. And unbound the rest, and then come in the other.

PRINCE. What, fought you with them all?

FAL. All! I know not what you call all, but if I fought not with fifty of them, I am a bunch of radish; if there were not two or three and fifty upon poor old Jack, then am I no two-legged creature.

PRINCE. Pray God you have not murdered some of them.

FAL. Nay, that's past praying for; I have peppered two of them. Two I am sure I have paid, two rogues in buckram suits. I tell thee what, Hal, if I tell thee a lie, spit in my face, call me horse. Thou knowest my old ward;[5] here I lay, and thus I bore my point. Four rogues in buckram let drive at me—

PRINCE. What, four? thou saidst but two even now.

FAL. Four, Hal; I told thee four.

POINS. Aye, aye, he said four.

FAL. These four came all a-front, and mainly[6] thrust at me. I made me no more ado but took all their seven points in my target,[7] thus.

PRINCE. Seven? why, there were but four even now.

FAL. In buckram?

POINS. Aye, four, in buckram suits.

FAL. Seven, by these hilts, or I am a villain else.

PRINCE. Prithee, let him alone; we shall have more anon.

FAL. Dost thou hear me, Hal?

PRINCE. Aye, and mark thee too, Jack.

FAL. Do so, for it is worth the listening to. These nine in buckram that I told thee of—

PRINCE. So, two more already.

FAL. Their points being broken—

POINS. Down fell their hose.[8]

FAL. Began to give me ground; but I followed me close, came in foot and hand, and with a thought[9] seven of the eleven I paid.

3. Breeches.
4. Here's the proof!
5. Defense; "here I lay": this was my stance.
6. Strongly.
7. Shield.
8. Poins puns on the other meaning of "points": the laces used to tie up trousers ("hose").
9. As quick as thought.

PRINCE. O monstrous! eleven buckram men grown out of two!

FAL. But, as the devil would have it, three misbegotten knaves in Kendal green came at my back and let drive at me, for it was so dark, Hal, that thou couldst not see thy hand.

PRINCE. These lies are like their father that begets them—gross as a mountain, open, palpable. Why, thou clay-brained guts, thou knotty-pated fool, thou whoreson, obscene, greasy tallow-catch[1]—

FAL. What, art thou mad? art thou mad? is not the truth the truth?

PRINCE. Why, how couldst thou know these men in Kendal green, when it was so dark thou couldst not see thy hand? come, tell us your reason. What sayest thou to this?

POINS. Come, your reason, Jack, your reason.

FAL. What, upon compulsion? Zounds, an I were at the strappado,[2] or all the racks in the world, I would not tell you on compulsion. Give you a reason on compulsion! if reasons[3] were as plentiful as blackberries, I would give no man a reason upon compulsion, I.

PRINCE. I'll be no longer guilty of this sin; this sanguine coward, this bed-presser, this horseback-breaker, this huge hill of flesh—

FAL. 'Sblood, you starveling, you eelskin, you dried neat's tongue, you bull's pizzle, you stockfish![4] O for breath to utter what is like thee! you tailor's yard, you sheath, you bow case, you vile standing-tuck[5]—

PRINCE. Well, breathe awhile, and then to it again; and when thou hast tired thyself in base comparisons, hear me speak but this.

POINS. Mark, Jack.

PRINCE. We two saw you four set on four and bound them, and were masters of their wealth. Mark now, how a plain tale shall put you down. Then did we two set on you four; and, with a word, outfaced you from your prize, and have it, yea, and can show it you here in the house; and, Falstaff, you carried your guts away as nimbly, with as quick dexterity, and roared for mercy and still run and roared, as ever I heard bullcalf. What a slave art thou, to hack thy sword as thou hast done, and then say it was in fight! What trick, what device, what starting-hole,[6] canst thou now find out to hide thee from this open and apparent shame?

POINS. Come, let's hear, Jack; what trick hast thou now?

FAL. By the Lord, I knew ye as well as he that made ye. Why, hear you, my masters: was it for me to kill the heir apparent? should I turn upon the true prince? why, thou knowest I am

1. Piece of tallow from which chandlers made candles.
2. A method of torture; "racks": another method.
3. A pun on the word "raisin," which was spelled and pronounced like "reason" in Elizabethan England.
4. I.e., you ox tongue, you bull's penis, you dried cod!
5. Stiff rapier.
6. Evasion.

as valiant as Hercules; but beware instinct; the lion will not touch the true prince.[7] Instinct is a great matter; I was now a coward on instinct. I shall think the better of myself and thee during my life; I for a valiant lion, and thou for a true prince. But, by the Lord, lads, I am glad you have the money. Hostess, clap to the doors; watch[8] tonight, pray tomorrow. Gallants, lads, boys, hearts of gold, all the titles of good fellowship come to you! What, shall we be merry? shall we have a play extempore?

PRINCE. Content; and the argument[9] shall be thy running away.

FAL. Ah, no more of that, Hal, an thou lovest me!

[*Enter* HOSTESS.]

HOST. O Jesu, my lord the prince!

PRINCE. How now, my lady the hostess! what sayest thou to me?

HOST. Marry, my lord, there is a nobleman of the court at door would speak with you; he says he comes from your father.

PRINCE. Give him as much as will make him a royal[1] man, and send him back again to my mother.

FAL. What manner of man is he?

HOST. An old man.

FAL. What doth gravity out of his bed at midnight? Shall I give him his answer?

PRINCE. Prithee, do, Jack.

FAL. Faith, and I'll send him packing. [*Exit.*]

PRINCE. Now, sirs. By 'r Lady, you fought fair; so did you, Peto; so did you, Bardolph; you are lions too, you ran away upon instinct, you will not touch the true prince; no, fie!

BARD. Faith, I ran when I saw others run.

PRINCE. Faith, tell me now in earnest, how came Falstaff's sword so hacked?

PETO. Why, he hacked it with his dagger, and said he would swear truth out of England but he would make you believe it was done in fight, and persuaded us to do the like.

BARD. Yea, and to tickle our noses with speargrass to make them bleed, and then to beslubber our garments with it and swear it was the blood of true men. I did that I did not this seven year before, I blushed to hear his monstrous devices.

PRINCE. O villain, thou stolest a cup of sack eighteen years ago, and wert taken with the manner,[2] and ever since thou hast blushed extempore. Thou hadst fire[3] and sword on thy side, and yet thou rannest away; what instinct hadst thou for it?

BARD. My lord, do you see these meteors? do you behold these exhalations?

PRINCE. I do.

BARD. What think you they portend?

PRINCE. Hot livers and cold purses.[4]

7. In many medieval romances the lion, as king of beasts, shows respect for royalty.
8. Stay up.
9. Plot or story.
1. A "royal" was half of a pound sterling, a "noble" was a third.
2. In the act.
3. "Fire" and the allusions to "meteors" and "exhalations" (shooting stars) refer to Bardolph's red nose.
4. I.e., drunkenness and poverty.

BARD. Choler, my lord, if rightly taken.

PRINCE. No, if rightly taken, halter.

[*Enter* FALSTAFF.]

Here comes lean Jack, here comes bare-bone. How now, my sweet creature of bombast,[5] how long is 't ago, Jack, since thou sawest thine own knee?

FAL. My own knee! when I was about thy years, Hal, I was not an eagle's talon in the waist; I could have crept into any alderman's thumb ring. A plague of sighing and grief—it blows a man up like a bladder. There's villainous news abroad; here was Sir John Bracy from your father; you must to the court in the morning. That same mad fellow of the north, Percy, and he of Wales, that gave Amamon[6] the bastinado and made Lucifer cuckold and swore the devil his true liegeman upon the cross of a Welsh hook[7]—what a plague call you him?

POINS. O, Glendower.

FAL. Owen, Owen, the same; and his son-in-law Mortimer, and old Northumberland, and that sprightly Scot of Scots, Douglas, that runs o' horseback up a hill perpendicular—

PRINCE. He that rides at high speed and with his pistol kills a sparrow flying.

FAL. You have hit it.

PRINCE. So did he never the sparrow.

FAL. Well, that rascal hath good mettle in him; he will not run.

PRINCE. Why, what a rascal art thou then, to praise him so for running!

FAL. O' horseback, ye cuckoo; but afoot he will not budge a foot.

PRINCE. Yes, Jack, upon instinct.

FAL. I grant ye, upon instinct. Well, he is there too, and one Mordake, and a thousand blue-caps[8] more. Worcester is stolen away tonight; thy father's beard is turned white with the news; you may buy land now as cheap as stinking mackerel.

PRINCE. Why then, it is like, if there come a hot June, and this civil buffeting hold, we shall buy maidenheads as they buy hobnails, by the hundreds.

FAL. By the mass, lad, thou sayest true; it is like we shall have good trading that way. But tell me, Hal, art not thou horrible afeard? thou being heir apparent, could the world pick thee out three such enemies again as that fiend Douglas, that spirit Percy, and that devil Glendower? Art thou not horribly afraid? doth not thy blood thrill at it?

PRINCE. Not a whit, i' faith; I lack some of thy instinct.

FAL. Well, thou wilt be horribly chid tomorrow when thou comest to thy father; if thou love me, practice an answer.

PRINCE. Do thou stand for[9] my father and examine me upon the particulars of my life.

FAL. Shall I? Content. This chair shall be my state,[1] this dagger

5. Padding, stuffing.
6. A devil. "Bastinado": a beating, cudgelling.
7. A long spear with a hook on it.
8. Scots.
9. Represent.
1. Throne.

my scepter, and this cushion my crown.

PRINCE. Thy state is taken for a joint-stool,[2] thy golden scepter for a leaden dagger, and thy precious rich crown for a pitiful bald crown!

FAL. Well, an the fire of grace be not quite out of thee, now shalt thou be moved. Give me a cup of sack to make my eyes look red, that it may be thought I have wept, for I must speak in passion, and I will do it in King Cambyses'[3] vein.

PRINCE. Well, here is my leg.[4]

FAL. And here is my speech. Stand aside, nobility.

HOST. O Jesu, this is excellent sport, i' faith!

FAL. Weep not, sweet queen, for trickling tears are vain.

HOST. O, the father, how he holds his countenance!

FAL. For God's sake, lords, convey my tristful queen,
For tears do stop the floodgates of her eyes.[5]

HOST. O Jesu, he doth it as like one of these harlotry players as ever I see!

FAL. Peace, good pint pot, peace, good ticklebrain. Harry, I do not only marvel where thou spendest thy time, but also how thou art accompanied, for though the camomile,[6] the more it is trodden on the faster it grows, so youth, the more it is wasted the sooner it wears. That thou art my son, I have partly thy mother's word, partly my own opinion, but chiefly a villainous trick of thine eye and a foolish hanging of thy nether lip that doth warrant[7] me. If then thou be son to me, here lies the point; why, being son to me, art thou so pointed at? Shall the blessed sun of heaven prove a micher[8] and eat blackberries? a question not to be asked. Shall the son of England prove a thief and take purses? a question to be asked. There is a thing, Harry, which thou hast often heard of and it is known to many in our land by the name of pitch. This pitch, as ancient writers do report, doth defile; so doth the company thou keepest: for, Harry, now I do not speak to thee in drink but in tears, not in pleasure but in passion, not in words only, but in woes also: and yet there is a virtuous man whom I have often noted in thy company, but I know not his name.

PRINCE. What manner of man, an it like your majesty?

FAL. A goodly portly man, i' faith, and a corpulent; of a cheerful look, a pleasing eye and a most noble carriage, and, as I think, his age some fifty, or, by 'r Lady, inclining to threescore; and now I remember me, his name is Falstaff. If that man should be lewdly given, he deceiveth me, for, Harry, I see virtue in his looks. If then the tree may be known by the fruit, as the fruit by the tree, then, peremptorily I speak it, there is virtue in that Falstaff; him keep with, the rest banish. And tell me

2. An ordinary stool, made by a joiner (carpenter).
3. Like the bombastic hero of the old play *Cambyses*.
4. I.e., he bows, makes an obeisance.
5. Falstaff's blank verse lines parody the old-fashioned tragedies of the 1570's and 80's.
6. An aromatic herb. The style in this speech is a parody of Euphuism, the ornate, elaborate, balanced style made popular by Lyly's *Euphues*.
7. Assure.
8. Truant.

now, thou naughty varlet, tell me, where hast thou been this month?

PRINCE. Dost thou speak like a king? Do thou stand for me, and I'll play my father.

FAL. Depose me? if thou dost it half so gravely, so majestically, both in word and matter, hang me up by the heels for a rabbit-sucker[9] or a poulter's hare.

PRINCE. Well, here I am set.[10]

FAL. And here I stand; judge, my masters.

PRINCE. Now, Harry, whence come you?

FAL. My noble lord, from Eastcheap.

PRINCE. The complaints I hear of thee are grievous.

FAL. 'Sblood, my lord, they are false: nay, I'll tickle ye for a young prince, i' faith.

PRINCE. Swearest thou, ungracious boy? thenceforth ne'er look on me. Thou art violently carried away from grace; there is a devil haunts thee in the likeness of an old fat man; a tun[1] of man is thy companion. Why dost thou converse with that trunk of humors, that bolting-hutch[2] of beastliness, that swollen parcel of dropsies, that huge bombard of sack, that stuffed cloak-bag of guts, that roasted Manningtree[3] ox with the pudding in his belly, that reverend vice, that gray iniquity, that father ruffian, that vanity in years? Wherein is he good, but to taste sack and drink it? wherein neat and cleanly, but to carve a capon and eat it? wherein cunning, but in craft? wherein crafty, but in villainy? wherein villainous, but in all things? wherein worthy, but in nothing?

FAL. I would your grace would take me with you; whom means your grace?

PRINCE. That villainous abominable misleader of youth, Falstaff, that old white-bearded Satan.

FAL. My lord, the man I know.

PRINCE. I know thou dost.

FAL. But to say I know more harm in him than in myself were to say more than I know. That he is old the more the pity, his white hairs do witness it; but that he is, saving your reverence, a whoremaster, that I utterly deny. If sack and sugar be a fault, God help the wicked! if to be old and merry be a sin, then many an old host that I know is damned; if to be fat be to be hated, then Pharaoh's lean kine[4] are to be loved. No, my good lord, banish Peto, banish Bardolph, banish Poins, but for sweet Jack Falstaff, kind Jack Falstaff, true Jack Falstaff, valiant Jack Falstaff, and therefore more valiant, being as he is old Jack Falstaff, banish not him thy Harry's company, banish not him thy Harry's company; banish plump Jack, and ban-

9. Suckling rabbit.
10. Seated.
1. Large barrel.
2. Trough; "bombard": leather wine vessel.
3. Town in Essex, noted for barbecues; "pudding": sausage. The "vice" was a comic character in the old morality plays. Falstaff is in some respects a descendant of this type-character.
4. In the dream Joseph interpreted. See Genesis xli.19–21.

ish all the world.

PRINCE. I do, I will. [⟨*A knocking heard.*⟩]

[⟨*Exeunt* HOSTESS *and* BARDOLPH.⟩]

[*Enter* BARDOLPH, *running.*]

BARD. O, my lord, my lord, the sheriff with a most monstrous watch is at the door.

FAL. Out, ye rogue! Play out the play; I have much to say in the behalf of that Falstaff.

[*Enter the* HOSTESS.]

HOST. O Jesu, my lord, my lord!

FAL. Heigh, heigh! the devil rides upon a fiddlestick;[5] what's the matter?

HOST. The sheriff and all the watch are at the door; they are come to search the house. Shall I let them in?

FAL. Dost thou hear, Hal? never call a true piece of gold a counterfeit; thou art essentially mad, without seeming so.[6]

PRINCE. And thou a natural coward, without instinct.

FAL. I deny your major;[7] if you will deny the sheriff, so; if not, let him enter. If I become not a cart as well as another man, a plague on my bringing up! I hope I shall as soon be strangled with a halter as another.[8]

PRINCE. Go hide thee behind the arras;[9] the rest walk up above. Now, my masters, for a true face and good conscience.

FAL. Both which I have had; but their date is out,[1] and therefore I'll hide me.

PRINCE. Call in the sheriff.

[*Exeunt* ⟨*all except the* PRINCE *and* POINS.⟩]

[*Enter* SHERIFF *and the* CARRIER.]

Now, master sheriff, what is your will with me?

SHER. First pardon me, my lord. A hue and cry
Hath followed certain men unto this house.

PRINCE. What men?

SHER. One of them is well known, my gracious lord,
A gross fat man.

CAR. As fat as butter.

PRINCE. The man, I do assure you, is not here,
For I myself at this time have employed him,
And, sheriff, I will engage my word to thee
That I will by tomorrow dinnertime
Send him to answer thee or any man
For anything he shall be charged withal;
And so let me entreat you leave the house.

SHER. I will, my lord. There are two gentlemen

5. I.e., there's a commotion.

6. I.e., don't give a true man (me, Falstaff) away as a thief. He goes on to accuse the prince, in his reversal of values in the play scene, of being out of his mind, though he appears rational.

7. Your major premise (that I, Falstaff, am a coward).

8. I.e., I hope my fat neck will not make the process of strangling on the gallows longer for me than for the rest of you. The "cart" is the wagon on which criminals were taken to be hanged.

9. The hangings or draperies which covered the walls. "Up above": on the balcony.

1. Lease has expired.

Have in this robbery lost three hundred marks.

PRINCE. It may be so; if he have robbed these men
He shall be answerable; and so farewell.

SHER. Good night, my noble lord.

PRINCE. I think it is good morrow, is it not?

SHER. Indeed, my lord, I think it be two o'clock.

[*Exeunt* ⟨SHERIFF *and* CARRIER.⟩]

PRINCE. This oily rascal is known as well as Paul's.[2] Go call him forth.

POINS. Falstaff!—Fast asleep behind the arras, and snorting like a horse.

PRINCE. Hark, how hard he fetches breath. Search his pockets. [*He searcheth his pockets, and findeth certain papers.*] What hast thou found?

POINS. Nothing but papers, my lord.

PRINCE. Let's see what they be: read them.

POINS. [*reads*] "Item, a capon. . . . . 2*s*. 2*d*.
Item, sauce. . . . . . 4*d*.
Item, sack, two gallons. . 5*s*. 8*d*.
Item, anchovies and sack
after supper. . . . . 2*s*. 6*d*.
Item, bread. . . . . . ob."[3]

PRINCE. O monstrous! but one halfpennyworth of bread to this intolerable deal of sack! What there is else, keep close; we'll read it at more advantage; there let him sleep till day. I'll to the court in the morning. We must all to the wars, and thy place shall be honorable. I'll procure this fat rogue a charge of foot,[4] and I know his death will be a march of twelvescore. The money shall be paid back again with advantage. Be with me betimes[5] in the morning, and so good morrow, Poins.

POINS. Good morrow, good my lord. [*Exeunt.*]

Act III

SCENE 1

[*Enter* HOTSPUR, WORCESTER, LORD MORTIMER, *and* OWEN GLENDOWER.]

MORT. These promises are fair, the parties sure,
And our induction[6] full of prosperous hope.

HOT. Lord Mortimer, and cousin Glendower,
Will you sit down?
And uncle Worcester; a plague upon it,
I have forgot the map.

GLEND. No, here it is.
Sit, cousin Percy, sit, good cousin Hotspur,
For by that name as oft as Lancaster[7]
Doth speak of you, his cheek looks pale and with

2. St. Paul's Cathedral.
3. Oble, a halfpenny.
4. Company of infantry. "Twelvescore": i.e., 240 yards.
5. Early.
6. Initial step.
7. I.e., King Henry IV. To call him by his lesser title is insulting.

A rising sigh he wisheth you in heaven.
HOT. And you in hell as often as he hears Owen Glendower spoke of.
GLEND. I cannot blame him; at my nativity
The front[8] of heaven was full of fiery shapes,
Of burning cressets, and at my birth
The frame and huge foundation of the earth
Shaked like a coward.
HOT. Why, so it would have done at the same season if your mother's cat had but kittened, though yourself had never been born.
GLEND. I say the earth did shake when I was born.
HOT. And I say the earth was not of my mind,
If you suppose as fearing you it shook.
GLEND. The heavens were all on fire, the earth did tremble.
HOT. O then the earth shook to see the heavens on fire,
And not in fear of your nativity.
Diseasèd nature oftentimes breaks forth
In strange eruptions; oft the teeming earth
Is with a kind of colic pinched and vexed
By the imprisoning of unruly wind
Within her womb, which for enlargement striving
Shakes the old beldam[9] earth and topples down
Steeples and moss-grown towers. At your birth
Our grandam earth, having this distemperature,[10]
In passion shook.
GLEND. Cousin, of many men
I do not bear these crossings. Give me leave
To tell you once again that at my birth
The front of heaven was full of fiery shapes,
The goats ran from the mountains, and the herds
Were strangely clamorous to the frighted fields.
These signs have marked me extraordinary,
And all the courses of my life do show
I am not in the roll of common men.
Where is he living, clipped in with[1] the sea
That chides the banks of England, Scotland, Wales,
Which calls me pupil or hath read to me?
And bring him out that is but woman's son
Can trace me in the tedious ways of art[2]
And hold me pace in deep experiments.
HOT. I think there's no man speaks better Welsh. I'll to dinner.
MORT. Peace, cousin Percy; you will make him mad.
GLEND. I can call spirits from the vasty deep.
HOT. Why, so can I, or so can any man;
But will they come when you do call for them?
GLEND. Why, I can teach you, cousin, to command
The devil.

8. The forehead. "Cressets": lamps.
9. Old woman.
10. Ailment.
1. Within the limits of.
2. Follow me in practicing difficult magic.

HOT. And I can teach thee, coz, to shame the devil
By telling truth; tell truth and shame the devil.[3]
If thou have power to raise him, bring him hither,
And I'll be sworn I have power to shame him hence.
O, while you live, tell truth and shame the devil!
MORT. Come, come, no more of this unprofitable chat.
GLEND. Three times hath Henry Bolingbroke made head
Against my power, thrice from the banks of Wye
And sandy-bottomed Severn have I sent him
Bootless[4] home and weather-beaten back.
HOT. Home without boots, and in foul weather too!
How 'scapes he agues,[5] in the devil's name?
GLEND. Come, here is the map; shall we divide our right
According to our threefold order ta'en?[6]
MORT. The archdeacon hath divided it
Into three limits very equally:
England, from Trent and Severn hitherto,
By south and east is to my part assigned;
All westward, Wales beyond the Severn shore,
And all the fertile land within that bound,
To Owen Glendower; and, dear coz, to you
The remnant northward lying off from Trent;
And our indentures tripartite are drawn,
Which being sealéd interchangeably,
A business that this night may execute,
Tomorrow, cousin Percy, you and I
And my good Lord of Worcester will set forth
To meet your father and the Scottish power,
As is appointed us, at Shrewsbury.
My father[7] Glendower is not ready yet,
Nor shall we need his help these fourteen days.
Within that space you may have drawn together
Your tenants, friends, and neighboring gentlemen.
GLEND. A shorter time shall send me to you, lords,
And in my conduct shall your ladies come,
From whom you now must steal and take no leave,
For there will be a world of water shed
Upon the parting of your wives and you.
HOT. Methinks my moiety,[8] north from Burton here,
In quantity equals not one of yours;
See how this river comes me cranking[9] in,
And cuts me from the best of all my land
A huge half-moon, a monstrous cantle[1] out.
I'll have the current in this place dammed up;
And here the smug[1a] and silver Trent shall run

3. A proverb.
4. Unsuccessful; but Hotspur takes it in the other sense.
5. Fevers and chills.
6. Divide our property according to the arrangement for division into three parts.
7. Father-in-law.
8. Part, share.
9. Curving.
1. Corner.
1a. Smooth.

In a new channel, fair and evenly;
It shall not wind with such a deep indent
To rob me of so rich a bottom[2] here.
GLEND. Not wind? it shall, it must; you see it doth.
MORT. Yea, but
Mark how he bears his course, and runs me up
With like advantage on the other side;
Gelding the opposéd continent[3] as much
As on the other side it takes from you.
WOR. Yea, but a little charge will trench him here
And on this north side win this cape of land,
And then he runs straight and even.
HOT. I'll have it so; a little charge will do it.
GLEND. I'll not have it altered.
HOT. Will not you?
GLEND. No, nor you shall not.
HOT. Who shall say me nay?
GLEND. Why, that will I.
HOT. Let me not understand you then; speak it in Welsh.
GLEND. I can speak English, lord, as well as you,
For I was trained up in the English court,
Where, being but young, I framéd to the harp
Many an English ditty lovely well
And gave the tongue a helpful ornament,
A virtue that was never seen in you.
HOT. Marry,
And I am glad of it with all my heart;
I had rather be a kitten and cry mew
Than one of these same meter ballad-mongers;
I had rather hear a brazen canstick turned,[4]
Or a dry wheel grate on the axletree,
And that would set my teeth nothing on edge,
Nothing so much as mincing[5] poetry;
'Tis like the forced gait of a shuffling nag.
GLEND. Come, you shall have Trent turned.
HOT. I do not care; I'll give thrice so much land
To any well-deserving friend;
But in the way of bargain, mark ye me,
I'll cavil[6] on the ninth part of a hair.
Are the indentures drawn? shall we be gone?
GLEND. The moon shines fair; you may be away by night.
I'll haste the writer, and withal
Break with[7] your wives of your departure hence.
I am afraid my daughter will run mad,
So much she doteth on her Mortimer. [*Exit.*]
MORT. Fie, cousin Percy, how you cross my father!
HOT. I cannot choose; sometime he angers me

2. Valley.
3. I.e., cutting off from the opposite side.
4. A brass candlestick turned on a lathe.
5. Affected. "Shuffling": hobbled.
6. Quibble.
7. Inform.

With telling me of the moldwarp[8] and the ant,
Of the dreamer Merlin and his prophecies,
And of a dragon and a finless fish,
A clip-winged griffin and a molten raven,
A couching lion and a ramping[9] cat,
And such a deal of skimble-skamble stuff
As puts me from my faith. I tell you what;
He held me last night at least nine hours
In reckoning up the several devils' names
That were his lackeys. I cried "hum" and "well, go to,"
But marked him not a word. O, he is as tedious
As a tired horse, a railing[1] wife,
Worse than a smoky house. I had rather live
With cheese and garlic in a windmill,[2] far,
Than feed on cates and have him talk to me
In any summer house in Christendom.

MORT. In faith, he is a worthy gentleman,
Exceedingly well read, and profited
In strange concealments,[3] valiant as a lion
And wondrous affable and as bountiful
As mines of India. Shall I tell you, cousin?
He holds your temper[4] in a high respect
And curbs himself even of his natural scope
When you come 'cross his humor; faith, he does.
I warrant you that man is not alive
Might so have tempted him as you have done
Without the taste of danger and reproof;
But do not use it oft, let me entreat you.

WOR. In faith, my lord, you are too willful-blame,
And since your coming hither have done enough
To put him quite beside his patience.
You must needs learn, lord, to amend this fault.
Though sometimes it show greatness, courage, blood[5]—
And that's the dearest grace it renders you—
Yet oftentimes it doth present harsh rage,
Defect of manners, want of government,[6]
Pride, haughtiness, opinion, and disdain;
The least of which haunting a nobleman
Loseth men's hearts and leaves behind a stain
Upon the beauty of all parts besides,
Beguiling them of commendation.

HOT. Well, I am schooled; good manners be your speed!
Here come our wives, and let us take our leave.

8. Mole. According to the chronicler Holinshed there were prophecies in which Henry IV was referred to as "a moldwarp, cursed of God." Merlin was the famous prophet of King Arthur's court; many later prophecies were attributed to him.

9. "Couching" and "ramping" are Hotspur's versions of the heraldic terms "couchant" (lying down) and "rampant" (erect, on hind feet).

1. Nagging.

2. Cheese and garlic would be smelly, and the living quarters in a mill would be noisy. "Cates": delicacies.

3. Experienced in secret mysteries.

4. Character.

5. Breeding, blood-lines.

6. Self-control. "Opinion": arrogance.

[*Enter* GLENDOWER *with the ladies.*]

MORT. This is the deadly spite that angers me;
My wife can speak no English, I no Welsh.

GLEND. My daughter weeps; she will not part with you,
She'll be a soldier too, she'll to the wars.

MORT. Good father, tell her that she and my aunt Percy
Shall follow in your conduct speedily.

[GLENDOWER SPEAKS *to her in Welsh, and she answers him in the same.*]

GLEND. She is desperate here; a peevish self-willed harlotry,[7] one that no persuasion can do good upon.

[*The lady speaks in Welsh.*]

MORT. I understand thy looks; that pretty Welsh
Which thou pour'st down from these swelling heavens[8]
I am too perfect in; and, but for shame,
In such a parley should I answer thee.

[*The lady speaks again in Welsh.*]

I understand thy kisses and thou mine,
And that's a feeling disputation,
But I will never be a truant, love,
Till I have learned thy language, for thy tongue
Makes Welsh as sweet as ditties highly penned,
Sung by a fair queen in a summer's bower,
With ravishing division,[9] to her lute.

GLEND. Nay, if you melt, then will she run mad.

[*The lady speaks again in Welsh.*]

MORT. O, I am ignorance itself in this!

GLEND. She bids you on the wanton rushes[10] lay you down
And rest your gentle head upon her lap,
And she will sing the song that pleaseth you
And on your eyelids crown the god of sleep,
Charming your blood with pleasing heaviness,[1]
Making such difference 'twixt wake and sleep
As is the difference betwixt day and night
The hour before the heavenly-harnessed team[2]
Begins his golden progress in the east.

MORT. With all my heart I'll sit and hear her sing;
By that time will our book,[3] I think, be drawn.

GLEND. Do so;
And those musicians that shall play to you
Hang in the air a thousand leagues from hence,
And straight they shall be here; sit, and attend.

HOT. Come, Kate, thou art perfect in lying down; come, quick, quick, that I may lay my head in thy lap.

LADY P. Go, ye giddy goose.

7. Wench; used affectionately, not seriously (Juliet's father applies the same phrase to her in *Romeo and Juliet*).
8. I.e., tears from her eyes. "Answer thee": cry likewise.
9. Musical variation.
10. The dry reeds used as a floor covering in Elizabethan England.
1. Drowsiness.
2. The horses of the sun.
3. The indenture.

[*The music plays.*]

HOT. Now I perceive the devil understands Welsh,
And 'tis no marvel, he is so humorous.[4]
By 'r Lady, he is a good musician.

LADY P. Then should you be nothing but musical, for you are altogether governed by humors. Lie still, ye thief, and hear the lady sing in Welsh.

HOT. I had rather hear Lady, my brach,[5] howl in Irish.

LADY P. Wouldst thou have thy head broken?

HOT. No.

LADY P. Then be still.

HOT. Neither; 'tis a woman's fault.[6]

LADY P. Now God help thee.

HOT. To the Welsh lady's bed.

LADY P. What's that?

HOT. Peace! she sings.

[*Here the lady sings a Welsh song.*]

HOT. Come, Kate, I'll have your song too.

LADY P. Not mine, in good sooth.[7]

HOT. Not yours, in good sooth! Heart! you swear like a comfit-maker's[8] wife. "Not you, in good sooth," and "as true as I live," and "as God shall mend me," and "as sure as day,"
And givest such sarcenet[9] surety for thy oaths
As if thou never walk'st further than Finsbury.
Swear me, Kate, like a lady as thou art,
A good mouth-filling oath, and leave "in sooth,"
And such protest of pepper-gingerbread,[1]
To velvet-guards and Sunday citizens.
Come, sing.

LADY P. I will not sing.

HOT. 'Tis the next way to turn tailor, or be redbreast teacher.[2] An the indentures be drawn, I'll away within these two hours; and so, come in when ye will. [*Exit.*]

GLEND. Come, come, Lord Mortimer, you are as slow
As hot Lord Percy is on fire to go.
By this our book is drawn; we will but seal,
And then to horse immediately.

MORT. With all my heart. [*Exeunt.*]

SCENE 2

[*Enter the* KING, PRINCE OF WALES, *and others.*]

KING. Lords, give us leave; the Prince of Wales and I

4. Capricious, governed by humors.
5. My bitch hound, Lady.
6. Hotspur sarcastically reverses the usual saying about women and talkativeness.
7. Truth.
8. Confectioner's.
9. Thin silk. Finsbury: a recreation ground outside London, frequented by citizens and their wives on Sundays, but not by ladies of Lady Percy's class.
1. I.e., such tame oaths, as crumbly and unsubstantial as gingerbread. "Velvet-guards": respectable people of the middle class, who wore velvet stripes on their clothes; "Sunday citizens": city folk out for a stroll on Sunday.
2. I.e., it is the easiest way to become a tailor (supposedly tailors sang at their work) or a person who teaches birds to sing. Hotspur is equally scornful of music and of people who work for a living.

Must have some private conference; but be near at hand,
For we shall presently have need of you. [*Exeunt* LORDS.]
I know not whether God will have it so
For some displeasing service I have done,
That, in his secret doom, out of my blood[3]
He'll breed revengement and a scourge for me;
But thou dost in thy passages[4] of life
Make me believe that thou art only marked
For the hot vengeance and the rod of heaven
To punish my mistreadings.[5] Tell me else,
Could such inordinate and low desires,
Such poor, such bare, such lewd,[6] such mean attempts,
Such barren pleasures, rude society
As thou art matched withal and grafted to
Accompany the greatness of thy blood
And hold their level with thy princely heart?

PRINCE. So please your majesty, I would I could
Quit[7] all offenses with as clear excuse
As well as I am doubtless I can purge
Myself of many I am charged withal;
Yet such extenuation let me beg,
As, in reproof of many tales devised
(Which oft the ear of greatness needs must hear)
By smiling pickthanks[8] and base newsmongers,
I may, for some things true, wherein my youth
Hath faulty wandered and irregular,
Find pardon on my true submissión.

KING. God pardon thee; yet let me wonder, Harry,
At thy affections, which doth hold a wing
Quite from the flight of all thy ancestors.
Thy place in council thou hast rudely lost,
Which by thy younger brother is supplied,
And art almost an alien to the hearts
Of all the court and princes of my blood.
The hope and expectation of thy time[9]
Is ruined, and the soul of every man
Prophetically do forethink thy fall.
Had I so lavish of my presence been,
So common-hackneyed[10] in the eyes of men,
So stale and cheap to vulgar company,
Opinion,[11] that did help me to the crown,
Had still kept loyal to possessión
And left me in reputeless banishment,
A fellow of no mark nor likelihood.
By being seldom seen, I could not stir

3. Unknown judgment, through my son.
4. Actions.
5. False steps, misdeeds.
6. Low.
7. Acquit myself of. "Doubtless": sure.
8. Flatterers; "newsmongers": tattletales.
9. Lifetime.
10. Cheapened, vulgarized.
11. Popularity, public opinion. "Possession, in the mood.

But like a comet I was wondered at,
That men would tell their children "This is he";
Others would say "Where, which is Bolingbroke?"
And then I stole all courtesy from heaven,
And dressed myself in such humility
That I did pluck allegiance from men's hearts,
Loud shouts and salutations from their mouths,
Even in the presence of the crownéd king.
Thus did I keep my person fresh and new,
My presence like a robe pontifical,
Ne'er seen but wondered at; and so my state,[1]
Seldom but sumptuous, showed like a feast
And wan[2] by rareness such solemnity.
The skipping king, he ambled up and down
With shallow jesters and rash bavin wits,[3]
Soon kindled and soon burnt, carded his state,
Mingled his royalty with capering fools,
Had his great name profanéd with their scorns
And gave his countenance[4] against his name
To laugh at gibing boys and stand the push
Of every beardless vain comparative,[5]
Grew a companion to the common streets,
Enfeoffed himself to popularity,[6]
That, being daily swallowed by men's eyes,
They surfeited with honey and began
To loathe the taste of sweetness, whereof a little
More than a little is by much too much.
So when he had occasion to be seen
He was but as the cuckoo is in June,[7]
Heard, not regarded, seen, but with such eyes
As, sick and blunted with community,[8]
Afford no extraordinary gaze
Such as is bent on sunlike majesty
When it shines seldom in admiring eyes,
But rather drowsed and hung their eyelids down,
Slept in his face[9] and rendered such aspéct
As cloudy men use to their adversaries,
Being with his presence glutted, gorged, and full.
And in that very line, Harry, standest thou,
For thou hast lost thy princely privilege
With vile participation.[1] Not an eye
But is a-weary of thy common sight,

1. Public ceremonial appearances.
2. Won. "Such solemnity": i.e., the greatest possible majestic effect (an intensive use of "such"). King Henry's theory of public relations is of course not based upon the assumption of a democratic society.
3. "Rash": quick; "bavin": brushwood; the image is explained in the next line. "Carded his state": degraded his royal dignity; "card" also means "to adulterate wine."
4. Authority; "name": reputation.
5. Shallow satirical pretender to wit.
6. Made himself the common property of the public.
7. The cuckoo is noticed in April, when its song is first heard; by June it is commonplace.
8. Commonness.
9. I.e., yawned in his face. "Aspect": looks; "cloudy": sullen.
1. Association with vile companions.

Save mine, which hath desired to see thee more,
Which now doth that I would not have it do,
Make blind itself with foolish tenderness.

PRINCE. I shall hereafter, my thrice gracious lord,
Be more myself.

KING. For all the world
As thou art to this hour was Richard then
When I from France set foot at Ravenspurgh,
And even as I was then is Percy now.
Now, by my scepter and my soul to boot,
He hath more worthy interest to the state
Than thou the shadow of successión;[2]
For of no right, nor color like to right,
He doth fill fields with harness in the realm,
Turns head against the lion's arméd jaws,[3]
And, being no more in debt to years than thou,
Leads ancient lords and reverend bishops on
To bloody battles and to bruising arms.
What never-dying honor hath he got
Against renownéd Douglas! whose high deeds,
Whose hot incursions and great name in arms
Holds from all soldiers chief majority
And military title capital[4]
Through all the kingdoms that acknowledge Christ.
Thrice hath this Hotspur, Mars in swaddling clothes,
This infant warrior, in his enterprises
Discomfited great Douglas, ta'en him once,
Enlargéd[5] him and made a friend of him,
To fill the mouth of deep defiance up[6]
And shake the peace and safety of our throne.
And what say you to this? Percy, Northumberland,
The Archbishop's grace of York, Douglas, Mortimer,
Capitulate[7] against us and are up.
But wherefore do I tell these news to thee?
Why, Harry, do I tell thee of my foes,
Which art my nearest and dearest enemy?
Thou that art like enough through vassal fear,
Base inclination and the start of spleen,[8]
To fight against me under Percy's pay,
To dog his heels and curtsy at his frowns,
To show how much thou art degenerate.

PRINCE. Do not think so; you shall not find it so;
And God forgive them that so much have swayed
Your majesty's good thoughts away from me.

2. I.e., Hotspur's claim to the throne is more solid, because of his achievements, than is Hal's, which rests only on shadowy rights of succession by birth. "Color": false pretense.
3. I.e., takes military action against the king's army. "Harness": armor.
4. Has the greatest reputation among soldiers. "Incursions": raids; "majority": superiority.
5. Freed.
6. I.e., to make the voice of defiance full in volume.
7. Raise a head, revolt.
8. Unreasoning impulse.

I will redeem all this on Percy's head
And in the closing of some glorious day
Be bold to tell you that I am your son,
When I will wear a garment all of blood
And stain my favors[9] in a bloody mask,
Which, washed away, shall scour my shame with it;
And that shall be the day, whene'er it lights,
That this same child of honor and renown,
This gallant Hotspur, this all-praiséd knight,
And your unthought-of Harry chance to meet.
For every honor sitting on his helm—
Would they were multitudes, and on my head
My shames redoubled!—for the time will come
That I shall make this northern youth exchange
His glorious deeds for my indignities.
Percy is but my factor,[1] good my lord,
To engross up glorious deeds on my behalf,
And I will call him to so strict account,
That he shall render every glory up,
Yea, even the slightest worship[2] of his time,
Or I will tear the reckoning from his heart.
This in the name of God I promise here,
The which if He be pleased I shall perform,
I do beseech your majesty, may salve
The long-grown wounds of my intemperance;
If not, the end of life cancels all bands,[3]
And I will die a hundred thousand deaths
Ere break the smallest parcel of this vow.

KING. A hundred thousand rebels die in this;
Thou shalt have charge and sovereign trust herein.
[*Enter* BLUNT.]
How now, good Blunt? thy looks are full of speed.

BLUNT. So hath the business that I come to speak of.
Lord Mortimer of Scotland hath sent word
That Douglas and the English rebels met
The eleventh of this month at Shrewsbury;
A mighty and a fearful head[4] they are,
If promises be kept on every hand,
As ever offered foul play in a state.

KING. The Earl of Westmoreland set forth today,
With him my son, Lord John of Lancaster,
For this advertisement[5] is five days old.
On Wednesday next, Harry, you shall set forward;
On Thursday we ourselves will march. Our meeting
Is Bridgenorth and, Harry, you shall march
Through Gloucestershire, by which account,[6]

9. Features.
1. Agent; "engross up": collect, acquire.
2. Honor.
3. Bonds, debts.
4. Power.
5. News.
6. Method. "Our business valued": according to estimates.

Our business valued, some twelve days hence
Our general forces at Bridgenorth shall meet.
Our hands are full of business: let's away;
Advantage feeds him fat while men delay.[7] [*Exeunt.*]

SCENE 3

[*Enter* FALSTAFF *and* BARDOLPH.]

FAL. Bardolph, am I not fallen away vilely since this last action?[8] do I not bate? do I not dwindle? Why, my skin hangs about me like an old lady's loose gown; I am withered like an old applejohn.[9] Well, I'll repent, and that suddenly, while I am in some liking; I shall be out of heart shortly, and then I shall have no strength to repent. An I have not forgotten what the inside of a church is made of, I am a peppercorn, a brewer's horse. The inside of a church! Company, villainous company, hath been the spoil of me.

BARD. Sir John, you are so fretful you cannot live long.

FAL. Why, there is it; come sing me a bawdy song, make me merry. I was as virtuously given as a gentleman need to be: virtuous enough; swore little; diced not above seven times a week; went to a bawdyhouse not above once in a quarter—of an hour; paid money that I borrowed three or four times; lived well and in good compass; and now I live out of all order, out of all compass.

BARD. Why, you are so fat, Sir John, that you must needs be out of all compass, out of all reasonable compass, Sir John.

FAL. Do thou amend thy face, and I'll amend my life; thou art our admiral,[1] thou bearest the lantern in the poop, but 'tis in the nose of thee; thou art the Knight of the Burning Lamp.

BARD. Why, Sir John, my face does you no harm.

FAL. No, I'll be sworn; I make as good use of it as many a man doth of a death's-head or a *memento mori*.[2] I never see thy face but I think upon hell-fire and Dives[3] that lived in purple, for there he is in his robes, burning, burning. If thou wert any way given to virtue, I would swear by thy face; my oath should be "By this fire, that's God's angel"; but thou art altogether given over, and wert indeed, but for the light in thy face, the son of utter darkness. When thou rannest up Gadshill in the night to catch my horse, if I did not think thou hadst been an *ignis fatuus*[4] or a ball of wildfire, there's no purchase in money. O, thou art a perpetual triumph,[5] an everlasting bonfire light! Thou hast saved me a thousand marks in links[6] and torches, walking with thee in the night betwixt tavern and tavern, but

7. I.e., the rebels' "advantage" (opportunity) grows as the king's men delay.
8. I.e., the Gadshill robbery; "bate": lose weight.
9. A keeping apple with a wrinkled skin. "In some liking": in good condition, in the mood.
1. Flagship.
2. I.e., a skull or some other reminder of death.
3. The rich man who would not give food to Lazarus and was punished in hell for it. See Luke xvi.19–31.
4. Will-o'-the-wisp; "wildfire": a firework used for military purposes.
5. Illumination at a public festival.
6. Small torches carried at night.

the sack that thou hast drunk me would have bought me lights as good cheap at the dearest chandler's[7] in Europe. I have maintained that salamander of yours with fire any time this two and thirty years, God reward me for it.

BARD. 'Sblood, I would my face were in your belly!

FAL. God-a-mercy! so should I be sure to be heartburned.

[*Enter* HOSTESS.]

How now, Dame Partlet[8] the hen! have you inquired yet who picked my pocket?

HOST. Why, Sir John, what do you think, Sir John? do you think I keep thieves in my house? I have searched, I have inquired, so has my husband, man by man, boy by boy, servant by servant; the tithe[9] of a hair was never lost in my house before.

FAL. Ye lie, hostess; Bardolph was shaved and lost many a hair, and I'll be sworn my pocket was picked. Go to, you are a woman, go.

HOST. Who, I? no, I defy thee; God's light, I was never called so in mine own house before.

FAL. Go to, I know you well enough.

HOST. No, Sir John; you do not know me, Sir John. I know you, Sir John; you owe me money, Sir John, and now you pick a quarrel to beguile me of it; I bought you a dozen of shirts to your back.

FAL. Dowlas,[1] filthy dowlas; I have given them away to bakers' wives, and they have made bolters of them.

HOST. Now, as I am a true woman, holland[2] of eight shillings an ell. You owe money here besides, Sir John, for your diet and by-drinkings,[3] and money lent you, four and twenty pound.

FAL. He had his part of it; let him pay.

HOST. He? alas, he is poor; he hath nothing.

FAL. How! poor? look upon his face; what call you rich? let them coin his nose, let them coin his cheeks; I'll not pay a denier.[4] What, will you make a younker of me? shall I not take mine ease in mine inn but I shall have my pocket picked? I have lost a seal ring of my grandfather's worth forty mark.[5]

HOST. O Jesu, I have heard the prince tell him I know not how oft that that ring was copper.

FAL. How! the prince is a Jack,[6] a sneak-up; 'sblood, an he were here, I would cudgel him like a dog if he would say so.

[*Enter the* PRINCE ⟨*and* POINS⟩, *marching, and* FALSTAFF *meets them playing upon his truncheon like a fife.*]

How now, lad, is the wind in that door, i' faith? must we all march?

7. Candlemaker's. "Salamanders" were lizards that supposedly lived in fire and ate it.
8. A nickname from the hen in Chaucer's Nun's Priest's Tale; in Shakespeare's time a conventional name for a scolding woman.
9. Tenth part.
1. A coarse cloth. "Bolters": sieves for flour.
2. Fine linen; "ell": 45 inches.
3. Drinks between meals.
4. French penny, worth a tenth of an English penny. "Younker": youngster, novice.
5. A mark was worth two-thirds of a pound.
6. Rascal; "sneak-up": a sneak.

BARD. Yea, two and two, Newgate fashion.[7]

HOST. My lord, I pray you hear me.

PRINCE. What sayest thou, Mistress Quickly? How doth thy husband? I love him well; he is an honest man.

HOST. Good my lord, hear me.

FAL. Prithee let her alone, and list to me.

PRINCE. What sayest thou, Jack?

FAL. The other night I fell asleep here behind the arras and had my pocket picked; this house is turned bawdyhouse, they pick pockets.

PRINCE. What didst thou lose, Jack?

FAL. Wilt thou believe me, Hal? three or four bonds of forty pound apiece, and a seal ring of my grandfather's.

PRINCE. A trifle, some eightpenny matter.

HOST. So I told him, my lord, and I said I heard your grace say so; and, my lord, he speaks most vilely of you, like a foul-mouthed man as he is, and said he would cudgel you.

PRINCE. What, he did not?

HOST. There's neither faith, truth, nor womanhood in me else.

FAL. There's no more faith in thee than in a stewed prune,[8] nor no more truth in thee than in a drawn fox, and for womanhood Maid Marian may be the deputy's wife of the ward to thee.[9] Go, you thing, go.

HOST. Say, what thing, what thing?

FAL. What thing! why, a thing to thank God on.

HOST. I am no thing to thank God on, I would thou shouldst know it; I am an honest man's wife, and, setting thy knighthood aside,[1] thou art a knave to call me so.

FAL. Setting thy womanhood aside, thou art a beast to say otherwise.

HOST. Say, what beast, thou knave, thou?

FAL. What beast? why, an otter.

PRINCE. An otter, Sir John, why an otter?

FAL. Why, she's neither fish nor flesh, a man knows not where to have her.[2]

HOST. Thou art an unjust man in saying so; thou or any man knows where to have me, thou knave, thou!

PRINCE. Thou sayest true, hostess, and he slanders thee most grossly.

HOST. So he doth you, my lord, and said this other day you ought[3] him a thousand pound.

PRINCE. Sirrah, do I owe you a thousand pound?

FAL. A thousand pound, Hal! A million. Thy love is worth a mil-

7. Chained together, like prisoners at Newgate.

8. Stewed prunes were commonly served in bawdyhouses, as a supposed protection against venereal disease. "Drawn": hunted.

9. "Maid Marian" was a female character of low morals in the popular Robin Hood plays; a "deputy's wife of the ward" would be a respectable woman.

1. I.e., ignoring, or intending no disrespect to, the rank of knighthood. Falstaff intentionally misunderstands the phrase.

2. I.e., how to understand her. But the Hostess' retort is, unconsciously, equivalent to saying that she is completely promiscuous.

3. Owed.

lion; thou owest me thy love.

HOST. Nay, my lord, he called you Jack, and said he would cudgel you.

FAL. Did I, Bardolph?

BARD. Indeed, Sir John, you said so.

FAL. Yea, if he said my ring was copper.

PRINCE. I say 'tis copper; darest thou be as good as thy word now?

FAL. Why, Hal, thou knowest, as thou art but man, I dare; but as thou art prince, I fear thee as I fear the roaring of the lion's whelp.

PRINCE. And why not as the lion?

FAL. The king himself is to be feared as the lion; dost thou think I'll fear thee as I fear thy father? Nay, an I do, I pray God my girdle[4] break.

PRINCE. O, if it should, how would thy guts fall about thy knees! But, sirrah, there's no room for faith, truth, nor honesty in this bosom of thine; it is all filled up with guts and midriff. Charge an honest woman with picking thy pocket! Why, thou whoreson, impudent, embossed rascal,[5] if there were anything in thy pocket but tavern-reckonings, memorandums of bawdyhouses, and one poor pennyworth of sugar candy to make thee long-winded, if thy pocket were enriched with any other injuries but these, I am a villain. And yet you will stand to it, you will not pocket up wrong; art thou not ashamed?

FAL. Dost thou hear, Hal? thou knowest in the state of innocency Adam fell, and what should poor Jack Falstaff do in the days of villainy? Thou seest I have more flesh than another man, and therefore more frailty. You confess then, you picked my pocket?

PRINCE. It appears so by the story.

FAL. Hostess, I forgive thee; go make ready breakfast, love thy husband, look to thy servants, cherish thy guests; thou shalt find me tractable to any honest reason; thou seest I am pacified still. Nay, prithee begone. [*Exit* HOSTESS.] Now, Hal, to the news at court; for the robbery, lad, how is that answered?

PRINCE. O, my sweet beef, I must still be good angel to thee; the money is paid back again.

FAL. O, I do not like that paying back; 'tis a double labor.

PRINCE. I am good friends with my father and may do anything.

FAL. Rob me the exchequer the first thing thou doest, and do it with unwashed hands too.

BARD. Do, my lord.

PRINCE. I have procured thee, Jack, a charge of foot.[6]

FAL. I would it had been of horse. Where shall I find one that can steal well? O for a fine thief, of the age of two and twenty or thereabouts! I am heinously unprovided. Well, God be thanked for these rebels, they offend none but the virtuous; I

4. Belt.

5. Swollen rascal; "embossed" was also a technical term in hunting, applied to a deer which was exhausted and foaming at the mouth.

6. Command of a company of foot-soldiers. "Horse": cavalry.

laud them, I praise them.
PRINCE. Bardolph!
BARD. My lord?
PRINCE. Go bear this letter to Lord John of Lancaster, to my brother John; this to my Lord of Westmoreland. [Exit BARDOLPH.] Go, Poins, to horse, to horse; for thou and I have thirty miles to ride yet ere dinnertime. [Exit POINS.] Jack, meet me tomorrow in the Temple Hall at two o'clock in the afternoon.
There shalt thou know thy charge, and there receive
Money and order for their furniture.[7]
The land is burning, Percy stands on high,
And either we or they must lower lie. [⟨Exit.⟩]
FAL. Rare words, brave world! Hostess, my breakfast, come.
O, I could wish this tavern were my drum![7a] [Exit.]

Act IV

SCENE 1

[Enter HOTSPUR, WORCESTER, and DOUGLAS.]

HOT. Well said, my noble Scot. If speaking truth
In this fine age were not thought flattery,
Such attribution should the Douglas have
As not a soldier of this season's stamp
Should go so general current[8] through the world.
By God, I cannot flatter; I do defy
The tongues of soothers,[9] but a braver place
In my heart's love hath no man than yourself;
Nay, task me to my word,[1] approve me, lord.
DOUG. Thou art the king of honor;
No man so potent breathes upon the ground
But I will beard him.[2]
HOT. Do so, and 'tis well.
[Enter a MESSENGER with letters.]
What letters hast thou there?—I can but thank you.
MESS. These letters come from your father.
HOT. Letters from him! why comes he not himself?
MESS. He cannot come, my lord; he is grievous sick.
HOT. Zounds! how has he the leisure to be sick
In such a justling[3] time? Who leads his power?
Under whose government come they along?
MESS. His letters bears his mind, not I, my lord.
WOR. I prithee tell me, doth he keep his bed?
MESS. He did, my lord, four days ere I set forth,
And at the time of my departure thence

7. Furnishings, equipment.
7a. Headquarters.
8. I.e., that not a soldier of this year's coinage should achieve such currency. "Attribution": praise.
9. Flatterers; "braver": more distinguished.
1. Compare my actions with my speech. "Approve": prove, test.
2. I.e., I will take on anybody, however powerful.
3. Turbulent.

He was much feared by[4] his physicians.
WOR. I would the state of time had first been whole
Ere he by sickness had been visited;
His health was never better worth than now.
HOT. Sick now! droop now! this sickness doth infect
The very lifeblood of our enterprise;
'Tis catching hither, even to our camp.
He writes me here that inward sickness—
And that his friends by deputation could not
So soon be drawn,[5] nor did he think it meet
To lay so dangerous and dear a trust
On any soul removed but on his own.
Yet doth he give us bold advertisement
That with our small conjunction[6] we should on
To see how fortune is disposed to us;
For, as he writes, there is no quailing now,
Because the king is certainly possessed[7]
Of all our purposes. What say you to it?
WOR. Your father's sickness is a maim to us.
HOT. A perilous gash, a very limb lopped off;
And yet in faith it is not; his present want[8]
Seems more than we shall find it. Were it good
To set the exact wealth of all our states
All at one cast, to set so rich a main[9]
On the nice hazard of one doubtful hour?
It were not good, for therein should we read
The very bottom and the soul of hope,[1]
The very list, the very utmost bound
Of all our fortunes.
DOUG. Faith, and so we should,
Where now remains a sweet reversion.[2]
We may boldly spend upon the hope of what
Is to come in;
A comfort of retirement[3] lives in this.
HOT. A rendezvous, a home to fly unto,
If that the devil and mischance look big
Upon the maidenhead of our affairs.[4]
WOR. But yet I would your father had been here.
The quality and hair[5] of our attempt
Brooks no division; it will be thought
By some that know not why he is away
That wisdom, loyalty, and mere dislike
Of our proceedings kept the earl from hence.

4. Feared for by. "State of time": public affairs.
5. Could not quickly be organized under a deputy. "Soul removed": other person.
6. Unified forces.
7. Informed.
8. Our present awareness of his absence.
9. Stake, in betting; "nice hazard": risky chance.
1. Foundation and essence of our expectations. "List": limit.
2. A fund to be inherited in the future.
3. Sustaining place to fall back on.
4. I.e., threaten the beginning of our affairs.
5. Character; "brooks": allows.

And think how such an apprehensión
May turn the tide of fearful factión[6]
And breed a kind of question in our cause,
For well you know we of the offering[7] side
Must keep aloof from strict arbitrement,
And stop all sight-holes, every loop[8] from whence
The eye of reason may pry in upon us.
This absence of your father's draws a curtain,
That shows the ignorant a kind of fear
Before not dreamt of.

HOT. You strain too far.
I rather of his absence make this use:
It lends a luster and more great opinion,
A larger dare to our great enterprise,
Than if the earl were here, for men must think,
If we without his help can make a head
To push against a kingdom, with his help
We shall o'erturn it topsy-turvy down.
Yet all goes well, yet all our joints are whole.

DOUG. As heart can think; there is not such a word
Spoke of in Scotland as this term of fear.

[*Enter* SIR RICHARD VERNON.]

HOT. My cousin Vernon, welcome, by my soul!

VER. Pray God my news be worth a welcome, lord.
The Earl of Westmoreland, seven thousand strong,
Is marching hitherwards; with him Prince John.

HOT. No harm; what more?

VER. And further I have learned
The king himself in person is set forth,
Or hitherwards intended speedily,
With strong and mighty preparatión.

HOT. He shall be welcome too. Where is his son,
The nimble-footed madcap Prince of Wales,
And his comrades that daft[9] the world aside
And bid it pass?

VER. All furnished, all in arms,
All plumed like estridges that with the wind
Bated, like eagles having lately bathed,[1]
Glittering in golden coats like images,
As full of spirit as the month of May,
And gorgeous as the sun at midsummer,
Wanton as youthful goats, wild as young bulls.
I saw young Harry, with his beaver[2] on,
His cushes on his thighs, gallantly armed,
Rise from the ground like feathered Mercury,
And vaulted with such ease into his seat,

6. Conspiracy.
7. Challenging. "Arbitrement": investigation.
8. Loophole.
9. Push.
1. Eagles were supposed to renew their youth by bathing in the ocean. "Estridges": ostriches; "bated": fluttering their wings.
2. Helmet. "Cushes": cuisses, armor for the thighs.

As if an angel dropped down from the clouds,
To turn and wind[3] a fiery Pegasus
And witch the world with noble horsemanship.
HOT. No more, no more. Worse than the sun in March
This praise doth nourish agues.[4] Let them come;
They come like sacrifices in their trim,
And to the fire-eyed maid of smoky war[5]
All hot and bleeding will we offer them;
The mailéd Mars shall on his altar sit
Up to the ears in blood. I am on fire
To hear this rich reprisal[6] is so nigh
And yet not ours. Come, let me taste my horse,
Who is to bear me like a thunderbolt
Against the bosom of the Prince of Wales;
Harry to Harry shall, hot horse to horse,
Meet and ne'er part till one drop down a corse.
O that Glendower were come!
VER. There is more news;
I learned in Worcester, as I rode along,
He cannot draw his power[7] this fourteen days.
DOUG. That's the worst tidings that I hear of yet.
WOR. Aye, by my faith, that bears a frosty sound.
HOT. What may the king's whole battle[8] reach unto?
VER. To thirty thousand.
HOT. Forty let it be;
My father and Glendower being both away,
The powers of us may serve so great a day.
Come, let us take a muster speedily;
Doomsday is near; die all, die merrily.
DOUG. Talk not of dying; I am out of fear
Of death or death's hand for this one-half year. [*Exeunt.*]

SCENE 2

[*Enter* FALSTAFF *and* BARDOLPH.]

FAL. Bardolph, get thee before to Coventry; fill me a bottle of sack, our soldiers shall march through. We'll to Sutton Co'fil'[9] tonight.

BARD. Will you give me money, captain?

FAL. Lay out, lay out.

BARD. This bottle makes an angel.[1]

FAL. An if it do, take it for thy labor; and if it make twenty, take them all; I'll answer the coinage. Bid my lieutenant Peto meet me at town's end.

BARD. I will, captain; farewell. [*Exit.*]

FAL. If I be not ashamed of my soldiers, I am a soused gurnet.[2] I have misused the king's press damnably. I have got in ex-

3. Direct. "Pegasus": winged horse.
4. Fevers. Malaria was thought to be caused by vapors from the marshes, drawn up by the sun in spring.
5. Bellona, goddess of war.
6. Prize.
7. Assemble his forces.
8. Army.
9. Sutton Coldfield, about 25 miles from Coventry.
1. Ten shillings' worth.
2. Pickled anchovy. "Press": the draft or impressment of soldiers into service.

change of a hundred and fifty soldiers three hundred and odd pounds. I press me none but good householders, yeomen's sons, inquire me out contracted bachelors, such as had been asked twice on the banns,[3] such a commodity[4] of warm slaves as had as lieve hear the devil as a drum, such as fear the report of a caliver worse than a struck fowl or a hurt wild duck. I pressed me none but such toasts-and-butter[5] with hearts in their bellies no bigger than pins' heads, and they have bought out their services, and now my whole charge consists of ancients,[6] corporals, lieutenants, gentlemen of companies, slaves as ragged as Lazarus in the painted cloth where the glutton's dogs licked his sores, and such as indeed were never soldiers, but discarded unjust serving-men, younger sons to younger brothers, revolted tapsters and ostlers trade-fallen,[7] the cankers of a calm world and a long peace, ten times more dishonorable ragged than an old-fac'd ancient,[8] and such have I to fill up the rooms of them that have bought out their services, that you would think that I had a hundred and fifty tattered prodigals lately come from swine-keeping, from eating draff[9] and husks. A mad fellow met me on the way and told me I had unloaded all the gibbets and pressed the dead bodies. No eye hath seen such scarecrows. I'll not march through Coventry with them, that's flat; nay, and the villains march wide betwixt the legs, as if they had gyves[1] on, for indeed I had the most of them out of prison. There's but a shirt and a half in all my company, and the half shirt is two napkins tacked together and thrown over the shoulders like a herald's coat without sleeves, and the shirt, to say the truth, stolen from my host at Saint Alban's, or the red-nose innkeeper of Daventry. But that's all one; they'll find linen enough on every hedge.[2]

[*Enter the* PRINCE *and the Lord of* WESTMORELAND.]

PRINCE. How now, blown Jack! how now, quilt!

FAL. What, Hal, how now, mad wag! what a devil dost thou in Warwickshire? My good Lord of Westmoreland, I cry you mercy; I thought your honor had already been at Shrewsbury.

WEST. Faith, Sir John, 'tis more than time that I were there, and you too; but my powers are there already. The king, I can tell you, looks for us all; we must away all night.

FAL. Tut, never fear me; I am as vigilant as a cat to steal cream.

PRINCE. I think, to steal cream indeed, for thy theft hath already made thee butter. But tell me, Jack, whose fellows are these that come after?

FAL. Mine, Hal, mine.

PRINCE. I did never see such pitiful rascals.

3. Notice of approaching marriage, announced three times publicly in church before the marriage could take place.
4. "Commodity": collection; "warm": well-to-do; "caliver": musket.
5. Sissies.
6. Ensigns.
7. Hostlers out of work; "cankers": canker worms.
8. Frayed flag.
9. Garbage. The prodigal son, in the Bible, fed on husks before returning to the paternal board.
1. Leg-irons.
2. Laundry was customarily hung on hedges to dry.

FAL. Tut, tut, good enough to toss,[3] food for powder, food for powder; they'll fill a pit as well as better; tush, man, mortal men, mortal men.

WEST. Aye, but, Sir John, methinks they are exceeding poor and bare, too beggarly.

FAL. Faith, for their poverty I know not where they had that, and for their bareness I am sure they never learned that of me.

PRINCE. No, I'll be sworn, unless you call three fingers[4] on the ribs bare. But, sirrah, make haste; Percy is already in the field.

FAL. What, is the king encamped?

WEST. He is, Sir John; I fear we shall stay too long.

FAL. Well,
To the latter end of a fray and the beginning of a feast
Fits a dull fighter and a keen guest. [*Exeunt.*]

SCENE 3

[*Enter* HOTSPUR, WORCESTER, DOUGLAS, *and* VERNON.]

HOT. We'll fight with him tonight.
WOR. It may not be.
DOUG. You give him then advantage.
VER. Not a whit.
HOT. Why say you so? looks he not for supply?
VER. So do we.
HOT. His is certain, ours is doubtful.
WOR. Good cousin, be advised; stir not tonight.
VER. Do not, my lord.
DOUG. You do not counsel well;
You speak it out of fear and cold heart.
VER. Do me no slander, Douglas; by my life,
And I dare well maintain it with my life,
If well-respected honor[5] bid me on,
I hold as little counsel with weak fear
As you, my lord, or any Scot that this day lives.
Let it be seen tomorrow in the battle
Which of us fears.
DOUG. Yea, or tonight.
VER. Content.
HOT. Tonight, say I.
VER. Come, come, it may not be. I wonder much,
Being men of such great leading as you are,
That you foresee not what impediments
Drag back our expedition;[6] certain horse
Of my cousin Vernon's are not yet come up,
Your uncle Worcester's horse came but today,
And now their pride and mettle is asleep,
Their courage with hard labor tame and dull,
That not a horse is half the half of himself.
HOT. So are the horses of the enemy

3. I.e., on a pike, or long spear.
4. Layers of fat. A finger was ¾ of an inch.
5. Well-considered (not rash, like Hotspur's).
6. Retard our speed.

In general, journey-bated[7] and brought low;
The better part of ours are full of rest.
WOR. The number of the king exceedeth ours;
For God's sake, cousin, stay till all come in.
[*The trumpet sounds a parley. Enter* SIR WALTER BLUNT.]
BLUNT. I come with gracious offers from the king,
If you vouchsafe me hearing and respect.
HOT. Welcome, Sir Walter Blunt; and would to God
You were of our determinatión!
Some of us love you well, and even those some
Envy your great deservings and good name
Because you are not of our quality,[8]
But stand against us like an enemy.
BLUNT. And God defend[9] but still I should stand so,
So long as out of limit and true rule
You stand against anointed majesty.
But to my charge. The king hath sent to know
The nature of your griefs, and whereupon
You conjure from the breast of civil peace
Such bold hostility, teaching his duteous land
Audacious cruelty. If that the king
Have any way your good deserts forgot,
Which he confesseth to be manifold,
He bids you name your griefs, and with all speed
You shall have your desires with interest
And pardon absolute for yourself and these
Herein misled by your suggestión.[1]
HOT. The king is kind, and well we know the king
Knows at what time to promise, when to pay
My father and my uncle and myself
Did give him that same royalty he wears;
And when he was not six and twenty strong,
Sick in the world's regard, wretched and low,
A poor unminded outlaw sneaking home,
My father gave him welcome to the shore;
And when he heard him swear and vow to God
He came but to be Duke of Lancaster,
To sue his livery[2] and beg his peace,
With tears of innocency and terms of zeal,
My father, in kind heart and pity moved,
Swore him assistance and performed it too.
Now when the lords and barons of the realm
Perceived Northumberland did lean to him,
The more and less came in with cap and knee,[3]
Met him in boroughs, cities, villages,
Attended him on bridges, stood in lanes,
Laid gifts before him, proffered him their oaths,

7. Tired from travel.
8. Fellowship, party.
9. Forbid; "still": always.
1. Temptation.
2. I.e., claim title to his late father's lands (held by King Richard II).
3. Cap in hand and on bended knee; i.e., offering homage.

Gave him their heirs as pages, followed him
Even at the heels in golden multitudes.
He presently, as greatness knows itself,
Steps me a little higher than his vow,
Made to my father while his blood was poor
Upon the naked shore at Ravenspurgh,
And now, forsooth, takes on him to reform
Some certain edicts and some strait[4] decrees
That lie too heavy on the commonwealth,
Cries out upon abuses, seems to weep
Over his country's wrongs, and by this face,[5]
This seeming brow of justice, did he win
The hearts of all that he did angle for;
Proceeded further, cut me off the heads
Of all the favorites that the absent king
In deputation left behind him here,
When he was personal[6] in the Irish war.

BLUNT. Tut, I came not to hear this.

HOT. Then to the point.
In short time after he deposed the king,
Soon after that deprived him of his life,
And in the neck of that tasked[7] the whole state;
To make that worse, suffered his kinsman March
(Who is, if every owner were well placed,
Indeed his king) to be engaged[8] in Wales,
There without ransom to lie forfeited;
Disgraced[1] me in my happy victories,
Sought to entrap me by intelligence,[2]
Rated mine uncle from the council board,
In rage dismissed my father from the court,
Broke oath on oath, committed wrong on wrong,
And in conclusion drove us to seek out
This head of safety,[3] and withal to pry
Into his title, the which we find
Too indirect for long continuance.

BLUNT. Shall I return this answer to the king?

HOT. Not so, Sir Walter; we'll withdraw awhile.
Go to the king, and let there be impawned[4]
Some surety for a safe return again,
And in the morning early shall mine uncle
Bring him our purposes; and so farewell.

BLUNT. I would you would accept of grace and love.

HOT. And may be so we shall.

BLUNT. Pray God you do. [*Exeunt.*]

4. Strict.
5. Pretense.
6. Actively participating in person.
7. I.e., immediately after that, (he) taxed.
8. Pawned as a hostage.
1. I.e., did not favor.
2. Spying; "rated": angrily dismissed.
3. Army for our safety.
4. Pledged; "surety": guarantee.

SCENE 4

[*Enter the* ARCHBISHOP OF YORK *and* SIR MICHAEL.]

ARCH. Hie, good Sir Michael; bear this sealéd brief[5]
With wingéd haste to the lord marshal,
This to my cousin Scroop, and all the rest
To whom they are directed. If you knew
How much they do import you would make haste.

SIR M. My good lord,
I guess their tenor.

ARCH. Like enough you do.
Tomorrow, good Sir Michael, is a day
Wherein the fortune of ten thousand men
Must bide the touch;[6] for, sir, at Shrewsbury,
As I am truly given to understand,
The king with mighty and quick-raiséd power
Meets with Lord Harry; and I fear, Sir Michael,
What with the sickness of Northumberland,
Whose power was in the first proportión,[7]
And what with Owen Glendower's absence thence,
Who with them was a rated[8] sinew too
And comes not in, o'er-ruled by prophecies—
I fear the power of Percy is too weak
To wage an instant trial with the king.

SIR M. Why, my good lord, you need not fear;
There is Douglas and Lord Mortimer.

ARCH. No, Mortimer is not there.

SIR M. But there is Mordake, Vernon, Lord Harry Percy,
And there is my Lord of Worcester and a head
Of gallant warriors, noble gentlemen.

ARCH. And so there is; but yet the king hath drawn
The special head[9] of all the land together:
The Prince of Wales, Lord John of Lancaster,
The noble Westmoreland, and warlike Blunt,
And many more corrivals [10] and dear men
Of estimation and command in arms.

SIR M. Doubt not, my lord, they shall be well opposed.

ARCH. I hope no less, yet needful 'tis to fear,
And to prevent[1] the worst, Sir Michael, speed;
For if Lord Percy thrive not, ere the king
Dismiss his power, he means to visit[2] us,
For he hath heard of our confederacy,
And 'tis but wisdom to make strong against him;
Therefore make haste. I must go write again
To other friends; and so farewell, Sir Michael. [*Exeunt.*]

5. Letter.
6. Stand the test.
7. The largest part.
8. Highly regarded.
9. Principal army.
10. Associates; "dear": noble.
1. Forestall.
2. Attack.

Act V

SCENE 1

[*Enter the* KING, PRINCE OF WALES, PRINCE JOHN OF LANCASTER, SIR WALTER BLUNT, *and* FALSTAFF.]

KING. How bloodily the sun begins to peer
Above yon busky[3] hill! The day looks pale
At his distemperature.[4]
PRINCE. The southern wind
Doth play the trumpet to his purposes,[5]
And by his hollow whistling in the leaves
Foretells a tempest and a blustering day.
KING. Then with the losers let it sympathize,
For nothing can seem foul to those that win.

[*The trumpet sounds. Enter* WORCESTER ⟨*and* VERNON.⟩]

How now, my lord of Worcester! 'Tis not well
That you and I should meet upon such terms
As now we meet. You have deceived our trust
And made us doff our easy robes of peace,
To crush[6] our old limbs in ungentle steel;
This is not well, my lord, this is not well.
What say you to it? will you again unknit
This churlish knot of all-abhorréd war
And move in that obedient orb[7] again
Where you did give a fair and natural light,
And be no more an exhaled meteor,[8]
A prodigy of fear and a portent
Of broachéd mischief to the unborn times?[9]
WOR. Hear me, my liege:
For mine own part I could be well content
To entertain the lag end of my life
With quiet hours, for I do protest
I have not sought the day of this dislike.
KING. You have not sought it! how comes it then?
FAL. Rebellion lay in his way, and he found it.
PRINCE. Peace, chewet,[1] peace!
WOR. It pleased your majesty to turn your looks
Of favor from myself and all our house,
And yet I must remember[2] you, my lord,
We were the first and dearest of your friends.
For you my staff of office did I break
In Richard's time, and posted day and night
To meet you on the way and kiss your hand

3. Wooded.
4. I.e., the sun's illness or malevolence.
5. I.e., the sun's intentions; the southern wind supports them.
6. Enfold, cramp.
7. Regular orbit, as of a planet.
8. Meteors were thought to be made of gas exhaled by a planet and were commonly associated with civil commotion.
9. I.e., of harm or disaster opened up ("broached") to plague the future. Note that "mischief" conveyed a stronger meaning to Shakespeare than it does to us.
1. Chattering bird.
2. Remind.

When yet you were in place and in account
Nothing so strong and fortunate as I.
It was myself, my brother, and his son
That brought you home and boldly did outdare
The dangers of the time. You swore to us,
And you did swear that oath at Doncaster,
That you did nothing purpose 'gainst the state
Nor claim no further than your new-fall'n[3] right,
The seat of Gaunt, dukedom of Lancaster.
To this we swore our aid. But in short space
It rained down fortune showering on your head
And such a flood of greatness fell on you,
What with our help, what with the absent king,
What with the injuries of a wanton time,
The seeming sufferances[4] that you had borne,
And the contrarious winds that held the king
So long in his unlucky Irish wars
That all in England did repute him dead;
And from this swarm of fair advantages
You took occasion to be quickly wooed
To gripe the general sway[5] into your hand,
Forgot your oath to us at Doncaster,
And being fed by us you used us so
As that ungentle gull[6] the cuckoo's bird
Useth the sparrow, did oppress our nest,
Grew by our feeding to so great a bulk
That even our love durst not come near your sight
For fear of swallowing;[7] but with nimble wing
We were enforced for safety sake to fly
Out of your sight and raise this present head,
Whereby we stand opposéd by such means
As you yourself have forged against yourself
By unkind usage, dangerous countenance,[8]
And violation of all faith and troth
Sworn to us in your younger enterprise.

KING. These things indeed you have articulate,[9]
Proclaimed at market crosses, read in churches,
To face[1] the garment of rebellión
With some fine color that may please the eye
Of fickle changelings and poor discontents,
Which gape and rub the elbow at the news
Of hurlyburly innovatión;
And never yet did insurrection want
Such water colors to impaint his cause,
Nor moody beggars starving for a time
Of pellmell havoc and confusión.

PRINCE. In both our armies there is many a soul

3. Recently inherited.
4. Sufferings.
5. Seize power over the whole state.
6. Rude nestling; the cuckoo hatches its young in other birds' nests.
7. Being swallowed.
8. Threatening looks.
9. Drawn up in detail.
1. Decorate.

Shall pay full dearly for this encounter;
If once they join in trial. Tell your nephew
The Prince of Wales doth join with all the world
In praise of Henry Percy; by my hopes,
This present enterprise set off his head,[2]
I do not think a braver gentleman,
More active-valiant or more valiant-young,
More daring or more bold, is now alive
To grace this latter age with noble deeds.
For my part, I may speak it to my shame,
I have a truant been to chivalry—
And so I hear he doth account me too—
Yet this before my father's majesty:
I am content that he shall take the odds
Of his great name and estimatión,
And will, to save the blood on either side,
Try fortune with him in a single fight.

KING. And, Prince of Wales, so dare we venture thee,
Albeit considerations infinite
Do make[3] against it. No, good Worcester, no,
We love our people well; even those we love
That are misled upon your cousin's part;
And, will they take the offer of our grace,
Both he and they and you, yea, every man
Shall be my friend again and I'll be his.
So tell your cousin, and bring me word
What he will do; but if he will not yield,
Rebuke and dread correction wait on[4] us
And they shall do their office. So, be gone;
We will not now be troubled with reply.
We offer fair; take it advisedly.

[*Exit* WORCESTER ⟨*and* VERNON.⟩]

PRINCE. It will not be accepted, on my life;
The Douglas and the Hotspur both together
Are confident against the world in arms.

KING. Hence, therefore, every leader to his charge,
For on their answer will we set on them,
And God befriend us, as our cause is just!

[*Exeunt all but the* PRINCE *and* FALSTAFF.]

FAL. Hal, if thou see me down in the battle and bestride me, so; 'tis a point of friendship.

PRINCE. Nothing but a colossus can do thee that friendship. Say thy prayers, and farewell.

FAL. I would 'twere bedtime, Hal, and all well.

PRINCE. Why, thou owest God a death. [⟨*Exit.*⟩]

FAL. 'Tis not due yet; I would be loath to pay him before his day. What need I be so forward with him that calls not on me? Well, 'tis no matter; honor pricks me on. Yea, but how if honor

2. Deducted from his account.
3. Weigh.
4. Accompany.

prick me off when I come on? How then? can honor set to a leg? No. Or an arm? No. Or take away the grief[5] of a wound? No. Honor hath no skill in surgery, then? No. What is honor? A word. What is in that word honor? what is that honor? Air. A trim reckoning![6] Who hath it? He that died o' Wednesday. Doth he feel it? No. Doth he hear it? No. 'Tis insensible,[7] then? Yea, to the dead. But will it not live with the living? No. Why? Detraction will not suffer it. Therefore I'll none of it; Honor is a mere scutcheon.[8] And so ends my catechism. [*Exit.*]

SCENE 2

[*Enter* WORCESTER *and* SIR RICHARD VERNON.]

WOR. O no, my nephew must not know, Sir Richard,
The liberal and kind offer of the king.
VER. 'Twere best he did.
WOR. Then are we all undone.
It is not possible, it cannot be,
The king should keep his word in loving us;
He will suspect us still and find a time
To punish this offense in other faults.
Suspicion all our lives shall be stuck full of eyes,
For treason is but trusted like the fox
Who, ne'er so tame, so cherished and locked up,
Will have a wild trick of his ancestors;
Look how we can, or sad or merrily,
Interpretation will misquote[9] our looks,
And we shall feed like oxen at a stall,
The better cherished, still the nearer death.
My nephew's trespass may be well forgot;
It hath the excuse of youth and heat of blood
And an adopted name of privilege,[1]
A harebrained Hotspur, governed by a spleen.
All his offenses live upon my head
And on his father's; we did train him on,
And, his corruption being ta'en from us,[2]
We, as the spring of all, shall pay for all.
Therefore, good cousin, let not Harry know
In any case the offer of the king.
VER. Deliver what you will; I'll say 'tis so.
Here comes your cousin.

[*Enter* HOTSPUR ⟨*and* DOUGLAS.⟩]

HOT. My uncle is returned;
Deliver up my Lord of Westmoreland.
Uncle, what news?
WOR. The king will bid you battle presently.[3]
DOUG. Defy him by the Lord of Westmoreland.

5. Pain.
6. A fine totaling of the bill.
7. Not capable of being felt.
8. A coat of arms, as often put on a tombstone.
9. Misinterpret.
1. A nickname which gives him privileges. "Spleen": impetuous temperament.
2. Being attributed to. "Train": entice.
3. Immediately.

HOT. Lord Douglas, go you and tell him so.
DOUG. Marry, and shall, and very willingly. [*Exit.*]
WOR. There is no seeming mercy in the king.
HOT. Did you beg any? God forbid!
WOR. I told him gently of our grievances,
Of his oath-breaking, which he mended thus,
By now forswearing[4] that he is forsworn;
He calls us rebels, traitors, and will scourge
With haughty arms this hateful name in us.
[*Enter* DOUGLAS.]
DOUG. Arm, gentlemen, to arms! for I have thrown
A brave defiance in King Henry's teeth,
And Westmoreland, that was engaged,[5] did hear it,
Which cannot choose but bring him quickly on.
WOR. The Prince of Wales stepped forth before the king,
And, nephew, challenged you to single fight.
HOT. O, would the quarrel lay upon our heads,
And that no man might draw short breath today
But I and Harry Monmouth! Tell me, tell me,
How showed his tasking?[6] seemed it in contempt?
VER. No, by my soul; I never in my life
Did hear a challenge urged more modestly,
Unless a brother should a brother dare
To gentle exercise and proof of arms.
He gave you all the duties[7] of a man,
Trimmed up your praises with a princely tongue,
Spoke your deservings like a chronicle,
Making you ever better than his praise
By still dispraising praise valued with[8] you;
And, which became him like a prince indeed,
He made a blushing cital[9] of himself,
And chid his truant youth with such a grace
As if he mastered there a double spirit
Of teaching and of learning instantly.
There did he pause; but let me tell the world,
If he outlive the envy[1] of this day,
England did never owe[2] so sweet a hope,
So much miscónstrued in his wantonness.[3]
HOT. Cousin, I think thou art enamoured
On his follies; never did I hear
Of any prince so wild a liberty.[4]
But be he as he will, yet once ere night
I will embrace him with a soldier's arm,
That he shall shrink under my courtesy.
Arm, arm with speed; and, fellows, soldiers, friends,
Better consider what you have to do
Than I, that have not well the gift of tongue,

4. Swearing falsely.
5. Held as a hostage.
6. Challenge.
7. Good qualities.
8. Compared to.
9. Mention, recital.
1. Malice.
2. Own.
3. Frivolity.
4. Reckless dissipation.

Can lift your blood up with persuasión.
[*Enter a* MESSENGER.]
MESS. My lord, here are letters for you.
HOT. I cannot read them now.
O gentlemen, the time of life is short!
To spend that shortness basely were too long,
If life did ride upon a dial's point,[5]
Still ending at the arrival of an hour;
And if we live, we live to tread on kings,
If die, brave death when princes die with us!
Now, for our consciences, the arms are fair,
When the intent of bearing them is just.
[*Enter another* MESSENGER.]
MESS. My lord, prepare; the king comes on apace.
HOT. I thank him that he cuts me from my tale;
For I profess not talking; only this—
Let each man do his best; and here draw I
A sword whose temper I intend to stain
With the best blood that I can meet withal
In the adventure of this perilous day.
Now, Esperance! Percy![6] and set on.
Sound all the lofty instruments of war,
And by that music let us all embrace;
For, heaven to earth,[7] some of us never shall
A second time do such a courtesy.
[*The trumpets sound. They embrace and exeunt.*]

SCENE 3

[*The* KING *enters with his power. Alarum*[8] *to the battle. Then enter* DOUGLAS *and* SIR WALTER BLUNT.]
BLUNT. What is thy name, that in the battle thus
Thou crossest me? what honor dost thou seek
Upon my head?
DOUG. Know then, my name is Douglas,
And I do haunt thee in the battle thus
Because some tell me that thou art a king.[9]
BLUNT. They tell thee true.
DOUG. The Lord of Stafford dear[1] today hath bought
Thy likeness, for instead of thee, King Harry,
This sword hath ended him; so shall it thee,
Unless thou yield thee as my prisoner.
BLUNT. I was not born a yielder, thou proud Scot,
And thou shalt find a king that will revenge
Lord Stafford's death. [*They fight.* DOUGLAS *kills* BLUNT.]
[*Enter* HOTSPUR.]

5. Hand of a clock; "still": always. Hotspur's meaning (in lines 83–85) is that a base life would be too long even if it lasted only an hour.
6. Hope, Percy! (the family motto).
7. I.e., the odds are heaven to earth that.
8. Trumpet signal.
9. Blunt and others are dressed to look like the king.
1. Expensively.

HOT. O Douglas, hadst thou fought at Holmedon thus,
I never had triumphed upon a Scot.

DOUG. All's done, all's won; here breathless lies the king.

HOT. Where?

DOUG. Here.

HOT. This, Douglas? No, I know this face full well;
A gallant knight he was, his name was Blunt;
Semblably furnished like the king himself.

DOUG. Ah fool, go with thy soul whither it goes!
A borrowed title hast thou bought too dear;
Why didst thou tell me that thou wert a king?

HOT. The king hath many marching in his coats.

DOUG. Now, by my sword, I will kill all his coats;
I'll murder all his wardrobe, piece by piece,
Until I meet the king.

HOT. Up and away!
Our soldiers stand full fairly for the day. [*Exeunt.*]

[*Alarum. Enter* FALSTAFF *alone.*]

FAL. Though I could 'scape shot-free[2] at London, I fear the shot here; here's no scoring but upon the pate. Soft, who are you? Sir Walter Blunt; there's honor for you, here's no vanity! I am as hot as molten lead, and as heavy too; God keep lead out of me! I need no more weight than mine own bowels. I have led my ragamuffins where they are peppered; there's not three of my hundred and fifty left alive, and they are for the town's end, to beg during life. But who comes here?

[*Enter the* PRINCE.]

PRINCE. What, stand'st thou idle here? lend me thy sword;
Many a nobleman lies stark and stiff
Under the hoofs of vaunting enemies,
Whose deaths are yet unrevenged; I prithee, lend me thy sword.

FAL. O Hal, I prithee give me leave to breathe awhile. Turk Gregory[3] never did such deeds in arms as I have done this day. I have paid Percy, I have made him sure.

PRINCE. He is indeed, and living to kill thee. I prithee, lend me thy sword.

FAL. Nay, before God, Hal, if Percy be alive, thou get'st not my sword; but take my pistol if thou wilt.

PRINCE. Give it me; what, is it in the case?

FAL. Aye, Hal; 'tis hot, 'tis hot; there's that will sack a city.

[*The* PRINCE *draws it out, and finds it to be a bottle of sack.*]

PRINCE. What, is it a time to jest and dally now?

[*He throws the bottle at him. Exit.*]

FAL. Well, if Percy be alive, I'll pierce him. If he do come in my way, so; if he do not, if I come in his willingly, let him make a

2. Scot-free, without paying the bill at a tavern; "scoring" continues the pun; it means (1) marking up a charge; (2) cutting with a sword.

3. Falstaff combines Pope Gregory VII, of whom fantastic stories were told, with "Turk" (the Turks were noted for ferocity).

carbonado[4] of me. I like not such grinning honor as Sir Walter hath; give me life, which if I can save, so; if not, honor comes unlooked for, and there's an end. [*Exit.*]

SCENE 4

[*Alarum. Excursions.*[5] *Enter the* KING, *the* PRINCE, PRINCE JOHN OF LANCASTER, *and* EARL OF WESTMORELAND.]

KING. I prithee,
Harry, withdraw thyself; thou bleed'st too much.
Lord John of Lancaster, go you with him.
LAN. Not I, my lord, unless I did bleed too.
PRINCE. I beseech your majesty, make up,[6]
Lest your retirement do amaze your friends.
KING. I will do so.
My Lord of Westmoreland, lead him to his tent.
WEST. Come, my lord, I'll lead you to your tent.
PRINCE. Lead me, my lord? I do not need your help,
And God forbid a shallow scratch should drive
The Prince of Wales from such a field as this,
Where stained nobility lies trodden on,
And rebels' arms triumph in massacres!
LAN. We breathe too long; come, cousin Westmoreland,
Our duty this way lies; for God's sake, come.
[⟨*Exeunt* PRINCE JOHN *and* WESTMORELAND.⟩]
PRINCE. By God, thou hast deceived me, Lancaster;
I did not think thee lord of such a spirit.
Before, I loved thee as a brother, John,
But now I do respect thee as my soul.
KING. I saw him hold Lord Percy at the point
With lustier maintenance than I did look for
Of such an ungrown warrior.
PRINCE. O, this boy
Lends mettle to us all! [*Exit.*]
[*Enter* DOUGLAS.]
DOUG. Another king! they grow like Hydra's heads.[7]
I am the Douglas, fatal to all those
That wear those colors on them; what art thou,
That counterfeit'st the person of a king?
KING. The king himself, who, Douglas, grieves at heart
So many of his shadows[8] thou hast met
And not the very king. I have two boys
Seek Percy and thyself about the field,
But seeing thou fall'st on me so luckily
I will assay thee; so defend thyself.
DOUG. I fear thou art another counterfeit,
And yet, in faith, thou bearest thee like a king;
But mine I am sure thou art, whoe'er thou be,

4. A cubed steak.
5. Brief appearances and exits of soldiers fighting.
6. Advance; "amaze": dismay.
7. The heads of this fabulous monster grew back faster than they could be cut off.
8. Likenesses.

And thus I win thee.

[*They fight; the* KING *being in danger, enter* PRINCE OF WALES.]

PRINCE. Hold up thy head, vile Scot, or thou art like
Never to hold it up again! the spirits
Of valiant Shirley, Stafford, Blunt, are in my arms;
It is the Prince of Wales that threatens thee,
Who never promiseth but he means to pay.

[*They fight;* DOUGLAS *flieth.*]

Cheerly, my lord; how fares your grace?
Sir Nicholas Gawsey hath for succor sent,
And so hath Clifton; I'll to Clifton straight.

KING. Stay, and breathe awhile.
Thou hast redeemed thy lost opinión,
And showed thou makest some tender of[9] my life
In this fair rescue thou hast brought to me.

PRINCE. O God, they did me too much injury
That ever said I hearkened for your death.
If it were so, I might have let alone
The insulting hand of Douglas over you,
Which would have been as speedy in your end
As all the poisonous potions in the world
And saved the treacherous labor of your son.

KING. Make up to Clifton; I'll to Sir Nicholas Gawsey. [*Exit.*]

[*Enter* HOTSPUR.]

HOT. If I mistake not, thou art Harry Monmouth.

PRINCE. Thou speak'st as if I would deny my name.

HOT. My name is Harry Percy.

PRINCE. Why then I see
A very valiant rebel of the name.
I am the Prince of Wales, and think not, Percy,
To share with me in glory any more:
Two stars keep not their motion in one sphere,[10]
Nor can one England brook a double reign
Of Harry Percy and the Prince of Wales.

HOT. Nor shall it, Harry, for the hour is come
To end the one of us; and would to God
Thy name in arms were now as great as mine!

PRINCE. I'll make it greater ere I part from thee,
And all the budding honors on thy crest
I'll crop to make a garland for my head.

HOT. I can no longer brook thy vanities. [*They fight.*]

[*Enter* FALSTAFF.]

FAL. Well said, Hal, to it, Hal! Nay, you shall find no boy's play here, I can tell you.

[*Enter* DOUGLAS; *he fighteth with* FALSTAFF, *who falls down as if he were dead.* ⟨*Exit* DOUGLAS.⟩ *The* PRINCE *killeth* PERCY.]

9. I.e., you have some concern for. "Opinion": reputation.

10. Orbit. "Brook": endure.

HOT. O Harry, thou hast robbed me of my youth!
I better brook the loss of brittle life
Than those proud titles thou hast won of me;
They wound my thoughts worse than thy sword my flesh;
But thought's the slave of life, and life time's fool,
And time, that takes survey of all the world,
Must have a stop. O, I could prophesy,
But that the earthy and cold hand of death
Lies on my tongue; no, Percy, thou art dust,
And food for— [⟨Dies.⟩]
PRINCE. For worms, brave Percy; fare thee well, great heart!
Ill-weaved ambition, how much art thou shrunk!
When that this body did contain a spirit
A kingdom for it was too small a bound,
But now two paces of the vilest earth
Is room enough; this earth that bears thee dead
Bears not alive so stout[1] a gentleman.
If thou wert sensible of courtesy,
I should not make so dear[2] a show of zeal;
But let my favors hide thy mangled face[3]
And, even in thy behalf, I'll thank myself
For doing these fair rites of tenderness.
Adieu, and take thy praise with thee to heaven;
Thy ignominy sleep with thee in the grave,
But not remembered in thy epitaph!
[*He spieth* FALSTAFF *on the ground.*]
What, old acquaintance, could not all this flesh
Keep in a little life? Poor Jack, farewell;
I could have better spared a better man.
O, I should have a heavy miss of thee,
If I were much in love with vanity![4]
Death hath not struck so fat a deer today,
Though many dearer,[5] in this bloody fray.
Emboweled will I see thee by and by;
Till then in blood by noble Percy lie. [*Exit.*]

FAL. [*rising up*] Emboweled! if thou embowel me today, I'll give you leave to powder[6] me and eat me tomorrow. 'Sblood, 'twas time to counterfeit, or that hot termagant[7] Scot had paid me scot and lot too. Counterfeit? I lie, I am no counterfeit; to die is to be a counterfeit, for he is but the counterfeit of a man who hath not the life of a man; but to counterfeit dying when a man thereby liveth is to be no counterfeit, but the true and perfect image of life indeed. The better part[8] of valor is discretion, in the which better part I have saved my life. Zounds, I am afraid of this gunpowder Percy, though he be dead; how if he should counterfeit too and rise? By my faith, I am afraid he would prove the better counterfeit. Therefore I'll make him

1. Valiant.
2. Open.
3. Prince Hal here covers Hotspur's face with a scarf.
4. Frivolity.
5. Nobler. "Emboweled": embalmed.
6. Pickle.
7. Violent; "scot and lot": completely.
8. Quality, not "portion."

sure; yea, and I'll swear I killed him. Why may not he rise as well as I? Nothing confutes me but eyes, and nobody sees me. Therefore, sirrah [*stabbing him*], with a new wound in your thigh, come you along with me.

[*He takes up* HOTSPUR *on his back.*]

[*Enter the* PRINCE *and* JOHN OF LANCASTER.]

PRINCE. Come, brother John, full bravely hast thou fleshed[9]
Thy maiden sword.

LAN. But soft, whom have we here?
Did you not tell me this fat man was dead?

PRINCE. I did; I saw him dead,
Breathless and bleeding on the ground. Art thou alive?
Or is it fantasy[10] that plays upon our eyesight?
I prithee speak; we will not trust our eyes
Without our ears; thou art not what thou seem'st.

FAL. No, that's certain, I am not a double man; but if I be not Jack Falstaff, then am I a Jack.[1] There is Percy [*throwing the body down*]; if your father will do me any honor, so; if not, let him kill the next Percy himself. I look to be either earl or duke, I can assure you.

PRINCE. Why, Percy I killed myself and saw thee dead.

FAL. Didst thou? Lord, Lord, how this world is given to lying! I grant you I was down and out of breath, and so was he; but we rose both at an instant and fought a long hour by Shrewsbury clock. If I may be believed, so; if not, let them that should reward valor bear the sin upon their own heads. I'll take it upon my death, I gave him this wound in the thigh; if the man were alive and would deny it, zounds, I would make him eat a piece of my sword.

LAN. This is the strangest tale that ever I heard.

PRINCE. This is the strangest fellow, brother John.
Come, bring your luggage nobly on your back;
For my part, if a lie may do thee grace,
I'll gild it with the happiest terms I have.

[*A retreat is sounded.*]

The trumpet sounds retreat;[2] the day is ours.
Come, brother, let us to the highest[3] of the field,
To see what friends are living, who are dead.

[*Exeunt* ⟨PRINCE OF WALES *and* LANCASTER.⟩]

FAL. I'll follow, as they say, for reward. He that rewards me, God reward him! If I do grow great,[4] I'll grow less, for I'll purge and leave sack, and live cleanly as a nobleman should do. [*Exit.*]

SCENE 5

[*The trumpets sound. Enter the* KING, PRINCE OF WALES, PRINCE JOHN OF LANCASTER, EARL OF WESTMORELAND, *with* WORCESTER *and* VERNON *prisoners.*]

9. Initiated.
10. Illusion.
1. I.e., a worthless fellow.
2. The signal to stop pursuit of the defeated enemy.
3. Highest part.
4. I.e., become "either earl or duke." "Purge": take cleansing medicines.

KING. Thus ever did rebellion find rebuke.
Ill-spirited Worcester, did not we send grace,
Pardon, and terms of love to all of you?
And wouldst thou turn our offers contrary,
Misuse the tenor of thy kinsman's trust?
Three knights upon our party slain today,
A noble earl and many a creature else
Had been alive this hour,
If like a Christian thou hadst truly borne
Betwixt our armies true intelligence.
WOR. What I have done my safety urged me to,
And I embrace this fortune patiently,
Since not to be avoided it falls on me.
KING. Bear Worcester to the death and Vernon too;
Other offenders we will pause upon.
[*Exeunt* WORCESTER *and* VERNON ⟨*guarded.*⟩]
How goes the field?
PRINCE. The noble Scot, Lord Douglas, when he saw
The fortune of the day quite turned from him,
The noble Percy slain, and all his men
Upon the foot of fear,[5] fled with the rest,
And falling from a hill he was so bruised
That the pursuers took him. At my tent
The Douglas is, and I beseech your grace
I may dispose of him.
KING. With all my heart.
PRINCE. Then, brother John of Lancaster, to you
This honorable bounty shall belong;
Go to the Douglas and deliver him
Up to his pleasure, ransomless and free;
His valor shown upon our crests today
Hath taught us how to cherish such high deeds
Even in the bosom of our adversaries.
LAN. I thank your grace for this high courtesy,
Which I shall give away immediately.
KING. Then this remains, that we divide our power.
You, son John and my cousin Westmoreland,
Towards York shall bend you with your dearest[6] speed
To meet Northumberland and the prelate Scroop,
Who, as we hear, are busily in arms;
Myself and you, son Harry, will towards Wales
To fight with Glendower and the Earl of March.
Rebellion in this land shall lose his sway,
Meeting the check of such another day;
And since this business so fair is done,
Let us not leave till all our own be won. [*Exeunt.*]

1598

5. Fleeing in panic.
6. Greatest.
7. (1) Hindrance (2) rebuke.

King Lear *King Lear* is one of Shakespeare's major tragedies, in the company of *Hamlet, Macbeth, Othello,* and *Antony and Cleopatra.* It is even on a grander scale than any of them, for it involves not only the world in which human events take place, but the elements themselves—the realm of Nature. Whether the cosmos is friendly to man, or indifferent to him, or hostile to his aims and aspirations is a subject which the writer of tragedy explores. From the Book of Job through the great Greek tragedies and on to Shakespeare the tragic dramatist shows man suffering and trying to find the meaning of his suffering. As Richard Sewall has put it (*Tragedy: Modern Essays in Criticism,* ed. Laurence Michel and Richard B. Sewall, p. 124), "the essence of his nature is brought out by suffering: 'I suffer, I will to suffer, I learn by suffering; therefore I am.' "

The anguish of the tragic hero arises from his uncertain knowledge of himself and of people around him; from his awareness that good and evil are distributed in no obvious or logical way, and that what seems at first to be good is in fact evil; and from his desperate question whether there are "justicers" above, and if so, how they can possibly allow the world to go on as it does.

King Lear was written sometime between 1603 and 1606, probably in 1604 or 1605. It, together with the other great tragedies, comes in a period after the sunny comedies *Much Ado About Nothing, As You Like It,* and *Twelfth Night,* and before the dramatic romances of Shakespeare's final period, *Cymbeline, The Winter's Tale,* and *The Tempest.* Although there is a certain concentration on a particular type of play in each of these three periods of Shakespeare's life, it would be rash to draw any conclusions about the dramatist's biography from this. Mozart wrote some of his happiest music when his personal life was miserable.

Structurally, *King Lear* has two plots, and more than in any other play of Shakespeare, the two plots reinforce each other. They both have to do with the relationship between parents and children. One plot involves three daughters and a father; the other displays a father and two sons, one legitimate and the other illegitimate. The plots are woven together intimately; they do not touch each other merely by coincidence. Shakespeare drew them from widely different sources: the main plot of King Lear and his three daughters came from an old chronicle play (not a tragedy) called *The True Chronicle History of King Leir and his Three Daughters,* supplemented by treatments of the story in Holinshed's *Chronicle,* Spenser's *Faerie Queene,* and perhaps others. The plot of Gloucester and his two sons comes from Sir Philip Sidney's popular romance, *The Countess of Pembroke's Arcadia.*

The play has many themes, persistently touched upon and handled in various ways. A major one is Nature, and the word has many meanings in the play. Nature was thought of in the Middle Ages as a goddess; she was also called (in Chaucer, for example) "Kind." The word "kind" and its derivatives have both senses in Shakespeare, and the words "nature" and "natural" have many connotations. "Natural" sometimes means "virtuous," as showing "natural" feelings for a parent or child. But "natural" may also mean the opposite of law and custom. "Nature" is not only the physical world, but also that part of nature that we call "human nature." What is truly "natural" in that sphere is a mystery. "Is there any cause in nature that makes these hard hearts?" asks Lear in his misery.

As he had done in some earlier plays, for example *Romeo and Juliet* and *Julius Caesar*, Shakespeare makes belief in astrology, the influence of the stars on human affairs, an important theme in *King Lear*. The characters take different points of view on this question, and we must not suppose that any one of them is necessarily giving the author's opinion. Belief in the stars is only one form of a great tragic dilemma: is what happens to us the result of fate or destiny, or do we bring our disasters upon ourselves?

Another great theme is the learning of wisdom. How is it done? By observation, using the eyes? By abandoning what we had supposed was wisdom and assuming that we are fools? By turning off the rational brain and trusting to the emotions? It has been suggested above that in tragedy man learns by suffering. In *King Lear* this suffering takes every form, physical and mental, and sometimes both. "How sharper than a serpent's tooth it is to have a thankless child!" says the old king. One of the ways the proud and arrogant must learn wisdom is by being stripped—stripped of their luxuries, their status, their power, and reduced to the level of beasts. It is noteworthy that this stripping process is one which can be done by one's enemies or by the elements, or by both.

The theme of "service" is a common one in Shakespeare. Service meant something different in the class society of the seventeenth century from what it means in our more democratic time. We are used to service stations and service industries, but in Shakespeare's time service was associated closely with rank, and it implied, or could imply, a degree of personal dedication which we would find strange. An earl, banished, disguises himself and applies to be a servant—a sensational situation in the eyes of Shakespeare's audience. Or servants resisting the evil actions of their masters—almost incredible. The roles of the Fool, Oswald, and Kent will not be clear unless we recall the earlier conception of service.

Though irony is very common in tragedy (that Gloucester doesn't "see" until he has lost his eyes is an example of irony) the comic element is not —except in Shakespeare. The porter in *Macbeth* is a famous instance. In *Lear* the Fool is partly comic, not in the free-hearted way of the fool Feste in *Twelfth Night*, but in the critical, satirical mode of Touchstone in *As You Like It*, only more so. The court jester, called "Fool" not because he was foolish, had a certain freedom which courtiers did not have. He could be threatened with whipping, as a child could, but he was treated affectionately by his master as long as he amused him. The Fool in *Lear* may be "a pestilent gall" to his master when he reminds him of his folly, but the King clearly loves him.

Love is a great force in the play, when it is finally discovered. It cannot be measured by numbers, as Lear first tries to do. Justice and pity may be relative, and they are vitally important in society, but in the great catastrophe at the end it is the love of Lear and Cordelia that surmounts even their destruction.

The Tragedy of King Lear

Dramatis Personae

KING LEAR
KING OF FRANCE
DUKE OF BURGUNDY
DUKE OF CORNWALL, *husband to* REGAN
DUKE OF ALBANY, *husband to* GONERIL
EARL OF KENT
EARL OF GLOUCESTER
EDGAR, *son to* GLOUCESTER
EDMUND, *bastard son to* GLOUCESTER
CURAN, *a courtier*
OLD MAN, *tenant to* GLOUCESTER
DOCTOR
FOOL
OSWALD, *steward to* GONERIL
A CAPTAIN *employed by* EDMUND
GENTLEMAN *attendant on* CORDELIA
A HERALD
SERVANTS *to* CORNWALL
GONERIL, REGAN, CORDELIA } *daughters to* LEAR
KNIGHTS *attending on* LEAR, OFFICERS, MESSENGERS, SOLDIERS, ATTENDANTS

Act I

SCENE 1

[*Enter* KENT, GLOUCESTER, *and* EDMUND.]

KENT. I thought the king had more affected[1] the Duke of Albany than Cornwall.

GLOU. It did always seem so to us: but now, in the division of the kingdom, it appears not which of the dukes he values most; for equalities are so weighed, that curiosity in neither can make choice of either's moiety.[2]

KENT. Is not this your son, my lord?

GLOU. His breeding, sir, hath been at my charge: I have so often blushed to acknowledge him, that now I am brazed[3] to it.

KENT. I cannot conceive[4] you.

GLOU. Sir, this young fellow's mother could: whereupon she grew round-wombed, and had, indeed, sir, a son for her cradle ere she had a husband for her bed. Do you smell a fault?

1. Regard for; "Albany" is Scotland.
2. I.e., shares are so evenly balanced that careful consideration cannot decide whose part is greater.
3. Hardened.
4. Understand, with a pun on "become pregnant."

KENT. I cannot wish the fault undone, the issue[5] of it being so proper.

GLOU. But I have, sir, a son by order of law, some year elder than this, who yet is no dearer in my account: though this knave[6] came something saucily into the world before he was sent for, yet was his mother fair; there was good sport at his making, and the whoreson must be acknowledged. Do you know this noble gentleman, Edmund?

EDM. No, my lord.

GLOU. My lord of Kent. Remember him hereafter as my honorable friend.

EDM. My services to your lordship.

KENT. I must love you, and sue to know you better.

EDM. Sir, I shall study deserving.

GLOU. He hath been out[7] nine years, and away he shall again. [*Sound a sennet.*[8]] The king is coming.

[*Enter one bearing a coronet, then* KING LEAR, CORNWALL, ALBANY, GONERIL, REGAN, CORDELIA, *and* ATTENDANTS.]

LEAR. Attend the lords of France and Burgundy, Gloucester.

GLOU. I shall, my liege. [*Exeunt* GLOUCESTER *and* EDMUND.]

LEAR. Meantime we shall express our darker[9] purpose.
Give me the map there. Know that we have divided
In three our kingdom; and 'tis our fast[1] intent
To shake all cares and business from our age;
Conferring them on younger strengths, while we
Unburthened crawl toward death. Our son of Cornwall,
And you, our no less loving son of Albany,
We have this hour a constant will to publish[2]
Our daughters' several dowers, that future strife
May be prevented now. The princes, France and Burgundy,
Great rivals in our youngest daughter's love,
Long in our court have made their amorous sojourn,
And here are to be answered. Tell me, my daughters,—
Since now we will divest us, both of rule,
Interest[3] of territory, cares of state,—
Which of you shall we say doth love us most?
That we our largest bounty may extend
Where nature doth with merit challenge.[4] Goneril,
Our eldest-born, speak first.

GON. Sir, I love you more than words can wield the matter;[5]
Dearer than eye-sight, space, and liberty;
Beyond what can be valued, rich or rare;
No less than life, with grace, health, beauty, honor;
As much as child e'er loved, or father found;

5. (1) Outcome (2) offspring; "proper": handsome.
6. Young fellow (not derogatory).
7. Abroad.
8. A distinctive set of notes on a trumpet, announcing the arrival of that particular person to whom the notes belong.
9. More secret.
1. Firm, unalterable.
2. Announce, make public.
3. Possession.
4. I.e., where nature plus merit can make the greatest claim for reward.
5. Handle the theme.

A love that makes breath poor, and speech unable;
Beyond all manner of so much I love you.
COR. [*aside*] What shall Cordelia speak? Love, and be silent.
LEAR. Of all these bounds, even from this line to this,
With shadowy forests and with champains[6] riched,
With plenteous rivers and wide-skirted meads,[7]
We make thee lady: to thine and Albany's issue
Be this perpetual. What says our second daughter,
Our dearest Regan, wife to Cornwall? Speak.
REG. Sir, I am made
Of the self-same metal[8] that my sister is,
And prize me at her worth. In my true heart
I find she names my very deed of love;
Only she comes too short, that I profess
Myself an enemy to all other joys,
Which the most precious square of sense[9] possesses,
And find I am alone felicitate[10]
In your dear highness' love.
COR. [*aside*] Then poor Cordelia!
And yet not so; since, I am sure, my love's
More richer than my tongue.
LEAR. To thee and thine hereditary ever
Remain this ample third of our fair kingdom;
No less in space, validity,[11] and pleasure,
Than that conferred on Goneril. Now, our joy,
Although the last, not least; to whose young love
The vines of France and milk of Burgundy
Strive to be interessed,[12] what can you say to draw
A third more opulent than your sisters? Speak.
COR. Nothing, my lord.
LEAR. Nothing?
COR. Nothing.
LEAR. Nothing can come of nothing. Speak again.
COR. Unhappy that I am, I cannot heave
My heart into my mouth. I love your majesty
According to my bond;[1] nor more nor less.
LEAR. How, how, Cordelia! mend your speech a little,
Lest it may mar your fortunes.
COR. Good my lord,
You have begot me, bred me, loved me; I
Return those duties back as are right fit,
Obey you, love you, and most honor you.
Why have my sisters husbands, if they say
They love you all? Haply, when I shall wed,
That lord whose hand must take my plight[2] shall carry

6. Unwooded plains.
7. Meadows.
8. The stuff (mettle) of which a person, or his character, is made.
9. Sensitive feeling.
10. I.e., can only be happy.
11. Value.
12. Closely united.
1. The word is ambiguous. It can mean filial obligation, one's "bounden duty," or it can mean the strict terms of a contract, as in *The Merchant of Venice*.
2. The pledge in the marriage service: "And thereto I plight thee my troth."

Half my love with him, half my care and duty.
Sure, I shall never marry like my sisters,
To love my father all.

LEAR. But goes thy heart with this?

COR. Ay, good my lord.

LEAR. So young, and so untender?

COR. So young, my lord, and true.

LEAR. Let it be so! Thy truth, then, be thy dower!
For, by the sacred radiance of the sun,
The mysteries of Hecate,[3] and the night;
By all the operation of the orbs[4]
From whom we do exist and cease to be;
Here I disclaim all my paternal care,
Propinquity and property of blood,[5]
And as a stranger to my heart and me
Hold thee, from this, for ever. The barbarous Scythian,[6]
Or he that makes his generation messes
To gorge his appetite,[7] shall to my bosom
Be as well neighbored, pitied, and relieved,
As thou my sometime daughter.

KENT. Good my liege,—

LEAR. Peace, Kent!
Come not between the dragon and his wrath.[8]
I loved her most, and thought to set my rest[9]
On her kind nursery. Hence, and avoid my sight!
So be my grave my peace, as here I give
Her father's heart from her! Call France; who stirs?
Call Burgundy. Cornwall and Albany,
With my two daughters' dowers digest[1] this third:
Let pride, which she calls plainness, marry her.
I do invest you jointly with my power,
Pre-eminence, and all the large effects
That troop with majesty. Ourself, by monthly course,
With reservation of an hundred knights,
By you to be sustained, shall our abode
Make with you by due turns. Only we still retain
The name, and all the additions to a king;[2]
The sway, revenue, execution of the rest,
Beloved sons, be yours; which to confirm,
This coronet part betwixt you.

KENT. Royal Lear,
Whom I have ever honored as my king,
Loved as my father, as my master followed,

3. The secret rites of the goddess of the lower world.
4. Planets.
5. Near relationship and identity of blood.
6. The nomadic Scythians were supposed to be the most barbarous people of antiquity.
7. A cannibal who eats his own children.
8. A dragon was on the crest of ancient British kings, and in Shakespeare the dragon is often a symbol of wrath.
9. Not only "to seek my repose" but also "to bet everything I have," an expression from the card game primero.
1. Absorb.
2. Royal titles, honors, ceremony. He intends to give up only his wealth and power.

As my great patron thought on in my prayers—
LEAR. The bow is bent and drawn, make from the shaft.[3]
KENT. Let it fall rather, though the fork[4] invade
The region of my heart: be Kent unmannerly,
When Lear is mad. What wilt thou do, old man?
Think'st thou that duty shall have dread to speak,
When power to flattery bows? To plainness honor's bound,
When majesty stoops to folly.[5] Reverse thy doom,[6]
And, in thy best consideration, check
This hideous rashness. Answer my life my judgment,
Thy youngest daughter does not love thee least;
Nor are those empty-hearted whose low sound
Reverbs no hollowness.[7]
LEAR. Kent, on thy life, no more.
KENT. My life I never held but as a pawn
To wage against thy enemies; nor fear to lose it,
Thy safety being the motive.
LEAR. Out of my sight!
KENT. See better, Lear; and let me still remain
The true blank of thine eye.[8]
LEAR. Now, by Apollo,—
KENT. Now, by Apollo, king,
Thou swear'st thy gods in vain.[9]
LEAR. O, vassal! miscreant!
[*Laying his hand on his sword.*]
ALB. / CORN. Dear sir, forbear.
KENT. Do;
Kill thy physician, and the fee bestow
Upon thy foul disease. Revoke thy doom;
Or, whilst I can vent clamor from my throat,
I'll tell thee thou dost evil.
LEAR. Hear me, recreant![1]
On thine allegiance, hear me!
Since thou hast sought to make us break our vow,
Which we durst never yet, and with strained[2] pride
To come between our sentence and our power,
Which nor our nature nor our place can bear,
Our potency made good, take thy reward.
Five days we do allot thee, for provision
To shield thee from diseases[3] of the world;
And on the sixth to turn thy hated back
Upon our kingdom: if, on the tenth day following,

3. I have drawn the bow; you had better avoid the arrow I am about to shoot at you.
4. An arrowhead with two prongs.
5. A common rhetorical device in Shakespeare, the substitution of the abstract for the concrete.
6. Judgment, sentence.
7. That Cordelia says little and speaks softly does not mean that she is hollow (insincere).
8. The bull's-eye of a target.
9. Classical gods are invoked throughout to heighten the pagan atmosphere. But there is frequent questioning as to whether those, or any, gods exist and if they do, whether they can be invoked. The word *miscreant*, which Lear calls Kent, used to mean "misbeliever."
1. Traitor.
2. Forced, unnatural.
3. Difficulties.

Thy banished trunk be found in our dominions,
The moment is thy death. Away! by Jupiter,
This shall not be revoked.

KENT. Fare thee well, king. Sith thus thou wilt appear,
Freedom lives hence, and banishment is here.[4]
[*To* CORDELIA.] The gods to their dear shelter take thee, maid,
That justly think'st, and hast most rightly said!
[*To* REGAN *and* GONERIL.] And your large speeches may your deeds approve,
That good effects may spring from words of love.[5]
Thus Kent, O princes, bids you all adieu;
He'll shape his old course in a country new. [*Exit.*]

[*Flourish. Re-enter* GLOUCESTER, *with* FRANCE, BURGUNDY, *and* ATTENDANTS.]

GLOU. Here's France and Burgundy, my noble lord.

LEAR. My lord of Burgundy,
We first address towards you, who with this king
Hath rivaled for our daughter. What, in the least,
Will you require in present dower with her,
Or cease your quest of love?

BUR. Most royal majesty,
I crave no more than what your highness offered,
Nor will you tender less.

LEAR. Right noble Burgundy,
When she was dear to us, we did hold her so;[6]
But now her price is fallen. Sir, there she stands;
If aught within that little seeming substance,[7]
Or all of it, with our displeasure pieced,[8]
And nothing more, may fitly like your grace,
She's there, and she is yours.

BUR. I know no answer.

LEAR. Will you, with those infirmities she owes,[9]
Unfriended, new-adopted to our hate,
Dowered with our curse, and strangered with our oath,
Take her, or leave her?

BUR. Pardon me, royal sir;
Election makes not up[1] on such conditions.

LEAR. Then leave her, sir; for, by the power that made me,
I tell you all her wealth. [*to* FRANCE] For you, great king,
I would not from your love make such a stray[2]
To match you where I hate; therefore beseech you
To avert your liking a more worthier way

4. I.e., to stay here would be a punishment like being banished, and going away is not a punishment, but an escape to freedom. "Sith": since.

5. May your actions correspond to your speeches, so words promising love may have good results. Kent's rhyming lines are ironical, moralistic, and constitute a kind of formal farewell.

6. Punning on the word "dear"—"beloved" and "expensive."

7. That small appearance of reality.

8. Attached to it.

9. Owns.

1. Choice is not made.

2. Stray so far.

Than on a wretch whom nature is ashamed
Almost to acknowledge hers.

FRANCE. This is most strange,
That she, whom even but now was your best object,
The argument[3] of your praise, balm of your age,
Most best, most dearest, should in this trice of time
Commit a thing so monstrous, to dismantle
So many folds of favor. Sure, her offense
Must be of such unnatural degree,
That monsters it, or your fore-vouched affection
Fall'n into taint;[4] which to believe of her,
Must be a faith that reason without miracle
Could never plant in me.

COR. I yet beseech your majesty—
If for I want that glib and oily art,
To speak and purpose not,—since what I well intend,
I'll do't before I speak —that you make known
It is no vicious blot, murder, or foulness,
No unchaste action, or dishonored step,
That hath deprived me of your grace and favor;
But even for want of that for which I am richer,
A still-soliciting[5] eye, and such a tongue
As I am glad I have not, though not to have it
Hath lost me in your liking.

LEAR. Better thou
Hadst not been born than not to have pleased me better.

FRANCE. Is it but this,—a tardiness in nature[6]
Which often leaves the history unspoke
That it intends to do? My lord of Burgundy,
What say you to the lady? Love's not love
When it is mingled with regards that stands
Aloof from th' entire point. Will you have her?
She is herself a dowry.

BUR. Royal Lear,
Give but that portion which yourself proposed,
And here I take Cordelia by the hand,
Duchess of Burgundy.

LEAR. Nothing! I have sworn; I am firm.

BUR. I am sorry, then, you have so lost a father
That you must lose a husband.

COR. Peace be with Burgundy!
Since that respects of fortune[7] are his love,
I shall not be his wife.

FRANCE. Fairest Cordelia, that art most rich, being poor;
Most choice, forsaken; and most loved, despised!

3. Main object of love and favor; "argument": subject.

4. Her offense must be unnatural and monstrous, or else your previously expressed affection for her must have been error.

5. Always pleading.

6. Natural shyness.

7. Considerations of money.

Thee and thy virtues here I seize upon:
Be it lawful I take up what's cast away.
Gods, gods! 't is strange that from their cold'st neglect
My love should kindle to inflamed respect.[8]
Thy dowerless daughter, king, thrown to my chance,
Is queen of us, of ours, and our fair France.
Not all the dukes of waterish Burgundy
Can buy this unprized precious maid of me.
Bid them farewell, Cordelia, though unkind;[9]
Thou losest here, a better where to find.

LEAR. Thou hast her, France; let her be thine; for we
Have no such daughter, nor shall ever see
That face of hers again. Therefore be gone
Without our grace, our love, our benison.[10]
Come, noble Burgundy.

[*Flourish. Exeunt all but* FRANCE, GONERIL, REGAN, *and* CORDELIA.]

FRANCE. Bid farewell to your sisters.

COR. The jewels of our father, with washed eyes[1]
Cordelia leaves you. I know you what you are,
And like a sister am most loath to call
Your faults as they are named. Love well our father.
To your professed bosoms[2] I commit him;
But yet, alas, stood I within his grace,
I would prefer him to a better place.
So, farewell to you both.

REG. Prescribe not us our duties.

GON. Let your study
Be to content your lord, who hath received you
At fortune's alms.[3] You have obedience scanted,
And well are worth the want that you have wanted.[4]

COR. Time shall unfold what pleated cunning hides:
Who cover faults, at last shame them derides.
Well may you prosper!

FRANCE. Come, my fair Cordelia.

[*Exeunt* FRANCE *and* CORDELIA.]

GON. Sister, it is not a little I have to say of what most nearly appertains to us both. I think our father will hence to-night.

REG. That's most certain, and with you; next month with us.

GON. You see how full of changes his age is; the observation we have made of it hath not been little: he always loved our sister most; and with what poor judgment he hath now cast her off appears too grossly.[5]

8. Passionate regard.
9. Unnatural and cruel. The rhyming lines here, as in Kent's farewell, are ceremonial and sententious.
10. Blessing.
1. Tears.
2. Referring to the love they claimed they felt.
3. As a petty charity, not a bounteous gift.
4. You have come short of obedience, and this lack is just about what you are worth.
5. Such chorus-like comments, a convention in Shakespeare, guide the audience's response; they are not intended to characterize the speakers.

REG. 'Tis the infirmity of his age; yet he hath ever but slenderly known himself.

GON. The best and soundest of his time hath been but rash; then must we look to receive from his age, not alone the imperfections of long-engraffed[6] condition, but therewithal the unruly waywardness that infirm and choleric years bring with them.

REG. Such unconstant starts[7] are we like to have from him as this of Kent's banishment.

GON. There is further compliment of leave-taking between France and him. Pray you, let's hit[8] together: if our father carry authority with such dispositions as he bears, this last[9] surrender of his will but offend us.

REG. We shall further think on 't.

GON. We must do something, and i' the heat.[10] [*Exeunt.*]

SCENE 2

[*Enter* EDMUND, *with a letter.*]

EDM. Thou, nature, art my goddess; to thy law
My services are bound. Wherefore should I
Stand in the plague of custom,[1] and permit
The curiosity[2] of nations to deprive me,
For that I am some twelve or fourteen moonshines
Lag of a brother? Why bastard? wherefore base?
When my dimensions are as well compact,[3]
My mind as generous[4] and my shape as true,
As honest[5] madam's issue? Why brand they us
With base? with baseness? bastardy? base, base?
Who, in the lusty stealth of nature, take
More composition and fierce quality[6]
Than doth, within a dull, stale, tired bed,
Go to creating a whole tribe of fops,
Got 'tween asleep and wake? Well, then,
Legitimate Edgar, I must have your land.
Our father's love is to the bastard Edmund
As to the legitimate. Fine word,—'legitimate'!
Well, my legitimate, if this letter speed,[7]
And my invention thrive, Edmund the base
Shall top the legitimate. I grow; I prosper.
Now, gods, stand up for bastards!
[*Enter* GLOUCESTER.]

GLOU. Kent banished thus? and France in choler parted?
And the king gone tonight? subscribed[8] his power?

6. Deeply rooted.
7. Sudden jerks (as from a skittish horse).
8. Agree.
9. Recent.
10. While the iron's hot (proverbial).
1. Be dependent on diseased custom.
2. Scrupulousness.
3. My proportions are as well made.
4. Noble, aristocratic.
5. Chaste.
6. A fuller mixture and more energy
7. Prosper; "invention": plot.
8. Surrendered.

Confined to exhibition?[9] All this done
Upon the gad?[1] Edmund, how now! what news?
EDM. So please your lordship, none. [*Putting up the letter.*]
GLOU. Why so earnestly seek you to put up that letter?
EDM. I know no news, my lord.
GLOU. What paper were you reading?
EDM. Nothing, my lord.
GLOU. No? What needed, then, that terrible dispatch of it into your pocket? the quality[2] of nothing hath not such need to hide itself. Let's see. Come, if it be nothing, I shall not need spectacles.
EDM. I beseech you, sir, pardon me. It is a letter from my brother, that I have not all o'er-read; and for so much as I have perused, I find it not fit for your o'er-looking.
GLOU. Give me the letter, sir.
EDM. I shall offend, either to detain or give it. The contents, as in part I understand them, are to blame.
GLOU. Let's see, let's see.
EDM. I hope, for my brother's justification, he wrote this but as an essay or taste[3] of my virtue.
GLOU. [*reads*] "This policy and reverence[4] of age makes the world bitter to the best of our times; keeps our fortunes from us till our oldness cannot relish them. I begin to find an idle and fond[5] bondage in the oppression of aged tyranny; who sways, not as it hath power, but as it suffered.[6] Come to me, that of this I may speak more. If our father would sleep till I waked him, you should enjoy half his revenue for ever, and live the beloved of your brother, EDGAR."
Hum—conspiracy!—"Sleep till I waked him,—you should enjoy half his revenue,"—My son Edgar! Had he a hand to write this? a heart and brain to breed it in?—When came this to you? who brought it?
EDM. It was not brought me, my lord; there's the cunning of it; I found it thrown in at the casement of my closet.[7]
GLOU. You know the character[8] to be your brother's?
EDM. If the matter were good, my lord, I durst swear it were his; but, in respect of that, I would fain think it were not.
GLOU. It is his.
EDM. It is his hand, my lord; but I hope his heart is not in the contents.
GLOU. Hath he never heretofore sounded[9] you in this business?
EDM. Never, my lord. But I have heard him oft maintain it to be fit, that, sons at perfect age, and fathers declining, the father should be as ward to the son, and the son manage his revenue.
GLOU. O villain, villain! His very opinion in the letter! Abhorred

9. A small allowance.
1. Suddenly.
2. Nature.
3. Test or trial.
4. Custom of reverencing.
5. Foolish.
6. Who rules not through power, but by our permission.
7. Private room.
8. Handwriting.
9. Tested the depth of (a nautical metaphor).

villain! Unnatural, detested, brutish villain! worse than brutish! Go, sirrah, seek him. I'll apprehend him. Abominable villain! Where is he?

EDM. I do not well know, my lord. If it shall please you to suspend your indignation against my brother till you can derive from him better testimony of his intent, you shall run a certain course; where, if you violently proceed against him, mistaking his purpose, it would make a great gap in your own honor and shake in pieces the heart of his obedience. I dare pawn down my life for him that he hath wrote this to feel my affection to your honor, and to no further pretense of danger.[1]

GLOU. Think you so?

EDM. If your honor judge it meet, I will place you where you shall hear us confer of this, and by an auricular assurance[2] have your satisfaction; and that without any further delay than this very evening.

GLOU. He cannot be such a monster—

EDM. Nor is not, sure.

GLOU. To his father, that so tenderly and entirely loves him. Heaven and earth! Edmund, seek him out; wind me into[3] him, I pray you; frame the business after your own wisdom. I would unstate myself, to be in a due resolution.[4]

EDM. I will seek him, sir, presently[5]; convey the business as I shall find means, and acquaint you withal.

GLOU. These late[6] eclipses in the sun and moon portend no good to us. Though the wisdom of nature can reason it thus and thus,[7] yet nature finds itself scourged by the sequent effects. Love cools, friendship falls off, brothers divide; in cities, mutinies;[8] in countries, discord; in palaces, treason; and the bond cracked 'twixt son and father. This villain of mine comes under the prediction; there's son against father. The king falls from bias of nature;[9] there's father against child. We have seen the best of our time. Machinations, hollowness, treachery, and all ruinous disorders, follow us disquietly to our graves. Find out this villain, Edmund; it shall lose thee nothing; do it carefully. And the noble and true-hearted Kent banished! his offence, honesty! 'Tis strange. [*Exit.*]

EDM. This is the excellent foppery[1] of the world, that, when we are sick in fortune, often the surfeit of our own behavior, we make guilty of[2] our disasters the sun, the moon, and the stars; as if we were villains by necessity; fools by heavenly compulsion; knaves, thieves, and treachers, by spherical predominance;[3] drunkards, liars, and adulterers, by an

1. Dangerous purpose.
2. Hearing directly.
3. Worm your way into his confidence.
4. Lose my rank (Lear has just "unstated" himself) to find out the real truth.
5. Immediately; "convey": manage.
6. Recent.
7. Though science can explain it in this or that way.
8. Riots.
9. Natural curve (a figure from bowling).
1. Stupidity.
2. Responsible for.
3. The dominating influence of a planet (in astrology).

enforced obedience of planetary influence; and all that we are evil in, by a divine thrusting on.[4] An admirable evasion of whore-master man, to lay his goatish[5] disposition to the charge of a star! My father compounded with my mother under the dragon's tail, and my nativity was under Ursa Major, so that it follows, I am rough and lecherous. Fut![6] I should have been that I am, had the maidenliest star in the firmament twinkled on my bastardizing. Edgar—

[*Enter* EDGAR.]

and pat he comes like the catastrophe of the old comedy.[7] My cue is villanous melancholy, with a sigh like Tom o' Bedlam.[8] O, these eclipses do portend these divisions![9] Fa, sol, la, mi.

EDG. How now, brother Edmund? What serious contemplation are you in?

EDM. I am thinking, brother, of a prediction I read this other day, what should follow these eclipses.

EDG. Do you busy yourself about that?

EDM. I promise you, the effects he writes of succeed[1] unhappily; as of unnaturalness between the child and the parent; death, dearth,[2] dissolutions of ancient amities; divisions in state, menaces and maledictions against king and nobles; needless diffidences,[3] banishment of friends, dissipation of cohorts,[4] nuptial breaches, and I know not what.

EDG. How long have you been a sectary astronomical?[5]

EDM. Come, come! When saw you my father last?

EDG. Why, the night gone by.

EDM. Spake you with him?

EDG. Ay, two hours together.

EDM. Parted you in good terms? Found you no displeasure in him by word or countenance?

EDG. None at all.

EDM. Bethink yourself wherein you may have offended him; and at my entreaty forbear his presence till some little time hath qualified[6] the heat of his displeasure; which at this instant so rageth in him, that with the mischief of your person it would scarcely allay.

EDG. Some villain hath done me wrong.

EDM. That's my fear. I pray you, have a continent[7] forbearance till the speed of his rage goes slower; and, as I say, retire with me to my lodging, from whence I will fitly[8] bring you to hear my lord speak. Pray ye, go! There's my key. If you do stir

4. Supernatural instigation.
5. Lecherous.
6. Christ's foot: an oath.
7. Like the conclusion in an old comedy, often hurriedly patched up to bring the play to an end.
8. A mad beggar. "Bedlam" comes from Bethlehem Hospital, an asylum for the insane in London.
9. Disunions. But "divisions" was also a musical term, meaning "runs."
1. Turn out.
2. Famine.
3. Distrusts.
4. Breaking up of army units, desertions.
5. Believer in astrology.
6. Lessened.
7. Restrained.
8. Suitably.

abroad, go armed.

EDG. Armed, brother?

EDM. Brother, I advise you to the best. Go armed. I am no honest man if there be any good meaning[9] towards you. I have told you what I have seen and heard; but faintly, nothing like the image and horror[10] of it. Pray you, away!

EDG. Shall I hear from you anon?

EDM. I do serve you in this business. [*Exit* EDGAR.]
A credulous father, and a brother noble,
Whose nature is so far from doing harms,
That he suspects none; on whose foolish honesty
My practices ride easy! I see the business.
Let me, if not by birth, have lands by wit:
All with me's meet that I can fashion fit.[1] [*Exit.*]

SCENE 3

[*Enter* GONERIL, *and* OSWALD, *her steward.*]

GON. Did my father strike my gentleman for chiding of his fool?

OSW. Yes, madam.

GON. By day and night[2] he wrongs me; every hour
He flashes into one gross crime[3] or other,
That sets us all at odds. I'll not endure it.
His knights grow riotous, and himself upbraids us
On every trifle. When he returns from hunting,
I will not speak with him. Say I am sick.
If you come slack of[4] former services,
You shall do well; the fault of it I'll answer.[5]

OSW. He's coming, madam; I hear him. [*Horns within.*]

GON. Put on what weary negligence you please,
You and your fellows. I'd have it come to question.[6]
If he dislike it, let him to our sister,
Whose mind and mine, I know, in that are one,
Not to be overruled. Idle old man,
That still would manage those authorities
That he hath given away! Now, by my life,
Old fools are babes again, and must be used
With checks as flatteries,—when they are seen abused.[7]
Remember what I tell you.

OSW. Well, madam.

GON. And let his knights have colder looks among you.
What grows of it, no matter; advise your fellows so.
I would breed from hence occasions,[8] and I shall,
That I may speak. I'll write straight[9] to my sister,
To hold my very course. Prepare for dinner. [*Exeunt.*]

9. Intention.
10. Horrible reality.
1. Manipulate to serve my purpose.
2. An oath; see I.i.106–22.
3. Offense, not necessarily a violation of law.
4. Fall short of.
5. Be answerable for.
6. Made an issue of.
7. Must be corrected by rebukes rather than flatteries when they are seen to be deluded.
8. Opportunities.
9. Immediately.

SCENE 4

[*Enter* KENT, *disguised.*]

KENT. If but as well I other accents borrow,
That can my speech defuse,[1] my good intent
May carry through itself to that full issue
For which I razed my likeness.[2] Now, banished Kent,
If thou canst serve where thou dost stand condemned,
So may it come, thy master, whom thou lovest,
Shall find thee full of labors.

[*Horns within. Enter* LEAR, KNIGHTS, *and* ATTENDANTS.]

LEAR. Let me not stay a jot[3] for dinner; go get it ready. [*Exit an* ATTENDANT.] How now! What art thou?

KENT. A man, sir.

LEAR. What dost thou profess?[4] What wouldst thou with us?

KENT. I do profess to be no less than I seem; to serve him truly that will put me in trust; to love him that is honest; to converse with him that is wise and says little; to fear judgment; to fight when I cannot choose; and to eat no fish.[5]

LEAR. What art thou?

KENT. A very honest-hearted fellow, and as poor as the king.

LEAR. If thou be as poor for a subject as he is for a king, thou art poor enough. What wouldst thou?

KENT. Service.

LEAR. Who wouldst thou serve?

KENT. You.

LEAR. Dost thou know me, fellow?

KENT. No, sir; but you have that in your countenance[6] which I would fain call master.

LEAR. What's that?

KENT. Authority.

LEAR. What services canst thou do?

KENT. I can keep honest counsel, ride, run, mar a curious[7] tale in telling it, and deliver a plain message bluntly. That which ordinary men are fit for, I am qualified in; and the best of me is diligence.

LEAR. How old art thou?

KENT. Not so young, sir, to love a woman for singing, nor so old to dote on her for anything. I have years on my back forty-eight.

LEAR. Follow me; thou shalt serve me. If I like thee no worse after dinner, I will not part from thee yet. Dinner, ho dinner! Where's my knave?[8] my fool? Go you, and call my fool hither.

[*Exit an* ATTENDANT.]

[*Enter* OSWALD.]

1. If I can speak like someone else, so that my voice is disguised.
2. Changed my appearance (put on this disguise).
3. Wait a moment.
4. What is your trade or calling? But Kent takes the word "profess" in another sense—to assert, believe.
5. To know that I must face judgment and act accordingly; to fight when I cannot avoid it; and to be a loyal Protestant.
6. Bearing.
7. Intricate, complicated.
8. Boy.

You, you, sirrah,[9] where's my daughter?

OSW. So please you,— [*Exit.*]

LEAR. What says the fellow there? Call the clotpoll[1] back. [*Exit a* KNIGHT.] Where's my fool, ho? I think the world's asleep.

[*Re-enter* KNIGHT.]

How now! where's that mongrel?

KNIGHT. He says, my lord, your daughter is not well.

LEAR. Why came not the slave back to me when I called him?

KNIGHT. Sir, he answered me in the roundest[2] manner, he would not.

LEAR. He would not!

KNIGHT. My lord, I know not what the matter is; but, to my judgment, your highness is not entertained[3] with that ceremonious affection as you were wont,[4] there's a great abatement of kindness appears as well in the general dependants as in the duke himself also and your daughter.

LEAR. Ha! sayest thou so?

KNIGHT. I beseech you pardon me, my lord, if I be mistaken; for my duty cannot be silent when I think your highness wronged.

LEAR. Thou but rememberest me of mine own conception. I have perceived a most faint neglect of late; which I have rather blamed as mine own jealous curiosity[5] than as a very pretence and purpose of unkindness. I will look further into 't. But where's my fool? I have not seen him this two days.

KNIGHT. Since my young lady's going into France, sir, the fool hath much pined away.

LEAR. No more of that; I have noted it well. Go you and tell my daughter I would speak with her. [*Exit* KNIGHT.] Go you, call hither my fool. [*Exit an* ATTENDANT.]

[*Re-enter* OSWALD.]

O, you sir, you! Come you hither, sir. Who am I, sir?

OSW. My lady's father.

LEAR. "My lady's father"! My lord's knave! You whoreson dog! you slave! you cur!

OSW. I am none of these, my lord; I beseech your pardon.

LEAR. Do you bandy[6] looks with me, you rascal? [*Striking him.*]

OSW. I'll not be struck, my lord.

KENT. Nor tripped neither, you base foot-ball player.[7] [*Tripping up his heels.*]

LEAR. I thank thee, fellow; thou servest me, and I'll love thee.

KENT. Come, sir, arise, away! I'll teach you differences.[8] Away, away! If you will measure your lubber's length[9] again, tarry; but away! Go to! Have you wisdom? so.

9. An address to a social inferior or stranger.
1. Clod-pate, blockhead.
2. Plainest, rudest.
3. Treated.
4. Accustomed.
5. Suspicious watchfulness.
6. Hit back and forth, as in tennis.
7. Elizabethan football, not the modern sport, was played only by lower-class ruffians, and, according to a contemporary, was marked by "fighting, brawling, contention, quarrel-picking, murder, homicide, and great effusion of blood."
8. Social rank and position.
9. Be knocked down.

[*Pushes* OSWALD *out*.]

LEAR. Now, my friendly knave, I thank thee: there's earnest[1] of thy service. [*Giving* KENT *money*.]

[*Enter* FOOL.]

FOOL. Let me hire him too. Here's my coxcomb. [*Offering* KENT *his cap*.]

LEAR. How now, my pretty knave! How dost thou?

FOOL. Sirrah, you were best take my coxcomb.

KENT. Why, fool?

FOOL. Why, for taking one's part that's out of favor. Nay, an thou canst not smile as the wind sits, thou'lt catch cold shortly.[2] There, take my coxcomb! Why, this fellow has banished two on's daughters, and did the third a blessing against his will. If thou follow him, thou must needs wear my coxcomb. How now, nuncle![3] Would I had two coxcombs and two daughters!

LEAR. Why, my boy?

FOOL. If I gave them all my living, I'd keep my coxcombs myself. There's mine; beg another of thy daughters.

LEAR. Take heed, sirrah; the whip.

FOOL. Truth's a dog must to kennel; he must be whipped out, when Lady the brach[4] may stand by the fire and stink.

LEAR. A pestilent gall to me!

FOOL. Sirrah, I'll teach thee a speech.

LEAR. Do.

FOOL. Mark it, nuncle:

Have more than thou showest,
Speak less than thou knowest,
Lend less than thou owest,[5]
Ride more than thou goest,
Learn more than thou trowest,
Set less than thou throwest;[6]
Leave thy drink and thy whore,
And keep in-a-door,
And thou shalt have more
Than two tens to a score.[7]

KENT. This is nothing, fool.

FOOL. Then 'tis like the breath of an unfeed lawyer; you gave me nothing for 't. Can you make no use of nothing, nuncle?

LEAR. Why, no, boy; nothing can be made out of nothing.

FOOL. [*to* KENT] Prithee, tell him, so much the rent of his land comes to. He will not believe a fool.

LEAR. A bitter fool!

FOOL. Dost thou know the difference, my boy, between a bitter

1. A small sum paid in advance.
2. If you can't please the party in power, you will be thrown out.
3. Contraction of "mine uncle"—a form of address used by fools to their male superiors.
4. Bitch. "Lady" was a common name for a female dog (see *1 Henry IV*, III.i.235).
5. Ownest; "goest': walk.
6. Don't put all your winnings on one cast of the dice.
7. You will have more than twenty shillings to the pound; i.e., you will save money.

fool and a sweet fool?

LEAR. No, lad; teach me.

FOOL.
That lord that counseled thee
To give away thy land,
Come place him here by me,
Do thou for him stand:
The sweet and bitter fool
Will presently appear;
The one in motley here,
The other found out there.

LEAR. Dost thou call me fool, boy?

FOOL. All thy other titles thou hast given away; that thou wast born with.

KENT. This is not altogether fool, my lord.

FOOL. No, faith, lords and great men will not let me; if I had a monopoly[8] out, they would have part on 't: and ladies too, they will not let me have all fool to myself; they 'll be snatching. Give me an egg, uncle, and I'll give thee two crowns.

LEAR. What two crowns shall they be?

FOOL. Why, after I have cut the egg i' the middle, and eat up the meat, the two crowns of the egg. When thou clovest thy crown i' the middle, and gavest away both parts, thou borest thy ass on thy back o'er the dirt.[9] Thou hadst little wit in thy bald crown, when thou gavest thy golden one away. If I speak like myself in this, let him be whipped that first finds it so.
[*singing*]
Fools had ne'er less wit in a year;
For wise men are grown foppish,
They know not how their wits to wear,
Their manners are so apish.

LEAR. When were you wont to be so full of songs, sirrah?

FOOL. I have used it, nuncle, ever since thou madest thy daughters thy mother; for when thou gavest them the rod, and put'st down thine own breeches,
[*singing*]
Then they for sudden joy did weep,
And I for sorrow sung,
That such a king should play bo-peep,[10]
And go the fools among.

Prithee, nuncle, keep a schoolmaster that can teach thy fool to lie. I would fain learn to lie.

LEAR. An[1] you lie, sirrah, we'll have you whipped.

FOOL. I marvel what kin thou and thy daughters are. They'll have me whipped for speaking true, thou'lt have me whipped for lying; and sometimes I am whipped for holding my peace. I had rather be any kind o' thing than a fool; and yet I would not be thee, nuncle; thou hast pared thy wit o' both sides, and

8. That monopolies on certain imports and raw materials were granted to courtiers was a source of common complaint.
9. Mud. In an Aesop fable, a man carries his ass instead of riding it.
10. Hide-and-go-seek.
1. If.

left nothing i' the middle. Here comes one o' the parings.

[*Enter* GONERIL.]

LEAR. How now, daughter! What makes that frontlet[2] on? Methinks you are too much of late i' the frown.

FOOL. Thou wast a pretty fellow when thou hadst no need to care for her frowning; now thou art an O without a figure.[3] I am better than thou art now; I am a fool, thou art nothing. [*To* GON.] Yes, forsooth, I will hold my tongue; so your face bids me, though you say nothing. Mum, mum,

He that keeps nor crust nor crum,
Weary of all, shall want some.

[*Pointing to* LEAR.] That's a shealed peascod.[4]

GON. Not only, sir, this your all-licensed[5] fool,
But other of your insolent retinue
Do hourly carp and quarrel, breaking forth
In rank[6] and not-to-be-endured riots. Sir,
I had thought, by making this well known unto you,
To have found a safe[7] redress; but now grow fearful,
By what yourself too late have spoke and done,
That you protect this course, and put it on[8]
By your allowance; which if you should, the fault
Would not 'scape censure, nor the redresses sleep,
Which, in the tender of a wholesome weal,[9]
Might in their working do you that offense,
Which else were shame, that then necessity
Will call discreet proceeding.

FOOL. For, you know, nuncle,
The hedge-sparrow fed the cuckoo so long,
That it had it[1] head bit off by it young.
So, out went the candle, and we were left darkling.[2]

LEAR. Are you our daughter?

GON. Come, sir.
I would you would make use of that good wisdom,
Whereof I know you are fraught,[3] and put away
These dispositions, that of late transform you
From what you rightly are.

FOOL. May not an ass know when the cart draws the horse? Whoop, Jug! I love thee.[4]

LEAR. Doth any here know me? This is not Lear.
Doth Lear walk thus? speak thus? Where are his eyes?
Either his notion[5] weakens, his discernings
Are lethargied—Ha! waking? 'Tis not so.

2. I.e., frown (literally, a band worn on the forehead).
3. A zero without a number before it.
4. A shelled or empty peapod.
5. Permitted to say or do anything.
6. Gross.
7. Sure.
8. Instigate it.
9. Out of our concern for a healthy society "redresses."
1. Its. The couplet sounds like a proverb.
2. In the dark.
3. Well furnished.
4. A bit of nonsense, probably accompanied by a caper. "Jug" is a nickname for "Joan."
5. Intellectual power.

Who is it that can tell me who I am?
FOOL. Lear's shadow.
LEAR. I would learn that;[6] for, by the marks of sovereignty, knowledge, and reason, I should be false—persuaded I had daughters.
FOOL. Which they will make an obedient father.
LEAR. Your name, fair gentlewoman?
GON. This admiration,[7] sir, is much o' the savor
Of other your new pranks. I do beseech you
To understand my purposes aright.
As you are old and reverend, you should be wise.
Here do you keep a hundred knights and squires;
Men so disordered, so deboshed[8] and bold,
That this our court, infected with their manners,
Shows[9] like a riotous inn. Epicurism and lust
Make it more like a tavern or a brothel
Than a graced[1] palace. The shame itself doth speak
For instant remedy; be then desired
By her, that else will take the thing she begs,
A little to disquantity[2] your train;
And the remainder that shall still depend,[3]
To be such men as may besort your age,
And know themselves and you.
LEAR. Darkness and devils!
Saddle my horses! call my train together!
Degenerate bastard! I'll not trouble thee.
Yet have I left a daughter.
GON. You strike my people, and your disordered rabble
Make servants of their betters.
[*Enter* ALBANY.]
LEAR. Woe that too late repents![4]—[*to* ALB.]
O, sir, are you come?
Is it your will? Speak, sir. Prepare my horses!
Ingratitude, thou marble-hearted fiend,
More hideous when thou show'st thee in a child
Than the sea-monster!
ALB. Pray, sir, be patient.
LEAR. [*to* GON.] Detested kite![5] thou liest:
My train are men of choice and rarest parts,
That all particulars of duty know,
And in the most exact regard support
The worships of their name. O most small fault,
How ugly didst thou in Cordelia show!
That, like an engine, wrench'd my frame of nature

6. The answer to his question. He ignores the Fool's answer.
7. Pretended astonishment, wondering who I am.
8. Debauched.
9. Appears.
1. Honorable.
2. Decrease in size.
3. Wait on you as dependents.
4. Woe to him who repents too late (a proverbial expression).
5. The carrion crow. In Shakespeare, a despicable creature symbolic of cowardice, meanness, cruelty, and death.

From the fixed place;[6] drew from my heart all love,
And added to the gall.[7] O Lear, Lear, Lear!
Beat at this gate, that let thy folly in, [*striking his head*]
And thy dear judgment out! Go, go, my people.

ALB. My lord, I am guiltless, as I am ignorant
Of what hath moved you.

LEAR. It may be so, my lord.
Hear, Nature, hear! dear goddess, hear!
Suspend thy purpose, if thou didst intend
To make this creature fruitful!
Into her womb convey sterility!
Dry up in her the organs of increase;
And from her derogate[8] body never spring
A babe to honor her! If she must teem,[9]
Create her child of spleen, that it may live
And be a thwart, disnatured [1]torment to her!
Let it stamp wrinkles in her brow of youth;
With cadent[2] tears fret channels in her cheeks;
Turn all her mother's pains and benefits[3]
To laughter and contempt, that she may feel
How sharper than a serpent's tooth it is
To have a thankless child! Away, away! [*Exit.*]

ALB. Now, gods that we adore, whereof comes this?

GON. Never afflict yourself to know the cause;
But let his disposition have that scope
That dotage gives it.

[*Re-enter* LEAR.]

LEAR. What, fifty of my followers at a clap?
Within a fortnight?

ALB. What's the matter, sir?

LEAR. I'll tell thee. [*to* GON.] Life and death! I am ashamed
That thou hast power to shake my manhood thus;
That these hot tears, which break from me perforce,
Should make thee worth them. Blasts and fogs upon thee!
The untented woundings[4] of a father's curse
Pierce every sense about thee! Old fond[5] eyes,
Beweep this cause again, I'll pluck ye out,
And cast you, with the waters that you lose,
To temper[6] clay. Yea, is it come to this?
Let it be so. Yet have I left a daughter,
Who, I am sure, is kind and comfortable.[7]
When she shall hear this of thee, with her nails
She'll flay thy wolvish visage. Thou shalt find
That I'll resume the shape which thou dost think

6. I.e., which, like a pulley or lever, moved a larger thing (my natural frame or disposition) from its regular place.
7. And put the bitter fluid, gall, there in place of love.
8. Debased.
9. Have children.
1. Perverse, unnatural.
2. Falling.
3. Maternal cares.
4. Wounds too deep to be cleaned with a "tent"—a roll of lint.
5. Foolish.
6. Moisten.
7. Willing to give comfort.

I have cast off for ever; thou shalt, I warrant thee.
[*Exeunt* LEAR, KENT, *and* ATTENDANTS.]

GON. Do you mark that, my lord?

ALB. I cannot be so partial, Goneril,
To the great love I bear you,—

GON. Pray you, content.[8] What, Oswald, ho! [*to the* FOOL]
You sir, more knave than fool, after your master!

FOOL. Nuncle Lear, nuncle Lear, tarry and take the fool with thee.

A fox, when one has caught her,
And such a daughter,
Should sure to the slaughter,
If my cap would buy a halter:
So the fool follows after.[9] [*Exit.*]

GON. This man hath had good counsel!—a hundred knights?
'Tis politic[1] and safe to let him keep
At point[2] a hundred knights? Yes, that on every dream,
Each buzz,[3] each fancy, each complaint, dislike,
He may enguard his dotage with their powers,
And hold our lives in mercy.[4] Oswald, I say!

ALB. Well, you may fear too far.

GON. Safer than trust too far:
Let me still[5] take away the harms I fear,
Not fear still to be taken. I know his heart.
What he hath uttered I have writ my sister.
If she sustain him and his hundred knights,
When I have showed the unfitness,—
[*Re-enter* OSWALD.]
How now, Oswald!
What, have you writ that letter to my sister?

OSW. Yes, madam.

GON. Take you some company, and away to horse!
Inform her full of my particular fear,
And thereto add such reasons of your own
As may compact[6] it more. Get you gone,
And hasten your return. [*Exit* OSWALD.] No, no, my lord,
This milky gentleness and course[7] of yours
Though I condemn not, yet, under pardon,
You are much more attaxed[8] for want of wisdom
Than praised for harmful mildness.[9]

ALB. How far your eyes may pierce I cannot tell:
Striving to better, oft we mar what's well.

GON. Nay, then—

ALB. Well, well; the event.[1] [*Exeunt.*]

8. Be quiet.
9. The rhyming words were pronounced "hauter" and "auter."
1. Prudent.
2. In armed readiness.
3. Rumor.
4. In jeopardy.
5. Always.
6. Confirm.
7. This mild and gentle course of action.
8. Criticized.
9. Dangerous lenity.
1. The outcome.

SCENE 5

[*Enter* LEAR, KENT, *and* FOOL.]

LEAR. Go you before to Gloucester with these letters.[2] Acquaint my daughter no further with any thing you know than comes from her demand out of[3] the letter. If your diligence be not speedy, I shall be there afore you.

KENT. I will not sleep, my lord, till I have delivered your letter. [*Exit.*]

FOOL. If a man's brains were in 's heels, were't not in danger of kibes?[4]

LEAR. Ay, boy.

FOOL. Then, I prithee, be merry; thy wit shall ne'er go slipshod.[5]

LEAR. Ha, ha, ha!

FOOL. Shalt see thy other daughter will use thee kindly;[6] for though she's as like this as a crab's[7] like an apple, yet I can tell what I can tell.

LEAR. Why, what canst thou tell, my boy?

FOOL. She will taste as like this as a crab does to a crab. Thou canst tell why one's nose stands i' the middle on's[8] face?

LEAR. No.

FOOL. Why, to keep one's eyes of either side's nose, that what a man cannot smell out, 'a may spy into.

LEAR. I did her wrong—

FOOL. Canst tell how an oyster makes his shell?

LEAR. No.

FOOL. Nor I neither; but I can tell why a snail has a house.

LEAR. Why?

FOOL. Why, to put his head in; not to give it away to his daughters, and leave his horns without a case.[9]

LEAR. I will forget my nature. So kind a father! Be my horses ready?

FOOL. Thy asses are gone about 'em. The reason why the seven stars are no moe[1] than seven is a pretty reason.

LEAR. Because they are not eight?

FOOL. Yes, indeed. Thou wouldst make a good fool.

LEAR. To take 't again perforce! Monster ingratitude!

FOOL. If thou wert my fool, nuncle, I'd have thee beaten for being old before thy time.

LEAR. How's that?

FOOL. Thou shouldst not have been old till thou hadst been wise.

LEAR. O, let me not be mad, not mad, sweet heaven!
Keep me in temper; I would not be mad!

2. This letter.
3. Question arising from.
4. Chilblains.
5. Wearing slippers, as would someone who was suffering from chilblains.
6. (1) Affectionately; (2) according to nature.
7. Crab apple, usually sour.
8. Of his.
9. The fool makes the cynical but common Elizabethan assumption that every married man is a cuckold.
1. More; "pretty": apt, cogent.

[*Enter* GENTLEMAN.]

How now! Are the horses ready?

GENT. Ready, my lord.

LEAR. Come, boy.

FOOL. She that's a maid now, and laughs at my departure,
Shall not be a maid long, unless things be cut shorter.[2]

[*Exeunt.*]

Act II

SCENE 1

[*Enter* EDMUND *and* CURAN *meeting.*]

EDM. Save thee, Curan.

CUR. And you, sir. I have been with your father, and given him notice that the Duke of Cornwall and Regan his duchess will be here with him this night.

EDM. How comes that?

CUR. Nay, I know not. You have heard of the news abroad—I mean the whispered ones, for they are yet but ear-bussing arguments?[3]

EDM. Not I. Pray you, what are they?

CUR. Have you heard of no likely wars toward,[4] 'twixt the Dukes of Cornwall and Albany?

EDM. Not a word.

CUR. You may do, then, in time. Fare you well, sir. [*Exit.*]

EDM. The duke be here tonight? The better! best!
This weaves itself perforce into my business.
My father hath set guard to take my brother;
And I have one thing, of a queasy[5] question,
Which I must act. Briefness and fortune, work!
Brother, a word! Descend! Brother, I say!

[*Enter* EDGAR.]

My father watches. O sir, fly this place!
Intelligence is given where you are hid.
You have now the good advantage of the night.
Have you not spoken 'gainst the Duke of Cornwall?
He's coming hither; now, i' the night, i' the haste,
And Regan with him: have you nothing said
Upon his party[6] 'gainst the Duke of Albany?
Advise yourself.

EDG. I am sure on't, not a word.

EDM. I hear my father coming. Pardon me!
In cunning[7] I must draw my sword upon you:

2. Addressed to the audience. An Elizabethan dirty joke: the maiden who laughs at me will lose her virginity soon unless all young men are castrated.
3. Whispered rumors.
4. Impending.
5. Requiring delicate management, but also rather nauseating.
6. On his side.
7. As a trick (to avoid suspicion of collusion).

Draw; seem to defend yourself; now quit you well.[8]
Yield! Come before my father. Light, ho, here!
Fly, brother. Torches, torches! So, farewell. [*Exit* EDGAR.]
Some blood drawn on me would beget opinion[9]
[*Wounds his arm.*]
Of my more fierce endeavor. I have seen drunkards
Do more than this in sport. Father, father!
Stop, stop! No help?
[*Enter* GLOUCESTER, *and* SERVANTS *with torches.*]

GLOU. Now, Edmund, where's the villain?

EDM. Here stood he in the dark, his sharp sword out,
Mumbling of wicked charms, conjuring the moon
To stand auspicious mistress,—

GLOU. But where is he?

EDM. Look, sir, I bleed.

GLOU. Where is the villain, Edmund?

EDM. Fled this way, sir. When by no means he could—

GLOU. Pursue him, ho! Go after. [*Exeunt some* SERVANTS.] By no means what?

EDM. Persuade me to the murder of your lordship;
But that[1] I told him, the revenging gods
'Gainst parricides did all their thunders bend;
Spoke, with how manifold and strong a bond
The child was bound to the father; sir, in fine,
Seeing how loathly opposite[2] I stood
To his unnatural purpose, in fell motion,[3]
With his prepared sword, he charges home
My unprovided body, lanched[4] mine arm:
But when he saw my best alarumed spirits,
Bold in the quarrel's right, roused to the encounter,
Or whether gasted[5] by the noise I made,
Full suddenly he fled.

GLOU. Let him fly far.
Not in this land shall he remain uncaught;
And found—dispatch.[6] The noble duke my master,
My worthy arch and patron,[7] comes to-night:
By his authority I will proclaim it,
That he which finds him shall deserve our thanks,
Bringing the murderous caitiff[8] to the stake;
He that conceals him, death.

EDM. When I dissuaded him from his intent,
And found him pight[9] to do it, with curst speech
I threatened to discover him. He replied,
"Thou unpossessing bastard! dost thou think
If I would stand against thee, would the reposal
Of any trust, virtue, or worth in thee

8. Fight vigorously.
9. Persuade people.
1. When.
2. Bitterly opposed.
3. Deadly thrust.
4. Wounded.
5. Frightened.
6. I.e., when he is captured, let him be killed.
7. Chief patron.
8. Wretch.
9. Determined; "curst": angry.

Make thy words faithed?[1] No. What I should deny,—
As this I would; ay, though thou didst produce
My very character,[2]—I'd turn it all
To thy suggestion, plot, and damned practice:
And thou must make a dullard of the world,
If they not thought the profits of my death
Were very pregnant and potential spurs
To make thee seek it."

GLOU. Strong and fast'ned[3] villain!
Would he deny his letter? I never got[4] him. [*Tucket within.*]
Hark, the Duke's trumpets! I know not why he comes.
All ports[5] I'll bar; the villain shall not 'scape;
The duke must grant me that. Besides, his picture
I will send far and near, that all the kingdom
May have due note of him; and of my land,
Loyal and natural[6] boy, I'll work the means
To make thee capable.[7]

[*Enter* CORNWALL, REGAN, *and* ATTENDANTS.]

CORN. How now, my noble friend! Since I came hither,
(Which I can call but now) I have heard strange news.

REG. If it be true, all vengeance comes too short
Which can pursue the offender. How dost, my lord?

GLOU. O, madam, my old heart is cracked, is cracked!

REG. What, did my father's godson seek your life?
He whom my father named? Your Edgar?

GLOU. O, lady, lady, shame would have it hid!

REG. Was he not companion with the riotous knights
That tend upon my father?

GLOU. I know not, madam. 'Tis too bad, too bad!

EDM. Yes, madam, he was of that consórt.[8]

REG. No marvel, then, though he were ill affected.[9]
'Tis they have put him on[1] the old man's death,
To have th' expense and waste of his revénues.
I have this present evening from my sister
Been well informed of them; and with such cautions
That if they come to sojourn at my house,
I'll not be there.

CORN. Nor I, assure thee, Regan.
Edmund, I hear that you have shown your father
A child-like[2] office.

EDM. 'Twas my duty, sir.

GLOU. He did bewray[3] his practice, and received
This hurt you see, striving to apprehend him.

CORN. Is he pursued?

GLOU. Ay, my good lord.

1. Believed.
2. Handwriting.
3. Hardened.
4. Begot.
5. Seaports, means of escape.
6. (1) Showing natural affection; (2) illegitimate.
7. I.e., of inheriting.
8. Gang.
9. Disloyal.
1. Incited him to procure.
2. Filial.
3. Reveal.

CORN. If he be taken, he shall never more
Be feared of doing harm.[4] Make your own purpose,
How in my strength you please. For you, Edmund,
Whose virtue and obedience doth this instant
So much commend itself, you shall be ours.
Natures of such deep trust we shall much need;
You we first seize on.
EDM. I shall serve you, sir,
Truly, however else.
GLOU. For him I thank your grace.
CORN. You know not why we came to visit you,—
REG. Thus out of season, threading[5] dark-eyed night.
Occasions, noble Gloucester, of some poise,[6]
Wherein we must have use of your advice:
Our father he hath writ, so hath our sister,
Of differences, which I least thought of fit
To answer from our home. The several messengers
From hence attend dispatch.[7] Our good old friend,
Lay comforts to your bosom, and bestow
Your needful counsel to our business,
Which craves the instant use.[8]
GLOU. I serve you, madam.
Your graces are right welcome. [*Exeunt.*]

SCENE 2

[*Enter* KENT *and* OSWALD, *severally.*]

OSW. Good dawning to thee, friend. Art of this house?
KENT. Ay.
OSW. Where may we set our horses?
KENT. I' the mire.
OSW. Prithee, if thou lovest me, tell me.
KENT. I love thee not.
OSW. Why, then, I care not for thee.
KENT. If I had thee in Lipsbury pinfold,[9] I would make thee care for me.
OSW. Why dost thou use me thus? I know thee not.
KENT. Fellow, I know thee.
OSW. What dost thou know me for?
KENT. A knave; a rascal; an eater of broken meats[1]; a base, proud, shallow, beggarly, three-suited, hundred-pound, filthy, worsted-stocking knave;[2] a lily-livered, action-taking[3] knave; a whoreson, glass-gazing, superserviceable, finical rogue; one-

4. Be a public danger.
5. Making our way through.
6. Weight, importance.
7. Are waiting to be sent off.
8. Must be done immediately.
9. An obscure expression, possibly meaning "between my teeth."
1. One who lives on scraps.
2. Servants were provided with three suits a year; Oswald's total resources would not be over a hundred pounds; he wears only worsted stockings (gentlemen wore silk).
3. One who goes to law instead of fighting; a coward.

trunk-inheriting[4] slave; one that wouldst be a bawd in way of good service, and art nothing but the composition of a knave, beggar, coward, pandar, and the son and heir of a mongrel bitch; one whom I will beat into clamorous whining, if thou deniest the least syllable of thy addition.[5]

OSW. Why, what a monstrous fellow art thou, thus to rail on one that is neither known of thee nor knows thee!

KENT. What a brazen-faced varlet art thou, to deny thou knowest me! Is it two days ago since I tripped up thy heels, and beat thee before the king? Draw, you rogue! For, though it be night, yet the moon shines. I'll make a sop of the moonshine[6] of you. Draw, you whoreson cullionly barber-monger, draw![7] *[Drawing his sword.]*

OSW. Away! I have nothing to do with thee.

KENT. Draw, you rascal! You come with letters against the king, and take Vanity the puppet's[8] part against the royalty of her father. Draw, you rogue, or I'll so carbonado[9] your shanks! Draw, you rascal! Come your ways!

OSW. Help, ho! murther! help!

KENT. Strike, you slave! Stand, rogue! Stand, you neat slave! Strike! *[Beating him.]*

OSW. Help, ho! murther! murther!

[Enter EDMUND *with his rapier drawn,* CORNWALL, REGAN, GLOUCESTER, *and* SERVANTS.*]*

EDM. How now! What's the matter? *[Parts them.]*

KENT. With you, goodman boy, an you please! Come, I'll flesh[1] ye! Come on, young master!

GLOU. Weapons! arms! What's the matter here?

CORN. Keep peace, upon your lives!
He dies that strikes again. What is the matter?

REG. The messengers from our sister and the king.

CORN. What is your difference? Speak.

OSW. I am scarce in breath, my lord.

KENT. No marvel, you have so bestirred your valor. You cowardly rascal, nature disclaims in thee; a tailor made thee.[2]

CORN. Thou art a strange fellow. A tailor make a man?

KENT. Ay, a tailor, sir. A stone-cutter or a painter could not have made him so ill, though he had been but two hours at the trade.

CORN. Speak yet, how grew your quarrel?

OSW. This ancient ruffian, sir, whose life I have spared at suit of[3] his gray beard —

4. One whose entire possessions would fit in one trunk.
5. Titles.
6. Full of holes, so the moon will shine through.
7. A base fellow who hangs around barber shops.
8. I.e., Goneril. Vanity was a character in the morality plays, which were often performed by puppets.
9. Score, cut cross-wise.
1. Initiate.
2. You are so cowardly that nature denies making you; a tailor made you (alluding to the proverb that it takes nine tailors to make a man).
3. Because of a plea by.

KENT. Thou whoreson zed! thou unnecessary letter![4] My lord, if you will give me leave, I will tread this unbolted[5] villain into mortar, and daub the walls of a jakes[6] with him. Spare my gray beard, you wagtail?[7]

CORN. Peace, sirrah!
You beastly knave, know you no reverence?

KENT. Yes, sir, but anger hath a privilege.

CORN. Why art thou angry?

KENT. That such a slave as this should wear a sword,[8]
Who wears no honesty. Such smiling rogues as these,
Like rats, oft bite the holy cords a-twain
Which are too intrinse t' unloose;[9] smooth every passion
That in the natures of their lords rebel;
Bring oil to fire, snow to their colder moods;
Renege, affirm, and turn their halcyon beaks[1]
With every gale and vary[2] of their masters,
Knowing nought, like dogs, but following.
A plague upon your epileptic visage!
Smile you my speeches, as I were a fool?
Goose, if I had you upon Sarum plain
I'ld drive ye cackling home to Camelot.[3]

CORN. What, art thou mad, old fellow?

GLOU. How fell you out? say that.

KENT. No contraries hold more antipathy
Than I and such a knave.

CORN. Why dost thou call him knave? What's his offense?

KENT. His countenance likes[4] me not.

CORN. No more, perchance, does mine, nor his, nor hers.

KENT. Sir, 'tis my occupation to be plain.
I have seen better faces in my time
Than stands on any shoulder that I see
Before me at this instant.

CORN. This is some fellow,
Who, having been praised for bluntness, doth affect
A saucy roughness, and constrains the garb
Quite from his nature.[5] He cannot flatter, he,
An honest mind and plain, he must speak truth!
An they will take it, so; if not, he's plain.
These kind of knaves I know, which in this plainness
Harbor more craft[6] and more corrupter ends

4. Zed, still the English name for the letter *z*, is unnecessary because its sound can be expressed by *s*.
5. Coarse, unsifted.
6. Privy.
7. A bird that bobs its head up and down constantly.
8. Swords were supposed to be worn only by gentlemen, and Oswald is a mere parasitic servant.
9. Bite in two the holy cords of affection (between daughter and father, for instance), which are too intricately tied to be undone in any natural way. "Smooth": flatter.
1. Deny, affirm, and turn with the wind, as a halcyon or kingfisher was supposed to when hung up by the neck.
2. Varying gale.
3. Salisbury (Sarum) Plain had flocks of geese on it. Camelot was the legendary castle of King Arthur, sometimes located at Winchester.
4. Pleases.
5. Distorts the nature of plain speech.
6. Deceit.

Than twenty silly ducking observants
That stretch their duties nicely.[7]
KENT. Sir, in good sooth, in sincere verity,
Under the allowance of your great aspect,
Whose influence, like the wreath of radiant fire
On flickering Phoebus' front,[8]
CORN. What mean'st by this?
KENT. To go out of my dialect, which you discommend so much. I know, sir, I am no flatterer. He that beguiled you in a plain accent was a plain knave; which for my part I will not be, though I should win your displeasure to entreat me to 't.
CORN. What was the offense you gave him?
OSW. I never gave him any:
It pleased the king his master very late
To strike at me, upon his misconstruction,[9]
When he, conjunct,[1] and flattering his displeasure,
Tripped me behind; being down, insulted, railed,
And put upon him such a deal of man,
That worthied him, got praises of the king
For him attempting who was self-subdued;[2]
And, in the fleshment[3] of this dread exploit,
Drew on me here again.
KENT. None of these rogues and cowards
But Ajax is their fool.[4]
CORN. Fetch forth the stocks!
You stubborn miscreant knave, you reverent braggart,
We'll teach you—
KENT. Sir, I am too old to learn.
Call not your stocks for me. I serve the king;
On whose employment I was sent to you:
You shall do small respect, show too bold malice
Against the grace and person of my master,
Stocking his messenger.
CORN. Fetch forth the stocks! As I have life and honor,
There shall he sit till noon.
REG. Till noon? Till night, my lord, and all night too!
KENT. Why, madam, if I were your father's dog,
You should not use me so.
REG. Sir, being his knave, I will.
CORN. This is a fellow of the self-same color
Our sister speaks of. Come, bring away the stocks!
[*Stocks brought out.*]
GLOU. Let me beseech your grace not to do so.
His fault is much, and the good king his master

7. Than twenty obsequious servants who precisely adopt the manners prescribed for them.
8. Kent, mimicking the flattery of servants like Oswald, addresses Cornwall as if he were a planet, comparable to the sun.
9. Misunderstanding.
1. Taking the king's side.
2. Made himself out to be a hero, won honor for himself . . . for attacking someone who wouldn't fight.
3. Furious excitement.
4. In Shakespeare's *Troilus and Cressida* the cowardly, malicious Thersites treats the plain-spoken warrior Ajax as a fool.

Will check[5] him for't. Your purposed low correction
Is such as basest and contemned'st wretches
For pilferings and most common trespasses
Are punished with: the king must take it ill,
That he, so slightly valued in his messenger,
Should have him thus restrained.

CORN. I'll answer[6] that.

REG. My sister may receive it much more worse,
To have her gentleman abused, assaulted,
For following her affairs. Put in his legs.

[KENT *is put in the stocks.*]

Come, my good lord, away.

[*Exeunt all but* GLOUCESTER *and* KENT.]

GLOU. I am sorry for thee, friend: 'tis the duke's pleasure,
Whose disposition, all the world well knows,
Will not be rubbed nor stopped: I'll entreat for thee.

KENT. Pray, do not, sir. I have watched[7] and traveled hard;
Some time I shall sleep out, the rest I'll whistle.
A good man's fortune may grow out at heels:
Give you good morrow!

GLOU. The duke's to blame in this; 't will be ill-taken. [*Exit.*]

KENT. Good king, that must approve the common saw,[8]
Thou out of heaven's benediction comest
To the warm sun!
Approach, thou beacon to this under globe,[9]
That by thy comfortable beams I may
Peruse this letter! Nothing almost sees miracles
But misery.[1] I know 'tis from Cordelia,
Who hath most fortunately been informed
Of my obscured course; [*reads*] "and shall find time
From this enormous state, seeking to give
Losses their remedies." All weary and o'er-watched,
Take vantage, heavy eyes, not to behold
This shameful lodging.
Fortune, good night; smile once more; turn thy wheel![2]

[*Sleeps.*]

SCENE 3

[*Enter* EDGAR.]

EDG. I heard myself proclaimed;
And by the happy hollow of a tree
Escaped the hunt. No port is free; no place,
That guard, and most unusual vigilance,
Does not attend my taking. Whiles I may 'scape,

5. Rebuke.
6. Be answerable for.
7. Gone without sleep.
8. Confirm the common saying.
9. I.e., the sun.

1. For those in misery, any relief seems almost miraculous.
2. Bring good fortune in place of the present bad. The goddess Fortuna was often portrayed turning a wheel.

I will preserve myself; and am bethought
To take the basest and most poorest shape
That ever penury, in contempt of man,
Brought near to beast.[3] My face I'll grime with filth,
Blanket my loins, elf[4] all my hair in knots,
And with presented nakedness out-face
The winds and persecutions of the sky.
The country gives me proof[5] and precedent
Of Bedlam beggars,[6] who, with roaring voices,
Strike in their numbed and mortified bare arms
Pins, wooden pricks, nails, sprigs of rosemary;
And with this horrible object,[7] from low farms,
Poor pelting[8] villages, sheep-cotes, and mills,
Sometime with lunatic bans,[9] sometime with prayers,
Enforce their charity. Poor Turlygod! poor Tom![1]
That's something yet! Edgar I nothing am. [*Exit.*]

SCENE 4

[*Enter* LEAR, FOOL, *and* GENTLEMAN.]

LEAR. 'Tis strange that they should so depart from home,
And not send back my messenger.

GENT. As I learned,
The night before there was no purpose in them
Of this remove.[2]

KENT. Hail to thee, noble master!

LEAR. Ha!
Makest thou this shame thy pastime?[3]

KENT. No, my lord.

FOOL. Ha, ha! he wears cruel garters.[4] Horses are tied by the heads, dogs and bears by the neck, monkeys by the loins, and men by the legs. When a man's over-lusty at legs, then he wears wooden nether-stocks.[5]

LEAR. What's he that hath so much thy place mistook
To set thee here?

KENT. It is both he and she;
Your son and daughter.

LEAR. No.

KENT. Yes.

LEAR. No, I say.

KENT. I say, yea.

LEAR. No, no, they would not!

KENT. Yes, yes, they have!

3. I have got the idea of taking the basest and poorest shape that poverty ever brought a man to, making him like a beast.
4. Tangle.
5. Example.
6. See note 8, p. 899, above.
7. Spectacle.
8. Paltry.
9. Curses.
1. Names assumed by beggars.
2. Change of residence.
3. Are you in this disgraceful situation as a joke?
4. A pun on "crewel," thin worsted yarn, which was used for garters.
5. Stockings.

LEAR. By Jupiter, I swear, no!
KENT. By Juno, I swear, aye!
LEAR. They durst not do 't;
They would not, could not do 't. 'Tis worse than murder,
To do upon respect[6] such violent outrage.
Resolve me, with all modest haste, which way
Thou mightst deserve, or they impose, this usage,
Coming from us.
KENT. My lord, when at their home
I did commend your highness' letters to them,
Ere I was risen from the place that showed
My duty kneeling, came there a reeking post,[7]
Stewed in his haste, half breathless, panting forth
From Goneril his mistress, salutations;
Delivered letters, spite of intermission,
Which presently they read; on whose contènts,[8]
They summoned up their meiny, straight took horse;
Commanded me to follow, and attend
The leisure of their answer, gave me cold looks,
And meeting here the other messenger,
Whose welcome, I perceived, had poisoned mine,—
Being the very fellow that of late
Displayed so saucily against your highness,—
Having more man than wit about me, drew.
He raised the house with loud and coward cries.
Your son and daughter found this trespass worth
The shame which here it suffers.
FOOL. Winter's not gone yet, if the wild-geese fly that way.[9]
Fathers that wear rags
Do make their children blind;
But fathers that bear bags[1]
Shall see their children kind.
Fortune, that arrant whore,
Ne'er turns the key[2] to the poor.
But, for all this, thou shalt have as many dolors for thy daughters as thou canst tell in a year.[3]
LEAR. O, how this mother swells up toward my heart!
Hysterica passio, down, thou climbing sorrow,
Thy element's below![4] Where is this daughter?
KENT. With the earl, sir, here within.
LEAR. Follow me not; stay here.
[*Exit.*]
GENT. Made you no more offenses but what you speak of?
KENT. None. How chance the king comes with so small a train?

6. (1) Upon the respect due a King's messenger; (2) deliberately.
7. Sweating messenger.
8. Getting the message; "meiny": household.
9. A pseudo-proverb meaning things are still in a bad way.
1. Hang on to the moneybags.
2. Opens the door.
3. Punning on dolors (sorrows) and dollars (coins) and on tell (narrate) and tell (count).
4. The mother, or *hysterica passio*, was a hysteria supposedly marked by a rising of wind from the belly to the heart and finally to the throat.

FOOL. An thou hadst been set i' the stocks for that question, thou hadst well deserved it.

KENT. Why, fool?

FOOL. We'll set thee to school to an ant, to teach thee there's no laboring i' the winter. All that follow their noses are led by their eyes but blind men, and there's not a nose among twenty but can smell him that's stinking. Let go thy hold when a great wheel runs down a hill, lest it break thy neck with following it; but the great one that goes up the hill, let him draw thee after. When a wise man gives thee better counsel, give me mine again. I would have none but knaves follow it, since a fool gives it.

> That sir which serves and seeks for gain,
> And follows but for form,
> Will pack[5] when it begins to rain,
> And leave thee in the storm.
> But I will tarry; the fool will stay,
> And let the wise man fly.
> The knave turns fool that runs away;
> The fool no knave, perdy.[6]

KENT. Where learned you this, fool?

FOOL. Not i' the stocks, fool.

[*Re-enter* LEAR, *with* GLOUCESTER.]

LEAR. Deny to speak with me? They are sick? they are weary?
They have traveled all the night? Mere fetches;[7]
The images of revolt and flying off.
Fetch me a better answer.

GLOU. My dear lord,
You know the fiery quality of the duke;
How unremoveable and fixed he is
In his own course.

LEAR. Vengeance! plague! death! confusion!
Fiery? what quality? Why, Gloucester, Gloucester,
I'd speak with the Duke of Cornwall and his wife.

GLOU. Well, my good lord, I have informed them so.

LEAR. Informed them! Dost thou understand me, man?

GLOU. Ay, my good lord.

LEAR. The king would speak with Cornwall; the dear father
Would with his daughter speak, commands her service.
Are they informed of this? My breath and blood!
Fiery? the fiery duke? Tell the hot duke that—
No, but not yet. May be he is not well.
Infirmity doth still neglect all office[8]
Whereto our health is bound; we are not ourselves
When nature, being oppressed, commands the mind
To suffer with the body. I'll forbear;
And am fallen out with my more headier will,[9]
To take[1] the indisposed and sickly fit

5. Be off.
6. Assuredly (*per Dieu*).
7. Tricks, ruses.
8. Duty.
9. Am at odds with my impetuous will.
1. For taking.

For the sound man. Death on my state![2] Wherefore
[*looking on* KENT]
Should he sit here? This act persuades me
That this remotion of the duke and her
Is practice only.[3] Give me my servant forth.
Go tell the duke and 's wife I'd speak with them,
Now, presently![4] Bid them come forth and hear me,
Or at their chamber-door I'll beat the drum
Till it cry sleep to death.[5]

GLOU. I would have all well betwixt you. [*Exit.*]

LEAR. O me, my heart, my rising heart! but, down!

FOOL. Cry to it, nuncle, as the cockney did to the eels when she put 'em i' the paste[6] alive; she knapped 'em o' the coxcombs with a stick, and cried "Down, wantons, down!" 'Twas her brother that, in pure kindness to his horse, buttered his hay.

[*Enter* CORNWALL, REGAN, GLOUCESTER, *and* SERVANTS.]

LEAR. Good morrow to you both.

CORN. Hail to your grace!
[KENT *is set at liberty.*]

REG. I am glad to see your highness.

LEAR. Regan, I think you are; I know what reason
I have to think so. If thou shouldst not be glad,
I would divorce me from thy mother's tomb,
Sepulchring an adultress. [*To* KENT.] O, are you free?
Some other time for that. Belovéd Regan,
Thy sister's naught. O Regan, she hath tied
Sharp-toothed unkindness, like a vulture, here![7]
[*Points to his heart.*]
I can scarce speak to thee; thou'lt not believe
With how depraved a quality—O Regan!

REG. I pray you, sir, take patience. I have hope
You less know how to value her desert
Than she to scant[8] her duty.

LEAR. Say, how is that?

REG. I cannot think my sister in the least
Would fail her obligation. If, sir, perchance
She have restrained the riots of your followers,
'Tis on such ground, and to such wholesome end,
As clears her from all blame.

LEAR. My curses on her!

REG. O, sir, you are old;
Nature in you stands on the very verge
Of her confine. You should be ruled and led
By some discretion,[9] that discerns your state
Better than you yourself. Therefore, I pray you,
That to our sister you do make return;

2. Royal power.
3. This removal of the Duke and Regan is a mere trick.
4. Immediately.
5. Until its sound kills sleep.
6. Meat pie.
7. Lear calls himself a kind of Prometheus, who suffered the punishment of having an eagle feed on his liver.
8. Be neglectful of.
9. I.e., some discreet person.

Say you have wronged her, sir.
LEAR. Ask her forgiveness?
Do you but mark how this becomes the house:[1]
"Dear daughter, I confess that I am old; [*kneeling*]
Age is unnecessary. On my knees I beg
That you'll vouchsafe me raiment, bed, and food."
REG. Good sir, no more! These are unsightly tricks.
Return you to my sister.
LEAR. [*Rising.*] Never, Regan!
She hath abated[2] me of half my train;
Looked black upon me; struck me with her tongue
Most serpent-like, upon the very heart.
All the stored vengeances of heaven fall
On her ingrateful top! Strike her young bones,[3]
You taking[4] airs, with lameness!
CORN. Fie, sir, fie!
LEAR. You nimble lightnings, dart your blinding flames
Into her scornful eyes! Infect her beauty,
You fen-sucked fogs, drawn by the powerful sun,
To fall and blast her pride!
REG. O the blest gods! so will you wish on me,
When the rash mood is on.
LEAR. No, Regan, thou shalt never have my curse.
Thy tender-hefted[5] nature shall not give
Thee o'er to harshness. Her eyes are fierce; but thine
Do comfort and not burn. 'Tis not in thee
To grudge my pleasures, to cut off my train,
To bandy hasty words, to scant my sizes,[6]
And in conclusion to oppose the bolt
Against my coming in. Thou better know'st
The offices[7] of nature, bond of childhood,
Effects of courtesy, dues of gratitude;
Thy half o' the kingdom hast thou not forgot,
Wherein I thee endowed.
REG. Good sir, to the purpose.
LEAR. Who put my man i' the stocks? [*Tucket within.*]
CORN. What trumpet's that?
REG. I know't, my sister's. This approves[8] her letter,
That she would soon be here.
[*Enter* OSWALD.]
Is your lady come?
LEAR. This is a slave, whose easy-borrowed pride
Dwells in the fickle grace of her he follows.
Out, varlet, from my sight!
CORN. What means your grace?

1. Our family, the royal family of Britain.
2. Deprived.
3. Unborn child (an expression from the old *King Leir*).
4. Infecting.
5. Gentle.
6. Allowances.
7. Duties.
8. Confirms.

LEAR. Who stocked my servant? Regan, I have good hope
Thou didst not know on 't. [*Enter* GONERIL.] Who comes here? O heavens,
If you do love old men, if your sweet sway
Allow obedience, if yourselves are old,
Make it your cause! Send down, and take my part!
[*To* GON.] Art not ashamed to look upon this beard?
O Regan, wilt thou take her by the hand?

GON. Why not by the hand, sir? How have I offended?
All's not offense that indiscretion finds
And dotage terms so.[9]

LEAR. O sides, you are too tough!
Will you yet hold? How came my man i' the stocks?

CORN. I set him there, sir; but his own disorders
Deserved much less advancement[1]

LEAR. You! did you?

REG. I pray you, father, being weak, seem so.
If, till the expiration of your month,
You will return and sojourn with my sister,
Dismissing half your train, come then to me.
I am now from home, and out of that provision
Which shall be needful for your entertainment.

LEAR. Return to her, and fifty men dismissed?
No, rather I abjure all roofs, and choose
To wage against the enmity o' the air;
To be a comrade with the wolf and owl,—
Necessity's sharp pinch! Return with her?
Why, the hot-blooded[2] France, that dowerless took
Our youngest born, I could as well be brought
To knee his throne, and, squire-like, pension beg
To keep base life afoot. Return with her?
Persuade me rather to be slave and sumpter[3]
To this detested groom. [*Pointing at* OSWALD.]

GON. At your choice, sir.

LEAR. I prithee, daughter, do not make me mad.
I will not trouble thee, my child; farewell.
We'll no more meet, no more see one another.
But yet thou art my flesh, my blood, my daughter;
Or rather a disease that's in my flesh,
Which I must needs call mine. Thou art a boil,
A plague-sore, an embossed carbuncle,[4]
In my corrupted blood. But I'll not chide thee;
Let shame come when it will, I do not call it.
I do not bid the Thunder-bearer[5] shoot,
Nor tell tales of thee to high-judging Jove.
Mend when thou canst; be better at thy leisure.

9. Not everything is an offense that poor judgment finds so and senility calls so.
1. His own misconduct deserved less promotion.
2. Passionate.
3. Packhorse.
4. Swollen tumor.
5. I.e., Jove.

I can be patient, I can stay with Regan,
I and my hundred knights.

REG. Not altogether so.
I looked not for you yet, nor am provided
For your fit welcome. Give ear, sir, to my sister;
For those that mingle reason with your passion
Must be content to think you old, and so—
But she knows what she does.

LEAR. Is this well spoken?

REG. I dare avouch it, sir. What, fifty followers?
Is it not well? What should you need of more?
Yea, or so many, sith that[6] both charge and danger
Speak 'gainst so great a number? How, in one house,
Should many people, under two commands,
Hold amity? 'T is hard; almost impossible.

GON. Why might not you, my lord, receive attendance
From those that she calls servants, or from mine?

REG. Why not, my lord? If then they chanced to slack you,
We could control them. If you will come to me,—
For now I spy a danger,—I entreat you
To bring but five-and-twenty. To no more
Will I give place or notice.

LEAR. I gave you all—

REG. And in good time you gave it.

LEAR. Made you my guardians, my depositaries;
But kept a reservation[7] to be followed
With such a number. What, must I come to you
With five-and-twenty, Regan? Said you so?

REG. And speak't again, my lord; no more with me.

LEAR. Those wicked creatures yet do look well-favored,
When others are more wicked; not being the worst
Stands in some rank of praise. [*To* GON.] I'll go with thee:
Thy fifty yet doth double five-and-twenty,
And thou art twice her love.

GON. Hear me, my lord.
What need you five-and-twenty, ten, or five,
To follow in a house where twice so many
Have a command to tend you?

REG. What need one?

LEAR. O, reason not the need! Our basest beggars
Are in the poorest thing superfluous.[8]
Allow not nature more than nature needs,
Man's life's as cheap as beast's. Thou art a lady;
If only to go warm were gorgeous,
Why, nature needs not what thou gorgeous wear'st,
Which scarcely keeps thee warm.[9] But, for true need,—

6. Since.
7. Made you my stewardesses and trustees, but kept a reserve clause.
8. Our poorest beggars, if they own anything at all, have more than they need.
9. I.e., if dressing warmly is to be gorgeous, you are both more and less than that; for the gorgeous lady's clothes you wear are too scanty to keep you warm.

You heavens, give me that patience, patience I need!
You see me here, you gods, a poor old man,
As full of grief as age; wretched in both!
If it be you that stirs these daughters' hearts
Against their father, fool me not so much[1]
To bear it tamely; touch me with noble anger,
And let not women's weapons, water-drops,
Stain my man's cheeks! No, you unnatural hags,
I will have such revenges on you both,
That all the world shall—I will do such things,—
What they are, yet I know not; but they shall be
The terrors of the earth! You think I'll weep;
No, I'll not weep.
I have full cause of weeping, but this heart
Shall break into a hundred thousand flaws[2]
Or ere I'll weep. O fool, I shall go mad!
[*Exeunt* LEAR, GLOUCESTER, KENT, *and* FOOL.
Storm and tempest.]

CORN. Let us withdraw; 't will be a storm.
REG. This house is little; the old man and his people
Cannot be well bestowed.
GON. 'Tis his own blame; hath put himself from rest,[3]
And must needs taste his folly.
REG. For his particular,[4] I'll receive him gladly,
But not one follower.
GON. So am I purposed.
Where is my lord of Gloucester?
CORN. Followed the old man forth. He is returned.
[*Re-enter* GLOUCESTER.]
GLOU. The king is in high rage.
CORN. Whither is he going?
GLOU. He calls to horse, but will I know not whither.
CORN. 'Tis best to give him way; he leads himself.
GON. My lord, entreat him by no means to stay.
GLOU. Alack, the night comes on, and the bleak winds
Do sorely ruffle.[5] For many miles about
There's scarce a bush.[6]
REG. O, sir, to willful men,
The injuries that they themselves procure
Must be their schoolmasters. Shut up your doors.
He is attended with a desperate train;[7]
And what they may incense him to, being apt
To have his ear abused, wisdom bids fear.
CORN. Shut up your doors, my lord; 'tis a wild night.
My Regan counsels well. Come out o' the storm. [*Exeunt.*]

1. Don't make me such a fool as.
2. Fragments.
3. He has separated himself from peace of mind.
4. As for himself alone.
5. Violently rage.
6. The Quarto reads "not a bush." The contradiction between either of these statements and Edgar's hollow tree in II.iii.2, has often been noticed.
7. There is no other indication that in these scenes Lear is accompanied by "a desperate train" (his knights).

Act III

SCENE 1

[*Storm still. Enter* KENT *and a* GENTLEMAN, *at several* doors.]

KENT. Who's there, besides foul weather?
GENT. One minded like the weather, most unquietly.
KENT. I know you. Where's the king?
GENT. Contending with the fretful elements;
Bids the wind blow the earth into the sea,
Or swell the curléd waters 'bove the main,[8]
That things might change or cease; tears his white hair,
Which the impetuous blasts, with eyeless rage,
Catch in their fury, and make nothing of;[9]
Strives in his little world of man[1] to out-scorn
The to-and-fro-conflicting wind and rain.
This night, wherein the cub-drawn bear would couch,[2]
The lion and the belly-pinchéd wolf
Keep their fur dry, unbonneted he runs,
And bids what will take all.[3]
KENT. But who is with him?
GENT. None but the fool, who labors to out-jest
His heart-struck injuries.[4]
KENT. Sir, I do know you;
And dare, upon the warrant of my note,
Commend a dear thing to you.[5] There is division,
Although as yet the face of it be covered
With mutual cunning, 'twixt Albany and Cornwall;
Who have—as who have not, that their great stars
Throned and set high?—servants, who seem no less,
Which are to France the spies and speculations
Intelligent of our state.[6] What hath been seen,
Either in snuffs and packings[7] of the dukes,
Or the hard rein which both of them have borne
Against the old kind king; or something deeper,
Whereof perchance these are but furnishings;[8]
But, true it is, from France there comes a power
Into this scattered kingdom; who already,
Wise in our negligence, have secret feet
In some of our best ports, and are at point[9]
To show their open banner. Now to you:

8. Land; "things": everything.
9. Show no respect for (opposite of "make much of").
1. I.e., microcosm.
2. The bear, sucked dry by its cubs and ravenously hungry, would nevertheless lie in its lair instead of seeking food.
3. A gambler's cry on the last throw of the dice—a cry of desperation.
4. To counter with his jests the injuries which have struck Lear to the heart.
5. Dare, on the basis of my knowledge of you, to entrust an important matter to you.
6. Who are France's spies and intelligence agents in our country.
7. Quarrels and plots against each other.
8. Trimmings.
9. Who already, taking advantage of our negligence, have gained a secret foothold and are ready.

If on my credit you dare build so far
To make your speed to Dover, you shall find
Some that will thank you, making just report
Of how unnatural and bemadding sorrow
The king hath cause to plain.[1]
I am a gentleman of blood and breeding;
And, from some knowledge and assurance,[2] offer
This office to you.

GENT. I will talk further with you.

KENT. No, do not.
For confirmation that I am much more
Than my out-wall, open this purse, and take
What it contains. If you shall see Cordelia,—
As fear not but you shall,—show her this ring,
And she will tell you who your fellow is
That yet you do not know. Fie on this storm!
I will go seek the king.

GENT. Give me your hand. Have you no more to say?

KENT. Few words, but, to effect,[3] more than all yet;
That, when we have found the king,—in which your pain
That way, I'll this,[4]—he that first lights on him
Holla the other. [*Exeunt severally.*]

SCENE 2

[*Enter* LEAR *and* FOOL. *Storm still.*]

LEAR. Blow, winds, and crack your cheeks![5] rage! blow!
You cataracts and hurricanoes,[6] spout
Till you have drenched our steeples, drowned the cocks![7]
You sulphurous and thought-executing fires,[8]
Vaunt-couriers to oak-cleaving thunderbolts,
Singe my white head! And thou, all-shaking thunder,
Smite flat the thick rotundity o' the world!
Crack Nature's molds, all germens spill at once,[9]
That make ingrateful man!

FOOL. O nuncle, court holy-water[1] in a dry house is better than this rain-water out o' door. Good nuncle, in, and ask thy daughters' blessing! Here's a night pities neither wise man nor fool.

LEAR. Rumble thy bellyful! Spit, fire! spout, rain!
Nor rain, wind, thunder, fire, are my daughters:
I tax not you, you elements, with unkindness;[2]

1. For making accurate report of the unnatural and maddening sorrow that the king can justifiably complain of.
2. Trustworthy information.
3. In importance.
4. In which troublesome task, you go that way, I'll go this.
5. In contemporary maps, winds were represented by faces with their cheeks puffed out, blowing.
6. Both words mean "waterspouts."
7. Weathercocks.
8. Lightning flashes which work ("execute") faster than thought.
9. Crack the molds Nature uses and destroy the seeds that make the ungrateful creature, man.
1. I.e., flattery.
2. I do not charge you elements with unnaturalness.

I never gave you kingdom, called you children,
You owe me no subscription.[3] Then let fall
Your horrible pleasure. Here I stand, your slave,
A poor, infirm, weak, and despised old man.
But yet I call you servile ministers,[4]
That have with two pernicious daughters joined
Your high engendered battles[5] 'gainst a head
So old and white as this. O! O! 't is foul!

FOOL. He that has a house to put 's head in has a good head-piece,[6]

The cod-piece that will house
  Before the head has any,
The head and he shall louse;
  So beggars marry many.[7]
The man that makes his toe
  What he his heart should make
Shall of a corn cry woe,
  And turn his sleep to wake.[8]

For there was never yet fair woman but she made mouths in a glass.[9]

LEAR. No, I will be the pattern of all patience; I will say nothing.

[*Enter* KENT.]

KENT. Who's there?

FOOL. Marry, here 's grace and a cod-piece;[1] that's a wise man and a fool.

KENT. Alas, sir, are you here? things that love night
Love not such nights as these; the wrathful skies
Gallow the very wanderers of the dark,[2]
And make them keep their caves. Since I was man,
Such sheets of fire, such bursts of horrid thunder,
Such groans of roaring wind and rain, I never
Remember to have heard. Man's nature cannot carry
The affliction nor the fear.

LEAR. Let the great gods,
That keep this dreadful pother o'er our heads,
Find out their enemies now.[3] Tremble, thou wretch,
That hast within thee undivulgéd crimes,
Unwhipped of justice. Hide thee, thou bloody hand;
Thou perjured, and thou simular of virtue
That are incestuous.[4] Caitiff, to pieces shake,

3. Submission, obedience.
4. Slavish agents.
5. Your heaven-born battalions.
6. (1) Helmet; (2) skull.
7. Codpiece: penis (from the piece of clothing covering it). "The man that begets children before he has a house will surely become a lousy vagabond. Thus it is that many beggars get married" (Kittredge's note).
8. The man who exchanges the place of his toe and his heart will get a corn on his heart that will hurt so he can't sleep at night.
9. A quasi-proverbial saying about the vanity of women. "Made mouths": made faces.
1. Grace refers to a noble person; the codpiece was prominent in a clown's costume.
2. Terrify the wild beasts.
3. By the terror inspired in guilty people.
4. You perjurer, and you incestuous man who pretends to be virtuous.

That under covert and convenient seeming
Hast practiced on man's life.[5] Close pent-up guilts
Rive your concealing continents, and cry
These dreadful summoners grace.[6] I am a man
More sinned against than sinning.

KENT. Alack, bare-headed?
Gracious my lord, hard by here is a hovel;
Some friendship will it lend you 'gainst the tempest.
Repose you there, while I to this hard house—
More harder than the stones whereof 'tis raised,
Which even but now, demanding after you,
Denied me to come in—return, and force
Their scanted courtesy.

LEAR. My wits begin to turn.
Come on, my boy. How dost, my boy? Art cold?
I am cold myself. Where is this straw, my fellow?
The art of our necessities is strange,
That can make vile things precious.[7] Come, your hovel.
Poor fool and knave, I have one part in my heart
That's sorry yet for thee.

FOOL. [*singing*]
He that has and a little tiny wit,—
With hey, ho, the wind and the rain,—
Must make content with his fortunes fit,
Though the rain it raineth every day.[8]

LEAR. True, boy. Come, bring us to this hovel.

[*Exeunt* LEAR *and* KENT.]

FOOL. This is a brave night to cool a courtesan.[9]
I'll speak a prophecy ere I go:
When priests are more in word than matter;
When brewers mar their malt with water;
When nobles are their tailors' tutors;
No heretics burned, but wenches' suitors;
When every case in law is right;
No squire in debt, nor no poor knight;
When slanders do not live in tongues,
Nor cutpurses come not to throngs;
When usurers tell their gold i' the field,
And bawds and whores do churches build;
Then shall the realm of Albion
Come to great confusion.
Then comes the time, who lives to see 't,

5. Wretch, who in clever and plausible deception has plotted a murder.
6. Carefully hidden crimes, burst out of the covering that hides you and beg mercy from these dreadful ministers of justice.
7. Necessity has a kind of strange magic which can make worthless things precious.
8. An adaptation of one verse of a song sung by Feste, the fool, at the end of Shakespeare's *Twelfth Night*. Lear's Fool alters it to emphasize the lack of wit of himself and his master.
9. A fine night to cool the lust of a courtesan.

That going shall be used with feet.
This prophecy Merlin shall make; for I live before his time.[1]
[*Exit.*]

SCENE 3

[*Enter* GLOUCESTER *and* EDMUND.]

GLOU. Alack, alack, Edmund, I like not this unnatural dealing.[2] When I desired their leave that I might pity him, they took from me the use of mine own house; charged me, on pain of their perpetual displeasure, neither to speak of him, entreat for him, nor any way sustain him.

EDM. Most savage and unnatural!

GLOU. Go to;[3] say you nothing. There's a division betwixt the dukes, and a worse matter than that. I have received a letter this night; 'tis dangerous to be spoken; I have locked the letter in my closet.[4] These injuries the king now bears will be revenged home; there's part of a power already footed; we must incline to the king.[5] I will seek him, and privily relieve him. Go you and maintain talk with the duke, that my charity be not of him perceived if he ask for me, I am ill, and gone to bed. Though I die for it, as no less is threatened me, the king my old master must be relieved. There is some strange thing toward, Edmund; pray you, be careful. [*Exit.*]

EDM. This courtesy, forbid thee,[6] shall the duke
Instantly know, and of that letter too.
This seems a fair deserving, and must draw me[7]
That which my father loses—no less than all.
The younger rises when the old doth fall. [*Exit.*]

SCENE 4

[*Enter* LEAR, KENT, *and* FOOL.]

KENT. Here is the place, my lord; good my lord, enter:
The tyranny of the open night's[8] too rough
For nature to endure. [*Storm still.*]

LEAR. Let me alone.

KENT. Good my lord, enter here.

LEAR. Wilt break my heart?

1. The "when . . . then" formula was a traditional medieval satiric mode in which the poet ticked off one abuse after another: when all are remedied, all will be well. One of the old "whens," erroneously thought to be by Chaucer, was called Merlin's Prophecy; the Fool, in identifying it, emphasizes the antiquity of the *Lear* setting.

2. I.e., unnatural behavior of Regan and Cornwall.

3. Enough.

4. Private room.

5. These injuries the king suffers will be revenged to the full; part of an army is already landed; we must be on the side of the king.

6. Forbidden to you.

7. This deserves reward and must get for me.

8. Night in the open.

KENT. I had rather break mine own. Good my lord, enter.

LEAR. Thou think'st 'tis much that this contentious storm
Invades us to the skin. So 'tis to thee;
But where the greater malady is fixed,[9]
The lesser is scarce felt. Thou'dst shun a bear;
But if thy flight lay toward the raging sea,
Thou'dst meet the bear i' the mouth. When the mind's free,
The body's delicate.[1] The tempest in my mind
Doth from my senses take all feeling else
Save what beats there. Filial ingratitude!
Is it not as this mouth should tear this hand
For lifting food to 't? But I will punish home.[2]
No, I will weep no more. In such a night
To shut me out! Pour on; I will endure.
In such a night as this! O Regan, Goneril!
Your old kind father, whose frank heart gave all,—
O, that way madness lies; let me shun that;
No more of that.

KENT. Good my lord, enter here.

LEAR. Prithee, go in thyself; seek thine own ease:
This tempest will not give me leave to ponder
On things would hurt me more. But I'll go in.
[*To the* FOOL.] In, boy; go first. You houseless poverty,[3]—
Nay, get thee in. I'll pray, and then I'll sleep.
[FOOL *goes in.*]

Poor naked wretches, whereso'er you are,
That bide[4] the pelting of this pitiless storm,
How shall your houseless heads and unfed sides,
Your looped and windowed raggedness,[5] defend you
From seasons such as these? O, I have ta'en
Too little care of this! Take physic, pomp;
Expose thyself to feel what wretches feel,
That thou mayst shake the superflux to them,
And show the heavens more just.[6]

EDG. [*within*] Fathom and half, fathom and half![7]
Poor Tom! [*The* FOOL *runs out from the hovel.*]

FOOL. Come not in here, nuncle, here's a spirit.
Help me, help me!

KENT. Give me thy hand. Who's there?

FOOL. A spirit, a spirit! He says his name's poor Tom.

KENT. What are thou that dost grumble there i' the straw? Come forth.

9. Chronic, incurable.
1. When the mind is at ease, the body is sensitive to physical pain.
2. Thoroughly.
3. The Fool is addressed.
4. Endure.
5. How shall your uncovered heads and unfed bodies, your tattered rags full of holes, like windows in a house.
6. Shake off the surplus you enjoy to the poor and show that the heavens distribute some kind of justice.
7. The rains are so heavy that Poor Tom pretends they are at sea and he is taking soundings.

[*Enter* EDGAR *disguised as a madman.*]

EDG. Away! the foul fiend follows me!
Through the sharp hawthorn blows the cold wind.
Humh! go to thy cold bed, and warm thee.[8]

LEAR. Hast thou given all to thy two daughters? And art thou come to this?

EDG. Who gives any thing to poor Tom? whom the foul fiend hath led through fire and through flame, through ford and whirlpool, o'er bog and quagmire; that hath laid knives under his pillow and halters in his pew; set ratsbane by his porridge;[9] made him proud of heart, to ride on a bay trotting-horse over four-inched bridges, to course[1] his own shadow for a traitor. Bless thy five wits! Tom's a-cold,—O, do, de, do de, do de. Bless thee from whirlwinds, star-blasting, and taking![2] Do poor Tom some charity, whom the foul fiend vexes: there could I have him now,—and there,—and there again, and there. [*Storm still.*]

LEAR. What, has his daughters brought him to this pass?
Couldst thou save nothing? Didst thou give them all?

FOOL. Nay, he reserved a blanket, else we had been all shamed.

LEAR. Now, all the plagues that in the pendulous air
Hang fated o'er men's faults light on thy daughters!

KENT. He hath no daughters, sir.

LEAR. Death, traitor! nothing could have subdued nature
To such a lowness but his unkind[3] daughters.
Is it the fashion that discarded fathers
Should have thus little mercy on their flesh?[4]
Judicious punishment! 't was this flesh begot
Those pelican daughters.[5]

EDG. Pillicock sat on Pillicock-hill.
Halloo, halloo, loo, loo!

FOOL. This cold night will turn us all to fools and madmen.

EDG. Take heed o' the foul fiend; obey thy parents; keep thy word justly; swear not; commit not with man's sworn spouse; set not thy sweet heart on proud array. Tom's a-cold.

LEAR. What hast thou been?

EDG. A serving-man, proud in heart and mind; that curled my hair; wore gloves in my cap;[6] served the lust of my mistress' heart, and did the act of darkness with her; swore as many oaths as I spake words, and broke them in the sweet face of heaven: one that slept in the contriving of lust, and waked to do it. Wine loved I deeply, dice dearly; and in woman out-

8. Poor Tom, pursued as he thinks by the devil, quotes snatches of old songs and plays. "Humh" signifies his shivering, as does "do de" in line 57.

9. The devil tried to capture souls of madmen by tempting them to the sin of suicide.

1. Chase.

2. Malign influences of planets and spirits. Lear picks up the theme in lines 64–65.

3. Unnatural.

4. Lear notices the pins and splinters Edgar has stuck into his arm.

5. In legend the pelican was supposed to feed its offspring with its own blood. The word reminds Edgar of a children's rhyme.

6. As a favor from his mistress.

paramoured the Turk. False of heart, light of ear, bloody of hand; hog in sloth, fox in stealth, wolf in greediness, dog in madness, lion in prey. Let not the creaking of shoes nor the rustling of silks betray thy poor heart to woman. Keep thy foot out of brothels, thy hand out of plackets,[7] thy pen from lenders' books, and defy the foul fiend. Still through the hawthorn blows the cold wind: Says suum, mun, ha, no, nonny. Dolphin my boy, my boy, sessa! let him trot by.[8] [*Storm still.*]

LEAR. Why, thou wert better in thy grave than to answer with thy uncovered body this extremity of the skies. Is man no more than this? Consider him well. Thou owest the worm no silk, the beast no hide, the sheep no wool, the cat[9] no perfume. Ha! here's three on's are sophisticated![1] Thou art the thing itself; unaccommodated[2] man is no more but such a poor, bare, forked animal as thou art. Off, off, you lendings! come, unbutton here. [*Tearing off his clothes.*]

FOOL. Prithee, nuncle, be contented; 'tis a naughty[3] night to swim in. Now a little fire in a wild field were like an old lecher's heart; a small spark, all the rest on's body cold. Look, here comes a walking fire.

[*Enter* GLOUCESTER, *with a torch.*]

EDG. This is the foul fiend Flibbertigibbet. He begins at curfew, and walks till the first cock.[4] He gives the web and the pin,[5] squinies[5] the eye, and makes the hare-lip; mildews the white[6] wheat, and hurts the poor creature of earth.

St. Withold footed thrice the old;
He met the night-mare and her nine-fold;
Bid her alight,
And her troth plight,
And, aroint thee, witch, aroint thee![7]

KENT. How fares your grace?

LEAR. What's he?

KENT. Who's there? What is't you seek?

GLOU. What are you there? Your names?

EDG. Poor Tom, that eats the swimming frog, the toad, the tadpole, the wall-newt and the water;[8] that in the fury of his heart, when the foul fiend rages, eats cow-dung for sallets;[9] swallows the old rat and the ditch-dog; drinks the green mantle of the standing-pool; who is whipped from tithing to tithing,[1] and stock-punished, and imprisoned; who hath had three suits to his back, six shirts to his body, horse to ride, and weapon to wear;

7. Slits or openings in petticoats.
8. Another line from an old ballad. "Sessa" is an interjection meaning something like "Off you go!"
9. Civet cat.
1. I.e., three of us (Lear, Kent, and the Fool) are artificial (adulterated, impure).
2. "Without the trappings of civilization" (Muir's note).
3. Wicked.
4. Midnight.
5. "Web and pin": cataract; "squinies": squints.
6. Nearly ripe.
7. A charm. "Old": wold (open country); "fold"; foals; "aroint": begone.
8. Water newt.
9. Salads.
1. Parish to parish.

But mice and rats, and such small deer,[2]
Have been Tom's food for seven long year.
Beware my follower. Peace, Smulkin; peace, thou fiend!
GLOU. What, hath your grace no better company?
EDG. The prince of darkness is a gentleman. Modo he's call'd, and Mahu.
GLOU. Our flesh and blood is grown so vile, my lord,
That it doth hate what gets [3] it.
EDG. Poor Tom's a-cold.
GLOU. Go in with me. My duty cannot suffer[4]
To obey in all your daughters' hard commands:
Though their injunction be to bar my doors,
And let this tyrannous night take hold upon you
Yet have I ventured to come seek you out.
And bring you where both fire and food is ready.
LEAR. First let me talk with this philosopher.[5]
What is the cause of thunder?
KENT. Good my lord, take his offer; go into the house.
LEAR. I'll take a word with this same learned Theban.[6]
What is your study?
EDG. How to prevent[7] the fiend, and to kill vermin.
LEAR. Let me ask you one word in private.
KENT. Importune him once more to go, my lord;
His wits begin to unsettle.
GLOU. Canst thou blame him? [*Storm still.*]
His daughters seek his death; ah, that good Kent!
He said it would be thus, poor banished man!
Thou say'st the king grows mad; I'll tell thee, friend,
I am almost mad myself. I had a son,
Now outlawed from my blood. He sought my life,
But lately, very late. I loved him, friend;
No father his son dearer. True to tell thee,
The grief hath crazed my wits. What a night's this!
I do beseech your grace,—
LEAR. O, cry you mercy,[8] sir.
Noble philosopher, your company.
EDG. Tom's a-cold.
GLOU. In, fellow, there, into the hovel; keep thee warm.
LEAR. Come, let's in all.
KENT. This way, my lord.
LEAR. With him!
I will keep still[9] with my philosopher.
KENT. Good my lord, soothe[10] him; let him take the fellow.
GLOU. Take him you on.
KENT. Sirrah, come on; go along with us.
LEAR. Come, good Athenian.

2. Animals.
3. Begets.
4. Allow me.
5. Natural philosopher, scientist.
6. Lear in his madness takes Poor Tom for a learned man from abroad: Thebes, Athens, or Persia (III.vi.74).
7. Avoid.
8. I beg your pardon.
9. Remain always.
10. Humor.

GLOU. No words, no words: hush.
EDG. Child Rowland to the dark tower came,[1]
His word was still,—Fie, foh, and fum,
I smell the blood of a British man. [*Exeunt.*]

SCENE 5

[*Enter* CORNWALL *and* EDMUND.]

CORN. I will have my revenge ere I depart his house.

EDM. How, my lord, I may be censured, that nature thus gives way to loyalty, something fears me to think of.[2]

CORN. I now perceive, it was not altogether your brother's evil disposition made him seek his death; but a provoking merit,[3] set a-work by a reproveable badness in himself.

EDM. How malicious is my fortune, that I must repent to be just! This is the letter he spoke of, which approves him an intelligent party[4] to the advantages of France. O heavens! that this treason were not, or not I the detector!

CORN. Go with me to the duchess.

EDM. If the matter of this paper be certain, you have mighty business in hand.

CORN. True or false, it hath made thee Earl of Gloucester. Seek out where thy father is, that he may be ready for our apprehension.[5]

EDM. [*aside*] If I find him comforting the king, it will stuff his suspicion more fully.—I will perséver in my course of loyalty, though the conflict be sore between that and my blood.[6]

CORN. I will lay trust upon thee, and thou shalt find a dearer father in my love. [*Exeunt.*]

SCENE 6

[*Enter* GLOUCESTER, LEAR, KENT, FOOL , *and* EDGAR.]

GLOU. Here is better than the open air; take it thankfully. I will piece out the comfort with what addition I can; I will not be long from you.

KENT. All the power of his wits have given sway to his impatience: the gods reward your kindness! [*Exit* GLOUCESTER.]

EDG. Frateretto calls me; and tells me Nero is an angler in the lake of darkness.[7] Pray, innocent, and beware the foul fiend.

FOOL. Prithee, nuncle, tell me whether a madman be a gentleman or a yeoman?

LEAR. A king, a king!

1. "Child": a candidate for knighthood. The line may be from a lost ballad; Browning built a notable poem on it. "Word": motto, which absurdly comes from *Jack the Giant Killer*.
2. "What people will think of me, since my natural feelings as a son thus give way to loyalty, rather frightens me" (Muir's note).
3. A quality in him deserved death.
4. Which proves him a spy.
5. Arrest.
6. Filial feelings.
7. Frateretto is the name of one of his demons. The Emperor Nero is a fisherman in Chaucer's *Monk's Tale*.

FOOL. No, he's a yeoman that has a gentleman to his son; for he's a mad yeoman that sees his son a gentleman before him.

LEAR. To have a thousand with red burning spits
Come hissing in upon 'em —

EDG. The foul fiend bites my back.

FOOL. He's mad that trusts in the tameness of a wolf, a horse's health,[8] a boy's love, or a whore's oath.

LEAR. It shall be done; I will arraign them straight.[9]
[*To* EDGAR.] Come, sit thou here, most learned justicer;
[*to the* FOOL] Thou, sapient sir, sit here. Now, you she foxes!

EDG. Look, where he stands and glares! Wantest thou eyes at trial, madam?[1]

Come o'er the bourn, Bessy, to me —

FOOL. Her boat hath a leak,
And she must not speak
Why she dares not come over to thee.

EDG. The foul fiend haunts poor Tom in the voice of a nightingale. Hopdance cries in Tom's belly for two white herring. Croak not, black angel; I have no food for thee.[2]

KENT. How do you, sir? Stand you not so amazed:
Will you lie down and rest upon the cushions?

LEAR. I'll see their trial first. Bring in the evidence.
[*To* EDGAR.] Thou robed man of justice, take thy place;
[*to the* FOOL] And thou, his yoke-fellow of equity,[3]
Bench by his side: [*to* KENT] you are o' the commission,
Sit you too,

EDG. Let us deal justly.

Sleepest or wakest thou, jolly shepherd?
Thy sheep be in the corn;
And for one blast of thy minikin mouth,
Thy sheep shall take no harm.[4]

Pur! the cat is gray.

LEAR. Arraign her first; 'tis Goneril. I here take my oath before this honorable assembly, she kicked the poor king her father.

FOOL. Come hither, mistress. Is your name Goneril?

LEAR. She cannot deny it.

FOOL. Cry you mercy, I took you for a joint-stool.[5]

LEAR. And here's another, whose warped looks proclaim
What store[6] her heart is made on. Stop her there!
Arms, arms, sword, fire! Corruption in the place!

8. Horses were supposed to be more subject to ailments than other animals.
9. I will legally try them (Goneril and Regan) right now.
1. Poor Tom points to Frateretto and asks the imaginary Goneril if she minds having onlookers at her trial. He then quotes (or sings) a line from a ballad which a lover addresses his sweetheart. "Bourn": brook.
2. The growling of his stomach from hunger Tom takes to be the croaking of the foul fiend.
3. I.e., judicial colleague.
4. Another ballad stanza. "Minikin": delicate, dainty.
5. The comment is a common one meaning "Pardon me; I didn't notice you," but the comedy is richer, and more like the Fool, if an actual stool is addressed. "Joint stool": a low stool made by joiner (carpenter).
6. Material.

False justicer, why hast thou let her 'scape?
EDG. Bless thy five wits!
KENT. O pity! Sir, where is the patience now,
That you so oft have boasted to retain?
EDG. [*aside*] My tears begin to take his part so much,
They'll mar my counterfeiting.[7]
LEAR. The little dogs and all,
Tray, Blanch, and Sweet-heart, see, they bark at me.[8]
EDG. Tom will throw his head at them. Avaunt, you curs!
Be thy mouth or black or white,
Tooth that poisons if it bite;
Mastiff, greyhound, mongrel grim,
Hound or spaniel, brach or lym,
Or bobtail tike or trundle-tail.
Tom will make them weep and wail:
For, with throwing thus my head,
Dogs leap the hatch, and all are fled.[9]

Do de, de, de. Sessa! Come, march to wakes and fairs and market-towns. Poor Tom, thy horn is dry.[1]

LEAR. Then let them anatomize[2] Regan; see what breeds about her heart. Is there any cause in nature that makes these hard hearts? [*To* EDGAR.] You, sir, I entertain for one of my hundred; I do not like the fashion of your garments. You will say they are Persian; but let them be changed.

KENT. Now, good my lord, lie there and rest awhile.

LEAR. Make no noise, make no noise; draw the curtains. So, so, so. We'll go to supper i' the morning.[3]

FOOL. And I'll go to bed at noon.

[*Re-enter* GLOUCESTER.]

GLOU. Come hither, friend. Where is the king my master?
KENT. Here, sir; but trouble him not; his wits are gone.
GLOU. Good friend, I prithee, take him in thy arms;
I have o'erheard a plot of death upon him:
There is a litter ready; lay him in 't
And drive towards Dover, friend, where thou shalt meet
Both welcome and protection. Take up thy master.
If thou shouldst dally half an hour, his life,
With thine, and all that offer to defend him,
Stand in assured loss. Take up, take up!
And follow me, that will to some provision
Give thee quick conduct.
KENT. Oppresséd nature sleeps:
This rest might yet have balmed thy broken sinews,
Which, if convenience will not allow,

7. Spoil my pretense.
8. Lear in his delirium thinks that his own dogs have sided with his daughters and now bark at him.
9. Another improvised charm. "Brach or lym": bitch or bloodhound; "hatch": the lower half of a divided door.
1. Beggars carried a horn to hold the drinks they begged.
2. Dissect.
3. The curtains are the curtains of his bed at home. He is aware that he should have supped before going to bed.

Stand in hard cure.[4] [*To the* FOOL.] Come, help to bear thy master:
Thou must not stay behind.

GLOU. Come come, away.

[*Exeunt all but* EDGAR.]

EDG. When we our betters see bearing our woes,
We scarcely think our miseries our foes.
Who alone suffers suffers most i' the mind,
Leaving free[5] things and happy shows behind:
But then the mind much sufferance doth o'erskip
When grief hath mates, and bearing[6] fellowship.
How light and portable my pain seems now,
When that which makes me bend makes the king bow;
He childed as I fathered! Tom, away!
Mark the high noises, and thyself bewray[7]
When false opinion, whose wrong thought defiles thee,
In thy just proof repeals and reconciles thee.[8]
What will hap more tonight, safe 'scape the king!
Lurk, lurk.[9] [*Exit.*]

SCENE 7

[*Enter* CORNWALL, REGAN, GONERIL, EDMUND, *and* SERVANTS.]

CORN. [*To* GONERIL] Post speedily to my lord your husband; show him this letter. The army of France is landed. Seek out the villain Gloucester. [*Exeunt some of the* SERVANTS.]

REG. Hang him instantly.

GON. Pluck out his eyes.

CORN. Leave him to my displeasure. Edmund, keep you our sister company. The revenges we are bound to[1] take upon your traitorous father are not fit for your beholding. Advise the duke, where you are going, to a most festinate[2] preparation. We are bound to the like. Our posts shall be swift and intelligent betwixt us. Farewell, dear sister: farewell, my lord of Gloucester.

[*Enter* OSWALD.]

How now! Where's the king?

OSW. My lord of Gloucester hath conveyed him hence.
Some five or six and thirty of his knights,
Hot questrists[3] after him, met him at gate;
Who, with some other of the lords dependants,
Are gone with him towards Dover; where they boast
To have well-armed friends.

4. This rest might have restored your racked nerves, which can hardly be cured without it.
5. Carefree.
6. Endurance, suffering.
7. Notice signs of discord among the powerful, and reveal yourself.
8. When the false charges which hurt you so much are proved unfounded and you are called back from exile and reconciled with your father.
9. Remain in hiding.
1. Ready to.
2. Rapid.
3. Seekers.

CORN. Get horses for your mistress.
GON. Farewell, sweet lord, and sister.
CORN. Edmund, farewell.
[*Exeunt* GONERIL, EDMUND, *and* OSWALD.]
Go seek the traitor Gloucester,
Pinion him like a thief, bring him before us.
[*Exeunt other* SERVANTS.]
Though well we may not pass upon his life
Without the form of justice, yet our power
Shall do a courtesy to[4] our wrath, which men
May blame, but not control. Who's there? the traitor?
[*Enter* GLOUCESTER, *brought in by two or three.*]
REG. Ingrateful fox! 'tis he.
CORN. Bind fast his corky[5] arms.
GLOU. What mean your graces? Good my friends, consider
You are my guests. Do me no foul play, friends.
CORN. Bind him, I say. [SERVANTS *bind him.*]
REG. Hard, hard. O filthy[6] traitor!
GLOU. Unmerciful lady as you are, I'm none.
CORN. To this chair bind him. Villain, thou shalt find—
[REGAN *plucks his beard.*]
GLOU. By the kind gods, 'tis most ignobly done
To pluck me by the beard.
REG. So white, and such a traitor!
GLOU. Naughty[7] lady,
These hairs, which thou dost ravish from my chin,
Will quicken,[8] and accuse thee. I am your host.
With robbers' hands my hospitable favors
You should not ruffle[9] thus. What will you do?
CORN. Come, sir, what letters had you late from France?
REG. Be simple answered,[1] for we know the truth.
CORN. And what confederacy have you with the traitors
Late footed[2] in the kingdom?
REG. To whose hands have you sent the lunatic king?
Speak.
GLOU. I have a letter guessingly set down,
Which came from one that's of a neutral heart,
And not from one opposed.
CORN. Cunning.
REG. And false.
CORN. Where hast thou sent the king?
GLOU. To Dover.
REG. Wherefore to Dover? Wast thou not charged at peril—
CORN. Wherefore to Dover? Let him first answer that.
GLOU. I am tied to the stake, and I must stand the course.[3]

4. Yield to.
5. Dry and withered.
6. Odious.
7. Wicked.
8. Come to life.
9. Do violence to.
1. I.e., frank.
2. Recently landed.
3. The image is of a bear tied to a stake and baited by dogs.

REG. Wherefore to Dover?
GLOU. Because I would not see thy cruel nails
  Pluck out his poor old eyes; nor thy fierce sister
  In his anointed[4] flesh stick boarish fangs.
  The sea, with such a storm as his bare head
  In hell-black night endured, would have buoyed up,
  And quenched the stellèd fires.[5]
  Yet, poor old heart, he holp the heavens to rage.
  If wolves had at thy gate howled that dern[6] time,
  Thou shouldst have said "Good porter, turn the key."
  All cruels else subscribed.[7] But I shall see
  The wingèd vengeance overtake such children.
CORN. See 't shalt thou never. Fellows, hold the chair.
  Upon these eyes of thine I'll set my foot.
GLOU. He that will think to live till he be old,
  Give me some help! O cruel! O ye gods!
REG. One side will mock another. The other too!
CORN. If you see vengeance,—
FIRST SERV. Hold your hand, my lord:
  I have served you ever since I was a child;
  But better service have I never done you
  Than now to bid you hold.
REG. How now, you dog!
FIRST SERV. If you did wear a beard upon your chin,
  I'd shake it on this quarrel.
REG. What do you mean?
CORN. My villain!
FIRST SERV. Why, then, come on, and take the chance of anger.
REG. Give me thy sword. A peasant stand up thus!
[CORNWALL *is wounded.*]
[*Takes a sword, and runs at him behind.*]
FIRST SERV. O, I am slain! My lord, you have one eye left
  To see some mischief on him. O! [*Dies.*]
CORN. Lest it see more, prevent it. Out, vile jelly!
  Where is thy luster now?
GLOU. All dark and comfortless. Where's my son Edmund?
  Edmund, enkindle all the sparks of nature,
  To quit this horrid act.[8]
REG. Out,[9] treacherous villain!
  Thou call'st on him that hates thee. It was he
  That made the overture[1] of thy treasons to us;
  Who is too good to pity thee.
GLOU. O my follies! Then Edgar was abused.
  Kind gods, forgive me that, and prosper him!
REG. Go thrust him out at gates, and let him smell
  His way to Dover. [*Exit one with* GLOUCESTER.]

4. As a king.
5. Would have risen up and quenched the fires of the stars.
6. Dire, dread.
7. I.e., all other cruel creatures submitted to the fury of the storm, but you did not.
8. Arouse all your filial feelings to revenge this horrid act.
9. Out upon you! (a curse).
1. Disclosure.

How is't, my lord? how look you?[2]
CORN. I have received a hurt. Follow me, lady;
Turn out that eyeless villain. Throw this slave
Upon the dunghill. Regan, I bleed apace.
Untimely comes this hurt. Give me your arm.
[*Exit* CORNWALL *led by* REGAN.]
SEC. SERV. I'll never care what wickedness I do,
If this man come to good.
THIRD SERV. If she live long,
And in the end meet the old[3] course of death,
Women will all turn monsters.
SEC. SERV. Let's follow the old earl, and get the Bedlam
To lead him where he would. His roguish madness
Allows itself to any thing.[4]
THIRD SERV. Go thou; I'll fetch some flax and whites of eggs[5]
To apply to his bleeding face. Now, heaven help him!
[*Exeunt severally.*]

Act IV

SCENE 1

[*Enter* EDGAR.]
EDG. Yet better thus, and known to be contemned
Than still contemned and flattered.[6] To be worst,
The lowest and most dejected thing of fortune,
Stands still in esperance, lives not in fear.[7]
The lamentable change is from the best;
The worst returns to laughter. Welcome, then,
Thou unsubstantial air that I embrace!
The wretch that thou hast blown unto the worst
Owes nothing to thy blasts. But who comes here?
[*Enter* GLOUCESTER, *led by an* OLD MAN.]
My father, poorly led? World, world, O world!
But that thy strange mutations make us hate thee,
Life would not yield to age.[8]
OLD MAN. O, my good lord, I have been your tenant, and your father's tenant, these fourscore years.
GLOU. Away, get thee away! Good friend, be gone.
Thy comforts can do me no good at all;
Thee they may hurt.
OLD MAN. Alack, sir, you cannot see your way.
GLOU. I have no way, and therefore want no eyes;

2. How do you seem to be?
3. Natural.
4. Since he is a mad vagabond (rogue) he will not be called to account.
5. The usual application for wounds in the eyes.
6. I.e., it is better to be a beggar, publicly known to be condemned, than always ("still") to be condemned by flattery, as a prince is.
7. The one cast to the bottom by fortune can hope to move up; he doesn't fear falling lower.
8. "The only thing that makes us grow old and die is our hatred of life in this world, and that hatred is caused by the strange vicissitudes of fortune" (Kittredge's note).

I stumbled when I saw. Full oft 'tis seen,
Our means secure us, and our mere defects
Prove our commodities.[9] O dear son Edgar,
The food of thy abuséd father's wrath![1]
Might I but live to see thee in my touch,
I'd say I had eyes again!
OLD MAN. How now! Who's there?
EDG. [*aside*] O gods! Who is't can say "I am at the worst"?
I am worse than e'er I was.
OLD MAN. 'Tis poor mad Tom.
EDG. [*aside*] And worse I may be yet: the worst is not
So long as we can say "This is the worst."
OLD MAN. Fellow, where goest?
GLOU. Is it a beggar-man?
OLD MAN. Madman and beggar too.
GLOU. He has some reason, else he could not beg.
I' the last night's storm I such a fellow saw;
Which made me think a man a worm.[2] My son
Came then into my mind, and yet my mind
Was then scarce friends with him. I have heard more since.
As flies to wanton[3] boys are we to the gods;
They kill us for their sport.
EDG. [*aside*] How should this be?
Bad is the trade that must play fool to sorrow,
Angering itself and others.—Bless thee, master!
GLOU. Is that the naked fellow?
OLD MAN. Ay, my lord.
GLOU. Then, prithee, get thee gone. If, for my sake,
Thou wilt o'ertake us, hence a mile or twain,
I' the way toward Dover, do it for ancient[4] love;
And bring some covering for this naked soul,
Who I'll entreat to lead me.
OLD MAN. Alack, sir, he is mad.
GLOU. 'Tis the times' plague, when madmen lead the blind.
Do as I bid thee, or rather do thy pleasure;
Above the rest,[5] be gone.
OLD MAN. I'll bring him the best 'parel that I have,
Come on 't what will. [*Exit.*]
GLOU. Sirrah, naked fellow,—
EDG. Poor Tom's a-cold. [*aside*] I cannot daub it further.[6]
GLOU. Come hither, fellow.
EDG. [*aside*] And yet I must.—Bless thy sweet eyes, they bleed.
GLOU. Know'st thou the way to Dover?
EDG. Both stile and gate, horse-way and foot-path. Poor Tom hath been scared out of his good wits. Bless thee, good man's

9. I.e., a truth often observed is that prosperity makes us careless but adversity proves to be our best possession.
1. The one on whom his father fed his anger.
2. "How much less man, that is a worm" (Job xxv.6).
3. Sportive, playful.
4. Former, bygone.
5. All.
6. Pretend anymore.

son, from the foul fiend! Five fiends have been in Poor Tom at once; of lust, as Obidicut; Hobbididance, prince of dumbness; Mahu, of stealing; Modo, of murder; Flibbertigibbet, of mopping and mowing,[7] who since possesses chambermaids and waiting-women. So, bless thee, master!

GLOU. Here, take this purse, thou whom the heavens' plagues
Have humbled to all strokes.[8] That I am wretched
Makes thee the happier. Heavens, deal so still!
Let the superfluous and lust-dieted[9] man,
That slaves your ordinance,[1] that will not see
Because he doth not feel, feel your power quickly;
So distribution should undo excess,
And each man have enough. Dost thou know Dover?

EDG. Ay, master.

GLOU. There is a cliff, whose high and bending[2] head
Looks fearfully in the confinéd deep.[3]
Bring me but to the very brim of it,
And I'll repair the misery thou dost bear
With something rich about me. From that place
I shall no leading need.

EDG. Give me thy arm.
Poor Tom shall lead thee. [*Exeunt.*]

SCENE 2

[*Enter* GONERIL *and* EDMUND.]

GON. Welcome, my lord. I marvel our mild husband
Not met us on the way.[4]

[*Enter* OSWALD.]

Now where's your master?

OSW. Madam, within, but never man so changed.
I told him of the army that was landed;
He smiled at it. I told him you were coming;
His answer was "The worse." Of Gloucester's treachery,
And of the loyal service of his son,
When I informed him, then he called me sot,[5]
And told me I had turned the wrong side out.
What most he should dislike seems pleasant to him;
What like, offensive.

GON. [*to* EDM.] Then shall you go no further.
It is the cowish[6] terror of his spirit,
That dares not undertake. He'll not feel wrongs
Which tie him to an answer.[7] Our wishes on the way

7. Making faces.
8. Have brought so low as to accept humbly the bitterest strokes of Fortune.
9. Overly self-indulgent.
1. Makes your law subject to him.
2. Beetling.
3. Look into the sea, hemmed in by cliffs.

4. I.e., from Gloucester's castle; they have arrived at Goneril and Albany's castle.
5. Fool.
6. Cowardly.
7. He will overlook offenses which would require him to punish.

May prove effects.[8] Back, Edmund, to my brother;
Hasten his musters and conduct his powers.
I must change arms at home, and give the distaff
Into my husband's hands. This trusty servant
Shall pass between us. Ere long you are like to hear,
If you dare venture in your own behalf,
A mistress's command. Wear this; spare speech;
[*Giving a favor.*]
Decline your head. This kiss, if it durst speak,
Would stretch thy spirits up into the air.
Conceive, and fare thee well.

EDM. Yours in the ranks of death.[9]

GON. My most dear Gloucester!
[*Exit* EDMUND.]
O, the difference of man and man!
To thee a woman's services are due:
My foot usurps my body.[1]

OSW. Madam, here comes my lord. [*Exit.*]

[*Enter* ALBANY.]

GON. I have been worth the whistle.[2]

ALB. O Goneril!
You are not worth the dust which the rude wind
Blows in your face. I fear your disposition.
That nature, which contemns it origin,
Cannot be bordered certain in itself.[3]
She that herself will sliver and disbranch
From her material sap, perforce must wither
And come to deadly use.[4]

GON. No more; the text is foolish.[5]

ALB. Wisdom and goodness to the vile seem vile;
Filths savor but themselves. What have you done?
Tigers, not daughters, what have you performed?
A father, and a gracious aged man,
Whose reverence even the head-lugged[6] bear would lick,
Most barbarous, most degenerate, have you madded.
Could my good brother suffer you to do it?
A man, a prince, by him so benefited!
If that the heavens do not their visible spirits[7]
Send quickly down to tame these vild[8] offenses,

8. Our desires expressed on the way here (that you might take Albany's place as my husband) may be fulfilled. "Brother": brother-in-law, Cornwall.
9. Some critics see sexual innuendoes in "spirits," "conceive," and "death."
1. I.e., "a woman might justly adore Edmund, but Albany in the role of husband is as if the foot presumed to control the whole body" (Brooke's note).
2. Goneril, commenting bitterly on Albany's failure to meet her on the way refers to a proverb, "It is a poor dog that is not worth the whistling."
3. I have fears concerning your disposition. The nature that renounces its source cannot be trusted to keep within natural or moral limits.
4. I.e., she who cuts herself off from the tree that gave her life must be a withered branch, ready for burning ("deadly use").
5. She suggests that Albany is starting to preach a sermon, and she will hear no more of it.
6. Tugged along by a chain around its head.
7. Lightning and thunderbolt, as distinguished from invisible spirits.
8. Vile.

It will come,
Humanity must perforce prey on itself,
Like monsters of the deep.

GON. Milk-livered man!
That bear'st a cheek for blows,[9] a head for wrongs:
Who hast not in thy brows an eye discerning
Thine honor from thy suffering; that not know'st
Fools do those villains pity who are punished
Ere they have done their mischief. Where's thy drum?
France spreads his banners in our noiseless[1] land,
With pluméd helm thy state[2] begins to threat;
Whiles thou, a moral[3] fool, sit'st still, and criest
"Alack, why does he so?"

ALB. See thyself, devil!
Proper deformity shows not in the fiend
So horrid as in woman.[4]

GON. O vain fool!

ALB. Thou changéd and self-covered thing, for shame,
Be-monster not thy feature.[5] Were't my fitness
To let these hands obey my blood,[6]
They are apt enough to dislocate and tear
Thy flesh and bones. Howe'er thou art a fiend,
A woman's shape doth shield thee.

GON. Marry, your manhood! mew!

[*Enter a* MESSENGER.]

ALB. What news?

MESS. O, my good lord, the Duke of Cornwall's dead;
Slain by his servant, going to put out
The other eye of Gloucester.

ALB. Gloucester's eyes?

MESS. A servant that he bred, thrilled with remorse,[7]
Opposed against the act, bending his sword
To his great master; who, thereat enraged,
Flew on him, and amongst them felled him dead;
But not without that harmful stroke, which since
Hath plucked him after.

ALB. This shows you are above,
You justicers, that these our nether crimes[8]
So speedily can venge! But, O poor Gloucester!
Lost he his other eye?

MESS. Both, both, my lord.
This letter, madam, craves a speedy answer;

9. To be understood in the light of Matthew v.39, "whosoever shall smite thee on thy right cheek, turn to him the other also," though *King Lear* has a pre-Christian setting.
1. Because the drum of Albany's army has not yet sounded.
2. Throne, power.
3. Moralizing.
4. The ugliness which is natural ("proper") in a demon is not so horrid as in a woman.
5. I.e., you hypocrite, do not allow your whole shape ("feature") to become that of a monster.
6. Passion.
7. A servant he had brought up, pierced by compassion.
8. I.e., you judges, that these crimes here below, on earth.

'T is from your sister.
GON. [*aside*] One way I like this well;
But being a widow, and my Gloucester with her,
May all the building in my fancy pluck
Upon my hateful life.[9] Another way,
The news is not so tart.—I'll read, and answer. [*Exit.*]
ALB. Where was his son when they did take his eyes?
MESS. Come with my lady hither.
ALB. He is not here.
MESS. No, my good lord; I met him back again.[1]
ALB. Knows he the wickedness?
MESS. Ay, my good lord; 'twas he informed against him;
And quit the house on purpose, that their punishment
Might have the freer course.
ALB. Gloucester, I live
To thank thee for the love thou show'dst the king,
And to revenge thine eyes. Come hither, friend.
Tell me what more thou know'st. [*Exeunt.*]

SCENE 3

[*Enter* KENT *and a* GENTLEMAN.]

KENT. Why the King of France is so suddenly gone back know you the reason?

GENT. Something he left imperfect in the state, which since his coming forth is thought of; which imports to the kingdom so much fear and danger, that his personal return was most required and necessary.

KENT. Who hath he left behind him general?

GENT. The Marshall of France, Monsieur LaFar.

KENT. Did your letters pierce[2] the queen to any demonstration of grief?

GENT. Ay, sir. She took them, read them in my presence;
And now and then an ample tear trilled[3] down
Her delicate cheek. It seemed she was a queen
Over her passion, who, most rebel-like,
Sought to be king o'er her.
KENT. O, then it moved her.
GENT. Not to a rage. Patience and sorrow strove
Who should express her goodliest. You have seen
Sunshine and rain at once: her smiles and tears
Were like, a better way.[4] Those happy smilets,
That played on her ripe lip, seemed not to know
What guests were in her eyes, which parted thence,
As pearls from diamonds dropped. In brief,
Sorrow would be a rarity most beloved,
If all could so become it.

9. May destroy all my castles in the air and make my life hateful to me.
1. On the way back.
2. Move.
3. Trickled.
4. But in a better fashion.

KENT. Made she no verbal question?
GENT. 'Faith, once or twice she heaved the name of "father"
Pantingly forth, as if it pressed her heart;
Cried "Sisters! sisters! Shame of ladies! sisters!
Kent! father! sisters! What, i' the storm? i' the night?
Let pity not be believed!" There she shook
The holy water from her heavenly eyes,
And clamor moistened.[5] Then away she started
To deal with grief alone.
KENT. It is the stars,
The stars above us, govern our conditions;[6]
Else one self mate and make[7] could not beget
Such different issues. You spoke not with her since?
GENT. No.
KENT. Was this before the king returned?
GENT. No, since.
KENT. Well, sir, the poor distressed Lear's i' the town;
Who sometime, in his better tune,[8] remembers
What we are come about, and by no means
Will yield to see his daughter.
GENT. Why, good sir?
KENT. A sovereign shame so elbows him; his own unkindness,
That stripped her from his benediction, turned her
To foreign casualties,[9] gave her dear rights
To his dog-hearted daughters, these things sting
His mind so venomously, that burning shame
Detains him from Cordelia.
GENT. Alack, poor gentleman!
KENT. Of Albany's and Cornwall's powers you heard not?
GENT. 'Tis so, they are afoot.
KENT. Well, sir, I'll bring you to our master Lear,
And leave you to attend him. Some dear cause[1]
Will in concealment wrap me up awhile;
When I am known aright, you shall not grieve
Lending me this acquaintance. I pray you, go
Along with me. [*Exeunt*.]

SCENE 4

[*Enter, with drum and colors,* CORDELIA, DOCTOR, *and* SOLDIERS.]

COR. Alack, 'tis he! Why, he was met even now
As mad as the vexed[2] sea; singing aloud;
Crowned with rank fumiter and furrow-weeds,
With hor-docks, hemlock, nettles, cuckoo-flowers,
Darnel,[3] and all the idle weeds that grow

5. "Followed her cries of sorrow with tears" (Kittredge's note).
6. Characters.
7. Mate.
8. In his lucid intervals.
9. Chances.
1. Important reason.
2. Turbulent.
3. All common weeds.

In our sustaining corn. A century[4] send forth;
Search every acre in the high-grown field,
And bring him to our eye. [*Exit an* OFFICER.] What can man's wisdom
In the restoring his bereaved sense?[5]
He that helps him take all my outward worth.
DOCT. There is means, madam.
Our foster-nurse of nature is repose,
The which he lacks. That to provoke in him,
Are many simples operative, whose power
Will close the eye of anguish.[6]
COR. All blest secrets,
All you unpublished virtues of the earth,
Spring with my tears![7] be aidant and remediate[8]
In the good man's distress! Seek, seek for him;
Lest his ungoverned rage dissolve the life
That wants the means to lead it.[9]
[*Enter a* MESSENGER.]
MESS. News, madam;
The British powers are marching hitherward.
COR. 'Tis known before; our preparation stands
In expectation of them. O dear father,
It is thy business that I go about;
Therefore great France
My mourning and importuned[1] tears hath pitied.
No blown[2] ambition doth our arms incite,
But love, dear love, and our aged father's right.
Soon may I hear and see him! [*Exeunt.*]

SCENE 5

[*Enter* REGAN *and* OSWALD.]
REG. But are my brother's powers set forth?
OSW. Ay, madam.
REG. Himself in person there?
OSW. Madam, with much ado.[3]
Your sister is the better soldier.
REG. Lord Edmund spake not with your lord at home?
OSW. No, madam.
REG. What might import my sister's letter to him?
OSW. I know not, lady.
REG. Faith, he is posted hence on serious matter.
It was great ignorance,[4] Gloucester's eyes being out,

4. A hundred soldiers.
5. I.e., what can medical science do to restore his lost sanity?
6. I.e., sleep, which he lacks, is nature's fostering nurse, and we have many powerful herbs ("simples") which will deaden his pain and put him to sleep.
7. May all unknown herb remedies spring up, watered by my tears.
8. Helpfully remedial.
9. Lest his mad frenzy take his life, since he is without the "means" (i.e., reason) to lead it.
1. Importuning.
2. Puffed up, inflated.
3. After much persuasion.
4. Folly.

To let him live. Where he arrives he moves
All hearts against us. Edmund, I think, is gone,
In pity of his misery, to dispatch
His nighted[5] life; moreover, to descry
The strength o' the enemy.

OSW. I must needs after him, madam, with my letter.

REG. Our troops set forth tomorrow. Stay with us;
The ways are dangerous.

OSW. I may not, madam:
My lady charged my duty in this business.

REG. Why should she write to Edmund? Might not you
Transport her purposes by word? Belike,
Something—I know not what. I'll love thee much,
Let me unseal the letter.

OSW. Madam, I had rather—

REG. I know your lady does not love her husband;
I am sure of that; and at her late being here
She gave strange oeillades[6] and most speaking looks
To noble Edmund. I know you are of her bosom.[7]

OSW. I, madam?

REG. I speak in understanding; y'are, I know't.
Therefore I do advise you, take this note:[8]
My lord is dead; Edmund and I have talked;
And more convenient is he for my hand
Than for your lady's. You may gather more.
If you do find him, pray you, give him this;[9]
And when your mistress hears thus much[10] from you,
I pray, desire her call her wisdom to her.
So, fare you well
If you do chance to hear of that blind traitor,
Preferment falls on him that cuts him off.

OSW. Would I could meet him, madam! I should show
What party I do follow.

REG. Fare thee well. [*Exeunt.*]

SCENE 6

[*Enter* GLOUCESTER, *and* EDGAR *dressed like a peasant.*]

GLOU. When shall we come to the top of that same hill?

EDG. You do climb up it now. Look how we labor.

GLOU. Methinks the ground is even.[1]

EDG. Horrible steep.
Hark, do you hear the sea?

GLOU. No, truly.

EDG. Why, then, your other senses grow imperfect
By your eyes' anguish.

GLOU. So may it be, indeed.
Methinks thy voice is altered, and thou speakest

5. Darkened through blindness.
6. Amorous glances.
7. In her confidence.
8. Take note of what I say.
9. A love-token.
10. What I have told her.
1. Flat.

In better phrase and matter than thou didst.
EDG. Y'are much deceived. In nothing am I changed
But in my garments.
GLOU. Methinks y'are better spoken.
EDG. Come on, sir; here's the place. Stand still. How fearful
And dizzy 'tis, to cast one's eyes so low!
The crows and choughs[2] that wing the midway air
Show scarce so gross[3] as beetles. Halfway down
Hangs one that gathers sampire,[4] dreadful trade!
Methinks he seems no bigger than his head.
The fishermen, that walk upon the beach,
Appear like mice; and yond tall anchoring bark,
Diminished to her cock;[5] her cock, a buoy
Almost too small for sight. The murmuring surge,
That on the unnumbered idle pebble[6] chafes,
Cannot be heard so high. I'll look no more,
Lest my brain turn, and the deficient sight[7]
Topple down headlong.
GLOU. Set me where you stand.
EDG. Give me your hand. You are now within a foot
Of th' extreme verge. For all beneath the moon
Would I not leap upright.
GLOU. Let go my hand.
Here, friend, 's another purse; in it a jewel
Well worth a poor man's taking. Fairies and gods
Prosper it with thee! Go thou farther off;
Bid me farewell, and let me hear thee going.
EDG. Now fare you well, good sir.
GLOU. With all my heart.
EDG. [*aside*] Why I do trifle thus with his despair
Is done to cure it.
GLOU. [*kneeling*] O you mighty gods!
This world I do renounce, and, in your sights,
Shake patiently my great affliction off.
If I could bear it longer, and not fall
To quarrel with your great opposeless[8] wills,
My snuff and loathéd part of nature[9] should
Burn itself out. If Edgar live, O, bless him!
Now, fellow, fare thee well. [*He falls forward and swoons.*]
EDG. Gone, sir; farewell.—
And yet I know not how conceit[1] may rob
The treasury of life, when life itself
Yields[2] to the theft. Had he been where he thought,
By this had thought been past. Alive or dead?

2. Jackdaws.
3. Large.
4. An aromatic plant used in pickling.
5. Cockboat.
6. Innumerable barren pebbles.
7. My vision being distorted.
8. Succumb to rebellion against. "Opposeless": irresistible.
9. Snuff: burnt part of a wick. The remainder of his life, loathsome to him, would be a snuff.
1. Imagination, delusion.
2. Consents.

Ho, you sir! friend! Hear you, sir? speak!
Thus might he pass indeed. Yet he revives.
What are you, sir?
GLOU. Away, and let me die.
EDG. Hadst thou been aught but gossamer, feathers, air,
So many fathom down precipitating,[3]
Thou'dst shivered like an egg; but thou dost breathe;
Hast heavy substance;[4] bleed'st not; speak'st; art sound.
Ten masts at each[5] make not the altitude
Which thou hast perpendicularly fell.
Thy life's a miracle. Speak yet again.
GLOU. But have I fallen, or no?
EDG. From the dread summit of this chalky bourn.[6]
Look up a-height; the shrill-gorged[7] lark so far
Cannot be seen or heard. Do but look up.
GLOU. Alack, I have no eyes.
Is wretchedness deprived that benefit,
To end itself by death? 'Twas yet some comfort,
When misery could beguile[8] the tyrant's rage,
And frustrate his proud will.
EDG. Give me your arm.
Up—so. How is 't? Feel you your legs? You stand.
GLOU. Too well, too well.
EDG. This is above all strangeness.
Upon the crown o' the cliff, what thing was that
Which parted from you?
GLOU. A poor unfortunate beggar.
EDG. As I stood here below, methought his eyes
Were two full moons; he had a thousand noses,
Horns whelked[9] and waved like the enridgéd sea:
It was some fiend. Therefore, thou happy father,[1]
Think that the clearest gods, who make them honors
Of men's impossibilities, have preserved thee.
GLOU. I do remember now. Henceforth I'll bear
Affliction till it do cry out itself
"Enough, enough," and die. That thing you speak of,
I took it for a man; often 't would say
"The fiend, the fiend"—he led me to that place.
EDG. Bear free[2] and patient thoughts. But who comes here?
[*Enter* LEAR, *fantastically dressed with wild flowers.*]
The safer sense will ne'er accommodate
His master thus.[3]
LEAR. No, they cannot touch me for coining; I am the king himself.[4]

3. Falling headlong.
4. Substantial weight.
5. End to end.
6. Boundary (i.e., the cliff).
7. Shrill-throated.
8. Cheat.
9. Twisted.

1. Old man (Edgar does not reveal his identity). "Clearest": glorious.
2. Happy.
3. A man in his right senses would never dress this way.
4. The king had the exclusive privilege of coining.

EDG. O thou side-piercing sight!

LEAR. Nature's above art in that respect. There's your press-money.[5] That fellow handles his bow like a crow-keeper.[6] Draw me a clothier's yard.[7] Look, look, a mouse! Peace, peace; this piece of toasted cheese will do 't. There's my gauntlet;[8] I'll prove it on a giant. Bring up the brown bills.[9] O, well flown, bird! i' the clout, i' the clout.[1] Hewgh! Give the word.[2]

EDG. Sweet marjoram.

LEAR. Pass.

GLOU. I know that voice.

LEAR. Ha! Goneril, with a white beard! They flattered me like a dog; and told me I had white hairs in my beard ere the black ones were there. To say "aye" and "no" to everything that I said![3]—"Aye" and "no" too was no good divinity. When the rain came to wet me once, and the wind to make me chatter; when the thunder would not peace at my bidding; there I found 'em, there I smelt 'em out. Go to, they are not men o' their words! They told me I was everything. 'Tis a lie, I am not ague-proof.

GLOU. The trick[4] of that voice I do well remember.
Is 't not the king?

LEAR. Aye, every inch a king!
When I do stare, see how the subject quakes.
I pardon that man's life. What was thy cause?[5]
Adultery?
Thou shalt not die. Die for adultery? No.
The wren goes to 't, and the small gilded fly
Does lecher in my sight.
Let copulation thrive; for Gloucester's bastard son
Was kinder to his father than my daughters
Got 'tween the lawful sheets. To 't luxury, pell-mell![6]
For I lack soldiers. Behold yond simpering dame,
Whose face between her forks presages snow;[7]
That minces virtue, and does shake the head
To hear of pleasure's name;
The fitchew, nor the soiléd horse, goes to 't
With a more riotous appetite.[8]
Down from the waist they are Centaurs,[9]

5. Money paid to recruits.
6. Scarecrow.
7. The standard English arrow was a cloth-yard long.
8. A glove thrown down as a challenge to a duel.
9. Halberds or pikes, painted brown to resist rust.
1. The bull's-eye.
2. Password. Edgar chooses the name of a herb supposed to be good for diseases of the brain.
3. I.e., to agree with me always, as flatterers do. "No good divinity": i.e., bad theology. Several Biblical texts say that your *aye* should mean aye, and your *no*, no.
4. Peculiarity.
5. Legal charge, offense.
6. Promiscuously: "luxury": lust.
7. I.e., whose face presages snow between her forks (legs).
8. I.e., neither the polecat nor the well-fed horse pursues sex more violently.
9. Creatures in Greek mythology, half human, half horse, supposed to be extremely lustful.

Though women all above.
But to the girdle do the gods inherit.[1]
Beneath is all the fiends'; there's hell, there's darkness,
There's the sulphurous pit, burning, scalding,
Stench, consumption! Fie, fie, fie! pah! pah!
Give me an ounce of civet,[2] good apothecary,
To sweeten my imagination.
There's money for thee.

GLOU. O, let me kiss that hand!

LEAR. Let me wipe it first; it smells of mortality.

GLOU. O ruined piece[3] of nature! This great world[4]
Shall so wear out to nought. Dost thou know me?

LEAR. I remember thine eyes well enough. Dost thou squiny[5] at me? No, do thy worst, blind Cupid; I'll not love. Read thou this challenge; mark but the penning of it.

GLOU. Were all the letters suns, I could not see one.

EDG. [*aside*] I would not take this from report. It is,
And my heart breaks at it.

LEAR. Read.

GLOU. What, with the case of eyes?[6]

LEAR. O, ho, are you there with me? No eyes in your head, nor no money in your purse? Your eyes are in a heavy case, your purse in a light.[7] Yet you see how this world goes.

GLOU. I see it feelingly.

LEAR. What, art mad? A man may see how this world goes with no eyes. Look with thine ears. See how yond justice rails upon yond simple[8] thief. Hark, in thine ear. Change places and, handy-dandy,[9] which is the justice, which is the thief? Thou hast seen a farmer's dog bark at a beggar?

GLOU. Aye, sir.

LEAR. And the creature[1] run from the cur? There thou mightst behold the great image of authority: a dog's obeyed in office.
Thou rascal beadle,[2] hold thy bloody hand!
Why dost thou lash that whore? Strip thine own back;
Thou hotly lusts to use her in that kind
For which thou whipp'st her. The usurer hangs the cozener.[3]
Through tattered clothes small vices do appear;
Robes and furred gowns hide all. Plate sin with gold,
And the strong lance of justice hurtless breaks;
Arm it in rags, a pigmy's straw does pierce it.

1. I.e., the gods rule only down to the belt.
2. Perfume.
3. Masterpiece. It was commonplace to consider man the masterpiece of Nature's creation.
4. The universe.
5. Squint.
6. Eye sockets.
7. I.e., your eyes are in a sad plight with a pun on "case" as socket) and your purse in a pleasant one (with a pun on "light" as "of little weight" and perhaps also "visible").
8. Low-class, ordinary.
9. A child's game in which one is asked to tell which closed fist contains an object.
1. Human being.
2. Minor constable.
3. The judge practices usury but hangs a small cheater.

None does offend, none, I say, none; I'll able 'em;[4]
Take that of me,[5] my friend, who have the power
To seal the accuser's lips. Get thee glass eyes;
And, like a scurvy politician,[6] seem
To see the things thou dost not. Now, now, now, now!
Pull off my boots. Harder, harder! So.[7]

EDG. O, matter and impertinency[8] mixed!
Reason in madness!

LEAR. If thou wilt weep[9] my fortunes, take my eyes.
I know thee well enough; thy name is Gloucester:
Thou must be patient. We came crying hither;
Thou knows't, the first time that we smell the air,
We wail and cry. I will preach to thee. Mark.

[LEAR *takes off his crown of weeds and flowers.*]

GLOU. Alack, alack the day!

LEAR. When we are born, we cry that we are come
To this great stage of fools. This' a good block;[1]
It were a delicate stratagem, to shoe
A troop of horse with felt. I'll put 't in proof;[2]
And when I have stol'n upon these sons-in-law,
Then, kill, kill, kill, kill, kill, kill!

[*Enter a* GENTLEMEN, *with* ATTENDANTS.]

GENT. O, here he is; lay hand upon him. Sir,
Your most dear daughter—

LEAR. No rescue? What, a prisoner? I am even
The natural fool of fortune. Use me well;
You shall have ransom. Let me have surgeons;
I am cut to the brains.

GENT. You shall have any thing.

LEAR. No seconds?[3] all myself?
Why, this would make a man a man of salt,[4]
To use his eyes for garden water-pots,
Aye, and laying autumn's dust.

GENT. Good sir—

LEAR. I will die bravely, like a smug bridegroom.[5] What!
I will be jovial. Come, come; I am a king,
My masters, know you that?

GENT. You are a royal one, and we obey you.

LEAR. Then there's life in't. Nay, if you get it, you shall get it with running. Sa, sa, sa, sa.[6]

[*Exit running;* ATTENDANTS *follow.*]

4. Authorize.
5. He hands him an imaginary pardon.
6. A vile trickster, a Machiavellian.
7. Lear imagines that he has just come in from hunting, as in I.iv.
8. Sense and nonsense.
9. Cry over.
1. "All the world's a stage" is a commonplace. Lear then thinks of the "stage" as a platform to preach from, but the word "block" suggests a mounting-block for getting on horseback, and, in another sense, hats, whence "felt."
2. Try the experiment.
3. Helpers.
4. Because of his tears.
5. "Bravely": (1) courageously; (2) in fine clothes. "Smug": neat.
6. I.e., the case is not yet desperate; but if you want me, you will have to catch me. "Sa, sa": a hunting cry, urging the hounds to greater speed.

GENT. A sight most pitiful in the meanest wretch,
Past speaking of in a king! Thou hast one daughter,
Who redeems nature from the general curse
Which twain have brought her to.
EDG. Hail, gentle[7] sir.
GENT. Sir, speed you. What's your will?
EDG. Do you hear aught, sir, of a battle toward?[8]
GENT. Most sure and vulgar.[9] Everyone hears that,
Which can distinguish sound.
EDG. But, by your favor,
How near's the other army?
GENT. Near and on speedy foot. The main descry
Stands on the hourly thought.[1]
EDG. I thank you, sir. That's all.
GENT. Though that the queen on special cause is here,
Her army is moved on.
EDG. I thank you, sir. [*Exit* GENT.]
GLOU. You ever-gentle gods, take my breath from me;
Let not my worser spirit[2] tempt me again
To die before you please!
EDG. Well pray you, father.
GLOU. Now, good sir, what are you?
EDG. A most poor man, made tame to fortune's blows;
Who, by the art of known and feeling sorrows,
Am pregnant to[3] good pity. Give me your hand,
I'll lead you to some biding.[4]
GLOU. Hearty thanks.
The bounty and the benison of heaven
To boot, and boot!
[*Enter* OSWALD.]
OSW. A proclaimed prize! Most happy!
That eyeless head of thine was first framed flesh
To raise my fortunes. Thou old unhappy traitor,
Briefly thyself remember.[5] The sword is out
That must destroy thee.
GLOU. Now let thy friendly hand
Put strength enough to 't. [EDGAR *interposes.*]
OSW. Wherefore, bold peasant.
Darest thou support a published[6] traitor? Hence,
Lest that the infection of his fortune take
Like hold on thee. Let go his arm.
EDG. Chill not let go, zir, without vurther 'casion.[7]
OSW. Let go, slave, or thou diest!
EDG. Good gentleman, go your gait, and let poor volk pass. An chud[8] ha' bin zwaggered out of my life, 't would not ha' bin

7. Noble.
8. In preparation.
9. Common knowledge.
1. We expect to descry the main force within the hour.
2. My evil genius.
3. Susceptible to.
4. Abode.
5. Remember your sins and repent.
6. Proclaimed.
7. Conventional rustic dialect, similar to that of Somersetshire. "Chill": I will.
8. If I should.

zo long as 'tis by a vortnight. Nay, come not near th' old man; keep out, che vor ye, or ise try whether your costard or my ballow be the harder.[9] Chill be plain with you.

OSW. Out, dunghill!

EDG. Chill pick your teeth, zir. Come! No matter vor your foins.[1]

[*They fight, and* EDGAR *knocks him down.*]

OSW. Slave, thou hast slain me. Villain, take my purse.
If ever thou wilt thrive, bury my body;
And give the letters[2] which thou find'st about me
To Edmund earl of Gloucester. Seek him out
Upon the British party. O, untimely death!
Death! [*He dies.*]

EDG. I know thee well: a serviceable villain;
As duteous to the vices of thy mistress
As badness would desire.

GLOU. What, is he dead?

EDG. Sit you down, father; rest you.
Let's see his pockets; the letters that he speaks of
May be my friends. He's dead; I am only sorry
He had no other death'sman. Let us see.
Leave, gentle wax;[3] and, manners blame us not.
To know our enemies' minds, we'd rip their hearts;
Their papers, is more lawful.

[*Reads.*] "Let our reciprocal vows be remembered. You have many opportunities to cut him off.[4] If your will want not, time and place will be fruitfully offered. There is nothing done, if he return the conqueror. Then am I the prisoner, and his bed my jail; from the loathed warmth wherof deliver me, and supply the place for your labor.

Your—wife, so I would say—
Affectionate servant,[5]
"GONERIL."

O undistinguished space of woman's will![6]
A plot upon her virtuous husband's life;
And the exchange my brother! Here, in the sands,
Thee I'll rake up, the post unsanctified[7]
Of murderous lechers; and in the mature time[8]
With this ungracious paper strike the sight
Of the death-practiced[9] duke. For him 'tis well
That of thy death and business I can tell.

GLOU. The king is mad. How stiff[1] is my vile sense,
That I stand up, and have ingenious feeling
Of my huge sorrows! Better I were distract;
So should my thoughts be severed from my griefs,

9. Keep out, I warrant you, or I'll see whether your head or my cudgel is harder.
1. Thrusts.
2. I.e., letter.
3. By your leave, gentle wax (as he unseals the letter).
4. I.e., kill Albany.
5. I.e., lover.
6. O limitless extent of woman's lust.
7. Unholy letter-carrier.
8. When time is ripe.
9. Whose death was plotted.
1. Unbending.

And woes by wrong imaginations lose
The knowledge of themselves.[2] [*Drum afar off.*]

EDG. Give me your hand.
Far off, methinks, I hear the beaten drum.
Come, father, I'll bestow you with a friend. [*Exeunt.*]

SCENE 7

[*Enter* CORDELIA, KENT, DOCTOR, *and a* GENTLEMAN.]

COR. O thou good Kent, how shall I live and work,
To match thy goodness? My life will be too short,
And every measure fail me.[3]

KENT. To be acknowledged, madam, is o'erpaid.
All my reports go with the modest truth;
Nor more nor clipped, but so.[4]

COR. Be better suited.
These weeds are memories of those worser hours.[5]
I prithee, put them off.

KENT. Pardon me, dear madam;
Yet to be known shortens my made intent.[6]
My boon I make it, that you know me not
Till time and I think meet.

COR. Then be 't so, my good lord. [*To the* DOCTOR.] How does the king?

DOCT. Madam, sleeps still.

COR. O you kind gods,
Cure this great breach in his abuséd nature!
The untuned and jarring senses, O, wind up
Of this child-changéd father![7]

DOCT. So please your majesty
That we may wake the king? He hath slept long.

COR. Be governed by your knowledge, and proceed
I' the sway of your own will. Is he arrayed?[8]

[*Enter* LEAR *in a chair carried by* SERVANTS.]

GENT. Aye, madam. In the heaviness of his sleep
We put fresh garments on him.

DOCT. Be by, good madam, when we do awake him;
I doubt not of his temperance.[9]

COR. Very well. [*Music.*]

DOCT. Please you, draw near. Louder the music there!

COR. O my dear father! Restoration hang
Thy medicine on my lips; and let this kiss
Repair those violent harms that my two sisters

2. I.e., I would be better off mad; then my troubles would be separated from my thoughts and accordingly would have no knowledge of themselves.
3. Since Kent's goodness is immeasurable.
4. Neither amplified nor abbreviated, but accurate.
5. Be better dressed. These clothes recall your hours of trouble.
6. I am not ready to be known yet.
7. Tune up the out-of-tune senses of this father who is changed into a child.
8. Dressed.
9. Normality.

Have in thy reverence made![1]
KENT. Kind and dear princess!
COR. Had you not been their father, these white flakes
Had challenged pity of them.[2] Was this a face
To be opposed against the warring winds?
To stand against the deep dread-bolted thunder?
In the most terrible and nimble stroke
Of quick, cross lightning? to watch—poor perdu!—
With this thin helm?[3] Mine enemy's dog,
Though he had bit me, should have stood that night
Against my fire; and wast thou fain, poor father,
To hovel thee with swine, and rogues forlorn,
In short and musty straw? Alack, alack!
'Tis wonder that thy life and wits at once
Had not concluded all. He wakes; speak to him.
DOCT. Madam, do you; 'tis fittest.
COR. How does my royal lord? How fares your majesty?
LEAR. You do me wrong to take me out o' the grave.
Thou art a soul in bliss; but I am bound
Upon a wheel of fire, that mine own tears
Do scald like molten lead.[4]
COR. Sir, do you know me?
LEAR. You are a spirit, I know. When did you die?
COR. Still, still, far wide![5]
DOCT. He's scarce awake. Let him alone awhile.
LEAR. Where have I been? Where am I? Fair daylight?
I am mightily abused.[6] I should e'en die with pity,
To see another thus. I know not what to say.
I will not swear these are my hands. Let's see.
I feel this pin prick. Would I were assured
Of my condition!
COR. O, look upon me, sir,
And hold your hands in benediction o'er me:
No, sir, you must not kneel.
LEAR. Pray, do not mock me.
I am a very foolish fond[7] old man,
Fourscore and upward, not an hour more nor less;
And, to deal plainly,
I fear I am not in my perfect mind.
Methinks I should know you, and know this man;
Yet I am doubtful; for I am mainly[8] ignorant
What place this is; and all the skill I have
Remembers not these garments; nor I know not
Where I did lodge last night. Do not laugh at me;

1. Have done to you, who should be treated with reverence.
2. These white hairs would have claimed pity from them.
3. Poor solitary sentinel, with this thin head protection (his hair).
4. In the New Testament Apocrypha the damned in hell are tormented on wheels of fire.
5. Wandering in the mind.
6. Deluded.
7. In his dotage.
8. Completely.

For, as I am a man, I think this lady
To be my child Cordelia.

COR. And so I am, I am.

LEAR. Be your tears wet? Yes, faith. I pray, weep not.
If you have poison for me, I will drink it.
I know you do not love me; for your sisters
Have, as I do remember, done me wrong.
You have some cause, they have not.

COR. No cause, no cause.

LEAR. Am I in France?

KENT. In your own kingdom, sir.

LEAR. Do not abuse[9] me.

DOCT. Be comforted, good madam. The great rage,[1]
You see, is killed in him; and yet it is danger
To make him even o'er the time he has lost.[2]
Desire him to go in. Trouble him no more
Till further settling.[3]

COR. Will't please your highness walk?

LEAR. You must bear with me:
Pray you now, forget and forgive. I am old and foolish.

[*Exeunt all but* KENT *and* GENTLEMAN.]

GENT. Holds it true, sir, that the Duke of Cornwall was so slain?

KENT. Most certain, sir.

GENT. Who is conductor[4] of his people?

KENT. As 'tis said, the bastard son of Gloucester.

GENT. They say Edgar, his banished son, is with the Earl of Kent in Germany.

KENT. Report is changeable.'Tis time to look about. The powers of the kingdom approach apace.[5]

GENT. The arbitrement[6] is like to be bloody. Fare you well, sir. [*Exit.*]

KENT. My point and period will be throughly wrought,[7]
Or well or ill, as this day's battle's fought. [*Exit.*]

Act V

SCENE 1

[*Enter, with drum and colors,* EDMUND, REGAN, GENTLEMEN, *and* SOLDIERS.]

EDM. Know of the duke if his last purpose hold,
Or whether since he is advised by aught
To change the course.[8] He's full of alteration
And self-reproving. Bring his constant pleasure.[9]

[*To a* GENTLEMAN, *who goes out.*]

9. Delude.
1. Violent delirium.
2. I.e., it is dangerous to make him go over his recent experiences.
3. Till he has calmed down.
4. Leader.
5. The British forces are approaching rapidly.
6. Decisive battle.
7. The end and purpose of my life will be completely worked out.
8. Find out from Albany if he still intends to fight or has changed his mind.
9. Fixed decision.

REG. Our sister's man is certainly miscarried.[1]
EDM. 'Tis to be doubted,[2] madam.
REG. Now, sweet lord,
You know the goodness I intend upon you.
Tell me—but truly—but then speak the truth,
Do you not love my sister?
EDM. In honored love.
REG. But have you never found my brother's way
To the forfended[3] place?
EDM. That thought abuses you.
REG. I am doubtful that you have been conjunct
And bosomed with her, as far as we call hers.[4]
EDM. No, by mine honor, madam.
REG. I never shall endure her. Dear my lord,
Be not familiar with her.
EDM. Fear me not.
She and the duke her husband!

[*Enter, with drum and colors,* ALBANY, GONERIL, *and* SOLDIERS.]

GON. [*aside*] I had rather lose the battle than that sister
Should loosen[5] him and me.
ALB. Our very loving sister, well be-met.
Sir, this I hear: the king is come to his daughter,
With others whom the rigor of our state[6]
Forced to cry out. Where I could not be honest,
I never yet was valiant. For this business,
It toucheth us, as France invades our land,
Not bolds the king, with others, whom, I fear,
Most just and heavy causes make oppose.[7]
EDM. Sir, you speak nobly.
REG. Why is this reasoned?[8]
GON. Combine together 'gainst the enemy;
For these domestic and particular broils
Are not the question here.
ALB. Let's then determine
With the ancient of war on our proceeding.[9]
EDM. I shall attend you presently at your tent.
REG. Sister, you'll go with us?
GON. No.
REG. 'Tis most convenient; pray you, go with us.
GON. [*aside*] O, ho, I know the riddle.—I will go.

[*As they are going out, enter* EDGAR *disguised.*]

EDG. If e'er your grace had speech with man so poor,
Hear me one word.

1. I.e., Oswald has certainly come to harm.
2. Feared.
3. Forbidden.
4. I am afraid you have been intimate with her, in every sense of the word.
5. Separate.
6. Harshness of our rule.
7. It concerns us because France invades our land, but not because it supports the king and others who have great and justified grievances and for that reason oppose us.
8. Why discuss it?
9. Consult with veterans on our strategy.

ALB. I'll overtake you. Speak.
[*Exeunt all but* ALBANY *and* EDGAR.]

EDG. Before you fight the battle, ope this letter.
If you have victory, let the trumpet sound
For him that brought it. Wretched though I seem,
I can produce a champion that will prove
What is avouched[1] there. If you miscarry,
Your business of the world hath so an end,
And machination[2] ceases. Fortune love you!

ALB. Stay till I have read the letter.

EDG. I was forbid it.
When time shall serve, let but the herald cry,
And I'll appear again.

ALB. Why, fare thee well. I will o'erlook[3] thy paper.
[*Exit* EDGAR.]

[*Re-enter* EDMUND.]

EDM. The enemy 's in view; draw up your powers.
Here is the guess of their true strength and forces
By diligent discovery; but your haste
Is now urged on you.

ALB. We will greet the time.[4] [*Exit.*]

EDM. To both these sisters have I sworn my love;
Each jealous of the other, as the stung
Are of the adder. Which of them shall I take?
Both? one? or neither? Neither can be enjoyed,
If both remain alive. To take the widow
Exasperates, makes mad her sister Goneril;
And hardly shall I carry out my side,
Her husband being alive. Now then we'll use
His countenance[5] for the battle; which being done,
Let her who would be rid of him devise
His speedy taking off.[6] As for the mercy
Which he intends to Lear and to Cordelia,
The battle done, and they within our power,
Shall never see his pardon; for my state
Stands on me to defend, not to debate.[7] [*Exit.*]

SCENE 2

[*Alarum within. Enter, with drum and colors,* LEAR, CORDELIA, *and* SOLDIERS, *over the stage; and exeunt.*]

[*Enter* EDGAR *and* GLOUCESTER.]

EDG. Here, father,[8] take the shadow of this tree
For your good host; pray that the right may thrive:

1. Asserted; "miscarry": are defeated.
2. Plotting.
3. Read.
4. Meet the emergency.
5. Authority.
6. Killing.
7. My interests require me to act, not discuss moral considerations.
8. Old man (Edgar has not revealed his identity).

If ever I return to you again,
I'll bring you comfort.

GLOU. Grace go with you, sir! [*Exit* EDGAR.]

[*Alarum and retreat within. Re-enter* EDGAR.]

EDG. Away, old man! give me thy hand! away!
King Lear hath lost, he and his daughter ta'en.
Give me thy hand! come on!

GLOU. No farther, sir; a man may rot even here.

EDG. What, in ill thoughts again? Men must endure
Their going hence, even as their coming hither;
Ripeness is all. Come on!

GLOU. And that's true, too. [*Exeunt.*]

SCENE 3

[*Enter, in conquest, with drum and colors,* EDMUND; LEAR *and* CORDELIA, *prisoners;* CAPTAIN, SOLDIERS, &c.]

EDM. Some officers take them away. Good guard,
Until their greater pleasures first be known
That are to censure them.[9]

COR. We are not the first
Who, with best meaning, have incurred the worst.
For thee, oppresséd king, am I cast down;
Myself could else out-frown false Fortune's frown.
Shall we not see these daughters and these sisters?

LEAR. No, no, no, no! Come, let's away to prison.
We two alone will sing like birds i' the cage.
When thou dost ask me blessing, I'll kneel down,[1]
And ask of thee forgiveness. So we'll live,
And pray, and sing, and tell old tales, and laugh
At gilded butterflies,[2] and hear poor rogues
Talk of court news; and we'll talk with them too,
Who loses and who wins; who 's in, and who 's out;
And take upon 's the mystery of things,[3]
As if we were Gods' spies; and we'll wear out,
In a walled prison, packs and sects of great ones,[4]
That ebb and flow by the moon.

EDM. Take them away.

LEAR. Upon such sacrifices,[5] my Cordelia,
The gods themselves throw incense. Have I caught thee?
He that parts us shall bring a brand from heavens,
And fire us hence like foxes.[6] Wipe thine eyes;
The good-years shall devour them, flesh and fell,[7]
Ere they shall make us weep! We'll see 'em starved first.

9. Until we know the wishes of the higher authorities who are to judge them.

1. It was considered shocking for a parent to kneel to his child.

2. Foppish courtiers.

3. Profess to understand the mysterious course of events.

4. We will outlast, in prison, cliques and parties.

5. As their renunciation of the world.

6. I.e., smoke us out as hunters smoke foxes from their holes.

7. Time shall devour them (Goneril and Regan), flesh and skin.

Come. [*Exeunt* LEAR *and* CORDELIA, *guarded*.]
EDM. Come hither, captain; hark.
Take thou this note [*giving a paper*]. Go follow them to prison:
One step I have advanced thee. If thou dost
As this instructs thee, thou dost make thy way
To noble fortunes. Know thou this, that men
Are as the time is. To be tender-minded
Does not become a sword. Thy great employment
Will not bear question.[8] Either say thou'lt do 't,
Or thrive by other means.
CAPT. I'll do 't, my lord.
EDM. About it; and write happy[9] when thou hast done.
Mark, I say, instantly; and carry it so
As I have set it down.[1]
CAPT. I cannot draw a cart, nor eat dried oats;
If it be a man's work, I'll do 't. [*Exit*.]
[*Flourish. Enter* ALBANY, GONERIL, REGAN, *another* CAPTAIN, *and* SOLDIERS.]
ALB. Sir, you have showed today your valiant strain,
And fortune led you well. You have the captives
That were the opposites of this day's strife.
I do require them of you, so to use them
As we shall find their merits and our safety
May equally determine.
EDM. Sir, I thought it fit
To send the old and miserable king
To some retention and appointed guard;
Whose age has charms in it, whose title more,
To pluck the common bosom on his side,
And turn our impressed lances in our eyes[2]
Which do command them. With him I sent the queen;
My reason all the same; and they are ready
Tomorrow, or at further space, t' appear
Where you shall hold your session. At this time
We sweat and bleed; the friend hath lost his friend;
And the best quarrels, in the heat, are cursed
By those that feel their sharpness.[3]
The question of Cordelia and her father
Requires a fitter place.
ALB. Sir, by your patience,
I hold you but a subject of this war,
Not as a brother.
REG. That's as we list to grace him.[4]

8. Cannot be discussed.
9. Consider yourself fortunate.
1. Do it immediately and do it just as I have written it down.
2. I.e., to win popular support and turn conscripted soldiers against us.
3. I.e., the best causes are injured by high feelings.
4. That depends on how much I please to honor him.

Methinks our pleasure might have been demanded,
Ere you had spoken so far. He led our powers;
Bore the commission of my place and person;
The which immediacy[5] may well stand up,
And call itself your brother.

GON. Not so hot!
In his own grace he doth exalt himself,
More than in your addition.[6]

REG. In my rights,
By me invested, he compeers the best.[7]

GON. That were the most, if he should husband you.

REG. Jesters do oft prove prophets.

GON. Holla, holla!
That eye that told you so looked but a-squint.

REG. Lady, I am not well; else I should answer
From a full-flowing stomach.[8] General,
Take thou my soldiers, prisoners, patrimony:
Dispose of them, of me; the walls[9] are thine.
Witness the world, that I create thee here
My lord and master.

GON. Mean you to enjoy him?

ALB. The let-alone lies not in your good will.

EDM. Nor in thine, lord.

ALB. Half-blooded fellow, yes.

REG. [*to* EDMUND] Let the drum strike, and prove my title thine.

ALB. Stay yet; hear reason. Edmund, I arrest thee
On[1] capital treason; and, in thine attaint,
This gilded serpent [*pointing to* GONERIL]. For your claim, fair sister,
I bar it in the interest of my wife;
'Tis she is sub-contracted to this lord,
And I, her husband, contradict your banes.[2]
If you will marry, make your loves to me,
My lady is bespoke.

GON. An interlude![3]

ALB. Thou art armed, Gloucester. Let the trumpet sound.
If none appear to prove upon thy head
Thy heinous, manifest, and many treasons,
There is my pledge [*throwing down a glove*]; I'll prove it on thy heart,
Ere I taste bread, thou art in nothing less
Than I have proclaimed thee.

5. I.e., being my immediate representative.
6. He ranks higher by his own qualities than by the titles you confer on him.
7. By virtue of the rights I have vested in him, he equals the highest rank.
8. From a tide of high resentment.
9. I.e., Regan's person, referring to the common conceit that the lady is a castle, besieged by her lover.
1. For.
2. Banns (announcements in church of an impending marriage).
3. I.e., what a drama this is!

REG. Sick, O, sick!
GON. [*aside*] If not, I'll ne'er trust medicine.[4]
EDM. There 's my exchange [*throwing down a glove*]. What in the world he is
That names me traitor, villain-like he lies.
Call by thy trumpet. He that dares approach,
On him, on you, who not? I will maintain[5]
My truth and honor firmly.
ALB. A herald, ho!
EDM. A herald, ho, a herald!
ALB. Trust to thy single virtue[6]; for thy soldiers,
All levied in my name, have in my name
Took their discharge.
REG. My sickness grows upon me.
ALB. She is not well; convey her to my tent. [*Exit* REGAN, *led.*]
[*Enter a* HERALD.]
Come hither, herald,—Let the trumpet sound,—
And read out this.
CAPT. Sound, trumpet! [A *trumpet sounds.*]
HER. [*reads*] "If any man of quality or degree within the lists of the army will maintain upon Edmund, supposed Earl of Gloucester, that he is a manifold traitor, let him appear by the third sound of the trumpet. He is bold in his defense."
EDM. Sound! [*First trumpet.*]
HER. Again! [*Second trumpet.*]
HER. Again! [*Third trumpet.*]
[*Trumpet answers within.*]
[*Enter* EDGAR, *at the third sound, armed, with a trumpet before him.*]
ALB. Ask him his purposes, why he appears
Upon this call o' the trumpet.
HER. What are you?
Your name, your quality? and why you answer
This present summons?
EDG. Know, my name is lost;
By treason's tooth bare-gnawn and canker-bit.[7]
Yet am I noble as the adversary
I come to cope.
ALB. Which is that adversary?
EDG. What's he that speaks for Edmund Earl of Gloucester?
EDM. Himself. What say'st thou to him?
EDG. Draw thy sword,
That, if my speech offend a noble heart,
Thy arm may do thee justice. Here is mine.
Behold, it is the privilege of mine honors,
My oath, and my profession. I protest,

4. Poison.
5. Prove in combat.
6. Your own personal strength.
7. I.e., gnawn and eaten by the tooth of the caterpillar, treason.

Maugre[8] thy strength, youth, place, and eminence,
Despite thy victor sword and fire-new[9] fortune,
Thy valor and thy heart, thou art a traitor;
False to thy gods, thy brother, and thy father;
Conspirant 'gainst this high-illustrious prince;
And, from the extremest upward of thy head
To the descent and dust below thy foot,
A most toad-spotted traitor. Say thou "No,"
This sword, this arm, and my best spirits, are bent
To prove upon thy heart, whereto I speak,
Thou liest.

EDM. In wisdom I should ask thy name;
But, since thy outside looks so fair and warlike
And that thy tongue some say[1] of breeding breathes,
What safe and nicely I might well delay
By rule of knighthood, I disdain and spurn.
Back do I toss these treasons to thy head;
With the hell-hated lie o'erwhelm thy heart;
Which, for they yet glance by and scarcely bruise,
This sword of mine shall give them instant way,
Where they shall rest for ever. Trumpets, speak!

[*Alarums. They fight.* EDMUND *falls.*]

ALB. Save him, save him![2]

GON. This is practice,[3] Gloucester:
By the law of arms thou wast not bound to answer
An unknown opposite. Thou art not vanquished,
But cozened and beguiled.

ALB. Shut your mouth, dame,
Or with this paper shall I stople it.[4]
Thou worse than any name, read thine own evil.
No tearing, lady! I perceive you know it.

[*Gives the letter to* EDMUND.]

GON. Say, if I do, the laws are mine, not thine.
Who can arraign me for 't?

ALB. Most monstrous! oh!
Know'st thou this paper?

GON. Ask me not what I know. [*Exit.*]

ALB. Go after her: she's desperate; govern her.

EDM. What you have charged me with, that have I done;
And more, much more; the time will bring it out.
'Tis past, and so am I. But what art thou
That hast this fortune[5] on me? If thou 'rt noble,
I do forgive thee.

EDG. Let's exchange charity.

8. Despite.
9. Brand new.
1. Smack.
2. A puzzle, variously explained. Dr. Johnson thought Albany wanted Edmund's life saved temporarily so he could be proved guilty; other editors give the line to Goneril.
3. Trickery.
4. Plug it up.
5. This downfall, turn of the wheel of Fortune. Cf. line 204, below.

I am no less in blood than thou art, Edmund;
If more, the more thou hast wronged me.
My name is Edgar, and thy father's son.
The gods are just, and of our pleasant[6] vices
Make instruments to plague us.
The dark and vicious place where thee he got[7]
Cost him his eyes.

EDM. Thou hast spoken right, 'tis true;
The wheel is come full circle! I am here.

ALB. Methought thy very gait did prophesy
A royal nobleness. I must embrace thee.
Let sorrow split my heart, if ever I
Did hate thee or thy father!

EDG. Worthy prince. I know 't.

ALB. Where have you hid yourself?
How have you known the miseries of your father?

EDG. By nursing them, my lord. List a brief tale;
And when 'tis told, O, that my heart would burst!
The bloody proclamation to escape,
That followed me so near,—O, our lives' sweetness!
That we the pain of death would hourly die
Rather than die at once![8]—taught me to shift
Into a madman's rags; to assume a semblance
That very dogs disdained; and in this habit
Met I my father with his bleeding rings,
Their precious stones new lost; became his guide,
Led him, begged for him, saved him from despair;
Never,—O fault!—revealed myself unto him,
Until some half-hour past, when I was armed:
Not sure, though hoping, of this good success,
I asked his blessing, and from first to last
Told him my pilgrimage. But his flawed heart,—
Alack, too weak the conflict to support!—
'Twixt two extremes of passion, joy and grief,
Burst smilingly.

EDM. This speech of yours hath moved me,
And shall perchance do good; but speak you on;
You look as you had something more to say.

ALB. If there be more, more woeful, hold it in;
For I am almost ready to dissolve,[9]
Hearing of this.

EDG. This would have seemed a period
To such as love not sorrow; but another,
To amplify too much would make much more,
And top extremity.[10]

6. Pleasure-giving.
7. Begot.
8. I.e., how sweet life must be to persuade us to go on dying every hour rather than dying once for all.
9. Melt in tears.
10. This would have seemed the end to those who don't love sorrow; only another sorrow, if I were to tell all about it, would go beyond that extreme limit.

Whilst I was big[1] in clamor came there in a man,
Who, having seen me in my worst estate,
Shunned my abhorred society; but then, finding
Who 'twas that so endured, with his strong arms
He fastened on my neck, and bellowed out
As he'd burst heaven; threw him on[2] my father;
Told the most piteous tale of Lear and him
That ever ear received; which in recounting
His grief grew puissant, and the strings of life
Began to crack. Twice then the trumpets sounded,
And there I left him tranced.[3]

ALB. But who was this?

EDG. Kent, sir, the banished Kent; who in disguise
Followed his enemy king, and did him service
Improper for a slave.[4]

[*Enter a* GENTLEMAN, *with a bloody knife.*]

GENT. Help, help, O, help!

EDG. What kind of help?

ALB. Speak, man.

EDG. What means that bloody knife?

GENT. 'Tis hot, it smokes,
It came even from the heart of—O, she's dead!

ALB. Who dead? speak, man.

GENT. Your lady, sir, your lady! and her sister
By her is poisoned; she hath confessed it.

EDM. I was contracted to them both. All three
Now marry in an instant.

[*Enter* KENT.]

EDG. Here comes Kent.

ALB. Produce their bodies, be they alive or dead:
This judgment of the heavens, that makes us tremble,
Touches us not with pity. [*Exit* GENTLEMAN.]
O, is this he?
The time will not allow the compliment[5]
Which very manners urges.

KENT. I am come
To bid my king and master aye good night.
Is he not here?

ALB. Great thing of us forgot!
Speak, Edmund, where's the king? and where's Cordelia?
See'st thou this object, Kent?

[*The bodies of* GONERIL *and* REGAN *are brought in.*]

KENT. Alack, why thus?

EDM. Yet Edmund was beloved.
The one the other poisoned for my sake,

1. Loud.
2. Embraced.
3. Senseless.
4. I.e., followed the king who was hostile to him and did service for him you wouldn't ask a slave to do.
5. Ceremony.

And after slew herself.
ALB. Even so. Cover their faces.
EDM. I pant for life. Some good I mean to do,
Despite of mine own nature. Quickly send,
Be brief in it, to the castle; for my writ
Is on the life of Lear and on Cordelia:
Nay, send in time.
ALB. Run, run, O, run!
EDG. To who, my lord? Who hath the office? send
Thy token of reprieve.
EDM. Well thought on. Take my sword,
Give it the captain.
ALB. Haste thee for thy life. [*Exit* EDGAR.]
EDM. He hath commission from thy wife and me
To hang Cordelia in the prison, and
To lay the blame upon her own despair,
That she fordid[6] herself.
ALB. The gods defend her! Bear him hence awhile.
[EDMUND *is borne off*.]
[*Re-enter* LEAR, *with* CORDELIA *dead in his arms;* EDGAR, CAPTAIN, *and others following*.]
LEAR. Howl, howl, howl, howl! O, you are men of stones:
Had I your tongues and eyes, I'd use them so
That heaven's vault should crack. She's gone forever!
I know when one is dead, and when one lives;
She's dead as earth. Lend me a looking-glass;
If that her breath will mist or strain the stone,[7]
Why, then she lives.
KENT. Is this the promised end?[8]
EDG. Or image of that horror?
ALB. Fall, and cease![9]
LEAR. This feather stirs; she lives! If it be so,
It is a chance which does redeem all sorrows
That ever I have felt.
KENT. [*kneeling*] O my good master!
LEAR. Prithee, away.
EDG. 'Tis noble Kent, your friend.
LEAR. A plague upon you, murderers, traitors all!
I might have saved her; now she's gone for ever!
Cordelia, Cordelia! stay a little. Ha!
What is 't thou say'st? Her voice was ever soft,
Gentle, and low, an excellent thing in woman.
I killed the slave that was a-hanging thee.
CAPT. 'Tis true, my lords, he did.
LEAR. Did I not, fellow?
I have seen the day, with my good biting falchion[1]

6. Destroyed.
7. Mirror (of polished crystal).
8. Doomsday, the Last Judgment.
9. Let the heavens fall, and everything come to an end.
1. Light sword.

I would have made them skip: I am old now,
And these same crosses[2] spoil me. Who are you?
Mine eyes are not o' the best. I'll tell you straight.[3]
KENT. If fortune brag of two she loved and hated,
One of them we behold.
LEAR. This is a dull sight. Are you not Kent?
KENT. The same,
Your servant Kent. Where is your servant Caius?
LEAR. He's a good fellow, I can tell you that;
He'll strike, and quickly too. He's dead and rotten.
KENT. No, my good lord; I am the very man,—
LEAR. I'll see that straight.[4]
KENT. That, from your first of difference and decay,[5]
Have followed your sad steps.
LEAR. You are welcome hither.
KENT. Nor no man else. All's cheerless, dark, and deadly.
Your eldest daughters have fordone themselves,
And desperately[6] are dead.
LEAR. Aye, so I think.
ALB. He knows not what he says; and vain it is
That we present us to him.
EDG. Very bootless.[7]

[*Enter a* CAPTAIN.]

CAPT. Edmund is dead, my lord.
ALB. That's but a trifle here.
You lords and noble friends, know our intent.
What comfort to this great decay[8] may come
Shall be applied. For us, we will resign,
During the life of this old majesty,
To him our absolute power; [*to* EDGAR *and* KENT] you, to your rights;
With boot, and such addition[9] as your honors
Have more than merited. All friends shall taste
The wages of their virtue, and all foes
The cup of their deserving. O, see, see!
LEAR. And my poor fool[1] is hanged! No, no, no life!
Why should a dog, a horse, a rat, have life,
And thou no breath at all? Thou'lt come no more,
Never, never, never, never, never!
Pray you, undo this button. Thank you, sir.
Do you see this? Look on her, look, her lips,
Look there, look there! [*Dies.*]
EDG. He faints! My lord, my lord!
KENT. Break, heart; I prithee, break!

2. Troubles, frustrations.
3. Straightway.
4. Look into it immediately.
5. Beginning of change and decline in fortunes.
6. From despair.
7. Futile.
8. This great man ruined.
9. More besides, and such titles.
1. An affectionate term, referring to Cordelia.

EDG. Look up, my lord.
KENT. Vex not his ghost.[2] O, let him pass! He hates him much
That would upon the rack of this tough world
Stretch him out longer.[3]
EDG. He is gone, indeed.
KENT. The wonder is, he hath endured so long.
He but usurped his life.
ALB. Bear them from hence. Our present business
Is general woe. [*to* KENT *and* EDGAR] Friends of my soul, you twain
Rule in this realm, and the gored[4] state sustain.
KENT. I have a journey, sir, shortly to go;
My master calls me, I must not say no.
EDG. The weight of this sad time we must obey;
Speak what we feel, not what we ought to say.
The oldest hath borne most; we that are young
Shall never see so much, nor live so long.[5]
[*Exeunt, with dead march.*]

1604–5 1608

2. Departing spirit.
3. The rack was an instrument of torture in which the victim's arms and legs were pulled, even to dislocation.
4. Wounded.
5. These lines are given to Albany in the Quarto, to Edgar in the Folio. Editors who follow the Quarto argue that Shakespeare always gives the concluding speech in a tragedy to the highest-ranking person who survives. Those who follow the Folio say that Edgar must reply to Albany's "Friends of my soul" and that "we that are young" suits Edgar better than Albany. In effect, Edgar tacitly accepts the commission to rule which Kent has had to decline, so he is the highest-ranking survivor.

THOMAS NASHE
(1567–1601)

Nashe, a Cambridge graduate, was a versatile writer of controversial pamphlets, satire, plays, a novel, and lyric verse. He was one of the university wits who came to London and wrote for the stage and the press. They lived short and precarious lives: Nashe was about 33 when he died; his friend Christopher Marlowe died at 29, George Peele at 30, and Robert Greene at 32. Nashe's personal enemy was an older man, Gabriel Harvey, Spenser's friend; with him he exchanged a series of vituperative and slanderous pamphlets in which Nashe's talent for invective was exploited to the fullest, until the ecclesiastical authorities ordered, in June, 1599, that "all Nashe's books and Doctor Harvey's books be taken wheresoever they may be found and that none of their books be ever printed hereafter."

Nashe's picaresque narrative, *The Unfortunate Traveler, or the Life of Jack Wilton*, is a rambling account of escapades all over Europe, including some fictional exploits attributed to the poet Surrey. He wrote a festive comedy, *Summer's Last Will and Testament*; an attack upon women called *The Anatomy of Absurdity*; an attack on social abuses of every kind entitled *Pierce Penniless His Supplication to the Devil*; and a strident comparison between the sins of the Jews which led to the destruction of Jerusalem and the current morals and manners of London, called *Christ's Tears Over Jerusalem*. Nashe's outlook, like that of many satirists, was conservative: he praised the past in comparison with the present. But his prose style sometimes sounds quite modern. It is headlong, impatient, colloquial, and vivid. One of his own phrases best describes it: "No wind that blows strong but is boisterous."

Spring, the Sweet Spring[1]

Spring, the sweet spring, is the year's pleasant king,
Then blooms each thing, then maids dance in a ring,
Cold doth not sting, the pretty birds do sing:
Cuckoo, jug-jug, pu-we, to-witta-woo![2]

The palm and may make country houses gay,
Lambs frisk and play, the shepherds pipe all day,
And we hear aye birds tune this merry lay:
Cuckoo, jug-jug, pu-we, to-witta-woo!

The fields breathe sweet, the daisies kiss our feet,
Young lovers meet, old wives a-sunning sit,
In every street these tunes our ears do greet:
Cuckoo, jug-jug, pu-we, to-witta-woo!
Spring, the sweet spring!

1592 1600

A Litany in Time of Plague

Adieu, farewell, earth's bliss;
This world uncertain is;
Fond[3] are life's lustful joys;
Death proves them all but toys;[4]
None from his darts can fly;
I am sick, I must die.
Lord, have mercy on us!

Rich men, trust not in wealth,
Gold cannot buy you health;
Physic himself must fade.
All things to end are made,
The plague full swift goes by;
I am sick, I must die.
Lord, have mercy on us!

1. This and the following lyric are from *A Pleasant Comedy Called Summer's Last Will and Testament*, acted before the Archbishop of Canterbury in his palace at Croydon in 1592, and published in 1600.

2. The calls of the cuckoo, the nightingale, the lapwing, and the owl respectively.

3. Foolish.

4. Trifles.

Beauty is but a flower
Which wrinkles will devour;
Brightness falls from the air;
Queens have died young and fair;
Dust hath closed Helen's eye.
I am sick, I must die.
Lord, have mercy on us!

Strength stoops unto the grave,
Worms feed on Hector brave;
Swords may not fight with fate,
Earth still holds ope her gate.
"Come, come!" the bells do cry.
I am sick, I must die.
Lord, have mercy on us.

Wit with his wantonness
Tasteth death's bitterness;
Hell's executioner
Hath no ears for to hear
What vain art can reply.
I am sick. I must die.
Lord, have mercy on us.

Haste, therefore, each degree,
To welcome destiny;
Heaven is our heritage,
Earth but a player's stage;
Mount we unto the sky.
I am sick, I must die.
Lord, have mercy on us.

1592 1600

From Pierce Penniless, His Supplication to the Devil

An Invective against Enemies of Poetry

With the enemies of poetry I care not if I have a bout, and those are they that term our best writers but babbling ballad-makers, holding them fantastical fools, that have wit but cannot tell how to use it. I myself have been so censured among some dull-headed divines,[1] who deem it no more cunning to write an exquisite poem than to preach pure Calvin or distill the juice of a commentary in a quarter sermon.[2] Prove it when you will, you slow-spirited Saturnists,[3] that have nothing but the pilferies of your pen to polish an exhortation withal; no eloquence but tautologies to tie the

1. Specifically, the Reverend Richard Harvey, brother of Gabriel, in an epistle prefixed to some copies of *The Lamb of God* (1590).
2. I.e., plagiarize from Calvin or another commentator on those rare (once a quarter) occasions when you preach at all.
3. Dull, morose persons.

ears of your auditory unto you; no invention but "here it is to be noted, I stole this note out of Beza or Marlorat";[4] no wit to move, no passion to urge, but only an ordinary form of preaching, blown up by use of often hearing and speaking; and you shall find there goes more exquisite pains and purity of wit to the writing of one such rare poem as *Rosamund*[5] than to a hundred of your dunstical sermons.

Should we (as you) borrow all out of others, and gather nothing of ourselves. our names should be baffuld[6] on every bookseller's stall, and not a chandler's mustard pot but would wipe his mouth with our waste paper. "New herrings, new!"[7] we must cry, every time we make ourselves public, or else we shall be christened with a hundred new titles of idiotism. Nor is poetry an art whereof there is no use in a man's whole life but to describe discontented thoughts and youthful desires; for there is no study but it doth illustrate and beautify. How admirably shine those divines above the common mediocrity, that have tasted the sweet springs of Parnassus!

Silver-tongued Smith,[8] whose well-tuned style hath made thy death the general tears of the Muses, quaintly couldst thou devise heavenly ditties to Apollo's lute, and teach stately verse to trip it as smoothly as if Ovid and thou had but one soul. Hence alone did it proceed that thou wert such a plausible pulpit man, that before thou enteredst into the rough ways of theology thou refinedst, preparedst, and purifiedst thy mind with sweet poetry. If a simple man's censure may be admitted to speak in such an open theater of opinions, I never saw abundant reading better mixed with delight, or sentences which no man can challenge of profane affectation sounding more melodious to the ear or piercing more deep to the heart.

To them that demand what fruits the poets of our time bring forth, or wherein they are able to prove themselves necessary to the state, thus I answer: first and foremost, they have cleansed our language from barbarism and made the vulgar sort[9] here in London (which is the fountain whose rivers flow round about England) to aspire to a richer purity of speech than is communicated with the commonality of any nation under heaven. The virtuous by their praises they encourage to be more virtuous; to vicious men they are as infernal hags to haunt their ghosts with eternal infamy after death. The soldier, in hope to have his high deeds celebrated by their pens, despiseth a whole army of perils, and acteth wonders exceeding all human conjecture. Those that care neither for God

4. Theodore Beza (1519–1605), successor of Calvin at Geneva; most eminent Protestant divine in Europe. Augustine Marlorat (1506–63), another of the Geneva reformers.

5. Samuel Daniel's *The Complaint of Rosamund* (1592).

6. Treated with scorn.

7. A fishmonger's street cry.

8. Henry Smith (1550–91), a very popular preacher. He published some verse in Latin.

9. Common people.

nor the devil, by their quills are kept in awe. *Multi famam,* saith one, *pauci conscientiam verentur.*[1]

Let God see what he will, they would be loath to have the shame of the world. What age will not praise immortal Sir Philip Sidney, whom noble Salustius[2] (that thrice singular French poet) hath famoused; together with Sir Nicholas Bacon, Lord Keeper, and merry Sir Thomas More, for the chief pillars of our English speech. Not so much but Chaucer's host, Bailly in Southwark, and his wife of Bath he keeps such a stir with, in his *Canterbury Tales,* shall be talked of whilst the Bath is used, or there be ever a bad house in Southwark.[3] Gentles, it is not your lay chronographers, that write of nothing but of mayors and sheriffs and the dear year[4] and the great frost, that can endow your names with never-dated glory; for they want the wings of choice words to fly to heaven, which we have; they cannot sweeten a discourse, or wrest admiration from men reading, as we can, reporting the meanest accident. Poetry is the honey of all flowers, the quintessence of all sciences, the marrow of wit, and the very phrase of angels. How much better is it, then, to have an elegant lawyer to plead one's cause, than a stutting townsman that loseth himself in his tale and doth nothing but make legs;[5] so much it is better for a nobleman or gentleman to have his honor's story related, and his deeds emblazoned, by a poet, than a citizen.

Alas, poor Latinless authors, they are so simple they know not what they do; they no sooner spy a new ballad, and his name to it that compiled it, but they put him in for one of the learned men of our time. I marvel how the masterless men, that set up their bills in Paul's[6] for services, and such as paste up their papers on every post, for arithmetic and writing schools, 'scape eternity amongst them. I believe both they and the knight marshal's men, that nail up mandates at the court gate for annoying the palace with filth or making water, if they set their names to the writing, will shortly make up the number of the learned men of our time, and be as famous as the rest. For my part, I do challenge[7] no praise of learning to myself, yet have I worn a gown in the University, and so hath *caret tempus non habet moribus;*[8] but this I dare presume, that if any Maecenas[9] bind me to him by his bounty or extend some sound liberality to me worth the speaking of, I will do him as much honor as any poet of my beardless years shall in England. Not that I am so

1. "Many respect fame; only a few, conscience," Pliny, *Epistles* III.20.
2. Guillaume de Saluste du Bartas (1544–90), an immensely popular religious poet, both in French and in English translation. It is in his *Second Sepmaine* that he praises Sidney, Bacon, and More.
3. Southwark was notorious for its brothels.
4. Year of high prices.
5. Bow and scrape.
6. Advertisements for jobs were commonly posted on the west door of the cathedral.
7. Claim.
8. (Bad Latin) i.e., even unlearned persons have worn a university gown.
9. Roman patron of poets, especially Virgil and Horace.

confident what I can do, but that I attribute so much to my thankful mind above others, which I am persuaded would enable me to work miracles.

On the contrary side, if I be evil intreated, or sent away with a flea in mine ear, let him look that I will rail on him soundly; not for an hour or a day, whiles the injury is fresh in my memory; but in some elaborate polished poem, which I will leave to the world when I am dead, to be a living image to all ages of his beggarly parsimony and ignoble illiberality; and let him not (whatsoever he be) measure the weight of my words by this book, where I write *quicquid in buccam venerit*,[1] as fast as my hand can trot; but I have terms (if I be vexed) laid in steep in *aqua fortis*[2] and gunpowder, that shall rattle through the skies and make an earthquake in a peasant's ears. Put case (since I am not yet out of the theme of wrath) that some tired jade belonging to the press, whom I never wronged in my life, hath named me expressly in print[3] (as I will not do him) and accuse me of want of learning, unbraiding me for reviving in an epistle of mine, the reverent memory of Sir Thomas More, Sir John Cheke, Doctor Watson, Doctor Haddon, Doctor Carr, Master Ascham,[4] as if they were no meat but for his mastership's mouth, or none but some such as the son of a ropemaker were worthy to mention them. To show how I can rail, thus would I begin to rail on him, "Thou that hadst thy hood turned over thy ears when thou wert a bachelor,[5] for abusing of Aristotle and setting him upon the school gates painted with ass's ears on his head, is it any discredit for me, thou great babound,[6] thou pygmy braggart, thou pamphleter of nothing but paeans,[7] to be censured by thee, that hast scorned the prince of philosophers? Thou that in thy dialogues sold'st honey for a halfpenny, and the choicest writers extant for cues[8] apiece, that camest to the logic schools when thou wert a freshman and writ'st phrases, off with thy gown and untruss, for I mean to lash thee mightily. Thou hast a brother,[9] hast thou not, student in almanacs, go to, I'll stand to it, fathered one of thy bastards (a book, I mean) which being of thy begetting was set forth under his name?"

* * *

The Defense of Plays

That state or kingdom that is in league with all the world, and hath no foreign sword to vex it, is not half so strong or confirmed to

1. Whatever occurs to me.
2. Soaking in nitric acid.
3. I.e., Richard Harvey in *The Lamb of God*. Nashe has a marginal note at this point which reads. "I would tell you in what book it is, but I am afraid it would make his book sell in his latter days, which hitherto hath lain dead and been a great loss to the printer."
4. Humanists praised by Nashe in his preface to Greene's *Menaphon* (1589).
5. Bachelor of Arts, recent graduate.
6. Baboon.
7. A reference to Richard Harvey's *Ephemeron, Sive Paean* (1583).
8. Quadrans, ⅛ of a penny.
9. John Harvey, who published almanacs for 1583 and 1589.

endure as that which lives every hour in fear of invasion. There is a certain waste of the people for whom there is no use but war; and these men must have some employment still to cut them off; *Nam si foras hostem non habent, domi invenient.*[1] If they have no service abroad, they will make mutinies at home. Or if the affairs of the state be such as cannot exhale all these corrupt excrements, it is very expedient they have some light toys to busy their heads withal, cast before them as bones to gnaw upon, which may keep them from having leisure to intermeddle with higher matters.

To this effect, the policy of plays is very necessary, howsoever some shallow-brained censurers (not the deepest searchers into the secrets of government) mightily oppugn them. For whereas the afternoon being idlest time of the day, wherein men that are their own masters (as gentlemen of the court, the Inns of the Court,[2] and the number of captains and soldiers about London) do wholly bestow themselves upon pleasure, and that pleasure they divide (how virtuously, it skills[3] not) either into gaming, following of harlots, drinking, or seeing a play; is it not then better (since of four extremes all the world cannot keep them but they will choose one) that they should betake them to the least, which is plays? Nay, what if I prove plays to be no extreme, but a rare exercise of virtue? First, for the subject of them, (for the most part) it is borrowed out of our English chronicles, wherein our forefathers' valiant acts (that have lain long buried in rusty brass and worm-eaten books) are revived, and they themselves raised from the grave of oblivion, and brought to plead their aged honors in open presence; than which, what can be a sharper reproof to these degenerate effeminate days of ours?

How would it have joyed brave Talbot,[4] the terror of the French, to think that after he had lain two hundred years in his tomb, he should triumph again on the stage, and have his bones new embalmed with the tears of ten thousand spectators at least (at several times) who in the tragedian that represents his person imagine they behold him fresh bleeding.

I will defend it against any collian[5] or clubfisted usurer of them all, there is no immortality can be given a man on earth like unto plays. What talk I to them of immortality, that are the only underminers of honor, and do envy any man that is not sprung up by base brokery like themselves. They care not if all the ancient houses were rooted out, so that like the burgomasters of the Low Countries they might share the government amongst them as states, and be quartermasters of our monarchy. All arts to them are vanity; and if

1. Adapted from Livy, Book XXX, xliv, 9. Nashe translates.
2. Law schools.
3. Matters.
4. In the play *Harey the VI* produced by Strange's men for Henslowe on March 3, 1592. What relation this play had to the Shakespearean *1 Henry VI* is uncertain, but Nashe's reference would fit I.iv.39–43, and II.iii.14–24.
5. Rascal (the usual form is "cullion").

you tell them what a glorious thing it is to have Henry the Fifth represented on the stage leading the French king prisoner, and forcing both him and the Dolphin[6] to swear fealty, "Aye, but," will they say, "what do we get by it?" Respecting neither the right of fame that is due to true nobility deceased, nor what hopes of eternity are to be proposed to adventurous minds, to encourage them forward, but only their execrable lucre and filthy unquenchable avarice.

They know when they are dead they shall not be brought upon the stage for any goodness, but in a merriment of the usurer and the devil, or buying arms of the herald, who gives them the lion without tongue, tail, or talons, because his master whom he must serve is a townsman and a man of peace, and must not keep any quarreling beasts to annoy his honest neighbors.

In plays, all cozenages,[7] all cunning drifts over-gilded with outward holiness, all stratagems of war, all the cankerworms that breed on the rust of peace, are most lively anatomized; they show the ill success of treason, the fall of hasty climbers, the wretched end of usurpers, the misery of civil dissension, and how just God is evermore in punishing of murther. And to prove every one of these allegations could I propound the circumstances of this play and that play, if I meant to handle this theme otherwise than *obiter*.[8] What should I say more? They are sour pills of reprehension wrapped up in sweet words. Whereas some petitioners of the counsel against them object,[9] they corrupt the youth of the city and withdraw prentices from their work; they heartily wish they might be troubled with none of their youth nor their prentices; for some of them (I mean the ruder handicrafts' servants) never come abroad but they are in danger of undoing; and as for corrupting them when they come, that's false; for no play they have encourageth any man to tumults or rebellion, but lays before such the halter and the gallows; or praiseth or approveth pride, lust, whoredom, prodigality, or drunkenness, but beats them down utterly. As for the hindrance of trades and traders of the city by them, that is an article foisted in by the vintners, alewives, and victualers, who surmise if there were no plays they should have all the company that resort to them lie boozing and beer-bathing in their houses every afternoon. Nor so, nor so, good brother bottle-ale, for there are other places besides where money can bestow itself; the sign of the smock[1] will wipe your mouth clean; and yet I have heard ye have made her a tenant to your taphouses. But what shall he do that hath spent himself? Where shall he haunt? Faith, when dice, lust, and drunkenness, and all, have dealt upon him, if there be never a play for him to go

6. Dauphin (son of the king of France).
7. Deceptions, cheats.
8. By the way.
9. "The confutation of citizens' objections against players" [Nashe's marginal note].
1. I.e., of a prostitute.

to for his penny, he sits melancholy in his chamber, devising upon felony or treason, and how he may best exalt himself by mischief.

In Augustus' time (who was the patron of all witty sports) there happened a great fray in Rome about a player, insomuch as all the city was in an uproar; whereupon, the emperor (after the broil was somewhat overblown) called the player before him, and asked what was the reason that a man of his quality durst presume to make such a brawl about nothing. He smilingly replied, "It is good for thee, Oh Caesar, that the people's heads are troubled with brawls and quarrels about us and our light matters; for otherwise they would look into thee and thy matters." Read Lipsius[2] or any profane or Christian politician, and you shall find him of this opinion. Our players are not as the players beyond sea, a sort of squirting bawdy comedians, that have whores and common courtesans to play women's parts, and forbear no immodest speech or unchaste action that may procure laughter; but our scene is more stately furnished than ever it was in the time of Roscius, our representations honorable and full of gallant resolution, not consisting like theirs of pantaloon, a whore, and a zany,[3] but of emperors, kings, and princes; whose true tragedies (*Sophocleo cothurno*)[4] they do vaunt.

Not Roscius nor Aesope,[5] those admired tragedians that have lived ever since before Christ was born, could ever perform more in action than famous Ned Allen.[6] I must accuse our poets of sloth and partiality that they will not boast in large impressions what worthy men (above all nations) England affords. Other countries cannot have a fiddler break a string but they will put it in print, and the old Romans in the writings they published thought scorn to use any but domestical examples of their own home-bred actors, scholars, and champions, and them they would extol to the third and fourth generation; cobblers, tinkers, fencers, none escaped them, but they mingled them all in one gallimaufry of glory.

Here I have used a like method, not of tying myself to mine own country, but by insisting in the experience of our time; and if I ever write anything in Latin (as I hope one day I shall), not a man of any desert here amongst us, but I will have up. Tarlton, Ned Allen, Knell, Bentley,[7] shall be made known to France, Spain, and Italy; and not a part that they surmounted in, more than other, but I will there note and set down, with the manner of their habits and attire.[8]

2. Justus Lipsius (1547–1606), Belgian scholar and historian.
3. Type parts in the *commedia dell' arte*.
4. "With Sophoclean dignity."
5. These two Roman actors flourished about 70 B.C.
6. Edward Alleyn (1566–1626), partner and son-in-law of Henslowe, the manager. He retired from the stage about 1603–4. He founded Dulwich College.
7. Actors older than Alleyn, and famous in the period before 1588. Richard Tarlton (d. 1588) was the most popular Elizabethan comedian.
8. Nashe never fulfilled this resolution.

Sixteenth-Century Lyrics

The 16th century was one of the great ages for lyric poetry in English. As J. J. Jusserand puts it, in his *Literary History of the English People,* "Indefatigable, the poets now sing verses worthy of remembrance, on every subject, amorous, religious, epic, satirical, pastoral, didactic, moving from the world of insects to the world of heroes. Songs rise naturally to their lips, no one knows why, they do not know why."

The lyrics written by courtiers, in the first half of the century as well as later, were poems intended to be set to music and sung. In the courts of all the Tudor sovereigns music flourished; skill in composition was an excellent qualification for a servant, and noblemen, even crowned heads themselves, pursued the art. Sometimes a courtly poet would compose new words to a popular tune. The songs of Wyatt and other courtiers collected in *Tottel's Miscellany* are only a remnant of the large amount of lyrical verse written in the courts of Henry VIII and Edward VI. The courtly "makers," as they have been called, were of course able to imitate and borrow foreign stanza forms and popular themes from the poetry of Italy and France. But at their best they wrote lyrics in the native English tradition also, and the fusing of native and foreign strains may well be the best reason for the flourishing of lyric poetry in the last decades of the century.

In Shakespeare's *Twelfth Night,* the Duke calls upon a court jester to repeat a song he has heard him sing:

> O fellow, come, the song we had last night.
> Mark it, Cesario; it is old and plain.
> The spinsters and the knitters in the sun,
> And the free maids that weave their thread with bones,
> Do use to chant it. It is silly sooth,
> And dallies with the innocence of love
> Like the old age.

Singing at court is pictured here; moreover, it is part of a play, thereby illustrating another source of lyric poetry in Elizabethan England: the drama. Acting companies used boys to play their female parts, and often these boys had been trained as singers; the playwright would provide them opportunities to display their talents. In Thomas Dekker's play of craftsmen's life, *The Shoemakers' Holiday*, the workers sing while they cobble shoes, and Shakespeare's gravedigger, in *Hamlet*, sings while he works.

The popular ballad, with its simple four-line stanza form, of anonymous or perhaps composite authorship, can be traced back to the 15th century, and, with the invention of printing, a more commercial form, the broadside ballad, became popular. Copies of broadside ballads were sold by traveling peddlers like Autolycus in Shakespeare's *Winter's Tale*; they were often crude affairs, and exploited the latest murder or scandal like the sensational newspaper of modern times.

At the other extreme were the two kinds of art song, the madrigal and the air. A madrigal is a song for two or more voices in counterpoint, usually a setting of a poem expressing the woes of the Petrarchan lover, although any subject is possible. The music is highly imitative of the meaning of the words, but since the separate voices are usually not on the same word at the same time, it is often difficult to understand a madrigal being sung. There is evidence that many Elizabethans could sing a part in a madrigal at sight—a feat which now requires a high degree of musical training. The words must be contained within one rather short stanza, since the music is so closely adapted to the meaning and since phrases are repeated many times in the different voices.

The air, a much less complicated musical form, used words arranged in stanzas; it was a single, recurring melody for the voice with a three-part accompaniment on the lute. Words written for the lute-song or air were much more frequently excellent lyric poems than the words written for madrigals, which tended to be not much more than epigrams. The finest poet of airs was Thomas Campion, who was also a composer. He had a remarkably sensitive ear and a thorough understanding of the problems of versification and musical setting. The genius of Campion and of Ben Jonson solved the vexed problem of whether English quantitative verse (verse which relies upon length and duration of syllables, rather than accent) could be successful.

The 16th century produced more anonymous lyrics than it did lyrics the authors of which can be identified. There are several reasons for this. The Elizabethan period shared the medieval idea that pride of individual authorship was unimportant. Moreover many poems circulated in manuscript and were copied into manuscript books one after the other, without particular care for identifying authorship. Sometimes publishers obtained such collections and printed them, either not knowing or not caring about the authorship of individual poems. The first great 16th-century anthology, *Tottel's Miscellany* (1557), has a large number of poems attributed to "Uncertain Authors," only a few of whom have been identified up to the present time; a very popular anthology at the end of the century, *The Phoenix Nest*, gives no name at all for some poems and attributes others to "Ignoto."

Another reason for the survival of anonymous poems was that they were often the lyrics for songs. The composer published his musical settings with the words, so that they could be sung, but few publishers gave credit to the author of the words. An exception was Thomas Campion. There was a casualness about authorship that seems strange to us. Aristocrats and courtiers, though they wrote poetry, often did not wish to be known as writers—it would seem beneath them. On the other hand, the art was less specialized in those days: lawyers, statesmen, explorers, parsons, soldiers, merchants—it was a rare Elizabethan who would not try his hand at a verse.

SIR WALTER RALEGH
(1552–1618)

The brilliant and versatile Ralegh was a soldier, courtier, poet, philosopher, explorer and colonizer, student of science, and historian. He is popularly known now as the founder of Virginia and the introducer of tobacco into Europe, but in his own time he was known for his skeptical mind, his great favor with the queen, his hatred of Spain, and, to Edmund Spenser and others, his poetry. The major part of his verse has not survived; it was a long poem to the queen called *Cynthia;* it was never printed and we have only a few stanzas in manuscript. Some of his shorter poems were very popular and were printed in anthologies or songbooks. His reply to Marlowe's *Passionate Shepherd* is only one of several such answers; both Donne and Herrick wrote them, but Ralegh's is the best. His poem *The Lie,* with its attacks upon social classes and institutions, in its turn provoked many answers. *Farewell, False Love* is an early poem of Ralegh's which was set to music by the composer William Byrd in 1588.

From 1603 to his execution in 1618 Ralegh was kept imprisoned in the Tower of London by King James, except for a period in 1617 when he made his ill-fated last voyage to Guiana. In prison he wrote his long, unfinished *History of the World*; it confines itself to the earliest times and does not deal with recent history because, as Ralegh remarked, he who follows truth too closely at the heels might get kicked in the teeth. The most famous passage in the *History* is at the end. An apostrophe to Death, it is a fine example of rotund 17th-century prose:

> O eloquent, just, and mighty Death! Whom none could advise, thou hast persuaded; what none hath dared, thou hast done; and whom the world hath flattered thou only hast cast out of the world and despised. Thou hast drawn together all the farfetched greatness, all the pride, cruelty, and ambition of man, and covered it all over with these two narrow words, *Hic jacet!* [Here lies]

Ralegh was a passionate man, like Hotspur and Hamlet, and of course he had enemies. Yet by 1618 popular sympathy was so much in his favor that, as Trevelyan said, "the ghost of Ralegh pursued the House of Stuart to the scaffold." Had he not earned a name as the founder of Virginia, the eloquent and grave historian, "a seafaring man, a soldier and a courtier," as he described himself on the scaffold, he would still be the poet Spenser praised, "the sommers nightingale" who

> tooke in hond
> My pipe, before that aemuléd [imitated] of many,
> And plaid thereon; (for well that skil he cond) [knew]
> Himself as skilfull in that art as any.

The Nymph's Reply to the Shepherd

If all the world and love were young,
And truth in every shepherd's tongue,

These pretty pleasures might me move
To live with thee and be thy love.

Time drives the flocks from field to fold
When rivers rage and rocks grow cold,
And Philomel[1] becometh dumb;
The rest complains of cares to come.

The flowers do fade, and wanton fields
To wayward winter reckoning yields;
A honey tongue, a heart of gall,
Is fancy's spring, but sorrow's fall.

Thy gowns, thy shoes, thy beds of roses,
Thy cap, thy kirtle,[2] and thy posies
Soon break, soon wither, soon forgotten—
In folly ripe, in reason rotten.

Thy belt of straw and ivy buds,
Thy coral clasps and amber studs,
All these in me no means can move
To come to thee and be thy love.

But could youth last and love still breed,
Had joys no date[3] nor age no need,
Then these delights my mind might move
To live with thee and be thy love.

[On the Life of Man]

What is our life? a play of passion;
Our mirth the music of division;[4]
Our mothers' wombs the tiring-houses[5] be
Where we are dressed for this short comedy.
Heaven the judicious sharp spectator is,

That sits and marks still who doth act amiss;
Our graves that hide us from the searching sun
Are like drawn curtains when the play is done.
Thus march we, playing, to our latest rest,
Only we die in earnest—that's no jest.

1612

[Sir Walter Ralegh to His Son]

Three things there be that prosper up apace
And flourish, whilst they grow asunder far,
But on a day, they meet all in one place,

1. The nightingale.
2. Skirt, outer petticoat.
3. Ending.
4. The more rapid accompaniment to, or variation on, a musical theme.
5. Dressing rooms in an Elizabethan theater.

And when they meet, they one another mar;
And they be these: the wood, the weed, the wag.
The wood is that which makes the gallow tree;
The weed is that which strings the hangman's bag;
The wag, my pretty knave, betokeneth thee.
Mark well, dear boy, whilst these assemble not,
Green springs the tree, hemp grows, the wag is wild,
But when they meet, it makes the timber rot;
It frets the halter, and it chokes the child.
Then bless thee, and beware, and let us pray
We part not with thee at this meeting day.

ca. 1600

Walsinghame[6]

"As you came from the holy land
  of Walsinghame,
Met you not with my true love
  by the way as you came?"

"How shall I know your true love,
  that have met many one
As I went to the holy land,
  that have come, that have gone?"

"She is neither white nor brown,
  but as the heavens fair:
There is none hath a form so divine
  in the earth or the air."

"Such an one did I meet, good sir,
  such an angelic face,
Who like a queen, like a nymph, did appear
  by her gait, by her grace."

"She hath left me here all alone,
  all alone as unknown,
Who sometimes did lead me with herself,
  and me loved as her own."

"What's the cause that she leaves you alone
  and a new way doth take,
Who loved you once as her own
  and her joy did you make?"

"I have loved her all my youth,
  but now, old, as you see;
Love likes not the falling fruit
  from the withered tree."

6. A priory popular for pilgrimages before its destruction in 1538. There were several traditional ballads on the subject; Ralegh's imitation is a dialogue between an old man and a pilgrim. They speak alternately, until the last four stanzas, when the pilgrim speaks.

"Know that love is a careless child
and forgets promise past;
He is blind, he is deaf when he list
and in faith never fast.

"His desire is a dureless[7] content
and a trustless joy;
He is won with a world of despair
and is lost with a toy.

"Of womenkind such indeed is the love,
(or the word 'love' abused)
Under which many childish desires
and conceits are excused.

"But Love is a durable fire
in the mind ever burning—
Never sick, never old, never dead,
from itself never turning."

The Lie

Go, soul, the body's guest,
Upon a thankless errand;
Fear not to touch the best;
The truth shall be thy warrant.
Go, since I needs must die,
And give the world the lie.

Say to the court, it glows
And shines like rotten wood;
Say to the church, it shows
What's good, and doth no good.
If church and court reply,
Then give them both the lie.

Tell potentates, they live
Acting by others' action;
Not loved unless they give,
Not strong but by a faction.
If potentates reply,
Give potentates the lie.

Tell men of high condition,
That manage the estate,
Their purpose is ambition,
Their practice only hate.
And if they once reply,
Then give them all the lie.

7. Transient.

Tell them that brave it[8] most,
They beg for more by spending,
Who, in their greatest cost,
Seek nothing but commending.
And if they make reply,
Then give them all the lie.

Tell zeal it wants devotion;
Tell love it is but lust;
Tell time it is but motion;
Tell flesh it is but dust.
And wish them not reply,
For thou must give the lie.

Tell age it daily wasteth;
Tell honor how it alters;
Tell beauty how she blasteth;
Tell favor how it falters.
And as they shall reply,
Give every one the lie.

Tell wit how much it wrangles
In tickle[9] points of niceness;
Tell wisdom she entangles
Herself in overwiseness.
And when they do reply,
Straight give them both the lie.

Tell physic of her boldness;
Tell skill it is pretension;
Tell charity of coldness;
Tell law it is contention.
And as they do reply,
So give them still the lie.

Tell fortune of her blindness;
Tell nature of decay;
Tell friendship of unkindness;
Tell justice of delay.
And if they will reply,
Then give them all the lie.

Tell arts they have no soundness,
But vary by esteeming;
Tell schools they want profoundness,
And stand too much on seeming.
If arts and schools reply,
Give arts and schools the lie.

Tell faith it's fled the city;
Tell how the country erreth;

8. I.e., those who spend much on clothes. 9. Delicate.

Tell manhood shakes off pity;
Tell virtue least preferreth.
And if they do reply,
Spare not to give the lie.

So when thou hast, as I
Commanded thee, done blabbing—
Although to give the lie
Deserves no less than stabbing—
Stab at thee he that will,
No stab the soul can kill.

ca. 1592

Farewell, False Love

Farewell, false love, the oracle of lies,
A mortal foe and enemy to rest;
An envious boy, from whom all cares arise,
A bastard vile, a beast with rage possessed;
A way of error, a temple full of treason,
In all effects contrary unto reason.

A poisoned serpent covered all with flowers,
Mother of sighs and murtherer of repose,
A sea of sorrows from whence are drawn such showers
As moisture lends to every grief that grows;
A school of guile, a net of deep deceit,
A gilded hook that holds a poisoned bait.

A fortress foiled[1] which reason did defend,
A siren song, a fever of the mind,
A maze wherein affection finds no end,
A raging cloud that runs before the wind,
A substance like the shadow of the sun,
A goal of grief for which the wisest run.

A quenchless fire, a nurse of trembling fear,
A path that leads to peril and mishap;
A true retreat of sorrow and despair,
An idle boy that sleeps in pleasure's lap,
A deep distrust of that which certain seems,
A hope of that which reason doubtful deems.

Sith[2] then thy trains my younger years betrayed,
And for my faith ingratitude I find,
And sith repentance hath my wrongs bewrayed[3]
Whose course was ever contrary to kind—
False love, desire, and beauty frail, adieu!
Dead is the root whence all these fancies grew.

1588

1. Overthrown.
2. Since; "trains": tricks, stratagems.
3 Revealed.

The Author's Epitaph, Made By Himself[4]

Even such is time, which takes in trust
Our youth, our joys, and all we have,
And pays us but with age and dust,
Who in the dark and silent grave
When we have wandered all our ways
Shuts up the story of our days,
And from which earth, and grave, and dust
The Lord shall raise me up, I trust.

1628

4. In the 17th century it was thought that Ralegh composed this poem the night before his execution and wrote it in his Bible. It is actually a version of the last stanza of a love poem, "Nature, That Washed Her Hands in Milk" (about 1592). Only the first three words and the final couplet are changed.

ROBERT SOUTHWELL
(1561–1595)

Father Robert Southwell, S.J., was the younger son of a prominent English family who went to the English seminary for Catholics at Douai as a youth, then to Rome, where he entered the Society of Jesus. In 1586 he returned to England. His mission was a dangerous one, and he probably foresaw the martyrdom he was to suffer in 1595. He wrote a good deal of religious prose and verse; the most famous of his lyrics is *The Burning Babe*. Ben Jonson remarked to William Drummond of Hawthornden that if he had written *The Burning Babe* he would have been willing to destroy many of his own poems.

The Burning Babe

As I in hoary winter's night stood shivering in the snow,
Surprised I was with sudden heat which made my heart to glow;
And lifting up a fearful eye to view what fire was near,
A pretty babe all burning bright did in the air appear;
Who, scorchéd with excessive heat, such floods of tears did shed
As though his floods should quench his flames which with his tears
were fed.
"Alas," quoth he, "but newly born in fiery heats I fry,[1]
Yet none approach to warm their hearts or feel my fire but I!
My faultless breast the furnace is, the fuel wounding thorns,
Love is the fire, and sighs the smoke, the ashes shame and scorns;
The fuel justice layeth on, and mercy blows the coals,
The metal in this furnace wrought are men's defiléd souls,
For which, as now on fire I am to work them to their good,
So will I melt into a bath to wash them in my blood."
With this he vanished out of sight and swiftly shrunk away,
And straight I calléd unto mind that it was Christmas day.

1602

1. Burn.

SAMUEL DANIEL
(1562–1619)

Samuel Daniel, translator, historian, and poet, was a follower of the Countess of Pembroke, Sidney's sister. He wrote classical tragedies, a verse history of the *Civil Wars Between the Two Houses of Lancaster and York* (1594–1609), a late defense of learning in *Musophilus*, and one of the better Elizabethan sonnet cycles, *Delia* (1592). His *Defense of Rhyme* (1603), written in answer to Thomas Campion's criticisms of the use of rhyme, is an important contribution to the critical debates of the time. As a lyric poet, Daniel is restrained, quiet, and eloquent.

From Delia

33

When men shall find thy flower, thy glory pass,
And thou, with careful brow sitting alone,
Receivéd hast this message from thy glass,
That tells thee truth, and says that all is gone,
Fresh shalt thou see in me the wounds thou madest,
Though spent thy flame, in me the heat remaining,
I that have loved thee thus before thou fadest,
My faith shall wax, when thou art in thy waning.
The world shall find this miracle in me,
That fire can burn when all the matter's spent;
Then what my faith hath been thyself shall see,
And that thou wast unkind thou mayst repent.
Thou mayst repent that thou hast scorned my tears,
When winter snows upon thy golden hairs.

34

When winter snows upon thy golden hairs,
And frost of age hath nipped thy flowers near;
When dark shall seem thy day that never clears,
And all lies with'red that was held so dear;
Then take this picture which I here present thee,
Limned with a pencil[1] not all unworthy.
Here see the gifts that God and nature lent thee;
Here read thy self and what I suff'red for thee.
This may remain thy lasting monument,
Which happily[2] posterity may cherish.
These colors with thy fading are not spent;
These may remain when thou and I shall perish.
If they remain, then thou shalt live thereby:
They will remain, and so thou canst not die.

1. I.e., painted with a brush. 2. Perhaps.

45

Care-charmer Sleep, son of the sable Night,
Brother to Death, in silent darkness born,
Relieve my languish and restore the light;
With dark forgetting of my cares, return.
And let the day be time enough to mourn
The shipwreck of my ill-adventured youth;
Let waking eyes suffice to wail their scorn
Without the torment of the night's untruth.
Cease, dreams, th' imagery of our day desires,
To model forth the passions of the morrow;
Never let rising sun approve you liars,
To add more grief to aggravate my sorrow.
Still let me sleep, embracing clouds in vain,
And never wake to feel the day's disdain.

46

Let others sing of knights and paladins
In aged accents and untimely[3] words,
Paint shadows in imaginary lines
Which well the reach of their high wits records;
But I must sing of thee and those fair eyes.
Authentic shall my verse in time to come,
When yet th' unborn shall say, "Lo where she lies,
Whose beauty made him speak that else was dumb."
These are the arks, the trophies I erect,
That fortify thy name against old age;
And these thy sacred virtues must protect
Against the dark and time's consuming rage.
Though th' error of my youth they shall discover,
Suffice, they show I lived and was thy lover.

1592

3. Obsolete.

MICHAEL DRAYTON
(1563–1631)

Drayton's long career as a poet extended from the early 1590's until well on in the 17th century. He was born about a year earlier than Shakespeare and in the same county, Warwickshire. He collaborated in plays, wrote sonnets, pastorals, odes, poetic epistles, and a versified history called *The Barons' Wars*, but he intended as his masterpiece a 30,000-line historical-geographical poem about the English countryside called *Poly-Olbion*. His lifelong devotion to Anne Goodere, Lady Rainsford, is memorialized in his sonnets to a lady called Idea. He revised his sonnets and added to them as they were republished, so one can trace his development from an Elizabethan to a 17th-century poet. He wrote of himself:

"My muse is rightly of the English strain
That cannot long one fashion entertain."

From Idea

6

How many paltry, foolish, painted things,
That now in coaches trouble every street,
Shall be forgotten, whom no poet sings,
Ere they be well wrapped in their winding sheet?
Where[1] I to thee eternity shall give
When nothing else remaineth of these days,
And queens hereafter shall be glad to live
Upon the alms of thy superfluous praise.
Virgins and matrons, reading these my rhymes,
Shall be so much delighted with thy story
That they shall grieve they lived not in these times
To have seen thee, their sex's only glory;
So shalt thou fly above the vulgar throng,
Still to survive in my immortal song.

1619

37

Dear, why should you command me to my rest
When now the night doth summon all to sleep?
Methinks this time becometh lovers best;
Night was ordained together friends to keep.
How happy are all other living things
Which, though the day disjoin by several flight,
The quiet evening yet together brings,
And each returns unto his love at night.
O thou, that art so courteous else to all,
Why shouldst thou, Night, abuse me only thus,
That every creature to his kind doth call
And yet 'tis thou dost only sever us.
Well could I wish it would be ever day
If when night comes you bid me go away.

1602

50

As in some countries far removed from hence
The wretched creature destinéd to die,
Having the judgment due to his offense,
By surgeons begged, their art on him to try;
Which on the living work without remorse,
First make incision on each mastering[2] vein,
Then staunch the bleeding, then trans-pierce the corse,
And with their balms recure the wounds again;
Then poison, and with physic him restore;
Not that they fear the hopeless man to kill,
But their experience to increase the more;

1. Whereas.

2. Master, principal.

Even so my mistress works upon my ill
By curing me and killing me each hour
Only to show her beauty's sovereign power.

1605

61

Since there's no help, come let us kiss and part;
Nay, I have done, you get no more of me,
And I am glad, yea glad with all my heart
That thus so cleanly I myself can free;
Shake hands forever, cancel all our vows,
And when we meet at any time again,
Be it not seen in either of our brows
That we one jot of former love retain.
Now at the last gasp of love's latest breath,
When, his pulse failing, passion speechless lies,
When faith is kneeling by his bed of death,
And innocence is closing up his eyes;
Now if thou wouldst, when all have given him over,
From death to life thou mightst him yet recover.

1619

THOMAS CAMPION
(1567–1620)

Thomas Campion was a law student, a physician, a composer, and a poet. His first poetic attempts were in Latin. His love of classical, quantitative versification carried over into his English poems and songs, as well as into his critical theory, which he expounded in his *Observations in the Art of English Poesy.* (In quantitative verse the syllables are arranged in pattern according to their length and duration, rather than according to accent or stress; cf. Campion's *Rose-Cheeked Laura.*) But his greatest achievement as a lyric poet—and he is one of the very best in the language—comes from the fact that he was both poet and composer. He says in the preface to one of his books, "I have chiefly aimed to couple my words and notes lovingly together, which will be much for him to do that hath not power over both."

My Sweetest Lesbia[1]

My sweetest Lesbia, let us live and love,
And though the sager sort our deeds reprove,

1. Imitated and partly translated from a poem by Catullus (87–ca. 54 B.C.), the Latin lyric poet who often celebrated the charms of Lesbia in his verses. This and the two lyrics which follow appeared in *A Book of Airs,* which contains Campion's first work as a composer.

Let us not weigh them. Heaven's great lamps do dive
Into their west, and straight again revive,
But soon as once set is our little light,
Then must we sleep one ever-during night.

If all would lead their lives in love like me,
Then bloody swords and armor should not be;
No drum nor trumpet peaceful sleeps should move,
Unless alarm came from the camp of love.
But fools do live, and waste their little light,
And seek with pain their ever-during night.

When timely death my life and fortune ends,
Let not my hearse be vexed with mourning friends,
But let all lovers, rich in triumph, come
And with sweet pastimes grace my happy tomb;
And Lesbia, close up thou my little light,
And crown with love my ever-during night.

1601

When to Her Lute Corinna Sings

When to her lute Corinna sings,
Her voice revives the leaden strings,
And doth in highest notes appear
As any challenged echo clear;
But when she doth of mourning speak,
Ev'n with her sighs the strings do break.

And as her lute doth live or die,
Led by her passion, so must I:
For when of pleasure she doth sing,
My thoughts enjoy a sudden spring,
But if she doth of sorrow speak,
Ev'n from my heart the strings do break.

1601

When Thou Must Home to Shades of Underground

When thou must home to shades of underground,
And there arrived, a new admiréd guest,
The beauteous spirits do engirt thee round,
White Iope,[2] blithe Helen, and the rest,
To hear the stories of thy finished love
From that smooth tongue whose music hell can move,

Then wilt thou speak of banqueting delights,
Of masques and revels which sweet youth did make,

2. Daughter of Aeolus, also known as Cassiopeia.

Of tourneys and great challenges of knights,
And all these triumphs for thy beauty's sake;
When thou hast told these honors done to thee,
Then tell, Oh tell, how thou didst murther me.

1601

Rose-cheeked Laura[3]

Rose-cheeked Laura, come,
Sing thou smoothly with thy beauty's
Silent music, either other
Sweetly gracing.

Lovely forms do flow
From concent[4] divinely framed;
Heav'n is music, and thy beauty's
Birth is heavenly.

These dull notes we sing
Discords need for helps to grace them;
Only beauty purely loving
Knows no discord,

But still moves delight,
Like clear springs renewed by flowing,
Ever perfect, ever in them-
Selves eternal.

1602

What If a Day

What if a day, or a month, or a year
Crown thy delights with a thousand sweet contentings?
Cannot a chance of a night or an hour
Cross thy desires with as many sad tormentings?
Fortune, honor, beauty, youth
Are but blossoms dying;
Wanton pleasure, doting love
Are but shadows flying.
All our joys are but toys,
Idle thoughts deceiving;
None have power of an hour
In their lives' bereaving.

Earth's but a point to the world, and a man
Is but a point to the world's comparéd centure;[5]

3. Written by Campion to illustrate his theories of versification in *Observations in the Art of English Poesy,* this song is a brilliant example of the way in which quantitative verse can be made musically effective in English.

4. Playing or singing together in harmony.

5. Circumference (literally, a belt or girdle).

Shall then the point of a point be so vain
As to triumph in a sely[6] point's adventure?
As is hazard that we have,
There is nothing biding;
Days of pleasure are like streams
Through fair meadows gliding.
Weal and woe, time doth go,
Time is never turning;
Secret fates guide our states,
Both in mirth and mourning.

1606

Never Love Unless You Can

Never love unless you can
Bear with all the faults of man;
Men sometimes will jealous be,
Though but little cause they see,
And hang the head, as discontent,
And speak what straight they will repent.

Men that but one saint adore
Make a show of love to more;
Beauty must be scorned in none,
Though but truly served in one;
For what is courtship but disguise?
True hearts may have dissembling eyes.

Men when their affairs require
Must a while themselves retire,
Sometimes hunt, and sometimes hawk,
And not ever sit and talk.
If these and such like you can bear,
Then like, and love, and never fear.

1617

There Is a Garden in Her Face

There is a garden in her face,
Where roses and white lilies grow,
A heavenly paradise is that place,
Wherein all pleasant fruits do flow.
There cherries grow, which none may buy
Till "Cherry ripe!"[7] themselves do cry.

Those cherries fairly do enclose
Of orient pearl a double row;
Which when her lovely laughter shows,
They look like rosebuds filled with snow.

6. Innocent, insignificant.

7. A familiar cry of London street vendors.

Yet them nor peer nor prince can buy,
Till "Cherry ripe!" themselves do cry.

Her eyes like angels watch them still;
Her brows like bended bows do stand,
Threatening with piercing frowns to kill
All that attempt with eye or hand
Those sacred cherries to come nigh,
Till "Cherry ripe!" themselves do cry.

1617

Think'st Thou to Seduce Me Then[1]

Think'st thou to seduce me then with words that have no meaning?
Parrots so can learn to prate, our speech by pieces gleaning;
Nurses teach their children so about the time of weaning.

Learn to speak first, then to woo; to wooing much pertaineth;
He that courts us, wanting art, soon falters when he feigneth,
Looks asquint on his discourse,[2] and smiles when he complaineth.

Skillful anglers hide their hooks, fit baits for every season;
But with crooked pins fish thou, as babes do that want reason:
Gudgeons[3] only can be caught with such poor tricks of treason.

Ruth[4] forgive me, if I erred from human heart's compassion,
When I laughed sometimes too much to see thy foolish fashion;
But, alas, who less could do that found so good occasion?

1617

Fain Would I Wed

Fain would I wed a fair young man that night and day could please me,
When my mind or body grieved that had the power to ease me.
Maids are full of longing thoughts that breed a bloodless sickness,
And that, oft I hear men say, is only cured by quickness.
Oft I have been wooed and praised, but never could be movéd;
Many for a day or so I have most dearly lovéd,
But this foolish mind of mine straight loathes the thing resolvéd;
If to love be sin in me, that sin is soon absolvéd.
Sure I think I shall at last fly to some holy order;
When I once am settled there, then can I fly no farther.
Yet I would not die a maid, because I had a mother,
As I was by one brought forth, I would bring forth another.

1617

1. In this poem and the one following, Campion assumes the voice of a female speaker; the procedure is rare enough among early poets to call for comment. Both poems are written in the old-fashioned metrical form known as "fourteeners"—verses of fourteen or fifteen syllables, with seven accented beats.
2. Looks away from the lady to check on his script.
3. Small fish.
4. Pity, which misled the girl into seeming too complaisant.

ANONYMOUS LYRICS[1]

Back and Side Go Bare, Go Bare[2]

Back and side go bare, go bare,
  Both foot and hand go cold;
But, belly, God send thee good ale enough,
  Whether it be new or old.

I cannot eat but little meat,
  My stomach is not good;
But sure I think that I can drink
  With him that wears a hood.[3]
Though I go bare, take ye no care,
  I am nothing a-cold;
I stuff my skin so full within
  Of jolly good ale and old.
Back and side go bare, go bare, etc.

I love no roast but a nut-brown toast,[4]
  And a crab laid in the fire;
A little bread shall do me stead,
  Much bread I not desire.
No frost nor snow, no wind, I trow,[5]
  Can hurt me if I would,
I am so wrapped, and throughly lapped
  Of jolly good ale and old.
Back and side go bare, etc.

And Tib my wife, that as her life
  Loveth well good ale to seek,
Full oft drinks she, till ye may see
  The tears run down her cheeks.
Then doth she troll[6] to me the bowl,
  Even as a maltworm should,
And saith, "Sweetheart, I took my part
  Of this jolly good ale and old."
Back and side go bare, etc.

Now let them drink, till they nod and wink,
  Even as good fellows should do;
They shall not miss to have the bliss
  Good ale doth bring men to;
And all poor souls that have scoured bowls
  Or have them lustily trolled,

1. For discussion, see the introduction to the Lyrics section.
2. One of the best of English drinking songs, this is sung in *Gammer Gurton's Needle*, a pioneer play in the development of native English comedy. The play is often ascribed to a "Mr. S., Master of Art," who probably wrote it for performance at Cambridge University.
3. Specifically, with a monk; generally, with anybody.
4. Toast was often dipped in beverages; "crab": crab apple.
5. Think, suppose.
6. Pass.

God save the lives of them and their wives,
  Whether they be young or old.

Back and side go bare, go bare,
  Both foot and hand go cold;
But, belly, God send thee good ale enough,
  Whether it be new or old.

1575

In Praise of a Contented Mind[1]

My mind to me a kingdom is;
  Such perfect joy therein I find
That it excels all other bliss
  That world affords or grows by kind.[2]
Though much I want[3] which most men have,
Yet still my mind forbids to crave.

No princely pomp, no wealthy store,
  No force to win the victory,
No wily wit to salve a sore,
  No shape to feed each gazing eye;
To none of these I yield as thrall.
For why[4] my mind doth serve for all.

I see how plenty suffers oft,
  How hasty climbers soon do fall;
I see that those that are aloft
  Mishap doth threaten most of all;
They get with toil, they keep with fear.
Such cares my mind could never bear.

Content I live, this is my stay;
  I seek no more than may suffice;
I press to bear no haughty sway;
  Look what[5] I lack my mind supplies;

1. One of the most popular of Elizabethan lyrics, *My Mind to Me a Kingdom Is,* is of uncertain authorship. It was long attributed to the courtier-poet and friend of Sidney, Sir Edward Dyer, but a recent study by Steven W. May has shown that it more probably is by Edward de Vere, seventeenth Earl of Oxford, also a courtier, poet, and patron of men of letters. Aristocratic poets did not publish their poems but allowed them to circulate in manuscript. Several manuscripts of this poem survive; May has printed from an Inner Temple manuscript the best text of the poem, which is followed, in modernized form, here. In 1588 the great Elizabethan composer William Byrd set it to music in his *Psalms, Sonnets, and Songs of Sadness and Pity.* There were other musical settings later; the poem was printed as a broadside ballad and remained popular down through the 17th century. It may be regarded as the culmination of the celebration in the 16th century of the ideal of *otium* or the contented mind. It is of course related to the idyllic simplicity of pastoral and to the glorification of the "mean estate" (moderate living) in such poems as Surrey's *My Friend, the Things That Do Attain.*

2. Nature.

3. Lack.

4. Because.

5. Whatever.

Lo, thus I triumph like a king,
Content with that my mind doth bring.

Some have too much, yet still do crave;
I little have, and seek no more.
They are but poor, though much they have,
And I am rich with little store.
They poor, I rich; they beg, I give;
They lack, I leave;[6] they pine, I live.

I laugh not at another's loss;
I grudge not at another's gain;
No worldly waves my mind can toss;
My state at one doth still remain.
I fear no foe, nor fawning friend;
I loathe not life, nor dread my end.

Some weigh their pleasure by their lust,[7]
Their wisdom by their rage of will,[8]
Their treasure is their only trust;
And cloakéd craft their store of skill.
But all the pleasure that I find
Is to maintain a quiet mind.

My wealth is health and perfect ease;
My conscience clear my chief defense;
I neither seek by bribes to please,
Nor by deceit to breed offense.
Thus do I live; thus will I die.
Would all did so as well as I!

1581 1588

Through Amaryllis Dance in Green[9]

Though Amaryllis dance in green
Like fairy queen;
And sing full clear
Corinna can, with smiling cheer.
Yet since their eyes make heart so sore,
Heigh ho, heigh ho, 'chill[1] love no more.

My sheep are lost for want of food,
And I so wood,[2]
That all the day

6. Bequeath, as in a will; "pine": dwindle away.
7. Sensual delight.
8. I.e., wild desires.
9. William Byrd set this anonymous lyric to music in his song book entitled *Psalms, Sonnets, and Songs of Sadness and Piety*. It is a "ballet"—a dance-song of short stanzas with refrain—an appropriate form for this quaint rustic song of the renunciation of love.
1. The rustic dialect form for "I will": (i)ch (w)ill.
2. Frantic.

I sit and watch a herdmaid gay,
Who laughs to see me sigh so sore,
Heigh ho, heigh ho, 'chill love no more.

Her loving looks, her beauty bright
    Is such delight,
    That all in vain
I love to like and lose my gain,
For her that thanks me not therefor,
Heigh ho, heigh ho, 'chill love no more.

Ah wanton eyes, my friendly foes,
    And cause of woes,
    Your sweet desire
Breeds flames of ice and freeze in fire.
Ye scorn to see me weep so sore,
Heigh ho, heigh ho, 'chill love no more.
Love ye who list, I force him not,
    Sith, God it wot,
    The more I wail,
The less my sighs and tears prevail.
What shall I do but say therefore,
Heigh ho, heigh ho, 'chill love no more.

1588

[The Queen's Champion Retires][1]

His golden locks time hath to silver turned;
O time too swift, O swiftness never ceasing!
His youth 'gainst time and age hath ever spurned,
But spurned in vain; youth waneth by increasing:[2]
Beauty, strength, youth are flowers but fading seen;
Duty, faith, love are roots, and ever green.

His helmet now shall make a hive for bees;
And lovers' sonnets turned to holy psalms;
A man-at-arms must now serve on his knees
And feed on prayers, which are age's alms:[3]
But though from court to cottage he depart,
His saint[4] is sure of his unspotted heart.

1. Sir Henry Lee, Master of the Armory, served as the Queen's Champion, undertaking to defend her honor against all comers, at an annual tournament or joust from 1559 to 1590. He then retired, at the age of 57, in favor of the Earl of Cumberland. On that occasion this lyric was sung by Robert Hales, the Queen's lutenist, on behalf of Lee. The authorship, sometimes ascribed to George Peele because the poem was first printed at the end of his *Polyhymnia,* is uncertain. It may be by Lee himself.

2. I.e., paradoxically, as one's growth increases, his youth decreases.

3. I.e., prayers are the only alms a retired, aged man can give.

4. Ladylove.

And when he saddest[5] sits in homely cell,
He'll teach his swains this carol for a song;
"Blessed be the hearts that wish my sovereign well;
Cursed be the souls that think her any wrong."
Goddess,[6] allow this agéd man his right
To be your beadsman[7] now, that was your knight.

1590

The Shepherd's Consort[8]

Hark, jolly shepherds, hark! Hark you yon lusty ringing!
How cheerfully the bells dance, whilst the jolly lads are springing!
Go then, why sit we here delaying,
And all you lads and merry lasses playing?
How gaily Flora leads it,
And how she sweetly treads it!
The woods and groves they ring loudly resounding,
With echo sweet rebounding!

1594

Come Away, Come, Sweet Love![1]

Come away, come, sweet love! The golden morning breaks;
All the earth, all the air of love and pleasure speaks.
Teach thine arms then to embrace,
And sweet rosy lips to kiss,
And mix our souls in mutual bliss;
Eyes were made for beauty's grace,
Viewing, rueing love-long pain,
Procured by beauty's rude disdain.

Come away, come, sweet love! The golden morning wastes,
While the sun from his sphere his fiery arrows casts
Making all the shadows fly,
Playing, staying in the grove
To entertain the stealth of love.
Thither, sweet love, let us hie,
Flying, dying in desire,
Winged with sweet hopes and heavenly fire.

Come away, come, sweet love! Do not in vain adorn
Beauty's grace, that should rise like to the naked morn.

5. "In serious mood," not "melancholy."
6. Queen Elizabeth, often honored as the moon goddess Diana (Cynthia).
7. One who offers prayers in behalf of someone.
8. Song. This poem is set to music in Thomas Morley's *Madrigals to Four Voices* (1594) and appears again as the final poem in the great pastoral anthology, *England's Helicon* (1600).
1. An aubade (or morning song to one's lady), set to music by John Dowland in his *First Book of Songs or Airs*. Dowland (1563–1626) was a famous composer and lutenist.

Lilies on the riverside
And fair Cyprian[2] flowers new-blown
Desire no beauties but their own,
Ornament is nurse of pride;
Pleasure measure love's delight.
Haste then, sweet love, our wishéd flight!

1597

Thule, the Period of Cosmography[3]

Thule, the period of cosmography,
  Doth vaunt of Hecla,[4] whose sulphurious fire
Doth melt the frozen clime and thaw the sky;
  Trinacrian Aetna's[5] flames ascend not higher.
These things seem wondrous, yet more wondrous I,
Whose heart with fear doth freeze, with love doth fry.

The Andalusian[6] merchant, that returns
  Laden with cochineal and China dishes,
Reports in Spain how strangely Fogo[7] burns
  Amidst an ocean full of flying fishes.
These things seem wondrous, yet more wondrous I,
Whose heart with fear doth freeze, with love doth fry.

1600

Madrigal[8]

My love in her attire doth show her wit,
  It doth so well become her;
For every season she hath dressings fit,
  For winter, spring, and summer.
  No beauty she doth miss
  When all her robes are on;
  But beauty's self she is
  When all her robes are gone.

1602

2. Pertaining to Venus, the Cyprian goddess; hence, spring flowers.

3. "Thule" or "Ultima Thule" was a general name for the Arctic; "period of cosmography" suggests the end point of navigation, a full stop. This remarkable poem, which draws upon Elizabethan interest in exploration and discovery to illustrate the conventional pangs of a lover, first appeared in a book of madrigals by Thomas Weelkes.

4. A volcano in Iceland.

5. Mt. Etna, a volcano on the island of Sicily. The poet is quoting Virgil, *Aeneid* III, 554: *e fluctu Trinacria cernitur Aetna* ("out of the waves appears Trinacrian [i.e., Sicilian] Aetna").

6. From southern Spain. "Cochineal": a red dye.

7. One of the Cape Verde Islands, 300

Weep You No More, Sad Fountains[9]

Weep you no more, sad fountains;
What need you flow so fast?
Look how the snowy mountains
Heaven's sun doth gently waste.
But my sun's heavenly eyes
View not your weeping,
That now lie sleeping
Softly, now softly lies
Sleeping.

Sleep is a reconciling,
A rest that peace begets.
Doth not the sun rise smiling
When fair at even he sets?
Rest you then, rest, sad eyes,
Melt not in weeping
While she lies sleeping
Softly, now softly lies
Sleeping.

1603

The Silver Swan[1]

The silver swan, who living had no note,
When death approached, unlocked her silent throat;
Leaning her breast against the reedy shore,
Thus sung her first and last, and sung no more:
"Farewell, all joys; Oh death, come close mine eyes;
More geese than swans now live, more fools than wise."

1612

miles off the coast of Africa, west of Dakar. Francis Drake visited it in 1578; the account in Hakluyt's *Principal Navigations* includes details used here: "The Isle of Fogo * * * called by the Portingals *Ila del fogo*, that is, the burning Island: in the Northside whereof is a consuming fire, the matter is sayd to bee of Sulphure * * * Being departed from these Islands, we drew towards the line [the Equator], where wee were becalmed the space of 3. weekes * * * we had the commoditie of great store [plenty] of fish, as Dolphin, Bonitas, and flying fishes, whereof some fell into our shippes, where hence they could not rise againe for want of moisture, for when their wings are drie, they cannot flie."

8. This sophisticated courtly lyric was printed in an anthology entitled *A Poetical Rhapsody* (1602).

9. This anonymous lyric comes from another song book of John Dowland's (his *Third and Last Book of Songs or Airs*). Like a number of other song-book lyrics which were apparently written only with the object of being set to music, its versification is quantitative.

1. From Orlando Gibbons' *First Set of Madrigals and Motets*. In this short lyric, Gibbons, who was one of the last of the madrigalists, may be mourning the demise of his art.

Prose of the Sixteenth Century

Three mind-shattering experiences struck England in quick succession during the first quarter of the 16th century. They were the humanism of the Italian Renaissance, which for a hundred years had been moving north across Europe, the Reformation of the Roman church set in motion by Martin Luther, and the discovery of the New World by Christopher Columbus. The broad impact of the Renaissance on English culture is richly represented in the poetry and drama of the Elizabethan age from Sidney, Spenser, and Marlowe to Shakespeare and Donne. But English prose, as it existed during most of the 15th and 16th centuries, was not an instrument in which anyone felt very much confidence; it was not, therefore, much exercised in works of "high" literature. Malory is the sole exception, but Malory writes a variety of English prose akin to early epic poetry—incantatory, evocative, indefinite. A modern English prose style was forged only gradually, in the exploration and exposition of urgent practical problems—among the chief of which were the issues posed by the Reformation of the church, and the speculations aroused by the discovery of new continents and unknown civilizations.

When Martin Luther nailed his 95 theses to the cathedral door at Wittenberg on the first of November, 1517, neither he nor anyone else knew what he was doing. Luther thought he was simply opening up some topics for academic discussion. But his ideas were hailed as, and immediately became, the slogans of a mass revolution, which swept Luther and the entire Christian world into deep waters of thought and feeling which had never before been sounded.

For medieval people, the Roman Catholic apostolic church was a universal, infallible, omnicompetent guide to the conduct of life from cradle to grave. They walked hand in hand with it, consulting its spokesmen at regular intervals, corrected by its discipline, comforted by its sacraments, sustained by its promises. The Bible, being in a special language which only clergymen could read, served to guide them, and they guided the laity. Ordinary people did not need to have a highly developed religious conscience (which is rather like a magnetic compass to navigate by) because they had something better—an infallible, divinely inspired, constant companion. Thus arose the vast system of confession, penance, and absolution, of indulgences and pardons and remission of sins, which gave the Catholic hierarchy so much power over their flock. Under the circumstances, it mattered hardly at all that the Bible, the order of the Mass, and most of the theological discussions were in Latin, which lay people could not understand. Understanding was not really part of their function.

But when Luther revolted against the ancient church, was cast out by it, and founded his own church, he did so in the name of a conscience—his own—enlightened by a personal reading of the Scriptures. Two consequences immediately followed. To decide rationally whether Luther, or the Pope, or some third party was right, everyone had to read the Bible for themselves. That is no light undertaking at best, for it is a long, hard book, confusing and apparently contradictory in many passages. Before most of us can even start to read this gigantic compendium of history, prophecy, and moral instruction, it has to be translated from the original Hebrew and Greek into the different vernaculars. That is a job of inconceivable complexity, at which scholars have been laboring from Luther's day to our own. And since membership in any particular church was now essentially voluntary, the whole focus of the religious service shifted, from adoration and lustration (as by the Mass) to persuasion and edification (as by the sermon). Finally, books of controversial and polemical divinity began to be written in the national languages, not only between Catholic and Protestant champions, but by different Protestant groups against one another. By studying these controversies, hearing these sermons, reading the Bible constantly, and purifying their consciences as much as possible, people (it was supposed) could decide for themselves what was the safest way to salvation.

Though the English Reformation under Henry VIII was more gradual, more moderate, and far less violent than it was on the Continent, the same basic changes took place nonetheless. The first reformers in England were among the first translators of the Bible; William Tyndale, boldest and most influential of the group, paid for his pioneer's assurance by being burned at the stake. Yet within three years of his death in 1536, an English Bible was on public sale everywhere in the land; and there can be no doubt that the impulse to read the Bible, and learn about one's eternal destination, was responsible for a tremendous forward leap in the basic literacy of the nation.

When people can read, there will be many interpretations of what is read, particularly if the subject matter is religious. A very large proportion of the books published in the second half of the 16th century were religious in content. Many of them were controversial, and there were, in very general terms, three parties to the controversy. First there was the "old religion," the Catholic church of Rome, which enjoyed a certain amount of toleration until 1570, when a papal bull declared Elizabeth to be not the rightful sovereign of England and absolved her subjects from obedience to her. After that, to publish anything expressing the Roman Catholic view was very dangerous. At the opposite extreme was the position of the protestants who had gone into exile during the reign of the Catholic Mary Tudor and returned when her protestant sister Elizabeth succeeded her. The most vigorous of these was John Foxe, whose *Acts and Monuments* (commonly called "The Book of Martyrs") fomented hatred for the church of Rome and all its actions under Queen Mary. The center position was that of the Church of England, which kept the bishops and other prelates of the Roman church, and some of its ceremonies, but denied the authority of the Pope. This position was attacked in a series of brilliant satiric underground pamphlets attributed to Martin Marprelate. The style of these was popular and colloquial, and from the point of view of the government, this made them all the more dangerous. The Elizabethan police sought out the secret press on which the tracts were printed (it was carried around the country on the back of a haywagon), and the men responsible disappeared into prison, where, conveniently, while waiting for trial, several of them died.

It came as the climax of an increasingly bitter controversy within the English church between puritan Presbyterians and conservative Episcopalians—a controversy which had already lasted almost fifty years—when Richard Hooker brought forth in 1594 the first part of his monumental treatise, *Of the Laws of Ecclesiastical Polity.* It is a forbidding title and a rigorous book; but it can still be read for pleasure, and it fully deserves its reputation as the first finished monument of modern English prose. *Suaviter in modo, fortiter in re* is the appropriate Latin tag: "softly as far as words go, but no compromise on principles." Gently, slowly, irresistibly, with manifold expressions of Christian charity, and with remorseless logic, Hooker crushes his antagonists like a boa constrictor enveloping a rabbit. His premises are laid so widely and deeply that one can hardly disagree with them and retain any pretense to rationality; then gradually he begins to tighten his conclusions. If the Puritan revolution, based on conscience, could have been stopped by careful logic or judicious common sense, Hooker's book would doubtless have stopped it. But conscience is a prickly, uncontrollable force, and the Puritans would not be argued out of their conscientious objections to the discipline of the English church.

The discovery of America was accomplished by an Italian in the service of the Spanish crown; Spaniards explored and conquered the great kingdoms of Mexico and Peru, while Portuguese navigators first turned the Cape of Good Hope on their way to India, and the tip of South America on their way around the world. The English were thus relative latecomers to the work of exploring and exploiting the New World. Sir Walter Ralegh attempted the first wretched and unsuccessful colony in Virginia fully a hundred years after Pope Alexander VI had categorically divided the New World between Spain and Portugal. By that time there were well-established Portuguese colonies up and down the coast of South America and India; and the Spanish were entrenched not only in Mexico and the American southwest, but in Florida and California. But though the English were slow in starting to compete with their Latin rivals, the voyages of discovery struck at English imaginations almost as soon as they were known. Gold and silver were the loot that stirred practical men to action: but the idea of a separate, remote civilization based on a new and different dispensation from God also deeply appealing. The language in which the conditions of the new world were described would have to be clear and straightforward, what Shakespeare called "a round, unvarnished tale."

Plain, practical prose, often on technical or scientific topics, and cast in the common, vernacular speech, flourished in England during the latter years of Elizabeth; it was a development largely unlike anything on the Continent. On the whole, the universities, which tended to be conservative, had little part on this activity. But the lectures established by Sir Thomas Gresham in the City of London were free for all to attend, and they were mostly in English. They provided the foundations for a practical vernacular technology, a pragmatic mingling of learned theory with homely practice, which could not fail to be profoundly influential, both on the material culture of England and on the language English people spoke. In 1600 Sir William Gilbert published in Latin his great treatise on magnetism, as Sir William Harvey in 1628 announced the circulation of the blood in the learned language. But Harvey's theory had been set forth in English lectures twelve years before he published to the learned world at large; and Gilbert worked closely with the navigators and mariners of English vessels in developing both his learned theories and some practical applications of them.

Meanwhile, scholars, clergymen, and courtiers were experimenting with literary ways to make English more sonorous and rhetorically more complex; and not all these experiments were without influence. During the last half of the century, English vocabulary was enormously enriched by a mass of words adapted from Greek and Latin originals; some evidently seemed artificial or pretentious, and were dropped, but many others were permanently adopted into the language. Whether Cicero or Seneca or some other classical author was the best model for an English prose stylist was much debated; the point was never conclusively settled, but the parties sometimes emerged from their dispute with a widened range of stylistic possibilities before them. The short-lived fad of "Euphuism"—an experiment in exaggerated, aphoristic, sententious prose begun by John Lyly in 1579 and concluded by the same author in 1580, was so out of fashion that it was parodied in 1598 by Shakespeare in 1 *Henry IV* II.iv.347–63.

The English language had been vindicated as a medium for God's word, as a vehicle for the sufferings of Protestant martyrs, as a suitable language for the instruction of an ambitious courtier, for the description of a newly explored country, or for the defense of poetry against its detractors. It could carry to every literate person the lives of the eminent Greeks and Romans and the chronicles of the English kings. It could make available to those who know no continental language the literary treasures of Italy and France and Spain, as well as those of what Ben Jonson called "insolent Greece" and "haughty Rome." It was a language still expanding rapidly, in vocabulary, with borrowings from other languages and new word-coinages, in syntax and in variety of styles. In fact Richard Mulcaster, Spenser's schoolmaster, saw in the expanding vocabulary of England a parallel to her growth in exploration and colonizing—her emergence as a world power. But the language remained, like the people who spoke and wrote it, close to the soil. Richard Carew, in his *Epistle on the Excellency of the English Tongue,* written in the last decade of the 16th century, commented on its variety: "Moreover, the copiousness of our language appeareth on the diversity of our dialects, for we have court, we have country English, we have northern and southern, gross and ordinary, which differ from each other, not only in the terminations, but also in many words, terms, and phrases, and express the same things in divers sorts, yet all right English alike; neither can any tongue (as I am persuaded) deliver a matter with more variety than ours, both plainly and by proverbs and metaphors."

TRANSLATING THE BIBLE (Isaiah liii.3–6)

The English Reformation made it imperative to read the Bible for oneself; hence fewer tasks were more important than rendering the Bible from its Greek and Hebrew originals into the vernacular. In England William Tyndale began his translation in 1523; he had to do it surreptitiously and outside the country; he finally suffered martyrdom for his efforts. In 1530 a royal proclamation condemned Tyndale's translation and all other versions in the vulgar tongue. Then in 1535 Miles Coverdale published, in Zürich, the first complete Bible in English. By this time the official attitude was changing, and in 1540 the so-called Great Bible was published, the first English Bible issued with official sanction—evidence of the extent of the breach between the English church and the Church of Rome.

The Geneva Bible (1560) was the work of Protestant refugees who fled to the Continent in the reign of the Catholic Queen Mary. It was the first Bible to divide the chapters into verses in the modern manner, and the first English Bible to be printed in Roman type rather than the old black letter or Gothic type. It was handy in size, and in many instances more accurate than its predecessors, but the marginal commentary was strongly biased in the Protestant direction. The Bishops' Bible (1568) was an attempt on the part of the Elizabethan church to counter the extreme Protestantism of the Geneva Bible. The bishops who sponsored it could indeed insist that their Bible be the official one used in churches, but the people continued to read the Geneva Bible at home, and its influence remained very great throughout the century. A Catholic translation into English, based upon the Latin Vulgate, was a belated concession to the demand for the scriptures in the vernacular. It was published by English refugees abroad, the New Testament at Rheims in 1582 and the Old Testament at Douai in 1609–10. Though it was outside the main English tradition, it was not without its influence upon the King James Version which was to follow.

King James did not like the popular Geneva Bible (some of its commentary was not highly favorable to kings). As a part of the religious settlement which took place early in his reign, he authorized a group of translators to make a new version of the Bible in English. The resulting work has been called "the noblest monument of English prose"; it owes more to Tyndale than to any other predecessor, but it has extraordinary beauties of its own. We have chosen to reprint versions of a passage from Isaiah that shows the King James Version at its most felicitous. Our last example comes from the New English Bible of 1970.

Translating the Bible (Isaiah liii.3–6)

From *The Great Bible*

He is despised and abhorred of men. He is such a man as is afull of sorrow and as hath good experience of infirmities. We have reckoned him so vile that we hid our faces from him. Yea, he was despised and therefore we regarded him not.

Howbeit he only hath taken on him our infirmities and borne our

pains. Yet we did judge him, as though he were plagued and cast down of God and punished.
Whereas he (notwithstanding) was wounded for our offenses and smitten for our wickedness. For the chastisement of our peace was laid upon him and with his stripes we are healed.
As for us, we have gone all astray, like sheep; every one hath turned his own way. But the Lord hath heaped together upon him the iniquity of us all.

1539–40

From *The Coverdale Bible*

He shall be the most simple and despised of all which yet hath good experience of sorrows and infirmities. We shall reckon him so simple and so vile that we shall hide our faces from him.
Howbeit of a truth he only taketh away our infirmity and beareth our pain, yet we shall judge him as though he were plagued and cast down of God.
Whereas he, notwithstanding, shall be wounded for our offenses and smitten for our wickedness. For the pain of our punishment shall be laid upon him and with his stripes shall we be healed.
As for us we go all astray, like sheep. Every one turneth his own way. But through him the Lord pardoneth all our sins.

1550

From *The Geneva Bible*

He is despised and rejected of men. He is a man full of sorrows and hath experience of infirmities. We hid as it were our faces from him. He was despised and we esteemed him not.
Surely he hath borne our infirmities and carried our sorrows; yet we did judge him as plagued, and smitten of God, and humbled.
But he was wounded for our transgressions; he was broken for our iniquities; the chastisement of our peace was upon him, and with his stripes we are healed.
All we like sheep have gone astray. We have turned every one to his own way, and the Lord hath laid upon him the iniquity of us all.

1560

From *The King James Bible*

He is despised and rejected of men; a man of sorrows, and acquainted with grief. And we hid as it were our faces from him. He was despised, and we esteemed him not.
Surely he hath borne our griefs and carried our sorrows; yet we did esteem him stricken, smitten of God, and afflicted.
But he was wounded for our transgressions; he was bruised for our iniquities. The chastisement of our peace was upon him, and with his stripes we are healed.
All we like sheep have gone astray; we have turned every one to his own way; and the Lord hath laid on him the iniquity of us all.

1611

From *The New English Bible*

He was despised, he shrank from the sight of men,
  tormented and humbled by suffering;
  we despised him, we held him of no account,
  a thing from which men turn away their eyes.

Yet on himself he bore our sufferings,
  our torments he endured,
  while we counted him smitten by God,
  struck down by disease and misery;

but he was pierced for our transgressions,
  tortured for our iniquities;
  the chastisement he bore is health for us
  and by his scourging we are healed.

We had all strayed like sheep,
  each of us had gone his own way;
  but the Lord laid upon him
  the guilt of us all.

1970

JOHN FOXE
(1516–1587)

John Foxe's career at Oxford University, where he had become a fellow of Magdalen College, was interrupted when his Puritan convictions led him to protest too energetically against some of the college rules and practices. For some years he then served as a tutor to the children of various great houses; but when Mary became queen in 1553, and the persecutions of Protestants began, he fled to the Continent. His great book was already under way, though it was in Latin and had not yet really focused on its main subject. In its first version (Strasbourg, 1554) it was a history of the persecutions suffered by the early Protestants, particularly Wycliffe and John Hus. But the book grew and grew under his hands, as he received from England accounts of the hideous tortures and persecutions being inflicted on the Protestants there. When Elizabeth came to the throne in 1558, Foxe returned at once to England, and there he translated his previous Latin volume, adding to it hundreds of stories (many true, some doubtful, some ridiculous) all tending to show the horrible malice of Catholic persecutors and the saintly sufferings of Protestant martyrs. The English edition was published in 1563; its title was *Acts and Monuments of these latter and perilous days, touching matters of the church, wherein are comprehended and described the great persecution and horrible troubles that have been wrought and practices by the Romish prelates from the year of Our Lord a thousand to the time now present*. It was immediately and enormously popular. Foxe saw life melodramatically, in terms of black and white; and he tended to believe without questioning it too closely any good story that confirmed his prejudices. As a result his book soon grew to enormous dimensions—in its final version, to over 6,000 folio pages, containing 4 million words. Apart from fanning the flames of anti-Catholic feeling, Foxe had an immense influence upon English nationalism; his stories tended to show that England was the land of the chosen people, and that, in passing through the fiery trials of Marian persecution, the Protestant martyrs were simply preparing the way for a glorious destiny in which England would lead the way toward the kingdom of God on earth. Foxe's second edition, in 1570, was so impressive that a copy of it was required to be placed, with the Bible, in every English church.

From Acts and Monuments

OF THESE LATTER AND PERILOUS DAYS, TOUCHING MATTERS OF THE CHURCH, WHEREIN ARE COMPREHENDED AND DESCRIBED THE GREAT PERSECUTION AND HORRIBLE TROUBLES THAT HAVE BEEN WROUGHT AND PRACTICES BY THE ROMISH PRELATES FROM THE YEAR OF OUR LORD A THOUSAND TO THE TIME NOW PRESENT

The Behavior of Dr. Ridley and Master Latimer,[1] at the Time of Their Death, which was the Sixteenth of October, an. 1555

Upon the north side of the town, in the ditch over against Balliol College, the place of execution was appointed; and for fear of any tumult that might arise, to let the burning of them, the Lord Williams was commanded by the queen's letters (and the householders of the city) to be there assistant, sufficiently appointed. And when everything was in a readiness, the prisoners were brought forth by the mayor and the bailiffs.

Master Ridley had a fair black gown furred, and faced with foins,[2] such as he was wont to wear being bishop, and a tippet of velvet furred likewise about his neck, a velvet nightcap upon his head, and a corner cap upon the same, going in a pair of slippers to the stake, and going between the mayor and an alderman, etc. After him came Master Latimer in a poor Bristol frieze frock all worn, with his buttoned cap, and a kerchief on his head all ready to the fire, a new long shroud hanging over his hose down to the feet; which at the first sight stirred men's hearts to rue upon them, beholding on the one side the honor they sometime had, and on the other, the calamity whereunto they were fallen.

Master Doctor Ridley, as he passed towards Bocardo,[3] looking up where Master Cranmer did lie, hoping belike to have seen him at the glass window and to have spoken unto him. But then Master Cranmer was busy with Friar Soto and his fellows, disputing

1. Nicholas Ridley (1500?–55) Bishop of London; Hugh Latimer (1492?–1555) former Bishop of Worcester, preacher to Edward VI.
2. Fur trimmings.
3. The prison in Oxford.

together, so that he could not see him through that occasion. Then Master Ridley, looking back, espied Master Latimer coming after, unto whom he said, "Oh, be ye there?" "Yea," said Master Latimer, "have after as fast as I can follow." So he following a pretty way off, at length they came both to the stake, one after the other, where first Dr. Ridley entering the place, marvelous earnestly holding up both his hands, looked towards heaven. Then shortly after espying Master Latimer, with a wondrous cheerful look, ran to him, embraced, and kissed him; and, as they that stood near reported, comforted him saying, "Be of good heart, brother, for God will either assuage the fury of the flame, or else strengthen us to abide it." With that went he to the stake, kneeled down by it, kissed it, and most effectuously[4] prayed, and behind him Master Latimer kneeled, as earnestly calling upon God as he. After they arose, the one talked with the other a little while, till they which were appointed to see the execution removed themselves out of the sun. What they said I can learn of no man.

Then Dr. Smith,[5] of whose recantation in King Edward's time ye heard before, began his sermon to them upon this text of St. Paul in the 13 chap. of the first epistle to the Corinthians: "*Si corpus meum tradam igni, charitatem autem non habeam, nihil inde utilitatis capio,*" that is, "If I yield my body to the fire to be burned and have not charity, I shall gain nothing thereby." Wherein he alleged that the goodness of the cause, and not the order of death, maketh the holiness of the person; which he confirmed by the examples of Judas, and of a woman in Oxford that of late hanged herself, for that they, and such like as he recited, might then be adjudged righteous, which desperately sundered their lives from their bodies, as he feared that those men that stood before him would do. But he cried still to the people to beware of them, for they were heretics, and died out of the church. And on the other side, he declared their diversities in opinions, as Lutherans, Oecolampadians, Zwinglians,[6] of which sect they were, he said, and that was the worst; but the old church of Christ and the Catholic faith believed far otherwise. At which place they lifted up both their hands and eyes to heaven, as it were calling God to witness of the truth; the which countenance they made in many other places of his sermon, whereas they thought he spake amiss. He ended with a very short exhortation to them to recant, and come home again to the church, and save their lives and souls, which else were condemned. His sermon was scant in all a quarter of an hour.

Dr. Ridley said to Master Latimer, "Will you begin to answer

4. With great effect.
5. Richard Smith, D.D. (1500–63); he had recanted in 1547 but later repudiated his recantation.
6. Followers, respectively, of Martin Luther (1483–1546), founder of the reformation in Germany; Johann Oecolampadius (1482–1531), organizer of Protestantism at Basle; Ulrich Zwingli (1484–1531), organizer of Protestantism in Zürich.

the sermon, or shall I?" Master Latimer said: "Begin you first, I pray you." "I will," said Master Ridley.

Then the wicked sermon being ended, Dr. Ridley and Master Latimer kneeled down upon their knees towards my Lord Williams of Tame, the vice-chancellor of Oxford, and divers other commissioners appointed for that purpose, which sat upon a form thereby. Unto whom Master Ridley said: "I beseech you, my lord, even for Christ's sake, that I may speak but two or three words." And whilst my lord bent his head to the mayor and vice-chancellor, to know (as it appeared) whether he might give him leave to speak, the bailiffs and Dr. Marshall, vice-chancellor, ran hastily unto him, and with their hands stopped his mouth, and said: "Master Ridley, if you will revoke your erroneous opinions, and recant the same, you shall not only have liberty so to do, but also the benefit of a subject; that is, have your life." "Not otherwise?" said Master Ridley. "No," quoth Dr. Marshall. "Therefore if you will not so do, then there is no remedy but you must suffer for your deserts." "Well," quoth Master Ridley, "so long as the breath is in my body, I will never deny my Lord Christ, and his known truth; God's will be done in me!" And with that he rose up and said with a loud voice: "Well then, I commit our cause to almighty God, which shall indifferently judge all." To whose saying, Master Latimer added his old posy,[7] "Well! There is nothing hid but it shall be opened." And he said he could answer Smith well enough, if he might be suffered.

Incontinently[8] they were commanded to make them ready, which they with all meekness obeyed. Master Ridley took his gown and his tippet,[9] and gave it to his brother-in-law Master Shipside, who all his time of imprisonment, although he might not be suffered to come to him, lay there at his own charges to provide him necessaries, which from time to time he sent him by the sergeant that kept him. Some other of his apparel that was little worth, he gave away; other the bailiffs took. He gave away besides divers other small things to gentlemen standing by, and divers of them pitifully weeping, as to Sir Henry Lea he gave a new groat; and to divers of my Lord Williams' gentlemen some napkins, some nutmegs, and races[1] of ginger; his dial,[2] and such other things as he had about him, to everyone that stood next him. Some plucked the points of his hose. Happy was he that might get any rag of him. Master Latimer gave nothing, but very quickly suffered his keeper to pull off his hose and his other array, which to look unto was very simple; and being stripped into his shroud, he seemed as comely a person to them that were present as one should lightly see; and whereas in his clothes he

7. Motto.
8. Immediately.
9. "This was no Popish tippet, but made only to keep his neck warm" [Foxe's note].
1. Roots.
2. Watch.

appeared a withered and crooked silly[3] old man, he now stood bolt upright, as comely a father as one might lightly behold.

Then Master Ridley, standing as yet in his truss,[4] said to his brother: "It were best for me to go in my truss still." "No," quoth his brother, "it will put you to more pain; and the truss will do a poor man good." Whereunto Master Ridley said: "Be it, in the name of God"; and so unlaced himself. Then being in his shirt, he stood upon the foresaid stone, and held up his hand and said: "Oh heavenly Father, I give unto thee most hearty thanks, for that thou hast called me to be a professor of[5] thee, even unto death. I beseech thee, Lord God, take mercy upon this realm of England, and deliver the same from all her enemies."

Then the smith took a chain of iron, and brought the same about both Dr. Ridley's and Master Latimer's middles; and as he was knocking in a staple, Dr. Ridley took the chain in his hand, and shaked the same, for it did gird in his belly, and looking aside to the smith, said: "Good fellow, knock it in hard, for the flesh will have his course." Then his brother did bring him gunpowder in a bag, and would have tied the same about his neck. Master Ridley asked what it was. His brother said, "Gunpowder." "Then," said he, "I take it to be sent of God; therefore I will receive it as sent of him. And have you any," said he, "for my brother?" meaning Master Latimer. "Yea, sir, that I have," quoth his brother. "Then give it unto him," said he, "betime; lest ye come too late." So his brother went, and carried of the same gunpowder unto Master Latimer.

In the meantime Dr. Ridley spake unto my Lord Williams, and said: "My lord, I must be a suitor unto your lordship in the behalf of divers poor men, and specially in the cause of my poor sister; I have made a supplication to the Queen's Majesty in their behalfs. I beseech your lordship for Christ's sake, to be a mean to her Grace for them. My brother here hath the supplication, and will resort to your lordship to certify you hereof. There is nothing in all the world that troubleth my conscience, I praise God, this only excepted. Whiles I was in the see of London divers poor men took leases of me, and agreed with me for the same. Now I hear say the bishop[6] that now occupieth the same room will not allow my grants unto them made, but contrary unto all law and conscience hath taken from them their livings, and will not suffer them to enjoy the same. I beseech you, my lord, be a mean for them; you shall do a good deed, and God will reward you."

Then they brought a faggot, kindled with fire, and laid the same

3. Innocent, harmless.
4. A close-fitting body garment or jacket.
5. Believer in, advocate of.
6. Edmund Bonner (ca. 1500–69); he had preceded Ridley as Bishop of London during the reign of Edward VI, and became Bishop again on Mary's accession.

down at Dr. Ridley's feet. To whom Master Latimer spake in this manner: "Be of good comfort, Master Ridley, and play the man. We shall this day light such a candle, by God's grace, in England, as I trust shall never be put out."

And so the fire being given unto them, when Dr. Ridley saw the fire flaming up toward him, he cried with a wonderful loud voice: "*In manus tuas, Domine, commendo spiritum meum; Domine, recipe, spiritum meum.*" And after, repeated this latter part often in English, "Lord, Lord, receive my spirit"; Master Latimer crying as vehemently on the other side, "Oh Father of heaven, receive my soul!" who received the flame as it were embracing of it. After, as he had stroked his face with his hands, and as it were bathed them a little in the fire, he soon died (as it appeared) with very little pain or none. And thus much concerning the end of this old and blessed servant of God, Master Latimer, for whose laborious travails, fruitful life, and constant death the whole realm hath cause to give great thanks to almighty God.

But Master Ridley, by reason of the evil making of the fire unto him, because the wooden faggots were laid about the gosse[7] and over-high built, the fire burned first beneath, being kept down by the wood; which when he felt, he desired them for Christ's sake to let the fire come unto him. Which when his brother-in-law heard, but not well understood, intending to rid him out of his pain (for the which cause he gave attendance), as one in such sorrow not well advised what he did, heaped faggots upon him, so that he clean covered him, which made the fire more vehement beneath, that it burned clean all his nether parts, before it once touched the upper; that that made him leap up and down under the faggots, and often desire them to let the fire come unto him, saying, "I cannot burn." Which indeed appeared well; for, after his legs were consumed by reason of his struggling through the pain (whereof he had no release, but only his contentation[8] in God), he showed that side toward us clean, shirt and all untouched with flame. Yet in all this torment he forgat not to call upon God still, having in his mouth, "Lord have mercy upon me," intermingling this cry, "Let the fire come unto me, I cannot burn." In which pains he labored till one of the standers-by with his bill[9] pulled off the faggots above, and where he saw the fire flame up, he wrested himself unto that side. And when the flame touched the gunpowder, he was seen stir no more, but burned on the other side, falling down at Master Latimer's feet. Which some said happened by reason that the chain loosed; other said that he fell over the chain by reason of the poise[1] of his body and the weakness of the nether limbs.

Some said that before he was like to fall from the stake, he

7. Gorse, used as kindling.
8. Satisfaction.
9. A long staff terminating in a hook-shaped blade.
1. Weight.

desired them to hold him to it with their bills. Howsoever it was, surely it moved hundreds to tears, in beholding the horrible sight; for I think there was none that had not clean exiled all humanity and mercy which would not have lamented to behold the fury of the fire so to rage upon their bodies. Signs there were of sorrow on every side. Some took it grievously to see their deaths, whose lives they held full dear; some pitied their persons, that thought their souls had no need thereof. His brother moved many men, seeing his miserable case, seeing (I say) him compelled to such infelicity, that he thought then to do him best service when he hastened his end. Some cried out of the luck, to see his endeavor (who most dearly loved him, and sought his release) turn to his greater vexation and increase of pain. But whoso considered their preferments in time past, the places of honor that they sometime occupied in this commonwealth, the favor they were in with their princes, and the opinion of learning they had, could not choose but sorrow with tears to see so great dignity, honor, and estimation, so necessary members sometime accounted, so many godly virtues, the study of so many years, such excellent learning, to be put into the fire and consumed in one moment. Well! dead they are, and the reward of this world they have already. What reward remaineth for them in heaven, the day of the Lord's glory, when he cometh with his saints, shall shortly, I trust, declare.

1563

SIR THOMAS HOBY
(1530–1566)

One of the great and influential books of the Renaissance was *Il Cortegiano* ("The Courtier") published in Italian by Count Baldasarre Castiglione (1478–1529) in 1528 and soon translated into all the other European languages. The English translation, by the humanist and diplomat Sir Thomas Hoby, was first published in 1561, but it was written earlier, probably during the reign of Queen Mary (1553–58) when Hoby lived abroad as a Protestant exile. The style of the translation makes it an important landmark in English prose; Hoby, like his master Sir John Cheke, prefers words from the native Anglo-Saxon element of the language, rather than borrowings from French or Italian.

The book attempts to present, in the form of dialogues between actual persons living at the court of the Duke of Urbino in the years 1504–8, a full description of the qualities and characteristics of the ideal courtier. Spenser's friend Gabriel Harvey, in his copy of Hoby's translation, summarized the contents of this great "courtesy book" as follows: "Above all things it importeth a courtier to be graceful and lovely in countenance and behavior; fine and discreet in discourse and entertainment; skillful and expert in letters and arms; active and gallant in every courtly exercise;

nimble and speedy of body and mind; resolute, industrious and valorous in action; as profound and invincible in action as is possible; and withal ever generously bold, wittily pleasant, and full of life in his sayings and doings." Shakespeare's Hamlet was such an ideal courtier, as Ophelia testifies when she attributes to him

> The courtier's, soldier's, scholar's eye, tongue, sword;
> The expectancy and rose of the fair state,
> The glass of fashion and the mold of form. (III.i.151–53)

The Elizabethans thought of Sir Philip Sidney as the example of an ideal courtier in real life.

Probably the most famous passage in *The Courtier* is Peter Bembo's discourse on love in Book IV. Its theme is essentially Platonic—that is, that love is not the mere gratification of the senses, but is the yearning of the soul after beauty. Furthermore, the beautiful is always ultimately identical with the good. Love properly understood is therefore a kind of ladder by which the soul progresses from lower to higher things. As he pursues his theme Bembo becomes more enraptured and ends with a prayer to Love as a god; although the dialogue form permits criticism of Bembo's doctrine, the eloquence of his speech carries the day.

From The Courtier

From *Book I*

[GRACE]

"Bound am I not," quoth the Count, "to teach you to have a good grace,[1] nor anything else, saving only to show you what a perfect Courtier ought to be. Neither will I take upon me to teach you this perfection, since a while ago I said that the Courtier ought to have the feat of wrestling and vaulting, and such other things, the which how I should be able to teach them, not having learned them myself? I am sure ye know it all. It sufficeth that as a good soldier can speak his mind to an armorer, of what fashion, of what temper and goodness he will have his harness,[2] and for all that cannot teach him to make it, nor to hammer or temper it, so perhaps I am able to tell you what a perfect Courtier ought to be, but not to teach you how ye should do to be one. Notwithstanding, to fulfill your request in what I am able, although it be (in manner) in a proverb that *Grace is not to be learned,* I say unto you, whoso mindeth to be gracious or to have a good grace in the exercises of the body (presupposing first that he be not of nature unapt) ought to begin betimes,[3] and to learn his principles of cunning men. The which thing

1. "Grace" had a wide range of meanings for Elizabethans, and many puns were made on the word. Most simply, it refers to a natural, easy manner, especially in doing something that is difficult. The Italian word is *sprezzatura.* The "Count" is Count Lodovico Canossa ("Count Lewis"), later Bishop of Bayeux.
2. Armor.
3. Early.

how necessary a matter Philip, king of Macedonia, thought it, a man may gather in that his will was that Aristotle, so famous a philosopher, and perhaps the greatest that ever hath been in the world, should be the man that should instruct Alexander, his son, in the first principles of letters. And of men whom we know nowadays, mark how well and with what a good grace Sir Galeazzo Sanseverino, master of the horse to the French king, doth all exercises of the body; and that because, beside the natural disposition of person that is in him, he hath applied all his study to learn of cunning men, and to have continually excellent men about him, and, of every one, to choose the best of that they have skill in. For as in wrestling, in vaulting, and in learning to handle sundry kind of weapons he hath taken for his guide our Master Peter Mount, who (as you know) is the true and only master of all artificial force and sleight, so in riding, in jousting, and in every other feat, he hath always had before his eyes the most perfectest that hath been known to be in those professions.

"He therefore that will be a good scholar, beside the practicing of good things, must evermore set all his diligence to be like his master, and, if it were possible, change himself into him. And when he hath had some entry, it profiteth him much to behold sundry men of that profession; and, governing himself with that good judgment that must always be his guide, go about to pick out, sometime of one and sometime of another, sundry matters. And even as the bee in the green meadows flieth always about the grass choosing out flowers, so shall our Courtier steal this grace from them that to his seeming[4] have it, and from each one that parcel that shall be most worthy praise. And not do as a friend of ours whom you all know, that thought he resembled much King Ferdinand the younger, of Aragon, and regarded not to resemble him in any other point but in the often lifting up his head, wrying[5] therewithal a part of his mouth, the which custom the king had gotten by infirmity. And many such there are that think they do much, so they resemble a great man in somewhat and take many times the thing in him that worst becometh him.

"But I, imagining with myself often times how this grace cometh, leaving apart such as have it from above, find one rule that is most general which in this part (methink) taketh place in all things belonging to a man in word or deed above all other. And that is to eschew as much as a man may, and as a sharp and dangerous rock, *Affectation* or curiosity,[6] and, to speak a new word, to use in everything a certain *Recklessness*,[7] to cover art withal, and seem what-

4. Opinion.
5. Twisting awry.
6. Over-fastidiousness.
7. Hoby translates badly here. The Italian word is *sprezzatura,* which means a natural, easy grace. "Art": artifice.

soever he doth and sayeth to do it without pain, and, as it were, not minding it. And of this do I believe grace is much derived, for in rare matters and well brought to pass every man knoweth the hardness of them, so that a readiness therein maketh great wonder. And contrariwise to use force, and, as they say, to hale by the hair, giveth a great disgrace and maketh everything, how great soever it be, to be little esteemed. Therefore that may be said to be a very art that appeareth not to be art; neither ought a man to put more diligence in anything than in covering it, for in case it be open, it loseth credit clean, and maketh a man little set by. And I remember that I have read in my days that there were some most excellent orators which among other their cares enforced themselves to make every man believe that they had no sight[8] in letters, and dissembling their cunning, made semblant their orations to be made very simply, and rather as nature and truth made them, than study and art, the which if it had been openly known would have put a doubt in the people's mind, for fear lest he beguiled them. You may see then how to show art and such bent study taketh away the grace of everything."

From *Book IV*

[LOVE]

Then the Lord Gaspar:[9] "I remember," quoth he, "that these lords yesternight, reasoning of the Courtier's qualities, did allow him to be a lover; and in making rehearsal[1] of as much as hitherto hath been spoken, a man may pick out a conclusion that the Courtier which with his worthiness and credit must incline his prince to virtue must in manner of necessity be aged, for knowledge cometh very seldom time before years, and specially in matters that be learned with experience. I cannot see, when he is well drawn[2] in years, how it will stand well with him to be a lover, considering, as it hath been said the other night, love frameth not with old men, and the tricks that in young men be gallantness, courtesy, and preciseness[3] so acceptable to women, in them are mere follies and fondness[4] to be laughed at, and purchase him that useth them hatred of women and mocks of others. Therefore, in case this your Aristotle, an old Courtier, were a lover and practiced the feats that young lovers do, as some that we have seen in our days, I fear me he would forget to teach his prince; and peradventure boys would mock him behind his back, and women would have none other delight in him but to make him a jesting-stock."

8. Knowledge, insight.
9. Gasparo Pallavicino, whose attitude in the dialogue is usually that of the woman-hater.
1. Reviewing.
2. Advanced.
3. Excessive neatness.
4. Foolishness.

Then said the Lord Octavian:[5] "Since all the other qualities appointed to the Courtier are meet for him, although he be old, methink we should not then bar him from this happiness to love."

"Nay rather," quoth the Lord Gaspar, "to take this love from him is a perfection over and above, and a making him to live happily out of misery and wretchedness."

M. Peter Bembo[6] said: "Remember you not, my Lord Gaspar, that the Lord Octavian declared the other night in his device of pastimes, although he be not skillful in love, to know yet that there be some lovers which reckon the disdains, the angers, the debates and torments which they receive of their ladies, sweet? Whereupon he required to be taught the cause of this sweetness. Therefore, in case our Courtier, though he be old, were kindled with those loves that be sweet without any bitter smack, he should feel no misery nor wretchedness at all. And being wise, as we set case[7] he is, he should not be deceived in thinking to be meet for him whatsoever were meet for young men, but in loving should perhaps love after a sort that might not only not bring him in slander, but to much praise and great happiness, without any loathsomeness at all, the which very seldom or in manner never happeneth to young men; and so should he neither lay aside the teaching of his prince, nor yet commit anything that should deserve the mocking of boys."

Then spake the Duchess:[8] "I am glad, M. Peter, that you have not been much troubled in our reasonings this night, for now we may be the bolder to give you in charge to speak, and to teach the Courtier this so happy a love, which bringeth with it neither slander nor any inconvenience; for perhaps it shall be one of the necessariest and profitablest qualities that hitherto hath been given him; therefore speak, of good fellowship, as much as you know therein."

M. Peter laughed and said: "I would be loath, madam, where I say it is lawful for old men to love, it should be an occasion for these ladies to think me old; therefore hardily[9] give ye this enterprise to another."

The Duchess answered: "You ought not to refuse to be counted old in knowledge, though ye be young in years. Therefore say on, and excuse yourself no more."

M. Peter said: "Surely, madam, if I must entreat upon this matter, I must first go ask counsel of my hermit[1] Lavinello."

The Lady Emilia[2] said then half in anger: "There is never a one

5. Ottaviano Fregoso, a soldier, later Doge of Genoa.
6. Poet. Platonist, grammarian, and historian; later a cardinal. He is here the philosopher of love. "M.": Master.
7. Assume.
8. Elizabetta Gonzaga, wife of the Duke of Urbino.
9. By all means.
1. I.e., spiritual advisor; cf. Friar Laurence in *Romeo and Juliet*.
2. Lady Emilia Pio, friend and confidante of the Duchess.

in all the company so disobedient as you be, M. Peter, therefore should the Duchess do well to chastise you somewhat for it."

M. Peter said smiling: "For love of God, madam, be not angry with me, for I will say whatever you will have me."

"Go to,[3] say on then," answered the Lady Emilia.

Then M. Peter after a while's silence, somewhat settling himself as though he should entreat upon a weighty matter, said thus: "My Lords, to show that old men may love not only without slander, but otherwhile[4] more happily than young men, I must be enforced to make a little discourse to declare what love is, and wherein consisteth the happiness that lovers may have. Therefore I beseech you give the hearing with heedfulness, for I hope to make you understand that it were not unfitting for any man here to be a lover, in case he were fifteen or twenty years elder than M. Morello."[5]

And here, after they had laughed awhile, M. Peter proceeded: "I say, therefore, that according as it is defined of the wise men of old time, love is nothing else but a certain coveting to enjoy beauty; and forsomuch as coveting longeth for nothing but for things known, it is requisite that knowledge go evermore before coveting, which of his own nature willeth the good, but of himself is blind and knoweth it not. Therefore hath nature so ordained that to every virtue of knowledge there is annexed a virtue of longing. And because in our soul there be three manner[6] ways to know, namely, by sense, reason, and understanding: of sense ariseth appetite or longing, which is common to us with brute beasts; of reason ariseth election or choice, which is proper to man; of understanding, by the which man may be partner with angels, ariseth will. Even as therefore the sense knoweth not but sensible matters and that which may be felt, so the appetite or coveting only desireth the same; and even as the understanding is bent but to behold things that may be understood, so is that will only fed with spiritual goods. Man of nature endowed with reason, placed, as it were, in the middle between these two extremities, may, through his choice inclining to sense or reaching to understanding, come nigh to the coveting, sometime of the one, sometime of the other part. In these sorts therefore may beauty be coveted, the general name whereof may be applied to all things, either natural or artificial, that are framed in good proportion and due temper,[7] as their nature beareth. But speaking of the beauty that we mean, which is only it that appeareth in bodies, and especially in the face of man, and moveth this fervent coveting which we call love, we will term it an influence of the heavenly

3. Very well.
4. Occasionally.
5. Morello da Ortona, a courtier and musician; later a speaker in the dialogue.
6. Kinds of.
7. The right mixture or combination of elements.

bountifulness, the which for all it stretcheth over all things that be created (like the light of the sun), yet when it findeth out a face well proportioned, and framed with a certain lively agreement of several colors, and set forth with lights and shadows, and with an orderly distance and limits of lines, thereinto it distilleth itself and appearth most well favored, and decketh out and lighteneth the subject where it shineth with a marvelous grace and glistering, like the sunbeams that strike against beautiful plate of fine gold wrought and set with precious jewels, so that it draweth unto it men's eyes with pleasure, and piercing through them imprinteth himself in the soul, and with an unwonted sweetness all to-stirreth[8] her and delighteth, and setting her on fire maketh her to covet him. When the soul then is taken with coveting to enjoy this beauty as a good thing, in case she suffer herself to be guided with the judgment of sense, she falleth into most deep errors, and judgeth the body in which beauty is discerned to be the principal cause thereof; whereupon to enjoy it she reckoneth it necessary to join as inwardly as she can with that body, which is false; and therefore whoso thinketh in possessing the body to enjoy beauty, he is far deceived, and is moved to it, not with true knowledge by the choice of reason, but with false opinion by the longing of sense. Whereupon the pleasure that followeth it is also false and of necessity full of errors. And therefore into one of the two vices run all those lovers that satisfy their unhonest lusts with the women whom they love; for either as soon as they come to the coveted end, they not only feel a fullness and loathsomeness, but also conceive a hatred against the right beloved, as though longing repented him of his offense and acknowledged the deceit wrought him by the false judgment of sense, that made him believe the ill to be good, or else they continue in the very same coveting and greediness, as though they were not indeed come to the end which they sought for. And albeit through the blind opinion that hath made them drunken (to their seeming) in that instant they feel a contentation,[9] as the diseased otherwhile, that dream they drink of some clear spring, yet they are not satisfied, nor leave off so. And because of possessing coveted goodness there arises always quietness and satisfaction in the possessor's mind, in case this were the true and right end of their coveting, when they possess it they would be at quietness and throughly satisfied, which they be not: but rather deceived through that likeness, they forthwith return again to unbridled coveting, and with the very same trouble which they felt at the first, they fall again into the raging and most burning thirst of the thing, that they hope in vain to possess perfectly. These kind of lovers therefore love most unluckily for either they never come by their covetings, which is a great un-

8. Moves violently.

9. Satisfied condition.

luckiness, or else if they do come by them, they find they come by their hurt and end their misery with other greater miseries, for both in the beginning and middle of this love, there is never other thing felt but afflictions, torments, griefs, pining travail, so that to be wan, vexed with continual tears and sighs, to live with a discontented mind, to be always dumb, or to lament, to covet death, in conclusion to be most unlucky are the properties which, they say, belong to lovers. The cause therefore of this wretchedness in men's minds is principally sense, which in youthful age beareth most sway, because the lustiness of the flesh and of the blood in that season addeth unto him even so much force as it withdraweth from reason. Therefore doth it easily train[1] the soul to follow appetite or longing, for when she seeth herself drowned in the earthly prison, because she is set in the office to govern the body, she cannot of herself understand plainly at the first the truth of spiritual beholding. Wherefore to compass the understanding of things, she must go beg the beginning at the senses, and therefore she believeth them and giveth ear to them, and is contented to be led by them, especially when they have so much courage, that (in a manner) they enforce her, and because they are deceitful they fill her with errors and false opinions. Whereupon most commonly it happeneth that young men be wrapped in this sensual love, which is a very rebel against reason, and therefore they make themselves unworthy to enjoy the favors and benefits which love bestows upon his true subjects, neither in love feel they any other pleasures than what beasts without reason do, but much more grievous afflictions. Setting case therefore this to be so, which is most true, I say that the contrary chanceth to them of a more ripe age. For in case they, when the soul is not now so much weighted down with the bodily burden, and when the natural burning assuageth and draweth to a warmth, if they be inflamed with beauty, and to it bend their coveting guided by reasonable choice, they be not deceived, and possess beauty perfectly, and therefore through the possessing of it, always goodness ensueth to them. Because beauty is good and consequently the true love of it is most good and holy, and evermore bringeth forth good fruits in the souls of them that with the bridle of reason restrain the ill disposition of sense, the which old men can much sooner do than young. It is not therefore out of reason to say that old men may also love without slander and more happily than young men, taking notwithstanding this name old, not for the age at the pit's brink, nor when the canals of the body be so feeble, that the soul cannot through them work her feats, but when knowledge in us is in his right strength. And I will not also hide this from you: namely, that I suppose where sensual love in every age is naught, yet in young

1. Entice.

men it deserveth excuse, and perhaps in some case leeful;[2] for although it puts them in afflictions, dangers, travails, and the unfortunateness that is said, yet are there many that to win them the goodwill of their ladies practice virtuous things, which for all they be not bent to a good end, yet are they good of themselves; and so of that much bitterness they pick out a little sweetness, and through the adversities which they sustain, in the end they acknowledge their error. As I judge therefore those young men that bridle their appetites, and love with reason, to be godly; so do I hold excused such as yield to sensual love, whereunto they be so inclined through the weakness and frailty of man—so they show therein meekness, courtesy, and prowess, and the other worthy conditions that these Lords have spoken of; and when those youthful years be gone and past, leave it off clean, keeping aloof from this sensual coveting as from the lowermost step of the stairs, by which a man may ascend to true love. But in case after they draw in years once, they reserve in their cold heart the fire of appetites, and bring stout reason in subjection to feeble sense, it cannot be said how much they are to be blamed: for like men without sense they deserve with an everlasting shame to be put in the number of unreasonable living creatures, because the thoughts and ways of sensual love be far unfitting for ripe age."

Here Bembo paused awhile, and when all things were whist[3] M. Morello of Ortona said: "And in case there were some old man more fresh and lusty and of a better complexion[4] than many young men, why would you not have it lawful for him to love with the love that young men love?"

The Duchess laughed, and said: "If the love of young men be so unlucky, why would you, M. Morello, that old men should also love with this unluckiness? But in case you were old, as these men say you be, you would not thus procure the hurt of old men."

M. Morello answered: "The hurt of old men, meseemeth, M. Peter Bembo procureth, who will have them to love after a sort that I for my part understand not; and, methink, the possessing of this beauty which he praiseth so much, without the body, is a dream."

"Do you believe, M. Morello," quoth then Count Lewis, "that beauty is always so good a thing as M. Peter Bembo speaketh of?"

"Not I, in good sooth," answered M. Morello. "But I remember rather that I have seen many beautiful women of a most ill inclination, cruel and spiteful, and it seemeth that, in a manner, it happeneth always so, for beauty maketh them proud, and pride, cruel."

2. Permissible.
3. Quiet.
4. Bodily vigor.

Count Lewis said, smiling: "To you perhaps they seem cruel, because they content you not with it that you would have. But cause M. Peter Bembo to teach you in what sort old men ought to covet beauty, and what to seek at their ladies' hands, and what to content themselves withal; and in not passing out of these bounds ye shall see that they shall be neither proud nor cruel, and will satisfy you with what you shall require."

M. Morello seemed then somewhat out of patience, and said: "I will not know the thing that toucheth[5] me not. But cause you to be taught how the young men ought to covet this beauty that are not so fresh and lusty as old men be."

Here Sir Frederick,[6] to pacify M. Morello and to break their talk, would not suffer Count Lewis to make answer, but interrupting him said: "Perhaps M. Morello is not altogether out of the way in saying that beauty is not always good, for the beauty of women is many times cause of infinite evils in the world—hatred, war, mortality, and destruction, whereof the razing of Troy can be a good witness; and beautiful women for the most part be either proud and cruel, as is said, or unchaste; but M. Morello would find no fault with that. There be also many wicked men that have the comeliness of a beautiful countenance, and it seemeth that nature hath so shaped them because they may be the readier to deceive, and that this amiable look were like a bait that covereth the hook."

Then M. Peter Bembo: "Believe not," quoth he, "but beauty is always good."

Here Count Lewis, because he would return again to his former purpose, interrupted him and said: "Since M. Morello passeth not to understand that which is so necessary for him, teach it me, and show me how old men may come by this happiness of love, for I will not care to be counted old, so it may profit me."

M. Peter Bembo laughed, and said: "First will I take the error out of these gentlemen's mind, and afterward will I satisfy you also." So beginning afresh: "My Lords," quoth he, "I would not that with speaking ill of beauty, which is a holy thing, any of us as profane and wicked should purchase him the wrath of God. Therefore, to give M. Morello and Sir Frederick warning, that they lose not their sight, as Stesichorus[7] did—a pain most meet for whoso dispraiseth beauty—I say that beauty cometh of God and is like a circle, the goodness whereof is the center. And therefore, as there can be no circle without a center, no more can beauty be without goodness. Whereupon doth very seldom an ill soul dwell in a

5. Concerns.
6. Federico Fregoso, later Archbishop of Salerno.
7. "A notable poet which lost his sight for writing against Helena [Helen of Troy] and recanting had his sight restored him again" [Hoby's note].

beautiful body. And therefore is the outward beauty a true sign of the inward goodness, and in bodies this comeliness is imprinted, more and less, as it were, for a mark of the soul, whereby she is outwardly known; as in trees, in which the beauty of the buds giveth a testimony of the goodness of the fruit. And the very same happeneth in bodies, as it is seen that palmisters by the visage know many times the conditions and otherwhile the thoughts of men. And, which is more, in beasts also a man may discern by the face the quality of the courage, which in the body declareth itself as much as it can. Judge you how plainly in the face of a lion, a horse, and an eagle, a man shall discern anger, fierceness, and stoutness; in lambs and doves, simpleness and very innocency; the crafty subtlety in foxes and wolves; and the like, in a manner, in all other living creatures. The foul,[8] therefore, for the most part be also evil, and the beautiful good. Therefore it may be said that beauty is a face pleasant, merry, comely, and to be desired for goodness; and foulness a face dark, uglesome, unpleasant, and to be shunned for ill. And in case you will consider all things, you shall find that whatsoever is good and profitable hath also evermore the comeliness of beauty. Behold the state of this great engine of the world,[9] which God created for the health and preservation of everything that was made: the heaven round beset with so many heavenly lights; and in the middle the earth environed with the elements and upheld with the very weight of itself; the sun, that compassing about giveth light to the whole, and in winter season draweth to the lowermost sign, afterward by little and little climbeth again to the other part; the moon, that of him taketh her light, according as she draweth nigh or goeth farther from him; and the other five stars that diversely keep the very same course. These things among themselves have such force by the knitting together of an order so necessarily framed that, with altering them any one jot, they should all be loosed and the world would decay. They have also such beauty and comeliness that all the wits men have cannot imagine a more beautiful matter.

"Think now of the shape of man, which may be called a little world, in whom every parcel of his body is seen to be necessarily framed by art and not by hap, and then the form altogether most beautiful, so that it were a hard matter to judge whether the members (as the eyes, the nose, the mouth, the ears, the arms, the breast, and in like manner the other parts) give either more profit to the countenance and the rest of the body, or comeliness. The

8. Ugly.
9. The following description is a summary of the Ptolemaic universe with the earth at the center; the elements of earth, water, air, fire surrounding the earth; the various crystalline spheres each containing sun, moon, or a planet; and the hard outer shell, the *Primum Mobile* (first mover).

like may be said of all other living creatures. Behold the feathers of fowls, the leaves and boughs of trees, which be given them of nature to keep them in their being, and yet have they withal a very great sightliness. Leave nature, and come to art. What thing is so necessary in sailing vessels as the forepart, the sides, the main yards, the mast, the sails, the stern, oars, anchors, and tacklings? All these things notwithstanding are so wellfavored in the eye that unto whoso beholdeth them they seem to have been found out as well for pleasure as for profit. Pillars and great beams uphold high buildings and palaces, and yet are they no less pleasureful unto the eyes of the beholders than profitable to the buildings. When men began first to build, in the middle of temples and houses they reared the ridge of the roof, not to make the works to have a better show, but because the water might the more commodiously avoid[1] on both sides; yet unto profit there was forthwith adjoined a fair sightliness, so that if, under the sky where there falleth neither hail nor rain, a man should build a temple without a reared ridge, it is to be thought that it could have neither a sightly show nor any beauty. Besides other things, therefore, it giveth a great praise to the world in saying that it is beautiful. It is praised in saying the beautiful heaven, beautiful earth, beautiful sea, beautiful rivers, beautiful woods, trees, gardens, beautiful cities, beautiful churches, houses, armies. In conclusion, this comely and holy beauty is a wondrous setting out of everything. And it may be said that good and beautiful be after a sort one self thing, especially in the bodies of men; of the beauty whereof the nighest cause, I suppose, is the beauty of the soul; the which, as a partner of the right and heavenly beauty, maketh sightly and beautiful whatever she toucheth, and most of all, if the body, where she dwelleth, be not of so vile a matter that she cannot imprint in it her property.[2] Therefore beauty is the true monument and spoil of the victory of the soul, when she with heavenly influence beareth rule over material and gross nature, and with her light overcometh the darkness of the body. It is not, then, to be spoken that beauty maketh women proud or cruel, although it seem so to M. Morello. Neither yet ought beautiful women to bear the blame of that hatred, mortality, and destruction which the unbridled appetites of men are the cause of. I will not now deny but it is possible also to find in the world beautiful women unchaste; yet not because beauty inclineth them to unchaste living, for it rather plucketh them from it, and leadeth them into the way of virtuous conditions, through the affinity that beauty hath with goodness; but otherwhile[3] ill bringing up, the continual provocations of lovers' tokens, poverty, hope, deceits, fear, and a thousand other matters,

1. Escape.
2. Attribute, quality.
3. Sometimes.

overcome the steadfastness, yea, of beautiful and good women; and for these and like causes may also beautiful men become wicked."

Then said the Lord Cesar:[4] "In case the Lord Gaspar's saying be true of yesternight, there is no doubt but the fair women be more chaste than the foul."

"And what was my saying?" quoth the Lord Gaspar.

The Lord Cesar answered: "If I do well bear in mind, your saying was that the women that are sued to always refuse to satisfy him that sueth to them, but those that are not sued to, sue to others. There is no doubt but the beautiful women have always more suitors, and be more instantly laid at[5] in love, than the foul. Therefore the beautiful always deny, and consequently be more chaste than the foul, which, not being sued to, sue unto others."

M. Peter Bembo laughed, and said: "This argument cannot be answered to."

Afterward he proceeded: "It chanceth also, oftentimes, that as the other senses, so the sight is deceived and judgeth a face beautiful which indeed is not beautiful. And because in the eyes and in the whole countenance of some woman a man beholdeth otherwhile a certain lavish wantonness painted, with dishonest flickerings, many, whom that manner delighteth because it promiseth them an easiness to come by the thing that they covet, call it beauty; but indeed it is a cloaked unshamefastness,[6] unworthy of so honorable and holy a name."

M. Peter Bembo held his peace, but those lords still were earnest upon him to speak somewhat more of this love and of the way to enjoy beauty aright, and at the last: "Methink," quoth he, "I have showed plainly enough that old men may love more happily than young, which was my drift; therefore it belongeth not to me to enter any farther."

Count Lewis answered: "You have better declared the unluckiness of young men than the happiness of old men, whom you have not as yet taught what way they must follow in this love of theirs; only you have said that they must suffer themselves to be guided by reason, and the opinion of many is that it is unpossible for love to stand with reason."

Bembo notwithstanding sought to make an end of reasoning, but the Duchess desired him to say on, and he began thus afresh: "Too unlucky were the nature of man, if our soul, in which this so fervent coveting may lightly arise, should be driven to nourish it with that only which is common to her with beasts, and could not turn it to the other noble part, which is proper to her.[7] Therefore, since it is so your pleasure, I will not refuse to reason upon this noble matter.

4. Lord Cesar Gonzaga, cousin of Castiglione.
5. Pursued.
6. Immodesty.
7. "I.e., Reason" [Hoby's note].

And because I know myself unworthy to talk of the most holy mysteries of Love, I beseech him to lead my thought and my tongue so that I may show this excellent Courtier how to love contrary to the wonted manner of the common ignorant sort. And even as from my childhood I have dedicated all my whole life unto him, so also now that my words may be answerable to the same intent, and to the praise of him: I say, therefore, that since the nature of man in youthful age is so much inclined to sense, it may be granted the Courtier, while he is young, to love sensually; but in case afterward also, in his riper years, he chance to be set on fire with this coveting of love, he ought to be good and circumspect, and heedful that he beguile not himself to be led willfully into the wretchedness that in young men deserveth more to be pitied than blamed and contrariwise in old men, more to be blamed than pitied. Therefore when an amiable countenance of a beautiful woman cometh in his sight, that is accompanied with noble conditions and honest behaviors, so that, as one practiced in love, he wotteth well that his hue hath an agreement with hers, as soon as he is aware that his eyes snatch that image and carry it to the heart, and that the soul beginneth to behold it with pleasure, and feeleth within herself the influence that stirreth her and by little and little setteth her in heat, and that those lively spirits that twinkle out through the eyes put continually fresh nourishment to the fire, he ought in this beginning to seek a speedy remedy and to raise up reason, and with her to fence the fortress of his heart, and to shut in such wise the passages against sense and appetites that they may enter neither with force nor subtle practice. Thus, if the flame be quenched, the jeopardy is also quenched. But in case it continue or increase, then must the Courtier determine, when he perceiveth he is taken, to shun throughly[8] all filthiness of common love, and so enter into the holy way of love with the guide of reason, and first consider that the body where that beauty shineth is not the fountain from whence beauty springeth, but rather because beauty is bodiless and, as we have said, an heavenly shining beam, she loseth much of her honor when she is coupled with that vile subject[9] and full of corruption, because the less she is partner thereof, the more perfect she is, and, clean sundered from it, is most perfect. And as a man heareth not with his mouth, nor smelleth with his ears, no more can he also in any manner wise enjoy beauty, nor satisfy the desire that she stirreth up in our minds, with feeling, but with the sense unto whom beauty is the very butt to level at,[1] namely, the virtue of seeing. Let him lay aside, therefore, the blind judgment of the sense, and enjoy with his eyes the brightness, the comeliness, the loving sparkles, laughters, gestures, and all the other pleasant furnitures of beauty, especially with hearing the sweetness

8. Completely.
9. I.e., the body.
1. Target to aim at.

of her voice, the tunableness[2] of her words, the melody of her singing and playing on instruments (in case the woman beloved be a musician), and so shall he with most dainty food feed the soul through the means of these two senses which have little bodily substance in them and be the ministers of reason, without entering farther toward the body with coveting unto any longing otherwise than honest. Afterward let him obey, please, and honor with all reverence his woman, and reckon her more dear to him than his own life, and prefer all her commodities[3] and pleasures before his own, and love no less in her the beauty of the mind than of the body. Therefore let him have a care not to suffer her to run into any error, but with lessons and good exhortations seek always to frame her to modesty, to temperance, to true honesty, and so to work that there may never take place in her other than pure thoughts and far wide from all filthiness of vices. And thus in sowing of virtue in the garden of that mind, he shall also gather the fruits of most beautiful conditions, and savor them with a marvelous good relish. And this shall be the right engendering and imprinting of beauty in beauty, the which some hold opinion to be the end of love. In this manner shall our Courtier be most acceptable to his lady, and she will always show herself toward him tractable, lowly,[4] and sweet in language, and as willing to please him as to be beloved of him; and the wills of them both shall be most honest and agreeable, and they consequently shall be most happy."

Here M. Morello: "The engendering," quoth he, "of beauty in beauty aright were the engendering of a beautiful child in a beautiful woman; and I would think it a more manifest token a great deal that she loved her lover, if she pleased him with this than with the sweetness of language that you speak of."

M. Peter Bembo laughed, and said: "You must not, M. Morello, pass your bounds. I may tell you it is not a small token that a woman loveth when she giveth unto her lover her beauty, which is so precious a matter; and by the ways that be a passage to the soul (that is to say, the sight and the hearing) sendeth the looks of her eyes, the image of her countenance, and the voice of her words, that pierce into the lover's heart and give a witness of her love."

M. Morello said: "Looks and words may be, and oftentimes are, false witnesses. Therefore whoso hath not a better pledge of love, in my judgment he is in an ill assurance. And surely I looked still that you would have made this woman of yours somewhat more courteous and free toward the Courtier than my Lord Julian[5] hath made his; but meseemeth ye be both of the property of those judges

2. Musical quality.
3. Conveniences.
4. Modest.
5. Giuliano de Medici, youngest son of Lorenzo the Magnificent, commander-in-chief of the papal armies, and a speaker in the dialogue.

that, to appear wise, give sentence against their own."

Bembo said: "I am well pleased to have this woman much more courteous toward my Courtier not young than the Lord Julian's is to the young; and that with good reason, because mine coveteth but honest matters, and therefore may the woman grant him them all without blame. But my Lord Julian's woman, that is not so assured of the modesty of the young man, ought to grant him the honest matters only, and deny him the dishonest. Therefore more happy is mine, that hath granted him whatsoever he requireth, than the other, that hath part granted and part denied. And because you may moreover the better understand that reasonable love is more happy than sensual, I say unto you that selfsame things in sensual ought to be denied otherwhile, and in reasonable granted; because in the one they be honest, and in the other dishonest. Therefore the woman, to please her good lover, besides the granting him merry countenances, familiar and secret talk, jesting, dallying, hand-in-hand, may also lawfully and without blame come to kissing, which in sensual love, according to the Lord Julian's rules, is not lawful. For since a kiss is a knitting together both of body and soul, it is to be feared lest the sensual lover will be more inclined to the part of the body than of the soul; but the reasonable lover wotteth[6] well that although the mouth be a parcel[7] of the body, yet is it an issue for the words that be the interpreters of the soul, and for the inward breath, which is also called the soul; and therefore hath a delight to join his mouth with the woman's beloved with a kiss—not to stir him to any unhonest desire, but because he feeleth that that bond is the opening of an entry to the souls, which, drawn with a coveting the one of the other, pour themselves by turn the one into the other's body, and be so mingled together that each of them hath two souls, and one alone so framed of them both ruleth, in a manner, two bodies. Whereupon a kiss may be said to be rather a coupling together of the soul than of the body, because it hath such force in her that it draweth her unto it, and, as it were, separateth her from the body. For this do all chaste lovers covet a kiss as a coupling of souls together. And therefore Plato, the divine lover, saith that in kissing his soul came as far as his lips to depart out of the body. And because the separating of the soul from the matters of the sense, and the thorough coupling of her with matters of understanding, may be betokened by a kiss, Solomon saith[8] in his heavenly book of ballads, 'Oh that he would kiss me with a kiss of his mouth,' to express the desire he had that his soul might be ravished through heavenly love to the beholding of heavenly beauty in such manner that, coupling herself inwardly with it, she might forsake the body."

* * *

6. Knows.
7. Part.
8. In Song of Solomon i.2.

When Bembo had hitherto spoken with such vehemency that a man would have thought him, as it were, ravished and beside himself, he stood still without once moving, holding his eyes toward heaven as astonied,[9] when the Lady Emilia, which together with the rest gave most diligent ear to this talk, took him by the plait[1] of his garment and, plucking him a little, said, "Take heed, M. Peter, that these thoughts make not your soul also to forsake the body." "Madam," answered M. Peter, it should not be the first miracle that love hath wrought in me."

1561

9. Enraptured.

1. Hem.

RICHARD HOOKER
(1554–1600)

Out of the long and bitter controversy over the government of the church in 16th-century England emerged one literary masterpiece. It is a long work in eight books called *Of the Laws of Ecclesiastical Polity* (that is, the governmental system of the church). The author was Richard Hooker, a scholar and minister who accomplished the extraordinary feat of engaging in the bitterest dispute of his time and maintaining a calm, reasonable manner. In 1585 Hooker was Master of the Temple (in modern terms, a dean of a law school); one of his subordinates was a Puritan lecturer named Walter Travers. Between them a running debate developed on the burning question of how the church should be governed. The Puritan view was that no organization or authority in the church was valid unless it was based clearly and specifically upon the Bible; the whole hierarchical system of the English church, with its deacons, priests, bishops, and archbishops, was accordingly wrong. The position Hooker undertook to defend was that the Scriptures, or divine revelation, are not the only guide given to men for organizing and administering the Christian church. A more important guide is the law of nature, which is also divinely given; this law can be discovered by the use of human reason.

In his great book, which grew out of his controversy with Travers, Hooker therefore had to explain how the law of nature justified the existing organization of the English church. Book I of *Ecclesiastical Polity* deals with laws in general and their various kinds, picturing a universe operating under natural and divine law and founded upon reason. Book II deals with the nature, authority, and adequacy of Scripture. Book III concerns the scriptural bases for worship and government. Book IV defends the rites and ceremonies of the English church, and Book V, longer than the first four together, is a commentary on *The Book of Common Prayer*. Books VI, VII, and VIII deal with various embodiments of authority—elders, bishops, kings, and popes.

Hooker was a close and effective reasoner; he relied not upon the fiery invective or impassioned rhetoric which characterized most disputants of his time, but rather upon a calm, reasonable, tolerant approach. His defense of existing ecclesiastical practices went back to fundamental principles, to a philosophy of nature and of man's place in it, of his relation to God and to his fellow men. It is this world view which makes Hooker's book of interest when the controversy over church organization has long since died down. And the prose in which Hooker sets forth his world view is the finest prose of the Elizabethan age. King James I is quoted by Izaak Walton, Hooker's 17th-century biographer, as saying, "I observe there is in Mr. Hooker no affected language; but a grave, comprehensive, clear manifestation of reason, and that backed with the authority of the Scriptures, the fathers and schoolmen, and with all law both sacred and civil. And, though others may write well, yet in the next age they will be forgotten; but doubtless there is in every page of Mr. Hooker's book the picture of a divine soul, such pictures of truth and reason, and drawn in so sacred colors, that they shall never fade but give an immortal memory to the author."

From Of the Laws of Ecclesiastical Polity

From *The Preface*

[ON MODERATION IN CONTROVERSY]

* * * Amongst ourselves, there was in King Edward's days some question moved by reason of a few men's scrupulosity touching certain things.[1] And beyond seas, of them which fled in the days of Queen Mary, some contenting themselves abroad with the use of their own service book at home authorized before their departure out of the realm, others liking better the common prayer book of the Church of Geneva translated, those smaller contentions before begun were by this mean somewhat increased. Under the happy reign of Her Majesty which now is, the greatest matter a while contended for was the wearing of the cap and surplice,[2] till there came *Admonitions Directed unto the High Court of Parliament,* by men who, concealing their names, thought it glory enough to discover their minds and affections, which were now universally bent even against all the orders and laws wherein this Church is found unconformable to the platform of Geneva. Concerning the defender of which admonitions, all that I mean to say is this: "There will come a time when three words uttered with charity and meekness shall

1. During the short reign of the boy king, Edward VI (1547–53), the reformation begun under Henry VIII was carried further. Services were held in English, images were banished from the church, and the use of holy water was forbidden. During the following reign of Mary, a Catholic, many Protestant reformers fled abroad and there were influenced by the Calvinist doctrines and practices of the "Church of Geneva."

2. The extreme Protestants or "Puritans" were opposed to the daily wearing of cap and gown by the clergy and the wearing of the surplice in church. This "Vestiarian controversy" was at its height in the 1560's. The *"Admonitions Directed unto the High Court of Parliament,"* by John Field and Thomas Wilcox (1572), attacked not only conventional clerical dress but the Prayer Book, episcopacy, and the whole structure of the Church of England.

receive a far more blessed reward than three thousand volumes written with disdainful sharpness of wit." But the manner of men's writing must not alienate our hearts from the truth if it appear they have the truth, as the followers of the same defender do think he hath, and in that persuasion they follow him no otherwise than himself doth Calvin, Beza[3] and others, with the like persuasion that they in this cause had the truth. We being as fully persuaded otherwise, it resteth that some kind of trial be used to find out which part is in error.

The first mean whereby Nature teacheth men to judge good from evil, as well in laws as in other things, is the force of their own discretion. Hereunto therefore Saint Paul referreth oftentimes his own speech to be considered by them that heard him, "I speak as to them which have understanding; judge ye what I say."[4] Again, afterward, "Judge in yourselves, is it comely that a woman pray uncovered?" The exercise of this kind of judgment our Saviour requireth in the Jews.[5] In them of Berea the Scripture commendeth it. Finally, whatsoever we do, if our own secret judgment consent not unto it as fit and good to be done, the doing of it, to us, is sin, although the thing itself be allowable. Saint Paul's rule therefore generally is, "Let every man in his own mind be fully persuaded of that thing which he either alloweth or doth."[6] Some things are so familiar and plain that truth from falsehood and good from evil is most easily discerned in them, even by men of no deep capacity. And of that nature, for the most part are things absolutely unto all men's salvation necessary, either to be held or denied, either to be done or avoided. For which cause Saint Augustine acknowledgeth that they are not only set down, but also plainly set down in scripture, so that he which heareth or readeth may, without any great difficulty, understand. Other things also there are belonging, though in a lower degree of importance, unto the offices of Christian men, which, because they are more obscure, more intricate and hard to be judged of, therefore God hath appointed some to spend their whole time principally in the study of things divine, to the end that in these more doubtful cases their understanding might be a light to direct others. "If the understanding power or faculty of the soul be," saith the Grand Physician,[7] "like unto the bodily sight, not of equal sharpness in all, what can be more convenient than that, even as the dark-sighted man is directed by the clear about

3. John Calvin (1509–64) and Theodore Beza (1519–1605), two leading Protestant reformers on the Continent.
4. I Corinthians x.15. The next quotation is from I Corinthians xi.13.
5. See Luke xii.57. "Them of Berea": the inhabitants of the Macedonian city of Berea who "received the word with all readiness of mind" when Paul preached to them, according to Acts xiv.10–11.
6. See Romans xiv.5.
7. I.e., Galen, Greek physician of the 2d century A.D., whose works were long accepted as the highest medical authority.

things visible, so likewise in matters of deeper discourse the wise in heart do show the simple where his way lieth?" In the doubtful cases of law, what man is there who seeth not how requisite it is that professors of skill in that faculty be our directors? So is it in all other kinds of knowledge. And even in this kind likewise the Lord hath himself appointed that "the Priest's lips should preserve knowledge, and that other men should seek the truth at his mouth, because he is the messenger of the Lord of Hosts."[8] Gregory Nazianzen, offended at the people's too great presumption in controlling the judgment of them to whom in such cases they should rather have submitted their own, seeketh by earnest entreaty to stay them within their bounds: "Presume not, ye that are sheep, to make yourselves guides of them that should guide you; neither seek ye to overskip the fold which they about you have pitched. It sufficeth for your part, if ye can well frame yourselves to be ordered. Take not upon you to judge your judges, nor to make them subject to your laws who should be a law to you. For God is not a God of sedition and confusion but of order and of peace." But ye will say that if the guides of the people be blind, the common sort of men must not close up their own eyes and be led by the conduct of such; if the priest be partial in the law, the flock must not therefore depart from the ways of sincere truth, and in simplicity yield to be followers of him for his place' sake and office over them. Which thing, though in itself most true, is in your defense notwithstanding weak; because the matter wherein ye think that ye see and imagine that your ways are sincere is of far deeper consideration than any one amongst five hundred of you conceiveth. Let the vulgar sort amongst you know that there is not the least branch of the cause wherein they are so resolute but to the trial of it a great deal more appertaineth than their concept doth reach unto. I write not this in disgrace of the simplest that way given,[9] but I would gladly they knew the nature of that cause wherein they think themselves thoroughly instructed and are not; by means whereof they daily run themselves, without feeling their own hazard, upon the dint of the Apostle's sentence against evil speakers as touching things wherein they are ignorant.[1] If it be granted a thing unlawful for private men, not called into public consultation, to dispute which is the best state of civil polity, with a desire of bringing in some other kind than that under which they already live, for of such disputes I take it his meaning was—if it be a thing confessed that of such questions they cannot determine without rashness, inasmuch as a great part of

8. See Malachi ii.7. "Gregory Nazianzen" is St. Gregory of Nazianzus, a 4th-century bishop.

9. I.e., I am not disparaging ordinary, uneducated people.

1. Ignorant people run the risk of the condemnation of the apostle Peter: "But these, as natural brute beasts, made to be taken and destroyed, speak evil of the things that they understand not; and shall utterly perish in their own corruption" (II Peter ii.12).

them consisteth in special circumstances, and for one kind as many reasons may be brought as for another—is there any reason in the world why they should better judge what kind of regiment[2] ecclesiastical is the fittest? For in the civil state more insight and, in those affairs, more experience a great deal needs be granted them, than in this they can possibly have. When they which write in defense of your discipline and commend it unto the highest[3] not in the least cunning manner, are forced notwithstanding to acknowledge that with whom the truth is they know not, they are not certain—what certainty or knowledge can the multitude have thereof? Weigh what doth move the common sort so much to favor this innovation and it shall soon appear unto you that the force of particular reasons which for your several opinions are alleged is a thing whereof the multitude never did nor could consider as to be therewith wholly carried; but certain general inducements are used to make salable your cause in gross; and when once men have cast a fancy towards it, any slight declaration of specialties will serve to lead forward men's inclinable and prepared minds. The method of winning the people's affection unto a general liking of "the Cause," for so ye term it, hath been this: First, in the hearing of the multitude, the faults, especially of higher callings, are ripped up with marvelous exceeding severity and sharpness of reproof, which being oftentimes done, begetteth a great good opinion of integrity, zeal, and holiness to such constant reprovers of sin as by likelihood would never be so much offended at that which is evil, unless themselves were singularly good. The next thing hereunto is to impute all faults and corruptions wherewith the world aboundeth unto the kind of ecclesiastical government established. Wherein, as by reproving faults, they purchased unto themselves with the multitude a name to be virtuous; so by finding out this kind of cause they obtain to be judged wise above others, whereas in truth unto the form even of Jewish government, which the Lord himself, they all confess, did establish, with like show of reason they might impute those faults which the prophets condemn in the governors of that commonwealth as to the English kind of regiment ecclesiastical (whereof also God himself though in other sort is author), the stains and blemishes found in our state, which springing from the root of human frailty and corruption, not only are, but have always been more or less—yea, and for anything we know to the contrary will be till the world's end—complained of, what form of government soever take place. Having gotten thus much sway in the hearts of men, a third step is to propose their own form of church government as the only sovereign

2. Government.
3. I.e., Queen Elizabeth. The *Humble Petition of the Commonalty* (1588) said, "we are very babes and children, not knowing our right hand from our left in matters that concern the Kingdom of Heaven." "Cunning": learned.

remedy of all evils, and to adorn it with all the glorious titles that may be. And the nature, as of men that have sick bodies, so likewise of the people in the crazedness of their minds possessed with dislike and discontentment at things present, is to imagine that anything the virtue whereof they hear commended would help them, but that most which they least have tried. The fourth degree of inducement is by fashioning the very notions and conceits[4] of men's minds in such sort that when they read the Scriptures they may think that everything soundeth towards the advancement of that discipline and to the utter disgrace of the contrary. Pythagoras, by bringing up his scholars in the speculative knowledge of numbers, made their conceits therein so strong that when they came to the contemplation of things natural they imagined that in every particular thing they even beheld, as it were with their eyes, how the elements of number gave essence and being to the works of nature. A thing in reason impossible, which notwithstanding through their misfashioned preconceit appeared unto them no less certain than if nature had written it in the very foreheads of all the creatures of God. * * *

From *Book I, Chapter 3*

[THE LAW OF NATURE FOR NATURAL AGENTS]

* * * Now if Nature should intermit her course and leave altogether, though it were but for a while, the observation of her own laws; if those principal and mother elements of the world, whereof all things in this lower world are made, should lose the qualities which they now have; if the frame of that heavenly arch erected over our heads should loosen and dissolve itself; if celestial spheres should forget their wonted motions and by irregular volubility turn themselves any way as it might happen; if the prince of the lights of heaven which now as a giant doth run his unwearied course, should as it were through a languishing faintness begin to stand and to rest himself; if the moon should wander from her beaten way, the times and seasons of the year blend themselves by disordered and confused mixture, the winds breathe out their last gasp, the clouds yield no rain, the earth be defeated of heavenly influence, the fruits of the earth pine away as children at the withered breasts of their mother no longer able to yield them relief, what would become of man himself, whom these things now do all serve? See we not plainly that obedience of creatures unto the law of Nature is the stay of the whole world? Notwithstanding with Nature it cometh sometimes to pass as with art. Let Phidias[5] have rude and obstinate stuff to carve, though his art do that it should, his work

4. Concepts.
5. The greatest of ancient Greek sculptors (5th century B.C.).

will lack that beauty which otherwise in fitter matter it might have had. He that striketh an instrument with skill may cause notwithstanding a very unpleasant sound if the string whereon he striketh chance to be uncapable of harmony. In the matter whereof natural things consist, that of Theophrastus[6] taketh place, "much of it is oftentimes such as will by no means yield to receive that impression which were best and most perfect." Which defect in the matter of things natural, they who gave themselves unto the contemplation of Nature among the heathen observed often; but the true original cause thereof divine malediction,[7] laid for the sin of man upon those creatures which God had made for the use of man. This, being an article of that saving truth which God hath revealed unto his church, was above the reach of their merely natural capacity and understanding. But howsoever these swervings are now and then incident into the course of Nature, nevertheless so constantly the laws of Nature are by natural agents observed, that no man denieth but those things which Nature worketh are wrought either always or for the most part after one and the same manner. * * *

From *Book I, Chapter 8*

[THE LAW OF NATURE FOR VOLUNTARY AGENTS]

* * * The general and perpetual voice of men is as the sentence[8] of God himself. For that which all men have at all times learned, Nature herself must needs have taught, and God being the author of Nature, her voice is but his instrument. By her from Him we receive whatsoever in such sort we learn. Infinite duties there are, the goodness whereof is by this rule sufficiently manifested, although we had no warrant besides to approve them. The apostle St. Paul having speech concerning the heathen saith of them "They are a law unto themselves."[9] His meaning is, that by force of the light of reason wherewith God illuminateth everyone which cometh into the world, men being enabled to know truth from falsehood, and good from evil, do thereby learn in many things what the will of God is; which will himself not revealing by any extraordinary means unto them, but they by natural discourse attaining the knowledge thereof, seem the makers of those laws which indeed are his, and they but only the finders of them out. A law therefore generally taken is a directive rule unto goodness of operation. The rule of divine operations outward is the definite appointment of God's own wisdom set down within himself. The rule of natural agents that work by simple necessity is the determination of the wisdom

6. Greek writer of the 3rd century B.C., a follower of Aristotle and inventor of the type of essay called the "character," which in concise form delineated a type of person.

7. God's curse in Eden, which fell not only upon sinful man but upon the earth as well.

8. Wisdom.

9. Romans ii.14.

of God, known to God himself, the principal director of them, but not unto them that are directed to execute the same. The rule of natural agents which work after a sort of their own accord, as the beasts do, is the judgment of common sense or fancy concerning the sensible[1] goodness of those objects wherewith they are moved. The rule of ghostly or immaterial natures, as spirits and angels, is their intuitive intellectual judgment concerning the amiable beauty and high goodness of that object, which with unspeakable joy and delight doth set them on work. The rule of voluntary agents on earth is the sentence that reason giveth concerning the goodness of those things which they are to do. And the sentences which reason giveth are some more, some less general, before it come to define in particular actions what is good. The main principles of reason are in themselves apparent. For to make nothing evident of itself unto man's understanding were to take away all possibility of knowing anything. And herein that of Theophrastus is true, "They that seek a reason of all things do utterly overthrow reason." * * *

From *Book I, Chapter* 9

[NATURE, RIGHTEOUSNESS, AND SIN]

Now the due observation of this law which reason teacheth us cannot but be effectual unto their great good that observe the same. For we see the whole world and each part thereof so compacted[2] that as long as each thing performeth only that work which is natural unto it, it thereby preserveth both other things and also itself. Contrariwise, let any principal thing, as the sun or moon, or any one of the heavens or elements, but once cease or fail, or swerve, and who does not easily conceive that the sequel thereof would be ruin both to itself and whatsoever dependeth upon it? And is it possible that man, being not only the noblest creature in the world, but even a very world in himself, his transgressing the law of his nature should draw no manner of harm after it? Yes, tribulation and anguish unto every soul that doth evil. Good doth follow unto all things by observing the course of their nature, and on the contrary side, evil by not observing it, but not unto natural agents that good which we call reward, not that evil which we properly term punishment. The reason whereof is because amongst creatures in this world, only man's observation of the law of his nature is Righteousness, only man's transgression Sin. And the reason of this is his manner of observing or transgressing the law of his nature. He doth not otherwise than voluntarily the one or the other. What we do against our wills, or constrainedly, we are not properly said to do it, because the motive cause of doing it is not in ourselves, but carrieth us, as if the

1. Perceptible by the senses.

2. Agreed.

wind should drive a feather in the air, we no whit furthering that whereby we are driven. In such cases therefore the evil which is done moveth compassion; men are pitied for it, as being rather miserable in such respect than culpable. * * *

From *Book I, Chapter 10*

[THE FOUNDATIONS OF SOCIETY]

That which hitherto we have set down is, I hope, sufficient to show their brutishness which imagine that religion and virtue are only as men will accompt of[3] them, that we might make as much accompt, if we would, of the contrary, without any harm unto ourselves, and that in Nature they are as indifferent one as the other. We see then how Nature itself teacheth laws and statutes to live by. The laws which have been hitherto mentioned do bind men absolutely, even as they are men, although they have never any settled fellowship, never any solemn agreement amongst themselves what to do or not to do. But forasmuch as we are not by ourselves sufficient to furnish ourselves with competent store of things needful for such a life as our nature doth desire, a life fit for the dignity of man, therefore to supply those defects and imperfections which are in us living single and solely, by ourselves, we are naturally induced to seek communion and fellowship with others. This was the cause of men's uniting themselves at the first in politic societies, which societies could not be without government, nor government without a distinct kind of law from that which hath been already declared. Two foundations there are which bear up public societies, the one a natural inclination whereby all men desire a sociable life and fellowship, the other an order expressly or secretly agreed upon, touching the manner of their union in living together. The latter is that which we call the law of a commonweal,[4] the very soul of a politic body, the parts whereof are by law animated, held together and set on work in such actions as the common good requireth. Laws politic, ordained for external order and regiment amongst men, are never framed as they should be, unless presuming the will of man to be inwardly obstinate, rebellious, and averse from all obedience unto the sacred laws of his nature—in a word, unless presuming man to be in regard of his depraved mind little better than a wild beast—they do accordingly provide notwithstanding so to frame his outward actions that they be no hindrance unto the common good for which societies are instituted; unless they do this, they are not perfect. It resteth therefore that we consider how Nature findeth out such laws of government as serve to direct even nature depraved to a right end. All men desired to lead in this world an happy life.

3. Value.
4. Commonwealth. Originally the "common good."

That life is led most happily, wherein all virtue is exercised without impediment or let. The Apostle[5] in exhorting men to contentment, although they have in this world no more than very bare food and raiment, giveth us thereby to understand that those are even the lowest of things necessary; that if we should be stripped of all those things without which we might possibly be, yet these must be left, that destitution in these is such an impediment, as till it be removed, suffereth not the mind of man to admit any other care. For this cause first God assigned Adam maintenance of life and then appointed him a law to observe. For this cause after men began to grow to a number, the first thing we read they gave themselves unto was the tilling of the earth and the feeding of cattle. Having by this mean whereon to live, the principal actions of their life afterward are noted by the exercise of their religion. True it is that the Kingdom of God must be the first thing in our purposes and desires. But inasmuch as righteous life presupposeth life, inasmuch as to live virtuously it is impossible except we live, therefore the first impediment which naturally we endeavor to remove is penury and want of things without which we cannot live. Unto life many implements are necessary; moe,[6] if we seek, as all men naturally do, such a life as hath in it joy, comfort, delight and pleasure. To this end we see how quickly sundry arts mechanical were found out in the very prime of the world. As things of greatest necessity are always first provided for, so things of greatest dignity are most accompted of by all such as judge rightly. Although therefore riches be a thing which every man wisheth, yet no man of judgment can esteem it better to be rich than wise, virtuous, and religious. If we be both or either of these, it is not because we are so born. For into the world we come as empty of the one as of the other, as naked in mind as we are in body. Both which necessities of man had at the first no other helps and supplies than only domestical, such as that which the prophet[7] implieth, saying, "Can a mother forget her child?", such as that which the Apostle[8] mentioneth, saying, "He that careth not for his own is worse than an infidel"; such as that concerning Abraham, "Abraham will command his sons and his household after him that they keep the way of the Lord."[9] But neither that which we learn of ourselves, nor that which others teach us, can prevail where wickedness and malice have taken deep root. If therefore when there was but as yet one only family in the world, no means of instruction human or divine could prevent effusion of blood, how could it be chosen but that when families were multiplied and increased upon earth, after separation each providing for itself, envy, strife, contention, and violence must grow amongst them? For hath

5. Paul, in I Timothy vi.8.
6. More.
7. Isaiah (xlix.17).
8. Paul, in I Timothy v.8.
9. Genesis xviii.19.

not Nature furnished man with wit and valor, as it were with armor, which may be used as well unto extreme evil as good? Yea, were they not used by the rest of the world unto evil, unto the contrary only by Seth, Enoch, and those few the rest in that line?[1] We all make complaint of the iniquity of our times; not unjustly, for the days are evil. But compare them with those times wherein there were no civil societies, with those times wherein there was as yet no manner of public regiment established, with those times wherein there were not above eight persons righteous living upon the face of the earth, and we have surely good cause to think that God hath blessed us exceedingly and hath made us behold most happy days. To take away all such mutual grievances, injuries, and wrongs, there was no way but only by growing into composition and agreement amongst themselves by ordaining some kind of government public and by yielding themselves subject thereunto, that unto whom they granted authority to rule and govern, by them the peace, tranquility, and happy estate of the rest might be procured. * * *

From *Book I, Chapter 12*

[THE NEED FOR REVEALED LAW]

* * * The first principles of the law of nature are easy: hard it were to find men ignorant of them; but concerning the duty which Nature's law doth require at the hands of men in a number of things particular, so far hath the natural understanding even of sundry whole nations been darkened, that they have not discerned—no, not gross iniquity—to be sin. Again, being so prone as we are to fawn upon ourselves, and to be ignorant as much as may be of our own deformities, without the feeling sense whereof we are most wretched, even so much the more because not knowing them we cannot as much as desire to have them taken away, how should our festered sores be cured but that God hath delivered a law as sharp as the two-edged sword, piercing the very closest and most unsearchable corners of the heart which the law of nature can hardly, human laws by no means possible, reach unto? Hereby we know even secret concupiscence to be sin, and are made fearful to offend, though it be but in a wandering cogitation.[2] * * *

1593

1. The virtuous line of Seth is described in Genesis iv.25–26. It was in the time of Seth and his son Enos that "men began to call upon the name of the Lord."

2. A reference to Hebrews iv.12: "For the word of God is quick, and powerful, and sharper than any two-edged sword, piercing even to the dividing asunder of soul and spirit and of the joints and marrow, and is a discerner of the thoughts and intents of the heart."

THOMAS HARIOT
(1560–1621)

Thomas Hariot, mathematician and scientist in the service of Sir Walter Ralegh, accompanied an expedition under Sir Richard Grenville, Ralegh's cousin, to Virginia in 1585, and wrote an account of it which was first published in 1588. Hariot was a careful observer and a competent "surveyor" or reporter. His account describes the geography, the climate, the vegetation, and the wild life of the country, but its main interest for us lies in his description of the natives. The English were very curious about the inhabitants of the new world: Shakespeare has one of his characters in *The Tempest* comment cynically on this trait of his countrymen: "When they will not give a doit [coin of small value] to relieve a lame beggar, they will lay out ten to see a dead Indian" (II.ii.31–33). Hariot of course shares the interest of his master, Ralegh, in colonization, so he gives as favorable an account of the strange country as he can. His prose is workmanlike and straightforward, as one might expect of a man whose interests were more scientific than literary.

Hariot's account, and many others of English voyages of discovery, were collected and published in the decade 1589–99 by Richard Hakluyt in a huge collection called *The Principal Navigations, Traffics, Voyages, and Discoveries of the English Nation.* This work the 19th-century historian J. A. Froude called "the prose epic of the modern English nation."

From A Brief and True Report of the Newfound Land of Virginia

Of the Commodities There Found, and to Be Raised, As Well Merchantable as Others. Written by Thomas Hariot, Servant to Sir Walter Ralegh, a Member of the Colony, and There Employed in Discovering a Full Twelve-Month

OF THE NATURE AND MANNERS OF THE PEOPLE

It resteth I speak a word or two of the natural inhabitants, their natures and manners, leaving large discourse thereof until time more convenient hereafter. Now only so far forth, as that you may know how they in respect of troubling our inhabiting and planting, are not to be feared, but that they shall have cause both to fear and love us, that shall inhabit with them.

They are a people clothed with loose mantles made of deerskins, and aprons of the same round about their middles, all else naked, of such a difference of statures only as we in England, having no edge tools or weapons of iron or steel to offend us withal, neither know they how to make any. Those weapons that they have, are only bows made of witch hazel and arrows of reeds, flat-edged truncheons also of wood about a yard long, neither have they anything to defend themselves but targets[1] made of barks, and some armors made of sticks wickered together with thread.

Their towns are but small, and near the seacoast but few, some containing but ten or twelve houses, some twenty; the greatest that we have seen has been but of thirty houses. If they be walled, it is only done with barks of trees made fast to stakes, or else with poles only fixed upright and close one by another.

Their houses are made of small poles, made fast at the tops in round form after the manner as is used in many arbories in our gardens of England, in most towns covered with barks, and in some with artificial mats made of long rushes, from the tops of the houses down to the ground. The length of them is commonly double to the breadth; in some places they are but twelve and sixteen yards long, and in some other we have seen of four-and-twenty.

In some places of the country, one only town belongs to the government of a *Wiróans* or chief Lord, in other some two or three, in some six, eight, and more. The greatest Wiroans that yet we had dealing with had but eighteen towns in his government and able to make not above seven or eight hundred fighting men at the most. The language of every government is different from any other, and the further they are distant, the greater is the difference.

Their manner of wars amongst themselves is either by sudden surprising one another most commonly about the dawning of the day, or moonlight, or else by ambushes, or some subtle devices. Set battles are very rare, except it fall out where there are many trees, where either party may have some hope of defense, after the delivery of every arrow, in leaping behind some or other.

If there fall out any wars between us and them, what their fight is likely to be, we having advantages against them so many manner of ways, as by our discipline, our strange weapons and devices else, especially ordnance great and small, it may easily be imagined, by the experience we have had in some places, the turning up of their heels against us in running away was their best defense.

In respect of us they are a people poor, and for want of skill and judgment in the knowledge and use of our things, do esteem our trifles before things of greater value. Notwithstanding, in their proper manner (considering the want of such means as we have), they seem very ingenious. For although they have no such tools, nor any such crafts, sciences, and arts as we, yet in those things they do, they show excellency of wit.[2] And by how much they upon due consideration shall find our manner of knowledges and crafts to

1. Shields.

2. I.e., intelligence.

exceed theirs in perfection, and speed for doing or execution, by so much the more is it probable that they should desire our friendship and love, and have the greater respect for pleasing and obeying us. Whereby may be hoped, if means of good government be used, that they may in short time be brought to civility and the embracing of true religion.

Some religion they have already, which although it be far from the truth, yet being as it is, there is hope it may be the easier and sooner reformed.

They believe that there are many gods, which they call *Mantóac*, but of different sorts and degrees, one only chief and great god, which hath been from all eternity. Who, as they affirm, when he purposed to make the world, made first other gods of a principal order to be as means and instruments to be used in the creation and government to follow, and after the sun, moon, and stars as petty gods, and the instruments of the other order more principal. First, they say, were made waters, out of which by the gods was made all diversity of creatures that are visible or invisible.

For mankind, they say a woman was made first which, by the working of one of the gods, conceived and brought forth children. And in such sort, they say, they had their beginning. But how many years or ages have passed since, they say they can make no relation, having no letters nor other such means as we to keep records of the particularities of times past, but only tradition from father to son.

They think that all the gods are of human shape, and therefore, they represent them by images in the forms of men, which they call *Kewasówok*, one alone is called *Kewás*. These they place in houses appropriate or temples, which they call *Machicómuck*, where they worship, pray, sing, and make many times offering unto them. In some Machicómuck, we have seen but one Kewas, in some two, and in other some three. The common sort think them to be also gods.

They believe also the immortality of the soul that, after this life as soon as the soul is departed from the body, according to the works it hath done, it is either carried to heaven, the habitacle of gods, there to enjoy perpetual bliss and happiness, or else to a great pit or hole, which they think to be in the furthest parts of their part of the world toward the sunset, there to burn continually. The place they call *Popogusso*.

For the confirmation of this opinion, they told me two stories of two men that had been lately dead and revived again. The one happened, but a few years before our coming into the country, of a wicked man, which having been dead and buried, the next day the earth of the grave being seen to move, was taken up again, who made declaration where his soul had been. That is to say, very near entering into Popogusso, had not one of the gods saved him, and gave him leave to return again and teach his friends what they should do to avoid that terrible place of torment. The other happened in the same year we were there, but in a town that was threescore miles from us, and it was told me for strange news, that one being dead, buried, and taken up again as the first, showed that although his body had lain dead in the grave, yet his soul was alive and had traveled far in a long broad way, on both sides whereof grew most delicate and pleasant trees, bearing more rare and excellent fruits, than ever he had seen before or was able to express, and at length came to most brave and fair houses, near which he met his father that had been dead before, who gave him great charge to go back again and show his friends what good they were to do to enjoy the pleasures of that place, which when he had done he should after come again.

What subtlety soever be in the Wiroances and priests, this opinion worketh so much in many of the common and simple sort of people, that it maketh them have great respect to their governors, and also great care what they do, to avoid torment after death, and to enjoy bliss, although notwithstanding there is punishment ordained for malefactors, as stealers, whoremongers, and other sort of wicked-doers, some punished with death, some with forfeitures,[3] some with beating, according to the greatness of the facts.

And this is the sum of their religion, which I learned by having special familiarity with some of their priests. Wherein they were not so sure grounded, nor gave such credit to their traditions and stories, but through conversing with us they were brought into great doubts of their own, and no small admiration of ours, with earnest desire in many, to learn more than we had means for want of perfect utterance in their language to express.

Most things they saw with us, as mathematical instruments, sea compasses, the virtue of the lodestone in drawing iron, a perspective glass whereby was showed many strange sights,[4] burning glasses, wild fireworks, guns, hooks, writing and reading, spring-clocks that seem to go of themselves, and many other things that we had were so strange unto them, and so far exceeded their capacities to comprehend the reason and means how they should be made and done, that they thought they were rather the works of gods than of men, or at the leastwise, they had been given and taught us of the gods. Which made many of them to have such opinion of us, as that if they knew not the truth of God and religion already, it was rather to be had from us whom God so specially loved, than from a people that were so simple as they found themselves to be in comparison of us. Whereupon greater credit was given unto that we spoke of, concerning such matters.

3. Fines.
4. The "perspective glass" was a telescope; the "burning glass" a mirror used to concentrate the sun's rays.

Many times and in every town where I came, according as I was able, I made declaration of the contents of the Bible, that therein was set forth the true and only God, and his mighty works, that therein was contained the true doctrine of salvation through Christ, with many particulars of miracles and chief points of religion, as I was able then to utter, and thought fit for the time. And although I told them the book materially and of itself was not of any such virtue, as I thought they did conceive, but only the doctrine therein contained, yet would many be glad to touch it, to embrace it, to kiss it, to hold it to their breasts and heads, and stroke over all their body with it, to show their hungry desire of that knowledge which was spoken of.

The Wiroans with whom we dwelt, called Wingina, and many of his people would be glad many times to be with us at our prayers, and many times call upon us both in his own town, as also in others whither he sometimes accompanied us, to pray and sing psalms, hoping thereby to be partaker of the same effects which we by that means also expected.

Twice this Wiroans was so grievously sick that he was like to die, and as he lay languishing, doubting of any help by his own priests, and thinking he was in such danger for offending us and thereby our God, sent for some of us to pray and be a means to our God that it would please him either that he might live, or after death dwell with him in bliss, so likewise were the requests of many others in the like case.

On a time also when their corn began to wither by reason of a drought which happened extraordinarily, fearing that it had come to pass by reason that in something they had displeased us, many would come to us and desire us to pray to our God of England, that he would preserve their corn, promising that when it was ripe we also should be partakers of the fruit.

* * * Some people could not tell whether to think us gods or men, and the rather because that all the space of their sickness, there was no man of ours known to die, or that was specially sick. They noted also that we had no women amongst us, neither that we did care for any of theirs.

Some, therefore, were of opinion that we were not born of women, and therefore not mortal, but that we were men of an old generation many years past, then risen again to immortality.

Some would likewise seem to prophesy that there were more of our generation yet to come to kill theirs and take their places as some thought the purpose was, by that which was already done. Those that were immediately to come after us they imagined to be in the air, yet invisible and without bodies, and that they by our entreaty and for the love of us did make the people to die in that sort as they did, by shooting invisible bullets into them.

To confirm this opinion, their physicians (to excuse their ignorance in curing the disease) would not be ashamed to say, but earnestly make the simple people believe that the strings of blood that they sucked out of the sick bodies, were the strings wherewithal the invisible bullets were tied and cast. Some also thought that we shot them ourselves out of our pieces, from the place where we dwelt, and killed the people in any town that had offended us, as we listed, how far distant from us soever it were. And other some said that it was the special work of God for our sakes, as we ourselves have cause in some sort to think no less, whatsoever some do, or may imagine to the contrary, specially some astrologers, knowing of the eclipse of the sun which we saw the same year before in our voyage thitherward, which unto them appeared very terrible. And also of a comet which began to appear but a few days before the beginning of the said sickness. But to exclude them from being the special causes of so special an accident, there are further reasons than I think fit at this present to be alleged. These their opinions I have set down the more at large, that it may appear unto you that there is good hope they may be brought through discreet dealing and government to the embracing of the truth, and consequently to honor, obey, fear, and love us.

And although some of our company towards the end of the year showed themselves too fierce in slaying some of the people in some towns, upon causes that on our part might easily enough have been borne withal, yet notwithstanding, because it was on their part justly deserved, the alteration of their opinions generally and for the most part concerning us is the less to be doubted. And whatsoever else they may be, by carefulness of ourselves need nothing at all to be feared.

1588

The Seventeenth Century

(1603-1660)

(1588: The Spanish Armada.)
1603: Death of Elizabeth Tudor, accession of James Stuart.
1605: The Gunpowder Plot; last effort of English Catholic extremists.
1620: First emigration of Pilgrims to the New World.
1625: Death of James I, accession of Charles I.
1641: Outbreak of Civil War: theaters closed, 1642.
1649: Execution of Charles I, beginning of Commonwealth and Protectorate, known inclusively as the Interregnum (1649–60).
1660: End of the Protectorate, Restoration of Charles II.
(1688: Abdication of James II, last Stuart king of England.)

In its narrowest definition, the "17th century" reaches from the accession of the first Stuart king (James I) in 1603 to the restoration of the third (Charles II) in 1660. But the events of those years are meaningful only if seen in a pattern extending from 1588 to 1688. Between these two outer dates occurred those massive social events which, in their cumulative effect, bridge the gap between the Tudor autocracy of the 16th century and the ill-defined but functioning constitutional monarchy of the 18th century. At the center of the period lies the Puritan Revolution of 1640–60. The quarrels and controversies which culminated in this upheaval began to make themselves felt shortly after 1588; its tremors and aftershocks largely subsided after 1688. In more senses than one, the Revolution was the central event of the century.

Armada year marked a decisive turning point in the reign of Elizabeth. Like most of her subjects, she had expected the nation's supreme triumph over a long-awaited, much-hated invader to release a tide of patriotic good feeling. Nothing of the sort happened; on the contrary. Social problems which had long lain suppressed in the interests of national unity suddenly surfaced when the nation was secure. They gave rise to bitter and divisive quarrels, fought out for the most part between the aging queen and her successive parliaments. There were disputes over the government of the church, disputes over foreign policy, disputes over monopolies and special forms of economic privilege, disputes over parliamentary rights and immunities.

These were conflicts too deep to be solved by the queen's traditional measures of cajolery and grandiose rhetoric; and they were not solved, nor even alleviated. Neither did the peaceful accession of James, the first English monarch of the Stuart family, serve to mollify these quarrels; they festered throughout his reign, and grew inflamed under the autocratic rule of his son, Charles I. By 1640 they were ready to flare into full-scale revolution, and flare they did. In the wars that followed, the forces of insurrection were successful in one of their aims (they rendered Charles powerless), but not in another (they failed to set up a stable government, free from the faults of the one they had destroyed). The military dictatorship (1649–60) established first by Oliver Cromwell under the name of Commonwealth and then maintained even after his death as a Protectorate was no more than a makeshift effort to contain a political instability that had got out of hand. When Charles II was recalled from exile (1660) and put back on his father's throne but without his father's powers, it became clear that England was bound to have, in religion and politics, some sort of organization looser than anyone had anticipated, looser than anyone really wanted. But its exact form was subject to constant pulling and hauling among the parties, and no solid settlement was reached till 1688, when Charles's brother and successor, James II, was ejected from the throne and sent into exile. After 1688, its social problems compromised if not solved, the country settled down to a long constitutional nap under a series of monarchs who made little trouble for their parliaments and therefore had little trouble with their thrones. The crisis was over.

Though infinitely complex in details, the main social problems which exercised the 17th century can be broadly stated, with their solutions, in two sentences. In the religious sphere, the basic issue was: How far should the reformation of the Protestant church be carried? and the solution accomplished in 1688 was, "As far as each individual self-defined religious group wants." In the sphere of constitutional politics, the basic issue was: How much authority should the monarch have independent of the parliament? and the solution accomplished in 1688 was, "Almost none."

BEFORE AND AFTER THE PURITAN REVOLT

To visualize the immense changes wrought by the crisis years of the Puritan Revolt, and their relation to the quality of English literature, it may be useful to anatomize very roughly the value-structure of English society before and after the event. Oversimplifications are inevitable, but necessary to point up a set of broad changes which actually took place; and definitions are possible because the Revolution was preceded and followed by periods of relative order and tranquillity. Under Elizabeth Tudor the court was the undisputed center of national authority, influence, power, reward, and intellectual inspiration. Careers were made and fortunes established through court connections. London was the center of the kingdom, and the court was the unchallenged center of London. Particularly was this true in matters of the intellect, of literature and the arts. The characteristic forms of literature under Elizabeth were courtly. Courtiers patronized the theater by attending plays (of which the middle class generally disapproved) and by lending the prestige of their names to different acting companies. The sonnet sequence, the pastoral romance (Sidney's *Arcadia*), the chivalric allegory (Spenser's *Faerie Queene*), the learned sermon, the erotic idyll (*Hero and Leander* or *Venus and Adonis*), the masque, the epic—all these were courtly forms, implying courtly readers. Patronage flowed, when it flowed at all, from courtly donors; and, apart from the precarious rewards of the theater, patronage was almost the only way for a man to live by his writing. The same pattern continued under the first two Stuarts, James I and Charles I. Whether in his sermons or in his poems, a man like Donne wrote primarily for courtiers. Versatile and various as he was, Ben Jonson channeled almost all his energies into writing for court and courtiers. Carew, Suckling, Lovelace, and a host of lesser writers were themselves courtiers, simply in the sense that they spent much of their time at court. A man like George Herbert was much remarked because he could have been a courtier and chose not to be. There were exceptions, of course; country doctors and rural parsons sometimes exercised themselves in literature. But the court influence was predominant, and so far as a literary society existed, it took its tone from the court. Because court circles were narrow, a poet did not have to wait for publication in order to be widely known among his fellow poets. Manuscript collections of poems by one author, or by several, circulated through the court; a poem could become popular, be set to music several times over, and yet never appear in print. The books that were printed generally appeared in small editions, and being destined for a particular audience, could take a good deal for granted in the way of special background and training. A court preacher like Lancelot Andrewes assumed in his hearers acquaintance with at least the rudiments of three ancient languages; Sir Philip Sidney in the *Arcadia* assumed familiarity with the traditions and conventions of courtly behavior. For court society had many characteristic and distinctive values. It implied a belief in hierarchical order within a strict framework of uniformity, involving obedience to the national church, loyalty to the national monarch. Within that framework, it tended to produce intricate, allusive, and highly decorative writing. Courtiers generally valued the heroic passions—love (but not necessarily marriage), warfare (largely free of a political context), and devotional piety (quite apart from practical morality). The controlling principle behind all these distinctions was an emphasis upon honor as the supreme principle in life, not to be estimated in any way by criteria of mere prudence. Literature written within this framework and primarily for readers who accepted it tended generally to reflect its arrangement of values.

After 1660, and even more strikingly after 1688, the pattern of values was quite different. For one thing, the court was no longer an unchallenged center of intellectual and literary influence. It did not have the power, social and financial, to be anything of the sort. For now money and influence no longer flowed exclusively from the court. London City (a network of banks and merchants, jobbers, financiers, brokers, tradesmen, and credit-managers) was one rival source of power and influence; Parliament itself, which in 1688 would assert decisive power over the throne by expelling James II and appointing a Dutchman to be his successor as William III, was another. Instead of standing above interest as the sole fountain of honor, the court thus became in effect one of several competing interests. The relatively conservative "landed interest" tended toward the court, as the more innovative "money interest" found its chief support in the City; and Parliament men, ranking themselves under the deliberately meaningless nicknames of "Tory" and "Whig," sided with either interest as they chose or with both as they found the occasion proper. One's connection with an interest was not through the inflexible principle of honor, but through the flexible one of . . . interest.

In precisely the same way, the established church, which had once claimed to be the sole guardian of men's spiritual welfare and therefore of their worldly behavior—the authoritative voice disciplining every Englishman's private interests—became after 1660 simply one of many possible religious communities. The Puritan sects, originally factions within the English church, had been freed to multiply and develop their independence during the Interregnum; after the Restoration, they could not be got back into the English (Anglican) church by force or persuasion. When several sects exist side by side in open competition, they are all voluntary. Each interprets Scripture after its own fashion, each follows its own moral code, each tries to attract proselytes, all agree in not trying to persecute one another. But that creates problems of discipline; if a member does not like the social code of his sect, he transfers to a more understanding sect, or out of them all. When neither monarch nor church could control social and economic behavior, most of it passed out of control altogether. For morality in a social or business sense applies mainly to people, considered as responsible economic agents; and the new forms of economic organization involved either artificial personalities or legal fictions to which moral laws do not apply. Corporations and joint-stock companies, cartels and syndicates, mutual-aid societies and credit unions, banks and bankers' combines (a whole gamut of anonymous voluntary associations) began to develop England piecemeal, amorphously, after the fashion of a modern capitalist nation. New money brought to the fore new men, enterprising and respectable, but with few pretensions to courtly manners or intellectual sophistication. The literature which appealed to them was less dogmatic and moralistic than the old hell-and-damnation puritanism; it was more serious than the frankly bawdy wit of the Restoration stage. Observing these and other divergencies of taste, enterprising publishers began to aim their products at a particular market, in which they specialized. Before long, they were hiring writers to turn out titles on order. The "booksellers," as they were called, thus replaced the older courtly patrons as makers of public taste. Authors who wrote to order at the bidding of publishers became known collectively, from the cheap lodgings where they congregated, as Grub Street authors. For them, at least, the change from a society organized around honor to one organized around interest was very palpable indeed.

Around the broad social changes sketched above there took place a set of intellectual and spiritual changes, no less striking and significant. The Elizabethan monarchy and church had been hierarchical in organization because that was thought to be the inevitable structure of things, the natural pattern of the world. Every creature had his place in the great order of divine appointments; and the different families of being were bound together by a chain of universal analogy. The king was to his subjects as Michael was to the other archangels, as the bishop was to his pastors, as the lion was to other beasts, as the eagle was to other birds, as the diamond was to other stones, as gold was to other metals. The head ruled the other parts of the body because, as the seat of reason, it was nobler. Reason, which ruled in man, made him natural head of the family because passion was thought to rule in woman. The king was head of the body politic; in him, reason ruled as it ought, over the passionate and tumultuous multitude. And all this ruling was necessary because of Adam's fall, as a result of which not only human psychology but the whole structure of the universe had been disordered. Though they differed over the form of the rule and the name of the ruler, almost all the contestants in the civil wars agreed that the people needed strict discipline of some sort, because in themselves they were radically imperfect. While the various leaders were disputing over details, the people, simply as a result of slow experience (by living under an "illegitimate" authority, without any sort of religious conformity), demonstrated that they were less imperfect, and needed less rigid discipline, than had been supposed.

One universal truth emerged from the Revolution and Civil Wars—that no one universal truth was to be had, whether by sword, by prayer, or by study. Nor was it really needed. Individuals, it seemed, could hold differing views about foreign policy, the nature of Christ's presence in the sacrament, or the lawfulness of infant baptism, without necessarily precipitating social chaos. A single true belief in these matters, and in many, many others, was evidently unnecessary. And thus the whole notion of human beings as radically fallen creatures, who needed a special saving truth and a dose of stiff discipline to redeem their faults began fading toward obsolescence. A reasonable person (one who behaved sensibly and didn't bother his or her neighbor) seemed to be almost as good as need be. In a long list of controversies, over which people had once been willing to slit throats, it turned out that nobody was right and nobody was wrong. And thus the English community changed from one founded on the concepts of hierarchy, uniformity, and personal relatedness, to one founded on the concepts of multiplicity, disparity, and toleration. In less than a hundred years, the nation had passed from enlightened, inept autocracy to a vigorous, materialistic pluralism.

LITERARY CROSS-CURRENTS

With the obvious and immensely important exception of Milton, hardly any of the high literature (*belles lettres*) of the 17th century was the work of Puritans or men sympathetic to the Puritan cause. This is hardly surprising. Many early Puritans looked with misgivings on the secular imagination. They mistrusted literature on the same principle that they mistrusted statues (graven idols), church music, and elaborate religious rituals. These were all allurements and enticings of the sensual world; they threatened to contaminate and diffuse the pure spiritual energy of divinely infused faith. Yet a sense of deep disquiet, of ancient traditions under challenge, is everywhere felt in the early 17th century; and it can hardly be accounted for except as a response to the growing challenge—social, political, and religious—which ultimately took form in the Revolt.

One may well think of the metaphysical poets who followed Donne (Herbert, Crashaw, Vaughan, Cowley, Cleveland) as trying to draw out the traditional lyric of love and devotion by stretching it, under deliberate mental pressure, to encompass new unities from which a sense of strain and violent effort was rarely absent. In the opposite direction, Jonson and his "sons" the Cavalier poets (Carew, Herrick, Suckling, Waller, Davenant) generally tried to compress and limit their poems, giving them a high finish and a strong sense of easy domination at the expense of their explicit intellectual content. Though these alternate "schools" do not by any means represent watertight compartments (Donne himself wrote some Jonsonian-style poems, Jonson some which sound quite like Donne), the broad contrast of "Cavalier" with "metaphysical" does describe two major poetic alternatives of the early century. Yet both styles were wholly inadequate containers for the sort of gigantic energy which Milton, for example, was seeking to express.

For Milton, with his deep sense of moral imperative, his heroic ambitions for poetry, his proud Englishness, all the fashionable verses of his contemporaries must have seemed unbearably constricting. Like any great poet, Milton was capable of profiting from the study of craftsmen whom he had no intention of imitating; and he did profit by a study of Donne and Jonson, we may be sure. But for his central inspiration he reached back beyond both metaphysicals and cavaliers, to the figure of Spenser. In his youth particularly his mind ran to Spenserian projects—chivalric romances based on Arthurian themes or sometimes on scriptural stories. Milton's style was thus fully formed by the period of the late 1630's—he found his voice, it is usual to say, in *Lycidas* (1637)—but what he defined as his "duty" kept him through the next twenty years at the uncongenial labor of producing topical prose pamphlets on public affairs. When he finally brought it forth in 1667, *Paradise Lost* appeared to be a poem written by a man formed in one civilization for an audience reared in another.

In fact, Milton's poem had some trouble finding even that "fit audience though few" which the poet hoped for it; the poem actually had to make its own audience, as it started to do toward the end of the century. (One of its strongest sponsors was Lord Somers, chief legal craftsman of the 1688 settlement.) Milton's gains were made partly at the expense, and partly with the help, of the Restoration's most representative poet, John Dryden. The heroic couplets which were Dryden's favored poetic vehicle had developed only gradually, in the hands of the Cavalier poets, from a rather jolting and irregular meter toward the poised and sinewy units out of which Dryden built his verse-paragraphs. These couplets were less choked with learning than Milton's blank verse; their sentence-units were shorter, and logical or pseudo-logical argumentation played a greater part in the structure. Dryden is more a poet of statement, Milton more a poet of suggestion. But both are architects in verse, though Milton builds a cathedral, Dryden an elegant townhouse. And it is pleasant to record that the lesser poet, who had received so much public acclaim, was generous in his appreciation of the greater poet, who knew so little of it.

During the twenty years of Puritan rule at mid-century, most of the theaters were closed and hardly anything was written for the stage; during this period, most of the old actors and playwrights died, and the revival of the English stage after 1660 depended very largely on the work of one man, Sir William Davenant, and on the example of the French stage, then at its height. Shakespeare's emulators and successors under the first two Stuarts were much influenced by the melancholy then so largely prevalent; the dark, oppressive mood is almost unbroken in the work of tragic writers such as Webster, Ford, Tourneur, and Middleton. But alongside this somber and sometimes morbid tragedy, almost serving as relief from it, flourished a great variety of tragicomic spectacles, romantic comedies, and pastoral fantasies. Very often these plays were influenced by the masques so popular at court

—that is, they included a great deal in the way of spectacle, display, pageant, music, and sometimes fantasy. Though Shakespeare was long dead, though Jonson was in his dotage, and though none of the successors to these two men met their measure, the stage continued vigorously active right up to the Civil War. But then the theaters were shut, abruptly and apparently forever. When they reopened in 1660, they were forced at first to rely on a backlog of twenty-year-old plays. But gradually they built up a repertoire of comedies (generally bawdy) and tragedies in the rhetorical, declamatory manner which gave them, quite as much as the heroic couplets in which they were cast, the name of "heroic tragedies." Both these fashions, like so much else in the Restoration were extreme and temporary. Dryden, who practiced both modes, lived to see them both at an end—the heroic tragedies under the weight of their own pomposity, the bawdy comedies under the attack of an infuriated clergyman, Jeremy Collier.

Beyond, perhaps outside, literature as such lies a change in the intellectual tone of the century which cannot be ignored, hard as it is to describe. The great minds of the early century were lawyers and theologians. Coke, Bacon, Selden, and Spelman among the lawyers, Laud, Andrewes, Cudworth, Ussher, and Chillingworth among the theologians were men famous in their generation. Among the lawyers, some are still consulted as authorities to this day—Coke is a name to conjure with in English law, and Selden's treatise on *Titles of Honor* is obsolete only because the subject itself is. As for the theologians, their work too has ceased to be "relevant"; but a brief browsing expedition through the "Library of Anglo-Catholic Theology" cannot fail to convince the student that they were men who worked—in their chosen trade—to very high standards of precise and authoritative scholarship. And yet, as the century's intellectual weather changed, these disciplines ceased to be at the center of things. There were great lawyers after 1660, but they were not the makers and shakers of society; there were famous clergymen, but they were not the builders of society's central codes of belief. Starting about mid-century, the great names belong to other disciplines—they are scientists like the astronomers Hooke and Halley, the physicist Robert Boyle, Locke the physician-philosopher, John Wallis and Sir Isaac Newton the mathematicians, William Harvey the anatomist. Few of them set out consciously to reconstruct an entire view of the cosmos, and Sir Isaac, who did so most successfully, retained to the end streaks and patches of the old beliefs. (He wrote a commentary on the Book of Revelation which has rather baffled those who admire his scientific work.) But the coming of a secular, materialist world view was in the air; even before the Puritans were forced to give up their dream of a community of saints, the tide had set and was ebbing rapidly another way.

BIRTH AND DEATH OF LITERARY FORMS

The stress and strain of a revolutionary age can thus be read at large in the century's literature, from the somber, sluggish melancholy of the early decades, through the hoarse, incoherent warfare of the middle years, to the slow firming up of new standards of decorum and correctness after 1660. Still another mark of violent change is provided by the number of literary forms which perished in the course of the century, even as others were being born.

Sonnets, for example, were all the rage in the last years of Elizabeth, the first years of James. Almost always they dealt with erotic themes, often they were linked together in sequences to suggest, if not to tell, a story. Donne turned the sonnet primarily to religious themes (of his *Songs and Sonnets,* only one, and it irregular, is actually a sonnet); Milton's sonnets are few, and none are erotic. And thereafter sonnets largely faded from the poetic repertory. Like epic poetry in our own day, sonnets just disappeared. Allegory suffered an even more curious fate. It was of course the essential method of Spenser's great poem, and a major ingredient in Milton's; the "highest" and most demanding poetry of the earlier age made use of it. But then again, in the last half of the century, it largely faded from view. Dryden did not accommodate his mind easily to allegory; when he did use it (as in *The Hind and the Panther*), there was a kind of grotesque comedy about it, as if the form were fundamentally a joke. Serious and explicit allegory had slid far down the social scale; it was now the natural mode for an inspired primitive like Bunyan.

Blighted by the killing frosts of Puritanism, the masque and madrigal both perished. The one was a courtly, the other a popular, form; but both were suspect as vain, sensual, and worldly. Madrigals, as a blend of folk- and art-songs deeply rooted in the indigenous culture, were particularly to be regretted. For many years they had been sung in the yeoman's home or merchant's parlor, to the accompaniment of a chest of viols, that is, a consort of stringed instruments. Many involved complex polyphonic harmonies; many had been composed by distinguished musicians. But because it was an art that tended to make men happy with their present state, instead of wretched and guilty as they should have been, the Puritans disapproved: they wanted, instead of a "nest of singing birds," a nation of psalm singers. So all the folk-arts and folk-customs faded—rounds and carols and madrigals, square-dancing, Maypoles, and rural games—to make way for the dreary, vacant English sabbath.

Despite the immense examples of Shakespeare and Milton, blank verse lost ground during the century to the rhymed couplet. Couplets had been written, in one form or another, since Chaucer's day, but only after mid-century did they take on the smooth, antithetical energy best exemplified in the opening lines of *Absalom and Achitophel.* They are a superb meter for argumentation—which was what Dryden did best. Alongside this regularizing of poetic surfaces went a vogue for extravagant and irregular odes after the manner of the Greek lyric poet Pindar. Jonson had known Pindar's work, and the *Ode on Cary and Morison* illustrates the rather severe conception he had of Pindaric form. Abraham Cowley in his *Pindarique Odes* (1656) set the example for greater irregularity in an effort to simulate greater violence of feeling, and his example was followed by Dryden, and later by Gray, not to speak of Wordsworth. Dryden's odes were sometimes set to music after a fashion imported from Italy and known by the Italian name of *oratorio.* He also wrote texts for operas, including one based on Milton's epic; opera too was an exotic form imported from Italy via France. After the indigenous madrigal and masque perished, their place was filled by imported oratorios and operas.

Satire, which had been a self-conscious novelty at the beginning of the century, was a well-established, almost a normal mode of poetry by the end; more explanation was called for when one didn't write satire than when one did. In the process, satire grew subtler and more various; the satirist recognized his responsibility to divert the reader as well as to insult his antagonist. Indeed, a whole new tone of gentlemanly discourse grew up after the Restoration; it went by the name of "raillery," or sometimes "banter"—and while silly things could be said in it, so too could serious and important truths, about which nonetheless a gentleman might not want to show himself too earnest. Below satire, burlesque was still another literary device to which the 17th century gave birth, with the aid of France. After the unrelieved earnestness of the Puritans, derision and buffoonery became the order of the day; and with the advent of burlesque, we find ourselves on the very threshold of the modern novel, which Henry Fielding was to define in memorable words as "a comic epic in prose." One reason why he felt that way was undoubtedly that he began his literary career as a writer of stage-burlesques.

Alongside dying forms, new ones naturally sprang up. The most striking of these were in the area of popular literature, and surely represented a response to the new freedom of the press. When the Puritans rose against the authoritarian government of Charles I in 1641, they broke the long-standing power of the Bishop of London to censor publications throughout the land. Immediately a flood of pamphlets, tracts, newsletters, satires, and propaganda of every description began pouring forth. In the nature of things, much of it was ephemeral, but it got people into the way of reading and disputing about public affairs. And once people were in the way of it, even though various efforts were made later in the century to reimpose censorship, none were really successful. For even when every faction wanted some form of censorship, they could not agree on who should exercise it, or how. As there were many religious sects after 1640, so there were many measures of truth, each individual being free to pursue truth as it might be individually defined, and to persuade others that this was, or that was not, true. The Restoration saw the portentous twin birth of periodical journalism and the two-party system, both reflecting in different ways the development of something like modern "public opinion." And though prose narrative had been practiced for a long time in the form of tales and romances, the Restoration saw the first growth of what was to become the novel. These developments were all predicated on a reading audience responsive to general ideas and nuances of social observation—not necessarily learned in the classical tongues or trained in courtly formalities, but able to follow a sustained discourse in plain, unrhetorical, commonsense English. Such an audience, so tuned and prepared, not expecting too much from its reading, but responsive to acute arguments or vivid touches of the imagination, is a first premise of modern literature. We are apt to think it as normal and natural a phenomenon as the air we breathe, but it is not. In fact it had to be created slowly, hesitantly, without much conscious intent on anyone's part, by a process of gradual accretion and expansion. Its existence is the foundation of the new age.

Being diverse out of harsh necessity and tolerant only reluctantly, the late 17th century was often halting and unsteady in its taste. It was forging new standards, not accepting the guidance of old ones; its hallmark is a widening eclecticism. Conscious efforts are made to reform the language itself by rendering it more light, lucid, and informal. Early prose fiction gropes to speak the voice and articulate the interests of the hitherto silent 50% of the nation which is female. A poem like John Dryden's *Annus Mirabilis* is an unprecedented medley of contemporary history and political argumentation; the audacious Abraham Cowley tries to write Pindaric odes on scientific topics; Milton's epic pours so much new wine into a very old bottle that it practically changes the definition of "bottle." Even apart from these internal developments, the Restoration was a strikingly cosmopolitan and international age. Strongly rationalist and quasi-mechanical philosophers from France, like René Descartes (1596–1650) and his follower Nicolas Malebranche (1638–1715), were read, translated, and vigorously discussed; less spectacular but in the long range just as important in his influence was the Jewish pantheist of Amsterdam, Baruch de Spinoza (1632–77). Seeing God as everywhere present in the universe, he developed a unified theory of mechanics, of ethics, and of theology which enabled him to dispense with all special forms of revelation. Though differing among themselves in various ways, these Continental philosophers all contributed to the growth of English deism—which is simply a form of belief that affirms a Supreme Being as the source of the world but denies, rejects, or remains neutral toward revelation and the supernatural doctrines of Christianity.

French manners, French styles, French tastes all invaded England when Charles II, after twenty years of wandering on the Continent, returned to his throne. French influence from the dramatists Pierre Corneille (1606–84), Jean Racine (1639–99), and the famous Molière (1622–73) made itself felt on the English stage; plays by these authors were translated and adapted to the English stage, while detailed comparisons were pursued between their work and that of English writers. Meanwhile, baroque and neoclassical buildings, inspired by French palaces like Versailles or Italian villas like those of the 16th-century architect Palladio, arose on English fields. Visitors from the Continent became more frequent, and young Englishmen, accompanied by their tutors, started to make that circuit of the Continental sights and monuments that was later to be known as the Grand Tour. Art-collectors—a species almost unknown in England before the 17th century—began to import Renaissance paintings and classical marbles and prints and manuscripts and rarities in general into English homes. Finally, a new age of translation began, with John Dryden at its center, second only in importance to the first age of Elizabethan translation. As it became simpler and clearer stylistically, the English language seemed to become ever richer in its vocabulary, more assured in its confidence that just about any clear concept could be expressed in English—and that any concept not that clear was not worth expressing in the first place.

In all these manifold ways, the 17th century changed not only the tone of literature, but the very definition of what literature could be. Like all great cultural shifts, this one was too complex to be captured in a single phrase or attributed to a single cause. It had neither a fixed beginning nor a precise end. Yet in the seamless web of history we can hardly fail to notice new colors and textures which, over the course of the 17th century, enter into the warp and woof of the nation's literary as of its social life, to make it look and feel like a whole new piece of cloth.

JOHN DONNE
(1572–1631)

Late 1601 or early 1602: Secret marriage to Ann More.
1615: Sacred orders.
1633: First publication of *Songs and Sonnets.*

There are two distinct but related authors known as John Donne. First is the scandalous young spark, who wrote bawdy and cynical verses—Jack Donne, the rake. Then there is the gravely witty, passionately religious divine, who wrote verses to his God as ardent as those he had once addressed to his mistresses. This is Dr. John Donne, the Dean of St. Paul's. Yet the key to both men is the same; it is a kind of restless, searching energy, which scorns the easy platitude and the smooth, empty phrase; which is vivid, immediate, troubling; and which makes the reading of Donne's poetry an imaginative and intellectual struggle and an all-absorbing experience.

Donne was born into an old Roman Catholic family, at a time when anti-Catholic feeling in England was near its height. His faith barred him from many of the usual avenues of success, and his point of view was always that of an insecure outsider. Though he attended both Oxford and Cambridge Universities, as well as Lincoln's Inn (where barristers got their training), he never took any academic degrees and never practiced law. After quietly abandoning Catholicism some time during the 1590's, he had scruples about becoming an Anglican. He had no gift for commerce, and though he inherited money from his father (who died when Donne was only 4), it was far from enough to render him independent. Hence he had to make his way in the world indirectly—by wit, charm, learning, valor, and above all, favor. Partly from sheer intellectual curiosity, he read enormously in divinity, medicine, law, and the classics; he wrote to display his learning and wit. He traveled on the Continent, especially, it would seem, to Spain; even in later years, he did a good deal of moving around. With Ralegh and Essex he took part in two hit-and-run expeditions against Cadiz and the Azores. He put himself in the way of court employment, danced attendance on great court ladies, and generally lived the life of a brilliant young man hopeful of preferment.

When in 1598 Donne was appointed private secretary to Sir Thomas Egerton, the Lord Keeper, his prospects for worldly advancement seemed good. He sat in Elizabeth's last parliament and moved in court circles. But in 1601 he secretly married Lady Egerton's niece, 17-year-old Ann More, and thereby ruined his own worldly hopes. The marriage turned out happily, but Donne's imprudence was never forgiven. Sir George More had Donne imprisoned and dismissed from his post; and for the next dozen years, the poet had to struggle at a series of makeshift employments to support his growing family. As a man of 35, Donne was no longer the brilliant young gallant of the 1590's; sick, poor, and unhappy, he was composing, but not publishing, a treatise on the lawfulness of suicide (*Biathanatos*). As he approached 40, he may have helped Thomas Morton, Dean of Gloucester, in composing anti-Catholic polemics (*Pseudo-Martyr*, 1610; *Ignatius his Conclave*, 1611). In return for patronage from Sir Robert Drury, he wrote in 1611 and 1612 a pair of long poems, *The Anniversaries*, on the death of Sir Robert's daughter Elizabeth. None of these activities represent a full employment of Donne's volcanic intellectual energy. To be sure, Donne's social position need not be painted too blackly. He had friends among the courtiers, politicians, poets, and clergy—Mrs. Magdalen Herbert and her sons George and Edward, Ben Jonson, Sir Henry Goodyere, and Sir Henry Wotton among them. He was never quite without resources. Yet, broadly speaking, the middle years of Donne's life were a period of searching, uncertainty, and unhappiness.

Though Donne had flatly refused in 1607 to take Anglican orders, King James was certain that he would some day make a great Anglican preacher. Hence he declared that Donne could have no preferment or employment from him, except in the church. Finally, in 1615, Donne overcame his scruples, not the least of which was the fear of seeming ambitious, and entered the ministry. He was in due course appointed Reader in Divinity at Lincoln's Inn. In the 17th century, among court circles and at the Inns of Court where lawyers congregated, preaching was at once a form of spiritual devotion, an intellectual exercise, and a dramatic entertainment. Donne's metaphorical style, bold erudition, and dramatic wit at once established him as a great preacher in an age of great preachers. Fully 160 of his sermons survive. In 1621 he was made Dean of St. Paul's, where he preached to great congregations of "City" lawyers, courtiers, merchants, and tradesmen. In addition, his private devotions were published in 1624, and he continued to write sacred poetry till within a few years of his death. Obsessed with the idea of death, Donne preached what was called his own funeral sermon just a few weeks before he died. It is a terrifyingly personal meditation on dissolution, as befits a man who arranged for a final portrait of himself to be taken, dressed in his shroud.

The poetry of Donne represents a sharp break with that written by his predecessors and most of his contemporaries. Much Elizabethan verse is decorative and flowery in its quality. Its images adorn, its meter is mellifluous. Image harmonizes with image, and line swells almost predictably into line. Donne's poetry, on the other hand, is written very largely in *conceits*—concentrated images which involve an element of dramatic contrast, of strain, or of intellectual difficulty. Most of the traditional "flowers of rhetoric" disappear completely. For instance, in his love poetry one never encounters bleeding hearts, cheeks like roses, lips like cherries, teeth like pearls, or Cupid shooting the arrows of love. The tears which flow in *A Valediction: of Weeping* are different from, and more complex than, the ordinary saline fluid of unhappy lovers; they are ciphers, naughts, symbols of the world's emptiness without the beloved; or else, suddenly reflecting her image, they are globes, worlds, they contain the sum of things. The poet who plays with conceits not only displays his own ingenuity; he may see into the nature of the world as deeply as the philosopher. Donne's conceits in particular leap continually in a restless orbit from the personal to the cosmic and back again.

Donne's rhythms are colloquial and various. He likes to twist and distort not only ideas, but metrical patterns and grammar itself. In the satires, which Renaissance writers understood to be "harsh" and "crabbed" as a genre, Donne's distortions often threaten to choke off the stream of expression entirely. But in the lyrics (both those which are worldly and those which are religious in theme), as in the elegies and sonnets, the verse never fails of a complex and memorable melody. Donne had an unusual gift, rather like that of a modern poet, T. S. Eliot, for striking off phrases which ring in the mind like a silver coin. They are two masters of the colloquial style, removed alike from the dignified, weighty manner of Milton and the sugared sweetness of the Elizabethans.

Donne and his followers are known to literary history as the "metaphysical school" of poets. Strictly speaking, this is a misnomer; there was no organized group of poets who imitated Donne, and if there had been, they would not have called themselves "metaphysical" poets. That term was invented by Dryden and Dr. Johnson. But the influence of Donne's poetic style was widely felt, especially by men whose taste was formed before 1660. George Herbert, Richard Crashaw, Henry Vaughan, Andrew Marvell, and Abraham Cowley are only the best known of those on whom Donne's influence is recognizable. The great change of taste which took place in 1660 threw Donne and the "conceited" style out of fashion; during the 18th and 19th centuries both he and his followers were rarely read and still more rarely appreciated. Finally, in the late 19th and early 20th centuries, three new editions of Donne appeared, of which Sir H. J. C. Grierson's, published in 1912, was quickly accepted as standard. By clarifying and purifying the often-garbled text, Grierson did a great deal to make Donne's poetry more available to the modern reader. Almost at once it started to exert an influence on modern poetic practice, the modern poets being hungry for a "tough" style which would free them from the worn-out rhetoric of late 19th-century romanticism. And Donne's status among the English poets quickly climbed from that of a curiosity to that of an acknowledged master.

No more than a couple of the poems on which Donne's modern reputation is built were published during his lifetime, though most of them were widely circulated through court and literary circles in handwritten copies. There were practical reasons for this halfway state of affairs. Many of the poems would have constituted black marks on Donne's reputation as an earnest and godly divine; and because they were difficult and allusive, only a few people wanted to read them. Thus Donne was known, outside the relatively limited circles which had access to manuscipt-collections, primarily as a preacher and devotional writer. But in these capacities he was tremendously productive and influential.

It has been said that there are two sorts of preachers—those who stand before us as representatives of God and explain His Word to us, and those who stand before God and explain our problems to Him. Certainly, John Donne belonged with the second group. He was a passionately human preacher, little interested in expounding dogma or laying down the rules of practical morality. What he presented to his hearers, in long, nervous periods, rich in poetic imagery and graphic detail, was a film in close-up of the

Christian drama—sin, guilt, contrition, repentance, faith, death, and transfiguration—with John Donne cast in the leading role. No other preacher in English could speak like Donne of the personal experience of entering heaven, and convey the sense that he had actually experienced in his own person every last detail of what he described.

Donne's acting impulses were not satisfied in the pulpit, though he preached an enormous number of immensely popular sermons; his whole life became a performance, upon which he commented, for public edification. Thus, his private prayers and devotions, written on the occasion of a serious sickness in 1623, promptly became a book (*Devotions upon Emergent Occasions*) in 1624. Readers of all sorts hastened to enjoy the pleasing anxieties and spiritual adventures of a devout and witty Christian wavering on the brink of eternity. To call the book a kind of existential soap-opera is doubtless too harsh, but it suggests some of the flamboyance with which Donne exploited his personal situation for purposes of pathetic and passionate instruction.

The basic text which follows is that of Sir Herbert Grierson (1912), but it has been modified, wherever sensible improvement seemed possible, and sometimes supplemented, by that of Dame Helen Gardner (*Divine Poems*, 1952, and *The Elegies and the Songs and Sonnets*, 1964).

The Good-Morrow

I wonder, by my troth, what thou and I
Did, till we loved? Were we not weaned till then,
But sucked on country pleasures, childishly?
Or snorted we in the seven sleepers' den?[1]
'Twas so; But this, all pleasures fancies be.
If ever any beauty I did see,
Which I desired, and got, 'twas but a dream of thee.

And now good morrow to our waking souls,
Which watch not one another out of fear;
For love all love of other sights controls,
And makes one little room an everywhere.
Let sea-discoverers to new worlds have gone,
Let maps to other,[2] worlds on worlds have shown,
Let us possess one world; each hath one, and is one.

My face in thine eye, thine in mine appears,[3]
And true plain hearts do in the faces rest;
Where can we find two better hemispheres
Without sharp North, without declining West?

1. Both Christian and Mohammedan authors recite the legend of seven youths of Ephesus, who hid in a cave from the persecutions of Decius, and slept there for 187 years. "Sucked" and "snorted" are words carefully chosen for their impact on the love poem. "But": except for.

2. I.e., let us concede that maps to other investigators have shown, etc. ("other" is an archaic plural form). In line 14 an alternative reading is "Let us possess *our* world" (from Dame Gardner).

3. Reflected in the pupils of one another's eyes, the lovers are, and possess, worlds of their own.

Whatever dies was not mixed equally;[4]
If our two loves be one, or thou and I
Love so alike that none do slacken, none can die.

1633

Song

Go and catch a falling star,
Get with child a mandrake root,[1]
Tell me where all past years are,
Or who cleft the Devil's foot,
Teach me to hear mermaids[2] singing,
Or to keep off envy's stinging,
And find
What wind
Serves to advance an honest mind.

If thou beest born to strange sights,
Things invisible to see,
Ride ten thousand days and nights,
Till age snow white hairs on thee,
Thou, when thou return'st, wilt tell me
All strange wonders that befell thee,
And swear
No where
Lives a woman true, and fair.

If thou find'st one, let me know,
Such a pilgrimage were sweet;
Yet do not, I would not go,
Though at next door we might meet;
Though she were true when you met her,
And last till you write your letter,
Yet she
Will be
False, ere I come, to two, or three.

1633

The Undertaking

I have done one braver thing
Than all the Worthies[1] did,
And yet a braver thence doth spring,
Which is, to keep that hid.

4. Scholastic philosophy taught that when the elements were imperfectly ("not equally") mixed, matter was mortal and mutable; but when they were perfectly mixed, it was undying and unchanging. The dividing line between these two natures was the sphere of the moon.

1. The mandrake root, or mandragora, forked like the lower part of the male body; to get one with child is a supreme impossibility.

2. Identified with the sirens, whose song only the wily Odysseus survived.

1. According to medieval legend, the Nine Worthies, or supreme heroes of history, included three Jews (Joshua, David, Judas Maccabeus), three pagans (Hector, Alexander, Julius Caesar), and three Christians (Arthur, Charlemagne, Godfrey of Bouillon).

It were but madness now t' impart
  The skill of specular stone,[2]
When he which can have learned the art
  To cut it, can find none.

So, if I now should utter this,
  Others (because no more
Such stuff to work upon, there is)
  Would love but as before.

But he who loveliness within
  Hath found, all outward loathes,
For he who color loves, and skin,
  Loves but their oldest clothes.

If, as I have, you also do
  Virtue attired in woman see,
And dare love that, and say so too,
  And forget the He and She;

And if this love, though placéd so,
  From profane men you hide,
Which will no faith on this bestow,
  Or, if they do, deride;

Then you have done a braver thing
  Than all the Worthies did;
And a braver thence will spring,
  Which is, to keep that hid.

1633

The Indifferent

I can love both fair and brown,[1]
Her whom abundance melts, and her whom want betrays,
Her who loves loneness best, and her who masks and plays,
Her whom the country formed, and whom the town,
Her who believes, and her who tries,[2]
Her who still weeps with spongy eyes,
And her who is dry cork, and never cries;
I can love her, and her, and you, and you,
I can love any, so she be not true.

Will no other vice content you?
Will it not serve your turn to do as did your mothers?
Or have you all old vices spent, and now would find out others?
Or doth a fear that men are true torment you?
O we are not, be not you so;

2. A transparent or translucent material, reputed to have been used in antiquity for mirrors (in Latin, *specula*), but no longer known.

1. Both blonde and brunette.
2. "Attempts to believe" and "tries things out."

Let me, and do you, twenty know.
Rob me, but bind me not, and let me go.
Must I, who came to travail[3] thorough you
Grow your fixed subject, because you are true?

Venus heard me sigh this song,
And by love's sweetest part, variety, she swore,
She heard not this till now; and that it should be so no more.
She went, examined, and returned ere long,
And said, Alas, some two or three
Poor heretics in love there be,
Which think to 'stablish dangerous constancy.
But I have told them, Since you will be true,
You shall be true to them who are false to you.

1633

The Canonization

For God's sake hold your tongue, and let me love,
Or chide my palsy, or my gout,
My five gray hairs, or ruined fortune, flout,
With wealth your state, your mind with arts improve,
Take you a course, get you a place,[1]
Observe His Honor, or His Grace,
Or the King's real, or his stamped face[2]
Contemplate; what you will, approve,[3]
So you will let me love.

Alas, alas, who's injured by my love?
What merchant's ships have my sighs drowned?
Who says my tears have overflowed his ground?
When did my colds a forward spring remove?[4]
When did the heats which my veins fill
Add one man to the plaguy bill?[5]
Soldiers find wars, and lawyers find out still
Litigious men, which quarrels move,
Though she and I do love.

Call us what you will, we are made such by love;
Call her one, me another fly,
We're tapers too, and at our own cost die,[6]

3. "Grief, sorrow," but also "journey, travel."

1. "Take you a course": not necessarily of physic or instruction, but in the general sense of "settling yourself in life." A "place" is an appointment, at court or elsewhere.

2. On coins.

3. Put to proof, find by experience.

4. By freezing a fountain or blighting a season.

5. Deaths from the hot-weather plague were recorded, by parish, in weekly lists.

6. Like the "fly," a symbol of transitory life, we are burned up in "tapers," which consume themselves. There is a hint here of the old superstition that every act of intercourse subtracts a day from one's life. (To "die," in the punning terminology of the 17th century, was to consummate the act of sex.)

And we in us find the eagle and the dove.[7]
The phoenix riddle hath more wit
By us: we two being one, are it.
So, to one neutral thing both sexes fit.
We die and rise the same, and prove
Mysterious by this love.

We can die by it, if not live by love,
And if unfit for tombs and hearse
Our legend be, it will be fit for verse;
And if no piece of chronicle we prove,
We'll build in sonnets pretty rooms;
As well a well-wrought urn becomes
The greatest ashes, as half-acre tombs,
And by these hymns,[8] all shall approve
Us canonized for love:

And thus invoke us: You whom reverend love
Made one another's hermitage;
You, to whom love was peace, that now is rage;
Who did the whole world's soul contract,[9] and drove
Into the glasses of your eyes
(So made such mirrors, and such spies,
That they did all to you epitomize)
Countries, towns, courts: Beg from above
A pattern of your love![10]

1633

A Nocturnal upon Saint Lucy's Day, Being the Shortest Day[1]

'Tis the year's midnight and it is the day's,
Lucy's, who scarce seven hours herself unmasks;

7. The eagle and the dove are symbols of earthly wisdom (strength) and heavenly meekness (purity), the latter paradoxically more powerful than the former. The phoenix, in general mythology, was a fabulous Arabian bird, only one of which existed at any one time. After living a thousand years, it lit its own funeral pyre, jumped in, and sang its funeral song as it was consumed—then rose triumphantly from its ashes, a new bird. Thus it was a symbol of immortality, as well as of desire rising from its own exhaustion. "Eagle" and "dove" are also alchemical terms for processes leading to the rise of "phoenix," a stage in the transmutation of metals.

8. Donne's own poems, transformed into hymns to a new love religion. "All" (posterity) shall "approve" (accept) us as love's saints.

9. In line 40 Dame Helen Gardner reads "extract" for "contract."

10. The poet and his mistress, turned to saints, are implored by the rest of the population to get from heaven ("above") a pattern of their love for general distribution. "Countries, towns, courts" are objects of the verb "drove"; the notion that eyes both see and reflect the outside world, and so "contain" it doubly, was very delightful to Donne.

1. A "nocturnal" seems to suggest a dreamy, meditative poem about dark thoughts; but the more common 17th-century usage alluded to an astronomical instrument, used for finding one's position or setting one's course at night. Donne probably wanted both meanings. St. Lucy's day falls on December 13, which under the old calendar was very close to the winter solstice (December 21 under our modern calendar). At this time of year the sun rises after eight in the latitude of London, and sets well before four.

The sun is spent, and now his flasks
Send forth light squibs,[2] no constant rays.
The world's whole sap is sunk;
The general balm th' hydroptic earth hath drunk,[3]
Whither, as to the bed's feet, life is shrunk,
Dead and interred; yet all these seem to laugh,
Compared with me, who am their epitaph.

Study me, then, you who shall lovers be
At the next world, that is, at the next spring;
For I am every dead thing
In whom love wrought new alchemy.
For his art did express[4]
A quintessence even from nothingness,
From dull privations and lean emptiness.
He ruined me, and I am re-begot
Of absence, darkness, death: things which are not.

All others from all things draw all that's good,
Life, soul, form, spirit, whence they being have;
I, by love's limbeck,[5] am the grave
Of all, that's nothing. Oft a flood
Have we two wept, and so
Drowned the whole world, us two; oft did we grow
To be two chaoses when we did show
Care to aught else; and often absences
Withdrew our souls, and made us carcasses.

But I am by her[6] death (which word wrongs her)
Of the first nothing the elixir grown;[7]
Were I a man, that I were one
I needs must know; I should prefer,
If I were any beast,
Some ends, some means; yea plants, yea stones detest
And love.[8] All, all some properties invest.
If I an ordinary nothing were,
As shadow, a light and body must be here.

But I am none, nor will my sun renew.
You lovers, for whose sake the lesser sun
At this time to the Goat[9] is run

2. The sun is compared to a gun shooting powder from powder flasks, but in small "squibs" like firecrackers.
3. The thirsty ("hydroptic") earth has drunk all the moisture in the world, as a dying person's vital heat was supposed to collect in one small part of the body.
4. Extract, draw forth.
5. Alembic, retort; a vessel used in distilling.
6. The fact that the mistress is now dead is very lightly touched on; Donne writes as from a great distance outside immediate experience. To speak of her death "wrongs" her by implying that she is not now among the immortals, a saint.
7. He is now "grown" (become) the "elixir of the first nothing," i.e., the quintessence of that absolute nothingness that existed even before the creation.
8. Beasts have intentions, plants instincts, even stones (like lodestones) attractions and antipathies.
9. Capricorn, in the zodiac, begins with the winter solstice; the goat is an emblem of sexual vigor.

To fetch new lust and give it you,
Enjoy your summer all.
Since she enjoys her long night's festival,
Let me prepare towards her, and let me call
This hour her vigil and her eve, since this
Both the year's and the day's deep midnight is.

1633

Love's Alchemy

Some that have deeper digged love's mine than I,
Say where his centric happiness doth lie;
I have loved, and got, and told,
But should I love, get, tell, till I were old,
I should not find that hidden mystery;
O, 'tis imposture all:
And as no chemic yet the elixir got,[1]
But glorifies his pregnant pot,[2]
If by the way to him befall
Some odoriferous thing, or medicinal;
So lovers dream a rich and long delight,
But get a winter-seeming summer's night.[3]

Our ease, our thrift, our honor, and our day,
Shall we for this vain bubble's shadow pay?
Ends love in this, that my man
Can be as happy as I can if he can
Endure the short scorn of a bridegroom's play?
That loving wretch that swears,
'Tis not the bodies marry, but the minds,
Which he in her angelic finds,
Would swear as justly that he hears,
In that day's rude hoarse minstrelsy, the spheres.[4]
Hope not for mind in women; at their best
Sweetness and wit they are, but mummy, possessed.[5]

1633

The Flea

Mark but this flea, and mark in this,
How little that which thou deniest me is;

1. "Chemic": alchemist; "the elixir": a magic medicine sought by alchemists and reputed to heal all ills.
2. Praises his fertile (and womb-shaped) retort.
3. A night cold as in winter and short as in summer.
4. The perfect harmony of the planets, moving in concentric crystalline spheres, is contrasted with the charivari, a boisterous serenade for pots, pans, and trumpets, performed on the wedding night.
5. Almost all punctuation for the last two lines represents conjectures by modern editors. There might equally well be commas after "best" and "wit." The last word, "possessed," may modify "mummy," meaning "mummy with a demon in it," or else "they," meaning "women who, when you have possessed them, are nothing but dried mummy."

Me it sucked first, and now sucks thee,
And in this flea our two bloods mingled be;
Thou know'st that this cannot be said
A sin, or shame, or loss of maidenhead,
Yet this enjoys before it woo,
And pampered swells with one blood made of two,
And this, alas, is more than we would do.[1]

Oh stay, three lives in one flea spare,
Where we almost, nay more than married, are.
This flea is you and I, and this
Our marriage bed and marriage temple is;
Though parents grudge, and you, we are met,
And cloistered in these living walls of jet,
Though use[2] make you apt to kill me
Let not to that, self-murder added be,
And sacrilege, three sins in killing three.

Cruel and sudden, hast thou since
Purpled thy nail, in blood of innocence?[3]
Wherein could this flea guilty be,
Except in that drop which it sucked from thee?
Yet thou triumph'st, and say'st that thou
Find'st not thy self nor me the weaker now;
'Tis true, then learn how false fears be;
Just so much honor, when thou yield'st to me,
Will waste, as this flea's death took life from thee.

1633

A Valediction: Forbidding Mourning[1]

As virtuous men pass mildly away,
And whisper to their souls to go,
Whilst some of their sad friends do say
The breath goes now, and some say, No;

So let us melt, and make no noise,
No tear-floods, nor sigh-tempests move,
'Twere profanation of our joys
To tell the laity our love.

Moving of th' earth brings harms and fears,
Men reckon what it did and meant;

1. I e., we, alas, don't dare hope for this consummation of our love, which the flea freely accepts. The idea of swelling suggests that of pregnancy.
2. Custom.
3. Like Herod, Donne's mistress has slaughtered the innocents, and is now clothed in imperial purple.
1. The particularly serious and steady tone of this poem may be due to the circumstances of its composition. Izaak Walton tells us it was addressed to Donne's wife on the occasion of his trip to the Continent in 1612. Donne had many forebodings of misfortune, which were verified when his wife gave birth to a stillborn child during his absence. Still, Walton's linkage of these events with this poem is only a speculation.

But trepidation of the spheres,
  Though greater far, is innocent.[2]

Dull sublunary[3] lovers' love
  (Whose soul[4] is sense) cannot admit
Absence, because it doth remove
  Those things which elemented[5] it.

But we by a love so much refined
  That our selves know not what it is,
Inter-assurèd of the mind,
  Care less, eyes, lips, and hands to miss.

Our two souls therefore, which are one,
  Though I must go, endure not yet
A breach, but an expansion,
  Like gold to airy thinness beat.

If they be two, they are two so
  As stiff twin compasses are two;
Thy soul, the fixed foot, makes no show
  To move, but doth, if th' other do.

And though it in the center sit,
  Yet when the other far doth roam,
It leans and hearkens after it,
  And grows erect, as that comes home.

Such wilt thou be to me, who must
  Like th' other foot, obliquely run;
Thy firmness makes my circle just,
  And makes me end where I begun.[6]

1633

The Ecstasy[1]

Where, like a pillow on a bed,
  A pregnant bank swelled up to rest
The violet's reclining head,
  Sat we two, one another's best.

2. I.e., earthquakes are thought to threaten evil consequences, but the variations of the spheres from true circularity, though they involve greater motions, are not considered sinister. "Trepidation of the spheres" (literally, "shuddering") was an additional arbitrary motion of the eighth sphere, introduced into the Ptolemaic system about the year 950 to account for certain celestial phenomena which were really due to the wobbling of the earth on its axis.

3. Beneath the moon, therefore mundane and subject to change.

4. Essence.

5. Composed.

6. The circle is an emblem of perfection; cf. also the motto of Mary, Queen of Scots, "In my end is my beginning." An excitingly complex, if perhaps overly medieval, reading of the poem is offered by John Freccero in *ELH*, XXX (December, 1963), 335–376.

1. For Donne's reader the word implies, not wild delight as it commonly does nowadays, but a standing apart, a movement of the soul outside of the body.

Our hands were firmly cemented
With a fast balm, which thence did spring.
Our eye-beams twisted, and did thread
Our eyes upon one double string;[1a]
So to intergraft our hands, as yet
Was all our means to make us one;
And pictures in our eyes to get
Was all our propagation.
As 'twixt two equal armies, Fate
Suspends uncertain victory,
Our souls (which to advance their state,
Were gone out) hung 'twixt her and me.
And whilst our souls negotiate there,
We like sepulchral statues lay;
All day the same our postures were,
And we said nothing all the day.
If any, so by love refined
That he soul's language understood,
And by good love were grown all mind,
Within convenient distance stood,
He (though he know not which soul spake,
Because both meant, both spake the same)
Might thence a new concoction[2] take,
And part far purer than he came.
This ecstasy doth unperplex,[3]
We said, and tell us what we love;
We see by this it was not sex;
We see we saw not what did move;[4]
But as all several souls contain
Mixture of things, they know not what,
Love these mixed souls doth mix again,
And makes both one, each this and that.
A single violet transplant,
The strength, the colour, and the size
(All which before was poor, and scant)
Redoubles still, and multiplies.
When love, with one another so
Interinanimates two souls,
That abler soul, which thence doth flow,
Defects of loneliness controls.[5]
We then, who are this new soul, know,
Of what we are composed, and made,
For, th' atomies[6] of which we grow,

1a. Joining hands and eyes is the only intercourse of the two lovers: "eye-beams" are invisible shafts of light, thought of as going out of the eyes and so enabling one to see things.

2. Purified mixture.

3. I.e., separate and clarify.

4. I.e., we see that we did not understand before what motivated ("did move") us.

5. The "abler soul" which derives from the union of two lesser ones can eliminate the defects with which each in itself is afflicted.

6. Atoms.

Are souls, whom no change can invade.
But O alas, so long, so far
Our bodies why do we forbear?
They are ours, though they are not we; we are
The intelligences, they the sphere.[7]
We owe them thanks because they thus,
Did us to us at first convey,
Yielded their forces, sense, to us,
Nor are dross to us, but allay.[8]
On man heaven's influence works not so
But that it first imprints the air,[9]
So soul into the soul may flow,
Though it to body first repair.
As our blood labors to beget
Spirits as like souls as it can,[1]
Because such fingers need to knit
That subtle knot which makes us man:
So must pure lovers' souls descend
T' affections, and to faculties
Which sense may reach and apprehend;
Else a great Prince in prison lies.
To our bodies turn we then, that so
Weak men on love revealed may look;
Love's mysteries in souls do grow,
But yet the body is his book.[2]
And if some lover, such as we,
Have heard this dialogue of one,[3]
Let him still mark us; he shall see
Small change when we are to bodies gone.

1633

Lovers' Infiniteness

If yet I have not all[1] thy love,
Dear, I shall never have it all;
I cannot breathe one other sigh to move,
Nor can entreat one other tear to fall;
All my treasure, which should purchase thee,

7. Medieval astronomers believed that the planets, set in crystalline spheres, were inhabited by "intelligences" which guided and controlled them. Similarly, Donne says, our bodies are guided and controlled by our souls.

8. "Dross" is an impurity which weakens metal, "allay" (alloy) an impurity which strengthens it. Our bodies contribute sensation ("sense") to the soul, and so reinforce it.

9. Astrological influences were thought to work on man through the surrounding air.

1. "Animal spirits" were thought to be begotten by the blood, to serve as intermediaries between body and soul.

2. I.e., love, a god within man, puts forth in the body a book where his mysteries may be read (as God the Creator put forth the book of Nature and the book of Scripture).

3. The characteristic Donne poem might be described as a "dialogue of one."

1. The influence of Donne's legal training is very clear here; the poem is a series of technical verbal quibbles on the word "all."

Sighs, tears, and oaths, and letters, I have spent.
Yet no more can be due to me
Than at the bargain made was meant;
If then thy gift of love were partial,
That some to me, some should to others fall,
  Dear, I shall never have thee all.

Or if then thou gavest me all,
All was but all which thou hadst then;
But if in thy heart since there be or shall
New love created be by other men,
Which have their stocks entire, and can in tears,
In sighs, in oaths, and letters outbid me,
This new love may beget new fears,
For this love was not vowed by thee.
And yet it was, thy gift being general;
The ground, thy heart, is mine; whatever shall
  Grow there, dear, I should have it all.

Yet I would not have all yet.
He that hath all can have no more;
And since my love doth every day admit
New growth, thou shouldst have new rewards in store.
Thou canst not every day give me thy heart;
If thou canst give it, then thou never gavest it.
Love's riddles are, that though thy heart depart,
It stays at home, and thou with losing savest it.
But we will have a way more liberal
Than changing hearts, to join them;[2] so we shall
  Be one, and one another's all.

1633

The Sun Rising

    Busy old fool, unruly sun,
    Why dost thou thus,
Through windows and through curtains call on us?
Must to thy motions lovers' seasons run?
    Saucy pedantic wretch, go chide
    Late school boys and sour prentices,
  Go tell court huntsmen that the King will ride,
  Call country ants to harvest offices;[1]
Love, all alike, no season knows nor clime,
Nor hours, days, months, which are the rags of time.

    Thy beams, so reverend and strong
    Why shouldst thou think?

2. To join hearts is more liberal than to "change" (exchange) them; "liberal" implies amorous generosity, also relief from legal hairsplitting.

1. Harvest chores, duties.

I could eclipse and cloud them with a wink,
But that I would not lose her sight so long;
If her eyes have not blinded thine,
Look, and tomorrow late, tell me,
Whether both th' Indias of spice and mine[2]
Be where thou leftst them, or lie here with me.
Ask for those kings whom thou saw'st yesterday,
And thou shalt hear, All here in one bed lay.

She is all states, and all princes, I,
Nothing else is.
Princes do but play us; compared to this,
All honor's mimic, all wealth alchemy.[3]
Thou, sun, art half as happy as we,
In that the world's contracted thus;
Thine age asks ease, and since thy duties be
To warm the world, that's done in warming us.
Shine here to us, and thou art everywhere;
This bed thy center is,[4] these walls, thy sphere.

1633

Air and Angels

Twice or thrice had I loved thee,
Before I knew thy face or name;
So in a voice, so in a shapeless flame,
Angels affect us oft, and worshipped be;
Still when, to where thou wert, I came,
Some lovely glorious nothing I did see.
But since my soul, whose child love is,
Takes limbs of flesh, and else could nothing do,[1]
More subtle than the parent is
Love must not be, but take a body too;
And therefore what thou wert, and who,
I bid love ask, and now
That it assume thy body I allow,
And fix itself in thy lip, eye, and brow.

Whilst thus to ballast love I thought,
And so more steadily to have gone,
With wares which would sink admiration,
I saw I had love's pinnace overfraught;[2]
Every thy hair for love to work upon
Is much too much, some fitter must be sought;
For, nor in nothing, nor in things

2. The India of "spice" is East India, that of "mine" (gold), the West Indies.
3. I.e., fraudulent.
4. The "center" of the sun's orbit.
1. As my soul could not function unless it were in a body, so love, which is the soul's child, must also be corporeal.
2. Her physical beauty (his "wares") would sink admiration—i.e., overwhelm wonder itself. This is too much ballast for love's "pinnace" (a small boat).

Extreme and scatt'ring[3] bright, can love inhere.
Then as an angel, face and wings
Of air, not pure as it, yet pure doth wear,
So thy love may be my love's sphere.[4]
Just such disparity
As is 'twixt air and angels' purity,
'Twixt women's love and men's will ever be.

1633

Break of Day[1]

'Tis true, 'tis day; what though it be?
O wilt thou therefore rise from me?
Why should we rise, because 'tis light?
Did we lie down, because 'twas night?
Love, which in spite of darkness brought us hither,
Should in despite of light keep us together.

Light hath no tongue, but is all eye;
If it could speak as well as spy,
This were the worst that it could say,
That being well, I fain would stay,
And that I loved my heart and honor so,
That I would not from him, that had them, go.

Must business thee from hence remove?
O, that's the worst disease of love.
The poor, the foul, the false, love can
Admit, but not the busied man.
He which hath business, and makes love, doth do
Such wrong, as when a married man doth woo.

1633

A Valediction: Of Weeping

Let me pour forth
My tears before thy face whilst I stay here,
For thy face coins them, and thy stamp they bear,
And by this mintage they are something worth,
For thus they be
Pregnant of thee;
Fruits of much grief they are, emblems of more—

3. Diffused, dazzling.
4. Some Scholastic philosophers held that angels, when they appeared to men, assumed a body of air. Such a body, though pure, was less so than the angel's spiritual being. Similarly, women's love, which Donne thinks *less* pure than that of men, may still serve as the receptacle ("sphere") for the love of men.

1. **Modeled on the Provençal aubade, or song of the lovers' parting at dawn, this poem is a departure for Donne in that it assumes a feminine point of view. As a rule, he is among the most consistently masculine of poets.**

When a tear falls, that Thou falls which it bore,
So thou and I are nothing then, when on a diverse shore.[1]

On a round ball
A workman that hath copies by, can lay
An Europe, Afric, and an Asia,
And quickly make that, which was nothing, all;[2]
So doth each tear
Which thee doth wear,
A globe, yea world, by that impression grow,
Till thy tears mixed with mine do overflow
This world; by waters sent from thee, my heaven dissolvéd so.[3]

O more than moon,
Draw not up seas to drown me in thy sphere;
Weep me not dead, in thine arms, but forbear
To teach the sea what it may do too soon.
Let not the wind
Example find
To do me more harm than it purposeth;
Since thou and I sigh one another's breath,
Whoe'er sighs most is cruelest, and hastes the other's death.[4]

1633

The Funeral

Whoever comes to shroud me, do not harm
Nor question much
That subtle wreath of hair which crowns my arm;
The mystery, the sign you must not touch,
For 'tis my outward soul,
Viceroy to that, which then to heaven being gone,
Will leave this to control,
And keep these limbs, her[1] provinces, from dissolution.

For if the sinewy thread[2] my brain lets fall
Through every part
Can tie those parts and make me one of all;
These hairs, which upward grew, and strength and art
Have from a better brain,
Can better do it; except she meant that I

1. The loss of the lovers in their separation is figured in the fall of a tear which contains the image of the mistress.
2. I.e., on a blank globe an artist can draw the world, and so convert a cipher, the image of nothingness, to the whole world.
3. In describing Creation, Genesis i.6–7 makes mention of certain heavenly waters, some above and some below the firmament. Their existence and function has been much debated by Bible scholars.
4. The breath of life has been interchanged between the lovers.
1. The soul's, but also the mistress's; compare "she," below, line 14.
2. The spinal cord and nervous system.

By this should know my pain,
As prisoners then are manacled, when they're condemned to die.

Whate'er she meant by it, bury it with me,
For since I am
Love's martyr, it might breed idolatry,
If into others' hands these relics came:
As 'twas humility[3]
To afford to it all that a soul can do,
So 'tis some bravery,
That since you would save none of me, I bury some of you.

1633

The Relic

When my grave is broke up again
Some second guest to entertain
(For graves have learned that woman-head[1]
To be to more than one a bed),
And he that digs it, spies
A bracelet of bright hair about the bone,
Will he not let us alone,
And think that there a loving couple lies,
Who thought that this device might be some way
To make their souls, at the last busy day,
Meet at this grave, and make a little stay?

If this fall in a time, or land,
Where mis-devotion[2] doth command,
Then he that digs us up, will bring
Us to the Bishop and the King,
To make us relics; then
Thou shalt be a Mary Magdalen, and I
A something else thereby;
All women shall adore us, and some men;
And since at such time, miracles are sought,
I would have that age by this paper taught
What miracles we harmless lovers wrought.

First, we loved well and faithfully,
Yet knew not what we loved, nor why,
Difference of sex no more we knew,
Than our guardian angels do;
Coming and going, we

3. It was humility to grant, in the first thirteen and a half lines of the poem, that her hair could act as a soul; it is also "bravery" (defiance) to bury a part of the mistress in revenge for her cruelty.

1. I.e., characteristic of women. On the re-use of graves, see Sir Thomas Browne's *Urn-Burial* and *Hamlet* V.i.

2. False devotion, superstition. Donne seems to have in mind Roman Catholicism.

Perchance might kiss, but not between those meals;[3]
Our hands ne'er touched the seals,
Which nature, injured by late law, sets free:
These miracles we did; but now, alas,
All measure and all language I should pass,
Should I tell what a miracle she was.

1633

3. The kiss of salutation and parting was, in the 17th century, a peculiarly English custom; the passage that follows seems to suggest some greater intimacy, permitted by nature, but unjustly abridged by "late law." It is hard to imagine what Donne had in mind here; he was not opposed to the sacrament of matrimony, and the laws of marriage could not be called "late," i.e., recent.

An Anatomy of the World

Donne composed this poem (later subtitled "The First Anniversary") to commemorate the death of a 14-year-old-girl, Elizabeth, younger daughter of his patron and friend Sir Robert Drury. Such formal elegies were much valued in Stuart society. The poet was expected not to dwell on the personal qualities of the deceased (and in fact Donne could not have done so because he had never seen the young lady) but to use the death of the individual as an occasion for religious and philosophical meditation on the meaning of life. Donne's *Anatomy of the World* is quite comparable in this respect to Milton's pastoral elegy, *Lycidas*. Both poems have been criticized for saying too little about their ostensible subject, and straying from it too far; whether this quality is a fault or a virtue, it must be recognized as a deliberate option of both poets.

The basic themes of Donne's poem are the decay and disintegration of the world (the word "anatomy" implies a post-mortem dissection) as a result of the breaking of those slender but precious lines of correspondent sympathy which used to hold it together (see above, the period introduction). An ancient harmony is gone, of which Elizabeth Drury is but one symbol; others, developed in the poem, are the story of the Garden of Eden and the Fall of Man, the myth of the Golden Age, and the disintegration (under the criticisms of Copernicus and Galileo) of the old geocentric cosmos, in which humanity and its moral life were the focus of universal attention.

The general view proposed by the poem, that the world used to be ideal and orderly but is rapidly getting worse, has a long history and has assumed many forms. It was particularly timely in the early 17th century when traditional patterns of belief and behavior were being so widely challenged, fractured, and discarded. As a man deeply rooted in Catholic traditions and scholastic philosophy, Donne was particularly sensitive to the challenges posed by science, by Puritanism, and by a money economy and the ethics implicit in it. Unity of being was Donne's lifelong obsession, no doubt because he directly experienced so little of it. This poem, lamenting loss of unity, is but the obverse of those witty and apparently perverse poems by Donne which tested unity by drawing out the bands of ingenious correspondence as far as possible. Though *An Anatomy of the World* is less compressed than those audacious, high-spirited stanzas, it rises quite gradually to a mournful magnificence which, like the very greatest elegiac poems, serves to depersonalize and universalize its subject.

An Anatomy of the World[1]

The First Anniversary

The entry into the work.

When that rich soul which to her heaven is gone,
Whom all do celebrate who know they have one
(For who is sure he hath a soul, unless
It see, and judge, and follow worthiness,
And by deeds praise it? He who doth not this,
May lodge an inmate soul, but 'tis not his);
When that queen ended here her progress time,[2]
And, as to her standing house,[3] to heaven did climb,
Where, loath to make the saints attend[4] her long,
She's now a part both of the choir and song,
This world in that great earthquake languishéd;
For in a common bath of tears it bled,
Which drew the strongest vital spirits out:
But succored then with a perplexéd doubt,
Whether the world did lose or gain in this
(Because since now no other way there is
But goodness to see her, whom all would see,
All must endeavor to be good as she),
This great consumption to a fever turned,
And so the world had fits; it joyed, it mourned.
And as men think that agues physic are,[5]
And the ague being spent, give over care,
So thou, sick world, mistak'st thyself to be
Well, when, alas, thou art in a lethargy.
Her death did wound and tame thee then, and then
Thou might'st have better spared the sun, or man;
That wound was deep, but 'tis more misery,
That thou hast lost thy sense and memory.
'Twas heavy[6] then to hear thy voice of moan,
But this is worse, that thou art speechless grown.
Thou hast forgot the name thou hadst; thou wast
Nothing but she, and her thou hast o'erpast.
For as a child kept from the font, until
A prince, expected long, come to fulfill
The ceremonies, thou unnamed had'st laid,

1. The marginal glosses alongside the poem are by Donne.
2. "That queen" is Elizabeth Drury, but it would naturally recall Queen Elizabeth as well, because she was immensely fond of "progresses," or brief formal visitations to country houses. "Her time on earth" is understood.
3. I.e., a house that stands open and empty waiting for its owner.
4. Await.
5. "Agues" (two syllables): fevers; "Physic": medicine. When you've had a fever, you're bound to get better (some people think).
6. Mournful, depressing.

Had not her coming, thee her palace made:[7]
Her name defined thee, gave thee form and frame,
And thou forget'st to celebrate thy name.
  Some months she hath been dead (but being dead,
Measures of times are all determinéd[8])
But long she hath been away, long, long, yet none
Offers to tell us who it is that's gone.
But as in states doubtful of future heirs,
When sickness without remedy impairs
The present prince, they're loath it should be said
The prince doth languish, or the prince is dead:
So mankind feeling now a general thaw,
A strong example gone, equal to law,
The cément which did faithfully compact
And glue all virtues, now resolved, and slacked,
Thought it some blasphemy to say she was dead,
Or that our weakness was discoveréd[9]
In that confession; therefore spoke no more
Than tongues, the soul being gone, the loss deplore.
But though it be too late to succor thee,
Sick world, yea, dead, yea, putrefied, since she,
Thy intrinsic balm and thy preservative,[1]
Can never be renewed, thou never live,
I (since no man can make thee live) will try
What we may gain by thy anatomy.[2]
Her death hath taught us dearly that thou art
Corrupt and mortal in thy purest part.
  Let no man say, the world itself being dead,
'Tis labor lost to have discoveréd
The world's infirmities, since there is none
Alive to study this dissection;
What life the world hath still.
For there's a kind of world remaining still,
Though she which did inanimate and fill
The world be gone, yet in this last long night,
Her ghost doth walk; that is, a glimmering light,
A faint weak love of virtue and of good
Reflects from her on them which understood
Her worth; and though she have shut in all day,
The twilight of her memory doth stay;
Which, from the carcass of the old world free,
Creates a new world; and new creatures be
Produced: the matter and the stuff of this,
Her virtue, and the form our practice is;
And though to be thus elemented,[3] arm
These creatures, from home-born intrinsic harm

7. The sick world is still being addressed; until it was made her palace, the world was nameless nothing.
8. I.e., since her death, time is at a stop.
9. Made evident.
1. I.e., a medicine that preserved one in perfect health forever.
2. I.e., by dissecting and analyzing the world's corpse, now its soul is gone.
3. I.e., lifted to her sphere.

(For all assumed[4] unto this dignity
So many weedless Paradises be,
Which of themselves produce no venomous sin,
Except some foreign serpent bring it in),
Yet, because outward storms the strongest break,
And strength itself by confidence grows weak,
This new world may be safer, being told

The sickness of the world.

The dangers and diseases of the old:
For with due temper[5] men do then forgo
Or covet things, when they their true worth know.

Impossibility of health.

There is no health; physicians say that we
At best enjoy but a neutrality.
And can there be worse sickness than to know
That we are never well, nor can be so?
We are born ruinous;[6] poor mothers cry
That children come not right, nor orderly,
Except they headlong come and fall upon
An ominous precipitation.
How witty's ruin! how importunate
Upon mankind! It labored to frustrate
Even God's purpose; and made women, sent
For man's relief, cause of his languishment.
They were to good ends, and they are so still,
But accessory, and principal in ill.
For that first marriage[7] was our funeral:
One woman at one blow then killed us all,
And singly, one by one, they kill us now.
We do delightfully ourselves allow
To that consumption; and profusely blind,
We kill ourselves to propagate our kind.[8]
And yet we do not that; we are not men:
There is not now that mankind which was then
When as the sun and man did seem to strive

Shortness of life.

(Joint tenants of the world) who should survive;
When stag, and raven,[9] and the long-lived tree,
Compared with man, died in minority;
When, if a slow-paced star had stolen away
From the observer's marking, he might stay
Two or three hundred years to see it again,
And then make up his observation plain;
When, as the age was long, the size was great;
Man's growth confessed and recompensed the meat;[1]
So spacious and large, that every soul

4. Raised.
5. Moderation.
6. Feeble, diseased; the Latin root, *ruina*, implies a falling down.
7. I.e., that of Adam and Eve.
8. Popular superstition had it that every act of sex shortened one's life by a day.
9. Stags and ravens were thought to live particularly long; but compared with early men, they, and even trees, died in their youth.
1. Early man was thought to have eaten better than modern man, lived longer, and grown to greater stature. Methuselah (below) is said to have lived 969 years (Genesis v.27).

Did a fair kingdom and large realm control;
And when the very stature, thus erect,
Did that soul a good way towards Heaven direct.
Where is this mankind now? who lives to age,
Fit to be made Methuselah his page?
Alas, we scarce live long enough to try
Whether a new-made clock run right, or lie.
Old grandsires talk of yesterday with sorrow,
And for our children we reserve tomorrow.
So short is life that every peasant strives,
In a torn house, or field, to have three lives.[2]
　And as in lasting, so in length is man
Contracted to an inch, who was a span;[3]
For had a man at first in forests strayed,
Or shipwrecked in the sea, one would have laid
A wager that an elephant or whale
That met him would not hastily assail
A thing so equal to him: now, alas,
The fairies and the pygmies well may pass
As credible; mankind decays so soon,
We're scarce our fathers' shadows cast at noon.
Only death adds to our length: nor are we grown
In stature to be men, till we are none.[4]
But this were light,[5] did our less volume hold
All the old text, or had we changed to gold
Their silver; or disposed into less glass
Spirits of virtue,[6] which then scattered was.
But 'tis not so: we're not retired, but damped;[7]
And as our bodies, so our minds are cramped:
'Tis shrinking, not close weaving, that hath thus
In mind and body both bedwarféd us.
We seem ambitious, God's whole work to undo;
Of nothing He made us, and we strive, too,
To bring ourselves to nothing back; and we
Do what we can to do it so soon as He.
With new diseases on ourselves we war,
And with new physic,[8] a worse engine far.
　Thus man, this world's vice-emperor, in whom
All faculties, all graces are at home—

Smallness of stature.

2. Leases of farmland were often made for "three lives," so the tenant would be encouraged to make improvements which his grandson at least might enjoy.
3. A "span" is the distance from tip of thumb to tip of little finger, about 9 inches.
4. Modern men are praised only after their death; they do not become proper men till they have ceased to be men at all.
5. I.e., this would be a trifle. "Volume": the word puns on both "bulk" and "book."
6. I.e., the distilled powers of virtue, which fit into a smaller bottle than the natural product does. Here and throughout, "virtue" includes not only the sense of "goodness," but that of "power," "efficacy."
7. I.e., not compressed, but deadened.
8. Medication. Modern medicine is said to be the worst enemy of human health.

And if in other creatures they appear,
They're but man's ministers, and legates there,
To work on their rebellions, and reduce
Them to civility, and to man's use—
This man, whom God did woo, and loath to attend[9]
Till man came up, did down to man descend,
This man, so great, that all that is, is his,
Oh what a trifle, and poor thing he is!
If man were anything, he's nothing now:
Help, or at least some time to waste, allow
To his other wants, yet when he did depart[1]
With her whom we lament, he lost his heart.
She, of whom the ancients seemed to prophesy
When they called virtues by the name of *she*;[2]
She in whom virtue was so much refined
That for alloy unto so pure a mind
She took the weaker sex,[3] she that could drive
The poisonous tincture, and the stain of Eve,
Out of her thoughts and deeds; and purify
All, by a true religious alchemy,
She, she is dead; she's dead: when thou knowest this,
Thou knowest how poor a trifling thing man is.
And learn'st thus much by our anatomy,
The heart being perished, no part can be free.
And that except thou feed (not banquet) on
The supernatural food, religion,
Thy better growth grows witheréd and scant;
Be more than man, or thou'rt less than an ant.
Then, as mankind, so is the world's whole frame
Quite out of joint, almost created lame:
For, before God had made up all the rest,
Corruption entered and depraved the best.
It seized the angels, and then first of all
The world did in her cradle take a fall,
And turned her brains, and took a general maim.
Wronging each joint of th' universal frame.
The noblest part, man, felt it first; and then
Both beasts and plants, cursed in the curse of man.[4]
So did the world from the first hour decay,
That evening was beginning of the day,
And now the springs and summers which we see
Like sons of women after fifty be.[5]

Decay of nature in other parts.

9. Wait. God wooed man by freely descending to earth and flesh in order to redeem His fellow creatures.
1. Part with, surrender, lose.
2. Latin *virtus* is a feminine noun.
3. Her mind was so pure that to make it bearable, she mingled it with the corruption and frailty of "the weaker sex."
4. For a similar account of the way man's fall corrupted the physical universe, see *Paradise Lost* X.706 ff.
5. Women giving birth after 50 were supposed to produce feeble or defective children.

And new philosophy calls all in doubt,
The element of fire is quite put out;[6]
The sun is lost, and the earth, and no man's wit
Can well direct him where to look for it.[7]
And freely men confess that this world's spent,
When in the planets and the firmament
They seek so many new; they see that this
Is crumbled out again to his atomies.[8]
'Tis all in pieces, all coherence gone;
All just supply, and all relation:
Prince, subject, father, son, are things forgot,
For every man alone thinks he hath got[9]
To be a phoenix, and that there can be
None of that kind, of which he is, but he.[1]
This is the world's condition now, and now
She that should all parts to reunion bow,
She that had all magnetic force alone,
To draw and fasten sundered parts in one;
She whom wise nature had invented then
When she observed that every sort of men
Did in their voyage in this world's sea stray,
And needed a new compass for their way;
She that was best, and first original
Of all fair copies, and the general
Steward to Fate;[2] she whose rich eyes and breast
Gilt the West Indies, and perfumed the East;[3]
Whose having breathed in this world did bestow
Spice on those isles, and bade them still smell so,
And that rich Indie which doth gold inter,
Is but as single money,[4] coined from her;
She to whom this world must itself refer,
As suburbs,[5] or the microcosm of her,
She, she is dead; she's dead: when thou know'st this,
Thou know'st how lame a cripple this world is.
And learn'st thus much by our anatomy,

6. The Polish astronomer Copernicus (1473–1543) and the Italian Galileo(1564–1642) led the argument of the "new philosophy" to show that the sun, not the earth, is the center of our galaxy. When this fact was established, a lot of traditional lore and some Biblical passages had to be reinterpreted or discarded. Among these discarded notions was that which required a rim of fire at the outer edge of the universe. That fire was "quite put out."

7. The idea of infinite space was unsettling to many people, especially when another speculation was added to it, that our world might be only one of several, all of which would have to be subject to divine providence. Cf. line 211, "They seek so many new"—new *worlds* is understood.

8. Atoms, the first principles of matter.

9. Achieved, arrived.

1. The fabulous phoenix was supposed to be unique; i.e., there was only one phoenix on earth at any one time. The loss of "relation" leaves each man thinking he is unique of his "kind" (variety).

2. Fate or Providence disposes of the world, but "she" was chief officer ("steward") under Fate.

3. The West Indies (i.e., the Americas) were a source of gold, the East Indies a source of spices and perfumes.

4. I.e., a single coin.

5. She is the center of everything, the world a mere appendage or suburb.

That this world's general sickness doth not lie
In any humor,[6] or one certain part;
But, as thou sawest it rotten at the heart,
Thou seest a hectic fever hath got hold
Of the whole substance, not to be controlled,
And that thou hast but one way not to admit
The world's infection, to be none of it.[7]
For the world's subtlest immaterial parts
Feel this consuming wound, and age's darts.

Disformity of parts.

For the world's beauty is decayed or gone;
Beauty, that's color and proportion.
We think the heavens enjoy their spherical,[8]
Their round proportion embracing all.
But yet their various and perplexéd course,
Observed in divers ages, doth enforce
Men to find out so many eccentric parts,[9]
Such divers downright lines, such overthwarts,
As disproportion that pure form. It tears
The firmament in eight and forty shares,
And in those constellations then arise
New stars,[1] and old do vanish from our eyes:
As though heav'n suffered earthquakes, peace, or war
When new towers rise, and old demolished are.
They have impaled[2] within a zodiac
The freeborn sun, and keep twelve signs awake
To watch his steps; the Goat and Crab control,[3]
And fright him back, who else to either pole
(Did not these tropics fetter him) might run:
For his course is not round, nor can the sun
Perfect a circle, or maintain his way
One inch direct; but where he rose today
He comes no more, but with a cozening line,
Steals by that point, and so is serpentine:
And seeming weary with his reeling thus,
He means to sleep, being now fall'n nearer us.
So, of the stars which boast that they do run
In circle still, none ends where he begun.
All their proportion's lame, it sinks, it swells.
For of meridians and parallels

6. The four bodily "humors" or dispositions combined to make up a temperament; when they were out of balance, a person was sick.

7. I.e., the only way to escape the world's infection is to die.

8. "Shape" or "proportion" is understood.

9. Over the centuries, the old Ptolemaic (geocentric) image of the universe had been patched up with many special theories (cycles, epicycles, eccentrics, and trepidations) designed to account for astronomical observations that could not be otherwise reconciled with the theory itself. The result of these various ("divers") amendments was, as Donne says, "disproportion."

1. The old astronomy had divided the heavens into 48 constellations, but new observations, especially with the just-developed telescope, were adding new stars to the list, even as Donne wrote.

2. Set within a pale, a fence.

3. The Tropics of Capricorn and Cancer, limits of the sun's northern and southern motion.

Man hath weaved out a net and this net thrown
Upon the heavens, and now they are his own.
Loath to go up the hill, or labor thus
To go to heaven, we make heaven come to us.
We spur, we rein the stars, and in their race
They're diversely content to obey our pace.
But keeps the earth her round proportion still?[4]
Doth not a Tenerife,[5] or higher hill
Rise so high like a rock, that one might think
The floating moon would shipwreck there and sink?
Seas are so deep that whales being struck today
Perchance tomorrow, scarce at middle way
Of their wished journey's end, the bottom, die.
And men, to sound depths, so much line untie,
As one might justly think that there would rise
At end thereof, one of the antipodes:[6]
If under all, a vault infernal be[7]
(Which sure is spacious, except that we
Invent another torment, that there must
Millions into a strait[8] hot room be thrust),
Then solidness and roundness have no place.
  Are these but warts and pock-holes in the face
Of the earth? Think so: but yet confess, in this
The world's proportion disfigured is,
That those two legs whereon it doth rely,
Reward and punishment, are bent awry.
And, Oh, it can no more be questionéd,
That beauty's best, proportion, is dead,
Since even grief itself, which now alone
Is left us, is without proportion.
She by whose lines proportion should be
Examined, measure of all symmetry,
Whom had that ancient seen, who thought souls made
Of harmony,[9] he would at next have said
That harmony was she, and thence infer
That souls were but resultances[1] from her,
And did from her into our bodies go,
As to our eyes, the forms from objects flow;
She, who if those great doctors truly said
That the ark[2] to man's proportions was made,

Disorder in the world.

4. I.e., is the earth still perfectly round, as it was created?
5. The peak of Teneriffe, in the Canary Islands, rises more than 12,000 feet above sea level.
6. Mythical islands on the other side of the world.
7. Hell is commonly represented as an immense cave at the center of the earth.
8. Narrow.
9. Aristoxenus was one of several ancient philosophers who held that the soul was a harmony of several elements; "at next": instantly.
1. Secondary productions, consequences.
2. Saint Augustine says, in *The City of God* (xv.26), that Noah's ark was constructed in proportion to the human body: all the animals lived peacefully in it, as the various passions are supposed to dwell peacefully in man. "She" was a "type" of the ark (i.e., analogous to it) because she was made to the proportions of mankind, as the ark was analogous to her because all

Had been a type for that, as that might be
A type of her in this, that contrary
Both elements and passions lived at peace
In her, who caused all civil war to cease;
She, after whom, what form soe'er we see,
Is discord, and rude incongruity,
She, she is dead, she's dead; when thou know'st this,
Thou know'st how ugly a monster this world is:
And learn'st thus much by our anatomy,
That here is nothing to enamor thee:
And that not only faults in inward parts,
Corruptions in our brains, or in our hearts,
Poisoning the fountains, whence our actions spring,
Endanger us: but that if everything
Be not done fitly and in proportion,
To satisfy wise and good lookers-on
(Since most men be such as most think they be),
They're loathsome too, by this deformity.[3]
For good and well must in our actions meet;
Wicked is not much worse than indiscreet.
  But beauty's other second element,
Color and luster, now is as near spent.
And had the world his just proportion.
Were it a ring still, yet the stone is gone.
As a compassionate turquoise which doth tell
By looking pale the wearer is not well,
As gold falls sick being stung with mercury,
All the world's parts of such complexion be.[4]
When nature was most busy, the first week,
Swaddling the newborn earth, God seemed to like
That she should sport herself sometimes and play,
To mingle and vary colors every day.
And then, as though she could not make enow,[5]
Himself His various rainbow did allow.
Sight is the noblest sense of any one,
Yet sight hath only color to feed on,
And color is decayed: summer's robe grows
Dusky, and like an oft dyed garment shows.
Our blushing red, which used in cheeks to spread,
Is inward sunk, and only our souls are red.[6]
Perchance the world might have recoveréd,
If she whom we lament had not been dead:
But she, in whom all white, and red, and blue
(Beauty's ingredients) voluntary grew,

the warring elements and contrary passions lived at peace within them both. This is an excellent example of the sort of "correspondence," or relation of one thing to another, the loss of which Donne is lamenting in the poem.

3. Most men behave as others expect them to behave; therefore when a man sins, not only he but all his "lookers-on" share in the blame.

4. I.e., evil has the power to contaminate good, especially now that the supreme good is gone, like a precious stone removed from a ring.

5. Enough.

6. Scarlet is the color of sin and shame.

As in an unvexed Paradise; from whom
Did all things' verdure and their luster come,
Whose composition was miraculous,
Being all color, all diaphanous
(For air and fire but thick gross bodies were,
And liveliest stones but drowsy and pale to her),
She, she is dead; she's dead: when thou know'st this,
Thou know'st how wan a ghost this our world is:
And learn'st thus much by our anatomy,
That it should more affright than pleasure thee.
And that, since all fair color then did sink,
'Tis now but wicked vanity to think
To color vicious deeds with good pretense,
Or with bought colors to illude[7] men's sense.

Weakness in the want of correspondence of heaven and earth.

  Nor in aught more this world's decay appears,
Than that her influence the heaven forbears,
Or that the elements do not feel this,
The father or the mother barren is.[8]
The clouds conceive not rain, or do not pour,
In the due birth time, down the balmy shower;
The air doth not motherly sit on the earth,
To hatch her seasons and give all things birth;
Springtimes were common cradles, but are tombs;
And false conceptions[9] fill the general wombs.
The air shows such meteors[1] as none can see
Not only what they mean, but what they be;
Earth such new worms[2] as would have troubled much
The Egyptian Mages to have made more such.
What artist[3] now dares boast that he can bring
Heaven hither, or constéllate anything,[4]
So as the influence of those stars may be
Imprisoned in an herb, or charm, or tree,
And do by touch all which those stars could do?
The art is lost, and correspondence too.
For heaven gives little, and the earth takes less,
And man least knows their trade and purposes.
  If this commerce 'twixt heaven and earth were not
Embarred, and all this traffic quite forgot,
She, for whose loss we have lamented thus,
Would work more fully and pow'rfully on us.
Since herbs and roots by dying lose not all,
But they, yea ashes too, are medicinal,
Death could not quench her virtue[5] so, but that

7. Deceive.
8. I.e., if the elements do not feel something amiss in the universe, and voluntarily forbear procreation, then the father (heaven) must be sterile or the mother (earth) barren.
9. Misbirths or absurd ideas.
1. Falling stars were supposed to be omens of good or bad events.
2. Monsters ("worms") spontaneously generated from the earth, like those created by the Egyptian Mages (magicians) in Exodus vii, are also portents.
3. I.e., a learned man, a fortune-teller or astrologist.
4. I.e., figure out its occult relations to the stars.
5. Alchemists often held that the life of a plant, for example, remained in its ashes, and could be regenerated from them; so the virtue of Elizabeth remains—if not strongly enough to attract followers, at least sufficiently to rouse admiration.

It would be (if not followed) wondered at:
And all the world would be one dying swan.
To sing her funeral praise, and vanish then.[6]
But as some serpents' poison hurteth not,
Except it be from the live serpent shot,
So doth her virtue need her here, to fit
That unto us; she working more than it.[7]
But she, in whom to such maturity
Virtue was grown, past growth, that it must die;
She, from whose influence all impressions came,
But, by receivers' impotencies, lame,[8]
Who, though she could not transubstantiate
All states to gold, yet gilded every state,
So that some princes have some temperance,
Some counselors some purpose to advance
The common profit, and some people have
Some stay, no more than kings should give, to crave,
Some women have some taciturnity,
Some nunneries some grains of chastity;
She that did thus much, and much more could do,
But that our age was iron,[9] and rusty too,
She, she is dead; she's dead: when thou know'st this,
Thou know'st how dry a cinder this world is.
And learn'st thus much by our anatomy,
That 'tis in vain to dew or mollify
It with thy tears, or sweat, or blood: nothing
Is worth our travail, grief, or perishing,
But those rich joys, which did possess her heart,
Of which she's now partaker and a part.

Conclusion. But as in cutting up a man that's dead,
The body will not last out[1] to have read
On every part, and therefore men direct
Their speech to parts that are of most effect,
So the world's carcass would not last if I
Were punctual[2] in this anatomy.
Nor smells it well to hearers,[3] if one tell
Them their disease, who fain would think they're well.
Here therefore be the end: and, blessèd maid,
Of whom is meant whatever hath been said,
Or shall be spoken well by any tongue,
Whose name refines coarse lines, and makes prose song,

6. The dying swan, foreseeing her own demise, sings (according to legend) one last song, her swan song, before perishing.
7. The poison of some snakes, Donne argues, is operative only while the beasts themselves are alive; so Elizabeth's virtue loses most of its power when she is not alive to administer it.
8. I.e., her influence is faulty ("lame") only because those on whom it is to work are impotent.
9. The ages of gold, silver, and bronze preceded (according to myth) the last and worst age, that of iron.
1. Endure.
2. Thorough, detailed.
3. I.e., it doesn't smell good, it's not fitting—Latinism (*non bene olet*), suggested by the metaphor of the world as a rotting corpse.

Accept this tribute, and his first year's rent,[4]
Who till his dark short taper's end be spent,
As oft as thy feast sees this widowed earth,
Will yearly celebrate thy second birth,
That is, thy death. For though the soul of man
Be got[5] when man is made, 'tis born but then
When man doth die; our body's as the womb,
And, as a midwife, death directs it home.
And you, her creatures,[6] whom she works upon,
And have your last and best concoction[7]
From her example and her virtue, if you
In reverence to her, do think it due
That no one should her praises thus rehearse,
As matter fit for chronicle, not verse,[8]
Vouchsafe to call to mind that God did make
A last, and lasting'st piece, a song. He spake
To Moses to deliver unto all
That song, because He knew they would let fall
The law, the prophets, and the history,
But keep the song still in their memory.[9]
Such an opinion (in due measure) made
Me this great office boldly to invade.
Nor could incomprehensibleness[10] deter
Me from thus trying to imprison her,
Which when I saw that a strict grave could do,
I saw not why verse might not do so too.
Verse hath a middle nature: heaven keeps souls,
The grave keeps bodies, verse the fame enrolls.

1611

Elegy XI. The Bracelet

UPON THE LOSS OF HIS MISTRESS'S CHAIN, FOR WHICH HE MADE SATISFACTION[1]

Not that in color it was like thy hair,
For armlets of that thou may'st let me wear;
Nor that thy hand it oft embraced and kissed,
For so it had that good which oft I missed;
Nor for that silly old morality[2]

4. I.e., annual payment. Donne had promised to write a poem every year on Elizabeth's death, and in fact wrote not only this first but a second "Anniversary."

5. Begotten.

6. Her creations.

7. Distillation. Readers of Donne's poem are rasied to the ultimate purity of which they are capable by the force of Elizabeth Drury's virtue.

8. A chronicle is a prose history, commonly of the more pedestrian sort. Donne may be implying that the story of Elizabeth belongs among the Saints' Lives.

9. The Song of Moses, delivered to the people just before his death, is in Deuteronomy xxxii.

10. I.e., the immense, incomprehensible quality of her virtue.

1. I.e., paid full value.

2. The jeer is at lovers' mottos of the "When this you see, remember me" variety.

That as these links were knit, our love should be—
Mourn I that I thy sevenfold chain have lost,
Nor for the luck's sake; but the bitter cost.
O, shall twelve righteous Angels,[3] which as yet
No leaven of vile solder did admit,
Nor yet by any way have strayed or gone
From the first state of their creation—
Angels which heaven commanded to provide
All things to me, and be my faithful guide,
To gain new friends, t' appease great enemies,
To comfort my soul when I lie or rise—
Shall these twelve innocents, by thy severe
Sentence (great judge), my sins' great burden bear?
Shall they be damned and in the furnace thrown
And punished for offenses not their own?
They save not me, they do not ease my pains,
When in that hell they're burnt and tied in chains.
  Were they but Crowns of France, I caréd not,
For most of these their natural country's rot[4]
I think possesseth, they come here to us
So pale, so lame, so lean, so ruinous;
And howsoe'er French kings most Christian be,
Their Crowns are circumcised most Jewishly.[5]
Or were they Spanish Stamps, still traveling,
That are become as catholic as their king,[6]
Those unlicked bear-whelps, unfiled pistolets
That (more than cannon shot) avails or lets;[7]
Which, negligently left unrounded, look
Like many-angled figures in the book
Of some great conjurer that would enforce
Nature, as these do justice, from her course;
Which, as the soul quickens head, feet, and heart,
As streams, like veins, run through th' earth's every part,
Visit all countries, and have slyly made
Gorgeous France ruined, ragged, and decayed;
Scotland, which knew no state, proud in one day;

3. These gold coins had on one side an image of St. Michael. "Vile solder" is lead, mixed with the original gold and recast as a form of counterfeiting.

3. The French louis had a crown on it, and was known by that name; syphilis was popularly known as "the French pox."

5. Since early times, kings of France have been known as "Most Christian" kings; their "circumcised" coins had little bits clipped off the edges.

6. The king of Spain is known as "the Most Catholic" king, but his money is catholic too, because it gets in everywhere. Donne is glancing throughout this passage at the fact that many English courtiers and officials were on the secret payroll of Spain.

7. Though crudely formed and apparently unfinished, Spanish coins are said to be very powerful, both positively ("avails," from the same root as "valiant") and negatively ("lets" in the sense of "releases"). The crude coins are compared to bear cubs unlicked by their mother (they were supposed to be born mere lumps and licked into shape by her.) "Pistolets" and *pistoles* are words applied indiscriminately to coins or handguns; however crudely made (many of the coins were minted in South America), their power is explosive.

And mangled seventeen-headed Belgia.[8]
Or were it such gold as that wherewithal
Almighty chemics from each mineral,
Having by subtle fire a soul out-pulled,
Are dirtily and desperately gulled.[9]
I would not spit to quench the fire they're in,
For they are guilty of much heinous sin.
But shall my harmless Angels perish? Shall
I lose my guard, my ease, my food, my all?
Much hope which they should nourish will be dead,
Much of my able youth and lustihead
Will vanish. If thou love, let them alone,
For thou wilt love me less when they are gone;
And be content that some loud squeaking crier,
Well-pleased with one lean, threadbare groat for hire,
May like a devil roar through every street[1]
And gall the finder's conscience if they meet.
Or let me creep to some dread conjurer
That with fantastic schemes fills full much paper,
Which hath divided heaven in tenements,
And with whores, thieves, and murderers stuffed his rents[2]
So full, that though he pass them all in sin,
He leaves himself no room to enter in.
But if, when all his art and time is spent,
He say 'twill ne'er be found, yet be content;
Receive from him that doom ungrudgingly,
Because he is the mouth of destiny.
Thou say'st (alas), the gold doth still remain
Though it be changed and put into a chain;
So in the first fall'n Angels[3] resteth still
Wisdom and knowledge, but 'tis turned to ill—
As these should do good works, and should provide
Necessities, but now must nurse thy pride.
And they are still bad Angels: mine are none,
For form gives being, and their form is gone.
Pity these Angels; yet their dignities
Pass Virtues, Powers, and Principalities.[4]

8. The inflation brought about by Spanish importation of American gold turned Europe topsy-turvy; France went from riches to rags, and Scotland, which had always been poor, became "proud in one day" perhaps when the Armada was shipwrecked there. "Belgia" (the Low Countries) had long consisted of 17 provinces (four duchies, seven counties, five lordships, and the margraviate of Antwerp).

9. "Chemics" are alchemists, who believed that gold was the "soul" of every other metal; having striven to extract it, they were "gulled" (i.e., disappointed).

1. Lost items were often called through the streets by the town crier; his price for this service was a mere groat, a coin so small as to be proverbial: "not worth a groat."

2. The conjurer, who can be hired to find a lost object, usually devotes his time to clients who want to cheat their way into heaven. "Pass": surpass.

3. I.e., Satan and his crew; but also the lost gold.

4. The theological doctrine here is that a good angel, though of the lowest rank, surpasses a bad angel of the highest; but Donne is also saying that money in the form of bribes can prevail over people of any rank.

But thou art resolute: thy will be done!
Yet with such anguish as her only son
The mother in the hungry grave doth lay,
Unto the fire these martyrs I betray.
Good souls (for you give life to everything),
Good Angels (for good messages you bring),
Destined you might have been to such an one
As would have loved and worshiped you alone,
One that would suffer hunger, nakedness,
Yea, death, ere he would make your number less.
But I am guilty of your sad decay;
May your few fellows longer with me stay.
But, oh, thou wretched finder, whom I hate
So that I almost pity thy estate;
Gold being the heaviest metal amongst all,
May my most heavy curse upon thee fall.
Here fettered, manacled, and hanged in chains
First may'st thou be; then chained to hellish pains;
Or be with foreign gold bribed to betray
Thy country, and fail both of that and thy pay.
May the next thing thou stoop'st to reach contain
Poison, whose nimble fume rot thy moist brain,
Or libels or some interdicted thing
Which, negligently kept, thy ruin bring.
Lust-bred diseases rot thee: and dwell with thee
Itching desire and no ability.
May all the evils that gold ever wrought;
All mischiefs that all devils ever thought;
Want after plenty; poor and gouty age;
The plagues of travelers; love; marriage
Afflict thee, and at thy life's last moment
May thy swoll'n sins themselves to thee present.
But I forgive: repent thee, honest man;
Gold is restorative,[5] restore it then.
But if from it thou beest loath to depart,
Because 'tis cordial,[6] would 'twere at thy heart.

1633

Elegy XIX. Going to Bed

Come, Madam, come, all rest my powers defy,
Until I labor, I in labor lie.[1]
The foe oft-times, having the foe in sight,
Is tired with standing though he never fight.
Off with that girdle, like heaven's zone glittering,
But a far fairer world encompassing.
Unpin that spangled breastplate which you wear

5. Healing, good to restore the health.
6. Good for diseases of the heart.

1. "Labor" in the sense of "get to work" and in the sense of "distress."

That th' eyes of busy fools may be stopped there.
Unlace yourself, for that harmonious chime
Tells me from you that now it is bed-time.
Off with that happy busk,[2] which I envy,
That still can be and still can stand so nigh.
Your gown going off, such beauteous state reveals
As when from flowery meads th' hill's shadow steals.
Off with that wiry coronet and show
The hairy diadem which on you doth grow:
Now off with those shoes, and then safely tread
In this love's hallowed temple, this soft bed.
In such white robes, heaven's angels used to be
Received by men; thou, angel, bring'st with thee
A heaven like Mahomet's paradise;[3] and though
Ill spirits walk in white, we easily know
By this these angels from an evil sprite,
Those set our hairs, but these our flesh upright.
License my roving hands, and let them go
Before, behind, between, above, below.
O my America! my new-found-land,
My kingdom, safeliest when with one man manned,
My mine of precious stones, my empery,
How blest am I in this discovering thee!
To enter in these bonds is to be free;
There where my hand is set, my seal shall be.[4]
Full nakedness! All joys are due to thee,
As souls unbodied, bodies unclothed must be,
To taste whole joys. Gems which you women use
Are like Atalanta's balls,[5] cast in men's views,
That when a fool's eye lighteth on a gem,
His earthly soul may covet theirs, not them.
Like pictures, or like books' gay coverings, made
For laymen, are all women thus arrayed;
Themselves are mystic books, which only we
(Whom their imputed grace will dignify)
Must see revealed.[6] Then since that I may know,
As liberally as to a midwife, show
Thyself: cast all, yea, this white linen hence,
There is no penance due to innocence.
To teach thee, I am naked first; why then
What need'st thou have more covering than a man?

1669

2. Corset.
3. Populated by seductive houris, for the delectation of the faithful.
4. The jokes mingle law with sex; having signed the document with his hand, he will now seal it, and in the bond of their relationship he will find freedom.
5. Atalanta, running a race against her suitor Hippomenes, was beaten when he dropped golden balls (apples) for her to pick up. Donne, for reasons of his own, reverses the story.
6. By granting favors to their lovers, women impute to them grace which they don't deserve, as God imputes grace to undeserving sinners. Laymen can only look at the covers of mystic books (women); but "we" who have saving grace can read them.

Satire III, Religion For the first time in English literary history, the mode of satire flourished in the last decade of Elizabeth's reign and under the first two Stuarts. Many social circumstances contributed to its popularity: a surplus of clever young men without jobs, bitter antipathies between social classes and groups, and a general spirit of disillusion and doubt which has been characterized as "Jacobean melancholy."

Out of this mood of prolonged doubt, search, and obstinate questioning came the five satires of John Donne. *Satire III, Religion* is not a satire in the customary sense of a mocking attack on some person or custom. It is a strenuous, inconclusive discussion of an acute theological problem: How may a man recognize the true church, to which all Christians claim to belong? The person to whom it is addressed is evidently a man without specific religious commitment, but with a great and anxious interest in religion, and a specially nervous feeling that the claims of Roman Catholicism may be justified. He has been a sailor, a soldier, a bit of a rake, a bit of a theologian; he has more than a smattering of law. In many small ways, he reminds us of young Jack Donne himself. But the most characteristic thing about this poem on the search for certainty is the toughness of mind which it evinces throughout. Donne's images have a raw, contemptuous force, his phrasing is clipped, his grammar and his meter are twisted by the energy of his argument. He has no easy answer for the question raised, and makes no effort to charm or lull the reader. His poem is sheer display of intellectual force, a pointed, inconclusive game of mind.

Satire III, Religion

Kind pity chokes my spleen; brave scorn forbids
Those tears to issue which swell my eyelids;
I must not laugh, nor weep sins, and be wise,
Can railing then cure these worn maladies?
Is not our mistress, fair Religion,
As worthy of all our souls' devotion,
As virtue was to the first blinded age?[1]
Are not heaven's joys as valiant to assuage
Lusts, as earth's honor was to them?[2] Alas,
As we do them in means, shall they surpass
Us in the end, and shall thy father's spirit
Meet blind philosophers in heaven, whose merit
Of strict life may be imputed faith,[3] and hear
Thee, whom he taught so easy ways and near
To follow, damned? O, if thou dar'st, fear this;
This fear great courage and high valor is.
Dar'st thou aid mutinous Dutch,[4] and dar'st thou lay

1. The age of paganism, blind to the light of Christianity, but capable of following natural morality ("virtue").
2. I.e., hope of heaven should be as powerful ("valiant") an antidote to sin in us as earthly honor was to "them"—the pagans.
3. Even without Christian faith, pagan philosophers may achieve heaven (see *The Divine Comedy, Paradiso* XX) by an extraordinary display of virtue which causes faith to be imputed to them.
4. The Dutch continually enlisted English volunteers in their rebellious wars against the Spaniards. Donne had never fought in Flanders, though he had sailed twice against the Spaniards, to Cadiz and the Azores.

Thee in ships, wooden sepulchers, a prey
To leaders' rage, to storms, to shot, to dearth?
Dar'st thou dive seas and dungeons of the earth?
Hast thou courageous fire to thaw the ice
Of frozen North discoveries? and thrice
Colder than salamanders,[5] like divine
Children in the oven,[6] fires of Spain, and the line,
Whose countries limbecks to our bodies be,
Canst thou for gain bear?[7] And must every he
Which cries not, "Goddess!" to thy mistress, draw,[8]
Or eat thy poisonous words? Courage of straw!
O desperate coward, wilt thou seem bold, and
To thy foes and his[9] (who made thee to stand
Sentinel in his world's garrison) thus yield,
And for forbidden wars, leave th' appointed field?
Know thy foes: The foul Devil (whom thou
Strivest to please) for hate, not love, would allow
Thee fain his whole realm to be quit;[1] and as
The world's all parts[2] wither away and pass,
So the world's self, thy other loved foe, is
In her decrepit wane, and thou, loving this,
Dost love a withered and worn strumpet; last,
Flesh (itself's death) and joys which flesh can taste,
Thou lovest; and thy fair goodly soul, which doth
Give this flesh power to taste joy, thou dost loathe.
Seek true religion. O, where? Mirreus,[3]
Thinking her unhoused here, and fled from us,
Seeks her at Rome; there, because he doth know
That she was there a thousand years ago.
He loves her rags so, as we here obey
The statecloth[4] where the Prince sat yesterday.
Crantz to such brave loves will not be enthralled,
But loves her only, who at Geneva is called
Religion—plain, simple, sullen, young,
Contemptuous, yet unhandsome; as among
Lecherous humors,[5] there is one that judges
No wenches wholesome but coarse country drudges.
Graius stays still at home here, and because

5. The salamander was traditionally so cold-blooded that it could live even in a fire.
6. The "divine children in the oven" are Shadrach, Meshach, and Abednego, rescued from the fiery furnace in Daniel iii.
7. The object of "bear" is "fires of Spain, and the line"—Inquisitorial and equatorial heats, which roast men as chemists heat materials in "limbecks" (alembics, or retorts for distilling).
8. I.e., fight a duel.
9. God's.
1. I.e., the Devil would gladly give you a free hand with his whole kingdom.
2. All parts of the world. It was a common belief in the 17th century that the world was getting old and decrepit.
3. The imaginary characters in this passage represent different creeds. "Mirreus" is a Roman Catholic, "Crantz" a Geneva Presbyterian, "Graius" an Erastian (i.e., believing in any religion sponsored by the state), "Phrygius" a skeptic, and "Graccus" a Universalist.
4. The royal canopy, a symbol of kingly power.
5. Tempers, temperaments.

Some preachers, vile ambitious bawds, and laws
Still new, like fashions, bid him think that she
Which dwells with us, is only perfect, he
Embraceth her whom his Godfathers will
Tender to him, being tender, as wards still
Take such wives as their guardians offer, or
Pay values.[6] Careless Phrygius doth abhor
All, because all cannot be good, as one
Knowing some women whores, dares marry none.
Graccus loves all as one, and thinks that so
As women do in divers countries go
In divers habits, yet are still one kind,
So doth, so is religion; and this blind-
ness too much light breeds; but unmoved thou
Of force must one, and forced but one allow;
And the right;[7] ask thy father which is she,
Let him ask his; though truth and falsehood be
Near twins, yet truth a little elder is;
Be busy to seek her, believe me this,
He's not of none, nor worst, that seeks the best.[8]
To adore, or scorn an image, or protest,
May all be bad; doubt wisely; in strange way
To stand inquiring right, is not to stray;
To sleep, or run wrong, is. On a huge hill,
Cragged and steep, Truth stands, and he that will
Reach her, about must, and about must go,
And what the hill's suddenness resists, win so;
Yet strive so, that before age, death's twilight,
Thy soul rest, for none can work in that night.
To will[9] implies delay, therefore now do.
Hard deeds, the body's pains; hard knowledge too
The mind's endeavors reach,[1] and mysteries
Are like the sun, dazzling, yet plain to all eyes.
Keep the truth which thou hast found; men do not stand
In so ill case here, that God hath with his hand
Signed kings' blank charters to kill whom they hate,
Nor are they vicars, but hangmen to fate.[2]
Fool and wretch, wilt thou let thy soul be tied
To man's laws, by which she shall not be tried
At the last day? O, will it then boot thee

6. Young men (of "tender" years) might reject the wives offered ("tendered") them by their guardians; but, if they did so, had to pay "values," i.e. fines.

7. I.e., being blind to the differences between religions, Graccus has too much light to see anything (lines 68–69). But the poet insists that without being swayed by human pressures, we must find just one true religion, "the right" true religion.

8. The man who seeks the best church is neither an unbeliever nor the worst sort of believer.

9. To intend a future action.

1. I.e., the body's pains achieve ("reach") hard deeds; the mind's endeavors will reach hard knowledge.

2. Human authority does not represent divine justice on earth; men are not God's vicars on earth (the hit here is at both the Pope and the secular monarch), but his hangmen at best—agents through whom his justice is fulfilled without carte blanche ("blank charters") to use their own judgments.

To say a Philip, or a Gregory,
A Harry, or a Martin taught thee this?[3]
Is not this excuse for mere contraries
Equally strong? Cannot both sides say so?
That thou mayest rightly obey power, her bounds know;
Those passed, her nature and name is changed; to be
Then humble to her is idolatry.[4]
As streams are, power is; those blest flowers that dwell
At the rough stream's calm head, thrive and do well,
But having left their roots, and themselves given
To the stream's tyrannous rage, alas, are driven
Through mills, and rocks, and woods, and at last, almost
Consumed in going, in the sea are lost.
So perish souls, which more choose men's unjust
Power from God claimed, than God himself to trust.

1633

Good Friday, 1613. Riding Westward

Let man's soul be a sphere, and then, in this,
The intelligence that moves, devotion is,[1]
And as the other spheres, by being grown
Subject to foreign motions, lose their own,
And being by others hurried every day,
Scarce in a year their natural form obey;
Pleasure or business, so, our souls admit
For their first mover, and are whirled by it.[2]
Hence is 't, that I am carried towards the West
This day, when my soul's form bends towards the East.
There I should see a Sun,[3] by rising, set,
And by that setting endless day beget:
But that Christ on this cross did rise and fall,
Sin had eternally benighted all.
Yet dare I almost be glad I do not see
That spectacle, of too much weight for me.
Who sees God's face, that is self-life, must die;
What a death were it then to see God die?
It made his own lieutenant, Nature, shrink;
It made his footstool crack, and the sun wink.[4]

3. "Philip" is Philip II of Spain, and "Gregory" any one of several Pope Gregories (VII, XIII, XIV); "Harry" is England's Henry VIII, and "Martin" is Martin Luther. Laymen and clergy, Protestants and Catholics, all are covered. "Boot": profit.

4. I.e., when the true limits of ecclesiastical power have been passed, obedience becomes idolatry.

1. As intelligences guide the visible planets, devotion is or should be the guiding principle of man's life.

2. I.e., spheres are deflected from their true orbits by outside influences; so our souls are deflected by business or pleasure.

3. The sun-Son pun was an ancient one. Christ, the Son of God, set when he rose on the Cross, and his setting (death) gave rise to the Christian era.

4. An earthquake and eclipse supposedly accompanied the Crucifixion.

Could I behold those hands which span the poles,
And tune all spheres at once, pierced with those holes?
Could I behold that endless height which is
Zenith to us, and our antipodes,[5]
Humbled below us? Or that blood which is
The seat of all our souls, if not of His,
Make dirt of dust, or that flesh which was worn
By God, for his apparel, ragg'd and torn?
If on these things I durst not look, durst I
Upon his miserable mother cast mine eye,
Who was God's partner here, and furnished thus
Half of that sacrifice which ransomed us?
Though these things, as I ride, be from mine eye,
They are present yet unto my memory,
For that looks towards them; and Thou look'st towards me,
O Saviour, as Thou hang'st upon the tree.
I turn my back to Thee but to receive
Corrections, till Thy mercies bid Thee leave.
O think me worth Thine anger; punish me;
Burn off my rusts and my deformity;
Restore Thine image so much, by Thy grace,
That Thou may'st know me, and I'll turn my face.

1633

From Holy Sonnets[1]

1

Thou hast made me, and shall Thy work decay?
Repair me now, for now mine end doth haste;
I run to death, and death meets me as fast,
And all my pleasures are like yesterday.
I dare not move my dim eyes any way,
Despair behind, and death before doth cast
Such terror, and my feeble flesh doth waste
By sin in it, which it towards hell doth weigh.
Only Thou art above, and when towards Thee
By Thy leave I can look, I rise again;
But our old subtle foe so tempteth me
That not one hour myself I can sustain.

5. "Zenith" and "antipodes" are the highest and farthest reach of heaven.

1. Several of the *Holy Sonnets* contain specific indications of date; number 17 makes reference to the recent death of Donne's wife (August 15, 1617) and number 18 may have been inspired by the Elector Palatine's defeat (October 29, 1620). But most are considerably earlier (1609–10). They are nineteen in number, conventional in their rhyme scheme and broad metrical pattern, but rhythmically bold, powerful in their imagery, and marked by deep emotional coloring. Donne's religion was never a secure or comfortable experience; his *Holy Sonnets* are documents which mingle anguished despair with no less anguished hope. And in a sonnet like *Holy Sonnet 14,* his faith rises to a series of knotted paradoxes involving coercion and submission, which would be revolting were it not for the full and evident sincerity of the mind to which they were inevitable.

Thy grace may wing me to prevent his art,
And Thou like adamant draw mine iron heart.[2]

1633

5

I am a little world made cunningly
Of elements, and an angelic sprite;[3]
But black sin hath betrayed to endless night
My world's both parts, and O, both parts must die.
You which beyond that heaven which was most high
Have found new spheres, and of new lands can write,[4]
Pour new seas in mine eyes, that so I might
Drown my world with my weeping earnestly,
Or wash it if it must be drowned no more.[5]
But O, it must be burnt! Alas, the fire
Of lust and envy have burnt it heretofore,
And made it fouler; let their flames retire,
And burn me, O Lord, with a fiery zeal
Of Thee and Thy house, which doth in eating heal.[6]

1635

7

At the round earth's imagined corners,[7] blow
Your trumpets, angels; and arise, arise
From death, you numberless infinities
Of souls, and to your scattered bodies go;
All whom the flood did, and fire shall, o'erthrow,
All whom war, dearth, age, agues, tyrannies,
Despair, law, chance hath slain, and you whose eyes
Shall behold God, and never taste death's woe.[8]
But let them sleep, Lord, and me mourn a space;
For, if above all these, my sins abound,
'Tis late to ask abundance of Thy grace
When we are there. Here on this lowly ground,
Teach me how to repent; for that's as good
As if Thou hadst sealed my pardon with Thy blood.

1633

2. "Wing": give wings to; "prevent": forestall; "adamant": loadstone. Note throughout the sonnets a combination of imperious energies and protestations of abject helplessness which determines the tone of Donne's religious feeling.

3. Both body and soul—the former made of "elements," the latter "angelic sprite" (spirit).

4. Donne asks the astronomers and explorers to find new oceans for tears to weep or waters to wash away his sins.

5. God promised (Genesis ix.11) after Noah's experience that the earth would never again be flooded.

6. See Psalm lxix.9: "For the zeal of thine house hath eaten me up." The passage involves three sorts of flame—those of the Last Judgment; those of lust and envy; and those of zeal, which alone heal.

7. Donne may have been thinking of the angels on old maps, who blow their trumpets to the four points of the compass. See also Revelation vii.1.

8. See Matthew xvi.28, Mark ix.1, and Luke ix.27, where the worthies are described who ascended directly to heaven from this life.

9

If poisonous minerals, and if that tree
Whose fruit threw death on else-immortal us,[9]
If lecherous goats, if serpents envious
Cannot be damned, alas! why should I be?
Why should intent or reason, born in me,
Make sins, else equal, in me more heinous?
And, mercy being easy and glorious
To God, in his stern wrath why threatens he?
But who am I that dare dispute with thee
O God? Oh, of thine only worthy blood
And my tears, make a heavenly Lethean[1] flood,
And drown in it my sin's black memory.
That thou remember them some claim as debt;
I think it mercy if thou wilt forget.

1633

10

Death, be not proud, though some have callèd thee
Mighty and dreadful, for thou art not so;
For those whom thou think'st thou dost overthrow
Die not, poor Death, nor yet canst thou kill me.
From rest and sleep, which but thy pictures be,
Much pleasure; then from thee much more must flow,
And soonest our best men with thee do go,
Rest of their bones, and soul's delivery.[2]
Thou art slave to fate, chance, kings, and desperate men,
And dost with poison, war, and sickness dwell,
And poppy[3] or charms can make us sleep as well
And better than thy stroke; why swell'st thou then?
One short sleep past, we wake eternally
And death shall be no more; Death, thou shalt die.

1633

14

Batter my heart, three-personed God; for You
As yet but knock, breathe, shine, and seek to mend;
That I may rise and stand, o'erthrow me, and bend
Your force to break, blow, burn, and make me new.
I, like an usurped town, to another due,
Labor to admit You, but O, to no end;
Reason, Your viceroy in me, me should defend,
But is captived, and proves weak or untrue.
Yet dearly I love You, and would be loved fain,
But am betrothed unto Your enemy.

9. The tree on which grew the apple eaten by Eve in the garden of Eden.

1. In classical mythology, the waters of the river Lethe caused instant forgetfulness.

2. I.e., our best men go with you to find rest for their bones and freedom ("delivery") for their souls.

3. Opium. "Why swell'st thou then?": why do you puff with pride?

Divorce me, untie or break that knot again;
Take me to You, imprison me, for I,
Except You enthrall me, never shall be free,
Nor ever chaste, except You ravish me.

1633

18

Show me, dear Christ, Thy spouse so bright and clear.[4]
What! is it she which on the other shore
Goes richly painted? or which, robbed and tore,
Laments and mourns in Germany and here?[5]
Sleeps she a thousand, then peeps up one year?
Is she self-truth, and errs? now new, now outwore?
Doth she, and did she, and shall she evermore
On one, on seven, or on no hill appear?[6]
Dwells she with us, or like adventuring knights
First travel[7] we to seek, and then make love?
Betray, kind husband, Thy spouse to our sights,
And let mine amorous soul court Thy mild dove,
Who is most true and pleasing to Thee then
When she is embraced and open to most men.

1899

A Hymn to Christ, at the Author's Last Going into Germany[8]

In what torn ship soever I embark,
That ship shall be my emblem of Thy ark;
What sea soever swallow me, that flood
Shall be to me an emblem of Thy blood;
Though Thou with clouds of anger do disguise
Thy face, yet through that mask I know those eyes,
  Which, though they turn away sometimes,
    They never will despise.

I sacrifice this island unto Thee,
And all whom I loved there, and who loved me;
When I have put our seas twixt them and me,
Put Thou Thy seas betwixt my sins and Thee.
As the tree's sap doth seek the root below
In winter, in my winter now I go

4. "What are the marks of a true church?" was a deeply fought field of interdenominational debate in the 17th century. Few Anglican clergymen would have expressed an indecision as universal as Donne's in this sonnet. Its skepticism, and a sense that versifying did not beseem a clergyman, kept the sonnet out of all 17th-century editions.

5. The Church of Rome is "she which goes richly painted on the other shore"; she is contrasted with the reformed churches "in Germany and here."

6. The Mount of Olives, the seven hills of Rome, and (perhaps) by Lake Geneva or in the town of Canterbury.

7. The 17th-century spelling, *travaile*, includes the idea of labor.

8. Donne went to Germany as chaplain to the Earl of Doncaster in 1619; the mission was a diplomatic one, to the King and Queen of Bohemia.

Where none but Thee, th' eternal root
Of true love, I may know.

Nor Thou nor Thy religion dost control
The amorousness of an harmonious soul,
But Thou would'st have that love Thyself; as Thou
Art jealous, Lord, so I am jealous now;
Thou lov'st not, till from loving more,[9] Thou free
My soul; whoever gives, takes liberty;
Oh, if Thou car'st not whom I love,
Alas, Thou lov'st not me.

Seal then this bill of my divorce to all
On whom those fainter beams of love did fall;
Marry those loves, which in youth scattered be
On fame, wit, hopes (false mistresses), to Thee.
Churches are best for prayer that have least light:
To see God only, I go out of sight;
And to 'scape stormy days, I choose
An everlasting night.

1633

Hymn to God My God, in My Sickness[1]

Since I am coming to that holy room
Where, with Thy choir of saints for evermore,
I shall be made Thy music; as I come
I tune the instrument here at the door,
And what I must do then, think here before.

Whilst my physicians by their love are grown
Cosmographers, and I their map, who lie
Flat on this bed, that by them may be shown
That this is my southwest discovery[2]
Per fretum febris,[3] by these straits to die,

I joy, that in these straits, I see my West;[4]
For, though their currents yield return to none,
What shall my West hurt me? As West and East
In all flat maps (and I am one) are one,
So death doth touch the resurrection.

Is the Pacific Sea my home? Or are
The Eastern riches? Is Jerusalem?
Anyan,[5] and Magellan, and Gibraltar,

9. From loving elsewhere. Donne is playing with the idea, "To give me true love you must take away my freedom to love elsewhere."

1. Though Izaak Walton, Donne's pious biographer, assigns this poem to the last days of his life, it was probably written in December, 1623.

2. The Straits of Magellan, or something spiritual which is analogous to them.

3. I.e., through the straits of fever.

4. Where the sun sets, hence where life ends.

5. The Bering Straits.

All straits, and none but straits, are ways to them,
Whether where Japhet dwelt, or Cham, or Shem.[6]

We think that Paradise and Calvary,
Christ's cross, and Adam's tree, stood in one place;
Look, Lord, and find both Adams met in me;
As the first Adam's sweat surrounds my face,
May the last Adam's blood my soul embrace.

So, in his purple wrapped,[7] receive me, Lord;
By these his thorns give me his other crown;
And, as to others' souls I preached Thy word,
Be this my text, my sermon to mine own;
Therefore that he may raise the Lord throws down.

1635

A Hymn to God the Father[1]

Wilt Thou forgive that sin where I begun,
Which is my sin, though it were done before?
Wilt Thou forgive that sin through which I run,
And do run still, though still I do deplore?
When Thou hast done, Thou hast not done,
For I have more.

Wilt Thou forgive that sin by which I have won
Others to sin? and made my sin their door?
Wilt Thou forgive that sin which I did shun
A year or two, but wallowed in a score?
When Thou hast done, Thou hast not done,
For I have more.

I have a sin of fear, that when I have spun
My last thread, I shall perish on the shore;
Swear by Thy self, that at my death Thy Son
Shall shine as he shines now and heretofore;
And, having done that, Thou hast done,
I fear no more.

1633

6. Japhet, Cham (Ham), and Shem were the three sons of Noah by whom the world was repopulated after the Flood (Genesis x). The descendants of Japhet were thought to inhabit Europe, those of Ham Africa, and those of Shem Asia.

7. The purple of Christ is his blood; also a royal garment.

1. Even in poetry of unquestioned seriousness, Donne's mind expressed itself naturally in puns; there are several in this short hymn, which Walton tells us was written during Donne's illness of 1623.

From Devotions upon Emergent Occasions[1]

Meditation IV

Medicusque vocatur.
The physician is sent for.

It is too little to call man a little world; except God, man is a diminutive to nothing.[2] Man consists of more pieces, more parts, than the world; than the world doth, nay, than the world is. And if these pieces were extended and stretched out in man as they are in the world, man would be the giant and the world the dwarf; the world but the map, and the man the world. If all the veins in our bodies were extended to rivers, and all the sinews to veins of mines, and all the muscles that lie upon one another to hills, and all the bones to quarries of stones, and all the other pieces to the proportion of those which correspond to them in the world, the air would be too little for this orb of man to move in, the firmament would be but enough for this star. For as the whole world hath nothing to which something in man doth not answer, so hath man many pieces of which the whole world hath no representation. Enlarge this meditation upon this great world, man, so far as to consider the immensity of the creatures this world produces. Our creatures are our thoughts, creatures that are born giants, that reach from east to west, from earth to heaven, that do not only bestride all the sea and land, but span the sun and firmament at once: my thoughts reach all, comprehend all.

Inexplicable mystery! I their creator am in a close prison, in a sick bed, anywhere, and any one of my creatures, my thoughts, is with the sun, and beyond the sun, overtakes the sun, and overgoes the sun in one pace, one step, everywhere. And then as the other world produces serpents and vipers, malignant and venomous creatures, and worms and caterpillars, that endeavor to devour that world which produces them, and monsters compiled and complicated of divers parents and kinds, so this world, our selves, produces all these in us, producing diseases and sicknesses of all those sorts;

1. Donne's private devotions were written during an attack of illness in the winter of 1623. They describe in detail the stages of Donne's disease and recovery; each stage comprises a meditation on the human condition, an expostulation and debate with God, and a prayer to Him. The book was published almost immediately it was written, and to great effect—the blend of private feeling and public moralizing rendering it particularly accessible to 17th-century readers. And its eloquent periods have provided a title for at least one major modern novel (see Meditation XVII). "Emergent" occasions are those which arise casually or unexpectedly.

Donne's Latin epigraphs are followed by his English translations, some of them very free ones indeed.

2. Donne's meditation is built on the Renaissance notion that man is a microcosm, a little world, analogous in every respect to the macrocosm, or big world, outside. But in playing with this notion, Donne paradoxically reverses it, arguing for a moment that man is a giant and the world his diminished representation.

venomous and infectious diseases, feeding and consuming diseases, and manifold and entangled diseases made up of many several ones. And can the other world name so many venomous, so many consuming, so many monstrous creatures, as we can diseases, of all these kinds? O miserable abundance, O beggarly riches! How much do we lack of having remedies for every disease when as yet we have not names for them?

But we have a Hercules against these giants, these monsters: that is the physician. He musters up all the resources of the other world to succor this, all nature to relieve man. We have the physician but we are not the physician. Here we shrink in our proportion, sink in our dignity in respect of very mean creatures who are physicians to themselves. The hart that is pursued and wounded, they say, knows an herb which, being eaten, throws off the arrow: a strange kind of vomit.[3] The dog that pursues it, though he be subject to sickness, even proverbially knows his grass that recovers him. And it may be true that the drugger is as near to man as to other creatures; it may be that obvious and present simples, easy to be had, would cure him; but the apothecary is not so near him, nor the physician so near him, as they two are to other creatures. Man hath not that innate instinct to apply these natural medicines to his present danger, as those inferior creatures have. He is not his own apothecary, his own physician, as they are. Call back therefore thy meditation again, and bring it down. What's become of man's great extent and proportion, when himself shrinks himself and consumes himself to a handful of dust? What's become of his soaring thoughts, his compassing thoughts, when himself brings himself to the ignorance, to the thoughtlessness of the grave? His diseases are his own, but the physician is not; he hath them at home, but he must send for the physician.

Meditation XIV

Idque notant criticis medici evenisse diebus.

The physicians observe these accidents to have fallen upon the critical days.

I would not make man worse than he is, nor his condition more miserable than it is. But could I though I would? As a man cannot flatter God nor overpraise him, so a man cannot injure man nor undervalue him. Thus much must necessarily be presented to his remembrance, that those false happinesses which he hath in this world have their times and their seasons and their critical days; and they are judged and denominated according to the times when they befall us. What poor elements are our happinesses made of

3. The deer who knows by instinct how to cure his poisoned wound by eating of an herb which is naturally antithetical to poison recurs frequently in Renaissance literature; a major source was Pliny's *Natural History* VIII.41. "Simples": herbs; "drugger": druggist.

if time, time which we can scarce consider to be anything, be an essential part of our happiness! All things are done in some place; but if we consider place to be no more but the next hollow superficies of the air, alas! how thin and fluid a thing is air, and how thin a film is a superficies, and a superficies of air! All things are done in time too; but if we consider time to be but the measure of motion, and howsoever it may seem to have three stations, past, present, and future, yet the first and last of these are not (one is not now, and the other is not yet) and that which you call *present* is not now the same that it was when you began to call it so in this line (before you sound that word *present* or that monosyllable *now*, the present and the now is past). If this imaginary half-nothing, time, be of the essence of our happinesses, how can they be thought durable? Time is not so; how can they be thought to be? Time is not so; not so considered in any of the parts thereof. If we consider eternity, into that time never entered; eternity is not an everlasting flux of time, but time is a short parenthesis in a long period; and eternity had been the same as it is, though time had never been. If we consider, not eternity, but perpetuity; not that which had no time to begin in, but which shall outlive time and be, when time shall be no more, what a minute is the life of the durablest creature compared to that! and what a minute is man's life in respect of the sun's or of a tree! and yet how little of our life is occasion, opportunity to receive good in; and how little of that occasion do we apprehend and lay hold of! How busy and perplexed a cobweb is the happiness of man here, that must be made up with a watchfulness to lay hold upon occasion, which is but a little piece of that which is nothing, time! And yet the best things are nothing without that. Honors, pleasures, possessions presented to us out of time, in our decrepit and distasted[4] and unapprehensive age, lose their office and lose their name; they are not honors to us that shall never appear nor come abroad into the eyes of the people to receive honor from them who give it; nor pleasures to us who have lost our sense to taste them; nor possessions to us who are departing from the possession of them. Youth is their critical day; that judges them, that denominates them, that inanimates and informs them, and makes them honors and pleasures and possessions; and when they come in an unapprehensive age, they come as a cordial when the bell rings out,[5] as a pardon when the head is off. We rejoice in the comfort of fire, but does any man cleave to it at midsummer? We are glad of the freshness and coolness of a vault, but does any man keep his Christmas there? or are the pleasures of the spring acceptable in autumn? If happiness be in the season or

4. Having lost the sense of taste.
5. A "cordial" (medicine) which arrives when the parish bell is already tolling is a bit too late.

in the climate, how much happier then are birds than men, who can change the climate and accompany and enjoy the same season ever.

Meditation XVII

Nunc lento sonitu dicunt, morieris.

Now this bell tolling softly for another, says to me, Thou must die.

Perchance he for whom this bell tolls may be so ill as that he knows not it tolls for him; and perchance I may think myself so much better than I am, as that they who are about me and see my state may have caused it to toll for me, and I know not that. The church is catholic, universal, so are all her actions; all that she does belongs to all. When she baptizes a child, that action concerns me; for that child is thereby connected to that body which is my head too,[6] and ingrafted into that body whereof I am a member. And when she buries a man, that action concerns me: all mankind is of one author and is one volume; when one man dies, one chapter is not torn out of the book, but translated[7] into a better language; and every chapter must be so translated. God employs several translators; some pieces are translated by age, some by sickness, some by war, some by justice; but God's hand is in every translation, and his hand shall bind up all our scattered leaves again for that library where every book shall lie open to one another. As therefore the bell that rings to a sermon calls not upon the preacher only, but upon the congregation to come, so this bell calls us all; but how much more me, who am brought so near the door by this sickness. There was a contention as far as a suit[8] (in which piety and dignity, religion and estimation,[9] were mingled) which of the religious orders should ring to prayers first in the morning; and it was determined that they should ring first that rose earliest. If we understand aright the dignity of this bell that tolls for our evening prayer, we would be glad to make it ours by rising early, in that application, that it might be ours as well as his whose indeed it is. The bell doth toll for him that thinks it doth; and though it intermit again, yet from that minute that that occasion wrought upon him, he is united to God. Who casts not up his eye to the sun when it rises? but who takes off his eye from a comet when that breaks out? Who bends not his ear to any bell which upon any occasion rings? but who can remove it from that bell which is passing a piece of himself out of this world? No man is an island, entire of itself; every man is a piece of the continent, a part of the main.[1] If a clod be washed away

6. I.e., the Christian church is the head of all men, as well as a body composed of its members.

7. Literally, "carried across"; hence, on the spiritual level, exalted from one sphere to another.

8. Controversy which went as far as a lawsuit.

9. Self-esteem.

1. Mainland.

by the sea, Europe is the less, as well as if a promontory were, as well as if a manor of thy friend's or of thine own were. Any man's death diminishes me because I am involved in mankind, and therefore never send to know for whom the bell tolls; it tolls for thee. Neither can we call this a begging of misery or a borrowing of misery, as though we were not miserable enough of ourselves but must fetch in more from the next house, in taking upon us the misery of our neighbors. Truly it were an excusable covetousness if we did; for affliction is a treasure, and scarce any man hath enough of it. No man hath affliction enough that is not matured and ripened by it and made fit for God by that affliction. If a man carry treasure in bullion, or in a wedge of gold, and have none coined into current money, his treasure will not defray him as he travels. Tribulation is treasure in the nature of it, but it is not current money in the use of it, except we get nearer and nearer our home, heaven, by it. Another man may be sick too, and sick to death, and this affliction may lie in his bowels as gold in a mine and be of no use to him; but this bell that tells me of his affliction digs out and applies that gold to me, if by this consideration of another's danger I take mine own into contemplation and so secure myself by making my recourse to my God, who is our only security.

1623 1624

From Sermon LXVI

[*On the Weight of Eternal Glory*]

All our life is a continual burden, yet we must not groan; a continual squeezing, yet we must not pant; and as in the tenderness of our childhood, we suffer and yet are whipped if we cry, so we are complained of if we complain, and made delinquents if we call the times ill. And that which adds weight to weight and multiplies the sadness of this consideration is this: that still the best men have had most laid upon them. As soon as I hear God say that he hath found "an upright man, that fears God and eschews evil," in the next lines I find a commission to Satan to bring in Sabeans and Chaldeans upon his cattle and servants, and fire and tempest upon his children, and loathsome diseases upon himself.[1] As soon as I hear God say that he hath found "a man according to his own heart," I see his sons ravish his daughters and then murder one another, and then rebel against the father and put him into straits for his life.[2] As soon as I hear God testify of Christ at his baptism, "This is my beloved Son in whom I am well pleased" I find that Son of his "led up by the Spirit, to be tempted of the devil."[3] And

1. This is the story of the Book of Job.
2. The story of David.
3. The temptation on the mount, Matthew iv.1–11.

after I hear God ratify the same testimony again, at his transfiguration ("This is my beloved Son in whom I am well pleased,"), I find that beloved Son of his deserted, abandoned, and given over to scribes, and Pharisees, and publicans, and Herodians,[4] and priests, and soldiers, and people, and judges, and witnesses, and executioners; and he that was called the beloved Son of God and made partaker of the glory of heaven, in this world, in his transfiguration, is made now the sewer of all the corruption, of all the sins of this world, as no Son of God but a mere man, as no man but a contemptible worm. As though the greatest weakness in this world were man, and the greatest fault in man were to be good, man is more miserable than other creatures, and good men more miserable than any other men.

But then there is *Pondus Gloriae*, an exceeding weight of eternal glory, that turns the scale; for as it makes all worldly prosperity as dung, so it makes all worldly adversity as feathers. And so it had need, for in the scale against it there are not only put temporal afflictions, but spiritual too; and to these two kinds we may accommodate those words, "He that falls upon this stone" (upon temporal afflictions) may be bruised, broken, "but he upon whom that stone falls" (spiritual afflictions) "is in danger to be ground to powder."[5] And then the great and yet ordinary danger is that these spiritual afflictions grow out of temporal: murmuring and diffidence in God and obduration, out of worldly calamities; and so against nature, the fruit is greater and heavier than the tree, spiritual heavier than temporal afflictions.

* * *

Let me wither and wear out mine age in a discomfortable, in an unwholesome, in a penurious prison, and so pay my debts with my bones and recompense the wastefulness of my youth with the beggary of mine age; let me wither in a spittle[6] under sharp and foul and infamous diseases, and so recompense the wantonness of my youth with that loathsomeness in mine age; yet if God withdraw not his spiritual blessings, his grace, his patience, if I can call my suffering his doing, my passion his action, all this that is temporal is but a caterpillar got into one corner of my garden, but a mildew fallen upon one acre of my corn; the body of all, the substance of all is safe as long as the soul is safe. But when I shall trust to that which we call a good spirit, and God shall deject and impoverish and evacuate that spirit, when I shall rely upon a moral constancy, and God shall shake, and enfeeble, and enervate, destroy and demolish that constancy, when I shall think to refresh myself in the serenity and sweet air of a good conscience, and God shall call up

4. Followers of Herod, listed among the enemies of Christ.
5. Matthew xxi.44. "Diffidence": mistrust, loss of faith.
6. Hospital.

the damps and vapors of hell itself and spread a cloud of diffidence and an impenetrable crust of desperation upon my conscience; when health shall fly from me and I shall lay hold upon riches to succor me and comfort me in my sickness, and riches shall fly from me, and I shall snatch after favor and good opinion to comfort me in my poverty; when even this good opinion shall leave me and calumnies and misinformations shall prevail against me; when I shall need peace because there is none but thou, O Lord, that should stand for me, and then shall find that all the wounds that I have, come from thy hand, all the arrows that stick in me, from thy quiver; when I shall see that because I have given myself to my corrupt nature, thou hast changed thine; and because I am all evil towards thee, therefore thou hast given over being good towards me: when it comes to this height, that the fever is not in the humors but in the spirits,[7] that mine enemy is not an imaginary enemy, fortune, nor a transitory enemy, malice in great persons, but a real and an irresistible and an inexorable and an everlasting enemy, The Lord of Hosts himself, The Almighty God himself, the Almighty God himself only knows the weight of this affliction, and except he put in that *Pondus Gloriae*, that exceeding weight of an eternal glory, with his own hand, into the other scale, we are weighed down, we are swallowed up, irreparably, irrevocably, irrecoverably, irremediably.

* * *

If you look upon this world in a map, you find two hemispheres, two half worlds. If you crush heaven into a map, you may find two hemispheres too, two half heavens; half will be joy, and half will be glory, for in these two (the joy of heaven and the glory of heaven) is all heaven often represented unto us. And as of those two hemispheres of the world, the first hath been known long before, but the other (that of America, which is the richer in treasure), God reserved for later discoveries; so though he reserve that hemisphere of heaven which is the glory thereof, to the resurrection, yet the other hemisphere, the joy of heaven, God opens to our discovery and delivers for our habitation even whilst we dwell in this world. * * * First think, that as a man must have some land or else he cannot be in wardship, so a man must have some of the love of God or else he could not fall under God's correction; God would not give him his physic, God would not study his cure, if he cared not for him. And then think also, that if God afford thee the shadow of his wings, that is, consolation, respiration, refreshing, though not a present and plenary deliverance in thy afflictions, not to thank God is a murmuring, and not to rejoice in God's ways is an unthankfulness. Howling is the noise of hell, singing the voice of

7. I.e., not superficial but in the root and marrow of my existence.

heaven; sadness the damp of hell, rejoicing the serenity of heaven. And he that hath not this joy here, lacks one of the best pieces of his evidence for the joys of heaven, and hath neglected or refused that earnest by which God uses to bind his bargain, that true joy in this world shall flow into the joy of heaven as a river flows into the sea; this joy shall not be put out in death and a new joy kindled in me in heaven; but as my soul, as soon as it is out of my body, is in heaven and does not stay for the possession of heaven nor for the fruition of the sight of God till it be ascended through air, and fire, and moon, and sun, and planets, and firmament, to that place which we conceive to be heaven, but without the thousandth part of a minute's stop, as soon as it issues, is in a glorious light, which is heaven (for all the way to heaven is heaven; and as those angels which came from heaven hither, bring heaven with them and are in heaven here, so that soul that goes to heaven meets heaven here; and as those angels do not divest heaven by coming, so these souls invest heaven, in their going). As my soul shall not go towards heaven but go by heaven to heaven, to the heaven of heavens, so the true joy of a good soul in this world is the very joy of heaven. * * *

1625 1640

BEN JONSON

(1572–1637)

1598: *Every Man in his Humor*, Jonson's first published play.
1606: *Volpone*
1616: Jonson appointed poet laureate; publishes his *Works*.
1618: *Pleasure Reconciled to Virtue*.
1630: Quarrel with Inigo Jones.

Ben Jonson did so many different things in the literary world of the early 17th century, and made use of so many different styles to do them, that he is very hard to see as a whole person. Actor, playwright, poet and poet laureate, scholar, critic, translator, man of letters, and head, for the first time in English, of a literary "school," the so-called "sons of Ben," he was a giant of a man. Yet we cannot easily take a perspective of him.

Jonson's life was tough and turbulent. After his father's early death, Ben was adopted in infancy by a bricklayer and educated by the great classical scholar and antiquarian William Camden, before necessity drove him to enter the army. In Flanders, where the Dutch with English help were warring against the Spaniards, he fought singlehanded with one of the enemy before the massed armies, and killed his man. Returning to England about 1595, he began to work as an actor and playwright but was drawn from one storm center to another. He killed a fellow-actor in a duel, and escaped the gallows only by pleading "benefit of clergy" (i.e., by proving he could read and write, which entitled him to plead before a more lenient court). He was jailed for insulting the Scottish nation at a time when King James was newly arrived from Scotland. He took furious part in an intricate set of literary wars with his fellow-playwrights. Having converted to Catholicism, he was the object of deep suspicion after the Gunpowder Plot of Guy Fawkes (1605), when the phobia against his religion reached its height. Yet he rode out all these troubles, growing mellower as he grew older, and in his latter years became the unofficial literary dictator of London, the king's pensioned poet, a favorite around the court, and the good friend of men like Shakespeare, Donne, Francis Beaumont, John Selden, Francis Bacon, dukes, diplomats, and distinguished folk generally. In addition, he engaged the affection of younger men (poets like Robert Herrick, Thomas Carew, and Sir John Suckling, speculative thinkers like Lord Falkland and Sir Kenelm Digby), who delighted to christen themselves "sons of Ben." Sons of Ben provided the nucleus of the entire "Cavalier school" of English poets.

The first of Jonson's great plays was *Every Man in His Humor,* in which Shakespeare acted a leading role. It was also the first of the so-called "comedies of humors," in which the prevailing eccentricities and ruling passions of men (i.e., their "humors") were exposed to satiric deflation. Though Jonson's classical tragedy *Sejanus* (1603) has not been much liked (it is gloomy in mood, static in action, and weighty with antiquarian lore), *Volpone* (1606) and *The Alchemist* (1610) are two supreme satiric comedies of the English stage. Both have been repeatedly "adapted" and "modernized," but even now the original texts are likely to seem more lively and vital than the versions. Meanwhile, starting in 1605, Jonson began writing for the court a series of masques—elaborate semi-theatrical displays involving spectacle, allegory, and compliment to the king or queen. Thus he became closely involved with the life of the court, a connection which was formalized in 1616, when he was appointed poet laureate with a substantial pension. In the same year, he published in a splendid volume his collected *Works,* a body of poetry to which he kept adding in the years before his death. Though his later plays were not very successful, he turned out many occasional poems, verse letters, translations, complimentary verses before other men's volumes—finding in all these different forms a grave, incisive pattern of formal speech through which the reverberations of his immense classical learning make themselves heard.

The bulk of Jonson's poetry falls, without undue strain, into five groups, based mostly on stylistic qualities. He wrote a number of poems of festive ceremony, poems which celebrate those qualities of ordered richness and dignified delight which represent his image of the good life. A poem like *To Penshurst* turns a physical building and its surrounding countryside into an emblem of modest yet noble opulence; the poem *On Inviting a Friend to Supper* is an imitation of Horace, yet its tonality is thoroughly English, and the "modest little supper" to which he invites his friend would scandalize a modern weight-watcher. Quite a different side of Jonson's talent is represented by his elegies and epitaphs; they are brief, full, simple poems, such as one could imagine being carved on a marble slab—direct, impersonal, inevitable. Allied to these are his compliments and tributes; often prefixed to his friends' books, but sometimes simple tributes of friendship and admiration, they summarize warmly yet judiciously a man's character and achievement. Jonson the pure poet finds expression in his songs, sometimes from the plays and masques but sometimes standing alone, often intended for musical accompaniment, but generally beautifully melodic, even without it. Finally, Jonson wrote (in imitation of the Roman poet Martial) a great number of epigrams, sometimes lewd, sometimes nasty, occasionally funny. We have lost the taste for this sort of thing today, but epigrams were a vital Renaissance genre, and Jonsons' profane epigrams can usefully be compared to Crashaw's sacred ones.

Jonson took his calling as a poet with the greatest seriousness, asserting the dignity of the profession with (sometimes) a kind of pedantry and emphasis that contrasts with Shakespeare's extraordinary anonymity. When Jonson published his collected works—*The Works of Benjamin Jonson*—in 1616, it was the first time an English author had been so presumptuous. Yet he succeeded in making the fact of professional authorship somehow respectable; an author like Dryden, who owed so much to Jonson on stylistic grounds, owed him a social debt as well. His career stood on foundations which Ben, with his pedantry and his pugnacity, was the first to lay down.

Volpone Though Jonson was reputed a slow composer, *Volpone* was created in little more than a month, and performed by the King's Men in the spring of 1606. It was a great success, and despite occasional lapses has held the stage ever since. (A recent Broadway adaptation, under the title of *Sly Fox*, transferred the action to San Francisco in the 1890's, but retained most of the original play's outlines; an adaptation for the French cinema, made by Stefan Zweig and featuring Harry Baur and Louis Jouvet, is by now technically old-fashioned but still dramatically superb.) The text was printed separately in a quarto of 1607 and reprinted with a few minor changes with the rest of Jonson's *Works* in the Folio of 1616 as well as the posthumous Folio of 1640. Our modernized text includes a number of stage directions first introduced by William Gifford in his edition of 1816, and a few more added by the present editor for the better understanding of the action.

Jonson's central topic—sordid greed deluded by ruthless guile—dictated the tonality of his play, which is cruelly funny. Classical satire, in the form of isolated passages in Horace, Juvenal, and Lucian, provided him with hints toward the basic action of legacy-chasing, and the reputation of Venice as a worldly, commercial, cosmopolitan center served to darken his comedy. But his own fondness for unscrupulous rascals, combined with deep indignation at the spreading prostitution of life to commercial interest, provided the real dynamic of the play. Because they prey on loathsome forms of life, Jonson's sharks are admired quite as much as they are despised; the murky social waters through which they cruise are not so ambiguous.

The play makes use of many traditional elements. Surely the medieval legend of Reynard the Fox contributed to the pervasive animal imagery; and figures like Mosca the wily parasite, old Corbaccio the miser, Voltore the shyster lawyer, and voluble Lady Would-Be all have definite analogues in Greek and Latin comedy. *Volpone*'s mode of cloaking serious moral points in voluminous comic exaggeration was practiced by many previous Renaissance authors, such as Erasmus (*The Praise of Folly*) and Rabelais (*Gargantua and Pantagruel*). Yet nowhere does the author triumph more splendidly over his materials than in *Volpone*: the play is instinct with a spirit of mischief and fun, a delight in the con game for its own sake, that renders all talk of sources and traditions very secondary indeed.

"The love of money is the root of all evil"—it had been the steady theme of preachers and teachers for thousands of years. But for Jonson, as for Shakespeare and Donne and for Thomas More before them all, the commercializing of life that began with the rise of a money economy and the development of an ethic dominated by self-interest, was particularly disturbing. Like his fellows, Jonson protested in *Volpone* the inhumanity, not just of greedy men, but of greedy laws—laws made by the greedy to protect the acquisitions of the greedy. In many ways the state of Venice is shown, in *Volpone*, to be a worse criminal than the criminals it prosecutes; and Jonson's vigorous social morality would not have rejected the implication that what Venice is in the play, England is about to become, in the city of London, the year of our lord 1606.

Volpone

OR
THE FOX

The Persons of the Play[1]

VOLPONE, *a magnifico*
MOSCA, *his parasite*
VOLTORE, *an advocate*
CORBACCIO, *an old gentleman*
CORVINO, *a merchant*
BONARIO, *son to Corbaccio*
SIR POLITIC WOULD-BE, *a knight*
PEREGRINE, *a gentleman traveller*
NANO, *a dwarf*
CASTRONE, *an eunuch*

1. Most of the names are Italian, and in that language many of them signify animals. Volpone: "fox." "Magnifico" is not a formal title; it simply means "gentleman." Mosca: "fly." The figure of the parasite implies scavenging, as well as fawning dependence. The client-patron relationship in Rome fostered parasitical dependents, and Jonson saw something similar, not only around the English court, but around the big money-men of London city. Voltore: "vulture." Corbaccio: "raven." Corvino: "crow." Bonario: "good-natured." Sir Politic Would-be: in the 17th century the word "politic" carried overtones of devious and subtle calculation. His name spells out, almost too explicitly, Sir Politic's character; and in its abbreviation ("Pol") suggests further the parrot he is. Peregrine: in English, "a falcon," but the world also associates with "pilgrim," i.e., "traveller." Nano: "dwarf." Castrone: "gelding." Androgyno: from the Greek, "man-woman," i.e., "hermaphrodite." Grege: from the Latin, "mob" or "crowd." Commendatori: a not very distinguished title of honor: Jonson assigns them a function akin to sergeants or marshals of a court. Mercatori: "merchants." Avocatori: properly, in Italian, "prosecutors"; Jonson makes them judges. Notario: "recorder." Celia: literally, "heavenly."

ANDROGYNO, *an hermaphrodite*

GREGE (*or Mob*)

COMMENDATORI, *officers of justice*
MERCATORI, *three merchants*
AVOCATORI, *four magistrates*
NOTARIO, *the register*

LADY WOULD-BE, SIR POLITIC'S *Wife*
CELIA, CORVINO'S *Wife*
SERVITORI, *Servants, two* WAITING-WOMEN, *&c.*

THE SCENE, *Venice*

The Argument[2]

Volpone, childless, rich, feigns sick, despairs,
Offers his state to hopes of several heirs,
Lies languishing; his parasite receives
Presents of all, assures, deludes; then weaves
Other cross plots, which ope themselves, are told.
New tricks for safety are sought; they thrive: when bold,
Each tempts the other again, and all are sold.[3]

Prologue

Now, luck yet send us, and a little wit
Will serve to make our play hit;
According to the palates of the season
Here is rhyme, not empty of reason.
This we were bid to credit from our poet,
Whose true scope, if you would know it,
In all his poems still hath been this measure,
To mix profit with your pleasure;[4]
And not as some, whose throats their envy failing,
Cry hoarsely, All he writes is railing;[5]
And when his plays come forth, think they can flout them,
With saying, he was a year about them.
To these there needs no lie,[6] *but this his creature,*
Which was two months since no feature;
And though he dares give them five lives to mend it,
'Tis known, five weeks fully penned it,
From his own hand, without a co-adjutor,
Novice, journey-man,[7] *or tutor.*
Yet thus much I can give you as a token
Of his play's worth, no eggs are broken,

2. A capsule summary of the plot.
3. Deceived.
4. That the task of the poet is to mix profit with pleasure was an idea dating back to Horace's *Art of Poetry*, lines 343–44.
5. Abuse, invective.
6. "To give the lie" was to deny flatly; we would use here the word "denial."
7. Piece-worker, apprentice, or assistant.

Nor quaking custards with fierce teeth affrighted,[8]
Wherewith your rout[9] *are so delighted;*
Nor hales he in a gull,[1] *old ends reciting,*
To stop gaps in his loose writing;
With such a deal of monstrous and forced action,
As might make Bedlam[2] *a faction:*
Nor made he his play for jests stolen from each table,
But makes jests to fit his fable;
And so presents quick comedy refined,
As best critics have designed;
The laws of time, place, persons he observeth,[3]
From no needful rule he swerveth.
All gall and copperas from his ink he draineth,
Only a little salt remaineth,[4]
Wherewith he'll rub your cheeks, till, red with laughter,
They shall look fresh a week after.

Act I

SCENE 1. *A Room in* VOLPONE'S *House.*

[*Enter* VOLPONE *and* MOSCA.]

VOLPONE. Good morning to the day; and next, my gold!
Open the shrine,[1] that I may see my saint.
[MOSCA *withdraws the curtain, and discovers piles of gold, plate, jewels, &c.*]
Hail the world's soul, and mine! more glad than is
The teeming earth to see the longed-for sun
Peep through the horns of the celestial ram,[2]
Am I, to view thy splendor darkening his;
That lying here, amongst my other hoards,
Show'st like a flame by night, or like the day
Struck out of chaos, when all darkness fled

8. Comic routines—thrown eggs or custard pies—which had popular success on the low Elizabethan stage. A giant custard pie was also served at city feasts inaugurating the Lord Mayor; sometimes an attendant fool jumped into it.
9. Mob, common herd.
1. Buffoon. Elizabethans were fond of wise saws and ancient adages, and often put characters into plays who recited them.
2. Bethlehem Hospital, the madhouse.
3. The so-called Aristotelian unities, actually imposed as prescripts by the Renaissance critics Castelvetro and Scaliger, placed limits of time and place on a dramatic action; the limitation on persons was less strict.
4. Gall and copperas (i.e., green vitriol) are traditional ingredients of ink: both are corrosive and bitter to the taste. Salt, though not an ingredient of ink, is a classical metaphor for wit, that which gives flavor to speech or writing.
1. Though there was no proscenium curtain in the Elizabethan theater, such as rises on a modern play, there was a small curtained inner area, and that is what Mosca unveils. By "the world's soul and mine" Volpone means the soul of the universe and his own immortal essence, both identified with gold.
2. The sun peeps through the horns of the constellation "Ram" in the zodiac about the middle of April; cf. Chaucer, at the opening of the *Canterbury Tales* (lines 5–8); "When Zephyrus eek with his sweete breeth / Inspired hath in every holt and heeth / The tendre croppes, and the yonge sonne / Hath in the Ram his halve cours yronne."

Unto the center. O thou son of Sol,[3]
But brighter than thy father, let me kiss,
With adoration, thee, and every relic
Of sacred treasure in this blesséd room.
Well did wise poets, by thy glorious name,
Title that age which they would have the best;[4]
Thou being the best of things, and far transcending
All style of joy, in children, parents, friends,
Or any other waking dream on earth.
Thy looks when they to Venus did ascribe,
They should have given her twenty thousand Cupids;[5]
Such are thy beauties and our loves! Dear saint,
Riches, the dumb god, that givest all men tongues,
That canst do nought, and yet mak'st men do all things;
The price of souls; even hell, with thee to boot,
Is made worth heaven. Thou art virtue, fame,
Honor and all things else. Who can get thee,
He shall be noble, valiant, honest, wise—

MOSCA. And what he will, sir. Riches are in fortune
A greater good than wisdom is in nature.

VOLPONE. True, my belovéd Mosca. Yet I glory
More in the cunning purchase[6] of my wealth
Than in the glad possession, since I gain
No common way; I use no trade, no venture;
I wound no earth with plough-shares, fat no beasts
To feed the shambles; have no mills for iron,
Oil, corn, or men, to grind them into powder;[7]
I blow no subtle glass, expose no ships
To threat'nings of the furrow-facéd sea;
I turn no moneys[8] in the public bank,
Nor usure private.

MOSCA. No, sir, nor devour
Soft prodigals. You shall have some will swallow
A melting heir as glibly as your Dutch
Will pills of butter, and ne'er purge[9] for it;

3. The circle of a gold coin is compared to the created cosmos, i.e., the world with sun, moon, and stars, created by God in Genesis i. When the sun illumined the outer universe, darkness "fled to the center," i.e., to hell, underground. Gold is said to be "the son of Sol" (the sun) because in Renaissance lore, the fertilizing rays of the sun, penetrating the ground, were supposed responsible for developing the "seeds of gold" naturally found there.

4. The "age of gold."

5. Lines 16–20 are translated from a fragment of Euripides; Seneca tells us that when they were pronounced onstage, the audience was so indignant that it would allow the play to continue only after Euripides provided assurance that the speakers would be badly punished in the course of the play. A traditional epithet of Venus is "golden"; but Volpone is not satisfied with her minting a single golden boy; he wants a lot of them.

6. I.e., acquisition.

7. As Jonson wrote, household industries were just starting to be converted, in a few places, to factory industries run by water power. Glass was a Venetian specialty, in Jonson's day as now, but in England it was just starting to be used for glazing.

8. I.e., take no interest. Banking and money-lending were more important in Venice, where long voyages were common mercantile practice, than in England.

9. Suffer indigestion. Many jokes were made in the 17th century on the Dutch appetite for butter. Loan-sharks swallowed up heirs by lending them money at exorbitant rates against their future inheritance.

Tear forth the fathers of poor families
Out of their beds, and coffin them alive
In some kind clasping prison, where their bones
May be forth-coming, when the flesh is rotten.
But your sweet nature doth abhor these courses;
You loathe the widow's or the orphan's tears
Should wash your pavements, or their piteous cries
Ring in your roofs, and beat the air for vengeance.

VOLPONE. Right, Mosca; I do loathe it.

MOSCA. And besides, sir,
You are not like the thresher that doth stand
With a huge flail, watching a heap of corn,
And, hungry, dares not taste the smallest grain,
But feeds on mallows, and such bitter herbs;
Nor like the merchant, who hath filled his vaults
With Romagnía, and rich Candian wines,
Yet drinks the lees of Lombard's vinegar.[1]
You will lie not in straw, whilst moths and worms
Feed on your sumptuous hangings and soft beds.
You know the use of riches, and dare give now
From that bright heap, to me, your poor observer,
Or to your dwarf, or your hermaphrodite,
Your eunuch, or what other household trifle
Your pleasure allows maintenance.

VOLPONE. Hold thee, Mosca, [*Gives him money.*]
Take of my hand; thou strik'st on truth in all,
And they are envious term thee parasite.
Call forth my dwarf, my eunuch, and my fool,
And let them make me sport. [*Exit* MOSCA.] What should I do,
But cocker up[2] my genius, and live free
To all delights my fortune calls me to?
I have no wife, no parent, child, ally,
To give my substance to, but whom I make
Must be my heir; and this makes men observe me.
This draws new clients daily to my house,
Women and men of every sex and age,
That bring me presents, send me plate, coin, jewels,
With hope that when I die (which they expect
Each greedy minute) it shall then return
Ten-fold upon them; whilst some, covetous
Above the rest, seek to engross me whole,[3]
And counter-work the one unto the other,
Contend in gifts, as they would seem in love.
All which I suffer, playing with their hopes,

1. Romagnía was a sweet wine from Greece; Candian is wine from Crete (Candia). During the Renaissance good wine was thought to come from the eastern Mediterranean, or else from Spain (sack and canary). French and Italian wines ("Lombard's vinegar") were not much appreciated, and the "lees" (dregs) were of course the worst part of any bottle.

2. Pamper, indulge.

3. An engrosser bought up an entire crop of grain, held it for hard times, then sold it at exorbitant prices.

And am content to coin them into profit,
And look upon their kindness, and take more,
And look on that; still bearing them in hand,
Letting the cherry knock against their lips,
And draw it by their mouths, and back again.[4]—How now!

SCENE 2

[*Enter* MOSCA *with* NANO, ANDROGYNO, *and* CASTRONE.]

NANO. *Now, room for fresh gamesters, who do will you to know,*
They do bring you neither play nor university show;
And therefore do entreat you, that whatsoever they rehearse,
May not fare a whit the worse, for the false pace of the verse.[5]
If you wonder at this, you will wonder more ere we pass,
For know, here[6] *is enclosed the soul of Pythagoras,*
That juggler divine, as hereafter shall follow;
Which soul, fast and loose, sir, came first from Apollo,
And was breathed into Æthalides,[7] *Mercurius his son,*
Where it had the gift to remember all that ever was done.
From thence it fled forth, and made quick transmigration
To goldy-locked Euphorbus,[8] *who was killed in good fashion,*
At the siege of old Troy, by the cuckold of Sparta.
Hermotimus was next (I find it in my charta)[9]
To whom it did pass, where no sooner it was missing,
But with one Pyrrhus of Delos it learned to go a fishing;
And thence did it enter the sophist of Greece.
From Pythagore, she went into a beautiful piece,
Hight Aspasia, the meretrix;[1] *and the next toss of her*
Was again of a whore, she became a philosopher,
Crates the cynic,[2] *as itself doth relate it:*
Since kings, knights, and beggars, knaves, lords, and fools gat it,
Besides ox and ass, camel, mule, goat, and brock,[3]
In all which it hath spoke, as in the cobbler's cock.
But I come not here to discourse of that matter,

4. "Chop-cherry" is a country game in which a cherry hung from a string is dangled before a player who tries to catch it with his teeth.

5. This little interlude tells us something about the tastes of the man for whom it is performed. The loose, jog-trot meter that the characters recite is reminiscent of the vices in the old morality plays.

6. He points at Androgyno. The Greek philosopher Pythagoras put forward the doctrine of transmigration of souls, and fantastic lineages were a frequent comic exercise in the Renaissance. Nano's comic story is copied from the life of Pythagoras, by Diogenes Laertius.

7. Herald of the Argonauts.

8. Trojan hero, killed by Menelaus, "the cuckold of Sparta"; Pythagoras specifically claimed to have been Euphorbus, and to recall the event.

9. Hermotimus is indeed mentioned in Nano's "charta," i.e., the text of Diogenes Laertius, but hardly anywhere else. Pyrrhus of Delos is an equally obscure figure, a fisherman mentioned only in Diogenes. The "sophist of Greece" is Pythagoras himself.

1. Whore; but Aspasia was simply the mistress of Pericles.

2. Crates was a philosopher of the Cynic school, a follower of Diogenes who professed a particularly bitter brand of scepticism.

3. Badger. Lucian's comic dialogue, "Gallus, or the Cock," which reproduces much of this material about Pythagoras, is a dialogue between a cobbler and a chicken.

Or his one, two, or three, or his great oath, BY QUATER!
His musics, his trigon, his golden thigh,[4]
Or his telling how elements shift; but I
Would ask, how of late thou hast suffered translation,
And shifted thy coat in these days of reformation.
ANDROGYNO. *Like one of the reformed, a fool, as you see,*
Counting all old doctrine heresy.
NANO. *But not on thine own forbid meats hast thou ventured?*
AND. *On fish, when first a Carthusian I entered.*[5]
NANO. *Why, then thy dogmatical silence hath left thee?*
AND. *Of that an obstreperous lawyer bereft me.*[6]
NANO. *O wonderful change, when sir lawyer forsook thee!*
For Pythagore's sake, what body then took thee?
ANDROGYNO. *A good dull mule.*
NANO. *And how! by that means*
Thou wert brought to allow of the eating of beans?[7]
ANDROGYNO. *Yes.*
NANO. *But from the mule into whom didst thou pass?*
ANDROGYNO. *Into a very strange beast, by some writers called an ass;*
By others, a precise, pure, illuminate brother,[8]
Of those devour flesh, and sometimes one another;
And will drop you forth a libel, or a sanctified lie,
Betwixt every spoonful of a nativity-pie.[9]
NANO. *Now quit thee, for heaven, of that profanenation,*
And gently report thy next transmigration.
ANDROGYNO. *To the same that I am.*
NANO. *A creature of delight,*
And, what is more than a fool, an hermaphrodite!
Now, prithee, sweet soul, in all thy variation,
Which body wouldst thou choose, to keep up thy station?
ANDROGYNO. *Troth, this I am in, even here would I tarry.*
NANO. *Cause here the delight of each sex thou canst vary?*
ANDROGYNO. *Alas, those pleasures be stale and forsaken;*
No, 'tis your fool wherewith I am so taken,
The only one creature that I can call blessed;[1]
For all other form I have proved most distressed.

4. Pythagorean theories about music and numerology, the Pythagorean theorem about right triangles, and the myth that Pythagoras had a golden thigh are glanced at here. A trigon is a triangle; the oath "by Quater" (four) is reported in Plutarch, *On the Sayings of the Philosophers*.
5. As a Carthusian monk (of a particularly strict sect), he learned to eat fish, which as a Pythagorean was forbidden to him.
6. Having taken a vow of silence as a Carthusian, he became a lawyer and learned to blabber.
7. Pythagoras forbade the eating of beans. All these prohibitions and special observances were supposed to have occult or mystical meaning.
8. All these adjectives would be understood as pointing at the Puritans, for whom Jonson had a standing aversion.
9. The Puritans did not like the old word "Christmas" because it included the "idolatrous" word "mass," so they began using the neutral word "Nativity," which Jonson here derides.
1. Jonson is drawing here on one of the wellsprings of Renaissance thought, Erasmus's mock-oration, *The Praise of Folly*.

NANO. *Spoke true, as thou wert in Pythagoras still.*
This learned opinion we celebrate will,
Fellow eunuch, as behooves us, with all our wit and art,
To dignify that whereof ourselves are so great and special a part.
VOLPONE. Now, very, very pretty! Mosca, this
Was thy invention?
MOSCA. If it please my patron,
Not else.
VOLPONE. It doth, good Mosca.
MOSCA. Then it was, sir.
[NANO *and* CASTRONE *sing.*[2]]
Fools, they are the only nation
Worth men's envy or admiration;
Free from care or sorrow-taking,
Selves and others merry making,
All they speak or do is sterling.
Your fool he is your great man's darling,
And your ladies' sport and pleasure;
Tongue and bauble are his treasure.
E'en his face begetteth laughter,
And he speaks truth free from slaughter;
He's the grace of every feast,
And sometimes the chiefest guest;
Hath his trencher[3] *and his stool.*
When wit waits upon the fool,
O, who would not be
He, he. he? [*Knocking without.*]
VOLPONE. Who's that? Away! [*Exeunt* NANO *and* CASTRONE.]
Look, Mosca.
MOSCA. Fool, begone! [*Exit* ANDROGYNO.] 'Tis signor Voltore, the advocate;
I know him by his knock.
VOLPONE. Fetch me my gown,
My furs, and night-caps; say, my couch is changing,
And let him entertain himself awhile
Without i' the gallery. [*Exit* MOSCA.] Now, now my clients
Begin their visitation! Vulture, kite,
Raven, and gor-crow, all my birds of prey,[4]
That think me turning carcass, now they come;
I am not for them yet.
[*Re-enter* MOSCA, *with the gown, &c.*]
How now? The news?
MOSCA. A piece of plate,[5] sir.
VOLPONE. Of what bigness?

2. The song is a patchwork of passages from Erasmus.
3. Dish.
4. Volpone foresees his visitors precisely in the order they come: Lady Politic is the kite, Corvino the gor-crow ("gor": filth). They are not, however, birds of prey, but all carrion-eaters.
5. A solid silver platter. In those days, when banks were uncertain and display important, families often put much of their wealth in massive silver dinnerware.

MOSCA. Huge,
Massy, and antique, with your name inscribed,
And arms engraven.
VOLPONE. Good! and not a fox
Stretched on the earth, with fine delusive sleights
Mocking a gaping crow?[6] ha, Mosca!
MOSCA. Sharp, sir.
VOLPONE. Give me my furs. [*Puts on his sick dress.*]
Why dost thou laugh so, man?
MOSCA. I cannot choose, sir, when I apprehend
What thoughts he has without now, as he walks:—
That this might be the last gift he should give;
That this would fetch you; if you died to-day,
And gave him all, what he should be to morrow;
What large return would come of all his ventures;
How he should worshipped be, and reverenced;
Ride with his furs and foot-cloths;[7] waited on
By herds of fools and clients; have clear way
Made for his mule, as lettered as himself;
Be called the great and learned advocate:
And then concludes, there's nought impossible.
VOLPONE. Yes, to be learned, Mosca.
MOSCA. O, no; rich
Implies it. Hood an ass with reverened purple,
So you can hide his two ambitious ears,
And he shall pass for a cathedral doctor.[8]
VOLPONE. My caps, my caps, good Mosca. Fetch him in.
MOSCA. Stay, sir; your ointment for your eyes.
VOLPONE. That's true;
Dispatch, dispatch.[9] I long to have possession
Of my new present.
MOSCA. That, and thousands more,
I hope to see you lord of.
VOLPONE. Thanks, kind Mosca.
MOSCA. And that, when I am lost in blended dust,
And hundred such as I am, in succession—
VOLPONE. Nay, that were too much, Mosca.
MOSCA. You shall live,
Still, to delude these harpies.
VOLPONE. Loving Mosca!
'Tis well. My pillow now, and let him enter. [*Exit* MOSCA.]

6. Volpone imagines an allegorical device, taken from one of Aesop's fables, engraved on the piece of plate. In essence, the story tells how the fox flattered the crow, sitting safely in a treetop with a piece of cheese, into trying to sing. When the foolish bird opened its mouth, the cheese fell to the ground for the fox to devour.
7. Ornate tapestries, laid upon the beast, not his rider; the furs would be for the lawyer.
8. The power of money to make the stupid wise, the ugly beautiful, and, in general, black white had been a satiric commonplace since antiquity. "Cathedral doctor": a doctor of theology (with the implication that he's not only the most pompous but the most stupid of the lot).
9. Hurry.

Now, my feigned cough, my phthisic, and my gout,
My apoplexy, palsy, and catarrhs,
Help, with your forcéd functions, this my posture,
Wherein, this three year, I have milked their hopes.
He comes; I hear him—Uh! [*coughing*] uh! uh! uh! O—

SCENE 3

[*Enter* MOSCA, *introducing* VOLTORE *with a piece of plate.*]

MOSCA. You still are what you were, sir. Only you,
Of all the rest, are he commands his love,
And you do wisely to preserve it thus,
With early visitation, and kind notes
Of your good meaning to him, which, I know,
Cannot but come most grateful. Patron! sir!
Here's signor Voltore is come—
VOLPONE. [*faintly*] What say you?
MOSCA. Sir, signor Voltore is come this morning
To visit you.
VOLPONE. I thank him.
MOSCA. And hath brought
A piece of antique plate, bought of St. Mark,[1]
With which he here presents you.
VOLPONE. He is welcome.
Pray him to come more often.
MOSCA. Yes.
VOLTORE. What says he?
MOSCA. He thanks you, and desires you see him often.
VOLPONE. Mosca.
MOSCA. My patron!
VOLPONE. Bring him near, where is he?
I long to feel his hand.
MOSCA. The plate is here, sir.
VOLTORE. How fare you, sir?
VOLPONE. I thank you, signor Voltore;
Where is the plate? mine eyes are bad.
VOLTORE. [*putting it into his hands*] I'm sorry,
To see you still thus weak.
MOSCA. [*aside*] That he's not weaker.
VOLPONE. You are too munificent.
VOLTORE. No, sir; would to heaven,
I could as well give health to you, as that plate!
VOLPONE. You give, sir, what you can; I thank you. Your love
Hath taste in this, and shall not be unanswered;
I pray you see me often.
VOLTORE. Yes, I shall, sir.
VOLPONE. Be not far from me.
MOSCA. Do you observe that, sir?

1. I.e., bought in Saint Mark's square.

VOLPONE. Hearken unto me still; it will concern you.
MOSCA. You are a happy man, sir; know your good.
VOLPONE. I cannot now last long—
MOSCA. You are his heir, sir.
VOLTORE. Am I?
VOLPONE. I feel me going; Uh! uh! uh! uh!
I'm sailing to my port, Uh! uh! uh! uh!
And I am glad I am so near my haven.
MOSCA. Alas, kind gentleman! Well, we must all go—
VOLTORE. But, Mosca—
MOSCA. Age will conquer.
VOLTORE. 'Pray thee, hear me:
Am I inscribed his heir for certain?
MOSCA. Are you!
I do beseech you, sir, you will vouchsafe
To write me in your family.[2] All my hopes
Depend upon your worship. I am lost,
Except the rising sun do shine on me.
VOLTORE. It shall both shine, and warm thee, Mosca.
MOSCA. Sir,
I am a man, that hath not done your love
All the worst offices.[3] Here I wear your keys,
See all your coffers and your caskets locked,
Keep the poor inventory of your jewels,
Your plate and moneys; am your steward, sir,
Husband[4] your goods here.
VOLTORE. But am I sole heir?
MOSCA. Without a partner, sir; confirmed this morning.
The wax is warm yet, and the ink scarce dry
Upon the parchment.
VOLTORE. Happy, happy, me!
By what good chance, sweet Mosca?
MOSCA. Your desert, sir;
I know no second cause.
VOLTORE. Thy modesty
Is loath to know it; well, we shall requite it.
MOSCA. He ever liked your course, sir; that first took him.
I oft have heard him say, how he admired
Men of your large profession, that could speak
To every cause, and things mere contraries,
Till they were hoarse again, yet all be law;
That, with most quick agility, could turn,
And return; make knots, and undo them;
Give forkéd counsel;[5] take provoking gold
On either hand, and put it up. These men,

2. I.e., inscribe me on the list of your servants.
3. Services.
4. Safeguard.
5. Ambiguous, ambivalent advice. This ironic praise of lawyers is probably from Cornelius Agrippa's book influential *On the uncertainty and vanity of the sciences and arts* (1531).

He knew, would thrive with their humility.
And, for his part, he thought he should be blessed
To have his heir of such a suffering spirit,
So wise, so grave, of so perplexed a tongue,
And loud withal, that would not wag, nor scarce
Lie still, without a fee; when every word
Your worship but lets fall, is a sequin!—[6]
[*Knocking without.*]
Who's that? one knocks; I would not have you seen, sir.
And yet—pretend you came, and went in haste;
I'll fashion an excuse—and, gentle sir,
When you do come to swim in golden lard,
Up to the arms in honey, that your chin
Is born up stiff, with fatness of the flood,
Think on your vassal; but remember me:
I have not been your worst of clients.

VOLTORE. Mosca—

MOSCA. When will you have your inventory brought, sir?
Or see a copy of the will? [*Knocking again.*] Anon![7]
I'll bring them to you, sir. Away, be gone;
Put business in your face. [*Exit* VOLTORE.]

VOLPONE. [*springing up*] Excellent Mosca!
Come hither, let me kiss thee.

MOSCA. Keep you still, sir.
Here is Corbaccio.

VOLPONE. Set the plate away.
The vulture's gone, and the old raven's come.

SCENE 4

MOSCA. Betake you to your silence and your sleep.
[*Puts the plate away.*] Stand there and multiply. Now shall we see
A wretch who is indeed more impotent
Than this can feign to be; yet hopes to hop
Over his grave. [*Enter* CORBACCIO.] Signor Corbaccio!
You're very welcome, sir.

CORBACCIO. How does your patron?

MOSCA. Troth, as he did, sir; no amends.

CORBACCIO. What! mends he?

MOSCA. No, sir, he's rather worse.

CORBACCIO. That's well. Where is he?

MOSCA. Upon his couch, sir, newly fallen asleep.

CORBACCIO. Does he sleep well?

MOSCA. No wink, sir, all this night.
Nor yesterday; but slumbers.[8]

6. Zecchino, a gold coin.
7. Said in response to a sharp rap at the door; a modern Mosca would say, "Coming!" See the game played by Prince Hal and Poins with a waiter who says nothing but "Anon!" in *1 Henry IV* II.iv.
8. Cat-naps.

CORBACCIO. Good! he should take
Some counsel of physicians. I have brought him
An opiate here, from mine own doctor.
MOSCA. He will not hear of drugs.
CORBACCIO. Why? I myself
Stood by while it was made, saw all the ingredients,
And know it cannot but most gently work.
My life for his, 'tis but to make him sleep.
VOLPONE. [*aside*] Ay, his last sleep, if he would take it.
MOSCA. Sir,
He has no faith in physic.
CORBACCIO. Say you, say you?
MOSCA. He has no faith in physic. He does think
Most of your doctors are the greater danger,
And worse disease, t'escape. I often have
Heard him protest, that your physician
Should never be his heir.
CORBACCIO. Not I his heir?
MOSCA. Not your physician, sir.
CORBACCIO. O, no, no, no,
I do not mean it.
MOSCA. No, sir, nor their fees
He cannot brook; he says, they flay a man,
Before they kill him.
CORBACCIO. Right, I do conceive you.
MOSCA. And then they do it by experiment;
For which the law not only doth absolve them,
But gives them great reward; and he is loath
To hire his death, so.
CORBACCIO. It is true, they kill
With as much license as a judge.
MOSCA. Nay, more;
For he but kills, sir, where the law condemns,
And these can kill him too.
CORBACCIO. Ay, or me,
Or any man. How does his apoplex?
Is that strong on him still?
MOSCA. Most violent.
His speech is broken, and his eyes are set,
His face drawn longer than 'twas wont—
CORBACCIO. How! how!
Stronger than he was wont?
MOSCA. No, sir: his face
Drawn longer than 'twas wont.
CORBACCIO. O, good!
MOSCA. His mouth
Is ever gaping, and his eyelids hang.
CORBACCIO. Good.
MOSCA. A freezing numbness stiffens all his joints,
And makes the color of his flesh like lead.

CORBACCIO. 'Tis good.
MOSCA. His pulse beats slow and dull.
CORBACCIO. Good symptoms still.
MOSCA. And from his brain—
CORBACCIO. Ha? how? not from his brain?
MOSCA. Yes, sir, and from his brain—
CORBACCIO. I conceive you; good.
MOSCA. Flows a cold sweat, with a continual rheum,
Forth the resolvéd corners of his eyes.
CORBACCIO. Is't possible? Yet I am better, ha!
How does he, with the swimming of his head?
MOSCA. O, sir, 'tis past the scotomy;[9] he now
Hath lost his feeling, and hath left to snort.
You hardly can perceive him, that he breathes.
CORBACCIO. Excellent, excellent! sure I shall outlast him!
This makes me young again, a score of years.
MOSCA. I was a coming for you, sir.
CORBACCIO. Has he made his will?
What has he given me?
MOSCA. No, sir.
CORBACCIO. Nothing? ha!
MOSCA. He has not made his will, sir.
CORBACCIO. Oh, oh, oh!
What then did Voltore, the lawyer, here?
MOSCA He smelt a carcass, sir, when he but heard
My master was about his testament;
As I did urge him to it for your good.
CORBACCIO. He came unto him, did he? I thought so.
MOSCA. Yes, and presented him this piece of plate.
CORBACCIO. To be his heir?
MOSCA. I do not know, sir.
CORBACCIO. True,
I know it too.
MOSCA. [*aside*] By your own scale, sir.[1]
CORBACCIO. Well,
I shall prevent him, yet. See, Mosca, look,
Here, I have brought a bag of bright sequins,
Will quite weigh down his plate.
MOSCA. [*taking the bag*] Yea, marry, sir.
This is true physic, this your sacred medicine;
No talk of opiates, to this great elixir![2]
CORBACCIO. 'Tis *aurum palpabile*,[3] if not *potabile*.
MOSCA. It shall be ministered to him, in his bowl.
CORBACCIO. Ay, do, do, do.

9. Dizziness, with dimness of sight.
1. The phrase seems to imply, "You think so because that's the sort of creature you are yourself."
2. No comparison of sedatives ("opiates") to this great medicine is possible. The elixir was supposed to be the supreme, universal medicine, capable of prolonging life indefinitely as well as of transforming baser metals to gold.
3. I.e., palpable, material gold; *aurum potabile*, or drinkable gold, was the elixir.

MOSCA. Most blesséd cordial!
This will recover him.
CORBACCIO. Yes, do, do, do.
MOSCA. I think it were not best, sir.
CORBACCIO. What?
MOSCA. To recover him.
CORBACCIO. O, no, no, no; by no means.
MOSCA. Why, sir, this
Will work some strange effect, if he but feel it.
CORBACCIO. 'Tis true, therefore forbear; I'll take my venture.
Give me it again.
MOSCA. At no hand; pardon me.
You shall not do yourself that wrong sir. I
Will so advise you, you shall have it all.
CORBACCIO. How?
MOSCA All, sir, 'tis your right, your own; no man
Can claim a part; 'tis yours without a rival,
Decreed by destiny.
CORBACCIO. How, how, good Mosca?
MOSCA. I'll tell you, sir. This fit he shall recover—
CORBACCIO. I do conceive you.
MOSCA. And, on first advantage
Of his gained sense, will I re-importune him
Unto the making of his testament.
And show him this. [*Pointing to the money.*]
CORBACCIO. Good, good.
MOSCA. 'Tis better yet,
If you will hear, sir.
CORBACCIO. Yes, with all my heart.
MOSCA. Now, would I counsel you, make home with speed;
There, frame a will, whereto you shall inscribe
My master your sole heir.
CORBACCIO. And disinherit
My son?
MOSCA. Oh, sir, the better: for that color
Shall make it much more taking.[4]
CORBACCIO. O, but color?
MOSCA. This will, sir, you shall send it unto me.
Now, when I come to enforce, as I will do,
Your cares, your watchings, and your many prayers,
Your more than many gifts, your this day's present,
And last, produce your will; where, without thought,
Or least regard unto your proper issue,
A son so brave and highly meriting,
The stream of your diverted love hath thrown you
Upon my master, and made him your heir:
He cannot be so stupid, or stone-dead,

4. That circumstance or appearance ("color") will make the trick more effective.

But out of conscience, and mere gratitude—
CORBACCIO. He must pronounce me his?
MOSCA. 'Tis true.
CORBACCIO. This plot
Did I think on before.
MOSCA. I do believe it.
CORBACCIO. Do you not believe it?
MOSCA. Yes, sir.
CORBACCIO. Mine own project.
MOSCA. Which, when he hath done, sir—
CORBACCIO. Published me his heir?
MOSCA. And you so certain to survive him—
CORBACCIO. Ay.
MOSCA. Being so lusty a man—
CORBACCIO. 'Tis true.
MOSCA. Yes, sir—
CORBACCIO. I thought on that too. See, how he should be
The very organ to express my thoughts!
MOSCA. You have not only done yourself a good—
CORBACCIO. But multiplied it on my son?
MOSCA. 'Tis right, sir.
CORBACCIO. Still, my invention.
MOSCA. 'Las, sir! heaven knows,
It hath been all my study, all my care
(I e'en grow gray withal), how to work things—
CORBACCIO. I do conceive, sweet Mosca.
MOSCA. You are he,
For whom I labor, here.
CORBACCIO. Ay, do, do, do:
I'll straight about it. [*Going.*]
MOSCA. Rook go with you, raven![5]
CORBACCIO. I know thee honest.
MOSCA. [*aside*] You do lie, sir!
CORBACCIO. And—
MOSCA. Your knowledge is no better than your ears, sir.
CORBACCIO. I do not doubt, to be a father to thee.
MOSCA. Nor I to gull my brother of his blessing.[6]
CORBACCIO. I may have my youth restored to me, why not?
MOSCA. Your worship is a precious ass!
CORBACCIO. What sayest thou?
MOSCA. I do desire your worship to make haste, sir.
CORBACCIO. 'Tis done, 'tis done; I go. [*Exit.*]
VOLPONE. [*leaping from his couch*] O, I shall burst!
Let out my sides, let out my sides—
MOSCA. Contain
Your flux of laughter, sir; you know this hope

5. The rook is a common crowlike bird, raucous and thievish; but Mosca is playing on a secondary meaning—cheat or deception: "May you be deceived, you raven!"

6. Jacob robbed Esau of his blessing by impersonating him before blind old Isaac (Genesis xxvii).

Is such a bait, it covers any hook.
VOLPONE. O, but thy working, and thy placing it!
I cannot hold; good rascal, let me kiss thee:
I never knew thee in so rare a humor.
MOSCA. Alas, sir, I but do as I am taught;
Follow your grave instructions; give them words;
Pour oil into their ears, and send them hence.
VOLPONE. 'Tis true, 'tis true. What a rare punishment
Is avarice to itself![7]
MOSCA. Ay, with our help, sir.
VOLPONE. So many cares, so many maladies,
So many fears attending an old age,
Yea, death so often called on, as no wish
Can be more frequent with them, their limbs faint,
Their senses dull, their seeing, hearing, going,
All dead before them; yea, their very teeth,
Their instruments of eating, failing them:
Yet this is reckoned life! nay, here was one,
Is now gone home, that wishes to live longer!
Feels not his gout, nor palsy; feigns himself
Younger by scores of years, flatters his age
With confident belying it, hopes he may,
With charms, like Æson,[8] have his youth restored;
And with these thoughts so battens, as if fate
Would be as easily cheated on, as he,
And all turns air! [*Knocking within.*] Who's that there, now? a third!
MOSCA. Close, to your couch again; I hear his voice:
It is Corvino, our spruce merchant.
VOLPONE. [*lies down as before*] Dead.[9]
MOSCA. Another bout, sir, with your eyes. [*Anointing them.*] —Who's there?

SCENE 5

[*Enter* CORVINO.]
Signor Corvino! come most wished for! O,
How happy were you, if you knew it, now!
CORVINO. Why? what? wherein?
MOSCA. The tardy hour is come, sir.
CORVINO. He is not dead?
MOSCA. Not dead, sir, but as good;
He knows no man.
CORVINO. How shall I do then?
MOSCA. Why, sir?
CORVINO. I have brought him here a pearl.

7. Seneca, Epistle 115, par. 16. Volpone is liberated, at least intellectually, from the vices on which he plays.
8. Aeson, Jason's father, was restored to life by the charms of Medea the witch.
9. I.e., "Pretend that I'm dead." The "bout . . . with your eyes" is a dose of gummy medicine.

MOSCA. Perhaps he has
So much remembrance left, as to know you, sir.
He still calls on you; nothing but your name
Is in his mouth. Is your pearl orient,[1] sir?
CORVINO. Venice was never owner of the like.
VOLPONE. [*faintly*] Signor Corvino!
MOSCA. Hark.
VOLPONE. Signor Corvino!
MOSCA. He calls you; step and give it him.—He's here, sir,
And he has brought you a rich pearl.
CORVINO. How do you, sir?
Tell him, it doubles the twelfth carat.[2]
MOSCA. Sir,
He cannot understand, his hearing's gone;
And yet it comforts him to see you—
CORVINO. Say,
I have a diamond for him, too.
MOSCA. Best show it, sir;
Put it into his hand; 'tis only there
He apprehends:[3] he has his feeling, yet.
See how he grasps it!
CORVINO. 'Las, good gentleman!
How pitiful the sight is!
MOSCA. Tut! forget, sir.
The weeping of an heir should still be laughter
Under a visor.[4]
CORVINO. Why, am I his heir?
MOSCA. Sir, I am sworn, I may not show the will
Till he be dead; but here has been Corbaccio,
Here has been Voltore, here were others too,
I cannot number 'em, they were so many,
All gaping here for legacies; but I,
Taking the vantage of his naming you,
Signor Corvino, Signor Corvino, took
Paper, and pen, and ink, and there I asked him,
Whom he would have his heir? *Corvino.* Who
Should be executor? *Corvino.* And,
To any question he was silent to,
I still interpreted the nods he made,
Through weakness, for consent; and sent home th' others,
Nothing bequeathed them, but to cry and curse.
CORVINO. O, my dear Mosca! [*They embrace.*] Does he not perceive us?
MOSCA. No more than a blind harper.[5] He knows no man,

1. Lustrous.
2. I.e., weighs 24 carats, or more than a third of an ounce—a huge pearl. "24-carat" has other overtones, as a measure of perfect purity in gold.
3. In English "apprehends" means "to understand intellectually," but the root Latin sense is "to grasp physically."
4. An heir should look sad by way of concealing his jubilation.
5. Playing the harp and singing ballads to it were traditional devices of blind beggars; but blindness in poets is sometimes accompanied by second sight, and Mosca knows that Volpone sees the situation clearly.

No face of friend, nor name of any servant,
Who 'twas that fed him last, or gave him drink;
Not those he hath begotten, or brought up,
Can he remember.

CORVINO. Has he children?

MOSCA. Bastards,
Some dozen, or more, that he begot on beggars,
Gypsies, and Jews, and black-moors, when he was drunk.
Knew you not that, sir? 'tis the common fable,
The dwarf, the fool, the eunuch, are all his;[6]
He's the true father of his family,
In all save me; but he has given them nothing.

CORVINO. That's well, that's well! Art sure he does not hear us?

MOSCA. Sure, sir! why, look you, credit your own sense.
[*Shouts in* VOLPONE'S *ear.*]
The pox approach, and add to your diseases,
If it would send you hence the sooner, sir.
For your incontinenence, it hath deserved it
Throughly and throughly, and the plague to boot!—
You may come near, sir—Would you would once close
Those filthy eyes of yours, that flow with slime,
Like two frog-pits; and those same hanging cheeks,
Covered with hide instead of skin—Nay, help, sir—
That look like frozen dish-clouts set on end!

CORVINO. Or like an old smoked wall, on which the rain
Ran down in streaks!

MOSCA. Excellent, sir! speak out.
You may be louder yet; a culverin[7]
Dischargéd in his ear would hardly bore it.

CORVINO. His nose is like a common sewer, still running.

MOSCA. 'Tis good! And what his mouth?

CORVINO. A very draught.[8]

MOSCA. O, stop it up—

CORVINO. By no means.

MOSCA. 'Pray you, let me:
Faith I could stifle him rarely with a pillow,
As well as any woman that should keep him.[9]

CORVINO. Do as you will; but I'll be gone.

MOSCA. Be so;
It is your presence makes him last so long.

CORVINO. I pray you, use no violence.

MOSCA. No, sir! why?
Why should you be thus scrupulous, pray you, sir?

CORVINO. Nay, at your discretion.

MOSCA. Well, good sir, be gone.

CORVINO. I will not trouble him now, to take my pearl?

6. The suggestion that Volpone's playmates are his own children is never really contradicted.
7. Horse-pistol.
8. Cesspool.
9. I.e., "I could smother him as well as a nurse."

MOSCA. Puh! nor your diamond. What a needless care
Is this afflicts you? Is not all here yours?
Am not I here? whom you have made your creature?
That owe my being to you?
CORVINO. Grateful Mosca!
Thou art my friend, my fellow, my companion,
My partner, and shalt share in all my fortunes.
MOSCA. Excepting one.
CORVINO. What's that?
MOSCA. Your gallant wife, sir.—
[*Exit* CORVINO.]
Now is he gone: we had no other means
To shoot him hence, but this.
VOLPONE. My divine Mosca!
Thou hast today outgone thyself. [*Knocking within.*]—
Who's there?
I will be troubled with no more. Prepare
Me music, dances, banquets, all delights;
The Turk is not more sensual in his pleasures,
Than will Volpone. [*Exit* MOSCA.] Let me see; a pearl!
A diamond! plate! sequins! Good morning's purchase.
Why, this is better than rob churches,[1] yet;
Or fat, by eating, once a month, a man—[*Enter* MOSCA.]
Who is't?
MOSCA. The beauteous Lady Would-be, sir,
Wife to the English knight, Sir Politic Would-be
(This is the style, sir, is directed me),[2]
Hath sent to know how you have slept tonight,
And if you would be visited?
VOLPONE. Not now:
Some three hours hence—
MOSCA. I told the squire so much.
VOLPONE. When I am high with mirth and wine, then, then.
'Fore heaven, I wonder at the desperate valor
Of the bold English, that they dare let loose
Their wives to all encounters!
MOSCA. Sir, this knight
Had not his name for nothing, he is *politic*,[3]
And knows, howe'er his wife affect strange airs,
She hath not yet the face to be dishonest:[4]
But had she Signor Corvino's wife's face—
VOLPONE. Has she so rare a face?
MOSCA. O, sir, the wonder,
The blazing star of Italy! a wench
Of the first year! a beauty ripe as harvest![5]

1. I.e., easy money.
2. I.e., "this is the way I've been told to announce her."
3. Devious, subtle.
4. I.e., "she's not beautiful enough to be unchaste."
5. A blazing star is literally a comet, hence a heavenly object of special attention. "A wench of the first year" seems to be a metaphor from wine-making, implying that the first crop of grapes makes the best wine.

Whose skin is whiter than a swan all over,
Than silver, snow, or lilies! a soft lip,
Would tempt you to eternity of kissing!
And flesh that melteth in the touch to blood!
Bright as your gold, and lovely as your gold!

VOLPONE. Why had not I known this before?

MOSCA. Alas, sir,
Myself but yesterday discovered it.

VOLPONE. How might I see her?

MOSCA. O, not possible;
She's kept as warily as is your gold;
Never does come abroad, never takes air,
But at a window. All her looks are sweet,
As the first grapes or cherries, and are watched
As near as they are.

VOLPONE. I must see her.

MOSCA. Sir,
There is a guard of ten spies thick upon her,
All his whole household; each of which is set
Upon his fellow, and have all their charge,
When he goes out, when he comes in, examined.

VOLPONE. I will go see her, though but at her window.

MOSCA. In some disguise, then.

VOLPONE. That is true; I must
Maintain mine own shape still the same; we'll think.
[*Exeunt.*]

Act II

SCENE 1. *St. Mark's Place, before* CORVINO'S *House.*

[*Enter* SIR POLITIC WOULD-BE, *and* PEREGRINE.]

SIR POLITIC. Sir, to a wise man, all the world's his soil.
It is not Italy, nor France, nor Europe,
That must bound me, if my fates call me forth.
Yet, I protest, it is no salt[6] desire
Of seeing countries, shifting a religion,
Nor any disaffection to the state
Where I was bred, and unto which I owe
My dearest plots,[7] hath brought me out; much less,
That idle, antique, stale, gray-headed project
Of knowing men's minds and manners, with Ulysses![8]
But a peculiar humor of my wife's,
Laid for this height of Venice, to observe,
To quote, to learn the language, and so forth.—
I hope you travel, sir, with license?[9]

PEREGRINE. Yes.

6. Wanton, frivolous.
7. Projects, notions.
8. Ulysses (Homer says) knew the minds of many men and saw many cities. The "humor" of Sir Politic's wife was exactly calculated, he thinks, to bring her to Venice.
9. I.e., special permission to travel abroad.

SIR POLITIC. I dare the safelier converse—How long, sir,
Since you left England?
PEREGRINE. Seven weeks.
SIR POLITIC. So lately!
You have not been with my lord ambassador?
PEREGRINE. Not yet, sir.
SIR POLITIC. Pray you, what news, sir, vents our climate?[1]
I heard last night a most strange thing reported
By some of my lord's followers, and I long
To hear how 'twill be seconded.
PEREGRINE. What was't, sir?
SIR POLITIC. Marry, sir, of a raven that should build
In a ship royal of the king's.[2]
PEREGRINE. This fellow,
Does he gull me,[3] trow? or is gulled?—Your name, sir?
SIR POLITIC. My name is Politic Would-be.
PEREGRINE. [*aside*] O, that speaks him.—
A knight, sir?
SIR POLITIC. A poor knight, sir.
PEREGRINE. Your lady
Lies here in Venice, for intelligence
Of tires and fashions, and behavior,
Among the courtesans?[4] the fine Lady Would-be?
SIR POLITIC. Yes, sir; the spider and the bee, oft-times
Suck from one flower.
PEREGRINE. Good Sir Politic,
I cry you mercy; I have heard much of you.
'Tis true, sir, of your raven.
SIR POLITIC. On your knowledge?
PEREGRINE. Yes, and your lion's whelping in the Tower.[5]
SIR POLITIC. Another whelp!
PEREGRINE. Another, sir.
SIR POLITIC. Now, heaven!
What prodigies be these? The fires at Berwick![6]
And the new star! these things concurring, strange
And full of omen! Saw you those meteors?
PEREGRINE. I did, sir.
SIR POLITIC. Fearful! Pray you, sir, confirm me,
Were there three porpoises seen above the bridge,
As they give out?[7]

1. I.e., "What news does our climate give off?"
2. A raven is a bird of ill omen.
3. To "gull" is constantly used in the sense of to fool or deceive; "trow?": do you think?
4. Attires, costumes. Venetian prostitutes were for hundreds of years reputed to be the most desirable in Europe, perhaps because Pietro Aretino advertised them so flatteringly in his pornographic poems.
5. Lions were in fact kept caged in the Tower of London, and cubs were whelped from time to time. Most of the events to which Sir Politic alludes had in fact occurred shortly before the time of the play's first production, and would have been familiar to the audience.
6. A new star appeared in October, 1604, and the aurora borealis over Berwick in January, 1605, was said to resemble armies of men fighting in the sky.
7. It was unusual for deep-sea creatures to venture up the Thames, past London Bridge.

PEREGRINE. Six, and a sturgeon, sir.
SIR POLITIC. I am astonished.
PEREGRINE. Nay, sir, be not so;
I'll tell you a greater prodigy than these.
SIR POLITIC. What should these things portend?
PEREGRINE. The very day
(Let me be sure) that I put forth from London,
There was a whale discovered in the river,
As high as Woolwich, that had waited there,
Few know how many months, for the subversion
Of the Stade fleet.[8]
SIR POLITIC. Is't possible? believe it,
'Twas either sent from Spain, or the Archduke's:
Spinola's whale, upon my life, my credit![9]
Will they not leave these projects? Worthy sir,
Some other news.
PEREGRINE. Faith, Stone the fool is dead,
And they do lack a tavern fool extremely.
SIR POLITIC. Is Mas' Stone dead?[1]
PEREGRINE. He's dead, sir; why, I hope
You thought him not immortal?—O, this knight,
Were he well known, would be a precious thing
To fit our English stage. He that should write
But such a fellow, should be thought to feign
Extremely, if not maliciously.
SIR POLITIC. Stone dead!
PEREGRINE. Dead. Lord! how deeply, sir, you apprehend it!
He was no kinsman to you?
SIR POLITIC. That I know of.
Well! that same fellow was an unknown fool.
PEREGRINE. And yet you knew him, it seems?
SIR POLITIC. I did so. Sir,
I knew him one of the most dangerous heads
Living within the state, and so I held him.
PEREGRINE. Indeed, sir?
SIR POLITIC. While he lived, in action.
He has received weekly intelligence,
Upon my knowledge, out of the Low Countries,
For all parts of the world, in cabbages;[2]
And those dispensed again to ambassadors,
In oranges, musk-melons, apricots,
Lemons, pome-citrons, and such-like; sometimes
In Colchester oysters, and your Selsey cockles.[3]

8. The Stade fleet was the Danish fleet at the mouth of the Elbe river. How a whale in the Thames could subvert it is not very clear.

9. Sir Politic's suggestions about the origin of the whale all involve Spain. It comes either from Spain itself, or from the Archduke Albert, ruler of the Spanish Netherlands in the name of Philip II, or from Ambrosio Spinola, general of the Spanish armies in Holland.

1. Stone the fool was an actual figure, about whom various anecdotes survive. "Mas' ": short for Master, the common denomination of fools and boys.

2. Cabbages were a recent importation from Holland.

3. "Pomecitrons" we would call simply "citrons." The oysters and cockles specified were the best shellfish to be had in England, and were often served to royalty.

PEREGRINE. You make me wonder.
SIR POLITIC. Sir, upon my knowledge.
Nay, I've observed him, at your public ordinary,[4]
Take his advertisement from a traveler
(A concealed statesman) in a trencher of meat;
And instantly, before the meal was done,
Convey an answer in a tooth-pick.
PEREGRINE. Strange!
How could this be, sir?
SIR POLITIC. Why, the meat was cut
So like his character, and so laid, as he
Must easily read the cipher.
PEREGRINE. I have heard,
He could not read, sir.
SIR POLITIC. So 'twas given out,
In polity,[5] by those that did employ him:
But he could read, and had your languages,
And to't,[6] as sound a noddle—
PEREGRINE. I have heard, sir,
That your baboons were spies, and that they were
A kind of subtle nation near to China.
SIR POLITIC. Ay, ay, your Mamaluchi.[7] Faith, they had
Their hand in a French plot or two; but they
Were so extremely given to women, as
They made discovery of all; yet I
Had my advices here, on Wednesday last,
From one of their own coat, they were returned,
Made their relations, as the fashion is,
And now stand fair for fresh employment.
PEREGRINE. [*aside*] 'Heart!
This Sir Politic will be ignorant of nothing.
—It seems, sir, you know all.
SIR POLITIC. Not all, sir; but
I have some general notions. I do love
To note and to observe; though I live out,
Free from the active torrent, yet I'd mark
The currents and the passages of things,
For mine own private use; and know the ebbs
And flows of state,
PEREGRINE. Believe it, sir, I hold
Myself in no small tie unto my fortunes,
For casting me thus luckily upon you,
Whose knowledge, if your bounty equal it,
May do me great assistance, in instruction
For my behavior, and my bearing, which

4. Common tavern. Advertisement: secret message, tip.
5. For political reasons, as part of his cover story.
6. In addition.
7. Mameluchi is the Italian form of *mamelukes*, a group of slaves and warriors originally from Circassia, in Asia Minor, who held or controlled the throne of Egypt for many years.

Is yet so rude and raw.
SIR POLITIC. Why? came you forth
Empty of rules for travel?
PEREGRINE. Faith, I had
Some common ones, from out that vulgar grammar,
Which he that cried Italian to me, taught me.[8]
SIR POLITIC. Why this it is that spoils all our brave bloods,
Trusting our hopeful gentry unto pedants,
Fellows of outside, and mere bark.[9] You seem
To be a gentleman, of ingenuous race:
I not profess it, but my fate hath been
To be, where I have been consulted with,
In this high kind, touching some great men's sons,
Persons of blood and honor.—
PEREGRINE. [*seeing people approach*] Who be these, sir?

SCENE II

[*Enter* MOSCA *and* NANO *disguised, followed by persons with materials for erecting a stage.*]

MOSCA. Under that window, there 't must be. The same.
SIR POLITIC. Fellows, to mount a bank. Did your instructor
In the dear tongues, never discourse to you
Of the Italian mountebanks?[1]
PEREGRINE. Yes, sir.
SIR POLITIC. Why,
Here you shall see one.
PEREGRINE. They are quacksalvers,
Fellows that live by venting[2] oils and drugs?
SIR POLITIC. Was that the character he gave you of them?
PEREGRINE. As I remember.
SIR POLITIC. Pity his ignorance.
They are the only knowing men of Europe!
Great general scholars, excellent physicians,
Most admired statesmen, professed favorites,
And cabinet counselors to the greatest princes;
The only languaged men of all the world![3]
PEREGRINE. And, I have heard, they are most lewd impostors;
Made all of terms and shreds; no less beliers
Of great men's favors, than their own vile medicines;
Which they will utter upon monstrous oaths,
Selling that drug for two-pence, ere they part,
Which they have valued at twelve crowns before.
SIR POLITIC. Sir, calumnies are answered best with silence.
Yourself shall judge—Who is it mounts, my friends?

8. Trained me in the pronunciation of Italian.
9. Superficial and ignorant teachers.
1. The word "mountebank" comes from the Italian *montambanco*, meaning "to mount the bench": other terms for the same fellow are *saltimbanco* and *charlatan*. They were a mixture of public entertainer and patent-medicine salesman who gave a very considerable semi-dramatic, improvised performance before delivering their pitch.
2. Vending.
3. The best talkers.

MOSCA. Scoto of Mantua, sir.[4]

SIR POLITIC. Is't he? Nay, then
I'll proudly promise, sir, you shall behold
Another man than has been phant'sied[5] to you.
I wonder yet, that he should mount his bank,
Here in this nook, that has been wont t'appear
In face of the Piazza!—Here he comes.

[*Enter* VOLPONE *disguised as a mountebank and followed by a crowd of people.*]

VOLPONE. [*to* NANO] Mount, zany.[6]

MOB. Follow, follow, follow, follow, follow!

SIR POLITIC. See how the people follow him! he's a man
May write ten thousand crowns in bank here. Note,

[VOLPONE *mounts the stage.*]

Mark but his gesture: I do use to observe
The state he keeps in getting up.

PEREGRINE. 'Tis worth it, sir.

VOLPONE. *Most noble gentlemen, and my worthy patrons! It may seem strange, that I, your Scoto Mantuano, who was ever wont to fix my bank in face of the public Piazza, near the shelter of the Portico to the Procuratia,*[7] *should now, after eight months' absence from this illustrious city of Venice, humbly retire myself into an obscure nook of the Piazza.*

SIR POLITIC. Did not I now object the same?

PEREGRINE. Peace, sir.

VOLPONE. *Let me tell you: I am not, as your Lombard proverb saith, cold on my feet;*[8] *or content to part with my commodities at a cheaper rate, than I accustomed: look not for it. Nor that the calumnious reports of that impudent detractor, and shame to our profession (Alessandro Buttone, I mean), who gave out, in public, I was condemned a* sforzato *to the galleys, for poisoning the cardinal Bembo's—*[9] *cook, hath at all attached, much less dejected me. No, no, worthy gentlemen; to tell you true, I cannot endure to see the rabble of these ground ciarlitani,*[1] *that spread their cloaks on the pavement, as if they meant to do feats of activity, and then come in*

4. Scoto of Mantua was a real person, a juggler, magician, and performer at legerdemain; he actually visited England and performed before Queen Elizabeth, about a quarter of a century before *Volpone* had its first performance.

5. Described to you.

6. Zany: from the Italian name *Giovanni*; a generic term for a fool, clown, performer. The speech of the crowd is intended to mimic a confused hubbub.

7. The arcade along the north side of Piazza San Marco, where the Procurators resided. Jonson takes great pains to make his Venetian details specific and accurate.

8. There is in fact an Italian proverb, "*Haver freddo a'piedi,*" meaning "to be so hard up that one has to sell one's goods at a loss."

9. Alessandro Buttone is an imaginary rival who has dreamed up a slander against Scoto—but the tale is most unlikely since Cardinal Bembo died in 1547, more than 50 years before the play is supposed to be taking place. A *sforzato* is a galley-slave; the dash before "cook" is supposed to indicate that the title of "cook" is just a euphemism.

1. Ground *ciarlatani* or charlatans put on their acts and sold their nostrums at street level.

lamely, with their moldy tales out of Boccaccio,[2] *like stale Tabarin, the fabulist: some of them discoursing their travels, and of their tedious captivity in the Turks' galley, when, indeed, were the truth known, they were the Christians' galleys, where very temperately they ate bread, and drunk water, as a wholesome penance, enjoined them by their confessors, for base pilferies.*[3]

SIR POLITIC. Note but his bearing, and contempt of these.

VOLPONE. *These turdy-facy-nasty-paty-lousy-fartical rogues, with one poor groat's-worth of unprepared antimony, finely wrapped up in several* scartoccios,[4] *are able, very well, to kill their twenty a week, and play; yet, these meager, starved spirits, who have half stopped the organs of their minds with earthy oppilations,*[5] *want not their favorers among your shrivelled salad-eating artisans, who are overjoyed that they may have their half-p'orth of physic; though it purge them into another world, it makes no matter.*

SIR POLITIC. Excellent! have you heard better language, sir?

VOLPONE. *Well, let them go. And, gentlemen, honorable gentlemen, know, that for this time, our bank, being thus removed from the clamors of the* canaglia,[6] *shall be the scene of pleasure and delight; for I have nothing to sell, little or nothing to sell.*

SIR POLITIC. I told you, sir, his end.

PEREGRINE. You did so, sir.

VOLPONE. *I protest, I, and my six servants, are not able to make of this precious liquor, so fast as it is fetched away from my lodging by gentlemen of your city; strangers of the* Terra-firma;[7] *worshipful merchants; ay, and senators too: who, ever since my arrival, have detained me to their uses, by their splendidous liberalities. And worthily; for, what avails your rich man to have his magazines stuffed with* moscadelli,[8] *or of the purest grape, when his physicians prescribe him, on pain of death, to drink nothing but water cocted*[9] *with aniseeds? O, health! health! the blessing of the rich! the riches of the poor! who can buy thee at too dear a rate, since there is no enjoying this world without thee? Be not then so sparing of your purses, honorable gentlemen, as to abridge the natural course of life—*

2. Boccaccio told in the *Decameron* a great many popular stories; as he lived in the 14th century, the tales were "moldy" by the 17th. Like Scoto, Tabarine was an actual Italian comedian of the time who performed in France (not, so far as we know, in England) during the 1570's.

3. Venetian galleys required many oars, often operated by captive Turks or condemned criminals, chained to the bench, fed miserable food, and whipped mercilessly.

4. Antimony was the basis of most common emetics; *scartoccios* were little paper envelopes in which drugs were placed.

5. Obstructions.

6. The common mob.

7. *Terra firma* is still the Venetian term for land across the lagoon, the mainland.

8. Muscadel or muscatel is wine made from certain grapes, in Italian *moscatini,* which seem to have the perfume of musk.

9. Flavored.

PEREGRINE. You see his end.

SIR POLITIC. Ay, is't not good?

VOLPONE. *For, when a humid flux, or catarrh, by the mutability of air, falls from your head into an arm or shoulder, or any other part; take you a ducat, or your sequin of gold, and apply to the place affected: see what good effect it can work.*[1] *No, no, 'tis this blessed* unguento, *this rare extraction, that hath only power to disperse all malignant humours, that proceed either of hot, cold, moist, or windy causes—*

PEREGRINE. I would he had put in dry too.[2]

SIR POLITIC. 'Pray you, observe.

VOLPONE. *To fortify the most indigest and crude stomach, ay, were it of one that, through extreme weakness, vomited blood, applying only a warm napkin to the place, after the unction and fricace;*[3]*—for the* vertigine *in the head, putting but a drop into your nostrils, likewise behind the ears; a most sovereign and approved remedy: the* Mal Caduco, *cramps, convulsions, paralyses, epilepsies,* Tremor-Cordia, *retired nerves, ill vapors of the spleen, stoppings of the liver, the stone, the strangury,* Hernia Ventosa, Iliaca Passio; *stops a* dysenteria *immediately; easeth the torsion of the small guts, and cures* Melancholia Hypocondriaca,[4] *being taken and applied, according to my printed receipt.* [Pointing to his bill and his vial.] *For, this is the physician, this the medicine; this counsels, this cures; this gives the direction, this works the effect; and, in sum, both together may be termed an abstract of the theoric and practic*[5] *in the Æsculapian art. 'Twill cost you eight crowns. And, Zan Fritada,*[6] *prithee sing a verse extempore in honor of it.*

SIR POLITIC. How do you like him, sir?

PEREGRINE. Most strangely, I!

SIR POLITIC. Is not his language rare?

PEREGRINE. But alchemy,[7]
I never heard the like; or Broughton's books.

[NANO *sings.*]

Had old Hippocrates, or Galen,[8]
That to their books put med'cines all in,
But known this secret, they had never
(Of which they will be guilty ever)

1. I.e., money won't cure your cold when you catch it (but my "blessed unguent" will).
2. Of the four "humours" or ingredients of a balanced human complexion, "Scoto" has left out one, as Peregrine drily observes.
3. Anointing and massage.
4. "*Melancholia Hypocondriaca*" is black depression. The other ailments are: *Mal Caduco,* falling sickness, epilepsy; *Tremor Cordia,* palpitations of the heart; strangury, painful urination; *Hernia Ventosa,* gassy hernia; *Iliaca Passio,* cramps of the small intestine.
5. Theory and practice. The Aesculapian art: medicine (from Aesculapius, Greek god of medicine).
6. Literally, "Johnny Omelet," obviously one of the mountebank's stooges.
7. Except for alchemy. Johnson had no use for the books of Hugh Broughton, a Puritan divine and rabbinical scholar.
8. Famous doctors of the Classical world.

Been murderers of so much paper,
Or wasted many a hurtless taper;
No Indian drug had e'er been famed,
Tobacco, sassafras not named;
Ne yet, of guacum[9] *one small stick, sir,*
Nor Raymond Lully's great elixir.
Ne had been known the Danish Gonswart,
Or Paracelsus, with his long sword.[1]

PEREGRINE. All this, yet, will not do; eight crowns is high.

VOLPONE. *No more. Gentlemen, if I had but time to discourse to you the miraculous effects of this my oil, surnamed* oglio del Scoto;[2] *with the countless catalogue of those I have cured of the aforesaid, and many more diseases; the patents and privileges of all the princes and commonwealths of Christendom; or but the depositions of those that appeared on my part, before the signory of the Sanita*[3] *and most learned College of Physicians; where I was authorized, upon notice taken of the admirable virtues of my medicaments, and mine own excellency in matter of rare and unknown secrets, not only to disperse them publicly in this famous city, but in all the territories, that happily joy under the government of the most pious and magnificent states of Italy. But may some other gallant fellow say, 'O, there be divers that make profession to have as good, and as experimented receipts as yours.' Indeed, very many have essayed, like apes, in imitation of that which is really and essentially in me, to make of this oil; bestowed great cost in furnaces, stills, alembics,*[4] *continual fires, and preparation of the ingredients, (as indeed there goes to it six hundred several simples,*[5] *besides some quantity of human fat, for the conglutination, which we buy of the anatomists) but, when these practitioners come to the last decoction, blow, blow, puff, puff, and all flies* in fumo:[6] *ha, ha, ha! Poor wretches, I rather pity their folly and indiscretion, than their loss of time and money; for those may be recovered by industry: but to be a fool born, is a disease incurable.*

For myself, I always from my youth have endeavored to get the rarest secrets, and book them, either in exchange, or for money: I spared nor cost nor labor, where anything was worthy to be learned. And, gentlemen, honorable gentlemen; I will undertake, by virtue of chemical art, out of the honorable hat that covers your head, to extract the four elements; that is to

9. Modern guaiacum, obtained from the bark of a South American tree.
1. Raymond Lully or Lull was a Spanish mystic philosopher of the 13th century who claimed to have discovered the elixir. "The Danish Gonswart": unidentifiable. Paracelsus, the famous German doctor of the 16th century, had a famous sword in the handle of which he kept, according to legend, familiar spirits, and according to history, medications and herbs.
2. Scoto's oil.
3. The Board of Medical Examiners in Venice.
4. Distilleries, retorts.
5. Herbs.
6. In smoke; "decoction": boiling down.

say, the fire, air, water, and earth, and return you your felt without burn or stain. For, whilst others have been at the balloo,[7] *I have been at my book; and am now past the craggy paths of study, and come to the flowery plains of honor and reputation.*

SIR POLITIC. I do assure you, sir, that is his aim.

VOLPONE. *But to our price—*

PEREGRINE. And that withal, sir Pol.

VOLPONE. *You all know, honorable gentlemen, I never valued this* ampulla, *or vial, at less than eight crowns; but for this time, I am content to be deprived of it for six: six crowns is the price, and less in courtesy I know you cannot offer me; take it or leave it, howsoever, both it and I am at your service. I ask you not as the value of the thing, for then I should demand of you a thousand crowns; so the cardinals Montalto, Farnese, the great duke of Tuscany, my gossip,*[8] *with divers other princes, have given me; but I despise money. Only to show my affection to you, honorable gentlemen, and your illustrious state here, I have neglected the messages of these princes, mine own offices, framed my journey hither, only to present you with the fruits of my travels.* [To NANO.]—*Tune your voices once more to the touch of your instruments, and give the honorable assembly some delightful recreation.*

PEREGRINE. What monstrous and most painful circumstance
Is here, to get some three or four *gazettes,*[9]
Some three-pence in the whole! for that 'twill come to.

[NANO *sings.*]

You that would last long, list to my song,
Make no more coil,[1] *but buy of this oil.*
Would you be ever fair and young?
Stout of teeth, and strong of tongue?
Tart of palate? quick of ear?
Sharp of sight? of nostril clear?
Moist of hand and light of foot?
Or, I will come nearer to't,
Would you live free from all diseases?
Do the act your mistress pleases,
Yet fright all aches from your bones?
Here's a medicine for the nones.[2]

VOLPONE. *Well, I am in a humor at this time to make a present of the small quantity my coffer contains; to the rich in courtesy, and to the poor for God's sake. Wherefore, now mark: I asked you six crowns; and six crowns, at other times, you have*

7. Balloon, ball; i.e., while others have been diverting themselves with ball games.
8. My good friend. Cardinal Montalto became Pope as Sixtus the Fifth in 1585; Alessandro Farnese had been Pope as Paul III in 1534; "the great duke of Tuscany" was Cosimo de Medici.
9. The smallest Venetian coins, worth less than an English penny.
1. Stir, fuss.
2. For the occasion.

paid me; you shall not give me six crowns, nor five, nor four, nor three, nor two, nor one; nor half a ducat; no, nor a mocenigo.[3] *Sixpence it will cost you, or six hundred pound—expect no lower price, for, by the banner of my front, I will not bate a* bagatine,[4]*—that I will have, only, a pledge of your loves, to carry something from amongst you, to show I am not contemned by you. Therefore, now, toss your handkerchiefs, cheerfully, cheerfully;*[5] *and be advertised, that the first heroic spirit that deigns to grace me with a handkerchief, I will give it a little remembrance of something, beside, shall please it better, than if I had presented it with a double pistolet.*[6]

PEREGRINE. Will you be that heroic spark, sir Pol?

[CELIA *at a window above, throws down her handkerchief.*]

O, see! the window has prevented[7] you.

VOLPONE. *Lady, I kiss your bounty; and for this timely grace you have done your poor Scoto of Mantua, I will return you, over and above my oil, a secret of that high and inestimable nature, shall make you for ever enamored on that minute, wherein your eye first descended on so mean, yet not altogether to be despised, an object. Here is a powder concealed in this paper, of which, if I should speak to the worth, nine thousand volumes were but as one page, that page as a line, that line as a word; so short is this pilgrimage of man (which some call life) to the expressing of it. Would I reflect on the price? why, the whole world were but as an empire, that empire as a province, that province as a bank, that bank as a private purse to the purchase of it. I will only tell you; it is the powder that made Venus a goddess, (given her by Apollo,) that kept her perpetually young, cleared her wrinkles, firmed her gums, filled her skin, colored her hair; from her derived to Helen, and at the sack of Troy unfortunately lost; till now, in this our age, it was as happily recovered, by a studious antiquary, out of some ruins of Asia, who sent a moiety*[8] *of it to the court of France, (but much sophisticated,) wherewith the ladies there now color their hair. The rest, at this present, remains with me; extracted to a quintessence, so that, wherever it but touches, in youth it perpetually preserves, in age restores the complexion; seats your teeth, did they dance like virginal jacks,*[9] *firm as a wall; makes them white as ivory, that were black as*———

3. A Venetian coin, worth about nine English pennies.
4. A tiny coin.
5. When business was brisk at the mountebank's stand, customers sometimes knotted their money in a handkerchief or glove and tossed it on stage; the money was taken out, replaced with the medicine, and the handkerchief tossed back to the purchaser.
6. A double pistolet was a Spanish coin of some value, worth not much less than an English pound.
7. Forestalled, anticipated.
8. Fraction; "sophisticated": refined, purified.
9. The quills that pluck the strings of a harpsichord ("virginal").

SCENE 3

[*Enter* CORVINO.]

CORVINO. Spite o' the devil, and my shame! come down, here;
Come down; [*To* VOLPONE.]—No house but mine to make your scene?
Signor Flaminio,[1] will you down, sir? down?
What, is my wife your Franciscina, sir?
No windows on the whole Piazza, here,
To make your properties, but mine? but mine? [*Beats away* VOLPONE, NANO, *&c.*]
Heart! ere to-morrow I shall be new-christened,
And called the *Pantalone di Bisognosi*,[2]
About the town.

PEREGRINE. What should this mean, sir Pol?

SIR POLITIC. Some trick of state, believe it; I will home.

PEREGRINE. It may be some design on you.

SIR POLITIC. I know not.
I'll stand upon my guard.

PEREGRINE. It is your best, sir.

SIR POLITIC. This three weeks, all my advices, all my letters,
They have been intercepted.

PEREGRINE. Indeed, sir!
Best have a care.

SIR POLITIC. Nay, so I will.

PEREGRINE. This knight,
I may not lose him, for my mirth, till night. [*Exeunt.*]

SCENE 4. *A Room in* VOLPONE'*s House.*

[*Enter* VOLPONE *and* MOSCA.]

VOLPONE. O, I am wounded!

MOSCA. Where, sir?

VOLPONE. Not without;
Those blows were nothing; I could bear them ever.
But angry Cupid, bolting from her eyes,
Hath shot himself into me like a flame,
Where, now, he flings about his burning heat,
As in a furnace an ambitious[3] fire,
Whose vent is stopped. The fight is all within me.
I cannot live, except thou help me, Mosca;
My liver melts, and I, without the hope
Of some soft air, from her refreshing breath,
Am but a heap of cinders.

MOSCA. 'Las, good sir,

1. Signor Flaminio was Flaminio Scala, a Venetian comic actor of the day; Franciscina is an always-available serving girl in popular Italian comedy (*commedia dell'arte*).

2. Pantaloon of the Paupers. Pantaloon, in the tradition of *commedia dell'arte*, is a doddering old fool in perpetual terror of being cuckolded.

3. Aspiring, growing. Most of Volpone's erotic torments are of the sort popularized 300 years before by Francesco Petrarca.

Would you had never seen her!
VOLPONE. Nay, would thou
Hadst never told me of her!
MOSCA. Sir, 'tis true;
I do confess I was unfortunate,
And you unhappy: but I'm bound in conscience,
No less than duty, to effect my best
To your release of torment, and I will, sir.
VOLPONE. Dear Mosca, shall I hope?
MOSCA. Sir, more than dear,
I will not bid you to despair of aught
Within a human compass.
VOLPONE. O, there spoke
My better angel. Mosca, take my keys,
Gold, plate, and jewels, all's at thy devotion;[4]
Employ them how thou wilt; nay, coin me too,
So thou, in this, but crown my longings. Mosca?
MOSCA. Use but your patience.
VOLPONE. So I have.
MOSCA. I doubt not
To bring success to your desires.
VOLPONE. Nay, then,
I not repent me of my late disguise.
MOSCA. If you can horn[5] him, sir, you need not.
VOLPONE. True:
Besides, I never meant him for my heir.—
Is not the color of my beard and eyebrows
To make me known?
MOSCA. No jot.
VOLPONE. I did it well.
MOSCA. So well, would I could follow you in mine,
With half the happiness!—and yet I would
Escape your epilogue.[6]
VOLPONE. But were they gulled
With a belief that I was Scoto?
MOSCA. Sir,
Scoto himself could hardly have distinguished!
I have not time to flatter you now, we'll part:
And as I prosper, so applaud my art. [*Exeunt.*]

SCENE 5. *A Room in* CORVINO*'s House.*

[*Enter* CORVINO, *sword in his hand, dragging in* CELIA.]
CORVINO. Death of mine honor, with the city's fool!
A juggling, tooth-drawing, prating mountebank!
And at a public window! where, whilst he,
With his strained action, and his dole[7] of faces,
To his drug-lecture draws your itching ears,

4. At your service.
5. Cuckold.
6. Avoid the beating you got.
7. Guile, trickery; the suggestion is of false faces or masks.

A crew of old, unmarried, noted lechers,
Stood leering up like satyrs: and you smile
Most graciously, and fan your favors forth,
To give your hot spectators satisfaction!
What, was your mountebank their call?[8] their whistle?
Or were you enamored on his copper rings,
His saffron jewel, with the toad-stone in't?
Or his embroidered suit, with the cope-stitch,
Made of a hearse cloth?[9] or his old tilt-feather?
Or his starched beard? Well! you shall have him, yes!
He shall come home, and minister unto you
The fricace for the mother.[1] Or, let me see,
I think you'd rather mount;[2] would you not mount?
Why, if you'll mount, you may; yes, truly, you may:
And so you may be seen, down to the foot.
Get you a cittern,[3] lady Vanity,
And be a dealer with the virtuous man;
Make one: I'll but protest myself a cuckold,
And save your dowry.[4] I'm a Dutchman, I!
For, if you thought me an Italian,
You would be damned, ere you did this, you whore!
Thou'dst tremble, to imagine, that the murder
Of father, mother, brother, all thy race,
Should follow, as the subject of my justice.

CELIA. Good sir, have patience.

CORVINO. What couldst thou propose
Less to thyself, than in this heat of wrath,
And stung with my dishonor, I should strike
This steel into thee, with as many stabs,
As thou wert gazed upon with goatish eyes?

CELIA. Alas, sir, be appeased! I could not think
My being at the window should more now
Move your impatience, than at other times.

CORVINO. No? not to seek and entertain a parley
With a known knave, before a multitude?
You were an actor with your handkerchief,
Which he most sweetly kissed in the receipt,
And might, no doubt, return it with a letter,
And 'point the place where you might meet; your sister's,
Your mother's, or your aunt's might serve the turn.

8. I.e., did you arrange the appearance of Scoto deliberately to draw a crowd?
9. Copper rings and toad-stone jewelry are Corvino's sneers at the cheap and flashy dress of the mountebank, whose suit (he imagines) is made of coarse brown burlap ("hearse-cloth") prettied up with embroidery.
1. Massage for the womb.
2. I.e., both on the man and on the stage.
3. A kind of guitar, with which she could set up with the mountebank as whore and pimp ("dealer"). "Lady Vanity" is a stock figure out of the old morality plays.
4. In the event of her infidelity, Celia's dowry would be forfeited to her husband. "I'm a Dutchman": the stolidity, not to say complacency, of Dutch men was a common theme of satire—Italians, on the other hand, were reputed to be fiercely jealous.

CELIA. Why, dear sir, when do I make these excuses,
Or ever stir abroad, but to the church?
And that so seldom—
CORVINO. Well, it shall be less;
And thy restraint before was liberty
To what I now decree: and therefore mark me.
First, I will have this bawdy light dammed up;[5]
And till't be done, some two or three yards off,
I'll chalk a line, o'er which if thou but chance
To set thy desperate foot, more hell, more horror,
More wild remorseless rage shall seize on thee,
Than on a conjuror, that had heedless left
His circle's safety ere his devil was laid.[6]
Then here's a lock which I will hang upon thee,
And, now I think on't, I will keep thee backwards;
Thy lodging shall be backwards; thy walks backwards;
Thy prospect, all be backwards; and no pleasure,
That thou shalt know but backwards. Nay, since you force
My honest nature, know, it is your own,
Being too open, makes me use you thus.
Since you will not contain your subtle nostrils
In a sweet room, but they must snuff the air
Of rank and sweaty passengers. [*Knocking within.*]—One knocks.
Away, and be not seen, pain of thy life;
Nor look toward the window: if thou dost—
Nay, stay, hear this: let me not prosper, whore,
But I will make thee an anatomy,[7]
Dissect thee mine own self, and read a lecture
Upon thee to the city, and in public.
Away!—[*Exit* CELIA.] Who's there? [*Enter* SERVANT.]
SERVANT. 'Tis signor Mosca, sir.

SCENE 6

CORVINO. Let him come in. [*Exit* SERVANT.] His master's dead: there's yet
Some good to help the bad. [*Enter* MOSCA.] My Mosca, welcome!
I guess your news.
MOSCA. I fear you cannot, sir.
CORVINO. Is't not his death?
MOSCA. Rather the contrary.
CORVINO. Not his recovery?
MOSCA. Yes, sir.
CORVINO. I am cursed,
I am bewitched, my crosses meet to vex me.

5. I.e., brick up the window.
6. When a warlock raised the devil, he was well advised to draw around himself a magic circle, over which the devil could not step.
7. A skeleton hung up in a medical laboratory for demonstration purposes.

How? how? how? how?
MOSCA. Why, sir, with Scoto's oil!
Corbaccio and Voltore brought of it,
Whilst I was busy in an inner room——
CORVINO. Death! that damned mountebank! but for the law
Now, I could kill the rascal: it cannot be,
His oil should have that virtue.[8] Have not I
Known him a common rogue, come fiddling in
To the *osteria*,[9] with a tumbling whore,
And, when he has done all his forced tricks, been glad
Of a poor spoonful of dead wine, with flies in't?
It cannot be. All his ingredients
Are a sheep's gall, a roasted bitch's marrow,
Some few sod[1] earwigs, pounded caterpillars,
A little capon's grease, and fasting spittle:
I know them to a dram.
MOSCA. I know not, sir;
But some on't, there, they poured into his ears,
Some in his nostrils, and recovered him;
Applying but the fricace.[2]
CORVINO. Pox o' that fricace!
MOSCA. And since, to seem the more officious
And flattering of his health, there, they have had,
At extreme fees, the college of physicians
Consulting on him, how they might restore him;
Where one would have a cataplasm[3] of spices,
Another a flayed ape clapped to his breast,
A third would have it a dog, a fourth an oil,
With wild cats' skins; at last, they all resolved
That, to preserve him, was no other means,
But some young woman must be straight sought out,
Lusty, and full of juice, to sleep by him;
And to this service, most unhappily,
And most unwillingly, am I now employed,
Which here I thought to pre-acquaint you with,
For your advice, since it concerns you most,
Because I would not do that thing might cross
Your ends, on whom I have my whole dependence, sir.
Yet, if I do it not, they may delate[4]
My slackness to my patron, work me out
Of his opinion; and there all your hopes,
Ventures, or whatsoever, are all frustrate!
I do but tell you, sir. Besides, they are all
Now striving, who shall first present him; therefore—
I could entreat you, briefly conclude somewhat;
Prevent[5] them if you can.

8. Efficacy.
9. The Italian word for "tavern."
1. Boiled; fasting spittle: as it implies, spit taken from a hungry man.
2. I.e., all they had to do was rub it in.
3. Poultice.
4. Denounce, complain of.
5. Forestall.

CORVINO. Death to my hopes,
This is my villainous fortune! Best to hire
Some common courtesan.
MOSCA. Ay, I thought on that, sir;
But they are all so subtle, full of art,
And age again doting and flexible,
So as—I cannot tell—we may, perchance,
Light on a quean[6] may cheat us all.
CORVINO. 'Tis true.
MOSCA. No, no: it must be one that has no tricks, sir,
Some simple thing, a creature made unto it;
Some wench you may command. Have you no kinswoman?
God's so—Think, think, think, think, think, think, think, sir.
One o' the doctors offered there his daughter.
CORVINO. How!
MOSCA. Yes, signor Lupo,[7] the physician.
CORVINO. His daughter!
MOSCA. And a virgin, sir. Why, alas,
He knows the state of's body, what it is;
That nought can warm his blood, sir, but a fever;
Nor any incantation raise his spirit:
A long forgetfulness hath seized that part.
Besides, sir, who shall know it? some one or two—
CORVINO. I pray thee give me leave. [*Walks aside.*] If any man
But I had had this luck—The thing in itself,
I know, is nothing—Wherefore should not I
As well command my blood and my affections,
As this dull doctor? In the point of honor,
The cases are all one of wife and daughter.
MOSCA. [*aside*] I hear him coming.
CORVINO. She shall do't: 'tis done.
Slight! if this doctor, who is not engaged,
Unless 't be for his counsel, which is nothing,
Offer his daughter, what should I, that am
So deeply in? I will prevent him: Wretch!
Covetous wretch![8]—Mosca, I have determined.
MOSCA. How, sir?
CORVINO. We'll make all sure. The party you wot of[9]
Shall be mine own wife, Mosca.
MOSCA. Sir, the thing,
But that I would not seem to counsel you,
I should have motioned[1] to you, at the first:
And, make your count, you have cut all their throats.
Why, 'tis directly taking a possession!
And in his next fit, we may let him go.
'Tis but to pull the pillow from his head,
And he is throttled: it had been done before,
But for your scrupulous doubts.

6. Trollop.
7. Doctor Wolf.
8. The words are spoken by Corvino to himself about himself.
9. Know about.
1. Suggested.

CORVINO. Ay, a plague on't,
My conscience fools my wit! Well, I'll be brief,
And so be thou, lest they should be before us:
Go home, prepare him, tell him with what zeal
And willingness I do it; swear it was
On the first hearing, as thou mayst do truly,
Mine own free motion.
MOSCA. Sir, I warrant you,
I'll so possess him with it, that the rest
Of his starved clients shall be banished all,
And only you received. But come not, sir,
Until I send, for I have something else
To ripen for your good, you must not know it.
CORVINO. But do not you forget to send now.
MOSCA. Fear not. [*Exit* MOSCA.]

SCENE 7

CORVINO. Where are you, wife? my Celia! wife!
[*Enter* CELIA, *weeping.*]
What, blubbering?
Come, dry those tears. I think thou thought'st me in earnest?
Ha! by this light I talked so but to try thee.
Methinks, the lightness of the occasion
Should have confirmed thee.[2] Come, I am not jealous.
CELIA. No?
CORVINO. Faith I am not, I, nor never was;
It is a poor unprofitable humor.
Do not I know, if women have a will,
They'll do 'gainst all the watches of the world,
And that the fiercest spies are tamed with gold?[3]
Tut, I am confident in thee, thou shalt see't;
And see, I'll give thee cause too, to believe it.
Come, kiss me. Go, and make thee ready straight,
In all thy best attire, thy choicest jewels,
Put them all on, and, with them, thy best looks:
We are invited to a solemn feast,
At old Volpone's, where it shall appear
How far I am free from jealousy or fear. [*Exeunt.*]

Act III

SCENE 1. *A Street.*

[*Enter* MOSCA.]
MOSCA. I fear, I shall begin to grow in love
With my dear self, and my most prosperous parts,
They do so spring and burgeon; I can feel
A whimsy in my blood: I know not how,
Success hath made me wanton. I could skip

2. You should have seen I was joking because the occasion was so trivial.

3. Immemorial commonplaces on the lust and treachery of women.

Out of my skin, now, like a subtle snake,
I am so limber. O! your parasite[4]
Is a most precious thing, dropped from above,
Not bred 'mongst clods and clodpoles, here on earth.
I muse the mystery[5] was not made a science,
It is so liberally professed! almost
All the wise world is little else, in nature,
But parasites or sub-parasites. And, yet,
I mean not those that have your bare town-art,
To know who's fit to feed them; have no house,
No family, no care, and therefore mold
Tales for men's ears, to bait[6] that sense; or get
Kitchen-invention, and some stale receipts
To please the belly, and the groin; nor those,
With their court dog-tricks, that can fawn and fleer,
Make their revénue out of legs and faces,[7]
Echo my lord, and lick away a moth:
But your fine elegant rascal, that can rise,
And stoop, almost together, like an arrow;
Shoot through the air as nimbly as a star;
Turn short as doth a swallow; and be here,
And there, and here, and yonder, all at once;
Present to any humor, all occasion;
And change a visor,[8] swifter than a thought!
This is the creature had the art born with him;
Toils not to learn it, but doth practice it
Out of most excellent nature: and such sparks
Are the true parasites, others but their zanies.

SCENE 2

[*Enter* BONARIO.]

MOSCA. Who's this? Bonario, old Corbaccio's son?
The person I was bound to seek.—Fair sir,
You are happily met.

BONARIO. That cannot be by thee.

MOSCA. Why, sir?

BONARIO. Nay, pray thee know thy way, and leave me:
I would be loath to interchange discourse
With such a mate as thou art.

MOSCA. Courteous sir,
Scorn not my poverty.

BONARIO. Not I, by heaven;
But thou shalt give me leave to hate thy baseness.

4. The comedies of Terence and Plautus, with which Jonson was thoroughly familiar, swarm with parasites; the very idea of the relationship was repugnant to his sturdy, Stoic independence of spirit.
5. Craft. Mosca is playing on the idea of the liberal arts and sciences.
6. The parasite who talks for a living "baits" (teases, gratifies) the sense of hearing; others gratify the bellies and groins of their patrons.
7. Scrapings and looks of admiration.
8. I.e., the mask of his expression.

MOSCA. Baseness!
BONARIO. Ay; answer me, is not thy sloth
Sufficient argument? thy flattery?
Thy means of feeding?
MOSCA. Heaven be good to me!
These imputations are too common, sir,
And easily stuck on virtue when she's poor.
You are unequal to me, and howe'er
Your sentence may be righteous, yet you are not,
That, ere you know me, thus proceed in censure:
St. Mark bear witness 'gainst you, 'tis inhuman. [*Weeps.*]
BONARIO. [*aside*] What! does he weep! the sign is soft and good;
I do repent me that I was so harsh.
MOSCA. 'Tis true, that, swayed by a strong necessity
I am enforced to eat my careful bread
With too much obsequy;[9] 'tis true, beside,
That I am fain to spin mine own poor raiment
Out of my mere observance,[1] being not born
To a free fortune: but that I have done
Base offices, in rending friends asunder,
Dividing families, betraying counsels,
Whispering false lies, or mining men with praises,
Trained their credulity with perjuries,
Corrupted chastity, or am in love
With mine own tender ease, but would not rather
Prove the most rugged, and laborious course,
That might redeem my present estimation,
Let me here perish, in all hope of goodness.
BONARIO. [*Aside.*] This cannot be a personated passion.—
I was to blame, so to mistake thy nature;
Prithee forgive me and speak out thy business.
MOSCA. Sir, it concerns you; and though I may seem,
At first to make a main offense in manners,
And in my gratitude unto my master;
Yet, for the pure love, which I bear all right,
And hatred of the wrong, I must reveal it.
This very hour your father is in purpose
To disinherit you—
BONARIO. How!
MOSCA. And thrust you forth,
As a mere stranger to his blood; 'tis true, sir.
The work no way engageth me, but, as
I claim an interest in the general state
Of goodness and true virtue, which I hear
T'abound in you; and, for which mere respect,
Without a second aim, sir, I have done it.
BONARIO. This tale hath lost thee much of the late trust
Thou hadst with me; it is impossible.

9. Flattery, obsequiousness. 1. Service.

I know not how to lend it any thought,
My father should be so unnatural.
MOSCA. It is a confidence that well becomes
Your piety; and formed, no doubt, it is
From your own simple innocence: which makes
Your wrong more monstrous and abhorred. But, sir,
I now will tell you more. This very minute,
It is, or will be doing; and, if you
Shall be but pleased to go with me, I'll bring you,
I dare not say where you shall see, but where
Your ear shall be a witness of the deed;
Hear yourself written bastard, and professed
The common issue of the earth.[2]
BONARIO. I'm 'mazed.
MOSCA. Sir, if I do it not, draw your just sword,
And score your vengeance on my front and face;
Mark me your villain: you have too much wrong,
And I do suffer for you, sir. My heart
Weeps blood in anguish—
BONARIO. Lead; I follow thee. [*Exeunt.*]

SCENE 3. *A Room in* VOLPONE*'s House.*

[*Enter* VOLPONE.]
VOLPONE. Mosca stays long, methinks. Bring forth your sports,
And help to make the wretched time more sweet.
[*Enter* NANO, ANDROGYNO, *and* CASTRONE.]
NANO. *Dwarf, fool, and eunuch, well met here we be.*
A question it were now, whether of us three,
Being all the known delicates[3] *of a rich man,*
In pleasing him, claim the precedency can?
CASTRONE. *I claim for myself.*
ANDROGYNO. *And so doth the fool.*
NANO. *'Tis foolish indeed: let me set you both to school.*
First for your dwarf, he's little and witty,
And every thing, as it is little, is pretty;
Else why do men say to a creature of my shape,
So soon as they see him, 'It's a pretty little ape?'
And why a pretty ape, but for pleasing imitation
Of greater men's actions, in a ridiculous fashion?
Beside, this feat[4] *body of mine doth not crave*
Half the meat, drink, and cloth, one of your bulks will have.
Admit your fool's face be the mother of laughter,
Yet, for his brain, it must always come after:
And though that do feed him, it's a pitiful case,
His body is beholding to such a bad face. [*Knocking within.*]
VOLPONE. Who's there? my couch; away! look, Nano, see:

2. A man without recognized father was known to the Romans as a *filius terrae,* "son of earth."
3. Favorites.
4. Trim.

[*Exeunt* ANDROGYNO *and* CASTRONE.]
Give me my caps, first—go, enquire. [*Exit* NANO.] Now, Cupid
Send it be Mosca, and with fair return!
NANO. [*within*] It is the beauteous madam—
VOLPONE. Would-be—is it?
NANO. The same.
VOLPONE. Now torment on me! Squire her in;
For she will enter, or dwell here forever:
Nay quickly. [*Retires to his couch.*]—That my fit were past! I fear
A second hell too, that my loathing this
Will quite expel my appetite to the other:[5]
Would she were taking now her tedious leave.
Lord, how it threats me what I am to suffer!

SCENE 4

[*Enter* NANO *with* LADY POLITIC WOULD-BE.]
LADY POLITIC. I thank you, good sir. 'Pray you signify
Unto your patron, I am here. This band
Shows not my neck enough. I trouble you, sir.
Let me request you, bid one of my women
Come hither to me. In good faith, I am dressed
Most favorably to-day. It is no matter;
'Tis well enough.[6]
[*Enter 1st* WAITING-WOMAN.]
Look, see, these petulant[7] things,
How they have done this!
VOLPONE. [*aside*] I do feel the fever
Entering in at mine ears; O, for a charm,
To fright it hence!
LADY POLITIC. Come nearer: is this curl
In his right place? or this? Why is this higher
Than all the rest? You have not washed your eyes, yet!
Or do they not stand even in your head?
Where is your fellow? call her. [*Exit 1st* WOMAN.]
NANO. [*aside*] Now, St. Mark
Deliver us! anon, she'll beat her women,
Because her nose is red.
[*Re-enter 1st with 2nd* WOMAN.]
LADY POLITIC. I pray you, view
This tire,[8] forsooth: are all things apt, or no?
1 WOMAN. One hair a little, here, sticks out, forsooth.
LADY POLITIC. Does't so, forsooth! and where was your dear sight,
When it did so, forsooth![9] What now! bird-eyed?

5. I.e., his loathing for Lady Politic may destroy his appetite for Celia.
6. The theme of talkative women was ancient and traditional; Jonson got a lot of Lady Politic's chatter from a Syrian sophist of the 4th century A.D., Libanius, who wrote a talkative book all about talkative women.
7. Troublesome.
8. Headdress, arrangement of hair.
9. She strikes at them both, and jeers at their flinching. "Bird-eyed": sharp of sight.

And you, too? Pray you, both approach and mend it.
Now, by that light, I muse you're not ashamed!
I, that have preached these things so oft unto you,
Read you the principles, argued all the grounds,
Disputed every fitness, every grace,
Called you to counsel of so frequent dressings—
NANO. [*aside*] More carefully than of your fame or honor.
LADY POLITIC. Made you acquainted, what an ample dowry
The knowledge of these things would be unto you,
Able, alone, to get you noble husbands
At your return; and you thus to neglect it!
Besides, you seeing what a curious[1] nation
The Italians are, what will they say of me?
The English lady cannot dress herself.—
Here's a fine imputation to our country!
Well, go your ways, and stay in the next room.
This fucus[2] was too coarse too; it's no matter.
Good sir, you'll give them entertainment?
[*Exeunt* NANO *and* WAITING-WOMEN.]
VOLPONE. The storm comes toward me.
LADY POLITIC. [*goes to the couch*] How does my Volpone?
VOLPONE. Troubled with noise; I cannot sleep; I dreamt
That a strange fury entered, now, my house,
And, with the dreadful tempest of her breath,
Did cleave my roof asunder.
LADY POLITIC. Believe me, and I
Had the most fearful dream, could I remember't—
VOLPONE. [*aside*] Out on my fate! I have given her the occasion
How to torment me: she will tell me hers.
LADY POLITIC. Methought, the golden mediocrity,[3]
Polite, and delicate—
VOLPONE O, if you do love me,
No more; I sweat, and suffer, at the mention
Of any dream: feel how I tremble yet.
LADY POLITIC. Alas, good soul! the passion of the heart.[4]
Seed-pearl were good now, boiled with syrup of apples,
Tincture of gold, and coral, citron-pills,
Your elecampane root, myrobalanes[5]—
VOLPONE. [*aside*] Ay me, I have ta'en a grass-hopper by the wing!
LADY POLITIC. Burnt silk, and amber; you have muscadel
Good in the house—
VOLPONE. You will not drink, and part?
LADY POLITIC. No, fear not that. I doubt we shall not get
Some English saffron, half a dram would serve;
Your sixteen cloves, a little musk, dried mints,

1. Fastidious, particular.
2. Makeup. The last sentence is spoken to Nano.
3. I.e., the golden rule or the golden mean.
4. Heartburn.
5. An Oriental drug used for diarrhea. "Elecampane": a stimulant.

Bugloss,[6] and barley-meal—
VOLPONE. [*aside*]   She's in again!
Before I feigned diseases, now I have one.
LADY POLITIC. And these applied with a right scarlet cloth.
VOLPONE. [*aside*] Another flood of words! a very torrent!
LADY POLITIC. Shall I, sir, make you a poultice?
VOLPONE.   No, no, no;
I'm very well, you need prescribe no more.
LADY POLITIC. I have a little studied physic; but now,
I'm all for music, save, in the forenoons,
An hour or two for painting. I would have
A lady, indeed, to have all letters and arts,
Be able to discourse, to write, to paint,
But principal, as Plato holds, your music
(And so does wise Pythagoras, I take it)
Is your true rapture; when there is consent[7]
In face, in voice, and clothes: and is, indeed,
Our sex's chiefest ornament.
VOLPONE.   The poet
As old in time as Plato, and as knowing,
Says, that your highest female grace is silence.[8]
LADY POLITIC. Which of your poets? Petrarch, or Tasso, or Dante?
Guarini? Ariosto? Aretine?
Cieco di Hadria?[9] I have read them all.
VOLPONE. [*aside*] Is everything a cause to my destruction?
LADY POLITIC. I think I have two or three of them about me.
VOLPONE. [*aside*] The sun, the sea, will sooner both stand still
Than her eternal tongue! nothing can 'scape it.
LADY POLITIC. Here's *Pastor Fido*—[1]
VOLPONE. [*aside*]   Profess obstinate silence;
That's now my safest.
LADY POLITIC.   All our English writers,
I mean such as are happy in th' Italian,
Will deign to steal out of this author, mainly;
Almost as much as from Montagnié:[2]
He has so modern and facile a vein,
Fitting the time, and catching the court-ear!
Your Petrarch is more passionate, yet he,
In days of sonneting, trusted them with much:
Dante is hard, and few can understand him.
But, for a desperate wit, there's Aretine;[3]

6. A common herb used as a mild stimulant.
7. Harmony, concord.
8. The poet as old as Plato is Sophocles (*Ajax*, line 293).
9. All Lady Politic's poets are well known today except Cieco di Hadria ("the blind man of Adria"), Luigi Groto; he was an actor as well as a poet, and made a tremendous impression by playing Oedipus (in Giustiniani's version of Sophocles' play) at the openi[illegible] Palladio's Teatro Olimpico at Vicenza (1585).
1. A pastoral by G. B. Guarini (1590), internationally popular.
2. Montaigne's name tended to be given three syllables by English tongues; his *Essays*, first published in 1580, were translated into English by Jonson's friend John Florio (1603).
3. Aretino's dirty poems, illustrated by Giulio Romano and engraved by M. Raimondi, were internationally notorious.

Only, his pictures are a little obscene—
You mark me not?
VOLPONE. Alas, my mind's perturbed.
LADY POLITIC. Why, in such cases, we must cure ourselves,
Make use of our philosophy—
VOLPONE. Oh me!
LADY POLITIC. And as we find our passions do rebel,
Encounter them with reason, or divert them,
By giving scope unto some other humor
Of lesser danger; as in politic bodies,
There's nothing more doth overwhelm the judgment,
And cloud the understanding, than too much
Settling and fixing, and, as 'twere, subsiding
Upon one object. For the incorporating
Of these same outward things, into that part,
Which we call mental, leaves some certain fæces[4]
That stop the organs, and, as Plato says,
Assassinate our knowledge.
VOLPONE. [*aside*] Now, the spirit
Of patience help me!
LADY POLITIC. Come, in faith, I must
Visit you more a days, and make you well;
Laugh and be lusty.
VOLPONE. [*aside*] My good angel save me!
LADY POLITIC. There was but one sole man in all the world,
With whom I e'er could sympathize; and he
Would lie you, often,[5] three, four hours together
To hear me speak; and be sometime so rapt,
As he would answer me quite from the purpose,
Like you, and you are like him, just. I'll discourse,
An't be but only, sir, to bring you asleep,
How we did spend our time and loves together,
For some six years.
VOLPONE. Oh, oh, oh, oh, oh, oh!
LADY POLITIC. For we were *coaetanei*,[6] and brought up—
VOLPONE. Some power, some fate, some fortune rescue me!

SCENE 5

[*Enter* MOSCA.]
MOSCA. God save you, madam!
LADY POLITIC. Good sir.
VOLPONE. Mosca! welcome,
Welcome to my redemption!
MOSCA. Why, sir?
VOLPONE. Oh,
Rid me of this my torture, quickly, there;
My madam, with the everlasting voice:
The bells, in time of pestilence, ne'er made
Like noise, or were in that perpetual motion!

4. Traces. Lady Politic is into orthodox, but very verbose, psychology.
5. Would often lie (if you please).
6. [illegible]an age.

The cock-pit comes not near it.[7] All my house,
But now, steamed like a bath with her thick breath.
A lawyer could not have been heard; nor scarce
Another woman, such a hail of words
She has let fall. For hell's sake, rid her hence.

MOSCA. Has she presented?

VOLPONE. O, I do not care;
I'll take her absence, upon any price,
With any loss.

MOSCA. Madam—

LADY POLITIC. I have brought your patron
A toy, a cap here, of mine own work.

MOSCA. 'Tis well.
I had forgot to tell you, I saw your knight,
Where you would little think it—

LADY POLITIC. Where?

MOSCA. Marry,
Where yet, if you make haste, you may apprehend him,
Rowing upon the water in a gondola,
With the most cunning courtesan of Venice.

LADY POLITIC. Is't true?

MOSCA. Pursue them, and believe your eyes:
Leave me to make your gift. [*Exit* LADY POLITIC *hastily.*]—I knew 'twould take:
For, lightly,[8] they that use themselves most license,
Are still most jealous.

VOLPONE. Mosca, hearty thanks,
For thy quick fiction, and delivery of me.
Now to my hopes, what sayest thou?

[*Re-enter* LADY POLITIC.]

LADY POLITIC. But do you hear, sir?—

VOLPONE. Again! I fear a paroxysm.

LADY POLITIC. Which way
Rowed they together?

MOSCA. Toward the Rialto.

LADY POLITIC. I pray you lend me your dwarf.

MOSCA. I pray you take him—
[*Exit* LADY POLITIC.]
Your hopes, sir, are like happy blossoms, fair,
And promise timely fruit, if you will stay
But the maturing; keep you at your couch,
Corbaccio will arrive straight, with the will;
When he is gone, I'll tell you more. [*Exit.*]

VOLPONE. My blood,
My spirits are returned; I am alive:
And, like your wanton gamester at primero,[9]

7. When the plague struck, church bells were constantly tolling; at the cockpit spectators constantly shouted bets and encouragement to the birds.

8. Commonly (an old sense of the word).

9. An early form of the Spanish card game later known as ombre (the game played in Pope's *Rape of the Lock*). The phrases "go less," "draw," and "encounter" are all used in primero.

Whose thought had whispered to him, not go less,
Methinks I lie, and draw—for an encounter.
[*The bed-curtains close upon* VOLPONE.]

SCENE 6. *The Passage Leading to* VOLPONE'S *Chamber.*

[*Enter* MOSCA *and* BONARIO.]

MOSCA. Sir, here concealed, [*shows him a closet*] you may hear all. But, pray you,
Have patience, sir. [*Knocking within.*]—The same's your father knocks:
I am compelled to leave you. [*Exit.*]

BONARIO. Do so. Yet
Cannot my thought imagine this a truth. [*Goes into the closet.*]

SCENE 7. *Another Part of the Same.*

[*Enter* MOSCA *and* CORVINO, CELIA *following.*]

MOSCA. Death on me! you are come too soon, what meant you?
Did not I say, I would send?

CORVINO. Yes, but I feared
You might forget it, and then they prevent us.

MOSCA. [*aside*] Prevent! did e'er man haste so, for his horns?
A courtier would not ply it so, for a place.
—Well, now there is no helping it, stay here;
I'll presently return.
[*Crosses stage to* BONARIO.]

CORVINO. Where are you, Celia?
You know not wherefore I have brought you hither?

CELIA. Not well, except you told me.

CORVINO. Now, I will: [*He leads her apart, and whispers to her.*]
Hark hither.

MOSCA. [*to* BONARIO] Sir your father hath sent word,
It will be half an hour ere he come;
And therefore, if you please to walk the while
Into that gallery—at the upper end,
There are some books to entertain the time;
And I'll take care no man shall come unto you, sir.

BONARIO. Yes, I will stay there. [*aside*] —I do doubt this fellow. [*Exit* BONARIO.]

MOSCA. [*Looking after him*] There; he is far enough; he can hear nothing:
And, for his father, I can keep him off. [*Exit.*]

CORVINO. [*to* CELIA] Nay, now, there is no starting back, and therefore,
Resolve upon it: I have so decreed.
It must be done. Nor would I move't afore,
Because I would avoid all shifts and tricks,
That might deny me.

CELIA. Sir, let me beseech you,

Affect not these strange trials;[1] if you doubt
My chastity, why, lock me up forever;
Make me the heir of darkness. Let me live,
Where I may please your fears, if not your trust.

CORVINO. Believe it, I have no such humor, I.
All that I speak I mean; yet I'm not mad;
Not horn-mad, see you? Go to, show yourself
Obedient, and a wife.

CELIA. O heaven!

CORVINO. I say it,
Do so.

CELIA. Was this the train?[2]

CORVINO. I've told you reasons;
What the physicians have set down; how much
It may concern me; what my engagements are;
My means; and the necessity of those means,
For my recovery:[3] wherefore, if you be
Loyal, and mine, be won, respect my venture.[4]

CELIA. Before your honor?

CORVINO. Honor! tut, a breath;[5]
There's no such thing in nature. A mere term
Invented to awe fools. What is my gold
The worse for touching, clothes for being looked on?
Why, this's no more. An old decrepit wretch,
That has no sense, no sinew; takes his meat
With others' fingers; only knows to gape,
When you do scald his gums;[6] a voice; a shadow;
And what can this man hurt you?

CELIA. [*aside*] Lord! what spirit
Is this hath entered him?

CORVINO. And for your fame,
That's such a jig;[7] as if I would go tell it,
Cry it on the Piazza! who shall know it,
But he that cannot speak it, and this fellow,[8]
Whose lips are in my pocket? save yourself
(If you'll proclaim't, you may), I know no other
Should come to know it.

CELIA. Are heaven and saints then nothing?
Will they be blind or stupid?

CORVINO. How!

CELIA. Good sir,
Be jealous still, emulate them;[9] and think
What hate they burn with toward every sin.

1. Don't tempt me so.
2. Is this what you had in mind all the time?
3. Corvino is evidently in financial straits.
4. In the sense of a commercial venture.
5. Like Falstaff (*1 Henry IV* V.i), Corvino disposes easily of honor.
6. I.e., the old man has to be fed by others, and doesn't even know enough to open his own mouth for food.
7. Farce, joke.
8. "He that cannot speak it": Volpone; "this fellow": Mosca.
9. I.e., God and the saints, who hate sin.

CORVINO. I grant you; if I thought it were a sin,
I would not urge you. Should I offer this
To some young Frenchman, or hot Tuscan blood
That had read Aretine,[1] conned all his prints,
Knew every quirk within lust's labyrinth,
And were professed critic in lechery;
And I would look upon him, and applaud him,
This were a sin: but here, 'tis contrary,
A pious work, mere charity, for physic,
And honest polity, to assure mine own.[2]
CELIA. O heaven! canst thou suffer such a change?
VOLPONE. Thou art mine honor, Mosca, and my pride,
My joy, my tickling, my delight! Go bring them.
MOSCA. [*advancing*] Please you draw near, sir.
CORVINO. Come on, what—
You will not be rebellious? by that light—
MOSCA. Sir,
Signor Corvino, here, is come to see you—
VOLPONE. Oh!
MOSCA. And hearing of the consultation had,
So lately, for your health, is come to offer,
Or rather, sir, to prostitute—
CORVINO. Thanks, sweet Mosca.
MOSCA. Freely, unasked, or unentreated—
CORVINO. Well.
MOSCA. As the true fervent instance of his love,
His own most fair and proper wife, the beauty
Only of price in Venice—
CORVINO. 'Tis well urged.
MOSCA. To be your comfortress, and to preserve you.
VOLPONE. Alas, I'm past, already! Pray you, thank him
For his good care and promptness; but for that,
'Tis a vain labor e'en to fight 'gainst heaven;
Applying fire to stone—uh, uh, uh, uh! [*Coughing.*]
Making a dead leaf grow again. I take
His wishes gently, though; and you may tell him,
What I have done for him: marry, my state is hopeless.
Will him to pray for me; and to use his fortune
With reverence, when he comes to't.
MOSCA. Do you hear, sir?
Go to him with your wife.
CORVINO. Heart of my father!
Wilt thou persist thus? come, I pray thee, come.
Thou seest 'tis nothing. Celia! By this hand,
I shall grow violent. Come, do't, I say.

1 Aretino was a notorious pornographer.

2. "Pious work" means it's good for your soul, "mere charity" says it's kindness to the neighbor, "for physic" says it's for the benefit of his health, "honest policy" means it's prudent self-interest, and "to assure mine own" gets down to the basic motivation—greed.

CELIA. Sir, kill me, rather: I will take down poison,
Eat burning coals, do anything.
CORVINO. Be damned!
Heart, I will drag thee hence, home, by the hair;
Cry thee a strumpet through the streets; rip up
Thy mouth unto thine ears; and slit thy nose,
Like a raw rochet![3]—Do not tempt me; come,
Yield, I am loath—Death! I will buy some slave
Whom I will kill, and bind thee to him, alive;
And at my window hang you forth, devising
Some monstrous crime which I, in capital letters,
Will eat into thy flesh with aquafortis,
And burning corsives,[4] on this stubborn breast.
Now, by the blood thou hast incensed, I'll do it!
CELIA. Sir, what you please you may, I am your martyr.
CORVINO. Be not thus obstinate, I have not deserved it:
Think who it is entreats you. 'Prithee, sweet;
Good faith, thou shalt have jewels, gowns, attires,
What thou wilt think, and ask. Do but go kiss him.
Or touch him, but. For my sake. At my suit.
This once. No? not! I shall remember this.
Will you disgrace me thus? Do you thirst my undoing?
MOSCA. Nay, gentle lady, be advised.
CORVINO. No, no.
She has watched her time. Ods precious, this is scurvy,[5]
'Tis very scurvy; and you are—
MOSCA. Nay, good sir.
CORVINO. An arrant locust, by heaven, a locust![6]
Crocodile, that hast thy tears prepared,
Expecting, how thou'lt bid them flow—
MOSCA. Nay, pray you, sir!
She will consider.
CELIA. Would my life would serve
To satisfy.
CORVINO. S'death! if she would but speak to him,
And save my reputation, it were somewhat;
But spitefully to effect my utter ruin!
MOSCA. Ay, now you have put your fortune in her hands.
Why, i'faith, it is her modesty; I must quit[7] her.
If you were absent, she would be more coming;
I know it, and dare undertake for her.
What woman can before her husband? Pray you,
Let us depart, and leave her here.
CORVINO. Sweet Celia,
Thou mayst redeem all, yet; I'll say no more:
If not, esteem yourself as lost. Nay, stay there.

3. Like a fish.
4. With acids and corrosives.
5. I.e., by God's precious blood, this is villainous.
6. I.e., a destructive plague. The lore of the crocodile says it sheds deceitful tears.
7. Acquit; coming: forthcoming.

[*Shuts the door, and exit with* MOSCA.]

CELIA. O God, and his good angels! whither, whither,
Is shame fled human breasts? that with such ease,
Men dare put off your honors, and their own?
Is that, which ever was a cause of life,
Now placed beneath the basest circumstance,
And modesty an exile made, for money?

VOLPONE. Ay, in Corvino, and such earth-fed minds, [*leaping from his couch*]
That never tasted the true heaven of love.
Assure thee, Celia, he that would sell thee,
Only for hope of gain, and that uncertain,
He would have sold his part of Paradise
For ready money, had he met a cope-man.[8]
Why are thou 'mazed to see me thus revived?
Rather applaud thy beauty's miracle;
'Tis thy great work:[9] that hath, not now alone,
But sundry times raised me, in several shapes,
And, but this morning, like a mountebank,
To see thee at thy window. Ay, before
I would have left my practice for thy love,
In varying figures I would have contended
With the blue Proteus, or the hornéd flood.[1]
Now art thou welcome.

CELIA. Sir!

VOLPONE. Nay, fly me not.
Nor let thy false imagination
That I was bed-rid, make thee think I am so:
Thou shalt not find it. I am now as fresh,
As hot, as high, and in as jovial plight,
As when, in that so celebrated scene,
At recitation of our comedy,
For entertainment of the great Valois,[2]
I acted young Antinous; and attracted
The eyes and ears of all the ladies present,
To admire each graceful gesture, note, and footing.

Song[3]

Come, my Celia, let us prove,
While we can, the sports of love,
Time will not be ours for ever,

8. Buyer.
9. "The great work" is always the philosopher's stone, which converts base metals to gold.
1. Proteus was a sea god who could take any shape at will; Virgil calls him "blue Proteus." Achelous was a river god with whom Hercules fought for possession of Deianira; he fought first as a river, then as a snake, and finally as a bull (hence "the hornéd flood"), but was beaten in all three shapes (Ovid, *Metamorphoses* IX).
2. Henry of Valois, Duke of Anjou, visited Venice in 1574, and was entertained with splendid festivities. Antinous was the favorite (catamite) of Emperor Hadrian, in Roman antiquity.
3. The opening lines are adapted from Catullus, boldest and bawdiest of Latin lyricists, and the whole song emphasises the theme of *"carpe diem"* (clutch the fleeting moment), which is a common erotic incitement.

He, at length, our good will sever;
Spend not then his gifts in vain:
Suns that set may rise again;
But if once we lose this light,
'Tis with us perpetual night.
Why should we defer our joys?
Fame and rumor are but toys.
Cannot we delude the eyes
Of a few poor household spies?
Or his easier ears beguile,
Thus removéd by our wile?—
'Tis no sin love's fruits to steal;
But the sweet thefts to reveal,
To be taken, to be seen,
These have crimes accounted been.

CELIA. Some sérene[4] blast me, or dire lightning strike
This my offending face!
VOLPONE. Why droops my Celia?
Thou hast, in place of a base husband, found
A worthy lover: use thy fortune well,
With secrecy and pleasure. See, behold,
What thou art queen of; not in expectation,
As I feed others: but possessed and crowned.
See here a rope of pearl; and each, more orient
Than that the brave Egyptian queen caroused:[5]
Dissolve and drink them. See, a carbuncle[6]
May put out both the eyes of our St. Mark;
A diamond, would have bought Lollia Paulina,
When she came in like star-light, hid with jewels,
That were the spoils of provinces;[7] take these,
And wear, and lose them: yet remains an earring
To purchase them again, and this whole state.
A gem but worth a private patrimony,
Is nothing: we will eat such at a meal.
The heads of parrots, tongues of nightingales,
The brains of peacocks, and of ostriches,
Shall be our food: and, could we get the phoenix,[8]
Though nature lost her kind, she were our dish.
CELIA. Good sir, these things might move a mind affected
With such delights; but I, whose innocence
Is all I can think wealthy, or worth th'enjoying,
And which, once lost, I have nought to lose beyond it,
Cannot be taken with these sensual baits:

4. Mist from heaven, malignant influence.
5. According to a common story, Cleopatra dissolved a precious pearl in wine and during a banquet with Antony drank it up.
6. Ruby.
7. Lollia Paulina, wife of a Roman governor, is said by Pliny (*Natural History* IX.117) to have worn in her hair jewels enough to represent the loot of several provinces.
8. Only one phoenix is said to be alive at any one time; eating him would eradicate the species.

If you have conscience—
VOLPONE. 'Tis the beggar's virtue;
If thou hast wisdom, hear me, Celia.
Thy baths shall be the juice of gilly-flowers,[9]
Spirit of roses, and of violets,
The milk of unicorns, and panthers' breath
Gathered in bags, and mixed with Cretan wines.[1]
Our drink shall be preparéd gold and amber;
Which we will take, until my roof whirl round
With the vertigo: and my dwarf shall dance,
My eunuch sing, my fool make up the antic,
Whilst we, in changéd shapes, act Ovid's tales,[2]
Thou, like Europa now, and I like Jove,
Then I like Mars, and thou like Erycine:
So, of the rest, till we have quite run through,
And wearied all the fables of the gods.
Then will I have thee in more modern forms,
Attiréd like some sprightly dame of France,
Brave Tuscan lady, or proud Spanish beauty;
Sometimes, unto the Persian Sophy's wife,[3]
Or the Grand Signor's mistress; and, for change,
To one of our most artful courtesans,
Or some quick Negro, or cold Russian;
And I will meet thee in as many shapes:
Where we may so transfuse our wandering souls
Out at our lips, and score up sums of pleasures, [*sings*]

That the curious shall not know
How to tell them as they flow;
And the envious, when they find
What their number is, be pined.[4]

CELIA. If you have ears that will be pierced; or eyes
That can be opened; a heart may be touched;
Or any part that yet sounds man about you;
If you have touch of holy saints, or heaven,
Do me the grace to let me 'scape. If not,
Be bountiful and kill me. You do know,
I am a creature, hither ill betrayed,
By one, whose shame I would forget it were.
If you will deign me neither of these graces,
Yet feed your wrath, sir, rather than your lust
(It is a vice comes nearer manliness),
And punish that unhappy crime of nature,

9. Clove-scented flowers used to flavor drinks and as a light perfume.
1. The most expensive known to Jonson's age.
2. I.e., to enact all the fables in the *Metamorphoses*. "Erycine" is one of the epithets of Venus.
3. The "Sophy" is the Shah of Persia, the "Grand Signor" the Sultan of Turkey.
4. Envious, depressed. The verses, once again, are adapted from Catullus.

Which you miscall my beauty; flay my face,
Or poison it with ointments, for seducing
Your blood to this rebellion. Rub these hands,
With what may cause an eating leprosy,
E'en to my bones and marrow: any thing,
That may disfavor[5] me, save in my honor—
And I will kneel to you, pray for you, pay down
A thousand hourly vows, sir, for your health;
Report, and think you virtuous—

VOLPONE. Think me cold,
Frozen and impotent, and so report me?
That I had Nestor's hernia,[6] thou wouldst think.
I do degenerate, and abuse my nation,
To play with opportunity thus long;
I should have done the act, and then have parleyed.
Yield, or I'll force thee. [*Seizes her.*]

CELIA. O! just God!

VOLPONE. In vain—

BONARIO. [*rushing in*] Forbear, foul ravisher! libidinous swine!
Free the forced lady, or thou diest, impostor!
But that I'm loath to snatch thy punishment
Out of the hand of justice, thou shouldst yet
Be made the timely sacrifice of vengeance
Before this altar, and this dross, thy idol.
Lady, let's quit the place, it is the den
Of villainy; fear nought, you have a guard:
And he, ere long, shall meet his just reward. [*Exeunt* BONARIO *and* CELIA.]

VOLPONE. Fall on me, roof, and bury me in ruin!
Become my grave, that wert my shelter! O!
I am unmasked, unspirited, undone,
Betrayed to beggary, to infamy—

SCENE 8

[*Enter* MOSCA, *wounded, and bleeding.*]

MOSCA. Where shall I run, most wretched shame of men,
To beat out my unlucky brains?

VOLPONE. Here, here.
What! dost thou bleed?

MOSCA. O that his well-driven sword
Had been so courteous to have cleft me down
Unto the navel, ere I lived to see
My life, my hopes, my spirits, my patron, all
Thus desperately engagéd, by my error!

VOLPONE. Woe on thy fortune!

MOSCA. And my follies, sir.

VOLPONE. Thou hast made me miserable.

5. Disfigure.
6. Senile impotence; the phrase is from Juvenal's sixth satire.

MOSCA. And myself, sir.
Who would have thought he would have hearkened so?
VOLPONE. What shall we do?
MOSCA. I know not; if my heart
Could expiate the mischance, I'd pluck it out.
Will you be pleased to hang me? or cut my throat?
And I'll requite you, sir. Let's die like Romans,
Since we have lived like Grecians.[7] [*Knocking within.*]
VOLPONE. Hark! who's there?
I hear some footing; officers, the Saffi,[8]
Come to apprehend us! I do feel the brand
Hissing already at my forehead; now
Mine ears are boring.[9]
MOSCA. To your couch, sir, you,
Make that place good, however. [VOLPONE *lies down, as before.*]—Guilty men
Suspect what they deserve still. Signor Corbaccio!

SCENE 9

[*Enter* CORBACCIO.]

CORBACCIO. Why, how now, Mosca?
MOSCA. O, undone, amazed, sir.
Your son, I know not by what accident,
Acquainted with your purpose to my patron,
Touching your will, and making him your heir,
Entered our house with violence, his sword drawn,
Sought for you, called you wretch, unnatural,
Vowed he would kill you.
CORBACCIO. Me!
MOSCA. Yes, and my patron.
CORBACCIO. This act shall disinherit him indeed:
Here is the will.
MOSCA. 'Tis well, sir.
CORBACCIO. Right and well;
Be you as careful now for me.
[*Enter* VOLTORE *behind.*]
MOSCA. My life, sir,
Is not more tendered; I am only yours.
CORBACCIO. How does he? will he die shortly, think'st thou?
MOSCA. I fear
He'll outlast May.
CORBACCIO. Today?
MOSCA. No, last out May, sir.
CORBACCIO. Couldst thou not give him a dram?
MOSCA. O, by no means, sir.

7. Greeks, especially Corinthians, were famous for living in luxury; Romans for committing suicide with dignity when life no longer appeared worthy of them.

8. Police officers, investigators.

9. Branding on the face and boring holes in the ears were common criminal punishments.

CORBACCIO. Nay, I'll not bid you.
VOLTORE. [*coming forward*] This is a knave, I see.
MOSCA. [*seeing* VOLTORE, *aside*] How! signor Voltore! did he hear me?
VOLTORE. Parasite!
MOSCA. Who's that? O, sir, most timely welcome—
VOLTORE. Scarce,
To the discovery of your tricks, I fear.
You are his, *only?* and mine also, are you not?
MOSCA. Who? I, sir!
VOLTORE. You, sir. What device is this
About a will?
MOSCA. A plot for you, sir.
VOLTORE. Come,
Put not your foists[1] upon me; I shall scent them.
MOSCA. Did you not hear it?
VOLTORE. Yes, I hear Corbaccio
Hath made your patron there his heir.
MOSCA. 'Tis true,
By my device, drawn to it by my plot,
With hope—
VOLTORE. Your patron should reciprocate?
And you have promised?
MOSCA. For your good, I did, sir.
Nay more, I told his son, brought, hid him here,
Where he might hear his father pass the deed;
Being persuaded to it by this thought, sir,
That the unnaturalness, first, of the act,
And then his father's oft disclaiming in him,
(Which I did mean t'help on), would sure enrage him
To do some violence upon his parent,
On which the law should take sufficient hold,
And you be stated[2] in a double hope:
Truth be my comfort, and my conscience,
My only aim was to dig you a fortune
Out of these two old rotten sepulchres—
VOLTORE. I cry thee mercy, Mosca.
MOSCA. Worth your patience,
And your great merit, sir. And see the change!
VOLTORE. Why, what success?[3]
MOSCA. Most hapless! you must help, sir.
Whilst we expected the old raven, in comes
Corvino's wife, sent hither by her husband—
VOLTORE. What, with a present?
MOSCA. No, sir, on visitation
(I'll tell you how anon); and staying long,
The youth he grows impatient, rushes forth,
Seizeth the lady, wounds me, makes her swear

1. Tricks, but also bad smells.
2. Installed.
3. Result, outcome.

(Or he would murder her, that was his vow)
To affirm my patron to have done her rape:
Which how unlike it is, you see! and hence,
With that pretext he's gone to accuse his father,
Defame my patron, defeat you—

VOLTORE. Where is her husband?
Let him be sent for straight.

MOSCA. Sir, I'll go fetch him.

VOLTORE. Bring him to the Scrutineo.[4]

MOSCA. Sir, I will.

VOLTORE. This must be stopped.

MOSCA. O, you do nobly, sir.
Alas, 'twas labored all, sir, for your good;
Nor was there want of counsel in the plot:
But fortune can, at any time, o'erthrow
The projects of a hundred learned clerks,[5] sir.

CORBACCIO. [*listening*] What's that?

VOLTORE. Will't please you, sir, to go along? [*Exit* CORBACCIO *followed by* VOLTORE.]

MOSCA. Patron, go in, and pray for our success.

VOLPONE. [*rising from his couch*] Need makes devotion: heaven your labor bless! [*Exeunt.*]

Act IV

SCENE 1. *A Street*.

[*Enter* SIR POLITIC WOULD-BE *and* PEREGRINE.]

SIR POLITIC. I told you, sir, it was a plot; you see
What observation is! You mentioned[6] me
For some instructions: I will tell you, sir
(Since we are met here in this height[7] of Venice),
Some few particulars I have set down,
Only for this meridian, fit to be known
Of your crude traveler; and they are these.
I will not touch, sir, at your phrase, or clothes,
For they are old.

PEREGRINE. Sir, I have better.

SIR POLITIC. Pardon,
I meant, as they are themes.

PEREGRINE. O, sir, proceed:
I'll slander you no more of wit, good sir.

SIR POLITIC. First, for your garb, it must be grave and serious,
Very reserved and locked; not tell a secret
On any terms, not to your father; scarce
A fable, but with caution; make sure choice
Both of your company, and discourse; beware
You never speak a truth—

4. The court of law. Jonson's court, like courts on the Continent generally, has power to look into abuses and investigate possible violations of the law, before any particular suit is filed.
5. Scholars.
6. Asked.
7. Climate, constitution.

PEREGRINE. How!
SIR POLITIC. Not to strangers,
For those be they you must converse with most;
Others I would not know, sir, but at distance,
So as I still might be a saver in them:[8]
You shall have tricks, else, passed upon you hourly.
And then, for your religion, profess none,
But wonder at the diversity of all;
And, for your part, protest, were there no other
But simply the laws o' th' land, you could content you.
Nick Machiavel, and Monsieur Bodin, both
Were of this mind.[9] Then must you learn the use
And handling of your silver fork at meals,[1]
The metal of your glass (these are main matters
With your Italian), and to know the hour
When you must eat your melons, and your figs.
PEREGRINE. Is that a point of state too?
SIR POLITIC. Here it is;
For your Venetian, if he see a man
Preposterous[2] in the least, he has him straight;
He has; he strips him. I'll acquaint you, sir.
I now have lived here, 'tis some fourteen months;
Within the first week of my landing here,
All took me for a citizen of Venice,
I knew the forms so well—
PEREGRINE. [*aside*] And nothing else.
SIR POLITIC. I had read Contarine,[3] took me a house,
Dealt with my Jews to furnish it with movables—
Well, if I could but find one man, one man
To mine own heart, whom I durst trust, I would—
PEREGRINE. What, what, sir?
SIR POLITIC. Make him rich; make him a fortune;
He should not think again. I would command it.
PEREGRINE. As how?
SIR POLITIC. With certain projects[4] that I have
Which I may not discover.
PEREGRINE. [*aside*] If I had
But one to wager with, I would lay odds now,

8. The implication is clear: Don't lend anybody money.
9. The abbreviation "Nick Machiavel" implies casual familiarity; the sentiment attributed to Machiavelli shows complete ignorance of him. Sir Politic Would-be is more nearly right in his estimate of Jean Bodin, the French political philosopher, who did advocate religious toleration.
1. Handling a fork was a new experience for Englishmen who traveled abroad in Jonson's time; back home, fingers were still the preferred instruments. "The metal of your glass": literally, the composition of your glass (perhaps to know what could or couldn't be put in it).
2. In its literal Latin sense, getting things back to front.
3. Contarini wrote a book on Venetian government, which Sir Politic would be quick to know. "My Jews": in the indefinite sense—the usual Jews that everybody goes to for furniture to set up a Venetian apartment.
4. Schemes for social improvement or making money (or preferably both) were favorite targets of 17th-century satire. "Discover": disclose.

He tells me instantly.
SIR POLITIC. One is (and that
I care not greatly who knows) to serve the state
Of Venice with red herrings for three years,
And at a certain rate, from Rotterdam,[5]
Where I have correspondence. There's a letter,
Sent me from one o' the States,[6] and to that purpose;
He cannot write his name, but that's his mark.
PEREGRINE. He is a chandler?
SIR POLITIC. No, a cheese monger.
There are some others too with whom I treat
About the same negotiation;
And I will undertake it: for, 'tis thus.
I'll do't with ease, I've cast it all. Your hoy[7]
Carries but three men in her, and a boy;
And she shall make me three returns a year.
So, if there come but one of three, I save;
If two, I can defalc[8]:—but this is now,
If my main project fail.
PEREGRINE. Then you have others?
SIR POLITIC. I should be loath to draw the subtle air
Of such a place, without my thousand aims.
I'll not dissemble, sir; where'er I come,
I love to be considerative; and 'tis true,
I have at my free hours thought upon
Some certain goods unto the state of Venice,
Which I do call my *Cautions*; and, sir, which
I mean, in hope of pension, to propound
To the Great Council, then unto the Forty,
So to the Ten.[9] My means are made already—
PEREGRINE. By whom?
SIR POLITIC. Sir, one that, though his place be obscure,
Yet he can sway, and they will hear him. He's
A *commendatore*.
PEREGRINE. What! a common sergeant?
SIR POLITIC. Sir, such as they are, put it in their mouths,
What they should say, sometimes, as well as greater.
I think I have my notes to show you—[*Searching his pockets.*]
PEREGRINE. Good, sir.
SIR POLITIC. But you shall swear unto me, on your gentry,[1]
Not to anticipate—
PEREGRINE. I, sir!

5. The Venetians have plenty of fresh fish in the Adriatic, and would not like salt herring in any case.
6. I.e., from one of the States-General in Holland.
7. A small North Sea fishing vessel; such a boat would have great trouble making a trip to Venice, let alone carrying a worthwhile cargo.
8. Reduce the amount, cut back, maybe even go into bankruptcy.
9. Representative legislative bodies, increasingly narrow and increasingly lofty, of the Venetian government. "My means": my approaches to these eminent bodies.
1. As you are a gentleman.

A circumstance—My paper is not with me.
PEREGRINE. O, but you can remember, sir.
SIR POLITIC. My first is
Concerning tinder-boxes.[2] You must know,
No family is here without its box.
Now, sir, it being so portable a thing,
Put case, that you or I were ill affected
Unto the state, sir; with it in our pockets,
Might not I go into the Arsenal,[3]
Or you? come out again? and none the wiser?
PEREGRINE. Except yourself, sir.
SIR POLITIC. Go to, then. I therefore
Advertise to the state, how fit it were,
That none but such as were known patriots,
Sound lovers of their country, should be suffered
To enjoy them in their houses; and even those
Sealed at some office, and at such a bigness
As might not lurk in pockets.
PEREGRINE. Admirable!
SIR POLITIC. My next is, how to inquire, and be resolved
By present demonstration, whether a ship,
Newly arrived from Syria, or from
Any suspected part of all the Levant,[4]
Be guilty of the plague; and where they use
To lie out forty, fifty days, sometimes,
About the Lazaretto,[5] for their trial,
I'll save that charge and loss unto the merchant,
And in an hour clear the doubt.
PEREGRINE. Indeed, sir!
SIR POLITIC. Or—I will lose my labor.
PEREGRINE. My faith, that's much.
SIR POLITIC. Nay, sir, conceive me. 'Twill cost me in onions,
Some thirty livres[6]—
PEREGRINE. Which is one pound sterling.
SIR POLITIC. Besides my water-works; for this I do, sir.
First, I bring in your ship 'twixt two brick-walls;
But those the state shall venture. On the one
I strain[7] me a fair tarpaulin, and in that
I stick my onions, cut in halves; the other
Is full of loop-holes, out at which I thrust
The noses of my bellows; and those bellows

2. As we would say, matchboxes or cigarette lighters.
3. Venice being largely a maritime power, the Arsenal where ships were built and repaired was (and still is) an important part of the city.
4. The Middle East.
5. Quarantine. Bubonic plague, carried by lice living on shipboard rats, was a constant peril in Venice, where trade with the Middle East was particularly busy. Ships had to wait several months in port before debarking crew, passengers, or cargo.
6. A French coin of small value. Onions were reputed to be good against the plague; cut open, they supposedly absorbed the plague germs from the air.
7. Stretch.

I keep, with water-works,[8] in perpetual motion,
Which is the easiest matter of a hundred.
Now, sir, your onion, which doth naturally
Attract the infection, and your bellows blowing
The air upon him, will show instantly,
By his changed color, if there be contagion,
Or else remain as fair as at the first.
—Now it is known, 'tis nothing.

PEREGRINE. You are right, sir.

SIR POLITIC. I would I had my note.

PEREGRINE. Faith, so would I:
But you have done well for once, sir.

SIR POLITIC. Were I false,
Or would be made so, I could show you reasons
How I could sell this state now to the Turk,[9]
Spite of their galleys, or their—[*Examining his papers.*]

PEREGRINE. Pray you, sir Pol.

SIR POLITIC. I have them not about me.

PEREGRINE. That I feared.
They are there, sir?

SIR POLITIC. No, this is my diary,
Wherein I note my actions of the day.

PEREGRINE. Pray you let's see, sir. What is here?
Notandum,[1]
[*Reads.*]
A rat had gnawn my spur-leathers; notwithstanding,
I put on new, and did go forth; but first
I threw three beans over the threshold. Item,
I went and bought two tooth-picks, whereof one
I burst immediately, in a discourse
With a Dutch merchant, 'bout ragion del stato.[2]
From him I went and paid a mocenigo
For piecing my silk stockings; by the way
I cheapened sprats;[3] *and at St. Mark's I urined.*
Faith, these are politic notes!

SIR POLITIC. Sir, I do slip
No action of my life, thus, but I quote it.

PEREGRINE. Believe me, it is wise!

SIR POLITIC. Nay, sir, read forth.

8. Sir Politic's waterworks are apparently a water wheel arranged to operate a bellows. Of course there is no spot in the flat country around Venice where streams have enough impetus to turn a wheel.

9. Here Sir Politic is verging on real subversion, and Peregrine quickly shuts him off.

1. Take special note.

2. Literally, "reason of state," but also the title of a famous book by Giovanni Botero, presenting a diluted version of Machiavelli's thought.

3. Bargained over some trifling fish; "piecing": mending.

SCENE 2

[*Enter, at a distance,* LADY POLITIC WOULD-BE, NANO, *and two* WAITING-WOMEN.]

LADY POLITIC. Where should this loose knight be, trow? sure he's housed.[4]
NANO. Why, then he's fast.
LADY POLITIC. Ay, he plays both with me.[5]
I pray you stay. This heat will do more harm
To my complexion, than his heart is worth.
(I do not care to hinder, but to take him.)
How it[6] comes off! [*Rubbing her cheeks.*]
1 WOMAN. My master's yonder.
LADY POLITIC. Where?
2 WOMAN. With a young gentleman.
LADY POLITIC. That same's the party,
In man's apparel! Pray you, sir, jog my knight;
I will be tender to his reputation,
However he demerit.
SIR POLITIC. [*seeing her*] My lady!
PEREGRINE. Where?
SIR POLITIC. 'Tis she indeed, sir; you shall know her. She is,
Were she not mine, a lady of that merit,
For fashion and behavior; and for beauty
I durst compare—
PEREGRINE. It seems you are not jealous,
That dare commend her.
SIR POLITIC. Nay, and for discourse—
PEREGRINE. Being your wife, she cannot miss that.
SIR POLITIC. [*introducing Peregrine*] Madam,
Here is a gentleman, pray you, use him fairly;
He seems a youth, but he is—
LADY POLITIC. None.
SIR POLITIC. Yes, one
Has put his face as soon into the world—
LADY POLITIC. You mean, as early? but today?
SIR POLITIC. How's this?
LADY POLITIC. Why, in this habit, sir; you apprehend me.
Well, Master Would-be, this doth not become you;
I had thought the odor, sir, of your good name
Had been more precious to you; that you would not
Have done this dire massacre on your honor;
One of your gravity, and rank besides!
But knights, I see, care little for the oath
They make to ladies, chiefly, their own ladies.
SIR POLITIC. Now, by my spurs, the symbol of my knighthood[7]—

4. Gone into somebody's house. "He's fast" implies that he's securely fastened and in fast company.
5. Both fast and loose.
6. I.e., her complexion.
7. Because King James created knights indiscriminately at his accession, knighthood was a broad joke in early 17th-century England.

PEREGRINE [*aside*] Lord, how his brain is humbled for an oath!
SIR POLITIC. I reach you not.
LADY POLITIC. Right, sir, your polity
May bear it through thus. [*To* PEREGRINE.]—Sir, a word with you.
I would be loath to contest publicly
With any gentlewoman, or to seem
Froward, or violent, as the courtier says;[8]
It comes too near rusticity in a lady,
Which I would shun by all means; and however
I may deserve from Master Would-be, yet
T'have one fair gentlewoman thus be made
The unkind instrument to wrong another,
And one she knows not, ay, and to perséver;
In my poor judgment, is not warranted
From being a solecism in our sex,
If not in manners.
PEREGRINE. How is this!
SIR POLITIC. Sweet madam,
Come nearer to your aim.
LADY POLITIC. Marry, and will, sir.
Since you provoke me with your impudence,
And laughter of your light land-siren here,
Your Sporus,[9] your hermaphrodite—
PEREGRINE. What's here?
Poetic fury, and historic[1] storms!
SIR POLITIC. The gentleman, believe it, is of worth,
And of our nation.
LADY POLITIC. Ay, your Whitefriars[2] nation!
Come, I blush for you, Master Would-be, ay;
And am ashamed you should have no more forehead,[3]
Than thus to be the patron, or St. George,
To a lewd harlot, a base fricatrice,[4]
A female devil, in a male outside.
SIR POLITIC. Nay,
An you be such a one, I must bid adieu
To your delights. The case appears too liquid. [*Exit.*]
LADY POLITIC. Ay, you may carry't clear, with your state-face![5]
But for your carnival concupiscence,
Who here is fled for liberty of conscience,
From furious persecution of the marshal,
Her will I dis'ple.[6]

8. I.e., Castiglione.
9. Sporus was a favorite catamite of Nero, who dressed him in drag and married him.
1. With reference to the historical allusion (Sporus), but "hysteric" is not far away.
2. Disreputable quarter of London, inhabited by whores.
3. Sense of shame.
4. Prostitute.
5. A solemn expression.
6. Discipline; specifically, whip. In England at least (though not in Venice) the marshal was directly charged with catching and punishing prostitutes.

PEREGRINE. This is fine, i'faith,
And do you use this often? Is this part
Of your wit's exercise, 'gainst you have occasion?
Madam——

LADY POLITIC. Go to, sir.

PEREGRINE. Do you hear me, lady?
Why, if your knight have set you to beg shirts,
Or to invite me home, you might have done it
A nearer way, by far.[7]

LADY POLITIC. This cannot work you
Out of my snare.

PEREGRINE. Why, am I in it, then?
Indeed your husband told me you were fair,
And so you are; only your nose inclines,
That side that's next the sun, to the queen-apple.[8]

LADY POLITIC. This cannot be endured, by any patience.

SCENE 3

[*Enter* MOSCA.]

MOSCA. What is the matter, madam?

LADY POLITIC. If the Senate
Right not my quest in this,[9] I will protest them
To all the world, no aristocracy.

MOSCA. What is the injury, lady?

LADY POLITIC. Why, the callet[1]
You told me of, here I have ta'en disguised.

MOSCA. Who? this! what means your ladyship? the creature
I mentioned to you is apprehended now,
Before the Senate; you shall see her—

LADY POLITIC. Where?

MOSCA. I'll bring you to her. This young gentleman,
I saw him land this morning at the port.

LADY POLITIC. Is't possible! how has my judgment wandered?
Sir, I must, blushing, say to you, I have erred;
And plead your pardon.

PEREGRINE. What, more changes yet!

LADY POLITIC. I hope you have not the malice to remember
A gentlewoman's passion. If you stay
In Venice here, please you to use me, sir—

MOSCA. Will you go, madam?

LADY POLITIC. 'Pray you, sir, use me; in faith,
The more you see me, the more I shall conceive
You have forgot our quarrel.

[*Exeunt* LADY WOULD-BE, MOSCA, NANO, *and* WAITING-WOMEN.]

PEREGRINE. This is rare!

7. Peregrine implies that the whole situation is a setup, the knight pimping for his wife.

8. Lady Politic has a fiery red nose.

9. Don't do me justice.

1. Slut.

Sir Politic Would-be? no; Sir Politic Bawd!
To bring me thus acquainted with his wife!
Well, wise Sir Pol, since you have practiced thus
Upon my freshman-ship,[2] I'll try your salt-head,
What proof it is against a counterplot. [*Exit.*]

SCENE 4. *The Scrutineo.*

[*Enter* VOLTORE, CORBACCIO, CORVINO, *and* MOSCA.]

VOLTORE. Well, now you know the carriage of the business,
Your constancy is all that is required
Unto the safety of it.

MOSCA. Is the lie[3]
Safely conveyed amongst us? is that sure?
Knows every man his burden?[4]

CORVINO. Yes.

MOSCA. Then shrink not.

CORVINO. [*aside to* MOSCA] But knows the advocate the truth?

MOSCA. O, sir,
By no means; I devised a formal tale
That salved your reputation. But be valiant, sir.

CORVINO. I fear no one but him, that this his pleading
Should make him stand for a co-heir—

MOSCA. Co-halter!
Hang him; we will but use his tongue, his noise,
As we do Croaker's[5] here.

CORVINO. Ay, what shall he do?

MOSCA. When we have done, you mean?

CORVINO. Yes.

MOSCA. Why, we'll think:
Sell him for mummia;[6] he's half dust already.
[*To* VOLTORE.] Do you not smile to see this buffalo,[7]
How he doth sport it with his head? [*aside*]—I should,
If all were well and past. [*To* CORBACCIO.] Sir, only you
Are he that shall enjoy the crop of all,
And these know not for whom they toil.

CORBACCIO. Ay, peace.

MOSCA. [*turning to* CORVINO] But you shall eat it. [*aside*]
Much![8] [*To* VOLTORE] Worshipful sir,
Mercury sit upon your thundering tongue,
Or the French Hercules,[9] and make your language
As conquering as his club, to beat along,

2. Innocence, as of a freshman, but in opposition to Sir Politic's "salt-head": salacity.
3. Untruth, but also the shape of things, as in the lie or lay of the land.
4. "Part," as in part-singing. Mosca must be sure everyone has his story straight.
5. I.e., Corbaccio's.
6. Allegedly the powdered remains of the Pharaohs, popularly sold as medicine.
7. An allusion to the cuckold's horns worn by Corvino.
8. I.e., "fat chance!"
9. Both Mercury, god of thieves, and the French Hercules were patrons of eloquence; the latter is specifically discussed by the classical burlesque-writer, Lucian.

As with a tempest, flat, our adversaries;
But much more yours, sir.

VOLTORE. Here they come, have done.

MOSCA. I have another witness, if you need, sir,
I can produce.

VOLTORE. Who is it?

MOSCA. Sir, I have her.

SCENE 5

[*Enter* AVOCATORI *and take their seats;* BONARIO, CELIA, NOTARIO, COMMENDATORI, SAFFI, *and other* OFFICERS OF JUSTICE.]

1 AVOCATORE. The like of this the Senate never heard of.

2 AVOCATORE. 'Twill come most strange to them when we report it.

4 AVOCATORE. The gentlewoman[1] has been ever held
Of unreprovéd name,

3 AVOCATORE. So has the youth.[2]

4 AVOCATORE. The more unnatural part that of his father.

2 AVOCATORE. More of the husband.[3]

1 AVOCATORE. I not know to give
His act a name, it is so monstrous!

4 AVOCATORE. But the impostor,[4] he's a thing created
To exceed example!

1 AVOCATORE. And all after-times!

2 AVOCATORE. I never heard a true voluptuary
Described, but him.

3 AVOCATORE. Appear yet those were cited?

NOTARIO. All but the old magnifico, Volpone.

1 AVOCATORE. Why is not he here?

MOSCA. Please your fatherhoods,
Here is his advocate: himself's so weak,
So feeble—

4 AVOCATORE. What are you?

BONARIO. His parasite,
His knave, his pander: I beseech the court,
He may be forced to come, that your grave eyes
May bear strong witness of his strange impostures.

VOLTORE. Upon my faith and credit with your virtues,
He is not able to endure the air.

2 AVOCATORE. Bring him, however.

3 AVOCATORE. We will see him.

4 AVOCATORE. Fetch him.

VOLTORE. Your fatherhoods' fit pleasures be obeyed; [*Exeunt* OFFICERS.]
But sure, the sight will rather move your pities
Than indignation. May it please the court,

1. I.e., Celia.
2. I.e., Bonario.
3. I.e., Corvino.
4. I.e., Volpone.

In the meantime, he may be heard in me.
I know this place most void of prejudice,
And therefore crave it, since we have no reason
To fear our truth should hurt our cause.

3 AVOCATORE. Speak free.

VOLTORE. Then know, most honored fathers, I must now
Discover to your strangely abuséd ears,
The most prodigious and most frontless[5] piece
Of solid impudence and treachery,
That ever vicious nature yet brought forth
To shame the state of Venice. This lewd woman,
That wants[6] no artificial looks or tears
To help the visor she has now put on,
Hath long been known a close adulteress
To that lascivious youth there; not suspected,
I say, but known, and taken in the act
With him; and by this man, the easy husband,
Pardoned; whose timeless[7] bounty makes him now
Stand here, the most unhappy, innocent person,
That ever man's own goodness made accused.
For these not knowing how to owe a gift
Of that dear grace, but with their shame; being placed
So above all powers of their gratitude,
Began to hate the benefit; and, in place
Of thanks, devise to extirp[8] the memory
Of such an act. Wherein, I pray your fatherhoods
To observe the malice, yea, the rage of creatures
Discovered in their evils; and what heart
Such take, even from their crimes. But that anon
Will more appear. This gentleman, the father,
Hearing of this foul fact, with many others,
Which daily struck at his too tender ears,
And grieved in nothing more than that he could not
Preserve himself a parent (his son's ills
Growing to that strange flood), at last decreed
To disinherit him.

1 AVOCATORE. These be strange turns!

2 AVOCATORE. The young man's fame was ever fair and honest.

VOLTORE. So much more full of danger is his vice,
That can beguile so under shade of virtue.
But, as I said, my honored sires, his father
Having this settled purpose, by what means
To him betrayed, we know not, and this day
Appointed for the deed; that parricide,
I cannot style him better, by confederacy[9]
Preparing this his paramour to be there,
Entered Volpone's house (who was the man,

5. Shameless.
6. Lacks; "visor": artificial features, outward appearance.
7. Ill-timed.
8. Wipe out, extirpate.
9. Conspiracy.

Your fatherhoods must understand, designed
For the inheritance), there sought his father;
But with what purpose sought he him, my lords?
I tremble to pronounce it, that a son
Unto a father, and to such a father,
Should have so foul, felonious intent!
It was to murder him; when, being prevented
By his more happy absence, what then did he?
Not check his wicked thoughts; no, now new deeds
(Mischief doth never[1] end where it begins);
An act of horror, fathers! he dragged forth
The agéd gentleman that had there lain bed-rid
Three years and more, out of his innocent couch,
Naked upon the floor, there left him; wounded
His servant in the face; and, with this strumpet,
The stale[2] to his forged practice, who was glad
To be so active (I shall here desire
Your fatherhoods to note but my collections,[3]
As most remarkable), thought at once to stop
His father's ends, discredit his free choice
In the old gentleman, redeem themselves,
By laying infamy upon this man,[4]
To whom, with blushing, they should owe their lives.

1 AVOCATORE. What proofs have you of this?
BONARIO. Most honored fathers,
I humbly crave there be no credit given
To this man's mercenary tongue.
2 AVOCATORE. Forbear.
BONARIO. His soul moves in his fee.
3 AVOCATORE. O, sir.
BONARIO. This fellow,
For six sols more,[5] would plead against his maker.
1 AVOCATORE. You do forget yourself.
VOLTORE. Nay, nay, grave fathers,
Let him have scope; can any man imagine
That he will spare his accuser, that would not
Have spared his parent?
1 AVOCATORE. Well, produce your proofs.
CELIA. I would I could forget I were a creature,
VOLTORE. Signor Corbaccio! [CORBACCIO *comes forward.*]
4 AVOCATORE. What is he?
VOLTORE. The father.
2 AVOCATORE. Has he had an oath?
NOTARIO. Yes.
CORBACCIO. What must I do now?
NOTARIO. Your testimony's craved.

1. Jonson's text reads "ever," and the sense is defensible, but the stronger meaning comes from "never."
2. Pretext.
3. Deductions.
4. I.e., Corvino.
5. Three pence.

CORBACCIO. Speak to the knave?
I'll have my mouth first stopped with earth; my heart
Abhors his knowledge:[6] I disclaim in him.
1 AVOCATORE. But for what cause?
CORBACCIO. The mere portent of nature!
He is an utter stranger to my loins.
BONARIO. Have they made you to this?
CORBACCIO. I will not hear thee,
Monster of men, swine, goat, wolf, parricide!
Speak not, thou viper.[7]
BONARIO. Sir, I will sit down,
And rather wish my innocence should suffer,
Than I resist the authority of a father.
VOLTORE. Signor Corvino! [CORVINO *comes forward.*]
2 AVOCATORE. This is strange.
1 AVOCATORE. Who's this?
NOTARIO. The husband.
4 AVOCATORE. Is he sworn?
NOTARIO. He is.
3 AVOCATORE. Speak, then.
CORVINO. This woman, please your fatherhoods, is a whore
Of most hot exercise, more than a partridge,[8]
Upon record—
1 AVOCATORE. No more.
CORVINO. Neighs like a jennet.[9]
NOTARIO. Preserve the honor of the court.
CORVINO. I shall,
And modesty of your most reverend ears.
And yet I hope that I may say, these eyes
Have seen her glued unto that piece of cedar,
That fine well-timbered gallant; and that here[1]
The letters may be read, through the horn,
That make the story perfect.
MOSCA. Excellent! sir.
CORVINO. [*aside to* MOSCA] There is no shame in this now, is there?
MOSCA. None.
CORVINO. Or if I said, I hoped that she were onward
To her damnation, if there be a hell
Greater than whore and woman; a good catholic
May make the doubt.[2]

6. Shudders to recognize him.
7. The parricide, as a creature wholly unnatural, was punished among the Romans by being whipped, sewed up in a sack with a dog, a cock, a viper, and an ape, and thrown into the sea.
8. The partridge vied with the sparrow as the most lustful of birds.
9. Mare.
1. Corvino holds two fingers over his head to make the horned sign of the cuckold.
2. If there's any hell worse than being a woman and a whore, Corvino thinks of saying Celia may be headed for it; because he doesn't say flatly that she *is* so headed, he can claim the virtue of charity, and remain a good Catholic. The 1607 quarto reads "Christian" instead of "catholic."

3 AVOCATORE. His grief hath made him frantic.
1 AVOCATORE. Remove him hence. [CELIA *swoons.*]
2 AVOCATORE. Look to the woman.
CORVINO. Rare!
Prettily feigned, again!
4 AVOCATORE. Stand from about her.
1 AVOCATORE. Give her the air.
3 AVOCATORE. [*to* MOSCA] What can you say?
MOSCA. My wound,
May it please your wisdoms, speaks for me, received
In aid of my good patron, when he missed
His sought-for father,[3] when that well-taught dame
Had her cue given her, to cry out, A rape!
BONARIO. O most laid impudence! Fathers—
3 AVOCATORE. Sir, be silent;
You had your hearing free, so must they theirs.
2 AVOCATORE. I do begin to doubt the imposture here.
4 AVOCATORE. This woman has too many moods.
VOLTORE. Grave fathers,
She is a creature of a most professed
And prostituted lewdness.
CORVINO. Most impetuous,
Unsatisfied, grave fathers!
VOLTORE. May her feignings
Not take your wisdoms: but this day she baited
A stranger, a grave knight, with her loose eyes,
And more lascivious kisses. This man saw them
Together on the water, in a gondola.
MOSCA. Here is the lady herself, that saw them too,
Without; who then had in the open streets
Pursued them, but for saving her knight's honor.
1 AVOCATORE. Produce that lady.
2 AVOCATORE. Let her come. [*Exit* MOSCA.]
4 AVOCATORE. These things,
They strike with wonder.
3 AVOCATORE. I am turned a stone.

SCENE 6

[*Enter* MOSCA *with* LADY WOULD-BE.]
MOSCA. Be resolute, madam.
LADY POLITIC. Ay, this same is she. [*Pointing to* CELIA.]
Out, thou chameleon[4] harlot! now thine eyes
Vie tears with the hyena. Dar'st thou look
Upon my wrongéd face?—I cry your pardons,
I fear I have forgettingly transgressed
Against the dignity of the court—
2 AVOCATORE. No, madam.

3. I.e., Corbaccio.
4. An animal that changes colors. The hyena is emblematic of treachery and an eater of carrion.

LADY POLITIC. And been exorbitant[5]—
2 AVOCATORE. You have not, lady.
4 AVOCATORE. These proofs are strong.
LADY POLITIC. Surely, I had no purpose
To scandalize your honors, or my sex's.
3 AVOCATORE. We do believe it.
LADY POLITIC. Surely, you may believe it.
2 AVOCATORE. Madam, we do.
LADY POLITIC. Indeed you may; my breeding
Is not so coarse——
4 AVOCATORE. We know it.
LADY POLITIC. To offend
With pertinacy——
3 AVOCATORE. Lady—
LADY POLITIC. Such a presence!
No, surely.
1 AVOCATORE. We well think it.
LADY POLITIC. You may think it.
1 AVOCATORE. Let her o'ercome. [*To* BONARIO.] What witnesses have you,
To make good your report?
BONARIO. Our consciences.
CELIA. And heaven, that never fails the innocent.
4 AVOCATORE. These are no testimonies.
BONARIO. Not in your courts,
Where multitude, and clamor overcomes.
1 AVOCATORE. Nay, then you do wax insolent.
[*Re-enter* OFFICERS, *bearing* VOLPONE *on a couch.*]
VOLTORE. Here, here,
The testimony comes, that will convince,
And put to utter dumbness their bold tongues!
See here, grave fathers, here's the ravisher,
The rider on men's wives, the great impostor,
The grand voluptuary! Do you not think
These limbs should affect venery?[6] or these eyes
Covet a concubine? pray you mark these hands;
Are they not fit to stroke a lady's breasts?
Perhaps he doth dissemble!
BONARIO. So he does.
VOLTORE. Would you have him tortured?
BONARIO. I would have him proved.
VOLTORE. Best try him then with goads, or burning irons;
Put him to the strappado.[7] I have heard
The rack hath cured the gout; 'faith, give it him,
And help him of a malady; be courteous.
I'll undertake, before these honored fathers,

5. Lady Politic doubtless means "excessive."
6. Be disposed to lust.
7. A common torture of the time: a man's hands were tied behind his back, and he was hoisted by his wrists on a gallows, to the common effect of dislocating his shoulders.

He shall have yet as many left diseases,
As she has known adulterers, or thou strumpets.
O, my most equal hearers, if these deeds,
Acts of this bold and most exorbitant strain,
May pass with sufferance, what one citizen
But owes the forfeit of his life, yea, fame,
To him that dares traduce him? which of you
Are safe, my honored fathers? I would ask,
With leave of your grave fatherhoods, if their plot
Have any face or color like to truth?
Or if, unto the dullest nostril here,
It smell not rank, and most abhorréd slander?
I crave your care of this good gentleman,
Whose life is much endangered by their fable;
And as for them, I will conclude with this,
That vicious persons, when they're hot, and fleshed
In impious acts, their constancy abounds:
Damned deeds are done with greatest confidence.

1 AVOCATORE. Take them to custody, and sever them. [CELIA *and* BONARIO *are taken out.*]

2 AVOCATORE. 'Tis pity two such prodigies should live.

1 AVOCATORE. Let the old gentleman be returned with care: [*Exeunt* OFFICERS *with* VOLPONE.]
I'm sorry our credulity hath wronged him.

4 AVOCATORE. These are two creatures!

3 AVOCATORE. I've an earthquake in me.[8]

2 AVOCATORE. Their shame, even in their cradles, fled their faces.

4 AVOCATORE. [*To* VOLTORE] You have done a worthy service to the state, sir,
In their discovery.

1 AVOCATORE. You shall hear, ere night,
What punishment the court decrees upon them.

VOLTORE. We thank your fatherhoods. [*Exeunt* AVOCATORI, NOTARIO, and OFFICERS.] [*To* MOSCA.]—How like you it?

MOSCA. Rare.
I'd have your tongue, sir, tipped with gold for this;
I'd have you be the heir to the whole city;
The earth I'd have want men, ere you want living:
They're bound to erect your statue in St. Mark's.
Signor Corvino, I would have you go
And show yourself, that you have conquered.

CORVINO. Yes.

MOSCA. It was much better that you should profess
Yourself a cuckold thus, than that the other
Should have been proved.

CORVINO. Nay, I considered that;
Now it is her fault.

MOSCA. Then it had been yours.

8. I'm overwhelmed.

CORVINO. True; I do doubt this advocate still.
MOSCA. I'faith,
You need not, I dare ease you of that care.
CORVINO. I trust thee, Mosca. [*Exit.*]
MOSCA. As your own soul, sir.
CORBACCIO. Mosca!
MOSCA. Now for your business, sir.
CORBACCIO. How! have you business?
MOSCA. Yes, yours sir.
CORBACCIO. O, none else?
MOSCA. None else, not I.
CORBACCIO. Be careful then.
MOSCA. Rest you with both your eyes, sir.
CORBACCIO. Dispatch it.[9]
MOSCA. Instantly.
CORBACCIO. And look that all,
Whatever, be put in, jewels, plate, moneys,
Household stuff, bedding, curtains.
MOSCA. Curtain-rings, sir:
Only the advocate's fee must be deducted.
CORBACCIO. I'll pay him now; you'll be too prodigal.
MOSCA. Sir, I must tender it.
CORBACCIO. Two sequins is well.
MOSCA. No, six, sir.
CORBACCIO. 'Tis too much.
MOSCA. He talked a great while;
You must consider that, sir.
CORBACCIO. Well, there's three—
MOSCA. I'll give it him.
CORBACCIO. Do so, and there's for thee. [*Exit.*]
MOSCA. Bountiful bones! What horrid strange offense
Did he commit 'gainst nature, in his youth,
Worthy this age? [*To* VOLTORE.]—You see, sir, how I work
Unto your ends; take you no notice.
VOLTORE. No,
I'll leave you. [*Exit.*]
MOSCA. All is yours, the devil and all,
Good advocate!—Madam, I'll bring you home.
LADY POLITIC. No, I'll go see your patron.
MOSCA. That you shall not.
I'll tell you why. My purpose is to urge
My patron to reform his will;[1] and for
The zeal you have shown today, whereas before
You were but third or fourth, you shall be now
Put in the first; which would appear as begged,
If you were present. Therefore—
LADY POLITIC. You shall sway me. [*Exeunt.*]

9. I.e., get the will made, with me in it.
1. Rewrite his testament, though always with the other connotation of improving his disposition.

Act V

SCENE 1. *A Room in* VOLPONE's *House.*

[*Enter* VOLPONE.]

VOLPONE. Well, I am here, and all this brunt[2] is past.
I ne'er was in dislike with my disguise
Till this fled moment:[3] here 'twas good, in private,
But in your public—*cave*[4] whilst I breathe.
'Fore God, my left leg 'gan to have the cramp,
And I apprehended[5] straight some power had struck me
With a dead palsy. Well! I must be merry,
And shake it off. A many of these fears
Would put me into some villainous disease,
Should they come thick upon me: I'll prevent 'em.
Give me a bowl of lusty wine, to fright
This humour from my heart. [*Drinks.*]—Hum, hum, hum!
'Tis almost gone already, I shall conquer.
Any device, now, of rare ingenious knavery,
That would possess me with a violent laughter,
Would make me up again. [*Drinks again.*]—So, so, so, so!
This heat is life; 'tis blood by this time! Mosca!

SCENE 2

[*Enter* MOSCA.]

MOSCA. How now, sir? does the day look clear again?
Are we recovered? and wrought out of error,
Into our way, to see our path before us?
Is our trade free once more?

VOLPONE. Exquisite Mosca!

MOSCA. Was it not carried learnedly?

VOLPONE. And stoutly.
Good wits are greatest in extremities.

MOSCA. It were a folly beyond thought, to trust
Any grand act unto a cowardly spirit.
You are not taken with it[6] enough, methinks.

VOLPONE. O, more than if I had enjoyed the wench;
The pleasure of all womankind's not like it.

MOSCA. Why now you speak, sir. We must here be fixed;
Here we must rest. This is our masterpiece;
We cannot think to go beyond this.

VOLPONE. True,
Thou'st played thy prize, my precious Mosca.

MOSCA. Nay, sir,
To gull the court—

VOLPONE. And quite divert the torrent
Upon the innocent.

2. Trouble.
3. Moment just past.
4. Beware, watch out.
5. The word is printed and pronounced "apprended."
6. Pleased, satisfied with it.

MOSCA. Yes, and to make
So rare a music out of discords—
VOLPONE. Right.
That yet to me's the strangest! how thou'st borne it
That these, being so divided 'mongst themselves,
Should not scent somewhat, or in me or thee,
Or doubt their own side.
MOSCA. True, they will not see't.
Too much light blinds them, I think.[7] Each of them
Is so possessed and stuffed with his own hopes,
That anything unto the contrary,
Never so true, or never so apparent,
Never so palpable, they will resist it—
VOLPONE. Like a temptation of the devil.
MOSCA. Right, sir.
Merchants may talk of trade, and your great signors
Of land that yields well; but if Italy
Have any glebe[8] more fruitful than these fellows,
I am deceived. Did not your advocate rare?[9]
VOLPONE. O—*My most honored fathers, my grave fathers,*
Under correction of your fatherhoods,
What face of truth is here? If these strange deeds
May pass, most honored fathers—I had much ado
To forbear laughing.
MOSCA. It seemed to me, you sweat, sir.
VOLPONE. In troth, I did a little.
MOSCA. But confess, sir,
Were you not daunted?
VOLPONE. In good faith, I was
A little in a mist, but not dejected;
Never; but still myself.
MOSCA. I think it, sir.
Now, so truth help me, I must needs say this, sir,
And out of conscience for your advocate,
He has taken pains, in faith, sir, and deserved,
In my poor judgment, I speak it under favor,
Not to contrary you, sir, very richly—
Well—to be cozened.
VOLPONE. Troth, and I think so too,
By that I heard him, in the latter end.
MOSCA. O, but before, sir: had you heard him first
Draw it to certain heads, then aggravate,
Then use his vehement figures[1]—I looked still
When he would shift a shirt;[2] and, doing this
Out of pure love, no hope of gain—
VOLPONE. 'Tis right.

7. An ancient adage.
8. Soil.
9. Did not your advocate (perform) rare(ly)?
1. Terms of legal oratory.
2. I.e., he sweated so much over his speech, it seemed he might have to change his linen.

I cannot answer him Mosca, as I would,
Not yet; but for thy sake, at thy entreaty,
I will begin e'en now to vex them all,
This very instant.

MOSCA. Good, sir.

VOLPONE. Call the dwarf
And eunuch forth.

MOSCA. Castrone, Nano!

[*Enter* CASTRONE *and* NANO.]

NANO. Here.

VOLPONE. Shall we have a jig now?

MOSCA. What you please, sir.

VOLPONE. Go,
Straight give out about the streets, you two,
That I am dead; do it with constancy,
Sadly, do you hear? impute it to the grief
Of this late slander. [*Exeunt* CASTRONE *and* NANO.]

MOSCA. What do you mean, sir?

VOLPONE. O,
I shall have instantly my vulture, crow,
Raven, come flying hither, on the news,
To peck for carrion, my she-wolf, and all,
Greedy, and full of expectation—

MOSCA. And then to have it ravished from their mouths!

VOLPONE. 'Tis true. I will have thee put on a gown,
And take upon thee, as thou wert mine heir;
Show them a will. Open that chest, and reach
Forth one of those that has the blanks; I'll straight
Put in thy name.

MOSCA. It will be rare, sir. [*Gives him a paper.*]

VOLPONE. Ay,
When they e'en gape, and find themselves deluded—

MOSCA. Yes.

VOLPONE. And thou use them scurvily! Dispatch,
Get on thy gown.

MOSCA. But what, sir, if they ask
After the body?

VOLPONE. Say, it was corrupted.

MOSCA. I'll say it stunk, sir; and was fain to have it
Coffined up instantly, and sent away.

VOLPONE. Anything, what thou wilt. Hold, here's my will.
Get thee a cap, a count-book,[3] pen and ink,
Papers afore thee; sit as thou wert taking
An inventory of parcels. I'll get up
Behind the curtain, on a stool, and hearken;
Sometime peep over, see how they do look,
With what degrees their blood doth leave their faces.
O, 'twill afford me a rare meal of laughter!

3. Ledger.

MOSCA. [*putting on a cap, and setting out the table, &c.*] Your advocate will turn stark dull upon it.
VOLPONE. It will take off his oratory's edge.
MOSCA. But your clarissimo, old round-back,[4] he
Will crump you like a hog-louse, with the touch.
VOLPONE. And what Corvino?
MOSCA. O, sir, look for him,
Tomorrow morning, with a rope and dagger,
To visit all the streets;[5] he must run mad.
My lady too, that came into the court
To bear false witness for your worship—
VOLPONE. Yes,
And kissed me 'fore the fathers, when my face
Flowed all with oils.
MOSCA. And sweat, sir. Why, your gold
Is such another medicine, it dries up
All those offensive savors; it transforms
The most deformed, and restores them lovely,
As 'twere the strange poetical girdle.[6] Jove
Could not invent t' himself a shroud more subtle
To pass Acrisius' guards.[7] It is the thing
Makes all the world her grace, her youth her beauty.
VOLPONE. I think she loves me.
MOSCA. Who? the lady, sir?
She's jealous of you.
VOLPONE. Dost thou say so? [*Knocking within.*]
MOSCA. Hark,
There's some already.
VOLPONE. Look.
MOSCA. It is the vulture;
He has the quickest scent.
VOLPONE. I'll to my place,
Thou to thy posture. [*Goes behind the curtain.*]
MOSCA. I am set.
VOLPONE. But, Mosca,
Play the artificer now, torture them rarely.

SCENE 3

[*Enter* VOLTORE.]
VOLTORE. How now, my Mosca?
MOSCA. [*writing*] *Turkey carpets, nine*[8]—
VOLTORE. Taking an inventory? that is well.

4. Corbaccio is a *clarissimo*, a distinguished man in Venice. "Crump you": curl up on you; there is a species of wood louse or hog louse (the names are interchangeable) which curls up in a ball when touched.
5. I.e., looking for a place to commit suicide.
6. The girdle of Venus (*cestus*) made any wearer irresistibly beautiful.
7. Acrisius was the father of Danae; he locked her up in a tower till Jove managed to get to her in the form of a shower of gold.
8. Turkey carpets (not necessarily from Turkey) were particularly thick and luxurious; cloth described as tissue often had threads of gold or silver interwoven.

MOSCA. *Two suits of bedding, tissue—*
VOLTORE. Where's the will?
Let me read that the while.
[*Enter* SERVANTS *with* CORBACCIO *in a chair.*]
CORBACCIO. So, set me down,
And get you home. [*Exeunt servants.*]
VOLTORE. Is he come now to trouble us?
MOSCA. *Of cloth of gold, two more—*
CORBACCIO. Is it done, Mosca?
MOSCA. *Of several velvets, eight—*
VOLTORE. I like his care.
CORBACCIO. Dost thou not hear?
[*Enter* CORVINO.]
CORVINO. Ha! is the hour come, Mosca?
VOLPONE. [*peeping over the curtain*] Ay, now they muster.
CORVINO. What does the advocate here,
Or this Corbaccio?
CORBACCIO. What do these here?
[*Enter* LADY POLITIC WOULD-BE.]
LADY POLITIC. Mosca!
Is his thread spun?
MOSCA. *Eight chests of linen—*
VOLPONE. O,
My fine dame Would-be, too!
CORVINO. Mosca, the will,
That I may show it these, and rid them hence.
MOSCA. *Six chests of diaper,*[9] *four of damask.*—There. [*Gives them the will carelessly, over his shoulder.*]
CORBACCIO. Is that the will?
MOSCA. *Down-beds, and bolsters—*
VOLPONE. Rare!
Be busy still. Now they begin to flutter:
They never think of me. Look, see, see, see!
How their swift eyes run over the long deed,
Unto the name, and to the legacies,
What is bequeathed them there—
MOSCA. *Ten suits of hangings*[1]*—*
VOLPONE. Ay, in their garters, Mosca. Now their hopes
Are at the gasp.
VOLTORE. Mosca the heir!
CORBACCIO. What's that?
VOLPONE. My advocate is dumb; look to my merchant,
He has heard of some strange storm, a ship is lost,
He faints; my lady will swoon. Old glazen-eyes,[2]
He hath not reached his despair yet.
CORBACCIO. All these

9. Fine linen cloth; "damask" (from Damascus): a silk fabric woven with many figures.
1. Sets of tapestries on the walls. But Volpone suggests garters, traditional means of suicide.
2. I.e., Corbaccio.

Are out of hope; I am, sure, the man. [*Takes the will.*]
CORVINO. But, Mosca—
MOSCA. *Two cabinets*—
CORVINO. Is this in earnest?
MOSCA. *One*
Of ebony—
CORVINO. Or do you but delude me?
MOSCA. *The other, mother of pearl*—I am very busy.
Good faith, it is a fortune thrown upon me—
Item, one salt[3] *of agate*—not my seeking.
LADY POLITIC. Do you hear, sir?
MOSCA. A *perfumed box*—'Pray you forbear,
You see I'm troubled—*made of an onyx*—
LADY POLITIC. How!
MOSCA. To-morrow or next day, I shall be at leisure
To talk with you all.
CORVINO. Is this my large hope's issue?
LADY POLITIC. Sir, I must have a fairer answer.
MOSCA. Madam!
Marry, and shall: pray you, fairly[4] quit my house.
Nay, raise no tempest with your looks; but hark you:
Remember what your ladyship offered me
To put you in an heir;[5] go to, think on it:
And what you said e'en your best madams did
For maintenance;[6] and why not you? Enough.
Go home, and use the poor Sir Pol, your knight, well,
For fear I tell some riddles; go, be melancholic. [*Exit* LADY POLITIC.]
VOLPONE. O, my fine devil!
CORVINO. Mosca, 'pray you a word.
MOSCA. Lord! will not you take your dispatch hence yet?
Methinks, of all, you should have been the example.
Why should you stay here? with what thought, what promise?
Hear you; do not you know, I know you an ass,
And that you would most fain have been a wittol,[7]
If fortune would have let you? that you are
A declared cuckold, on good terms? This pearl,
You'll say, was yours? Right. This diamond?
I'll not deny't, but thank you. Much here else?
It may be so. Why, think that these good works
May help to hide your bad. I'll not betray you;
Although you be but extraordinary,[8]
And have it only in title, it sufficeth;
Go home, be melancholic too, or mad. [*Exit* CORVINO.]
VOLPONE. Rare Mosca! how his villainy becomes him!

3. Salt-cellar.
4. Once and for all.
5. This aspect of Lady Politic Jonson has saved for the present moment.
6. Lady Politic would never say "for money."
7. A pimp for your own wife.
8. I.e., not a full-fledged pimp or cuckold, just one who did his best to be such.

VOLTORE. Certain he doth delude all these for me.
CORBACCIO. Mosca the heir!
VOLPONE. O, his four eyes have found it.[9]
CORBACCIO. I am cozened, cheated, by a parasite slave;
Harlot,[1] thou hast gulled me.
MOSCA. Yes, sir. Stop your mouth,
Or I shall draw the only tooth is left.
Are not you he, that filthy covetous wretch,
With the three legs,[2] that here, in hope of prey,
Have, any time this three years, snuffed about
With your most groveling nose, and would have hired
Me to the poisoning of my patron, sir?
Are not you he that have today in court
Professed the disinheriting of your son?
Perjured yourself? Go home, and die, and stink;
If you but croak a syllable, all comes out:
Away, and call your porters! [*Exit* CORBACCIO.]—
Go, go, stink.
VOLPONE. Excellent varlet!
VOLTORE. Now, my faithful Mosca,
I find thy constancy—
MOSCA. Sir?
VOLTORE. Sincere.
MOSCA. [*writing*] *A table*
Of porphyry—I mar'l you'll be thus troublesome.
VOLTORE. Nay, leave off now, they are gone.
MOSCA. Why, who are you?
What! Who did send for you? O, cry you mercy,
Reverend sir! Good faith, I am grieved for you,
That any chance of mine should thus defeat
Your (I must needs say) most deserving travails:
But I protest, sir, it was cast upon me,
And I could almost wish to be without it,
But that the will o' the dead must be observed.
Marry, my joy is that you need it not;
You have a gift, sir (thank your education),
Will never let you want, while there are men,
And malice, to breed causes. Would I had
But half the like, for all my fortune, sir!
If I have any suits (as I do hope,
Things being so easy and direct, I shall not)
I will make bold with your obstreperous aid—
Conceive me—for your fee, sir. In meantime,
You that have so much law, I know have the conscience
Not to be covetous of what is mine.
Good sir, I thank you for my plate; 'twill help

9. Corbaccio wears spectacles.
1. Frequently used of men, in the sense of "scoundrel."
2. I.e., two plus a cane or crutch.

To set up a young man.[3] Good faith, you look
As you were costive;[4] best go home and purge, sir. [*Exit* VOLTORE.]

VOLPONE. [*comes from behind the curtain*] Bid him eat lettuce well.[5] My witty mischief,
Let me embrace thee. O that I could now
Transform thee to a Venus!—Mosca, go,
Straight take my habit of clarissimo,[6]
And walk the streets; be seen, torment them more.
We must pursue, as well as plot. Who would
Have lost this feast?

MOSCA. I doubt it will lose them.

VOLPONE. O, my recovery shall recover all.
That I could now but think on some disguise
To meet them in, and ask them questions;
How I would vex them still at every turn!

MOSCA. Sir, I can fit you.

VOLPONE. Canst thou?

MOSCA. Yes, I know
One o' the commendatori, sir, so like you;
Him will I straight make drunk, and bring you his habit.[7]

VOLPONE. A rare disguise, and answering thy brain!
O, I will be a sharp disease unto them.

MOSCA. Sir, you must look for curses—

VOLPONE. Till they burst;
The fox fares ever best when he is cursed. [*Exeunt.*]

SCENE 4. *A Hall in* SIR POLITIC'*s House.*

[*Enter* PEREGRINE *disguised, and three* MERCHANTS.]

PEREGRINE. Am I enough disguised?

1 MERCHANT. I warrant you.

PEREGRINE. All my ambition is to fright him only.

2 MERCHANT. If you could ship him away, 'twere excellent.

3 MERCHANT. To Zant, or to Aleppo?[8]

PEREGRINE. Yes, and have his
Adventures put i' the Book of Voyages,
And his gulled story[9] registered for truth.
Well, gentlemen, when I am in a while,
And that you think us warm in our discourse,
Know your approaches.

1 MERCHANT. Trust it to our care. [*Exeunt* MERCHANTS.]

[*Enter* WAITING WOMAN.]

3. I.e., himself.
4. Constipated; "purge": take a laxative.
5. In classical days, lettuce was thought to have mild purgative powers.
6. Mosca, in putting on the distinctive dress of a nobleman (clarissímo) is running a big risk—laws about wearing the costume of one's rank were strict and severe.
7. Volpone now assumes a common sergeant's uniform, and over it a loose black robe, with a red cap and two brass buttons.
8. Zant is Byzantium, Constantinople, or (now) Istanbul; Aleppo, in Syria, still carries its old name.
9. The story of his gulling.

PEREGRINE. Save you, fair lady! Is Sir Pol within?
WOMAN. I do not know, sir.
PEREGRINE. Pray you say unto him,
Here is a merchant, upon earnest business,
Desires to speak with him.
WOMAN. I will see, sir. [*Exit*]
PEREGRINE. Pray you.—
I see the family is all female here.
[*Re-enter* WAITING WOMAN.]
WOMAN. He says, sir, he has weighty affairs of state,
That now require him whole; some other time
You may possess him.
PEREGRINE. Pray you say again.
If those require him whole, these will exact him,
Whereof I bring him tidings. [*Exit* WOMAN.]—What might be
His grave affair of state now? How to make
Bolognian sausages[1] here in Venice, sparing
One o' the ingredients?
[*Re-enter* WAITING WOMAN.]
WOMAN. Sir, he says, he knows
By your word *tidings*, that you are no statesman,[2]
And therefore wills you stay.
PEREGRINE. Sweet, pray you return him;
I have not read so many proclamations,
And studied them for words, as he has done—
But—here he deigns to come. [*Exit* WOMAN.]
[*Enter* SIR POLITIC.]
SIR POLITIC. Sir, I must crave
Your courteous pardon. There hath chanced today
Unkind disaster 'twixt my lady and me;
And I was penning my apology,
To give her satisfaction, as you came now.
PEREGRINE. Sir, I am grieved I bring you worse disaster:
The gentleman you met at the port today,
That told you, he was newly arrived—
SIR POLITIC. Ay, was
A fugitive punk?[3]
PEREGRINE. No, sir, a spy set on you;
And he has made relation to the senate,
That you professed to him to have a plot
To sell the state of Venice to the Turk.[4]
SIR POLITIC. O me!
PEREGRINE. For which, warrants are signed by this time,
To apprehend you, and to search your study
For papers—

1. Sausages of Bologna were so famous that *baloney* is still a word in general use.
2. "Tidings" were what normal people received; a secret-service operative would get "intelligence."
3. A runaway pimp (the "gentleman" was, of course, Peregrine himself).
4. See above, IV.1.

SIR POLITIC. Alas, sir, I have none but notes
Drawn out of play-books[5]—
PEREGRINE. All the better, sir.
SIR POLITIC. And some essays. What shall I do?
PEREGRINE. Sir, best
Convey yourself into a sugar-chest;
Or, if you could lie round, a frail[6] were rare,
And I could send you aboard.
SIR POLITIC. Sir, I but talked so,
For discourse' sake merely. [*Knocking within.*]
PEREGRINE. Hark! they are there.
SIR POLITIC. I am a wretch, a wretch!
PEREGRINE. What will you do, sir?
Have you ne'er a currant-butt[7] to leap into?
They'll put you to the rack; you must be sudden.
SIR POLITIC. Sir, I have an engine—
3 MERCHANT. [*within*] Sir Politic Would-be!
2 MERCHANT. [*within*] Where is he?
SIR POLITIC. That I have thought upon before time.
PEREGRINE. What is it?
SIR POLITIC. I shall ne'er endure the torture.
Marry, it is, sir, of a tortoise-shell,
Fitted for these extremities: pray you, sir, help me.
Here I've a place, sir, to put back my legs,
Please you to lay it on, sir, [*Lies down while* PEREGRINE *places the shell upon him.*]—With this cap,
And my black gloves, I'll lie, sir, like a tortoise,
Till they are gone.
PEREGRINE. And call you this an engine?
SIR POLITIC. Mine own device—Good sir, bid my wife's women
To burn my papers. [*Exit* PEREGRINE.]
[*The* MERCHANTS *rush in.*]
1 MERCHANT. Where is he hid?
3 MERCHANT. We must,
And will sure find him.
2 MERCHANT. Which is his study?
[*Re-enter* PEREGRINE.]
1 MERCHANT. What
Are you, sir?
PEREGRINE. I am a merchant, that came here
To look upon this tortoise.
3 MERCHANT. How!
1 MERCHANT. St. Mark!
What beast is this?
PEREGRINE. It is a fish.
2 MERCHANT. Come out here!

5. Sir Pol's exotic information turns out to be very common stuff. Play-books in particular had then about the reputation of comic books now.
6. Flimsy fruit-basket.
7. Cask for holding currants.

PEREGRINE. Nay, you may strike him, sir, and tread upon him:
He'll bear a cart.
1 MERCHANT. What, to run over him?
PEREGRINE. Yes.
3 MERCHANT. Let's jump upon him.
2 MERCHANT. Can he not go?
PEREGRINE. He creeps, sir.
1 MERCHANT. Let's see him creep. [*Pokes him.*]
PEREGRINE. No, good sir, you will hurt him.
2 MERCHANT. Heart, I will see him creep, or prick his guts.
3 MERCHANT. Come out here!
PEREGRINE. Pray you, sir! [*Aside to* SIR POLITIC.]
—Creep a little.
1 MERCHANT. Forth.
2 MERCHANT. Yet farther.
Good sir! [*Aside to* SIR POLITIC.]
—Creep.
2 MERCHANT. We'll see his legs.
[*They pull off the shell and discover him.*]
3 MERCHANT. Gods' so, he has garters!
1 MERCHANT. Ay, and gloves!
2 MERCHANT. Is this
Your fearful tortoise?
PEREGRINE. [*discovering himself*] Now, Sir Pol, we are even;
For your next project I shall be prepared.
I am sorry for the funeral of your notes, sir.
1 MERCHANT. 'Twere a rare motion[8] to be seen in Fleet Street.
2 MERCHANT. Ay, in the Term.
1 MERCHANT. Or Smithfield, in the fair.
3 MERCHANT. Methinks 'tis but a melancholic sight.
PEREGRINE. Farewell, most politic tortoise! [*Exeunt* PEREGRINE *and* MERCHANTS.]
[*Re-enter* WAITING-WOMAN.]
SIR POLITIC. Where's my lady?
Knows she of this?
WOMAN. I know not, sir.
SIR POLITIC. Inquire.
O, I shall be the fable of all feasts,
The freight of the gazetti,[9] ship-boys' tale;
And, which is worst, even talk for ordinaries.
WOMAN. My lady's come most melancholic home,
And says, sir, she will straight to sea, for physic.[1]
SIR POLITIC. And I, to shun this place and clime forever,
Creeping with house on back, and think it well
To shrink my poor head in my politic shell. [*Exeunt.*]

8. Puppet show. "Fleet Street": then as now a busy street in central London. "Smithfield": where Bartholomew Fair was held. All fairs were especially busy in Term, when lawyers, and their clients, were in residence. These Venetian *mercatori* are remarkably conversant with London manners.
9. Subject of the newsletters; "talk for the ordinaries": tavern gossip.
1. For her health.

SCENE 5. *A Room in* VOLPONE'S *House*.

[*Enter* MOSCA *in the habit of a* clarissimo, *and* VOLPONE *in that of a* commendatore.]

VOLPONE. Am I then like him?
MOSCA. O, sir, you are he.
No man can sever[2] you.
VOLPONE. Good.
MOSCA. But what am I?
VOLPONE. 'Fore heaven, a brave *clarissimo*; thou becom'st it!
Pity thou wert not born one.
MOSCA. If I hold
My made one, 'twill be well.
VOLPONE. I'll go and see
What news first at the court. [*Exit.*]
MOSCA. Do so. My fox
Is out of his hole,[3] and ere he shall re-enter,
I'll make him languish in his borrowed case,
Except he come to composition with me.—
Androgyno, Castrone, Nano!
[*Enter* ANDROGYNO, CASTRONE, *and* NANO.]
ALL. Here.
MOSCA. Go, recreate yourselves abroad; go, sport.— [*Exeunt.*]
So, now I have the keys, and am possessed.
Since he will needs be dead afore his time,
I'll bury him, or gain by him. I am his heir,
And so will keep me, till he share at least.
To cozen him of all, were but a cheat
Well placed; no man would cónstrue it a sin:
Let his sport pay for't. This is called the fox-trap. [*Exit.*]

SCENE 6. *A Street*.

[*Enter* CORBACCIO *and* CORVINO.]

CORBACCIO. They say the court is set.
CORVINO. We must maintain
Our first tale good, for both our reputations.
CORBACCIO. Why? mine's no tale; my son would there have killed me.
CORVINO. That's true, I had forgot. [*Aside.*]—Mine is, I'm sure.
But for your will, sir.
CORBACCIO. Ay, I'll come upon him
For that hereafter, now his patron's dead.
[*Enter* VOLPONE *in disguise.*]
VOLPONE. Signor Corvino! and Corbaccio! sir,
Much joy unto you.
CORVINO. Of what?
VOLPONE. The sudden good

2. Distinguish.
3. Children play a game called Fox-in-the-Hole. "His borrowed case": his false costume.

Dropped down upon you—
CORBACCIO. Where?
VOLPONE. And none knows how,
From old Volpone, sir.
CORBACCIO. Out, arrant knave!
VOLPONE. Let not your too much wealth, sir, make you furious.
CORBACCIO. Away, thou varlet.
VOLPONE. Why, sir?
CORBACCIO. Dost thou mock me?
VOLPONE. You mock the world, sir; did you not change[4] wills?
CORBACCIO. Out, harlot!
VOLPONE. O! belike you are the man,
Signor Corvino? Faith, you carry it well;
You grow not mad withal; I love your spirit.
You are not over-leavened[5] with your fortune.
You should have some would swell now, like a wine-vat.
With such an autumn—Did he give you all, sir?
CORVINO. Avoid, you rascal!
VOLPONE. Troth, your wife has shown
Herself a very woman;[6] but you are well,
You need not care, you have a good estate,
To bear it out, sir; better by this chance.
Except Corbaccio have a share.
CORBACCIO. Hence, varlet.
VOLPONE. You will not be a'known, sir; why, 'tis wise.
Thus do all gamesters, at all games, dissemble,
No man will seem to win. [*Exeunt* CORVINO *and* CORBACCIO.]
—Here comes my vulture,
Heaving his beak up in the air, and snuffing.

SCENE 7

[*Enter* VOLTORE.]
VOLTORE. Outstripped thus, by a parasite! a slave,
Would run on errands, and make legs[7] for crumbs!
Well, what I'll do—
VOLPONE. The court stays for your worship.
I' e'en rejoice, sir, at your worship's happiness,
And that it fell into so learnéd hands,
That understand the fingering—
VOLTORE. What do you mean?
VOLPONE. I mean to be a suitor to your worship
For the small tenement, out of reparations[8]—
That at the end of your long row of houses,
By the Pescheria[9]; it was, in Volpone's time,
Your predecessor, ere he grew diseased,

4. Exchange.
5. Too puffed up (like a loaf of bread).
6. I.e., promiscuous.
7. Bow and scrape.
8. Repair.
9. The fish market on the Grand Canal.

A handsome, pretty, customed[1] bawdy-house
As any was in Venice, none dispraised;
But fell with him. His body and that house
Decayed together.

VOLTORE. Come, sir, leave your prating.

VOLPONE. Why, if your worship give me but your hand
That I may have the refusal, I have done.
'Tis a mere toy to you, sir; candle-rents;[2]
As your learned worship knows—

VOLPONE. What do I know?

VOLPONE. Marry, no end of your wealth, sir; God decrease it!

VOLTORE. Mistaking knave! what, mock'st thou my misfortune?

VOLPONE. His blessing on your heart, sir; would 'twere more!— [*Exit* VOLTORE.]
—Now to my first again, at the next corner. [*Exit.*]

SCENE 8. [*Another part of the street.*]

[*Enter* CORBACCIO *and* CORVINO;—MOSCA *passes over the stage, before them.*]

CORBACCIO. See, in our habit![3] see the impudent varlet!

CORVINO. That I could shoot mine eyes at him, like gun-stones!

[*Enter* VOLPONE.]

VOLPONE. But is this true, sir, of the parasite?

CORBACCIO. Again, to afflict us! monster!

VOLPONE. In good faith, sir,
I'm heartily grieved, a beard of your grave length
Should be so over-reached. I never brooked[4]
That parasite's hair; methought his nose should cozen.
There still was somewhat in his look, did promise
The bane of a clarissimo.[5]

CORBACCIO. Knave—

VOLPONE. Methinks
Yet you, that are so traded in the world,
A witty merchant, the fine bird, Corvino,
That have such moral emblems on your name,
Should not have sung your shame, and dropped your cheese,
To let the fox laugh at your emptiness.[6]

CORVINO. Sirrah, you think the privilege of the place,
And your red saucy cap, that seems to me
Nailed to your jolt-head[7] with those two sequins,
Can warrant your abuses. Come you hither;
You shall perceive, sir, I dare beat you; approach.

VOLPONE. No haste, sir, I do know your valor well,
Since you durst publish what you are, sir.[8]

1. Well patronized; "none dispraised": without prejudice to any of the other splendid bawdy houses in Venice.
2. I.e., mere drippings and leftovers, enough to buy candles with.
3. I.e., in the clothes we aristocrats are accustomed to wear.
4. Could stand.
5. I.e., trouble for an aristocrat.
6. The recurrent refrain from Aesop's fable.
7. Blockhead.
8. A cuckold, liable to run "horn-mad."

CORVINO. Tarry,
I'd speak with you.
VOLPONE. Sir, sir, another time—
CORVINO. Nay, now.
VOLPONE. O lord, sir! I were a wise man,
Would stand the fury of a distracted cuckold. [*As he is running off, re-enter* MOSCA.]
CORBACCIO. What, come again!
VOLPONE. Upon 'em, Mosca; save me.
CORBACCIO. The air's infected where he breathes.
CORVINO. Let's fly him.
[*Exeunt* CORVINO *and* CORBACCIO.]
VOLPONE. Excellent basilisk![9] turn upon the vulture.

SCENE 9

[*Enter* VOLTORE.]
VOLTORE. Well, flesh-fly, it is summer with you now;
Your winter will come on.
MOSCA. Good advocate,
Prithee not rail, nor threaten out of place thus;
Thou'lt make a solecism, as madam says.[1]
Get you a biggen[2] more; your brain breaks loose. [*Exit.*]
VOLTORE. Well sir.
VOLPONE. Would you have me beat the insolent slave,
Throw dirt upon his first good clothes?
VOLTORE. This same
Is doubtless some familiar.
VOLPONE. Sir, the court,
In troth, stays for you. I am mad, a mule
That never read Justinian,[3] should get up,
And ride an advocate. Had you no quirk
To avoid gullage,[4] sir, by such a creature?
I hope you do but jest; he has not done it;
This's but confederacy,[5] to blind the rest.
You are the heir?
VOLTORE. A strange, officious,
Troublesome knave! thou dost torment me.
VOLPONE. I know—
It cannot be, sir, that you should be cozened;
'Tis not within the wit of man to do it;
You are so wise, so prudent; and 'tis fit
That wealth and wisdom still should go together.
[*Exeunt.*]

9. A mythical creature that kills with its glance.
1. The "solecism" of Lady Politic is above, IV 2.
2. A little skullcap worn by lawyers.
3. I.e., Mosca, wholly ignorant of the legal codes compiled by the Emperor Justinian.
4. Deceit.
5. Conspiracy, trickery.

SCENE 10. *The Scrutineo.*

[*Enter* AVOCATORI, NOTARIO, BONARIO, CELIA, CORBACCIO, CORVINO, COMMENDATORI, SAFFI, *&c.*]

1 AVOCATORE. Are all the parties here?

NOTARIO. All but the advocate.

2 AVOCATORE. And here he comes.

[*Enter* VOLTORE *and* VOLPONE.]

1 AVOCATORE. Then bring them forth to sentence.

VOLTORE. O, my most honored fathers, let your mercy
Once win upon your justice, to forgive—
I am distracted——

VOLPONE. [*Aside.*] What will he do now?

VOLTORE. O,
I know not which to address myself to first;
Whether your fatherhoods, or these innocents—

CORVINO. [*aside*] Will he betray himself?

VOLTORE. Whom equally
I have abused, out of most covetous ends—

CORVINO. The man is mad!

CORBACCIO. What's that?

CORVINO. He is possessed

VOLTORE. For which, now struck in conscience, here I prostrate
Myself at your offended feet, for pardon.

1, 2 AVOCATORI. Arise.

CELIA. O heaven, how just thou art!

VOLPONE. [*Aside.*] I am caught
In mine own noose—

CORVINO [*To* CORBACCIO] Be constant, sir; naught now
Can help, but impudence.

1 AVOCATORE. Speak forward.

COMMENDATORE. Silence!

VOLTORE. It is not passion in me, reverend fathers,
But only conscience, conscience, my good sires,
That makes me now tell truth. That parasite,
That knave, hath been the instrument of all.

1 AVOCATORE. Where is that knave? fetch him.

VOLPONE. I go. [*Exit.*]

CORVINO. Grave fathers,
This man's distracted; he confessed it now;
For, hoping to be old Volpone's heir,
Who now is dead—

3 AVOCATORE. How!

2 AVOCATORE. Is Volpone dead?

CORVINO. Dead since, grave fathers.

BONARIO. O sure vengeance!

1 AVOCATORE. Stay,
Then he was no deceiver.

VOLTORE. O no, none;

The parasite, grave fathers.
CORVINO. He does speak
Out of mere envy, 'cause the servant's made
The thing he gaped for. Please your fatherhoods,
This is the truth, though I'll not justify
The other,[6] but he may be some-deal faulty.
VOLTORE. Ay, to your hopes, as well as mine, Corvino.
But I'll use modesty. Pleaseth your wisdoms,
To view these certain notes, and but confer them;
As I hope favor, they shall speak clear truth.
CORVINO. The devil has entered him!
BONARIO. Or bides in you.
4 AVOCATORE. We have done ill, by a public officer
To send for him, if he be heir.
2 AVOCATORE. For whom?
4 AVOCATORE. Him that they call the parasite.
3 AVOCATORE. 'Tis true,
He is a man of great estate, now left.[7]
4 AVOCATORE. Go you, and learn his name, and say, the court
Entreats his presence here, but to the clearing
Of some few doubts. [*Exit* NOTARIO.]
2 AVOCATORE. This same's a labyrinth!
1 AVOCATORE. Stand you unto your first report?
CORVINO. My state,
My life, my fame—
BONARIO. Where is it?
CORVINO. Are at the stake.
1 AVOCATORE. Is yours so too?
CORBACCIO. The advocate's a knave,
And has a forkéd tongue—
2 AVOCATORE. Speak to the point.
CORBACCIO. So is the parasite too.
1 AVOCATORE. This is confusion.
VOLTORE. I do beseech your fatherhoods, read but those—
[*giving them papers.*]
CORVINO. And credit nothing the false spirit hath writ;
It cannot be, but he's possessed,[8] grave fathers.

SCENE 11. *A Street.*

[*Enter* VOLPONE.]
VOLPONE. To make a snare for mine own neck! and run
My head into it, wilfully! with laughter!
When I had newly 'scaped, was free, and clear!
Out of mere wantonness! O, the dull devil
Was in this brain of mine, when I devised it,
And Mosca gave it second; he must now

6. I.e., Mosca.
7. As an aristocrat (which he automatically is if he has a lot of money), Mosca is not to be summoned by a common official.
8. I.e., demonically possessed by a devil inside him (not wholly incredible in those days, when witchcraft was an accepted fact).

Help to sear up this vein,[9] or we bleed dead.
[*Enter* NANO, ANDROGYNO, *and* CASTRONE.]
How now! who let you loose? whither go you now?
What? to buy gingerbread, or to drown kitlings?
NANO. Sir, Master Mosca called us out of doors,
And bid us all go play, and took the keys.
ANDROGYNO. Yes.
VOLPONE. Did Master Mosca take the keys? why, so!
I'm farther in. These are my fine conceits!
I must be merry, with a mischief to me!
What a vile wretch was I, that could not bear
My fortune soberly! I must have my crotchets,
And my conundrums! Well, go you, and seek him.
His meaning may be truer than my fear.
Bid him, he straight come to me to the court;
Thither will I, and, if't be possible,
Unscrew my advocate, upon new hopes.
When I provoked him, then I lost myself. [*Exeunt.*]

SCENE 12. *The Scrutineo.*

[AVOCATORI, BONARIO, CELIA, CORBACCIO, CORVINO, COMMENDATORI, SAFFI, *&c. as before.*]

1 AVOCATORE. [*showing the papers*] These things can ne'er be reconciled. He here
Professeth that the gentleman was wronged,
And that the gentlewoman was brought thither,
Forced by her husband, and there left.
VOLTORE. Most true.
CELIA. How ready is heaven to those that pray!
1 AVOCATORE. But that
Volpone would have ravished her, he holds
Utterly false, knowing his impotence.
CORVINO. Grave fathers, he's possessed; again, I say,
Possessed; nay, if there be possession and
Obsession, he has both.[1]
3 AVOCATORE. Here comes our officer.
[*Enter* VOLPONE, *still in disguise.*]
VOLPONE. The parasite will straight be here, grave fathers.
4 AVOCATORE. You might invent some other name, sir varlet.
3 AVOCATORE. Did not the notary meet him?
VOLPONE. Not that I know.
4 AVOCATORE. His coming will clear all.
2 AVOCATORE. Yet, it is misty.
VOLTORE. May't please your fatherhoods.
VOLPONE. [*whispers to* VOLTORE] Sir, the parasite
Willed me to tell you, that his master lives;
That you are still the man; your hopes the same;

9. Cautery was frequent medical procedure in the days before antisepsis.

1. Possession is a devil attacking the mind from within, obsession is the same temptation from without.

And this was only a jest—

VOLTORE. How?

VOLPONE. Sir, to try
If you were firm, and how you stood affected.

VOLTORE. Art sure he lives?

VOLPONE. Do I live, sir?

VOLTORE. O me!
I was too violent.

VOLPONE. Sir, you may redeem it.
They said you were possessed; fall down, and seem so.
I'll help to make it good. [VOLTORE *falls.*] —God bless the man!
[*aside*] Stop your wind hard, and swell.—See, see, see, see!
He vomits crooked pins![2] his eyes are set,
Like a dead hare's hung in a poulter's[3] shop!
His mouth's running away! Do you see, signor?
Now it is in his belly.

CORVINO. Ay, the devil!

VOLPONE. Now in his throat.

CORVINO. Ay, I perceive it plain.

VOLPONE. 'Twill out, 'twill out! stand clear!
See where it flies,
In shape of a blue toad with a bat's wings!
Do not you see it, sir?

CORBACCIO. What? I think I do.

CORVINO. 'Tis too manifest.

VOLPONE. Look! he comes to himself!

VOLTORE. Where am I?

VOLPONE. Take good heart, the worst is past, sir.
You are dispossessed.

1 AVOCATORE. What accident is this?

2 AVOCATORE. Sudden and full of wonder!

3 AVOCATORE. If he were
Possessed, as it appears, all this is nothing. [*He waves the notes.*]

CORVINO. He has been often subject to these fits.

1 AVOCATORE. Show him that writing. —Do you know it, sir?

VOLPONE. [*whispers to* VOLTORE] Deny it, sir, forswear it; know it not.

VOLTORE. Yes, I do know it well, it is my hand;
But all that it contains is false.

BONARIO. O practice![4]

2 AVOCATORE. What maze is this?

1 AVOCATORE. Is he not guilty then,
Whom you there name the parasite?

VOLTORE. Grave fathers,
No more than his good patron, old Volpone.

2. The symptoms that Volpone "sees," and persuades others to see, were standard. The "blue toad with bat's wings" below is the demon himself.
3. A dealer in fowl and small game.
4. Deceit.

4 AVOCATORE. Why, he is dead.
VOLTORE. O no, my honored fathers,
He lives—
1 AVOCATORE. How! Lives?
VOLTORE. Lives.
2 AVOCATORE. This is subtler yet!
3 AVOCATORE. You said he was dead.
VOLTORE. Never.
AVOCATORE. [*To* CORVINO] You said so!
CORVINO. I heard so.
4 AVOCATORE. Here comes the gentleman; make him way.[5]
[*Enter* MOSCA *as a clarissimo.*]
3 AVOCATORE. A stool.
4 AVOCATORE. [*aside*] A proper man; and, were Volpone dead,
A fit match for my daughter.
3 AVOCATORE. Give him way.
VOLPONE. [*aside to* MOSCA] Mosca, I was almost lost; the advocate
Had betrayed all; but now it is recovered;
All's on the hinge again—say, I am living.
MOSCA. What busy knave is this! Most reverend fathers,
I sooner had attended your grave pleasures,
But that my order for the funeral
Of my dear patron did require me—
VOLPONE. [*aside*] Mosca!
MOSCA. Whom I intend to bury like a gentleman.
VOLPONE. [*aside*] Ay, quick,[6] and cozen me of all.
2 AVOCATORE. Still stranger!
More intricate!
1 AVOCATORE. And come about again!
4 AVOCATORE. [*aside*] It is a match, my daughter is bestowed.
MOSCA. [*aside to* VOLPONE] Will you give me half?
VOLPONE. First, I'll be hanged.
MOSCA. I know
Your voice is good, cry not so loud.
1 AVOCATORE. Demand
The advocate.—Sir, did you not affirm
Volpone was alive?
VOLPONE. Yes, and he is;
This gentleman[7] told me so. [*aside to* MOSCA] Thou shalt have half.
MOSCA. Whose drunkard is this same? speak, some that know him:
I never saw his face. [*aside to* VOLPONE] I cannot now
Afford it you so cheap.
VOLPONE. No!
1 AVOCATORE. [*To* VOLTORE] What say you?

5. Jonson's audience would be scandalized at the instant transformation of a parasite into a gentleman, partly because they had seen it happen frequently in their own land.
6. Alive.
7. I.e., Mosca.

The officer told me.

VOLTORE. I did, grave fathers,
And will maintain he lives, with mine own life,
And that this creature [*points to* MOSCA] told me. [*aside*] I was born
With all good stars my enemies.

MOSCA. Most grave fathers,
If such an insolence as this must pass
Upon me, I am silent: 'twas not this
For which you sent, I hope.

2 AVOCATORE. Take him away.

VOLPONE. [*aside*] Mosca!

3 AVOCATORE. Let him be whipped.

VOLPONE. Wilt thou betray me?
Cozen me?

3 AVOCATORE. And taught to bear himself
Toward a person of his rank.
Away. [*The* OFFICERS *seize* VOLPONE.]

MOSCA. I humbly thank your fatherhoods.

VOLPONE. [*aside*] Soft, soft. Whipped!
And lose all that I have! If I confess,
It cannot be much more.

4 AVOCATORE. Sir, are you married?[8]

VOLPONE. They'll be allied anon; I must be resolute.
The fox shall here uncase.[9] [*Throws off his disguise.*]

MOSCA. Patron!

VOLPONE. Nay, now
My ruins shall not come alone; your match
I'll hinder sure: my substance shall not glue you
Nor screw you into a family.

MOSCA. Why, patron!

VOLPONE. I am Volpone, and this [*pointing to* MOSCA] is my knave;
This, [*To* VOLTORE] his own knave; this, [*To* CORBACCIO] avarice's fool;
This, [*To* CORVINO] a chimera[1] of wittol, fool, and knave.
And, reverend fathers, since we all can hope
Nought but a sentence, let's not now despair it.
You hear me brief.

CORVINO. May it please your fatherhoods—

COMMENDATORE. Silence!

1 AVOCATORE. The knot is now undone by miracle.

2 AVOCATORE. Nothing can be more clear.

3 AVOCATORE. Or can more prove
These innocent.

1 ADVOCATORE. Give them their liberty.

BONARIO. Heaven could not long let such gross crimes be hid.

8. The question is addressed to Mosca.
9. Remove his mask.
1. The chimera was an unnatural imaginary creature compounded of lion, goat, and serpent.

2 AVOCATORE. If this be held the highway to get riches,
May I be poor!
3 AVOCATORE. This is not gain, but torment.
1 AVOCATORE. These possess wealth, as sick men possess fevers.
Which trulier may be said to possess them.[2]
2 AVOCATORE. Disrobe that parasite.
CORVINO, MOSCA. Most honored fathers!
1 AVOCATORE. Can you plead aught to stay the course of justice?
If you can, speak.
CORVINO, VOLTORE. We beg favor.
CELIA. And mercy.
1 AVOCATORE. You hurt your innocence, suing for the guilty.
Stand forth; and first, the parasite. You appear
T'have been the chiefest minister, if not plotter,
In all these lewd impostures; and now, lastly,
Have with your impudence abused the court,
And habit of a gentleman of Venice,
Being a fellow of no birth or blood:[3]
For which our sentence is, first, thou be whipped;
Then live perpetual prisoner in our galleys.
VOLPONE. I thank you for him.
MOSCA. Bane[4] to thy wolfish nature!
1 AVOCATORE. Deliver him to the Saffi. [MOSCA *is led out.*] —Thou, Volpone,
By blood and rank a gentleman, canst not fall
Under like censure; but our judgment on thee
Is, that thy substance all be straight confiscate
To the hospital of the Incurabili.[5]
And, since the most was gotten by imposture,
By feigning lame, gout, palsy, and such diseases,
Thou art to lie in prison, cramped with irons,
Till thou be'st sick and lame indeed. Remove him. [*He is taken away.*]
VOLPONE. This is called mortifying of a fox.
1 AVOCATORE. Thou, Voltore, to take away the scandal
Thou hast given all worthy men of thy profession,
Art banished from their fellowship, and our state.
Corbaccio!—bring him near—we here possess
Thy son of all thy state,[6] and confine thee
To the monastery of San Spirito;
Where, since thou knew'st not how to live well here,
Thou shalt be learned[7] to die well.

2. The aphorism is Seneca's (Epistle 119, par. 12).

3. Justice in Venice makes no pretense to equality; Mosca's sentence is most severe, and for snob reasons.

4. Poison. It was legitimate to poison wolves, not foxes. "Saffi": guards.

5. There was a Hospital of the Incurables in Venice, but the sentence carries an irony: these are the only people in Venice who can be trusted with money. The diseases to be picked up in Venetian jails were no joke; the Stinche, so called, were the most horrible dungeons in all Europe.

6. I.e., convey to your son your entire estate.

7. Taught.

CORBACCIO. Ha! what said he?
COMMENDATORE. You shall know anon, sir.
1 AVOCATORE. Thou, Corvino, shalt
Be straight embarked from thine own house, and rowed
Round about Venice, through the Grand Canal,
Wearing a cap with fair long ass's ears
Instead of horns; and so to mount, a paper
Pinned on thy breast, to the Berlina[8]——
CORVINO. Yes,
And have mine eyes beat out with stinking fish,
Bruised fruit, and rotten eggs—'Tis well. I'm glad
I shall not see my shame yet.
1 AVOCATORE. And to expiate
Thy wrongs done to thy wife, thou art to send her
Home to her father, with her dowry trebled:
And these are all your judgments—
ALL. Honored fathers.
1 AVOCATORE. Which may not be revoked. Now you begin,
When crimes are done, and past, and to be punished,
To think what your crimes are: away with them!
Let all that see these vices thus rewarded,
Take heart, and love to study 'em! Mischiefs feed
Like beasts, till they be fat, and then they bleed. [*Exeunt.*]
[VOLPONE *comes forward.*]
The seasoning of a play is the applause.
Now, though the fox be punished by the laws,
He yet doth hope, there is no suffering due,
For any fact which he hath done 'gainst you;
If there be, censure him; here he doubtful stands:
If not, fare jovially, and clap your hands. [*Exit.*]

1606

To Penshurst[1]

Thou art not, Penshurst, built to envious show,
Of touch[2] or marble; nor canst boast a row
Of polished pillars, or a roof of gold;
Thou hast no lantern, whereof tales are told,
Or stair, or courts; but stand'st an ancient pile,
And, these grudged at,[3] art reverenced the while.
Thou joy'st in better marks, of soil, of air,

8. Pillory.

1. The country seat of the Sidney family (famous for Sir Philip) in Kent; Jonson's is one of the first English poems celebrating a specific place (later examples are *Cooper's Hill* by John Denham and *Windsor Forest* by Alexander Pope).

2. Touchstone, i.e., basanite, a pure black, finely grained, and therefore expensive variety of basalt. "Lantern": cupola.

3. More pretentious houses are criticized.

Of wood, of water; therein thou art fair.
Thou hast thy walks for health, as well as sport;
Thy mount, to which the dryads[4] do resort,
Where Pan and Bacchus their high feasts have made,
Beneath the broad beech and the chestnut shade;
That taller tree, which of a nut was set
At his great birth where all the Muses met.[5]
There in the writhéd bark are cut the names
Of many a sylvan, taken with his flames;[6]
And thence the ruddy satyrs oft provoke
The lighter fauns to reach thy Lady's Oak.[7]
Thy copse too, named of Gamage,[8] thou hast there,
That never fails to serve thee seasoned deer
When thou wouldst feast or exercise thy friends.
The lower land, that to the river bends,
Thy sheep, thy bullocks, kine, and calves do feed;
The middle grounds thy mares and horses breed.
Each bank doth yield thee conies;[9] and the tops,
Fertile of wood, Ashore and Sidney's copse,[1]
To crown thy open table, doth provide
The purpled pheasant with the speckled side;
The painted partridge lies in every field,
And for thy mess is willing to be killed.
And if the high-swollen Medway[2] fail thy dish,
Thou hast thy ponds, that pay thee tribute fish,
Fat aged carps that run into thy net,
And pikes, now weary their own kind to eat,
As loath the second draught or cast to stay,
Officiously at first themselves betray;
Bright eels that emulate them, and leap on land
Before the fisher, or into his hand.
Then hath thy orchard fruit, thy garden flowers,
Fresh as the air, and new as are the hours.
The early cherry, with the later plum,
Fig, grape, and quince, each in his time doth come;
The blushing apricot and woolly peach
Hang on thy walls, that every child may reach.
And though thy walls be of the country stone,
They are reared with no man's ruin, no man's groan;
There's none that dwell about them wish them down;
But all come in, the farmer and the clown,[3]

4. Wood nymphs.
5. Sir Philip Sidney was born at Penshurst; an oak tree, planted the day of his birth, is still shown as "Sidney's oak."
6. Woodsman, in love because of reading Sidney's sonnets.
7. Lady Leicester's oak, named after a lady of the house who once entered into labor under its branches. "Provoke": challenge to a race.
8. Lady Barbara Gamage gave her name to a grove near the entrance of the park.
9. Rabbits.
1. "Ashore and Sidney's copse" are little woods and spinneys, lovingly enumerated by Jonson. They still survive, under their ancient names.
2. The local river.
3. Yokel.

And no one empty-handed, to salute
Thy lord and lady, though they have no suit.
Some bring a capon, some a rural cake,
Some nuts, some apples; some that think they make
The better cheeses bring them, or else send
By their ripe daughters, whom they would commend
This way to husbands, and whose baskets bear
An emblem of themselves in plum or pear.
But what can this (more than express their love)
Add to thy free provisions, far above
The need of such? whose liberal board doth flow
With all that hospitality doth know;
Where comes no guest but is allowed to eat,
Without his fear, and of thy lord's own meat;
Where the same beer and bread, and selfsame wine,
That is his lordship's shall be also mine,
And I not fain to sit (as some this day
At great men's tables), and yet dine away.[4]
Here no man tells[5] my cups; nor, standing by,
A waiter doth my gluttony envy,
But gives me what I call, and lets me eat;
He knows below he shall find plenty of meat.
Thy tables hoard not up for the next day;
Nor, when I take my lodging, need I pray
For fire, or lights, or livery;[6] all is there,
As if thou then wert mine, or I reigned here:
There's nothing I can wish, for which I stay.[7]
That found King James when, hunting late this way
With his brave son, the prince, they saw thy fires
Shine bright on every hearth, as the desires
Of thy Penates[8] had been set on flame
To entertain them; or the country came
With all their zeal to warm their welcome here.
What (great I will not say, but) sudden cheer
Didst thou then make 'em! and what praise was heaped
On thy good lady then, who therein reaped
The just reward of her high housewifery;
To have her linen, plate, and all things nigh,
When she was far; and not a room but dressed
As if it had expected such a guest!
These, Penshurst, are thy praise, and yet not all.
Thy lady's noble, fruitful, chaste withal.
His children thy great lord may call his own,
A fortune in this age but rarely known.
They are, and have been, taught religion; thence

4. Because the tables were so large, different courses might be served at different ends—hence the possibility of sitting at a man's table, yet dining away.
5. Counts.
6. Rations, food.
7. Wait.
8. Roman household gods. A room in the house is still known as "King James's room."

Their gentler spirits have sucked innocence.
Each morn and even they are taught to pray,
With the whole household, and may, every day,
Read in their virtuous parents' noble parts
The mysteries of manners, arms, and arts.
Now, Penshurst, they that will proportion[9] thee
With other edifices, when they see
Those proud, ambitious heaps, and nothing else,
May say their lords have built, but thy lord dwells.

1616

Inviting a Friend to Supper

Tonight, grave sir, both my poor house and I
Do equally desire your company:
Not that we think us worthy such a guest,
But that your worth will dignify our feast
With those that come; whose grace may make that seem
Something, which else could hope for no esteem.
It is the fair acceptance, Sir, creates
The entertainment perfect: not the cates.[1]
Yet shall you have, to rectify your palate,
An olive, capers, or some better salad
Ushering the mutton; with a short-legged hen,
If we can get her, full of eggs, and then
Lemons and wine for sauce; to these, a coney
Is not to be despaired of for our money;
And though fowl now be scarce, yet there are clerks,[2]
The sky not falling, think we may have larks.
I'll tell you of more, and lie, so you will come:
Of partridge, pheasant, wood-cock, of which some
May yet be there; and godwit if we can,
Knot, rail, and ruff, too.[3] Howsoe'er, my man
Shall read a piece of Virgil, Tacitus,
Livy, or of some better book to us,
Of which we'll speak our minds amidst our meat;
And I'll profess[4] no verses to repeat.
To this, if aught appear which I not know of,
That will the pastry, not my paper, show off.[5]
Digestive cheese and fruit there sure will be;
But that which most doth take my muse and me
Is a pure cup of rich Canary wine,
Which is the Mermaid's[6] now, but shall be mine;

9. Compare.
1. Dishes.
2. Scholars; pronounced "clarks." A "coney" is a rabbit.
3. The treat of the feast will be these various game-birds respectively curlew, snipe, sandpiper, and corn crake.
4. Undertake, promise.
5. Jonson's promise not to recite his poetry is ironically qualified; poems may appear, but they will be on sheets of paper under pies, not for declamation.
6. The Mermaid tavern, famous haunt of the poets; sweet wine from the Canary Islands was very popular in England. Horace and Anacreon (the one in Latin, the other in Greek) wrote many poems in praise of good wine.

Of which, had Horace or Anacreon tasted,
  Their lives, as do their lines, till now had lasted.
Tobacco, Nectar, or the Thespian spring
  Are all but Luther's beer to this I sing.[7]
Of this we will sup free but moderately,
  And we will have no Pooly or Parrot[8] by,
Nor shall our cups make any guilty men,
  But at our parting we shall be as when
We innocently met. No simple word
  That shall be uttered at our mirthful board
Shall make us sad next morning; or affright
  The liberty that we'll enjoy tonight.

1616

An Ode

High-spirited friend,
I send nor balms nor cor'sives[1] to your wound,
  Your fate hath found
A gentler and more agile hand to tend
The cure of that, which is but corporal;
And doubtful days (which were named "critical")
  Have made their fairest flight,
  And now are out of sight.
Yet doth some wholesome physic for the mind
  Wrapped in this paper lie,[2]
Which in the taking if you mis-apply,
  You are unkind.

Your covetous hand,
Happy in that fair honor it hath gained,
  Must now be reined.
True valor doth her own renown command
In one full action; nor have you now more
To do, than be a husband[3] of that store.
  Think but how dear you bought
  This same which you have caught,
Such thoughts will make you more in love with truth.
  'Tis wisdom, and that high,

7. The Thespian spring is Castalia, haunt of the muses; compared to Canary, all these other intoxicants are no better than Luther's beer, i.e.. weak stuff.

8. Pooly and Parrot were government spies though their conjunction also suggests a talkative bird, Poll Parrot. Jonson, as a Roman Catholic, had reason to be wary of undercover agents.

1. Balms would be soothing, as "cor'sives" (corrosives) would be irritating medications.

2. The situation is that the friend has been wounded in a duel. Now that the critical days are past, the lady over whom it was fought ("a gentler and more agile hand") will cure the wounded warrior's body. Jonson has a medication ("physic") for his mind.

3. Guardian, protector.

For men to use their fortune reverently,
Even in youth.

1640

To Lucy, Countess of Bedford, with Mr. Donne's Satires[4]

Lucy, you brightness of our sphere, who are
Life of the Muses' day, their morning star!
If works, not th' authors, their own grace should look,
Whose poems would not wish to be your book?
But these, desired by you, the maker's ends
Crown with their own. Rare poems ask rare friends.
Yet satires, since the most of mankind be
Their unavoided subject, fewest see:
For none e'er took that pleasure in sin's sense,
But, when they heard it taxed, took more offense.
They then that, living where the matter is bred,
Dare for these poems yet both ask and read
And like them too, must needfully, though few,
Be of the best: and 'mongst those, best are you;
Lucy, you brightness of our sphere, who are
The Muses' evening, as their morning star.

1616

Slow, Slow, Fresh Fount[1]

Slow, slow, fresh fount, keep time with my salt tears;
Yet slower, yet, O faintly, gentle springs!
List to the heavy part the music bears,
Woe weeps out her division,[2] when she sings.
Droop herbs and flowers;
Fall grief in showers;
Our beauties are not ours.
O, I could still,
Like melting snow upon some craggy hill,
Drop, drop, drop, drop,[3]
Since nature's pride is now a withered daffodil.

1600

4. Lucy, Countess of Bedford, was a famous patroness of the age, to whom both Jonson and Donne addressed a number of poems. Jonson's basic conceit is that you have to be a good person to read satire without twinges of conscience; since Lucy asks for the strongest satires, she must be the best person. What he was offering her was not, of course, a bound volume of Donne's satires; this was simply a manuscript collection, such as passed commonly from hand to hand in court circles.

1. From the satiric comedy *Cynthia's Revels* (1600). It deals with the sin of self-love, and this famous lyric is a lament sung by Echo for Narcissus, who was entranced by his own image and ultimately transformed into a flower.

2. Grief, but also a rapid, melodic passage of music.

3. This line shows how far Jonson could go in adapting his verse to the needs of a composer.

Queen and Huntress[1]

Queen and huntress, chaste and fair,
Now the sun is laid to sleep,
Seated in thy silver chair,
State in wonted manner keep;
Hesperus entreats thy light,
Goddess excellently bright.

Earth, let not thy envious shade
Dare itself to interpose;
Cynthia's shining orb was made
Heaven to clear, when day did close.
Bless us then with wishèd sight,
Goddess excellently bright.

Lay thy bow of pearl apart,
And thy crystal-shining quiver;
Give unto the flying hart
Space to breathe, how short soever.
Thou that mak'st a day of night,
Goddess excellently bright.

1600

Song: To Celia[2]

Drink to me only with thine eyes,
And I will pledge with mine;
Or leave a kiss but in the cup,
And I'll not look for wine.
The thirst that from the soul doth rise,
Doth ask a drink divine:
But might I of Jove's nectar sup,
I would not change for thine.

I sent thee late a rosy wreath,
Not so much honoring thee,
As giving it a hope, that there
It could not withered be.
But thou thereon did'st only breathe,
And sent'st it back to me;
Since when it grows and smells, I swear,
Not of itself, but thee.

1616

1. Also from *Cynthia's Revels*, this song is sung by Hesperus, the evening star, to Cynthia, or Diana, goddess of chastity and the moon—with whom Queen Elizabeth was, almost automatically, equated.

2. These famous lines are a patchwork of five separate passages in the *Epistles* of Philostratus, a Greek sophist of the 3rd century A.D. Jonson very carefully reworded the phrases (there are several early MS. versions of the poem) into this classic lyric.

In the Person of Woman-kind

A SONG APOLOGETIC

Men, if you love us, play no more
  The fools or tyrants with your friends,
To make us still sing o'er and o'er
  Our own false praises for your ends:
    We have both wits and fancies too,
    And if we must, let's sing of you.

Nor do we doubt but that we can,
  If we would search with care and pain,
Find some one good in some one man;
  So going thorough[1] all your strain,
    We shall at last of parcels make
    One good enough for a song's sake.

And as a cunning painter takes
  In any curious piece you see
More pleasure while the thing he makes
  Than when 'tis made, why so will we.
    And having pleased our art, we'll try
    To make a new, and hang that by.

On My First Daughter

Here lies, to each her parents' ruth,[2]
Mary, the daughter of their youth;
Yet all heaven's gifts being heaven's due,
It makes the father less to rue.
At six months' end she parted hence
With safety of her innocence;
Whose soul heaven's queen, whose name she bears,
In comfort of her mother's tears,
Hath placed amongst her virgin-train:
Where, while that severed doth remain,
This grave partakes the fleshly birth;
Which cover lightly, gentle earth!

1616

On My First Son

Farewell, thou child of my right hand,[3] and joy;
My sin was too much hope of thee, loved boy:

1. "Thorough" could be used for "through" in the 17th century when the meter required it.
2. Grief. There is no sure identification of Jonson's daughter, nor a positive date of composition for the poem.
3. "Child of the right hand" is a literal translation of the Hebrew name "Benjamin," which implies the meanings "dexterous" or "fortunate." The boy was born in 1596, and died on his birthday in 1603.

Seven years thou wert lent to me, and I thee pay,
Exacted by thy fate, on the just day.
O could I lose all father[4] now! for why
Will man lament the state he should envy,
To have so soon 'scaped world's and flesh's rage,
And, if no other misery, yet age?
Rest in soft peace, and asked, say, "Here doth lie
Ben Jonson his best piece of poetry."
For whose sake henceforth all his vows be such
As what he loves may never like too much.[5]

1616

Epitaph on Elizabeth, L. H.[6]

Wouldst thou hear what man can say
In a little? Reader, stay.
Underneath this stone doth lie
As much beauty as could die;
Which in life did harbor give
To more virtue than doth live.
If at all she had a fault,
Leave it buried in this vault.
One name was Elizabeth;
Th' other, let it sleep with death:
Fitter, where it died, to tell,
Than that it lived at all. Farewell!

1616

To the Memory of My Beloved Master William Shakespeare

AND WHAT HE HATH LEFT US[1]

To draw no envy, Shakespeare, on thy name,
Am I thus ample to thy book and fame,
While I confess thy writings to be such
As neither man nor Muse can praise too much.
'Tis true, and all men's suffrage.[2] But these ways
Were not the paths I meant unto thy praise:
For silliest ignorance on these may light,
Which, when it sounds at best, but echoes right;
Or blind affection,[3] which doth ne'er advance
The truth, but gropes, and urgeth all by chance;
Or crafty malice might pretend this praise,
And think to ruin where it seemed to raise.

4. Relinquish all thoughts of being a father.

5. The obscure grammar of the last lines seems to refer back to the feeling in line 2, that too much affection is fatal to the loved one.

6. The subject of this epitaph may have been Elizabeth, Lady Hatton; but, in fact, her name has slept with death.

1. This poem was prefixed to the first folio of Shakespeare's plays, published in 1623.

2. Agreement, consent.

3. Prejudice.

These are as some infamous bawd or whore
Should praise a matron. What could hurt her more?
But thou art proof against them, and, indeed,
Above th' ill fortune of them, or the need.
I therefore will begin. Soul of the age!
The applause! delight! the wonder of our stage!
My Shakespeare, rise; I will not lodge thee by
Chaucer or Spenser, or bid Beaumont lie
A little further to make thee a room:[4]
Thou art a monument without a tomb,
And art alive still while thy book doth live,
And we have wits to read and praise to give.
That I not mix thee so, my brain excuses,
I mean with great, but disproportioned[5] Muses;
For, if I thought my judgment were of years,
I should commit thee surely with thy peers,
And tell how far thou didst our Lyly outshine,
Or sporting Kyd, or Marlowe's mighty line.[6]
And though thou hadst small Latin and less Greek,[7]
From thence to honor thee I would not seek
For names, but call forth thund'ring Aeschylus,
Euripides, and Sophocles to us,
Pacuvius, Accius, him of Cordova dead,[8]
To life again, to hear thy buskin[9] tread
And shake a stage; or, when thy socks were on,
Leave thee alone for the comparison
Of all that insolent Greece or haughty Rome
Sent forth, or since did from their ashes come.
Triumph, my Britain; thou hast one to show
To whom all scenes[1] of Europe homage owe.
He was not of an age, but for all time!
And all the Muses still were in their prime
When like Apollo he came forth to warm
Our ears, or like a Mercury to charm.
Nature herself was proud of his designs,
And joyed to wear the dressing of his lines,
Which were so richly spun, and woven so fit,
As, since, she will vouchsafe no other wit:
The merry Greek, tart Aristophanes,

4. Chaucer, Spenser, and Francis Beaumont were buried in Westminster Abbey; Shakespeare, of course, in Stratford. Jonson endorses the separation; Shakespeare should not be crowded.

5. Not comparable.

6. John Lyly, Thomas Kyd, and Christopher Marlowe, Elizabethan dramatists put in the shade by Shakespeare.

7. Shakespeare had, by modern standards, a very adequate command of Latin; Jonson is speaking from the lofty height of his own remarkable scholarship. Shakespeare's French and Italian (he was competent in both tongues) Jonson does not think worthy of mention.

8. Marcus Pacuvius and Lucius Accius (2nd century B.C.) and "him of Cordova," Seneca the Younger (1st century A.D.), the greatest of the Latin tragedians. Only fragments survive of the plays of Pacuvius and Accius; Jonson's comparisons are more pedantic, in these instances, than relevant.

9. The symbol of tragedy, as contrasted with "socks" (in the next line), symbols of comedy.

1. Stages.

Neat Terence, witty Plautus[2] now not please,
But antiquated and deserted lie,
As they were not of Nature's family.
Yet must I not give Nature all; thy Art,
My gentle Shakespeare, must enjoy a part.
For though the poet's matter Nature be,
His Art doth give the fashion;[3] and that he
Who casts to write a living line must sweat
(Such as thine are) and strike the second heat
Upon the muses' anvil; turn the same,
And himself with it, that he thinks to frame,
Or for the laurel he may gain a scorn;
For a good poet's made as well as born.
And such wert thou! Look how the father's face
Lives in his issue; even so the race
Of Shakespeare's mind and manners brightly shines
In his well-turned and true-filed lines,
In each of which he seems to shake a lance,[4]
As brandished at the eyes of ignorance.
Sweet swan of Avon, what a sight it were
To see thee in our waters yet appear,
And make those flights upon the banks of Thames
That so did take Eliza and our James![5]
But stay; I see thee in the hemisphere
Advanced and made a constellation there![6]
Shine forth, thou star of poets, and with rage
Or influence[7] chide or cheer the drooping stage,
Which, since thy flight from hence, hath mourned like night,
And despairs day, but for thy volume's light.

1623

To John Donne

Donne, the delight of Phoebus and each Muse,
Who, to thy one, all other brains refuse;[1]
Whose every work, of thy most early wit,
Came forth example and remains so yet;
Longer a-knowing than most wits do live,
And which no affection praise enough can give.
To it[2] thy language, letters, arts, best life,
Which might with half mankind maintain a strife.

2. Aristophanes, the great Greek satirist and comic writer; Terence and Plautus (3rd and 2nd centuries B.C.), Roman writers of comedy.
3. Form, style. "Casts": undertakes.
a petty sum.
4. Pun on Shake-speare.
5. Queen Elizabeth and King James.
6. Heroes and demigods were typically exalted after death to a place among the stars.
7. "Rage" and "influence" describe the supposed effects of the planets on earthly affairs. "Rage" also implies poetic inspiration.
1. The word "refuse" could imply a reproach against Donne's obscurity, a notion of egotism ("refusal" involving preference of one over others), or the idea of welding (re-fusing) lesser minds to a greater.
2. The verb "add" is understood.

All which I meant to praise, and yet I would,
But leave, because I cannot as I should.

1616

To the Immortal Memory and Friendship of That Noble Pair, Sir Lucius Cary and Sir H. Morison[1]

The Turn

Brave infant of Saguntum, clear[2]
Thy coming forth in that great year
When the prodigious Hannibal did crown
His rage, with razing your immortal town.
Thou, looking then about
E'er thou wert half got out,
Wise child, didst hastily return
And mad'st thy mother's womb thine urn.
How summed a circle[3] didst thou leave mankind
Of deepest lore, could we the center find!

The Counter-Turn

Did wiser nature draw thee back
From out the horror of that sack,
Where shame, faith, honor, and regard of right
Lay trampled on?—the deeds of death and night
Urged, hurried forth, and hurled
Upon th' affrighted world?
Sword, fire, and famine, with fell fury met,
And all on utmost ruin set:
As, could they but life's miseries foresee,
No doubt all infants would return like thee.

The Stand

For what is life if measured by the space,
Not by the act?
Or maskéd man, if valued by his face,
Above his fact?
Here's one outlived his peers
and told forth fourscore years:
He vexéd time, and busied the whole state,
Troubled both foes and friends,
But ever to no ends:
What did this stirrer but die late?

1. Henry Morison died in 1629 at the age of only twenty; his good friend Lucius Cary was a year or two younger. Jonson's ode is modeled on those of Pindar, with their triple pattern of strophe, antistrophe, and epode, translated literally by Jonson as turn, counterturn, and stand. These divisions served, when the Greek odes were recited in a theater, to distinguish which part of the chorus chanted them; in English odes, they serve simply to formalize the structure.

2. Explain, describe. Pliny tells the story of the infant born while Sagunto, in Spain, was being assaulted by Hannibal; he dived back into his mother's womb (setting a record for brevity), and was buried there.

3. How complete a lesson.

How well at twenty had he fall'n or stood!
For three of his four-score, he did no good.

The Turn

He[4] entered well, by virtuous parts,
Got up and thrived with honest arts:
He purchased friends and fame and honors then,
And had his noble name advanced with men;
But, weary of that flight,
He stooped in all men's sight
To sordid flatteries, acts of strife,
And sunk in that dead sea of life
So deep, as he did then death's waters sup;
But that the cork of title buoyed him up.

The Counter-Turn

Alas, but Morison fell young;—
He never fell, thou fall'st,[5] my tongue.
He stood, a soldier, to the last right end,
A perfect patriot and a noble friend,
But most a virtuous son.
All offices[6] were done
By him, so ample, full, and round
In weight, in measure, number, sound,
As, though his age imperfect might appear,
His life was of humanity the sphere.

The Stand

Go now, and tell out[7] days summed up with fears,
And make them years;
Produce thy mass of miseries on the stage
To swell thine age;
Repeat of things a throng,
To show thou hast been long,
Not lived; for life doth her great actions spell,
By what was done and wrought
In season, and so brought
To light: her measures are, how well
Each syllab'e answered, and was formed how fair;
These make the lines of life, and that's her air.[8]

The Turn

It is not growing like a tree
In bulk, doth make man better be,

4. I.e., another man, a separate example.
5. Slip, with a latent pun on Latin *fallor*, "to make a slip of the tongue."
6. Duties of life.
7. Count, number.
8. Life is a poem set to music, the music of its meaning. Life's "measures" are its metrical patterns, as well as the standards by which it is judged.

Or standing long an oak, three hundred year,
To fall a log at last, dry, bald, and sere:
A lily of a day
Is fairer far in May
Although it fall and die that night;
It was the plant and flower of light.
In small proportions we just beauties see,
And in short measures life may perfect be.

The Counter-Turn

Call, noble Lucius, then for wine,
And let thy looks with gladness shine:
Accept this garland, plant it on thy head,
And think, nay, know, thy Morison's not dead.
He leaped the present age,
Possessed with holy rage,
To see that bright, eternal day,
Of which we priests and poets say
Such truths as we expect for happy men,
And there he lives with memory: and Ben

The Stand

Jonson, who sung this of him ere he went
Himself to rest,
Or taste a part of that full joy he meant
To have expressed
In this bright Asterism:[9]
Where it were friendship's schism
(Were not his Lucius long with us to tarry)
To separate these twi-
Lights, the Dioscuri;[1]
And keep the one half from his Harry.
But fate doth so alternate the design,
Whilst that in heaven, this light on earth must shine.

The Turn

And shine as you exalted are,
Two names of friendship, but one star,
Of hearts the union. And those not by chance
Made, or indentured, or leased out t' advance
The profits for a time.
No pleasures vain did chime
Of rhymes or riots at your feasts,
Orgies of drink, or feigned protests;
But simple love of greatness and of good
That knits brave minds and manners, more than blood.

9. Constellation.
1. Castor and Pollux, the Dioscuri, are stars comprising the constellation of Gemini, or the twins.

The Counter-Turn

This made you first to know the Why
You liked, then after to apply
That liking; and approach so one the tother,
Till either grew a portion of the other;
Each styled by his end,
The copy of his friend.
You lived to be the great surnames
And titles by which all made claims
Unto the Virtue. Nothing perfect done,
But as a Cary or a Morison.

The Stand

And such a force the fair example had,
As they that saw
The good and durst not practice it, were glad
That such a law
Was left yet to mankind,
Where they might read and find
Friendship in deed was written, not in words,
And with the heart, not pen,
Of two so early men,
Whose lives her rolls were, and records,
Who, ere the first down bloomèd on the chin
Had sowed these fruits, and got the harvest in.

1629 1640

Ode to Himself[1]

Come leave the loathèd stage,
And the more loathsome age,
Where pride and impudence, in faction knit,
Usurp the chair of wit!
Indicting and arraigning every day
Something they call a play.
Let their fastidious, vain
Commission of the brain
Run on and rage, sweat, censure, and condemn;
They were not made for thee, less thou for them.

Say that thou pour'st them wheat,
And they will acorns eat;
'Twere simple fury still thyself to waste
On such as have no taste!
To offer them a surfeit of pure bread,
Whose appetites are dead!
No, give them grains their fill,
Husks, draff to drink and swill:[2]

1. The failure of Jonson's *The New Inn* (1629) inspired this heroic assault on criticism and the public taste.

2. Jonson gets into one line three words which suggest pig-food.

If they love lees, and leave the lusty wine,
Envy them not; their palate's with the swine.

No doubt some moldy tale,
Like *Pericles*,[3] and stale
As the shrieve's crusts, and nasty as his fish—
Scraps, out every dish
Thrown forth and raked into the common tub,
May keep up the Play-club:
There, sweepings do as well
As the best-ordered meal;
For who the relish of these guests will fit
Needs set them but the alms basket of wit.

And much good do 't you then:
Brave plush and velvet men
Can feed on orts;[4] and, safe in your stage clothes,
Dare quit, upon your oaths,
The stagers and the stage-wrights too, your peers,[5]
Of larding your large ears
With their foul comic socks,
Wrought upon twenty blocks;
Which, if they are torn, and turned, and patched enough,
The gamesters share your guilt, and you their stuff.

Leave things so prostitute
And take th' Alcaic lute;[6]
Or thine own Horace, or Anacreon's lyre;
Warm thee by Pindar's fire:
And though thy nerves be shrunk, and blood be cold,
Ere years have made thee old,
Strike that disdainful heat
Throughout, to their defeat,
As curious fools, and envious of thy strain,
May, blushing, swear no palsy's in thy brain.

But when they hear thee sing
The glories of thy king,
His zeal to God and his just awe o'er men,
They may, blood-shaken then,
Feel such a flesh-quake to possess their powers
As they shall cry, "Like ours,
In sound of peace or wars,
No harp e'er hit the stars
In tuning forth the acts of his sweet reign,
And raising Charles his chariot 'bove his Wain."[7]

1631 1640

3. Shakespeare's play, at least in part (printed 1609), which Jonson compares to poorhouse fare.
4. Scraps.
5. This fourth stanza turns toward an attack on the players and playwrights themselves, whom Jonson holds responsible for the low state of public taste. His anger here comes close to incoherence, and the plain sense of the stanza is most unclear.
6. That of Alcaeus, who lived ca. 600 B.C., and became famous, along with Horace, Anacreon, and Pindar, among the greatest lyric poets.
7. Jonson's poetry will elevate the chariot of Charles I (symbol of his royal power) above Charles's Wain (the seven bright stars of Ursa Major) among the constellations.

Pleasure Reconciled to Virtue In the opening pages of his famous study, *The Civilization of the Renaissance in Italy*, Jacob Burckhardt eloquently describes the many pageants, tourneys, triumphs, and festal displays that were a striking feature of courtly and urban life in those days. England too, and as late as the first third of the 17th century, fostered these semi-dramatic ceremonials, under the title of masques. In its whole social and literary structure the masque stood quite apart from the stage play. It was performed by noble amateurs, not professional players, and performed, as a rule, only once, perhaps as the climax of "revels" which were tied strictly to a calendar date. The aim of the masque was not to make money, but to lose it, in great quantities and with maximum splendor. The masque did not try to create or maintain an intact illusion by separating the audience sharply from the action; rather, it mingled the audience off-stage with the actors on-stage, either inviting the audience to join the dance (as in *Pleasure Reconciled to Virtue*) or leading the players off the stage in an act of homage or deference to the chief person in the audience (as in Milton's *Comus*). The masque had many elements of an audience-participation game. Especially when produced at court, it made use of elaborate and expensive "machinery"—sets far more intricate than any the playhouses could afford. It involved many musicians, special dancers, and extravagant costumes; it jumbled the heraldic and mythical figures together in strange profusion; it was both comic and serious, and anything but realistic. The three constant elements of the masque were a rich spectacle (with both song and dance), a moral allegory, and a courtly compliment. In weaving these traditional ingredients together, Jonson, with his special gifts of learning, fantasy, and lucid eloquence, showed particular mastery. He wrote nearly thirty masques in all, of which *Pleasure Reconciled to Virtue* may be taken as typical.

The reader should not look for too much narrative logic in Jonson's masque, which shifts scenes and characters, not according to the sequences of a story, but to provide good "production numbers." Comus appears at the beginning of the masque, but only to sing a song and do a wild dance with his "crew." Hercules is present, because he once had to make a hard choice between pleasure and virtue; but as this choice is no longer necessary, he soon fades into the role of a spectator. There is another grotesque dance (an "antimasque" or "antic masque") of pygmies. This comic dance serves to prepare for, and contrast with, the elegant and polished dances performed by the gentry at the end of the masque; its specific form in Jonson's masque was probably determined by the presence of some dwarfs among the court jesters who wanted a part in the action. Finally, the true masquers take possession of the stage; they are a group of court lords, led by Prince Charles, richly dressed and wearing masks, but obviously recognizable in their own persons. They perform a series of intricate figures, descend into the audience to invite forth their ladies, and perform one other formal dance before the festivities become general.

These last dances of the masque are all under the guidance of Daedalus, the master-craftsman of ancient Greece, who is shown to be capable of reconciling pleasure with virtue, life with artifice, and the court with its own fantastic mirror-image in the masque. If Hercules in the masque reminds us of Jonson himself (teased by spiteful but impotent pygmies), the figure of Daedalus can scarcely fail to suggest Jonson's partner in masque-making, Inigo Jones. Jones was a student of continental art and architecture, a practicing architect under the special influence of Palladio, the Italian master, and an adviser to many aristocratic art-collectors; in his own line, he was quite as remarkable and influential a man as Jonson himself. The two men quarrelled violently and permanently in later years; but Jones was far and away the most sophisticated stage-designer and deviser of stage-effects in his time; we know he was responsible for the production of *Pleasure Reconciled to Virtue*; and Jonson would have enjoyed paying this elegant tribute to him as Daedalus, the fabulous artificer.

Pleasure Reconciled to Virtue

A MASQUE. AS IT WAS PRESENTED AT COURT BEFORE KING JAMES. 1618.

The scene was the mountain Atlas, who had his top ending in the figure of an old man, his head and beard all hoary and frost as if his shoulders were covered with snow; the rest wood and rock. A grove of ivy at his feet, out of which, to a wild music of cymbals, flutes and tabors, is brought forth Comus,[1] *the god of cheer, or the belly, riding in triumph, his head crowned with roses and other flowers, his hair curled; they that wait upon him crowned with ivy, their javelins done about with it; one of them going with Hercules his bowl bare before him, while the rest presented him with this*

HYMN

Room, room! make room for the bouncing belly.
First father of sauce, and deviser of jelly;
Prime master of arts, and the giver of wit,
That found out the excellent engine, the spit,
The plow and the flail, the mill and the hopper,
The hutch and the bolter, the furnace and copper,
The oven, the bavin, the mawkin, the peel,
The hearth and the range, the dog and the wheel.[2]
He, he first invented the hogshead and tun,
The gimlet and vice too, and taught them to run.
And since, with the funnel, an Hippocras bag
He's made of himself, that now he cries swag.[3]

1. Comus is the traditional classical and Renaissance figure of sensual indulgence; many of his properties here (ivy, wild music, and the flowing bowl) suggest his kinship with Dionysus. The bowl of Hercules, given him by the Sun-god, was so big that the hero sailed across the ocean in it. At the root of the masque is the ancient story that early in his life Hercules had to choose between a life of easy pleasure and one of strenuous virtue. But now, under King James, the two principles are at last going to be reconciled. Jonson's stage directions, being partly descriptive (for the reader), partly instructive (for the performer), are rather casual about observing consistency of tense.

2. "Hutch" (bin), "mill," and "hopper" were used in grinding grain; bavin, mawkin, and peel are different sorts of apparatus used in a bake-shop. A dog harnessed to a wheel served to keep a roasting-spit turning.

3. "Gimlet" and "vice" are tools for tapping a keg. A "Hippocras bag" is a cloth filter for clearing wine; and to "cry swag" is to reveal a drooping, pendulous belly.

Which shows, though the pleasure be but of four inches,
Yet he is a weasel, the gullet that pinches,
Of any delight, and not spares from the back
Whatever to make of the belly a sack.[4]
Hail, hail, plump paunch! O the founder of taste
For fresh meats, or powdered, or pickle, or paste;
Devourer of broiled, baked, roasted or sod,[5]
And emptier of cups, be they even or odd;
All which have now made thee so wide i' the waist
As scarce with no pudding thou art to be laced;
But eating and drinking until thou dost nod,
Thou break'st all thy girdles, and break'st forth a god.

To this, the Bowl-bearer.

Do you hear, my friends? to whom did you sing all this now? Pardon me only that I ask you, for I do not look for an answer; I'll answer myself. I know it is now such a time as the Saturnals[6] for all the world, that every man stands under the eaves of his own hat and sings what pleases him; that's the right and the liberty of it. Now you sing of god Comus here, the Belly-god. I say it is well, and I say it is not well. It is well as it is a ballad, and the belly worthy of it, I must needs say, an 'twere forty yards of ballad more—as much ballad as tripe. But when the belly is not edified by it, it is not well; for where did you ever read or hear that the belly had any ears? Come, never pump for an answer, for you are defeated. Our fellow Hunger there, that was as ancient a retainer to the belly as any of us, was turned away for being unseasonable—not unreasonable, but unseasonable—and now is he (poor thin-gut) fain to get his living with teaching of starlings, magpies, parrots and jackdaws, those things he would have taught the belly. Beware of dealing with the belly; the belly will not be talked to, especially when he is full. Then there is no venturing upon Venter;[7] he will blow you all up; he will thunder indeed, la: some in derision call him the father of farts. But I say he was the first inventor of great ordnance, and taught us to discharge them on festival days. Would we had a fit feast for him, i' faith, to show his activity: I would have something now fetched in to please his five senses, the throat; or the two senses, the eyes. Pardon me for my two senses; for I that carry Hercules' bowl[8] in the service may see double by my place, for I have drunk like a frog today. I would have a tun now brought in to dance, and so many bottles about him. Ha! You look as if you would make a problem of this. Do you see? Do you see? a problem: why bot-

4. The gullet, though only four inches long, is a harsh master; it imposes the belly's great weight on the back.
5. Boiled.
6. The Roman Saturnalia, which came about the end of the year, were a time of license; Jonson compares them to the twelfth-night festivities in the English court, at which this masque was produced.
7. Belly, in Latin.
8. To carry Hercules' bowl would clearly imply drinking a lot. "Tun": barrel.

tles? and why a tun? and why a tun? and why bottles to dance? I say that men that drink hard and serve the belly in any place of quality (as *The Jovial Tinkers,* or *The Lusty Kindred*[9]) are living measures of drink, and can transform themselves, and do every day, to bottles or tuns when they please; and when they have done all they can, they are, as I say again (for I think I said somewhat like it afore) but moving measures of drink; and there is a piece in the cellar can hold more than all they. This will I make good if it please our new god but to give a nod; for the belly does all by signs, and I am all for the belly, the truest clock in the world to go by.

Here the first antimasque[1] *danced by men in the shape of bottles, tuns, etc., after which,*

HERCULES. What rites are these? Breeds earth more monsters yet?
Antaeus[2] scarce is cold: what can beget
This store?—and stay! such contraries upon her?
Is earth so fruitful of her own dishonor?
Or 'cause his vice was inhumanity,
Hopes she by vicious hospitality
To work an expiation first?[3] and then
(Help, Virtue!) these are sponges and not men.
Bottles? mere vessels? half a tun of paunch?
How? and the other half thrust forth in haunch?
Whose feast? the belly's! Comus'! and my cup
Brought in to fill the drunken orgies up
And here abused! that was the crowned reward
Of thirsty heroes after labor hard!
Burdens and shames of nature, perish, die;
For yet you never lived, but in the sty
Of vice have wallowed, and in that swine's strife
Been buried under the offense of life.
Go, reel and fall under the load you make,
Till your swoll'n bowels burst with what you take.
Can this be pleasure, to extinguish man?
Or so quite change him in his figure? Can
The belly love his pain, and be content
With no delight but what's a punishment?
These monsters plague themselves, and fitly, too,
For they do suffer what and all they do.
But here must be no shelter, nor no shroud
For such: sink grove, or vanish into cloud!

9. These seem to be names of taverns.

1. The antimasque, or antic masque, was a group of dancers, grotesquely or comically dressed, who served to contrast with the main group of masquers.

2. Antaeus, an earth-born giant, whom Hercules destroyed in the course of his labors. As his favored sport was wrestling, and he grew stronger every time he touched the ground, Hercules had to kill him by holding him in the air till he died.

3. Hercules thinks that Comus is another child of earth. Earth, he supposes, is trying to expiate her guilt by producing one monster after another.

After this the whole grove vanished, and the whole music was discovered, sitting at the foot of the mountain, with Pleasure and Virtue seated above them. The choir invited Hercules to rest with this

SONG

Great friend and servant of the good,
Let cool awhile thy heated blood,
And from thy mighty labor cease.
Lie down, lie down,
And give thy troubled spirits peace,
Whilst Virtue, for whose sake
Thou dost this godlike travail take,
May of the choicest herbage[4] make,
Here on this mountain bred,
A crown, a crown
For thy immortal head.

Here Hercules lay down at their feet, and the second antimasque, which was of pygmies, appeared.

1ST PYGMY. Antaeus dead and Hercules yet live!
Where is this Hercules? What would I give
To meet him now? Meet him? nay three such other,
If they had hand in murder of our brother![5]
With three? with four, with ten, nay, with as many
As the name yields! Pray anger there be any
Whereon to feed my just revenge, and soon!
How shall I kill him? Hurl him 'gainst the moon,
And break him in small portions! Give to Greece
His brain, and every tract of earth a piece!
2ND PYGMY. He is yonder.
1ST PYGMY. Where?
3RD PYGMY. At the hill foot, asleep.
1ST PYGMY. Let one go steal his club.
2ND PYGMY. My charge; I'll creep.
4TH PYGMY. He's ours.
1ST PYGMY. Yes, peace.
3RD PYGMY. Triumph, we have him, boy.
4TH PYGMY. Sure, sure, he's sure.
1ST PYGMY. Come, let us dance for joy.

At the end of their dance they thought to surprise him, when sud-

4. Plants and branches; "travail": labor, trouble.

5. Pygmies and giants, minimals and maximals, are disproportioned offspring of mere earth, therefore brothers to one another. The pygmies don't know how many Hercules-figures there are, because so many tales were told about the hero that even Renaissance mythographers were forced to think there must have been several persons of that name.

denly, being awaked by the music, he roused himself, and they all ran into holes.

SONG

CHOIR. Wake, Hercules, awake: but heave up thy black eye,
'Tis only asked from thee to look and these will die,
Or fly.
Already they are fled,
Whom scorn had else left dead.

At which Mercury descended from the hill with a garland of poplar to crown him.

MERCURY. Rest still, thou active friend of Virtue: these
Should not disturb the peace of Hercules.
Earth's worms and honor's dwarfs, at too great odds,
Prove or provoke the issue of the gods.
See here a crown the agèd hill hath sent thee,
My grandsire Atlas, he that did present thee
With the best sheep that in his fold were found,
Or golden fruit in the Hesperian ground,
For rescuing his fair daughters, then the prey
Of a rude pirate, as thou cam'st this way;
And taught thee all the learning of the sphere,
And how, like him, thou might'st the heavens up-bear,
As that thy labor's virtuous recompense.[6]
He, though, a mountain now, hath yet the sense
Of thanking thee for more, thou being still
Constant to goodness, guardian of the hill;
Antaeus, by thee suffocated here,
And the voluptuous Comus, god of cheer,
Beat from his grove, and that defaced. But now
The time's arrived that Atlas told thee of: how
By unaltered law, and working of the stars,
There should be a cessation of all jars[7]
'Twixt Virtue and her noted opposite,
Pleasure; that both should meet here in the sight
Of Hesperus, the glory of the west,[8]
The brightest star, that from his burning crest
Lights all on this side the Atlantic seas
As far as to thy pillars, Hercules.[9]
See where he shines, Justice and Wisdom placed
About his throne, and those with Honor graced,

6. When Hercules was seeking the golden apples of the Hesperides, he took for a while Atlas' job of holding up the heavens, so the giant could wade out in the ocean and get the apples. Atlas himself was originally an astronomer, and thus knew "all the learning of the sphere."

7. Quarrels.

8. Jonson followed the mythographers in making Hesperus a brother of Atlas; as the evening star and guardian of the western isles, he identifies easily with King James.

9. The "pillars of Hercules" are the straits of Gibraltar.

Beauty and Love! It is not with his brother
Bearing the world, but ruling such another
Is his renown.[1] Pleasure, for his delight
Is reconciled to Virtue, and this night
Virtue brings forth twelve princes have been bred
In this rough mountain and near Atlas' head,
The hill of knowledge; one and chief of whom
Of the bright race of Hesperus is come,
Who shall in time the same that he is be,
And now is only a less light than he.[2]
These now she trusts with Pleasure, and to these
She gives an entrance to the Hesperides,
Fair Beauty's garden; neither can she fear
They should grow soft or wax effeminate here,
Since in her sight and by her charge all's done,
Pleasure the servant, Virtue looking on.[3]

Here the whole choir of music called the twelve masquers forth from the lap of the mountain, which then opened with this

SONG

Ope, agèd Atlas, open then thy lap,
And from thy beamy bosom strike a light,
That men may read in thy mysterious map
All lines
And signs
Of royal education and the right,
See how they come and show,
That are but born to know,
Descend,
Descend,
Though pleasure lead,
Fear not to follow:
They who are bred
Within the hill
Of skill
May safely tread
What path they will,
No ground of good is hollow.

In their descent from the hill Daedalus[4] came down before them.

1. As Hesperus, King James does not hold up the sky, like his brother Atlas, but rules over a special world of his own, England.
2. Tradition has it that Prince Charles was one of the masquers; he was just 18 at the time, and it was his first masque.
3. Having grown up inside Atlas itself, so that virtue comes naturally to them, the masquers can now be allowed to mingle freely with the daughters of Hesperus, in pursuit of pleasure.
4. Daedalus, the mythical Greek maker of mazes, acts here as master of the intricate steps of the dance which interweaves pleasure with virtue under the guidance of art.

HERCULES. But Hermes, stay a little, let me pause:
Who's this that leads?
MERCURY. A guide that gives them laws
To all their motions: Daedalus the wise.
HERCULES. And doth in sacred harmony comprise
His precepts?
MERCURY. Yes.
HERCULES. They may securely prove[5]
Then, any labyrinth, though it be of love.

Here, while they put themselves in form, Daedalus has his first

SONG

Come on, come on! and where you go,
So interweave the curious knot,
As ev'n th' observer scarce may know
Which lines are Pleasure's and which not.

First, figure out the doubtful way
At which awhile all youth should stay,[6]
Where she and Virtue did contend
Which should have Hercules to friend.

Then, as all actions of mankind.
Are but a labyrinth or maze,
So let your dances be entwined,
Yet not perplex men unto gaze;

But measured, and so numerous too,
As men may read each act you do,
And when they see the graces meet,
Admire the wisdom of your feet.

For dancing is an exercise
Not only shows the mover's wit,
But maketh the beholder wise,
As he hath power to rise to it.

The first dance.

After which Daedalus again.

SONG 2

O more, and more! this was so well
As praise wants half his voice to tell;

5. Experience.
6. The dancers are to "figure out" the doubtful moment of Hercules' choice in the sense of illustrating it; they are beyond the occasion of making it themselves, having already reconciled pleasure with virtue.

Again yourselves compose;
And now put all the aptness on
Of figure, that proportion
Or color can disclose.

That if those silent arts were lost,
Design and picture, they might boast
From you a newer ground;[7]
Instructed to the height'ning sense
Of dignity and reverence
In your true motions found:

Begin, begin; for look, the fair
Do longing listen to what air
You form your second touch;[8]
That they may vent their murmuring hymns
Just to the tune you move your limbs,
And wish their own were such.

Make haste, make haste, for this
The labyrinth of beauty is.

The second dance:

That ended, Daedalus.

SONG 3

It follows now you are to prove
The subtlest maze of all, that's love,
And if you stay too long,
The fair will think you do 'em wrong,

Go choose among—but with a mind
As gentle as the stroking wind
Runs o'er the gentler flowers.
And so let all your actions smile
As if they meant not to beguile
The ladies, but the hours.

Grace, laughter and discourse may meet,
And yet the beauty not go less:
For what is noble should be sweet,
But not dissolved in wantonness.

Will you that I give the law
To all your sport, and sum it?

7. Put on the "aptness of figure," i.e., significance of expression, of which art (proportion or color) is capable; thus, if design and picture, the silent arts, were lost, they could be rebuilt out of the dance alone.

8. Endeavor.

It should be such should envy draw,
But ever overcome it.

Here they danced with the ladies, and the whole revels followed;[9] *which ended, Mercury called to Daedalus in this following speech, which was after repeated in song by two trebles, two tenors, a bass, and the whole chorus.*

SONG 4

An eye of looking back were well,
Or any murmur that would tell
Your thoughts, how you were sent
And went,
To walk with Pleasure, not to dwell.

These, these are hours by Virtue spared
Herself, she being her own reward,
But she will have you know
That though
Her sports be soft, her life is hard.

You must return unto the hill,
And there advance
With labor, and inhabit still
That height and crown
From whence you ever may look down
Upon triúmphed Chance.

She, she it is, in darkness shines.
'Tis she that still herself refines
By her own light, to every eye
More seen, more known when Vice stands by.
And though a stranger here on earth,
In heaven she hath her right of birth.
There, there is Virtue's seat,
Strive to keep her your own;
'Tis only she can make you great,
Though place here make you known.

After which, they danced their last dance, and returned into the scene, which closed and was a mountain again as before.

And so it ended.

This pleased the king so well, as he would see it again; when it was presented with these additions.[1]

1618 1640

9. Group of onlookers and courtiers.
1. The "additions" were another short masque, *For the Honor of Wales*.

JOHN WEBSTER

(1580?–1625)

Though Shakespeare seems, in our eyes, to tower above all his contemporaries, and was by no means without honor in his own day, it is only by comparison with him that the Stuart playwrights look small. In any other age of English literature a group of writers which included not only Ben Jonson but John Ford, John Webster, Cyril Tourneur, Francis Beaumont, John Marston, John Fletcher, and Thomas Middleton would have been the climactic glory of the English stage. Such a galaxy of talent, working at a level just short of supreme, we shall not see again. Among them John Webster stands out as second only to Jonson himself—not as a contriver of well-articulated stage actions, but for the dark poetry of his tragic imagination. As a poet, he is scarcely less powerful than Shakespeare himself, though his range is more restricted. He is a poet of moods, and of certain specific moods, which his age tended to group under the heading of "melancholy." Melancholy is a state of psychic arrest, of morbid inwardness, of fixation and paralysis; and to the exploration of this mood Webster sacrificed some of the movement and even the logic of his plots. Like Hamlet, the central consciousness responds eloquently and imaginatively to his dark circumstances, but is incapable of decisive action to change them. In *The Duchess of Malfi*, Daniel de Bosola is such a man. His inclinations are basically virtuous, but he has been soured and embittered by failure; a soldier and a scholar by profession, he has been reduced to playing what he knows is the mean role of a household spy. Out of his diseased imagination he thus becomes a sardonic wit and a grotesque, violent poet. This poetry of his mirrors the world in which he has fallen, a foul, stagnant, sumptuous sink of corruption, such as 17th-century Englishmen, with their strong Protestant feelings, imagined 16th-century, pre-Reformation Italy to have been.

Webster was obviously fascinated by the diseased and sophisticated corruption which he attributed to the Italy of the Borgias; and he used it as a background against which to pose the figure of his Duchess, one of the freest and most positive women in all English drama. In boldly asserting her right to choose a husband without regard to her family or her social class, the Duchess far transcends the standards of her age. Webster clearly expects us to admire both the assured sensitivity of her impulses and the perfect self-command with which she meets her final fate.

Though his plots are less artfully put together than Shakespeare's, Webster is capable of tremendous poetic flashes. His scenes of brooding terror are lit by fitful lightnings of the imagination, as when Ferdinand, faced with his sister's corpse, at last sees what his insane furies have meant. As for the man who created these lurid nightmares, we know little or nothing about his personal life. He was the son of a tailor, and may himself have plied the needle for a time. He collaborated with other playwrights, but came into his own style when he emancipated himself from that dependence. He professed to be a slow writer, and he drew heavily on his reading in the course of composition. Modern scholarship has found a literary source for nearly every phrase and concept in his plays. But, trite though it is to say so, what he made of his reading is distinctively his own. His art is one of brilliant highlights and black shadows of furtive and dangerous intrigue carried out in the flickering light of hell-fire; it serves to illumine one unflawed character who accepts without faltering or cringing the ultimate test.

The Duchess of Malfi

Dramatis Personae

FERDINAND, *Duke of Calabria*
THE CARDINAL, *his brother*
ANTONIO BOLOGNA, *steward of the household to the* DUCHESS
DELIO, *his friend*
DANIEL DE BOSOLA, *gentleman of the horse to the* DUCHESS
CASTRUCCIO
MARQUIS OF PESCARA
COUNT MALATESTE
SILVIO, *a Lord, of Milan* } *gentlemen attending on the* DUCHESS
RODERIGO }
GRISOLAN
DOCTOR
Several MADMEN, PILGRIMS, EXECUTIONERS, OFFICERS, ATTENDANTS, *&c.*
THE DUCHESS OF MALFI, *sister of* FERDINAND *and the* CARDINAL
CARIOLA, *her woman*
JULIA, CASTRUCCIO'S *wife, and the* CARDINAL'S *mistress*
OLD LADY, LADIES, *and* CHILDREN

SCENE. *Amalfi, Rome, and Milan*

Act I

SCENE 1. *Amalfi; a hall in the* DUCHESS'S *palace.*

[*Enter* ANTONIO *and* DELIO.]

DELIO. You are welcome to your country, dear Antonio;
You have been long in France, and you return
A very formal Frenchman in your habit.[1]
How do you like the French court?
ANTONIO. I admire it:
In seeking to reduce both state and people
To a fixed order, their judicious king
Begins at home; quits[2] first his royal palace
Of flattering sycophants, of dissolute
And infamous persons, which he sweetly terms
His master's masterpiece, the work of Heaven;

1. An absolute Frenchman in your manners.

2. Liberates, frees.

Considering duly that a prince's court
Is like a common fountain, whence should flow
Pure silver drops in general, but if 't chance
Some cursed example poison't near the head,
Death and diseases through the whole land spread.
And what is 't makes this blessed government
But a most provident council; who dare freely
Inform him the corruption of the times?
Though some o' th' court hold it presumption
To instruct princes what they ought to do,
It is a noble duty to inform them
What they ought to foresee. Here comes Bosola.
The only court-gall;[3] yet I observe his railing
Is not for simple love of piety.
Indeed, he rails at those things which he wants;
Would be as lecherous, covetous, or proud,
Bloody, or envious, as any man,
If he had means to be so. Here's the Cardinal.

[*Enter the* CARDINAL *and* BOSOLA.]

BOSOLA. I do haunt you still.

CARDINAL. So.

BOSOLA. I have done you better service than to be slighted thus. Miserable age, where the only reward of doing well is the doing of it!

CARDINAL. You enforce your merit too much.

BOSOLA. I fell into the galleys[4] in your service; where, for two years together, I wore two towels instead of a shirt, with a knot on the shoulder, after the fashion of a Roman mantle. Slighted thus? I will thrive some way. Blackbirds fatten best in hard weather; why not I in these dog-days?[5]

CARDINAL. Would you could become honest!

BOSOLA. With all your divinity do but direct me the way to it. I have known many travel far for it, and yet return as arrant knaves as they went forth, because they carried themselves always along with them. [*Exit* CARDINAL.] Are you gone? Some fellows, they say, are possessed with the devil, but this great fellow were able to possess the greatest devil, and make him worse.

ANTONIO. He hath denied thee some suit?

BOSOLA. He and his brother are like plum-trees that grow crooked over standing-pools; they are rich and o'er-laden with fruit, but none but crows, pies, and caterpillars feed on them.[6] Could I be one of their flattering panders, I would hang on their ears

3. Court-satirist, but with the overtone of a disease, a blight.
4. Service at the oar of a Mediterranean galley was the last penalty this side of torture and execution, a 50-percent death sentence.
5. The hot, sultry season of midsummer. Being naturally an ill-omened creature, like a blackbird, Bosola thinks he may thrive under oppression.
6. "Standing-pools": stagnant, therefore poisonous, waters; "pies": magpies, birds of evil omen like blackbirds. By "panders," Bosola does not mean actual pimps, but slavish hangers-on, ready to perform any low office. The violence of these metaphors evidences the sickness of the speaker's mind.

like a horseleech till I were full and then drop off. I pray, leave me. Who would rely upon these miserable dependencies, in expectation to be advanced tomorrow? What creature ever fed worse than hoping Tantalus?[7] Nor ever died any man more fearfully than he that hoped for a pardon. There are rewards for hawks and dogs when they have done us service; but for a soldier that hazards his limbs in a battle, nothing but a kind of geometry is his last supportation.

DELIO. Geometry?

BOSOLA. Aye, to hang in a fair pair of slings, take his latter swing in the world upon an honorable pair of crutches, from hospital to hospital. Fare ye well, sir: and yet do not you scorn us; for places in the court are but like beds in the hospital, where this man's head lies at that man's foot, and so lower and lower. [*Exit.*]

DELIO. I knew this fellow seven years[8] in the galleys
For a notorious murder; and 'twas thought
The Cardinal suborned it. He was released
By the French general, Gaston de Foix,
When he recovered Naples.[9]

ANTONIO. 'Tis great pity
He should be thus neglected; I have heard
He's very valiant. This foul melancholy
Will poison all his goodness; for, I'll tell you,
If too immoderate sleep be truly said
To be an inward rust unto the soul,
It then doth follow want of action
Breeds all black malcontents; and their close rearing,
Like moths in cloth, do hurt for want of wearing.[1]

DELIO. The presence 'gins to fill: you promised me
To make me the partaker of the natures
Of some of your great courtiers.

ANTONIO. The Lord Cardinal's,
And other strangers that are now in court?
I shall. Here comes the great Calabrian duke.

[*Enter* FERDINAND, CASTRUCCIO, SILVIO, RODERIGO, GRISOLAN, *and* ATTENDANTS.]

FERDINAND. Who took the ring oftenest?[2]

SILVIO. Antonio Bologna, my lord.

FERDINAND. Our sister duchess' great-master of her household?

7. Tantalus, in classical mythology, was tantalized by the constant presence under his nose of delicious food and drink which, though he was starving, he could never reach.

8. In speaking to the Cardinal himself (above, line 35), Bosola mentions only two years.

9. Since Gaston de Foix was active in Italy during the early 1500's, this circumstance establishes the time of the tragedy as about 100 years before the time Webster wrote. Ferdinand and the Cardinal are Spaniards established in Italy, like the notorious house of Borgia (incestuous, simoniacal Pope Alexander VI and his two illegitimate children Cesare and Lucrezia), also active at the beginning of the 16th century.

1. Because they don't have anything to do, malcontents suffer from moths as do clothes which have not been worn for a long time. "The presence": the assemblage of the court.

2. A common game around court, used in training for tourneys, involved catching a hanging ring on the tip of a lance.

Give him the jewel. When shall we leave this sportive action, and fall to action indeed?

CASTRUCCIO. Methinks, my lord, you should not desire to go to war in person.

FERDINAND. Now for some gravity. Why, my lord?

CASTRUCCIO. It is fitting a soldier arise to be a prince, but not necessary a prince descend to be a captain.

FERDINAND. No?

CASTRUCCIO. No, my lord, he were far better do it by a deputy.

FERDINAND. Why should he not as well sleep or eat by a deputy? This might take idle, offensive, and base office from him, whereas the other deprives him of honor.

CASTRUCCIO. Believe my experience, that realm is never long in quiet where the ruler is a soldier.

FERDINAND. Thou told'st me thy wife could not endure fighting.

CASTRUCCIO. True, my lord.

FERDINAND. And of a jest she broke of a captain she met full of wounds. I have forgot it.

CASTRUCCIO. She told him, my lord, he was a pitiful fellow, to lie, like the children of Israel, all in tents.[3]

FERDINAND. Why, there's a wit were able to undo all the chirurgeons[4] o' the city; for although gallants should quarrel and had drawn their weapons and were ready to go to it, yet her persuasions would make them put up.

CASTRUCCIO. That she would, my lord.

FERDINAND. How do you like my Spanish gennet?[5]

RODERIGO. He is all fire.

FERDINAND. I am of Pliny's opinion, I think he was begot by the wind; he runs as if he were ballassed[6] with quicksilver.

SILVIO. True, my lord, he reels from the tilt often.[7]

RODERIGO *and* GRISOLAN. Ha, ha, ha!

FERDINAND. Why do you laugh? Methinks, you that are courtiers should be my touchwood, take fire when I give fire; that is, laugh but when I laugh, were the subject never so witty.

CASTRUCCIO. True, my lord, I myself have heard a very good jest, and have scorned to seem to have so silly a wit as to understand it.

FERDINAND. But I can laugh at your fool, my lord.

CASTRUCCIO. He cannot speak, you know, but he makes faces: my lady cannot abide him.

FERDINAND. No?

CASTRUCCIO. Nor endure to be in merry company, for she says too much laughing and too much company fills her too full of the wrinkle.

FERDINAND. I would, then, have a mathematical instrument

3. The lady's pun plays on the name for lint bandages, "tents."

4. Surgeons.

5. Sometimes "jennet": a small Spanish horse of Arabian stock.

6. Ballasted. Pliny in his natural history tells about some Spanish horses generated by a swift wind (VIII.lxvii).

7. "Reeling from the tilt" involves a double meaning: recoiling from the shock of a charge, and rolling about like quicksilver on a tilted table.

made for her face, that she might not laugh out of compass.[8]
I shall shortly visit you at Milan, Lord Silvio.

SILVIO. Your grace shall arrive most welcome.

FERDINAND. You are a good horseman, Antonio. You have excellent riders in France. What do you think of good horsemanship?

ANTONIO. Nobly, my lord: as out of the Grecian horse issued many famous princes, so out of brave horsemanship arise the first sparks of growing resolution that raise the mind to noble action.

FERDINAND. You have bespoke it worthily.

SILVIO. Your brother, the Lord Cardinal, and sister duchess.

[*Re-enter* CARDINAL, *with* DUCHESS, CARIOLA, *and* JULIA.]

CARDINAL. Are the galleys come about?

GRISOLAN. They are, my lord.

FERDINAND. Here's the Lord Silvio is come to take his leave.

DELIO. Now, sir, your promise. What's that Cardinal?
I mean his temper? They say he's a brave fellow,
Will play[9] his five thousand crowns at tennis, dance,
Court ladies, and one that hath fought single combats.

ANTONIO. Some such flashes superficially hang on him for form; but observe his inward character: he is a melancholy churchman; the spring in his face is nothing but the engendering of toads; where he is jealous of any man, he lays worse plots for them than ever was imposed on Hercules, for he strews in his way flatterers, panders, intelligencers, atheists, and a thousand such political monsters.[1] He should have been Pope; but instead of coming to it by the primitive decency of the Church, he did bestow bribes so largely and so impudently as if he would have carried it away without Heaven's knowledge. Some good he hath done——

DELIO. You have given too much of him. What's his brother?

ANTONIO. The duke there? A most perverse and turbulent nature.
What appears in him mirth is merely outside;
If he laugh heartily, it is to laugh
All honesty out of fashion.

DELIO. Twins?

ANTONIO. In quality.
He speaks with others' tongues, and hears men's suits
With others' ears; will seem to sleep o' th' bench
Only to entrap offenders in their answers;
Dooms men to death by information;[2]
Rewards by hearsay.

DELIO. Then the law to him
Is like a foul black cobweb to a spider:
He makes of it his dwelling and a prison
To entangle those shall feed him.

8. Excessively; with a pun on the draftsman's compass.
9. Wager.
1. "Intelligencers": spies. The Cardinal sets traps and dangers before his enemies as many and as formidable as the labors of Hercules.
2. On the basis of secret reports.

ANTONIO. Most true:
He never pays debts unless they be shrewd turns,[3]
And those he will confess that he doth owe.
Last, for his brother there, the Cardinal,
They that do flatter him most say oracles
Hang at his lips; and verily I believe them,
For the devil speaks in them.
But for their sister, the right noble duchess,
You never fixed your eye on three fair medals
Cast in one figure, of so different temper.
For her discourse, it is so full of rapture,
You only will begin then to be sorry
When she doth end her speech, and wish, in wonder,
She held it less vainglory to talk much,
Than your penance to hear her: whilst she speaks,
She throws upon a man so sweet a look,
That it were able to raise one to a galliard[4]
That lay in a dead palsy, and to dote
On that sweet countenance; but in that look
There speaketh so divine a continence
As cuts off all lascivious and vain hope.
Her days are practiced in such noble virtue
That sure her nights, nay, more, her very sleeps,
Are more in heaven than other ladies' shrifts.[5]
Let all sweet ladies break their flattering glasses,
And dress themselves in her.
DELIO. Fie, Antonio,
You play the wire-drawer[6] with her commendations.
ANTONIO. I'll case the picture up: only thus much;
All her particular worth grows to this sum,
She stains[7] the time past, lights the time to come.
CARDINAL. You must attend my lady in the gallery,
Some half an hour hence.
ANTONIO. I shall.
[*Exeunt* ANTONIO *and* DELIO.]
FERDINAND. Sister, I have a suit to you.
DUCHESS. To me, sir?
FERDINAND. A gentleman here, Daniel de Bosola,
One that was in the galleys—
DUCHESS. Yes, I know him.
FERDINAND. A worthy fellow he is. Pray, let me entreat for
The provisorship of your horse.
DUCHESS. Your knowledge of him.
Commends him and prefers him.
FERDINAND. Call him hither.
[*Exit* ATTENDANT.]
We are now upon parting. Good Lord Silvio,

3. Tricks to serve his own advantage.
4. A gay and lively dance.
5. Confessions.
6. Draw out her praises excessively; "case the picture": frame it.
7. Darkens (by comparison with her brilliance).

Do us commend to all our noble friends
At the leaguer.[8]
SILVIO. Sir, I shall.
DUCHESS. You are for Milan?
SILVIO. I am.
DUCHESS. Bring the caroches. We'll bring you down
To the haven.[9] [*Exeunt all but* FERDINAND *and the* CARDINAL.]
CARDINAL. Be sure you entertain that Bosola
For your intelligence:[1] I would not be seen in 't;
And therefore many times I have slighted him
When he did court our furtherance, as this morning.
FERDINAND. Antonio, the great-master of her household,
Had been far fitter.
CARDINAL. You are deceived in him:
His nature is too honest for such business.
He comes: I'll leave you. [*Exit.*]
[*Re-enter* BOSOLA.]
BOSOLA. I was lured to you.
FERDINAND. My brother, here, the Cardinal could never
Abide you.
BOSOLA. Never since he was in my debt.
FERDINAND. Maybe some oblique character in your face
Made him suspect you
BOSOLA. Doth he study physiognomy?
There's no more credit to be given to th' face
Than to a sick man's urine, which some call
The physician's whore because she cozens[2] him.
He did suspect me wrongfully.
FERDINAND. For that
You must give great men leave to take their times.
Distrust doth cause us seldom be deceived:
You see, the oft shaking of the cedar-tree
Fastens it more at root.
BOSOLA. Yet, take heed;
For to suspect a friend unworthily
Instructs him the next way to suspect you,
And prompts him to deceive you.
FERDINAND. [*giving him money*] There's gold.
BOSOLA. So:
What follows? Never rained such showers as these
Without thunderbolts i' th' tail of them. Whose throat must I cut?
FERDINAND. Your inclination to shed blood rides post
Before my occasion to use you. I give you that
To live i' th' court here, and observe the duchess;
To note all the particulars of her havior,
What suitors do solicit her for marriage,

8. A gathering of the armies, as at a siege.
9. Harbor; "caroches": carriages.
1. I.e., be sure to hire Bosola as your spy.
2. Tricks.

And whom she best affects. She's a young widow:
I would not have her marry again.
BOSOLA. No, sir?
FERDINAND. Do not you ask the reason, but be satisfied
I say I would not.
BOSOLA. It seems you would create me
One of your familiars.[3]
FERDINAND. Familiar? What's that?
BOSOLA. Why, a very quaint invisible devil in flesh,
An intelligencer.
FERDINAND. Such a kind of thriving thing
I would wish thee, and ere long thou may'st arrive
At a higher place by 't.
BOSOLA. Take your devils,
Which hell calls angels;[4] these cursed gifts would make
You a corrupter, me an impudent traitor;
And should I take these, they'd take me to hell.
FERDINAND. Sir, I'll take nothing from you that I have given:
There is a place that I procured for you
This morning, the provisorship o' th' horse;
Have you heard on 't?
BOSOLA. No.
FERDINAND. 'Tis yours. Is't not worth thanks?
BOSOLA. I would have you curse yourself now, that your bounty,
Which makes men truly noble, e'er should make me
A villain. Oh, that to avoid ingratitude
For the good deed you have done me, I must do
All the ill man can invent! Thus the devil
Candies all sins o'er; and what heaven terms vile,
That names he complimental.
FERDINAND. Be yourself;
Keep your old garb of melancholy; 'twill express
You envy those that stand above your reach,
Yet strive not to come near 'em: this will gain
Access to private lodgings, where yourself
May, like a politic dormouse—
BOSOLA. As I have seen some
Feed in a lord's dish, half asleep, not seeming
To listen to any talk; and yet these rogues
Have cut his throat in a dream. What's my place?
The provisorship o' th' horse? Say, then, my corruption
Grew out of horse-dung. I am your creature.
FERDINAND. Away! [*Exit.*]
BOSOLA. Let good men, for good deeds, covet good fame,
Since place and riches oft are bribes of shame:
Sometimes the devil doth preach. [*Exit.*]

3. Evil spirits, agents of the devil.
4. Gold coins were known, from the image on them, as angels.

SCENE 2

[*Enter* FERDINAND, DUCHESS, CARDINAL, *and* CARIOLA.]

CARDINAL. We are to part from you, and your own discretion
Must now be your director.
FERDINAND. You are a widow:
You know already what man is; and therefore
Let not youth, high promotion, eloquence—
CARDINAL. No,
Nor any thing without the addition, honor,
Sway your high blood.
FERDINAND. Marry! They are most luxurious
Will wed twice.
CARDINAL. Oh, fie!
FERDINAND. Their lives are more spotted
Than Laban's sheep.[5]
DUCHESS. Diamonds are of most value,
They say, that have passed through most jewelers' hands.
FERDINAND. Whores by that rule are precious.
DUCHESS. Will you hear me?
I'll never marry.
CARDINAL. So most widows say;
But commonly that motion[6] lasts no longer
Than the turning of an hour-glass; the funeral sermon
And it end both together.
FERDINAND. Now hear me:
You live in a rank pasture, here, i' th' court;
There is a kind of honey-dew[7] that's deadly;
'Twill poison your fame; look to't: be not cunning;
For they whose faces do belie their hearts
Are witches ere they arrive at twenty years,
Aye, and give the devil suck.
DUCHESS. This is terrible good counsel.
FERDINAND. Hypocrisy is woven of a fine small thread,
Subtler than Vulcan's engine:[8] yet, believe't,
Your darkest actions, nay, your privatest thoughts,
Will come to light.
CARDINAL. You may flatter yourself,
And take your own choice; privately be married
Under the eaves of night—
FERDINAND. Think't the best voyage
That e'er you made; like the irregular crab,
Which, though't goes backward, thinks that it goes right
Because it goes its own way; but observe,
Such weddings may more properly be said
To be executed than celebrated.

5. Dividing his flock with Jacob, Laban took the speckled sheep (Genesis xxx.31–33); the liver as seat of the passions was thought to be diseased when discolored.

6. Impulse, notion.

7. A sweet, sticky substance left on plants by aphids.

8. The net in which Vulcan, Venus' husband, caught her misbehaving with Mars.

CARDINAL. The marriage night
Is the entrance into some prison.
FERDINAND. And those joys,
Those lustful pleasures, are like heavy sleeps
Which do forerun man's mischief.
CARDINAL. Fare you well.
Wisdom begins at the end: remember it. [*Exit.*]
DUCHESS. I think this speech between you both was studied,
It came so roundly off.
FERDINAND. You are my sister;
This was my father's poniard,[9] do you see?
I'd be loth to see 't look rusty, 'cause 'twas his.
I would have you to give o'er these chargeable[1] revels:
A visor and a mask are whispering-rooms
That were never built for goodness—fare ye well—
And women like that part which, like the lamprey,[2]
Hath never a bone in 't.
DUCHESS. Fie, sir!
FERDINAND. Nay,
I mean the tongue; variety of courtship.
What cannot a neat knave with a smooth tale
Make a woman believe? Farewell, lusty widow. [*Exit.*]
DUCHESS. Shall this move me? If all my royal kindred
Lay in my way unto this marriage,
I'd make them my low footsteps; and even now,
Even in this hate, as men in some great battles,
By apprehending danger, have achieved
Almost impossible actions (I have heard soldiers say so),
So I through frights and threatenings will assay
This dangerous venture. Let old wives report
I winked and chose a husband. Cariola,
To thy known secrecy I have given up
More than my life—my fame.
CARIOLA. Both shall be safe,
For I'll conceal this secret from the world
As warily as those that trade in poison
Keep poison from their children.
DUCHESS. Thy protestation
Is ingenious and hearty:[3] I believe it.
Is Antonio come?
CARIOLA. He attends you.
DUCHESS. Good dear soul,
Leave me, but place thyself behind the arras,[4]
Where thou mayst overhear us. Wish me good speed,
For I am going into a wilderness

9. Dagger.
1. Expensive; "visor": a half-mask, worn by ladies at carnivals, theaters, and other dubious resorts.
2. "Lamprey": eel. They do, of course, have bones, but for the purposes of the Duke's insinuation they are better without.
3. Sincere and from the heart.
4. Tapestries were often hung in Renaissance palaces to moderate the chill of the bare walls.

Where I shall find nor path nor friendly clue
To be my guide. [CARIOLA *goes behind the arras.*]
[*Enter* ANTONIO.]
I sent for you: sit down;
Take pen and ink, and write. Are you ready?
ANTONIO. Yes.
DUCHESS. What did I say?
ANTONIO. That I should write somewhat.
DUCHESS. Oh, I remember.
After these triumphs and this large expense,
It's fit, like thrifty husbands,[5] we inquire
What's laid up for tomorrow.
ANTONIO. So please your beauteous excellence.
DUCHESS. Beauteous?
Indeed, I thank you: I look young for your sake;
You have ta'en my cares upon you.
ANTONIO. I'll fetch your grace
The particulars of your revenue and expense.
DUCHESS. Oh, you are an upright treasurer: but you mistook;
For when I said I meant to make inquiry
What's laid up for tomorrow, I did mean
What's laid up yonder for me.
ANTONIO. Where?
DUCHESS. In heaven.
I am making my will (as 'tis fit princes should,
In perfect memory), and I pray sir, tell me,
Were not one better make it smiling thus
Than in deep groans and terrible ghastly looks,
As if the gifts we parted with procured[6]
That violent distraction?
ANTONIO. O, much better.
DUCHESS. If I had a husband now, this care were quit:
But I intend to make you overseer.
What good deed shall we first remember? Say.
ANTONIO. Begin with that first good deed begun i' th' world
After man's creation, the sacrament of marriage:
I'd have you first provide for a good husband;
Give him all.
DUCHESS. All?
ANTONIO. Yes, your excellent self.
DUCHESS. In a winding-sheet?
ANTONIO. In a couple.
DUCHESS. Saint Winfred, that were a strange will![7]
ANTONIO. 'Twere stranger if there were no will in you
To marry again.
DUCHESS. What do you think of marriage?

5. Though used here in its original sense of one who preserves and safeguards property, the word shows where the Duchess' thoughts are tending.

6. Brought on.

7. Saint Winfred, Welsh virgin and martyr, is an odd saint for the Duchess of Malfi to swear on.

ANTONIO. I take't, as those that deny purgatory;
It locally contains or heaven or hell;
There's no third place in 't.
DUCHESS. How do you affect it?[8]
ANTONIO. My banishment, feeding my melancholy,
Would often reason thus—
DUCHESS. Pray, let's hear it.
ANTONIO. Say a man never marry, nor have children,
What takes that from him? Only the bare name
Of being a father, or the weak delight
To see the little wanton ride a-cock-horse
Upon a painted stick, or hear him chatter
Like a taught starling.
DUCHESS. Fie, fie, what's all this?
One of your eyes is bloodshot; use my ring to 't,
They say 'tis very sovereign.[9] 'Twas my wedding-ring,
And I did vow never to part with it
But to my second husband.
ANTONIO. You have parted with it now.
DUCHESS. Yes, to help your eyesight.
ANTONIO. You have made me stark blind.
DUCHESS. How?
ANTONIO. There is a saucy and ambitious devil
Is dancing in this circle.[1]
DUCHESS. Remove him.
ANTONIO. How?
DUCHESS. There needs small conjuration, when your finger
May do it: thus; is it fit?
[*She puts the ring upon his finger; he kneels.*]
ANTONIO. What said you?
DUCHESS. Sir,
This goodly roof of yours[2] is too low built;
I cannot stand upright in 't nor discourse,
Without I raise it higher: raise yourself;
Or, if you please, my hand to help you: so. [*Raises him.*]
ANTONIO. Ambition, madam, is a great man's madness,
That is not kept in chains and close-pent rooms,
But in fair lightsome lodgings, and is girt
With the wild noise of prattling visitants,
Which makes it lunatic beyond all cure.
Conceive not I am so stupid but I aim
Whereto your favors tend; but he's a fool
That, being a-cold, would thrust his hands i' th' fire
To warm them.
DUCHESS. So, now the ground's broke,
You may discover what a wealthy mine

8. Feel about it.
9. Healing, but with an additional overtone implying royal power.
1. To conjure up a devil, the necromancer first draws a charmed circle on the ground—like the duchess' ring.
2. His head as he kneels before her.

I make you lord of.
ANTONIO. O my unworthiness!
DUCHESS. You were ill to sell yourself:
This darkening of your worth is not like that
Which tradesmen use i' th' city, their false lights
Are to rid bad wares off[3] and I must tell you,
If you will know where breathes a complete man
(I speak it without flattery), turn your eyes,
And progress through yourself.
ANTONIO. Were there nor heaven
Nor hell, I should be honest: I have long served virtue,
And ne'er ta'en wages of her.
DUCHESS. Now she pays it.
The misery of us that are born great!
We are forced to woo, because none dare woo us;
And as a tyrant doubles with his words
And fearfully equivocates, so we
Are forced to express our violent passions
In riddles and in dreams, and leave the path
Of simple virtue, which was never made
To seem the thing it is not. Go, go brag
You have left me heartless; mine is in your bosom:
I hope 'twill multiply love there. You do tremble:
Make not your heart so dead a piece of flesh,
To fear more than to love me. Sir, be confident:
What is 't distracts you? This is flesh and blood, sir;
'Tis not the figure cut in alabaster
Kneels at my husband's tomb. Awake, awake, man!
I do here put off all vain ceremony,
And only do appear to you a young widow
That claims you for her husband, and, like a widow,
I use but half a blush in 't.
ANTONIO. Truth speak for me;
I will remain the constant sanctuary
Of your good name.
DUCHESS. I thank you, gentle love:
And 'cause you shall not come to me in debt,
Being now my steward, here upon your lips
I sign your *Quietus est*.[4] This you should have begged now;
I have seen children oft eat sweetmeats thus,
As fearful to devour them too soon.
ANTONIO. But for your brothers?
DUCHESS. Do not think of them.
All discord without this circumference[5]
Is only to be pitied, and not feared;
Yet, should they know it, time will easily
Scatter the tempest.

3. Tradesmen in the city display their goods in a poor light, so the defects won't be seen.

4. The legal formula for marking a bill "Paid" or "Acquitted."

5. Their arms around one another.

ANTONIO. These words should be mine,
And all the parts you have spoke, if some part of it
Would not have savored flattery.

DUCHESS. Kneel.

[CARIOLA *comes from behind the arras.*]

ANTONIO. Ha!

DUCHESS. Be not amazed; this woman's of my counsel:
I have heard lawyers say, a contract in a chamber
Per verba de presenti[6] is absolute marriage.

[*She and* ANTONIO *kneel.*]

Bless, heaven, this sacred gordian,[7] which let violence
Never untwine!

ANTONIO. And may our sweet affections, like the spheres,
Be still in motion!

DUCHESS. Quickening, and make
The like soft music!

ANTONIO. That we may imitate the loving palms,
Best emblem of a peaceful marriage, that ne'er
Bore fruit, divided!

DUCHESS. What can the Church force more?

ANTONIO. That fortune may not know an accident,
Either of joy or sorrow, to divide
Our fixéd wishes!

DUCHESS. How can the Church build faster?[8]
We now are man and wife, and 'tis the Church
That must but echo this. Maid, stand apart:
I now am blind.[9]

ANTONIO. What's your conceit in this?

DUCHESS. I would have you lead your fortune by the hand
Unto your marriage bed
(You speak in me this, for we now are one);
We'll only lie, and talk together, and plot
To appease my humorous kindred; and if you please,
Like the old tale in "Alexander and Lodowick,"
Lay a naked sword between us, keep us chaste.[1]
Oh, let me shroud my blushes in your bosom,
Since 'tis the treasury of all my secrets!

[*Exeunt* DUCHESS *and* ANTONIO.]

CARIOLA. Whether the spirit of greatness or of woman
Reign most in her, I know not; but it shows
A fearful madness: I owe her much of pity. [*Exit.*]

6. "Through words in the present tense"—not, as commonly supposed, and perhaps by Webster himself, "On the words of a witness." In canon law, the duchess is right; her agreement with Antonio to consider themselves married is a valid contract with or without priest, ceremony, or even the presence of a witness.

7. Knot.

8. More securely, with a pun on "swifter."

9. The phrase "Maid, stand apart" is addressed to Cariola. In shutting her eyes and rejecting all support, the Duchess dramatizes the quality of her choice.

1. Alexander and Lodowick were look-alike friends in an old ballad. For purely virtuous reasons, one slept with the wife of the other, but with the precaution indicated.

Act II

SCENE 1

[*Enter* BOSOLA *and* CASTRUCCIO.]

BOSOLA. You say you would fain be taken for an eminent courtier?

CASTRUCCIO. 'Tis the very main of my ambition.

BOSOLA. Let me see: you have a reasonable good face for 't already, and your nightcap expresses your ears sufficient largely. I would have you learn to twirl the strings of your band[2] with a good grace, and in a set speech, at th' end of every sentence, to hum three or four times, or blow your nose till it smart again, to recover your memory. When you come to be a president in criminal causes, if you smile upon a prisoner, hang him, but if you frown upon him and threaten him, let him be sure to 'scape the gallows.

CASTRUCCIO. I would be a very merry president.

BOSOLA. Do not sup o' night's; 'twill beget you an admirable wit.

CASTRUCCIO. Rather it would make me have a good stomach to quarrel; for they say, your roaring boys[3] eat meat seldom, and that makes them so valiant. But how shall I know whether the people take me for an eminent fellow?

BOSOLA. I will teach a trick to know it: give out you lie a-dying, and if you hear the common people curse you, be sure you are taken for one of the prime nightcaps.[4]

[*Enter an* OLD LADY.]

You come from painting now.

OLD LADY. From what?

BOSOLA. Why, from your scurvy face-physic. To behold thee not painted inclines somewhat near a miracle; these in thy face here were deep ruts and foul sloughs the last progress.[5] There was a lady in France that, having had the smallpox, flayed the skin off her face to make it more level; and whereas before she looked like a nutmeg-grater, after she resembled an abortive hedgehog.

OLD LADY. Do you call this painting?

BOSOLA. No, no, but you call it careening of an old morphewed lady, to make her disembogue again:[6] there's rough-cast phrase to your plastic.

OLD LADY. It seems you are well acquainted with my closet.

BOSOLA. One would suspect it for a shop of witchcraft, to find in it the fat of serpents, spawn of snakes, Jews' spittle, and their young children's ordure; and all these for the face. I would sooner eat a dead pigeon taken from the soles of the feet of

2. The elaborate ruff of the day had strings attached to it.

3. London town-bullies. (Webster's Amalfi has about it an occasional touch of Cheapside.)

4. Roughs who roamed the streets at night.

5. A progress was a formal royal journey of state.

6. Scraping ("careening") of an old, scaly ("morphewed") ship ("lady") to fit her for the ocean ("making her disembogue") again.

one sick of the plague than kiss one of you fasting.[7] Here are two of you, whose sin of your youth is the very patrimony of the physician; makes him renew his foot-cloth with the spring,[8] and change his high-priced courtesan with the fall of the leaf. I do wonder you do not loathe yourselves. Observe my meditation now.

What thing is in this outward form of man
To be beloved? We account it ominous,
If nature do produce a colt, or lamb,
A fawn, or goat, in any limb resembling
A man, and fly from 't as a prodigy:
Man stands amazed to see his deformity
In any other creature but himself.
But in our own flesh, though we bear diseases
Which have their true names only ta'en from beasts—
As the most ulcerous wolf and swinish measle[9]—
Though we are eaten up of lice and worms,
And though continually we bear about us
A rotten and dead body, we delight
To hide it in rich tissue: all our fear,
Nay, all our terror, is lest our physician
Should put us in the ground to be made sweet—
Your wife's gone to Rome: you two couple, and get you
To the wells at Lucca to recover your aches.[1]
I have other work on foot. [*Exeunt* CASTRUCCIO *and* OLD LADY.]
I observe our duchess
Is sick a-days: she pukes, her stomach seethes,
The fins of her eye-lids look most teeming blue,
She wanes i' th' cheek, and waxes fat i' th' flank,
And contrary to our Italian fashion,
Wears a loose-bodied gown: there's somewhat in 't.
I have a trick may chance discover it,
A pretty one; I have bought some apricocks,[2]
The first our spring yields.

[*Enter* ANTONIO *and* DELIO.]

DELIO. And so long since married?
You amaze me.

ANTONIO. Let me seal your lips for ever:
For, did I think that anything but th' air
Could carry these words from you, I should wish
You had no breath at all. [*turning to* BOSOLA] Now, sir, in your contemplation?

7. Centuries of traditional invective about women's cosmetic practices, and some contemporary practices and superstitions, lie behind this speech. Freshly killed pigeons were indeed applied to the feet of plague-victims, and fasting was supposed to cause bad breath.

8. The physician grows rich on those who have outworn their youth; every spring he buys a new harness for his horse and every fall a new mistress for himself.

9. "Wolf" and "measle": an ulcerous skin disease (lupus) and an infection of swine.

1. The wells at Lucca are the mineral springs at nearby Montecatini, then as now renowned as a place to "take the cure."

2. The old spelling "apricots," emphasizing the derivation of the name from Latin *praecox*, "early ripener."

You are studying to become a great wise fellow?

BOSOLA. Oh, sir, the opinion of wisdom is a foul tetter[3] that runs all over a man's body. If simplicity direct us to have no evil, it directs us to a happy being, for the subtlest folly proceeds from the subtlest wisdom. Let me be simply honest.

ANTONIO. I do understand your inside.

BOSOLA. Do you so?

ANTONIO. Because you would not seem to appear to th' world
Puffed up with your preferment, you continue
This out-of-fashion melancholy. Leave it, leave it.

BOSOLA. Give me leave to be honest in any phrase, in any compliment whatsoever. Shall I confess myself to you? I look no higher than I can reach: they are the gods that must ride on winged horses. A lawyer's mule of a slow pace will both suit my disposition and business; for, mark me, when a man's mind rides faster than his horse can gallop, they quickly both tire.

ANTONIO. You would look up to heaven, but I think
The devil, that rules i' th' air, stands in your light.

BOSOLA. Oh, sir, you are lord of the ascendant,[4] chief man with the duchess; a duke was your cousin-german removed. Say you were lineally descended from King Pepin,[5] or he himself, what of this? Search the heads of the greatest rivers in the world, you shall find them but bubbles of water. Some would think the souls of princes were brought forth by some more weighty cause than those of meaner persons: they are deceived, there's the same hand to them; the like passions sway them; the same reason that makes a vicar go to law for a tithe-pig,[6] and undo his neighbors, makes them spoil a whole province, and batter down goodly cities with the cannon.

[*Enter* DUCHESS *and* LADIES.]

DUCHESS. Your arm, Antonio; do I not grow fat?
I am exceeding short-winded. Bosola,
I would have you, sir, provide for me a litter,
Such a one as the Duchess of Florence rode in.

BOSOLA. The duchess used one when she was great with child.

DUCHESS. I think she did. Come hither, mend my ruff;
Here, when?
Thou art such a tedious lady, and thy breath smells
Of lemon-peels.[7] Would thou hadst done! Shall I swoon
Under thy fingers! I am so troubled
With the mother![8]

BOSOLA. [*aside*] I fear too much.

DUCHESS. I have heard you say

3. Scab.

4. In astrology, favored by the stars just coming into predominant influence.

5. Father of Charlemagne, and thus source of a great dynasty.

6. A parson was entitled to a tenth (tithe) of his parishioners' increase, but would be considered mean if he sued for a petty sum.

7. Lemon-peels were sometimes chewed to sweeten the breath. "Tedious": clumsy.

8. "The mother" is intestinal gas, sour stomach, but with a second meaning not lost on Bosola.

That the French courtiers wear their hats on 'fore
The king.
ANTONIO. I have seen it.
DUCHESS. In the presence?
ANTONIO. Yes.
DUCHESS. Why should not we bring up that fashion? 'Tis
Ceremony more than duty that consists
In the removing of a piece of felt.
Be you the example to the rest o' th' court;
Put on your hat first.
ANTONIO. You must pardon me.
I have seen, in colder countries than in France,
Nobles stand bare to th' prince, and the distinction
Methought showed reverently.
BOSOLA. I have a present for your grace.
DUCHESS. For me, sir?
BOSOLA. Apricocks, madam.
DUCHESS. O, sir, where are they?
I have heard of none to-year.
BOSOLA. [*aside*] Good; her color rises.
DUCHESS. Indeed, I thank you: they are wondrous fair ones.
What an unskillful fellow is our gardener!
We shall have none this month.
BOSOLA. Will not your grace pare them?
DUCHESS. No. They taste of musk, methinks; indeed they do.
BOSOLA. I know not: yet I wish your grace had pared 'em.
DUCHESS. Why?
BOSOLA. I forgot to tell you, the knave gardener,
Only to raise his profit by them the sooner,
Did ripen them in horse-dung.[9]
DUCHESS. O, you jest.
You shall judge: pray taste one.
ANTONIO. Indeed, madam,
I do not love the fruit.
DUCHESS. Sir, you are loath
To rob us of our dainties: 'tis a delicate fruit;
They say they are restorative.
BOSOLA. 'Tis a pretty art,
This grafting.
DUCHESS. 'Tis so; a bettering of nature.
BOSOLA. To make a pippin grow upon a crab,
A damson on a blackthorn. [*aside*] How greedily she eats them!
A whirlwind strike off these bawd farthingales![1]
For, but for that and the loose-bodied gown,
I should have discovered apparently[2]
The young springal[3] cutting a caper in her belly.

9. The heat of decomposing manure was widely supposed to have special virtues; but Bosola is thinking also of his post as provisor of the horse.

1. Early hoop-skirts, capable of concealing the figure.

2. Easily, certainly.

3. Colt, youngster.

DUCHESS. I thank you, Bosola. They were right good ones,
If they do not make me sick.
ANTONIO. How now, madam?
DUCHESS. This green fruit and my stomach are not friends;
How they swell me!
BOSOLA. [*aside*] Nay, you are too much swelled already.
DUCHESS. Oh, I am in an extreme cold sweat!
BOSOLA. I am very sorry.
DUCHESS. Lights to my chamber! O good Antonio,
I fear I am undone!
DELIO. Lights there, lights!
[*Exeunt* DUCHESS *and* LADIES. *Exit, on the other side,* BOSOLA.]
ANTONIO. O my most trusty Delio, we are lost!
I fear she's fall'n in labor; and there's left
No time for her remove.
DELIO. Have you prepared
Those ladies to attend her? and procured
That politic safe conveyance for the midwife
Your duchess plotted?
ANTONIO. I have.
DELIO. Make use, then, of this forced occasion:
Give out that Bosola hath poisoned her
With these apricocks; that will give some color
For her keeping close.
ANTONIO. Fie, fie, the physicians
Will then flock to her.
DELIO. For that you may pretend
She'll use some prepared antidote of her own,
Lest the physicians should re-poison her,
ANTONIO. I am lost in amazement: I know not what to think on 't. [*Exeunt.*]

SCENE 2

[*Enter* BOSOLA.]

BOSOLA. So, so, there's no question but her tetchiness[4] and most vulturous eating of the apricocks are apparent signs of breeding.

[*Enter an* OLD LADY.]

Now?

OLD LADY. I am in haste, sir.

BOSOLA. There was a young waiting-woman had a monstrous desire to see the glass-house[5]——

OLD LADY. Nay, pray let me go.

BOSOLA. And it was only to know what strange instrument it was should swell up a glass to the fashion of a woman's belly.

OLD LADY. I will hear no more of the glass-house. You are still

4. Irritability.
5. Where bottles were blown, near the theater in Blackfriars.

abusing women?

BOSOLA. Who, I? No; only, by the way now and then, mention your frailties. The orange-tree bears ripe and green fruit and blossoms all together; and some of you give entertainment for pure love, but more for more precious reward. The lusty spring smells well, but drooping autumn tastes well. If we have the same golden showers that rained in the time of Jupiter the thunderer, you have the same Danaës still,[6] to hold up their laps to receive them. Didst thou never study the mathematics?

OLD LADY. What's that sir?

BOSOLA. Why, to know the trick how to make a many lines meet in one center. Go, go, give your foster-daughters good counsel: tell them, that the devil takes delight to hang at a woman's girdle, like a false rusty watch, that she cannot discern how the time passes. [*Exit* OLD LADY.]

[*Enter* ANTONIO, DELIO, RODERIGO, *and* GRISOLAN.]

ANTONIO. Shut up the court-gates.
RODERIGO. Why, sir? what's the danger?
ANTONIO. Shut up the posterns[7] presently, and call
All the officers o' th' court.
GRISOLAN. I shall instantly. [*Exit.*]
ANTONIO. Who keeps the key o' th' park gate?
RODERIGO. Forobosco.
ANTONIO. Let him bring 't presently.

[*Re-enter* GRISOLAN *with* SERVANTS.]

1 SERVANT. O, gentlemen o' the court, the foulest treason!
BOSOLA. [*aside.*] If that these apricocks should be poisoned now.
Without my knowledge!
1 SERVANT. There was taken even now
A Switzer[8] in the duchess' bedchamber—
2 SERVANT. A Switzer?
1 SERVANT. With a pistol in his great cod-piece.[9]
BOSOLA. Ha, ha, ha!
1 SERVANT. The cod-piece was the case for 't.
2 SERVANT. There was
A cunning traitor: who would have searched his cod-piece?
1 SERVANT. True, if he had kept out of the ladies' chambers.
And all the molds of his buttons were leaden bullets.
2 SERVANT. O wicked cannibal!
A fire-lock in 's cod-piece!
1 SERVANT. 'Twas a French plot,
Upon my life.
2 SERVANT. To see what the devil can do!
ANTONIO. Are all the officers here?
SERVANTS. We are.
ANTONIO. Gentlemen,

6. Jupiter's success in wooing Danaë in a shower of gold traditionally illustrates female venality.
7. Outer gates of a castle or palace.
8. Swiss guard.
9. An outsize flap worn on the front of men's trunk hose.

We have lost much plate[1] you know, and but this evening
Jewels, to the value of four thousand ducats,
Are missing in the duchess' cabinet.
Are the gates shut?

SERVANT. Yes.

ANTONIO. 'Tis the duchess' pleasure
Each officer be locked into his chamber
Till the sun-rising; and to send the keys
Of all their chests and of their outward doors
Into her bed-chamber. She is very sick.

RODERIGO. At her pleasure.

ANTONIO. She entreats you take 't not ill:
The innocent shall be the more approved by it.

BOSOLA. Gentlemen o' th' wood-yard, where's your Switzer now?

1 SERVANT. By this hand, 'twas credibly reported by one o' th' black guard.[2] [*Exeunt all except* ANTONIO *and* DELIO.]

DELIO. How fares it with the duchess?

ANTONIO. She's exposed
Unto the worst of torture, pain, and fear.

DELIO. Speak to her all happy comfort.

ANTONIO. How I do play the fool with mine own danger!
You are this night, dear friend, to post to Rome;
My life lies in your service.

DELIO. Do not doubt me.

ANTONIO. Oh, 'tis far from me, and yet fear presents me
Somewhat that looks like danger.

DELIO. Believe it,
'Tis but the shadow of your fear, no more;
How superstitiously we mind our evils!
The throwing down salt, or crossing of a hare,
Bleeding at nose, the stumbling of a horse,
Or singing of a cricket, are of power
To daunt whole man in us. Sir, fare you well:
I wish you all the joys of a blessed father:
And, for my faith, lay this unto your breast,
Old friends, like old swords, still are trusted best. [*Exit.*]

[*Enter* CARIOLA.]

CARIOLA. Sir, you are the happy father of a son:
Your wife commends him to you.

ANTONIO. Blessed comfort!
For Heaven's sake tend her well: I'll presently
Go set a figure for 's nativity.[3] [*Exeunt.*]

SCENE 3

[*Enter* BOSOLA, *with a dark lantern.*]

BOSOLA. Sure I did hear a woman shriek: list, ha!

1. Massive gold and silver dishes, a frequent form of wealth in the days before banks.
2. Kitchen-scullions; the "wood-yard" is a source of firewood for kitchen and fireplaces.
3. Cast his horoscope.

And the sound came, if I received it right,
From the duchess' lodgings. There's some stratagem
In the confining all our courtiers
To their several wards: I must have part of it;
My intelligence will freeze else.[4] List, again!
It may be 'twas the melancholy bird,
Best friend of silence and of solitariness,
The owl, that screamed so. Ha! Antonio?

[*Enter* ANTONIO *with a candle, his sword drawn.*]

ANTONIO. I heard some noise. Who's there? What art thou?
Speak.

BOSOLA. Antonio? Put not your face nor body
To such a forced expression of fear.
I am Bosola, your friend.

ANTONIO. Bosola!
[*aside*] This mole does undermine me. Heard you not
A noise even now?

BOSOLA. From whence?

ANTONIO. From the duchess' lodging.

BOSOLA. Not I. Did you?

ANTONIO. I did, or else I dreamed.

BOSOLA. Let's walk towards it.

ANTONIO. No, it may be 'twas
But the rising of the wind.

BOSOLA. Very likely.
Methinks 'tis very cold, and yet you sweat:
You look wildly.

ANTONIO. I have been setting a figure[5]
For the duchess' jewels.

BOSOLA. Ah, and how falls your question?
Do you find it radical?[6]

ANTONIO. What's that to you?
'Tis rather to be questioned what design,
When all men were commanded to their lodgings,
Makes you a night-walker.

BOSOLA. In sooth, I'll tell you:
Now all the court's asleep, I thought the devil
Had least to do here; I came to say my prayers;
And if it do offend you I do so,
You are a fine courtier.

ANTONIO. [*aside*] This fellow will undo me.
You gave the duchess apricocks today:
Pray Heaven they were not poisoned!

BOSOLA. Poisoned? A Spanish fig[7]
For the imputation!

ANTONIO. Traitors are ever confident
Till they are discovered. There were jewels stolen, too;

4. All my news will be cold.
5. Establishing the loss involved. But Bosola takes the expression astrologically, as if Antonio were casting a horoscope.
6. Indicative, significant.
7. An obscene gesture, which Bosola doubtless makes onstage.

In my conceit, none are to be suspected
More than yourself.

BOSOLA. You are a false steward.

ANTONIO. Saucy slave, I'll pull thee up by the roots.

BOSOLA. Maybe the ruin will crush you to pieces.

ANTONIO. You are an impudent snake indeed, sir:
Are you scarce warm, and do you show your sting?
You libel well, sir.

BOSOLA. No, sir: copy it out,
And I will set my hand to 't.[8]

ANTONIO. [*aside*] My nose bleeds.
One that were superstitious would count
This ominous, when it merely comes by chance:
Two letters, that are wrought here for my name,
Are drowned in blood!
Mere accident. For you, sir, I'll take order
I' th' morn you shall be safe: [*aside*] 'tis that must color
Her lying-in: sir, this door you pass not:
I do not hold it fit that you come near
The duchess' lodgings, till you have quit yourself.
[*aside*] The great are like the base, nay, they are the same,
When they seek shameful ways to avoid shame. [*Exit.*]

BOSOLA. Antonio hereabout did drop a paper:
Some of your help, false friend: [*Opening his lantern.*] Oh, here it is.
What's here? A child's nativity calculated? [*Reads.*]

'The duchess was delivered of a son, 'tween the hours twelve and one in the night, *Anno Dom.* 1504,' that's this year—'*decimo nono Decembris.*'[9]—that's this night,—'taken according to the meridian of Malfi,'—that's our duchess: happy discovery! 'The lord of the first house being combust[1] in the ascendant, signifies short life; and Mars being in a human sign, joined to the tail of the Dragon, in the eighth house, doth threaten a violent death. *Caetera non scrutantur.*'[2]

Why, now 'tis most apparent: this precise[3] fellow
Is the duchess' bawd: I have it to my wish!
This is a parcel of intelligency
Our courtiers were cased up for: it needs must follow
That I must be committed on pretense
Of poisoning her; which I'll endure, and laugh at.
If one could find the father now! But that
Time will discover. Old Castruccio
I' th' morning posts to Rome: by him I'll send
A letter that shall make her brothers' galls
O'erflow their livers. This was a thrifty way.

8. Bosola denies the charge of underhanded malignancy, not by denying malignancy, but by offering to make it public.

9. The 19th of December.

1. Afire.

2. The rest is not to be seen. Mars and the Dragon are sinister signs, even separately; fatal together.

3. This very fellow, but also implying that Antonio acts like a Puritan, a "precisian." "Bawd": procurer.

Though lust do mask in ne'er so strange disguise,
She's oft found witty, but is never wise. [*Exit.*]

SCENE 4. *The palace of the* CARDINAL *at Rome.*

[*Enter* CARDINAL *and* JULIA.]

CARDINAL. Sit. Thou art my best of wishes. Prithee, tell me
What trick didst thou invent to come to Rome
Without thy husband.
JULIA. Why, my lord, I told him
I came to visit an old anchorite[4]
Here for devotion.
CARDINAL. Thou are a witty false one,
I mean, to him.
JULIA. You have prevailed with me
Beyond my strongest thoughts! I would not now
Find you inconstant.
CARDINAL. Do not put thyself
To such a voluntary torture, which proceeds
Out of your own guilt.
JULIA. How, my lord?
CARDINAL. You fear
My constancy, because you have approved[5]
Those giddy and wild turnings in yourself.
JULIA. Did you e'er find them?
CARDINAL. Sooth, generally for women;
A man might strive to make glass malleable,
Ere he should make them fixed.
JULIA. So, my lord.
CARDINAL. We had need go borrow that fantastic glass
Invented by Galileo the Florentine[6]
To view another spacious world i' th' moon,
And look to find a constant woman there.
JULIA. This is very well, my lord.
CARDINAL. Why do you weep?
Are tears your justification? The self-same tears
Will fall into your husband's bosom, lady,
With a loud protestation that you love him
Above the world. Come, I'll love you wisely,
That's jealously, since I am very certain
You cannot make me cuckold.
JULIA. I'll go home
To my husband.
CARDINAL. You may thank me, lady,
I have taken you off your melancholy perch,
Bore you upon my fist, and showed you game,

4. Hermit.
5. Experienced.
6. In 1504, Galileo's telescope was more than 100 years in the future, but the reference was topical for Webster's audience.

And let you fly at it.[7] I pray thee, kiss me.
When thou wast with thy husband, thou wast watched
Like a tame elephant: still you are to thank me:
Thou hadst only kisses from him and high feeding;
But what delight was that? 'Twas just like one
That hath a little fingering on the lute,
Yet cannot tune it: still you are to thank me.

JULIA. You told me of a piteous wound i' th' heart
And a sick liver, when you wooed me first,
And spake like one in physic.[8] [*A knock is heard.*]

CARDINAL. Who's that?

[*Enter* SERVANT.]

Rest firm, for my affection to thee,
Lightning moves slow to 't.[9]

SERVANT. Madam, a gentleman,
That's come post from Malfi, desires to see you.

CARDINAL. Let him enter. I'll withdraw. [*Exit.*]

SERVANT. He says
Your husband, old Castruccio, is come to Rome,
Most pitifully tired with riding post.[1] [*Exit.*]

[*Enter* DELIO.]

JULIA. Signior Delio! [*aside*] 'tis one of my old suitors.

DELIO. I was bold to come and see you.

JULIA. Sir, you are welcome.

DELIO. Do you lie here?

JULIA. Sure, your own experience
Will satisfy you no: our Roman prelates
Do not keep lodging for ladies.

DELIO. Very well.
I have brought you no commendations from your husband,
For I know none by him.

JULIA. I hear he's come to Rome.

DELIO. I never knew man and beast, of a horse and a knight,
So weary of each other: if he had had a good back,
He would have undertook to have borne his horse,
His breech was so pitifully sore.

JULIA. Your laughter
Is my pity.

DELIO. Lady, I know not whether
You want money, but I have brought you some.

JULIA. From my husband?

DELIO. No, from mine own allowance.

JULIA. I must hear the condition, ere I be bound to take it.

DELIO. Look on't, 'tis gold: hath it not a fine color?

JULIA. I have a bird more beautiful.

DELIO. Try the sound on 't.

7. The Cardinal speaks of himself as a falconer training a bird (Julia).
8. Like a man under a doctor's care.
9. By comparison.
1. When riding post, one changed horses at regular intervals without stopping to rest oneself.

JULIA. A lute-string far exceeds it:
It hath no smell, like cassia or civet;
Nor is it physical,[2] though some fond doctors
Persuade us seethe 't in cullises.[3] I'll tell you,
This is a creature bred by——

[*Re-enter* SERVANT.]

SERVANT. Your husband's come,
Hath delivered a letter to the Duke of Calabria
That, to my thinking, hath put him out of his wits. [*Exit.*]

JULIA. Sir, you hear:
Pray, let me know your business and your suit
As briefly as can be.

DELIO. With good speed: I would wish you,
At such time as you are non-resident
With your husband, my mistress.

JULIA. Sir, I'll go ask my husband if I shall,
And straight return your answer. [*Exit.*]

DELIO. Very fine!
Is this her wit, or honesty, that speaks thus?
I heard one say the duke was highly moved
With a letter sent from Malfi. I do fear
Antonio is betrayed: how fearfully
Shows his ambition now! Unfortunate fortune!
They pass through whirlpools, and deep woes do shun,
Who the event weigh ere the action's done.[4] [*Exit.*]

SCENE 5

[*Enter* CARDINAL, *and* FERDINAND *with a letter.*]

FERDINAND. I have this night digged up a mandrake.[5]

CARDINAL. Say you?

FERDINAND. And I am grown mad with 't.

CARDINAL. What's the prodigy?

FERDINAND. Read there—a sister damned: she's loose i' th' hilts;[6]
Grown a notorious strumpet.

CARDINAL. Speak lower.

FERDINAND. Lower?
Rogues do not whisper 't now, but seek to publish 't
(As servants do the bounty of their lords)
Aloud; and with a covetous searching eye,
To mark who note them. O, confusion seize her!
She hath had most cunning bawds to serve her turn,
And more secure conveyances for lust
Than towns of garrison for service.

CARDINAL. Is 't possible?

2. Medicinally valuable.
3. Boil it up in a broth.
4. I.e., who look ahead at the consequences of their actions.
5. A fabulous root, violently aphrodisiac but also deadly poison. Both aspects apply to Ferdinand.
6. I.e., promiscuous; literally, a sword which is too limber.

Can this be certain?

FERDINAND. Rhubarb, oh, for rhubarb[7]
To purge this choler! Here's the cursèd day
To prompt my memory, and here 't shall stick
Till of her bleeding heart I make a sponge
To wipe it out.

CARDINAL. Why do you make yourself
So wild a tempest?

FERDINAND. Would I could be one,
That I might toss her palace 'bout her ears,
Root up her goodly forests, blast her meads.[8]
And lay her general territory as waste
As she hath done her honors.

CARDINAL. Shall our blood,
The royal blood of Aragon and Castile,
Be thus attainted?

FERDINAND. Apply desperate physic:
We must not now use balsamum,[9] but fire,
The smarting cupping-glass, for that 's the mean
To purge infected blood, such blood as hers.
There is a kind of pity in mine eye,
I'll give it to my handkercher; and now 'tis here,
I'll bequeath this to her bastard.

CARDINAL. What to do?

FERDINAND. Why, to make soft lint for his mother's wounds,
When I have hewed her to pieces.

CARDINAL. Cursèd creature!
Unequal nature, to place women's hearts
So far upon the left side![1]

FERDINAND. Foolish men,
That e'er will trust their honor in a bark
Made of so slight weak bulrush as is woman,
Apt every minute to sink it!

CARDINAL. Thus ignorance, when it hath purchased honor,
It cannot wield it.

FERDINAND. Methinks I see her laughing—
Excellent hyena! Talk to me somewhat, quickly,
Or my imagination will carry me
To see her in the shameful act of sin.

CARDINAL. With whom?

FERDINAND. Happily[2] with some strong-thighed bargeman,
Or one o' the woodyard that can quoit the sledge
Or toss the bar, or else some lovely squire
That carries coals up to her privy lodgings.[3]

7. Rhubarb, as a laxative, was supposed to be good for the high pressures of choler, hot-burning rage.
8. Open fields.
9. Balm, a gentle remedy, gives way to cautery ("fire") and the "cupping-glass," by which people were bled.
1. The left is the sinister, or unlucky, side.
2. Probably, haply.
3. Beefy fellows employed in maintaining the supply of firewood, imagined as competing in gross tests of strength (throwing the sledge, tossing the bar), the winner to be promoted to the duchess's bed.

CARDINAL. You fly beyond your reason.
FERDINAND. Go to, mistress!
'Tis not your whore's milk that shall quench my wild fire,
But your whore's blood.
CARDINAL. How idly shows this rage, which carries you,
As men conveyed by witches through the air,
On violent whirlwinds! This intemperate noise
Fitly resembles deaf men's shrill discourse,
Who talk aloud, thinking all other men
To have their imperfection.
FERDINAND. Have not you
My palsy?
CARDINAL. Yes, I can be angry, but
Without this rupture: there is not in nature
A thing that makes man so deformed, so beastly,
As doth intemperate anger. Chide yourself.
You have divers men who never yet expressed
Their strong desire of rest but by unrest,
By vexing of themselves. Come, put yourself
In tune.
FERDINAND. So; I will only study to seem
The thing I am not. I could kill her now,
In you, or in myself; for I do think
It is some sin in us heaven doth revenge
By her.
CARDINAL. Are you stark mad?
FERDINAND. I would have their bodies
Burnt in a coal-pit with the ventage stopped,
That their cursed smoke might not ascend to heaven;
Or dip the sheets they lie in in pitch or sulphur,
Wrap them in 't, and then light them like a match;
Or else to-boil their bastard to a cullis,
And give 't his lecherous father to renew
The sin of his back.[4]
CARDINAL. I'll leave you.
FERDINAND. Nay, I have done.
I am confident, had I been damned in hell,
And should have heard of this, it would have put me
Into a cold sweat. In, in; I'll go sleep.
Till I know who leaps my sister, I'll not stir:
That known, I'll find scorpions to string my whips,[5]
And fix her in a general eclipse. [*Exeunt.*]

4. Only boiling down the bastard to a broth ("cullis") and feeding him to his father, as Atreus did to Thyestes in Greek legend, will satisfy Ferdinand. Thus the father will be made to "renew" (repair, atone for) the sin of his back in begetting the child.

5. Tipping the thongs of a whip with "scorpions" (tips of jagged steel or lead that sting and bite the flesh) is an old metaphor for aggravated punishment.

Act III

SCENE 1. *Amalfi.*

[*Enter* ANTONIO *and* DELIO.]

ANTONIO. Our noble friend, my most beloved Delio!
Oh, you have been a stranger long at court;
Came you along with the Lord Ferdinand?
DELIO. I did, sir. And how fares your noble duchess?
ANTONIO. Right fortunately well: she's an excellent
Feeder of pedigrees; since you last saw her,
She hath had two children more, a son and daughter.
DELIO. Methinks 'twas yesterday: let me but wink,
And not behold your face, which to mine eye
Is somewhat leaner, verily I should dream
It were within this half-hour.
ANTONIO. You have not been in law, friend Delio,
Nor in prison, nor a suitor at the court,
Nor begged the reversion of some great man's place,
Nor troubled with an old wife, which doth make
Your time so insensibly hasten.[6]
DELIO. Pray, sir, tell me.
Hath not this news arrived yet to the ear
Of the lord cardinal?
ANTONIO. I fear it hath:
The Lord Ferdinand, that's newly come to court,
Doth bear himself right dangerously.
DELIO. Pray, why?
ANTONIO. He is so quiet that he seems to sleep
The tempest out, as dormice do in winter.
Those houses that are haunted are most still
Till the devil be up.
DELIO. What say the common people?
ANTONIO. The common rabble do directly say
She is a strumpet.
DELIO. And your graver heads
Which would be politic, what censure they?
ANTONIO. They do observe I grow to infinite purchase,
The left hand way,[7] and all suppose the duchess
Would amend it, if she could; for, say they,
Great princes, though they grudge their officers
Should have such large and unconfinéd means
To get wealth under them, will not complain,
Lest thereby they should make them odious
Unto the people; for other obligation
Of love or marriage between her and me
They never dream of.
DELIO. The Lord Ferdinand
Is going to bed.

6. I.e., This is what makes your time pass imperceptibly ("insensibly") by.

7. I.e., they think I am getting rich dishonestly.

[*Enter* DUCHESS, FERDINAND, *and* BOSOLA.]

FERDINAND. I'll instantly to bed,
For I am weary.—I am to bespeak
A husband for you.
DUCHESS. For me, sir? Pray, who is't?
FERDINAND. The great Count Malateste.
DUCHESS. Fie upon him!
A count? He's a mere stick of sugar-candy;
You may look quite through him. When I choose
A husband, I will marry for your honor.
FERDINAND. You shall do well in 't. How is 't, worthy Antonio?
DUCHESS. But, sir, I am to have private conference with you
About a scandalous report is spread
Touching mine honor.
FERDINAND. Let me be ever deaf to 't:
One of Pasquil's paper bullets,[8] court-calumny,
A pestilent air, which princes' palaces
Are seldom purged of. Yet, say that it were true,
I pour it in your bosom, my fixed love
Would strongly excuse, extenuate, nay, deny
Faults, were they apparent in you. Go, be safe
In your own innocency.
DUCHESS. [*aside*] O blesséd comfort!
This deadly air is purged.
[*Exeunt* DUCHESS, ANTONIO, *and* DELIO.]
FERDINAND. Her guilt treads on
Hot-burning coulters.[9] Now, Bosola,
How thrives our intelligence?
BOSOLA. Sir, uncertainly
'Tis rumored she hath had three bastards, but
By whom we may go read i' th' stars.
FERDINAND. Why, some
Hold opinion all things are written there.
BOSOLA. Yes, if we could find spectacles to read them.
I do suspect there hath been some sorcery
Used on the duchess.
FERDINAND. Sorcery? To what purpose?
BOSOLA. To make her dote on some desertless fellow
She shames to acknowledge.
FERDINAND. Can your faith give way
To think there's power in potions or in charms,
To make us love whether we will or no?
BOSOLA. Most certainly.
FERDINAND. Away! These are mere gulleries,[1] horrid things,
Invented by some cheating mountebanks
To abuse us. Do you think that herbs or charms

8. Anonymous satires were traditionally pasted on the statue of Pasquillo, or Pasquino, near Piazza Navona in Rome, and attributed to his authorship.
9. Medieval virginity-inquests customarily required the questioned lady to walk barefoot over red-hot plowshares ("coulters").
1. Deceits.

Can force the will? Some trials have been made
In this foolish practice, but the ingredients
Were lenitive poisons,[2] such as are of force
To make the patient mad; and straight the witch
Swears by equivocation they are in love.
The witchcraft lies in her rank blood. This night
I will force confession from her. You told me
You had got, within these two days, a false key
Into her bedchamber.

BOSOLA. I have.

FERDINAND. As I would wish.

BOSOLA. What do you intend to do?

FERDINAND. Can you guess?

BOSOLA. No.

FERDINAND. Do not ask, then:
He that can compass me, and know my drifts,
May say he hath put a girdle 'bout the world,
And sounded all her quicksands.

BOSOLA. I do not
Think so.

FERDINAND. What do you think, then, pray?

BOSOLA. That you
Are your own chronicle too much, and grossly
Flatter yourself.

FERDINAND. Give me thy hand; I thank thee:
I never gave pension but to flatterers,
Till I entertained thee. Farewell.
That friend a great man's ruin strongly checks,
Who rails into his belief all his defects. [*Exeunt.*]

SCENE 2. *The Bedchamber of the* DUCHESS.

[*Enter* DUCHESS, ANTONIO, *and* CARIOLA.]

DUCHESS. Bring me the casket hither, and the glass.
You get no lodging here tonight, my lord.

ANTONIO. Indeed, I must persuade one.

DUCHESS. Very good:
I hope in time 'twill grow into a custom,
That noblemen shall come with cap and knee
To purchase a night's lodging of their wives.

ANTONIO. I must lie here.

DUCHESS. Must! You are a lord of misrule.[3]

ANTONIO. Indeed, my rule is only in the night.

DUCHESS. To what use will you put me?

ANTONIO. We'll sleep together.

DUCHESS. Alas, what pleasure can two lovers find in sleep!

2. Secret, slow-working poisons.
3. The mock-monarch of a carnival festival.

CARIOLA. My lord, I lie with her often, and I know
She'll much disquiet you.
ANTONIO. See, you are complained of.
CARIOLA. For she's the sprawling'st bedfellow.
ANTONIO. I shall like her
The better for that.
CARIOLA. Sir, shall I ask you a question?
ANTONIO. Oh, I pray thee, Cariola.
CARIOLA. Wherefore still, when you lie
With my lady, do you rise so early?
ANTONIO. Laboring men
Count the clock oftenest, Cariola, are glad
When their task's ended.
DUCHESS. I'll stop your mouth. [*Kisses him.*]
ANTONIO. Nay, that's but one; Venus had two soft doves
To draw her chariot; I must have another—
[*She kisses him again.*]
When wilt thou marry, Cariola?
CARIOLA. Never, my lord.
ANTONIO. Oh, fie upon this single life! Forgo it.
We read how Daphne, for her peevish flight,
Became a fruitless bay-tree; Syrinx turned
To the pale empty reed; Anaxarete
Was frozen into marble: whereas those
Which married, or proved kind unto their friends,
Were by a gracious influence transhaped
Into the olive, pomegranate, mulberry.
Became flowers, precious stones, or eminent stars.[4]
CARIOLA. This is a vain poetry, but I pray you tell me,
If there were proposed me, wisdom, riches, and beauty,
In three several young men, which should I choose?
ANTONIO. 'Tis a hard question: this was Paris' case,
And he was blind in 't, and there was great cause;
For how was 't possible he could judge right,
Having three amorous goddesses in view,
And they stark naked? 'Twas a motion[5]
Were able to benight the apprehension
Of the severest counsellor of Europe.
Now I look on both your faces so well formed,
It puts me in mind of a question I would ask.
CARIOLA. What is 't?
ANTONIO. I do wonder why hard-favored ladies,
For the most part, keep worse-favored waiting-women

4. The olive was created by Athene; the mulberry gained its color from the blood of Pyramus and Thisbe; the pomegranate seems to have no particular mythological origin. Most of the other stories of ladies being transformed for complying, or not complying, with the solicitations of a god are from Ovid, *Metamorphoses*.

5. Spectacle. Paris had to choose between Hera, Athena, and Aphrodite, goddesses of marriage, wisdom, and love; his selecting the latter led to the Trojan war.

To attend them, and cannot endure fair ones.
DUCHESS. Oh, that's soon answered.
Did you ever in your life know an ill painter
Desire to have his dwelling next door to the shop
Of an excellent picture-maker? 'Twould disgrace
His face-making, and undo him. I prithee,
When were we so merry?—My hair tangles.
ANTONIO. Pray thee, Cariola, let's steal forth the room,
And let her talk to herself: I have divers times
Served her the like, when she hath chafed extremely.
I love to see her angry. Softly, Cariola.
[*Exeunt* ANTONIO *and* CARIOLA.]
DUCHESS. Doth not the color of my hair 'gin to change?
When I wax gray, I shall have all the court
Powder their hair with arras,[6] to be like me.
You have cause to love me; I entered you into my heart
Before you would vouchsafe to call for the keys.
[*Enter* FERDINAND *behind.*]
We shall one day have my brothers take you napping;
Methinks his presence, being now in court,
Should make you keep your own bed; but you'll say
Love mixed with fear is sweetest. I'll assure you,
You shall get no more children till my brothers
Consent to be your gossips.[7] Have you lost your tongue?
[*She turns and sees* FERDINAND.]
'Tis welcome:
For know, whether I am doomed to live or die,
I can do both like a prince.
FERDINAND. Die, then, quickly! [*Giving her a poniard.*]
Virtue, where art thou hid? What hideous thing
Is it that doth eclipse thee?
DUCHESS. Pray, sir, hear me.
FERDINAND. Or is it true thou art but a bare name,
And no essential thing?
DUCHESS. Sir—
FERDINAND. Do not speak.
DUCHESS. No, sir: I will plant my soul in mine ears, to hear you.
FERDINAND. O most imperfect light of human reason,
That mak'st us so unhappy to foresee
What we can least prevent! Pursue thy wishes,
And glory in them: there's in shame no comfort
But to be past all bounds and sense of shame.
DUCHESS. I pray, sir, hear me. I am married.
FERDINAND. So!
DUCHESS. Haply,[8] not to your liking: but for that,
Alas, your shears do come untimely now

6. Orris-root, used in powdered form to make hair artificially gray.
7. Intimate friends, but also sponsors in baptism.
8. Perhaps.

To clip the bird's wings that's already flown!
Will you see my husband?

FERDINAND. Yes, if I could change
Eyes with a basilisk.[9]

DUCHESS. Sure, you came hither
By his confederacy.

FERDINAND. The howling of a wolf
Is music to thee, screech-owl: prithee, peace.
Whate'er thou art that hast enjoyed my sister,
For I am sure thou hear'st me, for thine own sake
Let me not know thee. I came hither prepared
To work thy discovery; yet am now persuaded
It would beget such violent effects
As would damn us both. I would not for ten millions
I had beheld thee: therefore use all means
I never may have knowledge of thy name;
Enjoy thy lust still, and a wretched life,
On that condition. And for thee, vile woman,
If thou do wish thy lecher may grow old
In thy embracements, I would have thee build
Such a room for him as our anchorites
To holier use inhabit. Let not the sun
Shine on him till he's dead; let dogs and monkeys
Only converse with him, and such dumb things
To whom nature denies use to sound his name;
Do not keep a paraquito,[1] lest she learn it;
If thou do love him, cut out thine own tongue,
Lest it bewray him.

DUCHESS. Why might not I marry?
I have not gone about in this to create
Any new world or custom.

FERDINAND. Thou art undone;
And thou hast ta'en that massy sheet of lead
That hid thy husband's bones, and folded it
About my heart.

DUCHESS. Mine bleeds for 't.

FERDINAND. Thine? Thy heart?
What should I name't unless a hollow bullet
Filled with unquenchable wild-fire?

DUCHESS. You are in this
Too strict, and were you not my princely brother,
I would say, too willful. My reputation
Is safe.

FERDINAND. Dost thou know what reputation is?
I'll tell thee—to small purpose, since the instruction
Comes now too late.
Upon a time Reputation, Love, and Death,

9. The mythical basilisk was fabled to kill with a glance.

1. Parrot.

Would travel o'er the world; and it was concluded
That they should part, and take three several ways.
Death told them, they should find him in great battles,
Or cities plagued with plagues. Love gives them counsel
To inquire for him 'mongst unambitious shepherds,
Where dowries were not talked of, and sometimes
'Mongst quiet kindred that had nothing left
By their dead parents. "Stay," quoth Reputation,
"Do not forsake me; for it is my nature,
If once I part from any man I meet,
I am never found again." And so for you:
You have shook hands with Reputation,
And made him invisible. So, fare you well.
I will never see you more.

DUCHESS. Why should only I,
Of all the other princes of the world,
Be cased up, like a holy relic? I have youth
And a little beauty.

FERDINAND. So you have some virgins
That are witches. I will never see thee more. [*Exit.*]

[*Enter* ANTONIO *with a pistol, and* CARIOLA.]

DUCHESS. You saw this apparition?

ANTONIO. Yes. We are
Betrayed. How came he hither? I should turn
This to thee, for that. [*Pointing the pistol at* CARIOLA.]

CARIOLA. Pray, sir, do; and when
That you have cleft my heart, you shall read there
Mine innocence.

DUCHESS. That gallery gave him entrance.

ANTONIO. I would this terrible thing would come again,
That, standing on my guard, I might relate
My warrantable[2] love. [*She shows the poniard.*]
Ha! What means this?

DUCHESS. He left this with me.

ANTONIO. And it seems did wish
You would use it on yourself.

DUCHESS. His action seemed
To intend so much.

ANTONIO. This hath a handle to 't
As well as a point: turn it towards him, and
So fasten the keen edge in his rank gall. [*Knocking within.*]
How now! Who knocks? More earthquakes?

DUCHESS. I stand
As if a mine beneath my feet were ready
To be blown up.

CARIOLA. 'Tis Bosola.

DUCHESS. Away!
O misery! Methinks unjust actions

2. Legitimate, defensible.

Should wear these masks and curtains, and not we.
You must instantly part hence: I have fashioned it
Already. [*Exit* ANTONIO.]

[*Enter* BOSOLA.]

BOSOLA. The duke your brother is ta'en up in a whirlwind,
Hath took horse, and 's rid post to Rome.

DUCHESS. So late?

BOSOLA. He told me, as he mounted into th' saddle,
You were undone.

DUCHESS. Indeed, I am very near it.

BOSOLA. What's the matter?

DUCHESS. Antonio, the master of our household,
Hath dealt so falsely with me in 's accounts:
My brother stood engaged with me for money
Ta'en up of certain Neapolitan Jews,
And Antonio lets the bonds be forfeit.[3]

BOSOLA. Strange!—[*aside*] This is cunning.

DUCHESS. And hereupon
My brother's bills at Naples are protested
Against.[4]—Call up our officers.

BOSOLA. I shall. [*Exit.*]

[*Re-enter* ANTONIO.]

DUCHESS. The place that you must fly to is Ancona:[5]
Hire a house there; I'll send after you
My treasure and my jewels. Our weak safety
Runs upon enginous wheels:[6] short syllables
Must stand for periods. I must now accuse you
Of such a feignèd crime as Tasso calls
Magnanima menzogna, a noble lie,
'Cause it must shield our honors. Hark! They are coming.

[*Re-enter* BOSOLA *and* OFFICERS.]

ANTONIO. Will your grace hear me?

DUCHESS. I have got well by you; you have yielded me
A million of loss: I am like to inherit
The people's curses for your stewardship.
You had the trick in audit-time to be sick,
Till I had signed your *quietus*;[7] and that cured you
Without help of a doctor. Gentlemen,
I would have this man be an example to you all;
So shall you hold my favor; I pray, let him;[8]
For h'as done that, alas, you would not think of,
And, because I intend to be rid of him,
I mean not to publish. [*to* ANTONIO] Use your fortune elsewhere.

3. I.e., my brother advanced me some money in the form of notes, which I sent to Neapolitan money-lenders; now Antonio has let them call on the Duke for payment.
4. I.e., the Duke of Calabria's checks have bounced.
5. Ancona lies on the Adriatic coast of Italy, across the peninsula from Amalfi and well to the north.
6. Automatic wheels.
7. Receipt.
8. Release him.

ANTONIO. I am strongly armed to brook my overthrow;
As commonly men bear with a hard year,
I will not blame the cause on 't; but do think
The necessity of my malevolent star
Procures this, not her humor. Oh, the inconstant
And rotten ground of service! You may see,
'Tis even like him, that in a winter night,
Takes a long slumber o'er a dying fire,
A-loth to part from 't; yet parts thence as cold
As when he first sat down.

DUCHESS. We do confiscate,
Towards the satisfying of your accounts,
All that you have.

ANTONIO. I am yours, and 'tis very fit
All mine should be so.

DUCHESS. So, sir, you have your pass.[9]

ANTONIO. You may see, gentlemen, what 'tis to serve
A prince with body and soul. [*Exit.*]

BOSOLA. Here's an example for extortion: what moisture is drawn out of the sea, when foul weather comes, pours down, and runs into the sea again.

DUCHESS. I would know what are your opinions of this Antonio.

SECOND OFFICER. He could not abide to see a pig's head gaping: I thought your grace would find him a Jew.[1]

THIRD OFFICER. I would you had been his officer, for your own sake.

FOURTH OFFICER. You would have had more money.

FIRST OFFICER. He stopped his ears with black wool, and to those came to him for money said he was thick of hearing.

SECOND OFFICER. Some said he was an hermaphrodite, for he could not abide a woman.

FOURTH OFFICER. How scurvy proud he would look when the treasury was full! Well, let him go!

FIRST OFFICER. Yes, and the chippings of the buttery fly after him, to scour his gold chain![2]

DUCHESS. Leave us. [*Exeunt* OFFICERS.] What do you think of these?

BOSOLA. That these are rogues that in 's prosperity, but to have waited on his fortune, could have wished his dirty stirrup riveted through their noses, and followed after 's mule, like a bear in a ring; would have prostituted their daughters to his lust; made their first-born intelligencers; thought none happy but such as were born under his blessed planet, and wore his livery: and do these lice drop off now? Well, never look to have the like again:[3] he hath left a sort of flattering rogues

9. Passport, leave to depart.

1. Jews were identified by their antipathy to pork; but the assumptions here are deliberately ridiculous.

2. A gold chain was the steward's traditional badge of office. Bread crumbs (the "chippings of the buttery") were used to polish gold and silver plate.

3. I.e., a servant as good as he was.

behind him; their doom must follow. Princes pay flatterers in their own money: flatterers dissemble their vices, and they dissemble their lies; that's justice. Alas, poor gentleman!

DUCHESS. Poor? He hath amply filled his coffers.

BOSOLA. Sure, he was too honest. Pluto, the god of riches, when he 's sent by Jupiter to any man, he goes limping, to signify that wealth that comes on God's name comes slowly; but when he 's sent on the devil's errand, he rides post and comes in by scuttles.[4] Let me show you what a most unvalued jewel you have in a wanton humor thrown away, to bless the man shall find him. He was an excellent courtier and most faithful; a soldier that thought it as beastly to know his own value too little as devilish to acknowledge it too much. Both his virtue and form deserved a far better fortune: his discourse rather delighted to judge itself than show itself; his breast was filled with all perfection, and yet it seemed a private whispering-room,[5] it made so little noise of 't.

DUCHESS. But he was basely descended.

BOSOLA. Will you make yourself a mercenary herald, rather to examine men's pedigrees than virtues? You shall want[6] him: for know, an honest statesman to a prince is like a cedar planted by a spring; the spring bathes the tree's root, the grateful tree rewards it with his shadow: you have not done so. I would sooner swim to the Bermoothes[7] on two politicians' rotten bladders, tied together with an intelligencer's heart-string, than depend on so changeable a prince's favor. Fare thee well, Antonio! Since the malice of the world would needs down with thee, it cannot be said yet that any ill happened unto thee, considering thy fall was accompanied with virtue.

DUCHESS. Oh, you render me excellent music!

BOSOLA. Say you?

DUCHESS. This good one that you speak of is my husband.

BOSOLA. Do I not dream? Can this ambitious age
Have so much goodness in 't as to prefer
A man merely for worth, without these shadows
Of wealth and painted honors? Possible?

DUCHESS. I have had three children by him.

BOSOLA. Fortunate lady!
For you have made your private nuptial bed
The humble and fair seminary of peace.
No question but many an unbeneficed scholar[8]
Shall pray for you for this deed, and rejoice
That some preferment in the world can yet
Arise from merit. The virgins of your land
That have no dowries shall hope your example
Will raise them to rich husbands. Should you want

4. In haste. Unvalued: invaluable.
5. Confessional-booth.
6. Miss.
7. The Bermudas, unknown in 1504, but very topical a hundred years later, when the play was written.
8. A scholar without an official appointment.

Soldiers, 'twould make the very Turks and Moors
Turn Christians, and serve you for this act.
Last, the neglected poets of your time,
In honor of this trophy of a man,
Raised by that curious engine, your white hand,
Shall thank you, in your grave, for 't; and make that
More reverend than all the cabinets[9]
Of living princes. For Antonio,
His fame shall likewise flow from many a pen,
When heralds shall want coats to sell to men.

DUCHESS. As I taste comfort in this friendly speech,
So would I find concealment.

BOSOLA. Oh, the secret of my prince,
Which I will wear on th' inside of my heart!

DUCHESS. You shall take charge of all my coin and jewels,
And follow him; for he retires himself
To Ancona.

BOSOLA. So.

DUCHESS. Whither, within few days,
I mean to follow thee.

BOSOLA. Let me think:
I would wish your grace to feign a pilgrimage
To our Lady of Loreto,[1] scarce seven leagues
From fair Ancona; so may you depart
Your country with more honor, and your flight
Will seem a princely progress, retaining
Your usual train about you.

DUCHESS. Sir, your direction
Shall lead me by the hand.

CARIOLA. In my opinion,
She were better progress to the baths at Lucca,
Or go visit the Spa in Germany;
For, if you will believe me, I do not like
This jesting with religion, this feigned
Pilgrimage.

DUCHESS. Thou art a superstitious fool.
Prepare us instantly for our departure.
Past sorrows, let us moderately lament them;
For those to come, seek wisely to prevent them.

[*Exit* DUCHESS, *with* CARIOLA.]

BOSOLA. A politician is the devil's quilted anvil;
He fashions all sins on him, and the blows
Are never heard: he may work in a lady's chamber,
As here for proof. What rests but I reveal
All to my lord? Oh, this base quality
Of intelligencer! Why, every quality i' th' world
Prefers but gain or commendation:

9. Reception-rooms. She will be more honored in her grave than living princes in their courts.

1. The shrine of the Virgin at Loreto was famous throughout Europe.

Now for this act I am certain to be raised,
And men that paint weeds to the life are praised.

SCENE 3. *Rome.*

[*Enter* CARDINAL, FERDINAND, MALATESTE, PESCARA, SILVIO, DELIO.]

CARDINAL. Must we turn soldier, then?
MALATESTE. The emperor,[2]
Hearing your worth that way, ere you attained
This reverend garment, joins you in commission
With the right fortunate soldier the Marquis of Pescara.
And the famous Lannoy.
CARDINAL. He that had the honor
Of taking the French king prisoner?[3]
MALATESTE. The same.
Here's a plot drawn for a new fortification
At Naples. [*They talk apart.*]
FERDINAND. This great Count Malateste, I perceive,
Hath got employment?
DELIO. No employment, my lord;
A marginal note in the muster-book, that he is
A voluntary lord.
FERDINAND. He 's no soldier?

DELIO. He has worn gunpowder in 's hollow tooth for the toothache.[4]

SILVIO. He comes to the leaguer[5] with a full intent
To eat fresh beef and garlic, means to stay
Till the scent be gone, and straight return to court.

DELIO. He hath read all the late service as the city chronicle relates it, and keeps two pewterers going, only to express battles in model.[6]

SILVIO. Then he'll fight by the book.

DELIO. By the almanac, I think, to choose good days and shun the critical. That's his mistress' scarf.

SILVIO. Yes, he protests he would do much for that taffeta.

DELIO. I think he would run away from a battle, to save it from taking prisoner.

SILVIO. He is horribly afraid gunpowder will spoil the perfume on 't.

DELIO. I saw a Dutchman break his pate once for calling him pot-gun;[7] he made his head have a bore in 't like a musket.

2. The Spanish Emperor, Charles V. The transformation of the Cardinal to a soldier (which has no consequence for the action of the play) again recalls Cesare Borgia, who was created a cardinal by his father, Alexander VI, before he resigned the office and became famous, or infamous, as a soldier.
3. Charles de Lannoy, Belgian by origin, did indeed capture Francis I at Pavia, but only in 1525, 21 years after the date of the play's supposed action.
4. Saltpeter was sometimes used against the toothache.
5. Assembly, muster of the troops.
6. He has studied all the recent military history as it's represented on pewter dishes, and employs two craftsmen of his own to keep him up to date.
7. Loudmouth.

SILVIO. I would he had made a touchhole to 't. He is indeed a guarded sumpter-cloth,[8] only for the remove of the court.

[*Enter* BOSOLA *and speaks to* FERDINAND *and the* CARDINAL.]

PESCARA. Bosola arrived? What should be the business?
Some falling-out amongst the cardinals.
These factions amongst great men, they are like
Foxes; when their heads are divided,
They carry fire in their tails, and all the country
About them goes to wrack for 't.[9]

SILVIO. What's that Bosola?

DELIO. I knew him in Padua—a fantastical scholar, like such who study to know how many knots were in Hercules' club, of what color Achilles' beard was, or whether Hector were not troubled with the toothache. He hath studied himself half blear-eyed to know the true symmetry of Caesar's nose by a shoeing-horn; and this he did to gain the name of a speculative man.[1]

PESCARA. Mark Prince Ferdinand:
A very salamander lives in 's eye,
To mock the eager violence of fire.[2]

SILVIO. That Cardinal hath made more bad faces with his oppression than ever Michael Angelo[3] made good ones: he lifts up 's nose, like a foul porpoise before a storm.

PESCARA. The Lord Ferdinand laughs.

DELIO. Like a deadly cannon that lightens ere it smokes.

PESCARA. These are your true pangs of death,
The pangs of life, that struggle with great statesmen.

DELIO. In such a deformed silence witches whisper
Their charms.

CARDINAL. Doth she make religion her riding-hood
To keep her from the sun and tempest?

FERDINAND. That,
That damns her. Methinks her fault and beauty,
Blended together, show like leprosy,
The whiter, the fouler. I make it a question
Whether her beggarly brats were ever christened.

CARDINAL. I will instantly solicit the state of Ancona.
To have them banished.

FERDINAND. You are for Loreto?
I shall not be at your ceremony; fare you well.
Write to the Duke of Malfi, my young nephew

8. He is an empty ceremony, a mere formality. "Touchhole": where the match was applied to set off a cannon.

9. Samson once tied some foxes together by the tail and set them afire to burn down the cornfields of the Philistines (Judges XV).

1. Scholarship was the traditional cause of melancholy, especially when exercised on impossible, useless questions like these.

2. The salamander, or water-lizard, was supposed to be so cold and wet of constitution that it could live in fire; Ferdinand is cold in his rage.

3. Michelangelo Buonarroti, the great Florentine painter and sculptor.

She had by her first husband, and acquaint him
With 's mother's honesty.

BOSOLA. I will.

FERDINAND. Antonio!
A slave that only smelled of ink and counters,
And never in 's life looked like a gentleman,
But in the audit-time. Go, go presently,[4]
Draw me out an hundred and fifty of our horse,
And meet me at the fort-bridge. [*Exeunt.*]

SCENE 4. *The Shrine of Our Lady of Loreto.*

[*Enter* TWO PILGRIMS.]

FIRST PILGRIM. I have not seen a goodlier shrine than this;
Yet I have visited many.

SECOND PILGRIM. The Cardinal of Aragon
Is this day to resign his cardinal's hat:
His sister duchess likewise is arrived
To pay her vow of pilgrimage. I expect
A noble ceremony.

FIRST PILGRIM. No question. They come.

[*Here the ceremony of the* CARDINAL'S *installment, in the habit of a soldier, is performed in delivering up his cross, hat, robes, and ring, at the shrine, and investing him with sword, helmet, shield, and spurs; then* ANTONIO, *the* DUCHESS, *and their children, having presented themselves at the shrine, are, by a form of banishment in dumb-show expressed towards them by the* CARDINAL *and the state of Ancona, banished: during all which ceremony, this ditty is sung, to very solumn music, by divers churchmen.*]

Arms and honors deck thy story,
To thy fame's eternal glory!
Adverse fortune ever fly thee;
No disastrous fate come nigh thee!

I alone will sing thy praises,
Whom to honor virtue raises;
And thy study, that divine is,
Bent to martial discipline is.
Lay aside all those robes lie by thee;
Crown thy arts with arms, they'll beautify thee.

O worthy of worthiest name, adorned in this manner,
Lead bravely thy forces on under war's warlike banner!
Oh, mayst thou prove fortunate in all martial courses!
Guide thou still by skill in arts and forces!

4. At once.

Victory attend thee nigh, whilst fame sings loud thy powers;
Triumphant conquest crown thy head, and blessings pour
down showers![5] [*Exeunt all except the* TWO PILGRIMS.]

FIRST PILGRIM. Here's a strange turn of state! Who would have thought
So great a lady would have matched herself
Unto so mean a person? Yet the Cardinal
Bears himself much too cruel.

SECOND PILGRIM. They are banished.

FIRST PILGRIM. But I would ask what power hath this state
Of Ancona to determine of a free prince?

SECOND PILGRIM. They are a free state, sir, and her brother showed
How that the Pope, fore-hearing of her looseness,
Hath seized into th' protection of the Church
The dukedom which she held as dowager.[6]

FIRST PILGRIM. But by what justice?

SECOND PILGRIM. Sure, I think by none,
Only her brother's instigation.

FIRST PILGRIM. What was it with such violence he took
Off from her finger?

SECOND PILGRIM. 'Twas her wedding-ring,
Which he vowed shortly he would sacrifice
To his revenge.

FIRST PILGRIM. Alas, Antonio!
If that a man be thrust into a well,
No matter who sets hands to 't, his own weight
Will bring him sooner to th' bottom. Come, let's hence.
Fortune makes this conclusion general,
All things do help th' unhappy man to fall. [*Exeunt.*]

SCENE 5. *Near Loreto.*

[*Enter* DUCHESS, ANTONIO, CHILDREN, CARIOLA, *and* SERVANTS.]

DUCHESS. Banished Ancona!

ANTONIO. Yes, you see what power
Lightens in great men's breath.

DUCHESS. Is all our train
Shrunk to this poor remainder?

ANTONIO. These poor men,
Which have got little in your service, vow
To take your fortune, but your wiser buntings,[7]
Now they are fledged, are gone.

DUCHESS. They have done wisely.

5. This song is not very suitable to the scene, and Webster, in the edition of 1623, denied writing it.

6. The Duchess held Malfi only as guardian for her son, the still youthful Duke.

7. Migratory birds; "take": accept.

This puts me in mind of death: physicians thus,
With their hands full of money, use to give o'er
Their patients.

ANTONIO. Right[8] the fashion of the world:
From decayed fortunes every flatterer shrinks;
Men cease to build where the foundation sinks.

DUCHESS. I had a very strange dream tonight.

ANTONIO. What was 't?

DUCHESS. Methought I wore my coronet of state,
And on a sudden all the diamonds
Were changed to pearls.

ANTONIO. My interpretation
Is, you'll weep shortly, for to me the pearls
Do signify your tears.

DUCHESS. The birds that live
I' th' field on the wild benefit of nature
Live happier than we; for they may choose their mates,
And carol their sweet pleasures to the spring.

[*Enter* BOSOLA *with a letter.*]

BOSOLA. You are happily o'erta'en.

DUCHESS. From my brother?

BOSOLA. Yes, from the Lord Ferdinand your brother
All love and safety.

DUCHESS. Thou dost blanch[9] mischief,
Wouldst make it white. See, see, like to calm weather
At sea before a tempest, false hearts speak fair
To those they intend most mischief.
"Send Antonio to me; I want his head in a business."
A politic equivocation!
He doth not want your counsel, but your head;
That is, he cannot sleep till you be dead.
And here's another pitfall that's strewed o'er
With roses: mark it, 'tis a cunning one:
"I stand engaged for your husband for several debts at Naples: let not that trouble him; I had rather have his heart than his money."
And I believe so too.

BOSOLA. What do you believe?

DUCHESS. That he so much distrusts my husband's love,
He will by no means believe his heart is with him
Until he see it: the devil is not cunning
Enough to circumvent us in riddles.

BOSOLA. Will you reject that noble and free league
Of amity and love which I present you?

DUCHESS. Their league is like that of some politic kings,
Only to make themselves of strength and power
To be our after-ruin: tell them so.

BOSOLA. And what from you?

ANTONIO. Thus tell him: I will not come.

8. Exactly.

9. Whitewash, cover up.

BOSOLA. And what of this? [*Pointing to the letter.*]
ANTONIO. My brothers have dispersed
Blood-hounds abroad; which till I hear are muzzled,
No truce, though hatched with ne'er such politic skill,
Is safe, that hangs upon our enemies' will.
I'll not come at them.
BOSOLA. This proclaims your breeding:
Every small thing draws a base mind to fear,
As the adamant draws iron.[1] Fare you well, sir;
You shall shortly hear from 's. [*Exit.*]
DUCHESS. I suspect some ambush;
Therefore, by all my love I do conjure you
To take your eldest son, and fly towards Milan.
Let us not venture all this poor remainder
In one unlucky bottom.[2]
ANTONIO. You counsel safely.
Best of my life, farewell. Since we must part,
Heaven hath a hand in 't, but no otherwise
Than as some curious artist[3] takes in sunder
A clock or watch, when it is out of frame,
To bring 't in better order.
DUCHESS. I know not
Which is best, to see you dead, or part with you.
Farewell, boy.
Thou art happy that thou hast not understanding
To know thy misery; for all our wit
And reading brings us to a truer sense
Of sorrow. In the eternal church, sir,
I do hope we shall not part thus.
ANTONIO. Oh, be of comfort!
Make patience a noble fortitude,
And think not how unkindly we are used:
Man, like to cassia, is proved best being bruised.[4]
DUCHESS. Must I, like to a slave-born Russian,
Account it praise to suffer tyranny?
And yet, O heaven, thy heavy hand is in 't!
I have seen my little boy oft scourge his top,[5]
And compared myself to 't: naught made me e'er
Go right but heaven's scourge-stick.
ANTONIO. Do not weep:
Heaven fashioned us of nothing, and we strive
To bring ourselves to nothing. Farewell, Cariola,
And thy sweet armful. If I do never see thee more,
Be a good mother to your little ones,
And save them from the tiger. Fare you well.

1. As the loadstone draws iron.
2. The metaphor is mercantile; let's not load all our cargo in one ship ("bottom").
3. Clever craftsman; "out of frame": not working.
4. Man, like cinnamon-bark, is most aromatic (virtuous) when pressed (oppressed).
5. Boys used to make tops spin by whipping them.

DUCHESS. Let me look upon you once more, for that speech
Came from a dying father. Your kiss is colder
Than that I have seen an holy anchorite
Give to a dead man's skull.

ANTONIO. My heart is turned to a heavy lump of lead,
With which I sound my danger. Fare you well.
[*Exeunt* ANTONIO *and his son.*]

DUCHESS. My laurel is all withered.

CARIOLA. Look, madam, what a troop of arméd men
Make toward us.

DUCHESS. Oh, they are very welcome:
When Fortune's wheel[6] is over-charged with princes,
The weight makes it move swift: I would have my ruin
Be sudden.
[Enter BOSOLA *vizarded,*[7] *with a guard.*]
I am your adventure,[8] am I not?

BOSOLA. You are. You must see your husband no more.

DUCHESS. What devil art thou that counterfeits heaven's thunder?

BOSOLA. Is that terrible? I would have you tell me whether
Is that note worse that frights the silly birds
Out of the corn, or that which doth allure them
To the nets? You have hearkened to the last too much.

DUCHESS. Oh, misery! Like to a rusty o'ercharged cannon,
Shall I never fly in pieces?—Come, to what prison?

BOSOLA. To none.

DUCHESS. Whither, then?

BOSOLA. To your palace.

DUCHESS. I have heard
That Charon's boat serves to convey all o'er[9]
The dismal lake, but brings none back again.

BOSOLA. Your brothers mean you safety and pity.

DUCHESS. Pity!
With such a pity men preserve alive
Pheasants and quails, when they are not fat enough
To be eaten.

BOSOLA. These are your children?

DUCHESS. Yes.

BOSOLA. Can they prattle?

DUCHESS. No.
But I intend, since they were born accursed,
Curses shall be their first language.

BOSOLA. Fie, madam!
Forget this base, low fellow—

DUCHESS. Were I a man,

6. The wheel of fortune is an ancient emblem of mutability; men have their fixed positions on it, and rise or fall as it turns.
7. Bosola wears a mask.
8. I.e., I am what you're looking for, am I not?
9. In classical mythology, Charon transports the souls of the dead across the river Styx to Hades.

I'd beat that counterfeit face into thy other.[1]
BOSOLA. One of no birth.[2]
DUCHESS. Say that he was born mean,
Man is most happy when 's own actions
Be arguments and examples of his virtue.
BOSOLA. A barren, beggarly virtue!
DUCHESS. I prithee, who is greatest? Can you tell?
Sad tales befit my woe: I'll tell you one.
A salmon, as she swam unto the sea,
Met with a dog-fish, who encounters her
With this rough language: "Why art thou so bold
To mix thyself with our high state of floods,
Being no eminent courtier, but one
That for the calmest and fresh time o' the year
Dost live in shallow rivers, rank'st thyself
With silly smelts and shrimps? And darest thou
Pass by our dog-ship without reverence?"
"Oh!" quoth the salmon, "sister, be at peace:
Thank Jupiter we both have passed the net!
Our value never can be truly known,
Till in the fisher's basket we be shown:
I' th' market then my price may be the higher,
Even when I am nearest to the cook and fire."
So to great men the moral may be stretchéd;
Men oft are valued high, when they're most wretched.
But come, whither you please. I am armed 'gainst misery;
Bent to all sways of the oppressor's will:
There's no deep valley but near some great hill. [*Exeunt.*]

Act IV

SCENE 1. *Amalfi.*

[*Enter* FERDINAND *and* BOSOLA.]
FERDINAND. How doth our sister duchess bear herself
In her imprisonment?
BOSOLA. Nobly. I'll describe her.
She's sad as one long used to 't, and she seems
Rather to welcome the end of misery
Than shun it; a behavior so noble
As gives a majesty to adversity:
You may discern the shape of loveliness
More perfect in her tears than in her smiles;
She will muse for hours together; and her silence,
Methinks, expresseth more than if she spake.
FERDINAND. Her melancholy seems to be fortified
With a strange disdain.

1. I.e., I'd push your mask down your throat.
2. Of low rank by birth.

BOSOLA. 'Tis so; and this restraint,
Like English mastiffs that grow fierce with tying,
Makes her too passionately apprehend
Those pleasures she's kept from.
FERDINAND. Curse upon her!
I will no longer study in the book
Of another's heart. Inform her what I told you. [*Exit.*]
[*Enter* DUCHESS.]
BOSOLA. All comfort to your grace!
DUCHESS. I will have none.
Pray thee, why dost thou wrap thy poisoned pills
In gold and sugar?
BOSOLA. Your elder brother, the Lord Ferdinand,
Is come to visit you, and sends you word,
'Cause once he rashly made a solemn vow
Never to see you more, he comes i' th' night,
And prays you gently neither torch nor taper
Shine in your chamber. He will kiss your hand
And reconcile himself, but for his vow
He dares not see you.
DUCHESS. At his pleasure. Take hence the lights.
He's come.
[*Enter* FERDINAND.]
FERDINAND. Where are you?
DUCHESS. Here, sir.
FERDINAND. This darkness suits you well.
DUCHESS. I would ask you pardon.
FERDINAND. You have it; for I account it
The honorabl'st revenge, where I may kill,
To pardon. Where are your cubs?
DUCHESS. Whom?
FERDINAND. Call them your children;
For though our national law distinguish bastards
From true legitimate issue, compassionate nature
Makes them all equal.
DUCHESS. Do you visit me for this?
You violate a sacrament o' th' Church
Shall make you howl in hell for 't.
FERDINAND. It had been well
Could you have lived thus always; for, indeed,
You were too much i' th' light—but no more—
I come to seal my peace with you. Here's a hand
[*Gives her a dead man's hand.*]
To which you have vowed much love; the ring upon 't
You gave.
DUCHESS. I affectionately kiss it.
FERDINAND. Pray, do, and bury the print of it in your heart.
I will leave this ring with you for a love-token,
And the hand as sure as the ring; and do not doubt
But you shall have the heart, too. When you need a friend,

Send it to him that owed[3] it; you shall see
Whether he can aid you.
DUCHESS. You are very cold;
I fear you are not well after your travel.
Ha! Lights! Oh, horrible!
FERDINAND. Let her have lights enough. [*Exit.*]
DUCHESS. What witchcraft doth he practice, that he hath left
A dead man's hand here?
[*Here is discovered, behind a traverse,*[4] *the artificial figures of Antonio and his children, appearing as if they were dead.*]
BOSOLA. Look you, here's the piece from which 'twas ta'en.
He doth present you this sad spectacle,
That, now you know directly they are dead,
Hereafter you may wisely cease to grieve
For that which cannot be recovered.
DUCHESS. There is not between heaven and earth one wish
I stay for after this: it wastes[5] me more
Than were't my picture, fashioned out of wax,
Stuck with a magical needle, and then buried
In some foul dunghill; and yond's an excellent property[6]
For a tyrant, which I would account mercy.
BOSOLA. What's that?
DUCHESS. If they would bind me to that lifeless trunk
And let me freeze to death.
BOSOLA. Come, you must live.
DUCHESS. That's the greatest torture souls feel in hell,
In hell, that they must live, and cannot die.
Portia,[7] I'll new-kindle thy coals again,
And revive the rare and almost dead example
Of a loving wife.
BOSOLA. Oh, fie! Despair? Remember
You are a Christian.
DUCHESS. The Church enjoins fasting:
I'll starve myself to death.
BOSOLA. Leave this vain sorrow.
Things being at the worst begin to mend: the bee
When he hath shot his sting into your hand, may then
Play with your eyelid.
DUCHESS. Good comfortable fellow,
Persuade a wretch that's broke upon the wheel
To have all his bones new set; entreat him live
To be executed again. Who must dispatch me?
I account this world a tedious theater,

3. Owned.
4. A translucent screen or curtain.
5. Consumes, as by secret disease; witches were supposed to be able to "waste" their enemies by making wax images and tormenting them as indicated below.
6. There's an excellent scheme.
7. Portia, the wife of Brutus, committed suicide by swallowing hot coals.

For I do play a part in 't 'gainst my will.
BOSOLA. Come, be of comfort; I will save your life,
DUCHESS. Indeed,
I have not leisure to tend so small a business.
BOSOLA. Now, by my life, I pity you.
DUCHESS. Thou art a fool, then,
To waste thy pity on a thing so wretched
As cannot pity itself. I am full of daggers.
Puff, let me blow these vipers from me.
[*Enter* SERVANT.]
What are you?
SERVANT. One that wishes you long life.
DUCHESS. I would thou wert hanged for the horrible curse
Thou hast given me. I shall shortly grow one
Of the miracles of pity. I'll go pray—
No, I'll go curse.
BOSOLA. Oh, fie!
DUCHESS. I could curse the stars—
BOSOLA. Oh, fearful!
DUCHESS. And those three smiling seasons of the year
Into a Russian winter, nay, the world
To its first chaos.[8]
BOSOLA. Look you, the stars shine still.
DUCHESS. Oh, but you must
Remember, my curse hath a great way to go.
Plagues, that make lanes through largest families,
Consume them!
BOSOLA. Fie, lady!
DUCHESS. Let them, like tyrants,
Never be remembered but for the ill they have done;
Let all the zealous prayers of mortified
Churchmen forget them!
BOSOLA. Oh, uncharitable!
DUCHESS. Let Heaven a little while cease crowning martyrs
To punish them!
Go, howl them this, and say, I long to bleed:
It is some mercy when men kill with speed.
[*Exeunt* DUCHESS *and* SERVANT.]
[*Re-enter* FERDINAND.]
FERDINAND. Excellent, as I would wish; she's plagued in art:
These presentations are but framed in wax
By the curious master in that quality,
Vincentio Lauriola,[9] and she takes them
For true substantial bodies.
BOSOLA. Why do you do this?
FERDINAND. To bring her to despair.

8. A Russian winter would last all year long.
9. The art of wax modeling was common enough, but the name of the artist seems to be imaginary.

BOSOLA. 'Faith, end here,
And go no farther in your cruelty.
Send her a penitential garment to put on
Next to her delicate skin, and furnish her
With beads and prayer-books.
FERDINAND. Damn her! That body of hers,
While that my blood ran pure in 't, was more worth
Than that which thou wouldst comfort, called a soul.
I will send her masks of common courtesans,
Have her meat served up by bawds and ruffians,
And, 'cause she'll needs be mad, I am resolved
To remove forth the common hospital
All the mad-folk, and place them near her lodging;
There let them practice together, sing and dance,
And act their gambols to the full o' th' moon:
If she can sleep the better for it, let her.
Your work is almost ended.
BOSOLA. Must I see her again?
FERDINAND. Yes.
BOSOLA. Never.
FERDINAND. You must.
BOSOLA. Never in mine own shape;
That's forfeited by my intelligence[1]
And this last cruel lie. When you send me next,
The business shall be comfort.
FERDINAND. Very likely.
Thy pity is nothing of kin to thee.[2] Antonio
Lurks about Milan: thou shalt shortly thither
To feed a fire as great as my revenge,
Which ne'er will slack till it have spent his fuel.
Intemperate agues make physicians cruel. [*Exeunt.*]

SCENE 2

[*Enter* DUCHESS *and* CARIOLA.]

DUCHESS. What hideous noise was that?
CARIOLA. 'Tis the wild consort
Of madmen, lady, which your tyrant brother
Hath placed about your lodging. This tyranny,
I think, was never practiced till this hour.
DUCHESS. Indeed, I thank him. Nothing but noise and folly
Can keep me in my right wits, whereas reason
And silence make me stark mad. Sit down;
Discourse to me some dismal tragedy.
CARIOLA. Oh, 'twill increase your melancholy.
DUCHESS. Thou are deceived:
To hear of greater grief would lessen mine.

1. I.e., I can't do that because she knows now I've played the spy on her.

2. I.e., pity doesn't suit you very well.

This is a prison?
CARIOLA. Yes, but you shall live
To shake this durance off.
DUCHESS. Thou art a fool:
The robin-redbreast and the nightingale
Never live long in cages.
CARIOLA. Pray, dry your eyes.
What think you of, madam?
DUCHESS. Of nothing; when I muse thus, I sleep.
CARIOLA. Like a madman, with your eyes open?
DUCHESS. Dost thou think we shall know one another in th' other world?
CARIOLA. Yes, out of question.
DUCHESS. Oh, that it were possible
We might but hold some two days' conference
With the dead! From them I should learn somewhat, I am sure,
I never shall know here. I'll tell thee a miracle;
I am not mad yet, to my cause of sorrow:
Th' heaven o'er my head seems made of molten brass,
The earth of flaming sulphur, yet I am not mad.
I am acquainted with sad misery
As the tanned galley-slave is with his oar;
Necessity makes me suffer constantly,
And custom makes it easy. Who do I look like now?
CARIOLA. Like to your picture in the gallery,
A deal of life in show, but none in practice,
Or rather like some reverend monument
Whose ruins are even pitied.
DUCHESS. Very proper.
And Fortune seems only to have her eyesight
To behold my tragedy.
How now! What noise is that?
[*Enter* SERVANT.]
SERVANT. I am come to tell you
Your brother hath intended you some sport.
A great physician, when the Pope was sick
Of a deep melancholy, presented him
With several sorts of madmen, which wild object
Being full of change and sport, forced him to laugh,
And so the imposthume[3] broke. The self-same cure
The duke intends on you.
DUCHESS. Let them come in.
SERVANT. There's a mad lawyer; and a secular priest;
A doctor that hath forfeited his wits
By jealousy; an astrologian
That in his works said such a day o' the' month
Should be the day of doom, and, failing of 't,
Ran mad; an English tailor crazed i' th' brain

3. Boil.

With the study of new fashions; a gentleman-usher[4]
Quite beside himself with care to keep in mind
The number of his lady's salutations
Or 'How do you's' she employed him in each morning;
A farmer, too, an excellent knave in grain,
Mad 'cause he was hindered transportation:
And let one broker that's mad loose to these,
You'd think the devil were among them.[5]

DUCHESS. Sit, Cariola. Let them loose when you please,
For I am chained to endure all your tyranny.

[*Enter* MADMEN.]

[*Here by a* MADMAN *this Song is sung to a dismal kind of music.*]

Oh, let us howl some heavy note,
Some deadly dogged howl,
Sounding as from the threatening throat
Of beasts and fatal fowl!
As ravens, screech-owls, bulls, and bears,
We'll bell, and bawl our parts,
Till irksome noise have cloyed your ears
And corrosived your hearts.
At last, whenas our choir wants breath,
Our bodies being blest,
We'll sing, like swans, to welcome death,
And die in love and rest.

FIRST MADMAN. Doom's-day not come yet? I'll draw it nearer by a perspective,[6] or make a glass that shall set all the world on fire upon an instant. I cannot sleep; my pillow is stuffed with a litter of porcupines.

SECOND MADMAN. Hell is a mere glass-house, where the devils are continually blowing up women's souls on hollow irons, and the fire never goes out.

THIRD MADMAN. I will lie with every woman in my parish the tenth night; I will tithe them over like haycocks.

FOURTH MADMAN. Shall my pothecary out-go me because I am a cuckold? I have found out his roguery; he makes alum of his wife's urine, and sells it to Puritans that have sore throats with overstraining.

FIRST MADMAN. I have skill in heraldry.

SECOND MADMAN. Hast?

FIRST MADMAN. You do give for your crest a woodcock's head with the brains picked out on 't; you are a very ancient gentleman.

THIRD MADMAN. Greek is turned Turk: we are only to be saved by the Helvetian translation.[7]

4. Doorkeeper.
5. All the madmen have lost their wits in the pursuit of their trades; lead them to a broker, who might get them back to work again, and they'll be madder than ever.
6. Telescope.
7. The Geneva Bible; but how it would help with the Greeks and Turks is clear only to the lunatic.

FIRST MADMAN. Come on, sir, I will lay the law to you.

SECOND MADMAN. Oh, rather lay a corrosive: the law will eat to the bone.

THIRD MADMAN. He that drinks but to satisfy nature is damned.

FOURTH MADMAN. If I had my glass[8] here, I would show a sight should make all the women here call me mad doctor.

FIRST MADMAN. What's he? A rope-maker?

SECOND MADMAN. No, no, no, a snuffling knave that, while he shows the tombs, will have his hand in a wench's placket.

THIRD MADMAN. Woe to the caroche[9] that brought home my wife from the masque at three o'clock in the morning! It had a large feather-bed in it.

FOURTH MADMAN. I have pared the devil's nails forty times, roasted them in raven's eggs, and cured agues with them.

THIRD MADMAN. Get me three hundred milchbats, to make possets to procure sleep.[1]

FOURTH MADMAN. All the college may throw their caps at me: I have made a soap boiler costive; it was my masterpiece.

[*Here the dance, consisting of eight* MADMEN, *with music answerable thereunto; after which* BOSOLA, *like an old man, enters.*]

DUCHESS. Is he mad too?

SERVANT. Pray, question him. I'll leave you.

[*Exeunt* SERVANT *and* MADMEN.]

BOSOLA. I am come to make thy tomb.

DUCHESS. Ha! My tomb?
Thou speak'st as if I lay upon my deathbed,
Gasping for breath. Dost thou perceive me sick?

BOSOLA. Yes, and the more dangerously, since thy sickness
Is insensible.[2]

DUCHESS. Thou art not mad, sure. Dost know me?

BOSOLA. Yes.

DUCHESS. Who am I?

BOSOLA. Thou art a box of worm-seed, at best but a salvatory of green mummy.[3] What's this flesh? A little crudded[4] milk, fantastical puff-paste. Our bodies are weaker than those paper-prisons boys use to keep flies in, more contemptible, since ours is to preserve earthworms. Didst thou ever see a lark in a cage? Such is the soul in the body: this world is like her little turf of grass, and the heaven o'er our heads, like her looking-glass, only gives us a miserable knowledge of the small compass of our prison.

DUCHESS. Am not I thy duchess?

BOSOLA. Thou art some great woman, sure, for riot[5] begins to sit

8. Looking-glass.
9. Carriage.
1. It is a mad idea indeed that toddies ("possets") made of bat's milk would put people to sleep.
2. Imperceptible.
3. "Worm-seed" is a matter whose ultimate end is the generation of worms. "A salvatory of green mummy": the substance of mummified bodies was considered medicinal. The living body is a box ("salvatory") of such medicine, only not yet ready for use.
4. Curdled.
5. Debauchery.

on thy forehead, clad in gray hairs, twenty years sooner than on a merry milkmaid's. Thou sleep'st worse than if a mouse should be forced to take up her lodging in a cat's ear: a little infant that breeds its teeth,[6] should it lie with thee, would cry out, as if thou wert the more unquiet bedfellow.

DUCHESS. I am Duchess of Malfi still.

BOSOLA. That makes thy sleep so broken:
Glories, like glow-worms, afar off shine bright,
But, looked to near, have neither heat nor light.

DUCHESS. Thou art very plain.

BOSOLA. My trade is to flatter the dead, not the living; I am a tomb-maker.

DUCHESS. And thou com'st to make my tomb?

BOSOLA. Yes.

DUCHESS. Let me be a little merry. Of what stuff wilt thou make it?

BOSOLA. Nay, resolve me first, of what fashion?

DUCHESS. Why, do we grow fantastical in our deathbed? Do we affect fashion in the grave?

BOSOLA. Most ambitiously. Princes' images on their tombs do not lie, as they were wont, seeming to pray up to heaven, but with their hands under their cheeks, as if they died of the toothache. They are not carved with their eyes fixed upon the stars, but as their minds were wholly bent upon the world, the selfsame way they seem to turn their faces.

DUCHESS. Let me know fully therefore the effect
Of this thy dismal preparation,
This talk fit for a charnel.

BOSOLA. Now I shall.

[*Enter* EXECUTIONERS, *with a coffin, cords, and a bell.*]

Here is a present from your princely brothers;
And may it arrive welcome, for it brings
Last benefit, last sorrow.

DUCHESS. Let me see it:
I have so much obedience in my blood,
I wish it in their veins to do them good.

BOSOLA. This is your last presence-chamber.[7]

CARIOLA. O my sweet lady!

DUCHESS. Peace; it affrights not me.

BOSOLA. I am the common bellman,
That usually is sent to condemned persons
The night before they suffer.

DUCHESS. Even now
Thou said'st thou wast a tomb-maker.

BOSOLA. 'Twas to bring you
By degrees to mortification.[8] Listen.

6. A teething infant.

7. The room in which a person of quality (duchess or prince) received courtiers and diplomats.

8. Repentance, but also death and decomposition.

Hark, now every thing is still
The screech-owl and the whistler[9] shrill
Call upon our dame aloud,
And bid her quickly don her shroud!
Much you had of land and rent:
Your length in clay's now competent:[1]
A long war disturbed your mind;
Here your perfect peace is signed.
Of what is 't fools make such vain keeping?
Sin their conception, their birth weeping,
Their life a general mist of error,
Their death a hideous storm of terror.
Strew your hair with powders sweet,
Don clean linen, bathe your feet,
And (the foul fiend more to check)
A crucifix let bless your neck:
'Tis now full tide 'tween night and day;
End your groan, and come away.

CARIOLA. Hence, villains, tyrants, murderers! Alas!
What will you do with my lady? Call for help.

DUCHESS. To whom? To our next neighbors? They are madfolks.

BOSOLA. Remove that noise.

DUCHESS. Farewell, Cariola.
In my last will I have not much to give:
A many hungry guests have fed upon me;
Thine will be a poor reversion.

CARIOLA. I will die with her.

DUCHESS. I pray thee, look thou giv'st my little boy
Some syrup for his cold, and let the girl
Say her prayers ere she sleep.

[CARIOLA *is forced out by the* EXECUTIONERS.]

Now what you please.
What death?

BOSOLA. Strangling;
Here are your executioners.

DUCHESS. I forgive them:
The apoplexy, catarrh, or cough o' th' lungs,
Would do as much as they do.

BOSOLA. Doth not death fright you?

DUCHESS. Who would be afraid on 't,
Knowing to meet such excellent company
In th' other world?

BOSOLA. Yet, methinks,
The manner of your death should much afflict you:
This cord should terrify you.

DUCHESS. Not a whit.
What would it pleasure me to have my throat cut

9. A bird premonitory of death.

1. Sufficient.

With diamonds? Or to be smothered
With cassia?[2] Or to be shot to death with pearls?
I know death hath ten thousand several doors
For men to take their exits, and 'tis found
They go on such strange geometrical hinges,
You may open them both ways.—Any way, for heaven sake,
So I were out of your whispering. Tell my brothers
That I perceive death, now I am well awake,
Best gift is they can give or I can take.
I would fain put off my last woman's fault,
I'd not be tedious to you.

EXECUTIONER. We are ready.

DUCHESS. Dispose my breath how please you, but my body
Bestow upon my women, will you?

EXECUTIONER. Yes.

DUCHESS. Pull, and pull strongly, for your able strength
Must pull down heaven upon me—
Yet stay; heaven-gates are not so highly arched
As princes' palaces; they that enter there
Must go upon their knees [*Kneels*]. Come, violent death.
Serve for mandragora[3] to make me sleep!
Go tell my brothers, when I am laid out,
They then may feed in quiet. [*They strangle her.*]

BOSOLA. Where's the waiting woman? Fetch her: some other
Strangle the children.

[*Exeunt* EXECUTIONERS, *some of whom return with* CARIOLA.]

Look you, there sleeps your mistress.

CARIOLA. Oh, you are damned
Perpetually for this! My turn is next.
Is 't not so ordered?

BOSOLA. Yes, and I am glad
You are so well prepared for 't.

CARIOLA. You are deceived, Sir,
I am not prepared for 't, I will not die;
I will first come to my answer, and know
How I have offended.

BOSOLA. Come, dispatch her.
You kept her counsel; now you shall keep ours.

CARIOLA. I will not die, I must not; I am contracted
To a young gentleman.

EXECUTIONER. Here's your wedding-ring.

CARIOLA. Let me but speak with the duke; I'll discover
Treason to his person.

BOSOLA. Delays! Throttle her.

EXECUTIONER. She bites and scratches.

CARIOLA. If you kill me now,
I am damned; I have not been at confession

2. Cinnamon.
3. The word is used loosely for a stupefying drug.

This two years.
BOSOLA. [*to* EXECUTIONERS] When!
CARIOLA. I am quick with child.
BOSOLA. Why, then,
Your credit's saved.[4] [*They strangle* CARIOLA.]
Bear her into th' next room;
Let this lie still.
[*Exeunt the* EXECUTIONERS *with the body of* CARIOLA.]
[*Enter* FERDINAND.]
FERDINAND. Is she dead?
BOSOLA. She is what
You'd have her. But here begin your pity.
[*Shows the children strangled.*]
Alas, how have these offended?
FERDINAND. The death
Of young wolves is never to be pitied.
BOSOLA. Fix
Your eye here.
FERDINAND. Constantly.
BOSOLA. Do you not weep?
Other sins only speak; murder shrieks out:
The element of water moistens the earth,
But blood flies upwards and bedews the heavens.
FERDINAND. Cover her face; mine eyes dazzle: she died young.
BOSOLA. I think not so; her infelicity
Seemed to have years too many.
FERDINAND. She and I were twins;
And should I die this instant, I had lived
Her time to a minute.
BOSOLA. It seems she was born first:
You have bloodily approved[5] the ancient truth,
That kindred commonly do worse agree
Than remote strangers.
FERDINAND. Let me see her face
Again. Why didst not thou pity her? What
An excellent honest man mightst thou have been,
If thou hadst borne her to some sanctuary!
Or, bold in a good cause, opposed thyself,
With thy advancéd sword above thy head,
Between her innocence and my revenge!
I bade thee, when I was distracted of my wits,
Go kill my dearest friend, and thou hast done 't.
For let me but examine well the cause:
What was the meanness of her match to me?
Only I must confess I had a hope,
Had she continued widow, to have gained
An infinite mass of treasure by her death:
And that was the main cause, her marriage,

4. Your reputation will now be safe.
5. Given proof of.

That drew a stream of gall quite through my heart.
For thee, as we observe in tragedies
That a good actor many times is cursed
For playing a villain's part, I hate thee for 't,
And, for my sake, say thou hast done much ill well.

BOSOLA. Let me quicken your memory, for I perceive
You are falling into ingratitude: I challenge
The reward due to my service.

FERDINAND. I'll tell thee
What I'll give thee.

BOSOLA. Do.

FERDINAND. I'll give thee a pardon
For this murder.

BOSOLA. Ha!

FERDINAND. Yes, and 'tis
The largest bounty I can study to do thee.
By what authority didst thou execute
This bloody sentence?

BOSOLA. By yours.

FERDINAND. Mine! Was I her judge?
Did any ceremonial form of law
Doom her to not-being? Did a complete jury
Deliver her conviction up i' th' court?
Where shalt thou find this judgment registered,
Unless in hell? See, like a bloody fool,
Thou'st forfeited thy life, and thou shalt die for 't.

BOSOLA. The office of justice is perverted quite
When one thief hangs another. Who shall dare
To reveal this?

FERDINAND. Oh, I'll tell thee;
The wolf shall find her grave, and scrape it up,
Not to devour the corpse, but to discover
The horrid murder.

BOSOLA. You, not I, shall quake for 't.

FERDINAND. Leave me.

BOSOLA. I will first receive my pension.

FERDINAND. You are a villain.

BOSOLA. When your ingratitude
Is judge, I am so.

FERDINAND. Oh, horror, that not the fear
Of Him which binds the devils can prescribe man
obedience! Never look upon me more.

BOSOLA. Why, fare thee well.
Your brother and yourself are worthy men:
You have a pair of hearts are hollow graves,
Rotten, and rotting others; and your vengeance,
Like two chained bullets, still goes arm in arm.
You may be brothers, for treason, like the plague,
Doth take much in a blood.[6] I stand like one

6. Treason and plague run in certain families.

That long hath ta'en a sweet and golden dream.
I am angry with myself, now that I wake.

FERDINAND. Get thee into some unknown part o' th' world,
That I may never see thee.

BOSOLA. Let me know
Wherefore I should be thus neglected. Sir,
I served your tyranny, and rather strove
To satisfy yourself than all the world,
And though I loathed the evil, yet I loved
You that did counsel it; and rather sought
To appear a true servant than an honest man.

FERDINAND. I'll go hunt the badger by owl-light:
'Tis a deed of darkness. [*Exit.*]

BOSOLA. He's much distracted. Off, my painted honor!
While with vain hopes our faculties we tire,
We seem to sweat in ice and freeze in fire.
What would I do, were this to do again?
I would not change my peace of conscience
For all the wealth of Europe.—She stirs; here's life.
Return, fair soul, from darkness, and lead mine
Out of this sensible[7] hell. She's warm, she breathes.
Upon thy pale lips I will melt my heart,
To store them with fresh color.—Who's there!
Some cordial[8] drink!—Alas! I dare not call:
So pity would destroy pity.—Her eye opes,
And heaven in it seems to ope, that late was shut,
To take me up to mercy.

DUCHESS. Antonio!

BOSOLA. Yes, madam, he is living;
The dead bodies you saw were but feigned statues:
He's reconciled to your brothers: the Pope hath wrought
The atonement.

DUCHESS. Mercy! [*She dies.*]

BOSOLA. Oh, she's gone again! There the cords of life broke.
Oh, sacred innocence, that sweetly sleeps
On turtles'[9] feathers, whilst a guilty conscience
Is a black register wherein is writ
All our good deeds and bad, a perspective[1]
That shows us hell! That we cannot be suffered
To do good when we have a mind to it!
This is manly sorrow; these tears, I am very certain,
Never grew in my mother's milk. My estate
Is sunk below the degree of fear. Where were
These penitent fountains while she was living?
Oh, they were frozen up! Here is a sight
As direful to my soul as is the sword
Unto a wretch hath slain his father. Come, I'll bear thee
Hence, and execute thy last will; that's deliver

7. Material, tangible.
8. Restorative.
9. Turtle doves, emblems of a loving couple.
1. Picture.

Thy body to the reverend dispose[2]
Of some good women: that the cruel tyrant
Shall not deny me. Then I'll post to Milan,
Where somewhat I will speedily enact
Worth my dejection. *[Exit with the body.]*

Act V

SCENE 1. *A Public Place in Milan.*

[Enter ANTONIO *and* DELIO.*]*

ANTONIO. What think you of my hope of reconcilement
To the Aragonian brethren?
DELIO. I misdoubt it;
For though they have sent their letters of safe-conduct
For your repair to Milan, they appear
But nets to entrap you. The Marquis of Pescara,
Under whom you hold certain land in cheat,[3]
Much 'gainst his noble nature hath been moved
To seize those lands, and some of his dependents
Are at this instant making it their suit
To be invested in your revenues.[4]
I cannot think they mean well to your life
That do deprive you of your means of life,
Your living.
ANTONIO. You are still an heretic
To any safety I can shape myself.[5]
DELIO. Here comes the marquis. I will make myself
Petitioner for some part of your land,
To know whither it is flying.
ANTONIO. I pray do. *[Withdraws.]*
[Enter PESCARA.*]*
DELIO. Sir, I have a suit to you.
PESCARA. To me?
DELIO. An easy one.
There is the citadel of Saint Bennet,[6]
With some demesnes, of late in the possession
Of Antonio Bologna; please you bestow them on me.
PESCARA. You are my friend, but this is such a suit,
Nor fit for me to give, nor you to take.
DELIO. No, sir?
PESCARA. I will give you ample reason for 't
Soon in private. Here's the Cardinal's mistress.
[Enter JULIA.*]*
JULIA. My lord, I am grown your poor petitioner,
And should be an ill beggar, had I not

2. Disposition.
3. Escheat, in default of legal heirs.
4. I.e., to be given your rents.
5. I.e., you still don't give me any hope of safety that I can believe in. "Heretic": unbeliever.
6. Saint Benedict; "demesnes": associated estates.

A great man's letter here, the Cardinal's,
To court you in my favor. [*Gives a letter.*]

PESCARA. He entreats for you
The citadel of Saint Bennet, that belonged
To the banished Bologna.

JULIA. Yes.

PESCARA. I could not
Have thought of a friend I could rather pleasure with it;
'Tis yours.

JULIA. Sir, I thank you; and he shall know
How doubly I am engaged both in your gift,
And speediness of giving, which makes your grant
The greater. [*Exit.*]

ANTONIO. [*aside*] How they fortify themselves
With my ruin!

DELIO. Sir, I am little bound to you.

PESCARA. Why?

DELIO. Because you denied this suit to me, and gave 't
To such a creature.

PESCARA. Do you know what it was?
It was Antonio's land, not forfeited
By course of law, but ravished from his throat
By the Cardinal's entreaty. It were not fit
I should bestow so main a piece of wrong
Upon my friend; 'tis a gratification
Only due to a strumpet, for it is injustice.
Shall I sprinkle the pure blood of innocents
To make those followers I call my friends
Look ruddier upon me? I am glad
This land, ta'en from the owner by such wrong,
Returns again unto so foul an use
As salary for his lust. Learn, good Delio,
To ask noble things of me, and you shall find
I'll be a noble giver.

DELIO. You instruct me well.

ANTONIO. [*aside*] Why, here's a man now would fright impudence
From sauciest beggars.

PESCARA. Prince Ferdinand's come to Milan,
Sick, as they give out, of an apoplexy,
But some say 'tis a frenzy. I am going
To visit him. [*Exit.*]

ANTONIO. 'Tis a noble old fellow.

DELIO. What course do you mean to take, Antonio?

ANTONIO. This night I mean to venture all my fortune,
Which is no more than a poor lingering life,
To the Cardinal's worst of malice. I have got
Private access to his chamber, and intend
To visit him about the mid of night,
As once his brother did our noble duchess.
It may be that the sudden apprehension

Of danger—for I'll go in mine own shape—
When he shall see it fraught with love and duty,
May draw the poison out of him, and work
A friendly reconcilement. If it fail,
Yet it shall rid me of this infamous calling,
For better fall once than be ever falling.

DELIO. I'll second you in all danger, and, howe'er,
My life keeps rank with yours.

ANTONIO. You are still my loved
And best friend. [*Exeunt.*]

SCENE 2

[*Enter* PESCARA *and* DOCTOR.]

PESCARA. Now, doctor, may I visit your patient?

DOCTOR. If 't please your lordship: but he's instantly[7]
To take the air here in the gallery
By my direction.

PESCARA. Pray thee, what's his disease?

DOCTOR. A very pestilent disease, my lord,
They call lycanthropia.[8]

PESCARA. What's that?
I need a dictionary to 't.

DOCTOR. I'll tell you.
In those that are possessed with 't there o'erflows
Such melancholy humor, they imagine
Themselves to be transformed into wolves;
Steal forth to churchyards in the dead of night,
And dig dead bodies up: as two nights since
One met the duke 'bout midnight in a lane
Behind Saint Mark's Church, with the leg of a man
Upon his shoulder; and he howled fearfully;
Said he was a wolf, only the difference
Was, a wolf's skin was hairy on the outside,
His on the inside; bade them take their swords,
Rip up his flesh, and try. Straight I was sent for,
And, having ministered to him, found his grace
Very well recovered.

PESCARA. I'm glad on 't.

DOCTOR. Yet not without some fear
Of a relapse. If he grow to his fit again,
I'll go a nearer way to work with him
Than ever Paracelsus[9] dreamed of: if
They'll give me leave, I'll buffet his madness
Out of him. Stand aside; he comes.

[*Enter* FERDINAND, MALATESTE, CARDINAL, *and* BOSOLA.]

7. Very shortly.

8. The mental aberration that produces werewolves—as the Doctor will shortly explain.

9. Paracelsus, the great Swiss alchemist, famous for his cures by sympathetic magic. Though anachronistic in this play, he would be well known to Webster's audience.

FERDINAND. Leave me.

MALATESTE. Why doth your lordship love this solitariness?

FERDINAND. Eagles commonly fly alone: they are crows, daws, and starlings that flock together. Look, what's that follows me?

MALATESTE. Nothing, my lord.

FERDINAND. Yes.

MALATESTE. 'Tis your shadow.

FERDINAND. Stay it; let it not haunt me.

MALATESTE. Impossible, if you move, and the sun shine.

FERDINAND. I will throttle it. [*Throws himself on the ground.*]

MALATESTE. O, my lord, you are angry with nothing.

FERDINAND. You are a fool: how is 't possible I should catch my shadow, unless I fall upon 't? When I go to hell, I mean to carry a bribe; for, look you, good gifts evermore make way for the worst persons.

PESCARA. Rise, good my lord.

FERDINAND. I am studying the art of patience.

PESCARA. 'Tis a noble virtue.

FERDINAND. To drive six snails before me from this town to Moscow; neither use goad nor whip to them, but let them take their own time—the patient'st man i' th' world match me for an experiment—and I'll crawl after like a sheep-biter.[1]

CARDINAL. Force him up. [*They raise him.*]

FERDINAND. Use me well, you were best. What I have done, I have done: I'll confess nothing.

DOCTOR. Now let me come to him. Are you mad, my lord? Are you out of your princely wits?

FERDINAND. What's he?

PESCARA. Your doctor.

FERDINAND. Let me have his beard sawed off, and his eyebrows filed more civil.

DOCTOR. I must do mad tricks with him, for that's the only way on 't. I have brought your grace a salamander's skin to keep you from sunburning.[2]

FERDINAND. I have cruel sore eyes.

DOCTOR. The white of a cockatrix's[3] egg is present remedy.

FERDINAND. Let it be a new laid one, you were best. Hide me from him: physicians are like kings—they brook no contradiction.

DOCTOR. Now he begins to fear me: now let me alone with him.

CARDINAL. How now? Put off your gown?

DOCTOR. Let me have some forty urinals filled with rosewater: he and I'll go pelt one another with them. Now he begins to fear me. Can you fetch a frisk, sir?[4] Let him go, let him go, upon my peril: I find by his eye he stands in awe of me; I'll make

1. A sheepdog, nipping at the heels of his flock.
2. The ideas are deliberately crazy: the Doctor is trying to enter into Ferdinand's frenzy in order gradually to draw him out.
3. A fabulous, and deadly poisonous, serpent, supposed to be hatched of a cock's egg.
4. Cut a caper, dance a jig.

him as tame as a dormouse.

FERDINAND. Can you fetch your frisks, sir? I will stamp him into a cullis, flay off his skin, to cover one of the anatomies[5] this rogue hath set i' th' cold yonder in Barber-Chirurgeons'-Hall. Hence, hence! You are all of you like beasts for sacrifice: there's nothing left of you but tongue and belly, flattery and lechery. [*Exit.*]

PESCARA. Doctor, he did not fear you throughly.

DOCTOR. True;
I was somewhat too forward.

BOSOLA. Mercy upon me,
What a fatal judgment hath fall'n upon this Ferdinand!

PESCARA. Knows your grace what accident hath brought
Unto the prince this strange distraction?

CARDINAL. [*aside*] I must feign somewhat. Thus they say it grew.
You have heard it rumored, for these many years
None of our family dies but there is seen
The shape of an old woman, which is given
By tradition to us to have been murdered
By her nephews for her riches. Such a figure
One night, as the prince sat up late at 's book,
Appeared to him; when, crying out for help,
The gentlemen of's chamber found his grace
All on a cold sweat, altered much in face
And language; since which apparition,
He hath grown worse and worse, and I much fear
He cannot live.

BOSOLA. Sir, I would speak with you.

PESCARA. We'll leave your grace,
Wishing to the sick prince, our noble lord,
All health of mind and body.

CARDINAL. You are most welcome.
[*Exeunt* PESCARA, MALATESTE, *and* DOCTOR.]
Are you come? So. [*aside*] This fellow must not know
By any means I had intelligence[6]
In our duchess' death; for, though I counseled it,
The full of all th' engagement seemed to grow
From Ferdinand.—Now, sir, how fares our sister?
I do not think but sorrow makes her look
Like to an oft-dyed garment: she shall now
Taste comfort from me. Why do you look so wildly?
Oh, the fortune of your master here the prince
Dejects you, but be you of happy comfort:
If you'll do one thing for me I'll entreat,
Though he had a cold tombstone o'er his bones,
I'll make you what you would be.

BOSOLA. Anything;

5. Anatomical skeletons hung up in the surgeon's college, which Ferdinand proposes to cover with the Doctor's flayed skin.

6. Had a hand in.

Give it me in a breath, and let me fly to 't:
They that think long small expedition win,
For musing much o' th' end cannot begin.
[*Enter* JULIA.]
JULIA. Sir, will you come in to supper?
CARDINAL. I am busy;
Leave me.
JULIA. [*aside*] What an excellent shape hath that fellow! [Exit.]
CARDINAL. 'Tis thus. Antonio lurks here in Milan:
Inquire him out, and kill him. While he lives,
Our sister cannot marry, and I have thought
Of an excellent match for her. Do this, and style me
Thy advancement.[7]
BOSOLA. But by what means shall I find him out?
CARDINAL. There is a gentleman called Delio
Here in the camp, that hath been long approved
His loyal friend. Set eye upon that fellow;
Follow him to mass; maybe Antonio,
Although he do account religion
But a school-name,[8] for fashion of the world
May accompany him; or else go inquire out
Delio's confessor, and see if you can bribe
Him to reveal it. There are a thousand ways
A man might find to trace him; as to know
What fellows haunt the Jews for taking up
Great sums of money, for sure he's in want;
Or else to go to th' picture-makers, and learn
Who bought her picture lately. Some of these
Haply may take.
BOSOLA. Well, I'll not freeze i' th' business:
I would see that wretched thing, Antonio,
Above all sights i' th' world.
CARDINAL. Do, and be happy. [*Exit.*]
BOSOLA. This fellow doth breed basilisks in 's eyes,
He's nothing else but murder; yet he seems
Not to have notice of the duchess' death.
'Tis his cunning: I must follow his example;
There cannot be a surer way to trace
Than that of an old fox.
[*Re-enter* JULIA, *with a pistol.*]
JULIA. So, sir, you are well met.
BOSOLA. How now?
JULIA. Nay, the doors are fast enough.
Now, sir,
I will make you confess your treachery.
BOSOLA. Treachery?
JULIA. Yes,
Confess to me which of my women 'twas

7. Look to me for your promotion.
8. Just an idle phrase.

You hired to put love-powder into my drink?
BOSOLA. Love-powder?
JULIA. Yes, when I was at Malfi.
Why should I fall in love with such a face else?
I have already suffered for thee so much pain,
The only remedy to do me good
Is to kill my longing.
BOSOLA. Sure, your pistol holds
Nothing but perfumes or kissing-comfits.[9]
Excellent lady! You have a pretty way on 't
To discover your longing. Come, come, I'll disarm you,
And arm you thus:[1] yet this is wondrous strange.
JULIA. Compare thy form and my eyes together, you'll find
My love no such great miracle. Now you'll say
I am wanton: this nice modesty in ladies
Is but a troublesome familiar[2] that haunts them.
BOSOLA. Know you me, I am a blunt soldier.
JULIA. The better:
Sure, there wants[3] fire where there are no lively sparks
Of roughness.
BOSOLA. And I want compliment.[4]
JULIA. Why, ignorance
In courtship cannot make you do amiss,
If you have a heart to do well.
BOSOLA. You are very fair.
JULIA. Nay, if you lay beauty to my charge,
I must plead unguilty.
BOSOLA. Your bright eyes carry
A quiver of darts in them sharper than sunbeams.
JULIA. You will mar me with commendation,
Put yourself to the charge of courting me,
Whereas now I woo you.
BOSOLA. [*aside*] I have it, I will work upon this creature.—
Let us grow most amorously familiar.
If the great Cardinal now should see me thus,
Would he not count me a villain?
JULIA. No; he might
Count me a wanton, not lay a scruple
Of offence on you; for if I see and steal
A diamond, the fault is not i' th' stone,
But in me the thief that purloins it. I am sudden
With you: we that are great women of pleasure
Use to cut off these uncertain wishes
And unquiet longings, and in an instant join
The sweet delight and the pretty excuse together.
Had you been i' th' street, under my chamber-window,

9. Candies to sweeten the breath.
1. Disarm (by taking away her pistol and kissing her); arm (by embracing her).
2. An irksome ghost.
3. Lacks, is missing.
4. I don't have the gift of flattery.

Even there I should have courted you.
BOSOLA. Oh, you are
An excellent lady!
JULIA. Bid me do somewhat for you
Presently[5] to express I love you.
BOSOLA. I will;
And if you love me, fail not to effect it.
The Cardinal is grown wondrous melancholy;
Demand the cause, let him not put you off
With feigned excuse; discover the main ground on 't.
JULIA. Why would you know this?
BOSOLA. I have depended on him,
And I hear that he is fallen in some disgrace
With the emperor: if he be, like the mice
That forsake falling houses, I would shift
To other dependence.
JULIA. You shall not need
Follow the wars: I'll be your maintenance.
BOSOLA. And I your loyal servant: but I cannot
Leave my calling.
JULIA. Not leave an ungrateful
General for the love of a sweet lady?
You are like some cannot sleep in feather-beds,
But must have blocks for their pillows.
BOSOLA. Will you do this?
JULIA. Cunningly.
BOSOLA. Tomorrow I'll expect th' intelligence.
JULIA. Tomorrow? Get you into my cabinet;
You shall have it with you. Do not delay me,
No more than I do you: I am like one
That is condemned; I have my pardon promised,
But I would see it sealed. Go, get you in:
You shall see me wind my tongue about his heart
Like a skein of silk. [*Exit* BOSOLA.]
[*Re-enter* CARDINAL.]
CARDINAL. Where are you?
[*Enter* SERVANTS.]
SERVANTS. Here.
CARDINAL. Let none, upon your lives, have conference
With the Prince Ferdinand, unless I know it.
[*aside*] In this distraction he may reveal
The murder.— [*Exeunt* SERVANTS.]
Yond's my lingering consumption:
I am weary of her, and by any means
Would be quit of.
JULIA. How now, my lord? What ails you?
CARDINAL. Nothing.
JULIA. Oh, you are much altered: come, I must be

5. Immediately.

Your secretary, and remove this lead
From off your bosom.[6] What's the matter?
CARDINAL. I may not
Tell you.
JULIA. Are you so far in love with sorrow
You cannot part with part of it? Or think you
I cannot love your grace when you are sad
As well as merry? Or do you suspect
I, that have been a secret to your heart
These many winters, cannot be the same
Unto your tongue?
CARDINAL. Satisfy thy longing—
The only way to make thee keep my counsel
Is not to tell thee.
JULIA. Tell your echo this,
Or flatterers, that like echoes still report
What they hear though most imperfect, and not me;
For if that you be true unto yourself,
I'll know.
CARDINAL. Will you rack[7] me?
JULIA. No, judgment shall
Draw it from you: it is an equal fault,
To tell one's secrets unto all or none.
CARDINAL. The first argues folly.
JULIA. But the last, tyranny.
CARDINAL. Very well. Why, imagine I have committed
Some secret deed which I desire the world
May never hear of.
JULIA. Therefore may not I know it?
You have concealed for me as great a sin
As adultery. Sir, never was occasion
For perfect trial of my constancy
Till now: sir, I beseech you——
CARDINAL. You'll repent it.
JULIA. Never.
CARDINAL. It hurries thee to ruin: I'll not tell thee.
Be well advised, and think what danger 'tis
To receive a prince's secrets: they that do,
Had need have their breasts hooped with adamant
To contain them. I pray thee, yet be satisfied;
Examine thine own frailty; 'tis more easy
To tie knots than unloose them: 'tis a secret
That, like a lingering poison, may chance lie
Spread in thy veins, and kill thee seven year hence.
JULIA. Now you dally with me.
CARDINAL. No more; thou shalt know it.
By my appointment the great Duchess of Malfi
And two of her young children, four nights since,

6. Secretaries opened letters addressed to their masters by removing the heavy lead seals.
7. Will you put me to the torture?

Were strangled.
JULIA. O Heaven! Sir, what have you done!
CARDINAL. How now? How settles this? Think you your bosom
Will be a grave dark and obscure enough
For such a secret?
JULIA. You have undone yourself, sir.
CARDINAL. Why?
JULIA. It lies not in me to conceal it.
CARDINAL. No?
Come, I will swear you to 't upon this book.
JULIA. Most religiously.
CARDINAL. Kiss it. [*She kisses the book.*]
Now you shall
Never utter it; thy curiosity
Hath undone thee: thou'rt poisoned with that book.
Because I knew thou couldst not keep my counsel,
I have bound thee to 't by death.
[*Re-enter* BOSOLA.]
BOSOLA. For pity sake,
Hold!
CARDINAL. Ha! Bosola?
JULIA. I forgive you
This equal piece of justice you have done;
For I betrayed your counsel to that fellow:
He overheard it; that was the cause I said
It lay not in me to conceal it.
BOSOLA. O foolish woman,
Couldst not thou have poisoned him?
JULIA. 'Tis weakness,
Too much to think what should have been done. I go
I know not whither. [*Dies.*]
CARDINAL. Wherefore com'st thou hither?
BOSOLA. That I might find a great man like yourself,
Not out of his wits as the Lord Ferdinand,
To remember my service.
CARDINAL. I'll have thee hewed in pieces.
BOSOLA. Make not yourself such a promise of that life
Which is not yours to dispose of.
CARDINAL. Who placed thee here?
BOSOLA. Her lust, as she intended.
CARDINAL. Very well.
Now you know me for your fellow-murderer.
BOSOLA. And wherefore should you lay fair marble colors[8]
Upon your rotten purposes to me?
Unless you imitate some that do plot great treasons,
And when they have done, go hide themselves i' th' graves
Of those were actors in 't?
CARDINAL. No more; there is

8. Plaster was often painted to look like marble.

A fortune attends thee.

BOSOLA. Shall I go sue
To Fortune any longer? 'Tis the fool's
Pilgrimage.

CARDINAL. I have honors in store for thee.

BOSOLA. There are a many ways that conduct to seeming
Honor, and some of them very dirty ones.

CARDINAL. Throw
To the devil thy melancholy. The fire burns well;
What need we keep a stirring of 't, and make
A greater smother? Thou wilt kill Antonio?

BOSOLA. Yes.

CARDINAL. Take up that body.

BOSOLA. I think I shall
Shortly grow the common bearer for churchyards.

CARDINAL. I will allow thee some dozen of attendants
To aid thee in the murder.

BOSOLA. Oh, by no means. Physicians that apply horse-leeches to any rank swelling use to cut off their tails, that the blood may run through them the faster: let me have no train[9] when I go to shed blood, lest it make me have a greater when I ride to the gallows.

CARDINAL. Come to me after midnight, to help to remove
That body to her own lodging: I'll give out
She died o' th' plague; 'twill breed the less inquiry
After her death.

BOSOLA. Where's Castruccio her husband?

CARDINAL. He's rode to Naples, to take possession
Of Antonio's citadel.

BOSOLA. Believe me, you have done
A very happy turn.

CARDINAL. Fail not to come.
There is the master-key of our lodgings, and by that
You may conceive what trust I plant in you.

BOSOLA. You shall find me ready. [*Exit* CARDINAL.]
O poor Antonio,
Though nothing be so needful to thy estate
As pity, yet I find nothing so dangerous;
I must look to my footing:
In such slippery ice-pavements men had need
To be frost-nailed well; they may break their necks else;
The precedent's here afore me. How this man
Bears up in blood! Seems fearless! Why, 'tis well:
Security some men call the suburbs of hell,
Only a dead wall between.[1] Well, good Antonio,
I'll seek thee out, and all my care shall be

9. Followers. Criminals, dragged through the streets to be hanged at Tyburn, were followed by crowds of the idle, the sadistic, and their own fellow criminals.

1. When men are close to hell, with only a dead wall between—but the wall isn't altogether dead, as we soon see—they can live securely there.

To put thee into safety from the reach
Of these most cruel biters that have got
Some of thy blood already. It may be,
I'll join with thee in a most just revenge:
The weakest arm is strong enough that strikes
With the sword of justice. Still methinks the duchess
Haunts me. There, there, 'tis nothing but my melancholy.
O Penitence, let me truly taste thy cup.
That throws men down only to raise them up! [*Exit.*]

SCENE 3. *A Fortification at Milan.*

[*Enter* ANTONIO *and* DELIO. *Echo from the* DUCHESS' *grave.*]

DELIO. Yond's the Cardinal's window. This fortification
Grew from the ruins of an ancient abbey;
And to yond side o' th' river lies a wall,
Piece of a cloister, which in my opinion
Gives the best echo that you ever heard,
So hollow and so dismal, and withal
So plain in the distinction of our words,
That many have supposed it is a spirit
That answers.

ANTONIO. I do love these ancient ruins.
We never tread upon them but we set
Our foot upon some reverend history:
And, questionless, here in this open court,
Which now lies naked to the injuries
Of stormy weather, some men lie interred
Loved the church so well, and gave so largely to 't,
They thought it should have canopied their bones
Till doomsday; but all things have their end:
Churches and cities, which have diseases
Like to men, must have like death that we have.

ECHO. "Like death that we have."

DELIO. Now the echo hath caught you.

ANTONIO. It groaned, methought, and gave
A very deadly accent.

ECHO. "Deadly accent."

DELIO. I told you 'twas a pretty one: you may make it
A huntsman, or a falconer, a musician
Or a thing of sorrow.

ECHO. "A thing of sorrow."

ANTONIO. Aye, sure, that suits it best.

ECHO. "That suits it best."

ANTONIO. 'Tis very like my wife's voice.

ECHO. "Aye, wife's voice."

DELIO. Come, let's walk further from 't. I would not have you
Go to th' Cardinal's tonight: do not.

ECHO. "Do not."

DELIO. Wisdom doth not more moderate wasting sorrow
Than time: take time for 't; be mindful of thy safety.
ECHO. "Be mindful of thy safety."
ANTONIO. Necessity compels me:
Make scrutiny throughout the passes of
Your own life, you'll find it impossible
To fly your fate.
ECHO. "Oh, fly your fate."
DELIO. Hark!
The dead stones seem to have pity on you, and give you
Good counsel.
ANTONIO. Echo, I will not talk with thee,
For thou art a dead thing.
ECHO. "Thou art a dead thing."
ANTONIO. My duchess is asleep now,
And her little ones, I hope sweetly: O Heaven,
Shall I never see her more?
ECHO. "Never see her more."
ANTONIO. I marked not one repetition of the echo
But that, and on the sudden a clear light
Presented me a face folded in sorrow.
DELIO. Your fancy merely.
ANTONIO. Come, I'll be out of this ague,
For to live thus is not indeed to live;
It is a mockery and abuse of life.
I will not henceforth save myself by halves;
Lose all, or nothing.
DELIO. Your own virtue save you!
I'll fetch your eldest son, and second[2] you:
It may be that the sight of his own blood
Spread in so sweet a figure[3] may beget
The more compassion. However, fare you well.
Though in our miseries Fortune have a part,
Yet in our noble sufferings she hath none:
Contempt of pain, that we may call our own. [*Exeunt.*]

SCENE 4. *A Room in the* CARDINAL'S *Palace.*

[*Enter* CARDINAL, PESCARA, MALATESTE, RODERIGO, *and* GRISOLAN.]

CARDINAL. You shall not watch tonight by the sick prince;
His grace is very well recovered.
MALATESTE. Good my lord, suffer[4] us.
CARDINAL. Oh, by no means;
The noise and change of object in his eye
Doth more distract him. I pray, all to bed;

2. Back you up.
3. Face.
4. Allow.

And though you hear him in his violent fit,
Do not rise, I entreat you.

PESCARA. So, sir; we shall not.

CARDINAL. Nay, I must have you promise upon your honors,
For I was enjoined to 't by himself; and he seemed
To urge it sensibly.[5]

PESCARA. Let our honors bind
This trifle.

CARDINAL. Nor any of your followers.

MALATESTE. Neither.

CARDINAL. It may be, to make trial of your promise,
When he's asleep, myself will rise and feign
Some of his mad tricks, and cry out for help,
And feign myself in danger.

MALATESTE. If your throat were cutting,
I'd not come at you, now I have protested against it.

CARDINAL. Why, I thank you.

GRISOLAN. 'Twas a foul storm tonight.

RODERIGO. The Lord Ferdinand's chamber shook like an osier.[6]

MALATESTE. 'Twas nothing but pure kindness in the devil,
To rock his own child. [*Exeunt all except the* CARDINAL.]

CARDINAL. The reason why I would not suffer these
About my brother, is, because at midnight
I may with better privacy convey
Julia's body to her own lodging. Oh, my conscience!
I would pray now, but the devil takes away my heart
For having any confidence in prayer.
About this hour I appointed Bosola
To fetch the body: when he hath served my turn,
He dies. [*Exit.*]

[*Enter* BOSOLA.]

BOSOLA. Ha! 'Twas the Cardinal's voice; I heard him name
Bosola and my death. Listen! I hear
One's footing.

[*Enter* FERDINAND.]

FERDINAND. Strangling is a very quiet death.

BOSOLA. [*aside*] Nay, then, I see I must stand upon my guard.

FERDINAND. What say to that? Whisper softly; do you agree to 't? So; it must be done i' th' dark: the Cardinal would not for a thousand pounds the doctor should see it. [*Exit.*]

BOSOLA. My death is plotted; here's the consequence of murder.
We value not desert nor Christian breath,
When we know black deeds must be cured with death.

[*Enter* ANTONIO *and* SERVANT.]

SERVANT. Here stay, sir and be confident, I pray:
I'll fetch you a dark lantern. [*Exit.*]

ANTONIO. Could I take him
At his prayers, there were hope of pardon.

5. With real feeling.

6. Reed.

BOSOLA. Fall right, my sword! [*Stabs him.*]
I'll not give thee so much leisure as to pray.
ANTONIO. Oh, I am gone! Thou hast ended a long suit[7]
In a minute.
BOSOLA. What art thou?
ANTONIO. A most wretched thing,
That only have thy benefit in death,
To appear myself.
[*Re-enter* SERVANT *with a lantern.*]
SERVANT. Where are you, sir?
ANTONIO. Very near my home. Bosola?
SERVANT. Oh, misfortune!
BOSOLA. Smother thy pity; thou art dead else. Antonio?
The man I would have saved 'bove mine own life!
We are merely the stars' tennis-balls, struck and bandied
Which way please them.[8] O good Antonio,
I'll whisper one thing in thy dying ear
Shall make thy heart break quickly! Thy fair duchess
And two sweet children——
ANTONIO. Their very names
Kindle a little life in me.
BOSOLA. Are murdered.
ANTONIO. Some men have wished to die
At the hearing of sad tidings; I am glad
That I shall do 't in sadness: I would not now
Wish my wounds balmed nor healed, for I have no use
To put my life to. In all our quest of greatness,
Like wanton boys, whose pastime is their care,
We follow after bubbles blown in th' air.
Pleasure of life, what is 't? Only the good
Hours of an ague; merely a preparative
To rest, to endure vexation. I do not ask
The process of my death; only commend me
To Delio.
BOSOLA. Break, heart!
ANTONIO. And let my son
Fly the courts of princes. [*Dies.*]
BOSOLA. Thou seem'st
To have loved Antonio?
SERVANT. I brought him hither,
To have reconciled him to the Cardinal.
BOSOLA. I do not ask thee that.
Take him up, if thou tender thine own life,
And bear him where the lady Julia
Was wont to lodge. Oh, my fate moves swift;

7. Antonio thinks it is the Cardinal, to whom he was addressing his "suit" (plea for reconciliation), who has murdered him.

8. The power of the stars over men's lives was a Renaissance commonplace.

I have this Cardinal in the forge already;
Now I'll bring him to th' hammer. Oh direful misprision![9]
I will not imitate things glorious,
No more than base; I'll be mine own example.
On, on, and look thou represent, for silence,
The thing thou bear'st.[1] [*Exeunt.*]

SCENE 5

[*Enter* CARDINAL, *with a book.*]

CARDINAL. I am puzzled in a question about hell:
He says, in hell there's one material fire,
And yet it shall not burn all men alike.
Lay him by. How tedious is a guilty conscience!
When I look into the fish-ponds in my garden,
Methinks I see a thing armed with a rake,
That seems to strike at me.

[*Enter* BOSOLA, *and* SERVANT *bearing* ANTONIO's *body.*]

Now, art thou come?
Thou look'st ghastly:
There sits in thy face some great determination
Mixed with some fear.

BOSOLA. Thus it lightens into action:
I am come to kill thee.

CARDINAL. Ha! Help! Our guard!

BOSOLA. Thou art deceived; they are out of thy howling.

CARDINAL. Hold; and I will faithfully divide
Revenues with thee.

BOSOLA. Thy prayers and proffers
Are both unseasonable.

CARDINAL. Raise the watch!
We are betrayed!

BOSOLA. I have confined your flight:[2]
I'll suffer your retreat to Julia's chamber,
But no further.

CARDINAL. Help! We are betrayed!

[*Enter, above,* PESCARA, MALATESTE, RODERIGO, *and* GRISOLAN.]

MALATESTE. Listen.

CARDINAL. My dukedom for rescue!

RODERIGO. Fie upon
His counterfeiting!

MALATESTE. Why, 'tis not the Cardinal.

RODERIGO. Yes, yes, 'tis he, but I'll see him hanged
Ere I'll go down to him.

CARDINAL. Here's a plot upon me;
I am assaulted! I am lost, unless some rescue.

9. Error.
1. I.e., be as still as the corpse you're carrying.
2. Cut off your escape.

GRISOLAN. He doth this pretty well, but it will not serve
To laugh me out of mine honor.
CARDINAL. The sword's at my throat!
RODERIGO. You would not bawl so loud then.
MALATESTE. Come, come,
Let's go to bed. He told us thus much aforehand.
PESCARA. He wished you should not come at him; but, believe't,
The accent of the voice sounds not in jest:
I'll down to him, howsoever, and with engines[3]
Force ope the doors. [*Exit above.*]
RODERIGO. Let's follow him aloof,[4]
And note how the Cardinal will laugh at him.
[*Exeunt, above,* MALATESTE, RODERIGO, *and* GRISOLAN.]
BOSOLA. There's for you first, [*He kills the* SERVANT.]
'Cause you shall not unbarricade the door
To let in rescue.
CARDINAL. What cause hast thou to pursue my life?
BOSOLA. Look there.
CARDINAL. Antonio?
BOSOLA. Slain by my hand unwittingly.
Pray, and be sudden: when thou killed'st thy sister,
Thou took'st from Justice her most equal balance,
And left her naught but her sword.
CARDINAL. Oh, mercy!
BOSOLA. Now, it seems thy greatness was only outward;
For thou fall'st faster of thyself than calamity
Can drive thee. I'll not waste longer time; there! [*Stabs him.*]
CARDINAL. Thou hast hurt me.
BOSOLA. Again! [*Stabs him again.*]
CARDINAL. Shall I die like a leveret,[5]
Without any resistance? Help, help, help!
I am slain!
[*Enter* FERDINAND.]
FERDINAND. Th' alarum? Give me a fresh horse;
Rally the vaunt-guard, or the day is lost.
Yield, yield! I give you the honor of arms,
Shake my sword over you; will you yield?[6]
CARDINAL. Help me; I am your brother!
FERDINAND. The devil!
My brother fight upon the adverse party?
[*He wounds the* CARDINAL, *and, in the scuffle, gives* BOSOLA *his death-wound.*]
There flies your ransom.
CARDINAL. O justice!
I suffer now for what hath former been:

3. Bars and beams.
4. At a distance.
5. A baby hare, a defenseless creature.
6. It won't do to look for too much sense in Ferdinand's wild cries; he thinks he's on the field of battle and offering the "honor of arms" (liberal surrender terms) to his foes.

Sorrow is held the eldest child of sin.

FERDINAND. Now you're brave fellows. Caesar's fortune was harder than Pompey's; Caesar died in the arms of prosperity, Pompey at the feet of disgrace. You both died in the field. The pain's nothing: pain many times is taken away with the apprehension of greater, as the toothache with the sight of a barber that comes to pull it out: there's philosophy for you.

BOSOLA. Now my revenge is perfect. Sink, thou main cause
[*He kills* FERDINAND.]
Of my undoing! The last part of my life
Hath done me best service.

FERDINAND. Give me some wet hay; I am broken-winded. I do account this world but a dog-kennel: I will vault credit and affect high pleasures beyond death.[7]

BOSOLA. He seems to come to himself, now he's so near
The bottom.

FERDINAND. My sister, O my sister! There's the cause on 't.
Whether we fall by ambition, blood, or lust,
Like diamonds we are cut with our own dust. [*Dies.*]

CARDINAL. Thou hast thy payment, too.

BOSOLA. Yes, I hold my weary soul in my teeth.
'Tis ready to part from me. I do glory
That thou, which stood'st like a huge pyramid
Begun upon a large and ample base,
Shalt end in a little point, a kind of nothing.

[*Enter, below,* PESCARA, MALATESTE, RODERIGO, *and* GRISOLAN.]

PESCARA. How now, my lord?

MALATESTE. O sad disaster!

RODERIGO. How
Comes this?

BOSOLA. Revenge for the Duchess of Malfi murdered
By th' Aragonian brethren; for Antonio
Slain by this hand; for lustful Julia
Poisoned by this man; and lastly for myself,
That was an actor in the main of all,
Much 'gainst mine own good nature, yet i' th' end
Neglected.

PESCARA. How now, my lord?

CARDINAL. Look to my brother: he gave us these large wounds
As we were struggling here i' the rushes.[8] And now,
I pray, let me be laid by and never thought of. [*Dies.*]

PESCARA. How fatally, it seems, he did withstand
His own rescue!

MALATESTE. Thou wretched thing of blood,
How came Antonio by his death?

7. Worn-out horses are said to be broken-winded. The last sentence implies that he expects no more of this life and looks forward only to the next one.

8. Reed mats laid down over Elizabethan floors in lieu of carpets.

BOSOLA. In a mist;
I know not how: such a mistake as I
Have often seen in a play. Oh, I am gone!
We are only like dead walls or vaulted graves,
That, ruined, yield no echo. Fare you well.
It may be pain, but no harm, to me to die
In so good a quarrel. Oh, this gloomy world!
In what a shadow, or deep pit of darkness,
Doth, womanish and fearful, mankind live!
Let worthy minds ne'er stagger in distrust
To suffer death or shame for what is just:
Mine is another voyage. [*Dies.*]
PESCARA. The noble Delio, as I came to the palace,
Told me of Antonio's being here, and showed me
A pretty gentleman, his son and heir.
[*Enter* DELIO *and* ANTONIO'S SON.]
MALATESTE. O sir,
You come too late!
DELIO. I heard so, and was armed[9] for 't
Ere I came. Let us make noble use
Of this great ruin; and join all our force
To establish this young hopeful gentleman
In 's mother's right. These wretched eminent things
Leave no more fame behind 'em, than should one
Fall in a frost, and leave his print in snow;
As soon as the sun shines, it ever melts,
Both form and matter. I have ever thought
Nature doth nothing so great for great men
As when she's pleased to make them lords of truth:
Integrity of life is fame's best friend,
Which nobly, beyond death, shall crown the end. [*Exeunt.*]

performed, 1614 *published*, 1623

9. Inwardly prepared.

ROBERT HERRICK

(1591–1674)

What little personal history Robert Herrick had was always too much for him; the decisions he had to take were mostly forced on him, and he accepted them as misfortunes. Yet he is the happiest of English poets. The son of a prosperous London goldsmith, he was slow in taking his degrees, slower still in finding himself a career. Clearly he would have liked nothing better than a life of leisured study in London, talking literature and drinking sack with his hero Ben Jonson, while polishing his verses. But social pressures were insistent; he took orders in the church and moved reluctantly to a parish at Dean Prior, in Devonshire.

As a Londoner, he did not much like the rough West Country or its people, but he gradually adapted to both, settling placidly into his bachelor quarters and secreting poems as a hen lays eggs. For the purposes of these poems, he invented for himself dozens of imaginary mistresses—hectic, bewitching creatures with exotic names; but the maid who kept house for him was prophetically named Prudence. At the top of his poetic bent, in *Corinna's Going A-Maying*, Herrick produced a truly major lyric on the central theme of his life, the happy reconciliation of nature and nature's god. But much of his poetic work seems casual, even trivial, though one can easily be misled by his apparent off-handedness into overlooking a serious strain that lies subsurface. He wrote against Devonshire, and then for it; about his cat, and his spaniel Tracy, and his maid Prudence; a farewell to sack (heart-rending) and a return to it (joyous). A recurrent theme in his work is a deftly balanced personal paganism—private sacrifices to household gods, tiny rituals and allusions to ancient creeds only half-seriously taken. The Puritans would have been scandalized had they realized that this minister of the holy gospel was at least half a pagan, and didn't even have the grace to be ashamed of the fact.

Herrick himself did not advertise his beliefs; but when the storm of civil war broke, and the Puritans came to power, they dispossessed him anyhow, and Herrick came down to London with the fruits of his exile. They were published early in 1648 in a fat little octavo volume with two titles, *Hesperides* for the secular poems, and *Noble Numbers* for those with sacred subjects. Altogether, there were over 1,200 poems in this one volume, the only publication of Herrick's life. But the time was not right for tiny, playful lyrics; nobody noticed *Hesperides*, either to applaud or deplore; and Herrick disappeared in silence and oblivion, not to be restored to English literature till the 19th century. He did manage to survive the harsh weather of Puritanism till King Charles was restored in 1660; and that restoration brought him back to Dean Prior, where he lived out his last years quietly, dying at the ripe age of 83.

Jonson taught Herrick the art of the polished trifle, the light touch, and the quiet mood. For both of them life was a sacrament—and Herrick brought to that sometimes portentous view of things a modesty and sense of proportion that are uniquely his own.

The Argument[1] of His Book

I sing of brooks, of blossoms, birds, and bowers,
Of April, May, of June, and July flowers.
I sing of Maypoles, hock carts, wassails, wakes,[2]
Of bridegrooms, brides, and of their bridal cakes.
I write of youth, of love, and have access
By these to sing of cleanly wantonness.[3]
I sing of dews, of rains, and, piece by piece,

1. Subject matter.
2. "Hock carts" carried home the last load of the harvest; therefore adorned and celebrated. "Wakes": festive, not funerary occasions, to commemorate the dedication of a parish church.
3. Good fun, but already tinged with the lascivious overtone the word carries today.

Of balm, of oil, of spice, and ambergris.[4]
I sing of times trans-shifting, and I write
How roses first came red and lilies white.
I write of groves, of twilights, and I sing
The court of Mab and of the fairy king.[5]
I write of hell; I sing (and ever shall)
Of heaven, and hope to have it after all.

1648

His Prayer to Ben Jonson

When I a verse shall make,
Know I have prayed thee,
For old religion's sake,[6]
Saint Ben to aid me.

Make the way smooth for me
When I, thy Herrick,
Honoring thee, on my knee,
Offer my lyric.

Candles I'll give to thee
And a new altar;
And thou Saint Ben shalt be
Writ in my psalter.

1648

To the Water Nymphs Drinking at the Fountain

Reach with your whiter hands to me
  Some crystal of the spring;
And I about the cup shall see
  Fresh lilies flourishing.

Or else, sweet nymphs, do you but this—
  To the glass your lips incline;
And I shall see by that one kiss
  The water turned to wine.

1648

The Lily in a Crystal

You have beheld a smiling rose
  When virgin hands have drawn

4. Ambergris is used in making perfumes; hence it carries the overtone of something rare and delectable.
5. Mab was by long-standing tradition queen of the fairies and wife of King Oberon. See Shakespeare, *A Midsummer Night's Dream.*
6. The Puritans were hostile to the invocation of saints, above all such "saints" as Ben Jonson. Herrick plays on the fact that Jonson was a Catholic (of the "old religion"), as well as a saint in the mock-religion of poetry.

O'er it a cobweb-lawn;[1]
And here you see, this lily shows,
Tombed in a crystal stone,
More fair in this transparent case
Than when it grew alone
And had but single grace.

You see how cream but naked is,
Nor dances in the eye
Without a strawberry;
Or some fine tincture,[2] like to this,
Which draws the sight thereto,
More by that wantoning[3] with it
Than when the paler hue
No mixture did admit.

You see how amber through the streams
More gently strokes the sight
With some concealed delight[4]
Than when he darts his radiant beams
Into the boundless air,
Where either too much life his worth
Doth all at once impair
Or set it little forth.

Put purple grapes or cherries in-
To glass, and they will send
More beauty to commend
Them from that clean and subtle skin
Than if they naked stood,
And had no other pride at all
But their own flesh and blood
And tinctures natural.

Thus lily, rose, grape, cherry, cream,
And strawberry do stir
More love when they transfer
A weak, a soft, a broken beam,
Than if they should discover
At full their proper excellence
Without some scene cast over
To juggle with the sense.

Thus let this crystaled lily be
A rule how far to teach
Your nakedness must reach,
And that no further than we see

1. A very fine, transparent linen.
2. Slight coloration.
3. Toying, sporting.
4. Some varieties of cloudy amber do in fact look more attractive under water.

Those glaring colors laid
By art's wise hand, but to this end
They should obey a shade
Lest they too far extend.

So, though you're white as swan or snow
And have the power to move
A world of men to love,
Yet when your lawns and silks shall flow
And that white cloud divide
Into a doubtful twilight, then,
Then will your hidden pride
Raise greater fires in men.

1648

To Blossoms

Fair pledges of a fruitful tree,
Why do ye fall so fast?
Your date is not so past
But you may stay yet here a while,
To blush and gently smile,
And go at last.

What, were ye born to be
An hour or half's delight,
And so to bid good night?
'Twas pity Nature brought you forth
Merely to show your worth,
And lose you quite.

But you are lovely leaves, where we
May read how soon things have
Their end, though ne'er so brave;
And after they have shown their pride
Like you a while, they glide
Into the grave.

1648

To the Virgins, to Make Much of Time

Gather ye rosebuds while ye may,
Old time is still a-flying;
And this same flower that smiles today
Tomorrow will be dying.

The glorious lamp of heaven, the sun,
The higher he's a-getting,

The sooner will his race be run,
And nearer he's to setting.

That age is best which is the first,
When youth and blood are warmer;
But being spent, the worse, and worst
Times still succeed the former.

Then be not coy, but use your time,
And, while ye may, go marry;
For, having lost but once your prime,
You may forever tarry.

1648

Corinna's Going A-Maying

Get up! get up for shame! the blooming morn
Upon her wings presents the god unshorn.[1]
See how Aurora throws her fair
Fresh-quilted colors through the air:[2]
Get up, sweet slug-a-bed, and see
The dew bespangling herb and tree.
Each flower has wept and bowed toward the east
Above an hour since, yet you not dressed;
Nay, not so much as out of bed?
When all the birds have matins said,
And sung their thankful hymns, 'tis sin,
Nay, profanation to keep in,
Whenas a thousand virgins on this day
Spring, sooner than the lark, to fetch in May.[3]

Rise, and put on your foliage, and be seen
To come forth, like the springtime, fresh and green,
And sweet as Flora.[4] Take no care
For jewels for your gown or hair;
Fear not; the leaves will strew
Gems in abundance upon you;
Besides, the childhood of the day has kept,
Against you come, some orient[5] pearls unwept;
Come and receive them while the light
Hangs on the dew-locks of the night,
And Titan[6] on the eastern hill

1. Apollo, the sun god, whose hair (the rays of the sun) is never cut. For a discussion of the poem, and Apollo's rôle in it, see Cleanth Brooks, *The Well-Wrought Urn* (New York, 1947), Ch. 4.

2. Aurora, goddess of the dawn, is both tossing her blankets aside, like one anxious to be up, and spreading over the earth a freshly composed coverlet of light.

3. On May Day morning, it was the custom to gather whitethorn blossoms and trim the house with them (see below, lines 30–35).

4. Flora, the Roman goddess of flowers and vegetation, had her festival in the spring.

5. Eastern, as pearls come from the Orient, but also rosy and glowing like the rising sun. "Against": until.

6. The sun.

    Retires himself, or else stands still
Till you come forth. Wash, dress, be brief in praying:
Few beads[7] are best when once we go a-Maying.

Come, my Corinna, come; and, coming, mark
How each field turns a street,[8] each street a park
    Made green and trimmed with trees; see how
    Devotion gives each house a bough
    Or branch: each porch, each door ere this,
    An ark, a tabernacle is,[9]
Made up of whitethorn neatly interwove,
As if here were those cooler shades of love.
    Can such delights be in the street
    And open fields, and we not see 't?
    Come, we'll abroad; and let's obey
    The proclamation made for May,
And sin no more, as we have done, by staying;
But, my Corinna, come, let's go a-Maying.

There's not a budding boy or girl this day
But is got up and gone to bring in May;
    A deal of youth, ere this, is come
    Back, and with whitethorn laden home.
    Some have dispatched their cakes and cream
    Before that we have left to dream;
And some have wept, and wooed, and plighted troth,
And chose their priest, ere we can cast off sloth.
    Many a green-gown[1] has been given,
    Many a kiss, both odd and even;[2]
    Many a glance, too, has been sent
    From out the eye, love's firmament;
Many a jest told of the keys betraying
This night, and locks picked; yet we're not a-Maying.

Come, let us go while we are in our prime,
And take the harmless folly of the time.
    We shall grow old apace, and die
    Before we know our liberty.
    Our life is short, and our days run
    As fast away as does the sun;
And, as a vapor or a drop of rain
Once lost, can ne'er be found again;
    So when or you or I are made
    A fable, song, or fleeting shade,
    All love, all liking, all delight

7. A casual term for prayers, but with overtones of the old (Catholic) religion, which in the next stanza is playfully converted into, and identified with, the worship of nature.
8. Turns into a street.
9. The doorways, ornamented with whitethorn, are like the Hebrew Ark of the Covenant; May sprigs are the central mystery of the religion of nature.
1. Got by rolling in the grass.
2. Kisses are odd and even in kissing games.

Lies drowned with us in endless night.
Then while time serves, and we are but decaying,
Come, my Corinna, come, let's go a-Maying.

1648

Delight in Disorder

A sweet disorder in the dress
Kindles in clothes a wantonness.[3]
A lawn[4] about the shoulders thrown
Into a fine distractión;
An erring[5] lace, which here and there
Enthralls the crimson stomacher;[6]
A cuff neglectful, and thereby
Ribbons to flow confusedly;
A winning wave, deserving note,
In the tempestuous petticoat;
A careless shoestring, in whose tie
I see a wild civility;
Do more bewitch me than when art
Is too precise[7] in every part.

1648

Upon Julia's Clothes

Whenas in silks my Julia goes,
Then, then, methinks, how sweetly flows
That liquefaction of her clothes.

Next, when I cast mine eyes, and see
That brave[8] vibration, each way free,
O, how that glittering taketh me!

1648

Upon Prue, His Maid

In this little urn is laid
Prudence Baldwin, once my maid,
From whose happy spark here let
Spring the purple violet.

1648

3. Most of the terms used to describe the ladies' clothing have an ethical or social overtone.
4. A scarf of fine linen.
5. Wandering, floating.
6. The lower part of the bodice.
7. "Precise" and "precision" were terms used freely of Puritans; Herrick, in praising feminine disarray, is defining the "sprezzatura," or careless grace, of his own cavalier art.
8. Glorious, splendid.

Upon His Spaniel Tracy

Now thou art dead, no eye shall ever see,
For shape and service, spaniel like to thee.
This shall my love do, give thy sad death one
Tear, that deserves of me a millión.

1648

Dreams

Here we are all, by day; by night, we're hurled
By dreams, each one into a several[1] world.

1648

To Lar[2]

No more shall I, since I am driven hence,
Devote to thee my grains of frankincense.
No more shall I from mantle-trees[3] hang down,
To honor thee, my little parsley crown:
No more shall I (I fear me) to thee bring
My chives of garlic for an offering.
No more shall I, from henceforth, hear a choir
Of merry crickets by my country fire.
Go where I will, thou lucky Lar stay here,
Warm by a glittering chimney all the year.

1648

His Return to London

From the dull confines of the drooping West,
To see the day spring from the pregnant East,
Ravished in spirit, I come, nay more, I fly
To thee, blest place of my nativity!
Thus, thus with hallowed foot I touch the ground
With thousand blessings by thy fortune crowned.
O fruitful genius! that bestowest here
An everlasting plenty, year by year;
O place! O people! Manners framed to please
All nations, customs, kindreds, languages!
I am a free-born Roman;[4] suffer then
That I amongst you live a citizen.

1. Separate.
2. The Roman Lar was a household god associated with the hearth and the family-center; he would normally be paid just such familiar, homely honors as Herrick describes—a bit of incense, an occasional bit of herb or savory seasoning. The poem was evidently written when Herrick was ejected from his living by the Puritans.
3. Mantlepiece.
4. A Roman born in the city was said to be "free of it," i.e., entitled to its liberties.

London my home is: though by hard fate sent
Into a long and irksome banishment;
Yet since called back; henceforward let me be,
O native country, repossessed by thee!
For, rather than I'll to the West return,
I'll beg of thee first here to have mine urn.
Weak I am grown, and must in short time fall;
Give thou my sacred relics burial.[5]

1648

5. As a priest and a poet, Herrick might without immodesty claim that his "relics" were sacred.

GEORGE HERBERT
(1593–1633)

George Herbert was the fifth son of an ancient and distinguished Welsh family. His father died when he was young, and he was brought up by his mother, Magdalen Herbert, a friend of Donne's, and a lady eminent both for her piety and her love of letters. After taking his degrees with distinction at the University of Cambridge, George Herbert was elected Public Orator of the university. It was a post carrying dignity and even some authority: its incumbent was called on to express, in the florid Latin of the day, the sentiments of the university on public occasions. Other men had used the post as a steppingstone to high political office; and Herbert seems to have had this idea, at least briefly, in mind. But the death of his patrons, and the bent of his own temper, soon drew him in another direction. In 1626 he took a minor office in the church; in 1629 he married Jane Danvers; and in 1630 he accepted the living of Bemerton, in Salisbury, and took orders.

Many younger sons of highly connected houses entered the church in those days—picking up a sinecure here and a nonresident ministry there; accepting the pay, and letting the work be done by underpaid curates; filling the offices of the church, perhaps without scandal, but also without the least breath of spiritual fervor. At Bemerton, on the contrary, George Herbert became at once what the age delighted to recognize as "a learned, godly, and painful divine." He preached and prayed; he rebuilt the church out of his own pocket; he visited the poor, consoled the sick, and sat by the bed of the dying—administering true pastoral care to the plowman and the peer alike. "Holy Mr. Herbert" became the talk of the countryside in the three short years of his ministry, before he died of consumption. And during these years, he completed the volume of poems known as *The Temple,* which was published shortly after his death, in 1633, by the friend to whom it had been left. His fame rests on this volume, and all our selections are taken from it.

As a poet, Herbert is quiet, inward, subtle, graceful, and neat. Working within the great tradition of Christian types and imagery, he delights in using quaint devices and homely images. But his spiritual feeling is to an extraordinary degree pure and fresh and free. Donne may be described as the poet of religious doubt, of strain, of anxiety; Herbert is the poet of religious faith, of submission, of acceptance. Both are classified as "metaphysical" poets; both use "conceited" and ingenious images; but Herbert, in a poem like *Love*, for example, allows his meaning to unfold from the situation gently like a flower, where Donne would be tugging at it or arguing with a mock opponent. Herbert is never flashy, nor even strongly dramatic; like the church he served, he is devoted to the quiet middle way. Yet his quiet is never the quiet of emotional poverty or torpor. Herbert's moods are as changeable as the English weather; but underneath them one hears the uninterrupted murmur of prayer, the serene wisdom of a thousand years of faith. The ancient forms were ever George Herbert's chief delight; his poetry, from which the concept of "freshness" is rarely absent, is like the parish church—an intricate, ancient structure, rich in traditional designs, which is open for the humblest and simplest person to enter.

Virtue

Sweet day, so cool, so calm, so bright,
The bridal of the earth and sky:
The dew shall weep thy fall tonight;
    For thou must die.

Sweet rose, whose hue, angry and brave,[1]
Bids the rash gazer wipe his eye:
Thy root is ever in its grave,
    And thou must die.

Sweet spring, full of sweet days and roses,
A box where sweets[2] compacted lie;
My music shows ye have your closes,[3]
    And all must die.

Only a sweet and virtuous soul,
Like seasoned timber, never gives;
But though the whole world turn to coal,[4]
    Then chiefly lives.

1633

Man

My God, I heard this day
That none doth build a stately habitation,
  But he that means to dwell therein.
  What house more stately hath there been,
Or can be, than is man? to whose creation
    All things are in decay.[1]

1. "Angry": having the hue of anger, red. "Brave": splendid. Both adjectives indicate the arrogant yet pathetic defiance of beauty in the face of time.
2. Perfumes.
3. Concluding cadences. The expression shows that Herbert intended his poem to be sung—as it has, in fact, often been.
4. Be reduced to a cinder at the Last Judgment. See II Peter iii.10.

1. By comparison with created man, and as a result of their service to him, all other things are in decay.

For man is every thing
And more; he is a tree, yet bears more fruit;
A beast, yet is or should be more;
Reason and speech we only bring.
Parrots may thank us, if they are not mute:
They go upon the score.[2]

Man is all symmetry,
Full of proportions, one limb to another,
And all to all the world besides;
Each part may call the farthest, brother;
For head with foot hath private amity,
And both with moons and tides.

Nothing hath got so far
But man hath caught and kept it as his prey.
His eyes dismount the highest star:
He is in little all the sphere.
Herbs gladly cure our flesh; because that they
Find their acquaintance there.

For as the winds do blow,
The earth doth rest, heav'n move, and fountains flow;
Nothing we see but means our good,
As our delight, or as our treasure.
The whole is either our cupboard of food,
Or cabinet of pleasure.

The stars have us to bed;
Night draws the curtain which the sun withdraws,
Music and light attend our head.
All things unto our flesh are kind
In their descent and being; to our mind
In their ascent and cause.

Each thing is full of duty.
Waters united are our navigation,
Distinguished, our habitation;
Below, our drink; above, our meat;
Both are our cleanliness. Hath one such beauty?[3]
Then how are all things neat!

2. Man has a vegetable, an animal, and a spiritual nature; he's the only creature which speaks and reasons. Parrots may seem to be an exception to the first of these rules, but they talk on credit (because we taught them how).

3. All the elements serve us multiply, for instance water. Oceans are valuable for navigation; the earth was created by dividing waters from waters (Genesis i.6–7); on earth water is drink, from above (as dew or manna), food. If one element can serve so richly, how beautiful is the sum of things.

More servants wait on man
Than he'll take notice of; in every path,
He treads down that which doth befriend him,
When sickness makes him pale and wan.[4]
O mighty love! Man is one world, and hath
Another to attend him.

Since then, my God, thou hast
So brave a palace built: O, dwell in it,
That it may dwell with thee at last!
Till then, afford us so much wit,
That, as the world serves us, we may serve thee,
And both, thy servants be.

1633

The Pilgrimage

I traveled on, seeing the hill where lay
My expectation.
A long it was and weary way.
The gloomy cave of desperation
I left on th'one, and on the other side
The rock of pride.[1]

And so I came to fancy's meadow, strowed
With many a flower;
Fain would I here have made abode,
But I was quickened by my hour.
So to care's copse I came, and there got through
With much ado.

That led me to the wild of passion, which
Some call the wold[2]—
A wasted place but sometimes rich.
Here I was robbed of all my gold
Save one good angel,[3] which a friend had tied
Close to my side.

At length I got unto the gladsome hill
Where lay my hope,
Where lay my heart; and, climbing still,
When I had gained the brow and top,
A lake of brackish waters on the ground
Was all I found.

4. Man thoughtlessly treads down the herb that will cure him when he's sick.

1. The spiritual pilgrimage or search through allegorical perils was a frequent literary motif long before Bunyan's *Pilgrim's Progress*; compare Henry Vaughan's *Regeneration*, below.

2. Upland moor country.

3. A golden coin as well as (punningly) a guardian angel.

With that abashed, and struck with many a sting
Of swarming fears,
I fell, and cried, "Alas, my king!
Can both the way and end be tears?"
Yet taking heart I rose, and then perceived
I was deceived:

My hill was further; so I flung away,
Yet heard a cry,
Just as I went: *None goes that way*
And lives: "If that be all," said I,
"After so foul a journey, death is fair,
And but a chair."[4]

1633

Easter Wings[1]

Lord, who createdst man in wealth and store,[2]
Though foolishly he lost the same,
Decaying more and more
Till he became
Most poor:
With thee
O let me rise
As larks, harmoniously,
And sing this day thy victories:
Then shall the fall further the flight in me.

My tender age in sorrow did begin:
And still with sicknesses and shame
Thou didst so punish sin,
That I became
Most thin.
With thee
Let me combine,
And feel this day thy victory;
For, if I imp[3] my wing on thine,
Affliction shall advance the flight in me.

1633

4. "Chair" implies rest and immobility, but also, in the sense of "sedan chair," a conveyance.

1. This poem and *The Altar* (below) are "shaped verses," which represent, by the typographical shape of the poem on the page, some part of the subject. Though sometimes condemned as "false wit," this sort of poem has appealed to an occasional author from Hellenistic times to the present. Among recent examples are *Vision and Prayer* by Dylan Thomas and *Un Coup de Dés* by Stéphane Mallarmé. The most amazing poet in this mode was a Byzantine pedant, Publius Optatian Porphyry, who printed his poems in two colors of ink, and got them to represent triremes and other complicated objects. Early editions of Herbert print *Easter Wings* with the lines running vertically.

2. Abundance.

3. Graft (a technical term from falconry).

The Altar

A broken ALTAR, Lord, thy servant rears,
Made of a heart, and cemented with tears:
Whose parts are as thy hand did frame;
No workman's tool hath touched the same.[4]
A HEART alone
Is such a stone,
As nothing but
Thy power doth cut.
Wherefore each part
Of my hard heart
Meets in this frame,
To praise thy Name:
That, if I chance to hold my peace,
These stones to praise thee may not cease.[5]
Oh let thy blessed SACRIFICE be mine,
And sanctify this ALTAR to be thine.

1633

The Flower

How fresh, oh Lord, how sweet and clean
Are thy returns! even as the flowers in spring;
To which, besides their own demesne,[1]
The late-past frosts tributes of pleasure bring.
Grief melts away
Like snow in May,
As if there were no such cold thing.

Who would have thought my shriveled heart
Could have recovered greenness? It was gone
Quite underground; as flowers depart
To see their mother-root, when they have blown,[2]
Where they together
All the hard weather,
Dead to the world, keep house unknown.

These are thy wonders, Lord of power,
Killing and quickening, bringing down to hell
And up to heaven in an hour;

4. A reference to Exodus xx.25, in which the Lord enjoins Moses to build an altar without using cut stone or any tools. Herbert's book was titled *The Temple*, and many individual poems are about particular parts of a church—tne porch, the windows, the floor, the lock and key, or the altar.

5. Herbert wants his poem to praise God whether or not it is being read or spoken. There is also a reference to Luke xix.40: "I tell you that, if these should hold their peace, the stones would immediately cry out." Herbert's poetry, like Milton's, is rich to overflowing in Scriptural echoes.

1. Estate of one's own (here, beauty or pleasure). The word, spelled *demean* in the original text, may also be a short form of "demeanor," i.e., bearing.

2. Bloomed.

Making a chiming of a passing-bell.[3]
We say amiss
This or that is:[4]
Thy word is all, if we could spell.

Oh that I once past changing were,
Fast in thy Paradise, where no flower can wither!
Many a spring I shoot up fair,
Offering[5] at heaven, growing and groaning thither;
Nor doth my flower
Want a spring shower,[6]
My sins and I joining together.

But while I grow in a straight line,
Still upwards bent, as if heaven were mine own,
Thy anger comes, and I decline:
What frost to that? what pole is not the zone
Where all things burn,
When thou dost turn,
And the least frown of thine is shown?[7]

And now in age I bud again,
After so many deaths I live and write;
I once more smell the dew and rain,
And relish versing. Oh, my only light,
It cannot be
That I am he
On whom thy tempests fell all night.

These are thy wonders, Lord of love,
To make us see we are but flowers that glide;[8]
Which when we once can find and prove,[9]
Thou hast a garden for us where to bide;
Who would be more,
Swelling through store,
Forfeit their Paradise by their pride.

1633

The Forerunners

The harbingers are come: see, see their mark;
White is their color, and behold my head.[1]

3. The passing-bell, intended to mark the death of a parishioner, is tolled in a monotone; a chiming offers pleasant variety.
4. I.e., that a thing exists in its own nature. "Spell": decipher the letters, but also cast a spell.
5. Aiming.
6. The tears of contrition produced by the "joining together" of the poet's conscience and his sins.
7. Lines 32–35 may be paraphrased: "What cold compares to God's anger? Compared to God's wrath, what polar chill would not seem like the heat of the equator?"
8. Pass silently away.
9. Experience.
1. Great men when they traveled in the 17th century often had "harbingers" (cf. French, *auberge*, lodging), who rode ahead of the main party to comman-

But must they have my brain? must they dispark
Those sparkling notions which therein were bred?
   Must dullness turn me to a clod?
Yet have they left me "Thou art still my God."

Good men ye be to leave me my best room,
Even all my heart and what is lodgéd there:
I pass not,[2] I, what of the rest become,
So "Thou art still my God" be out of fear.
   He will be pleaséd with that ditty;
And if I please Him, I write fine and witty.

Farewell, sweet phrases, lovely metaphors:
But will ye leave me thus? when ye before
Of stews and brothels only knew the doors,
Then did I wash you with my tears, and more,
   Brought you to Church well-dressed and clad:
My God must have my best, even all I had.

Lovely enchanting language, sugarcane,
Honey of roses, whither wilt thou fly?
Hath some fond lover 'ticed thee to thy bane?
And wilt thou leave the Church and love a sty?
   Fie! thou wilt soil thy 'broidered coat,
And hurt thyself and him that sings the note.

Let foolish lovers, if they will love dung,
With canvas, not with arras,[3] clothe their shame;
Let Folly speak in her own native tongue.
True Beauty dwells on high; ours is a flame
   But borrowed thence to light us thither:
Beauty and beauteous words should go together.

Yet, if you go, I pass not; take your way.
For "Thou art still my God" is all that ye
Perhaps with more embellishment can say.
Go, birds of Spring; let Winter have his fee;[4]
   Let a bleak paleness chalk the door,
So all within be livelier than before.

1633

deer resting places for the night. Customarily they marked the doors of the houses they had selected with chalk. Herbert's conceit is that he has been so marked, by the appearance of his first white hairs—a sign that all his fine language must be dispossessed, to make room for the great Lord to come.

2. I.e., I don't care. All the other thoughts in my house (my mind, my soul) can be turned out of doors, as long as you leave "my best room," my heart, and its one inhabitant, the thought "Thou art still my God."

3. I.e., with coarse cloth, not with fine tapestry.

4. The "birds of Spring" are the language of secular or erotic poetry; Winter with its snowy whiteness prefigures death, heralded by the chalk marks on the door.

Redemption[5]

Having been tenant long to a rich Lord,
Not thriving, I resolvéd to be bold,
And make a suit unto Him, to afford
A new small-rented lease, and cancel th' old.[6]

In heaven at His manor I Him sought:
They told me there that He was lately gone
About some land which He had dearly bought
Long since on earth, to take possession.

I straight returned, and knowing His great birth,
Sought Him accordingly in great resorts—
In cities, theaters, gardens, parks, and courts:
At length I heard a raggéd noise and mirth

Of thieves and murderers; there I Him espied,
Who straight, "Your suit is granted," said, and died.

1633

Love Unknown

Dear friend, sit down; the tale is long and sad,
And in my faintings I presume your love
Will more comply than help: a Lord I had,
And have, of Whom some grounds, which may improve,
I hold for two lives, and both lives in me.[7]
To Him I brought a dish of fruit one day,
And in the middle placed my heart. But He,
I sigh to say,
Looked on a servant who did know His eye
Better than you know me, or which is one,
Than I myself. The servant, instantly
Quitting the fruit, seized on my heart alone,
And threw it in a font, wherein did fall
A stream of blood which issued from the side
Of a great rock—I well remember all,
And have good cause—there it was dipped and dyed
And washed and wrung; the very wringing yet

5. "Redemption" means literally "buying back." In this beautifully concise sonnet, Herbert figures God as a landlord, himself as a discontented tenant.

6. I.e., to ask him for a new lease, involving a smaller rent, and to cancel the old lease. Herbert is often concerned to put spiritual relationships in terms of very humble, everyday business transactions, over which he casts a sacramental coloring.

7. The terminology is from legal contracts for leasing ground for a fixed number of "lives" or generations. God has leased a soul to Herbert for two lives, one in this world, one in the next.

Enforceth tears. *Your heart was foul, I fear.*
Indeed, 'tis true: I did and do commit
Many a fault more than my lease will bear,
Yet still asked pardon and was not denied.
But you shall hear. After my heart was well
And clean and fair, as I one even-tide,
I sigh to tell,
Walked by myself abroad, I saw a large
And spacious furnace flaming, and thereon
A boiling caldron, round about whose verge
Was in great letters set, *Affliction.*
The greatness showed the owner. So I went
To fetch a sacrifice out of my fold,
Thinking with that which I did thus present
To warm His love, which I did fear grew cold.
But as my heart did tender it, the man
Who was to take it from me slipped his hand,
And threw my heart into the scalding pan;
My heart that brought it (do you understand?),
The offerer's heart. *Your heart was hard, I fear.*
Indeed, 'tis true. I found a callous matter
Began to spread and to expatiate there;
But with a richer drug than scalding water
I bathed it often, ev'n with holy blood,
Which at a board, while many drank bare wine,
A friend did steal into my cup for good,
Ev'n taken inwardly, and most divine
To supple hardnesses. But at the length,
Out of the caldron getting, soon I fled
Unto my house, where to repair the strength
Which I had lost, I hasted to my bed.
But when I thought to sleep out all these faults,
I sigh to speak,
I found that some had stuffed the bed with thoughts,
I would say thorns. Dear, could my heart not break,
When with my pleasures, ev'n my rest was gone?
Full well I understood who had been there,
For I had given the key to none but one:
It must be He. *Your heart was dull, I fear.*
Indeed, a slack and sleepy state of mind
Did oft possess me, so that when I prayed,
Though my lips went, my heart did stay behind;
But all my scores were by another paid,
Who took the debt upon Him. *'Truly, friend,*
For aught I hear, your Master shows to you
More favor than you wot of: mark the end.
The Font did only what was old renew,
The Caldron suppled what was grown too hard,
The Thorns did quicken what was grown too dull:

All did but strive to mend what you had marred.
Wherefore be cheered, and praise Him to the full,
Each day, each hour, each moment of the week,
Who fain would have you be new, tender, quick.[8]

1633

Time

Meeting with Time, "Slack thing," said I,
"Thy scythe is dull; whet it for shame."
"No marvel, sir," he did reply,
"If it at length deserve some blame;
But where one man would have me grind it,
Twenty for one too sharp do find it."

"Perhaps some such of old did pass[1]
Who above all things loved this life;
To whom thy scythe a hatchet was
Which now is but a pruning knife.[2]
Christ's coming hath made man thy debtor,
Since by thy cutting he grows better.

"And in his blessing thou art blessed,
For where thou only wert before
An executioner at best,
Thou art a gardener now, and more,
An usher to convey our souls
Beyond the utmost stars and poles.

"And this is that makes life so long,
While it detains us from our God.
Ev'n pleasures here increase the wrong,
And length of days lengthens the rod.[3]
Who wants the place where God doth dwell
Partakes already half of hell.

"Of what strange length must that needs be,
Which ev'n eternity excludes!"[4]—
Thus far Time heard me patiently,
Then chafing said, "This man deludes:
What do I here before his door?
He doth not crave less time, but more."[5]

1633

8. "Quick" carries the meaning of sensitive, as in the "quick" under our fingernails.

1. Herbert is understood to be the speaker in stanzas 2, 3, 4, and the first two lines of stanza 5.

2. A hatchet kills, a pruning knife improves growing things like souls.

3. I.e., long life on earth is a punishment because it keeps us from bliss. "Wants": lacks, does not enjoy.

4. I.e., earthly time, however long or short it seems to be, has no real dimensions, since only after it has come to an end does man enter into eternity.

5. Time as a scythesman thinks he will cut men off; paradoxical Herbert welcomes him as a doorman to eternal life.

Death

Death, thou wast once an uncouth, hideous thing,
Nothing but bones,
The sad effect of sadder groans:
Thy mouth was open, but thou couldst not sing.

For we considered thee as at some six
Or ten years hence,
After the loss of life and sense,
Flesh being turned to dust and bones to sticks.

We looked on this side of thee, shooting short,
Where we did find
The shells of fledge-souls left behind[6]—
Dry dust, which sheds no tears, but may extort.

But since our Saviour's death did put some blood
Into thy face,
Thou art grown fair and full of grace,
Much in request, much sought for as a good.

For we do now behold thee gay and glad
As at doomsday,
When souls shall wear their new array,
And all thy bones with beauty shall be clad.

Therefore we can go die as sleep, and trust
Half that we have
Unto an honest faithful grave,
Making our pillows either down or dust.

1633

The Collar

I struck the board[1] and cried, "No more;
I will abroad!
What? shall I ever sigh and pine?
My lines and life are free, free as the road,
Loose as the wind, as large as store.
Shall I be still in suit?[2]
Have I no harvest but a thorn
To let me blood, and not restore
What I have lost with cordial[3] fruit?

6. Souls which have left the body and gone to heaven are like fledgling chicks which have left the shell behind. That shell (the corpse), though it sheds no tears itself, can draw ("extort") them from the survivors.

1. Table.

2. In attendance, waiting on someone for a favor.

3. Giving heart's ease, restorative.

Sure there was wine
Before my sighs did dry it; there was corn
Before my tears did drown it.
Is the year only lost to me?
Have I no bays[4] to crown it,
No flowers, no garlands gay? all blasted?
All wasted?
Not so, my heart; but there is fruit,
And thou hast hands.
Recover all thy sigh-blown age
On double pleasures: leave thy cold dispute
Of what is fit and not. Forsake thy cage,
Thy rope of sands,[5]
Which petty thoughts have made, and made to thee
Good cable, to enforce and draw,
And be thy law,
While thou didst wink[6] and wouldst not see.
Away! take heed;
I will abroad.
Call in thy death's-head[7] there; tie up thy fears.
He that forbears
To suit and serve his need,
Deserves his load."
But as I raved and grew more fierce and wild
At every word,
Methought I heard one calling, *Child!*
And I replied, *My Lord.*

1633

The Pulley

When God at first made man,
Having a glass of blessings standing by,
"Let us," said he, "pour on him all we can.
Let the world's riches, which dispersèd lie,
Contract into a span."

So strength first made a way;
Then beauty flowed, then wisdom, honor, pleasure.
When almost all was out, God made a stay,
Perceiving that, alone of all his treasure,
Rest in the bottom lay.[1]

4. The poet's wreath, here used as a general symbol of festivity.
5. Christian restrictions on behavior, which the "petty thoughts" of the docile believer have made "good cable," i.e., strong.
6. Shut your eyes (to the real weakness of the church's injunctions).
7. The skull which reminds the penitent of approaching death.
1. "Rest" in the poem has two senses ("remainder" and "repose"); Herbert works them against one another. This seesaw suggests the pulley, which can draw us to God one way or the other.

"For if I should," said he,
"Bestow this jewel also on my creature,
He would adore my gifts instead of me,
And rest in Nature, not the God of Nature;
So both should losers be.

"Yet let him keep the rest,
But keep them with repining restlessness.
Let him be rich and weary, that at least,
If goodness lead him not, yet weariness
May toss him to my breast."

Discipline

Throw away thy rod,
Throw away thy wrath:
O my God,
Take the gentle path.

For my heart's desire
Unto thine is bent:
I aspire
To a full consent.

Not a word or look
I affect to own,
But by book,
And thy book alone.[2]

Though I fail, I weep:
Though I halt in pace,
Yet I creep
To the throne of grace.

Then let wrath remove;
Love will do the deed:
For with love
Stony hearts will bleed.

Love is swift of foot;
Love's a man of war,[3]
And can shoot,
And can hit from far.

Who can 'scape his bow?
That which wrought on thee,
Brought thee low,
Needs must work on me.

2. Disclaiming all independence, Herbert describes himself as an actor, who will speak only "by the book."
3. The jubilant song sung by Moses in Exodus xv calls the Lord "a man of war"; but Herbert is thinking also, and without any apparent sense of contradiction, about Cupid, another divine bowman.

Throw away thy rod;
Though man frailties hath,
Thou art God:
Throw away thy wrath.

1633

Jordan (I)[1]

Who says that fictions only and false hair
Become a verse? Is there in truth no beauty?
Is all good structure in a winding stair?
May no lines pass, except they do their duty
Not to a true, but painted chair?[2]

Is it no verse, except enchanted groves
And sudden arbors shadow coarse-spun lines?[3]
Must purling streams refresh a lover's loves?
Must all be veiled while he that reads, divines,
Catching the sense at two removes?

Shepherds are honest people; let them sing:
Riddle who list, for me, and pull for prime:[4]
I envy no man's nightingale or spring;
Nor let them punish me with loss of rhyme,
Who plainly say, *My God, My King.*

1633

Jordan (II)

When first my lines of heavenly joys made mention,
Such was their luster, they did so excel,
That I sought out quaint words, and trim invention;
My thoughts began to burnish,[1] sprout, and swell,
Curling with metaphors a plain intention,
Decking the sense, as if it were to sell.[2]

1. Both poems titled *Jordan* are about complexity and simplicity; "crossing Jordan" is of course a symbol for entering into the Promised Land, and it seems likely that Herbert means to indicate by his title that for one who has crossed the river (i.e., come into God's country), many worldly complexities cease to be necessary or desirable.

2. May no poems ("lines") pass as good unless they make a reverence ("do their duty") to a false throne? It has often been the custom for men to bow before a throne, whether it was occupied or not (see Donne, *Satire III*, lines 47–48); but to require bowing to a throne in a painting (i.e., an artificial throne), would be excessive. Herbert implies that earthly love is a mere painted imitation of divine love.

3. "Sudden": i.e., that appear unexpectedly (an artificial effect much sought after in landscape gardening). "Shadow": overshadow, cause to be overlooked. Herbert is suggesting that flashy dramatic effects obscure poor craftsmanship.

4. To draw a lucky card in the card game of "primero." Herbert implies that anyone who understands one of the complex poems he is describing (and parodying) has made a wild and lucky guess.

1. Expand, burgeon.

2. For sale.

Thousands of notions in my brain did run,
 Offering their service, if I were not sped:[3]
I often blotted what I had begun;
 This was not quick[4] enough, and that was dead.
Nothing could seem too rich to clothe the sun,
 Much less those joys which trample on his head.[5]

As flames do work and wind when they ascend,
 So did I weave myself into the sense;
But while I bustled, I might hear a friend
 Whisper, "How wide[6] is all this long pretense!
There is in love a sweetness ready penned:
 Copy out only that, and save expense."

1633

Denial

When my devotions could not pierce
  Thy silent ears;
Then was my heart broken, as was my verse:
 My breast was full of fears
  And disorder:

My bent thoughts, like a brittle bow,
  Did fly asunder:
Each took his way; some would to pleasure go,
 Some to the wars and thunder
  Of alarms.

As good go anywhere, they say,
  As to benumb
Both knees and heart in crying night and day,
 Come, come, my God, O come!
  But no hearing.

O that thou shouldst give dust a tongue
  To cry to thee,
And then not hear it crying! All day long
 My heart was in my knee,[1]
  But no hearing.

Therefore my soul lay out of sight,
  Untuned, unstrung:
My feeble spirit, unable to look right,
 Like a nipped blossom, hung
  Discontented.

O cheer and tune my heartless breast;
  Defer no time,

3. Supplied, satisfied.
4. Lively, alive.
5. The "joys which trample on" the sun's head are those of the Son.
6. Irrelevant, "wide of the mark."
1. I.e., my heart was bowed and bent, like my knee, in reverence.

That so thy favors granting my request,
They and my mind may chime,[2]
And mend my rhyme.

1633

Aaron

Holiness on the head,
Light and perfections on the breast,
Harmonious bells below, raising the dead
To lead them unto life and rest:
Thus are true Aarons dressed.[3]

Profaneness in my head,
Defects and darkness in my breast,
A noise of passions ringing me for dead
Unto a place where is no rest:
Poor priest, thus am I dressed.

Only another head
I have, another heart and breast,
Another music, making live, not dead,
Without whom I could have no rest:
In him I am well dressed.

Christ is my only head,
My alone only heart and breast,
My only music, striking me even dead,
That to the old man I may rest,
And be in him new dressed.[4]

So, holy in my head,
Perfect and light in my dear breast,
My doctrine tuned by Christ, who is not dead,
But lives in me while I do rest,
Come, people; Aaron's dressed.

1633

Love (III)

Love bade me welcome: yet my soul drew back,
Guilty of dust and sin.
But quick-eyed Love, observing me grow slack[5]
From my first entrance in,

2. Agree. The rhyming of the last two lines, coming to restore the harmony of this stanza, illustrates Herbert's hope of harmony with God.
3. Exodus xxviii describes in great detail the garments to be worn by Aaron as high priest. Note that there are five letters in the name "Aaron," five stanzas in the poem, and five lines in each stanza.
4. As the clapper strikes the bell and makes music of it, Christ strikes the priest, killing the Old Adam (the "old man," i.e., human frailty) in him, and raising the regenerate soul.
5 Backward.

Drew nearer to me, sweetly questioning
If I lacked anything.[6]

"A guest," I answered, "worthy to be here":
Love said, "You shall be he."
"I, the unkind, ungrateful? Ah, my dear,
I cannot look on thee."
Love took my hand, and smiling did reply,
"Who made the eyes but I?"

"Truth, Lord; but I have marred them; let my shame
Go where it doth deserve."
"And know you not," says Love, "who bore the blame?"
"My dear, then I will serve."
"You must sit down," says Love, "and taste my meat."
So I did sit and eat.

1633

6. The first question of shopkeepers and tavern waiters to an entering customer would be "What d'ye lack?" (i.e., want).

RICHARD CRASHAW

(ca. 1613–1649)

Richard Crashaw is a phenomenon unique in Anglo-Saxon taste; there is really no other English poet who is much like him. His roots seem to be sunk less in English literature than in Italian and neo-Latin writings. His personal background was thoroughly English (his father was a noted Puritan clergyman, and his academic training was at Cambridge), but from the first he was devoted to ritual, ceremony, and ecclesiastical exercise. This habit of mind ultimately led him out of the English church altogether, and into Roman Catholicism—the church, as many Englishmen considered it, of the scarlet woman and of Antichrist himself. But, for one of Crashaw's ardent devotional temperament, it was a natural home. In terms of chronological time, Crashaw spent only the last five or six years of his life on the Continent and in the church of Rome; but in terms of his spiritual development, he never belonged anywhere else.

Poetically, Crashaw was a follower of George Herbert, as the title of his second volume *(Steps to the Temple)* suggests. But the feeling one gets from the two poets is altogether different. There is a little streak of quaint and homely imagery in Herbert; Crashaw exaggerates it toward the grotesque. In this practice he was following the writers of emblem-books—volumes in which a picture with allegorical meanings stood at the head of a poem explaining those meanings. He was also influenced by a widespread school of Jesuit writers of sacred Latin epigrams, and by the great Italian writer of conceits (*concetti*) Giambattista Marino, the first book of whose poem *The Massacre of the Innocents* Crashaw translated. All these influences—plus, of course, his own ardent temperament—pushed Crashaw toward the exploitation of far-fetched, almost perverse parallels, in which familiar physical objects not only stood for, but were sometimes distorted by, extravagant spiritual pressures. The method hardly allowed for any interest in "decorum," in the traditional sense of tonal harmony—and that, of course, is an assumption about the proper character of poetry that has prevailed very generally, until recent times. Thus Crashaw was bitterly ridiculed during the 19th and early 20th centuries for lines like those in *The Weeper*, his poem on the tears of Saint Mary Magdalen:

> And now where'er he strays
> Among the Galilean mountains
> Or more unwelcome ways,
> He's followed by two faithful fountains,
> Two walking baths; two weeping motions;
> Portable and compendious oceans.

The ludicrous effect produced by these lines isn't open to much question, any more than is the macabre effect produced by that little epigram on Luke 11 (below). But in seeking these effects, it is evident that Crashaw was a conscious and deliberate craftsman working in an established tradition which on the Continent often goes by the name of "baroque." Whether this term is worth importing into English literary history in order to take care of a largely isolated figure like Crashaw may be argued. Undeniably, it opens the way to make suggestive parallels, with Continental poetry and with developments in the sister arts. In any event, we of the modern world, with the violent and unresolved images of modern literature and the surrealist phantasmagoria behind us, seem better equipped to appreciate the poetry of Crashaw than readers have been for several hundred years past.

Since the image is so violent in Crashaw, the structure of his poems is often less strict than an English reader is used to; they wander from image to image, without seeming to "get anywhere." He wrote many of his poems several times over, in differing versions; the same images and stanzas will recur, but in an entirely different order, without any sign that the poem "as a whole" (if it is a whole) has suffered in any way. For the effect at which he aims is a phantasmagoria, a blurring together of erotic and spiritual, tortured and ecstatic, infantile and sadistic themes. This doesn't preclude wit, even cheerful wit, but it's wit under the impulsion of a more consuming religious passion than English devotional writers before Gerard Manley Hopkins generally display. Like Saint Teresa of Avila, the Spanish mystic whom Crashaw admired so much, he yearned to be eaten up by the zeal of God's house—a spiritual act of faith to whose ecstatic paradoxes his best poetry does spectacular justice.

Crashaw's publications were not many. In 1634 he published a book of *Sacred Epigrams* in Greek and Latin; a volume titled *Steps to the Temple (with Other Delights of the Muses)* appeared in 1646; and in 1652, a volume published in Paris under the title of *Carmen Deo Nostro* collected his final writings. Some new material has since been added from manuscript collections; and Crashaw has enjoyed, of late years, a genuine revival of popular favor, after long years of hostility, neglect, and, at best, condescension.

A special feature of Crashaw's poetry, in the manuscripts as well as the printed volumes, is the styling of his poem's titles. They are elaborately constructed in different sorts of lettering, the lines piled on top of one another to create outsize typographical façades, like the weighty fronts of baroque churches. The titles to *The Flaming Heart* and the poem *To the Countess of Denbigh* are reproduced here from the 1652 edition.

The Flaming Heart Saint Teresa of Avila, a 16th-century Spanish mystic, was one of the great figures of the Catholic counter-reformation. Her autobiography, describing not only her practical problems in establishing her ascetic order of barefoot Carmelites, but a series of ecstatic trances and visions which brought her close to the Heavenly Vision itself, was immediately popular throughout all Europe. Gian Lorenzo Bernini, the great Italian sculptor and architect, created the ultimate baroque statue of Saint Teresa, which stands to this day in the church of Santa Maria della Vittoria, in Rome. It shows the saint in an attitude of ecstatic, swooning abandonment, while a somewhat juvenile seraph stands over her, in the act of plunging a golden arrow into her heart. The statue is based on a famous passage of the autobiography.

Bernini's statue was not actually unveiled till after Crashaw's death, and though the poet was in Rome and could easily have learned about the statue, or seen it by visiting Bernini's studio, there is no definite proof that he actually did so. In any case, what he says in the poem about a "picture" applies perfectly to Bernini's statue: the seraph *is* a weak and childish figure, the saint an embodiment of sensual and religious passion. The reversal of roles with which the poet plays in the first part of his poem makes an effective literary game; but it isn't clear what sort of picture or statue would express his preferred conception of the saint. What excites him—and Bernini too, for that matter—is the moment of total absorption in the divine, the ecstatic union. For Puritans this is too fleshly an experience to be sacred, but for those who respond to imaginative challenge, holding these two elements in balance is a special and perilous delight.

The Flaming Heart
Vpon the Book and
picture of the seraphicall saint

TERESA,
(AS SHE IS VSVALLY EX-
pressed with a SERAPHIM
biside her.)[1]

Well-meaning readers! you that come as friends,
And catch the precious name this piece pretends;[2]
Make not too much haste to admire
That fair-cheeked fallacy of fire.

1. Crashaw does not know (or perhaps care) that "seraphim" is the plural form of the singular "seraph"; "seraphs" are distinguished among angels by dwelling continually in the fire of divine love.
2. Puts forward.

That is a Seraphim, they say,
And this the great Teresia.
Readers, be ruled by me, and make
Here a well-placed and wise mistake:
You must transpose the picture quite
And spell it wrong to read it right;
Read *him* for *her* and *her* for *him*,
And call the Saint the Seraphim.
  Painter, what didst thou understand,
To put her dart into his hand!
See, even the years and size of him
Shows this the Mother Seraphim.
This is the mistress-flame; and duteous he,
Her happy fire-works here comes down to see.
O most poor-spirited of men!
Had thy cold pencil kissed her pen[3]
Thou couldst not so unkindly err
To show us this faint shade for her.
Why, man, this speaks pure mortal frame,
And mocks with female frost love's manly frame.
One would suspect thou mean'st to paint
Some weak, inferior, woman saint.
But had thy pale-faced purple took
Fire from the burning cheeks of that bright book,
Thou wouldst on her have heaped up all
That could be found seraphical:
Whate'er this youth of fire wears fair,
Rosy fingers, radiant hair,
Glowing cheek and glistering wings,
All those fair and flagrant[4] things,
But before all, that fiery dart
Had filled the hand of this great heart.
  Do then as equal right requires,
Since his the blushes be, and hers the fires,
Resume and rectify thy rude design,
Undress thy seraphim into mine.
Redeem this injury of thy art,
Give him the veil, give her the dart.
  Give him the veil, that he may cover
The red cheeks of a rivaled lover,
Ashamed that our world now can show
Nests of new Seraphims here below.[5]
  Give her the dart, for it is she
(Fair youth) shoots both thy shaft and thee.
Say, all ye wise and well-pierced hearts
That live and die amidst her darts,
What is it your tasteful spirits do prove

3. I.e., if you'd only been properly inspired by her book.
4. Burning (from Latin *flagrare*).
5. Teresa burns on earth in the element of fire, as seraphim do in heaven.

In that rare life of her and love?
Say and bear witness. Sends she not
A Seraphim at every shot?
What magazines of immortal arms there shine!
Heaven's great artillery in each love-spun line.
Give then the dart to her who gives the flame,
Give him the veil who kindly takes the shame.
  But if it be the frequent fate
Of worst faults to be fortunate;
If all's prescription, and proud wrong
Hearkens not to an humble song,
For all the gallantry of him,
Give me the suffering Seraphim.[6]
His be the bravery of all those bright things,
The glowing cheeks, the glistering wings,
The rosy hand, the radiant dart;
Leave her alone the Flaming Heart.
  Leave her that, and thou shalt leave her
Not one loose shaft, but love's whole quiver.
For in love's field was never found
A nobler weapon than a wound.
Love's passives are his activ'st part,
The wounded is the wounding heart.
O heart! the equal poise of love's both parts,
Big alike with wounds and darts,
Live in these conquering leaves,[7] live all the same;
And walk through all tongues one triumphant flame.
Live here, great heart; and love and die and kill,
And bleed and wound; and yield and conquer still.
Let this immortal life, where'er it comes,
Walk in a crowd of loves and martyrdoms.
Let mystic deaths wait on 't, and wise souls be
The love-slain witnesses of this life of thee:
O sweet incendiary! show here thy art,
Upon this carcass of a hard, cold heart;[8]
Let all thy scattered shafts of light, that play
Among the leaves of thy large books of day,[9]
Combined against this breast, at once break in
And take away from me myself and sin!
This gracious robbery shall thy bounty be,
And my best fortunes such fair spoils of me.[1]
O thou undaunted daughter of desires!
By all thy dower of lights and fires;
By all the eagle in thee, all the dove;[2]

6. If Teresa can't be transformed into the angel, as he would like, Crashaw still prefers her as the "suffering Seraphim."
7. I.e., the leaves of St. Teresa's book.
8. After being Saint Teresa's, the heart is now Crashaw's.
9. Books filled with intellectual and spiritual light.
1. I.e., my best fortune will be to be despoiled in this way.
2. The eagle symbolizes wisdom, for its lofty flight and ability to look into the sun's eye; the dove symbolizes mercy. Cf. Donne's *Canonization*, line 22.

By all thy lives and deaths of love;
By thy large draughts of intellectual day,
And by thy thirsts of love more large than they;
By all thy brim-filled bowls of fierce desire,
By thy last morning's draught of liquid fire;
By the full kingdom of that final kiss
That seized thy parting soul, and sealed thee His;
By all the heavens thou hast in Him,
Fair sister of the seraphim,
By all of Him we have in thee,
Leave nothing of myself in me!
Let me so read thy life that I
Unto all life of mine may die!

1652

Non Vi.[1]

'Tis not the work of force but skill
To find the way into man's will.
'Tis loue alone can hearts unlock.
Who knowes the WORD, *he needs not knock.*

To the Noblest & best of Ladyes, the Countesse of Denbigh.

Perswading her to Resolution in Religion, & to render her selfe without further delay into the Communion of the Catholick Church.[2]

1. Not by force. The emblem, which expresses a moral question and answer through a picture and appended poem, was popular throughout Europe in the late Renaissance. The heart here has a hinge on the right to show that it can be opened, but it is sealed on the left with a scroll or phylactery inscribed with certain Biblical phrases, standing for the Word or the Law. Only knowledge of the Word enables one to open the heart.

2. Lords and ladies with religious doubts and scruples were the object of tremendous attention during the 17th century. Anxious conferences were held, with priests of all faiths eager to put their views before a possible influential convert; accounts of these conferences were published, disputed, analyzed, and pre-

What heaven-entreated heart is this,
Stands trembling at the gate of bliss,
Holds fast the door, yet dares not venture
Fairly to open it, and enter?
Whose definition is a doubt
'Twixt life and death, 'twixt in and out.
Say, lingering fair! why comes the birth
Of your brave soul so slowly forth?
Plead your pretenses (O you strong
In weakness!) why you choose so long
In labor of your self to lie,
Not daring quite to live nor die.
Ah, linger not, loved soul! a slow
And late consent was a long no;
Who grants at last, long time tried,
And did his best to have denied.
What magic bolts, what mystic bars,
Maintain the will in these strange wars!
What fatal yet fantastic bands
Keep the free heart from its own hands!
So when the year takes cold, we see
Poor waters their own prisoners be.
Fettered and locked up fast they lie
In a sad self-captivity.
Th' astonished nymphs their flood's strange fate deplore,
To see themselves their own severer shore.
  Thou that alone canst thaw this cold,
And fetch the heart from its stronghold,
Almighty Love! end this long war,
And of a meteor make a star.
O fix this fair Indefinite;
And 'mongst thy shafts of sovereign light
Choose out that sure decisive dart
Which has the key of this close heart,
Knows all the corners of 't, and can control
The self-shut cabinet of an unsearched soul.
O let it be at last love's hour!
Raise this tall trophy of thy power;
Come once the conquering way, not to confute,
But kill this rebel-word, *irresolute,*
That so, in spite of all this peevish strength
Of weakness, she may write, *resolved at length.*
  Unfold at length, unfold, fair flower,
And use the season of love's shower.

---

sented to the perplexed for their guidance. Susan, Countess of Denbigh, had been widowed in 1643, when her husband was killed fighting for the king; she had gone with the queen to Paris in 1644, and there, in a thoroughly Catholic environment, had begun contemplating conversion. The queen was a lifelong Catholic, Crashaw, though simply another member of the court in exile, was a new convert; pressure on the lady was therefore very strong to abjure her Anglicanism. As is his wont, Crashaw uses all the imagery of erotic persuasion in urging the Countess to "yield the fort and let life in."

Meet his well-meaning wounds, wise heart,
And haste to drink the wholesome dart,
That healing shaft which heaven till now
Hath in love's quiver hid for you.
O dart of love! arrow of light!
O happy you, if it hit right;
It must not fall in vain, it must
Not mark the dry, regardless dust.
Fair one, it is your fate, and brings
Eternal worlds upon its wings.
Meet it with wide-spread arms, and see
Its seat your soul's just center be.
Disband dull fears; give faith the day.
To save your life, kill your delay.
It is love's siege, and sure to be
Your triumph, though his victory.
'Tis cowardice that keeps this field,
And want of courage not to yield.
Yield, then, O yield, that love may win
The fort at last, and let life in.
Yield quickly, lest perhaps you prove
Death's prey before the prize of love.
This fort of your fair self, if 't be not won,
He is repulsed indeed; but you are undone.

1652

On Our Crucified Lord, Naked and Bloody

Th' have left Thee naked, Lord, O that they had;
This garment too I would they had denied.
Thee with Thyself they have too richly clad,
Opening the purple wardrobe of Thy side.
O never could be found garments too good
For Thee to wear, but these, of Thine own blood.

1646

To the Infant Martyrs[1]

Go, smiling souls, your new-built cages[2] break,
In heaven you'll learn to sing, ere here to speak,
Nor let the milky fonts that bathe your thirst
Be your delay;
The place that calls you hence is, at the worst,
Milk all the way.[3]

1646

1. This poem, and the five which follow, were originally published in Latin, as sacred epigrams; but also appeared in *Steps to the Temple,* translated into English.
2. I.e., the bodies which confine them to an earthly existence.
3. The Milky Way will replace their mothers' milk, at the worst; at best, they may rise even higher in the heavens.

I Am the Door

And now Th' art set wide ope, the spear's sad art,
Lo! hath unlocked Thee at the very heart;
He to himself (I fear the worst)
And his own hope
Hath shut these doors of heaven, that durst
Thus set them ope.

1646

Luke 11

Blessed be the paps which Thou hast sucked.

Suppose He had been tabled at thy teats,
Thy hunger feels not what He eats;
He'll have his teat ere long (a bloody one),
The Mother then must suck the Son.

1646

Upon the Infant Martyrs

To see both blended in one flood,
The mothers' milk, the children's blood,
Make me doubt if heaven will gather
Roses hence, or lilies rather.

1646

Luke 7

She began to wash His feet with tears and wipe them with the hairs of her head.

Her eyes' flood licks His feet's fair stain,
Her hairs' flame licks that up again.
This flame thus quenched hath brighter beams;
This flood thus stained fairer streams.

1646

On the Wounds of Our Crucified Lord

O these wakeful wounds of Thine!
Are they mouths? or are they eyes?
Be they mouths, or be they eyne,[1]
Each bleeding part some one supplies.[2]

Lo! a mouth, whose full-bloomed lips
At too dear a rate are roses.

1. An old plural form of "eyes."

2. I.e., each wound of Christ's supplies either an eye or a mouth.

Lo! a bloodshot eye! that weeps
And many a cruel tear discloses.

O thou that on this foot hast laid
Many a kiss and many a tear,
Now thou shalt have all repaid,
Whatsoe'er thy charges were.

This foot hath got a mouth and lips
To pay the sweet sum of thy kisses;
To pay thy tears, an eye that weeps
Instead of tears such gems as this is.

The difference only this appears
(Nor can the change offend),
The debt is paid in ruby-tears
Which thou in pearls didst lend.

1646

HENRY VAUGHAN

(1621–1695)

The doctrines of mystic correspondence (that is, of analogical relations between the world of creatures and the world of spirits), which had been publicly accepted philosophy during the Middle Ages, and which the genius of Donne had daringly revitalized in the late 16th century, faded during the 17th century before the rising rationalism and materialism which culminated in Hobbes, Locke, and Newton. One of the last figures to give full-voiced expression to it was a Welsh country doctor with special interest in the occult, Henry Vaughan.

Like Herrick, Vaughan enjoyed only a brief interlude of poetry in his long life. His career as a student at Oxford was interrupted by the civil wars, in which he took a brief part on the king's side. But after the royal defeat, he retired to his native Wales and began to practice medicine—as men could do in those days, without many preliminaries. (A treatise of *Hermetical Physic,* which he published in 1655, is reproduced in L. C. Martin's edition of Vaughan's *Works,* Vol. II; it gives some curious notions of his medical practice. But fortunately the Welsh are by nature a sturdy race.) In 1650 he published a thin volume of verse titled *Silex Scintillans,* The Fiery Flint; this was followed immediately by a second book called *Olor Iscanus,* or The Swan of Usk (1651). Both titles make rather erudite reference to Vaughan's Welsh ancestry and habitat: Wales is rough, rocky country, the home of hard men as well as of flinty hearts; and Usk is a little brook that flows near Vaughan's native town of Scethrog hard by Llansantffraed. *Silex Scintillans* was reprinted in 1655, with the addition of a second part—and that was, effectually, Vaughan's poetic career.

The major influences on Vaughan were evidently two. George Herbert's poetry made a great impression on the poet, and his verses are full of echoes from *The Temple*. More remarkably, Vaughan's twin brother Thomas was an esoteric, hermetic philosopher, an alchemist and a student of the occult correspondences of things. Vaughan's poems often imply some knowledge of these "secret doctrines" of the alchemical philosophers—doctrines in which folklore, sympathetic magic, religion, and the rudiments of scientific method rub elbows under the aegis of the mythical Egyptian teacher Hermes Trismegistus.

But though they are "occult" in their undertones and overtones, Vaughan's best poems are direct and untangled in their expression. They tend to start with a brilliant phrase or set of phrases and trail off into relatively prosaic meditations. Sparkles of poetic brightness attend most of his writings; but they glow irregularly and fade under the unsteady breath of the poet's personal inspiration. When that inspiration is up, he sees, or tries to see, through the veil of things, to the spiritual quick of life lying just under its commonplace, material surface. There is a kind of silver-gray purity in Vaughan's finest work, which, though comparable to Herbert's and tangibly influenced by it, is more nervous and restive, more apt to dissolve the physical book under our hands (as his last poem does), turning it into the living mind and immediate soul of a man.

The Retreat

Happy those early days! when I
Shined in my angel infancy.
Before I understood this place
Appointed for my second race,[1]
Or taught my soul to fancy aught
But a white, celestial thought;
When yet I had not walked above
A mile or two from my first love,
And looking back, at that short space,
Could see a glimpse of His bright face;
When on some gilded cloud or flower
My gazing soul would dwell an hour,
And in those weaker glories spy
Some shadows of eternity;
Before I taught my tongue to wound
My conscience with a sinful sound,
Or had the black art to dispense
A several[2] sin to every sense,
But felt through all this fleshly dress
Bright shoots of everlastingness.
  O, how I long to travel back,
And tread again that ancient track!
That I might once more reach that plain

1. The "second race" suggests, dimly, a doctrine of pre-existence. Comparisons are often made with Wordsworth's *Ode: Intimations of Immortality*.

2. Different.

Where first I left my glorious train,
From whence th' enlightened spirit sees
That shady city of palm trees.[3]
But, ah! my soul with too much stay[4]
Is drunk, and staggers in the way.
Some men a forward motion love;
But I by backward steps would move,
And when this dust falls to the urn,
In that state I came, return.

1650

Regeneration

A ward, and still in bonds, one day
I stole abroad;
It was high spring, and all the way
Primrosed and hung with shade;
Yet was it frost within,
And surly winds
Blasted my infant buds, and sin
Like clouds eclipsed my mind.

Stormed thus, I straight perceived my spring
Mere stage and show,
My walk a monstrous, mountained thing,
Roughcast with rocks and snow;
And as a pilgrim's eye,
Far from relief,
Measures the melancholy sky,
Then drops and rains for grief,

So sighed I upwards still; at last
'Twixt steps and falls
I reached the pinnacle, where placed
I found a pair of scales;
I took them up and laid
In th' one, late pains;
The other smoke and pleasures weighed,
But proved the heavier grains.[1]

With that some cried, "Away!" Straight I
Obeyed, and led
Full east, a fair, fresh field could spy;
Some called it Jacob's bed,[2]
A virgin soil which no

3. The New Jerusalem, the Heavenly City (see Deuteronomy xxxiv.3).
4. Delay.
1. Vaughan's spiritual adventure can only be described darkly. After his purgatorial ascent, smoke and pleasures prove heavier than "late pains"; i.e., the vanity of his mind outweighs its recent turning to repentance.
2. Jacob, who wrestled with an angel and ascended directly to heaven on a ladder, is here a type of the mystical visionary.

Rude feet ere trod,
Where, since he stepped there, only go
Prophets and friends of God.

Here I reposed; but scarce well set,
A grove descried
Of stately height, whose branches met
And mixed on every side;
I entered, and once in,
Amazed to see 't,
Found all was changed, and a new spring
Did all my senses greet.

The unthrift sun shot vital gold,
A thousand pieces,
And heaven its azure did unfold,
Checkered with snowy fleeces;
The air was all in spice,
And every bush
A garland wore; thus fed my eyes,
But all the ear lay hush.[3]

Only a little fountain lent
Some use for ears,
And on the dumb shades language spent,
The music of her tears;
I drew her near, and found
The cistern full
Of divers stones, some bright and round,
Others ill-shaped and dull.[4]

The first, pray mark, as quick as light
Danced through the flood,
But the last, more heavy than the night,
Nailed to the center stood;
I wondered much, but tired
At last with thought,
My restless eye that still desired
As strange an object brought.

It was a bank of flowers, where I descried,
Though 'twas midday,
Some fast asleep, others broad-eyed
And taking in the ray;
Here, musing long, I heard
A rushing wind
Which still increased, but whence it stirred
No where I could not find.

3. Quiet.
4. The stones may be thoughts, images, and concepts in the "little fountain" of inspiration; the imagery is no doubt tinged with alchemical symbolism, as well.

I turned me round, and to each shade
Dispatched an eye
To see if any leaf had made
Least motion or reply,
But while I listening sought
My mind to ease
By knowing where 'twas, or where not,
It whispered, "Where I please."[5]

"Lord," then said I, "on me one breath,
And let me die before my death!"

1650

Corruption

Sure it was so. Man in those early days
Was not all stone and earth;
He shined a little, and by those weak rays
Had some glimpse of his birth.
He saw heaven o'er his head, and knew from whence
He came, condemnéd, hither;
And, as first love draws strongest, so from hence
His mind sure progressed thither.
Things here were strange unto him: sweat and till,
All was a thorn or weed:
Nor did those last, but (like himself) died still
As soon as they did seed.
They seemed to quarrel with him, for that act
That felled him foiled them all:
He drew the curse upon the world, and cracked
The whole frame with his fall.[1]
This made him long for home, as loath to stay
With murmurers and foes;
He sighed for Eden, and would often say,
"Ah! what bright days were those!"
Nor was heaven cold unto him; for each day
The valley or the mountain
Afforded visits, and still paradise lay
In some green shade or fountain.
Angels lay leiger[2] here; each bush and cell,
Each oak and highway knew them;
Walk but the fields, or sit down at some well,
And he was sure to view them.
Almighty Love! where art Thou now? Mad man

5. John iii.8: "The wind bloweth where it listeth, and thou hearest the sound thereof, but canst not tell whence it cometh, and whither it goeth: so is every one that is born of the Spirit." Cf. also the inspiring breath by which God breathed life into man (Genesis ii.7).

1. Compare *Paradise Lost* X.650 ff.

2. As resident ambassadors (from heaven).

Sits down and freezeth on;
He raves, and swears to stir nor fire, nor fan,
But bids the thread be spun.[3]
I see, Thy curtains are close-drawn; Thy bow
Looks dim, too, in the cloud;
Sin triumphs still, and man is sunk below
The center, and his shroud.
All's in deep sleep and night: thick darkness lies
And hatcheth o'er Thy people—
But hark! what trumpet's that? what angel cries,
"Arise! thrust in Thy sickle"?[4]

1650

The World

I saw eternity the other night
Like a great ring of pure and endless light,
All calm as it was bright;
And round beneath it, Time, in hours, days, years,
Driven by the spheres,[1]
Like a vast shadow moved, in which the world
And all her train were hurled.
The doting lover in his quaintest[2] strain
Did there complain;
Near him, his lute, his fancy, and his flights,[3]
Wit's sour delights,
With gloves and knots,[4] the silly snares of pleasure,
Yet his dear treasure,
All scattered lay, while he his eyes did pour
Upon a flower.

The darksome statesman, hung with weights and woe,
Like a thick midnight fog, moved there so slow
He did nor stay nor go;
Condemning thoughts, like sad eclipses, scowl
Upon his soul,
And clouds of crying witnesses without
Pursued him with one shout.
Yet digged the mole, and, lest his ways be found,
Worked underground,
Where he did clutch his prey. But One did see
That policy:[5]

3. Man is willing to do none of the work of salvation, but expects all the rewards.
4. Revelation xiv.15: "And another angel came out of the temple, crying with a loud voice to him that sat on the cloud, 'Thrust in thy sickle and reap * * * '" The time to harvest is now.
1. The concentric spheres of Ptolemaic astronomy.
2. Most elaborate.
3. Light arrows, as used by Cupid.
4. Love knots.
5. Strategy. The "mole" (i.e., the "darksome statesman," line 16) worked underground to avoid detection: but He who marks the fall of a sparrow was not deceived.

Churches and altars fed him; perjuries
Were gnats and flies;
It rained about him blood and tears; but he
Drank them as free.[6]

The fearful miser on a heap of rust
Sat pining all his life there, did scarce trust
His own hands with the dust;
Yet would not place[7] one piece above, but lives
In fear of thieves.
Thousands there were as frantic as himself,
And hugged each one his pelf:
The downright epicure placed heaven in sense,[8]
And scorned pretense;
While others, slipped into a wide excess,
Said little less;
The weaker sort, slight, trivial wares enslave,
Who think them brave;[9]
And poor, despiséd Truth sat counting by[1]
Their victory.

Yet some, who all this while did weep and sing,
And sing and weep, soared up into the ring;
But most would use no wing.
"O fools!" said I, "thus to prefer dark night
Before true light!
To live in grots and caves, and hate the day
Because it shows the way,
The way which from this dead and dark abode
Leads up to God,
A way where you might tread the sun and be
More bright than he!"
But, as I did their madness so discuss,
One whispered thus:
"This ring the bridegroom did for none provide,
But for His bride."[2]

1650

They Are All Gone into the World of Light!

They are all gone into the world of light!
And I alone sit lingering here;
Their very memory is fair and bright,
And my sad thoughts doth clear.[1]

It glows and glitters in my cloudy breast
Like stars upon some gloomy grove,

6. I.e., as freely as they rained.
7. Invest.
8. Found his heaven in the senses.
9. Fine, flashy.
1. Watching.
2. See Revelation xix.7–9 and xxi for the marriage of the Lamb and the bride (Christ and His church).
1. Brighten.

Or those faint beams in which this hill is dressed
After the sun's remove.

I see them walking in an air of glory,
Whose light doth trample on my days;
My days, which are at best but dull and hoary,
Mere glimmering and decays.

O holy hope, and high humility,
High as the heavens above!
These are your walks, and you have showed them me
To kindle my cold love.

Dear, beauteous death! the jewel of the just,
Shining nowhere but in the dark;
What mysteries do lie beyond thy dust,
Could man outlook that mark![2]

He that hath found some fledged bird's nest may know
At first sight if the bird be flown;
But what fair well[3] or grove he sings in now,
That is to him unknown.

And yet, as angels in some brighter dreams
Call to the soul when man doth sleep,
So some strange thoughts transcend our wonted themes,
And into glory peep.

If a star were confined into a tomb,
Her captive flames must needs burn there;
But when the hand that locked her up gives room,
She'll shine through all the sphere.

O Father of eternal life, and all
Created glories under Thee!
Resume Thy spirit from this world of thrall[4]
Into true liberty!

Either disperse these mists, which blot and fill
My perspective[5] still as they pass;
Or else remove me hence unto that hill[6]
Where I shall need no glass.

1655

Man

Weighing the steadfastness and state
Of some mean things which here below reside,
Where birds, like watchful clocks, the noiseless date
And intercourse of times divide,
Where bees at night get home and hive, and flowers,

2. Limit.
3. Spring.
4. I.e., take back the spirit which you have made from this world of slavery.
5. Literally, "telescope," but more freely, "distant vision."
6. Sion hill (figuratively, Abraham's bosom).

Early as well as late,
Rise with the sun and set in the same bowers;

I would (said I) my God would give
The staidness of these things to man! for these
To His divine appointments ever cleave,
And no new business breaks their peace;
The birds nor sow nor reap, yet sup and dine;
The flowers without clothes live,
Yet Solomon was never dressed so fine.[1]

Man hath still either toys or care;[2]
He hath no root, nor to one place is tied,
But ever restless and irregular
About this earth doth run and ride.
He knows he hath a home, but scarce knows where;
He says it is so far
That he hath quite forgot how to go there.

He knocks at all doors, strays and roams,
Nay, hath not so much wit as some stones[3] have,
Which in the darkest nights point to their homes,
By some hid sense their Maker gave;
Man is the shuttle, to whose winding quest
And passage through these looms
God ordered motion, but ordained no rest.

1650

Silence and Stealth of Days!

Silence and stealth of days! 'tis now
Since thou art gone[1]
Twelve hundred hours, and not a brow
But clouds hang on.
As he that in some cave's thick damp,
Locked from the light,
Fixeth a solitary lamp
To brave the night,
And walking from his sun, when past
That glimmering ray,
Cuts through the heavy mists in haste
Back to his day,[2]
So o'er fled minutes I retreat
Unto that hour
Which showed thee last, but did defeat
Thy light and power;
I search and rack my soul to see

1. Cf. Matthew vi.26–29.
2. Diversions or grief.
3. Loadstones.

1. As indicated below, lines 27–28, the poem is on the loss of Vaughan's brother—not his twin brother Thomas, the hermetic philosopher, who did not die till 1666, but his younger brother William, who died in July, 1648.
2. The miner fixes his lamp halfway down the dark shaft, ventures a little beyond it, but then beats a hasty retreat.

Those beams again,
But nothing but the snuff[3] to me
Appeareth plain,
That dark and dead sleeps in its known
And common urn;
But those[4] fled to their maker's throne,
There shine and burn.
O could I track them! but souls must
Track one the other,
And now the spirit, not the dust,
Must be thy brother.
Yet I have one Pearl,[5] by whose light
All things I see,
And in the heart of earth and night,
Find heaven and thee.

1655

Unprofitableness

How rich, O Lord! how fresh thy visits are!
'Twas but just now my bleak leaves hopeless hung,
Sullied with dust and mud;
Each snarling blast shot through me, and did share[1]
Their youth and beauty; cold showers nipped and wrung
Their spiciness and blood.
But since thou didst in one sweet glance survey
Their sad decays, I flourish, and once more
Breathe all perfumes and spice;
I smell a dew like myrrh, and all the day
Wear in my bosom a full sun; such store
Hath one beam from thy eyes.
But, ah, my God! what fruit hast thou of this?
What one poor leaf did ever I let[2] fall
To wait upon thy wreath?
Thus thou all day a thankless weed dost dress,
And when th' hast done, a stench or fog is all
The odor I bequeath.

1650

3. The wick of the lamp; also, metaphorically, the bodily form of the brother.
4. The reference is back to "light and power."
5. The Bible.

1. Cut away; the word "share" derives from, and is here used for, "shear."
2. The original printed text reads "yet"; corrected to avoid a strained construction.

ANDREW MARVELL

(1621–1678)

Andrew Marvell was one of those quiet men of wit and spirit whose voices generally go unheard during the storm and turmoil of revolution. He attended Cambridge; but after graduating B.A. in 1638 and traveling abroad for some years, he disappears from the biographer's view, turning up around 1650 as tutor to the daughter of Sir Thomas Fairfax, Lord-General of the Parliamentary forces. Here, at the family seat in Yorkshire, Nun Appleton House, Marvell seems to have written many if not most of his English poems. They are playful miniatures, for the most part, which display a genius for catching in a phrase some glancing overtone of serious, almost profound, reflection. Yet their learning, like their serious intent, is hidden beneath a graceful, humorous surface, and they suggest that Marvell must have been a delightful tutor to the little girl who was growing up to be the daughter of a great house.

In 1657 Marvell was appointed assistant to the blind Latin Secretary for the Commonwealth, John Milton; and in his quiet way, he seems to have been responsible after the Restoration for saving Milton from imprisonment and possible execution. Starting in 1659, Marvell was returned M.P. for his home town of Hull, and he continued to represent it in a businesslike way until his death. He was a good committee man, though not a public speaker, and devoted to the interests of Hull. His letters to his constituents are valuable historical documents; but one would never guess from reading them that their author was an accomplished poet.

And in fact, when Marvell died, he was known to the world simply as the author of a few rough-and-ready satires in prose and verse which had been printed during the Restoration. His "serious" verse was only published three years after his death, by a woman who gave herself out as his widow but had really been his housekeeper. The reputation of these poems has made its way slowly, but steadily; and it has never stood higher than in our own time. For it is now clear that Marvell's is the most major minor verse in English. Playful, casual, and witty in tone, always light on its metrical feet and exact in its diction, it displays depth and intellectual hardness in unexpected places; its tèxture is extraordinarily rich. For example, the four poems about a mower seem almost to mock the tiny, conventional figures of Damon the susceptible mower and his hardhearted girl Juliana. They are conventional figures, and Damon voices the conventional complaints about her chilly responses to his ardent proposals. Yet the poems move so persistently and allusively around the old metaphor that all flesh is grass that we can hardly avoid sensing the presence of those other sinister scythemen, Old Father Time and the Grim Reaper. The poems have no more unity than is implied in the phrase "variations on a theme"; but their combination of a light touch, a view of mockery, and the shadow of a dark thought is perfectly Marvellian.

To His Coy Mistress

Had we but world enough, and time,
This coyness, lady, were no crime.
We would sit down, and think which way
To walk, and pass our long love's day.
Thou by the Indian Ganges' side
Shouldst rubies find; I by the tide
Of Humber would complain.[1] I would
Love you ten years before the flood,
And you should, if you please, refuse
Till the conversion of the Jews.[2]
My vegetable love should grow
Vaster than empires and more slow;
An hundred years should go to praise
Thine eyes, and on thy forehead gaze;
Two hundred to adore each breast,
But thirty thousand to the rest;
An age at least to every part,
And the last age should show your heart.
For, lady, you deserve this state,[3]
Nor would I love at lower rate.
But at my back I always hear
Time's wingéd chariot hurrying near;
And yonder all before us lie
Deserts of vast eternity.
Thy beauty shall no more be found,
Nor, in thy marble vault, shall sound
My echoing song; then worms shall try
That long-preserved virginity,
And your quaint honor turn to dust,
And into ashes all my lust:
The grave's a fine and private place,
But none, I think, do there embrace.
Now therefore, while the youthful hue
Sits on thy skin like morning dew,[4]
And while thy willing soul transpires[5]
At every pore with instant fires,
Now let us sport us while we may,
And now, like amorous birds of prey,
Rather at once our time devour
Than languish in his slow-chapped[6] power.

1. Compared to the gorgeous Oriental Ganges, the Humber (which flows past Marvell's home town of Hull) is a muddy estuary, where one is more likely to encounter herring-boats and coal scows than rubies. "Complain" implies ditties of plaintive, unavailing love.
2. According to popular chronology, the Jews were to be converted just before the Last Judgment.
3. Dignity.
4. The text reads "glew"—an odious reading. "Lew" (meaning "warmth") has also been suggested, but it was obsolete long before Marvell wrote.
5. Breathes forth. "Instant fires": immediate, present enthusiasm.
6. Slow-jawed. Time is envisaged as slowly chewing up the world and the people in it.

Let us roll all our strength and all
Our sweetness up into one ball,
And tear our pleasures with rough strife
Thorough the iron gates of life:
Thus, though we cannot make our sun
Stand still, yet we will make him run.[7]

1681

The Garden

How vainly men themselves amaze
To win the palm, the oak, or bays,[1]
And their incessant labors see
Crowned from some single herb, or tree,
Whose short and narrow-vergéd shade
Does prudently their toils upbraid;
While all flowers and all trees do close[2]
To weave the garlands of repose!

Fair Quiet, have I found thee here,
And Innocence, thy sister dear?
Mistaken long, I sought you then
In busy companies of men.
Your sacred plants, if here below,
Only among the plants will grow;
Society is all but rude
To this delicious solitude.

No white nor red was ever seen
So amorous as this lovely green.
Fond lovers, cruel as their flame,
Cut in these trees their mistress' name:
Little, alas, they know or heed
How far these beauties hers exceed!
Fair trees, wheresoe'er your barks I wound,
No name shall but your own be found.[3]

When we have run our passion's heat,
Love hither makes his best retreat.
The gods, that mortal beauty chase,
Still in a tree did end their race:
Apollo hunted Daphne so,
Only that she might laurel grow;[4]

7. In the final lines, lover and mistress triumphantly reverse their relation to time, eating it avidly like birds of prey instead of being eaten by it, forcing the sun to race after them instead of fruitlessly imploring it to stand still.

1. Crowns, respectively, for athletics, civic merit, and poetry. "Amaze": bewilder.

2. Unite.

3. Marvell proposes to carve on the bark of trees, not "Sylvia" or "Laura," but "Beech" and "Oak."

4. Ovid tells (in *Metamorphoses*) how Apollo hunted Daphne until she turned into a laurel, and how Pan pursued Syrinx until she became a reed, out of which he made Panpipes.

And Pan did after Syrinx speed,
Not as a nymph, but for a reed.

What wondrous life is this I lead!
Ripe apples drop about my head;
The luscious clusters of the vine
Upon my mouth do crush their wine;
The nectarine and curious[5] peach
Into my hands themselves do reach;
Stumbling on melons, as I pass,
Insnared with flowers, I fall on grass.

Meanwhile the mind, from pleasure less,[6]
Withdraws into its happiness;
The mind, that ocean where each kind
Does straight its own resemblance find;[7]
Yet it creates, transcending these,
Far other worlds and other seas,
Annihilating all that's made
To a green thought in a green shade.[8]

Here at the fountain's sliding foot,
Or at some fruit tree's mossy root,
Casting the body's vest[9] aside,
My soul into the boughs does glide:
There, like a bird, it sits and sings,
Then whets[1] and combs its silver wings,
And, till prepared for longer flight,
Waves in its plumes the various light.[2]

Such was that happy garden-state,
While man there walked without a mate:
After a place so pure and sweet,
What other help could yet be meet![3]
But 'twas beyond a mortal's share
To wander solitary there:
Two paradises 'twere in one
To live in paradise alone.

How well the skillful gardener drew
Of flowers and herbs this dial[4] new,
Where, from above, the milder sun

5. Exquisite.
6. Diminished and drawn in on itself to savor the pleasure.
7. Every creature on earth was popularly supposed to have its counterpart in the ocean; thus the mind is an ocean because it contains a counterpart to everything on earth.
8. The garden is a symbol of the contemplative life as contrasted with the active life; and green, distinguished from the white of innocence and the red of passion (line 17), connotes a way of life which is cool and detached from human concerns.
9. Vestment, garment.
1. Preens.
2. The many-colored light of this world, contrasted with the white radiance of eternity.
3. Genesis ii.18 records the Lord's decision to make "an help meet" for Adam—*i.e.*, Eve.
4. Clock. While the growth and decline of the garden measure the passage of time, the sun, a milder clock, runs through the zodiac, or constellation of the seasons.

Does through a fragrant zodiac run;
And as it works, th' industrious bee
Computes its time as well as we!
How could such sweet and wholesome hours
Be reckoned but with herbs and flowers?

1681

The Mower, Against Gardens

Luxurious man,[1] to bring his vice in use,
 Did after him the world seduce,
And from the fields the flowers and plants allure,
 Where Nature was most plain and pure.
He first enclosed within the gardens square
 A dead and standing pool of air,
And a more luscious earth for them did knead,
 Which stupefied them while it fed.
The pink grew then as double as his mind;[2]
 The nutriment did change the kind.
With strange perfumes he did the roses taint;
 And flowers themselves were taught to paint.
The tulip white did for complexion seek,
 And learned to interline its cheek;
Its onion root they then so high did hold,
 That one was for a meadow sold:[3]
Another world was searched through oceans new,
 To find the marvel of Peru;[4]
And yet these rarities might be allowed
 To man, that sovereign thing and proud,
Had he not dealt between the bark and tree,[5]
 Forbidden mixtures there to see.
No plant now knew the stock from which it came;
 He grafts upon the wild the tame,
That the uncertain and adulterate fruit
 Might put the palate in dispute.
His green seraglio has its eunuchs too,
 Lest any tyrant him outdo;
And in the cherry he does Nature vex,
 To procreate without a sex.
'Tis all enforced, the fountain and the grot,
 While the sweet fields do lie forgot,
Where willing Nature does to all dispense
 A wild and fragrant innocence;

1. Luxury-loving, voluptuous man, who wants to popularize ("bring in use") his own vices.
2. The double pink or carnation is a product of sophisticated, therefore hypocritical ("double"), minds.
3. A great boom in tulip bulbs took place in Holland during the 17th century; Marvell's line was therefore, on occasion, strictly accurate.
4. *Mirabilis Jalapa*, the four o'clock, a flower found originally in South America.
5. By grafting.

And fauns and fairies do the meadows till
  More by their presence than their skill.
Their statues polished by some ancient hand,
  May to adorn the gardens stand;
But, howsoe'er the figures do excel,
  The gods themselves with us do dwell.

1681

Damon the Mower

Hark how the mower Damon[1] sung,
With love of Juliana stung!
While everything did seem to paint
The scene more fit for his complaint.[2]
Like her fair eyes the day was fair,
But scorching like his amorous care;
Sharp, like his scythe, his sorrow was,
And withered, like his hopes, the grass.

"Oh what unusual heats are here,
Which thus our sunburnt meadows fear!
The grasshopper its pipe gives o'er,
And hamstringed frogs can dance no more;
But in the brook the green frog wades,
And grasshoppers seek out the shades;
Only the snake, that kept within,
Now glitters in its second skin.

"This heat the sun could never raise,
Nor dog star so inflame the days;[3]
It from an higher beauty grow'th,
Which burns the fields and mower both;
Which made the dog, and makes the sun
Hotter than his own Phaeton;[4]
Not July causeth these extremes,
But Juliana's scorching beams.

"Tell me where I may pass the fires
Of the hot day or hot desires,
To what cool cave shall I descend,
Or to what gelid[5] fountain bend?

1. Damon is a pastoral name familiar since Virgil's time; Juliana gets her name, if anywhere from July (lines 23–24).

2. Love song. The word "complaint" in this context carries a certain mockery with it; a shepherd who has nothing but love pangs to complain about is not really in much pain.

3. The dog star (Sirius in the constellation of Canis Major) is seen from July to September; coincidentally this is the period when dogs most often develop hydrophobia (i.e., rabies).

4. Son of Helios, the sun god of Greek mythology, he tried to drive his father's chariot, but let the horses run away, and scorched the world.

5. Icy.

Alas! I look for ease in vain,
When remedies themselves complain:[6]
No moisture but my tears do rest,
No cold but in her icy breast.

"How long wilt thou, fair shepherdess,
Esteem me and my presents less?
To thee the harmless snake I bring,
Disarméd of its teeth and sting;
To thee chameleons, changing hue,
And oak leaves tipped with honey dew;
Yet thou, ungrateful, hast not sought
Nor what they are, nor who them brought.

"I am the mower Damon, known
Through all the meadows I have mown.
On me the morn her dew distills
Before her darling daffodils,
And if at noon my toil me heat,
The sun himself licks off my sweat;
While, going home, the evening sweet
In cowslip-water bathes my feet.

"What though the piping shepherd stock
The plains with an unnumbered flock,
This scythe of mine discovers wide
More ground than all his sheep do hide.
With this the golden fleece I shear
Of all these closes every year,[7]
And though in wool more poor than they,
Yet I am richer far in hay.

"Nor am I so deformed to sight
If in my scythe I lookéd right;
In which I see my picture done
As in a crescent moon the sun.
The deathless fairies take me oft
To lead them in their dances soft,
And when I tune myself to sing,
About me they contract their ring.[8]

"How happy might I still have mowed,
Had not Love here his thistle sowed!
But now I all the day complain,
Joining my labor to my pain;

6. I.e., the fountain and cave themselves complain of unusual heat.

7. Hay is the "wool" of the fields ("closes"); it is a "golden" fleece simply because it is the mower's cash crop.

8. British folklore has it that the circular "raths" or earthen forts surviving from Druid days are fairy "rings" around which the little people dance at night. "Contract": the word means, not "tighten" or "squeeze," but simply "form."

And with my scythe cut down the grass,
Yet still my grief is where it was;
But when the iron blunter grows,
Sighing, I whet my scythe and woes."

While thus he drew his elbow round,
Depopulating all the ground,
And with his whistling scythe does cut
Each stroke between the earth and root,
The edgéd steel, by careless chance,
Did into his own ankle glance,
And there among the grass fell down
By his own scythe the mower mown.

"Alas!" said he, "these hurts are slight
To those that die by Love's despite.
With shepherd's purse and clown's all-heal[9]
The blood I stanch and wound I heal.
Only for him no cure is found
Whom Juliana's eyes do wound;
'Tis Death alone that this must do;
For, Death, thou art a mower too."

1681

The Mower to the Glowworms

Ye living lamps, by whose dear light
The nightingale does sit so late,
And studying all the summer night
Her matchless songs does meditate;[1]

Ye country comets, that portend
No war nor prince's funeral,
Shining unto no higher end
Than to presage the grass's fall;

Ye glowworms, whose officious flame
To wandering mowers shows the way,
That in the night have lost their aim,
And after foolish fires[2] do stray;

Your courteous fires in vain you waste,
Since Juliana here is come,
For she my mind hath so displaced
That I shall never find my home.

1681

9. Folk-names for popular remedies found in fields and hedges. Like a good Petrarchan lover, the mower falls with an erotic conceit and a sentimental morality on his lips.

1. The root word of "meditate" carries in Latin, the secondary meaning "to sing."

2. Will-o-the-wisps, swampfires.

The Mower's Song

My mind was once the true survey
Of all these meadows fresh and gay,
And in the greenness of the grass
Did see its hopes as in a glass;[1]
When Juliana came, and she,
What I do to the grass, does to my thoughts and me.

But these, while I with sorrow pine,
Grew more luxuriant still and fine,
That not one blade of grass you spied,
But had a flower on either side;
When Juliana came, and she,
What I do to the grass, does to my thoughts and me.

Unthankful meadows, could you so
A fellowship so true forego,
And in your gaudy May-games[2] meet,
While I lay trodden under feet?
When Juliana came, and she,
What I do to the grass, does to my thoughts and me.

But what you in compassion ought
Shall now by my revenge be wrought,
And flowers, and grass, and I, and all,
Will in one common ruin fall;
For Juliana comes, and she,
What I do to the grass, does to my thoughts and me.

And thus ye meadows, which have been
Companions of my thoughts more green,
Shall now the heraldry become
With which I shall adorn my tomb.
For Juliana came, and she,
What I do to the grass, does to my thoughts and me.

1681

The Picture of Little T. C. in a Prospect of Flowers[1]

See with what simplicity
This nymph begins her golden days!

1. Looking glass, mirror.
2. Festivals and merrymaking marked the first of May—and still do for the heartless grass, though not for the melancholy mower.

1. We do not know who T. C. was, though speculation has not been idle; all we need know is that she was a little girl. "Prospect": landscape, background scene.

In the green grass she loves to lie,
And there with her fair aspect tames
The wilder flowers and gives them names,
But only with the roses plays,
    And them does tell
What color best becomes them and what smell.

Who can foretell for what high cause
This darling of the gods was born?
Yet this is she whose chaster laws
The wanton Love shall one day fear,
And under her command severe
See his bow broke and ensign[2] torn.
    Happy who can
Appease this virtuous enemy of man!

O then let me in time compound
And parley with those conquering eyes
Ere they have tried their force to wound,
Ere with their glancing wheels they drive
In triumph over hearts that strive
And them that yield but more despise:
    Let me be laid
Where I may see the glories from some shade.

Meantime, whilst every verdant thing
Itself does at thy beauty charm,
Reform the errors of the spring;
Make that the tulips may have share
Of sweetness, seeing they are fair;
And roses of their thorns disarm:
    But most procure
That violets may a longer time endure.

But O, young beauty of the woods,
Whom Nature courts with fruit and flowers,
Gather the flowers but spare the buds,
Lest Flora,[3] angry at thy crime
To kill her infants in their prime,
Do quickly make th' example yours;
    And ere we see,
Nip in the blossom all our hopes and thee.

1681

2. Flag, pennant.

3. Roman goddess of flowers and plants.

The Coronet

When for the thorns with which I long, too long,
With many a piercing wound,
My Saviour's head have crowned,
I seek with garlands to redress that wrong,
Through every garden, every mead,
I gather flowers (my fruits are only flowers),
Dismantling all the fragrant towers
That once adorned my shepherdess's head:
And now, when I have summed up all my store,
Thinking (so I myself deceive)
So rich a chaplet[1] thence to weave
As never yet the King of Glory wore,
Alas! I find the serpent old,[2]
That, twining in his speckled breast,
About the flowers disguised does fold
With wreaths of fame and interest.[3]
Ah, foolish man, that wouldst debase with them
And mortal glory, Heaven's diadem!
But Thou who only couldst the serpent tame,
Either his slippery knots at once untie,
And disentangle all his winding snare,
Or shatter too with him my curious frame,[4]
And let these wither, so that he may die,
Though set with skill and chosen out with care;
That they, while thou on both their spoils dost tread,
May crown Thy feet, that could not crown Thy head.[5]

1681

A Dialogue Between the Soul and Body

SOUL. O, who shall from this dungeon raise
A soul enslaved so many ways? [1]
With bolts of bones, that fettered stands
In feet; and manacled in hands.
Here blinded with an eye; and there
Deaf with the drumming of an ear;
A soul hung up, as 'twere, in chains
Of nerves, and arteries, and veins;
Tortured, besides each other part,
In a vain head and double heart?

1. Garland.
2. Satan.
3. Self-glorification and self-interest.
4. I.e., my wreath of flowers. "These" in the next line refers to the flowers again.
5. Cf. the curse of Genesis iii.15, that the seed of Eve shall bruise the serpent's head.

1. The soul speaks almost in the words of St. Paul's epistle to the Romans vii.24: "O wretched man that I am! who shall deliver me from the body of this death?" The body's speech mirrors or parodies that of the soul.

BODY. O, who shall me deliver whole
From bonds of this tyrannic soul?
Which, stretched upright, impales me so
That mine own precipice[2] I go;
And warms and moves this needless frame[3]
(A fever could but do the same),
And, wanting where[4] its spite to try,
Has made me live to let me die.
A body that could never rest
Since this ill spirit it possessed.

SOUL. What magic could me thus confine
Within another's grief to pine?
Where, whatsoever it complain,
I feel, that cannot feel,[5] the pain;
And all my care itself employs,
That to preserve which me destroys;
Constrained not only to endure
Diseases, but, what's worse, the cure;
And, ready oft the port to gain,
Am shipwrecked into health again.

BODY. But Physic[6] yet could never reach
The maladies thou me dost teach;
Whom first the cramp of hope does tear,
And then the palsy shakes of fear;
The pestilence of love does heat,
Or hatred's hidden ulcer eat;
Joy's cheerful madness does perplex,
Or sorrow's other madness vex;
Which knowledge forces me to know,
And memory will not forego;
What but a soul could have the wit
To build me up for sin so fit?
So architects do square and hew
Green trees that in the forest grew.[7]

1681

The Definition of Love

My Love is of a birth as rare
As 'tis, for object, strange and high;

2. Possession of a soul is the reason why man walks erect, facing the heavens, instead of prowling the earth like a brute; but it is also the reason why he can fall and be damned, as brutes cannot; so the soul is an interior precipice.
3. This frame, which does not need it.
4. Lacking an object.
5. The soul can "feel" (sympathize) even though it "cannot feel" (has no power of physical sensation).
6. Medicine.
7. The body asserts that it has been trimmed and squared to an alien purpose, instead of being allowed to grow freely and naturally, as in the forest.

It was begotten by Despair
Upon Impossibility.

Magnanimous Despair alone
Could show me so divine a thing,
Where feeble Hope could ne'er have flown
But vainly flapped its tinsel wing.

And yet I quickly might arrive
Where my extended soul is fixed;[1]
But Fate does iron wedges drive,
And always crowds itself betwixt.

For Fate with jealous eye does see
Two perfect loves, nor lets them close;[2]
Their union would her ruin be,
And her tyrannic power depose.[3]

And therefore her decrees of steel
Us as the distant poles have placed
(Though Love's whole world on us doth wheel),
Not by themselves to be embraced,

Unless the giddy heaven fall,
And earth some new convulsion tear,
And, us to join, the world should all
Be cramped into a planisphere.[4]

As lines, so loves oblique may well
Themselves in every angle greet;[5]
But ours, so truly parallel,
Though infinite, can never meet.

Therefore the love which us doth bind,
But Fate so enviously debars,
Is the conjunction of the mind,
And opposition of the stars.[6]

1681

Bermudas

Where the remote Bermudas ride,
In th' ocean's bosom unespied,

1. Marvell thinks of his soul as having gone out of his body ("extended") and attached ("fixed") itself to his mistress.
2. Unite.
3. Fate, and its agents Time and Change, would none of them have any power against a perfect mixture of the elements.
4. A flat sphere, literally absurd, but describing a kind of astrological projection in which the world was represented in two dimensions and the poles were united.
5. "Oblique" includes the meaning of "deviating from right conduct or thought"; oblique loves, like oblique lines, touch in angles (corners), but Marvell's love and the lady's, being parallel and perfect, can never touch.
6. "Conjunction" and "opposition" are technical terms from astronomy, here yoked to Marvell's "definition."

From a small boat that rowed along,
The listening winds received this song:

"What should we do but sing His praise,
That led us through the watery maze
Unto an isle so long unknown,
And yet far kinder than our own?
Where He the huge sea monsters wracks,
That lift the deep upon their backs;[1]
He lands us on a grassy stage,
Safe from the storms, and prelate's rage.[2]
He gave us this eternal spring
Which here enamels everything,
And sends the fowls to us in care,
On daily visits through the air;
He hangs in shades the orange bright,
Like golden lamps in a green night,
And does in the pomegranates close
Jewels more rich than Ormus[3] shows;
He makes the figs our mouths to meet,
And throws the melons at our feet;
But apples[4] plants of such a price,
No tree could ever bear them twice;
With cedars, chosen by His hand,
From Lebanon, He stores the land;
And makes the hollow seas, that roar,
Proclaim the ambergris[5] on shore;
He cast (of which we rather boast)
The Gospel's pearl upon our coast,
And in these rocks for us did frame
A temple, where to sound His name.
O! let our voice His praise exalt,
Till it arrive at heaven's vault,
Which, thence (perhaps) rebounding, may
Echo beyond the Mexique Bay."[6]

Thus sung they in the English boat,
An holy and a cheerful note;
And all the way, to guide their chime,
With falling oars they kept the time.

1681

1. See Milton's use of the same sea fable in *Paradise Lost* I.203 ff. "Wracks": shipwrecks, destroys.
2. Storms at sea are quietly equated with bishops as sources of peril.
3. Pearl- and jewel-trading center in the Persian Gulf.
4. Pineapples.
5. "Proclaim," a kind of learned joke, suggests the seas roaring to announce their bounty. Ambergris is an expensive, mysterious, soapy substance found in sperm whales and used in the manufacture of perfumes (see *Moby-Dick,* Chapter XCII).
6. The Gulf of Mexico.

An Horatian Ode

UPON CROMWELL'S RETURN FROM IRELAND[1]

The forward youth that would appear,
Must now forsake his Muses dear,
Nor in the shadows sing
His numbers languishing:

'Tis time to leave the books in dust,
And oil the unuséd armor's rust;
Removing from the wall
The corselet of the hall.[2]

So restless Cromwell could not cease
In the inglorious arts of peace,
But through adventurous war
Urgéd his active star;

And, like the three-forked lightning, first
Breaking the clouds where it was nursed,
Did thorough his own side
His fiery way divide:[3]

For 'tis all one to courage high,
The emulous, or enemy;
And with such, to enclose,
Is more than to oppose;

Then burning through the air he went,
And palaces and temples rent;
And Caesar's head at last
Did through his laurels blast.[4]

1. Cromwell returned from conquering Ireland in May, 1650, about 18 months after the execution of Charles I. The two events were vaguely but persistently connected: Cromwell's victory over the Irish was somehow a "vindication" of his career to this point, a sign that God did not disapprove of his laying violent hands on the sacred person of the monarch. The title phrase, "An Horatian Ode," promises a poem of cool and balanced judgment, not "enthusiastic" or heroic like the odes of Pindar. For the political background of Marvell's poem, see John M. Wallace, "Marvell's Horatian Ode," *PMLA* 77 (1962), 33–45.

2. The "forward youth" who removes armor from the wall owes something to a similar figure in the first book of Lucan's ***Pharsalia,*** which is also a poem about force, justice, and civil war. Andrew Marvell was not by any means dropping books and picking up armor in 1650.

3. Cromwell had begun as a relatively inconspicuous Presbyterian, but soon became the leader of the more radical group variously known as the "Rump" or the "Independents." The "three-forked lightning" he wields identifies him with Zeus; and his giving birth (to himself, presumably) through his own side (party, of course, but a part of the body, too) might remind a reader of Athena's birth through Zeus's ear.

4. Laurels were used for royal crowns precisely because they were supposed to protect from lightning. "Caesar," of course, is Charles I. Cromwell's acts with his thunderbolt (smashing palaces, temples, and at last Caesar's head through its laurels) suggest a tyrannical God. Yet Caesar was a tyrant too.

'Tis madness to resist or blame
The face of angry Heaven's flame;
And if we would speak true,
Much to the man is due,

Who from his private gardens, where
He lived reservéd and austere,
As if his highest plot
To plant the bergamot;[5]

Could by industrious valor climb
To ruin the great work of Time,
And cast the kingdom old,
Into another mold;

Though Justice against Fate complain,
And plead the ancient rights in vain;
But those do hold or break,
As men are strong or weak.

Nature that hateth emptiness,
Allows of penetration less,
And therefore must make room
Where greater spirits come.

What field of all the civil wars
Where his were not the deepest scars?
And Hampton shows what part
He had of wiser art;[6]

Where, twining subtle fears with hope,
He wove a net of such a scope
That Charles himself might chase
To Caresbrooke's narrow case,

That thence the royal actor borne,
The tragic scaffold might adorn;
While round the arméd bands
Did clap their bloody hands.

He nothing common did or mean
Upon that memorable scene,
But with his keener eye
The ax's edge did try;[7]

5. Bergamot is a variety of pear; but its etymology (from the Turkish, "prince's pear") may conceal the insinuation that Cromwell had been plotting for power even in his early days of "private" life. The whole poem is full of puns (cf. "enclose," line 19, "mold," line 36) for the reader to seek out.

6. Hampton Court, where Charles I was confined shortly before his execution. It was popularly said that Cromwell connived at his momentary escape to Carisbrooke Castle on the Isle of Wight in order to convince the doubtful Parliament that the king could not be trusted and must be executed.

7. Latin uses one word, *acies*, for the front of a battle line, the edge of a sword- or ax-blade, and the beam of an eye.

Nor called the gods with vulgar spite
To vindicate his helpless right;
But bowed his comely head
Down, as upon a bed.

This was that memorable hour,
Which first assured the forcéd power;
So when they did design
The capitol's first line,

A bleeding head where they begun,
Did fright the architects to run;
And yet in that the state
Foresaw its happy fate.[8]

And now the Irish are ashamed
To see themselves in one year tamed;
So much one man can do,
That does both act and know.

They can affirm his praises best,
And have, though overcome, confessed
How good he is, how just,
And fit for highest trust.

Nor yet grown stiffer with command,
But still in the republic's hand—
How fit he is to sway,
That can so well obey.

He to the Commons' feet presents
A kingdom for his first year's rents;
And, what he may, forbears
His fame to make it theirs;

And has his sword and spoils ungirt,
To lay them at the public's skirt:
So, when the falcon high
Falls heavy from the sky,

She, having killed, no more does search,
But on the next green bough to perch;
Where, when he first does lure,
The falconer has her sure.

What may not then our isle presume,
While victory his crest does plume!
What may not others fear,
If thus he crown each year!

8. When foundations were being dug for the temple of Jupiter at Rome, Pliny tells us, the workmen uncovered a bloody head. They at first thought it an ill omen but then were persuaded to consider it a token that Rome would be the head (*caput*) of an empire; hence the name of the temple, Jupiter Capitolinus, and of the hill on which it stood, the Capitoline. The tale may well imply a generic relation between civilization and violence.

A Caesar he ere long to Gaul,
To Italy an Hannibal,
And to all states not free,
Shall climactéric be.[9]

The Pict no shelter now shall find
Within his party-colored mind,
But from this valor sad,
Shrink underneath the plaid;[1]

Happy if in the tufted brake
The English hunter him mistake,
Nor lay his hounds in near
The Caledonian[2] deer.

But thou, the war's and fortune's son,
March indefatigably on;
And for the last effect,
Still keep thy sword erect;[3]

Besides the force it has to fright
The spirits of the shady night,
The same arts that did gain
A power must it maintain.[4]

c. 1650 1681

9. Neither Caesar nor Hannibal brought, or pretended to bring, freedom to the lands they attacked. "Climactéric": a period of crucial change in human life (for better or worse), popularly supposed to occur when 9 joined with 7 in man's age, i.e., in his 63rd year.
1. Early inhabitants of Scotland were called Picts because their warriors painted themselves many colors (Latin, *pictus*: painted); Marvell is playing with an image of the Scotch as divided by factions (parties) into as many colors as Scotch plaids.
2. Scotch.
3. The sword is being carried "erect," i.e., with the bare blade up, not the cross of the handle. Naked power, not religion, is to be the ensign of Cromwell's rule.
4. The last lines of the poem seem to paraphrase a saying of Christ's to the effect that they who take the sword shall perish with the sword (Matthew xxvi.52); from Cromwell's point of view, it is not a very reassuring ending to the poem. Yet when the poem was printed, in 1681, the censor of Charles II thought it politically subversive, and had it physically cut out of all the copies of Marvell's poems except (fortunately) one.

JOHN MILTON
(1608–1674)

1637: *Lycidas.*
1640–60: The pamphlet wars.
1651: Blindness.
1667: *Paradise Lost.*

The life of John Milton falls conveniently into three divisions. There is a period of youthful education and apprenticeship, which culminates in the writing of *Lycidas* (1637) and Milton's foreign travels (1638–39).

There is a period of prose and controversy (1640–60), when almost all his verse was occasional, and when his major preoccupations were political and social; and finally, there are the last fourteen years of his life, when he returned to literature, a mature and somewhat embittered figure, to publish his three great poems, *Paradise Lost* (1667), *Paradise Regained* (1671), and *Samson Agonistes* (1671).

Milton was born at Bread Street in Cheapside, the elder son of what we would nowadays probably call a real-estate man. From the beginning, Milton showed prodigious gifts as a student of languages. At St. Paul's School he mastered Latin and Greek, and before long he was adept in most modern European tongues, as well as Hebrew. Sent to Christ's College, Cambridge, he proceeded B.A. in 1629 and M.A. in 1632, meanwhile continuing to read voraciously and writing (too infrequently for his own satisfaction) an occasional poem. In the normal course of events, a career like this would have culminated in ordination to the ministry and a position in the church. Both Milton and his parents seem to have anticipated this. But after taking his M.A., Milton, who disliked the trend of civil and religious affairs in England, did not take orders; instead, he retired to his father's country house at Horton in Buckinghamshire, and for five more years, under his own direction, read day and night. It seems likely that Milton, in his time, read just about everything that was ever written in English, Latin, Greek, and Italian. (Of course, he had the Bible by heart.) In 1634 he wrote, at the invitation of a nearby noble family, the masque known as *Comus;* and in 1637 he contributed to a volume memorializing a college classmate the elegy of *Lycidas*. Finally, in 1638, his most indulgent father sent this most voracious of students abroad, to put the finishing touches on an already splendid education. For two years, Milton traveled on the Continent, visiting famous literary figures and scenes; then, hearing rumors of impending troubles in England, he returned home in 1639.

Of Milton's complex and troubled career in controversy we need not say much. It too is divided in three phases. He began by publishing antiprelatical tracts, against the government of the church by bishops. These are rough, knockabout, name-calling tracts in the style of the times, which take a popular position on a relatively popular issue. But Milton's next venture procured him a reputation as a radical. In June, 1642, he married Mary Powell. Within six weeks, she left him, to return to her parents' house; and from 1643 to 1645, Milton published a series of pamphlets advocating that divorce be granted on the grounds of incompatibility. Clearly his personal situation had influenced his social judgment; just as clearly, respectable Englishmen, who were disturbed by the troubles of the time, were bound to feel that "divorce at pleasure" represented the end of all social order, the coming of complete anarchy. Though the position he took is moderate, even traditional, in many modern societies, it was too scandalous for his day, and Milton was much embittered by the rejection of his ideas. After the execution of Charles I, in 1649, he published a series of Latin disputations against Continental critics of the regime, defending the actions of Parliament in executing Charles. In the middle of this work, he went blind, as the result of eyestrain continued over many years. By the use of secretaries and amanuenses, however, he was able to fulfill his duties as

Latin Secretary to Cromwell's Council of State, and to contribute very substantially to the diplomatic dignity of the new government.

Meanwhile, his wife returned to him, and having borne him three daughters, died in 1652. In 1656 Milton married Katharine Woodcock, who died in childbirth, in 1658. Finally, in 1660, the whole political movement for which Milton had sacrificed so much, went to smash. Though Milton boldly published pamphlets in its support to the very last minute, the Good Old Cause was defeated, and Charles II recalled from his travels. For a time under the Restoration, Milton was imprisoned and in danger of his life; but friends intervened, and he escaped with a fine and the loss of most of his property.

In 1663 Milton married his third wife, Elizabeth Minshull; and in blindness, poverty, defeat, and relative isolation, he set about completing a poem "justifying the ways of God to men," which he had first envisaged many years before. It was published in 1667, as *Paradise Lost;* and despite the many difficulties which it presented, despite its unfamiliar meter (blank verse was rare outside drama), despite the unpopularity of its attitudes and Milton's reputation as a dangerous man, it was recognized at once as a supreme epic achievement. In 1671 Milton published *Paradise Regained,* an epic poem in four books describing Christ's temptation in the wilderness, and *Samson Agonistes,* a "closet" tragedy (i.e., not intended for the stage). He died, of complications arising from gout, in 1674.

In the writings of Milton, the work of two tremendous intellectual and social movements comes to a head. The Renaissance is responsible for the rich and complex texture of Milton's style, the multiplicity of its classical references, its wealth of ornament and decoration. *Paradise Lost,* being an epic, not only challenges comparison with Homer and Virgil, it undertakes to encompass the whole life of mankind—war, love, religion, Hell, Heaven, the cosmos. It is a poem vastly capacious of worldly experience. On the other hand, the Reformation speaks with equal, if not greater, authority in Milton's earnest and individually-minded Christianity. The great epic, which resounds with the grandeur and multiplicity of the world, is also a poem the central actions of which take place inwardly, at the core of man's conscience. Adam's fate culminates in an act of passive suffering, not of active heroism. He does not kill Hector or Turnus, much less Satan, he picks up the burden of worldly existence, and triumphs over his guilt by admitting it and repenting of it.

These two contrasting aspects of Milton's life and thought place him among the Christian humanists. His literary art places him in the small circle of great epic writers.

On Shakespeare[1]

What needs my Shakespeare for his honored bones
The labor of an age in pilèd stones,
Or that his hallowed relics should be hid

1. Milton's tribute to Shakespeare appeared in the Second Folio of the plays.

Under a star-ypointing pyramid?[2]
Dear son of memory, great heir of fame,
What need'st thou such weak witness of thy name?
Thou in our wonder and astonishment
Hast built thyself a livelong monument.
For whilst to th' shame of slow-endeavoring art,
Thy easy numbers flow, and that each heart
Hath from the leaves of thy unvalued book[3]
Those delphic lines with deep impression took,
Then thou, our fancy of itself bereaving,
Dost make us marble with too much conceiving;[4]
And so sepulchered in such pomp dost lie,
That kings for such a tomb would wish to die.

1632

L'Allegro[1]

Hence loathéd Melancholy
Of Cerberus[2] and blackest midnight born,
In Stygian[3] cave forlorn
'Mongst horrid shapes, and shrieks, and sights unholy,

2. "Star-ypointing" uses one of Spenser's archaic "y-" prefixes to eke out the meter. (Note also the interpolated "that" in line 10, serving the same purpose.) Milton's poem begins by answering the common complaint of the day, that Shakespeare should have been buried in some place more splendid than Stratford. Shakespeare is described as the "son of memory" because that makes him a brother of the muses, daughters of Mnemosyne ("memory") by Zeus.

3. Beyond all value, invaluable book.

4. The monuments of Shakespeare's tomb are all the enchanted and motionless readers of his book.

1. *L'Allegro* and *Il Penseroso* are a pair of companion-poems, probably written around 1630 or 1631, in those dancing tetrameter couplets which are so hard to keep from degenerating into singsong, and so delightful when controlled. Milton's handling of this difficult meter may be compared with virtuoso performances like those of Marvell (*To His Coy Mistress*), Keats (*Lines on the Mermaid Tavern*) and A. E. Housman (*Terence, This Is Stupid Stuff*).

The titles are almost untranslatable, which is why Milton did not translate them. But within the framework of two contrasted days, we see the cheerful, sociable man, and the melancholy, contemplative man in their typical spiritual attitudes. Milton's interest in the typical accounts for the striking generality of the pictures: "And every shepherd tells his tale / Under the hawthorn in the dale"—there is no effort to create an individual shepherd in a particular setting. All the shepherds in all the dales for miles around are telling one story or another, each under his own hawthorn bush. But Milton's focus is on the mind that sees, and on the tone which it casts over a landscape. The cheerful man infuses his world with contagious cheerfulness; the melancholy man casts over the events of his day (which, as events, are not very different) a pervasive veil of melancholy. The backgrounds of this complex contemplative mood may be explored in Burton's famous *Anatomy of Melancholy;* in a more recent book, Erwin Panofsky's study, *Albrecht Dürer,* where it occurs in connection with Dürer's magnificent engraving of Melancholia; or in Saxl, Panofsky, and Klibansky's immense study, *Saturn and Melancholy* (1964). There is a history of literary cheerfulness, too—*The Happy Man,* by Maren Sofie Røstvig (1954).

Milton's poems stand in contrast to one another, but the contrasts are shaded, not glaring; there is no effort to "decide" the conflict, or to make melancholy black and cheerfulness convivial. Both poems exist in a reflective half-light, as little idyls of description which for sheer elegance and charm have rarely been equaled.

2. The three-headed hell-hound of classical mythology.

3. I.e., near the river Styx, the river of the underworld.

Find out some uncouth cell,
  Where brooding Darkness spreads his jealous wings,
And the night-raven sings;
  There under ebon shades, and low-browed rocks,
As ragged as thy locks,
  In dark Cimmerian[4] desert ever dwell.
But come thou goddess fair and free,
In Heaven yclept Euphrosyne,[5]
And by men, heart-easing Mirth,
Whom lovely Venus at a birth
With two sister Graces more
To ivy-crownéd Bacchus bore;[6]
Or whether (as some sager sing)[7]
The frolic wind that breathes the spring,
Zephyr with Aurora playing,
As he met her once a-Maying,
There on beds of violets blue,
And fresh-blown[8] roses washed in dew,
Filled her with thee a daughter fair,
So buxom,[9] blithe, and debonair.
Haste thee nymph, and bring with thee
Jest and youthful Jollity,
Quips and Cranks,[1] and wanton Wiles,
Nods, and Becks, and wreathéd Smiles,
Such as hang on Hebe's[2] cheek,
And love to live in dimple sleek;
Sport that wrinkled Care derides,
And Laughter, holding both his sides.
Come, and trip it as ye go
On the light fantastic toe,
And in thy right hand lead with thee,
The mountain nymph, sweet Liberty;
And if I give thee honor due,
Mirth, admit me of thy crew
To live with her and live with thee,
In unreprovéd pleasures free;
To hear the lark begin his flight,
And, singing, startle the dull night,
From his watch-tower in the skies,
Till the dappled dawn doth rise;
Then to come[3] in spite of sorrow,
And at my window bid good morrow,
Through the sweetbriar, or the vine,

4. The Cimmerians, who gave their name to Crimea, were supposed to live on the outer edge of the world, in perpetual twilight.

5. Euphrosyne, Aglaia, and Thalia were the Graces, daughters (according to one story) of Zeus himself, and goddesses of beauty and delight. "Yclept": called.

6. Bacchus is god of wine.

7. The "sager" (poets) who describe the Graces as born of Zephyr and Aurora are in fact John Milton himself; he invented this version of the myth.

8. Newly opened.

9. Lively.

1. Jokes. "Becks": curtseys.

2. Goddess of youth and cupbearer to the other gods. Pronounced *Hee-bee*.

3. I.e., then admit me to come.

Or the twisted eglantine.
While the cock with lively din,
Scatters the rear of darkness thin,
And to the stack, or the barn door,
Stoutly struts his dames before;
Oft listening how the hounds and horn
Cheerly rouse the slumbering morn,
From the side of some hoar hill,
Through the high wood echoing shrill.
Sometime walking not unseen
By hedgerow elms, on hillocks green,
Right against the eastern gate,
Where the great sun begins his state,[4]
Robed in flames, and amber light,
The clouds in thousand liveries dight;[5]
While the plowman near at hand,
Whistles o'er the furrowed land,
And the milkmaid singeth blithe,
And the mower whets his scythe,
And every shepherd tells his tale,
Under the hawthorn in the dale.
Straight mine eye hath caught new pleasures
Whilst the landscape round it measures,
Russet lawns and fallows gray,
Where the nibbling flocks do stray,
Mountains on whose barren breast
The laboring clouds do often rest;
Meadows trim with daisies pied,[6]
Shallow brooks, and rivers wide.
Towers and battlements it sees
Bosomed high in tufted trees,
Where perhaps some beauty lies,
The cynosure[7] of neighboring eyes.
Hard by, a cottage chimney smokes,
From betwixt two aged oaks,
Where Corydon and Thyrsis[8] met,
Are at their savory dinner set
Of herbs, and other country messes,
Which the neat-handed Phyllis dresses;
And then in haste her bower she leaves,
With Thestylis to bind the sheaves;
Or if the earlier season lead
To the tanned haycock in the mead.
Sometimes with secure delight
The upland hamlets will invite,
When the merry bells ring round

4. Procession.
5. Dressed.
6. Dappled.
7. Literally, the bright polestar, by which mariners steer; here, a splendid, eminent object, much gazed at.
8. Since the days of Theocritus, the names "Corydon," "Thyrsis," "Phyllis," and "Thestylis" have been traditional shepherds' names.

And the jocund rebecks[9] sound
To many a youth and many a maid,
Dancing in the checkered shade;
And young and old come forth to play
On a sunshine holiday,
Till the livelong daylight fail;
Then to the spicy nut-brown ale,
With stories told of many a feat,
How fairy Mab[1] the junkets eat;
She was pinched and pulled, she said,
And he, by Friar's lantern led,
Tells how the drudging goblin[2] sweat
To earn his cream-bowl, duly set,
When in one night, ere glimpse of morn,
His shadowy flail hath threshed the corn
That ten day-laborers could not end;
Then lies him down the lubber fiend,[3]
And, stretched out all the chimney's length,
Basks at the fire his hairy strength;
And crop-full out of doors he flings
Ere the first cock his matin rings.
Thus done the tales, to bed they creep,
By whispering winds soon lulled asleep.
Towered cities please us then,
And the busy hum of men,
Where throngs of knights and barons bold,
In weeds[4] of peace high triumphs hold,
With store of ladies, whose bright eyes
Rain influence,[5] and judge the prize
Of wit, or arms, while both contend
To win her grace, whom all commend.
There let Hymen[6] oft appear
In saffron robe, with taper clear,
And pomp, and feast, and revelry,
With masque, and antique pageantry;
Such sights as youthful poets dream
On summer eves by haunted stream.
Then to the well-trod stage anon,
If Jonson's learned sock[7] be on,
Or sweetest Shakespeare, fancy's child,
Warble his native wood-notes wild.

9. A rebeck is a small three-stringed fiddle; "jocund" implies a festive occasion.

1. Queen Mab, wife of Oberon, the fairy king. "She" and "he" in the next two lines are country folk, telling of their experiences with the fairies.

2. Robin Goodfellow, alias Puck, Pook, or Hobgoblin. "Friar's lantern": will-o'-the-wisp.

3. Oafish spirit.

4. Garments. "Triumphs": festive ceremonies.

5. The ladies' eyes are stars, and so have astrological influence over the men.

6. Roman god of marriage, wearing a yellow ("saffron") robe.

7. A low-heeled slipper, worn by actors in classical comedy, and often contrasted with the buskin (high-heeled boot) appropriate to tragedy. The contrast of Jonson as a "learned" poet with Shakespeare as a "natural" one was conventional.

And ever against eating cares[8]
Lap me in soft Lydian airs,[9]
Married to immortal verse
Such as the meeting soul may pierce
In notes, with many a winding bout[1]
Of linkéd sweetness long drawn out,
With wanton heed, and giddy cunning,
The melting voice through mazes running;
Untwisting all the chains that tie
The hidden soul of harmony;
That Orpheus' self[2] may heave his head
From golden slumber on a bed
Of heaped Elysian flowers, and hear
Such strains as would have won the ear
Of Pluto, to have quite set free
His half-regained Eurydice.
These delights if thou canst give,
Mirth, with thee I mean to live.

ca. 1631 1645

Il Penseroso

Hence vain deluding Joys,
  The brood of Folly without father bred.
How little you bestead,[3]
  Or fill the fixéd mind with all your toys;[4]
Dwell in some idle brain,
  And fancies fond[5] with gaudy shapes possess,
As thick and numberless
  As the gay motes that people the sunbeams,
Or likest hovering dreams,
  The fickle pensioners[6] of Morpheus' train.
But hail thou Goddess, sage and holy,
Hail, divinest Melancholy,
Whose saintly visage is too bright
To hit[7] the sense of human sight;
And therefore to our weaker view,
O'erlaid with black, staid Wisdom's hue.
Black, but such as in esteem,

8. "Eating cares" is but one of many classical phrases in the poem; it is from Horace, *Odes* II.xi.18 (*curas edaces*).
9. "Lydian" airs in music would be soft, languishing, sensual—unlike the chaste Dorian and brisk Ionian.
1. A musical "run" passage.
2. Orpheus went to the underworld to regain his wife Eurydice, and by his music dissolved the guardians of Hades in tears. But as they left, he violated the condition of her release by looking back at her, and so lost her again. Milton uses the Orpheus story again in *Il Penseroso*, *Lycidas*, and *Paradise Lost* VII.32 ff.
3. Avail, help.
4. Trifles.
5. Foolish.
6. Followers. Morpheus is the god of sleep; the melancholy man feels the cheerful man lives in a dream.
7. Suit, agree with.

Prince Memnon's sister[8] might beseem,
Or that starred Ethiope queen[9] that strove
To set her beauty's praise above
The sea nymphs, and their powers offended.
Yet thou art higher far descended;
Thee bright-haired Vesta long of yore
To solitary Saturn bore;[1]
His daughter she (in Saturn's reign
Such mixture was not held a stain).
Oft in glimmering bowers and glades
He met her, and in secret shades
Of woody Ida's inmost grove,
While yet there was no fear of Jove.
Come pensive nun, devout and pure,
Sober, steadfast, and demure,
All in a robe of darkest grain,[2]
Flowing with majestic train,
And sable stole of cypress lawn[3]
Over thy decent shoulders drawn.
Come, but keep thy wonted state,
With even step and musing gait,
And looks commercing with the skies,
Thy rapt soul sitting in thine eyes:
There held in holy passion still,
Forget thyself to marble, till
With a sad leaden downward cast,
Thou fix them on the earth as fast.
And join with thee calm Peace and Quiet,
Spare Fast, that oft with gods doth dict,
And hears the Muses in a ring
Aye round about Jove's altar sing.
And add to these retired Leisure,
That in trim gardens takes his pleasure;
But first, and chiefest, with thee bring,
Him that yon soars on golden wing,
Guiding the fiery-wheeléd throne,
The cherub Contemplation;[4]
And the mute Silence hist along

8. Memnon in *Odyssey* XI was a handsome Ethiopian prince who fought for Troy; his sister, mentioned not by Homer but by later commentators, was Hemera.

9. Cassiopeia, who was "starred" (i.e., turned into a constellation) for bragging that her daughter Andromeda or she herself (Milton follows this second version) was more beautiful than the sea nymphs.

1. Vesta was a goddess of purity; Milton invented the story of her connection with Saturn on Mt. Ida in Crete, and of her giving birth to Melancholy. But Saturn helps out the poem because he was a primitive deity (hence melancholy is "natural") and because a saturnine complexion is said to show a dark and melancholy disposition.

2. Color.

3. "Cypress": a dark, delicate cloth (originally Cyprus, from the island; but the cypress is also the tree of death). "Lawn": a transparent, gauzy material, much like crape. "Decent": comely, proper.

4. The cherub Contemplation is suggested by the Biblical vision of Ezekiel.

'Less Philomel[5] will deign a song,
In her sweetest, saddest plight,
Smoothing the rugged brow of night,
While Cynthia[6] checks her dragon yoke
Gently o'er th' accustomed oak;
Sweet bird that shunn'st the noise of folly,
Most musical, most melancholy!
Thee chantress oft the woods among,
I woo to hear thy evensong;
And missing thee, I walk unseen
On the dry smooth-shaven green,
To behold the wandering moon,
Riding near her highest noon,
Like one that had been led astray
Through the Heaven's wide pathless way;
And oft as if her head she bowed,
Stooping through a fleecy cloud.
Oft on a plat[7] of rising ground,
I hear the far-off curfew sound,
Over some wide-watered shore,
Swinging slow with sullen roar;
Or if the air will not permit,
Some still removéd place will fit,
Where glowing embers through the room
Teach light to counterfeit a gloom
Far from all resort of mirth,
Save the cricket on the hearth,
Or the bellman's[8] drowsy charm,
To bless the doors from nightly harm;
Or let my lamp at midnight hour
Be seen in some high lonely tower,
Where I may oft outwatch the Bear,[9]
With thrice great Hermes,[1] or unsphere
The spirit of Plato to unfold
What worlds, or what vast regions hold
The immortal mind that hath forsook
Her mansion in this fleshly nook;
And of those demons[2] that are found
In fire, air, flood, or underground,
Whose power hath a true consent[3]
With planet, or with element.

5. The nightingale, whose song is traditionally one of grief. "Hist": summon.
6. Goddess of the moon, and of the underworld as well, she drives a pair of sleepless dragons.
7. Plot, flat open space.
8. The night watchman in little villages rang a bell to call the hours.
9. Since the Great Bear never sets, outwatching it is a major enterprise.
1. The Egyptian god Thoth or Hermes, to whom were attributed various esoteric books of the 3rd and 4th centuries A.D.; under the name of Hermes Trismegistus he later became a patron of magicians and alchemists. To "unsphere" Plato is to call Plato by magical means back to earth from the sphere he now inhabits.
2. Not devils, but classical beings akin to heroes, halfway between gods and men. There were four sorts of demons, corresponding to the four elements, each with a corresponding planet.
3. Mysterious agreement.

Some time let gorgeous Tragedy
In sceptered pall[4] come sweeping by,
Presenting Thebes', or Pelops' line,
Or the tale of Troy divine.[5]
Or what (though rare) of later age
Ennobled hath the buskined[6] stage.
But, O sad virgin, that thy power
Might raise Musaeus[7] from his bower,
Or bid the soul of Orpheus[8] sing
Such notes as, warbled to the string,
Drew iron tears down Pluto's cheek,
And made Hell grant what Love did seek.
Or call up him[9] that left half told
The story of Cambuscan bold,
Of Camball, and of Algarsife,
And who had Canacee to wife,
That owned the virtuous[1] ring and glass,
And of the wondrous horse of brass,
On which the Tartar king did ride;
And if aught else great bards beside
In sage and solemn tunes have sung,
Of tourneys and of trophies hung,
Of forests and enchantments drear,
Where more is meant than meets the ear.[2]
Thus, Night, oft see me in thy pale career,
Till civil-suited morn appear,[3]
Not tricked and frounced as she was wont,
With the Attic boy to hunt,
But kerchiefed in a comely cloud,
While rocking winds are piping loud,
Or ushered with a shower still,
When the gust hath blown his fill,
Ending on the rustling leaves,
With minute-drops from off the eaves.
And when the sun begins to fling
His flaring beams, me, Goddess, bring
To archéd walks of twilight groves,
And shadows brown that Sylvan[4] loves
Of pine or monumental oak,
Where the rude ax with heavéd stroke,
Was never heard the nymphs to daunt,

4. Royal robe (from Latin *palla*, the robe of tragic actors).
5. Tragedies about the royal line of Thebes would include Sophocles' Oedipus cycle; those about the line of Pelops, Aeschylus' *Oresteia;* and those about Troy, Euripides' *Trojan Women*.
6. The buskin of tragedy, contrasted with the sock of comedy.
7. A mythical poet-priest of the pre-Homeric age, supposedly son or pupil of the equally mythical Orpheus.
8. For the story of Orpheus, see *L'Allegro*, line 145, and note.
9. I.e., Chaucer, who in the Squire's Tale left the tale of Cambuscan half told.
1. Having special power.
2. A capsule description of allegory.
3. The goddess Aurora, who once fell in love with Cephalus ("the Attic boy," line 124), and used to go hunting with him. "Tricked and frounced": adorned and frizzled.
4. Roman god of the woodlands.

Or fright them from their hallowed haunt.
There in close covert by some brook,
Where no profaner eye may look,
Hide me from day's garish eye,
While the bee with honeyed thigh,
That at her flowery work doth sing,
And the waters murmuring
With such consort[5] as they keep,
Entice the dewy-feathered sleep;
And let some strange mysterious dream,
Wave at his wings in airy stream,
Of lively portraiture displayed,
Softly on my eyelids laid.[6]
And as I wake, sweet music breathe
Above, about, or underneath,
Sent by some spirit to mortals good,
Or th' unseen genius[7] of the wood.
But let my due feet never fail
To walk the studious cloister's pale,[8]
And love the high embowéd roof,
With antic[9] pillars massy proof,
And storied windows[1] richly dight,
Casting a dim religious light.
There let the pealing organ blow,
To the full-voiced choir below,
In service high, and anthems clear,
As may with sweetness, through mine ear,
Dissolve me into ecstasies,
And bring all heaven before mine eyes.
And may at last my weary age
Find out the peaceful hermitage,
The hairy gown and mossy cell,
Where I may sit and rightly spell[2]
Of every star that Heaven doth show,
And every herb that sips the dew
Till old experience do attain
To something like prophetic strain.
These pleasures, Melancholy, give,
And I with thee will choose to live.

ca. 1631 1645

5. Accompaniment.
6. Milton's syntax gets loose and dreamy too, here. He means, "Let some strange dream wave at the wings of sleep, while a stream of vivid pictures passes softly over my eyelids."
7. Guardian angel.
8. Enclosure.
9. I.e., covered with quaint, grotesque, or antic carvings; but "antique," which derives from the same Latin root, was not excluded from the sense. "Massy proof": massive and strong.
1. I.e., with stories told by stained-glass images. "Dight": dressed.
2. Study. The melancholy man wants to think his way into the cosmos until he becomes a prophet.

Lycidas This poem is a pastoral elegy; that is, it uses the sometimes artificial imagery supplied by an idyllic shepherd's existence to bewail the loss of a friend. Among its many predecessors in the Renaissance and in classical antiquity are poems by Spenser, Ronsard, Castiglione, Mantuan, Petrarch, Virgil, Theocritus, Moschus, and Bion; its successors include poems like *Adonais* by Shelley and *Thyrsis* by Matthew Arnold. T. P. Harrison and H. J. Leon have collected in *The Pastoral Elegy* (1939) a selection of poems from the tradition.

All pastoral poems enjoy the privilege of saying something about the world as a whole while seeming to talk simply of an artificial play-society; they are irresistibly allegorical. They have certain conventions—the swain (i.e., the shepherd) is ignorant but unspoiled, naturally virtuous, inherently poetic; life is pleasant and easy, yet just for this reason the basic human preoccupations stand out. The pastoral elegy has a further list of conventions—a history of past friendship, a questioning of destiny, a procession of mourners, a laying-on of flowers, a consolation, and usually a refrain. Milton adapted all but the last of these to *Lycidas*.

Edward King, who was the occasion of the poem if not its subject, was a fellow student of Milton's at Cambridge. Milton says he was a poet, and he was in the church. While proceeding to his new parish in Ireland, he was drowned, in 1637; and Milton joined with his schoolfellows, the following year, to produce a little memorial volume. *Justa Edouardo King* includes 35 poems, mostly in Latin; only *Lycidas* is of literary consequence.

It is written in a flowing, extended manner, with many run-on lines and great impetus, predominantly in pentameter, but with many variations of line length, and an irregular rhyme scheme including ten unrhymed lines and two perfectly formed stanzas of ottava rima. Many of these technical qualities are reminiscent of the Italian *canzone* or song, but most of them had been exemplified previously in Spenser's *Epithalamion*.

There are usually taken to be three explicit climaxes in *Lycidas*, each having to do with an aspect of the shepherd's life and with a problem which Milton wished to pose regarding the meaning of existence. Apollo answers his first question about the reward of poetry; St. Peter answers a second question, about the spiritual shepherd who betrays his flock; and finally Lycidas is translated into the Christian Paradise, to be at one with the Lamb of God, the Good Shepherd, the supreme giver of poetic fame, and the proper subject of all song. Subordinate patterns of imagery include vegetation and nature deities, water and water gods, who serve an immense variety of purposes.

Lycidas

IN THIS MONODY[1] THE AUTHOR BEWAILS A LEARNED FRIEND, UNFORTUNATELY DROWNED IN HIS PASSAGE FROM CHESTER ON THE IRISH SEAS, 1637. AND BY OCCASION FORETELLS THE RUIN OF OUR CORRUPTED CLERGY, THEN IN THEIR HEIGHT.

Yet once more, O ye laurels, and once more
Ye myrtles brown, with ivy never sere,[2]
I come to pluck your berries harsh and crude,[3]
And with forced fingers rude,
Shatter your leaves before the mellowing year.
Bitter constraint, and sad occasion dear,[4]
Compels me to disturb your season due;
For Lycidas is dead, dead ere his prime,
Young Lycidas, and hath not left his peer.
Who would not sing for Lycidas? He knew
Himself to sing, and build the lofty rhyme.
He must not float upon his watery bier
Unwept, and welter to the parching wind,
Without the meed[5] of some melodious tear.
Begin then, sisters of the sacred well[6]
That from beneath the seat of Jove doth spring,
Begin, and somewhat loudly sweep the string.
Hence with denial vain, and coy excuse;
So may some gentle Muse
With lucky words favor my destined urn,[7]
And as he passes turn,
And bid fair peace be to my sable shroud.
For we were nursed upon the selfsame hill,
Fed the same flock, by fountain, shade, and rill.
Together both, ere the high lawns[8] appeared
Under the opening eyelids of the morn,
We drove afield, and both together heard
What time the grayfly winds her sultry horn,[9]
Battening our flocks with the fresh dews of night,
Oft till the star that rose at evening bright

1. A song sung in Greek drama by a single voice. This Miltonic headnote was added in the edition of 1645.
2. "Laurels" for the crown of poetry given by Apollo; "myrtles" for the undying love granted by Venus; "ivy," the plant of Bacchus, also the reward of learning. All three plants are evergreens associated with poetic inspiration.
3. Unripe.
4. Heartfelt, profoundly moving; but also, in the 17th century, with overtones of "dire."
5. Reward.
6. The nine sister Muses were reported to dwell by various springs or "wells"; most likely Milton had in mind that of Aganippe near Mt. Helicon.
7. The speaker suggests that if he sings for Lycidas, "some gentle Muse" (i.e., poet) may some day sing for him.
8. Upland pastures.
9. I.e., heard the grayfly when she buzzes ("winds her sultry horn"). "Battening": feeding.

Toward Heaven's descent had sloped his westering wheel.
Meanwhile the rural ditties were not mute,
Tempered to th' oaten flute,[1]
Rough satyrs danced, and fauns with cloven heel
From the glad sound would not be absent long,
And old Damoetas[2] loved to hear our song.
But O the heavy change, now thou art gone,
Now thou art gone, and never must return!
Thee, shepherd, thee the woods and desert caves,
With wild thyme and the gadding[3] vine o'ergrown,
And all their echoes mourn.
The willows and the hazel copses green
Shall now no more be seen,
Fanning their joyous leaves to thy soft lays.
As killing as the canker[4] to the rose,
Or taint-worm to the weanling herds that graze,
Or frost to flowers that their gay wardrobe wear,
When first the white thorn blows;[5]
Such, Lycidas, thy loss to shepherd's ear.
Where were ye, nymphs,[6] when the remorseless deep
Closed o'er the head of your loved Lycidas?
For neither were ye playing on the steep,
Where your old Bards, the famous Druids[7] lie,
Nor on the shaggy top of Mona high,[8]
Nor yet where Deva spreads her wizard stream:
Ay me! I fondly dream—
Had ye been there—for what could that have done?
What could the Muse[9] herself that Orpheus bore,
The Muse herself, for her inchanting[1] son
Whom universal Nature did lament,
When by the rout[2] that made the hideous roar,
His gory visage down the stream was sent,
Down the swift Hebrus to the Lesbian shore?
Alas! What boots[3] it with incessant care
To tend the homely slighted shepherd's trade,
And strictly meditate the thankless Muse?[4]

1. Traditional Panpipes, played by shepherds.
2. A type name from pastoral poetry, possibly referring to some specific tutor at Cambridge.
3. Straggling.
4. Cankerworm.
5. Blossoms (as in the surviving expression, "full-blown").
6. Nature deities.
7. The Druids, priestly poet-kings of Celtic Britain, worshiped the forces of nature. They lie dead in their burying ground on the mountain ("steep") Kerig-y-Druidion in Wales.
8. "Mona" is the island of Anglesey. "Deva" is the river Dee in Cheshire. The Dee was magic ("wizard") because the size and position of its shifting stream foretold prosperity or dearth for the land. All the places mentioned in lines 52–55 are in the West Country, near where King drowned.
9. Calliope, Muse of epic poetry, was the mother of Orpheus.
1. "Inchanting" implies both song and magic; the root word survives as "incantation."
2. Orpheus was torn to pieces by a mob ("rout") of screaming Thracian women, who threw his gory head into the river Hebrus, down which it floated, still singing, and out to Lesbos in the Aegean. The fate of Orpheus and the Druids suggests that nature everywhere is indifferent to the destruction of the poet.
3. Profits.
4. Study to write poetry (the phrase is Virgil's).

Were it not better done as others use,
To sport with Amaryllis in the shade,
Or with the tangles of Neaera's hair?[5]
Fame is the spur that the clear spirit doth raise
(That last infirmity of noble mind)
To scorn delights, and live laborious days;
But the fair guerdon[6] when we hope to find,
And think to burst out into sudden blaze,
Comes the blind Fury[7] with th' abhorréd shears,
And slits the thin spun life. "But not the praise,"
Phoebus[8] replied, and touched my trembling ears;
"Fame is no plant that grows on mortal soil,
Not in the glistering foil[9]
Set off to th' world, nor in broad rumor lies,
But lives and spreads aloft by those pure eyes,
And perfect witness of all-judging Jove;
As he pronounces lastly on each deed,
Of so much fame in Heaven expect thy meed."
O fountain Arethuse,[1] and thou honored flood,
Smooth-sliding Mincius, crowned with vocal reeds,
That strain I heard was of a higher mood.
But now my oat[2] proceeds,
And listens to the herald of the sea[3]
That came in Neptune's plea.
He asked the waves, and asked the felon winds,
"What hard mishap hath doomed this gentle swain?"
And questioned every gust of rugged wings
That blows from off each beakéd promontory;
They knew not of his story,
And sage Hippotades[4] their answer brings,
That not a blast was from his dungeon strayed,
The air was calm, and on the level brine,
Sleek Panope[5] with all her sisters played.
It was that fatal and perfidious bark
Built in th' eclipse,[6] and rigged with curses dark,

5. "Amaryllis" and "Neaera," conventional names for pretty nymphs, a passing hour's diversion for idle shepherds.
6. Reward.
7. Atropos, one of the three Fates, bearing scissors with which she cuts the thread of human life. Milton, to suggest the bitterness of death, makes her an avenging Fury.
8. Phoebus Apollo, god of poetic inspiration. Touching the ears of one's hearers was a traditional Roman way of asking them to remember something that had been said (Virgil, *Eclogues* VI; Horace, *Satires* I.ix.77).
9. Cheap, flashy metal, used to add glitter to glass gems.
1. Arethusa was a fountain in Sicily, Mincius a river in Lombardy, the former associated with the pastorals of Theocritus, the latter with those of Virgil. Arethusa was originally a nymph who went bathing in the river Alpheus, in Arcadian Greece. The river god grew enamored, and gave chase; she dove into the ocean and fled undersea to Sicily, where she came up as a fountain. Milton plays here with the idea of his pastoral going underground while the "strain of a higher mood" (line 87) is heard.
2. Pipe, hence song.
3. Neptune's "herald" is Triton, pleading his master's innocence in the death of Lycidas.
4. Aeolus, god of winds, and son of Hippotas.
5. The chief Nereid or sea nymph.
6. I.e., time of the worst possible luck.

That sunk so low that sacred head of thine.
Next Camus,[7] reverend sire, went footing slow,
His mantle hairy, and his bonnet sedge,
Inwrought with figures dim, and on the edge
Like to that sanguine flower inscribed with woe.[8]
"Ah! who hath reft," quoth he, "my dearest pledge?"
Last came and last did go
The pilot of the Galilean lake,[9]
Two massy keys he bore of metals twain
(The golden opes, the iron shuts amain[1]).
He shook his mitered locks,[2] and stern bespake:
"How well could I have spared for thee, young swain,
Enow[3] of such as for their bellies' sake,
Creep and intrude, and climb into the fold!
Of other care they little reckoning make,
Than how to scramble at the shearers' feast,
And shove away the worthy bidden guest.
Blind mouths![4] That scarce themselves know how to hold
A sheep-hook,[5] or have learned aught else the least
That to the faithful herdsman's art belongs!
What recks it them?[6] What need they? They are sped;
And when they list,[7] their lean and flashy songs
Grate on their scrannel[8] pipes of wretched straw.
The hungry sheep look up, and are not fed,
But swoln with wind, and the rank mist they draw,
Rot inwardly, and foul contagion spread,
Besides what the grim wolf with privy paw[9]
Daily devours apace, and nothing said.
But that two-handed engine at the door[1]
Stands ready to smite once, and smite no more."
Return, Alpheus,[2] the dread voice is past,
That shrunk thy streams; return, Sicilian muse,

7. God of the river Cam (properly, Granta), representing the ancient University of Cambridge, but slow and shaggy like the stream.
8. The bonnet and mantle of Camus have marks of woe on the edge like the *AI AI* supposedly found on the hyacinth, a "sanguine flower" sprung from the blood of a youth killed accidentally by Apollo.
9. St. Peter, originally a fisherman on Lake Tiberias in Galilee, was first founder and bishop of the Christian church; his keys open and shut the gates to heaven.
1. Literally "in full force," "exceedingly"; in this context, "for good," "once and for all."
2. He wears the bishop's miter.
3. An old plural form of "enough," used here with contemptuous intensification, as if to say, "enough and more than enough."
4. This audacious metaphor, as of tapeworms, takes on new depth when one notes that the word *episcopus* (bishop) originally meant "over-seer" and a "pastor" is properly one who feeds his flock.
5. The bishop's staff, or crozier, is made in the form of a shepherd's crook.
6. What do they care? "They are sped": i.e., they have prospered in a worldly sense; but also, "their doom is sealed."
7. Choose (that is, choose to play on their pipes, as shepherds should); but with the secondary meaning of "listen."
8. Harsh, meager. Milton's is the first recorded literary use of the word in English; it existed previously only in a North-Country dialect.
9. I.e., Roman Catholicism, whose agents operated in secret.
1. Many guesses as to the specific meaning of the "two-handed engine" are on record; it may be St. Peter's keys, the two houses of Parliament, or a big sword, but there is no harm in letting it remain an indistinct, apocalyptic instrument of revenge.
2. With the return of Alpheus, the pastoral mode of the poem revives (see

And call the vales, and bid them hither cast
Their bells and flowerets of a thousand hues.
Ye valleys low where the mild whispers use,[3]
Of shades and wanton winds, and gushing brooks,
On whose fresh lap the swart star[4] sparely looks,
Throw hither all your quaint enameled eyes,
That on the green turf suck the honeyed showers,
And purple all the ground with vernal flowers.
Bring the rathe[5] primrose that forsaken dies.
The tufted crow-toe, and pale jessamine,
The white pink, and the pansy freaked[6] with jet,
The glowing violet,
The musk-rose, and the well attired woodbine.
With cowslips wan that hang the pensive head,
And every flower that sad embroidery wears:
Bid amaranthus[7] all his beauty shed,
And daffadillies fill their cups with tears,
To strew the laureate hearse[8] where Lycid lies.
For so to interpose a little ease,
Let our frail thoughts dally with false surmise.[9]
Ay me! Whilst thee the shores and sounding seas
Wash far away, where'er thy bones are hurled,
Whether beyond the stormy Hebrides,[1]
Where thou perhaps under the whelming tide
Visit'st the bottom of the monstrous world;
Or whether thou, to our moist vows denied,
Sleep'st by the fable of Bellerus old,[2]
Where the great vision of the guarded mount
Looks toward Namancos and Bayona's hold;[3]
Look homeward angel now, and melt with ruth:[4]
And, O ye dolphins,[5] waft the hapless youth.
   Weep no more, woeful shepherds, weep no more,
For Lycidas your sorrow is not dead,

above, lines 85–87), and a catalogue of flowers serves, as in Castiglione's *Alcon,* to "interpose a little ease."

3. I.e., are used or accustomed to be heard.

4. The Dog Star, Sirius, which during the heats of late summer "looks sparely" (witheringly) on the vegetation.

5. Early.

6. Flecked (the early verb survives in our word "freckle").

7. The amaranth is an imaginary flower that never fades; but for Lycidas it will.

8. Bier decked with laurels (see line 1).

9. The "false surmise" is that the body of Lycidas has been recovered and can receive Christian burial.

1. Islands off the coast of Scotland, representing the northern terminus of the Irish Sea.

2. The fabulous giant Bellerus is supposed to lie buried on Land's End in Cornwall.

3. St. Michael's Mount, in Cornwall, from which the archangel is envisioned as looking south, over miles of open Atlantic, across the Bay of Biscay, to Bayona and the stronghold of Namancos in northern Spain, where the historical Catholic enemy of Protestant England lay entrenched.

4. Michael is implored to look homeward, relaxing his stern guard for a moment of grief and pity ("ruth").

5. Dolphins, admirable sea beasts, brought the Greek poet Arion safely ashore for love of his verses, and also wafted the dead body of Melicertes to land, where he was promptly transformed to a sea god, Palaemon.

Sunk though he be beneath the watery floor,
So sinks the day-star[6] in the ocean bed,
And yet anon repairs his drooping head,
And tricks[7] his beams, and with new-spangled ore,
Flames in the forehead of the morning sky:
So Lycidas sunk low, but mounted high,
Through the dear might of him that walked the waves,
Where other groves, and other streams along,
With nectar pure his oozy locks he laves,
And hears the unexpressive nuptial song,[8]
In the blest kingdoms meek of joy and love.
There entertain him all the saints above,
In solemn troops and sweet societies
That sing, and singing in their glory move,
And wipe the tears forever from his eyes.
Now, Lycidas, the shepherds weep no more;
Henceforth thou art the genius[9] of the shore,
In thy large recompense, and shalt be good
To all that wander in that perilous flood.
Thus sang the uncouth swain[1] to th' oaks and rills,
While the still morn went out with sandals gray;
He touched the tender stops of various quills,[2]
With eager thought warbling his Doric[3] lay:
And now the sun had stretched out all the hills,
And now was dropped into the western bay;
At last he rose, and twitched his mantle blue:
Tomorrow to fresh woods, and pastures new.

1637

How Soon Hath Time

How soon hath Time, the subtle thief of youth,
Stoln on his wing my three and twentieth year!
My hasting days fly on with full career,
But my late spring no bud or blossom show'th.
Perhaps my semblance might deceive the truth,
That I to manhood am arrived so near,
And inward ripeness doth much less appear,
That some more timely-happy spirits endu'th.[1]

6. The sun.
7. Dresses.
8. Inexpressible hymn of joy, sung at "the marriage supper of the Lamb" (Revelation xix).
9. One who by divine appointment haunts a locality (in this case, "the shore") where he suffered and died, protecting others who might undergo a fate like his own.
1. Unlettered shepherd (a stock convention of this supremely literary form).
2. The oaten stalks of Panpipes.
3. Rustic, simple.
1. Endoweth.

Yet be it less or more, or soon or slow,
It shall be still in strictest measure even[2]
To that same lot, however mean or high,
Toward which Time leads me, and the will of Heaven;
All is, if I have grace to use it so,
As ever in my great Taskmaster's eye.[3]

1631 1645

On the New Forcers of Conscience Under the Long Parliament[1]

Because you have thrown off your prelate lord,[2]
And with stiff vows renounced his liturgy,
To seize the widowed whore Plurality[3]
From them whose sin ye envied, not abhorred,
Dare ye for this adjure the civil sword
To force our consciences that Christ set free,
And ride us with a classic hierarchy[4]
Taught ye by mere A. S. and Rutherford?[5]
Men whose life, learning, faith, and pure intent
Would have been held in high esteem with Paul
Must now be named and printed heretics
By shallow Edwards and Scotch what d'ye call:[6]
But we do hope to find out all your tricks,
Your plots and packing worse than those of Trent,[7]
That so the Parliament
May with their wholesome and preventive shears
Clip your phylacteries,[8] though balk your ears,

2. Equal, adequate. Whenever it appears and however much it amounts to, Milton's inner growth will be adequate to the destiny which time and heaven are preparing.
3. The last two lines are enigmatic; their sense depends on whether one reads the "all" of line 13 as referring to time or talent.
1. "The new forcers of conscience" are Presbyterians, whom Milton at first supported against the Episcopalians (Church-of-England men). Now, under the Puritan-dominated Long Parliament, he finds them as bad as their predecessors ("whose sin ye envied, not abhorred"). The sonnet proper has 14 lines followed by two "tails" of three lines each; in Italy, where it was common, this was called a *sonnetto caudato*, or "tailed sonnet."
2. Bishop.
3. I.e., the comfortable, and sometimes necessary, practice of one priest's holding several livings at once.
4. A church discipline made up on the Presbyterian model of synods or classes, ecclesiastical governing boards with strong powers over the laity.
5. Adam Stuart and Samuel Rutherford, Presbyterian pamphleteers, whose full names Milton does not deign to give.
6. Thomas Edwards, alarmed by the spread of heresies, began to describe them in a book picturesquely titled *Gangraena* (1645–46). Before giving up in despair, he wrote three fat volumes, including a denunciation of Milton, whom he described unjustly as an advocate of "divorce at pleasure." "Scotch what d'ye call" is Milton's humanistic sneer at the unpronounceability of Scottish names.
7. I.e., of the Council of Trent, held by the Papacy in consequence of the Reformation; it was widely reported to have been the scene of political jockeying.
8. Little scrolls, containing texts from the Pentateuch, worn by orthodox Jews to remind them of the Law. Milton uses them here as symbols of superstition. Mutilation by having one's ears cut

And succor our just fears
When they shall read this clearly in your charge:
New presbyter is but *old priest* writ large.

ca. 1646 1673

On the Late Massacre in Piedmont[1]

Avenge, O Lord, thy slaughtered saints, whose bones
Lie scattered on the Alpine mountains cold,
Even them who kept thy truth so pure of old
When all our fathers worshiped stocks and stones,
Forget not: in thy book record their groans
Who were thy sheep and in their ancient fold
Slain by the bloody Piemontese that rolled
Mother with infant down the rocks. Their moans
The vales redoubled to the hills, and they
To Heaven. Their martyred blood and ashes sow
O'er all th' Italian fields where still doth sway
The triple tyrant:[2] that from these may grow
A hundredfold, who having learnt thy way
Early may fly the Babylonian woe.[3]

1655 1673

When I Consider How My Light Is Spent[1]

When I consider how my light is spent
Ere half my days, in this dark world and wide,
And that one talent which is death to hide,
Lodged with me useless, though my soul more bent
To serve therewith my Maker, and present
My true account, lest he returning chide;
"Doth God exact day-labor, light denied?"
I fondly[2] ask; but Patience to prevent

---

off was a common punishment for sedition, and several Presbyterian leaders had suffered it. Milton's MS. read, "Clip ye as close as marginal P——'s ears," but the jeer was too brutal. William Prynne, whose books had many footnotes in the margins, and whose ears had twice been cropped, had suffered for a cause in which Milton at the time believed; and his final version of the line is gentler.

1. The Waldenses were a heretical sect, probably of Eastern origin by way of Venice: they lived in the valleys of northern Italy ("the Piedmont") and southern France, professing a creed which was particularly akin to Protestantism in its avoidance of graven images ("stocks and stones"). The understanding which had allowed them freedom of worship was terminated in 1655, and the massacre which ensued was widely protested by the Protestant powers of Europe. Milton, as Latin secretary to Cromwell, wrote several indignant letters.

2. I.e., the Pope, wearing his tiara with three crowns.

3. Protestants in Milton's day frequently identified the Roman Church with the "whore of Babylon" (Revelation xvii, xviii).

1. Milton's sonnet on his blindness is very close, in theme, to that on his 23rd birthday. But the absolute repose of the latter sonnet's final line is beyond anything in the earlier one.

2. Foolishly. "Prevent": forestall.

That murmur, soon replies, "God doth not need
Either man's work or his own gifts; who best
Bear his mild yoke, they serve him best. His state
Is kingly. Thousands at his bidding speed
And post o'er land and ocean without rest:
They also serve who only stand and wait."

1655 1673

Methought I Saw My Late Espouséd Saint

Methought I saw my late espouséd saint
Brought to me like Alcestis[1] from the grave,
Whom Jove's great son to her glad husband gave,
Rescued from death by force though pale and faint.
Mine, as whom washed from spot of childbed taint,
Purification in the old law did save,[2]
And such, as yet once more I trust to have
Full sight of her in Heaven without restraint,
Came vested all in white, pure as her mind.
Her face was veiled, yet to my fancied sight,
Love, sweetness, goodness, in her person shined
So clear, as in no face with more delight.
But O, as to embrace me she inclined,
I waked, she fled, and day brought back my night.

1658 1673

To My Friend, Mr. Henry Lawes, on His Airs[1]

Harry, whose tuneful and well measur'd song
First taught our English music how to span
Words with just note and accent, not to scan
With Midas' ears,[2] committing short and long,
Thy worth and skill exempts thee from the throng,
With praise enough for envy to look wan;
To after age thou shalt be writ the man
That with smooth air couldst humor best our tongue.
Thou honor'st verse, and verse must lend her wing
To honor thee, the priest of Phoebus' choir[3]

1. Alcestis, wife of Admetus, was rescued from the underworld by Hercules ("Jove's great son").
2. The old law, prescribing periods for the purification of women after childbirth, is found in Leviticus xii. The compression of line 5 is perhaps extreme; expanded, it would read, "My wife, like the woman whom when washed from spot of childbed taint," etc.

1. Henry Lawes, who composed the original music for Milton's *Comus*, was a real innovator in the art of setting poems to music; he brought the two elements into closer harmony than anyone had achieved before.
2. Ovid tells, in *Metamorphoses* XI, how Midas was given ass's ears because he preferred Pan's pipes to the music of Apollo. "Committing": confusing, setting into conflict with one another.
3. The choir of Phoebus consists of the muses.

That tun'st their happiest lines in hymn, or story.
Dante shall give fame leave to set thee higher
Than his Casella,[4] whom he woo'd to sing,
Met in the milder shades of Purgatory.

1648

From Areopagitica[1]

* * * In Athens, where books and wits were ever busier than in any other part of Greece, I find but only two sorts of writings which the magistrate cared to take notice of: those either blasphemous and atheistical, or libelous. Thus the books of Protagoras were by the judges of Areopagus commanded to be burnt, and himself banished the territory for a discourse begun with his confessing not to know *whether there were gods, or whether not.*[2] And against defaming, it was decreed that none should be traduced by name, as was the manner of Vetus Comoedia,[3] whereby we may guess how they censured libeling: and this course was quick enough, as Cicero writes, to quell both the desperate wits of other atheists, and the open way of defaming, as the event showed. Of other sects and

4. Dante met Casella (*Purgatory* II) on the lower slopes of the mountain, and persuaded him to sing.

1. *Areopagitica* appeared on November 24, 1644. The title means "things to be said before the Areopagus." The Areopagus was an ancient, powerful, and much-respected tribunal in Athens, before which Isocrates, in 355 B.C., delivered a famous speech. Milton's title implies a comparison between the Areopagus and the English Parliament, and this comparison may be thought to validate, in some degree, the florid, oratorical tone of the tract.

Areopagitica is a plea for the liberty of unlicensed printing; its occasion was a severe ordinance for the control of printing which had been passed by Parliament on June 14, 1643. This ordinance, however disagreeable at the moment, was no striking novelty in English history. On the contrary, control of the press had been actively exercised by all the Tudors and both the early Stuarts. The aim of this government regulation was traditionally defined as the preservation of order and uniformity in church and state; but it also had an economic motive. Unlicensed printers threatened a monopoly enjoyed by the twenty licensed printers of London. Thus the censorship laws familiar to Englishmen had generally been strictly defined and had bristled with penalties. But to enforce them was another matter entirely. Tudor and Stuart police forces being what they were, few printers or authors had to worry about the consequences of going to print without a license. As a matter of fact, *Areopagitica* was itself unlicensed, Milton's third unlicensed pamphlet since the passage of the Ordinance for Printing only seventeen months before.

Thus the practical effects of the Ordinance for Printing were less important (particularly, we may be sure, in Milton's eyes) than the principle involved. Having taken the lead in destroying the licensing system of the Stuarts, Parliament was now setting up a censorship of its own. After a long prologue, Milton's first approach to his subject was to undertake a condensed history of censorship intended to discredit the institution by showing that only degenerate cultures ever made use of it.

2. It was in the 5th century B.C. that the sophist Protagoras of Abdera was censured in the manner described; Cicero wrote approvingly of this action in his treatise *On the Nature of the Gods* I.xxiii.

3. The "Old Comedy" of Aristophanes dealt with individuals, unlike the "New Comedy" of Menander, which dealt with types.

opinions, though tending to voluptuousness and the denying of Divine Providence, they took no heed. Therefore we do not read that either Epicurus, or that libertine school of Cyrene, or what the Cynic impudence uttered, was ever questioned by the laws.[4] Neither is it recorded that the writings of those old comedians were suppressed, though the acting of them were forbid; and that Plato commended the reading of Aristophanes, the loosest of them all, to his royal scholar Dionysius,[5] is commonly known, and may be excused, if holy Chrysostom, as is reported, nightly studied so much the same author and had the art to cleanse a scurrilous vehemence into the style of a rousing sermon.[6] * * *

And that the primitive councils and bishops were wont only to declare what books were not commendable, passing no further, but leaving it to each one's conscience to read or to lay by, till after the year 800, is observed already by Padre Paolo, the great unmasker of the Trentine Council.[7] After which time the Popes of Rome, engrossing what they pleased of political rule into their own hands, extended their dominion over men's eyes, as they had before over their judgments, burning and prohibiting to be read what they fancied not; yet sparing in their censures, and the books not many which they so dealt with: till Martin the Fifth, by his bull, not only prohibited, but was the first that excommunicated the reading of heretical books; for about that time Wycliffe and Huss[8] growing terrible, were they who first drove the papal court to a stricter policy of prohibiting. Which course Leo the Tenth and his successors followed, until the Council of Trent and the Spanish Inquisition engendering together brought forth, or perfected, those catalogues and expurging indexes,[9] that rake through the entrails of many an old good author with a violation worse than any could

4. Epicurus (4th and 3rd centuries B.C.) thought the gods had no influence on human affairs, but he did not deny their existence; therefore he was free of censorship. Aristippus of Cyrene, the pupil of Socrates, was like Epicurus in making pleasure the end of life. His school was known, from the Greek word for "pleasure," as the school of Hedonism; but, like Epicurus, he is misunderstood as a sensualist. Diogenes was the most famous of the Cynics, who often affected a rude and truculent disposition ("Cynic impudence"). All these philosophers flourished in and about the 4th century B.C.

5. That Plato told Dionysius, tyrant of Syracuse, to read Aristophanes is an ancient tradition. St. John Chrysostom, archbishop of Constantinople in the 4th century, is said to have hated the stage plays of his own day but profited from a constant perusal of Aristophanes.

6. After working his way through the various cities of Greece and the meager records of Roman censorship, Milton takes his readers to the ages of primitive Christianity, where he finds no positive censorship, merely an occasional recommendation of certain books to be read or not to be read.

7. Father Paolo Sarpi (d. 1623) was a Venetian historian who opposed papal claims to secular authority. His *History of the Council of Trent* was favorite reading matter for Protestants, since it described in graphic detail the "plots and packing" which went on behind the scenes of the Counter-Reformation. See Milton's sonnet *On the New Forcers of Conscience,* line 14.

8. John Wycliffe (d. 1384) was an English church reformer and translator of the Bible; John Huss (burned at the stake in 1415) was a Bohemian reformer of similar tendencies.

9. Literally from the Latin, *indices expurgatorii,* lists of books forbidden to Catholics.

be offered to his tomb.

Nor did they stay in matters heretical, but any subject that was not to their palate, they either condemned in a Prohibition, or had it straight into the new purgatory of an Index. To fill up the measure of encroachment, their last invention was to ordain that no book, pamphlet, or paper should be printed (as if St. Peter had bequeathed them the keys of the press also out of paradise) unless it were approved and licensed under the hands of two or three glutton friars. For example:[1]

Let the Chancellor Cini be pleased to see if in this present work be contained aught that may withstand the printing.

Vincent Rabatta, Vicar of Florence.

I have seen this present work, and find nothing athwart the Catholic faith and good manners: in witness whereof I have given, etc.

Nicolò Cini, Chancellor of Florence.

Attending the precedent relation, it is allowed that this present work of Davanzati may be printed.

Vincent Rabatta, etc.

It may be printed, July 15.

Friar Simon Mompei d'Amelia, Chancellor of the holy office in Florence.

Sure they have a conceit,[2] if he of the bottomless pit had not long since broke prison, that this quadruple exorcism would bar him down. I fear their next design will be to get into their custody the licensing of that which they say Claudius intended,[3] but went not through with. Vouchsafe to see another of their forms, the Roman stamp:

Imprimatur, If it seem good to the reverend master of the holy palace.

Belcastro, Vicegerent.

Imprimatur, Friar Nicolò Rodolphi, Master of the holy palace.

Sometimes five Imprimaturs are seen together dialogue-wise in the piazza of one title page, complimenting and ducking each to other with their shaven reverences, whether the author, who stands by in perplexity at the foot of his epistle, shall to the press or to the sponge.[4] These are the pretty responsories, these are the dear antiphonies, that so bewitched of late our prelates and their chaplains

1. Milton's examples come from a book on *The English Schism*, translated by Bernardo Davanzati from the original of an English Jesuit.
2. Notion.
3. The Roman historian Suetonius says that Claudius once planned to tax the act of breaking wind. Milton's note refers to this impractical scheme in the decent obscurity of a learned language.
4. I.e., the eraser. In the next sentence, "responsories" and "antiphonies" are ecclesiastical services after the pattern of a dialogue.

with the goodly echo they made; and besotted us to the gay imitation of a lordly Imprimatur, one from Lambeth House, another from the west end of Paul's;[5] so apishly Romanizing, that the word of command still was set down in Latin; as if the learned grammatical pen that wrote it would cast no ink without Latin; or perhaps, as they thought, because no vulgar tongue was worthy to express the pure conceit of an Imprimatur; but rather, as I hope, for that our English, the language of men ever famous and foremost in the achievements of liberty, will not easily find servile letters enow to spell such a dictatory presumption English.[6] * * *

Good and evil we know in the field of this world grow up together almost inseparably; and the knowledge of good is so involved and interwoven with the knowledge of evil, and in so many cunning resemblances hardly to be discerned, that those confused seeds which were imposed on Psyche as an incessant labor to cull out and sort asunder,[7] were not more intermixed. It was from out the rind of one apple tasted, that the knowledge of good and evil, as two twins cleaving together, leaped forth into the world. And perhaps this is that doom which Adam fell into of knowing good and evil, that is to say of knowing good by evil.

As therefore the state of man now is, what wisdom can there be to choose, what continence to forbear without the knowledge of evil? He that can apprehend and consider vice with all her baits and seeming pleasures, and yet abstain, and yet distinguish, and yet prefer that which is truly better, he is the true wayfaring[8] Christian. I cannot praise a fugitive and cloistered virtue, unexercised and unbreathed, that never sallies out and sees her adversary, but slinks out of the race where that immortal garland[9] is to be run for, not without dust and heat. Assuredly we bring not innocence into the world, we bring impurity much rather; that which purifies us is trial, and trial is by what is contrary. That virtue therefore which is but a youngling in the contemplation of evil, and knows not the utmost that vice promises to her followers, and rejects it, is but a blank virtue, not a pure; her whiteness is but an excremental[1] whiteness; which was the reason why our sage and serious poet Spenser (whom I dare be known to think a better teacher than Scotus or Aquinas),[2]

5. Lambeth House is the Archbishop of Canterbury's London home. "Paul's" is St. Paul's Cathedral, headquarters of the Bishop of London. Under the prerogative government of Charles, these were the two chief censors.
6. Having finished with the history of censorship, Milton proceeds to argue more generally that the institution itself is evil and unchristian. As God left man free to choose among the many physical foods of this world, urging only temperance, so he left him free to pick and choose among ideas.
7. Angry at her son Cupid's love for Psyche, Venus set Psyche to sorting out a vast mound of mixed seeds; but the ants took pity on her, and did the work. See Apuleius, *The Golden Ass*.
8. There has been debate whether this word should be read "wayfaring" or "warfaring," but in the image of Christian life as a pilgrimage, a crusade, the two ideas are united.
9. The crown of righteousness, the garland of virtue.
1. Exterior (like a whited sepulcher, covering corruption within).
2. Duns Scotus and Thomas Aquinas, taken as types of the Scholastic theo-

describing true temperance under the person of Guyon, brings him in with his palmer through the cave of Mammon and the bower of earthly bliss, that he might see and know, and yet abstain.

Since therefore the knowledge and survey of vice is in this world so necessary to the constituting of human virtue, and the scanning of error to the confirmation of truth, how can we more safely, and with less danger, scout into the regions of sin and falsity than by reading all manner of tractates and hearing all manner of reason? And this is the benefit which may be had of books promiscuously read.

But of the harm that may result hence, three kinds are usually reckoned. First, is feared the infection that may spread; but then all human learning and controversy in religious points must remove out of the world, yea, the Bible itself; for that ofttimes relates blasphemy not nicely,[3] it describes the carnal sense of wicked men not unelegantly, it brings in holiest men passionately murmuring against Providence through all the arguments of Epicurus:[4] in other great disputes it answers dubiously and darkly to the common reader: and ask a Talmudist what ails the modesty of his marginal Keri, that Moses and all the prophets cannot persuade him to pronounce the textual Chetiv.[5] For these causes we all know the Bible itself put by the papist into the first rank of prohibited books. The ancientest Fathers must be next removed, as Clement of Alexandria, and that Eusebian book of evangelic preparation, transmitting our ears through a hoard of heathenish obscenities to receive the Gospel.[6] Who finds not that Irenaeus, Epiphanius, Jerome, and others discover[7] more heresies than they well confute, and that oft for heresy which is the truer opinion?[8] * * *

Impunity and remissness, for certain, are the bane of a commonwealth; but here the great art lies, to discern in what the law is to bid restraint and punishment, and in what things persuasion only is to work. If every action which is good or evil in man at ripe years were to be under pittance[9] and prescription and compulsion, what were virtue but a name, what praise could be then due to

logian. The passage of Spenser referred to is *Faerie Queene* II.vii.

3. Daintily.

4. See the Book of Ecclesiastes.

5. "Keri" are the marginal comments of rabbinical scholars on the "Chetiv" of the Bible, the text itself. When the text was too free-spoken for later commentators, Keri was sometimes read in place of Chetiv.

6. Eusebius' *Preparatio Evangelica*, like many early Christian books of polemic, describes heathen wickedness in fascinating detail, as an encouragement to Christan faith. St. Irenaeus, St. Epiphanius, St. Jerome, and even that ancient and edifying convert, Clement of Alexandria, are all subject to this charge.

7. Describe (and so preserve, report).

8. Milton now argues that books cannot pervert men unless they are given force and vitality by a teacher, who, if he is a good teacher, needs no books. A fool, he urges, can find material for his folly in the best books, and a wise man material for his wisdom in the worst. Plato, indeed, recommended censorship in his *Republic;* but in real life one cannot censor books without censoring ballads, fiddlers, clothing, conversation, and social life as a whole.

9. Rationing.

well-doing, what gramercy[1] to be sober, just, or continent?

Many there be that complain of Divine Providence for suffering Adam to transgress; foolish tongues! when God gave him reason, he gave him freedom to choose, for reason is but choosing; he had been else a mere artificial Adam, such an Adam as he is in the motions.[2] We ourselves esteem not of that obedience, or love, or gift, which is of force: God therefore left him free, set before him a provoking object, ever almost in his eyes; herein consisted his merit, herein the right of his reward, the praise of his abstinence. Wherefore did he create passions within us, pleasures round about us, but that these rightly tempered are the very ingredients of virtue? They are not skillful considerers of human things, who imagine to remove sin by removing the matter of sin; for, besides that it is a huge heap increasing under the very act of diminishing, though some part of it may for a time be withdrawn from some persons, it cannot from all, in such a universal thing as books are; and when this is done, yet the sin remains entire. Though ye take from a covetous man all his treasure, he has yet one jewel left, ye cannot bereave him of his covetousness. Banish all objects of lust, shut up all youth into the severest discipline that can be exercised in any hermitage, ye cannot make them chaste that came not thither so: such great care and wisdom is required to the right managing of this point.

Suppose we could expel sin by this means; look how much we thus expel of sin, so much we expel of virtue: for the matter of them both is the same; remove that, and ye remove them both alike. This justifies the high providence of God, who, though he commands us temperance, justice, continence, yet pours out before us, even to a profuseness, all desirable things, and gives us minds that can wander beyond all limit and satiety. Why should we then affect a rigor contrary to the manner of God and of nature, by abridging or scanting those means, which books freely permitted are, both to the trial of virtue and the exercise of truth?[3] * * *

Well knows he who uses to consider, that our faith and knowledge thrives by exercise, as well as our limbs and complexion.[4] Truth is compared in Scripture to a streaming fountain; if her waters flow not in a perpetual progression, they sicken into a muddy pool of conformity and tradition. A man may be a heretic in the truth; and if he believe things only because his pastor says so, or the Assembly so determines, without knowing other reason, though his

1. Reward, thanks.
2. Puppet shows.
3. Censorship, Milton urges, is a vulgar, mechanical job; no man of intelligence will undertake it, and a dunderhead will make serious blunders. Finally, to put stupid men in authority over intelligent ones will discourage the pursuit of learning on every hand, except so far as censorship, by giving authority to banned books, will encourage men to seek out and cling to perverse opinions.
4. Constitution, regarded as the proper mingling of certain qualities in one's body.

belief be true, yet the very truth he holds becomes his heresy. There is not any burden that some would gladlier post off to another than the charge and care of their religion. There be, who knows not that there be, of Protestants and professors[5] who live and die in as arrant an implicit faith as any lay papist of Loretto.[6] A wealthy man, addicted to his pleasure and to his profits, finds religion to be a traffic so entangled, and of so many piddling accounts, that of all mysteries he cannot skill[7] to keep a stock going upon that trade. What should he do? Fain he would have the name to be religious, fain he would bear up with his neighbors in that. What does he therefore, but resolves to give over toiling, and to find himself out some factor,[8] to whose care and credit he may commit the whole managing of his religious affairs; some divine of note and estimation that must be. To him he adheres, resigns the whole warehouse of his religion, with all the locks and keys, into his custody; and indeed makes the very person of that man his religion; esteems his associating with him a sufficient evidence and commendatory of his own piety. So that a man may say his religion is now no more within himself, but is become a dividual[9] movable, and goes and comes near him, according as that good man frequents the house. He entertains him, gives him gifts, feasts him, lodges him; his religion comes home at night, prays, is liberally supped, and sumptuously laid to sleep, rises, is saluted, and after the malmsey, or some well-spiced brewage, and better breakfasted than He whose morning appetite would have gladly fed on green figs between Bethany and Jerusalem,[1] his religion walks abroad at eight, and leaves his kind entertainer in the shop trading all day without his religion.

Another sort there be who, when they hear that all things shall be ordered, all things regulated and settled, nothing written but what passes through the custom-house of certain publicans that have the tonnaging and poundaging[2] of all free-spoken truth, will straight give themselves up into your hands, make 'em and cut 'em out what religion ye please: there be delights, there be recreations and jolly pastimes that will fetch the day about from sun to sun, and rock the tedious year as in a delightful dream. What need they torture their heads with that which others have taken so strictly and so unalterably into their own purveying? These are the fruits which a dull ease and cessation of our knowledge will bring forth among the people. How goodly and how to be wished were

5. "Professors" in this context are people professing the Protestant faith.
6. A famous Catholic shrine.
7. Trades he cannot manage.
8. Agent.
9. I.e., separate or separable. Milton is describing the common institution of the household chaplain.
1. Mark xi.12–13. Jesus, hungry, found nothing but leaves on the fig tree, for the time of the figs was not yet.
2. "Publicans": tax collectors. Tonnage and poundage were excise taxes levied illegally by the king before 1641, and therefore specially odious to Milton's readers.

such an obedient unanimity as this, what a fine conformity would it starch us all into! Doubtless a staunch and solid piece of framework, as any January could freeze together.[3] * * *

Truth indeed came once into the world with her Divine Master, and was a perfect shape most glorious to look on: but when he ascended, and his apostles after him were laid asleep, then straight arose a wicked race of deceivers, who, as that story goes of the Egyptian Typhon with his conspirators, how they dealt with the good Osiris,[4] took the virgin Truth, hewed her lovely form into a thousand pieces, and scattered them to the four winds. From that time ever since, the sad friends of Truth, such as durst appear, imitating the careful search that Isis made for the mangled body of Osiris, went up and down gathering up limb by limb, still as they could find them. We have not yet found them all, Lords and Commons, nor ever shall do, till her Master's second coming; he shall bring together every joint and member, and shall mold them into an immortal feature of loveliness and perfection. Suffer not these licensing prohibitions to stand at every place of opportunity, forbidding and disturbing them that continue seeking, that continue to do our obsequies to the torn body of our martyred saint. We boast our light; but if we look not wisely on the sun itself, it smites us into darkness. Who can discern those planets that are oft combust,[5] and those stars of brightest magnitude that rise and set with the sun, until the opposite motion of their orbs bring them to such a place in the firmament where they may be seen evening or morning? The light which we have gained was given us, not to be ever staring on, but by it to discover onward things more remote from our knowledge. It is not the unfrocking of a priest, the unmitering of a bishop, and the removing him from off the Presbyterian shoulders, that will make us a happy nation. No, if other things as great in the church, and in the rule of life both economical[6] and political, be not looked into and reformed, we have looked so long upon the blaze that Zwinglius[7] and Calvin hath beaconed up to us, that we are stark blind.

There be who perpetually complain of schisms and sects, and make it such a calamity that any man dissents from their maxims. 'Tis their own pride and ignorance which causes the disturbing, who neither will hear with meekness, nor can convince; yet all must be suppressed which is not found in their syntagma.[8] They are the

3. To set barriers in the way of fresh truths implies that a nation has all the truth it needs; but this, Milton argues, is far from the case. England has no grounds for smugness; the nation needs every bit of truth it can discover.

4. Plutarch tells, in his *Isis and Osiris*, of Typhon's scattering the fragments of his brother Osiris, and of Isis' efforts to recover them.

5. Literally, burned up; in astrology, so close to the sun as not to be visible.

6. Domestic.

7. Zwingli and Calvin, both radical Swiss reformers, were mainstays of the Presbyterian cause, which Milton was already feeling to be a little narrow.

8. Compilation of beliefs, creed.

troublers, they are the dividers of unity, who neglect and permit not others to unite those dissevered pieces which are yet wanting to the body of Truth. To be still searching what we know not by what we know, still closing up truth to truth as we find it (for all her body is homogeneal and proportional), this is the golden rule in theology as well as in arithmetic, and makes up the best harmony in a church; not the forced and outward union of cold and neutral and inwardly divided minds.

Lords and Commons of England, consider what nation it is whereof ye are, and whereof ye are the governors: a nation not slow and dull, but of a quick, ingenious and piercing spirit, acute to invent, subtle and sinewy to discourse, not beneath the reach of any point, the highest that human capacity can soar to. Therefore the studies of learning in her deepest sciences have been so ancient and so eminent among us, that writers of good antiquity and ablest judgment have been persuaded that even the school of Pythagoras and the Persian wisdom took beginning from the old philosophy of this island.[9] And that wise and civil Roman, Julius Agricola, who governed once here for Caesar, preferred the natural wits of Britain before the labored studies of the French. Nor is it for nothing that the grave and frugal Transylvanian sends out yearly from as far as the mountainous borders of Russia, and beyond the Hercynian wilderness, not their youth, but their staid men, to learn our language and our theologic arts.

Yet that which is above all this, the favor and the love of heaven, we have great argument[1] to think in a peculiar manner propitious and propending towards us. Why else was this nation chosen before any other, that out of her, as out of Zion,[2] should be proclaimed and sounded forth the first tidings and trumpet of Reformation to all Europe? And had it not been the obstinate perverseness of our prelates against the divine and admirable spirit of Wycliffe, to suppress him as a schismatic and innovator, perhaps neither the Bohemian Huss and Jerome,[3] no, nor the name of Luther or of Calvin, had been ever known: the glory of reforming all our neighbors had been completely ours. But now, as our obdurate clergy have with violence demeaned[4] the matter, we are become hitherto the latest and backwardest scholars of whom God offered to have made us the teachers. Now once again by all concurrence of signs, and by the general instinct of holy and devout men, as they daily

9. So far as it concerns Pythagoras and the Persians, this sentence is better patriotism than it is intellectual history. Agricola's opinion of the British intellect (referred to next), is found in Tacitus' *Life of Agricola;* "civil" means "cultured, civilized." The Transylvanians, being Protestants, did sometimes come to England from "beyond the Hercynian wilderness" (the Harz mountains) to study.

1. Reason. "Propending": inclining, favorable.

2. Mt. Zion, in Jerusalem, the site of the temple, the holy of holies.

3. Jerome of Prague (martyred in 1416) was a follower of Huss and so of Wycliffe.

4. Conducted.

and solemnly express their thoughts, God is decreeing to begin some new and great period in his church, even to the reforming of Reformation itself; what does he then but reveal himself to his servants, and as his manner is, first to his Englishmen? I say, as his manner is, first to us, though we mark not the method of his counsels, and are unworthy. Behold now this vast city: a city of refuge, the mansion house of liberty, encompassed and surrounded with his protection; the shop of war hath not there more anvils and hammers waking, to fashion out the plates[5] and instruments of armed justice in defense of beleaguered truth, than there be pens and heads there, sitting by their studious lamps, musing, searching, revolving new notions and ideas wherewith to present, as with their homage and their fealty, the approaching Reformation: others as fast reading, trying all things, assenting to the force of reason and convincement.

What could a man require more from a nation so pliant and so prone to seek after knowledge? What wants there to such a towardly[6] and pregnant soil, but wise and faithful laborers, to make a knowing people, a nation of prophets, of sages, and of worthies? We reckon more than five months yet to harvest; there need not be five weeks; had we but eyes to lift up, the fields are white already.[7] Where there is much desire to learn, there of necessity will be much arguing, much writing, many opinions; for opinion in good men is but knowledge in the making. Under these fantastic terrors of sect and schism we wrong the earnest and zealous thirst after knowledge and understanding which God hath stirred up in this city.

What some lament of, we rather should rejoice at, should rather praise this pious forwardness among men, to reassume the ill-deputed care of their religion into their own hands again. A little generous prudence, a little forbearance of one another, and some grain of charity might win all these diligences to join, and unite into one general and brotherly search after truth; could we but forgo this prelatical tradition of crowding free consciences and Christian liberties into canons and precepts of men. I doubt not, if some great and worthy stranger should come among us, wise to discern the mold and temper of a people, and how to govern it, observing the high hopes and aims, the diligent alacrity of our extended thoughts and reasonings in the pursuance of truth and freedom, but that he would cry out as Pyrrhus did, admiring the Roman docility and courage: "If such were my Epirots, I would not despair the greatest design that could be attempted, to make a church or kingdom happy."[8] Yet these are the men cried out against for schismat-

5. Plate mail, armor plate.
6. Favorable.
7. Milton is paraphrasing Christ's words to the disciples (John iv.35).
8. Though King Pyrrhus of Epirus beat the Roman armies at Heraclea in 280 B.C., he was much impressed by their discipline.

ics and sectaries;[9] as if, while the temple of the Lord was building, some cutting, some squaring the marble, others hewing the cedars, there should be a sort of irrational men, who could not consider there must be many schisms and many dissections[1] made in the quarry and in the timber, ere the house of God can be built. And when every stone is laid artfully together, it cannot be united into a continuity, it can but be contiguous in this world; neither can every piece of the building be of one form; nay rather the perfection consists in this, that out of many moderate varieties and brotherly dissimilitudes that are not vastly disproportional, arises the goodly and the graceful symmetry that commends the whole pile and structure. Let us therefore be more considerate builders, more wise in spiritual architecture, when great reformation is expected. For now the time seems come, wherein Moses the great prophet may sit in heaven rejoicing to see that memorable and glorious wish of his fulfilled, when not only our seventy elders, but all the Lord's people, are become prophets.[2] * * *

Methinks I see in my mind a noble and puissant nation rousing herself like a strong man after sleep, and shaking her invincible locks: methinks I see her as an eagle mewing[3] her mighty youth, and kindling her undazzled eyes at the full midday beam; purging and unscaling her long-abused sight at the fountain itself of heavenly radiance; while the whole noise of timorous and flocking birds, with those also that love the twilight, flutter about, amazed at what she means, and in their envious gabble would prognosticate a year of sects and schisms.[4] * * *

1644

9. Sectarians, dividers of the church.
1. Milton puns on the literal meanings of "schisms" and "dissections" ("split" and "cut up") to press the image of the church as a temple built of believers.
2. In Numbers xi.29, Moses expressed the wish that all the Lord's people (not just the council of "seventy," or Sanhedrin) were prophets.
3. Molting, shaking off. Or the word may be "newing," i.e., renewing.
4. With this vigorous expression of idealistic optimism, Milton's argument subsides into a few last repetitions and afterthoughts. In practical terms, it was not a successful argument; the ordinance against which it protested was not repealed, though it was never effectively enforced, being, in effect, unenforceable. In time, Milton himself became, temporarily, a licenser of news sheets under Cromwell. But this biographical fact need not and must not be taken as a retraction or limitation of the position assumed in *Areopagitica*, which moves throughout on a plane of policy far removed from mundane considerations of practical politics.

Paradise Lost

The entry into *Paradise Lost* is easy—deceptively so. Carried along by the impetus of Satan's tremendous adventures, readers are apt to forget there is any other part to the poem. Indeed, while we are getting acclimated to the Miltonic world, there is no reason to hold back our sympathy with Satan, our admiration for his heroic energy. It is energy in a bad cause, clearly; but it is energy, it is heroically exercised, and there is as yet no source of virtuous power to oppose or offset it. With the appearance of Christ the Son, at the opening of Book III, we begin to see in heavenly Love the counterpoise of Satan's hellish Hate; and in Book IV, as we are introduced not only to Adam and Eve but to Paradise, our sympathies gradually shift. Satan is no longer a glamorous underdog, fighting his adventurous way through the universe against enormous odds; he is a menacing vulture, a cormorant, a toad, a snake. He is not only dangerous, he is dull; whatever richness and variety he discovers in the universe serve only to produce in him envious hatred and destructiveness. His sin is incestuous, as the allegory of Sin and Death points out; it breeds out of itself ever fresh occasions of sin. Adam and Eve, who are weaker, less active, and less spectacular in every way, finally outweigh Satan in our interest and sympathy simply because they can respond to life, and to the terrifying experience of guilt, more vigorously than Satan can.

Seen overall—from above, as it were—*Paradise Lost* is a vast but delicately balanced structure. The adventure of Satan in Books I–III balances the history of mankind in Books X–XII. Book IV, the entry of Satan (and the reader) into Paradise, balances Book IX, describing the loss of Paradise. Books V and VI, describing the destructive war in Heaven, balance as on a fulcrum against Books VII and VIII, which describe the Creation and deal with the problems of understanding it.

Within the poem's larger structure, there are all sorts of secondary balances which the knowing reader will recognize for himself. The consult in Hell (Book II) is paralleled by a consult in Heaven (Book III); the Heavenly Trinity of Father, Son, and Holy Ghost is paralleled by a diabolic trinity of Satan, Sin, and Death. Satan's fall parallels Adam's fall, and the parallel is prolonged into that extended series of falls and recoveries which is the history of mankind. Moloch contrasts with Mammon; the Son's mercy with the Father's justice; Raphael's affability with Michael's severity; and so on, almost without limit.

The structure of the poem is at once massive and delicate; its language is also both rich and strong. Milton's range of classical reference and gift for epithet are undoubtedly staggering at first view, and his long, complexly subordinated sentences are sometimes hard to follow. Footnotes, alas, provide the only proper solution to this problem. But one need not equal, or even follow, all Milton's learning in order to appreciate his poem, especially at a first reading. The poem progresses as through a garden of metaphor and reference which stretches away on either side of one, as far as the eye can see; on a first tour, it is enough to get the general prospect clear, without learning the name of each particular blossom. Ultimately, the reader who is experienced in the poem comes to appreciate its details—epic similes like Leviathan the seabeast (I.201), no less than the one-eyed Arimaspians and the gryphon (II.944)—its epithets and circumlocutions like Mulciber (I.740), who is Vulcan, and Amram's son (I.339) who is Moses—without sense of strain or strangeness. Milton himself moved securely through the literatures of half a dozen languages and as many cultures; it is one of the supreme rewards of literary study to be able to follow him with an equivalent security.

Paradise Lost is at once a deeply traditional and a boldly original poem. Milton takes pains to fulfill the traditional prescriptions of the epic form; he gives us love, war, supernatural characters, a descent into Hell, a catalogue of warriors, all the conventional items of epic machinery. Yet no poem in which the climax of the central action is a woman eating a piece of fruit can be a conventional epic. Similarly, Milton himself defined his own moral purpose as being to "justify the ways of God to man." This seems no more than conventionally meek. Yet we cannot even think of equating the message of Milton's poem with Pope's injunction to "submit" because "whatever is is right." The way of life which Adam and Eve take up as the poem ends is that of the Christian pilgrimage through this world. Paradise was no place or condition in which to exercise Christian heroism as Milton conceives it. Expelled from Eden, our first "grand parents" pick up the burdens of humanity as we know them, sustained by a faith which we also know, and go forth to seek a blessing which we do not know yet. They are to become wayfaring, warfaring Christians, like John Milton; and in this condition, with its weaknesses and strivings and inevitable defeats, there is a glory that no devil can ever understand. Thus Milton strikes, humanly as well as artistically, a grand resolving chord. It is the careful, triumphant balancing and tempering of this conclusion which makes Milton's poem the noble architecture it is; and which makes of the end a richer, if not a more exciting, experience than the beginning.

From PARADISE LOST

Book I

The Argument[1]

This first book proposes, first in brief, the whole subject, man's disobedience, and the loss thereupon of Paradise, wherein he was placed: then touches the prime cause of his fall, the serpent, or rather Satan in the serpent; who, revolting from God, and drawing to his side many legions of angels, was, by the command of God, driven out of Heaven, with all his crew, into the great deep. Which action passed over, the poem hastens into the midst of things;[2] presenting Satan, with his angels, now fallen into Hell—described here not in the center (for heaven and earth may be supposed as yet not made, certainly not yet accursed), but in a place of utter darkness, fitliest called Chaos. Here Satan with his angels lying on the burning lake, thunderstruck and astonished, after a certain space recovers, as from confusion; calls up him who, next in order and dignity, lay by him: they confer of their miserable fall. Satan awakens all his legions, who lay till then in the same manner confounded. They rise: their numbers; array of battle; their

1. *Paradise Lost* appeared originally without any sort of prose aid to the reader; but, since many readers found the poem hard going, the printer asked Milton for some prose "Arguments" or summary explanations of the action in the various books, and prefixed them to later issues of the poem. We reprint those for the first three books and the ninth.

2. Adapted from Horace's prescription that the epic poet should start *"in medias res."*

chief leaders named, according to the idols known afterwards in Canaan and the countries adjoining. To these Satan directs his speech; comforts them with hope yet of regaining Heaven; but tells them, lastly, of a new world and new kind of creature to be created, according to an ancient prophecy, or report, in Heaven; for that angels were long before this visible creation was the opinion of many ancient fathers.[3] To find out the truth of this prophecy, and what to determine[4] thereon, he refers to a full council. What his associates thence attempt. Pandemonium, the palace of Satan, rises, suddenly built out of the deep: the infernal peers there sit in council.

Of man's first disobedience, and the fruit[5]
Of that forbidden tree whose mortal[6] taste
Brought death into the world, and all our woe,
With loss of Eden, till one greater Man[7]
Restore us, and regain the blissful seat,
Sing, Heavenly Muse,[8] that, on the secret top
Of Oreb, or of Sinai, didst inspire
That shepherd who first taught the chosen seed
In the beginning how the Heavens and Earth
Rose out of Chaos: or, if Sion hill[9]
Delight thee more, and Siloa's brook that flowed
Fast[1] by the oracle of God, I thence
Invoke thy aid to my adventurous song,
That with no middle flight intends to soar
Above th' Aonian mount,[2] while it pursues
Things unattempted yet in prose or rhyme.
And chiefly thou, O Spirit,[3] that dost prefer
Before all temples th' upright heart and pure,
Instruct me, for thou know'st; thou from the first
Wast present, and, with mighty wings outspread,
Dovelike sat'st brooding[4] on the vast abyss,

3. I.e., Church Fathers, the Christian writers of the first three centuries of the church.
4. I.e., what action to take upon their information.
5. Eve's apple, of course; but also all the consequences of eating it.
6. Deadly; but also "to mortals" (i.e., human beings).
7. Christ, the second Adam.
8. In Greek mythology, Urania, Muse of astronomy and epic poetry; but here identified, by references to Oreb and Sinai, with the Holy Spirit of the Bible, which inspired Moses ("that shepherd") to write Genesis and the other four books of the Pentateuch for the instruction of the Jews ("the chosen seed").
9. The hill of Sion and the brook of Siloa are two features of the landscape around Jerusalem likely to appeal to a Muse, whose natural haunts are springs and mountains (see *Lycidas,* line 15). Milton's aim is to show that poetry is everywhere recognized as an inspiration close to that of religion.
1. Close.
2. Helicon, home of the classical Muses; Milton is deliberately courting comparison with Homer and Virgil.
3. The Spirit is an impulse or voice of God, by which the Hebrew prophets were directly inspired.
4. A composite of phrases and ideas from Genesis i.2 ("And the earth was without form, and void; and darkness was upon the face of the deep. And the Spirit of God moved upon the face of the waters"); Matthew iii.16 ("and he saw the Spirit of God descending like a dove, and lighting upon him"); and Luke iii.22 ("and the Holy Ghost descended in a bodily shape like a dove upon him"). Milton's mind as he wrote was impregnated with expressions from the King James Bible, only a few of which can be indicated in the notes.

And mad'st it pregnant: what in me is dark
Illumine; what is low, raise and support;
That, to the height of this great argument,[5]
I may assert Eternal Providence,
And justify the ways of God to men.
  Say first (for Heaven hides nothing from thy view,
Nor the deep tract of Hell), say first what cause
Moved our grand[6] parents, in that happy state,
Favored of Heaven so highly, to fall off
From their Creator, and transgress his will
For[7] one restraint, lords of the world besides?[8]
Who first seduced them to that foul revolt?
  Th' infernal serpent; he it was, whose guile,
Stirred up with envy and revenge, deceived
The mother of mankind, what time[9] his pride
Had cast him out from Heaven, with all his host
Of rebel angels, by whose aid, aspiring
To set himself in glory above his peers,[1]
He trusted to have equaled the Most High,
If he opposed; and with ambitious aim
Against the throne and monarchy of God,
Raised impious war in Heaven and battle proud,
With vain attempt. Him the Almighty Power
Hurled headlong flaming from th' ethereal sky,
With hideous ruin and combustion, down
To bottomless perdition, there to dwell
In adamantine chains and penal fire,
Who durst defy th' Omnipotent to arms.
  Nine times the space that measures day and night
To mortal men, he with his horrid crew,
Lay vanquished, rolling in the fiery gulf,
Confounded though immortal. But his doom
Reserved him to more wrath; for now the thought
Both of lost happiness and lasting pain
Torments him; round he throws his baleful[2] eyes,
That witnessed huge affliction and dismay,
Mixed with obdúrate pride and steadfast hate.
At once, as far as angels ken,[3] he views
The dismal situation waste and wild:
A dungeon horrible, on all sides round,
As one great furnace flamed; yet from those flames
No light,[4] but rather darkness visible

5. Theme.
6. First in importance; by implication, in time also.
7. Because of.
8. In every other respect.
9. I.e., at the time when.
1. His equals. The sentence mimics Satan's action, piling clause loosely upon clause, and building ever higher, till "with vain attempt" (line 44) brings the whole structure crashing down. It is a dramatic entry into "the midst of things," where epics begin. Book VI will recount more largely the war in Heaven, in the full narrative form which Aeneas used to tell Dido of the last days of Troy.
2. Malignant, as well as suffering.
3. As far as angels can see.
4. Omitting the verb conveys abruptly the paradox: fire-without-light.

Served only to discover sights of woe,
Regions of sorrow, doleful shades, where peace
And rest can never dwell, hope never comes
That comes to all,[5] but torture without end
Still urges,[6] and a fiery deluge, fed
With ever-burning sulphur unconsumed.
Such place Eternal Justice had prepared
For those rebellious; here their prison ordained
In utter[7] darkness, and their portion set,
As far removed from God and light of Heaven
As from the center[8] thrice to th' utmost pole.
O how unlike the place from whence they fell!
There the companions of his fall, o'erwhelmed
With floods and whirlwinds of tempestuous fire,
He soon discerns; and, weltering by his side,
One next himself in power, and next in crime,
Long after known in Palestine, and named
Beëlzebub.[9] To whom th' arch-enemy,
And thence in Heaven called Satan,[1] with bold words
Breaking the horrid silence, thus began:
"If thou beëst he—but O how fallen! how changed
From him who, in the happy realms of light
Clothed with transcendent brightness, didst outshine
Myriads, though bright! if he whom mutual league,
United thoughts and counsels, equal hope
And hazard in the glorious enterprise,
Joined with me once, now misery hath joined
In equal ruin; into what pit thou seest[2]
From what height fallen, so much the stronger proved
He with his thunder:[3] and till then who knew
The force of those dire arms? Yet not for those,
Nor what the potent Victor in his rage
Can else inflict, do I repent, or change,
Though changed in outward luster, that fixed mind,
And high disdain from sense of injured merit,

5. The phrase echoes an expression in Dante ("All hope abandon, ye who enter here"), but Milton expresses it as a logical absurdity. Hope comes to "all" but not to Helldwellers; they are not included in "all."

6. Afflicts.

7. "Complete" but also "outer."

8. The earth. Milton makes use in *Paradise Lost* of two images of the cosmos: (1) the earth is the center of the *created* (Ptolemaic) cosmos of nine concentric spheres; but (2) the earth and the whole created cosmos are a mere appendage, hanging from Heaven by a golden chain, in the larger, aboriginal, and less shapely cosmos. In the present passage, the fall from Heaven to Hell (through the aboriginal universe) is described as thrice as far as the distance (in the created universe) from the center (earth) to the outermost sphere.

9. A Phoenician deity, or Baal (the name means "Lord of flies"); traditionally, a prince of devils and enemy of Jehovah. The Phoenician Baal, a sun god, had many aspects and so many names; most Baals were nature deities. But in the poem's time scheme all this lies in the future; Beelzebub's angelic name, whatever it was, has been erased from the Book of Life, and as he has not yet got another one, he must be called by the name he will have later on.

1. In Hebrew, the name means "Adversary."

2. Satan's syntax, like that of a man recovering from a stunning blow, is not of the clearest.

3. God with his thunderbolts.

That with the Mightiest raised me to contend,
And to the fierce contentions brought along
Innumerable force of spirits armed,
That durst dislike his reign, and, me preferring,
His utmost power with adverse power opposed
In dubious battle on the plains of Heaven,
And shook his throne. What though the field be lost?
All is not lost: the unconquerable will,
And study[4] of revenge, immortal hate,
And courage never to submit or yield:
And what is else not to be overcome?[5]
That glory never shall his wrath or might
Extort from me. To bow and sue for grace
With suppliant knee, and deify his power[6]
Who, from the terror of this arm, so late
Doubted his empire[7]—that were low indeed;
That were an ignominy and shame beneath
This downfall; since, by fate, the strength of gods,[8]
And this empyreal substance, cannot fail;
Since, through experience of this great event,
In arms not worse, in foresight much advanced,
We may with more successful hope resolve
To wage by force or guile eternal war,
Irreconcilable to our grand Foe,
Who now triúmphs, and in th' excess of joy
Sole reigning holds the tyranny[9] of Heaven."
  So spake th' apostate angel, though in pain,
Vaunting aloud, but racked with deep despair;
And him thus answered soon his bold compeer:[1]
  "O prince, O chief of many thronéd powers,
That led th' embattled seraphim[2] to war
Under thy conduct, and, in dreadful deeds
Fearless, endangered Heaven's perpetual King,
And put to proof his high supremacy,
Whether upheld by strength, or chance, or fate![3]
Too well I see and rue the dire event[4]

4. Pursuit.

5. I.e., what else does it mean not to be beaten? "That glory" is the glory of hearing Satan confess himself overcome.

6. I.e., deify the power of him who. Milton sometimes writes English as if it were an inflected language.

7. I.e., doubted whether he could maintain his empire. In the next line, "ignominy" is pronounced "ignomy."

8. The essence of Satan's fault is his claim to the position of a god, subject to fate but to nothing else. His substance is "empyreal" (heavenly, from the empyrean), and cannot be destroyed; but, as he learns in the poem, it can be confounded by God's greater power and weakened by its own corruption and self-contradictions. "Fail": cease to exist.

9. The accusation is bold, but one of the aims of the poem is to show that Satan is a tyrant and God is not. The next two lines start this dramatic process by suggesting that Satan's brave exterior is merely a front.

1. Comrade and equal.

2. According to tradition, there were nine orders of angels—seraphim, cherubim, thrones, dominions, virtues, powers, principalities, archangels, and angels; but Milton does not use these systematic categories systematically.

3. The devils can conceive of any reason for God's continuing rule, except goodness and justice.

4. Outcome.

That with sad overthrow and foul defeat
Hath lost us Heaven, and all this mighty host
In horrible destruction laid thus low,
As far as gods and heavenly essences
Can perish: for the mind and spirit remains
Invincible, and vigor soon returns,
Though all our glory extinct, and happy state
Here swallowed up in endless misery.
But what if he our Conqueror (whom I now
Of force[5] believe almighty, since no less
Than such could have o'erpowered such force as ours)
Have left us this our spirit and strength entire,
Strongly to suffer and support our pains,
That we may so suffice[6] his vengeful ire,
Or do him mightier service as his thralls
By right of war, whate'er his business be,
Here in the heart of Hell to work in fire,
Or do his errands in the gloomy deep?
What can it then avail though yet we feel
Strength undiminished, or eternal being
To undergo eternal punishment?"
    Whereto with speedy words th' arch-fiend[7] replied:
"Fallen cherub, to be weak is miserable,
Doing or suffering:[8] but of this be sure,
To do aught good never will be our task,
But ever to do ill our sole delight,
As being the contrary to his high will
Whom we resist. If then his providence
Out of our evil seek to bring forth good,
Our labor must be to pervert that end,
And out of good still to find means of evil;
Which oft times may succeed, so as perhaps
Shall grieve him, if I fail not,[9] and disturb
His inmost counsels from their destined aim.
But see! the angry Victor hath recalled
His ministers of vengeance and pursuit
Back to the gates of Heaven; the sulphurous hail,
Shot after us in storm, o'erblown hath laid
The fiery surge that from the precipice
Of Heaven received us falling; and the thunder,
Winged with red lightning and impetuous rage,
Perhaps hath spent his shafts, and ceases now
To bellow through the vast and boundless deep.
Let us not slip[1] th' occasion, whether scorn
Or satiate fury yield it from our Foe.
Seest thou yon dreary plain, forlorn and wild,
The seat of desolation, void of light,

5. Perforce, necessarily.
6. Satisfy.
7. A fiend is an enemy, one who hates; the word is an antonym of "friend."
8. Whether one is active or passive.
9. "Unless I'm mistaken" (direct from the Latin, *nisi fallor*).
1. I.e., let slip.

Save what the glimmering of these livid flames
Casts pale and dreadful? Thither let us tend
From off the tossing of these fiery waves;
There rest, if any rest can harbor there;
And, reassembling our afflicted powers,[2]
Consult how we may henceforth most offend
Our enemy, our own loss how repair,
How overcome this dire calamity,
What reinforcement we may gain from hope,
If not, what resolution from despair."[3]
  Thus Satan, talking to his nearest mate,
With head uplift above the wave, and eyes
That sparkling blazed; his other parts besides,
Prone on the flood, extended long and large,
Lay floating many a rood,[4] in bulk as huge
As whom[5] the fables name of monstrous size,
Titanian or Earth-born, that warred on Jove,
Briareos or Typhon,[6] whom the den
By ancient Tarsus held, or that sea beast
Leviathan,[7] which God of all his works
Created hugest that swim th' ocean-stream.
Him, haply, slumbering on the Norway foam,
The pilot of some small night-foundered[8] skiff,
Deeming some island, oft, as seamen tell,
With fixéd anchor in his scaly rind,
Moors by his side under the lee, while night
Invests[9] the sea, and wishéd morn delays.
So stretched out huge in length the arch-fiend lay,
Chained on the burning lake; nor ever thence
Had risen or heaved his head, but that the will
And high permission of all-ruling Heaven
Left him at large to his own dark designs,
That with reiterated crimes he might
Heap on himself damnation, while he sought
Evil to others, and enraged might see
How all his malice served but to bring forth
Infinite goodness, grace, and mercy shown
On man by him seduced, but on himself

2. Stricken armies.
3. Of the last nine lines of Satan's speech, no less than five rhyme. Milton may have felt the need for something like the couplet with which blank-verse dramatists cut off their scenes.
4. An old unit of measure, between six and eight yards.
5. I.e., as those whom.
6. Both the Titans, led by Briareos, and the earth-born Giants, represented by Typhon (who lived in Cilicia near Tarsus), fought with Jove. Briareos was said to have a hundred hands, and Typhon a hundred heads; and both were said, by different authors, to have been punished for their rebellion (like Satan for his) by being thrown into the underworld. Briareos and Typhon are still heard grumbling from time to time under Mt. Etna.
7. The great sea monster of Isaiah xxvii.1 or Job xli; for Milton and us, simply a whale, but scaly (line 206).
8. Overtaken by darkness.
9. Wraps, covers. The story of sailors mooring to whales was an old one, but the reference to Norway suggests that Milton was thinking of a recently translated version by Olaus Magnus, the Swedish historian.

Treble confusion, wrath, and vengeance poured.
  Forthwith upright he rears from off the pool
His mighty stature; on each hand the flames
Driven backward slope their pointing spires,[1] and, rolled
In billows, leave i' th' midst a horrid[2] vale.
Then with expanded wings he steers his flight
Aloft, incumbent on[3] the dusky air,
That felt unusual weight; till on dry land
He lights, if it were land that ever burned
With solid, as the lake with liquid fire,
And such appeared in hue; as when the force
Of subterranean wind transports a hill
Torn from Pelorus,[4] or the shattered side
Of thundering Etna, whose combustible
And fueled entrails, thence conceiving fire,
Sublimed[5] with mineral fury, aid the winds,
And leave a singéd bottom all involved[6]
With stench and smoke. Such resting found the sole
Of unblest feet. Him followed his next mate,
Both glorying to have 'scaped the Stygian[7] flood
As gods, and by their own recovered strength,
Not by the sufferance[8] of supernal power.
  "Is this the region, this the soil, the clime,"
Said then the lost archangel, "this the seat
That we must change for Heaven? this mournful gloom
For that celestial light? Be it so, since he
Who now is sovereign can dispose and bid
What shall be right: farthest from him is best,
Whom reason hath equaled, force hath made supreme
Above his equals.[9] Farewell, happy fields,
Where joy forever dwells! Hail, horrors! hail,
Infernal world! and thou, profoundest Hell,
Receive thy new possessor, one who brings
A mind not to be changed by place or time.
The mind is its own place, and in itself
Can make a Heaven of Hell, a Hell of Heaven.[1]
What matter where, if I be still the same,
And what I should be, all but less[2] than he
Whom thunder hath made greater? Here at least
We shall be free; th' Almighty hath not built
Here for his envy, will not drive us hence:
Here we may reign secure; and, in my choice,

1. Points of flame.
2. Not simply "ghastly," but in the Latin sense, "bristling."
3. Resting upon.
4. Pelorus and Etna are volcanic mountains in Sicily, which Milton pictures as exploding under pressure of underground winds.
5. Vaporized.
6. Wrapped.
7. Of the river Styx, i.e., demonic, hellish.
8. Permission.
9. Satan likes to think that by "reason" he is God's equal; this only shows how far he is from "right reason."
1. Satan's heroic resolution here, where he is converting Hell into a kind of plastic Heaven, takes another turn when in Book IV we find him bringing the Hell of his own mind into Paradise.
2. Second only to. The expression "all but less than" telescopes "all but equal to" and "only less than."

To reign is worth ambition, though in Hell:
Better to reign in Hell than serve in Heaven.
But wherefore let we then our faithful friends,
Th' associates and copartners of our loss,
Lie thus astonished[3] on th' oblivious pool,
And call them not to share with us their part
In this unhappy mansion, or once more
With rallied arms to try what may be yet
Regained in Heaven, or what more lost in Hell?"
  So Satan spake; and him Beëlzebub
Thus answered: "Leader of those armies bright
Which, but th' Omnipotent, none could have foiled!
If once they hear that voice, their liveliest pledge
Of hope in fears and dangers, heard so oft
In worst extremes, and on the perilous edge[4]
Of battle, when it raged, in all assaults
Their surest signal, they will soon resume
New courage and revive, though now they lie
Groveling and prostrate on yon lake of fire,
As we erewhile, astounded and amazed;
No wonder, fallen such a pernicious height!"
  He scarce had ceased when the superior fiend
Was moving toward the shore; his ponderous shield,
Ethereal temper,[5] massy, large, and round,
Behind him cast. The broad circumference
Hung on his shoulders like the moon, whose orb
Through optic glass the Tuscan artist[6] views
At evening, from the top of Fesolè,
Or in Valdarno, to descry new lands,
Rivers, or mountains, in her spotty globe.
His spear, to equal which the tallest pine
Hewn on Norwegian hills, to be the mast
Of some great admiral,[7] were but a wand,
He walked with, to support uneasy steps
Over the burning marl,[8] not like those steps
On Heaven's azure; and the torrid clime
Smote on him sore besides, vaulted with fire.
Nathless[9] he so endured, till on the beach
Of that inflamèd[1] sea he stood, and called
His legions, angel forms, who lay entranced,
Thick as autumnal leaves that strow the brooks
In Vallombrosa,[2] where th' Etrurian shades

3. Stunned. The epithet "oblivious" is transferred from the fallen angels to the pool in which they have fallen.
4. Not the fringe of battle but the front line (Latin *acies*).
5. With the qualities of ether, which, being the fifth element, is not subject to change, corruption, or decay.
6. Galileo, who looked through a telescope ("optic glass") from the hill town of Fiesole outside Florence in the Val d'Arno, is the only contemporary mentioned by Milton in *Paradise Lost*.
7. Not the naval commander, but his flagship, usually the biggest of the fleet.
8. Soil.
9. A compressed, archaic form of "not the less."
1. Flaming, of course, but also fevered.
2. "Shady Valley," high in the Apennines about twenty miles from Florence. "Etruria" is Etruscan land, i.e., Tuscany.

High over-arched embower;[3] or scattered sedge
Afloat, when with fierce winds Orion armed
Hath vexed the Red-Sea coast, whose waves o'erthrew
Busiris and his Memphian chivalry,
While with perfidious hatred they pursued
The sojourners of Goshen, who beheld
From the safe shore their floating carcasses
And broken chariot wheels.[4] So thick bestrown,
Abject and lost, lay these, covering the flood,
Under amazement of their hideous change.
He called so loud that all the hollow deep
Of Hell resounded: "Princes, potentates,
Warriors, the flower of Heaven, once yours, now lost,
If such astonishment as this can seize
Eternal spirits! or have ye chosen this place
After the toil of battle to repose
Your wearied virtue,[5] for the ease you find
To slumber here, as in the vales of Heaven?
Or in this abject posture have ye sworn
To adore the Conqueror, who now beholds
Cherub and seraph rolling in the flood
With scattered arms and ensigns,[6] till anon
His swift pursuers from Heaven-gates discern
Th' advantage, and descending tread us down
Thus drooping, or with linkéd thunderbolts
Transfix us to the bottom of this gulf?
Awake, arise, or be forever fallen!"
  They heard, and were abashed, and up they sprung
Upon the wing, as when men wont to watch
On duty, sleeping found by whom they dread,
Rouse and bestir themselves ere well awake.
Nor did they not perceive[7] the evil plight
In which they were, or the fierce pains not feel;
Yet to their general's voice they soon obeyed
Innumerable. As when the potent rod
Of Amram's son,[8] in Egypt's evil day,
Waved round the coast, up called a pitchy cloud
Of locusts, warping[9] on the eastern wind,
That o'er the realm of impious Pharaoh hung
Like night, and darkened all the land of Nile;

3. I.e., form bowers by enclosing space.
4. Orion is a constellation, visible chiefly in late summer and autumn, hence associated with storms; in the Red Sea, where sedge grows thick, these storms result in much floating seaweed. This reminds Milton of how the sea must have looked after the Israelites ("sojourners of Goshen") passed through it while escaping from Egypt, when it was covered with the littered corpses of Pharaoh ("Busiris") and his pursuing horsemen ("Memphian chivalry").
5. Strength, but Satan's sarcasm makes use of the other connotation too.
6. Standards, battle flags.
7. The double negatives make a positive: they did indeed perceive both plight and pains. (Latin, *neque non*, "nor . . . not," "and.")
8. Moses, who drew down a plague of locusts on Egypt (Exodus x.12–15). Milton's learned locution is designed to keep Moses out of Hell, as well as from appearing too often in the poem (cf. above, 307–11).
9. Swarming (a technical term from bee-culture).

So numberless were those bad angels seen
Hovering on wing under the cope[1] of Hell,
'Twixt upper, nether, and surrounding fires;
Till, as a signal given, th' uplifted spear
Of their great sultan[2] waving to direct
Their course, in even balance down they light
On the firm brimstone, and fill all the plain:
A multitude like which the populous North[3]
Poured never from her frozen loins to pass
Rhene or the Danaw, when her barbarous sons
Came like a deluge on the South, and spread
Beneath Gibraltar to the Libyan sands.
Forthwith, from every squadron and each band,
The heads and leaders thither haste where stood
Their great commander; godlike shapes, and forms
Excelling human; princely dignities,
And powers that erst in Heaven sat on thrones,
Though of their names in Heavenly records now
Be no memorial, blotted out and rased[4]
By their rebellion from the Books of Life.
Nor had they yet among the sons of Eve
Got them new names, till, wandering o'er the Earth,
Through God's high sufferance for the trial of man,
By falsities and lies the greatest part
Of mankind they corrupted to forsake
God their Creator, and th' invisible
Glory of him that made them to transform
Oft to the image of a brute, adorned
With gay religions[5] full of pomp and gold,
And devils to adore for deities.
Then were they known to men by various names,
And various idols through the heathen world.
　Say, Muse, their names then known, who first, who last,[6]
Roused from the slumber on that fiery couch,
At their great emperor's call, as next in worth
Came singly[7] where he stood on the bare strand,
While the promiscuous crowd stood yet aloof.
　The chief were those who, from the pit of Hell
Roaming to seek their prey on Earth, durst fix
Their seats, long after, next the seat of God,[8]

1. Roof.
2. A first use of the image, which will be reinforced later, of Satan as an Oriental despot.
3. The barbarian invasions of falling Rome began with crossings of the Rhine ("Rhene") and Danube ("Danaw") Rivers, and spread across Spain, via Gibraltar, to North Africa.
4. Erased. See above, line 81. Though reluctant to state the view strongly, Milton believed all the pagan deities had been devils in disguise.
5. Ceremonies.
6. The catalogue of gods here is an epic convention; Homer catalogues ships, Virgil warriors.
7. One at a time. The diabolical aristocrats rally round Satan, while the "promiscuous crowd," the vulgar gods, stand apart.
8. The first group of devils come from the Near East, close neighbors and intimate enemies of Jehovah at Jerusalem.

Their altars by his altar, gods adored
Among the nations round, and durst abide
Jehovah thundering out of Sion, throned
Between the cherubim; yea, often placed
Within his sanctuary itself their shrines,
Abominations; and with cursèd things
His holy rites and solemn feasts profaned,
And with their darkness durst affront his light.
First, Moloch,[9] horrid king, besmeared with blood
Of human sacrifice, and parents' tears;
Though, for the noise of drums and timbrels loud,
Their children's cries unheard, that passed through fire
To his grim idol. Him the Ammonite[1]
Worshiped in Rabba and her watery plain,
In Argob and in Basan, to the stream
Of utmost Arnon. Nor content with such
Audacious neighborhood, the wisest heart
Of Solomon he led by fraud to build
His temple right against the temple of God
On that opprobrious hill,[2] and made his grove
The pleasant valley of Hinnom, Tophet thence
And black Gehenna called, the type of Hell.
Next Chemos,[3] th' obscene dread of Moab's sons,
From Aroar to Nebo and the wild
Of southmost Abarim; in Hesebon
And Horonaim, Seon's realm, beyond
The flowery dale of Sibma clad with vines,
And Elealè to th' Asphaltic pool:
Peor[4] his other name, when he enticed
Israel in Sittim, on their march from Nile,
To do him wanton rites, which cost them woe.
Yet thence his lustful orgies he enlarged
Even to that hill of scandal, by the grove
Of Moloch homicide,[5] lust hard by hate,
Till good Josiah drove them thence to Hell.
With these came they who, from the bordering flood
Of old Euphrates to the brook that parts

9. A sun god, sometimes represented as a roaring bull or with a calf's head, within whose brazen image living children were often burned as sacrifices (for a lurid fictional account, see Flaubert's *Salammbô*). "Timbrels": tambourines.

1. The Ammonites lived east of the Jordan, and Milton uses uncouth place names ("Rabba," "Argob," "Basan," "utmost Arnon") to suggest wildness.

2. The rites of Moloch on "that opprobrious hill" (the Mount of Olives) right opposite the Jewish temple, and in the valley of Hinnom, so polluted these places that they were turned into the refuse dump of Jerusalem. Thus they became "types" (analogies) of Hell, under the names "Tophet" and "Gehenna."

3. Chemos or Chemosh was another name for Moloch, used in Moab, a nation lying south and east of the Dead Sea ("th' Asphaltic pool"). Many of the geographical names clustered here come from Isaiah xv–xvi.

4. For the story of how Peor seduced "Israel in Sittim," see Numbers xxv.

5. An epithet was often joined to a god's name as a surname (e.g., *Jupiter Tonans*, Jove the Thunderer); Milton's epithet involves almost a parody, Moloch the Mankiller. The story of "good Josiah" and his campaign against pagan gods is told in II Kings xxiii and in II Chronicles xxxiv.

Egypt from Syrian ground,[6] had general names
Of Baalim and Ashtaroth, those male,
These feminine.[7] For spirits, when they please,
Can either sex assume, or both; so soft
And uncompounded is their essence pure,
Not tied or manacled with joint or limb,
Nor founded on the brittle strength of bones,
Like cumbrous flesh; but, in what shape they choose,
Dilated or condensed, bright or obscure,
Can execute their airy purposes,
And works of love or enmity fulfill.
For those the race of Israel oft forsook
Their Living Strength,[8] and unfrequented left
His righteous altar, bowing lowly down
To bestial gods; for which their heads as low
Bowed down in battle, sunk before the spear
Of despicable foes. With these in troop
Came Astoreth, whom the Phoenicians called
Astarté, queen of heaven, with crescent horns;
To whose bright image nightly by the moon
Sidonian virgins[9] paid their vows and songs;
In Sion also not unsung, where stood
Her temple on th' offensive mountain,[1] built
By that uxorious king[2] whose heart, though large,
Beguiled by fair idolatresses, fell
To idols foul. Thammuz[3] came next behind,
Whose annual wound in Lebanon allured
The Syrian damsels to lament his fate
In amorous ditties all a summer's day,
While smooth Adonis[4] from his native rock
Ran purple to the sea, supposed with blood
Of Thammuz yearly wounded: the love tale
Infected Sion's daughters with like heat,
Whose wanton passions in the sacred porch
Ezekiel[5] saw, when, by the vision led,
His eye surveyed the dark idolatries
Of alienated Judah. Next came one
Who mourned in earnest, when the captive ark

6. Palestine lies between the Euphrates and "the brook Besor" (I Samuel xxx.10).
7. I.e., plural forms, masculine and feminine respectively, for Baal and Astarte. As Baals were aspects of the sun god, Astartes (Ishtars) were manifestations of the moon goddess.
8. The Jews lost battles, Milton says, when they neglected Jehovah.
9. Sidon and Tyre were the chief cities of Phoenicia.
1. The Mount of Olives again (see above, lines 403 and 416).
2. Solomon, who "loved many strange women" (I Kings xi.1–8).
3. A Syrian god, who was supposed to have been killed by a boar in Lebanon; annual festivals mourned his death and celebrated his revival, imitating the cycle of vegetable life. In his Greek form he was Adonis, god of the solar year.
4. A Lebanese river, named after the deity because every spring it turned blood-red with sedimentary mud.
5. Ezekiel complained that the Jewish women of his day were worshiping Thammuz (Ezekiel viii.14).

Maimed his brute image, head and hands lopped off,
In his own temple, on the grunsel-edge,[6]
Where he fell flat, and shamed his worshipers:
Dagon his name, sea monster, upward man
And downward fish; yet had his temple high
Reared in Azotus, dreaded through the coast
Of Palestine, in Gath and Ascalon,
And Accaron and Gaza's frontier bounds.[7]
Him followed Rimmon, whose delightful seat
Was fair Damascus, on the fertile banks
Of Abbana and Pharphar, lucid streams.
He also 'gainst the house of God was bold:
A leper once he lost, and gained a king,
Ahaz,[8] his sottish conqueror, whom he drew
God's altar to disparage and displace
For one of Syrian mode, whereon to burn
His odious offerings, and adore the gods
Whom he had vanquished. After these appeared
A crew who, under names of old renown,
Osiris, Isis, Orus,[9] and their train,
With monstrous shapes[1] and sorceries abused
Fanatic Egypt and her priests to seek
Their wandering gods disguised in brutish forms
Rather than human. Nor did Israel 'scape
Th' infection, when their borrowed gold composed
The calf in Oreb;[2] and the rebel king
Doubled that sin in Bethel and in Dan,
Likening his Maker to the grazéd ox[3]—
Jehovah, who, in one night, when he passed
From Egypt marching, equaled[4] with one stroke
Both her first-born and all her bleating gods.
Belial[5] came last; than whom a spirit more lewd
Fell not from Heaven, or more gross to love
Vice for itself. To him no temple stood
Or altar smoked; yet who more oft than he

6. When the Philistines stole the ark of God, they tried to store it in the temple of their sea god, Dagon; but in the morning the mutilated statue of Dagon was found on the threshold ("grunsel-edge"). See I Samuel v.1–5.

7. Milton names the five chief cities of the Philistines as places where Dagon was worshiped.

8. A Syrian general, Naaman, was cured of leprosy and converted from worship of Rimmon by the waters of the Jordan (II Kings v). King Ahaz, on the other hand, an Israelite monarch who conquered Damascus, was converted there to worship of Rimmon (II Kings xvi).

9. The second group of devils includes those from Egypt, driven in terror from heaven by the revolt of the giants (so Ovid tells us in *Metamorphoses* V), and forced to wander through Egypt in animal disguises.

1. Monstrous, because often represented with animals' heads.

2. Aaron made a golden calf in the wilderness (Exodus xxxii); Milton thought it an idol of the Egyptian god Apis because the gold of which it was made had been borrowed from the Egyptians.

3. Jeroboam, "the rebel king," doubled Aaron's sin by making *two* golden calves (I Kings xii.28–30).

4. Leveled. See Exodus xii.12 for Jehovah's vengeance on the first-born of Egypt and their gods.

5. Belial was never worshiped as a god; his name was originally an abstract noun meaning "wickedness"; hence used mainly in set phrases like "sons of Belial." He comes last, because weak and slothful.

In temples and at altars, when the priest
Turns atheist, as did Eli's sons,[6] who filled
With lust and violence the house of God?
In courts and palaces he also reigns,
And in luxurious cities, where the noise
Of riot ascends above their loftiest towers,
And injury and outrage; and, when night
Darkens the streets, then wander forth the sons
Of Belial, flown[7] with insolence and wine.
Witness the streets of Sodom,[8] and that night
In Gibeah, when the hospitable door
Exposed a matron, to avoid worse rape.
These were the prime in order and in might;
The rest were long to tell, though far renowned,
Th' Ionian gods, of Javan's issue held
Gods, yet confessed later than Heaven and Earth,
Their boasted parents;[9] Titan, Heaven's first-born,
With his enormous brood, and birthright seized
By younger Saturn; he from mightier Jove,
His own and Rhea's son, like measure found;
So Jove usurping reigned.[1] These, first in Crete
And Ida known, thence on the snowy top
Of cold Olympus ruled the middle air,
Their highest heaven; or on the Delphian cliff,
Or in Dodona, and through all the bounds
Of Doric land; or who with Saturn old
Fled over Adria to th' Hesperian fields,
And o'er the Celtic roamed the utmost isles.
All these and more came flocking; but with looks
Downcast and damp,[2] yet such wherein appeared
Obscure some glimpse of joy, to have found their chief
Not in despair, to have found themselves not lost
In loss itself; which on his countenance cast
Like doubtful hue.[3] But he, his wonted pride
Soon recollecting, with high words, that bore
Semblance of worth, not substance, gently raised
Their fainting courage, and dispelled their fears:
Then straight commands that, at the warlike sound

6. The misdeeds of Eli's sons, and the epithet "sons of Belial" applied to them, will be found in I Samuel ii. 12–17.

7. Flushed.

8. In Sodom and Gibeah ancient outrages befell, described in Genesis xix and Judges xix.

9. Though considered ancient by the Greeks ("Javan's issue," i.e., offspring of Javan, son of Japhet, son of Noah) and worshiped as the first children of "Heaven" (Uranus) and "Earth" (Ge), the Titans, Milton says, were actually confessed to be of a later age.

1. Cronos or Saturn, one of the Titans, deposed his elder brother, married his sister Rhea, and ruled until Zeus, who had been reared in secret on Mt. Ida in Crete, overthrew his own father and came to rule on Mt. Olympus. Zeus was also worshiped in Delphi, Dodona, and throughout the "Doric (Grecian) land." Meanwhile Saturn (lines 519–21), after his downfall, fled across the Adriatic Sea ("Adria") to Italy ("th' Hesperian fields"), crossed "the Celtic" (fields) of France, and finally reached Britain ("the utmost isles").

2. Depressed.

3. Their comfort is the chilly one of finding themselves not completely annihilated; and at first it is reflected in Satan's face.

Of trumpets loud and clarions,[4] be upreared
His mighty standard. That proud honor claimed
Azazel[5] as his right, a cherub tall:
Who forthwith from the glittering staff unfurled
Th' imperial ensign; which, full high advanced,
Shone like a meteor streaming to the wind,
With gems and golden luster rich emblazed,
Seraphic arms and trophies; all the while
Sonorous metal[6] blowing martial sounds:
At which the universal host up sent
A shout that tore Hell's concave,[7] and beyond
Frighted the reign of Chaos and old Night.[8]
All in a moment through the gloom were seen
Ten thousand banners rise into the air,
With orient[9] colors waving: with them rose
A forest huge of spears; and thronging helms
Appeared, and serried[1] shields in thick array
Of depth immeasurable. Anon they move
In perfect phalanx to the Dorian[2] mood
Of flutes and soft recorders; such as raised
To height of noblest temper heroes old
Arming to battle, and instead of rage
Deliberate valor breathed, firm, and unmoved
With dread of death to flight or foul retreat;
Nor wanting power to mitigate and swage[3]
With solemn touches troubled thoughts, and chase
Anguish and doubt and fear and sorrow and pain
From mortal or immortal minds. Thus they,
Breathing united force with fixéd thought,
Moved on in silence to soft pipes that charmed
Their painful steps o'er the burnt soil. And now
Advanced in view they stand, a horrid[4] front
Of dreadful length and dazzling arms, in guise
Of warriors old, with ordered spear and shield,
Awaiting what command their mighty chief
Had to impose. He through the arméd files
Darts his experienced eye, and soon traverse[5]
The whole battalion views, their order due,
Their visages and stature as of gods;
Their number last he sums. And now his heart
Distends with pride, and hardening in his strength
Glories: for never, since created man,[6]
Met such embodied force as, named with these,

4. Small, shrill, treble trumpets.
5. Among the historians of angels and devils, a traditional diabolic leader.
6. Reverberant trumpets.
7. Vault.
8. Disorder and darkness, the first materials of the cosmos, still maintain a kingdom between Heaven and Hell.
9. Lustrous, like the colors of a pearl.
1. Locked together.
2. Severe, simple. The shrill trumpet, which first roused the courage of the devils, now gives way to firm, martial tones, played on instruments of softer timbre, in the Spartan manner.
3. Assuage.
4. Bristling.
5. Across. Satan glances, like a reviewing officer, down the files and columns.
6. I.e., since the creation of man.

Could merit more than that small infantry
Warred on by cranes:[7] though all the giant brood
Of Phlegra with th' heroic race were joined
That fought at Thebes and Ilium, on each side
Mixed with auxiliar[8] gods; and what resounds
In fable or romance of Uther's son,
Begirt with British and Armoric knights;
And all who since, baptized or infidel,
Jousted in Aspramont, or Montalban,
Damasco, or Marocco, or Trebisond;
Or whom Biserta sent from Afric shore
When Charlemagne with all his peerage fell
By Fontarabbia.[9] Thus far these beyond
Compare of mortal prowess, yet observed[1]
Their dread commander. He, above the rest
In shape and gesture proudly eminent,
Stood like a tower. His form had yet not lost
All her[2] original brightness, nor appeared
Less than archangel ruined, and th' excess
Of glory obscured: as when the sun new-risen
Looks through the horizontal[3] misty air
Shorn of his beams, or from behind the moon,
In dim eclipse,[4] disastrous twilight sheds
On half the nations, and with fear of change
Perplexes monarchs. Darkened so, yet shone
Above them all th' archangel; but his face
Deep scars of thunder had entrenched, and care
Sat on his faded cheek, but under brows
Of dauntless courage, and considerate[5] pride
Waiting revenge. Cruel his eye, but cast
Signs of remorse and passion,[6] to behold
The fellows of his crime, the followers rather
(Far other once beheld in bliss), condemned
Forever now to have their lot in pain;
Millions of spirits for his fault amerced[7]
Of Heaven, and from eternal splendors flung

7. The pygmies had periodic fights with the cranes, which (according to Pliny) they won by riding to battle on pigs and goats. This would make them cavalry; but Milton wanted the pun on "infants." His idea is that, compared with the devils, all other armies that ever were would look puny.
8. Allied.
9. The Giants of Greek mythology were born at Phlegra (line 577); Milton imagines them joined with the Seven who fought against Thebes, and the whole Greek host that besieged Troy ("Ilium"), plus the various gods who helped on both sides. He even adds the knights "British or Armoric" (from Brittany) who fought with King Arthur ("Uther's son"), and includes a list of proper names taken from the cycles of romance and suggesting vast, remote armies. Fontarabbia, the best known, was reputed to be the scene of Roland's last stand in the *Chanson de Roland;* Milton thus mingles the fall of Charlemagne with that of his best-known knight.
1. Obeyed.
2. *Forma,* in Latin, is feminine; hence "her."
3. The rays of the sun, as it first rises over the horizon, are almost horizontal.
4. Time of ill omen. "Disastrous": threatening disaster.
5. Thoughtful, conscious.
6. Compassion.
7. Deprived.

For his revolt; yet faithful how they stood,
Their glory withered; as, when Heaven's fire
Hath scathed the forest oaks or mountain pines,
With singéd top their stately growth, though bare,
Stands on the blasted heath. He now prepared
To speak; whereat their doubled ranks they bend
From wing to wing, and half enclose him round
With all his peers: attention held them mute.
Thrice he essayed, and thrice, in spite of scorn,
Tears, such as angels weep, burst forth: at last
Words interwove with sighs found out their way:
"O myriads of immortal spirits! O powers
Matchless, but with th' Almighty!—and that strife
Was not inglorious, though th' event[8] was dire,
As this place testifies, and this dire change,
Hateful to utter. But what power of mind,
Foreseeing or presaging, from the depth
Of knowledge past or present, could have feared
How such united force of gods, how such
As stood like these, could ever know repulse?
For who can yet believe, though after loss,
That all these puissant[9] legions, whose exile
Hath emptied Heaven, shall fail to reascend,
Self-raised, and repossess their native seat?
For me, be witness all the host of Heaven,
If counsels different,[1] or danger shunned
By me, have lost our hopes. But he who reigns
Monarch in Heaven, till then as one secure
Sat on his throne, upheld by old repute,
Consent or custom, and his regal state
Put forth at full, but still his strength concealed,
Which tempted our attempt,[2] and wrought our fall.
Henceforth his might we know, and know our own,
So as not either to provoke, or dread
New war provoked: our better part remains
To work in close design,[3] by fraud or guile,
What force effected not; that he no less
At length from us may find, who overcomes
By force hath overcome but half his foe.
Space may produce new worlds; whereof so rife
There went a fame[4] in Heaven that he ere long
Intended to create, and therein plant
A generation whom his choice regard
Should favor equal to the sons of Heaven.
Thither, if but to pry, shall be perhaps
Our first eruption—thither, or elsewhere;

8. Outcome, result.
9. Potent, powerful.
1. Contradictory or even selfish, but also, in an obsolete sense, delaying.
2. Satan is an inveterate punster and player on words.
3. I.e., our best choice is to achieve by secret schemes.
4. Rumor. "Rife": common.

For this infernal pit shall never hold
Celestial spirits in bondage, nor th' abyss
Long under darkness cover. But these thoughts
Full counsel must mature. Peace is despaired,
For who can think submission? War, then, war
Open or understood,[5] must be resolved."
He spake; and, to confirm his words, outflew
Millions of flaming swords, drawn from the thighs
Of mighty cherubim; the sudden blaze
Far round illumined Hell. Highly they raged
Against the Highest, and fierce with graspéd arms
Clashed on their sounding shields the din of war,[6]
Hurling defiance toward the vault of Heaven.
There stood a hill not far, whose grisly[7] top
Belched fire and rolling smoke; the rest entire
Shone with a glossy scurf,[8] undoubted sign
That in his womb was hid metallic ore,
The work of sulphur.[9] Thither, winged with speed,
A numerous brígade hastened: as when bands
Of pioneers,[1] with spade and pickax armed,
Forerun the royal camp, to trench a field,
Or cast a rampart. Mammon led them on,
Mammon, the least erected[2] spirit that fell
From Heaven; for even in Heaven his looks and thoughts
Were always downward bent, admiring more
The riches of Heaven's pavement, trodden gold,
Than aught divine or holy else enjoyed
In vision beatific. By him first
Men also, and by his suggestion taught,
Ransacked the center, and with impious hands
Rifled the bowels of their mother Earth
For treasures better hid. Soon had his crew
Opened into the hill a spacious wound,
And digged out ribs[3] of gold. Let none admire
That riches grow in Hell; that soil may best
Deserve the precious bane. And here let those
Who boast in mortal things, and wondering tell
Of Babel, and the works of Memphian kings,
Learn how their greatest monuments of fame
And strength, and art, are easily outdone
By spirits reprobate,[4] and in an hour
What in an age they, with incessant toil
And hands innumerable, scarce perform.

5. Agreed-upon, tacit, hence secret.
6. Like Roman legionaries, the fallen angels applaud by beating swords on shields.
7. Horrible.
8. Crust.
9. Sulphur and mercury were considered the basic substances of all metals.
1. Sappers, engineers.
2. Elevated. Mammon is not a god but an abstract word meaning "wealth"; cf. Belial.
3. Bars, of course, but also with a hit at Eve, who was a "precious bane" (sweet poison) dug out of Adam's side. "Admire": wonder.
4. The tower of Babel and the Pyramids of Egypt ("works of Memphian kings") are easily outdone by the devils ("spirits reprobate").

Nigh on the plain, in many cells prepared,
That underneath had veins of liquid fire
Sluiced from the lake, a second multitude
With wondrous art founded the massy ore,
Severing each kind, and scummed the bullion-dross.
A third as soon had formed within the ground
A various mold, and from the boiling cells
By strange conveyance filled each hollow nook;[5]
As in an organ, from one blast of wind,
To many a row of pipes the soundboard breathes.
Anon out of the earth a fabric huge
Rose like an exhalation, with the sound
Of dulcet symphonies and voices sweet,
Built like a temple, where pilasters[6] round
Were set, and Doric pillars[7] overlaid
With golden architrave; nor did there want
Cornice or frieze, with bossy[8] sculptures graven;
The roof was fretted[9] gold. Not Babylon
Nor great Alcairo such magnificence
Equaled in all their glories,[1] to enshrine
Belus or Serapis their gods, or seat
Their kings, when Egypt with Assyria strove
In wealth and luxury. Th' ascending pile
Stood fixed[2] her stately height; and straight the doors,
Opening their brazen folds, discover, wide
Within, her ample spaces o'er the smooth
And level pavement: from the archéd roof,
Pendent by subtle magic, many a row
Of starry lamps and blazing cressets,[3] fed
With naphtha and asphaltus, yielded light
As from a sky. The hasty multitude
Admiring entered; and the work some praise,
And some the architect. His hand was known
In Heaven by many a towered structure high,
Where sceptered angels held their residence,
And sat as princes, whom the súpreme King
Exalted to such power, and gave to rule,
Each in his hierarchy, the orders bright.
Nor was his name unheard or unadored
In ancient Greece; and in Ausonian land
Men called him Mulciber;[4] and how he fell

5. After melting the gold with fire from the lake and pouring it into molds, the devils cause their building to rise by a sort of spiritual-musical magic.
6. Columns set in a wall.
7. Doric pillars are severe and plain.
8. Embossed.
9. Patterned.
1. At Babylon in Assyria there were temples to "Belus" or Baal; at Alcairo (modern Cairo, ancient Memphis) in Egypt, they were to Osiris, one of whose names was Serapis (here, but not ordinarily, accented on the first syllable).
2. Complete; "straight": straightway.
3. Basketlike lamps, hung from the ceiling.
4. Hephaestus, or Vulcan, was sometimes known in "Ausonian land" (Italy) by the secondary epithet of "Mulciber." The story of Jove's tossing him out of Heaven is told, to the accompaniment of much Homeric laughter, in *Iliad* I. Milton calls him by a secondary name because he is a little uneasy at having to put a "good" Greek deity in Hell.

From Heaven they fabled, thrown by angry Jove
Sheer o'er the crystal battlements: from morn
To noon he fell, from noon to dewy eve,
A summer's day, and with the setting sun
Dropped from the zenith, like a falling star,
On Lemnos, th' Aegean isle. Thus they relate,
Erring;[5] for he with this rebellious rout
Fell long before; nor aught availed him now
To have built in Heaven high towers; nor did he 'scape
By all his engines, but was headlong sent,
With his industrious crew, to build in Hell.
  Meanwhile the wingéd heralds, by command
Of sovereign power, with awful ceremony
And trumpet's sound, throughout the host proclaim
A solemn council forthwith to be held
At Pandemonium,[6] the high capital
Of Satan and his peers.[7] Their summons called
From every band and squaréd regiment
By place or choice the worthiest; they anon
With hundreds and with thousands trooping came
Attended. All access was thronged, the gates
And porches wide, but chief the spacious hall
(Though like a covered field, where champions bold
Wont ride in armed, and at the soldan's[8] chair
Defied the best of paynim chivalry
To mortal combat, or career with lance),
Thick swarmed, both on the ground and in the air,
Brushed with the hiss of rustling wings. As bees
In springtime, when the sun with Taurus[9] rides,
Pour forth their populous youth about the hive
In clusters; they among fresh dews and flowers
Fly to and fro, or on the smoothéd plank,
The suburb of their straw-built citadel,
New rubbed with balm, expatiate, and confer[1]
Their state-affairs: so thick the airy crowd
Swarmed and were straitened; till, the signal given,
Behold a wonder! They but now who seemed
In bigness to surpass Earth's giant sons,
Now less than smallest dwarfs, in narrow room
Throng numberless—like that pygmean race
Beyond the Indian mount;[2] or faery elves,
Whose midnight revels, by a forest side
Or fountain, some belated peasant sees,

5. Milton tells the story, and gives it six lines of splendid poetry (740–46), but in the end condemns it as a corrupt version of the Biblical truth.

6. "Pandemonium" (a Miltonic coinage) means literally "All-Demons"; an inversion of Pantheon, "All-Gods."

7. Nobility.

8. Sultan's. "Paynim": pagan.

9. The sun is in the Zodiacal sign of Taurus from April 19 to May 20.

1. Spread out and discuss, bring together. The simile of bees prepares for the sudden contraction of the devils' size; they can shrink or dilate at will.

2. The pygmies were supposed to live beyond the Himalayas, "the Indian mount."

Or dreams he sees, while overhead the Moon
Sits arbitress,[3] and nearer to the Earth
Wheels her pale course; they, on their mirth and dance
Intent, with jocund[4] music charm his ear;
At once with joy and fear his heart rebounds.
Thus incorporeal spirits to smallest forms
Reduced their shapes immense, and were at large,
Though without number still, amidst the hall
Of that infernal court. But far within,
And in their own dimensions like themselves,
The great seraphic lords and cherubim
In close recess and secret conclave sat,
A thousand demigods on golden seats,
Frequent and full.[5] After short silence then,
And summons read, the great consult began.

Book II

The Argument

The consultation begun, Satan debates whether another battle be to be hazarded for the recovery of Heaven: some advise it, others dissuade. A third proposal is preferred, mentioned before by Satan —to search the truth of that prophecy or tradition in Heaven concerning another world, and another kind of creature, equal or not much inferior to themselves, about this time to be created. Their doubt who shall be sent on this difficult search: Satan, their chief, undertakes alone the voyage; is honored and applauded. The council thus ended, the rest betake them several ways and to several employments, as their inclinations lead them, to entertain[1] the time till Satan return. He passes on his journey to Hell-gates; finds them shut, and who sat there to guard them; by whom at length they are opened, and discover[2] to him the great gulf between Hell and Heaven. With what difficulty he passes through, directed by Chaos, the power of that place, to the sight of this new world which he sought.

High on a throne of royal state, which far
Outshone the wealth of Ormus[3] and of Ind,
Or where the gorgeous East with richest hand
Showers on her kings barbaric pearl and gold,
Satan exalted sat, by merit raised
To that bad eminence; and, from despair

3. Witness.
4. Merry.
5. Crowded ("frequent") and in full complement ("full"); all present and accounted for.

1. Pass.
2. Disclose.
3. An island in the Persian Gulf, modern Hormuz, famous for pearls. "Ind": India

Thus high uplifted beyond hope, aspires
Beyond thus high, insatiate to pursue
Vain war with Heaven; and, by success[4] untaught,
His proud imaginations thus displayed:
"Powers and dominions, deities of Heaven!
For since no deep within her gulf can hold
Immortal vigor, though oppressed and fallen,
I give not Heaven for lost: from this descent
Celestial virtues rising will appear
More glorious and more dread than from no fall,
And trust themselves to fear no second fate.
Me though just right, and the fixed laws of Heaven
Did first create your leader, next, free choice,
With what besides, in council or in fight,
Hath been achieved of merit, yet this loss
Thus far at least recovered, hath much more
Established in a safe unenvied throne
Yielded with full consent.[5] The happier state
In Heaven, which follows dignity, might draw
Envy from each inferior; but who here
Will envy whom the highest place exposes
Foremost to stand against the Thunderer's aim,
Your bulwark, and condemns to greatest share
Of endless pain? Where there is then no good
For which to strive, no strife can grow up there
From faction; for none sure will claim in Hell
Precédence, none, whose portion is so small
Of present pain, that with ambitious mind
Will covet more. With this advantage then
To union, and firm faith, and firm accord,
More than can be in Heaven, we now return
To claim our just inheritance of old,
Surer to prosper than prosperity
Could have assured us;[6] and by what best way,
Whether of open war or covert guile,
We now debate; who can advise, may speak."
He ceased, and next him Moloch, sceptered king,
Stood up, the strongest and the fiercest spirit
That fought in Heaven, now fiercer by despair.
His trust was with th' Eternal to be deemed
Equal in strength, and rather than be less
Cared not to be at all; with that care lost
Went all his fear: of God, or Hell, or worse
He recked[7] not, and these words thereafter spake:

4. Outcome, result; experience of either sort, good or bad.
5. He lays claim to the throne by just right, fixed laws, free choice—and the fact that no one else will want such a dangerous job.
6. Note the play on "sure—prosper—prosperity—assured." An Elizabethan critic famous for his picturesque terminology, George Puttenham, calls this figure "*epanalepsis*, or the echo sound, otherwise the slow return." It is a favorite device of Milton's.
7. Cared.

"My sentence[8] is for open war: of wiles,
More unexpert,[9] I boast not: them let those
Contrive who need, or when they need, not now.
For while they sit contriving, shall the rest,
Millions that stand in arms, and longing wait
The signal to ascend, sit lingering here
Heaven's fugitives, and for their dwelling place
Accept this dark opprobrious den of shame,
The prison of his tyranny who reigns
By our delay? No! let us rather choose,
Armed with Hell-flames and fury, all at once
O'er Heaven's high towers to force resistless way,
Turning our tortures into horrid arms
Against the Torturer; when to meet the noise
Of his almighty engine[1] he shall hear
Infernal thunder, and for lightning see
Black fire and horror shot with equal rage
Among his angels, and his throne itself
Mixed with Tartarean[2] sulphur, and strange fire,
His own invented torments. But perhaps
The way seems difficult and steep to scale
With upright wing against a higher foe.
Let such bethink them, if the sleepy drench[3]
Of that forgetful lake benumb not still,
That in our proper motion[4] we ascend
Up to our native seat; descent and fall
To us is adverse. Who but felt of late,
When the fierce foe hung on our broken rear
Insulting,[5] and pursued us through the deep,
With what compulsion and laborious flight
We sunk thus low? Th' ascent is easy then;
Th' event[6] is feared: should we again provoke
Our stronger,[7] some worse way his wrath may find
To our destruction; if there be in Hell
Fear to be worse destroyed! What can be worse
Than to dwell here, driven out from bliss, condemned
In this abhorréd deep to utter woe;
Where pain of unextinguishable fire
Must exercise us without hope of end,
The vassals[8] of his anger, when the scourge
Inexorably, and the torturing hour,
Calls us to penance? More destroyed than thus,
We should be quite abolished, and expire.
What fear we then? what[9] doubt we to incense

8. Judgment.
9. Inexperienced. Moloch never had to be clever, and is proud of it.
1. The thunderbolt.
2. Tartarus is a classical name for Hell.
3. A draught of physic, as for animals; hence, used contemptuously here.
4. Natural impulse.
5. With the Latin sense of stamping or dancing on.
6. Outcome.
7. The word "enemy" is understood.
8. Servants, underlings; but perhaps also—or alternatively—"vessels."
9. Why.

His utmost ire? Which, to the height enraged,
Will either quite consume us, and reduce
To nothing this essential,[1] happier far
Than miserable to have eternal being!
Or if our substance be indeed divine,
And cannot cease to be, we are at worst
On this side nothing;[2] and by proof we feel
Our power sufficient to disturb his Heaven,
And with perpetual inroads to alarm,
Though inaccessible, his fatal throne:
Which, if not victory, is yet revenge."
He ended frowning, and his look denounced
Desperate revenge, and battle dangerous
To less than gods.[3] On th' other side up rose
Belial, in act more graceful and humane;
A fairer person lost not Heaven; he seemed
For dignity composed, and high exploit.
But all was false and hollow; though his tongue
Dropped manna,[4] and could make the worse appear
The better reason, to perplex and dash
Maturest counsels: for his thoughts were low,
To vice industrious, but to nobler deeds
Timorous and slothful: yet he pleased the ear,
And with persuasive accent thus began:
"I should be much for open war, O peers,
As not behind in hate, if what was urged
Main reason to persuade immediate war,
Did not dissuade me most, and seem to cast
Ominous conjecture on the whole success;[5]
When he who most excels in fact of arms,
In what he counsels, and in what excels
Mistrustful, grounds his courage on despair
And utter dissolution, as the scope
Of all his aim, after some dire revenge.
First, what revenge? The towers of Heaven are filled
With armèd watch, that render all access
Impregnable; oft on the bordering deep
Encamp their legions, or with óbscure wing
Scout far and wide into the realm of Night,
Scorning surprise. Or could we break our way
By force, and at our heels all Hell should rise
With blackest insurrection, to confound
Heaven's purest light, yet our great enemy
All incorruptible would on his throne

1. Essence.
2. I.e., we are now as badly off as we can be without being nothing, and so need have no fear.
3. Only gods could have withstood Moloch.
4. His tongue was honeyed. To "make the worse appear / The better reason" was characteristic of Sophists—hollow, mercenary logic-choppers of ancient Greece. "Dash": confuse.
5. As above, line 9, outcome. "Fact": feat.

Sit unpolluted, and th' ethereal mold[6]
Incapable of stain would soon expel
Her mischief, and purge off the baser fire,
Victorious. Thus repulsed, our final hope
Is flat despair: we must exasperate
Th' almighty Victor to spend all his rage,
And that must end us, that must be our cure,
To be no more. Sad cure! for who would lose,
Though full of pain, this intellectual being,
Those thoughts that wander through eternity,
To perish rather, swallowed up and lost
In the wide womb of uncreated Night,
Devoid of sense and motion? And who knows,
Let this be good,[7] whether our angry Foe
Can give it, or will ever? How he can
Is doubtful; that he never will is sure.
Will he, so wise, let loose at once his ire,
Belike[8] through impotence, or unaware,
To give his enemies their wish, and end
Them in his anger, whom his anger saves
To punish endless? 'Wherefore cease we then?'
Say they who counsel war, 'we are decreed,
Reserved and destined to eternal woe;
Whatever doing, what can we suffer more,
What can we suffer worse?' Is this then worst,
Thus sitting, thus consulting, thus in arms?
What when we fled amain,[9] pursued and strook
With Heaven's afflicting thunder, and besought
The deep to shelter us? this Hell then seemed
A refuge from those wounds. Or when we lay
Chained on the burning lake? that sure was worse.
What if the breath that kindled those grim fires,
Awaked, should blow them into sevenfold rage,
And plunge us in the flames? or from above
Should intermitted[1] vengeance arm again
His red right hand to plague us? What if all
Her[2] stores were opened, and this firmament
Of Hell should spout her cataracts of fire,
Impendent[3] horrors, threatening hideous fall
One day upon our heads; while we perhaps
Designing or exhorting glorious war,
Caught in a fiery tempest shall be hurled,
Each on his rock transfixed, the sport and prey
Of racking whirlwinds, or forever sunk
Under yon boiling ocean, wrapped in chains;

6. Substance. "Ethereal" substance, derived from "ether," is thought to be incorruptible.
7. I.e., suppose it is good to be destroyed.
8. Ironically, in the sense of "I dare say."
9. Headlong. "Strook": struck.
1. Momentarily suspended.
2. Those of Hell.
3. In the Latin sense, hanging down, threatening.

There to converse with everlasting groans,
Unrespited, unpitied, unreprieved,
Ages of hopeless end! This would be worse.
War therefore, open or concealed, alike
My voice dissuades; for what can force or guile[4]
With him, or who deceive his mind, whose eye
Views all things at one view? He from Heaven's height
All these our motions[5] vain, sees and derides,
Not more almighty to resist our might
Than wise to frustrate all our plots and wiles.
Shall we then live thus vile, the race of Heaven
Thus trampled, thus expelled to suffer here
Chains and these torments? Better these than worse,
By my advice; since fate inevitable
Subdues us, and omnipotent decree,
The Victor's will. To suffer, as to do,
Our strength is equal,[6] nor the law unjust
That so ordains: this was at first resolved,
If we were wise, against so great a foe
Contending, and so doubtful what might fall.
I laugh, when those who at the spear are bold
And venturous, if that fail them, shrink and fear
What yet they know must follow, to endure
Exile, or ignominy, or bonds, or pain,
The sentence of their Conqueror. This is now
Our doom; which if we can sustain and bear,
Our súpreme Foe in time may much remit
His anger, and perhaps, thus far removed,
Not mind us not offending, satisfied
With what is punished;[7] whence these raging fires
Will slacken, if his breath stir not their flames.
Our purer essence then will overcome
Their noxious vapor, or inured[8] not feel,
Or changed at length, and to the place conformed
In temper and in nature, will receive
Familiar the fierce heat, and void of pain;
This horror will grow mild, this darkness light;
Besides what hope the never-ending flight
Of future days may bring, what chance, what change
Worth waiting, since our present lot appears
For happy though but ill, for ill not worst,[9]
If we procure not to ourselves more woe."
Thus Belial, with words clothed in reason's garb,

4. The verb "accomplish" or "achieve" is omitted.

5. Proposals, plots.

6. I.e., passive endurance and active energy are both in the devils' power. Belial points out, with dangerous good sense, that they must have known from the beginning that they might have to exercise both (lines 201–3).

7. A Latinism, *quod punitum est;* God will be satisfied with the punishment that has been inflicted.

8. Accustomed.

9. I.e., from the point of view of happiness, the devils are but ill off; from the point of view of evil, they could be worse. This is diabolic relativism.

Counseled ignoble ease and peaceful sloth,
Not peace; and after him thus Mammon spake:
"Either to disenthrone the King of Heaven
We war, if war be best, or to regain
Our own right lost: him to unthrone we then
May hope, when everlasting Fate shall yield
To fickle Chance, and Chaos judge the strife.
The former, vain to hope, argues[1] as vain
The latter; for what place can be for us
Within Heaven's bound, unless Heaven's Lord supreme
We overpower? Suppose he should relent
And publish grace to all, on promise made
Of new subjection; with what eyes could we
Stand in his presence humble, and receive
Strict laws imposed, to celebrate his throne
With warbled hymns, and to his Godhead sing
Forced Halleluiahs; while he lordly sits
Our envied Sovereign, and his altar breathes
Ambrosial odors and ambrosial flowers,
Our servile offerings? This must be our task
In Heaven, this our delight; how wearisome
Eternity so spent in worship paid
To whom we hate! Let us not then pursue,
By force impossible, by leave obtained
Unácceptable, though in Heaven, our state
Of spendid vassalage;[2] but rather seek
Our own good from ourselves, and from our own
Live to ourselves, though in this vast recess,
Free, and to none accountable, preferring
Hard liberty before the easy yoke
Of servile pomp. Our greatness will appear
Then most conspicuous, when great things of small,
Useful of hurtful, prosperous of adverse,
We can create, and in what place soe'er
Thrive under evil, and work ease out of pain
Through labor and endurance. This deep world
Of darkness do we dread? How oft amidst
Thick clouds and dark doth Heaven's all-ruling Sire
Choose to reside, his glory unobscured,
And with the majesty of darkness round
Covers his throne; from whence deep thunders roar,
Mustering their rage, and Heaven resembles Hell!
As he our darkness, cannot we his light
Imitate when we please? This desert soil
Wants[3] not her hidden luster, gems, and gold;
Nor want we skill or art, from whence to raise
Magnificence; and what can Heaven show more?

1. Proves.
2. Servitude.
3. Lacks. Mammon proposes a tawdry imitation-Heaven in Hell; this is the ultimate in diabolic degradation.

Our torments also may in length of time
Become our elements, these piercing fires
As soft as now severe, our temper changed
Into their temper; which must needs remove
The sensible[4] of pain. All things invite
To peaceful counsels, and the settled state
Of order, how in safety best we may
Compose our present evils, with regard
Of what we are and where, dismissing quite
All thoughts of war. Ye have what I advise."
He scarce had finished, when such murmur filled
Th' assembly, as when hollow rocks retain
The sound of blustering winds, which all night long
Had roused the sea, now with hoarse cadence lull
Seafaring men o'erwatched,[5] whose bark by chance,
Or pinnace, anchors in a craggy bay
After the tempest: such applause was heard
As Mammon ended, and his sentence pleased,
Advising peace; for such another field
They dreaded worse than Hell; so much the fear
Of thunder and the sword of Michaël[6]
Wrought still within them; and no less desire
To found this nether empire, which might rise
By policy, and long process of time,
In emulation opposite to Heaven.
Which when Beëlzebub perceived, than whom,
Satan except, none higher sat, with grave
Aspect he rose, and in his rising seemed
A pillar of state; deep on his front[7] engraven
Deliberation sat and public care;
And princely counsel in his face yet shone,
Majestic though in ruin. Sage he stood
With Atlantean[8] shoulders fit to bear
The weight of mightiest monarchies; his look
Drew audience and attention still as night
Or summer's noontide air, while thus he spake:
"Thrones and imperial powers, offspring of Heaven,
Ethereal virtues; or these titles now
Must we renounce, and, changing style, be called
Princes of Hell? For so the popular vote
Inclines, here to continue, and build up here
A growing empire—Doubtless! while we dream,
And know not that the King of Heaven hath doomed
This place our dungeon, not our safe retreat
Beyond his potent arm, to live exempt
From Heaven's high jurisdiction, in new league

4. Sense, sensation.
5. Tired out with watching.
6. The warrior angel, chief stay of the angelic armies.
7. Forehead, brow.
8. Worthy of Atlas, one of the Titans, who as a punishment for rebellion was condemned to stand in North Africa and hold up the heavens.

Banded against his throne, but to remain
In strictest bondage, though thus far removed,
Under th' inevitable curb, reserved
His captive multitude. For he, be sure,
In height or depth, still first and last will reign
Sole King, and of his kingdom lose no part
By our revolt, but over Hell extend
His empire, and with iron scepter rule
Us here, as with his golden those in Heaven.
What[9] sit we then projecting peace and war?
War hath determined us,[1] and foiled with loss
Irreparable; terms of peace yet none
Vouchsafed or sought; for what peace will be given
To us enslaved, but custody severe,
And stripes, and arbitrary punishment
Inflicted? and what peace can we return,
But, to our power,[2] hostility and hate,
Untamed reluctance,[3] and revenge, though slow,
Yet ever plotting how the Conqueror least
May reap his conquest, and may least rejoice
In doing what we most in suffering feel?[4]
Nor will occasion want, nor shall we need
With dangerous expedition to invade
Heaven, whose high walls fear no assault or siege,
Or ambush from the deep. What if we find
Some easier enterprise? There is a place
(If ancient and prophetic fame[5] in Heaven
Err not), another world, the happy seat
Of some new race called *Man*, about this time
To be created like to us,[6] though less
In power and excellence, but favored more
Of him who rules above; so was his will
Pronounced among the gods, and by an oath,
That shook Heaven's whole circumference, confirmed.
Thither let us bend all our thoughts, to learn
What creatures there inhabit, of what mold,
Or substance, how endued,[7] and what their power,
And where their weakness, how attempted[8] best,
By force or subtlety. Though Heaven be shut,
And Heaven's high Arbitrator sit secure
In his own strength, this place may lie exposed,
The utmost border of his kingdom, left
To their defense who hold it;[9] here, perhaps,

9. Why.
1. I.e., war has decided the question for (but also, limited) us.
2. I.e., to the best of our power.
3. Resistance (in the Latin sense, struggling back).
4. How God may get least pleasure from our pain—a devil's view of the deity.
5. Report, rumor.
6. The created (Ptolemaic) cosmos came into existence only after the fall of Satan, and the fallen angels, being otherwise occupied, could not know of it.
7. Endowed.
8. Attacked, but also "tempted."
9. To be defended by the occupants.

Some advantageous act may be achieved
By sudden onset: either with Hell-fire
To waste[1] his whole creation, or possess
All as our own, and drive, as we were driven,
The puny habitants; or if not drive,
Seduce them to our party, that their God
May prove their foe, and with repenting hand
Abolish his own works. This would surpass
Common revenge, and interrupt his joy
In our confusion, and our joy upraise
In his disturbance; when his darling sons,
Hurled headlong to partake with us, shall curse
Their frail original,[2] and faded bliss,
Faded so soon! Advise if this be worth
Attempting, or to sit in darkness here
Hatching vain empires." Thus Beëlzebub
Pleaded his devilish counsel, first devised
By Satan, and in part proposed; for whence,
But from the author of all ill could spring
So deep a malice, to confound[3] the race
Of mankind in one root, and Earth with Hell
To mingle and involve, done all to spite
The great Creator? But their spite still serves
His glory to augment. The bold design
Pleased highly those infernal states, and joy
Sparkled in all their eyes; with full assent
They vote: whereat his speech he thus renews:
"Well have ye judged, well ended long debate,
Synod of gods, and, like to what ye are,
Great things resolved; which from the lowest deep
Will once more lift us up, in spite of Fate,
Nearer our ancient seat; perhaps in view
Of those bright confines, whence with neighboring arms
And opportune excursion we may chance
Re-enter Heaven; or else in some mild zone
Dwell not unvisited of Heaven's fair light,
Secure, and at the brightening orient beam
Purge off this gloom; the soft delicious air,
To heal the scar of these corrosive fires,
Shall breathe her balm. But first, whom shall we send
In search of this new world? whom shall we find
Sufficient? who shall tempt[4] with wandering feet
The dark, unbottomed, infinite abyss,
And through the palpable obscure[5] find out
His uncouth way, or spread his airy flight
Upborn with indefatigable wings

1. Lay waste.
2. Originator, parent; or, perhaps, "their original condition."
3. Destroy, ruin. Adam, the first man, is the "root" of mankind.
4. Try, attempt (from Latin *temptare*).
5. Darkness so thick it can be felt. "Uncouth": strange, new.

Over the vast abrupt,[6] ere he arrive
The happy isle?[7] What strength, what art, can then
Suffice, or what evasion bear him safe
Through the strict senteries[8] and stations thick
Of angels watching round? Here he had need
All circumspection, and we now no less
Choice in our suffrage;[9] for on whom we send
The weight of all, and our last hope, relies."
   This said, he sat; and expectation held
His look suspense,[1] awaiting who appeared
To second, or oppose, or undertake
The perilous attempt; but all sat mute,
Pondering the danger with deep thoughts; and each
In others' countenance read his own dismay,
Astonished. None among the choice and prime
Of those Heaven-warring champions could be found
So hardy as to proffer or accept
Alone the dreadful voyage; till at last
Satan, whom now transcendent glory raised
Above his fellows, with monarchal pride
Conscious of highest worth, unmoved thus spake:
   "O progeny of Heaven, empyreal thrones!
With reason hath deep silence and demur[2]
Seized us, though undismayed. Long is the way
And hard, that out of Hell leads up to light;
Our prison strong, this huge convex[3] of fire,
Outrageous to devour, immures us round
Ninefold,[4] and gates of burning adamant,
Barred over us, prohibit all egress.
These passed, if any pass, the void profound
Of unessential[5] Night receives him next,
Wide gaping, and with utter loss of being
Threatens him, plunged in that abortive gulf.
If thence he 'scape into whatever world,
Or unknown region, what remains him less[6]
Than unknown dangers and as hard escape?
But I should ill become this throne, O peers,
And this imperial sovereignty, adorned
With splendor, armed with power, if aught proposed
And judged of public moment,[7] in the shape
Of difficulty or danger, could deter
Me from attempting. Wherefore do I assume

6. Chaos; a striking example of sound imitating sense.
7. Wherever man is (for the fallen angels do not yet know of Earth).
8. Old spelling of *sentries*, necessary here for the meter.
9. Care in our voting.
1. I.e., everyone sat waiting in suspense.
2. Delay.
3. Vault.
4. Walls us in with nine thicknesses. See below, lines 645 ff.
5. Without real being, darkness being merely the absence of light. The "abortive gulf" expresses again this completely negative quality of Chaos and Night.
6. I.e., what awaits him except.
7. Importance.

These royalties,[8] and not refuse to reign,
Refusing to accept as great a share
Of hazard as of honor, due alike
To him who reigns, and so much to him due
Of hazard more, as he above the rest
High honored sits?[9] Go therefore, mighty powers,
Terror of Heaven, though fallen; intend[1] at home,
While here shall be our home, what best may ease
The present misery, and render Hell
More tolerable; if there be cure or charm
To respite, or deceive, or slack the pain
Of this ill mansion; intermit no watch
Against a wakeful foe, while I abroad
Through all the coasts of dark destruction seek
Deliverance for us all: this enterprise
None shall partake with me." Thus saying, rose
The monarch, and prevented[2] all reply;
Prudent, lest, from his resolution raised,[3]
Others among the chief might offer now
(Certain to be refused) what erst they feared,
And, so refused, might in opinion stand
His rivals, winning cheap the high repute
Which he through hazard huge must earn. But they
Dreaded not more th' adventure than his voice
Forbidding; and at once with him they rose;
Their rising all at once was as the sound
Of thunder heard remote. Towards him they bend
With awful[4] reverence prone; and as a god
Extol him equal to the Highest in Heaven.
Nor failed they to express how much they praised,
That for the general safety he despised
His own; for neither do the spirits damned
Lose all their virtue; lest bad men should boast
Their specious deeds on Earth, which glory excites,
Or close ambition varnished o'er with zeal.[5]
  Thus they their doubtful consultations dark
Ended, rejoicing in their matchless chief:
As when from mountain tops the dusky clouds
Ascending, while the north wind sleeps, o'erspread
Heaven's cheerful face, the lowering element
Scowls o'er the darkened landscape snow or shower;
If chance the radiant sun with farewell sweet
Extend his evening beam, the fields revive,

8. Insignia of royalty. "Refusing": i.e., if I refuse.
9. Satan's argument, simple though entangled in rhetoric, is that rulers must share in the dangers as well as the rewards of an enterprise.
1. Undertake, endeavor.
2. Forestalled, anticipated.
3. After their courage had been raised by his resolution.
4. Full of respect and awe.
5. The sense is that damned spirits still retain some virtues; lest bad men boast of good deeds they have done out of glory and ambition, Milton has shown us that devils do just as much. "Specious": pretending virtue. "Close": secret.

The birds their notes renew, and bleating herds
Attest their joy, that hill and valley rings.
O shame to men! Devil with devil damned
Firm concord holds, men only disagree
Of creatures rational, though under hope
Of heavenly grace; and, God proclaiming peace,[6]
Yet live in hatred, enmity, and strife
Among themselves, and levy cruel wars,
Wasting the earth, each other to destroy:
As if (which might induce us to accord)
Man had not hellish foes enow[7] besides,
That day and night for his destruction wait!
   The Stygian council thus dissolved; and forth
In order came the grand infernal peers.
Midst came their mighty paramount,[8] and seemed
Alone th' antagonist of Heaven, nor less
Than Hell's dread emperor, with pomp supreme,
And godlike imitated state; him round
A globe[9] of fiery seraphim enclosed
With bright emblazonry,[1] and horrent arms.
Then of their session ended they bid cry
With trumpets' regal sound the great result:
Toward the four winds four speedy cherubim
Put to their mouths the sounding alchemy[2]
By herald's voice explained; the hollow abyss
Heard far and wide, and all the host of Hell
With deafening shout, returned them loud acclaim.
Thence more at ease their minds and somewhat raised
By false presumptuous hope, the rangéd[3] powers
Disband; and, wandering, each his several way
Pursues, as inclination or sad choice
Leads him perplexed where he may likeliest find
Truce to his restless thoughts, and entertain
The irksome hours, till his great chief return.
Part on the plain, or in the air sublime,[4]
Upon the wing, or in swift race contend,
As at th' Olympian games or Pythian fields;[5]
Part curb their fiery steeds, or shun the goal
With rapid wheels, or fronted brígades form.
As when, to warn proud cities, war appears
Waged in the troubled sky, and armies rush
To battle in the clouds;[6] before each van
Prick forth the airy knights, and couch their spears

6. I.e., though God proclaims peace.
7. I.e., enough; the old plural emphatic form.
8. Champion, chief.
9. Band or crowd.
1. Decorated shields. "Horrent": bristling.
2. I.e., resonant trumpets (made of the alloy brass by a marriage of metals which Milton associates with alchemy).
3. Arrayed in ranks.
4. Aloft, uplifted (the adjective modifies the flyer, not the air).
5. The Olympic games were held at Olympia, the Pythian games at Delphi. To "shun the goal" is to drive a chariot as close as possible around a column without hitting it.
6. Warfare in the skies at night, portending trouble on earth. "Prick": spur.

Till thickest legions close; with feats of arms
From either end of Heaven the welkin[7] burns.
Others with vast Typhoean[8] rage more fell
Rend up both rocks and hills, and ride the air
In whirlwind; Hell scarce holds the wild uproar.
As when Alcides, from Oechalia crowned
With conquest, felt th' envenomed robe, and tore
Through pain up by the roots Thessalian pines,
And Lichas from the top of Oeta threw
Into th' Euboic sea.[9] Others more mild,
Retreated in a silent valley, sing
With notes angelical to many a harp
Their own heroic deeds and hapless fall
By doom of battle; and complain that Fate
Free Virtue should enthrall to Force or Chance.
Their song was partial,[1] but the harmony
(What could it less when spirits immortal sing?)
Suspended[2] Hell, and took with ravishment
The thronging audience. In discourse more sweet
(For eloquence the soul, song charms the sense)
Others apart sat on a hill retired,
In thoughts more elevate, and reasoned high
Of providence, foreknowledge, will, and fate,
Fixed fate, free will, foreknowledge absolute,
And found no end, in wandering mazes lost.
Of good and evil much they argued then,
Of happiness and final misery,
Passion and apathy,[3] and glory and shame,
Vain wisdom all, and false philosophy![4]
Yet with a pleasing sorcery could charm
Pain for a while or anguish, and excite
Fallacious hope, or arm th' obdurèd[5] breast
With stubborn patience as with triple steel.
Another part, in squadrons and gross[6] bands,
On bold adventure to discover wide
That dismal world, if any clime perhaps
Might yield them easier habitation, bend
Four ways their flying march, along the banks
Of four infernal rivers that disgorge

7. Sky.
8. Like that of Typhon, the hundred-headed Titan. See above, I.199.
9. Hercules, returning in triumph from Oechalia, prepared to sacrifice to the gods on top of Mt. Oeta, and sent to his wife Dejanira for a new robe. She had been told by the dying Nessus, a centaur whom Hercules had killed, that centaur's blood would preserve her husband's love. So she sent Hercules a robe anointed with the blood of Nessus. The "envenomed robe" tortured him into a frenzy, and before he died, he threw Lichas, who had brought it, together with a good part of Mt. Oeta itself, into the sea of Euboea.
1. Prejudiced.
2. Held in suspense.
3. Feeling and lack of feeling; the angels are dabbling in Stoicism.
4. Milton means, not that the subjects themselves are vain (he himself, in the present poem, has a good deal to say on these topics), but that the very premises with which devils start are bound to land them in error.
5. Hardened.
6. Solid, dense.

Into the burning lake their baleful streams:[7]
Abhorréd Styx, the flood of deadly hate;
Sad Acheron of sorrow, black and deep;
Cocytus, named of lamentation loud
Heard on the rueful stream; fierce Phlegethon
Whose waves of torrent fire inflame with rage.
Far off from these a slow and silent stream,
Lethe, the river of oblivion, rolls
Her watery labyrinth, whereof who drinks
Forthwith his former state and being forgets,
Forgets both joy and grief, pleasure and pain.
Beyond this flood a frozen continent
Lies dark and wild, beat with perpetual storms
Of whirlwind and dire hail, which on firm land
Thaws not, but gathers heap,[8] and ruin seems
Of ancient pile; all else deep snow and ice,
A gulf profound as that Serbonian bog[9]
Betwixt Damiata and Mount Casius old,
Where armies whole have sunk: the parching air
Burns frore,[1] and cold performs th' effect of fire.
Thither by harpy-footed[2] Furies haled,
At certain revolutions[3] all the damned
Are brought; and feel by turns the bitter change
Of fierce extremes, extremes by change more fierce,
From beds of raging fire to starve[4] in ice
Their soft ethereal warmth, and there to pine
Immovable, infixed, and frozen round
Periods of time; thence hurried back to fire.
They ferry over this Lethean sound
Both to and fro, their sorrow to augment,
And wish and struggle, as they pass, to reach
The tempting stream, with one small drop to lose
In sweet forgetfulness all pain and woe,
All in one moment, and so near the brink;
But Fate withstands, and to oppose th' attempt
Medusa[5] with Gorgonian terror guards
The ford, and of itself the water flies
All taste of living wight, as once it fled
The lips of Tantalus.[6] Thus roving on
In cónfused march forlorn, th' adventurous bands

7. The four rivers are traditional in hellish geography; Milton takes pains to distinguish them by the original meanings of their Greek names (Styx means "hateful," Acheron "woeful," etc.). Lethe is "far off" and very different from the others, oblivion being relatively a blessed state in hell.
8. In a heap, so that it looks like the ruin of an old building ("ancient pile").
9. Lake Serbonis, once famous for its quicksands but today dried up, used to lie on the coast of Egypt, just east of the Nile, between Damiata and Mt. Cassius.
1. Frosty.
2. With hooked claws.
3. I.e., of time.
4. Benumb.
5. One of the three Gorgons, women with snaky hair, scaly bodies, and boar's tusks, the very sight of whose faces changed men to stone.
6. Tantalus, afflicted with a raging thirst, stood in the middle of a lake, the water of which always eluded his grasp (hence, "tantalize").

With shuddering horror pale, and eyes aghast
Viewed first their lamentable lot, and found
No rest. Through many a dark and dreary vale
They passed, and many a region dolorous,
O'er many a frozen, many a fiery alp,[7]
Rocks, caves, lakes, fens, bogs, dens, and shades of death,
A universe of death, which God by curse
Created evil, for evil only good,
Where all life dies, death lives, and Nature breeds,
Perverse, all monstrous, all prodigious things,
Abominable, unutterable, and worse
Than fables yet have feigned, or fear conceived,
Gorgons, and Hydras, and Chimeras[8] dire.
  Meanwhile the adversary of God and man,
Satan with thoughts inflamed of highest design,
Puts on swift wings,[9] and toward the gates of Hell
Explores his solitary flight; sometimes
He scours the right hand coast, sometimes the left;
Now shaves with level wing the deep, then soars
Up to the fiery concave[1] towering high.
As when far off at sea a fleet descried
Hangs in the clouds, by equinoctial winds
Close sailing from Bengala,[2] or the isles
Of Ternate and Tidore,[3] whence merchants bring
Their spicy drugs; they on the trading flood
Through the wide Ethiopian[4] to the Cape
Ply stemming nightly toward the pole: so seemed
Far off the flying fiend. At last appear
Hell bounds, high reaching to the horrid roof,
And thrice threefold the gates; three folds were brass,
Three iron, three of adamantine rock,
Impenetrable, impaled with circling fire,
Yet unconsumed. Before the gates there sat
On either side a formidable shape;[5]
The one seemed woman to the waist, and fair,
But ended foul in many a scaly fold
Voluminous and vast, a serpent armed
With mortal sting. About her middle round
A cry[6] of Hellhounds never-ceasing barked

7. A "fiery alp" is a volcano.
8. The Hydra was a serpent with nine heads, which was slain by Hercules; the Chimera was a fire-breathing creature, part lion, part dragon, part goat. They exemplify abominations of nature.
9. Satan does not fasten on his wings; he takes swiftly to wing.
1. Vault.
2. An old form of "Bengal."
3. Two of the Molucca or "Spice" Islands, modern Indonesia.
4. The Indian Ocean, east of Africa. "The Cape" is of course the Cape of Good Hope; "the pole," the South Pole.
5. The allegorical figures of Sin and Death are founded on James i.15: "Then when lust hath conceived, it bringeth forth sin: and sin, when it is finished, bringeth forth death." But the incestuous relations of Sin and Death are Milton's own invention. Physically, Sin is modeled on Virgil's or Ovid's Scylla, with some touches adopted from Spenser's Error; Death is a traditional figure, vague and vast.
6. Pack.

With wide Cerberean[7] mouths full loud, and rung
A hideous peal; yet, when they list, would creep,
If aught disturbed their noise, into her womb,
And kennel there, yet there still barked and howled
Within unseen. Far less abhorred than these
Vexed Scylla,[8] bathing in the sea that parts
Calabria from the hoarse Trinacrian shore;
Nor uglier follow the night-hag,[9] when, called
In secret, riding through the air she comes,
Lured with the smell of infant blood, to dance
With Lapland witches, while the laboring moon
Eclipses at their charms. The other shape,
If shape it might be called that shape had none
Distinguishable in member, joint, or limb,
Or substance might be called that shadow seemed,
For each seemed either; black it stood as night,
Fierce as ten Furies, terrible as Hell,
And shook a dreadful dart; what seemed his head
The likeness of a kingly crown had on.
Satan was now at hand, and from his seat
The monster moving onward came as fast,
With horrid strides; Hell trembled as he strode.
Th' undaunted fiend what this might be admired,[1]
Admired, not feared; God and his Son except,
Created thing nought valued he nor shunned;
And with disdainful look thus first began:
"Whence and what art thou, execrable shape,
That dar'st, though grim and terrible, advance
Thy miscreated front[2] athwart my way
To yonder gates? Through them I mean to pass,
That be assured, without leave asked of thee.
Retire, or taste thy folly, and learn by proof,
Hell-born, not to contend with spirits of Heaven."
To whom the goblin, full of wrath, replied:
"Art thou that traitor angel, art thou he,
Who first broke peace in Heaven, and faith, till then
Unbroken, and in proud rebellious arms
Drew after him the third part of Heaven's sons
Conjured[3] against the Highest, for which both thou
And they, outcast from God, are here condemned
To waste eternal days in woe and pain?
And reckon'st thou thyself with spirits of Heaven,
Hell-doomed, and breath'st defiance here and scorn,
Where I reign king, and, to enrage thee more,

7. Like Cerberus, the traditional hound of Hell.
8. Circe out of jealousy threw poison into the water where Scylla bathed, in the straits between Calabria and Sicily ("Trinacria"); as a result of the poisons, Scylla developed a ring of barking, snapping dogs around her waist.
9. Hecate, goddess of sorcery. She attends the orgies of witches in the home of all witchcraft, Lapland, whither she is drawn by the blood of babies sacrificed for the occasion.
1. Wondered.
2. Misshapen forehead, or face.
3. Sworn together by an oath.

Thy king and lord? Back to thy punishment,
False fugitive, and to thy speed add wings,
Lest with a whip of scorpions I pursue
Thy ling'ring, or with one stroke of this dart
Strange horror seize thee, and pangs unfelt before."
So spake the grisly terror, and in shape,
So speaking and so threatening, grew tenfold
More dreadful and deform. On th' other side,
Incensed with indignation, Satan stood
Unterrified, and like a comet burned
That fires the length of Ophiucus[4] huge
In th' Arctic sky, and from his horrid hair
Shakes pestilence and war. Each at the head
Leveled his deadly aim; their fatal hands
No second stroke intend,[5] and such a frown
Each cast at th' other, as when two black clouds,
With Heaven's artillery fraught,[6] come rattling on
Over the Caspian,[7] then stand front to front
Hovering a space, till winds the signal blow
To join their dark encounter in mid-air:
So frowned the mighty combatants, that Hell
Grew darker at their frown; so matched they stood;
For never but once more was either like
To meet so great a foe.[8] And now great deeds
Had been achieved, whereof all Hell had rung,
Had not the snaky sorceress that sat
Fast by Hell-gate, and kept the fatal key,
Ris'n, and with hideous outcry rushed between.
"O father, what intends thy hand," she cried,
"Against thy only son?[9] What fury, O son,
Possesses thee to bend that mortal dart
Against thy father's head? and know'st for whom?
For Him who sits above and laughs the while
At thee ordained his drudge, to execute
Whate'er his wrath, which he calls Justice, bids;
His wrath which one day will destroy ye both!"
She spake, and at her words the hellish pest
Forbore, then these to her Satan returned:
"So strange thy outcry, and thy words so strange
Thou interposest, that my sudden hand,
Prevented,[1] spares to tell thee yet by deeds
What it intends, till first I know of thee,
What thing thou art, thus double-formed, and why,
In this infernal vale first met, thou call'st

4. A vast Northern constellation, "The Serpent-Holder" (also called "Serpentarius"). Satan will soon appear as a snake; and, like a comet, he portends "pestilence and war."
5. I.e., the first stroke will do the business.
6. Loaded with thunderbolts.
7. The Caspian is a particularly stormy area.
8. I.e., the Son of God.
9. Sin, Death, and Satan, in their various interrelations, parody obscenely the relations between God and the Son, Adam and Eve.
1. Forestalled.

Me father, and that phantasm call'st my son?
I know thee not, nor ever saw till now
Sight more detestable than him and thee."
T' whom thus the portress of Hell-gate replied:
"Hast thou forgot me then, and do I seem
Now in thine eye so foul? once deemed so fair
In Heaven, when at th' assembly, and in sight
Of all the seraphim with thee combined
In bold conspiracy against Heaven's King,
All on a sudden miserable pain
Surprised thee; dim thine eyes, and dizzy swum
In darkness, while thy head flames thick and fast
Threw forth, till on the left side opening wide,
Likest to thee in shape and countenance bright,
Then shining heavenly-fair, a goddess armed
Out of thy head I sprung.[2] Amazement seized
All th' host of Heaven; back they recoiled afraid
At first, and called me *Sin*, and for a sign
Portentous held me; but, familiar grown,
I pleased, and with attractive graces won
The most averse, thee chiefly, who full oft
Thyself in me thy perfect image viewing
Becam'st enamored;[3] and such joy thou took'st
With me in secret, that my womb conceived
A growing burden. Meanwhile war arose,
And fields were fought in Heaven; wherein remained
(For what could else?) to our almighty Foe
Clear victory, to our part loss and rout
Through all the empyrean. Down they fell,
Driven headlong from the pitch[4] of Heaven, down
Into this deep, and in the general fall
I also; at which time this powerful key
Into my hand was given, with charge to keep
These gates forever shut, which none can pass
Without my opening. Pensive here I sat
Alone, but long I sat not, till my womb
Pregnant by thee, and now excessive grown,
Prodigious motion felt and rueful throes.
At last this odious offspring whom thou seest,
Thine own begotten, breaking violent way,
Tore through my entrails, that, with fear and pain
Distorted, all my nether shape thus grew
Transformed; but he, my inbred enemy,
Forth issued, brandishing his fatal dart,
Made to destroy. I fled, and cried out *Death!*
Hell trembled at the hideous name, and sighed
From all her caves, and back resounded *Death!*

2. As Athena sprang full-grown from the head of Zeus.
3. Sin looks attractive at first, being a lovely woman at the top of her body; but she is a serpent below, and ends in a "mortal sting," i.e., death. See James i.14, "when lust hath conceived, it bringeth forth sin, and sin, when it is finished, bringeth forth death."
4. Peak.

I fled; but he pursued (though more, it seems,
Inflamed with lust than rage) and, swifter far,
Me overtook, his mother, all dismayed,
And in embraces forcible and foul
Engendering with me, of that rape begot
These yelling monsters, that with ceaseless cry
Surround me, as thou sawest, hourly conceived
And hourly born, with sorrow infinite
To me; for when they list, into the womb
That bred them they return, and howl, and gnaw
My bowels, their repast; then, bursting forth
Afresh, with conscious terrors vex me round,
That rest or intermission none I find.
Before mine eyes in opposition sits
Grim Death, my son and foe, who sets them on,
And me his parent would full soon devour
For want of other prey, but that he knows
His end with mine involved; and knows that I
Should prove a bitter morsel, and his bane,
Whenever that shall be; so Fate pronounced.
But thou, O father, I forewarn thee, shun
His deadly arrow; neither vainly hope
To be invulnerable in those bright arms,
Though tempered heavenly; for that mortal dint,
Save he who reigns above, none can resist."[5]
  She finished, and the subtle fiend his lore
Soon learned, now milder, and thus answered smooth:
"Dear daughter, since thou claimest me for thy sire,
And my fair son here show'st me, the dear pledge
Of dalliance had with thee in Heaven, and joys
Then sweet, now sad to mention, through dire change
Befallen us unforeseen, unthought of; know
I come no enemy, but to set free
From out this dark and dismal house of pain,
Both him and thee, and all the Heavenly host
Of spirits that, in our just pretenses[6] armed,
Fell with us from on high. From them I go
This uncouth errand sole,[7] and one for all
Myself expose, with lonely steps to tread
Th' unfounded deep, and through the void immense
To search with wandering quest a place foretold
Should be, and, by concurring signs, ere now
Created vast and round, a place of bliss
In the purlieus[8] of Heaven, and therein placed
A race of upstart creatures, to supply
Perhaps our vacant room, though more removed,
Lest Heaven, surcharged[9] with potent multitude,

5. I.e., only God is immune to death.
6. Grievances.
7. Alone on a desolate journey.
8. Outskirts, suburbs.
9. Too full. "Broils": controversies.

Might hap to move new broils. Be this, or aught
Than this more secret, now designed, I haste
To know; and, this once known, shall soon return,
And bring ye to the place where thou and Death
Shall dwell at ease, and up and down unseen
Wing silently the buxom[1] air, embalmed
With odors: there ye shall be fed and filled
Immeasurably; all things shall be your prey."
He ceased, for both seemed highly pleased, and Death
Grinned horrible a ghastly smile, to hear
His famine[2] should be filled, and blessed his maw
Destined to that good hour. No less rejoiced
His mother bad, and thus bespake her sire:
"The key of this infernal pit, by due
And by command of Heaven's all-powerful King
I keep, by him forbidden to unlock
These adamantine gates; against all force
Death ready stands to interpose his dart,
Fearless to be o'ermatched by living might.
But what owe I to his commands above
Who hates me, and hath hither thrust me down
Into this gloom of Tartarus profound,
To sit in hateful office here confined,
Inhabitant of Heaven and heavenly-born,
Here in perpetual agony and pain,
With terrors and with clamors compassed round
Of mine own brood that on my bowels feed?
Thou art my father, thou my author, thou
My being gav'st me; whom should I obey
But thee? whom follow? Thou wilt bring me soon
To that new world of light and bliss, among
The gods who live at ease, where I shall reign
At thy right hand voluptuous,[3] as beseems
Thy daughter and thy darling, without end."
Thus saying, from her side the fatal key,
Sad instrument of all our woe, she took;
And, towards the gate rolling her bestial train,[4]
Forthwith the huge portcullis high up-drew,
Which but herself not all the Stygian powers[5]
Could once have moved; then in the keyhole turns
Th' intricate wards, and every bolt and bar
Of massy iron or solid rock with ease
Unfastens: on a sudden open fly
With impetuous recoil and jarring sound
Th' infernal doors, and on their hinges grate

1. Yielding. "Embalmed": made fragrant, but also with a thought of the process associated with death.
2. Hunger, belly.
3. As the Son sits at God's right hand, Sin will sit at Satan's; a blasphemous parody of the Creed, showed up by the word "voluptuous."
4. I.e., accompanied by her yelping offspring.
5. The powers of Hell.

Harsh thunder, that the lowest bottom shook
Of Erebus.[6] She opened, but to shut
Excelled[7] her power; the gates wide open stood,
That with extended wings a bannered host,
Under spread ensigns[8] marching, might pass through
With horse and chariots ranked in loose array;
So wide they stood, and like a furnace-mouth
Cast forth redounding[9] smoke and ruddy flame.
Before their eyes in sudden view appear
The secrets of the hoary deep, a dark
Illimitable ocean, without bound,
Without dimension; where length, breadth, and height,
And time and place are lost; where eldest Night
And Chaos, ancestors of Nature, hold
Eternal anarchy, amidst the noise
Of endless wars, and by confusion stand.
For Hot, Cold, Moist, and Dry, four champions fierce
Strive here for mastery, and to battle bring
Their embryon atoms;[1] they around the flag
Of each his faction, in their several clans,
Light-armed or heavy, sharp, smooth, swift, or slow,
Swarm populous, unnumbered as the sands
Of Barca or Cyrene's torrid soil,[2]
Levied to side with warring winds, and poise[3]
Their lighter wings. To whom these most adhere,
He rules a moment; Chaos[4] umpire sits,
And by decision more embroils the fray
By which he reigns: next him, high arbiter,
Chance governs all. Into this wild abyss,
The womb of Nature and perhaps her grave,
Of neither sea, nor shore, nor air, nor fire,
But all these in their pregnant causes[5] mixed
Confusedly, and which thus must ever fight,
Unless th' Almighty Maker them ordain
His dark materials to create more worlds,[6]
Into this wild abyss the wary fiend
Stood on the brink of Hell and looked awhile,
Pondering his voyage; for no narrow frith[7]
He had to cross. Nor was his ear less pealed[8]
With noises loud and ruinous (to compare
Great things with small) than when Bellona[9] storms,

6. Another classical name for Hell.
7. Exceeded. That Sin cannot shut Hell gate, though she can open it, is symbolical.
8. Standards, flags.
9. Billowing.
1. The four elements, fire, earth, water, and air, struggle endlessly in Chaos. "Embryon": embryo, unformed.
2. Barca and Cyrene were cities built on the shifting sands of North Africa.
3. Give weight to.
4. Chaos is both the place where confusion reigns and personified confusion itself.
5. Chaos is not organized to the point of being matter; it is the seeds of all forms of matter.
6. God must impose order on Chaos to create worlds from it.
7. Channel, firth.
8. Rung.
9. Goddess of war.

With all her battering engines bent to raze
Some capital city; or less than if this frame
Of Heaven were falling, and these elements
In mutiny had from her axle torn
The steadfast Earth. At last his sail-broad vans[1]
He spreads for flight, and in the surging smoke
Uplifted spurns the ground; thence many a league,
As in a cloudy chair ascending, rides
Audacious; but that seat soon failing, meets
A vast vacuity: all unawares,
Fluttering his pennons[2] vain, plumb down he drops
Ten thousand fathom deep, and to this hour
Down had been falling, had not by ill chance
The strong rebuff[3] of some tumultuous cloud,
Instinct[4] with fire and niter, hurried him
As many miles aloft; that fury stayed,
Quenched in a boggy Syrtis,[5] neither sea,
Nor good dry land, nigh foundered on he fares,
Treading the crude consistence, half on foot,
Half flying; behoves[6] him now both oar and sail.
As when a gryphon through the wilderness
With wingéd course o'er hill or moory dale,
Pursues the Arimaspian, who by stealth
Had from his wakeful custody purloined
The guarded gold:[7] so eagerly the fiend
O'er bog or steep, through strait, rough, dense, or rare,
With head, hands, wings, or feet pursues his way,
And swims, or sinks, or wades, or creeps, or flies.
At length a universal hubbub wild
Of stunning sounds and voices all confused
Borne through the hollow dark, assaults his ear
With loudest vehemence. Thither he plies
Undaunted, to meet there whatever power
Or spirit of the nethermost abyss
Might in that noise reside, of whom to ask
Which way the nearest coast of darkness lies
Bordering on light; when straight behold the throne
Of Chaos, and his dark pavilion spread
Wide on the wasteful deep! With him enthroned
Sat sable-vested Night, eldest of things,
The consort of his reign; and by them stood
Orcus and Ades,[8] and the dreaded name

1. Wings.
2. Pinions, from Latin *pennae*, "wings."
3. Puff or blast.
4. Filled. "Niter": saltpeter.
5. Quicksand, from the North African gulfs, famous for their shifting sandbars.
6. Befits.
7. Gryphons, fabulous creatures, half-eagle, half-dragon, lived in northern Europe, and were said to hoard gold. When it was stolen from them by the one-eyed Arimaspians, they pursued these curious malefactors, hopping, flapping, and squawking. The story is a piece of moralized natural history, directed against the love of money.
8. Latin and Greek names of Pluto, god of Hell.

Of Demogorgon;[9] Rumor next and Chance,
And Tumult and Confusion all embroiled,
And Discord with a thousand various mouths.
  T' whom Satan, turning boldly, thus: "Ye powers
And spirits of this nethermost abyss,
Chaos and ancient Night, I come no spy,
With purpose to explore or to disturb
The secrets of your realm; but by constraint
Wandering this darksome desert, as my way
Lies through your spacious empire up to light,
Alone and without guide, half lost, I seek
What readiest path leads where your gloomy bounds
Confine with[1] Heaven; or if some other place
From your dominion won, th' Ethereal King
Possesses lately, thither to arrive
I travel this profound.[2] Direct my course:
Directed, no mean recompense it brings
To your behoof,[3] if I that region lost,
All usurpation thence expelled, reduce
To their original darkness and your sway
(Which is my present journey[4]), and once more
Erect the standard there of ancient Night.
Yours be th' advantage all, mine the revenge!"
  Thus Satan; and him thus the anarch[5] old,
With faltering speech and visage incomposed,[6]
Answered: "I know thee, stranger, who thou art,
That mighty leading angel, who of late
Made head against Heaven's King, though overthrown.
I saw and heard; for such a numerous host
Fled not in silence through the frighted deep
With ruin upon ruin, rout on rout,
Confusion worse confounded; and Heaven-gates
Poured out by millions her victorious bands,
Pursuing. I upon my frontiers here
Keep residence; if all I can will serve,
That little which is left so to defend
Encroached on still through our intestine broils[7]
Weakening the scepter of old Night: first Hell,
Your dungeon, stretching far and wide beneath;
Now lately Heaven and Earth,[8] another world
Hung o'er my realm, linked in a golden chain
To that side Heaven from whence your legions fell.
If that way be your walk, you have not far;

9. A mysterious subdeity, stronger than Fate itself, first invented by Boccaccio. Cf. Shelley's *Prometheus Unbound*.
1. Border on.
2. Deep pit.
3. On your behalf.
4. I.e., the purpose of my present journey.
5. Chaos is not "monarch" of his realm, but "anarch," i.e., nonruler.
6. Disturbed.
7. I.e., our territory is continually shrinking because of our civil wars ("intestine broils").
8. Our human world and its sky have been carved out of Chaos. The sky is distinguished from "Heaven" as used in line 1006, meaning the abode of the blessed, the Empyrean.

So much the nearer danger. Go, and speed!
Havoc and spoil and ruin are my gain."
He ceased; and Satan stayed not to reply,
But, glad that now his sea should find a shore,
With fresh alacrity and force renewed
Springs upward, like a pyramid of fire,
Into the wild expanse, and through the shock
Of fighting elements, on all sides round
Environed, wins his way; harder beset
And more endangered, than when Argo[9] passed
Through Bosporus betwixt the jostling rocks;
Or when Ulysses on the larboard shunned
Charybdis, and by th' other whirlpool steered:
So he with difficulty and labor hard
Moved on: with difficulty and labor he;
But, he once past, soon after when man fell,
Strange alteration! Sin and Death amain,[1]
Following his track (such was the will of Heaven),
Paved after him a broad and beaten way
Over the dark abyss, whose boiling gulf
Tamely endured a bridge of wondrous length
From Hell continued reaching th' utmost orb[2]
Of this frail world; by which the spirits perverse
With easy intercourse pass to and fro
To tempt or punish mortals, except whom
God and good angels guard by special grace.
But now at last the sacred influence
Of light appears, and from the walls of Heaven
Shoots far into the bosom of dim Night
A glimmering dawn. Here Nature first begins
Her farthest verge,[3] and Chaos to retire,
As from her outmost works a broken foe
With tumult less and with less hostile din;
That[4] Satan with less toil, and now with ease
Wafts on the calmer wave by dubious light,
And, like a weather-beaten vessel, holds[5]
Gladly the port, though shrouds and tackle torn;
Or in the emptier waste, resembling air,
Weighs his spread wings, at leisure to behold
Far off th' empyreal Heaven, extended wide
In circuit, undetermined[6] square or round,

9. Jason and his fifty Argonauts, sailing through the Bosporus to the Black Sea in pursuit of the Golden Fleece, had to pass through the Symplegades, or clashing rocks. Ulysses also had a tight squeeze to pass between Scylla and Charybdis, where Italy almost touches Sicily. Charybdis was a whirlpool, but Scylla, the dog-monster who ate alive six of Ulysses' best men, is called by Milton "th' other whirlpool."
1. At full speed, vigorously.
2. The world is surrounded by nine spheres, the whole construction comprising the created universe. The bridge built by Sin and Death ends on the outermost of these spheres.
3. Threshold. The end of Chaos is the beginning of (created) Nature.
4. So that.
5. Makes for.
6. Heaven is so vast that simply by looking at it one cannot tell its shape. Of course it is really round, the circle being an emblem of perfection.

With opal towers and battlements adorned
Of living sapphire, once his native seat;
And fast by, hanging in a golden chain,
This pendant world,[7] in bigness as a star
Of smallest magnitude close by the moon.
Thither, full fraught with mischievous revenge,
Accursed, and in a curséd hour, he hies.

Book III

The Argument

God sitting on his throne sees Satan flying towards this world, then newly created; shows him to the Son who sat at his right hand; foretells the success of Satan in perverting mankind; clears his own justice and wisdom from all imputation, having created man free and able enough to have withstood his tempter; yet declares his purpose of grace towards him, in regard he fell not of his own malice, as did Satan, but by him seduced. The Son of God renders praises to his Father for the manifestations of his gracious purpose towards man; but God again declares, that Grace cannot be extended towards man without the satisfaction of divine justice; man hath offended the majesty of God by aspiring to godhead, and therefore with all his progeny devoted to death must die, unless some one can be found sufficient to answer for his offense, and undergo his punishment. The Son of God freely offers himself a ransom for man: the Father accepts him, ordains his incarnation, pronounces his exaltation above all names in Heaven and earth; commands all the angels to adore him; they obey, and hymning to their harps in full choir, celebrate the Father and the Son. Meanwhile Satan alights upon the bare convex of this world's outermost orb; where wandering he first finds a place since called the Limbo of Vanity; what persons and things fly up thither; thence comes to the gate of Heaven, described ascending by stairs, and the waters above the firmament that flow about it: His passage thence to the orb of the sun; he finds there Uriel the regent of that orb, but first changes himself into the shape of a meaner angel; and pretending a zealous desire to behold the new creation and man whom God placed here, inquires of him the place of his habitation, and is directed; alights first on mount Niphates.

Hail, holy Light, offspring of Heaven first-born!
Or of th' Eternal coeternal beam,
May I express thee unblamed?[1] since God is light,

7. Homer first showed the world as hanging from Heaven by a golden chain (*Iliad* VIII). As Milton uses the image, it has a symbolic meaning as well; earth is dependent on Heaven. The world which hangs from Heaven is not just our earth, but earth and all its nine spheres, the created cosmos, as described by Ptolemy.

1. Milton feels some hesitation at calling Light coeternal with God himself; his reasons follow.

And never but in unapproachéd light
Dwelt from eternity, dwelt then in thee,
Bright effluence of bright essence increate![2]
Or hear'st thou rather[3] pure ethereal stream,
Whose fountain who shall tell? Before the sun,
Before the heavens, thou wert, and at the voice
Of God, as with a mantle, didst invest[4]
The rising world of waters dark and deep,
Won from the void and formless infinite!
Thee I revisit now with bolder wing,
Escaped the Stygian pool, though long detained
In that obscure sojourn, while in my flight,
Through utter and through middle darkness[5] borne,
With other notes than to th' Orphean lyre[6]
I sung of Chaos and eternal Night;
Taught by the Heavenly Muse[7] to venture down
The dark descent, and up to reascend,
Though hard and rare. Thee I revisit safe,
And feel thy sovereign vital lamp; but thou
Revisit'st not these eyes, that roll in vain
To find thy piercing ray, and find no dawn;
So thick a drop serene[8] hath quenched their orbs,
Or dim suffusion veiled. Yet not the more
Cease I to wander where the Muses haunt
Clear spring, or shady grove, or sunny hill,
Smit with the love of sacred song;[9] but chief
Thee, Sion,[1] and the flowery brooks beneath,
That wash thy hallowed feet, and warbling flow,
Nightly I visit: nor sometimes forget[2]
Those other two equaled with me in fate,[3]
So were I equaled with them in renown,
Blind Thamyris and blind Maeonides,
And Tiresias and Phineus, prophets old:[4]
Then feed on thoughts that voluntary move
Harmonious numbers; as the wakeful bird[5]
Sings darkling, and, in shadiest covert hid,
Tunes her nocturnal note. Thus with the year

2. Uncreated, i.e., eternal.
3. I.e., would you rather be called. The construction is a Latinism.
4. Occupy.
5. Hell and Chaos.
6. One of the so-called Orphean Hymns is *To Night*. But Milton's darkness, being Christian, is deeper and wider.
7. Urania.
8. One medical theory about blindness attributed it to a *gutta serena*, another to a *suffusio nigra*.
9. The phrase is Virgilian, "[*Musarum*] *ingenti percussus amore*" (*Georgics* II.476), but the adjective "sacred" is Milton's own reservation.
1. The mountain of Scriptural inspiration, with its brooks Siloa and Kidron.
2. I.e., and never forget: therefore always remember.
3. Blind like me.
4. Thamyris was a blind Thracian poet, who lived before Homer. "Maeonides" is an epithet of Homer, either as a son of Maeon or as a native of Maeonia. Tiresias was the blind prophet of Thebes (cf. *Oedipus Rex*); Phineus was another blind prophet and soothsayer (*Aeneid* III). For Milton poetry and prophesy were intimately joined; blindness of the outer eye rendered more acute the sight of the inner eye; and the very thought of these matters moved him, as he says, spontaneously to verse.
5. The nightingale. "Darkling": at night.

Seasons return; but not to me returns
Day, or the sweet approach of even or morn,
Or sight of vernal bloom, or summer's rose,
Or flocks, or herds, or human face divine;
But cloud instead and ever-during dark
Surrounds me, from the cheerful ways of men
Cut off, and, for the book of knowledge fair,
Presented with a universal blank
Of Nature's works, to me expunged and rased,[6]
And wisdom at one entrance quite shut out.
So much the rather thou, Celestial Light,
Shine inward, and the mind through all her powers
Irradiate; there plant eyes; all mist from thence
Purge and disperse, that I may see and tell
Of things invisible to mortal sight.
   Now had th' Almighty Father from above,
From the pure empyrean where he sits
High throned above all height, bent down his eye,
His own works and their works at once to view:
About him all the sanctities of Heaven
Stood thick as stars, and from his sight[7] received
Beatitude past utterance; on his right
The radiant image of his glory sat,
His only Son. On Earth he first beheld
Our two first parents, yet the only two
Of mankind, in the happy garden placed,
Reaping immortal fruits of joy and love,
Uninterrupted joy, unrivaled love,
In blissful solitude. He then surveyed
Hell and the gulf between, and Satan there
Coasting the wall of Heaven on this side Night,
In the dun air sublime,[8] and ready now
To stoop, with wearied wings and willing feet,
On the bare outside of this world, that seemed
Firm land embosomed without firmament,
Uncertain which, in ocean or in air.
Him God beholding from his prospect high,
Wherein past, present, future, he beholds,
Thus to his only Son foreseeing spake:
   "Only-begotten Son, seest thou what rage
Transports our adversary? whom no bounds
Prescribed, no bars of Hell, nor all the chains
Heaped on him there, nor yet the main abyss
Wide interrupt,[9] can hold; so bent he seems
On desperate revenge, that shall redound

6. Shaved off (like a Roman tablet), erased.
7. From sight of him.
8. From the aspect of God's radiance the air is "dun," i.e., dusky; Satan is literally "sublime" in it, i.e., lifted up, aloft. But from where Satan hangs, outside the world's outer shell, he cannot be sure the world and its nine concentric spheres are not a single solid (line 75). The points of view are precisely distinguished.
9. Dividing, in between.

Upon his own rebellious head. And now,
Through all restraint broke loose, he wings his way
Not far off Heaven, in the precincts of light,
Directly towards the new-created world,
And man there placed, with purpose to essay
If him by force he can destroy, or, worse,
By some false guile pervert: and shall pervert;
For man will hearken to his glozing[1] lies,
And easily transgress the sole command,
Sole pledge of his obedience; so will fall
He and his faithless progeny. Whose fault?
Whose but his own? Ingrate, he had of me
All he could have; I made him just and right,
Sufficient to have stood, though free to fall.
Such I created all th' ethereal powers
And spirits, both them who stood and them who failed:
Freely they stood who stood, and fell who fell.
Not free, what proof could they have given sincere[2]
Of true allegiance, constant faith, or love,
Where only what they needs must do appeared,
Not what they would? What praise could they receive,
What pleasure I, from such obedience paid,
When Will and Reason (Reason also is Choice),
Useless and vain, of freedom both despoiled,
Made passive both, had served Necessity,
Not me? They, therefore, as to right belonged,
So were created, nor can justly accuse
Their Maker, or their making, or their fate,
As if predestination overruled
Their will, disposed by absolute decree
Or high foreknowledge. They themselves decreed
Their own revolt, not I. If I foreknew,
Foreknowledge had no influence on their fault,
Which had no less proved certain unforeknown[3]
So without least impulse or shadow of fate,
Or aught by me immutably foreseen,
They trespass, authors to themselves in all,
Both what they judge and what they choose; for so
I formed them free, and free they must remain
Till they enthrall themselves: I else must change
Their nature, and revoke the high decree
Unchangeable, eternal, which ordained
Their freedom; they themselves ordained their fall.
The first sort[4] by their own suggestion fell,
Self-tempted, self-depraved; man falls, deceived
By the other first: man, therefore, shall find grace;

1. Flattering.
2. The delayed modifer is a favorite stylistic device of Milton's. "Sincere" goes with "proof."
3. I.e., if I had not foreknown it.
4. The bad angels, Satan and his crew.

The other, none. In mercy and justice both,[5]
Through Heaven and Earth, so shall my glory excel;
But mercy, first and last, shall brightest shine."
Thus while God spake ambrosial fragrance filled
All Heaven, and in the blessed spirits elect
Sense of new joy ineffable diffused.
Beyond compare the Son of God was seen
Most glorious; in him all his Father shone
Substantially expressed;[6] and in his face
Divine compassion visibly appeared,
Love without end, and without measure grace;
Which uttering, thus he to his Father spake:
"O Father, gracious was that word which closed
Thy sovereign sentence, that man should find grace;
For which both Heaven and Earth shall high extol
Thy praises, with th' innumerable sound
Of hymns and sacred songs, wherewith thy throne
Encompassed shall resound thee ever blest.
For, should man finally be lost, should man,
Thy creature late so loved, thy youngest son,
Fall circumvented thus by fraud, though joined
With his own folly? That be from thee far,
That far be from thee, Father, who art judge
Of all things made, and judgest only right!
Or shall the adversary[7] thus obtain
His end, and frustrate thine? shall he fulfill
His malice, and thy goodness bring to naught
Or proud return, though to his heavier doom,
Yet with revenge accomplished, and to Hell
Draw after him the whole race of mankind,
By him corrupted? Or wilt thou thyself
Abolish thy creation, and unmake,
For him, what for thy glory thou hast made?
So should thy goodness and thy greatness both
Be questioned and blasphemed without defense."
To whom the great Creator thus replied:
"O Son, in whom my soul hath chief delight,
Son of my bosom, Son who art alone
My word, my wisdom, and effectual might,
All hast thou spoken as my thoughts are, all
As my eternal purpose hath decreed.[8]
Man shall not quite be lost, but saved who will;
Yet not of will in him, but grace in me
Freely vouchsafed. Once more I will renew

5. Mercy and justice are two key terms in the poem. Their personifications here are separate: God is justice (he claims to be merciful, but his speech does not have this tone at all), the Son is mercy; but by Book XII Milton intends to show their identity.

6. God himself cannot be directly apprehended, except through the Son.

7. "Satan" in Hebrew means "Adversary."

8. The Lord's speech is notably rhythmic and even rhymed.

His lapsèd powers, though forfeit, and enthralled
By sin to foul exorbitant desires:
Upheld by me, yet once more he shall stand
On even ground against his mortal foe,
By me upheld,[9] that he may know how frail
His fallen condition is, and to me owe
All his deliverance, and to none but me.
Some I have chosen of peculiar grace,
Elect above the rest; so is my will:
The rest shall hear me call, and oft be warned
Their sinful state,[1] and to appease betimes
Th' incensèd Deity, while offered grace
Invites; for I will clear their senses dark
What may suffice,[2] and soften stony hearts
To pray, repent, and bring obedience due.
To prayer, repentance, and obedience due,
Though but endeavored with sincere intent,
Mine ear shall not be slow, mine eye not shut.
And I will place within them as a guide
My umpire Conscience; whom if they will hear,
Light after light well used they shall attain,[3]
And to the end persisting, safe arrive.
This my long sufferance, and my day of grace,
They who neglect and scorn shall never taste;
But hard be hardened, blind be blinded more,
That they may stumble on, and deeper fall;
And none but such from mercy I exclude.
But yet all is not done. Man, disobeying,
Disloyal, breaks his fealty, and sins
Against the high supremacy of Heaven,
Affecting[4] godhead, and so, losing all,
To expiate his treason hath naught left,
But, to destruction sacred and devote,
He with his whole posterity must die;
Die he or Justice must; unless for him
Some other, able and as willing,[5] pay
The rigid satisfaction, death for death.
Say, heavenly powers, where shall we find such love?
Which of ye will be mortal, to redeem
Man's mortal crime,[6] and just, th' unjust to save?
Dwells in all Heaven charity so dear?"
    He asked, but all the heavenly choir stood mute,[7]

9. Note the ambiguity: the second "by me upheld" (line 180) may modify either "he" (line 178) or "his mortal foe" (line 179). Both divine and hellish energy are ultimately divine.
1. I.e., warned about their sinful state.
2. I.e., as much as need be.
3. By using light well, they will reach even more light, and, in the end, salvation.
4. Pretending to. "Devote": dedicated, given up to.
5. I.e., able to pay, and as willing as he is able.
6. Note that "mortal" means "human" (line 214) but "deadly" (line 215).
7. The silence of the good angels in face of a difficult task parallels that of the devils in the "great consult" (II. 420–26).

And silence was in Heaven: on man's behalf
Patron or intercessor none appeared,
Much less that durst upon his own head draw
The deadly forfeiture, and ransom set.
And now without redemption all mankind
Must have been lost, adjudged to Death and Hell
By doom severe, had not the Son of God,
In whom the fullness dwells of love divine,
His dearest mediation[8] thus renewed:
  "Father, thy word is passed, man shall find grace;
And shall Grace not find means, that finds her way,
The speediest of thy wingéd messengers,
To visit all thy creatures, and to all
Comes unprevented,[9] unimplored, unsought?
Happy for man, so coming! He her aid
Can never seek, once dead in sins and lost;
Atonement for himself, or offering meet,
Indebted and undone, hath none to bring.
Behold me, then: me for him, life for life,
I offer; on me let thine anger fall;
Account me man: I for his sake will leave
Thy bosom, and this glory next to thee
Freely put off, and for him lastly die
Well pleased; on me let Death wreak all his rage.
Under his gloomy power I shall not long
Lie vanquished. Thou hast given me to possess
Life in myself forever; by thee I live;
Though now to Death I yield, and am his due,
All that of me can die, yet, that debt paid,
Thou wilt not leave me in the loathsome grave
His prey, nor suffer my unspotted soul
Forever with corruption there to dwell;
But I shall rise victorious, and subdue
My vanquisher, spoiled of his vaunted spoil.
Death his death's wound shall then receive, and stoop[1]
Inglorious, of his mortal sting disarmed;
I through the ample air in triumph high
Shall lead Hell captive maugre[2] Hell, and show
The powers of darkness bound. Thou, at the sight
Pleased, out of Heaven shalt look down and smile,
While, by thee raised, I ruin[3] all my foes,
Death last, and with his carcass glut the grave;
Then, with the multitude of my redeemed,
Shall enter Heaven, long absent, and return,
Father, to see thy face, wherein no cloud
Of anger shall remain, but peace assured

8. Intercession.
9. Unforestalled.
1. Be humbled, fall.
2. In spite of (French, *malgré*). The Son's triumph is represented in a series of fantastic paradoxes—a vanquisher vanquished, a spoiler spoiled, death dead, Hell captured in all Hell's despite.
3. In the Latin sense, throw down.

And reconcilement: wrath shall be no more
Thenceforth, but in thy presence joy entire."
His words here ended; but his meek aspéct
Silent yet spake, and breathed immortal love
To mortal men, above which only shone
Filial obedience: as a sacrifice
Glad to be offered, he attends the will
Of his great Father. Admiration[4] seized
All Heaven, what this might mean, and whither tend,
Wondering; but soon th' Almighty thus replied:
"O thou in Heaven and Earth the only peace
Found out for mankind under wrath,[5] O thou
My sole complacence![6] well thou know'st how dear
To me are all my works; nor man the least,
Though last created, that for him I spare
Thee from my bosom and right hand, to save,
By losing thee a while, the whole race lost!
Thou, therefore, whom thou only canst redeem,
Their nature also to thy nature join;[7]
And be thyself man among men on Earth,
Made flesh, when time shall be, of virgin seed,
By wondrous birth; be thou in Adam's room
The head of all mankind, though Adam's son.[8]
As in him perish all men, so in thee,
As from a second root, shall be restored
As many as are restored; without thee, none.
His crime makes guilty all his sons;[9] thy merit,
Imputed, shall absolve them who renounce
Their own both righteous and unrighteous deeds,[1]
And live in thee transplanted, and from thee
Receive new life. So man, as is most just,
Shall satisfy for man, be judged and die,
And dying rise, and, rising, with him raise
His brethren, ransomed with his own dear life.
So heavenly love shall outdo hellish hate,
Giving to death, and dying to redeem,
So dearly to redeem, what hellish hate
So easily destroyed, and still destroys
In those who, when they may, accept not grace.

4. Wonder, curiosity.
5. The Lord is looking to the future, when mankind will be under his wrath.
6. Contentment.
7. I.e., join the nature of those people (mankind) whom you alone can save to your own nature; in other words, "Become a man and suffer the pains of mortality." The antecedent of "whom" is, loosely construed, the "their" which follows it.
8. Adam is, properly, the "Old Adam"; Christ is the Second Adam (there was an old tradition that the Forbidden Tree and the Cross of Christ stood on the same spot). The Son of God, who long antedates the creation of Adam, and who is actually the first created being (III.383), is historical Jesus Christ in one sense, an eternal spiritual principle in another.
9. The intense legalism of the Deity is apparent.
1. I.e., the merit of Christ, imputed to men, frees from original sin those who renounce their own deeds both good and bad and hope to be saved by faith.

Nor shalt thou, by descending to assume
Man's nature, lessen or degrade thine own.
Because thou hast, though throned in highest bliss
Equal to God, and equally enjoying
Godlike fruition,[2] quitted all to save
A world from utter loss, and hast been found
By merit more than birthright Son of God,[3]
Found worthiest to be so by being good,
Far more than great or high; because in thee
Love hath abounded more than glory abounds;
Therefore thy humiliation shall exalt
With thee thy manhood also to this throne:
Here shalt thou sit incarnate, here shalt reign
Both God and man, Son both of God and man,
Anointed[4] universal King. All power
I give thee; reign forever, and assume
Thy merits; under thee, as Head Supreme,
Thrones, princedoms, powers, dominions, I reduce:
All knees to thee shall bow of them that bide
In Heaven, or Earth, or under Earth in Hell.
When thou, attended gloriously from Heaven,
Shalt in the sky appear, and from thee send
The summoning archangels to proclaim
Thy dread tribunal, forthwith from all winds[5]
The living, and forthwith the cited dead
Of all past ages, to the general doom
Shall hasten; such a peal shall rouse their sleep.
Then, all thy saints assembled, thou shalt judge
Bad men and angels; they arraigned shall sink
Beneath thy sentence; Hell, her numbers full,
Thenceforth shall be forever shut. Meanwhile
The world shall burn, and from her ashes spring
New Heaven and Earth, wherein the just shall dwell,[6]
And, after all their tribulations long,
See golden days, fruitful of golden deeds,
With Joy and Love triúmphing, and fair Truth.
Then thou thy regal scepter shalt lay by;
For regal scepter then no more shall need;[7]
God shall be all in all. But all ye gods,[8]
Adore him who, to compass all this, dies;
Adore the Son, and honor him as me."
No sooner had th' Almighty ceased, but all
The multitude of angels, with a shout

2. Godlike pleasures, rewards.
3. An audacious doctrine, that Christ was Son of God by merit. Satan, one notes, was sultan of Hell on the same principle.
4. "The Anointed," in Hebrew, is the Messiah.
5. From all directions. "Cited": summoned.
6. The burning of the earth is based on II Peter iii.12, 13.
7. Be needed.
8. In addressing the angels as gods, the Lord is merely indicating their share in his divinity; the word is not literal.

Loud as from numbers without number, sweet
As from blest voices, uttering joy, Heaven rung[9]
With jubilee, and loud hosannas filled
Th' eternal regions. Lowly reverent
Towards either throne[1] they bow, and to the ground
With solemn adoration down they cast
Their crowns, inwove with amarant[2] and gold;
Immortal amarant, a flower which once
In Paradise, fast by the Tree of Life,
Began to bloom, but soon for man's offense
To Heaven removed, where first it grew, there grows
And flowers aloft, shading the Fount of Life,
And where the River of Bliss through midst of Heaven
Rolls o'er Elysian[3] flowers her amber stream.
With these, that never fade, the spirits elect
Bind their resplendent locks, enwreathed with beams.
Now in loose garlands thick thrown off, the bright
Pavement, that like a sea of jasper shone,
Empurpled with celestial roses smiled.
Then, crowned again, their golden harps they took,
Harps ever tuned, that glittering by their side
Like quivers hung; and with preamble sweet
Of charming symphony they introduce
Their sacred song, and waken raptures high:
No voice exempt,[4] no voice but well could join
Melodious part; such concord is in Heaven.
   Thee, Father, first they sung, Omnipotent,
Immutable, Immortal, Infinite,[5]
Eternal King; thee, Author of all being,
Fountain of light, thyself invisible
Amidst the glorious brightness where thou sitt'st
Throned inaccessible, but when thou shad'st
The full blaze of thy beams, and through a cloud
Drawn round about thee like a radiant shrine
Dark with excessive bright thy skirts appear,[6]
Yet dazzle Heaven, that brightest seraphim
Approach not, but with both wings veil their eyes.
Thee next they sang, of all creation first,

9. "Multitude" (line 345) is subject of the sentence, "rung" the verb, and "Heaven" the object.
1. Those of God and the Son.
2. Or "amaranth"; in Greek, "unwithering"—an unfading flower and hence a type of immortality, which could not continue on earth after man became subject to death.
3. Milton draws freely, and with no sense of incongruity, on pagan properties for his Christian Heaven. "Amber": not "yellow," but "clear." Milton's epithets are not always visually strong.
4. Abstaining.
5. Joshua Sylvester, in translating the long, pedestrian poem of Du Bartas on the creation, makes use of this line. It is the only example, and not a very striking one, of Milton's paralleling an English predecessor for ten consecutive syllables.
6. In this hymn, for the first time, we get a sense of the majesty and mystery of the Godhead; hitherto, he has been rather querulous and legalistic.

Begotten Son, divine similitude,
In whose conspicuous countenance, without cloud
Made visible, th' Almighty Father shines,
Whom else[7] no creature can behold: on thee
Impressed th' effulgence of his glory abides;
Transfused on thee his ample spirit rests.
He Heaven of Heavens, and all the powers therein,
By thee created; and by thee threw down
Th' aspiring dominations.[8] Thou that day
Thy Father's dreadful thunder didst not spare,
Nor stop thy flaming chariot wheels, that shook
Heaven's everlasting frame, while o'er the necks
Thou drov'st of warring angels disarrayed.
Back from pursuit, thy powers with loud acclaim
Thee only extolled, Son of thy Father's might,
To execute fierce vengeance on his foes.
Not so on man: him, through their malice fallen,
Father of mercy and grace, thou didst not doom
So strictly, but much more to pity incline.
No sooner did thy dear and only Son
Perceive thee purposed not to doom frail man
So strictly, but much more to pity inclined,[9]
He, to appease thy wrath, and end the strife
Of mercy and justice in thy face discerned,
Regardless of the bliss wherein he sat
Second to thee, offered himself to die
For man's offense. O unexampled love!
Love nowhere to be found less than divine!
Hail, Son of God, Savior of men! Thy name
Shall be the copious matter of my[1] song
Henceforth, and never shall my harp thy praise
Forget, nor from thy Father's praise disjoin!
  Thus they in Heaven, above the starry sphere,
Their happy hours in joy and hymning spent.
Meanwhile, upon the firm opacous globe
Of this round world, whose first convex divides
The luminous inferior orbs, enclosed
From chaos and th' inroad of darkness old,
Satan alighted walks.[2] A globe far off
It seemed; now seems a boundless continent,

7. Except for whom (if it were not for the Son. no creature could see God).

8. I.e., the rebel angels.

9. A "than" or "but" is understood at the end of line 405. The repetition (lines 402, 405) suggests the choral nature of the psalm. Note in 407 the re-emphasis on a conflict of mercy and justice.

1. Either the angels are singing as a single chorus, or Milton wishes to associate himself with them; possibly both. The change of pronoun is deliberate and striking.

2. Satan is not on the earth's surface but on the outermost of the nine concentric spheres that make up the created cosmos. This sphere is "opacous" (opaque) by contrast with the inner eight (containing seven planets and the fixed stars), which are crystalline and transparent.

Dark, waste, and wild, under the frown of night
Starless exposed, and ever-threatening storms
Of chaos blustering round, inclement sky,
Save on that side which from the wall of Heaven,
Though distant far, some small reflection gains
Of glimmering air less vexed with tempest loud.
Here walked the fiend at large in spacious field.
As when a vulture, on Imaus bred,
Whose snowy ridge the roving Tartar bounds,[3]
Dislodging from a region scarce of prey,
To gorge the flesh of lambs or veanling[4] kids
On hills where flocks are fed, flies toward the springs
Of Ganges or Hydaspes, Indian streams,
But in his way lights on the barren plains
Of Sericana, where Chineses drive
With sails and wind their cany wagons light;[5]
So, on this windy sea of land, the fiend
Walked up and down alone, bent on his prey:
Alone, for other creature in this place,
Living or lifeless, to be found was none;—
None yet; but store hereafter from the earth
Up hither like aerial vapors flew
Of all things transitory and vain, when sin
With vanity had filled the works of men—
Both all things vain, and all who in vain things
Built their fond hopes of glory or lasting fame,
Or happiness in this or th' other life.[6]
All who have their reward on earth, the fruits
Of painful superstition and blind zeal,
Naught seeking but the praise of men, here find
Fit retribution, empty as their deeds;
All th' unaccomplished works of nature's hand,
Abortive, monstrous, or unkindly[7] mixed,
Dissolved on earth, fleet hither, and in vain,
Till final dissolution, wander here—
Not in the neighboring moon, as some have dreamed:
Those argent fields more likely habitants,[8]

3. Imaus, a ridge of mountains beyond the modern Himalayas, is described by Pliny (*Natural History*, VI.17), and shown in Mercator's *Atlas*, as running north through Asia from modern Afghanistan to the Arctic Circle.

4. Newborn.

5. Both the Ganges and Hydaspes (a tributary of the river Indus) rise from the mountains of northern India; Sericana is an area (known only vaguely to Milton through the *Pilgrimage* of Purchas the traveler) in what is now Sinkiang province, in China. Milton got his memory of wind-driven land-carts from Peter Heylyn's *Cosmography*.

6. Milton's Paradise of Fools (named in line 496) was probably inspired by Ariosto's equivalent valley on the moon (*Orlando Furioso*, Canto 34; see below, line 459); it serves much the same function as Dante's Limbo, to dispose of those who deserve neither salvation nor damnation. But, instead of indifferents, Milton's region is reserved for deluded victims of misplaced devotion, chiefly Roman Catholics.

7. Against "kind," against their own natures.

8. Argent: silver. The moon Milton imagines, though only briefly, as a kind of middle Paradise.

Translated saints, or middle spirits hold,
Betwixt th' angelical and human kind.
Hither, of ill-joined sons and daughters born,
First from the ancient world those giants came,
With many a vain exploit, though then renowned:[9]
The builders next of Babel on the plain
Of Sennaar,[1] and still with vain design
New Babels, had they wherewithal, would build:
Others came single; he who, to be deemed
A god, leaped fondly into Etna flames,
Empedocles, and he who, to enjoy
Plato's Elysium, leaped into the sea,
Cleombrotus;[2] and many more, too long,
Embryos and idiots, eremites and friars,
White, black, and gray, with all their trumpery.[3]
Here pilgrims roam, that strayed so far to seek
In Golgotha him dead who lives in Heaven;
And they who, to be sure of paradise,
Dying put on the weeds of Dominic,
Or in Franciscan think to pass disguised.[4]
They pass the planets seven, and pass the fixed,
And that crystálline sphere whose balance weighs
The trepidation talked, and that first moved;[5]
And now Saint Peter at heaven's wicket seems
To wait them with his keys, and now at foot
Of heaven's ascent they lift their feet, when, lo!
A violent cross wind from either coast
Blows them transverse ten thousand leagues awry,
Into the devious air. Then might ye see
Cowls, hoods, and habits, with their wearers, tossed
And fluttered into rags; then relics, beads,
Indulgences, dispenses, pardons, bulls,[6]
The sport of winds: all these, upwhirled aloft,
Fly o'er the backside of the world far off

9. The "giants in the earth," born of unnatural marriages between the sons of God and the daughters of men, are creatures "unkindly mixed," therefore sent to the Paradise of Fools, "though then renowned," as Genesis vi.4 tells us.

1. Shinär, the plain of Babel, as in Genesis xi. 2–9. Babel for Milton is an emblem of human pride and folly

2. Both Empedocles and Cleombrotus carried piety to the point of folly and suicide. Hell is reserved for the wilfully malicious, the Paradise of Fools for the merely misguided.

3. Unnatural mixtures produce embryos and idiots; Milton adds to them hermits and friars (the white are Carmelites, the black Dominicans, and the gray Franciscans); he thinks they exemplify unnatural piety, frustrated by its very nature.

4. Pilgrims also are unnatural in their piety, since they worship the relic and forget the spirit; so are those who try to trick God into granting them salvation by wearing religious garb on their deathbeds.

5. Milton follows their souls through the spheres of the seven then-known planets, that of the fixed stars, and through the outermost sphere responsible for what astronomers call "the trepidation," a periodic corrective shudder of the cosmos. This is, or is right next to, the prime mover, or *primum mobile*—the next step seems to be the pearly gates themselves.

6. All that Milton considered the "trumpery", that is, the exterior and legal manifestations, of ecclesiasticism, is here cast aside as vanity. Milton certainly means "backside" (line 494) to have its vulgar connotation.

Into a limbo large and broad, since called
The Paradise of Fools; to few unknown
Long after, now unpeopled and untrod.
  All this dark globe the fiend found as he passed;
And long he wandered, till at last a gleam
Of dawning light turned thitherward in haste
His traveled steps. Far distant he descries,
Ascending by degrees magnificent
Up the wall of Heaven, a structure high;
At top whereof, but far more rich, appeared
The work as of a kingly palace-gate,
With frontispiece[7] of diamond and gold
Embellished; thick with sparkling orient gems
The portal shone, inimitable on earth
By model, or by shading pencil drawn.
The stairs were such as whereon Jacob saw
Angels ascending and descending, bands
Of guardians bright, when he from Esau fled
To Padan-Aram, in the field of Luz
Dreaming by night under the open sky,
And waking cried, *This is the gate of Heaven.*
Each stair mysteriously was meant, nor stood
There always, but drawn up to heaven sometimes
Viewless;[8] and underneath a bright sea flowed
Of jasper, or of liquid pearl, whereon
Who after came from earth sailing arrived
Wafted by angels, or flew o'er the lake
Rapt in a chariot drawn by fiery steeds.
The stairs were then let down, whether to dare
The fiend by easy ascent, or aggravate
His sad exclusion from the doors of bliss.[9]
Direct against which opened from beneath,
Just o'er the blissful seat of paradise,
A passage down to th' earth—a passage wide;
Wider by far than that of after-times
Over Mount Sion, and, though that were large,
Over the promised land to God so dear,
By which, to visit oft those happy tribes,
On high behests his angels to and fro
Passed frequent,[1] and his eye with choice regard

7. Façade.
8. Invisible. The story of Jacob's vision is summarized from Genesis xxviii.1–19. The stairs of the ladder were meant "mysteriously"—each represented a stage of spiritual growth.
9. In either case, Milton implies, heavenly authorities were aware of Satan's approach.
1. The crystalline spheres would be impenetrable if there weren't passages, or holes, in them, through which heavenly—and, alas, diabolic—spirits could make their way. The visiting angels "act as" his eye and "keep a" close regard on the chosen people. Cf., below, lines 650 and 660.

From Paneas, the fount of Jordan's flood,
To Beërsaba, where the holy land
Borders on Egypt and the Arabian shore.[2]
So wide the opening seemed, where bounds were set
To darkness, such as bound the ocean wave.
Satan from hence, now on the lower stair,
That scaled by steps of gold to heaven-gate,
Looks down with wonder at the sudden view
Of all this world at once. As when a scout,
Through dark and desert ways with peril gone
All night, at last by break of cheerful dawn
Obtains the brow of some high-climbing hill,
Which to his eye discovers unaware
The goodly prospect of some foreign land
First seen, or some renowned metropolis
With glistering spires and pinnacles adorned,
Which now the rising sun gilds with his beams;
Such wonder seized, though after heaven seen,
The spirit malign, but much more envy seized,
At sight of all this world beheld so fair.
Round he surveys (and well might, where he stood
So high above the circling canopy
Of night's extended shade) from eastern point
Of Libra to the fleecy star that bears
Andromeda far off Atlantic seas[3]
Beyond th' horizon; then from pole to pole
He views in breadth,—and, without longer pause,
Down right into the world's first region throws
His flight precipitant, and winds with ease
Through the pure marble air his oblique way[4]
Amongst innumerable stars, that shone
Stars distant, but nigh-hand seemed other worlds.
Or other worlds they seemed, or happy isles,
Like those Hesperian gardens famed of old,
Fortunate fields, and groves, and flowery vales;[5]
Thrice happy isles! But who dwelt happy there
He stayed not to inquire: above them all
The golden sun, in splendor likest heaven,
Allured his eye. Thither his course he bends,
Through the calm firmament (but up or down,
By center or eccentric, hard to tell,

2. From Paneas (or Dan) in northern Palestine to Beersaba, or Beersheba, near the Egyptian border—the whole land.

3. In the zodiac, Libra or the Scales are diametrically opposite the Ram ("the fleecy star"), which seems to carry the constellation Andromeda on its back.

4. "Marble" derives from the Greek word for "shining", but there's also a sense of solidity in the adjective to contrast with Satan's "oblique" approach.

5. The gardens of the Hesperides and the "fortunate isles" of Greek mythology lay far out in the Atlantic, almost like separate miniature worlds.

Or longitude)[6] where the great luminary,
Aloof the vulgar constellations thick,
That from his lordly eye keep distance due,
Dispenses light from far. They, as they move
Their starry dance in numbers that compute
Days, months, and years, towards his all-cheering lamp
Turn swift their various motions, or are turned
By his magnetic beam, that gently warms
The universe, and to each inward part
With gentle penetration, though unseen,
Shoots invisible virtue even to the deep;[7]
So wondrously was set his station bright.
There lands the fiend, a spot like which perhaps
Astronomer in the sun's lucent orb
Through his glazed optic tube yet never saw.[8]
The place he found beyond expression bright,
Compared with aught on earth,[9] metal or stone—
Not all parts like, but all alike informed
With radiant light, as glowing iron with fire.
If metal, part seemed gold, part silver clear;
If stone, carbuncle most or chrysolite,
Ruby or topaz, to the twelve that shone
In Aaron's breast-plate,[1] and a stone besides,
Imagined rather oft than elsewhere seen—
That stone, or like to that, which here below
Philosophers in vain so long have sought;
In vain, though by their powerful art they bind
Volatile Hermes, and call up unbound
In various shapes old Proteus from the sea,
Drained through a limbec to his native form.[2]
What wonder then if fields and regions here
Breathe forth elixir pure, and rivers run
Potable gold, when, with one virtuous touch,
Th' arch-chemic sun, so far from us remote,

6. Milton is cautious about saying whether the sun or the earth is at the center of the created cosmos. Like any educated man of his day, he knew that the earth goes around the sun, not vice versa, but poetically it was better for him to leave the option open.

7. "Virtue" in the sense of "influence," "strength": it was commonly thought that the "influence" of the sun caused seeds of gold to grow in the depths of the earth (see below, lines 608–612).

8. Galileo had discovered sun-spots in 1609; the possibility that the telescope might lead to an actual sighting of devils or angels was not yet extinct in Milton's day.

9. Strictly speaking, Satan has not been to the earth yet, but Milton cannot lose sight of the reader, who's been nowhere else.

1. Exodus xxviii lists the twelve precious stones in the breastplate of Aaron, the high-priest; "to" means "comparable to" or "to the number of."

2. The philosopher's stone had been sought by "binding" or fixing mercury ("volatile Hermes," i.e., quicksilver) or calling up Proteus to catch him in a limbec (alembic) in order to reduce both changeable deities to their natural forms. "Proteus" here stands for the gold which alchemists supposed to be hidden, in dilute form, within all other matter; their art aimed at extracting it.

Produces, with terrestrial humor mixed,
Here in the dark so many precious things
Of color glorious and effect so rare?[3]
Here matter new to gaze the devil met
Undazzled. Far and wide his eye commands;
For sight no obstacle found here, nor shade,
But all sunshine, as when his beams at noon
Culminate from th' equator, as[4] they now
Shot upward still direct, whence no way round
Shadow from body opaque can fall; and the air,
Nowhere so clear, sharpened his visual ray
To objects distant far, whereby he soon
Saw within ken a glorious angel stand,
The same whom John saw also in the sun.[5]
His back was turned, but not his brightness hid;
Of beaming sunny rays a golden tiar[6]
Circled his head, nor less his locks behind
Illustrious[7] on his shoulders fledge with wings
Lay waving round: on some great charge employed
He seemed, or fixed in cogitation deep.
Glad was the spirit impure, as now in hope
To find who might direct his wandering flight
To paradise, the happy seat of man,
His journey's end, and our beginning woe.
But first he casts to change his proper shape,
Which else might work him danger or delay:
And now a stripling cherub he appears,
Not of the prime, yet such as in his face
Youth smiled celestial, and to every limb
Suitable grace diffused; so well he feigned.
Under a coronet his flowing hair
In curls on either cheek played; wings he wore
Of many a colored plume sprinkled with gold,
His habit fit for speed succinct,[8] and held
Before his decent steps a silver wand.
He drew not nigh unheard; the angel bright,
Ere he drew nigh, his radiant visage turned,
Admonished by his ear, and straight was known
Th' archangel Uriel—one of the seven
Who in God's presence, nearest to his throne,

3. Milton argues that if the sun can cause gold to grow in mines, it must be itself full of "virtue" (power) to produce chemical changes—it is the "archchemic."

4. The sense of the passage will be clearer if for this second "as" we read "so." Satan, standing in the sun itself, can neither cast a shadow nor see one.

5. John of Patmos, author of the book of Revelation, saw an angel standing in the sun (xix.17).

6. Tiara, crown.

7. Lustrous and illuminated. "Fledge": fledged, feathered.

8. From the Latin *succingere*, "to draw in, tuck up." Satan, in disguise, wears some sort of light cloak that can be gathered up to leave his legs (and wings) free for speed.

Stand ready at command, and are his eyes
That run through all the heavens, or down to th' earth
Bear his swift errands over moist and dry,
O'er sea and land. Him Satan thus accosts:—
"Uriel! for thou of those seven spirits that stand
In sight of God's high throne, gloriously bright,
The first art wont his great authentic will
Interpreter through highest heaven to bring,
Where all his sons thy embassy attend,
And here art likeliest by supreme decree
Like honor to obtain, and as his eye
To visit oft this new creation round—
Unspeakable desire to see and know
All these his wondrous works, but chiefly man,
His chief delight and favor, him for whom
All these his works so wondrous he ordained,
Hath brought me from the choirs of cherubim[9]
Alone thus wandering. Brightest seraph, tell
In which of all these shining orbs hath man
His fixéd seat—or fixéd seat hath none,
But all these shining orbs his choice to dwell—
That I may find him, and with secret gaze
Or open admiration him behold
On whom the great creator hath bestowed
Worlds, and on whom hath all these graces poured;
That both in him and all things, as is meet,
The universal maker we may praise;
Who justly hath driven out his rebel foes
To deepest hell, and, to repair that loss,
Created this new happy race of men
To serve him better: wise are all his ways!"
So spake the false dissembler unperceived;
For neither man nor angel can discern
Hypocrisy, the only evil that walks
Invisible, except to God alone,
By his permissive will, through Heaven and earth;[1]
And oft, though wisdom wake, suspicion sleeps
At wisdom's gate, and to simplicity
Resigns her charge, while goodness thinks no ill
Where no ill seems: which now for once beguiled
Uriel, though regent of the sun, and held
The sharpest-sighted spirit of all in heaven;
Who to the fraudulent imposter foul,

9. Uriel is one of the seraphim, the first order of angelic beings; cherubim would be of the second rank.

1. God has two wills—one active, by which he does, perforce, only good things, the other permissive, by which he allows things to take their course, whether for good or for evil.

In his uprightness, answer thus returned:—
"Fair angel, thy desire, which tends to know
The works of God, thereby to glorify
The great work-master, leads to no excess
That reaches blame, but rather merits praise
The more it seems excess, that led thee hither
From thy empyreal mansion thus alone,
To witness with thine eyes what some perhaps,
Contented with report, hear only in Heaven:
For wonderful indeed are all his works,
Pleasant to know, and worthiest to be all
Had in remembrance always with delight!
But what created mind can comprehend
Their number, or the wisdom infinite
That brought them forth, but hid their causes deep?
I saw when, at his word, the formless mass,
This world's material mould, came to a heap:
Confusion heard his voice, and wild uproar
Stood ruled, stood vast infinitude confined;
Till, at his second bidding, darkness fled,
Light shone, and order from disorder sprung.
Swift to their several quarters hasted then
The cumbrous elements—earth, flood, air, fire;
And this etheral quintessence of Heaven
Flew upward, spirited[2] with various forms,
That rolled orbicular, and turned to stars
Numberless, as thou seest, and how they move:
Each had his place appointed, each his course;
The rest in circuit walls this universe.[3]
Look downward on that globe, whose hither side
With light from hence, though but reflected, shines:
That place is earth, the seat of man; that light
His day, which else, as th' other hemisphere,
Night would invade, but there the neighboring moon
(So call that opposite fair star) her aid
Timely interposes and, her monthly round
Still ending, still renewing, through mid-heaven,
With borrowed light her countenance triform[4]
Hence fills and empties, to enlighten th' earth,
And in her pale dominion checks the night.
That spot to which I point is paradise,
Adam's abode; those lofty shades his bower.

2. Informed with spiritual energy.

3. The rest of the stars became fixed in the outermost sphere, that which walls off the created universe from the immensity of Chaos outside.

4. Though the moon's cycle is divided into quarters, there are, strictly, only three of them: crescent, full, and waning (the dark of the moon, when it's invisible, is the fourth quarter); in addition, the moon has three classical names—Luna, Diana, and Hecate.

Thy way thou canst not miss; me mine requires."
  Thus said, he turned; and Satan, bowing low,
As to superior spirits is wont in Heaven,
Where honor due and reverence none neglects,
Took leave, and toward the coast of earth beneath,
Down from th' ecliptic, sped with hoped success,
Throws his steep flight in many an airy wheel,
Nor stayed, till on Niphates'[5] top he lights.

From Book IV

[*Satan's Entry into Paradise*]

  O for that warning voice, which he who saw
Th' Apocalypse heard cry in Heaven aloud,
Then when the dragon, put to second rout,
Came furious down to be revenged on men,
Woe to the inhabitants on Earth![1] that now,
While time was, our first parents had been warned
The coming of their secret foe, and scaped,
Haply so scaped, his mortal snare![2] For now
Satan, now first inflamed with rage, came down,
The tempter, ere th' accuser, of mankind,
To wreak on innocent frail man his loss
Of that first battle, and his flight to hell.
Yet not rejoicing in his speed, though bold
Far off and fearless, nor with cause to boast,
Begins his dire attempt; which, nigh the birth
Now rolling, boils in his tumultuous breast,
And like a devilish engine back recoils
Upon himself. Horror and doubt distract
His troubled thoughts, and from the bottom stir
The Hell within him; for within him Hell
He brings, and round about him, nor from Hell
One step, no more than from himself, can fly
By change of place.[3] Now conscience wakes despair
That slumbered; wakes the bitter memory
Of what he was, what is, and what must be
Worse; of worse deeds worse sufferings must ensue.

5. Mt. Niphates lies in the northwest corner of modern Iran, not far from the Turkish border—it was an ideal spot from which to spy on Paradise, which lay in the plain below, between the Tigris and Euphrates rivers.

1. John of Patmos, in Revelation xii, describes a war in heaven between dragon and angels, in the course of which a voice cries from heaven, "Woe to the inhabitants of the earth and of the sea!"

2. "Haply": by good luck, happily. "Mortal": deadly. "First" in line 9 refers back to "second" in line 3; Milton wants us to remember that his story was the first of all the Bible stories, and is, as it were, their root.

3. Satan's proud statement that "the mind is its own place" (I, 254) finds here its bitter ironic echo.

Sometimes towards Eden, which now in his view
Lay pleasant, his grieved look he fixes sad;
Sometimes towards heaven and the full-blazing sun,
Which now sat high in his meridian tower:[4]
Then, much revolving, thus in sighs began:—
  "O thou that, with surpassing glory crowned,
Look'st from thy sole dominion like the god
Of this new world—at whose sight all the stars
Hide their diminished heads—to thee I call,
But with no friendly voice, and add thy name,
O sun, to tell thee how I hate thy beams,
That bring to my remembrance from what state
I fell, how glorious once above thy sphere,
Till pride and worse ambition threw me down,
Warring in Heaven against Heaven's matchless king!
Ah, wherefore? He deserved no such return
From me, whom he created what I was
In that bright eminence, and with his good
Upbraided none;[5] nor was his service hard.
What could be less than to afford him praise,
The easiest recompense, and pay him thanks,
How due! Yet all his good proved ill in me,
And wrought but malice. Lifted up so high,
I 'sdained[6] subjection, and thought one step higher
Would set me highest, and in a moment quit
The debt immense of endless gratitude,
So burdensome, still paying, still to owe;
Forgetful what from him I still received;
And understood not that a grateful mind
By owing owes not, but still pays, at once
Indebted and discharged—what burden then?
Oh, had his powerful destiny ordained
Me some inferior angel, I had stood
Then happy; no unbounded hope had raised
Ambition. Yet why not? Some other power
As great might have aspired, and me, though mean,
Drawn to his part. But other powers as great
Fell not, but stand unshaken, from within
Or from without to all temptations armed!
Hadst thou[7] the same free will and power to stand?
Thou hadst. Whom hast thou then, or what, to accuse,
But Heaven's free love dealt equally to all?

4. Midday, the height of noon. Milton's nephew Edward Phillips tells us that the speech which follows was the first part of the poem that existed, when Milton still thought of making it into the drama of "Adam Unparadised."

5. Demanded no return for his benefits; the phrase echoes James i.5.

6. Disdained. "Quit": acquit, pay off.

7. Satan addresses himself directly, as Adam will do under parallel circumstances in Book X, line 758.

Be then his love accursed, since, love or hate,
To me alike it deals eternal woe.
Nay, cursed be thou; since against his thy will
Chose freely what it now so justly rues.
Me miserable![8] which way shall I fly
Infinite wrath and infinite despair?
Which way I fly is Hell; myself am Hell;
And, in the lowest deep, a lower deep
Still threatening to devour me opens wide,
To which the Hell I suffer seems a Heaven.
O, then, at last relent! Is there no place
Left for repentance, none for pardon left?
None left but by submission; and that word
Disdain forbids me, and my dread of shame
Among the spirits beneath, whom I seduced
With other promises and other vaunts
Than to submit, boasting I could subdue
Th' omnipotent. Ay me! they little know
How dearly I abide that boast so vain,
Under what torments inwardly I groan.
While they adore me on the throne of Hell,
With diadem and scepter high advanced,
The lower still I fall, only supreme
In misery: such joy ambition finds!
But say I could repent, and could obtain,
By act of grace,[9] my former state, how soon
Would height recall high thoughts, how soon unsay
What feigned submission swore! Ease would recant
Vows made in pain, as violent and void
For never can true reconcilement grow
Where wounds of deadly hate have pierced so deep;
Which would but lead me to a worse relapse
And heavier fall: so should I purchase dear
Short intermission, bought with double smart.
This knows my punisher; therefore as far
From granting he, as I from begging, peace.
All hope excluded thus, behold, instead
Of us, outcast, exiled, his new delight,
Mankind, created, and for him this world!
So farewell hope, and, with hope, farewell fear,
Farewell remorse! All good to me is lost;
Evil, be thou my good: by thee at least
Divided empire with Heaven's king I hold,
By thee, and more than half perhaps will reign;

8. "Me miserable!": an exact Latinism, *"me miserum!"* "Myself am hell" makes brilliantly clear what can be meant by "The mind is its own place," I.254.

9. The correct technical term for a formal pardon is an "act of grace."

As man ere long, and this new world, shall know."
  Thus while he spake, each passion dimmed his face,
Thrice changed with pale—ire, envy, and despair;
Which marred his borrowed visage, and betrayed
Him counterfeit, if any eye beheld:
For heavenly minds from such distempers foul
Are ever clear. Whereof he soon aware
Each perturbation smoothed with outward calm,
Artificer of fraud; and was the first
That practiced falsehood under saintly show,
Deep malice to conceal, couched with revenge:
Yet not enough had practiced to deceive
Uriel, once warned; whose eye pursued him down
The way he went, and on th' Assyrian mount
Saw him disfigured, more than could befall
Spirit of happy sort: his gestures fierce
He marked and mad demeanor, then alone,
As he supposed, all unobserved, unseen.
  So on he fares, and to the border comes
Of Eden, where delicious Paradise,
Now nearer, crowns with her enclosure green,
As with a rural mound, the champaign[1] head
Of a steep wilderness, whose hairy sides
With thicket overgrown, grotesque[2] and wild,
Access denied; and overhead up grew
Insuperable height of loftiest shade,
Cedar, and pine, and fir, and branching palm,
A sylvan scene, and, as the ranks ascend
Shade above shade, a woody theater[3]
Of stateliest view. Yet higher than their tops
The verdurous wall of Paradise up sprung;
Which to our general sire[4] gave prospect large
Into his nether empire neighboring round.
And higher than that wall a circling row
Of goodliest trees, laden with fairest fruit,
Blossoms and fruits at once of golden hue,
Appeared, with gay enameled colors mixed;
On which the sun more glad impressed his beams
Than in fair evening cloud, or humid bow,[5]
When God hath showered the earth: so lovely seemed
That landscape. And of pure now purer air[6]

1. From French *champs*, open countryside. Paradise is an open garden on top of a hill straddling a river in the east of Eden.
2. One of the earliest uses of the word in English to mean "romantic" or "picturesque."
3. As if in a Greek amphitheater, the trees are set row on row.
4. Adam.
5. The rainbow. There is a thick wall of trees around Paradise, which "access denied"; then above them, the shaggy sides of Paradise itself ("the verdurous wall"), and above it the garden of fruit trees.
6. After breathing pure air, Satan now breathes even purer.

Meets his approach, and to the heart inspires
Vernal delight and joy, able to drive[7]
All sadness but despair. Now gentle gales,
Fanning their odoriferous wings, dispense
Native perfumes, and whisper whence they stole
Those balmy spoils. As when to them who sail
Beyond the Cape of Hope, and now are past
Mozambic, off at sea northeast winds blow
Sabean odors from the spicy shore
Of Araby the Blest,[8] with such delay
Well pleased they slack their course, and many a league
Cheered with the grateful smell old Ocean smiles;
So entertained those odorous sweets the fiend
Who came their bane, though with them better pleased
Than Asmodëus with the fishy fume
That drove him, though enamored, from the spouse
Of Tobit's son,[9] and with a vengeance sent
From Media post to Egypt, there fast bound.
Now to th' ascent of that steep savage[1] hill
Satan had journeyed on, pensive and slow;
But further way found none; so thick entwined,
As one continued brake, the undergrowth
Of shrubs and tangling bushes had perplexed
All path of man or beast that passed that way.
One gate there only was, and that looked east
On th' other side. Which when th' arch-felon saw,
Due entrance he disdained, and, in contempt,
At one slight bound high overleaped all bound[2]
Of hill or highest wall, and sheer within
Lights on his feet. As when a prowling wolf,
Whom hunger drives to seek new haunt for prey,
Watching where shepherds pen their flocks at eve,
In hurdled cotes[3] amid the field secure,
Leaps o'er the fence with ease into the fold;
Or as a thief, bent to unhoard the cash
Of some rich burgher, whose substantial doors,
Cross-barred and bolted fast, fear no assault,
In at the window climbs, or o'er the tiles;

7. Scatter.
8. Coasting up East Africa after doubling the Cape of Good Hope, Milton supposes off "Mozambic" (Mozambique) one might meet "Sabean" (i.e., as from Sheba) odors coming from "Araby the Blest" (Arabia Felix). This is the fantasy of a man who learned his geography from medieval atlases and Diodorus Siculus, for the distance between Mozambique and Arabia is close to 2,000 miles.
9. Milton retells briefly here the story of Tobias, Tobit's son, who married Sara and was saved from the fate of her seven previous husbands by the advice of Raphael, who showed him how to make a fishy smell that would drive away the devil Asmodeus. See the Book of Tobit among the Apocrypha.
1. Wooded, entangled (from Latin, *silvaticus*, through Italian *selvaggio*, and French *sauvage*).
2. Satan enters Paradise, not only illegally, but with a contemptuous pun.
3. Pens made of woven reeds.

So clomb[4] this first grand thief into God's fold:
So since into his church lewd hirelings[5] climb.
Thence up he flew, and on the Tree of Life,
The middle tree and highest there that grew,
Sat like a cormorant; yet not true life
Thereby regained, but sat devising death
To them who lived; nor on the virtue thought
Of that life-giving plant, but only used
For prospect,[6] what, well used, had been the pledge
Of immortality. So little knows
Any, but God alone, to value right
The good before him, but perverts best things
To worst abuse, or to their meanest use.
Beneath him, with new wonder, now he views,
To all delight of human sense exposed,
In narrow room Nature's whole wealth; yea, more,
A Heaven on Earth; for blissful Paradise
Of God the garden was, by him in the east
Of Eden planted. Eden stretched her line
From Auran eastward to the royal towers
Of great Seleucia, built by Grecian kings,
Or where the sons of Eden long before
Dwelt in Telassar.[7] In this pleasant soil
His far more pleasant garden God ordained.
Out of the fertile ground he caused to grow
All trees of noblest kind for sight, smell, taste;
And all amid them stood the Tree of Life,
High eminent, blooming ambrosial fruit
Of vegetable gold; and next to life,
Our death, the Tree of Knowledge, grew fast by—
Knowledge of good, bought dear by knowing ill.
Southward through Eden went a river large,
Nor changed his course, but through the shaggy hill
Passed underneath engulfed; for God had thrown
That mountain, as his garden-mold,[8] high raised
Upon the rapid current, which, through veins
Of porous earth with kindly[9] thirst up drawn,

4. Old past tense of "climb," but used with a special feeling of ungainly energy. The whole metaphor, of God as a rich citizen hoarding Adam and Eve from Satan the second-story-man, is instinct with comic feeling. On the devil as a thief, see John x.1.

5. Base men interested only in money; Milton felt strongly that churchmen should be unsalaried to insure the purity of their motives.

6. Perspective, lookout.

7. By suggesting alternate boundaries of Eden, Milton invokes a hazy sense of the richness, vastness, and antiquity of the Middle East. "Auran" is an area in Syria, to the south of Damascus; "Seleucia" lies near modern Bagdad, a powerful city founded by one of Alexander's generals (hence, "built by Grecian kings"); and "Telassar" is another Near Eastern kingdom, this one probably on the east bank of the Euphrates.

8. The mountain is God's topsoil, out of which grows Paradise. The river (traditionally Tigris) flowed under the hill.

9. Natural.

Rose a fresh fountain, and with many a rill
Watered the garden; thence united fell
Down the steep glade, and met the nether flood,
Which from his darksome passage now appears,
And now, divided into four main streams,
Runs diverse, wandering many a famous realm
And country, whereof here needs no account;[1]
But rather to tell how, if art could tell,
How, from that sapphire fount the crispéd[2] brooks,
Rolling on orient pearl and sands of gold,
With mazy error[3] under pendant shades
Ran nectar, visiting each plant, and fed
Flowers worthy of Paradise; which not nice[4] art
In beds and curious knots, but Nature boon[5]
Poured forth profuse on hill, and dale, and plain,
Both where the morning sun first warmly smote
The open field, and where the unpierced shade
Embrowned[6] the noontide bowers. Thus was this place,
A happy rural seat of various view:[7]
Groves whose rich trees wept odorous gums and balm;
Others whose fruit, burnished with golden rind,
Hung amiable[8]—Hesperian fables true,
If true, here only—and of delicious taste.
Betwixt them lawns, or level downs, and flocks
Grazing the tender herb, were interposed,
Or palmy hillock; or the flowery lap
Of some irriguous[9] valley spread her store,
Flowers of all hue, and without thorn the rose.[1]
Another side, umbrageous[2] grots and caves
Of cool recess, o'er which the mantling vine
Lays forth her purple grape, and gently creeps
Luxuriant; meanwhile murmuring waters fall
Down the slope hills dispersed, or in a lake,
That to the fringéd bank with myrtle crowned
Her crystal mirror holds, unite their streams.
The birds their choir apply;[3] airs, vernal airs,
Breathing the smell of field and grove, attune
The trembling leaves, while universal Pan,[4]

1. Milton has in mind Genesis ii.10; but the expression "whereof here needs no account" dodges many questions about the correct translation of this passage.
2. Wavy, ruffled.
3. From Latin *errare*, "wandering."
4. Particular, careful.
5. Liberal, bounteous.
6. Darkened.
7. Aspect.
8. Lovely. These were real golden apples like those said to have existed in the Hesperides, fabulous islands of the Western Ocean; Paradise was the only place where the fable of the Hesperides was literally true.
9. Well-watered.
1. Figuratively and literally, there was no need for thorns in Paradise.
2. Shady.
3. Practice their song. "Airs" may be either "breezes" or "melodies," and probably are both.
4. The god of all nature. "Pan" in Greek means "all" but it is also the name of the goat-legged nature god.

Knit with the Graces and the Hours in dance,
Led on th' eternal spring.[5] Not that fair field
Of Enna, where Proserpin gathering flowers,
Herself a fairer flower, by gloomy Dis
Was gathered, which cost Ceres all that pain
To seek her through the world; nor that sweet grove
Of Daphne,[6] by Orontes and th' inspired
Castalian spring, might with this Paradise
Of Eden strive; nor that Nyseian isle,
Girt with the river Triton, where old Cham,
Whom Gentiles Ammon call and Libyan Jove,
Hid Amalthea, and her florid son,
Young Bacchus, from his stepdame Rhea's eye;[7]
Nor, where Abassin kings their issue guard,
Mount Amara[8] (though this by some supposed
True Paradise) under the Ethiop line
By Nilus' head, enclosed with shining rock,
A whole day's journey high, but wide remote
From this Assyrian garden, where the fiend
Saw undelighted all delight, all kind
Of living creatures, new to sight and strange.
Two of far nobler shape, erect and tall,
Godlike erect,[9] with native honor clad
In naked majesty, seemed lords of all,
And worthy seemed; for in their looks divine,
The image of their glorious Maker, shone
Truth, wisdom, sanctitude severe and pure—
Severe, but in true filial freedom[1] placed,
Whence true authority in men; though both
Not equal, as their sex not equal seemed.
For contemplation he and valor formed,

5. The god of nature dances with the Graces and Hours, an image of perfect harmony.

6. Milton is comparing Paradise with the famous beauty spots of antiquity. Enna in Sicily was a lovely meadow from which "Proserpin" was kidnapped by "gloomy Dis" (i.e., Pluto); her mother Ceres sought her throughout the world. The grove of Daphne, near Antioch and the Orontes river in the Near East, had a spring called "Castalia" in imitation of the Muses' fountain near Delphi.

7. The isle of Nysa in the river Triton in Tunisia was where Ammon hid Bacchus, his bastard child by Amalthea, from the eye of his wife Rhea. "Florid" (wine-flushed) Bacchus, when he grew up, received the name of Dionysus in honor of his birthplace. The identification of the Egyptian god Ammon or Hammon with Cham or Ham, the son of Noah, is a piece of comparative anthropology on Milton's part.

8. Finally, Paradise ("this Assyrian garden," line 285) is finer than the palaces atop Mt. Amara, where the "Abassin" (Abyssinian) kings had a splendid palace. Milton's authority for this exotic scene was Peter Heylyn (*Cosmographie* IV.lxiv), from whom he took several phrases direct. His passage then had a continuing influence on the names and phrasings of Coleridge's *Kubla Khan*.

9. By emphasizing the word "erect," Milton means to distinguish man from the beasts of the field, who went "prone."

1. Though almost a paradox, the phrase suggests Milton's idea that true freedom always involves respect for authority and hierarchy. Cf. Eve's foolish question, "For, inferior, who is free?" (IX.825).

For softness she and sweet attractive grace;
He for God only, she for God in him.[2]
His fair large front[3] and eye sublime declared
Absolute rule; and hyacinthine[4] locks
Round from his parted forelock manly hung
Clustering, but not beneath his shoulders broad:
She, as a veil down to the slender waist,
Her unadornéd golden tresses wore
Disheveled, but in wanton ringlets waved
As the vine curls her tendrils,[5] which implied
Subjection, but required with gentle sway,
And by her yielded, by him best received,
Yielded with coy[6] submission, modest pride,
And sweet, reluctant, amorous delay.
Nor those mysterious parts were then concealed;
Then was not guilty shame. Dishonest shame
Of Nature's works, honor dishonorable,
Sin-bred, how have ye troubled all mankind
With shows instead, mere shows of seeming pure,
And banished from man's life his happiest life,
Simplicity and spotless innocence!
So passed they naked on, nor shunned the sight
Of God or angel; for they thought no ill;
So hand in hand they passed, the loveliest pair
That ever since in love's embraces met:
Adam the goodliest man of men since born
His sons; the fairest of her daughters Eve.[7]
Under a tuft of shade that on a green
Stood whispering soft, by a fresh fountain-side,
They sat them down; and, after no more toil
Of their sweet gardening labor than sufficed
To recommend cool Zephyr,[8] and make ease
More easy, wholesome thirst and appetite
More grateful, to their supper fruits they fell,
Nectarine fruits, which the compliant boughs
Yielded them, sidelong as they sat recline
On the soft downy bank damasked with flowers.
The savory pulp they chew, and in the rind,
Still as they thirsted scoop the brimming stream;
Nor gentle purpose,[9] nor endearing smiles

2. Milton's ideas on the relations between the sexes were strict for his day, though not as strict as they now appear.
3. Forehead.
4. A classical metaphor, often applied to hair, and implying "brown" or perhaps "flowing," but actually not very definite in its import.
5. Eve's hair is curly, abundant, uncontrolled; like the vegetation in Paradise, it clings seductively about a severe and masculine virtue.
6. Shy.
7. Logically these constructions are absurd; Adam was not born since his day, Eve was not one of her own daughters. Milton combines comparative with superlative forms for emphatic effect.
8. I.e., to make a cool breeze welcome.
9. Conversation. "Wanted": lacked.

Wanted, nor youthful dalliance, as beseems
Fair couple linked in happy nuptial league,
Alone as they. About them frisking played
All beasts of th' earth, since wild, and of all chase[1]
In wood or wilderness, forest or den.
Sporting the lion ramped,[2] and in his paw
Dandled the kid; bears, tigers, ounces, pards,[3]
Gamboled before them; th' unwieldly elephant,
To make them mirth, used all his might, and wreathed
His lithe proboscis; close the serpent sly,
Insinuating,[4] wove with Gordian twine
His braided train,[5] and of his fatal guile
Gave proof unheeded. Others on the grass
Couched and now filled with pasture, gazing sat,
Or bedward ruminating;[6] for the sun,
Declined, was hasting now with prone career
To th' ocean isles,[7] and in th' ascending scale
Of Heaven the stars that usher evening rose:
When Satan, still in gaze as first he stood,
Scarce thus at length failed speech recovered sad:[8]
"O Hell! what do mine eyes with grief behold?
Into our room of bliss thus high advanced
Creatures of other mold, Earth-born perhaps,
Not spirits, yet to heavenly spirits bright
Little inferior; whom my thoughts pursue
With wonder, and could love; so lively shines
In them divine resemblance, and such grace
The hand that formed them on their shape hath poured.[9]
Ah! gentle pair, ye little think how nigh
Your change approaches, when all these delights
Will vanish, and deliver ye to woe,
More woe, the more your taste is now of joy:
Happy, but for so happy[1] ill secured
Long to continue, and this high seat, your Heaven,
Ill fenced for Heaven to keep out such a foe
As now is entered; yet no purposed foe
To you, whom I could pity thus forlorn,
Though I unpitied. League with you I seek,
And mutual amity, so strait, so close,
That I with you must dwell, or you with me,

1. Who lurk in every sort of cover.
2. Reared up.
3. Lynxes and leopards.
4. Writhing and twisting, but with a glance at the Tempter's rhetorical techniques.
5. Checkered body. "Gordian twine": knots, like the Gordian knot, cut by Alexander the Great.
6. The animals are chewing their cuds before bedtime; in Paradise, where the animal kingdom is not yet subject to death, they are perforce vegetarians.
7. The Azores.
8. The choked, laborious line mirrors Satan's heavy, congested mind.
9. Though Satan's moral values are topsy-turvy ("Evil, be thou my Good," he has said in the first part of Book IV), his aesthetic values are strictly orthodox.
1. Such happiness.

Henceforth.[2] My dwelling, haply, may not please,
Like this fair Paradise, your sense; yet such
Accept your Maker's work; he gave it me,
Which I as freely give. Hell shall unfold,
To entertain you two, her widest gates,
And send forth all her kings; there will be room,
Not like these narrow limits, to receive
Your numerous offspring; if no better place,
Thank him who puts me, loath, to this revenge
On you, who wrong me not, for him who wronged.[3]
And, should I at your harmless innocence
Melt, as I do, yet public reason just—
Honor and empire with revenge enlarged
By conquering this new world—compels me now
To do what else, though damned, I should abhor."[4]
  So spake the fiend, and with necessity,
The tyrant's plea, excused his devilish deeds.
Then from his lofty stand on that high tree
Down he alights among the sportful herd
Of those four-footed kinds, himself now one,
Now other, as their shape served best his end
Nearer to view his prey, and unespied,
To mark what of their state he more might learn
By word or action marked. About them round
A lion now he stalks with fiery glare;
Then as a tiger, who by chance hath spied
In some purlieu[5] two gentle fawns at play,
Straight couches close; then, rising, changes oft
His couchant watch, as one who chose his ground,
Whence rushing he might surest seize them both
Griped in each paw * * *

2. Though it starts in simple admiration, Satan's friendship for mankind is, at the end, rather grisly and sardonic. The turning point seems to be "though I unpitied" (line 375)—the reaction of a spoiled child.
3. I.e., it is not my fault; Satan's favorite phrase.
4. Satan's final reason for destroying Adam and Eve is thoroughly Satanic; it is *ragione di stato*, reason of state, the public interest.
5. The outskirt of a forest. Note that Satan can and does enter any animal he wants; it is only for the special purposes of the temptation that he finds the serpent specially convenient.

Summary By eavesdropping on Adam and Eve, Satan learns of the prohibited Tree of Knowledge; this weakness he resolves to exploit. Meanwhile Uriel, rendered suspicious by Satan's fierce demeanor outside Paradise, reports to Gabriel, the angel specially assigned to guard mankind, that a diabolic intruder may be near. Gabriel promises to search him out. After Adam and Eve say their evening prayers and retire, Gabriel divides his night watch into groups, assigning Ithuriel and Zephon to guard closely the bower of Adam and Eve. They find Satan whispering in the ear of the sleeping Eve, and bring him before Gabriel. A battle impends, but is averted by a heavenly signal, and Satan flees out of Paradise.

Book V

Summary In the morning, Eve is distressed by her dreams of the previous night, which she relates to Adam; he comforts her. Meanwhile God dispatches Raphael to warn man of the approaching danger. Adam sees him in the distance, and while Eve readies more lunch for her guest, goes forth to meet the heavenly visitant.

[*The Full and Ordered Universe*]

* * * So to the sylvan lodge
They came, that like Pomona's arbor[1] smiled
With flowerets decked and fragrant smells; but Eve,
Undecked save with herself, more lovely fair
Than wood nymph or the fairest goddess feigned
Of three that on Mount Ida naked strove,[2]
Stood t' entertain her guest from Heaven; no veil
She needed, virtue-proof, no thought infirm
Altered her cheek. On whom the Angel "Hail"
Bestowed, the holy salutation used
Long after to blessed Mary, second Eve.
"Hail mother of mankind, whose fruitful womb
Shall fill the world more numerous with thy sons
Than with these various fruits the trees of God
Have heaped this table." Raised of grassy turf
Their table was, and mossy seats had round,
And on her ample square from side to side
All autumn piled, though spring and autumn here
Danced hand in hand. A while discourse they hold—
No fear lest dinner cool—when thus began
Our author.[3] "Heavenly stranger, please to taste
These bounties which our nourisher, from whom
All perfect good, unmeasured-out, descends,
To us for food and for delight hath caused
The earth to yield;[4] unsavory food perhaps
To spiritual natures; only this I know,
That one celestial Father gives to all."
To whom the Angel: "Therefore what he gives
(Whose praise be ever sung) to man in part
Spiritual, may of purest spirits be found
No ungrateful food;[5] and food alike those pure

1. Pomona, Roman goddess of fruits and flowers, dwelt in an orchard.
2. Aphrodite, Hera, and Athena were judged for their beauty on Mount Ida by Paris, son of Priam. Milton reminds us that the goddesses were only "feigned," i.e., not true in the sense that the Christian god is true.
3. Our creator (i.e., Adam).
4. I.e., please to taste these bounties which God ("our nourisher") has caused the earth to yield to us for food and for delight.
5. I.e., food that is proper for man, who is partly spiritual, will be proper also for the very purest spirits. The idea that within the hierarchical universe higher powers include and comprehend lower powers is the key to the entire passage that follows.

Intelligential substances require
As doth your rational; and both contain
Within them every lower faculty
Of sense, whereby they hear, see, smell, touch, taste,
Tasting concoct,[6] digest, assimilate,
And corporeal to incorporeal turn.
For know, whatever was created needs
To be sustained and fed; of elements
The grosser feeds the purer, earth the sea,
Earth and the sea feed air, the air those fires
Ethereal, and as lowest first the moon—
Whence in her visage round those spots, unpurged
Vapors not yet into her substance turned.[7]
Nor doth the moon no nourishment exhale
From her moist continent to higher orbs.
The sun, that light imparts to all, receives
From all his alimental recompense
In humid exhalations, and at even
Sups with the ocean.[8] Though in Heaven the trees
Of life ambrosial[9] fruitage bear, and vines
Yield nectar, though from off the boughs each morn
We brush mellifluous dews, and find the ground
Covered with pearly grain, yet God hath here
Varied his bounty so with new delights
As may compare with Heaven; and to taste
Think not I shall be nice."[1] So down they sat,
And to their viands fell, nor seemingly
The Angel, nor in mist (the common gloss
Of theologians),[2] but with keen dispatch
Of real hunger and concoctive heat
To transubstantiate;[3] what redounds, transpires
Through spirits with ease: nor wonder: if by fire
Of sooty coal, the empiric alchemist
Can turn, or holds it possible to turn,
Metals of drossiest ore to perfect gold
As from the mine. Meanwhile, at table Eve

6. Make ready by heat, warm up.
7. Spots on the moon, which we now know to be extinct volcanic craters or the marks of large meteorites, were hard for early astronomers to explain; Milton's notion is that they are still-undigested food drawn up from the inferior planet, earth.
8. The phenomenon of evaporation Milton interprets as the sun dining off the moisture exhaled from oceans.
9. Ambrosia and nectar are the traditional diet of angelic creatures.
1. Scrupulous, finicky.
2. Theologians intent on maintainng the pure spirituality of angels say they experience only the likeness of eating or loving—seemingly, or in a mist; Milton will have none of this evasion: the angel ate with real hunger.
3. In common theological use, transubstantiation is the Roman Catholic doctrine that the bread and wine of the eucharist really become the body and blood of Christ; Milton would vigorously have denied that doctrine as it applied to the sacrament, but says that here, by transforming material food to spiritual substance, the angel performed an act of true transubstantiation. The excess ("what redounds") is exhaled through spiritual pores.

Ministered naked, and their flowing cups
With pleasant liquors crowned. O innocence
Deserving paradise! if ever, then,
Then had the sons of God excuse t' have been
Enamored at that sight; but in those hearts
Love unlibidinous reigned, nor jealousy
Was understood, the injured lover's hell.
  Thus when with meats and drinks they had sufficed,
Not burdened nature, sudden mind arose
In Adam, not to let th' occasion pass
Giv'n him by this great conference to know
Of things above his world, and of their being
Who dwell in Heaven, whose excellence he saw
Transcend his own so far, whose radiant forms
Divine effulgence,[4] whose high power so far
Exceeded human, and his wary speech
Thus to th' empyreal[5] minister he framed.
  "Inhabitant with God, now know I well
Thy favor in this honor done to man,
Under whose lowly roof thou hast vouchsafed
To enter and these earthly fruits to taste,
Food not of angels, yet accepted so
As that more willingly thou couldst not seem
At Heav'n's high feasts t' have fed: yet what compare?"
  To whom the wingéd hierarch replied:
"O Adam, one Almighty is, from whom
All things proceed and up to him return,
If not depraved from good, created all
Such to perfection, one first matter all,
Endued with various forms, various degrees
Of substance, and in things that live, of life;[6]
But more refined, more spiritous, and pure,
As nearer to him placed or nearer tending,
Each in their several active spheres assigned,
Till body up to spirit work, in bounds
Proportioned to each kind. So from the root
Springs lighter the green stalk, from thence the leaves
More airy, last the bright consummate flower
Spirits odorous breathes:[7] flowers and their fruit,
Man's nourishment, by gradual scale sublimed,[8]

4. A verb to the general effect of "diffused" or "radiated" is omitted.

5. A minister from the empyrean, the highest or fiery level of heaven, with a perhaps accidental touch on "imperial," as well.

6. Behind Raphael's speech lies the traditional division of natural things into inanimate objects, vegetable, animal, human, and angelic natures; they all derive from one matter, created by God, but are differentiated by Him into distinct levels of purity.

7. As the flower is the consummation of a plant's existence, its odors are efflorescences analogous to man's spiritual life, the consummation of *his* existence.

8. Purified.

To vital spirits aspire, to animal,
To intellectual—give both life and sense,
Fancy[9] and understanding, whence the soul
Reason receives, and reason is her being,
Discursive or intuitive;[1] discourse
Is oftest yours, the latter most is ours,
Differing but in degree, of kind the same.
Wonder not then, what God for you saw good
If I refuse not,[2] but convert, as you,
To proper substance; time may come when men
With angels may participate, and find
No inconvenient diet, nor too light fare;
And from these corporal nutriments perhaps
Your bodies may at last turn all to spirit,
Improved by tract of time, and winged ascend,
Ethereal as we,[3] or may at choice
Here or in heavenly paradises dwell;
If ye be found obedient, and retain
Unalterably firm his love entire
Whose progeny you are. Meanwhile, enjoy
Your fill what happiness this happy state
Can comprehend, incapable of more."

9. Imagination.

1. For Milton, discursive human reason, which must be learned by rules and study, is quite different from the intuitive reason planted from the beginning in the essential being of angels.

2. I.e., don't be surprised if I accept ("refuse not") what God thought would be good for you.

3. Raphael is talking to unfallen man, who in time might very well turn all to spirit; Milton's views on the ultimate pefectibility of man on earth altered considerably during his lifetime, and must be carefully calculated in the light of the dramatic situation.

Summary After this mingled explanation and warning, Raphael, by way of emphasizing the danger that threatens Adam and Eve, enters upon the story of Satan's revolt and fall. Satan, pretending that God's exaltation of the Son was an offense to angelic dignity, persuaded a host of his fellow angels to withdraw their allegiance to God and set up a camp in the north. When open war on God was declared, however, one of these angels was able to repent. The seraph Abdiel, though scorned by his fellow rebels, denounced the rebellion, and returned, heroically alone, to the ranks of God's followers.

Book VI. Summary **Continuing the story of the war in Heaven, Raphael describes the assembling of the armies and a first skirmish in which Satan is both insulted and wounded by Abdiel. After the first day's battle, the evil angels retire discomfited; but overnight Satan invents cannon with which, on the second day, the good angels are put to some disorder. In**

the fury of the fight, however, they pull up mountains by the roots and bury the cannon beneath them; thus the issue remains inconclusive. On the third day, God withdraws all his armies and sends the Son alone into battle; the Son drives his enemies irresistibly over the wall of Heaven, and after falling nine days through Chaos they are swallowed up in Hell.

From Book VII

[*The Invocation*][1]

Descend from Heaven, Urania, by that name
If rightly thou art called,[2] whose voice divine
Following, above th' Olympian hill I soar,
Above the flight of Pegasean wing![3]
The meaning, not the name I call: for thou
Nor of the Muses nine, nor on the top
Of old Olympus dwell'st, but heavenly born,
Before the hills appeared, or fountain flowed,
Thou with eternal Wisdom didst converse,
Wisdom thy sister, and with her didst play
In presence of th' Almighty Father,[4] pleased
With thy celestial song. Up led by thee
Into the Heaven of Heavens I have presumed,
An earthly guest, and drawn empyreal air,
Thy tempering;[5] with like safety guided down,
Return me to my native element:
Lest from this flying steed unreined (as once
Bellerophon,[6] though from a lower clime),
Dismounted, on th' Aleian field I fall,
Erroneous[7] there to wander and forlorn.
Half yet remains unsung, but narrower bound
Within the visible diurnal sphere;
Standing on Earth, not rapt above the pole,

1. To start the second half of his poem, Milton must counterbalance the destruction of the war in Heaven with the creation by God of a new universe, centering on the Earth. Book VII is devoted to this topic; and to approach so vast a subject, Milton once more invokes his Muse.
2. Milton has only the names of classical Muses with which to invoke the spiritual principles of Christian theology. Properly the Muse of astronomy, Urania is also the symbol of heavenly love and of divine wisdom; Milton here renews the invocation he made in Book I.
3. Pegasus, the flying horse of poetry, suggests (in connection with Bellerophon, line 18) Milton's sense of his own perilous audacity in writing so vast a poem.
4. In Proverbs viii.30, Wisdom is made to speak of "playing always before God" previous even to the Creation. Milton makes his Muse coeval with divine wisdom.
5. Tempered (i.e., mixed and softened) by thee.
6. Bellerophon tried to explore the stars astride Pegasus the flying horse; but Zeus sent a gadfly to sting Pegasus, and his rider, after falling onto the Aleian plain in Lycia, wandered about there till he died.
7. From Latin *errare,* "to wander," as well as "to be mistaken."

More safe I sing with mortal voice, unchanged
To hoarse or mute, though fall'n on evil days,
On evil days though fall'n, and evil tongues;
In darkness, and with dangers compassed round,
And solitude; yet not alone, while thou
Visit'st my slumbers nightly, or when morn
Purples the east:[8] still govern thou my song,
Urania, and fit audience find, though few.
But drive far off the barbarous dissonance
Of Bacchus and his revelers, the race
Of that wild rout that tore the Thracian bard[9]
In Rhodope, where woods and rocks had ears
To rapture, till the savage clamor drowned
Both harp and voice; nor could the Muse defend
Her son. So fail not thou, who thee implores:
For thou art heavenly, she an empty dream.

8. Milton composed mostly at night or very early in the morning.
9. The Thracian Bacchantes, female worshipers of Bacchus, tore Orpheus to pieces in Rhodope, though even the rocks and trees were so impressed with his music that they refused to be used against the poet. See *Lycidas*, lines 58–63. Orpheus was son of Calliope, the epic Muse.

Summary At Adam's request, Raphael continues his narration and describes how God, to replace the fallen angels, created the world, its creatures, and finally man, in the course of six days; the story of the creation concludes, on the seventh day, with a chorus of thanksgiving by the angels.

Book VIII. Summary Adam asks Raphael why so many and such splendid stars seem to be at the service of the earth, which appears smaller and less noble than they; at this point Eve leaves her husband and his guest to continue the discussion alone. Raphael proposes various astronomical possibilities but gives no conclusive answer to Adam's question, urging him instead to confine his curiosity to more practical matters. Adam now, at Raphael's request, describes his own recollections of his creation, as well as his first meeting and marriage with Eve. In the course of the story, he shows a somewhat exaggerated deference for Eve, which the angel rebukes; Adam is to be the head of the family, and follow his own judgment, not his wife's. Repeating his admonitions to beware of temptation, Raphael departs.

Book IX

The Argument

Satan, having compassed the Earth, with meditated guile returns as a mist by night into Paradise; enters into the serpent sleeping. Adam and Eve in the morning go forth to their labors, which Eve proposes to divide in several places, each laboring apart: Adam consents not, alleging the danger lest that enemy of whom they were forewarned should attempt her found alone. Eve, loath to be thought not circumspect or firm enough, urges her going apart, the rather desirous to make trial of her strength; Adam at last yields. The serpent finds her alone: his subtle approach, first gazing, then speaking, with much flattery extolling Eve above all other creatures. Eve, wondering to hear the serpent speak, asks how he attained to human speech and such understanding not till now; the serpent answers that by tasting of a certain tree in the garden he attained both to speech and reason, till then void of both. Eve requires him to bring her to that tree, and finds it to be the Tree of Knowledge forbidden: the serpent, now grown bolder, with many wiles and arguments induces her at length to eat. She, pleased with the taste, deliberates a while whether to impart thereof to Adam or not; at last brings him of the fruit; relates what persuaded her to eat thereof. Adam, at first amazed, but perceiving her lost, resolves, through vehemence of love, to perish with her, and, extenuating[1] the trespass, eats also of the fruit. The effects thereof in them both; they seek to cover their nakedness; then fall to variance and accusation of one another.

No more of talk where God[2] or angel guest
With man, as with his friend, familiar used
To sit indulgent, and with him partake
Rural repast, permitting him the while
Venial[3] discourse unblamed. I now must change
Those notes to tragic; foul distrust, and breach
Disloyal, on the part of man, revolt
And disobedience; on the part of Heaven,
Now alienated, distance and distaste,
Anger and just rebuke, and judgment given,
That brought into this world a world of woe,
Sin and her shadow Death, and Misery,
Death's harbinger. Sad task! yet argument
Not less but more heroic than the wrath
Of stern Achilles on his foe pursued
Thrice fugitive about Troy wall; or rage
Of Turnus for Lavinia disespoused;
Or Neptune's ire, or Juno's, that so long
Perplexed the Greek, and Cytherea's son:[4]

1. Not "diminishing" or "excusing" as in customary English usage, but carrying further, drawing out.
2. God, of course, has not been lunching with Adam; but since man is about to fall, the age is now over when such an occasion could be contemplated.
3. Permissible.
4. In the *Iliad* (XXII), Achilles pursues Hector three times around Troy wall before catching him. In the *Aeneid*, Aeneas must fight with Turnus for the hand of Lavinia. Neptune (or Poseidon) was unfriendly to Odysseus (the Greek); Juno (or Hera) to Aeneas, who was Cytherea's, i.e., Aphrodite's, son by Anchises.

If answerable style I can obtain
Of my celestial Patroness,[5] who deigns
Her nightly visitation unimplored,
And dictates to me slumbering, or inspires
Easy my unpremeditated verse,[6]
Since first this subject for heroic song
Pleased me, long choosing and beginning late,[7]
Not sedulous by nature to indite
Wars, hitherto the only argument
Heroic deemed, chief mastery to dissect[8]
With long and tedious havoc fabled knights
In battles feigned (the better fortitude
Of patience and heroic martyrdom
Unsung), or to describe races and games,
Or tilting furniture,[9] emblazoned shields,
Impresses quaint, caparisons and steeds,
Bases and tinsel trappings, gorgeous knights
At joust and tournament; then marshaled feast
Served up in hall with sewers and seneschals:[1]
The skill of artifice or office mean;
Not that which justly gives heroic name
To person or to poem. Me, of these
Nor skilled nor studious, higher argument
Remains,[2] sufficient of itself to raise
That name,[3] unless an age too late, or cold
Climate, or years, damp my intended wing
Depressed; and much they may if all be mine,
Not hers who brings it nightly to my ear.
The sun was sunk, and after him the star
Of Hesperus, whose office is to bring
Twilight upon the Earth, short arbiter
'Twixt day and night, and now from end to end
Night's hemisphere had veiled the horizon round,
When Satan, who late fled before the threats
Of Gabriel out of Eden,[4] now improved
In meditated fraud and malice, bent
On man's destruction, mauger what might hap
Of heavier on himself,[5] fearless returned.

5. The muse, Urania.

6. Milton, we are told by his nephew Edward Phillips, used to wake up in the morning with lines of poetry full-formed in his head; he would then dictate them to an amanuensis.

7. Milton's early plans for epics, preserved in manuscript, did center on national heroes; his choice of a sacred subject is a novelty within the epic tradition. "Sedulous": eager.

8. I.e., in describing wars one's chief task is to dissect; dissect, in its strict Latin sense of "cut apart," but perhaps also with a comic overtone from the anatomy table.

9. The equipment of tournaments; "impresses quaint": elaborate devices on shields; "bases": trappings for horses.

1. Waiters and stewards, who also dissect.

2. I.e., for me, when these things are set aside which I neither can nor want to do, there remains a higher argument.

3. I.e., the name heroic poet. "Age too late": not Milton's age, but the age of the world. Milton felt a "cold climate," by forcing people to keep their mouths shut and mumble, was inimical to epic poetry. "Damp": stupefy, benumb.

4. At the end of Book IV.

5. Despite the peril of heavier (punishments).

By night he fled, and at midnight returned
From compassing the Earth—cautious of day
Since Uriel, regent of the sun, descried
His entrance, and forewarned the Cherubim
That kept their watch.[6] Thence, full of anguish, driven,
The space of seven continued nights he rode
With darkness; thrice the equinoctial line[7]
He circled, four times crossed the car of Night
From pole to pole, traversing each colure;
On the eighth returned, and on the coast averse
From entrance or cherubic watch by stealth
Found unsuspected way. There was a place
(Now not, though sin, not time, first wrought the change)
Where Tigris, at the foot of Paradise,
Into a gulf shot under ground, till part
Rose up a fountain by the Tree of Life.
In with the river sunk, and with it rose,
Satan, involved in rising mist; then sought
Where to lie hid. Sea he had searched and land
From Eden over Pontus, and the pool
Maeotis, up beyond the river Ob;[8]
Downward as far antarctic; and, in length,
West from Orontes to the ocean barred
At Darien, thence to the land where flows
Ganges and Indus.[9] Thus the orb he roamed
With narrow search, and with inspection deep
Considered every creature, which of all
Most opportune might serve his wiles, and found
The serpent subtlest beast of all the field.[1]
Him, after long debate, irresolute
Of thoughts revolved,[2] his final sentence chose
Fit vessel, fittest imp[3] of fraud, in whom
To enter, and his dark suggestions hide
From sharpest sight; for in the wily snake
Whatever sleights none would suspicious mark,
As from his wit and native subtlety
Proceeding, which, in other beasts observed,
Doubt[4] might beget of diabolic power
Active within beyond the sense of brute.

6. At the beginning of Book IV. These connections with Book IV not only bridge the intervening narration, but emphasize a balancing of the whole epic; see the headnote.
7. The equator. The colures are the two great circles of the celestial sphere which intersect at the poles. By circling the globe, either from east to west or over the north and south poles, Satan can remain continually hidden in darkness.
8. Pontus is the Black Sea, the pool Maeotis the swamps of the Sea of Azov; the river Ob flows north through Siberia into the Arctic Ocean.
9. Flying west from Orontes in Syria, Satan crossed the Atlantic to the Isthmus of Panama (Darien), then the Pacific and southeast Asia to India.
1. Genesis iii.1 describes the serpent as the subtlest beast of the field.
2. I.e., unable to decide among his revolving thoughts. "Sentence": decision.
3. Graft, offshoot.
4. Suspicion.

Thus he resolved, but first from inward grief
His bursting passion into plaints thus poured:
"O Earth, how like to Heaven, if not preferred
More justly, seat worthier of Gods, as built
With second thought, reforming what was old!
For what God, after better, worse would build?
Terrestrial Heaven, danced round by other Heavens,
That shine, yet bear their bright officious lamps,
Light above light, for thee alone, as seems,
In thee concent'ring all their precious beams
Of sacred influence![5] As God in Heaven
Is center, yet extends to all, so thou
Cent'ring receiv'st from all those orbs; in thee,
Not in themselves, all their known virtue appears,
Productive in herb, plant, and nobler birth
Of creatures animate with gradual life
Of growth, sense, reason,[6] all summed up in man.
With what delight could I have walked thee round,
If I could joy in aught; sweet interchange
Of hill and valley, rivers, woods, and plains,
Now land, now sea, and shores with forest crowned,
Rocks, dens, and caves! But I in none of these
Find place or refuge; and the more I see
Pleasures about me, so much more I feel
Torment within me, as from the hateful siege[7]
Of contraries; all good to me becomes
Bane,[8] and in Heaven much worse would be my state.
But neither here seek I, no, nor in Heaven,
To dwell, unless by mastering Heaven's Supreme;
Nor hope to be myself less miserable
By what I seek, but others to make such
As I, though thereby worse to me redound.
For only in destroying I find ease
To my relentless thoughts, and him [9] destroyed,
Or won to what may work his utter loss,
For whom all this was made, all this [1] will soon
Follow, as to him linked in weal or woe:
In woe then, that destruction wide may range!
To me shall be the glory sole among
The infernal Powers, in one day to have marred
What he, Almighty styled, six nights and days
Continued making, and who knows how long
Before had been contriving? though perhaps
Not longer than since I in one night freed

5. Satan, like Adam in Book VIII, is impressed that so many heavenly bodies center on (and "serve") the earth—as the old Ptolemaic astronomy taught that they did. "Officious": dutiful.

6. Life on earth is gradual, or graduated, from the herb which merely grows, to the animal which grows and feels, to man, who grows, feels, and thinks.

7. Conflict.

8. Poison. This is exactly what he willed in IV.110.

9. I.e., man.

1. I.e., the created cosmos.

From servitude inglorious well-nigh half
Th' angelic name, and thinner left the throng
Of his adorers. He, to be avenged,
And to repair his numbers thus impaired,
Whether such virtue,[2] spent of old, now failed
More angels to create (if they at least
Are his created),[3] or to spite us more,
Determined to advance into our room
A creature formed of earth, and him endow,
Exalted from so base original,
With heavenly spoils, our spoils. What he decreed
He effected; man he made, and for him built
Magnificent this World, and Earth his seat,
Him lord pronounced, and, O indignity!
Subjected to his service angel-wings
And flaming ministers, to watch and tend
Their earthy charge. Of these the vigilance
I dread, and to elude, thus wrapt in mist
Of midnight vapor, glide obscure, and pry
In every bush and brake, where hap may find
The serpent sleeping, in whose mazy folds
To hide me, and the dark intent I bring.
O foul descent! that I, who erst contended
With Gods to sit the highest, am now constrained
Into a beast, and, mixed with bestial slime,
This essence to incarnate and imbrute,[4]
That to the height of deity aspired!
But what will not ambition and revenge
Descend to? Who aspires must down as low
As high he soared, obnoxious,[5] first or last,
To basest things. Revenge, at first though sweet,
Bitter ere long back on itself recoils.
Let it; I reck not, so it light well aimed,
Since higher I fall short, on him who next
Provokes my envy, this new favorite
Of Heaven, this man of clay, son of despite,
Whom, us the more to spite,[6] his Maker raised
From dust: spite then with spite is best repaid."
So saying, through each thicket, dank or dry,
Like a black mist low-creeping, he held on
His midnight search, where soonest he might find
The serpent. Him fast sleeping soon he found,
In labyrinth of many a round self-rolled,
His head the midst, well stored with subtle wiles:
Not yet in horrid shade or dismal den,

2. Strength, energy.
3. Satan never raises this question, whether angels are created or independent beings, without hesitating over it.
4. Satan's incarnation in a snake is a grotesque parody of the Son of God's incarnation in Christ.
5. Subject to.
6. Satan sees God in his own image, as a spiteful creature.

Nor nocent[7] yet, but on the grassy herb,
Fearless, unfeared, he slept. In at his mouth
The devil entered, and his brutal sense,
In heart or head, possessing soon inspired
With act intelligential; but his sleep
Disturbed not, waiting close[8] th' approach of morn.
Now, whenas sacred light began to dawn
In Eden on the humid flowers, that breathed
Their morning incense, when all things that breathe
From th' Earth's great altar send up silent praise
To the Creator, and his nostrils fill
With grateful smell, forth came the human pair,
And joined their vocal worship to the choir
Of creatures wanting voice; that done, partake
The season,[9] prime for sweetest scents and airs;
Then cómmune how that day they best may ply
Their growing work; for much their work outgrew
The hands' dispatch of two gardening so wide:
And Eve first to her husband thus began:
"Adam, well may we labor still[1] to dress
This garden, still to tend plant, herb, and flower,
Our pleasant task enjoined; but, till more hands
Aid us, the work under our labor grows,
Luxurious by restraint: what we by day
Lop overgrown, or prune, or prop, or bind,
One night or two with wanton growth derides,
Tending to wild. Thou, therefore, now advise,
Or hear what to my mind first thoughts present.
Let us divide our labors; thou where choice
Leads thee, or where most needs, whether to wind
The woodbine round this arbor, or direct
The clasping ivy where to climb; while I
In yonder spring[2] of roses intermixed
With myrtle find what to redress till noon.
For, while so near each other thus all day
Our task we choose, what wonder if so near
Looks intervene and smiles, or objects new
Casual discourse draw on, which intermits
Our day's work, brought to little, though begun
Early, and th' hour of supper comes unearned!"
To whom mild answer Adam thus returned:
"Sole Eve, associate sole, to me beyond
Compare above all living creatures dear!
Well hast thou motioned,[3] well thy thoughts employed
How we might best fulfil the work which here
God hath assigned us, nor of me shalt pass

7. Harmful.
8. In secret.
9. I.e., go forth into the morning air. "Prime": the best.
1. Continually.
2. Growth.
3. Suggested.

Unpraised; for nothing lovelier can be found
In woman than to study household good,
And good works in her husband to promote.[4]
Yet not so strictly hath our Lord imposed
Labor as to debar us when we need
Refreshment, whether food or talk between,
Food of the mind, or this sweet intercourse
Of looks and smiles; for smiles from reason flow,
To brute denied, and are of love the food,
Love, not the lowest end of human life.
For not to irksome toil, but to delight,
He made us, and delight to reason joined.
These paths and bowers doubt not but our joint hands
Will keep from wilderness with ease, as wide
As we need walk, till younger hands ere long
Assist us. But, if much converse perhaps
Thee satiate, to short absence I could yield;
For solitude sometimes is best society,
And short retirement urges sweet return.
But other doubt possesses me, lest harm
Befall thee, severed from me; for thou know'st
What hath been warned us, what malicious foe,
Envying our happiness, and of his own
Despairing, seeks to work us woe and shame
By sly assault, and somewhere nigh at hand
Watches, no doubt, with greedy hope to find
His wish and best advantage, us asunder,[5]
Hopeless to circumvent us joined, where each
To other speedy aid might lend at need.
Whether his first design be to withdraw
Our fealty from God, or to disturb
Conjugal love, than which perhaps no bliss
Enjoyed by us excites his envy more;
Or this, or worse,[6] leave not the faithful side
That gave thee being, still shades thee and protects.
The wife, where danger or dishonor lurks,
Safest and seemliest by her husband stays,
Who guards her, or with her the worst endures."
   To whom the virgin[7] majesty of Eve,
As one who loves, and some unkindness meets,
With sweet austere composure thus replied:
   "Offspring of Heaven and Earth, and all Earth's lord!
That such an enemy we have, who seeks
Our ruin, both by thee informed I learn,
And from the parting angel overheard,

4. Proverbs xxxi is devoted to the praise of a good wife, and Milton doubtless had it in mind here.
5. I.e., to find us apart, which will answer his wishes and serve his advantage.
6. I.e., whether this or something worse be his intent.
7. Unspotted.

As in a shady nook I stood behind,
Just then returned at shut of evening flowers.
But that thou shouldst my firmness therefore doubt
To God or thee, because we have a foe
May tempt it, I expected not to hear.
His violence thou fear'st not, being such
As we, not capable of death or pain,
Can either not receive, or can repel.
His fraud is, then, thy fear; which plain infers
Thy equal fear that my firm faith and love
Can by his fraud be shaken or seduced:
Thoughts, which how found they harbor in thy breast,
Adam, misthought of her to thee so dear?" [8]
To whom, with healing words, Adam replied:
"Daughter of God and man, immortal Eve,
For such thou art, from sin and blame entire; [9]
Not diffident of thee do I dissuade
Thy absence from my sight, but to avoid
Th' attempt itself, intended by our foe.
For he who tempts, though in vain, at least asperses [1]
The tempted with dishonor foul, supposed
Not incorruptible of faith, not proof
Against temptation. Thou thyself with scorn
And anger wouldst resent the offered wrong,
Though ineffectual found; misdeem not, then,
If such affront I labor to avert
From thee alone, which on us both at once
The enemy, though bold, will hardly dare;
Or, daring, first on me th' assault shall light.
Nor thou his malice and false guile contemn—
Subtle he needs must be who could seduce
Angels—nor think superfluous others' aid.
I from the influence of thy looks receive
Access[2] in every virtue; in thy sight
More wise, more watchful, stronger, if need were
Of outward strength; while shame, thou looking on,
Shame to be overcome or overreached,[3]
Would utmost vigor raise, and raised unite.
Why shouldst not thou like sense within thee feel
When I am present, and thy trial choose
With me, best witness of thy virtue tried?"
So spake domestic Adam in his care
And matrimonial love; but Eve, who thought
Less[4] áttributed to her faith sincere,

8. I.e., these thoughts were misthought of (misapplied to) her to thee so dear (me).

9. "Entire" is from Latin *integer*, untouched. "Diffident": the usual English meaning is "shy," "timid"; Milton emphasizes the Latin roots, *dis* + *fides* = mistrustful.

1. The word is from Latin *spargere*, to sprinkle, with overtones from English "aspersion," an ugly insinuation.

2. Extra strength.

3. Overpowered or outwitted.

4. Too little.

Thus her reply with accent sweet renewed:
"If this be our condition, thus to dwell
In narrow circuit straitened by a foe,
Subtle or violent, we not endued
Single with like defence wherever met,
How are we happy, still in fear of harm?
But harm precedes not sin: only our foe
Tempting affronts us with his foul esteem
Of our integrity: his foul esteem
Sticks no dishonor on our front,[5] but turns
Foul on himself; then wherefore shunned or feared
By us, who rather double honor gain
From his surmise proved false, find peace within,
Favor from Heaven, our witness, from th' event?
And what is faith, love, virtue, unassayed
Alone, without exterior help sustained?
Let us not then suspect our happy state
Left so imperfect by the Maker wise
As not secure to single or combined.
Frail is our happiness, if this be so;
And Eden were no Eden, thus exposed."
To whom thus Adam fervently replied:
"O woman, best are all things as the will
Of God ordained them; his creating hand
Nothing imperfect or deficient left
Of all that he created, much less man,
Or aught that might his happy state secure,
Secure from outward force. Within himself
The danger lies, yet lies within his power;
Against his will he can receive no harm.
But God left free the will; for what obeys
Reason is free; and reason he made right,
But bid her well beware, and still erect,[6]
Lest, by some fair appearing good surprised,
She dictate false, and misinform the will
To do what God expressly hath forbid.
Not then mistrust, but tender love, enjoins
That I should mind [7] thee oft; and mind thou me.
Firm we subsist, yet possible to swerve,
Since reason not impossibly may meet
Some specious object by the foe suborned,
And fall into deception unaware,
Not keeping strictest watch, as she was warned.
Seek not temptation, then, which to avoid
Were better, and most likely if from me

5. Forehead.
6. Remain alert.
7. Remind; in the next phrase, "mind" means "obey."

Thou sever not: trial will come unsought.
Wouldst thou approve thy constancy, approve[8]
First thy obedience; th' other who can know,
Not seeing thee attempted, who attest?
But if thou think trial unsought may find
Us both securer[8a] than thus warned thou seem'st,
Go; for thy stay, not free, absents thee more.
Go in thy native innocence; rely
On what thou hast of virtue; summon all;
For God towards thee hath done his part: do thine.'
So spake the patriarch of mankind; but Eve
Persisted; yet submiss, though last, replied:
"With thy permission,[9] then, and thus forewarned,
Chiefly by what thy own last reasoning words
Touched only, that our trial, when least sought,
May find us both perhaps far less prepared,
The willinger I go, nor much expect
A foe so proud will first the weaker seek;
So bent, the more shall shame him his repulse."
Thus saying, from her husband's hand her hand
Soft she withdrew, and like a wood nymph light,
Oread or dryad, or of Delia's train,[1]
Betook her to the groves, but Delia's self
In gait surpassed and goddesslike deport,
Though not as she with bow and quiver armed,
But with such gardening tools as art yet rude,
Guiltless of fire[2] had formed, or angels brought.
To Pales, or Pomona, thus adorned,
Likest she seemed, Pomona when she fled
Vertumnus, or to Ceres in her prime,
Yet virgin of Proserpina from Jove.[3]
Her long with ardent look his eye pursued
Delighted, but desiring more her stay.
Oft he to her his charge of quick return
Repeated; she to him as oft engaged
To be returned by noon amid the bower,
And all things in best order to invite
Noontide repast, or afternoon's repose.
O much deceived, much failing, hapless Eve,

8. Prove, give evidence of

8a. The Latin word *securus* can mean either "safe" or "free from care," i.e., "careless." Adam's warning is at once reassuring and ominous.

9. Eve takes a reluctant and extorted permission as free leave to do what she wants. Though apparently submissive, she gets the last word.

1. An "oread" is a nymph of the mountain, a "dryad" one of the wood. "Delia" is Diana or Artemis, goddess of the chase, who when she hunted was accompanied by a train of nymphs.

2. There was no need of fire in Paradise; but that fire is a possession which renders one guilty suggests an overtone of the Prometheus myth.

3. Pales is a Roman goddess of flocks, Pomona a Roman divinity of fruits and orchards. Pomona was wooed by Vertumnus, god of the turning year, who assumed all sorts of shapes to win her. Ceres, the Mother Nature of the ancients (hence, the word "cereal"), bore Proserpina to Jupiter. All three goddesses are patrons of agriculture, like Eve.

Of thy presumed return![4] Event perverse!
Thou never from that hour in Paradise
Found'st either sweet repast, or sound repose;
Such ambush hid among sweet flowers and shades
Waited with hellish rancor imminent[5]
To intercept thy way, or send thee back
Despoiled of innocence, of faith, of bliss.
For now, and since first break of dawn, the fiend,
Mere serpent in appearance, forth was come,
And on his quest, where likeliest he might find
The only two of mankind, but in them
The whole included race, his purposed prey.
In bower and field he sought, where any tuft
Of grove or garden-plot more pleasant lay,
Their tendance[6] or plantation for delight;
By fountain or by shady rivulet
He sought them both, but wished his hap might find
Eve separate; he wished, but not with hope
Of what so seldom chanced; when to his wish,
Beyond his hope, Eve separate he spies,
Veiled in a cloud of fragrance, where she stood,
Half spied, so thick the roses bushing round
About her glowed, oft stooping to support
Each flower of slender stalk, whose head though gay
Carnation, purple, azure, or specked with gold,
Hung drooping unsustained, them she upstays
Gently with myrtle band, mindless the while
Herself, though fairest unsupported flower,
From her best prop so far, and storm so nigh.[7]
Nearer he drew, and many a walk traversed
Of stateliest covert, cedar, pine, or palm;
Then voluble[8] and bold, now hid, now seen
Among thick-woven arborets[9] and flowers
Embordered on each bank, the hand of Eve:
Spot more delicious than those gardens feigned
Or of revived Adonis,[1] or renowned
Alcinous, host of old Laertes' son,
Or that, not mystic, where the sapient king[2]
Held dalliance with his fair Egyptian spouse.
Much he the place admired, the person more.
As one who long in populous city pent,

4. "Much deceived" carries over; Eve was "much deceived of" (about) her "presumed return."
5. Threatening.
6. Object of their tending.
7. The conceit of the flower-gatherer who is herself gathered is repeated here from IV.270, where it was applied to Proserpina.
8. Rolling (a Latinism).
9. Bushes. "Hand": handiwork.
1. The garden of Adonis was a heavenly bower where Venus' lover was supposed still to lie in secret, recovering from his wound received on earth (Venus would not allow him to die). Alcinous was king of the Phaeacians. His garden, visited by Odysseus ("old Laertes' son"), is described in the *Odyssey*.
2. Solomon; his "fair Egyptian spouse" is Pharaoh's daughter: Milton is referring to the Song of Solomon vi.2. The fact that it is "not mystic" (i.e., not mythical) distinguishes the Scriptural garden from the "feigned" (line 439) ones of classical legend.

Where houses thick and sewers annoy[3] the air,
Forth issuing on a summer's morn to breathe
Among the pleasant villages and farms
Adjoined, from each thing met conceives delight,
The smell of grain, or tedded[4] grass, or kine,
Or dairy, each rural sight, each rural sound:
If chance with nymphlike step fair virgin pass,[5]
What pleasing seemed, for her now pleases more,
She most, and in her look sums all delight.[6]
Such pleasure took the serpent to behold
This flowery plat,[7] the sweet recess of Eve
Thus early, thus alone; her heavenly form
Angelic, but more soft, and feminine,
Her graceful innocence, her every air
Of gesture or least action overawed
His malice, and with rapine[8] sweet bereaved
His fierceness of the fierce intent it brought:
That space the evil one abstracted stood
From his own evil, and for the time remained
Stupidly good,[9] of enmity disarmed,
Of guile, of hate, of envy, of revenge.
But the hot Hell that always in him burns,
Though in mid Heaven, soon ended his delight,
And tortures him now more, the more he sees
Of pleasure not for him ordained: then soon
Fierce hate he recollects, and all his thoughts
Of mischief, gratulating,[1] thus excites:
  "Thoughts, whither have ye led me? with what sweet
Compulsion thus transported to forget
What hither brought us? hate, not love, nor hope
Of Paradise for Hell, hope here to taste
Of pleasure, but all pleasure to destroy,
Save what is in destroying;[2] other joy
To me is lost. Then let me not let pass
Occasion which now smiles; behold alone
The woman, opportune to all attempts,
Her husband, for I view far round, not nigh,
Whose higher intellectual more I shun,
And strength, of courage haughty, and of limb
Heroic built, though of terrestrial mold;[3]
Foe not informidable, exempt from wound,[4]
I not; so much hath Hell debased, and pain

3. Make noisome, befoul.
4. Tossed and drying in the sun.
5. I.e., if it chance that with nymphlike step a fair virgin should pass.
6. I.e., in her look sums up, or epitomizes, all delight.
7. Plot.
8. It is a deliberate paradox that her sweetness can ravish his malice; the word is deliberately overviolent.
9. Without his evil, Satan (like many wicked people) is quite dull and ordinary. But at the moment he is stunned.
1. Exulting.
2. What brought Satan to Paradise was not hope of pleasure, but the wish to destroy all pleasure except the pleasure of destruction itself.
3. Made of earth.
4. Adam in the state of innocence is invulnerable.

Enfeebled me, to what I was in Heaven.
She fair, divinely fair, fit love for gods,
Not terrible, though terror be in love
And beauty, not approached by stronger hate,
Hate stronger, under show of love well feigned,
The way which to her ruin now I tend."[5]
So spake the enemy of mankind, enclosed
In serpent, inmate bad, and toward Eve
Addressed his way, not with indented wave,
Prone on the ground, as since, but on his rear,
Circular base of rising folds, that towered
Fold above fold a surging maze; his head
Crested aloft, and carbuncle[6] his eyes;
With burnished neck of verdant gold, erect
Amidst his circling spires,[7] that on the grass
Floated redundant. Pleasing was his shape,
And lovely; never since of serpent kind
Lovelier, not those that in Illyria changed
Hermione and Cadmus,[8] or the god
In Epidaurus;[9] nor to which transformed
Ammonian Jove, or Capitoline was seen,
He with Olympias, this with her who bore
Scipio, the height of Rome.[1] With tract oblique
At first, as one who sought access, but feared
To interrupt, sidelong he works his way.
As when a ship by skillful steersman wrought
Nigh river's mouth or foreland, where the wind
Veers oft, as oft so steers, and shifts her sail:
So varied he, and of his tortuous train
Curled many a wanton wreath in sight of Eve,
To lure her eye: she busied heard the sound
Of rustling leaves, but minded not, as used
To such disport before her through the field,
From every beast, more duteous at her call,
Than at Circean call the herd disguised.[2]
He bolder now, uncalled before her stood:
But as in gaze admiring; oft he bowed
His turret crest, and sleek enameled neck,
Fawning, and licked the ground whereon she trod.
His gentle dumb expression turned at length

5. I.e., love and beauty are terrible unless counteracted by hate—as they are being counteracted in Satan, to the ruin of Eve.
6. Deep red, inflamed.
7. Coils. "Redundant": abundantly, to excess.
8. Ovid tells how Cadmus and Harmonia (Milton's "Hermione") were changed to serpents after they retired (in despair at the misfortunes of their children) to Illyria.
9. Aesculapius, god of medicine, had a temple at Epidaurus, from which he sometimes emerged in the form of a serpent.
1. Jupiter Ammon ("Ammonian Jove"), in the form of a snake, was said to have consorted with Olympias to beget Alexander the Great; and in the same way, the Jupiter of the Roman capitol (Jove "Capitoline") was thought to have begotten Scipio Africanus, the savior and leader ("height") of Rome.
2. Circe, who enchanted men into the shape of swine, was attended by an obedient herd in the *Odyssey*.

The eye of Eve to mark his play: he, glad
Of her attention gained, with serpent tongue
Organic, or impulse of vocal air,[3]
His fraudulent temptation thus began.
"Wonder not, sovereign mistress, if perhaps
Thou canst, who art sole wonder; much less arm
Thy looks, the heaven of mildness, with disdain,
Displeased that I approach thee thus, and gaze
Insatiate, I thus single, nor have feared
Thy awful brow, more awful thus retired.
Fairest resemblance of thy Maker fair,
Thee all things living gaze on, all things thine
By gift, and thy celestial beauty adore
With ravishment beheld, there best beheld
Where universally admired: but here
In this enclosure wild, these beasts among,
Beholders rude, and shallow to discern
Half what in thee is fair, one man except,
Who sees thee?[4] (and what is one?) who shouldst be seen
A goddess among gods, adored and served
By angels numberless, thy daily train."
So glozed[5] the tempter, and his proem tuned;
Into the heart of Eve his words made way,
Though at the voice much marveling: at length,
Not unamazed, she thus in answer spake.
"What may this mean? Language of man pronounced
By tongue of brute, and human sense expressed?
The first at least of these I thought denied
To beasts, whom God on their creation-day
Created mute to all articulate sound;
The latter I demur,[6] for in their looks
Much reason, and in their actions oft appears.
Thee, serpent, subtlest beast of all the field
I knew, but not with human voice endued:[7]
Redouble then this miracle, and say,
How cam'st thou speakable of mute,[8] and how
To me so friendly grown above the rest
Of brutal kind, that daily are in sight?
Say, for such wonder claims attention due."
To whom the guileful tempter thus replied:
"Empress of this fair world, resplendent Eve!
Easy to me it is to tell thee all
What thou command'st and right thou shouldst be obeyed:
I was at first as other beasts that graze
The trodden herb, of abject thoughts and low,

3. I.e., Satan either used the actual tongue of the serpent or himself impressed the air with speech.
4. The beasts cannot see the beauty of Eve's soul, only Adam can. Satan's entire speech is couched in the extravagant phrases of the Petrarchan love convention.
5. Flattered. "Proem": introduction.
6. I.e., as to whether rational sense was denied to brutes, I am doubtful.
7. Endowed.
8. To have speech after being dumb.

As was my food, nor aught but food discerned
Or sex, and apprehended nothing high:
Till on a day, roving the field, I chanced
A goodly tree far distant to behold
Loaden with fruit of fairest colors mixed,
Ruddy and gold; I nearer drew to gaze;
When from the boughs a savory odor blown,
Grateful to appetite, more pleased my sense
Than smell of sweetest fennel,[9] or the teats
Of ewe or goat dropping with milk at even,
Unsucked of lamb or kid, that tend their play.
To satisfy the sharp desire I had
Of tasting those fair apples, I resolved
Not to defer: hunger and thirst at once,
Powerful persuaders, quickened at the scent
Of that alluring fruit, urged me so keen.
About the mossy trunk I wound me soon,
For, high from ground, the branches would require
Thy utmost reach, or Adam's: round the tree
All other beasts that saw, with like desire
Longing and envying stood, but could not reach.
Amid the tree now got, where plenty hung
Tempting so nigh, to pluck and eat my fill
I spared not;[1] for such pleasure till that hour
At feed or fountain never had I found.
Sated at length, ere long I might perceive
Strange alteration in me, to degree
Of reason in my inward powers, and speech
Wanted not long, though to this shape retained.[2]
Thenceforth to speculations high or deep
I turned my thoughts, and with capacious mind
Considered all things visible in Heaven,
Or Earth, or middle, all things fair and good:
But all that fair and good in thy divine
Semblance, and in thy beauty's heavenly ray
United I beheld: no fair[3] to thine
Equivalent or second, which compelled
Me thus, though importune perhaps, to come
And gaze, and worship thee of right declared
Sovereign of creatures, universal dame."
  So talked the spirited[4] sly snake: and Eve
Yet more amazed, unwary thus replied:
  "Serpent, thy overpraising leaves in doubt
The virtue of that fruit, in thee first proved.
But say, where grows the tree, from hence how far?

9. Milton learned probably from Pliny, the natural historian, that serpents were fond of fennel; popular superstition had it that they drank the milk of sheep and goats.

1. Refrained not.

2. His inward powers, his mental constitution and gift of speech, were changed; but he retained his exterior shape as before.

3. Beauty.

4. Possessed by a spirit, inspired.

For many are the trees of God that grow
In Paradise, and various, yet unknown
To us; in such abundance lies our choice,
As leaves a greater store of fruit untouched,
Still hanging incorruptible, till men
Grow up to their provision, and more hands
Help to disburden Nature of her bearth."[5]
To whom the wily adder, blithe and glad:
"Empress, the way is ready, and not long,
Beyond a row of myrtles, on a flat,
Fast by a fountain, one small thicket past
Of blowing[6] myrrh and balm: if thou accept
My conduct, I can bring thee thither soon."
"Lead then," said Eve. He leading swiftly rolled
In tangles, and made intricate seem straight,
To mischief swift.[7] Hope elevates, and joy
Brightens his crest; as when a wandering fire
Compact of unctuous vapor,[8] which the night
Condenses, and the cold environs round,
Kindled through agitation to a flame
(Which oft, they say, some evil spirit attends),
Hovering and blazing with delusive light,
Misleads th' amazed night-wanderer from his way
To bogs and mires, and oft through pond or pool,
There swallowed up and lost, from succor far:
So glistered the dire snake, and into fraud
Led Eve our credulous mother, to the tree
Of prohibition,[9] root of all our woe:
Which when she saw, thus to her guide she spake:
"Serpent, we might have spared our coming hither,
Fruitless to me, though fruit be here to excess,
The credit of whose virtue rest with thee;[1]
Wondrous indeed, if cause of such effects!
But of this tree we may not taste nor touch:
God so commanded, and left that command
Sole daughter of his voice;[2] the rest, we live
Law to ourselves; our reason is our law."
To whom the Tempter guilefully replied:
"Indeed? Hath God then said that of the fruit
Of all these garden trees ye shall not eat,
Yet lords declared of all in Earth or air?"
To whom thus Eve, yet sinless: "Of the fruit
Of each tree in the garden we may eat,
But of the fruit of this fair tree amidst

5. So spelled to pun on the idea of trees bearing fruit and thus in a way giving birth to young.
6. Blooming.
7. Milton's physical descriptions of the serpent often have distinct moral overtones, as here.
8. Composed of oily vapor; Milton's theory of the *ignis fatuus*, or will-o'-the-wisp, is strikingly material and "scientific."
9. Prohibited tree (a Hebraism).
1. I.e., you must remain the only evidence of the fruit's power.
2. His one injunction (a literal Hebraism). "The rest": in everything else.

The garden, God hath said, 'Ye shall not eat
Thereof, nor shall ye touch it, lest ye die.' "
  She scarce had said, though brief, when now more bold,
The tempter, but with show of zeal and love
To man, and indignation at his wrong,
New part puts on, and as to passion moved,
Fluctuates disturbed, yet comely, and in act
Raised,[3] as of some great matter to begin.
As when of old some orator renowned
In Athens or free Rome, where eloquence
Flourished, since mute, to some great cause addressed,
Stood in himself collected, while each part,
Motion, each act, won audience ere the tongue,
Sometimes in height began, as no delay
Of preface brooking,[4] through his zeal of right.
So standing, moving, or to height upgrown
The tempter all impassioned thus began:
  "O sacred, wise, and wisdom-giving plant,
Mother of science![5] now I feel thy power
Within me clear, not only to discern
Things in their causes, but to trace the ways
Of highest agents, deemed however wise.
Queen of this universe! do not believe
Those rigid threats of death. Ye shall not die;
How should ye? By the fruit? it gives you life
To knowledge;[6] by the Threatener? look on me,
Me who have touched and tasted, yet both live,
And life more perfect have attained than Fate
Meant me, by venturing higher than my lot.
Shall that be shut to man, which to the beast
Is open? Or will God incense his ire
For such a petty trespass, and not praise
Rather your dauntless virtue, whom the pain
Of death denounced, whatever thing death be,
Deterred not from achieving what might lead
To happier life, knowledge of good and evil?
Of good, how just![7] Of evil, if what is evil
Be real, why not known, since easier shunned?
God therefore cannot hurt ye, and be just;
Not just, not God; not feared then, nor obeyed:
Your fear itself of death removes the fear.[8]
Why then was this forbid? Why but to awe,
Why but to keep ye low and ignorant,
His worshipers? He knows that in the day
Ye eat thereof, your eyes that seem so clear,

3. Poised in posture.
4. The orator, as if too much moved to be bothered with a preface, bursts into the middle of his speech.
5. Knowledge.
6. Life in addition to knowledge; or, life with which to enlarge your knowledge.
7. I.e., how just to have knowledge of good!
8. I.e., your fear of death removes your fear of God; since if God inflicts death, he will not be just and hence not God. The serpent's sophism is visible.

Yet are but dim, shall perfectly be then
Opened and cleared, and ye shall be as gods,
Knowing both good and evil, as they know.
That ye should be as gods, since I as man,
Internal man,[9] is but proportion meet,
I, of brute, human; ye, of human, gods.
So ye shall die perhaps, by putting off
Human, to put on gods:[1] death to be wished,
Though threatened, which no worse than this can bring.
And what are gods that man may not become
As they, participating godlike food?
The gods are first, and that advantage use
On our belief, that all from them proceeds.
I question it; for this fair Earth I see,
Warmed by the sun, producing every kind,
Them nothing: If they all things,[2] who enclosed
Knowledge of good and evil in this tree,
That whoso eats thereof forthwith attains
Wisdom without their leave? And wherein lies
Th' offense, that man should thus attain to know?
What can your knowledge hurt him, or this tree
Impart against his will if all be his?
Or is it envy, and can envy dwell
In heavenly breasts?[3] These, these, and many more
Causes import your need of this fair fruit.
Goddess humane,[4] reach then, and freely taste!"
He ended, and his words, replete with guile,
Into her heart too easy entrance won:
Fixed on the fruit she gazed, which to behold
Might tempt alone, and in her ears the sound
Yet rung of his persuasive words, impregned[5]
With reason, to her seeming, and with truth;
Meanwhile the hour of noon drew on, and waked
An eager appetite, raised by the smell
So savory of that fruit, which with desire,
Inclinable now grown to touch or taste,
Solicited her longing eye;[6] yet first
Pausing a while, thus to herself she mused:
"Great are thy virtues, doubtless, best of fruits,
Though kept from man, and worthy to be admired,
Whose taste, too long forborne, at first essay
Gave elocution to the mute, and taught
The tongue not made for speech to speak thy praise:
Thy praise he also who forbids thy use,

9. Man in intellectual powers.

1. The devil can quote scripture to his purpose, and here he is perverting Saint Paul, who told the Colossians (iii. 9–10) to put off the old man and put on the new. "Participating" (line 717): sharing.

2. The verb "produced" is understood. Satan is telling now, not about "God," but "the gods."

3. Adapted from Virgil, *Aeneid* I.15. "Import": imply, suggest.

4. Not so much "human goddess" (a Satanic paradox) as "kindly," "gracious" goddess.

5. Impregnated.

6. The five senses of Eve—sight, hearing, smell, taste, and touch—are all solicited by the fruit.

Conceals not from us,[7] naming thee the Tree
Of Knowledge, knowledge both of good and evil;
Forbids us then to taste; but his forbidding
Commends thee more, while it infers the good
By thee communicated, and our want:
For good unknown, sure is not had, or had
And yet unknown, is as not had at all.[8]
In plain then, what forbids he but to know?
Forbids us good, forbids us to be wise!
Such prohibitions bind not. But if Death
Bind us with after-bands, what profits then
Our inward freedom? In the day we eat
Of this fair fruit, our doom is, we shall die.
How dies the serpent? He hath eaten and lives,
And knows, and speaks, and reasons, and discerns,
Irrational till then. For us alone
Was death invented? Or to us denied
This intellectual food, for beasts reserved?
For beasts it seems: yet that one beast which first
Hath tasted, envies not, but brings with joy
The good befallen him, author unsuspect,[9]
Friendly to man, far from deceit or guile.
What fear I then, rather what know to fear[1]
Under this ignorance of good and evil,
Of God or death, of law or penalty?
Here grows the cure of all, this fruit divine,
Fair to the eye, inviting to the taste,
Of virtue[2] to make wise: what hinders then
To reach, and feed at once both body and mind?"
  So saying, her rash hand in evil hour,
Forth reaching to the fruit, she plucked, she eat.[3]
Earth felt the wound, and Nature from her seat[4]
Sighing through all her works gave signs of woe,
That all was lost. Back to the thicket slunk
The guilty serpent, and well might, for Eve
Intent now wholly on her taste, naught else
Regarded; such delight till then, as seemed,
In fruit she never tasted, whether true
Or fancied so, through expectation high
Of knowledge; nor was godhead from her thought.[5]
Greedily she engorged without restraint,
And knew not eating death:[6] satiate at length,
And heightened as with wine, jocund and boon,[7]

7. God himself, by naming it, has called attention to the tree's magic powers.
8. An unknown good is like no good at all. "In plain": i.e., in plain language.
9. A witness beyond suspicion.
1. In her ignorance, Eve does not really know what to fear and what not to fear.
2. Power.
3. In the 17th century, an accepted past tense of "eat."
4. Wherever Nature is hidden, in the heart of things, she sighs.
5. She expected to achieve godhead immediately.
6. A grim pun. She is eating death and does not know it; but death is eating her too. Compare "eating cares" (*L'Allegro*, line 135).
7. Joyous and liberal.

Thus to herself she pleasingly began:
"O sovereign, virtuous, precious of all trees
In Paradise! of operation blest
To sapience,[8] hitherto obscured, infamed,
And thy fair fruit let hang, as to no end
Created; but henceforth my early care,
Not without song each morning, and due praise
Shall tend thee, and the fertile burden ease
Of thy full branches offered free to all;
Till dieted by thee I grow mature
In knowledge, as the gods who all things know;
Though others[9] envy what they cannot give:
For had the gift been theirs, it had not here
Thus grown. Experience, next to thee I owe,
Best guide; not following thee I had remained
In ignorance; thou open'st Wisdom's way,
And giv'st access, though secret she retire.
And I perhaps am secret; Heaven is high,
High and remote to see from thence distinct
Each thing on Earth; and other care perhaps
May have diverted from continual watch
Our great Forbidder,[1] safe with all his spies
About him. But to Adam in what sort[2]
Shall I appear? Shall I to him make known
As yet my change, and give him to partake
Full happiness with me, or rather not,
But keep the odds[3] of knowledge in my power
Without copartner? so to add what wants
In female sex, the more to draw his love,
And render me more equal, and perhaps,
A thing not undesirable, sometime
Superior: for, inferior, who is free?[4]
This may be well: but what if God have seen
And death ensue? Then I shall be no more,
And Adam, wedded to another Eve,
Shall live with her enjoying, I extinct;
A death to think. Confirmed then I resolve,
Adam shall share with me in bliss or woe:
So dear I love him, that with him all deaths
I could endure, without him live no life."[5]
So saying, from the tree her step she turned,
But first low reverence done,[6] as to the power

8. To wisdom, for the wise and those of good taste. (Latin *sapere,* to be wise, has its root in the verb "to taste.") "Infamed": without fear, but also defamed, i.e., maligned.
9. The gods, i.e., other gods. In saying that God did not give the tree, Eve is merely echoing a lesson learned from the serpent.
1. Now that Eve has fallen, God is a "great Forbidder," and all his gifts in Paradise are forgotten.
2. Guise.
3. Balance.
4. Eve's fatal foolishness implies that the only person in the world who can ever be free is an absolute tyrant.
5. Her affection is not unlike Satan's (IV.374–385) in its destructiveness.
6. Eve's first physical act after falling is idolatry.

That dwelt within, whose presence had infused
Into the plant sciental[7] sap, derived
From nectar, drink of gods. Adam the while
Waiting desirous her return, had wove
Of choicest flowers a garland to adorn
Her tresses, and her rural labors crown,
As reapers oft are wont their harvest queen.
Great joy he promised to his thoughts, and new
Solace in her return, so long delayed:
Yet oft his heart, divine[8] of something ill,
Misgave him; he the faltering measure[9] felt;
And forth to meet her went, the way she took
That morn when first they parted. By the Tree
Of Knowledge he must pass; there he her met,
Scarce from the tree returning; in her hand
A bough of fairest fruit that downy smiled,
New gathered, and ambrosial smell diffused.
To him she hastened, in her face excuse
Came prologue, and apology to prompt,[1]
Which with bland words at will she thus addressed:
"Hast thou not wondered, Adam, at my stay?
Thee I have missed, and thought it long, deprived
Thy presence, agony of love till now
Not felt, nor shall be twice; for never more
Mean I to try, what rash untried I sought,
The pain of absence from thy sight. But strange
Hath been the cause, and wonderful to hear:
This tree is not as we are told, a tree
Of danger tasted,[2] nor to evil unknown
Opening the way, but of divine effect
To open eyes, and make them gods who taste;
And hath been tasted such. The serpent wise,
Or not restrained as we, or not obeying,
Hath eaten of the fruit, and is become,
Not dead, as we are threatened, but thenceforth
Endued with human voice and human sense,
Reasoning to admiration,[3] and with me
Persuasively hath so prevailed, that I
Have also tasted, and have also found
Th' effects to correspond, opener mine eyes
Dim erst, dilated spirits, ampler heart,
And growing up to godhead;[4] which for thee
Chiefly I sought, without thee can despise.
For bliss, as thou hast part, to me is bliss,
Tedious, unshared with thee, and odious soon.
Thou therefore also taste, that equal lot

7. Knowledge-giving.
8. Foreboding, suspicious.
9. I.e., of his pulse.
1. Her face had an excuse in it, as prologue to an apology which followed after.
2. If tasted.
3. Admirably. "Persuasively": by persuasion.
4. Everything that Eve says she feels is what Satan has told her she will feel.

May join us, equal joy, as equal love;
Lest, thou not tasting, different degree[5]
Disjoin us, and I then too late renounce
Deity for thee, when Fate will not permit."[6]
Thus Eve with countenance blithe her story told;
But in her cheek distemper[7] flushing glowed.
On th' other side, Adam, soon as he heard
The fatal trespass done by Eve, amazed,
Astonied[8] stood and blank, while horror chill
Ran through his veins, and all his joints relaxed;
From his slack hand the garland wreathed for Eve
Down dropped, and all the faded roses shed.
Speechless he stood and pale, till thus at length
First to himself he inward silence broke:
"O fairest of creation, last and best
Of all God's works, creature in whom excelled
Whatever can to sight or thought be formed,
Holy, divine, good, amiable, or sweet!
How art thou lost, how on a sudden lost,
Defaced, deflowered, and now to death devote?[9]
Rather how hast thou yielded to transgress
The strict forbiddance, how to violate
The sacred fruit forbidden! Some cursèd fraud
Of enemy hath beguiled thee, yet unknown,[1]
And me with thee hath ruined, for with thee
Certain my resolution is to die.
How can I live without thee, how forgo
Thy sweet converse and love so dearly joined,
To live again in these wild woods forlorn?[2]
Should God create another Eve, and I
Another rib afford, yet loss of thee
Would never from my heart; no, no! I feel
The link of nature draw me: flesh of flesh,
Bone of my bone thou art, and from thy state
Mine never shall be parted, bliss or woe."
So having said, as one from sad dismay
Recomforted, and after thoughts disturbed
Submitting to what seemed remediless,
Thus in calm mood his words to Eve he turned:
"Bold deed thou hast presumed, adventurous Eve
And peril great provoked, who thus hath dared
Had it been only coveting to eye
That sacred fruit, sacred[3] to abstinence,
Much more to taste it, under ban to touch.

5. Differing rank in the hierarchy of creatures.
6. Contrast Eve's logic when she is alone (lines 817–825).
7. The proportion of Eve's humors—which, in the state of innocence, gave her perfect health—has been disturbed, and she is running a fever.
8. Astonished, perhaps even "petrified." "Blank": empty of mind.
9. Doomed.
1. "Yet unknown" modifies "enemy."
2. Without Eve, Paradise itself is wild and forlorn.
3. Devoted.

But past who can recall, or done undo?
Not God omnipotent, nor Fate! Yet so
Perhaps thou shalt not die, perhaps the fact[4]
Is not so heinous now, foretasted fruit,
Profaned first by the serpent, by him first
Made common and unhallowed ere our taste,
Nor yet on him found deadly; he yet lives,
Lives, as thou saidst, and gains to live as man
Higher degree of life: inducement strong
To us, as likely, tasting, to attain
Proportional ascent, which cannot be
But to be gods, or angels, demigods.[5]
Nor can I think that God, Creator wise,
Though threatening, will in earnest so destroy
Us his prime creatures, dignified so high,
Set over all his works, which in our fall,
For us created, needs with us must fail,
Dependent made; so God shall uncreate,
Be frustrate, do, undo, and labor lose;
Not well conceived of God,[6] who, though his power
Creation could repeat, yet would be loath
Us to abolish, lest the adversary
Triúmph and say: 'Fickle their state whom God
Most favors; who can please him long? Me first
He ruined, now mankind; whom will he next?'
Matter of scorn, not to be given the foe.
However, I with thee have fixed my lot,
Certain to undergo like doom: if death
Consort with thee, death is to me as life;
So forcible within my heart I feel
The bond of nature draw me to my own,
My own in thee, for what thou art is mine;
Our state cannot be severed; we are one,
One flesh; to lose thee were to lose myself."
    So Adam, and thus Eve to him replied:
"O glorious trial of exceeding love,
Illustrious evidence, example high!
Engaging me to emulate; but short
Of thy perfection, how shall I attain,
Adam? from whose dear side I boast me sprung,
And gladly of our union hear thee speak,
One heart, one soul in both; whereof good proof
This day affords, declaring thee resolved,
Rather than death or aught than death more dread
Shall separate us, linked in love so dear,
To undergo with me one guilt, one crime,
If any be, of tasting this fair fruit;

4. Act.
5. Note how Adam agrees first in Eve's harmless errors about the serpent, then in her sinful ambition to achieve a higher form of life.
6. I.e., not a proper conception of God (as making his actions dependent on those of an inferior).

Whose virtue (for of good still good proceeds,
Direct, or by occasion[7]) hath presented
This happy trial of thy love, which else
So eminently never had been known.
Were it I thought death menaced would ensue[8]
This my attempt, I would sustain alone
The worst, and not persuade thee, rather die
Deserted, than oblige[9] thee with a fact
Pernicious to thy peace, chiefly assured
Remarkably so late of thy so true,
So faithful love unequaled;[1] but I feel
Far otherwise th' event; [2] not death, but life
Augmented, opened eyes, new hopes, new joys,
Taste so divine, that what of sweet before
Hath touched my sense, flat seems to this, and harsh.
On my experience, Adam, freely taste,
And fear of death deliver to the winds."
  So saying, she embraced him, and for joy
Tenderly wept, much won that he his love
Had so ennobled, as of choice to incur
Divine displeasure for her sake, or death.
In recompense (for such compliance bad
Such recompense best merits), from the bough
She gave him of that fair enticing fruit
With liberal hand; he scrupled not to eat,
Against his better knowledge, not deceived,
But fondly overcome with female charm.[3]
Earth trembled from her entrails, as again
In pangs, and Nature gave a second groan,
Sky lowered, and muttering thunder, some sad drops
Wept at completing of the mortal sin
Original; while Adam took no thought,
Eating his fill, nor Eve to iterate
Her former trespass feared, the more to soothe
Him with her loved society; that now
As with new wine intoxicated both,
They swim in mirth, and fancy that they feel
Divinity within them breeding wings
Wherewith to scorn the Earth. But that false fruit
Far other operation first displayed,
Carnal desire inflaming; he on Eve
Began to cast lascivious eyes, she him
As wantonly repaid; in lust they burn,
Till Adam thus 'gan Eve to dalliance move:
  "Eve, now I see thou art exact[4] of taste,

7. Indirectly.
8. Result from.
9. Render liable, involve.
1. Now that she knows Adam loves her, Eve has more misgivings than ever about involving him in her crime.
2. Result (of eating the apple).
3. See I Timothy ii.14: "And Adam was not deceived, but the woman being deceived was in the transgression."
4. Exacting, demanding.

And elegant, of sapience[5] no small part,
Since to each meaning savor we apply,
And palate call judicious. I the praise
Yield thee, so well this day thou hast purveyed.[6]
Much pleasure we have lost, while we abstained
From this delightful fruit, nor known till now
True relish, tasting; if such pleasure be
In things to us forbidden, it might be wished,
For this one tree had been forbidden ten.
But come; so well refreshed, now let us play,
As meet is, after such delicious fare;
For never did thy beauty, since the day
I saw thee first and wedded thee, adorned
With all perfections, so enflame my sense
With ardor to enjoy thee, fairer now
Than ever, bounty of this virtuous tree."
  So said he, and forbore not glance or toy[7]
Of amorous intent, well understood
Of[8] Eve, whose eye darted contagious fire.
Her hand he seized, and to a shady bank,
Thick overhead with verdant roof embowered
He led her, nothing loath; flowers were the couch,
Pansies, and violets, and asphodel,
And hyacinth, Earth's freshest, softest lap.
There they their fill of love and love's disport
Took largely, of their mutual guilt the seal,
The solace of their sin, till dewy sleep
Oppressed them, wearied with their amorous play.
  Soon as the force of that fallacious fruit,
That with exhilarating vapor bland
About their spirits had played, and inmost powers
Made err, was now exhaled, and grosser sleep
Bred of unkindly fumes,[9] with conscious dreams
Encumbered, now had left them, up they rose
As from unrest, and each the other viewing,
Soon found their eyes how opened, and their minds
How darkened. Innocence, that as a veil
Had shadowed them from knowing ill, was gone;
Just confidence, and native righteousness,
And honor from about them, naked left
To guilty Shame; he covered, but his robe
Uncovered more.[1] So rose the Danite strong,
Herculean Samson, from the harlot-lap
Of Philistean Dalilah, and waked
Shorn of his strength;[2] they destitute and bare

5. Wisdom, but the word comes from Latin *sapere*, "to taste," which gives rise, via another etymology, to the word "savor." Adam's sentence plays rather heavily on these two meanings of *sapere*.
6. Provided for us, provisioned us.
7. Caress.
8. By.
9. Unnatural vapors.
1. They were covered with shame, which made them conscious of their nakedness as they had never been before.
2. See the story of Samson and Delilah, Judges xvi.4–20.

Of all their virtue. Silent, and in face
Confounded, long they sat, as strucken mute;
Till Adam, though not less than Eve abashed,
At length gave utterance to these words constrained:
"O Eve, in evil hour[3] thou didst give ear
To that false worm,[4] of whomsoever taught
To counterfeit man's voice, true in our fall,
False in our promised rising; since our eyes
Opened we find indeed, and find we know
Both good and evil, good lost, and evil got:
Bad fruit of knowledge, if this be to know,
Which leaves us naked thus, of honor void,
Of innocence, of faith, of purity,
Our wonted ornaments now soiled and stained,
And in our faces evident the signs
Of foul concupiscence; whence evil store,[5]
Even shame, the last of evils; of the first
Be sure then.[6] How shall I behold the face
Henceforth of God or angel, erst with joy
And rapture so oft beheld? Those heavenly shapes
Will dazzle now this earthly[7] with their blaze
Insufferably bright. O might I here
In solitude live savage, in some glade
Obscured, where highest woods, impenetrable
To star or sunlight, spread their umbrage broad,
And brown[8] as evening! Cover me, ye pines,
Ye cedars, with innumerable boughs
Hide me, where I may never see them more![9]
But let us now, as in bad plight, devise
What best may for the present serve to hide
The parts of each from other, that seem most
To shame obnoxious,[1] and unseemliest seen;
Some tree whose broad smooth leaves together sewed,
And girded on our loins, may cover round
Those middle parts, that this newcomer, Shame,
There sit not, and reproach us as unclean."
So counseled he, and both together went
Into the thickest wood; there soon they chose
The figtree,[2] not that kind for fruit renowned,
But such as at this day, to Indians known,
In Malabar or Deccan[3] spreads her arms

3. Even in his misery, Adam cannot resist the word-play on Eve-evil.
4. Serpent, with a connotation of disgust. "Of": by.
5. A store of evil.
6. I.e., since we now feel shame, the last and worst of evils, we shall soon experience the first and lesser ones.
7. The noun "eyes" or "vision" is understood.
8. Dark.
9. Cf. Revelation vi.16: "And said to the mountains and rocks, Fall on us, and hide us from the face of him that sitteth on the throne, and from the wrath of the Lamb."
1. Vulnerable, liable.
2. The banyan, or Indian fig. It has, in fact, small leaves, but Milton's knowledge of it came from Gerard's *Herball*, where all the details of lines 1104–10 may be found.
3. Sections of southern India.

Branching so broad and long, that in the ground
The bended twigs take root, and daughters grow
About the mother tree, a pillared shade
High overarched, and echoing walks between;
There oft the Indian herdsman, shunning heat,
Shelters in cool, and tends his pasturing herds
At loopholes cut through thickest shade. Those leaves
They gathered, broad as Amazonian targe,[4]
And with what skill they had, together sewed,
To gird their waist; vain covering, if to hide
Their guilt and dreaded shame! O how unlike
To that first naked glory! Such of late
Columbus found th' American, so girt
With feathered cincture,[5] naked else and wild
Among the trees on isles and woody shores.
Thus fenced, and, as they thought, their shame in part
Covered, but not at rest or ease of mind,
They sat them down to weep; nor only tears
Rained at their eyes, but high winds worse within
Began to rise, high passions, anger, hate,
Mistrust, suspicion, discord, and shook sore
Their inward state of mind, calm region once
And full of peace, now tossed and turbulent:
For Understanding ruled not, and the Will
Heard not her lore, both in subjection now
To sensual Appetite, who, from beneath
Usurping over sovereign Reason, claimed
Superior sway.[6] From thus distempered breast,
Adam, estranged in look and altered style,
Speech intermitted thus to Eve renewed:
"Would thou hadst hearkened to my words, and stayed
With me, as I besought thee, when that strange
Desire of wandering, this unhappy morn,
I know not whence possessed thee! we had then
Remained still happy, not as now, despoiled
Of all our good, shamed, naked, miserable.
Let none henceforth seek needless cause to approve[7]
The faith they owe; when earnestly they seek
Such proof, conclude, they then begin to fail."
To whom, soon moved with touch of blame, thus Eve:
"What words have passed thy lips, Adam severe?
Imput'st thou that to my default, or will
Of wandering, as thou call'st it, which who knows
But might as ill have happened, thou being by,
Or to thyself perhaps? Hadst thou been there,
Or here th' attempt, thou couldst not have discerned

4. Shield. The Amazons, mythical female warriors, carried large crescent-shaped shields.
5. Belt.
6. The psychology of the Fall is made explicit here. The higher faculties of reason, represented by the brain, are in subjection to the lower faculties of appetite, represented by sensuality. Moreover, Adam has lost his superiority over Eve.
7. Test, prove. "Owe": own.

Fraud in the serpent, speaking as he spake;
No ground of enmity between us known,
Why he should mean me ill, or seek to harm?
Was I to have never parted from thy side?
As good have grown there still a lifeless rib.
Being as I am, why didst not thou, the head,[8]
Command me absolutely not to go,
Going into such danger, as thou saidst?
Too facile[9] then, thou didst not much gainsay,
Nay, didst permit, approve, and fair dismiss.
Hadst thou been firm and fixed in thy dissent,
Neither had I transgressed, nor thou with me."
  To whom, then first incensed, Adam replied:
"Is this the love, is this the recompense
Of mine to thee, ingrateful Eve, expressed
Immutable[1] when thou were lost, not I,
Who might have lived and joyed immortal bliss,
Yet willingly chose rather death with thee?
And am I now upbraided as the cause
Of thy transgressing? not enough severe,
It seems, in thy restraint! What could I more?
I warned thee, I admonished thee, foretold
The danger, and the lurking enemy
That lay in wait; beyond this had been force,
And force upon free will hath here no place.
But confidence then bore thee on, secure
Either to meet no danger, or to find
Matter of glorious trial; and perhaps
I also erred in overmuch admiring
What seemed in thee so perfect, that I thought
No evil durst attempt thee! but I rue
That error now, which is become my crime,
And thou th' accuser. Thus it shall befall
Him who, to worth in women overtrusting,
Lets her will rule; restraint she will not brook,[2]
And, left to herself, if evil thence ensue,
She first his weak indulgence will accuse."
  Thus they in mutual accusation spent
The fruitless hours, but neither self-condemning;[3]
And of their vain contést appeared no end.

8. Head of the family, but also the rational director, as the head is to the rest of the body. Cf. I Corinthians xi.3, "the head of the woman is the man."
9. Easy, permissive.
1. Shown to be unchangeable.
2. Accept.
3. Sterile recrimination is an early fruit of the forbidden tree; only self-condemnation can turn the fall from a mind-closing to a mind-opening event.

From Book X

Summary When it is known in Heaven that man has fallen, God sends his Son to pass judgment on the sinners. Having found them in the garden, he hears their confession and passes instant sentence, cursing the serpent, condemning Eve to the pains of childbirth and Adam to those of daily toil; but in mercy he clothes the human couple both outwardly with the skins of beasts and inwardly with his righteousness. Meanwhile Sin and Death, sitting by Hell-gate, feel new strength, and pass across Chaos, leaving a great bridge behind them. On their way they meet with their parent, Satan, learn of his success on earth, and press eagerly forward in hopes of destroying man altogether. Satan, on the other hand, continues his flight back toward Hell, where he is to report to his constituents.

[*Consequences of the Fall*]

* * * Th' other way Satan went down
The causey[1] to Hell-gate; on either side
Disparted Chaos overbuilt exclaimed,
And with rebounding surge the bars assailed,
That scorned his indignation.[2] Through the gate,
Wide open and unguarded, Satan passed,
And all about found desolate; for those
Appointed to sit there[3] had left their charge,
Flown to the upper world; the rest were all
Far to the inland retired, about the walls
Of Pandemonium, city and proud seat
Of Lucifer, so by allusion called
Of that bright star to Satan paragoned.[4]
There kept their watch the legions, while the Grand
In council sat, solicitous what chance
Might intercept their emperor sent; so he
Departing gave command, and they observed.
As when the Tartar from his Russian foe,
By Astracan, over the snowy plains,
Retires, or Bactrian Sophi, from the horns
Of Turkish crescent, leaves all waste beyond
The realm of Aladule, in his retreat

1. Causeway.
2. Chaos, as the instinctive enemy of order, is hostile to the bridge built across its gulf by Sin and Death, even though it means an increase in the kingdom of Chaos itself.
3. I.e., Sin and Death.
4. Satan is called Lucifer, the light-bringer, because bright as the morning star (before he fell). The Grand (line 427) are the superior angels. "Grandee" was a new word in English, adapted from Spanish; it implied a man of large, undefined economic and social power.

To Tauris or Casbeen;[5] so these, the late
Heaven-banished host, left desert utmost Hell
Many a dark league, reduced in careful watch
Round their metropolis, and now expecting
Each hour their great adventurer from the search
Of foreign worlds. He through the midst unmarked,
In show plebeian angel militant[6]
Of lowest order, passed, and, from the door
Of that plutonian hall, invisible
Ascended his high throne, which, under state[7]
Of richest texture spread, at th' upper end
Was placed in regal luster. Down a while
He sat, and round about him saw, unseen.
At last, as from a cloud, his fulgent[8] head
And shape star-bright appeared, or brighter, clad
With what permissive glory since his fall
Was left him, or false glitter. All amazed
At that so sudden blaze, the Stygian throng
Bent their aspéct, and whom they wished beheld,
Their mighty chief returned: loud was th' acclaim.
Forth rushed in haste the great consulting peers,
Raised from their dark divan,[9] and with like joy
Congratulant approached him, who with hand
Silence, and with these words attention, won:
"Thrones, Dominations, Princedoms, Virtues, Powers!
For in possession such, not only of right,[1]
I call ye, and declare ye now, returned,
Successful beyond hope, to lead ye forth
Triumphant out of this infernal pit
Abominable, accursed, the house of woe,
And dungeon of our tyrant! Now possess,
As lords, a spacious world, to our native Heaven
Little inferior, by my adventure hard
With peril great achieved. Long were to tell
What I have done, what suffered, with what pain
Voyaged th' unreal, vast, unbounded deep
Of horrible confusion, over which
By Sin and Death a broad way now is paved

5. The comparison is with the Persians and Tartars retreating across the Eastern wastes before the attacking Turks. "Bactrian": Persian, "Tauris," "Casbeen": Tabriz, Kazvin. Milton wants his simile to convey a mingled sense of barbaric Oriental splendor, cruelty, and desolation in Hell.

6. Literally, an angelic footsoldier or private, but with an ironic overtone from the phrase "church militant."

7. Canopy.

8. Glittering, refulgent.

9. The Turkish council of state; the Oriental theme continues.

1. Satan makes a distinction much in men's minds since the days of Cromwell and Charles I; a kingdom could be claimed either by right (in law, *de jure*) or in fact (by possession, *de facto*). The devils now have both claims to their titles. "Returned" (line 462) modifies "I" at the beginning of the line: "now that I have returned."

To expedite your glorious march; but I
Toiled out my uncouth passage, forced to ride
Th' untractable abyss, plunged in the womb
Of unoriginal[2] night and chaos wild,
That, jealous of their secrets, fiercely opposed
My journey strange, with clamorous uproar
Protesting fate supreme; thence how I found
The new-created world, which fame in Heaven
Long had foretold, a fabric wonderful,
Of absolute perfection; therein man
Placed in a paradise, by our exile
Made happy. Him by fraud I have seduced
From his creator, and, the more to increase
Your wonder, with an apple! He,[3] thereat
Offended—worth your laughter!—hath given up
Both his belovéd man and all his world
To Sin and Death a prey, and so to us,
Without our hazard, labor, or alarm,
To range in, and to dwell, and over man
To rule, as over all he should have ruled.
True is, me also he hath judged; or rather
Me not, but the brute serpent, in whose shape
Man I deceived. That which to me belongs
Is enmity, which he will put between
Me and mankind: I am to bruise his heel;
His seed (when, is not set) shall bruise my head.[4]
A world who would not purchase with a bruise,
Or much more grievous pain? Ye have th' account
Of my performance; what remains, ye gods,
But up and enter now into full bliss?"
   So having said, a while he stood, expecting
Their universal shout and high applause
To fill his ear; when, contrary, he hears,
On all sides, from innumerable tongues
A dismal universal hiss, the sound
Of public scorn. He wondered, but not long
Had leisure, wondering at himself now more.
His visage drawn he felt to sharp and spare,
His arms clung to his ribs, his legs entwining
Each other, till, supplanted,[5] down he fell,

2. Without source or origin, primeval.

3. God.

4. Satan seems to have overheard or understood the curse pronounced by God on the serpent, even though he was not present at the time.

5. The word is used with its Latin force of "tripped up by the heels." Ovid (*Metamorphosis* IV. 575 ff.), Lucan (*Pharsalia* IX. 700 ff.), and Dante (*Inferno* XXV) had made set pieces about people being transformed into serpents. This whole scene has been the occasion of much critical dispute. A. J. A. Waldock (*Paradise Lost and Its Critics*) denounced it as a "cartoon scene" in which Milton's editorial hand is much too heavily felt; various defenders have propounded alternative justifications.

A monstrous serpent on his belly prone,
Reluctant,[6] but in vain; a greater power
Now ruled him, punished in the shape he sinned,
According to his doom. He would have spoke,
But hiss for hiss returned with forkéd tongue
To forkéd tongue; for now were all transformed
Alike, to serpents all, as accessories
To his bold riot.[7] Dreadful was the din
Of hissing through the hall, thick-swarming now
With complicated monsters, head and tail—
Scorpion, and asp, and amphisbaena dire,[8]
Cerastes horned, hydrus, and ellops drear,
And dipsas (not so thick swarmed once the soil
Bedropped with blood of Gorgon, or the isle
Ophiusa); but still greatest he the midst,
Now dragon grown, larger than whom the sun
Engendered in the Pythian vale on slime,
Huge Python;[9] and his power no less he seemed
Above the rest still to retain. They all
Him followed, issuing forth to th' open field,
Where all yet left of that revolted rout,
Heaven-fallen, in station or just array,
Sublime[1] with expectation when to see
In triumph issuing forth their glorious chief.
They saw, but other sight instead, a crowd
Of ugly serpents. Horror on them fell,
And horrid sympathy; for what they saw
They felt themselves now changing. Down their arms,
Down fell both spear and shield; down they as fast,
And the dire hiss renewed, and the dire form
Catched by contagion, like in punishment
As in their crime. Thus was th' applause they meant
Turned to exploding hiss, triumph to shame
Cast on themselves from their own mouths. There stood
A grove hard by, sprung up with this their change,
His will who reigns above,[2] to aggravate
Their penance, laden with fair fruit, like that

6. The Latin sense is felt again, "struggling against the change."
7. Revolt.
8. "Complicated": again a Latinism, meaning "twined together." The "amphisbaena" was alleged to have a head at each end of its body; "cerastes" was a horned snake, "hydrus" a water-snake, "ellops" perhaps the swordfish, and "dipsas" a snake whose bite was supposed to create outrageous thirst. When Perseus flew over Libya with the head of the snaky-haired Gorgon, the drops of her blood fell to the ground and became serpents. The "isle Ophiusa" is Snake Island, in the Balearics.
9. Python was a gigantic mythological serpent engendered by Apollo, the sun god, from the slime left by Deucalion's flood, and slain by Apollo in a great contest.
1. On tiptoes. The ordinary devils are standing in ranks outside Pandemonium, trying to catch a glimpse of Satan.
2. "By the will of him who reigns above."

Which grew in paradise, the bait of Eve
Used by the tempter. On that prospect strange
Their earnest eyes they fixed, imagining
For one forbidden tree a multitude
Now risen, to work them further woe or shame;[3]
Yet, parched with scalding thirst and hunger fierce,
Though to delude them sent, could not abstain,
But on they rolled in heaps, and, up the trees
Climbing, sat thicker than the snaky locks
That curled Megaera.[4] Greedily they plucked
The fruitage fair to sight, like that which grew
Near that bituminous lake where Sodom flamed;[5]
This, more delusive, not the touch, but taste
Deceived; they, fondly[6] thinking to allay
Their appetite with gust, instead of fruit
Chewed bitter ashes, which th' offended taste
With spattering noise rejected. Oft they assayed,
Hunger and thirst constraining: drugged as oft,
With hatefulest disrelish writhed their jaws
With soot and cinders filled: so oft they fell
Into the same illusion, not as man
Whom they triúmphed once lapsed.[7] Thus were they plagued,
And worn with famine long, and ceaseless hiss,
Till their lost shape, permitted, they resumed—
Yearly enjoined, some say, to undergo
This annual humbling certain numbered days,
To dash their pride, and joy for man seduced.[8]
However, some tradition they dispersed
Among the heathen of their purchase got,
And fabled how the serpent, whom they called
Ophion, with Eurynome (the wide-
Encroaching Eve perhaps),[9] had first the rule
Of high Olympus, thence by Saturn driven
And Ops, ere yet Dictaean[1] Jove was born.

3. The punishment of the devils not only fits the crime, it *is* the crime (the eating of forbidden fruit) repeated again and again, in disgust and loathing.
4. Megaera, like her sister Furies, had snakes instead of hair on her head.
5. Sodom apples grew (legend had it) on the spot where that accursed city once stood; though good to look at, they dissolved into ashes when plucked.
6. Foolishly. "Gust": taste.
7. They fell again and again into delusion, though they had felt superior to man, who fell just once.
8. There are many folktales about fairies, devils, incubi, and the like, who are forced periodically to take on the shape of some loathsome creature.
9. There is a mythological story about the Titan Ophion (the name means "snake") and his wife Eurynome ("the wide-reacher"), who ruled Olympus till Saturn and his wife Rhea (or Ops) drove them away. Milton feels this story may be a vague, pagan reminiscence of the real truth, the fall of Satan. But there is an unresolved suggestion here that Eve fell with Satan, becoming a kind of Proserpina to his role as Pluto, King of Hell.
1. Zeus was raised in a cave on Mount Dicte, in Crete; hence, "Dictaean Jove."

Summary Sin and Death proceed without further interruption to the earth, and enter into possession of it. God sees their arrival and declines to interfere, but prophesies that their triumph will be only temporary; in due course they will be forced back to hell again, and forever. Meanwhile, the angels are ordered to twist the earth on its axis, disorder the planets so their influence will in future be bad as well as good, and rearrange the cosmos generally. In consequence, the temperate climate of Paradise at once gives way to extremes of heat and cold, and furious winds begin to blow across the ruined planet.

* * * Thus began
Outrage from lifeless things; but Discord, first
Daughter of Sin, among th' irrational,
Death introduced through fierce antipathy:[1]
Beast now with beast 'gan war, and fowl with fowl,
And fish with fish: to graze the herb[2] all leaving,
Devoured each other; nor stood much in awe
Of man, but fled him, or with countenance grim
Glared on him passing. These were from without
The growing miseries, which Adam saw
Already in part, though hid in gloomiest shade,
To sorrow abandoned, but worse felt within,
And in a troubled sea of passion tossed,
Thus to disburden sought with sad complaint:
"O miserable of happy![3] Is this the end
Of this new glorious world, and me so late
The glory of that glory? who now, become
Accursed of blessed, hide me from the face
Of God, whom to behold was then my height
Of happiness! Yet well, if here would end
The misery; I deserved it, and would bear
My own deservings; but this will not serve.
All that I eat or drink, or shall beget,
Is propagated curse.[4] O voice, once heard
Delightfully, 'Increase and multiply,'
Now death to hear! for what can I increase
Or multiply, but curses on my head?
Who, of all ages to succeed, but, feeling
The evil on him brought by me, will curse
My head: "Ill fare our ancestor impure!
For this we may thank Adam!' but his thanks
Shall be the execration;[5] so, besides

1. "Discord" is the subject of the sentence, "Death" the object. "Th' irrational" are the beasts.
2. Grass.
3. I.e., change, to misery from happiness.
4. Whatever prolongs life extends the curse.
5. The only thanks for Adam will be mankind's curses.

Mine own that bide upon me, all from me
Shall with a fierce reflux on me redound,
On me, as on their natural center, light
Heavy, though in their place.[6] O fleeting joys
Of Paradise, dear bought with lasting woes!
Did I request thee, Maker, from my clay
To mold me man? Did I solicit thee
From darkness to promote me, or here place
In this delicious garden? As my will
Concurred not to my being, it were but right
And equal[7] to reduce me to my dust,
Desirous to resign and render back
All I received, unable to perform
Thy terms too hard, by which I was to hold
The good I sought not. To the loss of that,
Sufficient penalty, why hast thou added
The sense of endless woes? Inexplicable
Thy justice seems; yet, to say truth, too late
I thus contest; then should have been refused
Those terms whatever, when they were proposed.
Thou[8] didst accept them; wilt thou enjoy the good,
Then cavil the conditions? And though God
Made thee without thy leave, what if thy son
Prove disobedient, and reproved, retort,
'Wherefore didst thou beget me? I sought it not.'
Wouldst thou admit for his contempt of thee
That proud excuse? Yet him not thy election,[9]
But natural necessity begot.
God made thee of choice his own, and of his own
To serve him; thy reward was of his grace;
Thy punishment then justly is at his will.
Be it so, for I submit; his doom is fair,
That dust I am and shall to dust return.
O welcome hour whenever! Why delays
His hand to execute what his decree
Fixed on this day? Why do I overlive?
Why am I mocked with death, and lengthened out
To deathless pain? How gladly would I meet
Mortality, my sentence, and be earth
Insensible! how glad would lay me down
As in my mother's lap![1] There I should rest
And sleep secure; his dreadful voice no more

6. Adam plays with the notion that natural objects have weight only as long as they are above their "natural" positions; so all curses will flow naturally to him, but they will still be heavy when they have lighted.
7. Just.
8. "Thou," which referred to God in lines 753 and 755, here shifts as Adam suddenly addresses himself.
9. Choice.
1. Adam's lamentations owe a good deal to the Book of Job iii.

Would thunder in my ears; no fear of worse
To me and to my offspring would torment me
With cruel expectation. Yet one doubt
Pursues me still, lest all I cannot die;[2]
Lest that pure breath of life, the spirit of man
Which God inspired, cannot together perish
With this corporeal clod; then, in the grave,
Or in some other dismal place, who knows
But I shall die a living death? O thought
Horrid, if true! Yet why? It was but breath
Of life that sinned; what dies but what had life
And sin? the body properly hath neither.
All of me then shall die: let this appease
The doubt, since human reach no further knows.[3]
For though the Lord of all be infinite,
Is his wrath also? Be it, man is not so,
But mortal doomed. How can he exercise
Wrath without end on man whom death must end?
Can he make deathless death? That were to make
Strange contradiction, which to God himself
Impossible is held, as argument
Of weakness, not of power.[4] Will he draw out,
For anger's sake, finite to infinite
In punished man, to satisfy his rigor
Satisfied never? That were to extend
His sentence beyond dust and Nature's law;
By which all causes else according still
To the reception of their matter act,
Not to th' extent of their own sphere.[5] But say
That death be not one stroke, as I supposed,
Bereaving[6] sense, but endless misery
From this day onward, which I feel begun
Both in me and without me, and so last
To perpetuity—Ay me! that fear
Comes thundering back with dreadful revolution
On my defenseless head! Both death and I
Am found eternal, and incorporate[7] both:
Nor I on my part single; in me all
Posterity stands cursed. Fair patrimony

2. Direct from Horace, *Odes* III.xxx.6: *non omnis moriar*.
3. Adam convinces himself, as Milton was apparently convinced, that both soul and body die at death; the corollary is that they are resurrected together.
4. For a man in a state of nature, Adam displays a fine command of medieval theology. He holds that if God contradicts himself, it is a sign of weakness.
5. A maxim of 17th-century physics; all agents (other than God) act according to the capacity of the object, not to the extent of their inherent powers.
6. Taking away.
7. In the same body. Adam is appalled to find that he has become death incarnate; the grammar ("both death and I/*Am*") displays his shock.

That I must leave ye, sons! O, were I able
To waste it all myself, and leave ye none!
So disinherited, how would ye bless
Me, now your curse! Ah, why should all mankind
For one man's fault thus guiltless be condemned,
If guiltless? But from me what can proceed,
But all corrupt, both mind and will depraved,
Not to do only, but to will the same
With me?[8] How can they then acquitted stand
In sight of God? Him, after all disputes,
Forced[9] I absolve. All my evasions vain
And reasonings, though through mazes, lead me still
But to my own conviction: first and last
On me, me only, as the source and spring
Of all corruption, all the blame lights due;[1]
So might the wrath! Fond[2] wish! Couldst thou support
That burden, heavier than the earth to bear;
Than all the world much heavier, though divided
With that bad woman? Thus, what thou desir'st,
And what thou fear'st, alike destroys all hope
Of refuge, and concludes thee miserable[3]
Beyond all past example and future;
To Satan only like, both crime and doom.
O Conscience! into what abyss of fears
And horrors hast thou driven me; out of which
I find no way, from deep to deeper plunged!"
  Thus Adam to himself lamented loud
Through the still night, not now, as ere man fell,
Wholesome and cool and mild, but with black air
Accompanied, with damps and dreadful gloom;
Which to his evil conscience represented
All things with double terror. On the ground
Outstretched he lay, on the cold ground, and oft
Cursed his creation; Death as oft accused
Of tardy execution, since denounced
The day of his offense. "Why comes not Death,"
Said he, "with one thrice-acceptable stroke
To end me? Shall Truth fail to keep her word,
Justice divine not hasten to be just?
But Death comes not at call; Justice divine
Mends not her slowest pace for prayers or cries.
O woods, O fountains, hillocks, dales, and bowers!

8. Not only will men repeat Adam's sin; their will is corrupted and they will *want* to be fallen like Adam.
9. Perforce.
1. In this discovery that he alone must accept the guilt of mankind, Adam has chosen crucially to be like Christ and unlike Satan—at the very moment when he feels exactly the opposite.
2. Foolish.
3. Shows thee to be miserable.

With other echo late I taught your shades
To answer, and resound far other song."
Whom thus afflicted when sad Eve beheld,
Desolate where she sat, approaching nigh,
Soft words to his fierce passion she essayed;
But her with stern regard he thus repelled:
"Out of my sight, thou serpent! that name best
Befits thee, with him leagued, thyself as false
And hateful: nothing wants, but that thy shape,
Like his, and color serpentine, may show
Thy inward fraud, to warn all creatures from thee
Henceforth; lest that too heavenly form, pretended[4]
To hellish falsehood, snare them. But for thee
I had persisted happy, had not thy pride
And wandering vanity, when least was safe,
Rejected my forewarning, and disdained
Not to be trusted, longing to be seen
Though by the devil himself, him overweening[5]
To overreach, but, with the serpent meeting,
Fooled and beguiled; by him thou, I by thee,
To trust thee from my side, imagined wise,
Constant, mature, proof against all assaults;
And understood not all was but a show
Rather than solid virtue, all but a rib
Crooked by nature—bent, as now appears,
More to the part sinister[6]—from me drawn;
Well if thrown out, as supernumerary
To my just number found![7] Oh, why did God,
Creator wise, that peopled highest Heaven
With spirits masculine, create at last
This novelty on earth, this fair defect
Of nature, and not fill the world at once
With men, as angels, without feminine;
Or find some other way to generate
Mankind?[8] This mischief had not then befallen,
And more that shall befall—innumerable
Disturbances on earth through female snares,
And strait conjunction[9] with this sex. For either
He never shall find out fit mate, but such
As some misfortune brings him, or mistake;
Or whom he wishes most shall seldom gain,
Through her perverseness, but shall see her gained
By a far worse, or, if she love, withheld
By parents, or his happiest choice too late

4. Serving as a mask.
5. Overconfident.
6. "On the left hand," as in Latin; also "unlucky."
7. Since men visibly have twelve ribs on both sides, it was supposed that Adam originally had thirteen ribs on his left side, so that he could give up one and still have twelve, an even ("just") number.
8. Ancient traditions of antifeminist thought lie behind these ungenerous speculations.
9. Close connections, i.e., matrimony.

Shall meet, already linked and wedlock-bound
To a fell[1] adversary, his hate or shame:
Which infinite calamity shall cause
To human life, and household peace confound."
He added not, and from her turned; but Eve,
Not so repulsed, with tears that ceased not flowing,
And tresses all disordered, at his feet
Fell humble, and, embracing them, besought
His peace, and thus proceeded in her plaint:
"Forsake me not thus, Adam! witness Heaven
What love sincere and reverence in my heart
I bear thee, and unweeting[2] have offended,
Unhappily deceived! Thy suppliant[3]
I beg, and clasp thy knees; bereave me not,
Whereon I live, thy gentle looks, thy aid,
Thy counsel in this uttermost distress,
My only strength and stay: forlorn of thee,
Whither shall I betake me, where subsist?
While yet we live, scarce one short hour perhaps,
Between us two let there be peace; both joining,
As joined in injuries, one enmity
Against a foe by doom express assigned us,
That cruel serpent. On me exercise not
Thy hatred for this misery befallen;
On me already lost, me than thyself
More miserable. Both have sinned, but thou
Against God only; I against God and thee,
And to the place of judgement will return,
There with my cries importune Heaven, that all
The sentence, from thy head removed, may light
On me, sole cause to thee of all this woe,
Me, me only, just object of his ire."[4]
She ended weeping; and her lowly plight,
Immovable till peace obtained from fault
Acknowledged and deplored,[5] in Adam wrought
Commiseration. Soon his heart relented
Towards her, his life so late and sole delight,
Now at his feet submissive in distress,
Creature so fair his reconcilement seeking,
His counsel, whom she had displeased, his aid;
As one disarmed, his anger all he lost,
And thus with peaceful words upraised her soon:
"Unwary, and too desirous, as before,
So now, of what thou know'st not,[6] who desir'st

1. Bitter.
2. Unintentionally.
3. As a suppliant to thee.
4. Eve too now offers to accept the blame for the Fall; and the moral regeneration of man is henceforth possible.
5. Her suppliant posture ("lowly plight") would not be changed till she obtained forgiveness ("peace") from her admission of her fault, and repentance for it.
6. Adam's remark is rueful but affectionate; Eve is still looking for more trouble than she knows how to handle.

The punishment all on thyself! Alas!
Bear thine own first, ill able to sustain
His full wrath, whose thou feel'st as yet least part,[7]
And my displeasure bear'st so ill. If prayers
Could alter high decrees, I to that place
Would speed before thee, and be louder heard,
That on my head all might be visited,
Thy frailty and infirmer sex forgiven,
To me committed, and by me exposed.
But rise; let us no more contend, nor blame
Each other, blamed enough elsewhere, but strive
In offices of love, how we may lighten
Each other's burden in our share of woe;
Since this day's death denounced, if aught I see,
Will prove no sudden, but a slow-paced evil,
A long day's dying to augment our pain,
And to our seed (O hapless seed!) derived."[8]
To whom thus Eve, recovering heart, replied:
"Adam, by sad experiment I know
How little weight my words with thee can find,
Found so erroneous, thence by just event
Found so unfortunate; nevertheless,
Restored by thee, vile as I am, to place
Of new acceptance, hopeful to regain
Thy love, the sole contentment of my heart
Living or dying, from thee I will not hide
What thoughts in my unquiet breast are risen.
Tending to some relief of our extremes,
Or end, though sharp and sad, yet tolerable,
As in our evils,[9] and of easier choice.
If care of our descent perplex us most,
Which must be born to certain woe, devoured
By Death at last—and miserable it is
To be to others cause of misery,
Our own begotten, and of our loins to bring
Into this cursèd world a woeful race
That after wretched life must be at last
Food for so foul a monster—in thy power
It lies yet ere conception to prevent[1]
The race unblessed, to being yet unbegot.
Childless thou art, childless remain: so Death
Shall be deceived his glut, and with us two
Be forced to satisfy his ravenous maw.
But if thou judge it hard and difficult,
Conversing, looking, loving, to abstain

7. I.e., ill able to sustain the full wrath of God—of whose wrath, so far, you have felt only the least part.
8. Handed down.
9. A Latinism. The English meaning is something like "given the evil plight in which we find ourselves."
1. Literally, in the Latin root, come before, forestall.

From love's due rites, nuptial embraces sweet,
And with desire to languish without hope
Before the present object[2] languishing
With like desire, which would be misery
And torment less than none of what we dread,
Then both our selves and seed at once to free
From what we fear for both, let us make short;
Let us seek Death, or he not found, supply
With our own hands his office on ourselves.
Why stand we longer shivering under fears
That show no end but Death, and[3] have the power,
Of many ways to die the shortest choosing,
Destruction with destruction to destroy."
  She ended here, or vehement despair
Broke off the rest; so much of Death her thoughts
Had entertained as dyed her cheeks with pale.
But Adam, with such counsel nothing swayed,
To better hopes his more attentive mind
Laboring had raised, and thus to Eve replied:
  "Eve, thy contempt of life and pleasure seems
To argue in thee something more sublime
And excellent than what thy mind contemns;[4]
But self-destruction therefore[5] sought refutes
That excellence thought in thee, and implies,
Not thy contempt, but anguish and regret
For loss of life and pleasure overloved.
Or if thou covet Death as utmost end
Of misery, so thinking to evade
The penalty pronounced, doubt not but God
Hath wiselier armed his vengeful ire than so
To be forestalled; much more I fear lest Death
So snatched will not exempt us from the pain
We are by doom to pay; rather such acts
Of contumacy[6] will provoke the Highest
To make Death in us live. Then let us seek
Some safer resolution, which methinks
I have in view, calling to mind with heed
Part of our sentence, that thy seed shall bruise
The serpent's head; piteous amends, unless
Be meant, whom I conjecture, our grand foe
Satan, who in the serpent hath contrived
Against us this deceit. To crush his head
Would be revenge indeed, which will be lost
By Death brought on ourselves or childless days
Resolved, as thou proposest; so our foe
Shall 'scape his punishment ordained, and we

2. The present object is of course Eve herself, referring to herself obliquely because she is ashamed to admit that she would pine for Adam, as he for her.

3. I.e., when we.

4. Despises.

5. For this motive.

6. Contempt.

Instead shall double ours upon our heads.
No more be mentioned then of violence
Against ourselves and willful barrenness,
That cuts us off from hope, and savors only
Rancor and pride, impatience and despite,
Reluctance[7] against God and his just yoke
Laid on our necks. Remember with what mild
And gracious temper he both heard and judged
Without wrath or reviling; we expected
Immediate dissolution, which we thought
Was meant by Death that day, when lo, to thee
Pains only in childbearing were foretold,
And bringing forth, soon recompensed with joy,
Fruit of thy womb. On me the curse aslope
Glanced on the ground,[8] with labor I must earn
My bread. What harm? Idleness had been worse.
My labor will sustain me; and lest cold
Or heat should injure us, his timely care
Hath unbesought provided, and his hands
Clothed us unworthy, pitying while he judged.
How much more, if we pray him, will his ear
Be open and his heart to pity incline,
And teach us further by what means to shun
Th' inclement seasons, rain, ice, hail, and snow,
Which now the sky with various face begins
To show us in this mountain, while the winds
Blow moist and keen, shattering the graceful locks
Of these fair spreading trees—which bids us seek
Some better shroud, some better warmth to cherish
Our limbs benumbed, ere this diurnal star[9]
Leave cold the night, how we his gathered beams,
Reflected, may with matter sere foment,
Or by collision of two bodies grind
The air attrite to fire,[1] as late the clouds,
Justling or pushed with winds rude in their shock,
Tine[2] the slant lightning, whose thwart flame driven down
Kindles the gummy bark of fir or pine,
And sends a comfortable heat from far,
Which might supply the sun. Such fire to use,
And what may else be remedy or cure
To evils which our own misdeeds have wrought,
He will instruct us praying, and of grace
Beseeching him, so as we need not fear

7. From Latin, *luctare,* to struggle; here, to oppose (the will of God).
8. The curse, like a spear that almost missed its target, glanced aside and stuck in the ground.
9. The sun.
1. Adam is inventing the burning glass ("matter sere" is dry leaves, twigs, etc.) and the use of flint and steel to start fires. "Attrite": rubbed or worn down; in this sense, the word is more Latin than English.
2. Kindle, light.

To pass commodiously this life, sustained
By him with many comforts, till we end
In dust, our final rest and native home.
"What better can we do than to the place
Repairing where he judged us, prostrate fall
Before him reverent, and there confess
Humbly our faults, and pardon beg, with tears
Watering the ground, and with our sighs the air
Frequenting,[3] sent from hearts contrite, in sign
Of sorrow unfeigned, and humiliation meek?
Undoubtedly he will relent and turn
From his displeasure; in whose look serene,
When angry most he seemed and most severe,
What else but favor, grace, and mercy shone?"
So spake our father penitent, nor Eve
Felt less remorse: they forthwith to the place
Repairing where he judged them, prostrate fell
Before him reverent, and both confessed
Humbly their faults, and pardon begged, with tears
Watering the ground, and with their sighs the air
Frequenting, sent from hearts contrite, in sign
Of sorrow unfeigned, and humiliation meek.[4]

3. Filling.
4. The deliberate repetition of six consecutive lines, almost word for word, with only six lines in between, is a very strong mark of closure. Adam and Eve have reached most of the major decisions which will separate their fate from that of Satan.

Book XI. Summary The prayers of Adam and Eve prove acceptable to God. But while man may now hope for ultimate redemption, he may no longer dwell in Paradise; and Michael, the warrior archangel, is dispatched to explain the sentence, offer some hope for the future, and dismiss mankind from the happy garden. Adam is at first overcome with grief; but the angel encourages him, and while Eve is put in a trance, Adam is raised to the peak of a high hill and shown in a vision the future of the human race as far as the flood of Noah.

From Book XII

Summary Continuing his instruction of Adam, Michael relates the history of the world from the time of Noah through the coming of Christ, whose ascent into Heaven and triumph over Death after the Crucifixion he describes. The Church which Christ and his apostles leave behind, however, will not be free from troubles caused by greedy and ambitious men; it will require reform. But the reformers will be persecuted and their road will be hard, until at length, in the Last Judgment, Satan and his kingdom will be dissolved, and new heavens and new earths created to exist in eternal bliss.

[*The Departure from Eden*]

So spake th' archangel Michaël; then paused,
As at the world's great period;[1] and our sire,
Replete with joy and wonder, thus replied:
"O goodness infinite, goodness immense!
That all this good of evil shall produce,
And evil turn to good; more wonderful
Than that which by creation first brought forth
Light out of darkness! Full of doubt I stand,
Whether I should repent me now of sin
By me done and occasioned, or rejoice
Much more that much more good thereof shall spring;
To God more glory, more good will to men
From God, and over wrath grace shall abound.
But say, if our Deliverer up to Heaven
Must reascend, what will betide the few,
His faithful, left among th' unfaithful herd,
The enemies of truth? Who then shall guide
His people, who defend? Will they not deal
Worse with his followers than with him they dealt?"
"Be sure they will," said th' angel; "but from Heaven
He to his own a Comforter will send,
The promise of the Father, who shall dwell,
His Spirit, within them, and the law of faith,
Working through love, upon their hearts shall write,
To guide them in all truth, and also arm
With spiritual armor, able to resist
Satan's assaults, and quench his fiery darts,
What[2] man can do against them, not afraid,
Though to the death; against such cruelties
With inward consolations recompensed,
And oft supported so as shall amaze
Their proudest persecutors.[3] For the Spirit,
Poured first on his Apostles, whom he sends
To evangelize the nations, then on all
Baptized, shall them with wondrous gifts endue[4]
To speak all tongues, and do all miracles,
As did their Lord before them. Thus they win
Great numbers of each nation to receive
With joy the tidings brought from Heaven: at length,
Their ministry performed, and race well run,
Their doctrine and their story written left,

1. Conclusion.
2. As much as.
3. Milton briefly summarizes here the story of the Christian martyrs.
4. Endow.

They die; but in their room, as they forewarn,
Wolves shall succeed for teachers, grievous wolves,[5]
Who all the sacred mysteries of Heaven
To their own vile advantages shall turn
Of lucre and ambition, and the truth
With superstitions and traditions taint,
Left only in those written records pure,
Though not but by the Spirit understood.
Then shall they seek to avail themselves of names,
Places, and titles,[6] and with these to join
Secular power, though feigning still to act
By spiritual; to themselves appropriating
The Spirit of God, promised alike and given
To all believers; and, from that pretense,
Spiritual laws by carnal[7] power shall force
On every conscience, laws which none shall find
Left them enrolled, or what the Spirit within
Shall on the heart engrave.[8] What will they then,
But force the Spirit of Grace itself, and bind
His consort, Liberty? what but unbuild
His living temples,[9] built by faith to stand,
Their own faith, not another's? for, on Earth,
Who against faith and conscience can be heard
Infallible? Yet many will presume:
Whence heavy persecution shall arise
On all who in the worship persevere
Of Spirit and Truth; the rest, far greater part,
Will deem in outward rites and specious[1] forms
Religion satisfied; Truth shall retire
Bestuck with slanderous darts, and works of faith
Rarely be found. So shall the world go on,
To good malignant, to bad men benign,
Under her own weight groaning,[2] till the day
Appear of respiration[3] to the just
And vengeance to the wicked, at return
Of Him so lately promised to thy aid,
The Woman's Seed,[4] obscurely then foretold,
Now amplier known thy Savior and thy Lord;
Last in the clouds from Heaven to be revealed

5. To profit by religion was for Milton the lowest of crimes; he felt that priests should serve without pay. In addition, he regularly uses the wolf as an emblem of the Papacy; see *Lycidas*, line 128.
6. The name "Catholic," the place of court preacher, and the title of "bishop," for example.
7. Fleshly, i.e., secular, of this world.
8. I.e., the wolves will enforce laws which have no ancient authority or appeal to the conscience.
9. Individual believers. Milton's strict Protestant individualism speaks throughout this passage of protest against persecution.
1. Fair-seeming.
2. This passage, which in isolation appears to offer some justification for viewing the end of the poem as essentially pessimistic, should be set against Adam's earlier statement (lines 470–78) that the Fall was really a fortunate event, and gave rise to more good than evil.
3. Relief, refreshment.
4. Christ, whose Second Coming is here foreseen.

In glory of the Father, to dissolve
Satan with his perverted world; then raise
From the conflagrant mass,[5] purged and refined,
New Heavens, new Earth, ages of endless date
Founded in righteousness and peace and love,
To bring forth fruits, joy and eternal bliss."
He ended, and thus Adam last replied:
"How soon hath thy prediction, seer blest,
Measured this transient world, the race of Time,
Till Time stand fixed! Beyond is all abyss,
Eternity, whose end no eye can reach.
Greatly instructed I shall hence depart,
Greatly in peace of thought, and have my fill
Of knowledge, what[6] this vessel can contain;
Beyond which was my folly to aspire.
Henceforth I learn that to obey is best,
And love with fear the only God, to walk
As in his presence, ever to observe
His providence, and on him sole depend,
Merciful over all his works, with good
Still overcoming evil, and by small
Accomplishing great things, by things deemed weak
Subverting worldly-strong, and worldly-wise
By simply meek; that suffering for truth's sake
Is fortitude to highest victory,
And to the faithful, death the gate of life;
Taught this by his example whom I now
Acknowledge my Redeemer ever blest."
To whom thus also th' angel last replied:
"This having learned, thou hast attained the sum[7]
Of wisdom; hope no higher, though all the stars
Thou knew'st by name,[8] and all th' ethereal powers,
All secrets of the deep, all Nature's works,
Or works of God in heaven, air, earth, or sea,
And all the riches of this world enjoy'dst,
And all the rule, one empire. Only add
Deeds to thy knowledge answerable;[9] add faith,
Add virtue, patience, temperance; add love,
By name to come called charity, the soul
Of all the rest: then wilt thou not be loath
To leave this Paradise, but shalt possess
A Paradise within thee, happier far.
Let us descend now, therefore, from this top
Of speculation;[1] for the hour precise
Exacts[2] our parting hence; and, see! the guards,
By me encamped on yonder hill, expect

5. The burning world.
6. As much as.
7. Total.
8. Michael glances back at the rebuke administered by Raphael in Book VIII to Adam's astronomical curiosity.
9. Corresponding.
1. Hill of vision.
2. Requires.

Their motion, at whose front[3] a flaming sword,
In signal of remove, waves fiercely round.
We may no longer stay. Go, waken Eve;
Her also I with gentle dreams have calmed,
Portending good, and all her spirits composed
To meek submission: thou, at season fit,
Let her with thee partake what thou hast heard;
Chiefly what may concern her faith to know,
The great deliverance by her seed to come
(For by the Woman's Seed) on all mankind;
That ye may live, which will be many days,[4]
Both in one faith unanimous; though sad
With cause for evils past, yet much more cheered
With meditation on the happy end."
He ended, and they both descend the hill.
Descended, Adam to the bower where Eve
Lay sleeping ran before, but found her waked;
And thus with words not sad she him received:
"Whence thou return'st and whither went'st, I know;
For God is also in sleep, and dreams advise,
Which he hath sent propitious, some great good
Presaging, since, with sorrow and heart's distress
Wearied, I fell asleep. But now lead on;
In me is no delay; with thee to go
Is to stay here; without thee here to stay
Is to go hence unwilling; thou to me
Art all things under Heaven, all places thou,
Who for my willful crime art banished hence.
This further consolation yet secure
I carry hence: though all by me is lost,
Such favor I unworthy am vouchsafed,
By me the Promised Seed shall all restore."
So spake our mother Eve; and Adam heard
Well pleased, but answered not; for now too nigh
Th' archangel stood, and from the other hill
To their fixed station, all in bright array,
The cherubim descended; on the ground
Gliding meteorous, as evening mist
Risen from a river o'er the marish[5] glides,
And gathers ground fast at the laborer's heel
Homeward returning. High in front advanced,
The brandished sword of God before them blazed,
Fierce as a comet; which with torrid heat,
And vapor as the Libyan air adust,[6]
Began to parch that temperate clime; whereat
In either hand the hastening angel caught
Our lingering parents, and to th' eastern gate
Led them direct, and down the cliff as fast

3. Before whom.
4. Adam lived to be 930 (Genesis v.5).
5. Marsh (an old form).
6. The scorched climate of Libya, in North Africa, was proverbial.

To the subjected[7] plain; then disappeared.
They, looking back, all th' eastern side beheld
Of Paradise, so late their happy seat,[8]
Waved over by that flaming brand;[9] the gate
With dreadful faces thronged and fiery arms.
Some natural tears they dropped, but wiped them soon;
The world was all before them, where to choose
Their place of rest, and Providence their guide.
They, hand in hand, with wandering steps and slow,
Through Eden took their solitary way.

1662–67 1667, 1674

7. Low-lying.
8. Home.
9. "Sword," with the extra overtone of "burning."

Samson Agonistes The figure of Samson, as one finds him in the Book of Judges, does not seem at first glance particularly adaptable to the elevated mode of tragedy. He is a promiscuous, violent fellow, given to riddles and practical jokes—the last of which puts a gruesome end to himself and his enemies. His long shaggy hair, his name (Samson, in Hebrew *Shimshun*), which includes the Hebrew word for "sun," and a persistent association with fire, all suggest a connection with some primitive solar cult, such as can be seen behind the equivalent figure of Hercules. A burly, truculent, and not-very-clever giant, in short; one would not easily see in him the dignified and purifying figure of the tragic sufferer.

But though Samson's rude vigor and vengeful nature appealed to Milton on one level; the story of his fall through the treachery of a woman on another; and the fact of his blindness on still another; there was a last level on which he could in fact be represented as the type and precursor of the Christian hero. He suffered for his people; in the very pit of despair he was rendered suddenly capable of God's revivifying grace; long exercised in physical warfare, he gave evidence in his last heroic action of having learned the principles of spiritual warfare.

Milton approached the idea of tragedy with hesitations and misgivings; for a Puritan of his day, the very idea of a stage play was instinct with moral danger. But the example of the Greeks and of his much-admired Tasso prevailed; he wrote a "closet drama," a drama intended not for the actual stage but for reading. As a play, Dr. Johnson proclaimed it deficient; it had, he said, a beginning and an end but no proper middle. Modern criticism, dissenting as usual from Dr. Johnson and stimulated as usual by his judgment, has exercised itself to find in Samson's spiritual progression during the successive visits of Manoa, Dalila, and Harapha ample psychological movement to sustain both action and interest. This is beyond doubt a useful exercise; but it is useful also to reflect that Samson acts in the end by direction of an inward spirit, a private, intimate inspiration; and that for the coming of this spirit there is no sufficient preparation. "The wind bloweth where it listeth, and thou hearest the sound thereof, but canst not tell whence it cometh, and whither it goeth: so is every one that is born of the Spirit" (John iii.8).

The story of Samson is told in Judges xiii-xvi. "Agonistes" means "in struggle" or "under trial"; it is a term derived from the Greek word for a wrestler and suggests not only that Samson is an athlete of the Lord but that he will wrestle with the pillars.

Samson Agonistes

A DRAMATIC POEM

Of That Sort of Dramatic Poem Which Is Called Tragedy

Tragedy, as it was anciently composed, hath been ever held the gravest, moralest, and most profitable of all other poems: therefore said by Aristotle to be of power, by raising pity and fear, or terror, to purge the mind of those and such-like passions, that is, to temper and reduce them to just measure with a kind of delight, stirred up by reading or seeing those passions well imitated.[1] Nor is Nature wanting in her own effects to make good his assertion; for so, in physic, things of melancholic hue and quality are used against melancholy, sour against sour, salt to remove salt humors.[2] Hence philosophers and other gravest writers, as Cicero, Plutarch, and others, frequently cite out of tragic poets, both to adorn and illustrate their discourse. The Apostle Paul himself thought it not unworthy to insert a verse of Euripides into the text of Holy Scripture, I Cor. xv. 33; and Paraeus, commenting on the Revelation, divides the whole book, as a tragedy, into acts, distinguished each by a chorus of heavenly harpings and song between.[3] Heretofore men in highest dignity have labored not a little to be thought able to compose a tragedy. Of that honor Dionysius the elder was no less ambitious than before of his attaining to the tyranny.[4] Augustus Caesar also had begun his *Ajax*, but unable to please his own judgment with what he had begun, left it unfinished. Seneca the philosopher is by some thought the author of those tragedies (at least the best of them) that go under that name. Gregory Nazianzen, a Father of the Church, thought it not unbeseeming the sanctity of his person to write a tragedy, which he entitled *Christ Suffering*.[5] This is mentioned to vindicate tragedy from the small esteem, or rather infamy, which in the account of many it undergoes at this

1. Milton is paraphrasing Aristotle's *Poetics* 6.
2. Italian critics like Minturno had applied notions of homeopathic medicine (like cures like) to tragedy; the idea is not Aristotelean. "Physic": medicine.
3. David Paraeus, a 17th-century German Calvinist.
4. Dionysius (4th century B.C.) won a prize at Athens for tragedy, after becoming tyrant of Syracuse.
5. Seneca the philosopher was indeed the author of tragedies; but Gregory Nazianzen, a Greek ecclesiastic of the 4th century, did not write the tragedy *Christ Suffering*, which scholarly opinion of Milton's day attributed to him.

day, with other common interludes—happening through the poet's error of intermixing comic stuff with tragic sadness and gravity, or introducing trivial and vulgar persons—which by all judicious hath been counted absurd, and brought in without discretion, corruptly to gratify the people. And, though ancient tragedy use no prologue,[6] yet using sometimes, in case of self-defense or explanation, that which Martial calls an epistle,[7] in behalf of this tragedy, coming forth after the ancient manner, much different from what among us passes for best, thus much beforehand may be epistled, that chorus is here introduced after the Greek manner, not ancient only, but modern, and still in use among the Italians.[8] In the modeling therefore of this poem, with good reason, the ancients and Italians are rather followed, as of much more authority and fame. The measure of verse used in the chorus is of all sorts, called by the Greeks *Monostrophic*,[9] or rather *Apolelymenon*,[1] without regard had to strophe, antistrophe, or epode, which were a kind of stanzas framed only for the music, then used with the chorus that sung; not essential to the poem, and therefore not material; or, being divided into stanzas or pauses, they may be called *alloeostropha*.[2] Division into act and scene, referring chiefly to the stage (to which this work never was intended), is here omitted.[3]

It suffices if the whole drama be found not produced[4] beyond the fifth act. Of the style and uniformity, and that commonly called the plot, whether intricate or explicit—which is nothing indeed but such economy, or disposition of the fable, as may stand best with verisimilitude and decorum[5]—they only will best judge who are not unacquainted with Aeschylus, Sophocles, and Euripides, the three tragic poets unequaled yet by any, and the best rule to all who endeavor to write tragedy. The circumscription of time wherein the whole drama begins and ends is, according to ancient rule and best example, within the space of twenty-four hours.[6]

6. Prologues and epilogues were frequent on the Restoration stage; Milton sets himself apart from contemporary styles.
7. Martial, the Roman epigrammatist of the 1st century A.D., prefixed an epistle to his book of epigrams.
8. Tasso's tragedy *Re Torrismondo* was modeled closely on classical examples.
9. Not divided into strophe, antistrophe, and epode.
1. Free from stanzaic patterns altogether.
2. With various forms of strophe, irregular.
3. The reader who cares will not find Milton's drama hard to divide into the customary five acts, each ending with a chorus: Act I (Samson and chorus) lines 1–325; II (Samson and Manoa) 326–709; III (Samson and Dalila) 710–1060; IV (Samson and Harapha) 1061–1296; V (Catastrophe) 1297–the end.
4. Led along, drawn out.
5. Decorum, for a Renaissance writer, is not simply solemn or sedate behavior but the use of appropriate and suitable style, depending on speaker, subject, setting, genre, and so on.
6. The so-called "unity of time," limiting dramatic action to 24 hours, was derived from Aristotle's *Poetics* by the Renaissance critic Castelvetro.

The Argument

Samson, made captive, blind, and now in the prison at Gaza,[7] there to labor as in a common workhouse, on a festival day, in the general cessation from labor, comes forth into the open air, to a place nigh, somewhat retired, there to sit a while and bemoan his condition. Where he happens at length to be visited by certain friends and equals of his tribe, which make the chorus, who seek to comfort him what they can; then by his old father, Manoa, who endeavors the like, and withal tells him his purpose to procure his liberty by ransom; lastly, that this feast was proclaimed by the Philistines as a day of thanksgiving for their deliverance from the hands of Samson—which yet more troubles him. Manoa then departs to prosecute his endeavor with the Philistian lords for Samson's redemption; who, in the meanwhile, is visited by other persons, and, lastly, by a public officer to require his coming to the feast before the lords and people, to play or show his strength in their presence. He at first refuses, dismissing the public officer with absolute denial to come; at length persuaded inwardly that this was from God, he yields to go along with him, who came now the second time with great threatenings to fetch him. The chorus yet remaining on the place, Manoa returns full of joyful hope to procure ere long his son's deliverance: in the midst of which discourse an Ebrew[8] comes in haste, confusedly at first, and afterwards more distinctly, relating the catastrophe—what Samson had done to the Philistines, and by accident to himself; wherewith the tragedy ends.

The Persons

SAMSON
MANOA, *the father of Samson*
DALILA, *his wife*
HARAPHA *of Gath*
Public Officer
Messenger
Chorus of Danites[9]

The Scene, before the Prison in Gaza.

SAMSON. A little onward lend thy guiding hand
To these dark steps, a little further on;
For yonder bank hath choice of sun or shade.
There I am wont to sit, when any chance
Relieves me from my task of servile toil,
Daily in the common prison else enjoined me,[1]

7. The Philistines, warlike and commercial, lived in Southwest Palestine (the southern coast of modern Israel between, approximately, Tel Aviv and Gaza) in five great cities splendidly named Ashdod, Eshkol, Gaza, Gath, and Ashkalon. They were a wholly urban people as against the largely rural Israelites.

8. Milton follows an old English tradition in transliterating the name "Ebrew."

9. Hebrews of the tribe of Dan, Samson's tribe. When the land of Canaan was divided among the twelve tribes, they received the southern portion, adjacent to the Philistines.

1. The metrical pattern of this line, with its many unaccented syllables and careful placement of the strong word "else," merits careful study.

Where I, a prisoner chained, scarce freely draw
The air, imprisoned also, close and damp,
Unwholesome draught. But here I feel amends—
The breath of heaven fresh blowing, pure and sweet,
With day-spring[2] born; here leave me to respire.
This day a solemn feast the people hold
To Dagon,[3] their sea-idol, and forbid
Laborious works. Unwillingly this rest
Their superstition yields me; hence, with leave
Retiring from the popular noise, I seek
This unfrequented place, to find some ease—
Ease to the body some, none to the mind
From restless thoughts, that, like a deadly swarm
Of hornets armed, no sooner found alone
But rush upon me thronging, and present
Times past, what once I was, and what am now.
Oh, wherefore was my birth from Heaven foretold
Twice by an angel,[4] who at last, in sight
Of both my parents, all in flames ascended
From off the altar where an offering burned,
As in a fiery column charioting
His godlike presence, and from some great act
Or benefit revealed to Abraham's race?
Why was my breeding ordered and prescribed
As of a person separate to God,
Designed for great exploits,[5] if I must die
Betrayed, captived, and both my eyes put out,
Made of my enemies the scorn and gaze,
To grind in brazen fetters under task
With this heaven-gifted strength? O glorious strength,
Put to the labor of a beast, debased
Lower than bondslave! Promise was that I
Should Israel from Philistian yoke deliver;
Ask for this great deliverer now, and find him
Eyeless in Gaza, at the mill with slaves,
Himself in bonds under Philistian yoke.
Yet stay; let me not rashly call in doubt
Divine prediction. What if all foretold
Had been fulfilled but through mine own default?
Whom have I to complain of but myself,
Who this high gift of strength committed to me,
In what part lodged, how easily bereft me,
Under the seal of silence could not keep,[6]

2. Break of day.

3. Dagon's name comes from *dag*, fish, and he seems to have had a fishy shape. His would thus be a marine cult to correspond with that of the many Baals, or land gods of the Philistines. See *Paradise Lost* I.457–66.

4. Before Samson was born an angel foretold that he would begin the delivery of Israel from the Philistines (Judges xiii.5).

5. Samson was a Nazarite, member of an ascetic group specially dedicated to the service of God. See Numbers vi.

6. I.e., who could not keep silent about the high gift of strength committed to me, or about where it was located, or about how easily it could be taken from me.

But weakly to a woman must reveal it,
O'ercome with importunity and tears?
O impotence of mind in body strong!
But what is strength without a double share
Of wisdom? Vast, unwieldy, burdensome,
Proudly secure,[7] yet liable to fall
By weakest subtleties; not made to rule,
But to subserve where wisdom bears command.
God, when he gave me strength, to show withal,
How slight the gift was, hung it in my hair.
But peace! I must not quarrel with the will
Of highest dispensation,[8] which herein
Haply had ends above my reach to know.
Suffices that to me strength is my bane,
And proves the source of all my miseries—
So many, and so huge, that each apart
Would ask a life to wail. But, chief of all,
O loss of sight, of thee I most complain!
Blind among enemies! O worse than chains,
Dungeon, or beggary, or decrepit age!
Light, the prime work of God,[9] to me is extinct,
And all her various objects of delight
Annulled, which might in part my grief have eased.
Inferior to the vilest now become
Of man or worm, the vilest here excel me:
They creep, yet see; I, dark in light, exposed
To daily fraud, contempt, abuse, and wrong,
Within doors, or without, still as a fool,
In power of others, never in my own—
Scarce half I seem to live, dead more than half.
O dark, dark, dark, amid the blaze of noon,
Irrecoverably dark, total eclipse
Without all hope of day!
O first-created beam, and thou great Word,
"Let there be light, and light was over all,"
Why am I thus bereaved thy prime decree?[1]
The sun to me is dark
And silent[2] as the moon,
When she deserts the night,
Hid in her vacant interlunar cave.[3]
Since light so necessary is to life,
And almost life itself, if it be true
That light is in the soul,
She all in every part,[4] why was the sight

7. Confident, free from care (Latin, *cura*).
8. Providence.
9. God's first ("prime") act in creating the world was to say "Let there be light" (Genesis i.3), a phrase Milton paraphrases below.
1. I.e., why am I thus deprived of the first-created (and most important) thing?
2. Unperceived.
3. Ancient astronomers supposed that during the daytime the moon hid in a cave.
4. A famous formula of Plotinus (*Ennead* IV.ii.1) describes the soul as "all in all and all in every part."

To such a tender ball as th' eye confined,
So obvious[5] and so easy to be quenched,
And not, as feeling, through all parts diffused,
That she might look at will through every pore?
Then had I not been thus exiled from light,
As in the land of darkness, yet in light,
To live a life half dead, a living death,
And buried; but, O yet more miserable!
Myself my sepulcher, a moving grave;
Buried, yet not exempt,
By privilege of death and burial,
From worst of other evils, pains, and wrongs;
But made hereby obnoxious[6] more
To all the miseries of life,
Life in captivity
Among inhuman foes.
But who are these? for with joint pace I hear
The tread of many feet steering this way;
Perhaps my enemies, who come to stare
At my affliction, and perhaps to insult,
Their daily practice to afflict me more.
CHORUS. This, this is he; softly a while;
Let us not break in upon him.
O change beyond report, thought, or belief!
See how he lies at random, carelessly diffused,[7]
With languished head unpropped,
As one past hope, abandoned,
And by himself given over,
In slavish habit, ill-fitted weeds[8]
O'er-worn and soiled.
Or do my eyes misrepresent? Can this be he,
That heroic, that renowned,
Irresistible Samson? whom, unarmed,
No strength of man, or fiercest wild beast, could withstand:[9]
Who tore the lion as the lion tears the kid;
Ran on embattled armies clad in iron,
And, weaponless himself,
Made arms ridiculous, useless the forgery[1]
Of brazen shield and spear, the hammered cuirass,
Chalybean-tempered[2] steel, and frock of mail
Adamantean proof;
But safest he who stood aloof,
When insupportably[3] his foot advanced,
In scorn of their proud arms and warlike tools,

5. Exposed.
6. Vulnerable, subject.
7. Literally, "poured forth," outstretched.
8. Rags.
9. Judges xiv.5–6 tells the story of Samson ripping apart a lion with his bare hands.
1. Weapons of forged steel, but also fraudulent, exterior protections.
2. The Chalybes lived on the Black Sea and were famous ironworkers. "Adamantean proof": hard as adamant, i.e., diamond.
3. Irresistibly.

Spurned them to death by troops. The bold Ascalonite[4]
Fled from his lion ramp; old warriors turned
Their plated backs under his heel,
Or groveling soiled their crested helmets in the dust.
Then with what trivial weapon came to hand,
The jaw of a dead ass, his sword of bone,
A thousand foreskins fell, the flower of Palestine,
In Ramath-lechi, famous to this day;[5]
Then by main force pulled up, and on his shoulders bore,
The gates of Azza, post and massy bar,
Up to the hill by Hebron, seat of giants old,
No journey of a Sabbath day, and loaded so,
Like whom the Gentiles feign to bear up Heaven.[6]
Which shall I first bewail,
Thy bondage or lost sight,
Prison within prison
Inseparably dark?
Thou art become (O worst imprisonment!)
The dungeon of thyself; thy soul
(Which men enjoying sight oft without cause complain),
Imprisoned now indeed,
In real darkness of the body dwells,
Shut up from outward light
To incorporate with gloomy night;
For inward light, alas!
Puts forth no visual beam.[7]
O mirror of our fickle state,
Since man on earth unparalleled![8]
The rarer thy example stands,
By how much from the top of wondrous glory,
Strongest of mortal men,
To lowest pitch of abject fortune thou art fallen!
For him I reckon not in high estate
Whom long descent of birth,
Or the sphere[9] of fortune, raises;
But thee, whose strength, while virtue was her mate,
Might have subdued the Earth,

4. A man from Ascalon, or Ashkalon, one of the five great Philistine cities. "Lion ramp": a lion in the act of attacking its prey, rampant.

5. On one occasion Samson killed a thousand Philistines (i.e., "foreskins", uncircumcised warriors), using the jawbone of an ass (Judges xv.15–17). Judges xvi.3 tells how Samson, to escape his enemies, picked up and carried off the gates of Gaza (Azza).

6. In Greek (or, as Milton calls it, Gentile) mythology, Atlas supports the heavens. From Gaza to Hebron would be about forty miles—no journey for the day of rest.

7. Renaissance physiologists supposed the eye saw by sending forth a "visual beam" which it directed at various objects.

8. I.e., no such example (has been seen) since man (was) on earth. "Fickle": changeable.

9. "Sphere": wheel. Fortune was described as possessing a wheel which merely by rotating automatically interchanged the highest and lowest social positions. Milton's definition of "high estate" is interior and spiritual; he has no interest in the old "Fall of Princes" theme. In fact, the play exactly reverses that theme.

Universally crowned with highest praises.
SAMSON. I hear the sound of words; their sense the air
Dissolves unjointed ere it reach my ear.
CHORUS. He speaks: let us draw nigh. Matchless in might,
The glory late of Israel, now the grief!
We come, thy friends and neighbors not unknown,
From Eshtaol and Zora's fruitful vale,
To visit or bewail thee; or, if better,
Counsel or consolation we may bring,
Salve to thy sores: apt words have power to swage[1]
The tumors of a troubled mind,
And are as balm to festered wounds.
SAMSON. Your coming, friends, revives me; for I learn
Now of my own experience, not by talk,
How counterfeit a coin they are who "friends"
Bear in their superscription (of the most
I would be understood). In prosperous days
They swarm, but in adverse withdraw their head,
Not to be found, though sought. Ye see, O friends,
How many evils have enclosed me round;
Yet that which was the worst now least afflicts me,
Blindness; for, had I sight, confused with shame,
How could I once look up, or heave[2] the head,
Who, like a foolish pilot, have shipwrecked
My vessel trusted to me from above,
Gloriously rigged, and for a word, a tear,
Fool! have divulged the secret gift of God
To a deceitful woman? Tell me, friends,
Am I not sung and proverbed for a fool
In every street? Do they not say, "How well
Are come upon him his deserts"? Yet why?
Immeasurable strength they might behold
In me; of wisdom nothing more than mean.[3]
This with the other should at least have paired;[4]
These two, proportioned ill, drove me transverse.[5]
CHORUS. Tax not divine disposal. Wisest men
Have erred, and by bad women been deceived;
And shall again, pretend they ne'er so wise.[6]
Deject not, then, so overmuch thyself,
Who hast of sorrow thy full load besides.
Yet, truth to say, I oft have heard men wonder
Why thou should'st wed Philistian women rather
Than of thine own tribe fairer, or as fair,
At least of thy own nation, and as noble.
SAMSON. The first I saw at Timna, and she pleased
Me, not my parents, that I sought to wed

1. Assuage.
2. Lift.
3. Average.
4. Been equal.
5. Off the true course.
6. I.e., intend they never so wisely.

The daughter of an infidel.[7] They knew not
That what I motioned[8] was of God; I knew
From intimate impulse, and therefore urged
The marriage on, that, by occasion hence,[9]
I might begin Israel's deliverance—
The work to which I was divinely called.
She proving false, the next I took to wife
(O that I never had! fond wish too late!)
Was in the vale of Sorec, Dálila,[1]
That specious monster, my accomplished snare.
I thought it lawful from my former act
And the same end, still watching to oppress
Israel's oppressors. Of what now I suffer
She was not the prime cause, but I myself,
Who, vanquished with a peal of words (O weakness!),
Gave up my fort of silence to a woman.

CHORUS. In seeking just occasion to provoke
The Philistine, thy country's enemy,
Thou never wast remiss, I bear thee witness;
Yet Israel still serves with all his sons.[2]

SAMSON. That fault I take not on me, but transfer
On Israel's governors and heads of tribes,
Who, seeing those great acts which God had done
Singly by me against their conquerors,
Acknowledged not, or not at all considered
Deliverance offered. I, on th' other side,
Used no ambition to commend my deeds;[3]
The deeds themselves, though mute, spoke loud the doer.
But they persisted deaf, and would not seem
To count them things worth notice, till at length
Their lords, the Philistines, with gathered powers,
Entered Judea seeking me, who then
Safe to the rock of Etham was retired,
Not flying, but forecasting in what place
To set upon them, what advantaged best.
Meanwhile the men of Judah, to prevent
The harass of their land, beset me round;
I willingly on some conditions came
Into their hands, and they as gladly yield me
To the uncircumcised[4] a welcome prey,
Bound with two cords. But cords to me were threads
Touched with the flame: on their whole host I flew
Unarmed, and with a trivial weapon felled
Their choicest youth; they only lived who fled.[5]

7. Judges xiv.1–4 tells the story of Samson's first decision to marry outside his own tribe and nation.
8. Intended.
9. I.e., so that it might provide an occasion for me to begin Israel's deliverance.
1. Judges xvi.4.
2. I.e., Israel and the children of Israel are still in servitude.
3. I.e., sought for no testimonials to my actions.
4. Foreigners, the people outside the covenant of Abraham.
5. Judges xv.8–17 tells the tale of Samson's single-handed victory, using a "trivial weapon," the jawbone of an ass.

Had Judah that day joined, or one whole tribe,
They had by this[6] possessed the towers of Gath,
And lorded over them whom now they serve.
But what more oft, in nations grown corrupt,
And by their vices brought to servitude,
Than to love bondage more than liberty,
Bondage with ease than strenuous liberty,[7]
And to despise, or envy, or suspect,
Whom God hath of his special favor raised
As their deliverer? If he aught begin,
How frequent to desert him, and at last
To heap ingratitude on worthiest deeds!

CHORUS. Thy words to my remembrance bring
How Succoth and the fort of Penuel
Their great deliverer contemned,
The matchless Gideon, in pursuit
Of Madian, and her vanquished kings;[8]
And how ingrateful Ephraim
Had dealt with Jephtha, who by argument,
Not worse than by his shield and spear,
Defended Israel from the Ammonite,
Had not his prowess quelled their pride
In that sore battle when so many died
Without reprieve, adjudged to death
For want of well pronouncing *Shibboleth*.[9]

SAMSON. Of such examples add me to the roll.
Me easily indeed mine[1] may neglect,
But God's proposed deliverance not so.

CHORUS. Just are the ways of God,
And justifiable to men,
Unless there be who think not God at all.
If any be, they walk obscure;
For of such doctrine never was there school,
But the heart of the fool,
And no man therein doctor but himself.[2]
Yet more there be who doubt his ways not just,
As to his own edícts found contradicting;
Then give the reins to wandering thought,
Regardless of his glory's diminution,
Till, by their own perplexities involved,
They ravel[3] more, still less resolved,
But never find self-satisfying solution.
As if they would confine th' Interminable,[4]
And tie him to his own prescript,

6. By this time.
7. Milton obviously has in mind, not only early Israel, but also contemporary England.
8. Judges viii: Succoth and Penuel refused aid to Gideon when he was pursuing the common foe, and he punished them.
9. Judges xi and xii.
1. My people.
2. Psalm xiv deals with the fool who says in his heart there is no God. "Doctor": teacher.
3. Become entangled.
4. Infinite.

Who made our laws to bind us, not himself,
And hath full right to exempt
Whomso it pleases him by choice
From national obstriction,[5] without taint
Of sin, or legal debt;
For with his own laws he can best dispense.
He would not else, who never wanted means,
Nor in respect of the enemy just cause,
To set his people free,
Have prompted this heroic Nazarite,
Against his vow of strictest purity,
To seek in marriage that fallacious bride,
Unclean, unchaste.
Down, Reason, then; at least, vain reasonings down;
Though Reason here aver
That moral verdict quits her of unclean:
Unchaste was subsequent; her stain, not his.[6]
But see! here comes thy reverend sire,
With careful step, locks white as down,[7]
Old Manoa: advise [8]
Forthwith how thou ought'st to receive him.

SAMSON. Ay me! another inward grief, awaked
With mention of that name, renews th' assault.

MANOA. Brethren and men of Dan (for such ye seem,
Though in this uncouth[9] place), if old respect,
As I suppose, towards your once gloried friend,
My son, now captive, hither hath informed[1]
Your younger feet, while mine, cast back with age,
Came lagging after, say if he be here.

CHORUS. As signal[2] now in low dejected state
As erst in highest, behold him where he lies.

MANOA. O miserable change! Is this the man,
That ínvincible Samson, far renowned,
The dread of Israel's foes, who with a strength
Equivalent to angels' walked their streets,
None offering fight; who, single combatant,
Dueled their armies ranked in proud array,
Himself an army—now unequal match
To save himself against a coward armed
At one spear's length? O ever-failing trust
In mortal strength! and, oh, what not in man
Deceivable and vain? [3] Nay, what thing good

5. Obligation, i.e., the law against marrying Gentiles (Deuteronomy vii.3). The chorus here accepts Samson's argument that God had prompted him inexplicably to marry the woman of Timna.
6. The chorus, having accused the woman of Timna of being unclean (i.e., Gentile and taboo) and unchaste, now admits that since Samson married her at God's instigation she was not unclean to him; and that she was unchaste only after Samson left her. Reason is therefore puzzled.
7. "Careful": full of care; "down": swan's down.
8. Reflect, consider inwardly.
9. Unknown, unfamiliar.
1. Directed.
2. Notable, eminent.
3. I.e., what is there in man that is not deceivable and vain?

Prayed for, but often proves our woe, our bane?
I prayed for children, and thought barrenness
In wedlock a reproach; I gained a son,
And such a son as all men hailed me happy:
Who would be now a father in my stead?
Oh, wherefore did God grant me my request,
And as a blessing with such pomp adorned?
Why are his gifts desirable, to tempt
Our earnest prayers, then, given with solemn hand
As graces, draw a scorpion's tail behind?
For this did the angel twice descend?[4] for this
Ordained thy nurture holy, as of a plant
Select and sacred? glorious for a while,
The miracle of men; then in an hour
Ensnared, assaulted, overcome, led bound,
Thy foes' derision, captive, poor and blind,
Into a dungeon thrust, to work with slaves!
Alas! methinks whom God hath chosen once
To worthiest deeds, if he through frailty err,
He should not so o'erwhelm, and as a thrall
Subject him to so foul indignities,
Be it but for honor's sake of former deeds.

SAMSON. Appoint not heavenly disposition,[5] father.
Nothing of all these evils hath befallen me
But justly; I myself have brought them on;
Sole author I, sole cause.[6] If aught seem vile,
As vile hath been my folly, who have profaned
The mystery of God, given me under pledge
Of vow, and have betrayed it to a woman,
A Canaanite, my faithless enemy.
This well I knew, nor was at all surprised,
But warned by oft experience. Did not she
Of Timna first betray me, and reveal
The secret wrested from me in her height
Of nuptial love professed, carrying it straight
To them who had corrupted her, my spies
And rivals? [7] In this other was there found
More faith, who, also in her prime of love,
Spousal embraces, vitiated with gold,
Though offered only, by the scent conceived,
Her spurious first-born, treason against me? [8]
Thrice she assayed, with flattering prayers and sighs,
And amorous reproaches, to win from me

4. The angel who announced Samson's birth was sent a second time, in answer to Manoa's request, to give instructions concerning his education and training.

5. I.e., do not presume to control heaven's decisions.

6. Like Adam, *Paradise Lost* X, Samson proves his own resurgent virtue by accepting responsibility for his own faults.

7. Samson's first wife, the woman of Timna, revealed Samson's riddle to his enemies (Judges xiv.8–19).

8. At the mere scent of gold, Dalila conceived a bastard ("spurious") offspring for Samson—treason.

My capital secret,[9] in what part my strength
Lay stored, in what part summed, that she might know;
Thrice I deluded her, and turned to sport
Her importunity, each time perceiving
How openly and with what impudence
She purposed to betray me, and (which was worse
Than undissembled hate) with what contempt
She sought to make me traitor to myself.[1]
Yet, the fourth time, when, mustering all her wiles,
With blandished parleys, feminine assaults,
Tongue-batteries, she surceased[2] not day nor night
To storm me, over-watched and wearied out,
At times when men seek most repose and rest,
I yielded, and unlocked her all my heart,
Who, with a grain of manhood well resolved,
Might easily have shook off all her snares;
But foul effeminacy [3] held me yoked
Her bondslave. O indignity, O blot
To honor and religion! servile mind
Rewarded well with servile punishment!
The base degree to which I now am fallen,
These rags, this grinding, is not yet so base
As was my former servitude, ignoble,
Unmanly, ignominious, infamous,
True slavery; and that blindness worse than this,
That saw not how degenerately I served.

MANOA. I cannot praise thy marriage-choices, son,
Rather approved them not; but thou didst plead
Divine impulsion[4] prompting how thou might'st
Find some occasion to infest our foes.
I state not that; this I am sure, our foes
Found soon occasion thereby to make thee
Their captive, and their triumph; thou the sooner
Temptation found'st, or over-potent charms,
To violate the sacred trust of silence
Deposited within thee; which to have kept
Tacit was in thy power. True; and thou bear'st
Enough, and more, the burden of that fault;
Bitterly hast thou paid, and still art paying,
That rigid score.[5] A worse thing yet remains:
This day the Philistines a popular feast
Here celebrate in Gaza, and proclaim
Great pomp, and sacrifice, and praises loud,
To Dagon, as their god who hath delivered
Thee, Samson, bound and blind, into their hands—

9. The secret Dalila learned was of capital importance; also, it involved the hair on Samson's head (*caput*).
1. Judges xvi.5–20.
2. Forbore.
3. "Effeminacy": uxoriousness, overfondness, the fault of Adam.
4. Prudent Manoa mistrusts the inner impulse which is Samson's conscience and the first principle of his life. "Infest": attack.
5. Debt.

Them out of thine, who slew'st them many a slain.[6]
So Dagon shall be magnified,[7] and God,
Besides whom is no god, compared with idols,
Disglorified, blasphemed, and had in scorn
By th' idolatrous rout amidst their wine;
Which to have come to pass by means of thee,
Samson, of all thy sufferings think the heaviest,
Of all reproach the most with shame that ever
Could have befallen thee and thy father's house.

SAMSON. Father, I do acknowledge and confess
That I this honor, I this pomp, have brought
To Dagon, and advanced his praises high
Among the heathen round; to God have brought
Dishonor, obloquy, and oped the mouths
Of idolists and atheists; have brought scandal
To Israel, diffidence[8] of God, and doubt
In feeble hearts, propense[9] enough before
To waver, or fall off and join with idols:
Which is my chief affliction, shame and sorrow,
The anguish of my soul, that suffers not
Mine eye to harbor sleep, or thoughts to rest.
This only hope relieves me, that the strife
With me hath end. All the contést is now
'Twixt God and Dagon. Dagon hath presumed,
Me overthrown, to enter lists[1] with God,
His deity comparing and preferring
Before the God of Abraham. He, be sure,
Will not connive,[2] or linger, thus provoked,
But will arise, and his great name assert.
Dagon must stoop, and shall ere long receive
Such a discomfit as shall quite despoil him
Of all these boasted trophies won on me,
And with confusion blank[3] his worshipers.

MANOA. With cause this hope relieves thee; and these words
I as a prophecy receive; for God
(Nothing more certain) will not long defer
To vindicate the glory of his name
Against all competition, nor will long
Endure it doubtful whether God be Lord
Or Dagon. But for thee what shall be done?
Thou must not in the meanwhile, here forgot,
Lie in this miserable loathsome plight
Neglected. I already have made way
To some Philistian lords, with whom to treat
About thy ransom. Well they may by this[4]
Have satisfied their utmost of revenge,

6. I.e., who slew many a one for them.
7. Glorified.
8. Mistrust.
9. Inclined.
1. Jousting courts as in medieval tourneys.
2. Hesitate, palter.
3. Confound, turn pale.
4. By this time.

By pains and slaveries, worse than death, inflicted
On thee, who now no more canst do them harm.
SAMSON. Spare that proposal, father; spare the trouble
Of that solicitation. Let me here,
As I deserve, pay on my punishment,
And expiate, if possible, my crime,
Shameful garrulity. To have revealed
Secrets of men, the secrets of a friend,
How heinous had the fact been, how deserving
Contempt and scorn of all; to be excluded
All friendship, and avoided as a blab,
The mark of fool set on his front![5] But I
God's counsel have not kept, his holy secret
Presumptuously have published, impiously,
Weakly at least and shamefully: a sin
That Gentiles in their parables condemn
To their abyss and horrid pains confined.[6]
MANOA. Be penitent, and for thy fault contrite;
But act not in thy own affliction, son.
Repent the sin; but, if the punishment
Thou canst avoid, self-preservation bids;
Or th' execution leave to high disposal,
And let another hand, not thine, exact
Thy penal forfeit from thyself. Perhaps
God will relent, and quit[7] thee all his debt;
Who ever more approves and more accepts
(Best pleased with humble and filial submission)
Him who, imploring mercy, sues for life,
Than who, self-rigorous, chooses death as due;[8]
Which argues over-just, and self-displeased
For self-offense more than for God offended.
Reject not, then, what offered means who knows
But God hath set before us to return thee
Home to thy country and his sacred house,
Where thou may'st bring thy offerings, to avert
His further ire, with prayers and vows renewed.
SAMSON. His pardon I implore; but, as for life,
To what end should I seek it? When in strength
All mortals I excelled, and great in hopes,
With youthful courage, and magnanimous thoughts
Of birth from Heaven foretold and high exploits,
Full of divine instinct, after some proof
Of acts indeed heroic, far beyond
The sons of Anak,[9] famous now and blazed,
Fearless of danger, like a petty god

5. Forehead.
6. In classical legend, Tantalus was confined to hell and torment because he betrayed the secrets of the gods, and Prometheus was savagely punished for giving to mankind the secret of fire.
7. Cancel.
8. This is very similar to Adam's argument against suicide in *Paradise Lost* X.1013–30.
9. Giants, described in Numbers xiii.

I walked about, admired of all, and dreaded
On hostile ground, none daring my affront.
Then, swoll'n with pride, into the snare I fell
Of fair fallacious looks, venereal trains,[1]
Softened with pleasure and voluptuous life;
At length to lay my head and hallowed pledge
Of all my strength in the lascivious lap
Of a deceitful concubine, who shore me,
Like a tame wether,[2] all my precious fleece,
Then turned me out ridiculous, despoiled,
Shaven, and disarmed among my enemies.
CHORUS. Desire of wine and all delicious drinks,
Which many a famous warrior overturns,
Thou could'st repress; nor did the dancing ruby,
Sparkling out-poured, the flavor or the smell,
Or taste, that cheers the heart of gods and men,
Allure thee from the cool crystalline stream.
SAMSON. Wherever fountain or fresh current flowed
Against the eastern ray, translucent, pure
With touch ethereal of Heaven's fiery rod,[3]
I drank, from the clear milky juice allaying
Thirst, and refreshed; nor envied them the grape
Whose heads that turbulent liquor fills with fumes.
CHORUS. O madness! to think use of strongest wines
And strongest drinks our chief support of health,
When God with these forbidden made choice to rear
His mighty champion, strong above compare,
Whose drink was only from the liquid brook! [4]
SAMSON. But what availed this temperance, not complete
Against another object more enticing?
What boots it at one gate to make defense,
And at another to let in the foe,
Effeminately vanquished? by which means,
Now blind, disheartened, shamed, dishonored, quelled,
To what can I be useful? wherein serve
My nation, and the work from Heaven imposed?
But to sit idle on the household hearth,
A burdenous drone; to visitance a gaze,[5]
Or pitied object; these redundant [6] locks,
Robustious to no purpose, clustering down,
Vain monument of strength; till length of years
And sedentary numbness craze [7] my limbs
To a contemptible old age obscure.

1. Sensual, sexual lures.
2. A castrated male sheep.
3. The rays of the sun. Samson is saying that wherever water was purest and cleanest, he drank of it—never of wine; "rod" intimates a parallel with Moses, who like Samson brought forth a spring in the middle of the desert.
4. Samson's calling as a Nazarite forbade him the use of wine.
5. A spectacle for visitors.
6. In its Latin sense, "redundant" means "flowing," in the English sense "unnecessary," "unemployed." "**Robustious**": strong.
7. Weaken, twist.

Here rather let me drudge, and earn my bread,
Till vermin, or the draff of servile food,[8]
Consume me, and oft-invocated death
Hasten the welcome end of all my pains.

MANOA. Wilt thou then serve the Philistines with that gift
Which was expressly given thee to annoy them?
Better at home lie bed-rid, not only idle,
Inglorious, unemployed, with age outworn.
But God, who caused a fountain at thy prayer
From the dry ground to spring, thy thirst to allay
After the brunt of battle,[9] can as easy
Cause light again within thy eyes to spring,
Wherewith to serve him better than thou hast.
And I persuade me so. Why else this strength
Miraculous yet remaining in those locks?
His might continues in thee not for naught,
Nor shall his wondrous gifts be frustrate thus.

SAMSON. All otherwise to me my thoughts portend,
That these dark orbs no more shall treat with light,
Nor th' other light of life continue long,
But yield to double darkness nigh at hand;
So much I feel my genial spirits[1] droop,
My hopes all flat: Nature within me seems
In all her functions weary of herself;
My race of glory run, and race of shame,
And I shall shortly be with them that rest.

MANOA. Believe not these suggestions, which proceed
From anguish of the mind, and humors black
That mingle with thy fancy.[2] I, however,
Must not omit a father's timely care
To prosecute the means of thy deliverance
By ransom or how else: meanwhile be calm,
And healing words from these thy friends admit.

SAMSON. Oh, that torment should not be confined
To the body's wounds and sores,
With maladies innumerable
In heart, head, breast, and reins,
But must secret passage find
To th' inmost mind,
There exercise all his fierce accidents,[3]
And on her purest spirits prey,
As on entrails, joints, and limbs,
With answerable pains, but more intense,
Though void of corporal sense!

8. Garbage given to slaves as food.
9. The story of how Samson, with divine aid, created a spring in the desert after the battle with the ass's jawbone, is told in Judges xv.18–19.
1. Life forces, vital energy.
2. Black bile, the melancholy humor, was supposed to have specially ill effects on the imagination.
3. I.e., there put into effect all the fierce qualities (of torment).

My griefs not only pain me
As a lingering disease,
But, finding no redress, ferment and rage;
Nor less than wounds immedicable
Rankle, and fester, and gangrene,
To black mortification.[4]
Thoughts, my tormentors, armed with daily stings,
Mangle my apprehensive tenderest parts,
Exasperate, exulcerate, and raise
Dire inflammation, which no cooling herb
Or med'cinal liquor can assuage,
Nor breath of vernal air from snowy Alp.
Sleep hath forsook and given me o'er
To death's benumbing opium as my only cure;
Thence faintings, swoonings of despair,
And sense of Heaven's desertion.[5]
I was his nursling once and choice delight,
His destined from the womb,
Promised by heavenly message [6] twice descending.
Under his special eye
Abstemious I grew up and thrived amain;
He led me on to mightiest deeds,
Above the nerve [7] of mortal arm,
Against the uncircumcised, our enemies:
But now hath cast me off as never known,
And to those cruel enemies,
Whom I by his appointment had provoked,
Left me, all helpless with th' irreparable loss
Of sight, reserved alive to be repeated [8]
The subject of their cruelty or scorn.
Nor am I in the list of them that hope;
Hopeless are all my evils, all remediless.
This one prayer yet remains, might I be heard,
No long petition—speedy death,
The close of all my miseries and the balm.

CHORUS. Many are the sayings of the wise,
In ancient and in modern books enrolled,
Extolling patience as the truest fortitude,
And to the bearing well of all calamities,
All chances incident to man's frail life,
Consolatories writ
With studied argument, and much persuasion sought,
Lenient [9] of grief and anxious thought.
But with th' afflicted in his pangs their sound
Little prevails, or rather seems a tune

4. A medical term for decay.
5. Samson comes close here to suggesting that religious despair is the symptom of a physical condition; cf. Burton's *Anatomy of Melancholy*.
6. Messenger.
7. Sinew, hence, strength.
8. Repeatedly, continually.
9. Soothing (from Latin, *leniens*).

Harsh, and of dissonant mood [1] from his complaint,
Unless he feel within
Some source of consolation from above,
Secret refreshings that repair his strength
And fainting spirits uphold.[2]
God of our fathers! what is man,
That thou towards him with hand so various—
Or might I say contrarious?—
Temper'st thy providence through his short course:
Not evenly, as thou rul'st
The angelic orders, and inferior creatures mute,
Irrational and brute? [3]
Nor do I name of men the common rout,
That, wandering loose about,
Grow up and perish as the summer fly,
Heads without name, no more remembered;
But such as thou hast solemnly elected,
With gifts and graces eminently adorned,
To some great work, thy glory,
And people's safety, which in part they effect.
Yet toward these, thus dignified, thou oft,
Amidst their height of noon,
Changest thy countenance and thy hand, with no regard
Of highest favors past
From thee on them, or them to thee of service.[4]
Nor only dost degrade them, or remit
To life obscured, which were a fair dismission,
But throw'st them lower than thou didst exalt them high,
Unseemly falls in human eye,
Too grievous for the trespass or omission;
Oft leav'st them to the hostile sword
Of heathen and profane, their carcasses
To dogs and fowls a prey, or else captívod,
Or to the unjust tribunals, under change of times,
And condemnation of the ingrateful multitude.[5]
If these they 'scape, perhaps in poverty
With sickness and disease thou bow'st them down,
Painful diseases and deformed,
In crude [6] old age;
Though not disordinate,[7] yet causeless suffering
The punishment of dissolute days. In fine,

1. The musical mode, or psychological mood, of the comforter jars on that of the sufferer.
2. Compare Job's answers to his comforters, especially xiv.
3. The chorus feels that the beings above and below man on the Great Chain of Being (the nine orders of angels above, the many mute beasts below) are ruled by a less capricious code than is man.
4. Manoa has already voiced this plaint, lines 368–72.
5. After the Restoration, many Puritan leaders were executed, jailed, or exiled, while even the corpses of some who were dead were exhumed, beheaded, and publicly exhibited.
6. Literally, "raw," but, figuratively, "premature."
7. I.e., though they have not been dissipated (disordinate). Milton resented having the gout, supposed to be a disease of the luxurious.

Just or unjust alike seem miserable,
For oft alike both come to evil end.
So deal not with this once thy glorious champion,
The image of thy strength, and mighty minister.[8]
What do I beg? how hast thou dealt already!
Behold him in this state calamitous, and turn
His labors, for thou canst, to peaceful end.
But who is this? what thing of sea or land—
Female of sex it seems—
That, so bedecked, ornate, and gay,
Comes this way sailing,
Like a stately ship
Of Tarsus, bound for th' isles
Of Javan or Gadire,[9]
With all her bravery on, and tackle trim,
Sails filled, and streamers waving,
Courted by all the winds that hold them play;
An amber [1] scent of odorous perfume
Her harbinger, a damsel train behind?
Some rich Philistian matron she may seem;
And now, at nearer view, no other certain
Than Dálila thy wife.[2]

SAMSON. My wife! my traitress! let her not come near me.

CHORUS. Yet on she moves; now stands and eyes thee fixed,
About t'have spoke; but now, with head declined,
Like a fair flower surcharged with dew, she weeps,
And words addressed seem into tears dissolved,
Wetting the borders of her silken veil.
But now again she makes address to speak.

DALILA. With doubtful feet and wavering resolution
I came, still dreading thy displeasure, Samson;
Which to have merited, without excuse,
I cannot but acknowledge. Yet, if tears
May expiate (though the fact more evil drew
In the perverse event than I foresaw),[3]
My penance hath not slackened, though my pardon
No way assured. But conjugal affection,
Prevailing over fear and timorous doubt,
Hath led me on, desirous to behold
Once more thy face, and know of thy estate,[4]
If aught in my ability may serve
To lighten what thou suffer'st, and appease
Thy mind with what amends is in my power—

8. Agent, but with a religious connotation as well.

9. Tarsus (the birthplace of St. Paul) is a trading city in modern Turkey; the isles of Javan are the isles of Greece, supposed to be populated by descendants of Javan, son of Noah's son Japhet. Gadire is modern Cadiz in Spain. Many of these geographical details are to be found in Isaiah II.lxvi, etc.

1. Ambergris.

2. The circling, mocking, derisive description of the chorus carefully holds Samson in suspense till the last minute.

3. I.e., my action turned out worse than I intended.

4. Condition.

Though late, yet in some part to recompense
My rash but more unfortunate misdeed.
SAMSON. Out, out, hyena![5] These are thy wonted arts,
And arts of every woman false like thee,
To break all faith, all vows, deceive, betray;
Then, as repentant, to submit, beseech,
And reconcilement move with feigned remorse,
Confess, and promise wonders in her change—
Not truly penitent, but chief to try
Her husband, how far urged his patience bears,
His virtue or weakness which way to assail:
Then, with more cautious and instructed skill,
Again transgresses, and again submits;
That wisest and best men, full oft beguiled,
With goodness principled not to reject
The penitent, but ever to forgive,
Are drawn to wear out miserable days,
Entangled with a poisonous bosom-snake,
If not by quick destruction soon cut off,
As I by thee, to ages an example.
DALILA. Yet hear me, Samson, not that I endeavor
To lessen or extenuate my offense,
But that, on th' other side, if it be weighed
By itself, with aggravations not surcharged,
Or else with just allowance counterpoised,
I may, if possible, thy pardon find
The easier towards me, or thy hatred less.
First granting, as I do, it was a weakness
In me, but incident to all our sex,
Curiosity, inquisitive, importune
Of secrets, then with like infirmity
To publish them, both common female faults,
Was it not weakness also to make known,
For importunity, that is for naught,
Wherein consisted all thy strength and safety?
To what I did thou show'dst me first the way.
But I to enemies revealed, and should not!
Nor should'st thou have trusted that to woman's frailty:[6]
Ere I to thee, thou to thyself wast cruel.
Let weakness, then, with weakness come to parle,[7]
So near related, or the same of kind;
Thine forgive mine, that men may censure thine
The gentler, if severely thou exact not
More strength from me than in thyself was found.

5. Apart from being an animal of odious habits and appearance, the hyena was a traditional beast of hypocrisy, supposed to entice men to destruction by its power of imitating the human voice.

6. Like Eve, who wore down Adam with importunity, then blamed him for giving in (*Paradise Lost* IX.1155–61) Dalila blames Samson for doing what she herself has demanded.

7. Parley, agreement.

And what if love, which thou interpret'st hate,
The jealousy of love, powerful of sway
In human hearts, nor less in mine towards thee,
Caused what I did? I saw thee mutable
Of fancy; feared lest one day thou would'st leave me,
As her at Timna; sought by all means, therefore,
How to endear, and hold thee to me firmest:
No better way I saw than by importuning
To learn thy secrets, get into my power
Thy key of strength and safety. Thou wilt say,
"Why, then, revealed?" I was assured by those
Who tempted me that nothing was designed
Against thee but safe custody and hold.
That made for me; I knew that liberty
Would draw thee forth to perilous enterprises,
While I at home sat full of cares and fears,
Wailing thy absence in my widowed bed;
Here I should still enjoy thee, day and night,
Mine and love's prisoner, not the Philistines',
Whole to myself, unhazarded abroad,
Fearless at home of partners in my love.
These reasons in love's law have passed for good,
Though fond [8] and reasonless to some perhaps;
And love hath oft, well meaning, wrought much woe,
Yet always pity or pardon hath obtained.
Be not unlike all others, not austere
As thou art strong, inflexible as steel.
If thou in strength all mortals dost exceed,
In uncompassionate anger do not so.

SAMSON. How cunningly the sorceress displays
Her own transgressions, to upbraid me mine!
That malice, not repentance, brought thee hither,
By this appears. I gave, thou say'st, th' example,
I led the way—bitter reproach, but true;
I to myself was false ere thou to me.
Such pardon, therefore, as I give my folly
Take to thy wicked deed; which when thou seest
Impartial, self-severe, inexorable,
Thou wilt renounce thy seeking, and much rather
Confess it feigned. Weakness is thy excuse,
And I believe it, weakness to resist
Philistian gold. If weakness may excuse,
What murderer, what traitor, parricide,
Incestuous, sacrilegious, but may plead it?
All wickedness is weakness; that plea, therefore,
With God or man will gain thee no remission.
But love constrained thee! Call it furious rage
To satisfy thy lust. Love seeks to have love;

8. Foolish.

My love how could'st thou hope, who took'st the way
To raise in me inexpiable [9] hate,
Knowing, as needs I must, by thee betrayed?
In vain thou striv'st to cover shame with shame,
Or by evasions thy crime uncover'st more.

DALILA. Since thou determin'st weakness for no plea
In man or woman, though to thy own condemning,
Hear what assaults I had, what snares besides,
What sieges girt me round, ere I consented;
Which might have awed the best resolved of men,
The constantest, to have yielded without blame.
It was not gold, as to my charge thou lay'st,
That wrought with me.[1] Thou know'st the magistrates
And princes of my country came in person,
Solicited, commanded, threatened, urged,
Adjured by all the bonds of civil duty
And of religion—pressed how just it was,
How honorable, how glorious, to entrap
A common enemy, who had destroyed
Such numbers of our nation: and the priest
Was not behind, but ever at my ear,
Preaching how meritorious with the gods
It would be to ensnare an irreligious
Dishonorer of Dagon. What had I
To oppose against such powerful arguments?
Only my love of thee held long debate,
And combated in silence all these reasons
With hard contest. At length, that grounded maxim,
So rife and celebrated in the mouths
Of wisest men, that to the public good
Private respects must yield,[2] with grave authority
Took full possession of me, and prevailed;
Virtue, as I thought, truth, duty, so enjoining.

SAMSON. I thought where all thy circling wiles would end,
In feigned religion, smooth hypocrisy!
But, had thy love, still odiously pretended,
Been, as it ought, sincere, it would have taught thee
Far other reasonings, brought forth other deeds.
I, before all the daughters of my tribe
And of my nation, chose thee from among
My enemies, loved thee, as too well thou knew'st;
Too well; unbosomed all my secrets to thee,
Not out of levity, but overpowered
By thy request, who could deny thee nothing;
Yet now am judged an enemy. Why, then,

9. Inextinguishable.

1. Judges xvi is very explicit that Dalila betrayed Samson for money—eleven hundred pieces of silver offered her by each one of the Philistine lords.

2. Reason of state, political expediency, was in Milton's eyes the worst of all possible motives for an action. Cf. *Paradise Lost* IV. 393–94.

Didst thou at first receive me for thy husband,
Then, as since then, thy country's foe professed?
Being once a wife, for me thou wast to leave
Parents and country; nor was I their subject,
Nor under their protection, but my own;
Thou mine, not theirs.[3] If aught against my life
Thy country sought of thee, it sought unjustly,
Against the law of nature, law of nations;
No more thy country, but an impious crew
Of men conspiring to uphold their state
By worse than hostile deeds, violating the ends
For which our country is a name so dear;
Not therefore to be obeyed. But zeal moved thee;
To please thy gods thou didst it! Gods unable
To acquit themselves and prosecute their foes
But by ungodly deeds, the contradiction
Of their own deity, gods cannot be;
Less therefore to be pleased, obeyed, or feared.
These false pretexts and varnished colors failing,
Bare in thy guilt, how foul must thou appear!

DALILA. In argument with men a woman ever
Goes by the worse,[4] whatever be her cause.

SAMSON. For want of words, no doubt, or lack of breath!
Witness when I was worried with thy peals.

DALILA. I was a fool, too rash, and quite mistaken
In what I thought would have succeeded best.
Let me obtain forgiveness of thee, Samson;
Afford me place to show what recompense
Towards thee I intend for what I have misdone,
Misguided. Only what remains past cure
Bear not too sensibly,[5] nor still insist
To afflict thyself in vain. Though sight be lost,
Life yet hath many solaces, enjoyed
Where other senses want not their delights—
At home, in leisure and domestic ease,
Exempt from many a care and chance to which
Eyesight exposes, daily, men abroad.
I to the lords will intercede, not doubting
Their favorable ear, that I may fetch thee
From forth this loathsome prison house, to abide
With me, where my redoubled love and care,
With nursing diligence, to me glad office,
May ever tend about thee to old age,
With all things grateful cheered, and so supplied
That what by me thou hast lost thou least shalt miss.

SAMSON. No, no; of my condition take no care;

3. I.e., you were under my protection, not theirs.
4. Comes off second best.
5. "Too sensibly": with too great sensitivity.

It fits not; thou and I long since are twain;
Nor think me so unwary or accursed [6]
To bring my feet again into the snare
Where once I have been caught. I know thy trains,
Though dearly to my cost, thy gins, and toils.[7]
Thy fair enchanted cup, and warbling charms,
No more on me have power; their force is nulled;
So much of adder's wisdom I have learned,
To fence my ear against thy sorceries.[8]
If in my flower of youth and strength, when all men
Loved, honored, feared me, thou alone could hate me,
Thy husband, slight me, sell me, and forgo me,
How would'st thou use me now, blind, and thereby
Deceivable, in most things as a child
Helpless, thence easily contemned and scorned,
And last neglected! How would'st thou insult,
When I must live uxorious to thy will
In perfect thraldom! how again betray me,
Bearing my words and doings to the lords
To gloss upon, and, censuring, frown or smile! [9]
This jail I count the house of liberty
To thine, whose doors my feet shall never enter.

DALILA. Let me approach at least, and touch thy hand.

SAMSON. Not for thy life, lest fierce remembrance wake
My sudden rage to tear thee joint by joint.[1]
At distance I forgive thee, go with that;
Bewail thy falsehood, and the pious works
It hath brought forth to make thee memorable
Among illustrious women, faithful wives;
Cherish thy hastened widowhood with the gold
Of matrimonial treason: so farewell.

DALILA. I see thou art implacable, more deaf
To prayers than winds and seas. Yet winds to seas
Are reconciled at length, and sea to shore:
Thy anger, unappeasable, still rages,
Eternal tempest never to be calmed.
Why do I humble thus myself, and, suing
For peace, reap nothing but repulse and hate,
Bid go with evil omen,[2] and the brand
Of infamy upon my name denounced?
To mix with thy concernments I desist
Henceforth, nor too much disapprove my own.

6. I.e., so neglectful or bewitched.

7. "Trains": tricks; "gins": snares; "toils": nets. The traditional images for female wiles are heightened by reference to an enchanting cup and warbled charms reminiscent of Homer's Circe (*Odyssey*, X).

8. Psalm lviii verses 4 and 5 describes the "deaf adder that stoppeth her ear; which will not hearken to the voice of charmers, charming never so wisely."

9. Milton's libertarian hatred of censorship and managed liberty is very apparent.

1. What Samson might remember, at the touch of Dalila, which would lead him to tear her to pieces, is a problem in domestic psychology.

2. I.e., dismissed with threats of ill fame.

Fame, if not double-faced, is double-mouthed,
And with contrary blast proclaims most deeds;[3]
On both his wings, one black, th' other white,
Bears greatest names in his wild airy flight.
My name, perhaps, among the circumcised
In Dan, in Judah, and the bordering tribes,
To all posterity may stand defamed,
With malediction mentioned, and the blot
Of falsehood most unconjugal traduced.
But in my country, where I most desire,
In Ecron, Gaza, Asdod, and in Gath,
I shall be named among the famousest
Of women, sung at solemn festivals,
Living and dead recorded, who to save
Her country from a fierce destroyer chose
Above the faith of wedlock bands; my tomb
With odors[4] visited and annual flowers;
Not less renowned than in Mount Ephraim
Jael, who, with inhospitable guile,
Smote Sisera sleeping,[5] through the temples nailed.
Nor shall I count it heinous to enjoy
The public marks of honor and reward
Conferred upon me for the piety
Which to my country I was judged to have shown.
At this whoever envies or repines,
I leave him to his lot, and like my own.

CHORUS. She's gone, a manifest serpent by her sting
Discovered in the end, till now concealed.

SAMSON. So let her go. God sent her to debase me,
And aggravate my folly, who committed
To such a viper his most sacred trust
Of secrecy, my safety, and my life.

CHORUS. Yet beauty, though injurious, hath strange power,
After offense returning, to regain
Love once possessed, nor can be easily
Repulsed, without much inward passion[6] felt,
And secret sting of amorous remorse.

SAMSON. Love-quarrels oft in pleasing concord end;
Not wedlock-treachery, endangering life.

CHORUS. It is not virtue, wisdom, valor, wit,
Strength, comeliness of shape, or amplest merit.
That woman's love can win, or long inherit;[7]
But what it is hard is to say,
Harder to hit,

3. The figure of Fame, in Milton's youthful poem *On the Fifth of November*, does indeed have a double tongue, one for truth and one for lies. Fame or Rumor was a favorite grotesque allegorical figure in classical poets like Ovid (*Metamorphoses* XII.43 ff.) and Virgil (*Aeneid* IV.173 ff.).

4. Perfumes.

5. Jael lured Sisera, who saw in her the wife of his ally and friend, into a tent, and there drove a large nail into his head (Judges iv.17–21).

6. Suffering.

7. Possess.

Which way soever men refer it
(Much like thy riddle, Samson),[8] in one day
Or seven though one should musing sit.
If any of these, or all, the Timnian bride
Had not so soon preferred
Thy paranymph, worthless to thee compared,
Successor in thy bed,[9]
Nor both so loosely disallied
Their nuptials,[1] nor this last so treacherously
Had shorn the fatal harvest of thy head.
Is it for that[2] such outward ornament
Was lavished on their sex, that inward gifts
Were left for haste unfinished, judgment scant,
Capacity not raised to apprehend
Or value what is best
In choice, but oftest to affect[3] the wrong?
Or was too much of self-love mixed,
Of constancy no root infixed,
That either they love nothing, or not long?
Whate'er it be, to wisest men and best,
Seeming at first all heavenly under virgin veil,
Soft, modest, meek, demure,
Once joined, the contrary she proves, a thorn
Intestine,[4] far within defensive arms
A cleaving[5] mischief, in his way to virtue
Adverse and turbulent; or by her charms
Draws him awry, enslaved
With dotage, and his sense depraved
To folly and shameful deeds, which ruin ends.
What pilot so expert but needs must wreck,
Embarked with such a steers-mate at the helm?
Favored of Heaven who finds
One virtuous, rarely found,
That in domestic good combines:
Happy that house! his way to peace is smooth:
But virtue which breaks through all opposition,
And all temptation can remove,
Most shines and most is acceptable above.
Therefore God's universal law
Gave to the man despotic power
Over his female in due awe,
Nor from that right to part an hour,
Smile she or lour:
So shall he least confusion draw
On his whole life, not swayed

8. Samson's riddle is propounded and answered in Judges xiv, verses 14 and 18.
9. I.e., if any of these ("virtue, . . . ," lines 1010–11) sufficed, Samson's first wife (the Timnian bride) would not have preferred to marry his "paranymph" (best man). See Judges xiv.
1. I.e., nor would both your wives have been so careless about their marriage vows.
2. Because.
3. Desire.
4. An inward thorn, a viper in the bosom.
5. Clinging; a traditional emblem of marriage was the elm and the vine.

By female usurpation, nor dismayed.
But had we best retire? I see a storm.
SAMSON. Fair days have oft contracted [6] wind and rain.
CHORUS. But this another kind of tempest brings.
SAMSON. Be less abstruse; my riddling days are past.
CHORUS. Look now for no enchanting voice, nor fear
The bait of honeyed words; a rougher tongue
Draws hitherward, I know him by his stride,
The giant Harapha [7] of Gath, his look
Haughty, as is his pile [8] high-built and proud.
Comes he in peace? What wind hath blown him hither
I less conjecture than when first I saw
The sumptuous Dalila floating this way: [9]
His habit carries peace, his brow defiance.
SAMSON. Or peace or not, alike to me he comes.
CHORUS. His fraught [1] we soon shall know: he now arrives.
HARAPHA. I come not, Samson, to condole thy chance,
As these [2] perhaps, yet wish it had not been,
Though for no friendly intent. I am of Gath;
Men call me Harapha, of stock renowned
As Og, or Anak, and the Emims old
That Kiriathaim held.[3] Thou know'st me now,
If thou at all art known.[4] Much I have heard
Of thy prodigious might and feats performed,
Incredible to me, in this displeased,
That I was never present on the place
Of those encounters, where we might have tried
Each other's force in camp or listed field; [5]
And now am come to see of whom such noise
Hath walked about, and each limb to survey,
If thy appearance answer loud report.
SAMSON. The way to know were not to see, but taste.[6]
HARAPHA. Dost thou already single [7] me? I thought
Gyves and the mill had tamed thee. O that fortune
Had brought me to the field where thou art famed
To have wrought such wonders with an ass's jaw!
I should have forced thee soon wish [8] other arms,

6. Drawn after them.
7. Harapha does not appear at all within the story told in the Book of Judges; Milton invented him with the help of some hints from the image of Goliath in I Samuel xvii and some other giants in II Samuel xxi. *Rapha* means giant in Hebrew.
8. Body; with the suggestion that he is tall as a tower.
9. That the various visitors of Samson are blown hither and yon by the winds of occasion serves to emphasize the deep steadiness of Samson's final resolution.
1. Intent.
2. The chorus of Danites, naturally sympathetic to Samson.
3. Og was a giant King of Bashan in Deuteronomy iii.11; Anak and his sons were giants in Numbers xiii.33; the Emims were giants in Deuteronomy ii. 10–11 and Genesis xiv.5.
4. I.e., you know me now if you know anything; but also "if you are anyone worth knowing." Compare Satan's brag to Zephon and Ithuriel, "Not to know me argues yourselves unknown." *Paradise Lost* IV.830.
5. "Camp": field of battle (from Latin, *campus*); "listed field": lists, tourney-ground.
6. Make a trial of.
7. Challenge; "gyves": chains.
8. Eighteenth-century editors changed "wish" to "with", easing the grammar at the expense of the sense.

Or left thy carcass where the ass lay thrown;
So had the glory of prowess been recovered
To Palestine, won by a Philistine
From the unforeskinned race, of whom thou bear'st
The highest name for valiant acts. That honor,
Certain to have won by mortal duel from thee,
I lose, prevented by thy eyes put out.

SAMSON. Boast not of what thou would'st have done, but do
What then thou would'st; thou seest it in thy hand.

HARAPHA. To combat with a blind man I disdain,
And thou hast need much washing to be touched.

SAMSON. Such usage as your honorable lords
Afford me, assassinated [9] and betrayed;
Who durst not with their whole united powers
In fight withstand me single and unarmed,
Nor in the house with chamber ambushes [1]
Close-banded durst attack me, no, not sleeping,
Till they had hired a woman with their gold,
Breaking her marriage-faith, to circumvent me.
Therefore, without feigned shifts, let be assigned
Some narrow place enclosed, where sight may give thee,
Or rather flight, no great advantage on me;
Then put on all thy gorgeous arms, thy helmet
And brigandine of brass, thy broad habergeon,
Vant-brace and greaves and gauntlet; [2] add thy spear,
A weaver's beam, and seven-times-folded shield:
I only with an oaken staff will meet thee,
And raise such outcries on thy clattered iron,
Which long shall not withhold me from thy head,
That in a little time, while breath remains thee,
Thou oft shalt wish thyself at Gath, to boast
Again in safety what thou would'st have done
To Samson, but shalt never see Gath more.

HARAPHA. Thou durst not thus disparage glorious arms,
Which greatest heroes have in battle worn,
Their ornament and safety, had not spells
And black enchantments, some magician's art,
Armed thee or charmed thee strong, which thou from Heaven
Feign'dst at thy birth was given thee in thy hair,
Where strength can least abide, though all thy hairs
Were bristles ranged like those that ridge the back
Of chafed wild boars or ruffled porcupines.

SAMSON. I know no spells, use no forbidden arts;
My trust is in the Living God, who gave me,

9. Treacherously assailed.

1. Samson refers to the four occasions on which Philistines hid in his bedroom while Dalila tried unsuccessfully to betray him to them.

2. "Brigandine": a padded chest-protector, covered with iron scales or rings; "habergeon": a coat of mail, a hauberk; "vant-brace": a steel cuff for the forearm; greaves protect the shins and thighs, and gauntlets the hands. A weaver's beam, emblem of weightiness, is used to keep threads hanging tautly in a loom. All these military details are from the description of Goliath, I Samuel xvii.4–7.

At my nativity, this strength, diffused
No less through all my sinews, joints, and bones,
Than thine, while I preserved these locks unshorn,
The pledge of my unviolated vow.
For proof hereof, if Dagon be thy god,
Go to his temple, invocate his aid
With solemnest devotion, spread before him
How highly it concerns his glory now
To frustrate and dissolve these magic spells,
Which I to be the power of Israel's God
Avow, and challenge Dagon to the test,
Offering to combat thee, his champion bold,
With th' utmost of his godhead seconded:
Then thou shalt see, or rather to thy sorrow
Soon feel, whose God is strongest, thine or mine.
HARAPHA. Presume not on thy God. Whate'er he be,
Thee he regards not, owns not, hath cut off
Quite from his people, and delivered up
Into thy enemies' hand; permitted them
To put out both thine eyes, and fettered send thee
Into the common prison, there to grind
Among the slaves and asses, thy comrádes,
As good for nothing else, no better service
With those thy boisterous locks; no worthy match
For valor to assail, nor by the sword
Of noble warrior, so to stain his honor,
But by the barber's razor best subdued.
SAMSON. All these indignities, for such they are
From thine,[3] these evils I deserve and more,
Acknowledge them from God inflicted on me
Justly, yet despair not of his final pardon,
Whose ear is ever open, and his eye
Gracious to re-admit the suppliant;
In confidence whereof I once again
Defy thee to the trial of mortal fight,
By combat to decide whose god is God,
Thine, or whom I with Israel's sons adore.
HARAPHA. Fair honor that thou dost thy God, in trusting
He will accept thee to defend his cause,
A murderer, a revolter, and a robber!
SAMSON. Tongue-doughty giant, how dost thou prove me these?
HARAPHA. Is not thy nation subject to our lords?
Their magistrates confessed it when they took thee
As a league-breaker, and delivered bound
Into our hands; [4] for hadst not committed

3. Thy people.

4. Judges xiv.8–20 and xv.9–15 describe the episode. Samson when he came to Timna to be married proposed a riddle and a bet to the marriage guests; they got his intended bride to reveal the riddle, and in revenge he killed thirty of their people and left the lady to the "paranymph," or best man. Old Testament Samson is indeed a rude and savage figure; Milton, with characteristic confidence, undertakes his legal defense in everything.

Notorious murder on those thirty men
At Ascalon, who never did thee harm,
Then, like a robber, stripp'dst them of their robes?
The Philistines, when thou hadst broke the league,
Went up with armèd powers thee only seeking,
To others did no violence nor spoil.

SAMSON. Among the daughters of the Philistines
I chose a wife, which argued me no foe,
And in your city held my nuptial feast;
But your ill-meaning politician lords,
Under pretense of bridal friends and guests,
Appointed to await me thirty spies,
Who, threatening cruel death, constrained the bride
To wring from me, and tell to them, my secret,
That solved the riddle which I had proposed.
When I perceived all set on enmity,
As on my enemies, wherever chanced,
I used hostility, and took their spoil,
To pay my underminers in their coin.
My nation was subjected to your lords! [5]
It was the force of conquest; force with force
Is well ejected when the conquered can.
But I, a private person, whom my country
As a league-breaker gave up bound, presumed
Single rebellion, and did hostile acts!
I was no private,[6] but a person raised,
With strength sufficient, and command from Heaven,
To free my country. If their servile minds
Me, their deliverer sent, would not receive,
But to their masters gave me up for nought,
Th' unworthier they; whence to this day they serve.
I was to do my part from Heaven assigned,
And had performed it if my known offense
Had not disabled me, not all your force.
These shifts refuted, answer thy appellant,[7]
Though by his blindness maimed for high attempts,
Who now defies thee thrice to single fight,
As a petty enterprise of small enforce.[8]

HARAPHA. With thee, a man condemned, a slave enrolled,
Due by the law to capital punishment?
To fight with thee no man of arms will deign.

SAMSON. Cam'st thou for this, vain boaster, to survey me,
To descant on my strength, and give thy verdict?
Come nearer; part not hence so slight informed;
But take good heed my hand survey not thee.

HARAPHA. O Baal-zebub! [9] can my ears unused

5. I.e., you argue that my nation was subjected to your lords.
6. Outlaw.
7. I.e., now that we've disposed of these dodges, answer your challenger. "Apellant": literally, caller, one who calls you out.
8. Difficulty.
9. Baal-zebub is Beelzebub, god of the flies.

Hear these dishonors, and not render death?
SAMSON. No man withholds thee; nothing from thy hand
Fear I incurable; bring up thy van; [1]
My heels are fettered, but my fist is free.
HARAPHA. This insolence other kind of answer fits.
SAMSON. Go, baffled coward, lest I run upon thee,
Though in these chains, bulk without spirit vast,
And with one buffet lay thy structure low,
Or swing thee in the air, then dash thee down,
To the hazard of thy brains and shattered sides.
HARAPHA. By Astaroth,[2] ere long thou shalt lament
These braveries,[3] in irons loaden on thee.
CHORUS. His giantship is gone somewhat crestfallen,
Stalking with less unconscionable [4] strides,
And lower looks, but in a sultry chafe.
SAMSON. I dread him not, nor all his giant brood,
Though fame divulge him father of five sons,
All of gigantic size, Goliath chief.[5]
CHORUS. He will directly to the lords, I fear,
And with malicious counsel stir them up
Some way or other yet further to afflict thee.
SAMSON. He must allege some cause, and offered fight
Will not dare mention, lest a question rise
Whether he durst accept the offer or not;
And that he durst not plain enough appeared.
Much more affliction than already felt
They cannot well impose, nor I sustain,
If they intend advantage of my labors,
The work of many hands, which earns my keeping,
With no small profit daily to my owners.
But come what will; my deadliest foe will prove
My speediest friend, by death to rid me hence;
The worst that he can give to me the best.
Yet so it may fall out, because their end
Is hate, not help to me, it may with mine
Draw their own ruin who attempt the deed.
CHORUS. O, how comely it is, and how reviving
To the spirits of just men long oppressed,
When God into the hands of their deliverer
Puts invincible might,
To quell the mighty of the earth, th' oppressor,
The brute and boisterous force of violent men,
Hardy and industrious to support
Tyrannic power, but raging to pursue
The righteous, and all such as honor truth!

1. The vanguard of an army was, naturally, the first group engaged. Samson invites Harapha to start the fight.
2. Moon-goddess of the Philistines, consort of Dagon. See *Paradise Lost* I.437–46.
3. Boasts.
4. Excessive.
5. II Samuel xxi describes four giants "born to the giant in Gath" and slain by David; Milton makes the identification with Harapha on his own.

He all their ammunition
And feats of war defeats,[6]
With plain heroic magnitude of mind
And celestial vigor armed;
Their armories and magazines contemns,
Renders them useless, while
With wingéd expedition [7]
Swift as the lightning glance he executes
His errand on the wicked, who, surprised,
Lose their defense, distracted and amazed.
  But patience is more oft the exercise
Of saints, the trial of their fortitude,
Making them each his own deliverer,
And victor over all
That tyranny or fortune can inflict.
Either of these is in thy lot,[8]
Samson, with might endued
Above the sons of men; but sight bereaved
May chance to number thee with those
Whom patience finally must crown.[9]
  This Idol's day hath been to thee no day of rest,
Laboring thy mind
More than the working day thy hands.
And yet, perhaps, more trouble is behind;
For I descry this way
Some other tending; in his hand
A scepter or quaint [1] staff he bears,
Comes on amain, speed in his look.
By his habit I discern him now
A public officer, and now at hand
His message will be short and voluble.[2]
OFFICER. Ebrews, the prisoner Samson here I seek.
CHORUS. His manacles remark [3] him; there he sits.
OFFICER. Samson, to thee our lords thus bid me say:
This day to Dagon is a solemn feast,
With sacrifices, triumph, pomp, and games;
Thy strength they know surpassing human rate,
And now some public proof thereof require
To honor this great feast, and great assembly.
Rise, therefore, with all speed, and come along,
Where I will see thee heartened and fresh clad,
To appear as fits before th' illustrious lords.
SAMSON. Thou know'st I am an Ebrew; therefore tell them
Our law forbids at their religious rites
My presence; for that cause I cannot come.

6. A touch of the pervasive Miltonic punning.
7. Haste.
8. Fate.
9. The Christian tragedy, like the Christian epic, must center ultimately on an act of passive, not active, fortitude. It is the special achievement of Samson to combine in a single action both qualities.
1. Ornamented.
2. To the point.
3. Distinguish.

OFFICER. This answer, be assured, will not content them.
SAMSON. Have they not sword-players, and every sort
Of gymnic artists, wrestlers, riders, runners,
Jugglers and dancers, antics, mummers, mimics,[4]
But they must pick me out, with shackles tired,
And over-labored at their public mill,
To make them sport with blind activity?
Do they not seek occasion of new quarrels,
On my refusal, to distress me more,
Or make a game of my calamities?
Return the way thou cam'st; I will not come.
OFFICER. Regard thyself; this will offend them highly.
SAMSON. Myself? my conscience, and internal peace.
Can they think me so broken, so debased
With corporal servitude, that my mind ever
Will condescend to such absurd commands?
Although their drudge, to be their fool or jester,
And, in my midst of sorrow and heart-grief,
To show them feats, and play before their god,
The worst of all indignities, yet on me
Joined [5] with supreme contempt! I will not come.
OFFICER. My message was imposed on me with speed,
Brooks no delay: is this thy resolution?
SAMSON. So take it with what speed thy message needs.
OFFICER. I am sorry what this stoutness [6] will produce.
SAMSON. Perhaps thou shalt have cause to sorrow indeed.
CHORUS. Consider, Samson; matters now are strained
Up to the height, whether to hold or break.
He's gone, and who knows how he may report
Thy words by adding fuel to the flame?
Expect another message, more imperious,
More lordly thundering than thou well wilt bear.
SAMSON. Shall I abuse this consecrated gift
Of strength, again returning with my hair
After my great transgression, so requite
Favor renewed, and add a greater sin
By prostituting holy things to idols,
A Nazarite, in place abominable,
Vaunting my strength in honor to their Dagon?
Besides how vile, contemptible, ridiculous,
What act more execrably unclean,[7] profane?
CHORUS. Yet with this strength thou serv'st the Philistines,
Idolatrous, uncircumcised, unclean.
SAMSON. Not in their idol-worship, but by labor
Honest and lawful to deserve my food
Of those who have me in their civil power.
CHORUS. Where the heart joins not, outward acts defile not.

4. "Gymnic artists": gymnasts; "antics": clowns; "mummers": actors.
5. Enjoined, ordered.
6. Defiance.
7. Taboo.

SAMSON. Where outward force constrains, the sentence holds:[8]
But who constrains me to the temple of Dagon,
Not dragging? The Philistian lords command:
Commands are no constraints. If I obey them,
I do it freely, venturing to displease
God for the fear of man, and man prefer,
Set God behind; which, in his jealousy,
Shall never, unrepented, find forgiveness.
Yet that he may dispense with me, or thee,
Present in temples at idolatrous rites
For some important cause,[9] thou need'st not doubt.
CHORUS. How thou wilt here come off surmounts my reach.
SAMSON. Be of good courage; I begin to feel
Some rousing motions in me, which dispose
To something extraordinary my thoughts.
I with this messenger will go along—
Nothing to do, be sure, that may dishonor
Our Law, or stain my vow of Nazarite.
If there be aught of presage in the mind,
This day will be remarkable in my life
By some great act, or of my days the last.[1]
CHORUS. In time thou hast resolved: the man returns.
OFFICER. Samson, this second message from our lords
To thee I am bid say: Art thou our slave,
Our captive, at the public mill our drudge,
And dar'st thou, at our sending and command,
Dispute thy coming? Come without delay;
Or we shall find such engines to assail
And hamper thee, as thou shalt come of force,
Though thou wert firmlier fastened than a rock.
SAMSON. I could be well content to try their art,
Which to no few of them would prove pernicious;
Yet, knowing their advantages too many,
Because[2] they shall not trail me through their streets
Like a wild beast, I am content to go.
Masters' commands come with a power resistless
To such as owe them absolute subjection;
And for a life who will not change his purpose?
(So mutable are all the ways of men!)
Yet this be sure, in nothing to comply
Scandalous or forbidden in our Law.
OFFICER. I praise thy resolution.[3] Doff these links:
By this compliance thou wilt win the lords
To favor, and perhaps to set thee free.

8. I.e., where outward force constrains, your motto may be right.
9. God will make a special dispensation for Samson to attend idolatrous ceremonies "for some important cause," which Samson cannot yet define but which he intuits.
1. By a classic device of dramatic irony, Samson proposes as alternatives two events which will both simultaneously come true. "Presage": premonition, presight
2. So that.
3. Decision. "Doff these links": take off these chains.

SAMSON. Brethren, farewell. Your company along
I will not wish, lest it perhaps offend them
To see me girt with friends; and how the sight
Of me, as of a common enemy,
So dreaded once, may now exasperate them
I know not. Lords are lordliest in their wine;
And the well-feasted priest then soonest fired
With zeal, if aught religion seem concerned;[4]
No less the people, on their holy-days,
Impetuous, insolent, unquenchable.
Happen what may, of me expect to hear
Nothing dishonorable, impure, unworthy
Our God, our Law, my nation, or myself;
The last of me or no I cannot warrant.
CHORUS. Go, and the Holy One
Of Israel be thy guide
To what may serve his glory best, and spread his name
Great among the heathen round;
Send thee the angel of thy birth, to stand
Fast by thy side, who from thy father's field
Rode up in flames after his message told
Of thy conception, and be now a shield
Of fire; that Spirit that first rushed on thee
In the camp of Dan,
Be efficacious in thee now at need![5]
For never was from Heaven imparted
Measure of strength so great to mortal seed
As in thy wondrous actions hath been seen.
But wherefore comes old Manoa in such haste
With youthful steps? Much livelier than erewhile
He seems: supposing here to find his son,
Or of him bringing to us some glad news?
MANOA. Peace with you, brethren! My inducement hither
Was not at present here to find my son,
By order of the lords new parted hence
To come and play before them at their feast.
I heard all as I came; the city rings,
And numbers thither flock: I had no will,
Lest I should see him forced to things unseemly.
But that which moved my coming now was chiefly
To give ye part with me[6] what hope I have
With good success to work his liberty.
CHORUS. That hope would much rejoice us to partake
With thee. Say, reverend sire; we thirst to hear.
MANOA. I have attempted, one by one, the lords,

4. Milton's animus against paid priests, whom he considers particularly likely to contaminate the Word of God with their own private interests and worldly desires, comes out plainly here.

5. Samson's angel, appearing before his birth and at various crises during his life (Judges xiv.6,19; xv.14) is here invoked almost as a tutelary spirit or guardian angel.

6. I.e., to impart to you.

Either at home, or through the high street passing,
With supplication prone and father's tears,
To accept of ransom for my son, their prisoner.
Some much averse I found, and wondrous harsh,
Contemptuous, proud, set on revenge and spite;
That part most reverenced Dagon and his priests:
Others more moderate seeming, but their aim
Private reward, for which both God and State
They easily would set to sale: a third
More generous far and civil, who confessed
They had enough revenged having reduced
Their foe to misery beneath their fears;
The rest was magnanimity to remit,
If some convenient ransom were proposed.[7]
What noise or shout was that? It tore the sky.

CHORUS. Doubtless the people shouting to behold
Their once great dread, captive and blind before them,
Or at some proof of strength before them shown.

MANOA. His ransom, if my whole inheritance
May compass it, shall willingly be paid
And numbered down. Much rather I shall choose
To live the poorest in my tribe, than richest
And he in that calamitous prison left.
No, I am fixed not to part hence without him.
For his redemption all my patrimony,
If need be, I am ready to forgo
And quit. Not wanting him, I shall want nothing.

CHORUS. Fathers are wont to lay up for their sons;
Thou for thy son art bent to lay out all:
Sons wont to nurse their parents in old age,
Thou in old age car'st how to nurse thy son,
Made older than thy age through eyesight lost.

MANOA. It shall be my delight to tend his eyes,
And view him sitting in his house, ennobled
With all those high exploits by him achieved,
And on his shoulders waving down those locks
That of a nation armed the strength contained.
And I persuade me God hath not permitted
His strength again to grow up with his hair
Garrisoned round about him like a camp
Of faithful soldiery, were not his purpose
To use him further yet in some great service—
Not to sit idle with so great a gift
Useless, and thence ridiculous, about him.[8]
And, since his strength with eyesight was not lost,

7. The three parties are in effect bigots, swindlers, and gentlemen—three types common enough in Restoration England, with whom Milton and the defeated Puritans must have had frequently to deal.

8. A good deal of the play deals with the concept of relevance and irrelevance; outward weapons and outward strength are often beside the point ("ridiculous") in the face of inward and spiritual powers.

God will restore him eyesight to[9] his strength.
CHORUS. Thy hopes are not ill founded, nor seem vain,
Of his delivery, and thy joy thereon
Conceived, agreeable to a father's love;
In both which we, as next,[1] participate.
MANOA. I know your friendly minds, and—O, what noise!
Mercy of Heaven! what hideous noise was that?
Horribly loud, unlike the former shout.
CHORUS. Noise call you it, or universal groan,
As if the whole inhabitation perished?
Blood, death, and deathful deeds, are in that noise,
Ruin,[2] destruction at the utmost point.
MANOA. Of ruin indeed methought I heard the noise.
Oh! it continues; they have slain my son.
CHORUS. Thy son is rather slaying them; that outcry
From slaughter of one foe could not ascend.
MANOA. Some dismal accident it needs must be.
What shall we do, stay here, or run and see?
CHORUS. Best keep together here, lest, running thither,
We unawares run into danger's mouth.
This evil on the Philistines is fallen:
From whom could else a general cry be heard?
The sufferers then will scarce molest us here;
From other hands we need not much to fear.
What if, his eyesight (for to Israel's God
Nothing is hard) by miracle restored,
He now be dealing dole[3] among his foes,
And over heaps of slaughtered walk his way?
MANOA. That were a joy presumptuous to be thought.
CHORUS. Yet God hath wrought things as incredible
For his people of old; what hinders now?
MANOA. He can, I know, but doubt to think he will;
Yet hope would fain subscribe, and tempts belief.
A little stay will bring some notice hither.
CHORUS. Of good or bad so great, of bad the sooner;
For evil news rides post, while good news baits.[4]
And to our wish I see one hither speeding—
An Ebrew, as I guess, and of our tribe.
MESSENGER.[5] O, whither shall I run, or which way fly
The sight of this so horrid spectacle,
Which erst[6] my eyes beheld, and yet behold?
For dire imagination still pursues me.
But providence or instinct of nature seems,
Or reason, though disturbed, and scarce consulted,
To have guided me aright, I know not how,

9. To accompany.
1. "As next": as kinsmen.
2. From Latin *ruina*, downfall.
3. Wreaking havoc.
4. Pauses to renew (bait) the horses.
5. Greek tragedy forbade the representation on stage of actual bloodshed; a messenger is therefore a frequent figure at the end of the Greek tragedy, arriving posthaste from the scene of the final catastrophe, to deliver in a long set speech a descriptive report.
6. A moment ago.

To thee first, reverend Manoa, and to these
My countrymen, whom here I knew remaining,
As[7] at some distance from the place of horror,
So in the sad event too much concerned.

MANOA. The accident was loud, and here before thee
With rueful cry; yet what it was we hear not.
No preface needs; thou seest we long to know.

MESSENGER. It would burst forth; but I recover breath,
And sense distract, to know well what I utter.

MANOA. Tell us the sum; the circumstance defer.

MESSENGER. Gaza yet stands; but all her sons are fallen,
All in a moment overwhelmed and fallen.

MANOA. Sad, but thou know'st to Israelites not saddest
The desolation of a hostile city.

MESSENGER. Feed on that first; there may in grief be surfeit.[8]

MANOA. Relate by whom.

MESSENGER. By Samson.

MANOA. That still lessens
The sorrow, and coverts it nigh to joy.

MESSENGER. Ah! Manoa, I refrain too suddenly
To utter what will come at last too soon,
Lest evil tidings, with too rude irruption
Hitting thy agéd ear, should pierce too deep.

MANOA. Suspense in news is torture; speak them out.

MESSENGER. Then take the worst in brief: Samson is dead.

MANOA. The worst indeed! O, all my hopes defeated
To free him hence! but Death, who sets all free,
Hath paid his ransom now and full discharge.
What windy[9] joy this day had I conceived,
Hopeful of his delivery, which now proves
Abortive as the first-born bloom of spring
Nipped with the lagging rear of winter's frost!
Yet, ere I give the reins to grief, say first
How died he; death to life is crown or shame.
All by him fell, thou say'st; by whom fell he?
What glorious hand gave Samson his death's wound?

MESSENGER. Unwounded of his enemies he fell.

MANOA. Wearied with slaughter, then, or how? explain.

MESSENGER. By his own hands.

MANOA. Self-violence! What cause
Brought him so soon at variance with himself
Among his foes?

MESENGER. Inevitable cause
At once both to destroy and be destroyed.
The edifice, where all were met to see him,
Upon their heads and on his own he pulled.

MANOA. O lastly over-strong against thyself!
A dreadful way thou took'st to thy revenge.

7. The construction "As . . . So . . ." is equivalent to a "Though . . . Yet . . .".

8. I.e., there may be all too much grief to follow.

9. Empty and talky.

More than enough we know; but, while things yet
Are in confusion, give us, if thou canst,
Eyewitness of what first or last was done,
Relation more particular and distinct.

MESSENGER. Occasions drew me early to this city;
And, as the gates I entered with sunrise,
The morning trumpets festival proclaimed
Through each high street. Little I had dispatched,
When all abroad was rumored that this day
Samson should be brought forth, to show the people
Proof of his mighty strength in feats and games.
I sorrowed at his captive state, but minded
Not to be absent at that spectacle.
The building was a spacious theater,
Half round on two main pillars vaulted high,
With seats where all the lords, and each degree
Of sort,[1] might sit in order to behold;
The other side was open, where the throng
On banks and scaffolds under sky might stand: [2]
I among these aloof obscurely stood.
The feast and noon grew high, and sacrifice
Had filled their hearts with mirth, high cheer, and wine,
When to their sports they turned. Immediately
Was Samson as a public servant brought,
In their state livery clad: before him pipes
And timbrels; [3] on each side went arméd guards;
Both horse and foot before him and behind,
Archers and slingers, cataphracts [4] and spears.
At sight of him the people with a shout
Rifted the air, clamoring their god with praise,
Who had made their dreadful enemy their thrall.
He patient, but undaunted, where they led him,
Came to the place; and what was set before him,
Which without help of eye might be assayed,[5]
To heave, pull, draw, or break, he still performed
All with incredible, stupendous force,
None daring to appear antagonist.
At length, for intermission sake, they led him
Between the pillars; he his guide requested
(For so from such as nearer stood we heard),
As over-tired, to let him lean a while
With both his arms on those two massy pillars,
That to the archéd roof gave main support.
He unsuspicious led him; which when Samson
Felt in his arms, with head a while inclined,

1. Of rank.
2. The temple at Gaza comprised a covered pavilion or shell for the gentry, semi-circular in shape and supported at the center of the semi-circle by two pillars; on the open side, under the hot sun, and behind the stage, as it were, sat the common people.
3. Tambourines.
4. Armored horsemen on armored horses.
5. Attempted.

And eyes fast fixed, he stood, as one who prayed,
Or some great matter in his mind revolved:
At last, with head erect, thus cried aloud:
"Hitherto, Lords, what your commands imposed
I have performed, as reason was, obeying,
Not without wonder or delight beheld;
Now, of my own accord,[6] such other trial
I mean to show you of my strength yet greater
As with amaze shall strike all who behold."
This uttered, straining all his nerves,[7] he bowed;
As with the force of winds and waters pent
When mountains tremble,[8] those two massy pillars
With horrible convulsion to and fro
He tugged, he shook, till down they came, and drew
The whole roof after them with burst of thunder
Upon the heads of all who sat beneath,
Lords, ladies, captains, counselors, or priests,
Their choice nobility and flower, not only
Of this, but each Philistian city round,
Met from all parts to solemnize this feast.
Samson, with these immixed, inevitably
Pulled down the same destruction on himself;
The vulgar [9] only 'scaped, who stood without.

CHORUS. O dearly bought revenge, yet glorious!
Living or dying thou hast fulfilled
The work for which thou wast foretold
To Israel, and now li'st victorious
Among thy slain self-killed;
Not willingly, but tangled in the fold
Of dire Necessity,[1] whose law in death conjoined
Thee with thy slaughtered foes, in number more
Than all thy life had slain before.

SEMICHORUS. While their hearts were jocund and sublime,[2]
Drunk with idolatry, drunk with wine
And fat regorged [3] of bulls and goats,
Chaunting their idol, and preferring
Before our living Dread, who dwells
In Silo, his bright sanctuary,[4]
Among them he a spirit of frenzy sent,
Who hurt their minds,
And urged them on with mad desire
To call in haste for their destroyer.
They, only set on sport and play,

6. Latin, *mea sponte*, on spontaneous impulse of conscience.
7. Muscles.
8. Earthquakes in Milton's day were supposed to be the effect of escaping winds and waters imprisoned (pent) beneath the earth.
9. The common people.
1. Samson must not be supposed guilty of suicide. See above, lines 1586–87.
2. Joyous and exalted.
3. Greedily devoured.
4. Shiloh, where the Israelites established their tabernacle (Joshua xviii.1).

Unweetingly[5] importuned
Their own destruction to come speedy upon them.
So fond are mortal men,
Fallen into wrath divine,
As their own ruin on themselves to invite,
Insensate left, or to sense reprobate,
And with blindness internal[6] struck.

SEMICHORUS. But he, though blind of sight,
Despised, and thought extinguished quite,
With inward eyes illuminated,
His fiery virtue roused
From under ashes into sudden flame,
And as an evening dragon[7] came,
Assailant on the perchéd roosts
And nests in order ranged
Of tame villatic[8] fowl, but as an eagle
His cloudless thunder bolted on their heads.
So Virtue, given for lost,[9]
Depressed and overthrown, as seemed,
Like that self-begotten bird,[1]
In the Arabian woods embossed,[2]
That no second knows nor third,
And lay erewhile a holocaust,[3]
From out her ashy womb now teemed,
Revives, reflourishes, then vigorous most
When most unactive deemed;
And, though her body die, her fame survives,
A secular[4] bird, ages of lives.

MANOA. Come, come; no time for lamentation now,
Nor much more cause. Samson hath quit[5] himself
Like Samson, and heroicly hath finished
A life heroic, on his enemies
Fully revenged; hath left them years of mourning
And lamentation to the sons of Caphtor[6]
Through all Philistian bounds; to Israel
Honor hath left and freedom, let but them
Find courage to lay hold on this occasion;
To himself and father's house eternal fame;
And, which is best and happiest yet, all this
With God not parted from him, as was feared,
But favoring and assisting to the end.
Nothing is here for tears, nothing to wail

5. Unwittingly.
6. The play accomplishes itself by showing the internal blindness of the Philistines at the very moment of Samson's spiritual illumination.
7. Serpent (from Latin, *draco*).
8. Farmyard (from Latin, *villaticus*); "bolted": cast as a thunderbolt.
9. "Given up for lost."
1. The mythical phoenix begets itself out of its own ashes; it is unique, that is, there is only one phoenix alive at any one time, and it lives in the deserts of Arabia.
2. Enclosed, hidden.
3. A sacrifice burned whole on the altar.
4. Living through the centuries (Latin, *saecula*).
5. Acquitted.
6. In Amos ix.7 the Philistines are described as immigrants from Caphtor, i.e. Crete.

Or knock the breast; no weakness, no contempt,
Dispraise, or blame; nothing but well and fair,
And what may quiet us in a death so noble.
Let us go find the body where it lies
Soaked in his enemies' blood, and from the stream
With lavers [7] pure, and cleansing herbs, wash off
The clotted gore. I, with what speed the while [8]
(Gaza is not in plight to say us nay),
Will send for all my kindred, all my friends,
To fetch him hence, and solemnly attend,
With silent obsequy and funeral train,
Home to his father's house. There will I build him
A monument, and plant it round with shade
Of laurel ever green and branching palm,[9]
With all his trophies hung, and acts enrolled
In copious legend, or sweet lyric song.
Thither shall all the valiant youth resort,
And from his memory inflame their breasts
To matchless valor and adventures high;
The virgins also shall, on feastful days,
Visit his tomb with flowers, only bewailing
His lot unfortunate in nuptial choice,
From whence captivity and loss of eyes.
CHORUS.[1] All is best, though we oft doubt
What th' unsearchable dispose [2]
Of Highest Wisdom brings about,
And ever best found in the close.
Oft he seems to hide his face,
But unexpectedly returns,
And to his faithful champion hath in place [3]
Bore witness gloriously; whence Gaza mourns,
And all that band them to resist
His uncontrollable intent.
His servants he, with new acquist [4]
Of true experience from this great event,
With peace and consolation hath dismissed,
And calm of mind, all passion spent.

1671

7. Basins.
8. I.e., with what speed (I may) in the meanwhile.
9. Leaves of laurel were worn by civic conquerors on triumphal occasions; wreaths of palm were given to victors in the Olympic games. Samson, as both an athletic victor in his *agon* and the favored of Heaven, gets both.
1. The final chorus of the play is cast in the form of a sonnet.
2. Appointment, disposition.
3. On this very spot, at this very instant.
4. Increase, acquisition.

Seventeenth-Century Lyrics

More than most literary periods, the first half of the 17th century was rich in first-rate poets of the second rank (the phrase means simply that they were writers of evident talent with limited range or scope). There were as many as 50 or 60 of them, including some who in a less prolific age might have passed for major figures. Any narrow selection from so large a chorus is bound to appear arbitrary. The tithing who follow have been chosen to illustrate the diversity of the century, to make possible several sorts of grouping for comparison or contrast, and because they are attractive poets in their own right.

Across the arc of our chosen era, the lyric voice steadily diminished in force. Verse satire, verse argumentation, and the steadily expanding field of prose gained ground—not necessarily at the expense of lyric poetry, but by striking contrast with the diminution of the lyric. Heroic couplets and non-dramatic blank verse dominated the scene at the end of the century; they had been unknown at the beginning. Farce, travesty, burlesque, and parody rose in importance, while sonnets fell; odes were in and allegories out. Behind this constant rise and fall of forms lay fluctuations in the meaning of an ill-defined, much-used word, "wit." In the early century "wit" had been an intellectual and spiritual principle of crucial value: it aimed at binding together, at least imaginatively or metaphorically, the fragments of a disintegrating universe. Its proper work was to discover, if not to create, the chords of sympathy binding things together. Its earlier ability to do this, its present failure to cope with the new developments of the age (the new science and the new ethics) formed the theme of Donne's anxious, agonized *Anatomy of the World*. Then, during the middle of the century, the word began to diminish, to mean something like smart, antithetical writing. Under the Restoration it tended to mean raillery or repartee, and it often carried the overtone of bawdy double-entendre. It no longer held, and could not pretend to hold, the world together by the bonds of imaginative sympathy, especially when that job was already being done, far more neatly and efficiently, by Newton's three laws of motion. And so, during the last part of the 17th century, voices began to be heard, suggesting that "wit" be replaced altogether as a literary principle, its place to be taken by something called "sense" or "good sense." Much interesting literature can be produced under the aegis of good sense; but it is not likely to take the form of intense lyric utterance. Two contrasting poets of the later century cast light on the point.

Abraham Cowley, though Doctor Johnson thought him the major metaphysical poet, was so only in terms of manner. By temperament, by choice of subject, by the texture of his mind, he belongs with the argumentative and scientific poets of the age of Dryden. The "new philosophy," which so distressed Donne, formed the basis of Cowley's confident assurance; the religion which bulked so large in Donne's life is nowhere in Cowley's. He has been domesticated in the world of material evidence and rational analysis; his wit involves no spiritual dynamic. On the other hand, Thomas Traherne pursued a private vision of an innocent world so ecstatically that tensions with the real world hardly seemed to exist for him. The wit and tension of the metaphysical style, at its high points in Donne, Herbert, Crashaw and Marvell, had involved a double vision, a deep sense of strain and anxiety. Cowley, one might say, retained the metaphysical manner without its animating vision. Traherne so lost himself in the vision that he discarded the manner. In any event, the metaphysical style, like the lyric impulse as a whole, had largely faded well before the end of the 17th century.

FRANCIS BEAUMONT *and* JOHN FLETCHER
(1584–1616) (1579–1625)

Francis Beaumont and John Fletcher collaborated so intimately, on so many different plays, that they were long thought of as a single consolidated author, "Beaumont-and-Fletcher." Modern scholarship and modern analytical techniques have done much and will surely do more to disentangle the separate contributions of the two fluent, facile young men to the mass of stagecraft that still passes under their joint names. For during the few short years of their collaboration, they wrote—either together, or separately, or with other collaborators—dozens of plays of every different kind—romantic comedies, pastoral tragedies, classical-historical melodramas, broad farces, heroic romances, and a whole inventory of other types. Tradition has it that Beaumont was more the theatrical architect, who laid out the structure of the plays and ordered the action, while Fletcher specialized in dramatic set-speeches and fanciful, extravagant scenes. But in one respect, they were equally matched—as lyric poets, and it is in this capacity that they are represented here.

On the stage, where it passes quickly over the audience and cannot be recalled for second thoughts or further study, poetry must charm at first hearing. It cannot tease the audience into prolonged meditation, or test its power to catch a distant allusion. A musical accompaniment will help enormously to give the poem weight, to make it stand out against the texture of the play proper as something special. But poetry must always be very discreet in the presence of music; if it makes too many demands of its own, it will end up choking and obstructing the mood that the music aims to create. The poetry of Beaumont and Fletcher, with its clear debt to Ben Jonson, is a model of poetic work which reconciles these various demands. Simple of syntax, and undemanding in its assertions, it builds toward the creation of a mood—effortless, liquid, and poised.

Songs from *The Faithful Shepherdess*[1]

Sing His Praises That Doth Keep

Sing his praises that doth keep
  Our flocks from harm,
Pan,[2] the father of our sheep;
  And arm in arm
Tread we softly in a round,
Whilst the hollow neighboring ground
Fills the music with her sound.

Pan, O great god Pan, to thee
  Thus do we sing:
Thou that keep'st us chaste and free
  As the young spring,
Ever be thy honor spoke,
From that place the morn is broke
To that place day doth unyoke.

Shepherds All and Maidens Fair

Shepherds all and maidens fair,
Fold[3] your flocks up, for the air
'Gins to thicken, and the sun
Already his great course hath run.
See the dewdrops how they kiss
Every little flower that is,
Hanging on their velvet heads
Like a rope of crystal beads.
See the heavy clouds low falling
And bright Hesperus[4] down calling
The dead night from underground,
At whose rising mists unsound
Damps and vapors fly apace,
Hovering o'er the wanton face
Of these pastures, where they come
Striking dead doth bud and bloom.

Therefore from such danger lock
Everyone his lovéd flock,
And let your dogs lie loose without,
Lest the wolf come as a scout
From the mountain, and ere day
Bear a lamb or kid away,
Or the crafty thievish fox
Break upon your simple flocks.

1. By John Fletcher.
2. The Roman god of nature, of fields, flocks, and streams.
3. Gather into the sheepfold.
4. The evening star.

To secure yourself from these
Be not too secure in ease;
Let one eye his watches keep
Whilst the t' other eye doth sleep.
So you shall good shepherds prove
And for ever hold the love
Of our great god. Sweetest slumbers
And soft silence fall in numbers[5]
On your eyelids: so farewell,
Thus I end my evening's knell.

Do Not Fear to Put Thy Feet

Do not fear to put thy feet
Naked in the river, sweet;
Think not leech or newt or toad
Will bite thy foot when thou hast trod;
Nor let the water, rising high
As thou wad'st in, make thee cry
And sob; but ever live with me,
And not a wave shall trouble thee.

See the Day Begins to Break

See the day begins to break,
And the light shoots like a streak
Of subtle fire, the wind blows cold,
Whilst the morning doth unfold.
Now the birds begin to rouse,
And the squirrel from the boughs
Leaps to get him nuts and fruit.
The early lark, that erst[6] was mute,
Carols to the rising day
Many a note and many a lay.

1610

Songs from *Valentinian*[1]

Care-Charming Sleep

Care-charming sleep, thou easer of all woes,
Brother to death, sweetly thyself dispose
On this afflicted prince;[2] fall like a cloud
In gentle showers; give nothing that is loud
Or painful to his slumbers; easy, sweet,
And as a purling stream, thou son of Night,
Pass by his troubled senses; sing his pain
Like hollow murmuring wind or silver rain.

5. In cadence, metrically.
6. Once, formerly.
1. By John Fletcher.
2. The song is sung over Valentinian ("this afflicted prince") in the play.

Into this prince gently, oh gently slide,
And kiss him into slumbers like a bride.

Hear, Ye Ladies That Despise

Hear, ye ladies that despise
What the mighty Love has done;
Fear examples, and be wise:
Fair Callisto was a nun;
Leda, sailing on the stream
To deceive the hopes of man,
Love accounting but a dream,
Doted on a silver swan;
Danaë, in a brazen tower
Where no love was, loved a shower.[3]

Hear, ye ladies that are coy,
What the mighty Love can do,
Fear the fierceness of the boy:[4]
The chaste Moon he makes to woo;
Vesta, kindling holy fires,
Circled round about with spies,
Never dreaming loose desires,
Doting at the altar dies.[5]
Ilion, in a short hour, higher
He can build, and once more fire.[6]

ca. 1612

Lovers, Rejoice![7]

Lovers, rejoice! your pains shall be rewarded,
The god of Love himself grieves at your crying;
No more shall frozen honor be regarded,
Nor the coy faces of a maid denying.
No more shall virgins sigh, and say, "We dare not,
For men are false and what they do they care not."
All shall be well again; then do not grieve,
Men shall be true, and women shall believe.

3. All three ladies were victims of Zeus. Callisto was vowed to the service of Diana, who demanded chastity of her followers; Zeus raped her, then, in the shape of a swan, seduced Leda, and in the shape of a shower of gold overcame Danaë, who had been locked up in a brass tower.

4. I.e., Cupid, who made Diana herself, goddess of the moon and of chastity, fall in love with Endymion.

5. Here not the Roman goddess of that name, but a Vestal Virgin, vowed to chastity and faithful to her vows, who fades away as a result of longings unknown even to herself.

6. Set on fire. Troy ("Ilion") is said to have been destroyed by Cupid because he instigated the act of Paris in stealing Helen of Troy from her husband Menelaus, thereby setting off the Trojan War.

7. From *Cupid's Revenge* by Beaumont or Fletcher or both, with the help of Philip Massinger and perhaps Nathaniel Field.

Lovers, rejoice! what you shall say henceforth
When you have caught your sweethearts in your arms
Shall be accounted oracle and worth;
No more fainthearted girls shall dream of harms,
And cry they are too young; the god hath said,
Fifteen shall make a mother of a maid:
Then, wise men, pull your roses yet unblown,
Love hates the too-ripe fruit that falls alone.

ca. 1612

Songs from *The Masque of the Inner Temple and Gray's Inn*[1]

Shake Off Your Heavy Trance

Shake off your heavy trance,
  And leap into a dance,
Such as no mortals use[2] to tread,
  Fit only for Apollo[3]
To play to, for the moon to lead,
  And all the stars to follow.

Ye Should Stay Longer If We Durst

Ye should stay longer if we durst.
Away! Alas, that he that first
Gave Time wild wings to fly away
Hath now no power to make him stay.
But though these games must needs be played,
I would this pair, when they are laid,[4]
  And not a creature nigh them,
Could catch his scythe as he doth pass,
And cut his wings and break his glass,[5]
  And keep him ever by them.

Peace and Silence Be the Guide

Peace and silence be the guide
To the man and to the bride!
If there be a joy yet new
In marriage, let it fall on you,
  That all the world may wonder.
If we should stay, we should do worse,
And turn our blessing to a curse,
  By keeping you asunder.

1613

1. By Francis Beaumont.
2. Are accustomed.
3. God of poetry in Greek mythology.
4. I.e., laid to rest.
5. Time traditionally carries a scythe and an hourglass, and flies on swift wings, because he mows things down, measures their duration, and flees away much too fast.

The Passionate Man's Song[1]

Hence all you vain delights,
As short as are the nights
Wherein you spend your folly:
There's naught in this life sweet,
If man were wise to see't,
But only melancholy,
Oh sweetest melancholy.
Welcome, folded arms and fixéd eyes,
A sigh that, piercing, mortifies,
A look that's fastened to the ground,
A tongue chained up without a sound.

Fountain heads and pathless groves,
Places which pale passion loves,
Moonlight walks, when all the fowls
Are warmly housed, save bats and owls,
A midnight bell, a parting groan,
These are the sounds we feed upon.
Then stretch our bones in a still-gloomy valley,
Nothing's so dainty sweet as lovely melancholy.

ca. 1620 1647

1. From *The Nice Valor,* by John Fletcher. This song clearly had an influence on both the form and thought of Milton's *L'Allegro* and *Il Penseroso.*

THOMAS CAREW

(1595–1640)

Bright, talented, and idle, Thomas Carew (pronounced *Carey*) carefully avoided serious work of all sorts; everything he did, and writing poetry particularly, seemed to be the diversion of his empty hours. Yet he was the first poet (and remains, with Marvell, one of the two poets) to unite the intellectual toughness of metaphysical verse with the polish and elegant lightness cultivated by the followers of Jonson.

As the son of a distinguished lawyer, Carew was himself destined for the law, but the Middle Temple dismissed him for idleness. He tried the diplomatic corps, but was sent home in disgrace for "levity." He became a hanger-on around the court, and ultimately (his most solemn employment) a gentleman of the bedchamber; his diversions were pretty girls, bowling, and versifying—apparently in that order. Yet when his poems were collected, after his death, they turned out to include some of the wittiest and most elegant verses of the century.

Everything that the Puritans despised in "wit" was epitomized in Carew. He had no high spiritual seriousness at all; he was not, in the solemn sense, "sincere." Many of his poems were obvious bits of light persiflage, "mere" amusements. He was not only clever, he was by 17th-century standards (and even more by those of the 19th century) obscene. Yet somehow this libidinous trifler managed to say more true things in his *Elegy on the Death of Doctor Donne* than criticism would be able to enunciate in the next three hundred years. And in *A Rapture* he expressed, naturally and joyously, a side of life that Puritanism would, to the best of its ability, swathe in black crape and hypocrisy for an equivalent length of time.

An Elegy upon the Death of the Dean of Paul's, Dr. John Donne[1]

Can we not force from widowed poetry,
Now thou art dead, great Donne, one elegy
To crown thy hearse? Why yet did we not trust,
Though with unkneaded dough-baked prose, thy dust,
Such as the unscissored[2] lect'rer from the flower
Of fading rhetoric, short-lived as his hour,
Dry as the sand that measures it,[3] should lay
Upon the ashes on the funeral day?
Have we nor tune, nor voice? Didst thou dispense
Through all our language both words and sense?
'Tis sad truth. The pulpit may her plain
And sober Christian precepts still retain;
Doctrines it may, and wholesome uses, frame,
Grave homilies and lectures; but the flame
Of thy brave soul, that shot such heat and light
As burnt our earth and made our darkness bright,
Committed holy rapes upon our will,
Did through the eye the melting heart distil,
And the deep knowledge of dark truths so teach
As sense might judge what fancy could not reach,[4]
Must be desired forever. So the fire
That fills with spirit and heat the Delphic choir,[5]
Which, kindled first by thy Promethean[6] breath,
Glowed here a while, lies quenched now in thy death.
The Muses' garden, with pedantic weeds
O'erspread, was purged by thee; the lazy seeds
Of servile imitation thrown away,

1. First appearing in the 1633 edition of Donne's poems, this elegy was described as by "Mr. Tho: Carie." It was reprinted in the 1640 edition of Carew's poems, from which our text is taken.
2. I.e., with uncut hair. Whether from grief, poverty, or in imitation of Apollo is not clear.
3. The hourglass was used by preachers to keep track of time.
4. I.e., so that things too abstract and elevated even to be imagined might be made plain to sense. "Desired": missed.
5. The choir of poets, inspired by Apollo, whose oracle used to be at Delphi.
6. Donne stole fire from heaven, like Prometheus, and used it to fill with spirit and heat the choir of poets.

And fresh invention planted; thou didst pay
The debts of our penurious bankrupt age—
Licentious thefts, that make poetic rage
A mimic fury, when our souls must be
Possessed, or with Anacreon's ecstasy,
Or Pindar's,[7] not their own. The subtle cheat
Of sly exchanges, and the juggling feat
Of two-edged words,[8] or whatsoever wrong
By ours was done the Greek or Latin tongue,
Thou hast redeemed, and opened us a mine
Of rich and pregnant fancy, drawn a line
Of masculine expression, which had good
Old Orpheus[9] seen, or all the ancient brood
Our superstitious fools admire, and hold
Their lead more precious than thy burnished gold,
Thou hadst been their exchequer, and no more
They in each other's dung had raked for ore.
Thou shalt yield no precedence, but of time
And the blind fate of language, whose tuned chime
More charms the outward sense; yet thou mayest claim
From so great disadvantage greater fame,
Since to the awe of thy imperious wit
Our troublesome language bends, made only fit
With her tough thick-ribbed hoops, to gird about
Thy giant fancy, which had proved too stout
For their soft melting phrases. As in time
They had the start, so did they cull the prime
Buds of invention many a hundred year,
And left the rifled fields, besides the fear
To touch their harvest; yet from those bare lands
Of what is only thine, thy only hands
(And that their smallest work) have gleaned more
Than all those times and tongues could reap before.
  But thou art gone, and thy strict laws will be
Too hard for libertines in poetry.
They will repeal[1] the goodly exiled train
Of gods and goddesses, which in thy just reign
Were banished nobler poems; now with these
The silenced tales in the *Metamorphoses*[2]
Shall stuff their lines and swell the windy page,
Till verse, refined by thee in this last age,

7. Anacreon (6th and 5th centuries B.C.) and Pindar (first half of the 5th century B.C.) were famous Greek lyric poets.

8. "Sly exchanges": Carew seems to refer to the habit, frequent in Jonsonian and Miltonic style, of using English words in their Latin senses, e.g., "horrid (bristling) spears." "Two-edged words" might be puns; but as these were a favorite device of Donne's, this cannot be the sense. Perhaps "two-edged words" are not far from "sly exchanges" in meaning.

9. Ancient Greek poet and prophet, so mythical that he is often used as the type of all poets.

1. Recall, as from banishment.

2. Ovid's tales in the *Metamorphoses* had been a favorite stockpile of poetical properties for Renaissance poets; Donne forwent them, but soon they will return.

Turn ballad-rhyme, or those old idols be
Adored again with new apostasy.
O pardon me, that break with untuned verse
The reverend silence that attends thy hearse,
Whose awful[3] solemn murmurs were to thee,
More than these faint lines, a loud elegy,
That did proclaim in a dumb eloquence
The death of all the arts, whose influence,
Grown feeble, in these panting numbers lies
Gasping short-winded accents, and so dies:
So doth the swiftly turning wheel not stand
In th' instant we withdraw the moving hand,
But some small time retain a faint weak course
By virtue of the first impulsive force;
And so whilst I cast on thy funeral pile
Thy crown of bays,[4] oh, let it crack awhile
And spit disdain, till the devouring flashes
Suck all the moisture up; then turn to ashes.
I will not draw the envy to engross
All thy perfections, or weep all the loss;
Those are too numerous for one elegy,
And this too great to be expressed by me.
Let others carve the rest; it shall suffice
I on thy grave this epitaph incise:

Here lies a king, that ruled as he thought fit
The universal monarchy of wit;
Here lie two flamens,[5] *and both those the best:*
Apollo's[6] *first, at last the true God's priest.*

1633, 1640

Disdain Returned

He that loves a rosy cheek,
Or a coral lip admires,
Or from starlike eyes doth seek
Fuel to maintain his fires;
As old Time makes these decay,
So his flames must waste away.

But a smooth and steadfast mind,
Gentle thoughts and calm desires,
Hearts with equal love combined,
Kindle never-dying fires.
Where these are not, I despise
Lovely cheeks, or lips, or eyes.

3. I.e., awed.
4. The poet's crown.
5. Priests of the Roman religion.
6. I.e., of the god of poetry.

No tears, Celia, now shall win
  My resolved heart to return;
I have searched thy soul within,
  And find naught but pride and scorn;
I have learned thy arts, and now
  Can disdain as much as thou.
Some power, in my revenge convey
That love to her I cast away.[7]

1640

A Song

Ask me no more where Jove bestows,
When June is past, the fading rose;
For in your beauties orient deep,[1]
These flowers, as in their causes, sleep.[2]

Ask me no more whither do stray
The golden atoms of the day;
For in pure love heaven did prepare
Those powders to enrich your hair.

Ask me no more whither doth haste
The nightingale when May is past;
For in your sweet dividing[3] throat
She winters, and keeps warm her note.

Ask me no more where those stars light,
That downwards fall in dead of night;
For in your eyes they sit, and there
Fixéd become, as in their sphere.

Ask me no more if east or west
The phoenix builds her spicy nest;[4]
For unto you at last she flies,
And in your fragrant bosom dies.

1640

7. I.e., to a previous mistress.

1. The text permits two readings here: "in your beauties which are orient deep" or "in the orient depths of your beauty." In addition to its reference to the Far East, "orient" implies "pearly" or "lustrous."

2. Aristotelian philosophy suggested that objects often lay latent in their causes—e.g., that in the seed creating man there was a little man (*homunculus*). In Carew's compliment, the lady is a summation of last summer and cause of the next one.

3. Harmonious (from the "division," or musical trill).

4. The phoenix, an Arabian bird, builds her nest from spicy shrubs. She dies every thousand years and a new bird springs from her ashes.

To Ben Jonson

Upon occasion of his Ode of Defiance annexed to his play of The New Inn[1]

'Tis true, dear Ben, thy just chastising hand
Hath fixed upon the sotted age a brand
To their swoll'n pride and empty scribbling due.
It can nor judge nor write; and yet 'tis true
Thy comic Muse from the exalted line
Touched by thy *Alchemist*[2] doth since decline
From that her zenith, and foretells a red
And blushing evening when she goes to bed—
Yet such as shall outshine the glimmering light
With which all stars shall gild the following night.
Nor think it much (since all thy eaglets may
Endure the sunny trial)[3] if we say,
This hath the stronger wing, or that doth shine
Tricked up in fairer plumes, since all are thine.
Who hath his flock of cackling geese compared
With thy tuned choir of swans? or else who dared
To call thy births deformed? But if thou bind
By city-custom, or by gavel-kind,[4]
In equal shares thy love on all thy race,
We may distinguish of their sex and place:
Though one hand form them and though one brain strike
Souls into all, they are not all alike.
Why should the follies then of this dull age
Draw from thy pen such an immodest rage
As seems to blast thy else-immortal bays,[5]
When thine own tongue proclaims thy itch of praise?
Such thirst will argue drought. No, let be hurled
Upon thy works by the detracting world
What malice can suggest; let the rout say
The running sands that, ere thou make a play,
Count the slow minutes might a Goodwin frame[6]
To swallow when th' hast done thy shipwrecked name.

1. Jonson's late play *The New Inn* was hissed from the stage in 1629 and published in 1631 with an angry "Ode of Defiance" prefixed. Carew's remonstration must have been written close upon that event.
2. Jonson's play (1610) about three confidence tricksters.
3. To make sure the young birds in his nest are genuine eaglets, the eagle is reputed to fly with them up toward the sun; any bird that isn't an authentic eagle is blinded by the rays.
4. "City-custom" (i.e., London city custom) and "gavel-kind" (a system of land tenure once common in Kent) were two legal ways of dividing an estate equally among all the heirs—as opposed to the normal English rule of primogeniture (everything to the eldest son).
5. Bays or laurel make up the poet's crown.
6. Goodwin Sands were a sandbar, shifty and treacherous, on which many ships were lost. Jonson's slowness in composition was proverbial.

Let them the dear[7] expense of oil upbraid,
Sucked by thy watchful lamp that hath betrayed
To theft the blood of martyred authors, spilt
Into thy ink, while thou growest pale with guilt.[8]
Repine not at the taper's thrifty waste,
That sleeks thy terser poems; nor is haste
Praise, but excuse; and if thou overcome
A knotty writer, bring the booty home;
Nor think it theft if the rich spoils so torn
From conquered authors be as trophies worn.
Let others glut on the extorted praise
Of vulgar breath: trust thou to after days.
Thy labored works shall live when Time devours
Th' abortive offspring of their hasty hours.
Thou art not of their rank, the quarrel lies
Within thine own verge[9]—then let this suffice,
The wiser world doth greater thee confess
Than all men else, than thy self only less.

ca. 1631 1640

A Rapture

I will enjoy thee now, my Celia, come
And fly with me to love's Elysium.[1]
The giant, Honor, that keeps cowards out,
Is but a masquer,[2] and the servile rout
Of baser subjects only bend in vain
To the vast idol, whilst the nobler train
Of valiant lovers daily sail between
The huge Colossus' legs,[3] and pass unseeen
Unto the blissful shore. Be bold and wise,
And we shall enter; the grim Swiss[4] denies
Only tame fools a passage, that not know
He is but form and only frights in show
The duller eyes that look from far; draw near,
And thou shalt scorn what we were wont to fear.
We shall see how the stalking pageant[5] goes
With borrowed legs, a heavy load to those
That made and bear him—not as we once thought
The seed of gods, but a weak model wrought

7. Extravagant.
8. The other great charge against Jonson was that he copied or translated too liberally from other authors.
9. I.e., within your own territory, against yourself. Duels cannot properly take place between two men of different rank, and as Jonson is out of everyone else's class, he can only fight himself.
1. In classical mythology, the abode of the blessed spirits.
2. I.e., a play-actor. "Rout": crowd.
3. The ancient Colossus of Rhodes bestrode the entrance to that harbor, so that ships entering or leaving passed between its legs.
4. The Pope's Swiss Guard were so picturesque that the adjective came in time to stand for the noun.
5. Figure in a pageant, make-believe giant.

By greedy men, that seek to enclose the common,
And within private arms empale free woman.[6]
  Come then, and mounted on the wings of love,
We'll cut the flitting air and soar above
The monster's head, and in the noblest seats
Of those blessed shades, quench and renew our heats.
There shall the Queen of Love, and Innocence,
Beauty, and Nature banish all offense
From our close ivy twines, there I'll behold
Thy baréd snow and thy unbraided gold.
There my enfranchised hand on every side
Shall o'er thy naked polished ivory slide.
No curtain there, though of transparent lawn,[7]
Shall be before thy virgin treasure drawn,
But the rich mine to the enquiring eye
Exposed, shall ready still for mintage lie,
And we will coin young Cupids.[8] There a bed
Of roses and fresh myrtles shall be spread
Under the cooler shade of cypress groves;
Our pillows, of the down of Venus' doves,[9]
Whereon our panting limbs we'll gently lay
In the faint respites of our active play,
That so our slumbers may in dreams have leisure
To tell the nimble fancy our past pleasure,
And so our souls that cannot be embraced
Shall the embraces of our bodies taste.
Meanwhile the bubbling stream shall court the shore,
Th' enamored chirping wood-choir shall adore
In varied tunes the Deity of Love;
The gentle blasts of western winds shall move
The trembling leaves, and through their close boughs breathe
Still music, while we rest ourselves beneath
Their dancing shade; till a soft murmur, sent
From souls entranced in amorous languishment
Rouse us, and shoot into our veins fresh fire
Till we in their sweet ecstasy expire.
  Then, as the empty bee, that lately bore
Into the common treasure all her store,
Flies 'bout the painted field with nimble wing,
Deflowering the fresh virgins of the spring,
So will I rifle all the sweets that dwell
In my delicious paradise, and swell
My bag with honey, drawn forth by the power
Of fervent kisses from each spicy flower.
I'll seize the rose buds in their perfumed bed,

6. To "empale" is to surround with a fence, but the word has phallic overtones as well.

7. Fine linen.

8. Behind this metaphor of mine-mint-and-coin lies the ancient belief that in the creation of children woman contributes matter, man form (*materia* and *forma*).

9. Venus, when she travels, rides in a chariot drawn by a yoke of doves.

The violet knots, like curious mazes spread
O'er all the garden, taste the ripened cherry,
The warm, firm apple, tipped with coral berry.
Then will I visit with a wandering kiss
The vale of lilies and the bower of bliss,
And where the beauteous region both divide
Into two milky ways, my lips shall slide
Down those smooth alleys, wearing as I go
A track for lovers on the printed snow.
Thence climbing o'er the swelling Apennine,
Retire into thy grove of eglantine,
Where I will all those ravished sweets distill
Through love's alembic,[1] and with chemic skill
From the mixed mass one sovereign balm[2] derive,
Then bring that great elixir to thy hive.
Now in more subtle wreaths I will entwine
My sinewy thighs, my legs and arms with thine;
Thou like a sea of milk shalt lie displayed,
Whilst I the smooth, calm Océan invade
With such a tempest as when Jove of old
Fell down on Danaë in a storm of gold.[3]
Yet my tall pine shall in the Cyprian strait
Ride safe at anchor and unlade her freight;
My rudder with thy bold hand like a tried
And skillful pilot thou shalt steer, and guide
My bark[4] into love's channel, where it shall
Dance as the bounding waves do rise or fall.
Then shall thy circling arms embrace and clip
My willing body, and thy balmy lip
Bathe me in juice of kisses, whose perfume
Like a religious incense shall consume
And send up holy vapors to those powers
That bless our loves and crown our sportful hours,
That with such halcyon calmness fix our souls
In steadfast peace, as no affright controls.
There no rude sounds shake us with sudden starts,
No jealous ears, when we unrip our hearts,
Suck our discourse in, no observing spies
This blush, that glance traduce; no envious eyes
Watch our close meetings, nor are we betrayed
To rivals by the bribéd chambermaid.
No wedlock bonds unwreathe our twisted loves,
We seek no midnight arbor, no dark groves

1. I.e., retort—a vessel used for distilling.
2. According to alchemical doctrine, skilled distillation could extract from common metals not only the philosopher's stone but a supreme ointment ("sovereign balm"), good to prevent as well as to cure all diseases whatever.
3. In ancient mythology Zeus (or Jove) wooed Danaë in a shower of gold, thereby begetting Perseus. "Pine": mast, and by metonymy, ship; "Cyprian": Cyprus was reputed the birthplace of the goddess of love, sometimes called simply "the Cyprian."
4. Vessel.

To hide our kisses; there the hated name
Of husband, wife, lust, modest, chaste, or shame
Are vain and empty words, whose very sound
Was never heard in the Elysian ground.
All things are lawful there that may delight
Nature or unrestrainéd appetite.
Like and enjoy, to will and act is one;
We only sin when love's rites are not done.
  The Roman Lucrece there reads the divine
Lectures of love's great master, Aretine,
And knows as well as Laïs how to move
Her pliant body in the act of love.[5]
To quench the burning ravisher, she hurls
Her limbs into a thousand winding curls,
And studies artful postures, such as be
Carved on the bark of every neighboring tree
By learned hands, that so adorned the rind
Of those fair plants, which, as they lay entwined
Have fanned their glowing fires. The Grecian dame
That in her endless web toiled for a name
As fruitless as her work doth there display
Herself before the youth of Ithaca,
And th' amorous sport of gamesome nights prefer
Before dull dreams of the lost traveler.[6]
Daphne hath broke her bark, and that swift foot
Which th' angry gods had fastened with a root
To the fixed earth, doth now unfettered run
To meet th' embraces of the youthful sun.[7]
She hangs upon him like his Delphic lyre,[8]
Her kisses blow the old and breath new fire;
Full of her god, she sings inspired lays,
Sweet odes of love, such as deserve the bays
Which she herself was.[9] Next her, Laura lies
In Petrarch's learnéd arms, drying those eyes
That did in such sweet smooth-paced numbers flow,
As made the world enamored of his woe.[1]

5. In Elysium, Lucrece (chastest of Roman matrons, who committed suicide to atone for the disgrace of her rape by Tarquin) reads Aretino (bawdiest of Italian pornographers), to provoke her attacker to new efforts. Laïs was a famous prostitute of Corinth.

6. Penelope was the faithful wife of Odysseus ("the lost traveler"); during the twenty years he was away (at Troy, and on the way back), she fended off her importunate suitors by weaving an endless web—she unwove by night what she wove by day—which she said she had to finish before she could marry again. But in Elysium, she welcomes "the youth of Ithaca" (the suitors) and enjoys "gamesome nights" with them.

7. Closely pursued by Apollo, god of poetry and the sun, Daphne with the help of Zeus turned into a laurel bush or bay tree to get away from him.

8. The shrine of Apollo was at Delphi; he carries a lyre as an emblem of poetic harmony.

9. The songs she sings deserve the crown of poetry, woven of laurel or bays; but she herself was a laurel or bay tree.

1. Whether Laura was a real lady or a laurel bush (hence an emblem of poetry) is still in dispute; but Petrarch (1304–74) wrote melancholy poems to and about her, and she was a martyr to honor.

These and ten thousand beauties more, that died
Slave to the tyrant,[2] now enlarged, deride
His canceled laws, and for their time misspent
Pay into love's exchequer double rent.
  Come then, my Celia, we'll no more forbear
To taste our joys, struck with a panic fear,
But will depose from his imperious sway
This proud usurper and walk free as they,
With necks unyoked; nor is it just that he
Should fetter your soft sex with chastity
Which nature made unapt for abstinence;
When yet this false impostor can dispense
With human justice and with sacred right,
And maugre[3] both their laws, command me fight
With rivals or with emulous loves, that dare
Equal with thine their mistress' eyes or hair.
If thou complain of wrong, and call my sword
To carve out thy revenge, upon that word
He[4] bids me fight and kill, or else he brands
With marks of infamy my coward hands.
And yet religion bids from bloodshed fly,
And damns me for that act. Then tell me why
This goblin Honor which the world adores
Should make men atheists and not women whores.[5]

1640

2. The tyrant is Honor; the inhabitants of Elysium are "enlarged" (i.e., liberated) from him.
3. In spite of.
4. I.e., Honor.
5. These last two and a half lines of the poem cast some curious reflections on the first 164.

EDMUND WALLER
(1606–1687)

Edmund Waller was born to money, and through his long life got steadily richer; he went to parliament very early, and stayed there (when the distractions of the times permitted) till he was a very old man. In politics he was a moderate Royalist, but without the strength of character or intellect to play a leading role in public affairs.

In poetry too, Waller was a moderating and softening influence. His verses, first published in 1645 while he was in exile, then republished and expanded just before his death, enjoyed an enormous popularity which nowadays we find hard to explain. At first glance they seem mostly remarkable for their negative qualities. A poem like *The Story of Phoebus and Daphne Applied* is not ingenious or strained in its thinking, but it is not "natural" either—on the contrary, it is highly artificial. Its diction is formal, almost mannered. Its couplets are metrically smooth, frequently end-stopped, and full of balanced antitheses; the caesura is used artfully from time to time to break up the roll of the pentameters, and balance one half-line against another. The poem has "point" in the sense that one word or locution constantly works against another; occasionally it rises to a kind of verbal "counter-point." Waller was one of the first Englishmen to write this way. Though his style drew a little from Donne and a lot from Jonson, though in his lighter lyric moments he sounds a good deal like Carew, he really was a pioneer. And thus the Restoration poets were quite right when they honored old Mr. Waller as one of the chief "improvers of our numbers"—by which they meant that he had brought a new correctness to English metrics and diction. Perhaps Waller had less intellectual energy to be mastered than did earlier poets; but the degree and manner of his mastery were in themselves widely influential.

The Story of Phoebus and Daphne Applied[1]

Thyrsis, a youth of the inspiréd train,
Fair Sacharissa loved, but loved in vain;[2]
Like Phoebus sung the no less amorous boy;
Like Daphne she, as lovely and as coy.
With numbers[3] he the flying nymph pursues,
With numbers such as Phoebus' self might use.
Such is the chase when love and fancy leads
O'er craggy mountains and through flowery meads,[4]
Invoked to testify the lover's care
Or form some image of his cruel fair.
Urged with his fury, like a wounded deer,
O'er these he fled; and now approaching near,
Had reached the nymph with his harmonious lay,
Whom all his charms could not incline to stay.
Yet what he sung in his immortal strain,
Though unsuccessful, was not sung in vain.
All but the nymph that should redress his wrong
Attend his passion and approve his song.
Like Phoebus thus, acquiring unsought praise,
He catched at love, and filled his arms with bays.

1645

1. Phoebus (Apollo, god of poetry) fell in love with Daphne, and pursued her till Zeus, to save her, turned her into a laurel tree; the laurel, or bay tree is, accordingly, an emblem of poetic fame, and successful poets are crowned with laurel leaves ("bays").

2. Since Sacharissa is the constant name of Waller's beloved, it is a fair presumption that Thyrsis is himself. "A youth of the inspiréd train" is poetic diction for a poet, as "cruel fair," below, is for a mistress. The boy is "no less amorous" than Phoebus, the girl just as "coy" (unwilling) as Daphne.

3. Poetic diction for verses.

4. Meadows. The craggy mountains represent the lover's griefs, the flowery meadows (by neat antithesis) his mistress's beauty.

Song

Go, lovely rose!
Tell her that wastes her time and me
That now she knows,
When I resemble[1] her to thee,
How sweet and fair she seems to be.

Tell her that's young,
And shuns to have her graces spied,
That hadst thou sprung
In deserts, where no men abide,
Thou must have uncommended died.

Small is the worth
Of beauty from the light retired;
Bid her come forth,
Suffer herself to be desired,
And not blush so to be admired.

Then die! that she
The common fate of all things rare
May read in thee;
How small a part of time they share
That are so wondrous sweet and fair!

1645

On a Girdle

That which her slender waist confined,
Shall now my joyful temples bind;
No monarch but would give his crown,
His arms might do what this has done.

It was my heaven's extremest sphere,[2]
The pale[3] which held that lovely deer;
My joy, my grief, my hope, my love
Did all within this circle move!

A narrow compass! and yet there
Dwelt all that's good, and all that's fair;
Give me but what this ribbon bound,
Take all the rest the sun goes round! [4]

1686

1. Compare.
2. The last of the nine concentric crystalline spheres which, according to Ptolemaic astronomy, made up the universe. Hence, the lady's outermost garment.
3. Fence encircling a park. There is, of course. a pun on "deer" in this line.
4. The version of this poem printed in 1645 substituted "Do" for "Did" in line 8, and gave the last couplet as: "Give me but what this ribbon tied, / Take all the sun goes round beside."

Of English Verse[1]

Poets may boast, as safely vain,
Their works shall with the world remain;
Both bound together live and die,
The verses and the prophecy.

But who can hope his lines should long
Last in a daily changing tongue?
While they are new, envy prevails,
And as that dies, our language fails.

When architects have done their part,
The matter may betray their art;
Time, if we use ill-chosen stone,
Soon brings a well-built palace down.

Poets that lasting marble seek
Must carve in Latin or in Greek;
We write in sand, our language grows,
And like the tide our work o'erflows.

Chaucer his sense can only boast,
The glory of his numbers[2] lost!
Years have defaced his matchless strain;
And yet he did not sing in vain.

The beauties which adorned that age,
The shining subjects of his rage,[3]
Hoping they should immortal prove,
Rewarded with success his love.

This was the generous poet's scope,
And all an English pen can hope,
To make the fair approve his flame
That can so far extend their name.

Verse thus designed has no ill fate
If it arrive but at the date
Of fading beauty, if it prove
But as long-lived as present love.

1686

1. To understand Waller's deprecatory attitude toward English poetry, we must recall that in his day modern English was very new, and was still acquiring new words, forms, and usages at a rapid pace. We write in sand, he says, the tide of language rises, and overflows our work. In those days it was true.

2. Metrics, versification. The belief that Chaucer's versification was hopelessly obsolete led to such ventures as Dryden's "translation" of some of his *Canterbury Tales* into modern (i.e., 17th-century) English.

3. Poetic fury, inspiration. As it calls attention to its own artifice, the word "rage" is a piece of poetic diction.

Of the Last Verses in the Book

When we for age could neither read nor write,
The subject made us able to indite;
The soul, with nobler resolutions decked,
The body stooping, does herself erect.
No mortal parts are requisite to raise
Her that, unbodied, can her Maker praise.
The seas are quiet when the winds give o'er;
So calm are we when passions are no more!
For then we know how vain it was to boast
Of fleeting things, so certain to be lost.
Clouds of affection[4] from our younger eyes
Conceal that emptiness which age descries.
The soul's dark cottage, battered and decayed,
Lets in new light through the chinks that time has made;
Stronger by weakness, wiser men become,
As they draw near to their eternal home.
Leaving the old, both worlds at once they view,
That stand upon the threshold of the new.

1686

4. Passion.

SIR JOHN SUCKLING
(1609–1642)

"Natural, easy Suckling," says Millamant rapturously, in Congreve's comedy, *The Way of the World*; he is her ideal of a poet, one who does not take the whole business very seriously. "Brisk" was the adjective that his contemporaries generally applied to Sir John. He was a small man physically, a wit, a gamester, and a courtier, who when he turned to poetry imitated and exaggerated the informal, colloquial qualities of Donne. Many years before, Baldassare Castiglione in his dialogue *The Courtier* (1528) had emphasized a certain fine carelessness ("*sprezzatura*") as the natural quality of a great gentleman. It meant that no matter how hard one had worked on some accomplishment—a poem, a costume, swordsmanship—one should treat it always as if it were a natural, easy, spontaneous action. Sir John Suckling, above all the other "Cavalier" poets who gallantly supported the lost cause of Charles Stuart, cultivated this special quality of instinctive, careless poise. Sometimes, indeed, like a Restoration fop, he seems so careful about being careless that the substance of his discourse goes by the board. But his gay trifles have remained current in the language as some others have not; he is the prototype of the Cavalier playboy.

Song

Why so pale and wan, fond lover?
Prithee, why so pale?
Will, when looking well can't move her,
Looking ill prevail?
Prithee, why so pale?

Why so dull and mute, young sinner?
Prithee, why so mute?
Will, when speaking well can't win her,
Saying nothing do't?
Prithee, why so mute?

Quit, quit, for shame; this will not move,
This cannot take her.
If of herself she will not love,
Nothing can make her:
The devil take her!

1638

Loving and Beloved

There never yet was honest man
That ever drove the trade of love.
It is impossible, nor can
Integrity our ends promove;[1]
For kings and lovers are alike in this,
That their chief art in reign dissembling is.

Here we are loved and there we love,
Good nature now and passion strive
Which of the two should be above
And laws unto the other give.
So we false fire with art sometimes discover,
And the true fire with the same art do cover.

What rack[2] can fancy find so high?
Here we must court and here engage,
Though in the other place we die.
O! 'tis torture all and cozenage:
And which the harder is I cannot tell,
To hide true love, or make false love look well.

Since it is thus, God of desire,
Give me my honesty again,

1. Promote, move forward.
2. Torture. The thought is, what agony can we imagine so extreme as this, to be obliged by the affections of one girl while ourselves loving another?

And take thy brands back and thy fire;
I'm weary of the state I'm in:
Since (if the very best should now befall),
Love's triumph must be Honor's funeral.

1646

Out upon It!

Out upon it! I have loved
Three whole days together;
And am like to love three more,
If it prove fair weather.

Time shall molt away his wings,
Ere he shall discover
In the whole wide world again
Such a constant lover.

But the spite on 't is, no praise
Is due at all to me:
Love with me had made no stays
Had it any been but she.

Had it any been but she,
And that very face,
There had been at least ere this
A dozen dozen in her place.

1659

RICHARD LOVELACE
(1618–1657)

Richard Lovelace and Sir John Suckling are commonly bracketed together as the leaders of the "Cavalier" poets; and though they were quite different, both as men and as writers, there is no injustice in the conjunction. Both men fought and suffered for the king; both wrote gallant verses. Perhaps one feels a little more substance in the work of Lovelace; but perhaps that is simply because he was lucky enough to live a little longer. He is best known for his poems of clarion resolution:

Stone walls do not a prison make,
Nor iron bars a cage,

but he is also an affectionate observer of, and gentle moralizer upon, the little creatures—snails, ants, grasshoppers.

Lovelace was born of an old and wealthy Kentish family, and educated at Oxford; he was an attractive, handsome, and witty young man, the very model of a courtier. King Charles and Queen Henrietta Maria admired his demeanor so much, when they visited Oxford in 1636, that they had him created M.A. on the spot. But the Civil Wars were hard on him; he fought bravely, was imprisoned, exiled, wounded while serving as a soldier of fortune abroad, imprisoned again in England, and finally released, penniless and unemployed. His death followed shortly. Lovelace published *Lucasta* in 1649, and a posthumous volume appeared in 1659, with his remaining writings. A special point of interest about Lovelace is that he was one of the few English writers of the 17th century to be seriously concerned with the art of painting and the appreciation of good pictures, to which he thought his countrymen disgracefully blind.

To Althea, from Prison

When Love with unconfinéd wings
Hovers within my gates,
And my divine Althea brings
To whisper at the grates;
When I lie tangled in her hair
And fettered to her eye,
The gods[1] that wanton in the air
Know no such liberty.

When flowing cups run swiftly round,
With no allaying Thames,[2]
Our careless heads with roses bound,
Our hearts with loyal flames;
When thirsty grief in wine we steep,
When healths and draughts go free,
Fishes, that tipple in the deep,
Know no such liberty.

When, like committed linnets,[3] I
With shriller throat shall sing
The sweetness, mercy, majesty,
And glories of my King;
When I shall voice aloud how good
He is, how great should be,
Enlargéd winds, that curl the flood,
Know no such liberty.

Stone walls do not a prison make,
Nor iron bars a cage;
Minds innocent and quiet take
That for an hermitage.
If I have freedom in my love,
And in my soul am free,
Angels alone, that soar above,
Enjoy such liberty.

1649

1. Some versions read "birds" instead of "gods."
2. No mixture of water in the wine.
3. Caged finches.

To Lucasta, Going to the Wars

Tell me not, Sweet, I am unkind
That from the nunnery
Of thy chaste breast and quiet mind,
To war and arms I fly.

True, a new mistress now I chase,
The first foe in the field;
And with a stronger faith embrace
A sword, a horse, a shield.

Yet this inconstancy is such
As you too shall adore;
I could not love thee, Dear, so much,
Loved I not honor more.

1649

The Grasshopper

TO MY NOBLE FRIEND, MR. CHARLES COTTON[4]

Oh, thou that swing'st upon the waving hair
Of some well-filled oaten beard,
Drunk every night with a delicious tear
Dropped thee from heav'n, where now th' art reared,

The joys of earth and air are thine entire,
That with thy feet and wings dost hop and fly;
And when thy poppy[5] works thou dost retire
To thy carved acorn bed to lie.

Up with the day, the sun thou welcom'st then,
Sport'st in the gilt-plats[6] of his beams,
And all these merry days mak'st merry men,
Thyself, and melancholy streams.[7]

But ah, the sickle! golden ears are cropped,
Ceres and Bacchus[8] bid goodnight;
Sharp frosty fingers all your flow'rs have topped,
And what scythes spared, winds shave off quite.

4. Lovelace's friend Mr. Charles Cotton, scholar, man of letters, and father of Montaigne's translator, may have appeared to the poet an industrious and prudent ant, compared with himself, the melodious and improvident grasshopper. (Lovelace lost his entire fortune in the Civil Wars.) The circumstances of the poem are evidently those of the interregnum, when a winter of Puritanism seemed to be settling over all civilized feeling in England. For a copious explication of the poem's backgrounds and overtones, see D. C. Allen's article in *Modern Language Quarterly,* XVIII (1957). 35–43.

5. Opiate, sleeping potion.

6. Golden meadows.

7. The three objects of "mak'st merry" are "men," "thyself," and "melancholy streams."

8. The grain and the grape.

Poor verdant fool! and now green ice! thy joys
  Large and as lasting as thy perch of grass,
Bid us lay in 'gainst winter rain, and poise
  Their floods with an o'erflowing glass.

Thou best of men and friends! we will create
  A genuine summer in each other's breast;
And spite of this cold time and frozen fate
  Thaw us a warm seat to our rest.

Our sacred hearths shall burn eternally
  As vestal flames;[9] the North wind, he
Shall strike his frost-stretched wings, dissolve, and fly
  This Etna in epitome.[1]

Dropping December shall come weeping in,
  Bewail th'usurping of his reign;
But when in showers of old Greek[2] we begin,
  Shall cry, he hath his crown again!

Night as clear Hesper[3] shall our tapers whip
  From the light casements where we play,
And the dark hag from her black mantle strip,
  And stick there everlasting day.

Thus richer than untempted kings are we,
  That asking nothing, nothing need:
Though lord of all that seas embrace, yet he
  That wants himself is poor indeed.

1649

The Snail

Wise emblem of our politic world,
Sage snail, within thine own self curled,
Instruct me softly to make haste,
Whilst these my feet go slowly fast.[1]
  Compendious snail! thou seem'st to me
Large Euclid's strict epitome,[2]

9. The vestal virgins, in Rome, were responsible for tending an eternal flame.
1. Boreas, the North wind, "striking" (i.e., folding up) his wings, flees from the underground warmth of Etna, an emblem of the flame of friendship.
2. Greek wine was especially favored in the classical world; drinkers, in classical times, often wore festive crowns at their carousals; and December "crowns," i.e., terminates the year.
3. The tapers are compared to Hesperus, the morning star, which whips night from the sky. Hecate, the dark hag, was sometimes described as the daughter of Night.

1. "Politic" carries a slight implication of low cleverness: the snail is an emblem of those who "take care of Number One," as Lovelace's biography shows he was conspicuously unable to do. Lines 3 and 4 play with a Latinism: the way to get ahead is to *festina lente*, to make haste slowly, as Lovelace intends to do on his (poetic) feet.
2. Euclid the Greek mathematician wrote a complete book on geometry, of which the snail, with his convoluted structure, is a tiny abridgement.

And in each diagram dost fling
Thee from the point unto the ring—
A figure now triangular,
An oval now, and now a square,
And then a serpentine dost crawl,
Now a straight line, now crooked, now all.
  Preventing[3] rival of the day,
Th' art up, and openest thy ray
And ere the morn cradles the moon,
Th' art broke into a beauteous noon.
Then when the sun sups in the deep,
Thy silver horns o'er Cynthia's[4] peep,
And thou from thine own liquid bed,
New Phoebus,[5] heav'st thy pleasant head.
  Who shall a name for thee create,
Deep riddle of mysterious state?
Bold nature that gives common birth
To all products of sea and earth,
Of thee, as earthquakes, is afraid,
Nor will thy dire delivery aid.
  Thou thine own daughter, then, and sire,
That son and mother art entire,[6]
That big still with thy self dost go,
And liv'st an agéd embryo,
That like the cubs of India,
Thou from thy self a while dost play,
But frighted with a dog or gun,
In thine own belly thou dost run,[7]
And as thy house was thine own womb,
So thine own womb concludes thy tomb.
  But now I must (analyzéd king)[8]
Thy economic virtues sing;
Thou great staid husband,[9] still within
Thou, thee, that's thine, dost discipline;
And when thou art to progress bent,
Thou movest thyself and tenement;
As warlike Scythians traveled,[1] you
Remove your men and city too,

3. Forestalling.

4. The moon's.

5. Phoebus is the sun god. As the sun rises every morning from the ocean, so the snail rises from his liquid bed inside his shell.

6. Many snails are in fact hermaphroditic; like gastropods in general, their inner organs are in a state of disarray compared with what we vertebrates consider "normal."

7. Popular natural histories described a creature, living in India and named Su; its young were carried in a pouch from which they emerged to play, and to which they retreated when threatened.

8. The snail is king of his own nation (shell), and Lovelace, having analyzed his sex life, is about to discuss his "economy" (i.e., his management of household affairs).

9. Frugal or provident person.

1. According to Herodotus, the nomadic Scythians pitched their tents on their wagons, and had no other dwellings. "Progress" (line 41) implies a formal royal journey, such as Queen Elizabeth used to enjoy so much, from country house to country house.

Then after a sad dearth and rain,
Thou scatterest thy silver train;
And when the trees grow naked and old,
Thou clothest them with cloth of gold
Which from thy bowels thou dost spin,
And draw from the rich mines within.
  Now hast thou changed thee saint, and made
Thyself a fane[2] that's cupola'ed,
And in thy wreathéd cloister thou
Walkest thine own gray friar[3] too;
Strict and locked up, th' art hood all o'er,
And ne'er eliminat'st[4] thy door.
On salads thou dost feed severe,
And 'stead of beads[5] thou drop'st a tear.
And when to rest each calls the bell,
Thou sleep'st within thy marble cell,
Where in dark contemplation placed,
The sweets of nature thou dost taste,
Who[6] now with time thy days resolve,
And in a jelly thee dissolve,
Like a shot star,[7] which doth repair
Upward and rarefy the air.

1659

2. Shrine.
3. Franciscan monk.
4. From Latin *limen*, threshold: i.e., you never go out of doors (though the Franciscans themselves had sometimes been rebuked as wandering or vagabond friars).
5. The rosary is a mnemonic device popular with monks, who use its 150 beads as a way of keeping track of their prayers. The meditative snail drops a bit of slime instead of a bead.
6. Nature.
7. Shooting stars were popularly supposed to dissolve to jelly when they landed on earth. But the pure spirit of the star was then carried aloft, rising to the upper atmosphere, which it purified.

THOMAS TRAHERNE
(1637–1674)

Though the short, obscure life of Thomas Traherne fell squarely in the middle of the 17th century, this retiring clergyman did not become known as an English author till the first years of the 20th century, when a manuscript volume of his poems and prose meditations fell into the hands of a perceptive bookseller, who published it. Another volume followed within a few years, and Traherne took his place among the English poets. Though it is sometimes uneven, there is a freshness and visionary innocence in Traherne's work at its best that might not have proved uncongenial to the mind of William Blake, had Traherne's poetry been discovered a hundred years earlier.

Wonder

How like an angel came I down!
How bright are all things here!
When first among his works I did appear,
O how their glory did me crown!
The world resembled his eternity,
In which my soul did walk,
And everything that I did see
Did with me talk.

The skies in their magnificence,
The lively, lovely air;
O how divine, how soft, how sweet, how fair!
The stars did entertain my sense,
And all the works of God so bright and pure,
So rich and great did seem,
As if they ever must endure,
In my esteem.

A native health and innocence
Within my bones did grow,
And while my God did all his glories show,
I felt a vigor in my sense
That was all SPIRIT. I within did flow
With seas of life like wine;
I nothing in the world did know
But 'twas divine.

Harsh ragged objects were concealed,
Oppression's tears and cries,
Sins, griefs, complaints, dissensions, weeping eyes,
Were hid; and only things revealed
Which heavenly spirits and the angels prize.
The state of innocence
And bliss, not trades and poverties,
Did fill my sense.

The streets were paved with golden stones,
The boys and girls were mine,
O how did all their lovely faces shine!
The sons of men were holy ones.
In joy and beauty then appeared to me
And everything which here I found
While like an angel I did see,
Adorned the ground.

Rich diamond and pearl and gold
In every place was seen;

Rare splendors, yellow, blue, red, white, and green,
Mine eyes did everywhere behold.
Great wonders clothed with glory did appear,
Amazement was my bliss.
That and my wealth was everywhere:
No joy to this![1]

Cursed and devised proprieties,[2]
With envy, avarice,
And fraud, those fiends that spoil even paradise,
Fled from the splendor of mine eyes.
And so did hedges, ditches, limits, bounds,
I dreamed not aught of those,
But wandered over all men's grounds,
And found repose.

Proprieties themselves were mine,
And hedges ornaments;
Walls, boxes, coffers, and their rich contents
Did not divide my joys, but all combine.
Clothes, ribbons, jewels, laces, I esteemed
My joys by others worn;
For me they all to wear them seemed
When I was born.

1903

On News

News from a foreign country came;
As if my treasurer and my wealth lay there,
So much it did my heart inflame!
'Twas wont to call my soul into mine ear
Which thither went to meet
The approaching sweet,
And on the threshold stood
To entertain the unknown good.
It hovered there
As if 'twould leave mine ear,
And was so eager to embrace
The joyful tidings as they came,
'Twould almost leave its dwelling place
To entertain the same.

As if the tidings were the things,
My very joys themselves, my foreign treasure,

1. Compared to this.

2. Properties. It is not simply private property, but more importantly the individual self from which Traherne in his vision has escaped.

Or else did bear them on their wings,
With so much joy they came, with so much pleasure.
My soul stood at the gate
To recreate[3]
Itself with bliss, and to
Be pleased with speed. A fuller view
It fain would take,
Yet journeys back would make
Unto my heart, as if 'twould fain
Go out to meet, yet stay within
To fit a place, to entertain,
And bring the tidings in.

What sacred instinct did inspire
My soul in childhood with a hope so strong?
What secret force moved my desire
To expect my joys beyond the seas so young?
Felicity I knew
Was out of view;
And being here alone,
I saw that happiness was gone
From me! for this
I thirsted—absent bliss,
And thought that sure beyond the seas
Or else in something near at hand[4]
I knew not yet (since naught did please
I knew), my bliss did stand.

But little did the infant dream
That all the treasures of the world were by,
And that himself was so the cream
And crown of all which round about did lie.[5]
Yet thus it was. The gem,
The diadem,
The ring enclosing all
That stood upon this earthy ball,
The heavenly eye,
Much wider than the sky,
Wherein they all included were,
The glorious soul that was the king
Made to possess them, did appear
A small and little thing!

1908

3. Divert.
4. The word "that" is understood at the end of lines 40 and 41.
5. The soul of the little child, though he does not yet know it, is the climax of creation, and its epitome—that is, it contains within itself the forms of all the forms in the world.

On Leaping over the Moon[1]

I saw new worlds beneath the water lie,
New people, yea, another sky
And sun, which seen by day,
Might things more clear display.
Just such another
Of late my brother[2]
Did in his travel see, and saw by night,
A much more strange and wondrous sight;
Nor could the world exhibit such another
So great a sight, but in a brother.

Adventure strange! no such in story we
New or old, true or feignéd see.
On earth he seemed to move,
Yet Heaven went above;
Up in the skies
His body flies,
In open, visible, yet magic sort:
As he along the way did sport,
Over the flood he takes his nimble course
Without the help of feignéd horse.[3]

As he went tripping o'er the king's highway.
A little pearly river lay
O'er which, without a wing
Or oar, he dared to swim,
Swim through the air
On body fair;
He would not use or trust Icarian wings[4]
Lest they should prove deceitful things;
For had he fallen, it had been wondrous high,
Not from, but from above the sky.

He might have dropped through that thin element
Into a fathomless descent
Unto the nether sky
That did beneath him lie
And there might tell
What wonders dwell
On earth above. Yet doth he briskly run,
And bold the danger overcome,

1. At one time toward the end of the 17th century, this poem seems to have been intended for the press, but did not appear in print till the 20th century.
2. Traherne's brother Philip.
3. Perhaps Bellerophon's Pegasus or the hippogriff which Astolfo rode to the moon in Ariosto's *Orlando Furioso*.
4. I.e., like those of wax, made for Icarus by his father Dedalus. They melted in the sun's heat.

Who, as he leapt, with joy related soon
How happy he o'erleaped the moon.

What wondrous things upon the earth are done
Beneath and yet above the sun?
Deeds all appear again
In higher spheres; remain
In clouds as yet:
But there they get
Another light, and in another way
Themselves to us above display.
The skies themselves this earthly globe surround;
We're even here within them found.

On heavenly ground within the skies we walk,
And in this middle center talk:
Did we but wisely move
On earth in heaven above,
Then soon should we
Exalted be
Above the sky: from whence whoever falls,
Through a long dismal precipice,
Sinks to the deep abyss where Satan crawls,
Where horrid Death and Despair lies.

As much as others thought themselves to lie
Beneath the moon, so much more high
Himself he thought to fly
Above the starry sky,
As that he spied
Below the tide.
Thus did he yield me in the shady night
A wondrous and instructive light,
Which taught me that under our feet there is,
As o'er our heads, a place of bliss.

1910

ABRAHAM COWLEY
(1618–1667)

Abraham Cowley, a precocious young person, picked up the metaphysical mode in his early teens, and could never really get rid of it—though in fact it suited neither his peaceful temper nor his rational, mechanical philosophy. Metaphysical poetry is the poetry of anxiety; though he often tried to mime anxiety, Cowley was too sensible and too secure in the plain sense of things really to feel it.

Like most of his generation, the poet suffered from the Civil Wars, which uprooted him from his quiet fellowship at Trinity College, Cambridge, forced him into politics, and finally drove him into exile with the royal family, to which he was devoted. But the flow of his pen never ceased. He wrote a learned epic on the life of King David; he wrote a set of love poems to an entirely imaginary mistress; he wrote a stage comedy; he wrote some satires, and a set of "Pindaric" odes, in imitation of the enthusiastic, highly charged, and irregular style of the Greek poet Pindar. He also wrote a number of quiet, attractive informal essays.

Most of these writings found a sympathetic audience, and Cowley was admired, in his day, far above Milton. With the benefit of our hindsight, we find this hard to imagine, but Milton had not published his two epics or *Samson Agonistes* while Cowley was alive; and the Restoration had a particularly hard time swallowing Milton's connections with Cromwell and the regicides. In any case, and for whatever reasons, almost immediately after Cowley's death, his reputation suffered a catastrophic decline, from which it has never recovered. Still, as our selections indicate, Cowley commanded a good deal of plain, intellectual vigor, which rendered him accessible to his own time and of interest to ours as an early adventurer in the difficult task of giving scientific thought a literary shape.

To Mr. Hobbes[1]

Vast bodies of philosophy
I oft have seen and read,
But all are bodies dead,
Or bodies by Art fashionèd;
I never yet the living soul could see
But in thy books and thee.
'Tis only God can know
Whether the fair idea thou dost show
Agree entirely with his own or no.
This I dare boldly tell,
'Tis so like truth, 'twill serve our turn as well.
Just, as in nature, thy proportions be,
As full of concord their variety,
As firm the parts upon their center rest,
And all so solid are, that they, at least
As much as nature, emptiness detest.

1. The poem is addressed to Thomas Hobbes, the Malmesbury philosopher, a friend of Cowley's; in form, it is a loose imitation of the Greek odes written by the Theban poet Pindar. Cowley understood these odes to be irregular and sublime (in which he was right), and that this was the character of his own genius (in which he was hopelessly wrong). His effort here to work up an artificial "sublime" is not very impressive; but his sense that a new world of philosophy is just opening before men is characteristic of his age. Cowley had an amateur's interest in science, and great admiration for the Royal Society; but the problem of accommodating scientific rationalism within a rhetoric of poetic enthusiasm was too hard for him to handle.

Long did the mighty Stagirite[2] retain
The universal intellectual reign,
Saw his own country's short-lived leopard[3] slain;
The stronger Roman eagle did out-fly,
Oftener renewed his age, and saw that die.
Mecca itself, in spite of Mahomet possessed,
And chased by a wild deluge from the east,
His monarchy new planted in the west.[4]
But as in time each great imperial race
Degenerates, and gives some new one place,
So did this noble empire waste,
Sunk by degrees from glories past,
And in the school-men's[5] hands, it perished quite at last.
Then nought but words it grew,
And those all barbarous too.
It perished and it vanished there,
The life and soul breathed out, became but empty air.

The fields which answered well the ancients' plow,
Spent and outworn, return no harvest now;
In barren age wild and inglorious lie,
And boast of past fertility,
The poor relief of present poverty.
Food and fruit we now must want
Unless new lands we plant.
We break up tombs with sacrilegious hands;
Old rubbish we remove;
To walk in ruins, like vain ghosts, we love,
And with fond divining wands,
We search among the dead
For treasures buriéd,
Whilst still the liberal earth does hold
So many virgin mines of undiscovered gold.

The Baltic, Euxine, and the Caspian
And slender-limbed Mediterranean,
Seem narrow creeks to thee,[6] and only fit
For the poor wretched fisher-boats of wit.
Thy nobler vessel the vast ocean tries,
And nothing sees but seas and skies,
Till unknown regions it descries,

2. Aristotle (who came from the town of Stagira, in Greece).

3. Alexander the Great, Aristotle's pupil. Cowley is here tracing the history of Aristotelian philosophy through the ages.

4. Arabian thinkers like Avicenna and Averroes were largely responsible for transmitting Aristotle's work to the Western world. The "monarchy new planted in the west" is the Moorish regime in Spain.

5. Cowley's contempt for the scholastic philosophers (Scotus, Occam, Aquinas, and the rest) is unbounded.

6. Hobbes himself. Cowley's conviction that the new philosophy of "things" rather than "words" represents a whole new world for exploration and discovery echoes the confident affirmations of Bacon.

Thou great Columbus of the golden lands of new philosophies.
Thy task was harder much than his,
For thy learned America is
Not only found out first by thee,
And rudely left to future industry,
But thy eloquence and thy wit
Has planted, peopled, built, and civilized it.

I little thought before,
(Nor, being my own self so poor,
Could comprehend so vast a store)
That all the wardrobe of rich eloquence
Could have afforded half enough
Of bright, of new and lasting stuff,
To clothe the mighty limbs of thy gigantic sense.
Thy solid reason, like the shield from heaven
To the Trojan hero given,[7]
Too strong to take a mark from any mortal dart,
Yet shines with gold and gems in every part,
And wonders on it graved by the learned hand of art,
A shield that gives delight
Even to the enemy's sight,
Then when they're sure to lose the combat by 't.

Nor can the snow which now cold age does shed
Upon thy reverend head[8]
Quench or allay the noble fires within;
But all which thou hast been,
And all that youth can be thou 'rt yet,
So fully still dost thou
Enjoy the manhood and the bloom of wit,
And all the natural heat, but not the fever too.
So contraries on Etna's[9] top conspire,
Here hoary frosts, and by them breaks out fire.
A secure peace the faithful neighbors keep,
Th' emboldened snow next to the flame does sleep.
And if we weigh, like thee,
Nature and causes, we shall see
That thus it needs must be;
To things immortal time can do no wrong,
And that which never is to die, forever must be young.

1656

7. In Book VIII of the *Aeneid*, Aeneas gets from his mother, Venus, a splendid shield made by her husband, Vulcan.

8. Hobbes was born in 1588, the year of the Spanish Armada; he was therefore 68 when Cowley's poem first appeared.

9. Mount Etna, a volcano in Sicily, is so high that in winter it is sometimes snow-capped.

To the Royal Society[1]

1

Philosophy,[2] the great and only heir
Of all that human knowledge which has been
Unforfeited by man's rebellious sin,
Though full of years he do appear
(Philosophy, I say, and call it *He*
For whatsoe'er the painter's fancy be,[3]
It a male virtue seems to me),
Has still been kept in nonage[4] till of late,
Nor managed or enjoyed his vast estate.
Three or four thousand years, one would have thought,
To ripeness and perfection might have brought
A science so well bred and nursed,
And of such hopeful parts too at the first.
But, oh, the guardians and the tutors then
(Some negligent and some ambitious men)
Would ne'er consent to set him free,
Or his own natural powers to let him see,
Lest that should put an end to their authority.

2

That his own business he might quite forget,
They amused him with the sports of wanton wit;
With the desserts of poetry they fed him,
Instead of solid meats t' increase his force;
Instead of vigorous exercise, they led him
Into the pleasant labyrinths of ever-fresh discourse.[5]
Instead of carrying him to see
The riches which do hoarded for him lie
In Nature's endless treasury,
They chose his eye to entertain
(His curious but not covetous eye),
With painted scenes and pageants of the brain.
Some few exalted spirits this latter age has shown,
That labored to assert the liberty
(From guardians who were now usurpers grown)
Of this old minor still, captived philosophy;
But 'twas rebellion called to fight
For such a long-oppresséd right.
Bacon at last, a mighty man, arose

1. John Evelyn the diarist, an enthusiast for the Royal Society, suggested to Cowley that he write this poem, which he did in the last year of his life.
2. Though he does not make the point immediately clear, Cowley means by "Philosophy" natural philosophy, i.e., scientific investigation. The definition comes clear below when he distinguishes Philosophy from Authority, the latter understood to represent primarily Aristotle and his interpreters.
3. Painters and writers commonly represented Philosophy as a woman.
4. The period of legal minority, when one is not of age (non-age).
5. A standard complaint against scholastic philosophy was that it consisted too largely of merely verbal exercises.

Whom a wise king and Nature chose
Lord Chancellor of both their laws,
And boldly undertook the injured pupil's cause.[6]

3

Authority,[7] which did a body boast,
Though 'twas but air condensed, and stalked about
Like some old giant's more gigantic ghost
To terrify the learnéd rout,[8]
With the plain magic of true reason's light
He chased out of our sight,
Nor suffered living men to be misled
By the vain shadows of the dead.
To graves, from whence it rose, the conquered phantom[9] fled;
He broke the monstrous god which stood
In midst of th' orchard, and the whole did claim,
Which, with a useless scythe of wood
And something else not worth a name
(Both vast for show, yet neither fit
Or to defend or to beget—
Ridiculous and senseless terrors!) made
Children and superstitious men afraid.
The orchard's open now and free,
Bacon has broke that scarecrow deity;
Come, enter all that will,
Behold the ripened fruit, come gather now your fill.
Yet still, methinks, we fain would be
Catching at the forbidden tree;
We would be like the deity,
When truth and falsehood, good and evil, we
Without the senses' aid within ourselves would see;
For 'tis God only who can find
All Nature in his mind.

4

From words, which are but pictures of the thought
(Though we our thoughts from them perversely drew),
To things, the mind's right object, he it brought.[1]
Like foolish birds, to painted grapes we flew;[2]
He sought, and gathered for our use, the true;
And when in heaps the chosen bunches lay,
He pressed them wisely the mechanic[3] way,

6. Francis Bacon (1561–1626) was both Lord Chancellor of England and a leading scientific thinker.

7. Early scientific investigators were constantly running up against the "authority" of the ancients, particularly Aristotle, to whose judgment they were sometimes asked to make their scientific findings conform.

8. Crowd, mob.

9. I.e., Authority. In the following lines it is compared, as an empty threat, to statues of the Roman nature god Pan, which were set in orchards with a wooden scythe and a giant phallus to scare away birds and evil spirits.

1. I.e., he called the mind away from words to things.

2. The Greek painter Zeuxis was said to have painted grapes so realistically that the birds came and pecked at them.

3. Mechanical, materialistic.

Till all their juice did in one vessel join,
Ferment into a nourishment divine,
  The thirsty soul's refreshing wine.
Who to the life an exact piece would make
Must not from others' work a copy take;
  No, not from Rubens or Van Dyck:[4]
Much less content himself to make it like
The ideas and the images which lie
In his own fancy or his memory.
  No, he before his sight must place
  The natural and living face;
  The real object must command
Each judgment of his eye, and motion of his hand.

5

From these and all long errors of the way
In which our wandering predecessors went,
And like th' old Hebrews many years did stray
  In deserts but of small extent,
Bacon, like Moses, led us forth at last,
  The barren wilderness he passed,
  Did on the very border stand
  Of the blessèd promised land,
And from the mountain's top of his exalted wit
  Saw it himself, and showed us it.[5]
But life did never to one man allow
Time to discover worlds and conquer too,
Nor can so short a line[6] sufficient be
To fathom the vast depths of Nature's sea.
  The work he did we ought t' admire,
And were unjust if we should more require
From his few years, divided 'twixt th' excess
Of low affliction and high happiness.[7]
For who on things remote can fix his sight,
That's always in a triumph or a fight?

6

From you, great champions,[8] we expect to get
These spacious countries but discovered yet;
Countries where yet instead of Nature, we
Her images and idols worshiped see.
These large and wealthy regions to subdue,
Though learning has whole armies at command,
  Quartered about in every land,
A better troop she ne'er together drew.

4. The work of Peter Paul Rubens (1577–1640) and his pupil Antony Van Dyck (1599–1641) was well known and much admired in England.
5. Like Moses, who had a remote view of the promised land from the top of Mount Pisgah, but could never himself get there, Bacon foresaw but never experienced the triumphs of science.
6. I.e., the line of man's life.
7. Bacon knew great success ("happiness") as Lord Chancellor, and great "affliction" when he was impeached for accepting bribes.
8. The members of the Royal Society, to whom the poem is addressed.

Methinks, like Gideon's little band[9]
God with design has picked out you
To do these noble wonders by a few.
When the whole host he saw, "They are," said he,
"Too many to o'ercome for me";
And now he chooses out his men
Much in the way that he did then—
Not those many whom he found
Idly extended on the ground
To drink with their dejected head
The stream just so as by their mouths it fled;
No, but those few who took the waters up,
And made of their laborious hands the cup.

7

Thus you prepared; and in the glorious fight,
Their wondrous pattern too you take:
Their old and empty pitchers first they brake,
And with their hands then lifted up the light.
Io![1] Sound too the trumpets here!
Already your victorious lights appear;
New scenes of heaven already we espy,
And crowds of golden worlds on high,
Which from the spacious plains of earth and sea
Could never yet discovered be
By sailor's or Chaldean's watchful eye.[2]
Nature's great works no distance can obscure,
No smallness her near objects can secure.
You've taught the curious sight to press
Into the privatest recess
Of her imperceptible littleness;
You've learned to read her smallest hand,
And well begun her deepest sense to understand.

8

Mischief and true dishonor fall on those
Who would to laughter or to scorn expose
So virtuous and so noble a design,
So human for its use, for knowledge so divine.
The things which these proud men despise, and call
Impertinent and vain and small,
Those smallest things of Nature let me know
Rather than all their greatest actions do.
Whoever would deposéd truth advance
Into the throne usurped from it
Must feel at first the blows of ignorance
And the sharp points of envious wit.

9. For the story of Gideon and his little band, see Judges, especially vi and vii. The story of how Gideon selected his warriors is substantially as told by Cowley in stanzas 6 and 7.

1. Greek and Roman cry of triumph.

2. Sailors watch the sky to take their bearings; Chaldeans were the famous astronomers of antiquity.

So when, by various turns of the celestial dance
   In many thousand years,
   A star, so long unknown, appears,
Though heaven itself more beauteous by it grow,
It troubles and alarms the world below,
Does to the wise a star, to fools a meteor[3] show.

9

With courage and success you the bold work begin;
   Your cradle has not idle been.
None e'er but Hercules and you could be
At five years' age worthy a history.[4]
   And ne'er did fortune better yet
   Th' historian to the story fit.
   As you from all old errors free
And purge the body of philosophy,
   So from all modern follies he
Has vindicated eloquence and wit.
His candid style like a clean stream does slide,
   And his bright fancy all the way
   Does like the sunshine in it play.
It does like Thames, the best of rivers, glide
Where the god does not rudely overturn
   But gently pour the crystal urn,
And with judicious hand does the whole current guide.
It has all the beauties Nature can impart,
And all the comely dress without the paint of art.

1667

3. Meteors were thought to be omens of ill fortune.

4. I.e., the *History of the Royal Society* by Thomas Sprat. After Cowley's death, Sprat edited a splendid volume of his collected works, and wrote his biography.

Prose of the Seventeenth Century

The history of English prose up to the end of the 16th century is by no means simple, but it can be written and has been written; after a long, slow development and a number of experiments in both ornate and colloquial styles, the tongue produced its first prose masterpiece in Richard Hooker's massive polemic *Of the Laws of Ecclesiastical Polity* (1593). Hooker is so much respected because he is both dignified and colloquial, learned and direct, strong and gentle; in many respects he represents what the genius of the language was or was becoming—clear, sinewy, consecutive, rational. There had been nothing like him before. But after Hooker, English prose went so many different ways, and was applied to so many different tasks, that tracing or describing them all is very hard indeed.

In the early part of the century, two broad classes of prose can be observed. Francis Bacon, whose philosophical bias was against metaphors, rhetorical adornments, and artificial figures of speech, cultivated a plain style, using short, clear sentences and pithy apothegms. The mode was known, to contrast it with the longer and more florid periods of Ciceronian style, as "the Senecan amble." (Cicero the orator used the extended, suspended, decorated sentence; Seneca the philosopher used the short, direct, simple one.) Robert Burton was another exponent of the plain style, though his arrangement of detail is considerably more helterskelter than Bacon's; and of course plain prose was very much the accepted thing in the writings of practical men like lawyers, travelers, scholars, and popular moralists. On the other hand, a good deal of ecclesiastical prose tended to a rhetorical ornateness reminiscent of Cicero—for example, the sermons of John Donne and Jeremy Taylor. Also ornate, though in somewhat different ways, were the prose styles of the historian Sir Walter Raleigh and the learned controversialist John Milton. But Sir Thomas Browne, who in effect wrote metaphysical poems in prose, can only be placed in a class by himself. And increasingly, as prose was turned to more different ends by more different classes of people—to explain, to persuade, to define, to describe, to explore complex psychological states, to play with ironic nuances, or simply to entertain, the variety of prose styles expanded, until one finds it impossible or at least idle to classify prose styles. For writers have started to have, as we say, "styles of their own."

For all this variety, a general tendency to write less formal, less ornate prose makes itself felt in the later century. Partly this was because the pamphlet and publicity battles that accompanied the Civil Wars taught men the persuasive powers of plain style. Partly also the lessons of scientific clarity and simplicity, taught by Bacon and repeated by many others, from the respectable Royal Society to the less respectable Thomas Hobbes, began to take hold. More important than the positive achievements of science (these tended to be detailed and not immediately impressive) was the gradual disintegration of all those occult correspondences and ingenious analogies which had furnished the material of so many metaphysical conceits and pulpit-parables. The phoenix ceased to be an emblem of the resurrection and became a bird that nobody had ever seen, a mere superstition; the pelican was not a bird to be doubted out of existence, but people ceased to believe that it re-enacted the sacrifice of Christ by drawing blood from its chest to feed its young. All those ingenious games of cross-reference and sympathetic correspondence, dear to the hearts of medieval moralists, went abruptly out of fashion. Prose got deliberately plain and literal as it was applied to more plain and literal tasks. But it did not for that reason cease to have literary value, not even when applied to a task as severe as the description of a scientific experiment. Our concluding report from the laboratory of Isaac Newton suffices to demonstrate that.

FRANCIS BACON

(1561–1626)

1597: First edition of the *Essays* (augmented and revised editions in 1612 and 1625).
1605: *The Advancement of Learning*.
1620: *Novum Organum*.
1621: Bacon's disgrace and retirement.

Francis Bacon, the younger son of a highly placed Elizabethan civil servant, studied law at Cambridge and Gray's Inn, entered the legal bureaucracy of Elizabeth, and rose steadily through it until, under James, he stood at the head of his profession, as Lord Chancellor of England. But after barely three years in this office, he fell from power and reputation, accused of taking bribes in office, and confessing himself guilty of corruption and neglect. The last five years of his life were spent in retirement.

Bacon's only predecessor in the field of the essay was Michel de Montaigne (1533–92), the French country squire who wrote so volubly, intimately, charmingly—and at such immense length—about himself. Concentration on self was not for Montaigne simply a matter of egotistic display; he thought himself a fair specimen of the whole human race, and proposed that we can learn a good deal about mankind in general by stripping a single example morally as well as physically naked. But Bacon when he set out to write essays had no intention of imitating his unbuttoned predecessor. As a man with a judicial position to maintain, he was not out to discover himself or explore unknown thoughts. His training in law and his reading in the Roman moralists had given him the habit of thinking in axioms; and axioms of prudent, practical conduct were what he laid down. Montaigne, in titling his writings *Essais*, emphasized the tentative and exploratory nature of his thought; he didn't care about developing a consistent, defensible philosophy, only about tracing the quirky track of his changing moods. Bacon laid down the law like a magistrate or a Dutch uncle, and largely concealed his "self"—at least in the way Montaigne defined "self"—under the official robes of worldly wisdom.

Only the bookish side of Montaigne came out in Bacon's *Essays*; reading them, you would imagine that he was born at the age of thirty-eight, with a volume of moral epistles for one parent and a treatise of English law for the other. Neither do his *Essays* provide much of a guide to human nature; you would scarcely learn from them, any more than from the writings of Emerson, that the human race is divided into two sexes. What one could pick up are certain prudential, practical rules about the successful conduct of business life. Philadelphia lawyers were once famous for giving this kind of advice, and Bacon phrased it in crisp, compressed phrases, easy for a busy man to remember. Axioms and adages are the kernels of legal wisdom, and Bacon's essays often read like a string of walnut sayings, hard to crack, but meaty and nourishing enough, once one has got inside them.

Bacon's reticence—not to say inhibition—when writing personal essays contrasts strikingly with the sweep and boldness of his directly philosophical work. Here the importance of what he says and implies is almost impossible to overstate. He was not himself much of a practical scientist, and anyone who tries can comb from his works an amazing collection of superstitious and unfounded beliefs. But his vision of intellectual method was wide as well as deep, and its emphasis on verifiable experiment held immense promise for the future. In fact, simple emphasis on "experience" and "experiment" (the former word was sometimes used where we would employ the latter) was not a novel principle when Bacon put it forth. A man like Paracelsus, the Swiss alchemist of the 16th century, had insisted on following his own experience against the authority of the great Galen and other doctors of classical antiquity. That was why Paracelsus and his alchemical followers were called "empirics." But their observations were uncontrolled. They noted the effects of what they called occult sympathies (for example, the peculiar affinity of the sunflower for the sun), and generalized from that single observation by analogy. Bacon recommended controlled and repeated experiments, in which theory worked to direct and focus experience, and in which all experiments were coordinated with one another. And this vision, as most memorably outlined in *The New Atlantis*, represented the ideal of the future. If anything, the great chancellor did not give enough weight to the concept of the controlling hypothesis; a modern scientist would give more, reducing the role of experiment to simple verification. But in most other respects, Bacon was centuries ahead of his time.

Yet, before anything could be built out of scientific hypothesis and verification, there was a major work of demolition to be accomplished. That was simply the mass of things that men already knew, under the name of "science," which weren't so. Bacon attacked such errors and their causes in the *Novum Organum*, or "New Instrument of Knowledge," (1620), under the heading of "idols," or false images of the mind.

From Essays

Of Truth

"What is truth?" said jesting Pilate; and would not stay for an answer.[1] Certainly there be that delight in giddiness,[2] and count it a bondage to fix a belief; affecting free-will in thinking, as well as in acting. And though the sects of philosophers of that kind[3] be gone, yet there remain certain discoursing wits, which are of the same veins, though there be not so much blood in them as was in those of the ancients. But it is not only the difficulty and labor which men take in finding out of truth; nor again, that when it is found, it imposeth upon[4] men's thoughts, that doth bring lies in favor; but a natural though corrupt love of the lie itself. One of the later school of the Grecians examineth the matter, and is at a stand to think what should be in it, that men should love lies; where neither they make for pleasure, as with poets; nor for advantage, as with the merchant, but for the lie's sake. But I cannot tell:[5] this same truth is a naked and open daylight, that doth not show the masks and mummeries and triumphs of the world half so stately and daintily as candle lights. Truth may perhaps come to the price of a pearl, that showeth best by day, but it will not rise to the price of a diamond or carbuncle,[6] that showeth best in varied lights. A mixture of a lie doth ever add pleasure. Doth any man doubt that if there were taken out of men's minds vain opinions, flattering hopes, false valuations, imaginations as one would, and the like, but it would leave the minds of a number of men poor shrunken things, full of melancholy and indisposition, and unpleasing to themselves? One of the fathers, in great severity, called poesy *vinum daemonum,*[7] because it filleth the imagination, and yet it is but with the shadow of a lie. But it is not the lie that passeth through the mind, but the lie that sinketh in, and settleth in it, that doth the hurt, such as we spake of before. But howsoever these things are thus in men's depraved judgments and affections, yet truth, which only doth judge itself, teacheth that the inquiry of truth, which is the love-making, or wooing of it, the knowledge of truth, which is the presence of it, and the belief of truth, which is the enjoying of it, is the sovereign good of human nature. The first creature[8] of God, in the works of the days, was the light of the sense; the last was the light of reason; and His sabbath work ever since is the illumination of His Spirit.

1. See John xviii.38 for Pilate's idle query to Jesus.
2. Changeability, insecurity of ideas. "That": those who.
3. The Greek Skeptics, who taught the uncertainty of all knowledge. "Discoursing wits": discursive minds.
4. Restricts, limits.
5. "I cannot tell," says Bacon, and tells.
6. Ruby.
7. The wine of devils; St. Augustine is probably being cited.
8. Creation.

First, He breathed light upon the face of the matter, or chaos; then He breathed light into the face of man; and still He breatheth and inspireth light into the face of His chosen. The poet that beautified the sect that was otherwise inferior to the rest[9] saith yet excellently well: "It is a pleasure to stand upon the shore, and to see ships tossed upon the sea: a pleasure to stand in the window of a castle, and to see a battle, and the adventures thereof below: but no pleasure is comparable to the standing upon the vantage ground of truth" (a hill not to be commanded,[1] and where the air is always clear and serene), "and to see the errors, and wanderings, and mists, and tempests, in the vale below": so always that this prospect[2] be with pity, and not with swelling or pride. Certainly, it is heaven upon earth to have a man's mind move in charity, rest in providence, and turn upon the poles of truth.

To pass from theological and philosophical truth to the truth of civil business; it will be acknowledged even by those that practice it not, that clear and round dealing[3] is the honor of man's nature, and that mixture of falsehood is like alloy in coin of gold and silver, which may make the metal work the better, but it embaseth[4] it. For these winding and crooked courses are the goings of the serpent; which goeth basely upon the belly, and not upon the feet. There is no vice that doth so cover a man with shame as to be found false and perfidious; and therefore Montaigne saith prettily, when he inquired the reason why the word of the lie should be such a disgrace, and such an odious charge, saith he, "If it be well weighed, to say that a man lieth is as much as to say that he is brave towards God and a coward towards men."[5] For a lie faces God, and shrinks from man. Surely the wickedness of falsehood and breach of faith cannot possibly be so highly expressed, as in that it shall be the last peal to call the judgments of God upon the generations of men, it being foretold that when Christ cometh, he shall not "find faith upon the earth."[6]

1625

Of Marriage and Single Life[1]

He that hath wife and children hath given hostages to fortune; for they are impediments to great enterprises, either of virtue or mischief. Certainly the best works, and of greatest merit for the public, have proceeded from the unmarried or childless men, which

9. Lucretius' *On the Nature of Things* expressed the Epicurean creed, which Bacon thought inferior because it emphasized pleasure. The passage cited comprises the first words of Book I.
1. Dominated.
2. I.e., provided always that this contemplation.
3. The dealing that Bacon calls "round" we should describe as "square."
4. Debases.
5. *Essays* II.18.
6. Luke xviii.8.
1. The text is that of the 1625 edition.

both in affection and means have married and endowed the public. Yet it were great reason that those that have children should have greatest care of future times, unto which they know they must transmit their dearest pledges. Some there are who, though they lead a single life, yet their thoughts do end with themselves, and account future times impertinences.[2] Nay, there are some other that account wife and children but as bills of charges. Nay more, there are some foolish rich covetous men that take a pride in having no children, because they may be thought so much the richer. For perhaps they have heard some talk, "Such an one is a great rich man," and another except to it, "Yea, but he hath a great charge of children"; as if it were an abatement to his riches. But the most ordinary cause of a single life is liberty, especially in certain self-pleasing and humorous[3] minds, which are so sensible of every restraint, as they will go near to think their girdles and garters to be bonds and shackles. Unmarried men are best friends, best masters, best servants, but not always best subjects, for they are light to run away, and almost all fugitives are of that condition. A single life doth well with churchmen, for charity will hardly water the ground where it must first fill a pool. It is indifferent for judges and magistrates, for if they be facile[4] and corrupt, you shall have a servant five times worse than a wife. For soldiers, I find the generals commonly in their hortatives[5] put men in mind of their wives and children; and I think the despising of marriage amongst the Turks maketh the vulgar soldier more base. Certainly wife and children are a kind of discipline of humanity; and single men, though they be many times more charitable, because their means are less exhaust,[6] yet, on the other side, they are more cruel and hard-hearted (good to make severe inquisitors), because their tenderness is not so oft called upon. Grave natures, led by custom, and therefore constant, are commonly loving husbands, as was said of Ulysses, *Vetulam suam praetulit immortalitati*.[7] Chaste women are often proud and froward, as presuming upon the merit of their chastity. It is one of the best bonds, both of chastity and obedience, in the wife if she think her husband wise, which she will never do if she find him jealous. Wives are young men's mistresses, companions for middle age, and old men's nurses, so as a man may have a quarrel[8] to marry when he will. But yet he was reputed one of the wise men that made answer to the question when a man should marry: "A young man not yet, an elder man not at all."[9] It is often seen that bad husbands have very good

2. Irrelevant concerns.
3. Unbalanced, whimsical.
4. Pliable.
5. Exhortations.
6. Exhausted, drained.
7. "He preferred his old wife to immortality." Ulysses might have had immortality in the company of the nymph Calypso, but preferred to go back to Penelope.
8. Pretext.
9. Thales (6th century B.C.) was the confirmed bachelor who made this remark. He was one of the Seven Sages of Greece.

wives; whether it be that it raiseth the price of their husbands' kindness when it comes, or that the wives take a pride in their patience. But this never fails, if the bad husbands were of their own choosing, against their friends' consent; for then they will be sure to make good their own folly.

1612, 1625

Of Studies[1]

Studies serve for delight, for ornament, and for ability. Their chief use for delight is in privateness[2] and retiring; for ornament, is in discourse; and for ability, is in the judgment and disposition of business. For expert men[3] can execute, and perhaps judge of particulars, one by one; but the general counsels, and the plots and marshaling of affairs, come best from those that are learned. To spend too much time in studies is sloth; to use them too much for ornament is affectation; to make judgment wholly by their rules is the humor[4] of a scholar. They perfect nature, and are perfected by experience; for natural abilities are like natural plants, that need pruning by study; and studies themselves do give forth directions too much at large, except they be bounded in by experience. Crafty men contemn studies, simple men admire them, and wise men use them, for they teach not their own use; but that is a wisdom without them, and above them, won by observation. Read not to contradict and confute, nor to believe and take for granted, nor to find talk and discourse, but to weigh and consider. Some books are to be tasted, others to be swallowed, and some few to be chewed and digested; that is, some books are to be read only in parts; others to be read, but not curiously;[5] and some few to be read wholly, and with diligence and attention. Some books also may be read by deputy and extracts made of them by others, but that would be only in the less important arguments and the meaner sort of books; else distilled books are like common distilled waters,[6] flashy things. Reading maketh a full man, conference[7] a ready man, and writing an exact man. And therefore, if a man write little, he had need have a great memory; if he confer little, he had need have a present wit;[8] and if he read little, he had need have more cunning, to seem to know that[9] he doth not. Histories make men wise; poets, witty;[1] the mathematics, subtle; natural philosophy, deep; moral, grave; logic and rhetoric, able to contend. *Abeunt studia in mores.*[2] Nay, there is no stond or

1. The text is that of the 1625 edition.
2. Private life.
3. Men of experience, the English adjective being used in its Latin sense, *experti*.
4. Mannerism, implying absurd error.
5. Not with care.
6. Infusions of herbs, etc., used as home remedies.
7. Conversation, meetings.
8. Lively intelligence.
9. That which.
1. Imaginative, inventive.
2. "Studies culminate in manners" (Ovid, *Heroides*). "Stond": difficulty.

impediment in the wit but may be wrought out by fit studies, like as diseases of the body may have appropriate exercises. Bowling is good for the stone and reins,[3] shooting for the lungs and breast, gentle walking for the stomach, riding for the head, and the like. So if a man's wit be wandering, let him study the mathematics; for in demonstrations, if his wit be called away never so little, he must begin again. If his wit be not apt to distinguish or find differences, let him study the schoolmen,[4] for they are *Cymini sectores*. If he be not apt to beat over matters[5] and to call up one thing to prove and illustrate another, let him study the lawyer's cases. So every defect of the mind may have a special receipt.[6]

1597, 1625

Of Negotiating[7]

It is generally better to deal by speech than by letter, and by the mediation of a third than by a man's self. Letters are good when a man would draw an answer by letter back again, or when it may serve for a man's justification afterwards to produce his own letter, or where it may be danger to be interrupted or heard by pieces. To deal in person is good when a man's face breedeth regard, as commonly with inferiors, or in tender[1] cases, where a man's eye upon the countenance of him with whom he speaketh may give him a direction how far to go; and generally, where a man will reserve to himself liberty either to disavow or to expound. In choice of instruments, it is better to choose men of a plainer sort, that are like to do that that is committed to them, and to report back again faithfully the success, than those that are cunning to contrive out of other men's business somewhat to grace themselves, and will help the matter in report for satisfaction sake. Use also such persons as affect[2] the business wherein they are employed, for that quickeneth much; and such as are fit for the matter, as bold men for expostulation, fair-spoken men for persuasion, crafty men for inquiry and observation, froward and absurd men for business that doth not well bear out itself.[3] Use also such as have been lucky, and prevailed before in things wherein you have employed them; for that breeds confidence, and they will strive to maintain their prescription.[4] It is better to sound a person with whom one deals afar off, than to fall upon the point at first, except you mean to sur-

3. Gall bladder and kidneys.
4. Medieval theologians. The Latin means "dividers of cuminseed," i.e., hairsplitters.
5. Discuss a subject thoroughly.
6. Cure, prescription.
7. The text is that of the 1625 edition.

1. Difficult, complex.
2. Like.
3. Bacon suggests that when you have an unjust demand to make, you select a fool to make it.
4. Keep up their reputation.

prise him by some short question. It is better dealing with men in appetite,[5] than with those that are where they would be. If a man deal with another upon conditions, the start or first performance is all,[6] which a man cannot reasonably demand, except either the nature of the thing be such which must go before, or else a man can persuade the other party that he shall still need him in some other thing, or else that he be counted the honester man. All practice is to discover or to work.[7] Men discover themselves in trust, in passion, at unawares, and of necessity, when they would have somewhat done and cannot find an apt pretext. If you would work any man, you must either know his nature and fashions, and so lead him; or his ends, and so persuade him; or his weakness and disadvantages, and so awe him; or those that have interest in him, and so govern him. In dealing with cunning persons, we must ever consider their ends, to interpret their speeches; and it is good to say little to them, and that which they least look for. In all negotiations of difficulty, a man may not look to sow and reap at once; but must prepare business, and so ripen it by degrees.

1612, 1625

Of Masques and Triumphs[1]

These things are but toys to come amongst such serious observations. But yet, since princes will have such things, it is better they should be graced with elegancy than daubed with cost. Dancing to song is a thing of great state and pleasure. I understand it that the song be in choir,[2] placed aloft, and accompanied with some broken music; and the ditty fitted to the device.[3] Acting in song, especially in dialogues, hath an extreme good grace; I say acting, not dancing (for that is a mean and vulgar thing); and the voices of the dialogue would be strong and manly (a bass and a tenor; no treble), and the ditty high and tragical, not nice or dainty. Several choirs placed one over against another and taking the voice by catches, anthem-wise,[4] give great pleasure. Turning dances into figure is a childish curiosity.[5] And generally let it be noted that those things which I here set down are such as do naturally take the sense and not respect petty wonderments. It is true the alterations of scenes,

5. Hungry men.
6. If you're arguing over details, they will have to be settled by reference to the basic agreement, or to some other power relationship.
7. All sharp bargaining aims to find out what men are up to or to make use of them. "Discover": reveal.
1. Two varieties of amateur theatricals performed at court—ceremonial celebrations.
2. The singers should be placed as a choir in a gallery; the instrumental accompaniment is to be "broken," i.e., intermittent.
3. I.e., the song should be suited to the action.
4. I.e., the choirs should sing responsively.
5. Making the pattern of the dance an emblem of some sort is, according to Bacon, an idle oddity.

so it be quietly and without noise, are things of great beauty and pleasure, for they feed and relieve the eye before it be full of the same object. Let the scenes abound with light, specially colored and varied, and let the masquers or any other that are to come down from the scene have some motions upon the scene itself before their coming down; for it draws the eye strangely and makes it with great pleasure to desire to see that[6] it cannot perfectly discern. Let the songs be loud and cheerful, and not chirpings or pulings.[7] Let the music likewise be sharp and loud and well placed. The colors that show best by candle light are white, carnation, and a kind of sea-water green; and oes or spangs,[8] as they are of no great cost, so they are of most glory. As for rich embroidery, it is lost and not discerned. Let the suits of the masquers be graceful, and such as become the person when the vizards[9] are off, not after examples of known attires—Turks, soldiers, mariners, and the like. Let antimasques[1] not be long; they have been commonly of fools, satyrs, baboons, wild men, antics, beasts, sprites, witches, Ethiops, pygmies, turquets,[2] nymphs, rustics, Cupids, statua's moving, and the like. As for angels, it is not comical enough to put them in antimasques; and anything that is hideous, as devils, giants, is on the other side as unfit. But chiefly let the music of them be recreative and with some strange changes. Some sweet odors suddenly coming forth, without any drops falling, are, in such a company as there is steam and heat, things of great pleasure and refreshment. Double masques, one of men, another of ladies, addeth state and variety. But all is nothing except the room be kept clear and neat.

For jousts and tourneys and barriers,[3] the glories of them are chiefly in the chariots, wherein the challengers make their entry, especially if they be drawn with strange beasts, as lions, bears, camels, and the like; or in the devices of their entrance, or in the bravery of their liveries,[4] or in the goodly furniture of their horses and armor. But enough of these toys.

1625

6. What.
7. I.e., not squeaky or wailing.
8. Sequins or spangles.
9. Masks.
1. Grotesque dances of odd or macabre characters, who served in masques to contrast with the noble and beautiful masquers.
2. Actors disguised in Turkish costumes.
3. These are all varieties of mock combats or tournaments.
4. Attire.

From Novum Organum[1]

[*The Idols*]

50

But by far the greatest hindrance and aberration of the human understanding proceeds from the dullness, incompetency, and deceptions of the senses; in that things which strike the sense outweigh things which do not immediately strike it, though they[2] be more important. Hence it is that speculation commonly ceases where sight ceases; insomuch that of things invisible there is little or no observation. Hence all the working of the spirits enclosed in tangible bodies lies hid and unobserved of men.[3] So also all the more subtle changes of form in the parts of coarser substances (which they commonly call alteration, though it is in truth local motion through exceedingly small spaces) is in like manner unobserved. And yet unless these two things just mentioned be searched out and brought to light, nothing great can be achieved in nature, as far as the production of works is concerned. So again the essential nature of our common air, and of all bodies less dense than air (which are very many), is almost unknown. For the sense by itself is a thing infirm and erring; neither can instruments for enlarging or sharpening the senses do much; but all the truer kind of interpretation of nature is effected by instances and experiments fit and apposite; wherein the sense decides touching the experiment only, and the experiment touching the point in nature and the thing itself.

51

The human understanding is of its own nature prone to abstractions and gives a substance and reality to things which are fleeting. But to resolve nature into abstractions is less to our purpose than to dissect her into parts; as did the school of Democritus,[4] which

1. *Novum Organum,* or "The New Instrument of Learning," does not properly represent a work of English literature, since it was written in Latin, for an international scholarly audience. (Bacon rather mistrusted the modern languages, thinking they would "wear away" in time; but Latin was safe.) Still, no history of English ideas can afford to ignore this book; for it was the keystone of Bacon's vast project to renovate the structure of human learning from the ground up. The translation is that of Spedding, Ellis, and Heath, from their edition of the *Works* (1860–64).

Observation was the essential process of Bacon's new method; he felt that only observation, long continued and carefully directed, was capable of producing certainty about the operations of nature. As against the true intellectual mean produced by careful observation and controlled experiment, he set the frivolity of the skeptics and the unwarranted confidence of the dogmatists. This argument rises to its height about halfway through the first (destructive) part of the book, in an extended account of the various Idols, or delusive ideas, which mislead and bewilder the human understanding.

2. The latter.

3. Though his views on scientific method were amazingly modern, Bacon's ideas about physical phenomena were those of his age; he believed in subtle spiritual principles which might lie concealed in physical objects, unobserved by men.

4. The school of Democritus, the "laughing philosopher" of ancient Greece (5th century B.C.), held that the world was composed of atoms. Democritus developed the atomic theory, of which Leucippus was the originator; Lucretius (four centuries later) became the great literary exponent of this school.

went further into nature than the rest. Matter rather than forms should be the object of our attention, its configurations and changes of configuration, and simple action, and law of action or motion; for forms are figments of the human mind, unless you will call those laws of action forms.

52

Such then are the idols which I call *Idols of the Tribe*;[5] and which take their rise either from the homogeneity of the substance of the human spirit, or from its preoccupation, or from its narrowness, or from its restless motion, or from an infusion of the affections, or from the incompetency of the senses, or from the mode of impression.

53

The *Idols of the Cave* take their rise in the peculiar constitution, mental or bodily, of each individual; and also in education, habit, and accident. Of this kind there is a great number and variety; but I will instance those the pointing out of which contains the most important caution, and which have most effect in disturbing the clearness of the understanding.

54

Men become attached to certain particular sciences[6] and speculations, either because they fancy themselves the authors and inventors thereof, or because they have bestowed the greatest pains upon them and become most habituated to them. But men of this kind, if they betake themselves to philosophy and contemplations of a general character, distort and color them in obedience to their former fancies; a thing especially to be noticed in Aristotle, who made his natural philosophy a mere bondservant to his logic, thereby rendering it contentious and well nigh useless. The race of chemists[7] again out of a few experiments of the furnace have built up a fantastic philosophy, framed with reference to a few things; and Gilbert also, after he had employed himself most laboriously in the study and observation of the loadstone, proceeded at once to construct an entire system in accordance with his favorite subject.[8]

55

There is one principal and, as it were, radical distinction between different minds, in respect of philosophy and the sciences, which is this: that some minds are stronger and apter to mark the differences of things, others to mark their resemblances. The steady and acute mind can fix its contemplations and dwell and fasten on the subtlest

5. By "Idols" Bacon means delusive images of truth, leading men away from the exact knowledge of science. By "Idols of the Tribe" he denotes particularly generalizations based on inadequate facts—a fault to which all men are prone.

6. Ideas, bits of information.

7. Alchemists.

8. William Gilbert, author of a famous treatise on the magnet (1600), serves Bacon (rather unfairly) as an example of dogmatism founded on a few limited experiments.

distinctions: the lofty and discursive mind recognizes and puts together the finest and most general resemblances. Both kinds however easily err in excess, by catching the one at gradations, the other at shadows.

56

There are found some minds given to an extreme admiration of antiquity, others to an extreme love and appetite for novelty; but few so duly tempered that they can hold the mean, neither carping at what has been well laid down by the ancients, nor despising what is well introduced by the moderns. This however turns to the great injury of the sciences and philosophy; since these affectations of antiquity and novelty are the humors of partisans rather than judgments; and truth is to be sought for not in the felicity of any age, which is an unstable thing, but in the light of nature and experience, which is eternal. These factions therefore must be abjured, and care must be taken that the intellect be not hurried by them into assent.

57

Contemplations of nature and of bodies in their simple form break up and distract the understanding, while contemplations of nature and bodies in their composition and configuration overpower and dissolve the understanding:[9] a distinction well seen in the school of Leucippus and Democritus as compared with the other philosophies. For that school is so busied with the particles that it hardly attends to the structure; while the others are so lost in admiration of the structure that they do not penetrate to the simplicity of nature. These kinds of contemplation should therefore be alternated and taken by turns; that so the understanding may be rendered at once penetrating and comprehensive, and the inconveniences above mentioned, with the idols which proceed from them, may be avoided.

58

Let such then be our provision and contemplative prudence for keeping off and dislodging the *Idols of the Cave*, which grow for the most part either out of the predominance of a favorite subject, or out of an excessive tendency to compare or to distinguish, or out of partiality for particular ages, or out of the largeness or minuteness of the objects contemplated. And generally let every student of nature take this as a rule—that whatever his mind seizes and dwells upon with peculiar satisfaction is to be held in suspicion, and that so much the more care is to be taken in dealing with such questions to keep the understanding even and clear.

59

But the *Idols of the Market-place* are the most troublesome of all: idols which have crept into the understanding through the alliances

9. I.e., reducing nature to first principles is, intellectually, as dangerous as trying to observe all its particulars.

of words and names. For men believe that their reason governs words; but it is also true that words react on the understanding; and this it is that has rendered philosophy and the sciences sophistical and inactive. Now words, being commonly framed and applied according to the capacity of the vulgar, follow those lines of division which are most obvious to the vulgar understanding. And whenever an understanding of greater acuteness or a more diligent observation would alter those lines to suit the true divisions of nature, words stand in the way and resist the change. Whence it comes to pass that the high and formal discussions of learned men end oftentimes in disputes about words and names; with which (according to the use[1] and wisdom of the mathematicians) it would be more prudent to begin, and so by means of definitions reduce them to order. Yet even definitions cannot cure this evil in dealing with natural and material things; since the definitions themselves consist of words, and those words beget others: so that it is necessary to recur to individual instances, and those in due series and order; as I shall say presently when I come to the method and scheme for the formation of notions and axioms.[2]

60

The idols imposed by words on the understanding are of two kinds. They are either names of things which do not exist (for as there are things left unnamed through lack of observation, so likewise are there names which result from fantastic suppositions and to which nothing in reality responds), or they are names of things which exist, but yet confused and ill-defined, and hastily and irregularly derived from realities. Of the former kind are Fortune, the Prime Mover, Planetary Orbits, Element of Fire, and like fictions which owe their origin to false and idle theories.[3] And this class of idols is more easily expelled, because to get rid of them it is only necessary that all theories should be steadily rejected and dismissed as obsolete.[4]

But the other class, which springs out of a faulty and unskillful abstraction, is intricate and deeply rooted. Let us take for example such a word as *humid*; and see how far the several things which

1. Custom.

2. Bacon's mistrust of words, evident here, led the Royal Society to cultivate a plain, stripped prose style for purposes of scientific communication.

3. The "Prime Mover" was a transparent sphere on the outside of the universe, supposed to move all the other spheres; the "Element of Fire" was an area of pure, invisible fire, supposed to exist above the atmosphere. In the nature of things, these concepts could be based on no observation. "Planetary Orbits," on the other hand, are very real; Bacon may be referring to the old notion of crystalline spheres in which the planets were supposed to be set.

4. Bacon does not really mean "theories" in the inclusive modern sense, but "abstractions loosely invoked to explain particular facts." He is actually restating William of Occam's famous 14th-century principle, known as "Occam's razor," to the effect that "essences must not be multiplied beyond necessity."

the word is used to signify agree with each other; and we shall find the word *humid* to be nothing else than a mark loosely and confusedly applied to denote a variety of actions which will not bear to be reduced to any constant meaning. For it both signifies that which easily spreads itself round any other body; and that which in itself is indeterminate and cannot solidize; and that which readily yields in every direction; and that which easily divides and scatters itself; and that which easily unites and collects itself; and that which readily flows and is put in motion; and that which readily clings to another body and wets it; and that which is easily reduced to a liquid, or being solid easily melts. Accordingly when you come to apply the word—if you take it in one sense, flame is humid; if in another, air is not humid; if in another, fine dust is humid; if in another, glass is humid. So that it is easy to see that the notion is taken by abstraction only from water and common and ordinary liquids, without any due verification.

There are however in words certain degrees of distortion and error. One of the least faulty kinds is that of names of substances, especially of lowest species and well-deduced (for the notion of *chalk* and of *mud* is good, of *earth* bad); a more faulty kind is that of actions, as *to generate, to corrupt, to alter;* the most faulty is of qualities (except such as are the immediate objects of the sense), as *heavy, light, rare, dense,* and the like. Yet in all these cases some notions are of necessity a little better than others, in proportion to the greater variety of subjects that fall within the range of the human sense.

61

But the *Idols of the Theater*[5] are not innate, nor do they steal into the understanding secretly, but are plainly impressed and received into the mind from the play-books of philosophical systems and the perverted rules of demonstration. To attempt refutations in this case would be merely inconsistent with what I have already said: for since we agree neither upon principles nor upon demonstrations, there is no place for argument. And this is so far well, inasmuch as it leaves the honor of the ancients untouched. For they are no wise disparaged—the question between them and me being only as to the way. For as the saying is, the lame man who keeps the right road outstrips the runner who takes a wrong one. Nay, it is obvious that when a man runs the wrong way, the more active and swift he is the further he will go astray.

But the course I propose for the discovery of sciences is such as leaves but little to the acuteness and strength of wits, but places all

5. I.e., those derived from previous philosophical systems, which misrepresent life by overdramatizing it and mislead men by pretending to show them reality itself.

wits and understandings nearly on a level. For as in the drawing of a straight line or a perfect circle, much depends on the steadiness and practice of the hand, if it be done by aim of hand only, but if with the aid of rule or compass, little or nothing; so is it exactly with my plan. But though particular confutations would be of no avail, yet touching the sects and general divisions of such systems I must say something; something also touching the external signs which show that they are unsound; and finally something touching the causes of such great infelicity and of such lasting and general agreement in error; that so the access to truth may be made less difficult, and the human understanding may the more willingly submit to its purgation and dismiss its idols.

62

Idols of the Theater, or of systems, are many, and there can be and perhaps will be yet many more. For were it not that now for many ages men's minds have been busied with religion and theology; and were it not that civil governments, especially monarchies, have been averse to such novelties, even in matters speculative; so that men labor therein to the peril and harming of their fortunes—not only unrewarded, but exposed also to contempt and envy; doubtless there would have arisen many other philosophical sects like to those which in great variety flourished once among the Greeks. For as on the phenomena of the heavens many hypotheses may be constructed, so likewise (and more also) many various dogmas may be set up and established on the phenomena of philosophy. And in the plays of this philosophical theater you may observe the same thing which is found in the theater of the poets, that stories invented for the stage are more compact and elegant, and more as one would wish them to be, than true stories out of history.

In general, however, there is taken for the material of philosophy either a great deal out of a few things, or a very little out of many things; so that on both sides philosophy is based on too narrow a foundation of experiment and natural history, and decides on the authority of too few cases. For the rational school of philosophers snatches from experience a variety of common instances, neither duly ascertained nor diligently examined and weighed, and leaves all the rest to meditation and agitation of wit.[6]

There is also another class of philosophers, who having bestowed much diligent and careful labor on a few experiments, have thence made bold to educe and construct systems; wresting all other facts in a strange fashion to conformity therewith.

6. Bacon's thought contained a concealed element of anti-intellectualism: his enthusiasm for experiment led him to denigrate the value of reason, as very few modern scientists would feel it necessary to do. What he is opposing here is an excessive concern with the forms of logic, as exemplified, he would say, in "the schoolmen."

And there is yet a third class, consisting of those who out of faith and veneration mix their philosophy with theology and traditions; among whom the vanity of some has gone so far aside as to seek the origin of sciences among spirits and genii. So that this parent stock of errors—this false philosophy—is of three kinds; the sophistical, the empirical, and the superstitious. * * *

68

So much concerning the several classes of idols, and their equipage: all of which must be renounced and put away with a fixed and solemn determination, and the understanding thoroughly freed and cleansed; the entrance into the kingdom of man, founded on the sciences, being not much other than the entrance into the kingdom of heaven, whereinto none may enter except as a little child.

1620

From The New Atlantis[1]

[*Solomon's House*]

We came at our day and hour, and I was chosen by my fellows for the private access.[2] We found him in a fair chamber, richly hanged, and carpeted under foot, without any degrees to the state.[3] He was set upon a low throne richly adorned, and a rich cloth of state over his head, of blue satin embroidered. He was alone, save that he had two pages of honor, on either hand one, finely attired in white. His undergarments were the like that we saw him wear in the chariot; but instead of his gown, he had on him a mantle with a cape of the same fine black, fastened about him. When we came in, as we were taught, we bowed low at our first entrance, and when we were come near his chair, he stood up, holding forth his hand ungloved and in posture of blessing; and we every one of us stooped down, and kissed the hem of his tippet.[4] That done, the rest departed, and I remained. Then he warned the pages forth of

1. Sir Thomas More's *Utopia* (1516) set a fashion for imaginary communities with ideal forms of government which was suddenly taken up in the early 17th century. The German Johann Andreae published in 1619 his *Christianopolis;* Thomas Campanella, languishing in a Neapolitan jail, wrote his *City of the Sun* in 1623. Bacon's contribution to the discussion, perhaps because he never completed it, is really tangential to the concept of an ideal commonwealth. His *New Atlantis* is in effect a research establishment which could exist in any society that would tolerate it. Perhaps for that reason, it had an immediate influence beyond that of most full-fledged Utopias; and was largely realized, within thirty years of its publication, in the shape of the Philosophical Society which in 1662 became the Royal Society. Bacon begins by describing an imaginary voyage to the island of Bensalem, supposed to lie in the vicinity of the Bering Straits. Here, after learning about the miraculous diffusion of Christianity to the island, he is invited to visit their most interesting institution, Solomon's House.

2. Audience.

3. I.e., without stairs leading up to the dais.

4. Scarf.

the room, and caused me to sit down beside him, and spake to me thus in the Spanish tongue:

"God bless thee, my son; I will give thee the greatest jewel I have. For I will impart unto thee, for the love of God and men, a relation of the true state of Solomon's House. Son, to make you know the true state of Solomon's House, I will keep this order. First, I will set forth unto you the end of our foundation. Secondly, the preparations and instruments we have for our works. Thirdly, the several employments and functions whereto our fellows are assigned. And fourthly, the ordinances and rites which we observe.

"The end of our foundation is the knowledge of causes, and secret motions of things; and the enlarging of the bounds of human empire, to the effecting of all things possible.

"The preparations and instruments are these. We have large and deep caves of several depths: the deepest are sunk six hundred fathoms; and some of them are digged and made under great hills and mountains; so that if you reckon together the depth of the hill, and the depth of the cave, they are, some of them, above three miles deep. For we find that the depth of a hill, and the depth of a cave from the flat, is the same thing; both remote alike from the sun and heaven's beams, and from the open air. These caves we call the lower region, and we use them for all coagulations, indurations,[5] refrigerations, and conservations of bodies. We use them likewise for the imitation of natural mines, and the producing also of new artificial metals, by compositions and materials which we use, and lay there for many years. We use them also sometimes (which may seem strange) for curing of some diseases, and for prolongation of life in some hermits that choose to live there, well accommodated of[6] all things necessary, and indeed live very long; by whom also we learn many things.

"We have burials in several earths, where we put divers cements,[7] as the Chinese do their porcelain. But we have them in greater variety, and some of them more fine. We also have great variety of composts[8] and soils, for the making of the earth fruitful.

"We have high towers, the highest about half a mile in height, and some of them likewise set upon high mountains, so that the vantage of the hill, with the tower, is in the highest of them three miles at least. And these places we call the upper region, accounting the air between the high places and the low as a middle region. We use these towers, according to their several heights and situations, for insolation,[9] refrigeration, conservation, and for the view of divers meteors—as winds, rain, snow, hail;[1] and some of the fiery me-

5. Hardenings.
6. Provided with.
7. Clays and pottery mixtures.
8. Manures.
9. Exposure to the sun.
1. Anything that fell from the sky was, in Renaissance terminology, a meteor.

teors also. And upon them, in some places, are dwellings of hermits, whom we visit sometimes, and instruct what to observe.

"We have great lakes, both salt and fresh, whereof we have use for the fish and fowl. We use them also for burials of some natural bodies, for we find a difference in things buried in earth, or in air below the earth, and things buried in water. We have also pools, of which some do strain fresh water out of salt, and others by art do turn fresh water into salt. We have also some rocks in the midst of the sea, and some bays upon the shore, for some works wherein is required the air and vapor of the sea. We have likewise violent streams and cataracts, which serve us for many motions; and likewise engines for multiplying and enforcing[2] of winds to set also on going divers motions.

"We have also a number of artificial wells and fountains, made in imitation of the natural sources and baths, as tincted upon[3] vitriol, sulphur, steel, brass, lead, nitre, and other minerals; and again, we have little wells for infusions of many things, where the waters take the virtue[4] quicker and better than in vessels or basins. And amongst them we have a water, which we call Water of Paradise, being by that we do to it, made very sovereign[5] for health and prolongation of life.

"We have also great and spacious houses, where we imitate and demonstrate meteors—as snow, hail, rain, some artificial rains of bodies, and not of water, thunders, lightnings; also generations of bodies in air—as frogs, flies, and divers others.

"We have also certain chambers, which we call chambers of health, where we qualify[6] the air as we think good and proper for the cure of divers diseases, and preservation of health.

"We have also fair and large baths, of several mixtures, for the cure of diseases, and the restoring of a man's body from arefaction;[7] and others for the confirming of it in strength of sinews, vital parts, and the very juice and substance of the body.

"We have also large and various orchards and gardens, wherein we do not so much respect beauty as variety of ground and soil, proper for divers trees and herbs, and some very spacious, where trees and berries are set, whereof we make divers kinds of drinks, besides the vineyards. In these we practice likewise all conclusions[8] of grafting and inoculating, as well of wild-trees as fruit-trees, which produceth many effects. And we make (by art) in the same orchards and gardens trees and flowers to come earlier or later than their seasons, and to come up and bear more speedily than by their natural course they do. We make them also by art greater much than their

2. Re-enforcing, strengthening.
3. Tinctured with.
4. Property (of the substances put into water).
5. Efficacious.
6. Modify.
7. Drying up.
8. Theories.

nature; and their fruit greater and sweeter, and of differing taste, smell, color, and figure, from their nature. And many of them we so order as they become of medicinal use.

"We have also means to make divers plants rise by mixtures of earths without seeds, and likewise to make divers new plants, differing from the vulgar,[9] and to make one tree or plant turn into another.

"We have also parks, and enclosures of all sorts, of beasts and birds; which we use not only for view or rareness, but likewise for dissections and trials,[1] that thereby we may take light what may be wrought upon the body of man. Wherein we find many strange effects: as continuing life in them, though divers parts, which you account vital, be perished and taken forth; resuscitating of some that seem dead in appearance, and the like. We try also all poisons, and other medicines upon them, as well of chirurgery[2] as physic. By art likewise, we make them greater or taller than their kind is, and contrariwise dwarf them and stay their growth; we make them more fruitful and bearing than their kind is, and contrariwise barren and not generative. Also we make them differ in color, shape, activity, many ways. We find means to make commixtures and copulations of divers kind, which have produced many new kinds,[3] and them not barren, as the general opinion is. We make a number of kinds of serpents, worms, fishes, flies, of putrefaction, whereof some are advanced (in effect) to be perfect creatures, like beasts or birds, and have sexes, and do propagate. Neither do we this by chance, but we know beforehand of what matter and commixture what kind of those creatures will arise.

"We have also particular pools where we make trials upon fishes, as we have said before of beasts and birds.

"We have also places for breed and generation of those kinds of worms and flies which are of special use; such as are with you your silkworms and bees.

"I will not hold you long with recounting of our brew-houses, bake-houses, and kitchens, where are made divers drinks, breads, and meats, rare and of special effects. Wines we have of grapes, and drinks of other juice of fruits, of grains, and of roots, and of mixtures with honey, sugar, manna, and fruits dried and decocted;[4] also of the tears or woundings of trees, and of the pulp of canes. And these drinks are of several ages, some to the age or last[5] of forty years. We have drinks also brewed with several herbs, and roots and spices; yea, with several fleshes and whitemeats;[6] whereof some of the drinks are such as they are in effect meat and drink both, so that

9. Ordinary.
1. Experiments.
2. Surgery.
3. Species.
4. Dissolved in water, by boiling.
5. Duration.
6. Breast of chicken, fish, sometimes cheese.

divers, especially in age, do desire to live with them, with little or no meat or bread. And above all, we strive to have drinks of extreme thin parts, to insinuate into the body, and yet without all biting, sharpness, or fretting; insomuch as some of them, put upon the back of your hand, will with a little stay[7] pass through to the palm, and yet taste mild to the mouth. We have also waters, which we ripen in that fashion, as they become nourishing, so that they are indeed excellent drink, and many will use no other. Bread we have of several grains, roots, and kernels; yea, and some of flesh, and fish, dried; with divers kinds of leavenings and seasonings; so that some do extremely move appetites; some do nourish so, as divers do live of them, without any other meat, who live very long. So for meats, we have some of them so beaten, and made tender, and mortified,[8] yet without all corrupting, as a weak heat of the stomach will turn them into good chylus,[9] as well as a strong heat would meat otherwise prepared. We have some meats also, and breads, and drinks, which taken by men, enable them to fast long after; and some other, that used[1] make the very flesh of men's bodies sensibly more hard and tough, and their strength far greater than otherwise it would be.

"We have dispensatories, or shops of medicines; wherein you may easily think, if we have such variety of plants and living creatures more than you have in Europe (for we know what you have), the simples,[2] drugs, and ingredients of medicines, must likewise be in so much the greater variety. We have them likewise of divers ages, and long fermentations. And for their preparations, we have not only all manner of exquisite distillations and separations, and especially by gentle heats, and percolations through divers strainers, yea, and substances; but also exact forms of composition,[3] whereby they incorporate almost as they were natural simples.

"We have also divers mechanical arts, which you have not; and stuffs made by them, as papers, linen, silks, tissues, dainty works of feathers of wonderful luster, excellent dyes, and many others. and shops likewise, as well for such as are not brought into vulgar use amongst us, as for those that are. For you must know, that of the things before recited, many of them are grown into use throughout the kingdom, but yet, if they did flow from our invention, we have of them also for patterns and principals.[4]

"We have also furnaces of great diversities, and that keep great diversity of heats: fierce and quick, strong and constant, soft and

7. Delay.
8. Softened.
9. Chyle, food in its emulsified and digestible form. Bacon thinks of the stomach as a furnace, which softens food by heat.
1. The word "when" is understood here.
2. Herbs.
3. Ways of putting the ingredients of medicines together, making compounds.
4. Models.

mild; blown, quiet; dry, moist; and the like. But above all we have heats, in imitations of the sun's and heavenly bodies' heats, that pass divers inequalities, and (as it were) orbs, progresses, and returns,[5] whereby we produce admirable effects. Besides, we have heats of dungs, and of bellies and maws of living creatures and of their bloods and bodies, and of hays and herbs laid up moist, of lime unquenched, and such like. Instruments also which generate heat only by motion. And farther, places for strong insolations; and again, places under the earth, which by nature or art yield heat. These divers heats we use as the nature of the operation which we intend requireth.

"We have also perspective houses,[6] where we make demonstrations of all lights and radiations, and of all colors; and out of things uncolored and transparent we can represent unto you all several colors, not in rainbows (as it is in gems and prisms), but of themselves single. We represent also all multiplications of light, which we carry to great distance, and make so sharp, as to discern small points and lines. Also all colorations of light; all delusions and deceits of the sight, in figures, magnitudes, motions, colors; all demonstrations of shadows. We find also divers means, yet unknown to you, of producing of light originally from divers bodies. We procure means of seeing objects afar off, as in the heaven and remote places; and represent things near as afar off, and things afar off as near, making feigned distances. We have also helps for the sight, far above spectacles and glasses in use. We have also glasses and means to see small and minute bodies, perfectly and distinctly; as the shapes and colors of small flies and worms, grains and flaws in gems which cannot otherwise be seen, observations in urine and blood not otherwise to be seen. We make artificial rainbows, halos, and circles about light. We represent also all manner of reflections, refractions, and multiplications of visual beams of objects.

"We have also precious stones of all kinds, many of them of great beauty and to you unknown; crystals likewise; and glasses of divers kinds; and amongst them some of metals vitrificated,[7] and other materials besides those of which you make glass. Also a number of fossils and imperfect minerals, which you have not. Likewise loadstones of prodigious virtue:[8] and other rare stones, both natural and artificial.

"We have also sound-houses, where we practice and demonstrate all sounds and their generation. We have harmonies which you have not, of quarter sounds and lesser slides of sounds. Divers instruments of music likewise to you unknown, some sweeter than any you have;

5. I.e.. the furnaces produce various heats at will.
6. For optical experiments.
7. Turned to glass.
8. Strength.

together with bells and rings that are dainty and sweet. We represent small sounds as great and deep; likewise great sounds, extenuate[9] and sharp; we make divers tremblings and warblings of sounds, which in their original are entire.[1] We represent and imitate all articulate sounds and letters, and the voices and notes of beasts and birds. We have certain helps, which set to the ear do further the hearing greatly. We have also divers strange and artificial echoes, reflecting the voice many times, and as it were tossing it; and some that give back the voice louder than it came, some shriller and some deeper; yea, some rendering[2] the voice, differing in the letters or articulate sound from that they receive. We have also means to convey sounds in trunks[3] and pipes, in strange lines and distances.

"We have also perfume-houses, wherewith we join also practices of taste. We multiply smells, which may seem strange: we imitate smells, making all smells to breathe out of other mixtures than those that give them. We make divers imitations of taste likewise, so that they will deceive any man's taste. And in this house we contain also a confiture-house, where we make all sweetmeats, dry and moist, and divers pleasant wines, milks, broths, and salads, far in greater variety than you have.

"We have also engine-houses, where are prepared engines and instruments for all sorts of motions. There we imitate and practice to make swifter motions than any you have, either out of your muskets or any engine that you have; and to make them and multiply them more easily and with small force, by wheels and other means, and to make them stronger and more violent than yours are, exceeding your greatest cannons and basilisks.[4] We represent also ordnance and instruments of war and engines of all kinds; and likewise new mixtures and compositions of gunpowder, wildfires burning in water and unquenchable; also fireworks of all variety, both for pleasure and use. We imitate also flights of birds; we have some degrees of flying[5] in the air. We have ships and boats for going under water and brooking[6] of seas, also swimming girdles and supporters. We have divers curious clocks, and other like motions of return, and some perpetual motions. We imitate also motions of living creatures by images of men, beasts, birds, fishes, and serpents; we have also a great number of other various motions, strange for equality,[7] fineness, and subtlety.

"We have also a mathematical-house, where are represented all instruments, as well of geometry as astronomy, exquisitely made.

"We have also houses of deceits of the senses, where we represent

9. Drawn out thin.
1. I.e., we can vary notes which in nature are single.
2. Transforming.
3. Tubes.
4. Cannon, named after the fabulous beast that killed by a beam from its eye.
5. I.e., rudimentary forms of flying.
6. Withstanding.
7. Unusual for their evenness.

all manners of feats of juggling, false apparitions, impostures and illusions, and their fallacies. And surely you will easily believe that we, that have so many things truly natural which induce admiration, could in a world of particulars deceive the senses if we would disguise those things, and labor to make them seem more miraculous. But we do hate all impostures and lies, insomuch as we have severely forbidden it to all our fellows, under pain of ignominy and fines, that they do not show any natural work or thing adorned or swelling, but only pure as it is, and without all affectation of strangeness.

"These are, my son, the riches of Solomon's House.

"For the several employments and offices of our fellows, we have twelve that sail into foreign countries under the names of other nations (for our own we conceal), who bring us the books and abstracts and patterns of experiments of all other parts. These we call Merchants of Light.

"We have three that collect the experiments which are in all books. These we call Depredators.

"We have three that collect the experiments of all mechanical arts, and also of liberal sciences, and also of practices which are not brought into arts. These we call Mystery-men.

"We have three that try new experiments, such as themselves think good. These we call Pioneers or Miners.

"We have three that draw the experiments of the former four into titles and tables, to give the better light for the drawing of observations and axioms out of them. These we call Compilers.

"We have three that bend themselves, looking into the experiments of their fellows, and cast about how to draw out of them things of use and practice for man's life and knowledge, as well for works as for plain demonstration of causes, means of natural divinations, and the easy and clear discovery of the virtues and parts of bodies. These we call Dowry-men or Benefactors.

"Then after divers meetings and consults of our whole number, to consider of the former labors and collections, we have three that take care out of them to direct new experiments, of a higher light, more penetrating into Nature than the former. These we call Lamps.

"We have three others that do execute the experiments so directed, and report them. These we call Inoculators.

"Lastly, we have three that raise the former discoveries by experiments into greater observations, axioms, and aphorisms. These we call Interpreters of Nature.[8]

"We have also, as you must think, novices and apprentices, that the succession of the former employed men do not fail; besides a

8. The total staff of Solomon's House is 36; a generous allowance, by Bacon's estimate, for the project of understanding the natural cosmos. Modern researchers would want a little more staff.

great number of servants and attendants, men and women. And this we do also: we have consultations, which of the inventions and experiences which we have discovered shall be published, and which not; and take all an oath of secrecy for the concealing of those which we think fit to keep secret; though some of those we do reveal sometimes to the State, and some not.[9]

"For our ordinances and rites, we have two very long and fair galleries: in one of these we place patterns and samples of all manner of the more rare and excellent inventions; in the other we place the statues of all principal inventors. There we have the statue of your Columbus, that discovered the West Indies; also the inventor of ships; your monk that was the inventor of ordnance and of gunpowder;[1] the inventor of music; the inventor of letters; the inventor of printing; the inventor of observations of astronomy; the inventor of works in metal; the inventor of glass; the inventor of silk of the worm; the inventor of wine; the inventor of corn and bread; the inventor of sugars; and all these by more certain tradition than you have. Then we have divers inventors of our own, of excellent works, which since you have not seen, it were too long to make descriptions of them; and besides, in the right understanding of those descriptions you might easily err. For upon every invention of value we erect a statue to the inventor, and give him a liberal and honorable reward. These statues are some of brass, some of marble and touchstone,[2] some of cedar and other special woods gilt and adorned; some of iron, some of silver, some of gold.

"We have certain hymns and services, which we say daily of laud and thanks to God for His marvelous works. And forms of prayer, imploring His aid and blessing for the illumination of our labors, and the turning of them into good and holy uses.

"Lastly, we have circuits or visits, of divers principal cities of the kingdom; where, as it cometh to pass, we do publish such new profitable inventions as we think good. And we do also declare natural divinations of diseases, plagues, swarms of hurtful creatures, scarcity, tempests, earthquakes, great inundations, comets, temperature of the year, and divers other things; and we give counsel thereupon, what the people shall do for the prevention and remedy of them."

And when he had said this he stood up; and I, as I had been taught, kneeled down; and he laid his right hand upon my head, and said, "God bless thee, my son, and God bless this relation which I have made. I give thee leave to publish it, for the good of other nations; for we here are in God's bosom, a land unknown." And

9. Observe Bacon's suspicion of the body politic, and the freedom which he allows to Solomon's House from political pressure.

1. Tradition credits Roger Bacon, a 13th-century monk, with the discovery of gunpowder. Bacon tactfully avoids his name.

2. A hard basaltic-type rock.

so he left me; having assigned a value of about two thousand ducats for a bounty to me and my fellows. For they give great largesses, where they come, upon all occasions.

The rest was not perfected.

1627

ROBERT BURTON

(1577–1640)

Robert Burton was a scholar at Christ Church, Oxford, where he matriculated in 1593 and stayed for the rest of his life. He never traveled, never married, never sought "success" or attained it; he existed exclusively among books—old, crabbed books by preference. All this absorption in books was supposed (according to the lore of traditional medicine and the theory of "humors" dating back to the Greeks) to throw his constitution out of balance and produce a "melancholy" temperament in which black bile predominated. And in Burton's case, sure enough, that was what happened. His cure for the desperate condition afflicting him was to write a book about his disease; this project occupied the rest of his life.

It wasn't altogether an eccentric project. There had been many books on melancholy before: because of their sedentary life, it was the favorite disease of scholars, and so got a lot of attention. And the age was interested in taking man apart, in finding out what makes him tick. Sir John Davies wrote a long poem on normal psychology, in 1599; it was called *Nosce Teipsum*, or "Know Thyself." Somewhat later, Phineas Fletcher expanded on some Spenserian hints, particularly the "House of Alma" passage in the *Faerie Queene* (Book II, Canto ix), to create an allegorical anatomy of man, called *The Purple Island*. (Man's body is an island, rather like England, floating in the purple sea of his own blood: James Joyce was fascinated with the poem, and used it in the composition of *Ulysses*.) Thus Burton was in good company when he began his *Anatomy*. But nobody ever put so much energy into the subject, or handled it in such an epic way. The first edition came out in 1621; later editions, each augmented over the previous one, appeared in 1624, 1628, 1632, and 1638. When he died, in 1640, Burton left behind materials for still another, and bigger edition: the book continued to grow, even after the author's death, as if it had acquired a queer, unnatural vitality of its own.

These cumulative additions do not generally deepen the thought of the book or advance its argument into new territory; they are verbal tags from Burton's immense reading, stuck into the text of the book, after Montaigne's fashion, wherever they seemed more or less appropriate. For though he was perfectly serious in trying to understand the disease of melancholy, Burton wrote like a man afflicted with logorrhea. He poured forth words, his own and other people's, as if he were using them to relieve an inner pressure, rather than to express something. He never used one word where fifty would do, never refrained from an erudite citation just because he had said the same thing three times already. He was a humorist and a bit of a buffoon; the role he assumes in his *Anatomy* is that of a mad scholar choked on his own erudition and in danger of exploding from its inner pressures. When he thinks of all things that can make a man melancholy (or, as we would say, "neurotic"), Burton envisages "a stupend, vast, infinite Ocean of incredible madness and folly: a Sea full of shelves and rocks, sands, gulfs, Euripuses [currents] and contrary tides, full of fearful monsters, uncouth shapes, roaring waves, tempests, and Siren calms, Halcyonian Seas, unspeakable misery, such absurd and ridiculous, feral and lamentable fits, that I know not whether they are more to be pitied or derided, or may be believed, but that we daily see the same practiced in our days, fresh examples, new news, fresh objects of misery and madness in this kind, that are still represented to us, abroad, at home, in the midst of us, in our bosoms."

All that seething turmoil in the bosom of a retiring Oxford scholar! To relieve the pressure of it, Burton prescribed (among many, many other things) exercise and study, more and more study, more and more books, difficult but not necessarily useful projects, in a word, distractions—projects like the very book we are reading. Hysteria is diverted by giving it a toy to play with, a trifle to agitate: the mechanism is that described later by Swift in *A Tale of a Tub*. Burton describes the remedy at such vociferous length that it's clear he is practicing what he preaches in the very act of preaching it. But at the end of our selection, the whole exercise is stood on its head when the recommended cure turns out to be nothing less than the disease itself. It is a joke worthy of Burton's great predecessor in the field of medical clowning, François Rabelais.

From The Anatomy of Melancholy

From *Exercise Rectified*[1]

But amongst those exercises or recreations of the mind within doors, there is none so general, so aptly to be applied to all sorts of men, so fit and proper to expel idleness and melancholy, as that of study: "Study is the delight of old age, the support of youth, the ornament of prosperity, the solace and refuge of adversity, the delight of the household," etc., find the rest in Tully, *Pro Archia Poeta*.[2] What so full of content as to read, walk, and see maps, pictures, statues, jewels, marbles, which some so much magnify, as those that Phidias made of old so exquisite and pleasing to be beheld, that, as Chrysostom thinketh, "if any man be sickly, troubled in mind, or that cannot sleep for grief, and shall but stand over against one of Phidias's images, he will forget all care, or what-

1. Part II, Sect. 2, Mem. 4. Burton's book is elaborately subdivided into Parts, Sections, and Members; these are more formal than real, since he clearly writes whatever occurs to him next.
2. Tully is Cicero, the oration that in behalf of Archias the poet. In general, the footnotes for this selection will make no effort to follow Burton through the incredible mazes of the Bodleian library and his own memory.

soever else may molest him, in an instant?"[3] There be those as much taken with Michael Angelo's, Raphael de Urbino's, Francesco Francia's pieces, and many of those Italian and Dutch painters, which were excellent in their ages; and esteem of it as a most pleasing sight to view those neat architectures, devices, escutcheons, coats of arms, read such books, to peruse old coins of several sorts in a fair gallery; artificial works, perspective glasses, old relics, Roman antiquities, variety of colors. A good picture is *falsa veritas et muta poesis*[4] and though (as Vives saith)[5] *artificia delectant, sed mox fastidimus,* artificial toys please but for a time; yet who is he that will not be moved with them for the present?

* * * To most kind of men it is an extraordinary delight to study. For what a world of books offers itself, in all subjects, arts, and sciences, to the sweet content and capacity of the reader? In arithmetic, geometry, perspective, optics, astronomy, architecture, sculpture, painting, of which so many and such elaborate treatises are of late written; in mechanics and their mysteries, military matters, navigation, riding of horses, fencing, swimming, gardening, planting, great tomes of husbandry, cookery, falconry, hunting, fishing, fowling, &c., with exquisite pictures of all sports, games, and what not? In music, metaphysics, natural and moral philosophy, philology, in policy, heraldry, genealogy, chronology, &c., they afford great tomes, or those studies of antiquity, &c., *et quid subtilius Arithmeticis inventionibus, quid jucundius Musicis rationibus, quid divinius Astronomicis, quid rectius Geometricis demonstrationibus?*[6] What so sure, what so pleasant? He that shall but see that geometrical tower of Garezenda at Bologna in Italy, the steeple and clock at Strasburg, will admire the effects of art, or that engine of Archimedes, to remove the earth itself, if he had but a place to fasten his instrument; Archimedis Cochlea,[7] and the rare devices to corrivate waters, musical instruments, and trisyllable echoes again, again, and again repeated, with myriads of such. What vast tomes are extant in law, physic, and divinity for profit, pleasure, practice, speculation, in verse or prose, &c.! their names alone are the subject of great volumes, we have thousands of authors of all sorts, many great libraries full well furnished, like so many dishes of meat, served out for several palates; and he is a very block that is affected with none of them. Some take an infinite delight to study the very

3. St. John Chrysostom, an early Christian saint famous for his eloquence; Burton cites from his 12th oration.
4. "False truth and silent poetry."
5. Juan Luis Vives, 16th-century Spanish humanist: Burton cites from his commentary on *De Anima*.
6. "And what is subtler than arithmetical discoveries, what more pleasant than musical harmonies, what more divine than astronomical or more certain than geometrical demonstrations?" From Girolamo Cardano, 16th-century Italian physician-philosopher. The tower at Bologna and the steeple at Strasburg are about as real to Burton as the imaginary lever with which Archimedes said he could move the earth.
7. Archimedes' water screw.

languages wherein these books are written, Hebrew, Greek, Syriac, Chaldee, Arabic, &c. Methinks it would please any man to look upon a geographical map, *suavi animum delectatione allicere, ob incredibilem rerum varietatem et jucunditatem, et ad pleniorem sui cognitionem excitare,*[8] chorographical, topographical delineations, to behold, as it were, all the remote provinces, towns, cities of the world, and never to go forth to the limits of his study, to measure by the scale and compass their extent, distance, examine their site. Charles the Great, as Platina writes, had three fair silver tables, in one of which superficies was a large map of Constantinople, in the second, Rome neatly engraved, in the third an exquisite description of the whole world, and much delight he took in them. What greater pleasure can there now be, than to view those elaborate maps of Ortelius, Mercator, Hondius, &c.? To peruse those books of cities, put out by Braunus and Hogenbergius? To read those exquisite descriptions of Maginus, Munster, Herrera, Laet, Merula, Boterus, Leander, Albertus, Camden, Leo Afer, Adricomius, Nic. Gerbelius, &c.! Those famous expeditions of Christoph. Columbus, Americus Vespucius, Marcus Polus the Venetian, Lod. Vertomannus, Aloysius Cadamustus, &c.? Those accurate diaries of Portuguese, Hollanders, of Bartison, Oliver à Nort, &c., Hakluyt's Voyages, Pet. Martyr's Decades, Benzo, Lerius, Linschoten's relations, those Hodaeporicons of Jod. a Meggen, Brocard the monk, Bredenbachius, Jo. Dublinius, Sands, &c., to Jerusalem, Egypt, and other remote places of the world? Those pleasant itineraries of Paulus Hentzerus, Jodocus Sincerus, Dux Polonus, &c., to read Bellonius's observations, P. Gillius his surveys; those parts of America set out and curiously cut in pictures by Fratres a Bry. To see a well-cut herbal, herbs, trees, flowers, plants, all vegetables expressed in their proper colors to the life, as that of Matthiolus upon Dioscorides, Delacampius, Lobel, Bauhinus, and that last voluminous and mighty herbal of Beslar of Nuremberg, wherein almost every plant is to his own bigness. To see birds, beasts, and fishes of the sea, spiders, gnats, serpents, flies, &c., all creatures set out by the same art, and truly expressed in lively colors, with an exact description of their natures, qualities, &c., as hath been accurately performed by Aelian, Gesner, Ulysses Aldrovandus, Bellonius, Rondoletius, Hippolytus Salvianus, &c. * * *

King James, 1605, when he came to see our University of Oxford, and amongst other edifices now went to view that famous library renewed by Sir Thomas Bodley, in imitation of Alexander at his departure brake out into that noble speech, If I were not a king, I would be a university man; "and if it were so that I must be a pris-

8. "It allures the mind with profound pleasure, on account of the incredible variety and beauty of the subjects, and excites it to further knowledge." From the preface to Mercator's *Geography*.

oner, if I might have my wish, I would desire to have no other prison than that library, and to be chained together with so many good authors *et mortuis magistris* (and dead teachers)." So sweet is the delight of study, the more learning they have (as he that hath a dropsy. The more he drinks the thirstier he is), the more they covet to learn, and the last day is *prioris discipulus* (the student of the day before); harsh at first learning is, *radices amarae* (bitter roots), but *fructus dulces* (sweet fruits), according to that of Isocrates, pleasant at last; the longer they live, the more they are enamored with the Muses. Heinsius, the keeper of the library at Leyden in Holland, was mewed up in it all the year long; and that which to thy thinking should have bred a loathing caused in him a greater liking. "I no sooner (saith he) come into the library, but I bolt the door to me, excluding lust, ambition, avarice, and all such vices, whose nurse is idleness, the mother of ignorance, and melancholy herself, and in the very lap of eternity, amongst so many divine souls, I take my seat, with so lofty a spirit and sweet content, that I pity all our great ones, and rich men that know not this happiness."[9] * * *

Whosoever he is therefore that is overrun with solitariness, or carried away with pleasing melancholy and vain conceits, and for want of employment knows not how to spend his time, or crucified with worldly care, I can prescribe him no better remedy than this of study, to compose himself to the learning of some art or science. Provided always that this malady proceed not from overmuch study; for in such case he adds fuel to the fire, and nothing can be more pernicious; let him take heed he do not overstretch his wits, and make a skeleton of himself; or such inamoratos as read nothing but playbooks, idle poems, jests, Amadis de Gaul, the Knight of the Sun, the Seven Champions, Palmerin de Oliva, Huon of Bordeaux, &c. Such many times prove in the end as mad as Don Quixote. Study is only prescribed to those that are otherwise idle, troubled in mind, or carried headlong with vain thoughts and imaginations, to distract their cogitations (although variety of study, or some serious subject, would do the former no harm), and divert their continual meditations another way. Nothing in this case better than study. * * *

1621

9. From the letters of Daniel Heinsius. Burton in his last paragraph gets thoroughly entangled, for the people who can't be cured by study include not only those who've already studied too much, but those who haven't studied at all, who have read nothing but "playbooks, idle poems, jests." In short, study is a good cure for anyone who's cured by study, but not for anyone who isn't.

THOMAS HOBBES

(1588–1679)

Thomas Hobbes, the second great philosopher of the 17th century, was the acknowledged pupil of the first, Francis Bacon, and the unacknowledged instructor of the third, John Locke. Born in 1588 (Armada year), he had attended Oxford and then served as tutor and secretary to various noblemen, including several members of the Cavendish family, and Bacon. When the civil wars broke out in 1641 he took the Royalist side, though not very actively, and when the king's party was defeated, he went off to Paris with the royal court-in-exile. His plan as a philosopher was to publish one book on physical bodies, one on human nature, and one on the state; and in fact he wrote books under these three titles, both in English and Latin. But in reality his career is less symmetrical and orderly than that fact implies, because the English texts are often quite different from the Latin, and the book for which he is best known, *Leviathan,* does not fit into the scheme at all. *Leviathan* appeared in Paris in 1651, scandalizing Puritans by its frankly secular tone, and disturbing Royalists because it seemed to make no real distinction between a legal king and an established usurper. When Hobbes left Paris shortly after the book's publication, returned to England, and made his peace with Cromwell, the worst fears of the Royalists were realized. But their fury hit a peak after the Restoration, when Hobbes not only went unpunished for his "treason," but was pensioned by his old friend and former pupil, Charles II. Throughout the Restoration, his outspoken materialism made him a cause of scandal around the court; but his caustic tongue made him feared, and the indolent, cynical king was fond of him. Toward the end of his life he began gathering disciples, some of whom he would just as gladly have done without; for lewd, swearing, sceptical fellows sometimes took delight in being known as "Hobbists," not because they had studied or understood his philosophy, but because it was a name of scandal. He had a deeper influence on his enemies. A whole generation of theologians and moralists trained themselves by thundering against Hobbes. And in the meanwhile, the quiet, capacious mind of Locke absorbed what it wanted from the thought of Hobbes and, without getting involved in the Hobbist controversies, built a structure of incomparable solidity using many of the older philosopher's materials.

From Leviathan

Part I, Chapter 13. Of the Natural Condition of Mankind as Concerning Their Felicity and Misery

Nature hath made men so equal in the faculties of body and mind as that, though there be found one man sometimes manifestly stronger in body or of quicker mind than another, yet when all is reckoned together, the difference between man and man is not so considerable as that one man can thereupon claim to himself any benefit, to which another may not pretend as well as he. For as to the strength of body, the weakest has strength enough to kill the strongest, either by secret machination, or by confederacy with others that are in the same danger with himself.

And as to the faculties of the mind—setting aside the arts grounded upon words, and especially that skill of proceeding upon general and infallible rules, called science; which very few have, and but in few things; as being not a native faculty, born with us; nor attained, as prudence, while we look after somewhat else—I find yet a greater equality amongst men than that of strength. For prudence is but experience, which equal time equally bestows on all men, in those things they equally apply themselves unto. That which may perhaps make such equality incredible is but a vain conceit of one's own wisdom, which almost all men think they have in a greater degree than the vulgar—that is, than all men but themselves and a few others, whom by fame, or for concurring with themselves, they approve. For such is the nature of men, that howsoever they may acknowledge many others to be more witty, or more eloquent, or more learned, yet they will hardly believe there be many so wise as themselves; for they see their own wit at hand, and other men's at a distance. But this proveth rather that men are in that point equal, than unequal. For there is not ordinarily a greater sign of the equal distribution of anything than that every man is contented with his share.

From this equality of ability ariseth equality of hope in the attaining of our ends. And therefore if any two men desire the same thing, which nevertheless they cannot both enjoy, they become enemies; and in the way to their end (which is principally their own conservation, and sometimes their delectation only) endeavor to destroy or subdue one another. And from hence it comes to pass that where an invader hath no more to fear than another man's single power; if one plant, sow, build, or possess a convenient seat, others may probably be expected to come prepared with forces united, to dispossess and deprive him, not only of the fruit of his labor, but also of his life or liberty. And the invader again is in the like danger of another.

And from this diffidence[1] of one another, there is no way for any man to secure himself so reasonable as anticipation; that is, by force or wiles to master the persons of all men he can, so long, till he see no other power great enough to endanger him, and this is no more than his own conservation requireth, and is generally allowed. Also because there be some, that taking pleasure in contemplating their own power in the acts of conquest, which they pursue farther than their security requires; if others that otherwise would be glad to be

1. Lack of faith, mistrust.

at ease within modest bounds, should not by invasion increase their power, they would not be able long time, by standing only on their defense, to subsist. And by consequence, such augmentation of dominion over men being necessary to a man's conservation, it ought to be allowed him.

Again, men have no pleasure, but on the contrary a great deal of grief, in keeping company, where there is no power able to overawe them all. For every man looketh that his companion should value him at the same rate he sets upon himself; and upon all signs of contempt, or undervaluing, naturally endeavors, as far as he dares (which amongst them that have no common power to keep them in quiet, is far enough to make them destroy each other), to extort a greater value from his contemners by damage, and from others by the example.

So that in the nature of man, we find three principal causes of quarrel. First, competition; second, diffidence; thirdly, glory.

The first maketh men invade for gain; the second, for safety; and the third, for reputation. The first use violence to make themselves masters of other men's persons, wives, children, and cattle; the second, to defend them; the third, for trifles, as a word, a smile, a different opinion, and any other sign of undervalue, either direct in their persons, or by reflection in their kindred, their friends, their nation, their profession, or their name.

Hereby it is manifest that during the time men live without a common power to keep them all in awe, they are in that condition which is called war; and such a war as is of every man against every man. For war consisteth not in battle only, or the act of fighting, but in a tract of time wherein the will to contend by battle is sufficiently known, and therefore the notion of time is to be considered in the nature of war, as it is in the nature of weather. For as the nature of foul weather lieth not in a shower or two of rain, but in an inclination thereto of many days together; so the nature of war consisteth not in actual fighting, but in the known disposition thereto, during all the time there is no assurance to the contrary. All other time is peace.

Whatsoever therefore is consequent to a time of war, where every man is enemy to every man; the same is consequent to the time wherein men live without other security than what their own strength and their own invention shall furnish them withal. In such condition there is no place for industry, because the fruit thereof is uncertain, and consequently no culture of the earth; no navigation, nor use of the commodities that may be imported by sea; no commodious building; no instruments of moving, and removing, such things as require much force; no knowledge of the face of the earth; no account of time; no arts; no letters; no society; and which is worst of all, continual fear, and danger of violent death;

and the life of man, solitary, poor, nasty, brutish, and short.

It may seem strange to some man that has not well weighed these things, that nature should thus dissociate, and render men apt to invade and destroy one another; and he may therefore, not trusting to this inference, made from the passions, desire perhaps to have the same confirmed by experience. Let him therefore consider with himself, when taking a journey, he arms himself and seeks to go well accompanied; when going to sleep, he locks his doors; when even in his house he locks his chests; and this when he knows there be laws, and public officers, armed, to revenge all injuries shall be done him; what opinion he has of his fellow subjects, when he rides armed; of his fellow citizens, when he locks his doors; and of his children, and servants, when he locks his chests. Does he not there as much accuse mankind by his actions, as I do by my words? But neither of us accuse man's nature in it. The desires and other passions of man are in themselves no sin. No more are the actions that proceed from those passions, till they know a law that forbids them, which, till laws be made, they cannot know; nor can any law be made, till they have agreed upon the person that shall make it.

It may peradventure be thought there was never such a time nor condition of war as this; and I believe it was never generally so, over all the world; but there are many places where they live so now. For the savage people in many places of America, except the government of small families, the concord whereof dependeth on natural lust, have no government at all and live at this day in that brutish manner, as I said before. Howsoever, it may be perceived what manner of life there would be, where there were no common power to fear; by the manner of life which men that have formerly lived under a peaceful government use to degenerate into in a civil war.[2]

But though there had never been any time wherein particular men were in a condition of war one against another; yet in all times, kings and persons of sovereign authority, because of their independency, are in continual jealousies, and in the state and posture of gladiators; having their weapons pointing, and their eyes fixed on one another; that is, their forts, garrisons, and guns upon the frontiers of their kingdoms; and continual spies upon their neighbors; which is a posture of war. But because they uphold thereby the industry of their subjects, there does not follow from it that misery which accompanies the liberty of particular men.

To this war of every man against every man, this also is consequent: that nothing can be unjust. The notions of right and wrong, justice and injustice, have there no place. Where there is no com-

2. Hobbes may well be thinking of such famous accounts of savage civil wars as that of Thucydides (whom he translated).

mon power, there is no law; where no law, no injustice. Force and fraud are in war the two cardinal virtues. Justice and injustice are none of the faculties neither of the body nor mind. If they were, they might be in a man that were alone in the world, as well as his senses and passions. They are qualities that relate to men in society, not in solitude. It is consequent also to the same conditions that there be no propriety,[3] no dominion, no *mine* and *thine* distinct; but only that to be every man's, that he can get; and for so long as he can keep it. And thus much for the ill condition which man by mere nature is actually placed in; though with a possibility to come out of it, consisting partly in the passions, partly in his reason.

The passions that incline men to peace are fear of death, desire of such things as are necessary to commodious living, and a hope by their industry to obtain them. And reason suggesteth convenient articles of peace, upon which men may be drawn to agreement. These articles are they which otherwise are called the Laws of Nature whereof I shall speak more particularly in the two following chapters.

From *Part I, Chapter 14. Of the First and Second Natural Laws*

The Right of Nature, which writers commonly call *jus naturale,* is the liberty each man hath to use his own power as he will himself for the preservation of his own nature, that is to say, of his own life; and consequently of doing anything which in his own judgment and reason he shall conceive to be the aptest means thereunto.

By Liberty is understood, according to the proper signification of the word, the absence of external impediments, which impediments may oft take away part of a man's power to do what he would, but cannot hinder him from using the power left him according as his judgment and reason shall dictate to him.

A Law of Nature (*lex naturalis*) is a precept or general rule found out by reason, by which a man is forbidden to do that which is destructive of his life or taketh away the means of preserving the same; and to omit that by which he thinketh it may be best preserved. For though they that speak of this subject use to confound[4] *Jus* and *Lex*, *Right* and *Law*; yet they ought to be distinguished, because Right consisteth in liberty to do or to forbear, whereas Law determineth and bindeth to one of them: so that Law and Right differ as much as obligation and liberty, which in one and the same matter are inconsistent.

And because the condition of man (as hath been declared in the precedent chapter) is a condition of war of every one against every one, in which case every one is governed by his own reason, and

3. Property.

4. Customarily confuse.

there is nothing he can make use of that may not be a help unto him in preserving his life against his enemies: it followeth that in such a condition every man has a right to every thing, even to one another's body. And therefore as long as this natural right of every man to every thing endureth, there can be no security to any man (how strong or wise soever he be) of living out the time which nature ordinarily alloweth men to live. And consequently it is a precept, or general rule of reason, *That every man ought to endeavor peace as far as he has hope of obtaining it; and when he cannot obtain it, that he may seek and use all helps and advantages of war.* The first branch of which rule containeth the first and fundamental law of nature, which is *to seek peace and follow it.* The second, the sum of the right of nature, which is, *by all means we can to defend ourselves.*

From this fundamental law of nature, by which men are commanded to endeavor peace, is derived this second law: *That a man be willing, when others are so too, as far-forth as*[5] *for peace and defence of himself he shall think necessary, to lay down this right to all things, and be contented with so much liberty against other men as he would allow other men against himself.* For as long as any man holdeth this right of doing anything he liketh, so long are all men in the condition of war. But if other men will not lay down their right, as well as he, then there is no reason for anyone to divest himself of his. For that were to expose himself to prey (which no man is bound to) rather than to dispose himself to peace. This is that law of the Gospel: *Whatsoever you require that others should do to you, that do ye to them.*[6] * * *

From *Part I, Chapter 15. Of Other Laws of Nature*

From that law of nature by which we are obliged to transfer to another such rights as, being retained, hinder the peace of mankind, there followeth a third, which is this: *That men perform their covenants made.* Without which covenants are in vain, and but empty words; and, the right of all men to all things remaining, we are still in the condition of war.

And in this law of nature consisteth the fountain and original of Justice. For where no covenant hath preceded, there hath no right been transferred, and every man has right to every thing; and consequently no action can be unjust. But when a covenant is made, then to break it is unjust; and the definition of injustice is no other than *the not performance of covenant.* And whatsoever is not unjust is just.

But because covenants of mutual trust, where there is a fear of

5. Insofar as.
6. The golden rule: Matthew vii.12, Luke vi.31.

not performance on either part * * * are invalid; though the original of justice be the making of covenants, yet injustice actually there can be none, till the cause of such fear be taken away; which while men are in the natural condition of war, cannot be done. Therefore, before the names of just and unjust can have place, there must be some coercive power, to compel men equally to the performance of their covenants by the terror of some punishment greater than the benefit they expect by the breach of their covenant, and to make good that propriety[7] which by mutual contract men acquire in recompense of the universal right they abandon: and such power there is none before the erection of a commonwealth. And this is also to be gathered out of the ordinary definition of justice in the schools;[8] for they say that *Justice is the constant will of giving to every man his own*. And therefore where there is no *own*, that is, no propriety, there is no injustice; and where there is no coercive power erected, that is, where there is no commonwealth, there is no propriety, all men having right to all things. Therefore where there is no commonwealth, there nothing is unjust. So that the nature of justice consisteth in keeping of valid covenants; but the validity of covenants begins not but with the constitution of a civil power, sufficient to compel men to keep them. And then it is also that propriety begins.

The fool hath said in his heart, there is no such thing as justice, and sometimes also with his tongue;[9] seriously alleging that every man's conservation and contentment being committed to his own care, there could be no reason why every man might not do what he thought conduced thereunto: and therefore also, to make or not make, keep or not keep covenants was not against reason, when it conduced to one's benefit. He does not therein deny that there be covenants, and that they are sometimes broken, sometimes kept, and that such breach of them may be called injustice, and the observance of them, justice: but he questioneth whether injustice, taking away the fear of God (for the same fool hath said in his heart there is no God), may not sometimes stand with that reason which dictateth to every man his own good; and particularly then when it conduceth to such a benefit as shall put a man in a condition to neglect, not only the dispraise and revilings, but also the power of other men. The kingdom of God is gotten by violence; but what if it could be gotten by unjust violence? were it against reason so to get it, when it is impossible to receive hurt by it? and if it be not against reason, it is not against justice, or else justice is not

7. Property, in the sense of right or privilege.
8. I.e., among the schoolmen, medieval Aristotelians like St. Thomas Aquinas.
9. It is by no means a common fool who speaks up at this point; what he is saying is that a man who breaks his covenant (as Cromwell broke his oath of allegiance to Charles I) does not act unreasonably, as long as he serves his own interest. Though Hobbes tries to answer this fool, it is not clear that he succeeds.

to be approved for good. From such reasoning as this, successful wickedness hath obtained the name of virtue; and some that in all other things have disallowed the violation of faith, yet have allowed it when it is for the getting of a kingdom. And the heathen that believed that *Saturn* was deposed by his son *Jupiter* believed nevertheless the same *Jupiter* to be the avenger of injustice:[1] somewhat like to a piece of law in Coke's commentaries on Littleton, where he says, if the right heir of the crown be attainted of treason, yet the crown shall descend to him, and *eo instante*[2] the attainder be void. From which instances a man will be very prone to infer that when the heir apparent of a kingdom shall kill him that is in possession, though his father; you may call it injustice or by what other name you will; yet it can never be against reason, seeing all the voluntary actions of men tend to the benefit of themselves, and those actions are most reasonable that conduce most to their ends. This specious reasoning is nevertheless most false.

For the question is not of promises mutual where there is no security of performance on either side, as when there is no civil power erected over the parties promising; for such promises are no covenants. But either where one of the parties has performed already, or where there is a power to make him perform: there is the question whether it be against reason, that is against the benefit of the other, to perform or not. And I say it is not against reason (to perform the promise). For the manifestation whereof, we are to consider: first, that when a man doth a thing which (notwithstanding anything that can be foreseen and reckoned on) tendeth to his own destruction, howsoever[3] some accident which he could not expect arriving may turn it to his benefit; yet such events do not make it reasonably or wisely done. Secondly, that in a condition of war, wherein every man to every man, for want of a common power to keep them all in awe, is an enemy, there is no man can hope by his own strength or wit to defend himself from destruction without the help of confederates; where everyone expects the same defence by the confederation that anyone else does. And therefore he which declares he thinks it reason to deceive those that help him can in reason expect no other means of safety than what can be had from his own single power. He therefore that breaketh his covenant, and subsequently declareth that he thinks he may with reason do so,

1. In Greek mythology, Saturn was deposed by Zeus (Jupiter), his son; yet Zeus, though himself a usurper, became father of the gods and the spokesman of justice. In all this discussion, the parallel with Cromwell (a usurper, yet perhaps the creator of a new justice) is strongly felt. Compare Marvell's *Horatian Ode*.

2. In that very instant. The heir to a throne is a traitor when he conspires against his father; but the instant he is successful, the king is dead, he is the new king, he cannot commit treason against himself, so the attainder of treason is void. "Coke upon Littleton" (the commentaries of Sir Edward Coke on Sir Thomas Littleton's 15th-century law-treatise) is a famous legal authority.

3. Even though.

cannot be received into any society that unite themselves for peace and defence, but by the error of them that receive him; nor when he is received be retained in it without seeing the danger of their error; which errors a man cannot reasonably reckon upon as the means of his security. And therefore if he be left or cast out of society, he perisheth; and if he live in society, it is by the errors of other men, which he could not foresee nor reckon upon; and consequently against the reason of his preservation; and so as all men that contribute not to his destruction forbear him only out of ignorance of what is good for themselves.

As for the instance of gaining the secure and perpetual felicity of heaven by any way, it is frivolous; there being but one way imaginable, and that is not breaking, but keeping of covenant.

And for the other instance of attaining sovereignty by rebellion, it is manifest that though the event follow, yet because it cannot reasonably be expected, but rather the contrary; and because by gaining it so others are taught to gain the same in like manner, the attempt thereof is against reason. Justice therefore, that is to say, keeping of covenant, is a rule of reason, by which we are forbidden to do anything destructive to our life, and consequently a law of nature. * * *

1651

IZAAK WALTON
(1593–1683)

Izaak Walton, who was a member of the ironmongers' company, is remembered these days as the author of *The Complete Angler*. This is an early treatise on the art of angling, woven artfully into a quaintly humorous dialogue; it is consulted nowadays not so much by people who want to catch fish as by people who want to think about fishing from the placid perspective of a library. But to his own generation, Izaak was essentially a pious biographer. A devout Anglican himself, he first turned to biography in the late 30's, just as the Civil Wars were looming; and all his biographical work was done at a time when the English church was under attack from the Puritans, or struggling to re-establish itself after the Restoration. The men whose lives he wrote were ideally suited to be saints and martyrs in a roster of Anglican worthies; or, if they were not ideally suited for the role, Izaak's happy imagination and faculty of forgetting inconvenient details did much to make them so. But if they are not models of scholarly objectivity—how could they be, in that age?—the biographies of Walton are warm and moving compositions of literary art. Certainly he has not been the last man to feel that a good cause justified a little liberty with exact truth.

From The Life of Dr. John Donne[1]

[*Donne Takes Holy Orders*]

I return from my account of the vision to tell the reader that both before Mr. Donne's going into France, at his being there, and after his return, many of the nobility and others that were powerful at court were watchful and solicitous to the king for some secular employment for him. The king had formerly both known and put a value upon his company, and had also given him some hopes of a state-employment; being always much pleased when Mr. Donne attended him, especially at his meals, where there were usually many deep discourses of general learning and very often friendly disputes or debates of religion betwixt His Majesty and those divines whose places required their attendance on him at those times: particularly the Dean of the Chapel, who then was Bishop Montague (the publisher of the learned and eloquent works of His Majesty) and the most Reverend Doctor Andrewes the late learned Bishop of Winchester, who then was the king's almoner.[2]

About this time there grew many disputes that concerned the Oath of Supremacy and Allegiance,[3] in which the king had appeared, and engaged himself by his public writings now extant: and His Majesty discoursing with Mr. Donne concerning many of the reasons which are usually urged against the taking of those oaths, apprehended such a validity and clearness in his stating the questions, and his answers to them, that His Majesty commanded him to bestow some time in drawing the arguments into a method, and then to write his answers to them; and, having done that, not to send, but be his own messenger and bring them to him. To this he presently and diligently applied himself, and within six weeks brought them to him under his own handwriting, as they be now printed; the book bearing the name of *Pseudo-Martyr*, printed *anno* 1610.

1. The present selection begins with Donne in middle life. Walton has broken his account of these middle years with a digression on second sight, occasioned by a vision which Donne is said to have had in France when his wife was ill at home. Izaak then picks up the thread of his narrative with Donne on the threshold of his career in the church. The text is from the fourth edition (1675); "Feb. 15, 1640," the date at the end of the *Life*, is misleading.

2. Donne's friends were Richard Montague, later Bishop of Chichester, and famous as an Anglican controversialist and historian; and Lancelot Andrewes, eminent divine, preacher, and translator of the Bible. Both were members of the High-Church, anti-Calvinist wing of the church; both were men of vast learning. As "king's almoner," Andrewes was his Majesty's official almsgiver; Montague, as the king's "publisher," prepared for the press the literary works of which James was so proud.

3. A requirement that they swear unequivocal allegiance to the Crown, under pain of fines and imprisonment, was troubling to the Roman Catholics of England, who claimed that they were being persecuted for following their consciences in upholding Papal supremacy. The title of Donne's book, *Pseudo-Martyr*, shows the line he took with this argument.

When the king had read and considered that book, he persuaded Mr. Donne to enter into the ministry; to which, at that time, he was, and appeared, very unwilling, apprehending it (such was his mistaking modesty) to be too weighty for his abilities: and though His Majesty had promised him a favor, and many persons of worth mediated with His Majesty for some secular employment for him (to which his education had apted[4] him), and particularly the Earl of Somerset[5] when in his greatest height of favor; who being then at Theobald's with the king, where one of the clerks of the council died that night, the Earl posted a messenger for Mr. Donne to come to him immediately, and at Mr. Donne's coming, said, "Mr. Donne, to testify the reality of my affection, and my purpose to prefer you, stay in this garden till I go up to the king, and bring you word that you are clerk of the council: doubt not my doing this, for I know the king loves you, and know the king will not deny me." But the king gave a positive denial to all requests, and, having a discerning spirit, replied, "I know Mr. Donne is a learned man, has the abilities of a learned divine, and will prove a powerful preacher; and my desire is to prefer him that way, and in that way I will deny you nothing for him." After that time, as he professeth, "the king descended to a persuasion, almost to a solicitation, of him to enter into sacred orders":[6] which, although he then denied not, yet he deferred it for almost three years. All which time he applied himself to an incessant study of textual divinity, and to the attainment of a great perfection in the learned languages, Greek and Hebrew.

In the first and most blessed times of Christianity, when the clergy were looked upon with reverence, and deserved it, when they overcame their opposers by high examples of virtue, by a blessed patience and long suffering, those only were then judged worthy the ministry whose quiet and meek spirits did make them look upon that sacred calling with an humble adoration and fear to undertake it; which indeed requires such great degrees of humility, and labor, and care, that none but such were then thought worthy of that celestial dignity. And such only were then sought out and solicited to undertake it. This I have mentioned because forwardness and inconsideration could not in Mr. Donne, as in many others, be an argument of insufficiency or unfitness;[7] for he had considered long, and had many

4. Fitted.
5. Robert Carr, a handsome young page about court, had been raised by King James's favor to the rank of Earl of Somerset; and thus had reason to think the king would deny him nothing. He was later disgraced by the scandal surrounding the mysterious death of Sir Thomas Overbury. "Theobald's" was Lord Burghley's country house in Herts, acquired by James as a royal recreation-spot.
6. A quotation from Donne himself, in the *Devotions upon Emergent Occasions.*
7. I.e., in many men, the fact that they sought a job eagerly might be evidence of their unfitness for it; but not in Donne, for he did not seek it.

strifes within himself concerning the strictness of life and competency of learning required in such as enter into sacred orders; and doubtless, considering his own demerits, did humbly ask God with St. Paul, "Lord, who is sufficient for these things?" and with meek Moses, "Lord, who am I?"[8] And sure, if he had consulted with flesh and blood, he had not for these reasons put his hand to that holy plow. But God, who is able to prevail, wrestled with him, as the angel did with Jacob, and marked him; marked him for his own; marked him with a blessing, a blessing of obedience to the motions of his blessed spirit. And then, as he had formerly asked God with Moses, "Who am I?" so now, being inspired with an apprehension of God's particular mercy to him, in the king's and other solicitations of him, he came to ask King David's thankful question, "Lord, who am I, that thou art so mindful of me?"[9] So mindful of me as to lead me for more than forty years through this wilderness of the many temptations and various turnings of a dangerous life; so merciful to me as to move the learnedest of kings to descend to move me to serve at the altar; so merciful to me as at last to move my heart to embrace this holy motion! Thy motions I will and do embrace: and I now say with the blessed Virgin, "Be it with thy servant as seemeth best in thy sight";[1] and so, blessed Jesus, I do take the cup of salvation and will call upon thy name and will preach thy gospel.

Such strifes as these St. Austin[2] had, when St. Ambrose endeavored his conversion to Christianity; with which he confesseth he acquainted his friend Alipius. Our learned author (a man fit to write after no mean copy) did the like. And declaring his intentions to his dear friend Dr. King,[3] then Bishop of London, a man famous in his generation and no stranger to Mr. Donne's abilities (for he had been chaplain to the Lord Chancellor at the time of Mr. Donne's being his lordship's secretary), that reverend man did receive the news with much gladness; and, after some expressions of joy, and a persuasion to be constant in his pious purpose, he proceeded with all convenient speed to ordain him first deacon, and then priest not long after.

Now the English Church had gained a second St. Austin; for I think none was so like him before his conversion, none so like St. Ambrose after it:[4] and if his youth had the infirmities of the one,

8. II Corinthians ii.16 and Exodus iii.11.
9. A paraphrase of Psalm viii.4. Donne's "soliloquy" is, naturally, the work of Walton's imagination—an effort to render vividly the character in conflict.
1. Cf. Luke i.38.
2. Augustine. The reference is to Augustine's conversion, described in the *Confessions*.
3. This is John King (father of Henry King, the poet); he was created bishop of London in 1611.
4. Augustine, though his literary gifts were never in question, was tainted in his youth with libertinism and the Manichaean heresy; St. Ambrose, bishop of Milan, though less eloquent, was a steady pillar of the church against heretics, particularly the Arians. These great prototypes from the 4th century A.D. were widely known and imitated as a result of Augustine's *Confessions*.

his age had the excellencies of the other; the learning and holiness of both.

And now all his studies, which had been occasionally diffused, were all concentered in divinity. Now he had a new calling, new thoughts, and a new employment for his wit and eloquence. Now, all his earthly affections were changed into divine love; and all the faculties of his own soul were engaged in the conversion of others: in preaching the glad tidings of remission to repenting sinners and peace to each troubled soul. To these he applied himself with all care and diligence: and now such a change was wrought in him that he could say with David, "O how amiable are thy tabernacles, O Lord God of Hosts!"[5] Now he declared openly, "That when he required a temporal, God gave him a spiritual blessing." And that "he was now gladder to be a doorkeeper in the House of God, than he could be to enjoy the noblest of all temporal employments."

Presently after he entered into his holy profession, the king sent for him, and made him his Chaplain in Ordinary,[6] and promised to take a particular care for his preferment.

And though his long familiarity with scholars and persons of greatest quality was such as might have given some men boldness enough to have preached to any eminent auditory; yet his modesty in this employment was such that he could not be persuaded to it, but went, usually accompanied with some one friend, to preach privately in some village not far from London; his first sermon being preached at Paddington. This he did till His Majesty sent and appointed him a day to preach to him at Whitehall;[7] and, though much were expected from him, both by His Majesty and others, yet he was so happy (which few are) as to satisfy and exceed their expectations: preaching the Word so, as showed his own heart was possessed with those very thoughts and joys that he labored to distill into others: a preacher in earnest; weeping sometimes for his auditory, sometimes with them; always preaching to himself, like an angel from a cloud, but in none; carrying some, as St. Paul was, to heaven in holy raptures, and enticing others by a sacred art and courtship to amend their lives: here picturing a vice so as to make it ugly to those that practiced it; and a virtue so as to make it be beloved, even by those that loved it not; and all this with a most particular grace and an unexpressible addition of comeliness.[8]

[*Donne on His Deathbed*]

It is observed that a desire of glory or commendation is rooted in the very nature of man; and that those of the severest and most

5. Cf. Psalm lxxxiv.1.
6. One of the king's regular staff of chaplains.
7. At court.
8. Having described Donne's decision to take holy orders, Walton proceeds to represent him as a perfect priest—eloquent, laborious, patient, and cheerful. At last, however, he sickened and grew ill; the stage is set for a protracted deathbed scene, such as Donne, Walton, and the 17th century relished enthusiastically.

mortified lives, though they may become so humble as to banish self-flattery, and such weeds as naturally grow there; yet they have not been able to kill this desire of glory, but that like our radical heat,[9] it will both live and die with us; and many think it should do so; and we want not sacred examples to justify the desire of having our memory to outlive our lives; which I mention, because Dr. Donne, by the persuasion of Dr. Fox, easily yielded at this very time[1] to have a monument made for him; but Dr. Fox undertook not to persuade him how, or what monument it should be; that was left to Dr. Donne himself.

A monument being resolved upon, Dr. Donne sent for a carver to make for him in wood the figure of an urn, giving him directions for the compass and height of it; and to bring with it a board, of the just[2] height of his body. These being got, then without delay a choice painter was got to be in readiness to draw his picture, which was taken as followeth. Several charcoal fires being first made in his large study, he brought with him into that place his winding-sheet in his hand, and having put off all his clothes, had this sheet put on him, and so tied with knots at his head and feet, and his hands so placed as dead bodies are usually fitted to be shrouded and put into their coffin or grave. Upon this urn he thus stood with his eyes shut and with so much of the sheet turned aside as might show his lean, pale, and deathlike face, which was purposely turned towards the east, from whence he expected the second coming of his and our Saviour Jesus. In this posture he was drawn at his just height; and when the picture was fully finished, he caused it to be set by his bedside, where it continued and became his hourly object till his death, and was then given to his dearest friend and executor Dr. Henry King,[3] then chief residentiary of St. Paul's, who caused him to be thus carved in one entire piece of white marble, as it now stands in that church;[4] and by Dr. Donne's own appointment, these words were to be affixed to it as his epitaph:

JOHANNES DONNE
Sac. Theol. Profess.

Post varia studia quibus ab annis tenerrimis
fideliter, nec infeliciter incubuit,
instinctu et impulsu Sp. Sancti, monitu
et hortatu

9. Bodily warmth.
1. Toward the end of his life, in 1631. Dr. Simeon Fox was Donne's physician.
2. Exact.
3. This is the poet, son of the Bishop of London who had advised Donne to enter holy orders, and himself later Bishop of Chichester. A reproduction of the portrait may be found in Grierson's edition of the poems, Vol. I, opp. p. 369.
4. Donne's tomb was destroyed in the great fire of 1666; only the statue survived, and is still seen in St. Paul's.

REGIS JACOBI, *ordines sacros*
amplexus, anno sui Jesu, 1614, *et suae aetatis* 42,
decanatu hujus ecclesiae indutus 27
Novembris, 1621,
exutus morte ultimo die Martii, 1631,
hic licet in occiduo cinere aspicit eum
cujus nomen est Oriens.[5]

And now, having brought him through the many labyrinths and perplexities of a various life, even to the gates of death and the grave, my desire is, he may rest till I have told my reader that I have seen many pictures of him in several habits and at several ages and in several postures; and I now mention this, because I have seen one picture of him, drawn by a curious[6] hand, at his age of eighteen, with his sword, and what other adornments might then suit with the present fashions of youth and the giddy gaieties of that age;[7] and his motto then was—

How much shall I be changed,
Before I am changed![8]

And if that young and his now dying picture were at this time set together, every beholder might say, "Lord! how much is Dr. Donne already changed, before he is changed!" And the view of them might give my reader occasion to ask himself with some amazement, "Lord! how much may I also, that am now in health, be changed before I am changed; before this vile, this changeable body shall put off mortality!" and therefore to prepare for it. But this is not writ so much for my reader's memento as to tell him that Dr. Donne would often in his private discourses, and often publicly in his sermons, mention the many changes both of his body and mind; especially of his mind from a vertiginous giddiness; and would as often say, "his great and most blessed change was from a temporal to a spiritual employment"; in which he was so happy, that he accounted the former part of his life to be lost; and the beginning of it to be from his first entering into sacred orders and serving his most merciful God at his altar.

Upon Monday, after the drawing this picture, he took his last leave of his beloved study; and, being sensible of his hourly decay, retired himself to his bedchamber; and that week sent at several[9]

5. "John Donne, Professor of Sacred Theology. After various studies, which he plied from his tenderest youth faithfully and not unsuccessfully, moved by the instinct and impulse of the Holy Spirit and the admonition and encouragement of King James, he took holy orders in the year of his Jesus 1614 and the year of his age 42. On the 27th of November, 1621, he was invested as dean of this church; and divested by death, the last day of March, 1631. Here in the decline of ashes he looks to One whose name is a Rising Sun."
6. Skillful.
7. See the portrait reproduced in Grierson, Vol. I, opp. p. 7.
8. Transformed (i.e., by death).
9. Separate.

times for many of his most considerable friends, with whom he took a solemn and deliberate farewell, commending to their considerations some sentences useful for the regulation of their lives; and then dismissed them, as good Jacob did his sons, with a spiritual benediction. The Sunday following, he appointed his servants, that if there were any business yet undone that concerned him or themselves, it should be prepared against Saturday next; for after that day he would not mix his thoughts with anything that concerned this world; nor ever did; but, as Job, so he "waited for the appointed day of his dissolution."

And now he was so happy as to have nothing to do but to die, to do which he stood in need of no longer time; for he had studied it long and to so happy a perfection that in a former sickness he called God to witness, "he was that minute ready to deliver his soul into his hands, if that minute God would determine his dissolution."[1] In that sickness he begged of God the constancy to be preserved in that estate forever; and his patient expectation to have his immortal soul disrobed from her garment of mortality makes me confident that he now had a modest assurance that his prayers were then heard and his petition granted. He lay fifteen days earnestly expecting his hourly change; and in the last hour of his last day, as his body melted away and vapored into spirit, his soul having, I verily believe, some revelation of the beatifical vision, he said, "I were miserable if I might not die"; and after those words, closed many periods of his faint breath by saying often, "Thy kingdom come, thy will be done." His speech, which had long been his ready and faithful servant, left him not till the last minute of his life, and then forsook him, not to serve another master (for who speaks like him) but died before him; for that it was then become useless to him that now conversed with God on earth as angels are said to do in heaven, only by thoughts and looks. Being speechless, and seeing heaven by that illumination by which he saw it, he did, as St. Stephen, "look steadfastly into it, till he saw the Son of Man standing at the right hand of God his Father";[2] and being satisfied with this blessed sight, as his soul ascended and his last breath departed from him, he closed his own eyes; and then disposed his hands and body into such a posture as required not the least alteration by those that came to shroud him.

Thus variable, thus virtuous was the life: thus excellent, thus exemplary was the death of this memorable man.

He was buried in that place of St. Paul's Church which he had appointed for that use some years before his death; and by which he passed daily to pay his public devotions to Almighty God (who

1. Walton again quotes from the *Devotions*.

2. Cf. Acts vii.55.

was then served twice a day by a public form of prayer and praises in that place):[3] but he was not buried privately, though he desired it; for, besides an unnumbered number of others, many persons of nobility, and of eminency for learning, who did love and honor him in his life, did show it at his death by a voluntary and sad attendance of his body to the grave, where nothing was so remarkable as a public sorrow.

To which place of his burial some mournful friends repaired, and, as Alexander the Great did to the grave of the famous Achilles, so they strewed his with an abundance of curious and costly flowers; which course, they (who were never yet known) continued morning and evening for many days, not ceasing, till the stones that were taken up in that church to give his body admission into the cold earth (now his bed of rest) were again by the mason's art so leveled and firmed as they had been formerly, and his place of burial undistinguishable to common view.

The next day after his burial, some unknown friend, some one of the many lovers and admirers of his virtue and learning, wrote this epitaph with a coal on the wall over his grave:

Reader! I am to let thee know,
Donne's body only lies below;
For, could the grave his soul comprise,
Earth would be richer than the skies!

Nor was this all the honor done to his reverend ashes; for, as there be some persons that will not receive a reward for that for which God accounts himself a debtor, persons that dare trust God with their charity and without a witness; so there was by some grateful unknown friend that thought Dr. Donne's memory ought to be perpetuated, an hundred marks sent to his two faithful friends and executors,[4] towards the making of his monument. It was not for many years known by whom; but after the death of Dr. Fox, it was known that it was he that sent it; and he lived to see as lively a representation of his dead friend as marble can express: a statue indeed so like Dr. Donne, that (as his friend Sir Henry Wotton hath expressed himself) "it seems to breathe faintly, and posterity shall look upon it as a kind of artificial miracle."

He was of stature moderately tall; of a straight and equally proportioned body, to which all his words and actions gave an unexpressible addition of comeliness.

The melancholy and pleasant humor were in him so contempered that each gave advantage to the other, and made his company one of the delights of mankind.

3. This phrase clearly shows up as one of Walton's later additions to the *Life;* Walton originally wrote when the forms of liturgy had not been changed.

4. "Dr. King and Dr. Monfort" [marginal note].

His fancy was unimitably high, equaled only by his great wit; both being made useful by a commanding judgment.

His aspect was cheerful, and such as gave a silent testimony of a clear knowing soul, and of a conscience at peace with itself.

His melting eye showed that he had a soft heart, full of noble compassion; of too brave a soul to offer injuries and too much a Christian not to pardon them in others.

He did much contemplate (especially after he entered into his sacred calling) the mercies of Almighty God, the immortality of the soul, and the joys of heaven: and would often say in a kind of sacred ecstasy—"Blessed be God that he is God, only and divinely like himself."

He was by nature highly passionate, but more apt to reluct at[5] the excesses of it. A great lover of the offices of humanity, and of so merciful a spirit that he never beheld the miseries of mankind without pity and relief.

He was earnest and unwearied in the search of knowledge, with which his vigorous soul is now satisfied, and employed in a continual praise of that God that first breathed it into his active body: that body, which once was a temple of the Holy Ghost and is now become a small quantity of Christian dust:

But I shall see it reanimated.

Feb. 15, 1640.

I. W.

1640, 1675

5. Oppose.

SIR THOMAS BROWNE

(1605–1682)

Though his life was long, Browne's biography contains few events. Born in London, he attended Oxford and then medical schools on the Continent—at Montpellier in France, Padua in Italy, and Leyden in Holland. Rubbing elbows with people of different religions encouraged Browne to reflect on his own religious stance, and shortly after his return to England (about 1635) he wrote a little essay called *Religio Medici* ("A Doctor's Faith"). Not being intended for publication, it wasn't published for several years, till a printer (prophetically named Andrew Crook) brought out a pirated edition in 1642. Browne had by then married and settled down to practice medicine at the remote little town of Norwich in the marshy countryside of Norfolk. His book was thought witty and ingenious, perhaps because it managed to talk at length about religion without ever discussing or even facing any of the great religious issues which were tearing the country apart. What fascinated Browne was a private game he was playing between faith and doubt; he would think of all the most intricate and perplexing questions that his "philosophy" could invent, and then solve them by means of his faith. Absorbed in this curious inner drama of his, Browne never entered the literary "world" (such as it was) of London, and never took active sides in the civil war. Like Thoreau, one of his later admirers, he did not need to move around because he was traveling widely in Norwich.

Some of his investigations were published in 1646 under the forbidding title of *Pseudodoxia Epidemica,* or "Vulgar Errors." They consisted of immense researches into all the foolish ideas entertained by mankind over the ages—superstitions and oddities of opinion, mythical animals, pious legends, hexes, hoaxes, assorted nonsense of every description. It was characteristic of Browne's mind that he was always more interested in what wasn't knowable than in what was. His thought instinctively moved toward the mysterious, the remote, the legendary; and though, for his day, he was an enlightened man, he accepted almost as many vulgar errors as he exposed. He enjoyed the mysteries of ancient wisdom; he enjoyed even more thinking about the unthinkable. Thus when some workmen near Norwich accidentally dug up some funeral urns dating back hundreds, and probably thousands of years, Doctor Browne took occasion to visit the site, inspect the find, and write (in 1658) a private meditation on death and burial practices. The subject might have produced a morbid (or, worse, a dull) document; but Browne's agile metaphysical wit, and gorgeous, polysyllabic rhetoric, gave an immense, resonant poetry to his treatise *Hydriotaphia, Urn-Burial.*

Whatever the ostensible topic of which he was treating, Browne always turned it toward that curious inward balance of faith and scepticism which fascinated him. "We carry with us," he wrote, "the wonders we seek without us: there is all Africa and her prodigies within us. We are that bold and adventurous piece of nature which he that studies wisely learns in a compendium what others labor at in a divided piece and endless volume." His focus was on himself, rarely on those areas of material, factual information where his age was learning, at a furious pace and with ruthless precision, to discriminate truth from falsehood. During his lifetime, the modern scientific outlook, the modern scientific method, established themselves beyond serious challenge at the center of intellectual life. Browne as a philosopher of the old school hardly gave the new developments a thought. What song the sirens sang, and what name Achilles assumed when he hid himself among women, were subjects more congenial for his speculative, inward mind. No doubt he knew that they were funny subjects to think about; the prose in which he discussed these matters, always polysyllabic and Latinate, sometimes gets so elaborate that one can't help suspecting self-mockery. But these were all essential ingredients in the alchemy of a personality, and it is the fascination of that personality—darker and more mysterious than Burton's, but just as much the deliberate creation of an artist—that has kept Browne's name and books alive over the centuries.

From Religio Medici[1]

* * *

40. I am naturally bashful, nor hath conversation, age, or travel been able to effront or enharden me; yet I have one part of modesty which I have seldom discovered in another; that is (to speak truly) I am not so much afraid of death as ashamed thereof. 'Tis the very disgrace and ignominy of our natures, that in a moment can so disfigure us that our nearest friends, wife, and children stand afraid and start at us. The birds and beasts of the field that before in a natural fear obeyed us, forgetting all allegiance begin to prey upon us. This very conceit hath in a tempest disposed and left me willing to be swallowed up in the abyss of waters, wherein I had perished unseen, unpitied, without wondering eyes, tears of pity, lectures of mortality, and none had said, "*Quantum mutatus ab illo!*"[2] Not that I am ashamed of the anatomy of my parts or can accuse nature for playing the bungler in any part of me or my own vicious life for contracting any shameful disease up on me, whereby I might not call myself as wholesome a morsel for the worms as any.

41. Some, upon the courage of a fruitful issue[3] wherein, as in the truest chronicle, they seem to outlive themselves, can with greater patience away with death. This conceit and counterfeit subsisting in our progenies seems to me a mere fallacy, unworthy the desires of a man that can but conceive a thought of the next world; who, in a nobler ambition, should desire to live in his substance in heaven

1. Browne wrote *Religio Medici* about 1635, when he was a little short of 30 years old (see Section 41); he had just returned from his medical studies on the continent, where he had been forced to worship—if he was to worship at all—with communities of different faiths. The essay was written as a form of personal stock-taking, in the shape of a letter to a friend; in 1642 it was printed without Browne's permission, and in 1643 reprinted in an authorized and corrected version. Our text follows the 1643 printing with a few additions, in brackets, from M. Jean-Jacques Denonain's edition based on manuscript copies (Cambridge, 1953).

The title means "A Doctor's Faith," and one might well ask why a doctor should have a special religion of his own, different from a lawyer's or a merchant's. By "faith," however, Browne does not simply mean "creed." He disposes, almost casually, of all the things his age usually meant by "faith"—doctrinal and dogmatic tenets, ceremonies and public observances, an ecclesiastical organization. Not that he is a doubter or a heretic; he accepts the establishment in every detail. But he is interested in something more mysterious and personal, which most of his essay is devoted to exploring; this is a relation to the Christian mystery of faith and resurrection, in which he believes, not because he can explain or defend it but because he cannot. Browne's position, known as "fideism," vigorously separates philosophy from faith and exempts faith from criticism by reason, while at the same time depriving it of reason's support. Previous speculators along these lines, like Montaigne, had explicitly recognized that "fideism" was a dangerous weapon of intellectual foilplay. But for Browne it answered a deep temperamental need.

2. "How greatly changed from what he was!" The phrase was used by Aeneas of Hector, *Aeneid* II.274; Browne may be referring to an occasion when he was shipwrecked between Ireland and England in 1630.

3. Emboldened by having had children.

rather than his name and shadow in the earth. And therefore at my death I mean to take a total adieu of the world, not caring for a monument, history, or epitaph, not so much as the bare memory of my name to be found anywhere but in the universal register of God. I am not yet so cynical as to approve the testament of Diogenes,[4] nor do I altogether allow that *rodomontado* of Lucan—

> *Caelo tegitur, qui non habet urnam.*[5]
> He that unburied lies wants not his hearse,
> For unto him a tomb's the universe.

but commend in my calmer judgment those ingenuous intentions that desire to sleep by the urns of their fathers and strive to go the nearest way unto corruption. I do not envy the temper of crows and daws,[6] nor the numerous and weary days of our fathers before the flood. If there be any truth in astrology, I may outlive a jubilee;[7] as yet I have not seen one revolution of Saturn,[8] nor hath my pulse beat thirty years; and yet, excepting one, have seen the ashes and left underground all the kings of Europe, have been contemporary to three emperors, four Grand Seignieurs,[9] and as many popes. Methinks I have outlived myself and begin to be weary of the sun. I have shaken hands with delight in my warm blood and canicular days.[1] I perceive I do anticipate the vices of age. The world to me is but a dream or mock-show, and we all therein but pantaloons and antics[2] to my severer contemplations.

42. It is not, I confess, an unlawful prayer to desire to surpass the days of our Savior, or wish to outlive that age wherein He thought fittest to die; yet if (as divinity affirms) there shall be no gray hairs in heaven, but all shall rise in the perfect state of men, we do but outlive those perfections in this world to be recalled unto them by a greater miracle in the next, and run on here but to be retrograde hereafter. Were there any hopes to outlive vice or a point to be superannuated from sin, it were worthy our knees to implore the days of Methuselah. But age doth not rectify but incurvate our natures, turning bad dispositions into worser habits, and, like diseases, brings on incurable vices. For every day as we grow weaker in age, we grow stronger in sin, and the number of our days doth but make our sins innumerable. The same vice committed at sixteen is not the same, though it agree in all other circumstances, at forty, but swells and doubles from the circumstance of our ages, wherein,

4. Diogenes asked his friends not to bury him but to hang him out for a scarecrow.
5. *Pharsalia* VII.819.
6. Traditionally long-lived creatures, linked here with patriarchs like Noah and Methuselah.
7. Fifty years. Browne lived to 77.
8. Browne was born under Saturn (October 19); he was saturnine (melancholy and philosophical) by temperament; and Saturn completes a heavenly cycle in a little less than thirty years.
9. Sultans of Turkey.
1. Dog days, of July and early August, when summer heat is often at its height.
2. Jokers and clowns.

besides the constant and inexcusable habit of transgressing, the maturity of our judgment cuts off pretence unto excuse or pardon.

Every sin, the oftener it is committed the more it acquireth in the quality of evil; as it succeeds in time, so it proceeds in degrees of badness, for as they proceed they ever multiply and, like figures in arithmetic, the last stands for more than all that went before it. [The course and order of my life would be a very death unto another. I use [3] myself to all diets, humors, airs, hunger, thirst, cold, heat, want, plenty, necessity, dangers, hazards. When I am cold I cure not myself by heat; when sick, not by physic. Those that know how I live may justly say I regard not life, nor stand in fear of death.] [4] And though I think no man can live well once but he that could live twice, yet for my own part I would not live over my hours past, or begin again the thread of my days—not upon Cicero's ground [5] because I have lived them well, but for fear I should live them worse. I find my growing judgment daily instructs me how to be better, but my untamed affections and confirmed vitiosity makes me daily do worse. I find in my confirmed age the same sins I discovered in my youth. I committed many then because I was a child, and because I commit them still I am yet an infant. Therefore, I perceive a man may be twice a child before the days of dotage, and stand in need of Aeson's bath [6] before threescore.

43. And truly there goes a great deal of providence to produce a man's life unto threescore. There is more required than an able temper for those years. Though the radical humor contain in it sufficient oil for seventy, yet I perceive in some it gives no light past thirty.[7] Men assign not all the causes of long life that write whole books thereof. They that found themselves[8] on the radical balsam or vital sulphur of the parts determine not why Abel lived not so long as Adam. There is, therefore, a secret gloom or bottom of our days. 'Twas His wisdom to determine them, but His perpetual and waking providence that fulfills and accomplishes them, wherein the spirits, ourselves, and all the creatures of God in a secret and disputed way do execute His will. Let them not therefore complain of immaturity that die about thirty; they fall but like the whole world, whose solid and well composed substance must not expect the duration and period of its constitution; when all things are completed in it, its age is accomplished, and the last and general fever may as naturally destroy it before six thousand as me before forty. There is therefore some

3. Accustom.
4. This passage was substituted for most of section 42 and all of section 43 in the manuscript copies and unauthorized editions.
5. In *De Senectute* 23, Cicero supposes the philosopher will be ready to die because he has lived well.
6. A classical fountain of youth.
7. A man's "radical humor" is the basic constitution governing his disposition—phlegm, choler, and so on; Browne compares it to the oil feeding the lamp of life.
8. Base their judgments (as to a man's longevity). Abel, of course, failed to live as long as Adam because Cain killed him.

other hand that twines the thread of life than that of nature. We are not only ignorant in antipathies and occult qualities, our ends are as obscure as our beginnings. The line of our days is drawn by night, and the various effects therein by a pencil that is invisible, wherein, though we confess our ignorance, I am sure we do not err if we say it is the hand of God.

44. I am much taken with two verses of Lucan since I have been able not only, as we do at school to construe, but understand them:

> *Victurosque Dei celant ut vivere durent,*
> *Felix esse mori.*[9]
> We're all deluded, vainly searching ways
> To make us happy by the length of days;
> For, cunningly to make's protract this breath
> The Gods conceal the happiness of death.

There be many excellent strains in that poet, wherewith his Stoical genius hath liberally supplied him; and truly there are singular pieces in the philosophy of Zeno and doctrine of the Stoics,[1] which, I perceive, delivered in a pulpit pass for current divinity. Yet herein are they in extremes that can allow a man to be his own assassin and so highly extol the end and suicide of Cato.[2] This is indeed not to fear death but yet to be afraid of life. It is a brave act of valor to contemn death; but where life is more terrible than death, it is then the truest valor to dare to live, and herein religion hath taught us a noble example. For, all the valiant acts of Curtius, Scevola, or Codrus[3] do not parallel or match that one of Job; and sure there is no torture to the rack of a disease, nor any poniards in death itself like those in the way or prologue unto it. *Emori nolo, sed me esse mortuum nihil curo*—"I would not die but care not if I am dead."[4]

Were I of Caesar's religion I should be of his desires, and wish rather to go off at one blow than to be sawed in pieces by the grating torture of a disease. Men that look no further than their outsides think health an appurtenance unto life, and quarrel with their constitutions for being sick. But I that have examined the parts of man and know upon what tender filaments that fabric hangs, do wonder that we are not always so; and, considering the thousand doors that lead to death, do thank my God that we can die but once. 'Tis not only the mischief of diseases and the villainy of poisons that make an end of us; we vainly accuse the fury of guns and the new inventions of death. 'Tis in the power of every hand to destroy us, and we are beholding unto every one we meet he doth

9. *Pharsalia* IV.519.
1. Zeno was the first of the Stoic philosophers, who taught avoidance of passion and submission to necessity.
2. The younger Cato ("of Utica" from the place of his death) committed suicide (46 B.C.) rather than compromise with Caesar.
3. Curtius, Scevola, and Codrus all suffered (Curtius and Codrus death, Scevola mutilation) in behalf of their country.
4. Cicero, *Tusculan Disputations* I.8.

not kill us. There is therefore but one comfort left, that, though it be in the power of the weakest arm to take away life, it is not in the strongest to deprive us of death. God would not exempt Himself from that; the misery of immortality in the flesh He undertook not That was in it immortal.[5] Certainly there is no happiness within this circle of flesh, nor is it in the optics of these eyes to behold felicity. The first day of our jubilee is death. The devil hath therefore failed of his desires: we are happier with death than we should have been without it. There is no misery but in himself, where there is no end of misery; and so indeed in his own sense the Stoic is in the right. He forgets that he can die who complains of misery: we are in the power of no calamity while death is in our own.

45. Now, besides this literal and positive kind of death, there are others whereof divines make mention, and those, I think, not merely metaphorical—as mortification, dying unto sin and the world. Therefore I say every man hath a double horoscope: one of his humanity, his birth; another of his Christianity, his baptism. And from this do I compute or calculate my nativity, not reckoning those *horae combustae*[6] and odd days, or esteeming myself anything before I was my Savior's and enrolled in the register of Christ. Whosoever enjoys not this life, I count him but an apparition, though he wear about him the sensible affections of flesh. In these moral acceptions, the way to be immortal is to die daily; nor can I think I have the true theory of death when I contemplate a skull or behold a skeleton with those vulgar imaginations it casts upon us. I have therefore enlarged that common *memento mori* into a more Christian memorandum: *memento quatuor novissima*,[7] those four inevitable points of us all—death, judgment, heaven, and hell. Neither did the contemplations of the heathens rest in their graves without a further thought of Rhadamanth[8] or some judicial proceeding after death, though in another way and upon suggestion of their natural reasons. I cannot but marvel from what sybil or oracle they stole the prophesy of the world's destruction by fire, or whence Lucan learned to say,

> *Communis mundo superest rogus, ossibus astra*
> *Misturus*—[9]
> There yet remains to th' world one common fire
> Wherein our bones with stars shall make one pyre.

I believe the world grows near its end, yet is neither old nor decayed, nor will ever perish upon the ruins of its own principles. As the work of creation was above nature, so is its adversary, annihilation, without which the world hath not its end but its mutation.

5. Christ, who was an immortal in mortal garb, never undertook the burden of physical immortality.
6. Literally, burnt hours, hours when the moon is obscured by the sun; used here as a metaphor for the period between birth and baptism.
7. Remember the four last things. A *memento mori* is a reminder of death, generally a skull.
8. Greek judge of the underworld.
9. *Pharsalia* VII.814.

Now what fire should be able to consume it thus far without the breath of God, which is the truest consuming flame, my philosophy cannot inform me. Some believe there went not a minute to the world's creation, nor shall there go to its destruction; those six days, so punctually described, make not to them one moment but rather seem to manifest the method and idea of that great work in the intellect of God than the manner how He proceeded in its operation. I cannot dream that there should be at the last day any such judicial proceeding or calling to the bar as indeed the Scripture seems to imply and the literal commentators do conceive. For unspeakable mysteries in the Scripture are often delivered in a vulgar and illustrative way, and, being written unto man, are delivered not as they truly are but as they may be understood. Wherein, notwithstanding, the different interpretations according to different capacities may stand firm with our devotion, nor be any way prejudicial to each single edification.

46. Now, to determine the day and year of this inevitable time is not only convincible and statute-madness but also manifest impiety. How shall we interpret Elias' six thousand years [1] or imagine the secret communicated to a rabbi which God hath denied unto His angels? [2] It had been an excellent query to have posed the devil of Delphos, and must needs have forced him to some strange amphibology.[3] It hath not only mocked the predictions of sundry astrologers in ages past but the prophecies of many melancholy heads in these present, who, neither understanding reasonably things past or present, pretend a knowledge of things to come, heads ordained only to manifest the incredible effects of melancholy and to fulfill old prophecies rather than be the authors of new. "In those days there shall come wars and rumors of wars" [4] to me seems no prophecy but a constant truth, in all times verified since it was pronounced. "There shall be signs in the moon and stars." [5] How comes He, then, like a thief in the night when He gives an item of his coming? That common sign drawn from the revelation of Antichrist is as obscure as any; in our common compute he hath been come these many years. But, for my own part, to speak freely, omitting those ridiculous anagrams, I am half of Paracelsus' opinion, and think that Antichrist is the philosopher's stone in divinity,[6]

1. According to Jewish tradition, Elijah (Elias) prophesied that 6,000 years would be the ultimate age of the world.
2. In Matthew xxiv.36, Christ says no man knows the hour of the Last Judgment; the "rabbi" is any rabbinical commentator, type of the esoteric exegete.
3. Pagan oracles like that at Delphos (Delphi) were often attributed by Christian writers to the work of daemons or devils; an amphibology is an ambiguous pronouncement, in which the oracles specialized.
4. Matthew xxiv.6.
5. Luke xxi.25.
6. The coming of Antichrist was supposed to foreshadow the Last Judgment; Paracelsus was a doubter. Browne uses the "philosopher's stone" as an emblem of fantastic illusion. The "ridiculous anagrams" were arguments made from the names of the Popes, which, being translated into Greek or Hebrew (where every letter has a numerical value), were sometimes triumphantly added up to the number of the Beast in the Book of Revelation, i.e., 666.

for the discovery and invention whereof, though there be prescribed rules and probable inductions, yet hath hardly any man attained the perfect discovery thereof. That general opinion that the world grows near its end hath possessed all ages past as nearly as ours. I am afraid that the souls that now depart cannot escape that lingering expostulation of the saints under the altar, "*Quousque Domine?* How long, O Lord?"[7] and groan in the expectation of the great jubilee.

* * *

50. I cannot tell how to say that fire is the essence of hell; I know not what to make of purgatory, or conceive a flame that can either prey upon or purify the substance of a soul. Those flames of sulphur mentioned in the Scriptures[8] I take not to be understood of this present hell but of that to come, where fire shall make up the complement of our tortures and have a body or subject wherein to manifest its tyranny. Some who have had the honor to be textuary in divinity are of opinion it shall be the same specifical fire with ours. This is hard to conceive, yet I can make good how even that may prey upon our bodies and yet not consume us; for in this material world there are bodies that persist invincible in the powerfullest flames, and though by the action of fire they fall into ignition and liquation, yet will they never suffer a destruction. I would gladly know how Moses with an actual fire calcined or burned the golden calf into powder,[9] for that mystical metal of gold, whose solary and celestial nature I admire, exposed unto the violence of fire, grows only hot and liquifies but consumeth not. So, when the consumable and volatile pieces of our bodies shall be defined into a more impregnable and fixed temper like gold, though they suffer from the action of flames, they shall never perish but lie immortal in the arms of fire.

And surely if this frame must suffer only by the action of this element, there will many bodies escape, and not only heaven but earth will not be at an end but rather a beginning. For, at present it is not earth but a composition of fire, water, earth, and air;[1] but at that time, spoiled of these ingredients, it shall appear in a substance more like itself, its ashes. Philosophers that opinioned the world's destruction by fire did never dream of annihilation, which is beyond the power of sublunary causes, for the last and proper action of that element is but vitrification or a reduction of a body into glass. And therefore some of our chemists facetiously affirm, yea, and urge Scripture for it, that at the last fire all shall be crystallized

7. Revelation vi.9–10.
8. Revelation xxi.8.
9. Exodus xxxii.20 says that Moses not only burnt the golden calf and ground it to powder, but strewed it on the water and made the children of Israel drink of it.
1. The four Aristotelian elements.

and reverberated into glass, which is the utmost action of that element. Nor need we fear this term of annihilation or wonder that God will destroy the works of His creation. For, man subsisting, who is and will then truly appear a microcosm, the world cannot be said to be destroyed. For the eyes of God and perhaps also of our glorified selves shall as really behold and contemplate the world in its epitome or contracted essence, as now they do at large and in its dilated substance. In the seed of a plant, to the eyes of God and to the understanding of man, there exist, though in an invisible way, the perfect leaves, flowers, and fruit thereof; for things that are *in posse* [2] to the sense are actually existent to the understanding. Thus God beholds all things, Who contemplates as fully His works in their epitome as in their full volume, and beheld as amply the whole world in that little compendium of the sixth day [3] as in the scattered and dilated pieces of those five before.

51. Men commonly set forth the torments of hell by fire and the extremity of corporal afflictions, and describe hell in the same method that Mahomet doth heaven. This indeed makes a noise and drums in popular ears; but if this be the terrible piece thereof, it is not worthy to stand in diameter with heaven, whose happiness consists in that part that is best able to comprehend it, that immortal essence, that translated divinity and colony of God, the soul. Surely, though we place hell under earth, the devil's walk and purlieu is about it. Men speak too popularly who place it in those flaming mountains [4] which to grosser apprehensions represent hell. The heart of man is the place the devil dwells in. I feel sometimes a hell within myself; Lucifer keeps his court in my breast, Legion is revived in me.[5] There are as many hells as Anaxagoras' conceited worlds.[6] There was more than one hell in Magdalen when there were seven devils,[7] for every devil is an hell unto himself. He holds enough of torture in his own *ubi* [8] and needs not the misery of circumference to afflict him; and thus a distracted conscience here is a shadow or introduction unto hell hereafter. Who can but pity the merciful intention of those hands that do destroy themselves? The devil, were it in his power, would do the like; which being impossible, his miseries are endless, and he suffers most in that attribute wherein he is impassable,[9] his immortality.

2. A state of potential being.
3. Man was made on the sixth day as a summary (microcosm) of the work of the first five.
4. Volcanoes.
5. Lucifer is the devil, Legion (from Mark v.9) the assembly of unclean spirits.
6. Browne has apparently confused Anaxagoras with Anaximander who "conceited" (i.e., imagined) an indefinite number of worlds.
7. Luke viii.2 tells the story of Christ's driving seven devils out of Mary Magdalene.
8. Literally, in Latin, *where;* in context, his own self.
9. Inassailable.

52. I thank God, and with joy I mention it, I was never afraid of hell nor never grew pale at the description of that place. I have so fixed my contemplations on heaven that I have almost forgot the idea of hell, and am afraid rather to lose the joys of the one than endure the misery of the other. To be deprived of them is a perfect hell and needs, methinks, no addition to complete our afflictions. That terrible term hath never detained me from sin, nor do I owe any good action to the name thereof. I fear God, yet am not afraid of Him; His mercies make me ashamed of my sins before His judgments afraid thereof. These are the forced and secondary method of His wisdom, which He useth but as the last remedy and upon provocation; a course rather to deter the wicked than incite the virtuous to His worship. I can hardly think there was ever any scared into heaven. They go the fairest way to heaven that would serve God without a hell; other mercenaries that crouch unto Him in fear of hell, though they term themselves the servants, are indeed but the slaves of the Almighty.

53. And to be true and speak my soul, when I survey the occurrences of my life and call into account the finger of God, I can perceive nothing but an abyss and mass of mercies, either in general to mankind or in particular to myself. And, whether out of the prejudice of my affection or an inverting and partial conceit of His mercies, I know not, but those which others term crosses, afflictions, judgments, misfortunes, to me, who enquire farther into them than their visible effects, they both appear and in event have ever proved the secret and dissembled favors of His affection. It is a singular piece of wisdom to apprehend truly and without passion the works of God, and so well to distinguish His justice from His mercy as not to miscall those noble attributes. Yet it is likewise an honest piece of logic so to dispute and argue the proceedings of God as to distinguish even His judgments into mercies. For God is merciful unto all because better to the worst than the best deserve, and to say He punisheth none in this world, though it be a paradox, is no absurdity. To one that hath committed murder, if the judge should only ordain a fine, it were a madness to call this a punishment and to repine at the sentence rather than admire the clemency of the judge. Thus, our offences being mortal, and deserving not only death but damnation, if the goodness of God be content to traverse and pass them over with a loss, misfortune, or disease, what frenzy were it to term this a punishment rather than an extremity of mercy, and to groan under the rod of His judgments rather than admire the scepter of His mercies!

Therefore to adore, honor, and admire Him is a debt of gratitude due from the obligation of our nature, states, and conditions; and with these thoughts, he that knows them best will not deny that I adore Him. That I obtain heaven and the bliss thereof is accidental and not the intended work of my devotion, it being a felicity I can neither think to deserve nor scarce in modesty to expect. For these two ends of us all, either as rewards or punishments, are mercifully ordained and disproportionally disposed unto our actions; the one being so far beyond our deserts, the other so infinitely below our demerits.

* * *

1635 1642 (*surreptitious*)
1643 (*authentic*)

From Hydriotaphia, Urn-Burial

Chapter V

Now since these dead bones have already outlasted the living ones of Methuselah,[1] and in a yard under ground, and thin walls of clay, outworn all the strong and specious buildings above it, and quietly rested under the drums and tramplings of three conquests;[2] what prince can promise such diuturnity unto his relics, or might not gladly say,

Sic ego componi versus in ossa velim?[3]

Time, which antiquates antiquities, and hath an art to make dust of all things, hath yet spared these minor monuments.

In vain we hope to be known by open and visible conservatories, when to be unknown was the means of their continuation, and obscurity their protection. If they died by violent hands, and were thrust into their urns, these bones become considerable, and some old philosophers would honor them, whose souls they conceived most pure, which were thus snatched from their bodies, and to retain a stronger propension[4] unto them; whereas they weariedly left a languishing corpse, and with faint desires of reunion. If they fell by long and aged decay, yet wrapped up in the bundle of time, they fall into indistinction, and make but one blot with infants. If we begin to die when we live, and long life be but a prolongation of death, our life is a sad composition; we live with death, and die not in a moment. How many pulses made up the life of Methuselah, were work for Archimedes: common counters sum up the life of Moses his man.[5] Our days become considerable, like petty sums, by

1. Methuselah lived 969 years (Genesis v.27).
2. Roman, Saxon, and Norman. "Diuturnity": long life.
3. "Thus I, when dead, should wish to go to rest" (Tibullus).
4. Attraction. "They" are the philosophers, who traditionally die in bed.
5. I.e., the ordinary man, alluded to in Psalm xc, supposed to be by Moses; it says (verse 10), "The days of our years are three-score years and ten."

minute accumulations; where numerous fractions make up but small round numbers; and our days of a span long make not one little finger.[6]

If the nearness of our last necessity[7] brought a nearer conformity unto it, there were a happiness in hoary hairs, and no calamity in half-senses. But the long habit of living indisposeth us for dying; when avarice makes us the sport of death, when even David grew politicly cruel, and Solomon could hardly be said to be the wisest of men.[8] But many are too early old, and before the date of age. Adversity stretcheth our days, misery makes Alcmena's nights,[9] and time hath no wings unto it. But the most tedious being is that which can unwish itself, content to be nothing, or never to have been, which was beyond the malcontent of Job, who cursed not the day of his life, but his nativity:[1] content to have so far been as to have a title to future being; although he had lived here but in an hidden state of life, and as it were an abortion.

What song the Sirens sang, or what name Achilles assumed when he hid himself among women, though puzzling questions, are not beyond all conjecture.[2] What time the persons of these ossuaries entered the famous nations of the dead, and slept with princes and counselors, might admit a wide[3] solution. But who were the proprietaries of these bones, or what bodies these ashes made up, were a question above antiquarism; not to be resolved by man, nor easily perhaps by spirits, except we consult the provincial guardians, or tutelary observators.[4] Had they made as good provision for their names as they have done for their relics, they had not so grossly erred in the art of perpetuation. But to subsist in bones, and be but pyramidally extant,[5] is a fallacy in duration. Vain ashes, which in the oblivion of names, persons, times, and sexes, have found unto themselves a fruitless continuation, and only arise unto late posterity, as emblems of mortal vanities, antidotes against pride, vainglory, and madding vices. Pagan vainglories, which thought the world might last forever, had encouragement for ambition; and, finding no Atropos[6] unto the immortality of their names, were never damped with the necessity of oblivion. Even old ambitions had

6. In certain ancient arithmetics, Browne's note tells us, "the little finger of the right hand, contracted, signified an hundred."
7. I.e., death.
8. David suffered in his last years from the rebellion and death of his son Absalom; Solomon was seduced by fair idolatresses to the service of alien gods.
9. Sleeping with Alcmena to beget Hercules, Jove enjoyed himself so much that he forbade the sun to rise for one day; thus there were three nights in a row.
1. Job iii.
2. Suetonius (*Lives of the Twelve Caesars*) says that Tiberius went to the "silly and laughable extreme" of testing grammarians (whom he admired) with these questions.
3. Approximate.
4. Browne, who believed in witches, also believed in angelic protectors, both personal ("tutelary observators") and of more extended jurisdiction ("provincial guardians").
5. Like a pyramid, famous though the person buried within it is long forgotten.
6. Of the three Fates, Clotho, Lachesis, and Atropos, the last-named held the scissors. They cut the threads of mortal life.

the advantage of ours, in the attempts of their vainglories, who, acting early and before the probable meridian[7] of time, have by this time found great accomplishment of their designs, whereby the ancient heroes have already outlasted their monuments and mechanical preservations. But in this latter scene of time, we cannot expect such mummies unto our memories, when ambition may fear the prophecy of Elias,[8] and Charles the Fifth can never hope to live within two Methuselahs of Hector.[9]

And therefore, restless inquietude for the diuturnity of our memories unto present considerations seems a vanity almost out of date, and superannuated piece of folly. We cannot hope to live so long in our names as some have done in their persons; one face of Janus[1] holds no proportion unto the other. 'Tis too late to be ambitious. The great mutations of the world are acted, or time may be too short for our designs. To extend our memories by monuments, whose death we daily pray for,[2] and whose duration we cannot hope, without injury to our expectations in the advent of the last day, were a contradiction to our beliefs. We whose generations are ordained in this setting part of time[3] are providentially taken off from such imaginations; and, being necessitated to eye the remaining particle of futurity, are naturally constituted unto thoughts of the next world, and cannot excusably decline the consideration of that duration, which maketh pyramids pillars of snow, and all that's past a moment.

Circles and right lines limit and close all bodies, and the mortal right-lined circle must conclude and shut up all.[4] There is no antidote against the opium of time, which temporally considereth all things: our fathers find their graves in our short memories, and sadly tell us how we may be buried in our survivors. Gravestones tell truth scarce forty years.[5] Generations pass while some trees stand, and old families last not three oaks. To be read by bare inscriptions like many in Gruter,[6] to hope for eternity by enigmatical epithets or first letters of our names, to be studied by antiquaries, who we were, and have new names given us like many of the mummies, are cold consolations unto the students of perpetuity, even by everlasting languages.

To be content that times to come should only know there was

7. Noon, midday.
8. "That the earth will last but 6,000 years" [Browne's note]. There is no warrant for this in the Bible.
9. Since Methuselah lived to be 969, Browne's estimate is conservative: Hector, the hero of Troy, had more than three 'Methuselahs" head start on Charles V (1500–58).
1. Janus, Roman god of doorways and beginnings (hence "January"), had two heads facing in opposite directions, the past and the future.
2. We pray for the "death" and destruction of our graves at the Last Judgment.
3. The image is from the sunset.
4. Θ (*theta*), the first letter of Θάνατος ("death"), symbolizes it.
5. Because old corpses are dug up and replaced with new; see *Hamlet* V.i; and Donne, *The Relic,* lines 3–4.
6. Jan Gruter (1560–1627) was a Dutch scholar who published a collection of Latin inscriptions.

such a man, not caring whether they knew more of him, was a frigid ambition in Cardan;[7] disparaging his horoscopal inclination and judgment of himself. Who cares to subsist like Hippocrates' patients, or Achilles' horses in Homer, under naked nominations, without deserts and noble acts, which are the balsam of our memories, the *entelechia*[8] and soul of our subsistences? To be nameless in worthy deeds exceeds[9] an infamous history. The Canaanitish woman lives more happily without a name than Herodias with one. And who had not rather have been the good thief than Pilate?[1]

But the iniquity of oblivion blindly scattereth her poppy, and deals with the memory of men without distinction to merit of perpetuity. Who can but pity the founder of the pyramids? Herostratus lives that burnt the temple of Diana;[2] he is almost lost that built it. Time hath spared the epitaph of Adrian's horse,[3] confounded that of himself. In vain we compute our felicities by the advantage of our good names, since bad have equal durations, and Thersites is like to live as long as Agamemnon.[4] Who knows whether the best of men be known, or whether there be not more remarkable persons forgot than any that stand remembered in the known account of time? Without the favor of the everlasting register, the first man had been as unknown as the last, and Methuselah's long life had been his only chronicle.

Oblivion is not to be hired: the greater part must be content to be as though they had not been, to be found in the register of God, not in the record of man. Twenty-seven names make up the first story, and the recorded names ever since contain not one living century.[5] The number of the dead long exceedeth all that shall live. The night of time far surpasseth the day, and who knows when was the equinox? Every hour adds unto that current arithmetic,[6] which scarce stands one moment. And since death must be the Lucina[7] of life, and even pagans could doubt whether thus to live were to die; since our longest sun sets at right descensions, and makes but winter arches, and therefore it cannot be long before we lie down in darkness, and have our light in ashes;[8] since the brother of death

7. Girolamo Cardano, a famous Italian mathematician and occultist of the 16th century. Taking his own horoscope, he found himself destined to great things.
8. Essence, perfection.
9. Is better than.
1. The woman of Canaan had faith in Jesus; Herodias asked for the head of John the Baptist (Matthew xv.27–28; Mark vi.22–25). The good thief, crucified beside Christ, had his blessing; Pontius Pilate, the procurator of Judea, typifies the sanctimonious villain.
2. Herostratus of Ephesus set fire to the great temple in that city simply in order to gain a stupid immortality.
3. Adrian (Hadrian) was emperor of Rome in the 2nd century A.D.
4. Thersites, the scurrilous scoffer of the *Iliad*, is contrasted with Agamemnon, the royal leader.
5. Genesis i–v tells the story of the human race from the creation to the flood in 27 names; of all the names since the flood, not 100 ("century") are really living ones.
6. That continual addition.
7. Roman goddess of childbirth, hence, "the deliverance."
8. At funerals, Browne's note says, the Jews place a wax candle in a pot of ashes beside the corpse. The "brother of death" is sleep.

daily haunts us with dying mementos, and time that grows old in itself bids us hope no long duration; diuturnity is a dream and folly of expectation.

Darkness and light divide the course of time, and oblivion shares with memory a great part even of our living beings; we slightly remember our felicities, and the smartest strokes of affliction leave but short smart upon us. Sense endureth no extremities, and sorrows destroy us or themselves. To weep into stones are fables.[9] Afflictions induce callosities;[1] miseries are slippery, or fall like snow upon us, which notwithstanding is no unhappy stupidity. To be ignorant of evils to come, and forgetful of evils past, is a merciful provision in nature, whereby we digest the mixture of our few and evil days, and, our delivered senses not relapsing into cutting remembrances, our sorrows are not kept raw by the edge of repetitions. A great part of antiquity contented their hopes of subsistency with a transmigration of their souls: a good way to continue memories, while having the advantage of plural successions, they could not but act something remarkable in such variety of beings, and enjoying the fame of their passed selves, make accumulation of glory unto their last durations. Others, rather than be lost in the uncomfortable night of nothing, were content to recede into the common being, and make one particle of the public soul of all things, which was no more than to return into their unknown and divine original again. Egyptian ingenuity[2] was more unsatisfied, contriving their bodies in sweet consistencies, to attend the return of their souls. But all was vanity, feeding the wind, and folly. The Egyptian mummies, which Cambyses or time hath spared, avarice now consumeth.[3] Mummy is become merchandise, Mizraim cures wounds, and Pharaoh is sold for balsams.

In vain do individuals hope for immortality, or any patent[4] from oblivion, in preservations below the moon; men have been deceived even in their flatteries above the sun, and studied conceits to perpetuate their names in heaven. The various cosmography of that part hath already varied the names of contrived constellations: Nimrod is lost in Orion, and Osiris in the Dog Star.[5] While we look for incorruption in the heavens, we find they are but like the earth, durable in their main bodies, alterable in their parts: whereof beside comets and new stars, perspectives[6] begin to tell tales, and the

9. Like Niobe, whose grief turned her to stone.
1. Callouses, hardness, indifference.
2. The reference is to embalming practices.
3. The story of Cambyses ravaging Egypt is told in Herodotus, Book III. Powdered mummy was sold in the 17th century as medicine (see Donne, *Love's Alchemy*, line 24). "Mizraim": i.e., Egypt; Mizraim was a son of Ham (Genesis x.6–14).
4. Protection.
5. I.e., the names of the stars change—Osiris to Sirius, Nimrod the mighty hunter (Genesis x.9) to Orion.
6. Telescopes.

spots that wander about the sun, with Phaethon's favor,[7] would make clear conviction.

There is nothing strictly immortal but immortality. Whatever hath no beginning may be confident of no end; all others have a dependent being and within the reach of destruction; which is the peculiar[8] of that necessary essence that cannot destroy itself; and the highest strain of omnipotency, to be so powerfully constituted as not to suffer even from the power of itself. But the sufficiency of Christian immortality frustrates all earthly glory, and the quality of either state after death makes a folly of posthumous memory. God, who can only[9] destroy our souls, and hath assured our resurrection, either of our bodies or names hath directly promised no duration. Wherein there is so much of chance that the boldest expectants have found unhappy frustration; and to hold long subsistence seems but a scape in oblivion.[1] But man is a noble animal, splendid in ashes, and pompous in the grave, solemnizing nativities and deaths with equal luster, nor omitting ceremonies of bravery[2] in the infamy of his nature.

Life is a pure flame, and we live by an invisible sun within us. A small fire sufficeth for life, great flames seemed too little after death, while men vainly affected precious pyres, and to burn like Sardanapalus;[3] but the wisdom of funeral laws found the folly of prodigal blazes, and reduced undoing fires unto the rule of sober obsequies, wherein few could be so mean as not to provide wood, pitch, a mourner, and an urn.

Five languages secured not the epitaph of Gordianus.[4] The man of God[5] lives longer without a tomb than any by one, invisibly interred by angels, and adjudged to obscurity, though not without some marks directing human discovery. Enoch and Elias,[6] without either tomb or burial, in an anomalous state of being, are the great examples of perpetuity, in their long and living memory, in strict account being still on this side death, and having a late part yet to act upon this stage of earth. If in the decretory term of the world[7] we shall not all die but be changed, according to received translation, the last day will make but few graves; at least quick resurrections will anticipate lasting sepultures; some graves will be opened

7. Phaethon was an unfortunate son of the Sun, who tried to drive his father's chariot and nearly set the universe on fire. His erratic course reminds Browne of spots which wander across the sun's face, and which had only recently been charted by astronomers, starting with Galileo.
8. Characteristic.
9. Who alone can.
1. Weak trick against forgetfulness.
2. Proud ceremonies.
3. Sardanapalus burned up a palace full of eunuchs, concubines, and treasures as his funeral pyre; later civilizations often forbade such lavish displays.
4. The epitaph of Gordianus, emperor of Rome (238–244), was written in five languages; but it was obliterated in all of them by his successor, Licinius.
5. Moses (see Deuteronomy xxxiv).
6. Enoch and "Elias" (Elijah) were translated straight to heaven (Genesis v.24; II Kings ii.11).
7. The Last Judgment.

before they be quite closed, and Lazarus be no wonder.[8] When many that feared to die shall groan that they can die but once, the dismal state is the second and living death, when life puts despair on the damned; when men shall wish the coverings of mountains, not of monuments, and annihilations shall be courted.[9]

While some have studied monuments, others have studiously declined them; and some have been so vainly boisterous that they durst not acknowledge their graves, wherein Alaricus[1] seems most subtle, who had a river turned to hide his bones at the bottom. Even Sulla,[2] that thought himself safe in his urn, could not prevent revenging tongues, and stones thrown at his monument. Happy are they whom privacy makes innocent, who deal so with men in this world that they are not afraid to meet them in the next; who, when they die, make no commotion among the dead, and are not touched with that poetical taunt of Isaiah.[3]

Pyramids, arches, obelisks were but the irregularities of vainglory, and wild enormities of ancient magnanimity. But the most magnanimous resolution rests in the Christian religion, which trampleth upon pride, and sits on the neck of ambition, humbly pursuing that infallible perpetuity unto which all others must diminish their diameters, and be poorly seen in angles of contingency.[4]

Pious spirits who passed their days in raptures of futurity made little more of this world than the world that was before it, while they lay obscure in the chaos of pre-ordination, and night of their fore-beings. And if any have been so happy as truly to understand Christian annihilation, ecstasies, exolution,[5] liquefaction, transformation, the kiss of the spouse, gustation of God, and ingression into the divine shadow, they have already had an handsome anticipation of heaven; the glory of the world is surely over, and the earth in ashes unto them.

To subsist in lasting monuments, to live in their productions, to exist in their names and predicament of chimeras,[6] was large satisfaction unto old expectations, and made one part of their Elysiums.[7] But all this is nothing in the metaphysics of true belief. To live indeed is to be again ourselves, which being not only an hope but an evidence in noble believers, 'tis all one to lie in St. Innocent's

8. Lazarus, the dead man raised by Christ (John xi).
9. The damned soul shrieking for mountains to shield him from the wrath of God was a figure beloved of preachers. See Luke xxiii.30 and Revelation vi.16.
1. Alaric, the Gothic invader, was buried in the bed of the river Busento (A.D. 410).
2. Roman politician and general, who died 78 B.C.
3. In Isaiah xiv the mighty ones of the earth are taunted with their approaching downfall into hell.
4. The angle of contingency is the smallest possible angle; Browne puns on the idea that all these lesser perpetuities are subject to accident ("contingency").
5. The loosening or freeing of the spirit from the bonds of the body.
6. In the condition of phantasms.
7. The pagan afterworld.

churchyard,[8] as in the sands of Egypt: ready to be anything, in the ecstasy of being ever, and as content with six foot as the *moles* of Adrianus.[9]

—Tabesne cadavera solvat,
An rogus, haud refert.
—LUCAN

1658

8. In Paris, where bodies soon consume; contrasted with the desert, where they last a long time.
9. Adrian's (Hadrian's) tomb, now Castel San Angelo in Rome, the type of a magnificent mausoleum. The Latin tag is translated, "By the swift funeral pyre or slow decay / (No matter which) the bodies pass away" (Lucan, *Pharsalia* VII.809).

JOHN LOCKE

(1632–1704)

1667: Physician to the first Earl of Shaftesbury
1684: Expelled from Oxford post as part of intrigues against Shaftesbury
1689–90: Publication of the *Essay, Letter Concerning Toleration,* and *Treatise of Government*

Locke's *Essay Concerning Human Understanding,* which is a pretty formidable book of technical philosophy, drew some protests over its title, and others of a contrary tendency over its method. It seemed too heavy, hard, and long to be a mere essay. On the other hand, its basic material was described as too trifling to merit so much analysis. For all Mr. Locke proposed to do in 600 knotty pages was to analyze a few ideas that he found lying about in his own mind.

As usual, the philosopher, who was nothing if not a long-headed man, had considered these criticisms already and had devised a single answer for both. His book was an essay because, like that of Montaigne, it aimed to explore the mind of mankind in general through a discriminating analysis of one mind in particular. When Locke analyzed the ideas of his mind, the ways they were acquired and put together, he found they were clear when they were based on direct experience, and adequate when they were clear. Usually, it appeared, problems occurred when the basic ideas with which he was trying to calculate were blurred or confused or did not refer to anything determinate. Thus a critical analysis of the ideas in an individual mind could lead straight to a rule about adequate ideas in general and the sort of subject where adequate ideas were possible. On the basis of such a limitation, individuals might reach rational agreement with one another, and so set up an area of natural law, within which a common rule of understanding was available.

The clergy were naturally upset over Locke's new "way of ideas," which invited people to discard from their minds any ideas that they could not reduce to clear, distinct, i.e., determinate, form. "Mysteries of faith" were essential to the mental economy of churchmen. How could the Trinity or the doctrine of predestination be reduced to clear, distinct ideas? If they couldn't, must one then discard them? On this last point, Locke was polite but very firm. Yes, if one wanted to discourse reasonably and understandably, one really must discard any idea which could not be given a determinate shape and meaning. The philosopher had evidently performed this operation on any unclear and indistinct ideas he found in his own mind. What was left of Christianity when one got rid of all its "unreasonable" elements was a cool, general, undemanding creed, which did not commit one to much more than a belief in the existence of God, and was therefore known as "Deism." Locke did not like labels, but he was a kind of Deist. Though a scandalous idea in the late 17th century, Deism was a perfectly respectable creed by the time of Pope.

Like most philosophers, Locke had a minimum of personal history. His background and connections were all with the Puritan movement, but he was early disillusioned with the enthusiastic moods and dogmatic persecutions to which he found the Puritans prone. Having a small but steady private income, he became a student, chiefly at Oxford, learning enough medicine to act as a physician, holding an occasional appointive office, but never allowing any of these activities to limit his controlling passion, which was simply for thought. After 1667, he was personal physician and tutor in the household of a violent, crafty politician, the first Earl of Shaftesbury (Dryden's "Achitophel"). But Locke himself was always a grave, dispassionate man, almost frighteningly judicious. On one occasion, Shaftesbury's political enemies at Oxford had Locke watched for several years on end, during which he was not heard to say one word either critical of the government or favorable to it. When times are turbulent, so much discretion is suspicious in itself; and Locke found it convenient to go abroad for several years during the 1680's. He lived quietly in Holland, and pursued his thoughts. The Glorious Revolution and the accession of William III brought him back to England, and made possible the publication of the *Essay*, on which he had been working for many years. Its publication foreshadowed the coming Age of Reason, not only in the positive ideas that the book advanced, but in the quiet way it set aside as insoluble a range of problems about absolute authority and absolute assurance to which the 17th century had prodigally sacrificed its best resources of mind and heart.

From An Essay Concerning Human Understanding

From *The Epistle to the Reader*

Reader,

I here put into thy hands what has been the diversion of some of my idle and heavy hours; if it has the good-luck to prove so of any of thine, and thou hast but half so much pleasure in reading as I had in writing it, thou wilt as little think thy money, as I do my pains, ill bestowed. Mistake not this for a commendation of my work; nor conclude, because I was pleased with the doing of it, that therefore I am fondly taken with it now it is done. He that hawks at larks and sparrows, has no less sport, though a much less considerable quarry, than he that flies at nobler game: and he is little acquainted with the subject of this treatise, the Understanding, who does not know, that as it is the most elevated faculty of the soul, so it is employed with a greater and more constant delight than any of the other. Its searches after truth are a sort of hawking and hunting, wherein the very pursuit makes a great part of the pleasure. Every step the mind takes in its progress towards knowledge makes some discovery, which is not only new, but the best, too, for the time at least.

For the understanding, like the eye, judging of objects only by its own sight, cannot but be pleased with what it discovers, having less regret for what has escaped it, because it is unknown. Thus he who has raised himself above the alms-basket, and not content to live lazily on scraps of begged opinions, sets his own thoughts on work, to find and follow truth, will (whatever he lights on) not miss the hunter's satisfaction; every moment of his pursuit will reward his pains with some delight, and he will have reason to think his time not ill spent, even when he cannot much boast of any great acquistion.

This, reader, is the entertainment of those who let loose their own thoughts, and follow them in writing; which thou oughtest not to envy them, since they afford thee an opportunity of the like diversion, if thou wilt make use of thy own thoughts in reading. It is to them, if they are thy own, that I refer myself; but if they are taken upon trust from others, it is no great matter what they are, they not following truth, but some meaner consideration; and it is not worth while to be concerned what he says or thinks, who says or thinks only as he is directed by another. If thou judgest for thyself, I know thou wilt judge candidly; and then I shall not be harmed or offended, whatever be thy censure. For, though it be certain that there is nothing in this treatise of the truth whereof I am not fully persuaded, yet I consider myself as liable to mistakes as I can think thee; and know that this book must stand or fall with thee, not by any opinion I have of it, but thy own. If thou findest little in it new or instructive to thee, thou art not to blame me for it. It was not meant for those that had already mastered this subject, and made a thorough acquaintance with their own understandings, but for my own information, and the satisfaction of a few friends, who acknowledged themselves not to have sufficiently considered it. Were it fit to trouble thee with the history of this Essay, I should tell thee, that five or six friends, meeting at my chamber, and discoursing on a subject very remote from this, found themselves quickly at a stand by the difficulties that rose on every side. After we had awhile puzzled ourselves, without coming any nearer a resolution of those doubts which perplexed us, it came into my thoughts, that we took a wrong course; and that, before we set ourselves upon inquiries of that nature, it was necessary to examine our own abilities, and see what objects our understandings were or were not fitted to deal with. This I proposed to the company, who all readily assented; and thereupon it was agreed, that this should be our first inquiry. Some hasty and undigested thoughts, on a subject I had never before considered, which I set down against our next meeting, gave the first entrance into this discourse, which, having been thus begun by chance, was continued by entreaty; written by incoherent parcels; and, after long intervals of neglect, resumed again, as my humor or occasions permitted; and at last, in a retirement, where an attendance on my health gave me leisure, it was brought into that order thou now seest it.

This discontinued way of writing may have occasioned, besides others, two contrary faults; viz., that too little and too much may be said in it. If thou findest anything wanting, I shall be glad, that what I have writ gives thee any desire that I should have gone farther: if it seems too much to thee, thou must blame the subject; for when I first put pen to paper, I thought all I should have to say on this matter would have been contained in one sheet of paper; but the farther I went, the larger prospect I had: new discoveries led me still on, and so it grew insensibly to the bulk it now appears in. I will not deny but possibly it might be reduced to a narrower compass than it is; and that some parts of it might be contracted; the way it has been writ in, by catches, and many long intervals of interruption, being apt to cause some repetitions. But, to confess the truth, I am now too lazy or too busy to make it shorter.

I am not ignorant how little I herein consult my own reputation, when I knowingly let it go with a fault so apt to disgust the most judicious, who are always the nicest[1] readers. But they who know sloth is apt to content itself with any excuse, will pardon me, if mine has prevailed on me where I think I have a very good one. I will not, therefore, allege in my defense, that the same notion, having different respects,[2] may be convenient or necessary to prove or illustrate several parts of the same discourse; and that so it has happened in many parts of this: but, waiving that, I shall frankly avow, that I have sometimes dwelt long upon the same argument, and expressed it different ways, with a quite different design. I pretend not to publish this Essay for the information of men of large thoughts and quick apprehensions; to such masters of knowledge, I profess myself a scholar, and therefore warn them beforehand not

1. Most critical.

2. Aspects.

to expect any thing here but what, being spun out of my own coarse thoughts,[3] is fitted to men of my own size, to whom, perhaps, it will not be unacceptable that I have taken some pains to make plain and familiar to their thoughts some truths, which established prejudice or the abstractness of the ideas themselves, might render difficult. Some objects had need be turned on every side; and when the notion is new, as I confess some of these are to me, or out of the ordinary road, as I suspect they will appear to others, it is not one simple view of it that will gain it admittance into every understanding, or fix it there with a clear and lasting impression. There are few, I believe, who have not observed in themselves or others, that what in one way of proposing was very obscure, another way of expressing it has made very clear and intelligible; though afterward the mind found little difference in the phrases, and wondered why one failed to be understood more than the other. But every thing does not hit alike upon every man's imagination. We have our understandings no less different than our palates; and he that thinks the same truth shall be equally relished by every one in the same dress, may as well hope to feast every one with the same sort of cookery; the meat may be the same and the nourishment good, yet every one not be able to receive it with that seasoning; and it must be dressed another way, if you will have it go down with some even of strong constitutions. The truth is, those who advised me to publish it, advised me, for this reason, to publish it as it is; and since I have been brought to let it go abroad, I desire it should be understood by whoever gives himself the pains to read it. I have so little affection to be in print, that if I were not flattered this Essay might be of some use to others, as I think it has been to me, I should have confined it to the view of some friends, who gave the first occasion to it. My appearing therefore in print being on purpose to be as useful as I may, I think it necessary to make what I have to say as easy and intelligible to all sorts of readers as I can. And I had much rather the speculative and quick-sighted should complain of my being in some parts tedious, than that anyone, not accustomed to abstract speculations, or prepossessed with different notions, should mistake or not comprehend my meaning.

It will possibly be censured as a great piece of vanity or insolence in me, to pretend to instruct this our knowing age, it amounting to little less when I own that I publish this Essay with hopes that it may be useful to others. But if it may be permitted to speak freely of those who, with a feigned modesty, condemn as useless what they themselves write, methinks it savors much more of vanity or insolence to publish a book for any other end; and he fails very

3. Locke's mock-modest confession that his philosophy had been "spun out of his own coarse thoughts" gave rise to a good deal of critical ridicule, echoes of which are heard in the debate between the spider and the bee in Swift's *Battle of the Books*.

much of that respect he owes the public, who prints, and consequently expects that men should read, that wherein he intends not they should meet with any thing of use to themselves or others: and should nothing else be found allowable in this treatise, yet my design will not cease to be so; and the goodness of my intention ought to be some excuse for the worthlessness of my present. It is that chiefly which secures me from the fear of censure, which I expect not to escape more than better writers. Men's principles, notions, and relishes are so different, that it is hard to find a book which pleases or displeases all men. I acknowledge the age we live in is not the least knowing, and therefore not the most easy to be satisfied. If I have not the good luck to please, yet nobody ought to be offended with me. I plainly tell all my readers, except half a dozen, this treatise was not at first intended for them; and therefore they need not be at the trouble to be of that number. But yet if any one thinks fit to be angry, and rail at it, he may do it securely; for I shall find some better way of spending my time than in such kind of conversation. I shall always have the satisfaction to have aimed sincerely at truth and usefulness, though in one of the meanest ways. The commonwealth of learning is not at this time without master-builders, whose mighty designs in advancing the sciences will leave lasting monuments to the admiration of posterity: but every one must not hope to be a Boyle or a Sydenham; and in an age that produces such masters as the great Huygenius, and the incomparable Mr. Newton, with some other of that strain,[4] it is ambition enough to be employed as an under-laborer in clearing ground a little, and removing some of the rubbish that lies in the way to knowledge; which certainly had been very much more advanced in the world, if the endeavors of ingenious and industrious men had not been much cumbered with the learned but frivolous use of uncouth, affected, or unintelligible terms introduced into the sciences, and there made an art of to that degree, that philosophy, which is nothing but the true knowledge of things was thought unfit or uncapable to be brought into well-bred company and polite conversation.[5] Vague and insignificant forms of speech, and abuse of language, have so long passed for mysteries of science; and hard or misapplied words, with little or no meaning, have, by prescription, such a right to be mistaken for deep learning and height of

4. Robert Boyle is the great Anglo-Irish chemist and physicist; Thomas Sydenham, a physician and authority on the cure of fevers; Christiaan Huygens was a Dutch mathematician and astronomer; and Newton is of course Sir Isaac. Locke's choice of scientists to illustrate the great minds of his time is certainly tendentious. A generation or two earlier a list of "great men" would have consisted largely of theologians and perhaps lawyers.

5. Locke was tutor to Anthony Ashley Cooper, third Earl of Shaftesbury, whose philosophical writings make of genteel social conversation and civilized good humor something like guides to ultimate truth. Whatever can't be spoken in a drawing room without exposing a gentleman to ridicule—so Shaftesbury comes close to saying—is not likely to be true. Locke's basic hostility to cant and jargon has been extended by Shaftesbury, but its original source is apparent.

speculation; that it will not be easy to persuade either those who speak or those who hear them, that they are but the covers of ignorance, and hindrance of true knowledge. To break in upon the sanctuary of vanity and ignorance, will be, I suppose, some service to human understanding: though so few are apt to think they deceive or are deceived in the use of words, or that the language of the sect they are of has any faults in it which ought to be examined or corrected, that I hope I shall be pardoned if I have in the third book dwelt long on this subject; and endeavored to make it so plain, that neither the inveterateness of the mischief, nor the prevalency of the fashion, shall be any excuse for those who will not take care about the meaning of their own words, and will not suffer the significancy of their expressions to be inquired into. * * *

The booksellers, preparing for the fourth edition of my Essay, gave me notice of it, that I might, if I had leisure, make any additions or alterations I should think fit. Whereupon I thought it convenient to advertise the reader, that besides several corrections I had made here and there, there was one alteration which it was necessary to mention, because it ran through the whole book, and is of consequence to be rightly understood. What I thereupon said, was this:—

"Clear and distinct ideas" are terms which, though familiar and frequent in men's mouths, I have reason to think every one who uses does not perfectly understand. And possibly it is but here and there one who gives himself the trouble to consider them so far as to know what he himself or others precisely mean by them. I have therefore, in most places, chose to put "determinate" or "determined," instead of "clear" and "distinct," as more likely to direct men's thoughts to my meaning in this matter. By those denominations, I mean some object in the mind, and consequently determined, i.e., such as it is there seen and perceived to be. This, I think, may fitly be called a "determinate" or "determined" idea, when such as it is at any time objectively in the mind, and so determined there, it is annexed, and without variation determined, to a name or articulate sound which is to be steadily the sign of that very same object of the mind, or determinate idea.

To explain this a little more particularly: By "determinate," when applied to a simple idea, I mean that simple appearance which the mind has in its view, or perceives in itself, when that idea is said to be in it. By "determinate," when applied to a complex idea, I mean such an one as consists of a determinate number of certain simple or less complex ideas, joined in such a proportion and situation as the mind has before its view, and sees in itself, when that idea is present in it, or should be present in it when a man gives a name to it. I say "should be;" because it is not every one, nor perhaps any one, who is so careful of his language as to use no word till he views in his mind the precise determined idea which he resolves to make it the sign of. The want of this is the cause of no small obscurity and confusion in men's thoughts and discourses.

I know there are not words enough in any language to answer all the variety of ideas that enter into men's discourses and reasonings. But this hinders not but that when anyone uses any term, he may have in his mind a determined idea which he makes it the sign of, and to which he should keep it steadily annexed during that present discourse. Where he does not or cannot do this, he in vain pretends to clear or distinct ideas: it is plain his are not so; and therefore there can be expected nothing but obscurity and confusion, where such terms are made use of which have not such a precise determination.

Upon this ground I have thought "determined ideas" a way of speaking less liable to mistake than "clear and distinct"; and where men have got such determined ideas of all that they reason, inquire, or argue about, they will find a great part of their doubts and disputes at an end. The greatest part of the questions and controversies that perplex mankind, depending on the doubtful and uncertain use of words, or (which is the same) indetermined ideas, which they are made to stand for: I have made choice of these terms to signify, 1. Some immediate object of the mind, which it perceives and has before it, distinct from the sound it uses as a sign of it. 2. That this idea, thus determined, i.e., which the mind has in itself, and knows and sees there, be determined without any change to that name, and that name determined to that precise idea. If men had such determined ideas in their inquiries and discourses, they would both discern how far their own inquiries and discourses went, and avoid the greatest part of the disputes and wranglings they have with others.

1689

SAMUEL PEPYS

(1633–1703)

Samuel Pepys (pronounced "Peeps") was a bureaucrat in the London office of the Royal Navy, docile if not very enthusiastic in his attachment to the church of England, energetic and ultimately very influential in his office. The spirit of Puritanism touched him only tangentially, but touch him it did, not on the revivalist side but on the sober, bookkeeping side of his functionary's soul. In 1660, when he was about 27 years old, married, and solidly settled in office, he started to keep a private diary of his daily life;

and, being a methodical, persistent man, he kept it going in minute detail for nine years, covering the most colorful and turbulent period of the Restoration. For the social historian, it provides an unparalleled record of London life, its plays and plagues, vulgarities, executions, wars, fires, scandals and intrigues. It is also a great human document *à la* Montaigne; an epic of the ordinary. The hero is Mr. Pepys; the epic action is his rise in the world to affluence and influence.

Because he wrote in shorthand, only recently invented and not very widely known, Pepys felt safe in recording all the undignified and squalid episodes of his existence. As a result the *Diary* acquired, during the prudish 19th century, a false reputation for obscenity. Only recently has it been deciphered in its unexpurgated entirety, and revealed itself as a remarkably sane and full record of a man's life. Pepys recorded his life as it happened and completely because he was a truthful man, and because he wanted a record of his spiritual and material progress through this world. The *Diary* served him as an aid to navigation through life's ocean; Pepys used it to take recurrent fixes on his social latitude and longitude. A normal time for this review of things was year's end, when practicality and piety were apt to blend in a singular amalgam of complacency and good practical sense.

Our text is from *The Diary of Samuel Pepys*, transcribed and edited by Robert Latham and William Matthews (University of California Press, 1970).

From The Diary

January 28, 1661

At the office all morning. Dined at home. And after dinner to Fleet street with my sword to Mr. Brigden (lately made Captain of the Auxiliaries) to be refreshed.[1] And with him to an alehouse, where I met Mr. Damport; and after some talk of Cromwell, Ireton, and Bradshaw's bodies being taken out of their graves today,[2] I went to Mr. Crew's and thence to the theater, where I saw again *The Lost Lady*,[3] which doth now please me better than before. And here, I sitting behind in a dark place, a lady spat backward upon me by a mistake, not seeing me. But after seeing her to be a very pretty lady, I was not troubled at it at all. Thence to Mr. Crew's; and there met Mr. Moore, who came lately to town, and went with me to my father's and with him to Standing's—whither came to us Dr. Fairbrother,[4] who I took and my father to the Bear and gave a pint of sack and a pint of claret. He doth still continue his expressions of respect and love to me. And tells me my brother John will make a good scholar.

1. Pepys was evidently enrolled in some sort of militia, and had to renew his oath.
2. The bodies of Cromwell, Ireton, and Bradshaw, all men who had taken part in the execution of Charles I, were exhumed, hanged, and disgraced as traitors.
3. Pepys had seen this play, first acted in 1638, only nine days before. He did not like it at all the first time.
4. Dr. Fairbrother, of King's College, Cambridge, was in charge of the education of Pepys' younger brother, John.

Thence to see the Doctor at his lodgings at Mr. Holden's, where I bought a hat, cost me 35*s.* So home by moonshine, and by the way was overtaken by the Comptroller's[5] coach; and so home to his house with him. So home and to bed. This noon I had my press set up in my chamber for papers to be put in.

October 28, 1661

At the office all day, and dined at home; and so to Paul's churchyard to Hunt's, and there find my Therobo[6] done. Which pleases me very well, and costs me 26s. to the altering—but now he tells me it is as good a lute as any is in England, and is worth well 10*l.* Hither I sent for Captain Ferrers to me, who comes with a friend of his, and they and I to the theater and there saw *Argalus and Parthenia;*[7] where a woman acted Parthenia and came afterward on the stage in man's clothes, and had the best legs that ever I saw; and I was very well pleased with it. Thence to the Ringo ale house, and thither sent for a belt-maker and bought of him a handsome belt for second mourning,[8] which cost me 24*s.* and is very neat. So home and to bed.

December 31, 1662

Thus ended this year, with great mirth to me and my wife. Our condition being thus—we are at present spending a night or two at my Lord's[9] lodgings at Whitehall. Our home at the Navy office, which is and hath a pretty while been in good condition, finished and made very convenient. My purse is worth about 650*l.*—besides my goods of all sorts—which yet might have been more but for my late layings-out upon my house and public assessment, and yet would not have been so much if I had not lived a very orderly life all this year, by virtue of the oaths that God put into my heart to take against wine, plays, and other expenses, and to observe for these last twelve months—and which I am now going to renew, I under God owing my present content thereunto.[1] My family is myself and wife; William my clerk; Jane, my wife's upper-maid, but I think growing proud and negligent upon it, we must part, which

5. The Comptroller of the Navy, Sir Robert Slingsby; as a high-level bureaucrat, he is riding in a coach, and picks up Pepys; within a few years, Pepys will have his own coach. Press: chest of drawers.

6. Theorbo, a kind of early guitar. Pepys was an enthusiastic amateur musician, not only singing and playing, but also composing an occasional song of his own. Shillings and pounds are represented in the *Diary* by *s. and l.*

7. This romantic pastoral play had been written and published during the 1630's, but was being revived during the Restoration, for lack of other dramatic fare. The appearance of women on the stage was still a novelty, female parts having previously been taken by boys.

8. Pepys' Uncle Robert had died three months earlier; second mourning was evidently less austere than first.

9. My Lord Sandwich, after whose descendant the snack was named; as chief Lord of the Admiralty, he was Pepys's administrative superior, his patron, and on occasion his financial guide.

1. Pepys had found himself going to the theater too often in 1661, and getting drunk too often; he took great oaths, and reduced both habits sharply.

troubles me; Susan our cook-maid, a pretty willing wench but no good cook; and Waynman my boy,[2] who I am now turning away for his naughty tricks. We have had from the beginning our healths to this day very well, blessed be God. Our late maid Sarah going from us (though put away by us) to live with Sir W. Penn[3] doth trouble me, though I love the wench—so that we do make ourselves a little strange to him and his family for it, and resolve to do so.

December 31, 1663

* * * And so home; and after a little while at my office, I home and supped; and so had a good fire in my chamber, and there sat till 4 o'clock in the morning, making up my accounts and writing this past Journal of the year. And first I bless God, I do, after a large expense, even this month by reason of Christmas and some payments to my father and other things extraordinary, find that I am worth in money, besides all my household stuff or anything of Brampton,[4] above 800*l.*; whereof, in my Lord Sandwich's hand, 700*l.*, and the rest in my hand; so that there is not above 15*l.* of all my estate in money at this minute out of my hands and my Lord's —for which the good God be pleased to give me a thankful heart and a mind careful to preserve this and increase it.

I do live at my lodgings in the Navy Office—my family being, besides my wife and I, Jane Gentleman, Bess our excellent/good-natured cook-maid, and Susan a little girl—having neither man nor boy, nor like to have again a good while—living now in most perfect content and quiet and very frugally also. My health pretty good, but only that I have been much troubled with a costiveness[5] which I am laboring to get away, and have hopes of doing it. At the office I am well, though envied to the devil by Sir W. Batten, who hates me to death but cannot hurt me. The rest either love or at least do not show otherwise, though I know Sir W. Penn to be a false knave touching me, though he seems fair.

December 31, 1664

At the office all morning, and after dinner there again; despatched first my letters, and then to my accounts, not of the month but of the whole year also, and was at it till past 12 at night—it being bitter cold; but yet I was well satisfied with my work and, above all, to find myself, by the great blessing of God, worth 1349*l.* —by which, as I have spent very largely, so I have laid up above 500*l.* this year above what I was worth this day twelvemonth. The

2. Waynman was a very bad boy indeed, though we know only a few of his specific faults. Pepys beat him savagely to reform his character, and when that did not work, had him shipped off to the Barbadoes. To be known as a bad boy could have thoroughly disagreeable consequences in those days.

3. Sir W. Penn was the father of the Quaker leader.

4. Pepys had inherited some property at Brampton near Huntingdon.

5. Constipation.

Lord make me for ever thankful to his holy name for it.

Thence home to eat a little, and so to bed. As soon as ever the clock struck one, I kissed my wife in the kitchen by the fireside, wishing her a merry New Year, observing that I believe I was the first proper wisher of it this year, for I did it as soon as ever the clock struck one.

So ends the old year, I bless God with great joy to me; not only from my having made so good a year of profit, as having spent 420*l.* and laid up 540*l.* and upward.

But I bless God, I have never been in so good plight as to my health in so very cold weather as this is, nor indeed in any hot weather these ten years, as I am at this day and have been these four or five months. But I am at a great loss to know whether it be my hare's foot,[6] or taking every morning of a pill of turpentine, or my having left off the wearing of a gown.

My family is my wife, in good health, and happy with her—her woman Mercer, a pretty modest quiet maid—her chambermaid Bess—her cook-maid Jane—the little girl Susan, and my boy which I have had about half a year, Tom Edwards, which I took from the King's chapel. And a pretty and loving quiet family I have as any man in England.

January 23, 1665

Thence to Jervas's,[7] my mind, God forgive me, running too much after sa fille,[8] but elle[9] not being within, I away by coach to the Change[1]—and thence home to dinner; and finding Mrs. Bagwell[2] waiting at the office after dinner, away elle and I to a cabaret where elle and I have été[3] before; and there I had her company toute l'après-dîner and had mon plein plaisir of elle[4]—but strange, to see how a woman, notwithstanding her greatest pretences of love à son mari[5] and religion, may be vaincue.[6] Thence to the Court of the Turkey Company at Sir Andr. Rickard's, to treat about carrying some men of ours to Tangiers,[7] and had there a very civil reception, though a denial of the thing, as not practicable with them, and I think so too. So to my office a little; but being minded to make an end of my pleasure today, that I might fallow[8] my business, I did

6. Pepys carried a hare's foot as a protection against colic.
7. An alehouse where Pepys knew from experience casual female companionship could easily be picked up. His French phrases are for extra security—though, as a matter of fact, his wife was French by birth, and knew the language perfectly.
8. Her daughter.
9. She.
1. The Exchange, where merchants met to transact business.
2. The wife of a ship's carpenter, with whom Pepys had earlier reached an understanding.
3. She and I have been.
4. The whole afternoon and I had my fill of pleasure with her.
5. To her husband.
6. Overcome.
7. Pepys, an official of the Navy, was shrewdly trying to arrange some cheap transportation for naval personnel to the base at Tangiers aboard the vessels of a private company.
8. Follow.

take a coach and to Jervas's again, thinking to avoir recontré[9] Jane; mais elle n'était pas dedans.[1] So I back again and to my office, where I did with great content faire[2] a vow to mind my business and laisser aller les femmes[3] for a month; and am with all my heart glad to find myself able to come to so good a resolution, that thereby I may fallow my business, which, and my honor thereby, lies a-bleeding. So home to supper and to bed.

December 31, 1666

* * * Thence to the New Exchange to clear my wife's score;[4] and so going back again, I met Doll Lane (Mrs. Martin's sister) with another young woman of the Hall, one Scott, and took them to the Half-Moon tavern and there drank some burned wine with them, without more pleasure; and so away home by coach,[5] and there to dinner and then to my accounts, wherein at last I find them clear and right; but to my great discontent, do find that my gettings this year have been 573*l.* less than my last—it being this year in all but 2986*l.*; whereas the last I got 3560*l.* And then again my spendings this year have exceeded my spendings the last by 644*l.*—my whole spendings last year being but 509*l.*; whereas this year it appears I have spent 1154*l.*—which is a sum not fit to be said that ever I should spend in one year, before I am master of a better estate than I am. Yet, blessed be God, and I pray God make me thankful for it, I do find myself worth in money, all good, above 6,200*l.*; which is above 1800*l.* more than I was the last year. This, I trust in God, will make me thankful for what I have, and careful to make up by care next year what by my negligence and prodigality I have lost and spent this year.

9. Have met.
1. But she was not in.
2. Make.
3. Leave women alone.
4. At the New Exchange one could buy fabrics, dress materials, laces, etc. Pepys was clearing up his wife's charge account at the end of the year.
5. The coach, to which Pepys has now graduated, is doubtless one of the expenses that appall him. In earlier days, he walked: see entry for January 28, 1661, above.

THOMAS SPRAT
(1635–1713)

The Royal Society—or, as its full title reads, The Royal Society of London for Improving Natural Knowledge—began without royal patronage as a group of private gentlemen who started to meet, about the middle of the century, at Oxford or in London. As a group, the members were neither Anglican nor Puritan in their sympathies; and they avoided political as well as religious labels. Taking advantage of a strong interest in scientific observation which had been fostered by the Gresham lectures—under the terms of the original grant, they were to be delivered in the English language, and in London city, and were free for all to attend—the members of the Society concerned themselves with "natural knowledge," that is, scientific experiments and observations. Often the details with which they were concerned struck outsiders as ridiculously trivial; Charles II learned they had spent an entire meeting discussing the weight of air, and laughed himself inarticulate over it. (As it happened, the subject was one of the most serious and important with which they could have been concerned.) But the king agreed to grant the group a royal charter, and the Society began to flourish at once. It remains to this day one of the most distinguished scientific academies in the world.

Yet from the beginning a good many of the clergy had an uneasy sense that scientific investigation of nature might lead to neglect of the God who created nature. And so, to answer that criticism and others, the Society enlisted the pen of Thomas Sprat, a bright young clergyman very much in tune with the times, who was later to rise in the church and become Bishop of Rochester. He was an able young man with a flair for argumentation, and though the Royal Society of which he was writing a "history" was less than ten years old, he at least produced a vigorous defense of it. About the rest of Sprat's career there is not very much to say; nothing that he ever did in the rest of his long life equaled the significance of this one book in behalf of the Society. Not the least effective of its arguments concerned the merits of a plain English prose style, uncontrived and unadorned, devoted to a bare recital of the facts. This argument took effect far beyond the narrow range of professed scientists. Even fine gentlemen and wits, who indulged in what they called "raillery" at the expense of the Royal Society, were touched by the steady resolution of its members to talk only about those matters for which they had demonstrable evidence. And the middle classes, as they gradually surrendered their Puritan dream of establishing the Kingdom of God on earth, found in the practical exploitation of scientific knowledge an alternative outlet for their stirring and restless ambitions. For them too a doctrine of plain sense and methodical accumulation turned out to have its attractions. Our selections are from Part II, section xx, and Part III, section xxxv, of *The History of the Royal Society*.

From The History of the Royal Society

[*On the Language of the Members*]

Thus they have directed, judged, conjectured upon, and improved experiments. But lastly, in these and other businesses that have come under their care, there is one thing more about which the Society has been most solicitous, and that is the manner of their discourse; which, unless they had been very watchful to keep in due temper, the whole spirit and vigor of their design had been soon eaten out by the luxury and redundance of speech. The ill effects of this superfluity of talking have already overwhelmed most other arts and professions, insomuch that when I consider the means of happy living and the causes of their corruption, I can hardly forbear recanting what I said before, and concluding that eloquence ought to be banished out of all civil societies as a thing fatal to peace and good manners. To this opinion I should wholly incline if I did not find that it is a weapon which may be as easily procured by bad men as good, and that if these should only cast it away, and those retain it, the naked innocence of virtue would be upon all occasions exposed to the armed malice of the wicked. This is the chief reason that should now keep up the ornaments of speaking in any request, since they are so much degenerated from their original usefulness. They were at first, no doubt, an admirable instrument in the hands of wise men, when they were only employed to describe goodness, honesty, obedience in larger, fairer, and more moving images; to represent truth clothed with bodies; and to bring knowledge back again to our very senses, from whence it was at first derived to our understandings. But now they are generally changed to worse uses. They make the fancy[1] disgust the best things if they come sound and unadorned; they are in open defiance against reason, professing not to hold much correspondence with that, but with its slaves, the passions; they give the mind a motion too changeable and bewitching to consist with right practice. Who can behold without indignation how many mists and uncertainties these specious tropes and figures[2] have brought on our knowledge? How many rewards which are due to more profitable and difficult arts have been still snatched away by the easy vanity of fine speaking?[3] For now I am warmed with this just anger, I cannot withhold myself from betraying the shallowness of all these seeming mysteries upon which we writers and speakers look so big.[4] And, in few words, I dare say that of all the studies of men, nothing may be sooner obtained than this vicious abundance of phrase, this trick of metaphors, this volubility of tongue, which makes so great a noise in the world. But I spend words in vain, for the evil is now so inveterate that it is hard to know whom to blame or where to begin reform. We all value one another so much on this beautiful deceit, and labor so long after it in the years of our education, that we cannot but ever after think

1. Words like "fancy," "humor," and "judgment" were very loosely used in the 17th century, and a great deal of their meaning comes from the individual context. In this sentence "fancy" means the impression we have of a thing before we have actually experienced it.

2. Figures of speech, rhetorical "flowers" such as the ancient Greek sophists used; many of the objections raised by Sprat against rhetoric go back to charges laid against the sophists primarily by Plato.

3. Probably without realizing it, Sprat has fallen here into one of the oldest of rhetorical topics, the argument between the pen and the sword, the man of words and the man of deeds.

4. I.e., pride ourselves.

kinder of it than it deserves. And indeed in most other parts of learning I look on it to be a thing almost utterly desperate in its cure; and I think it may be placed amongst those "general mischiefs," such as the dissension of Christian princes, the want of practice in religion, and the like, which have been so long spoken against, that men are become insensible about them, every one shifting off the fault from himself to others, and so they are only made bare commonplaces of complaint. It will suffice my present purpose to point out what has been done by the Royal Society toward the correcting of its excesses in natural philosophy, to which it is, of all others, a most professed enemy.

They have therefore been most rigorous in putting in execution the only remedy that can be found for this extravagance: and that has been a constant resolution to reject all the amplifications, digressions, and swellings of style, to return back to the primitive purity and shortness, when men delivered so many things almost in an equal number of words.[5] They have exacted from all their members a close, naked, natural way of speaking; positive expressions, clear senses, a native easiness bringing all things as near the mathematical plainness as they can; and preferring the language of artisans, countrymen, and merchants before that of wits or scholars.

And here there is one thing not to be passed by, which will render this established custom of the Society well-nigh everlasting: and that is the general constitution of the minds of the English. I have already often insisted on some of the prerogatives of England, whereby it may justly lay claim to be the head of a philosophical league above all other countries in Europe. I have urged its situation, its present genius, and the disposition of its merchants; and many more such arguments to encourage us still remain to be used. But of all others, this which I am now urging is of the most weighty and important consideration. If there can be a true character given of the universal temper of any nation under heaven, then certainly this must be ascribed to our countrymen: that they have commonly an unaffected sincerity; that they love to deliver their minds with a sound simplicity; that they have the middle qualities between the reserved subtle southern and the rough unhewn northern people; that they are not extremely prone to speak; that they are more concerned what others will think of the strength than of the fineness of what they say; and that a universal modesty possesses them. These qualities are so conspicuous and proper to our soil that we often hear them objected to us by some of our neighbor satirists in more disgraceful expressions. For they are wont to revile the English with

5. Again Sprat falls back on a rhetorical formula: the contrast of words and things goes back to Quintilian and before that to Cato the Elder. "So many words, so many things" is a favorite catch-phrase of some language reformers, but it describes a state that never was and never will be.

a want of familiarity, with a melancholy dumpishness, with slowness, silence, and with the unrefined sullenness of their behavior. But these are only the reproaches of partiality or ignorance; for they ought rather to be commended for an honorable integrity; for a neglect of circumstances and flourishes; for regarding things of greater moment more than less; for a scorn to deceive as well as to be deceived—which are all the best endowments that can enter into a philosophical mind. So that even the position of our climate, the air, the influence of the heaven, the composition of the English blood, as well as the embraces of the ocean, seem to join with the labors of the Royal Society to render our country a land of experimental knowledge. And it is a good sign that nature will reveal more of its secrets to the English than to others,[6] because it has already furnished them with a genius so well proportioned for the receiving and retaining its mysteries.

[*Wit Less to be Prized than Sound Sense*]

To this address which I have made to our nobility and gentry, I will add as an appendix another benefit of experiments, which perhaps it will scarce become me to name amidst so many matters of greater weight: and that is that their discoveries will be very serviceable to the wits and writers of this and all future ages. But this I am provoked to mention by the consideration of the present genius of the English nation; wherein the study of wit and humor of writing[7] prevails so much that there are very few conditions or degrees or ages of men who are free from its infection. I will therefore declare to all those whom this spirit has possessed that there is in the works of nature an inexhaustible treasure of fancy and invention which will be revealed proportionably to the increase of their knowledge.

To this purpose I must premise that it is required in the best and most delightful wit that it be founded on such images which are generally known, and are able to bring a strong and sensible impression on the mind. The several subjects from which it has been raised in all times are the fables and religions of the ancients, the civil histories of all countries, the customs of nations, the Bible, the sciences and manners of men, the several arts of their hands, and the works of nature. In all these, where there may be a resemblance of one thing to another, as there may be in all, there is a sufficient foundation for wit. This in all its kinds has its increases, heights,

6. Sprat echoes Milton's conviction in *Areopagitica* that God will reveal himself, "as his manner is, first to his Englishmen." Behind such cadences lie generations of belief in the special destiny of England, as traced by William Haller in *The Elect Nation* (New York, 1963).

7. I.e., wit as modified by humor and limited to writing: ingenuity in making comparisons between things apparently unlike or unrelated.

and decays, as well as all other things. Let us then examine what parts of it are already exhausted, and what remain new and untouched and are still likely to be farther advanced.

The wit of the fables and religions of the ancient world is well nigh consumed.[8] They have already served the poets long enough, and it is now high time to dismiss them, especially seeing they have this peculiar imperfection, that they were only fictions at first; whereas truth is never so well expressed or amplified as by those ornaments which are true and real in themselves.

The wit which is raised from civil histories and the customs of countries is solid and lasting. The similitudes it affords are substantial and equal to the minds of men, being drawn from themselves and their own actions. Of this the wittiest nations have always made the greatest use; their writings being adorned with a wit that was free of their own cities, consisting of examples and apothegms and proverbs derived from their ancestors. This I allege because this kind is scarce yet begun in the English language, though our own civil history abounds as much as any other with great examples and memorable events which may serve for the ornament of comparison.

The manners and tempers and extravagances of men are a standing and eternal foundation of wit. This, if it be gathered from particular observations, is called humor; and the more particular they are, they are still the pleasanter. In this kind I may well affirm that our nation excels all others, as our dramatic poetry may witness.

The wit that may be borrowed from the Bible is magnificent, and, as all the other treasures of knowledge it contains, inexhaustible. This may be used and allowed without any danger of profaneness. The ancient heathens did the same. They made their divine ceremonies the chief subjects of their fancies. By that means their religions had a more awful[9] impression, became more popular, and lasted longer in force, than else they would have done. And why may not Christianity admit the same thing, if it be practiced with sobriety and reverence? What irreligion can there be in applying some Scripture-expressions to natural things? Why are not the one rather exalted and purified than the other defiled by such applications? The very enthusiasts[1] themselves, who are wont to start at such wit as atheistical, are more guilty of its excesses than any other sort of men. For whatever they allege out of the historical, prophetical, or evangelical writings, and apply it to themselves, their enemies, or their country, though they call it the mind of God, yet it is nothing else but Scripture-comparison and similitude.

8. Once again Sprat is following a well-trodden path; complaints about the exhaustion of classical mythology had been voiced by many, including, for example, Thomas Carew in his *Elegy on the Death of Dr. Donne*.

9. Awe-inspiring.

1. The Puritans, so called because they laid so much stress on the individual conscience as enlightened by direct inspiration from God, or enthusiasm. "Start at": object to.

The sciences of men's brains are none of the best materials for this kind of wit. Very few have happily succeeded in logical, metaphysical, grammatical, nay even scarce in mathematical comparisons; and the reason is, because they are most of them conversant about things removed from the senses, and so cannot surprise the fancy with very obvious or quick or sensible delights.

The wit that is founded on the arts of men's hands is masculine and durable; it consists of images that are generally observed, and such visible things which are familiar to men's minds. This therefore I will reckon as the first sort, which is still improvable by the advancement of experiments.

And to this I will add the works of nature, which are one of the best and most fruitful soils for the growth of wit. It is apparent that the defect of the ancients in natural knowledge did also straiten[2] their fancies. Those few things which they knew they used so much, and applied so often, that they even almost wore them away by their using. The sweetness of flowers and fruits and herbs they had quite devoured; they had tired out the sun and moon and stars with their similitudes, more than they fancy them to be wearied by their daily journeys round the heavens.

It is now therefore seasonable for natural knowledge to come forth and to give us the understanding of new virtues and qualities of things; which may relieve their fellow creatures that have long borne the burden alone and have long been vexed by the imaginations of poets. This charitable assistance experiments will soon bestow. The comparisons which these may afford will be intelligible to all, because they proceed from things that enter into all men's senses. These will make the most vigorous impression on men's fancies, because they do even touch their eyes and are nearest to their nature. Of these the variety will be infinite, for the particulars are so from whence they may be deduced. These may be always new and unsullied, seeing there is such a vast number of natural and mechanical things not yet fully known or improved, and by consequence not yet sufficiently applied.

The use of experiments to this purpose is evident, by the wonderful advantage that my Lord Bacon received from them. This excellent writer was abundantly recompensed for his noble labors in that philosophy by a vast treasure of admirable imaginations which it afforded him, wherewith to express and adorn his thoughts about other matters. But I will not confine this observation to one single author, though he was one of the first and most artificial[3] managers of this way of wit. I will venture to declare in general of the English tongue, that as it contains a greater stock of natural and mechanical discoveries, so it is also more enriched with beautiful conceptions

2. Limit.

3. Artful, dexterous.

and inimitable similitudes, gathered from the arts of men's hands and the works of nature, than ever any other language could produce.

And now I hope what I have here said will prevail something with the wits and *railleurs*[4] of this age, to reconcile their opinions and discourses to these studies. For now they may behold that if they shall decry the promoting of experiments, they will deprive themselves of the most fertile subject of fancy. And indeed it has been with respect to these terrible men that I have made this long digression. I acknowledge that we ought to have a great dread of their power; I confess I believe that new philosophy need not (as Caesar) fear the pale or the melancholy as much as the humorous and the merry.[5] For they perhaps, by making it ridiculous because it is new, and because they themselves are unwilling to take pains about it, may do it more injury than all the arguments of our severe and frowning and dogmatical adversaries.

But to gain their good will, I must acquaint them, that the family of the *railleurs* is derived from the same original with the philosophers. The founder of philosophy is confessed by all to be Socrates;[6] and he also was the famous father of all irony. They ought therefore to be tender in this matter, wherein the honor of their common parent is concerned; it becomes them to remember that it is the fault, and not the excellence of wit, to defile its own nest, and not to spare its own friends and relations for the sake of a jest.

The truth is, the extremes of raillery are more offensive than those of stupidity. It is a work of such a tender and subtle spirit, that it cannot be decently performed by all pretenders to it; nor does it always agree well with the temper of our nation, which as it has a greater courage than to suffer derision, so it has a firmer virtue than to be wholly taken up about deriding of others. Such men are therefore to know that all things are capable of abuse from the same topics by which they may be commended. They are to consider that laughter is the easiest and the slenderest fruit of wit. They are to understand that it proceeds from the observation of the deformity of things, but that there is a nobler and more masculine pleasure which is raised from beholding their order and beauty. From thence they may conclude how great the difference is between

4. The word, like the quality it denotes, is French. It implies a vein of superficial, sarcastic humor in a person who talks to show off his cleverness, and who expects to be answered in kind. Being relatively new in England, this sort of talking and writing was just gaining its own name (adapted from the French) of "raillery."

5. Julius Caesar, in Shakespeare's play as in Plutarch's *Life of Caesar*, mistrusted Brutus and Cassius for their lean and hungry looks.

6. Socrates, the protagonist of many of Plato's dialogues, was by no means the founder of philosophy; but even without this detail, the argument that jokers shouldn't deride philosophers because Socrates was a joker and a philosopher, is flimsy enough.

them and the real philosophers; for while nature has only formed them to be pleased with its irregularities and monsters, it has given the other the delight of knowing and studying its most beautiful works.

In plain terms, a universal abuse of everything, though it may tickle the fancy never so much, is inhuman madness, as one of the ancients well expresses it, who calls such mirth *humanis Bacchari rebus*.[7] If all things were made the subjects of such humor, all worthy designs would soon be laughed out of the world; and for our present sport, our posterity would become barbarous. All good enterprises ought to find assistance when they are begun, applause when they succeed, and even pity and praise if they fail. The true raillery should be a defense for good and virtuous works, and should only intend the derision of extravagant, and the disgrace of vile and dishonorable things. This kind of wit ought to have the nature of salt, to which it is usually compared, which preserves and keeps sweet the good and the sound parts of all bodies, and only frets,[8] dries up, and destroys those humors which putrefy and corrupt.

1667

7. "Sporting riotously with human affairs" (Claudian, xviii.25).
8. Eats away, corrodes. Wit was frequently compared to salt by the ancients, on the score that it gives flavor to discourse.

SIR ISAAC NEWTON
(1642–1727)

Isaac Newton was the posthumous son of a small farmer in Lincolnshire; as a boy, he invented machines, as an undergraduate he was making discoveries in optics and the higher mathematics, and in 1667, aged barely 25, he was elected a fellow of Trinity College, Cambridge. It would be generous to describe intellectual life in Restoration universities as "torpid," and Newton got little in the way of stimulus from his colleagues. But he was a man whose mind worked incessantly and at the very highest level of insight; apart from specific discoveries in the fields of optics, mathematics, physics, and astronomy, he generated an entire world view which was outdated only in the 20th century by the work of Einstein. The importance of Newton's thought cannot be described or even indicated here: interested readers should refer to a suitable history of philosophy or of scientific thought.

Much of Sir Isaac's scientific work was reported in Latin, still the language of international scholarship; but when he chose, the great thinker could express himself in notably lucid and trenchant English. The first of his important experiments, having to do with light and color, took form as a letter to the Royal Society, which appeared in the Society's *Journal*, dated February 19, 1672. The experiments and reasoning are described in language of perfect clarity; and when, as the last word of his account, he drops a very heavy word indeed, it clinches the point like a hammer driving home a spike.

From A Letter of Mr. Isaac Newton, Professor of the Mathematics in the University of Cambridge, Containing His New Theory about Light and Colors

Sent by the Author to the Publisher from Cambridge, Febr. 6. 1672, in order to Be Communicated to the Royal Society

Sir,

To perform my late promise to you, I shall without further ceremony acquaint you that in the beginning of the year 1666 (at which time I applied myself to the grinding of optic glasses of other figures than spherical) I procured me a triangular glass prism to try therewith the celebrated phenomena of colors. And in order thereto having darkened my chamber and made a small hole in my window-shuts to let in a convenient quantity of the sun's light, I placed my prism at his entrance that it might be thereby refracted to the opposite wall. It was at first a very pleasing divertissement to view the vivid and intense colors produced thereby; but after a while, applying myself to consider more circumspectly, I became surprised to see them in an *oblong* form, which according to the received laws of refraction I expected should have been *circular*.

They were terminated at the sides with straight lines, but at the ends the decay of light was so gradual that it was difficult to determine justly what was their figure; yet they seemed *semicircular*.

Comparing the length of this colored spectrum with its breadth, I found it about five times greater, a disproportion so extravagant that it excited me to a more than ordinary curiosity of examining from whence it might proceed. I could scarce think that the various thickness of the glass or the termination with shadow or darkness could have any influence on light to produce such an effect; yet I thought it not amiss first to examine those circumstances, and so tried what would happen by transmitting light through parts of the glass of divers thicknesses, or by setting the prism without so that the light might pass through it and be refracted before it was terminated by the hole. But I found none of those circumstances material. The fashion of the colors was in all these cases the same.

Then I suspected whether by any unevenness in the glass or other contingent irregularity these colors might be thus dilated. And to try this, I took another prism like the former and so placed it that the light, passing through them both, might be refracted contrary ways, and so by the latter returned into that course from which the former had diverted it. For by this means I thought the regular effects of the first prism would be destroyed by the second prism but the irregular ones more augmented by the multiplicity of refractions. The event was that the light which by the first prism was diffused into an oblong form was by the second reduced into an orbicular one with as much regularity as when it did not at all pass through them. So that, whatever was the cause of that length, 'twas not any contingent irregularity.[1]

* * *

The gradual removal of these suspicions at length led me to the *experimentum crucis*,[2] which was this: I took two boards, and placed one of them close behind the prism at the window, so that the light might pass through a small hole made in it for the purpose and fall on the other board, which I placed at about 12 feet distance, having first made a small hole in it also, for some of that incident[3] light to pass through. Then I placed another prism behind this second board so that the light, trajected through both the boards, might pass through that also, and be again refracted before it arrived at the wall. This done, I took the first prism in my hand, and turned it to and fro slowly about its axis, so much as to make the several parts of the image cast on the second board successively pass through the hole in it, that I might observe to what places on the wall the second prism would refract them. And I saw by the variation of those places that the light tending to that end of the image towards which the refraction of the first prism was made did in the second prism suffer a refraction considerably greater than the light tending to the other end. And so the true cause of the length of that image was detected to be no other than that light consists of *rays differently refrangible*, which, without any respect to a difference in their incidence, were, according to their degrees of refrangibility, transmitted towards divers parts of the wall.[4]

* * *

I shall now proceed to acquaint you with another more notable difformity in its rays, wherein the *origin of color* is unfolded: concerning which I shall lay down the doctrine first and then for its examination give you an instance or two of the experiments, as a specimen of the rest.

1. Newton goes on to describe several experiments and calculations by which he disposed of alternative theories—such as that rays coming from different parts of the sun caused the diffusion of light into an oblong, or that the rays of light were bent after they left the prism. Neither idea proved viable.
2. Crucial experiment, turning point.
3. From Latin *incidere*, to fall into or onto. Newton uses it of light striking an obstacle.
4. At this point Newton digresses to a discussion of the optical consequences of his view of light, adding in passing that his experiments were interrupted for two years by the plague; but at last he returns to some further and even more important characteristics of light.

The doctrine you will find comprehended and illustrated in the following propositions.

1. As the rays of light differ in degrees of refrangibility, so they also differ in their disposition to exhibit this or that particular color. Colors are not qualifications of light, derived from refractions or reflections of natural bodies (as 'tis generally believed), but original and connate properties which in divers rays are divers. Some rays are disposed to exhibit a red color and no other; some a yellow and no other, some a green and no other, and so of the rest. Nor are there only rays proper and particular to the more eminent colors, but even to all their intermediate gradations.

2. To the same degree of refrangibility ever belongs the same color, and to the same color ever belongs the same degree of refrangibility. The least refrangible rays are all disposed to exhibit a red color, and contrarily those rays which are disposed to exhibit a red color are all the least refrangible. So the most refrangible rays are all disposed to exhibit a deep violet color, and contrarily those which are apt to exhibit such a violet color are all the most refrangible. And so to all the intermediate colors in a continued series belong intermediate degrees of refrangibility. And this analogy 'twixt colors and refrangibility is very precise and strict; the rays always exactly agreeing in both or proportionally disagreeing in both.

3. The species of color and degree of refrangibility proper to any particular sort of rays is not mutable by refraction nor by reflection from natural bodies nor by any other cause that I could yet observe. When any one sort of rays hath been well parted from those of other kinds, it hath afterwards obstinately retained its color, notwithstanding my utmost endeavors to change it. I have refracted it with prisms and reflected it with bodies which in daytime were of other colors; I have intercepted it with the colored film of air interceding two compressed plates of glass; transmitted it through colored mediums and through mediums irradiated with other sorts of rays, and diversely terminated it; and yet could never produce any new color out of it. It would by contracting or dilating become more brisk or faint and by the loss of many rays in some cases very obscure and dark; but I could never see it changed *in specie*.[5]

4. Yet seeming transmutations of colors may be made, where there is any mixture of divers sorts of rays. For in such mixtures, the component colors appear not, but by their mutual allaying each other constitute a middling color. And therefore if by refraction or any other of the aforesaid causes the difform rays latent in such a mixture be separated, there shall emerge colors different from the color of the composition. Which colors are not new generated, but only made apparent by being parted; for if they be again entirely mixed

5. In kind.

and blended together, they will again compose that color which they did before separation. And for the same reason, transmutations made by the convening of divers colors are not real; for when the difform rays are again severed, they will exhibit the very same colors which they did before they entered the composition—as you see blue and yellow powders when finely mixed appear to the naked eye green, and yet the colors of the component corpuscles are not thereby transmuted, but only blended. For, when viewed with a good microscope, they still appear blue and yellow interspersedly.

5. There are therefore two sorts of colors. The one original and simple, the other compounded of these. The original or primary colors are red, yellow, green, blue, and a violet-purple, together with orange, indigo, and an indefinite variety of intermediate graduations.

6. The same colors *in specie* with these primary ones may be also produced by composition. For a mixture of yellow and blue makes green; or red and yellow makes orange; of orange and yellowish green makes yellow. And in general if any two colors be mixed which, in the series of those generated by the prism, are not too far distant from one another, they by their mutual alloy compound that color which in the said series appeareth in the mid-way between them. But those which are situated at too great a distance, do not so. Orange and indigo produce not the intermediate green, nor scarlet and green the intermediate yellow.

7. But the most surprising and wonderful composition was that of whiteness. There is no one sort of rays which alone can exhibit this. 'Tis ever compounded, and to its composition are requisite all the aforesaid primary colors, mixed in a due proportion. I have often with admiration beheld that, all the colors of the prism being made to converge and thereby to be again mixed as they were in the light before it was incident upon the prism, reproduced light, entirely and perfectly white, and not at all sensibly differing from a direct light of the sun, unless when the glasses I used were not sufficiently clear; for then they would a little incline it to *their* color.

8. Hence therefore it comes to pass that whiteness is the usual color of light, for light is a confused aggregate of rays endued with all sorts of colors, as they are promiscuously darted from the various parts of luminous bodies. And of such a confused aggregate, as I said, is generated whiteness, if there be a due proportion of the ingredients; but if any one predominate, the light must incline to that color, as it happens in the blue flame of brimstone, the yellow flame of a candle, and the various colors of the fixed stars.

9. These things considered, the manner how colors are produced by the prism is evident. For of the rays constituting the incident

light, since those which differ in color proportionally differ in refrangibility, they by their unequal refractions must be severed and dispersed into an oblong form in an orderly succession from the least refracted scarlet to the most refracted violet. And for the same reason it is that objects, when looked upon through a prism, appear colored. For the difform rays, by their unequal refractions, are made to diverge towards several parts of the retina, and there express the images of things colored, as in the former case they did the sun's image upon a wall. And by this inequality of refractions they become not only colored, but also very confused and indistinct.

10. Why the colors of the rainbow appear in falling drops of rain is also from hence evident. For those drops which refract the rays disposed to appear purple in greatest quantity to the spectator's eye, refract the rays of other sorts so much less as to make them pass beside it;[6] and such are the drops on the inside of the primary bow and on the outside of the secondary or exterior one. So those drops which refract in greatest plenty the rays apt to appear red toward the spectator's eye, refract those of other sorts so much more as to make them pass beside it; and such are the drops on the exterior part of the primary and interior part of the secondary bow.

* * *

13. I might add more instances of this nature, but I shall conclude with this general one, that the colors of all natural bodies have no other origin than this, that they are variously qualified to reflect one sort of light in greater plenty than another. And this I have experimented in a dark room by illuminating those bodies with uncompounded light of divers colors. For by that means any body may be made to appear of any color. They have there no appropriate color, but ever appear of the color of the light cast upon them, but yet with this difference, that they are most brisk and vivid in the light of their own daylight color. *Minium*[7] appeareth there of any color indifferently with which 'tis illuminated, but yet most luminous in red, and so *Bise*[8] appeareth indifferently of any color with which 'tis illustrated, but yet most luminous in blue. And therefore *minium* reflecteth rays of any color, but most copiously those endued with red; and consequently when illustrated with daylight, that is, with all sorts of rays promiscuously blended, those qualified with red shall abound most in the reflected light, and by their prevalence cause it to appear of that color. And for the same reason *bise*, reflecting blue most copiously, shall appear blue by the excess of those rays in its reflected light; and the like of other bodies. And that this is the entire and adequate cause of their

6. I.e., disappear alongside it.
7. Red lead.
8. Azurite blue.

colors is manifest, because they have no power to change or alter the colors of any sort of rays incident apart, but put on all colors indifferently with which they are enlightened.

These things being so, it can no longer be disputed whether there be colors in the dark, nor whether they be the qualities of the objects we see, no, nor perhaps whether light be a body. For since colors are the qualities of light, having its rays for their entire and immediate subject, how can we think those rays qualities also, unless one quality may be the subject of and sustain another—which in effect is to call it substance. We should not know bodies for substances were it not for their sensible qualities, and the principal of those being now found due to something else, we have as good reason to believe that to be a substance also.[9]

Besides, who ever thought any quality to be a heterogeneous aggregate, such as light is discovered to be? But to determine more absolutely what light is, after what manner refracted, and by what modes or actions it produceth in our minds the phantasms of colors, is not so easy. And I shall not mingle conjectures with certainties.

1672

9. I.e., the only way we know bodies are substances is that our senses perceive their qualities. The chief of these qualities, color, is now known to be a quality of light, not body; our conclusion can perfectly well be that light is a form of substance, as well as body, and that we know it to be so through its quality, color.

The Restoration and the Eighteenth Century

(1660-1798)

1660:	Charles II restored to the English throne.
1688–89:	The Glorious Revolution: deposition of James II and accession of William of Orange.
1700:	Death of John Dryden.
1707:	Act of Union unites Scotland and England, which thus become "Great Britain."
1714:	Rule by house of Hanover begins with accession of George I.
1744–45:	Deaths of Pope and Swift.
1784:	Death of Samuel Johnson.
1789:	The French Revolution begins.

The England to which Charles Stuart returned in 1660 was a nation divided against itself, exhausted by twenty years of civil war and revolution. Early in Charles's reign, the people were visited by two frightful calamities that seemed to the superstitious to be the work of a divine Providence outraged by rebellion and regicide: the plague of 1665, ravaging the country, carried off over 70,000 souls in London alone; and in September, 1666, a fire which raged for five days destroyed a large part of the City (more than 13,000 houses), leaving about two-thirds of the population homeless. Yet the nation rose from its ashes, in the century that followed, to become an empire. Within two decades of the king's return, the Royal Navy had defeated the navy of Holland, England's greatest maritime and commercial rival; and, in a series of wars fought between 1689 and 1763 against France, the British acquired dominions that stretched around the world, from Canada in the west to India in the east. Internally, moreover, the nation became whole again. The Glorious Revolution of 1689 established a rule of law, and the Act of Union of 1707 a political alliance, under which England was transformed into Great Britain in fact as well as name—a larger country to which men of widely differing backgrounds and origins felt they owed allegiance. Many of the great British writers of the 18th century came from Ireland, like Swift, Burke, Sheridan, and Goldsmith; many came from

Scotland, like Thomson, Boswell, and Hume. Strengthened from without and from within, Great Britain was able to endure the loss of her thirteen American colonies and to enter the final struggle with Revolutionary and Napoleonic France as a world power.

RELIGION AND POLITICS

Charles came home to the almost universal satisfaction of his subjects, for after the abdication of Richard Cromwell in 1659 the country had seemed at the brink of chaos, and Britons were eager to believe that the king would bring order, peace, freedom under law, and a spirit of mildness back into the national life. But no political settlement could be stable until the religious issues of the age had been resolved. The restoration of the monarchy meant, inevitably, the restoration of the Established Church; and though Charles had promised mildness toward all but a few of his late father's enemies, the bishops and Anglican clergy felt anything but Christian charity toward their Dissenting brothers. In 1662 Parliament reimposed the Book of Common Prayer on all ministers and congregations, and in 1664 religious meetings in which the forms of the Established Church were not followed were declared illegal. Thousands of clergymen resigned their livings, and the jails were filled with Nonconformist preachers who, like John Bunyan, refused to be silenced. In 1673 the triumph of the Establishment was completed by the Test Act, which required all holders of civil and military offices to receive the sacrament according to the Anglican rite and to declare their disbelief in transubstantiation. Thus the two adversaries of the Anglican Church, Protestant Dissenters and Roman Catholics, were alike excluded from public life, though the practice of occasional conformity (i.e., receiving the sacrament in an Anglican church at rare intervals) enabled many Dissenters to comply with the law. Throughout the closing decades of the 17th century, Anglicans associated Nonconformity with revolution, regicide, republicanism, and the rule of the Puritan Saints—hence, with subversion; and with excessive zeal, "enthusiasm" (i.e., belief in private revelation), and irrationality—hence, with absurdity. The scorn and detestation in which Dissenters were held may be measured by the delight that readers took in Samuel Butler's caricature of Presbyterians and Independents in *Hudibras* (1663), an attitude that persisted unchanged for the rest of the century, as Jonathan Swift's *Tale of a Tub*, written about 1697, makes clear. As for the English Catholics, they appeared always as potential traitors of whom anything evil could be believed. Few doubted, for example, that the Great Fire of 1666 had been set by Catholics.

Although ecclesiastical problems seemed to have been quickly and effectively solved, the constitutional issues which had divided Charles I and Parliament were not so readily settled. Charles II had promised to govern through Parliament, but like other members of his family he held strong views on the power and prerogatives of the Crown. Nevertheless, he was content to avoid crises whenever he could, and since he was an astute politician he frequently could. He concealed from his subjects his Catholic sympathies (on his deathbed he received the last rites of the Roman Church), for he had no wish "to go on his travels" again. The one great religious and constitutional crisis of his reign was the Popish Plot and its political consequences (1678–81)—the unsuccessful attempt of a faction in

Parliament to force Charles to accept a bill excluding his Catholic brother, James, Duke of York, from the succession. Except in this instance, where he was successful because of his courage, duplicity, and political skill, Charles allowed no opportunity for a test of strength between Crown and Parliament.

One important result of the political and religious turmoils of the decade following the Popish Plot was the emergence of two clearly defined political parties, Whig and Tory. The party of the court, which supported the king in 1681, came to be called Tories; the king's opponents, Whigs. By the end of the century the two parties had developed opposed attitudes on other important issues. The Tories drew their strength largely from the landed gentry and the country clergy. They were the conservatives of the period: strong supporters of the Crown and of the Established Church as the two great sources of political and social stability, they bitterly (though futilely) opposed toleration of Dissenters and successfully supported the Test Act. They were hostile to the new moneyed interests, whether among the newer nobility or the increasingly well-to-do middle class, for they held that landed wealth is the only responsible wealth. The Whigs were a less homogeneous group: many powerful nobles, jealous of the powers of the Crown, the merchants and financiers of London, a number of bishops and Low Church clergymen, and the Dissenters; these varied groups were united by their policies of toleration and support of commerce.

After James II came to the throne in 1685, determined to advance the cause of the Roman Church in England, an atmosphere of crisis rapidly developed. Claiming the right to set aside laws and to overrule Parliament, he issued in 1687 a Declaration of Indulgence, suspending the Tests and penal laws against both Catholics and Dissenters, and he began to fill the army and government—not to mention the universities—with his coreligionists. Matters came to a crisis in the summer of 1688, when a son was born to the queen and the prospect of a succession of Catholic monarchs confronted the nation. Secret negotiations paved the way for the arrival in England of the Dutchman William of Orange at the head of a small armed force. He was the leading champion of Protestantism on the Continent and the husband of James's Protestant daughter Mary. Finding resistance to his hostile subjects impossible, James, after sending his wife and the infant prince out of the country, fled to France on December 11. There he was cordially received by Louis XIV, granted a subsidy, and established with his court at St. Germain. For over half a century the possibility of invasion and the forcible restoration first of James, later of his son "the Old Pretender," and finally of his grandson Prince Charles Edward, was a source of anxiety to the English government. Adherents of the exiled family are called Jacobites (from the Latin *Jacobus*, James). Many Englishmen and a great many more Scots remained loyal to the house of Stuart until there was nothing left of the Jacobite cause but a pleasant sentiment. Two serious Jacobite rebellions actually occurred: in 1715, when the Old Pretender arrived in Scotland to support an uprising against the newly crowned Hanoverian, George I, and more threateningly in 1745, when Prince Charles Edward (the "Bonnie Prince Charlie" of romantic story) came dangerously close to success in his invasion of England, an event which affects the fortunes of the hero in Henry Fielding's novel *Tom Jones*.

It was only with the flight of James that England could begin to bury the past and to turn toward her destiny in the next age. The coming in of William and Mary and the settlement achieved in 1689 were known as the Glorious or Bloodless Revolution, all the more glorious for being bloodless. A more tolerant era was opening, as was made apparent in important acts passed by Parliament in the first year of the new reign. Since the Revolution had been largely achieved by Whigs, Whig principles prevailed during William's reign. In 1689 the Bill of Rights limited the powers of the Crown, reaffirmed the supremacy of Parliament, and guaranteed important legal rights to individuals. Moreover, the Toleration Act, although it did not repeal the Test, did grant freedom of worship to Dissenters. A number of the conflicting elements in the national life were thus reconciled through what proved to be a workable compromise; and with the passage of the Act of Settlement in 1701, settling the succession to the throne upon Sophia, Electress of Hanover, and her descendants (as the granddaughter of James I, she was the closest Protestant relative of the Princess Anne, James II's younger daughter, whose sole surviving child died in that year), the difficult problems that had so long divided England seemed resolved. The principles established in 1689 brought stability and order into English life and endured unaltered in essentials until the Reform Bill of 1832.

During the reign of Anne, the last Stuart monarch (1702–14), a renewal of tension embittered the political atmosphere. On the Continent England led her allies, Holland, Austria, and Bavaria, to victory in the War of the Spanish Succession against France and Spain (1702–13). The hero of the war was the brilliant Captain-General John Churchill, Duke of Marlborough, who, with his duchess, dominated the queen until 1710. The war was a Whig war, supported by powerful Whig lords and the Whig merchants of London, who grew increasingly rich on war profits and who stood to gain by any weakening of the power of France and Spain. The Whigs were anxious to reward the Dissenters for their loyalty by removing the Test. Unfortunately for them, Anne was especially devoted to the church, and when, in 1710, they were made to appear to threaten the health of the Establishment, she dismissed her Whig ministers and called in Robert Harley as Lord Treasurer and the brilliant young Henry St. John as Secretary of State (in charge of foreign relations) to form the Tory ministry which governed England during the last four years of her reign. The Marlboroughs were dismissed, the duke even losing his command in 1711, but not before the royal favor and a grateful nation had made him immensely rich and had given him the land on which he built his famous palace, Blenheim (pronounced *Blen'm*) in memory of the most brilliant victory (pronounced *Blén-hime*) of the war.

It was these Tory ministers whom Defoe and Swift served in their different ways; it was for them that Matthew Prior negotiated the Peace of Utrecht, ratified in 1713. To Swift's despair, a bitter rivalry developed between Harley (then Earl of Oxford) and St. John (then Viscount Bolingbroke) during 1713–14, and as the queen's life faded in the summer of 1714, Bolingbroke succeeded in ousting Oxford, only to have his own ambitions thwarted by the death of Anne and the return to power of the vindictive Whigs with the accession of George I, son of the late Sophia, Electress of Hanover. For a moment it seemed as if this event might not occur without bloodshed, but the crisis quickly passed, the Protestant succession was not immediately opposed by Jacobites, and the Whigs turned happily to investigating the conduct of the former ministers. Harley was imprisoned in the Tower of London (where he remained until 1717), and Bolingbroke, charged with treasonable correspondence with the Pretender, fled to France, where he actually became, for a while, Secretary of State to the Jacobite court. Pardoned in 1723, but denied his seat in the House of Lords, he returned to England and directed the opposition to Robert Walpole, while seeing much of Pope and playing the gentleman-farmer-philosopher at Dawley Farm.

The three Georges who occupied the throne during the rest of the century presided over a nation that grew increasingly prosperous through war, trade, and the beginnings of industrialism. George I (reigned 1714–27) and George II (reigned 1727–60) spoke broken English, had little interest in the affairs of the country. In their hearts they remained petty German princelings even when they were kings of Great Britain, spending as much time as possible in Hanover. Under such circumstances it was inevitable that ministers should become more important and more independent of the Crown than they had been under stronger and more intelligent monarchs. Through the indifference of two kings and the ambition and great abilities of the Whig Prime Minister Sir Robert Walpole, the modern system of ministerial government began to develop. This was the last important contribution of the age to British political institutions. Walpole's long ascendency (1721–42) brought a period of peace and prosperity and of capable government based, paradoxically, on flagrant political corruption. Although Walpole strengthened the importance of the House of Commons in British politics, he nonetheless continued, if he did not increase, the corruption of its members through bribery. He was a practical man and cared little for literature, preferring to spend money on useful journalists and voting Members of Parliament rather than on poets. Thus with two kings who knew nothing of literature and a prime minister who was indifferent to it, English writers could not expect the shower of offices and government sinecures that had made the age of Anne the great age of patronage: Congreve, Steele, Addison, Prior, Swift had expected and obtained such rewards both for their literary eminence and for their service to party. But after 1715, as patronage declined, authors found that they must turn to the publishers, who could pay them well because of the growing reading public. Indeed, Johnson was accustomed to declare that the booksellers of the midcentury had become the patrons of literature.

The long reign of George III (1760–1820), the first Hanoverian monarch born in England, somewhat retarded the development of government through parties and responsible ministers, for the king was determined to rule personally, and he succeeded in doing so to a remarkable degree. This was a dangerous policy for a man who, as a politician, was neither wise nor liberal. He brought the Tories back into power after they had been excluded from office for 46 years, and he did all that he could to crush the long-powerful Whig oligarchy.

INTELLECTUAL BACKGROUND

The political turbulence of the 17th century subsided only gradually during the last decades of the century, and the "peace of the Augustans" did not settle over England until the Protestant succession had been safely accomplished. Analogously, the literature of the Restoration period (1660–1700) did not at once attain the measured pace and disciplined order that we associate with "classic" art. John Dryden himself, the principal writer of the period, delighted, as Johnson remarked, "in wild and daring sallies of sentiment, in the irregular and eccentric violence of wit." The period is remarkable for variety: Milton's major poems, relics of an earlier age, appeared in 1667 (*Paradise Lost*) and 1671 (*Paradise Regained* and *Samson Agonistes*). The age that produced Bunyan's *Pilgrim's Progress,* perhaps the greatest literary expression of the Nonconformist conscience, produced also the libertine poems of such court wits as Rochester, Sedley, and Etherege, savage satire like Butler's, the brilliant depiction of the dissolute but elegant manners of the upper classes in the comedies of Etherege, Wycherley, and Congreve, and the rant and bombast of Dryden's rhymed heroic plays. But the general drift was toward classic restraint and good sense; and both Dryden's example, in the works of his maturity, and his numerous critical essays helped to formulate standards and to make the period the foundation on which the neoclassical art of the next century was erected.

Perhaps most people think of the Restoration as a period wholly given over to frivolity and debauchery. It is true that Puritan rigidities (never enforced quite as rigorously as sometimes has been made out) were quickly repudiated by the upper classes. It is true that the king was easy-going, pleasure-loving, and amorous, more fond of the society of boon companions—and mistresses—than he was of business of state. It is true that the court itself was luxurious, immoral, full of intrigue. It is true that all this is vividly reflected in lampoons, satires, and comedies. But the ordinary life of the nation did not radically change. Rural manners, then as now, were conservative and old-fashioned. The London citizens, middle-class and respectable, cherishing much of the independence and piety of Dissent, were scandalized by the behavior of such lewd young men as Rochester and Etherege, who regarded them with contempt and considered their wives and daughters fair game. Even good royalists like John Evelyn and Samuel Pepys often speak anxiously in their diaries of the moral laxness of the court and the danger to the country of the king's example.

Charles himself had serious intellectual interests and was a patron of the arts. He dabbled in chemistry and was interested in the progress of science. A characteristic act was his chartering in 1662 the Royal Society of London for the Improving of Natural Knowledge, thus giving official approval to the scientific movement that Francis Bacon had initiated early in the century and that was just then coming to maturity. The king's love of music and painting led him to import from the Continent composers, musicians, new musical instruments, the French and Italian opera, and painting and painters largely from the Low Countries. His interest in the theater was demonstrated by the chartering of two companies of actors in 1660, both under royal patronage, the King's Players, and the Duke's—the Duke being James, Duke of York.

It is natural, therefore, that the most characteristic art of the period reflected the interests and tastes of those who supported it, as is the case today. Artists addressed themselves to court and "town," the western suburbs which were the center of fashion. The middle-class tradesmen who lodged over their shops in the City (i.e., that part of greater London which was once within the city walls and which was then thickly populated) were scorned as tasteless barbarians. Except in the theater, literature was not in itself a gainful profession (as it was to become in the 18th century), and writers looked for patronage from the court and the great nobles. Milton, for example, received only £10 for the first edition of *Paradise Lost*. By the end of the century, however, thanks to the enterprise of the bookseller Jacob Tonson and the new device of publishing books through subscription (i.e., soliciting payment in advance for de luxe copies of a work, in addition to publishing a regular trade edition), Dryden was able to earn between £1000 and £1200 by his translation of the works of Virgil (1697). And Pope's Homer, similarly published between 1715 and 1726, was to prove even more profitable.

Perhaps the most important aspect of the Restoration period is the increasing challenge of various forms of secular thought to the old religious orthodoxies which had been matters of life and death since the Reformation. As the contentious voices of Roman, Anglican, and Dissenter grew more and more subdued, other interests attracted adventurous minds. Thomas Hobbes, in *Leviathan* (1651), had taught a philosophic materialism and advocated an absolute government as the most efficacious check to human nature, which he described as wholly driven by egoistic and predatory passions. Detested by the church and attacked on all sides, these ideas nonetheless played their role in the lives and writings of some of the more advanced young men, and they provoked by way of reaction in the next century an optimistic insistence on the natural goodness of man. A soberer and more ancient tradition was philosophic skepticism. Originating in ancient Greece, skepticism had found its most persuasive recent statement in the essays of the Frenchman Michel de Montaigne (1533–92), whose influence was widespread throughout 17th-century Europe. The skeptic argued that all our knowledge is derived from our senses, but that our senses do not report the world around us accurately, and that therefore reliable knowledge is an impossibility. The safest course is to affirm nothing as absolutely true, to remember that most beliefs are mere opinions, and, where possible, to be guided by the traditional in matters intellectual, political, and ethical. Butler, Dryden, and Rochester, among others, more or less adhered to this doctrine. But though the skeptic remained in doubt about the results of human reasoning, he was not precluded from religious beliefs, for he could assert (as did Dryden after his conversion to Catholicism) that faith alone is necessary for accepting the mysteries of the Christian religion.

The new science, advanced by members of the Royal Society, was rapidly altering men's view of nature. Science in the 17th century was principally concerned with the physical sciences—with astronomy, physics, and, to a lesser degree, chemistry; and the discoveries in these sciences were reassuring in their revelation of universal and immutable law and order, clear revelations of the wisdom and goodness of God in His creation. Such laws of nature as Boyle's law of the behavior of gases under pressure or Newton's law of gravitation seemed obviously to support the idea that a beneficent, divine intelligence created and directs the universe. The whole creation appeared a revelation of the mind, intent, and nature of the Creator. The truest truths proved to be the clearest, the simplest, the most general. Such truths, while they confirmed the existence of a Deity, seemed at the same time to render unnecessary, even preposterous, the intricate a priori reasoning of Scholastic philosophy, and to promise a time, not remote, when mystery would be banished entirely from nature. Indeed, the new religion, Deism or Natural Religion, which had an increasingly wide appeal to "enlightened" minds, deduced its simple rationalistic creed from the Book of Nature, God's first and, to many 18th-century men, only valid revelation. The Deists deduced the existence of a Supreme Being or First Cause from the existence of the universe: a creature presupposes a Creator. The laws of nature, the structure of the universe—its regularity, order, and purposefulness—sufficiently proved the reasonableness, goodness, and wisdom of this Creator. Him we can and must revere; but, good though He is, it is demonstrable that He does not punish vice and reward virtue in this life; and therefore, being good and just, He must do so in some future life: hence, we must believe in immortality. Meanwhile, here on earth, it is our duty to co-operate with Nature and the Deity, cultivating as best we can wisdom, virtue, and benevolence. This creed is as simple and as rational as one of Newton's laws; but its complete omission of the "second revelation" of the Scriptures, the scheme of salvation through the vicarious atonement, made it unacceptable to many Christians, although many found it possible to accept both Natural Religion and revealed Christianity.

As the 17th century drew to a close, its temper became more secular, tolerant, and moderate. If it is not quite possible to talk sensibly of an "Age of Reason" in England, it is possible to think of the early decades of the 18th century as a period of good sense, restraint, and reasonableness. "Enthusiasm," that state of mind which asserted the validity of private inspiration and which had fostered a dangerous zeal among the Saints of Dissent, was decried. The new age was willing to settle for the possible within the limits of human intelligence and of the material world. Its temper was expressed by its most influential philosopher, John Locke (1632–1704), in his *Essay Concerning Human Understanding* (1690):

> If by this inquiry into the nature of the understanding, I can discover the powers thereof; how far they reach; to what things they are in any degree proportionate; and where they fail us, I suppose it may be of use to prevail with the busy mind of man to be more cautious in meddling with things exceeding its comprehension; to stop when it is at the utmost extent of its tether; and to sit down in a quiet ignorance of those things which, upon examination, are found to be beyond the reach of our capacities. * * * Our business here is not to know all things, but those which concern our conduct.

These words might be taken as the creed of 18th-century England. Such a position is Swift's, when he inveighs against metaphysics, abstract logical deductions, and theoretical science; it is similar to Pope's in the *Essay on Man*; it prompts Dr. Johnson to talk of "the business of living"; it helps to account for the emphasis that the Anglican clergy put on good works, rather than faith, as the way to salvation, and for their dislike of emotion and "enthusiasm" in religion.

But if the 18th century brought a recognition of the limitations of man, it also took an optimistic view of his moral nature. Rejecting Hobbes, 18th-century philosophers asserted that man is naturally good and that he finds his highest happiness in the exercise of virtue and benevolence. Such a view of human nature we describe as "sentimental." It found the source of virtue in men's instinctive and social impulses rather than in a code of conduct sanctioned by divine law. And men began to feel—or to fancy that they felt—exquisite pleasure in the exercise of benevolent impulses. Sentimentalism fostered a benevolism that led to social reforms seldom envisioned in earlier times—to the improvement of jails, to the relief of imprisoned debtors, to the establishment of foundling hospitals and of homes for penitent prostitutes, and ultimately to the abolition of the slave trade; but it also encouraged a ready flow of feeling and tears and a capacity to respond to the joys and sorrows of others. The doctrine of the natural goodness of man seemed to many to suggest that it is civilization which corrupts us and that primitive men, "noble savages" who live according to nature, are models of innocence and virtue. Such notions encouraged an interest in primitive societies and even helped to prepare for the enthusiastic reception given the peasant poet Robert Burns, an "original genius," as well as for William Wordsworth's interest in children and in simple, rural people.

As the wave of sentimentalism mounted, a parallel rise of religious feeling occurred after about 1740. The great religious revival known as Methodism was led by John Wesley (1703–91), his brother Charles (1707–88), and George Whitefield (1714–70), all Oxford graduates. The Methodists took their gospel to the common people, preaching the necessity of a conviction of sin, and of conversion, and the joy of the "blessed assurance" of being saved. Often denied the privilege of preaching in village churches, they preached to thousands in the open fields and in barns. The somnolent Anglican Church and the self-assured upper classes were repelled by the emotionalism aroused by Methodist preachers among the lower orders. It seemed as if the irrationality, zeal, and enthusiasm of the Puritan sects were being revived. But the religious awakening persisted, and affected many clergymen and laymen within the Establishment, who, as "Evangelicals," reanimated the church and promoted unworldliness and piety. And yet the insistence of Methodists on faith over works as the way to salvation did not prevent them or their Anglican counterparts from playing important roles in many of the social reforms of the time, especially in helping to abolish slavery and the slave trade.

NEOCLASSICAL LITERARY THEORY

The literature of the period between 1660 and 1785 can conveniently, though perhaps too schematically, be considered as falling into three lesser periods of about forty years each: the first, extending to the death of Dryden in 1700, may be thought of as the period in which English "neoclassical" literature came into being and its critical principles were formulated; the second, ending with the death of Pope in 1744 and of Swift in 1745, brought to its culmination the literary movement initiated by Dryden and his generation; the third, concluding with the death of Johnson in 1784 and the publication of William Cowper's *The Task* in 1785, was a period in which neoclassical principles were confronted by new ideas which contained within themselves the origins of the Romantic movement of the early 19th century.

Apparently a sudden change of taste took place about 1660; but the change was not so sudden as it appears. Like the English Renaissance, it was part of a general movement in European culture, seen perhaps at its most impressive in 17th-century France. Described most simply, it was a reaction against the intricacy and occasional obscurity, boldness, and extravagance of European literature of the late Renaissance, in favor of greater simplicity, clarity, restraint, regularity, and good sense. This tendency is most readily to be observed in the preference of Dryden and his contemporaries for "easy, natural" wit, which aims to surprise rather than to shock. It accompanied, though it was not necessarily caused by, the development of certain rationalistic philosophies and the rise of experimental science, as well as a desire for peace and order after an era of violent extremism.

This movement produced in France the impressive body of classical literature that distinguished the age of Louis XIV. In England it produced a literature that we term "neoclassical," or "Augustan," because it was strongly influenced by the writers of the reign of the first Roman emperor, Augustus Caesar, just before the beginning of the Christian era. Rome's Augustan Age was a period of stability and peace after the civil war that followed the death of Julius Caesar. Its chief poets, Virgil, Horace, and Ovid, addressed their carefully ordered, disciplined, and polished works to a sophisticated aristocracy, among whom they found generous patrons. Dryden's generation was aware of an analogy between the situations of post-Civil War England and Augustan Rome. Later generations would be suspicious of that analogy; after 1700 most writers stressed that Augustus had been a tyrant who thought himself greater than the law. But in 1660 there was hope that Charles would be a better Augustus, bringing to England civilized order and enlightened patronage of the arts, a self-consciously Augustan age.

Charles and his followers inevitably brought back from France an admiration of contemporary French literature as well as of French fashions and elegance. But it is a mistake to regard the Restoration, as many historians have done, as a period in which the court and its poets betrayed English genius to French rules and taste. The French critics were of course known and studied in England, and the theories of such writers as Pierre Corneille, René Rapin, and Nicolas Boileau were influential. But English literature remained stubbornly English: English writers took what they required from France, but used it for their own ends. It was not Dryden's aim merely to imitate the French poets or for that matter the Latin, but to produce in England works that would be worthy to stand beside theirs. He knew that this could be done only if English literature remained true to its living tradition: Chaucer, Spenser, Shakespeare, Jonson, Donne entered into his literary consciousness as well as Virgil, Horace, Longinus, or Corneille.

It is likely that, had Charles never lived abroad, the English neoclassical period would have come into existence pretty much in the form that it actually assumed. Ben Jonson's poems and criticism brought the classicizing tendencies of the English Renaissance to a focus. His closed heroic couplets are the model for those of Edmund Waller and Sir John Denham, whom Dryden considered the principal "refiners" of English metrics. One of the lesser "Sons of Ben," Sir John Beaumont, at least as early as 1625—and incidentally in couplets that might have been the very pattern of those of Dryden and Pope—proposed critical standards that became dominant after 1660:

> Pure phrase, fit epithets, a sober care
> Of metaphors, descriptions clear, yet rare,
> Similitudes contracted, smooth and round,
> Not vexed by learning, but with Nature crowned:
> Strong figures drawn from deep inventions, springs,
> Consisting less in words, and more in things:
> A language not affecting ancient times,
> Nor Latin shreds, by which the pedant climbs.
>
> [*To His Late Majesty, Concerning the True Form of English Poetry*]

Such standards, alien to the poetry of Donne, Crashaw, or Milton, prefigure the poetry of the Augustans, and make evident the fact that a native "classicism" existed side by side with metaphysical poetry. The emphasis on the correct ("pure"), the appropriate ("fit"), restraint and discipline ("sober care"), clarity, the fresh and surprising ("rare"), Nature, strength, freedom from pedantry—these indicate exactly the direction English literature was to take after the Restoration.

What was the prevalent idea of the nature of the poet? He must, of course, be a genius, for all agreed with Horace that the poet is born, not made. But even genius must be trained and disciplined if it is to produce art. The word *poet* is derived from a Greek word meaning "maker," and this notion dominated the Augustans' idea of the poet: he is the maker of an object, a poem. He must have "invention," the gift of finding materials for his poems—fictional, but representative, images of human actions and of the world in which those actions take place; and he must so vivify, heighten, and order those materials that they seem true pictures of what is, or might or ought to be, or of the evil and folly that we should avoid. For the poet makes this image of life in order to teach, not so much by precept and moral sentences as by examples that move our love and admiration or evoke our fear and detestation. And to teach effectively he must please us by his fictions and by all the ornaments of language, metrics, and rhetoric that belong to his craft.

The materials of poetry must derive from, conform to, and recognizably represent "Nature," a word of many meanings in the neoclassic or any age. The Augustans were especially conscious of one meaning: Nature as the universal, permanent, and representative elements in the moral and intellectual experience of men. External nature—the landscape—both as a source of aesthetic pleasure and as an object of scientific inquiry or religious contemplation attracted the attention of Englishmen throughout the 18th century. But Pope's injunction to the critic, "First follow Nature," has primarily *human* nature and *human* experience in view. Nature is truth in the sense that it includes the permanent, enduring, general truths which have been, are, and will be true for all men, in all times, everywhere. The poet exists not to take us on long voyages to discover the new and unique, but to reveal the permanent and the representative in human experience through what becomes for us an act of recognition. Johnson, in Chapter X of *Rasselas,* says that the poet is to examine "not the individual, but the species; to remark general properties and large appearances * * * to exhibit in his portraits of nature such prominent and striking features as recall the original to every mind." Historians during this period studied the particulars of history in order to observe the universal human nature which those particulars reveal; and scientists formulated, after experiment and observation of particulars, universal and permanent laws of nature. Indeed, Sir Isaac Newton's *Principia* (1687) did much to reinforce scientifically the idea of Nature as order, which underlies such a typical 18th-century work as Pope's *Essay on Man.*

But it would be erroneous to assume that this emphasis on the general and the representative excluded the particular from the arts and reduced their material to the merely obvious, typical, and familiar. If human nature was held to be uniform, men were known to be infinitely varied; and the task of the artist was so to treat the particular as to render it representative. Thus Pope, after praising the characters of Shakespeare because they are "Nature herself," continued: "But every single character in Shakespeare is as much an individual as those in life itself; it is * * * impossible to find any two alike * * * " And Johnson praised the poet James Thomson because he looked on external nature "with a mind that at once comprehends the vast, and attends to the minute."

But although Nature was "at once the source, and end, and test of art," the poet could learn much from the ancients—the great writers, philosophers, critics, sculptors, and architects of Greece and especially of Rome. They were useful guides not because they were ancient, but because they had so truly expressed Nature that, despite changes as radical as those wrought by the establishment of Christianity in Europe, they had lost none of their relevance to the experience of modern men. As Pope said, Homer and Nature were the same; and both Pope and his readers found Horace's satires on Roman society thoroughly applicable to their own world, for Horace had followed Nature, "one clear, unchanged, and universal light."

And how did a poet come to know Nature? Not, certainly, by a life of solitude or rural retirement, or by the intermittent light of visionary gleams. The poet was to be a member of society, an important and functional part of a civilized community that would not be civilized without his presence. Only by living among men and by ceaseless and sympathetic observation of them could he gain the knowledge of Nature required of him as a poet. He was also to supplement his own inevitably limited experience by the wisdom of the past, by studying Nature wherever truthfully represented: in Homer, Virgil, Horace, or Shakespeare.

He could learn also from the ancients how to practice his craft. If a poem is an object to be made, the maker, like an architect or a cabinetmaker, must follow sound principles or botch the job. The ancients—Aristotle in his *Poetics,* Horace in his *Ars Poetica,* Quintilian in his *Institutio Oratoria,* for instance—had left more or less systematized principles (or to use the word current among the Augustans, "rules") by which to order "Nature"—the material of art—into an epic, a tragedy, a dramatic character, an oration. They had deduced these rules from the practice of earlier masters—Homer, Sophocles, the Greek and Roman orators. Italian and French critics during the 16th and 17th centuries invented new rules of their own and refined on and further codified those of the ancients. The rules directed the planning and executing of one or another of the literary "kinds," or genres: epic, tragedy, comedy, pastoral, satire, ode; the choice of language, which must differ from genre to genre; the use of figures and tropes; tone, style, characters. They could serve as a short cut to Nature, for as Pope said, they "are Nature methodized."

In England, actually, the rules were followed in rather a casual way. Most readers were prepared to admit that mere correctness could not recommend a poem which was commonplace in thought and sentiment and unanimated by the vital force of genius. Almost everyone acknowledged that Shakespeare had written the greatest body of drama in modern literature without following the rules of the ancients or the moderns. Indeed, the presence of Shakespeare and the native English suspicion of mere theory prevented English neoclassical literature from being shackled by pedantic critics. In 1765 Samuel Johnson was to brush aside in the name of Shakespeare and good sense two hundred years of critical reverence for the three unities of action, place, and time, a reverence which had not, however, much affected the plotting of English plays during that period.

The idea that each of the literary kinds is distinct and has its own proper material, characters, language, and style, was influential throughout our period. Epic and tragedy, the loftiest and most serious of the kinds, demand noble English, stately verse, heightened diction, splendor of figures and ornaments. (This can be readily understood by examining a few pages of *Paradise Lost.*) Comedy, on the other hand, since it deals with ordinary people in daily life, calls for a lower style and natural, unadorned language. This principle was known as the principle of "decorum" or the appropriate; it determined Dryden's definition of wit as "a propriety of thoughts and words; or, in other terms, thoughts and words elegantly adapted to the subject."

Examining the psychological faculties that distinguish the artist from other men, critics fixed upon "wit" as his most important and characteristic endowment. "Wit," like "Nature," is a complicated word of many meanings. Here it implies quickness and liveliness of mind, inventiveness, a readiness to perceive resemblances between things apparently unlike and so to enliven literary discourse with appropriate images, similes, and metaphors. This faculty was often identified with "fancy" or "imagination," and was thought to be irregular, wayward, extravagant, unless curbed and disciplined by another and soberer faculty, "judgment." An excess of imagination was considered dangerous to sanity, and in literature to lead away from Nature and truth to falsehood and such violent and farfetched conceits as we find in the poetry of Donne or Crashaw at their boldest. One task of the age was to tame what seemed the wildness of metaphysical wit into the more reasonable and decorous wit that Dryden described in the passage quoted above. So Pope insists in the *Essay on Criticism*, lines 80–83, on the necessity of a harmonious union of judgment and fancy (which he calls "wit") in a work of literature. Though judgment was to tame, it was not to suppress passion, energy, or originality, but to make them more effective through discipline: "The winged courser, like a generous horse, / Shows most true mettle when you check his course."

Two more general observations must be made. When Wordsworth, in the Preface to *Lyrical Ballads* (1800), declared that the poems were written "in a selection of the language really used by men," he went on to attack 18th-century poets for their use of an artificial and stock "diction." Coleridge, in *Biographia Literaria* (1817), also had a good deal to say on the subject. Although the bulk of good poetry in the 18th century, as in other times, is written in "a selection of the language really used by men," the special and stylized diction to which the two early Romantics objected did exist, especially in heroic, descriptive, pastoral, and lyric poetry. It is characterized by periphrasis (a roundabout and elegant way of avoiding homely words: "finny tribe" for "fish," or "household feathery people" for "chickens"); frequently used stock phrases, such as "shining sword," "verdant mead," "bounding main," "checkered shade"; words used in their original Latin sense, such as "genial," "gelid," "horrid"; and a fondness for adjectives ending in *y*. This language originated in the attempt of Renaissance poets all over Europe to rival the elegant and golden diction of Virgil and other Roman writers. Milton depended on it to help him obtain "answerable style" for the lofty theme of *Paradise Lost*. Dryden used it in his translation of Virgil. Thomson found it suitable in passages of generalized description in *The Seasons*, and Pope employed it, not always happily, in his versions of Homer. Used with discretion it could be both subtle and expressive; but when it became a mannerism, or a dead and conventional language used mechanically, as it did with scores of mere versifiers, it properly became an object of contempt. "Hay and straw were burned in the fields of Thessaly," for instance, was translated into poetic diction:

> There at his words devouring Vulcan feasts
> On all the tribute which Thessalian meads
> Yield to the scythe, and riots on the heaps
> Of Ceres, emptied of the ripened grain.
>
> [Glover's *Leonidas*, 1737]

But such extremes of mannerism are seldom to be found in the works of the good poets of the century.

Finally, there is the matter of versification. Everyone associates the neoclassical period with the "closed" heroic couplet—i.e., a pentameter couplet which more often than not contains within itself a complete statement and so is closed by a semicolon, period, question mark, or exclamation point. Within these two lines it was possible to attain certain rhetorical or witty effects by the use of parallelism, balance, or antithesis within the couplet as a whole or the individual line. The second line of the couplet might be made closely parallel in structure and meaning to the first, or the two could be played off against each other in antithesis; taking advantage of the fact that normally a pentameter line of English verse contains at some point a slight pause called a "caesura," one part of a line so divided can be made parallel with or antithetical to the other or even to one of the two parts of the following line. This can be illustrated by a passage from Sir John Denham's *Cooper Hill* (1642), which was quoted and parodied *ad nauseam* for many years. The poem addresses the Thames and builds up a witty comparison between the flow of a river and the flow of verse (italics are ours, to illustrate the rhetorical effects):

	O could I flow like thee, | | and make thy stream
Parallelism:	*My great example,* | | as it is *my theme!*
Double balance:	*Though deep, yet clear,* | | *though gentle,* yet not *dull,*
Double balance:	*Strong* without *rage,* | | without *o'erflowing, full.*

It only remained for Dryden and Pope to bind such passages more tightly together with alliteration and assonance, and the typical metrical-rhetorical wit of the new age had been perfected.

Shortly after the beginning of the 18th century began the vogue of blank verse—the other metrical form most favored by the age. Philosophical poems, descriptive poems, meditative poems, and original or translated epics employed blank verse of one sort or another from Thomson's *Seasons* (1726–30) to Cowper's *The Task* (1785); and the tradition determined Wordsworth's use of the form in *Tintern Abbey* and *The Prelude*. The two chief patterns of blank verse available to the age were the blank verse of Milton in *Paradise Lost* and the dramatic blank verse of Dryden and other Restoration tragic poets. The influence of Milton is easily detected, not by the success with which his manner was imitated, but by the amateur performance of most of those who try to play on his instrument. The dramatic blank verse of the Restoration too often led in 18th-century poetry to a rather disagreeably declamatory and rhetorical manner. But gradually a more lyrical blank verse developed, of which William Cowper is the master; and this more plastic metrical line had a formative influence on the blank verse of William Wordsworth.

RESTORATION LITERATURE, 1660–1700

The period between 1660 and 1700 was remarkably varied and vigorous. Dryden was the dominant figure, of course, writing in all the important contemporary forms—occasional verse, comedy, tragedy, heroic play, ode, satire, translation, and critical essay—and the variety of Dryden suggests the variety of his age. Both his example and his precepts had great infleunce, but that influence did not enforce a sterile and pedantic conformity to the rules of critics, but instead gave to the England of his day a *modern* literature, cosmopolitan, to be sure, but possessing the richness and variety that he admired in the Elizabethans, the "God's plenty" that he praised in Chaucer's *Canterbury Tales*.

The prose of the Restoration is a clear indication of the direction in which literature was moving. The styles of Donne's sermons, of Milton's pamphlets, of Sir Thomas Browne's writings, and of the character books (to select four different kinds of earlier 17th-century prose) were quite unsuitable to serve the ends of the new age. They were too elaborate, too involved, too ornate, too insistently musical, or too wittily rhetorical and pointed for mere exposition or social intercourse. The Royal Society decreed that its members must employ only a plain, concise, and utilitarian prose style suitable to the clear communication of scientific truths. Metaphors, similes, and rhetorical flourishes were disapproved because they engaged the emotions, not the reason, and though they were tolerable in poetry, they had no place in rational discourse. Similarly the learned, often pedantic language, the rhetoric and imagery and emotional intensity of earlier 17th-century pulpit oratory gradually gave way to a simplicity and plainness of diction and style entirely appropriate to sermons which sought mainly to inculcate in both the ignorant and the learned a rational morality in the conduct of life, and to avoid anything smacking of religious "enthusiasm." In polite literature, thanks to the example of such writers as Abraham Cowley, Dryden, and Sir William Temple, the ideal of good prose came to be a clear, simple, and natural style which has the ease and poise of well-bred urbane conversation. This is a social prose, designed for a social age. Later, it was available to the writers of periodical essays, such as Addison or Steele, to the novelists of the 18th century, and to the many practitioners of the delightful art of letter-writing, one of the minor literary achievements of the 18th century; the brilliant but intimate letters of Horace Walpole, and of the poets Thomas Gray and William Cowper, have never been surpassed. This movement toward clarity and simplicity in prose accompanied a similar movement away from the intricacies of metaphysical wit in verse, which found an early statement in Dryden's *Essay of Dramatic Poesy*.

But if prose was simplified and wit was tamed, the Restoration did not break wholly with the immediate past. It retained the Renaissance admiration for the typically aristocratic heroic ideal as expressed in the "heroic poem" or epic. *Paradise Lost*, carefully modeled though it is on the structure and conventions of ancient epic poetry, did not meet the expectations of most Restoration readers, who associated the heroic poem with "fierce wars and faithful loves" and expected it to offer patterns of ideal virtue and heroism for the emulation of princes and generals. General enthusiasm for Milton's epic did not develop until the early 18th century. The romantic idealism of the heroic mode was most characteristically expressed during the Restoration not in the heroic poem (except for Dryden's translations of the *Aeneid* and of Chaucer's Knight's Tale), but in the heroic play, which Dryden, its foremost practitioner, defined as "a heroic poem in little." The theme of these plays (their vogue lasted from about 1664 to about 1675) was the conflict between love and honor in the hearts of impossibly valorous heroes and impossibly high-minded and attractive ladies.

Dryden's one undoubted masterpiece in serious drama is his blank verse tragedy *All for Love* (produced 1677), based on the story of Antony and Cleopatra. In this play we can observe the effect of neoclassic taste on the drama: Dryden kept the three unities of action, place, and time more exactly, as he remarked, than "the English theater requires." Instead of Shakespeare's world-wide panorama, his rapid shifts of scene, his complex characters, we have the last hours of the tragic lovers presented in a static though grand manner and in a plot that is almost too neatly symmetrical. But though not Shakespeare, *All for Love* is a noble tragedy. The two other eminent tragic poets of the period were Nathaniel Lee (ca. 1649–92), known for violent plots, the wild emotions of his characters, and the extravagance of his rhetoric; and Thomas Otway (1652–85), who excelled in pathos. Not one enduring tragedy was written during the 18th century. Addison's *Cato* (produced in 1713) is a museum piece, illustrating the frigidity of "correct" and rule-bound tragedy. The long succession of verse tragedy thereafter was cursed by hollow rhetoric, stilted declamation, forced emotion, and conventional diction. George Lillo's *London Merchant* (produced in 1731) in prose, dealing with commonplace characters in mercantile life, took a feeble step in the direction of the sort of realistic, middle-class tragedy with which we are familiar today.

The real distinction of Restoration drama was comedy, which, like its cousin satire, is concerned with criticism of man as a moral and social being. Although Dryden had no great talent for the comic, he produced a number of successful comedies, the best of which have well-constructed plots and amusing dialogue, spiced with quick repartee between gay and emancipated rakes, male and female (as in *Marriage à la Mode*, produced ca. 1672). Thomas Shadwell (ca. 1642–92), later the unhappy object of Dryden's satire, specialized in comedies of humor, following his master Ben Jonson in his own rather clumsy but not incompetent way. But the finest comedies of the period are those of Sir George Etherege (ca. 1635–91), William Wycherley (ca. 1640–1716), William Congreve, and the less accomplished but witty Sir John Vanbrugh (pronounced *Vánbroo* or *Vanbróok*, 1664–1726) and George Farquhar (ca. 1677–1707). These writers excelled in representing—and critically evaluating—the social behavior of the fashionable upper classes of the town, though of course their version of that life is heightened and stylized, not a literal transcript. This sort of comedy—brilliantly witty, cynical in its view of the nature of man, whom it shows to be sensual, egoistic, and predatory—is known as "the comedy of manners," since its concern is to bring the moral and social behavior of its familiar social types to the test of comic laughter. The principal male character is a hero who lives not for military glory but for pleasure and the conquests that he can achieve in his amorous campaigns. The object of his very practical game of sexual intrigue is a beautiful, witty, pleasure-loving, and emancipated lady, every bit his equal in the strategies of love. The two are distinguished not for virtue, but for the good taste, aristocratic good breeding, true wit, sophisticated charm, and well-bred grace with which they conduct the often complicated intrigue that makes up the plot of such comedies. The best examples of the comedy of manners before William Congreve's *The Way of the World* (produced in 1700) are Etherege's *The Man of Mode* (produced in 1676), William Wycherley's *The Country Wife* (produced ca. 1672–74), and Congreve's earlier *Love for Love* (produced in 1695).

During the 1690's a considerable demand arose for moral reform in both literature and daily life, partly because of the nature of Restoration comedy. "Societies for the Reformation of Manners" were founded with the support of the soberer Anglicans and the resurgent Nonconformists. Their members served not only as propagandists of moral respectability, but also less pleasingly as spies and informers who brought offenders to trial for blasphemy, obscenity, and sexual immorality. The most effective attack on the indecencies of language and situation in comedy was made by the Anglican clergyman Jeremy Collier, whose *Short View of the Immorality and Profaneness of the English Stage* (1698) bore hard on Dryden and Congreve, among others. Collier spoke for the outraged moral sense of the godly middle classes as well as for the church, and his attack helped to discredit "wit" and the wits as subversive of religion and morals. One of the tasks that Steele and Addison undertook in the *Tatler* and *Spectator* and Pope in his *Essay on Criticism*, early in the next century, was to rehabilitate "wit" by making it the servant of social and moral decorum. When Dryden died, a better ordered and more respectable (if not actually more virtuous) society was coming into being.

The literary life of Restoration and 18th-century London differs from that of our own time in no more striking way than in its semipublic and social character. From 1652 and increasingly during the first half of the 18th century, the coffeehouses of London served as informal meeting places for men of all classes, and their popularity did much to promote conversation and the exchange of opinion. At the coffeehouses men could smoke, drink chocolate or coffee, read the newspapers, write and receive letters, exchange news, gossip, and opinions, and observe the oddities of character that the English have always been happy to cultivate. Like-minded men tended to congregate at certain coffeehouses: literary men at Will's in Covent Garden, where Dryden ruled during most of his life in London; scholars and the learned professions at the Grecian; Whigs at St. James's, and so on. Thus the clubs which played an important role in English masculine society came into being, from Addison's imaginary Spectator Club to the brilliant men who formed Johnson's famous Club. The men who frequented the coffeehouses formed an influential element among the reading public and helped to determine the tone of literature, the critical reputation of writers, the success or failure of plays, and the character of such periodicals as the *Tatler* and the *Spectator*. After the middle of the century, certain literary ladies known as bluestockings, led by the wealthy Mrs. Elizabeth Montague, established the salon and the *conversazione* as a means of encouraging literary conversation between the sexes.

EIGHTEENTH-CENTURY LITERATURE, 1700–1745

During the 45 years between the deaths of Dryden and Swift, the literature that Dryden and his contemporaries had created attained full maturity. A new and brilliant group of writers took the stage: Swift, with *A Tale of a Tub* (1704–10); Addison, with his overpraised and vastly popular poetic celebration of Marlborough's victory at Blenheim, *The Campaign* (1705); Prior, with *Poems on Several Occasions* (1707); Steele, with the *Tatler* (1709); and the youthful Pope, in the same year, with his *Pastorals*. On the whole, the literature of this period is chiefly a literature of wit, concerned with civilization, with man in his social relationships; and consequently it is critical and in some degree moral or satiric. It preserves the earlier period's interest in the heroic, but apart from Pope's translations of Homer, no writer succeeded in heroic poetry. It is revealing and characteristic that on the other hand some of the finest works of the period are mock-heroic (individual passages in Swift's *Battle of the Books* and *A Description of a City Shower* and Pope's *Rape of the Lock* and *The Dunciad*) or humorous burlesques of serious classic or modern modes (John

Gay's delightful town mock-Georgic, *Trivia, or the Art of Walking the Streets of London*, 1716, or his burlesque of the heroics of Italian opera, *The Beggar's Opera*, produced in 1728). Such literature is addressed to highly sophisticated and cultivated readers, and it reminds us that earlier 18th-century literature retained the aristocratic bias that had marked the literature of the 17th century.

Nevertheless a body of writing that reached a wider audience was coming into being. The reading public expanded steadily throughout the 18th century, and its new recruits were upper-class women and the increasingly numerous rich and leisured people of both sexes in the trading middle class. The popular press flourished, producing a succession of newspapers, literary periodicals in the manner of the *Tatler*, miscellanies of various sorts, and finally, in 1731, the first magazine in the modern sense, the *Gentleman's Magazine*, which was to be followed not only by imitations but also by the appearance of such successful literary reviews as the *Monthly Review* (1749) and the *Critical Review* (1756). The new journalism satisfied the hunger of the less well-educated among the literate for all sorts of information about politics, science, philosophy, literature, as well as for such less edifying materials as scandal and gossip. It also created a demand for writers—not necessarily for geniuses—and, though often on harsh terms, men began to subsist as hack writers and compilers in a milieu that came to be called Grub Street, from the name of an actual street, just as we can speak of the whole sphere of speculative finance and banking as Wall Street. To such writers as Pope and Swift, Grub Street with all its denizens (it was to gain the services of both Johnson and Oliver Goldsmith!) represented a serious threat to humanistic learning, urbane enlightenment, and good taste. But literature became in this period of expanding publication and increasingly numerous readers a gainful profession. Something will shortly be said of the novel, but it may be remarked here that the novel as we know it—a long prose narrative concerned with the actual world and the men and women who inhabit it—very probably could not have come into existence had not these new readers existed. The 18th-century novel supplied the place in the life of the common reader that the heroic poem had occupied in the life of the courtly reader of the past.

During this period certain literary kinds changed very much for the worse. The lyric, one of the glories of the Elizabethan age and the first half of the 17th century, had become in the Restoration a minor and graceful mode, appropriate to a song or a "paper of verses" addressed to a mistress. The wits of Charles II's court could turn out accomplished, conventional poems of this sort which do not lack distinction; and Matthew Prior was their counterpart in the time of William of Orange and Queen Anne. But between 1700 and 1740 lyric poetry became increasingly trivial and empty. Comedy, too, underwent a deplorable change. The moral reform of the 1690's, together with the increasingly optimistic and flattering view of human nature, made the rakes of Restoration comedy seem distasteful libels on humanity. A new sort of comedy, "sentimental comedy," began to replace the old comedy of manners; not only because it is based on the sentimental notion that man is naturally good and that, given a chance, his virtuous feelings and his good heart will triumph over his accidentally acquired vices and follies, but also because its dialogue deals in high moral sentiments rather than wit, and because its virtuous heroines and virtuous (or penitent) heroes suffer misfortunes which move the audience not to laughter, but to tears. One of the pleasures invented in 18th-century Europe was the delicious pleasure of weeping, and sentimental comedy (or, as the French phrased it, *la comédie larmoyante,* "weeping comedy") brought that pleasure to playgoers through many decades. As tragedy froze into rhetoric, comedy dissolved in tears. And the successes enjoyed by John Gay's comic ballad opera *The Beggar's Opera* (1728), or the laughing comedies of Goldsmith and Sheridan later in the century, could not eradicate the taste for sentimentality. It is a curious fact that although during the 18th century the *theater* prospered and the stage was adorned by a succession of great actors and actresses (the finest being Johnson's pupil and friend, David Garrick), the *drama* declined into a depressing nullity.

On the other hand, of course, satire flourished, its most distinguished practitioners being Pope and Swift, though they are only two among many effective writers. The satirist is usually a conservative, who uses his weapon against those deviations from norms of conduct which threaten to undermine traditional and socially approved behavior. Both Pope and Swift wrote their major satires as Tories, at a time when Britain was dominated by the Whig party. The Tories resisted, but resisted futilely, the social and economic changes which were taking place as England grew from an island kingdom into a world power, and transformed its agrarian into a mercantile economy. They looked with gloomy forebodings on the rising tide of popular taste, on what they considered the invasion and debasement of the polite world by the barbarians from the middle classes and by vulgar and luxurious rich and noble families, and on the increase of corruption in public life. The satire of both Swift and Pope is great because it was animated by moral urgency and heightened by a tragic sense of doom. Pope saw the issue as a struggle between Darkness and Light, Chaos and Order, Barbarism and Civilization: a vision which he expressed in his greatest work, *The Dunciad.* For Swift the issue was one between "right reason" and "madness"—not clinical insanity, of course, but a blindness to anything but one's own private illusions, which is an abandonment of practical reality.

But the great age of satire also produced a wholly different sort of poetry from that which Pope was writing in the 1730's. After 1726, when James Thomson published the first of his nature poems, *Winter,* the poetry of natural description flourished and the characteristic 18th-century English taste for natural and picturesque beauty found expression—not only in poetry, but also in that typical Georgian art, landscape gardening, and finally in the beginning of the art of landscape in water color or oils, which has been England's principal achievement in painting. Nothing could be further from the truth than the assumption of most 19th-century critics and literary historians that a love of external nature was unknown to English literature until the coming of the Romantic poets, a view encouraged by some not disinterested remarks of Coleridge and Wordsworth. But Wordsworth was the heir of 18th-century nature poets: *Tintern Abbey*

(1798) not only was written *within* the century, but in most respects is very much a poem *of* the century.

In the course of the century, Englishmen not only admired tamed and ordered nature, in large landscape gardens or cultivated fields, but also early learned to enjoy the more thrilling, emotional pleasure which they began to feel in the presence of what they called "the sublime" in nature: vast spaces, mountainous country, wild and untamed landscape. Whether the enthusiast of nature went to landscape for evidence of the presence of the Deity or merely to enjoy natural beauty, he inevitably learned to feel emotions in the presence of external nature and to examine the quality of his feelings. Before the death of Pope and Swift, in the poetry of Thomson and others, a literature of feeling had come into existence alongside the dominant literature of wit. The development of such a literature of sentiment is perhaps the crucial fact in the literary history of the century after the deaths of Pope and Swift.

THE EMERGENCE OF NEW LITERARY THEMES AND MODES, 1740–1785

When Matthew Arnold, speaking for Victorian taste, called the 18th century an "Age of Prose," he meant to cast doubt upon its poetry; but the later part of the century might indeed be honored as an age of prose. Never before nor since have so many great writers of prose flourished at once, nor so many kinds of intellectual prose been perfected: literary criticism, with Samuel Johnson; biography, James Boswell; philosophy, David Hume; politics, Edmund Burke; history, Edward Gibbon; aesthetics, Sir Joshua Reynolds; economics, Adam Smith; natural history, Gilbert White. Each of these authors is a master stylist, whose effort to express himself clearly and fully creates an art as difficult to achieve, and as precise, as poetry. Indeed, the prose style of the period often seems to build upon the principles of neoclassical verse: its elaborately balanced use of parallels and antitheses, its elegant allusions to classical literature, its public, rhetorical manner, its craving for generality. At its best, however, such prose depends less on formal virtues than on its weight of thought. Unlike the earlier masters of simplicity in prose—Addison, Swift, Defoe—the authors of the Age of Johnson have little confidence in plain speaking. Readers will not be convinced of the truth, they suspect, merely by having the facts laid before them; they must be offered scientific demonstration or passionate eloquence. Some comments by Johnson on the prose of Swift make the point by example as well as precept:

> His style was well suited to his thoughts, which are never subtilized by nice disquisitions, decorated by sparkling conceit, elevated by ambitious sentences, or variegated by far-sought learning. He pays no court to the passions, he excites neither surprise nor admiration; he always understands himself, and his readers always understand him. * * * This easy and safe conveyance of meaning it was Swift's desire to attain, and for having attained he deserves praise, though perhaps not the highest praise. For purposes merely didactic, when something is to be told that was not known before, it is the best mode; but against that inattention by which known truths are suffered to lie neglected, it makes no provision; it instructs, but does not persuade.

Johnson's prose bristles with long words, qualifications of thought, and "ambitious sentences" that are the very opposite of the style he describes; he attempts not merely to be understood, not merely to instruct, but to persuade. And similar ambitions motivate many of the authors of his time. An unprecedented effort to formulate the first principles of philosophy, history, psychology, and art required a whole new language of persuasion, more subtle, logical, and accurate than English had ever been before.

An age of great prose, however, can put a burden on its poets. Many of the generation of talented young poets who emerged about the time of Pope's death, a group that includes William Collins, Thomas Gray, and the brothers Joseph and Thomas Warton, are haunted by the fear that the spirit of poetry may have passed away—driven out by the spirit of prose, by an ideal of mere "correctness," by the end of superstitions that had once peopled the landscape with fairies and demons, the stuff of poetry. In an age barren of magic, they ask, where is poetry to be found? That question becomes obsessive in many poems of the period, suffusing them with melancholy. Indeed, more and more poetry itself was associated with melancholy, a sweet sadness, a yearning for another time and place. The prototype of the mid-18th-century melancholy poet was Milton's *Il Penseroso*, a night-loving solitary, who sucks pensive sadness from the "far-off curfew" or the swelling organ in the twilight of a Gothic church. Such a figure is most unlike the Augustan poet, a social being, living in a crowded world and little given to the impropriety of the public confession of private feelings. He is rather a not very remote ancestor of such typically Romantic figures as Wordsworth, wandering "lonely as a cloud," of Byron's Childe Harold, brooding over the ruins of Rome, or of the speaker of Keats's sonnet, who, contemplating his own mortal day and the transitoriness of love and beauty, exclaims:

> on the shore
> Of the wide world I stand alone and think,
> Till love and fame to nothingness do sink.

The "pilgrim" in William Collins' *Ode to Evening* and the speaker in Thomas Gray's *Elegy Written in a Country Churchyard* are typical 18th-century Penserosos. The idea of the poet was changing from that of a maker to that of an introspective, brooding confessor; the materials of poetry were becoming rather the inner life and private vision of the poet than the public, social affairs of men.

Poets who brood in silence are never far from thoughts of death; and an often morbid fascination with death, suicide, and the grave preoccupies the poets of midcentury. The clergyman Edward Young (1683–1765) wrote an immensely long and popular poem in blank verse, *The Complaint: or Night Thoughts on Life, Death, and Immortality* (1742–46), to supplement the Christian optimism of Pope's *Essay on Man* with a darker view of Christianity based on fear of the life to come. But the "graveyard school" is less concerned with religion than with horror and decay. Within an elaborate stage-setting of medieval ruins and fleshless bodies, the soul of the graveyard poet self-consciously acts out its secret fears. The revival of

Gothic architectural styles, most famously Horace Walpole's tiny and precious pseudo-Gothic castle, Strawberry Hill, helped influence literary styles as well. The Gothic vogue, like a similar vogue for Chinese decor, seemed to suggest that old-fashioned canons of taste—proportion, balance, simplicity, and harmony—might count for less in art than the pleasures of fancy and extravagance—intricacy, asymmetry, a willful excess. Poets began to cultivate archaic language and dead literary forms; especially, after Thomas Percy's edition of *Reliques of Ancient English Poetry* (1765), the ballad. Thus Thomas Chatterton (1752–1770), whom the Romantics later idolized for his precocious genius and his tragic early death, composed sham medieval ballads he pretended to have found in an old manuscript. The most remarkable literary consequence of such medievalizing, however, was the invention of the Gothic romance. Horace Walpole's *Castle of Otranto* (1765), a dreamlike tale of terror inspired by the physical appearance of Strawberry Hill, created a mode of fiction that retains its popularity to the present day. In the typical Gothic romance, set amidst the glooms and intricacies of a medieval castle, the laws of nightmare replace the laws of probability. Forbidden themes—incest, murder, necrophilia, atheism, the torments of sexual desire—are allowed free play; repressed feelings, morbid fears rise to the surface of the narrative. Although most such romances, like William Beckford's *Vathek* (1786) and Matthew Lewis's *The Monk* (1796), depend on sensationalism and the grotesque, Gothicism also influenced serious novels of social purpose, like William Godwin's *Caleb Williams* (1794); and Godwin's daughter, Mary Shelley, eventually composed a romantic nightmare, *Frankenstein* (1816), that continues to haunt our dreams.

Ultimately, it was not to a medieval revival that poets looked for a renewal of poetry, but to their own imaginations and feelings. In his *Ode to Fancy* (1746), Joseph Warton associated "fancy" with the natural, the wild and spontaneous, with solitude, and with enthusiasm and the passions. Such a concept of the fancy or imagination emphasizes not rules and crafts of the maker, but original genius, the poet as the seer, as nature's priest. True poets, Warton suggests, should not be conversationalists or orators but singers. A sublime excess, a visionary fervor, became the mark of poetry. "The public has seen all that art can do," William Shenstone wrote in 1761, welcoming James Macpherson's bardic *Ossian*, "and they want the more striking efforts of wild, original, enthusiastic genius." But genius is easier to call for than to recognize; when it does come, people are apt to call it madness. Many of the best poets of the period—Collins, Christopher Smart, later William Cowper—suffered from mental illness, and others, like Chatterton, were scorned by society. Nor did many readers so much as notice the extraordinary work of Smart, or later of William Blake. The apocalyptic strain of poetry, bursting the bonds of logical transition, of grammar, and even of the natural world, proved difficult to approach. Cowper, the most popular poet of the latter part of the century, won his readers with a more modest, intimate kind of verse, never departing far from the accents of friendly conversation. Nevertheless, it was to visionary poetry, and to genius, that the future belonged. "The road of excess," Blake notes in a Proverb of Hell, "leads to the palace of wisdom." As the

18th century drew to an end amid revolutions in society and thought, poets began to travel that road.

THE BEGINNING OF THE NOVEL

To say that the modern novel came into existence in the 18th century is not to say that there was no prose fiction before 1700. There were the ancient Greek romances and their modern European imitators; the courtly *Arcadia* of Sidney and the humbler fiction of Deloney and Nashe and other Elizabethans; the interminable French romances of the 17th century and their English translations and imitations, loosely constructed, blending aristocratic refinement, chivalric adventure, and courtly love; the tales of the adventures of rogues and the careers of famous criminals; and, in a world apart, Bunyan's vivid allegories of the spiritual adventures of wayfaring and militant Christians and their adversaries. But it remains true that, if we except Daniel Defoe, the creator of the modern novel was Samuel Richardson (1689–1761). It is interesting to observe that both Defoe and Richardson belonged to the middle class and expressed in their works middle-class interests and attitudes. Defoe simply ignored the sentimental and aristocratic refinements of the earlier romances and was content to show his readers not a world as it might be, a heroic world, but their world as it was, populated with believable people who were motivated by the practical concerns that dominate our daily lives. He did not seek—and except through *Robinson Crusoe* (1719) did not often find—readers among the upper classes. He was content to interest shopkeepers, apprentices, and servants, who were already avid readers of tales of crime and adventure, usually heavily laced with pious moral observations.

Richardson, however, caught the attention of all literate Europe, and once for all established the novel as we know it, a solid and enduring object in the literary landscape. His three novels were strikingly new in their minute and subtle analysis of emotions and states of mind. It was while he was compiling a little book of model letters that he conceived the idea of *Pamela*, or *Virtue Rewarded* (1740), a story told in a series of letters, in which a virtuous servant girl who resists her master's base designs on her virtue eventually wins him as her husband. Richardson's masterpiece, *Clarissa* (1747–48), carries the same epistolary method, moral instruction, and sexual titillation to new heights. In the conflict between the libertine Lovelace, an attractive and diabolical aristocrat, and the angelic Clarissa, the perfection of middle-class values, Richardson created a fiction that embodied the ideals and the tensions of his society. No earlier author had involved his readers so fully in the thoughts and emotions of his characters; nor had any author paid such close attention to the pressures on women. His final novel turns to a model of male perfection, *Sir Charles Grandison* (1753–54), with less success.

Henry Fielding (1707–54), who loved virtue as much as Richardson did, but to whom goodness was a matter of spontaneity and fellow feeling, not of mere propriety or conformity to a code, considered *Pamela* a misleading image of virtue; therefore, in 1742, he published *Joseph Andrews*, which begins as an hilarious burlesque of *Pamela* by describing the staunch resistance offered to the lewd advances of Lady Booby by her servant, the virtuous Joseph, brother of Pamela. Expelled for his chastity from Lady

Booby's household, he takes to the road, joining the guileless Parson Adams, who is walking to London to try to sell a bundle of his sermons to a publisher. Their adventures make up what Fielding called "a comic epic in prose." His great novel is *The History of Tom Jones, A Foundling* (1749). The protagonist became the pattern of the good-natured hero of the age: a young man of manly virtues, generous, high-spirited, loyal, and courageous, but impulsive, wanting prudence, full of animal spirits and sensuality. The novel is crowded with incident and with varied types of men and women; and critics have agreed with Coleridge's praise of its brilliantly constructed plot. Fielding's sentimentality is not the sentimentality of Richardson, whose dying heroine Clarissa gives full expression to every shade of feeling as she writes her letters, using her coffin as an escritoire; rather it is the sentimentality of a man—of most English men and women of his time—who accepted the doctrine that most people are naturally good and that our innate love of truth and virtue can in the end save us from our baser selves. Fielding's other important novel, *Amelia* (1751), having as its heroine a long-suffering woman, almost wholly passive, is an example of pathos rather than of Fielding's comic vigor and healthy gusto.

Two other novelists must be mentioned: Tobias Smollett (1721–71) and Laurence Sterne (1713–68). Smollett was a gifted caricaturist, a dealer in grotesque humor and rather strongly flavored comedy. He delighted to depict the seamier side of 18th-century life, its brutality, coarse practical jokes, and strong odors. *Roderick Random* (1748), *Peregrine Pickle* (1751), and *Ferdinand, Count Fathom* (1753), owe something to the picaresque tradition, as, of course, did Fielding's first two novels. Smollett's one masterpiece is an epistolary novel, *Humphry Clinker* (1771), which recounts, through letters written by several members of a traveling party, the comic incidents of a journey through England and Scotland, from the differing points of view of the travelers, somc of them "originals" in a high degree.

Sterne, an unclerical clergyman, a humorist, a wit, a consumptive whose disease gave a hectic, heightened quality to his senses and emotions, a masterly recorder of the refinements of sensation, feeling, and thought, produced between 1760 and 1767 his long, brilliant, sentimental-comic, and eccentric novel, *The Life and Opinions of Tristram Shandy*. He deliberately frustrated all the stock expectations of his readers. The plot has not the logical order of a beginning, a middle, and an end; instead it abandons clock time for psychological time, interrupts scenes in order to digress or to recount past or future events, follows whimsically any apparently chance association, digresses for several chapters—in fact, it is designed as an elaborate joke at the reader's expense. And yet the method gets us inside the consciousness of the narrator and the other characters, and into a world peopled by the most engaging of comic characters.

Fielding, Smollett, and Sterne gave to English literature not only vivid scenes from the life of their times, but a gallery of eccentric and original characters that illustrate the interest of the age not only in the ideal and the general, but also in the individual and the unique. The novels of Dickens and of Thackeray in the 19th century owe much to their forerunners in the 18th.

THE CONTINUITY OF THE AUGUSTAN TRADITION

Despite the emergence of new literary forms, materials, and methods after the death of Pope and Swift, the Augustan line continued vigorously throughout the last half of the 18th and even into the 19th century. If the years between 1745 and 1784 were years of change and experiment, they were also the period of Samuel Johnson's greatest achievement and influence. A conservative in literature as in politics and religion, Johnson defended in conversation and in his critical writings the humanistic neoclassicism which he had inherited from the older generation. His two major poems, *London* (1738) and *The Vanity of Human Wishes* (1749), are satirical and ethical and show little influence of the new sensibility of the midcentury. He was loyal to the heroic couplet and to the use of generalized diction. His *Dictionary* (1755) was designed not to fix our language permanently but certainly to retard the process of change and to censure words which he considered superfluous. His critical writings sufficiently reveal his devotion to the standards of Dryden and Pope, though his judgments of particular writers and works were often personal, even idiosyncratic. But his conservatism was saved from pedantry by the empirical bent of his mind and his broad and humanistic learning.

If Johnson speaks for his age, the reason is partly that he shares a faith, with many of his contemporaries, in common sense and the common reader. "By the common sense of readers uncorrupted with literary prejudices," he wrote in the last of his great *Lives of the Poets* (1780), " * * * must be finally decided all claim to poetical honors." A similar respect for common sense, and for standards of taste and behavior based upon universal principles of mind that all men share, marks many of the grandest achievements of the century; for instance, the political writings of Edmund Burke, the great Whig statesman and orator, or the *Discourses on Art* (1769–90) of Sir Joshua Reynolds, who drew the best aesthetic theory of his day into an elegant whole. Moreover, the poets whom everyone read relied less upon apocalyptic visions than upon a verse that could do justice to the ordinary feelings of ordinary people. Gray's *Elegy*, Goldsmith's *The Deserted Village*, Crabbe's *The Village*, and the lyrics of Robert Burns are only a few of the poems that strive to make poetry from and for the lives of the common man. Nor did Goldsmith, Crabbe, and Burns, for all their attachment to the growing wave of sentimentalism, desert the verse forms—the careful craftsmanship, the rhyming couplets—developed by the earlier Augustan masters. Even Cowper's *The Task* (1785), which brings us to the threshold of the Romantic movement, belongs most definitely in the 18th century. Indeed, the Augustan age did not die on that day in 1798 when a small and unsuccessful volume of poems, *Lyrical Ballads*, was published by Wordsworth and Coleridge. We hear the accents of that age from time to time in the poems of both Wordsworth and Coleridge, in many of the poems of Byron, and in Byron's ardent defense of Pope and Dryden, when the new age finally brought those masters to judgment. And we hear its old verities expressed in its own vocabulary in the criticism of that arch-enemy of the Romantic movement, Francis Jeffrey, editor of the *Edinburgh Review*, as when, for example, in a review (1808) of a volume of poems by George Crabbe, he paused to rebuke the (as he believed) affectedly eccentric poet Wordsworth for having written *The Thorn* and one of the Lucy poems:

> Now we leave it to any reader of common candor and discernment to say whether these representations of character and sentiment are drawn from the eternal and universal standard of truth and nature, which every one is knowing enough to recognize, and no one great enough to depart from with impunity; or whether they are not formed * * * upon certain fantastic and affected peculiarities in the mind or fancy of the author, into which it is most improbable that many of his readers will enter, and which cannot, in some cases, be comprehended without much effort and explanation.

JOHN DRYDEN
(1631–1700)

1668: Made poet laureate.
1681: *Absalom and Achitophel.*
ca. 1686: Conversion to Catholicism.
1689: Loss of court offices upon accession of William and Mary.
1697: Translation of Virgil.

Although John Dryden's parents seem to have sided with Parliament against the king, there is no evidence that the poet grew up in a strict Puritan family. His father, a country gentleman of moderate fortune, gave his son a gentleman's education at Westminster School, under the renowned Dr. Richard Busby, who used the rod as a pedagogical aid in imparting a sound knowledge of the learned languages and literatures to his charges (among others John Locke and Matthew Prior). From Westminster, Dryden went to Trinity College, Cambridge, where he took his A.B. in 1654. He probably held a minor post in Cromwell's government, and if he did so, it was obtained through the influence of his cousin Sir Gilbert Pickering, a member of the Protector's Council. His first important and impressive poem, *Heroic Stanzas* (1659), was written to commemorate the death of Cromwell. It was followed in the next year by *Astraea Redux*, celebrating the return of Charles II to his throne. Years later Dryden's political and religious enemies taunted him with this sudden change of position, as if he had been a political turncoat, ready to change sides whenever he could serve his own interests. The charge has often been repeated, but it is both malicious and stupid: as Dr. Johnson long ago said, "if he changed, he changed with the nation," for in 1660 most Englishmen enthusiastically welcomed the Restoration. During the rest of his life Dryden was to remain entirely loyal to Charles and to his successor James II.

Dryden is the commanding literary figure of the last four decades of the 17th century. He is that rare phenomenon, the man of letters in whose work the image of an age can be discerned. Every important aspect of the life of his times—political, religious, philosophical, artistic—finds expression somewhere in his writings. Dryden is the least personal of our poets. He is not at all the solitary, subjective poet listening to the murmur of his own voice and preoccupied with his own personal view of experience, but rather a citizen of the world commenting publicly on matters of public concern.

From the beginning to the end of his literary career, Dryden's original nondramatic poems are most typically occasional poems, i.e., poems which celebrate particular events of a public character—a coronation, a military victory, a death, a political crisis. Such poems are social and ceremonial, and they demand of the writer tact as well as talent. They are public and formal, blending poetry with rhetoric and oratory, and their tone is that of the forum, not of intimate conversation or private meditation. In varying degrees Dryden's occasional poems have these qualities. His earliest published poem, to be sure, *Upon the Death of Lord Hastings* (1649), belongs stylistically to the tradition of metaphysical poetry, but ten years later, when his next ambitious poem appeared, the *Heroic Stanzas* on the death of Cromwell, he had mastered the tone, language, and manner of grave public speech. His principal achievements in this form are the two poems on the king's return and his coronation; *Annus Mirabilis* (1667), which celebrates the English naval victory over the Dutch and the fortitude of the people of London and the king during the Great Fire, both events of that "wonderful year," 1666; the political poems, the lines on the death of Oldham (1684), the odes, and the masque printed below.

Between 1664 and 1681, however, Dryden was mainly and most seriously a playwright. The newly chartered theaters needed a modern repertory, and Dryden was foremost among those who set vigorously about supplying the need. As his *Essay of Dramatic Poesy* (1668) shows, he studied the works of the great playwrights of Greece and Rome, of the English Renaissance, and of contemporary France, seeking sound theoretical principles on which to construct the new drama that the age demanded. Indeed his fine critical intelligence always supported his creative powers, and because he took literature seriously and enjoyed discussing it, he became, it appears almost casually, what Dr. Johnson called him: "the father of English criticism." His abilities as both poet and dramatist brought him to the attention of the king, who in 1668 made him poet laureate. Two years later the post of Historiographer Royal was added to the laureateship at a combined stipend of £200, well over £2000 in modern money.

Dryden is not a great playwright, but he was influential in his own time. He wrote his plays, as he frankly confessed, to please his audiences, which were not heterogeneous, like Shakespeare's, but were largely drawn from the court and from the fashionable world that took its standard from the court. He followed rather than formed the taste of his audiences, producing rhymed heroic plays, in which incredibly noble heroes and heroines face incredibly difficult choices between their mutual love and the claims of honor, and the dialogue is conducted in a boldly rhetorical style; comedies of busy intrigue and bright, witty repartee, especially between a male and female rake; and, later, libretti for the newly introduced dramatic form, the opera. His one great tragedy—on Antony and Cleopatra—is *All for Love* (1677), in blank verse, written more in emulation than in imitation of Shakespeare.

Between 1678 and 1681, when he was nearing 50, Dryden discovered his great gift for writing formal verse satire. A quarrel with Thomas Shadwell, a playwright of some talent, prompted the mock-heroic episode *Mac Flecknoe,* which was probably written about 1678 but which was not published until 1682. Out of the stresses occasioned by the Popish Plot (1678) and its political aftermath came his major political satires, *Absalom and Achitophel* (1681), and *The Medal* (1682), his final attack on the villain of *Absalom and Achitophel*, the Earl of Shaftesbury. Twenty years' experience as poet and playwright had prepared him technically for the triumphant achievement that *Absalom and Achitophel* undoubtedly is. He had completely mastered the heroic couplet, having fashioned it into an instrument suitable in his hands for every sort of discourse from the thrust and parry of quick logical argument, to lyric feeling, rapid narrative, or forensic declamation. And he had fashioned a noble, resonant, and malleable language as well. Thanks to this long discipline, he was able in one stride to assume his proper place beside the masters of verse satire: Horace, Juvenal, Persius, in ancient Rome, and Boileau, his French contemporary.

The consideration of religious and political questions that the events of 1678–81 forced on Dryden brought a new seriousness to his mind and works. In 1682 he published *Religio Laici,* a poem in which he examined the grounds of his religious faith and defended the *via media* of the Anglican Church against the rationalism of Deism on the one hand and the authoritarianism of Rome on the other. But he had moved closer to Rome than he perhaps realized when he wrote the poem. Charles II died in 1685 and was succeeded by his Catholic brother, James II. Within less than a year Dryden and his two sons were converted to Catholicism. Just when, by whom, and under what circumstances the poet was converted we do not know, but once again his enemies were loud in denouncing his apparent venality. Again the accusation does not survive serious scrutiny. Dryden's court appointments had been renewed promptly on the accession of James, certainly before his conversion. Moreover, as Louis Bredvold has shown, Dryden's early philosophic skepticism (the conviction that the human reason cannot arrive at truth) gave way to fideism (the acceptance by faith alone of Christian mysteries as interpreted by some valid tradition). The development was slow and consistent, and his sincerity is borne out by his steadfast loyalty to the Roman Church after James abdicated and the Protestant William and Mary came in; as a result he was to lose his offices and their much-needed stipends. From his new position as a Roman Catholic, Dryden wrote in 1687 *The Hind and the Panther,* in which he defended the doctrines of his church and the policies (which he knew to be ruinous for the king and his coreligionists) that James was pursuing. Though full of splendid passages, this poem is a rather odd performance. The various religious sects of England are represented by appropriate animals, and, surprisingly enough, we listen to a prolonged theological debate between two of them, the milk-white Hind (the Roman Church) and the spotted Panther (the Anglican Church).

Dryden was now nearing 60, with a family to support on a much-diminished income. With quiet dignity he once more undertook to earn his living. He easily resumed his career as a playwright, producing five more plays before his death. He had occasionally practiced translation in the past and to this minor but, in his time, highly esteemed art he now returned. In 1693 appeared his translations from Juvenal and Persius, with the long dedicatory epistle on satire; and in 1697, his greatest achievement in this mode, the magnificent folio, illustrated, of the works of Virgil. At the very end, two months before his death, came the *Fables Ancient and Modern,* prefaced by one of the finest of his critical essays and made up of superb translations from Ovid, Boccaccio, and Chaucer.

What was the nature of Dryden's achievement? His drama, by and large, belongs entirely to his age, though its influence persisted into the next century. His critical writings established canons of taste and theoretical principles that determined the character of neoclassic literature in the next century. He helped establish a new sort of prose—easy, lucid, plain, and shaped to the cadences of natural speech. This is the prose that we like to think of as "modern," although it is not everywhere evident in our modern age. Johnson praised it for its informality and apparent artlessness:

> * * * every word seems to drop by chance, though it falls into its proper place. Nothing is cold or languid; the whole is airy, animated, and vigorous * * * though all is easy, nothing is feeble; though all seems careless, there is nothing harsh * * *

His satire, as vital today as it was nearly 300 years ago, exerted a fruitful influence on the most brilliant verse satirist of the next century, Alexander Pope. The vigor and variety of his metrics made inevitable the long-enduring vogue of the heroic couplet among his successors. At the same time, he created a poetic language that remained the basic language of poetry until the early 19th century and that even the Romantic movement did not wholly destroy. This is not to say that he created the stock "poetic diction" to which Wordsworth and Coleridge justly objected later on, though he added to it and used it judiciously. His language is the superbly civilized language of the Augustan style at its best: dignified, unaffected, precise and always musical—a noble instrument of public speech. Johnson's final estimate remains valid:

> By him we were taught *sapere et fari,* to think naturally and express forcibly * * * What was said of Rome, adorned by Augustus, may be applied by an easy metaphor to English poetry embellished by Dryden, *lateritiam invenit, marmoream reliquit,* he found it brick, and he left it marble.

From Annus Mirabilis[1]

[*London Reborn*]

Yet London, empress of the northern clime,
    By an high fate thou greatly didst expire;
Great as the world's, which at the death of time
    Must fall, and rise a nobler frame by fire.[2]

As when some dire usurper Heaven provides,
    To scourge his country with a lawless sway:[3]
His birth, perhaps, some petty village hides,
    And sets his cradle out of fortune's way:

1. 1666 was a "year of wonders" (*annus mirabilis*): war, plague, the great fire of London. According to the enemies of Charles II, God was visiting His wrath upon the English people to signify that the reign of an unholy king would soon come to an end. Dryden's long "historical poem" *Annus Mirabilis,* written the same year, interprets the wonders differently: as trials sent by God to punish rebellious spirits and to bind the king and his people together. "Never had prince or people more mutual reason to love each other," Dryden wrote, "if suffering for each other can endear affection." Charles had endured rejection and exile, England had been torn by civil war. Dryden views these sufferings as a covenant, pledge of better times to come. Out of Charles' troubles, he predicts in heroic stanzas modeled on Virgil, the king shall arise like a new Augustus, the ruler of a great empire; and out of fire London shall arise like the phoenix, ready to take her place as trade center for the world, in the glory of a new Augustan age.

2. Ovid, whom Dryden quotes, foretells, in Book I of *The Metamorphoses,* that the world will be purged by fire.

3. Probably a reference to Oliver Cromwell.

Till fully ripe his swelling fate breaks out,
    And hurries him to mighty mischiefs on:
His Prince, surprised at first, no ill could doubt,[4]
    And wants the power to meet it when 'tis known:

Such was the rise of this prodigious fire,
    Which in mean buildings first obscurely bred,
From thence did soon to open streets aspire,
    And straight to palaces and temples spread.

* * *

Me-thinks already, from this chymic[5] flame,
    I see a city of more precious mold:
Rich as the town which gives the Indies name,[6]
    With silver paved, and all divine with gold.

Already, laboring with a mighty fate,
    She shakes the rubbish from her mounting brow,
And seems to have renewed her charter's date,
    Which Heaven will to the death of time allow.

More great than human, now, and more August,[7]
    New deified she from her fires does rise:
Her widening streets on new foundations trust,
    And, opening, into larger parts she flies.

Before, she like some shepherdess did show,
    Who sat to bathe her by a river's side:
Not answering to her fame, but rude and low,
    Nor taught the beauteous arts of modern pride.

Now, like a Maiden Queen, she will behold,
    From her high turrets, hourly suitors come:
The East with incense, and the West with gold,
    Will stand, like suppliants, to receive her doom.[8]

The silver Thames, her own domestic flood,
    Shall bear her vessels like a sweeping train;
And often wind (as of his mistress proud)
    With longing eyes to meet her face again.

The wealthy Tagus, and the wealthier Rhine,
    The glory of their towns no more shall boast;
And Seine, that would with Belgian rivers join,[9]
    Shall find her luster stained, and traffic lost.

The venturous merchant, who designed[1] more far,
    And touches on our hospitable shore,

4. Fear.
5. Alchemic or transmuting. The fire of London, which utterly consumed the central city, burned for four days, September 2–6. By September 10 Christopher Wren had already submitted a plan, much of it later adopted, for rebuilding the city on a grander scale.
6. Mexico.
7. Augusta, the old name of London [Dryden's note].
8. Judgment, decree.
9. France and Holland (which then included Belgium) had made an alliance for trade, as well as war, against England. The river Tagus flows into the Atlantic at Lisbon.
1. Intended to go.

Charmed with the splendor of this northern star,
  Shall here unlade him, and depart no more.

Our powerful navy shall no longer meet,
  The wealth of France or Holland to invade;
The beauty of this Town, without a fleet,
  From all the world shall vindicate[2] her trade.

And while this famed emporium we prepare,
  The British ocean shall such triumphs boast,
That those who now disdain our trade to share,
  Shall rob like pirates on our wealthy coast.

Already we have conquered half the war,
  And the less dangerous part is left behind:
Our trouble now is but to make them dare,
  And not so great to vanquish as to find.

Thus to the eastern wealth through storms we go,
  But now, the Cape once doubled,[3] fear no more;
A constant trade-wind will securely blow,
  And gently lay us on the spicy shore.

1666   1667

Song from *Marriage à la Mode*

1

Why should a foolish marriage vow,
  Which long ago was made,
Oblige us to each other now,
  When passion is decayed?
We loved, and we loved, as long as we could,
  Till our love was loved out in us both;
But our marriage is dead when the pleasure is fled:
  'Twas pleasure first made it an oath.

2

If I have pleasures for a friend,
  And farther love in store,
What wrong has he whose joys did end,
  And who could give no more?
'Tis a madness that he should be jealous of me,
  Or that I should bar him of another:
For all we can gain is to give ourselves pain,
  When neither can hinder the other.

ca. 1672   1673

2. Defend, protect.

3. Sailed around.

Absalom and Achitophel In 1678 a dangerous crisis, both religious and political, threatened to undo the Restoration settlement and to precipitate England once again into civil war. The Popish Plot and its aftermath not only whipped up extreme anti-Catholic passions, but led between 1679 and 1681 to a bitter political struggle between Charles II (whose adherents came to be called Tories) and the Earl of Shaftesbury (whose followers were termed Whigs). The issues were nothing less than the prerogatives of the Crown and the possible exclusion of the king's Catholic brother, James, Duke of York, from his rightful position as heir-presumptive to the throne: Charles's cool courage and brilliant, if unscrupulous, political genius saved the throne for his brother and gave at least temporary peace to his people.

Charles was a Catholic at heart—he received the last rites of that Church on his deathbed—and was eager to do what he could do discreetly for the relief of his Catholic subjects, who suffered severe civil and religious disabilities imposed by their numerically superior Protestant countrymen. James openly professed the Catholic religion, an awkward fact politically, for he was next in line of succession since Charles had no legitimate children. The household of the duke, as well as that of Charles's neglected queen, Catherine of Braganza, inevitably became the center of Catholic life and intrigue at court and consequently of Protestant prejudice and suspicion.

No one understood, however, that the situation was explosive until 1678, when Titus Oates (a renegade Catholic convert and a man of the most infamous character) offered sworn testimony of the existence of a Jesuit plot to assassinate the king, burn London, massacre Protestants, and re-establish the Roman Church.

The country might have kept its head and come to realize (what no historian has doubted) that Oates and his confederates were perjured rascals, as Charles himself quickly perceived. But panic was created by the discovery of the murdered body of a prominent London Justice of the Peace, Sir Edmund Berry Godfrey, who a few days before had received for safekeeping a copy of Oates's testimony. The crime, immediately ascribed to the Catholics, has never been solved. Fear and indignation reached a hysterical pitch when the seizure of the papers of the Duke of York's secretary revealed that he had been in correspondence with the confessor of Louis XIV regarding the re-establishment of the Roman Church in England. Before the terror subsided many innocent men were executed on the increasingly bold and always false evidence of Oates and his fellows.

The Earl of Shaftesbury, the Duke of Buckingham, and others quickly took advantage of the situation. With the support of the Commons and the City of London, they moved to exclude the Duke of York from the succession. Between 1679 and 1681 Charles and Shaftesbury were engaged in a mighty struggle. The Whigs found a candidate of their own in the king's favorite illegitimate son, the handsome and engaging Duke of Monmouth, whom they advanced as a proper successor to his father. They urged Charles to legitimize him, and when he refused they whispered that there was proof that the king had secretly married Monmouth's mother. The young man allowed himself to be used against his father. He was sent on a triumphant progress through western England, where he was enthusiastically received. Twice an Exclusion Bill nearly passed both Houses. But by early 1681 Charles had secured his own position by secretly accepting from Louis XIV a three-year subsidy that made him independent of Parliament, which had tried to force his hand by refusing to vote him funds. He summoned Parliament to meet at Oxford in the spring of 1681, and, a few moments after the Commons had passed the Exclusion Bill, in a bold stroke he abruptly dissolved Parliament, which never met again during his reign. Already, as Charles was aware, a reaction had set in against the violence of the Whigs. In midsummer, when he felt it safe to move against his enemies, Shaftesbury was sent to the Tower, charged with high treason. In November the Grand Jury, packed with Whigs, threw out the indictment, and the earl was free; but his power was broken, and he lived only two more years.

Shortly before the Grand Jury acted, Dryden published anonymously the first part of *Absalom and Achitophel,* apparently hoping to influence their verdict. It is worthy of the occasion which produced it. The issues in question were grave; the chief actors, the most important men in the realm. Dryden, therefore, could not use burlesque and caricature as had Butler, or the mock-heroic as he himself had done in *Mac Flecknoe*. Only a heroic style and manner were appropriate to his weighty material, and the poem is most original in its blending of the heroic and the satiric. Dryden's task called for all his tact and literary skill; he had to mention, but to gloss over, the king's faults: his indolence and love of pleasure; his neglect of his wife and his devotion to his mistresses—conduct which had left him with many children, but no heir except his Catholic brother. He had to deal gently with Monmouth, whom Charles still loved. And he had to present, or appear to present, the king's case objectively.

The remarkable parallels between the rebellion of Absalom against his father King David (II Samuel xiii–xviii) had already been remarked in sermons, satires, and pamphlets. Dryden took the hint and gave contemporary events a due distance and additional dignity by approaching them indirectly through their Biblical analogues. The poem is famous for its brilliant portraits of the king's enemies and friends; but equally admirable are the temptation scene (which, like other passages, is indebted to *Paradise Lost*) and the remarkably astute analysis of the Popish Plot itself.

A second part of *Absalom and Achitophel* appeared in 1682. Most of it is the work of Nahum Tate, but lines 310–509, which include the devastating portraits of Doeg and Og (two Whig poets, Elkanah Settle and Thomas Shadwell) are certainly by Dryden.

Absalom and Achitophel: A Poem

In pious times, ere priestcraft did begin,
Before polygamy was made a sin;
When man on many multiplied his kind,
Ere one to one was cursedly confined;
When nature prompted and no law denied
Promiscuous use of concubine and bride;
Then Israel's monarch after Heaven's own heart,[1]
His vigorous warmth did variously impart
To wives and slaves; and, wide as his command,
Scattered his Maker's image through the land.
Michal,[2] of royal blood, the crown did wear,
A soil ungrateful to the tiller's care:
Not so the rest; for several mothers bore
To godlike David several sons before.
But since like slaves his bed they did ascend,
No true succession could their seed attend.

1. David ("a man after [God's] own heart," according to I Samuel xiii.14) represents Charles II.

2. "Michal," one of David's wives, represents the childless queen, Catherine of Braganza.

Of all this numerous progeny was none
So beautiful, so brave, as Absalom:[3]
Whether, inspired by some diviner lust,
His father got him with a greater gust,[4]
Or that his conscious destiny made way,
By manly beauty, to imperial sway.
Early in foreign fields he won renown,
With kings and states allied to Israel's crown:[5]
In peace the thoughts of war he could remove,
And seemed as he were only born for love.
Whate'er he did, was done with so much ease,
In him alone 'twas natural to please;
His motions all accompanied with grace;
And paradise was opened in his face.
With secret joy indulgent David viewed
His youthful image in his son renewed:
To all his wishes nothing he denied;
And made the charming Annabel[6] his bride.
What faults he had (for who from faults is free?)
His father could not, or he would not see.
Some warm excesses which the law forbore,
Were cónstrued youth that purged by boiling o'er:
And Amnon's murther,[7] by a specious name,
Was called a just revenge for injured fame.
Thus praised and loved the noble youth remained,
While David, undisturbed, in Sion[8] reigned.
But life can never be sincerely[9] blest;
Heaven punishes the bad, and proves[1] the best.
The Jews,[2] a headstrong, moody, murmuring race,
As ever tried the extent and stretch of grace;
God's pampered people, whom, debauched with ease,
No king could govern, nor no God could please
(Gods they had tried of every shape and size
That god-smiths could produce, or priests devise);[3]
These Adam-wits,[4] too fortunately free,
Began to dream they wanted liberty;
And when no rule, no precedent was found,
Of men by laws less circumscribed and bound,
They led their wild desires to woods and caves,
And thought that all but savages were slaves.
They who, when Saul[5] was dead, without a blow,

3. James Scott, Duke of Monmouth (1649–85).
4. Relish, pleasure.
5. Monmouth had won repute as a soldier fighting for France against Holland and for Holland against France.
6. Anne Scott, Duchess of Buccleuch (pronounced *Bue-cloo*), a beauty and a great heiress.
7. Absalom killed his half-brother Amnon, who had raped Absalom's sister Tamar (II Samuel xiii.28–29). The parallel with Monmouth is vague. He is known to have committed acts of violence in his youth, but certainly not fratricide.
8. London.
9. Wholly.
1. Tests.
2. The English.
3. Dryden recalls the political and religious controversies which, since the Reformation, had divided England and finally caused civil war.
4. Adam rebelled because he felt that he lacked ("wanted") liberty, since he was forbidden to eat the fruit of one tree.
5. Oliver Cromwell. "Ishbosheth": Saul's son; he stands for Richard Cromwell, who succeeded his father as Lord Protector.

Made foolish Ishbosheth the crown forgo;
Who banished David did from Hebron[6] bring,
And with a general shout proclaimed him king:
Those very Jews, who, at their very best,
Their humor[7] more than loyalty expressed,
Now wondered why so long they had obeyed
An idol monarch, which their hands had made;
Thought they might ruin him they could create,
Or melt him to that golden calf,[8] a state.
But these were random bolts;[9] no formed design
Nor interest made the factious crowd to join:
The sober part of Israel, free from stain,
Well knew the value of a peaceful reign;
And, looking backward with a wise affright,
Saw seams of wounds, dishonest[1] to the sight:
In contemplation of whose ugly scars
They cursed the memory of civil wars.
The moderate sort of men, thus qualified,[2]
Inclined the balance to the better side;
And David's mildness managed it so well,
The bad found no occasion to rebel.
But when to sin our biased[3] nature leans,
The careful Devil is still at hand with means;
And providently pimps for ill desires:
The Good Old Cause[4] revived, a plot requires.
Plots, true or false, are necessary things,
To raise up commonwealths and ruin kings.
  The inhabitants of old Jerusalem
Were Jebusites;[5] the town so called from them;
And theirs the native right.
But when the chosen people[6] grew more strong,
The rightful cause at length became the wrong;
And every loss the men of Jebus bore,
They still were thought God's enemies the more.
Thus worn and weakened, well or ill content,
Submit they must to David's government:
Impoverished and deprived of all command,
Their taxes doubled as they lost their land;
And, what was harder yet to flesh and blood,
Their gods disgraced, and burnt like common wood.[7]
This set the heathen priesthood[8] in a flame;
For priests of all religions are the same:
Of whatsoe'er descent their godhead be,

6. Where David reigned over Judah after the death of Saul and before he became king of Israel (II Samuel i–v). Charles had been crowned in Scotland in 1651.
7. Caprice.
8. The image worshiped by the Children of Israel during the period that Moses spent on Mt. Sinai, receiving the law from God. "A state": a republic.
9. Shots.
1. Disgraceful.
2. Assuaged.
3. Inclined. Cf. *Mac Flecknoe,* line 189 and note.
4. The Commonwealth. Dryden stigmatizes the Whigs by associating them with subversion.
5. Roman Catholics. The original name of Jerusalem (here, London) was Jebus.
6. Protestants.
7. Such oppressive laws against Roman Catholics date from the time of Elizabeth I.
8. Roman Catholic clergy.

Stock, stone, or other homely pedigree,
In his defense his servants are as bold,
As if he had been born of beaten gold.
The Jewish rabbins,[9] though their enemies,
In this conclude them honest men and wise:
For 'twas their duty, all the learned think,
To espouse his cause, by whom they eat and drink.
From hence began that Plot, the nation's curse,
Bad in itself, but represented worse;
Raised in extremes, and in extremes decried;
With oaths affirmed, with dying vows denied;
Not weighed or winnowed by the multitude;
But swallowed in the mass, unchewed and crude.
Some truth there was, but dashed[1] and brewed with lies,
To please the fools, and puzzle all the wise.
Succeeding times did equal folly call,
Believing nothing, or believing all.
The Egyptian[2] rites the Jebusites embraced,
Where gods were recommended by their taste.
Such savory deities must needs be good,
As served at once for worship and for food.
By force they could not introduce these gods,
For ten to one in former days was odds;
So fraud was used (the sacrificer's trade):
Fools are more hard to conquer than persuade.
Their busy teachers mingled with the Jews,
And raked for converts even the court and stews:[3]
Which Hebrew priests the more unkindly took,
Because the fleece accompanies the flock.[4]
Some thought they God's anointed [4a] meant to slay
By guns, invented since full many a day:
Our author swears it not; but who can know
How far the Devil and Jebusites may go?
This Plot, which failed for want of common sense,
Had yet a deep and dangerous consequence:
For, as when raging fevers boil the blood,
The standing lake soon floats into a flood,
And every hostile humor, which before
Slept quiet in its channels, bubbles o'er;
So several factions from this first ferment
Work up to foam, and threat the government.
Some by their friends, more by themselves thought wise,
Opposed the power to which they could not rise.
Some had in courts been great, and thrown from thence,
Like fiends were hardened in impenitence;
Some, by their monarch's fatal mercy, grown
From pardoned rebels kinsmen to the throne,
Were raised in power and public office high;

9. Anglican clergy.
1. Adulterated.
2. French, therefore Catholic. In the next line Dryden sneers at the doctrine of transubstantiation.
3. Brothels.
4. Dryden charges that the Anglican clergy ("Hebrew priests") resented proselytizing by Catholics chiefly because they stood to lose their tithes ("fleece").
4a. The King.

Strong bands, if bands ungrateful men could tie.
Of these the false Achitophel[5] was first;
A name to all succeeding ages cursed:
For close designs, and crooked counsels fit;
Sagacious, bold, and turbulent of wit;[6]
Restless, unfixed in principles and place;
In power unpleased, impatient of disgrace:
A fiery soul, which, working out its way,
Fretted the pygmy body to decay,
And o'er-informed the tenement of clay.[7]
A daring pilot in extremity;
Pleased with the danger, when the waves went high,
He sought the storms; but, for a calm unfit,
Would steer too nigh the sands, to boast his wit.
Great wits[8] are sure to madness near allied,
And thin partitions do their bounds divide;
Else why should he, with wealth and honor blest,
Refuse his age the needful hours of rest?
Punish a body which he could not please;
Bankrupt of life, yet prodigal of ease?
And all to leave what with his toil he won,
To that unfeathered two-legged thing,[9] a son;
Got, while his soul did huddled[1] notions try;
And born a shapeless lump, like anarchy.
In friendship false, implacable in hate,
Resolved to ruin or to rule the state.
To compass this the triple bond[2] he broke,
The pillars of the public safety shook,
And fitted Israel for a foreign yoke;
Then seized with fear, yet still affecting fame,
Usurped a patriot's all-atoning name.
So easy still it proves in factious times,
With public zeal to cancel private crimes.
How safe is treason, and how sacred ill,
Where none can sin against the people's will!
Where crowds can wink, and no offense be known,
Since in another's guilt they find their own!
Yet fame deserved, no enemy can grudge;
The statesman we abhor, but praise the judge.
In Israel's courts ne'er sat an Abbethdin[3]

5. Anthony Ashley Cooper, 1st Earl of Shaftesbury (1621–83). He had served in the Parliamentary army and been a member of Cromwell's Council of State. He later helped bring back Charles, and in 1670 was made a member of the notorious Cabal Ministry, which formed an alliance with Louis XIV in which England betrayed her ally, Holland, and joined France in war against that country. In 1672 he became Lord Chancellor, but with the dissolution of the Cabal in 1673 he was removed from office. Lines 146–49 apply perfectly to him.

6. Unruly imagination.

7. The soul is thought of as the animating principle, the force that puts the body in motion. Shaftesbury's body seemed too small to house his fiery, energetic soul.

8. Men of genius. That genius and madness are akin is a very old idea.

9. Cf. Plato's definition of man: "a featherless biped."

1. Confused, hurried.

2. The Triple Alliance of England, Sweden, and Holland against France, 1668. Shaftesbury helped to bring about the war against Holland in 1672.

3. The chief of the seventy elders who composed the Jewish supreme court. The allusion is to Shaftesbury's serving as Lord Chancellor in 1672–73. Dry-

With more discerning eyes, or hands more clean;
Unbribed, unsought, the wretched to redress;
Swift of dispatch, and easy of access.
Oh, had he been content to serve the crown,
With virtues only proper to the gown;
Or had the rankness of the soil been freed
From cockle, that oppressed the noble seed;
David for him his tuneful harp had strung,
And Heaven had wanted one immortal song.[4]
But wild Ambition loves to slide, not stand,
And Fortune's ice prefers to Virtue's land.
Achitophel, grown weary to possess
A lawful fame, and lazy happiness,
Disdained the golden fruit to gather free,
And lent the crowd his arm to shake the tree.
Now, manifest of[5] crimes contrived long since,
He stood at bold defiance with his prince;
Held up the buckler of the people's cause
Against the crown, and skulked behind the laws.
The wished occasion of the Plot he takes;
Some circumstances finds, but more he makes.
By buzzing emissaries fills the ears
Of listening crowds with jealousies[6] and fears
Of arbitrary counsels brought to light,
And proves the king himself a Jebusite.
Weak arguments! which yet he knew full well
Were strong with people easy to rebel.
For, governed by the moon, the giddy Jews
Tread the same track when she the prime renews;[7]
And once in twenty years, their scribes record,
By natural instinct they change their lord.
Achitophel still wants a chief, and none
Was found so fit as warlike Absalom:
Not that he wished his greatness to create
(For politicians neither love nor hate),
But, for he knew his title not allowed,
Would keep him still depending on the crowd,
That kingly power, thus ebbing out, might be
Drawn to the dregs of a democracy.[8]
Him he attempts with studied arts to please,
And sheds his venom in such words as these:
"Auspicious prince, at whose nativity
Some royal planet[9] ruled the southern sky;
Thy longing country's darling and desire;

den's praise of Shaftesbury's integrity in this office, by suggesting a balanced judgment, makes his condemnation of the statesman more effective than it might otherwise have been.

4. I.e., David would have had occasion to write one less song of praise to Heaven. The reference may be to II Samuel xxii or to Psalm iv.

5. Detected in.

6. Suspicions.

7. The moon "renews her prime" when her several phases recur on the same day of the solar calendar—i.e., complete a cycle—as happens approximately every twenty years. The crisis between Charles I and Parliament began to grow acute about 1640; Charles II returned in 1660; it is now 1680 and a full cycle has been completed.

8. To Dryden, "democracy" meant popular government. The "dregs of a democracy" would be mob rule.

9. A planet whose influence destines him to kingship.

Their cloudy pillar and their guardian fire:[1]
Their second Moses, whose extended wand
Divides the seas, and shows the promised land;
Whose dawning day in every distant age
Has exercised the sacred prophet's rage:
The people's prayer, the glad diviners' theme,
The young men's vision, and the old men's dream![2]
Thee, savior, thee, the nation's vows[3] confess,
And, never satisfied with seeing, bless:
Swift unbespoken pomps thy steps proclaim,
And stammering babes are taught to lisp thy name.
How long wilt thou the general joy detain,
Starve and defraud the people of thy reign?
Content ingloriously to pass thy days
Like one of Virtue's fools that feeds on praise;
Till thy fresh glories, which now shine so bright,
Grow stale and tarnish with our daily sight.
Believe me, royal youth, thy fruit must be
Or gathered ripe, or rot upon the tree.
Heaven has to all allotted, soon or late,
Some lucky revolution of their fate;
Whose motions if we watch and guide with skill
(For human good depends on human will),
Our Fortune rolls as from a smooth descent,
And from the first impression takes the bent;
But, if unseized, she glides away like wind,
And leaves repenting Folly far behind.
Now, now she meets you with a glorious prize,
And spreads her locks before her as she flies.[4]
Had thus old David, from whose loins you spring,
Not dared, when Fortune called him, to be king,
At Gath[5] an exile he might still remain,
And heaven's anointing[6] oil had been in vain.
Let his successful youth your hopes engage;
But shun the example of declining age;
Behold him setting in his western skies,
The shadows lengthening as the vapors rise.
He is not now, as when on Jordan's sand[7]
The joyful people thronged to see him land,
Covering the beach, and blackening all the strand;
But, like the Prince of Angels, from his height
Comes tumbling downward with diminished light;[8]

1. After their exodus from Egypt under the leadership of Moses, whose "extended wand" separated the waters of the Red Sea so that they crossed over on dry land, the Israelites were led in their forty-year wandering in the wilderness by a pillar of cloud by day and a pillar of fire by night. See Exodus xiii–xiv.
2. Cf. Joel ii.28.
3. Solemn promises of fidelity.
4. Achitophel gives to Fortune the traditional attributes of the allegorical personification of Opportunity: bald except for a forelock, she can be seized only as she approaches.
5. Brussels, where Charles spent his last years in exile. David took refuge from Saul in Gath (I Samuel xxvii.4).
6. After God rejected Saul, He sent Samuel to anoint the boy David, as a token that he should finally come to the throne (I Samuel xvi.1–13).
7. The seashore at Dover, where Charles landed (May 25, 1660).
8. Cf. the fall of Satan in *Paradise Lost,* which dims the brightness of the archangel. The choice of the undignified word "tumbling" is deliberate.

Betrayed by one poor plot to public scorn
(Our only blessing since his cursed return),
Those heaps of people which one sheaf did bind,
Blown off and scattered by a puff of wind.
What strength can he to your designs oppose,
Naked of friends, and round beset with foes?
If Pharaoh's[9] doubtful succor he should use,
A foreign aid would more incense the Jews:
Proud Egypt would dissembled friendship bring;
Foment the war, but not support the king:
Nor would the royal party e'er unite
With Pharaoh's arms to assist the Jebusite;
Or if they should, their interest soon would break,
And with such odious aid make David weak.
All sorts of men by my successful arts,
Abhorring kings, estrange their altered hearts
From David's rule: and 'tis the general cry,
'Religion, commonwealth, and liberty.'[1]
If you, as champion of the public good,
Add to their arms a chief of royal blood,
What may not Israel hope, and what applause
Might such a general gain by such a cause?
Not barren praise alone, that gaudy flower
Fair only to the sight, but solid power;
And nobler is a limited command,
Given by the love of all your native land,
Than a successive title,[2] long and dark,
Drawn from the moldy rolls of Noah's ark."
   What cannot praise effect in mighty minds,
When flattery soothes, and when ambition blinds!
Desire of power, on earth a vicious weed,
Yet, sprung from high, is of celestial seed:
In God 'tis glory; and when men aspire,
'Tis but a spark too much of heavenly fire.
The ambitious youth, too covetous of fame,
Too full of angels' metal[3] in his frame,
Unwarily was led from virtue's ways,
Made drunk with honor, and debauched with praise.
Half loath, and half consenting to the ill
(For loyal blood within him struggled still),
He thus replied: "And what pretense have I
To take up arms for public liberty?
My father governs with unquestioned right;
The faith's defender, and mankind's delight,
Good, gracious, just, observant of the laws:
And heaven by wonders has espoused his cause.
Whom has he wronged in all his peaceful reign?
Who sues for justice to his throne in vain?
What millions has he pardoned of his foes,

9. Louis XIV of France.
1. Cf. line 82 and note.
2. A title to the crown based on succession.
3. An alternative spelling of *mettle,* (i.e., spirit). But a pun on "metal" is intended, as is obvious from the pun "angel" (a purely intellectual being and a coin). Ambition caused the revolt of the angels in heaven.

Whom just revenge did to his wrath expose?
Mild, easy, humble, studious of our good,
Inclined to mercy, and averse from blood;
If mildness ill with stubborn Israel suit,
His crime is God's beloved attribute.
What could he gain, his people to betray,
Or change his right for arbitrary sway?
Let haughty Pharaoh curse with such a reign
His fruitful Nile, and yoke a servile train.
If David's rule Jerusalem displease,
The Dog Star[4] heats their brains to this disease.
Why then should I, encouraging the bad,
Turn rebel and run popularly mad?
Were he a tyrant, who, by lawless might
Oppressed the Jews, and raised the Jebusite,
Well might I mourn; but nature's holy bands
Would curb my spirits and restrain my hands:
The people might assert[5] their liberty,
But what was right in them were crime in me.
His favor leaves me nothing to require,
Prevents my wishes, and outruns desire.
What more can I expect while David lives?
All but his kingly diadem he gives:
And that"— But there he paused; then sighing, said—
"Is justly destined for a worthier head.
For when my father from his toils shall rest
And late augment the number of the blest,
His lawful issue shall the throne ascend,
Or the collateral line,[6] where that shall end.
His brother, though oppressed with vulgar spite,
Yet dauntless, and secure of native right,
Of every royal virtue stands possessed;
Still dear to all the bravest and the best.
His courage foes, his friends his truth proclaim;
His loyalty the king, the world his fame.
His mercy even the offending crowd will find,
For sure he comes of a forgiving kind.[7]
Why should I then repine at heaven's decree,
Which gives me no pretense to royalty?
Yet O that fate, propitiously inclined,
Had raised my birth, or had debased my mind;
To my large soul not all her treasure lent,
And then betrayed it to a mean descent!
I find, I find my mounting spirits bold,
And David's part disdains my mother's mold.
Why am I scanted by a niggard birth?[8]

4. Sirius, which in midsummer rises and sets with the sun and is thus associated with the maddening heat of the "dog days."
5. Claim.
6. In the event of Charles's dying without legitimate issue, the throne would constitutionally pass to his brother James, or his descendants, the "collateral line."
7. Race, in the sense of family.
8. I.e., why am I limited by a sordid birth?

My soul disclaims the kindred of her earth;
And, made for empire, whispers me within,
'Desire of greatness is a godlike sin.' "
Him staggering so when hell's dire agent found,[9]
While fainting Virtue scarce maintained her ground,
He pours fresh forces in, and thus replies:
"The eternal God, supremely good and wise,
Imparts not these prodigious gifts in vain:
What wonders are reserved to bless your reign!
Against your will, your arguments have shown,
Such virtue's only given to guide a throne.
Not that your father's mildness I contemn,
But manly force becomes the diadem.
'Tis true he grants the people all they crave;
And more, perhaps, than subjects ought to have:
For lavish grants suppose a monarch tame,
And more his goodness than his wit[1] proclaim.
But when should people strive their bonds to break,
If not when kings are negligent or weak?
Let him give on till he can give no more,
The thrifty Sanhedrin[2] shall keep him poor;
And every shekel which he can receive,
Shall cost a limb of his prerogative.[3]
To ply him with new plots shall be my care;
Or plunge him deep in some expensive war;
Which when his treasure can no more supply,
He must, with the remains of kingship, buy.
His faithful friends our jealousies and fears
Call Jebusites, and Pharaoh's pensioners;
Whom when our fury from his aid has torn,
He shall be naked left to public scorn.
The next successor, whom I fear and hate,
My arts have made obnoxious to the state;
Turned all his virtues to his overthrow,
And gained our elders[4] to pronounce a foe.
His right, for sums of necessary gold,
Shall first be pawned, and afterward be sold;
Till time shall ever-wanting David draw,
To pass your doubtful title into law:
If not, the people have a right supreme
To make their kings; for kings are made for them.
All empire is no more than power in trust,
Which, when resumed, can be no longer just.
Succession, for the general good designed,
In its own wrong a nation cannot bind;
If altering that the people can relieve,
Better one suffer than a nation grieve.

9. Observe the Miltonic inversion, which helps to maintain the epic tone.

1. Intelligence.

2. The highest judicial counsel of the Jews; here, Parliament.

3. The Whigs hoped to limit the special privileges of the Crown (the royal "prerogative") by refusing to vote money to Charles. He circumvented them by living on French subsidies and refusing to summon Parliament.

4. The chief magistrates and rulers of the Jews. Shaftesbury had won over ("gained") country gentlemen and nobles to his hostile view of James.

The Jews well know their power: ere Saul they chose,[5]
God was their king, and God they durst depose.
Urge now your piety,[6] your filial name,
A father's right, and fear of future fame;
The public good, that universal call,
To which even heaven submitted, answers all.
Nor let his love enchant your generous mind;
'Tis Nature's trick to propagate her kind.
Our fond begetters, who would never die,
Love but themselves in their posterity.
Or let his kindness by the effects be tried,
Or let him lay his vain pretense aside.
God said he loved your father; could he bring
A better proof than to anoint him king?
It surely showed he loved the shepherd well,
Who gave so fair a flock as Israel.
Would David have you thought his darling son?
What means he then, to alienate[7] the crown?
The name of godly he may blush to bear:
'Tis after God's own heart[8] to cheat his heir.
He to his brother gives supreme command;
To you a legacy of barren land,[8a]
Perhaps the old harp, on which he thrums his lays,
Or some dull Hebrew ballad in your praise.
Then the next heir, a prince severe and wise,
Already looks on you with jealous eyes;
Sees through the thin disguises of your arts,
And marks your progress in the people's hearts.
Though now his mighty soul its grief contains,
He meditates revenge who least complains;
And, like a lion, slumbering in the way,
Or sleep dissembling, while he waits his prey,
His fearless foes within his distance draws,
Constrains his roaring, and contracts his paws;
Till at the last, his time for fury found,
He shoots with sudden vengeance from the ground;
The prostrate vulgar[9] passes o'er and spares,
But with a lordly rage his hunters tears.
Your case no tame expedients will afford:
Resolve on death, or conquest by the sword,
Which for no less a stake than life you draw;
And self-defense is nature's eldest law.
Leave the warm people no considering time;
For then rebellion may be thought a crime.
Prevail yourself of what occasion gives,
But try your title while your father lives;
And that your arms may have a fair pretense,[1]

5. Before Saul, the first king of Israel, came to the throne, the Jews were governed by judges. Similarly Oliver Cromwell ("Saul") as Lord Protector took over the reins of government, after he had dissolved the Rump Parliament in 1653.
6. Dutifulness to a parent.
7. In law, to convey the title to property to another person.
8. An irony: cf. line 7, note.
8a. James was given the title of generalissimo in 1678. In 1679 Monmouth was banished and withdrew to Holland.
9. Common people.
1. Pretext.

Proclaim you take them in the king's defense;
Whose sacred life each minute would expose
To plots, from seeming friends, and secret foes.
And who can sound the depth of David's soul?
Perhaps his fear his kindness may control.
He fears his brother, though he loves his son,
For plighted vows too late to be undone.
If so, by force he wishes to be gained,
Like women's lechery, to seem constrained.[2]
Doubt not; but when he most affects the frown,
Commit a pleasing rape upon the crown.
Secure his person to secure your cause:
They who possess the prince, possess the laws."
He said, and this advice above the rest
With Absalom's mild nature suited best:
Unblamed of life (ambition set aside),
Not stained with cruelty, nor puffed with pride,
How happy had he been, if destiny
Had higher placed his birth, or not so high!
His kingly virtues might have claimed a throne,
And blest all other countries but his own.
But charming greatness since so few refuse,
'Tis juster to lament him than accuse.
Strong were his hopes a rival to remove,
With blandishments to gain the public love;
To head the faction while their zeal was hot,
And popularly prosecute the Plot.
To further this, Achitophel unites
The malcontents of all the Israelites;
Whose differing parties he could wisely join,
For several ends, to serve the same design:
The best (and of the princes some were such),
Who thought the power of monarchy too much;
Mistaken men, and patriots in their hearts;
Not wicked, but seduced by impious arts.
By these the springs of property were bent,
And wound so high, they cracked the government.
The next for interest sought to embroil the state,
To sell their duty at a dearer rate;
And make their Jewish markets of the throne,
Pretending public good, to serve their own.
Others thought kings an useless heavy load,
Who cost too much, and did too little good.
These were for laying honest David by,
On principles of pure good husbandry.[3]
With them joined all the haranguers of the throng,
That thought to get preferment by the tongue.
Who follow next, a double danger bring,
Not only hating David, but the king:
The Solymaean rout,[4] well-versed of old
In godly faction, and in treason bold;

2. Forced.
3. Economy.
4. I.e., London rabble. Solyma was a name for Jerusalem.

Cowering and quaking at a conqueror's sword,
But lofty to a lawful prince restored;
Saw with disdain an ethnic[5] plot begun,
And scorned by Jebusites to be outdone.
Hot Levites[6] headed these; who, pulled before
From the ark, which in the Judges' days they bore,
Resumed their cant, and with a zealous cry
Pursued their old beloved theocracy:
Where Sanhedrin and priest enslaved the nation,
And justified their spoils by inspiration:[7]
For who so fit for reign as Aaron's race,[8]
If once dominion they could found in grace?
These led the pack; though not of surest scent,
Yet deepest-mouthed[9] against the government.
A numerous host of dreaming saints[1] succeed,
Of the true old enthusiastic breed:
'Gainst form and order they their power employ,
Nothing to build, and all things to destroy.
But far more numerous was the herd of such,
Who think too little, and who talk too much.
These out of mere instinct, they knew not why,
Adored their fathers' God and property;
And, by the same blind benefit of fate,
The Devil and the Jebusite did hate:
Born to be saved, even in their own despite,
Because they could not help believing right.
Such were the tools; but a whole Hydra more
Remains, of sprouting heads too long to score.
Some of their chiefs were princes of the land:
In the first rank of these did Zimri[2] stand;
A man so various, that he seemed to be
Not one, but all mankind's epitome:
Stiff in opinions, always in the wrong;

5. Gentile; here, Roman Catholic.

6. I.e., Presbyterian clergymen. The tribe of Levi, assigned to duties in the tabernacle, carried the ark of the covenant during the forty-year sojourn in the wilderness (Numbers iv). Under the Commonwealth ("in the Judges' days") Presbyterianism became the state religion, and its clergy therefore "bore the ark." The Act of Uniformity (1662) forced the Presbyterian clergy out of their livings: in short, before the Popish Plot, they had been "pulled from the ark." They are represented here as joining the Whigs in the hope of restoring the Commonwealth, "their old beloved theocracy."

7. Observe in these lines the cluster of disparaging words: "cant," "zealous," "inspiration." Dryden shared Samuel Butler's contempt for the irrationality of Dissenters.

8. Priests had to be descendants of Aaron (Exodus xxviii.1; Numbers xviii.7).

9. Loudest. The phrase is applied to hunting dogs. "Pack" and "scent" sustain the image.

1. A term used by certain Dissenters for those elected to salvation. The extreme fanaticism of the "saints" and their claims to inspiration are characterized as a form of religious madness ("enthusiastic").

2. George Villiers, 2nd Duke of Buckingham (1628–87), wealthy, brilliant, dissolute, unstable. He had been an influential member of the Cabal, but after 1673 had joined Shaftesbury in opposition to the Court party. This is the least political of the satirical portraits in the poem. Buckingham had been the chief author of *The Rehearsal* (1671), the play which satirized the heroic play and ridiculed Dryden in the character of Mr. Bayes. Politics gave Dryden an opportunity to retaliate. He comments on this portrait in his *Discourse Concerning the Original and Progress of Satire.* Dryden had two Biblical Zimris in mind: the Zimri destroyed for his lustfulness and blasphemy (Numbers xxv) and the conspirator and regicide of I Kings xvi.8–20 and II Kings ix.31.

Was everything by starts, and nothing long;
But, in the course of one revolving moon,
Was chymist,[3] fiddler, statesman, and buffoon:
Then all for women, painting, rhyming, drinking,
Besides ten thousand freaks that died in thinking.
Blest madman, who could every hour employ,
With something new to wish, or to enjoy!
Railing[4] and praising were his usual themes;
And both (to show his judgment) in extremes:
So over-violent, or over-civil,
That every man, with him, was God or Devil.
In squandering wealth was his peculiar art:
Nothing went unrewarded but desert.
Beggared by fools, whom still he found[5] too late,
He had his jest, and they had his estate.
He laughed himself from court; then sought relief
By forming parties, but could ne'er be chief;
For, spite of him, the weight of business fell
On Absalom and wise Achitophel:
Thus, wicked but in will, of means bereft,
He left not faction, but of that was left.
　Titles and names 'twere tedious to rehearse
Of lords, below the dignity of verse.
Wits, warriors, Commonwealth's men, were the best;
Kind husbands, and mere nobles, all the rest.
And therefore, in the name of dullness, be
The well-hung Balaam and cold Caleb, free;
And canting Nadab[6] let oblivion damn,
Who made new porridge for the paschal lamb.
Let friendship's holy band some names assure;
Some their own worth, and some let scorn secure.
Nor shall the rascal rabble here have place,
Whom kings no titles gave, and God no grace:
Not bull-faced Jonas,[7] who could statutes draw
To mean rebellion, and make treason law.
But he, though bad, is followed by a worse,
The wretch who heaven's anointed dared to curse:
Shimei,[8] whose youth did early promise bring
Of zeal to God and hatred to his king,

3. Chemist.
4. Reviling, abusing.
5. Found out; "still": constantly.
6. The identities of Balaam, Caleb, and Nadab have not been certainly established, although various Whig nobles have been suggested. For Balaam see Numbers xxii–xxiv; for Caleb, Numbers xiii–xiv; for Nadab, Leviticus x.1–2. "Well-hung" may mean "fluent of speech" or "sexually potent" or both; "cold" would contrast with the second meaning of "well-hung." "Canting" points to a Nonconformist, as does the obscure line 576, for Dissenters referred to the Book of Common Prayer contemptuously as "porridge," a hodgepodge, unsubstantial stuff. The "paschal lamb," the lamb slain at the Passover, is Christ.
7. Sir William Jones, Attorney General, had been largely responsible for the passage of the first Exclusion Bill by the House of Commons. He prosecuted the accused in the Popish Plot.
8. Shimei cursed and stoned David when he fled into the wilderness during Absalom's revolt (II Samuel xvi.5–14); his name is used here for one of the two sheriffs of London, Slingsby Bethel, a Whig, former republican, and virulent enemy of Charles. He packed juries with Whigs and so secured the acquittal of enemies of the court, among them Shaftesbury himself.

Did wisely from expensive sins refrain,
And never broke the Sabbath, but for gain;
Nor ever was he known an oath to vent,
Or curse, unless against the government.
Thus heaping wealth, by the most ready way
Among the Jews, which was to cheat and pray,
The city, to reward his pious hate
Against his master, chose him magistrate.
His hand a vare[9] of justice did uphold;
His neck was loaded with a chain of gold.
During his office, treason was no crime;
The sons of Belial[1] had a glorious time;
For Shimei, though not prodigal of pelf,
Yet loved his wicked neighbor as himself.
When two or three were gathered to declaim
Against the monarch of Jerusalem,
Shimei was always in the midst of them;
And if they cursed the king when he was by,
Would rather curse than break good company.
If any durst his factious friends accuse,
He packed a jury of dissenting Jews;
Whose fellow-feeling in the godly cause
Would free the suffering saint from human laws.
For laws are only made to punish those
Who serve the king, and to protect his foes.
If any leisure time he had from power
(Because 'tis sin to misemploy an hour),
His business was, by writing, to persuade
That kings were useless, and a clog to trade;
And, that his noble style he might refine,
No Rechabite[2] more shunned the fumes of wine.
Chaste were his cellars, and his shrieval board[3]
The grossness of a city feast abhorred:
His cooks, with long disuse, their trade forgot;
Cool was his kitchen, though his brains were hot.
Such frugal virtue malice may accuse,
But sure 'twas necessary to the Jews:
For towns once burnt[4] such magistrates require
As dare not tempt God's providence by fire.
With spiritual food he fed his servants well,
But free from flesh that made the Jews rebel;
And Moses' laws he held in more account,
For forty days of fasting in the mount.[5]
To speak the rest, who better are forgot,
Would tire a well-breathed witness of the Plot.
Yet, Corah,[6] thou shalt from oblivion pass:

9. Staff.

1. Sons of wickedness. Cf. Milton, *Paradise Lost* I.490–505. Dryden probably intended a pun on Balliol, the Oxford college in which leading Whigs stayed during the brief and fateful meeting of Parliament at Oxford in 1681.

2. An austere Jewish sect that drank no wine (Jeremiah xxxv.2–19).

3. Sheriff's dinner table.

4. London burned in 1666.

5. Mt. Sinai, where, during a fast of forty days, Moses received the law (Exodus xxxiv.28).

6. Or Korah, a rebellious Levite, swallowed up by the earth because of his

Erect thyself, thou monumental brass,
High as the serpent of thy metal made,[7]
While nations stand secure beneath thy shade.
What though his birth were base, yet comets rise
From earthy vapors, ere they shine in skies.
Prodigious actions may as well be done
By weaver's issue,[8] as by prince's son.
This arch-attestor for the public good
By that one deed ennobles all his blood.
Who ever asked the witnesses' high race
Whose oath with martyrdom did Stephen grace?[9]
Ours was a Levite, and as times went then,
His tribe were God Almighty's gentlemen.
Sunk were his eyes, his voice was harsh and loud,
Sure signs he neither choleric[1] was nor proud:
His long chin proved his wit; his saintlike grace
A church vermilion, and a Moses' face.[2]
His memory, miraculously great,
Could plots, exceeding man's belief, repeat;
Which therefore cannot be accounted lies,
For human wit could never such devise.
Some future truths are mingled in his book;
But where the witness failed, the prophet spoke:
Some things like visionary flights appear;
The spirit caught him up, the Lord knows where,
And gave him his rabbinical degree,
Unknown to foreign university.[3]
His judgment yet his memory did excel;
Which pieced his wondrous evidence so well,
And suited to the temper of the times,
Then groaning under Jebusitic crimes.
Let Israel's foes suspect his heavenly call,
And rashly judge his writ apocryphal;[4]
Our laws for such affronts have forfeits made:
He takes his life, who takes away his trade.
Were I myself in witness Corah's place,
The wretch who did me such a dire disgrace
Should whet my memory, though once forgot,
To make him an appendix of my plot.
His zeal to heaven made him his prince despise,
And load his person with indignities;
But zeal peculiar privilege affords,

crimes (Numbers xvi). Corah is Titus Oates, the self-appointed, perjured, and "well-breathed" (long-winded) witness of the Plot.

7. Moses erected a brazen serpent to heal the Jews bitten by fiery serpents (Numbers xxi.4–9). "Brass" also means "impudence" or "shamelessness."

8. Oates's father, a clergyman, belonged to an obscure family of ribbon weavers.

9. The first Christian martyr, accused by false witnesses (Acts vi–vii).

1. Prone to anger.

2. Moses' face shone when he came down from Mt. Sinai with the tables of the law (Exodus xxxiv.29–30). Oates's face suggests high living, not spiritual illumination.

3. Oates falsely claimed to be a Doctor of Divinity in the University of Salamanca.

4. Not inspired, and hence excluded from Holy Writ.

Indulging latitude to deeds and words;
And Corah might for Agag's murder[5] call,
In terms as coarse as Samuel used to Saul.
What others in his evidence did join
(The best that could be had for love or coin),
In Corah's own predicament will fall;
For *witness* is a common name to all.
  Surrounded thus with friends of every sort,
Deluded Absalom forsakes the court:
Impatient of high hopes, urged with renown,
And fired with near possession of a crown.
The admiring crowd are dazzled with surprise,
And on his goodly person feed their eyes:
His joy concealed, he sets himself to show,
On each side bowing popularly[6] low;
His looks, his gestures, and his words he frames,
And with familiar ease repeats their names.
Thus formed by nature, furnished out with arts,
He glides unfelt into their secret hearts.
Then, with a kind compassionating look,
And sighs, bespeaking pity ere he spoke,
Few words he said; but easy those and fit,
More slow than Hybla-drops,[7] and far more sweet.
  "I mourn, my countrymen, your lost estate;
Though far unable to prevent your fate:
Behold a banished man, for your dear cause
Exposed a prey to arbitrary laws!
Yet oh! that I alone could be undone,
Cut off from empire, and no more a son!
Now all your liberties a spoil are made,
Egypt and Tyrus[8] intercept your trade,
And Jebusites your sacred rites invade.
My father, whom with reverence yet I name,
Charmed into ease, is careless of his fame;
And, bribed with petty sums of foreign gold,
Is grown in Bathsheba's[9] embraces old;
Exalts his enemies, his friends destroys;
And all his power against himself employs.
He gives, and let him give, my right away;
But why should he his own, and yours betray?
He only, he can make the nation bleed,
And he alone from my revenge is freed.
Take then my tears (with that he wiped his eyes),

5. Agag is probably one of the five Catholic peers executed for the Popish Plot in 1680, most likely Lord Stafford, against whom Oates fabricated testimony; almost certainly not, as is usually suggested, Sir Edmund Berry Godfrey (cf. title note). For "Agag's murder" and Samuel's coarse terms to Saul, see I Samuel xv.

6. "So as to please the crowd" (Johnson's *Dictionary*).

7. The famous honey of Hybla in Sicily.

8. France and Holland.

9. With whom David committed adultery (II Samuel xi); here, Charles II's French mistress, Louise de Keroualle, Duchess of Portsmouth.

'Tis all the aid my present power supplies:
No court-informer can these arms accuse;
These arms may sons against their fathers use:
And 'tis my wish, the next successor's reign
May make no other Israelite complain."
  Youth, beauty, graceful action seldom fail;
But common interest always will prevail;
And pity never ceases to be shown
To him who makes the people's wrongs his own.
The crowd (that still believe their kings oppress),
With lifted hands their young Messiah bless:
Who now begins his progress to ordain
With chariots, horsemen, and a numerous train;
From east to west his glories he displays,[1]
And, like the sun, the promised land surveys.
Fame runs before him as the morning star,
And shouts of joy salute him from afar:
Each house receives him as a guardian god,
And consecrates the place of his abode:
But hospitable treats did most commend
Wise Issachar,[2] his wealthy western friend.
This moving court, that caught the people's eyes,
And seemed but pomp, did other ends disguise:
Achitophel had formed it, with intent
To sound the depths, and fathom where it went,
The people's hearts; distinguish friends from foes,
And try their strength, before they came to blows.
Yet all was colored with a smooth pretense
Of specious love, and duty to their prince.
Religion, and redress of grievances,
Two names that always cheat and always please,
Are often urged; and good King David's life
Endangered by a brother and a wife.[3]
Thus, in a pageant show, a plot is made,
And peace itself is war in masquerade.
O foolish Israel! never warned by ill,
Still the same bait, and circumvented still!
Did ever men forsake their present ease,
In midst of health imagine a disease;
Take pains contingent mischiefs to foresee,
Make heirs for monarchs, and for God decree?
What shall we think! [4] Can people give away
Both for themselves and sons, their native sway?
Then they are left defenseless to the sword
Of each unbounded, arbitrary lord:

1. In 1680 Monmouth made a progress through the west of England, seeking popular support for his cause.
2. Thomas Thynne of Longleat. He entertained Monmouth on his journey in the west. "Wise" is, of course, ironic.
3. Titus Oates had sworn that both James, Duke of York, and the Queen were involved in a plot to poison Charles II.
4. In the passage that follows, Dryden states his political philosophy. He bases the royal authority on a covenant entered into by the governor and the governed.

And laws are vain, by which we right enjoy,
If kings unquestioned can those laws destroy.
Yet if the crowd be judge of fit and just,
And kings are only officers in trust,
Then this resuming covenant was declared
When kings were made, or is forever barred.
If those who gave the scepter could not tie
By their own deed their own posterity,
How then could Adam bind his future race?
How could his forfeit on mankind take place?
Or how could heavenly justice damn us all,
Who ne'er consented to our father's fall?
Then kings are slaves to those whom they command,
And tenants to their people's pleasure stand.
Add, that the power for property allowed
Is mischievously seated in the crowd;
For who can be secure of private right,
If sovereign sway may be dissolved by might?
Nor is the people's judgment always true:
The most may err as grossly as the few;
And faultless kings run down, by common cry,
For vice, oppression, and for tyranny.
What standard is there in a fickle rout,
Which, flowing to the mark,[5] runs faster out?
Nor only crowds, but Sanhedrins may be
Infected with this public lunacy,
And share the madness of rebellious times,
To murder monarchs for imagined crimes.[6]
If they may give and take whene'er they please,
Not kings alone (the Godhead's images),
But government itself at length must fall
To nature's state, where all have right to all.
Yet, grant our lords the people kings can make,
What prudent men a settled throne would shake?
For whatsoe'er their sufferings were before,
That change they covet makes them suffer more.
All other errors but disturb a state,
But innovation is the blow of fate.
If ancient fabrics nod, and threat to fall,
To patch the flaws, and buttress up the wall,
Thus far 'tis duty; but here fix the mark;
For all beyond it is to touch our ark.[7]
To change foundations, cast the frame anew,
Is work for rebels, who base ends pursue,
At once divine and human laws control,
And mend the parts by ruin of the whole.

5. An obscure couplet, rare in Dryden. George R. Noyes paraphrases it thus: "The fickle crowd is apparently compared to water, which, after rising to the *mark,* or boundary, it was intended to reach, overflows all the faster."

6. An allusion to the execution of Charles I.

7. Uzzah was struck dead because he sacrilegiously touched the Ark of the Covenant. II Samuel vi. 6–7.

The tampering world is subject to this curse,
To physic their disease into a worse.
  Now what relief can righteous David bring?
How fatal 'tis to be too good a king!
Friends he has few, so high the madness grows:
Who dare be such, must be the people's foes:
Yet some there were, even in the worst of days;
Some let me name, and naming is to praise.
  In this short file Barzillai [8] first appears;
Barzillai, crowned with honor and with years:
Long since, the rising rebels he withstood
In regions waste, beyond the Jordan's flood:
Unfortunately brave to buoy the State;
But sinking underneath his master's fate:
In exile with his godlike prince he mourned;
For him he suffered, and with him returned.
The court he practiced, not the courtier's art:
Large was his wealth, but larger was his heart:
Which well the noblest objects knew to choose,
The fighting warrior, and recording Muse.
His bed could once a fruitful issue boast;
Now more than half a father's name is lost.
His eldest hope,[9] with every grace adorned,
By me (so Heaven will have it) always mourned,
And always honored, snatched in manhood's prime
By unequal fates, and Providence's crime:
Yet not before the goal of honor won,
All parts fulfilled of subject and of son;
Swift was the race, but short the time to run.
O narrow circle, but of power divine,
Scanted in space, but perfect in thy line!
By sea, by land, thy matchless worth was known,
Arms thy delight, and war was all thy own:
Thy force, infused, the fainting Tyrians [1] propped;
And haughty Pharaoh found his fortune stopped.
Oh ancient honor! Oh unconquered hand,
Whom foes unpunished never could withstand!
But Israel was unworthy of thy name:
Short is the date of all immoderate fame.
It looks as Heaven our ruin had designed,
And durst not trust thy fortune and thy mind.
Now, free from earth, thy disencumbered soul
Mounts up, and leaves behind the clouds and starry pole:
From thence thy kindred legions mayst thou bring,
To aid the guardian angel of thy king.
Here stop my Muse, here cease thy painful flight;

8. James Butler, Duke of Ormond (1610–88). He was famous for his loyalty to the Stuart cause. He fought for Charles I in Ireland, and when that cause was hopeless, he joined Charles II in his exile abroad. He spent a large fortune in behalf of the King and continued to serve him loyally after the Restoration.

9. Ormond's son, Thomas, Earl of Ossory (1634–80), a famous soldier, and like his father devoted to Charles II.

1. The Dutch.

No pinions can pursue immortal height:
Tell good Barzillai thou canst sing no more,
And tell thy soul she should have fled before:
Or fled she with his life, and left this verse
To hang on her departed patron's hearse?
Now take thy steepy flight from heaven, and see
If thou canst find on earth another *he:*
Another *he* would be too hard to find;
See then whom thou canst see not far behind.
Zadoc the priest,[2] whom, shunning power and place,
His lowly mind advanced to David's grace:
With him the Sagan of Jerusalem,
Of hospitable soul, and noble stem;
Him of the western dome, whose weighty sense
Flows in fit words and heavenly eloquence.
The prophets' sons, by such example led,
To learning and to loyalty were bred:
For colleges on bounteous kinds depend,
And never rebel was to arts a friend.
To these succeed the pillars of the laws,
Who best could plead, and best can judge a cause.
Next them a train of loyal peers ascend;
Sharp-judging Adriel, the Muses' friend,
Himself a Muse—in Sanhedrin's debate
True to his prince, but not a slave of state:
Whom David's love with honors did adorn,
That from his disobedient son were torn.
Jotham of piercing wit, and pregnant thought,
Indued by nature, and by learning taught
To move assemblies, who but only tried
The worse a while, then chose the better side;
Nor chose alone, but turned the balance too;
So much the weight of one brave man can do.
Hushai, the friend of David in distress,
In public storms, of manly steadfastness:
By foreign treaties he informed his youth,
And joined experience to his native truth.
His frugal care supplied the wanting throne,
Frugal for that, but bounteous of his own:
'Tis easy conduct when exchequers flow,
But hard the task to manage well the low;
For sovereign power is too depressed or high,
When kings are forced to sell, or crowds to buy.
Indulge one labor more, my weary Muse,
For Amiel: who can Amiel's praise refuse?
Of ancient race by birth, but nobler yet

2. William Sancroft, Archbishop of Canterbury; the Sagan is Henry Compton, Bishop of London; "Him of the western dome" is John Dolben, Dean of Westminster; "The prophets' sons" are the boys of Westminster School, which Dryden had attended; Adriel is John Sheffield, Earl of Mulgrave; Jotham, George Savile, Marquis of Halifax; Hushai, Laurence Hyde, Earl of Rochester; and Amiel is Edward Seymour, Speaker of the House of Commons.

In his own worth, and without title great:
The Sanhedrin long time as chief he ruled,
Their reason guided, and their passion cooled:
So dexterous was he in the crown's defence,
So formed to speak a loyal nation's sense,
That, as their band was Israel's tribes in small,
So fit was he to represent them all.
Now rasher charioteers the seat ascend,
Whose loose careers his steady skill commend:
They like the unequal ruler of the day,
Misguide the seasons, and mistake the way;
While he withdrawn at their mad labor smiles,
And safe enjoys the sabbath of his toils.
These were the chief, a small but faithful band
Of worthies, in the breach who dared to stand,
And tempt the united fury of the land.
With grief they viewed such powerful engines bent,
To batter down the lawful government:
A numerous faction, with pretended frights,
In Sanhedrins to plume the regal rights;
The true successor from the court removed: [3]
The Plot, by hireling witnesses, improved.
These ills they saw, and, as their duty bound,
They showed the king the danger of the wound:
That no concessions from the throne would please,
But lenitives [4] fomented the disease;
That Absalom, ambitious of the crown,
Was made the lure to draw the people down;
That false Achitophel's pernicious hate
Had turned the Plot to ruin Church and State:
The council violent, the rabble worse;
That Shimei taught Jerusalem to curse.
With all these loads of injuries oppressed,
And long revolving in his careful breast,
The event of things, at last, his patience tired,
Thus from his royal throne, by Heaven inspired,
The godlike David spoke: with awful fear
His train their Maker in their master hear.
"Thus long have I, by native mercy swayed,
My wrongs dissembled, my revenge delayed:
So willing to forgive the offending age,
So much the father did the king assuage.
But now so far my clemency they slight,
The offenders question my forgiving right.
That one was made for many, they contend;
But 'tis to rule; for that's a monarch's end.
They call my tenderness of blood, my fear;
Though manly tempers can the longest bear.
Yet, since they will divert my native course,

3. The Duke of York had been banished from England.

4. Any medicine that relieves pain.

'Tis time to show I am not good by force.
Those heaped affronts that haughty subjects bring,
Are burdens for a camel, not a king:
Kings are the public pillars of the State,
Born to sustain and prop the nation's weight:
If my young Samson will pretend a call
To shake the column, let him share the fall:[5]
But, oh, that yet he would repent and live!
How easy 'tis for parents to forgive!
With how few tears a pardon might be won
From nature, pleading for a darling son!
Poor pitied youth, by my paternal care
Raised up to all the height his frame could bear:
Had God ordained his fate for empire born,
He would have given his soul another turn:
Gulled[6] with a patriot's name, whose modern sense
Is one that would by law supplant his prince:
The people's brave, the politician's tool;
Never was patriot yet, but was a fool.
Whence comes it that religion and the laws
Should more be Absalom's than David's cause?
His old instructor, ere he lost his place,
Was never thought indued with so much grace.[7]
Good heavens, how faction can a patriot paint!
My rebel ever proves my people's saint:
Would *they* impose an heir upon the throne?
Let Sanhedrins be taught to give their own.
A king's at least a part of government,
And mine as requisite as their consent;
Without my leave a future king to choose,
Infers a right the present to depose:
True, they petition me to approve their choice;
But Esau's hands suit ill with Jacob's voice.[8]
My pious subjects for my safety pray,
Which to secure, they take my power away.
From plots and treasons Heaven preserve my years,
But save me most from my petitioners.
Unsatiate as the barren womb or grave;
God cannot grant so much as they can crave.
What then is left but with a jealous eye
To guard the small remains of royalty?
The law shall still direct my peaceful sway,
And the same law teach rebels to obey:
Votes shall no more established power control—
Such votes as make a part exceed the whole:
No groundless clamors shall my friends remove,
Nor crowds have power to punish ere they prove:
For gods and godlike kings, their care express,
Still to defend their servants in distress.

5. Judges xvi.
6. Deceived.
7. The Earl of Shaftesbury.
8. Genesis xxvii. 22.

O that my power to saving were confined:
Why am I forced, like Heaven, against my mind,
To make examples of another kind?
Must I at length the sword of justice draw?
O curst effects of necessary law!
How ill my fear they by my mercy scan!
Beware the fury of a patient man.
Law they require, let Law then show her face;
They could not be content to look on Grace,
Her hinder parts, but with a daring eye
To tempt the terror of her front and die.[9]
By their own arts, 'tis righteously decreed,
Those dire artificers of death shall bleed.
Against themselves their witnesses will swear,
Till viper-like their mother Plot they tear:
And suck for nutriment that bloody gore,
Which was their principle of life before.
Their Belial with their Belzebub[10] will fight;
Thus on my foes, my foes shall do me right:
Nor doubt the event; for factious crowds engage,
In their first onset, all their brutal rage.
Then let 'em take an unresisted course,
Retire and traverse, and delude their force:
But when they stand all breathless, urge the fight,
And rise upon 'em with redoubled might:
For lawful power is still superior found,
When long driven back, at length it stands the ground."
He said. The Almighty, nodding, gave consent;
And peals of thunder shook the firmament.
Henceforth a series of new time began,
The mighty years in long procession ran:
Once more the godlike David was restored,
And willing nations knew their lawful lord.

1681

Mac Flecknoe[1]

OR A SATIRE UPON THE TRUE-BLUE-PROTESTANT POET, T. S.

All human things are subject to decay,
And when fate summons, monarchs must obey.

9. Moses was not allowed to see the countenance of Jehovah. Exodus xxxiii. 20–23.

10. Belial, the incarnation of all evil; Beelzebub, a god of the Philistines.

1. The victim of this superb satire, which is cast in the form of a mock-heroic episode, is Thomas Shadwell (1640–92), the playwright, with whom Dryden had been on good terms for a number of years, certainly as late as March, 1678. Shadwell considered himself the successor of Ben Jonson and the champion of the type of comedy that Jonson had written, the "comedy of humors," in which each character is presented under the domination of a single psychological trait or eccentricity, his humor. His plays are not without merit, but they are often clumsy and prolix, and certainly much inferior to Jonson's. For many years he had conducted a public argument with Dryden on the merits of Jonson's comedies, which he thought Dryden undervalued. Exactly what moved Dry-

This Flecknoe found, who, like Augustus,[2] young
Was called to empire, and had governed long;
In prose and verse, was owned, without dispute,
Through all the realms of Nonsense, absolute.
This aged prince, now flourishing in peace,
And blest with issue of a large increase,
Worn out with business, did at length debate
To settle the succession of the state;
And, pondering which of all his sons was fit
To reign, and wage immortal war with wit,
Cried: " 'Tis resolved; for nature pleads that he
Should only rule, who most resembles me.
Sh——[3] alone my perfect image bears,
Mature in dullness from his tender years:
Sh—— alone, of all my sons, is he
Who stands confirmed in full stupidity.
The rest to some faint meaning make pretense,
But Sh—— never deviates into sense.
Some beams of wit on other souls may fall,
Strike through, and make a lucid interval;
But Sh——'s genuine night admits no ray,
His rising fogs prevail upon the day.
Besides, his goodly fabric[4] fills the eye,
And seems designed for thoughtless majesty:
Thoughtless as monarch oaks that shade the plain,
And, spread in solemn state, supinely reign.

den to attack him is a matter of conjecture: he may simply have grown progressively bored and irritated by Shadwell and his tedious argument. The poem seems to have been written in late 1678 or 1679 and to have circulated only in manuscript, until it was printed in 1682 in a pirated edition by an obscure publisher. By that time, the two playwrights were alienated by politics as well as by literary quarrels. Shadwell was a violent Whig and the reputed author of a sharp attack on Dryden as the Tory author of *Absalom and Achitophel* and *The Medal*. It was probably for this reason that the printer added the subtitle referring to Shadwell's Whiggism in the phrase "true-blue-Protestant poet." Political passions were running high and sales would be helped if the poem seemed to refer to the events of the day.

Whereas Butler had debased and degraded his victims by using burlesque, caricature, and the grotesque, Dryden exposed Shadwell to ridicule by using the devices of mock-epic, which treats the low, mean, or absurd in the grand language, lofty style, and solemn tone of epic poetry. The obvious disparity between subject and style makes the satiric point. In 1678 an execrable Irish poet and playwright, Richard Flecknoe, died. Dryden conceived the idea of presenting Shadwell (the self-proclaimed heir of Ben Jonson, the laureate) as the son and successor of Flecknoe—hence *Mac* (i.e., son of) *Flecknoe*—from whom he interits the throne of dullness. Flecknoe in the triple role of king, priest, and poet hails his successor, pronounces a panegyric on his perfect fitness for the throne, anoints and crowns him, foretells his glorious reign, and, as he sinks (leaden dullness cannot soar), leaves his mantle to fall symbolically upon Shadwell's shoulders. The poem abounds in literary allusions—to Roman legend and history and to the *Aeneid;* to Cowley's fragmentary epic, *The Davideis*, and to *Paradise Lost;* and to Shadwell's own plays. Biblical allusions add an unexpected dimension of incongruous dignity to the low scene. The coronation takes place in the City, to the plaudits of the citizens, who are fit to admire only what is dull. In 217 lines Dryden created an image of Shadwell which has fixed his reputation to this day.

2. In 31 B.C. Octavian became the first Roman emperor at the age of 32. He assumed the title Augustus in 27 B.C.

3. Thomas Shadwell. The initial and second letter of the name followed by a dash give the appearance, but only the appearance, of protecting Dryden's victim by concealing his name. A common device in the satire of the period.

4. His body. Shadwell was a corpulent man.

Heywood and Shirley[5] were but types of thee,
Thou last great prophet of tautology.[6]
Even I, a dunce of more renown than they,
Was sent before but to prepare thy way;
And, coarsely clad in Norwich drugget,[7] came
To teach the nations in thy greater name.[8]
My warbling lute, the lute I whilom[9] strung,
When to King John of Portugal I sung,
Was but the prelude to that glorious day,
When thou on silver Thames didst cut thy way,
With well-timed oars before the royal barge,
Swelled with the pride of thy celestial charge;
And big with hymn, commander of a host,
The like was ne'er in Epsom blankets tossed.[1]
Methinks I see the new Arion[2] sail,
The lute still trembling underneath thy nail.
At thy well-sharpened thumb from shore to shore
The treble squeaks for fear, the basses roar;
Echoes from Pissing Alley Sh—— call,
And Sh—— they resound from Aston Hall.
About thy boat the little fishes throng,
As at the morning toast[3] that floats along.
Sometimes, as prince of thy harmonious band,
Thou wield'st thy papers in thy threshing hand.
St. André's[4] feet ne'er kept more equal time,
Not ev'n the feet of thy own *Psyche's* rhyme;
Though they in number as in sense excel:
So just, so like tautology, they fell,
That, pale with envy, Singleton[5] forswore
The lute and sword, which he in triumph bore,
And vowed he ne'er would act Villerius[6] more."
Here stopped the good old sire, and wept for joy
In silent raptures of the hopeful boy.
All arguments, but most his plays, persuade,
That for anointed[7] dullness he was made.

5. Thomas Heywood (ca. 1570–1641) and James Shirley (1596–1666), playwrights popular before the closing of the theaters in 1642 but now out of fashion. They are introduced here as "types" (i.e., prefigurings) of Shadwell, in the sense that Solomon was regarded as an Old Testament prefiguring of Christ, the "last [final] great prophet."
6. Unnecessary repetition of meaning in different words.
7. A coarse woolen cloth.
8. The parallel between Flecknoe, as forerunner of Shadwell, and John the Baptist, as forerunner of Jesus, is made plain in lines 32–34 by the use of details and even words taken from Matthew iii.3–4 and John i.23.
9. Formerly. Flecknoe boasted of the patronage of the Portuguese king.
1. A reference to Shadwell's comedy *Epsom Wells* and to the farcical scene in his *Virtuoso,* in which Sir Samuel Hearty is tossed in a blanket.
2. A legendary Greek poet. Returning home by sea, he was robbed and thrown overboard by the sailors, but was saved by a dolphin which had been charmed by his music.
3. Sewage.
4. A French dancer who designed the choreography of Shadwell's opera *Psyche* (1675). Dryden's sneer in the next line at the mechanical metrics of the songs in *Psyche* is justified.
5. John Singleton (d. 1686), a musician at the Theatre Royal.
6. A character in Sir William Davenant's *Siege of Rhodes* (1656), the first English opera.
7. The anticipated phrase is "anointed *majesty.*" English kings are anointed with oil at their coronations.

Close to the walls which fair Augusta[8] bind
(The fair Augusta much to fears inclined),
An ancient fabric[9] raised to inform the sight,
There stood of yore, and Barbican it hight:
A watchtower once; but now, so fate ordains,
Of all the pile an empty name remains.
From its old ruins brothel houses rise,
Scenes of lewd loves, and of polluted joys,
Where their vast courts the mother-strumpets keep,
And, undisturbed by watch, in silence sleep.
Near these a Nursery[1] erects its head,
Where queens are formed, and future heroes bred;
Where unfledged actors learn to laugh and cry,
Where infant punks[2] their tender voices try,
And little Maximins[3] the gods defy.
Great Fletcher[4] never treads in buskins here,
Nor greater Jonson dares in socks appear;
But gentle Simkin[5] just reception finds
Amidst this monument of vanished minds:
Pure clinches[6] the suburbian Muse affords,
And Panton[7] waging harmless war with words.
Here Flecknoe, as a place to fame well known,
Ambitiously design'd his Sh——'s throne;
For ancient Dekker[8] prophesied long since,
That in this pile would reign a mighty prince,
Born for a scourge of wit, and flail of sense;
To whom true dullness should some *Psyches* owe,
But worlds of *Misers* from his pen should flow;
Humorists and *Hypocrites*[9] it should produce,
Whole Raymond families, and tribes of Bruce.
Now Empress Fame had published the renown
Of Sh——'s coronation through the town.
Roused by report of Fame, the nations meet,
From near Bunhill, and distant Watling Street.[1]
No Persian carpets spread the imperial way,
But scattered limbs of mangled poets lay;
From dusty shops neglected authors come,
Martyrs of pies, and relics of the bum.[2]

8. London. The next line alludes to the fears excited by the Popish Plot (cf. *Absalom and Achitophel*).
9. Building.
1. The name of a training school for young actors.
2. Prostitutes.
3. Maximin is the cruel emperor in Dryden's *Tyrannic Love* (1669), notorious for his bombast.
4. John Fletcher (1579–1625), the playwright and collaborator with Francis Beaumont (ca. 1584–1616). "Buskins" and "socks" were the symbols of tragedy and comedy.
5. A popular character in low farces.
6. Puns.
7. Said to have been a celebrated punster.
8. Thomas Dekker (ca. 1572–1632), the playwright, whom Jonson had satirized in *The Poetaster*.
9. Three of Shadwell's plays; *The Hypocrite,* a failure, was not published. "Raymond" and "Bruce" (line 94) are characters in *The Humorists* and *The Virtuoso* respectively.
1. Since Bunhill is about a quarter of a mile and Watling Street little more than half a mile from the site of the Nursery, where the coronation is held, Shadwell's fame is narrowly circumscribed. Moreover, his subjects live in the heart of the City, regarded by men of wit and fashion as the abode of bad taste and middle-class vulgarity.
2. Unsold books eventually went to bakers' shops and privies.

Much Heywood, Shirley, Ogilby[3] there lay,
But loads of Sh—— almost choked the way.
Bilked stationers[4] for yeomen stood prepared,
And Herringman was captain of the guard.
The hoary prince in majesty appeared,
High on a throne of his own labors reared.
At his right hand our young Ascanius[5] sate,
Rome's other hope, and pillar of the state.
His brows thick fogs, instead of glories, grace,
And lambent dullness played around his face.
As Hannibal did to the altars come,
Sworn by his sire a mortal foe to Rome,[6]
So Sh—— swore, nor should his vow be vain,
That he till death true dullness would maintain;
And, in his father's right, and realm's defense,
Ne'er to have peace with wit, nor truce with sense.
The king himself the sacred unction[7] made,
As king by office, and as priest by trade.
In his sinister[8] hand, instead of ball,
He placed a mighty mug of potent ale;
Love's Kingdom to his right he did convey,
At once his scepter, and his rule of sway;
Whose righteous lore the prince had practiced young,
And from whose loins recorded *Psyche* sprung.
His temples, last, with poppies were o'erspread,
That nodding seemed to consecrate his head.
Just at that point of time, if fame not lie,
On his left hand twelve reverend owls did fly.[9]
So Romulus, 'tis sung, by Tiber's brook,
Presage of sway from twice six vultures took.
The admiring throng loud acclamations make,
And omens of his future empire take.
The sire then shook the honors[1] of his head,
And from his brows damps of oblivion shed
Full on the filial dullness: long he stood,
Repelling from his breast the raging god;
At length burst out in this prophetic mood:

3. John Ogilby, a translator of Homer and Virgil, ridiculed by both Dryden and Pope as a bad poet.
4. Cheated publishers, who acted as "yeomen" of the guard, led by Henry Herringman, who until 1679 was the publisher of both Shadwell and Dryden.
5. Or Iulus, son of Aeneas; Virgil referred to him as "*spes altera Romae*" ("Rome's other hope"; *Aeneid* XII. 168). As Troy fell, he was marked as favored by the gods when a flickering ("lambent") flame played round his head (*Aeneid* II.680–84).
6. Hannibal, who almost conquered Rome in 216 B.C., during the 2nd Punic War, took this oath at the age of 9 (Livy xxi.1).
7. The sacramental oil, used in the coronation.
8. Left. During his coronation a British monarch holds two symbols of kingship: a globe ("ball") representing the world in his left hand, a scepter in his right. In lines 121–27, Shadwell's symbols of monarchy—a mug of ale; Flecknoe's dreary play, *Love's Kingdom;* a crown of poppies—suggest heaviness, dullness, drowsiness. The poppies also refer obliquely to Shadwell's addiction to opium.
9. Birds of night, appropriate substitutes for the twelve vultures whose flight confirmed to Romulus the destined site of Rome, of which he was founder and king.
1. Ornaments, hence locks.

"Heavens bless my son, from Ireland let him reign
To far Barbadoes on the western main;[2]
Of his dominion may no end be known,
And greater than his father's be his throne;
Beyond *Love's Kingdom* let him stretch his pen!"
He paused, and all the people cried, "Amen."
Then thus continued he: "My son, advance
Still in new impudence, new ignorance.
Success let others teach, learn thou from me
Pangs without birth, and fruitless industry.
Let *Virtuosos* in five years be writ;
Yet not one thought accuse thy toil of wit.
Let gentle George[3] in triumph tread the stage,
Make Dorimant betray, and Loveit rage;
Let Cully, Cockwood, Fopling, charm the pit,
And in their folly show the writer's wit.
Yet still thy fools shall stand in thy defense,
And justify their author's want of sense.
Let 'em be all by thy own model made
Of dullness, and desire no foreign aid;
That they to future ages may be known,
Not copies drawn, but issue of thy own.
Nay, let thy men of wit too be the same,
All full of thee, and differing but in name.
But let no alien S—dl—y[4] interpose,
To lard with wit[5] thy hungry *Epsom* prose.
And when false flowers of rhetoric thou wouldst cull,
Trust nature, do not labor to be dull;
But write thy best, and top; and, in each line,
Sir Formal's[6] oratory will be thine:
Sir Formal, though unsought, attends thy quill,
And does thy northern dedications[7] fill.
Nor let false friends seduce thy mind to fame,
By arrogating Jonson's hostile name.
Let father Flecknoe fire thy mind with praise,
And uncle Ogilby thy envy raise.
Thou art my blood, where Jonson has no part:
What share have we in nature, or in art?
Where did his wit on learning fix a brand,
And rail at arts he did not understand?
Where made he love in Prince Nicander's vein,[8]
Or swept the dust in *Psyche's* humble strain?

2. Shadwell's empire is vast but empty.
3. Sir George Etherege (ca. 1635–91), a writer of brilliant comedies. In the next couplet Dryden names characters from his plays.
4. Sir Charles Sedley (1638–1701), wit, rake, poet, playwright. Dryden hints that he contributed more than the prologue to Shadwell's *Epsom Wells*.
5. The phrase "lard with wit" recalls a sentence in Burton's *Anatomy of Melancholy:* "They lard their lean books with the fat of others' works * * * "
6. Sir Formal Trifle, the ridiculous and vapid orator in *The Virtuoso*.
7. Shadwell frequently dedicated his works to the Duke of Newcastle and members of his family.
8. In *Psyche*.

Where sold he bargains,[9] 'whip-stitch, kiss my arse,'
Promised a play and dwindled to a farce?[1]
When did his Muse from Fletcher scenes purloin,
As thou whole Eth'rege dost transfuse to thine?
But so transfused, as oil on water's flow,
His always floats above, thine sinks below.
This is thy province, this thy wondrous way,
New humors to invent for each new play:
This is that boasted bias[2] of thy mind,
By which one way, to dullness, 'tis inclined;
Which makes thy writings lean on one side still,
And, in all changes, that way bends thy will.
Nor let thy mountain-belly make pretense
Of likeness; thine's a tympany[3] of sense.
A tun[4] of man in thy large bulk is writ,
But sure thou'rt but a kilderkin of wit.
Like mine, thy gentle numbers feebly creep;
Thy tragic Muse gives smiles, thy comic sleep.
With whate'er gall thou sett'st thyself to write,
Thy inoffensive satires never bite.
In thy felonious heart though venom lies,
It does but touch thy Irish pen,[5] and dies.
Thy genius calls thee not to purchase fame
In keen iambics,[6] but mild anagram.
Leave writing plays, and choose for thy command
Some peaceful province in acrostic land.
There thou may'st wings display and altars raise,
And torture one poor word ten thousand ways.[7]
Or, if thou wouldst thy different talent suit,
Set thy own songs, and sing them to thy lute."
He said: but his last words were scarcely heard
For Bruce and Longville had a trap prepared,
And down they sent the yet declaiming bard.[8]
Sinking he left his drugget robe behind,
Borne upwards by a subterranean wind.

9. To "sell bargains" is to answer an innocent question with a coarse or indecent phrase as in this line. "Whipstitch" is a nonsense word frequently used by Sir Samuel Hearty in *The Virtuoso*.
1. Low comedy which depends largely on situation rather than wit, consistently condemned by Dryden and other serious playwrights.
2. In bowling, the spin given to the bowl that causes it to swerve. Dryden closely parodies a passage in Shadwell's epilogue to *The Humorists*.
3. A swelling in some part of the body caused by wind.
4. A large wine cask. "Kilderkin": a very small cask.
5. Flecknoe was Irish, and so his son must be Irish. Ireland suggested only poverty, superstition, and barbarity to 17th-century Londoners.
6. Sharp satire.
7. "Anagram": the transposition of letters in a word so as to make a new one; "acrostic": a poem in which the first letter of each line, read downward, makes up the name of the person or thing that is the subject of the poem; "wings" and "altars" refer to poems in the shape of these objects as in George Herbert's *Easter Wings* and *The Altar*. Dryden is citing instances of triviality and overingenuity in literature.
8. In *The Virtuoso*, Bruce and Longville play this trick on Sir Formal Trifle while he makes a speech.

The mantle fell to the young prophet's part,[9]
With double portion of his father's art.

ca. 1679 1682

To the Memory of Mr. Oldham[1]

Farewell, too little, and too lately known,
Whom I began to think and call my own:
For sure our souls were near allied, and thine
Cast in the same poetic mold with mine.
One common note on either lyre did strike,
And knaves and fools[2] we both abhorred alike.
To the same goal did both our studies drive;
The last set out the soonest did arrive.
Thus Nisus[3] fell upon the slippery place,
While his young friend performed and won the race.
O early ripe! to thy abundant store
What could advancing age have added more?
It might (what nature never gives the young)
Have taught the numbers[4] of thy native tongue.
But satire needs not those, and wit will shine
Through the harsh cadence of a rugged line:[5]
A noble error, and but seldom made,
When poets are by too much force betrayed.
Thy generous fruits, though gathered ere their prime,
Still showed a quickness;[6] and maturing time
But mellows what we write to the dull sweets of rhyme.
Once more, hail and farewell;[7] farewell, thou young,
But ah too short, Marcellus[8] of our tongue;
Thy brows with ivy, and with laurels bound;[9]
But fate and gloomy night encompass thee around.

1684

9. When the prophet Elijah was carried to heaven in a chariot of fire borne on a whirlwind, his mantle fell on his successor, the younger prophet Elisha (II Kings.ii.8–14). Flecknoe, prophet of dullness, naturally cannot ascend, but must sink.

1. John Oldham (1653–83), the young poet whose *Satires upon the Jesuits* (1681) won Dryden's admiration. This elegy was published in Oldham's *Remains in Verse and Prose* (1684).

2. The objects of satire.

3. Nisus, on the point of winning a foot race, slipped in a pool of blood; his "young friend" was Euryalus (Virgil, *Aeneid* V.315–39).

4. Metrics, verse.

5. Dryden repeats the Renaissance idea that the satirist should avoid smoothness and affect rough meters ("harsh cadence").

6. Sharpness of flavor.

7. Dryden echoes the famous words that conclude Catullus' elegy to his brother: "*Atque in perpetuum, frater, ave atque vale*" ("And forever, brother, hail and farewell!").

8. The nephew of Augustus, adopted by him as his successor. After winning military fame as a youth, he died at the age of 20. Virgil celebrated him in the *Aeneid* VI.854–86; the last line of Dryden's poem is a reminiscence of *Aeneid* VI.866.

9. The poet's wreath. Cf. Milton's *Lycidas*, lines 1–2.

To the Pious Memory of the Accomplished Young Lady Mrs. Anne Killigrew[1]

EXCELLENT IN THE TWO SISTER ARTS OF POESY AND PAINTING.

An Ode

1

Thou youngest virgin-daughter of the skies,
Made in the last promotion of the blest,
Whose palms,[2] new plucked from paradise,

1. Like Milton's *Lycidas,* Dryden's ode to Anne Killigrew is not so much the expression of private grief as it is a decorous ceremonial gesture dignifying a public occasion. In both poems the death of an individual becomes the point of departure for the treatment of larger topics. The fact that Mrs. Killigrew was not a distinguished poet or painter is irrelevant: her death prompted the poet to consider the arts themselves, their present state in a corrupt age, their central role in civilization, their service to virtue and religion. In the course of the poem, the dead woman is transformed into a symbol of the sister arts themselves, what they are, and what, on earth, they might become. *Lycidas* is an elegy; Dryden's ode combines the elegiac with the lyric and the heroic. Although *Lycidas* is cast in the traditional mode of the pastoral lament, and *Anne Killigrew* in the form of a eulogistic memorial, both poems develop classical and Christian themes which had become conventions of the funeral poem: the death of the young and promising, the praise of his genius and virtues, a lament for the times which suffer such loss, and a consolation, offered by describing the reception of the soul of the dead into heaven.

Dryden's poem, in form, is an irregular ode, a lyric poem which develops a serious theme in a dignified or exalted manner. Two kinds of ode were recognized during the 18th century. To quote Johnson: " * * * the ode is either of the greater or less kind. The less is characterized by sweetness and ease; the greater by sublimity, rapture, and quickness of transition." The greater ode, of which this is the finest example in 17th-century poetry, was associated with the odes of Pindar, the lyric poet of 5th-century Greece, whose intricate metrics, bold imagery, and intense and energetic power were aspired to (seldom with success) by English poets throughout our period. Pindar's odes were rigorously constructed: each was divided into long stanzas, which in turn were subdivided into three parts—called in Greek strophe, antistrophe, and epode—whose metrical structure was repeated throughout the whole poem. Strophes and antistrophes were identical but the epodes followed a different metrical pattern. Such symmetry is not easily attained in English verse because of the paucity of rhymes in our language, but Ben Jonson's *To the Immortal Memory * * * of * * * Sir Lucius Cary and Sir Henry Morison* is strictly Pindaric, as are Thomas Gray's *The Progress of Poesy* and *The Bard* (1757).

In 1656 Abraham Cowley published loose paraphrases of two of Pindar's odes in which he abandoned the formal structure of the originals in favor of irregular meters and irregularly constructed stanzas, while trying to preserve Pindar's rapture, boldness, and sublimity. Thanks to Cowley's popularity, his irregular Pindarics became the standard of what the age considered the loftiest sort of lyric poetry. It was a tempting form for poets who wished to achieve (or to simulate) the loftiest lyric rapture, for the apparent structural disorder could suggest inspired improvisation. The result was a plague of turgid rhetoric in uninteresting irregular meter.

Dryden declared that Cowley's Pindarics lacked "somewhat of a finer turn and more lyrical verse" and that such odes should consist in "the warmth and vigor of fancy, the masterly figures, and the copiousness of imagination" (Ker, *Essays* I.267–268). His superb ear and gift for melodious eloquence enabled him in this poem to raise the greater ode to heights not to be equaled again until Wordsworth wrote his *Ode: Intimations of Immortality.*

The lesser ode, often in this period associated with the odes of Horace, is more quiet and contemplative, more lyrical in mood, and it usually employs an uncomplicated, rather short stanza.

"Mrs." means "Mistress," used at this time for our "Miss."

2. The symbol of victory (cf. Revelation vii.9).

In spreading branches more sublimely rise,
Rich with immortal green above the rest;
Whether, adopted to some neighboring star,
Thou roll'st above us in thy wandering race,
 Or in procession fixed and regular,
 Moved with the heavens' majestic pace,
 Or called to more superior bliss,
Thou tread'st with seraphims the vast abyss:[3]
Whatever happy region is thy place,
Cease thy celestial song a little space;
Thou wilt have time enough for hymns divine,
 Since heaven's eternal year is thine.
Hear then a mortal Muse thy praise rehearse,
 In no ignoble verse;
But such as thy own voice did practice here,
When thy first fruits of poesy were given,
To make thyself a welcome inmate there,
 While yet a young probationer,
 And candidate of heaven.

2

 If by traduction came thy mind,
 Our wonder is the less to find
A soul so charming from a stock so good;
Thy father was transfused into thy blood:[4]
So wert thou born into the tuneful strain
(An early, rich, and inexhausted vein).
 But if thy pre-existing soul
 Was formed at first with myriads more,
It did through all the mighty poets roll
 Who Greek or Latin laurels wore,
And was that Sappho last, which once it was before.[5]
 If so, then cease thy flight, O heaven-born mind!
 Thou hast no dross to purge from thy rich ore;
 Nor can thy soul a fairer mansion find
 Than was the beauteous frame she left behind:
Return, to fill or mend the choir of thy celestial kind.

3

 May we presume to say that at thy birth
New joy was sprung in heaven, as well as here on earth?
 For sure the milder planets did combine

3. Dryden is speculating on where the soul of the dead poetess has come to rest: is she the tutelary deity of a planet ("neighboring star")? or of one of the remote "fixed" stars? or does she enjoy the higher ("superior") bliss of having joined the "seraphim," the guardians of the throne of God? (cf. Isaiah vi). Like Milton, Dryden makes use of the Ptolemaic universe of concentric spheres moving around the earth "in procession fixed and regular."

4. The idea that the soul is transmitted by the father at the moment of conception. Since Henry Killigrew had written a tragedy, his daughter is said to have inherited a poet's soul from him. In lines 29–32, Dryden proposes the theory that the soul exists before birth, and less seriously that through the ages it transmigrates from body to body.

5. Mrs. Killigrew is said to have been Sappho (the Greek lyric poetess of the 7th century B.C.) twice: "once before," when her soul transmigrated into Sappho's body, and most recently ("last"), when it inhabited the body of the modern Sappho, Anne Killigrew.

On thy auspicious horoscope to shine,[6]
And even the most malicious were in trine.
Thy brother-angels at thy birth
Strung each his lyre, and tuned it high,
That all the people of the sky
Might know a poetess was born on earth.
And then, if ever, mortal ears
Had heard the music of the spheres!
And if no clustering swarm of bees
On thy sweet mouth distilled their golden dew,[7]
'Twas that such vulgar miracles
Heaven had not leisure to renew:
For all the blest fraternity of love
Solemnized there thy birth, and kept thy holiday above.

4

O gracious God! how far have we
Profaned thy heavenly gift of poesy!
Made prostitute and profligate the Muse,
Debased to each obscene and impious use,
Whose harmony was first ordained above
For tongues of angels, and for hymns of love!
O wretched we! why were we hurried down
This lubric and adulterate[8] age
(Nay, added fat pollutions of our own)
To increase the steaming ordures of the stage?
What can we say to excuse our second fall?
Let this thy vestal,[9] Heaven, atone for all:
Her Arethusan stream remains unsoiled,
Unmixed with foreign filth, and undefiled;
Her wit was more than man, her innocence a child!

5

Art she had none, yet wanted none,
For nature did that want supply;
So rich in treasures of her own,
She might our boasted stores defy:
Such noble vigor did her verse adorn
That it seemed borrowed where 'twas only born.
Her morals too were in her bosom bred,
By great examples daily fed,
What in the best of books, her father's life, she read.
And to be read herself she need not fear;
Each test and every light her Muse will bear,

6. The familiar idea that character and destiny are determined by the position of the planets at the moment of birth ("horoscope"). Mrs. Killigrew's horoscope was fortunate ("auspicious"): even those planets that are usually baleful ("malicious") were "in trine"—120 degrees apart and hence favorable in their influence.

7. It was said that bees clustered on the lips of the infant Pindar, thus foretelling his greatness as a lyric poet.

8. Lewd and corrupted.

9. I.e., thy virgin. The Roman "vestal" virgins guarded the fire in the Temple of Vesta, goddess of the hearth. For "Arethusan stream," cf. Milton's *Lycidas*, line 85.

Though Epictetus with his lamp were there.[1]
Even love (for love sometimes her Muse expressed)
Was but a lambent flame[2] which played about her breast,
Light as the vapors of a morning dream;
So cold herself, whilst she such warmth expressed,
'Twas Cupid bathing in Diana's stream.

6

Born to the spacious empire of the Nine,[3]
One would have thought she should have been content
To manage well that mighty government;
But what can young ambitious souls confine?
To the next realm she stretched her sway,
For Painture[4] near adjoining lay,
A plenteous province, and alluring prey.
A chamber of dependences[5] was framed
(As conquerors will never want pretense,
When armed, to justify the offense)
And the whole fief in right of Poetry she claimed.
The country open lay without defense;
For poets frequent inroads there had made,
And perfectly could represent
The shape, the face, with every lineament;
And all the large demains[6] which the dumb Sister swayed,
All bowed beneath her government,
Received in triumph wheresoe'er she went.
Her pencil[7] drew whate'er her soul designed,
And oft the happy draft surpassed the image in her mind.
The sylvan scenes[8] of herds and flocks
And fruitful plains and barren rocks;
Of shallow brooks that flowed so clear
The bottom did the top appear;
Of deeper too and ampler floods,
Which, as in mirrors, showed the woods;
Of lofty trees, with sacred shades
And pérspectives[9] of pleasant glades,
Where nymphs of brightest form appear,
And shaggy satyrs standing near,

1. A collector is said to have paid a large sum for the lamp of the philosopher Epictetus in the faith that owning it would make him wise. Dryden merely means that Anne Killigrew's poems would appear pure even if judged in the light of the most severe Stoic ethical standards.
2. I.e., "a flickering flame." Cf. Dryden's *Mac Flecknoe*, line 111 and note on line 108.
3. The nine Muses, who preside over the arts of literature, the dance, music, and astronomy.
4. The art of painting (a Gallicism).
5. In the elaborate figure that dominates lines 95–98, Dryden alludes to recent peaceful annexations by Louis XIV of France, who in 1679 added most of Alsace, Lorraine, and Luxembourg to his realm through his policy of *"réunions,"* by setting up *"Chambres de Réunions."* These chambers by quasi-legal means awarded to Louis, as overlord, towns, cities, and estates with all their "dependences" or fiefs, i.e., estates held under the feudal system from overlords, to whom the holders owed services and rents.
6. I.e., an estate held in one's own right, as opposed to "fief" (line 98). The "dumb Sister" is the Muse of painting.
7. Painter's brush.
8. Cf. Milton, *Paradise Lost* IV.140.
9. Vistas.

Which them at once admire and fear;
The ruins, too, of some majestic piece,
Boasting the power of ancient Rome or Greece,
Whose statues, friezes, columns broken lie,
And, though defaced, the wonder of the eye:[1]
What nature, art, bold fiction e'er durst frame,
Her forming hand gave feature to the name.
So strange a concourse ne'er was seen before
But when the peopled ark the whole creation bore.[2]

7

The scene then changed: with bold erected look
Our martial king[3] the sight with reverence strook;
For, not content to express his outward part,
Her hand called out the image of his heart:
His warlike mind, his soul devoid of fear,
His high-designing thoughts were figured there,
As when by magic, ghosts are made appear.
Our phoenix queen[4] was portrayed, too, so bright,
Beauty alone could beauty take[5] so right:
Her dress, her shape, her matchless grace
Were all observed, as well as heavenly face.
With such a peerless majesty she stands
As in that day she took the crown from sacred hands;[6]
Before a train of heroines was seen,
In beauty foremost, as in rank the queen.
Thus nothing to her genius was denied,
But like a ball of fire, the further thrown,
Still with a greater blaze she shone,
And her bright soul broke out on every side.
What next she had designed, heaven only knows;[7]
To such immoderate growth her conquest rose
That fate alone its progress could oppose.

8

Now all those charms, that blooming grace,
The well-proportioned shape, and beauteous face,
Shall never more be seen by mortal eyes:
In earth the much-lamented virgin lies!
Not wit nor piety could fate prevent;
Nor was the cruel destiny content
To finish all the murder at a blow,
To sweep at once her life and beauty too;
But, like a hardened felon, took a pride

1. Mrs. Killigrew's landscapes are typical of the ideal classical landscape of 17th-century Italian painters: contrasts of fruitful plains and barren rocks, water that reflects trees, vistas, classical ruins, and mythological figures.
2. Noah's ark, which contained all that survived of created beings.
3. James II, who, as Duke of York, had won a reputation for courage and skill while fighting as a soldier with the French armies in the 1650's and serving as an admiral during the English-Dutch wars of the 1660's.
4. Mary of Modena, wife of James II, whose unique beauty is expressed by the reference to the "phoenix," the fabulous bird, only one of which exists during each thousand years.
5. I.e., take the likeness of.
6. The queen was crowned by the "sacred hands" of the Archbishop of Canterbury.
7. God alone knows.

To work more mischievously slow,
And plundered first, and then destroyed.
O double sacrilege on things divine,
To rob the relic, and deface the shrine!
But thus Orinda died:[8]
Heaven, by the same disease, did both translate;
As equal were their souls, so equal was their fate.

9

Meantime her warlike brother[9] on the seas
His waving streamers to the winds displays,
And vows for his return with vain devotion pays.
Ah, generous youth, that wish forbear;
The winds too soon will waft thee here!
Slack all thy sails, and fear to come,
Alas, thou know'st not thou art wrecked at home!
No more shalt thou behold thy sister's face;
Thou hast already had her last embrace.
But look aloft, and if thou kenn'st[1] from far,
Among the Pleiads,[2] a new-kindled star,
If any sparkles than the rest more bright,
'Tis she that shines in that propitious light.

10

When in mid-air the golden trump shall sound,
To raise the nations under ground;
When in the Valley of Jehosaphat[3]
The judging God shall close the book of fate,
And there the last assizes[4] keep
For those who wake and those who sleep;
When rattling bones together fly
From the four corners of the sky;
When sinews o'er the skeletons are spread,
Those clothed with flesh, and life inspires the dead;
The sacred poets first shall hear the sound,
And foremost from the tomb shall bound,
For they are covered with the lightest ground,
And straight, with inborn vigor, on the wing,
Like mounting larks, to the new morning sing.
There thou, sweet saint, before the choir shalt go,
As harbinger[5] of heaven, the way to show,
The way which thou so well hast learned below.

1686

8. The poetess Katharine Philips (1631–64), fancifully referred to by her admirers as "the matchless Orinda," who, like Anne Killigrew, died of the disfiguring disease, smallpox.
9. Henry Killigrew, an officer in the Royal Navy. Pennons ("streamers") fly from the mast of his ship.
1. Perceivest.
2. The Pleiades, a cluster of stars (six are visible to the unaided eye) in the constellation Taurus.
3. Joel iii.12; Ezekiel xxxvii.
4. Periodical sessions of superior courts held in each county in England; here, of course, the Last Judgment—at which some will be alive on earth ("wake") and many will have already died ("sleep").
5. One who goes ahead to provide a lodging.

A Song for St. Cecilia's Day[1]

1

From harmony, from heavenly harmony
This universal frame began:
When Nature[2] underneath a heap
Of jarring atoms lay,
And could not heave her head,
The tuneful voice was heard from high:
"Arise, ye more than dead."
Then cold, and hot, and moist, and dry,
In order to their stations leap,
And Music's power obey.
From harmony, from heavenly harmony
This universal frame began:
From harmony to harmony
Through all the compass of the notes it ran,
The diapason[3] closing full in man.

2

What passion cannot Music raise and quell![4]
When Jubal[5] struck the corded shell,
His listening brethren stood around,
And, wondering, on their faces fell
To worship that celestial sound.
Less than a god they thought there could not dwell
Within the hollow of that shell
That spoke so sweetly and so well.
What passion cannot Music raise and quell!

1. St. Cecilia, a Roman lady, was an early Christian martyr. She has long been regarded as the patroness of music and the supposed inventor of the organ. Celebrations of her festival day (November 22) in England were usually devoted to music and the praise of music, and from about 1683 to 1703 a "Musical Society" in London annually commemorated it with a religious service and a public concert. This concert always included an ode written and set to music for the occasion, of which the two by Dryden (*A Song for St. Cecilia's Day*, 1687, and *Alexander's Feast*, 1697) are the most distinguished. G. B. Draghi, an Italian brought to England by Charles II, set this ode to music, but Handel's fine score, composed in 1739, has completely obscured the original setting. Like the ode to Mrs. Killigrew, this is an irregular ode in the manner of Cowley. In stanzas 3–6 Dryden boldly attempted to suggest in the sounds of his words the characteristic tones of the instruments mentioned.

2. Created nature, ordered by the Divine Wisdom out of chaos, which Dryden, adopting the physics of the Greek philosopher Epicurus, describes as composed of the warring and discordant ("jarring") atoms of the four elements: earth, fire, water, air ("cold," "hot," "moist," "dry").

3. The entire compass of tones in the scale. Dryden is thinking of the Chain of Being, the ordered creation from inanimate nature up to man, God's latest and final work. The just gradations of notes in a scale is analogous to the equally just gradations in the ascending scale of created beings. Both are the result of harmony.

4. The power of music to describe, evoke, or subdue emotion ("passion") is a frequent theme in 17th-century literature. In stanzas 2–6 the poet considers music as awakening religious awe, warlike courage, sorrow for unrequited love, jealousy and fury, and the impulse to worship God.

5. According to Genesis iv.21, the inventor of the lyre and the pipe. Dryden imagines Jubal's lyre to have been made of a tortoise shell ("corded shell").

3

The trumpet's loud clangor
Excites us to arms,
With shrill notes of anger,
And mortal alarms.
The double double double beat
Of the thundering drum
Cries: "Hark! the foes come;
Charge, charge, 'tis too late to retreat."

4

The soft complaining flute
In dying notes discovers
The woes of hopeless lovers,
Whose dirge is whispered by the warbling lute.

5

Sharp violins[6] proclaim
Their jealous pangs, and desperation,
Fury, frantic indignation,
Depth of pains, and height of passion,
For the fair, disdainful dame.

6

But O! what art can teach,
What human voice can reach,
The sacred organ's praise?
Notes inspiring holy love,
Notes that wing their heavenly ways
To mend the choirs above.

7

Orpheus[7] could lead the savage race;
And trees unrooted left their place,
Sequacious of the lyre;
But bright Cecilia raised the wonder higher:
When to her organ vocal breath was given,
An angel heard, and straight appeared,[8]
Mistaking earth for heaven.

GRAND CHORUS

As from the power of sacred lays
The spheres began to move,[9]
And sung the great Creator's praise
To all the blest above;
So, when the last and dreadful hour

6. A reference to the bright tone of the modern violin, introduced into England at the Restoration. The tone of the old-fashioned viol is much duller (Bronson).

7. A legendary poet, son of one of the Muses, who played so wonderfully on the lyre that wild beasts ("the savage race") grew tame and followed him, as did even rocks and trees. "Sequacious of": following.

8. According to the legend, it was Cecilia's piety, not her music, that brought an angel to visit her.

9. As it was harmony which ordered the universe, so it was angelic song ("sacred lays") which put the celestial bodies ("spheres") in motion. The harmonious chord which results from the traditional "music of the spheres" is a hymn of "praise" sung by created nature to its "Creator."

This crumbling pageant[1] shall devour,
The trumpet shall be heard on high,[2]
The dead shall live, the living die,
And Music shall untune the sky.

1687

Epigram on Milton[3]

Three poets, in three distant ages born,
Greece, Italy, and England did adorn.
The first in loftiness of thought surpassed,
The next in majesty, in both the last:
The force of Nature could no farther go;
To make a third, she joined the former two.

1688

Alexander's Feast[1]

OR THE POWER OF MUSIC; AN ODE IN HONOR OF ST. CECILIA'S DAY

1

'Twas at the royal feast, for Persia won
By Philip's[2] warlike son:
Aloft in awful state
The godlike hero sate
On his imperial throne;
His valiant peers were placed around;
Their brows with roses and with myrtles[3] bound:
(So should desert in arms be crowned).
The lovely Thaïs, by his side,
Sate like a blooming Eastern bride
In flower of youth and beauty's pride.
Happy, happy, happy pair!
None but the brave,
None but the brave,
None but the brave deserves the fair.

1. The universe: the stage on which the drama of man's salvation has been acted out.

2. The "last trump" of I Corinthians xv.52, which will announce the Resurrection and the Last Judgment. Dryden develops his theme of harmony as order in such a way as to give full emphasis of the splendid paradox ("Music shall *untune*") in the final line of the ode.

3. Engraved beneath the portrait of Milton in Jacob Tonson's edition of *Paradise Lost* (1688). The "three poets" are Homer, Virgil, Milton.

1. In Dryden's earlier poem for St. Cecilia's Day, music was celebrated primarily as harmony and order, though its power over the passions was also praised. *Alexander's Feast* is devoted entirely to the second theme. It is based upon a well-known episode in the life of Alexander the Great. After the defeat of the Persian Emperor Darius III and the fall of the Persian capital, Persepolis (331 B.C.), Alexander held a great feast for his officers. Thaïs, his Athenian mistress, persuaded him to set fire to the palace in revenge for the burning of Athens by the Persians under Xerxes in 480 B.C. According to Plutarch, Alexander was moved by love and wine, not by music; but Dryden, perhaps altering an old tradition that Alexander's musician Timotheus once caused the hero by his flute-playing to start up and arm himself, attributes the burning of Persepolis to the power of music. The original music was by Jeremiah Clarke, but Handel's score of 1736 is better known.

2. King Philip II of Macedonia, father of Alexander the Great.

3. The Greeks and Romans wore wreaths of flowers at banquets. Roses and myrtles are emblems of love.

CHORUS

Happy, happy, happy pair!
None but the brave,
None but the brave,
None but the brave deserves the fair.

2

Timotheus, placed on high
Amid the tuneful choir,
With flying fingers touched the lyre:
The trembling notes ascend the sky,
And heavenly joys inspire.
The song began from Jove,
Who left his blissful seats above
(Such is the power of mighty love).[4]
A dragon's fiery form belied the god:
Sublime on radiant spires[5] he rode,
When he to fair Olympia pressed;
And while he sought her snowy breast:
Then, round her slender waist he curled,
And stamped an image of himself, a sovereign of the world.
The listening crowd admire[6] the lofty sound:
"A present deity," they shout around;
"A present deity," the vaulted roofs rebound.
With ravished ears
The monarch hears,
Assumes the god,
Affects to nod,
And seems to shake the spheres.[7]

CHORUS

With ravished ears
The monarch hears,
Assumes the god,
Affects to nod,
And seems to shake the spheres.

3

The praise of Bacchus[8] then the sweet musician sung,
Of Bacchus ever fair and ever young:
The jolly god in triumph comes;
Sound the trumpets; beat the drums;
Flushed with a purple grace
He shows his honest face:
Now give the hautboys[9] breath; he comes, he comes!
Bacchus, ever fair and young
Drinking joys did first ordain;

4. An oracle had declared that Alexander was the son of Zeus ("Jove") by Philip's wife Olympias (not, as Dryden calls her in line 30, "Olympia"), thus conferring on him that semi-divinity often claimed by heroes. Zeus habitually conducted his amours with mortals in the guise of an animal: in this case a dragon.

5. High on shining coils ("radiant spires"). "Spires" for the coils of a serpent is derived from the Latin word *spira,* which Virgil uses in this sense, *Aeneid* II.217. Cf. *Paradise Lost* IX.502.

6. Wonder at.

7. According to Virgil (*Aeneid* X.115) the nod of Jove causes earthquakes.

8. The god of wine.

9. Oboes.

Bacchus' blessings are a treasure,
Drinking is a soldier's pleasure;
Rich the treasure,
Sweet the pleasure,
Sweet is pleasure after pain.

CHORUS

Bacchus' blessings are a treasure,
Drinking is the soldier's pleasure;
Rich the treasure,
Sweet the pleasure,
Sweet is pleasure after pain.

4

Soothed with the sound, the king grew vain;
Fought all his battles o'er again,
And thrice he routed all his foes, and thrice he slew the slain.
The master saw the madness rise,
His glowing cheeks, his ardent eyes;
And, while he[1] heaven and earth defied,
Changed his hand, and checked his pride.
He chose a mournful Muse,
Soft pity to infuse:
He sung Darius great and good,
By too severe a fate
Fallen, fallen, fallen, fallen,
Fallen from his high estate,
And weltering in his blood;
Deserted at his utmost need
By those his former bounty fed;
On the bare earth exposed he lies,
With not a friend to close his eyes.[2]
With downcast looks the joyless victor sate,
Revolving[3] in his altered soul
The various turns of chance below;
And, now and then, a sigh he stole,
And tears began to flow.

CHORUS

Revolving in his altered soul
The various turns of chance below;
And, now and then, a sigh he stole,
And tears began to flow.

5

The mighty master smiled to see
That love was in the next degree;
'Twas but[4] a kindred sound to move,
For pity melts the mind to love.
Softly sweet, in Lydian[5] measures,

1. Alexander; in line 72, "his hand" is the hand of Timotheus, "his pride," the pride of Alexander.
2. After his final defeat by Alexander, Darius was assassinated by his own followers.
3. Pondering.
4. I.e., it was necessary only.
5. In Greek music the Lydian mode expressed the plaintive and the sad.

Soon he soothed his soul to pleasures.
"War," he sung, "is toil and trouble;
Honor, but an empty bubble.
Never ending, still beginning,
Fighting still, and still destroying:
If the world be worth thy winning,
Think, O think it worth enjoying.
Lovely Thais sits beside thee,
Take the good the gods provide thee."
The many[6] rend the skies with loud applause;
So Love was crowned, but Music won the cause.
The prince, unable to conceal his pain,
Gazed on the fair
Who caused his care,
And sighed and looked, sighed and looked,
Sighed and looked, and sighed again:
At length, with love and wine at once oppressed,
The vanquished victor sunk upon her breast.

CHORUS

The prince, unable to conceal his pain,
Gazed on the fair
Who caused his care,
And sighed and looked, sighed and looked,
Sighed and looked, and sighed again:
At length, with love and wine at once oppressed,
The vanquished victor sunk upon her breast.

6

Now strike the golden lyre again:
A louder yet, and yet a louder strain.
Break his bands of sleep asunder,
And rouse him, like a rattling peal of thunder.
Hark, hark, the horrid[7] sound
Has raised up his head:
As waked from the dead,
And amazed, he stares around.
"Revenge, revenge!" Timotheus cries,
"See the Furies[8] arise!
See the snakes that they rear,
How they hiss in their hair,
And the sparkles that flash from their eyes!
Behold a ghastly band,
Each a torch in his hand!
Those are Grecian ghosts, that in battle were slain,
And unburied remain[9]
Inglorious on the plain:

6. As G. R. Noyes points out, "many" means *meiny*, "a retinue," a spelling that Dryden used elsewhere in his work.
7. Rough, from Latin *horridus*.
8. The Erinyes of the Greeks, avengers of crimes against the natural and the social orders. They are described as women with snakes in their hair and around their waists and arms.
9. According to Greek beliefs, the shades of the dead could not rest until their bodies were buried.

Give the vengeance due
To the valiant crew.
Behold how they toss their torches on high,
How they point to the Persian abodes,
And glittering temples of their hostile gods!"
The princes applaud, with a furious joy;
And the king seized a flambeau[1] with zeal to destroy;
Thaïs led the way,
To light him to his prey,
And, like another Helen, fired another Troy.[2]

CHORUS

And the king seized a flambeau with zeal to destroy;
Thaïs led the way,
To light him to his prey,
And, like another Helen, fired another Troy.

7

Thus long ago,
Ere heaving bellows learned to blow,
While organs yet were mute;
Timotheus, to his breathing flute,
And sounding lyre,
Could swell the soul to rage, or kindle soft desire.
At last, divine Cecilia came,
Inventress of the vocal frame;[3]
The sweet enthusiast,[4] from her sacred store,
Enlarged the former narrow bounds,
And added length to solemn sounds,
With nature's mother wit, and arts unknown before.
Let old Timotheus yield the prize,
Or both divide the crown:
He raised a mortal to the skies;
She drew an angel down.

GRAND CHORUS

At last, divine Cecilia came,
Inventress of the vocal frame;
The sweet enthusiast, from her sacred store,
Enlarged the former narrow bounds,
And added length to solemn sounds,
With nature's mother wit, and arts unknown before.
Let old Timotheus yield the prize,
Or both divide the crown:
He raised a mortal to the skies;
She drew an angel down.

1697

1. Torch.
2. Helen's elopement to Troy with Paris brought on the Trojan War and the ultimate destruction of the city by the Greeks.
3. Organ.
4. Usually at this time a disparaging word, frequently, though not always, applied to a religious zealot or fanatic. Here it is used approvingly and in its literal sense, "possessed by a god," an allusion to Cecilia's angelic companion referred to in line 170. But see note on *Song for St. Cecilia's Day,* line 53.

The Secular Masque[1]

[*Enter* JANUS.[2]]

JANUS. Chronos,[3] Chronos, mend thy pace;
An hundred times the rolling sun
Around the radiant belt[4] has run
In his revolving race.
Behold, behold, the goal in sight;
Spread thy fans,[5] and wing thy flight.

[*Enter* CHRONOS, *with a scythe in his hand, and a great globe on his back, which he sets down at his entrance.*]

CHRONOS. Weary, weary of my weight,
Let me, let me drop my freight,
And leave the world behind.
I could not bear
Another year
The load of humankind.

[*Enter* MOMUS,[6] *laughing.*]

MOMUS. Ha! ha! ha! ha! ha! ha! well hast thou done
To lay down thy pack,
And lighten thy back;
The world was a fool, e'er since it begun,
And since neither Janus, nor Chronos, nor I
Can hinder the crimes,
Or mend the bad times,
'Tis better to laugh than to cry.

CHORUS OF ALL THREE.
'Tis better to laugh than to cry.

JANUS. Since Momus comes to laugh below,
Old Time, begin the show,
That he may see, in every scene,
What changes in this age have been.

CHRONOS. Then, goddess of the silver bow,[7] begin.

[*Horns, or hunting music within.*]

[*Enter* DIANA.]

DIANA. With horns and with hounds I waken the day,

1. A masque is a dramatic performance, usually mythological in character, that combines poetry, music, dance, and spectacle. Distinctly a courtly form of art, it flourished at the courts of James I and Charles I. This masque, however, was written for public performance as an afterpiece to the revival of Fletcher's *The Pilgrim*, revised by Sir John Vanbrugh, and produced for the financial benefit of Dryden himself. It is a "secular masque" because it celebrates the end of the century, "secular" being derived from the Latin *saeculares*, applied to the games, plays, and shows celebrated in Rome once an "age," a period of 120 years. It is not certain that Dryden lived to see his masque performed.

2. The god of beginnings, who here presides over the opening of the new century.

3. God of time.

4. The sun, in the course of a year, passes through all twelve signs of the zodiac ("the radiant belt").

5. Wings.

6. God of mockery and faultfinding.

7. Diana, the virgin goddess of the moon, a huntress. She symbolizes England before the Civil War, an allusion to James I's passion for the chase.

And hie to my woodland walks away;
I tuck up my robe, and am buskined[8] soon,
And tie to my forehead a wexing[9] moon.
I course the fleet stag, unkennel the fox,
And chase the wild goats o'er summits of rocks;
With shouting and hooting we pierce through the sky,
And Echo turns hunter, and doubles the cry.

CHORUS OF ALL.
With shouting and hooting we pierce through the sky,
And Echo turns hunter, and doubles the cry.

JANUS. Then our age was in its prime:
CHRONOS. Free from rage:
DIANA. And free from crime:
MOMUS. A very merry, dancing, drinking,
Laughing, quaffing, and unthinking time.

CHORUS OF ALL.
Then our age was in its prime,
Free from rage, and free from crime;
A very merry, dancing, drinking,
Laughing, quaffing, and unthinking time.

[*Dance of* DIANA'S *attendants.*]

[*Enter* MARS.[1]]

MARS. Inspire[2] the vocal brass, inspire;
The world is past its infant age:
Arms and honor,
Arms and honor,
Set the martial mind on fire,
And kindle manly rage.
Mars has looked the sky to red;
And Peace, the lazy good, is fled.
Plenty, Peace, and Pleasure fly;
The sprightly green
In woodland walks no more is seen;
The sprightly green has drunk the Tyrian dye.[3]

CHORUS OF ALL.
Plenty, Peace, etc.

MARS. Sound the trumpet, beat the drum;
Through all the world around,
Sound a reveille, sound, sound,
The warrior god is come.

CHORUS OF ALL.
Sound the trumpet, etc.

MOMUS. Thy sword within the scabbard keep,
And let mankind agree;
Better the world were fast asleep,

8. Wearing hunting boots.
9. Waxing (i.e., increasing, because in the first quarter).
1. God of war, who represents the period of the Civil War and the Commonwealth.
2. Breathe into.
3. I.e., the costume has changed from the green of the hunter to the crimson of the soldier (at once the color of blood and of "Tyrian dye," known to the ancients as "purple").

Than kept awake by thee.
The fools are only thinner,
With all our cost and care;
But neither side a winner,
For things are as they were.

CHORUS OF ALL.
The fools are only, etc.

[*Enter* VENUS.[4]]

VENUS. Calms appear when storms are past,
Love will have his hour at last:
Nature is my kindly care;
Mars destroys, and I repair;
Take me, take me, while you may;
Venus comes not every day.

CHORUS OF ALL.
Take her, take her, etc.

CHRONOS. The world was then so light,
I scarcely felt the weight;
Joy ruled the day, and Love the night.
But since the Queen of Pleasure left the ground,[5]
I faint, I lag,
And feebly drag
The ponderous orb around.

MOMUS. All, all of a piece throughout:
[*Pointing to* DIANA.]
Thy chase had a beast in view;
[*To* MARS.]
Thy wars brought nothing about;
[*To* VENUS.]
Thy lovers were all untrue.

JANUS. 'Tis well an old age is out:

CHRONOS. And time to begin a new.

CHORUS OF ALL.
All, all of a piece throughout:
Thy chase had a beast in view;
Thy wars brought nothing about;
Thy lovers were all untrue.
'Tis well an old age is out,
And time to begin a new.

[*Dance of huntsmen, nymphs, warriors, and lovers.*]

1700

4. Goddess of love and beauty, representing the licentious reigns of Charles II and James II.

5. Sir Walter Scott suggested that this line refers to the exiled Queen Mary of Modena, wife of James II.

Criticism Because Dryden liked to talk about literature, he became a critic, indeed the first comprehensive critic in England. The Elizabethans, largely impelled by the example of Italian humanists, had produced an interesting and unsystematic body of critical writings. Dryden could look back to such pioneer works as George Puttenham's *Art of English Poesy* (1589), Sir Philip Sidney's *Apology for Poetry* (1595), Samuel Daniel's *Defense of Rhyme* (ca. 1603), and Ben Jonson's *Timber, or Discoveries* (1641), which is more Jonson's commonplace book than a collection of critical essays. These and later writings Dryden knew, as he knew the ancient critics, especially Aristotle, Horace, Quintilian, and Longinus, and the important contemporary French critics, notably Corneille, Rapin, and Boileau. Taken as a whole, his critical prefaces and dedications, which appeared between 1664 and 1700, are the work of a man of independent mind who has made his own synthesis of critical canons from wide reading, a great deal of thinking, and the constant practice of the art of writing. As a critic he is no man's disciple, and he has the saving grace of being always willing to change his mind. This unwillingness to construct a rigid and dogmatic critical system has been regarded by many as mere inconsistency, but recent students of Dryden have held that it is actually the sign of a lively mind, always capable of growth.

All but a very few of Dryden's critical works (most notably the *Essay of Dramatic Poesy*) grew out of the works to which they served as prefaces: comedies, heroic plays, tragedies, translations, poems of various sorts. Each work posed problems which Dryden was eager to discuss with his readers, and the topics that he treated proved to be important in the development of the new literature of which he was the principal apologist. Little that was pertinent escaped his attention: the processes of literary creation fascinated him and led him to talk of wit, fancy, imagination, and judgment; the question of the relation of the poet to tradition prompted him to explore earlier literatures in search of safe guides and models; the problems posed by the new theater and the new drama made it desirable that he, as a playwright, should reassess the achievement of Shakespeare's generation and should theorize about the nature of the forms of modern drama from tragedy down to farce; his interest in poetry as a craft started discussions of metrics, language, imagery, metaphors, poetic license, methods of translation, the literary kinds, the decorum of styles; and always his ready enthusiasm for great writers evoked warm and generous characterizations of the genius of other poets: Shakespeare, Jonson, Chaucer, Juvenal, Horace, Homer, Virgil. For nearly forty years this voice was heard in the land, and when it was finally silenced, a set of critical standards had come into existence and the Augustan age was approaching maturity. The representative selections below may give some insight into how Dryden helped to order taste and critical standards, while he sacrificed nothing of that freedom without which the English literary genius could not function.

From An Essay of Dramatic Poesy[1]

[*Two Sorts of Bad Poetry*]

" * * * I have a mortal apprehension of two poets,[2] whom this victory, with the help of both her wings, will never be able to escape." " 'Tis easy to guess whom you intend," said Lisideius; "and without naming them, I ask you if one of them does not perpetually pay us with clenches[3] upon words, and a certain clownish kind of raillery?[4] if now and then he does not offer at a catachresis[5] or Clevelandism, wresting and torturing a word into another meaning: in fine, if he be not one of those whom the French would call *un mauvais buffon;*[6] one who is so much a well-willer to the satire, that he spares no man; and though he cannot strike a blow to hurt any, yet ought to be punished for the malice of the action, as our witches are justly hanged, because they think themselves so, and suffer deservedly for believing they did mischief, because they meant it." "You have described him," said Crites, "so exactly that I am afraid to come after you with my other extremity of poetry. He is one of those who, having had some advantage of education and converse, knows better than the other what a poet should be,

1. With the reopening of the theaters in 1660, older plays were revived, but, despite their power and charm, they seemed old-fashioned. Although new playwrights, ambitious to create a modern English drama, soon appeared, they were uncertain of their direction. What, if anything, useful could they learn from the dramatic practice of the ancients? Should they ignore the English dramatists of the late 16th and early 17th centuries? Should they make their example the vigorous contemporary drama of France? Dryden addresses himself to these and other problems in this essay, his first extended piece of criticism. Its purpose, he tells us, was "chiefly to vindicate the honor of our English writers from the censure of those who unjustly prefer the French before them." Its method is skeptical: Dryden presents several points of view, but imposes none. The form is a dialogue among friends, like the *Tusculan Disputations* or the *Brutus* of Cicero. Crites praises the drama of the ancients; Eugenius protests against their authority and argues for the idea of progress in the arts; Lisideius urges the excellence of French plays; Neander, speaking in the climactic position, defends the native tradition and the greatness of Shakespeare, Fletcher, and Jonson. The dialogue takes place on June 3, 1665, in a boat on the Thames. The four friends are rowed downstream to listen to the cannonading of the English and Dutch fleets, engaged in battle off the Suffolk coast. As the gunfire recedes they are assured of victory and order their boatman to return to London, and naturally enough they fall to discussing the number of bad poems that the victory will evoke.

2. Probably Robert Wilde and possibly Richard Flecknoe, whom Dryden later ridiculed in *Mac Flecknoe*. Their actual identity is unimportant, for they merely represent two extremes in poetry, both deplorable: the fantastic and extravagant manner of decadent metaphysical wit and its opposite, the flat and the dull. The new poetry was to seek a mean between these extremes. Cf. Pope, *Essay on Criticism* II.239–42 and 289–300.

3. Puns.

4. Boorish banter.

5. The use of a word in a sense remote from its normal meaning: a legitimate figure of speech used by all poets, it had been abused by John Cleveland (1613–58), who was at first admired for his ingenuity, but whose reputation declined rapidly after the Restoration. A Clevelandism: "The marigold, whose courtier's face / *Echoes* the sun * * * "

6. A malicious jester.

but puts it into practice more unluckily than any man; his style and matter are everywhere alike: he is the most calm, peaceable writer you ever read: he never disquiets your passions[7] with the least concernment, but still[8] leaves you in as even a temper as he found you; he is a very Leveler[9] in poetry: he creeps along with ten little words in every line, and helps out his numbers with *for to*, and *unto*, and all the pretty expletives[1] he can find, till he drags them to the end of another line; while the sense is left tired halfway behind it: he doubly starves all his verses, first for want of thought, and then of expression; his poetry neither has wit in it, nor seems to have it; like him in Martial:

Pauper videri Cinna vult, et est pauper.[2]

"He affects plainness, to cover his want of imagination: when he writes the serious way, the highest flight of his fancy is some miserable antithesis, or seeming contradiction; and in the comic he is still reaching at some thin conceit, the ghost of a jest, and that too flies before him, never to be caught; these swallows which we see before us on the Thames are the just resemblance of his wit: you may observe how near the water they stoop, how many proffers they make to dip, and yet how seldom they touch it; and when they do, it is but the surface: they skim over it but to catch a gnat, and then mount into the air and leave it."

[*The Wit of the Ancients: The Universal*]

" * * * A thing well said will be wit in all languages; and though it may lose something in the translation, yet to him who reads it in the original, 'tis still the same: he has an idea of its excellency, though it cannot pass from his mind into any other expression or words than those in which he finds it. When Phaedria, in the *Eunuch*,[3] had a command from his mistress to be absent two days, and, encouraging himself to go through with it, said, '*Tandem ego non illa caream, si sit opus, vel totum triduum?*'[4]—Parmeno, to mock the softness of his master, lifting up his hands and eyes, cries out, as it were in admiration,[5] '*Hui! universum triduum!*' the elegancy of which *universum*, though it cannot be rendered in our language, yet leaves an impression on our souls: but this happens seldom in him; in Plautus[6] oftener, who is infinitely too bold

7. Emotions.
8. Always.
9. The Levelers were radical egalitarians and republicans, a powerful political force in the Puritan Army about 1648. They were suppressed by Cromwell.
1. Words used merely to fill out a line of verse. Cf. Pope, *Essay on Criticism* II.346–47.
2. "Cinna wishes to seem poor, and he is poor" (*Epigrams* VIII.xix).
3. A comedy by the Roman poet Terence (ca. 185–159 B.C.).
4. "Shall I not then do without her, if need be, for three whole days?"
5. Wonder. The wit of Parmeno's exclamation, "Oh, three entire days," depends on *universum*, which suggests that a lover may regard three days as an eternity.
6. Titus Maccus Plautus, Roman comic poet (ca. 254–184 B.C.).

in his metaphors and coining words, out of which many times his wit is nothing; which questionless was one reason why Horace falls upon him so severely in those verses:

Sed proavi nostri Plautinos et numeros et
Laudavere sales, nimium patienter utrumque,
Ne dicam stolide.[7]

For Horace himself was cautious to obtrude a new word on his readers, and makes custom and common use the best measure of receiving it into our writings:

Multa renascentur quae nunc cecidere, cadentque
Quae nunc sunt in honore vocabula, si volet usus,
Quem penes arbitrium est, et jus, et norma loquendi.[8]

"The not observing this rule is that which the world has blamed in our satirist, Cleveland: to express a thing hard and unnaturally is his new way of elocution. 'Tis true no poet but may sometimes use a catachresis: Virgil does it—

Mistaque ridenti colocasia fundet acantho[9]—

in his eclogue of Pollio; and in his seventh *Aeneid:*

mirantur et undae,
Miratur nemus insuetum fulgentia longe
Scuta virum fluvio pictasque innare carinas.[1]

And Ovid once so modestly that he asks leave to do it:

quem, si verbo audacia detur,
Haud metuam summi dixisse Palatia caeli.[2]

calling the court of Jupiter by the name of Augustus his palace; though in another place he is more bold, where he says, '*et longas visent Capitolia pompas.*'[3] But to do this always, and never be able to write a line without it, though it may be admired by some few pedants, will not pass upon those who know that wit is best conveyed to us in the most easy language; and is most to be admired when a great thought comes dressed in words so commonly received that it is understood by the meanest apprehensions, as the

7. "But our ancestors too tolerantly (I do not say foolishly) praised both the verse and the wit of Plautus" (*Ars Poetica,* lines 270–72). Dryden misquotes slightly.
8. "Many words that have perished will be born again, and those shall perish that are now esteemed, if usage wills it, in whose power are the judgment, the law, and the pattern of speech" (*Ars Poetica,* lines 70–72).
9. "[The earth] shall give forth the Egyptian bean, mingled with the smiling acanthus" (*Eclogues* IV.20). "*Smiling* acanthus" is a catachresis.
1. Actually *Aeneid* VIII.91–93. Dryden's paraphrase makes the point clearly: "The woods and waters wonder at the gleam / Of shields and painted ships that stem the stream" (*Aeneis* VIII.125–26). "Wonder" is a catachresis.
2. "[This is the place] which, if boldness of expression be permitted, I shall not hesitate to call the Palace of high heaven" (*Metamorphoses* I.175–76).
3. "And the Capitol shall see the long processions" (*Metamorphoses* I.561).

best meat is the most easily digested: but we cannot read a verse of Cleveland's without making a face at it, as if every word were a pill to swallow: he gives us many times a hard nut to break our teeth, without a kernel for our pains. So that there is this difference betwixt his satires and Doctor Donne's; that the one gives us deep thoughts in common language, though rough cadence; the other gives us common thoughts in abstruse words: 'tis true in some places his wit is independent of his words, as in that of the *Rebel Scot:*

> Had Cain been Scot, God would have changed his doom;
> Not forced him wander, but confined him home.[4]

"*Si sic omnia dixisset!*[5] This is wit in all languages: it is like mercury, never to be lost or killed:[6] and so that other—

> For beauty, like white powder, makes no noise,
> And yet the silent hypocrite destroys.

You see the last line is highly metaphorical, but it is so soft and gentle that it does not shock us as we read it."

[*Shakespeare and Ben Jonson Compared*]

"To begin, then, with Shakespeare. He was the man who of all modern, and perhaps ancient poets, had the largest and most comprehensive soul. All the images of Nature were still present to him, and he drew them, not laboriously, but luckily; when he describes anything, you more than see it, you feel it too. Those who accuse him to have wanted learning, give him the greater commendation: he was naturally learned; he needed not the spectacles of books to read Nature; he looked inwards, and found her there. I cannot say he is everywhere alike; were he so, I should do him injury to compare him with the greatest of mankind. He is many times flat, insipid; his comic wit degenerating into clenches, his serious swelling into bombast. But he is always great when some great occasion is presented to him; no man can say he ever had a fit subject for his wit and did not then raise himself as high above the rest of poets,

> *Quantum lenta solent inter viburna cupressi*[7]

The consideration of this made Mr. Hales of Eton[8] say that there was no subject of which any poet ever writ, but he would produce it much better treated of in Shakespeare; and however others are now generally preferred before him, yet the age wherein he lived,

4. Lines 63–64.
5. "Had he said everything thus!" (Juvenal, *Satires* X.123–24).
6. Mercury is said to be "killed" if its fluidity is destroyed. The couplet quoted below is from *Rupertismus*, lines 39–40.
7. "As do cypresses among the bending shrubs" (Virgil, *Eclogues* I.25).
8. The learned John Hales (1584–1656), provost of Eton. He is reputed to have said this to Jonson himself.

which had contemporaries with him Fletcher and Jonson, never equaled them to him in their esteem: and in the last king's[9] court, when Ben's reputation was at highest, Sir John Suckling,[1] and with him the greater part of the courtiers, set our Shakespeare far above him. * * *

"As for Jonson, to whose character I am now arrived, if we look upon him while he was himself (for his last plays were but his dotages), I think him the most learned and judicious writer which any theater ever had. He was a most severe judge of himself, as well as others. One cannot say he wanted wit, but rather that he was frugal of it. In his works you find little to retrench[2] or alter. Wit, and language, and humor also in some measure, we had before him; but something of art[3] was wanting to the drama till he came. He managed his strength to more advantage than any who preceded him. You seldom find him making love in any of his scenes or endeavoring to move the passions; his genius was too sullen and saturnine[4] to do it gracefully, especially when he knew he came after those who had performed both to such an height. Humor was his proper sphere:[5] and in that he delighted most to represent mechanic people.[6] He was deeply conversant in the ancients, both Greek and Latin, and he borrowed boldly from them: there is scarce a poet or historian among the Roman authors of those times whom he has not translated in *Sejanus* and *Catiline*.[7] But he has done his robberies so openly, that one may see he fears not to be taxed by any law. He invades authors like a monarch; and what would be theft in other poets is only victory in him. With the spoils of these writers he so represents old Rome to us, in its rites, ceremonies, and customs, that if one of their poets had written either of his tragedies, we had seen less of it than in him. If there was any fault in his language, 'twas that he weaved it too closely and laboriously, in his serious plays:[8] perhaps, too, he did a little too much Romanize our tongue, leaving the words which he translated almost as much Latin as he found them: wherein, though he learnedly followed the idiom of their language, he did not enough comply with the idiom of ours. If I would compare him with Shakespeare, I must acknowledge him the more correct poet, but Shakespeare the greater wit.[9] Shakespeare was the Homer, or father of our dramatic poets; Jonson was the Virgil, the pattern of elaborate writing; I admire him, but I love Shakespeare. To

9. Charles I.
1. Courtier, poet, playwright, much admired in Dryden's time for his wit and the easy naturalness of his style.
2. Delete.
3. Craftsmanship.
4. Heavy.
5. In Jonson's comedies the characters are seen under the domination of some psychological trait, ruling passion, or affectation—i.e., some "humor"—which makes them unique and ridiculous.
6. I.e., artisans.
7. Jonson's two Roman plays, dated 1605 and 1611 respectively.
8. This is the reading of the first edition. Curiously enough, in the second edition Dryden altered the phrase to "in his comedies especially."
9. Genius.

conclude of him; as he has given us the most correct plays, so in the precepts which he has laid down in his *Discoveries,* we have as many and profitable rules for perfecting the stage, as any wherewith the French can furnish us."

1668

From The Author's Apology for Heroic Poetry and Heroic License[1]

[*"Boldness" of Figures and Tropes Defended: The Appeal to "Nature"*]

* * * They, who would combat general authority with particular opinion, must first establish themselves a reputation of understanding better than other men. Are all the flights of heroic poetry to be concluded bombast, unnatural, and mere madness, because they are not affected with their excellencies? It is just as reasonable as to conclude there is no day, because a blind man cannot distinguish of light and colors. Ought they not rather, in modesty, to doubt of their own judgments, when they think this or that expression in Homer, Virgil, Tasso, or Milton's *Paradise* to be too far strained, than positively to conclude that 'tis all fustian and mere nonsense? 'Tis true there are limits to be set betwixt the boldness and rashness of a poet; but he must understand those limits who pretends to judge as well as he who undertakes to write: and he who has no liking to the whole ought, in reason, to be excluded from censuring of the parts. He must be a lawyer before he mounts the tribunal; and the judicature of one court, too, does not qualify a man to preside in another. He may be an excellent pleader in the Chancery, who is not fit to rule the Common Pleas. But I will presume for once to tell them that the boldest strokes of poetry, when they are managed artfully, are those which most delight the reader.

Virgil and Horace, the severest writers of the severest age, have made frequent use of the hardest metaphors and of the strongest hyperboles; and in this case the best authority is the best argument, for generally to have pleased, and through all ages, must bear the force of universal tradition. And if you would appeal from thence to right reason, you will gain no more by it in effect than,

1. This essay was prefixed to Dryden's *State of Innocence,* the libretto for an opera (never produced), based on *Paradise Lost.* Dryden had been ridiculed for the extravagant and bold imagery and rhetorical figures that are typical of the style of his rhymed heroic plays. This preface is a defense not only of his own predilection for what Samuel Johnson described as "wild and daring sallies of sentiment, in the irregular and eccentric violence of wit," but also of the theory that heroic and idealized materials should be treated in lofty and boldly metaphorical style; hence his definition of "wit" as propriety.

first, to set up your reason against those authors, and, secondly, against all those who have admired them. You must prove why that ought not to have pleased which has pleased the most learned and the most judicious; and, to be thought knowing, you must first put the fool upon all mankind. If you can enter more deeply than they have done into the causes and resorts[2] of that which moves pleasure in a reader, the field is open, you may be heard: but those springs of human nature are not so easily discovered by every superficial judge: it requires philosophy, as well as poetry, to sound the depth of all the passions, what they are in themselves, and how they are to be provoked; and in this science the best poets have excelled. * * * From hence have sprung the tropes[3] and figures, for which they wanted a name who first practiced them and succeeded in them. Thus I grant you that the knowledge of Nature was the original rule, and that all poets ought to study her, as well as Aristotle and Horace, her interpreters.[4] But then this also undeniably follows, that those things which delight all ages must have been an imitation of Nature—which is all I contend. Therefore is rhetoric made an art; therefore the names of so many tropes and figures were invented, because it was observed they had such and such effect upon the audience. Therefore catachreses and hyperboles[5] have found their place amongst them; not that they were to be avoided, but to be used judiciously and placed in poetry as heightenings and shadows are in painting, to make the figure bolder, and cause it to stand off to sight. * * *

[*Wit as "Propriety"*]

* * * [Wit] is a propriety of thoughts and words; or, in other terms, thought and words elegantly adapted to the subject. If our critics will join issue on this definition, that we may *convenire in aliquo tertio*;[6] if they will take it as a granted principle, it will be easy to put an end to this dispute. No man will disagree from another's judgment concerning the dignity of style in heroic poetry; but all reasonable men will conclude it necessary that sublime subjects ought to be adorned with the sublimest, and, consequently, often with the most figurative expressions. * * *

1677

2. Mechanical springs which set something in motion.
3. The use of a word in a figurative sense; "figures," in this phrase, means such figures of speech as metaphors and similes.
4. In the words of the French critic René Rapin, the rules (largely derived from Aristotle's *Poetics* and Horace's *Ars Poetica*) were made in order to "reduce Nature to method." Cf. Pope, *Essay on Criticism* I.88–89.
5. "Catachresis" is the use of a word in a sense remote from its normal meaning; "hyperbole," deliberate overstatement or exaggeration.
6. "To find some means of agreement, in a third term, between the two opposites" [W. P. Ker's note].

From A Discourse Concerning the Original and Progress of Satire[1]

[*The Art of Satire*]

* * * How easy is it to call rogue and villain, and that wittily! But how hard to make a man appear a fool, a blockhead, or a knave without using any of those opprobrious terms! To spare the grossness of the names, and to do the thing yet more severely, is to draw a full face, and to make the nose and cheeks stand out, and yet not to employ any depth of shadowing.[2] This is the mystery of that noble trade, which yet no master can teach to his apprentice; he may give the rules, but the scholar is never the nearer in his practice. Neither is it true that this fineness of raillery[3] is offensive. A witty man is tickled while he is hurt in this manner, and a fool feels it not. The occasion of an offense may possibly be given, but he cannot take it. If it be granted that in effect this way does more mischief; that a man is secretly wounded, and though he be not sensible himself, yet the malicious world will find it out for him; yet there is still a vast difference betwixt the slovenly butchering of a man, and the fineness of a stroke that separates the head from the body, and leaves it standing in its place. A man may be capable, as Jack Ketch's[4] wife said of his servant, of a plain piece of work, a bare hanging; but to make a malefactor die sweetly was only belonging to her husband. I wish I could apply it to myself, if the reader would be kind enough to think it belongs to me. The character of Zimri in my *Absalom*[5] is, in my opinion, worth the whole poem: it is not bloody, but it is ridiculous enough; and he, for whom it was intended, was too witty to resent it as an injury. If I had railed,[6] I might have suffered for it justly; but I managed my own work more happily, perhaps more dexterously. I avoided the mention of great crimes, and applied myself to the representing of blindsides, and little extravagancies; to which, the wittier a man is, he is generally the more obnoxious.[7] It succeeded as I

1. This passage is an excerpt from the long and rambling preface which served as the dedication of a translation of the satires of the Roman satirists Juvenal and Persius to Charles Sackville, 6th Earl of Dorset. The translations were made by Dryden and other writers, among them William Congreve. Dryden traces the origin and development of verse satire in Rome, and in a very fine passage contrasts Horace and Juvenal as satiric poets. It is plain that he prefers the "tragic" satire of Juvenal to the urbane and laughing satire of Horace. But in the passage printed here he praises his own satiric character of Zimri (the Duke of Buckingham) in *Absalom and Achitophel* for the very reason that it is modeled on Horatian "raillery," not Juvenalian invective.
2. Early English miniaturists prided themselves on the art of giving roundness to the full face without painting in shadows.
3. Satirical mirth, good-natured satire.
4. A notorious public executioner of Dryden's time (d. 1686). His name later became a generic term for all members of his profession.
5. See *Absalom and Achitophel* I.544–68.
6. Reviled, abused. Observe that the verb differed in meaning from its noun, defined above.
7. Liable.

wished; the jest went round, and he was laughed at in his turn who began the frolic. * * *

1693

From The Preface to *Fables Ancient and Modern*[1]

[*In Praise of Chaucer*]

In the first place, as he is the father of English poetry, I hold him in the same degree of veneration as the Grecians held Homer, or the Romans Virgil. He is a perpetual fountain of good sense; learned in all sciences;[2] and, therefore, speaks properly on all subjects. As he knew what to say, so he knows also when to leave off; a continence which is practiced by few writers, and scarcely by any of the ancients, excepting Virgil and Horace. * * *

Chaucer followed Nature everywhere, but was never so bold to go beyond her; and there is a great difference of being *poeta* and *nimis poeta*,[3] if we may believe Catullus, as much as betwixt a modest behavior and affectation. The verse of Chaucer, I confess, is not harmonious to us; but 'tis like the eloquence of one whom Tacitus commends, it was *auribus istius temporis accommodata:*[4] they who lived with him, and some time after him, thought it musical; and it continues so, even in our judgment, if compared with the numbers[5] of Lydgate and Gower, his contemporaries; there is the rude sweetness of a Scotch tune in it, which is natural and pleasing, though not perfect. 'Tis true I cannot go so far as he who published the last edition of him;[6] for he would make us believe the fault is in our ears, and that there were really ten syllables in a verse where we find but nine; but this opinion is not worth confuting; 'tis so gross and obvious an error that common sense (which is a rule in everything but matters of faith and revelation) must convince the reader that equality of numbers in every verse which we call heroic[7] was either not known, or not always practiced in Chaucer's age. It were an easy matter to produce some thousands

1. Dryden's final work, published in the year of his death, was a collection of translations from Homer, Ovid, Boccaccio, and Chaucer, and one or two other pieces. The Preface, in many ways, is Dryden's ripest and finest critical essay. In it, he is not concerned with critical theory or with a formalistic approach to literature; he is simply a man, grown old in the reading and writing of poetry, who is eager to talk informally with his readers about some of his favorite authors. His praise of Chaucer (unusually sympathetic and perceptive for 1700) is animated by that love of great literature which is manifest in everything that Dryden wrote.

2. Branches of learning.

3. A poet ("*poeta*") and too much of a poet ("*nimis poeta*"). The phrase is not from Catullus but from Martial (*Epigrams* III.44).

4. "Suitable to the ears of that time." Tacitus was a Roman historian and writer on oratory (A.D. ca. 55–ca. 117).

5. Versification. John Lydgate (ca. 1370–ca. 1449) wrote poetry which shows the influence of Chaucer. John Gower (d. 1408), poet and friend of Chaucer.

6. Thomas Speght's Chaucer, which Dryden used, was first published in 1598; the second edition, published in 1602, was reprinted in 1687.

7. The pentameter line. In Dryden's time few readers knew how to pronounce Middle English, especially the syllabic *e*. Moreover, Chaucer's works were

of his verses which are lame for want of half a foot, and sometimes a whole one, and which no pronunciation can make otherwise. We can only say that he lived in the infancy of our poetry, and that nothing is brought to perfection at the first. * * *

He must have been a man of a most wonderful comprehensive nature, because, as it has been truly observed of him, he has taken into the compass of his *Canterbury Tales* the various manners and humors (as we now call them) of the whole English nation in his age. Not a single character has escaped him. All his pilgrims are severally distinguished from each other; and not only in their inclinations but in their very physiognomies and persons. Baptista Porta[8] could not have described their natures better than by the marks which the poet gives them. The matter and manner of their tales, and of their telling, are so suited to their different educations, humors, and callings that each of them would be improper in any other mouth. Even the grave and serious characters are distinguished by their several sorts of gravity: their discourses are such as belong to their age, their calling, and their breeding; such as are becoming of them, and of them only. Some of his persons are vicious, and some virtuous; some are unlearned, or (as Chaucer calls them) lewd, and some are learned. Even the ribaldry of the low characters is different: the Reeve, the Miller, and the Cook are several[9] men, and distinguished from each other as much as the mincing Lady Prioress and the broad-speaking, gap-toothed Wife of Bath. But enough of this; there is such a variety of game springing up before me that I am distracted in my choice, and know not which to follow. 'Tis sufficient to say, according to the proverb, that here is God's plenty. * * *

1700

known only in corrupt printed texts. As a consequence Chaucer's verse seemed rough and irregular.

8. Giambattista della Porta (ca. 1535–1615), author of a Latin treatise on physiognomy.

9. Different.

JOHN BUNYAN
(1628–1688)

1653: Conversion.
1660–72: Imprisoned in Bedford jail.
1675: Second imprisonment in Bedford jail; *The Pilgrim's Progress* composed.

Bunyan is one of the most remarkable figures in 17th-century literature. The son of a poor Bedfordshire tinker (a maker and mender of metal pots), he received only meager schooling and then learned his father's craft. Nothing in the circumstances of his early life could have suggested that he would become a writer known the world over in translations too numerous to reckon, many of them in languages and dialects of which he had never heard.

His inner life is fully chronicled in his spiritual autobiography, *Grace Abounding to the Chief of Sinners* (1666). Here we learn of his humble parentage, his marriage to a woman (he does not tell us her name) whose dowry consisted only of two pious tracts, and of his military service—in the Parliamentary army (though he neglects to say so). But such details scarcely interest him except as he can use them to reveal the purposes of Divine Providence. *Grace Abounding* was written to show the way by which a man, convinced of his sins, is led by God's grace through the agonies of spiritual crises to a new birth and the assurance of salvation; and to record how the obscure and sinful tinker was transformed into the eloquent and fearless preacher. Such books abounded in Puritan England and followed a conventional formula; but Bunyan's psychological insight and vivid narrative gifts make *Grace Abounding* one of the most enthralling autobiographies in the language.

As a result of his spiritual struggle and triumph, he joined one of the several groups of Baptists and began his career as a preacher and religious writer. Preachers, both male and female, often even less educated than Bunyan, were common phenomena among the sects during the Commonwealth. They wished no ordination but the "call," and they could dispense with learning since they abounded in inspiration, inner light, and the gifts conferred by the Holy Spirit. In November, 1660, despite Charles II's promised policy of mildness, the Anglican Church began to persecute and silence the Dissenting sects. Jails filled with unlicensed Nonconformist preachers, and John Bunyan was one of the prisoners. Refusing to keep silent, he chose imprisonment and so for twelve years remained in Bedford jail, preaching to his fellow prisoners and writing religious books. Upon his release, he was called to the pastorate of a Nonconformist group in Bedford. It was during a second imprisonment, in 1675, when the Test Act was once again rigorously enforced against Nonconformists, that he wrote his greatest work, *The Pilgrim's Progress from This World to That Which Is to Come* (1678), revised and augmented in the third edition (1679). Bunyan was a prolific writer: Part II of *The Pilgrim's Progress*, dealing with the journey of Christian's wife and children, appeared in 1684; *The Life and Death of Mr. Badman*, in 1680; *The Holy War*, in 1682. But these major works form only a small part of all his writings.

The Pilgrim's Progress is the most successful allegory in our literature. Its basic metaphor—life is a journey—is simple and familiar; the objects that the pilgrim Christian meets are homely and commonplace: a quagmire, the highway, the bypaths and short cuts through pleasant meadows; the inn, the steep hill, the town fair on market day; the river that must be forded—such objects were familiar then, and *mutatis mutandis*, are familiar even in our automotive age. They have the immediacy of daily experience, a quality that recalls the equally homely parables of Jesus, but Bunyan's allegorizing of these details charges them with spiritual significance. Moreover, Bunyan is a superb storyteller: this is, after all, a tale of adventure; he knows how to keep his reader in suspense, and because he was of the folk, how to mingle the romantic and the strange with the familiar. If the road that Christian travels is the King's Highway, it is also a perilous path along which we encounter giants, wild beasts, hobgoblins, and the terrible Apollyon, "the angel of the bottomless pit," with whom Christian must fight. Bunyan's knowledge of human nature keeps the tale firmly based on universal experience—whether in the brilliant and sometimes humorous characterization of other travelers along the way (who represent states of the soul and intellectual or moral attitudes) or in the inevitably right arrangement of Christian's own experiences, from the unforgettable first sight that we catch of him as his reading in the book convinces him of his sins and evokes his cry of terror, to the moving account of his death with Hopeful in the river. Finally, Bunyan's style, modeled on the prose of the English Bible, together with his concrete and living language and carefully observed and vividly rendered details, enable even the simplest reader to share the experiences of the characters. What could be better than the following sentence? "Some cry out against sin even as the mother cries out against her child in her lap, when she calleth it slut and naughty girl, and then falls to hugging and kissing it." Even the conversations on doctrinal matters, tedious though they are, cannot seriously damage so human and dramatic a tale. In a secular age like the present, *The Pilgrim's Progress* is no longer a household book; but it survives in the speech of men who have never read it, for it gave to our language phrases that will doubtless always live: "the slough of despond," "the house beautiful," "Mr. Worldly-Wiseman," "Vanity Fair." And it lives again for anyone who reads beyond the first page.

From Grace Abounding to the Chief of Sinners

It would be too long for me here to stay, to tell you in particular how God did set me down in all the things of Christ, and how he did, that he might so do, lead me into his words, yea and also how he did open them unto me, make them shine before me, and cause them to dwell with me and comfort me over and over, both of his own being, and the being of his Son, and Spirit, and Word, and Gospel.

Only this, as I said before I will say unto you again, that in general he was pleased to take this course with me, first, to suffer me to be afflicted with temptation concerning them, and then reveal them to me; as sometimes I should lie under great guilt for sin, even crushed to the ground therewith, and then the Lord would shew me the death of Christ, yea and so sprinkle my Conscience with his Blood, that I should find, and that before I was aware, that in that Conscience where but just now did reign and rage the Law, even there would rest and abide the Peace and Love of *God* through Christ.

Now had I an evidence, as I thought, of my salvation from Heaven, with many golden Seals thereon, all hanging in my sight; now could I remember this manifestation, and the other discovery of grace with comfort; and should often long and desire that the last day were come, that I might forever be inflamed with the sight, and joy, and communion of him, whose Head was crowned with Thorns, whose Face was spit on, and Body broken, and Soul made an offering for my sins: for whereas before I lay continually trembling at the mouth of Hell; now me thought I was got so far therefrom, that I could not, when I looked back, scarce discern it; and O thought I, that I were fourscore years old now, that I might die quickly, that my soul might be gone to rest.

But before I had got thus far out of these my temptations, I did greatly long to see some ancient Godly man's Experience, who had writ some hundred of years before I was born; for, for those who had writ in our days, I thought (but I desire them now to pardon me) that they had Writ only that which others felt, or else had, through the strength of their Wits and Parts, studied to answer such Objections as they perceived others were perplexed with, without going down themselves into the deep. Well, after many such longings in my mind, the God in whose hands are all our days and ways, did cast into my hand, one day, a book of *Martin Luther*, his comment on the *Galathians*, so old that it was ready to fall piece from piece, if I did but turn it over. Now I was pleased much that such an old book had fallen into my hand; the which, when I had but a little way perused, I found my condition in his experience, so largely and profoundly handled, as if his Book had been written out of my heart; this made me marvel: for thus thought I, this man could not know anything of the state of Christians now, but must needs write and speak of the Experience of former days.

Besides, he doth most gravely also, in that book debate of the rise of these temptations, namely, Blasphemy, Desperation, and the like, shewing that the law of *Moses*, as well as the Devil, Death, and Hell, hath a very great hand therein; the which at first was very strange to me, but considering and watching, I found it so indeed. But of Particulars here I intend nothing, only this methinks I must let fall before all men, I do prefer this book of Mr. *Luther* upon the *Galathians*, (excepting the Holy Bible) before all the books that ever I have seen, as most fit for a wounded Conscience.

* * *

And now I found, as I thought, that I loved Christ dearly. O me thought my soul cleaved unto him, my affections cleaved unto him. I felt love to him as hot as fire, and now, as Job said, I thought I should die in my nest; but I did quickly find that my great love was but little, and that I, who had as I thought such burning love to Jesus Christ, could let him go again for a trifle. God can tell how to abase us, and can hide pride from man. Quickly after this my love was tried to purpose.

For after the Lord had in this manner thus graciously delivered me from this great and sore temptation, and had set me down so sweetly in the faith of his holy gospel, and had given me such strong consolation and blessed evidence from heaven touching my interest in his love through Christ; the Tempter came upon me again, and that with a more grievous and dreadful temptation than before.

And that was to sell and part with this most blessed Christ, to exchange him for the things of this life, for any thing: the temptation lay upon me for the space of a year, and did follow me so continally that I was not rid of it one day in a month, no not sometimes one hour in many days together, unless I was asleep.

And though in my judgment I was persuaded that those who were once effectually in Christ (as I hoped, through his grace, I had seen myself) could never lose him forever . . . yet it was a continual vexation to me to think I should have so much as one such thought within me against a Christ, a Jesus, that had done for me as he had done; and yet then I had almost none others, but such blasphemous ones.

But it was neither my dislike of the thought, nor yet any desire and endeavor to resist it, that in the least did shake or abate the continuation or force and strength thereof; for it did always in almost whatever I thought intermix itself therewith, in such sort that I could neither eat my food, stoop for a pin, chop a stick, or cast mine eye to look on this or that, but still the temptation would come, *Sell Christ for this, or sell Christ for that; sell him, sell him.*

Sometimes it would run in my thoughts not so little as a hundred times together, Sell him, sell him, sell him; against which, I may say, for whole hours together, I have been forced to stand as continually leaning and forcing my spirit against it, lest haply before I were aware, some wicked thought might arise in my heart that might consent thereto; and sometimes also the Tempter would make me believe I had consented to it, then should I be as tortured on a rack for whole days together.

This temptation did put me to such scares lest I should sometimes, I say, consent thereto and be overcome therewith, that by the very force of my mind in laboring to gainsay and resist this wickedness, my very body also would be put into action or motion, by way of pushing or thrusting with my hands or elbows; still answering, as fast as the destroyer said *Sell him*: I will not, I will not, I will not, I will not, no, not for thousands, thousands, thousands of worlds, thus reckoning lest I should in the midst of these assaults set too low a value of him, even until I scarce well knew where I was, or how to be composed again.

At these seasons he would not let me eat my food at quiet, but forsooth when I was set at the table at my meat, I must go hence to pray, I must leave my food now, just now, so counterfeit holy would this Devil be. When I was thus tempted, I should say in myself, *Now I am at my meat, let me make an end.* No, said he, *you must do it now, or you will displease God and despise Christ.* Wherefore

I was much afflicted with these things; and because of the sinfulness of my nature (imagining that these things were impulses from God), I should deny to do it as if I denied God; and then should I be as guilty because I did not obey a temptation of the Devil, as if I had broken the law of God indeed.

But to be brief, one morning, as I did lie in my bed, I was, as at other times, most fiercely assaulted with this temptation, to *sell and part with Christ*; the wicked suggestion still running in my mind, *Sell him, sell him, sell him,* as fast as a man could speak; against which also in my mind, as at other times, I answered, No, no, not for thousands, thousands, thousands, at least twenty times together; but at last, after much striving, even until I was almost out of breath, I felt this thought pass through my heart, *Let him go if he will!* and I thought also that I felt my heart freely consent thereto. Oh, the diligence of Satan! Oh, the desperateness of man's heart!

Now was the battle won, and down I fell, as a bird that is shot from the top of a tree, into great guilt and fearful despair; thus getting out of my bed, I went moping into the field; but God knows with as heavy a heart as mortal man, I think, could bear; where for the space of two hours, I was like a man bereft of life, and as now past all recovery, and bound over to eternal punishment.

* * *

Now was I as one bound, I felt myself shut up unto the judgment to come; nothing now for two years together would abide with me but damnation and an expectation of damnation: I say nothing now would abide with me but this, save some few moments for relief, as in the sequel you will see.

These words were to my soul like fetters of brass to my legs, in the continual sound of which I went for several months together. But about ten or eleven a clock one day, as I was walking under a hedge, full of sorrow and guilt, God knows, and bemoaning myself for this hard hap, that such a thought should arise within me, suddenly this sentence bolted in upon me, *The blood of Christ remits all guilt*; at this I made a stand in my spirit: with that, this word took hold upon me, *The blood of Jesus Christ his son cleanseth us from all sin.*

Now I began to conceive peace in my soul, and methought I saw as if the tempter did leer and steal away from me, as being ashamed of what he had done. At the same time also I had my sin and the blood of Christ thus represented to me, That my sin when compared to the blood of Christ was no more to it than this little clot or stone before me is to this vast and wide field that here I see. This gave me good encouragement for the space of two or three hours, in which time also methought I saw by faith the son of God as suffering for my sins. But because it tarried not, I therefore sunk in my spirit under exceeding guilt again.

* * *

And now I was both a burden and a terror to myself, nor did I ever so know, as now, what it was to be weary of my life and yet afraid to die. Oh, how gladly now would I have been anybody but myself! Anything but a man! and in any condition but mine own! for there was nothing did pass more frequently over my mind, than that it was impossible for me to be forgiven my transgression, and to be saved from the wrath to come.

* * *

Once as I was walking to and fro in a good man's shop, bemoaning to myself in my sad and doleful state, afflicting myself with self-abhorrence for this wicked and ungodly thought, lamenting also for this hard hap of mine, for that I should commit so great a sin, greatly fearing I should not be pardoned; praying also in my heart, That if this sin of mine did differ from that against the Holy Ghost, the Lord would show it to me: and being now ready to sink with fear, suddenly there was as if there had rushed in at the window the noise of wind upon me, but very pleasant, and as if I had heard a voice speaking, *Didst ever refuse to be justified by the blood of Christ?* and withal my whole life of profession[1] past was in a moment opened to me, wherein I was made to see that designedly I had not; so my heart answered groaningly, *No.* Then fell with power that word of God upon me, *See that ye refuse not him that speaketh* (Hebrews 12.25). This made a strange seizure upon my spirit; it brought light with it, and commanded a silence in my heart of all those tumultuous thoughts that before did use, like masterless hellhounds to roar and bellow and make a hideous noise within me. It showed me also that Jesus Christ had yet a work of grace and mercy for me, that he had not, as I had feared, quite forsaken and cast off my soul; yea, this was a kind of chide for my proneness to desperation; a kind of threatening me if I did not, notwithstanding my sins and the heinousness of them, venture my salvation upon the son of God. * * * This lasted in the savor of it, for about three or four days, and then I began to mistrust and to despair again.

* * *

At another time I remember I was again much under the question, Whether the blood of Christ was sufficient to save my soul? In which doubt I continued from morning till about seven or eight at night; and at last when I was, as it were, quite worn out with fear lest it should not lay hold on me, these words did sound suddenly within me, *He is able*: but me thought this word *able* was spoke so loud unto me, it showed such a *great* word, it seemed to be writ in *great* letters, and gave such a justle to my fear and doubt (I mean for the time it tarried with me, which was about a day) as I never

1. My life as a believing (professing) Christian.

had from that, all my life either before or after that.

But one morning when I was again at prayer and trembling under the fear of this, that no word of God could help me, that piece of a sentence darted in upon me, *My grace is sufficient.* At this me thought I felt some stay, as if there might be hopes. But O how good a thing is it for God to send his word! for about a fortnight before, I was looking on this very place, and then I thought it could not come near my soul with comfort, and threw down my book in a pet. Then I thought it was not large enough for me; no, not large enough; but now it was as if it had arms of grace so wide that it could not only enclose me, but many more besides.

By these words I was sustained, yet not without exceeding conflicts, for the space of seven or eight weeks: for my peace would be in and out sometimes twenty times a day. Comfort now and trouble presently; peace now, and before I could go a furlong, as full of fear and guilt as ever heart could hold. And this was not only now and then, but my whole seven weeks' experience; for this about the sufficiency of grace and that of Esau's parting with his birthright[2] would be like a pair of scales within my mind, sometimes one end would be uppermost and sometimes again the other, according to which would be my peace or trouble.

1666

From The Pilgrim's Progress

From This World to That Which Is to Come: Delivered Under the Similitude of a Dream

[*Christian Sets out for the Celestial City*]

As I walked through the wilderness of this world, I lighted on a certain place where was a Den, and I laid me down in that place to sleep; and, as I slept, I dreamed a dream. I dreamed, and behold I saw a man clothed with rags, standing in a certain place, with his face from his own house, a book in his hand, and a great burden upon his back (*Isaiah lxiv.6; Luke xiv.33; Psalms xxxviii.4; Habakkuk ii.2; Acts xvi.31*). I looked and saw him open the book and read therein; and, as he read, he wept, and trembled; and not being able longer to contain, he brake out with a lamentable cry, saying, "What shall I do?" (*Acts ii.37*).

In this plight, therefore, he went home and refrained himself as long as he could, that his wife and children should not perceive his distress; but he could not be silent long, because that his trouble increased. Wherefore at length he brake his mind to his wife

2. Bunyan believed that when the fatal phrase about "letting Christ go if he would" flashed through his mind, all power to share in the Christian blessing was eternally lost to him, as Esau sold his birthright irrevocably, irretrievably, forever.

and children; and thus he began to talk to them. O my dear wife, said he, and you the children of my bowels, I your dear friend am in myself undone by reason of a burden that lieth hard upon me; moreover, I am for certain informed that this our city will be burned with fire from heaven, in which fearful overthrow both myself, with thee, my wife, and you, my sweet babes, shall miserably come to ruin, except (the which yet I see not) some way of escape can be found, whereby we may be delivered. At this his relations were sore amazed; not for that they believed that what he had said to them was true, but because they thought that some frenzy distemper[1] had got into his head; therefore, it drawing towards night, and they hoping that sleep might settle his brains, with all haste they got him to bed; but the night was as troublesome to him as the day; wherefore, instead of sleeping, he spent it in sighs and tears. So when the morning was come, they would know how he did. He told them, Worse and worse; he also set to talking to them again, but they began to be hardened. They also thought to drive away his distemper by harsh and surly carriages[2] to him: sometimes they would deride, sometimes they would chide, and sometimes they would quite neglect him. Wherefore he began to retire himself to his chamber, to pray for and pity them, and also to condole his own misery; he would also walk solitarily in the fields, sometimes reading, and sometimes praying; and thus for some days he spent his time.

Now I saw, upon a time, when he was walking in the fields, that he was (as he was wont) reading in this book, and greatly distressed in his mind; and as he read, he burst out, as he had done before, crying, "What shall I do to be saved?"

I saw also that he looked this way and that way, as if he would run; yet he stood still, because (as I perceived) he could not tell which way to go. I looked then, and saw a man named Evangelist[3] coming to him, who asked, Wherefore dost thou cry? (*Job xxxiii.23*). He answered, Sir, I perceive by the book in my hand that I am condemned to die, and after that to come to judgment (*Hebrews ix.27*), and I find that I am not willing to do the first (*Job xvi.21*), nor able to do the second (*Ezekiel xxii.14*). * * *

Then said Evangelist, Why not willing to die, since this life is attended with so many evils? The man answered, Because I fear that this burden that is upon my back will sink me lower than the grave, and I shall fall into Tophet[4] (*Isaiah xxx.33*). And, sir, if I be not fit to go to prison, I am not fit to go to judgment, and from thence to execution; and the thoughts of these things make me cry.[5]

1. A malady causing madness; the use of "frenzy" as an adjective was not uncommon in the 17th century.
2. Behavior.
3. A preacher of the Gospel; literally, a bearer of good news.
4. The place near Jerusalem where bodies and filth were burned; hence, by association, a name for hell.
5. Cry out.

Then said Evangelist, If this be thy condition, why standest thou still? He answered, Because I know not whither to go. Then he gave him a parchment roll, and there was written within, "Fly from the wrath to come" (*Matthew iii.7*).

The man therefore read it, and looking upon Evangelist very carefully,[6] said, Whither must I fly? Then said Evangelist, pointing with his finger over a very wide field, Do you see yonder wicket-gate?[7] (*Matthew vii.13, 14.*) The man said, No. Then said the other, Do you see yonder shining light? (*Psalms cxix.105; II Peter i.19.*) He said, I think I do. Then said Evangelist, Keep that light in your eye, and go up directly thereto; so shalt thou see the gate; at which when thou knockest it shall be told thee what thou shalt do.

So I saw in my dream that the man began to run. Now, he had not run far from his own door, but his wife and children perceiving it, began to cry after him to return; but the man put his fingers in his ears, and ran on, crying, Life! life! eternal life! (*Luke xiv.26.*) So he looked not behind him, but fled towards the middle of the plain (*Genesis xix.17*).

The neighbors also came out to see him run (*Jeremiah xx.10*); and as he ran some mocked, others threatened, and some cried after him to return; and, among those that did so, there were two that resolved to fetch him back by force. The name of the one was Obstinate, and the name of the other Pliable. Now by this time the man was got a good distance from them; but, however, they were resolved to pursue him, which they did, and in a little time they overtook him. Then said the man, Neighbors, wherefore are ye come? They said, To persuade you to go back with us. But he said, That can by no means be; you dwell, said he, in the City of Destruction (the place also where I was born) I see it to be so; and, dying there, sooner or later, you will sink lower than the grave, into a place that burns with fire and brimstone; be content, good neighbors, and go along with me.

OBST. What! said Obstinate, and leave our friends and our comforts behind us?

CHR. Yes, said Christian (for that was his name), because that ALL which you shall forsake is not worthy to be compared with a little of that which I am seeking to enjoy (*II Corinthians v.17*); and, if you will go along with me, and hold it, you shall fare as I myself; for there, where I go, is enough and to spare (*Luke xv.17*). Come away, and prove my words.

OBST. What are the things you seek, since you leave all the world to find them?

CHR. I seek an inheritance incorruptible, undefiled, and that fad-

6. Sorrowfully.
7. A small gate in or beside a larger gate.

eth not away (*I Peter i.4*), and it is laid up in heaven, and safe there (*Hebrews xi.16*), to be bestowed, at the time appointed, on them that diligently seek it. Read it so, if you will, in my book.

OBST. Tush! said Obstinate, away with your book; will you go back with us or no?

CHR. No, not I, said the other, because I have laid my hand to the plow (*Luke ix.62*).

OBST. Come, then, neighbor Pliable, let us turn again, and go home without him; there is a company of these crazed-headed coxcombs,[8] that, when they take a fancy by the end, are wiser in their own eyes than seven men that can render a reason (*Proverbs xxvi.16*).

PLI. Then said Pliable, Don't revile; if what the good Christian says is true, the things he looks after are better than ours; my heart inclines to go with my neighbor.

OBST. What! more fools still? Be ruled by me, go back; who knows whither such a brain-sick fellow will lead you? Go back, go back, and be wise.

CHR. Nay, but do thou come with thy neighbor, Pliable; there are such things to be had which I spoke of, and many more glories besides. If you believe not me, read here in this book; and for the truth of what is expressed therein, behold, all is confirmed by the blood of Him that made it (*Hebrews ix.17–22; xiii.20*).

PLI. Well, neighbour Obstinate, said Pliable, I begin to come to a point,[9] I intend to go along with this good man, and to cast in my lot with him: but, my good companion, do you know the way to this desired place?

CHR. I am directed by a man, whose name is Evangelist, to speed me to a little gate that is before us, where we shall receive instructions about the way.

PLI. Come, then, good neighbor, let us be going. Then they went both together. * * *

[*The Slough of Despond*]

Now I saw in my dream, that just as they had ended this talk they drew near to a very miry slough,[1] that was in the midst of the plain; and they, being heedless, did both fall suddenly into the bog. The name of the slough was Despond. Here, therefore, they wallowed for a time, being grievously bedaubed with dirt; and Christian, because of the burden that was on his back, began to sink in the mire.

PLI. Then said Pliable, Ah, neighbor Christian, where are you now?

CHR. Truly, said Christian, I do not know.

PLI. At that Pliable began to be offended, and angrily said to his

8. Fools: "fancy": delusion.
9. Decision.

1. Pronounce to rhyme with *now*.

fellow, Is this the happiness you have told me all this while of? If we have such ill speed at our first setting out, what may we expect 'twixt this and our journey's end? May I get out again with my life, you shall possess the brave country alone for me. And, with that, he gave a desperate struggle or two, and got out of the mire on that side of the slough which was next[2] to his own house: so away he went, and Christian saw him no more.

Wherefore Christian was left to tumble in the Slough of Despond alone: but still he endeavored to struggle to that side of the slough that was further from his own house, and next to the wicket-gate; the which he did, but could not get out, because of the burden that was upon his back: but I beheld in my dream, that a man came to him, whose name was Help, and asked him what he did there?

CHR. Sir, said Christian, I was bid go this way by a man called Evangelist, who directed me also to yonder gate, that I might escape the wrath to come; and as I was going thither I fell in here.

HELP. But why did not you look for the steps?

CHR. Fear followed me so hard that I fled the next way, and fell in.

HELP. Then said he, Give me thy hand; so he gave him his hand, and he drew him out, and set him upon sound ground, and bid him go on his way.

Then I stepped to him that plucked him out, and said, Sir, wherefore, since over this place is the way from the City of Destruction to yonder gate, is it that this plat[3] is not mended, that poor travelers might go thither with more security? And he said unto me, This miry slough is such a place as cannot be mended; it is the descent whither the scum and filth that attends conviction for sin doth continually run, and therefore it was called the Slough of Despond; for still, as the sinner is awakened about his lost condition, there ariseth in his soul many fears, and doubts, and discouraging apprehensions, which all of them get together, and settle in this place. And this is the reason of the badness of this ground. * * *

[*Vanity Fair*][4]

Then I saw in my dream, that when they were got out of the wilderness, they presently saw a town before them, and the name

2. Nearest.
3. A plot of ground.
4. In this, perhaps the best-known episode in the book, Bunyan characteristically turns one of the most familiar institutions in contemporary England—annual fairs—into an allegory of universal spiritual significance. Christian and his companion Faithful pass through the town of Vanity at the season of the local fair. "Vanity" means "emptiness" or "worthlessness," and hence the fair is an allegory of worldliness and the corruption of the religious life through the attractions of the world. From earliest times numerous fairs were held for stated periods throughout Britain; to them the most important merchants from all over Europe brought their wares. The serious business of buying and selling was accompanied by all sorts of diversions—eating, drinking, and other fleshly pleasures, as well as spectacles of strange animals, acrobats, and other wonders.

of that town is Vanity; and at the town there is a fair kept, called Vanity Fair; it is kept all the year long; it beareth the name of Vanity Fair because the town where it is kept is lighter than vanity; and also because all that is there sold, or that cometh thither, is vanity. As is the saying of the wise, "All that cometh is vanity" (*Ecclesiastes i.2, 14; ii.11, 17; xi.8; Isaiah xl.17*).

This fair is no new-erected business, but a thing of ancient standing; I will show you the original of it.

Almost five thousand years agone, there were pilgrims walking to the Celestial City, as these two honest persons are; and Beelzebub, Apollyon, and Legion,[5] with their companions, perceiving by the path that the pilgrims made, that their way to the city lay through this town of Vanity, they contrived here to set up a fair; a fair wherein should be sold all sorts of vanity, and that it should last all the year long. Therefore at this fair are all such merchandise sold, as houses, lands, trades, places, honors, preferments,[6] titles, countries, kingdoms, lusts, pleasures, and delights of all sorts, as whores, bawds, wives, husbands, children, masters, servants, lives, blood, bodies, souls, silver, gold, pearls, precious stones, and what not.

And, moreover, at this fair there is at all times to be seen jugglings, cheats, games, plays, fools, apes, knaves, and rogues, and that of every kind.

Here are to be seen, too, and that for nothing, thefts, murders, adulteries, false swearers, and that of a blood-red color.

And as in other fairs of less moment, there are the several rows and streets, under their proper names, where such and such wares are vended; so here likewise you have the proper places, rows, streets (viz., countries and kingdoms), where the wares of this fair are soonest to be found. Here is the Britain Row, the French Row, the Italian Row, the Spanish Row, the German Row, where several sorts of vanities are to be sold. But, as in other fairs, some one commodity is as the chief of all the fair, so the ware of Rome and her merchandise[7] is greatly promoted in this fair; only our English nation, with some others, have taken a dislike thereat.

Now, as I said, the way to the Celestial City lies just through this town where this lusty[8] fair is kept; and he that will go to the City, and yet not go through this town, must needs "go out of the world" (*I Corinthians v.10*). The Prince of princes himself, when here, went through this town to his own country, and that upon a fair-day too;[9] yea, and as I think, it was Beelzebub, the chief lord of this fair, that invited him to buy of his vanities; yea, would have

5. Beelzebub, prince of the devils (Matthew xii.24); Apollyon, the Destroyer, "the Angel of the bottomless pit" (Revelation ix.11); Legion, the "unclean spirit" sent by Jesus into the Gadarene swine (Mark v.9).
6. Appointments and promotions to political or ecclesiastical positions.
7. The usages and the temporal power of the Roman Catholic Church.
8. Merry.
9. The temptation of Jesus in the wilderness (Matthew iv.1–11).

made him lord of the fair, would he but have done him reverence as he went through the town. (*Matthew iv.8; Luke iv.5–7.*) Yea, because he was such a person of honor, Beelzebub had him from street to street, and showed him all the kingdoms of the world in a little time, that he might, if possible, allure the Blessed One to cheapen[1] and buy some of his vanities; but he had no mind to the merchandise, and therefore left the town, without laying out so much as one farthing upon these vanities. This fair, therefore, is an ancient thing, of long standing, and a very great fair.

Now these pilgrims, as I said, must needs go through this fair. Well, so they did; but, behold, even as they entered into the fair, all the people in the fair were moved, and the town itself as it were in a hubbub about them; and that for several reasons: for

First, The pilgrims were clothed with such kind of raiment as was diverse from the raiment of any that traded in that fair. The people, therefore, of the fair, made a great gazing upon them: some said they were fools, some they were bedlams,[2] and some they are outlandish men. (*I Corinthians ii.7*, 8.)

Secondly, And as they wondered at their apparel, so they did likewise at their speech; for few could understand what they said; they naturally spoke the language of Canaan,[3] but they that kept the fair were the men of this world; so that, from one end of the fair to the other, they seemed barbarians[4] each to the other.

Thirdly, But that which did not a little amuse the merchandisers was that these pilgrims set very light by all their wares; they cared not so much as to look upon them; and if they called upon them to buy, they would put their fingers in their ears, and cry, "Turn away mine eyes from beholding vanity," and look upwards, signifying that their trade and traffic was in heaven. (*Psalms cxix.37; Philippians iii.19*, 20.)

One chanced mockingly, beholding the carriages of the men, to say unto them, What will ye buy? But they, looking gravely upon him, said, "We buy the truth" (*Proverbs xxiii.23*). At that there was an occasion taken to despise the men the more; some mocking, some taunting, some speaking reproachfully, and some calling upon others to smite them. At last things came to an hubbub and great stir in the fair, insomuch that all order was confounded. Now was word presently brought to the great one of the fair, who quickly came down, and deputed some of his most trusty friends to take these men into examination, about whom the fair was almost overturned. So the men were brought to examination; and they that sat

1. Ask the price of.
2. Lunatics from Bethlehem Hospital, the insane asylum in London. "Outlandish": foreign.
3. The Promised Land, ultimately conquered by the Children of Israel (Joshua iv) and settled by them: hence the pilgrims speak the language of the Bible and of the true religion. Dissenters were notorious for their habitual use of Biblical language.
4. The Greeks and Romans so designated all those who spoke a foreign tongue.

upon them[5] asked them whence they came, whither they went, and what they did there, in such an unusual garb? The men told them that they were pilgrims and strangers in the world, and that they were going to their own country, which was the Heavenly Jerusalem (*Hebrews xi.13–16*); and that they had given no occasion to the men of the town, nor yet to the merchandisers, thus to abuse them, and to let[6] them in their journey, except it was for that, when one asked them what they would buy, they said they would buy the truth. But they that were appointed to examine them did not believe them to be any other than bedlams and mad, or else such as came to put all things into a confusion in the fair. Therefore they took them and beat them, and besmeared them with dirt, and then put them into the cage, that they might be made a spectacle to all the men of the fair. * * *

[*The River of Death and the Celestial City*]

So I saw that when they[7] awoke, they addressed themselves to go up to the City; but, as I said, the reflection of the sun upon the City (for the City was pure gold, *Revelation xxi.18*) was so extremely glorious, that they could not, as yet, with open face behold it, but through an instrument made for that purpose. (*II Corinthians iii.18.*) So I saw that as I went on, there met them two men, in raiment that shone like gold; also their faces shone as the light.

These men asked the pilgrims whence they came; and they told them. They also asked them where they had lodged, what difficulties and dangers, what comforts and pleasures they had met in the way; and they told them. Then said the men that met them, You have but two difficulties more to meet with, and then you are in the City.

Christian then and his companion asked the men to go along with them; so they told them they would. But, said they, you must obtain it by your own faith. So I saw in my dream that they went on together till they came in sight of the gate.

Now I further saw that betwixt them and the gate was a river, but there was no bridge to go over; the river was very deep. At the sight, therefore, of this river, the pilgrims were much stunned;[8] but the men that went with them said, You must go through, or you cannot come at the gate.

The pilgrims then began to inquire if there was no other way to the gate; to which they answered, Yes; but there hath not any, save two, to wit, Enoch and Elijah,[9] been permitted to tread that path, since the foundation of the world, nor shall, until the last

5. Interrogated and tried them.
6. Hinder.
7. Christian and his companion, Hopeful. Ignorance, who appears tragically in the final paragraph, had tried to accompany the two pilgrims, but had dropped behind because of his hobbling gait.
8. Amazed.
9. Both were "translated" alive to heaven (Genesis v.24, Hebrews xi.5, II Kings ii.11–12).

trumpet shall sound. (*I Corinthians xv.51, 52.*) The pilgrims then, especially Christian, began to despond in his mind, and looked this way and that, but no way could be found by them by which they might escape the river. Then they asked the men if the waters were all of a depth. They said no; yet they could not help them in that case; for, said they, you shall find it deeper or shallower, as you believe in the King of the place.

They then addressed themselves to the water; and entering, Christian began to sink, and crying out to his good friend Hopeful, he said, I sink in deep waters; the billows go over my head, all his waves go over me! Selah.[1]

Then said the other, Be of good cheer, my brother, I feel the bottom, and it is good. Then said Christian, Ah, my friend, the sorrows of death have compassed me about; I shall not see the land that flows with milk and honey. And with that a great darkness and horror fell upon Christian, so that he could not see before him. Also here he in great measure lost his senses, so that he could neither remember nor orderly talk of any of those sweet refreshments that he had met with in the way of his pilgrimage. But all the words that he spake still tended to discover that he had horror of mind, and heart-fears that he should die in that river, and never obtain entrance in at the gate. Here also, as they that stood by perceived, he was much in the troublesome thoughts of the sins that he had committed, both since and before he began to be a pilgrim. 'Twas also observed that he was troubled with apparitions of hobgoblins and evil spirits; for ever and anon he would intimate so much by words. Hopeful, therefore, here had much ado to keep his brother's head above water; yea, sometimes he would be quite gone down, and then, ere a while, he would rise up again half dead. Hopeful also would endeavor to comfort him, saying, Brother, I see the gate and men standing by to receive us; but Christian would answer, 'Tis you, 'tis you they wait for; you have been Hopeful ever since I knew you. And so have you, said he to Christian. Ah, brother, said he, surely if I was right he would now arise to help me; but for my sins he hath brought me into the snare, and hath left me. Then said Hopeful, My brother, you have quite forgot the text, where it is said of the wicked, "There are no bands in their death, but their strength is firm. They are not in trouble as other men, neither are they plagued like other men" (*Psalms lxxiii.4, 5*). These troubles and distresses that you go through in these waters are no sign that God hath forsaken you, but are sent to try you, whether you will call to mind that which heretofore you have received of his goodness, and live upon him in your distresses.

Then I saw in my dream that Christian was as in a muse[2] a

1. A word of uncertain meaning that occurs frequently at the end of a verse in the Psalms. Bunyan may have supposed it to signify the end.

2. A deep meditation.

while, to whom also Hopeful added this word, Be of good cheer. Jesus Christ maketh thee whole. And with that Christian brake out with a loud voice, Oh, I see him again! and he tells me, "When thou passest through the waters, I will be with thee; and through the rivers, they shall not overflow thee" (*Isaiah xliii.2*). Then they both took courage, and the Enemy was after that as still as a stone, until they were gone over. Christian therefore presently found ground to stand upon, and so it followed that the rest of the river was but shallow. Thus they got over. Now, upon the bank of the river on the other side, they saw the two Shining Men again, who there waited for them. Wherefore, being come out of the river, they saluted them saying, We are ministering spirits, sent forth to minister for those that shall be heirs of salvation. Thus they went along towards the gate. * * *

Now when they were come up to the gate, there was written over it in letters of gold, "Blessed are they that do his commandments, that they may have right to the tree of life, and may enter in through the gates into the city" (*Revelation xxii.14*).

Then I saw in my dream, that the Shining Men bid them call at the gate; the which, when they did, some from above looked over the gate, to wit, Enoch, Moses, and Elijah, etc., to whom it was said, These pilgrims are come from the City of Destruction, for the love that they bear to the King of this place; and then the pilgrims gave in unto them each man his certificate, which they had received in the beginning; those, therefore, were carried in to the King, who, when he had read them, said, Where are the men? To whom it was answered, They are standing without the gate. The King then commanded to open the gate, "That the righteous nation," said he, "which keepeth the truth, may enter in" (*Isaiah xxvi.2*).

Now I saw in my dream that these two men went in at the gate; and lo, as they entered, they were transfigured, and they had raiment put on that shone like gold. There was also that met them with harps and crowns, and gave them to them: the harps to praise withal, and the crowns in token of honor. Then I heard in my dream that all the bells in the city rang again for joy, and that it was said unto them, "ENTER YE INTO THE JOY OF OUR LORD" (*Matthew xxv.21*). I also heard the men themselves, that they sang with a loud voice, saying, "BLESSING AND HONOR, GLORY AND POWER, BE TO HIM THAT SITTETH UPON THE THRONE, AND TO THE LAMB FOREVER AND EVER" (*Revelation v.13*).

Now just as the gates were opened to let in the men, I looked in after them, and, behold, the City shone like the sun; the streets also were paved with gold, and in them walked many men, with crowns on their heads, palms in their hands, and golden harps to sing praises withal.

There were also of them that had wings, and they answered one another without intermission, saying, "Holy, holy, holy is the Lord" (*Revelation iv.8*). And after that they shut up the gates, which when I had seen I wished myself among them.

Now while I was gazing upon all these things, I turned my head to look back, and saw Ignorance come up to the riverside; but he soon got over, and that without half that difficulty which the other two men met with. For it happened that there was then in that place one Vain-hope, a ferryman, that with his boat helped him over; so he, as the other, I saw, did ascend the hill to come up to the gate, only he came alone; neither did any man meet him with the least encouragement. When he was come up to the gate, he looked up to the writing that was above, and then began to knock, supposing that entrance should have been quickly administered to him; but he was asked by the men that looked over the top of the gate, Whence came you? and what would you have? He answered, I have eat and drank in the presence of the King, and he has taught in our streets. Then they asked him for his certificate, that they might go in and show it to the King; so he fumbled in his bosom for one, and found none. Then said they, Have you none? But the man answered never a word. So they told the King, but he would not come down to see him, but commanded the two Shining Ones that conducted Christian and Hopeful to the City, to go out and take Ignorance, and bind him hand and foot, and have him away. Then they took him up, and carried him through the air, to the door that I saw in the side of the hill, and put him in there. Then I saw that there was a way to hell, even from the gates of heaven, as well as from the City of Destruction. So I awoke, and behold it was a dream. 1678

WILLIAM CONGREVE

(1670–1729)

1693: First play, *The Old Bachelor*, produced.
1695: *Love for Love*, a successful comedy.
1700: Failure of *The Way of the World;* Congreve retires from the stage.

On both sides of his family Congreve was descended from well-to-do and prominent county families. His father, a younger son, obtained a commission as lieutenant in the army and removed with his family to Ireland in 1674. There the future playwright was educated at Kilkenny School and Trinity College, Dublin; at both places he was a younger contemporary of Swift, with whom he was always on friendly terms. In 1691 he took rooms in the Middle Temple and began to study law, but like other Templars of fact and fiction he preferred the wit of the coffeehouses and the theater to the aridity of the law. Within a year he had so distinguished himself at Will's Coffeehouse that he had become intimate with the great Dryden himself; and his brief career as a dramatist began shortly thereafter.

The success of *The Old Bachelor* (produced in 1693) immediately established him as the most promising young dramatist in London. It had the then phenomenally long run of fourteen days, and Dryden declared it the best first play he had ever read. *The Double Dealer* (produced in 1693) was a near failure, though it evoked one of Dryden's most graceful and gracious poems, in which he praised Congreve as the superior of Jonson and Fletcher and the equal of Shakespeare. *Love for Love* (produced in 1695) was an unqualified success and remains Congreve's most frequently revived play. In 1697 he brought out a tragedy, *The Mourning Bride,* which enjoyed great popular esteem. Congreve's most elegant work, *The Way of the World,* received a brilliant production in 1700. But it did not succeed with audiences, and subsequently Congreve gave up the stage. He held a minor government post, which, though a Whig, he was allowed to keep during the Tory ministry of Oxford and Bolingbroke; after the accession of George I he was given a more lucrative government sinecure. Despite the political animosities of the first two decades of the century, he managed to remain on friendly terms with Swift and Pope, and Pope dedicated to him his translation of the *Iliad*. His final years were perplexed by poor health, but were made bearable by the love of Henrietta, Duchess of Marlborough, whose last child, a daughter, was in all probability the playwright's.

Love for Love is Congreve's most humorous play—humorous not only in the sparkle of its wit and its infectious good nature but according to the author's own definition of *humor*: "a singular and unavoidable manner of doing or saying anything, peculiar and natural to one man only, by which his speech and actions are distinguished from those of other men." Like Ben Jonson, Congreve writes a comedy of humors. Each character represents a single trait, exaggerated and sharpened until it dominates every response to life. Thus Foresight puts all his faith in astrology; Sir Sampson Legend thinks that world travel has made him a man of the world; Tattle prides himself on kissing and telling, and Scandal on plain speaking; Ben is at sea wherever he goes; Miss Prue, like her name, is short of prudence; and Valentine gives all for love. Even the servants are brilliantly characterized: Jeremy, the clever survivor, steals the first scene, and the silly Nurse has fine moments in Act II. The wit of the play depends on its truth to type; few if any of the speeches could be assigned to another person. Life supplied Congreve with some of his humors; astrology, for instance, was popular at court. But the art of *Love for Love* consists of its fresh use of the stock of stage comedy. Few plays contain more good roles for actors: vivid in themselves, and nicely contrasted to allow the give-and-take that is the life of drama.

Power, sex, and money are the stars that guide most Restoration comedies; and the marriage market, where power, sex, and money are in conjunction, lends *Love for Love* its plot. In an age when marriages still had far more to do with social and commercial alliances than with romance, the question asked by many plays amounts to no more than "Who will catch the heiress?" Thus Valentine, deprived of his inheritance, must recoup his fortunes by landing Angelica. But Congreve, writing late in the period, plays down the elements of libertinism and self-interest, and emphasizes instead the values of honesty and affection. The title of *Love for Love* was probably intended to recall another play, D'Urfey's *Love for Money* (1691); and the contrast forcefully reminds us that marriage should be more than a financial transaction. Many of the characters in Congreve's comedy share a common weakness: the desire to get something for nothing. Foresight's belief that he can rule his fate through astrology, Sir Sampson's readiness to think that a beautiful, rich woman will trade her youth for his lecherous old age, Tattle's plot to trap an heiress, all involve the same greedy logic. But the play also involves a different logic, just as the successful suitor in Shakespeare's *Merchant of Venice* "must give and hazard all he hath." Even while feigning madness, Valentine plays the part of Truth; and he wins his lady not through plotting but through an act of generosity and self-sacrifice. "I never valued fortune, but as it was subservient to my pleasure; and my only pleasure was to please this lady." Love is rewarded by love, and deception by deception. Behind the poetic justice of this ending, it is possible to see not only the hand of the author but the hand of Providence. Valentine, whose name invokes the saint of love, is saved by an Angel. Yet the true guardian spirit of *Love for Love* is not so much Christian grace as the muse of comedy, who exposes every solemn lie and dissolves all problems in laughter.

Love for Love

Dramatis Personae

SIR SAMPSON LEGEND, *father to* VALENTINE *and* BEN

VALENTINE, *fallen under his father's displeasure by his expensive way of living, in love with* ANGELICA

SCANDAL, *his friend, a free speaker*

TATTLE, *a half-witted beau, vain of his amours, yet valuing himself for secrecy*

BEN, SIR SAMPSON'S *younger son, half home-bred and half sea-bred, designed to marry* MISS PRUE

FORESIGHT, *an illiterate old fellow, peevish and positive, superstitious, and pretending to understand astrology, palmistry, physiognomy,*[1] *omens, dreams, etc., uncle to* ANGELICA

JEREMY, *servant to* VALENTINE

TRAPLAND, *a scrivener*[2]

BUCKRAM, *a lawyer*

1. Telling fortunes from the lines of the face.

2. Broker or money-lender.

ANGELICA, *niece to* FORESIGHT, *of a considerable fortune in her own hands*

MRS. FORESIGHT, *second wife to* FORESIGHT

MRS. FRAIL, *sister to* MRS. FORESIGHT, *a woman of the town*

MISS PRUE, *daughter to* FORESIGHT *by a former wife, a silly, awkward country girl*

NURSE, *to* MISS PRUE

JENNY, *maid to* ANGELICA

A STEWARD, OFFICERS, SAILORS, *and several* SERVANTS

SCENE—*London*

Prologue Spoken at the opening of the New House

BY MR. BETTERTON[3]

The husbandman[4] in vain renews his toil,
To cultivate each year a hungry soil;
And fondly hopes for rich and generous fruit,
When what should feed the tree devours the root.
Th'unladen boughs he sees, bode certain dearth,
Unless transplanted to more kindly earth.
So the poor husbands of the stage, who found
Their labors lost upon the ungrateful ground,
This last and only remedy have proved;
And hope new fruit from ancient stocks[5] removed.
Well may they hope, when you so kindly aid,
And plant a soil which you so rich have made.
As Nature gave the world to man's first age,
So from your bounty we receive this stage;
The freedom man was born to, you've restored,
And to our world such plenty you afford,
It seems like Eden, fruitful of its own accord.
But since in Paradise frail flesh gave way,
And when but two were made, both went astray;
Forbear your wonder and the fault forgive,
If in our larger family we grieve
One falling Adam, and one tempted Eve.[6]
We who remain would gratefully repay
What our endeavors can, and bring this day,
The first-fruit offering of a virgin play.
We hope there's something that may please each taste,
And though of homely fare we make the feast,
Yet you will find variety at least.
There's humor, which for cheerful friends we got,
And for the thinking party there's a plot.

3. Thomas Betterton (ca. 1635–1710), the great actor who originated the role of Valentine, had quarreled with the Theater Royal and founded a new playhouse in Lincoln's Inn Fields, taking most of the company with him. *Love for Love* was their opening production.

4. Farmer.

5. Trunks or stems, with a play on theatrical "stock companies."

6. A reference to two members of the company who had gone back to the rival Theater Royal.

We've something too, to gratify ill nature
(If there be any here), and that is satire.
Though satire scarce dares grin, 'tis grown so mild;
Or only shows its teeth, as if it smiled.
As asses thistles, poets mumble wit,
And dare not bite, for fear of being bit.
They hold their pens, as swords are held by fools,
And are afraid to use their own edge-tools.
Since *The Plain Dealer's* scenes of manly rage,[7]
Not one has dared to lash this crying[8] age.
This time the poet owns the bold essay,
Yet hopes there's no ill manners in his play:
And he declares by me, he has designed
Affront to none, but frankly speaks his mind.
And should the ensuing scenes not chance to hit,
He offers but this one excuse, 'twas writ
Before your late encouragement of wit.[9]

Act One

SCENE ONE

VALENTINE *in his chamber reading.* JEREMY *waiting.*[1] *Several books upon the table.*

VALENTINE. Jeremy.

JEREMY. Sir.

VALENTINE. Here, take away; I'll walk a turn, and digest what I have read.

JEREMY. [*aside, and taking away the books*] You'll grow devilish fat upon this paper diet.

VALENTINE. And d'ye hear, go you to breakfast.—There's a page doubled down in Epictetus that is a feast for an emperor.

JEREMY. Was Epictetus a real cook, or did he only write receipts?[2]

VALENTINE. Read, read, sirrah, and refine your appetite. Learn to live upon instruction; feast your mind, and mortify your flesh; read, and take your nourishment in at your eyes; shut up your mouth and chew the cud of understanding. So Epictetus advises.

JEREMY. O Lord! I have heard much of him when I waited upon a gentleman at Cambridge. Pray, what was that Epictetus?

VALENTINE. A very rich man—not worth a groat.

JEREMY. Humph, and so he has made a very fine feast where there is nothing to be eaten.

VALENTINE. Yes.

JEREMY. Sir, you're a gentleman, and probably understand this fine

7. Manly, the title character of William Wycherley's *The Plain Dealer*, was famous for his belligerent honesty.
8. Plays could be "cried down," or hissed off the stage, by offended audiences.
9. I.e., the granting of the license for the new theater.
1. Attending.
2. Recipes. Epictetus (ca. 55–135 A.D.), the Stoic philosopher, taught that reliance on worldly things was folly.

feeding. But if you please, I had rather be at board wages.[3] Does your Epictetus, or your Seneca here, or any of these poor rich rogues, teach you how to pay your debts without money? Will they shut up the mouths of your creditors? Will Plato be bail for you? Or Diogenes, because he understands confinement, and lived in a tub, go to prison for you? 'Slife,[4] sir, what do you mean, to mew your self up here with three or four musty books in commendation of starving and poverty?

VALENTINE. Why, sirrah, I have no money, you know it; and therefore resolve to rail at all that have. And in that I but follow the examples of the wisest and wittiest men in all ages; these poets and philosophers whom you naturally hate, for just such another reason; because they abound in sense, and you are a fool.

JEREMY. Ay, sir, I am a fool, I know it. And yet, heav'n help me, I'm poor enough to be a wit. But I was always a fool, when I told you what your expenses would bring you to: your coaches and your liveries, your treats and your balls: your being in love with a lady that did not care a farthing for you in your prosperity, and keeping company with wits, that cared for nothing but your prosperity, and now when you are poor, hate you as much as they do one another.

VALENTINE. Well, and now I am poor, I have an opportunity to be revenged on 'em all. I'll pursue Angelica with more love than ever, and appear more notoriously her admirer in this restraint than when I openly rivaled the rich fops that made court to her. So shall my poverty be a mortification to her pride, and perhaps make her compassionate[5] that love which has principally reduced me to this lowness of fortune. And for the wits, I'm sure I'm in a condition to be even with them.

JEREMY. Nay, your condition is pretty even with theirs, that's the truth on't.

VALENTINE. I'll take some of their trade out of their hands.

JEREMY. Now Heav'n of mercy continue the tax upon paper! You don't mean to write!

VALENTINE. Yes, I do; I'll write a play.

JEREMY. Hem! Sir, if you please to give me a small certificate of three lines—only to certify those whom it may concern that the bearer hereof, Jeremy Fetch by name, has for the space of seven years truly and faithfully served Valentine Legend Esq., and that he is not now turned away for any misdemeanor, but does voluntarily dismiss his master from any future authority over him—

VALENTINE. No, sirrah, you shall live with me still.

JEREMY. Sir, it's impossible—I may die with you, starve with you, or be damned with your works; but to live even three days, the life of a play,[6] I no more expect it than to be canonized for a muse after my decease.

VALENTINE. You are witty, you rogue. I shall want your help. I'll

3. Wages paid servants for food.
4. An oath (short for "God's life").
5. Pity.
6. Plays often closed after the third night, when the profits went to the author.

have to learn to make couplets to tag the ends of acts.[7] D'ye hear, get the maids to crambo in an evening, and learn the knack of rhyming. You may arrive at the height of a song sent by an unknown hand, or a chocolate house lampoon.

JEREMY. But sir, is this the way to recover your father's favor? Why, Sir Sampson will be irreconcilable. If your younger brother should come from sea, he'd never look upon you again. You're undone, sir, you're ruined; you won't have a friend left in the world if you turn poet. Ah, pox confound that Will's coffeehouse,[8] it has ruined more young men than the Royal Oak Lottery. Nothing thrives that belongs to't. The man of the house would have been an alderman by this time with half the trade, if he had set up in the city. For my part, I never sit at the door that I don't get double the stomach[9] that I do at a horse race. The air upon Banstead Downs[1] is nothing to it for a whetter. Yet I never see it but the spirit of famine appears to me; sometimes like a decayed porter, worn out with pimping and carrying *billet-doux* and songs, not like other porters for hire, but for the jest's sake; now like a thin chairman,[2] melted down to half his proportion with carrying a poet upon tick[3] to visit some great fortune, and his fare to be paid him like the wages of sin, either at the day of marriage, or the day of death.

VALENTINE. Very well, sir. Can you proceed?

JEREMY. Sometimes like a bilked bookseller, with a meager terrified countenance, that looks as if he had written for himself, or were resolved to turn author and bring the rest of his brethren into the same condition; and lastly, in the form of a worn-out punk,[4] with verses in her hand, which her vanity had preferred to settlements, without a whole tatter to her tail, but as ragged as one of the muses, or as if she were carrying her linen to the paper mill, to be converted into folio books of warning to all young maids not to prefer poetry to good sense, or lying in the arms of a needy wit before the embraces of a wealthy fool.

[*Enter* SCANDAL.]

SCANDAL. What, Jeremy holding forth?

VALENTINE. The rogue has, with all the wit he could muster up, been declaiming against wit.

SCANDAL. Ay? Why then I'm afraid Jeremy has wit, for wherever it is, it's always contriving its own ruin.

JEREMY. Why, so I have been telling my master, sir. Mr. Scandal, for Heaven's sake, sir, try if you can dissuade him from turning poet.

SCANDAL. Poet! He shall turn soldier first, and rather depend upon

7. A rhymed couplet signified the end of an act. "To crambo": to play at capping verses.

8. Congreve, like Dryden and other literary lions, spent much of his time at Will's. Literary life, Jeremy suggests, is a form of gambling (the Royal Oak, the only legal English lottery, was suppressed in 1699).

9. Appetite or courage.

1. A racecourse (now Epsom Downs).

2. Someone who carries or wheels others in a chair.

3. On credit.

4. Prostitute.

the outside of his head than the lining. Why, what the devil! Has not your poverty made you enemies enough? Must you needs show your wit to get more?

JEREMY. Ay, more indeed. For who cares for anybody that has more wit than himself?

SCANDAL. Jeremy speaks like an oracle. Don't you see how worthless great men and dull rich rogues avoid a witty man of small fortune? Why, he looks like a writ of inquiry[5] into their titles and estates, and seems commissioned by Heav'n to seize the better half.

VALENTINE. Therefore I would rail in my writings, and be revenged.

SCANDAL. Rail? At whom? The whole world? Impotent and vain! Who would die a martyr to sense in a country where the religion is folly? You may stand at bay for a while, but when the full cry is against you, you won't have fair play for your life. If you can't be fairly run down by the hounds, you will be treacherously shot by the huntsmen.—No, turn pimp, flatterer, quack, lawyer, parson, be chaplain to an atheist, or stallion to an old woman, anything but poet. A modern poet is worse, more servile, timorous, and fawning than any I have named: without[6] you could retrieve the ancient honors of the name, recall the stage of Athens, and be allowed the force of open honest satire.

VALENTINE. You are as inveterate against our poets as if your character had been lately exposed upon the stage. Nay, I am not violently bent upon the trade. — [*One knocks.*] Jeremy, see who's there.

[*Exit* JEREMY.]

But tell me what you would have me do. What do the world say of me, and of my forced confinement?

SCANDAL. The world behaves itself as it used to do on such occasions; some pity you and condemn your father; others excuse him, and blame you. Only the ladies are merciful and wish you well, since love and pleasurable expense have been your greatest faults.

[*Enter* JEREMY.]

VALENTINE. How now?

JEREMY. Nothing new, sir. I have dispatched some half a dozen duns[7] with as much dexterity as a hungry judge does causes at dinner time.

VALENTINE. What answer have you given 'em?

SCANDAL. Patience, I suppose, the old receipt.

JEREMY. No, faith, sir. I have put 'em off so long with patience and forbearance and other fair words that I was forced now to tell 'em in plain downright English—

VALENTINE. What?

JEREMY. That they should be paid.

VALENTINE. When?

5. Legal investigation.
6. Unless.
7. Bill-collectors.

JEREMY. Tomorrow.

VALENTINE. And how the devil do you mean to keep your word?

JEREMY. Keep it? Not at all; it has been so very much stretched that I reckon it will break of course by tomorrow, and nobody be surprised at the matter.—[*Knocking*] Again! Sir, if you don't like my negotiation, will you be pleased to answer these yourself?

VALENTINE. See who they are.

[*Exit* JEREMY.]

By this, Scandal, you may see what it is to be great; Secretaries of State, presidents of the council, and generals of an army lead just such a life as I do; have just such crowds of visitants in a morning, all soliciting of past promises, which are but a civiler sort of duns, that lay claim to voluntary debts.

SCANDAL. And you, like a true great man, having engaged their attendance and promised more than ever you intend to perform, are more perplexed to find evasions than you would be to invent the honest means of keeping your word and gratifying your creditors.

VALENTINE. Scandal, learn to spare your friends, and do not provoke your enemies; this liberty of your tongue will one day bring a confinement on your body, my friend.

[*Re-enter* JEREMY.]

JEREMY. O sir, there's Trapland the scrivener, with two suspicious fellows like lawful pads,[8] that would knock a man down with pocket-tipstaves, and there's your father's steward, and the nurse with one of your children from Twitnam.[9]

VALENTINE. Pox on her, could she find no other time to fling my sins in my face? Here, give her this [*gives money*], and bid her trouble me no more. A thoughtless two-handed[1] whore, she knows my condition well enough, and might have overlaid[2] the child a fortnight ago if she had had any forecast in her.

SCANDAL. What, is it bouncing Margery and my godson?

JEREMY. Yes, sir.

SCANDAL. My blessing to the boy, with this token [*gives money*] of my love. And d'ye hear, bid Margery put more flocks in her bed, shift[3] twice a week, and not work so hard, that she may not smell so vigorously. I shall take the air shortly.

VALENTINE. Scandal, don't spoil my boy's milk. [*To* JEREMY] Bid Trapland come in.

[*Exit* JEREMY.]

If I can give that Cerberus a sop,[4] I shall be at rest for one day.

[*Enter* TRAPLAND *and* JEREMY.]

O Mr. Trapland! My old friend! Welcome! Jeremy, a chair, quickly. A bottle of sack and a toast—fly!—a chair first.

TRAPLAND. A good morning to you Mr. Valentine, and to you Mr.

8. Footpads. "Pocket-tipstaves": truncheons carried by bailiffs.
9. Twickenham, a suburb of London.
1. Strapping.
2. Concealed or smothered; "forecast": foresight.
3. Change clothes.
4. Cerberus, the watchdog of Hades, could be put to sleep by a bit of drugged food.

Scandal.

SCANDAL. The morning's a very good morning, if you don't spoil it.

VALENTINE. Come, sit down, you know his way.

TRAPLAND. [*sits*] There is a debt, Mr. Valentine, of £1,500, of pretty long standing—

VALENTINE. I cannot talk about business with a thirsty palate. [*To* JEREMY] Sirrah, the sack.

TRAPLAND. And I desire to know what course you have taken for the payment.

VALENTINE. Faith and troth, I am heartily glad to see you. My service to you. Fill, fill, to honest Mr. Trapland, fuller.

TRAPLAND. Hold, sweetheart. This is not to our business. My service to you, Mr. Scandal—[*drinks*]—I have forborne as long—

VALENTINE. T'other glass, and then we'll talk. Fill, Jeremy.

TRAPLAND. No more, in truth. I have forborne, I say—

VALENTINE. Sirrah, fill when I bid you. And how does your handsome daughter? Come, a good husband to her. [*Drinks.*]

TRAPLAND. Thank you; I have been out of this money—

VALENTINE. Drink first. Scandal, why do you not drink? [*They drink.*]

TRAPLAND. And in short, I can be put off no longer.

VALENTINE. I was much obliged to you for your supply. It did me signal service in my necessity. But you delight in doing good—Scandal, drink to me, my friend Trapland's health. An honester man lives not, nor one more ready to serve his friend in distress, though I say it to his face. Come, fill each man his glass.

SCANDAL. What! I know Trapland has been a whoremaster, and loves a wench still. You never knew a whoremaster that was not an honest fellow.

TRAPLAND. Fie, Mr. Scandal, you never knew—

SCANDAL. What don't I know? I know the buxom black widow in the Poultry[5]—£800 a year jointure, and £20,000 in money. Aha! Old Trap!

VALENTINE. Say you so, i'faith. Come, we'll remember the widow. I know whereabouts you are. Come, to the widow—

TRAPLAND. No more indeed.

VALENTINE. What, the widow's health! Give it him—off with it. [*They drink.*] A lovely girl, i'faith; black sparkling eyes, soft pouting ruby lips! Better sealing there than a bond for a million, hah?

TRAPLAND. No, no, there's no such thing. We'd better mind our business. You're a wag.

VALENTINE. No faith, we'll mind the widow's business, fill again. Pretty round heaving breasts, a Barbary shape,[6] and a jut with her bum, would stir an anchoret. And the prettiest foot! Oh, if a man could but fasten his eyes to her feet as they steal in and out and play at Bo-peep under her petticoats, ah, Mr. Trapland?

5. A London street. "Jointure": property inherited by a wife on her husband's death.

6. I.e., graceful as an Arab mare; "anchoret": hermit.

TRAPLAND. Verily, give me a glass—you're a wag—and here's to the widow. [*Drinks.*]

SCANDAL. [*to* VALENTINE] He begins to chuckle. Ply him close, or he'll relapse into a dun.

[*Enter* OFFICER.]

OFFICER. By your leave, gentlemen. Mr. Trapland, if we must do our office, tell us. We have half a dozen gentlemen to arrest in Pall Mall and Covent Garden, and if we don't make haste the chairmen will be abroad and block up the chocolate houses, and then our labor's lost.

TRAPLAND. Udso, that's true. Mr. Valentine, I love mirth, but business must be done. Are you ready to—

JEREMY. Sir, your father's steward says he comes to make proposals concerning your debts.

VALENTINE. Bid him come in. Mr. Trapland, send away your officer. You shall have an answer presently.[7]

MR. TRAPLAND. Mr. Snap, stay within call.

[*Exit* OFFICER.]

[*Enter* STEWARD *and whispers to* VALENTINE.]

SCANDAL. Here's a dog now, a traitor in his wine. [*To* TRAPLAND] Sirrah, refund the sack: Jeremy, fetch him some warm water, or I'll rip up his stomach, and go the shortest way to his conscience.

TRAPLAND. Mr. Scandal, you are uncivil. I did not value your sack, but you cannot expect it again, when I have drunk it.

SCANDAL. And how do you expect to have your money again, when a gentleman has spent it?

VALENTINE. [*to* STEWARD] You need say no more, I understand the conditions. They are very hard, but my necessity is very pressing. I agree to 'em. Take Mr. Trapland with you, and let him draw the writing.—Mr. Trapland, you know this man. He shall satisfy you.

TRAPLAND. Sincerely, I am loath to be thus pressing, but my necessity—

VALENTINE. No apology, good Mr. Scrivener, you shall be paid.

TRAPLAND. I hope you forgive me. My business requires—

[*Exeunt* STEWARD, TRAPLAND *and* JEREMY.]

SCANDAL. He begs pardon like a hangman at an execution.

VALENTINE. But I have got a reprieve.

SCANDAL. I am surprised. What, does your father relent?

VALENTINE. No; he has sent me the hardest conditions in the world. You have heard of a booby brother of mine that was sent to sea three years ago? This brother, my father hears, is landed; whereupon he very affectionately sends me word, if I will make a deed of conveyance of my right to his estate after his death to my younger brother, he will immediately furnish me with four thousand pound to pay my debts and make my fortune. This was once proposed before, and I refused it; but the present impatience of my creditors for their money, and my own impatience of

7. At once.

confinement and absence from Angelica, force me to consent.

SCANDAL. A very desperate demonstration of your love to Angelica; and I think she has never given you any assurance of hers.

VALENTINE. You know her temper; she never gave me any great reason either for hope or despair.

SCANDAL. Women of her airy temper, as they seldom think before they act, so they rarely give us any light to guess at what they mean. But you have little reason to believe that a woman of this age, who has had an indifference for you in your prosperity, will fall in love with your ill fortune; besides, Angelica has a great fortune of her own, and great fortunes either expect another great fortune, or a fool.

[*Enter* JEREMY.]

JEREMY. More misfortunes, sir.

VALENTINE. What, another dun?

JEREMY. No sir, but Mr. Tattle is come to wait upon you.

VALENTINE. Well, I can't help it. You must bring him up; he knows I don't go abroad.

[*Exit* JEREMY.]

SCANDAL. Pox on him, I'll be gone.

VALENTINE. No, prithee stay. Tattle and you should never be asunder; you are light and shadow; and show one another. He is perfectly thy reverse both in humor and understanding, and as you set up for defamation, he is a mender of reputations.

SCANDAL. A mender of reputations! Ay, just as he is a keeper of secrets, another virtue that he sets up for in the same manner. For the rogue will speak aloud in the posture of a whisper, and deny a woman's name while he gives you the marks of her person. He will forswear receiving a letter from her, and at the same time show you her hand upon the superscription. And yet perhaps he has counterfeited the hand too, and sworn to a truth. But he hopes not to be believed and refuses the reputation of a lady's favor, as a Doctor[8] says "No" to a bishopric, only that it may be granted him. In short, he is a public professor of secrecy, and makes proclamation that he holds private intelligence.—He's here.

[*Enter* TATTLE.]

TATTLE. Valentine, good morrow, Scandal, I am yours—that is, when you speak well of me.

SCANDAL. That is, when I am yours; for while I am my own, or anybody's else, that will never happen.

TATTLE. How inhumane!

VALENTINE. Why, Tattle, you need not be much concerned at anything that he says, for to converse with Scandal is to play at Losing Loadum;[9] you must lose a good name to him before you can win it for yourself.

TATTLE. But how barbarous that is, and how unfortunate for him, that the world shall think the better of any person for his calum-

8. A learned divine or clergyman.

9. A card game won by losing tricks.

niation! I thank heaven it has always been a part of my character to handle the reputation of others very tenderly.

SCANDAL. Ay, such rotten reputations as you have to deal with are to be handled tenderly indeed.

TATTLE. Nay, but why rotten? Why should you say rotten, when you know not the persons of whom you speak? How cruel that is!

SCANDAL. Not know 'em? Why, thou never hadst to do with anybody that did not stink to all the town.

TATTLE. Ha, ha, ha; nay, now you make a jest of it indeed. For there is nothing more known than that nobody knows anything of that nature of me. As I hope to be saved, Valentine, I never exposed a woman since I knew what woman was.

VALENTINE. And yet you have conversed with several.

TATTLE. To be free with you, I have. I don't care if I own that. Nay more, I'm going to say a bold word now, I never could meddle with a woman that had to do with anybody else.

SCANDAL. How!

VALENTINE. Nay faith, I'm apt to believe him. Except her husband, Tattle.

TATTLE. Oh that—

SCANDAL. What think you of that noble commoner, Mrs. Drab?[1]

TATTLE. Pooh, I know Madam Drab has made her brags in three or four places, that I said this and that, and writ to her, and did I know not what. But, upon my reputation, she did me wrong. Well, well, that was malice. But I know the bottom of it. She was bribed to that by one that we all know—a man too. Only to bring me into disgrace with a certain woman of quality—

SCANDAL. Whom we all know.

TATTLE. No matter for that. Yes, yes, everybody knows. No doubt on't, everybody knows my secrets. But I soon satisfied the lady of my innocence. For I told her: Madam, says I, there are some persons who make it their business to tell stories, and say this and that of one and t'other, and everything in the world, and, says I, if your Grace—

SCANDAL. Grace!

TATTLE. O Lord, what have I said? My unlucky tongue!

VALENTINE. Ha, ha, ha!

SCANDAL. Why, Tattle, thou hast more impudence than one can in reason expect. I shall have an esteem for thee. Well, and—ha, ha, ha—well, go on, and what did you say to her Grace?

VALENTINE. I confess this is something extraordinary.

TATTLE. Not a word as I hope to be saved; an errant *lapsus linguae*.[2]—Come, let's talk of something else.

VALENTINE. Well, but how did you acquit yourself?

TATTLE. Pooh, pooh, nothing at all, I only rallied with you. A woman of ord'nary rank was a little jealous of me, and I told her something or other—faith, I know not what.—Come, let's talk of something else. [*Hums a song.*]

1. Name for a whore or strumpet.
2. Slip of the tongue.

SCANDAL. Hang him, let him alone, he has a mind we should inquire.

TATTLE. Valentine, I supped last night with your mistress,[3] and her uncle, Old Foresight: I think your father lies at Foresight's.

VALENTINE. Yes.

TATTLE. Upon my soul, Angelica's a fine woman, and so is Mrs. Foresight, and her sister Mrs. Frail.

SCANDAL. Yes, Mrs. Frail is a very fine woman, we all know her.

TATTLE. Oh, that is not fair.

SCANDAL. What?

TATTLE. To tell.

SCANDAL. To tell what? Well, what do you know of Mrs. Frail?

TATTLE. Who, I? Upon honor I don't know whether she be man or woman, but by the smoothness of her chin and roundness of her lips.

SCANDAL. No?

TATTLE. No.

SCANDAL. She says otherwise.

TATTLE. Impossible!

SCANDAL. Yes faith. Ask Valentine else.

TATTLE. Why then, as I hope to be saved, I believe a woman only obliges a man to secrecy that she may have the pleasure of telling herself.

SCANDAL. No doubt on't. Well, but has she done you wrong, or no? You have had her, ha?

TATTLE. Though I have more honor than to tell first, I have more manners than to contradict what a lady has declared.

SCANDAL. Well, you own it?

TATTLE. I am strangely surprised! Yes, yes, I can't deny't, if she taxes me with it.

SCANDAL. She'll be here by and by, she sees Valentine every morning.

TATTLE. How?

VALENTINE. She does me the favor—I mean of a visit sometimes. I did not think she had granted more to anybody.

SCANDAL. Nor I, faith. But Tattle does not use to belie a lady; it is contrary to his character. How one may be deceived in a woman, Valentine!

TATTLE. Nay, what do you mean, gentlemen?

SCANDAL. I'm resolved I'll ask her.

TATTLE. O barbarous! Why, did you not tell me—

SCANDAL. No, you told us.

TATTLE. And bid me ask Valentine?

VALENTINE. What did I say? I hope you won't bring me to confess an answer when you never asked me the question.

TATTLE. But, gentlemen, this is the most inhumane proceeding.

VALENTINE. Nay, if you have known Scandal thus long, and cannot avoid such a palpable decoy as this was, the ladies have a fine time whose reputations are in your keeping.

3. I.e., a woman who is courted.

[*Enter* JEREMY.]

JEREMY. Sir, Mrs. Frail has sent to know if you are stirring.

VALENTINE. Show her up when she comes.

[*Exit* JEREMY.]

TATTLE. I'll be gone.

VALENTINE. You'll meet her.

TATTLE. Have you not a back way?

VALENTINE. If there were, you have more discretion than to give Scandal such an advantage. Why, your running away will prove all that he can tell her.

TATTLE. Scandal, you will not be so ungenerous.—Oh, I shall lose my reputation of secrecy forever—I shall never be received but upon public days, and my visits will never be admitted beyond a drawing room. I shall never see a bedchamber again, never be locked in a closet, nor run behind a screen or under a table; never be distinguished among the waiting-women by the name of Trusty Mr. Tattle more. You will not be so cruel?

VALENTINE. Scandal, have pity on him, he'll yield to any conditions.

TATTLE. Any, any terms.

SCANDAL. Come then, sacrifice half a dozen women of good reputation to me presently. Come, where are you familiar? And see that they are women of quality too, the first quality.

TATTLE. 'Tis very hard. Won't a baronet's lady pass?

SCANDAL. No, nothing under a Right Honorable.

TATTLE. O inhumane! You don't expect their names?

SCANDAL. No, their titles shall serve.

TATTLE. Alas, that's the same thing. Pray spare me their titles—I'll describe their persons.

SCANDAL. Well, begin then. But take notice, if you are so ill a painter that I cannot know the person by your picture of her, you must be condemned, like other bad painters, to write the name at the bottom.

TATTLE. Well, first then—

[*Enter* MRS. FRAIL.]

O unfortunate! she's come already; will you have patience till another time—I'll double the number.

SCANDAL. Well, on that condition. Take heed you don't fail me.

MRS. FRAIL. Heyday! I shall get a fine reputation by coming to see fellows in a morning. Scandal, you devil, are you here too? Oh Mr. Tattle, everything is safe with you, we know.

SCANDAL. Tattle?

TATTLE. Mum—O madam, you do me too much honor.

VALENTINE. Well, Lady Galloper, how does Angelica?

MRS. FRAIL. Angelica? Manners![4]

VALENTINE. What, you will allow an absent lover—

MRS. FRAIL. No, I'll allow a lover present with his mistress to be particular. But otherwise I think his passion ought to give place to his manners.

4. I.e., Valentine's use of Angelica's first name is impolite or "particular."

VALENTINE. But what if he have more passion than manners?

MRS. FRAIL. Then let him marry and reform.

VALENTINE. Marriage indeed may qualify the fury of his passion, but it very rarely mends a man's manners.

MRS. FRAIL. You are the most mistaken in the world. There is no creature perfectly civil but a husband. For in a little time he grows only rude to his wife, and that is the highest good breeding, for it begets his civility to other people. Well, I'll tell you news; but I suppose you hear your brother Benjamin is landed. And my brother Foresight's daughter is come out of the country —I assure you, there's a match talked of by the old people. Well, if he be but as great a sea beast as she is a land monster, we shall have a most amphibious breed. The progeny will be all otters; he has been bred at sea, and she has never been out of the country.

VALENTINE. Pox take 'em, their conjunction bodes no good, I'm sure.

MRS. FRAIL. Now you talk of conjunction, my brother Foresight has cast both their nativities, and prognosticates an admiral and an eminent justice of the peace to be the issue male of their two bodies; 'tis the most superstititious old fool! He would have persuaded me that this was an unlucky day, and would not let me come abroad. But I invented a dream, and sent him to Artimodorus[5] for interpretation, and so stole out to see you. Well, and what will you give me now? Come, I must have something.

VALENTINE. Step into the next room and I'll give you something.

SCANDAL. Ay, we'll all give you something.

MRS. FRAIL. Well, what will you all give me?

VALENTINE. Mine's a secret.

MRS. FRAIL. I thought you would give me something that would be a trouble to you to keep.

VALENTINE. And Scandal shall give you a good name.

MRS. FRAIL. That's more than he has for himself. And what will you give me, Mr. Tattle?

TATTLE. I? My soul, madam.

MRS. FRAIL. Pooh, no, I thank you. I have enough to do to take care of my own. Well, but I'll come and see you one of these mornings. I hear you have a great many pictures.

TATTLE. I have a pretty good collection at your service, some originals.

SCANDAL. Hang him, he has nothing but the Seasons and the Twelve Caesars, paltry copies, and the Five Senses,[6] as ill represented as they are in himself. And he himself is the only original you will see there.

MRS. FRAIL. Ay, but I hear he has a closet of beauties.

SCANDAL. Yes, all that have done him favors, if you will believe him.

5. Ancient authority on the meaning of dreams.

6. Popular prints from old masters.

MRS. FRAIL. Ay, let me see those, Mr. Tattle.

TATTLE. Oh, madam, those are sacred to love and contemplation. No man but the painter and myself was ever blessed with the sight.

MRS. FRAIL. Well, but a woman—

TATTLE. Nor woman, till she consented to have her picture there too, for then she is obliged to keep the secret.

SCANDAL. No, no. Come to me if you would see pictures.

MRS. FRAIL. You?

SCANDAL. Yes faith, I can show you your own picture and most of your acquaintance to the life, and as like as at Kneller's.[7]

MRS. FRAIL. O lying creature! Valentine, does not he lie? I can't believe a word he says.

VALENTINE. No indeed, he speaks truth now. For as Tattle has pictures of all that have granted him favors, he has the pictures of all that have refused him—if satires, descriptions, characters, and lampoons are pictures.

SCANDAL. Yes, mine are most in black and white. And yet there are some set out in their true colors, both men and women. I can show you Pride, Folly, Affectation, Wantonness, Inconstancy, Covetousness, Dissimulation, Malice, and Ignorance, all in one piece. Then I can show you Lying, Foppery, Vanity, Cowardice, Bragging, Lechery, Impotence and Ugliness in another piece; and yet one of these is a celebrated beauty, and t'other a professed beau. I have paintings too, some pleasant enough.

MRS. FRAIL. Come, let's hear 'em.

SCANDAL. Why, I have a beau in a bagnio,[8] cupping for a complexion, and sweating for a shape.

MRS. FRAIL. So.

SCANDAL. Then I have a lady burning of brandy in a cellar with a hackney coachman.

MRS. FRAIL. O devil! Well, but that story is not true.

SCANDAL. I have some hieroglyphics[9] too. I have a lawyer with a hundred hands, two heads and but one face; a divine with two faces and one head; and I have a soldier with his brains in his belly and his heart where his head should be.

MRS. FRAIL. And no head?

SCANDAL. No head.

MRS. FRAIL. Pooh, this is all invention. Have you ne'er a poet?

SCANDAL. Yes, I have a poet weighing words, and selling praise for praise, and a critic picking his pocket. I have another large piece too, representing a school where there are huge proportioned critics, with long wigs, laced coats, Steinkirk cravats,[1] and terrible faces, with catcalls in their hands, and hornbooks about their necks. I have many more of this kind, very well painted, as you shall see.

7. Sir Godfrey Kneller (1646?–1723) was the leading portrait painter of the day.

8. Bathhouse; "cupping": drawing off blood.

9. I.e., pictures with hidden meanings.

1. Fashionably loose neckties. "Catcalls": whistles used to hoot plays; "hornbooks": primers.

MRS. FRAIL. Well, I'll come, if it be only to disprove you.

[*Enter* JEREMY.]

JEREMY. Sir, here's the steward again from your father.

VALENTINE. I'll come to him. Will you give me leave? I'll wait on you again presently.

MRS. FRAIL. No, I'll be gone. Come, who squires me to the Exchange?[2] I must call my sister Foresight there.

SCANDAL. I will. I have a mind to your sister.

MRS. FRAIL. Civil!

TATTLE. I will, because I have a tender for your ladyship.

MRS. FRAIL. That's somewhat the better reason, to my opinion.

SCANDAL. Well, if Tattle entertains you, I have the better opportunity to engage your sister.

VALENTINE. Tell Angelica I am about making hard conditions to come abroad and be at liberty to see her.

SCANDAL. I'll give an account of you and your proceedings. If indiscretion be a sign of love, you are the most a lover of anybody that I know. You fancy that parting with your estate will help you to your mistress. In my mind he is a thoughtless adventurer,
Who hopes to purchase wealth, by selling land,
Or win a mistress with a losing hand.

[*Exeunt.*]

THE END OF THE FIRST ACT

Act Two

SCENE ONE

A room in FORESIGHT'*s house.*

[FORESIGHT *and* SERVANT.]

FORESIGHT. Heyday! What, are all the women of my family abroad? Is not my wife come home, nor my sister, nor my daughter?

SERVANT. No, sir.

FORESIGHT. Mercy on us, what can be the meaning of it? Sure the moon is in all her fortitudes.[3] Is my niece Angelica at home?

SERVANT. Yes, sir.

FORESIGHT. I believe you lie, sir.

SERVANT. Sir?

FORESIGHT. I say you lie, sir. It is impossible that anything should be as I would have it; for I was born, sir, when the crab was ascending, and all my affairs go backward.

SERVANT. I can't tell indeed, sir.

FORESIGHT. No, I know you can't, sir. But I can tell, sir, and foretell, sir.

[*Enter* NURSE.]

Nurse, where's your young mistress?

NURSE. Wee'st heart,[4] I know not, they're none of 'em come home

2. A shopping arcade or trading center in the Strand.
3. I.e., astrologically, her greatest strength.
4. Woe's my heart (dialect).

yet. Poor child, I warrant she's fond o' seeing the town. Marry, pray Heav'n they ha' given her any dinner. Good lackaday! Ha, ha, ha! O strange! I'll vow and swear now. Ha, ha, ha! Marry, and did you ever see the like?

FORESIGHT. Why, how now, what's the matter?

NURSE. Pray Heav'n send your worship good luck, marry, and amen with all my heart, for you have put on one stocking with the wrong side outward.

FORESIGHT. Ha, now? Faith and troth I'm glad of it, and so I have; that may be good luck in troth, in troth it may, very good luck. Nay, I have had some omens: I got out of bed backwards too this morning, without premeditation; pretty good that too. But then I stumbled coming down stairs, and met a weasel; bad omens those. Some bad, some good, our lives are checkered. Mirth and sorrow, want and plenty, night and day, make up our time.—But in troth I am pleased at my stocking, very well pleased at my stocking.—Oh, here's my niece!—

[*Enter* ANGELICA.]

Sirrah, go tell Sir Sampson Legend I'll wait on him, if he's at leisure—'tis now three a clock, a very good hour for business; Mercury[5] governs this hour.

[*Exit* SERVANT.]

ANGELICA. Is not it a good hour for pleasure too? Uncle, pray lend me your coach, mine's out of order.

FORESIGHT. What, would you be gadding too? Sure all females are mad today. It is of evil portent, and bodes mischief to the master of a family. I remember an old prophecy written by Messahalah the Arabian,[6] and thus translated by a Reverend Buckinghamshire bard.

> When housewifes all the house forsake,
> And leave good man to brew and bake,
> Withouten guile, then be it said,
> That house doth stand upon its head;
> And when the head is set in grond,
> Ne marl[7] if it be fruitful fond.

Fruitful, the head fruitful, that bodes horns; the fruit of the head is horns.[8] Dear niece, stay at home, for by the head of the house is meant the husband. The prophecy needs no explanation.

ANGELICA. Well, but I can neither make you a cuckold, uncle, by going abroad, nor secure you from being one by staying at home.

FORESIGHT. Yes, yes. While there's one woman left, the prophecy is not in full force.

ANGELICA. But my inclinations are in force. I have a mind to go abroad, and if you won't lend me your coach, I'll take a hackney, or a chair, and leave you to erect a scheme,[9] and find who's in

5. The planet that presides over traders.
6. Astrologer (ca. 9th century). The "Buckinghamshire bard," John Mason, had died the previous year, but his disciples refused to believe it.
7. No marvel. "Grond": ground; "fond": found.
8. The mark of a cuckolded husband.
9. To set up an astrological chart. Many of Angelica's words ("inclinations," "conjunction," "retrograde," "ascendant") involve puns on astrology.

conjunction with your wife. Why don't you keep her at home, if you're jealous when she's abroad? You know my aunt is a little retrograde (as you call it) in her nature. Uncle, I'm afraid you are not lord of the ascendant, ha, ha, ha.

FORESIGHT. Well, jill-flirt, you are very pert, and always ridiculing that celestial science.

ANGELICA. Nay, uncle, don't be angry. If you are, I'll reap up all your false prophecies, ridiculous dreams, and idle divinations. I'll swear you are a nuisance to the neighborhood. What a bustle did you keep against the last invisible eclipse, laying in provision as 'twere for a siege! What a world of fire and candle, matches and tinderboxes did you purchase! One would have thought we were ever after to live underground, or at least making a voyage to Greenland, to inhabit there all the dark season.

FORESIGHT. Why, you malapert[1] slut—

ANGELICA. Will you lend me your coach, or I'll go on. Nay, I'll declare how you prophesied popery was coming, only because the butler had mislaid some of the apostle spoons,[2] and thought they were lost. Away went religion and spoon-meat together.—Indeed, uncle, I'll indite you for a wizard.

FORESIGHT. How, hussy? Was there ever such a provoking minx?

NURSE. O merciful Father, how she talks!

ANGELICA. Yes, I can make oath of your unlawful midnight practices; you and the old nurse there.

NURSE. Marry, Heaven defend—I at midnight practices! O Lord, what's here to do? I in unlawful doings with my master's worship! Why, did you ever hear the like now? Sir, did ever I do any thing of your midnight concerns but warm your bed and tuck you up, and set the candle and your tobacco box and your urinal by you, and now and then rub the soles of your feet?—O Lord, I!

ANGELICA. Yes, I saw you together, through the keyhole of the closet one night, like Saul and the Witch of Endor,[3] turning the sieve and shears, and pricking your thumbs to write poor innocent servants' names in blood about a little nutmeg grater which she had forgot in the caudle cup.[4] Nay, I know something worse, if I would speak of it.

FORESIGHT. I defy you, hussy; but I'll remember this, I'll be revenged on you, cockatrice;[5] I'll hamper you. You have your fortune in your own hands, but I'll find a way to make your lover, your prodigal spendthrift gallant, Valentine, pay for all, I will.

ANGELICA. Will you? I care not, but all shall out then. Look to it, nurse. I can bring witness that you have a great unnatural teat under your left arm, and he another, and that you suckle a young devil in the shape of a tabby cat by turns, I can.

1. Impudent.
2. Old-fashioned spoons whose handles end in figures of the apostles; "spoon-meat": broth. Angelica is playing on the idea that some English people still feared a Catholic rebellion.
3. Saul tried to see into the future by having a witch call up the spirit of the prophet Samuel (I Samuel xxviii). "Sieve and shears" were used for divination.
4. A warm spiced drink.
5. Legendary serpent, supposed to grow unnaturally from a cock's egg.

NURSE. A teat, a teat, I an unnatural teat! O the false slanderous thing; feel, feel here, if I have anything but like another Christian [*crying*] or any teats, but two that ha'n't given suck this thirty years.

FORESIGHT. I will have patience, since it is the will of the stars I should be thus tormented. This is the effect of the malicious conjunctions and oppositions in the third house[6] of my nativity. There the curse of kindred was foretold. But I will have my doors locked up. I'll punish you. Not a man shall enter my house.

ANGELICA. Do, uncle, lock 'em up quickly before my aunt come home. You'll have a letter for alimony tomorrow morning. But let me be gone first, and then let no mankind come near the house, but converse with spirits and the celestial signs, the bull, and the ram, and the goat. Bless me! there are a great many horned beasts among the twelve signs, uncle. But cuckolds go to Heav'n.

FORESIGHT. But there's but one virgin among the twelve signs, spitfire, but one virgin.

ANGELICA. Nor there had not been that one, if she had had to do with anything but astrologers, uncle. That makes my aunt go abroad.

FORESIGHT. How, how? Is that the reason? Come, you know something. Tell me, and I'll forgive you. Do, good niece. Come, you shall have my coach and horses, faith and troth you shall. Does my wife complain? Come, I know women tell one another. She is young and sanguine, has a wanton hazel eye, and was born under Gemini,[7] which may incline her to society. She has a mole upon her lip, with a moist palm, and an open liberality on the Mount of Venus.

ANGELICA. Ha, ha, ha!

FORESIGHT. Do you laugh? Well, gentlewoman, I'll—But come, be a good girl, don't perplex your poor uncle, tell me. Won't you speak? Odd, I'll—

[*Enter* SERVANT,]

SERVANT. Sir Sampson is coming down to wait upon you.

ANGELICA. Goodbye, uncle. Call me a chair. I'll find out my aunt, and tell her she must not come home.

[*Exit* ANGELICA *and* SERVANT.]

FORESIGHT. I'm so perplexed and vexed, I am not fit to receive him. I shall scarce recover myself before the hour be past. Go, nurse, tell Sir Sampson I'm ready to wait on him.

NURSE. Yes, sir.

FORESIGHT. Well—Why, if I was born to be a cuckold, there's no more to be said.

[*Enter* SIR SAMPSON LEGEND *with a paper*.]

SIR SAMPSON. Nor no more to be done, old boy, that's plain. Here 'tis, I have it in my hand, old Ptolomee.[8] I'll make the un-

6. The third section of the zodiac signifies brethren.

7. A "hot and moist" sign. All these characteristics warn of sensuality.

8. The *Almagest* of Ptolemy of Alexandria (2nd century) was the standard account of Greek astronomy. "Nostrodamus": a famous 16th-century prophet.

gracious prodigal know who begat him, I will, old Nostrodamus. What, I warrant my son thought nothing belonged to a father but forgiveness and affection. No authority, no correction, no arbitrary power, nothing to be done, but for him to offend and me to pardon. I warrant you, if he danced till dooms-day, he thought I was to pay the piper. Well, but here it is under black and white, *signatum, sigillatum,* and *deliberatum;*[9] that as soon as my son Benjamin is arrived, he is to make over to him his right of inheritance. Where's my daughter that is to be? Ha! Old Merlin![1] body o' me, I'm so glad I'm revenged on this undutiful rogue.

FORESIGHT. Odso, let me see. Let me see the paper. Ay, faith and troth, here 'tis, if it will but hold. I wish things were done, and the conveyance made. When was this signed, what hour? Odso, you should have consulted me for the time. Well, but we'll make haste.

SIR SAMPSON. Haste, ay, ay, haste enough. My son Ben will be in town tonight. I have ordered my lawyer to draw up writings of settlement and jointure. All shall be done tonight. No matter for the time. Prithee, brother Foresight, leave superstition. Pox o' th' time! There's no time but the time present; there's no more to be said of what's past, and all that is to come will happen. If the sun shine by day, and the stars by night, why, we shall know one another's faces without the help of a candle, and that's all the stars are good for.

FORESIGHT. How, how, Sir Sampson, that all? Give me leave to contradict you, and tell you you are ignorant.

SIR SAMPSON. I tell you I am wise, and *sapiens dominabitur astris;*[2] there's Latin for you to prove it, and an argument to confound your Ephemeris.[3] Ignorant! I tell you, I have traveled, old Fircu, and know the globe. I have seen the antipodes,[4] where the sun rises at midnight and sets at noonday.

FORESIGHT. But I tell you, I have traveled, and traveled in the celestial spheres, know the signs and the planets, and their houses, can judge of motions direct and retrograde, of sextiles, quadrates, trines, and oppositions, fiery trigons and aquatical trigons,[5] know whether life shall be long or short, happy or unhappy, whether diseases are curable or incurable, if journeys shall be prosperous, undertakings successful, or goods stol'n recovered. I know—

SIR SAMPSON. I know the length of the Emperor of China's foot, have kissed the Great Mogul's slipper, and rid a hunting upon an elephant with the Cham of Tartary. Body of me, I have made a cuckold of a king, and the present Majesty of Bantam[6] is the issue of these loins.

FORESIGHT. I know when travelers lie or speak truth, when they don't know it themselves.

SIR SAMPSON. I have known an astrologer made a cuckold in the

9. Signed, sealed, and delivered.
1. King Arthur's legendary wizard.
2. The wise will rule over the stars.
3. Astrological almanac.
4. The opposite side of the earth.
5. All these terms refer to various positions of celestial bodies in the zodiac.
6. A port in Java.

twinkling of a star, and seen a conjurer that could not keep the devil out of his wife's circle.

FORESIGHT. [*aside*] What, does he twit me with my wife too? I must be better informed of this.—Do you mean my wife, Sir Sampson? Though you made a cuckold of the king of Bantam, yet by the body of the sun—

SIR SAMPSON. By the horns of the moon, you would say, Brother Capricorn.[7]

FORESIGHT. Capricorn in your teeth, thou modern Mandevil;[8] Ferdinand Mendez Pinto was but a type of thee, thou liar of the first magnitude. Take back your paper of inheritance; send your son to sea again. I'll wed my daughter to an Egyptian mummy ere she shall incorporate with a contemner of sciences, and a defamer of virtue.

SIR SAMPSON. [*aside*] Body of me, I have gone too far. I must not provoke honest Albumazar.[9] [*Aloud*] An Egyptian mummy is an illustrious creature, my trusty hieroglyphic, and may have significations of futurity about him. Odsbud, I would my son were an Egyptian mummy for thy sake. What, thou art not angry for a jest, my good Haly? I reverence the sun, moon, and stars with all my heart. What, I'll make thee a present of a mummy. Now I think on't, body of me, I have a shoulder of an Egyptian king, that I purloined from one of the pyramids, powdered with hieroglyphics. Thou shalt have it sent home to thy house, and make an entertainment for all the philomaths,[1] and students in physic and astrology in and about London.

FORESIGHT. But what do you know of my wife, Sir Sampson?

SIR SAMPSON. Thy wife is a constellation of virtues. She's the moon, and thou art the man in the moon. Nay, she is more illustrious than the moon, for she has her chastity without her inconstancy. 'S'bud,[2] I was but in jest.

[*Enter* JEREMY.]

How now, who sent for you? Ha! What would you have?

FORESIGHT. Nay, if you were but in jest. Who's that fellow? I don't like his physiognomy. [JEREMY *whispers to* SIR SAMPSON.]

SIR SAMPSON. My son, sir; what son, sir? My son Benjamin, ho?

JEREMY. No, sir, Mr. Valentine, my master. 'Tis the first time he has been abroad since his confinement, and he comes to pay his duty to you.

SIR SAMPSON. Well, sir.

[*Enter* VALENTINE.]

JEREMY. He is here, sir.

VALENTINE. Your blessing, sir.

SIR SAMPSON. You've had it already, sir, I think I sent it you today in a bill of four thousand pound. A great deal of money, brother Foresight.

7. Sign of the goat—with horns.
8. Sir John Mandeville and Ferdinand Pinto both wrote famous tales of travel.
9. Arabian astrologer, as is Haly.
1. Lovers of learning, especially astrologers.
2. An oath (short for "God's blood").

FORESIGHT. Ay indeed, Sir Sampson, a great deal of money for a young man. I wonder what he can do with it!

SIR SAMPSON. Body o' me, so do I. Hark ye, Valentine, if there is too much, refund the superfluity, do'st hear, boy?

VALENTINE. Superfluity, sir, it will scarce pay my debts. I hope you will have more indulgence than to oblige me to those hard conditions which my necessity signed to.

SIR SAMPSON. Sir, how, I beseech you, what were you pleased to intimate concerning indulgence?

VALENTINE. Why, sir, that you would not go to the extremity of the conditions, but release me at least from some part—

SIR SAMPSON. Oh, sir, I understand you. That's all, ha?

VALENTINE. Yes, sir, all that I presume to ask. But what you, out of fatherly fondness, will be pleased to add, shall be doubly welcome.

SIR SAMPSON. No doubt of it, sweet sir, but your filial piety and my fatherly fondness would fit like two tallies. Here's a rogue, brother Foresight, makes a bargain under hand and seal in the morning, and would be released from it in the afternoon! Here's a rogue, dog, here's conscience and honesty! This is your wit now, this is the morality of your wits! You are a wit, and have been a beau, and may be a—Why sirrah, is it not here under hand and seal? Can you deny it?

VALENTINE. Sir, I don't deny it.

SIR SAMPSON. Sirrah, you'll be hanged. I shall live to see you go up Holborn Hill.[3] Has he not a rogue's face? Speak, brother, you understand physiognomy; a hanging look to me; of all my boys the most unlike me. He has a damned Tyburn face, without the benefit of the clergy.

FORESIGHT. Hum. Truly I don't care to discourage a young man. He has a violent death in his face; but I hope no danger of hanging.

VALENTINE. Sir, is this usage for your son? For that old, weather-headed fool, I know how to laugh at him; but you, sir—

SIR SAMPSON. You, sir; and you, sir! Why, who are you, sir?

VALENTINE. Your son, sir.

SIR SAMPSON. That's more than I know, sir, and I believe not.

VALENTINE. Faith, I hope not.

SIR SAMPSON. What, would you have your mother a whore? Did you ever hear the like! Did you ever hear the like! Body o' me—

VALENTINE. I would have an excuse for your barbarity and unnatural usage.

SIR SAMPSON. Excuse! Impudence! Why sirrah, mayn't I do what I please? Are not you my slave? Did not I beget you? And might not I have chosen whether I would have begot you or no? 'Ouns, who are you? Whence came you? What brought you into the world? How came you here, sir? Here, to stand here, upon those two legs, and look erect with that audacious face, hah! Answer

3. The way to the gallows at Tyburn.

me that! Did you come a volunteer into the world? Or did I beat up[4] for you with the lawful authority of a parent, and press you to the service?

VALENTINE. I know no more why I came than you do why you called me. But here I am, and if you don't mean to provide for me, I desire you would leave me as you found me.

SIR SAMPSON. With all my heart. Come, uncase, strip, and go naked out of the world as you came into't.

VALENTINE. My clothes are soon put off; but you must also deprive me of reason, thought, passions, inclinations, affections, appetites, senses, and the huge train of attendants that you begot along with me.

SIR SAMPSON. Body o' me, what a many-headed monster have I propagated!

VALENTINE. I am of myself, a plain easy simple creature, and to be kept at small expense, but the retinue that you gave me are craving and invincible. They are so many devils that you have raised, and will have employment.

SIR SAMPSON. 'Ouns, what had I to do to get children? Can't a private man be born without all these followers? Why, nothing under an emperor should be born with appetites. Why, at this rate a fellow that has but a groat in his pocket may have a stomach capable of a ten-shilling ordinary.[5]

JEREMY. Nay, that's as clear as the sun; I'll make oath of it before any justice in Middlesex.

SIR SAMPSON. Here's a cormorant too. 'S'heart, this fellow was not born with you? I did not beget him, did I?

JEREMY. By the provision that's made for me, you might have begot me too. Nay, and to tell your worship another truth, I believe you did, for I find I was born with those same whoreson appetites, too, that my master speaks of.

SIR SAMPSON. Why, look you there now, I'll maintain it that by the rule of right reason this fellow ought to have been born without a palate. 'S'heart, what should he do with a distinguishing taste? I warrant now he'd rather eat a pheasant than a piece of poor John.[6] And smell, now, why, I warrant he can smell, and loves perfumes above a stink. Why, there's it. And music, don't you love music, scoundrel?

JEREMY. Yes, I have a reasonable good ear, sir, as to jigs and country dances and the like. I don't much matter[7] your solas or sonatas, they give me the spleen.

SIR SAMPSON. The spleen! Ha, ha, ha! A pox confound you—solas and sonatas? 'Ouns, whose son are you? How were you engendered, muckworm?

JEREMY. I am by my father, the son of a chairman; my mother sold oysters in winter and cucumbers in summer; and I came upstairs into the world, for I was born in a cellar.

4. Call to service by a drum (with a pun).
5. Meal.
6. Dry salt fish.
7. Care for; "solas": solos; "spleen": fashionable feelings of depression.

FORESIGHT. By your looks, you should go upstairs out of the world[8] too, friend.

SIR SAMPSON. And if this rogue were anatomized now, and dissected, he has his vessels of digestion and concoction and so forth, large enough for the inside of a cardinal, this son of a cucumber. These things are unaccountable and unreasonable. Body o' me, why was not I a bear, that my cubs might have lived upon sucking their paws? Nature has been provident only to bears and spiders; the one has its nutriment in his own hands, and t'other spins his habitation out of his entrails.

VALENTINE. Fortune was provident enough to supply all the necessities of my nature, if I had my right of inheritance.

SIR SAMPSON. Again! 'Ouns, han't you four thousand pound? If I had it again, I would not give thee a groat. What, wouldst thou have me turn pelican, and feed thee out of my own vitals?[9] 'S'heart, live by your wits. You were always fond of the wits; now let's see if you have wit enough to keep yourself. Your brother will be in town tonight or tomorrow morning, and then look you perform covenants—and so your friend and servant. Come, brother Foresight.

[*Exeunt* SIR SAMPSON *and* FORESIGHT.]

JEREMY. I told you what your visit would come to.

VALENTINE. 'Tis as much as I expected. I did not come to see him, I came to Angelica. But since she was gone abroad, it was easily turned another way, and at least looked well on my side. What's here? Mrs. Foresight and Mrs. Frail? They are earnest—I'll avoid 'em. Come this way, and go and enquire when Angelica will return.

[*Exeunt.*]

[*Enter* MRS. FORESIGHT *and* MRS. FRAIL.]

MRS. FRAIL. What have you to do to watch me? 'S'life. I'll do what I please.

MRS. FORESIGHT. You will?

MRS. FRAIL. Yes, marry will I. A great piece of business to go to Covent Garden Square in a hackney coach[1] and take a turn with one's friend.

MRS. FORESIGHT. Nay, two or three turns, I'll take my oath.

MRS. FRAIL. Well, what if I took twenty? I'll warrant if you had been there, it had been only innocent recreation. Lord, where's the comfort of this life, if we can't have the happiness of conversing where we like?

MRS. FORESIGHT. But can't you converse at home? I own it, I think there's no happiness like conversing with an agreeable man. I don't quarrel at that, nor I don't think but your conversation was very innocent; but the place is public, and to be seen with a man in a hackney coach is scandalous. What if anybody else should have seen you alight as I did? How can anybody be happy while they're in perpetual fear of being seen and censured? Besides, it

8. I.e., to the gallows.

9. Pelicans, according to legend, tore their own breasts to feed their young.

1. A two-horse carriage, kept for hire.

would not only reflect upon you, sister, but me.

MRS. FRAIL. Pooh, here's a clutter. Why should it reflect upon you? I don't doubt but you have thought yourself happy in a hackney coach before now. If I had gone to Knightsbridge, or to Chelsea, or to Spring Garden, or Barn Elms[2] with a man alone, something might have been said.

MRS. FORESIGHT. Why, was I ever in any of these places? What do you mean, sister?

MRS. FRAIL. Was I? What do you mean?

MRS. FORESIGHT. You have been at a worse place.

MRS. FRAIL. I at a worse place, and with a man!

MRS. FORESIGHT. I suppose you would not go alone to the World's End.[3]

MRS. FRAIL. The World's End! What, do you mean to banter me?

MRS. FORESIGHT. Poor innocent! You don't know that there's a place called the World's End? I'll swear you can keep your countenance purely, you'd make an admirable player.

MRS. FRAIL. I'll swear you have a great deal of impudence, and in my mind too much for the stage.

MRS. FORESIGHT. Very well, that will appear who has most. You never were at the World's End?

MRS. FRAIL. No.

MRS. FORESIGHT. You deny it positively to my face?

MRS. FRAIL. Your face, what's your face?

MRS. FORESIGHT. No matter for that, it's as good a face as yours.

MRS. FRAIL. Not by a dozen years' wearing. But I do deny it positively to your face then.

MRS. FORESIGHT. I'll allow you now to find fault with my face; for I'll swear your impudence has put me out of countenance. But look you here now, where did you lose this gold bodkin?[4] O sister, sister!

MRS. FRAIL. My bodkin!

MRS. FORESIGHT. Nay, 'tis yours, look at it.

MRS. FRAIL. Well, if you go to that, where did you find this bodkin? O sister, sister! Sister every way!

MRS. FORESIGHT. [*aside*] O devil on't, that I could not discover[5] her without betraying myself!

MRS. FRAIL. I have heard gentlemen say, sister, that one should take great care when one makes a thrust in fencing, not to lie open oneself.

MRS. FORESIGHT. It's very true, sister. Well, since all's out, and as you say, since we are both wounded, let us do that is often done in duels, take care of one another, and grow better friends than before.

MRS. FRAIL. With all my heart. Ours are but slight flesh wounds, and if we keep 'em from air, not at all dangerous. Well, give me your hand in token of sisterly secrecy and affection.

MRS. FORESIGHT. Here 'tis, with all my heart.

2. Disreputable suburban resorts.
3. An inn in Chelsea.
4. Long hairpin.
5. Expose.

MRS. FRAIL. Well, as an earnest of friendship and confidence, I'll acquaint you with a design that I have. To tell truth, and speak openly one to another, I'm afraid the world have observed us more than we have observed one another. You have a rich husband, and are provided for; I am at a loss, and have no great stock either of fortune or reputation, and therefore must look sharply about me. Sir Sampson has a son that is expected tonight, and by the account I have heard of his education can be no conjurer. The estate you know is to be made over to him. Now if I could wheedle him, sister, ha? You understand me?

MRS. FORESIGHT. I do, and will help you to the utmost of my power. And I can tell you one thing that falls out luckily enough; my awkward daughter-in-law,[6] who you know is designed for his wife, is grown fond of Mr. Tattle. Now if we can improve that, and make her have an aversion for the booby, it may go a great way towards his liking of you. Here they come together; and let us contrive some way or other to leave 'em together.

[*Enter* TATTLE *and* MISS PRUE.]

MISS PRUE. Mother, mother, mother, look you here.

MRS. FORESIGHT. Fie, fie, Miss, how you bawl! Besides, I have told you, you must not call me mother.

MISS PRUE. What must I call you then? Are not you my father's wife?

MRS. FORESIGHT. Madam, you must say madam. By my soul, I shall fancy myself old indeed, to have this great girl call me mother. Well, but Miss, what are you so overjoyed at?

MISS PRUE. Look you here, madam, then, what Mr. Tattle has given me. Look you here, cousin, here's a snuffbox; nay, there's snuff in't. Here, will you have any? Oh, good! How sweet it is! Mr. Tattle is all over sweet: his peruke[7] is sweet, and his gloves are sweet, and his handkerchief is sweet, pure sweet, sweeter than roses. Smell him, mother, madam, I mean. He gave me this ring for a kiss.

TATTLE. O fie, Miss, you must not kiss and tell.

MISS PRUE. Yes; I may tell my mother. And he says he'll give me something to make me smell so. Oh pray lend me your handkerchief. Smell, cousin; he says, he'll give me something that will make my smocks smell this way. Is not it pure? It's better than lavender, mun.[8] I'm resolved I won't let nurse put any more lavender among my smocks. Ha, cousin?

MRS. FRAIL. Fie, Miss, amongst your linen, you must say. You must never say smock.

MISS PRUE. Why, it is not bawdy, is it cousin?

TATTLE. Oh, madam, you are too severe upon Miss. You must not find fault with her pretty simplicity, it becomes her strangely. Pretty Miss, don't let 'em persuade you out of your innocency.

MRS. FORESIGHT. Oh, demm[9] you, toad. I wish you don't persuade her out of her innocency.

6. I.e., stepdaughter.
7. Wig.
8. Term of address.
9. I.e., damn (dialect).

TATTLE. Who, I madam? O Lord, how can your ladyship have such a thought? Sure you don't know me.

MRS. FRAIL. Ah devil, sly devil. He's as close, sister, as a confessor. He thinks we don't observe him.

MRS. FORESIGHT. A cunning cur. How soon he could find out a fresh harmless creature; and left us, sister, presently.

TATTLE. Upon reputation—

MRS. FORESIGHT. They're all so, sister, these men. They love to have the spoiling of a young thing, they are as fond of it as of being first in the fashion or of seeing a new play the first day. I warrant it would break Mr. Tattle's heart to think that anybody else should be beforehand with him.

TATTLE. O Lord, I swear I would not for the world.

MRS. FRAIL. O hang you, who'll believe you? You'd be hanged before you'd confess. We know you. She's very pretty. Lord, what pure red and white! She looks so wholesome. Ne'er stir, I don't know, but I fancy, if I were a man—

MISS PRUE. How you love to jeer one, cousin.

MRS. FORESIGHT. Hark'ee, sister, by my soul the girl is spoiled already. D'ye think she'll ever endure a great lubberly tarpaulin?[1] Gad, I warrant you she won't let him come near her, after Mr. Tattle.

MRS. FRAIL. O' my soul, I'm afraid not. Eh! filthy creature, that smells all of pitch and tar! [*To* TATTLE] Devil take you, you confounded toad! Why did you see her before she was married?

MRS. FORESIGHT. Nay, why did we let him? My husband will hang us. He'll think we brought 'em acquainted.

MRS. FRAIL. Come, faith, let us be gone. If my brother Foresight should find us with them, he'd think so sure enough.

MRS. FORESIGHT. So he would. But then, leaving 'em together is as bad. And he's such a sly devil, he'll never miss an opportunity.

MRS. FRAIL. I don't care; I won't be seen in't.

MRS. FORESIGHT. Well, if you should, Mr. Tattle, you'll have a world to answer for, remember I wash my hands of it, I'm thoroughly innocent.

[*Exeunt* MRS. FORESIGHT *and* MRS. FRAIL.]

MISS PRUE. What makes 'em go away, Mr. Tattle? What do they mean, do you know?

TATTLE. Yes, my dear, I think I can guess. But hang me if I know the reason of it.

MISS PRUE. Come, must not we go too?

TATTLE. No, no, they don't mean that.

MISS PRUE. No! What then? What shall you and I do together?

TATTLE. I must make love to you, pretty Miss. Will you let me make love to you?

MISS PRUE. Yes, if you please.

TATTLE. [*aside*] Frank, egad, at least. What a pox does Mrs. Foresight mean by this civility? Is it to make a fool of me? Or does she leave us together out of good morality, and do as she would be

1. Nickname for a sailor.

done by? Gad, I'll understand it so.

MISS PRUE. Well, and how will you make love to me? Come, I long to have you begin. Must I make love too? You must tell me how.

TATTLE. You must let me speak, Miss, you must not speak first. I must ask you questions, and you must answer.

MISS PRUE. What, is it like the catechism? Come then, ask me.

TATTLE. De'e you think you can love me?

MISS PRUE. Yes.

TATTLE. Pooh, pox, you must not say yes already. I shan't care a farthing for you then in a twinkling.

MISS PRUE. What must I say then?

TATTLE. Why you must say no, or you believe not, or you can't tell.

MISS PRUE. Why, must I tell a lie then?

TATTLE. Yes, if you would be well-bred. All well-bred persons lie. Besides, you are a woman, you must never speak what you think. Your words must contradict your thoughts, but your actions may contradict your words. So, when I ask you if you can love me, you must say no, but you must love me too. If I tell you you are handsome, you must deny it, and say I flatter you. But you must think yourself more charming than I speak you, and like me, for the beauty which I say you have, as much as if I had it myself. If I ask you to kiss me, you must be angry, but you must not refuse me. If I ask you for more, you must be more angry, but more complying. And as soon as ever I make you say you'll cry out, you must be sure to hold your tongue.

MISS PRUE. O Lord, I swear this is pure. I like it better than our old-fashioned country way of speaking one's mind. And must not you lie too?

TATTLE. Hum—yes. But you must believe I speak truth.

MISS PRUE. O Gemini! Well, I always had a great mind to tell lies, but they frighted me, and said it was a sin.

TATTLE. Well, my pretty creature, will you make me happy by giving me a kiss?

MISS PRUE. No, indeed, I'm angry at you. [*Runs and kisses him.*]

TATTLE. Hold, hold, that's pretty well, but you should not have given it me, but have suffered me to take it.

MISS PRUE. Well, we'll do it again.

TATTLE. With all my heart. Now then, my little angel. [*Kisses her.*]

MISS PRUE. Pish.

TATTLE. That's right. Again, my charmer. [*Kisses again.*]

MISS PRUE. O fie, nay, now I can't abide you.

TATTLE. Admirable! That was as well as if you had been born and bred in Covent Garden all the days of your life. And won't you show me, pretty Miss, where your bed-chamber is?

MISS PRUE. No, indeed won't I. But I'll run there, and hide myself from you behind the curtains.

TATTLE. I'll follow you.

MISS PRUE. Ah, but I'll hold the door with both hands and be angry—and you shall push me down before you come in.

TATTLE. No, I'll come in first, and push you down afterwards.

MISS PRUE. Will you? Then I'll be more angry, and more complying.

TATTLE. Then I'll make you cry out.

MISS PRUE. Oh, but you shan't, for I'll hold my tongue.

TATTLE. O my dear apt scholar.

MISS PRUE. Well, now I'll run and make more haste than you.

[*Exit* MISS PRUE.]

TATTLE. You shall not fly so fast as I'll pursue.

[*Exit after her.*]

THE END OF THE SECOND ACT

Act Three

SCENE ONE

A room in FORESIGHT'S *house.*

[*Enter* NURSE.]

NURSE. Miss, Miss, Miss Prue. Mercy on me, marry and amen. Why, what's become of the child? Why Miss, Miss Foresight. Sure she has not locked herself up in her chamber, and gone to sleep, or to prayers. Miss, Miss! I hear her. Come to your father, child. Open the door. Open the door, Miss. I hear you cry husht. O Lord, who's there? [*Peeps.*] What's here to do? O the Father! a man with her! Why, Miss I say, God's my life, here's fine doings towards. O Lord, we're all undone. O you young harlotry! [*Knocks.*] Ods my life, won't you open the door? I'll come in the back way.

[*Exit.*]

[TATTLE *and* MISS PRUE *at the door.*]

MISS PRUE. O Lord, she's coming—and she'll tell my father. What shall I do now?

TATTLE. Pox take her! If she had stayed two minutes longer, I should have wished for her coming.

MISS PRUE. O dear, what shall I say? Tell me, Mr. Tattle, tell me a lie.

TATTLE. There's no occasion for a lie; I could never tell a lie to no purpose. But since we have done nothing, we must say nothing, I think. I hear her. I'll leave you together, and come off as you can. [*Thrusts her in and shuts the door.*]

[*Enter* VALENTINE, SCANDAL, *and* ANGELICA.]

ANGELICA. You can't accuse me of inconstancy; I never told you that I loved you.

VALENTINE. But I can accuse you of uncertainty, for not telling me whether you did or no.

ANGELICA. You mistake indifference for uncertainty; I never had concern enough to ask myself the question.

SCANDAL. Nor good nature enough to answer him that did ask you, I'll say that for you, madam.

ANGELICA. What, are you setting up for good nature?

SCANDAL. Only for the affectation of it, as the women do for ill nature.

ANGELICA. Persuade your friend that it is all affectation.

VALENTINE. I shall receive no benefit from the opinion, for I know no effectual difference between continued affectation and reality.

TATTLE. [*coming up, aside to* SCANDAL] Scandal, are you in private discourse, anything of secrecy?

SCANDAL. Yes, but I dare trust you. We were talking of Angelica's love for Valentine. You won't speak of it?

TATTLE. No, no, not a syllable. I know that's a secret, for it's whispered everywhere.

SCANDAL. Ha, ha ha!

ANGELICA. What is, Mr. Tattle? I heard you say something was whispered everywhere.

SCANDAL. Your love of Valentine.

ANGELICA. How!

TATTLE. No, madam, his love for your ladyship. Gad take me, I beg your pardon, for I never heard a word of your ladyship's passion till this instant.

ANGELICA. My passion! And who told you of my passion, pray, sir?

SCANDAL. [*to* TATTLE] Why, is the devil in you? Did not I tell it you for a secret?

TATTLE. Gadso, but I thought she might have been trusted with her own affairs.

SCANDAL. Is that your discretion? Trust a woman with herself?

TATTLE. You say true. I beg your pardon, I'll bring all off. [*To* ANGELICA] It was impossible, madam, for me to imagine that a person of your ladyship's wit and gallantry could have so long received the passionate addresses of the accomplished Valentine, and yet remain insensible; therefore you will pardon me, if from a just weight of his merit, with your ladyship's good judgment, I formed the balance of a reciprocal affection.

VALENTINE. O the devil, what damned costive[2] poet has given thee this lesson of fustian to get by rote?

ANGELICA. I dare swear you wrong him, it is his own. And Mr. Tattle only judges of the success of others from the effects of his own merit. For certainly Mr. Tattle was never denied anything in his life.

TATTLE. O Lord! Yes indeed madam, several times.

ANGELICA. I swear I don't think 'tis possible.

TATTLE. Yes, I vow and swear I have. Lord, madam, I'm the most unfortunate man in the world, and the most cruelly used by the ladies.

ANGELICA. Nay, now you're ungrateful.

TATTLE. No, I hope not. 'Tis as much ingratitude to own some favors as to conceal others.

VALENTINE. There, now it's out.

ANGELICA. I don't understand you now. I thought you had never asked anything but what a lady might modestly grant and you confess.

2. Constipated; "fustian": lofty, inflated language.

SCANDAL. So faith, your business is done here. Now you may go brag somewhere else.

TATTLE. Brag! O heavens! Why, did I name anybody?

ANGELICA. No; I suppose that is not in your power; but you would if you could, no doubt on't.

TATTLE. Not in my power, madam! What does your ladyship mean, that I have no woman's reputation in my power?

SCANDAL. [*aside*] 'Ouns, why, you won't own it, will you?

TATTLE. Faith, madam, you're in the right. No more I have, as I hope to be saved. I never had it in my power to say anything to a lady's prejudice in my life. For as I was telling you, madam, I have been the most unsuccessful creature living in things of that nature, and never had the good fortune to be trusted once with a lady's secret, not once.

ANGELICA. No?

VALENTINE. Not once, I dare answer for him.

SCANDAL. And I'll answer for him, for I'm sure if he had he would have told me. I find, madam, you don't know Mr. Tattle.

TATTLE. No indeed, madam, you don't know me at all, I find. For sure my intimate friends would have known.

ANGELICA. Then it seems you would have told, if you had been trusted.

TATTLE. O pox, Scandal, that was too far put.—Never have told particulars, madam. Perhaps I might have talked as of a third person, or have introduced an amour of my own, in conversation, by way of novel,[3] but never have explained particulars.

ANGELICA. But whence comes the reputation of Mr. Tattle's secrecy, if he was never trusted?

SCANDAL. Why thence it arises. The thing is proverbially spoken, but may be applied to him. As if we should say in general terms, he only is secret who never was trusted; a satirical proverb upon our sex. There's another upon yours: as she is chaste, who was never asked the question. That's all.

VALENTINE. A couple of very civil proverbs, truly. 'Tis hard to tell whether the lady or Mr. Tattle be the more obliged to you. For you found her virtue upon the backwardness of the men, and his secrecy upon the mistrust of the women.

TATTLE. Gad, it's very true, madam, I think we are obliged to acquit ourselves. And for my part—But your ladyship is to speak first.

ANGELICA. Am I? Well, I freely confess I have resisted a great deal of temptation.

TATTLE. And egad, I have given some temptation that has not been resisted.

VALENTINE. Good.

ANGELICA. I cite Valentine there to declare to the court how fruitless he has found his endeavors, and to confess all his solicitations and my denials.

3. I.e., novelty.

VALENTINE. I am ready to plead not guilty for you, and guilty for myself.

SCANDAL. So, why this is fair. Here's demonstration with a witness.

TATTLE. Well, my witnesses are not present, but I confess I have had favors from persons. But as the favors are numberless, so the persons are nameless.

SCANDAL. Pooh, pox, this proves nothing.

TATTLE. No? I can show letters, lockets, pictures and rings; and if there be occasion for witnesses, I can summon the maids at the chocolate houses, all the porters of Pall Mall and Covent Garden, the doorkeepers at the Playhouse, the drawers[4] at Locket's, Pontack's, the Rummer, Spring Garden; my own landlady and *valet de chambre*, all who shall make oath that I receive more letters than the secretary's office, and that I have more visor-masks[5] to enquire for me than ever went to see the hermaphrodite or the naked prince.[6] And it is notorious that in a country church once, an inquiry being made who I was, it was answered I was the famous Tattle, who had ruined so many women.

VALENTINE. It was there, I suppose, you got the nickname of the Great Turk.

TATTLE. True: I was called Turk Tattle all over the parish. The next Sunday all the old women kept their daughters at home, and the parson had not half his congregation. He would have brought me into the Spiritual Court,[7] but I was revenged upon him, for he had a handsome daughter whom I initiated into the science. But I repented it afterwards, for it was talked of in town. And a lady of quality that shall be nameless, in a raging fit of jealousy, came down in her coach and six horses and exposed herself upon my account. Gad, I was sorry for it with all my heart—you know whom I mean. You know where we raffled—

SCANDAL. Mum, Tattle.

VALENTINE. 'Sdeath, are not you ashamed?

ANGELICA. O barbarous! I never heard so insolent a piece of vanity. Fie, Mr. Tattle, I'll swear I could not have believed it. Is this your secrecy?

TATTLE. Gadso, the heat of my story carried me beyond my discretion, as the heat of the lady's passion hurried her beyond her reputation. But I hope you don't know whom I mean; for there were a great many ladies raffled. Pox on't, now could I bite off my tongue.

SCANDAL. No, don't; for then you'll tell us no more. Come, I'll recommend a song to you upon the hint of my two proverbs, and I see one in the next room that will sing it. [*Goes to the door.*]

TATTLE. For Heav'n's sake, if you do guess, say nothing. Gad, I'm very unfortunate.

[*Re-enter* SCANDAL, *with one to sing.*]

SCANDAL. Pray sing the first song in the last new play.

4. Tapsters or bartenders at London restaurants.
5. I.e., women of the town, who disguised themselves with masks.
6. London sideshows of the time included hermaphrodites and a tattooed man, "Prince Giolo, son of King of Moangis."
7. A court with authority over ecclesiastical disputes.

SONG

1

A nymph and a swain to Apollo once prayed,
The swain had been jilted, the nymph been betrayed.
Their intent was to try if his oracle knew
E'er a nymph that was chaste, or a swain that was true.

2

Apollo was mute, and had like t' have been posed,[8]
But sagely at length he this secret disclosed:
He alone won't betray in whom none will confide,
And the nymph may be chaste that has never been tried.

[*Exit* SINGER.]

[*Enter* SIR SAMPSON, MRS. FRAIL, MISS PRUE *and* SERVANT.]

SIR SAMPSON. Is Ben come? Odso, my son Ben come? Odd, I'm glad on't. Where is he? I long to see him. Now, Mrs. Frail, you shall see my son Ben. Body o' me, he's the hopes of my family. I ha'n't seen him these three years. I warrant he's grown. Call him in, bid him make haste. I'm ready to cry for joy.

[*Exit* SERVANT.]

MRS. FRAIL. Now, Miss, you shall see your husband.

MISS PRUE. [*aside to* MRS. FRAIL] Pish, he shall be none of my husband.

MRS. FRAIL. Hush. Well! he shan't, leave that to me. I'll beckon Mr. Tattle to us.

ANGELICA. Won't you stay and see your brother?

VALENTINE. We are the twin stars, and cannot shine in one sphere; when he rises I must set.[9] Besides, if I should stay, I don't know but my father in good nature may press me to the immediate signing the deed of conveyance of my estate, and I'll defer it as long as I can. Well, you'll come to a resolution.

ANGELICA. I can't. Resolution must come to me, or I shall never have one.

SCANDAL. Come, Valentine, I'll go with you; I've something in my head to communicate to you.

[*Exit* VALENTINE *and* SCANDAL.]

SIR SAMPSON. What, is my son Valentine gone? What, is he sneaked off, and would not see his brother? There's an unnatural whelp! There's an ill-natured dog! What, were you here too, madam, and could not keep him? Could neither love, nor duty, nor natural affection oblige him? Odsbud, madam, have no more to say to him; he is not worth your consideration. The rogue has not a drachm[1] of generous love about him. All interest, all interest. He's an undone scoundrel, and courts your estate. Body o' me, he does not care a doit for your person.

ANGELICA. I'm pretty even with him, Sir Sampson; for if ever I

8. Puzzled.

9. Castor and Pollux, twin brothers and twin stars, were allowed by Zeus to live forever, but only on alternate days.

1. Tiny amount (after a Greek coin). "Doit": smallest Dutch coin.

could have liked anything in him, it should have been his estate too. But since that's gone, the bait's off, and the naked hook appears.

SIR SAMPSON. Odsbud, well spoken! And you are a wiser woman than I thought you were. For most young women nowadays are to be tempted with a naked hook.

ANGELICA. If I marry, Sir Sampson, I'm for a good estate with any man, and for any man with a good estate. Therefore if I were obliged to make a choice, I declare I'd rather have you than your son.

SIR SAMPSON. Faith and troth, you're a wise woman, and I'm glad to hear you say so. I was afraid you were in love with the reprobate. Odd, I was sorry for you with all my heart. Hang him, mungrel! Cast him off, you shall see the rogue show himself, and make love to some desponding cadua[2] of fourscore for sustenance. Odd, I love to see a young spendthrift forced to cling to an old woman for support, like ivy round a dead oak, faith I do. I love to see 'em hug and cotton together, like down upon a thistle.

[*Enter* BEN LEGEND *and* SERVANT.]

BEN. Where's father?

SERVANT. There, sir, his back's toward you.

SIR SAMPSON. My son Ben! Bless thee, my dear boy. Body o' me, thou art heartily welcome.

BEN. Thank you, father, and I'm glad to see you.

SIR SAMPSON. Odsbud, and I'm glad to see thee. Kiss me, boy, kiss me again and again, dear Ben [*Kisses him.*]

BEN. So, so, enough, father. Mess,[3] I'd rather kiss these gentlewomen.

SIR SAMPSON. And so thou shalt. Mrs. Angelica, my son Ben.

BEN. Forsooth, an you please. [*Salutes her.*] Nay, mistress, I'm not for dropping anchor here. About ship, i'faith. [*Kisses* MRS. FRAIL.] Nay, and you too, my little cock-boat.[4] So! [*Kisses* MISS PRUE.]

TATTLE. Sir, you're welcome ashore.

BEN. Thank you, thank you, friend.

SIR SAMPSON. Thou hast been many a weary league, Ben, since I saw thee.

BEN. Ey, ey, been! Been far enough, an[5] that be all. Well father, and how do all at home? How does brother Dick, and brother Val?

SIR SAMPSON. Dick? Body o' me, Dick has been dead these two years! I writ you word when you were at Leghorn.[6]

BEN. Mess, and that's true; marry, I had forgot. Dick's dead, as you say. Well, and how? I have a many questions to ask you. Well, you be'nt married again, father, be you?

SIR SAMPSON. No, I intend you shall marry, Ben. I would not marry

2. Something decrepit.
3. An oath ("by the mass").
4. A small ship's boat.
5. If (old-fashioned usage).
6. Livorno, a port on the northwest coast of Italy.

for thy sake.

BEN. Nay, what does that signify? An you marry again, why then, I'll go to sea again, so there's one for t'other, an that be all. Pray don't let me be your hindrance. E'en marry a God's name an the wind sit that way. As for my part, mayhap I have no mind to marry.

MRS. FRAIL. That would be pity, such a handsome young gentleman.

BEN. Handsome! He, he, he! Nay forsooth, an you be for joking, I'll joke with you, for I love my jest, an the ship were sinking, as we sayn at sea. But I'll tell you why I don't much stand towards matrimony. I love to roam about from port to port, and from land to land. I could never abide to be port-bound as we call it. Now a man that is married has as it were, d'ye see, his feet in the bilboes,[7] and mayhap mayn't get 'em out again when he would.

SIR SAMPSON. Ben's a wag.

BEN. A man that is married, d'ye see, is no more like another man than a galley slave is like one of us free sailors. He is chained to an oar all his life, and mayhap forced to tug a leaky vessel into the bargain.

SIR SAMPSON. A very wag, Ben's a very wag. Only a little rough, he wants a little polishing.

MRS. FRAIL. Not at all. I like his humor mightily, it's plain and honest. I should like such a humor in a husband extremely.

BEN. Sayn you so forsooth? Marry and I should like such a handsome gentlewoman for a bed-fellow hugely. How say you, mistress, would you like going to sea? Mess, you're a tight vessel, and well rigged, an you were but as well manned.

MRS. FRAIL. I should not doubt that, if you were master of me.

BEN. But I'll tell you one thing, an you come to sea in a high wind, or that, lady, you mayn't carry so much sail o'your head. Top and topgallant,[8] by the Mess.

MRS. FRAIL. No, why so?

BEN. Why an you do, you may run the risk to be overset, and then you'll carry your keels above water, he, he, he!

ANGELICA. I swear, Mr. Benjamin is the veriest wag in nature, an absolute sea-wit.

SIR SAMPSON. Nay, Ben has parts, but as I told you before, they want a little polishing. You must not take anything ill, madam.

BEN. No, I hope the gentlewoman is not angry. I mean all in good part, for if I give a jest, I'll take a jest, and so forsooth you may be as free with me.

ANGELICA. I thank you, sir, I am not at all offended. But methinks, Sir Sampson, you should leave him alone with his mistress. Mr. Tattle, we must not hinder lovers.

TATTLE. [*aside to* MISS PRUE] Well, Miss, I have your promise.

SIR SAMPSON. Body o' me, madam, you say true. Look you, Ben, this is your mistress. Come, Miss, you must not be shamefaced,

7. Shackles.
8. Sails above the mainmast (referring to her hairstyle).

we'll leave you together.

MISS PRUE. I can't abide to be left alone. Mayn't my cousin stay with me?

SIR SAMPSON. No, no. Come, let's away.

BEN. Look you, father, mayhap the young woman mayn't take a liking to me.

SIR SAMPSON. I warrant thee, boy. Come, come, we'll be gone. I'll venture that.

[*Exeunt all but* BEN *and* MISS PRUE.]

BEN. Come mistress, will you please to sit down? For an you stand a stern a that'n,[9] we shall never grapple together. Come, I'll haul a chair. There, an you please to sit, I'll sit by you.

MISS PRUE. You need not sit so near one. If you have anything to say, I can hear you farther off, I an't deaf.

BEN. Why, that's true as you say, nor I an't dumb; I can be heard as far as another. I'll heave off to please you. [*Sits farther off.*] An we were a league asunder, I'd undertake to hold discourse with you, an 'twere not a main high wind indeed, and full in my teeth. Look you forsooth, I am as it were bound for the land of matrimony. 'Tis a voyage d'ye see that was none of my seeking. I was commanded by father, and if you like of it, mayhap I may steer into your harbor. How say you, mistress? The short of the thing is this, that if you like me, and I like you, we may chance to swing in a hammock together.

MISS PRUE. I don't know what to say to you, nor I don't care to speak with you at all.

BEN. No? I'm sorry for that. But pray, why are you so scornful?

MISS PRUE. As long as one must not speak one's mind, one had better not speak at all, I think, and truly I won't tell a lie for the matter.

BEN. Nay, you say true in that, it's but a folly to lie. For to speak one thing and to think just the contrary way is, as it were, to look one way and to row another. Now for my part d'ye see, I'm for carrying things above board. I'm not for keeping anything under hatches. So that if you ben't as willing as I, say so a God's name, there's no harm done. Mayhap you may be shamefaced. Some maidens, though'f they love a man well enough, yet they don't care to tell'n so to's face. If that's the case, why, silence gives consent.

MISS PRUE. But I'm sure it is not so, for I'll speak sooner than you should believe that. And I'll speak truth, though one should always tell a lie to a man. And I don't care, let my father do what he will. I'm too big to be whipped, so I'll tell you plainly, I don't like you, nor love you at all, nor never will, that's more. So, there's your answer for you, and don't trouble me no more, you ugly thing.

BEN. Look you, young woman. You may learn to give good words, however. I spoke you fair, d'ye see, and civil. As for your love or

9. I.e., with your back turned.

your liking, I don't value it of a rope's end. And mayhap I like you as little as you do me. What I said was in obedience to father. Gad, I fear a whipping no more than you do. But I tell you one thing, if you should give such language at sea, you'd have a cat-o'-nine-tails[1] laid 'cross your shoulders. Flesh, who are you? You heard t'other handsome young woman speak civilly to me, of her own accord. Whatever you think of yourself, Gad I don't think you are any more to compare to her than a can of small beer to a bowl of punch.

MISS PRUE. Well, and there's a handsome gentleman, and a fine gentleman, and a sweet gentleman, that was here that loves me, and I love him; and if he sees you speak to me any more, he'll thrash your jacket for you, he will, you great sea-calf.

BEN. What, do you mean that fair-weather spark that was here just now? Will he thrash my jacket? Let'n, let'n. But an he comes near me, mayhap I may giv'n a salt eel[2] for's supper for all that. What does father mean to leave me alone as soon as I come home with such a dirty dowdy? Sea calf! I an't calf enough to lick your chalked face, you cheese-curd you. Marry thee! Ouns! I'll marry a Lapland witch[3] as soon, and live upon selling of contrary winds, and wracked vessels.

MISS PRUE. I won't be called names, nor I won't be abused thus, so I won't. If I were a man—[*cries*]—you durst not talk at this rate. No you durst not, you stinking tar-barrel.

[*Enter* MRS. FORESIGHT *and* MRS. FRAIL.]

MRS. FORESIGHT. They have quarreled just as we could wish.

BEN. Tar-barrel? Let your sweetheart there call me so, if he'll take your part, your Tom Essence,[4] and I'll say something to him. Gad I'll lace his musk-doublet for him! I'll make him stink! He shall smell more like a weasel than a civet cat afore I ha'done with 'en.

MRS. FORESIGHT. Bless me, what's the matter, Miss? What, does she cry? Mr. Benjamin, what have you done to her?

BEN. Let her cry: the more she cries, the less she'll—she has been gathering foul weather in her mouth, and now it rains out at her eyes.

MRS. FORESIGHT. Come, Miss, come along with me, and tell me, poor child.

MRS. FRAIL. Lord, what shall we do, there's my brother Foresight, and Sir Sampson coming. Sister, do you take Miss down into the parlor, and I'll carry Mr. Benjamin into my chamber, for they must not know that they are fall'n out. Come, sir, will you venture yourself with me? [*Looks kindly on him.*]

BEN. Venture? Mess, and that I will, 'twere to sea in a storm.

[*Exeunt.*]

[*Enter* SIR SAMPSON *and* FORESIGHT.]

SIR SAMPSON. I left 'em together here. What, are they gone? Ben's

1. Whip with nine lashes.
2. Rope used for flogging.
3. Fabled to send winds and tempests.
4. Perfume-loving coxcomb in a play (1676) by Thomas Rawlins.

a brisk boy. He has got her into a corner. Father's own son, faith, he'll touzle her, and mouzle[5] her. The rogue's sharp set, coming from sea; if he should not stay for saying grace, old Foresight, but fall to without the help of a parson, ha? Odd, if he should I could not be angry with him. 'Twould be but like me, a chip of the old block. Ha! Thou'rt melancholy, old Prognostication, as melancholy as if thou hadst spilt the salt, or pared thy nails of a Sunday. Come, cheer up, look about thee. Look up, old stargazer. Now is he poring upon the ground for a crooked pin, or an old horse-nail, with the head towards him.

FORESIGHT. Sir Sampson, we'll have the wedding tomorrow morning.

SIR SAMPSON. With all my heart.

FORESIGHT. At ten a clock, punctually at ten.

SIR SAMPSON. To a minute, to a second. Thou shall set thy watch, and the bridegroom shall observe its motions. They shall be married to a minute, go to bed to a minute, and when the alarm strikes, they shall keep time like the figures of St. Dunstan's clock, and *consummatum est*[6] shall ring all over the parish.

[*Enter* SCANDAL.]

SCANDAL. Sir Sampson, sad news.

FORESIGHT. Bless us!

SIR SAMPSON. Why, what's the matter?

SCANDAL. Can't you guess at what ought to afflict you and him, and all of us, more than anything else?

SIR SAMPSON. Body o' me, I don't know any universal grievance but a new tax, and the loss of the Canary Fleet,[7] without popery should be landed in the West, or the French fleet were at anchor at Blackwall.

SCANDAL. No. Undoubtedly Mr. Foresight knew all this, and might have prevented it.

FORESIGHT. 'Tis no earthquake!

SCANDAL. No, not yet, nor whirlwind. But we don't know what it may come to. But it has had a consequence already that touches us all.

SIR SAMPSON. Why, body o' me, out with't.

SCANDAL. Something has appeared to your son Valentine. He's gone to bed upon't, and very ill. He speaks little, yet says he has a world to say. Asks for his father and the wise Foresight; talks of Raymond Lully,[8] and the ghost of Lilly. He has secrets to impart, I suppose, to you two. I can get nothing out of him but sighs. He desires he may see you in the morning, but would not be disturbed tonight, because he has some business to do in a dream.

5. "To fondle with the mouth close. A low word" (Johnson's *Dictionary*). "Sharp set": with sails trimmed to the wind; in a hurry.

6. "It is finished," Christ's last words on the cross (John xix.30), here adapted to the consummation of the marriage.

7. The French treasure fleet, pursued by British ships in the war. "Without": unless; "Blackwall": on the Thames near London.

8. 13th-century Spanish philosopher, whose followers, the Lullists, turned to alchemy. William Lilly, a famous astrologer, had died in 1681.

SIR SAMPSON. Hoity toity, what have I to do with his dreams or his divination? Body o' me, this is a trick to defer signing the conveyance. I warrant the devil will tell him in a dream that he must not part with his estate. But I'll bring him a parson to tell him that the devil's a liar. Or if that won't do, I'll bring a lawyer that shall out-lie the devil. And so I'll try whether my blackguard or his shall get the better of the day. [*Exit.*]

SCANDAL. Alas, Mr. Foresight, I'm afraid all is not right. You are a wise man, and a conscientious man, a searcher into obscurity and futurity, and if you commit an error, it is with a great deal of consideration, and discretion, and caution.

FORESIGHT. Ah, good Mr. Scandal—

SCANDAL. Nay, nay, 'tis manifest; I do not flatter you. But Sir Sampson is hasty, very hasty. I'm afraid he is not scrupulous enough, Mr. Foresight. He has been wicked, and heaven grant he may mean well in his affair with you. But my mind gives me, these things cannot be wholly insignificant. You are wise, and should not be overreached, methinks you should not—

FORESIGHT. Alas, Mr. Scandal—*Humanum est errare.*

SCANDAL. You say true, man will err, mere man will err; but you are something more. There have been wise men, but they were such as you, men who consulted the stars, and were observers of omens. Solomon was wise, but how? By his judgment in astrology. So says Pineda[9] in his third book and eighth chapter.

FORESIGHT. You are learned, Mr. Scandal.

SCANDAL. A trifler, but a lover of art. And the wise men of the East owed their instruction to a star, which is rightly observed by Gregory the Great[1] in favor of astrology. And Albertus Magnus makes it the most valuable science, because, says he, it teaches us to consider the causation of causes in the causes of things.

FORESIGHT. I protest I honor you, Mr. Scandal. I did not think you had been read in these matters. Few young men are inclined—

SCANDAL. I thank my stars that have inclined me. But I fear this marriage and making over this estate, this transferring of a rightful inheritance, will bring judgments upon us. I prophesy it, and I would not have the fate of Cassandra,[2] not to be believed. Valentine is disturbed; what can be the cause of that? And Sir Sampson is hurried on by an unusual violence. I fear he does not act wholly from himself; methinks he does not look as he used to do.

FORESIGHT. He was always of an impetuous nature. But as to this marriage, I have consulted the stars; and all appearances are prosperous.

SCANDAL. Come, come, Mr. Foresight, let not the prospect of worldly lucre carry you beyond your judgment, nor against your conscience. You are not satisfied that you act justly.

9. Spanish author of a commentary on King Solomon (1609).

1. Pope from 590 to 604. Albertus Magnus, the teacher of St. Thomas Aquinas, helped to make alchemy and astrology respectable.

2. Legendary Trojan prophetess whose prophecies, though always true, were never believed.

FORESIGHT. How?

SCANDAL. You are not satisfied, I say. I am loath to discourage you. But it is palpable that you are not satisfied.

FORESIGHT. How does it appear, Mr. Scandal? I think I am very well satisfied.

SCANDAL. Either you suffer yourself to deceive yourself, or you do not know yourself.

FORESIGHT. Pray explain yourself.

SCANDAL. Do you sleep well o'nights?

FORESIGHT. Very well.

SCANDAL. Are you certain? You do not look so.

FORESIGHT. I am in health, I think.

SCANDAL. So was Valentine this morning, and looked just so.

FORESIGHT. How? Am I altered any way? I don't perceive it.

SCANDAL. That may be, but your beard is longer than it was two hours ago.

FORESIGHT. Indeed? Bless me!

[*Enter* MRS. FORESIGHT.]

MRS. FORESIGHT. Husband, will you go to bed? It's ten a clock. Mr. Scandal, your servant.

SCANDAL. [*aside*] Pox on her, she has interrupted my design. But I must work her into the project. [*Aloud*] You keep early hours, madam.

MRS. FORESIGHT. Mr. Foresight is punctual, we sit up after him.

FORESIGHT. My dear, pray lend me your glass, your little looking glass.

SCANDAL. Pray lend it him, madam. I'll tell you the reason. [*She gives him the glass:* SCANDAL *and she whisper.*] My passion for you is grown so violent that I am no longer master of my self. I was interrupted this morning, when you had charity enough to give me your attention, and I had hopes of finding another opportunity of explaining myself to you, but was disappointed all this day, and the uneasiness that has attended me ever since brings me now hither at this unseasonable hour.

MRS. FORESIGHT. Was there ever such impudence? To make love to me before my husband's face. I'll swear I'll tell him.

SCANDAL. Do, I'll die a martyr rather than disclaim my passion. But come a little farther this way, and I'll tell you what project I had to get him out of the way, that I might have an opportunity of waiting upon you. [*Whispers.*]

FORESIGHT. [*looking in the glass*] I do not see any revolution here. Methinks I look with a serene and benign aspect[3]—pale, a little pale—but the roses of these cheeks have been gathered many years. Ha! I do not like that sudden flushing. Gone already! Hem, hem, hem! Faintish. My heart is pretty good, yet it beats; and my pulses? Ha! I have none. Mercy on me! Hum. Yes, here they are. Gallop, gallop, gallop, gallop, gallop, gallop. Hey, whither will they hurry me? Now they're gone again, and now

3. Countenance, with a play on the relative position of a planet as it appears on earth.

I'm faint again, and pale again, and hem! and my—hem?—breath, hem!—grows short. Hem, hem! He, he, hem!

SCANDAL. [*aside to* MRS. FORESIGHT] It takes. Pursue it in the name of love and pleasure.

MRS. FORESIGHT. How do you do, Mr. Foresight?

FORESIGHT. Hum, not so well as I thought I was. Lend me your hand.

SCANDAL. Look you there now. Your lady says your sleep has been unquiet of late.

FORESIGHT. Very likely.

MRS. FORESIGHT. Oh, mighty restless, but I was afraid to tell him so. He has been subject to talking and starting.

SCANDAL. And did not use to be so?

MRS. FORESIGHT. Never, never, till within these three nights. I cannot say that he has once broken my rest since we have been married.

FORESIGHT. I will go to bed.

SCANDAL. Do so, Mr. Foresight, and say your prayers. He looks better than he did.

MRS. FORESIGHT. [*calls*] Nurse, nurse!

FORESIGHT. Do you think so, Mr. Scandal?

SCANDAL. Yes, yes, I hope this will be gone by morning, taking it in time.

FORESIGHT. I hope so.

[*Enter* NURSE.]

MRS. FORESIGHT. Nurse, your master is not well; put him to bed.

SCANDAL. I hope you will be able to see Valentine in the morning. You had best take a little diacodion[4] and cowslip water, and lie upon your back. Maybe you may dream.

FORESIGHT. I thank you, Mr. Scandal, I will. Nurse, let me have a watch-light, and lay the *Crumbs of Comfort*[5] by me.

NURSE. Yes, sir.

FORESIGHT. And—Hem, hem! I am very faint.

SCANDAL. No, no, you look much better.

FORESIGHT. Do I? And d'ye hear, bring me, let me see, within a quarter of twelve—hem—he, hem!—just upon the turning of the tide, bring me the urinal. And I hope neither the lord of my ascendants nor the moon will be combust,[6] and then I may do well.

SCANDAL. I hope so. Leave that to me; I will erect a scheme; and I hope I shall find both Sol and Venus in the sixth house.[7]

FORESIGHT. I thank you, Mr. Scandal. Indeed, that would be a great comfort to me. Hem, hem! Good night. [*Exit.*]

SCANDAL. Good night, good Mr. Foresight. And I hope Mars and Venus will be in conjunction while your wife and I are together.

MRS. FORESIGHT. Well, and what use do you hope to make of this project? You don't think that you are ever like to succeed in your

4. An opiate.
5. A popular manual of devotion.
6. I.e., extinguished by the light of the sun.
7. Virgo, a sign of good health in astrology.

design upon me?

SCANDAL. Yes, faith, I do. I have a better opinion both of you and myself than to despair.

MRS. FORESIGHT. Did you ever hear such a toad? Hark'ee devil, do you think any woman honest?

SCANDAL. Yes, several, very honest. They'll cheat a little at cards sometimes, but that's nothing.

MRS. FORESIGHT. Pshaw! but virtuous, I mean?

SCANDAL. Yes, faith, I believe some women are virtuous too; but 'tis as I believe some men are valiant, through fear. For why should a man court danger, or a woman shun pleasure?

MRS. FORESIGHT. O monstrous! What are conscience and honor?

SCANDAL. Why, honor is a public enemy, and conscience a domestic thief; and he that would secure his pleasure must pay a tribute to one and go halves with the other. As for honor, that you have secured, for you have purchased a perpetual opportunity for pleasure.

MRS. FORESIGHT. An opportunity for pleasure?

SCANDAL. Ay, your husband. A husband is an opportunity for pleasure, so you have taken care of honor; and 'tis the least I can do to take care of conscience.

MRS. FORESIGHT. And so you think we are free for one another?

SCANDAL. Yes faith, I think so. I love to speak my mind.

MRS. FORESIGHT. Why then, I'll speak my mind. Now as to this affair between you and me: Here you make love to me. Why, I'll confess it does not displease me. Your person is well enough and your understanding is not amiss.

SCANDAL. I have no great opinion of myself, yet I think I'm neither deformed nor a fool.

MRS. FORESIGHT. But you have a villainous character. You are a libertine in speech as well as practice.

SCANDAL. Come, I know what you would say. You think it more dangerous to be seen in conversation with me than to allow some other men the last favor. You mistake; the liberty I take in talking is purely affected for the service of your sex. He that first cries out "stop thief" is often he that has stolen the treasure. I am a juggler, that act by confederacy; and if you please, we'll put a trick upon the world.

MRS. FORESIGHT. Ay, but you are such an universal juggler that I'm afraid you have a great many confederates.

SCANDAL. Faith, I'm sound.

MRS. FORESIGHT. O fie, I'll swear you're impudent.

SCANDAL. I'll swear you're handsome.

MRS. FORESIGHT. Pish, you'd tell me so, though you did not think so.

SCANDAL. And you'd think so, though I should not tell you so. And now I think we know one another pretty well.

MRS. FORESIGHT. O Lord, who's here?

[*Enter* MRS. FRAIL *and* BEN.]

BEN. Mess, I love to speak my mind. Father has nothing to do with me. Nay, I can't say that neither, he has something to do with me. But what does that signify? If so be that I ben't minded to be steered by him, 'tis as though'f he should drive against wind and tide.

MRS. FRAIL. Ay, but my dear, we must keep it secret till the estate be settled. For, you know, marrying without an estate is like sailing in a ship without ballast.

BEN. He, he, he! Why, that's true. Just so for all the world it is indeed, as like as two cable ropes.

MRS. FRAIL. And though I have a good portion, you know one would not venture all in one bottom.[8]

BEN. Why, that's true again, for mayhap one bottom may spring a leak. You have hit it indeed; Mess, you've nicked[9] the channel.

MRS. FRAIL. Well, but if you should forsake me after all, you'd break my heart.

BEN. Break your heart? I'd rather the *Mary-gold* should break her cable in a storm, as well as I love her. Flesh, you don't think I'm false-hearted, like a land-man. A sailor will be honest, though'f mayhap he has never a penny of money in his pocket. Mayhap I may not have so fair a face as a citizen or a courtier, but for all that I've as good blood in my veins, and a heart as sound as a biscuit.

MRS. FRAIL. And will you love me always?

BEN. Nay, an I love once, I'll stick like pitch, I'll tell you that. Come, I'll sing you a song of a sailor.

MRS. FRAIL. Hold, there's my sister. I'll call her to hear it.

MRS. FORESIGHT. Well, I won't go to bed to my husband tonight, because I'll retire to my own chamber and think of what you have said.

SCANDAL. Well, you'll give me leave to wait upon you to your chamber door and leave you my last instructions?

MRS. FORESIGHT. Hold, here's my sister coming toward us.

MRS. FRAIL. If it won't interrupt you, I'll entertain you with a song.

BEN. The song was made upon one of our ship's crew's wife; our boatswain made the song. Mayhap you may know her, sir. Before she was married, she was called buxom Joan of Deptford.

SCANDAL. I have heard of her.

BEN. [*sings*]

1

A soldier and a sailor,
A tinker, and a tailor,
Had once a doubtful strife, sir,
To make a maid a wife, sir,
Whose name was buxom Joan.
For now the time was ended,
When she no more intended,
To lick her lips at men, sir,

8. Hull of a ship.

9. Hit exactly.

And gnaw the sheets in vain, sir,
  And lie o'nights alone.

2

The soldier swore like thunder,
He loved her more than plunder,
And showed her many a scar, sir,
That he had brought from far, sir,
  With fighting for her sake.
The tailor thought to please her,
With off'ring her his measure.
The tinker, too, with mettle,
Said he could mend her kettle,
  And stop up ev'ry leak.

3

But while these three were prating,
The sailor, slyly waiting,
Thought if it came about, sir,
That they should all fall out, sir,
  He then might play his part.
And just e'en as he meant, sir,
To loggerheads they went, sir,
And then he let fly at her,
A shot 'twixt wind and water,
  That won this fair maid's heart.

BEN. If some of our crew that came to see me are not gone, you shall see that we sailors can dance sometimes, as well as other folks. [*Whistles.*] I warrant that brings 'em, an they be within hearing.

[*Enter* SEAMEN.]

O here they be, and fiddles along with 'em. Come my lads, let's have a round, and I'll make one.

[*Dance.*]

We're merry folk, we sailors, we han't much to care for. Thus we live at sea; eat biscuit, and drink flip,[1] put on a clean shirt once a quarter, come home and lie with our landladies once a year, get rid of a little money, and then put off with the next fair wind. How d'ye like us?

MRS. FRAIL. Oh, you are the happiest, merriest men alive.

MRS. FORESIGHT. We're beholding to Mr. Benjamin for this entertainment. I believe it's late.

BEN. Why, forsooth, an you think so, you had best go to bed. For my part, I mean to toss a can[2] and remember my sweetheart afore I turn in. Mayhap I may dream of her.

MRS. FORESIGHT. Mr. Scandal, you had best go to bed and dream too.

SCANDAL. Why, faith, I have a good lively imagination, and can dream as much to the purpose as another, if I set about it. But

1. Beer with brandy, sweetened and spiced.

2. Drink a cup.

dreaming is the poor retreat of a lazy, hopeless, and imperfect lover. 'Tis the last glimpse of love to worn-out sinners, and the faint dawning of a bliss to wishing girls and growing boys.

There's naught but willing, waking love that can
Make blessed the ripened maid, and finished man.

[*Exeunt.*]

THE END OF THE THIRD ACT

Act Four

SCENE ONE

VALENTINE'S *lodging.*

[*Enter* SCANDAL *and* JEREMY.]

SCANDAL. Well, is your master ready? Does he look madly and talk madly?

JEREMY. Yes, sir, you need make no great doubt of that. He that was so near turning poet yesterday morning can't be much to seek in playing the madman today.

SCANDAL. Would he have Angelica acquainted with the reason of his design?

JEREMY. No sir, not yet. He has a mind to try whether his playing the madman won't make her play the fool and fall in love with him, or at least own that she has loved him all this while, and concealed it.

SCANDAL. I saw her take coach just now with her maid, and think I heard her bid the coachman drive hither.

JEREMY. Like enough, sir, for I told her maid this morning my master was run stark mad only for love of her mistress. I hear a coach stop; if it should be she, sir, I believe he would not see her till he hears how she takes it.

SCANDAL. Well, I'll try her. 'Tis she, here she comes.

[*Enter* ANGELICA *with* JENNY.]

ANGELICA. Mr. Scandal, I suppose you don't think it a novelty to see a woman visit a man at his own lodgings in a morning?

SCANDAL. Not upon a kind occasion, madam. But when a lady comes tyrannically to insult a ruined lover, and make manifest the cruel triumphs of her beauty, the barbarity of it something surprises me.

ANGELICA. I don't like raillery from a serious face. Pray tell me what is the matter.

JEREMY. No strange matter, madam; my master's mad, that's all. I suppose your ladyship has thought him so a great while?

ANGELICA. How d'you mean, mad?

JEREMY. Why faith, madam, he's mad for want of his wits, just as he was poor for want of money. His head is e'en as light as his pockets, and anybody that has a mind to a bad bargain can't do better than to beg him for his estate.

ANGELICA. If you speak truth, your endeavoring at wit is very unseasonable.

SCANDAL. [*aside*] She's concerned, and loves him.

ANGELICA. Mr. Scandal, you can't think me guilty of so much inhumanity as not to be concerned for a man I must own myself obliged to. Pray tell me truth.

SCANDAL. Faith, madam, I wish telling a lie would mend the matter. But this is no new effect of an unsuccessful passion.

ANGELICA. [*aside*] I know not what to think—yet I should be vexed to have a trick put upon me. [*Aloud*] May I not see him?

SCANDAL. I'm afraid the physician is not willing you should see him yet. Jeremy, go in and inquire.

[*Exit* JEREMY.]

ANGELICA. Ha! I saw him wink and smile—I fancy 'tis a trick. I'll try[3]—I would disguise to all the world a failing, which I must own to you. I fear my happiness depends upon the recovery of Valentine. Therefore I conjure you as you are his friend, and as you have compassion upon one fearful of affliction, to tell me what I am to hope for. I cannot speak, but you may tell me. Tell me, for you know what I would ask.

SCANDAL. [*aside*] So, this is pretty plain. [*Aloud*] Be not too much concerned, madam; I hope his condition is not desperate. An acknowledgement of love from you, perhaps, may work a cure, as the fear of your aversion occasioned his distemper.

ANGELICA. [*aside*] Say you so? Nay, then I'm convinced, and if I don't play trick for trick, may I never taste the pleasure of revenge. [*Aloud*] Acknowledgement of love! I find you have mistaken my compassion, and think me guilty of a weakness I am a stranger to. But I have too much sincerity to deceive you, and too much charity to suffer him to be deluded with vain hopes. Good nature and humanity oblige me to be concerned for him, but to love is neither in my power nor inclination, and if he can't be cured without I suck the poison from his wounds, I'm afraid he won't recover his senses till I lose mine.

SCANDAL. Hey, brave woman, i'faith. Won't you see him, then, if he desire it?

ANGELICA. What signify a madman's desires? Besides, 'twould make me uneasy. If I don't see him, perhaps my concern for him may lessen. If I forget him, 'tis no more than he has done by himself; and now the surprise is over, methinks I am not half so sorry for him as I was.

SCANDAL. So, faith, good nature works apace; you were confessing just now an obligation to his love.

ANGELICA. But I have considered that passions are unreasonable and involuntary. If he loves, he can't help it, and if I don't love, I can't help it; no more than he can help his being a man, or I my being a woman; or no more than I can help my want of inclination to stay longer here. Come, Jenny.

[*Exit* ANGELICA *and* JENNY.]

SCANDAL. Humh! An admirable composition, faith, this same womankind.

3. Find out.

[*Enter* JEREMY.]

JEREMY. What, is she gone, sir?

SCANDAL. Gone? Why, she was never here, nor anywhere else, nor I don't know her if I see her, nor you neither.

JEREMY. Good lack! What's the matter now? Are any more of us to be mad! Why, sir, my master longs to see her, and is almost mad in good earnest with the joyful news of her being here.

SCANDAL. We are all under a mistake. Ask no questions, for I can't resolve you; but I'll inform your master. In the meantime, if our project succeed no better with his father than it does with his mistress, he may descend from his exaltation of madness into the road of commonsense and be content only to be made a fool with other reasonable people. I hear Sir Sampson. You know your cue; I'll to your master. [*Exit.*]

[*Enter* SIR SAMPSON LEGEND *with a* LAWYER.]

SIR SAMPSON. D'ye see, Mr. Buckram, here's the paper signed with his own hand.

BUCKRAM. Good, sir. And the conveyance is ready drawn in this box, if he be ready to sign and seal.

SIR SAMPSON. Ready? Body o' me, he must be ready. His sham sickness shan't excuse him. Oh, here's his scoundrel. Sirrah, where's your master?

JEREMY. Ah, sir, he's quite gone.

SIR SAMPSON. Gone! What, he is not dead?

JEREMY. No, sir, not dead.

SIR SAMPSON. What, is he gone out of town, run away, ha? Has he tricked me? Speak, varlet.

JEREMY. No, no, sir, he's safe enough, sir, an he were but as sound, poor gentleman. He is indeed here, sir, and not here, sir.

SIR SAMPSON. Heyday, rascal, do you banter me? Sirrah, d'ye banter me? Speak, sirrah, where is he, for I will find him.

JEREMY. Would you could sir, for he has lost himself. Indeed, sir, I have a'most broke my heart about him. I can't refrain tears when I think of him, sir. I'm as melancholy for him as a passing-bell, sir, or a horse in a pound.

SIR SAMPSON. A pox confound your similitudes, sir. Speak to be understood, and tell me in plain terms what the matter is with him, or I'll crack your fool's skull.

JEREMY. Ah, you've hit it, sir. That's the matter with him, sir. His skull's cracked, poor gentleman; he's stark mad, sir.

SIR SAMPSON. Mad!

BUCKRAM. What, is he *non compos?*[4]

JEREMY. Quite *non compos*, sir.

BUCKRAM. Why, then all's obliterated, Sir Sampson. If he be *non compos mentis,* his act and deed will be of no effect, it is not good in law.

SIR SAMPSON. Ouns, I won't believe it. Let me see him, sir. Mad! I'll make him find his senses.

JEREMY. Mr. Scandal is with him, sir; I'll knock at the door.

4. Not in control (of one's mind).

[*Goes to the scene,*[5] *which opens and discovers* VALENTINE *upon a couch disorderly dressed,* SCANDAL *by him.*]

SIR SAMPSON. How now, what's here to do?

VALENTINE. [*starting*] Ha! Who's that?

SCANDAL. For Heav'ns sake softly, sir, and gently. Don't provoke him.

VALENTINE. Answer me. Who is that? And that?

SIR SAMPSON. Gads-bobs, does he not know me? Is he mischievous? I'll speak gently. Val, Val, dost thou not know me, boy? Not know thy own father, Val? I am thy own father, and this is honest Brief Buckram, the lawyer.

VALENTINE. It may be so. I did not know you. The world is full. There are people that we do know, and people that we do not know; and yet the sun shines upon all alike. There are fathers that have many children, and there are children that have many fathers. 'Tis strange! But I am Truth, and come to give the world the lie.

SIR SAMPSON. Body o' me, I know not what to say to him.

VALENTINE. Why does that lawyer wear black? Does he carry his conscience without-side? Lawyer, what art thou? Dost thou know me?

BUCKRAM. O Lord, what must I say? Yes, sir.

VALENTINE. Thou liest, for I am Truth. 'Tis hard, I cannot get a livelihood amongst you. I have been sworn out of Westminster Hall[6] the first day of every term. Let me see—no matter how long—But I'll tell you one thing; it's a question that would puzzle an arithmetician, if you should ask him, whether the Bible saves more souls in Westminster Abbey, or damns more in Westminster Hall. For my part, I am Truth, and can't tell; I have very few acquaintance.

SIR SAMPSON. Body o' me, he talks sensibly in his madness. Has he no intervals?

JEREMY. Very short, sir.

BUCKRAM. Sir, I can do you no service while he's in this condition. Here's your paper, sir. He may do me a mischief if I stay. The conveyance is ready, sir, if he recover his senses. [*Exit.*]

SIR SAMPSON. Hold, hold, don't you go yet.

SCANDAL. You'd better let him go, sir, and send for him if there be occasion, for I fancy his presence provokes him more.

VALENTINE. Is the lawyer gone? 'Tis well, then we may drink about without going together by the ears.[7] Heigh ho! What a clock is't? My father here? Your blessing, sir.

SIR SAMPSON. He recovers. Bless thee, Val. How dost thou do, boy?

VALENTINE. Thank you, sir, pretty well. I have been a little out of order. Won't you please to sit, sir?

SIR SAMPSON. Ay, boy. Come, thou shalt sit down by me.

VALENTINE. Sir, 'tis my duty to wait.

5. Curtained recess or "inner stage."
6. I.e., the law courts.
7. I.e., fighting.

SIR SAMPSON. No, no; come, come, sit you down, honest Val. How dost thou do? Let me feel thy pulse. Oh, pretty well now, Val. Body o' me, I was sorry to see thee indisposed. But I'm glad thou'rt better, honest Val.

VALENTINE. I thank you, sir.

SCANDAL. [*aside*] Miracle! the monster grows loving.

SIR SAMPSON. Let me feel thy hand again, Val. It does not shake. I believe thou canst write, Val. Ha, boy? Thou can'st write thy name, Val? [*In whisper to* JEREMY] Jeremy, step and overtake Mr. Buckram, bid him make haste back with the conveyance. Quick, quick!

[*Exit* JEREMY.]

SCANDAL. [*aside*] That ever I should suspect such a heathen of any remorse!

SIR SAMPSON. Dost thou know this paper, Val? I know thou'rt honest, and wilt perform articles.

[*Shows him the paper but holds it out of his reach.*]

VALENTINE. Pray let me see it, sir. You hold it so far off that I can't tell whether I know it or no.

SIR SAMPSON. See it, boy? Ay, ay, why thou dost see it. 'Tis thy own hand, Val. Why let me see, I can read it as plain as can be. Look you here [*reads*]: *The condition of this obligation*—Look you, as plain as can be, so it begins. And then at the bottom, *As witness my hand*, VALENTINE LEGEND, in great letters. Why, 'tis as plain as the nose in one's face. What, are my eyes better than thine? I believe I can read it farther off yet. Let me see. [*Stretches his arm as far as he can.*]

VALENTINE. Will you please to let me hold it, sir?

SIR SAMPSON. Let thee hold it, say'st thou? Ay, with all my heart. What matter is it who holds it? What need anybody hold it? I'll put it up in my pocket, Val. And then nobody need hold it. [*Puts the paper in his pocket.*] There, Val: it's safe enough, boy. But thou shalt have it as soon as thou hast set thy hand to another paper, little Val.

[*Re-enter* JEREMY *with* BUCKRAM.]

VALENTINE. What, is my bad genius here again? Oh no, 'tis the lawyer with an itching palm, and he's come to be scratched. My nails are not long enough. Let me have a pair of red-hot tongs quickly, quickly, and you shall see me act St. Dunstan, and lead the devil by the nose.[8]

BUCKRAM. O Lord, let me be gone; I'll not venture myself with a madman. [*Exit* BUCKRAM.]

VALENTINE. Ha, ha, ha! you need not run so fast, honesty will not overtake you. Ha, ha, ha! The rogue found me out to be in *forma pauperis*[9] presently.

SIR SAMPSON. Ouns! What a vexation is here! I know not what to do or say, nor which way to go.

8. Pictured on a tavern sign near St. Dunstan's church.

9. Bankrupt.

VALENTINE. Who's that, that's out of his way? I am Truth, and can set him right. Harkee, friend, the straight road is the worst way you can go. He that follows his nose always will very often be led into a stink. *Probatum est.*[1] But what are you for? Religion or politics? There's a couple of topics for you, no more like one another than oil and vinegar. And yet those two beaten together by a state-cook[2] make sauce for the whole nation.

SIR SAMPSON. What the devil had I to do, ever to beget sons! Why did I ever marry?

VALENTINE. Because thou wert a monster, old boy. The two greatest monsters in the world are a man and a woman. What's thy opinion?

SIR SAMPSON. Why, my opinion is that those two monsters joined together make yet a greater, that's a man and his wife.

VALENTINE. Aha! Old truepenny, say'st thou so? thou hast nicked it. But it's wonderful strange, Jeremy!

JEREMY. What is, sir?

VALENTINE. That gray hairs should cover a green head—and I make a fool of my father.

[*Enter* FORESIGHT, MRS. FORESIGHT, *and* FRAIL.]

VALENTINE. What's here! Erra Pater?[3] or a bearded sybil? If prophecy comes, Truth must give place. [*Exit with* JEREMY.]

FORESIGHT. What says he? What, did he prophesy? Ha, Sir Sampson, bless us! How are we?

SIR SAMPSON. Are we? A pox o'your prognostication. Why, we are fools as we use to be. Ouns, that you could not foresee that the moon would predominate; and my son be mad.—Where's your oppositions, your trines, and your quadrates? What did your Cardan and your Ptolomee tell you? Your Messahalah and your Longomontanus,[4] your harmony of chiromancy with astrology? Ah! pox on't, that I that know the world, and men and manners, that don't believe a syllable in the sky and stars, and sun and almanacs, and trash, should be directed by a dreamer, an omen-hunter, and defer business in expectation of a lucky hour. When, body o' me, there never was a lucky hour after the first opportunity. [*Exit* SIR SAMPSON.]

FORESIGHT. Ah, Sir Sampson, heaven help your head. This is none of your lucky hour; *nemo omnibus horis sapit.*[5] What, is he gone, and in contempt of science? Ill stars and unconverted ignorance attend him!

SCANDAL. You must excuse his passion, Mr. Foresight, for he has been heartily vexed. His son is *non compos mentis*, and thereby incapable of making any conveyance in law, so that all his measures are disappointed.

FORESIGHT. Ha! say you so?

MRS. FRAIL. [*aside to* MRS. FORESIGHT] What, has my sea lover lost his anchor of hope then?

1. It is proven.
2. I.e., politician.
3. A legendary astrologer.
4. All were mathematicians and astrologers; "chiromancy": palmistry.
5. No one is wise at every hour.

MRS. FORESIGHT. Oh, sister, what will you do with him?

MRS. FRAIL. Do with him? Send him to sea again in the next foul weather. He's used to an inconstant element, and won't be surprised to see the tide turned.

FORESIGHT. [*considers*] Wherein was I mistaken, not to foresee this?

SCANDAL. [*aside to* MRS. FORESIGHT] Madam, you and I can tell him something else that he did not foresee, and more particularly relating to his own fortune.

MRS. FORESIGHT. What do you mean? I don't understand you.

SCANDAL. Hush, softly. The pleasures of last night, my dear, too considerable to be forgot so soon.

MRS. FORESIGHT. Last night! And what would your impudence infer from last night? Last night was like the night before, I think.

SCANDAL. 'S'death, do you make no difference between me and your husband?

MRS. FORESIGHT. Not much; he's superstitious, and you are mad, in my opinion.

SCANDAL. You make me mad. You are not serious. Pray recollect yourself.

MRS. FORESIGHT. Oh, yes, now I remember. You were very impertinent and impudent, and would have come to bed with me.

SCANDAL. And did not?

MRS. FORESIGHT. Did not! With that face can you ask the question?

SCANDAL. [*aside*] This I have heard of before, but never believed. I have been told she had that admirable quality of forgetting to a man's face in the morning that she had lain with him all night, and denying favors with more impudence than she could grant 'em. [*Aloud*] Madam, I'm your humble servant, and honor you. You look pretty well, Mr. Foresight. How did you rest last night?

FORESIGHT. Truly Mr. Scandal, I was so taken up with broken dreams and distracted visions that I remember little.

SCANDAL. 'Twas a very forgetting night. But would you not talk with Valentine? Perhaps you may understand him. I'm apt to believe there is something mysterious in his discourses, and sometimes rather think him inspired than mad.

FORESIGHT. You speak with singular good judgment, Mr. Scandal, truly. I am inclining to your Turkish[6] opinion in this matter, and do reverence a man whom the vulgar think mad. Let us go in to him.

MRS. FRAIL. Sister, do you stay with them; I'll find out my lover and give him his discharge, and come to you. O'my conscience, here he comes.

[*Exeunt* FORESIGHT, MRS. FORESIGHT *and* SCANDAL.]

[*Enter* BEN.]

BEN. All mad, I think. Flesh, I believe all the calentures[7] of the sea are come ashore, for my part.

6. I.e., esoteric or occult; "vulgar": common people.

7. Tropical fevers.

MRS. FRAIL. Mr. Benjamin in choler?

BEN. No, I'm pleased well enough, now I have found you. Mess, I've had such a hurricane upon your account yonder.

MRS. FRAIL. My account? Pray, what's the matter?

BEN. Why, father came and found me squabbling with yon chitty-faced[8] thing, as he would have me marry, so he asked what was the matter. He asked in a surly sort of a way. (It seems brother Val is gone mad, and so that put'n into a passion; but what did I know that, what's that to me?) So he asked in a surly sort of manner, and gad, I answered 'n as surlily. What though'f he be my father, I an't bound prentice to 'n. So, faith I told 'n in plain terms, if I were minded to marry, I'd marry to please myself, not him. And for the young woman that he provided for me, I thought it more fitting for her to learn her sampler,[9] and make dirt-pies, than to look after a husband. For my part I was none of her man. I had another voyage to make, let him take it as he will.

MRS. FRAIL. So then you intend to go to sea again?

BEN. Nay, nay, my mind run upon you, but I would not tell him so much. So he said he'd make my heart ache, and if so be that he could get a woman to his mind, he'd marry himself. Gad, says I, an you play the fool and marry at these years, there's more danger of your head's aching than my heart. He was woundy angry when I gav'n that wipe.[1] He hadn't a word to say, and so I left'n, and the green girl together. Mayhap the bee may bite, and he'll marry her himself, with all my heart.

MRS. FRAIL. And were you this undutiful and graceless wretch to your father?

BEN. Then why was he graceless first? If I am undutiful and graceless, why did he beget me so? I did not get myself.

MRS. FRAIL. O impiety! How have I been mistaken! What an inhumane merciless creature have I set my heart upon? Oh, I am happy to have discovered the shelves and quicksands that lurk beneath that faithless smiling face.

BEN. Hey toss! What's the matter now? Why, you ben't angry, be you?

MRS. FRAIL. Oh, see me no more, for thou wert born amongst rocks, suckled by whales, cradled in a tempest, and whistled to by winds; and thou art come forth with fins and scales, and three rows of teeth, a most outrageous fish of prey.

BEN. O Lord, O Lord, she's mad, poor young woman. Love has turned her senses, her brain is quite overset. Welladay, how shall I do to set her to rights?

MRS. FRAIL. No, no, I am not mad, monster, I am wise enough to find you out. Hadst thou the impudence to aspire at being a husband with that stubborn and disobedient temper? You that know not how to submit to a father, presume to have a sufficient stock of duty to undergo a wife? I should have been finely fobbed[2]

8. Baby-faced.
9. Embroidery of the alphabet or other lessons for children.
1. Swipe or cutting remark; "woundy": extremely.
2. Cheated.

indeed, very finely fobbed.

BEN. Harkee, forsooth. If so be that you are in your right senses, d'ye see, for ought as I perceive I'm like to be finely fobbed, if I have got anger here upon your account, and you are tacked about[3] already. What d'ye mean, after all your fair speeches, and stroking my cheeks, and kissing and hugging, what, would you sheer off so? Would you, and leave me aground?

MRS. FRAIL. No, I'll leave you adrift, and go which way you will.

BEN. What, are you false-hearted then?

MRS. FRAIL. Only the wind's changed.

BEN. More shame for you! The wind's changed? It's an ill wind blows nobody good. Mayhap I have good riddance on you, if these be your tricks. What d'ye mean all this while, to make a fool of me?

MRS. FRAIL. Any fool, but a husband.

BEN. Husband! Gad I would not be your husband if you would have me, now I know your mind, though'f you had your weight in gold and jewels, and though'f I loved you never so well.

MRS. FRAIL. Why, canst thou love, porpoise?

BEN. No matter what I can do, don't call names. I don't love you so well as to bear that, whatever I did. I'm glad you show yourself, mistress. Let them marry you as don't know you. Gad, I know you too well, by sad experience. I believe he that marries you will go to sea in a henpecked frigate—I believe that, young woman—and mayhap may come to an anchor at Cuckold's Point. So there's a dash for you, take it as you will. Mayhap you may holla after me when I won't come too. [*Exit.*]

MRS. FRAIL. Ha, ha, ha! No doubt on't. [*Sings.*] *My true love is gone to sea.—*

[*Enter* MRS. FORESIGHT.]

O sister, had you come a minute sooner, you would have seen the resolution of a lover. Honest Tar and I are parted; and with the same indifference that we met. O' my life, I am half vexed at the insensibility of a brute that I despised.

MRS. FORESIGHT. What then, he bore it most heroically?

MRS. FRAIL. Most tyrannically, for you see he has got the start of me, and I, the poor forsaken maid, am left complaining on the shore. But I'll tell you a hint that he has given me. Sir Sampson is enraged, and talks desperately of committing matrimony himself. If he has a mind to throw himself away, he can't do it more effectually than upon me, if we could bring it about.

MRS. FORESIGHT. Oh, hang him old fox, he's too cunning; besides, he hates both you and me. But I have a project in my head for you, and I have gone a good way towards it. I have almost made a bargain with Jeremy, Valentine's man, to sell his master to us.

MRS. FRAIL. Sell him, how?

MRS. FORESIGHT. Valentine raves upon Angelica, and took me for her, and Jeremy says will take anybody for her that he imposes on

3. Changed in direction (sailing against the wind). "Sheer off": swerve away.

him. Now I have promised him mountains, if in one of his mad fits he will bring you to him in her stead, and get you married together, and put to bed together; and after consummation, girl, there's no revoking. And if he should recover his senses, he'll be glad at least to make you a good settlement. Here they come, stand aside a little, and tell me how you like the design.

[*Enter* VALENTINE, SCANDAL, FORESIGHT, *and* JEREMY.]

SCANDAL. [*to* JEREMY] And have you given your master a hint of their plot upon him?

JEREMY. Yes, sir; he says he'll favor it, and mistake her for Angelica.

SCANDAL. It may make sport.

FORESIGHT. Mercy on us!

VALENTINE. Husht. Interrupt me not. I'll whisper prediction to thee, and thou shalt prophesy. I am Truth, and can teach thy tongue a new trick. I have told thee what's past; now I tell what's to come. Dost thou know what will happen tomorrow? Answer me not, for I will tell thee. Tomorrow, knaves will thrive through craft, and fools through fortune; and honesty will go as it did, frost-nipped in a summer suit. Ask me questions concerning tomorrow.

SCANDAL. Ask him, Mr. Foresight.

FORESIGHT. Pray what will be done at court?

VALENTINE. Scandal will tell you. I am Truth, I never come there.

FORESIGHT. In the city?

VALENTINE. Oh, prayers will be said in empty churches at the usual hours. Yet you will see such zealous faces behind counters, as if religion were to be sold in every shop. Oh, things will go methodically in the city, the clocks will strike twelve at noon, and the horned herd buzz in the Exchange at two. Wives and husbands will drive distinct trades, and care and pleasure separately occupy the family. Coffee houses will be full of smoke and stratagem. And the cropped[4] prentice, that sweeps his master's shop in the morning, may, ten to one, dirty his sheets before night. But there are two things that you will see very strange; which are wanton wives, with their legs at liberty, and tame cuckolds, with chains about their necks. But hold, I must examine you before I go farther, you look suspiciously. Are you a husband?

FORESIGHT. I am married.

VALENTINE. Poor creature! Is your wife of Covent Garden parish?

FORESIGHT. No. St. Martins-in-the-Fields.

VALENTINE. Alas, poor man! His eyes are sunk, and his hands shriveled; his legs dwindled, and his back bowed. Pray, pray, for a metamorphosis. Change thy shape, and shake off age; get thee Medea's kettle,[5] and be boiled anew, come forth with lab'ring callous hands, a chine of steel, and Atlas shoulders. Let Taliacotus[6] trim the calves of twenty chairmen, and make thee pedestals

4. Short-haired; i.e., in training.

5. According to Ovid's *Metamorphoses*, Medea's potions made Jason's father young again; "chine": spine.

6. Tagliacozzi was a famous Italian plastic surgeon.

to stand erect upon, and look matrimony in the face. Ha, ha, ha! That a man should have a stomach to a wedding supper, when the pigeons ought rather to be laid to his feet,[7] ha, ha, ha!

FORESIGHT. His frenzy is very high now, Mr. Scandal.

SCANDAL. I believe it is a spring tide.

FORESIGHT. Very likely, truly. You understand these matters, Mr. Scandal. I shall be very glad to confer with you about these things which he has uttered. His sayings are very mysterious and hieroglyphical.

VALENTINE. Oh, why would Angelica be absent from my eyes so long?

JEREMY. She's here, sir.

MRS. FORESIGHT. Now, sister.

MRS. FRAIL. O Lord, what must I say?

SCANDAL. Humor him, madam, by all means.

VALENTINE. Where is she? Oh, I see her. She comes, like riches, health, and liberty at once, to a despairing, starving, and abandoned wretch. Oh, welcome, welcome.

MRS. FRAIL. How de'e you, sir? Can I serve you?

VALENTINE. Harkee; I have a secret to tell you. Endymion[8] and the moon shall meet us upon Mount Latmos, and we'll be married in the dead of night. But say not a word. Hymen[9] shall put his torch into a dark lantern, that it may be secret; and Juno shall give her peacock poppy-water, that he may fold his ogling tail, and Argus's hundred eyes be shut, ha?[1] Nobody shall know, but Jeremy.

MRS. FRAIL. No, no, we'll keep it secret. It shall be done presently.

VALENTINE. The sooner the better. Jeremy, come hither; closer, that none may overhear us. Jeremy, I can tell you news. Angelica is turned nun, and I am turning friar, and yet we'll marry one another in spite of the Pope. Get me a cowl and beads, that I may play my part, for she'll meet me two hours hence in black and white, and a long veil to cover the project, and we won't see one another's faces, till we have done something to be ashamed of; and then we'll blush once for all.

[*Enter* TATTLE *and* ANGELICA.]

JEREMY. I'll take care, and—

VALENTINE. Whisper.

ANGELICA. Nay, Mr. Tattle, if you make love to me you spoil my design, for I intended to make you my confidant.

TATTLE. But, madam, to throw away your person—such a person! —and such a fortune, on a madman!

ANGELICA. I never loved him till he was mad; but don't tell anybody so.

SCANDAL. [*aside*] How's this? Tattle making love to Angelica!

7. Treatment administered to the dying.
8. Legendary shepherd loved by the goddess of the moon on Mount Latmos, in Asia Minor.
9. God of marriage.
1. When Argus, Juno's watchman, was killed, she put his hundred eyes into the peacock's tail. "Poppy-water": a narcotic.

TATTLE. Tell, madam? Alas, you don't know me. I have much ado to tell your ladyship how long I have been in love with you. But encouraged by the impossibility of Valentine's making any more addresses to you, I have ventured to declare the very inmost passion of my heart. Oh madam, look upon us both. There you see the ruins of a poor decayed creature. Here, a complete and lively figure, with youth and health, and all his five senses in perfection, madam, and to all this, the most passionate lover—

ANGELICA. O fie, for shame, hold your tongue. A passionate lover, and five senses in perfection! When you are as mad as Valentine, I'll believe you love me, and the maddest shall take me.

VALENTINE. It is enough. Ha, who's here?

MRS. FRAIL. [*to* JEREMY] O Lord, her coming will spoil all.

JEREMY. No, no, madam, he won't know her; if he should, I can persuade him.

VALENTINE. [*whispers*] Scandal, who are all these? Foreigners? If they are, I'll tell you what I think. Get away all the company but Angelica, that I may discover my design to her.

SCANDAL. [*whispers*] I will. I have discovered something of Tattle, that is of a piece with Mrs. Frail. He courts Angelica. If we could contrive to couple 'em together.—Hark'ee—

MRS. FORESIGHT. He won't know you, cousin, he knows nobody.

FORESIGHT. But he knows more than anybody. O niece, he knows things past and to come, and all the profound secrets of time.

TATTLE. Look you, Mr. Foresight, it is not my way to make many words of matters, and so I shan't say much, but in short, d'ye see, I will hold you a hundred pound now that I know more secrets than he.

FORESIGHT. How? I cannot read that knowledge in your face, Mr. Tattle. Pray, what do you know?

TATTLE. Why, d'ye think I'll tell you, sir? Read it in my face? No sir, 'tis written in my heart. And safer there, sir, than letters writ in juice of lemon, for no fire can fetch it out. I am no blab, sir.

VALENTINE. [*to* SCANDAL] Acquaint Jeremy with it, he may easily bring it about. They are welcome, and I'll tell 'em so myself. [*Aloud*] What, do you look strange upon me? Then I must be plain. [*Coming up to them.*] I am Truth, and hate an old acquaintance with a new face.

[SCANDAL *goes aside with* JEREMY.]

TATTLE. Do you know me, Valentine?

VALENTINE. You? Who are you? No, I hope not.

TATTLE. I am Jack Tattle, your friend.

VALENTINE. My friend, what to do? I am no married man, and thou canst not lie with my wife; I am very poor, and thou canst not borrow money of me. Then what employment have I for a friend?

TATTLE. Hah! A good open speaker, and not to be trusted with a secret.

ANGELICA. Do you know me, Valentine?

VALENTINE. Oh, very well.

ANGELICA. Who am I?

VALENTINE. You're a woman; one to whom heaven gave beauty, when it grafted roses on a brier. You are the reflection of heaven in a pond, and he that leaps at you is sunk. You are all white, a sheet of lovely spotless paper, when you first are born; but you are to be scrawled and blotted by every goose's quill. I know you; for I loved a woman, and loved her so long, that I found out a strange thing: I found out what a woman was good for.

TATTLE. Ay, prithee, what's that?

VALENTINE. Why, to keep a secret.

TATTLE. O Lord!

VALENTINE. O exceeding good to keep a secret. For though she should tell, yet she is not to be believed.

TATTLE. Hah! good again, faith.

VALENTINE. I would have music. Sing me the song that I like.

SONG

1

I tell thee, Charmion, could I time retrieve,
And could again begin to love and live,
To you I should my earliest off'ring give;
    I know my eyes would lead my heart to you,
    And I should all my vows and oaths renew,
    But to be plain, I never would be true.

2

For by our weak and weary truth, I find,
Love hates to center in a point assigned,
But runs with joy the circle of the mind.
    Then never let us chain what should be free,
    But for relief of either sex agree,
    Since women love to change, and so do we.

No more, for I am melancholy. [*Walks musing.*]

JEREMY. [*to* SCANDAL] I'll do't, sir.

SCANDAL. Mr. Foresight, we had best leave him. He may grow outrageous, and do mischief.

FORESIGHT. I will be directed by you.

JEREMY. [*to* MRS. FRAIL] You'll meet, Madam; I'll take care everything shall be ready.

MRS. FRAIL. Thou shalt do what thou wilt, have what thou wilt; in short, I will deny thee nothing.

TATTLE. [*to* ANGELICA] Madam, shall I wait upon you?

ANGELICA. No, I'll stay with him. Mr. Scandal will protect me. Aunt, Mr. Tattle desires you would give him leave to wait on you.

TATTLE. [*aside*] Pox on't, there's no coming off, now she has said that. [*Aloud*] Madam, will you do me the honor?

MRS. FORESIGHT. Mr. Tattle might have used less ceremony.

[*Exeunt* FORESIGHT, MRS. FORESIGHT, TATTLE, MRS. FRAIL, JEREMY.]

SCANDAL. Jeremy, follow Tattle.

ANGELICA. Mr. Scandal, I only stay till my maid comes, and because I had a mind to be rid of Mr. Tattle.

SCANDAL. Madam, I am very glad that I overheard a better reason, which you gave to Mr. Tattle; for his impertinence forced you to acknowledge a kindness for Valentine, which you denied to all his sufferings and my solicitations. So I'll leave him to make use of the discovery, and your ladyship to the free confession of your inclinations.

ANGELICA. O heavens! You won't leave me alone with a madman?

SCANDAL. No, madam; I only leave a madman to his remedy.
[*Exit* SCANDAL.]

VALENTINE. Madam, you need not be very much afraid, for I fancy I begin to come to myself.

ANGELICA. [*aside*] Ay, but if I don't fit[2] you, I'll be hanged.

VALENTINE. You see what disguises love makes us put on. Gods have been in counterfeited shapes for the same reason; and the divine part of me, my mind, has worn this mask of madness, and this motley livery[3] only as the slave of love, and menial creature of your beauty.

ANGELICA. Mercy on me, how he talks! Poor Valentine!

VALENTINE. Nay, faith, now let us understand one another, hypocrisy apart. The comedy draws toward an end, and let us think of leaving acting, and be ourselves; and since you have loved me, you must own I have at length deserved you should confess it.

ANGELICA. [*sighs*] I would I had loved you, for Heaven knows I pity you; and could I have foreseen the sad effects, I would have striven. But that's too late. [*Sighs.*]

VALENTINE. What sad effects? What's too late? My seeming madness has deceived my father, and procured me time to think of means to reconcile me to him, and preserve the right of my inheritance to his estate; which otherwise, by articles, I must this morning have resigned. And this I had informed you of today, but you were gone before I knew you had been here.

ANGELICA. How? I thought your love of me had caused this transport in your soul, which it seems you only counterfeited for mercenary ends and sordid interest.

VALENTINE. Nay, now you do me wrong, for if any interest was considered, it was yours, since I thought I wanted more than love to make me worthy of you.

ANGELICA. Then you thought me mercenary. But how am I deluded by this interval of sense, to reason with a madman?

VALENTINE. Oh, 'tis barbarous to misunderstand me longer.
[*Enter* JEREMY.]

ANGELICA. Oh, here's a reasonable creature; sure he will not have the impudence to persevere. Come, Jeremy, acknowledge your trick, and confess your master's madness counterfeit.

JEREMY. Counterfeit, madam? I'll maintain him to be as absolutely

2. Get back at.

3. I.e., fool's clothing.

and substantially mad as any freeholder in Bethlehem.[4] Nay, he's as mad as any projector, fanatic, chemist, lover, or poet in Europe.

VALENTINE. Sirrah, you lie. I am not mad.

ANGELICA. Ha, ha, ha! You see, he denies it.

JEREMY. O Lord, madam, did you ever know any madman mad enough to own it?

VALENTINE. Sot, can't you apprehend?[5]

ANGELICA. Why, he talked very sensibly just now.

JEREMY. Yes, madam, he has intervals: but you see he begins to look wild again now.

VALENTINE. Why, you thick-skulled rascal, I tell you the farce is done, and I will be mad no longer. [*Beats him.*]

ANGELICA. Ha, ha, ha! Is he mad or no, Jeremy?

JEREMY. Partly, I think, for he does not know his mind two hours. I'm sure I left him just now in a humor to be mad. And I think I have not found him very quiet at this present. [*One knocks.*] Who's there?

VALENTINE. Go see, you sot. [*Exit* JEREMY.] I'm very glad that I can move your mirth, though not your compassion.

ANGELICA. I did not think you had apprehension enough to be exceptious.[6] But madmen show themselves most by overpretending to a sound understanding, as drunken men do by overacting sobriety. I was half inclining to believe you, till I accidentally touched upon your tender part. But now you have restored me to my former opinion and compassion.

[*Enter* JEREMY.]

JEREMY. Sir, your father has sent to know if you are any better yet. Will you please to be mad, sir, or how?

VALENTINE. Stupidity! You know the penalty of all I'm worth must pay for the confession of my senses. I'm mad, and will be mad to everybody but this lady.

JEREMY. So: just the very backside of truth. But lying is a figure in speech that interlards the greatest part of my conversation. Madam, your ladyship's woman. [*Goes to the door.*]

[*Enter* JENNY.]

ANGELICA. Well, have you been there? Come hither.

JENNY. [*aside to* ANGELICA] Yes, madam, Sir Sampson will wait upon you presently.

VALENTINE. You are not leaving me in this uncertainty?

ANGELICA. Would anything but a madman complain of uncertainty? Uncertainty and expectation are the joys of life. Security is an insipid thing, and the overtaking and possessing of a wish discovers the folly of the chase. Never let us know one another better, for the pleasure of a masquerade is done when we come to show faces. But I'll tell you two things before I leave you. I am not the fool you take me for, and you are mad and don't know it. [*Exeunt* ANGELICA *and* JENNY.]

4. Bedlam, the madhouse. "Projector": schemer or inventor.

5. Understand.

6. Disposed to make objections.

VALENTINE. From a riddle you can expect nothing but a riddle. There's my instruction and the moral of my lesson.

JEREMY. What, is the lady gone again, sir? I hope you understood one another before she went.

VALENTINE. Understood! She is harder to be understood than a piece of Egyptian antiquity, or an Irish manuscript; you may pore till you spoil your eyes, and not improve your knowledge.

JEREMY. I have heard 'em say, sir, they read hard Hebrew books backwards; maybe you begin to read at the wrong end.

VALENTINE. They say so of a witches' prayer, and dreams and Dutch almanacs are to be understood by contraries. But there's regularity and method in that. She is a medal without a reverse or inscription, for indifference has both sides alike. Yet while she does not seem to hate me, I will pursue her, and know her if it be possible, in spite of the opinion of my satirical friend, Scandal, who says,

That women are like tricks by sleight of hand,
Which, to admire, we should not understand.

[*Exeunt.*]

THE END OF THE FOURTH ACT

Act Five

SCENE ONE

A room in FORESIGHT's *house.*

[*Enter* ANGELICA *and* JENNY.]

ANGELICA. Where is Sir Sampson? Did you not tell me he would be here before me?

JENNY. He's at the great glass in the dining room, madam, setting his cravat and wig.

ANGELICA. How! I'm glad on't. If he has a mind I should like him, it's a sign he likes me; and that's more than half my design.

JENNY. I hear him, madam.

ANGELICA. Leave me, and d'ye hear, if Valentine should come or send, I am not to be spoken with.

[*Exit* JENNY.]

[*Enter* SIR SAMPSON.]

SIR SAMPSON. I have not been honored with the commands of a fair lady a great while.—Odd, madam, you have revived me—not since I was five and thirty.

ANGELICA. Why, you have no great reason to complain, Sir Sampson, that is not long ago.

SIR SAMPSON. Zooks, but it is, madam, a very great while to a man that admires a fine woman as much as I do.

ANGELICA. You're an absolute courtier, Sir Sampson.

SIR SAMPSON. Not at all, madam. Odsbud, you wrong me; I am not so old neither to be a bare courtier, only a man of words. Odd, I have warm blood about me yet, I can serve a lady any way. Come, come, let me tell you, you women think a man old too soon, faith and troth you do. Come, don't despise fifty; odd, fifty, in a hale constitution, is no such contemptible age.

ANGELICA. Fifty a contemptible age! Not at all, a very fashionable age I think. I assure you I know very considerable beaux that set a good face upon fifty. Fifty! I have seen fifty in a side box[7] by candelight out-blossom five and twenty.

SIR SAMPSON. O pox, outsides, outsides, a pize[8] take 'em, mere outsides. Hang your side box beaux; no, I'm none of those, none of your forced trees that pretend to blossom in the fall, and bud when they should bring forth fruit. I am of a long-lived race, and inherit vigor. None of my family married till fifty, yet they begot sons and daughters till fourscore. I am of your patriarchs, I, a branch of one of your antediluvian[9] families, fellows that the flood could not wash away. Well, madam, what are your commands? Has any young rogue affronted you, and shall I cut his throat? Or—

ANGELICA. No, Sir Sampson, I have no quarrel upon my hands. I have more occasion for your conduct than your courage at this time. To tell you the truth, I'm weary of living single, and want a husband.

SIR SAMPSON. Odsbud, and 'tis a pity you should. [*Aside*] Odd, would she would like me, then I should hamper my young rogues. Odd, would she would; faith and troth she's devilish handsome. [*Aloud*] Madam, you deserve a good husband, and 'twere a pity you should be thrown away upon any of these young idle rogues about the town. Odd, there's ne'er a young fellow worth hanging, that is, a very young fellow. Pize on 'em, they never think beforehand of anything; and if they commit matrimony, 'tis as they commit murder, out of a frolic; and are ready to hang themselves, or to be hanged by the law, the next morning. Odso, have a care, madam.

ANGELICA. Therefore I ask your advice, Sir Sampson. I have fortune enough to make any man easy that I can like, if there were such a thing as a young agreeable man, with a reasonable stock of good nature and sense—for I would neither have an absolute wit nor a fool.

SIR SAMPSON. Odd, you are hard to please madam. To find a young fellow that is neither a wit in his own eye nor a fool in the eye of the world is a very hard task. But, faith and troth, you speak very discreetly; for I hate both a wit and a fool.

ANGELICA. She that marries a fool, Sir Sampson, commits the reputation of her honesty or understanding to the censure of the world. And she that marries a very witty man submits both to the severity and insolent conduct of her husband. I should like a man of wit for a lover, because I would have such an one in my power; but I would no more be his wife than his enemy. For his malice is not a more terrible consequence of his aversion than his jealousy is of his love.

SIR SAMPSON. None of old Foresight's sybils[1] ever uttered such a

7. Enclosed seat at the side of a theater.
8. Pox.
9. I.e., before the flood ("patriarchs" were the heads of tribal families in the Old Testament).
1. Prophetesses.

truth. Odsbud, you have won my heart. I hate a wit. I had a son that was spoiled among 'em; a good hopeful lad, till he learned to be a wit—and might have risen in the state—But a pox on't, his wit run him out of his money, and now his poverty has run him out of his wits.

ANGELICA. Sir Sampson, as your friend I must tell you you are very much abused in that matter. He's no more mad than you are.

SIR SAMPSON. How, madam? Would I could prove it.

ANGELICA. I can tell you how that may be done. But it is a thing that would make me appear to be too much concerned in your affairs.

SIR SAMPSON. [*aside*] Odsbud, I believe she likes me. [*Aloud*] Ah, madam, all my affairs are scarce worthy to be laid at your feet; and I wish, madam, they stood in a better posture, that I might make a more becoming offer to a lady of your incomparable beauty and merit. If I had Peru in one hand, and Mexico in t'other, and the Eastern empire under my feet, it would make me only a more glorious victim to be offered at the shrine of your beauty.

ANGELICA. Bless me, Sir Sampson, what's the matter?

SIR SAMPSON. Odd, madam, I love you. And if you would take my advice in a husband—

ANGELICA. Hold, hold, Sir Sampson. I asked your advice for a husband, and you are giving me your consent. I was indeed thinking to propose something like it in a jest, to satisfy you about Valentine. For if a match were seemingly carried on, between you and me, it would oblige him to throw off his disguise of madness, in apprehension of losing me. For you know he has long pretended a passion for me.

SIR SAMPSON. Gadzooks, a most ingenious contrivance, if we were to go through with it. But why must the match only be seemingly carried on? Odd, let it be a real contract.

ANGELICA. O fie, Sir Sampson, what would the world say?

SIR SAMPSON. Say? They would say you were a wise woman, and I a happy man. Odd, madam, I'll love you as long as I live, and leave you a good jointure when I die.

ANGELICA. Ay, but that is not in your power, Sir Sampson; for when Valentine confesses himself in his senses, he must make over his inheritance to his younger brother.

SIR SAMPSON. Odd, you're cunning, a wary baggage! Faith and troth, I like you the better. But I warrant you, I have a proviso in the obligation in favor of myself. Body o' me, I have a trick to turn the settlement upon the issue male of our two bodies begotten. Odsbud, let us find children, and I'll find an estate.

ANGELICA. Will you? Well, do you find the estate, and leave the other to me.

SIR SAMPSON. O rogue! But I'll trust you. And will you consent? Is it a match then?

ANGELICA. Let me consult my lawyer concerning this obligation, and if I find what you propose practicable, I'll give you my answer.

SIR SAMPSON. With all my heart. Come in with me and I'll lend you the bond. You shall consult your lawyer and I'll consult a parson. Odzooks, I'm a young man. Odzooks I'm a young man, and I'll make it appear. Odd, you're devilish handsome. Faith and troth, you're very handsome, and I'm very young, and very lusty. Odsbud, hussy, you know how to choose, and so do I. Odd, I think we are very well met: Give me your hand, odd, let me kiss it. 'Tis as warm and as soft—as what? Odd, as t'other hand. Give me t'other hand, and I'll mumble 'em, and kiss 'em till they melt in my mouth.

ANGELICA. Hold, Sir Sampson, you're profuse of your vigor before your time. You'll spend your estate before you come to it.

SIR SAMPSON. No, no, only give you a rent-roll[2] of my possessions. Ah, baggage! I warrant you for little Sampson. Odd, Sampson's a very good name for an able fellow. Your Sampsons were strong dogs from the beginning.

ANGELICA. Have a care, and don't overact your part. If you remember, the strongest Sampson of your name pulled an old house over his head at last.[3]

SIR SAMPSON. Say you so, hussy? Come, let's go then. Odd, I long to be pulling down too; come away. Odso, here's somebody coming.

[*Exeunt.*]

[*Enter* TATTLE *and* JEREMY.]

TATTLE. Is not that she, gone out just now?

JEREMY. Ay, sir, she's just going to the place of appointment. Ah sir, if you are not very faithful and close in this business, you'll certainly be the death of a person that has a most extraordinary passion for your honor's service.

TATTLE. Ay, who's that?

JEREMY. Even my unworthy self, sir. Sir, I have had an appetite to be fed with your commands a great while. And now, sir, my former master having much troubled the fountain of his understanding, it is a very plausible occasion for me to quench my thirst at the spring of your bounty. I thought I could not recommend myself better to you, sir, than by the delivery of a great beauty and fortune into your arms, whom I have heard you sigh for.

TATTLE. I'll make thy fortune; say no more. Thou art a pretty fellow, and canst carry a message to a lady in a pretty soft kind of phrase, and with a good persuading accent.

JEREMY. Sir, I have the seeds of rhetoric and oratory in my head. I have been at Cambridge.

TATTLE. Ay. 'Tis well enough for a servant to be bred at an university, but the education is a little too pedantic for a gentleman. I hope you are secret in your nature, private, close, ha?

JEREMY. O sir, for that sir, 'tis my chief talent. I'm as secret as the head of Nilus.[4]

2. Inventory.
3. See Judges xvi.30.
4. The source of the river Nile was not yet known.

TATTLE. Ay? Who's he, though? A Privy Counselor?

JEREMY. [*aside*] O ignorance! [*Aloud*] A cunning Egyptian, sir, that with his arms would overrun the country, yet nobody could ever find out his headquarters.

TATTLE. Close dog! A good whoremaster, I warrant him. The time draws nigh, Jeremy. Angelica will be veiled like a nun, and I must be hooded like a friar. Ha, Jeremy?

JEREMY. Ay, sir, hooded like a hawk, to seize at first sight upon the quarry. It is the whim of my master's madness to be so dressed. And she is so in love with him, she'll comply with anything to please him. Poor lady, I'm sure she'll have reason to pray for me, when she finds what a happy exchange she has made, between a madman and so accomplished a gentleman.

TATTLE. Ay, faith, so she will, Jeremy. You're a good friend to her, poor creature. I swear I do it hardly so much in consideration of myself as compassion to her.

JEREMY. 'Tis an act of charity, sir, to save a fine woman with thirty thousand pound from throwing herself away.

TATTLE. So 'tis, faith. I might have saved several others in my time. But i'Gad I could never find in my heart to marry anybody before.

JEREMY. Well, sir, I'll go and tell her my master's coming, and meet you in half a quarter of an hour, with your disguise, at your own lodgings. You must talk a little madly, she won't distinguish the tone of your voice.

TATTLE. No, no, let me alone for a counterfeit. I'll be ready for you.

[*Enter* MISS PRUE.]

MISS PRUE. O Mr. Tattle, are you here! I'm glad I have found you. I have been looking up and down for you, like anything, till I'm as tired as anything in the world.

TATTLE. [*aside*] O pox, how shall I get rid of this foolish girl?

MISS PRUE. Oh I have pure[5] news, I can tell you pure news. I must not marry the seaman now—my father says so. Why won't you be my husband? You say you love me, and you won't be my husband. And I know you may be my husband now if you please.

TATTLE. O fie, Miss. Who told you so, child?

MISS PRUE. Why, my father. I told him that you loved me.

TATTLE. O fie, Miss, why did you do so? And who told you so, child?

MISS PRUE. Who? Why, you did, did not you?

TATTLE. O pox, that was yesterday, Miss, that was a great while ago, child. I have been asleep since; slept a whole night, and did not so much as dream of the matter.

MISS PRUE. Pshaw! Oh, but I dreamt that it was so, though.

TATTLE. Ay, but your father will tell you that dreams come by contraries, child. O fie! What, we must not love one another now. Pshaw! That would be a foolish thing indeed. Fie, fie, you're a woman now, and must think of a new man every morning, and

5. Good.

forget him every night. No, no, to marry is to be a child again, and play with the same rattle always. O fie, marrying is a paw[6] thing.

MISS PRUE. Well, but don't you love me as well as you did last night then?

TATTLE. No, no, child, you would not have me.

MISS PRUE. No? Yes, but I would, though.

TATTLE. Pshaw, but I tell you, you would not. You forget you're a woman, and don't know your own mind.

MISS PRUE. But here's my father, and he knows my mind.

[*Enter* FORESIGHT.]

FORESIGHT. Oh, Mr. Tattle, your servant; you are a close man. But methinks your love to my daughter was a secret I might have been trusted with. Or had you a mind to try if I could discover it by my art, hum, ha? I think there is something in your physiognomy that has a resemblance of her, and the girl is like me.

TATTLE. [*aside*] And so you would infer that you and I are alike. What does the old prig mean? I'll banter him, and laugh at him, and leave him. [*Aloud*] I fancy you have a wrong notion of faces.

FORESIGHT. How? What? A wrong notion? How so?

TATTLE. In the way of art. I have some taking[7] features, not obvious to vulgar eyes, that are indications of a sudden turn of good fortune in the lottery of wives, and promise a great beauty and great fortune reserved alone for me by a private intrigue of destiny, kept secret from the piercing eye of perspicuity, from all astrologers, and the stars themselves.

FORESIGHT. How? I will make it appear that what you say is impossible.

TATTLE. Sir, I beg your pardon, I'm in haste.

FORESIGHT. For what?

TATTLE. To be married, sir, married.

FORESIGHT. Ay, but pray take me along with you, sir.

TATTLE. No, sir, 'tis to be done privately. I never make confidants.

FORESIGHT. Well, but my consent I mean. You won't marry my daughter without my consent?

TATTLE. Who, I, sir? I'm an absolute stranger to you and your daughter, sir.

FORESIGHT. Heyday! What time of the moon is this?

TATTLE. Very true, sir, and desire to continue so. I have no more love for your daughter than I have likeness of you; and I have a secret in my heart which you would be glad to know, and shan't know; and yet you shall know it too, and be sorry for't afterwards. I'd have you to know, sir, that I am as knowing as the stars and as secret as the night. And I'm going to be married just now, yet did not know of it half an hour ago, and the lady stays for me, and does not know of it yet. There's a mystery for you. I know you love to untie difficulties. Or if you can't solve this, stay

6. Naughty.

7. Attractive.

here a quarter of an hour, and I'll come and explain it to you. [*Exit.*]

MISS PRUE. O father, why will you let him go? Won't you make him be my husband?

FORESIGHT. Mercy on us, what do these lunacies portend? Alas, he's mad, child, stark wild.

MISS PRUE. What, and must not I have e'er a husband then? What, must I go to bed to nurse again, and be a child as long as she's an old woman? Indeed but I won't. For now my mind is set upon a man, I will have a man some way or other. Oh! methinks I'm sick when I think of a man, and if I can't have one, I would go to sleep all my life. For when I'm awake, it makes me wish and long, and I don't know for what. And I'd rather be always asleeping than sick with thinking.

FORESIGHT. O fearful! I think the girl's influenced too. Hussy, you shall have a rod.

MISS PRUE. A fiddle of a rod, I'll have a husband, and if you won't get me one, I'll get one for myself. I'll marry our Robin the butler; he says he loves me, and he's a handsome man, and shall be my husband. I warrant he'll be my husband and thank me too, for he told me so.

[*Enter* SCANDAL, MRS. FORESIGHT, *and* NURSE.]

FORESIGHT. Did he so? I'll dispatch him for't presently. Rogue! O nurse, come hither.

NURSE. What is your worship's pleasure?

FORESIGHT. Here, take your young mistress and lock her up presently, till farther orders from me. Not a word, hussy. Do what I bid you, no reply, away! And bid Robin make ready to give an account of his plate and linen, d'ye hear, be gone when I bid you.

[*Exit* NURSE *and* MISS PRUE.]

MRS. FORESIGHT. What's the matter, husband?

FORESIGHT. 'Tis not convenient to tell you now. Mr. Scandal, heav'n keep us all in our senses. I fear there is a contagious frenzy abroad. How does Valentine?

SCANDAL. Oh, I hope he will do well again. I have a message from him to your niece Angelica.

FORESIGHT. I think she has not returned since she went abroad with Sir Sampson.

[*Enter* BEN.]

MRS. FORESIGHT. Here's Mr. Benjamin; he can tell us if his father be come home.

BEN. Who, father? Ay, he's come home with a vengeance.

MRS. FORESIGHT. Why, what's the matter?

BEN. Matter! Why, he's mad.

FORESIGHT. Mercy on us, I was afraid of this.

BEN. And there's the handsome young woman, she as they say Brother Val went mad for, she's mad too, I think.

FORESIGHT. O my poor niece, my poor niece, is she gone too? Well, I shall run mad next.

MRS. FORESIGHT. Well, but how mad? How d'ye mean?

BEN. Nay, I'll give you leave to guess. I'll undertake to make a voyage to Antigua.[8] No, hold, I mayn't say so neither—but I'll sail as far as Leghorn and back again before you shall guess at the matter, and do nothing else. Mess, you may take in all the points of the compass and not hit right.

MRS. FORESIGHT. Your experiment will take up a little too much time.

BEN. Why, then I'll tell you, there's a new wedding upon the stocks;[9] and they two are a going to be married to rights.

SCANDAL. Who?

BEN. Why father and—the young woman. I can't hit of her name.

SCANDAL. Angelica?

BEN. Ay, the same.

MRS. FORESIGHT. Sir Sampson and Angelica? Impossible!

BEN. That may be, but I'm sure it is as I tell you.

SCANDAL. 'S'death, it's a jest. I can't believe it.

BEN. Look you, friend, it's nothing to me, whether you believe it or no. What I say is true, d'ye see? They are married, or just going to be married, I know not which.

FORESIGHT. Well, but they are not mad, that is, not lunatic?

BEN. I don't know what you may call madness, but she's mad for a husband, and he's horn-mad, I think, or they'd ne'er make a match together. Here they come.

[*Enter* SIR SAMPSON, ANGELICA, *with* BUCKRAM.]

SIR SAMPSON. Where is this old soothsayer? This uncle of mine elect? Aha, old Foresight, uncle Foresight, wish me joy uncle Foresight, double joy, both as uncle and astrologer. Here's a conjunction that was not foretold in all your Ephemeris. The brightest star in the blue firmament is shot from above in a jelly of love,[1] and so forth; and I'm lord of the ascendant. Odd, you're an old fellow, Foresight; uncle I mean, a very old fellow, uncle Foresight; and yet you shall live to dance at my wedding, faith and troth you shall. Odd, we'll have the music of the spheres for thee, old Lilly, that we will, and thou shalt lead up a dance in *via Lactea*.[2]

FORESIGHT. I'm thunder-strook! You are not married to my niece?

SIR SAMPSON. Not absolutely married, uncle, but very near it, within a kiss of the matter, as you see. [*Kisses* ANGELICA.]

ANGELICA. 'Tis very true indeed, uncle. I hope you'll be my father, and give me.

SIR SAMPSON. That he shall, or I'll burn his globes. Body o' me, he shall be thy father, I'll make him thy father, and thou shalt make me a father, and I'll make thee a mother, and we'll beget sons and daughters enough to put the weekly bills[3] out of countenance.

SCANDAL. Death and hell! Where's Valentine? [*Exit.*]

MRS. FORESIGHT. This is so surprising—

8. In the West Indies.
9. In preparation.
1. Quoted from Dryden's *Tyrannic Love* (1669).
2. The Milky Way.
3. Official lists of births and deaths.

SIR SAMPSON. How! What does my aunt say? Surprising, aunt? Not at all, for a young couple to make a match in winter? Not at all. It's a plot to undermine cold weather, and destroy that usurper of a bed called a warming pan.

MRS. FORESIGHT. I'm glad to hear you have so much fire in you, Sir Sampson.

BEN. Mess, I fear his fire's little better than tinder. Mayhap it will only serve to light up a match for somebody else. The young woman's a handsome young woman, I can't deny it. But, father, if I might be your pilot in this case, you should not marry her. It's just the same thing as if so be you should sail so far as the Straits[4] without provision.

SIR SAMPSON. Who gave you authority to speak, sirrah? To your element, fish, be mute, fish, and to sea. Rule your helm, sirrah, don't direct me.

BEN. Well, well, take you care of your own helm, or you mayn't keep your own vessel steady.

SIR SAMPSON. Why, you impudent tarpaulin! Sirrah, do you bring your forecastle jests upon your father? But I shall be even with you, I won't give you a groat. Mr. Buckram, is the conveyance so worded that nothing can possibly descend to this scoundrel? I would not so much as have him have the prospect of an estate, though there were no way to come to it but by the northeast passage.[5]

BUCKRAM. Sir, it is drawn according to your directions; there is not the least cranny of the law unstopped.

BEN. Lawyer, I believe there's many a cranny and leak unstopped in your conscience. If so be that one had a pump to your bosom, I believe we should discover a foul hold. They say a witch will sail in a sieve. But I believe the devil would not venture aboard o'your conscience. And that's for you.

SIR SAMPSON. Hold your tongue, sirrah. How now, who's there.

[*Enter* TATTLE *and* MRS. FRAIL.]

MRS. FRAIL. Oh, sister, the most unlucky accident!

MRS. FORESIGHT. What's the matter?

TATTLE. Oh, the two most unfortunate poor creatures in the world we are!

FORESIGHT. Bless us! How so?

MRS. FRAIL. Ah, Mr. Tattle and I, poor Mr. Tattle and I are—I can't speak it out.

TATTLE. Nor I. But poor Mrs. Frail and I are—

MRS. FRAIL. Married.

MRS. FORESIGHT. Married! How?

TATTLE. Suddenly—before we knew where we were—that villain Jeremy, by the help of disguises, tricked us into one another.

FORESIGHT. Why, you told me just now you went hence in haste to be married.

4. I.e., of Gibraltar.
5. An impossible route to the east, sailing north of Russia.

ANGELICA. But I believe Mr. Tattle meant the favor to me; I thank him.

TATTLE. I did, as I hope to be saved, madam, my intentions were good. But this is the most cruel thing, to marry one does not know how, nor why, nor wherefore. The devil take me if ever I was so much concerned at anything in my life.

ANGELICA. 'Tis very unhappy, if you don't care for one another.

TATTLE. The least in the world. That is for my part, I speak for myself. Gad, I never had the least thought of serious kindness. I never liked anybody less in my life. Poor woman! Gad, I'm sorry for her too, for I have no reason to hate her neither; but I believe I shall lead her a damned sort of a life.

MRS. FORESIGHT. [*aside to* MRS. FRAIL] He's better than no husband at all, though he's a coxcomb.

MRS. FRAIL. [*to her*] Ay, ay, it's well it's no worse. Nay, for my part I always despised Mr. Tattle of all things. Nothing but his being my husband could have made me like him less.

TATTLE. Look you there, I thought as much. Pox on't, I wish we could keep it secret. Why, I don't believe any of this company would speak of it.

MRS. FRAIL. But, my dear, that's impossible. The parson and that rogue Jeremy will publish it.

TATTLE. Ay, my dear, so they will, as you say.

ANGELICA. Oh, you'll agree very well in a little time. Custom will make it easy to you.

TATTLE. Easy! Pox on't, I don't believe I shall sleep tonight.

SIR SAMPSON. Sleep, quotha? No, why, you would not sleep o'your wedding night? I'm an older fellow than you, and don't mean to sleep.

BEN. Why there's another match now, as though'f a couple of privateers were looking for a prize, and should fall foul of one another. I'm sorry for the young man with all my heart. Look you, friend, if I may advise you, when she's going—for that you must expect, I have experience of her—when she's going, let her go. For no matrimony is tough enough to hold her, and if she can't drag her anchor along with her, she'll break her cable, I can tell you that. Who's here, the madman?

[*Enter* VALENTINE *dressed*, SCANDAL, *and* JEREMY.]

VALENTINE. No; here's the fool; and if occasion be, I'll give it under my hand.

SIR SAMPSON. How now?

VALENTINE. Sir, I'm come to acknowledge my errors, and ask your pardon.

SIR SAMPSON. What, have you found your senses at last, then? In good time, sir.

VALENTINE. You were abused, sir, I never was distracted.

FORESIGHT. How? Not mad, Mr. Scandal?

SCANDAL. No, really, sir; I'm his witness, it was all counterfeit.

VALENTINE. I thought I had reasons. But it was a poor contrivance, the effect has shown it such.

SIR SAMPSON. Contrivance! What, to cheat me? To cheat your father? Sirrah, could you hope to prosper?

VALENTINE. Indeed, I thought, sir, when the father endeavored to undo the son, it was a reasonable return of nature.

SIR SAMPSON. Very good, sir. Mr. Buckram, are you ready? Come, sir, will you sign and seal?

VALENTINE. If you please, sir. But first I would ask this lady one question.

SIR SAMPSON. Sir, you must ask my leave first. That lady? No, sir, you shall ask that lady no questions till you have asked her blessing, sir. That lady is to be my wife.

VALENTINE. I have heard as much, sir, but I would have it from her own mouth.

SIR SAMPSON. That's as much as to say, I lie, sir, and you don't believe what I say.

VALENTINE. Pardon me, sir. But I reflect that I very lately counterfeited madness. I don't know but the frolic may go round.

SIR SAMPSON. Come, chuck, satisfy him, answer him.—Come, come, Mr. Buckram, the pen and ink.

BUCKRAM. Here it is, sir, with the deed, all is ready.

[VALENTINE *goes to* ANGELICA.]

ANGELICA. 'Tis true, you have a great while pretended love to me; nay, what if you were sincere? Still you must pardon me if I think my own inclinations have a better right to dispose of my person than yours.

SIR SAMPSON. Are you answered now, sir?

VALENTINE. Yes, sir.

SIR SAMPSON. Where's your plot, sir, and your contrivance now, sir? Will you sign, sir? Come, will you sign and seal?

VALENTINE. With all my heart, sir.

SCANDAL. 'S'death, you are not mad indeed, to ruin yourself?

VALENTINE. I have been disappointed of my only hope, and he that loses hope may part with anything. I never valued fortune but as it was subservient to my pleasure, and my only pleasure was to please this lady. I have made many vain attempts, and find at last that nothing but my ruin can effect it, which for that reason I will sign to. Give me the paper.

ANGELICA. [*aside*] Generous Valentine!

BUCKRAM. Here is the deed, sir.

VALENTINE. But where is the bond by which I am obliged to sign this?

BUCKRAM. Sir Sampson, you have it.

ANGELICA. No, I have it. And I'll use it, as I would everything that is an enemy to Valentine. [*Tears the paper.*]

SIR SAMPSON. How now?

VALENTINE. Ha!

ANGELICA. [*to* VALENTINE] Had I the world to give you, it could not make me worthy of so generous and faithful a passion. Here's my hand, my heart was always yours, and struggled very hard to make this utmost trial of your virtue.

VALENTINE. Between pleasure and amazement I am lost. But on my knees I take the blessing.

SIR SAMPSON. Ouns, what is the meaning of this?

BEN. Mess, here's the wind changed again. Father, you and I may make a voyage together now.

ANGELICA. Well, Sir Sampson, since I have played you a trick, I'll advise you how you may avoid such another. Learn to be a good father, or you'll never get a second wife. I always loved your son, and hated your unforgiving nature. I was resolved to try him to the utmost. I have tried you too, and know you both. You have not more faults than he has virtues, and 'tis hardly more pleasure to me that I can make him and myself happy than that I can punish you.

VALENTINE. If my happiness could receive addition, this kind surprise would make it double.

SIR SAMPSON. Ouns, you're a crocodile.

FORESIGHT. Really, Sir Sampson, this is a sudden eclipse.

SIR SAMPSON. You're an illiterate fool, and I'm another, and the stars are liars; and if I had breath enough, I'd curse them and you, myself and everybody. Ouns! Cullied, bubbled, jilted, woman-bobbed[6] at last—I have not patience. [*Exit* SIR SAMPSON.]

TATTLE. If the gentleman is in this disorder for want of a wife, I can spare him mine. [*To* JEREMY] Oh, are you there, sir? I'm indebted to you for my happiness.

JEREMY. Sir, I ask you ten thousand pardons, 'twas an errant mistake. You see, sir, my master was never mad, or anything like it. Then how could it be otherwise?

VALENTINE. Tattle, I thank you, you would have interposed between me and heaven, but Providence laid purgatory in your way. You have but justice.

SCANDAL. I hear the fiddles that Sir Sampson provided for his own wedding. Methinks 'tis pity they should not be employed when the match is so much mended. Valentine, though it be morning, we may have a dance.

VALENTINE. Anything, my friend, everything that looks like joy and transport.

SCANDAL. Call 'em, Jeremy.

ANGELICA. I have done dissembling now, Valentine, and if that coldness which I have always worn before you should turn to an extreme fondness, you must not suspect it.

VALENTINE. I'll prevent that suspicion, for I intend to dote on at that immoderate rate, that your fondness shall never distinguish itself enough to be taken notice of. If ever you seem to love too much, it must be only when I can't love enough.

ANGELICA. Have a care of large promises; you know you are apt to run more in debt than you are able to pay.

VALENTINE. Therefore I yield my body as your prisoner, and make your best on't.

SCANDAL. The music stays for you.

[*Dance*]

6. Made a fool; "cullied": duped.

Well, madam, you have done exemplary justice, in punishing an inhumane father and rewarding a faithful lover. But there is a third good work, which I, in particular, must thank you for. I was an infidel to your sex, and you have converted me. For now I am convinced that all women are not like fortune, blind in bestowing favors, either on those who do not merit, or who do not want 'em.

ANGELICA. 'Tis an unreasonable accusation that you lay upon our sex. You tax us with injustice, only to cover your own want of merit. You would all have the reward of love, but few have the constancy to stay till it becomes your due. Men are generally hypocrites and infidels. They pretend to worship, but have neither zeal nor faith. How few, like Valentine, would persevere even unto martyrdom, and sacrifice their interest to their constancy. In admiring me you misplace the novelty.

The miracle today is that we find
A lover true, not that a woman's kind.

[*Exeunt omnes.*]

FINIS

Epilogue Spoken at the Opening of the New House

BY MRS. BRACEGIRDLE[7]

Sure Providence at first designed this place
To be the player's refuge in distress;
For still in every storm they all run hither,
As to a shed that shields 'em from the weather.
But thinking of this change which last befell us,
It's like what I have heard our poets tell us:
For when behind our scenes their suits are pleading,
To help their love, sometimes they show their reading;
And wanting ready cash to pay for hearts,
They top[8] their learning on us, and their parts.
Once of philosophers they told us stories,
Whom, as I think they called—Py—Pythagories,
I'm sure 'tis some such Latin name they give 'em,
And we, who know no better, must believe 'em.
Now to these men (say they) such souls were given,
That after death, ne'er went to hell, nor heaven,
But lived, I know not how, in beasts; and then
When many years were past, in men again.
Methinks, we players resemble such a soul,
That does from bodies, we from houses[9] stroll.
Thus Aristotle's soul, of old that was,
May now be damned to animate an ass;

7. Anne Bracegirdle (ca. 1663–1748), a leading actress as well as Congreve's mistress, created the role of Angelica.
8. Complete or surmount. "To top a part" is to play a role to its utmost; here with a pun ("top": cover; "parts": private parts).
9. I.e., playhouses. The actors migrate from one house to another as, according to the Greek philosopher Pythagoras, souls move from body to body.

Or in this very house, for ought we know,
Is doing painful penance in some beau;
And this our audience, which did once resort
To shining theaters to see our sport,
Now find us tossed into a tennis court.[1]
These walls but t'other day were filled with noise
Of roaring gamesters, and your damme boys.[2]
Then bounding balls and rackets they encompassed,
And now they're filled with jests, and flights, and bombast!
I vow I don't much like this transmigration,
Strolling from place to place by circulation.
Grant Heaven, we don't return to our first station.
I know not what these think, but for my part
I can't reflect without an aching heart,
How we should end in our original, a cart.[3]
But we can't fear, since you're so good to save us,
That you have only set us up, to leave us.
Thus from the past, we hope for future grace,
I beg it—
And some here know I have a begging face.
Then pray continue this your kind behavior,
For a clear[4] stage won't do, without your favor.

1695

1. The new theater was located in a former tennis court.
2. Swearing rowdies.
3. Where the first plays were performed.
4. Without debt.

DANIEL DEFOE
(ca. 1660–1731)

1703: Pilloried and jailed for political pamphleteering.
1704–13: Editor of the *Review*.
1719: *Robinson Crusoe*, first of his adventure tales.

By birth, education, and occupations Daniel Defoe was a stranger to the sphere of refined tastes and classical learning that determined the course of English literature during his lifetime. Middle-class in his birth, Presbyterian in his religion, he belonged to the vigorous and durable group of Nonconformist tradesmen who, after the Restoration, slowly increased their wealth and toward the end of the 17th century began to achieve political importance.

He began life as a small merchant and for a while prospered; but he was not overscrupulous in his dealings, and in 1692 he found himself bankrupt, with debts amounting to £17,000. This was the first of his many financial crises, crises which drove him to make his way, like his own heroes and heroines, by whatever means presented themselves to his clever mind and abundant energy. And however double his dealings, he seems always to have found the way to reconcile them with his genuine Nonconformist piety. His restless mind was fertile in "projects," both for himself and for the country; and his itch for politics made the role of passive observer impossible for him.

An ardent Whig, he first gained notoriety by political verses and pamphlets, and for one of them, in which he ironically defended the Anglican's hostility to the Dissenter, *The Shortest Way with the Dissenters*, he stood in the pillory three times and was sentenced to jail. He was released through the influence of that astute politician, Robert Harley (later Earl of Oxford), who recognized in Defoe, as he was to do in Swift, a useful ally. For the next eleven years Defoe served his benefactor secretly as a political spy and confidential agent, traveling throughout England and Scotland, reporting and perhaps influencing opinion. As founder and editor of the *Review*, his job was to gain support for Harley's policies, and his Whiggism did not seem to make it difficult for him to follow Harley's lead, even when, in 1710, his master became head of a Tory ministry. It is characteristic of Defoe that, after the fall of the Tories in 1714, he went over to the triumphant Whigs and served them as loyally as he had their enemy.

When he was nearly 60, Defoe's energy and inventiveness enabled him to break new ground, indeed to begin a new career. One of the few books of the century that belong to world literature is *Robinson Crusoe*, which appeared in 1719. It is the first of a series of tales of adventure for which Defoe is now admired, but which brought him little esteem from the polite world, however much they gratified the less cultivated readers in the City or the servants' hall. In this and other tales which followed, Defoe was able to use all his greatest gifts: the ability to re-create a milieu vividly, through the cumulative effect of carefully observed, often petty details; a special skill in writing relaxed and careless prose which seems to reveal the consciousness of the first-person narrator and which comes alive because the language is the language of actual speech; his wide knowledge of the society in which he lived, both the trading bourgeoisie and the rogues who preyed on them; and his absorption in the spectacle of the lonely human being, whether Crusoe on his island or Moll Flanders in England and Virginia, somehow bending a stubborn and indifferent environment to his own ends of survival or profits. He was interested in the mere processes of living, and there is something of himself in all his protagonists: enormous vitality, ultimate humanity, a scheming and not always edifying ingenuity. In these fictitious autobiographies of adventurers or rogues—*Captain Singleton* (1720), *Moll Flanders* (1722), *Colonel Jack* (1722), and *Roxana* (1724)—Defoe spoke for and to the members of his own class. Like them, he was engrossed by property and success; and his way of writing made all he touched seem true.

The Apparition of Mrs. Veal (1706) is similarly "true." Once thought pure fiction, an early example of the ghost story, it is now known to be based on fact. There was a Mrs. Bargrave, and there was—or had been, at least until September 7, 1705—a Mrs. Veal. Like the later *Journal of the Plague Year* (1722), however, Defoe's account of the apparition is a remarkable example of reporting transformed by art. To make the story credible, he calls upon most of the techniques his novels were to develop: the authority of the first-person narrator, the swiftness and suspense of the action, the matter-of-fact style. Defoe himself was willing to believe in ghosts—he later wrote an essay on *The History and Reality of Apparitions* (1727)—and he induces us to suspend any disbelief of our own. Most of all, he directs us to the facts. The apparition of Mrs. Veal walks through a world of concrete details; an elbow chair, a scoured silk gown, an averted kiss, the striking of a clock. It is these details, not the world of spirits, that absorb our interest. Modestly but irresistibly, with the magic of the storyteller's art, they revive the sense of a place, a moment of time, people we can touch.

A True Relation of the Apparition of One Mrs. Veal,

The Next Day after Her Death: To One Mrs. Bargrave At Canterbury. The 8th of September, 1705.

The Preface

This relation is matter of fact, and attended with such circumstances as may induce any reasonable man to believe it. It was sent by a gentleman, a justice of peace at Maidstone in Kent, and a very intelligent person, to his friend in London, as it is here worded;[1] which discourse is attested by a very sober and understanding gentlewoman, a kinswoman of the said gentleman's, who lives in Canterbury, within a few doors of the house in which the within-named Mrs. Bargrave lives; who believes his kinswoman to be of so discerning a spirit, as not to be put upon by any fallacy, and who positively assured him that the whole matter, as it is here related and laid down, is what is really true, and what she herself had in the same words (as near as may be) from Mrs. Bargrave's own mouth, who she knows had no reason to invent and publish such a story, nor any design to forge and tell a lie, being a woman of much honesty and virtue, and her whole life a course, as it were, of piety. The use which we ought to make of it is to consider that there is a life to come after this, and a just God who will retribute to every one according to the deeds done in the body; and therefore to reflect upon our past course of life we have led in the world, that our time is short and uncertain, and that if we would escape the punishment of the ungodly and receive the reward of the righteous, which is the laying hold of eternal life, we ought, for the time to come, to return to God by a speedy repentance, ceasing to do evil and learning to do well; to seek after God early, if happily he may be found of us, and lead such lives for the future as may be well pleasing in his sight.

A *Relation of the Apparition of Mrs. Veal*

This thing is so rare in all its circumstances, and on so good

1. No source has been found for Defoe's "relation," though several earlier accounts of the apparition were available to him.

authority, that my reading and conversation has not given me anything like it. It is fit to gratify the most ingenious and serious inquirer. Mrs. Bargrave is the person to whom Mrs. Veal appeared after her death; she is my intimate friend, and I can avouch for her reputation, for these last fifteen or sixteen years, on my own knowledge; and I can confirm the good character she had from her youth to the time of my acquaintance. Though since this relation she is calumniated by some people that are friends to the brother of Mrs. Veal who appeared; who think the relation of this appearance to be a reflection, and endeavor what they can to blast Mrs. Bargrave's reputation, and to laugh the story out of countenance. But the circumstances thereof, and the cheerful disposition of Mrs. Bargrave, notwithstanding the unheard-of ill usage of a very wicked husband, there is not the least sign of dejection in her face; nor did I ever hear her let fall a desponding or murmuring expression; nay, not when actually under her husband's barbarity; which I have been witness to, and several other persons of undoubted reputation.

Now you must know, that Mrs.[2] Veal was a maiden gentlewoman of about thirty years of age, and for some years last past had been troubled with fits, which were perceived coming on her by her going off from her discourse very abruptly, to some impertinence.[3] She was maintained by an only brother, and kept his house in Dover. She was a very pious woman, and her brother a very sober man, to all appearance; but now he does all he can to null or quash the story. Mrs. Veal was intimately acquainted with Mrs. Bargrave from her childhood. Mrs. Veal's circumstances were then mean; her father did not take care of his children as he ought, so that they were exposed to hardships; and Mrs. Bargrave in those days had as unkind a father, though she wanted for neither food nor clothing, whilst Mrs. Veal wanted for both; so that it was in the power of Mrs. Bargrave to be very much her friend in several instances, which mightily endeared Mrs. Veal; insomuch that she would often say, "Mrs. Bargrave, you are not only the best, but the only friend I have in the world; and no circumstances of life shall ever dissolve my friendship." They would often condole each other's adverse fortune, and read together *Drelincourt upon Death*,[4] and other good books; and so, like two Christian friends, they comforted each other under their sorrow.

Sometime after, Mr. Veal's friends got him a place in the custom-house at Dover, which occasioned Mrs. Veal, by little and little, to fall off from her intimacy with Mrs. Bargrave, though there was never any such thing as a quarrel; but an indifferency came on

2. "Mrs."—pronounced "Mistress"—designated any woman, married or unmarried, with no superior title.
3. Irrelevancy.
4. *The Christian's Consolations Against the Fears of Death*. Defoe's story, which mentions Drelincourt's popular book several times, was regularly printed as a foreword to it in the 18th century.

by degrees, till at last Mrs. Bargrave had not seen her in two years and a half, though above a twelvemonth of the time Mrs. Bargrave had been absent from Dover, and this last half-year has been in Canterbury about two months of the time, dwelling in a house of her own.

In this house, on the eighth of September last, *viz.* 1705, she was sitting alone in the forenoon, thinking over her unfortunate life, and arguing herself into a due resignation to Providence, though her condition seemed hard. "And," said she, "I have been provided for hitherto, and doubt not but I shall be still; and am well satisfied that my afflictions shall end, when it is most fit for me"; and then took up her sewing-work, which she had no sooner done but she hears a knocking at the door; she went to see who it was there, and this proved to be Mrs. Veal, her old friend, who was in a riding-habit: at that moment of time the clock struck twelve at noon.

"Madam," says Mrs. Bargrave, "I am surprised to see you, you have been so long a stranger," but told her she was glad to see her and offered to salute[5] her, which Mrs. Veal complied with, till their lips almost touched, and then Mrs. Veal drew her hand across her own eyes and said, "I am not very well," and so waived it. She told Mrs. Bargrave she was going a journey, and had a great mind to see her first. "But," says Mrs. Bargrave, "how came you to take a journey alone? I am amazed at it, because I know you have so fond a brother." "O!" says Mrs. Veal, "I gave my brother the slip, and came away, because I had so great a mind to see you before I took my journey." So Mrs. Bargrave went in with her, into another room within the first, and Mrs. Veal sat herself down in an elbow-chair, in which Mrs. Bargrave was sitting when she heard Mrs. Veal knock. Then says Mrs. Veal, "My dear friend, I am come to renew our old friendship again, and to beg your pardon for my breach of it, and if you can forgive me you are one of the best of women." "O!" says Mrs. Bargrave, "don't mention such a thing, I have not had an uneasy thought about it, I can easily forgive it." "What did you think of me?" says Mrs. Veal. Says Mrs. Bargrave, "I thought you were like the rest of the world, and that prosperity had made you forget yourself and me." Then Mrs. Veal reminded Mrs. Bargrave of the many friendly offices she did her in former days, and much of the conversation they had with each other in the time of their adversity; what books they read, and what comfort in particular they received from Drelincourt's *Book of Death*, which was the best, she said, on that subject, was ever wrote. She also mentioned Dr. Sherlock,[6] and two Dutch books which were translated, wrote upon death, and several others: but Drelincourt, she said, had the clearest notions of death, and of the future state, of any who have

5. Tried to kiss.

6. William Sherlock, *A Practical Discourse Concerning Death* (1689).

handled that subject. Then she asked Mrs. Bargrave whether she had Drelincourt; she said yes. Says Mrs. Veal, "Fetch it," and so Mrs. Bargrave goes upstairs, and brings it down. Says Mrs. Veal, "Dear Mrs. Bargrave, if the eyes of our faith were as open as the eyes of our body, we should see numbers of angels about us for our guard. The notions we have of heaven now are nothing like what it is, as Drelincourt says. Therefore be comforted under your afflictions, and believe that the Almighty has a particular regard to you, and that your afflictions are marks of God's favor; and when they have done the business they were sent for, they shall be removed from you. And believe me, my dear friend, believe what I say to you, one minute of future happiness will infinitely reward you for all your sufferings. For I can never believe" (and claps her hand upon her knee with a great deal of earnestness, which indeed ran through all her discourse) "that ever God will suffer you to spend all your days in this afflicted state; but be assured that your afflictions shall leave you, or you them in a short time." She spake in that pathetical and heavenly manner, that Mrs. Bargrave wept several times, she was so deeply affected with it. Then Mrs. Veal mentioned Dr. Horneck's *Ascetick*,[7] at the end of which he gives an account of the lives of the primitive Christians. Their pattern she recommended to our imitation; and said, "their conversation was not like this of our age. For now" (says she) "there is nothing but frothy vain discourse, which is far different from theirs. Theirs was to edification, and to build one another up in the faith: so that they were not as we are, nor are we as they are; but," said she, "we might do as they did. There was a hearty friendship among them, but where is it now to be found?" Says Mrs. Bargrave, " 'Tis hard indeed to find a true friend in these days." Says Mrs. Veal, "Mr. Norris has a fine copy of verses, called 'Friendship in Perfection,' which I wonderfully admire, have you seen the book?" says Mrs. Veal. "No," says Mrs. Bargrave, "but I have the verses of my own writing out." "Have you?" says Mrs. Veal, "then fetch them"; which she did from above stairs, and offered them to Mrs. Veal to read, who refused, and waived the thing, saying holding down her head would make it ache, and then desired Mrs. Bargrave to read them to her, which she did. As they were admiring Friendship, Mrs. Veal said, "Dear Mrs. Bargrave, I shall love you forever."[8] In the verses there is twice used the word "Elysium." "Ah!" says Mrs. Veal, "these poets have such names for heaven." She would often draw her hand cross her own eyes; and say, "Mrs. Bargrave, don't you think I am mightily impaired by my fits?" "No," says Mrs. Bar-

7. Anthony Horneck, *The Happy Ascetick* (1681).

8. In John Norris' poem (1687), Damon assures Pythias that even death will not sever their friendship: "I then will be/Your friend and guardian angel too./And though with more refined society/I'll leave Elysium to converse with you."

grave, "I think you look as well as ever I knew you."

After all this discourse, which the apparition put in words much finer than Mrs. Bargrave said she could pretend to, and was much more than she can remember (for it cannot be thought that an hour and three-quarters' conversation could all be retained, though the main of it, she thinks she does), she said to Mrs. Bargrave, she would have her write a letter to her brother, and tell him, she would have him give rings to such and such; and that there was a purse of gold in her cabinet, and that she would have two broad pieces given to her cousin Watson. Talking at this rate, Mrs. Bargrave thought that a fit was coming upon her, and so placed herself in a chair just before her knees, to keep her from falling to the ground, if her fits should occasion it; for the elbow chair, she thought, would keep her from falling on either side. And to divert Mrs. Veal, as she thought, she took hold of her gown sleeve several times, and commended it. Mrs. Veal told her it was a scoured silk, and newly made up. But for all this Mrs. Veal persisted in her request, and told Mrs. Bargrave she must not deny her; and she would have her tell her brother all their conversation, when she had an opportunity. "Dear Mrs. Veal," says Mrs. Bargrave, "this seems so impertinent that I cannot tell how to comply with it; and what a mortifying story will our conversation be to a young gentleman?" "Well," says Mrs. Veal, "I must not be denied." "Why," says Mrs. Bargrave, " 'tis much better methinks to do it yourself." "No," says Mrs. Veal, "though it seems impertinent to you now, you will see more reason for it hereafter." Mrs. Bargrave then, to satisfy her importunity, was going to fetch a pen and ink; but Mrs. Veal said, "Let it alone now, and do it when I am gone; but you must be sure to do it"; which was one of the last things she enjoined her at parting; and so she promised her.

Then Mrs. Veal asked for Mrs. Bargrave's daughter. She said she was not at home, "but if you have a mind to see her," says Mrs. Bargrave, "I'll send for her." "Do," says Mrs. Veal. On which she left her, and went to a neighbor's, to send for her; and by the time Mrs. Bargrave was returning, Mrs. Veal was got without the door in the street, in the face of the beast-market on a Saturday (which is market day) and stood ready to part as soon as Mrs. Bargrave came to her. She asked her, why she was in such haste? She said, she must be going, though perhaps she might not go her journey till Monday. And told Mrs. Bargave she hoped she should see her again at her cousin Watson's before she went whither she was agoing. Then she said, she would not take her leave of her, and walked from Mrs. Bargrave in her view, till a turning interrupted the sight of her, which was three-quarters after one in the afternoon.

Mrs. Veal died the 7th of September, at twelve o'clock at noon, of her fits, and had not above four hours' senses before her death, in which time she received the sacrament. The next day after Mrs. Veal's appearing, being Sunday, Mrs. Bargrave was mightily indisposed with a cold and a sore throat, that she could not go out that day; but on Monday morning she sends a person to Captain Watson's to know if Mrs. Veal were there. They wondered at Mrs. Bargrave's inquiry, and sent her word that she was not there, nor was expected. At this answer Mrs. Bargrave told the maid she had certainly mistook the name, or made some blunder. And though she was ill, she put on her hood, and went herself to Captain Watson's, though she knew none of the family, to see if Mrs. Veal was there or not. They said, they wondered at her asking, for that she had not been in town; they were sure, if she had, she would have been there. Says Mrs. Bargrave, "I am sure she was with me on Saturday almost two hours." They said it was impossible, for they must have seen her if she had. In comes Captain Watson, while they were in dispute, and said that Mrs. Veal was certainly dead, and her escutcheons[9] were making. This strangely surprised Mrs. Bargrave, who went to the person immediately who had the care of them, and found it true. Then she related the whole story to Captain Watson's family, and what gown she had on, and how striped. And that Mrs. Veal told her it was scoured. Then Mrs. Watson cried out, "You have seen her indeed, for none knew but Mrs. Veal and myself, that the gown was scoured"; and Mrs. Watson owned that she described the gown exactly; "for," said she, "I helped her to make it up." This Mrs. Watson blazed all about the town, and avouched the demonstration of the truth of Mrs. Bargrave's seeing Mrs. Veal's apparition. And Captain Watson carried two gentlemen immediately to Mrs. Bargrave's house, to hear the relation from her own mouth. And then it spread so fast that gentlemen and persons of quality, the judicious and skeptical part of the world, flocked in upon her, which at last became such a task, that she was forced to go out of the way. For they were in general extremely satisfied of the truth of the thing; and plainly saw that Mrs. Bargrave was no hypochondriac,[1] for she always appears with such a cheerful air, and pleasing mien, that she has gained the favor and esteem of all the gentry. And it's thought a great favor if they can but get the relation from her own mouth. I should have told you before, that Mrs. Veal told Mrs. Bargrave that her sister and brother-in-law were just come down from London to see her. Says Mrs. Bargrave, "How came you to order things so strangely?" "It could not be helped," said Mrs. Veal; and her sister and brother did come to see her, and entered the town of Dover just as Mrs. Veal was expiring. Mrs. Bargrave asked her whether she would not drink some tea. Says Mrs. Veal, "I do not care if I do; but I'll warrant this mad fellow" (meaning Mrs. Bargrave's husband) "has broke all your trinkets."[2]

9. An armorial panel placed on the house of a dead person.
1. Someone given to melancholy and fantasies.
2. That is, her tea-set.

"But," says Mrs. Bargrave, "I'll get something to drink in for all that"; but Mrs. Veal waived it, and said, "It is no matter, let it alone," and so it passed.

All the time I sat with Mrs. Bargrave, which was some hours, she recollected fresh sayings of Mrs. Veal. And one material thing more she told Mrs. Bargrave, that old Mr. Breton allowed Mrs. Veal ten pounds a year, which was a secret, and unknown to Mrs. Bargrave, till Mrs. Veal told it her. Mrs. Bargrave never varies in her story, which puzzles those who doubt of the truth, or are unwilling to believe it. A servant in a neighbor's yard adjoining to Mrs. Bargrave's house heard her talking to somebody, an hour of the time Mrs. Veal was with her. Mrs. Bargrave went out to her next neighbor's the very moment she parted with Mrs. Veal, and told what ravishing conversation she had with an old friend, and told the whole of it. Drelincourt's *Book of Death* is, since this happened, bought up strangely. And it is to be observed, that notwithstanding all this trouble and fatigue Mrs. Bargrave has undergone upon this account, she never took the value of a farthing, nor suffered her daughter to take anything of anybody, and therefore can have no interest[3] in telling the story.

But Mr. Veal does what he can to stifle the matter, and said he would see Mrs. Bargrave; but yet it is certain matter of fact that he has been at Captain Watson's since the death of his sister, and yet never went near Mrs. Bargrave; and some of his friends report her to be a great liar, and that she knew of Mr. Breton's ten pounds a year. But the person who pretends to say so has the reputation of a notorious liar, among persons which I know to be of undoubted repute. Now Mr. Veal is more a gentleman than to say she lies; but says a bad husband has crazed her. But she needs only to present herself, and it will effectually confute that pretense. Mr. Veal says he asked his sister on her deathbed whether she had a mind to dispose of anything, and she said no. Now the things which Mrs. Veal's apparition would have disposed of were so trifling, and nothing of justice aimed at in their disposal, that the design of it appears to me to be only in order to make Mrs. Bargrave so to demonstrate the truth of her appearance, as to satisfy the world of the reality thereof, as to what she had seen and heard; and to secure her reputation among the reasonable and understanding part of mankind. And then again, Mr. Veal owns that there was a purse of gold; but it was not found in her cabinet, but in a comb-box. This looks improbable, for that Mrs. Watson owned that Mrs. Veal was so very careful of the key of her cabinet, that she would trust nobody with it. And if so, no doubt she would not trust her gold out of it. And Mrs. Veal's often drawing her hand over her eyes, and asking Mrs. Bargrave whether her fits had not impaired her, looks to me as if she did it on purpose to remind Mrs. Bargrave of

3. Financial advantage or profit.

her fits, to prepare her not to think it strange that she should put her upon writing to her brother to dispose of rings and gold, which looked so much like a dying person's bequest; and it took accordingly with Mrs. Bargrave, as the effect of her fits coming upon her; and was one of the many instances of her wonderful love to her, and care of her, that she should not be affrighted: which indeed appears in her whole management; particularly in her coming to her in the daytime, waiving the salutation, and when she was alone; and then the manner of her parting, to prevent a second attempt to salute her.

Now, why Mr. Veal should think this relation a reflection (as 'tis plain he does by his endeavoring to stifle it) I can't imagine, because the generality believe her to be a good spirit, her discourse was so heavenly. Her two great errands were to comfort Mrs. Bargrave in her affliction, and to ask her forgiveness for her breach of friendship, and with a pious discourse to encourage her. So that after all, to suppose that Mrs. Bargrave could hatch such an invention as this from Friday noon till Saturday noon (supposing that she knew of Mrs. Veal's death the very first moment) without jumbling circumstances, and without any interest too, she must be more witty, fortunate, and wicked too, than any indifferent person, I dare say, will allow. I asked Mrs. Bargrave several times if she was sure she felt the gown. She answered modestly, "If my senses be to be relied on, I am sure of it." I asked her if she heard a sound, when she clapped her hand upon her knee. She said, she did not remember she did; and she said, "She appeared to be as much a substance as I did, who talked with her. And I may," said she, "be as soon persuaded that your apparition is talking to me now, as that I did not really see her; for I was under no manner of fear. I received her as a friend, and parted with her as such. I would not," says she, "give one farthing to make anyone believe it, I have no interest in it; nothing but trouble is entailed upon me for a long time, for aught that I know; and had it not come to light by accident, it would never have been made public." But now, she says, she will make her own private use of it, and keep herself out of the way as much as she can. And so she has done since. She says, she had a gentleman who came thirty miles to her to hear the relation; and that she had told it to a room full of people at a time. Several particular gentlemen have had the story from Mrs. Bargrave's own mouth.

This thing has very much affected me, and I am as well satisfied as I am of the best grounded matter of fact. And why we should dispute matter of fact because we cannot solve things of which we have no certain or demonstrative notions, seems strange to me. Mrs. Bargrave's authority and sincerity alone would have been undoubted in any other case.

1706

Poetry: Augustan Modes

SAMUEL BUTLER
(1612–1680)

Butler passed his middle years during the "fury" of the Civil War and under the Commonwealth, sardonically observing the behavior and lovingly memorizing the faults of the Puritan rulers. He despised them and found relief for his feelings by satirizing them, though, naturally enough, he could not publish while they were in power. He served as clerk to several Puritan justices of the peace in the west of England, one of whom, according to tradition, was the original of Sir Hudibras (the *s* is pronounced). To Butler these men were fanatics, rapacious rascals, and hypocrites, inhabiting a world populated by only two classes: knaves and their preordained victims, fools.

Hudibras, Part I, was published late in 1662 (the edition bears the date 1663) and pleased the triumphant Royalists. King Charles II admired and often quoted the poem and rewarded its author with a gift of £300; it was, after all, a relief to laugh at what he had earlier hated and feared. The first part, attacking Presbyterians and Independents, proved more vigorous and effective than Parts II and III, which followed in 1664 and 1678 respectively, and which are less unified, since they aim at several different objects: romantic love, sex, astrology, and the new science, among others. After his initial success, Butler was neglected by the men he had pleased. He died in poverty, and not until 1721 was a monument erected in Westminster Abbey to his memory.

Hudibras is a travesty, or burlesque, i.e., it takes a serious subject and debases it by using a low style or distorts it by grotesque exaggeration. Butler carried this mode even into his verse, for he reduced the iambic tetrameter line (used subtly and seriously by such 17th-century poets as John Donne, John Milton, and Andrew Marvell) to something approaching doggerel, and his boldly comic rhymes add to the effect of broad comedy which he sought to create. Burlesque was a popular form of satire during the 17th century, especially after the French poet Paul Scarron published his *Virgile Travesti* (1648), which provoked mirth by retelling the heroic fable of the *Aeneid* in the most vulgar terms. Butler's use of burlesque expresses his contempt for the Puritans and their Commonwealth. Their theology he reduced to absurdity, their religious practices to pretense and self-deception, their morality to imposture and hypocrisy. In short, the history of England from 1642 to 1660 is made to appear mere sound and fury.

Butler took his hero's name from Spenser's *Faerie Queene*, II.ii, where

Sir Huddibras appears briefly as the lover of Elissa, who represents sullenness as opposed to high spirits. To a mind like Butler's, chivalric romance seemed contemptibly absurd, and therefore a suitable vehicle for his satiric narrative: Hudibras, the pedantic Presbyterian and his squire Ralph, the Independent, who relies on inner light and inspiration and who talks a deal of mystical nonsense, move in a romantic and hence an irrational world. The questing knight of chivalric romance is degraded into the meddling, hypocritical busybody Hudibras, who goes out, like an officer in Cromwell's army, "a-coloneling" against the popular sport of bearbaiting. The knight and the squire suggest Don Quixote and Sancho Panza, but the temper of Butler's mind is as remote from Cervantes' warm humanity as it is from Spenser's ardent idealism.

Butler had no illusions; he was skeptical in philosophy and conservative in politics, distrusting theoretical reasoning and the new science, disdainful of claims of inspiration and illumination, contemptuous of Catholicism and dubious of bishops, Anglican no less than Roman. It is difficult to think of anything which he approved unless it was peace, common sense, and the wisdom that emerges from the experience of mankind through the ages.

From Hudibras

From *Part I, Canto I*

THE ARGUMENT

Sir Hudibras, his passing worth,
The manner how he sallied forth,
His arms and equipage are shown,
His horse's virtues and his own:
The adventure of the Bear and Fiddle
Is sung, but breaks off in the middle.

When civil fury[1] first grew high,
And men fell out, they knew not why;
When hard words, jealousies, and fears
Set folks together by the ears
And made them fight, like mad or drunk,
For Dame Religion as for punk,[2]
Whose honesty they all durst swear for,
Though not a man of them knew wherefore;
When gospel-trumpeter,[3] surrounded
With long-eared rout, to battle sounded,
And pulpit, drum ecclesiastic,[4]

1. The Civil War between Royalists and Parliamentarians (1642–1649).
2. I.e., a prostitute.
3. A Presbyterian minister, vehemently preaching rebellion. The "long-eared rout" is a mob of Puritans or Roundheads, so called because they wore their hair short instead of in flowing curls and thus exposed their ears, which to many satirists suggested the long ears of the ass.
4. The Presbyterian clergy were said to have preached the country into civil war. Hence, in pounding their pulpits with their fists, they are said to beat their ecclesiastical drums.

Was beat with fist instead of a stick;
Then did Sir Knight abandon dwelling,
And out he rode a-coloneling.[5]
  A wight he was whose very sight would
Entitle him Mirror of Knighthood;
That never bent his stubborn knee
To anything but chivalry,
Nor put up blow but that which laid
Right worshipful on shoulder blade;[6]
Chief of domestic knights and errant,
Either for chartel or for warrant;[7]
Great on the bench, great in the saddle,
That could as well bind o'er as swaddle.[8]
Mighty he was at both of these,
And styled of war as well as peace.
(So some rats of amphibious nature
Are either for the land or water.)
But here our authors make a doubt
Whether he were more wise or stout.
Some hold the one and some the other;
But howsoe'er they make a pother,
The difference was so small his brain
Outweighed his rage but half a grain;
Which made some take him for a tool
That knaves do work with, called a fool,
And offer to lay wagers that,
As Montaigne, playing with his cat,
Complains she thought him but an ass,[9]
Much more she would Sir Hudibras
(For that's the name our valiant knight
To all his challenges did write).
But they're mistaken very much,
'Tis plain enough he was no such.
We grant, although he had much wit,
He was very shy of using it;
As being loath to wear it out,
And therefore bore it not about,
Unless on holidays, or so,
As men their best apparel do.
Beside, 'tis known he could speak Greek

5. Here pronounced *có-lo-nel-ing.* "Wight:" a creature.
6. When a man is knighted he kneels and is tapped on the shoulder by his overlord's sword.
7. "Chartel," a written challenge to combat, such as a knight errant sends. But Hudibras, as Justice of the Peace ("domestic knight"), could also issue a "warrant" (a writ authorizing an arrest, a seizure, or a search). Hence he is satirically called "great on the [Justice's] bench" as well as in the saddle. "Errant" was spelled and pronounced *arrant.*
8. Both Justice of the Peace and soldier, he is equally able to "bind over" a malefactor to be tried at the next sessions or in his role of colonel, to beat ("swaddle") him.
9. In his *Apology for Raymond Sebond,* Michel de Montaigne (1533–92), French skeptic and essayist, wondered whether he played with his cat or his cat played with him.

As naturally as pigs squeak;
That Latin was no more difficile
Than to a blackbird 'tis to whistle.
Being rich in both, he never scanted
His bounty unto such as wanted,
But much of either would afford
To many that had not one word.
For Hebrew roots, although they're found
To flourish most in barren ground,[1]
He had such plenty as sufficed
To make some think him circumcised;
And truly so perhaps he was,
'Tis many a pious Christian's case.
He was in logic a great critic,
Profoundly skilled in analytic.
He could distinguish and divide
A hair 'twixt south and southwest side;
On either which he would dispute,
Confute, change hands, and still confute.
He'd undertake to prove, by force
Of argument, a man's no horse;
He'd prove a buzzard is no fowl,
And that a lord may be an owl,
A calf an alderman, a goose a justice,
And rooks committee-men and trustees.[2]
He'd run in debt by disputation,
And pay with ratiocination.
All this by syllogism true,
In mood and figure,[3] he would do.
For rhetoric, he could not ope
His mouth but out there flew a trope;[4]
And when he happened to break off
In the middle of his speech, or cough,[5]
He had hard words ready to show why,
And tell what rules he did it by.
Else, when with greatest art he spoke,
You'd think he talked like other folk;
For all a rhetorician's rules
Teach nothing but to name his tools.
His ordinary rate of speech
In loftiness of sound was rich,
A Babylonish dialect,[6]

1. Hebrew, the language of Adam, was thought of as the primitive language, the one which men in a state of nature would naturally speak.
2. Committees were set up in the counties by Parliament and given authority to imprison Royalists and to sequestrate their estates. "Rooks": a kind of blackbird; slang for "cheats."
3. "Mood" is the form of an argument. The "figure" of a syllogism is "the proper disposition of the middle term with the parts of the question."
4. Figure of speech.
5. Some pulpit orators regarded hemming and coughing as ornaments of speech.
6. Pedants affected the use of foreign words. The allusion is to the Tower of Babel (Genesis xi.4–9).

Which learned pedants much affect.
It was a parti-colored dress
Of patched and piebald languages;
'Twas English cut on Greek and Latin,
Like fustian heretofore on satin.[7]
It had an odd promiscuous tone,
As if he had talked three parts in one;
Which made some think, when he did gabble,
They had heard three laborers of Babel,
Or Cerberus himself pronounce
A leash of languages at once.[8]
This he as volubly would vent
As if his stock would ne'er be spent;
And truly, to support that charge,
He had supplies as vast and large.
For he could coin or counterfeit
New words with little or no wit;[9]
Words so debased and hard no stone
Was hard enough to touch them on.
And when with hasty noise he spoke 'em,
The ignorant for current took 'em;
That had the orator, who once
Did fill his mouth with pebble-stones
When he harangued,[1] but known his phrase,
He would have used no other ways.
  In mathematics he was greater
Than Tycho Brahe,[2] or Erra Pater:
For he, by geometric scale,
Could take the size of pots of ale;
Resolve by sines and tangents straight,
If bread or butter wanted weight;
And wisely tell what hour o' the day
The clock does strike, by algebra.
  Beside, he was a shrewd philosopher,
And had read every text and gloss over;
Whate'er the crabbed'st author hath,
He understood by implicit faith;
Whatever skeptic could inquire for,
For every *why* he had a *wherefore*;
Knew more than forty of them do,
As far as words and terms could go.
All which he understood by rote

7. Clothes made of coarse cloth ("fustian") were slashed so as to display the richer satin lining.
8. The sporting term "leash" denotes a group of three dogs, hawks, deer, etc.; hence, *three* in general. Cerberus was the three-headed dog that guarded the entrance to Hades.
9. The Presbyterians and other sects invented a special religious vocabulary, much ridiculed by Anglicans: "outgoings," "workings-out," "gospel-walking-times," etc.
1. Demosthenes cured a stutter by speaking with pebbles in his mouth.
2. A Danish astronomer (1546–1601). "Erra Pater": Butler's contemptuous name for the popular astrologer William Lilly (1602–81).

And, as occasion served, would quote,
No matter whether right or wrong;
They might be either said or sung.
His notions fitted things so well
That which was which he could not tell,
But oftentimes mistook the one
For the other, as great clerks have done.[3]
He could reduce all things to acts,
And knew their natures by abstracts;
Where entity and quiddity,[4]
The ghosts of defunct bodies, fly;
Where truth in person does appear,
Like words congealed in northern air.[5]
He knew what's what, and that's as high
As metaphysic wit can fly.
In school-divinity[6] as able
As he that hight Irrefragable;[7]
Profound in all the nominal
And real ways beyond them all;
And with as delicate a hand
Could twist as tough a rope of sand.
And weave fine cobwebs, fit for skull
That's empty when the moon is full;[8]
Such as take lodgings in a head
That's to be let unfurnishéd
He could raise scruples dark and nice,[9]
And after solve 'em in a trice;
As if divinity had catched
The itch on purpose to be scratched,
Or, like a mountebank,[1] did wound
And stab herself with doubts profound,
Only to show with how small pain
The sores of faith are cured again;
Although by woeful proof we find
They always leave a scar behind.
He knew the seat of paradise,[2]

3. Elsewhere Butler wrote: "Notions are but pictures of things in the imagination of man, and if they agree with their originals in nature, they are true, and if not, false." "Clerks": scholars.

4. In the hair-splitting logic of medieval Scholastic philosophy, a distinction was drawn between the "entity" or *being* and the "quiddity" or *essence* of bodies. Butler calls entity and quiddity "ghosts" because they were held to be independent realities and so to survive the bodies in which they lodge.

5. The notion, as old as the Greek wit Lucian, that in arctic regions words freeze as they are uttered and become audible only when they thaw.

6. Scholastic theology.

7. Alexander of Hales (d. 1245) was called "Irrefragable," i.e., unanswerable, because his system seemed incontrovertible. The next couplet refers to the debate, continuous throughout the Middle Ages, as to whether the objects of our concepts exist in nature or are mere intellectual abstractions. The "nominalists" denied their objective reality, the "realists" affirmed it.

8. The frenzies of madmen were supposed to wax and wane with the moon (hence "lunatic").

9. Obscure ("dark") and subtle ("nice") intellectual perplexities ("scruples").

1. A seller of quack medicines.

2. The problem of the precise location of the Garden of Eden and the similar problems listed in the ensuing dozen lines had all been the subject of controversy among theologians.

Could tell in what degree it lies;
And, as he was disposed, could prove it
Below the moon, or else above it;
What Adam dreamt of when his bride
Came from her closet in his side;
Whether the devil tempted her
By a High Dutch interpreter;
If either of them had a navel;
Who first made music malleable; [2a]
Whether the serpent at the fall
Had cloven feet or none at all:
All this without a gloss or comment
He could unriddle in a moment,
In proper terms, such as men smatter
When they throw out and miss the matter.
  For his religion, it was fit
To match his learning and his wit:
'Twas Presbyterian true blue,[3]
For he was of that stubborn crew
Of errant[4] saints whom all men grant
To be the true church militant,
Such as do build their faith upon
The holy text of pike and gun;
Decide all controversies by
Infallible artillery,
And prove their doctrine orthodox
By apostolic blows and knocks;
Call fire, and sword, and desolation
A godly, thorough reformation,
Which always must be carried on
And still be doing, never done;
As if religion were intended
For nothing else but to be mended.
A sect whose chief devotion lies
In odd, perverse antipathies;[5]
In falling out with that or this,
And finding somewhat still amiss;
More peevish, cross, and splénetic
Than dog distract or monkey sick;

2a. Capable of being fashioned into form. Pythagoras is said to have organized sounds into the musical scale.
3. The Scotch Covenanters adopted blue as their color, in contrast to the Royalist red. Blue is the color of constancy; hence, "true blue," staunch, unwavering. This and the next five couplets bitterly recall the violence and fanaticism of the Parliamentary armies in attempting to reform the Anglican Church.
4. A pun: "arrant," meaning "unmitigated," and "errant," meaning "wandering," were both spelled and pronounced *arrant*. The Puritans frequently called themselves "saints."
5. The hostility of the sects to everything Anglican or Roman Catholic laid them open to the charge of opposing innocent practices out of mere perverse antipathy. Some extreme Presbyterians fasted at Christmas, instead of following the old custom of feasting and rejoicing. Cf. lines 211–12.

That with more care keep holiday
The wrong, than others the right way;
Compound for sins they are inclined to
By damning those they have no mind to;
Still so perverse and opposite
As if they worshiped God for spite.
The selfsame thing they will abhor
One way and long another for.
Free-will they one way disavow,[6]
Another, nothing else allow:
All piety consists therein
In them, in other men all sin.
Rather than fail, they will defy
That which they love most tenderly;
Quarrel with minced pies and disparage
Their best and dearest friend, plum-porridge;
Fat pig and goose itself oppose,
And blaspheme custard through the nose.[7]

* * *

1663

6. By the doctrine of predestination.

7. A reference to the nasal whine of the pious sectarians.

JOHN WILMOT, SECOND EARL OF ROCHESTER (1647–1680)

John Wilmot, Second Earl of Rochester, was the precocious son of one of Charles II's most loyal followers in exile. He won the king's favor at the Restoration and, in 1664, after education at Oxford and on the continent, took a place at court, at the age of seventeen. There he soon distinguished himself as "the man who has the most wit and the least honor in England." For one escapade, the abduction of Elizabeth Malet, an heiress, he was imprisoned in the Tower. But he regained his position by courageous service in the naval war against the Dutch; and in 1667 he married Miss Malet. The rest of his career was no less stormy. His satiric wit, directed not only at ordinary mortals but at Dryden and Charles II himself, embroiled him in constant quarrels and exiles; his practical jokes, his affairs, his dissipation were legendary. He told his biographer, Gilbert Burnet, that "for five years together he was continually drunk." Just before his death, however, he was converted to Christian repentance; and for posterity Rochester became a favorite moral topic: the libertine who had seen the error of his ways.

"Wit," in the Restoration, meant not only a clever turn of phrase but mental capacity, intellectual power. Rochester was famous for both kinds of wit. His fierce intelligence, impatient of sham and convention, helped design a way of life based on style, cleverness, self-interest—a way of life observable in Restoration plays (Dorimant, in Etherege's *The Man of*

Mode, strongly resembles Rochester). Philosophically, such behavior may be seen as an experiment in living the life of a "natural man," in accord with Hobbes's doctrine that all laws, even our notions of good and evil, are artificial social checks upon natural human desires. *The Disabled Debauchee,* composed in "heroic stanzas" like those of Dryden's *Annus Mirabilis,* subverts the very notion of heroism by turning conventions upside-down. Yet everything is kept plausible by Rochester's special gift for impersonation, the same talent, according to one enemy, that made him a dangerous seducer—"He enters into all your tastes and your feelings, and makes you believe everything he says, though not a single word is sincere."

The Disabled Debauchee

As some brave admiral, in former war
  Deprived of force, but pressed with courage still,
Two rival fleets appearing from afar,
  Crawls to the top of an adjacent hill;

From whence, with thoughts full of concern, he views
  The wise and daring conduct of the fight,
Whilst each bold action to his mind renews
  His present glory and his past delight;

From his fierce eyes flashes of fire he throws,
  As from black clouds when lightning breaks away;
Transported, thinks himself amidst the foes,
  And absent, yet enjoys the bloody day;

So, when my days of impotence approach,
  And I'm by pox[1] and wine's unlucky chance
Forced from the pleasing billows of debauch
  On the dull shore of lazy temperance,

My pains at least some respite shall afford
  While I behold the battle you maintain
When fleets of glasses sail about the board,[2]
  From whose broadsides[3] volleys of wit shall rain.

Nor let the sight of honorable scars,
  Which my too forward valor did procure,
Frighten new-listed[4] soldiers from the wars:
  Past joys have more than paid what I endure.

Should any youth (worth being drunk) prove nice,[5]
  And from his fair inviter meanly shrink,

1. Venereal disease.
2. Table.
3. The sides of the table; artillery on a ship; sheets on which satirical verses were printed.
4. Newly enlisted.
5. Coy, fastidious.

'Twill please the ghost of my departed vice
If, at my counsel, he repent and drink.

Or should some cold-complexioned sot forbid,
With his dull morals, our bold night-alarms,
I'll fire his blood by telling what I did
When I was strong and able to bear arms.

I'll tell of whores attacked, their lords at home;
Bawds' quarters beaten up, and fortress won;
Windows demolished, watches[6] overcome;
And handsome ills by my contrivance done.

Nor shall our love-fits, Chloris, be forgot,
When each the well-looked linkboy[7] strove t' enjoy,
And the best kiss was the deciding lot
Whether the boy used you, or I the boy.

With tales like these I will such thoughts inspire
As to important mischief shall incline:
I'll make him long some ancient church to fire,
And fear no lewdness he's called to by wine.

Thus, statesmanlike, I'll saucily impose,
And safe from action, valiantly advise;
Sheltered in impotence, urge you to blows,
And being good for nothing else, be wise.

1680

6. Watchmen.
7. Good-looking boy employed to light the way with a link or torch.

ANNE FINCH, COUNTESS OF WINCHILSEA (1661–1720)

Born into an ancient country family, Anne Kingsmill became a maid of honor at the court of Charles II. There she met Colonel Heneage Finch; in 1684 they married. During the short reign of James II they prospered at court, but at the king's fall in 1688 they were forced to retire, eventually settling on a beautiful family estate at Eastwell, in Kent, near the south coast of England. Here Colonel Finch became, in 1712, Earl of Winchilsea; and here Lady Winchilsea wrote most of her poems, influenced, she said, by "the solitude & security of the country," and by "objects naturally inspiring soft and poetical imaginations." Her *Miscellany Poems on Several Occasions, Written by a Lady* were published in 1713; one poem, *The Spleen,* a description of the mysterious melancholic illness from which she and many other fashionable people suffered, achieved some fame. But her larger reputation only began a century later, when Wordsworth praised her for keeping her eye upon external nature, and for a style "often admirable, chaste, tender, and vigorous."

Three things conspired to keep Lady Winchilsea's poems in the shade: she was an aristocrat; her nature was retiring; and she was a woman. Any one of these might have made her shrink from exposing herself to the jeers that still, at the turn of the century, greeted any effort by a "scribbling lady." Many of her best poems, for instance *The Petition for an Absolute Retreat,* celebrate the joys of solitude. Nevertheless, remarkably, she chose to publish. The reason may be found in her contempt for the notion that women are fit for nothing but trivial pursuits. "Women are education's and not nature's fools," she once wrote. Lady Winchilsea, like the blue-stockings who became so prominent later in the century, is a serious woman, and proud of it. Against the scoffers, she offers herself as an example of what a woman can be: thoughtful, sensitive, observant; able to find strength in her own mind and quiet joy in her musings in the night.

On Myself

Good heaven, I thank thee, since it was designed
I should be framed but of the weaker kind,
That yet my soul is rescued from the love
Of all those trifles, which their[1] passions move.
Pleasures, and praise, and plenty have with me
But their just value. If allowed they be,
Freely and thankfully as much I taste,
As will not reason or religion waste.[2]
If they're denied, I on my self can live,
And slight those aids unequal chance does give.
When in the sun, my wings can be displayed,
And in retirement, I can bless the shade.

1713

A Nocturnal Reverie

In such a night,[3] when every louder wind
Is to its distant cavern safe confined;
And only gentle Zephyr fans his wings,
And lonely Philomel,[4] still waking, sings;
Or from some tree, famed for the owl's delight,
She, hollowing clear, directs the wanderer right:
In such a night, when passing clouds give place,

1. I.e., most women's.
2. As will not destroy reason or religion.
3. This phrase, repeated twice below, echoes the same repeated phrase in the night-piece that opens Act V of *The Merchant of Venice*.
4. The nightingale.

Or thinly veil the heavens' mysterious face;
When in some river, overhung with green,
The waving moon and trembling leaves are seen;
When freshened grass now bears itself upright,
And makes cool banks to pleasing rest invite,
Whence springs the woodbind, and the bramble-rose,
And where the sleepy cowslip sheltered grows;
Whilst now a paler hue the foxglove takes,
Yet checkers still with red the dusky brakes:
When scattered glow-worms, but in twilight fine,
Show trivial beauties watch their hour to shine;
Whilst Salisbury[5] stands the test of every light,
In perfect charms, and perfect virtue bright:
When odors, which declined repelling day,
Through temperate air uninterrupted stray;
When darkened groves their softest shadows wear,
And falling waters we distinctly hear;
When through the gloom more venerable shows
Some ancient fabric,[6] awful in repose,
While sunburnt hills their swarthy looks conceal,
And swelling haycocks thicken up the vale:
When the loosed horse now, as his pasture leads,
Comes slowly grazing through the adjoining meads,
Whose stealing pace, and lengthened shade we fear,
Till torn-up forage in his teeth we hear:
When nibbling sheep at large pursue their food,
And unmolested kine rechew the cud;
When curlews cry beneath the village walls,
And to her straggling brood the partridge calls;
Their shortlived jubilee the creatures keep,
Which but endures, whilst tyrant man does sleep;
When a sedate content the spirit feels,
And no fierce light disturbs, whilst it reveals;
But silent musings urge the mind to seek
Something, too high for syllables to speak;
Till the free soul to a composedness charmed,
Finding the elements of rage disarmed,
O'er all below a solemn quiet grown,
Joys in the inferior world,[7] and thinks it like her own:
In such a night let me abroad remain,
Till morning breaks, and all's confused again;
Our cares, our toils, our clamors are renewed,
Or pleasures, seldom reached, again pursued.

1713

5. Probably Lady Salisbury, the daughter of a friend. The sense is that this lady differs from others more trivial, who like glow-worms look fine only one hour a day.

6. Edifice.

7. The world of nature (compared to the world of the soul).

MATTHEW PRIOR
(1664–1721)

Prior's distinguished diplomatic achievements cannot concern us here. He became a diplomat through the patronage of Dryden's friend the Earl of Dorset, wit, courtier, and poet, when he was appointed secretary to the embassy at The Hague. His public career culminated in his negotiating for Oxford's Tory ministry the Treaty of Utrecht (1713), which ended the War of the Spanish Succession; but after the fall of the Tories in 1714, Prior was recalled from Paris, placed under house arrest for over a year, and frequently interrogated in the hope that his evidence could be used to bring Oxford to trial as a traitor. Upon his release he found himself out of place and broken in fortune. But the extraordinary success of such friends as Swift and Pope in supporting the publication by subscription of his *Poems on Several Occasions* (1718) secured him a profit of 4,000 guineas, a very large sum at that time, which enabled him to end his life in comfort.

Prior was a representative man of his time: philosophically a skeptic; in public life ambitious and self-seeking, but not corruptible; a wit who entertained no illusions about life and who accepted its darker side and the fallibility of man with grace and irony. In his own words:

> Now in equipage stately, now humbly on foot,
> Both fortunes he tried, but to neither would trust,
> And whirled in the round, as the wheel turned about,
> He found riches had wings, and knew man was but dust.

His poetry was the by-product of a busy life—"the fruits of [his] vacant hours," as he once wrote. This pose of being the gentleman amateur he inherited from the Restoration court poets—naturally enough, considering his early association with Dorset and others. And indeed as a lyric poet he stands at the end of the long tradition of *vers de société,* such as was written by the "mob of gentlemen who wrote with ease" at the courts of Charles and James. But Prior was no careless writer: his grace and colloquial simplicity of language are the effects of studied art. His finest pieces are his lyrics, not his official odes and panegyrics. Of his two philosophical poems it is not the serious *Solomon* in weighty language and heroic couplets that attracts readers today, but rather the skeptical and delightfully witty *Alma* (written during his arrest in 1715) in deft octosyllabic couplets and homely conversational language that suggest Swift at his best. William Cowper admired Prior's ability to "make verse speak the language of prose, without being prosaic—to marshal the words of it in such an order as they might naturally take in falling from the lips of an extemporary speaker, yet without meanness, harmoniously, elegantly, and without seeming to displace a syllable for the sake of the rhyme * * *"

No poems were more popular, in the 17th and 18th centuries, than those which praised the virtues of a modest, retired life, sequestered from the ambitions of city and court. According to Dr. Johnson, "Perhaps no composition in our language has been oftener perused than Pomfret's *Choice*" (1700), which chooses the Golden Mean: a small estate, old books and wines, a few friends, a prudent female companion, a peaceful death. Yet Prior, who knew well enough the disappointments of public life, also knew that simple country living did not guarantee virtue. *An Epitaph* satirizes not the quiet but the unexamined life. For an epigraph, Prior took a chorus from Seneca's *Thyestes*—"All I seek is to lie still"—to which we might add Tolstoy's judgment of Ivan Ilych, whose "life was most ordinary and most simple and therefore most terrible."

An Epitaph

Interred beneath this marble stone
Lie sauntering Jack and idle Joan.
While rolling threescore years and one
Did round this globe their courses run;
If human things went ill or well;
If changing empires rose or fell;
The morning passed, the evening came,
And found this couple still the same.
They walked and ate, good folks: what then?
Why then they walked and ate again.
They soundly slept the night away;
They did just nothing all the day;
And having buried children four,
Would not take pains to try for more.
Nor sister either had, nor brother:
They seemed just tallied for each other.
  Their moral and economy[1]
Most perfectly they made agree:
Each virtue kept its proper bound,
Nor trespassed on the other's ground.
Nor fame, nor censure they regarded:
They neither punished, nor rewarded.
He cared not what the footmen did;
Her maids she neither praised, nor chid:
So every servant took his course;
And bad at first, they all grew worse.
Slothful disorder filled his stable,
And sluttish plenty decked her table.
Their beer was strong; their wine was port;
Their meal was large; their grace was short.
They gave the poor the remnant-meat
Just when it grew not fit to eat.
  They paid the church and parish rate,[2]
And took, but read not the receipt;

1. Morality and household management. 2. Tax.

For which they claimed their Sunday's due
Of slumbering in an upper pew.
  No man's defects sought they to know,
So never made themselves a foe.
No man's good deeds did they commend,
So never raised themselves a friend.
Nor cherished they relations poor:
That might decrease their present store;
Nor barn nor house did they repair:
That might oblige their future heir.
  They neither added, nor confounded;[3]
They neither wanted, nor abounded.
Each Christmas they accompts[4] did clear;
And wound their bottom[5] round the year.
Nor tear nor smile did they employ
At news of public grief or joy.
When bells were rung and bonfires made,
If asked, they ne'er denied their aid:
Their jug was to the ringers carried,
Whoever either died, or married.
Their billet[6] at the fire was found,
Whoever was deposed, or crowned.
  Nor good, nor bad, nor fools, nor wise;
They would not learn, nor could advise;
Without love, hatred, joy, or fear,
They led—a kind of—as it were;
Nor wished, nor cared, nor laughed, nor cried:
And so they lived; and so they died.

1718

3. Wasted.
4. Accounts.
5. Wound up their skein of thread; that is, they set the year nicely to rights.
6. Firewood.

JOHN GAY

(1685–1732)

The career of John Gay encompasses most of the ways that a talented but indigent author of the early 18th century could try to make a living: publication, patronage, odd jobs at court, the theater. Having been well educated at school in Devon, he came to London at seventeen to try his luck as apprentice to a silk mercer. Five years later he became secretary to his friend Aaron Hill, who introduced him to the publishing world and literary circles. Eventually most of the leading authors in London adopted him as a favorite; with Pope, Swift, and Arbuthnot he helped found the Scriblerus Club, famous for its literary satires and practical jokes. Through the offices of friends like these he obtained the patrons and political appointments that supported him. The same Scriblerian influence may be discerned in his first successful poem, *The Shepherd's Week* (1714), a burlesque pastoral. Two years later a mock-georgic, *Trivia, or the Art of Walking the Streets of London,* showed that the town could be as rough as, and more corrupting than, the country. Gay's popularity and financial security, however, were confirmed only by later works: two sets of verse *Fables*, published in 1727 and 1738; and above all *The Beggar's Opera* (1728). This ballad-opera, suggested by Swift—"what think you of a Newgate pastoral, among the thieves and whores there?"—satirized political corruption and Italian opera; the vitality of its raffish characters, and of its theme that vice is the same in high places as in low, maintains its popularity.

Gay seldom seems to take his verse seriously, yet few poets have looked with deeper irony upon the social fabric; life, not as poets would gild it, but as it is. The playfulness of his mock forms and literary parodies, as in *The Birth of the Squire,* exposes the disparity between high poetic expectations and coarse human reality. The squire, expected to bring about a new Golden Age, will waste his life in hunting and drink. For all his lightness of touch, Gay views society with a clarity and a complexity that many greater poets might envy.

Pope's epitaph on Gay, inscribed in Westminster Abbey, begins this way:

Of manners gentle, of affections mild;
In wit, a man; simplicity, a child;
With native humor tempering virtuous rage,
Formed to delight at once and lash the age.

But Gay wrote an epitaph of his own.

Life is a jest, and all things show it;
I thought so once, but now I know it.

The Birth of the Squire. An Eclogue

IN IMITATION OF THE POLLIO OF VIRGIL[1]

Ye sylvan Muses, loftier strains recite,
Not all in shades and humble cots[2] delight.
Hark! the bells ring; along the distant grounds
The driving gales convey the swelling sounds;
Th' attentive swain, forgetful of his work,
With gaping wonder leans upon his fork.
What sudden news alarms the waking morn?
To the glad squire a hopeful heir is born.
Mourn, mourn, ye stags, and all ye beasts of chase,
This hour destruction brings on all your race.
See the pleased tenants duteous offerings bear,
Turkeys, and geese, and grocer's sweetest ware;

1. Virgil's famous Fourth Eclogue (dedicated to Consul Pollio) foretells the birth of a marvelous child, the hope of Rome. In the Middle Ages it was assumed that the poet had foreseen the birth of Christ, and he became known as a great magician.
2. Cottages.

With the new health[3] the ponderous tankard flows,
And old October[4] reddens every nose.
Beagles and spaniels round his cradle stand,
Kiss his moist lip and gently lick his hand.
He joys to hear the shrill horn's echoing sounds,
And learns to lisp the names of all the hounds.
With frothy ale to make his cup o'erflow,
Barley shall in paternal acres grow;
The bee shall sip the fragrant dew from flowers,
To give metheglin[5] for his morning hours;
For him the clustering hop shall climb the poles,
And his own orchard sparkle in his bowls.

His sire's exploits he now with wonder hears,
The monstrous tales indulge his greedy ears:
How when youth strung his nerves and warmed his veins,
He rode, the mighty Nimrod[6] of the plains.
He leads the staring infant through the hall,
Points out the horny spoils that grace the wall;
Tells how this stag through three whole counties fled,
What rivers swam, where bayed, and where he bled.
Now he the wonders of the fox repeats,
Describes the desperate chase, and all his cheats;
How in one day, beneath his furious speed,
He tired seven coursers of the fleetest breed;
How high the pale he leapt, how wide the ditch,
When the hound tore the haunches of the witch![7]
These stories, which descend from son to son,
The forward boy shall one day make his own.

Ah, too fond mother, think the time draws nigh
That calls the darling from thy tender eye;
How shall his spirit brook the rigid rules,
And the long tyranny of grammar schools?
Let younger brothers o'er dull authors plod,
Lashed into Latin by the tingling rod;
No, let him never feel that smart disgrace:
Why should he wiser prove than all his race?

When ripening youth with down o'ershades his chin,
And every female eye incites to sin,
The milkmaid (thoughtless of her future shame)
With smacking lip shall raise his guilty flame;
The dairy, barn, the hayloft, and the grove
Shall oft be conscious of their stolen love.
But think, Priscilla, on that dreadful time
When pangs and watery qualms shall own[8] thy crime;

3. Toast.
4. Ale.
5. Mead (made from honey).
6. A great hunter (*Genesis* 10.9).
7. "The most common accident to sportsmen; to hunt a witch in the shape of a hare" [Gay's note].
8. Confess.

How wilt thou tremble when thy nipple's pressed
To see the white drops bathe thy swelling breast!
Nine moons shall publicly divulge her shame,
And the young squire forestall a father's name.

When twice twelve times the reaper's sweeping hand
With leveled harvests has bestrewn the land,
On famed St. Hubert's feast[9] his winding horn
Shall cheer the joyful hound and wake the morn.
This memorable day his eager speed
Shall urge with bloody heel the rising steed.
O check the foamy bit, nor tempt thy fate;
Think on the murders of a five-bar gate!
Yet prodigal of life, the leap he tries,
Low in the dust his groveling honor lies,
Headlong he falls, and on the rugged stone
Distorts[1] his neck, and cracks the collarbone.
O venturous youth, thy thirst of game allay;
May'st thou survive the perils of this day!
He shall survive; and in late years be sent
To snore away debates in Parliament.

The time shall come, when his more solid sense
With nod important shall the laws dispense;
A justice, with grave justices shall sit,
He praise their wisdom, they admire his wit.
No greyhound shall attend the tenant's pace,
No rusty gun the farmer's chimney grace;
Salmons shall leave their covers void of fear,
Nor dread the thievish net or triple spear;
Poachers shall tremble at his awful name,
Whom vengeance now o'ertakes for murdered game.

Assist me, Bacchus, and ye drunken powers,
To sing his friendships and his midnight hours!

Why dost thou glory in thy strength of beer,
Firm-corked and mellowed till the twentieth year;
Brewed or when Phoebus warms the fleecy sign
Or when his languid rays in Scorpio shine?[2]
Think on the mischiefs which from hence have sprung!
It arms with curses dire the wrathful tongue;
Foul scandal to the lying lip affords,
And prompts the memory with injurious words.
O where is wisdom, when by this o'erpowered?
The state is censured, and the maid deflowered!
And wilt thou still, O squire, brew ale so strong?
Hear then the dictates of prophetic song.

9. November 3, which opens the hunting season.
1. Wrenches.
2. Either in spring (Aries) or fall (Scorpio).

Methinks I see him in his hall appear,
Where the long table floats in clammy beer,
'Midst mugs and glasses shattered o'er the floor,
Dead-drunk, his servile crew supinely snore;
Triumphant, o'er the prostrate brutes he stands,
The mighty bumper trembles in his hands;
Boldly he drinks, and like his glorious sires,
In copious gulps of potent ale expires.

1720

LADY MARY WORTLEY MONTAGU
(1689–1762)

In her early teens Lady Mary Pierrepont did something that well-bred young women were not supposed to do: she secretly taught herself Latin. The act reveals many of the traits that would also characterize her as a mature woman: curiosity, love of learning, intelligence, ambition, independence of mind. The eldest daughter of a wealthy Whig peer (he later became Marquess of Dorchester), she grew up amid a glittering London circle that included Addison, Steele, Congreve, and later Pope and Gay. But she was not content to live the life of a dutiful aristocratic daughter. Unlike most women in her time, she married for love; and when her husband, Edward Wortley Montagu, was appointed ambassador to Constantinople in 1716, she took advantage of the opportunity by traveling through Europe, studying the language and customs of Turkey, and even visiting Turkish harems. She also pioneered in introducing smallpox inoculation to England (her own son and daughter were among the first to be inoculated). Returning home in 1718, she spent unhappy years that included bitter political quarrels with Pope and the gradual failure of her marriage. Then, in middle age, she fell in love with a young Italian author, Francesco Algarotti. In 1739 she followed him to Italy; but the passion that had kindled in their letters was soon quenched at their meeting. The rest of her life was passed abroad, in Avignon, Brescia, and Venice. She died soon after her return to London in 1762.

As an author Lady Mary is remembered chiefly for her letters. In a century that included most of the great letter-writers in English—Gray, Horace Walpole, Cowper, and others—she is one of the greatest. "What fire, what ease, what knowledge of Europe and Asia!" Edward Gibbon commented when her Turkish correspondence was published. But from an early age she had also tried her hand at other literary forms: essays, poems, even a translated play. In her own time she was especially admired as a poet. When Pope, after their quarrel, gave her the name of "Sappho" (see *Epistle II. To a Lady*, lines 24–26), he was doubtless betraying the nervousness that most men felt in the presence of intelligent women (the Greek poet Sappho, after all, preferred women to men); yet he was also associating her with the classic author of lyric verse. Lady Mary's verse, though often casual, reveals the mind of a woman who is not willing to accept the stereotypes imposed on her by men. Mary Astell (1668–1731), an important early feminist and a friend of Lady Mary, had strongly urged women to preserve their freedom of choice—it was education, not marriage, that would set them free—and many of Lady Mary's poems reflect a similar theme. A woman, they suggest, need not defer to a man who is less than her equal; she must look to her own satisfaction before she looks to his; and she always has the right to say no. The verse demands respect by virtue of its sexual candor and punishing wit. Like Lady Mary herself, it is never dull; and at its best it places her in that ideal community defined by E. M. Forster: "Not an aristocracy of power, based upon rank and influence, but an aristocracy of the sensitive, the considerate, and the plucky."

The Lover: A Ballad

At length, by so much importunity pressed,
Take, C——,[1] at once, the inside of my breast;
This stupid indifference so often you blame
Is not owing to nature, to fear, or to shame;
I am not as cold as a Virgin in lead,[2]
Nor is Sunday's sermon so strong in my head;
I know but too well how time flies along,
That we live but few years and yet fewer are young.

But I hate to be cheated, and never will buy
Long years of repentance for moments of joy.
Oh was there a man (but where shall I find
Good sense and good nature so equally joined?)
Would value his pleasure, contribute to mine,
Not meanly would boast, nor would lewdly design,[3]
Not over severe, yet not stupidly vain,
For I would have the power though not give the pain;

No pedant yet learnéd, not rakehelly gay
Or laughing because he has nothing to say,
To all my whole sex obliging and free,
Yet never be fond of any but me;
In public preserve the decorum that's just,
And show in his eyes he is true to his trust,
Then rarely approach, and respectfully bow,
Yet not fulsomely pert, nor yet foppishly low.

But when the long hours of public are past
And we meet with champagne and a chicken at last,
May every fond pleasure that hour endear,
Be banished afar both discretion and fear,

1. Probably Richard Chandler, a friend of Lady Mary. The ideal "lover" of the title, however, is not to be identified with any particular person.

2. I.e., an image of the Virgin Mary, either as a leaden statue or as a stained glass window framed in lead.

3. Plot.

Forgetting or scorning the airs of the crowd
He may cease to be formal, and I to be proud,
Till lost in the joy we confess that we live,
And he may be rude, and yet I may forgive.

And that my delight may be solidly fixed,
Let the friend and the lover be handsomely mixed,
In whose tender bosom my soul might confide,
Whose kindness can sooth me, whose counsel could guide.
From such a dear lover as here I describe
No danger should fright me, no millions should bribe;
But till this astonishing creature I know,
As I long have lived chaste, I will keep myself so.

I never will share with the wanton coquette,
Or be caught by a vain affectation of wit.
The toasters and songsters may try all their art
But never shall enter the pass of my heart.
I loathe the lewd rake, the dressed fopling despise;
Before such pursuers the nice[4] virgin flies;
And as Ovid has sweetly in parables told
We harden like trees, and like rivers are cold.[5]

1747

Epistle from Mrs. Yonge to Her Husband[1]

Think not this paper comes with vain pretense
To move your pity, or to mourn th' offense
Too well I know that hard obdurate heart;
No softening mercy there will take my part,
Nor can a woman's arguments prevail,

4. Fastidious.

5. In Ovid's *Metamorphoses* Daphne, to escape Apollo, was turned into a laurel; and Arethusa, escaping Alpheus, became a fountain.

1. In 1724 the notorious libertine William Yonge, separated from his wife Mary, discovered that she (like him) had committed adultery. He sued her lover, Colonel Norton, for damages and collected £1,500. Later that year, according to the law of the time, he petitioned the Houses of Parliament for a divorce. The case was tried in public, Mrs. Yonge's love letters were read aloud, and two men testified that they had found her and Norton "together in naked bed." Yonge was granted the divorce, his wife's dowry, and the greater part of her fortune.

Though the *Epistle* is obviously based on this sensational affair, it is also a work of imagination. Like Pope's *Eloisa to Abelard*—addressed to Lady Mary herself—it takes the form of an heroic epistle, the passionate outcry of an abandoned woman. The poet, entering into the feelings of Mrs. Yonge, justifies her conduct with reasons both of the heart and head. The objects of her attack include the institution of marriage, which binds wives in "eternal chains"; the double standard of morality, which requires chastity from women but not men; the hypocrisy of society, which condemns the very behavior it secretly lusts after; and the craven greed and cruelty of the husband himself. But 18th-century women seldom dared to speak like this in public, and the *Epistle* was never published until the 1970's.

When even your patron's wise example fails.[2]
But this last privilege I still retain;
Th' oppressed and injured always may complain.
   Too, too severely laws of honor bind
The weak submissive sex of womankind.
If sighs have gained or force compelled our hand,
Deceived by art, or urged by stern command,
Whatever motive binds the fatal tie,
The judging world expects our constancy.
   Just heaven! (for sure in heaven does justice reign,
Though tricks below that sacred name profane)
To you appealing I submit my cause,
Nor fear a judgment from impartial laws.
All bargains but conditional[3] are made;
The purchase void, the creditor unpaid;
Defrauded servants are from service free;
A wounded slave regains his liberty.
For wives ill used no remedy remains,
To daily racks condemned, and to eternal chains.
   From whence is this unjust distinction grown?
Are we not formed with passions like your own?
Nature with equal fire our souls endued,
Our minds as haughty, and as warm our blood;
O'er the wide world your pleasures you pursue,
The change is justified by something new;
But we must sigh in silence—and be true.
Our sex's weakness you expose and blame
(Of every prattling fop the common theme),
Yet from this weakness you suppose is due
Sublimer virtue than your Cato[4] knew.
Had heaven designed us trials so severe,
It would have formed our tempers then to bear.
   And I have borne (oh what have I not borne!)
The pang of jealousy, the insults of scorn.
Wearied at length, I from your sight remove,
And place my future hopes in secret love.
In the gay bloom of glowing youth retired,
I quit the woman's joy to be admired,
With that small pension your hard heart allows,
Renounce your fortune, and release your vows.
To custom (though unjust) so much is due;
I hide my frailty from the public view.
My conscience clear, yet sensible of shame,
My life I hazard, to preserve my fame.

2. Sir Robert Walpole, Yonge's friend at court, was rumored to tolerate his own wife's infidelities.
3. Only conditionally.
4. The asceticism and self-discipline of the Roman statesman Cato had been emphasized in Addison's famous tragedy *Cato* (1713).

And I prefer this low inglorious state
To vile dependence on the thing I hate—
But you pursue me to this last retreat.
Dragged into light, my tender crime is shown
And every circumstance of fondness known.
Beneath the shelter of the law you stand,
And urge my ruin with a cruel hand,
While to my fault thus rigidly severe,
Tamely submissive to the man you fear.[5]
  This wretched outcast, this abandoned wife,
Has yet this joy to sweeten shameful life:
By your mean conduct, infamously loose,
You are at once my accuser and excuse.
Let me be damned by the censorious prude
(Stupidly dull, or spiritually lewd),
My hapless case will surely pity find
From every just and reasonable mind.
When to the final sentence I submit,
The lips condemn me, but their souls acquit.
  No more my husband, to your pleasures go,
The sweets of your recovered freedom know.
Go: court the brittle friendship of the great,
Smile at his board,[6] or at his levee wait;
And when dismissed, to madam's toilet fly,[7]
More than her chambermaids, or glasses, lie,
Tell her how young she looks, how heavenly fair,
Admire the lilies and the roses there.
Your high ambition may be gratified,
Some cousin of her own be made your bride,
And you the father of a glorious race
Endowed with Ch——l's strength and Low——r's face.[8]

1724 1977

5. I.e., Walpole. Lady Mary suggests that the whole political establishment of England takes sides against Mrs. Yonge.
6. Dining table; "levee": morning reception of visitors.
7. It was fashionable for women like Lady Walpole to receive visitors during the last stages of dressing (their "toilet"). "Glasses": mirrors.
8. General Churchill was rumored to have had an affair with Lady Walpole; Antony Lowther was a notorious gallant. The author implies that Yonge's next wife may be as untrue as his first. Mrs. Yonge remarried immediately after her divorce; five years later Yonge himself (whose divorce had made him rich) married the daughter of a baron.

JONATHAN SWIFT
(1667–1745)

1704: *A Tale of a Tub* and *The Battle of the Books*.
1710–14: Alignment with Tories; political writings in defense of the Tory ministry.
1713: Made Dean of St. Patrick's Cathedral, Dublin.
1726: Publication of *Gulliver's Travels*.

Swift—a posthumous child—was born of English parents in Dublin. Through the generosity of an uncle he was educated at Kilkenny School and Trinity College, Dublin; but before he could fix on a career, the troubles that followed upon James II's abdication and his subsequent invasion of Ireland drove him along with other Anglo-Irish to England. Between 1689 and 1699 he was more or less continuously a member of the household of his kinsman Sir William Temple, an urbane, civilized man, a retired diplomat, and a friend of King William. During these years Swift read widely; rather reluctantly decided on the church as a career and so took orders; and discovered his astonishing gifts as a satirist. About 1696–97 he wrote his powerful satires on corruptions in religion and learning, *A Tale of a Tub* and *The Battle of the Books*, which were published in 1704 and reached their final form only in the fifth edition of 1710. These were the years in which he slowly came to maturity. When at the age of 32, he returned to Ireland as chaplain to the Lord Justice, the Earl of Berkeley, he had a clear sense of his genius.

It was at Temple's that Swift met and learned to love the woman whose role in his life has been the cause of much conjecture. Esther Johnson (Swift's "Stella") was the daughter of Temple's steward, and when Swift first knew her she was little more than a child. He educated her, formed her character, and came to love her as he was to love no other person. After Temple's death she removed (at Swift's suggestion) with her lifelong companion, Rebecca Dingley, to Dublin, where she and Swift met constantly, but never alone. To her he wrote the famous journal-letters, later published (1766) as *The Journal to Stella*, during his four-year residence in London when he was working with the Tories; and to her he wrote charming poems. Whether they were secretly married or whether they never married—and in either case why—has been often debated. A marriage of any sort seems most unlikely; and however perplexing their relationship was to others, it was obviously satisfying to each of them. Not even the violent passion that Swift awakened, no doubt unwittingly, in a much younger woman, Hester Vanhomrigh (pronounced *Van-úm-mer-y*), her pleadings and reproaches and early death, could unsettle his devotion to Stella. An enigmatic account of his relations with "Vanessa," as he called Miss Vanhomrigh, is given in his poem *Cadenus and Vanessa*.

The man who gained the lifelong devotion of Stella and evoked the romantic passion of Vanessa was also admired and loved by many of the distinguished men of his time. His friendships with Addison, Pope, Dr. Arbuthnot, John Gay, Prior, Oxford, Bolingbroke, not to mention those with his less brilliant, but pleasant, Irish circle, bear witness to his moral integrity and social charm. The dark side of Swift's nature has been exaggerated at the cost of neglecting the wit and gaiety, the playful humor, and the consciously assumed eccentricities which marked his social behavior. Nor is it tenable that his satires are the product of a diseased mind which was gradually disintegrating throughout his life. Swift suffered most of his adult life from what we now recognize as Ménière's syndrome, which affects the inner ear, causing dizziness, nausea, and deafness. By all these ills he was greatly afflicted, but he was never in any sense insane. After 1739, when he was 72 years old, his infirmities and deafness cut him off from social life and his duties as Dean, and from then on senility advanced inexorably. In 1742 guardians were appointed to administer his affairs, and his last three years were spent in gloom and lethargy. But the writer of the satires was a man in full control of very great intellectual powers.

Because Swift was a clergyman, a spirited controversialist, and a devoted supporter of the Anglican Church as an institution no less important than the Crown itself, he was drawn into politics in both England and Ireland. He was hostile to all who seemed to threaten the Established Church—Deists, freethinkers, Roman Catholics, Nonconformists, or merely Whig politicians. In 1710 he abandoned his old party, the Whig, because he disapproved of its indifference to the welfare of the Anglican Church in Ireland and of its desire to repeal the Test Act, which required all holders of offices of state to take the Sacrament according to the Anglican rites, thus excluding Roman Catholics and Dissenters. Welcomed by the Tories, he became the most brilliant political journalist of the day, serving the government of Oxford and Bolingbroke as editor of the party organ, the *Examiner*, and as author of its most powerful articles, as well as writing longer pamphlets in support of important policies, such as that favoring the Peace of Utrecht (1713). He was greatly valued by the two ministers, who admitted him to social intimacy, though never to their counsels. The reward of his services was not the English bishopric which he had a right to expect, but the Deanship of St. Patrick's Cathedral in Dublin, which came to him in 1713, a year before the death of Queen Anne and the fall of the Tories put an end to all his hopes of preferment in England.

In Ireland, where he lived unwillingly, he became not only an efficient ecclesiastical administrator, but also, in 1724, the leader of Irish resistance to English oppression. Under the pseudonym of "M. B., Drapier," he published the famous series of public letters that aroused the country to refuse to accept £100,000 in new copper coins (minted in England by William Wood, who had obtained his patent through court corruption) which, it was feared, would further debase the coinage of the already poverty-stricken kingdom. Although his authorship of the letters was known to all Dublin, no one could be found to earn the £300 offered by the government for information as to the identity of the Drapier. Swift is still venerated in Ireland as a national hero. He earned the right to refer to himself in the epitaph that he wrote for his tomb as a vigorous defender of liberty.

For all his involvement in public affairs, Swift seems to stand apart from his contemporaries—a striking figure even among the statesmen of the time, a man who towered above other writers by reason of his more profound imagination, mordant wit, and emotional intensity. He has been called a misanthrope, a hater of mankind; and *Gulliver's Travels* has been considered an expression of savage misanthropy. It is true that Swift proclaimed himself a misanthrope in a letter to Pope, declaring that though he loved individuals, he hated mankind in general, and offering a new definition of man as not *animal rationale* ("a rational animal"), but as merely *animal rationis capax* ("an animal *capable* of reason"). This, he declared, is the "great foundation" upon which his "misanthropy" was erected. Swift was stating not his hatred of his fellowmen, but his antagonism to the current optimistic view that human nature is essentially good. To the "philanthropic" flattery that sentimentalism and Deistic rationalism were paying to human nature, Swift opposed a more ancient and plausible view: that human nature is deeply and permanently flawed, and that we can do nothing with or for the human race until we recognize its moral and intellectual limitations. This attitude he was pleased to call "misanthropy." In his epitaph he spoke of the "fierce indignation" which had torn his heart, an indignation that found superb expression in his greatest satires. It was provoked by the constant spectacle of creatures capable of reason, and therefore of reasonable conduct, steadfastly refusing to live up to their capabilities.

Swift is one of our greatest writers of prose. He defined a good style as "proper words in proper places," a more complex and difficult saying than at first appears. Clear, simple, concrete diction, uncomplicated syntax, economy and conciseness of language mark all of his writings. His is a style that shuns ornaments and singularity of all kinds, a style that grows more tense and controlled the more fierce the indignation that it is called upon to express. The virtues of his prose are those of his poetry, which only lately has come to be much valued. It is unpoetic poetry, devoid of, indeed as often as not mocking at, inspiration, romantic love, easily assumed literary attitudes, and conventional poetic language. Like the prose it is predominantly satiric in purpose, but not without its moments of comedy and light-heartedness, though written most often not so much to divert as to reform mankind.

A Description of a City Shower

Careful observers may foretell the hour
(By sure prognostics) when to dread a shower:
While rain depends,[1] the pensive cat gives o'er
Her frolics, and pursues her tail no more.
Returning home at night, you'll find the sink[2]
Strike your offended sense with double stink.
If you be wise, then go not far to dine;
You'll spend in coach hire more than save in wine.

1. Impends, is imminent. An example of elevated diction used frequently throughout the poem in order to gain a mock dignity, comically inappropriate to the homely and realistic subject.
2. Sewer.

A coming shower your shooting corns presage,
Old achés throb, your hollow tooth will rage.
Sauntering in coffeehouse is Dulman[3] seen;
He damns the climate and complains of spleen.
  Meanwhile the South, rising with dabbled wings,
A sable cloud athwart the welkin flings,
That swilled more liquor than it could contain,
And, like a drunkard, gives it up again.
Brisk Susan whips her linen from the rope,
While the first drizzling shower is borne aslope:
Such is that sprinkling which some careless quean[4]
Flirts on you from her mop, but not so clean:
You fly, invoke the gods; then turning, stop
To rail; she singing, still whirls on her mop.
Not yet the dust had shunned the unequal strife,
But, aided by the wind, fought still for life,
And wafted with its foe by violent gust,
'Twas doubtful which was rain and which was dust.
Ah! where must needy poet seek for aid,
When dust and rain at once his coat invade?
Sole coat, where dust cemented by the rain
Erects the nap, and leaves a mingled stain.
  Now in contiguous drops the flood comes down,
Threatening with deluge this devoted town.
To shops in crowds the daggled[5] females fly,
Pretend to cheapen goods, but nothing buy.
The Templar[6] spruce, while every spout's abroach,
Stays till 'tis fair, yet seems to call a coach.
The tucked-up sempstress walks with hasty strides,
While streams run down her oiled umbrella's sides.
Here various kinds, by various fortunes led,
Commence acquaintance underneath a shed.
Triumphant Tories and desponding Whigs
Forget their feuds,[7] and join to save their wigs.
Boxed in a chair[8] the beau impatient sits,
While spouts run clattering o'er the roof by fits,
And ever and anon with frightful din
The leather sounds;[9] he trembles from within.
So when Troy chairmen bore the wooden steed,
Pregnant with Greeks impatient to be freed
(Those bully Greeks, who, as the moderns do,

3. A type name (from "dull man"), like Congreve's "Petulant" or "Witwoud." It was commonly believed at this time that the Englishman's tendency to melancholy ("the spleen") was attributable to the rainy climate.

4. Wench, slut.

5. Spattered with mud. "To cheapen": to bargain for.

6. A young man engaged in studying law. In the literature of the period the Templar is usually depicted as neglecting his professional studies for the sake of dissipation and the pursuit of literature. Cf. the Member of the Inner Temple in *Spectator* 2. "Abroach": pouring out water.

7. The Whig ministry had just fallen and the Tories, led by Harley and St. John, were forming the government with which Swift was to be closely associated until the death of the Queen in 1714.

8. Sedan chair.

9. The roof of the sedan chair was made of leather.

Instead of paying chairmen, run them through[1]),
Laocoön struck the outside with his spear,
And each imprisoned hero quaked for fear.[2]
Now from all parts the swelling kennels[3] flow,
And bear their trophies with them as they go:
Filth of all hues and odors seem to tell
What street they sailed from, by their sight and smell.
They, as each torrent drives with rapid force,
From Smithfield or St. Pulchre's shape their course,
And in huge confluence joined at Snow Hill ridge,
Fall from the conduit prone to Holborn Bridge.[4]
Sweepings from butchers' stalls, dung, guts, and blood,
Drowned puppies, stinking sprats,[5] all drenched in mud,
Dead cats, and turnip tops, come tumbling down the flood.[6]

1710

Stella's Birthday, 1721[1]

All travelers at first incline
Wheree'er they see the fairest sign,
And if they find the chambers neat,
And like the liquor and the meat,[2]
Will call again and recommend
The Angel Inn to every friend:
And though the painting grows decayed
The house will never lose its trade;
Nay, though the treacherous rascal Thomas
Hangs a new Angel two doors from us[3]
As fine as daubers' hands can make it
In hopes that strangers may mistake it,
They think it both a shame and sin
To quit the true old Angel Inn.

1. Run them through with their swords. The bully, always prone to violence, was a familiar figure in London streets and places of amusement.
2. *Aeneid* II.40–53.
3. The open gutters in the middle of the street.
4. An accurate description of the drainage system of this part of London—the eastern edge of Holborn and West Smithfield, which lie outside the old walls west and east of Newgate. The great cattle and sheep markets were in Smithfield. The church of St. Sepulchre ("St. Pulchre's") stood opposite Newgate Prison. Holborn Conduit was at the foot of Snow Hill. It drained into Fleet Ditch, an evil-smelling open sewer, at Holborn Bridge.
5. Small herrings.
6. In Falkner's edition of Swift's *Works* (Dublin, 1735) a note almost certainly suggested by Swift points to the concluding triplet, with its resonant final Alexandrine, as a burlesque of a mannerism of Dryden and other Restoration poets, and claims that Swift's ridicule banished the triplet from contemporary poetry.

1. This is the second of Swift's seven birthday poems to "Stella," his dear friend Esther Johnson (see the introduction).
2. The beverages and the food.
3. Thomas Sheridan and his wife Elizabeth (the "new Angel") had recently befriended Swift and often entertained him at their home. Sheridan (1687–1738) was a schoolmaster and grandfather of the playwright Richard Brinsley Sheridan.

Now, this is Stella's case in fact;
An angel's face, a little cracked
(Could poets or could painters fix
How angels look at thirty-six);[4]
This drew us in at first to find
In such a form an angel's mind,
And every virtue now supplies[5]
The fainting rays of Stella's eyes.
See, at her levee[6] crowding swains
Whom Stella freely entertains
With breeding, humor, wit, and sense,
And puts them to so small expense,
Their minds so plentifully fills,
And makes such reasonable bills,
So little gets for what she gives,
We really wonder how she lives;
And, had her stock been less, no doubt
She must have long ago run out.
Then, who can think we'll quit the place
When Doll hangs out a newer face,
Or stop and light at Cloe's head[7]
With scraps and leavings to be fed.
Then, Cloe, still go on to prate
Of thirty-six, and thirty-eight;
Pursue thy trade of scandal picking,
Thy hints that Stella is no chicken,
Your innuendos when you tell us
That Stella loves to talk with fellows;
But let me warn thee to believe
A truth for which thy soul should grieve:
That, should you live to see the day
When Stella's locks must all be gray,
When age must print a furrowed trace
On every feature of her face;
Though you and all your senseless tribe
Could art or time or nature bribe
To make you look like beauty's queen
And hold forever at fifteen,
No bloom of youth can ever blind
The cracks and wrinkles of your mind;
All men of sense will pass your door
And crowd to Stella's at fourscore.[8]

1721 1727

4. Though Stella admitted to 36, Swift knew that her real age was 40.
5. Compensates for.
6. Reception of visitors.
7. The picture of a head was often the sign of an inn.
8. I.e., 80. Later that year Stella replied with a poem on Swift's birthday, acknowledging his good influence: "You taught how I might youth prolong / By knowing what was right and wrong; * * * / Your lectures could my fancy fix, / And I can please at thirty-six."

Verses on the Death of Dr. Swift

OCCASIONED BY READING A MAXIM IN ROCHEFOUCAULD[1]

Dans l'adversité de nos meilleurs amis nous trouvons toujours quelque chose, qui ne nous déplaît pas.[2]

As Rochefoucauld his maxims drew
From nature, I believe 'em true:
They argue no corrupted mind
In him; the fault is in mankind.
This maxim more than all the rest
Is thought too base for human breast:
"In all distresses of our friends
We first consult our private ends,
While Nature, kindly bent to ease us,
Points out some circumstance to please us."
If this perhaps your patience move,[3]
Let reason and experience prove.
We all behold with envious eyes
Our equal raised above our size.
Who would not at a crowded show
Stand high himself, keep others low?
I love my friend as well as you,
But why should he obstruct my view?
Then let me have the higher post;
Suppose it but an inch at most.
If in a battle you should find
One, whom you love of all mankind,
Had some heroic action done,
A champion killed, or trophy won;
Rather than thus be overtopped,
Would you not wish his laurels cropped?
Dear honest Ned is in the gout,
Lies racked with pain, and you without:
How patiently you hear him groan!
How glad the case is not your own!
What poet would not grieve to see
His brethren write as well as he?
But rather than they should excel,
He'd wish his rivals all in hell.
Her end when Emulation misses,
She turns to envy, stings, and hisses:
The strongest friendship yields to pride,
Unless the odds be on our side.

1. François de La Rochefoucauld (1613–80), writer of witty, cynical maxims. Writing to Pope (November 26, 1725), Swift, opposing the optimistic philosophy that Pope and Bolingbroke were at that time developing, professed to have founded his whole character on these maxims.

2. "In the misfortune of our best friends we always find something that does not displease us."

3. Should agitate.

Vain humankind! fantastic race!
Thy various follies who can trace?
Self-love, ambition, envy, pride,
Their empire in our hearts divide.
Give others riches, power, and station;
'Tis all on me an usurpation;
I have no title to aspire,
Yet, when you sink, I seem the higher.
In Pope I cannot read a line,
But with a sigh I wish it mine:
When he can in one couplet fix
More sense than I can do in six,
It gives me such a jealous fit,
I cry, "Pox take him and his wit!"
I grieve to be outdone by Gay[4]
In my own humorous biting way.
Arbuthnot is no more my friend,
Who dares to irony pretend,
Which I was born to introduce,
Refined it first, and showed its use.
St. John,[5] as well as Pulteney, knows
That I had some repute for prose;
And, till they drove me out of date,
Could maul a minister of state.
If they have mortified my pride,
And made me throw my pen aside;
If with such talents Heaven hath blessed 'em,
Have I not reason to detest 'em?
To all my foes, dear Fortune, send
Thy gifts, but never to my friend:
I tamely can endure the first,
But this with envy makes me burst.
Thus much may serve by way of proem;
Proceed we therefore to our poem.
The time is not remote, when I
Must by the course of nature die;
When, I foresee, my special friends
Will try to find their private ends:
Though it is hardly understood
Which way my death can do them good;
Yet thus, methinks, I hear 'em speak:

4. John Gay (1685–1732), author of the famous *Beggar's Opera* (1728), intimate friend of Swift and Pope. His *Trivia, or the Art of Walking the Streets of London* (1716) owes something to Swift's *City Shower*. Dr. John Arbuthnot, physician and wit, friend of Swift and Pope. See Pope's *Epistle to Dr. Arbuthnot*.

5. Henry St. John, Lord Bolingbroke (see note, Pope's *Essay on Man*. I.1), though debarred from the House of Lords and from public office, had become the center of a group of Tories and discontented young Whigs (of whom William Pulteney was one) who united in opposing Sir Robert Walpole, the chief minister. They published a political periodical, the *Craftsman*, thus rivaling Swift in his role of political pamphleteer and enemy of Sir Robert.

"See how the Dean begins to break!
Poor gentleman! he droops apace!
You plainly find it in his face.
That old vertigo[6] in his head
Will never leave him till he's dead.
Besides, his memory decays;
He recollects not what he says;
He cannot call his friends to mind;
Forgets the place where last he dined;
Plies you with stories o'er and o'er;
He told them fifty times before.
How does he fancy we can sit
To hear his out-of-fashion wit?
But he takes up with younger folks,
Who for his wine will bear his jokes.
Faith, he must make his stories shorter,
Or change his comrades once a quarter;
In half the time he talks them round,
There must another set be found.
"For poetry, he's past his prime;
He takes an hour to find a rhyme;
His fire is out, his wit decayed,
His fancy sunk, his Muse a jade.[7]
I'd have him throw away his pen—
But there's no talking to some men."
And then their tenderness appears
By adding largely to my years:
"He's older than he would be reckoned,
And well remembers Charles the Second.
He hardly drinks a pint of wine;
And that, I doubt, is no good sign.
His stomach, too, begins to fail;
Last year we thought him strong and hale;
But now he's quite another thing;
I wish he may hold out till spring."
They hug themselves, and reason thus:
"It is not yet so bad with us."
In such a case they talk in tropes,[8]
And by their fears express their hopes.
Some great misfortune to portend
No enemy can match a friend.
With all the kindness they profess,
The merit of a lucky guess
(When daily how-d'ye's come of course,
And servants answer, "Worse and worse!")
Would please 'em better, than to tell
That God be praised! the Dean is well.

6. Johnson in his *Dictionary* authorizes Swift's pronounciation: *ver-ti-go.*
7. A worn-out horse, in contrast to Pegasus, the winged horse of Greek mythology, emblem of poetic inspiration.
8. Figures of speech.

Then he who prophesied the best,
Approves his foresight to the rest:
"You know I always feared the worst,
And often told you so at first."
He'd rather choose that I should die,
Than his prediction prove a lie.
Not one foretells I shall recover,
But all agree to give me over.
  Yet, should some neighbor feel a pain
Just in the parts where I complain,
How many a message would he send!
What hearty prayers that I should mend!
Inquire what regimen I kept;
What gave me ease, and how I slept,
And more lament, when I was dead,
Then all the snivelers round my bed.
  My good companions, never fear;
For though you may mistake a year,
Though your prognostics run too fast,
They must be verified at last.
  Behold the fatal day arrive!
  "How is the Dean?"—"He's just alive."
Now the departing prayer is read.
"He hardly breathes"—"The Dean is dead."
Before the passing bell begun,
The news through half the town has run.
"Oh! may we all for death prepare!
What has he left? and who's his heir?"
"I know no more than what the news is;
'Tis all bequeathed to public uses."
"To public use! a perfect whim!
What had the public done for him?
Mere envy, avarice, and pride:
He gave it all—but first he died.
And had the Dean in all the nation
No worthy friend, no poor relation?
So ready to do strangers good,
Forgetting his own flesh and blood?"
Now Grub Street [9] wits are all employed;
With elegies the town is cloyed;
Some paragraph in every paper
To curse the Dean, or bless the Drapier.[1]
  The doctors, tender of their fame,
Wisely on me lay all the blame.
"We must confess his case was nice; [2]
But he would never take advice.

9. Originally a street in London largely inhabited by hack writers; later, a generic term applied to all such writers.
1. It was in the character of "M. B.," a Dublin drapier, that Swift aroused the Irish people to resistance against the importation of Wood's halfpence. See biographical introduction.
2. Delicate; hence demanding careful diagnosis and treatment.

Had he been ruled, for aught appears,
He might have lived these twenty years:
For, when we opened him, we found,
That all his vital parts were sound."
  From Dublin soon to London spread,
'Tis told at court, "The Dean is dead."
Kind Lady Suffolk,[3] in the spleen,
Runs laughing up to tell the Queen.
The Queen, so gracious, mild and good,
Cries, "Is he gone? 'tis time he should.
He's dead, you say; why, let him rot:
I'm glad the medals were forgot.[4]
I promised him, I own; but when?
I only was the Princess then;
But now, as consort of the King,
You know, 'tis quite a different thing."
  Now Chartres,[5] at Sir Robert's levee,
Tells with a sneer the tidings heavy:
"Why, is he dead without his shoes?"
Cries Bob, "I'm sorry for the news:
Oh, were the wretch but living still,
And in his place my good friend Will! [6]
Or had a miter on his head,
Provided Bolingbroke were dead!"
  Now Curll his shop from rubbish drains: [7]
Three genuine tomes of Swift's remains!
And then, to make them pass the glibber,
Revised by Tibbalds, Moore, and Cibber.[8]
He'll treat me as he does my betters,
Publish my will, my life, my letters;
Revive the libels born to die,
Which Pope must bear, as well as I.
  Here shift the scene, to represent
How those I love my death lament.
Poor Pope will grieve a month, and Gay
A week, and Arbuthnot a day.
  St. John himself will scarce forbear
To bite his pen, and drop a tear.

3. George II's mistress, with whom Swift became friendly during his visit to Pope in 1726. "In the spleen": in low spirits. The phrase is ironic, as "laughing" in the next line makes clear.

4. Queen Caroline had promised Swift some medals when she was Princess of Wales during the same year.

5. Col. Francis Chartres, a debauchee often satirized by Pope; Sir Robert Walpole.

6. William Pulteney (see line 59 and its note.)

7. Edmund Curll, shrewd and disreputable bookseller, published pirated works, scandalous biographies, and works falsely ascribed to notable writers of the time.

8. Lewis Theobald (1688–1744), Shakespeare scholar and editor, already enthroned as King of the Dunces in Pope's *Dunciad* (1728). Like Pope, Swift spells the name phonetically. James Moore-Smyth, poetaster and playwright, an enemy of Pope. Colley Cibber (1671–1757), comic actor, playwright, and supremely untalented poet laureate. He succeeded Theobald as King of the Dunces in the *Dunciad* of 1743.

The rest will give a shrug, and cry,
"I'm sorry—but we all must die!"
Indifference clad in wisdom's guise
All fortitude of mind supplies:
For how can stony bowels melt
In those who never pity felt?
When *we* are lashed, *they* kiss the rod,
Resigning to the will of God.
The fools, my juniors by a year,
Are tortured with suspense and fear;
Who wisely thought my age a screen,
When death approached, to stand between:
The screen removed, their hearts are trembling;
They mourn for me without dissembling.
My female friends, whose tender hearts
Have better learned to act their parts,
Receive the news in doleful dumps:
"The Dean is dead (and what is trumps?)
Then, Lord have mercy on his soul!
(Ladies, I'll venture for the vole.[9])
Six deans, they say, must bear the pall.
(I wish I knew what king to call.)
Madam, your husband will attend
The funeral of so good a friend?"
"No, madam, 'tis a shocking sight;
And he's engaged tomorrow night:
My Lady Club would take it ill,
If he should fail her at quadrille.
He loved the Dean—(I lead a heart)
But dearest friends, they say, must part.
His time was come; he ran his race;
We hope he's in a better place."
Why do we grieve that friends should die?
No loss more easy to supply.
One year is past; a different scene!
No further mention of the Dean,
Who now, alas! no more is missed,
Than if he never did exist.
Where's now this favorite of Apollo?
Departed—and his works must follow,
Must undergo the common fate;
His kind of wit is out of date.
Some country squire to Lintot[1] goes,
Inquires for Swift in verse and prose.
Says Lintot, "I have heard the name;
He died a year ago."—"The same."
He searches all the shop in vain.

9. The equivalent in the card game quadrille of bidding a grand slam in bridge.

1. Bernard Lintot, the publisher of Pope's Homer and some of his early poems.

"Sir, you my find them in Duck Lane:[2]
I sent them, with a load of books,
Last Monday to the pastry-cook's.[3]
To fancy they could live a year!
I find you're but a stranger here.
The Dean was famous in his time,
And had a kind of knack at rhyme.
His way of writing now is past:
The town has got a better taste.
I keep no antiquated stuff;
But spick and span I have enough.
Pray do but give me leave to show 'em:
Here's Colley Cibber's birthday poem.
This ode you never yet have seen
By Stephen Duck[4] upon the Queen.
Then here's a letter finely penned
Against the *Craftsman*[5] and his friend;
It clearly shows that all reflection
On ministers is disaffection.
Next, here's Sir Robert's vindication,[6]
And Mr. Henley's last oration.[7]
The hawkers have not got them yet:
Your honor please to buy a set?
"Here's Woolston's tracts,[8] the twelfth edition;
'Tis read by every politician:
The country members, when in town,
To all their boroughs send them down;
You never met a thing so smart;
The courtiers have them all by heart;
Those maids of honor (who can read)
Are taught to use them for their creed.
The reverend author's good intention
Has been rewarded with a pension.
He does an honor to his gown,
By bravely running priestcraft down;
He shows, as sure as God's in Gloucester,[9]
That Jesus was a grand impostor;
That all his miracles were cheats,
Performed as jugglers do their feats:

2. London street where second-hand books and publishers' "remainders" were sold.
3. To be used as waste paper for lining baking dishes and wrapping parcels.
4. Stephen Duck, "the thresher poet," an agricultural laborer, whose mild poetic gifts brought him to the notice and patronage of Queen Caroline.
5. See line 59 and its note.
6. "Walpole hires a string of party scribblers who do nothing else but write in his defense" [Swift's note].
7. "Orator" John Henley, an Independent preacher, who dazzled unlearned audiences with his oratory and who wrote treatises on elocution.
8. Thomas Woolston (1670–1733), a freethinker, whose *Discourses on the Miracles of Our Saviour* had recently earned him notoriety.
9. Proverbially, Gloucestershire was full of monks.

The Church had never such a writer;
A shame he has not got a miter!"
Suppose me dead; and then suppose
A club assembled at the Rose;[10]
Where, from discourse of this and that,
I grow the subject of their chat.
And while they toss my name about,
With favor some, and some without,
One, quite indifferent in the cause,
My character impartial draws:
"The Dean, if we believe report,
Was never ill received at court.
As for his works in verse and prose,
I own myself no judge of those;
Nor can I tell what critics thought 'em:
But this I know, all people bought 'em,
As with a moral view designed
To cure the vices of mankind.
"His vein, ironically grave,
Exposed the fool and lashed the knave,
To steal a hint was never known,
But what he writ was all his own.
"He never thought an honor done him,
Because a duke was proud to own him,
Would rather slip aside and choose
To talk with wits in dirty shoes;
Despised the fools with stars and garters,
So often seen caressing Chartres.
He never courted men in station,
Nor persons held in admiration;
Of no man's greatness was afraid,
Because he sought for no man's aid.
Though trusted long in great affairs,
He gave himself no haughty airs;
Without regarding private ends,
Spent all his credit for his friends;
And only chose the wise and good;
No flatterers, no allies in blood;
But succored virtue in distress,
And seldom failed of good success;
As numbers in their hearts must own,
Who, but for him, had been unknown.
"With princes kept a due decorum,
But never stood in awe before 'em.
He followed David's lesson just;
In princes never put thy trust:[11]

10. A fashionable tavern in Covent Garden.

11. Psalm cxlvi.3.

And would you make him truly sour,
Provoke him with a slave in power.
The Irish senate if you named,
With what impatience he declaimed!
Fair Liberty was all his cry,
For her he stood prepared to die;
For her he boldly stood alone;
For her he oft exposed his own.
Two kingdoms, just as faction led,
Had set a price upon his head,
But not a traitor could be found,
To sell him for six hundred pound.[1]
"Had he but spared his tongue and pen,
He might have rose like other men;
But power was never in his thought,
And wealth he valued not a groat:
Ingratitude he often found,
And pitied those who meant the wound;
But kept the tenor of his mind,
To merit well of human kind:
Nor made a sacrifice of those
Who still were true, to please his foes.
He labored many a fruitless hour,
To reconcile his friends in power;
Saw mischief by a faction brewing,
While they pursued each other's ruin.
But finding vain was all his care,
He left the court in mere despair.[2]
"And, oh! how short are human schemes!
Here ended all our golden dreams.
What St. John's skill in state affairs,
What Ormonde's [3] valor, Oxford's cares,
To save their sinking country lent,
Was all destroyed by one event.[4]
Too soon that precious life was ended,
On which alone our weal depended.

1. In 1714 the government offered £300 for the discovery of the author of Swift's *Public Spirit of the Whigs,* and in 1724 the Irish government offered a similar amount for the discovery of the author of the fourth of Swift's *Drapier's Letters.*

2. The antagonism between the two chief ministers (his dear friends), Robert Harley, Earl of Oxford, and Bolingbroke paralyzed the Tory ministry in the crucial last months of Queen Anne's life and drove Swift to retirement in Ireland, whence he returned in 1714 to make a final effort to heal the breach and save the government. He failed and retired to the country in despair. There he received the news of Anne's death on August 1. The Hanoverian succession brought the Whigs back in triumph, ruined Swift's friends, and brought Swift's public life to a close.

3. James Butler, Duke of Ormonde, who succeeded to the command of the English armies on the Continent, when, in 1711, the Duke of Marlborough was stripped of his offices by Anne. He went into exile in 1714 and was active in Jacobite intrigue.

4. The death of Queen Anne.

When up a dangerous faction starts,[5]
With wrath and vengeance in their hearts;
By solemn League and Covenant bound,
To ruin, slaughter, and confound;
To turn religion to a fable,
And make the government a Babel;
Pervert the laws, disgrace the gown,
Corrupt the senate, rob the crown;
To sacrifice old England's glory,
And make her infamous in story:
When such a tempest shook the land,
How could unguarded Virtue stand?
With horror, grief, despair, the Dean
Beheld the dire destructive scene:
His friends in exile, or the Tower,[6]
Himself within the frown of power,
Pursued by base envenomed pens,
Far to the land of slaves and fens;[7]
A servile race in folly nursed,
Who truckle most, when treated worst.
"By innocence and resolution,
He bore continual persecution;
While numbers to preferment rose,
Whose merits were to be his foes;
When even his own familiar friends,
Intent upon their private ends,
Like renegadoes now he feels,
Against him lifting up their heels.
"The Dean did, by his pen, defeat
An infamous destructive cheat;[8]
Taught fools their interest how to know,
And gave them arms to ward the blow.
Envy has owned it was his doing,
To save that hapless land from ruin;
While they who at the steerage [9] stood,
And reaped the profit, sought his blood.
"To save them from their evil fate,
In him was held a crime of state.
A wicked monster on the bench,[1]

5. Swift's view of the policies of the "dangerous faction" (the Whig party) is hardly impartial. He feared it especially because of its toleration of Dissenters, and so as an enemy of the Church of England.
6. Bolingbroke was in exile; Oxford was sent to the Tower by the Whigs.
7. Ireland.
8. The scheme to introduce Wood's copper halfpence into Ireland in 1723–24.
9. Literally the steering of a ship. Here the direction and management of public affairs in Ireland.
1. William Whitshed, Lord Chief Justice of the King's Bench of Ireland. In 1720, when the jury refused to find Swift's anonymous pamphlet *Proposal for the Universal Use of Irish Manufacture* wicked and seditious, Whitshed sent them back nine times, hoping to force them to another verdict. In 1724 he presided over the trial of Harding, the printer of Swift's fourth *Drapier's Letter,* but again was unable, despite bullying, to force a verdict of guilty.

Whose fury blood could never quench;
As vile and profligate a villain,
As modern Scroggs, or old Tresilian;[2]
Who long all justice had discarded,
Nor feared he God, nor man regarded;
Vowed on the Dean his rage to vent,
And make him of his zeal repent:
But Heaven his innocence defends,
The grateful people stand his friends;
Not strains of law, nor judge's frown,
Nor topics brought to please the crown,
Nor witness hired, nor jury picked,
Prevail to bring him in convict.
"In exile, with a steady heart,
He spent his life's declining part;
Where folly, pride, and faction sway
Remote from St. John, Pope, and Gay.
"His friendships there, to few confined,
Were always of the middling kind;
No fools of rank, a mongrel breed,
Who fain would pass for lords indeed:
Where titles give no right or power,
And peerage is a withered flower;
He would have held it a disgrace,
If such a wretch had known his face.
On rural squires, that kingdom's bane,
He vented oft his wrath in vain;
Biennial squires [3] to market brought:
Who sell their souls, and votes for naught;
The nation stripped, go joyful back,
To rob the church, their tenants rack,
Go snacks with rogues and rapparees;[4]
And keep the peace to pick up fees;
In every job to have a share,
A jail or barrack to repair;
And turn the tax for public roads,
Commodious to their own abodes.
"Perhaps I may allow the Dean
Had too much satire in his vein;
And seemed determined not to starve it,
Because no age could more deserve it.
Yet malice never was his aim;
He lashed the vice, but spared the name;
No individual could resent,

2. Sir William Scroggs, Lord Chief Justice of England at the time of the Popish Plot, 1678 (see Dryden's *Absalom and Achitophel*), was impeached for his misdemeanors in office in 1680. Sir Robert Tresilian punished with great severity in 1381 men who had participated in the Peasants' Revolt; he was impeached and in 1387 was hanged.

3. Members of the Irish Parliament.

4. Highwaymen.

Where thousands equally were meant;
His satire points at no defect,
But what all mortals may correct;
For he abhorred that senseless tribe
Who call it humor when they gibe:
He spared a hump, or crooked nose,
Whose owners set not up for beaux.
True genuine dullness moved his pity,
Unless it offered to be witty.
Those who their ignorance confessed,
He ne'er offended with a jest;
But laughed to hear an idiot quote
A verse from Horace learned by rote.
"He knew an hundred pleasant stories,
With all the turns of Whigs and Tories:
Was cheerful to his dying day;
And friends would let him have his way.
"He gave the little wealth he had
To build a house for fools and mad;[5]
And showed by one satiric touch,
No nation wanted it so much.
That kingdom he hath left his debtor,
I wish it soon may have a better."

1731 1739

From A Tale of a Tub

A *Digression Concerning the Original, the Use, and Improvement of Madness in a Commonwealth*[1]

Nor shall it any ways detract from the just reputation of this famous sect,[2] that its rise and institution are owing to such an author as I have described Jack to be, a person whose intellectuals were overturned, and his brain shaken out of its natural position; which we commonly suppose to be a distemper, and call by the

5. Swift left funds to endow a hospital for the insane.

1. *A Tale of a Tub*, Swift's first major work, recounts the adventures of three brothers: Peter (Roman Catholicism), Martin (Luther, here regarded as inspiring the Church of England), and Jack (Calvin, the spirit of Protestant dissent). But the most memorable character of the book is its narrator, who interrupts the story with numerous digressions (including even "A Digression in Praise of Digressions"), and whose pride in learning and lack of common sense represent the zealous modern insanity that Swift takes as his target for satire. "A Digression Concerning Madness," this narrator's masterpiece, is based on Swift's ironical doctrine of "the mechanical operation of the spirit": the notion that all spiritual and mental states derive from physical causes—in this case, the ascent of "vapors" to the brain. Beneath his whimsy, however, the author raises a fearful question: what right has any human being to trust that he is sane?

2. The Aeolists, who "maintain the original cause of all things to be wind," are equated by Swift with religious dissenters who believe themselves to be inspired.

name of madness or frenzy. For, if we take a survey of the greatest actions that have been performed in the world, under the influence of single men, which are the establishment of new empires by conquest, the advance and progress of new schemes in philosophy, and the contriving, as well as the propagating, of new religions, we shall find the authors of them all to have been persons whose natural reason had admitted great revolutions from their diet, their education, the prevalency of some certain temper, together with the particular influence of air and climate. Besides, there is something individual in human minds, that easily kindles at the accidental approach and collision of certain circumstances, which, though of paltry and mean appearance, do often flame out into the greatest emergencies of life. For great turns are not always given by strong hands, but by lucky adaption, and at proper seasons; and it is of no import where the fire was kindled, if the vapor has once got up into the brain. For the upper region of man is furnished like the middle region of the air; the materials are formed from causes of the widest difference, yet produce at last the same substance and effect. Mists arise from the earth, steams from dunghills, exhalations from the sea, and smoke from fire; yet all clouds are the same in composition as well as consequences, and the fumes issuing from a jakes[3] will furnish as comely and useful a vapor as incense from an altar. Thus far, I suppose, will easily be granted me; and then it will follow, that as the face of nature never produces rain but when it is overcast and disturbed, so human understanding, seated in the brain, must be troubled and overspread by vapors, ascending from the lower faculties to water the invention and render it fruitful. Now, although these vapors, (as it hath been already said) are of as various original as those of the skies, yet the crop they produce differs both in kind and degree, merely according to the soil. I will produce two instances to prove and explain what I am now advancing.

A certain great prince[4] raised a mighty army, filled his coffers with infinite treasures, provided an invincible fleet, and all this without giving the least part of his design to his greatest ministers or his nearest favorites. Immediately the whole world was alarmed; the neighboring crowns in trembling expectation towards what point the storm would burst; the small politicians everywhere forming profound conjectures. Some believed he had laid a scheme for universal monarchy; others, after much insight, determined the matter to be a project for pulling down the Pope, and setting up the reformed religion, which had once been his own. Some again, of a deeper sagacity, sent him into Asia to subdue the Turk, and recover Palestine. In the midst of all these projects and prepara-

3. Latrine.

4. "This was Harry the Great of France" [Swift's note]. Henry IV (1553–1610), infatuated with the Princesse de Condé, whose husband had removed her to the Spanish Netherlands, prepared an expedition to bring her back.

tions, a certain state-surgeon,[5] gathering the nature of the disease by these symptoms, attempted the cure, at one blow performed the operation, broke the bag, and out flew the vapor; nor did anything want to render it a complete remedy, only that the prince unfortunately happened to die in the performance. Now, is the reader exceeding curious to learn whence this vapor took its rise, which had so long set the nations at a gaze? What secret wheel, what hidden spring, could put into motion so wonderful an engine? It was afterwards discovered that the movement of this whole machine had been directed by an absent female, whose eyes had raised a protuberancy, and before emission, she was removed into an enemy's country. What should an unhappy prince do in such ticklish circumstances as these? He tried in vain the poet's never-failing receipt of *corpora quaeque;*[6] for,

Idque petit corpus mens unde est saucia amore:
Unde feritur, eo tendit, gestitque coire.—LUCRETIUS[7]

Having to no purpose used all peaceable endeavors, the collected part of the semen, raised and inflamed, became adust, converted to choler, turned head upon the spinal duct, and ascended to the brain. The very same principle that influences a bully to break the windows of a whore who has jilted him, naturally stirs up a great prince to raise mighty armies, and dream of nothing but sieges, battles, and victories.

——*Teterrima belli*
Causa——[8]

The other instance is what I have read somewhere in a very ancient author, of a mighty king,[9] who, for the space of above thirty years, amused himself to take and lose towns, beat armies, and be beaten, drive princes out of their dominions; fright children from their bread and butter; burn, lay waste, plunder, dragoon, massacre subject and stranger, friend and foe, male and female. 'Tis recorded, that the philosophers of each country were in grave dispute upon causes natural, moral, and political, to find out where they should assign an original solution of this phenomenon. At last the vapor or spirit, which animated the hero's brain, being in perpetual circulation, seized upon that region of the human body, so renowned for furnishing the *zibeta occidentalis,*[1] and gathering

5. "Ravillac, who stabbed Henry the Great in his coach" [Swift's note].
6. "Any available bodies."
7. "The body strives for that which sickens the mind with love. . . . Stretches out toward that which smites it, and yearns to couple" (*De Rerum Natura* IV. 1048 ff.). "Adust": burned up.
8. "The most abominable cause of war" in olden days, according to Horace, *Satires* I. iii. 107–8, was a whore.
9. "This is meant of the present French king" [Louis XIV] [Swift's note].
1. "Paracelsus, who was so famous for chemistry, tried an experiment upon human excrement, to make a perfume of it, which when he had brought to perfection, he called *zibeta occidentalis,* or western-civet, the back parts of man . . . being the west" [Swift's note].

there into a tumor, left the rest of the world for that time in peace. Of such mighty consequence it is where those exhalations fix, and of so little from whence they proceed. The same spirits which, in their superior progress, would conquer a kingdom, descending upon the anus, conclude in a fistula.[2]

Let us next examine the great introducers of new schemes in philosophy, and search till we can find from what faculty of the soul the disposition arises in mortal man, of taking it into his head to advance new systems with such an eager zeal, in things agreed on all hands impossible to be known; from what seeds this disposition springs, and to what quality of human nature these grand innovators have been indebted for their number of disciples. Because it is plain, that several of the chief among them, both ancient and modern, were usually mistaken by their adversaries, and indeed by all except their own followers, to have been persons crazed, or out of their wits; having generally proceeded, in the common course of their words and actions, by a method very different from the vulgar dictates of unrefined reason; agreeing for the most part in their several models, with their present undoubted successors in the academy of modern Bedlam[3] (whose merits and principles I shall farther examine in due place). Of this kind were *Epicurus, Diogenes, Apollonius, Lucretius, Paracelsus, Descartes,*[4] and others, who, if they were now in the world, tied fast, and separate from their followers, would, in this our undistinguishing age, incur manifest danger of phlebotomy,[5] and whips, and chains, and dark chambers, and straw. For what man, in the natural state or course of thinking, did ever conceive it in his power to reduce the notions of all mankind exactly to the same length, and breadth, and height of his own? Yet this is the first humble and civil design of all innovators in the empire of reason. Epicurus modestly hoped, that one time or other a certain fortuitous concourse of all men's opinions, after perpetual justlings, the sharp with the smooth, the light and the heavy, the round and the square, would by certain *clinamina*[6] unite in the notions of atoms and void, as these did in the originals of all things. Cartesius reckoned to see, before he died, the sentiments of all philosophers, like so many lesser stars in his romantic system, wrapped and drawn within his own vortex.[7] Now, I would gladly be informed, how it is possible to account for such imaginations as

2. Ulcer shaped like a pipe.
3. Bethlehem hospital, London's lunatic asylum.
4. Each of these famous speculative thinkers was known as a materialist, hence suspected by Swift of encouraging atheism.
5. Medical blood-letting.
6. Swerves. The Greek philosopher Epicurus held that the universe was formed by atoms swerving together; Swift implies that a similar miracle would be required for men to join in agreement with Epicurus.
7. The physics of René Descartes (1596–1650) is based on a theory of vortices; Swift considered the theory pure romance.

these in particular men without recourse to my phenomenon of vapors, ascending from the lower faculties to overshadow the brain, and there distilling into conceptions for which the narrowness of our mother-tongue has not yet assigned any other name beside that of madness or frenzy. Let us therefore now conjecture how it comes to pass, that none of these great prescribers do ever fail providing themselves and their notions with a number of implicit disciples. And, I think, the reason is easy to be assigned: for there is a peculiar string in the harmony of human understanding, which in several individuals is exactly of the same tuning. This, if you can dexterously screw up to its right key, and then strike gently upon it, whenever you have the good fortune to light among those of the same pitch, they will, by a secret necessary sympathy, strike exactly at the same time. And in this one circumstance lies all the skill or luck of the matter; for if you chance to jar the string among those who are either above or below your own height, instead of subscribing to your doctrine, they will tie you fast, call you mad, and feed you with bread and water. It is therefore a point of the nicest conduct to distinguish and adapt this noble talent, with respect to the differences of persons and of times. Cicero understood this very well, when writing to a friend in England, with a caution, among other matters, to beware of being cheated by our hackney-coachmen (who, it seems, in those days were as arrant rascals as they are now), has these remarkable words: *Est quod gaudeas te in ista loca venisse, ubi aliquid sapere viderere.*[8] For, to speak a bold truth, it is a fatal miscarriage so ill to order affairs, as to pass for a fool in one company, when in another you might be treated as a philosopher. Which I desire some certain gentlemen of my acquaintance to lay up in their hearts, as a very seasonable *innuendo.*

This, indeed, was the fatal mistake of that worthy gentleman, my most ingenious friend, Mr. W—tt—n,[9] a person, in appearance, ordained for great designs, as well as performances; whether you will consider his notions or his looks. Surely no man ever advanced into the public with fitter qualifications of body and mind, for the propagation of a new religion. Oh, had those happy talents, misapplied to vain philosophy, been turned into their proper channels of dreams and visions, where distortion of mind and countenance are of such sovereign use, the base detracting world would not then have dared to report that something is amiss, that his brain has undergone an unlucky shake; which even his brother modernists

8. "It is ground for rejoicing that you have come to such places, where anyone can seem wise" (Cicero, *Familiar Epistles* vii. 10).

9. William Wotton (who had championed modern authors against Swift's patron, Sir William Temple, a spokesman for the ancients) is ridiculed in Swift's *Battle of the Books,* published in the same volume as *A Tale of a Tub* (1704).

themselves, like ungrates, do whisper so loud, that it reaches up to the very garret I am now writing in.

Lastly, whosoever pleases to look into the fountains of enthusiasm,[1] from whence, in all ages, have eternally proceeded such fattening streams, will find the springhead to have been as troubled and muddy as the current. Of such great emolument is a tincture of this vapor, which the world calls madness, that without its help, the world would not only be deprived of those two great blessings, conquests and systems, but even all mankind would unhappily be reduced to the same belief in things invisible. Now, the former *postulatum* being held, that it is of no import from what originals this vapor proceeds, but either in what angles it strikes and spreads over the understanding, or upon what species of brain it ascends; it will be a very delicate point to cut the feather, and divide the several reasons to a nice and curious reader, how this numerical difference in the brain can produce effects of so vast a difference from the same vapor, as to be the sole point of individuation between Alexander the Great, Jack of Leyden[2] and Monsieur Descartes. The present argument is the most abstracted that ever I engaged in; it strains my faculties to their highest stretch; and I desire the reader to attend with utmost perpensity; for I now proceed to unravel this knotty point.

There is in mankind a certain[3] * * * * *
* * * * * * * * *
Hic multa * * * * * *
desiderantur. * * * * * *
* * * * * And this I take to be a clear solution of the matter.

Having therefore so narrowly passed through this intricate difficulty, the reader will, I am sure, agree with me in the conclusion, that if the moderns mean by madness, only a disturbance or transposition of the brain, by force of certain vapors issuing up from the lower faculties, then has this madness been the parent of all those mighty revolutions that have happened in empire, in philosophy, and in religion. For the brain, in its natural position and state of serenity, disposeth its owner to pass his life in the common forms, without any thought of subduing multitudes to his own power, his reasons, or his visions; and the more he shapes his under-

1. For much of the 18th century the word "enthusiasm" (literally, "possessed by a god") signified a deluded belief in personal revelation.

2. John of Leyden, a tailor and prophet, briefly established a revolutionary Anabaptist community, the "New Jerusalem," in the city of Münster early in the 16th century.

3. "Here is another defect in the manuscript, but I think the author did wisely, and that the matter which thus strained his faculties, was not worth a solution; and it were well if all metaphysical cobweb problems were no otherwise answered" [Swift's note]. The Latin phrase ("Much is missing here") indicates a gap in the text Swift pretends to be "editing."

standing by the pattern of human learning, the less he is inclined to form parties after his particular notions, because that instructs him in his private infirmities, as well as in the stubborn ignorance of the people. But when a man's fancy gets astride on his reason, when imagination is at cuffs with the senses, and common understanding, as well as common sense, is kicked out of doors, the first proselyte he makes is himself; and when that is once compassed, the difficulty is not so great in bringing over others; a strong delusion always operating from without as vigorously as from within. For cant[4] and vision are to the ear and the eye, the same that tickling is to the touch. Those entertainments and pleasures we most value in life, are such as dupe and play the wag with the senses. For, if we take an examination of what is generally understood by happiness, as it has respect either to the understanding or the senses, we shall find all its properties and adjuncts will herd under this short definition, that it is a perpetual possession of being well deceived. And first, with relation to the mind or understanding, 'tis manifest what mighty advantages fiction has over truth; and the reason is just at our elbow, because imagination can build nobler scenes, and produce more wonderful revolutions, than fortune or nature will be at expense to furnish. Nor is mankind so much to blame in his choice thus determining him, if we consider that the debate merely lies between things past and things conceived; and so the question is only this: whether things that have place in the imagination, may not as properly be said to exist, as those that are seated in the memory; which may be justly held in the affirmative, and very much to the advantage of the former, since this is acknowledged to be the womb of things, and the other allowed to be no more than the grave. Again, if we take this definition of happiness, and examine it with reference to the senses, it will be acknowledged wonderfully adapt. How fading and insipid do all objects accost us, that are not conveyed in the vehicle of delusion! How shrunk is everything, as it appears in the glass of nature! So that if it were not for the assistance of artificial mediums, false lights, refracted angles, varnish, and tinsel, there would be a mighty level in the felicity and enjoyments of mortal men. If this were seriously considered by the world, as I have a certain reason to suspect it hardly will, men would no longer reckon among their high points of wisdom, the art of exposing weak sides, and publishing infirmities; an employment, in my opinion, neither better nor worse than that of unmasking, which, I think, has never been allowed[5] fair usage, either in the world, or the playhouse.

In the proportion that credulity is a more peaceful possession of

4. "Sudden exclamations, whining, unusual tones, and in fine all praying and preaching like the unlearned of the Presbyterians" (*Spectator* 147).

5. Admitted to be.

the mind than curiosity, so far preferable is that wisdom, which converses about the surface, to that pretended philosophy which enters into the depth of things, and then comes gravely back with informations and discoveries, that in the inside they are good for nothing. The two senses, to which all objects first address themselves, are the sight and the touch; these never examine farther than the color, the shape, the size, and whatever other qualities dwell, or are drawn by art upon the outward of bodies; and then comes reason officiously with tools for cutting, and opening, and mangling, and piercing, offering to demonstrate, that they are not of the same consistence quite through. Now I take all this to be the last degree of perverting nature; one of whose eternal laws it is, to put her best furniture forward. And therefore, in order to save the charges of all such expensive anatomy for the time to come, I do here think fit to inform the reader, that in such conclusions as these, reason is certainly in the right, and that in most corporeal beings, which have fallen under my cognizance, the outside has been infinitely preferable to the in; whereof I have been farther convinced from some late experiments. Last week I saw a woman flayed, and you will hardly believe how much it altered her person for the worse. Yesterday I ordered the carcass of a beau to be stripped in my presence; when we were all amazed to find so many unsuspected faults under one suit of clothes. Then I laid open his brain, his heart, and his spleen; but I plainly perceived at every operation, that the farther we proceeded, we found the defects increase upon us in number and bulk; from all which, I justly formed this conclusion to myself: that whatever philosopher or projector[6] can find out an art to solder and patch up the flaws and imperfections of nature, will deserve much better of mankind, and teach us a more useful science, than that so much in present esteem, of widening and exposing them (like him who held anatomy to be the ultimate end of physic).[7] And he, whose fortunes and dispositions have placed him in a convenient station to enjoy the fruits of this noble art; he that can with Epicurus content his ideas with the films and images that fly off upon his senses from the superficies[8] of things; such a man, truly wise, creams off nature, leaving the sour and the dregs for philosophy and reason to lap up. This is the sublime and refined point of felicity, called the possession of being well deceived; the serene peaceful state of being a fool among knaves.

But to return to madness. It is certain, that according to the system I have above deduced, every species thereof proceeds from a redundancy of vapors; therefore, as some kinds of frenzy give double strength to the sinews, so there are of other species, which add

6. Someone given to speculative experiments.
7. Medical practice.
8. Surfaces. Epicurus considered the senses, directly affected by objects, more trustworthy than reason.

vigor, and life, and spirit to the brain. Now, it usually happens, that these active spirits, getting possession of the brain, resemble those that haunt other waste and empty dwellings, which for want of business, either vanish, and carry away a piece of the house, or else stay at home and fling it all out of the windows. By which are mystically displayed the two principal branches of madness, and which some philosophers, not considering so well as I, have mistaken to be different in their causes, over-hastily assigning the first to deficiency, and the other to redundance.

I think it therefore manifest, from what I have here advanced, that the main point of skill and address is to furnish employment for this redundancy of vapor, and prudently to adjust the season of it; by which means it may certainly become of cardinal and catholic emolument, in a commonwealth. Thus one man, choosing a proper juncture, leaps into a gulf, from thence proceeds a hero, and is called the saver of his country; another achieves the same enterprise, but unluckily timing it, has left the brand of madness fixed as a reproach upon his memory; upon so nice a distinction, are we taught to repeat the name of Curtius[9] with reverence and love, that of Empedocles with hatred and contempt. Thus also it is usually conceived, that the elder Brutus only personated the fool and madman for the good of the public; but this was nothing else than a redundancy of the same vapor long misapplied, called by the Latins, *ingenium par negotiis;*[1] or (to translate it as nearly as I can) a sort of frenzy, never in its right element, till you take it up in business of the state.

Upon all which, and many other reasons of equal weight, though not equally curious, I do here gladly embrace an opportunity I have long sought for, of recommending it as a very noble undertaking to Sir Edward Seymour, Sir Christopher Musgrave, Sir John Bowls, John How, Esq.,[2] and other patriots concerned, that they would move for leave to bring in a bill for appointing commissioners to inspect into Bedlam, and the parts adjacent; who shall be empowered to send for persons, papers, and records, to examine into the merits and qualifications of every student and professor, to observe with utmost exactness their several dispositions and behavior, by which means, duly distinguishing and adapting their talents, they might produce admirable instruments for the several offices in a state, * * * * *,[3] civil, and military, proceeding in such methods as I shall here humbly propose. And I hope the gentle reader will give some allowance to my great solicitudes in this important affair,

9. The Roman hero Marcus Curtius appeased the gods by hurling himself into an ominous crack in the earth of the Forum; Empedocles committed suicide by leaping into the crater of Mount Etna.
1. "A talent for business." Lucius Junius Brutus, like Hamlet, pretended madness to deceive his murderous uncle, Tarquin the Proud.
2. Members of Parliament.
3. Swift omits the third office, Ecclesiastical. "Instruments": useful persons.

upon account of the high esteem I have borne that honorable society, whereof I had some time the happiness to be an unworthy member.

Is any student tearing his straw in piece-meal, swearing and blaspheming, biting his grate, foaming at the mouth, and emptying his piss-pot in the spectators' faces? Let the right worshipful the commissioners of inspection give him a regiment of dragoons, and send him into Flanders among the rest. Is another eternally talking, sputtering, gaping, bawling in a sound without period or article? What wonderful talents are here mislaid! Let him be furnished immediately with a green bag and papers, and threepence in his pocket,[4] and away with him to Westminster Hall. You will find a third gravely taking the dimensions of his kennel, a person of foresight and insight, though kept quite in the dark; for why, like Moses, *ecce cornuta erat ejus facies.*[5] He walks duly in one pace, entreats your penny with due gravity and ceremony, talks much of hard times, and taxes, and the whore of Babylon, bars up the wooden window of his cell constantly at eight o'clock, dreams of fire, and shoplifters, and court-customers, and privileged places. Now, what a figure would all these acquirements amount to, if the owner were sent into the city[6] among his brethren! Behold a fourth, in much and deep conversation with himself, biting his thumbs at proper junctures, his countenance checkered with business and design, sometimes walking very fast, with his eyes nailed to a paper that he holds in his hands; a great saver of time, somewhat thick of hearing, very short of sight, but more of memory; a man ever in haste, a great hatcher and breeder of business, and excellent at the famous art of whispering nothing; a huge idolator of monosyllables and procrastination, so ready to give his word to everybody, that he never keeps it; one that has forgot the common meaning of words, but an admirable retainer of the sound; extremely subject to the looseness,[7] for his occasions are perpetually calling him away. If you approach his grate in his familiar intervals, "Sir," says he, "give me a penny, and I'll sing you a song; but give me the penny first." (Hence comes the common saying, and commoner practice, of parting with money for a song.) What a complete system of court skill is here described in every branch of it, and all utterly lost with wrong application! Accost the hole of another kennel, first stopping your nose, you will behold a surly, gloomy, nasty, slovenly mortal, raking in his own dung, and dabbling in his urine. The best part of his diet is the reversion of his own ordure, which expiring into steams, whirls

4. "A lawyers coach-hire" [Swift's note] from the Inns of Court to Westminster. Most lawyers carried green bags.

5. "Cornutus is either horned or shining, and by this term, Moses is described in the vulgar Latin of the Bible" [Swift's note]. Swift puns on the Latin phrase ("Behold his face was shining") by suggesting someone kept in the dark through being "horned," i. e., a cuckold.

6. The commercial center of London.

7. Diarrhea.

perpetually about, and at last re-infunds. His complexion is of a dirty yellow, with a thin scattered beard, exactly agreeable to that of his diet upon its first declination, like other insects, who having their birth and education in an excrement, from thence borrow their color and their smell. The student of this apartment is very sparing of his words, but somewhat over-liberal of his breath; he holds his hand out ready to receive your penny, and immediately upon receipt withdraws to his former occupations. Now, is it not amazing to think, the society of Warwick-lane[8] should have no more concern for the recovery of so useful a member, who, if one may judge from these appearances, would become the greatest ornament to that illustrious body? Another student struts up fiercely to your teeth, puffing with his lips, half squeezing out his eyes, and very graciously holds you out his hand to kiss. The keeper desires you not to be afraid of this professor, for he will do you no hurt; to him alone is allowed the liberty of the antechamber, and the orator of the place gives you to understand, that this solemn person is a tailor run mad with pride. This considerable student is adorned with many other qualities, upon which at present I shall not farther enlarge.——*Hark in your ear*[9]——I am strangely mistaken, if all his address, his motions, and his airs, would not then be very natural, and in their proper element.

I shall not descend so minutely, as to insist upon the vast number of beaux, fiddlers, poets, and politicians, that the world might recover by such a reformation; but what is more material, besides the clear gain redounding to the commonwealth, by so large an acquisition of persons to employ, whose talents and acquirements, if I may be so bold as to affirm it, are now buried, or at least misapplied; it would be a mighty advantage accruing to the public from this inquiry, that all these would very much excel, and arrive at great perfection in their several kinds; which, I think, is manifest from what I have already shown, and shall enforce by this one plain instance: that even I myself, the author of these momentous truths, am a person, whose imaginations are hard-mouthed,[1] and exceedingly disposed to run away with his reason, which I have observed from long experience to be a very light rider, and easily shook off; upon which account, my friends will never trust me alone, without a solemn promise to vent my speculations in this, or the like manner, for the universal benefit of human kind; which perhaps the gentle, courteous, and candid reader, brimful of that modern charity and tenderness usually annexed to his office, will be very hardly persuaded to believe.

1704

8. Royal College of Physicians.
9. "I cannot conjecture what the author means here, or how this chasm could be filled, though it is capable of more than one interpretation" [Swift's note].
1. (Of a horse) apt to reject control by the bit.

AN ARGUMENT TO PROVE THAT THE

Abolishing of Christianity in England

MAY, AS THINGS NOW STAND, BE ATTENDED WITH SOME INCONVENIENCES, AND PERHAPS NOT PRODUCE THOSE MANY GOOD EFFECTS PROPOSED THEREBY.[1]

I am very sensible what a weakness and presumption it is, to reason against the general humor and disposition of the world. I remember it was with great justice, and a due regard to the freedom both of the public and the press, forbidden upon several penalties to write, or discourse, or lay wagers against the Union,[2] even before it was confirmed by Parliament, because that was looked upon as a design to oppose the current of the people, which, besides the folly of it, is a manifest breach of the fundamental law that makes this majority of opinion the voice of God. In like manner, and for the very same reasons, it may perhaps be neither safe nor prudent to argue against the abolishing of Christianity at a juncture when all parties appear so unanimously determined upon the point, as we cannot but allow from their actions, their discourses, and their writings. However, I know not how, whether from the affectation of singularity, or the perverseness of human nature, but so it unhappily falls out that I cannot be entirely of this opinion. Nay, though I were sure an order were issued for my immediate prosecution by the attorney-general, I should still confess that in the present posture of our affairs at home or abroad, I do not yet see the absolute necessity of extirpating the Christian religion from among us.

This perhaps may appear too great a paradox even for our wise and paradoxical age to endure: therefore I shall handle it with all tenderness, and with the utmost deference to that great and profound majority which is of another sentiment.

And yet the curious may please to observe how much the genius of a nation is liable to alter in half an age: I have heard it affirmed for certain by some very old people that the contrary opin-

1. The Test Act of 1673 required all holders of public office to take the sacrament of the Lord's Supper according to the usage of the Church of England; it was directed against Dissenters and Roman Catholics. In 1708 the Whigs (with whom Swift was then allied) were seeking to repeal the Test in Ireland and eventually in England, in an effort to consolidate the support of the Dissenters. Swift believed that repeal would do great harm to the Established Church, and as a good Anglican priest he opposed it with this essay.

Swift's technique is to assume blandly that to argue against the Test Act is to argue against Christianity and the Church, and he constructs his essay accordingly. The basic satiric principle is therefore that of the *reductio ad absurdum,* but this device is surrounded by a host of other ironies.

2. The union of Scotland and England under one crown in 1707.

ion was even in their memories as much in vogue as the other is now; and that a project for the abolishing of Christianity would then have appeared as singular, and been thought as absurd, as it would be at this time to write or discourse in its defense.

Therefore I freely own that all appearances are against me. The system of the Gospel, after the fate of other systems, is generally antiquated and exploded; and the mass or body of the common people, among whom it seems to have had its latest credit, are now grown as much ashamed of it as their betters; opinions, like fashions, always descending from those of quality to the middle sort, and thence to the vulgar, where at length they are dropped and vanish.

But here I would not be mistaken, and must therefore be so bold as to borrow a distinction from the writers on the other side, when they make a difference between nominal and real Trinitarians. I hope no reader imagines me so weak to stand up in the defense of real Christianity, such as used in primitive times (if we may believe the authors of those ages) to have an influence upon men's belief and actions: to offer at the restoring of that would indeed be a wild project; it would be to dig up foundations; to destroy at one blow all the wit, and half the learning of the kingdom; to break the entire frame and constitution of things; to ruin trade, extinguish arts and sciences with the professors of them; in short, to turn our courts, exchanges, and shops into deserts; and would be full as absurd as the proposal of Horace,[3] where he advises the Romans all in a body to leave their city and seek a new seat in some remote part of the world, by way of cure for the corruption of their manners.

Therefore I think this caution was in itself altogether unnecessary (which I have inserted only to prevent all possibility of caviling), since every candid reader will easily understand my discourse to be intended only in defense of nominal Christianity, the other having been for some time wholly laid aside by general consent as utterly inconsistent with all other present schemes of wealth and power.

But why we should therefore cast off the name and title of Christians, although the general opinion and resolution be so violent for it, I confess I cannot (with submission) apprehend the consequence necessary. However, since the undertakers propose such wonderful advantages to the nation by this project, and advance many plausible objections against the system of Christianity, I shall briefly consider the strength of both, fairly allow them their greatest weight, and offer such answers as I think most reasonable. After which I will beg leave to show what inconveniences may possibly happen by such an innovation, in the present posture of our affairs.

3. *Epode* xvi.

First, one great advantage proposed by the abolishing of Christianity is that it would very much enlarge and establish liberty of conscience, that great bulwark of our nation, and of the protestant religion, which is still too much limited by priestcraft, notwithstanding all the good intentions of the legislature, as we have lately found by a severe instance. For it is confidently reported that two young gentlemen of real hopes, bright wit, and profound judgment, who upon a thorough examination of causes and effects, and by the mere force of natural abilities, without the least tincture of learning, having made a discovery that there was no God, and generously communicating their thoughts for the good of the public, were some time ago, by an unparalleled severity, and upon I know not what obsolete law, broke only for blasphemy. And as it hath been wisely observed, if persecution once begins, no man alive knows how far it may reach, or where it will end.

In answer to all which, with deference to wiser judgments, I think this rather shows the necessity of a nominal religion among us. Great wits love to be free with the highest objects; and if they cannot be allowed a God to revile or renounce, they will speak evil of dignities, abuse the government, and reflect upon the ministry; which I am sure few will deny to be of much more pernicious consequence, according to the saying of Tiberius, *Deorum offensa diis curae.*[4] As to the particular fact related, I think it is not fair to argue from one instance; perhaps another cannot be produced; yet (to the comfort of all those who may be apprehensive of persecution) blasphemy we know is freely spoken a million of times in every coffeehouse and tavern, or wherever else good company meet. It must be allowed indeed, that to break an English freeborn officer only for blasphemy, was, to speak the gentlest of such an action, a very high strain of absolute power. Little can be said in excuse for the general; perhaps he was afraid it might give offense to the allies[5] among whom, for aught we know, it may be the custom of the country to believe a God. But if he argued, as some have done, upon a mistaken principle, that an officer who is guilty of speaking blasphemy may some time or other proceed so far as to raise a mutiny, the consequence is by no means to be admitted: for, surely the commander of an English army is likely to be but ill obeyed whose soldiers fear and reverence him as little as they do a deity.

It is further objected against the gospel system that it obliges men to the belief of things too difficult for freethinkers, and such who have shaken off the prejudices that usually cling to a confined

4. "Offenses against the gods are the concern of the gods" (Tacitus, *Annals* I.lxxiii).

5. England's principal allies against France in the War of the Spanish Succession were Holland, Austria, Prussia, Portugal, and Savoy.

education. To which I answer that men should be cautious how they raise objections which reflect upon the wisdom of the nation. Is not everybody freely allowed to believe whatever he pleases, and to publish his belief to the world whenever he thinks fit, especially if it serves to strengthen the party which is in the right? Would any indifferent foreigner who should read the trumpery lately written by Asgil, Tindal, Toland, Coward,[6] and forty more, imagine the Gospel to be our rule of faith, and confirmed by parliaments? Does any man either believe, or say he believes, or desire to have it thought that he says he believes one syllable of the matter? And is any man worse received upon that score, or does he find his want of nominal faith a disadvantage to him in the pursuit of any civil or military employment? What if there be an old dormant statute or two against him? Are they not now obsolete to a degree that Empson and Dudley [7] themselves, if they were now alive, would find it impossible to put them in execution?

It is likewise urged that there are by computation in this kingdom above ten thousand parsons whose revenues, added to those of my lords the bishops, would suffice to maintain at least two hundred young gentlemen of wit and pleasure, and freethinking enemies to priestcraft, narrow principles, pedantry, and prejudices; who might be an ornament to the court and town. And then again, so great a number of able (-bodied) divines might be a recruit to our fleet and armies. This indeed appears to be a consideration of some weight; but then, on the other side, several things deserve to be considered likewise: as, first, whether it may not be thought necessary that in certain tracts of country, like what we call parishes, there shall be one man at least of abilities to read and write. Then it seems a wrong computation that the revenues of the Church throughout this island would be large enough to maintain two hundred young gentlemen, or even half that number, after the present refined way of living; that is, to allow each of them such a rent [8] as, in the modern form of speech, would make them easy. But still there is in this project a greater mischief behind; and we ought to beware of the woman's folly who killed the hen that every morning laid her a golden egg. For, pray, what would become of the race of men in the next age if we had nothing to trust to beside the scrofulous, consumptive productions, furnished by our men of wit and pleasure, when, having squandered away their vigor, health, and estates, they are forced by some disagreeable marriage to piece up their broken fortunes, and entail rottenness and politeness on their posterity? Now here are ten thousand persons reduced by the wise

6. Deistic writers.
7. Two corrupt ministers of Henry VII, notorious for reviving obsolete statutes in subservience to that king's greed.
8. Income.

regulations of Henry the Eighth to the necessity of a low diet and moderate exercise,[9] who are the only great restorers of our breed, without which the nation would in an age or two become one great hospital.

Another advantage proposed by the abolishing of Christianity is the clear gain of one day in seven, which is now entirely lost, and consequently the kingdom one-seventh less considerable in trade, business, and pleasure; besides the loss to the public of so many stately structures now in the hands of the clergy, which might be converted into playhouses, exchanges, markethouses, common dormitories, and other public edifices.

I hope I shall be forgiven a hard word, if I call this a perfect cavil. I readily own there hath been an old custom, time out of mind, for people to assemble in the churches every Sunday, and that shops are still frequently shut, in order, as it is conceived, to preserve the memory of that ancient practice; but how this can prove a hindrance to business or pleasure is hard to imagine. What if the men of pleasure are forced, one day in the week, to game at home instead of the chocolatehouse? Are not the taverns and coffeehouses open? Can there be a more convenient season for taking a dose of physic? Are fewer claps got upon Sundays than other days? Is not that the chief day for traders to sum up the accounts of the week and for lawyers to prepare their briefs? But I would fain know how it can be pretended that the churches are misapplied? Where are more appointments and rendezvouses of gallantry? Where more care to appear in the foremost box with greater advantage of dress? Where more meetings for business? Where more bargains driven of all sorts? And where so many conveniences or incitements to sleep?

There is one advantage greater than any of the foregoing proposed by the abolishing of Christianity: that it will utterly extinguish parties among us by removing those factious distinctions of High and Low Church, of Whig and Tory, Presbyterian and Church of England, which are now so many mutual clogs upon public proceedings, and dispose men to prefer the gratifying themselves, or depressing their adversaries, before the most important interest of the state.

I confess, if it were certain that so great an advantage would redound to the nation by this expedient, I would submit and be silent: but will any man say that if the words *whoring, drinking, cheating, lying, stealing,* were by act of Parliament ejected out of the English tongue and dictionaries, we should all awake next morn-

9. Swift refers ironically to Henry VIII's expropriation of church lands at the time of the Reformation. Instead of giving them to the church for the support of the clergy, as Swift thought he should have done, he bestowed them on laymen, thus impoverishing the lower clergy, who were deprived of the tithes that would otherwise have been their due.

ing chaste and temperate, honest and just, and lovers of truth? Is this a fair consequence? Or, if the physicians would forbid us to pronounce the words *pox, gout, rheumatism,* and *stone,* would that expedient serve like so many talismans to destroy the diseases themselves? Are party and faction rooted in men's hearts no deeper than phrases borrowed from religion, or founded upon no firmer principles? And is our language so poor that we cannot find other terms to express them? Are *envy, pride, avarice,* and *ambition* such ill nomenclators that they cannot furnish appellations for their owners? Will not *heydukes* and *mamalukes, mandarins* and *patshaws,* or any other words formed at pleasure, serve to distinguish those who are in the ministry from others who would be in it if they could? What, for instance, is easier than to vary the form of speech, and instead of the *church,* make it a question in politics whether the Monument [1] be in danger? Because religion was nearest at hand to furnish a few convenient phrases, is our invention so barren we can find no others? Suppose, for argument sake, that the Tories favored Margarita, the Whigs Mrs. Tofts, and the Trimmers Valentini,[2] would not *Margaritians, Toftians,* and *Valentinians* be very tolerable marks of distinction? The *Prasini* and *Veniti,*[3] two most virulent factions in Italy, began (if I remember right) by a distinction of colors in ribbons, which we might do with as good a grace about the dignity of the blue and the green, and would serve as properly to divide the court, the Parliament, and the kingdom between them, as any terms of art whatsoever borrowed from religion. Therefore I think there is little force in this objection against Christianity, or prospect of so great an advantage as is proposed in the abolishing of it.

'Tis again objected as a very absurd, ridiculous custom that a set of men should be suffered, much less employed and hired, to bawl one day in seven against the lawfulness of those methods most in use toward the pursuit of greatness, riches, and pleasure, which are the constant practice of all men alive on the other six. But this objection is, I think, a little unworthy so refined an age as ours. Let us argue this matter calmly; I appeal to the breast of any polite freethinker whether in the pursuit of gratifying a predominant passion he hath not always felt a wonderful incitement, by reflecting it was a thing forbidden; and therefore we see, in order to cultivate this taste, the wisdom of the nation hath taken special care that the ladies should be furnished with prohibited silks and the men with prohibited wine. And indeed, it were to be wished that some other prohibitions were promoted in order to improve the pleasures of the town; which, for want of such expedients begin already, as I am

1. The column that commemorates the great fire of London, 1666.
2. Singers in the popular Italian opera.
3. Rival factions in the Roman chariot races, violently supported by the populace.

told, to flag and grow languid, giving way daily to cruel inroads from the spleen.[4]

'Tis likewise proposed as a great advantage to the public that if we once discard the system of the Gospel, all religion will of course be banished for ever; and consequently, along with it, those grievous prejudices of education, which under the names of *virtue, conscience, honor, justice*, and the like, are so apt to disturb the peace of human minds, and the notions whereof are so hard to be eradicated by right reason or freethinking, sometimes during the whole course of our lives.

Here first I observe how difficult it is to get rid of a phrase which the world is once grown fond of, though the occasion that first produced it be entirely taken away. For several years past, if a man had but an ill-favored nose, the deep thinkers of the age would some way or other contrive to impute the cause to the prejudice of his education. From this fountain were said to be derived all our foolish notions of justice, piety, love of our country, all our opinions of God, or a future state, heaven, hell, and the like: and there might formerly perhaps have been some pretense for this charge. But so effectual care hath been since taken to remove those prejudices by an entire change in the methods of education that (with honor I mention it to our polite innovators) the young gentlemen who are now on the scene, seem to have not the least tincture of those infusions, or string of those weeds; and, by consequence, the reason for abolishing nominal Christianity upon that pretext is wholly ceased.

For the rest, it may perhaps admit a controversy whether the banishing of all notions of religion whatsoever would be convenient for the vulgar. Not that I am in the least of opinion with those who hold religion to have been the invention of politicians to keep the lower part of the world in awe by the fear of invisible powers; unless mankind were then very different from what it is now: for I look upon the mass or body of our people here in England to be as freethinkers, that is to say, as staunch unbelievers, as any of the highest rank. But I conceive some scattered notions about a superior power to be of singular use for the common people, as furnishing excellent materials to keep children quiet when they grow peevish, and providing topics of amusement in a tedious winter night.

Lastly, it is proposed as a singular advantage that the abolishing of Christianity will very much contribute to the uniting of Protestants, by enlarging the terms of communion so as to take in all sorts of Dissenters, who are now shut out of the pale upon account of a few ceremonies which all sides confess to be things indifferent;

4. Melancholy; often a real affliction, but as often affected as a fashionable ailment.

that this alone will effectually answer the great ends of a scheme for comprehension, by opening a large noble gate, at which all bodies may enter: whereas the chaffering with Dissenters, and dodging about this or t'other ceremony, is but like opening a few wickets[5] and leaving them at jar, by which no more than one can get in at a time, and that, not without stooping, and sideling, and squeezing his body.

To all this I answer that there is one darling inclination of mankind, which usually affects to be a retainer to religion, though she be neither its parent, its godmother, or its friend; I mean the spirit of opposition, that lived long before Christianity, and can easily subsist without it. Let us, for instance, examine wherein the opposition of sectaries[6] among us consists; we shall find Christianity to have no share in it at all. Does the Gospel any where prescribe a starched, squeezed countenance, a stiff, formal gait, a singularity of manners and habit, or any affected modes of speech different from the reasonable part of mankind? Yet, if Christianity did not lend its name to stand in the gap, and to employ or divert these humors, they must of necessity be spent in contraventions to the laws of the land, and disturbance of the public peace. There is a portion of enthusiasm assigned to every nation, which, if it hath not proper objects to work on, will burst out, and set all in a flame. If the quiet of state can be bought by only flinging men a few ceremonies to devour, it is a purchase no wise man would refuse. Let the mastiffs amuse themselves about a sheepskin stuffed with hay, provided it will keep them from worrying the flock. The institution of convents abroad seems in one point a strain of great wisdom, there being few irregularities in human passions that may not have recourse to vent themselves in some of those orders, which are so many retreats for the speculative, the melancholy, the proud, the silent, the politic and the morose, to spend themselves, and evaporate the noxious particles; for each of whom we in this island are forced to provide a several sect of religion, to keep them quiet. And whenever Christianity shall be abolished, the legislature must find some other expedient to employ and entertain them. For what imports it how large a gate you open if there will be always left a number who place a pride and merit in refusing to enter?

Having thus considered the most important objections against Christianity and the chief advantages proposed by the abolishing thereof, I shall now with equal deference and submission to wiser judgments as before, proceed to mention a few inconveniences that may happen if the Gospel should be repealed; which perhaps the projectors may not have sufficiently considered.

And first, I am very sensible how much the gentlemen of wit and

5. Small gates.

6. Adherents of one of the dissenting sects.

pleasure are apt to murmur, and be choked at the sight of so many daggled-tail parsons who happen to fall in their way, and offend their eyes. But at the same time, these wise reformers do not consider what an advantage and felicity it is for great wits to be always provided with objects of scorn and contempt, in order to exercise and improve their talents, and divert their spleen from falling on each other or on themselves; especially when all this may be done without the least imaginable danger to their persons.

And to urge another argument of a parallel nature: if Christianity were once abolished, how could the freethinkers, the strong reasoners, and the men of profound learning, be able to find another subject so calculated in all points whereon to display their abilities? What wonderful productions of wit should we be deprived of from those whose genius by continual practice hath been wholly turned upon raillery and invectives against religion, and would therefore never be able to shine or distinguish themselves upon any other subject! We are daily complaining of the great decline of wit among us, and would we take away the greatest, perhaps the only, topic we have left? Who would ever have suspected Asgil for a wit, or Toland for a philosopher, if the inexhaustible stock of Christianity had not been at hand to provide them with materials? What other subject, through all art or nature, could have produced Tindal for a profound author, or furnished him with readers? It is the wise choice of the subject that alone adorns and distinguishes the writer. For had a hundred such pens as these been employed on the side of religion, they would have immediately sunk into silence and oblivion.

Nor do I think it wholly groundless, or my fears altogether imaginary, that the abolishing of Christianity may perhaps bring the Church in danger, or at least put the senate to the trouble of another securing vote. I desire I may not be mistaken; I am far from presuming to affirm or think that the Church is in danger at present, or as things now stand; but we know not how soon it may be so when the Christian religion is repealed. As plausible as this project seems, there may a dangerous design lurk under it. Nothing can be more notorious than that the atheists, deists, Socinians,[7] Antitrinitarians, and other subdivisions of freethinkers are persons of little zeal for the present ecclesiastical establishment: their declared opinion is for repealing the Sacramental Test; they are very indifferent with regard to ceremonies; nor do they hold the *jus divinum* of Episcopacy.[8] Therefore this may be intended as one politic step toward altering the constitution of the Church estab-

7. The Socinians denied the divinity of Jesus.

8. The divine authority of Anglican bishops, derived from apostolic succession.

lished, and setting up Presbytery[9] in the stead, which I leave to be further considered by those at the helm.

In the last place, I think nothing can be more plain than that by this expedient, we shall run into the evil we chiefly pretend to avoid; and that the abolishment of the Christian religion will be the readiest course we can take to introduce popery. And I am the more inclined to this opinion because we know it has been the constant practice of the Jesuits to send over emissaries with instructions to personate themselves members of the several prevailing sects among us. So it is recorded that they have at sundry times appeared in the guise of Presbyterians, Anabaptists, Independents, and Quakers, according as any of these were most in credit; so, since the fashion hath been taken up of exploding religion, the popish missionaries have not been wanting to mix with the freethinkers; among whom, Toland, the great oracle of the Antichristians, is an Irish priest, the son of an Irish priest; and the most learned and ingenious author of a book called *The Rights of the Christian Church*, was in a proper juncture reconciled to the Romish faith, whose true son, as appears by an hundred passages in his treatise, he still continues. Perhaps I could add some others to the number; but the fact is beyond dispute, and the reasoning they proceed by is right: for, supposing Christianity to be extinguished, the people will never be at ease till they find out some other method of worship; which will as infallibly produce superstition as this will end in popery.

And therefore, if notwithstanding all I have said, it still be thought necessary to have a bill brought in for repealing Christianity, I would humbly offer an amendment; that instead of the word *Christianity* may be put *religion* in general; which I conceive will much better answer all the good ends proposed by the projectors of it. For, as long as we leave in being a God and his providence, with all the necessary consequences which curious and inquisitive men will be apt to draw from such premises, we do not strike at the root of the evil, though we should ever so effectually annihilate the present scheme of the Gospel. For of what use is freedom of thought, if it will not produce freedom of action, which is the sole end, how remote soever in appearance, of all objections against Christianity? And, therefore, the freethinkers consider it as a sort of edifice wherein all the parts have such a mutual dependence on each other that if you happen to pull out one single nail, the whole fabric must fall to the ground. This was happily expressed by him who had heard of a text brought for proof of the Trinity, which in an ancient manuscript was differently read; he thereupon immedi-

9. The Presbyterians opposed episcopacy and set up a democratic form of church government.

ately took the hint, and by a sudden deduction of a long *sorites*, [1] most logically concluded, "Why, if it be as you say, I may safely whore and drink on, and defy the parson." From which, and many the like instances easy to be produced, I think nothing can be more manifest than that the quarrel is not against any particular points of hard digestion in the Christian system, but against religion in general; which, by laying restraints on human nature, is supposed the great enemy to the freedom of thought and action.

Upon the whole, if it shall still be thought for the benefit of Church and State that Christianity be abolished, I conceive, however, it may be more convenient to defer the execution to a time of peace, and not venture in this conjuncture to disoblige our allies, who, as it falls out, are all Christians; and many of them, by the prejudices of their education, so bigoted as to place a sort of pride in the appellation. If upon being rejected by them, we are to trust to an alliance with the Turk, we shall find ourselves much deceived: for, as he is too remote, and generally engaged in war with the Persian emperor, so his people would be more scandalized at our infidelity than our Christian neighbors. Because the Turks are not only strict observers of religious worship, but what is worse, believe a God; which is more than is required of us even while we preserve the name of Christians.

To conclude: whatever some may think of the great advantages to trade by this favorite scheme, I do very much apprehend that in six months time after the act is passed for the extirpation of the Gospel, the Bank and East-India Stock may fall at least one per cent. And since that is fifty times more than ever the wisdom of our age thought fit to venture for the preservation of Christianity, there is no reason we should be at so great a loss merely for the sake of destroying it.

1708 1711

1. "An argument when one proposition is accumulated on another" (Johnson's *Dictionary*).

Gulliver's Travels

Gulliver's Travels is Swift's most universal satire. Although it is full of allusions to recent and contemporary historical events, it is as valid today as it was in 1726, for its objects are man's moral nature and the defective political, economic, and social institutions which human imperfections call into being. Swift adopts an ancient satirical device: the imaginary voyage. Lemuel Gulliver, the narrator, is a ship's surgeon, a reasonably well-educated man, kindly, resourceful, cheerful, inquiring, patriotic, truthful, and rather unimaginative. He is, in short, a reasonably decent example of humanity, with whom we identify ourselves readily enough. He undertakes four voyages, all of which end disastrously among "several remote nations of the world." In the first, Gulliver is shipwrecked in the empire of Lilliput, where he finds himself a giant among a diminutive people, charmed by their miniature city and amused by their toylike prettiness. But in the end they prove to be treacherous, malicious, ambitious, vengeful, and cruel. As we read we grow disenchanted with the inhabitants of this fanciful kingdom, and then gradually we begin to recognize our likeness to them, especially in the disproportion between our natural pettiness and our boundless and destructive passions. In the second voyage, Gulliver is abandoned by his shipmates in Brobdingnag, a land of giants, creatures ten times as large as Europeans. Naturally enough, he assumes that such monsters must be brutes, but the reverse proves to be the case. Brobdingnag is something of a utopia, governed by a humane and enlightened prince who is the embodiment of moral and political wisdom. In the long interview in which Gulliver pridefully enlarges on the glories of England and her political institutions, the King reduces him to resentful silence by asking questions which reveal the difference between what is and what ought to be in human, especially British, institutions. In Brobdingnag, Gulliver finds himself a Lilliputian, his pride humbled by his helpless state and his human vanity diminished by the realization that his body must have seemed as disgusting to the Lilliputians as do the bodies of the Brobdingnagians to him.

In the third voyage, to Laputa, Swift is chiefly concerned with attacking extremes of theoretical and speculative reasoning, whether in science, politics, or economics. Much of this voyage is an allegory of political life under the administration of the Whig minister, Sir Robert Walpole. The final voyage sets Gulliver between a race of horses, Houyhnhnms (pronounced *Hwin-ims*), who live entirely by reason except for a few well-controlled and muted social affections, and their slaves, the Yahoos, whose bodies are obscene caricatures of the human body, and who have no glimmer of reason, but are mere creatures of appetite and passion.

When *Gulliver's Travels* first appeared, everyone read it—children for the story, politicians for the satire of current affairs—and ever since it has retained a hold on readers of every kind. Almost unique in world literature, it is simple enough for a child, complex enough to carry an adult beyond his depth. Swift's art works on many levels. First of all, there is the sheer playfulness of the narrative. Through Gulliver's eyes, we gaze on marvel after marvel: a tiny girl who threads an invisible needle with invisible silk, or a white mare who threads a needle between pastern and hoof. The travels, like a fairy story, transport us to imaginary worlds that function with a perfect, fantastic logic different from our own; Swift exercises our sense of vision. But beyond that, he exercises our perceptions of meaning. In *Gulliver's Travels*, things are seldom what they seem; irony, probing or corrosive, underlies almost every word. During the last chapter, Gulliver insists that the example of the Houyhnhnms has made him incapable of telling a lie—but the oath he swears is quoted from Sinon, whose lies to the Trojans persuaded them to accept the Trojan *horse*. Swift trains us to read alertly, to look beneath the surface. Yet on its deepest level, the book does not offer final meanings, but a question: what sort of thing is man? Voyaging through imaginary worlds, we try to find ourselves. Are we prideful insects, or lords of creation? brutes, or reasonable beings? In the last voyage, Swift pushes such questions, and Gulliver himself, almost beyond endurance; hating his own humanity, Gulliver forgets who he is. For the reader, however, the outcome cannot be so clear. Swift does not set out to satisfy our minds, but to vex and unsettle them. And he leaves us at the moment when the mixed face of humanity—the pettiness of the Lilliputians, the savagery of the Yahoos, the innocence of Gulliver himself—begins to look strangely familiar, like our own faces in a mirror.

From Gulliver's Travels[1]

A Letter from Captain Gulliver to His Cousin Sympson

I hope you will be ready to own publicly, whenever you shall be called to it, that by your great and frequent urgency you prevailed on me to publish a very loose and uncorrect account of my travels; with direction to hire some young gentlemen of either University to put them in order, and correct the style, as my Cousin Dampier[2] did by my advice, in his book called *A Voyage round the World*. But I do not remember I gave you power to consent that anything should be omitted, and much less that anything should be inserted: therefore, as to the latter, I do here renounce everything of that kind; particularly a paragraph about her Majesty the late Queen Anne, of most pious and glorious memory; although I did reverence and esteem her more than any of human species. But you, or your interpolator, ought to have considered that as it was not my inclination, so was it not decent to praise any animal of our composition before my master Houyhnhnm; and besides, the fact was altogether false; for to my knowledge, being in England during some part of her Majesty's reign, she did govern by a chief Minister; nay, even by two successively; the first whereof was the Lord of Godolphin, and the second the Lord of Oxford; so that you have made me *say the thing that was not*. Likewise, in the account of the Academy of Projectors, and several passages of my discourse to my master Houyhnhnm, you have either omitted some material circumstances, or minced or changed them in such a manner, that I do hardly know mine own work. When I formerly hinted to you some-

1. Swift's full title for this work was *Travels into Several Remote Nations of the World. In Four Parts. By Lemuel Gulliver, First a Surgeon, and then a Captain of several Ships*. In the first edition (1726), either the bookseller or Swift's friends Charles Ford, Pope, and others, who were concerned in getting the book anonymously into print, altered and omitted so much of the original manuscript (because of its dangerous political implications) that Swift was seriously annoyed. When, in 1735, the Dublin bookseller George Faulkner brought out an edition of Swift's works, the Dean seems to have taken pains, surreptitiously, to see that a more authentic version of the work was published. This text is the basis of modern editions.

In this letter, first published in 1735, Swift complains, among other matters, of the alterations in his original text made by the publisher, Benjamin Motte, in the interest of what he considered political discretion.

2. William Dampier (1652–1715), the explorer, whose account of his circumnavigation of the globe Swift had read.

thing of this in a letter, you were pleased to answer that you were afraid of giving offense; that people in power were very watchful over the press; and apt not only to interpret, but to punish everything which looked like an *innuendo* (as I think you called it). But pray, how could that which I spoke so many years ago, and at above five thousand leagues distance, in another reign, be applied to any of the Yahoos, who now are said to govern the herd; especially, at a time when I little thought on or feared the unhappiness of living under them. Have not I the most reason to complain, when I see these very Yahoos carried by Houyhnhnms in a vehicle, as if these were brutes, and those the rational creatures? And, indeed, to avoid so monstrous and detestable a sight was one principal motive of my retirement hither.[3]

Thus much I thought proper to tell you in relation to yourself, and to the trust I reposed in you.

I do in the next place complain of my own great want of judgment, in being prevailed upon by the intreaties and false reasonings of you and some others, very much against mine own opinion, to suffer my travels to be published. Pray bring to your mind how often I desired you to consider, when you insisted on the motive of public good, that the Yahoos were a species of animals utterly incapable of amendment by precepts or examples; and so it hath proved; for instead of seeing a full stop put to all abuses and corruptions, at least in this little island, as I had reason to expect, behold, after above six months warning. I cannot learn that my book hath produced one single effect according to mine intentions; I desired you would let me know by a letter, when party and faction were extinguished; judges learned and upright; pleaders honest and modest, with some tincture of common sense; and Smithfield[4] blazing with pyramids of law books; the young nobility's education entirely changed; the physicians banished; the female Yahoos abounding in virtue, honor, truth, and good sense; courts and levees of great ministers thoroughly weeded and swept; wit, merit, and learning rewarded; all disgracers of the press in prose and verse, condemned to eat nothing but their own cotton,[5] and quench their thirst with their own ink. These, and a thousand other reformations, I firmly counted upon by your encouragement; as indeed they were plainly deducible from the precepts delivered in my book. And, it must be owned that seven months were a sufficient time to correct every vice and folly to which Yahoos are subject; if their natures had been capable of the least disposition to virtue or wisdom; yet so far have you been from answering mine expectation in any of your letters, that on the contrary, you are loading our carrier every week with libels, and keys, and reflections, and memoirs, and second

3. To Nottinghamshire.
4. A part of London containing many bookshops.
5. Presumably their paper.

parts; wherein I see myself accused of reflecting upon great statesfolk; of degrading human nature (for so they have still the confidence to style it) and of abusing the female sex. I find likewise, that the writers of those bundles are not agreed among themselves; for some of them will not allow me to be author of mine own travels; and others make me author of books to which I am wholly a stranger.

I find likewise that your printer hath been so careless as to confound the times, and mistake the dates of my several voyages and returns; neither assigning the true year, or the true month, or day of the month; and I hear the original manuscript is all destroyed, since the publication of my book. Neither have I any copy left; however, I have sent you some corrections, which you may insert, if ever there should be a second edition; and yet I cannot stand to them, but shall leave that matter to my judicious and candid readers, to adjust it as they please.

I hear some of our sea Yahoos find fault with my sea language, as not proper in many parts, nor now in use. I cannot help it. In my first voyages, while I was young, I was instructed by the oldest mariners, and learned to speak as they did. But I have since found that the sea Yahoos are apt, like the land ones, to become new fangled in their words; which the latter change every year; insomuch, as I remember upon each return to mine own country, their old dialect was so altered, that I could hardly understand the new. And I observe, when any Yahoo comes from London out of curiosity to visit me at mine own house, we neither of us are able to deliver our conceptions in a manner intelligible to the other.[6]

If the censure of Yahoos could any way affect me, I should have great reason to complain that some of them are so bold as to think my book of travels a mere fiction out of mine own brain; and have gone so far as to drop hints that the Houyhnhnms, and Yahoos have no more existence than the inhabitants of Utopia.

Indeed I must confess that as to the people of Lilliput, Brobdingrag (for so the word should have been spelled, and not erroneously Brobdingnag) and Laputa, I have never yet heard of any Yahoo so presumptuous as to dispute their being, or the facts I have related concerning them; because the truth immediately strikes every reader with conviction. And, is there less probability in my account of the Houyhnhnms or Yahoos, when it is manifest as to the latter, there are so many thousands even in this city, who only differ from their brother brutes in Houyhnhnmland, because they use a sort of a jabber, and do not go naked. I wrote for their amendment, and not their approbation. The united praise of the whole race would be of less consequence to me, than the neighing of those two degenerate Houyhnhnms I keep in my stable; because, from

6. Swift was the inveterate enemy of slang.

these, degenerate as they are, I still improve in some virtues, without any mixture of vice.

Do these miserable animals presume to think that I am so far degenerated as to defend my veracity; Yahoo as I am, it is well known through all Houyhnhnmland, that by the instructions and example of my illustrious master, I was able in the compass of two years (although I confess with the utmost difficulty) to remove that infernal habit of lying, shuffling, deceiving, and equivocating, so deeply rooted in the very souls of all my species; especially the Europeans.

I have other complaints to make upon this vexatious occasion; but I forbear troubling myself or you any further. I must freely confess that since my last return, some corruptions of my Yahoo nature have revived in me by conversing with a few of your species, and particularly those of mine own family, by an unavoidable necessity; else I should never have attempted so absurd a project as that of reforming the Yahoo race in this kingdom; but I have now done with all such visionary schemes for ever.

1727? 1735

The Publisher to the Reader

The author of these travels, Mr. Lemuel Gulliver, is my ancient and intimate friend; there is likewise some relation between us by the mother's side. About three years ago Mr. Gulliver, growing weary of the concourse of curious people coming to him at his house in Redriff,[1] made a small purchase of land, with a convenient house, near Newark, in Nottinghamshire, his native country; where he now lives retired, yet in good esteem among his neighbors. Although Mr. Gulliver were born in Nottinghamshire, where his father dwelt, yet I have heard him say his family came from Oxfordshire; to confirm which, I have observed in the churchyard at Banbury, in that county, several tombs and monuments of the Gullivers.

Before he quitted Redriff, he left the custody of the following papers in my hands, with the liberty to dispose of them as I should think fit. I have carefully perused them three times; the style is very plain and simple; and the only fault I find is that the author, after the manner of travelers, is a little too circumstantial. There is an air of truth apparent through the whole; and indeed the author was so distinguished for his veracity, that it became a sort of proverb among his neighbors at Redriff, when anyone affirmed a thing, to say, it was as true as if Mr. Gulliver had spoke it.

1. Rotherhithe, a district in southern London, below Tower Bridge, then frequented by sailors.

By the advice of several worthy persons, to whom, with the author's permission, I communicated these papers, I now venture to send them into the world; hoping they may be, at least for some time, a better entertainment to our young noblemen, than the common scribbles of politics and party.

This volume would have been at least twice as large, if I had not made bold to strike out innumerable passages relating to the winds and tides, as well as to the variations and bearings in the several voyages; together with the minute descriptions of the management of the ship in storms, in the style of sailors; likewise the account of the longitudes and latitudes, wherein I have reason to apprehend that Mr. Gulliver may be a little dissatisfied; but I was resolved to fit the work as much as possible to the general capacity of readers. However, if my own ignorance in sea affairs shall have led me to commit some mistakes, I alone am answerable for them; and if any traveler hath a curiosity to see the whole work at large, as it came from the hand of the author, I will be ready to gratify him.

As for any further particulars relating to the author, the reader will receive satisfaction from the first pages of the book.

RICHARD SYMPSON

Part I. A Voyage to Lilliput

CHAPTER I. *The author gives some account of himself and family; his first inducements to travel. He is shipwrecked, and swims for his life; gets safe on shore in the country of Lilliput; is made a prisoner, and carried up the country.*

My father had a small estate in Nottinghamshire; I was the third of five sons. He sent me to Emanuel College in Cambridge, at fourteen years old, where I resided three years, and applied myself close to my studies: but the charge of maintaining me (although I had a very scanty allowance) being too great for a narrow fortune, I was bound apprentice to Mr. James Bates, an eminent surgeon in London, with whom I continued four years; and my father now and then sending me small sums of money, I laid them out in learning navigation, and other parts of the mathematics, useful to those who intend to travel, as I always believed it would be some time or other my fortune to do. When I left Mr. Bates, I went down to my father; where, by the assistance of him and my uncle John, and some other relations, I got forty pounds, and a promise of thirty pounds a year to maintain me at Leyden:[1] there I studied physic two years and seven months, knowing it would be useful in long voyages.

1. The University of Leyden, in Holland, a center for the study of "physic" (medicine).

Soon after my return from Leyden, I was recommended by my good master Mr. Bates, to be surgeon to the *Swallow*, Captain Abraham Pannell commander; with whom I continued three years and a half, making a voyage or two into the Levant[2] and some other parts. When I came back, I resolved to settle in London, to which Mr. Bates, my master, encouraged me; and by him I was recommended to several patients. I took part of a small house in the Old Jury; and being advised to alter my condition, I married Mrs.[3] Mary Burton, second daughter to Mr. Edmond Burton, hosier, in Newgate Street, with whom I received four hundred pounds for a portion.

But, my good master Bates dying in two years after, and I having few friends, my business began to fail; for my conscience would not suffer me to imitate the bad practice of too many among my brethren. Having therefore consulted with my wife, and some of my acquaintance, I determined to go again to sea. I was surgeon successively in two ships, and made several voyages, for six years, to the East and West Indies; by which I got some addition to my fortune. My hours of leisure I spent in reading the best authors, ancient and modern, being always provided with a good number of books; and when I was ashore, in observing the manners and dispositions of the people, as well as learning their language; wherein I had a great facility by the strength of my memory.

The last of these voyages not proving very fortunate, I grew weary of the sea, and intended to stay at home with my wife and family. I removed from the Old Jury to Fetter Lane, and from thence to Wapping, hoping to get business among the sailors; but it would not turn to account. After three years' expectation that things would mend, I accepted an advantageous offer from Captain William Prichard, master of the *Antelope*, who was making a voyage to the South Sea. We set sail from Bristol, May 4th, 1699, and our voyage at first was very prosperous.

It would not be proper, for some reasons, to trouble the reader with the particulars of our adventures in those seas: let it suffice to inform him, that in our passage from thence to the East Indies we were driven by a violent storm to the northwest of Van Diemen's Land.[4] By an observation, we found ourselves in the latitude of 30 degrees 2 minutes south. Twelve of our crew were dead by immoderate labor, and ill food, the rest were in a very weak condition. On the fifth of November, which was the beginning of summer in those parts, the weather being very hazy, the seamen spied a rock, within half a cable's length of the ship; but the wind was so strong, that we were driven directly upon it, and immediately split. Six of the

2. The eastern Mediterranean.
3. "Mrs." (pronounced "Mistress") designated any woman, married or unmarried. "Old Jury": a street (once "Old Jewry") in the City of London.
4. Tasmania.

crew, of whom I was one, having let down the boat into the sea, made a shift to get clear of the ship, and the rock. We rowed by my computation about three leagues, till we were able to work no longer, being already spent with labor while we were in the ship. We therefore trusted ourselves to the mercy of the waves; and in about half an hour the boat was overset by a sudden flurry from the north. What became of my companions in the boat, as well as of those who escaped on the rock, or were left in the vessel, I cannot tell; but conclude they were all lost. For my own part, I swam as fortune directed me, and was pushed forward by wind and tide. I often let my legs drop, and could feel no bottom; but when I was almost gone, and able to struggle no longer, I found myself within my depth; and by this time the storm was much abated. The declivity was so small, that I walked near a mile before I got to the shore, which I conjectured was about eight o'clock in the evening. I then advanced forward near half a mile, but could not discover any sign of houses or inhabitants; at least I was in so weak a condition, that I did not observe them. I was extremely tired, and with that, and the heat of the weather, and about half a pint of brandy that I drank as I left the ship, I found myself much inclined to sleep. I lay down on the grass, which was very short and soft, where I slept sounder than ever I remember to have done in my life, and as I reckoned, above nine hours; for when I awaked, it was just daylight. I attempted to rise, but was not able to stir: for as I happened to lie on my back, I found my arms and legs were strongly fastened on each side to the ground; and my hair, which was long and thick, tied down in the same manner. I likewise felt several slender ligatures across my body, from my armpits to my thighs. I could only look upwards; the sun began to grow hot, and the light offended my eyes. I heard a confused noise about me, but in the posture I lay, could see nothing except the sky. In a little time I felt something alive moving on my left leg, which advancing gently forward over my breast, came almost up to my chin; when bending my eyes downwards as much as I could, I perceived it to be a human creature not six inches high,[5] with a bow and arrow in his hands, and a quiver at his back. In the meantime, I felt at least forty more of the same kind (as I conjectured) following the first. I was in the utmost astonishment, and roared so loud, that they all ran back in a fright; and some of them, as I was afterwards told, were hurt with the falls they got by leaping from my sides upon the ground. However, they soon returned; and one of them, who ventured so far as to get a full sight of my face, lifting up his hands and eyes by way of admiration,[6] cried out in a shrill, but distinct voice, *Hekinah*

5. Lilliput is scaled, fairly consistently, at one-twelfth of Gulliver's world.

6. Wonderment.

Degul: the others repeated the same words several times, but I then knew not what they meant. I lay all this while, as the reader may believe, in great uneasiness; at length, struggling to get loose, I had the fortune to break the strings, and wrench out the pegs that fastened my left arm to the ground; for, by lifting it up to my face, I discovered the methods they had taken to bind me; and, at the same time, with a violent pull, which gave me excessive pain, I a little loosened the strings that tied down my hair on the left side; so that I was just able to turn my head about two inches. But the creatures ran off a second time, before I could seize them; whereupon there was a great shout in a very shrill accent; and after it ceased, I heard one of them cry aloud, *Tolgo phonac;* when in an instant I felt above an hundred arrows discharged on my left hand, which pricked me like so many needles; and besides they shot another flight into the air, as we do bombs in Europe, whereof many, I suppose, fell on my body (though I felt them not) and some on my face, which I immediately covered with my left hand. When this shower of arrows was over, I fell a groaning with grief and pain; and then striving again to get loose, they discharged another volley larger than the first, and some of them attempted with spears to stick me in the sides; but, by good luck, I had on me a buff jerkin,[7] which they could not pierce. I thought it the most prudent method to lie still; and my design was to continue so till night, when, my left hand being already loose, I could easily free myself: and as for the inhabitants, I had reason to believe I might be a match for the greatest armies they could bring against me, if they were all of the same size with him that I saw. But fortune disposed otherwise of me. When the people observed I was quiet, they discharged no more arrows: but by the noise increasing, I knew their numbers were greater; and about four yards from me, over-against my right ear, I heard a knocking for above an hour, like people at work; when turning my head that way, as well as the pegs and strings would permit me, I saw a stage erected about a foot and a half from the ground, capable of holding four of the inhabitants, with two or three ladders to mount it: from whence one of them, who seemed to be a person of quality, made me a long speech, whereof I understood not one syllable. But I should have mentioned, that before the principal person began his oration, he cried out three times, *Langro Dehul san*: (these words and the former were afterwards repeated and explained to me). Whereupon immediately about fifty of the inhabitants came, and cut the strings that fastened the left side of my head, which gave me the liberty of turning it to the right, and of observing the person and gesture of him who was to speak. He appeared to be of a middle age, and taller than any of

7. Leather jacket.

the other three who attended him; whereof one was a page who held up his train, and seemed to be somewhat longer than my middle finger; the other two stood one on each side to support him. He acted every part of an orator, and I could observe many periods[8] of threatenings, and others of promises, pity and kindness. I answered in a few words, but in the most submissive manner, lifting up my left hand and both my eyes to the sun, as calling him for a witness; and being almost famished with hunger, having not eaten a morsel for some hours before I left the ship, I found the demands of nature so strong upon me, that I could not forbear showing my impatience (perhaps against the strict rules of decency) by putting my finger frequently on my mouth, to signify that I wanted food. The Hurgo (for so they call a great lord, as I afterwards learned) understood me very well. He descended from the stage, and commanded that several ladders should be applied to my sides, on which above an hundred of the inhabitants mounted, and walked towards my mouth, laden with baskets full of meat, which had been provided and sent thither by the King's orders upon the first intelligence he received of me. I observed there was the flesh of several animals, but could not distinguish them by the taste. There were shoulders, legs, and loins shaped like those of mutton, and very well dressed, but smaller than the wings of a lark. I eat them by two or three at a mouthful, and took three loaves at a time, about the bigness of musket bullets. They supplied me as fast as they could, showing a thousand marks of wonder and astonishment at my bulk and appetite. I then made another sign that I wanted drink. They found by my eating that a small quantity would not suffice me; and being a most ingenious people, they slung up with great dexterity one of their largest hogsheads; then rolled it towards my hand, and beat out the top; I drank it off at a draught, which I might well do, for it hardly held half a pint, and tasted like a small wine of Burgundy, but much more delicious. They brought me a second hogshead, which I drank in the same manner, and made signs for more, but they had none to give me. When I had performed these wonders, they shouted for joy, and danced upon my breast, repeating several times as they did at first, *Hekinah Degul*. They made me a sign that I should throw down the two hogsheads, but first warned the people below to stand out of the way, crying aloud, *Borach Mivola*, and when they saw the vessels in the air, there was an universal shout of *Hekinah Degul*. I confess I was often tempted, while they were passing backwards and forwards on my body, to seize forty or fifty of the first that came in my reach, and dash them against the ground. But the remembrance of what I had felt, which probably might not be the worst they could do; and the promise of

8. In rhetoric, complete, well-constructed sentences.

honor I made them, for so I interpreted my submissive behavior, soon drove out those imaginations. Besides, I now considered myself as bound by the laws of hospitality to a people who had treated me with so much expense and magnificence. However, in my thoughts I could not sufficiently wonder at the intrepidity of these diminutive mortals, who durst venture to mount and walk on my body, while one of my hands was at liberty, without trembling at the very sight of so prodigious a creature as I must appear to them. After some time, when they observed that I made no more demands for meat, there appeared before me a person of high rank from his Imperial Majesty. His Excellency, having mounted on the small of my right leg, advanced forwards up to my face, with about a dozen of his retinue. And producing his credentials under the Signet Royal, which he applied[9] close to my eyes, spoke about ten minutes, without any signs of anger, but with a kind of determinate resolution; often pointing forwards, which, as I afterwards found, was towards the capital city, about half a mile distant, whither it was agreed by his Majesty in council that I must be conveyed. I answered in a few words, but to no purpose, and made a sign with my hand that was loose, putting it to the other (but over his Excellency's head, for fear of hurting him or his train) and then to my own head and body, to signify that I desired my liberty. It appeared that he understood me well enough; for he shook his head by way of disapprobation, and held his hand in a posture to show that I must be carried as a prisoner. However, he made other signs to let me understand that I should have meat and drink enough, and very good treatment. Whereupon I once more thought of attempting to break my bonds; but again, when I felt the smart of their arrows upon my face and hands, which were all in blisters, and many of the darts still sticking in them; and observing likewise that the number of my enemies increased; I gave tokens to let them know that they might do with me what they pleased. Upon this the *Hurgo* and his train withdrew, with much civility and cheerful countenances. Soon after I heard a general shout, with frequent repetitions of the words, *Peplom Selan,* and I felt great numbers of the people on my left side relaxing the cords to such a degree, that I was able to turn upon my right, and to ease myself with making water; which I very plentifully did, to the great astonishment of the people, who conjecturing by my motions what I was going to do, immediately opened to the right and left on that side, to avoid the torrent which fell with such noise and violence from me. But before this, they had daubed my face and both my hands with a sort of ointment very pleasant to the smell, which in a few minutes removed all the smart of their arrows. These circumstances, added

9. Brought.

to the refreshment I had received by their victuals and drink, which were very nourishing, disposed me to sleep. I slept about eight hours, as I was afterwards assured; and it was no wonder; for the physicians, by the Emperor's order, had mingled a sleeping potion in the hogsheads of wine.

It seems that upon the first moment I was discovered sleeping on the ground after my landing, the Emperor had early notice of it by an express; and determined in council that I should be tied in the manner I have related (which was done in the night while I slept), that plenty of meat and drink should be sent me, and a machine prepared to carry me to the capital city.

This resolution perhaps may appear very bold and dangerous, and I am confident would not be imitated by any prince in Europe on the like occasion; however, in my opinion it was extremely prudent as well as generous. For supposing these people had endeavored to kill me with their spears and arrows while I was asleep; I should certainly have awaked with the first sense of smart, which might so far have roused my rage and strength, as to enable me to break the strings wherewith I was tied; after which, as they were not able to make resistance, so they could expect no mercy.

These people are most excellent mathematicians, and arrived to a great perfection in mechanics by the countenance and encouragement of the Emperor, who is a renowned patron of learning. This prince hath several machines fixed on wheels, for the carriage of trees and other great weights. He often builds his largest men of war, whereof some are nine foot long, in the woods where the timber grows, and has them carried on these engines[1] three or four hundred yards to the sea. Five hundred carpenters and engineers were immediately set at work to prepare the greatest engine they had. It was a frame of wood raised three inches from the ground, about seven foot long and four wide, moving upon twenty-two wheels. The shout I heard was upon the arrival of this engine, which it seems set out in four hours after my landing. It was brought parallel to me as I lay. But the principal difficulty was to raise and place me in this vehicle. Eighty poles, each of one foot high, were erected for this purpose, and very strong cords of the bigness of packthread were fastened by hooks to many bandages, which the workmen had girt round my neck, my hands, my body, and my legs. Nine hundred of the strongest men were employed to draw up these cords by many pulleys fastened on the poles; and thus, in less than three hours, I was raised and slung into the engine, and there tied fast. All this I was told, for while the whole operation was performing, I lay in a profound sleep, by the force of that soporiferous[2] medicine infused into my liquor. Fifteen hundred of

1. Contrivances.

2. Inducing unnatural sleep.

the Emperor's largest horses, each about four inches and a half high, were employed to draw me towards the metropolis, which, as I said, was half a mile distant.

About four hours after we began our journey, I awaked by a very ridiculous accident; for, the carriage being stopped a while to adjust something that was out of order, two or three of the young natives had the curiosity to see how I looked when I was asleep; they climbed up into the engine, and advancing very softly to my face, one of them, an officer in the guards, put the sharp end of his half-pike a good way up into my left nostril, which tickled my nose like a straw, and made me sneeze violently: whereupon they stole off unperceived, and it was three weeks before I knew the cause of my awaking so suddenly. We made a long march the remaining part of the day, and rested at night with five hundred guards on each side of me, half with torches, and half with bows and arrows, ready to shoot me if I should offer to stir. The next morning at sunrise we continued our march, and arrived within two hundred yards of the city gates about noon. The Emperor and all his court came out to meet us, but his great officers would by no means suffer his Majesty to endanger his person by mounting on my body.

At the place where the carriage stopped, there stood an ancient temple, esteemed to be the largest in the whole kingdom, which having been polluted some years before by an unnatural murder,[3] was, according to the zeal of those people, looked on as profane, and therefore had been applied to common use, and all the ornaments and furniture carried away. In this edifice it was determined I should lodge. The great gate fronting to the north was about four foot high, and almost two foot wide, through which I could easily creep. On each side of the gate was a small window not above six inches from the ground: into that on the left side, the King's smiths conveyed fourscore and eleven chains, like those that hang to a lady's watch in Europe, and almost as large, which were locked to my left leg with six and thirty padlocks. Over against this temple, on the other side of the great highway, at twenty foot distance, there was a turret at least five foot high. Here the Emperor ascended with many principal lords of his court, to have an opportunity of viewing me, as I was told, for I could not see them. It was reckoned that above an hundred thousand inhabitants came out of the town upon the same errand; and in spite of my guards, I believe there could not be fewer than ten thousand, at several times, who mounted upon my body by the help of ladders. But a proclamation was soon issued to forbid it upon pain of death. When the workmen found it was impossible for me to break loose, they cut all the strings that bound me; whereupon I rose up with as melancholy a

3. Presumably a reference to the execution of Charles I, who was sentenced in Westminster Hall.

disposition as ever I had in my life. But the noise and astonishment of the people at seeing me rise and walk are not to be expressed. The chains that held my left leg were about two yards long, and gave me not only the liberty of walking backwards and forwards in a semicircle; but, being fixed within four inches of the gate, allowed me to creep in, and lie at my full length in the temple.

Chapter II. *The Emperor of Lilliput, attended by several of the nobility, comes to see the author in his confinement. The Emperor's person and habit described. Learned men appointed to teach the author their language. He gains favor by his mild disposition. His pockets are searched, and his sword and pistols taken from him.*

When I found myself on my feet, I looked about me, and must confess I never beheld a more entertaining prospect. The country round appeared like a continued garden, and the inclosed fields, which were generally forty foot square, resembled so many beds of flowers. These fields were intermingled with woods of half a stang,[4] and the tallest trees, as I could judge, appeared to be seven foot high. I viewed the town on my left hand, which looked like the painted scene of a city in a theater.

I had been for some hours extremely pressed by the necessities of nature; which was no wonder, it being almost two days since I had last disburthened myself. I was under great difficulties between urgency and shame. The best expedient I could think on, was to creep into my house, which I accordingly did; and shutting the gate after me, I went as far as the length of my chain would suffer; and discharged my body of that uneasy load. But this was the only time I was ever guilty of so uncleanly an action; for which I cannot but hope the candid reader will give some allowance, after he hath maturely and impartially considered my case, and the distress I was in. From this time my constant practice was, as soon as I rose, to perform that business in open air, at the full extent of my chain, and due care was taken every morning before company came, that the offensive matter should be carried off in wheelbarrows by two servants appointed for that purpose. I would not have dwelt so long upon a circumstance, that perhaps at first sight may appear not very momentous, if I had not thought it necessary to justify my character in point of cleanliness to the world; which I am told some of my maligners have been pleased, upon this and other occasions, to call in question.

When this adventure was at an end, I came back out of my house, having occasion for fresh air. The Emperor was already descended from the tower, and advancing on horseback towards me, which had like to have cost him dear; for the beast, although very

4. A quarter of an acre.

well trained, yet wholly unused to such a sight, which appeared as if a mountain moved before him, reared up on his hinder feet: but that prince, who is an excellent horseman, kept his seat, until his attendants ran in, and held the bridle, while his Majesty had time to dismount. When he alighted, he surveyed me round with great admiration, but kept beyond the length of my chains. He ordered his cooks and butlers, who were already prepared, to give me victuals and drink, which they pushed forward in a sort of vehicles upon wheels until I could reach them. I took these vehicles, and soon emptied them all; twenty of them were filled with meat, and ten with liquor; each of the former afforded me two or three good mouthfuls, and I emptied the liquor of ten vessels, which was contained in earthen vials, into one vehicle, drinking it off at a draught; and so I did with the rest. The Empress, and young princes of the blood, of both sexes, attended by many ladies, sat at some distance in their chairs; but upon the accident that happened to the Emperor's horse, they alighted, and came near his person; which I am now going to describe. He is taller, by almost the breadth of my nail, than any of his court, which alone is enough to strike an awe into the beholders. His features are strong and masculine, with an Austrian lip, and arched nose, his complexion olive, his countenance[5] erect, his body and limbs well proportioned, all his motions graceful, and his deportment majestic. He was then past his prime, being twenty-eight years and three quarters old, of which he had reigned about seven, in great felicity, and generally victorious. For the better convenience of beholding him, I lay on my side, so that my face was parallel to his, and he stood but three yards off: however, I have had him since many times in my hand, and therefore cannot be deceived in the description. His dress was very plain and simple, the fashion of it between the Asiatic and the European; but he had on his head a light helmet of gold, adorned with jewels, and a plume on the crest. He held his sword drawn in his hand, to defend himself, if I should happen to break loose; it was almost three inches long, the hilt and scabbard were gold enriched with diamonds. His voice was shrill, but very clear and articulate, and I could distinctly hear it when I stood up. The ladies and courtiers were all most magnificently clad, so that the spot they stood upon seemed to resemble a petticoat spread on the ground, embroidered with figures of gold and silver. His Imperial Majesty spoke often to me, and I returned answers, but neither of us could understand a syllable. There were several of his priests and lawyers present (as I conjectured by their habits) who were commanded to address themselves to me, and I spoke to them in as many languages as I had the least smattering of, which were High and Low

5. Bearing, appearance. Swift is satirically idealizing George I, whom most of the British thought gross.

Dutch,[6] Latin, French, Spanish, Italian, and Lingua Franca; but all to no purpose. After about two hours the court retired, and I was left with a strong guard, to prevent the impertinence, and probably the malice of the rabble, who were very impatient to crowd about me as near as they durst; and some of them had the impudence to shoot their arrows at me as I sat on the ground by the door of my house, whereof one very narrowly missed my left eye. But the colonel ordered six of the ringleaders to be seized, and thought no punishment so proper as to deliver them bound into my hands, which some of his soldiers accordingly did, pushing them forwards with the butt-ends of their pikes into my reach; I took them all in my right hand, put five of them into my coat-pocket; and as to the sixth, I made a countenance as if I would eat him alive. The poor man squalled terribly, and the colonel and his officers were in much pain, especially when they saw me take out my penknife: but I soon put them out of fear; for, looking mildly, and immediately cutting the strings he was bound with, I set him gently on the ground, and away he ran. I treated the rest in the same manner, taking them one by one out of my pocket, and I observed both the soldiers and people were highly obliged at this mark of my clemency, which was represented very much to my advantage at court.

Towards night I got with some difficulty into my house, where I lay on the ground, and continued to do so about a fortnight; during which time the Emperor gave orders to have a bed prepared for me. Six hundred beds of the common measure were brought in carriages, and worked up in my house; an hundred and fifty of their beds sewn together made up the breadth and length, and these were four double, which however kept me but very indifferently from the hardness of the floor, that was of smooth stone. By the same computation they provided me with sheets, blankets, and coverlets, tolerable enough for one who had been so long enured to hardships as I.

As the news of my arrival spread through the kingdom, it brought prodigious numbers of rich, idle, and curious people to see me; so that the villages were almost emptied, and great neglect of tillage and household affairs must have ensued, if his Imperial Majesty had not provided by several proclamations and orders of state against this inconveniency. He directed that those who had already beheld me should return home, and not presume to come within fifty yards of my house without license from court; whereby the secretaries of state got considerable fees.

In the mean time, the Emperor held frequent councils to debate what course should be taken with me; and I was afterwards assured by a particular friend, a person of great quality, who was as much in

6. German and Dutch; "lingua franca": a jargon, based on Italian, used by traders in the Mediterranean.

the secret as any, that the court was under many difficulties concerning me. They apprehended[7] my breaking loose, that my diet would be very expensive, and might cause a famine. Sometimes they determined to starve me, or at least to shoot me in the face and hands with poisoned arrows, which would soon dispatch me: but again they considered, that the stench of so large a carcass might produce a plague in the metropolis, and probably spread through the whole kingdom. In the midst of these consultations, several officers of the army went to the door of the great council chamber; and two of them being admitted, gave an account of my behavior to the six criminals above-mentioned; which made so favorable an impression in the breast of his Majesty, and the whole board, in my behalf, that an imperial commission was issued out, obliging all the villages nine hundred yards round the city to deliver in every morning six beeves, forty sheep, and other victuals for my sustenance; together with a proportionable quantity of bread and wine, and other liquors: for the due payment of which his Majesty gave assignments[8] upon his treasury. For this prince lives chiefly upon his own demesnes; seldom except upon great occasions raising any subsidies upon his subjects, who are bound to attend him in his wars at their own expense. An establishment was also made of six hundred persons to be my domestics, who had board-wages allowed for their maintenance, and tents built for them very conveniently on each side of my door. It was likewise ordered, that three hundred tailors should make me a suit of clothes after the fashion of the country: that six of his Majesty's greatest scholars should be employed to instruct me in their language: and, lastly, that the Emperor's horses, and those of the nobility, and troops of guards, should be exercised in my sight, to accustom themselves to me. All these orders were duly put in execution; and in about three weeks I made a great progress in learning their language; during which time the Emperor frequently honored me with his visits, and was pleased to assist my masters in teaching me. We began already to converse together in some sort; and the first words I learned, were to express my desire that he would please to give me my liberty; which I every day repeated on my knees.[9] His answer, as I could apprehend, was, that this must be a work of time, not to be thought on without the advice of his council; and that first I must *Lumos kelmin pesso desmar lon emposo*; that is, swear a peace with him and his kingdom. However, that I should be used with all kindness; and he advised me to acquire by my patience and discreet behavior, the good opinion of himself and his subjects. He desired I would not

7. Anticipated with fear.
8. Formal mandates of revenue.
9. Gulliver's plea for liberty, and the threat of starvation or rebellion he represents to his captors, suggest the situation of Ireland with respect to England.

take it ill, if he gave orders to certain proper officers to search me; for probably I might carry about me several weapons, which must needs be dangerous things, if they answered the bulk of so prodigious a person.[1] I said, his Majesty should be satisfied, for I was ready to strip myself, and turn up my pockets before him. This I delivered part in words, and part in signs. He replied, that by the laws of the kingdom, I must be searched by two of his officers; that he knew this could not be done without my consent and assistance; that he had so good an opinion of my generosity and justice, as to trust their persons in my hands; that whatever they took from me should be returned when I left the country, or paid for at the rate which I would set upon them. I took up the two officers in my hands, put them first into my coat-pockets, and then into every other pocket about me, except my two fobs, and another secret pocket which I had no mind should be searched, wherein I had some little necessaries of no consequence to any but myself. In one of my fobs there was a silver watch, and in the other a small quantity of gold in a purse. These gentlemen, having pen, ink, and paper about them, made an exact inventory of every thing they saw; and when they had done, desired I would set them down, that they might deliver it to the Emperor. This inventory I afterwards translated into English, and is word for word as follows.

> Imprimis, In the right coat-pocket of the Great Man-Mountain (for so I interpret the words *Quinbus Flestrin*) after the strictest search, we found only one great piece of coarse cloth, large enough to be a foot-cloth for your Majesty's chief room of state. In the left pocket, we saw a huge silver chest, with a cover of the same metal, which we the searchers were not able to lift. We desired it should be opened; and one of us, stepping into it, found himself up to the mid leg in a sort of dust, some part whereof flying up to our faces, set us both a sneezing for several times together. In his right waistcoat-pocket, we found a prodigious bundle of white thin substances, folded one over another, about the bigness of three men, tied with a strong cable, and marked with black figures; which we humbly conceive to be writings; every letter almost half as large as the palm of our hands. In the left there was a sort of engine, from the back of which were extended twenty long poles, resembling the palisados[2] before your Majesty's court; wherewith we conjecture the Man-Mountain combs his head; for we did not always trouble him with questions, because we found it a great difficulty to make him understand us. In the large pocket on the right side of his middle cover (so I translate the word *ranfu-lo*, by which they meant my

1. When the Whigs came into power in 1715, the leading Tories, who included Swift's friends Oxford and Bolingbroke (Robert Harley and Henry St. John) as well as Swift himself, were investigated by a Committee of Secrecy.

2. Fences of stakes.

breeches) we saw a hollow pillar of iron, about the length of a man, fastened to a strong piece of timber, larger than the pillar; and upon one side of the pillar were huge pieces of iron sticking out, cut into strange figures; which we know not what to make of. In the left pocket, another engine of the same kind. In the smaller pocket on the right side, were several round flat pieces of white and red metal, of different bulk; some of the white, which seemed to be silver, were so large and heavy, that my comrade and I could hardly lift them. In the left pocket were two black pillars irregularly shaped: we could not, without difficulty, reach the top of them as we stood at the bottom of his pocket. One of them was covered, and seemed all of a piece; but at the upper end of the other, there appeared a white round substance, about twice the bigness of our heads. Within each of these was inclosed a prodigious plate of steel; which, by our orders, we obliged him to show us, because we apprehended they might be dangerous engines. He took them out of their cases, and told us, that in his own country his practice was to shave his beard with one of these, and to cut his meat with the other. There were two pockets which we could not enter: these he called his fobs; they were two large slits cut into the top of his middle cover, but squeezed close by the pressure of his belly. Out of the right fob hung a great silver chain, with a wonderful kind of engine at the bottom. We directed him to draw out whatever was at the end of the chain, which appeared to be a globe, half silver, and half of some transparent metal: for on the transparent side we saw certain strange figures circularly drawn, and thought we could touch them, until we found our fingers stopped with that lucid substance. He put this engine to our ears, which made an incessant noise like that of a watermill. And we conjecture it is either some unknown animal, or the god that he worships: but we are more inclined to the latter opinion, because he assured us (if we understood him right, for he expressed himself very imperfectly), that he seldom did any thing without consulting it. He called it his oracle, and said it pointed out the time for every action of his life. From the left fob he took out a net almost large enough for a fisherman, but contrived to open and shut like a purse, and served him for the same use: we found therein several massy pieces of yellow metal, which if they be of real gold, must be of immense value.

Having thus, in obedience to your Majesty's commands, diligently searched all his pockets, we observed a girdle[3] about his waist made of the hide of some prodigious animal; from which, on the left side, hung a sword of the length of five men; and on the right, a bag or pouch divided into two cells; each cell capable of holding three of your Majesty's subjects. In one of these cells were several globes or balls of a most ponderous metal, about the bigness of our heads, and required a strong hand to lift them: the

3. Belt.

other cell contained a heap of certain black grains, but of no great bulk or weight, for we could hold above fifty of them in the palms of our hands.

This is an exact inventory of what we found about the body of the Man-Mountain; who used us with great civility, and due respect to your Majesty's commission. Signed and sealed on the fourth day of the eighty-ninth moon of your Majesty's auspicious reign.

CLEFREN FRELOCK, MARSI FRELOCK.

When this inventory was read over to the Emperor, he directed me to deliver up the several particulars. He first called for my scimitar, which I took out, scabbard and all. In the meantime he ordered three thousand of his choicest troops (who then attended him) to surround me at a distance, with their bows and arrows just ready to discharge: but I did not observe it; for my eyes were wholly fixed upon his Majesty. He then desired me to draw my scimitar, which, although it had got some rust by the sea water, was in most parts exceeding bright. I did so, and immediately all the troops gave a shout between terror and surprise; for the sun shone clear, and the reflection dazzled their eyes, as I waved the scimitar to and fro in my hand. His Majesty, who is a most magnanimous[4] prince, was less daunted than I could expect; he ordered me to return it into the scabbard, and cast it on the ground as gently as I could, about six foot from the end of my chain. The next thing he demanded was one of the hollow iron pillars, by which he meant my pocket-pistols. I drew it out, and at his desire, as well as I could, expressed to him the use of it, and charging it only with powder, which by the closeness of my pouch happened to escape wetting in the sea (an inconvenience that all prudent mariners take special care to provide against), I first cautioned the Emperor not to be afraid; and then I let it off in the air. The astonishment here was much greater than at the sight of my scimitar. Hundreds fell down as if they had been struck dead; and even the Emperor, although he stood his ground, could not recover himself in some time. I delivered up both my pistols in the same manner as I had done my scimitar, and then my pouch of powder and bullets; begging him that the former might be kept from fire; for it would kindle with the smallest spark, and blow up his imperial palace into the air. I likewise delivered up my watch, which the Emperor was very curious to see; and commanded two of his tallest yeomen of the guards to bear it on a pole upon their shoulders, as draymen in England do a barrel of ale. He was amazed at the continual noise it made, and the motion of the minute-hand, which he could easily discern; for their sight is much

4. Courageous, great-spirited. Magnanimity, the relation (direct or inverse) between the size of the body and the soul, is a central concern of the first two parts of the *Travels*.

more acute than ours: he asked the opinions of his learned men about him, which were various and remote, as the reader may well imagine without my repeating; although indeed I could not very perfectly understand them. I then gave up my silver and copper money, my purse with nine large pieces of gold, and some smaller ones; my knife and razor, my comb and silver snuffbox, my handkerchief and journal book. My scimitar, pistols, and pouch, were conveyed in carriages to his Majesty's stores; but the rest of my goods were returned me.

I had, as I before observed, one private pocket which escaped their search, wherein there was a pair of spectacles (which I sometimes use for the weakness of my eyes), a pocket perspective,[5] and several other little conveniences; which, being of no consequence to the Emperor, I did not think myself bound in honor to discover, and I apprehended they might be lost or spoiled if I ventured them out of my possession.

Chapter III. *The author diverts the Emperor and his nobility of both sexes in a very uncommon manner. The diversions of the court of Lilliput described. The author hath his liberty granted him upon certain conditions.*

My gentleness and good behavior had gained so far on the Emperor and his court, and indeed upon the army and people in general, that I began to conceive hopes of getting my liberty in a short time. I took all possible methods to cultivate this favorable disposition. The natives came by degrees to be less apprehensive of any danger from me. I would sometimes lie down, and let five or six of them dance on my hand. And at last the boys and girls would venture to come and play at hide-and-seek in my hair. I had now made a good progress in understanding and speaking their language. The Emperor had a mind one day to entertain me with several of the country shows; wherein they exceed all nations I have known, both for dexterity and magnificence. I was diverted with none so much as that of the rope-dancers, performed upon a slender white thread, extended about two foot, and twelve inches from the ground. Upon which I shall desire liberty, with the reader's patience, to enlarge a little.

This diversion is only practiced by those persons who are candidates for great employments, and high favor, at court. They are trained in this art from their youth, and are not always of noble birth, or liberal education. When a great office is vacant either by death or disgrace (which often happens) five or six of those candidates petition the Emperor to entertain his Majesty and the court

5. Telescope.

with a dance on the rope; and whoever jumps the highest without falling, succeeds in the office. Very often the chief ministers themselves are commanded to show their skill, and to convince the Emperor that they have not lost their faculty. Flimnap,[6] the Treasurer, is allowed to cut a caper on the strait rope, at least an inch higher than any other lord in the whole empire. I have seen him do the summerset several times together upon a trencher[7] fixed on the rope, which is no thicker than a common packthread in England. My friend Reldresal, Principal Secretary for Private Affairs, is, in my opinion, if I am not partial, the second after the Treasurer; the rest of the great officers are much upon a par.

These diversions are often attended with fatal accidents, whereof great numbers are on record. I myself have seen two or three candidates break a limb. But the danger is much greater when the ministers themselves are commanded to show their dexterity; for, by contending to excel themselves and their fellows, they strain so far, that there is hardly one of them who hath not received a fall; and some of them two or three. I was assured, that a year or two before my arrival, Flimnap would have infallibly broke his neck, if one of the King's cushions,[8] that accidentally lay on the ground, had not weakened the force of his fall.

There is likewise another diversion, which is only shown before the Emperor and Empress, and first minister, upon particular occasions. The Emperor lays on a table three fine silken threads of six inches long. One is blue, the other red, and the third green.[9] These threads are proposed as prizes for those persons whom the Emperor hath a mind to distinguish by a peculiar mark of his favor. The ceremony is performed in his Majesty's great chamber of state; where the candidates are to undergo a trial of dexterity very different from the former, and such as I have not observed the least resemblance of in any other country of the old or the new world. The Emperor holds a stick in his hands, both ends parallel to the horizon, while the candidates, advancing one by one, sometimes leap over the stick, sometimes creep under it backwards and forwards several times, according as the stick is advanced or depressed. Sometimes the Emperor holds one end of the stick, and his first minister the other; sometimes the minister has it entirely to himself. Whoever performs his part with most agility, and holds out the longest in *leaping* and *creeping*, is rewarded with the blue-colored silk; the red is given to the next, and the green to the third, which they all wear girt twice round about the middle; and you see few great persons about this court who are not adorned with one of these girdles.

6. Sir Robert Walpole, the Whig head of the government, notorious in Swift's circle for his political acrobatics.

7. Plate; "summerset": somersault.

8. A mistress of George I was supposed to have helped restore Walpole to office in 1721.

9. The Orders of the Garter, the Bath, and the Thistle, conferred for services to the King.

The horses of the army, and those of the royal stables, having been daily led before me, were no longer shy, but would come up to my very feet, without starting. The riders would leap them over my hand as I held it on the ground; and one of the Emperor's huntsmen, upon a large courser, took[1] my foot, shoe and all; which was indeed a prodigious leap. I had the good fortune to divert the Emperor one day after a very extraordinary manner. I desired he would order several sticks of two foot high, and the thickness of an ordinary cane, to be brought me; whereupon his Majesty commanded the master of his woods to give directions accordingly; and the next morning six woodmen arrived with as many carriages, drawn by eight horses to each. I took nine of these sticks, and fixing them firmly in the ground in a quadrangular figure, two foot and a half square, I took four other sticks, and tied them parallel at each corner, about two foot from the ground; then I fastened my handkerchief to the nine sticks that stood erect, and extended it on all sides till it was as tight as the top of a drum; and the four parallel sticks, rising about five inches higher than the handkerchief, served as ledges on each side. When I had finished my work, I desired the Emperor to let a troop of his best horse, twenty-four in number, come and exercise upon this plain. His Majesty approved of the proposal, and I took them up one by one in my hands, ready mounted and armed, with the proper officers to exercise them. As soon as they got into order, they divided into two parties, performed mock skirmishes, discharged blunt arrows, drew their swords, fled and pursued, attacked and retired; and in short discovered the best military discipline I ever beheld. The parallel sticks secured them and their horses from falling over the stage; and the Emperor was so much delighted, that he ordered this entertainment to be repeated several days; and once was pleased to be lifted up, and give the word of command; and, with great difficulty, persuaded even the Empress herself to let me hold her in her close chair[2] within two yards of the stage, from whence she was able to take a full view of the whole performance. It was my good fortune that no ill accident happened in these entertainments, only once a fiery horse that belonged to one of the captains pawing with his hoof struck a hole in my handkerchief, and his foot slipping, he overthrew his rider and himself; but I immediately relieved them both; for covering the hole with one hand, I set down the troop with the other, in the same manner as I took them up. The horse that fell was strained in the left shoulder, but the rider got no hurt, and I repaired my handkerchief as well as I could; however, I would not trust to the strength of it any more in such dangerous enterprises.

About two or three days before I was set at liberty, as I was enter-

1. Jumped over.

2. An enclosed or sedan chair.

taining the court with these kinds of feats, there arrived an express to inform his Majesty that some of his subjects, riding near the place where I was first taken up, had seen a great black substance lying on the ground, very oddly shaped, extending its edges round as wide as his Majesty's bedchamber, and rising up in the middle as high as a man; that it was no living creature, as they at first apprehended, for it lay on the grass without motion, and some of them had walked round it several times; that by mounting upon each others' shoulders, they had got to the top, which was flat and even; and stamping upon it they found it was hollow within; that they humbly conceived it might be something belonging to the Man-Mountain, and if his Majesty pleased, they would undertake to bring it with only five horses. I presently[3] knew what they meant; and was glad at heart to receive this intelligence. It seems upon my first reaching the shore after our shipwreck, I was in such confusion, that before I came to the place where I went to sleep, my hat, which I had fastened with a string to my head while I was rowing, and had stuck on all the time I was swimming, fell off after I came to land; the string, as I conjecture, breaking by some accident which I never observed, but thought my hat had been lost at sea. I intreated his Imperial Majesty to give orders it might be brought to me as soon as possible, describing to him the use and the nature of it: and the next day the wagoners arrived with it, but not in a very good condition; they had bored two holes in the brim, within an inch and half of the edge, and fastened two hooks in the holes; these hooks were tied by a long cord to the harness, and thus my hat was dragged along for above half an English mile: but the ground in that country being extremely smooth and level, it received less damage than I expected.

Two days after this adventure, the Emperor, having ordered that part of his army which quarters in and about his metropolis to be in a readiness, took a fancy of diverting himself in a very singular manner. He desired I would stand like a colossus, with my legs as far asunder as I conveniently could. He then commanded his general (who was an old experienced leader, and a great patron of mine) to draw up the troops in close order, and march them under me; the foot[4] by twenty-four in a breast, and the horse by sixteen, with drums beating, colors flying, and pikes advanced. This body consisted of three thousand foot, and a thousand horse. His Majesty gave orders, upon pain of death, that every soldier in his march should observe the strictest decency with regard to my person; which, however, could not prevent some of the younger officers from turning up their eyes as they passed under me. And, to confess

3. Immediately.

4. Foot-soldiers or infantry.

the truth, my breeches were at that time in so ill a condition, that they afforded some opportunities for laughter and admiration.

I had sent so many memorials and petitions for my liberty, that his Majesty at length mentioned the matter first in the cabinet, and then in a full council; where it was opposed by none, except Skyresh Bolgolam,[5] who was pleased, without any provocation, to be my mortal enemy. But it was carried against him by the whole board, and confirmed by the Emperor. That minister was *Galbet*, or Admiral of the Realm; very much in his master's confidence, and a person well versed in affairs, but of a morose and sour complexion.[6] However, he was at length persuaded to comply; but prevailed that the articles and conditions upon which I should be set free, and to which I must swear, should be drawn up by himself. These articles were brought to me by Skyresh Bolgolam in person, attended by two under-secretaries, and several persons of distinction. After they were read, I was demanded to swear to the performance of them; first in the manner of my own country, and afterwards in the method prescribed by their laws; which was to hold my right foot in my left hand, to place the middle finger of my right hand on the crown of my head, and my thumb on the tip of my right ear. But because the reader may perhaps be curious to have some idea of the style and manner of expression peculiar to that people, as well as to know the articles upon which I recovered my liberty, I have made a translation of the whole instrument,[7] word for word, as near as I was able; which I here offer to the public.

> Golbasto Momaren Evlame Gurdilo Shefin Mully Ully Gue, most mighty Emperor of Lilliput, delight and terror of the universe, whose dominions extend five thousand blustrugs (about twelve miles in circumference) to the extremities of the globe; Monarch of all Monarchs; taller than the sons of men; whose feet press down to the center, and whose head strikes against the sun; at whose nod the princes of the earth shake their knees; pleasant as the spring, comfortable as the summer, fruitful as autumn, dreadful as winter. His most sublime Majesty proposeth to the Man-Mountain, lately arrived at our celestial dominions, the following articles, which by a solemn oath he shall be obliged to perform.
>
> First, The Man-Mountain shall not depart from our dominions, without our license under our great seal.
>
> Secondly, He shall not presume to come into our metropolis, without our express order; at which time the inhabitants shall have two hours warning, to keep within their doors.
>
> Thirdly, The said Man-Mountain shall confine his walks to our

5. The Earl of Nottingham, an enemy of Swift.

6. Disposition.

7. A formal legal document.

principal high roads; and not offer to walk or lie down in a meadow, or field of corn.

Fourthly, As he walks the said roads, he shall take the utmost care not to trample upon the bodies of any of our loving subjects, their horses, or carriages, nor take any of our said subjects into his hands, without their own consent.

Fifthly, If an express require extraordinary dispatch, the Man-Mountain shall be obliged to carry in his pocket the messenger and horse, a six days' journey once in every moon, and return the said messenger back (if so required) safe to our Imperial Presence.

Sixthly, He shall be our ally against our enemies in the island of Blefuscu, and do his utmost to destroy their fleet, which is now preparing to invade us.

Seventhly, That the said Man-Mountain shall, at his times of leisure, be aiding and assisting to our workmen, in helping to raise certain great stones, towards covering the wall of the principal park, and other our royal buildings.

Eighthly, That the said Man-Mountain shall, in two moons' time, deliver in an exact survey of the circumference of our dominions by a computation of his own paces round the coast.

Lastly, That upon his solemn oath to observe all the above articles, the said Man-Mountain shall have a daily allowance of meat and drink sufficient for the support of 1,728 of our subjects; with free access to our Royal Person, and other marks of our favor. Given at our palace at Belfaborac the twelfth day of the ninety-first moon of our reign.

I swore and subscribed to these articles with great cheerfulness and content, although some of them were not so honorable as I could have wished; which proceeded wholly from the malice of Skyresh Bolgolam the High Admiral: whereupon my chains were immediately unlocked, and I was at full liberty: the Emperor himself in person did me the honor to be by at the whole ceremony. I made my acknowledgements by prostrating myself at his Majesty's feet: but he commanded me to rise; and after many gracious expressions, which, to avoid the censure of vanity, I shall not repeat, he added, that he hoped I should prove a useful servant, and well deserve all the favors he had already conferred upon me, or might do for the future.

The reader may please to observe, that in the last article for the recovery of my liberty, the Emperor stipulates to allow me a quantity of meat and drink, sufficient for the support of 1,728 Lilliputians. Some time after, asking a friend at court how they came to fix on that determinate number, he told me, that his Majesty's mathematicians, having taken the height of my body by the help of a quadrant, and finding it to exceed theirs in the proportion of twelve to one, they concluded from the similarity of their bodies, that mine must contain at least 1,728 of theirs, and consequently would require as much food as was necessary to support that number of Lilliputians. By which, the reader may conceive an idea of the ingenuity of that people, as well as the prudent and exact economy of so great a prince.

Chapter IV. *Mildendo, the metropolis of Lilliput, described, together with the Emperor's palace. A conversation between the author and a principal secretary, concerning the affairs of that empire; the author's offers to serve the Emperor in his wars.*

The first request I made after I had obtained my liberty, was, that I might have license to see Mildendo, the metropolis; which the Emperor easily granted me, but with a special charge to do no hurt, either to the inhabitants, or their houses. The people had notice by proclamation of my design to visit the town. The wall which encompassed it is two foot and an half high, and at least eleven inches broad, so that a coach and horses may be driven very safely round it; and it is flanked with strong towers at ten foot distance. I stepped over the great western gate, and passed very gently, and sideling[8] through the two principal streets, only in my short waistcoat, for fear of damaging the roofs and eaves of the houses with the skirts of my coat. I walked with the utmost circumspection, to avoid treading on any stragglers, who might remain in the streets, although the orders were very strict, that all people should keep in their houses, at their own peril. The garret windows and tops of houses were so crowded with spectators, that I thought in all my travels I had not seen a more populous place. The city is an exact square, each side of the wall being five hundred foot long. The two great streets, which run cross and divide it into four quarters, are five foot wide. The lanes and alleys, which I could not enter, but only viewed them as I passed, are from twelve to eighteen inches. The town is capable of holding five hundred thousand souls. The houses are from three to five stories. The shops and markets well provided.

The Emperor's palace is in the center of the city, where the two great streets meet. It is enclosed by a wall of two foot high, and twenty foot distant from the buildings. I had his Majesty's permission to step over this wall; and the space being so wide between that and the palace, I could easily view it on every side. The outward court is a square of forty foot, and includes two other courts: in the inmost are the royal apartments, which I was very desirous to see, but found it extremely difficult; for the great gates, from one square into another, were but eighteen inches high, and seven inches wide. Now the buildings of the outer court were at least five foot high; and it was impossible for me to stride over them, without

8. Sideways.

infinite damage to the pile, although the walls were strongly built of hewn stone, and four inches thick. At the same time the Emperor had a great desire that I should see the magnificence of his palace; but this I was not able to do till three days after, which I spent in cutting down with my knife some of the largest trees in the royal park, about an hundred yards distant from the city. Of these trees I made two stools, each about three foot high, and strong enough to bear my weight. The people having received notice a second time, I went again through the city to the palace, with my two stools in my hands. When I came to the side of the outer court, I stood upon one stool, and took the other in my hand: this I lifted over the roof, and gently set it down on the space between the first and second court, which was eight foot wide. I then stepped over the buildings very conveniently from one stool to the other, and drew up the first after me with a hooked stick. By this contrivance I got into the inmost court; and lying down upon my side, I applied my face to the windows of the middle stories, which were left open on purpose, and discovered the most splendid apartments that can be imagined. There I saw the Empress, and the young princes in their several lodgings, with their chief attendants about them. Her Imperial Majesty was pleased to smile very graciously upon me and gave me out of the window her hand to kiss.

But I shall not anticipate the reader with farther descriptions of this kind, because I reserve them for a greater work, which is now almost ready for the press; containing a general description of this empire, from its first erection, through a long series of princes, with a particular account of their wars and politics, laws, learning, and religion; their plants and animals, their peculiar manners and customs, with other matters very curious and useful; my chief design at present being only to relate such events and transactions as happened to the public, or to myself, during a residence of about nine months in that empire.

One morning, about a fortnight after I had obtained my liberty, Reldresal, Principal Secretary (as they style him) of Private Affairs, came to my house, attended only by one servant. He ordered his coach to wait at a distance, and desired I would give him an hour's audience; which I readily consented to, on account of his quality, and personal merits, as well as of the many good offices he had done me during my solicitations at court. I offered to lie down, that he might the more conveniently reach my ear; but he chose rather to let me hold him in my hand during our conversation. He began with compliments on my liberty, said he might pretend to some merit in it; but, however, added, that if it had not been for the present situation of things at court, perhaps I might not have obtained it so soon. For, said he, as flourishing a condition as we appear to be in to foreigners, we labor under two mighty evils; a violent faction at home, and the danger of an invasion by a most potent enemy from abroad. As to the first, you are to understand, that for above seventy moons past, there have been two struggling parties in the empire, under the names of *Tramecksan*, and *Slamecksan*,[9] from the high and low heels on their shoes, by which they distinguish themselves.

It is alleged indeed, that the high heels are most agreeable to our ancient constitution: but however this be, his Majesty hath determined to make use of only low heels in the administration of the government and all offices in the gift of the crown; as you cannot but observe; and particularly, that his Majesty's imperial heels are lower at least by a *drurr* than any of his court; (*drurr* is a measure about the fourteenth part of an inch). The animosities between these two parties run so high, that they will neither eat nor drink, nor talk with each other. We compute the *Tramecksan*, or High-Heels, to exceed us in number; but the power is wholly on our side. We apprehend his Imperial Highness, the heir to the crown, to have some tendency towards the High-Heels; at least we can plainly discover one of his heels higher than the other, which gives him a hobble in his gait.[1] Now, in the midst of these intestine disquiets, we are threatened with an invasion from the island of Blefuscu,[2] which is the other great empire of the universe, almost as large and powerful as this of his Majesty. For as to what we have heard you affirm, that there are other kingdoms and states in the world, inhabited by human creatures as large as yourself, our philosophers are in much doubt; and would rather conjecture that you dropped from the moon, or one of the stars; because it is certain, that an hundred mortals of your bulk would, in a short time, destroy all the fruits and cattle of his Majesty's dominions. Besides, our histories of six thousand moons make no mention of any other regions, than the two great empires of Lilliput and Blefuscu. Which two mighty powers have, as I was going to tell you, been engaged in a most obstinate war for six and thirty moons past. It began upon the following occasion. It is allowed on all hands, that the primitive way of breaking eggs before we eat them, was upon the larger end: but his present Majesty's grandfather, while he was a boy, going to eat an egg, and breaking it according to the ancient practice, happened to cut one of his fingers. Whereupon the Emperor his father published an edict, commanding all his subjects, upon great penalties, to break the smaller end of their eggs. The people so highly resented this law, that our histories tell us there have been six rebellions raised on that account; wherein one emperor lost his life, and another his crown.[3] These civil commotions were constantly

9. Tory (High Church) and Whig (Low Church).
1. The Prince of Wales (later George II) had friends in both parties.
2. France.
3. Swift's satirical allegory of the strife between Catholics (Big-Endians) and Protestants (Little-Endians) touches on Henry VIII (who "broke" with the Pope), Charles I (who lost his life), and James II (who lost his crown).

fomented by the monarchs of Blefuscu; and when they were quelled, the exiles always fled for refuge to that empire. It is computed, that eleven thousand persons have, at several times, suffered death, rather than submit to break their eggs at the smaller end. Many hundred large volumes have been published upon this controversy: but the books of the Big-Endians have been long forbidden, and the whole party rendered incapable by law of holding employments.[4] During the course of these troubles, the emperors of Blefuscu did frequently expostulate by their ambassadors, accusing us of making a schism in religion, by offending against a fundamental doctrine of our great prophet Lustrog, in the fifty-fourth chapter of the *Brundecral* (which is their Alcoran). This, however, is thought to be a mere strain upon the text: for the words are these; *That all true believers shall break their eggs at the convenient end:* and which is the convenient end, seems, in my humble opinion, to be left to every man's conscience, or at least in the power of the chief magistrate[5] to determine. Now the Big-Endian exiles have found so much credit in the Emperor of Blefuscu's court, and so much private assistance and encouragement from their party here at home, that a bloody war hath been carried on between the two empires for six and thirty moons with various success;[6] during which time we have lost forty capital ships, and a much greater number of smaller vessels, together with thirty thousand of our best seamen and soldiers; and the damage received by the enemy is reckoned to be somewhat greater than ours. However, they have now equipped a numerous fleet, and are just preparing to make a descent upon us; and his Imperial Majesty, placing great confidence in your valor and strength, hath commanded me to lay this account of his affairs before you.

I desired the Secretary to present my humble duty to the Emperor, and to let him know, that I thought it would not become me, who was a foreigner, to interfere with parties; but I was ready, with the hazard of my life, to defend his person and state against all invaders.

Chapter V. *The author by an extraordinary stratagem prevents an invasion. A high title of honor is conferred upon him. Ambassadors arrive from the Emperor of Blefuscu, and sue for peace. The Empress's apartment on fire by an accident; the author instrumental in saving the rest of the palace.*

The empire of Blefuscu is an island situated to the north northeast side of Lilliput, from whence it is parted only by a channel of

4. The Test Act (1673) prevented Catholics and Nonconformists from holding office unless they accepted the Anglican sacrament.

5. Ruler, sovereign. Swift himself accepted the right of the king to determine religious observances.

6. Reminiscent of the War of the Spanish Succession (1701–1713).

eight hundred yards wide. I had not yet seen it, and upon this notice of an intended invasion, I avoided appearing on that side of the coast, for fear of being discovered by some of the enemy's ships, who had received no intelligence of me; all intercourse between the two empires having been strictly forbidden during the war, upon pain of death; and an embargo laid by our Emperor upon all vessels whatsoever. I communicated to his Majesty a project I had formed of seizing the enemy's whole fleet; which, as our scouts assured us, lay at anchor in the harbor ready to sail with the first fair wind. I consulted the most experienced seamen upon the depth of the channel, which they had often plumbed; who told me, that in the middle at high water it was seventy *glumgluffs* deep, which is about six foot of European measure; and the rest of it fifty *glumgluffs* at most. I walked to the northeast coast over against Blefuscu; where, lying down behind a hillock, I took out my small pocket perspective glass, and viewed the enemy's fleet at anchor, consisting of about fifty men of war, and a great number of transports: I then came back to my house, and gave order (for which I had a warrant) for a great quantity of the strongest cable and bars of iron. The cable was about as thick as packthread, and the bars of the length and size of a knitting-needle. I trebled the cable to make it stronger, and for the same reason I twisted three of the iron bars together, bending the extremities into a hook. Having thus fixed fifty hooks to as many cables, I went back to the northeast coast, and putting off my coat, shoes, and stockings, walked into the sea in my leathern jerkin, about half an hour before high water. I waded with what haste I could, and swam in the middle about thirty yards until I felt the ground; I arrived at the fleet in less than half an hour. The enemy was so frighted when they saw me, that they leaped out of their ships, and swam to shore, where there could not be fewer than thirty thousand souls. I then took my tackling, and fastening a hook to the hole at the prow of each, I tied all the cords together at the end. While I was thus employed, the enemy discharged several thousand arrows, many of which stuck in my hands and face; and besides the excessive smart, gave me much disturbance in my work. My greatest apprehension was for my eyes, which I should have infallibly lost, if I had not suddenly thought of an expedient. I kept, among other little necessaries, a pair of spectacles in a private pocket, which, as I observed before, had escaped the Emperor's searchers. These I took out, and fastened as strongly as I could upon my nose; and thus armed went on boldly with my work in spite of the enemy's arrows; many of which struck against the glasses of my spectacles, but without any other effect, further than a little to discompose them. I had now fastened all the hooks, and taking the knot in my hand, began to pull; but not a ship would stir, for they were all too fast by their anchors, so that the boldest part of my enterprise remained. I therefore let go the cord, and leaving the hooks fixed to the ships, I resolutely cut with my knife the cables that fastened the anchors, receiving above two hundred shots in my face and hands; then I took up the knotted end of the cables to which my hooks were tied; and with great ease drew fifty of the enemy's largest men-of-war after me.

The Blefuscudians, who had not the least imagination of what I intended, were at first confounded with astonishment. They had seen me cut the cables, and thought my design was only to let the ships run adrift, or fall foul on each other: but when they perceived the whole fleet moving in order, and saw me pulling at the end, they set up such a scream of grief and despair, that it is almost impossible to describe or conceive. When I had got out of danger, I stopped a while to pick out the arrows that stuck in my hands and face, and rubbed on some of the same ointment that was given me at my first arrival, as I have formerly mentioned. I then took off my spectacles, and waiting about an hour until the tide was a little fallen, I waded through the middle with my cargo, and arrived safe at the royal port of Lilliput.

The Emperor and his whole court stood on the shore, expecting the issue of this great adventure. They saw the ships move forward in a large half-moon, but could not discern me, who was up to my breast in water. When I advanced to the middle of the channel, they were yet more in pain, because I was under water to my neck. The Emperor concluded me to be drowned, and that the enemy's fleet was approaching in a hostile manner: but he was soon eased of his fears, for the channel growing shallower every step I made, I came in a short time within hearing; and holding up the end of the cable by which the fleet was fastened, I cried in a loud voice, Long live the most puissant Emperor of Lilliput! This great prince received me at my landing with all possible encomiums, and created me a *Nardac* upon the spot, which is the highest title of honor among them.

His Majesty desired I would take some other opportunity of bringing all the rest of his enemy's ships into his ports. And so unmeasurable is the ambition of princes, that he seemed to think of nothing less than reducing the whole empire of Blefuscu into a province, and governing it by a viceroy; of destroying the Big-Endian exiles, and compelling that people to break the smaller end of their eggs, by which he would remain sole monarch of the whole world. But I endeavored to divert him from this design, by many arguments drawn from the topics of policy as well as justice: and I plainly protested, that I would never be an instrument of bringing a free and brave people into slavery. And when the matter was debated in council, the wisest part of the ministry were of my opinion.

This open bold declaration of mine was so opposite to the

schemes and politics of his Imperial Majesty, that he could never forgive me; he mentioned it in a very artful manner at council, where I was told that some of the wisest appeared, at least by their silence, to be of my opinion; but others, who were my secret enemies, could not forbear some expressions, which by a side-wind[7] reflected on me. And from this time began an intrigue between his Majesty and a junta of ministers maliciously bent against me, which broke out in less than two months, and had like to have ended in my utter destruction. Of so little weight are the greatest services to princes, when put into the balance with a refusal to gratify their passions.[8]

About three weeks after this exploit, there arrived a solemn embassy frrom Blefuscu, with humble offers of a peace; which was soon concluded upon conditions very advantageous to our Emperor; wherewith I shall not trouble the reader. There were six ambassadors, with a train of about five hundred persons; and their entry was very magnificent, suitable to the grandeur of their master, and the importance of their business. When their treaty was finished, wherein I did them several good offices by the credit I now had, or at least appeared to have at court, their Excellencies, who were privately told how much I had been their friend, made me a visit in form. They began with many compliments upon my valor and generosity; invited me to that kingdom in the Emperor their master's name; and desired me to show them some proofs of my prodigious strength, of which they had heard so many wonders; wherein I readily obliged them, but shall not interrupt the reader with the particulars.

When I had for some time entertained their Excellencies to their infinite satisfaction and surprise, I desired they would do me the honor to present my most humble respects to the Emperor their master, the renown of whose virtues had so justly filled the whole world with admiration, and whose royal person I resolved to attend before I returned to my own country. Accordingly, the next time I had the honor to see our Emperor, I desired his general license to wait on the Blefuscudian monarch, which he was pleased to grant me, as I could plainly perceive, in a very cold manner; but could not guess the reason, till I had a whisper from a certain person, that Flimnap and Bolgolam had represented my intercourse with those ambassadors as a mark of disaffection, from which I am sure my heart was wholly free. And this was the first time I began to conceive some imperfect idea of courts and ministers.

It is to be observed, that these ambassadors spoke to me by an interpreter; the languages of both empires differing as much from

7. Indirectly.

8. After a series of British naval victories, the Treaty of Utrecht (1713) had ended the war with France, but the Tory ministers who engineered the peace were subsequently accused of having sold out to the enemy.

each other as any two in Europe, and each nation priding itself upon the antiquity, beauty, and energy of their own tongues, with an avowed contempt for that of their neighbor; yet our Emperor, standing upon the advantage he had got by the seizure of their fleet, obliged them to deliver their credentials, and make their speech, in the Lilliputian tongue. And it must be confessed, that from the great intercourse of trade and commerce between both realms, from the continual reception of exiles, which is mutual among them, and from the custom in each empire to send their young nobility and richer gentry to the other, in order to polish themselves, by seeing the world, and understanding men and manners, there are few persons of distinction, or merchants, or seamen, who dwell in the maritime parts, but what can hold conversation in both tongues; as I found some weeks after, when I went to pay my respects to the Emperor of Blefuscu, which in the midst of great misfortunes, through the malice of my enemies, proved a very happy adventure to me, as I shall relate in its proper place.

The reader may remember, that when I signed those articles upon which I recovered my liberty, there were some which I disliked upon account of their being too servile, neither could any thing but an extreme necessity have forced me to submit. But being now a *Nardac*, of the highest rank in that empire, such offices[9] were looked upon as below my dignity, and the Emperor (to do him justice) never once mentioned them to me. However, it was not long before I had an opportunity of doing his Majesty, at least as I then thought, a most signal service. I was alarmed at midnight with the cries of many hundred people at my door; by which being suddenly awaked, I was in some kind of terror. I heard the word *burglum* repeated incessantly; several of the Emperor's court, making their way through the crowd, intreated me to come immediately to the palace, where her Imperial Majesty's apartment was on fire, by the carelessness of a maid of honor, who fell asleep while she was reading a romance. I got up in an instant; and orders being given to clear the way before me, and it being likewise a moonshine night, I made a shift to get to the palace without trampling on any of the people. I found they had already applied ladders to the walls of the apartment, and were well provided with buckets, but the water was at some distance. These buckets were about the size of a large thimble, and the poor people supplied me with them as fast as they could; but the flame was so violent, that they did little good. I might easily have stifled it with my coat, which I unfortunately left behind me for haste, and came away only in my leathern jerkin. The case seemed wholly desperate and deplorable; and this magnificent palace would have infallibly been burnt down to the ground, if, by a presence of mind, unusual to me, I had not suddenly thought of an expedient. I had the evening before drank plentifully

9. Duties.

of a most delicious wine, called *glimigrim* (the Blefuscudians call it *flunec*, but ours is esteemed the better sort), which is very diuretic. By the luckiest chance in the world, I had not discharged myself of any part of it. The heat I had contracted by coming very near the flames, and by my laboring to quench them, made the wine begin to operate by urine; which I voided in such a quantity, and applied so well to the proper places, that in three minutes the fire was wholly extinguished; and the rest of that noble pile, which had cost so many ages in erecting, preserved from destruction.

It was now daylight, and I returned to my house, without waiting to congratulate with the Emperor; because, although I had done a very eminent piece of service, yet I could not tell how his Majesty might resent the manner by which I had performed it: for, by the fundamental laws of the realm, it is capital[1] in any person, of what quality soever, to make water within the precincts of the palace. But I was a little comforted by a message from his Majesty, that he would give orders to the Grand Justiciary for passing my pardon in form; which, however, I could not obtain. And I was privately assured, that the Empress, conceiving the greatest abhorrence of what I had done,[2] removed to the most distant side of the court, firmly resolved that those buildings should never be repaired for her use; and, in the presence of her chief confidents, could not forbear vowing revenge.

CHAPTER VI. *Of the inhabitants of Lilliput; their learning, laws, and customs, the manner of educating their children. The author's way of living in that country. His vindication of a great lady.*

Although I intend to leave the description of this empire to a particular treatise, yet in the mean time I am content to gratify the curious reader with some general ideas. As the common size of the natives is somewhat under six inches, so there is an exact proportion in all other animals, as well as plants and trees: for instance, the tallest horses and oxen are between four and five inches in height, the sheep an inch and a half, more or less; their geese about the bigness of a sparrow; and so the several gradations downwards, till you come to the smallest, which, to my sight, were almost invisible; but nature hath adapted the eyes of the Lilliputians to all objects proper for their view: they see with great exactness, but at no great distance. And to show the sharpness of their sight towards objects that are near, I have been much pleased with observing a cook pulling[3] a lark, which was not so large as a common fly; and a young girl threading an invisible needle with invisible silk. Their tallest trees are about seven foot high; I mean some of those in the great royal park, the tops whereof I could but just reach with my

1. Punishable by death.
2. Queen Anne, whom Swift called "a royal prude," strongly objected to the coarseness of *A Tale of a Tub*.
3. Plucking.

fist clinched. The other vegetables[4] are in the same proportion; but this I leave to the reader's imagination.

I shall say but little at present of their learning, which for many ages hath flourished in all its branches among them: but their manner of writing is very peculiar; being neither from the left to the right, like the Europeans; nor from the right to the left, like the Arabians; nor from up to down, like the Chinese; nor from down to up, like the Cascagians;[5] but aslant from one corner of the paper to the other, like ladies in England.

They bury their dead with their heads directly downwards; because they hold an opinion that in eleven thousand moons they are all to rise again; in which period, the earth (which they conceive to be flat) will turn upside down, and by this means they shall, at their resurrection, be found ready standing on their feet. The learned among them confess the absurdity of this doctrine; but the practice still continues, in compliance to the vulgar.

There are some laws and customs in this empire very peculiar; and if they were not so directly contrary to those of my own dear country, I should be tempted to say a little in their justification. It is only to be wished, that they were as well executed. The first I shall mention relateth to informers. All crimes against the state are punished here with the utmost severity; but if the person accused make his innocence plainly to appear upon his trial, the accuser is immediately put to an ignominious death; and out of his goods or lands, the innocent person is quadruply recompensed for the loss of his time, for the danger he underwent, for the hardship of his imprisonment, and for all the charges he hath been at in making his defense. Or, if that fund be deficient, it is largely[6] supplied by the crown. The Emperor doth also confer on him some public mark of his favor; and proclamation is made of his innocence through the whole city.

They look upon fraud as a greater crime than theft, and therefore seldom fail to punish it with death; for they allege, that care and vigilance, with a very common understanding, may preserve a man's goods from thieves; but honesty hath no fence against superior cunning: and since it is necessary that there should be a perpetual intercourse of buying and selling, and dealing upon credit, where fraud is permitted or connived at, or hath no law to punish it, the honest dealer is always undone, and the knave gets the advantage. I remember when I was once interceding with the King for a criminal who had wronged his master of a great sum of money, which he had received by order, and ran away with; and happening to tell his Majesty, by way of extenuation, that it was only a breach of trust, the Emperor thought it monstrous in me to offer, as a defense, the greatest aggravation of the crime: and truly, I had little to say in

4. Plants.
5. Swift's invention.
6. Fully.

return, farther than the common answer, that different nations had different customs; for, I confess, I was heartily ashamed.

Although we usually call reward and punishment the two hinges upon which all government turns, yet I could never observe this maxim to be put in practice by any nation, except that of Lilliput. Whoever can there bring sufficient proof that he hath strictly observed the laws of his country for seventy-three moons, hath a claim to certain privileges, according to his quality[7] and condition of life, with a proportionable sum of money out of a fund appropriated for that use: he likewise acquires the title of *Snilpall*, or *Legal*, which is added to his name, but doth not descend to his posterity. And these people thought it a prodigious defect of policy among us, when I told them that our laws were enforced only by penalties, without any mention of reward. It is upon this account that the image of Justice, in their courts of judicature, is formed with six eyes, two before, as many behind, and on each side one, to signify circumspection; with a bag of gold open in her right hand, and a sword sheathed in her left, to show she is more disposed to reward than to punish.

In choosing persons for all employments, they have more regard to good morals than to great abilities; for, since government is necessary to mankind, they believe that the common size of human understandings is fitted to some station or other; and that Providence never intended to make the management of public affairs a mystery, to be comprehended only by a few persons of sublime genius, of which there seldom are three born in an age: but they suppose truth, justice, temperance, and the like, to be in every man's power; the practice of which virtues, assisted by experience and a good intention, would qualify any man for the service of his country, except where a course of study is required. But they thought the want of moral virtues was so far from being supplied by superior endowments of the mind, that employments could never be put into such dangerous hands as those of persons so qualified; and at least, that the mistakes committed by ignorance in a virtuous disposition would never be of such fatal consequence to the public weal, as the practices of a man whose inclinations led him to be corrupt, and had great abilities to manage, to multiply, and defend his corruptions.

In like manner, the disbelief of a divine Providence renders a man uncapable of holding any public station; for since kings avow themselves to be the deputies of Providence, the Lilliputians think nothing can be more absurd than for a prince to employ such men as disown the authority under which he acteth.

In relating these and the following laws, I would only be understood to mean the original institutions, and not the most scandalous

7. Social position.

corruptions into which these people are fallen by the degenerate nature of man. For as to that infamous practice of acquiring great employments by dancing on the ropes, or badges of favor and distinction by leaping over sticks, and creeping under them, the reader is to observe, that they were first introduced by the grandfather of the Emperor now reigning; and grew to the present height by the gradual increase of party and faction.

Ingratitude is among them a capital crime, as we read it to have been in some other countries; for they reason thus, that whoever makes ill returns to his benefactor, must needs be a common enemy to the rest of mankind, from whom he hath received no obligation; and therefore such a man is not fit to live.

Their notions relating to the duties of parents and children differ extremely from ours. For, since the conjunction of male and female is founded upon the great law of nature, in order to propagate and continue the species, the Lilliputians will needs have it, that men and women are joined together like other animals, by the motives of concupiscence; and that their tenderness towards their young proceedeth from the like natural principle: for which reason they will never allow, that a child is under any obligation to his father for begetting him, or to his mother for bringing him into the world; which, considering the miseries of human life, was neither a benefit in itself, nor intended so by his parents, whose thoughts in their love-encounters were otherwise employed. Upon these, and the like reasonings, their opinion is, that parents are the last of all others to be trusted with the education of their own children: and therefore they have in every town public nurseries, where all parents, except cottagers[8] and laborers, are obliged to send their infants of both sexes to be reared and educated when they come to the age of twenty moons; at which time they are supposed to have some rudiments of docility. These schools are of several kinds, suited to different qualities, and to both sexes. They have certain professors[9] well skilled in preparing children for such a condition of life as befits the rank of their parents, and their own capacities as well as inclinations. I shall first say something of the male nurseries, and then of the female.

The nurseries for males of noble or eminent birth are provided with grave and learned professors, and their several deputies. The clothes and food of the children are plain and simple. They are bred up in the principles of honor, justice, courage, modesty, clemency, religion, and love of their country; they are always employed in some business, except in the times of eating and sleeping, which are very short, and two hours for diversions, consisting of bodily exercises.[1] They are dressed by men until four years of age, and then are obliged to dress themselves, although their quality be ever so great; and the women attendants, who are aged proportionably to

8. Agricultural workers, peasants.
9. Professional teachers.
1. Activities.

ours at fifty, perform only the most menial offices. They are never suffered to converse with servants, but go together in small or greater numbers to take their diversions, and always in the presence of a professor, or one of his deputies; whereby they avoid those early bad impressions of folly and vice to which our children are subject. Their parents are suffered to see them only twice a year; the visit is not to last above an hour; they are allowed to kiss the child at meeting and parting; but a professor, who always standeth by on those occasions, will not suffer them to whisper, or use any fondling expressions, or bring any presents of toys, sweetmeats, and the like.

The pension from each family for the education and entertainment[2] of a child, upon failure of due payment, is levied by the Emperor's officers.

The nurseries for children of ordinary gentlemen, merchants, traders, and handicrafts, are managed proportionably after the same manner; only those designed for trades are put out apprentices at seven years old; whereas those of persons of quality continue in their exercises until fifteen, which answers to one and twenty with us: but the confinement is gradually lessened for the last three years.

In the female nurseries, the young girls of quality are educated much like the males, only they are dressed by orderly servants of their own sex, but always in the presence of a professor or deputy, until they come to dress themselves, which is at five years old. And if it be found that these nurses ever presume to entertain the girls with frightful or foolish stories, or the common follies practiced by chambermaids among us, they are publicly whipped thrice about the city, imprisoned for a year, and banished for life to the most desolate parts of the country. Thus the young ladies there are as much ashamed of being cowards and fools as the men; and despise all personal ornaments beyond decency and cleanliness: neither did I perceive any difference in their education, made by their difference of sex, only that the exercises of the females were not altogether so robust; and that some rules were given them relating to domestic life, and a smaller compass of learning was enjoined them: for their maxim is, that among people of quality, a wife should be always a reasonable and agreeable companion, because she cannot always be young. When the girls are twelve years old, which among them is the marriageable age, their parents or guardians take them home, with great expressions of gratitude to the professors, and seldom without tears of the young lady and her companions.

In the nurseries of females of the meaner sort, the children are instructed in all kinds of works proper for their sex, and their several degrees:[3] those intended for apprentices are dismissed at seven years old, the rest are kept to eleven.

The meaner families who have children at these nurseries are

2. Sustenance.

3. Various social ranks.

obliged, besides their annual pension, which is as low as possible, to return to the steward of the nursery a small monthly share of their gettings, to be a portion for the child; and therefore all parents are limited in their expenses by the law. For the Lilliputians think nothing can be more unjust, than that people, in subservience to their own appetites, should bring children into the world, and leave the burthen of supporting them on the public. As to persons of quality, they give security to appropriate a certain sum for each child, suitable to their condition; and these funds are always managed with good husbandry, and the most exact justice.

The cottagers and laborers keep their children at home, their business being only to till and cultivate the earth; and therefore their education is of little consequence to the public; but the old and diseased among them are supported by hospitals: for begging is a trade unknown in this empire.

And here it may perhaps divert the curious reader, to give some account of my domestic,[4] and my manner of living in this country, during a residence of nine months and thirteen days. Having a head mechanically turned, and being likewise forced by necessity, I had made for myself a table and chair convenient enough, out of the largest trees in the royal park. Two hundred sempstresses were employed to make me shirts, and linen for my bed and table, all of the strongest and coarsest kind they could get; which, however, they were forced to quilt together in several folds; for the thickest was some degrees finer than lawn. Their linen is usually three inches wide, and three foot make a piece. The sempstresses took my measure as I lay on the ground, one standing at my neck, and another at my mid-leg, with a strong cord extended, that each held by the end, while the third measured the length of the cord with a rule of an inch long. Then they measured my right thumb, and desired no more; for by a mathematical computation, that twice round the thumb is one round the wrist, and so on to the neck and the waist; and by the help of my old shirt, which I displayed on the ground before them for a pattern, they fitted me exactly. Three hundred tailors were employed in the same manner to make me clothes; but they had another contrivance for taking my measure. I kneeled down, and they raised a ladder from the ground to my neck; upon this ladder one of them mounted, and let fall a plumb-line from my collar to the floor, which just answered the length of my coat; but my waist and arms I measured myself. When my clothes were finished, which was done in my house (for the largest of theirs would not have been able to hold them), they looked like the patchwork made by the ladies in England, only that mine were all of a color.

I had three hundred cooks to dress my victuals, in little convenient huts built about my house, where they and their families lived,

4. Household.

and prepared me two dishes apiece. I took up twenty waiters in my hand, and placed them on the table; an hundred more attended below on the ground, some with dishes of meat, and some with barrels of wine, and other liquors, slung on their shoulders; all which the waiters above drew up as I wanted, in a very ingenious manner, by certain cords, as we draw the bucket up a well in Europe. A dish of their meat was a good mouthful, and a barrel of their liquor a reasonable draught. Their mutton yields to ours, but their beef is excellent. I have had a sirloin so large, that I have been forced to make three bites of it; but this is rare. My servants were astonished to see me eat it bones and all, as in our country we do the leg of a lark. Their geese and turkeys I usually eat at a mouthful, and I must confess they far exceed ours. Of their smaller fowl I could take up twenty or thirty at the end of my knife.

One day his Imperial Majesty, being informed of my way of living, desired that himself and his royal consort, with the young princes of the blood of both sexes, might have the happiness (as he was pleased to call it) of dining with me. They came accordingly, and I placed them upon chairs of state on my table, just over against me, with their guards about them. Flimnap the Lord High Treasurer attended there likewise, with his white staff; and I observed he often looked on me with a sour countenance, which I would not seem to regard, but eat more than usual, in honor to my dear country, as well as to fill the court with admiration. I have some private reasons to believe, that this visit from his Majesty gave Flimnap an opportunity of doing me ill offices to his master. That minister had always been my secret enemy, although he outwardly caressed me more than was usual to the moroseness of his nature. He represented to the Emperor the low condition of his treasury; that he was forced to take up money at great discount; that exchequer bills[5] would not circulate under nine per cent below par; that I had cost his Majesty above a million and a half of *sprugs* (their greatest gold coin, about the bigness of a spangle); and upon the whole, that it would be advisable in the Emperor to take the first fair occasion of dismissing me.

I am here obliged to vindicate the reputation of an excellent lady, who was an innocent sufferer upon my account. The Treasurer took a fancy to be jealous of his wife, from the malice of some evil tongues, who informed him that her Grace had taken a violent affection for my person; and the court-scandal ran for some time that she once came privately to my lodging. This I solemnly declare to be a most infamous falsehood, without any grounds, farther than that her Grace was pleased to treat me with all innocent marks of freedom and friendship. I own she came often to my house, but always publicly, nor ever without three more in the coach, who were usually her sister and young daughter, and some particular acquaint-

5. Government bills of credit. Walpole was noted as a canny financier.

ance; but this was common to many other ladies of the court. And I still appeal to my servants round, whether they at any time saw a coach at my door without knowing what persons were in it. On those occasions, when a servant had given me notice, my custom was to go immediately to the door; and, after paying my respects, to take up the coach and two horses very carefully in my hands (for if there were six horses, the postillion always unharnessed four) and place them on a table, where I had fixed a moveable rim quite round, of five inches high, to prevent accidents. And I have often had four coaches and horses at once on my table full of company, while I sat in my chair leaning my face towards them; and when I was engaged with one set, the coachmen would gently drive the others round my table. I have passed many an afternoon very agreeably in these conversations. But I defy the Treasurer, or his two informers (I will name them, and let them make their best of it) Clustril and Drunlo, to prove that any person ever came to me *incognito*, except the Secretary Reldresal, who was sent by express command of his Imperial Majesty, as I have before related. I should not have dwelt so long upon this particular, if it had not been a point wherein the reputation of a great lady is so nearly concerned, to say nothing of my own; although I had the honor to be a *Nardac*, which the Treasurer himself is not; for all the world knows he is only a *Clumglum*, a title inferior by one degree, as that of a marquis is to a duke in England; yet I allow he preceded me in right of his post. These false informations, which I afterwards came to the knowledge of, by an accident not proper to mention, made the Treasurer show his lady for some time an ill countenance, and me a worse; for although he was at last undeceived and reconciled to her, yet I lost all credit with him; and found my interest decline very fast with the Emperor himself, who was indeed too much governed by that favorite.

CHAPTER VII. *The author, being informed of a design to accuse him of high treason, makes his escape to Blefuscu. His reception there.*

Before I proceed to give an account of my leaving this kingdom, it may be proper to inform the reader of a private intrigue which had been for two months forming against me.

I had been hitherto all my life a stranger to courts, for which I was unqualified by the meanness of my condition. I had indeed heard and read enough of the dispositions of great princes and ministers; but never expected to have found such terrible effects of them in so remote a country, governed, as I thought, by very different maxims from those in Europe.

When I was just preparing to pay my attendance on the Emperor of Blefuscu, a considerable person at court (to whom I had been very serviceable at a time when he lay under the highest displeasure of his Imperial Majesty) came to my house very privately at night in a close chair, and without sending his name, desired admittance. The chairmen were dismissed; I put the chair, with his Lordship in it, into my coat-pocket; and giving orders to a trusty servant to say I was indisposed and gone to sleep, I fastened the door of my house, placed the chair on the table, according to my usual custom, and sat down by it. After the common salutations were over, observing his Lordship's countenance full of concern, and enquiring into the reason, he desired I would hear him with patience, in a matter that highly concerned my honor and my life. His speech was to the following effect, for I took notes of it as soon as he left me.

You are to know, said he, that several committees of council have been lately called in the most private manner on your account: and it is but two days since his Majesty came to a full resolution.

You are very sensible that Skyresh Bolgolam (*Galbet*, or High Admiral) hath been your mortal enemy almost ever since your arrival. His original reasons I know not; but his hatred is much increased since your great success against Blefuscu, by which his glory, as Admiral, is obscured. This lord, in conjunction with Flimnap the High Treasurer, whose enmity against you is notorious on account of his lady, Limtoc the General, Lalcon the Chamberlain, and Balmuff the Grand Justiciary, have prepared articles of impeachment against you, for treason, and other capital crimes.[6]

This preface made me so impatient, being conscious of my own merits and innocence, that I was going to interrupt; when he entreated me to be silent, and thus proceeded.

Out of gratitude for the favors you have done me, I procured information of the whole proceedings, and a copy of the articles, wherein I venture my head for your service.

Articles of Impeachment against Quinbus Flestrin
(*the* Man-Mountain).

ARTICLE I

Whereas, by a statute made in the reign of his Imperial Majesty Calin Deffar Plune, it is enacted, that whoever shall make water within the precincts of the royal palace shall be liable to the pains and penalties of high treason: notwithstanding, the said Quinbus Flestrin, in open breach of the said law, under color of extinguishing the fire kindled in the apartment of his Majesty's most dear imperial consort, did maliciously, traitorously, and devilishly, by discharge of his urine, put out the said fire kindled in the said apartment, lying and being within the precincts of the said royal palace; against the statute in that case provided, etc., against the duty, etc.

6. After the Whigs had investigated Oxford and Bolingbroke, both were impeached for high treason, on charges of being sympathetic to the Jacobites and the French.

ARTICLE II

That the said Quinbus Flestrin, having brought the imperial fleet of Blefuscu into the royal port, and being afterwards commanded by his Imperial Majesty to seize all the other ships of the said empire of Blefuscu, and reduce that empire to a province, to be governed by a viceroy from hence; and to destroy and put to death not only all the Big-Endian exiles, but likewise all the people of that empire who would not immediately forsake the Big-Endian heresy: he, the said Flestrin, like a false traitor against his most auspicious, serene, Imperial Majesty, did petition to be excused from the said service, upon pretense of unwillingness to force the consciences, or destroy the liberties and lives of an innocent people.

ARTICLE III

That, whereas certain ambassadors arrived from the court of Blefuscu to sue for peace in his Majesty's court: he the said Flestrin did, like a false traitor, aid, abet, comfort, and divert the said ambassadors; although he knew them to be servants to a prince who was lately an open enemy to his Imperial Majesty, and in open war against his said Majesty.

ARTICLE IV

That the said Quinbus Flestrin, contrary to the duty of a faithful subject, is now preparing to make a voyage to the court and empire of Blefuscu, for which he hath received only verbal license from his Imperial Majesty; and under color of the said license, doth falsely and traitorously intend to take the said voyage, and thereby to aid, comfort, and abet the Emperor of Blefuscu, so late an enemy, and in open war with his Imperial Majesty aforesaid.

There are some other articles, but these are the most important, of which I have read you an abstract.

In the several debates upon this impeachment, it must be confessed that his Majesty gave many marks of his great *lenity*; often urging the services you had done him, and endeavoring to extenuate your crimes. The Treasurer and Admiral insisted that you should be put to the most painful and ignominious death, by setting fire on your house at night; and the General was to attend with twenty thousand men armed with poisoned arrows, to shoot you on the face and hands. Some of your servants were to have private orders to strew a poisonous juice on your shirts and sheets, which would soon make you tear your own flesh, and die in the utmost torture. The General came into the same opinion; so that for a long time there was a majority against you. But his Majesty resolving, if possible, to spare your life, at last brought off[7] the Chamberlain.

Upon this incident, Reldresal, Principal Secretary for Private

7. Won over.

Affairs, who always approved[8] himself your true friend, was commanded by the Emperor to deliver his opinion, which he accordingly did; and therein justified the good thoughts you have of him. He allowed your crimes to be great; but that still there was room for mercy, the most commendable virtue in a prince, and for which his Majesty was so justly celebrated. He said, the friendship between you and him was so well known to the world, that perhaps the most honorable board might think him partial: however, in obedience to the command he had received, he would freely offer his sentiments. That if his Majesty, in consideration of your services, and pursuant to his own merciful disposition, would please to spare your life, and only give order to put out both your eyes, he humbly conceived, that by this expedient justice might in some measure be satisfied, and all the world would applaud the *lenity* of the Emperor, as well as the fair and generous proceedings of those who have the honor to be his counselors. That the loss of your eyes would be no impediment to your bodily strength, by which you might still be useful to his Majesty. That blindness is an addition to courage, by concealing dangers from us; that the fear you had for your eyes was the greatest difficulty in bringing over the enemy's fleet; and it would be sufficient for you to see by the eyes of the ministers, since the greatest princes do no more.

This proposal was received with the utmost disapprobation by the whole board. Bolgolam, the Admiral, could not preserve his temper; but rising up in fury, said, he wondered how the Secretary durst presume to give his opinion for preserving the life of a traitor: that the services you had performed were, by all true reasons of state, the great aggravation of your crimes; that you, who were able to extinguish the fire by discharge of urine in her Majesty's apartment (which he mentioned with horror), might, at another time, raise an inundation by the same means, to drown the whole palace; and the same strength which enabled you to bring over the enemy's fleet might serve, upon the first discontent, to carry it back: that he had good reasons to think you were a Big-Endian in your heart; and as treason begins in the heart before it appears in overt acts, so he accused you as a traitor on that account, and therefore insisted you should be put to death.

The Treasurer was of the same opinion; he showed to what straits his Majesty's revenue was reduced by the charge of maintaining you, which would soon grow insupportable: that the Secretary's expedient of putting out your eyes was so far from being a remedy against this evil, that it would probably increase it; as it is manifest from the common practice of blinding some kind of fowl, after which they fed the faster, and grew sooner fat: that his sacred Majesty, and the council, who are your judges, were in their own consciences fully convinced of your guilt; which was a sufficient argu-

8. Proved.

ment to condemn you to death, without the formal proofs required by the strict letter of the law.

But his Imperial Majesty, fully determined against capital punishment, was graciously pleased to say, that since the council thought the loss of your eyes too easy a censure, some other may be inflicted hereafter. And your friend the Secretary humbly desiring to be heard again, in answer to what the Treasurer had objected concerning the great charge his Majesty was at in maintaining you, said, that his Excellency, who had the sole disposal of the Emperor's revenue, might easily provide against this evil, by gradually lessening your establishment; by which, for want of sufficient food, you would grow weak and faint, and lose your appetite, and consequently decay and consume in a few months; neither would the stench of your carcass be then so dangerous, when it should become more than half diminished; and immediately upon your death, five or six thousand of his Majesty's subjects might, in two or three days, cut your flesh from your bones, take it away by cart-loads, and bury it in distant parts to prevent infection; leaving the skeleton as a monument of admiration to posterity.

Thus by the great friendship of the Secretary, the whole affair was compromised. It was strictly enjoined, that the project of starving you by degrees should be kept a secret; but the sentence of putting out your eyes was entered on the books; none dissenting except Bolgolam the Admiral, who being a creature of the Empress, was perpetually instigated by her Majesty to insist upon your death; she having borne perpetual malice against you, on account of that infamous and illegal method you took to extinguish the fire in her apartment.

In three days your friend the Secretary will be directed to come to your house, and read before you the articles of impeachment; and then to signify the great lenity and favor of his Majesty and council; whereby you are only condemned to the loss of your eyes, which his Majesty doth not question you will gratefully and humbly submit to; and twenty of his Majesty's surgeons will attend, in order to see the operation well performed, by discharging very sharp-pointed arrows into the balls of your eyes, as you lie on the ground.

I leave to your prudence what measures you will take; and to avoid suspicion, I must immediately return in as private a manner as I came.

His Lordship did so, and I remained alone, under many doubts and perplexities of mind.

It was a custom introduced by this prince and his ministry (very different, as I have been assured, from the practices of former times), that after the court had decreed any cruel execution, either to gratify the monarch's resentment, or the malice of a favorite, the Emperor always made a speech to his whole council, expressing his great lenity and tenderness, as qualities known and confessed by all the world. This speech was immediately published through the kingdom; nor did any thing terrify the people so much as those encomiums on his Majesty's mercy; because it was observed, that the more these praises were enlarged and insisted on, the more inhuman was the punishment, and the sufferer more innocent. Yet as to myself, I must confess, having never been designed for a courtier, either by my birth or education, I was so ill a judge of things, that I could not discover the lenity and favor of this sentence, but conceived it (perhaps erroneously) rather to be rigorous than gentle. I sometimes thought of standing my trial; for although I could not deny the facts alleged in the several articles, yet I hoped they would admit of some extenuations. But having in my life perused many state trials, which I ever observed to terminate as the judges thought fit to direct, I durst not rely on so dangerous a decision, in so critical a juncture, and against such powerful enemies. Once I was strongly bent upon resistance: for while I had liberty, the whole strength of that empire could hardly subdue me, and I might easily with stones pelt the metropolis to pieces; but I soon rejected that project with horror, by remembering the oath I had made to the Emperor, the favors I received from him, and the high title of *Nardac* he conferred upon me. Neither had I so soon learned the gratitude of courtiers, to persuade myself that his Majesty's present severities acquitted me of all past obligations.

At last I fixed upon a resolution, for which it is probable I may incur some censure, and not unjustly; for I confess I owe the preserving my eyes, and consequently my liberty, to my own great rashness and want of experience: because if I had then known the nature of princes and ministers, which I have since observed in many other courts, and their methods of treating criminals less obnoxious than myself, I should with great alacrity and readiness have submitted to so *easy* a punishment. But hurried on by the precipitancy of youth, and having his Imperial Majesty's license to pay my attendance upon the Emperor of Blefuscu, I took this opportunity, before the three days were elapsed, to send a letter to my friend the Secretary, signifying my resolution of setting out that morning for Blefuscu,[9] pursuant to the leave I had got; and without waiting for an answer, I went to that side of the island where our fleet lay. I seized a large man of war, tied a cable to the prow, and lifting up the anchors, I stripped myself, put my clothes (together with my coverlet, which I carried under my arm) into the vessel; and drawing it after me, between wading and swimming, arrived at the royal port of Blefuscu, where the people had long expected me. They lent me two guides to direct me to the capital city, which is

9. Before his trial for treason could be held, Bolingbroke had escaped to France.

of the same name; I held them in my hands until I came within two hundred yards of the gate; and desired them to signify my arrival to one of the secretaries, and let him know, I there waited his Majesty's commands. I had an answer in about an hour, that his Majesty, attended by the royal family, and great officers of the court, was coming out to receive me. I advanced a hundred yards; the Emperor, and his train, alighted from their horses, the Empress and ladies from their coaches; and I did not perceive they were in any fright or concern. I lay on the ground to kiss his Majesty's and the Empress's hand. I told his Majesty that I was come according to my promise, and with the license of the Emperor my master, to have the honor of seeing so mighty a monarch, and to offer him any service in my power, consistent with my duty to my own prince; not mentioning a word of my disgrace, because I had hitherto no regular information of it, and might suppose myself wholly ignorant of any such design; neither could I reasonably conceive that the Emperor would discover the secret while I was out of his power: wherein, however, it soon appeared I was deceived.

I shall not trouble the reader with the particular account of my reception at this court, which was suitable to the generosity of so great a prince; nor of the difficulties I was in for want of a house and bed, being forced to lie on the ground, wrapped up in my coverlet.

CHAPTER VIII. *The author, by a lucky accident, finds means to leave Blefuscu; and, after some difficulties, returns safe to his native country.*

Three days after my arrival, walking out of curiosity to the northeast coast of the island, I observed, about half a league off, in the sea, somewhat that looked like a boat overturned. I pulled off my shoes and stockings, and wading two or three hundred yards, I found the object to approach nearer by force of the tide; and then plainly saw it to be a real boat, which I supposed might, by some tempest, have been driven from a ship. Whereupon I returned immediately towards the city, and desired his Imperial Majesty to lend me twenty of the tallest vessels he had left after the loss of his fleet, and three thousand seamen under the command of his Vice Admiral. This fleet sailed round, while I went back the shortest way to the coast where I first discovered the boat; I found the tide had driven it still nearer; the seamen were all provided with cordage, which I had beforehand twisted to a sufficient strength. When the ships came up, I stripped myself, and waded till I came within an hundred yards of the boat; after which I was forced to swim till I got up to it. The seamen threw me the end of the cord, which I fastened to a hole in the fore-part of the boat, and the other end to a man of war: but I found all my labor to little purpose; for being out of my depth, I was not able to work. In this necessity, I was forced to swim behind, and push the boat forwards as often as I could, with one of my hands; and the tide favoring me, I advanced so far, that I could just hold up my chin and feel the ground. I rested two or three minutes, and then gave the boat another shove, and so on till the sea was no higher than my armpits. And now the most laborious part being over, I took out my other cables which were stowed in one of the ships, and fastening them first to the boat, and then to nine of the vessels which attended me, the wind being favorable, the seamen towed, and I shoved till we arrived within forty yards of the shore; and waiting till the tide was out, I got dry to the boat, and by the assistance of two thousand men, with ropes and engines,[1] I made a shift to turn it on its bottom, and found it was but little damaged.

I shall not trouble the reader with the difficulties I was under by the help of certain paddles, which cost me ten days making, to get my boat to the royal port of Blefuscu; where a mighty concourse of people appeared upon my arrival, full of wonder at the sight of so prodigious a vessel. I told the Emperor that my good fortune had thrown this boat in my way, to carry me to some place from whence I might return into my native country; and begged his Majesty's orders for getting materials to fit it up, together with license to depart; which, after some kind expostulations, he was pleased to grant.

I did very much wonder, in all this time, not to have heard of any express relating to me from our Emperor to the court of Blefuscu. But I was afterwards given privately to understand, that his Imperial Majesty, never imagining I had the least notice of his designs, believed I was only gone to Blefuscu in performance of my promise, according to the license he had given me, which was well known at our court; and would return in a few days when that ceremony was ended. But he was at last in pain at my long absence; and, after consulting with the Treasurer, and the rest of that cabal, a person of quality was dispatched with the copy of the articles against me. This envoy had instructions to represent to the monarch of Blefuscu the great lenity of his master, who was content to punish me no further than with the loss of my eyes; that I had fled from justice, and if I did not return in two hours, I should be deprived of my title of *Nardac*, and declared a traitor. The envoy further added, that in order to maintain the peace and amity between both empires, his master expected, that his brother of Blefuscu would give orders to have me sent back to Lilliput, bound hand and foot, to be punished as a traitor.

The Emperor of Blefuscu, having taken three days to consult, returned an answer consisting of many civilities and excuses. He

1. Mechanical contrivances.

said, that as for sending me bound, his brother knew it was impossible; that although I had deprived him of his fleet, yet he owed great obligations to me for many good offices I had done him in making the peace. That however, both their Majesties would soon be made easy; for I had found a prodigious vessel on the shore, able to carry me on the sea, which he had given order to fit up with my own assistance and direction; and he hoped in a few weeks both empires would be freed from so insupportable an incumbrance.

With this answer the envoy returned to Lilliput, and the monarch of Blefuscu related to me all that had passed, offering me at the same time (but under the strictest confidence) his gracious protection, if I would continue in his service; wherein although I believed him sincere, yet I resolved never more to put any confidence in princes or ministers, where I could possibly avoid it; and therefore, with all due acknowledgements for his favorable intentions, I humbly begged to be excused. I told him, that since fortune, whether good or evil, had thrown a vessel in my way, I was resolved to venture myself in the ocean, rather than be an occasion of difference between two such mighty monarchs. Neither did I find the Emperor at all displeased; and I discovered by a certain accident, that he was very glad of my resolution, and so were most of his ministers.

These considerations moved me to hasten my departure somewhat sooner than I intended; to which the court, impatient to have me gone, very readily contributed. Five hundred workmen were employed to make two sails to my boat, according to my directions, by quilting thirteen fold of their strongest linen together. I was at the pains of making ropes and cables, by twisting ten, twenty or thirty of the thickest and strongest of theirs. A great stone that I happened to find, after a long search by the seashore, served me for an anchor. I had the tallow of three hundred cows for greasing my boat, and other uses. I was at incredible pains in cutting down some of the largest timber trees for oars and masts, wherein I was, however, much assisted by his Majesty's ship-carpenters, who helped me in smoothing them, after I had done the rough work.

In about a month, when all was prepared, I sent to receive his Majesty's commands, and to take my leave. The Emperor and royal family came out of the palace; I lay down on my face to kiss his hand, which he very graciously gave me: so did the Empress, and young princes of the blood. His Majesty presented me with fifty purses of two hundred *sprugs* apiece, together with his picture at full length, which I put immediately into one of my gloves, to keep it from being hurt. The ceremonies at my departure were too many to trouble the reader with at this time.

I stored the boat with the carcasses of an hundred oxen, and three hundred sheep, with bread and drink proportionable, and as much meat ready dressed as four hundred cooks could provide. I took with me six cows and two bulls alive, with as many ewes and rams, intending to carry them into my own country, and propagate the breed. And to feed them on board, I had a good bundle of hay, and a bag of corn.[2] I would gladly have taken a dozen of the natives; but this was a thing the Emperor would by no means permit; and besides a diligent search into my pockets, his Majesty engaged my honor not to carry away any of his subjects, although with their own consent and desire.

Having thus prepared all things as well as I was able, I set sail on the twenty-fourth day of September, 1701, at six in the morning; and when I had gone about four leagues to the northward, the wind being at southeast, at six in the evening, I descried a small island about half a league to the northwest. I advanced forward, and cast anchor on the lee-side of the island, which seemed to be uninhabited. I then took some refreshment, and went to my rest. I slept well, and as I conjecture at least six hours; for I found the day broke in two hours after I awaked. It was a clear night; I eat my breakfast before the sun was up; and heaving anchor, the wind being favorable, I steered the same course that I had done the day before, wherein I was directed by my pocket compass. My intention was to reach, if possible, one of those islands which I had reason to believe lay to the northeast of Van Diemen's Land. I discovered nothing all that day; but upon the next, about three in the afternoon, when I had by my computation made twenty-four leagues from Blefuscu, I descried a sail steering to the southeast; my course was due east. I hailed her, but could get no answer; yet I found I gained upon her, for the wind slackened. I made all the sail I could, and in half an hour she spied me, then hung out her ancient,[3] and discharged a gun. It is not easy to express the joy I was in upon the unexpected hope of once more seeing my beloved country, and the dear pledges[4] I had left in it. The ship slackened her sails, and I came up with her between five and six in the evening, September 26; but my heart leapt within me to see her English colors. I put my cows and sheep into my coat-pockets and got on board with all my little cargo of provisions. The vessel was an English merchantman, returning from Japan by the North and South Seas;[5] the captain, Mr. John Biddel of Deptford, a very civil man, and an excellent sailor. We were now in the latitude of 30 degrees south; there were about fifty men in the ship; and here I met an old comrade of mine, one Peter Williams, who gave me a good character to the captain. This gentleman treated me with kindness, and desired I

2. Wheat.
3. Flag.
4. Hostages (i.e., his family).
5. North and South Pacific.

would let him know what place I came from last, and whither I was bound; which I did in few words; but he thought I was raving, and that the dangers I underwent had disturbed my head; whereupon I took my black cattle and sheep out of my pocket, which, after great astonishment, clearly convinced him of my veracity. I then showed him the gold given me by the Emperor of Blefuscu, together with his Majesty's picture at full length, and some other rarities of that country. I gave him two purses of two hundred *sprugs* each, and promised, when we arrived in England, to make him a present of a cow and a sheep big with young.

I shall not trouble the reader with a particular account of this voyage; which was very prosperous for the most part. We arrived in the Downs[6] on the 13th of April, 1702. I had only one misfortune, that the rats on board carried away one of my sheep; I found her bones in a hole, picked clean from the flesh. The rest of my cattle I got safe on shore, and set them a grazing in a bowling-green at Greenwich, where the fineness of the grass made them feed very heartily, though I had always feared the contrary; neither could I possibly have preserved them in so long a voyage, if the captain had not allowed me some of his best biscuit, which rubbed to powder, and mingled with water, was their constant food. The short time I continued in England, I made a considerable profit by showing my cattle to many persons of quality, and others: and before I began my second voyage, I sold them for six hundred pounds. Since my last return, I find the breed is considerably increased, especially the sheep; which I hope will prove much to the advantage of the woolen manufacture, by the fineness of the fleeces.

I stayed but two months with my wife and family; for my insatiable desire of seeing foreign countries would suffer me to continue no longer. I left fifteen hundred pounds with my wife, and fixed her in a good house at Redriff. My remaining stock I carried with me, part in money, and part in goods, in hopes to improve my fortunes. My eldest uncle, John, had left me an estate in land, near Epping, of about thirty pounds a year; and I had a long lease of the Black Bull in Fetter Lane, which yielded me as much more: so that I was not in any danger of leaving my family upon the parish.[7] My son Johnny, named so after his uncle, was at the grammar school, and a towardly[8] child. My daughter Betty (who is now well married, and has children) was then at her needlework. I took leave of my wife, and boy and girl, with tears on both sides; and went on board the *Adventure*, a merchant-ship of three hundred tons, bound for Surat, Captain John Nicholas of Liverpool, Commander. But my account of this voyage must be referred to the second part of my *Travels*.

6. A rendezvous for ships off the southeast coast of England.
7. On welfare (living on charity given by the parish).
8. Promising.

Part II. A Voyage to Brobdingnag

Chapter I. *A great storm described. The longboat*[1] *sent to fetch water; the Author goes with it to discover the country. He is left on shore, is seized by one of the natives, and carried to a farmer's house. His reception there, with several accidents that happened there. A description of the inhabitants.*

Having been condemned by nature and fortune to an active and restless life, in ten months after my return I again left my native country, and took shipping in the Downs on the 20th day of June, 1702, in the *Adventure*, Captain John Nicholas, a Cornish man, Commander, bound for Surat.[2] We had a very prosperous gale till we arrived at the Cape of Good Hope, where we landed for fresh water, but discovering a leak we unshipped our goods and wintered there; for the Captain falling sick of an ague, we could not leave the Cape till the end of March. We then set sail, and had a good voyage till we passed the Straits of Madagascar; but having got northward of that island, and to about five degrees south latitude, the winds, which in those seas are observed to blow a constant equal gale between the north and west from the beginning of December to the beginning of May, on the 19th of April began to blow with much greater violence and more westerly than usual, continuing so for twenty days together, during which time we were driven a little to the east of the Molucca Islands and about three degrees northward of the Line, as our Captain found by an observation he took the 2nd of May, at which time the wind ceased, and it was a perfect calm, whereat I was not a little rejoiced. But he, being a man well experienced in the navigation of those seas, bid us all prepare against a storm, which accordingly happened the day following: for a southern wind, called the southern monsoon, began to set in.

Finding it was likely to overblow,[3] we took in our spritsail, and stood by to hand the foresail; but making foul weather, we looked the guns were all fast, and handed the mizzen. The ship lay very broad off, so we thought it better spooning before the sea, than trying or hulling. We reefed the foresail and set him, we hauled aft the foresheet; the helm was hard aweather. The ship wore bravely. We belayed the fore-downhaul; but the sail was split, and we hauled down the yard and got the sail into the ship, and unbound all the things clear of it. It was a very fierce storm; the sea broke

1. The largest boat carried by a merchant sailing vessel.

2. In India. The geography of the voyage is simple: The *Adventure*, after sailing up the east coast of Africa to about 5° south of the equator (the "Line"), is blown past India into the Malay Archipelago, north of the islands of Buru and Ceram. The storm then drives the ship northward and eastward, away from the coast of Siberia ("Great Tartary") into the northeast Pacific, at that time unexplored. Brobdingnag lies somewhere in the vicinity of Alaska.

3. This paragraph is taken almost literally from Samuel Sturmy's *Mariner's Magazine* (1669). Swift is ridiculing the use of technical terms by writers of popular voyages.

strange and dangerous. We hauled off upon the lanyard of the whipstaff, and helped the man at helm. We would not get down our topmast, but let all stand, because she scudded before the sea very well, and we knew that the topmast being aloft, the ship was the wholesomer, and made better way through the sea, seeing we had searoom. When the storm was over, we set foresail and mainsail, and brought the ship to. Then we set the mizzen, main topsail and the fore topsail. Our course was east-northeast, the wind was at southwest. We got the starboard tacks aboard, we cast off our weather braces and lifts; we set in the lee braces, and hauled forward by the weather bowlings, and hauled them tight, and belayed them, and hauled over the mizzen tack to windward, and kept her full and by as near as she would lie.

During this storm, which was followed by a strong wind west-southwest, we were carried by my computation about five hundred leagues to the east, so that the oldest sailor on board could not tell in what part of the world we were. Our provisions held out well, our ship was stanch, and our crew all in good health; but we lay in the utmost distress for water. We thought it best to hold on the same course rather than turn more northerly, which might have brought us to the northwest parts of Great Tartary, and into the frozen sea.

On the 16th day of June, 1703, a boy on the topmast discovered land. On the 17th we came in full view of a great island or continent (for we knew not whether) on the south side whereof was a small neck of land jutting out into the sea, and a creek[4] too shallow to hold a ship of above one hundred tons. We cast anchor within a league of this creek, and our Captain sent a dozen of his men well armed in the longboat, with vessels for water if any could be found. I desired his leave to go with them that I might see the country and make what discoveries I could. When we came to land we saw no river or spring, nor any sign of inhabitants. Our men therefore wandered on the shore to find out some fresh water near the sea, and I walked alone about a mile on the other side, where I observed the country all barren and rocky. I now began to be weary, and seeing nothing to entertain my curiosity, I returned gently down towards the creek; and the sea being full in my view, I saw our men already got into the boat, and rowing for life to the ship. I was going to hollow after them, although it had been to little purpose, when I observed a huge creature walking after them in the sea as fast as he could; he waded not much deeper than his knees and took prodigious strides, but our men had the start of him half a league, and the sea thereabouts being full of sharp-pointed rocks, the monster was not able to overtake the boat. This I was afterwards told, for I durst not stay to see the issue of that adventure, but ran as fast as I could the way I first went, and

4. A small bay or cove, affording anchorage.

then climbed up a steep hill, which gave me some prospect of the country. I found it fully cultivated; but that which first surprised me was the length of the grass, which, in those grounds that seemed to be kept for hay, was about twenty foot high.[5]

I fell into a highroad, for so I took it to be, although it served to the inhabitants only as a footpath through a field of barley. Here I walked on for some time, but could see little on either side, it being now near harvest, and the corn[6] rising at least forty foot. I was an hour walking to the end of this field, which was fenced in with a hedge of at least one hundred and twenty foot high, and the trees so lofty that I could make no computation of their altitude. There was a stile to pass from this field into the next: it had four steps, and a stone to cross over when you came to the utmost. It was impossible for me to climb this stile, because every step was six foot high, and the upper stone above twenty. I was endeavoring to find some gap in the hedge when I discovered one of the inhabitants in the next field advancing towards the stile, of the same size with him whom I saw in the sea pursuing our boat. He appeared as tall as an ordinary spire-steeple, and took about ten yards at every stride, as near as I could guess. I was struck with the utmost fear and astonishment, and ran to hide myself in the corn, from whence I saw him at the top of the stile, looking back into the next field on the right hand; and heard him call in a voice many degrees louder than a speaking trumpet; but the noise was so high in the air that at first I certainly thought it was thunder. Whereupon seven monsters like himself came towards him with reaping hooks in their hands, each hook about the largeness of six scythes. These people were not so well clad as the first, whose servants or laborers they seemed to be. For, upon some words he spoke, they went to reap the corn in the field where I lay. I kept from them at as great a distance as I could, but was forced to move with extreme difficulty, for the stalks of the corn were sometimes not above a foot distant, so that I could hardly squeeze my body betwixt them. However, I made a shift to go forward till I came to a part of the field where the corn had been laid by the rain and wind; here it was impossible for me to advance a step, for the stalks were so interwoven that I could not creep through, and the beards of the fallen ears so strong and pointed that they pierced through my clothes into my flesh. At the same time I heard the reapers not above an hundred yards behind me. Being quite dispirited with toil, and wholly overcome by grief and despair, I lay down between two ridges and heartily wished I might there end my days. I bemoaned my desolate widow and fatherless children; I lamented my own folly and willfulness in attempting a second voyage against the advice of all my friends and relations. In this terrible agitation of mind, I could not forbear

5. Swift's intention, not always carried out accurately, is that everything in Brobdingnag should be, in relation to our familiar world, on a scale of ten to one.

6. Wheat, not maize.

thinking of Lilliput, whose inhabitants looked upon me as the greatest prodigy that ever appeared in the world; where I was able to draw an imperial fleet in my hand, and perform those other actions which will be recorded forever in the chronicles of that empire, while posterity shall hardly believe them, although attested by millions. I reflected what a mortification it must prove to me to appear as inconsiderable in this nation as one single Lilliputian would be among us. But this I conceived was to be the least of my misfortunes; for as human creatures are observed to be more savage and cruel in proportion to their bulk, what could I expect but to be a morsel in the mouth of the first among these enormous barbarians who should happen to seize me? Undoubtedly philosophers are in the right when they tell us that nothing is great or little otherwise than by comparison. It might have pleased fortune to let the Lilliputians find some nation where the people were as diminutive with respect to them as they were to me. And who knows but that even this prodigious race of mortals might be equally overmatched in some distant part of the world, whereof we have yet no discovery?

Scared and confounded as I was, I could not forbear going on with these reflections; when one of the reapers approaching within ten yards of the ridge where I lay, made me apprehend that with the next step I should be squashed to death under his foot, or cut in two with his reaping hook. And therefore when he was again about to move, I screamed as loud as fear could make me. Whereupon the huge creature trod short, and looking round about under him for some time, at last espied me as I lay on the ground. He considered a while with the caution of one who endeavors to lay hold on a small dangerous animal in such a manner that it shall not be able either to scratch or to bite him, as I myself have sometimes done with a weasel in England. At length he ventured to take me up behind by the middle between his forefinger and thumb, and brought me within three yards of his eyes, that he might behold my shape more perfectly. I guessed his meaning, and my good fortune gave me so much presence of mind that I resolved not to struggle in the least as he held me in the air about sixty foot from the ground, although he grievously pinched my sides, for fear I should slip through his fingers. All I ventured was to raise mine eyes towards the sun, and place my hands together in a supplicating posture, and to speak some words in an humble melancholy tone, suitable to the condition I then was in. For I apprehended every moment that he would dash me against the ground, as we usually do any little hateful animal which we have a mind to destroy. But my good star would have it that he appeared pleased with my voice and gestures, and began to look upon me as a curiosity, much wondering to hear me pronounce articulate words, although he could not understand them. In the meantime I was not able to forbear groaning and shedding tears and turning my head towards my sides, letting him know, as well as I could, how cruelly I was hurt by the pressure of his thumb and finger. He seemed to apprehend my meaning; for, lifting up the lappet[7] of his coat, he put me gently into it, and immediately ran along with me to his master, who was a substantial farmer, and the same person I had first seen in the field.

The farmer having (as I supposed by their talk) received such an account of me as his servant could give him, took a piece of a small straw about the size of a walking staff, and therewith lifted up the lappets of my coat, which it seems he thought to be some kind of covering that nature had given me. He blew my hairs aside to take a better view of my face. He called his hinds[8] about him, and asked them (as I afterwards learned) whether they had ever seen in the fields any little creature that resembled me. He then placed me softly on the ground upon all four; but I got immediately up, and walked slowly backwards and forwards, to let those people see I had no intent to run away. They all sat down in a circle about me, the better to observe my motions. I pulled off my hat, and made a low bow towards the farmer; I fell on my knees, and lifted up my hands and eyes, and spoke several words as loud as I could; I took a purse of gold out of my pocket, and humbly presented it to him. He received it on the palm of his hand, then applied it close to his eye to see what it was, and afterwards turned it several times with the point of a pin (which he took out of his sleeve), but could make nothing of it. Whereupon I made a sign that he should place his hand on the ground; I then took the purse, and opening it, poured all the gold into his palm. There were six Spanish pieces of four pistoles each, beside twenty or thirty smaller coins. I saw him wet the tip of his little finger upon his tongue, and take up one of my largest pieces, and then another; but he seemed to be wholly ignorant what they were. He made me a sign to put them again into my purse, and the purse again into my pocket, which after offering to him several times, I thought it best to do.

The farmer by this time was convinced I must be a rational creature. He spoke often to me, but the sound of his voice pierced my ears like that of a water mill, yet his words were articulate enough. I answered as loud as I could in several languages, and he often laid his ear within two yards of me, but all in vain, for we were wholly unintelligible to each other. He then sent his servants to their work, and taking his handkerchief out of his pocket, he doubled and spread it on his hand, which he placed flat on the ground with the palm upwards, making me a sign to step into it, as I could easily do, for it was not above a foot in thickness. I thought it my part to obey, and for fear of falling, laid myself at full length upon the handkerchief, with the remainder of which

7. Flap or fold.

8. Farm servants.

he lapped me up to the head for further security, and in this manner carried me home to his house. There he called his wife, and showed me to her; but she screamed and ran back as women in England do at the sight of a toad or a spider. However, when she had a while seen my behavior, and how well I observed the signs her husband made, she was soon reconciled, and by degrees grew extremely tender of me.

It was about twelve at noon, and a servant brought in dinner. It was only one substantial dish of meat (fit for the plain condition of an husbandman) in a dish of about four-and-twenty foot diameter. The company were the farmer and his wife, three children, and an old grandmother. When they were sat down, the farmer placed me at some distance from him on the table, which was thirty foot high from the floor. I was in a terrible fright, and kept as far as I could from the edge, for fear of falling. The wife minced a bit of meat, then crumbled some bread on a trencher,[9] and placed it before me. I made her a low bow, took out my knife and fork, and fell to eat; which gave them exceeding delight. The mistress sent her maid for a small dram cup, which held about two gallons, and filled it with drink; I took up the vessel with much difficulty in both hands, and in a most respectful manner drank to her ladyship's health, expressing the words as loud as I could in English; which made the company laugh so heartily that I was almost deafened with the noise. This liquor tasted like a small cider,[1] and was not unpleasant. Then the master made me a sign to come to his trencher side; but as I walked on the table, being in great surprise all the time, as the indulgent reader will easily conceive and excuse, I happened to stumble against a crust, and fell flat on my face, but received no hurt. I got up immediately, and observing the good people to be in much concern, I took my hat (which I held under my arm out of good manners) and waving it over my head, made three huzzas to show I had got no mischief by my fall. But advancing forwards toward my master (as I shall henceforth call him), his youngest son who sat next him, an arch[2] boy of about ten years old, took me up by the legs, and held me so high in the air that I trembled every limb; but his father snatched me from him, and at the same time gave him such a box on the left ear as would have felled an European troop of horse to the earth, ordering him to be taken from the table. But being afraid the boy might owe me a spite, and well remembering how mischievous all children among us naturally are to sparrows, rabbits, young kittens, and puppy dogs, I fell on my knees, and pointing to the boy, made my master to understand, as well as I could, that I desired his son might be pardoned. The father complied, and the lad took his seat again; whereupon I went to him and kissed his hand, which my master took, and made him stroke me gently with it.

9. A platter.

1. I.e., weak cider.

2. Mischievous.

In the midst of dinner, my mistress's favorite cat leaped into her lap. I heard a noise behind me like that of a dozen stocking weavers at work; and turning my head, I found it proceeded from the purring of this animal, who seemed to be three times larger than an ox, as I computed by the view of her head and one of her paws, while her mistress was feeding and stroking her. The fierceness of this creature's countenance altogether discomposed me, although I stood at the farther end of the table, above fifty foot off, and although my mistress held her fast for fear she might give a spring and seize me in her talons. But it happened there was no danger, for the cat took not the least notice of me when my master placed me within three yards of her. And as I have been always told, and found true by experience in my travels, that flying or discovering[3] fear before a fierce animal is a certain way to make it pursue or attack you, so I resolved in this dangerous juncture to show no manner of concern. I walked with intrepidity five or six times before the very head of the cat, and came within half a yard of her; whereupon she drew herself back, as if she were more afraid of me; I had less apprehension concerning the dogs, whereof three or four came into the room, as it is usual in farmers' houses; one of which was a mastiff, equal in bulk to four elephants, and a greyhound, somewhat taller than the mastiff, but not so large.

When dinner was almost done, the nurse came in with a child of a year old in her arms, who immediately spied me, and began a squall that you might have heard from London Bridge to Chelsea, after the usual oratory of infants, to get me for a plaything. The mother out of pure indulgence took me up, and put me towards the child, who presently seized me by the middle, and got my head in his mouth, where I roared so loud that the urchin was frighted and let me drop; and I should infallibly have broke my neck if the mother had not held her apron under me. The nurse to quiet her babe made use of a rattle, which was a kind of hollow vessel filled with great stones, and fastened by a cable to the child's waist: but all in vain, so that she was forced to apply the last remedy by giving it suck. I must confess no object ever disgusted me so much as the sight of her monstrous breast, which I cannot tell what to compare with so as to give the curious reader an idea of its bulk, shape, and color. It stood prominent six foot, and could not be less than sixteen in circumference. The nipple was about half the bigness of my head, and the hue both of that and the dug so varified with spots, pimples, and freckles that nothing could appear more nauseous: for I had a near sight of her, she sitting down the more conveniently to give suck, and I standing on the table. This made me reflect upon the fair skins of our English ladies, who appear so beautiful to us, only because they are of our own size, and their defects not to be seen but through a magnifying glass, where

3. Revealing.

we find by experiment that the smoothest and whitest skins look rough and coarse and ill colored.

I remember when I was at Lilliput, the complexion of those diminutive people appeared to me the fairest in the world; and talking upon this subject with a person of learning there, who was an intimate friend of mine, he said that my face appeared much fairer and smoother when he looked on me from the ground than it did upon a nearer view when I took him up in my hand and brought him close, which he confessed was at first a very shocking sight. He said he could discover great holes in my skin; that the stumps of my beard were ten times stronger than the bristles of a boar, and my complexion made up of several colors altogether disagreeable: although I must beg leave to say for myself that I am as fair as most of my sex and country and very little sunburnt by all my travels. On the other side, discoursing of the ladies in that Emperor's court, he used to tell me one had freckles, another too wide a mouth, a third too large a nose; nothing of which I was able to distinguish. I confess this reflection was obvious enough; which however I could not forbear, lest the reader might think those vast creatures were actually deformed: for I must do them justice to say they are a comely race of people; and particularly the features of my master's countenance, although he were but a farmer, when I beheld him from the height of sixty foot, appeared very well proportioned.

When dinner was done, my master went out to his laborers; and as I could discover by his voice and gesture, gave his wife a strict charge to take care of me. I was very much tired and disposed to sleep, which my mistress perceiving, she put me on her own bed, and covered me with a clean white handkerchief, but larger and coarser than the mainsail of a man-of-war.

I slept about two hours, and dreamed I was at home with my wife and children, which aggravated my sorrows when I awaked and found myself alone in a vast room, between two and three hundred foot wide, and above two hundred high, lying in a bed twenty yards wide. My mistress was gone about her household affairs, and had locked me in. The bed was eight yards from the floor. Some natural necessities required me to get down; I durst not presume to call, and if I had, it would have been in vain with such a voice as mine at so great a distance from the room where I lay to the kitchen where the family kept. While I was under these circumstances, two rats crept up the curtains, and ran smelling backwards and forwards on the bed. One of them came up almost to my face; whereupon I rose in a fright, and drew out my hanger[4] to defend myself. These horrible animals had the boldness to attack me on both sides, and one of them held his forefeet at my collar; but I had the good fortune to rip up his belly before he

4. A short, broad sword.

could do me any mischief. He fell down at my feet; and the other seeing the fate of his comrade, made his escape, but not without one good wound on the back, which I gave him as he fled, and made the blood run trickling from him. After this exploit I walked gently to and fro on the bed, to recover my breath and loss of spirits. These creatures were of the size of a large mastiff, but infinitely more nimble and fierce; so that if I had taken off my belt before I went to sleep, I must have infallibly been torn to pieces and devoured. I measured the tail of the dead rat, and found it to be two yards long, wanting an inch; but it went against my stomach to drag the carcass off the bed, where it lay still bleeding; I observed it had yet some life, but with a strong slash cross the neck, I thoroughly dispatched it.

Soon after, my mistress came into the room, who seeing me all bloody, ran and took me up in her hand. I pointed to the dead rat, smiling and making other signs to show I was not hurt, whereat she was extremely rejoiced, calling the maid to take up the dead rat with a pair of tongs, and throw it out of the window. Then she set me on a table, where I showed her my hanger all bloody, and wiping it on the lappet of my coat, returned it to the scabbard. I was pressed to do more than one thing, which another could not do for me, and therefore endeavored to make my mistress understand that I desired to be set down on the floor; which after she had done, my bashfulness would not suffer me to express myself farther than by pointing to the door, and bowing several times. The good woman with much difficulty at last perceived what I would be at, and taking me up again in her hand, walked into the garden, where she set me down. I went on one side about two hundred yards; and beckoning to her not to look or to follow me, I hid myself between two leaves of sorrel, and there discharged the necessities of nature.

I hope the gentle reader will excuse me for dwelling on these and the like particulars, which however insignificant they may appear to groveling vulgar[5] minds, yet will certainly help a philosopher to enlarge his thoughts and imagination, and apply them to the benefit of public as well as private life, which was my sole design in presenting this and other accounts of my travels to the world; wherein I have been chiefly studious of truth, without affecting any ornaments of learning or of style. But the whole scene of this voyage made so strong an impression on my mind, and is so deeply fixed in my memory, that in committing it to paper I did not omit one material circumstance; however, upon a strict review, I blotted out several passages of less moment which were in my first copy, for fear of being censured as tedious and trifling, whereof travelers are often, perhaps not without justice, accused.

5. Commonplace, uncultivated, in contrast to the scientist ("philosopher"); an irony.

Chapter II. *A description of the farmer's daughter. The Author carried to a market town, and then to the metropolis. The particulars of his journey.*

My mistress had a daughter of nine years old, a child of towardly parts for her age, very dexterous at her needle, and skillful in dressing her baby.[6] Her mother and she contrived to fit up the baby's cradle for me against night: the cradle was put into a small drawer of a cabinet, and the drawer placed upon a hanging shelf for fear of the rats. This was my bed all the time I stayed with those people, although made more convenient by degrees as I began to learn their language, and make my wants known. This young girl was so handy, that after I had once or twice pulled off my clothes before her, she was able to dress and undress me, although I never gave her that trouble when she would let me do either myself. She made me seven shirts, and some other linen of as fine cloth as could be got, which indeed was coarser than sackcloth, and these she constantly washed for me with her own hands. She was likewise my schoolmistress to teach me the language: when I pointed to anything, she told me the name of it in her own tongue, so that in a few days I was able to call for whatever I had a mind to. She was very good-natured, and not above forty foot high, being little for her age. She gave me the name of *Grildrig,* which the family took up, and afterwards the whole kingdom. The word imports what the Latins call *nanunculus,* the Italian *homunceletino,*[7] and the English *mannikin.* To her I chiefly owe my preservation in that country: we never parted while I was there; I called her my *Glumdalclitch,* or little nurse: and I should be guilty of great ingratitude if I omitted this honorable mention of her care and affection towards me, which I heartily wish it lay in my power to requite as she deserves, instead of being the innocent but unhappy instrument of her disgrace, as I have too much reason to fear.

It now began to be known and talked of in the neighborhood that my master had found a strange animal in the field, about the bigness of a *splacknuck,* but exactly shaped in every part like a human creature, which it likewise imitated in all its actions: seemed to speak in a little language of its own, had already learned several words of theirs, went erect upon two legs, was tame and gentle, would come when it was called, do whatever it was bid, had the finest limbs in the world, and a complexion fairer than a nobleman's daughter of three years old. Another farmer who lived hard by, and was a particular friend of my master, came on a visit on purpose to inquire into the truth of this story. I was immediately produced, and placed upon a table, where I walked as I was commanded, drew my hanger, put it up again, made my reverence to my master's

6. Doll.

7. The Latin and Italian words are Swift's own coinages, as, of course, are the various words from the Brobdingnagian language.

guest, asked him in his own language how he did, and told him he was welcome, just as my little nurse had instructed me. This man, who was old and dimsighted, put on his spectacles to behold me better, at which I could not forbear laughing very heartily, for his eyes appeared like the full moon shining into a chamber at two windows. Our people, who discovered the cause of my mirth, bore me company in laughing, at which the old fellow was fool enough to be angry and out of countenance. He had the character of a great miser, and to my misfortune he well deserved it by the cursed advice he gave my master to show me as a sight upon a market day in the next town, which was half an hour's riding, about two and twenty miles from our house. I guessed there was some mischief contriving when I observed my master and his friend whispering long together, sometimes pointing at me; and my fears made me fancy that I overheard and understood some of their words. But the next morning Glumdalclitch, my little nurse, told me the whole matter, which she had cunningly picked out from her mother. The poor girl laid me on her bosom, and fell a weeping with shame and grief. She apprehended some mischief would happen to me from rude vulgar folks, who might squeeze me to death, or break one of my limbs by taking me in their hands. She had also observed how modest I was in my nature, how nicely I regarded my honor, and what an indignity I should conceive it to be exposed for money as a public spectacle to the meanest of the people. She said her papa and mamma had promised that Grildrig should be hers; but now she found they meant to serve her as they did last year, when they pretended to give her a lamb, and yet, as soon as it was fat, sold it to a butcher. For my own part, I may truly affirm that I was less concerned than my nurse. I had a strong hope, which never left me, that I should one day recover my liberty; and as to the ignominy of being carried about for a monster, I considered myself to be a perfect stranger in the country, and that such a misfortune could never be charged upon me as a reproach, if ever I should return to England; since the King of Great Britain himself, in my condition, must have undergone the same distress.

My master, pursuant to the advice of his friend, carried me in a box the next market day to the neighboring town, and took along with him his little daughter, my nurse, upon a pillion[8] behind him. The box was close on every side, with a little door for me to go in and out, and a few gimlet holes to let in air. The girl had been so careful to put the quilt of her baby's bed into it, for me to lie down on. However, I was terribly shaken and discomposed in this journey, although it were but of half an hour. For the horse went about forty foot at every step, and trotted so high that the agitation was equal to the rising and falling of a ship in a great storm, but much more frequent. Our journey was somewhat further than

8. A pad attached to the hinder part of a saddle, on which a second person, usually a woman, could ride.

from London to St. Albans. My master alighted at an inn which he used to frequent; and after consulting a while with the innkeeper, and making some necessary preparations, he hired the *Grultrud,* or crier, to give notice through the town of a strange creature to be seen at the Sign of the Green Eagle, not so big as a *splacknuck* (an animal in that country very finely shaped, about six foot long), and in every part of the body resembling an human creature, could speak several words and perform an hundred diverting tricks.

I was placed upon a table in the largest room of the inn, which might be near three hundred foot square. My little nurse stood on a low stool close to the table, to take care of me, and direct what I should do. My master, to avoid a crowd, would suffer only thirty people at a time to see me. I walked about on the table as the girl commanded; she asked me questions as far as she knew my understanding of the language reached, and I answered them as loud as I could. I turned about several times to the company, paid my humble respects, said they were welcome, and used some other speeches I had been taught. I took up a thimble filled with liquor, which Glumdalclitch had given me for a cup, and drank their health. I drew out my hanger, and flourished with it after the manner of fencers in England. My nurse gave me part of a straw, which I exercised as a pike, having learned the art in my youth. I was that day shown to twelve sets of company, and as often forced to go over again with the same fopperies, till I was half dead with weariness and vexation. For those who had seen me made such wonderful reports that the people were ready to break down the doors to come in. My master for his own interest would not suffer anyone to touch me except my nurse; and, to prevent danger, benches were set round the table at such a distance as put me out of everybody's reach. However, an unlucky schoolboy aimed a hazelnut directly at my head, which very narrowly missed me; otherwise, it came with so much violence that it would have infallibly knocked out my brains, for it was almost as large as a small pumpion:[9] but I had the satisfaction to see the young rogue well beaten, and turned out of the room.

My master gave public notice that he would show me again the next market day, and in the meantime he prepared a more convenient vehicle for me, which he had reason enough to do; for I was so tired with my first journey, and with entertaining company for eight hours together, that I could hardly stand upon my legs or speak a word. It was at least three days before I recovered my strength; and that I might have no rest at home, all the neighboring gentlemen from an hundred miles round, hearing of my fame, came to see me at my master's own house. There could not be fewer than thirty persons with their wives and children (for the country is very populous); and my master demanded the rate of a

9. Pumpkin.

full room whenever he showed me at home, although it were only to a single family. So that for some time I had but little ease every day of the week (except Wednesday, which is their Sabbath) although I were not carried to the town.

My master finding how profitable I was like to be, resolved to carry me to the most considerable cities of the kingdom. Having therefore provided himself with all things necessary for a long journey, and settled his affairs at home, he took leave of his wife; and upon the 17th of August, 1703, about two months after my arrival, we set out for the metropolis, situated near the middle of that empire, and about three thousand miles distance from our house. My master made his daughter Glumdalclitch ride behind him. She carried me on her lap in a box tied about her waist. The girl had lined it on all sides with the softest cloth she could get, well quilted underneath, furnished it with her baby's bed, provided me with linen and other necessaries, and made everything as convenient as she could. We had no other company but a boy of the house, who rode after us with the luggage.

My master's design was to show me in all the towns by the way, and to step out of the road for fifty or an hundred miles to any village or person of quality's house where he might expect custom. We made easy journeys of not above seven or eight score miles a day: for Glumdalclitch, on purpose to spare me, complained she was tired with the trotting of the horse. She often took me out of my box at my own desire, to give me air and show me the country, but always held me fast by leading strings. We passed over five or six rivers many degrees broader and deeper than the Nile or the Ganges; and there was hardly a rivulet so small as the Thames at London Bridge. We were ten weeks in our journey, and I was shown in eighteen large towns, besides many large villages and private families.

On the 26th day of October, we arrived at the metropolis, called in their language *Lorbrulgrud*, or Pride of the Universe. My master took a lodging in the principal street of the city, not far from the royal palace, and put out bills in the usual form, containing an exact description of my person and parts. He hired a large room between three and four hundred foot wide. He provided a table sixty foot in diameter, upon which I was to act my part, and palisadoed it round three foot from the edge, and as many high, to prevent my falling over. I was shown ten times a day to the wonder and satisfaction of all people. I could now speak the language tolerably well, and perfectly understood every word that was spoken to me. Besides, I had learned their alphabet, and could make a shift to explain a sentence here and there; for Glumdalclitch had been my instructor while we were at home, and at leisure hours during our journey. She carried a little book in her pocket, not much larger than a Sanson's *Atlas;*[1] it was a common treatise for the use of young girls, giving a short account of their religion: out of this she taught me my letters, and interpreted the words.

CHAPTER III. *The Author sent for to Court. The Queen buys him of his master, the farmer, and presents him to the King. He disputes with his Majesty's great scholars. An apartment at Court provided for the Author. He is in high favor with the Queen. He stands up for the honor of his own country. His quarrels with the Queen's dwarf.*

The frequent labors I underwent every day made in a few weeks a very considerable change in my health: the more my master got by me, the more unsatiable he grew. I had quite lost my stomach, and was almost reduced to a skeleton. The farmer observed it, and concluding I soon must die, resolved to make as good a hand of me as he could. While he was thus reasoning and resolving with himself, a *Slardral,* or Gentleman Usher, came from Court, commanding my master to carry me immediately thither for the diversion of the Queen and her ladies. Some of the latter had already been to see me and reported strange things of my beauty, behavior, and good sense. Her Majesty and those who attended her were beyond measure delighted with my demeanor. I fell on my knees and begged the honor of kissing her Imperial foot; but this gracious princess held out her little finger towards me (after I was set on a table), which I embraced in both my arms, and put the tip of it, with the utmost respect, to my lip. She made me some general questions about my country and my travels, which I answered as distinctly and in as few words as I could. She asked whether I would be content to live at Court. I bowed down to the board of the table, and humbly answered that I was my master's slave, but if I were at my own disposal, I should be proud to devote my life to her Majesty's service. She then asked my master whether he were willing to sell me at a good price. He, who apprehended I could not live a month, was ready enough to part with me, and demanded a thousand pieces of gold, which were ordered him on the spot, each piece being about the bigness of eight hundred moidores;[2] but, allowing for the proportion of all things between that country and Europe, and the high price of gold among them, was hardly so great a sum as a thousand guineas would be in England. I then said to the Queen, since I was now her Majesty's most humble creature and vassal, I must beg the favor that Glumdalclitch, who had always tended me with so much care and kindness, and understood to do it so well, might be admitted into her service, and continue to be my nurse and instructor. Her Majesty agreed to my petition, and easily got the farmer's consent, who was glad enough to have his daughter preferred at Court; and the poor girl herself was not able to hide her

1. I.e., over two feet long and about two feet wide. 2. Portuguese coins.

joy. My late master withdrew, bidding me farewell, and saying he had left me in a good service; to which I replied not a word, only making him a slight bow.

The Queen observed my coldness, and when the farmer was gone out of the apartment, asked me the reason. I made bold to tell her Majesty that I owed no other obligation to my late master than his not dashing out the brains of a poor harmless creature found by chance in his field; which obligation was amply recompensed by the gain he had made in showing me through half the kingdom, and the price he had now sold me for. That the life I had since led was laborious enough to kill an animal of ten times my strength. That my health was much impaired by the continual drudgery of entertaining the rabble every hour of the day; and that if my master had not thought my life in danger, her Majestry would not have got so cheap a bargain. But as I was out of all fear of being ill treated under the protection of so great and good an Empress, the Ornament of Nature, the Darling of the World, the Delight of her Subjects, the Phoenix of the Creation; so I hoped my late master's apprehensions would appear to be groundless, for I already found my spirits to revive by the influence of her most august presence.

This was the sum of my speech, delivered with great improprieties and hesitation; the latter part was altogether framed in the style peculiar to that people, whereof I learned some phrases from Glumdalclitch, while she was carrying me to Court.

The Queen, giving great allowance for my defectiveness in speaking, was however surprised at so much wit and good sense in so diminutive an animal. She took me in her own hand, and carried me to the King, who was then retired to his cabinet.[3] His Majesty, a prince of much gravity, and austere countenance, not well observing my shape at first view, asked the Queen after a cold manner how long it was since she grew fond of a *splacknuck*; for such it seems he took me to be, as I lay upon my breast in her Majesty's right hand. But this princess, who hath an infinite deal of wit and humor, set me gently on my feet upon the scrutore,[4] and commanded me to give his Majesty an account of myself, which I did in a very few words; and Glumdalclitch, who attended at the cabinet door, and could not endure I should be out of her sight, being admitted, confirmed all that had passed from my arrival at her father's house.

The King, although he be as learned a person as any in his dominions, had been educated in the study of philosophy and particularly mathematics; yet when he observed my shape exactly, and saw me walk erect, before I began to speak, conceived I might be a piece of clockwork (which is in that country arrived to a very great perfection) contrived by some ingenious artist. But when he heard my voice, and found what I delivered to be regular and ra-

3. A private apartment. **4. Writing desk.**

tional, he could not conceal his astonishment. He was by no means satisfied with the relation I gave him of the manner I came into his kingdom, but thought it a story concerted between Glumdalclitch and her father, who had taught me a set of words to make me sell at a higher price. Upon this imagination he put several other questions to me, and still received rational answers, no otherwise defective than by a foreign accent, and an imperfect knowledge in the language, with some rustic phrases which I had learned at the farmer's house, and did not suit the polite style of a court.

His Majesty sent for three great scholars who were then in their weekly waiting (according to the custom in that country). These gentlemen, after they had a while examined my shape with much nicety, were of different opinions concerning me. They all agreed that I could not be produced according to the regular laws of nature, because I was not framed with a capacity of preserving my life, either by swiftness, or climbing of trees, or digging holes in the earth. They observed by my teeth, which they viewed with great exactness, that I was a carnivorous animal; yet most quadrupeds being an overmatch for me, and field mice, with some others, too nimble, they could not imagine how I should be able to support myself, unless I fed upon snails and other insects; which they offered, by many learned arguments, to evince that I could not possibly do. One of them seemed to think that I might be an embryo, or abortive birth. But this opinion was rejected by the other two, who observed my limbs to be perfect and finished, and that I had lived several years, as it was manifest from my beard, the stumps whereof they plainly discovered through a magnifying glass. They would not allow me to be a dwarf, because my littleness was beyond all degrees of comparison; for the Queen's favorite dwarf, the smallest ever known in that kingdom, was nearly thirty foot high. After much debate, they concluded unanimously that I was only *relplum scalcath*, which is interpreted literally, *lusus naturae*;[5] a determination exactly agreeable to the modern philosophy of Europe, whose professors, disdaining the old evasion of *occult causes*, whereby the followers of Aristotle endeavor in vain to disguise their ignorance, have invented this wonderful solution of all difficulties, to the unspeakable advancement of human knowledge.

After this decisive conclusion, I entreated to be heard a word or two. I applied myself to the King, and assured his Majesty that I came from a country which abounded with several millions of both sexes, and of my own stature, where the animals, trees, and houses were all in proportion, and where by consequence I might be as able to defend myself, and to find sustenance, as any of his Majesty's subjects could do here; which I took for a full answer to

5. One of nature's sports, or, roughly, freaks. Swift had contempt for both the medieval schoolmen, who discussed "occult causes," the unknown causes of observable effects, and modern scientists, who, he believed, often concealed their ignorance by using equally meaningless terms.

those gentlemen's arguments. To this they only replied with a smile of contempt, saying that the farmer had instructed me very well in my lesson. The King, who had a much better understanding, dismissing his learned men, sent for the farmer, who by good fortune was not yet gone out of town; having therefore first examined him privately, and then confronted him with me and the young girl, his Majesty began to think that what we told him might possibly be true. He desired the Queen to order that a particular care should be taken of me, and was of opinion that Glumdalclitch should still continue in her office of tending me, because he observed we had a great affection for each other. A convenient apartment was provided for her at Court; she had a sort of governess appointed to take care of her education, a maid to dress her, and two other servants for menial offices; but the care of me was wholly appropriated to herself. The Queen commanded her own cabinet-maker to contrive a box that might serve me for a bedchamber, after the model that Glumdalclitch and I should agree upon. This man was a most ingenious artist, and according to my directions, in three weeks finished for me a wooden chamber of sixteen foot square and twelve high, with sash windows, a door, and two closets, like a London bedchamber. The board that made the ceiling was to be lifted up and down by two hinges, to put in a bed ready furnished by her Majesty's upholsterer, which Glumdalclitch took out every day to air, made it with her own hands, and letting it down at night, locked up the roof over me. A nice[6] workman, who was famous for little curiosities, undertook to make me two chairs, with backs and frames, of a substance not unlike ivory, and two tables, with a cabinet to put my things in. The room was quilted on all sides, as well as the floor and the ceiling, to prevent any accident from the carelessness of those who carried me, and to break the force of a jolt when I went in a coach. I desired a lock for my door to prevent rats and mice from coming in: the smith, after several attempts, made the smallest that ever was seen among them, for I have known a larger at the gate of a gentleman's house in England. I made a shift[7] to keep the key in a pocket of my own, fearing Glumdalclitch might lose it. The Queen likewise ordered the thinnest silks that could be gotten, to make me clothes, not much thicker than an English blanket, very cumbersome till I was accustomed to them. They were after the fashion of the kingdom, partly resembling the Persian, and partly the Chinese, and are a very grave, decent habit.

The Queen became so fond of my company that she could not dine without me. I had a table placed upon the same at which her Majesty ate, just at her left elbow, and a chair to sit on. Glumdalclitch stood upon a stool on the floor, near my table, to assist and take care of me. I had an entire set of silver dishes and plates, and

6. Exact.

7. Contrived.

other necessaries, which, in proportion to those of the Queen, were not much bigger than what I have seen of the same kind in a London toyshop,[8] for the furniture of a baby-house: these my little nurse kept in her pocket in a silver box and gave me at meals as I wanted them, always cleaning them herself. No person dined with the Queen but the two Princesses Royal, the elder sixteen years old, and the younger at that time thirteen and a month. Her Majesty used to put a bit of meat upon one of my dishes, out of which I carved for myself; and her diversion was to see me eat in miniature. For the Queen (who had indeed but a weak stomach) took up at one mouthful as much as a dozen English farmers could eat at a meal, which to me was for some time a very nauseous sight. She would craunch the wing of a lark, bones and all, between her teeth, although it were nine times as large as that of a full-grown turkey; and put a bit of bread into her mouth as big as two twelve-penny loaves. She drank out of a golden cup, above a hogshead at a draught. Her knives were twice as long as a scythe set straight upon the handle. The spoons, forks, and other instruments were all in the same proportion. I remember when Glumdalclitch carried me out of curiosity to see some of the tables at Court, where ten or a dozen of these enormous knives and forks were lifted up together, I thought I had never till then beheld so terrible a sight.

It is the custom that every Wednesday (which, as I have before observed, was their Sabbath) the King and Queen, with the royal issue of both sexes, dine together in the apartment of his Majesty, to whom I was now become a favorite; and at these times my little chair and table were placed at his left hand, before one of the salt-cellars. This prince took a pleasure in conversing with me, inquiring into the manners, religion, laws, government, and learning of Europe; wherein I gave him the best account I was able. His apprehension was so clear, and his judgment so exact, that he made very wise reflections and observations upon all I said. But I confess that after I had been a little too copious in talking of my own beloved country, of our trade and wars by sea and land, of our schisms in religion and parties in the state, the prejudices of his education prevailed so far that he could not forbear taking me up in his right hand, and stroking me gently with the other, after an hearty fit of laughing, asked me whether I were a Whig or a Tory. Then turning to his first minister, who waited behind him with a white staff, near as tall as the mainmast of the *Royal Sovereign*,[9] he observed how contemptible a thing was human grandeur, which could be mimicked by such diminutive insects as I: "and yet," said he, "I dare engage, these creatures have their titles and distinctions of honor; they contrive little nests and burrows, that they call houses and cities; they make a figure in dress and equipage;[1] they love, they

8. A shop for selling knickknacks.
9. At the English court the Lord Treasurer bore a white staff as the symbol of his office. The *Royal Sovereign* was one of the largest ships in the Royal Navy.
1. A carriage and horses, with attendant footmen.

fight, they dispute, they cheat, they betray." And thus he continued on, while my color came and went several times with indignation to hear our noble country, the mistress of arts and arms, the scourge of France, the arbitress of Europe, the seat of virtue, piety, honor, and truth, the pride and envy of the world, so contemptuously treated.

But as I was not in a condition to resent injuries, so, upon mature thoughts, I began to doubt whether I were injured or no. For, after having been accustomed several months to the sight and converse of this people, and observed every object upon which I cast my eyes to be of proportionable magnitude, the horror I had first conceived from their bulk and aspect was so far worn off that if I had then beheld a company of English lords and ladies in their finery and birthday clothes,[2] acting their several parts in the most courtly manner of strutting and bowing and prating, to say the truth, I should have been strongly tempted to laugh as much at them as this King and his grandees did at me. Neither indeed could I forbear smiling at myself when the Queen used to place me upon her hand towards a looking glass, by which both our persons appeared before me in full view together; and there could be nothing more ridiculous than the comparison; so that I really began to imagine myself dwindled many degrees below my usual size.

Nothing angered and mortified me so much as the Queen's dwarf, who being of the lowest stature that was ever in that country (for I verily think he was not full thirty foot high) became so insolent at seeing a creature so much beneath him that he would always affect to swagger and look big as he passed by me in the Queen's antechamber, while I was standing on some table talking with the lords or ladies of the court; and he seldom failed of a smart word or two upon my littleness, against which I could only revenge myself by calling him brother, challenging him to wrestle, and such repartees as are usual in the mouths of Court pages. One day at dinner this malicious little cub was so nettled with something I had said to him that, raising himself upon the frame of Her Majesty's chair, he took me up by the middle, as I was sitting down, not thinking any harm, and let me drop into a large silver bowl of cream, and then ran away as fast as he could. I fell over head and ears, and if I had not been a good swimmer, it might have gone very hard with me; for Glumdalclitch in that instant happened to be at the other end of the room, and the Queen was in such a fright that she wanted presence of mind to assist me. But my little nurse ran to my relief, and took me out, after I had swallowed above a quart of cream. I was put to bed; however, I received no other damage than the loss of a suit of clothes, which was utterly spoiled. The dwarf was soundly whipped, and as a further punishment, forced to drink up the bowl of cream into which he had

2. **Courtiers dressed with especial splendor on the monarch's birthday.**

thrown me; neither was he ever restored to favor: for soon after the Queen bestowed him to a lady of high quality, so that I saw him no more, to my very great satisfaction; for I could not tell to what extremity such a malicious urchin might have carried his resentment.

He had before served me a scurvy trick, which set the Queen a laughing, although at the same time she were heartily vexed, and would have immediately cashiered him,[3] if I had not been so generous as to intercede. Her Majesty had taken a marrow bone upon her plate, and after knocking out the marrow, placed the bone again in the dish, erect as it stood before; the dwarf watching his opportunity, while Glumdalclitch was gone to the sideboard, mounted upon the stool she stood on to take care of me at meals, took me up in both hands, and squeezing my legs together, wedged them into the marrow bone above my waist, where I stuck for some time, and made a very ridiculous figure. I believe it was near a minute before anyone knew what was become of me, for I thought it below me to cry out. But, as princes seldom get their meat hot, my legs were not scalded, only my stockings and breeches in a sad condition. The dwarf at my entreaty had no other punishment than a sound whipping.

I was frequently rallied by the Queen upon account of my fearfulness, and she used to ask me whether the people of my country were as great cowards as myself. The occasion was this. The kingdom is much pestered with flies in summer, and these odious insects, each of them as big as a Dunstable lark, hardly gave me any rest while I sat at dinner, with their continual humming and buzzing about my ears. They would sometimes alight upon my victuals, and leave their loathsome excrement or spawn behind, which to me was very visible, although not to the natives of that country, whose large optics were not so acute as mine in viewing smaller objects. Sometimes they would fix upon my nose or forehead, where they stung me to the quick, smelling very offensively; and I could easily trace that viscous matter, which our naturalists tell us enables those creatures to walk with their feet upwards upon a ceiling. I had much ado to defend myself against these destable animals, and could not forbear starting when they came on my face. It was the common practice of the dwarf to catch a number of these insects in his hand, as schoolboys do among us, and let them out suddenly under my nose, on purpose to frighten me, and divert the Queen. My remedy was to cut them in pieces with my knife as they flew in the air, wherein my dexterity was much admired.

I remember one morning when Glumdalclitch had set me in my box upon a window, as she usually did in fair days to give me air (for I durst not venture to let the box be hung on a nail out of the window, as we do with cages in England), after I had lifted up one

3. Dismissed him.

of my sashes, and sat down at my table to eat a piece of sweet cake for my breakfast, above twenty wasps, allured by the smell, came flying into the room, humming louder than the drones of as many bagpipes. Some of them seized my cake, and carried it piecemeal away; others flew about my head and face, confounding me with the noise, and putting me in the utmost terror of their stings. However, I had the courage to rise and draw my hanger, and attack them in the air. I dispatched four of them, but the rest got away, and I presently shut my window. These insects were as large as partridges; I took out their stings, found them an inch and a half long, and as sharp as needles. I carefully preserved them all, and having since shown them with some other curiosities in several parts of Europe, upon my return to England I gave three of them to Gresham College,[4] and kept the fourth for myself.

CHAPTER IV. *The country described. A proposal for correcting modern maps. The King's palace, and some account of the metropolis. The Author's way of traveling. The chief temple described.*

I now intend to give the reader a short description of this country, as far as I have traveled in it, which was not above two thousand miles round Lorbrulgrud the metropolis. For the Queen, whom I always attended, never went further when she accompanied the King in his progresses, and there stayed till his Majesty returned from viewing his frontiers. The whole extent of this prince's dominions reacheth about six thousand miles in length, and from three to five in breadth. From whence I cannot but conclude that our geographers of Europe are in a great error by supposing nothing but sea between Japan and California: for it was ever my opinion that there must be a balance of earth to counterpoise the great continent of Tartary; and therefore they ought to correct their maps and charts by joining this vast tract of land to the northwest parts of America, wherein I shall be ready to lend them my assistance.

The kingdom is a peninsula, terminated to the northeast by a ridge of mountains thirty miles high, which are altogether impassable by reason of the volcanoes upon the tops. Neither do the most learned know what sort of mortals inhabit beyond those mountains, or whether they be inhabited at all. On the three other sides it is bounded by the ocean. There is not one seaport in the whole kingdom; and those parts of the coasts into which the rivers issue are so full of pointed rocks, and the sea generally so rough, that there is no venturing with the smallest of their boats; so that these people are wholly excluded from any commerce with the rest of the world. But the large rivers are full of vessels, and abound with excellent fish, for they seldom get any from the sea, because the sea fish are of the same size with those in Europe, and consequently

4. The Royal Society, in its earliest years, met in Gresham College.

not worth catching; whereby it is manifest that nature, in the production of plants and animals of so extraordinary a bulk, is wholly confined to this continent, of which I leave the reasons to be determined by philosophers. However, now and then they take a whale that happens to be dashed against the rocks, which the common people feed on heartily. These whales I have known so large that a man could hardly carry one upon his shoulders; and sometimes for curiosity they are brought in hampers to Lorbrulgrud: I saw one of them in a dish at the King's table, which passed for a rarity, but I did not observe he was fond of it; for I think indeed the bigness disgusted him, although I have seen one somewhat larger in Greenland.

The country is well inhabited, for it contains fifty-one cities, near an hundred walled towns, and a great number of villages. To satisfy my curious reader, it may be sufficient to describe Lorbrulgrud. This city stand upon almost two equal parts on each side the river that passes through. It contains above eighty thousand houses, and about six hundred thousand inhabitants. It is in length three *glongluns* (which make about fifty-four English miles) and two and a half in breadth, as I measured it myself in the royal map made by the King's order, which was laid on the ground on purpose for me, and extended an hundred feet; I paced the diameter and circumference several times barefoot, and computing by the scale, measured it pretty exactly.

The King's palace is no regular edifice, but an heap of buildings about seven miles round: the chief rooms are generally two hundred and forty foot high, and broad and long in proportion. A coach was allowed to Glumdalclitch and me, wherein her governess frequently took her out to see the town, or go among the shops; and I was always of the party, carried in my box, although the girl at my own desire would often take me out, and hold me in her hand, that I might more conveniently view the houses and the people as we passed along the streets. I reckoned our coach to be about a square of Westminster Hall,[5] but not altogether so high; however, I cannot be very exact. One day the governess ordered our coachman to stop at several shops, where the beggars, watching their opportunity, crowded to the sides of the coach, and gave me the most horrible spectacles that ever an English eye beheld. There was a woman with a cancer in her breast, swelled to a monstrous size, full of holes, in two or three of which I could have easily crept, and covered my whole body. There was a fellow with a wen in his neck, larger than five woolpacks, and another with a couple of wooden legs, each about twenty foot high. But the most hateful sight of all was the lice crawling on their clothes. I could see distinctly the limbs of these vermin with my naked eye, much better than those

5. The ancient hall, now incorporated into the Houses of Parliament, where the Law Courts then sat. Swift presumably means the square of its breadth (just under 68 feet).

of an European louse through a microscope, and their snouts with which they rooted like swine. They were the first I had ever beheld; and I should have been curious enough to dissect one of them if I had proper instruments (which I unluckily left behind me in the ship), although indeed the sight was so nauseous that it perfectly turned my stomach.

Besides the large box in which I was usually carried, the Queen ordered a smaller one to be made for me, of about twelve foot square and ten high, for the convenience of traveling, because the other was somewhat too large for Glumdalclitch's lap, and cumbersome in the coach; it was made by the same artist, whom I directed in the whole contrivance. This traveling closet was an exact square with a window in the middle of three of the squares, and each window was latticed with iron wire on the outside, to prevent accidents in long journeys. On the fourth side, which had no window, two strong staples were fixed, through which the person that carried me, when I had a mind to be on horseback, put in a leathern belt, and buckled it about his waist. This was always the office of some grave trusty servant in whom I could confide, whether I attended the King and Queen in their progresses, or were disposed to see the gardens, or pay a visit to some great lady or minister of state in the court, when Glumdalclitch happened to be out of order: for I soon began to be known and esteemed among the greatest officers, I suppose more upon account of their Majesties' favor than any merit of my own. In journeys, when I was weary of the coach, a servant on horseback would buckle my box, and place it on a cushion before him; and there I had a full prospect of the country on three sides from my three windows. I had in this closet a field bed and a hammock hung from the ceiling, two chairs and a table, neatly screwed to the floor to prevent being tossed about by the agitation of the horse or the coach. And having been long used to sea voyages, those motions, although sometimes very violent, did not much discompose me.

When I had a mind to see the town, it was always in my traveling closet, which Glumdalclitch held in her lap in a kind of open sedan, after the fashion of the country, borne by four men, and attended by two others in the Queen's livery. The people, who had often heard of me, were very curious to crowd about the sedan; and the girl was complaisant enough to make the bearers stop, and to take me in her hand that I might be more conveniently seen.

I was very desirous to see the chief temple, and particularly the tower belonging to it, which is reckoned the highest in the kingdom. Accordingly one day my nurse carried me thither, but I may truly say I came back disappointed; for the height is not above three thousand foot, reckoning from the ground to the highest pinnacle top; which, allowing for the difference between the size of those people and us in Europe, is no great matter for admiration, nor at all equal in proportion (if I rightly remember) to Salisbury steeple.[6] But, not to detract from a nation to which during my life I shall acknowledge myself extremely obliged, it must be allowed that whatever this famous tower wants in height is amply made up in beauty and strength. For the walls are near an hundred foot thick, built of hewn stone, whereof each is about forty foot square, and adorned on all sides with statues of gods and emperors cut in marble larger than the life, placed in their several niches. I measured a little finger which had fallen down from one of these statues, and lay unperceived among some rubbish, and found it exactly four foot and an inch in length. Glumdalclitch wrapped it up in a handkerchief, and carried it home in her pocket to keep among other trinkets, of which the girl was very fond, as children at her age usually are.

The King's kitchen is indeed a noble building, vaulted at top, and about six hundred foot high. The great oven is not so wide by ten paces as the cupola at St. Paul's:[7] for I measured the latter on purpose after my return. But if I should describe the kitchen grate, the prodigious pots and kettles, the joints of meat turning on the spits, with many other particulars, perhaps I should be hardly believed; at least a severe critic would be apt to think I enlarged a little, as travelers are often suspected to do. To avoid which censure, I fear I have run too much into the other extreme, and that if this treatise should happen to be translated into the language of Brobdingnag (which is the general name of that kingdom) and transmitted thither, the King and his people would have reason to complain that I had done them an injury by a false and diminutive representation.

His Majesty seldom keeps above six hundred horses in his stables: they are generally from fifty-four to sixty foot high. But when he goes abroad on solemn days, he is attended for state by a militia guard of five hundred horse, which indeed I thought was the most splendid sight that could be ever beheld, till I saw part of his army in battalia;[8] whereof I shall find another occasion to speak.

CHAPTER V. *Several adventures that happened to the Author. The execution of a criminal. The Author shows his skill in navigation.*

I should have lived happy enough in that country if my littleness had not exposed me to several ridiculous and troublesome accidents, some of which I shall venture to relate. Glumdalclitch often carried me into the gardens of the court in my smaller box, and would sometimes take me out of it and hold me in her hand, or set me down to walk. I remember, before the dwarf left the Queen, he followed us one day into those gardens; and my nurse having set me down, he and I being close together near some dwarf apple

6. One of the most beautiful Gothic steeples in England is that of Salisbury Cathedral, 404 feet high.

7. The cupola of St. Paul's Cathedral in London is 108 feet in diameter.

8. Battle array.

trees, I must needs show my wit by a silly allusion between him and the trees, which happens to hold in their language as it doth in ours. Whereupon, the malicious rogue watching his opportunity, when I was walking under one of them, shook it directly over my head, by which a dozen apples, each of them near as large as a Bristol barrel, came tumbling about my ears; one of them hit me on the back as I chanced to stoop, and knocked me down flat on my face, but I received no other hurt; and the dwarf was pardoned at my desire, because I had given the provocation.

Another day Glumdalclitch left me on a smooth grassplot to divert myself while she walked at some distance with her governess. In the meantime there suddenly fell such a violent shower of hail that I was immediately by the force of it struck to the ground: and when I was down, the hailstones gave me such cruel bangs all over the body as if I had been pelted with tennis balls;[9] however I made a shift to creep on all four, and shelter myself by lying on my face on the lee side of a border of lemon thyme, but so bruised from head to foot that I could not go abroad in ten days. Neither is this at all to be wondered at, because nature in that country observing the same proportion through all her operations, a hailstone is near eighteen hundred times as large as one in Europe; which I can assert upon experience, having been so curious to weigh and measure them.

But a more dangerous accident happened to me in the same garden when my little nurse, believing she had put me in a secure place, which I often entreated her to do that I might enjoy my own thoughts, and having left my box at home to avoid the trouble of carrying it, went to another part of the garden with her governess and some ladies of her acquaintance. While she was absent and out of hearing, a small white spaniel belonging to one of the chief gardeners, having got by accident into the garden, happened to range near the place where I lay. The dog following the scent, came directly up, and taking me in his mouth, ran straight to his master, wagging his tail, and set me gently on the ground. By good fortune he had been so well taught that I was carried between his teeth without the least hurt, or even tearing my clothes. But the poor gardener, who knew me well, and had a great kindness for me, was in a terrible fright. He gently took me up in both his hands, and asked me how I did; but I was so amazed and out of breath that I could not speak a word. In a few minutes I came to myself, and he carried me safe to my little nurse, who by this time had returned to the place where she left me, and was in cruel agonies when I did not appear nor answer when she called; she severely reprimanded the gardener on account of his dog. But the thing was hushed up and never known at court; for the girl was afraid of the Queen's anger; and truly, as to myself, I thought it

9. 18th-century tennis balls, unlike the modern, were very hard.

would not be for my reputation that such a story should go about.

This accident absolutely determined Glumdalclitch never to trust me abroad for the future out of her sight. I had been long afraid of this resolution, and therefore concealed from her some little unlucky adventures that happened in those times when I was left by myself. Once a kite[1] hovering over the garden made a swoop at me, and if I had not resolutely drawn my hanger, and run under a thick espalier,[2] he would have certainly carried me away in his talons. Another time walking to the top of a fresh molehill, I fell to my neck in the hole through which that animal had cast up the earth, and coined some lie, not worth remembering, to excuse myself for spoiling my clothes. I likewise broke my right shin against the shell of a snail, which I happened to stumble over, as I was walking alone, and thinking on poor England.

I cannot tell whether I were more pleased or mortified to observe in those solitary walks that the smaller birds did not appear to be at all afraid of me; but would hop about within a yard distance, looking for worms and other food with as much indifference and security as if no creature at all were near them. I remember a thrush had the confidence to snatch out of my hand with his bill a piece of cake that Glumdalclitch had just given me for my breakfast. When I attempted to catch any of these birds, they would boldly turn against me, endeavoring to pick my fingers, which I durst not venture within their reach; and then they would hop back unconcerned to hunt for worms or snails, as they did before. But one day I took a thick cudgel, and threw it with all my strength so luckily at a linnet that I knocked him down, and seizing him by the neck with both my hands, ran with him in triumph to my nurse. However, the bird, who had only been stunned, recovering himself, gave me so many boxes with his wings on both sides of my head and body, though I held him at arm's length, and was out of the reach of his claws, that I was twenty times thinking to let him go. But I was soon relieved by one of our servants, who wrung off the bird's neck, and I had him next day for dinner, by the Queen's command. This linnet, as near as I can remember, seemed to be somewhat larger than an English swan.

The Maids of Honor often invited Glumdalclitch to their apartments, and desired she would bring me along with her, on purpose to have the pleasure of seeing and touching me. They would often strip me naked from top to toe and lay me at full length in their bosoms; wherewith I was much disgusted, because, to say the truth, a very offensive smell came from their skins, which I do not mention or intend to the disadvantage of those excellent ladies, for whom I have all manner of respect; but I conceive that my sense was more acute in proportion to my littleness, and that those illus-

1. A bird of prey.

2. A trellis on which fruit trees are trained.

trious persons were no more disagreeable to their lovers, or to each other, than people of the same quality are with us in England. And, after all, I found their natural smell was much more supportable than when they used perfumes, under which I immediately swooned away. I cannot forget that an intimate friend of mine in Lilliput took the freedom in a warm day, when I had used a good deal of exercise, to complain of a strong smell about me, although I am as little faulty that way as most of my sex: but I suppose his faculty of smelling was as nice with regard to me as mine was to that of this people. Upon this point, I cannot forbear doing justice to the Queen, my mistress, and Glumdalclitch, my nurse, whose persons were as sweet as those of any lady in England.

That which gave me most uneasiness among these Maids of Honor, when my nurse carried me to visit them, was to see them use me without any manner of ceremony, like a creature who had no sort of consequence. For they would strip themselves to the skin and put on their smocks in my presence, while I was placed on their toilet[3] directly before their naked bodies; which, I am sure, to me was very far from being a tempting sight, or from giving me any other emotions than those of horror and disgust. Their skins appeared so coarse and uneven, so variously colored, when I saw them near, with a mole here and there as broad as a trencher, and hairs hanging from it thicker than pack-threads, to say nothing further concerning the rest of their persons. Neither did they at all scruple, while I was by, to discharge what they had drunk, to the quantity of at least two hogsheads, in a vessel that held above three tuns. The handsomest among these Maids of Honor, a pleasant frolicsome girl of sixteen, would sometimes set me astride upon one of her nipples, with many other tricks, wherein the reader will excuse me for not being over particular. But I was so much displeased that I entreated Glumdalclitch to contrive some excuse for not seeing that young lady any more.

One day a young gentleman, who was nephew to my nurse's governess, came and pressed them both to see an execution. It was of a man who had murdered one of that gentleman's intimate acquaintance. Glumdalclitch was prevailed on to be of the company, very much against her inclination, for she was naturally tender-hearted: and as for myself, although I abhorred such kind of spectacles, yet my curiosity tempted me to see something that I thought must be extraordinary. The malefactor was fixed in a chair upon a scaffold erected for the purpose, and his head cut off at a blow with a sword of about forty foot long. The veins and arteries spouted up such a prodigious quantity of blood, and so high in the air, that the great *jet d'eau*[4] at Versailles was not equal for the time it lasted; and the head, when it fell on the scaffold floor, gave such a bounce,[5]

3. Toilet table.
4. This fountain rose over forty feet in the air.
5. A sudden noise.

as made me start, although I were at least half an English mile distant.

The Queen, who often used to hear me talk of my sea voyages, and took all occasions to divert me when I was melancholy, asked me whether I understood how to handle a sail or an oar, and whether a little exercise of rowing might not be convenient for my health. I answered that I understood both very well. For although my proper employment had been to be surgeon or doctor to the ship, yet often, upon a pinch, I was forced to work like a common mariner. But I could not see how this could be done in their country, where the smallest wherry was equal to a first-rate man-of-war among us, and such a boat as I could manage would never live in any of their rivers. Her Majestry said, if I would contrive a boat, her own joiner[6] should make it, and she would provide a place for me to sail in. The fellow was an ingenious workman and, by my instructions, in ten days finished a pleasure boat with all its tackling, able conveniently to hold eight Europeans. When it was finished, the Queen was so delighted that she ran with it in her lap to the King, who ordered it to be put in a cistern full of water, with me in it, by way of trial; where I could not manage my two sculls, or little oars, for want of room. But the Queen had before contrived another project. She ordered the joiner to make a wooden trough of three hundred foot long, fifty broad, and eight deep; which being well pitched to prevent leaking, was placed on the floor along the wall in an outer room of the palace. It had a cock near the bottom to let out the water when it began to grow stale, and two servants could easily fill it in half an hour. Here I often used to row for my own diversion, as well as that of the Queen and her ladies, who thought themselves well entertained with my skill and agility. Sometimes I would put up my sail, and then my business was only to steer, while the ladies gave me a gale with their fans; and when they were weary, some of the pages would blow my sail forward with their breath, while I showed my art by steering starboard or larboard as I pleased. When I had done, Glumdalclitch always carried my boat into her closet, and hung it on a nail to dry.

In this exercise I once met an accident which had like to have cost me my life. For one of the pages having put my boat into the trough, the governess who attended Glumdalclitch very officiously[7] lifted me up to place me in the boat; but I happened to slip through her fingers, and should have infallibly fallen down forty feet upon the floor, if by the luckiest chance in the world I had not been stopped by a corking-pin[8] that stuck in the good gentlewoman's stomacher; the head of the pin passed between my shirt and the waistband of my breeches, and thus I was held by the middle in the air until Glumdalclitch ran to my relief.

6. A skilled woodworker.
7. Kindly, dutifully.
8. A pin of the largest size. "Stomacher": an ornamental covering for the front and upper part of the body.

Another time, one of the servants, whose office it was to fill my trough every third day with fresh water, was so careless to let a huge frog (not perceiving it) slip out of his pail. The frog lay concealed till I was put into my boat, but then seeing a resting place, climbed up, and made it lean so much on one side that I was forced to balance it with all my weight on the other, to prevent overturning. When the frog was got in, it hopped at once half the length of the boat, and then over my head, backwards and forwards, daubing my face and clothes with its odious slime. The largeness of its features made it appear the most deformed animal that can be conceived. However, I desired Glumdalclitch to let me deal with it alone. I banged it a good while with one of my sculls, and at last forced it to leap out of the boat.

But the greatest danger I ever underwent in that kingdom was from a monkey, who belonged to one of the clerks of the kitchen. Glumdalclitch had locked me up in her closet, while she went somewhere upon business or a visit. The weather being very warm, the closet window was left open, as well as the windows in the door of my bigger box, in which I usually lived, because of its largeness and conveniency. As I sat quietly meditating at my table, I heard something bounce in at the closet window, and skip about from one side to the other, whereat, although I was much alarmed, yet I ventured to look out, but stirred not from my seat; and then I saw this frolicsome animal, frisking and leaping up and down, till at last he came to my box, which he seemed to view with great pleasure and curiosity, peeping in at the door and every window. I retreated to the farther corner of my room, or box, but the monkey looking in at every side, put me into such a fright that I wanted presence of mind to conceal myself under the bed, as I might easily have done. After some time spent in peeping, grinning, and chattering, he at last espied me, and reaching one of his paws in at the door, as a cat does when she plays with a mouse, although I often shifted place to avoid him, he at length seized the lappet of my coat (which, being made of that country cloth, was very thick and strong) and dragged me out. He took me up in his right forefoot, and held me as a nurse does a child she is going to suckle, just as I have seen the same sort of creature do with a kitten in Europe: and when I offered to struggle, he squeezed me so hard that I thought it more prudent to submit. I have good reason to believe that he took me for a young one of his own species, by his often stroking my face very gently with his other paw. In these diversions he was interrupted by a noise at the closet door, as if somebody were opening it, whereupon he suddenly leaped up to the window at which he had come in, and thence upon the leads and gutters, walking upon three legs, and holding me in the fourth, till he clambered up to a roof that was next to ours. I heard Glumdalclitch give a shriek at the moment he was carrying me out. The poor girl was almost distracted: that quarter of the palace was all in an uproar; the servants ran for ladders; the monkey was seen by hundreds in the court, sitting upon the ridge of a building, holding me like a baby in one of his forepaws and feeding me with the other, by cramming into my mouth some victuals he had squeezed out of the bag on one side of his chaps, and patting me when I would not eat; whereat many of the rabble below could not forbear laughing; neither do I think they justly ought to be blamed, for without question the sight was ridiculous enough to everybody but myself. Some of the people threw up stones, hoping to drive the monkey down; but this was strictly forbidden, or else very probably my brains had been dashed out.

The ladders were now applied, and mounted by several men; which the monkey observing, and finding himself almost encompassed, not being able to make speed enough with his three legs, let me drop on a ridge tile, and made his escape. Here I sat for some time three hundred yards from the ground, expecting every moment to be blown down by the wind, or to fall by my own giddiness, and come tumbling over and over from the ridge to the eaves. But an honest lad, one of my nurse's footmen, climbed up, and putting me into his breeches pocket, brought me down safe.

I was almost choked with the filthy stuff the monkey had crammed down my throat; but my dear little nurse picked it out of my mouth with a small needle, and then I fell a vomiting, which gave me great relief. Yet I was so weak and bruised in the sides with the squeezes given me by this odious animal that I was forced to keep my bed a fortnight. The King, Queen, and all the Court sent every day to inquire after my health, and her Majesty made me several visits during my sickness. The monkey was killed, and an order made that no such animal should be kept about the palace.

When I attended the King after my recovery, to return him thanks for his favors, he was pleased to rally me a good deal upon this adventure. He asked me what my thoughts and speculations were while I lay in the monkey's paw, how I liked the victuals he gave me, his manner of feeding, and whether the fresh air on the roof had sharpened my stomach. He desired to know what I would have done upon such an occasion in my own country. I told his Majesty that in Europe we had no monkeys, except such as were brought for curiosities from other places, and so small that I could deal with a dozen of them together, if they presumed to attack me. And as for that monstrous animal with whom I was so lately engaged (it was indeed as large as an elephant), if my fears had suffered me to think so far as to make use of my hanger (looking fiercely and clapping my hand upon the hilt as I spoke) when he poked his paw into my chamber, perhaps I should have given him such a wound as would have made him glad to withdraw it with more haste than he put it in. This I delivered in a firm tone, like a person who was jealous lest his courage should be called in question. However, my speech produced nothing else besides a loud laughter, which all the respect due to his Majesty from those about him could not make them contain. This made me reflect how vain an attempt it is for a man to endeavor doing himself honor among those who are out of all degree of equality or comparison with him. And yet I have seen the moral of my own behavior very frequent in England since my return, where a little contemptible varlet, without the least title to birth, person, wit, or common sense, shall presume to look with importance, and put himself upon a foot with the greatest persons of the kingdom.

I was every day furnishing the court with some ridiculous story; and Glumdalclitch, although she loved me to excess, yet was arch enough to inform the Queen whenever I committed any folly that she thought would be diverting to her Majesty. The girl, who had been out of order, was carried by her governess to take the air about an hour's distance, or thirty miles from town. They alighted out of the coach near a small footpath in a field, and Glumdalclitch setting down my traveling box, I went out of it to walk. There was a cow dung in the patch, and I must needs try my activity by attempting to leap over it. I took a run, but unfortunately jumped short, and found myself just in the middle up to my knees. I waded through with some difficulty, and one of the footmen wiped me as clean as he could with his handkerchief; for I was filthily bemired, and my nurse confined me to my box till we returned home, where the Queen was soon informed of what had passed and the footmen spread it about the Court, so that all the mirth, for some days, was at my expense.

CHAPTER VI. *Several contrivances of the Author to please the King and Queen. He shows his skill in music. The King inquires into the state of Europe, which the Author relates to him. The King's observations thereon.*

I used to attend the King's levee[9] once or twice a week, and had often seen him under the barber's hand, which indeed was at first very terrible to behold. For the razor was almost twice as long as an ordinary scythe. His Majesty, according to the custom of the country, was only shaved twice a week. I once prevailed on the barber to give me some of the suds or lather, out of which I picked forty or fifty of the strongest stumps of hair. I then took a piece of fine wood, and cut it like the back of a comb, making several holes in it at equal distance with as small a needle as I could get from Glumdalclitch. I fixed in the stumps so artificially,[1] scraping

9. A morning reception held by a prince or nobleman, sometimes while dressing for the day.

1. Skillfully.

and sloping them with my knife towards the points, that I made a very tolerable comb; which was a seasonable supply, my own being so much broken in the teeth that it was almost useless; neither did I know any artist in that country so nice and exact as would undertake to make me another.

And this puts me in mind of an amusement wherein I spent many of my leisure hours. I desired the Queen's woman to save for me the combings of her Majesty's hair, whereof in time I got a good quantity; and consulting with my friend the cabinetmaker, who had received general orders to do little jobs for me, I directed him to make two chair frames, no larger than those I had in my box, and then to bore little holes with a fine awl round those parts where I designed the backs and seats; through these holes I wove the strongest hairs I could pick out, just after the manner of cane chairs in England. When they were finished, I made a present of them to her Majesty, who kept them in her cabinet, and used to show them for curiosities, as indeed they were the wonder of every one that beheld them. The Queen would have made me sit upon one of these chairs, but I absolutely refused to obey her, protesting I would rather die a thousand deaths than place a dishonorable part of my body on those precious hairs that once adorned her Majesty's head. Of these hairs (as I had always a mechanical genius) I likewise made a neat little purse above five foot long, with her Majesty's name deciphered in gold letters, which I gave to Glumdalclitch by the Queen's consent. To say the truth, it was more for show than use, being not of strength to bear the weight of the larger coins; and therefore she kept nothing in it but some little toys[2] that girls are fond of.

The King, who delighted in music, had frequent consorts[3] at court, to which I was sometimes carried, and set in my box on a table to hear them; but the noise was so great that I could hardly distinguish the tunes. I am confident that all the drums and trumpets of a royal army, beating and sounding together just at your ears, could not equal it. My practice was to have my box removed from the places where the performers sat, as far as I could, then to shut the doors and windows of it, and draw the window curtains, after which I found their music not disagreeable.

I had learned in my youth to play a little upon the spinet. Glumdalclitch kept one in her chamber, and a master attended twice a week to teach her: I call it a spinet, because it somewhat resembled that instrument, and was played upon in the same manner. A fancy came into my head that I would entertain the King and Queen with an English tune upon this instrument. But this appeared extremely difficult: for the spinet was near sixty foot long, each key being almost a foot wide; so that, with my arms extended, I could

2. Trifles.

3. Concerts.

not reach to above five keys, and to press them down required a good smart stroke with my fist, which would be too great a labor and to no purpose. The method I contrived was this: I prepared two round sticks about the bigness of common cudgels; they were thicker at one end than the other, and I covered the thicker ends with a piece of a mouse's skin, that by rapping on them I might neither damage the tops of the keys, nor interrupt the sound. Before the spinet a bench was placed, about four foot below the keys, and I was put upon the bench. I ran sideling upon it that way and this, as fast as I could, banging the proper keys with my two sticks; and made a shift to play a jig, to the great satisfaction of both their Majesties: but it was the most violent exercise I ever underwent, and yet I could not strike above sixteen keys, nor, consequently, play the bass and treble together, as other artists do; which was a great disadvantage to my performance.

The King, who, as I before observed, was a prince of excellent understanding, would frequently order that I should be brought in my box and set upon the table in his closet. He would then command me to bring one of my chairs out of the box, and sit down within three yards distance upon the top of the cabinet, which brought me almost to a level with his face. In this manner I had several conversations with him. I one day took the freedom to tell his Majesty that the contempt he discovered towards Europe, and the rest of the world, did not seem answerable to those excellent qualities of mind that he was master of. That reason did not extend itself with the bulk of the body: on the contrary, we observed in our country that the tallest persons were usually least provided with it. That among other animals, bees and ants had the reputation of more industry, art, and sagacity than many of the larger kinds; and that, as inconsiderable as he took me to be, I hoped I might live to do his Majesty some signal service. The King heard me with attention, and began to conceive a much better opinion of me than he had before. He desired I would give him as exact an account of the government of England as I possibly could; because, as fond as princes commonly are of their own customs (for so he conjectured of other monarchs, by my former discourses), he should be glad to hear of anything that might deserve imitation.

Imagine with thyself, courteous reader, how often I then wished for the tongue of Demosthenes or Cicero, that might have enabled me to celebrate the praise of my own dear native country in a style equal to its merits and felicity.

I began my discourse by informing his Majesty that our dominions consisted of two islands, which composed three mighty kingdoms under one sovereign, beside our plantations in America. I dwelt long upon the fertility of our soil, and the temperature[4] of

4. Temperateness.

our climate. I then spoke at large upon the constitution of an English Parliament, partly made up of an illustrious body called the House of Peers, persons of the noblest blood, and of the most ancient and ample patrimonies. I described that extraordinary care always taken of their education in arts and arms, to qualify them for being counselors born to the king and kingdom; to have a share in the legislature, to be members of the highest Court of Judicature, from whence there could be no appeal; and to be champions always ready for the defense of their prince and country, by their valor, conduct, and fidelity. That these were the ornament and bulwark of the kingdom, worthy followers of their most renowned ancestors, whose honor had been the reward of their virtue, from which their posterity were never once known to degenerate. To these were joined several holy persons, as part of that assembly, under the title of Bishops, whose peculiar business it is to take care of religion, and of those who instruct the people therein. These were searched and sought out through the whole nation, by the prince and his wisest counselors, among such of the priesthood as were most deservedly distinguished by the sanctity of their lives and the depth of their erudition, who were indeed the spiritual fathers of the clergy and the people.

That the other part of the Parliament consisted of an assembly called the House of Commons, who were all principal gentlemen, freely picked and culled out by the people themselves, for their great abilities and love of their country, to represent the wisdom of the whole nation. And these two bodies make up the most august assembly in Europe, to whom, in conjunction with the prince, the whole legislature is committed.

I then descended to the Courts of Justice, over which the Judges, those venerable sages and interpreters of the law, presided, for determining the disputed rights and properties of men, as well as for the punishment of vice, and protection of innocence. I mentioned the prudent management of our treasury, the valor and achievements of our forces by sea and land. I computed the number of our people, by reckoning how many millions there might be of each religious sect, or political party among us. I did not omit even our sports and pastimes, or any other particular which I thought might redound to the honor of my country. And I finished all with a brief historical account of affairs and events in England for about an hundred years past.

This conversation was not ended under five audiences, each of several hours, and the King heard the whole with great attention, frequently taking notes of what I spoke, as well as memorandums of several questions he intended to ask me.

When I had put an end to these long discourses, his Majesty in a sixth audience consulting his notes, proposed many doubts, queries, and objections, upon every article. He asked what methods were used to cultivate the minds and bodies of our young nobility, and in what kind of business they commonly spent the first and teachable part of their lives. What course was taken to supply that assembly when any noble family became extinct. What qualifications were necessary in those who were to be created new lords. Whether the humor[5] of the prince, a sum of money to a Court lady or a prime minister, or a design of strengthening a party opposite to the public interest, ever happened to be motives in those advancements. What share of knowledge these lords had in the laws of their country, and how they came by it, so as to enable them to decide the properties of their fellow subjects in the last resort. Whether they were always so free from avarice, partialities, or want that a bribe or some other sinister view could have no place among them. Whether those holy lords I spoke of were constantly promoted to that rank upon account of their knowledge in religious matters, and the sanctity of their lives, had never been compliers with the times while they were common priests, or slavish prostitute chaplains to some nobleman, whose opinions they continued servilely to follow after they were admitted into that assembly.

He then desired to know what arts were practiced in electing those whom I called Commoners. Whether a stranger with a strong purse might not influence the vulgar voters to choose him before their own landlord or the most considerable gentleman in the neighborhood. How it came to pass that people were so violently bent upon getting into this assembly, which I allowed to be a great trouble and expense, often to the ruin of their families, without any salary or pension: because this appeared such an exalted strain of virtue and public spirit that his Majesty seemed to doubt it might possibly not be always sincere; and he desired to know whether such zealous gentlemen could have any views of refunding themselves for the charges and trouble they were at, by sacrificing the public good to the designs of a weak and vicious prince in conjunction with a corrupted ministry. He multiplied his questions, and sifted me thoroughly upon every part of this head, proposing numberless inquiries and objections, which I think it not prudent or convenient to repeat.

Upon what I said in relation to our Courts of Justice, his Majesty desired to be satisfied in several points: and this I was the better able to do, having been formerly almost ruined by a long suit in chancery, which was decreed for me with costs. He asked what time was usually spent in determining between right and wrong, and what degree of expense. Whether advocates and orators had liberty to plead in causes manifestly known to be unjust, vexatious, or oppressive. Whether party in religion or politics were observed

5. Whim.

to be of any weight in the scale of justice. Whether those pleading orators were persons educated in the general knowledge of equity, or only in provincial, national, and other local customs. Whether they or their judges had any part in penning those laws which they assumed the liberty of interpreting and glossing upon at their pleasure. Whether they had ever at different times pleaded for and against the same cause, and cited precedents to prove contrary opinions. Whether they were a rich or a poor corporation. Whether they received any pecuniary reward for pleading or delivering their opinions. And particularly whether they were ever admitted as members in the lower senate.

He fell next upon the management of our treasury, and said he thought my memory had failed me, because I computed our taxes at about five or six millions a year, and when I came to mention the issues,[6] he found they sometimes amounted to more than double, for the notes he had taken were very particular in this point; because he hoped, as he told me, that the knowledge of our conduct might be useful to him, and he could not be deceived in his calculations. But if what I told him were true, he was still at a loss how a kingdom could run out of its estate like a private person. He asked me, who were our creditors? and where we should find money to pay them? He wondered to hear me talk of such chargeable and extensive wars; that certainly we must be a quarrelsome people, or live among very bad neighbors, and that our generals must needs be richer than our kings.[7] He asked what business we had out of our own islands, unless upon the score of[8] trade or treaty or to defend the coasts with our fleet. Above all, he was amazed to hear me talk of a mercenary standing army[9] in the midst of peace, and among a free people. He said if we were governed by our own consent in the persons of our representatives, he could not imagine of whom we were afraid, or against whom we were to fight; and would hear my opinion whether a private man's house might not better be defended by himself, his children, and family, than by half a dozen rascals picked up at a venture[1] in the streets for small wages, who might get an hundred times more by cutting their throats.

He laughed at my odd kind of arithmetic (as he was pleased to call it) in reckoning the numbers of our people by a computation drawn from the several sects among us in religion and politics. He said he knew no reason why those who entertain opinions prejudicial to the public should be obliged to change, or should not be obliged

6. Expenditures.
7. An allusion to the enormous fortune gained by the Duke of Marlborough, formerly Captain-General of the army, whom Swift detested.
8. For the sake of.
9. Since the declaration of the Bill of Rights (1689), a standing army without authorization by Parliament had been illegal. Swift and the Tories in general were vigilant in their opposition to such an army.
1. By chance.

to conceal them. And as it was tyranny in any government to require the first, so it was weakness not to enforce the second: for a man may be allowed to keep poisons in his closet, but not to vend them about for cordials.[2]

He observed that among the diversions of our nobility and gentry I had mentioned gaming.[3] He desired to know at what age this entertainment was usually taken up, and when it was laid down; how much of their time it employed; whether it ever went so high as to affect their fortunes; whether mean, vicious people, by their dexterity in that art, might not arrive at great riches, and sometimes keep our very nobles in dependence, as well as habituate them to vile companions, wholly take them from the improvement of their minds, and force them, by the losses they have received, to learn and practice that infamous dexterity upon others.

He was perfectly astonished with the historical account I gave him of our affairs during the last century, protesting it was only an heap of conspiracies, rebellions, murders, massacres, revolutions, banishments, the very worst effects that avarice, faction, hypocrisy, perfidiousness, cruelty, rage, madness, hatred, envy, lust, malice, or ambition could produce.

His Majesty in another audience was at the pains to recapitulate the sum of all I had spoken; compared the questions he made with the answers I had given; then taking me into his hands, and stroking me gently, delivered himself in these words, which I shall never forget nor the manner he spoke them in. "My little friend Grildrig, you have made a most admirable panegyric[4] upon your country. You have clearly proved that ignorance, idleness, and vice are the proper ingredients for qualifying a legislator. That laws are best explained, interpreted, and applied by those whose interests and abilities lie in perverting, confounding, and eluding them. I observe among you some lines of an institution which in its original might have been tolerable; but these half erased, and the rest wholly blurred and blotted by corruptions. It doth not appear from all you have said how any one virtue is required towards the procurement of any one station among you; much less that men are ennobled on account of their virtue, that priests are advanced for their piety or learning, soldiers for their conduct or valor, judges for their integrity, senators for the love of their country, or counselors for their wisdom. As for yourself," continued the King, "who have spent the greatest part of your life in traveling, I am well disposed to hope you may hitherto have escaped many vices of your country. But by what I have gathered from your own relation, and the answers I have with much pains wringed and extorted from you, I cannot but conclude the bulk of your natives to be the most pernicious race

2. Medicines to stimulate the heart, or, equally commonly, liqueurs.
3. Gambling.
4. A formal oration in praise of someone or something.

of little odious vermin that nature ever suffered to crawl upon the surface of the earth."

Chapter VII. *The Author's love of his country. He makes a proposal of much advantage to the King; which is rejected. The King's great ignorance in politics. The learning of that country very imperfect and confined. Their laws, and military affairs, and parties in the State.*

Nothing but an extreme love of truth could have hindered me from concealing this part of my story. It was in vain to discover my resentments, which were always turned into ridicule: and I was forced to rest with patience while my noble and most beloved country was so injuriously treated. I am heartily sorry as any of my readers can possibly be that such an occasion was given, but this prince happened to be so curious and inquisitive upon every particular that it could not consist either with gratitude or good manners to refuse giving him what satisfaction I was able. Yet thus much I may be allowed to say in my own vindication: that I artfully eluded many of his questions, and gave to every point a more favorable turn by many degrees than the strictness of truth would allow. For I have always borne that laudable partiality to my own country, which Dionysius Halicarnassensis[5] with so much justice recommends to an historian. I would hide the frailties and deformities of my political mother, and place her virtues and beauties in the most advantageous light. This was my sincere endeavor in those many discourses I had with that mighty monarch, although it unfortunately failed of success.

But great allowances should be given to a King who lives wholly secluded from the rest of the world, and must therefore be altogether unacquainted with the manners and customs that most prevail in other nations: the want of which knowledge will ever produce many *prejudices*, and a certain *narrowness of thinking*, from which we and the politer countries of Europe are wholly exempted. And it would be hard indeed if so remote a prince's notions of virtue and vice were to be offered as a standard for all mankind.

To confirm what I have now said, and further, to show the miserable effects of a *confined education*, I shall here insert a passage which will hardly obtain belief. In hopes to ingratiate myself farther into his Majesty's favor, I told him of an invention discovered between three and four hundred years ago, to make a certain powder, into an heap of which the smallest spark of fire falling would kindle the whole in a moment, although it were as big as a mountain, and make it all fly up in the air together, with a noise and agitation

5. A Greek rhetorician and historian, who flourished ca. 25 B.C. His history of Rome was written to reconcile the Greeks to their Roman masters.

greater than thunder. That a proper quantity of this powder rammed into an hollow tube of brass or iron, according to its bigness, would drive a ball of iron or lead with such violence and speed as nothing was able to sustain its force. That the largest balls thus discharged would not only destroy whole ranks of an army at once, but batter the strongest walls to the ground; sink down ships with a thousand men in each, to the bottom of the sea; and, when linked together by a chain, would cut through masts and rigging; divide hundreds of bodies in the middle, and lay all waste before them. That we often put this powder into large hollow balls of iron, and discharged them by an engine into some city we were besieging; which would rip up the pavements, tear the houses to pieces, burst and throw splinters on every side, dashing out the brains of all who came near. That I knew the ingredients very well, which were cheap and common; I understood the manner of compounding them, and could direct his workmen how to make those tubes of a size proportionable to all other things in his Majesty's kingdom, and the largest need not be above two hundred foot long; twenty or thirty of which tubes, charged with the proper quantity of powder and balls, would batter down the walls of the strongest town in his dominions in a few hours; or destroy the whole metropolis, if ever it should pretend to dispute his absolute commands. This I humbly offered to his Majesty as a small tribute of acknowledgment in return of so many marks that I had received of his royal favor and protection.

The King was struck with horror at the description I had given of those terrible engines and the proposal I had made. He was amazed how so impotent and groveling an insect as I (these were his expressions) could entertain such inhuman ideas, and in so familiar a manner as to appear wholly unmoved at all the scenes of blood and desolation which I had painted as the common effects of those destructive machines; whereof he said some evil genius, enemy to mankind, must have been the first contriver. As for himself, he protested that although few things delighted him so much as new discoveries in art or in nature, yet he would rather lose half his kingdom than be privy[6] to such a secret, which he commanded me, as I valued my life, never to mention any more.

A strange effect of *narrow principles* and *short views!* that a prince possessed of every quality which procures veneration, love, and esteem; of strong parts, great wisdom, and profound learning; endued with admirable talents for government, and almost adored by his subjects; should from a *nice, unnecessary scruple,* whereof in Europe we can have no conception, let slip an opportunity put into his hands that would have made him absolute master of the lives, the liberties, and the fortunes of his people. Neither do I say this with the least intention to detract from the many virtues of that

6. To share secret knowledge.

excellent King, whose character I am sensible will on this account be very much lessened in the opinion of an English reader: but I take this defect among them to have risen from their ignorance; they not having hitherto reduced politics into a science, as the more acute wits of Europe have done. For I remember very well, in a discourse one day with the King, when I happened to say there were several thousand books among us written upon the art of government, it gave him (directly contrary to my intention) a very mean opinion of our understandings. He professed both to abominate and despise all *mystery, refinement,* and *intrigue,* either in a prince or a minister. He could not tell what I meant by *secrets of state,* where an enemy or some rival nation were not in the case. He confined the knowledge of governing within very *narrow bounds:* to common sense and reason, to justice and lenity,[7] to the speedy determination of civil and criminal causes, with some other obvious topics which are not worth considering. And he gave it for his opinion that whoever could make two ears of corn or two blades of grass to grow upon a spot of ground where only one grew before would deserve better of mankind and do more essential service to his country than the whole race of politicians [7a] put together.

The learning of this people is very defective, consisting only in morality, history, poetry, and mathematics; wherein they must be allowed to excel. But the last of these is wholly applied to what may be useful in life, to the improvement of agriculture and all mechanical arts; so that among us it would be little esteemed. And as to ideas, entities, abstractions, and transcendentals,[8] I could never drive the least conception into their heads.

No law of that country must exceed in words the number of letters in their alphabet, which consists only in two and twenty. But indeed few of them extend even to that length. They are expressed in the most plain and simple terms, wherein those people are not mercurial[9] enough to discover above one interpretation. And to write a comment upon any law is a capital crime. As to the decision of civil causes, or proceedings against criminals, their precedents[1] are so few that they have little reason to boast of any extraordinary skill in either.

They have had the art of printing as well as the Chinese, time out of mind. But their libraries are not very large; for that of the King's, which is reckoned the biggest, doth not amount to above a thousand volumes, placed in a gallery of twelve hundred foot long, from whence I had liberty to borrow what books I pleased. The

7. Mildness.
7a. By "politicians" Swift means something like our modern "political scientists"—theorists.
8. In Swift's time, "transcendental" was practically synonymous with "metaphysical."
9. Changeable.
1. A legal decision or a course of action which comes to serve as a rule in determining similar cases in the future. In the Fourth Voyage of *Gulliver's Travels,* Gulliver is made to say: "It is a maxim among these lawyers that whatever hath been done before may legally be done again. * * * "

Queen's joiner had contrived in one of the Glumdalclitch's rooms a kind of wooden machine five and twenty foot high, formed like a standing ladder; the steps were each fifty foot long. It was indeed a movable pair of stairs, the lowest end placed at ten foot distance from the wall of the chamber. The book I had a mind to read was put up leaning against the wall. I first mounted to the upper step of the ladder, and turning my face towards the book, began at the top of the page, and so walking to the right and left about eight or ten paces according to the length of the lines, till I had gotten a little below the level of mine eyes, and then descending gradually till I came to the bottom: after which I mounted again, and began the other page in the same manner, and so turned over the leaf, which I could easily do with both my hands, for it was as thick and stiff as a pasteboard, and in the largest folios[2] not above eighteen or twenty foot long.

Their style is clear, masculine, and smooth, but not florid; for they avoid nothing more than multiplying unnecessary words or using various expressions. I have perused many of their books, especially those in history and morality. Among the rest, I was much diverted with a little old treatise, which always lay in Glumdalclitch's bedchamber, and belonged to her governess, a grave elderly gentlewoman, who dealt in writings of morality and devotion. The book treats of the weakness of human kind, and is in little esteem, except among the women and the vulgar. However, I was curious to see what an author of that country could say upon such a subject. This writer went through all the usual topics of European moralists: showing how diminutive, contemptible, and helpless an animal was man in his own nature; how unable to defend himself from the inclemencies of the air, or the fury of wild beasts; how much he was excelled by one creature in strength, by another in speed, by a third in foresight, by a fourth in industry. He added that nature was degenerated in these latter declining ages of the world, and could now produce only small abortive births in comparison of those in ancient times. He said it was very reasonable to think, not only that the species of men were originally much larger, but also that there must have been giants in former ages; which, as it is asserted by history and tradition, so it hath been confirmed by huge bones and skulls casually dug up in several parts of the kingdom, far exceeding the common dwindled race of man in our days. He argued that the very laws of nature absolutely required we should have been made in the beginning of a size more large and robust, not so liable to destruction from every little accident of a tile falling from a house, or a stone cast from the hand of a boy, or of being drowned in a little brook. From this way of reasoning, the author drew several moral applications useful in the

2. A book of the largest size.

conduct of life, but needless here to repeat. For my own part, I could not avoid reflecting how universally this talent was spread, of drawing lectures in morality, or indeed rather matter of discontent and repining, from the quarrels we raise with nature. And I believe, upon a strict inquiry, those quarrels might be shown as ill grounded among us as they are among that people.

As to their military affairs, they boast that the King's army consists of an hundred and seventy-six thousand foot and thirty-two thousand horse: if that may be called an army which is made up of tradesmen in the several cities, and farmers in the country, whose commanders are only the nobility and gentry, without pay or reward. They are indeed perfect enough in their exercises, and under very good discipline, wherein I saw no great merit; for how should it be otherwise, where every farmer is under the command of his own landlord, and every citizen under that of the principal men in his own city, chosen after the manner of Venice by ballot?

I have often seen the militia of Lorbrulgrud drawn out to exercise in a great field near the city, of twenty miles square. They were in all not above twenty-five thousand foot, and six thousand horse; but it was impossible for me to compute their number, considering the space of ground they took up. A cavalier mounted on a large steed might be about an hundred foot high. I have seen this whole body of horse, upon a word of command, draw their swords at once, and brandish them in the air. Imagination can figure nothing so grand, so surprising, and so astonishing. It looked as if ten thousand flashes of lightning were darting at the same time from every quarter of the sky.

I was curious to know how this prince, to whose dominions there is no access from any other country, came to think of armies, or to teach his people the practice of military discipline. But I was soon informed, both by conversation and reading their histories. For in the course of many ages they have been troubled with the same disease to which the whole race of mankind is subject: the nobility often contending for power, the people for liberty, and the King for absolute dominion. All which, however happily tempered by the laws of the kingdom, have been sometimes violated by each of the three parties, and have more than once occasioned civil wars, the last whereof was happily put an end to by this prince's grandfather in a general composition;[3] and the militia, then settled with common consent, hath been ever since kept in the strictest duty.

Chapter VIII. *The King and Queen make a progress to the frontiers. The Author attends them. The manner in which he leaves the country very particularly related. He returns to England.*

3. A political settlement based upon general agreement of all parties.

I had always a strong impulse that I should some time recover my liberty, though it were impossible to conjecture by what means, or to form any project with the least hope of succeeding. The ship in which I sailed was the first ever known to be driven within sight of that coast; and the King had given strict orders that if at any time another appeared, it should be taken ashore, and with all its crew and passengers brought in a tumbrel[4] to Lorbrulgrud. He was strongly bent to get me a woman of my own size, by whom I might propagate the breed: but I think I should rather have died than undergone the disgrace of leaving a posterity to be kept in cages like tame canary birds, and perhaps in time sold about the kingdom to persons of quality for curiosities. I was indeed treated with much kindness: I was the favorite of a great King and Queen, and the delight of the whole Court, but it was upon such a foot as ill became the dignity of human kind. I could never forget those domestic pledges[5] I had left behind me. I wanted to be among people with whom I could converse upon even terms, and walk about the streets and fields without fear of being trod to death like a frog or a young puppy. But my deliverance came sooner than I expected, and in a manner not very common; the whole story and circumstances of which I shall faithfully relate.

I had now been two years in this country; and about the beginning of the third, Glumdalclitch and I attended the King and Queen in progress to the south coast of the kingdom. I was carried as usual in my traveling box, which, as I have already described, was a very convenient closet of twelve foot wide. I had ordered a hammock to be fixed by silken ropes from the four corners at the top, to break the jolts when a servant carried me before him on horseback, as I sometimes desired; and would often sleep in my hammock while we were upon the road. On the roof of my closet, set not directly over the middle of the hammock, I ordered the joiner to cut out a hole of a foot square to give me air in hot weather as I slept, which hole I shut at pleasure with a board that drew backwards and forwards through a groove.

When we came to our journey's end, the King thought proper to pass a few days at a palace he hath near Flanflasnic, a city within eighteen English miles of the seaside. Glumdalclitch and I were much fatigued; I had gotten a small cold, but the poor girl was so ill as to be confined to her chamber. I longed to see the ocean, which must be the only scene of my escape, if ever it should happen. I pretended to be worse than I really was, and desired leave to take the fresh air of the sea with a page whom I was very fond of, and who had sometimes been trusted with me. I shall never forget with what unwillingness Glumdalclitch consented, nor the strict charge she gave the page to be careful of me, bursting at the

4. A farm wagon.

5. His wife and children.

same time into a flood of tears, as if she had some foreboding of what was to happen. The boy took me out in my box about half an hour's walk from the palace, towards the rocks on the seashore. I ordered him to set me down, and lifting up one of my sashes, cast many a wistful melancholy look towards the sea. I found myself not very well, and told the page that I had a mind to take a nap in my hammock, which I hoped would do me good. I got in, and the boy shut the window close down, to keep out the cold. I soon fell asleep: and all I can conjecture is that while I slept, the page, thinking no danger could happen, went among the rocks to look for birds' eggs; having before observed him from my window searching about, and picking up one or two in the clefts. Be that as it will, I found myself suddenly awaked with a violent pull upon the ring which was fastened at the top of my box for the conveniency of carriage. I felt my box raised very high in the air, and then borne forward with prodigious speed. The first jolt had like to have shaken me out of my hammock, but afterwards the motion was easy enough. I called out several times as loud as I could raise my voice, but all to no purpose. I looked towards my windows, and could see nothing but the clouds and sky. I heard a noise just over my head like the clapping of wings, and then began to perceive the woeful condition I was in; that some eagle had got the ring of my box in his beak, with an intent to let it fall on a rock, like a tortoise in a shell, and then pick out my body and devour it. For the sagacity and smell of this bird enable him to discover his quarry at a great distance, although better concealed than I could be within a two-inch board.

In a little time I observed the noise and flutter of wings to increase very fast, and my box was tossed up and down like a signpost in a windy day. I heard several bangs or buffets, as I thought, given to the eagle (for such I am certain it must have been that held the ring of my box in his beak), and then all on a sudden felt myself falling perpendicularly down for above a minute, but with such incredible swiftness that I almost lost my breath. My fall was topped by a terrible squash, that sounded louder to mine ears than the cataract of Niagara; after which I was quite in the dark for another minute, and then my box began to rise so high that I could see light from the tops of my windows. I now perceived that I was fallen into the sea. My box, by the weight of my body, the goods that were in, and the broad plates of iron fixed for strength at the four corners of the top and bottom, floated about five foot deep in water. I did then and do now suppose that the eagle which flew away with my box was pursued by two or three others, and forced to let me drop while he was defending himself against the rest, who hoped to share in the prey. The plates of iron fastened at the bottom of the box (for those were the strongest) preserved the balance while it fell, and hindered it from being broken on the surface of the water. Every joint of it was well grooved, and the door did not move on hinges, but up and down like a sash; which kept my closet so tight that very little water came in. I got with much difficulty out of my hammock, having first ventured to draw back the slip-board on the roof already mentioned, contrived on purpose to let in air, for want of which I found myself almost stifled.

How often did I then wish myself with my dear Glumdalclitch, from whom one single hour had so far divided me! And I may say with truth that in the midst of my own misfortune, I could not forbear lamenting my poor nurse, the grief she would suffer for my loss, the displeasure of the Queen, and the ruin of her fortune. Perhaps many travelers have not been under greater difficulties and distress than I was at this juncture, expecting every moment to see my box dashed in pieces, or at least overset by the first violent blast or a rising wave. A breach in one single pane of glass would have been immediate death, nor could anything have preserved the windows but the strong lattice wires placed on the outside against accidents in traveling. I saw the water ooze in at several crannies, although the leaks were not considerable, and I endeavored to stop them as well as I could. I was not able to lift up the roof of my closet, which otherwise I certainly should have done, and sat on the top of it, where I might at least preserve myself from being shut up, as I may call it, in the hold. Or, if I escaped these dangers for a day or two, what could I expect but a miserable death of cold and hunger! I was four hours under these circumstances, expecting and indeed wishing every moment to be my last.

I have already told the reader that there were two strong staples fixed upon that side of my box which had no window and into which the servant, who used to carry me on horseback, would put a leathern belt, and buckle it about his waist. Being in this disconsolate state, I heard, or at least thought I heard, some kind of grating noise on that side of my box where the staples were fixed; and soon after I began to fancy that the box was pulled or towed along in the sea; for I now and then felt a sort of tugging, which made the waves rise near the tops of my windows, leaving me almost in the dark. This gave me some faint hopes of relief, although I was not able to imagine how it could be brought about. I ventured to unscrew one of my chairs, which were always fastened to the floor; and having made a hard shift to screw it down again directly under the slipping-board that I had lately opened, I mounted on the chair, and putting my mouth as near as I could to the hole, I called for help in a loud voice, and in all the languages I understood. I then fastened my handkerchief to a stick I usually carried, and thrusting it up the hole, waved it several times in the air, that if any boat or ship were near, the seamen might conjecture some unhappy mortal to be shut up in the box.

I found no effect from all I could do, but plainly perceived my closet to be moved along; and in the space of an hour or better, that side of the box where the staples were, and had no window, struck against something that was hard. I apprehended it to be a rock, and found myself tossed more than ever. I plainly heard a noise upon the cover of my closet, like that of a cable, and the grating of it as it passed through the ring. I then found myself hoisted up by degrees at least three foot higher than I was before. Whereupon I again thrust up my stick and handkerchief, calling for help till I was almost hoarse. In return to which, I heard a great shout repeated three time, giving me such transports of joy as are not to be conceived but by those who feel them. I now heard a trampling over my head, and somebody calling through the hole with a loud voice in the English tongue: "If there be anybody below, let them speak." I answered, I was an Englishman, drawn by ill fortune into the greatest calamity that ever any creature underwent, and begged, by all that was moving, to be delivered out of the dungeon I was in. The voice replied, I was safe, for my box was fastened to their ship; and the carpenter should immediately come and saw an hole in the cover, large enough to pull me out. I answered, that was needless and would take up too much time, for there was no more to be done but let one of the crew put his finger into the ring, and take the box out of the sea into the ship, and so into the captain's cabin. Some of them, upon hearing me talk so wildly, thought I was mad; others laughed; for indeed it never came into my head that I was now got among people of my own stature and strength. The carpenter came, and in a few minutes sawed a passage about four foot square; then let down a small ladder, upon which I mounted, and from thence was taken into the ship in a very weak condition.

The sailors were all in amazement, and asked me a thousand questions, which I had no inclination to answer. I was equally confounded at the sight of so many pygmies, for such I took them to be, after having so long accustomed my eyes to the monstrous objects I had left. But the Captain, Mr. Thomas Wilcocks, an honest, worthy Shropshire man, observing I was ready to faint, took me into his cabin, gave me a cordial to comfort me, and made me turn in upon his own bed, advising me to take a little rest, of which I had great need. Before I went to sleep I gave him to understand that I had some valuable furniture in my box, too good to be lost, a fine hammock, an handsome field bed, two chairs, a table, and a cabinet; that my closet was hung on all sides, or rather quilted with silk and cotton; that if he would let one of the crew bring my closet into his cabin, I would open it before him and show him my goods. The Captain, hearing me utter these absurdities, concluded I was raving; however (I suppose to pacify me), he promised to give order as I desired, and going upon deck, sent some of his men down into my closet, from whence (as I afterwards found) they drew up all my goods and stripped off the quilting; but the chairs, cabinet, and bedstead, being screwed to the floor, were much damaged by the ignorance of the seamen, who tore them up by force. Then they knocked off some of the boards for the use of the ship; and when they had got all they had a mind for, let the hulk drop into the sea, which, by reason of many breaches made in the bottom and sides, sunk to rights.[6] And indeed I was glad not to have been a spectator of the havoc they made, because I am confident it would have sensibly touched me, by bringing former passages into my mind, which I had rather forget.

I slept some hours, but perpetually disturbed with dreams of the place I had left, and the dangers I had escaped. However, upon waking, I found myself much recovered. It was now about eight o'clock at night, and the Captain ordered supper immediately, thinking I had already fasted too long. He entertained me with great kindness, observing me not to look wildly, or talk inconsistently; and when we were left alone, desired I would give him a relation of my travels, and by what accident I came to be set adrift in that monstrous wooden chest. He said that about twelve o'clock at noon, as he was looking through his glass, he spied it at a distance, and thought it was a sail, which he had a mind to make,[7] being not much out of his course, in hopes of buying some biscuit, his own beginning to fall short. That, upon coming nearer, and finding his error, he sent out his longboat to discover what I was; that his men came back in a fright, swearing they had seen a swimming house. That he laughed at their folly, and went himself in the boat, ordering his men to take a strong cable along with them. That the weather being calm, he rowed round me several times, observed my windows, and the wire lattices that defended them. That he discovered two staples upon one side, which was all of boards, without any passage for light. He then commanded his men to row up to that side, and fastening a cable to one of the staples, ordered his men to tow my chest (as he called it) towards the ship. When it was there, he gave directions to fasten another cable to the ring fixed in the cover, and to raise up my chest with pulleys, which all the sailors were not able to do above two or three foot. He said they saw my stick and handkerchief thrust out of the hole, and concluded that some unhappy man must be shut up in the cavity. I asked whether he or the crew had seen any prodigious birds in the air about the time he first discovered me. To which he answered that, discoursing this matter with the sailors while I was asleep, one of them said he had observed three eagles flying towards the

6. At once; altogether.

7. Overtake.

north, but remarked nothing of their being larger than the usual size (which I suppose must be imputed to the great height they were at), and he could not guess the reason of my question. I then asked the Captain how far he reckoned we might be from land; he said, by the best computation he could make, we were at least an hundred leagues. I assured him that he must be mistaken by almost half; for I had not left the country from whence I came above two hours before I dropped into the sea. Whereupon he began again to think that my brain was disturbed, of which he gave me a hint, and advised me to go to bed in a cabin he had provided. I assured him I was well refreshed with his good entertainment and company, and as much in my senses as ever I was in my life. He then grew serious and desired to ask me freely whether I were not troubled in mind by the consciousness of some enormous crime, for which I was punished at the command of some prince, by exposing me in that chest, as great criminals in other countries have been forced to sea in a leaky vessel without provisions; for although he should be sorry to have taken so ill[8] a man into his ship, yet he would engage his word to set me safe on shore in the first port where we arrived. He added that his suspicions were much increased by some very absurd speeches I had delivered at first to the sailors, and afterwards to himself, in relation to my closet or chest, as well as by my odd looks and behavior while I was at supper.

I begged his patience to hear me tell my story, which I faithfully did from the last time I left England to the moment he first discovered me. And as truth always forceth its way into rational minds, so this honest, worthy gentleman, who had some tincture of learning, and very good sense, was immediately convinced of my candor and veracity. But further to confirm all I had said, I entreated him to give order that my cabinet should be brought, of which I kept the key in my pocket (for he had already informed me how the seamen disposed of my closet). I opened it in his presence and showed him the small collection of rarities I made in the country from whence I had been so strangely delivered. There was the comb I had contrived out of the stumps of the King's beard, and another of the same materials, but fixed into a paring of her Majesty's thumbnail, which served for the back. There was a collection of needles and pins from a foot to half a yard long; four wasp-stings, like joiners' tacks; some combings of the Queen's hair; a gold ring which one day she made me a present of in a most obliging manner, taking it from her little finger, and throwing it over my head like a collar. I desired the Captain would please to accept this ring in return for his civilities, which he absolutely refused. I showed him a corn that I had cut off with my own hand from a Maid of Honor's toe; it was about the bigness of a Kentish pippin,[9] and grown so

8. Evil.

9. Apple.

hard that, when I returned to England, I got it hollowed into a cup and set in silver. Lastly, I desired him to see the breeches I had then on, which were made of a mouse's skin.

I could force nothing on him but a footman's tooth, which I observed him to examine with great curiosity, and found he had a fancy for it. He received it with abundance of thanks, more than such a trifle could deserve. It was drawn by an unskillful surgeon in a mistake from one of Glumdalclitch's men, who was afflicted with the toothache; but it was as sound as any in his head. I got it cleaned, and put it into my cabinet. It was about a foot long, and four inches in diameter.

The Captain was very well satisfied with this plain relation I had given him, and said he hoped when we returned to England I would oblige the world by putting it in paper and making it public. My answer was that I thought we were already overstocked with books of travels; that nothing could now pass which was not extraordinary; wherein I doubted some authors less consulted truth than their own vanity or interest, or the diversion of ignorant readers. That my story could contain little besides common events, without those ornamental descriptions of strange plants, trees, birds, and other animals, or the barbarous customs and idolatry of savage people, with which most writers abound. However, I thanked him for his good opinion, and promised to take the matter into my thoughts.

He said he wondered at one thing very much, which was to hear me speak so loud, asking me whether the King or Queen of that country were thick of hearing. I told him it was what I had been used to for above two years past, and that I admired[1] as much at the voices of him and his men, who seemed to me only to whisper, and yet I could hear them well enough. But, when I spoke in that country, it was like a man talking in the street to another looking out from the top of a steeple, unless when I was placed on a table, or held in any person's hand. I told him I had likewise observed another thing: that when I first got into the ship, and the sailors stood all about me, I thought they were the most little contemptible creatures I had ever beheld. For indeed while I was in that prince's country, I could never endure to look in a glass after mine eyes had been accustomed to such prodigious objects, because the comparison gave me so despicable a conceit[2] of myself. The Captain said that while we were at supper he observed me to look at everything with a sort of wonder, and that I often seemed hardly able to contain my laughter; which he knew not well how to take, but imputed it to some disorder in my brain. I answered, it was very true; and I wondered how I could forbear, when I saw his dishes of the size of a silver threepence, a leg of pork hardly a

1. Wondered at.

2. Notion.

mouthful, a cup not so big as a nutshell; and so I went on, describing the rest of his household stuff and provisions after the same manner. For, although the Queen had ordered a little equipage[3] of all things necessary for me while I was in her service, yet my ideas were wholly taken up with what I saw on every side of me, and I winked at my own littleness, as people do at their own faults. The Captain understood my raillery very well, and merrily replied with the old English proverb, that he doubted[4] mine eyes were bigger than my belly, for he did not observe my stomach so good, although I had fasted all day; and continuing in his mirth, protested he would have gladly given an hundred pounds to have seen my closet in the eagle's bill, and afterwards in its fall from so great an height into the sea; which would certainly have been a most astonishing object, worthy to have the description of it transmitted to future ages: and the comparison of Phaeton[5] was so obvious, that he could not forbear applying it, although I did not much admire the conceit.

The Captain having been at Tonquin,[6] was in his return to England driven northeastward to the latitude of 44 degrees, and of longitude 143. But meeting a trade wind two days after I came on board him, we sailed southward a long time, and coasting New Holland[7] kept our course west-southwest, and then south-southwest till we doubled the Cape of Good Hope. Our voyage was very prosperous, but I shall not trouble the reader with a journal of it. The Captain called in at one or two ports, and sent in his longboat for provisions and fresh water; but I never went out of the ship till we came into the Downs,[8] which was on the third day of June, 1706, about nine months after my escape. I offered to leave my goods in security for payment of my freight; but the Captain protested he would not receive one farthing. We took kind leave of each other, and I made him promise he would come to see me at my house in Redriff.[9] I hired a horse and guide for five shillings, which I borrowed of the Captain.

As I was on the road, observing the littleness of the houses, the trees, the cattle, and the people, I began to think myself in Lilliput. I was afraid of trampling on every traveler I met, and often called aloud to have them stand out of the way, so that I had like to have gotten one or two broken heads for my impertinence.

When I came to my own house, for which I was forced to inquire, one of the servants opening the door, I bent down to go in

3. Furnishings.
4. Feared.
5. The son of Apollo, whose unsuccessful attempt to drive the chariot of the sun god resulted in his death, when he was hurled by Zeus from the sky and fell into the river Eridanus, where he drowned.
6. Tonkin, in Indo-China.
7. Australia.
8. The sheltered anchorage between Goodwin Sands and the coast of Kent, near Deal.
9. Rotherhithe, on the south bank of the Thames, slightly below the City.

(like a goose under a gate) for fear of striking my head. My wife ran out to embrace me, but I stooped lower than her knees, thinking she could otherwise never be able to reach my mouth. My daughter kneeled to ask my blessing, but I could not see her till she arose, having been so long used to stand with my head and eyes erect to above sixty foot; and then I went to take her up with one hand by the waist. I looked down upon the servants and one or two friends who were in the house, as if they had been pygmies and I a giant. I told my wife she had been too thrifty; for I found she had starved herself and her daughter to nothing. In short, I behaved myself so unaccountably that they were all of the Captain's opinion when he first saw me, and concluded I had lost my wits. This I mention as an instance of the great power of habit and prejudice.

In a little time I and my family and friends came to a right understanding; but my wife protested I should never go to sea any more, although my evil destiny so ordered that she had not power to hinder me; as the reader may know hereafter. In the meantime I here conclude the second part of my unfortunate voyages.

From *Part III. A Voyage to Laputa, Balnibarbi, Glubbdubdrib, Luggnagg, and Japan*

[*The Flying Island of Laputa*]

CHAPTER I. *The author sets out on his third voyage. Is taken by pirates. The malice of a Dutchman. His arrival at an island. He is received into Laputa.*

I had not been at home above ten days, when Captain William Robinson, a Cornish man, commander of the *Hopewell*, a stout ship of three hundred tons, came to my house. I had formerly been surgeon of another ship where he was master, and a fourth part owner, in a voyage to the Levant. He had always treated me more like a brother than an inferior officer; and hearing of my arrival made me a visit, as I apprehended, only out of friendship, for nothing passed more than what is usual after long absence. But repeating his visits often, expressing his joy to find me in good health, asking whether I were now settled for life, adding that he intended a voyage to the East Indies, in two months, at last he plainly invited me, although with some apologies, to be surgeon of the ship; that I should have another surgeon under me, besides our two mates; that my salary should be double to the usual pay; and that having experienced my knowledge in sea-affairs to be at least equal to his, he would enter into any engagement to follow my advice, as much as if I had share in the command.

He said so many other obliging things, and I knew him to be so honest a man, that I could not reject his proposal; the thirst I had of seeing the world, notwithstanding my past misfortunes, continuing as violent as ever. The only difficulty that remained, was to persuade my wife, whose consent however I at last obtained, by the prospect of advantage she proposed to her children.

We set out the 5th day of August, 1706, and arrived at Fort St. George,[1] the 11th day of April, 1707. We stayed there three weeks to refresh our crew, many of whom were sick. From thence we went to Tonquin, where the captain resolved to continue some time, because many of the goods he intended to buy were not ready, nor could he expect to be dispatched in several months. Therefore in hopes to defray some of the charges he must be at, he bought a sloop, loaded it with several sorts of goods, wherewith the Tonquinese usually trade to the neighboring islands; and putting fourteen men on board, whereof three were of the country, he appointed me master of the sloop, and gave me power to traffic, while he transacted his affairs at Tonquin.

We had not sailed above three days, when a great storm arising, we were driven five days to the north-northeast, and then to the east; after which we had fair weather, but still with a pretty strong gale from the west. Upon the tenth day we were chased by two pirates, who soon overtook us; for my sloop was so deep loaden, that she sailed very slow; neither were we in a condition to defend our selves.

We were boarded about the same time by both the pirates, who entered furiously at the head of their men; but finding us all prostrate upon our faces (for so I gave order), they pinioned us with strong ropes, and setting a guard upon us, went to search the sloop.

I observed among them a Dutchman, who seemed to be of some authority, although he was not commander of either ship. He knew us by our countenances to be Englishmen, and jabbering to us in his own language, swore we should be tied back to back, and thrown into the sea. I spoke Dutch tolerably well; I told him who we were, and begged him in consideration of our being Christians and Protestants, of neighboring countries, in strict alliance, that he would move the captains to take some pity on us. This inflamed his rage; he repeated his threatenings, and turning to his companions, spoke with great vehemence, in the Japanese language, as I suppose; often using the word *Christianos*.[2]

The largest of the two pirate ships was commanded by a Japanese captain, who spoke a little Dutch, but very imperfectly. He came up to me, and after several questions, which I answered in great humility, he said we should not die. I made the captain a very low bow, and then turning to the Dutchman, said, I was sorry to find more

1. Madras, in India.

2. Swift was prejudiced against Holland: as a republic that practiced religious tolerance, it represented an alternative to England's establishment of Church and state. Though military allies against France, in 1707, the two countries remained commercial rivals.

mercy in a heathen, than in a brother Christian. But I had soon reason to repent those foolish words; for the malicious reprobate, having often endeavored in vain to persuade both the captains that I might be thrown into the sea (which they would not yield to after the promise made me, that I should not die), however prevailed so far as to have a punishment inflicted on me, worse in all human appearance than death itself. My men were sent by an equal division into both the pirate ships, and my sloop new manned. As to myself, it was determined that I should be set adrift in a small canoe, with paddles and a sail, and four days' provisions; which last the Japanese captain was so kind to double out of his own stores, and would permit no man to search me. I got down into the canoe, while the Dutchman, standing upon the deck, loaded me with all the curses and injurious terms his language could afford.

About an hour before we saw the pirates, I had taken an observation, and found we were in the latitude of 46 N. and of longitude 183. When I was at some distance from the pirates, I discovered by my pocket-glass several islands to the southeast. I set up my sail, the wind being fair, with a design to reach the nearest of those islands, which I made a shift to do in about three hours. It was all rocky; however I got many birds' eggs, and striking fire I kindled some heath and dry seaweed, by which I roasted my eggs. I eat no other supper, being resolved to spare my provisions as much as I could. I passed the night under the shelter of a rock, strowing some heath under me, and slept pretty well.

The next day I sailed to another island, and thence to a third and fourth, sometimes using my sail, and sometimes my paddles. But not to trouble the reader with a particular account of my distresses, let it suffice that on the 5th day I arrived at the last island in my sight, which lay south-southeast to the former.

This island was at a greater distance than I expected, and I did not reach it in less than five hours. I encompassed it almost round before I could find a convenient place to land in, which was a small creek, about three times the wideness of my canoe. I found the island to be all rocky, only a little intermingled with tufts of grass, and sweet-smelling herbs. I took out my small provisions, and after having refreshed myself, I secured the remainder in a cave, whereof there were great numbers. I gathered plenty of eggs upon the rocks, and got a quantity of dry seaweed, and parched grass, which I designed to kindle the next day, and roast my eggs as well as I could. (For I had about me my flint, steel, match, and burning glass.) I lay all night in the cave where I had lodged my provisions. My bed was the same dry grass and seaweed which I intended for fuel. I slept very little, for the disquiets of my mind prevailed over my weariness, and kept me awake. I considered how impossible it was to preserve my life in so desolate a place; and how miserable my end must be. Yet I found my self so listless and desponding, that I had not the heart to rise; and before I could get spirits enough to creep out of my cave, the day was far advanced. I walked a while among the rocks; the sky was perfectly clear, and the sun so hot, that I was forced to turn my face from it: when all on a sudden it became obscured, as I thought, in a manner very different from what happens by the interposition of a cloud. I turned back, and perceived a vast opaque body between me and the sun, moving forwards towards the island: it seemed to be about two miles high, and hid the sun six or seven minutes, but I did not observe the air to be much colder, or the sky more darkened, than if I had stood under the shade of a mountain. As it approached nearer over the place where I was, it appeared to be a firm substance, the bottom flat, smooth, and shining very bright from the reflection of the sea below. I stood upon a height about two hundred yards from the shore, and saw this vast body descending almost to a parallel with me, at less than an English mile distance. I took out my pocket perspective, and could plainly discover numbers of people moving up and down the sides of it, which appeared to be sloping, but what those people were doing I was not able to distinguish.

The natural love of life gave me some inward motions of joy, and I was ready to entertain a hope, that this adventure might some way or other help to deliver me from the desolate place and condition I was in. But at the same time, the reader can hardly conceive my astonishment, to behold an island in the air, inhabited by men, who were able (as it should seem) to raise, or sink, or put it into a progressive motion, as they pleased. But not being, at that time, in a disposition to philosophize upon this phenomenon, I rather chose to observe what course the island would take; because it seemed for a while to stand still. Yet soon after it advanced nearer; and I could see the sides of it, encompassed with several gradations of galleries and stairs, at certain intervals, to descend from one to the other. In the lowest gallery, I beheld some people fishing with long angling rods, and others looking on. I waved my cap (for my hat was long since worn out) and my handkerchief towards the island; and upon its nearer approach, I called and shouted with the utmost strength of my voice; and then looking circumspectly,[3] I beheld a crowd gathered to that side which was most in my view. I found by their pointing towards me and to each other, that they plainly discovered me, although they made no return to my shouting. But I could see four or five men running in great haste up the stairs to the top of the island, who then disappeared. I happened rightly to conjecture, that these were sent for orders to some person in authority upon this occasion.

The number of people increased, and in less than half an hour the island was moved and raised in such a manner, that the lowest gallery appeared in a parallel of less than an hundred yards' distance

3. Attentively around.

from the height where I stood. I then put myself into the most supplicating postures, and spoke in the humblest accent, but received no answer. Those who stood nearest over against me seemed to be persons of distinction, as I supposed by their habit. They conferred earnestly with each other, looking often upon me. At length one of them called out in a clear, polite, smooth dialect, not unlike in sound to Italian; and therefore I returned an answer in that language, hoping at least that the cadence might be more agreeable to his ears. Although neither of us understood the other, yet my meaning was easily known, for the people saw the distress I was in.

They made signs for me to come down from the rock, and go towards the shore, which I accordingly did; and the flying island being raised to a convenient height, the verge directly over me, a chain was let down from the lowest gallery, with a seat fastened to the bottom, to which I fixed myself, and was drawn up by pulleys.

Chapter II. *The humors and dispositions of the Laputans described. An account of their learning. Of the King and his court. The author's reception there. The inhabitants subject to fears and disquietudes. An account of the women.*

At my alighting I was surrounded by a crowd of people, but those who stood nearest seemed to be of better quality. They beheld me with all the marks and circumstances of wonder; neither indeed was I much in their debt, having never till then seen a race of mortals so singular in their shapes, habits, and countenances. Their heads were all reclined to the right, or the left; one of their eyes turned inward, and the other directly up to the zenith. Their outward garments were adorned with the figures of suns, moons, and stars, interwoven with those of fiddles, flutes, harps, trumpets, guitars, harpsichords, and many more instruments of music, unknown to us in Europe.[4] I observed here and there many in the habits of servants, with a blown bladder fastened like a flail to the end of a short stick, which they carried in their hands. In each bladder was a small quantity of dried pease or little pebbles (as I was afterwards informed). With these bladders they now and then flapped the mouths and ears of those who stood near them, of which practice I could not then conceive the meaning. It seems, the minds of these people are so taken up with intense speculations, that they neither can speak, or attend to the discourses of others, without being roused by some external taction[5] upon the organs of speech and hearing; for which reason those persons who are able to afford it always keep a flapper (the original is *climenole*) in their family, as one of their domestics; nor ever walk abroad or make visits without him. And the business of this officer is, when two or more persons

4. The Laputans represent contemporary speculation, deplored by Swift, about abstract theories of science, mathematics, and music. Both the Royal Society and Sir Isaac Newton took an interest in the mathematical basis of music.

5. Touch.

are in company, gently to strike with his bladder the mouth of him who is to speak, and the right ear of him or them to whom the speaker addresseth himself. This flapper is likewise employed diligently to attend his master in his walks, and upon occasion to give him a soft flap on his eyes, because he is always so wrapped up in cogitation, that he is in manifest danger of falling down every precipice, and bouncing his head against every post; and in the streets, of jostling others, or being jostled himself into the kennel.[6]

It was necessary to give the reader this information, without which he would be at the same loss with me, to understand the proceedings of these people, as they conducted me up the stairs to the top of the island, and from thence to the royal palace. While we were ascending, they forgot several times what they were about, and left me to myself, till their memories were again roused by their flappers; for they appeared altogether unmoved by the sight of my foreign habit and countenance, and by the shouts of the vulgar, whose thoughts and minds were more disengaged.

At last we entered the palace, and proceeded into the chamber of presence; where I saw the King seated on his throne, attended on each side by persons of prime quality. Before the throne was a large table filled with globes and spheres, and mathematical instruments of all kinds. His Majesty took not the least notice of us, although our entrance was not without sufficient noise, by the concourse of all persons belonging to the court. But he was then deep in a problem, and we attended at least an hour before he could solve it. There stood by him on each side a young page, with flaps in their hands, and when they saw he was at leisure, one of them gently struck his mouth, and the other his right ear; at which he started like one awaked on the sudden, and looking towards me, and the company I was in, recollected the occasion of our coming, whereof he had been informed before. He spoke some words, whereupon immediately a young man with a flap came up to my side, and flapped me gently on the right ear; but I made signs as well as I could, that I had no occasion for such an instrument; which as I afterwards found gave his Majesty and the whole court a very mean opinion of my understanding. The King, as far as I could conjecture, asked me several questions, and I addressed myself to him in all the languages I had. When it was found that I could neither understand nor be understood, I was conducted by his order to an apartment in his palace (this prince being distinguished above all his predecessors for his hospitality to strangers),[7] where two servants were appointed to attend me. My dinner was brought, and four persons of quality, whom I remembered to have seen very near the King's person, did me the honor to dine with me. We had two courses, of three dishes each. In the first course there was a shoul-

6. Gutter.

7. George I, a patron of music and science, had filled his court with Hanoverians when he came to England in 1714.

der of mutton, cut into an equilateral triangle; a piece of beef into a rhomboid; and a pudding into a cycloid. The second course was two ducks, trussed up into the form of fiddles; sausages and pudding resembling flutes and hautboys,[8] and a breast of veal in the shape of a harp. The servants cut our bread into cones, cylinders, parallelograms, and several other mathematical figures.

While we were at dinner, I made bold to ask the names of several things in their language, and those noble persons, by the assistance of their flappers, delighted to give me answers, hoping to raise my admiration of their great abilities, if I could be brought to converse with them. I was soon able to call for bread and drink, or whatever else I wanted.

After dinner my company withdrew, and a person was sent to me by the King's order, attended by a flapper. He brought with him pen, ink, and paper, and three or four books; giving me to understand by signs, that he was sent to teach me the language. We sat together four hours, in which time I wrote down a great number of words in columns, with the translations over against them. I likewise made a shift to learn several short sentences. For my tutor would order one of my servants to fetch something, to turn about, to make a bow, to sit, or stand, or walk, and the like. Then I took down the sentence in writing. He showed me also in one of his books the figures of the sun, moon, and stars, the zodiac, the tropics and polar circles, together with the denominations of many figures of planes and solids. He gave me the names and descriptions of all the musical instruments, and the general terms of art in playing on each of them. After he had left me, I placed all my words with their interpretations in alphabetical order. And thus in a few days, by the help of a very faithful memory, I got some insight into their language.

The word, which I interpret the *Flying* or *Floating Island*, is in the original *Laputa;* whereof I could never learn the true etymology. *Lap* in the old obsolete language signifieth *high*, and *untuh* a *governor;* from which they say by corruption was derived *Laputa*, from *Lapuntuh*. But I do not approve of this derivation, which seems to be a little strained. I ventured to offer to the learned among them a conjecture of my own, that *Laputa* was *quasi Lap outed; Lap* signifying properly the dancing of the sunbeams in the sea, and *outed* a wing, which however I shall not obtrude, but submit to the judicious reader.[9]

Those to whom the King had entrusted me, observing how ill I was clad, ordered a tailor to come next morning, and take my measure for a suit of clothes. This operator did his office after a different manner from those of his trade in Europe. He first took my altitude by a quadrant, and then, with rule and compasses, described the

8. Oboes.
9. Gulliver overlooks a likelier etymology: Spanish *la puta*, "the whore".

dimensions and outlines of my whole body; all which he entered upon paper, and in six days brought my clothes very ill made, and quite out of shape, by happening to mistake a figure in the calculation. But my comfort was, that I observed such accidents very frequent, and little regarded.

During my confinement for want of clothes, and by an indisposition that held me some days longer, I much enlarged my dictionary; and when I went next to court, was able to understand many things the King spoke, and to return him some kind of answers. His Majesty had given orders that the island should move northeast and by east, to the vertical point over Lagado, the metropolis of the whole kingdom, below upon the firm earth. It was about ninety leagues distant, and our voyage lasted four days and a half. I was not in the least sensible of the progressive motion made in the air by the island. On the second morning, about eleven o'clock, the King himself in person, attended by his nobility, courtiers, and officers, having prepared all their musical instruments, played on them for three hours without intermission, so that I was quite stunned with the noise; neither could I possibly guess the meaning, till my tutor informed me. He said, that the people of their island had their ears adapted to hear the music of the spheres, which always played at certain periods; and the court was now prepared to bear their part in whatever instrument they most excelled.

In our journey towards Lagado, the capital city, his Majesty ordered that the island should stop over certain towns and villages, from whence he might receive the petitions of his subjects. And to this purpose, several packthreads were let down with small weights at the bottom. On these packthreads the people strung their petitions, which mounted up directly like the scraps of paper fastened by schoolboys at the end of the string that holds their kite.[1] Sometimes we received wine and victuals from below, which were drawn up by pulleys.

The knowledge I had in mathematics gave me great assistance in acquiring their phraseology, which depended much upon that science and music; and in the latter I was not unskilled. Their ideas are perpetually conversant in lines and figures. If they would, for example, praise the beauty of a woman, or any other animal, they describe it by rhombs, circles, parallelograms, ellipses, and other geometrical terms; or else by words of art drawn from music, needless here to repeat. I observed in the King's kitchen all sorts of mathematical and musical instruments, after the figures of which they cut up the joints that were served to his Majesty's table.

Their houses are very ill built, the walls bevil, without one right angle in any apartment; and this defect ariseth from the contempt they bear for practical geometry; which they despise as vulgar and

1. Petitioners, that is, might as well go fly a kite. Throughout this section Swift satirizes the "distance" of George I (who spent much of his time in Hanover) from his English subjects.

mechanic, those instructions they give being too refined for the intellectuals of their workmen; which occasions perpetual mistakes. And although they are dextrous enough upon a piece of paper, in the management of the rule, the pencil, and the divider, yet in the common actions and behavior of life I have not seen a more clumsy, awkward, and unhandy people, nor so slow and perplexed in their conceptions upon all other subjects, except those of mathematics and music. They are very bad reasoners, and vehemently given to opposition, unless when they happen to be of the right opinion, which is seldom their case. Imagination, fancy, and invention, they are wholly strangers to, nor have any words in their language by which those ideas can be expressed; the whole compass of their thoughts and mind being shut up within the two forementioned sciences.

Most of them, and especially those who deal in the astronomical part, have great faith in judicial astrology, although they are ashamed to own it publicly. But what I chiefly admired,[2] and thought altogether unaccountable, was the strong disposition I observed in them towards news and politics; perpetually enquiring into public affairs, giving their judgments in matters of state; and passionately disputing every inch of a party opinion. I have indeed observed the same disposition among most of the mathematicians I have known in Europe; although I could never discover the least analogy between the two sciences; unless those people suppose, that because the smallest circle hath as many degrees as the largest, therefore the regulation and management of the world require no more abilities than the handling and turning of a globe. But I rather take this quality to spring from a very common infirmity of human nature, inclining us to be more curious and conceited in matters where we have least concern, and for which we are least adapted either by study or nature.

These people are under continual disquietudes, never enjoying a minute's peace of mind; and their disturbances proceed from causes which very little affect the rest of mortals. Their apprehensions arise from several changes they dread in the celestial bodies. For instance; that the earth, by the continual approaches of the sun towards it, must in course of time be absorbed or swallowed up. That the face of the sun will by degrees be encrusted with its own effluvia,[3] and give no more light to the world. That the earth very narrowly escaped a brush from the tail of the last comet, which would have infallibly reduced it to ashes; and that the next, which they have calculated for one and thirty years hence, will probably destroy us.[4] For, if in its perihelion it should approach within a certain degree of the sun (as by their calculations they have reason to

2. Wondered at.
3. Sunspots.
4. Halley's comet, some astronomers had feared, might strike the earth on its next appearance (1758). All the disasters that disquiet the Laputans had occurred to English scientists as possible implications of Newtonian theory.

dread), it will conceive a degree of heat ten thousand times more intense than that of red-hot glowing iron; and in its absence from the sun, carry a blazing tail ten hundred thousand and fourteen miles long; through which if the earth should pass at the distance of one hundred thousand miles from the nucleus, or main body of the comet, it must in its passage be set on fire, and reduced to ashes. That the sun daily spending its rays without any nutriment to supply them, will at last be wholly consumed and annihilated; which must be attended with the destruction of this earth, and of all the planets that receive their light from it.

They are so perpetually alarmed with the apprehensions of these and the like impending dangers, that they can neither sleep quietly in their beds, nor have any relish for the common pleasures or amusements of life. When they meet an acquaintance in the morning, the first question is about the sun's health, how he looked at his setting and rising, and what hopes they have to avoid the stroke of the approaching comet. This conversation they are apt to run into with the same temper that boys discover in delighting to hear terrible stories of sprites and hobgoblins, which they greedily listen to, and dare not go to bed for fear.

The women of the island have abundance of vivacity; they contemn their husbands, and are exceedingly fond of strangers, whereof there is always a considerable number from the continent below, attending at court, either upon affairs of the several towns and corporations, or their own particular occasions; but are much despised, because they want the same endowments. Among these the ladies choose their gallants: but the vexation is, that they act with too much ease and security; for the husband is always so rapt in speculation, that the mistress and lover may proceed to the greatest familiarities before his face, if he be but provided with paper and implements, and without his flapper at his side.

The wives and daughters lament their confinement to the island, although I think it the most delicious spot of ground in the world; and although they live here in the greatest plenty and magnificence, and are allowed to do whatever they please, they long to see the world, and take the diversions of the metropolis, which they are not allowed to do without a particular license from the King; and this is not easy to be obtained, because the people of quality have found by frequent experience, how hard it is to persuade their women to return from below. I was told that a great court lady, who had several children, is married to the prime minister, the richest subject in the kingdom, a very graceful person, extremely fond of her, and lives in the finest palace of the island, went down to Lagado, on the pretense of health, there hid herself for several months, till the King sent a warrant to search for her, and she was found in an obscure eating-house all in rags, having pawned her clothes to maintain an old deformed footman, who beat her every day, and in whose company she was taken much against her will. And although her husband received her with all possible kindness, and without the least reproach, she soon after contrived to steal down again with all her jewels, to the same gallant, and hath not been heard of since.

This may perhaps pass with the reader rather for an European or English story, than for one of a country so remote. But he may please to consider, that the caprices of womankind are not limited by any climate or nation; and that they are much more uniform than can be easily imagined.

In about a month's time I had made a tolerable proficiency in their language, and was able to answer most of the King's questions, when I had the honor to attend him. His Majesty discovered not the least curiosity to enquire into the laws, government, history, religion, or manners of the countries where I had been; but confined his questions to the state of mathematics, and received the account I gave him with great contempt and indifference, though often roused by his flapper on each side.

[*The Struldbruggs*]

Chapter X. *The Luggnaggians commended. A particular description of the struldbruggs, with many conversations between the author and some eminent persons upon that subject.*

The Luggnaggians are a polite[1] and generous people, and although they are not without some share of that pride which is peculiar to all eastern countries, yet they show themselves courteous to strangers, especially such who are countenanced by the court. I had many acquaintance among persons of the best fashion, and being always attended by my interpreter, the conversation we had was not disagreeable.

One day in much good company, I was asked by a person of quality, whether I had seen any of their *struldbruggs* or *immortals*. I said I had not; and desired he would explain to me what he meant by such an appellation, applied to a mortal creature. He told me, that sometimes, although very rarely, a child happened to be born in a family with a red circular spot in the forehead, directly over the left eyebrow, which was an infallible mark that it should never die. The spot, as he described it, was about the compass of a silver threepence, but in the course of time grew larger, and changed its color; for at twelve years old it became green, so continued till five and twenty, then turned to a deep blue; at five and forty it grew coal black, and as large as an English shilling; but never admitted any farther alteration. He said these births were so rare, that he did not believe there could be above eleven hundred *struldbruggs* of

1. Refined, cultivated.

both sexes in the whole kingdom, of which he computed about fifty in the metropolis, and among the rest a young girl born about three years ago. That these productions were not peculiar to any family, but a mere effect of chance; and the children of the *struldbruggs* themselves were equally mortal with the rest of the people.

I freely own myself to have been struck with inexpressible delight upon hearing this account: and the person who gave it me happening to understand the Balnibarbian language, which I spoke very well, I could not forbear breaking out into expressions perhaps a little too extravagant. I cried out as in a rapture: Happy nation, where every child hath at least a chance for being immortal! Happy people who enjoy so many living examples of ancient virtue, and have masters ready to instruct them in the wisdom of all former ages! But happiest beyond all comparison are those excellent *struldbruggs*, who being born exempt from that universal calamity of human nature, have their minds free and disengaged, without the weight and depression of spirits caused by the continual apprehension of death. I discovered my admiration[2] that I had not observed any of these illustrious persons at court; the black spot on the forehead being so remarkable a distinction, that I could not have easily overlooked it; and it was impossible that his Majesty, a most judicious prince, should not provide himself with a good number of such wise and able counselors. Yet perhaps the virtue of those reverend sages was too strict for the corrupt and libertine manners of a court. And we often find by experience that young men are too opinionative[3] and volatile to be guided by the sober dictates of their seniors. However, since the King was pleased to allow me access to his royal person, I was resolved upon the very first occasion to deliver my opinion to him on this matter freely, and at large by the help of my interpreter; and whether he would please to take my advice or no, yet in one thing I was determined, that his Majesty having frequently offered me an establishment in this country, I would with great thankfulness accept the favor, and pass my life here in the conversation of those superior beings the *struldbruggs*, if they would please to admit me.

The gentleman to whom I addressed my discourse, because (as I have already observed) he spoke the language of Balnibarbi, said to me with a sort of a smile, which usually ariseth from pity to the ignorant, that he was glad of any occasion to keep me among them, and desired my permission to explain to the company what I had spoke. He did so; and they talked together for some time in their own language, whereof I understood not a syllable, neither could I observe by their countenances what impression my discourse had made on them. After a short silence the same person told me, that his friends and mine (so he thought fit to express himself) were

2. Wonder.
3. Speculative, impractical. Note, in the next sentence, Gulliver's own resolve to deliver his opinion.

very much pleased with the judicious remarks I had made on the great happiness and advantages of immortal life; and they were desirous to know in a particular manner, what scheme of living I should have formed to myself, if it had fallen to my lot to have been born a *struldbrugg*.

I answered, it was easy to be eloquent on so copious and delightful a subject, especially to me who have been often apt to amuse myself with visions of what I should do if I were a king, a general, or a great lord; and upon this very case I had frequently run over the whole system how I should employ myself, and pass the time if I were sure to live forever.

That, if it had been my good fortune to come into the world a *struldbrugg*, as soon as I could discover my own happiness by understanding the difference between life and death, I would first resolve by all arts and methods whatsoever to procure myself riches: in the pursuit of which, by thrift and management, I might reasonably expect in about two hundred years to be the wealthiest man in the kingdom. In the second place, I would from my earliest youth apply myself to the study of arts and sciences, by which I should arrive in time to excel all others in learning. Lastly, I would carefully record every action and event of consequence that happened in the public, impartially draw the characters of the several successions of princes, and great ministers of state; with my own observations on every point. I would exactly set down the several changes in customs, languages, fashions of dress, diet and diversions. By all which acquirements, I should be a living treasury of knowledge and wisdom, and certainly become the oracle of the nation.

I would never marry after threescore, but live in an hospitable manner, yet still on the saving side. I would entertain myself in forming and directing the minds of hopeful young men, by convincing them from my own remembrance, experience and observation, fortified by numerous examples, of the usefulness of virtue in public and private life. But my choice and constant companions should be a set of my own immortal brotherhood, among whom I would elect a dozen from the most ancient down to my own contemporaries. Where any of these wanted fortunes, I would provide them with convenient lodges round my own estate, and have some of them always at my table, only mingling a few of the most valuable among you mortals, whom length of time would harden me to lose with little or no reluctance, and treat your posterity after the same manner; just as a man diverts himself with the annual succession of pinks and tulips in his garden, without regretting the loss of those which withered the preceding year.

These *struldbruggs* and I would mutually communicate our observations and memorials[4] through the course of time; remark the several gradations by which corruption steals into the world, and

4. Memories.

oppose it in every step, by giving perpetual warning and instruction to mankind; which, added to the strong influence of our own example, would probably prevent that continual degeneracy of human nature, so justly complained of in all ages.

Add to all this, the pleasure of seeing the various revolutions of states and empires; the changes in the lower and upper world;[5] ancient cities in ruins; and obscure villages become the seats of kings. Famous rivers lessening into shallow brooks; the ocean leaving one coast dry, and overwhelming another; the discovery of many countries yet unknown. Barbarity overrunning the politest nations, and the most barbarous becoming civilized. I should then see the discovery of the longitude, the perpetual motion, the universal medicine,[6] and many other great inventions brought to the utmost perfection.

What wonderful discoveries should we make in astronomy, by outliving and confirming our own predictions, by observing the progress and returns of comets, with the changes of motion in the sun, moon and stars.

I enlarged upon many other topics, which the natural desire of endless life and sublunary happiness could easily furnish me with. When I had ended, and the sum of my discourse had been interpreted as before to the rest of the company, there was a good deal of talk among them in the language of the country, not without some laughter at my expense. At last the same gentleman who had been my interpreter said, he was desired by the rest to set me right in a few mistakes, which I had fallen into through the common imbecility[7] of human nature, and upon that allowance was less answerable for them. That this breed of *struldbruggs* was peculiar to their country, for there were no such people either in Balnibarbi or Japan, where he had the honor to be ambassador from his Majesty, and found the natives in both those kingdoms very hard to believe that the fact was possible; and it appeared from my astonishment when he first mentioned the matter to me, that I received it as a thing wholly new, and scarcely to be credited. That in the two kingdoms above mentioned, where during his residence he had conversed very much, he observed long life to be the universal desire and wish of mankind. That whoever had one foot in the grave was sure to hold back the other as strongly as he could. That the oldest had still hopes of living one day longer, and looked on death as the greatest evil, from which nature always prompted him to retreat; only in this island of Luggnagg the appetite for living was not so eager, from the continual example of the *struldbruggs* before their eyes.

5. Earth and heaven; figuratively, common people and the ruling class. "Revolutions": cycles.
6. The *elixir vitae*, an alchemical formula to preserve life forever, was considered by Swift an impossible dream, like a method for calculating longitude at sea, or a perpetual motion machine.
7. Weakness.

That the system of living contrived by me was unreasonable and unjust, because it supposed a perpetuity of youth, health, and vigor, which no man could be so foolish to hope, however extravagant he might be in his wishes. That the question therefore was not whether a man would choose to be always in the prime of youth, attended with prosperity and health; but how he would pass a perpetual life under all the usual disadvantages which old age brings along with it. For although few men will avow their desires of being immortal upon such hard conditions, yet in the two kingdoms before mentioned of Balnibarbi and Japan, he observed that every man desired to put off death for some time longer, let it approach ever so late; and he rarely heard of any man who died willingly, except he were incited by the extremity of grief or torture. And he appealed to me whether in those countries I had traveled, as well as my own, I had not observed the same general disposition.

After this preface he gave me a particular account of the *struldbruggs* among them. He said they commonly acted like mortals, till about thirty years old, after which by degrees they grew melancholy and dejected, increasing in both till they came to fourscore. This he learned from their own confession; for otherwise there not being above two or three of that species born in an age, they were too few to form a general observation by. When they came to fourscore years, which is reckoned the extremity of living in this country, they had not only all the follies and infirmities of other old men, but many more which arose from the dreadful prospect of never dying. They were not only opinionative, peevish, covetous, morose, vain, talkative; but uncapable of friendship, and dead to all natural affection, which never descended below their grandchildren. Envy and impotent desires are their prevailing passions. But those objects against which their envy seems principally directed, are the vices of the younger sort, and the deaths of the old. By reflecting on the former, they find themselves cut off from all possibility of pleasure; and whenever they see a funeral, they lament and repine that others are gone to an harbor of rest, to which they themselves never can hope to arrive. They have no remembrance of anything but what they learned and observed in their youth and middle age, and even that is very imperfect. And for the truth or particulars of any fact, it is safer to depend on common traditions than upon their best recollections. The least miserable among them appear to be those who turn to dotage, and entirely lose their memories; these meet with more pity and assistance, because they want[8] many bad qualities which abound in others.

If a *struldbrugg* happen to marry one of his own kind, the marriage is dissolved of course by the courtesy of the kingdom, as soon as the younger of the two comes to be fourscore. For the law thinks it a reasonable indulgence, that those who are condemned without

8. Lack.

any fault of their own to a perpetual continuance in the world, should not have their misery doubled by the load of a wife.

As soon as they have completed the term of eighty years, they are looked on as dead in law; their heirs immediately succeed to their estates, only a small pittance is reserved for their support; and the poor ones are maintained at the public charge. After that period they are held incapable of any employment of trust or profit; they cannot purchase lands, or take leases, neither are they allowed to be witnesses in any cause, either civil or criminal, not even for the decision of meers[9] and bounds.

At ninety they lose their teeth and hair; they have at that age no distinction of taste, but eat and drink whatever they can get, without relish or appetite. The diseases they were subject to still continue without increasing or diminishing. In talking they forget the common appellation of things, and the names of persons, even of those who are their nearest friends and relations. For the same reason they never can amuse themselves with reading, because their memory will not serve to carry them from the beginning of a sentence to the end, and by this defect they are deprived of the only entertainment whereof they might otherwise be capable.

The language of this country being always upon the flux, the *struldbruggs* of one age do not understand those of another; neither are they able after two hundred years to hold any conversation (farther than by a few general words) with their neighbors the mortals; and thus they lie under the disadvantage of living like foreigners in their own country.

This was the account given me of the *struldbruggs*, as near as I can remember. I afterwards saw five or six of different ages, the youngest not above two hundred years old, who were brought to me at several times by some of my friends; but although they were told that I was a great traveler, and had seen all the world, they had not the least curiosity to ask me a question; only desired I would give them *slumskudask*, or a token of remembrance; which is a modest way of begging, to avoid the law that strictly forbids it, because they are provided for by the public, although indeed with a very scanty allowance.

They are despised and hated by all sorts of people; when one of them is born, it is reckoned ominous, and their birth is recorded very particularly; so that you may know their age by consulting the registry, which however hath not been kept above a thousand years past, or at least hath been destroyed by time or public disturbances. But the usual way of computing how old they are, is by asking them what kings or great persons they can remember, and then consulting history; for infallibly the last prince in their mind did not begin his reign after they were fourscore years old.

They were the most mortifying sight I ever beheld; and the

9. Boundaries.

women more horrible than the men. Besides the usual deformities in extreme old age, they acquired an additional ghastliness in proportion to their number of years, which is not to be described; and among half a dozen I soon distinguished which was the oldest, although there were not above a century or two between them.

The reader will easily believe, that from what I had heard and seen, my keen appetite for perpetuity of life was much abated. I grew heartily ashamed of the pleasing visions I had formed; and thought no tyrant could invent a death into which I would not run with pleasure from such a life. The King heard of all that had passed between me and my friends upon this occasion, and rallied[1] me very pleasantly; wishing I would send a couple of *struldbruggs* to my own country, to arm our people against the fear of death; but this it seems is forbidden by the fundamental laws of the kingdom; or else I should have been well content with the trouble and expense of transporting them.

I could not but agree, that the laws of this kingdom relating to the *struldbruggs*, were founded upon the strongest reasons, and such as any other country would be under the necessity of enacting in the like circumstances. Otherwise, as avarice is the necessary consequent of old age, those immortals would in time become proprietors of the whole nation, and engross[2] the civil power; which, for want of abilities to manage, must end in the ruin of the public.

Part IV. A Voyage to the Country of the Houyhnhnms [1]

CHAPTER I. *The Author sets out as Captain of a ship. His men conspire against him, confine him a long time to his cabin, set him on shore in an unknown land. He travels up into the country. The Yahoos, a strange sort of animal, described. The Author meets two Houyhnhnms.*

I continued at home with my wife and children about five months in a very happy condition, if I could have learned the lesson of knowing when I was well. I left my poor wife big with child, and accepted an advantageous offer made me to be Captain of the *Adventure*, a stout merchantman of 350 tons; for I understood navigation well, and being grown weary of a surgeon's employment at sea, which however I could exercise upon occasion, I took a skillful young man of that calling, one Robert Purefoy, into my ship. We set sail from Portsmouth upon the 7th day of September, 1710; on the 14th we met with Captain Pocock of Bristol, at Tenariff,[2] who was going to the Bay of Campeachy [3] to cut logwood. On the 16th he was parted from us by a storm; I heard since my return that his ship foundered and none escaped, but one

1. Ridiculed.
2. Absorb, monopolize.

1. Pronounced Hwín-ims. The word suggests the neigh characteristic of a horse.
2. Teneriffe, one of the Canary Islands.
3. In the Gulf of Mexico.

cabin boy. He was an honest man and a good sailor, but a little too positive in his own opinions, which was the cause of his destruction, as it hath been of several others. For if he had followed my advice, he might at this time have been safe at home with his family as well as myself.

I had several men died in my ship of calentures,[4] so that I was forced to get recruits out of Barbadoes and the Leeward Islands, where I touched by the direction of the merchants who employed me; which I had soon too much cause to repent, for I found afterwards that most of them had been buccaneers. I had fifty hands on board; and my orders were that I should trade with the Indians in the South Sea, and make what discoveries I could. These rogues whom I had picked up debauched my other men, and they all formed a conspiracy to seize the ship and secure me; which they did one morning, rushing into my cabin, and binding me hand and foot, threatening to throw me overboard, if I offered to stir. I told them I was their prisoner, and would submit. This they made me swear to do, and then unbound me, only fastening one of my legs with a chain near my bed, and placed a sentry at my door with his piece charged, who was commanded to shoot me dead if I attempted my liberty. They sent me down victuals and drink, and took the government of the ship to themselves. Their design was to turn pirates and plunder the Spaniards, which they could not do, till they got more men. But first they resolved to sell the goods in the ship, and then go to Madagascar for recruits, several among them having died since my confinement. They sailed many weeks, and traded with the Indians; but I knew not what course they took, being kept close prisoner in my cabin, and expecting nothing less than to be murdered, as they often threatened me.

Upon the 9th day of May, 1711, one James Welch came down to my cabin; and said he had orders from the Captain to set me ashore. I expostulated with him, but in vain; neither would he so much as tell me who their new Captain was. They forced me into the long-boat, letting me put on my best suit of clothes, which were as good as new, and a small bundle of linen, but no arms except my hanger; and they were so civil as not to search my pockets, into which I conveyed what money I had, with some other little necessaries. They rowed about a league, and then set me down on a strand. I desired them to tell me what country it was; they all swore, they knew no more than myself, but said that the Captain (as they called him) was resolved, after they had sold the lading, to get rid of me in the first place where they discovered land. They pushed off immediately, advising me to make haste, for fear of being overtaken by the tide, and bade me farewell.

In this desolate condition I advanced forward, and soon got upon

4. "A distemper peculiar to sailors, in hot climates; wherein they imagine the sea to be green fields, and will throw themselves into it, if not restrained" (Johnson's *Dictionary*).

firm ground, where I sat down on a bank to rest myself, and consider what I had best to do. When I was a little refreshed, I went up into the country, resolving to deliver myself to the first savages I should meet, and purchase my life from them by some bracelets, glass rings, and other toys, which sailors usually provide themselves with in those voyages, and whereof I had some about me. The land was divided by long rows of trees, not regularly planted, but naturally growing; there was great plenty of grass, and several fields of oats. I walked very circumspectly for fear of being surprised, or suddenly shot with an arrow from behind, or on either side. I fell into a beaten road, where I saw many tracks of human feet, and some of cows, but most of horses. At last I beheld several animals in a field, and one or two of the same kind sitting in trees. Their shape was very singular, and deformed, which a little discomposed me, so that I lay down behind a thicket to observe them better. Some of them coming forward near the place where I lay, gave me an opportunity of distinctly marking their form. Their heads and breasts were covered with a thick hair, some frizzled and others lank; they had beards like goats, and a long ridge of hair down their backs, and the fore parts of their legs and feet; but the rest of their bodies were bare, so that I might see their skins, which were of a brown buff color. They had no tails, nor any hair at all on their buttocks, except about the anus; which, I presume Nature had placed there to defend them as they sat on the ground; for this posture they used, as well as lying down, and often stood on their hind feet. They climbed high trees, as nimbly as a squirrel, for they had strong extended claws before and behind, terminating in sharp points, and hooked. They would often spring, and bound, and leap with prodigious agility. The females were not so large as the males; they had long lank hair on their heads, and only a sort of down on the rest of their bodies, except about the anus, and pudenda. Their dugs hung between their forefeet, and often reached almost to the ground as they walked. The hair of both sexes was of several colors, brown, red, black, and yellow. Upon the whole, I never beheld in all my travels so disagreeable an animal, or one against which I naturally conceived so strong an antipathy. So that thinking I had seen enough, full of contempt and aversion, I got up and pursued the beaten road, hoping it might direct me to the cabin of some Indian: I had not gone far when I met one of these creatures full in my way, and coming up directly to me. The ugly monster, when he saw me, distorted several ways every feature of his visage, and stared as at an object he had never seen before; then approaching nearer, lifted up his forepaw, whether out of curiosity or mischief, I could not tell; but I drew my hanger, and gave him a good blow with the flat side of it; for I durst not strike him with the edge, fearing the inhabitants might be provoked against me, if they should come to know that I had killed or maimed any of their cattle. When the beast felt the smart, he drew back, and roared so loud, that a herd of at least forty came flocking about me from the next field, howling and making odious faces; but I ran to the body of a tree, and leaning my back against it, kept them off, by waving my hanger. Several of this cursed brood getting hold of the branches behind, leaped up into the tree, from whence they began to discharge their excrements on my head; however, I escaped pretty well, by sticking close to the stem of the tree, but was almost stifled with the filth, which fell about me on every side.

In the midst of this distress, I observed them all to run away on a sudden as fast as they could; at which I ventured to leave the tree, and pursue the road, wondering what it was that could put them into this fright. But looking on my left hand, I saw a horse walking softly in the field; which my persecutors having sooner discovered, was the cause of their flight. The horse started a little when he came near me, but soon recovering himself, looked full in my face with manifest tokens of wonder; he viewed my hands and feet, walking round me several times. I would have pursued my journey, but he placed himself directly in the way, yet looking with a very mild aspect, never offering the least violence. We stood gazing at each other for some time; at last I took the boldness, to reach my hand towards his neck, with a design to stroke it; using the common style and whistle of jockies when they are going to handle a strange horse. But, this animal seeming to receive my civilities with disdain, shook his head, and bent his brows, softly raising up his left forefoot to remove my hand. Then he neighed three or four times, but in so different a cadence, that I almost began to think he was speaking to himself in some language of his own.

While he and I were thus employed, another horse came up; who applying himself to the first in a very formal manner, they gently struck each others right hoof before, neighing several times by turns, and varying the sound, which seemed to be almost articulate. They went some paces off, as if it were to confer together, walking side by side, backward and forward, like persons deliberating upon some affair of weight; but often turning their eyes towards me, as it were to watch that I might not escape. I was amazed to see such actions and behavior in brute beasts; and concluded with myself that if the inhabitants of this country were endued with a proportionable degree of reason, they must needs be the wisest people upon earth. This thought gave me so much comfort, that I resolved to go forward until I could discover some house or village, or meet with any of the natives, leaving the two horses to discourse together as they pleased. But the first, who was a dapple grey, observing me to steal off, neighed after me in so expressive a tone that I fancied myself to understand what he meant; whereupon I turned back, and came near him, to expect his farther commands; but concealing my fear as much as I could; for I began to be in some pain, how this adventure might terminate; and the reader will easily believe I did not much like my present situation.

The two horses came up close to me, looking with great earnestness upon my face and hands. The grey steed rubbed my hat all round with his right fore hoof, and discomposed it so much that I was forced to adjust it better, by taking it off, and settling it again; whereat both he and his companion (who was a brown bay) appeared to be much surprised; the latter felt the lappet of my coat, and finding it to hang loose about me, they both looked with new signs of wonder. He stroked my right hand, seeming to admire the softness, and color; but he squeezed it so hard between his hoof and his pastern, that I was forced to roar; after which they both touched me with all possible tenderness. They were under great perplexity about my shoes and stockings, which they felt very often, neighing to each other, and using various gestures, not unlike those of a philosopher, when he would attempt to solve some new and difficult phenomenon.

Upon the whole, the behavior of these animals was so orderly and rational, so acute and judicious, that I at last concluded, they must needs be magicians, who had thus metamorphosed themselves upon some design; and seeing a stranger in the way, were resolved to divert themselves with him; or perhaps were really amazed at the sight of a man so very different in habit, feature, and complexion from those who might probably live in so remote a climate. Upon the strength of this reasoning, I ventured to address them in the following manner: "Gentlemen, if you be conjurers, as I have good cause to believe, you can understand any language; therefore I make bold to let your worships know that I am a poor distressed Englishman, driven by his misfortunes upon your coast; and I entreat one of you, to let me ride upon his back, as if he were a real horse, to some house or village, where I can be relieved. In return of which favor, I will make you a present of this knife and bracelet" (taking them out of my pocket). The two creatures stood silent while I spoke, seeming to listen with great attention; and when I had ended, they neighed frequently towards each other, as if they were engaged in serious conversation. I plainly observed, that their language expressed the passions very well, and the words might with little pains be resolved into an alphabet more easily than the Chinese.

I could frequently distinguish the word *Yahoo*,[5] which was repeated by each of them several times; and although it were impossible for me to conjecture what it meant, yet while the two horses were busy in conversation, I endeavored to practice this word upon my tongue; and as soon as they were silent, I boldly pronounced "Yahoo" in a loud voice, imitating, at the same time, as near as I could, the neighing of a horse; at which they were both visibly sur-

5. Morley suggested that *Yahoo* was compounded from two expressions of disgust, *yah* and *ugh* (or *hoo*) common in the 18th century [Case's note].

prised, and the grey repeated the same word twice, as if he meant to teach me the right accent, wherein I spoke after him as well as I could, and found myself perceivably to improve every time, although very far from any degree of perfection. Then the bay tried me with a second word, much harder to be pronounced; but reducing it to the English orthography, may be spelt thus, *Houyhnhnm*. I did not succeed in this so well as the former, but after two or three farther trials, I had better fortune; and they both appeared amazed at my capacity.

After some farther discourse, which I then conjectured might relate to me, the two friends took their leaves, with the same compliment of striking each other's hoof; and the grey made me signs that I should walk before him; wherein I thought it prudent to comply, till I could find a better director. When I offered to slacken my pace, he would cry, "Hhuun, Hhuun"; I guessed his meaning, and gave him to understand, as well as I could that I was weary, and not able to walk faster; upon which, he would stand a while to let me rest.

CHAPTER II. *The Author conducted by a Houyhnhnm to his house. The house described. The Author's reception. The food of the Houyhnhnms. The Author in distress for want of meat is at last relieved. His manner of feeding in that country.*

Having traveled about three miles, we came to a long kind of building, made of timber, stuck in the ground, and wattled across; the roof was low, and covered with straw. I now began to be a little comforted, and took out some toys, which travelers usually carry for presents to the savage Indians of America and other parts, in hopes the people of the house would be thereby encouraged to receive me kindly. The horse made me a sign to go in first; it was a large room with a smooth clay floor, and a rack and manger extending the whole length on one side. There were three nags, and two mares, not eating, but some of them sitting down upon their hams, which I very much wondered at; but wondered more to see the rest employed in domestic business; the last seemed but ordinary cattle; however this confirmed my first opinion, that a people who could so far civilize brute animals must needs excel in wisdom all the nations of the world. The grey came in just after, and thereby prevented any ill treatment, which the others might have given me. He neighed to them several times in a style of authority, and received answers.

Beyond this room there were three others, reaching the length of the house, to which you passed through three doors, opposite to each other, in the manner of a vista; we went through the second room towards the third; here the grey walked in first, beckoning me to attend;[6] I waited in the second room, and got ready my presents,

6. To wait.

for the master and mistress of the house; they were two knives, three bracelets of false pearl, a small looking glass and a bead necklace. The horse neighed three or four times, and I waited to hear some answers in a human voice, but I heard no other returns than in the same dialect, only one or two a little shriller than his. I began to think that this house must belong to some person of great note among them, because there appeared so much ceremony before I could gain admittance. But, that a man of quality should be served all by horses, was beyond my comprehension. I feared my brain was disturbed by my sufferings and misfortunes; I roused myself, and looked about me in the room where I was left alone; this was furnished as the first, only after a more elegant manner. I rubbed my eyes often, but the same objects still occurred. I pinched my arms and sides, to awake myself, hoping I might be in a dream. I then absolutely concluded that all these appearances could be nothing else but necromancy and magic. But I had no time to pursue these reflections; for the grey horse came to the door, and made me a sign to follow him into the third room; where I saw a very comely mare, together with a colt and foal, sitting on their haunches, upon mats of straw, not unartfully made, and perfectly neat and clean.

The mare soon after my entrance, rose from her mat, and coming up close, after having nicely observed my hands and face, gave me a most contemptuous look; then turning to the horse, I heard the word Yahoo often repeated betwixt them; the meaning of which word I could not then comprehend, although it were the first I had learned to pronounce; but I was soon better informed, to my everlasting mortification: for the horse beckoning to me with his head, and repeating the word, "Hhuun, Hhuun," as he did upon the road, which I understood was to attend him, led me out into a kind of court, where was another building at some distance from the house. Here we entered, and I saw three of those detestable creatures, which I first met after my landing, feeding upon roots, and the flesh of some animals, which I afterwards found to be that of asses and dogs, and now and then a cow dead by accident or disease. They were all tied by the neck with strong withes, fastened to a beam; they held their food between the claws of their forefeet, and tore it with their teeth.

The master horse ordered a sorrel nag, one of his servants, to untie the largest of these animals, and take him into a yard. The beast and I were brought close together; and our countenances diligently compared, both by master and servant, who thereupon repeated several times the word "Yahoo." My horror and astonishment are not to be described, when I observed, in this abominable animal, a perfect human figure; the face of it indeed was flat and broad, the nose depressed, the lips large, and the mouth wide; but these differences are common to all savage nations, where the lineaments of the countenance are distorted by the natives suffering their infants to lie groveling on the earth, or by carrying them on their backs, nuzzling with their face against the mother's shoulders. The forefeet of the Yahoo differed from my hands in nothing else but the length of the nails, the coarseness and brownness of the palms, and the hairiness on the backs. There was the same resemblance between our feet, with the same differences, which I knew very well, although the horses did not, because of my shoes and stockings; the same in every part of our bodies, except as to hairiness and color, which I have already described.

The great difficulty that seemed to stick with the two horses was to see the rest of my body so very different from that of a Yahoo, for which I was obliged to my clothes, whereof they had no conception; the sorrel nag offered me a root, which he held (after their manner, as we shall describe in its proper place) between his hoof and pastern; I took it in my hand, and having smelled it, returned it to him again as civilly as I could. He brought out of the Yahoo's kennel a piece of ass's flesh, but it smelled so offensively that I turned from it with loathing; he then threw it to the Yahoo, by whom it was greedily devoured. He afterwards showed me a wisp of hay, and a fetlock full of oats; but I shook my head, to signify that neither of these were food for me. And indeed, I now apprehended that I must absolutely starve, if I did not get to some of my own species; for as to those filthy Yahoos, although there were few greater lovers of mankind, at that time, than myself, yet I confess I never saw any sensitive being so detestable on all accounts; and the more I came near them, the more hateful they grew, while I stayed in that country. This the master horse observed by my behavior, and therefore sent the Yahoo back to his kennel. He then put his forehoof to his mouth, at which I was much surprised, although he did it with ease, and with a motion that appeared perfectly natural; and made other signs to know what I would eat; but I could not return him such an answer as he was able to apprehend; and if he had understood me, I did not see how it was possible to contrive any way for finding myself nourishment. While we were thus engaged, I observed a cow passing by; whereupon I pointed to her, and expressed a desire to let me go and milk her. This had its effect; for he led me back into the house, and ordered a mare-servant to open a room, where a good store of milk lay in earthen and wooden vessels, after a very orderly and cleanly manner. She gave me a large bowl full, of which I drank very heartily, and found myself well refreshed.

About noon I saw coming towards the house a kind of vehicle, drawn like a sledge by four Yahoos. There was in it an old steed, who seemed to be of quality; he alighted with his hind feet forward, having by accident got a hurt in his left forefoot. He came to dine with our horse, who received him with great civility. They dined in the best room, and had oats boiled in milk for the second course, which the old horse eat warm, but the rest cold. Their mangers were placed circular in the middle of the room, and divided into several partitions, round which they sat on their haunches upon bosses of straw. In the middle was a large rack with angles answering to every partition of the manger. So that each horse and mare eat their own hay, and their own mash of oats and milk, with much decency and regularity. The behavior of the young colt and foal appeared very modest; and that of the master and mistress extremely cheerful and complaisant to their guest. The grey ordered me to stand by him; and much discourse passed between him and his friend concerning me, as I found by the stranger's often looking on me, and the frequent repetition of the word Yahoo.

I happened to wear my gloves; which the master grey observing, seemed perplexed; discovering signs of wonder what I had done to my forefeet; he put his hoof three or four times to them, as if he would signify, that I should reduce them to their former shape, which I presently did, pulling off both my gloves, and putting them into my pocket. This occasioned farther talk, and I saw the company was pleased with my behavior, whereof I soon found the good effects. I was ordered to speak the few words I understood; and while they were at dinner, the master taught me the names for oats, milk, fire, water, and some others which I could readily pronounce after him, having from my youth a great facility in learning languages.

When dinner was done, the master horse took me aside, and by signs and words made me understand the concern he was in that I had nothing to eat. Oats in their tongue are called *hlunnh*. This word I pronounced two or three times; for although I had refused them at first, yet upon second thoughts, I considered that I could contrive to make a kind of bread, which might be sufficient with milk to keep me alive, till I could make my escape to some other country, and to creatures of my own species. The horse immediately ordered a white mare-servant of his family to bring me a good quantity of oats in a sort of wooden tray. These I heated before the fire as well as I could, and rubbed them till the husks came off, which I made a shift to winnow from the grain; I ground and beat them between two stones, then took water, and made them into a paste or cake, which I toasted at the fire, and eat warm with milk. It was at first a very insipid diet, although common enough in many parts of Europe, but grew tolerable by time; and having been often reduced to hard fare in my life, this was not the first experiment I had made how easily nature is satisfied. And I cannot but observe that I never had one hour's sickness, while I staid in this island. It is true, I sometimes made a shift to catch a rabbit, or bird, by springes [7] made of Yahoos' hairs; and I often gathered wholesome herbs, which I boiled, or eat as salads with my bread; and now and then, for a rarity, I made a little butter, and drank the whey. I was

7. Snares.

at first at a great loss for salt; but custom soon reconciled the want of it; and I am confident that the frequent use of salt among us is an effect of luxury, and was first introduced only as a provocative to drink; except where it is necessary for preserving of flesh in long voyages, or in places remote from great markets. For we observe no animal to be fond of it but man; [8] and as to myself, when I left this country, it was a great while before I could endure the taste of it in anything that I eat.

This is enough to say upon the subject of my diet, wherewith other travelers fill their books, as if the readers were personally concerned whether we fare well or ill. However, it was necessary to mention this matter, lest the world should think it impossible that I could find sustenance for three years in such a country, and among such inhabitants.

When it grew towards evening, the master horse ordered a place for me to lodge in; it was but six yards from the house, and separated from the stable of the Yahoos. Here I got some straw, and covering myself with my own clothes, slept very sound. But I was in a short time better accommodated, as the reader shall know hereafter, when I come to treat more particularly about my way of living.

CHAPTER III. *The Author studious to learn the language, the Houyhnhnm his master assists in teaching him. The language described. Several Houyhnhnms of quality come out of curiosity to see the Author. He gives his master a short account of his voyage.*

My principal endeavor was to learn the language, which my master (for so I shall henceforth call him) and his children, and every servant of his house were desirous to teach me. For they looked upon it as a prodigy, that a brute animal should discover such marks of a rational creature. I pointed to everything, and enquired the name of it, which I wrote down in my journal book when I was alone, and corrected my bad accent, by desiring those of the family to pronounce it often. In this employment, a sorrel nag, one of the under servants, was very ready to assist me.

In speaking, they pronounce through the nose and throat, and their language approaches nearest to the High Dutch or German, of any I know in Europe; but is much more graceful and significant. The Emperor Charles V made almost the same observation, when he said, that if he were to speak to his horse, it should be in High Dutch.[9]

The curiosity and impatience of my master were so great, that he spent many hours of his leisure to instruct me. He was convinced (as he afterwards told me) that I must be a Yahoo, but my

8. Gulliver is, of course, in error. Many animals require salt.

9. The Emperor is supposed to have said that he would speak to his God in Spanish, to his mistress in Italian, and to his horse in German.

teachableness, civility, and cleanliness astonished him; which were qualities altogether so opposite to those animals. He was most perplexed about my clothes, reasoning sometimes with himself whether they were a part of my body; for I never pulled them off till the family were asleep, and got them on before they waked in the morning. My master was eager to learn from whence I came; how I acquired those appearances of reason, which I discovered in all my actions; and to know my story from my own mouth, which he hoped he should soon do by the great proficiency I made in learning and pronouncing their words and sentences. To help my memory, I formed all I learned into the English alphabet, and writ the words down with the translations. This last, after some time, I ventured to do in my master's presence. It cost me much trouble to explain to him what I was doing; for the inhabitants have not the least idea of books or literature.

In about ten weeks time I was able to understand most of his questions; and in three months could give him some tolerable answers. He was extremely curious to know from what part of the country I came, and how I was taught to imitate a rational creature; because the Yahoos (whom he saw I exactly resembled in my head, hands, and face, that were only visible) with some appearance of cunning, and the strongest disposition to mischief, were observed to be the most unteachable of all brutes. I answered that I came over the sea, from a far place, with many others of my own kind, in a great hollow vessel made of the bodies of trees; that my companions forced me to land on this coast, and then left me to shift for myself. It was with some difficulty, and by the help of many signs, that I brought him to understand me. He replied that I must needs be mistaken, or that I *said the thing which was not.* (For they have no word in their language to express lying or falsehood.) He knew it was impossible that there could be a country beyond the sea, or that a parcel of brutes could move a wooden vessel whither they pleased upon water. He was sure no Houyhnhnm alive could make such a vessel, or would trust Yahoos to manage it.

The word Houyhnhnm, in their tongue, signifies a Horse; and in its etymology, the Perfection of Nature. I told my master that I was at a loss for expression, but would improve as fast as I could; and hoped in a short time I should be able to tell him wonders; he was pleased to direct his own mare, his colt, and foal, and the servants of the family to take all opportunities of instructing me; and every day for two or three hours, he was at the same pains himself; several horses and mares of quality in the neighborhood came often to our house, upon the report spread of a wonderful Yahoo, that could speak like a Houyhnhnm, and seemed in his words and actions to discover some glimmerings of reason. These delighted to converse with me; they put many questions, and received such answers as I was able to return. By all which advantages,

I made so great a progress, that in five months from my arrival, I understood whatever was spoke, and could express myself tolerably well.

The Houyhnhnms who came to visit my master, out of a design of seeing and talking with me, could hardly believe me to be a right Yahoo, because my body had a different covering from others of my kind. They were astonished to observe me without the usual hair or skin, except on my head, face, and hands; but I discovered that secret to my master, upon an accident, which happened about a fortnight before.

I have already told the reader, that every night when the family were gone to bed, it was my custom to strip and cover myself with my clothes; it happened one morning early, that my master sent for me, by the sorrel nag, who was his valet; when he came, I was fast asleep, my clothes fallen off on one side, and my shirt above my waist. I awaked at the noise he made, and observed him to deliver his message in some disorder; after which he went to my master, and in a great fright gave him a very confused account of what he had seen; this I presently discovered; for going as soon as I was dressed, to pay my attendance upon his honor, he asked me the meaning of what his servant had reported; that I was not the same thing when I slept as I appeared to be at other times; that his valet assured him, some part of me was white, some yellow, at least not so white, and some brown.

I had hitherto concealed the secret of my dress, in order to distinguish myself as much as possible, from that cursed race of Yahoos; but now I found it in vain to do so any longer. Besides, I considered that my clothes and shoes would soon wear out, which already were in a declining condition, and must be supplied by some contrivance from the hides of Yahoos, or other brutes; whereby the whole secret would be known. I therefore told my master, that in the country from whence I came, those of my kind always covered their bodies with the hairs of certain animals prepared by art, as well for decency, as to avoid inclemencies of air both hot and cold; of which, as to my own person I would give him immediate conviction, if he pleased to command me; only desiring his excuse, if I did not expose those parts that nature taught us to conceal. He said, my discourse was all very strange, but especially the last part; for he could not understand why Nature should teach us to conceal what Nature had given. That neither himself nor family were ashamed of any parts of their bodies; but however I might do as I pleased. Whereupon, I first unbuttoned my coat, and pulled it off. I did the same with my waistcoat; I drew off my shoes, stockings, and breeches. I let my shirt down to my waist, and drew up the bottom, fastening it like a girdle about my middle to hide my nakedness.

My master observed the whole performance with great signs of curiosity and admiration. He took up all my clothes in his pastern, one piece after another, and examined them diligently; he then stroked my body very gently, and looked round me several times; after which he said, it was plain I must be a perfect Yahoo; but that I differed very much from the rest of my species, in the whiteness and smoothness of my skin, my want of hair in several parts of my body, the shape and shortness of my claws behind and before, and my affectation of walking continually on my two hinder feet. He desired to see no more; and gave me leave to put on my clothes again, for I was shuddering with cold.

I expressed my uneasiness at his giving me so often the appellation of Yahoo, an odious animal, for which I had so utter an hatred and contempt. I begged he would forbear applying that word to me, and take the same order in his family, and among his friends whom he suffered to see me. I requested likewise, that the secret of my having a false covering to my body might be known to none but himself, at least as long as my present clothing should last; for as to what the sorrel nag his valet had observed, his honor might command him to conceal it.

All this my master very graciously consented to; and thus the secret was kept till my clothes began to wear out, which I was forced to supply by several contrivances, that shall hereafter be mentioned. In the meantime, he desired I would go on with my utmost diligence to learn their language, because he was more astonished at my capacity for speech and reason, than at the figure of my body, whether it were covered or no; adding that he waited with some impatience to hear the wonders which I promised to tell him.

From thenceforward he doubled the pains he had been at to instruct me; he brought me into all company, and made them treat me with civility, because, as he told them privately, this would put me into good humor, and make me more diverting.

Every day when I waited on him, beside the trouble he was at in teaching, he would ask me several questions concerning myself, which I answered as well as I could; and by those means he had already received some general ideas, although very imperfect. It would be tedious to relate the several steps, by which I advanced to a more regular conversation, but the first account I gave of myself in any order and length was to this purpose:

That, I came from a very far country, as I already had attempted to tell him, with about fifty more of my own species; that we traveled upon the seas, in a great hollow vessel made of wood, and larger than his honor's house. I described the ship to him in the best terms I could; and explained by the help of my handkerchief displayed, how it was driven forward by the wind. That, upon a quarrel among us, I was set on shore on this coast, where I walked forward without knowing whither, till he delivered me from the persecution of those execrable Yahoos. He asked me who made the ship, and how it was possible that the Houyhnhnms of my country would leave it to the management of brutes? My answer was that I durst proceed no farther in my relation, unless he would give me his word and honor that he would not be offended; and then I would tell him the wonders I had so often promised. He agreed; and I went on by assuring him, that the ship was made by creatures like myself, who in all the countries I had traveled, as well as in my own, were the only governing, rational animals; and that upon my arrival hither, I was as much astonished to see the Houyhnhnms act like rational beings, as he or his friends could be in finding some marks of reason in a creature he was pleased to call a Yahoo; to which I owned my resemblance in every part, but could not account for their degenerate and brutal nature. I said farther, that if good fortune ever restored me to my native country, to relate my travels hither, as I resolved to do; everybody would believe that I *said the thing which was not*; that I invented the story out of my own head; and with all possible respect to himself, his family, and friends, and under his promise of not being offended, our countrymen would hardly think it probable, that a Houyhnhnm should be the presiding creature of a nation, and a Yahoo the brute.

Chapter IV. *The Houyhnhnms' notion of truth and falsehood. The author's discourse disapproved by his master. The author gives a more particular account of himself, and the accidents of his voyage.*

My master heard me with great appearances of uneasiness in his countenance; because *doubting* or *not believing* are so little known in this country, that the inhabitants cannot tell how to behave themselves under such circumstances. And I remember in frequent discourses with my master concerning the nature of manhood, in other parts of the world, having occasion to talk of *lying* and *false representation,* it was with much difficulty that he comprehended what I meant; although he had otherwise a most acute judgment. For he argued thus: that the use of speech was to make us understand one another, and to receive information of facts; now if anyone *said the thing which was not,* these ends were defeated; because I cannot properly be said to understand him; and I am so far from receiving information, that he leaves me worse than in ignorance; for I am led to believe a thing *black* when it is *white,* and *short* when it is *long.* And these were all the notions he had concerning that faculty of *lying,* so perfectly well understood, and so universally practiced among human creatures.

To return from this digression; when I asserted that the Yahoos were the only governing animals in my country, which my master said was altogether past his conception, he desired to know, whether we had Houyhnhnms among us, and what was their employment; I told him we had great numbers; that in summer they grazed in the fields, and in winter were kept in houses, with hay and oats, where Yahoo servants were employed to rub their skins smooth, comb their manes, pick their feet, serve them with food, and make their beds. "I understand you well," said my master; "it is now very plain from all you have spoken, that whatever share of reason the Yahoos pretend to, the Houyhnhnms are your masters; I heartily wish our Yahoos would be so tractable." I begged his honor would please to excuse me from proceeding any farther, because I was very certain that the account he expected from me would be highly displeasing. But he insisted in commanding me to let him know the best and the worst; I told him he should be obeyed. I owned that the Houyhnhnms among us, whom we called Horses, were the most generous [1] and comely animal we had; that they excelled in strength and swiftness; and when they belonged to persons of quality, employed in traveling, racing, and drawing chariots, they were treated with much kindness and care, till they fell into diseases, or became foundered in the feet; but then they were sold, and used to all kind of drudgery till they died; after which their skins were stripped and sold for what they were worth, and their bodies left to be devoured by dogs and birds of prey. But the common race of horses had not so good fortune, being kept by farmers and carriers, and other mean people, who put them to greater labor, and feed them worse. I described as well as I could, our way of riding; the shape and use of a bridle, a saddle, a spur, and a whip; of harness and wheels. I added, that we fastened plates of a certain hard substance called iron at the bottom of their feet, to preserve their hoofs from being broken by the stony ways on which we often traveled.

My master, after some expressions of great indignation, wondered how we dared to venture upon a Houyhnhnm's back; for he was sure, that the weakest servant in his house would be able to shake off the strongest Yahoo; or by lying down, and rolling upon his back, squeeze the brute to death. I answered that our horses were trained up from three or four years old to the several uses we intended them for; that if any of them proved intolerably vicious, they were employed for carriages; that they were severely beaten while they were young for any mischievous tricks; that the males, designed for the common use of riding or draught, were generally castrated about two years after their birth, to take down their spirits, and make them more tame and gentle; that they were indeed sensible of rewards and punishments; but his honor would please to consider that they had not the least tincture of reason any more than the Yahoos in this country.

It put me to the pains of many circumlocutions to give my master a right idea of what I spoke; for their language doth not abound in variety of words, because their wants and passions are fewer than

1. Noble.

among us. But it is impossible to express his noble resentment at our savage treatment of the Houyhnhnm race; particularly after I had explained the manner and use of castrating horses among us, to hinder them from propagating their kind, and to render them more servile. He said, if it were possible there could be any country where Yahoos alone were endued with reason, they certainly must be the governing animal, because reason will in time always prevail against brutal strength. But, considering the frame of our bodies, and especially of mine, he thought no creature of equal bulk was so ill-contrived for employing that reason in the common offices of life; whereupon he desired to know whether those among whom I lived resembled me or the Yahoos of his country. I assured him that I was as well shaped as most of my age; but the younger and the females were much more soft and tender, and the skins of the latter generally as white as milk. He said I differed indeed from other Yahoos, being much more cleanly, and not altogether so deformed; but in point of real advantage, he thought I differed for the worse. That my nails were of no use either to my fore or hinder feet; as to my forefeet, he could not properly call them by that name, for he never observed me to walk upon them; that they were too soft to bear the ground; that I generally went with them uncovered, neither was the covering I sometimes wore on them of the same shape, or so strong as that on my feet behind. That I could not walk with any security; for if either of my hinder feet slipped, I must inevitably fall. He then began to find fault with other parts of my body; the flatness of my face, the prominence of my nose, my eyes placed directly in front, so that I could not look on either side without turning my head; that I was not able to feed myself without lifting one of my forefeet to my mouth; and therefore nature had placed those joints to answer that necessity. He knew not what could be the use of those several clefts and divisions in my feet behind; that these were too soft to bear the hardness and sharpness of stones without a covering made from the skin of some other brute; that my whole body wanted a fence against heat and cold, which I was forced to put on and off every day with tediousness and trouble. And lastly, that he observed every animal in his country naturally to abhor the Yahoos, whom the weaker avoided, and the stronger drove from them. So that supposing us to have the gift of reason, he could not see how it were possible to cure that natural antipathy which every creature discovered against us; nor consequently, how we could tame and render them serviceable. However, he would (as he said) debate the matter no farther, because he was more desirous to know my own story, the country where I was born, and the several actions and events of my life before I came hither.

I assured him how extremely desirous I was that he should be satisfied in every point; but I doubted much whether it would be possible for me to explain myself on several subjects whereof his honor could have no conception, because I saw nothing in his country to which I could resemble them. That however, I would do my best, and strive to express myself by similitudes, humbly desiring his assistance when I wanted proper words; which he was pleased to promise me.

I said, my birth was of honest parents, in an island called England, which was remote from this country, as many days journey as the strongest of his honor's servants could travel in the annual course of the sun. That I was bred a surgeon, whose trade it is to cure wounds and hurts in the body, got by accident or violence. That my country was governed by a female man, whom we called a queen. That I left it to get riches, whereby I might maintain myself and family when I should return. That in my last voyage, I was Commander of the ship and had about fifty Yahoos under me, many of which died at sea, and I was forced to supply them by others picked out from several nations. That our ship was twice in danger of being sunk; the first time by a great storm, and the second, by striking against a rock. Here my master interposed, by asking me, how I could persuade strangers out of different countries to venture with me, after the losses I had sustained, and the hazards I had run. I said, they were fellows of desperate fortunes, forced to fly from the places of their birth, on account of their poverty or their crimes. Some were undone by lawsuits; others spent all they had in drinking, whoring, and gaming; others fled for treason; many for murder, theft, poisoning, robbery, perjury, forgery, coining false money; for committing rapes or sodomy; for flying from their colors, or deserting to the enemy; and most of them had broken prison. None of these durst return to their native countries for fear of being hanged, or of starving in a jail; and therefore were under a necessity of seeking a livelihood in other places.

During this discourse, my master was pleased often to interrupt me. I had made use of many circumlocutions in describing to him the nature of the several crimes, for which most of our crew had been forced to fly their country. This labor took up several days conversation before he was able to comprehend me. He was wholly at a loss to know what could be the use or necessity of practicing those vices. To clear up which I endeavored to give him some ideas of the desire of power and riches; of the terrible effects of lust, intemperance, malice, and envy. All this I was forced to define and describe by putting of cases, and making suppositions. After which, like one whose imagination was struck with something never seen or heard of before, he would lift up his eyes with amazement and indignation. Power, government, war, law, punishment, and a thousand other things had no terms, wherein that language could express them; which made the difficulty almost insuperable to give my master any conception of what I meant; but being of an excellent understanding, much improved by contemplation and converse, he at last arrived at a competent knowledge of what human nature in our parts of the world is capable to perform; and desired I would give him some particular account of that land, which we call Europe, especially, of my own country.

CHAPTER V. *The Author, at his master's commands, informs him of the state of England. The causes of war among the princes of Europe. The Author begins to explain the English Constitution.*

The reader may please to observe that the following extract of many conversations I had with my master contains a summary of the most material points, which were discoursed at several times for above two years; his honor often desiring fuller satisfaction as I farther improved in the Houyhnhnm tongue. I laid before him, as well as I could, the whole state of Europe; I discoursed of trade and manufactures, of arts and sciences; and the answers I gave to all the questions he made, as they arose upon several subjects, were a fund of conversation not to be exhausted. But I shall here only set down the substance of what passed between us concerning my own country, reducing it into order as well as I can, without any regard to time or other circumstances, while I strictly adhere to truth. My only concern is that I shall hardly be able to do justice to my master's arguments and expressions; which must needs suffer by my want of capacity, as well as by a translation into our barbarous English.

In obedience therefore to his honor's commands, I related to him the Revolution under the Prince of Orange; the long war with France entered into by the said Prince, and renewed by his successor the present queen; wherein the greatest powers of Christendom were engaged, and which still continued. I computed at his request, that about a million of Yahoos might have been killed in the whole progress of it; and perhaps a hundred or more cities taken, and five times as many ships burned or sunk.[2]

He asked me what were the usual causes or motives that made one country to go to war with another. I answered, they were innumerable; but I should only mention a few of the chief. Sometimes the ambition of princes, who never think they have land or people enough to govern; sometimes the corruption of ministers, who engage their master in a war in order to stifle or divert the clamor of the subjects against their evil administration. Difference in opinions hath cost many millions of lives; for instance, whether flesh be bread, or bread be flesh; whether the juice of a certain berry be blood or wine; whether whistling be a vice or a virtue; whether it be better to kiss a post, or throw it into the fire; what is the best color for a coat, whether black, white, red, or grey; and

2. Gulliver relates recent English history: the Glorious Revolution of 1688 and the War of Spanish Succession (1703–13). He greatly exaggerates the casualties in the war.

whether it should be long or short, narrow or wide, dirty or clean;[3] with many more. Neither are any wars so furious and bloody, or of so long continuance, as those occasioned by difference in opinion, especially if it be in things indifferent.[4]

Sometimes the quarrel between two princes is to decide which of them shall dispossess a third of his dominions, where neither of them pretend to any right. Sometimes one prince quarreleth with another, for fear the other should quarrel with him. Sometimes a war is entered upon, because the enemy is too strong, and sometimes because he is too weak. Sometimes our neighbors want the things which we have, or have the things which we want; and we both fight, till they take ours or give us theirs. It is a very justifiable cause of war to invade a country after the people have been wasted by famine, destroyed by pestilence, or embroiled by factions amongst themselves. It is justifiable to enter into a war against our nearest ally, when one of his towns lies convenient for us, or a territory of land, that would render our dominions round and compact. If a prince send forces into a nation, where the people are poor and ignorant, he may lawfully put half of them to death, and make slaves of the rest, in order to civilize and reduce them from their barbarous way of living. It is a very kingly, honorable, and frequent practice, when one prince desires the assistance of another to secure him against an invasion, that the assistant, when he hath driven out the invader, should seize on the dominions himself, and kill, imprison, or banish the prince he came to relieve. Alliance by blood or marriage is a sufficient cause of war between princes; and the nearer the kindred is, the greater is their disposition to quarrel; poor nations are hungry, and rich nations are proud; and pride and hunger will ever be at variance. For these reasons, the trade of a soldier is held the most honorable of all others: because a soldier is a Yahoo hired to kill in cold blood as many of his own species, who have never offended him, as possibly he can.

There is likewise a kind of beggarly princes in Europe, not able to make war by themselves, who hire out their troops to richer nations for so much a day to each man; of which they keep three fourths to themselves, and it is the best part of their maintenance; such are those in many northern parts of Europe.[5]

"What you have told me," said my master, "upon the subject of war, doth indeed discover most admirably the effects of that reason you pretend to; however, it is happy that the shame is greater than the danger; and that Nature hath left you utterly uncapable of doing much mischief; for your mouths lying flat with your faces, you can hardly bite each other to any purpose, unless by

3. Gulliver refers to the religious controversies of the Reformation and Counter Reformation: the doctrine of transubstantiation, the use of music in church services, the veneration of the crucifix, and the wearing of priestly vestments.

4. Of little consequence.

5. A satiric glance at George I, who, as Elector of Hanover, had dealt in this trade.

consent. Then, as to the claws upon your feet before and behind, they are so short and tender, that one of our Yahoos would drive a dozen of yours before him. And therefore in recounting the numbers of those who have been killed in battle, I cannot but think that you have *said the thing which is not.*"

I could not forbear shaking my head and smiling a little at his ignorance. And, being no stranger to the art of war, I gave him a description of cannons, culverins, muskets, carabines, pistols, bullets, powder, swords, bayonets, battles, sieges, retreats, attacks, undermines, countermines, bombardments, sea fights; ships sunk with a thousand men; twenty thousand killed on each side; dying groans, limbs flying in the air; smoke, noise, confusion, trampling to death under horses' feet; flight, pursuit, victory; fields strewed with carcasses left for food to dogs, and wolves, and birds of prey; plundering, stripping, ravishing, burning, and destroying. And, to set forth the valor of my own dear countrymen, I assured him that I had seen them blow up a hundred enemies at once in a siege, and as many in a ship; and beheld the dead bodies drop down in pieces from the clouds, to the great diversion of all the spectators.

I was going on to more particulars, when my master commanded me silence. He said, whoever understood the nature of Yahoos might easily believe it possible for so vile an animal, to be capable of every action I had named, if their strength and cunning equaled their malice. But, as my discourse had increased his abhorrence of the whole species, so he found it gave him a disturbance in his mind, to which he was wholly a stranger before. He thought his ears being used to such abominable words, might by degrees admit them with less detestation. That, although he hated the Yahoos of this country, yet he no more blamed them for their odious qualities, than he did a *gnnayh* (a bird of prey) for its cruelty, or a sharp stone for cutting his hoof. But, when a creature pretending to reason could be capable of such enormities, he dreaded lest the corruption of that faculty might be worse than brutality itself. He seemed therefore confident, that instead of reason, we were only possessed of some quality fitted to increase our natural vices; as the reflection from a troubled stream returns the image of an ill-shapen body, not only larger, but more distorted.

He added that he had heard too much upon the subject of war, both in this and some former discourses. There was another point which a little perplexed him at present. I had said that some of our crew left their country on account of being ruined by law: that I had already explained the meaning of the word; but he was at a loss how it should come to pass, that the law which was intended for every man's preservation, should be any man's ruin. Therefore he desired to be farther satisfied what I meant by law, and the dispensers thereof, according to the present practice in my own country; because he thought nature and reason were sufficient guides for a reasonable animal, as we pretended to be, in showing us what we ought to do, and what to avoid.

I assured his honor that law was a science wherein I had not much conversed, further than by employing advocates, in vain, upon some injustices that had been done me. However, I would give him all the satisfaction I was able.

I said there was a society of men among us, bred up from their youth in the art of proving by words multiplied for the purpose, that white is black, and black is white, according as they are paid. To this society all the rest of the people are slaves.

"For example. If my neighbor hath a mind to my cow, he hires a lawyer to prove that he ought to have my cow from me. I must then hire another to defend my right; it being against all rules of law that any man should be allowed to speak for himself. Now in this case, I who am the true owner lie under two great disadvantages. First, my lawyer being practiced almost from his cradle in defending falsehood is quite out of his element when he would be an advocate for justice, which as an office unnatural, he always attempts with great awkwardness, if not with ill-will. The second disadvantage is that my lawyer must proceed with great caution, or else he will be reprimanded by the judges, and abhorred by his brethren, as one who would lessen the practice of the law. And therefore I have but two methods to preserve my cow. The first is to gain over my adversary's lawyer with a double fee; who will then betray his client, by insinuating that he hath justice on his side. The second way is for my lawyer to make my cause appear as unjust as he can; by allowing the cow to belong to my adversary; and this if it be skillfully done, will certainly bespeak the favor of the bench.

"Now, your honor is to know that these judges are persons appointed to decide all controversies of property, as well as for the trial of criminals; and picked out from the most dextrous lawyers who are grown old or lazy; and having been biased all their lives against truth and equity, lie under such a fatal necessity of favoring fraud, perjury, and oppression, that I have known some of them to have refused a large bribe from the side where justice lay, rather than injure the faculty,[6] by doing anything unbecoming their nature or their office.

"It is a maxim among these lawyers, that whatever hath been done before may legally be done again; and therefore they take special care to record all the decisions formerly made against common justice and the general reason of mankind. These, under the name of *precedents*, they produce as authorities to justify the most iniquitous opinions; and the judges never fail of directing accordingly.

6. Profession.

"In pleading, they studiously avoid entering into the merits of the cause; but are loud, violent, and tedious in dwelling upon all circumstances which are not to the purpose. For instance, in the case already mentioned, they never desire to know what claim or title my adversary hath to my cow; but whether the said cow were red or black; her horns long or short; whether the field I graze her in be round or square; whether she were milked at home or abroad; what diseases she is subject to, and the like. After which they consult precedents, adjourn the cause, from time to time, and in ten, twenty, or thirty years come to an issue.

"It is likewise to be observed, that this society hath a peculiar cant and jargon of their own, that no other mortal can understand, and wherein all their laws are written, which they take special care to multiply; whereby they have wholly confounded the very essence of truth and falsehood, of right and wrong; so that it will take thirty years to decide whether the field, left me by my ancestors for six generations, belong to me, or to a stranger three hundred miles off.

"In the trial of persons accused for crimes against the state, the method is much more short and commendable: the judge first sends to sound the disposition of those in power; after which he can easily hang or save the criminal, strictly preserving all the forms of law."

Here my master interposing said it was a pity that creatures endowed with such prodigious abilities of mind as these lawyers, by the description I gave of them must certainly be, were not rather encouraged to be instructors of others in wisdom and knowledge. In answer to which, I assured his honor that in all points out of their own trade, they were usually the most ignorant and stupid generation among us, the most despicable in common conversation, avowed enemies to all knowledge and learning; and equally disposed to pervert the general reason of mankind, in every other subject of discourse as in that of their own profession.

CHAPTER VI. *A continuation of the state of England, under Queen Anne. The character of a first minister in the courts of Europe.*

My master was yet wholly at a loss to understand what motives could incite this race of lawyers to perplex, disquiet, and weary themselves by engaging in a confederacy of injustice, merely for the sake of injuring their fellow animals; neither could he comprehend what I meant in saying they did it for hire. Whereupon I was at much pains to describe to him the use of money, the materials it was made of, and the value of the metals; that when a Yahoo had got a great store of his precious substance, he was able to purchase whatever he had a mind to; the finest clothing, the noblest houses, great tracts of land, the most costly meats and drinks; and have his choice of the most beautiful females. Therefore since money alone was able to perform all these feats, our Yahoos thought they could never have enough of it to spend or to save, as they found themselves inclined from their natural bent either to profusion or avarice. That the rich man enjoyed the fruit of the poor man's labor, and the latter were a thousand to one in proportion to the former. That the bulk of our people was forced to live miserably, by laboring every day for small wages to make a few live plentifully. I enlarged myself much on these and many other particulars to the same purpose, but his honor was still to seek,[7] for he went upon a supposition that all animals had a title to their share in the productions of the earth; and especially those who presided over the rest. Therefore he desired I would let him know what these costly meats were, and how any of us happened to want[8] them. Whereupon I enumerated as many sorts as came into my head, with the various methods of dressing them, which could not be done without sending vessels by sea to every part of the world, as well for liquors to drink, as for sauces, and innumerable other conveniencies. I assured him, that this whole globe of earth must be at least three times gone round, before one of our better female Yahoos could get her breakfast, or a cup to put it in. He said, "That must needs be a miserable country which cannot furnish food for its own inhabitants." But what he chiefly wondered at, was how such vast tracts of ground as I described, should be wholly without fresh water, and the people put to the necessity of sending over the sea for drink. I replied that England (the dear place of my nativity) was computed to produce three times the quantity of food, more than its inhabitants are able to consume, as well as liquors extracted from grain, or pressed out of the fruit of certain trees, which made excellent drink; and the same proportion in every other convenience of life. But, in order to feed the luxury and intemperance of the males, and the vanity of the females, we sent away the greatest part of our necessary things to other countries, from whence in return we brought the materials of diseases, folly, and vice, to spend among ourselves. Hence it follows of necessity, that vast numbers of our people are compelled to seek their livelihood by begging, robbing, stealing, cheating, pimping, forswearing, flattering, suborning, forging, gaming, lying, fawning, hectoring, voting, scribbling, star gazing, poisoning, whoring, canting, libeling, freethinking, and the like occupations; every one of which terms, I was at much pains to make him understand.

That, wine was not imported among us from foreign countries, to supply the want of water or other drinks, but because it was a sort of liquid which made us merry, by putting us out of our senses; diverted all melancholy thoughts, begat wild extravagant imaginations in the brain, raised our hopes, and banished our

7. Still did not understand.
8. Lack.

fears; suspended every office of reason for a time, and deprived us of the use of our limbs, until we fell into a profound sleep; although it must be confessed, that we always awaked sick and dispirited; and that the use of this liquor filled us with diseases, which made our lives uncomfortable and short.

But beside all this, the bulk of our people supported themselves by furnishing the necessities or conveniencies of life to the rich, and to each other. For instance, when I am at home and dressed as I ought to be, I carry on my body the workmanship of an hundred tradesmen; the building and furniture of my house employ as many more; and five times the number to adorn my wife.

I was going on to tell him of another sort of people, who get their livelihood by attending the sick; having upon some occasions informed his honor that many of my crew had died of diseases. But here it was with the utmost difficulty that I brought him to apprehend what I meant. He could easily conceive that a Houyhnhnm grew weak and heavy a few days before his death; or by some accident might hurt a limb. But that nature, who worketh all things to perfection, should suffer any pains to breed in our bodies, he thought impossible; and desired to know the reason of so unaccountable an evil. I told him, we fed on a thousand things which operated contrary to each other; that we eat when we were not hungry, and drank without the provocation of thirst; that we sat whole nights drinking strong liquors without eating a bit, which disposed us to sloth, inflamed our bodies, and precipitated or prevented digestion. That, prostitute female Yahoos acquired a certain malady, which bred rottenness in the bones of those who fell into their embraces; that this and many other diseases were propagated from father to son; so that great numbers come into the world with complicated maladies upon them; that it would be endless to give him a catalogue of all diseases incident to human bodies; for they could not be fewer than five or six hundred, spread over every limb, and joint; in short, every part, external and intestine, having diseases appropriated to each. To remedy which, there was a sort of people bred up among us, in the profession or pretense of curing the sick. And because I had some skill in the faculty, I would in gratitude to his honor let him know the whole mystery and method by which they proceed.

Their fundamental is that all diseases arise from repletion; from whence they conclude, that a great evacuation of the body is necessary, either through the natural passage, or upwards at the mouth. Their next business is, from herbs, minerals, gums, oils, shells, salts, juices, seaweed, excrements, barks of trees, serpents, toads, frogs, spiders, dead men's flesh and bones, birds, beasts and fishes, to form a composition for smell and taste the most abominable, nauseous, and detestable, that they can possibly contrive, which the stomach immediately rejects with loathing, and this they call a vomit. Or else from the same storehouse, with some other poisonous additions, they command us to take in at the orifice above or below (just as the physician then happens to be disposed) a medicine equally annoying and disgustful to the bowels; which relaxing the belly, drives down all before it; and this they call a purge, or a clyster. For nature (as the physicians allege) having intended the superior anterior orifice only for the intromission of solids and liquids, and the inferior posterior for ejection, these artists ingeniously considering that in all diseases nature is forced out of her seat; therefore to replace her in it, the body must be treated in a manner directly contrary, but interchanging the use of each orifice; forcing solids and liquids in at the anus, and making evacuations at the mouth.

But, besides real diseases, we are subject to many that are only imaginary, for which the physicians have invented imaginary cures; these have their several names, and so have the drugs that are proper for them; and with these our female Yahoos are always infested.

One great excellency in this tribe is their skill at prognostics, wherein they seldom fail; their predictions in real diseases, when they rise to any degree of malignity, generally portending death, which is always in their power, when recovery is not, and therefore, upon any unexpected signs of amendment, after they have pronounced their sentence rather than be accused as false prophets, they know how to approve[9] their sagacity to the world by a seasonable dose.

They are likewise of special use to husbands and wives, who are grown weary of their mates; to eldest sons, to great ministers of state, and often to princes.

I had formerly upon occasion discoursed with my master upon the nature of government in general, and particularly of our own excellent constitution, deservedly the wonder and envy of the whole world. But having here accidently mentioned a minister of state, he commanded me some time after to inform him what species of Yahoo I particularly meant by that appellation.

I told him that a first or chief minister of state, whom I intended to describe, was a creature wholly exempt from joy and grief, love and hatred, pity and anger; at least makes use of no other passions but a violent desire of wealth, power, and titles; that he applies his words to all uses, except to the indication of his mind; that he never tells a truth, but with an intent that you should take it for a lie; nor a lie, but with a design that you should take it for a truth; that those he speaks worst of behind their backs are in the surest way to preferment; and whenever he begins to praise you to others or to yourself, you are from that day forlorn. The worst mark you can receive is a promise, especially when it is confirmed

9. Prove.

with an oath; after which every wise man retires, and gives over all hopes.

There are three methods by which a man may rise to be chief minister: the first is by knowing how with prudence to dispose of a wife, a daughter, or a sister; the second, by betraying or undermining his predecessor; and the third is by a furious zeal in public assemblies against the corruptions of the court. But a wise prince would rather choose to employ those who practice the last of these methods; because such zealots prove always the most obsequious and subservient to the will and passions of their master. That, these ministers having all employments at their disposal, preserve themselves in power by bribing the majority of a senate or great council; and at last by an expedient called an Act of Indemnity[1] (whereof I described the nature to him) they secure themselves from after reckonings, and retire from the public, laden with the spoils of the nation.

The palace of a chief minister is a seminary to breed up others in his own trade; the pages, lackies, and porter, by imitating their master, become ministers of state in their several districts, and learn to excel in the three principal ingredients, of insolence, lying, and bribery. Accordingly, they have a subaltern court paid to them by persons of the best rank; and sometimes by the force of dexterity and impudence, arrive through several gradations to be successors to their lord.

He is usually governed by a decayed wench, or favorite footman, who are the tunnels through which all graces are conveyed, and may properly be called, in the last resort, the governors of the kingdom.

One day, my master, having heard me mention the nobility of my country, was pleased to make me a compliment which I could not pretend to deserve: that, he was sure, I must have been born of some noble family, because I far exceeded in shape, color, and cleanliness, all the Yahoos of his nation, although I seemed to fail in strength, and agility, which must be imputed to my different way of living from those other brutes; and besides, I was not only endowed with the faculty of speech, but likewise with some rudiments of reason, to a degree, that with all his acquaintance I passed for a prodigy.

He made me observe, that among the Houyhnhnms, the white, the sorrel, and the iron grey were not so exactly shaped as the bay, the dapple grey, and the black; nor born with equal talents of mind, or a capacity to improve them; and therefore continued always in the condition of servants, without ever aspiring to match out of their own race, which in that country would be reckoned monstrous and unnatural.

1. An act passed at each session of Parliament to protect ministers of state who in good faith might have acted illegally.

I made his honor my most humble acknowledgments for the good opinion he was pleased to conceive of me; but assured him at the same time, that my birth was of the lower sort, having been born of plain, honest parents, who were just able to give me a tolerable education; that, nobility among us was altogether a different thing from the idea he had of it; that, our young noblemen are bred from their childhood in idleness and luxury; that, as soon as years will permit, they consume their vigor, and contract odious diseases among lewd females; and when their fortunes are almost ruined, they marry some woman of mean birth, disagreeable person, and unsound constitution, merely for the sake of money, whom they hate and despise. That, the productions of such marriages are generally scrofulous, rickety or deformed children; by which means the family seldom continues above three generations, unless the wife take care to provide a healthy father among her neighbors, or domestics, in order to improve and continue the breed. That a weak diseased body, a meager countenance, and sallow complexion are the true marks of noble blood; and a healthy robust appearance is so disgraceful in a man of quality, that the world concludes his real father to have been a groom or a coachman. The imperfections of his mind run parallel with those of his body; being a composition of spleen, dullness, ignorance, caprice, sensuality, and pride.

Without the consent of this illustrious body, no law can be enacted, repealed, or altered, and these nobles have likewise the decision of all our possessions without appeal.

CHAPTER VII. *The Author's great love of his native country. His master's observations upon the constitution and administration of England, as described by the Author, with parallel cases and comparisons. His master's observations upon human nature.*

The reader may be disposed to wonder how I could prevail on myself to give so free a representation of my own species, among a race of mortals who were already too apt to conceive the vilest opinion of humankind, from that entire congruity betwixt me and their Yahoos. But I must freely confess that the many virtues of those excellent quadrupeds placed in opposite view to human corruptions had so far opened my eyes, and enlarged my understanding, that I began to view the actions and passions of man in a very different light; and to think the honor of my own kind not worth managing;[2] which, besides, it was impossible for me to do before a person of so acute a judgment as my master, who daily convinced me of a thousand faults in myself, whereof I had not the least perception before, and which with us would never be numbered even among human infirmities. I had likewise learned from his example an utter detestation of all falsehood or disguise; and

2. Taking care of.

truth appeared so amiable to me, that I determined upon sacrificing everything to it.

Let me deal so candidly with the reader as to confess that there was yet a much stronger motive for the freedom I took in my representation of things. I had not been a year in this country, before I contracted such a love and veneration for the inhabitants, that I entered on a firm resolution never to return to humankind, but to pass the rest of my life among these admirable Houyhnhnms in the contemplation and practice of every virtue; where I could have no example or incitement to vice. But it was decreed by fortune, my perpetual enemy, that so great a felicity should not fall to my share. However, it is now some comfort to reflect that in what I said of my countrymen, I extenuated their faults as much as I durst before so strict an examiner; and upon every article, gave as favorable a turn as the matter would bear. For, indeed, who is there alive that will not be swayed by his bias and partiality to the place of his birth?

I have related the substance of several conversations I had with my master, during the greatest part of the time I had the honor to be in his service; but have indeed for brevity sake omitted much more than is here set down.

When I had answered all his questions, and his curiosity seemed to be fully satisfied; he sent for me one morning early, and commanding me to sit down at some distance (an honor which he had never before conferred upon me), he said he had been very seriously considering my whole story, as far as it related both to myself and my country; that, he looked upon us as a sort of animals to whose share, by what accident he could not conjecture, some small pittance of reason had fallen, whereof we made no other use than by its assistance to aggravate our natural corruptions, and to acquire new ones which nature had not given us. That we disarmed ourselves of the few abilities she had bestowed; had been very successful in multiplying our original wants, and seemed to spend our whole lives in vain endeavors to supply them by our own inventions. That, as to myself, it was manifest I had neither the strength or agility of a common Yahoo; that I walked infirmly on my hinder feet; had found out a contrivance to make my claws of no use or defense, and to remove the hair from my chin, which was intended as a shelter from the sun and the weather. Lastly, that I could neither run with speed, nor climb trees like my brethren (as he called them) the Yahoos in this country.

That our institutions of government and law were plainly owing to our gross defects in reason, and by consequence, in virtue; because reason alone is sufficient to govern a rational creature; which was therefore a character we had no pretense to challenge, even from the account I had given of my own people; although he manifestly perceived, that in order to favor them, I had concealed many particulars, and often *said the thing which was not.*

He was the more confirmed in this opinion, because he observed that I agreed in every feature of my body with other Yahoos, except where it was to my real disadvantage in point of strength, speed, and activity, the shortness of my claws, and some other particulars where nature had no part; so, from the representation I had given him of our lives, our manners, and our actions, he found as near a resemblance in the disposition of our minds. He said the Yahoos were known to hate one another more than they did any different species of animals; and the reason usually assigned was the odiousness of their own shapes, which all could see in the rest, but not in themselves. He had therefore begun to think it not unwise in us to cover our bodies, and by that invention, conceal many of our deformities from each other, which would else be hardly supportable. But he now found he had been mistaken; and that the dissentions of those brutes in his country were owing to the same cause with ours, as I had described them. For, if (said he) you throw among five Yahoos as much food as would be sufficient for fifty, they will, instead of eating peaceably, fall together by the ears, each single one impatient to have all to itself; and therefore a servant was usually employed to stand by while they were feeding abroad, and those kept at home were tied at a distance from each other. That, if a cow died of age or accident, before a Houyhnhnm could secure it for his own Yahoos, those in the neighborhood would come in herds to seize it, and then would ensue such a battle as I had described, with terrible wounds made by their claws on both sides, although they seldom were able to kill one another, for want of such convenient instruments of death as we had invented. At other times the like battles have been fought between the Yahoos of several neighborhoods without any visible cause; those of one district watching all opportunities to surprise the next before they are prepared. But if they find their project hath miscarried, they return home, and for want of enemies, engage in what I call a civil war among themselves.

That, in some fields of his country, there are certain shining stones of several colors, whereof the Yahoos are violently fond; and when part of these stones are fixed in the earth, as it sometimes happeneth, they will dig with their claws for whole days to get them out, and carry them away, and hide them by heaps in their kennels; but still looking round with great caution, for fear their comrades should find out their treasure. My master said he could never discover the reason of this unnatural appetite, or how these stones could be of any use to a Yahoo; but now he believed it might proceed from the same principle of avarice, which I had ascribed to mankind. That he had once, by way of experiment, privately removed a heap of these stones from the place where one of his Yahoos had buried it, whereupon, the sordid animal missing his treasure, by his loud lamenting brought the whole herd to the place, there miserably howled, then fell to biting and tearing the rest; began to pine away, would neither eat nor sleep, nor work, till he ordered a servant privately to convey the stones into the same hole, and hide them as before; which when his Yahoo had found, he presently recovered his spirits and good humor; but took care to remove them to a better hiding place; and hath ever since been a very serviceable brute.

My master farther assured me, which I also observed myself; that in the fields where these shining stones abound, the fiercest and most frequent battles are fought, occasioned by perpetual inroads of the neighboring Yahoos.

He said it was common when two Yahoos discovered such a stone in a field, and were contending which of them should be the proprietor, a third would take the advantage, and carry it away from them both; which my master would needs contend to have some resemblance with our suits at law; wherein I thought it for our credit not to undeceive him; since the decision he mentioned was much more equitable than many decrees among us; because the plaintiff and defendant there lost nothing beside the stone they contended for; whereas our courts of equity would never have dismissed the cause while either of them had anything left.

My master continuing his discourse said there was nothing that rendered the Yahoos more odious, than their undistinguished appetite to devour everything that came in their way, whether herbs, roots, berries, corrupted flesh of animals, or all mingled together; and it was peculiar in their temper, that they were fonder of what they could get by rapine or stealth at a greater distance, than much better food provided for them at home. If their prey held out, they would eat till they were ready to burst, after which nature had pointed out to them a certain root that gave them a general evacuation.

There was also another kind of root very juicy, but something rare and difficult to be found, which the Yahoos fought for with much eagerness, and would suck it with great delight; it produced the same effects that wine hath upon us. It would make them sometimes hug, and sometimes tear one another; they would howl and grin, and chatter, and reel, and tumble, and then fall asleep in the mud.

I did indeed observe that the Yahoos were the only animals in this country subject to any diseases; which however, were much fewer than horses have among us, and contracted not by any ill treatment they meet with, but by the nastiness and greediness of that sordid brute. Neither has their language any more than a general appellation for those maladies; which is borrowed from the name of the beast, and called *Hnea Yahoo*, or the Yahoo's Evil; and the cure prescribed is a mixture of their own dung and urine, forcibly put down the Yahoo's throat. This I have since often known to have been taken with success, and do here freely recommend it to my countrymen, for the public good, as an admirable specific against all diseases produced by repletion.

As to learning, government, arts, manufactures, and the like, my master confessed he could find little or no resemblance between the Yahoos of that country and those in ours. For he only meant to observe what parity there was in our natures. He had heard indeed some curious Houyhnhnms observe that in most herds there was a sort of ruling Yahoo (as among us there is generally some leading or principal stag in a park) who was always more deformed in body, and mischievous in disposition, than any of the rest. That this leader had usually a favorite as like himself as he could get, whose employment was to lick his master's feet and posteriors, and drive the female Yahoos to his kennel; for which he was now and then rewarded with a piece of ass's flesh. This favorite is hated by the whole herd; and therefore to protect himself, keeps always near the person of his leader. He usually continues in office till a worse can be found; but the very moment he is discarded, his successor, at the head of all the Yahoos in that district, young and old, male and female, come in a body, and discharge their excrements upon him from head to foot. But how far this might be applicable to our courts and favorites, and ministers of state, my master said I could best determine.

I durst make no return to this malicious insinuation, which debased human understanding below the sagacity of a common hound, who hath judgment enough to distinguish and follow the cry of the ablest dog in the pack, without being ever mistaken.

My master told me there were some qualities remarkable in the Yahoos, which he had not observed me to mention, or at least very slightly, in the accounts I had given him of humankind. He said, those animals, like other brutes, had their females in common; but in this they differed, that the she-Yahoo would admit the male while she was pregnant; and that the hes would quarrel and fight with the females as fiercely as with each other. Both which practices were such degrees of infamous brutality, that no other sensitive creature ever arrived at.

Another thing he wondered at in the Yahoos was their strange disposition to nastiness and dirt; whereas there appears to be a natural love of cleanliness in all other animals. As to the two former accusations, I was glad to let them pass without any reply, because I had not a word to offer upon them in defense of my species, which otherwise I certainly had done from my own inclinations. But I could have easily vindicated humankind from the imputation of singularity upon the last article, if there had been any swine in that country (as unluckily for me there were not) which although it may be a sweeter quadruped than a Yahoo, cannot I humbly conceive in justice pretend to more cleanliness; and so his honor himself must have owned, if he had seen their filthy way of feeding, and their custom of wallowing and sleeping in the mud.

My master likewise mentioned another quality, which his servants had discovered in several Yahoos, and to him was wholly unaccountable. He said, a fancy would sometimes take a Yahoo, to retire into a corner, to lie down and howl, and groan, and spurn away all that came near him, although he were young and fat, and wanted neither food nor water; nor did the servants imagine what could possibly ail him. And the only remedy they found was to set him to hard work, after which he would infallibly come to himself. To this I was silent out of partiality to my own kind; yet here I could plainly discover the true seeds of spleen,[3] which only seizeth on the lazy, the luxurious, and the rich; who, if they were forced to undergo the same regimen, I would undertake for the cure.

His Honor had farther observed, that a female Yahoo would often stand behind a bank or a bush, to gaze on the young males passing by, and then appear, and hide, using many antic gestures and grimaces; at which time it was observed, that she had a most offensive smell; and when any of the males advanced, would slowly retire, looking back, and with a counterfeit show of fear, run off into some convenient place where she knew the male would follow her.

At other times, if a female stranger came among them, three or four of her own sex would get about her, and stare and chatter, and grin, and smell her all over; and then turn off with gestures that seemed to express contempt and disdain.

Perhaps my master might refine a little in these speculations, which he had drawn from what he observed himself, or had been told by others; however, I could not reflect without some amazement, and much sorrow, that the rudiments of lewdness, coquetry, censure, and scandal, should have place by instinct in womankind.

I expected every moment that my master would accuse the Yahoos of those unnatural appetites in both sexes, so common among us. But nature it seems hath not been so expert a schoolmistress; and these politer pleasures are entirely the productions of art and reason, on our side of the globe.

Chapter VIII. *The Author relateth several particulars of the Yahoos. The great virtues of the Houyhnhnms. The education and exercises of their youth. Their general assembly.*

As I ought to have understood human nature much better than I supposed it possible for my master to do, so it was easy to apply

3. Hypochondria.

the character he gave of the Yahoos to myself and my countrymen; and I believed I could yet make farther discoveries from my own observation. I therefore often begged his honor to let me go among the herds of Yahoos in the neighborhood; to which he always very graciously consented, being perfectly convinced that the hatred I bore those brutes would never suffer me to be corrupted by them; and his honor ordered one of his servants, a strong sorrel nag, very honest and good-natured, to be my guard; without whose protection I durst not undertake such adventures. For I have already told the reader how much I was pestered by those odious animals upon my first arrival. I afterwards failed very narrowly three or four times of falling into their clutches, when I happened to stray at any distance without my hanger. And I have reason to believe, they had some imagination that I was of their own species, which I often assisted myself, by stripping up my sleeves, and shewing my naked arms and breast in their sight, when my protector was with me; at which times they would approach as near as they durst, and imitate my actions after the manner of monkeys, but ever with great signs of hatred; as a tame jackdaw with cap and stockings is always persecuted by the wild ones, when he happens to be got among them.

They are prodigiously nimble from their infancy; however, I once caught a young male of three years old, and endeavored by all marks of tenderness to make it quiet; but the little imp fell a squalling, scratching, and biting with such violence, that I was forced to let it go; and it was high time, for a whole troop of old ones came about us at the noise; but finding the cub was safe (for away it ran) and my sorrel nag being by, they durst not venture near us. I observed the young animal's flesh to smell very rank, and the stink was somewhat between a weasel and a fox, but much more disagreeable. I forgot another circumstance (and perhaps I might have the reader's pardon, if it were wholly omitted) that while I held the odious vermin in my hands, it voided its filthy excrements of a yellow liquid substance, all over my clothes; but by good fortune there was a small brook hard by, where I washed myself as clean as I could; although I durst not come into my master's presence until I were sufficiently aired.

By what I could discover, the Yahoos appear to be the most unteachable of all animals, their capacities never reaching higher than to draw or carry burdens. Yet I am of opinion, this defect ariseth chiefly from a perverse, restive disposition. For they are cunning, malicious, treacherous and revengeful. They are strong and hardy, but of a cowardly spirit, and by consequence insolent, abject, and cruel. It is observed that the red-haired of both sexes are more libidinous and mischievous than the rest, whom yet they much exceed in strength and activity.

The Houyhnhnms keep the Yahoos for present use in huts not far from the house; but the rest are sent abroad to certain fields, where they dig up roots, eat several kinds of herbs, and search about for carrion, or sometimes catch weasels and *luhimuhs* (a sort of wild rat) which they greedily devour. Nature hath taught them to dig deep holes with their nails on the side of a rising ground, wherein they lie by themselves; only the kennels of the females are larger, sufficient to hold two or three cubs.

They swim from their infancy like frogs, and are able to continue long under water, where they often take fish, which the females carry home to their young. And upon this occasion, I hope the reader will pardon my relating an odd adventure.

Being one day abroad with my protector the sorrel nag, and the weather exceeding hot, I entreated him to let me bathe in a river that was near. He consented, and I immediately stripped myself stark naked, and went down softly into the stream. It happened that a young female Yahoo standing behind a bank, saw the whole proceeding; and inflamed by desire, as the nag and I conjectured, came running with all speed, and leaped into the water within five yards of the place where I bathed. I was never in my life so terribly frighted; the nag was grazing at some distance, not suspecting any harm; she embraced me after a most fulsome manner; I roared as loud as I could, and the nag came galloping towards me, whereupon she quitted her grasp, with the utmost reluctancy, and leaped upon the opposite bank, where she stood gazing and howling all the time I was putting on my clothes.

This was matter of diversion to my master and his family, as well as of mortification to myself. For now I could no longer deny that I was a real Yahoo, in every limb and feature, since the females had a natural propensity to me as one of their own species; neither was the hair of this brute of a red color (which might have been some excuse for an appetite a little irregular) but black as a sloe, and her countenance did not make an appearance altogether so hideous as the rest of the kind; for I think, she could not be above eleven years old.

Having already lived three years in this country, the reader I suppose will expect that I should, like other travelers, give him some account of the manners and customs of its inhabitants, which it was indeed my principal study to learn.

As these noble Houyhnhnms are endowed by Nature with a general disposition to all virtues, and have no conceptions or ideas of what is evil in a rational creature; so their grand maxim is to cultivate reason, and to be wholly governed by it. Neither is reason among them a point problematical as with us, where men can argue with plausibility on both sides of a question; but strikes you with immediate conviction; as it must needs do where it is not mingled, obscured, or discolored by passion and interest. I remember it was with extreme difficulty that I could bring my master to understand the meaning of the word "opinion," or how a point could be disputable; because reason taught us to affirm or deny only where we are certain; and beyond our knowledge we cannot do either. So that controversies, wranglings, disputes, and positiveness in false or dubious propositions are evils unknown among the Houyhnhnms. In the like manner when I used to explain to him our several systems of natural philosophy, he would laugh that a creature pretending to reason should value itself upon the knowledge of other people's conjectures, and in things, where that knowledge, if it were certain, could be of no use. Wherein he agreed entirely with the sentiments of Socrates, as Plato delivers them, which I mention as the highest honor I can do that prince of philosophers. I have often since reflected what destruction such a doctrine would make in the libraries of Europe; and how many paths to fame would be then shut up in the learned world.

Friendship and benevolence are the two principal virtues among the Houyhnhnms; and these not confined to particular objects, but universal to the whole race. For a stranger from the remotest part is equally treated with the nearest neighbor, and wherever he goes, looks upon himself as at home. They preserve decency and civility in the highest degrees, but are altogether ignorant of ceremony. They have no fondness for their colts or foals; but the care they take in educating them proceedeth entirely from the dictates of reason. And I observed my master to show the same affection to his neighbor's issue that he had for his own. They will have it that nature teaches them to love the whole species, and it is reason only that maketh a distinction of persons, where there is a superior degree of virtue.

When the matron Houyhnhnms have produced one of each sex, they no longer accompany with their consorts, except they lose one of their issue by some casualty, which very seldom happens; but in such a case they meet again; or when the like accident befalls a person whose wife is past bearing, some other couple bestows on him one of their own colts, and then go together a second time, until the mother be pregnant. This caution is necessary to prevent the country from being overburdened with numbers. But the race of inferior Houyhnhnms bred up to be servants is not so strictly limited upon this article; these are allowed to produce three of each sex, to be domestics in the noble families.

In their marriages they are exactly careful to choose such colors as will not make any disagreeable mixture in the breed. Strength is chiefly valued in the male, and comeliness in the female; not upon the account of love, but to preserve the race from degenerating; for, where a female happens to excel in strength, a consort is chosen with regard to comeliness. Courtship, love, presents, jointures, settlements, have no place in their thoughts, or terms whereby to express them in their language. The young couple meet and are joined, merely because it is the determination of their parents and friends; it is what they see done every day; and they look upon it as one of the necessary actions in a reasonable being. But the violation of marriage, or any other unchastity, was never heard of; and the married pair pass their lives with the same friendship and mutual benevolence that they bear to all others of the same species who come in their way, without jealousy, fondness, quarreling, or discontent.

In educating the youth of both sexes, their method is admirable, and highly deserveth our imitation. These are not suffered to taste a grain of oats, except upon certain days, till eighteen years old; nor milk, but very rarely; and in summer they graze two hours in the morning, and as many in the evening, which their parents likewise observe; but the servants are not allowed above half that time; and a great part of the grass is brought home, which they eat at the most convenient hours, when they can be best spared from work.

Temperance, industry, exercise, and cleanliness are the lessons equally enjoined to the young ones of both sexes; and my master thought it monstrous in us to give the females a different kind of education from the males, except in some articles of domestic management; whereby, as he truly observed, one half of our natives were good for nothing but bringing children into the world; and to trust the care of their children to such useless animals, he said was yet a greater instance of brutality.

But the Houyhnhnms train up their youth to strength, speed, and hardiness, by exercising them in running races up and down steep hills, or over hard stony grounds; and when they are all in a sweat, they are ordered to leap over head and ears into a pond or a river. Four times a year the youth of certain districts meet to show their proficiency in running, and leaping, and other feats of strength or agility; where the victor is rewarded with a song made in his or her praise. On this festival the servants drive a herd of Yahoos into the field, laden with hay, and oats, and milk for a repast to the Houyhnhnms; after which these brutes are immediately driven back again, for fear of being noisome to the assembly.

Every fourth year, at the vernal equinox, there is a representative council of the whole nation, which meets in a plain about twenty miles from our house, and continueth about five or six days. Here they inquire into the state and condition of the several districts; whether they abound or be deficient in hay or oats, or cows or Yahoos? And wherever there is any want (which is but seldom) it is immediately supplied by unanimous consent and contribution. Here likewise the regulation of children is settled: as for instance, if a Houyhnhnm hath two males, he changeth one of them with another who hath two females, and when a child hath been lost by any casualty, where the mother is past breeding, it is determined what family in the district shall breed another to supply the loss.

Chapter IX. *A grand debate at the general assembly of the Houyhnhnms, and how it was determined. The learning of the Houyhnhnms. Their buildings. Their manner of burials. The defectiveness of their language.*

One of these grand assemblies was held in my time, about three months before my departure, whither my master went as the representative of our district. In this council was resumed their old debate, and indeed, the only debate that ever happened in their country; whereof my master after his return gave me a very particular account.

The question to be debated was whether the Yahoos should be exterminated from the face of the earth. One of the members for the affirmative offered several arguments of great strength and weight, alleging that, as the Yahoos were the most filthy, noisome, and deformed animal which nature ever produced, so they were the most restive and indocible, mischievous, and malicious; they would privately suck the teats of the Houyhnhnms' cows; kill and devour their cats, trample down their oats and grass, if they were not continually watched; and commit a thousand other extravagancies. He took notice of a general tradition, that Yahoos had not been always in their country, but that many ages ago, two of these brutes appeared together upon a mountain; whether produced by the heat of the sun upon corrupted mud and slime, or from the ooze and froth of the sea, was never known. That these Yahoos engendered, and their brood in a short time grew so numerous as to overrun and infest the whole nation. That the Houyhnhnms to get rid of this evil, made a general hunting, and at last enclosed the whole herd; and destroying the older, every Houyhnhnm kept two young ones in a kennel, and brought them to such a degree of tameness as an animal so savage by nature can be capable of acquiring, using them for draft and carriage. That there seemed to be much truth in this tradition, and that those creatures could not be *ylnhniamshy* (or aborigines of the land) because of the violent hatred the Houyhnhnms as well as all other animals bore them; which although their evil disposition sufficiently deserved, could never have arrived at so high a degree, if they had been aborigines, or else they would have long since been rooted out. That the inhabitants taking a fancy to use the service of the Yahoos, had very imprudently neglected to cultivate the breed of asses, which were a comely animal, easily kept, more tame and orderly, without any offensive smell, strong enough for labor, although they yield to the other in agility of body; and if their braying be no agreeable sound, it is far preferable to the horrible howlings of the Yahoos.

Several others declared their sentiments to the same purpose, when my master proposed an expedient to the assembly, whereof he had indeed borrowed the hint from me. He approved of the tradition, mentioned by the honorable member, who spoke before; and affirmed, that the two Yahoos said to be first seen among them, had been driven thither over the sea; that coming to land, and being forsaken by their companions, they retired to the mountains, and degenerating by degrees, became in process of time much more savage than those of their own species in the country from whence these two originals came. The reason of his assertion was that he had now in his possession a certain wonderful Yahoo (meaning myself) which most of them had heard of, and many of them had seen. He then related to them how he first found me; that my body was all covered with an artificial composure of the skins and hairs of other animals; that I spoke in a language of my own, and had thoroughly learned theirs; that I had related to him the accidents which brought me thither; that when he saw me without my covering, I was an exact Yahoo in every part, only of a whiter color, less hairy and with shorter claws. He added how I had endeavored to persuade him that in my own and other countries the Yahoos acted as the governing, rational animal, and held the Houyhnhnms in servitude; that he observed in me all the qualities of a Yahoo, only a little more civilized by some tincture of reason, which however was in a degree as far inferior to the Houyhnhnm race as the Yahoos of their country were to me; that among other things, I mentioned a custom we had of castrating Houyhnhnms when they were young, in order to render them tame; that the operation was easy and safe; that it was no shame to learn wisdom from brutes, as industry is taught by the ant, and building by the swallow (for so I translate the world *lyhannh*, although it be a much larger fowl). That this invention might be practiced upon the younger Yahoos here, which, besides rendering them tractable and fitter for use, would in an age put an end to the whole species without destroying life. That in the meantime the Houyhnhnms should be exhorted to cultivate the breed of asses, which, as they are in all respects more valuable brutes, so they have this advantage, to be fit for service at five years old, which the others are not till twelve.

This was all my master thought fit to tell me at that time, of what passed in the grand council. But he was pleased to conceal one particular, which related personally to myself, whereof I soon felt the unhappy effect, as the reader will know in its proper place, and from whence I date all the succeeding misfortunes of my life.

The Houyhnhnms have no letters, and consequently, their knowledge is all traditional. But there happening few events of any moment among a people so well united, naturally disposed to every virtue, wholly governed by reason, and cut off from all commerce with other nations, the historical part is easily preserved without burdening their memories. I have already observed that they are subject to no diseases, and therefore can have no need of physicians. However, they have excellent medicines composed of herbs, to cure accidental bruises and cuts in the pastern or frog of the foot by sharp stones, as well as other maims and hurts in the several parts of the body.

They calculate the year by the revolution of the sun and the moon, but use no subdivisions into weeks. They are well enough acquainted with the motions of those two luminaries, and understand the nature of eclipses; and this is the utmost progress of their astronomy.

In poetry they must be allowed to excell all other mortals; wherein the justness of their similes, and the minuteness, as well as exactness of their descriptions, are indeed inimitable. Their verses abound very much in both of these, and usually contain either some exalted notions of friendship and benevolence, or the praises of those who were victors in races and other bodily exercises. Their buildings, although very rude and simple, are not inconvenient, but well contrived to defend them from all injuries of cold and heat. They have a kind of tree, which at forty years old loosens in the root, and falls with the first storm; it grows very straight, and being pointed like stakes with a sharp stone (for the Houyhnhnms know not the use of iron), they stick them erect in the ground about ten inches asunder, and then weave in oat straw, or sometimes wattles, betwixt them. The roof is made after the same manner, and so are the doors.

The Houyhnhnms use the hollow part between the pastern and the hoof of their forefeet as we do our hands, and this with greater dexterity than I could at first imagine. I have seen a white mare of our family thread a needle (which I lent her on purpose) with that joint. They milk their cows, reap their oats, and do all the work which requires hands in the same manner. They have a kind of hard flints, which by grinding against other stones they form into instruments that serve instead of wedges, axes, and hammers. With tools made of these flints, they likewise cut their hay, and reap their oats, which there groweth naturally in several fields; the Yahoos draw home the sheaves in carriages, and the servants tread them in certain covered huts, to get out the grain, which is kept in stores. They make a rude kind of earthen and wooden vessels, and bake the former in the sun.

If they can avoid casualties, they die only of old age, and are buried in the obscurest places that can be found, their friends and relations expressing neither joy nor grief at their departure; nor does the dying person discover the least regret that he is leaving the world, any more than if he were upon returning home from a visit to one of his neighbors; I remember my master having once made an appointment with a friend and his family to come to his house upon some affair of importance; on the day fixed, the mistress and her two children came very late; she made two excuses, first for her husband, who, as she said, happened that very morning to *lhnuwnh.* The word is strongly expressive in their language, but not easily rendered into English; it signifies, *to retire to his first Mother.* Her excuse for not coming sooner was that her husband dying late in the morning, she was a good while consulting her servants about a convenient place where his body should be laid; and I observed she behaved herself at our house, as cheerfully as the rest; she died about three months after.

They live generally to seventy or seventy-five years, very seldom to fourscore; some weeks before their death they feel a gradual decay, but without pain. During this time they are much visited by their friends, because they cannot go abroad with their usual ease and satisfaction. However, about ten days before their death, which they seldom fail in computing, they return the visits that have been made by those who are nearest in the neighborhood, being carried in a convenient sledge drawn by Yahoos; which vehicle they use, not only upon this occasion, but when they grow old, upon long journeys, or when they are lamed by any accident. And therefore when the dying Houyhnhnms return those visits, they take a solemn leave of their friends, as if they were going to some remote part of the country, where they designed to pass the rest of their lives.

I know not whether it may be worth observing, that the Houyhnhnms have no word in their language to express anything that is evil, except what they borrow from the deformities or ill qualities of the Yahoos. Thus they denote the folly of a servant, an omission of a child, a stone that cuts their feet, a continuance of foul or unseasonable weather, and the like, by adding to each the epithet of Yahoo. For instance, *hhnm Yahoo, whnaholm Yahoo, ynlhmndwihlma Yahoo,* and an ill-contrived house, *ynholmhnmrohlnw Yahoo.*

I could with great pleasure enlarge farther upon the manners and virtues of this excellent people; but intending in a short time to publish a volume by itself expressly upon that subject, I refer the reader thither. And in the meantime, proceed to relate my own sad catastrophe.

CHAPTER X. *The Author's economy, and happy life among the Houyhnhnms. His great improvement in virtue, by conversing with them. Their conversations. The Author hath notice given him by his master that he must depart from the country. He falls into a swoon for grief, but submits. He contrives and finishes a canoe, by the help of a fellow servant, and puts to sea at a venture.*

I had settled my little economy to my own heart's content. My master had ordered a room to be made for me after their manner, about six yards from the house; the sides and floors of which I plastered with clay, and covered with rush mats of my own contriving; I had beaten hemp, which there grows wild, and made of it a sort of ticking; this I filled with the feathers of several birds I had taken with springes made of Yahoos' hairs, and were excellent food. I had worked two chairs with my knife, the sorrel nag helping me in the grosser and more laborious part. When my clothes were worn to rags, I made myself others with the skins of rabbits, and of a certain beautiful animal about the same size, called *nnuhnoh,* the skin of which is covered with a fine down. Of these I likewise made very tolerable stockings. I soled my shoes with wood which I cut from a tree, and fitted to the upper leather, and when this was worn out, I supplied it with the skins of Yahoos, dried in the sun. I often got honey out of hollow trees, which I mingled with water, or eat it with my bread. No man could more verify the truth of these two maxims, that *Nature is very easily satisfied;* and, that *Necessity is the mother of invention.* I enjoyed perfect health of body, and tranquility of mind; I did not feel the treachery or inconstancy of a friend, nor the inquiries of a secret or open enemy. I had no occasion of bribing, flattering, or pimping to procure the favor of any great man, or of his minion. I wanted no fence against fraud or oppression; here was neither physician to destroy my body, nor lawyer to ruin my fortune; no informer to watch my words and actions, or forge accusations against me for hire; here were no gibers, censurers, backbiters, pickpockets, highwaymen, housebreakers, attorneys, bawds, buffoons, gamesters, politicians, wits, splenetics, tedious talkers, controvertists, ravishers, murderers, robbers, virtuosos; no leaders or followers of party and faction; no encouragers to vice, by seducement or examples; no dungeons, axes, gibbets, whipping posts, or pillories; no cheating shopkeepers or mechanics; no pride, vanity or affectation; no fops, bullies, drunkards, strolling whores, or poxes; no ranting, lewd, expensive wives; no stupid, proud pedants; no importunate, overbearing, quarrelsome, noisy, roaring, empty, conceited, swearing companions; no scoundrels raised from the dust upon the merit of their vices; or nobility thrown into it on account of their virtues; no lords, fiddlers, judges, or dancing masters.

I had the favor of being admitted to several Houyhnhnms, who came to visit or dine with my master; where his honor graciously suffered me to wait in the room, and listen to their discourse. Both he and his company would often descend to ask me questions, and receive my answers. I had also sometimes the honor of attending my master in his visits to others. I never presumed to speak, except in answer to a question; and then I did it with inward regret, because it was a loss of so much time for improving myself; but I was infinitely delighted with the station of an humble auditor in such conversations, where nothing passed but what was useful, expressed in the fewest and most significant words; where (as I have already said) the greatest decency was observed, without the least degree of ceremony; where no person spoke without being pleased himself, and pleasing his companions; where there was no interruption, tediousness, heat, or difference of sentiments. They have a notion, that when people are met together, a short silence doth much improve conversation; this I found to be true; for during those little intermissions of talk, new ideas would arise in their minds, which very much enlivened the discourse. Their subjects are generally on friendship and benevolence; on order and economy; sometimes upon the visible operations of nature, or ancient traditions; upon the bounds and limits of virtue; upon the unerring rules of reason; or upon some determinations, to be taken at the next great assembly; and often upon the various excellencies of poetry. I may add, without vanity, that my presence often gave them sufficient matter for discourse, because it afforded my master an occasion of letting his friends into the history of me and my country, upon which they were all pleased to discant in a manner not very advantageous to human kind; and for that reason I shall not repeat what they said; only I may be allowed to observe that his honor, to my great admiration, appeared to understand the nature of Yahoos much better than myself. He went through all our vices and follies, and discovered many which I had never mentioned to him; by only supposing what qualities a Yahoo of their country, with a small proportion of reason, might be capable of exerting; and concluded, with too much probability, how vile as well as miserable such a creature must be.

I freely confess, that all the little knowledge I have of any value was acquired by the lectures I received from my master, and from hearing the discourses of him and his friends; to which I should be prouder to listen, than to dictate to the greatest and wisest assembly in Europe. I admired the strength, comeliness, and speed of the inhabitants; and such a constellation of virtues in such amiable persons produced in me the highest veneration. At first, indeed, I did not feel that natural awe which the Yahoos and all other animals bear towards them; but it grew upon me by degrees, much sooner than I imagined, and was mingled with a respectful love and gratitude, that they would condescend to distinguish me from the rest of my species.

When I thought of my family, my friends, my countrymen, or human race in general, I considered them as they really were, Yahoos in shape and disposition, perhaps a little more civilized, and qualified with the gift of speech; but making no other use of reason than to improve and multiply those vices, whereof their brethren in this country had only the share that nature allotted them. When I happened to behold the reflection of my own form in a lake or fountain, I turned away my face in horror and detestation of myself, and could better endure the sight of a common Yahoo than of my own person. By conversing with the Houyhnhnms, and looking upon them with delight, I fell to imitate their gait and gesture, which is now grown into a habit; and my friends often tell me in a blunt way, that I trot like a horse; which, however, I take for a great compliment; neither shall I disown, that in speaking I am apt to fall into the voice and manner of the Houyhnhnms, and hear myself ridiculed on that account without the least mortification.

In the midst of this happiness, when I looked upon myself to be fully settled for life, my master sent for me one morning a little earlier than his usual hour. I observed by his countenance that he was in some perplexity, and at a loss how to begin what he had to speak. After a short silence, he told me, he did not know how I would take what he was going to say; that, in the last general assembly, when the affair of the Yahoos was entered upon, the representatives had taken offense at his keeping a Yahoo (meaning myself) in his family more like a Houyhnhnm than a brute animal. That he was known frequently to converse with me, as if he could receive some advantage of pleasure in my company; that such a practice was not agreeable to reason or nature, or a thing ever heard of before among them. The assembly did therefore exhort him, either to employ me like the rest of my species, or command me to swim back to the place from whence I came. That the first of these expedients was utterly rejected by all the Houyhnhnms who had ever seen me at his house or their own; for, they alleged, that because I had some rudiments of reason, added to the natural pravity of those animals, it was to be feared, I might be able to seduce them into the woody and mountainous parts of the country, and bring them in troops by night to destroy the Houyhnhnms' cattle, as being naturally of the ravenous kind, and averse from labor.

My master added that he was daily pressed by the Houyhnhnms of the neighborhood to have the assembly's exhortation executed, which he could not put off much longer. He doubted it would be impossible for me to swim to another country; and therefore wished I would contrive some sort of vehicle resembling those I had described to him, that might carry me on the sea; in which work I should have the assistance of his own servants, as well as those of his neighbors. He concluded that for his own part he could have been content to keep me in his service as long as I lived; because he found I had cured myself of some bad habits and dispositions, by endeavoring, as far as my inferior nature was capable, to imitate the Houyhnhnms.

I should here observe to the reader, that a decree of the general assembly in this country is expressed by the word *hnhloayn*, which signifies an exhortation, as near as I can render it; for they have no conception how a rational creature can be compelled, but only advised, or exhorted; because no person can disobey reason without giving up his claim to be a rational creature.

I was struck with the utmost grief and despair at my master's discourse; and being unable to support the agonies I was under, I fell into a swoon at his feet; when I came to myself, he told me that he concluded I had been dead (for these people are subject to no such imbecilities of nature). I answered, in a faint voice, that death would have been too great an happiness; that although I could not blame the assembly's exhortation, or the urgency of his friends; yet in my weak and corrupt judgment, I thought it might consist with reason to have been less rigorous. That I could not swim a league, and probably the nearest land to theirs might be distant above an hundred; that many materials, necessary for making a small vessel to carry me off, were wholly wanting in this country, which, however, I would attempt in obedience and gratitude to his honor, although I concluded the thing to be impossible, and therefore looked on myself as already devoted [4] to destruction. That the certain prospect of an unnatural death was the least of my evils; for, supposing I should escape with life by some strange adventure, how could I think with temper [5] of passing my days among Yahoos, and relapsing into my old corruptions, for want of examples to lead and keep me within the paths of virtue. That I knew too well upon what solid reasons all the determinations of the wise Houyhnhnms were founded, not to be shaken by arguments of mine, a miserable Yahoo; and therefore after presenting him with my humble thanks for the offer of his servants' assistance in making a vessel, and desiring a reasonable time for so difficult a work, I told him I would endeavor to preserve a wretched being; and, if ever I returned to England, was not without hopes of being useful to my own species by celebrating the praises of the renowned Houyhnhnms, and proposing their virtues to the imitation of mankind.

My master in a few words made me a very gracious reply, allowed me the space of two months to finish my boat, and ordered the sorrel nag, my fellow servant (for so at this distance I may presume to call him), to follow my instructions, because I told my master that his help would be sufficient, and I knew he had a tenderness for me.

In his company my first business was to go to that part of the coast where my rebellious crew had ordered me to be set on shore. I got upon a height, and looking on every side into the sea, fancied I saw a small island towards the northeast; I took out my pocket glass, and could then clearly distinguish it about five leagues off, as I computed; but it appeared to the sorrel nag to be only a blue cloud; for, as he had no conception of any country besides his own, so he

4. Doomed.

5. Equanimity.

could not be as expert in distinguishing remote objects at sea, as we who so much converse in that element.

After I had discovered this island, I considered no farther; but resolved, it should, if possible, be the first place of my banishment, leaving the consequence to fortune.

I returned home, and consulting with the sorrel nag, we went into a copse at some distance, where I with my knife, and he with a sharp flint fastened very artificially,[6] after their manner, to a wooden handle, cut down several oak wattles about the thickness of a walking staff, and some larger pieces. But I shall not trouble the reader with a particular description of my own mechanics; let it suffice to say, that in six weeks time, with the help of the sorrel nag, who performed the parts that required most labor, I finished a sort of Indian canoe; but much larger, covering it with the skins of Yahoos, well stitched together, with hempen threads of my own making. My sail was likewise composed of the skins of the same animal; but I made use of the youngest I could get, the older being too tough and thick; and I likewise provided myself with four paddles. I laid in a stock of boiled flesh, of rabbits and fowls; and took with me two vessels, one filled with milk, and the other with water.

I tried my canoe in a large pond near my master's house, and then corrected in it what was amiss, stopping all the chinks with Yahoo's tallow, till I found it staunch, and able to bear me and my freight. And when it was as complete as I could possibly make it, I had it drawn on a carriage very gently by Yahoos, to the seaside, under the conduct of the sorrel nag and another servant.

When all was ready, and the day came for my departure, I took leave of my master and lady, and the whole family, my eyes flowing with tears and my heart quite sunk with grief. But his honor, out of curiosity, and perhaps (if I may speak it without vanity) partly out of kindness, was determined to see me in my canoe; and got several of his neighboring friends to accompany him. I was forced to wait above an hour for the tide, and then observing the wind very fortunately bearing towards the island to which I intended to steer my course, I took a second leave of my master; but as I was going to prostrate myself to kiss his hoof, he did me the honor to raise it gently to my mouth. I am not ignorant how much I have been censured for mentioning this last particular. Detractors are pleased to think it improbable that so illustrious a person should descend to give so great a mark of distinction to a creature so inferior as I. Neither have I forgot how apt some travelers are to boast of extraordinary favors they have received. But, if these censurers were better acquainted with the noble and courteous disposition of the Houyhnhnms, they would soon change their opinion. I paid my respects to the rest of the Houyhnhnms in his honor's company; then getting into my canoe, I pushed off from shore.

6. **Artfully**.

CHAPTER XI. *The Author's dangerous voyage. He arrives at New Holland, hoping to settle there. Is wounded with an arrow by one of the natives. Is seized and carried by force into a Portuguese ship. The great civilities of the Captain. The Author arrives at England.*

I began this desperate voyage on February 15, 1714/5,[7] at 9 o'clock in the morning. The wind was very favorable; however, I made use at first only of my paddles; but considering I should soon be weary, and that the wind might probably chop about, I ventured to set up my little sail; and thus, with the help of the tide, I went at the rate of a league and a half an hour, as near as I could guess. My master and his friends continued on the shore, till I was almost out of sight; and I often heard the sorrel nag (who always loved me) crying out, "*Hnuy illa nyha maiah Yahoo,*" ("Take care of thyself, gentle Yahoo").

My design was, if possible, to discover some small island uninhabited, yet sufficient by my labor to furnish me with necessaries of life, which I would have thought a greater happiness than to be first minister in the politest court of Europe, so horrible was the idea I conceived of returning to live in the society and under the government of Yahoos. For in such a solitude as I desired, I could at least enjoy my own thoughts, and reflect with delight on the virtues of those inimitable Houyhnhnms, without any opportunity of degenerating into the vices and corruptions of my own species.

The reader may remember what I related when my crew conspired against me, and confined me to my cabin, how I continued there several weeks, without knowing what course we took; and when I was put ashore in the longboat, how the sailors told me with oaths, whether true or false, that they knew not in what part of the world we were. However, I did then believe us to be about 10 degrees southward of the Cape of Good Hope, or about 45 degrees southern latitude, as I gathered from some general words I overheard among them, being I supposed to the southeast in their intended voyage to Madagascar. And although this were but little better than conjecture, yet I resolved to steer my course eastward, hoping to reach the southwest coast of New Holland, and perhaps some such island as I desired, lying westward of it. The wind was full west, and by six in the evening I computed I had gone eastward at least eighteen leagues; when I spied a very small island about half a league off, which I soon reached. It was nothing but a rock with one creek,[8] naturally arched by the force of tempests. Here I put in my canoe, and climbing a part of the rock, I could plainly discover land to the east, extending from south to north. I lay all night in my canoe; and repeating my voyage early in the morning, I arrived in seven hours to the southeast point of New Holland. This confirmed me in the opinion I have long entertained, that the maps and

7. I.e., 1714. The year began on March 25th.

8. A bay.

charts place this country at least three degrees more to the east than it really is; which thought I communicated many years ago to my worthy friend Mr. Herman Moll,[9] and gave him my reasons for it, although he hath rather chosen to follow other authors.

I saw no inhabitants in the place where I landed; and being unarmed, I was afraid of venturing far into the country. I found some shellfish on the shore, and eat them raw, not daring to kindle a fire, for fear of being discovered by the natives. I continued three days feeding on oysters and limpets, to save my own provisions; and I fortunately found a brook of excellent water, which gave me great relief.

On the fourth day, venturing out early a little too far, I saw twenty or thirty natives upon a height, not above five hundred yards from me. They were stark naked, men, women, and children round a fire, as I could discover by the smoke. One of them spied me, and gave notice to the rest; five of them advanced towards me, leaving the women and children at the fire. I made what haste I could to the shore, and getting into my canoe, shoved off; the savages observing me retreat, ran after me; and before I could get far enough into the sea, discharged an arrow, which wounded me deeply on the inside of my left knee. (I shall carry the mark to my grave.) I apprehended the arrow might be poisoned; and paddling out of the reach of their darts (being a calm day) I made a shift to suck the wound, and dress it as well as I could.

I was at a loss what to do, for I durst not return to the same landing place, but stood to the north, and was forced to paddle; for the wind, although very gentle, was against me, blowing northwest. As I was looking about for a secure landing place, I saw a sail to the north northeast, which appearing every minute more visible, I was in some doubt whether I should wait for them or no; but at last my detestation of the Yahoo race prevailed; and turning my canoe, I sailed and paddled together to the south, and got into the same creek from whence I set out in the morning, choosing rather to trust myself among these barbarians than live with European Yahoos. I drew up my canoe as close as I could to the shore, and hid myself behind a stone by the little brook, which, as I have already said, was excellent water.

The ship came within half a league of this creek, and sent out her longboat with vessels to take in fresh water (for the place it seems was very well known), but I did not observe it until the boat was almost on shore; and it was too late to seek another hiding place. The seamen at their landing observed my canoe, and rummaging it all over, easily conjectured that the owner could not be far off. Four of them well armed searched every cranny and lurking hole, till at last they found me flat on my face behind the stone. They gazed a while in admiration[1] at my strange uncouth dress;

9. A famous contemporary map maker. 1. Wonder.

my coat made of skins, my wooden-soled shoes, and my furred stockings; from whence, however, they concluded I was not a native of the place, who all go naked. One of the seamen in Portuguese bid me rise, and asked who I was. I understood that language very well, and getting upon my feet, said I was a poor Yahoo, banished from the Houyhnhnms, and desired they would please to let me depart. They admired to hear me answer them in their own tongue, and saw by my complexion I must be an European; but were at a loss to know what I meant by Yahoos and Houyhnhnms, and at the same time fell a laughing at my strange tone in speaking, which resembled the neighing of a horse. I trembled all the while betwixt fear and hatred; I again desired leave to depart, and was gently moving to my canoe; but they laid hold on me, desiring to know what country I was of? whence I came? with many other questions. I told them I was born in England, from whence I came about five years ago, and then their country and ours was at peace. I therefore hoped they would not treat me as an enemy, since I meant them no harm, but was a poor Yahoo, seeking some desolate place where to pass the remainder of his unfortunate life.

When they began to talk, I thought I never heard or saw any thing so unnatural; for it appeared to me as monstrous as if a dog or a cow should speak in England, or a Yahoo in Houyhnhnmland. The honest Portuguese were equally amazed at my strange dress, and the odd manner of delivering my words, which however they understood very well. They spoke to me with great humanity, and said they were sure their Captain would carry me *gratis* to Lisbon, from whence I might return to my own country; that two of the seamen would go back to the ship, to inform the Captain of what they had seen, and receive his orders; in the meantime, unless I would give my solemn oath not to fly, they would secure me by force. I thought it best to comply with their proposal. They were very curious to know my story, but I gave them very little satisfaction; and they all conjectured, that my misfortunes had impaired my reason. In two hours the boat, which went laden with vessels of water, returned with the Captain's commands to fetch me on board. I fell on my knees to preserve my liberty; but all was in vain, and the men having tied me with cords, heaved me into the boat, from whence I was taken into the ship, and from thence into the Captain's cabin.

His name was Pedro de Mendez; he was a very courteous and generous person; he entreated me to give some account of myself, and desired to know what I would eat or drink; said I should be used as well as himself, and spoke so many obliging things, that I wondered to find such civilities from a Yahoo. However, I remained silent and sullen; I was ready to faint at the very smell of him and his men. At last I desired something to eat out of my own canoe; but he ordered me a chicken and some excellent wine, and then directed that I should be put to bed in a very clean cabin. I would not undress myself, but lay on the bedclothes; and in half an hour stole out, when I thought the crew was at dinner; and getting to the side of the ship, was going to leap into the sea, and swim for my life, rather than continue among Yahoos. But one of the seamen prevented me, and having informed the Captain, I was chained to my cabin.

After dinner Don Pedro came to me, and desired to know my reason for so desperate an attempt; assured me he only meant to do me all the service he was able; and spoke so very movingly, that at last I descended to treat him like an animal which had some little portion of reason. I gave him a very short relation of my voyage; of the conspiracy against me by my own men; of the country where they set me on shore, and of my five years residence there. All which he looked upon as if it were a dream or a vision; whereat I took great offense; for I had quite forgot the faculty of lying, so peculiar to Yahoos in all countries where they preside, and consequently the disposition of suspecting truth in others of their own species. I asked him whether it were the custom of his country to *say the thing that was not?* I assured him I had almost forgot what he meant by falsehood; and if I had lived a thousand years in Houyhnhnmland, I should never have heard a lie from the meanest servant. That I was altogether indifferent whether he believed me or no; but however, in return for his favors, I would give so much allowance to the corruption of his nature, as to answer any objection he would please to make; and he might easily discover the truth.

The Captain, a wise man, after many endeavors to catch me tripping in some part of my story, at last began to have a better opinion of my veracity. But he added that since I professed so inviolable an attachment to truth, I must give him my word of honor to bear him company in this voyage without attempting anything against my life; or else he would continue me a prisoner till we arrived at Lisbon. I gave him the promise he required; but at the same time protested that I would suffer the greatest hardships rather than return to live among Yahoos.

Our voyage passed without any considerable accident. In gratitude to the Captain I sometimes sat with him at his earnest request, and strove to conceal my antipathy against humankind, although it often broke out; which he suffered to pass without observation. But the greatest part of the day, I confined myself to my cabin, to avoid seeing any of the crew. The Captain had often entreated me to strip myself of my savage dress, and offered to lend me the best suit of clothes he had. This I would not be prevailed on to accept, abhorring to cover myself with anything that had been on the back of a Yahoo. I only desired he would lend me two clean shirts, which having been washed since he wore them, I believed would not so much defile me. These I changed every second day, and washed them myself.

We arrived at Lisbon, Nov. 5, 1715. At our landing, the Captain forced me to cover myself with his cloak, to prevent the rabble from crowding about me. I was conveyed to his own house; and at my earnest request, he led me up to the highest room backwards.[2] I conjured him to conceal from all persons what I had told him of the Houyhnhnms; because the least hint of such a story would not only draw numbers of people to see me, but probably put me in danger of being imprisoned, or burned by the Inquisition. The Captain persuaded me to accept a suit of clothes newly made; but I would not suffer the tailor to take my measure; however, Don Pedro being almost of my size, they fitted me well enough. He accoutred me with other necessaries, all new, which I aired for twenty-four hours before I would use them.

The Captain had no wife, nor above three servants, none of which were suffered to attend at meals; and his whole deportment was so obliging, added to very good human understanding, that I really began to tolerate his company. He gained so far upon me, that I ventured to look out of the back window. By degrees I was brought into another room, from whence I peeped into the street, but drew my head back in a fright. In a week's time he seduced me down to the door. I found my terror gradually lessened, but my hatred and contempt seemed to increase. I was at last bold enough to walk the street in his company, but kept my nose well stopped with rue, or sometimes with tobacco.

In ten days, Don Pedro, to whom I had given some account of my domestic affairs, put it upon me as a point of honor and conscience that I ought to return to my native country, and live at home with my wife and children. He told me there was an English ship in the port just ready to sail, and he would furnish me with all things necessary. It would be tedious to repeat his arguments, and my contradictions. He said it was altogether impossible to find such a solitary island as I had desired to live in; but I might command in my own house, and pass my time in a manner as recluse as I pleased.

I complied at last, finding I could not do better. I left Lisbon the 24th day of November, in an English merchantman, but who was the Master I never inquired. Don Pedro accompanied me to the ship, and lent me twenty pounds. He took kind leave of me, and embraced me at parting; which I bore as well as I could. During this last voyage I had no commerce with the Master, or any of his men; but pretending I was sick kept close in my cabin. On the fifth of December, 1715, we cast anchor in the Downs about nine in the morning, and at three in the afternoon I got safe to my house at Redriff.

My wife and family received me with great surprise and joy, because they concluded me certainly dead; but I must freely confess, the sight of them filled me only with hatred, disgust, and con-

2. At the rear.

tempt; and the more, by reflecting on the near alliance I had to them. For, although since my unfortunate exile from the Houyhnhnm country, I had compelled myself to tolerate the sight of Yahoos, and to converse with Don Pedro de Mendez; yet my memory and imaginations were perpetually filled with the virtues and ideas of those exalted Houyhnhnms. And when I began to consider that by copulating with one of the Yahoo species, I had become a parent of more, it struck me with the utmost shame, confusion, and horror.

As soon as I entered the house, my wife took me in her arms, and kissed me; at which, having not been used to the touch of that odious animal for so many years, I fell in a swoon for almost an hour. At the time I am writing, it is five years since my last return to England; during the first year I could not endure my wife or children in my presence, the very smell of them was intolerable; much less could I suffer them to eat in the same room. To this hour they dare not presume to touch my bread, or drink out of the same cup; neither was I ever able to let one of them take me by the hand. The first money I laid out was to buy two young stone-horses,[3] which I keep in a good stable, and next to them the groom is my greatest favorite; for I feel my spirits revived by the smell he contracts in the stable. My horses understand me tolerably well; I converse with them at least four hours every day. They are strangers to bridle or saddle; they live in great amity with me, and friendship to each other.

CHAPTER XII. *The Author's veracity. His design in publishing this work. His censure of those travelers who swerve from the truth. The Author clears himself from any sinister ends in writing. An objection answered. The method of planting colonies. His native country commended. The right of the crown to those countries described by the Author is justified. The difficulty of conquering them. The Author takes his last leave of the reader; proposeth his manner of living for the future; gives good advice, and concludeth.*

Thus, gentle reader, I have given thee a faithful history of my travels for sixteen years, and above seven months; wherein I have not been so studious of ornament as of truth. I could perhaps like others have astonished thee with strange improbable tales; but I rather chose to relate plain matter of fact in the simplest manner and style; because my principal design was to inform, and not to amuse thee.

It is easy for us who travel into remote countries, which are seldom visited by Englishmen or other Europeans, to form descriptions of wonderful animals both at sea and land. Whereas a traveler's chief aim should be to make men wiser and better, and to improve their minds by the bad as well as good example of

3. Stallions.

what they deliver concerning foreign places.

I could heartily wish a law were enacted, that every traveler, before he were permitted to publish his voyages, should be obliged to make oath before the Lord High Chancellor that all he intended to print was absolutely true to the best of his knowledge; for then the world would no longer be deceived as it usually is, while some writers, to make their works pass the better upon the public, impose the grossest falsities on the unwary reader. I have perused several books of travels with great delight in my younger days; but, having since gone over most parts of the globe, and been able to contradict many fabulous accounts from my own observation, it hath given me a great disgust against this part of reading, and some indignation to see the credulity of mankind so impudently abused. Therefore, since my acquaintance were pleased to think my poor endeavors might not be unacceptable to my country; I imposed on myself as a maxim, never to be swerved from, that I would *strictly adhere to truth;* neither indeed can I be ever under the least temptation to vary from it, while I retain in my mind the lectures and example of my noble master, and the other illustrious Houyhnhnms, of whom I had so long the honor to be an humble hearer.

——Nec si miserum Fortuna Sinonem
Finxit, vanum etiam, mendacemque improba finget.[4]

I know very well how little reputation is to be got by writings which require neither genius nor learning, nor indeed any other talent, except a good memory, or an exact *Journal.* I know likewise, that writers of travels, like dictionary-makers, are sunk into oblivion by the weight and bulk of those who come last, and therefore lie uppermost. And it is highly probable that such travelers who shall hereafter visit the countries described in this work of mine, may be detecting my errors (if there be any) and adding many new discoveries of their own, jostle me out of vogue, and stand in my place, making the world forget that ever I was an author. This indeed would be too great a mortification if I wrote for fame; but, as my sole intention was the PUBLIC GOOD, I cannot be altogether disappointed. For, who can read the virtues I have mentioned in the glorious Houyhnhnms, without being ashamed of his own vices, when he considers himself as the reasoning, governing animal of his country? I shall say nothing of those remote nations where Yahoos preside; amongst which the least corrupted are the Brobdingnagians, whose wise maxims in morality and government it would be our happiness to observe. But I forbear descanting further, and rather leave the judicious reader to his own remarks and applications.

4. Virgil, *Aeneid,* II, 79–80. "* * * nor if Fortune had moulded Sinon for misery, will she also in spite mould him as false and lying."

I am not a little pleased that this work of mine can possibly meet with no censurers; for what objections can be made against a writer who relates only plain facts that happened in such distant countries, where we have not the least interest with respect either to trade or negotiations? I have carefully avoided every fault with which common writers of travels are often too justly charged. Besides, I meddle not the least with any party, but write without passion, prejudice, or ill-will against any man or number of men whatsoever. I write for the noblest end, to inform and instruct mankind, over whom I may, without breach of modesty, pretend to some superiority, from the advantages I received by conversing so long among the most accomplished Houyhnhnms. I write without any view towards profit or praise. I never suffer a word to pass that may look like reflection, or possibly give the least offense even to those who are most ready to take it. So that, I hope, I may with justice pronounce myself an Author perfectly blameless; against whom the tribes of answerers, considerers, observers, reflectors, detecters, remarkers will never be able to find matter for exercising their talents.

I confess it was whispered to me that I was bound in duty as a subject of England, to have given in a memorial to a secretary of state, at my first coming over; because, whatever lands are discovered by a subject, belong to the Crown. But I doubt whether our conquests in the countries I treat of would be as easy as those of Ferdinando Cortez over the naked Americans. The Lilliputians, I think, are hardly worth the charge of a fleet and army to reduce them; and I question whether it might be prudent or safe to attempt the Brobdingnagians; or, whether an English army would be much at their ease with the Flying Island over their heads. The Houyhnhnms, indeed, appear not to be so well prepared for war, a science to which they are perfect strangers, and especially against missive weapons. However, supposing myself to be a minister of state, I could never give my advice for invading them. Their prudence, unanimity, unacquaintedness with fear, and their love of their country would amply supply all defects in the military art. Imagine twenty thousand of them breaking into the midst of an European army, confounding the ranks, overturning the carriages, battering the warriors' faces into mummy,[5] by terrible yerks[6] from their hinder hoofs: for they would well deserve the character given to Augustus, *Recalcitrat undique tutus.*[7] But instead of proposals for conquering that magnanimous nation, I rather wish they were in a capacity or disposition to send a sufficient number of their inhabitants for civilizing Europe; by teaching us the first principles of Honor, Justice, Truth, Temperance,

5. Pulp.
6. Kicks.
7. Horace, *Satires* II.i.20. "* * * he kicks backward, at every point on his guard."

public Spirit, Fortitude, Chastity, Friendship, Benevolence, and Fidelity. The names of all which Virtues are still retained among us in most languages, and are to be met with in modern as well as ancient authors, which I am able to assert from my own small reading.

But I had another reason which made me less forward to enlarge his majesty's dominions by my discoveries: to say the truth, I had conceived a few scruples with relation to the distributive justice of princes upon those occasions. For instance, a crew of pirates are driven by a storm they know not whither; at length a boy discovers land from the topmast; they go on shore to rob and plunder; they see an harmless people, are entertained with kindness, they give the country a new name, they take formal possession of it for the king, they set up a rotton plank or a stone for a memorial, they murder two or three dozen of the natives, bring away a couple more by force for a sample, return home, and get their pardon. Here commences a new dominion acquired with a title by Divine Right. Ships are sent with the first opportunity; the natives driven out or destroyed, their princes tortured to discover their gold; a free license given to all acts of inhumanity and lust; the earth reeking with the blood of its inhabitants: and this execrable crew of butchers employed in so pious an expedition is a *modern colony* sent to convert and civilize an idolatrous and barbarous people.

But this description, I confess, doth by no means affect the British nation, who may be an example to the whole world for their wisdom, care, and justice in planting colonies; their liberal endowments for the advancement of religion and learning; their choice of devout and able pastors to propagate Christianity; their caution in stocking their provinces with people of sober lives and conversations from this the Mother Kingdom; their strict regard to the distribution of justice, in supplying the civil administration through all their colonies with officers of the greatest abilities, utter strangers to corruption: and to crown all, by sending the most vigilant and virtuous governors, who have no other views than the happiness of the people over whom they preside, and the honor of the king their master.

But, as those countries which I have described do not appear to have any desire of being conquered, and enslaved, murdered, or driven out by colonies, nor abound either in gold, silver, sugar, or tobacco, I did humbly conceive they were by no means proper objects of our zeal, our valor, or our interest. However, if those whom it may concern, think fit to be of another opinion, I am ready to depose, when I shall be lawfully called, that no European did ever visit these countries before me. I mean, if the inhabitants ought to be believed.

But, as to the formality of taking possession in my sovereign's name, it never came once into my thoughts; and if it had, yet as my affairs then stood, I should perhaps in point of prudence and self-preservation have put it off to a better opportunity.

Having thus answered the only objection that can be raised against me as a traveler, I here take a final leave of my courteous readers, and return to enjoy my own speculations in my little garden at Redriff; to apply those excellent lessons of virtue which I learned among the Houyhnhnms; to instruct the Yahoos of my own family as far as I shall find them docible animals; to behold my figure often in a glass, and thus if possible habituate myself by time to tolerate the sight of a human creature; to lament the brutality of Houyhnhnms in my own country, but always treat their persons with respect, for the sake of my noble master, his family, his friends, and the whole Houyhnhnm race, whom these of ours have the honor to resemble in all their lineaments, however their intellectuals came to degenerate.

I began last week to permit my wife to sit at dinner with me, at the farthest end of a long table; and to answer (but with the utmost brevity) the few questions I ask her. Yet the smell of a Yahoo continuing very offensive, I always keep my nose well stopped with rue, lavender, or tobacco leaves. And although it be hard for a man late in life to remove old habits, I am not altogether out of hopes in some time to suffer a neighbor Yahoo in my company, without the apprehensions I am yet under of his teeth or his claws.

My reconcilement to the Yahoo kind in general might not be so difficult, if they would be content with those vices and follies only which nature hath entitled them to. I am not in the least provoked at the sight of a lawyer, a pickpocket, a colonel, a fool, a lord, a gamester, a politician, a whoremonger, a physician, an evidence, a suborner, an attorney, a traitor, or the like: this is all according to the due course of things. But when I behold a lump of deformity, and diseases both in body and mind, smitten with pride, it immediately breaks all the measures of my patience; neither shall I be ever able to comprehend how such an animal and such a vice could tally together. The wise and virtuous Houyhnhnms, who abound in all excellencies that can adorn a rational creature, have no name for this vice in their language, which hath no terms to express anything that is evil, except those whereby they describe the detestable qualities of their Yahoos, among which they were not able to distinguish this of pride, for want of thoroughly understanding human nature, as it showeth itself in other countries, where that animal presides. But I, who had more experience, could plainly observe some rudiments of it among the wild Yahoos.

But the Houyhnhnms, who live under the government of reason, are no more proud of the good qualities they possess, than I should be for not wanting a leg or an arm, which no man in his wits would boast of, although he must be miserable without them. I dwell the longer upon this subject from the desire I have to make the society of an English Yahoo by any means not insupportable; and therefore I here entreat those who have any tincture of this absurd vice, that they will not presume to appear in my sight.

1726, 1735

A Modest Proposal[1]

For Preventing the Children of Poor People in Ireland from Being a Burden to Their Parents or Country, and for Making Them Beneficial to the Public

It is a melancholy object to those who walk through this great town[2] or travel in the country, when they see the streets, the roads, and cabin doors, crowded with beggars of the female sex, followed by three, four, or six children, all in rags and importuning every passenger for an alms. These mothers, instead of being able to work for their honest livelihood, are forced to employ all their time in strolling to beg sustenance for their helpless infants, who, as they grow up, either turn thieves for want of work, or leave their dear native country to fight for the Pretender in Spain, or sell themselves to the Barbadoes.[3]

I think it is agreed by all parties that this prodigious number of children in the arms, or on the backs, or at the heels of their mothers, and frequently of their fathers, is in the present deplor-

1. *A Modest Proposal* is an example of Swift's favorite satiric devices used with superb effect. Irony (from the deceptive adjective "modest" in the title to the very last sentence) pervades the piece. A rigorous logic deduces ghastly arguments from a shocking premise so quietly assumed that the reader assents before he is aware of what his assent implies. Parody, at which Swift is adept, allows him to glance sardonically at the by then familiar figure of the benevolent humanitarian (forerunner of the modern sociologist, social worker, economic planner) concerned to correct a social evil by means of a theoretically conceived plan. The proposer, as naïve as he is apparently logical and kindly, ignores and therefore emphasizes for the reader the enormity of his plan. The whole is an elaboration of a rather trite metaphor: "The English are devouring the Irish." But there is nothing trite about the pamphlet, which expresses in Swift's most controlled style his pity for the oppressed, ignorant, populous, and hungry Catholic peasants of Ireland, and his anger at the rapacious English absentee landlords, who were bleeding the country white with the silent approbation of Parliament, ministers, and the Crown.

2. Dublin.

3. James Francis Edward Stuart (1688–1766), the son of James II, was claimant ("Pretender") to the throne of England from which the Glorious Revolution had barred his succession. Catholic Ireland was loyal to him, and Irishmen joined him in his exile on the Continent. Because of the poverty in Ireland, many Irishmen emigrated to the West Indies and other British colonies in America; they paid their passage by binding themselves to work for a stated period for one of the planters.

able state of the kingdom a very great additional grievance; and therefore whoever could find out a fair, cheap, and easy method of making these children sound, useful members of the commonwealth would deserve so well of the public as to have his statue set up for a preserver of the nation.

But my intention is very far from being confined to provide only for the children of professed beggars; it is of a much greater extent, and shall take in the whole number of infants at a certain age who are born of parents in effect as little able to support them as those who demand our charity in the streets.

As to my own part, having turned my thoughts for many years upon this important subject, and maturely weighed the several schemes of other projectors,[4] I have always found them grossly mistaken in their computation. It is true, a child just dropped from its dam may be supported by her milk for a solar year, with little other nourishment; at most not above the value of two shillings, which the mother may certainly get, or the value in scraps, by her lawful occupation of begging; and it is exactly at one year old that I propose to provide for them in such a manner as instead of being a charge upon their parents or the parish, or wanting food and raiment for the rest of their lives, they shall on the contrary contribute to the feeding, and partly to the clothing, of many thousands.

There is likewise another great advantage in my scheme, that it will prevent those voluntary abortions, and that horrid practice of women murdering their bastard children, alas, too frequent among us, sacrificing the poor innocent babes, I doubt, more to avoid the expense than the shame, which would move tears and pity in the most savage and inhuman breast.

The number of souls in this kingdom[5] being usually reckoned one million and a half, of these I calculate there may be about two hundred thousand couple whose wives are breeders; from which number I subtract thirty thousand couples who are able to maintain their own children, although I apprehend there cannot be so many under the present distresses of the kingdom; but this being granted, there will remain an hundred and seventy thousand breeders. I again subtract fifty thousand for those women who miscarry, or whose children die by accident or disease within the year. There only remain an hundred and twenty thousand children of poor parents annually born. The question therefore is, how this number shall be reared and provided for, which, as I have already said, under the present situation of affairs, is utterly impossible by all the methods hitherto proposed. For we can neither employ them in handicraft or agriculture; we neither build houses (I mean in the country) nor cultivate land. They can very seldom pick up a livelihood

4. Devisers of schemes.

5. Ireland.

by stealing till they arrive at six years old, except where they are of towardly[6] parts; although I confess they learn the rudiments much earlier, during which time they can however be looked upon only as probationers, as I have been informed by a principal gentleman in the county of Cavan, who protested to me that he never knew above one or two instances under the age of six, even in a part of the kingdom so renowned for the quickest proficiency in that art.

I am assured by our merchants that a boy or a girl before twelve years old is no salable commodity; and even when they come to this age they will not yield above three pounds, or three pounds and half a crown at most on the Exchange; which cannot turn to account either to the parents or the kingdom, the charge of nutriment and rags having been at least four times that value.

I shall now therefore humbly propose my own thoughts, which I hope will not be liable to the least objection.

I have been assured by a very knowing American of my acquaintance in London, that a young healthy child well nursed is at a year old a most delicious, nourishing, and wholesome food, whether stewed, roasted, baked, or boiled; and I make no doubt that it will equally serve in a fricassee or a ragout.[7]

I do therefore humbly offer it to public consideration that of the hundred and twenty thousand children, already computed, twenty thousand may be reserved for breed, whereof only one fourth part to be males, which is more than we allow to sheep, black cattle, or swine; and my reason is that these children are seldom the fruits of marriage, a circumstance not much regarded by our savages, therefore one male will be sufficient to serve four females. That the remaining hundred thousand may at a year old be offered in sale to the persons of quality and fortune through the kingdom, always advising the mother to let them suck plentifully in the last month, so as to render them plump and fat for a good table. A child will make two dishes at an entertainment for friends; and when the family dines alone, the fore or hind quarter will make a reasonable dish, and seasoned with a little pepper or salt will be very good boiled on the fourth day, especially in winter.

I have reckoned upon a medium that a child just born will weigh twelve pounds, and in a solar year if tolerably nursed increaseth to twenty-eight pounds.

I grant this food will be somewhat dear, and therefore very proper for landlords, who, as they have already devoured most of the parents, seem to have the best title to the children.

Infant's flesh will be in season throughout the year, but more plentiful in March, and a little before and after. For we are told by a grave author, an eminent French physician,[8] that fish being

6. Dutiful, tractable.

7. A highly seasoned meat stew.

8. François Rabelais (ca. 1494–1553), a humorist and a satirist, by no means grave.

a prolific diet, there are more children born in Roman Catholic countries about nine months after Lent than at any other season; therefore, reckoning a year after Lent, the markets will be more glutted than usual, because the number of popish infants is at least three to one in this kingdom; and therefore it will have one other collateral advantage, by lessening the number of Papists among us.

I have already computed the charge of nursing a beggar's child (in which list I reckon all cottagers, laborers, and four fifths of the farmers) to be about two shillings per annum, rags included; and I believe no gentleman would repine to give ten shillings for the carcass of a good fat child, which, as I have said, will make four dishes of excellent nutritive meat, when he hath only some particular friend or his own family to dine with him. Thus the squire will learn to be a good landlord, and grow popular among the tenants; the mother will have eight shillings net profit, and be fit for work till she produces another child.

Those who are more thrifty (as I must confess the times require) may flay the carcass; the skin of which artificially[9] dressed will make admirable gloves for ladies, and summer boots for fine gentlemen.

As to our city of Dublin, shambles[1] may be appointed for this purpose in the most convenient parts of it, and butchers we may be assured will not be wanting; although I rather recommend buying the children alive, and dressing them hot from the knife as we do roasting pigs.

A very worthy person, a true lover of his country, and whose virtues I highly esteem, was lately pleased in discoursing on this matter to offer a refinement upon my scheme. He said that many gentlemen of this kingdom, having of late destroyed their deer, he conceived that the want of venison might be well supplied by the bodies of young lads and maidens, not exceeding fourteen years of age nor under twelve, so great a number of both sexes in every county being now ready to starve for want of work and service; and these to be disposed of by their parents, if alive, or otherwise by their nearest relations. But with due deference to so excellent a friend and so deserving a patriot, I cannot be altogether in his sentiments; for as to the males, my American acquaintance assured me from frequent experience that their flesh was generally tough and lean, like that of our schoolboys, by continual exercise, and their taste disagreeable; and to fatten them would not answer the charge. Then as to the females, it would, I think with humble submission, be a loss to the public, because they soon would become breeders themselves: and besides, it is not improbable that some scrupulous people might be apt to censure such a practice (although indeed very unjustly) as a little bordering upon cruelty;

9. Skillfully.

1. Slaughterhouses.

which, I confess, hath always been with me the strongest objection against any project, how well soever intended.

But in order to justify my friend, he confessed that this expedient was put into his head by the famous Psalmanazar,[2] a native of the island Formosa, who came from thence to London above twenty years ago, and in conversation told my friend that in his country when any young person happened to be put to death, the executioner sold the carcass to persons of quality as a prime dainty; and that in his time the body of a plump girl of fifteen, who was crucified for an attempt to poison the emperor, was sold to his Imperial Majesty's prime minister of state, and other great mandarins of the court, in joints from the gibbet, at four hundred crowns. Neither indeed can I deny that if the same use were made of several plump young girls in this town, who without one single groat to their fortunes cannot stir abroad without a chair, and appear at the playhouse and assemblies in foreign fineries which they never will pay for, the kingdom would not be the worse.

Some persons of a desponding spirit are in great concern about that vast number of poor people who are aged, diseased, or maimed, and I have been desired to employ my thoughts what course may be taken to ease the nation of so grievous an encumbrance. But I am not in the least pain upon that matter, because it is very well known that they are every day dying and rotting by cold and famine, and filth and vermin, as fast as can be reasonably expected. And as to the younger laborers, they are now in almost as hopeful a condition. They cannot get work, and consequently pine away for want of nourishment to a degree that if at any time they are accidentally hired to common labor, they have not strength to perform it; and thus the country and themselves are happily delivered from the evils to come.

I have too long digressed, and therefore shall return to my subject. I think the advantages by the proposal which I have made are obvious and many, as well as of the highest importance.

For first, as I have already observed, it would greatly lessen the number of Papists, with whom we are yearly overrun, being the principal breeders of the nation as well as our most dangerous enemies; and who stay at home on purpose to deliver the kingdom to the Pretender, hoping to take their advantage by the absence of so many good Protestants, who have chosen rather to leave their country than stay at home and pay tithes against their conscience to an Episcopal curate.

Secondly, the poorer tenants will have something valuable of their own, which by law may be made liable to distress,[3] and help

2. George Psalmanazar (ca. 1679–1763), a famous imposter. A Frenchman, he imposed himself on English bishops, noblemen, and scientists as a Formosan. He wrote an entirely fictitious account of Formosa, in which he described human sacrifices and cannibalism.

3. Distraint, i.e., the seizing, through legal action, of property for the payment of debts and other obligations.

to pay their landlord's rent, their corn and cattle being already seized and money a thing unknown.

Thirdly, whereas the maintenance of an hundred thousand children, from two years old and upwards, cannot be computed at less than ten shillings a piece per annum, the nation's stock will be thereby increased fifty thousand pounds per annum, besides the profit of a new dish introduced to the tables of all gentlemen of fortune in the kingdom who have any refinement in taste. And the money will circulate among ourselves, the goods being entirely of our own growth and manufacture.

Fourthly, the constant breeders, besides the gain of eight shillings sterling per annum by the sale of their children, will be rid of the charge of maintaining them after the first year.

Fifthly, this food would likewise bring great custom to taverns, where the vintners will certainly be so prudent as to procure the best receipts for dressing it to perfection, and consequently have their houses frequented by all the fine gentlemen, who justly value themselves upon their knowledge in good eating; and a skillful cook, who understands how to oblige his guests, will contrive to make it as expensive as they please.

Sixthly, this would be a great inducement to marriage, which all wise nations have either encouraged by rewards or enforced by laws and penalties. It would increase the care and tenderness of mothers toward their children, when they were sure of a settlement for life to the poor babes, provided in some sort by the public, to their annual profit instead of expense. We should see an honest emulation among the married women, which of them could bring the fattest child to the market. Men would become as fond of their wives during the time of their pregnancy as they are now of their mares in foal, their cows in calf, or sows when they are ready to farrow; nor offer to beat or kick them (as is too frequent a practice) for fear of a miscarriage.

Many other advantages might be enumerated. For instance, the addition of some thousand carcasses in our exportation of barreled beef, the propagation of swine's flesh, and improvement in the art of making good bacon, so much wanted among us by the great destruction of pigs, too frequent at our tables, which are no way comparable in taste or magnificence to a well-grown, fat, yearling child, which roasted whole will make a considerable figure at a lord mayor's feast or any other public entertainment. But this and many others I omit, being studious of brevity.

Supposing that one thousand families in this city would be constant customers for infants' flesh, besides others who might have it at merry meetings, particularly weddings and christenings, I compute that Dublin would take off annually about twenty thousand carcasses, and the rest of the kingdom (where probably they will be sold somewhat cheaper) the remaining eighty thousand.

I can think of no one objection that will possibly be raised against this proposal, unless it should be urged that the number of people will be thereby much lessened in the kingdom. This I freely own, and it was indeed one principal design in offering it to the world. I desire the reader will observe, that I calculate my remedy for this one individual kingdom of Ireland and for no other that ever was, is, or I think ever can be upon earth. Therefore let no man talk to me of other expedients: of taxing our absentees at five shillings a pound: of using neither clothes nor household furniture except what is of our own growth and manufacture: of utterly rejecting the materials and instruments that promote foreign luxury: of curing the expensiveness of pride, vanity, idleness, and gaming in our women: of introducing a vein of parsimony, prudence, and temperance: of learning to love our country, in the want of which we differ even from Laplanders and the inhabitants of Topinamboo:[4] of quitting our animosities and factions, nor acting any longer like the Jews, who were murdering one another at the very moment their city was taken:[5] of being a little cautious not to sell our country and conscience for nothing: of teaching landlords to have at least one degree of mercy toward their tenants: lastly, of putting a spirit of honesty, industry, and skill into our shopkeepers; who, if a resolution could now be taken to buy only our native goods, would immediately unite to cheat and exact upon us in the price, the measure, and the goodness, nor could ever yet be brought to make one fair proposal of just dealing, though often and earnestly invited to it.[6]

Therefore I repeat, let no man talk to me of these and the like expedients, till he hath at least some glimpse of hope that there will ever be some hearty and sincere attempt to put them in practice.

But as to myself, having been wearied out for many years with offering vain, idle, visionary thoughts, and at length utterly despairing of success, I fortunately fell upon this proposal, which, as it is wholly new, so it hath something solid and real, of no expense and little trouble, full in our own power, and whereby we can incur no danger in disobliging England. For this kind of commodity will not bear exportation, the flesh being of too tender a consistence to admit a long continuance in salt, although perhaps I could name a country which would be glad to eat up our whole nation without it.[7]

After all, I am not so violently bent upon my own opinion as

4. I.e., even Laplanders love their frozen, infertile country and the savage tribes of Brazil their jungle more than the Anglo-Irish love Ireland.

5. During the siege of Jerusalem by the Roman Emperor Titus, who captured and destroyed the city in A.D. 70, the city was torn by bloody fights between factions of fanatics.

6. Swift himself had made all these proposals in various pamphlets. In editions printed during his lifetime the various proposals were italicized to indicate that Swift is no longer being ironic.

7. I.e., England.

to reject any offer proposed by wise men, which shall be found equally innocent, cheap, easy, and effectual. But before something of that kind shall be advanced in contradiction to my scheme, and offering a better, I desire the author or authors will be pleased maturely to consider two points. First, as things now stand, how they will be able to find food and raiment for an hundred thousand useless mouths and backs. And secondly, there being a round million of creatures in human figure throughout this kingdom, whose sole subsistence put into a common stock would leave them in debt two millions of pounds sterling, adding those who are beggars by profession to the bulk of farmers, cottagers, and laborers, with their wives and children who are beggars in effect; I desire those politicians who dislike my overture, and may perhaps be so bold to attempt an answer, that they will first ask the parents of these mortals whether they would not at this day think it a great happiness to have been sold for food at a year old in the manner I prescribe, and thereby have avoided such a perpetual scene of misfortunes as they have since gone through by the oppression of landlords, the impossibility of paying rent without money or trade, the want of common sustenance, with neither house nor clothes to cover them from the inclemencies of the weather, and the most inevitable prospect of entailing the like or greater miseries upon their breed forever.

I profess, in the sincerity of my heart, that I have not the least personal interest in endeavoring to promote this necessary work, having no other motive than the public good of my country, by advancing our trade, providing for infants, relieving the poor, and giving some pleasure to the rich. I have no children by which I can propose to get a single penny; the youngest being nine years old, and my wife past childbearing.

1729

JOSEPH ADDISON *and* SIR RICHARD STEELE
(1672–1719) (1672–1729)

1709–11: *Tatler* published.
1711–12: *Spectator* published.
1714: *Spectator* resumed (for 80 numbers).

The friendship of Joseph Addison and Richard Steele began when they were schoolboys together at the Charterhouse in London. Their careers ran parallel courses and brought them for a while into fruitful collaboration. Addison, though a man of infinite charm among intimates, was by nature reserved, rather chilly, calculating, ungenerous, and prudent. Steele was impulsive and rakish when young (but ardently devoted to his beautiful wife), imprudent to a degree, and consequently in frequent financial distress. Addison never stumbled in his progress to financial competence, a late marriage to a dowager countess, and a successful political career; walking less surely, Steele experienced many vicissitudes and faced serious financial problems during his last years.

Both men attended Oxford, where Addison took his degree, won a fellowship, and earned a reputation for Latin verse; the less scholarly Steele, however, had only moderate academic success and did not stay for a degree, but left the University to take a commission in the army. For a while he cut a dashing figure in London, even, to his horror, seriously wounding a man in a duel. Both men enjoyed the patronage of the great Whig magnates, and except during the last four years of Queen Anne's reign, when the Tories were in the ascendency, they were generously treated. Steele became editor of the *London Gazette*, an official newspaper that appeared twice a week during the greater part of his editorship, listing government appointments and reporting domestic and foreign news—in short, the first newspaper in the modern sense, for it was very much unlike the news pamphlets or the news letters, written by hand and sent out to subscribers, that one finds in the previous century. Much later, Steele became manager of the Theatre Royal, Drury Lane. Meanwhile he had served in Parliament and been knighted by George I. Addison held more important positions: he was secretary to the Lord Lieutenant of Ireland, and later an Under-Secretary of State; finally, toward the end of his life, he became Secretary of State. Both men wrote plays: Addison's *Cato*, a frigid and very "correct" tragedy, had great success in 1713 because it was received by the town as a political play; and Steele's later plays at Drury Lane (*The Conscious Lovers*, 1722, for instance) were instrumental in establishing the popularity of sentimental comedy throughout the 18th century.

Steele's debts and Addison's loss of office in 1710 were the efficient causes of their journalistic enterprises, through which they developed one of the most characteristic types of 18th-century literature, the periodical essay. Steele's experience as gazetteer had involved him in journalism, and in 1709, when in need of money, he launched the *Tatler* under the pseudonym Isaac Bickerstaff. He sought to attract the largest possible audience: the title was a bid for female readers, and the early fivefold division of each number into departments (dated from four appropriate coffeehouses and the editor's own apartment) dealing respectively with "gallantry, pleasure and entertainment," poetry, learning, news, and personal reflections gave the paper a wide appeal among men. The fifth department soon swallowed up the other four, as the lucubrations of Squire Bickerstaff won readers in coffeehouses and at breakfast tables. The paper appeared thrice weekly from April, 1709, to January, 1711. Steele wrote by far the greater number of *Tatlers*, but Addison contributed helpfully, as did other friends. The *Spectator*, which appeared daily except Sunday from March, 1711, to December, 1712 (and was briefly resumed by Addison in 1714), was the joint undertaking of the two friends, though it was dominated by Addison. The papers had many imitators in their own day and throughout the rest of the century; Johnson's *Rambler* and *Idler* and Goldsmith's brief *Bee* are distinguished instances.

The periodical essay as developed in these two papers admits of no strict definition. It is less formal and purely didactic than the essays of Bacon, less personal than those of Charles Lamb and William Hazlitt in the next century. It deals with the widest possible variety of topics: manners and morals, literature and philosophical ideas, types and characters, fads, fashions, foibles; and these it was necessary to treat lightly and in an agreeable manner. But one topic of the times was wisely steered around in both papers—politics.

Both Steele and Addison were conscious moralists and did not disguise their intention of improving the minds, morals, and manners of their readers. Moral reform had been in the air since the 1690's, and the new society that was coming into existence (and was certainly in some degree the creation of Addison and Steele) was attaining a balance between the morality and respectability of the old, rather Puritan middle class (which was too often narrowly Philistine in taste and outlook) and the wit, grace, and enlightenment of the older aristocratic and fashionable class (which, in the previous century, had too often been libertine in morals and thought). The new social ideal, which the two essayists themselves fostered, stressed moderation, reasonableness, self-control, urbanity, and good taste. Steele's *Tatler* essays on marriage and domestic life held up an ideal which would have provoked the wits of Charles's day to contemptuous laughter. He wrote on any topic that suggested itself as pleasing or useful: the theater, true breeding as against vulgar manners, education, simplicity in dress, the proper use of Sunday, and so on; and he lightly ridiculed common social types such as the prude, the coquette, the "pretty fellow," and the rake. Addison's best *Tatler* essays initiated his study of eccentric or affected characters (to be continued in the *Spectator*), cleverly observed and described with agreeable humor. These essays on social types were a development of the "characters" of the 17th century. The *Tatler* papers quickly won an appreciative audience, and when published in book form, they continued (like those of the *Spectator*) to sell throughout the century. Steele's style is informal, even careless, but for that very reason intimate and engaging. His generous, even sentimental, warmth imparts itself to his style and animates his subject when, as is most often the case, he writes from his heart. It was, he says, "a most exquisite pleasure * * * to trace human life through all its mazes and recesses, and to show much shorter methods than men ordinarily practice to be happy, agreeable, and great." Shortly after Steele discontinued the *Tatler*, John Gay in a pamphlet, *The Present State of Wit*, praised him for banishing or checking follies and persuading the town to virtue, religion, and learning. "In the dress he gives it [learning] 'tis a most welcome guest at tea tables and assemblies, and is relished and caressed by the merchants on the 'Change * * * "

The readers whom Steele had reached and influenced were at hand when the *Spectator* began to appear two months after the last *Tatler*. Steele played a more important role in the paper than Addison had in the *Tatler*, but the *Spectator* is throughout Addisonian. In the second number Steele introduces us to the members of Mr. Spectator's Club (male social life was dominated by clubs during the reign of Queen Anne), who prove to be a man about town, a student of law and literature, a churchman, a soldier, a Tory country squire, and, interestingly enough, a London merchant. These men suggest the readers (other than women) to whom the paper was primarily addressed. As a Whig, Steele was ardently sympathetic with the new moneyed class in the City, and it was evidently his intention to pit the merchant, Sir Andrew Freeport, the representative of the new order, against the Tory Sir Roger de Coverley, who is presented as belonging to a vanishing order. Addison, however, preferred to present Sir Roger in episodes set in town and in the country as an endearing, eccentric character, often absurd but always amiable and innocent. He is a prominent ancestor of a long line of similar characters in fiction during the next two centuries. The social criticism continued, with more wit and raillery than the *Tatler* had usually commanded. Addison's scholarly interests broadened the material to include the popularization of current philosophical notions about man and nature; and he wrote several important series of critical papers: among others, two recommending the ballad of *Chevy Chase* (old ballads had not yet come into fashion), a group distinguishing true and false wit, an extended series of Saturday essays evaluating *Paradise Lost*, and finally, an influential series on "the pleasures of the imagination" which treated the aesthetics of visual beauty in nature and art. Altogether, the *Spectator* fulfilled his ambition (see *Spectator* 10, below) to be considered a modern Socrates. Addison's contributions to the paper are the finest among the vast numbers of 18th-century periodical essays. If his tone is a little superior and his style a bit more fussy than we like today, his keen observation of the life around him, the graceful ease of his learning, his never cruel wit, and, despite the commonplaceness of most of his moral and philosophical reflections, his genuine if occasional originality made him the most agreeable, and consequently the most persuasive, instructor the age could have found.

The best description of Addison's prose is Dr. Johnson's in his *Life of Addison:* "His prose is the model of the middle style; on grave subjects not formal, on light occasions not groveling; pure without scrupulosity, and exact without apparent elaboration; always equable, and always easy, without glowing words or pointed sentences." And he concludes: "Whoever wishes to attain an English style, familiar but not coarse, and elegant but not ostentatious, must give his days and nights to the volumes of Addison," a course of study which a good many aspiring writers during the century seem to have undertaken with some success.

The Periodical Essay: Manners

STEELE: [The Gentleman; The Pretty Fellow]

From *The Tatler, No. 21, Saturday, May 28, 1709*

Quidquid agunt homines——
——nostri est farrago libelli.[1]
—JUVENAL, *Satire* I.85–86

White's Chocolate House,[2] May 26

A gentleman has writ to me out of the country a very civil letter, and said things which I suppress with great violence to my vanity.

1. "Whatever men do * * * shall form the motley subject of my book." Steele used this epigraph for all but a very few of the first 62 *Tatlers*.

2. One of the fashionable chocolate houses, from which Steele, in the earlier numbers of the *Tatler*, dated "accounts of gallantry, pleasure, and entertainment."

There are many terms in my narratives which he complains want explaining, and has therefore desired that, for the benefit of my country readers, I would let him know what I mean by a Gentleman, a Pretty Fellow, a Toast, a Coquette, a Critic, a Wit, and all other appellations of those now in the gayer world, who are in possession of these several characters; together with an account of those who unfortunately pretend to them. I shall begin with him we usually call a Gentleman, or man of conversation.

It is generally thought that warmth of imagination, quick relish of pleasure, and a manner of becoming it, are the most essential qualities for forming this sort of man. But anyone that is much in company will observe that the height of good breeding is shown rather in never giving offense, than in doing obliging things. Thus, he that never shocks you, though he is seldom entertaining, is more likely to keep your favor than he who often entertains, and sometimes displeases you. The most necessary talent therefore in a man of conversation, which is what we ordinarily intend by a fine gentleman, is a good judgment. He that has this in perfection is master of his companion, without letting him see it; and has the same advantage over men of any other qualifications whatsoever, as one that can see would have over a blind man of ten times his strength.

This is what makes Sophronius the darling of all who converse with him, and the most powerful with his acquaintance of any man in town. By the light of this faculty, he acts with great ease and freedom among the men of pleasure, and acquits himself with skill and dispatch among the men of business. All which he performs with so much success that, with as much discretion in life as any man ever had, he neither is, nor appears, cunning. But as he does a good office, if he ever does it, with readiness and alacrity, so he denies what he does not care to engage in, in a manner that convinces you that you ought not to have asked it. His judgment is so good and unerring, and accompanied with so cheerful a spirit, that his conversation is a continual feast, at which he helps some, and is helped by others, in such a manner that the equality of society is perfectly kept up, and every man obliges as much as he is obliged: for it is the greatest and justest skill in a man of superior understanding, to know how to be on a level with his companions. This sweet disposition runs through all the actions of Sophronius, and makes his company desired by women, without being envied by men. Sophronius would be as just as he is, if there were no law; and would be as discreet as he is, if there were no such thing as calumny.

In imitation of this agreeable being, is made that animal we call a Pretty Fellow; who being just able to find out that what makes Sophronius acceptable is a natural behavior, in order to the same reputation, makes his own an artificial one. Jack Dimple is his perfect mimic, whereby he is of course the most unlike him of all men living. Sophronius just now passed into the inner room directly forward: Jack comes as fast after as he can for the right and left looking glass, in which he had but just approved himself by a nod at each, and marched on. He will meditate within for half an hour, till he thinks he is not careless enough in his air, and come back to the mirror to recollect his forgetfulness. * * *

STEELE: [Dueling]

From *The Tatler, No. 25, Tuesday, June 7, 1709*

Quidquid agunt homines——
——nostri est farrago libelli.
—JUVENAL, *Satire* I.85–86

White's Chocolate House, June 6

A letter from a young lady, written in the most passionate terms, wherein she laments the misfortune of a gentleman, her lover, who was lately wounded in a duel, has turned my thoughts to that subject, and inclined me to examine into the causes which precipitate men into so fatal a folly. And as it has been proposed to treat of subjects of gallantry in the article from hence, and no one point in nature is more proper to be considered by the company who frequent this place than that of duels, it is worth our consideration to examine into this chimerical groundless humor, and to lay every other thought aside, until we have stripped it of all its false pretenses to credit and reputation amongst men.

But I must confess, when I consider what I am going about, and run over in my imagination all the endless crowd of men of honor who will be offended at such a discourse, I am undertaking, methinks, a work worthy an invulnerable hero in romance, rather than a private gentleman with a single rapier; but as I am pretty well acquainted by great opportunities with the nature of man, and know of a truth that all men fight against their will, the danger vanishes, and resolution rises upon this subject. For this reason, I shall talk very freely on a custom which all men wish exploded, though no man has courage enough to resist it.

But there is one unintelligible word, which I fear will extremely perplex my dissertation, and I confess to you I find very hard to explain, which is the term "satisfaction." An honest country gentleman had the misfortune to fall into company with two or three modern men of honor, where he happened to be very ill treated; and one of the company, being conscious of his offense, sends a note to him in the morning, and tells him he was ready to give him satisfaction. "This is fine doing," says the plain fellow; "last night he sent me away cursedly out of humor, and this morning he fancies it would be a satisfaction to be run through the body."

As the matter at present stands, it is not to do handsome actions denominates a man of honor; it is enough if he dares to defend ill ones. Thus you often see a common sharper in competition with a gentleman of the first rank; though all mankind is convinced that a fighting gamester is only a pickpocket with the courage of an highwayman. One cannot with any patience reflect on the unaccountable jumble of persons and things in this town and nation, which occasions very frequently that a brave man falls by a hand below that of a common hangman, and yet his executioner escapes the clutches of the hangman for doing it. I shall therefore hereafter consider how the bravest men in other ages and nations have behaved themselves upon such incidents as we decide by combat; and show, from their practice, that this resentment neither has its foundation from true reason or solid fame; but is an imposture, made of cowardice, falsehood, and want of understanding. For this work, a good history of quarrels would be very edifying to the public, and I apply myself to the town for particulars and circumstances within their knowledge, which may serve to embellish the dissertation with proper cuts.[1] Most of the quarrels I have ever known have proceeded from some valiant coxcomb's persisting in the wrong, to defend some prevailing folly, and preserve himself from the ingenuity[2] of owning a mistake.

By this means it is called "giving a man satisfaction" to urge your offense against him with your sword; which puts me in mind of Peter's order to the keeper, in *The Tale of a Tub*:[3] "If you neglect to do all this, damn you and your generation forever: and so we bid you heartily farewell." If the contradiction in the very terms of one of our challenges were as well explained and turned into downright English, would it not run after this manner?

"Sir,

"Your extraordinary behavior last night, and the liberty you were pleased to take with me, makes me this morning give you this, to tell you, because you are an ill-bred puppy, I will meet you in Hyde Park an hour hence; and because you want both breeding and humanity, I desire you would come with a pistol in your hand, on horseback, and endeavor to shoot me through the head to teach you more manners. If you fail of doing me this pleasure, I shall say you are a rascal, on every post in town: and so, sir, if you will not injure me more, I shall never forgive what you have done already. Pray, sir, do not fail of getting everything ready; and you will infinitely oblige, sir, your most obedient humble servant, etc." * * *

1. Either woodcuts or engravings on copper plates.
2. Honorable candor.
3. In Swift's satire, the Roman Church is attacked in the character of Peter. The passage (slightly misquoted) satirizes the Pope's practice of issuing indulgences.

ADDISON: [The Trial of the Petticoat]

The Tatler, No. 116, Thursday, January 5, 1709–10

——*Pars minima est ipsa puella sui.*—OVID[1]

The court being prepared for proceeding on the cause of the petticoat, I gave orders to bring in a criminal who was taken up as she went out of the puppet show about three nights ago, and was now standing in the street with a great concourse of people about her. Word was brought me, that she had endeavored twice or thrice to come in, but could not do it by reason of her petticoat, which was too large for the entrance of my house,[2] though I had ordered both the folding doors to be thrown open for its reception. Upon this, I desired the jury of matrons, who stood at my right hand, to inform themselves of her condition, and know whether there were any private reasons why she might not make her appearance separate from her petticoat. This was managed with great discretion, and had such an effect, that upon the return of the verdict from the bench of matrons, I issued out an order forthwith, that the criminal should be stripped of her encumbrances, till she became little enough to enter my house. I had before given directions for an engine[3] of several legs, that could contract or open itself like the top of an umbrella, in order to place the petticoat upon it, by which means I might take a leisurely survey of it, as it should appear in its proper dimensions. This was all done accordingly; and forthwith, upon the closing of the engine, the petticoat was brought into court. I then directed the machine to be set upon the table, and dilated in such a manner, as to show the garment in its utmost circumference; but my great hall was too narrow for the experiment; for before it was half unfolded, it described so immoderate a circle, that the lower part of it brushed upon my face as I sat in my chair of judicature. I then inquired for the person that belonged to the petticoat; and, to my great surprise, was directed to a very beautiful young damsel, with so pretty a face and shape, that I bid her come out of the crowd, and seated her upon a little crock[4] at my left hand. "My pretty maid," said I, "do you own yourself to have been the inhabitant of the garment before us?" The girl I found had good sense, and told me with a smile, "That notwithstanding it was her own petticoat, she should be very glad to see an example made of it; and that she wore it for no other reason, but that she had a mind to look as big and burly as other persons of her quality; that she had kept out of it as long as she could, and till she began to appear little in the eyes of all her acquaintance; that if she laid it aside, people would think she was not made like other women." I always

1. "The least part of her is the woman herself"—Ovid's *Remedia Amoris* ("The Cure of Love"), line 344.
2. Extravagant hoop-petticoats, stiffened by whalebone, had recently come into fashion.
3. Mechanical contrivance.
4. Stool.

give great allowances to the fair sex upon account of the fashion, and therefore was not displeased with the defense of the pretty criminal. I then ordered the vest[5] which stood before us to be drawn up by a pulley to the top of my great hall, and afterwards to be spread open by the engine it was placed upon, in such a manner, that it formed a very splendid and ample canopy over our heads, and covered the whole court of judicature with a kind of silken rotunda, in its form not unlike the cupola of St. Paul's. I entered upon the whole cause with great satisfaction, as I sat under the shadow of it.

The counsel for the petticoat was now called in, and ordered to produce what they had to say against the popular cry which was raised against it. They answered the objections with great strength and solidity of argument, and expatiated in very florid harangues, which they did not fail to set off and furbelow[6] (if I may be allowed the metaphor) with many periodical sentences and turns of oratory. The chief arguments for their client were taken, first, from the great benefit that might arise to our woolen manufactory from this invention, which was calculated as follows: the common petticoat has not above four yards in the circumference; whereas this over our heads had more in the semidiameter;[7] so that by allowing it twenty-four yards in the circumference, the five millions of woolen petticoats, which (according to Sir William Petty)[8] supposing what ought to be supposed in a well-governed state, that all petticoats are made of that stuff, would amount to thirty millions of those of the ancient mode. A prodigious improvement of the woolen trade! and what could not fail to sink the power of France in a few years.

To introduce the second argument, they begged leave to read a petition of the rope-makers, wherein it was represented, that the demand for cords, and the price of them, were much risen since this fashion came up. At this, all the company who were present lifted up their eyes into the vault; and I must confess, we did discover many traces of cordage which were interwoven in the stiffening of the drapery.

A third argument was founded upon a petition of the Greenland trade,[9] which likewise represented the great consumption of whalebone which would be occasioned by the present fashion, and the benefit which would thereby accrue to that branch of the British trade.

To conclude, they gently touched upon the weight and unwieldiness of the garment, which they insinuated might be of great use to preserve the honor of families.

These arguments would have wrought very much upon me (as I

5. Garment.
6. Ornament (like the flounce of a dress). "Periodical sentences" consist of several clauses, usually with elaborate rhetorical constructions.
7. Radius.
8. Economist (1623–87), famous for his exact calculations, who helped invent the science of statistics.
9. The whaling industry.

then told the company in a long and elaborate discourse), had I not considered the great and additional expense which such fashions would bring upon fathers and husbands; and therefore by no means to be thought of till some years after a peace. I further urged, that it would be a prejudice to the ladies themselves, who could never expect to have any money in the pocket, if they laid out so much on the petticoat. To this I added, the great temptation it might give to virgins, of acting in security like married women, and by that means give a check to matrimony, an institution always encouraged by wise societies.

At the same time, in answer to the several petitions produced on that side, I showed one subscribed by the women of several persons of quality, humbly setting forth, that since the introduction of this mode, their respective ladies had (instead of bestowing on them their cast[1] gowns) cut them into shreds, and mixed them with the cordage and buckram, to complete the stiffening of their under-petticoats. For which, and sundry other reasons, I pronounced the petticoat a forfeiture; but to show that I did not make that judgment for the sake of filthy lucre, I ordered it to be folded up, and sent it as a present to a widow gentlewoman, who has five daughters, desiring she would make each of them a petticoat out of it, and send me back the remainder, which I design to cut into stomachers, caps, facings of my waistcoat sleeves, and other garnitures suitable to my age and quality.

I would not be understood, that (while I discard this monstrous invention) I am an enemy to the proper ornaments of the fair sex. On the contrary, as the hand of nature has poured on them such a profusion of charms and graces, and sent them into the world more amiable and finished than the rest of her works; so I would have them bestow upon themselves all the additional beauties that art can supply them with, provided it does not interfere with, disguise, or pervert, those of nature.

I consider woman as a beautiful romantic animal, that may be adorned with furs and feathers, pearls and diamonds, ores and silks. The lynx shall cast its skin at her feet to make her a tippet;[2] the peacock, parrot, and swan, shall pay contributions to her muff; the sea shall be searched for shells, and the rocks for gems; and every part of nature furnish out its share towards the embellishment of a creature that is the most consummate work of it. All this I shall indulge them in; but as for the petticoat I have been speaking of, I neither can nor will allow it.[3]

1. Cast-off.
2. Stole.
3. On this paragraph, Virginia Woolf commented, "As for women—or 'the fair sex,' as Addison liked to call them—their follies were past counting. He did his best to count them, with a loving particularity which roused the ill-humor of Swift. But he did it very charmingly, with a natural relish for the task. * * * In all these matters Addison was on the side of sense and taste and civilization."

STEELE: [The Spectator's Club]

The Spectator, No. 2, Friday, March 2, 1711

——Haec alii sex
Vel plures uno conclamant ore.[1]
—JUVENAL, *Satire* VII.166–67

The first of our society is a gentleman of Worcestershire, of ancient descent, a baronet, his name Sir Roger de Coverley. His great-grandfather was inventor of that famous country-dance which is called after him. All who know that shire are very well acquainted with the parts and merits of Sir Roger. He is a gentleman that is very singular in his behavior, but his singularities proceed from his good sense, and are contradictions to the manners of the world only as he thinks the world is in the wrong. However, this humor creates him no enemies, for he does nothing with sourness or obstinacy; and his being unconfined to modes and forms makes him but the readier and more capable to please and oblige all who know him. When he is in town, he lives in Soho Square. It is said he keeps himself a bachelor by reason he was crossed in love by a perverse, beautiful widow of the next county to him. Before this disappointment, Sir Roger was what you call a fine gentleman, had often supped with my Lord Rochester and Sir George Etherege, fought a duel upon his first coming to town, and kicked Bully Dawson in a public coffeehouse for calling him "youngster."[2] But being ill used by the above-mentioned widow, he was very serious for a year and a half; and though, his temper being naturally jovial, he at last got over it, he grew careless of himself, and never dressed afterward. He continues to wear a coat and doublet of the same cut that were in fashion at the time of his repulse, which, in his merry humors, he tells us, has been in and out twelve times since he first wore it. 'Tis said Sir Roger grew humble in his desires after he had forgot this cruel beauty, insomuch that it is reported he has frequently offended in point of chastity with beggars and gypsies; but this is looked upon by his friends rather as matter of raillery than truth. He is now in his fifty-sixth year, cheerful, gay, and hearty; keeps a good house both in town and country; a great lover of mankind; but there is such a mirthful cast in his behavior that he is rather beloved than esteemed. His tenants grow rich, his servants look satisfied, all the young women profess love to him, and the young men are glad of his company; when he comes into a house he calls the servants by their names, and talks all the way upstairs to a visit. I must not omit that Sir Roger is a justice of the quorum;[3] that he fills the chair at a quarter-session with great abil-

1. "Six more at least join their consenting voice."
2. John Wilmot, Earl of Rochester (1647–80), the poet and rake, an intimate of Charles II; Sir George Etherege (ca. 1634–91), playwright, rake, and boon companion of the king and Rochester. Bully Dawson was a notorious sharper of the period.
3. A county justice of the peace, presiding over quarterly sessions of the court.

ities; and, three months ago, gained universal applause by explaining a passage in the Game Act.

The gentleman next in esteem and authority among us is another bachelor, who is a member of the Inner Temple;[4] a man of great probity, wit, and understanding; but he has chosen his place of residence rather to obey the direction of an old humorsome[5] father, than in pursuit of his own inclinations. He was placed there to study the laws of the land, and is the most learned of any of the house in those of the stage. Aristotle and Longinus are much better understood by him than Littleton or Coke.[6] The father sends up, every post, questions relating to marriage articles, leases, and tenures, in the neighborhood; all which questions he agrees with an attorney to answer and take care of in the lump. He is studying the passions themselves, when he should be inquiring into the debates among men which arise from them. He knows the argument of each of the orations of Demosthenes and Tully,[7] but not one case in the reports of our own courts. No one ever took him for a fool, but none, except his intimate friends, know he has a great deal of wit. This turn makes him at once both disinterested and agreeable; as few of his thoughts are drawn from business, they are most of them fit for conversation. His taste of books is a little too just[8] for the age he lives in; he has read all, but approves of very few. His familiarity with the customs, manners, actions, and writings of the ancients makes him a very delicate observer of what occurs to him in the present world. He is an excellent critic, and the time of the play is his hour of business; exactly at five he passes through New Inn, crosses through Russell Court, and takes a turn at Will's[9] till the play begins; he has his shoes rubbed and his periwig powdered at the barber's as you go into the Rose.[1] It is for the good of the audience when he is at a play, for the actors have an ambition to please him.

The person of next consideration is Sir Andrew Freeport, a merchant of great eminence in the city of London, a person of indefatigable industry, strong reason, and great experience. His notions of trade are noble and generous, and (as every rich man has usually some sly way of jesting which would make no great figure were he not a rich man) he calls the sea the British Common. He is acquainted with commerce in all its parts, and will tell you that it

4. One of the Inns of Court, where lawyers resided or had their offices and where students studied law.

5. Full of crotchets.

6. In other words, he is more familiar with the laws of literature than those of England. The *Poetics* of Aristotle and the Greek treatise *On the Sublime* (reputedly by Longinus) were in high favor among the critics of the time. Sir Thomas Littleton, 15th-century jurist, was author of a renowned treatise on *Tenures;* Sir Edward Coke (1552–1634) was the judge and writer whose *Reports* and *Institutes of the Laws of England* (known as *Coke upon Littleton*) have exerted a great influence on the interpretation of English law.

7. Marcus Tullius Cicero.

8. Exact.

9. The coffeehouse in Covent Garden associated with literature and criticism since Dryden had begun to frequent it in the 1660's.

1. A tavern near Drury Lane.

is a stupid and barbarous way to extend dominion by arms; for true power is to be got by arts and industry. He will often argue that if this part of our trade were well cultivated, we should gain from one nation; and if another, from another. I have heard him prove that diligence makes more lasting acquisitions than valor, and that sloth has ruined more nations than the sword. He abounds in several frugal maxims, among which the greatest favorite is, "A penny saved is a penny got." A general trader of good sense is pleasanter company than a general scholar; and Sir Andrew having a natural unaffected eloquence, the perspicuity of his discourse gives the same pleasure that wit would in another man. He has made his fortunes himself, and says that England may be richer than other kingdoms by as plain methods as he himself is richer than other men; though at the same time I can say this of him, that there is not a point in the compass but blows home a ship in which he is an owner.

Next to Sir Andrew in the clubroom sits Captain Sentry, a gentleman of great courage, good understanding, but invincible modesty. He is one of those that deserve very well, but are very awkward at putting their talents within the observation of such as should take notice of them. He was some years a captain, and behaved himself with great gallantry in several engagements and at several sieges; but having a small estate of his own, and being next heir to Sir Roger, he has quitted a way of life in which no man can rise suitably to his merit who is not something of a courtier as well as a soldier. I have heard him often lament that in a profession where merit is placed in so conspicuous a view, impudence should get the better of modesty. When he has talked to this purpose I never heard him make a sour expression, but frankly confess that he left the world because he was not fit for it. A strict honesty and an even, regular behavior are in themselves obstacles to him that must press through crowds who endeavor at the same end with himself—the favor of a commander. He will, however, in his way of talk, excuse generals for not disposing according to men's desert, or inquiring into it, "for," says he, "that great man who has a mind to help me, has as many to break through to come at me as I have to come at him"; therefore he will conclude that the man who would make a figure, especially in a military way, must get over all false modesty, and assist his patron against the importunity of other pretenders by a proper assurance in his own vindication. He says it is a civil cowardice to be backward in asserting[2] what you ought to expect, as it is a military fear to be slow in attacking when it is your duty. With this candor does the gentleman speak of himself and others. The same frankness runs through all his conversation. The military part of his life has furnished him with many adventures, in the relation of which he is very agreeable to the company; for he is never overbearing, though accustomed to command men

2. Claiming.

in the utmost degree below him; nor ever too obsequious from an habit of obeying men highly above him.

But that our society may not appear a set of humorists[3] unacquainted with the gallantries and pleasures of the age, we have among us the gallant Will Honeycomb, a gentleman who, according to his years, should be in the decline of his life, but having ever been very careful of his person, and always had a very easy fortune, time has made but very little impression either by wrinkles on his forehead or traces in his brain. His person is well turned and of a good height. He is very ready at that sort of discourse with which men usually entertain women. He has all his life dressed very well, and remembers habits[4] as others do men. He can smile when one speaks to him, and laughs easily. He knows the history of every mode, and can inform you from which of the French king's wenches our wives and daughters had this manner of curling their hair, that way of placing their hoods; whose frailty was covered by such a sort of petticoat, and whose vanity to show her foot made that part of the dress so short in such a year. In a word, all his conversation and knowledge has been in the female world. As other men of his age will take notice to you what such a minister said upon such and such an occasion, he will tell you when the Duke of Monmouth[5] danced at court such a woman was then smitten, another was taken with him at the head of his troop in the Park. In all these important relations, he has ever about the same time received a kind glance or a blow of a fan from some celebrated beauty, mother of the present Lord Such-a-one. If you speak of a young commoner that said a lively thing in the House, he starts up: "He has good blood in his veins; Tom Mirabell begot him. The rogue cheated me in that affair; that young fellow's mother used me more like a dog than any woman I ever made advances to." This way of talking of his very much enlivens the conversation among us of a more sedate turn; and I find there is not one of the company but myself, who rarely speak at all, but speaks of him as of that sort of man who is usually called a well-bred, fine gentleman. To conclude his character, where women are not concerned he is an honest, worthy man.

I cannot tell whether I am to account him whom I am next to speak of as one of our company, for he visits us but seldom; but when he does, it adds to every man else a new enjoyment of himself. He is a clergyman, a very philosophic man, of general learning, great sanctity of life, and the most exact good breeding. He has the misfortune to be of a very weak constitution, and consequently cannot accept of such cares and business as preferments in his function would oblige him to; he is therefore among divines what a chamber-counselor is among lawyers. The probity of his mind and the integrity of his life create him followers, as being eloquent or

3. Eccentrics.
4. Clothes.
5. The illegitimate son of Charles II, the ill-fated Absalom of Dryden's *Absalom and Achitophel.*

loud advances others. He seldom introduces the subject he speaks upon; but we are so far gone in years that he observes, when he is among us, an earnestness to have him fall on some divine topic, which he always treats with much authority, as one who has no interest in this world, as one who is hastening to the object of all his wishes and conceives hope from his decays and infirmities. These are my ordinary companions.

ADDISON: [The Royal Exchange]

The Spectator, No. 69, Saturday, May 19, 1711

> ***Hic segetes, illic veniunt felicius uvae;***
> ***Arborei foetus alibi, atque injussa virescunt***
> ***Gramina. Nonne vides, croceos ut Tmolus odores,***
> ***India mittit ebur, molles sua thura Sabaei?***
> ***At Chalybes nudi ferrum, virosaque Pontus***
> ***Castorea, Eliadum palmas Epirus equarum?***
> ***Continuo has leges aeternaque foedera certis***
> ***Imposuit Natura locis . . .*—Virg.**[1]

There is no place in the town which I so much love to frequent as the Royal Exchange.[2] It gives me a secret satisfaction, and, in some measure, gratifies my vanity, as I am an Englishman, to see so rich an assembly of countrymen and foreigners consulting together upon the private business of mankind, and making this metropolis a kind of emporium for the whole earth. I must confess I look upon high-change[3] to be a great council, in which all considerable nations have their representatives. Factors[4] in the trading world are what ambassadors are in the politic world; they negotiate affairs, conclude treaties, and maintain a good correspondence between those wealthy societies of men that are divided from one another by seas and oceans, or live on the different extremities of a continent. I have often been pleased to hear disputes adjusted between an inhabitant of Japan and an alderman of London, or to see a subject of the Great Mogul[5] entering into a league with one of the Czar of

1. "This ground with Bacchus, that with Ceres suits: / The other loads the trees with happy fruits. / A fourth with grass, unbidden, decks the ground: / Thus Tmolus is with yellow saffron crowned: / India, black ebon and white ivory bears: / And soft Idume weeps her odorous tears. / Thus Pontus sends her beaver stones from far; / And naked Spaniards temper steel for war. / Epirus for the Elean chariot breeds, / In hopes of palms, a race of running steeds. / This is the original contract; these the laws / Imposed by Nature, and by Nature's cause, / On sundry places"—Virgil's *Georgics*, I.54–61, in Dryden's translation.

Virgil's point is that different soils produce different crops, such as grapes (Bacchus) or grain (Ceres). Hence Rome must gather products from the far corners of its empire, just as London, according to Addison, trades with the whole world.

2. The Royal Exchange, built in 1669, was a large, two-story building in the City of London where merchants met to transact business. Inside was a paved court, surrounded by galleries, with a statue of Charles II at the center; upstairs there were nearly 200 shops. Because of the costs and the volume of business, a contemporary called it "perhaps the richest spot of ground in the world."

3. The busiest time of day.

4. Agents or brokers.

5. European name for the emperor of Delhi, who ruled over a large part of northern India.

Muscovy. I am infinitely delighted in mixing with these several ministers of commerce, as they are distinguished by their different walks and different languages; sometimes I am justled among a body of Armenians; sometimes I am lost in a crowd of Jews; and sometimes make one in a group of Dutchmen. I am a Dane, Swede, or Frenchman at different times; or rather fancy myself like the old philosopher, who upon being asked what countryman he was, replied, that he was a citizen of the world.[6]

Though I very frequently visit this busy multitude of people, I am known to nobody there but my friend Sir Andrew, who often smiles upon me as he sees me bustling in the crowd, but at the same time connives at my presence without taking any further notice of me. There is indeed a merchant of Egypt who just knows me by sight, having formerly remitted me some money to Grand Cairo; but as I am not versed in the modern Coptic, our conferences go no further than a bow and a grimace.[7]

This grand scene of business gives me an infinite variety of solid and substantial entertainments. As I am a great lover of mankind, my heart naturally overflows with pleasure at the sight of a prosperous and happy multitude, insomuch that at many public solemnities I cannot forbear expressing my joy with tears that have stolen down my cheeks. For this reason I am wonderfully delighted to see such a body of men thriving in their own private fortunes, and at the same time promoting the public stock; or in other words, raising estates for their own families, by bringing into their country whatever is wanting, and carrying out of it whatever is superfluous.

Nature seems to have taken a peculiar care to disseminate her blessings among the different regions of the world, with an eye to this mutual intercourse and traffic among mankind, that the natives of the several parts of the globe might have a kind of dependence upon one another, and be united together by their common interest. Almost every degree[8] produces something peculiar to it. The food often grows in one country, and the sauce in another. The fruits of Portugal are corrected by the products of Barbadoes; the infusion[9] of a China plant sweetened with the pith of an Indian cane. The Philippic Islands give a flavor to our European bowls. The single dress of a woman of quality is often the product of an hundred climates. The muff and the fan come together from the different ends of the earth. The scarf is sent from the torrid zone, and the tippet from beneath the pole. The brocade petticoat rises out of the mines of Peru, and the diamond necklace out of the bowels of Indostan.[1]

If we consider our own country in its natural prospect, without any of the benefits and advantages of commerce, what a barren

6. A remark variously attributed to Diogenes or Socrates.
7. A wry look.
8. Latitude.
9. Tea. The West Indies, India, and the Philippine Islands all exported sugar.
1. India.

uncomfortable spot of earth falls to our share! Natural historians tell us, that no fruit grows originally among us, besides hips and haws,[2] acorns and pignuts, with other delicacies of the like nature; that our climate of itself, and without the assistances of art, can make no further advances towards a plum than to a sloe, and carries an apple to no greater a perfection than a crab; that our melons, our peaches, our figs, our apricots, and cherries, are strangers among us, imported in different ages, and naturalized in our English gardens; and that they would all degenerate and fall away into the trash of our own country, if they were wholly neglected by the planter, and left to the mercy of our sun and soil. Nor has traffic more enriched our vegetable world, than it has improved the whole face of nature among us. Our ships are laden with the harvest of every climate; our tables are stored with spices, and oils, and wines; our rooms are filled with pyramids of China, and adorned with the workmanship of Japan; our morning's draft comes to us from the remotest corners of the earth; we repair our bodies by the drugs of America, and repose ourselves under Indian canopies. My friend Sir Andrew calls the vineyards of France our gardens; the Spice Islands our hotbeds; the Persians our silk-weavers, and the Chinese our potters. Nature indeed furnishes us with the bare necessaries of life, but traffic gives us a great variety of what is useful, and at the same time supplies us with everything that is convenient and ornamental. Nor is it the least part of this our happiness, that whilst we enjoy the remotest products of the north and south, we are free from those extremities of weather which give them birth; that our eyes are refreshed with the green fields of Britain, at the same time that our palates are feasted with fruits that rise between the tropics.

For these reasons there are not more useful members in a commonwealth than merchants. They knit mankind together in a mutual intercourse of good offices, distribute the gifts of nature, find work for the poor, add wealth to the rich, and magnificence to the great. Our English merchant converts the tin of his own country into gold, and exchanges his wool for rubies. The Mahometans are clothed in our British manufacture, and the inhabitants of the Frozen Zone warmed with the fleeces of our sheep.

When I have been upon the 'Change, I have often fancied one of our old kings standing in person, where he is represented in effigy,[3] and looking down upon the wealthy concourse of people with which that place is every day filled. In this case, how would he be surprised to hear all the languages of Europe spoken in this little spot of his former dominions, and to see so many private men, who in his time would have been the vassals of some powerful baron, negotiating like princes for greater sums of money than were for-

2. Fruits of the rose and hawthorn; like "pignuts" (edible tubers), the "sloe" (fruit of the blackthorn), and the "crab" (crabapple), they are considered barely edible.

3. The galleries of the Exchange held statues of all the British monarchs since the Norman Conquest.

merly to be met with in the royal treasury! Trade, without enlarging the British territories, has given us a kind of additional empire; it has multiplied the number of the rich, made our landed estates infinitely more valuable than they were formerly, and added to them an accession of other estates as valuable as the lands themselves.[4]

ADDISON: [Sir Roger at Church]

The Spectator, No. 112, Monday, July 9, 1711

> Ἀθανάτους μὲν πρῶτα θεοὺς, νόμῳ ὡς διάκειται,
> Τίμα.[1]
>
> —PYTHAGORAS

I am always very well pleased with a country Sunday, and think, if keeping holy the seventh day were only a human institution, it would be the best method that could have been thought of for the polishing and civilizing of mankind. It is certain the country people would soon degenerate into a kind of savages and barbarians were there not such frequent returns of a stated time, in which the whole village meet together with their best faces, and in their cleanliest habits, to converse with one another upon indifferent subjects, hear their duties explained to them, and join together in adoration of the Supreme Being. Sunday clears away the rust of the whole week, not only as it refreshes in their minds the notions of religion, but as it puts both the sexes upon appearing in their most agreeable forms, and exerting all such qualities are apt to give them a figure in the eye of the village. A country fellow distinguishes himself as much in the churchyard as a citizen[2] does upon the 'Change, the whole parish politics being generally discussed in that place either after sermon or before the bell rings.

My friend Sir Roger, being a good churchman, has beautified the inside of his church with several texts of his own choosing; he has likewise given a handsome pulpit cloth, and railed in the communion table at his own expense. He has often told me that, at his coming to his estate, he found his parishioners very irregular; and that, in order to make them kneel and join in the responses, he gave every one of them a hassock and a Common Prayer book, and at the same time employed an itinerant singing master, who goes about the country for that purpose, to instruct them rightly in the tunes of the Psalms; upon which they now very much value themselves, and indeed outdo most of the country churches that I have ever heard.

As Sir Roger is landlord to the whole congregation, he keeps

4. Addison's eulogy of trade became a classic Whig statement of the virtues of a free economy, as opposed to Tory warnings about the way that increasing luxury would destroy the British character.

1. "First worship the immortal gods as custom decrees." The first of the so-called Golden Verses of Pythagoras.

2. A citizen of the City of London, hence commonly a merchant. The " 'Change" is the Exchange in London, where merchants met to transact business.

them in very good order, and will suffer nobody to sleep in it besides himself; for if by chance he has been surprised into a short nap at sermon, upon recovering out of it he stands up and looks about him, and if he sees anybody else nodding, either wakes them himself, or sends his servant to them. Several other of the old knight's particularities break out upon these occasions; sometimes he will be lengthening out a verse in the Singing-Psalms half a minute after the rest of the congregation have done with it; sometimes, when he is pleased with the matter of his devotion, he pronounces "Amen" three or four times to the same prayer; and sometimes stands up when everybody else is upon their knees, to count the congregation, or see if any of his tenants are missing.

I was yesterday very much surprised to hear my old friend, in the midst of the service, calling out to one John Matthews to mind what he was about, and not disturb the congregation. This John Matthews, it seems, is remarkable for being an idle fellow, and at that time was kicking his heels for his diversion. This authority of the knight, though exerted in that odd manner which accompanies him in all circumstances of life, has a very good effect upon the parish, who are not polite[3] enough to see anything ridiculous in his behavior; besides that the general good sense and worthiness of his character makes his friends observe these little singularities as foils that rather set off than blemish his good qualities.

As soon as the sermon is finished, nobody presumes to stir till Sir Roger is gone out of the church. The knight walks down from his seat in the chancel between a double row of his tenants, that stand bowing to him on each side, and every now and then inquires how such an one's wife, or mother, or son, or father do, whom he does not see at church—which is understood as a secret reprimand to the person that is absent.

The chaplain has often told me that upon a catechizing day, when Sir Roger has been pleased with a boy that answers well, he has ordered a Bible to be given him next day for his encouragement, and sometimes accompanies it with a flitch of bacon to his mother. Sir Roger has likewise added five pounds a year to the clerk's place; and, that he may encourage the young fellows to make themselves perfect in the church service, has promised, upon the death of the present incumbent, who is very old, to bestow it according to merit.

The fair understanding between Sir Roger and his chaplain, and their mutual concurrence in doing good, is the more remarkable because the very next village is famous for the differences and contentions that rise between the parson and the squire, who live in a perpetual state of war. The parson is always preaching at the squire, and the squire, to be revenged on the parson, never comes to church. The squire has made all his tenants atheists and tithe-stealers;[4]

3. Refined.
4. Farmers who cheat the parson to whom they are bound to pay annual tithes (i.e., a tenth of the produce of their farms).

while the parson instructs them every Sunday in the dignity of his order, and insinuates to them almost in every sermon that he is a better man than his patron. In short, matters are come to such an extremity that the squire has not said his prayers either in public or private this half year; and that the parson threatens him, if he does not mend his manners, to pray for him in the face of the whole congregation.

Feuds of this nature, though too frequent in the country, are very fatal to the ordinary people, who are so used to be dazzled with riches that they pay as much deference to the understanding of a man of an estate as of a man of learning; and are very hardly brought to regard any truth, how important soever it may be, that is preached to them, when they know there are several men of five hundred a year who do not believe it.

ADDISON: [Sir Roger at the Assizes[1]]

The Spectator, No. 122, Friday, July 20, 1711

Comes jucundus in via pro vehiculo est.[2]
—PUBLILIUS SYRUS, *Fragments*

A man's first care should be to avoid the reproaches of his own heart; his next, to escape the censures of the world. If the last interferes with the former, it ought to be entirely neglected; but otherwise there cannot be a greater satisfaction to an honest mind than to see those approbations which it gives itself seconded by the applauses of the public. A man is more sure of his conduct when the verdict which he passes upon his own behavior is thus warranted and confirmed by the opinion of all that know him.

My worthy friend Sir Roger is one of those who is not only at peace within himself but beloved and esteemed by all about him. He receives a suitable tribute for his universal benevolence to mankind in the returns of affection and good will which are paid him by everyone that lives within his neighborhood. I lately met with two or three odd instances of that general respect which is shown to the good old knight. He would needs carry Will Wimble[3] and myself with him to the county assizes. As we were upon the road, Will Wimble joined a couple of plain men who rid before us, and conversed with them for some time, during which my friend Sir Roger acquainted me with their characters.

"The first of them," says he, "that has a spaniel by his side, is a yeoman[4] of about an hundred pounds a year, an honest man.

1. Periodic sessions of superior courts held by visiting judges throughout England.
2. "An agreeable companion upon the road is as good as a coach." Addison substituted *jucundus* for the original's *facundus* ("eloquent").
3. A character used by Addison to illustrate the injury done to younger sons of gentlemen by not educating them for a profession or to trade.
4. A man who owns and cultivates a small estate. His rank is just below that of gentleman.

He is just within the Game Act,[5] and qualified to kill an hare or a pheasant. He knocks down a dinner with his gun twice or thrice a week; and by that means lives much cheaper than those who have not so good an estate as himself. He would be a good neighbor if he did not destroy so many partridges; in short he is a very sensible man, shoots flying,[6] and has been several times foreman of the petty jury.[7]

"The other that rides along with him is Tom Touchy, a fellow famous for taking the law of everybody. There is not one in the town where he lives that he has not sued at a quarter sessions. The rogue had once the impudence to go to law with the widow.[8] His head is full of costs, damages, and ejectments; he plagued a couple of honest gentlemen so long for a trespass in breaking one of his hedges, till he was forced to sell the ground it enclosed to defray the charges of the prosecution. His father left him fourscore pounds a year, but he has cast[9] and been cast so often that he is not now worth thirty. I suppose he is going upon the old business of the willow tree."

As Sir Roger was giving me this account of Tom Touchy, Will Wimble and his two companions stopped short till we came up to them. After having paid their respects to Sir Roger, Will told him that Mr. Touchy and he must appeal to him upon a dispute that arose between them. Will, it seems, had been giving his fellow travelers an account of his angling one day in such a hole; when Tom Touchy, instead of hearing out his story, told him that Mr. Such-an-one, if he pleased, might take the law of him for fishing in that part of the river. My friend Sir Roger heard them both, upon a round trot;[1] and after having paused some time, told them, with an air of a man who would not give his judgment rashly, "that much might be said on both sides." They were neither of them dissatisfied with the knight's determination, because neither of them found himself in the wrong by it. Upon which we made the best of our way to the assizes.

The court was sat before Sir Roger came; but notwithstanding all the justices had taken their places upon the bench, they made room for the old knight at the head of them; who, for his reputation in the country, took occasion to whisper in the judge's ear that he was glad his lordship had met with so much good weather in his circuit. I was listening to the proceedings of the court with much attention, and infinitely pleased with that great appearance and solemnity which so properly accompanies such a public administration of our laws, when, after about an hour's sitting, I observed to my great surprise, in the midst of a trial, that my friend Sir Roger

5. This law restricted the right to kill game to owners of land whose annual income was £100 or more.
6. A true sportsman, he shoots birds only when they are on the wing.
7. The trial jury of twelve in an ordinary civil or criminal case.
8. The woman whom Sir Roger had loved in his youth. She is frequently mentioned in essays that deal with the old knight.
9. Defeated in a lawsuit.
1. While trotting briskly.

was getting up to speak. I was in some pain for him, till I found he had acquitted himself of two or three sentences, with a look of much business and great intrepidity.

Upon his first rising the court was hushed, and a general whisper ran among the country people that Sir Roger was up. The speech he made was so little to the purpose that I shall not trouble my readers with an account of it; and I believe was not so much designed by the knight himself to inform the court, as to give him a figure in my eye, and keep up his credit in the country.

I was highly delighted, when the court rose, to see the gentlemen of the country gathering about my old friend, and striving who should compliment him most; at the same time that the ordinary people gazed upon him at a distance, not a little admiring his courage that was not afraid to speak to the judge.

In our return home we met with a very odd accident which I cannot forbear relating, because it shows how desirous all who know Sir Roger are of giving him marks of their esteem. When we were arrived upon the verge of his estate, we stopped at a little inn to rest ourselves and our horses. The man of the house had, it seems, been formerly a servant in the knight's family; and to do honor to his old master, had some time since, unknown to Sir Roger, put him up in a signpost before the door; so that the knight's head had hung out upon the road about a week before he himself knew anything of the matter. As soon as Sir Roger was acquainted with it, finding that his servant's indiscretion proceeded wholly from affection and good will, he only told him that he had made him too high a compliment; and when the fellow seemed to think that could hardly be, added, with a more decisive look, that it was too great an honor for any man under a duke; but told him at the same time that it might be altered with a very few touches, and that he himself would be at the charge of it. Accordingly they got a painter, by the knight's directions, to add a pair of whiskers to the face, and by a little aggravation of the features to change it into the Saracen's Head. I should not have known this story had not the innkeeper, upon Sir Roger's alighting, told him in my hearing that his honor's head was brought back last night with the alterations that he had ordered to be made in it. Upon this my friend, with his usual cheerfulness, related the particulars above-mentioned, and ordered the head to be brought into the room. I could not forbear discovering greater expressions of mirth than ordinary upon the appearance of this monstrous face, under which, notwithstanding it was made to frown and stare in a most extraordinary manner, I could still discover a distant resemblance of my old friend. Sir Roger, upon seeing me laugh, desired me to tell him truly if I thought it possible for people to know him in that disguise. I at first kept my usual silence; but upon the knight's conjuring me to tell him whether it was not still more like himself than a Saracen, I composed my countenance in the best manner I could, and replied that much might be said on both sides.

These several adventures, with the knight's behavior in them, gave me as pleasant a day as ever I met with in any of my travels.

The Periodical Essay: Ideas

ADDISON: [The Aims of the Spectator]

The Spectator, No. 10, Monday, March 12, 1711

Non aliter quam qui adverso vix flumine lembum
Remigiis subigit, si bracchia forte remisit,
Atque illum in præceps prono rapit alveus amni.[1]
—VIRGIL, *Georgics* I.201–3

It is with much satisfaction that I hear this great city inquiring day by day after these my papers, and receiving my morning lectures with a becoming seriousness and attention. My publisher tells me that there are already three thousand of them distributed every day. So that if I allow twenty readers to every paper, which I look upon as a modest computation, I may reckon about three-score thousand disciples in London and Westminster, who I hope will take care to distinguish themselves from the thoughtless herd of their ignorant and unattentive brethren. Since I have raised to myself so great an audience, I shall spare no pains to make their instruction agreeable, and their diversion useful. For which reasons I shall endeavor to enliven morality with wit, and to temper wit with morality, that my readers may, if possible, both ways find their account in the speculation of the day. And to the end that their virtue and discretion may not be short, transient, intermitting starts of thought, I have resolved to refresh their memories from day to day, till I have recovered them out of that desperate state of vice and folly into which the age is fallen. The mind that lies fallow but a single day sprouts up in follies that are only to be killed by a constant and assiduous culture. It was said of Socrates that he brought philosophy down from heaven, to inhabit among men; and I shall be ambitious to have it said of me that I have brought philosophy out of closets and libraries, schools and colleges, to dwell in clubs and assemblies, at tea tables and in coffeehouses.

I would therefore in a very particular manner recommend these my speculations to all well-regulated families that set apart an hour in every morning for tea and bread and butter; and would earnestly advise them for their good to order this paper to be punctually

1. "Like him whose oars can hardly force his boat against the current, if by chance he relaxes his arms, the boat sweeps him headlong down the steam."

served up, and to be looked upon as a part of the tea equipage.

Sir Francis Bacon observes that a well-written book, compared with its rivals and antagonists, is like Moses' serpent, that immediately swallowed up and devoured those of the Egyptians.[2] I shall not be so vain as to think that where *The Spectator* appears the other public prints will vanish; but shall leave it to my reader's consideration whether is it not much better to be let into the knowledge of one's self, than to hear what passes in Muscovy or Poland; and to amuse ourselves with such writings as tend to the wearing out of ignorance, passion, and prejudice, than such as naturally conduce to inflame hatreds, and make enmities irreconcilable?

In the next place, I would recommend this paper to the daily perusal of those gentlemen whom I cannot but consider as my good brothers and allies, I mean the fraternity of spectators, who live in the world without having anything to do in it; and either by the affluence of their fortunes or laziness of their dispositions have no other business with the rest of mankind but to look upon them. Under this class of men are comprehended all contemplative tradesmen, titular physicians, fellows of the Royal Society, Templars[3] that are not given to be contentious, and statesmen that are out of business; in short, everyone that considers the world as a theater, and desires to form a right judgment of those who are the actors on it.

There is another set of men that I must likewise lay a claim to, whom I have lately called the blanks of society, as being altogether unfurnished with ideas, till the business and conversation of the day has supplied them. I have often considered these poor souls with an eye of great commiseration, when I have heard them asking the first man they have met with, whether there was any news stirring? and by that means gathering together materials for thinking. These needy persons do not know what to talk of till about twelve o'clock in the morning; for by that time they are pretty good judges of the weather, know which way the wind sits, and whether the Dutch mail be come in.[4] As they lie at the mercy of the first man they meet, and are grave or impertinent all the day long, according to the notions which they have imbibed in the morning, I would earnestly entreat them not to stir out of their chambers till they have read this paper, and do promise them that I will daily instil into them such sound and wholesome sentiments as shall

2. In *The Advancement of Learning*, II, "To the King." But it was the rod of Aaron, not of Moses, that turned into a devouring serpent (Exodus vii. 10–12).

3. Lawyers or students of the law who live or have their offices ("chambers") in the Middle or Inner Temple, one of the Inns of Court.

4. Bringing the latest war news.

have a good effect on their conversation for the ensuing twelve hours.

But there are none to whom this paper will be more useful than to the female world. I have often thought there has not been sufficient pains taken in finding out proper employments and diversions for the fair ones. Their amusements seem contrived for them, rather as they are women, than as they are reasonable creatures; and are more adapted to the sex than to the species. The toilet is their great scene of business, and the right adjusting of their hair the principal employment of their lives. The sorting of a suit of ribbons[5] is reckoned a very good morning's work; and if they make an excursion to a mercer's[6] or a toyshop, so great a fatigue makes them unfit for anything else all the day after. Their more serious occupations are sewing and embroidery, and their greatest drudgery the preparation of jellies and sweetmeats. This, I say, is the state of ordinary women; though I know there are multitudes of those of a more elevated life and conversation, that move in an exalted sphere of knowledge and virtue, that join all the beauties of the mind to the ornaments of dress, and inspire a kind of awe and respect, as well as love, into their male beholders. I hope to increase the number of these by publishing this daily paper, which I shall always endeavor to make an innocent if not an improving entertainment, and by that means at least divert the minds of my female readers from greater trifles. At the same time, as I would fain give some finishing touches to those which are already the most beautiful pieces in human nature, I shall endeavor to point all those imperfections that are the blemishes, as well as those virtues which are the embellishments, of the sex. In the meanwhile I hope these my gentle readers, who have so much time on their hands, will not grudge throwing away a quarter of an hour in a day on this paper, since they may do it without any hindrance to business.

I know several of my friends and well-wishers are in great pain for me, lest I should not be able to keep up the spirit of a paper which I oblige myself to furnish every day: but to make them easy in this particular, I will promise them faithfully to give it over as soon as I grow dull. This I know will be matter of great raillery to the small wits; who will frequently put me in mind of my promise, desire me to keep my word, assure me that it is high time to give over, with many other little pleasantries of the like nature, which men of a little smart genius cannot forbear throwing out against their best friends, when they have such a handle given them

5. A set of ribbons to be worn together.
6. A seller of such small-wares as tape, ribbon, fringe. A "toyshop" is a shop where baubles and trifles are sold.

of being witty. But let them remember that I do hereby enter my caveat against this piece of raillery.

ADDISON: [Wit: True, False, Mixed]

The Spectator, No. 62, Friday, May 11, 1711

Scribendi recte sapere est et principium et fons.[1]
—HORACE, *Ars Poetica* 309

Mr. Locke has an admirable reflection upon the difference of wit and judgment, whereby he endeavors to show the reason why they are not always the talents of the same person. His words are as follow: "And hence, perhaps, may be given some reason of that common observation, that men who have a great deal of wit and prompt memories, have not always the clearest judgment, or deepest reason. For wit lying most in the assemblage of ideas, and putting those together with quickness and variety, wherein can be found any resemblance or congruity, thereby to make up pleasant pictures and agreeable visions in the fancy; judgment, on the contrary, lies quite on the other side, in separating carefully one from another, ideas wherein can be found the least difference, thereby to avoid being misled by similitude, and by affinity to take one thing for another. This is a way of proceeding quite contrary to metaphor and allusion; wherein, for the most part, lies that entertainment and pleasantry of wit which strikes so lively on the fancy, and is therefore so acceptable to all people."[2]

This is, I think, the best and most philosophical account that I have ever met with of wit, which generally, though not always, consists in such a resemblance and congruity of ideas as this author mentions. I shall only add to it, by way of explanation, that every resemblance of ideas is not that which we call wit, unless it be such an one that gives delight and surprise to the reader. These two properties seem essential to wit, more particularly the last of them. In order therefore that the resemblance in the ideas be wit, it is necessary that the ideas should not lie too near one another in the nature of things; for where the likeness is obvious, it gives no surprise. To compare one man's singing to that of another, or to represent the whiteness of any object by that of milk and snow, or the variety of its colors by those of the rainbow, cannot be called wit, unless, besides this obvious resemblance, there be some further congruity discovered in the two ideas that is capable of giving the reader some surprise. Thus when a poet tells us, the bosom of his mistress is as white as snow, there is no wit in the comparison; but when he adds, with a sigh, that it is as cold too, it then grows into wit. Every reader's memory may supply him with innumerable

1. "Discernment is the source and fount of writing well."

2. John Locke, *Essay Concerning Human Understanding* (1690) II. 2.

instances of the same nature. For this reason, the similitudes in heroic poets, who endeavor rather to fill the mind with great conceptions, than to divert it with such as are new and surprising, have seldom anything in them that can be called wit. Mr. Locke's account of wit, with this short explanation, comprehends most of the species of wit, as metaphors, similtudes, allegories, enigmas, mottoes, parables, fables, dreams, visions, dramatic writings, burlesque, and all the methods of allusion:[3] as there are many other pieces of wit (how remote soever they may appear at first sight from the foregoing description) which upon examination will be found to agree with it.

As true wit generally consists in this resemblance and congruity of ideas, false wit chiefly consists in the resemblance and congruity sometimes of single letters, as in anagrams, chronograms,[4] lipograms, and acrostics; sometimes of syllables, as in echoes and doggerel rhymes; sometimes of words, as in puns and quibbles; and sometimes of whole sentences or poems, cast into the figures of eggs, axes, or altars:[5] nay, some carry the notion of wit so far, as to ascribe it even to external mimicry; and to look upon a man as an ingenious person, that can resemble the tone, posture, or face of another.

As true wit consists in the resemblance of ideas, and false wit in the resemblance of words, according to the foregoing instances; there is another kind of wit which consists partly in the resemblance of ideas, and partly in the resemblance of words; which for distinction's sake I shall call mixed wit. This kind of wit is that which abounds in Cowley, more than in any author that ever wrote. Mr. Waller has likewise a great deal of it. Mr. Dryden is very sparing in it. Milton had a genius much above it. Spenser is in the same class with Milton. The Italians, even in their epic poetry, are full of it. Monsieur Boileau, who formed himself upon the ancient poets, has everywhere rejected it with scorn. If we look after mixed wit among the Greek writers, we shall find it nowhere but in the epigrammatists. There are indeed some strokes of it in the little poem ascribed to Musaeus,[6] which by that, as well as many other marks, betrays itself to be a modern composition. If we look into the Latin writers, we find none of this mixed wit in Virgil, Lucretius, or Catullus; very little in Horace, but a great deal of it in Ovid, and scarce anything else in Martial.

Out of the innumerable branches of mixed wit, I shall choose one instance which may be met with in all the writers of this class. The passion of love in its nature has been thought to resemble fire; for which reason the words fire and flame are made use of to signify

3. Word-play; more broadly, any covert or symbolic use of language.
4. Phrase in which certain letters express a date; e.g., "LorD HaVe MerCIe Vpon Vs": the capital letters, in Roman numerals, add up to 1666, the *annus mirabilis* of fire, plague, and war. "Lipogram": a composition omitting all words that contain a certain letter or letters.
5. See *The Altar* and *Easter Wings* by George Herbert.
6. A poem called *Hero and Leander*, attributed to Musaeus, an ancient Greek poet, was first published in 1635.

love. The witty poets therefore have taken an advantage from the doubtful meaning of the word fire, to make an infinite number of witticisms. Cowley observing the cold regard of his mistress's eyes,[7] and at the same time their power of producing love in him, considers them as burning-glasses made of ice; and finding himself able to live in the greatest extremities of love, concludes the torrid zone to be habitable. When his mistress has read his letter written in juice of lemon by holding it to the fire, he desires her to read it over a second time by love's flames. When she weeps, he wishes it were inward heat that distilled those drops from the limbec.[8] When she is absent he is beyond eighty, that is, thirty degrees nearer the pole than when she is with him. His ambitious love is a fire that naturally mounts upwards; his happy love is the beams of heaven, and his unhappy love flames of hell. When it does not let him sleep, it is a flame that sends up no smoke; when it is opposed by counsel and advice, it is a fire that rages the more by the wind's blowing upon it. Upon the dying of a tree in which he had cut his loves, he observes that his written flames had burned up and withered the tree. When he resolves to give over his passion, he tells us that one burnt like him for ever dreads the fire. His heart is an Aetna, that instead of Vulcan's shop[9] encloses Cupid's forge in it. His endeavoring to drown his love in wine, is throwing oil upon the fire. He would insinuate to his mistress, that the fire of love, like that of the sun (which produces so many living creatures) should not only warm but beget. Love in another place cooks pleasure at his fire. Sometimes the poet's heart is frozen in every breast, and sometimes scorched in every eye. Sometimes he is drowned in tears, and burnt in love, like a ship set on fire in the middle of the sea.

The reader may observe in every one of these instances, that the poet mixes the qualities of fire with those of love; and in the same sentence speaking of it both as a passion, and as real fire, surprises the reader with those seeming resemblances or contradictions that make up all the wit in this kind of writing. Mixed wit therefore is a composition of pun and true wit, and is more or less perfect as the resemblance lies in the ideas or in the words: its foundations are laid partly in falsehood and partly in truth: reason puts in her claim for one half of it, and extravagance for the other. The only province therefore for this kind of wit, is epigram, or those little occasional poems that in their own nature are nothing else but a tissue of epigrams. I cannot conclude this head of mixed wit, without owning that the admirable poet out of whom I have taken the examples of it, had as much true wit as any author that ever writ; and indeed all other talents of an extraordinary genius.

7. In *The Mistress, or Several Copies of Love-Verses* (1647).
8. Alembic, an apparatus used in distilling.
9. Mount Etna was supposed to be the workshop of Vulcan, the Roman god of fire and metal-working.

It may be expected, since I am upon this subject, that I should take notice of Mr. Dryden's definition of wit; which, with all the deference that is due to the judgment of so great a man, is not so properly a definition of wit, as of good writing in general. Wit, as he defines it, is "a propriety of words and thoughts adapted to the subject."[1] If this be a true definition of wit, I am apt to think that Euclid[2] was the greatest wit that ever set pen to paper: it is certain there never was a greater propriety of words and thoughts adapted to the subject, than what that author has made use of in his elements. I shall only appeal to my reader, if this definition agrees with any notion he has of wit: if it be a true one, I am sure Mr. Dryden was not only a better poet, but a greater wit than Mr. Cowley; and Virgil a much more facetious man than either Ovid or Martial.

Bouhours,[3] whom I look upon to be the most penetrating of all the French critics, has taken pains to show that it is impossible for any thought to be beautiful which is not just, and has not its foundation in the nature of things; that the basis of all wit is truth; and that no thought can be valuable, of which good sense is not the groundwork. Boileau[4] has endeavored to inculcate the same notion in several parts of his writings, both in prose and verse. This is that natural way of writing, that beautiful simplicity, which we so much admire in the compositions of the ancients; and which nobody deviates from, but those who want strength of genius to make a thought shine in its own natural beauties. Poets who want this strength of genius to give that majestic simplicity to nature, which we so much admire in the works of the ancients, are forced to hunt after foreign ornaments, and not to let any piece of wit of what kind soever escape them. I look upon these writers as Goths in poetry, who, like those in architecture, not being able to come up to the beautiful simplicity of the old Greeks and Romans, have endeavored to supply its place with all the extravagances of an irregular fancy. Mr. Dryden makes a very handsome observation on Ovid's writing a letter from Dido to Aeneas, in the following words:[5] "Ovid" (says he, speaking of Virgil's fiction of Dido and Aeneas) "takes it up after him, even in the same age, and makes an ancient heroine of Virgil's new-created Dido; dictates a letter for her just before her death to the ungrateful fugitive; and, very unluckily for himself, is for measuring a sword with a man so much superior in force to him, on the same subject. I think I may be judge of this, because I have translated both. The famous author of the Art of Love[6] has nothing of his own; he borrows all from a greater master

1. Adapted from Dryden's *Apology for Heroic Poetry* (1677).
2. Hellenic mathematician (ca. 300 B.C.)
3. Dominique Bouhours (1628–1702), who wrote an *Art of Criticism*.
4. Nicholas Boileau (1636–1711), a famous French neoclassicist, wrote a verse *Art of Poetry* (1674) translated by Dryden.
5. From Dryden's Dedication to his translation of the *Aeneid* (1697).
6. Ovid.

in his own profession, and, which is worse, improves nothing which he finds: nature fails him, and being forced to his old shift, he has recourse to witticism. This passes indeed with his soft admirers, and gives him the preference to Virgil in their esteem."

Were not I supported by so great an authority as that of Mr. Dryden, I should not venture to observe, that the taste of most of our English poets, as well as readers, is extremely Gothic. He quotes Monsieur Segrais[7] for a threefold distinction of the readers of poetry: in the first of which he comprehends the rabble of readers, whom he does not treat as such with regard to their quality,[8] but to their numbers and the coarseness of their taste. His words are as follow: "Segrais has distinguished the readers of poetry, according to their capacity of judging, into three classes. [He might have said the same of writers too, if he had pleased.] In the lowest form he places those whom he calls *les petits esprits,*[9] such things as are our upper-gallery audience in a play-house; who like nothing but the husk and rind of wit, prefer a quibble, a conceit, an epigram, before solid sense and elegant expression: these are mob-readers. If Virgil and Martial stood for parliament-men, we know already who would carry it.[1] But though they make the greatest appearance in the field, and cry the loudest, the best on 't is they are but a sort of French Huguenots, or Dutch boors,[2] brought over in herds, but not naturalized; who have not lands of two pounds per annum in Parnassus, and therefore are not privileged to poll.[3] Their authors are of the same level, fit to represent them on a mountebank's stage, or to be masters of the ceremonies in a bear-garden: yet these are they who have the most admirers. But it often happens, to their mortification, that as their readers improve their stock of sense (as they may by reading better books, and by conversation with men of judgment), they soon forsake them."

I must not dismiss this subject without observing, that as Mr. Locke in the passage above-mentioned has discovered the most fruitful source of wit, so there is another of a quite contrary nature to it, which does likewise branch itself out into several kinds. For not only the resemblance but the opposition of ideas does very often produce wit; as I could show in several little points, turns, and antitheses, that I may possibly enlarge upon in some future speculation.[4]

7. Jean Regnauld de Segrais (1624-1701), who had translated Virgil into French, is quoted extensively by Dryden.
8. Social standing.
9. The small-minded.
1. That is, the witty Martial would easily defeat the weighty Virgil in an election.
2. Peasants. Huguenots and the Dutch were the largest class of immigrants in England. "On 't": that one can say.
3. Vote. Only freeholders worth two pounds a year could go to the polls; and these readers of little taste hold no land in Parnassus (where the Muses live).
4. For such an "enlargement," see Samuel Johnson's remarks on wit in the *Life of Cowley*.

ADDISON: [*Paradise Lost:* General Critical Remarks]

The Spectator, No. 267, Saturday, January 5, 1712

Cedite Romani scriptores, cedite Graii.[1]
—PROPERTIUS, *Elegies* II.xxxiv.65

There is nothing in nature so irksome as general discourses, especially when they turn chiefly upon words. For this reason I shall waive the discussion of that point which was started some years since, Whether Milton's *Paradise Lost* may be called an heroic poem? Those who will not give it that title may call it (if they please) a *divine poem.* It will be sufficient to its perfection, if it has in it all the beauties of the highest kind of poetry; and as for those who allege it is not an heroic poem, they advance no more to the diminution of it, than if they should say Adam is not Aeneas, nor Eve Helen.

I shall therefore examine it by the rules of epic poetry,[2] and see whether it falls short of the *Iliad* or *Aeneid,* in the beauties which are essential to that kind of writing. The first thing to be considered in an epic poem is the fable,[3] which is perfect or imperfect, according as the action which it relates is more or less so. This action should have three qualifications in it. First, it should be but one action. Secondly, it should be an entire action; and thirdly, it should be a great action. To consider the action of the *Iliad, Aeneid,* and *Paradise Lost,* in these three several lights. Homer to preserve the unity of his action hastens into the midst of things, as Horace has observed:[4] had he gone up to Leda's egg, or begun much later, even at the rape of Helen, or the investing of Troy, it is manifest that the story of the poem would have been a series of several actions. He therefore opens his poem with the discord of his princes, and with great art interweaves in the several succeeding parts of it, an account of everything material which relates to them and had passed before that fatal dissension. After the same manner Aeneas makes his first appearance in the Tyrrhene seas,[5] and within sight of Italy, because the action proposed to be celebrated was that of

1. "Yield place, ye Roman and ye Grecian writers, yield."
2. The rules for the conduct of an epic poem, derived out of the poems of Homer and Virgil, the *Poetics* of Aristotle, and the *Ars Poetica* of Horace, had been given their most systematic and complete statement in Père René Le Bossu's *Traité du poème épique* (1675), which was immediately absorbed into English critical thought. Addison writes of *Paradise Lost* with Le Bossu well in sight, but he is no slavish disciple.
3. The plot of a drama or poem.
4. *Ars Poetica,* 147–49. Helen, whose abduction from her husband Menelaus by the Trojan prince Paris brought on the Trojan War, was the daughter of Leda, who was visited by Zeus in the guise of a swan.
5. That part of the Mediterranean Sea west of Italy, bounded by the islands of Sicily, Sardinia, and Corsica.

his settling himself in Latium.[6] But because it was necessary for the reader to know what had happened to him in the taking of Troy, and in the preceding parts of his voyage, Virgil makes his hero relate it by way of episode[7] in the second and third books of the *Aeneid.* The contents of both which books come before those of the first book in the thread of the story, though for preserving of this unity of action, they follow them in the disposition of the poem. Milton, in imitation of these two great poets, opens his *Paradise Lost* with an infernal council plotting the fall of man, which is the action he proposed to celebrate; and as for those great action which preceded, in point of time, the battle of the angels, and the creation of the world (which would have entirely destroyed the unity of his principal action, had he related them in the same order that they happened), he cast them into the fifth, sixth, and seventh books, by way of episode to this noble poem.

Aristotle himself allows that Homer has nothing to boast of as to the unity of his fable, though at the same time that great critic and philosopher endeavors to palliate this imperfection in the Greek poet, by imputing it in some measure to the very nature of an epic poem. Some have been of opinion that the *Aeneid* labors also in this particular, and has episodes which may be looked upon as excrescences rather than as parts of the action. On the contrary, the poem which we have now under our consideration hath no other episodes than such as naturally arise from the subject, and yet is filled with such a multitude of astonishing incidents that it gives us at the same time a pleasure of the greatest variety, and of the greatest simplicity.

I must observe also that as Virgil, in the poem which was designed to celebrate the original of the Roman Empire, has described the birth of its great rival, the Carthaginian commonwealth, Milton with the like art in his poem on the Fall of Man, has related the fall of those angels who are his professed enemies. Besides the many other beauties in such an episode, its running parallel with the great action of the poem hinders it from breaking the unity so much as another episode would have done that had not so great an affinity with the principal subject. In short, this is the same kind of beauty which the critics admire in the *Spanish Friar, or The Double Discovery,*[8] where the two different plots look like counterparts and copies of one another.

The second qualification required in the action of an epic poem is, that it should be an *entire* action. An action is entire when it is complete in all its parts; or as Aristotle describes it, when it con-

6. The kingdom of the Latini, where Aeneas was hospitably received when he landed at the mouth of the Tiber. He married Lavinia, the daughter of King Latinus, and later ruled the kingdom.

7. An incidental narration or digression in an epic which arises naturally from the subject but is separable from the main action.

8. A comedy by Dryden.

sists of a beginning, a middle, and an end. Nothing should go before it, be intermixed with it, or follow after it, that is not related to it. As on the contrary, no single step should be omitted in that just and regular process which it must be supposed to take from its original to its consummation. Thus we see the anger of Achilles in its birth, its continuance, and effects; and Aeneas's settlement in Italy, carried on through all the oppositions in his way to it both by sea and land. The action in Milton excels (I think) both the former in this particular: we see it contrived in hell, executed upon earth, and punished by heaven. The parts of it are told in the most distinct manner, and grow out of one another in the most natural method.

The third qualification of an epic poem is its *greatness*. The anger of Achilles was of such consequence that it embroiled the kings of Greece, destroyed the heroes of Troy, and engaged all the gods in factions. Aeneas's settlement in Italy produced the Caesars, and gave birth to the Roman Empire. Milton's subject was still greater than either of the former; it does not determine the fate of single persons or nations, but of a whole species. The united powers of hell are joined together for the destruction of mankind, which they effected in part, and would have completed, had not Omnipotence itself interposed. The principal actors are man in his greatest perfection, and woman in her highest beauty. Their enemies are the fallen angels: the Messiah their friend, and the Almighty their protector. In short, everything that is great in the whole circle of being, whether within the verge of nature, or out of it, has a proper part assigned it in this noble poem.

In poetry, as in architecture, not only the whole, but the principal members, and every part of them, should be great. I will not presume to say, that the book of games in the *Aeneid*, or that in the *Iliad*, are not of this nature, nor to reprehend Virgil's simile of the top, and many other of the same nature in the *Iliad*, as liable to any censure in this particular; but I think we may say, without derogating from those wonderful performances, that there is an unquestionable magnificence in every part of *Paradise Lost*, and indeed a much greater than could have been formed upon any pagan system.

But Aristotle, by the greatness of the action, does not only mean that it should be great in its nature, but also in its duration, or in other words, that it should have a due length in it, as well as what we properly call greatness. The just measure of the kind of magnitude, he explains by the following similitude. An animal, no bigger than a mite, cannot appear perfect to the eye, because the sight takes it in at once, and has only a confused idea of the whole, and not a distinct idea of all its parts: if on the contrary you should suppose an animal of ten thousand furlongs in length, the eye would be so filled with a single part of it, that it could not give the mind an idea of the whole. What these animals are to the eye, a very short or a very long action would be to the memory. The first would be, as it were, lost and swallowed up by it, and the other difficult to be contained in it. Homer and Virgil have shown their principal art in this particular; the action of the *Iliad,* and that of the *Aeneid,* were in themselves exceeding short, but are so beautifully extended and diversified by the invention of episodes, and the machinery[9] of gods, with the like poetical ornaments, that they make up an agreeable story sufficient to employ the memory without overcharging it. Milton's action is enriched with such a variety of circumstances that I have taken as much pleasure in reading the contents of his books as in the best invented story I ever met with. It is possible that the traditions on which the *Iliad* and *Aeneid* were built had more circumstances in them than the history of the Fall of Man, as it is related in Scripture. Besides it was easier for Homer and Virgil to dash the truth with fiction, as they were in no danger of offending the religion of their country by it. But as for Milton, he had not only a very few circumstances upon which to raise his poem, but was also obliged to proceed with the greatest caution in everything that he added out of his own invention. And, indeed, notwithstanding all the restraints he was under, he has filled his story with so many surprising incidents, which bear so close an analogy with what is delivered in Holy Writ, that it is capable of pleasing the most delicate reader, without giving offense to the most scrupulous.

The modern critics have collected from several hints in the *Iliad* and *Aeneid* the space of time which is taken up by the action of each of those poems; but as a great part of Milton's story was transacted in regions that lie out of the reach of the sun and the sphere of day, it is impossible to gratify the reader with such a calculation, which indeed would be more curious than instructive; none of the critics, either ancient or modern, having laid down rules to circumscribe the action of an epic poem with any determined number of years, days, or hours.

This Piece of Criticism on Milton's Paradise Lost *shall be carried on in the following Saturdays' papers.*[1]

9. The technical term (from *deus ex machina*) in critical theory for the supernatural beings who oversee and intervene in the affairs of the characters in epic poems.

1. The series on *Paradise Lost* contains eighteen essays.

ADDISON: [On the Scale of Being]

The Spectator, No. 519, October 25, 1712

inde hominum pecudumque genus, vitaeque volantum,
et quae marmoreo fert monstra sub aequore pontus.[1]
—VIRGIL, *Aeneid* VI.728–29

Though there is a great deal of pleasure in contemplating the material world, by which I mean that system of bodies into which nature has so curiously wrought the mass of dead matter, with the several relations which those bodies bear to one another, there is still, methinks, something more wonderful and surprising in contemplations on the world of life, by which I mean all those animals with which every part of the universe is furnished. The material world is only the shell of the universe: the world of life are its inhabitants.

If we consider those parts of the material world which lie the nearest to us and are, therefore, subject to our observations and inquiries, it is amazing to consider the infinity of animals with which it is stocked. Every part of matter is peopled. Every green leaf swarms with inhabitants. There is scarce a single humor in the body of a man, or of any other animal, in which our glasses do not discover myriads of living creatures. The surface of animals is also covered with other animals which are, in the same manner, the basis of other animals that live upon it; nay, we find in the most solid bodies, as in marble itself, innumerable cells and cavities that are crowded with such imperceptible inhabitants as are too little for the naked eye to discover. On the other hand if we look into the more bulky parts of nature, we see the seas, lakes, and rivers teeming with numberless kinds of living creatures. We find every mountain and marsh, wilderness and wood, plentifully stocked with birds and beasts, and every part of matter affording proper necessaries and conveniences for the livelihood of multitudes which inhabit it.

The author of *The Plurality of Worlds*[2] draws a very good argument upon this consideration for the peopling of every planet, as indeed it seems very probable from the analogy of reason that, if no part of matter which we are acquainted with lies waste and useless, those great bodies, which are at such a distance from us, should not be desert and unpeopled, but rather that they should be furnished with beings adapted to their respective situations.

Existence is a blessing to those beings only which are endowed

1. "Thence the race of men and beasts, the life of flying creatures, and the monsters that ocean bears beneath her smooth surface."
2. Bernard de Fontenelle (1657–1757). This delightful book, a series of dialogues between a scientist and a countess concerning the possibility of other inhabited planets and the new astrophysics in general, was published in 1686 in France and beautifully translated by Joseph Glanvill in 1688.

with perception and is, in a manner, thrown away upon dead matter any further than as it is subservient to beings which are conscious of their existence. Accordingly we find from the bodies which lie under observation that matter is only made as the basis and support of animals and that there is no more of the one than what is necessary for the existence of the other.

Infinite Goodness is of so communicative a nature that it seems to delight in the conferring of existence upon every degree of perceptive being. As this is a speculation which I have often pursued with great pleasure to myself, I shall enlarge farther upon it, by considering that part of the scale of beings which comes within our knowledge.

There are some living creatures which are raised but just above dead matter. To mention only that species of shellfish, which are formed in the fashion of a cone, that grow to the surface of several rocks and immediately die upon their being severed from the place where they grow. There are many other creatures but one remove from these, which have no other sense besides that of feeling and taste. Others have still an additional one of hearing; others of smell, and others of sight. It is wonderful to observe by what a gradual progress the world of life advances through a prodigious variety of species before a creature is formed that is complete in all its senses; and, even among these, there is such a different degree of perfection in the sense which one animal enjoys, beyond what appears in another, that, though the sense in different animals be distinguished by the same common denomination, it seems almost of a different nature. If after this we look into the several inward perfections of cunning and sagacity, or what we generally call instinct, we find them rising after the same manner, imperceptibly, one above another, and receiving additional improvements, according to the species in which they are implanted. This progress in nature is so very gradual that the most perfect of an inferior species comes very near to the most imperfect of that which is immediately above it.

The exuberant and overflowing goodness of the Supreme Being, whose mercy extends to all his works, is plainly seen, as I have before hinted, from his having made so very little matter, at least what falls within our knowledge, that does not swarm with life. Nor is his goodness less seen in the diversity than in the multitude of living creatures. Had he only made one species of animals, none of the rest would have enjoyed the happiness of existence; he has, therefore, *specified* in his creation every degree of life, every capacity of being. The whole chasm in nature, from a plant to a man, is filled up with diverse kinds of creatures, rising one over another by such a gentle and easy ascent that the little transitions and deviations from one species to another are almost insensible. This intermediate space is so well husbanded and managed that there is scarce a degree of perception which does not appear in some one part of the world of life. Is the goodness or wisdom of the Divine Being more manifested in this his proceeding?

There is a consequence, besides those I have already mentioned, which seems very naturally deducible from the foregoing considerations. If the scale of being rises by such a regular progress so high as man, we may by a parity of reason suppose that it still proceeds gradually through those beings which are of a superior nature to him, since there is an infinitely greater space and room for different degrees of perfection between the Supreme Being and man than between man and the most despicable insect. This consequence of so great a variety of beings which are superior to us, from that variety which is inferior to us, is made by Mr. Locke[3] in a passage which I shall here set down after having premised that, notwithstanding there is such infinite room between man and his Maker for the creative power to exert itself in, it is impossible that it should ever be filled up, since there will be still an infinite gap or distance between the highest created being and the Power which produced him:

> That there should be more species of intelligent creatures above us than there are of sensible and material below, is probable to me from hence: That in all the visible corporeal world we see no chasms or no gaps. All quite down from us, the descent is by easy steps and a continued series of things that, in each remove, differ very little from the other. There are fishes that have wings and are not strangers to the airy region; and there are some birds that are inhabitants of the water, whose blood is cold as fishes and their flesh so like in taste that the scrupulous are allowed them on fish days. There are animals so near of kin both to birds and beasts that they are in the middle between both: amphibious animals link the terrestrial and aquatic together; seals live at land and at sea, and porpoises have the warm blood and entrails of a hog, not to mention what is confidently reported of mermaids or seamen. There are some brutes that seem to have as much knowledge and reason as some that are called men; and the animal and vegetable kingdoms are so nearly joined that, if you will take the lowest of one and the highest of the other, there will scarce be perceived any great difference between them; and so on, till we come to the lowest and the most inorganical parts of matter, we shall find everywhere that the several species are linked together and differ but in almost insensible degrees. And when we consider the infinite power and wisdom of the Maker, we have reason to think that it is suitable to the magnificent harmony of the universe and the great design and infinite goodness of the Architect, that the species of creatures should also, by gentle degrees,

3. John Locke, in his *Essay Concerning Human Understanding* (1690) III.vi. 12.

ascend upward from us toward his infinite perfection, as we see they gradually descend from us downward; which, if it be probable, we have reason to be persuaded that there are far more species of creatures above us than there are beneath, we being in degrees of perfection much more remote from the infinite being of God than we are from the lowest state of being and that which approaches nearest to nothing. And yet of all those distinct species we have no clear distinct ideas.

In this system of being, there is no creature so wonderful in its nature, and which so much deserves our particular attention, as man, who fills up the middle space between the animal and intellectual nature, the visible and invisible world, and is that link in the chain of beings which has been often termed the *nexus utriusque mundi*.[4] So that he who, in one respect, is associated with angels and archangels, may look upon a Being of infinite perfection as his father, and the highest order of spirits as his brethren, and may, in another respect, say to corruption, "Thou art my father," and to the worm, "Thou art my mother and my sister."[5]

4. "The binding together of both worlds."

5. Job xvii.14.

ALEXANDER POPE

(1688–1744)

1711: *Essay on Criticism*.
1712: First version of *The Rape of the Lock*.
1713–26: Translating Homer, editing Shakespeare.
1728: The *Dunciad* begins Pope's career as major verse satirist.
1733–34: The *Essay on Man* begins Pope's career as ethical and philosophical poet.

Pope is the only important writer of his generation who was solely a man of letters. Since he could not, as a Roman Catholic, attend a university, vote, or hold public office, he was excluded from the sort of patronage which was freely bestowed by statesmen on most writers during the reign of Anne. This disadvantage he turned into a positive good, for the translation of Homer's *Iliad* and *Odyssey*, which he undertook for profit as well as for fame, gave him ample means to live the life of an independent suburban gentleman. After 1718 he lived hospitably in his villa by the Thames at Twickenham (then pronounced *Twit'nam*), entertaining his friends and converting his five acres of land into a diminutive landscape garden. Almost exactly a century earlier, Shakespeare had earned enough to retire to a country estate at Stratford—but he had been an actor-manager as well as a playwright; Pope, therefore, was the first writer to demonstrate that literature alone could be a gainful profession.

Ill health plagued Pope almost from birth. Delicate as a child, he was early stunted and deformed by tuberculosis of the spine. His father, a well-to-do London merchant, retired from business in the year of the poet's birth, and about 1700 acquired a small property at Binfield in Windsor Forest. In rural surroundings, as the boy's health improved, he early acquired his lifelong taste for natural beauty and for gardening. There he completed by wide reading the desultory schooling that both his ill health and his religion had made inevitable, and, encouraged by his father, he began also to develop his precocious talent for poetry. The removal to Binfield, then, was in every way advantageous. But Pope was never to enjoy good health: in later life he was troubled by violent headaches, and he suffered from easily exacerbated nerves. This neurotic irritability was a price he had to pay for the sensitive and ardent temperament that helped make him one of our greatest poets. Because of it, he both hated and loved intensely; because of it his responsiveness to beauty in all its forms was unusually acute.

Pope's first striking success as a poet was the *Essay on Criticism* (1711), which earned him the fame of Addison's approval and the notoriety of an intemperate personal attack from the critic John Dennis, who was angered by a casual reference to himself in the poem. *The Rape of the Lock*, both in its original shorter version of 1712 and in its more elaborate version of 1714, established the author of the *Essay on Criticism* as a master not only of metrics and of language, but also of witty, urbane satire. In the earlier work, Pope had excelled all his predecessors in writing a didactic poem after the example of Horace; in the later, he had written the most brilliant mock epic in the language. But there was another vein in Pope's youthful poetry, much of which, concerned as it is with natural beauty and love, reveals a temperament that in a later poet might have been called "Romantic." The *Pastorals* (1709), Pope's first publication, and *Windsor Forest* (1713; much of it was written earlier) are essentially nature poems, abounding in visual imagery and descriptive passages of ideally ordered nature. They remind us that Pope was an amateur painter who delighted in the beauty of external nature, as well as in the artificial beauty of the world of *The Rape of the Lock*. The *Elegy to the Memory of an Unfortunate Lady*, published in the collected poems of 1717, presents the high heroics of romantic love. Looking back to his early poems, Pope said that he had wandered "in Fancy's maze." And even the long task of translating Homer, the "dull duty" of editing Shakespeare, and, in middle age, his preoccupation with ethical and satirical poetry did not extinguish this side of Pope's nature and art. He learned to subordinate, but he did not cease to use, this sensitive awareness of visual beauty in his later poetry.

Pope's early poetry brought him to the attention of literary men, with whom he began to associate in the masculine world of coffeehouse and tavern. His fragile health never permitted him to live the rakish life that he would have liked, but it did not prevent his enjoying the company of some of the most distinguished men of letters of the time. Between 1706 and 1711 he came to know, among many others, William Congreve, William Walsh, the critic and poet, and Richard Steele and Joseph Addison, who, after 1709, were two of the most admired writers of the day. As it happened, all these men were Whigs. Pope was probably indifferent to politics at this time, or at least he could readily ignore politics in the excitement of taking his place among the leading wits of the town. But after the fall of the Whigs in 1710, and the formation of the Tory government under Robert Harley (later Earl of Oxford) and Henry St. John (later Viscount Bolingbroke) party loyalties bred bitterness among the wits as among the politicians.

By 1712 Pope had made the acquaintance of another group of writers, all Tories, who soon became his intimate friends: Jonathan Swift, by then the close associate of Harley and St. John and the principal propagandist for their policies; Dr. John Arbuthnot, physician to the queen, a learned scientist, a wit of the first quality, and a man of deep humanity and utter integrity; John Gay, the poet, who in 1728 was to produce the *Beggar's Opera*, the greatest theatrical success of the century; and Thomas Parnell, a poet of some distinction, who died prematurely in 1718. It was among these men that Pope was to find his lifelong friends; and it was through them that he became the friend and admirer of Oxford, and later the intimate of Bolingbroke. As he grew more intimate with his new circle, he began to drift away from Addison and his earlier friends.

In 1714 this group, at the instigation of Pope, formed a club which was to cooperate in a scheme for satirizing all sorts of false learning and pedantry in philosophy, science, and other branches of knowledge. They were joined by the Earl of Oxford, who attended as often as business permitted. The friends proposed to write jointly the biography of a learned fool whom they named Martinus Scriblerus (Martin the Scribbler), whose life and opinions would be a running commentary on whatever they considered the abuses of learning and the follies of the learned. The death of the queen in August, 1714, brought the venture to a premature end, but not before some amusing episodes had been invented, as the published (probably very much rewritten) version of the *Memoirs of Martinus Scriblerus* (1741), makes plain. The real importance of the club, however, is that it fostered a satiric temper which was to find unexpected expression in such mature works of the friends as *Gulliver's Travels*, the *Dunciad*, and even, perhaps, the *Beggar's Opera*.

"The life of a wit is a warfare on earth," said Pope, generalizing from his own experience. His very success as a poet (and his astonishing precocity brought him success very early) made enemies among the less talented and consequently envious writers, who were to plague him in pamphlets, verse satires, and squibs in the journals throughout his entire literary career. He was to be attacked for his writings, his religion, and his physical deformity. Though he smarted under the jibes of his detractors, he was a fighter who struck back, always giving better than he got. The common notion that he was a malicious, treacherous, venomous man, motivated merely by personal vanity and malice, is the creation of his enemies, and can be accepted by no one who reads the vicious attacks on him published from 1711 to the end of his life. Usually he was not the aggressor, but he never forgot an insult or forgave an injury, and sooner or later he took his revenge—sometimes, it must be admitted, in rather unsavory ways. But he was loved and trusted by many of the most honorable, eminent, and gifted men of his time, and with only a few exceptions (aside from politicians), the objects of his satire are people who would be forgotten today had they not been so humiliatingly preserved to posterity.

Pope's literary warfare began in 1713, when he announced his intention of translating the *Iliad* and sought, with the support of his friends, subscribers to a de luxe edition of the work. Subscribers came in droves, but Pope had enemies as well. The Whig writers who surrounded Addison at Button's Coffee House did all they could through anonymous attacks to hinder the success of the venture, and even (with Addison's knowledge and perhaps encouragement) announced a rival translation by Thomas Tickell, one of Addison's Oxford friends. The eventual success of the first published installment of his *Iliad* in 1715 did not obliterate Pope's just resentment against Addison and his "little senate"; and this resentment found expression in the damaging portrait of Addison (under the name of Atticus), which, years after it was written, was included in Pope's *Epistle to Dr. Arbuthnot* (1735), lines 193–214. The not unjustified attacks on Pope's edition of Shakespeare (1725), especially those by the learned Shakespeare scholar Lewis Theobald (Pope always spelled and pronounced the name "Tibbald" in his satires), led to Theobald's appearance as king of the dunces in the *Dunciad* (1728). In this impressive poem Pope stigmatized his literary enemies as agents of all that he disliked and feared in the literary tendencies of his time—the vulgarization of taste and the arts consequent on the rapid growth of the reading public, the development of journalism, magazines, and other popular and cheap publications, which spread scandal, sensationalism, and political partisanship—in short the new commercial spirit of the nation, which was corrupting not only the arts, but, as Pope saw it, the national life itself.

In the 1730's Pope moved on to philosophical, ethical, and political subjects in the *Essay on Man*, the *Epistles to Several Persons*, and the *Imitations of Horace*. The reigns of George I and George II appeared to him, as to Swift and other Tories, a period of rapid moral, political, and cultural deterioration. The agents of decay seemed in one way or another related to the spread of moneyed (as opposed to landed) wealth, which accounted for the political corruption encouraged by Sir Robert Walpole and the court party, and the increasing influence in all aspects of the national life of a vulgar class of *nouveaux riches*. Pope assumed the role of the champion of traditional civilization: of right reason, humanistic learning, sound art, good taste, and public virtue. For him the supreme value was order —cosmic, political, social, aesthetic—which he saw (or believed he saw) threatened on all sides. It was fortunate that most of his enemies seem to have been designed by nature to illustrate various degrees of unreason, pedantry, bad art, vulgar taste, and, at best, indifferent morals. Personal malice edged his satire, but his art elevated his unhappy victims into symbols of Georgian barbarism.

The principal obstacle between the modern reader and Pope's satires is that they seem to require a vast amount of particular knowledge about a long-vanished age. This is not entirely the case. Although a certain amount of social and political history is helpful, the whole body of Pope's satire can be read and enjoyed without much biographical information. The satirist traditionally deals in generally prevalent evils and generally observable human types, and this is true of Pope, even when he named actual individuals. Usually in the late satires, as in the earlier *Rape*, he used fictional or type names, although he most often had an individual in mind —Sappho, Atossa, Atticus, Sporus; and when he named individuals (as he consistently did in the *Dunciad* and occasionally elsewhere), his purpose was to raise his victims to the bad eminence of typifying some sort of obliquity. Nor need we be concerned with whether or not the moral character of the speaker of the satires is identical with that of Alexander Pope of Twickenham. Pope created a clearly defined person (the "I" of the satires) with the character and personality of one who could freely censure the age. This fictional or semi-fictional figure is the detached observer, somewhat removed from City, town, and court, the centers of corruption; he is the friend of virtuous men, whose friendship for him testifies to his integrity; he is fond of peace, country life, the arts, morality, and truth, and he detests their opposites which flourish in the great world. In such an age, Pope implies, it is impossible for such a man—honest, truthful, blunt—not to write satire. Where even political power and law are subject to the corruptor wealth, no weapon remains to the guardian of the public weal but the "sacred weapon" of satire. This is the satirist whom Pope creates, and to move from him to the private character of Pope is to move away from the poems.

Something must be said about Pope's versification, and the varied styles of his poems. It takes only a little familiarity with his writings to discover how wrong has been the conventional judgment that they are artificial, mechanical, and monotonous. From first to last, the permanent elements of Pope's poetic style are his remarkable rhythmic variety, despite the apparently rigid metrical unit—the heroic couplet—in which he wrote; the precision of meaning and the harmony (or the expressive disharmony, when necessary) of his language; and his superb discipline, which enables him at his characteristic best to achieve maximum conciseness together with maximum complexity. Something of Pope's metrical variety and verbal harmony can be observed in even so short a passage as lines 71–76 of the pastoral *Summer* (1709), lines so lyrical that Handel set them to music. In the passage quoted below (as also in the following quotation), only those rhetorical stresses which distort the normal iambic flow of the verse have been marked; internal pauses within the line are indicated by single and double bars, alliteration and assonance by italics.

> Óh d*é*ign to visit our *f*ors*a*ken *s*e*a*ts,
> The mossy *fou*ntains || and the *green* retr*ea*ts!
> Where'er yóu wálk || cóol *gá*les shall *f*an the gl*a*de,
> Trées whére yóu sít || shall cro*w*d into a sh*a*de:
> Where'er yóu tréad || the bl*u*shing *f*lo*w*ers shall rise,
> And all thíngs *fló*urish where yóu t*ú*rn your eyes.

Pope has attained metrical variety here by the free substitution of trochees and spondees for the normal iambs; he has achieved rhythmic variety by arranging phrases and clauses (units of syntax and logic) of different lengths within single lines and couplets, so that the passage moves with the sinuous fluency of thought and feeling, not the mechanical regularity of a metronome; and he has not only chosen musical combinations of words, but has also subtly modulated the harmony of the passage by unobtrusive patterns of alliteration and assonance.

Contrast with this pastoral passage lines 16–25 of the *Epilogue to the Satires, Dialogue II* (1738), in which Pope is not making music, but is imitating actual conversation so realistically that the metrical pattern and the integrity of the couplet and individual line seem to be destroyed (though in fact they are very much present). The poet-satirist is engaged in a dialogue with a friend who warns him that his satire is too personal, indeed mere libel. The poet is speaking:

> Yé státesmen, | priests of one religion all!
> Yé trádesmen vile || in army, court, or hall!
> Yé réverend atheists. || F. Scandal! | name them, | Who?
>   P. Why that's the thing you bid me not to do.
> Whó stárved a sister, || who foreswore a debt,
> Í néver named; || the town's inquiring yet.
> The poisoning dame— | F. Yóu méan— | P. I don't— | F. Yóu dó.
>   P. Sée, nów Í kéep the secret, || and nót yóu!
> The bribing statesman— | F. Hóld, || tóo hígh you go.
>   P. The bribed elector— || F. There you stoop tóo lów.

In such a passage the language and rhythms of poetry merge with the language and rhythms of impassioned living speech.

A fine example of Pope's ability to derive the maximum of meaning from the most economic use of language and image is the description of the manor house in which lives old Cotta, the miser (*Epistle to Lord Bathurst*, lines 187–196):

> Like some lone Chartreuse stands the good old Hall,
> Silence without, and fasts within the wall;
> No raftered roofs with dance and tabor sound,
> No noontide bell invites the country round;
> Tenants with sighs the smokeless towers survey,
> And turn the unwilling steeds another way;
> Benighted wanderers, the forest o'er,
> Curse the saved candle and unopening door;
> While the gaunt mastiff growling at the gate,
> Affrights the beggar whom he longs to eat.

The first couplet of this passage, which associates the "Hall," symbol of English rural hospitality, with the Grande Chartreuse, the monastery in the French Alps, which, though a place of "silence" and "fasts" for the monks, afforded food and shelter to all travelers, clashes forcefully with the dismal details of Cotta's miserly dwelling; and the meaning of the scene is concentrated in the grotesque image of the last couplet: the half-starved watchdog and the frightened beggar confronting each other in mutual hunger.

But there is another sort of variety within Pope's work as a whole which derives from the poet's respect for the idea that the different kinds of literature have their different and appropriate styles. Thus the *Essay on Criticism*, an informal discussion of literary theory, is written, like Horace's *Ars Poetica*, a similarly didactic poem, in a plain style, relatively devoid of imagery and eloquence, and in the easy language of well-bred talk. *The Rape of the Lock*, being "a heroi-comical poem" (that is, a comic poem that treats trivial material in an epic style), employs the lofty heroic language that Dryden had perfected in his translation of Virgil, and introduces amusing parodies of passages in *Paradise Lost*; parodies raised to truly Miltonic sublimity and complexity by the conclusion of the *Dunciad*. *Eloisa to Abelard* renders the brooding, passionate voice of its heroine in a declamatory language, given to sudden outbursts and shifts of tone, that recalls the stage. The grave epistles that make up the *Essay on Man*, a philosophical discussion of such majestic themes as the Creator and his creation, the universe, and the nature of man, of human society, and of happiness, are written in a stately forensic language and tone and constantly employ the traditional rhetoric figures. The *Imitations of Horace*, and, above all, the *Epistle to Dr. Arbuthnot*, his finest poem "in the Horatian way," reveal Pope's final mastery of the plain style of Horace's epistles and satires and justify his image of himself as the heir of the Roman poet. In short no other poet of the century can equal Pope in the range of his materials, the diversity of his poetic styles, and the sheer mastery of the poet's craft.

An Essay on Criticism[1]

Part I

'Tis hard to say, if greater want of skill
Appear in writing or in judging ill;
But of the two less dangerous is the offense
To tire our patience than mislead our sense.
Some few in that, but numbers err in this,
Ten censure[2] wrong for one who writes amiss;

1. There is no pleasanter introduction to the canons of taste in the English Augustan age than Pope's *Essay on Criticism*. As Addison said in his review in *Spectator* 253, it assembles the "most known and most received observations on the subject of literature and criticism." Pope was attempting to do for his time what Horace, in his *Ars Poetica*, and what Nicolas Boileau (French poet of the age of Louis XIV), in his *L'Art Poëtique*, had done for theirs. Horace is not only one of Pope's instructors in the principles of criticism; he is also Pope's model in this poem, especially in the simple, conversational language, the tone of well-bred ease, and the deliberately plain style of the *Ars Poetica*—all of which qualities Pope reproduces.
In framing his critical creed, Pope did not try for novelty: he drew from the standard writings of classical antiquity, especially from the *Ars Poetica*, and the *Institutio Oratoria* of the Roman rhetorician Quintilian; from French critical theory of the preceding century; and from Ben Jonson's *Timber, or Discoveries* and the prefaces of John Dryden. He wished merely to give to generally accepted doctrines pleasing and memorable expression. Here one meets the key words of neoclassical criticism: *wit, Nature, ancients, rules, genius. Wit* in the poem is a word of many meanings—a clever remark, or the man who makes it; a conceit; liveliness of mind; inventiveness; fancy; genius; a genius; poetry itself, among others. *Nature* is an equally ambiguous word, meaning not "things out there," or "the outdoors," but most importantly that which is representative, universal, permanent in human experience as opposed to the idiosyncratic, the individual, the temporary. In line 21, the word comes close to meaning "intuitive knowledge." In line 52, it means that half-personified power manifested in the cosmic order, which in its modes of working is a model for art. The reverence felt by most Augustans for the works of the great writers of ancient Greece and Rome raised the question how far the authority of these *ancients* extended. Were their works to be received as models to be conscientiously imitated? Were the *rules* received from them or deducible from their works to be accepted as prescriptive laws or merely convenient guides? Was individual *genius* to be bound by what has been conventionally held to be *Nature*, by the authority of the *ancients*, and by the legalistic pedantry of *rules?* Or could it go its own way?
In Part I of the *Essay* Pope constructs a harmonious system in which he effects a compromise among all these conflicting forces—a compromise which is typically 18th century in spirit. Part II analyzes the causes of faulty criticism. Part III characterizes the good critic and praises the great critics of the past.

2. Judge.

A fool might once himself alone expose,
Now one in verse makes many more in prose.
'Tis with our judgments as our watches, none
Go just alike, yet each believes his own.
In poets as true genius is but rare,
True taste as seldom is the critic's share;
Both must alike from Heaven derive their light,
These born to judge, as well as those to write.
Let such teach others who themselves excel,
And censure freely who have written well.
Authors are partial to their wit, 'tis true,
But are not critics to their judgment too?
Yet if we look more closely, we shall find
Most have the seeds of judgment in their mind:
Nature affords at least a glimmering light;
The lines, though touched but faintly, are drawn right.
But as the slightest sketch, if justly traced,
Is by ill coloring but the more disgraced,
So by false learning is good sense defaced:
Some are bewildered in the maze of schools,
And some made coxcombs[3] Nature meant but fools.
In search of wit these lose their common sense,
And then turn critics in their own defense:
Each burns alike, who can, or cannot write,
Or with a rival's or an eunuch's spite.
All fools have still an itching to deride,
And fain would be upon the laughing side.
If Maevius[4] scribble in Apollo's spite,
There are who judge still worse than he can write.
Some have at first for wits, then poets passed,
Turned critics next, and proved plain fools at last.
Some neither can for wits nor critics pass,
As heavy mules are neither horse nor ass.
Those half-learn'd witlings, numerous in our isle,
As half-formed insects on the banks of Nile;[5]
Unfinished things, one knows not what to call,
Their generation's so equivocal:
To tell[6] them would a hundred tongues require,
Or one vain wit's, that might a hundred tire.
But you who seek to give and merit fame,
And justly bear a critic's noble name,
Be sure yourself and your own reach to know,
How far your genius, taste, and learning go;
Launch not beyond your depth, but be discreet,
And mark that point where sense and dullness meet.
Nature to all things fixed the limits fit,
And wisely curbed proud man's pretending wit.
As on the land while here the ocean gains,

3. Superficial pretenders to learning.
4. A silly poet alluded to contemptuously by Virgil in *Eclogue III* and by Horace in *Epode X*.
5. The ancients believed that many forms of life were spontaneously generated in the fertile mud of the Nile.
6. Reckon, count.

In other parts it leaves wide sandy plains;
Thus in the soul while memory prevails,
The solid power of understanding fails;
Where beams of warm imagination play,
The memory's soft figures melt away.
One science[7] only will one genius fit,
So vast is art, so narrow human wit.
Not only bounded to peculiar arts,
But oft in those confined to single parts.
Like kings we lose the conquests gained before,
By vain ambition still to make them more;
Each might his several province well command,
Would all but stoop to what they understand.
  First follow Nature, and your judgment frame
By her just standard, which is still the same;
Unerring Nature, still divinely bright,
One clear, unchanged, and universal light,
Life, force, and beauty must to all impart,
At once the source, and end, and test of art.
Art from that fund each just supply provides,
Works without show, and without pomp presides.
In some fair body thus the informing soul
With spirits feeds, with vigor fills the whole,
Each motion guides, and every nerve sustains;
Itself unseen, but in the effects remains.
Some, to whom Heaven in wit has been profuse,
Want as much more to turn it to its use;
For wit and judgment often are at strife,
Though meant each other's aid, like man and wife.
'Tis more to guide than spur the Muse's steed,
Restrain his fury than provoke his speed;
The wingéd courser,[8] like a generous horse,
Shows most true mettle when you check his course.
  Those rules of old discovered, not devised,
Are Nature still, but Nature methodized;
Nature, like liberty, is but restrained
By the same laws which first herself ordained.
  Hear how learn'd Greece her useful rules indites,
When to repress and when indulge our flights:
High on Parnassus' top her sons she showed,
And pointed out those arduous paths they trod;
Held from afar, aloft, the immortal prize,
And urged the rest by equal steps to rise.
Just precepts thus from great examples given,
She drew from them what they derived from Heaven.
The generous critic fanned the poet's fire,
And taught the world with reason to admire.
Then criticism the Muse's handmaid proved,

7. Branch of learning.
8. Pegasus, associated with the Muses and poetic inspiration; "generous": spirited, highly bred.

To dress her charms, and make her more beloved:
But following wits from that intention strayed,
Who could not win the mistress, wooed the maid;
Against the poets their own arms they turned,
Sure to hate most the men from whom they learned.
So modern 'pothecaries, taught the art
By doctors' bills[9] to play the doctor's part,
Bold in the practice of mistaken rules,
Prescribe, apply, and call their masters fools.
Some on the leaves of ancient authors prey,
Nor time nor moths e'er spoiled so much as they.
Some dryly plain, without invention's aid,
Write dull receipts[10] how poems may be made.
These leave the sense their learning to display,
And those explain the meaning quite away.
  You then whose judgment the right course would steer,
Know well each ancient's proper character;
His fable,[1] subject, scope in every page;
Religion, country, genius of his age:
Without all these at once before your eyes,
Cavil you may, but never criticize.
Be Homer's works your study and delight,
Read them by day, and meditate by night;
Thence form your judgment, thence your maxims bring,
And trace the Muses upward to their spring.
Still with itself compared, his text peruse;
And let your comment be the Mantuan Muse.[2]
  When first young Maro in his boundless mind
A work to outlast immortal Rome designed,
Perhaps he seemed above the critic's law,
And but from Nature's fountains scorned to draw;
But when to examine every part he came,
Nature and Homer were, he found, the same.
Convinced, amazed, he checks the bold design,
And rules as strict his labored work confine
As if the Stagirite[3] o'erlooked each line.
Learn hence for ancient rules a just esteem;
To copy Nature is to copy them.
  Some beauties yet no precepts can declare,
For there's a happiness as well as care.[4]

9. Prescriptions.

10. Formulas for preparing a dish; recipes. Pope himself wrote an amusing burlesque *Receipt to Make an Epic Poem*, first published in the *Guardian* 78 (1713).

1. Plot or story of a play or poem, "Scope": aim or purpose.

2. Virgil, the "young Maro" of the following line, was born in a village adjacent to Mantua in Italy; hence "Mantuan Muse." His epic, the *Aeneid*, was modeled on Homer's *Iliad* and *Odyssey* and was considered to be a refinement on the Greek poems. Thus it could be thought of as a commentary ("comment") on Homer's poems.

3. Aristotle, native of Stagira, from whose *Poetics* later critics formulated strict rules for writing tragedy and the epic.

4. I.e., no rules ("precepts") can explain ("declare") some beautiful effects in a work of art which can be the result only of inspiration or good luck ("happiness"), not of painstaking labor ("care").

Music resembles poetry, in each
Are nameless graces which no methods teach,
And which a master hand alone can reach.
If, where the rules not far enough extend
(Since rules were made but to promote their end)
Some lucky license answers to the full
The intent proposed, that license is a rule.
Thus Pegasus, a nearer way to take,
May boldly deviate from the common track.
From vulgar bounds with brave disorder part,
And snatch a grace beyond the reach of art,
Which without passing through the judgment, gains
The heart, and all its end at once attains.
In prospects thus, some objects please our eyes,
Which out of Nature's common order rise,
The shapeless rock, or hanging precipice.
Great wits sometimes may gloriously offend,
And rise to faults true critics dare not mend;
But though the ancients thus their rules invade
(As kings dispense with laws themselves have made)
Moderns, beware! or if you must offend
Against the precept, ne'er transgress its end;
Let it be seldom, and compelled by need;
And have at least their precedent to plead.
The critic else proceeds without remorse,
Seizes your fame, and puts his laws in force.
  I know there are, to whose presumptuous thoughts
Those freer beauties, even in them, seem faults.[5]
Some figures monstrous and misshaped appear,
Considered singly, or beheld too near,
Which, but proportioned to their light or place,
Due distance reconciles to form and grace.
A prudent chief not always must display
His powers in equal ranks and fair array,
But with the occasion and the place comply,
Conceal his force, nay seem sometimes to fly.
Those oft are stratagems which errors seem,
Nor is it Homer nods, but we that dream.
  Still green with bays each ancient altar stands
Above the reach of sacrilegious hands,
Secure from flames, from envy's fiercer rage,
Destructive war, and all-involving age.
See, from each clime the learn'd their incense bring!
Here in all tongues consenting[6] paeans ring!
In praise so just let every voice be joined,[7]
And fill the general chorus of mankind.
Hail, bards triumphant! born in happier days,
Immortal heirs of universal praise!

5. Pronounced *fawts*.
6. Agreeing, concurring.
7. Pronounced *jined*.

Whose honors with increase of ages grow,
As streams roll down, enlarging as they flow;
Nations unborn your mighty names shall sound,
And worlds applaud that must not yet be found!
Oh, may some spark of your celestial fire,
The last, the meanest of your sons inspire
(That on weak wings, from far, pursues your flights,
Glows while he reads, but trembles as he writes)
To teach vain wits a science little known,
To admire superior sense, and doubt their own!

Part II

Of all the causes which conspire to blind
Man's erring judgment, and misguide the mind,
What the weak head with strongest bias rules,
Is pride, the never-failing vice of fools.
Whatever Nature has in worth denied,
She gives in large recruits[8] of needful pride;
For as in bodies, thus in souls, we find
What wants in blood and spirits swelled with wind:
Pride, where wit fails, steps in to our defense,
And fills up all the mighty void of sense.
If once right reason drives that cloud away,
Truth breaks upon us with resistless day.
Trust not yourself: but your defects to know,
Make use of every friend—and every foe.
A little learning is a dangerous thing;
Drink deep, or taste not the Pierian spring.[9]
There shallow draughts intoxicate the brain,
And drinking largely sobers us again.
Fired at first sight with what the Muse imparts,
In fearless youth we tempt[1] the heights of arts,
While from the bounded level of our mind
Short views we take, nor see the lengths behind;
But more advanced, behold with strange surprise
New distant scenes of endless science rise!
So pleased at first the towering Alps we try,
Mount o'er the vales, and seem to tread the sky,
The eternal snows appear already past,
And the first clouds and mountains seem the last;
But, those attained, we tremble to survey
The growing labors of the lengthened way,
The increasing prospect tires our wandering eyes,
Hills peep o'er hills, and Alps on Alps arise!
A perfect judge will read each work of wit
With the same spirit that its author writ:
Survey the whole, nor seek slight faults to find
Where Nature moves, and rapture warms the mind;

8. Supplies.
9. The spring in Pieria on Mt. Olympus, sacred to the Muses.
1. Attempt.

Nor lose, for that malignant dull delight,
The generous pleasure to be charmed with wit.
But in such lays as neither ebb nor flow,
Correctly cold, and regularly low,
That, shunning faults, one quiet tenor keep,
We cannot blame indeed—but we may sleep.
In wit, as nature, what affects our hearts
Is not the exactness of peculiar parts;
'Tis not a lip, or eye, we beauty call,
But the joint force and full result of all.
Thus when we view some well-proportioned dome
(The world's just wonder, and even thine, O Rome![2]),
No single parts unequally surprise,
All comes united to the admiring eyes:
No monstrous height, or breadth, or length appear;
The whole at once is bold and regular.

Whoever thinks a faultless piece to see,
Thinks what ne'er was, nor is, nor e'er shall be.
In every work regard the writer's end,
Since none can compass more than they intend;
And if the means be just, the conduct true,
Applause, in spite of trivial faults, is due.
As men of breeding, sometimes men of wit,
To avoid great errors must the less commit,
Neglect the rules each verbal critic lays,
For not to know some trifles is a praise.
Most critics, fond of some subservient art,
Still make the whole depend upon a part:
They talk of principles, but notions prize,
And all to one loved folly sacrifice.

Once on a time La Mancha's knight,[3] they say,
A certain bard encountering on the way,
Discoursed in terms as just, with looks as sage,
As e'er could Dennis,[4] of the Grecian stage;
Concluding all were desperate sots and fools
Who durst depart from Aristotle's rules.
Our author, happy in a judge so nice,
Produced his play, and begged the knight's advice;
Made him observe the subject and the plot,
The manners, passions, unities; what not?
All which exact to rule were brought about,
Were but a combat in the lists left out.
"What! leave the combat out?" exclaims the knight.
"Yes, or we must renounce the Stagirite."
"Not so, by Heaven!" he answers in a rage,

2. The dome of St. Peter's, designed by Michelangelo.
3. Don Quixote. The story comes not from Cervantes' novel, but from a spurious sequel to it by Don Alonzo Fernandez de Avellaneda.
4. John Dennis (1657–1734), though one of the leading critics of the time, was frequently ridiculed by the wits for his irascibility and his rather solemn pomposity. Pope apparently did not know Dennis personally, but his jibe at him in Part III of this poem incurred the critic's lasting animosity.

"Knights, squires, and steeds must enter on the stage."
"So vast a throng the stage can ne'er contain."
"Then build a new, or act it in a plain."
Thus critics of less judgment than caprice,
Curious,[5] not knowing, not exact, but nice,
Form short ideas, and offend in arts
(As most in manners), by a love to parts.
Some to conceit[6] alone their taste confine,
And glittering thoughts struck out at every line;
Pleased with a work where nothing's just or fit,
One glaring chaos and wild heap of wit.
Poets, like painters, thus unskilled to trace
The naked nature and the living grace,
With gold and jewels cover every part,
And hide with ornaments their want of art.
True wit is Nature to advantage dressed,
What oft was thought, but ne'er so well expressed;
Something whose truth convinced at sight we find,
That gives us back the image of our mind.
As shades more sweetly recommend the light,
So modest plainness sets off sprightly wit;
For works may have more wit than does them good,
As bodies perish through excess of blood.
Others for language all their care express,
And value books, as women men, for dress.
Their praise is still—the style is excellent;
The sense they humbly take upon contént.[7]
Words are like leaves; and where they most abound,
Much fruit of sense beneath is rarely found.
False eloquence, like the prismatic glass,
Its gaudy colors spreads on every place;[8]
The face of Nature we no more survey,
All glares alike, without distinction gay.
But true expression, like the unchanging sun,
Clears and improves whate'er it shines upon;
It gilds all objects, but it alters none.
Expression is the dress of thought, and still
Appears more decent as more suitable.
A vile conceit in pompous words expressed
Is like a clown[9] in regal purple dressed:
For different styles with different subjects sort,
As several garbs with country, town, and court.
Some by old words to fame have made pretense,
Ancients in phrase, mere moderns in their sense.
Such labored nothings, in so strange a style,
Amaze the unlearn'd, and make the learned smile;

5. Laboriously careful. "Nice": minutely accurate, over refined.
6. Pointed wit, ingenuity and extravagance, or affectation in the use of figures, especially similes and metaphors.
7. Mere acquiescence.
8. A very up-to-date scientific reference. Newton's *Optics*, which treated of the prism and the spectrum, had been published in 1704, though his theories had been known earlier.
9. Rustic, boor.

Unlucky as Fungoso[1] in the play,
These sparks with awkward vanity display
What the fine gentleman wore yesterday;
And but so mimic ancient wits at best,
As apes our grandsires in their doublets dressed.
In words as fashions the same rule will hold,
Alike fantastic if too new or old:
Be not the first by whom the new are tried,
Nor yet the last to lay the old aside.
  But most by numbers[2] judge a poet's song,
And smooth or rough with them is right or wrong.
In the bright Muse though thousand charms conspire,
Her voice is all these tuneful fools admire,
Who haunt Parnassus but to please their ear,
Not mend their minds; as some to church repair,
Not for the doctrine, but the music there.
These equal syllables alone require,
Though oft the ear the open vowels tire,[3]
While expletives[4] their feeble aid do join,
And ten low words oft creep in one dull line:
While they ring round the same unvaried chimes,
With sure returns of still expected rhymes;
Where'er you find "the cooling western breeze,"
In the next line, it "whispers through the trees";
If crystal streams "with pleasing murmurs creep,"
The reader's threatened (not in vain) with "sleep";
Then, at the last and only couplet fraught
With some unmeaning thing they call a thought,
A needless Alexandrine[5] ends the song
That, like a wounded snake, drags its slow length along.
Leave such to tune their own dull rhymes, and know
What's roundly smooth or languishingly slow;
And praise the easy vigor of a line
Where Denham's strength and Waller's sweetness join.[6]
True ease in writing comes from art, not chance,
As those move easiest who have learned to dance.
'Tis not enough no harshness gives offense,
The sound must seem an echo to the sense.
Soft is the strain when Zephyr gently blows,
And the smooth stream in smoother numbers flows;
But when loud surges lash the sounding shore,
The hoarse, rough verse should like the torrent roar.
When Ajax strives some rock's vast weight to throw,

1. A character in Ben Jonson's comedy *Every Man out of His Humor* (1599).
2. Versification.
3. In lines 345–57 Pope cleverly contrives to make his own metrics or diction illustrate the faults that he is exposing.
4. Words used merely to achieve the necessary number of feet in a line of verse.
5. A line of verse containing six iambic feet; it is illustrated in the next line.
6. Dryden, whom Pope echoes here, considered Sir John Denham (1615–69) and Edmund Waller (1606–87) to have been the principal shapers of the closed pentameter couplet. He had distinguished the "strength" of the one and the "sweetness" of the other.

The line too labors, and the words move slow;
Not so when swift Camilla scours the plain,
Flies o'er the unbending corn, and skims along the main.
Hear how Timotheus'[7] varied lays surprise,
And bid alternate passions fall and rise!
While at each change the son of Libyan Jove[8]
Now burns with glory, and then melts with love;
Now his fierce eyes with sparkling fury glow,
Now sighs steal out, and tears begin to flow:
Persians and Greeks like turns of nature[9] found
And the world's victor stood subdued by sound!
The power of music all our hearts allow,
And what Timotheus was is Dryden now.
  Avoid extremes; and shun the fault of such
Who still are pleased too little or too much.
At every trifle scorn to take offense:
That always shows great pride, or little sense.
Those heads, as stomachs, are not sure the best,
Which nauseate all, and nothing can digest.
Yet let not each gay turn thy rapture move;
For fools admire,[1] but men of sense approve:
As things seem large which we through mists descry,
Dullness is ever apt to magnify.
  Some foreign writers, some our own despise;
The ancients only, or the moderns prize.
Thus wit, like faith, by each man is applied
To one small sect, and all are damned beside.
Meanly they seek the blessing to confine,
And force that sun but on a part to shine,
Which not alone the southern wit sublimes,
But ripens spirits in cold northern climes;
Which from the first has shone on ages past,
Enlights the present, and shall warm the last;
Though each may feel increases and decays,
And see now clearer and now darker days.
Regard not then if wit be old or new,
But blame the false and value still the true.
  Some ne'er advance a judgment of their own,
But catch the spreading notion of the town;
They reason and conclude by precedent,
And own stale nonsense which they ne'er invent.
Some judge of authors' names, not works, and then
Nor praise nor blame the writings, but the men.
Of all this servile herd the worst is he
That in proud dullness joins with quality,
A constant critic at the great man's board,
To fetch and carry nonsense for my lord.

7. The musician in Dryden's *Alexander's Feast*. Pope retells the story of that poem in the following lines.
8. Alexander the Great.
9. Alternations of feelings.
1. Wonder. "Approve": judge favorably only after due deliberation.

What woeful stuff this madrigal would be
In some starved hackney sonneteer or me!
But let a lord once own the happy lines,
How the wit brightens! how the style refines!
Before his sacred name flies every fault,
And each exalted stanza teems with thought!
The vulgar thus through imitation err;
As oft the learn'd by being singular;
So much they scorn the crowd, that if the throng
By chance go right, they purposely go wrong.
So schismatics[2] the plain believers quit,
And are but damned for having too much wit.
Some praise at morning what they blame at night,
But always think the last opinion right.
A Muse by these is like a mistress used,
This hour she's idolized, the next abused;
While their weak heads like towns unfortified,
'Twixt sense and nonsense daily change their side.
Ask them the cause; they're wiser still, they say;
And still tomorrow's wiser than today.
We think our fathers fools, so wise we grow;
Our wiser sons, no doubt, will think us so.
Once school divines[3] this zealous isle o'erspread;
Who knew most sentences was deepest read.
Faith, Gospel, all seemed made to be disputed,
And none had sense enough to be confuted.
Scotists and Thomists now in peace remain
Amidst their kindred cobwebs in Duck Lane.[4]
If faith itself has different dresses worn,
What wonder modes in wit should take their turn?
Oft, leaving what is natural and fit,
The current folly proves the ready wit;
And authors think their reputation safe,
Which lives as long as fools are pleased to laugh.
Some valuing those of their own side or mind,
Still make themselves the measure of mankind:
Fondly[5] we think we honor merit then,
When we but praise ourselves in other men.
Parties in wit attend on those of state,
And public faction doubles private hate.
Pride, Malice, Folly against Dryden rose,
In various shapes of parsons, critics, beaux;
But sense survived, when merry jests were past;
For rising merit will buoy up at last.

2. Those who have divided the church on points of theology. Pope stressed the first syllable, the pronunciation approved by Johnson in his *Dictionary*.

3. The medieval theologians, such as the followers of Duns Scotus and St. Thomas Aquinas mentioned in line 444; "sentences" alludes to Peter Lombard's *Book of Sentences*, a book esteemed by Scholastic philosophers.

4. Street where publishers' remainders and second-hand books were sold.

5. Foolishly.

Might he return and bless once more our eyes,
New Blackmores and new Milbourns must arise.[6]
Nay, should great Homer lift his awful head,
Zoilus[7] again would start up from the dead.
Envy will merit, as its shade, pursue,
But like a shadow, proves the substance true;
For envied wit, like Sol eclipsed, makes known
The opposing body's grossness, not its own.
When first that sun too powerful beams displays,
It draws up vapors which obscure its rays;
But even those clouds at last adorn its way,
Reflect new glories, and augment the day.
  Be thou the first true merit to befriend;
His praise is lost who stays till all commend.
Short is the date, alas! of modern rhymes,
And 'tis but just to let them live betimes.
No longer now that golden age appears,
When patriarch wits survived a thousand years:
Now length of fame (our second life) is lost,
And bare threescore is all even that can boast;
Our sons their fathers' failing language see,
And such as Chaucer is shall Dryden be.[8]
So when the faithful pencil has designed
Some bright idea of the master's mind,
Where a new world leaps out at his command,
And ready Nature waits upon his hand;
When the ripe colors soften and unite,
And sweetly melt into just shade and light;
When mellowing years their full perfection give,
And each bold figure just begins to live,
The treacherous colors the fair art betray,
And all the bright creation fades away!
  Unhappy wit, like most mistaken things,
Atones not for that envy which it brings.
In youth alone its empty praise we boast,
But soon the short-lived vanity is lost;
Like some fair flower the early spring supplies,
That gaily blooms, but even in blooming dies,
What is this wit, which must our cares employ?
The owner's wife, that other men enjoy;
Then most our trouble still when most admired,
And still the more we give, the more required;
Whose fame with pains we guard, but lose with ease,
Sure some to vex, but never all to please;

6. Sir Richard Blackmore, physician and poet, had attacked Dryden for the immorality of his plays; the Rev. Luke Milbourn had attacked his translation of Virgil.

7. A Greek critic of the 4th century B.C., who wrote a book of carping criticism of Homer.

8. The radical changes that took place in the English language between the death of Chaucer in 1400 and the death of Dryden in 1700 suggested that in another 300 years Dryden would be unintelligible. Latin seemed the only means of attaining enduring fame.

'Tis what the vicious fear, the virtuous shun,
By fools 'tis hated, and by knaves undone!
If wit so much from ignorance undergo,
Ah, let not learning too commence its foe!
Of old those met rewards who could excel,
And such were praised who but endeavored well;
Though triumphs were to generals only due,
Crowns were reserved to grace the soldiers too.
Now they who reach Parnassus' lofty crown
Employ their pains to spurn some others down;
And while self-love each jealous writer rules,
Contending wits become the sport of fools;
But still the worst with most regret commend,
For each ill author is as bad a friend.
To what base ends, and by what abject ways,
Are mortals urged through sacred[9] lust of praise!
Ah, ne'er so dire a thirst of glory boast,
Nor in the critic let the man be lost!
Good nature and good sense must ever join;
To err is human, to forgive divine.
But if in noble minds some dregs remain
Nor yet purged off, of spleen and sour disdain,
Discharge that rage on more provoking crimes,
Nor fear a dearth in these flagitious[1] times.
No pardon vile obscenity should find,
Though wit and art conspire to move your mind;
But dullness with obscenity must prove
As shameful sure as impotence in love.
In the fat age of pleasure, wealth, and ease
Sprung the rank weed, and thrived with large increase:
When love was all an easy monarch's[2] care,
Seldom at council, never in a war;
Jilts ruled the state, and statesmen farces writ;
Nay, wits had pensions, and young lords had wit;
The fair sat panting at a courtier's play,
And not a mask[3] went unimproved away;
The modest fan was lifted up no more,
And virgins smiled at what they blushed before.
The following license of a foreign reign
Did all the dregs of bold Socinus drain;[4]
Then unbelieving priests reformed the nation,
And taught more pleasant methods of salvation;
Where Heaven's free subjects might their rights dispute,
Lest God himself should seem too absolute;
Pulpits their sacred satire learned to spare,

9. Accursed. The phrase imitates Virgil's "*auri sacra fames,*" "accursed hunger for gold" (*Aeneid* III.57).
1. Scandalously wicked.
2. Charles II. The concluding lines of Part II discuss the corruption of wit and poetry under this monarch.
3. A woman wearing a mask.
4. The "foreign reign" refers to William III, a Dutchman. Socinus was the name of two Italian theologians of the 16th century who denied the divinity of Jesus.

And Vice admired to find a flatterer there!
Encouraged thus, wit's Titans braved the skies,
And the press groaned with licensed blasphemies.
These monsters, critics! with your darts engage,
Here point your thunder, and exhaust your rage!
Yet shun their fault, who, scandalously nice,
Will needs mistake an author into vice;
All seems infected that the infected spy,
As all looks yellow to the jaundiced eye.

Part III

Learn then what morals critics ought to show,
For 'tis but half a judge's task, to know.
'Tis not enough, taste, judgment, learning, join;
In all you speak, let truth and candor[5] shine:
That not alone what to your sense is due
All may allow; but seek your friendship too.
Be silent always when you doubt your sense;
And speak, though sure, with seeming diffidence:
Some positive, persisting fops we know,
Who, if once wrong, will needs be always so;
But you, with pleasure own your errors past,
And make each day a critic[6] on the last.
'Tis not enough, your counsel still be true;
Blunt truths more mischief than nice falsehoods do;
Men must be taught as if you taught them not,
And things unknown proposed as things forgot.
Without good breeding, truth is disapproved;
That only makes superior sense beloved.
Be niggards of advice on no pretense;
For the worst avarice is that of sense.
With mean complacence[7] ne'er betray your trust,
Nor be so civil as to prove unjust.
Fear not the anger of the wise to raise;
Those best can bear reproof, who merit praise.
'Twere well might critics still this freedom take;
But Appius reddens at each word you speak,
And stares, tremendous! with a threatening eye,
Like some fierce tyrant in old tapestry.[8]
Fear most to tax an honorable fool,
Whose right it is, uncensured to be dull;
Such, without wit, are poets when they please,
As without learning they can take degrees.[9]

5. Kindness, impartiality.
6. Critique.
7. Softness of manners; desire of pleasing.
8. "This picture was taken to himself by John Dennis, a furious old critic by profession, who, upon no other provocation, wrote against this Essay and its author, in a manner perfectly lunatic. * * *" [Pope's note, 1744]. Pope *did* intend to ridicule Dennis, whose *Appius and Virginia* had failed on the stage in 1709, and who was known for his stare and his use of the word "tremendous." See line 270 above.
9. Honorary degrees were granted to unqualified men of rank. "Satyrs": satires.

Leave dangerous truths to unsuccessful satyrs,
And flattery to fulsome dedicators,
Whom, when they praise, the world believes no more,
Than when they promise to give scribbling o'er.
'Tis best sometimes your censure to restrain,
And charitably let the dull be vain:
Your silence there is better than your spite,
For who can rail so long as they can write?
Still humming on, their drowsy course they keep,
And lashed so long, like tops, are lashed asleep.[1]
False steps but help them to renew the race,
As, after stumbling, jades[2] will mend their pace.
What crowds of these, impenitently bold,
In sounds and jingling syllables grown old,
Still run on poets, in a raging vein,
Even to the dregs and squeezings of the brain,
Strain out the last dull droppings of their sense,
And rhyme with all the rage of impotence.
  Such shameless bards we have, and yet 'tis true,
There are as mad, abandoned critics too.
The bookful blockhead, ignorantly read,
With loads of learned lumber[3] in his head,
With his own tongue still edifies his ears,
And always listening to himself appears.
All books he reads, and all he reads assails,
From Dryden's *Fables* down to Durfey's *Tales*.[4]
With him, most authors steal their works, or buy;
Garth did not write his own *Dispensary*.[5]
Name a new play, and he's the poet's friend,
Nay showed his faults—but when would poets mend?
No place so sacred from such fops is barred,
Nor is Paul's church more safe than Paul's churchyard:[6]
Nay, fly to altars; *there* they'll talk you dead:
For fools rush in where angels fear to tread.
Distrustful sense with modest caution speaks,
It still looks home, and short excursions makes;
But rattling nonsense in full volleys breaks,
And never shocked, and never turned aside,
Bursts out, resistless, with a thundering tide.
  But where's the man, who counsel can bestow,
Still pleased to teach, and yet not proud to know?
Unbiased, or[7] by favor, or by spite:
Not dully prepossessed, nor blindly right;
Though learned, well-bred; and though well-bred, sincere;

1. Tops "sleep" when they spin so rapidly that they seem not to move.
2. Worthless, worn-out horses.
3. Rubbish.
4. Dryden's *Fables* (1700), a set of translations, were among his most admired works; Thomas D'Urfey's *Tales* (1704) were notorious potboilers.
5. Samuel Garth (1661–1719), who had been accused of plagiarizing his mock-epic poem, *The Dispensary* (1699), was admired and defended by Pope.
6. Booksellers' district near St. Paul's Cathedral, whose aisles were used as a place to meet and do business.
7. Either.

Modestly bold, and humanly severe:
Who to a friend his faults can freely show,
And gladly praise the merit of a foe?
Blessed with a taste exact, yet unconfined;
A knowledge both of books and humankind;
Gen'rous converse;[8] a soul exempt from pride;
And love to praise, with reason on his side?
  Such once were critics; such the happy few,
Athens and Rome in better ages knew.
The mighty Stagirite[9] first left the shore,
Spread all his sails, and durst the deeps explore;
He steered securely, and discovered far,
Led by the light of the Maeonian star.[1]
Poets, a race long unconfined, and free,
Still fond and proud of savage liberty,
Received his laws; and stood convinced 'twas fit,
Who conquered nature, should preside o'er wit.
  Horace still charms with graceful negligence,
And without method talks us into sense;
Will, like a friend, familiarly convey
The truest notions in the easiest[2] way.
He, who supreme in judgment, as in wit,
Might boldly censure, as he boldly writ,
Yet judged with coolness, though he sung with fire;
His precepts teach but what his works inspire.
Our critics take a contrary extreme,
They judge with fury, but they write with fle'me.[3]
Nor suffers Horace more in wrong translations
By wits, than critics[4] in as wrong quotations.
  See Dionysius[5] Homer's thoughts refine,
And call new beauties forth from every line!
  Fancy and art in gay Petronius[6] please,
The scholar's learning, with the courtier's ease.
  In grave Quintilian's[7] copious work, we find
The justest rules, and clearest method joined:
Thus useful arms in magazines[8] we place,
All ranged in order, and disposed with grace,
But less to please the eye, than arm the hand,
Still fit for use, and ready at command.
  Thee, bold Longinus! [9] all the nine inspire,
And bless their critic with a poet's fire.

8. Well-bred conversation.
9. Aristotle, whose *Poetics* founded the art of literary criticism, was born at Stagira.
1. Homer, who was supposed to have been born in Maeonia.
2. Least formal.
3. Phlegmatically.
4. I.e., than by critics. Phrases from Horace's *Ars Poetica* were quoted incessantly by critics.
5. Dionysius of Halicarnassus (1st century B.C.) wrote an important treatise on the artistic arrangement of words.
6. Author of the *Satyricon* (1st century A.D.).
7. Author of the *Institutio Oratoria* (ca. 95 A.D.), a famous treatise on rhetoric. Here as elsewhere, Pope's terms of praise are drawn from the author he is praising.
8. Storehouses or arsenals.
9. Supposed author of the influential treatise *On the Sublime* (1st century A.D.), greatly in vogue at the time of Pope. "Nine": the muses.

An ardent judge, who, zealous in his trust,
With warmth gives sentence, yet is always just;
Whose own example strengthens all his laws,
And is himself that great sublime he draws.
  Thus long succeeding critics justly reigned,
License repressed, and useful laws ordained.
Learning and Rome alike in empire grew;
And arts still followed where her eagles[1] flew;
From the same foes, at last, both felt their doom,
And the same age saw learning fall, and Rome.
With tyranny, then superstition joined,
As that the body, this enslaved the mind;
Much was believed, but little understood,
And to be dull was construed to be good;
A second deluge learning thus o'errun,
And the monks finished what the Goths begun.[2]
  At length Erasmus, that great, injured name
(The glory of the priesthood, and the shame!),[3]
Stemmed the wild torrent of a barb'rous age,
And drove those holy Vandals off the stage.
  But see! each Muse, in Leo's[4] golden days,
Starts from her trance, and trims her withered bays!
Rome's ancient Genius, o'er its ruins spread,
Shakes off the dust, and rears his reverend head.
Then sculpture and her sister-arts revive;
Stones leaped to form, and rocks began to live;
With sweeter notes each rising temple rung;
A Raphael painted, and a Vida[5] sung.
Immortal Vida: on whose honored brow
The poet's bays and critic's ivy grow:
Cremona now shall ever boast thy name,
As next in place to Mantua, next in fame![6]
  But soon by impious arms[7] from Latium chased,
Their ancient bounds the banished Muses passed;
Thence arts o'er all the northern world advance,
But critic-learning flourished most in France:
The rules a nation, born to serve, obeys;
And Boileau still in right of Horace sways.[8]
But we, brave Britons, foreign laws despised,

1. Emblems on the standards of the Roman army.
2. Pope thought that the scholastic theologians of the Middle Ages were "holy Vandals" who had "sacked" learning as the Goths and Vandals had sacked Rome.
3. Erasmus (1466–1536), the great humanist scholar, was the "glory" of the priesthood because of his goodness and learning, and its "shame" because he was persecuted.
4 Leo X, pope from 1513 to 1521, was notable for his encouragement of artists. "Bays": the wreath of poetry.
5. "M. Hieronymus Vida, an excellent Latin poet, who writ an Art of Poetry in verse. He flourished in the time of Leo the Tenth" [Pope's note]. Raphael (1483–1520) painted many of his greatest works under the patronage of Leo X.
6. Vida came from Cremona, near Mantua, the birthplace of Virgil, his favorite poet.
7. German and Spanish troops sacked Rome in 1527. "Latium": Italy.
8. Boileau's *L'Art Poétique* (1674) regularized and modernized the lessons of Horace's *Ars Poetica*.

And kept unconquered—and uncivilized;
Fierce for the liberties of wit, and bold,
We still defied the Romans, as of old.
Yet some there were, among the sounder few
Of those who less presumed, and better knew,
Who durst assert the juster ancient cause,
And here restored wit's fundamental laws.
Such was the Muse, whose rules and practice tell,
"Nature's chief masterpiece is writing well."[9]
Such was Roscommon, not more learned than good,
With manners gen'rous as his noble blood;
To him the wit of Greece and Rome was known,
And every author's merit, but his own.
Such late was Walsh[10]—the Muse's judge and friend,
Who justly knew to blame or to commend;
To failings mild, but zealous for desert;
The clearest head, and the sincerest heart.
This humble praise, lamented shade! receive,
This praise at least a grateful Muse may give:
The Muse, whose early voice you taught to sing,
Prescribed her heights, and pruned her tender wing,
(Her guide now lost) no more attempts to rise,
But in low numbers[11] short excursions tries:
Content, if hence the unlearned their wants may view,
The learned reflect on what before they knew:
Careless of censure, nor too fond of fame;
Still pleased to praise, yet not afraid to blame;
Averse alike to flatter, or offend;
Not free from faults, nor yet too vain to mend.

1709 1711

9. Quoted from an *Essay on Poetry* by John Sheffield, Duke of Buckingham (1648–1721), who had befriended the young Pope. Wentworth Dillon, Earl of Roscommon, wrote an important *Essay on Translated Verse* (1684).

10. William Walsh (1663–1708), whom Dryden once called "the best critic of our nation," and who had advised Pope to work at becoming the first great "correct" poet in English. The "Muse" here is Pope himself.

11. Humble verses.

The Rape of the Lock

The Rape of the Lock is based upon an actual episode that provoked a quarrel between two prominent Catholic families. Pope's friend John Caryll, to whom the poem is addressed (line 3), suggested that Pope write it, in the hope that a little laughter might serve to soothe ruffled tempers. Lord Petre had cut off a lock of hair from the head of the lovely Arabella Fermor (often spelled "Farmer" and doubtless so pronounced), much to the indignation of the lady and her relatives. In its original version of two cantos and 334 lines, published in 1712, *The Rape of the Lock* was a great success. In 1713 a new version was undertaken against the advice of Addison, who considered the poem perfect as it was first written. Pope greatly expanded the earlier version, adding the delightful "machinery" (i.e., the supernatural agents in epic action) of the Sylphs, Belinda's toilet, the card game, and the visit to the Cave of Spleen in Canto IV. In 1717, with the addition of Clarissa's speech on good humor, the poem assumed its final form.

With supreme tact, delicate fancy, playful wit, and the gentlest satire, Pope elaborated the trivial episode which occasioned the poem into the semblance of an epic in miniature, the most nearly perfect "heroi-comical poem" in English. The poem abounds in parodies and echoes of the *Iliad*, the *Aeneid*, and *Paradise Lost*, thus constantly forcing the reader to compare small things with great. The familiar devices of epic are observed, but the incidents or characters are beautifully proportioned to the scale of mock epic. The *Rape* tells of war, but it is the drawing-room war between the sexes; it has its heroes and heroines, but they are beaux and belles; it has its supernatural characters ("machinery") but they are Sylphs (borrowed, as Pope tells us in his engaging dedicatory letter, from Rosicrucian lore)—creatures of the air, the souls of dead coquettes, with tasks appropriate to their nature—or the Gnome Umbriel, once a prude on earth; it has its epic game, played on the "velvet plain" of the card table, its feasting heroes, who sip coffee and gossip, its battle, fought with the clichés of compliment and conceits, with frowns and angry glances, with snuff and a bodkin; it has the traditional epic journey to the underworld—here the Cave of Spleen, emblematic of the peevish ill nature of spoiled and hypochondriacal women. And Pope creates a world in which these actions take place, a world that is dense with beautiful objects: brocades, ivory and tortoise shell, cosmetics and diamonds, lacquered furniture, silver teapot, delicate chinaware. It is a world that is constantly in motion and that sparkles and glitters with light, whether the light of the sun, or of Belinda's eyes, or that light into which the "fluid" bodies of the Sylphs seem to dissolve as they flutter in shrouds and around the mast of Belinda's ship. Though Pope laughs at this world and its creatures—and remembers that a grimmer, darker world surrounds it (III.19–24 and V. 145–48)—he makes us very much aware of its beauty and its charm.

The epigraph may be translated, "I was unwilling, Belinda, to ravish your locks; but I rejoice to have conceded this to your prayers" (Martial, *Epigrams* XII.lxxxiv.1–2). Pope substituted his heroine for Martial's Polytimus. The epigraph is intended to suggest that the poem was published at Miss Fermor's request.

The Rape of the Lock

AN HEROI-COMICAL POEM

Nolueram, Belinda, tuos violare capillos;
sed juvat hoc precibus me tribuisse tuis.
—MARTIAL

TO MRS. ARABELLA FERMOR

MADAM,

It will be in vain to deny that I have some regard for this piece, since I dedicate it to you. Yet you may bear me witness, it was intended only to divert a few young ladies, who have good sense and good humor enough to laugh not only at their sex's little unguarded follies, but at their own. But as it was communicated with the air of a secret, it soon found its way into the world. An imperfect copy having been offered to a bookseller, you had the good nature for my sake to consent to the publication of one more correct; this I was forced to, before I had executed half my design, for the machinery was entirely wanting to complete it.

The machinery, Madam, is a term invented by the critics, to signify that part which the deities, angels, or demons are made to act in a poem; for the ancient poets are in one respect like many modern ladies: let an action be never so trivial in itself, they always make it appear of the utmost importance. These machines I determined to raise on a very new and odd foundation, the Rosicrucian[1] doctrine of spirits.

I know how disagreeable it is to make use of hard words before a lady; but 'tis so much the concern of a poet to have his works understood, and particularly by your sex, that you must give me leave to explain two or three difficult terms.

The Rosicrucians are a people I must bring you acquainted with. The best account I know of them is in a French book called *Le Comte de Gabalis,*[2] which both in its title and size is so like a novel, that many of the fair sex have read it for one by mistake. According to these gentlemen, the four elements are inhabited by spirits, which they call Sylphs, Gnomes, Nymphs, and Salamanders. The Gnomes or Demons of earth delight in mischief; but the Sylphs, whose habitation is in the air, are the best-conditioned creatures imaginable. For they say, any mortals may enjoy the most intimate familiarities with these gentle spirits, upon a condition very easy to all true adepts, an inviolate preservation of chastity.

As to the following cantos, all the passages of them are as fabulous as the vision at the beginning, or the transformation at the end; (except the loss of your hair, which I always mention with reverence). The human persons are as fictitious as the airy ones; and the character of Belinda, as it is now managed, resembles you in nothing but in beauty.

If this poem had as many graces as there are in your person, or in your mind, yet I could never hope it should pass through the world half so uncensured as you have done. But let its fortune be what it will, mine is happy enough, to have given me this occasion of assuring you that I am, with the truest esteem,

MADAM,

Your most obedient, humble servant,

A. POPE

1. A system of arcane philosophy introduced into England from Germany in the 17th century.

2. By the Abbé de Montfaucon de Villars, published in 1670.

Canto I

What dire offense from amorous causes springs,
What mighty contests rise from trivial things,
I sing—This verse to Caryll, Muse! is due:
This, even Belinda may vouchsafe to view:
Slight is the subject, but not so the praise,
If she inspire, and he approve my lays.
Say what strange motive, Goddess! could compel
A well-bred lord to assault a gentle belle?
Oh, say what stranger cause, yet unexplored,
Could make a gentle belle reject a lord?
In tasks so bold can little men engage,
And in soft bosoms dwells such mighty rage?
Sol through white curtains shot a timorous ray,
And oped those eyes that must eclipse the day.
Now lapdogs give themselves the rousing shake,
And sleepless lovers just at twelve awake:
Thrice rung the bell, the slipper knocked the ground,[3]
And the pressed watch returned a silver sound.
Belinda still her downy pillow pressed,
Her guardian Sylph prolonged the balmy rest:
'Twas he had summoned to her silent bed
The morning dream that hovered o'er her head.
A youth more glittering than a birthnight beau[4]
(That even in slumber caused her cheek to glow)
Seemed to her ear his winning lips to lay,
And thus in whispers said, or seemed to say:
"Fairest of mortals, thou distinguished care
Of thousand bright inhabitants of air!
If e'er one vision touched thy infant thought,
Of all the nurse and all the priest have taught,
Of airy elves by moonlight shadows seen,
The silver token, and the circled green,[5]
Or virgins visited by angel powers,
With golden crowns and wreaths of heavenly flowers,
Hear and believe! thy own importance know,
Nor bound thy narrow views to things below.
Some secret truths, from learned pride concealed,
To maids alone and children are revealed:
What though no credit doubting wits may give?
The fair and innocent shall still believe.
Know, then, unnumbered spirits round thee fly,
The light militia of the lower sky:

3. Belinda thus summons her maid. A "pressed watch" chimes the hour and the quarter-hour when the stem is pressed down.
4. Courtiers wore especially fine clothes on the sovereign's birthday.
5. According to popular belief fairies skim off the cream from jugs of milk left standing overnight and leave a coin ("silver token") in payment. Rings of bright green grass, which are common in England even in winter, were held to be due to the round dances of fairies.

These, though unseen, are ever on the wing,
Hang o'er the box, and hover round the Ring.[6]
Think what an equipage thou hast in air,
And view with scorn two pages and a chair.[7]
As now your own, our beings were of old,
And once enclosed in woman's beauteous mold;
Thence, by a soft transition, we repair
From earthly vehicles to these of air.
Think not, when woman's transient breath is fled,
That all her vanities at once are dead:
Succeeding vanities she still regards,
And though she plays no more, o'erlooks the cards.
Her joy in gilded chariots, when alive,
And love of ombre,[8] after death survive.
For when the Fair in all their pride expire,
To their first elements[9] their souls retire:
The sprites of fiery termagants in flame
Mount up, and take a Salamander's name.[10]
Soft yielding minds to water glide away,
And sip, with Nymphs, their elemental tea.[11]
The graver prude sinks downward to a Gnome,
In search of mischief still on earth to roam.
The light coquettes in Sylphs aloft repair,
And sport and flutter in the fields of air.
"Know further yet; whoever fair and chaste
Rejects mankind, is by some Sylph embraced:
For spirits, freed from mortal laws, with ease
Assume what sexes and what shapes they please.[12]
What guards the purity of melting maids,
In courtly balls, and midnight masquerades,
Safe from the treacherous friend, the daring spark,
The glance by day, the whisper in the dark,
When kind occasion prompts their warm desires,
When music softens, and when dancing fires?
'Tis but their Sylph, the wise Celestials know,
Though Honor is the word with men below.
"Some nymphs there are, too conscious of their face,
For life predestined to the Gnomes' embrace.
These swell their prospects and exalt their pride,
When offers are disdained, and love denied:
Then gay ideas[1] crowd the vacant brain,

6. The "box" in the theater and the fashionable circular drive ("Ring") in Hyde Park.
7. Sedan chair.
8. The popular card game. See III.27 ff. and note.
9. The four elements out of which all things were believed to have been made were fire, water, earth, and air. One or another of these elements was supposed to be predominant in both the physical and psychological make-up of each human being. In this context they are spoken of as "humors."
10. Pope borrowed his supernatural beings from Rosicrucian mythology. Each element was inhabited by a spirit, as the following lines explain. The salamander is a lizardlike animal, in antiquity believed to live in fire.
11. Pronounce *tay*.
12. Cf. *Paradise Lost* I.427–31; this is one of many allusions to that poem in the *Rape*.
1. Showy images.

While peers, and dukes, and all their sweeping train,
And garters, stars, and coronets[2] appear,
And in soft sounds, 'your Grace' salutes their ear.
'Tis these that early taint the female soul,
Instruct the eyes of young coquettes to roll,
Teach infant cheeks a bidden blush to know,
And little hearts to flutter at a beau.
"Oft, when the world imagine women stray,
The Sylphs through mystic mazes guide their way,
Through all the giddy circle they pursue,
And old impertinence[3] expel by new.
What tender maid but must a victim fall
To one man's treat, but for another's ball?
When Florio speaks what virgin could withstand,
If gentle Damon did not squeeze her hand?
With varying vanities, from every part,
They shift the moving toyshop[4] of their heart;
Where wigs with wigs, with sword-knots sword-knots strive,
Beaux banish beaux, and coaches coaches drive.
This erring mortals levity may call;
Oh, blind to truth! the Sylphs contrive it all.
"Of these am I, who thy protection claim,
A watchful sprite, and Ariel is my name.
Late, as I ranged the crystal wilds of air,
In the clear mirror of thy ruling star
I saw, alas! some dread event impend,
Ere to the main this morning sun descend,
But Heaven reveals not what, or how, or where:
Warned by the Sylph, O pious maid, beware!
This to disclose is all thy guardian can:
Beware of all, but most beware of Man!"
He said; when Shock,[5] who thought she slept too long,
Leaped up, and waked his mistress with his tongue.
'Twas then, Belinda, if report say true,
Thy eyes first opened on a billet-doux;
Wounds, charms, and ardors were no sooner read,
But all the vision vanished from thy head.
And now, unveiled, the toilet stands displayed,
Each silver vase in mystic order laid.
First, robed in white, the nymph intent adores,
With head uncovered, the cosmetic powers.
A heavenly image in the glass appears;
To that she bends, to that her eyes she rears.
The inferior priestess, at her altar's side,
Trembling begins the sacred rites of Pride.
Unnumbered treasures ope at once, and here
The various offerings of the world appear;
From each she nicely culls with curious toil,

2. Emblems of nobility. "Your Grace" would be a duchess.
3. Trifle.
4. A shop stocked with baubles and trifles.
5. Belinda's lapdog; a "shock" was a long-haired poodle.

And decks the goddess with the glittering spoil.
This casket India's glowing gems unlocks,
And all Arabia breathes from yonder box.
The tortoise here and elephant unite,
Transformed to combs, the speckled and the white.
Here files of pins extend their shining rows,
Puffs, powders, patches, Bibles,[6] billet-doux.
Now awful Beauty puts on all its arms;
The fair each moment rises in her charms,
Repairs her smiles, awakens every grace,
And calls forth all the wonders of her face;
Sees by degrees a purer blush arise,
And keener lightnings quicken in her eyes.
The busy Sylphs surround their darling care,
These set the head, and those divide the hair,
Some fold the sleeve, whilst others plait the gown;
And Betty's[7] praised for labors not her own.

Canto II

Not with more glories, in the ethereal plain,
The sun first rises o'er the purpled main,
Than, issuing forth, the rival of his beams
Launched on the bosom of the silver Thames.
Fair nymphs and well-dressed youths around her shone,
But every eye was fixed on her alone.
On her white breast a sparkling cross she wore,
Which Jews might kiss, and infidels adore.
Her lively looks a sprightly mind disclose,
Quick as her eyes, and as unfixed as those:
Favors to none, to all she smiles extends;
Oft she rejects, but never once offends.
Bright as the sun, her eyes the gazers strike,
And, like the sun, they shine on all alike.
Yet graceful ease, and sweetness void of pride,
Might hide her faults, if belles had faults to hide:
If to her share some female errors fall,
Look on her face, and you'll forget 'em all.
This nymph, to the destruction of mankind,
Nourished two locks which graceful hung behind
In equal curls, and well conspired to deck
With shining ringlets the smooth ivory neck.
Love in these labyrinths his slaves detains,
And mighty hearts are held in slender chains.
With hairy springes[8] we the birds betray,
Slight lines of hair surprise the finny prey,
Fair tresses man's imperial race ensnare,
And beauty draws us with a single hair.
The adventurous Baron the bright locks admired,

6. It has been suggested that Pope intended here not "Bibles," but "bibelots," (trinkets), but this intepretation has not gained wide acceptance.

7. Belinda's maid, the "inferior priestess" mentioned in line 127.

8. Snares; pronounced *sprin-jez.*

He saw, he wished, and to the prize aspired.
Resolved to win, he meditates the way,
By force to ravish, or by fraud betray;
For when success a lover's toil attends,
Few ask if fraud or force attained his ends.
For this, ere Phoebus rose, he had implored
Propitious Heaven, and every power adored,
But chiefly Love—to Love an altar built,
Of twelve vast French romances, neatly gilt.
There lay three garters, half a pair of gloves,
And all the trophies of his former loves.
With tender billet-doux he lights the pyre,
And breathes three amorous sighs to raise the fire.
Then prostrate falls, and begs with ardent eyes
Soon to obtain, and long possess the prize:
The powers gave ear, and granted half his prayer,
The rest the winds dispersed in empty air.
But now secure the painted vessel glides,
The sunbeams trembling on the floating tides,
While melting music steals upon the sky,
And softened sounds along the waters die.
Smooth flow the waves, the zephyrs gently play,
Belinda smiled, and all the world was gay.
All but the Sylph—with careful thoughts oppressed,
The impending woe sat heavy on his breast.
He summons straight his denizens of air;
The lucid squadrons round the sails repair:
Soft o'er the shrouds aërial whispers breathe
That seemed but zephyrs to the train beneath.
Some to the sun their insect-wings unfold,
Waft on the breeze, or sink in clouds of gold.
Transparent forms too fine for mortal sight,
Their fluid bodies half dissolved in light,
Loose to the wind their airy garments flew,
Thin glittering textures of the filmy dew,
Dipped in the richest tincture of the skies,
Where light disports in ever-mingling dyes,
While every beam new transient colors flings,
Colors that change whene'er they wave their wings.
Amid the circle, on the gilded mast,
Superior by the head was Ariel placed;
His purple[9] pinions opening to the sun,
He raised his azure wand, and thus begun:
"Ye Sylphs and Sylphids, to your chief give ear!
Fays, Fairies, Genii, Elves, and Daemons, hear!
Ye know the spheres and various tasks assigned
By laws eternal to the aërial kind.
Some in the fields of purest ether play,

9. In 18th-century poetic diction the word might mean "blood-red," "purple," or simply (as is likely here) "brightly colored." The word derives from Virgil, *Eclogue* IX, 40 *purpurcum*. An example of the Latinate nature of some poetic diction of the period.

And bask and whiten in the blaze of day.
Some guide the course of wandering orbs on high,
Or roll the planets through the boundless sky.
Some less refined, beneath the moon's pale light
Pursue the stars that shoot athwart the night,
Or suck the mists in grosser air below,
Or dip their pinions in the painted bow,
Or brew fierce tempests on the wintry main,
Or o'er the glebe[1] distill the kindly rain.
Others on earth o'er human race preside,
Watch all their ways, and all their actions guide:
Of these the chief the care of nations own,
And guard with arms divine the British Throne.
"Our humbler province is to tend the Fair,
Not a less pleasing, though less glorious care:
To save the powder from too rude a gale,
Nor let the imprisoned essences exhale;
To draw fresh colors from the vernal flowers;
To steal from rainbows e'er they drop in showers
A brighter wash;[2] to curl their waving hairs,
Assist their blushes, and inspire their airs;
Nay oft, in dreams invention we bestow,
To change a flounce, or add a furbelow.
"This day black omens threat the brightest fair,
That e'er deserved a watchful spirit's care;
Some dire disaster, or by force or slight,
But what, or where, the Fates have wrapped in night:
Whether the nymph shall break Diana's law,[3]
Or some frail china jar receive a flaw,
Or stain her honor or her new brocade,
Forget her prayers, or miss a masquerade,
Or lose her heart, or necklace, at a ball;
Or whether Heaven has doomed that Shock must fall.
Haste, then, ye spirits! to your charge repair:
The fluttering fan be Zephyretta's care;
The drops[4] to thee, Brillante, we consign;
And, Momentilla, let the watch be thine;
Do thou, Crispissa,[5] tend her favorite Lock;
Ariel himself shall be the guard of Shock.
"To fifty chosen Sylphs, of special note,
We trust the important charge, the petticoat;
Oft have we known that sevenfold fence to fail,
Though stiff with hoops, and armed with ribs of whale.
Form a strong line about the silver bound,
And guard the wide circumference around.
"Whatever spirit, careless of his charge,
His post neglects, or leaves the fair at large,
Shall feel sharp vengeance soon o'ertake his sins,

1. Cultivated field.
2. Cosmetic lotion.
3. Diana was the goddess of chastity.
4. Diamond earrings. Observe the appropriateness of the names of the Sylphs to their assigned functions.
5. From Latin *crispere*, to curl.

Be stopped in vials, or transfixed with pins,
Or plunged in lakes of bitter washes lie,
Or wedged whole ages in a bodkin's eye;[6]
Gums and pomatums shall his flight restrain,
While clogged he beats his silken wings in vain,
Or alum styptics with contracting power
Shrink his thin essence like a riveled[7] flower:
Or, as Ixion[8] fixed, the wretch shall feel
The giddy motion of the whirling mill,
In fumes of burning chocolate shall glow,
And tremble at the sea that froths below!"
He spoke; the spirits from the sails descend;
Some, orb in orb, around the nymph extend;
Some thread the mazy ringlets of her hair;
Some hang upon the pendants of her ear:
With beating hearts the dire event they wait,
Anxious, and trembling for the birth of Fate.

Canto III

Close by those meads, forever crowned with flowers,
Where Thames with pride surveys his rising towers,
There stands a structure of majestic frame,
Which from the neighboring Hampton takes its name.[9]
Here Britain's statesmen oft the fall foredoom
Of foreign tyrants and of nymphs at home;
Here thou, great Anna! whom three realms obey,
Dost sometimes counsel take—and sometimes tea.
Hither the heroes and the nymphs resort,
To taste awhile the pleasures of a court;
In various talk the instructive hours they passed,
Who gave the ball, or paid the visit last;
One speaks the glory of the British Queen,
And one describes a charming Indian screen;
A third interprets motions, looks, and eyes;
At every word a reputation dies.
Snuff, or the fan, supply each pause of chat,
With singing, laughing, ogling, and all that.
Meanwhile, declining from the noon of day,
The sun obliquely shoots his burning ray;
The hungry judges soon the sentence sign,
And wretches hang that jurymen may dine;
The merchant from the Exchange returns in peace,
And the long labors of the toilet cease.
Belinda now, whom thirst of fame invites,
Burns to encounter two adventurous knights,

6. A "bodkin" is a blunt needle with a large eye, used for drawing ribbon through eyelets in the edging of women's garments.

7. To "rivel" is to "contract into wrinkles and corrugations" (Johnson's *Dictionary*).

8. In the Greek myth Ixion was punished in the underworld by being bound on an everturning wheel.

9. Hampton Court, the royal palace, about fifteen miles up the Thames from London.

At ombre[1] singly to decide their doom,
And swells her breast with conquests yet to come.
Straight the three bands prepare in arms to join,
Each band the number of the sacred nine.
Soon as she spreads her hand, the aërial guard
Descend, and sit on each important card:
First Ariel perched upon a Matadore,
Then each according to the rank they bore;
For Sylphs, yet mindful of their ancient race,
Are, as when women, wondrous fond of place.
   Behold, four Kings in majesty revered,
With hoary whiskers and a forky beard;
And four fair Queens whose hands sustain a flower,
The expressive emblem of their softer power;
Four Knaves in garbs succinct,[2] a trusty band,
Caps on their heads, and halberts in their hand;
And parti-colored troops, a shining train,
Draw forth to combat on the velvet plain.
   The skillful nymph reviews her force with care;
"Let Spades be trumps!" she said, and trumps they were.
   Now move to war her sable Matadores,
In show like leaders of the swarthy Moors.
Spadillio first, unconquerable lord!
Led off two captive trumps, and swept the board.
As many more Manillio forced to yield,
And marched a victor from the verdant field.
Him Basto followed, but his fate more hard
Gained but one trump and one plebeian card.
With his broad saber next, a chief in years,
The hoary Majesty of Spades appears,
Puts forth one manly leg, to sight revealed,
The rest his many-colored robe concealed.
The rebel Knave, who dares his prince engage,
Proves the just victim of his royal rage.
Even mighty Pam,[3] that kings and queens o'erthrew
And mowed down armies in the fights of loo,
Sad chance of war! now destitute of aid,
Falls undistinguished by the victor Spade.
   Thus far both armies to Belinda yield;
Now to the Baron fate inclines the field.
His warlike amazon her host invades,

1. The game of ombre which Belinda plays against the Baron and another young man is too complicated for complete explication here. Pope has carefully arranged the cards so that Belinda wins. The Baron's hand is strong enough to be a threat, but the third player's is of little account. The hand is played exactly according to the rules of ombre, and Pope's description of the cards is equally accurate. Each player holds nine cards (line 30). The "Matadores" (line 33), when spades are trumps, are "Spadillio" (line 49), the ace of spades; "Manillio" (line 51), the two of spades; "Basto" (line 53), the ace of clubs; Belinda holds all three of these. (For a more complete description of ombre, see Appendix C, *The Rape of the Lock and Other Poems*, ed. Geoffrey Tillotson, in the Twickenham Edition of Pope's poems, Vol. II.)

2. Girded up.

3. The knave of clubs, the highest trump in the game of loo.

The imperial consort of the crown of Spades.
The Club's black tyrant first her victim died,
Spite of his haughty mien and barbarous pride.
What boots the regal circle on his head,
His giant limbs, in state unwieldy spread?
That long behind he trails his pompous robe,
And of all monarchs only grasps the globe?
  The Baron now his Diamonds pours apace;
The embroidered King who shows but half his face,
And his refulgent Queen, with powers combined
Of broken troops an easy conquest find.
Clubs, Diamonds, Hearts, in wild disorder seen,
With throngs promiscuous strew the level green.
Thus when dispersed a routed army runs,
Of Asia's troops, and Afric's sable sons,
With like confusion different nations fly,
Of various habit, and of various dye,
The pierced battalions disunited fall
In heaps on heaps; one fate o'erwhelms them all.
  The Knave of Diamonds tries his wily arts,
And wins (oh, shameful chance!) the Queen of Hearts.
At this, the blood the virgin's cheek forsook,
A livid paleness spreads o'er all her look;
She sees, and trembles at the approaching ill,
Just in the jaws of ruin, and Codille,[4]
And now (as oft in some distempered state)
On one nice trick depends the general fate.
An Ace of Hearts steps forth: the King unseen
Lurked in her hand, and mourned his captive Queen.
He springs to vengeance with an eager pace,
And falls like thunder on the prostrate Ace.
The nymph exulting fills with shouts the sky,
The walls, the woods, and long canals reply.
  O thoughtless mortals! ever blind to fate,
Too soon dejected, and too soon elate:
Sudden these honors shall be snatched away,
And cursed forever this victorious day.
  For lo! the board with cups and spoons is crowned,
The berries crackle, and the mill turns round;[5]
On shining altars of Japan[6] they raise
The silver lamp; the fiery spirits blaze:
From silver spouts the grateful liquors glide,
While China's earth receives the smoking tide.
At once they gratify their scent and taste,
And frequent cups prolong the rich repast.
Straight hover round the fair her airy band;
Some, as she sipped, the fuming liquor fanned,

4. The term applied to losing a hand at cards.
5. I.e., coffee is roasted and ground.
6. I.e., small, lacquered tables. The word "altars" suggests the ritualistic character of coffee-drinking in Belinda's world.

Some o'er her lap their careful plumes displayed,
Trembling, and conscious of the rich brocade.
Coffee (which makes the politician wise,
And see through all things with his half-shut eyes)
Sent up in vapors to the Baron's brain
New stratagems, the radiant Lock to gain.
Ah, cease, rash youth! desist ere 'tis too late,
Fear the just Gods, and think of Scylla's fate![7]
Changed to a bird, and sent to flit in air,
She dearly pays for Nisus' injured hair!
　But when to mischief mortals bend their will,
How soon they find fit instruments of ill!
Just then, Clarissa drew with tempting grace
A two-edged weapon from her shining case:
So ladies in romance assist their knight,
Present the spear, and arm him for the fight.
He takes the gift with reverence, and extends
The little engine on his fingers' ends;
This just behind Belinda's neck he spread,
As o'er the fragrant steams she bends her head.
Swift to the Lock a thousand sprites repair,
A thousand wings, by turns, blow back the hair,
And thrice they twitched the diamond in her ear,
Thrice she looked back, and thrice the foe drew near.
Just in that instant, anxious Ariel sought
The close recesses of the virgin's thought;
As on the nosegay in her breast reclined,
He watched the ideas rising in her mind,
Sudden he viewed, in spite of all her art,
An earthly lover lurking at her heart.
Amazed, confused, he found his power expired,
Resigned to fate, and with a sigh retired.
　The Peer now spreads the glittering forfex[8] wide,
To enclose the Lock; now joins it, to divide.
Even then, before the fatal engine closed,
A wretched Sylph too fondly interposed;
Fate urged the shears, and cut the Sylph in twain
(But airy substance soon unites again):
The meeting points the sacred hair dissever
From the fair head, forever, and forever!
　Then flashed the living lightning from her eyes,
And screams of horror rend the affrighted skies.
Not louder shrieks to pitying heaven are cast,
When husbands, or when lapdogs breathe their last;
Or when rich china vessels fallen from high,
In glittering dust and painted fragments lie!

7. Scylla, daughter of Nisus, was turned into a sea bird because, for the sake of her love for Minos of Crete, who was besieging her father's city of Megara, she cut from her father's head the purple lock on which his safety depended. She is not the Scylla of "Scylla and Charybdis."

8. Scissors.

"Let wreaths of triumph now my temples twine,"
The victor cried, "the glorious prize is mine!
While fish in streams, or birds delight in air,
Or in a coach and six the British Fair,
As long as *Atalantis*[9] shall be read,
Or the small pillow grace a lady's bed,
While visits shall be paid on solemn days,
When numerous wax-lights in bright order blaze,
While nymphs take treats, or assignations give,
So long my honor, name, and praise shall live!
What Time would spare, from Steel receives its date,
And monuments, like men, submit to fate!
Steel could the labor of the Gods destroy,
And strike to dust the imperial towers of Troy;
Steel could the works of mortal pride confound,
And hew triumphal arches to the ground.
What wonder then, fair nymph! thy hairs should feel,
The conquering force of unresisted Steel?"

Canto IV

But anxious cares the pensive nymph oppressed,
And secret passions labored in her breast.
Not youthful kings in battle seized alive,
Not scornful virgins who their charms survive,
Not ardent lovers robbed of all their bliss,
Not ancient ladies when refused a kiss,
Not tyrants fierce that unrepenting die,
Not Cynthia when her manteau's[1] pinned awry,
E'er felt such rage, resentment, and despair,
As thou, sad virgin! for thy ravished hair.
For, that sad moment, when the Sylphs withdrew
And Ariel weeping from Belinda flew,
Umbriel,[2] a dusky, melancholy sprite
As ever sullied the fair face of light,
Down to the central earth, his proper scene,
Repaired to search the gloomy Cave of Spleen.[3]
Swift on his sooty pinions flits the Gnome,
And in a vapor reached the dismal dome.
No cheerful breeze this sullen region knows,
The dreaded east is all the wind that blows.
Here in a grotto, sheltered close from air,
And screened in shades from day's detested glare,
She sighs forever on her pensive bed,
Pain at her side, and Megrim[4] at her head.
Two handmaids wait the throne: alike in place
But differing far in figure and in face.
Here stood Ill-Nature like an ancient maid,

9. Mrs. Manley's *New Atalantis* (1709) was notorious for its thinly concealed allusions to contemporary scandals.
1. Negligee or loose robe.
2. The name suggests shade and darkness.
3. Ill humor.
4. Headache.

Her wrinkled form in black and white arrayed;
With store of prayers for mornings, nights, and noons,
Her hand is filled; her bosom with lampoons.
There Affectation, with a sickly mien,
Shows in her cheek the roses of eighteen,
Practiced to lisp, and hang the head aside,
Faints into airs, and languishes with pride,
On the rich quilt sinks with becoming woe,
Wrapped in a gown, for sickness and for show.
The fair ones feel such maladies as these,
When each new nightdress gives a new disease.
A constant vapor[5] o'er the palace flies,
Strange phantoms rising as the mists arise;
Dreadful as hermit's dreams in haunted shades,
Or bright as visions of expiring maids.
Now glaring fiends, and snakes on rolling spires,[6]
Pale specters, gaping tombs, and purple fires;
Now lakes of liquid gold, Elysian scenes,
And crystal domes, and angels in machines.[7]
Unnumbered throngs on every side are seen
Of bodies changed to various forms by Spleen.
Here living teapots stand, one arm held out,
One bent; the handle this, and that the spout:
A pipkin[8] there, like Homer's tripod, walks;
Here sighs a jar, and there a goose pie talks;
Men prove with child, as powerful fancy works,
And maids, turned bottles, call aloud for corks.
Safe passed the Gnome through this fantastic band,
A branch of healing spleenwort[9] in his hand.
Then thus addressed the Power: "Hail, wayward Queen!
Who rule the sex to fifty from fifteen:
Parent of vapors and of female wit,
Who give the hysteric or poetic fit,
On various tempers act by various ways,
Make some take physic, others scribble plays;
Who cause the proud their visits to delay,
And send the godly in a pet to pray.
A nymph there is that all your power disdains,
And thousands more in equal mirth maintains.
But oh! if e'er thy Gnome could spoil a grace,
Or raise a pimple on a beauteous face,
Like citron-waters[1] matrons' cheeks inflame,
Or change complexions at a losing game;

5. Emblematic of "the vapors," i.e., hypochondria, melancholy, peevishness, often affected by fashionable women.
6. Coils.
7. Mechanical devices used in the theaters for spectacular effects. The fantasies of neurotic women here merge with the sensational stage effects popular with contemporary audiences.
8. An earthen pot. In *Iliad* XVIII.373–77, Vulcan furnishes the gods with self-propelling "tripods" (three-legged stools).
9. An herb, efficacious against the spleen. Pope alludes to the golden bough that Aeneas and the Cumaean sybil carry with them for protection into the underworld in *Aeneid* VI.
1. Brandy flavored with orange or lemon peel.

If e'er with airy horns[2] I planted heads,
Or rumpled petticoats, or tumbled beds,
Or caused suspicion when no soul was rude,
Or discomposed the headdress of a prude,
Or e'er to costive lapdog gave disease,
Which not the tears of brightest eyes could ease,
Hear me, and touch Belinda with chagrin:[3]
That single act gives half the world the spleen."
The Goddess with a discontented air
Seems to reject him though she grants his prayer.
A wondrous bag with both her hands she binds,
Like that where once Ulysses held the winds;[4]
There she collects the force of female lungs,
Sighs, sobs, and passions, and the war of tongues.
A vial next she fills with fainting fears,
Soft sorrows, melting griefs, and flowing tears.
The Gnome rejoicing bears her gifts away,
Spreads his black wings, and slowly mounts to day.
Sunk in Thalestris'[5] arms the nymph he found,
Her eyes dejected and her hair unbound.
Full o'er their heads the swelling bag he rent,
And all the Furies issued at the vent.
Belinda burns with more than mortal ire,
And fierce Thalestris fans the rising fire.
"O wretched maid!" she spread her hands, and cried
(While Hampton's echoes, "Wretched maid!" replied),
"Was it for this you took such constant care
The bodkin, comb, and essence to prepare?
For this your locks in paper durance bound,
For this with torturing irons wreathed around?
For this with fillets strained your tender head,
And bravely bore the double loads of lead?[6]
Gods! shall the ravisher display your hair,
While the fops envy, and the ladies stare!
Honor forbid! at whose unrivaled shrine
Ease, pleasure, virtue, all, our sex resign.
Methinks already I your tears survey,
Already hear the horrid things they say,
Already see you a degraded toast,
And all your honor in a whisper lost!
How shall I, then, your helpless fame defend?
'Twill then be infamy to seem your friend!

2. Horns, the symbol of the cuckold, the man whose wife has been unfaithful to him; here "airy," because they exist only in the jealous suspicions of the husband, the victim of the mischievous Umbriel.
3. Ill humor.
4. Aeolus (later conceived of as god of the winds) gave Ulysses a bag containing all the winds adverse to his voyage home. When his ship was in sight of Ithaca, his companions opened the bag and the storms that ensued drove Ulysses far away (*Odyssey* X.19 ff.).
5. The name is borrowed from a queen of the Amazons, hence a fierce and warlike woman. Thalestris, according to legend, traveled 30 days in order to have a child by Alexander the Great. Plutarch denies the story.
6. The frame on which the elaborate coiffures of the day were arranged.

And shall this prize, the inestimable prize,
Exposed through crystal to the gazing eyes,
And heightened by the diamond's circling rays,
On that rapacious hand forever blaze?
Sooner shall grass in Hyde Park Circus grow,
And wits take lodgings in the sound of Bow;[7]
Sooner let earth, air, sea, to chaos fall,
Men, monkeys, lapdogs, parrots, perish all!"
She said; then raging to Sir Plume repairs,
And bids her beau demand the precious hairs
(Sir Plume of amber snuffbox justly vain,
And the nice conduct of a clouded cane),
With earnest eyes, and round unthinking face,
He first the snuffbox opened, then the case,
And thus broke out—"My Lord, why, what the devil!
Z——ds! damn the lock! 'fore Gad, you must be civil!
Plague on't! 'tis past a jest—nay prithee, pox!
Give her the hair"—he spoke, and rapped his box.
"It grieves me much," replied the Peer again,
"Who speaks so well should ever speak in vain.
But by this Lock, this sacred Lock I swear
(Which never more shall join its parted hair;
Which never more its honors shall renew,
Clipped from the lovely head where late it grew),
That while my nostrils draw the vital air,
This hand, which won it, shall forever wear."
He spoke, and speaking, in proud triumph spread
The long-contended honors[8] of her head.
But Umbriel, hateful Gnome, forbears not so;
He breaks the vial whence the sorrows flow.
Then see! the nymph in beauteous grief appears,
Her eyes half languishing, half drowned in tears;
On her heaved bosom hung her drooping head,
Which with a sigh she raised, and thus she said:
"Forever cursed be this detested day,
Which snatched my best, my favorite curl away!
Happy! ah, ten times happy had I been,
If Hampton Court these eyes had never seen!
Yet am not I the first mistaken maid,
By love of courts to numerous ills betrayed.
Oh, had I rather unadmired remained
In some lone isle, or distant northern land;
Where the gilt chariot never marks the way,
Where none learn ombre, none e'er taste bohea![9]
There kept my charms concealed from mortal eye,
Like roses that in deserts bloom and die.
What moved my mind with youthful lords to roam?
Oh, had I stayed, and said my prayers at home!

7. A person born within sound of the bells of St. Mary-le-Bow in Cheapside is said to be a cockney. No fashionable wit would have so vulgar an address.
8. Ornaments, hence locks; a Latinism.
9. A costly sort of tea.

'Twas this the morning omens seemed to tell,
Thrice from my trembling hand the patch box[1] fell;
The tottering china shook without a wind,
Nay, Poll sat mute, and Shock was most unkind!
A Sylph too warned me of the threats of fate,
In mystic visions, now believed too late!
See the poor remnants of these slighted hairs!
My hands shall rend what e'en thy rapine spares.
These in two sable ringlets taught to break,
Once gave new beauties to the snowy neck;
The sister lock now sits uncouth, alone,
And in its fellow's fate foresees its own;
Uncurled it hangs, the fatal shears demands,
And tempts once more thy sacrilegious hands.
Oh, hadst thou, cruel! been content to seize
Hairs less in sight, or any hairs but these!"

Canto V

She said: the pitying audience melt in tears.
But Fate and Jove had stopped the Baron's ears.
In vain Thalestris with reproach assails,
For who can move when fair Belinda fails?
Not half so fixed the Trojan[2] could remain,
While Anna begged and Dido raged in vain.
Then grave Clarissa graceful waved her fan;
Silence ensued, and thus the nymph began:
"Say why are beauties praised and honored most,
The wise man's passion, and the vain man's toast?
Why decked with all that land and sea afford,
Why angels called, and angel-like adored?
Why round our coaches crowd the white-gloved beaux,
Why bows the side box from its inmost rows?
How vain are all these glories, all our pains,
Unless good sense preserve what beauty gains;
That men may say when we the front box grace,
'Behold the first in virtue as in face!'
Oh! if to dance all night, and dress all day,
Charmed the smallpox, or chased old age away,
Who would not scorn what housewife's cares produce,
Or who would learn one earthly thing of use?
To patch, nay ogle, might become a saint,
Nor could it sure be such a sin to paint.
But since, alas! frail beauty must decay,
Curled or uncurled, since locks will turn to gray;
Since painted, or not painted, all shall fade,
And she who scorns a man must die a maid;

1. A box to hold the ornamental patches of court plaster worn on the face by both sexes. Cf. *Spectator* 81.
2. Aeneas, who forsook Dido at the bidding of the gods, despite her reproaches and the supplications of her sister Anna. Virgil compares him to a steadfast oak that withstands a storm (*Aeneid* IV.437–43).

What then remains but well our power to use,
And keep good humor still whate'er we lose?
And trust me, dear, good humor can prevail
When airs, and flights, and screams, and scolding fail.
Beauties in vain their pretty eyes may roll;
Charms strike the sight, but merit wins the soul."[3]
  So spoke the dame, but no applause ensued;
Belinda frowned, Thalestris called her prude.
"To arms, to arms!" the fierce virago cries,
And swift as lightning to the combat flies.
All side in parties, and begin the attack;
Fans clap, silks rustle, and tough whalebones crack;
Heroes' and heroines' shouts confusedly rise,
And bass and treble voices strike the skies.
No common weapons in their hands are found,
Like Gods they fight, nor dread a mortal wound.
  So when bold Homer makes the Gods engage,
And heavenly breasts with human passions rage;
'Gainst Pallas, Mars; Latona, Hermes arms;
And all Olympus rings with loud alarms:
Jove's thunder roars, heaven trembles all around,
Blue Neptune storms, the bellowing deeps resound:
Earth shakes her nodding towers, the ground gives way,
And the pale ghosts start at the flash of day!
  Triumphant Umbriel on a sconce's[4] height
Clapped his glad wings, and sat to view the fight:
Propped on the bodkin spears, the sprites survey
The growing combat, or assist the fray.
  While through the press enraged Thalestris flies,
And scatters death around from both her eyes,
A beau and witling perished in the throng,
One died in metaphor, and one in song.
"O cruel nymph! a living death I bear,"
Cried Dapperwit, and sunk beside his chair.
A mournful glance Sir Fopling upwards cast,
"Those eyes are made so killing"—was his last.
Thus on Maeander's flowery margin lies
The expiring swan, and as he sings he dies.
  When bold Sir Plume had drawn Clarissa down,
Chloe stepped in, and killed him with a frown;
She smiled to see the doughty hero slain,
But, at her smile, the beau revived again.
  Now Jove suspends his golden scales in air,
Weighs the men's wits against the lady's hair;
The doubtful beam long nods from side to side;
At length the wits mount up, the hairs subside.
  See, fierce Belinda on the Baron flies,

3. The speech is a close parody of Pope's own translation of the speech of Sarpedon to Glaucus, first published in 1709 and slightly revised in his version of the *Iliad* (XII.371–96).
4. Candlestick fastened on the wall.

With more than usual lightning in her eyes;
Nor feared the chief the unequal fight to try,
Who sought no more than on his foe to die.
But this bold lord with manly strength endued,
She with one finger and a thumb subdued:
Just where the breath of life his nostrils drew,
A charge of snuff the wily virgin threw;
The Gnomes direct, to every atom just,
The pungent grains of titillating dust.
Sudden, with starting tears each eye o'erflows,
And the high dome re-echoes to his nose.
"Now meet thy fate," incensed Belinda cried,
And drew a deadly bodkin[5] from her side.
(The same, his ancient personage to deck,
Her great-great-grandsire wore about his neck,
In three seal rings; which after, melted down,
Formed a vast buckle for his widow's gown:
Her infant grandame's whistle next it grew,
The bells she jingled, and the whistle blew;
Then in a bodkin graced her mother's hairs,
Which long she wore, and now Belinda wears.)
"Boast not my fall," he cried, "insulting foe!
Thou by some other shalt be laid as low.
Nor think to die dejects my lofty mind:
All that I dread is leaving you behind!
Rather than so, ah, let me still survive,
And burn in Cupid's flames—but burn alive."
"Restore the Lock!" she cries; and all around
"Restore the Lock!" the vaulted roofs rebound.
Not fierce Othello in so loud a strain
Roared for the handkerchief that caused his pain.[6]
But see how oft ambitious aims are crossed,
And chiefs contend till all the prize is lost!
The lock, obtained with guilt, and kept with pain,
In every place is sought, but sought in vain:
With such a prize no mortal must be blessed,
So Heaven decrees! with Heaven who can contest?
Some thought it mounted to the lunar sphere,
Since all things lost on earth are treasured there.
There heroes' wits are kept in ponderous vases,
And beaux' in snuffboxes and tweezer cases.
There broken vows and deathbed alms are found,
And lovers' hearts with ends of riband bound,
The courtier's promises, and sick man's prayers,
The smiles of harlots, and the tears of heirs,
Cages for gnats, and chains to yoke a flea,
Dried butterflies, and tomes of casuistry.
But trust the Muse—she saw it upward rise,

5. An ornamental pin shaped like a dagger, to be worn in the hair.

6. *Othello* III.iv.

Though marked by none but quick, poetic eyes
(So Rome's great founder to the heavens withdrew,[7]
To Proculus alone confessed in view);
A sudden star, it shot through liquid air,
And drew behind a radiant trail of hair.
Not Berenice's locks first rose so bright,[8]
The heavens bespangling with disheveled light.
The Sylphs behold it kindling as it flies,
And pleased pursue its progress through the skies.
 This the beau monde shall from the Mall[9] survey,
And hail with music its propitious ray.
This the blest lover shall for Venus take,
And send up vows from Rosamonda's Lake.[1]
This Partridge[2] soon shall view in cloudless skies,
When next he looks through Galileo's eyes;
And hence the egregious wizard shall foredoom
The fate of Louis, and the fall of Rome.
 Then cease, bright nymph! to mourn thy ravished hair,
Which adds new glory to the shining sphere!
Not all the tresses that fair head can boast,
Shall draw such envy as the Lock you lost.
For, after all the murders of your eye,
When, after millions slain, yourself shall die:
When those fair suns shall set, as set they must,
And all those tresses shall be laid in dust,
This Lock the Muse shall consecrate to fame,
And 'midst the stars inscribe Belinda's name.

1712 1714

Ode on Solitude[3]

Happy the man whose wish and care
 A few paternal acres bound,
Content to breathe his native air,
 In his own ground.

Whose herds with milk, whose fields with bread,
 Whose flocks supply him with attire,
Whose trees in summer yield him shade,
 In winter fire.

7. Romulus, the "founder" and first king of Rome, was snatched to heaven in a storm cloud while reviewing his army in the Campus Martius (Livy I. xvi).

8. Berenice, the wife of Ptolemy III, dedicated a lock of her hair to the gods to ensure her husband's safe return from war. It was turned into a constellation.

9. A walk laid out by Charles II in St. James's Park, a resort for strollers of all sorts.

1. In St. James's Park; associated with unhappy lovers.

2. John Partridge, the astrologer whose annually published predictions had been amusingly satirized by Swift and other wits in 1708. "Galileo's eyes": i.e., a telescope.

3. The hint for this poem was taken from Horace's well-known *Epode II*, which praises the simplicity and innocence of country life, a favorite literary theme in Pope's time.

Blest, who can unconcernedly find
Hours, days, and years slide soft away,
In health of body, peace of mind,
Quiet by day,

Sound sleep by night; study and ease,
Together mixed; sweet recreation;
And innocence, which most does please
With meditation.

Thus let me live, unseen, unknown;
Thus unlamented let me die;
Steal from the world, and not a stone
Tell where I lie.

ca. 1700–1709 1717, 1736

Epistle to Miss Blount[1]

ON HER LEAVING THE TOWN, AFTER THE CORONATION

As some fond virgin, whom her mother's care
Drags from the town to wholesome country air,
Just when she learns to roll a melting eye,
And hear a spark,[2] yet think no danger nigh;
From the dear man unwilling she must sever,
Yet takes one kiss before she parts forever:
Thus from the world fair Zephalinda[3] flew,
Saw others happy, and with sighs withdrew;
Not that their pleasures caused her discontent;
She sighed not that they stayed, but that she went.
She went to plain-work,[4] and to purling brooks,
Old-fashioned halls, dull aunts, and croaking rooks:
She went from opera, park, assembly, play,
To morning walks, and prayers three hours a day;
To part her time 'twixt reading and bohea,[5]
To muse, and spill her solitary tea, .
Or o'er cold coffee trifle with the spoon,
Count the slow clock, and dine exact at noon;[6]
Divert her eyes with pictures in the fire,
Hum half a tune, tell stories to the squire;
Up to her godly garret after seven,
There starve and pray, for that's the way to heaven.
Some squire, perhaps, you take delight to rack,
Whose game is whist, whose treat a toast in sack;
Who visits with a gun, presents you birds,

1. Teresa Blount, sister of Pope's lifelong friend Martha Blount. The "coronation" was that of George I (1714).
2. A fop, a beau.
3. A fanciful name adopted by Miss Blount.
4. "Needlework, as distinguished from embroidery" (Johnson's *Dictionary*).
5. A costly sort of tea.
6. The fashionable hour for dining in London was three or four o'clock. A noon dinner is a sign of old-fashioned rusticity.

Then gives a smacking buss, and cries—"No words!"
Or with his hounds comes hollowing from the stable,
Makes love with nods and knees beneath a table;
Whose laughs are hearty, though his jests are coarse,
And loves you best of all things—but his horse.
  In some fair evening, on your elbow laid,
You dream of triumphs in the rural shade;
In pensive thought recall the fancied scene,
See coronations rise on every green:
Before you pass the imaginary sights
Of lords and earls and dukes and gartered knights,
While the spread fan o'ershades your closing eyes;
Then give one flirt,[7] and all the vision flies.
Thus vanish scepters, coronets, and balls,
And leave you in lone woods, or empty walls!
  So when your slave,[8] at some dear idle time
(Not plagued with headaches or the want of rhyme)
Stands in the streets, abstracted from the crew,
And while he seems to study, thinks of you;
Just when his fancy points [9] your sprightly eyes,
Or sees the blush of soft Parthenia [1] rise,
Gay [2] pats my shoulder, and you vanish quite;
Streets, chairs, and coxcombs rush upon my sight;
Vexed to be still in town, I knit my brow,
Look sour, and hum a tune—as you may now.

1717

Eloisa to Abelard[1]

The Argument

Abelard and Eloisa flourished in the twelfth century; they were two of the most distinguished persons of their age in learning and

7. I.e., opens and closes her fan with a jerk.
8. I.e., Pope.
9. Notices
1. Martha Blount.
2. John Gay, the poet.

1. Like Ovid's *Sappho to Phaon*, which Pope had translated in his teens, *Eloisa to Abelard* is an heroic epistle: strictly defined, a versified love letter, involving historical persons, which dramatizes the feelings of a woman who has been forsaken. Pope took his subject from one of the most famous affairs of history. Peter Abelard (1079–1142), a brilliant scholastic theologian, seduced a young girl, his pupil Heloise; eventually she bore him a child, and they were secretly married. Enraged at the betrayal of trust, and what he regarded as the casting off of Heloise, her uncle Fulbert revenged himself by having Abelard castrated. The lovers separated; each of them entered a monastery, and went on to a distinguished career in the Church. Yet their greatest fame derives from the letters they are supposed to have exchanged late in their lives (modern scholars have cast doubt on the authenticity of Heloise's letters). It is this correspondence, made newly popular by French and English translations of the original Latin, that inspired Pope's poem.

The heroic epistle challenges an author in two ways: he must exert his historical imagination, projecting himself into another time and place; and he must enter the mind and passions of a woman, acting her part, and showing everything through her point of view. Historically, Pope draws on his knowledge of Roman Catholic ritual to envelop Eloisa in a rich medieval atmosphere. The dark beauty, but for nothing more famous than for their unfortunate passion. After a long course of calamities, they retired each to a several[2] convent, and consecrated the remainder of their days to religion. It was many years after this separation, that a letter of Abelard's to a friend which contained the history of his misfortune, fell into the hands of Eloisa. This awakening all her tenderness, occasioned those celebrated letters (out of which the following is partly extracted)[3] which give so lively a picture of the struggles of grace and nature, virtue and passion.

In these deep solitudes and awful cells,
Where heavenly-pensive contemplation dwells,
And ever-musing melancholy reigns;
What means this tumult in a vestal's[4] veins?
Why rove my thoughts beyond this last retreat?
Why feels my heart its long-forgotten heat?
Yet, yet I love!—From Abelard it[5] came,
And Eloisa yet must kiss the name.
  Dear fatal name! rest ever unrevealed,
Nor pass these lips in holy silence sealed.
Hide it, my heart, within that close disguise,
Where mixed with God's, his loved idea[6] lies.
O write it not, my hand—the name appears
Already written—wash it out, my tears!
In vain lost Eloisa weeps and prays,
Her heart still dictates, and her hand obeys.
  Relentless walls! whose darksome round contains
Repentant sighs, and voluntary pains:
Ye rugged rocks! which holy knees have worn;
Ye grots and caverns shagged with horrid[7] thorn!
Shrines! where their vigils pale-eyed virgins keep,
And pitying saints, whose statues learn to weep![8]

Gothic convent, situated in an imaginary landscape of grottos, mountains, and pine forests, embodies the 18th-century sense of the "romantic": fantastic, legendary, extravagant. Here Eloisa is cloistered, not only physically but mentally, by religious mysticism that surrounds her with a melancholy as palpable as the image of her lover. The greatest triumph of the poem, however, is psychological. In *Eloisa*, for the only time in his career, Pope tells a story wholly through another's voice. Confused and tormented, the heroine tosses between two kinds of love: an erotic passion for the earthly lover whose memory she cannot quell; and the divine, chaste love that must content a nun. Abelard and God, within her fantasy, compete for her soul. Pope brings these internal struggles to the surface by externalizing them in bold dramatic rhetoric, formal and intense as an aria in an opera (the poem was long a favorite for reading aloud). Eloisa views herself theatrically, if only because, in the letter, she is trying to make Abelard visualize the pathos of her situation. There is literally no way out for her; and at the end of the poem, she can break the static circle of desire and loneliness only by picturing herself in the peace of death. Yet the high reputation of the work, well into the Romantic era, owes less to its theatrics than to its convincing image of a mind in pain. "If you search for passion," Byron wrote more than a century later, "where is it to be found stronger than in the Epistle from Eloisa to Abelard?"

2. Separate.

3. Pope's source was a highly romanticized English version of the letters by John Hughes, published in 1713.

4. Nun's. Here, as elsewhere, Eloisa substitutes a pagan form for a Christian; nor is she in fact a virgin (vestal).

5. The letter to which Eloisa is replying.

6. Mental image or shape.

7. Bristling.

8. In damp places, stone "weeps" through condensation.

Tho' cold like you, unmoved, and silent grown,
I have not yet forgot myself to stone.
All is not Heaven's while Abelard has part,
Still rebel nature holds out half my heart;
Nor prayers nor fasts its stubborn pulse restrain,
Nor tears, for ages taught to flow in vain.
Soon as thy letters trembling I unclose,
That well-known name awakens all my woes.
Oh name for ever sad! for ever dear!
Still breathed in sighs, still ushered with a tear.
I tremble too, where'er my own I find,
Some dire misfortune follows close behind.
Line after line my gushing eyes o'erflow,
Led through a sad variety of woe:
Now warm in love, now withering in my bloom,
Lost in a convent's solitary gloom!
There stern religion quenched the unwilling flame,
There died the best of passions, love and fame.
Yet write, oh write me all, that I may join
Griefs to thy griefs, and echo sighs to thine.
Nor foes nor fortune take this power away.
And is my Abelard less kind than they?
Tears still are mine, and those I need not spare,
Love but demands what else were shed in prayer;
No happier task these faded eyes pursue,
To read and weep is all they now can do.
Then share thy pain, allow that sad relief;
Ah, more than share it! give me all thy grief.
Heaven first taught letters for some wretch's aid,
Some banished lover, or some captive maid;
They live, they speak, they breathe what love inspires,
Warm from the soul, and faithful to its fires,
The virgin's wish without her fears impart,
Excuse the blush, and pour out all the heart,
Speed the soft intercourse from soul to soul,
And waft a sigh from Indus[9] to the Pole.
Thou knowest how guiltless first I met thy flame,
When love approached me under friendship's name;
My fancy formed thee of angelic kind,
Some emanation of the all-beauteous Mind.[1]
Those smiling eyes, attempering[2] every ray,
Shone sweetly lambent with celestial day:
Guiltless I gazed; heaven listened while you sung;
And truths divine came mended from that tongue.[3]
From lips like those what precept failed to move?
Too soon they taught me 'twas no sin to love.
Back through the paths of pleasing sense I ran,
Nor wished an angel whom I loved a man.

9. A southern constellation.
1. God, conceived (as is proper to a student of philosophy) in Platonic terms.
2. Moderating, assuaging.
3. "He was her preceptor in philosophy and divinity" [Pope's note].

Dim and remote the joys of saints I see,
Nor envy them, that heaven I lose for thee.
How oft, when pressed to marriage, have I said,
Curse on all laws but those which love has made!
Love, free as air, at sight of human ties,
Spreads his light wings, and in a moment flies.
Let wealth, let honor, wait the wedded dame,
August her deed, and sacred be her fame;
Before true passion all those views remove,[4]
Fame, wealth, and honor! what are you to love?
The jealous god, when we profane his fires,
Those restless passions in revenge inspires,
And bids them make mistaken mortals groan,
Who seek in love for aught but love alone.
Should at my feet the world's great master fall,
Himself, his throne, his world, I'd scorn 'em all:
Not Caesar's empress would I deign to prove;[5]
No, make me mistress to the man I love;
If there be yet another name more free,
More fond than mistress, make me that to thee!
Oh happy state! when souls each other draw,
When love is liberty, and nature, law:
All then is full, possessing, and possessed,
No craving void left aching in the breast:
Even thought meets thought ere from the lips it part,
And each warm wish springs mutual from the heart.
This sure is bliss (if bliss on earth there be)
And once the lot of Abelard and me.
Alas how changed! what sudden horrors rise!
A naked lover bound and bleeding lies!
Where, where was Eloise? her voice, her hand,
Her poniard, had opposed the dire command.
Barbarian, stay! that bloody stroke restrain;
The crime was common,[6] common be the pain.
I can no more; by shame, by rage suppressed,
Let tears, and burning blushes speak the rest.
Canst thou forget that sad, that solemn day,
When victims at yon altar's foot we lay?
Canst thou forget what tears that moment fell,
When, warm in youth, I bade the world farewell?
As with cold lips I kissed the sacred veil,
The shrines all trembled, and the lamps grew pale:
Heaven scarce believed the conquest it surveyed,
And saints with wonder heard the vows I made.
Yet then, to those dread altars as I drew,
Not on the Cross my eyes were fixed, but you;
Not grace, or zeal, love only was my call,
And if I lose thy love, I lose my all.

4. Depart.
5. Try.
6. Shared; "pain": punishment.

Come! with thy looks, thy words, relieve my woe;
Those still at least are left thee to bestow.
Still on that breast enamored let me lie,
Still drink delicious poison from thy eye,
Pant on thy lip, and to thy heart be pressed;
Give all thou canst—and let me dream the rest.
Ah no! instruct me other joys to prize,
With other beauties charm my partial[7] eyes,
Full in my view set all the bright abode,
And make my soul quit Abelard for God.
 Ah think at least thy flock deserves thy care,
Plants of thy hand, and children of thy prayer.
From the false world in early youth they fled,
By thee to mountains, wilds, and deserts led.
You raised these hallowed walls;[8] the desert smiled,
And paradise was opened in the wild.
No weeping orphan saw his father's stores
Our shrines irradiate,[9] or emblaze the floors;
No silver saints, by dying misers given,
Here bribed the rage of ill-requited heaven:
But such plain roofs as piety could raise,
And only vocal with the Maker's[1] praise.
In these lone walls (their day's eternal bound)
These moss-grown domes with spiry turrets crowned,
Where awful arches make a noon-day night,
And the dim windows shed a solemn light,
Thy eyes diffused a reconciling ray,
And gleams of glory brightened all the day.
But now no face divine contentment wears,
'Tis all blank sadness, or continual tears.
See how the force of others' prayers I try,
(O pious fraud of amorous charity!)
But why should I on others' prayers depend?
Come thou, my father, brother, husband, friend!
Ah let thy handmaid, sister, daughter move,
And all those tender names in one, thy love!
The darksome pines that o'er yon rocks reclined
Wave high, and murmur to the hollow wind,
The wandering streams that shine between the hills,
The grots that echo to the tinkling rills,
The dying gales that pant upon the trees,
The lakes that quiver to the curling breeze;
No more these scenes my meditation aid,
Or lull to rest the visionary[2] maid.
But o'er the twilight groves and dusky caves,

7. Fond; seeing only a part.
8. "He founded the monastery" [Pope's note]. Abelard erected the "Paraclete," a modest oratory near Troyes, in 1122; seven years later, when the nunnery of which Heloise was prioress was evicted from its property, he ceded the lands of the Paraclete to her.
9. Adorn with splendor.
1. God's or Abelard's.
2. Given to visions.

Long-sounding isles,[3] and intermingled graves,
Black Melancholy sits, and round her throws
A death-like silence, and a dread repose:
Her gloomy presence saddens all the scene,
Shades every flower, and darkens every green,
Deepens the murmur of the falling floods,
And breathes a browner horror on the woods.[4]
  Yet here for ever, ever must I stay;
Sad proof how well a lover can obey!
Death, only death, can break the lasting chain;
And here, even then, shall my cold dust remain,
Here all its frailties, all its flames resign,
And wait, till 'tis no sin to mix with thine.
  Ah wretch! believed the spouse of God in vain,
Confessed within the slave of love and man.
Assist me, heaven! but whence arose that prayer?
Sprung it from piety, or from despair?
Even here, where frozen chastity retires,
Love finds an altar for forbidden fires.
I ought to grieve, but cannot what I ought;
I mourn the lover, not lament the fault;
I view my crime, but kindle at the view,
Repent old pleasures, and solicit new;
Now turned to heaven, I weep my past offense,
Now think of thee, and curse my innocence.
Of all affliction taught a lover yet,
'Tis sure the hardest science[5] to forget!
How shall I lose the sin, yet keep the sense,[6]
And love the offender, yet detest the offense?
How the dear object from the crime remove,
Or how distinguish penitence from love?
Unequal task! a passion to resign,
For hearts so touched, so pierced, so lost as mine.
Ere such a soul regains its peaceful state,
How often must it love, how often hate!
How often hope, despair, resent, regret,
Conceal, disdain—do all things but forget.
But let heaven seize it, all at once 'tis fired,
Not touched, but rapt; not wakened, but inspired![7]
Oh come! oh teach me nature to subdue,
Renounce my love, my life, my self—and you.
Fill my fond heart with God alone, for he
Alone can rival, can succeed to thee.
  How happy is the blameless vestal's lot!

3. Sounds reverberate over water as in the *aisles* of a church.
4. "The image of the Goddess Melancholy sitting over the convent, and, as it were, expanding her dreadful wings over its whole circuit, and diffusing her gloom all around it, is truly sublime, and strongly conceived" [Joseph Warton].
5. Knowledge.
6. Both perception and sensation.
7. I.e., when touched, at once rapt; when wakened, at once inspired.

The world forgetting, by the world forgot.
Eternal sun-shine of the spotless mind!
Each prayer accepted, and each wish resigned;
Labor and rest, that equal periods keep;
"Obedient slumbers that can wake and weep;"[8]
Desires composed, affections ever even;
Tears that delight, and sighs that waft to heaven.
Grace shines around her with serenest beams,
And whispering angels prompt her golden dreams.
For her the unfading rose of Eden blooms,
And wings of seraphs shed divine perfumes,
For her the Spouse prepares the bridal ring,
For her white virgins hymenaeals[9] sing,
To sounds of heavenly harps she dies away,
And melts in visions of eternal day.
Far other dreams my erring soul employ,
Far other raptures, of unholy joy:
When at the close of each sad, sorrowing day,
Fancy restores what vengeance snatched away,
Then conscience sleeps, and leaving nature free,
All my loose soul unbounded springs to thee.
O curst, dear horrors of all-conscious night![1]
How glowing guilt exalts the keen delight!
Provoking daemons all restraint remove,
And stir within me every source of love.
I hear thee, view thee, gaze o'er all thy charms,
And round thy phantom glue my clasping arms.
I wake—no more I hear, no more I view,
The phantom flies me, as unkind as you.
I call aloud; it hears not what I say;
I stretch my empty arms; it glides away:
To dream once more I close my willing eyes;
Ye soft illusions, dear deceits, arise!
Alas, no more!—methinks we wandering go
Through dreary wastes, and weep each other's woe;
Where round some moldering tower pale ivy creeps,
And low-browed rocks hang nodding o'er the deeps.
Sudden you mount! you beckon from the skies;
Clouds interpose, waves roar, and winds arise.
I shriek, start up, the same sad prospect find,
And wake to all the griefs I left behind.[2]
For thee the fates, severely kind, ordain
A cool suspense[3] from pleasure and from pain;
Thy life a long dead calm of fixed repose;

8. A quotation from *Description of a Religious House*, by Richard Crashaw.
9. Wedding hymns. Every nun is the bride of Christ, her spouse.
1. The night knows everything; and Eloisa is conscious (guiltily aware) all through the night.
2. Cf. the conclusion to the *Epistle to Miss Blount*, a comic companion-piece to this poem.
3. Suspension.

No pulse that riots, and no blood that glows.
Still as the sea, ere winds were taught to blow,
Or moving spirit bade the waters flow;
Soft as the slumbers of a saint forgiven,
And mild as opening gleams of promised heaven.
  Come, Abelard! for what hast thou to dread?
The torch of Venus burns not for the dead.
Nature stands checked; religion disapproves;
Even thou art cold—yet Eloisa loves.
Ah hopeless, lasting flames! like those that burn
To light the dead, and warm the unfruitful urn.[4]
  What scenes appear where'er I turn my view?
The dear ideas, where I fly, pursue,
Rise in the grove, before the altar rise,
Stain all my soul, and wanton in my eyes!
I waste the matin lamp in sighs for thee,
Thy image steals between my God and me,
Thy voice I seem in every hymn to hear,
With every bead I drop too soft a tear.
When from the censer clouds of fragrance roll,
And swelling organs lift the rising soul,
One thought of thee puts all the pomp to flight,
Priests, tapers, temples, swim before my sight:
In seas of flame[5] my plunging soul is drowned,
While altars blaze, and angels tremble round.
  While prostrate here in humble grief I lie,
Kind, virtuous drops just gathering in my eye,
While praying, trembling, in the dust I roll,
And dawning grace is opening on my soul:
Come, if thou dar'st, all charming as thou art!
Oppose thyself to heaven; dispute[6] my heart;
Come, with one glance of those deluding eyes
Blot out each bright idea of the skies.
Take back that grace, those sorrows, and those tears,
Take back my fruitless penitence and prayers,
Snatch me, just mounting, from the blest abode,
Assist the fiends and tear me from my God!
  No, fly me, fly me! far as pole from pole;
Rise Alps between us! and whole oceans roll!
Ah come not, write not, think not once of me,
Nor share one pang of all I felt for thee.
Thy oaths I quit,[7] thy memory resign,
Forget, renounce me, hate whate'er was mine.
Fair eyes, and tempting looks (which yet I view!)
Long loved, adored ideas! all adieu!
O grace serene! oh virtue heavenly fair!

4. Perpetual fires were placed in Roman tombs.
5. Love, or Hell.
6. Contend for.
7. Absolve.

Divine oblivion of low-thoughted care!
Fresh blooming hope, gay daughter of the sky!
And faith, our early immortality!
Enter, each mild, each amicable guest;
Receive, and wrap me in eternal rest!
  See in her cell sad Eloisa spread,
Propped on some tomb, a neighbor of the dead!
In each low wind methinks a spirit calls,
And more than echoes talk along the walls.
Here, as I watched the dying lamps around,
From yonder shrine I heard a hollow sound.
"Come, sister, come! (it said, or seemed to say)
Thy place is here, sad sister, come away!
Once like thyself, I trembled, wept, and prayed,
Love's victim then, tho' now a sainted maid:
But all is calm in this eternal sleep;
Here grief forgets to groan, and love to weep,
Even superstition loses every fear:
For God, not man, absolves our frailties here."
  I come, I come! prepare your roseate bowers,
Celestial palms, and ever-blooming flowers.
Thither, where sinners may have rest, I go,
Where flames refined in breasts seraphic glow.
Thou, Abelard! the last sad office pay,
And smooth my passage to the realms of day:
See my lips tremble, and my eyeballs roll,
Suck my last breath, and catch my flying soul!
Ah no—in sacred vestments may'st thou stand,
The hallowed taper trembling in thy hand,
Present the Cross before my lifted eye,
Teach me at once, and learn of[8] me to die.
Ah then, thy once-loved Eloisa see!
It will be then no crime to gaze on me.
See from my cheek the transient roses fly!
See the last sparkle languish in my eye!
Till every motion, pulse, and breath be o'er;
And even my Abelard be loved no more.
O death all-eloquent! you only prove
What dust we doat on, when 'tis man we love.
  Then too, when fate shall thy fair frame destroy,
(That cause of all my guilt, and all my joy)
In trance ecstatic may thy pangs be drowned,
Bright clouds descend, and angels watch thee round,
From opening skies may streaming glories shine,
And saints embrace thee with a love like mine.
  May one kind grave unite each hapless name,[9]

8. Learn from.

9. "Abelard and Eloisa were interred in the same grave, or in monuments adjoining, in the monastery of Paraclete" [Pope's note].

And graft my love immortal on thy fame!
Then, ages hence, when all my woes are o'er,
When this rebellious heart shall beat no more;
If ever chance two wandering lovers brings
To Paraclete's white walls, and silver springs,
O'er the pale marble shall they join their heads,
And drink the falling tears each other sheds,
Then sadly say, with mutual pity moved,
"Oh may we never love as these have loved!"
From the full choir when loud Hosannas rise,
And swell the pomp of dreadful sacrifice,[1]
Amid that scene if some relenting eye
Glance on the stone where our cold relics lie,
Devotion's self shall steal a thought from heaven,
One human tear shall drop, and be forgiven.
And sure if fate some future bard shall join
In sad similitude of griefs to mine,
Condemned whole years in absence to deplore,[2]
And image charms he must behold no more,
Such if there be, who loves so long, so well,
Let him our sad, our tender story tell;
The well-sung woes will sooth my pensive ghost;
He best can paint 'em, who shall feel 'em most.

1717

1. The celebration of the Eucharist (Mass).
2. Lament. Pope, imagining himself imagined by Eloisa, hints that he too is separated from a loved one; probably Lady Mary Wortley Montagu, who was in Turkey. Pope and Lady Mary later quarreled, and she appears as Sappho in Epistle II, *To a Lady*.

An Essay on Man

Pope's philosophical poem, *An Essay on Man*, is a fragment of an ambitious but never completed scheme for what the poet referred to as his "ethic work," which was to have been a large survey of man and of the society which he has created. The work is dedicated to Henry St. John (pronounced *Sín-jun*), Viscount Bolingbroke (1678–1751), the brilliant, though erratic, Secretary of State in the Tory ministry of 1710–14, whom Pope had come to know through Swift. After the accession of George I he fled to France, attainted of treason, but was pardoned and allowed to return in 1723. He settled near Pope at Dawley Farm and a close friendship developed between the two men. In their conversations Bolingbroke, who fancied himself a philosopher, helped Pope to formulate the optimistic system that is expounded in this poem, though the notion that Pope merely versified ideas that Bolingbroke furnished him in prose is no longer considered valid.

It is clear that the poem would have been pretty much what it is had the two men never met, for it expresses doctrines widely circulated and generally accepted at the time by enlightened minds throughout Europe.

The *Essay* gives memorable expression to ideas about the nature of the universe and man's place in it, ideas upon which 18th-century optimism rested. The evolutionary theories of the 19th century and the history of the first half of the 20th century have made such optimism untenable today; but this does not mean that the *Essay* is either trivial or cheap.

Pope's purpose is to "vindicate the ways of God to man," a phrase that consciously echoes *Paradise Lost* I.26. Like Milton, Pope faces the problem of the existence of evil in a world presumed to be the creation of a good God (a philosophical work that deals with this problem is called a "theodicy"). *Paradise Lost* is Biblical in content, Christian in doctrine; the *Essay on Man* avoids all specifically Christian doctrines, not because Pope disbelieved them, but because "man," the subject of the poem, includes millions who never heard of Christianity, and Pope is concerned with the universal. Milton tells a mythological story. Pope writes in abstract terms.

The *Essay* is divided into four Epistles. In the first Pope asserts the essential order and goodness of the universe and the rightness of man's place in it. The other Epistles deal with how man may emulate in his nature and in society the cosmic harmony revealed in the first Epistle. The second seeks to show how he may attain a psychological harmony which can become the basis of a virtuous life through the co-operation of self-love and the passions (both necessary to our complete humanity) with reason, the controller and director. The third is concerned with man in society, which, it teaches, was created through the co-operation of self-love (the egoistic drives that motivate us) and social love (our dependence on others, our inborn benevolence). The fourth is concerned with happiness, which lies within the reach of all, for it is dependent upon virtue, which becomes possible when—though only when—self-love is transmuted into love of man and love of God. Such, in brief summary, are Pope's main ideas in the poem. He has given them expression in splendid language, unforgettable phrases (many have detached themselves from the poem and have become a part of our daily speech), and astonishing metrical virtuosity; and though the poem is didactic, it is richly musical and is distinguished by subtly beautiful visual imagery.

From An Essay on Man

TO HENRY ST. JOHN, LORD BOLINGBROKE

Epistle I. Of the Nature and State of Man, With Respect to the Universe

Awake, my St. John! leave all meaner things
To low ambition, and the pride of kings.
Let us (since life can little more supply
Than just to look about us and to die)
Expatiate free[1] o'er all this scene of man;

1. Range freely.

A mighty maze! but not without a plan;
A wild, where weeds and flowers promiscuous shoot,
Or garden, tempting with forbidden fruit.
Together let us beat this ample field,
Try what the open, what the covert yield;
The latent tracts, the giddy heights, explore
Of all who blindly creep, or sightless soar;
Eye Nature's walks, shoot folly as it flies,
And catch the manners living as they rise;
Laugh where we must, be candid[2] where we can;
But vindicate the ways of God to man.[3]

1. Say first, of God above, or man below,
What can we reason, but from what we know?
Of man, what see we but his station here,
From which to reason, or to which refer?
Through worlds unnumbered though the God be known,
'Tis ours to trace him only in our own.
He, who through vast immensity can pierce,
See worlds on worlds compose one universe,
Observe how system into system runs,
What other planets circle other suns,
What varied Being peoples every star,
May tell why Heaven has made us as we are.
But of this frame the bearings, and the ties,
The strong connections, nice dependencies,
Gradations just, has thy pervading soul
Looked through? or can a part contain the whole?
Is the great chain, that draws all to agree,
And drawn supports, upheld by God, or thee?

2. Presumptuous man! the reason wouldst thou find,
Why formed so weak, so little, and so blind?
First, if thou canst, the harder reason guess,
Why formed no weaker, blinder, and no less!
Ask of thy mother earth, why oaks are made
Taller or stronger than the weeds they shade?
Or ask of yonder argent fields above,
Why Jove's satellites[4] are less than Jove?
Of systems possible, if 'tis confessed
That Wisdom Infinite must form the best,
Where all must full or not coherent be,
And all that rises, rise in due degree;
Then, in the scale of reasoning life, 'tis plain,
There must be, somewhere, such a rank as man:
And all the question (wrangle e'er so long)
Is only this, if God has placed him wrong?
Respecting man, whatever wrong we call,
May, must be right, as relative to all.

2. Kindly.
3. Pope deliberately echoes *Paradise Lost* I.26.
4. In his *Dictionary* Johnson notes and condemns Pope's giving his word four syllables, as in Latin.

In human works, though labored on with pain,
A thousand movements scarce one purpose gain;
In God's, one single can its end produce;
Yet serves to second too some other use.
So man, who here seems principal alone,
Perhaps acts second to some sphere unknown,
Touches some wheel, or verges to some goal;
'Tis but a part we see, and not a whole.
When the proud steed shall know why man restrains
His fiery course, or drives him o'er the plains;
When the dull ox, why now he breaks the clod,
Is now a victim, and now Egypt's god:
Then shall man's pride and dullness comprehend
His actions', passions', being's use and end;
Why doing, suffering, checked, impelled; and why
This hour a slave, the next a deity.
Then say not man's imperfect, Heaven in fault;
Say rather, man's as perfect as he ought:
His knowledge measured to his state and place,
His time a moment, and a point his space.
If to be perfect in a certain sphere,[5]
What matter, soon or late, or here or there?
The blest today is as completely so,
As who began a thousand years ago.

3. Heaven from all creatures hides the book of Fate,
All but the page prescribed, their present state:
From brutes what men, from men what spirits know:
Or who could suffer Being here below?
The lamb thy riot dooms to bleed today,
Had he thy reason, would he skip and play?
Pleased to the last, he crops the flowery food,
And licks the hand just raised to shed his blood.
O blindness to the future! kindly given,
That each may fill the circle marked by Heaven:
Who sees with equal eye, as God of all,
A hero perish, or a sparrow fall,
Atoms or systems[6] into ruin hurled,
And now a bubble burst, and now a world.
Hope humbly then; with trembling pinions soar;
Wait the great teacher Death, and God adore!
What future bliss, he gives not thee to know,
But gives that hope to be thy blessing now.
Hope springs eternal in the human breast:
Man never is, but always to be blest:
The soul, uneasy and confined from home,
Rests and expatiates in a life to come.
Lo! the poor Indian, whose untutored mind
Sees God in clouds, or hears him in the wind;
His soul proud Science never taught to stray

5. I.e., in one's "state and place."

6. Solar systems.

Far as the solar walk, or milky way;
Yet simple Nature to his hope has given,
Behind the cloud-topped hill, an humbler heaven;
Some safer world in depth of woods embraced,
Some happier island in the watery waste,
Where slaves once more their native land behold,
No fiends torment, no Christians thirst for gold!
To be, contents his natural desire,
He asks no angel's wing, no seraph's fire;
But thinks, admitted to that equal sky,
His faithful dog shall bear him company.

4. Go, wiser thou! and, in thy scale of sense,
Weigh thy opinion against Providence;
Call imperfection what thou fancy'st such,
Say, here he gives too little, there too much;
Destroy all creatures for thy sport or gust,[7]
Yet cry, if man's unhappy, God's unjust;
If man alone engross not Heaven's high care,
Alone made perfect here, immortal there:
Snatch from his hand the balance and the rod,
Rejudge his justice, be the God of God!
In pride, in reasoning pride, our error lies;
All quit their sphere, and rush into the skies.
Pride still is aiming at the blest abodes,
Men would be angels, angels would be gods.
Aspiring to be gods, if angels fell,
Aspiring to be angels, men rebel:
And who but wishes to invert the laws
Of order, sins against the Eternal Cause.

5. Ask for what end the heavenly bodies shine,
Earth for whose use? Pride answers, " 'Tis for mine:
For me kind Nature wakes her genial power,
Suckles each herb, and spreads out every flower;
Annual for me, the grape, the rose renew
The juice nectareous, and the balmy dew;
For me, the mine a thousand treasures brings;
For me, health gushes from a thousand springs;
Seas roll to waft me, suns to light me rise;
My footstool earth, my canopy the skies."
But errs not Nature from this gracious end,
From burning suns when livid deaths descend,
When earthquakes swallow, or when tempests sweep
Towns to one grave, whole nations to the deep?
"No," 'tis replied, "the first Almighty Cause
Acts not by partial, but by general laws;
The exceptions few; some change since all began,
And what created perfect?"—Why then man?
If the great end be human happiness,

7. "Sense of tasting" (Johnson's *Dictionary*).

Then Nature deviates; and can man do less?
As much that end a constant course requires
Of showers and sunshine, as of man's desires;
As much eternal springs and cloudless skies,
As men forever temperate, calm, and wise.
If plagues or earthquakes break not Heaven's design,
Why then a Borgia, or a Catiline?[8]
Who knows but he whose hand the lightning forms,
Who heaves old ocean, and who wings the storms,
Pours fierce ambition in a Caesar's mind,
Or turns young Ammon[9] loose to scourge mankind?
From pride, from pride, our very reasoning springs;
Account for moral, as for natural things:
Why charge we Heaven in those, in these acquit?
In both, to reason right is to submit.
Better for us, perhaps, it might appear,
Were there all harmony, all virtue here;
That never air or ocean felt the wind;
That never passion discomposed the mind:
But ALL subsists by elemental strife;
And passions are the elements of life.
The general ORDER, since the whole began,
Is kept in Nature, and is kept in man.

6. What would this man? Now upward will he soar,
And little less than angel, would be more;
Now looking downwards, just as grieved appears
To want the strength of bulls, the fur of bears.
Made for his use all creatures if he call,
Say what their use, had he the powers of all?
Nature to these, without profusion, kind,
The proper organs, proper powers assigned;
Each seeming want compénsated of course,
Here with degrees of swiftness, there of force;
All in exact proportion to the state;
Nothing to add, and nothing to abate.
Each beast, each insect, happy in its own;
Is Heaven unkind to man, and man alone?
Shall he alone, whom rational we call,
Be pleased with nothing, if not blessed with all?
The bliss of man (could pride that blessing find)
Is not to act or think beyond mankind;
No powers of body or of soul to share,
But what his nature and his state can bear.
Why has not man a microscopic eye?

8. The Renaissance Italian family of the Borgias were notorious for their crimes: ruthless lust for power, cruelty, rapaciousness, treachery, and murder (especially by poisoning); Cesare Borgia (1476–1507), son of Pope Alexander VI, is here referred to. Lucius Sergius Catiline (ca. 108–62 B.C.), an ambitious, greedy, and cruel conspirator against the Roman state, was denounced in Cicero's famous orations before the senate and in the Forum.

9. Alexander the Great.

For this plain reason, man is not a fly.
Say what the use, were finer optics given,
To inspect a mite, not comprehend the heaven?
Or touch, if tremblingly alive all o'er,
To smart and agonize at every pore?
Or quick effluvia[1] darting through the brain,
Die of a rose in aromatic pain?
If nature thundered in his opening ears,
And stunned him with the music of the spheres,
How would he wish that Heaven had left him still
The whispering zephyr, and the purling rill?
Who finds not Providence all good and wise,
Alike in what it gives, and what denies?

7. Far as creation's ample range extends,
The scale of sensual,[2] mental powers ascends:
Mark how it mounts, to man's imperial race,
From the green myriads in the peopled grass:
What modes of sight betwixt each wide extreme,
The mole's dim curtain, and the lynx's beam:[3]
Of smell, the headlong lioness between,
And hound sagacious[4] on the tainted green:
Of hearing, from the life that fills the flood,
To that which warbles through the vernal wood:
The spider's touch, how exquisitely fine!
Feels at each thread, and lives along the line:
In the nice[5] bee, what sense so subtly true
From poisonous herbs extracts the healing dew:
How instinct varies in the groveling swine,
Compared, half-reasoning elephant, with thine!
'Twixt that, and reason, what a nice barrier;[6]
Forever separate, yet forever near!
Remembrance and reflection how allied;
What thin partitions sense from thought divide:
And middle natures, how they long to join,
Yet never pass the insuperable line!
Without this just gradation, could they be
Subjected, these to those, or all to thee?
The powers of all subdued by thee alone,
Is not thy reason all these powers in one?

8. See, through this air, this ocean, and this earth,
All matter quick, and bursting into birth.
Above, how high progressive life may go!
Around, how wide! how deep extend below!

1. According to the philosophy of Epicurus (adopted by Robert Boyle, the chemist, and other 17th-century scientists), the senses are stirred to perception by being bombarded through the pores by steady streams of "effluvia," incredibly thin and tiny—but material—images of the objects which surround us.
2. Sensory.
3. One of several early theories of vision held that the eye casts a beam of light which makes objects visible.
4. Quick of scent.
5. Exact, accurate.
6. Pronounced *ba-réer.*

Vast Chain of Being! which from God began,
Natures ethereal, human, angel, man,
Beast, bird, fish, insect, what no eye can see,
No glass can reach! from Infinite to thee,
From thee to nothing.—On superior powers
Were we to press, inferior might on ours:
Or in the full creation leave a void,
Where, one step broken, the great scale's destroyed:
From Nature's chain whatever link you strike,
Tenth or ten thousandth, breaks the chain alike.
  And, if each system in gradation roll
Alike essential to the amazing Whole,
The least confusion but in one, not all
That system only, but the Whole must fall.
Let earth unbalanced from her orbit fly,
Planets and suns run lawless through the sky,
Let ruling angels from their spheres be hurled,
Being on being wrecked, and world on world,
Heaven's whole foundations to their center nod,
And Nature tremble to the throne of God:
All this dread ORDER break—for whom? for thee?
Vile worm!—oh, madness, pride, impiety!

  9. What if the foot, ordained the dust to tread,
Or hand, to toil, aspired to be the head?
What if the head, the eye, or ear repined
To serve mere engines to the ruling Mind?[7]
Just as absurd for any part to claim
To be another, in this general frame:
Just as absurd, to mourn the tasks or pains,
The great directing MIND of ALL ordains.
  All are but parts of one stupendous whole,
Whose body Nature is, and God the soul;
That, changed through all, and yet in all the same,
Great in the earth, as in the ethereal frame,
Warms in the sun, refreshes in the breeze,
Glows in the stars, and blossoms in the trees,
Lives through all life, extends through all extent,
Spreads undivided, operates unspent,
Breathes in our soul, informs our mortal part,
As full, as perfect, in a hair as heart;
As full, as perfect, in vile man that mourns,
As the rapt seraph that adores and burns;
To him no high, no low, no great, no small;
He fills, he bounds, connects, and equals all.

  10. Cease then, nor ORDER imperfection name:
Our proper bliss depends on what we blame.
Know thy own point: this kind, this due degree
Of blindness, weakness, Heaven bestows on thee.

7. Cf. I Corinthians xii.14–26.

Submit—In this, or any other sphere,
Secure to be as blest as thou canst bear:
Safe in the hand of one disposing Power,
Or in the natal, or the mortal hour.
All Nature is but art, unknown to thee;
All chance, direction, which thou canst not see;
All discord, harmony not understood;
All partial evil, universal good:
And, spite of pride, in erring reason's spite,
One truth is clear: Whatever IS, is RIGHT.

From *Epistle II. Of the Nature and State of Man With Respect to Himself, as an Individual*

1. Know then thyself, presume not God to scan;
The proper study of mankind is Man.
Placed on this isthmus of a middle state,
A being darkly wise, and rudely great:
With too much knowledge for the skeptic side,
With too much weakness for the Stoic's pride,
He hangs between; in doubt to act, or rest,
In doubt to deem himself a god, or beast;
In doubt his mind or body to prefer,
Born but to die, and reasoning but to err;
Alike in ignorance, his reason such,
Whether he thinks too little, or too much:
Chaos of thought and passion, all confused;
Still by himself abused, or disabused;
Created half to rise, and half to fall;
Great lord of all things, yet a prey to all;
Sole judge of truth, in endless error hurled:
The glory, jest, and riddle of the world!

* * *

1733

The Universal Prayer

Father of all! in every age,
In every clime adored,
By saint, by savage, and by sage,
Jehovah, Jove, or Lord!

Thou Great First Cause, least understood:
Who all my sense confined
To know but this—that thou art good,
And that myself am blind:

Yet gave me, in this dark estate,
To see the good from ill;

And binding Nature fast in fate,
  Left free the human will.

What conscience dictates to be done,
  Or warns me not to do,
This, teach me more than Hell to shun,
  That, more than Heaven pursue.

What blessings thy free bounty gives,
  Let me not cast away;
For God is paid when man receives,
  To enjoy is to obey.

Yet not to earth's contracted span,
  Thy goodness let me bound,
Or think thee Lord alone of man,
  When thousand worlds are round:

Let not this weak, unknowing hand
  Presume thy bolts to throw,
And deal damnation round the land,
  On each I judge thy foe.

If I am right, thy grace impart,
  Still in the right to stay;
If I am wrong, oh teach my heart
  To find that better way.

Save me alike from foolish pride,
  Or impious discontent,
At aught thy wisdom has denied,
  Or aught thy goodness lent.

Teach me to feel another's woe,
  To hide the fault I see;
That mercy I to others show,
  That mercy show to me.

Mean though I am, not wholly so
  Since quickened by thy breath;
Oh lead me wheresoe'er I go,
  Through this day's life or death.

This day, be bread and peace my lot:
  All else beneath the sun,
Thou know'st if best bestowed or not,
  And let thy will be done.

To thee, whose temple is all space,
  Whose altar, earth, sea, skies!
One chorus let all being raise!
  All Nature's incense rise!

ca. 1715 1738

Epistle II. To a Lady[1]

OF THE CHARACTERS OF WOMEN

Nothing so true as what you once let fall,
"Most women have no characters at all."
Matter too soft a lasting mark to bear,
And best distinguished by black, brown, or fair.
How many pictures[2] of one nymph we view,
All how unlike each other, all how true!
Arcadia's countess, here, in ermined pride,
Is, there, Pastora by a fountain side.
Here Fannia, leering on her own good man,
And there, a naked Leda with a swan.[3]
Let then the fair one beautifully cry,
In Magdalen's loose hair and lifted eye,
Or dressed in smiles of sweet Cecilia shine,[4]
With simpering angels, palms, and harps divine;
Whether the charmer sinner it, or saint it,
If folly grow romantic,[5] I must paint it.
Come then, the colors and the ground[6] prepare!

1. This is one of four poems that Pope grouped together under the title *Epistles to Several Persons*, but that have usually been known by the less appropriate title *Moral Essays*. They were conceived as parts of Pope's ambitious "ethic work," of which only the first part, the *Essay on Man*, was completed. *Epistle I* treats the characters of men, *Epistle II* the characters of women. The other two epistles are concerned with the use of riches, a subject that engaged Pope's attention during the 1730's, since he distrusted the influence on private morals and public life of the rapidly growing wealth of England under the first Hanoverians.

Epistle II contains a series of brilliantly executed portraits (the metaphor of portrait painting dominates the poem) which among them illustrate the thesis that women are consistent only in being inconsistent. As we move from portrait to portrait, we not only observe ladies who are changeable and fickle in their own nature, but we also meet a variety of female characters—the affected, the slatternly, the soft-natured, the silly, the lewd, for instance—who remind us that ladies are as variegated as tulips (line 41).

Are the portraits imaginary or do they represent women whom Pope knew and whom his readers could recognize? This question exercised the gossips of Pope's own time and after; and it has occupied the attention of Pope's editors and commentators ever since his death. Many of the portraits indubitably allude to actual women (Sappho); some doubtless are composite (Atossa); others are mere types. Questions of identity, however, pertain rather to Pope's biography and character than to his art. It should matter little if at all to the reader first approaching Pope's satire whether in fact Atossa is Sarah, Duchess of Marlborough, or, as is much more likely, Katherine, Duchess of Buckinghamshire, or, most likely of all, Katherine combined with a few traits of Sarah. Occasionally, perhaps, a lady's name might have hinted to some of Pope's contemporaries that a real person was intended. Today the reader who is not a specialist will do well to neglect particular applications of Pope's satire and to concern himself with the generally, the permanently human, which is always the center of Pope's works.

The "lady" of the title is Martha Blount (1690–1763), Pope's best-loved female friend, to whom he left the bulk of his property.

2. Ladies of the 17th and 18th centuries liked to have themselves painted in the costumes and attitudes of fanciful, mythological, or historical characters.

3. Leda was seduced by Zeus, who approached her in the form of a swan.

4. St. Mary Magdalen was often painted during the 17th century in the attitude described in line 12. St. Cecilia, the reputed inventor of the organ, was traditionally painted in the manner which Pope satirically glances at here.

5. Extravagant.

6. The first coatings of paint on the canvas before the figures in the picture are sketched in.

Dip in the rainbow, trick her off in air;
Choose a firm cloud, before it fall, and in it
Catch, ere she change, the Cynthia[7] of this minute.
Rufa, whose eye quick-glancing o'er the park,
Attracts each light gay meteor of a spark,
Agrees as ill with Rufa studying Locke,[8]
As Sappho's diamonds with her dirty smock,
Or Sappho at her toilet's greasy task,[9]
With Sappho fragrant at an evening masque:
So morning insects that in muck begun,
Shine, buzz, and flyblow in the setting sun.
How soft is Silia! fearful to offend,
The frail one's advocate, the weak one's friend:
To her, Calista proved her conduct nice,
And good Simplicius asks of her advice.
Sudden, she storms! she raves! You tip the wink,
But spare your censure; Silia does not drink.
All eyes may see from what the change arose,
All eyes may see—a pimple on her nose.
Papillia,[1] wedded to her amorous spark,
Sighs for the shades—"How charming is a park!"
A park is purchased, but the fair he sees
All bathed in tears—"Oh, odious, odious trees!"
Ladies, like variegated tulips, show;
'Tis to their changes half their charms we owe;
Fine by defect, and delicately weak,
Their happy spots the nice admirer take,
'Twas thus Calypso[2] once each heart alarmed,
Awed without virtue, without beauty charmed;
Her tongue bewitched as oddly as her eyes,
Less wit than mimic, more a wit than wise;
Strange graces still, and stranger flights she had,
Was just not ugly, and was just not mad;
Yet ne'er so sure our passion to create,
As when she touched the brink of all we hate.
Narcissa's[3] nature, tolerably mild,
To make a wash,[4] would hardly stew a child;
Has even been proved to grant a lover's prayer,
And paid a tradesman once to make him stare,
Gave alms at Easter, in a Christian trim,
And made a widow happy, for a whim.
Why then declare good nature is her scorn,
When 'tis by that alone she can be borne?

7. One of the names of Diana, goddess of the moon, a notoriously changeable heavenly body.
8. John Locke, author of *An Essay Concerning Human Understanding* (1690).
9. Lady Mary Wortley Montagu, though beautiful as a young woman, became notorious for her slatternly appearance and personal uncleanliness. Both Sappho and Lady Mary were female poets. "Flyblow": deposit their eggs.
1. The name comes from Latin for "butterfly."
2. The name is borrowed from the fascinating goddess who detained Odysseus on her island for seven years after the fall of Troy, thus preventing his return to his kingdom, Ithaca.
3. Type of extreme self-love. Narcissus, a beautiful youth, fell in love with his own image when he saw it reflected in a fountain.
4. Cosmetic lotion.

Why pique all mortals, yet affect a name?
A fool to pleasure, yet a slave to fame:
Now deep in Taylor and the *Book of Martyrs*,[5]
Now drinking citron[6] with his Grace and Chartres.
Now conscience chills her, and now passion burns;
And atheism and religion take their turns;
A very heathen in the carnal part,
Yet still a sad, good Christian at her heart.
  See Sin in state, majestically drunk;
Proud as a peeress, prouder as a punk;
Chaste to her husband, frank[6a] to all beside,
A teeming mistress, but a barren bride.
What then? let blood and body bear the fault,
Her head's untouched, that noble seat of thought:
Such this day's doctrine—in another fit
She sins with poets through pure love of wit.
What has not fired her bosom or her brain?
Caesar and Tallboy,[7] Charles and Charlemagne.
As Helluo,[8] late dictator of the feast,
The nose of hautgout,[9] and the tip of taste,
Criticked your wine, and analyzed your meat,
Yet on plain pudding deigned at home to eat;
So Philomedé,[1] lecturing all mankind
On the soft passion, and the taste refined,
The address, the delicacy—stoops at once,
And makes her hearty meal upon a dunce.
  Flavia's a wit, has too much sense to pray;
To toast our wants and wishes, is her way;
Nor asks of God, but of her stars, to give
The mighty blessing, "while we live, to live."
Then all for death, that opiate of the soul!
Lucretia's dagger,[2] Rosamonda's bowl.
Say, what can cause such impotence of mind?
A spark too fickle, or a spouse too kind.
Wise wretch! with pleasures too refined to please,
With too much spirit to be e'er at ease,
With too much quickness ever to be taught,

5. Jeremy Taylor, 17th-century Anglican divine, whose *Holy Living and Holy Dying* was often reprinted in the 18th century. John Foxe's *Acts and Monuments* (usually referred to as Foxe's *Book of Martyrs*), 1563, was a household book in most Protestant families in the 17th and 18th centuries; a record of the Protestants who perished for their faith under the persecution of Mary Tudor (1553–58), it was instrumental in keeping anti-Catholic sentiments alive.

6. I.e., citron-water, brandy flavored with lemon or orange peel. "His Grace" is usually said to be the Duke of Wharton, an old enemy of Swift's and a notorious libertine; Francis Chartres: a debauchee often mentioned by Pope.

6a. "Liberal; generous" (Johnson's *Dictionary*).

7. A crude young man in Richard Brome's comedy *The Jovial Crew* (1641) or the opera adapted from the play (1731); "Charles," as F. W. Bateson points out, was a generic name for a footman in the period.

8. Latin for "glutton."

9. "Anything with a strong relish or strong scent, as overkept venison" (Johnson's *Dictionary*).

1. The name is Pope's adaptation of a Greek epithet meaning "laughter-loving," frequently applied to Aphrodite, the goddess of love.

2. Lucretia, violated by Tarquin, committed suicide; according to tradition, the "fair Rosamonda," mistress of Henry II, was forced by Queen Eleanor to drink poison.

With too much thinking to have common thought:
You purchase pain with all that joy can give,
And die of nothing but a rage to live.
  Turn then from wits; and look on Simo's mate,
No ass so meek, no ass so obstinate.
Or her, that owns her faults, but never mends,
Because she's honest, and the best of friends:
Or her, whose life the Church and scandal share,
Forever in a passion, or a prayer:
Or her, who laughs at hell, but (like her Grace)
Cries, "Ah! how charming, if there's no such place!"
Or who in sweet vicissitude appears
Of mirth and opium, ratafie[3] and tears,
The daily anodyne, and nightly draught,
To kill those foes to fair ones, time and thought.
Woman and fool are two hard things to hit,
For true no-meaning puzzles more than wit.
  But what are these to great Atossa's mind?[4]
Scarce once herself, by turns all womankind!
Who, with herself, or others, from her birth
Finds all her life one warfare upon earth:
Shines in exposing knaves, and painting fools,
Yet is whate'er she hates and ridicules.
No thought advances, but her eddy brain
Whisks it about, and down it goes again.
Full sixty years the world has been her trade,
The wisest fool much time has ever made.
From loveless youth to unrespected age,
No passion gratified except her rage.
So much the fury still outran the wit,
The pleasure missed her, and the scandal hit.
Who breaks with her, provokes revenge from hell,
But he's a bolder man who dares be well:[5]
Her every turn with violence pursued,
Nor more a storm her hate than gratitude:
To that each passion turns, or soon or late;
Love, if it makes her yield, must make her hate:
Superiors? death! and equals? what a curse!
But an inferior not dependent? worse.
Offend her, and she knows not to forgive;
Oblige her, and she'll hate you while you live:
But die, and she'll adore you—Then the bust
And temple rise—then fall again to dust.
Last night, her lord was all that's good and great;
A knave this morning, and his will a cheat.
Strange! by the means defeated of the ends,
By spirit robbed of power, by warmth of friends,
By wealth of followers! without one distress

3. "A fine liquor, prepared from the kernels of apricots and spirits" (Johnson's *Dictionary*).

4. Atossa, daughter of Cyrus, Emperor of Persia (d. 529 B.C.). If the Duchess of Buckinghamshire is alluded to, the name is appropriate, for she was the natural daughter of James II.

5. Be in her favor.

Sick of herself through very selfishness!
Atossa, cursed with every granted prayer,
Childless with all her children, wants an heir.
To heirs unknown descends the unguarded store,
Or wanders, Heaven-directed, to the poor.
   Pictures like these, dear Madam, to design,
Asks no firm hand, and no unerring line;
Some wandering touches, some reflected light,
Some flying stroke alone can hit 'em right:
For how should equal colors do the knack?[6]
Chameleons who can paint in white and black?
   "Yet Chloe sure was formed without a spot—"
Nature in her then erred not, but forgot.
"With every pleasing, every prudent part,
Say, what can Chloe want?"—She wants a heart.
She speaks, behaves, and acts just as she ought;
But never, never, reached one generous thought.
Virtue she finds too painful an endeavor,
Content to dwell in decencies forever.
So very reasonable, so unmoved,
As never yet to love, or to be loved.
She, while her lover pants upon her breast,
Can mark[6a] the figures on an Indian chest;
And when she sees her friend in deep despair,
Observes how much a chintz exceeds mohair.
Forbid it Heaven, a favor or a debt
She e'er should cancel—but she may forget.
Safe is your secret still in Chloe's ear;
But none of Chloe's shall you ever hear.
Of all her dears she never slandered one,
But cares not if a thousand are undone.
Would Chloe know if you're alive or dead?
She bids her footman put it in her head.
Chloe is prudent—Would you too be wise?
Then never break your heart when Chloe dies.
   One certain portrait may (I grant) be seen,
Which Heaven has varnished out, and made a *Queen*:[7]
The same forever! and described by all
With Truth and Goodness, as with crown and ball.
Poets heap virtues, painters gems at will,
And show their zeal, and hide their want of skill.
'Tis well—but, artists! who can paint or write,
To draw the naked is your true delight.
That robe of quality so struts and swells,
None see what parts of Nature it conceals:
The exactest traits of body or of mind,
We owe to models of an humble kind.
If Queensberry[8] to strip there's no compelling,

6. Do the trick.
6a. Pay attention to.
7. Pope refers as usual to Queen Caroline with disapprobation.
8. The Duchess of Queensberry, whom Pope valued because of her kindness to his friend John Gay, had been a famous beauty.

'Tis from a handmaid we must take a Helen.
From peer or bishop 'tis no easy thing
To draw the man who loves his God, or king:
Alas! I copy (or my draft would fail)
From honest Mah'met[9] or plain Parson Hale.
But grant, in public men sometimes are shown,
A woman's seen in private life alone:
Our bolder talents in full light displayed;
Your virtues open fairest in the shade.
Bred to disguise, in public 'tis you hide;
There, none distinguish 'twixt your shame or pride,
Weakness or delicacy; all so nice,
That each may seem a virtue, or a vice.
In men, we various ruling passions find;
In women, two almost divide the kind;
Those, only fixed, they first or last obey,
The love of pleasure, and the love of sway.
That, Nature gives; and where the lesson taught
Is but to please, can pleasure seem a fault?
Experience, this; by man's oppression cursed,
They seek the second not to lose the first.
Men, some to business, some to pleasure take;
But every woman is at heart a rake;
Men, some to quiet, some to public strife;
But every lady would be queen for life.
Yet mark the fate of a whole sex of queens!
Power all their end, but beauty all the means:
In youth they conquer, with so wild a rage,
As leaves them scarce a subject in their age:
For foreign glory, foreign joy, they roam,
No thought of peace or happiness at home.
But wisdom's triumph is well-timed retreat,
As hard a science to the fair as great!
Beauties, like tyrants, old and friendless grown,
Yet hate repose, and dread to be alone,
Worn out in public, weary every eye,
Nor leave one sigh behind them when they die.
Pleasures the sex, as children birds, pursue,
Still out of reach, yet never out of view,
Sure, if they catch, to spoil the toy at most,
To covet flying, and regret when lost:
At last, to follies youth could scarce defend,
It grows their age's prudence to pretend;
Ashamed to own they gave delight before,
Reduced to feign it, when they give no more:
As hags hold sabbaths,[1] less for joy than spite,
So these their merry, miserable night;
Still round and round the ghosts of beauty glide,

9. Mahomet, a Turkish servant of George I; Dr. Stephen Hales was an Anglican clergyman and friend of Pope.

1. Obscene rites popularly supposed to be held by witches ("hags"); "night," in the next line, refers to evenings on which ladies entertained guests.

And haunt the places where their honor died.
See how the world its veterans rewards!
A youth of frolics, an old age of cards;
Fair to no purpose, artful to no end,
Young without lovers, old without a friend;
A fop their passion, but their prize a sot;
Alive, ridiculous, and dead, forgot!
Ah friend! to dazzle let the vain design;
To raise the thought, and touch the heart be thine!
That charm shall grow, while what fatigues the Ring[2]
Flaunts and goes down, an unregarded thing:
So when the sun's broad beam has tired the sight,
All mild ascends the moon's more sober light,
Serene in virgin modesty she shines,
And unobserved the glaring orb declines.
Oh! blest with temper, whose unclouded ray
Can make tomorrow cheerful as today;
She, who can love a sister's charms, or hear
Sighs for a daughter with unwounded ear;
She, who ne'er answers till a husband cools,
Or, if she rules him, never shows she rules;
Charms by accepting, by submitting sways,
Yet has her humor most, when she obeys;
Lets fops or fortune fly which way they will;
Disdains all loss of tickets[3] or Codille;
Spleen, vapors, or smallpox, above them all,
And mistress of herself, though China[4] fall.
And yet, believe me, good as well as ill,
Woman's at best a contradiction still.
Heaven, when it strives to polish all it can
Its last best work, but forms a softer man;
Picks from each sex, to make the favorite blest,
Your love of pleasure, our desire of rest:
Blends, in exception to all general rules,
Your taste of follies, with our scorn of fools:
Reserve with frankness, art with truth allied,
Courage with softness, modesty with pride;
Fixed principles, with fancy ever new;
Shakes all together, and produces—you.
Be this a woman's fame: with this unblest,
Toasts live a scorn, and queens may die a jest.
This Phoebus promised (I forget the year)
When those blue eyes first opened on the sphere;
Ascendant Phoebus watched that hour with care,
Averted half your parents' simple prayer;
And gave you beauty, but denied the pelf
That buys your sex a tyrant o'er itself.
The generous god, who wit and gold refines,

2. The fashionable drive in Hyde Park.
3. I.e., lottery tickets; "Codille": the loss of a hand at the card games of ombre or quadrille.
4. Pope refers punningly to the chinaware which fashionable women collected enthusiastically.

And ripens spirits as he ripens mines,[5]
Kept dross for duchesses, the world shall know it,
To you gave sense, good humor, and a poet.

1735, 1744

Epistle to Dr. Arbuthnot[1]

Advertisement

TO THE FIRST PUBLICATION OF THIS *Epistle*

This paper is a sort of bill of complaint, begun many years since, and drawn up by snatches, as the several occasions offered. I had no thoughts of publishing it, till it pleased some persons of rank and fortune (the authors of *Verses to the Imitator of Horace*, and of an *Epistle to a Doctor of Divinity from a Nobleman at Hampton Court*) to attack, in a very extraordinary manner, not only my writings (of which, being public, the public is judge) but my person, morals, and family, whereof, to those who know me

5. Phoebus Apollo, as god of poetry "ripens wit"; as god of the sun, he "ripens mines," for respectable scientific theory held that the sun's rays mature precious metals in the earth.

1. Dr. John Arbuthnot (1667–1735), to whom Pope addressed his best-known verse epistle, was distinguished both as a physician and as a man of wit. He had been one of the liveliest members of the Martinus Scriblerus Club, helping his friends to create the character and shape the career of the learned pedant whose *Memoirs* the Club had undertaken to write.

Pope had long been meditating such a poem, which was to be both an attack on his detractors and a defense of his own character and career. In his usual way he had jotted down hints, lines, couplets, fragments over a period of two decades, but the poem might never have been completed had it not been for two events: Arbuthnot, from his deathbed, wrote to urge Pope to continue his abhorrence of vice and to express it in his writings; and, during 1733, Pope was the victim of two bitter attacks by "persons of rank and fortune," as the "Advertisement" has it. The *Verses Addressed to the Imitator of Horace* was the work of Lady Mary Wortley Montagu, helped by her friend Lord Hervey (pronounced "Harvey"), a close friend and confidant of Queen Caroline; *An Epistle to a Doctor of Divinity from a Nobleman at Hampton Court* was the work of Lord Hervey alone. Lady Mary, it must be admitted, had provocation enough, especially in Pope's recent reference to her in *The First Satire of the Second Book of Horace,* lines 83–84; but Hervey had little to complain of beyond occasional covert references to him as "Lord Fanny." At any rate, the two scurrilous attacks goaded Pope into action, and the poem was completed by the end of the summer of 1734.

The *Epistle* is a masterpiece of poetic rhetoric. The very fact that it is addressed to Dr. Arbuthnot, a man who had the general approbation of the world because of his kindliness and probity, in some degree seems to guarantee the integrity of the "I" of the poem and to diminish the moral stature of his enemies. This acquisition of virtue through association, an effective stroke, is supported by every device of persuasive rhetoric: reasonable argument and emotional appeals, subtly suggestive imagery, and superbly controlled shifts in tone and style which help to sway the reader's judgment to the side of the speaker. The poem opens in the flat language of commonplace prose discourse, tinged with a wry humor and a tone of exasperation: "Shut, shut the door, good John! (fatigued, I said)" and as it progresses it rises or falls in language and style according to the emotions which the speaker expresses—anger, contempt, amusement, sarcasm, mock self-pity, indignation, hatred, affection, gratitude, tenderness—to return at the end to the homely tone of the opening.

It is not clear that Pope intended the poem to be thought of as a dialogue, as it has usually been printed since Warburton's edition of 1751. The original edition, while suggesting interruptions in the flow of the monologue, kept entirely to the form of a letter. The introduction of the friend, who speaks from time to time, of course converts the original letter into a dramatic dialogue.

not, a truer information may be requisite. Being divided between the necessity to say something of myself, and my own laziness to undertake so awkward a task, I thought it the shortest way to put the last hand to this epistle. If it have anything pleasing, it will be that by which I am most desirous to please, the truth and the sentiment; and if anything offensive, it will be only to those I am least sorry to offend, the vicious or the ungenerous.

Many will know their own pictures in it, there being not a circumstance but what is true; but I have, for the most part, spared their names, and they may escape being laughed at, if they please.

I would have some of them know, it was owing to the request of the learned and candid friend to whom it is inscribed, that I make not as free use of theirs as they have done of mine. However, I shall have this advantage, and honor, on my side, that whereas, by their proceeding, any abuse may be directed at any man, no injury can possibly be done by mine, since a nameless character can never be found out, but by its truth and likeness. P.

P. Shut, shut the door, good John![2] (fatigued, I said),
Tie up the knocker, say I'm sick, I'm dead.
The Dog Star[3] rages! nay 'tis past a doubt
All Bedlam,[4] or Parnassus, is let out:
Fire in each eye, and papers in each hand,
They rave, recite, and madden round the land.
What walls can guard me, or what shades can hide?
They pierce my thickets, through my grot[5] they glide,
By land, by water, they renew the charge,
They stop the chariot, and they board the barge.
No place is sacred, not the church is free;
Even Sunday shines no Sabbath day to me:
Then from the Mint[6] walks forth the man of rhyme,
Happy to catch me just at dinner time.
Is there a parson, much bemused in beer,
A maudlin poetess, a rhyming peer,
A clerk foredoomed his father's soul to cross,
Who pens a stanza when he should engross?[7]
Is there who,[7a] locked from ink and paper, scrawls
With desperate charcoal round his darkened walls?
All fly to Twit'nam,[8] and in humble strain
Apply to me to keep them mad or vain.
Arthur,[9] whose giddy son neglects the laws,

2. John Serle, Pope's gardener.
3. Sirius, associated with the period of greatest heat (and hence of madness) because it sets with the sun in late summer. August, in ancient Rome, was the season for reciting poetry.
4. Bethlehem Hospital for the insane in London.
5. The subterranean passage under the road that separated his house at Twickenham from his garden became, in Pope's hands, a romantic grotto ornamented with shells and mirrors.
6. A place in Southwark where debtors were free from arrest (they could not be arrested anywhere on Sundays).
7. Write out legal documents.
7a. Is there some madman who, locked up without ink or paper* * * ?
8. I.e., Twickenham, Pope's villa on the bank of the Thames, a few miles above Hampton Court.
9. Arthur Moore, whose son, James Moore Smythe, dabbled in literature. Moore Smythe had earned Pope's enmity by using in one of his plays some unpublished lines from Pope's ***Epistle***

Imputes to me and my damned works the cause:
Poor Cornus[1] sees his frantic wife elope,
And curses wit, and poetry, and Pope.
Friend to my life (which did not you prolong,
The world had wanted many an idle song)
What drop or nostrum[2] can this plague remove?
Or which must end me, a fool's wrath or love?
A dire dilemma! either way I'm sped,[2a]
If foes, they write, if friends, they read me dead.
Seized and tied down to judge, how wretched I!
Who can't be silent, and who will not lie.
To laugh were want of goodness and of grace,
And to be grave exceeds all power of face.
I sit with sad civility, I read
With honest anguish and an aching head,
And drop at last, but in unwilling ears,
This saving counsel, "Keep your piece nine years."[3]
"Nine years!" cries he, who high in Drury Lane,[4]
Lulled by soft zephyrs through the broken pane,
Rhymes ere he wakes, and prints before term[5] ends,
Obliged by hunger and request of friends:
"The piece, you think, is incorrect? why, take it,
I'm all submission, what you'd have it, make it."
Three things another's modest wishes bound,
My friendship, and a prologue, and ten pound.
Pitholeon[6] sends to me: "You know his Grace,
I want a patron; ask him for a place."
Pitholeon libeled me—"but here's a letter
Informs you, sir, 'twas when he knew no better.
Dare you refuse him? Curll[7] invites to dine,
He'll write a *Journal*, or he'll turn divine."[8]
Bless me! a packet.—" 'Tis a stranger sues,
A virgin tragedy, an orphan Muse."
If I dislike it, "Furies, death, and rage!"
If I approve, "Commend it to the stage."
There (thank my stars) my whole commission ends,
The players and I are, luckily, no friends.
Fired that the house reject him, " 'Sdeath, I'll print it,
And shame the fools—Your interest, sir, with Lintot!"[9]
Lintot, dull rogue, will think your price too much.
"Not, sir, if you revise it, and retouch."

to a Lady in spite of Pope's objections.
1. Latin for "horn," the traditional emblem of the cuckold.
2. Medicine.
2a. Destroyed; killed (Johnson's *Dictionary*).
3. The advice of Horace in *Ars Poetica* (line 388).
4. I.e., living in a garret in Drury Lane, site of one of the theaters and the haunt of the profligate.
5. One of the four annual periods in which the law courts are in session and with which the publishing season coincided.
6. "A foolish poet of Rhodes, who pretended much to Greek" [Pope's note]; he is Leonard Welsted, who translated Longinus and had attacked and slandered Pope. See line 375.
7. Edmund Curll, shrewd and disreputable bookseller, published pirated works, works falsely ascribed to reputable writers, scandalous biographies, and other ephemera. Pope had often attacked him and had assigned to him a low role in the *Dunciad*.
8. I.e., he will attack Pope in the *London Journal* or write a treatise on theology, as Welsted in fact did.
9. Bernard Lintot, publisher of Pope's Homer and other early works.

All my demurs but double his attacks;
At last he whispers, "Do; and we go snacks."[1]
Glad of a quarrel, straight I clap the door,
"Sir, let me see your works and you no more."
'Tis sung, when Midas' ears began to spring
(Midas, a sacred person and a king),
His very minister who spied them first,
(Some say his queen) was forced to speak, or burst.[2]
And is not mine, my friend, a sorer case,
When every coxcomb perks them in my face?
A. Good friend, forbear! you deal in dangerous things.
I'd never name queens, ministers, or kings;
Keep close to ears, and those let asses prick;
'Tis nothing—— P. Nothing? if they bite and kick?
Out with it, *Dunciad!* let the secret pass,
That secret to each fool, that he's an ass:
The truth once told (and wherefore should we lie?)
The queen of Midas slept, and so may I.
You think this cruel? take it for a rule,
No creature smarts so little as a fool.
Let peals of laughter, Codrus! round thee break,
Thou unconcerned canst hear the mighty crack.
Pit, box, and gallery in convulsions hurled,
Thou stand'st unshook amidst a bursting world.
Who shames a scribbler? break one cobweb through,
He spins the slight, self-pleasing thread anew:
Destroy his fib or sophistry, in vain;
The creature's at his dirty work again,
Throned in the center of his thin designs,
Proud of a vast extent of flimsy lines.
Whom have I hurt? has poet yet or peer
Lost the arched eyebrow or Parnassian sneer?
And has not Colley[3] still his lord and whore?
His butchers Henley? his freemasons Moore?
Does not one table Bavius[4] still admit?
Still to one bishop Philips seem a wit?
Still Sappho[5]—— A. Hold! for God's sake—you'll offend.
No names—be calm—learn prudence of a friend.
I too could write, and I am twice as tall;
But foes like these!—— P. One flatterer's worse than all.

1. Go shares.

2. Midas, king of ancient Lydia, had the bad taste to prefer the flute-playing of Pan to that of Apollo, whereupon the god endowed him with ass's ears. It was his barber (not his wife or his minister) who discovered the secret and whispered it into a hole in the earth. The reference to "queen" and "minister" makes it plain that Pope is alluding to George II, Queen Caroline, and Walpole.

3. Colley Cibber. The laureate John Henley, known as "Orator" Henley, an independent preacher of marked eccentricity, was popular among the lower orders, especially for his elocution.

4. The bad poet alluded to in Virgil's *Eclogues* III. The "Bishop" is Hugh Boulter, Bishop of Armagh; he had employed as his secretary Ambrose Philips (1674–1749), whose insipid and babbling simplicity of manner in poetry earned him the nickname of "Namby-Pamby."

5. Lady Mary Wortley Montagu.

Of all mad creatures, if the learn'd are right,
It is the slaver kills, and not the bite.
A fool quite angry is quite innocent:
Alas! 'tis ten times worse when they repent.
One dedicates in high heroic prose,
And ridicules beyond a hundred foes;
One from all Grub Street[6] will my fame defend,
And, more abusive, calls himself my friend.
This prints my letters,[7] that expects a bribe,
And others roar aloud, "Subscribe, subscribe!"[8]
There are, who to my person pay their court:
I cough like Horace, and, though lean, am short;
Ammon's great son[9] one shoulder had too high,
Such Ovid's nose, and "Sir! you have an eye—"
Go on, obliging creatures, make me see
All that disgraced my betters met in me.
Say for my comfort, languishing in bed,
"Just so immortal Maro[1] held his head":
And when I die, be sure you let me know
Great Homer died three thousand years ago.
Why did I write? what sin to me unknown
Dipped me in ink, my parents', or my own?
As yet a child, nor yet a fool to fame,
I lisped in numbers, for the numbers came.
I left no calling for this idle trade,
No duty broke, no father disobeyed.
The Muse but served to ease some friend, not wife,
To help me through this long disease, my life,
To second, Arbuthnot! thy art and care,
And teach the being you preserved, to bear.[2]
A. But why then publish? P. Granville the polite,
And knowing Walsh, would tell me I could write;
Well-natured Garth inflamed with early praise,
And Congreve loved, and Swift endured my lays;
The courtly Talbot, Somers, Sheffield, read;
Even mitered Rochester would nod the head,
And St. John's self (great Dryden's friends before)
With open arms received one poet more.[3]

6. A term denoting the whole society of literary, political, and journalistic hack writers.
7. In 1726 Curll had surreptitiously acquired and published without permission some of Pope's letters to Henry Cromwell.
8. To ensure the financial success of a work, the public was often asked to "subscribe" to it by taking a certain number of copies before printing was undertaken. Pope's Homer was published thus.
9. Alexander the Great. "Ovid's nose": Ovid's family name Naso suggests the Latin word *nasus* ("nose"), hence the pun.
1. Virgil.
2. Endure.
3. The purpose of this list is to establish Pope as the successor of Dryden and thus to place him far above his Grub-Street persecutors. George Granville, Lord Lansdowne, poet and statesman; William Walsh, poet and critic; Sir Samuel Garth, physician and mock-epic poet; William Congreve, the playwright; the statesmen Charles Talbot, Duke of Shrewsbury; Lord Sommers; John Sheffield, Duke of Buckinghamshire; and Francis Atterbury, Bishop of Rochester, had all been associated with Dryden in his later years and had all encouraged the young Pope.

Happy my studies, when by these approved!
Happier their author, when by these beloved!
From these the world will judge of men and books,
Not from the Burnets, Oldmixons, and Cookes.[4]
  Soft were my numbers; who could take offense
While pure description held the place of sense?
Like gentle Fanny's[5] was my flowery theme,
A painted mistress, or a purling stream.
Yet then did Gildon[6] draw his venal quill;
I wished the man a dinner, and sat still.
Yet then did Dennis[7] rave in furious fret;
I never answered, I was not in debt.
If want provoked, or madness made them print,
I waged no war with Bedlam or the Mint.
  Did some more sober critic come abroad?
If wrong, I smiled; if right, I kissed the rod.
Pains, reading, study are their just pretense,
And all they want is spirit, taste, and sense.
Commas and points they set exactly right,
And 'twere a sin to rob them of their mite.
Yet ne'er one sprig of laurel graced these ribalds,
From slashing Bentley down to piddling Tibbalds.[8]
Each wight who reads not, and but scans and spells,
Each word-catcher that lives on syllables,
Even such small critics some regard may claim,
Preserved in Milton's or in Shakespeare's name.
Pretty! in amber to observe the forms
Of hairs, or straws, or dirt, or grubs, or worms!
The things, we know, are neither rich nor rare,
But wonder how the devil they got there.
  Were others angry? I excused them too;
Well might they rage; I gave them but their due.
A man's true merit 'tis not hard to find;
But each man's secret standard in his mind,
That casting weight[9] pride adds to emptiness,
This, who can gratify? for who can guess?
The bard[1] whom pilfered pastorals renown,

4. Thomas Burnet, John Oldmixon, and Thomas Cooke; Pope identifies them in a note as "authors of secret and scandalous history."

5. John, Lord Hervey, whom Pope satirizes in the character of Sporus, lines 305–33 below.

6. Charles Gildon, minor critic and scribbler, who, Pope believed, early attacked him at the instigation of Addison; hence "venal quill."

7. John Dennis (see *Essay on Criticism*, line 270 and its note).

8. Richard Bentley (1662–1742), the eminent classical scholar, seemed to both Pope and Swift the perfect type of the pedant: he is called "slashing" because, in his edition of *Paradise Lost* (1732), he had set in square brackets all passages which he disliked on the grounds they had been slipped into the poem without the blind poet's knowledge. Lewis Theobald (1688–1744), whose minute learning in Elizabethan literature had enabled him to expose Pope's defects as an editor of Shakespeare in 1726. Pope made him King of the Dunces in the *Dunciad* (1728).

9. The weight that turns the scale; here, the "deciding factor."

1. Ambrose Philips, Pope's rival in pastoral poetry in 1709, when their pastorals were published in Tonson's sixth *Miscellany*. Philips had also translated some Persian tales. Cf. line 100.

Who turns a Persian tale for half a crown,
Just writes to make his barrenness appear,
And strains from hard-bound brains eight lines a year:
He, who still wanting, though he lives on theft,
Steals much, spends little, yet has nothing left;
And he who now to sense, now nonsense leaning,
Means not, but blunders round about a meaning:
And he whose fustian's so sublimely bad,
It is not poetry, but prose run mad:
All these, my modest satire bade translate,
And owned that nine such poets made a Tate.[2]
How did they fume, and stamp, and roar, and chafe!
And swear, not Addison himself was safe.

Peace to all such! but were there one whose fires
True Genius kindles, and fair Fame inspires;
Blessed with each talent and each art to please,
And born to write, converse, and live with ease:
Should such a man, too fond to rule alone,
Bear, like the Turk, no brother near the throne;
View him with scornful, yet with jealous eyes,
And hate for arts that caused himself to rise;
Damn with faint praise, assent with civil leer,
And without sneering, teach the rest to sneer;
Willing to wound, and yet afraid to strike,
Just hint a fault, and hesitate dislike;
Alike reserved to blame or to commend,
A timorous foe, and a suspicious friend;
Dreading even fools; by flatterers besieged,
And so obliging that he ne'er obliged;
Like Cato, give his little senate[3] laws,
And sit attentive to his own applause;
While wits and Templars[4] every sentence raise,
And wonder with a foolish face of praise—
Who but must laugh, if such a man there be?
Who would not weep, if Atticus[5] were he?

What though my name stood rubric[6] on the walls
Or plastered posts, with claps, in capitals?
Or smoking forth, a hundred hawkers' load,
On wings of winds came flying all abroad?
I sought no homage from the race that write;
I kept, like Asian monarchs, from their sight:

2. Nahum Tate (1652–1715), poet laureate (1692–1715). His popular re-writing of Shakespeare's *King Lear* provided a happy ending; he wrote most of Part II of *Absalom and Achitophel*. The line refers to the old adage that it takes nine tailors to make one man.

3. Addison's tragedy *Cato* had been a sensational success in 1713. Pope had written the prologue, in which occurs the line, "While Cato gives his little senate laws." The satirical reference here is to Addison in the role of arbiter of taste among his friends and admirers, mostly Whigs, at Button's Coffee House. It was these people who had worked against the success of Pope's Homer.

4. Law students.

5. Pope's satiric pseudonym for Addison; Atticus (109–32 B.C.) was a wealthy man of letters and a friend of Cicero, known as a wise and disinterested man.

6. In red letters. "Claps": posters.

Poems I heeded (now berhymed so long)
No more than thou, great George! a birthday song.
I ne'er with wits or witlings passed my days
To spread about the itch of verse and praise;
Nor like a puppy daggled through the town
To fetch and carry sing-song up and down;
Nor at rehearsals sweat, and mouthed, and cried,
With handkerchief and orange at my side;
But sick of fops, and poetry, and prate,
To Bufo[7] left the whole Castalian state.
   Proud as Apollo on his forkéd hill,[8]
Sat full-blown Bufo, puffed by every quill;
Fed with soft dedication all day long,
Horace and he went hand in hand in song.
His library (where busts of poets dead
And a true Pindar stood without a head)
Received of wits an undistinguished race,
Who first his judgment asked, and then a place:
Much they extolled his pictures, much his seat,[9]
And flattered every day, and some days eat:
Till grown more frugal in his riper days,
He paid some bards with port, and some with praise;
To some a dry rehearsal was assigned,
And others (harder still) he paid in kind.
Dryden alone (what wonder?) came not nigh;
Dryden alone escaped this judging eye:
But still the great have kindness in reserve;
He helped to bury whom he helped to starve.
   May some choice patron bless each gray goose quill!
May every Bavius have his Bufo still!
So when a statesman wants a day's defense,
Or Envy holds a whole week's war with Sense,
Or simple Pride for flattery makes demands,
May dunce by dunce be whistled off my hands!
Blessed be the great! for those they take away,
And those they left me—for they left me Gay;[1]
Left me to see neglected genius bloom,
Neglected die, and tell it on his tomb;
Of all thy blameless life the sole return
My verse, and Queensberry weeping o'er thy urn!
Oh, let me live my own, and die so too!
("To live and die is all I have to do")
Maintain a poet's dignity and ease,

7. A type of tasteless patron of the arts. (*Bufo* means "toad" in Latin). The Castalian spring on Mt. Parnassus was sacred to Apollo and the Muses.
8. Mt. Parnassus had two peaks, one sacred to Apollo, one to Bacchus.
9. Pronounced *sate,* and rhymed in next line with "eat" (*ate*). *Seat* means "estate."
1. John Gay (1685–1732), author of the *Beggar's Opera* (1728) and other delightful works, dear friend of Swift and Pope. His failure to obtain patronage from the court intensified Pope's hostility to the Whig administration and the queen. Gay spent the last years of his life under the protection of the Duke and Duchess of Queensberry.

And see what friends, and read what books I please;
Above a patron, though I condescend
Sometimes to call a minister my friend.
I was not born for courts or great affairs;
I pay my debts, believe, and say my prayers,
Can sleep without a poem in my head,
Nor know if Dennis be alive or dead.
  Why am I asked what next shall see the light?
Heavens! was I born for nothing but to write?
Has life no joys for me? or (to be grave)
Have I no friend to serve, no soul to save?
"I found him close with Swift"—"Indeed? no doubt"
Cries prating Balbus, "something will come out."
'Tis all in vain, deny it as I will.
"No, such a genius never can lie still,"
And then for mine obligingly mistakes
The first lampoon Sir Will or Bubo makes.[2]
Poor guiltless I! and can I choose but smile,
When every coxcomb knows me by my style?
  Cursed be the verse, how well soe'er it flow,
That tends to make one worthy man my foe,
Give Virtue scandal, Innocence a fear,
Or from the soft-eyed virgin steal a tear!
But he who hurts a harmless neighbor's peace,
Insults fallen worth, or Beauty in distress,
Who loves a lie, lame Slander helps about,
Who writes a libel, or who copies out:
That fop whose pride affects a patron's name,
Yet absent, wounds an author's honest fame;
Who can your merit selfishly approve,
And show the sense of it without the love;
Who has the vanity to call you friend,
Yet wants the honor, injured, to defend;
Who tells whate'er you think, whate'er you say,
And, if he lie not, must at least betray:
Who to the dean and silver bell can swear,
And sees at Cannons what was never there:[3]
Who reads but with a lust to misapply,
Make satire a lampoon, and fiction, lie:
A lash like mine no honest man shall dread,
But all such babbling blockheads in his stead.
  Let Sporus[4] tremble—— A. What? that thing of silk,
Sporus, that mere white curd of ass's milk?[5]
Satire or sense, alas! can Sporus feel?

2. Sir William Yonge, Whig politician and poetaster; George Bubb ("Bubo") Dodington was a Whig patron of letters.

3. Pope's enemies had accused him of satirizing Cannons, the ostentatious estate of the Duke of Chandos, in his description of Timon's villa in the *Epistle to Burlington*. This Pope quite justly denied. The bell of Timon's chapel was of silver, and there preached a dean who "never mentions Hell to ears polite."

4. John, Lord Hervey, effeminate courtier and confidant of Queen Caroline; see title footnote. The original Sporus was a boy, whom the Emperor Nero publicly married (see Suetonius' life of Nero in *The Twelve Caesars*).

5. Ass's milk was drunk by invalids.

Who breaks a butterfly upon a wheel?
  P. Yet let me flap this bug with gilded wings,
This painted child of dirt, that stinks and stings;
Whose buzz the witty and the fair annoys,
Yet wit ne'er tastes, and beauty ne'er enjoys;
So well-bred spaniels civilly delight
In mumbling of the game they dare not bite.
Eternal smiles his emptiness betray,
As shallow streams run dimpling all the way.
Whether in florid impotence he speaks,
And, as the prompter breathes, the puppet squeaks;
Or at the ear of Eve,[6] familiar toad,
Half froth, half venom, spits himself abroad,
In puns, or politics, or tales, or lies,
Or spite, or smut, or rhymes, or blasphemies.
His wit all seesaw between *that* and *this*,
Now high, now low, now master up, now miss,
And he himself one vile antithesis.
Amphibious thing! that acting either part,
The trifling head or the corrupted heart,
Fop at the toilet, flatterer at the board,
Now trips a lady, and now struts a lord.
Eve's tempter thus the rabbins[7] have expressed,
A cherub's face, a reptile all the rest;
Beauty that shocks you, parts that none will trust,
Wit that can creep, and pride that licks the dust.
  Not Fortune's worshiper, nor Fashion's fool,
Not Lucre's madman, nor Ambition's tool,
Not proud, nor servile, be one poet's praise,
That if he pleased, he pleased by manly ways:
That flattery, even to kings, he held a shame,
And thought a lie in verse or prose the same:
That not in fancy's maze he wandered long,
But stooped[8] to truth, and moralized his song:
That not for fame, but Virtue's better end,
He stood the furious foe, the timid friend,
The damning critic, half approving wit,
The coxcomb hit, or fearing to be hit;
Laughed at the loss of friends he never had,
The dull, the proud, the wicked, and the mad;
The distant threats of vengeance on his head,
The blow unfelt, the tear he never shed;
The tale revived, the lie so oft o'erthrown,
The imputed trash, and dullness not his own;
The morals blackened when the writings 'scape,
The libeled person, and the pictured shape;[9]

6. "Eve" is the queen. The allusion is to *Paradise Lost* IV.799–809.
7. Scholars of and authorities on Jewish law and doctrine.
8. The falcon is said to "stoop" to its prey when it swoops down and seizes it in flight.
9. Pope's deformity was frequently ridiculed and occasionally caricatured.

Abuse on all he loved, or loved him, spread,
A friend in exile, or a father dead;
The whisper, that to greatness still too near,
Perhaps yet vibrates on his Sovereign's ear—
Welcome for thee, fair Virtue! all the past!
For thee, fair Virtue! welcome even the last!
  A. But why insult the poor, affront the great?
P. A knave's a knave to me in every state:
Alike my scorn, if he succeed or fail,
Sporus at court, or Japhet[1] in a jail,
A hireling scribbler, or a hireling peer,
Knight of the post[2] corrupt, or of the shire,
If on a pillory, or near a throne,
He gain his prince's ear, or lose his own.
  Yet soft by nature, more a dupe than wit,
Sappho[3] can tell you how this man was bit:
This dreaded satirist Dennis will confess
Foe to his pride, but friend to his distress:[4]
So humble, he has knocked at Tibbald's door,
Has drunk with Cibber, nay, has rhymed for Moore.
Full ten years slandered, did he once reply?
Three thousand suns went down on Welsted's lie.
To please a mistress one aspersed his life;
He lashed him not, but let her be his wife.
Let Budgell charge low Grub Street on his quill,
And write whate'er he pleased, except his will;[5]
Let the two Curlls of town and court,[6] abuse
His father, mother, body, soul, and muse.
Yet why? that father held it for a rule,
It was a sin to call our neighbor fool;
That harmless mother thought no wife a whore:
Hear this, and spare his family, James Moore!
Unspotted names, and memorable long,
If there be force in virtue, or in song.
  Of gentle blood (part shed in honor's cause,
While yet in Britain honor had applause)
Each parent sprung—— A. What fortune, pray?—— P. Their own,
And better got than Bestia's[7] from the throne.
Born to no pride, inheriting no strife,
Nor marrying discord in a noble wife,
Stranger to civil and religious rage,
The good man walked innoxious through his age.
No courts he saw, no suits would ever try,

1. Japhet Crook, a notorious forger.
2. One who lives by selling false evidence.
3. Lady Mary Wortley Montagu. "Bit": taken in; deceived.
4. Pope wrote the prologue to Cibber's *Provoked Husband* when that play was performed for Dennis's benefit, shortly before the old critic died.
5. Eustace Budgell attacked the *Grub Street Journal* for publishing what he took to be a squib by Pope charging him with having forged the will of Dr. Matthew Tindal.
6. I.e., the publisher and Lord Hervey.
7. Probably the Duke of Marlborough, whose vast fortune was made through the favor of Queen Anne. The actual Bestia was a corrupt Roman consul.

Nor dared an oath,[8] nor hazarded a lie.
Unlearn'd, he knew no schoolman's subtle art,
No language but the language of the heart.
By nature honest, by experience wise,
Healthy by temperance, and by exercise;
His life, though long, to sickness passed unknown,
His death was instant, and without a groan.
Oh, grant me thus to live, and thus to die!
Who sprung from kings shall know less joy than I.
O friend! may each domestic bliss be thine!
Be no unpleasing melancholy mine:
Me, let the tender office long engage,
To rock the cradle of reposing Age,
With lenient arts extend a mother's breath,
Make Languor smile, and smooth the bed of Death,
Explore the thought, explain the asking eye,
And keep a while one parent from the sky![9]
On cares like these if length of days attend,
May Heaven, to bless those days, preserve my friend,
Preserve him social, cheerful, and serene,
And just as rich as when he served a Queen![1]
A. Whether that blessing be denied or given,
Thus far was right—the rest belong to Heaven.

1735

8. As a Catholic, Pope's father refused to take the Oaths of Allegiance and Supremacy, and the oath against the Pope. He thus rendered himself vulnerable to the many repressive anti-Catholic laws then in force.

9. Pope was a tender and devoted son. His mother had died in 1733, and the earliest version of these lines dates from 1731, when the poet was nursing her through a serious illness.

1. Pope alludes to the fact that Arbuthnot, a man of strict probity, left the queen's service no wealthier than when he entered it.

The Dunciad: Book the Fourth

The Fourth Book of *The Dunciad*, Pope's last major work, was originally intended as a continuation of *An Essay on Man*. To Swift, the spiritual ancestor of the poem, Pope confided in 1736 that he was at work on a series of epistles on the uses of human reason and learning, to conclude with "a satire against the misapplication of all these, exemplified by pictures, characters, and examples." But the epistles never appeared; instead, the satire grew until it took their place. As Pope surveyed England in his last years, the complex literary and social order that had sustained him seemed to be crumbling. It was a time for desperate measures, for satire. And the means of retribution was at hand, in the structure of Pope's own *Dunciad*, the long work that had already impaled so many enemies.

The first *Dunciad*, published in three books in 1728, is a mock-epic reply to Pope's critics and other petty authors. Its hero and victim, Lewis Theobald, had attacked Pope's edition of Shakespeare (1725); other victims had offended Pope either by personal abuse or simply by ineptitude. Inspired by

Dryden's *Mac Flecknoe*, the *Dunciad* celebrates the triumph of the hordes of Grub Street. Indeed, so many obscure hacks were mentioned that a *Dunciad Variorum* (1729) was soon required, in which mock-scholarly notes identify the victims, "since it is only in this monument that they must expect to survive." But a modern reader need not catch every reference to enjoy the dazzling wit of the poem, or the sheer sense of fun with which Pope remakes the London literary world into a tiny insane fair-ground of his own.

The New Dunciad (1742), however, plays a far more serious game: here Pope takes aim at the rot of the whole social fabric. The satire goes deep, and works at many levels. For convenience, these may be divided into four. 1) Politics: From 1721 to 1742 England had been ruled by the Whig supremacy of Robert Walpole, First Minister. To Pope and his circle, the immensely powerful Walpole (no friend of poets) seemed a crass and greedy vulgarian, like his monarch George II. It is no accident, in the kingdom of the *Dunciad*, that Dulness personified sits on a throne. 2) Society: Just as the action of the *Aeneid* had been the removal of the empire of Troy to Latium, the action of the *Dunciad*, according to Pope, is "the removal of the empire of Dulness from the City of London to the polite world, Westminster"; that is, the abdication of civility in favor of commerce and financial interests. In modern England authors write for money, and ministers govern for profit; conspicuous consumption (especially the consumption of paper by scribblers) has replaced the old values of the yeoman and the aristocrat. In 1743 Pope revised the original *Dunciad*, substituting the actor and poet laureate Colley Cibber for Theobald as the hero, and incorporating *The New Dunciad* as Book Four (the version printed here). Dulness, he implies, has achieved her final triumph; Cibber is laureate in England. 3) Education: The word "dunce" is derived from the scholastic philosopher John Duns Scotus (ca. 1265–1308), whose name had come to stand for silly and useless subtlety, logical hair-splitting. Pope, as an heir of the Renaissance, believes that the central subject of education must always be its relevance for human behavior: "The proper study of mankind is Man," and moral philosophy, the relation of men to each other and to the world, should be the teacher's first and last concern. By contrast, Dunces waste their time on grammar (words alone) or the "science" of the collector (things alone); they never comprehend that word and thing, like spirit and matter, are essentially dead unless they join. 4) Religion: At its deepest level, the subject of the *Dunciad* is the undoing of God's creation. Many passages from Book Four echo *Paradise Lost*, and one of Pope's starting places seems to be Satan's threat (*Paradise Lost* II. 968–87) to return the world to its original darkness, chaos, and ancient night. The *Dunciad* ends in a great apocalypse, with a yawn that signals the death of *Logos*; as words have become meaningless, so has the whole creation, which the Lord called forth with words. Here Pope invokes, with terrifying intensity, the old idea that God was the first poet, whose poem was the world, and suggests that the sickness of the word has infected all nature. But there is one consolation: out of non-art itself, out of matter without spirit and substance without essence, the poet creates his own final artistic triumph, and makes a poem.

From The Dunciad

From *Book the Fourth*

Yet, yet a moment, one dim ray of light
Indulge, dread Chaos, and eternal Night!
Of darkness visible[1] so much be lent,
As half to show, half veil the deep intent.
Ye Powers![2] whose mysteries restored I sing,
To whom Time bears me on his rapid wing,
Suspend a while your force inertly strong,
Then take at once the poet and the song.
  Now flamed the Dog-star's[3] unpropitious ray,
Smote every brain, and withered every bay,[4]
Sick was the sun, the owl forsook his bower,
The moon-struck prophet felt the madding hour:
Then rose the seed[5] of Chaos, and of Night,
To blot out Order, and extinguish Light,
Of dull and venal a new world to mold,
And bring Saturnian[6] days of lead and gold.
  She mounts the throne: her head a cloud concealed,
In broad effulgence all below revealed,
('Tis thus aspiring Dulness ever shines)
Soft on her lap her Laureate son[7] reclines.
  Beneath her foot-stool, Science groans in chains,
And Wit dreads exile, penalties and pains.
There foamed rebellious Logic, gagged and bound,
There, stripped, fair Rhetoric languished on the ground;
His blunted arms by Sophistry are born,
And shameless Billingsgate[8] her robes adorn.
Morality, by her false guardians drawn,
Chicane in furs, and Casuistry in lawn,[9]
Gasps, as they straighten at each end the cord,
And dies, when Dulness gives her Page[1] the word.

[THE EDUCATOR]

  Now crowds on crowds around the Goddess press,
Each eager to present the first Address.[2]
Dunce scorning dunce beholds the next advance,
But fop shows fop superior complaisance.

1. Cf. *Paradise Lost* I. 63.
2. Chaos and Night, invoked in place of the Muse, since "the restoration of their empire is the action of the poem" [Pope].
3. Sirius, associated with the heat of summer and the madness of poets (see *Epistle to Dr. Arbuthnot*, line 3).
4. The laurel, whose garlands are bestowed on poets.
5. The Goddess Dulness.
6. Saturn ruled during the golden age; the new age of "gold" will be re-established by the dull and venal.
7. Colley Cibber, the poet laureate.
8. Fishmarket slang, which now covers the noble science of rhetoric.
9. Chicanery (legal trickery) wears the ermine robe of a judge; casuistry wears the linen sleeves of a bishop.
1. Sir Francis Page, a notorious "hanging judge"; court page, used to strangle criminals in Turkey; page of writing on which a dull author "kills" moral sentiments.
2. The Goddess, newly enthroned, is receiving petitions and congratulations.

When lo! a Specter[3] rose, whose index-hand
Held forth the virtue of the dreadful wand;
His beavered brow a birchen garland wears,[4]
Dropping with infant's blood, and mother's tears.
O'er every vein a shuddering horror runs;
Eton and Winton shake through all their sons.
All flesh is humbled, Westminster's bold race[5]
Shrink, and confess the Genius[6] of the place:
The pale boy-Senator yet tingling stands,
And holds his breeches close with both his hands.
Then thus. "Since Man from beast by words is known,
Words are Man's province, words we teach alone.
When reason doubtful, like the Samian letter,[7]
Points him two ways, the narrower is the better.
Placed at the door of learning, youth to guide,
We never suffer it to stand too wide.
To ask, to guess, to know, as they commence,
As fancy opens the quick springs of sense,
We ply the memory, we load the brain,
Bind rebel wit, and double chain on chain,
Confine the thought, to exercise the breath;[8]
And keep them in the pale of words till death.
Whate'er the talents, or howe'er designed,
We hang one jingling padlock on the mind:
A poet the first day, he dips his quill;
And what the last? a very poet still.
Pity! the charm works only in our wall,
Lost, lost too soon in yonder House or Hall."[9]

[THE CARNATION AND THE BUTTERFLY]

Then thick as locusts blackening all the ground,
A tribe,[1] with weeds and shells fantastic crowned,
Each with some wondrous gift approached the Power,
A nest, a toad, a fungus, or a flower.
But far the foremost, two, with earnest zeal,
And aspect ardent to the throne appeal.
The first thus opened: "Hear thy suppliant's call,
Great Queen, and common Mother of us all!
Fair from its humble bed I reared this flower,
Suckled, and cheer'd, with air, and sun, and shower,
Soft on the paper ruff its leaves I spread,
Bright with the gilded button tipped its head,

3. The ghost of Dr. Busby, stern headmaster of Westminster School.
4. He wears a hat (beaver) and a garland of birch twigs, used for flogging. "Wand": cane used for beating.
5. Alumni of Westminster School, with a play on the justices and members of Parliament who meet at Westminster Hall.
6. I.e., admit that Dr. Busby is the presiding deity (Genius).
7. The letter *Y*, which Pythagoras (a native of Samos) used as an emblem of the different roads of virtue and vice.
8. Students are taught only to recite the classic poets by heart.
9. The House of Commons and Westminster Hall, where law cases were heard. The eloquence learned by rote disappears on occasions for public speaking.
1. The Virtuosi, or amateur scientists and collectors.

Then throned in glass, and named it CAROLINE[2]
Each maid cried, charming! and each youth, divine!
Did Nature's pencil ever blend such rays,
Such varied light in one promiscuous blaze?
Now prostrate! dead! behold that Caroline:
No maid cries, charming! and no youth, divine!
And lo the wretch! whose vile, whose insect lust
Laid this gay daughter of the Spring in dust.
Oh punish him, or to th' Elysian shades
Dismiss my soul, where no carnation fades."
He ceased, and wept. With innocence of mien,
The accused stood forth, and thus addressed the Queen.
"Of all th' enameled race,[3] whose silvery wing
Waves to the tepid zephyrs of the spring,
Or swims along the fluid atmosphere,
Once brightest shined this child of heat and air.
I saw, and started from its vernal bower
The rising game, and chased from flower to flower.
It fled, I followed; now in hope, now pain;
It stopped, I stopped; it moved, I moved again.
At last it fixed, 'twas on what plant it pleased,
And where it fixed, the beauteous bird[4] I seized:
Rose or carnation was below my care;
I meddle, Goddess! only in my sphere.
I tell the naked fact without disguise,
And, to excuse it, need but show the prize;
Whose spoils this paper offers to your eye,
Fair even in death! this peerless Butterfly."
"My sons!" she answered, "both have done your parts;
Live happy both, and long promote our arts.
But hear a mother, when she recommends
To your fraternal care, our sleeping friends.
The common soul, of heaven's more frugal make,
Serves but to keep fools pert, and knaves awake:
A drowsy watchman, that just gives a knock,
And breaks our rest, to tell us what's a clock.[5]
Yet by some object every brain is stirred;
The dull may waken to a hummingbird;
The most recluse, discreetly opened, find
Congenial matter in the cockle-kind;[6]
The mind, in metaphysics at a loss,
May wander in a wilderness of moss;
The head that turns at super-lunar things,
Poised with a tail, may steer on Wilkins' wings.[7]

2. Queen Caroline, an enthusiastic gardener, is an appropriate choice to lend her name to the perfect carnation.
3. Colored insects.
4. Insect.
5. Eighteenth-century watchmen kept guard in the streets and announced the hours.
6. Cockle-shells, popular with collectors, as were hummingbirds and varieties of moss.
7. John Wilkins (1614–72), one of the founders of the Royal Society, had speculated "that a man may be able to fly, by the application of wings to his own body."

"O! would the Sons of Men once think their eyes
And reason given them but to study *flies!*[8]
See Nature in some partial narrow shape,
And let the Author of the whole escape:
Learn but to trifle; or, who most observe,
To wonder at their Maker, not to serve."

[THE TRIUMPH OF DULNESS]

Then blessing all,[9] "Go children of my care!
To practice now from theory repair.
All my commands are easy, short, and full:
My sons! be proud, be selfish, and be dull.
Guard my prerogative, assert my throne:
This nod confirms each privilege your own.
The cap and switch be sacred to his Grace;[1]
With staff and pumps[2] the Marquis lead the race;
From stage to stage the licensed[3] Earl may run,
Paired with his fellow-charioteer the Sun;
The learned Baron butterflies design,
Or draw to silk Arachne's subtle line;[4]
The Judge to dance his brother Sergeant[5] call;
The Senator at cricket urge the ball;
The Bishop stow (pontific luxury!)
An hundred souls of turkeys in a pie;[6]
The sturdy squire to Gallic masters[7] stoop,
And drown his lands and manors in a Soup.
Others import yet nobler arts from France,
Teach kings to fiddle, and make senates dance.
Perhaps more high some daring son may soar,[8]
Proud to my list to add one monarch more;
And nobly conscious, Princes are but things
Born for First Ministers, as slaves for kings,
Tyrant supreme! shall three estates command,
And MAKE ONE MIGHTY DUNCIAD OF THE LAND!"
More she had spoke, but yawned—All Nature nods:
What mortal can resist the Yawn of Gods?
Churches and chapels instantly it reached;
(St. James's first, for leaden Gilbert[9] preached)
Then catched the schools; the Hall scarce kept awake;
The Convocation gaped,[1] but could not speak:

8. Cf. *An Essay on Man* I.189–96: "Say what the use, were finer optics given / T' inspect a mite, not comprehend the heaven?"
9. Having conferred her titles, Dulness bids each of the rulers of England to indulge in the triviality closest to his heart.
1. His Grace, a duke who loves horse-racing, is to use the cap and switch of a jockey.
2. Footmen, who wore pumps (low-cut shoes for running), were matched in races.
3. The license required by the owner of a stagecoach; also, privileged or licentious.
4. A spiderweb.
5. A lawyer or legislative officer; formal ceremonies at the Inns of Court are said to have resembled a country dance, "a call of sergeants."
6. According to Pope, a hundred turkeys had been "not unfrequently deposited in one Pye in the Bishopric of Durham."
7. French chefs.
8. A bold, direct attack on Walpole.
9. Dr. John Gilbert, Dean of Exeter.
1. The Convocation, an assembly of clergy consulting on ecclesiastical affairs, had been adjourned since 1717.

Lost was the Nation's Sense,[2] nor could be found,
While the long solemn unison went round:
Wide, and more wide, it spread o'er all the realm;
Even Palinurus[3] nodded at the helm:
The vapor mild o'er each committee crept;
Unfinished treaties in each office slept;
And chiefless armies dozed out the campaign;
And navies yawned for orders on the main.
O Muse! relate (for you can tell alone,
Wits have short memories, and dunces none)
Relate, who first, who last resigned to rest;
Whose heads she partly, whose completely blessed;
What charms could faction, what ambition lull,
The venal quiet, and entrance the dull;
'Till drowned was sense, and shame, and right, and wrong—
O sing, and hush the nations with thy song!

. . . . .

In vain, in vain,—the all-composing Hour
Resistless falls: The Muse obeys the Power.
She comes! she comes![4] the sable throne behold
Of Night primeval, and of Chaos old!
Before her, Fancy's gilded clouds decay,
And all its varying rainbows die away.
Wit shoots in vain its momentary fires,
The meteor drops, and in a flash expires.
As one by one, at dread Medea's strain,
The sickening stars fade off the ethereal plain;[5]
As Argus' eyes by Hermes' wand oppressed,
Closed one by one to everlasting rest;[6]
Thus at her felt approach, and secret might,
Art after Art goes out, and all is Night.
See skulking Truth to her old cavern fled,[7]
Mountains of casuistry heaped o'er her head!
Philosophy, that leaned on Heaven before,
Shrinks to her second cause,[8] and is no more.
Physic[9] of Metaphysic begs defense,
And Metaphysic calls for aid on Sense!
See Mystery[1] to Mathematics fly!
In vain! they gaze, turn giddy, rave, and die.
Religion blushing veils her sacred fires,
And unawares Morality expires.

2. A term for Parliament.
3. The pilot of Aeneas' ship; here Walpole.
4. Having triumphed in the contemporary world of affairs, Dulness (like her antitype Christ) has a Second Coming, a prophetic vision in which she extinguishes the light of the arts and sciences.
5. In Seneca's *Medea*, the stars obey the curse of Medea, a magician and avenger.
6. Argus, Hera's hundred-eyed watchman, was charmed to sleep and slain by Hermes.
7 "Alluding to the saying of Democritus, that Truth lay at the bottom of a deep well" [Pope's note].
8. Science (philosophy) no longer accepts God as the first cause, or final explanation of how all things came to be; instead, it accepts only the second or material cause, and tries to account for all things by physical principles alone.
9. Natural science in general.
1. A religious truth known only through divine revelation.

Nor public flame, nor private, dares to shine;
Nor human spark is left, nor glimpse divine!
Lo! thy dread Empire, CHAOS is restored;
Light dies before thy uncreating word:[2]
Thy hand, great Anarch! lets the curtain fall;
And Universal Darkness buries All.

1743

2. Cf. God's first creating words in Genesis, "Let there be light."

SAMUEL JOHNSON
(1709–1784)

1737: Settles in London.
1747–55: At work on the *Dictionary*.
1762: Pensioned by the Crown.
1765: Edition of Shakespeare.
1779, 1781: *Lives of the Poets.*

Throughout the 19th century it was generally agreed that although Johnson himself was interesting, especially as a conversationalist, most of his works were unreadable. His poems were condemned as prosaic, his essays as tritely moralistic, his criticism as wrongheaded and tasteless. The case is altered today: a few of the poems, it is agreed, belong with the best of the century; the grave *Rambler* essays, which in his own time established his reputation as a stylist and a moralist, prove not so forbidding as we have been told they are; and the criticism is ranked with that of Dryden and Samuel Taylor Coleridge as the best in English. Boswell's Johnson is chiefly a conversationalist whose talk came hot from a mind that was wise, humane, honest, truthful, and well stored with knowledge drawn from books and experience. The talk is that of a wit and a poet who was quick to seize and to use the unexpected but appropriate image to illuminate truth as it was apprehended by a deeply moral imagination. Any fair examination of Johnson's best writings will demonstrate that for all its studied formality, Johnson's prose surpasses the virtues of his conversation. The object of the talker and of the moral essayist or critic proves in general to be the same—the search for truth in the wide field of human experience; and the wit and wisdom and energy of Johnson's spontaneous talk are also present in his prose.

Two examples must suffice here. When Mrs. Anna Williams wondered why a man should make a beast of himself through drunkenness, Johnson answered that "he who makes a beast of himself gets rid of the pain of being a man." In this reply Mrs. Williams' tired metaphor is so charged with an awareness of the dark aspects of human life that it comes almost unbearably alive. Such moments characterize Johnson's writings as well. For instance, in reviewing the book of a fatuous would-be philosopher who blandly explained away the pains of poverty by declaring that a kindly providence compensates the poor by making them more hopeful, more healthy, more capable of relishing small pleasures and less sensitive to small annoyances than the rich, Johnson, who had known extreme poverty, retorted: "The poor indeed are insensible of many little vexations which sometimes embitter the possessions and pollute the enjoyment of the rich. They are not pained by casual incivility, or mortified by the mutilation of a compliment; but this happiness is like that of the malefactor who ceases to feel the cords that bind him when the pincers are tearing his flesh."

Johnson had himself known the pains of poverty. During his boyhood and youth, his father's financial circumstances steadily worsened, so that he was forced to leave Oxford before he had taken a degree. An early marriage drove him to open a school which was unsuccessful; and the failure of the school prompted him to attempt to make his way as a writer in London. The years between 1737, when he first arrived there with his pupil David Garrick (later to become the leading actor of his generation), and 1755, when the publication of the *Dictionary* established his reputation, were very difficult. He supported himself at first as best he could by doing hack work for the *Gentleman's Magazine*, but gradually his own original writings began to attract attention, though hardly to support his wife and himself.

In 1747 Johnson published the *Plan* of his *Dictionary*, and the next seven years were occupied in compiling it—although he had been sanguine enough to count on finishing it in three years. Boswell remarks that "the world contemplated with wonder" a work "achieved by one man, while other countries had thought such undertakings fit only for whole academies." When in 1748 Dr. Adams, a friend from Oxford days, questioned his ability to carry out such a work alone in so short a time, and reminded him that the *Dictionary* of the French Academy had been compiled by forty academicians working for forty years, Johnson replied with humorous jingoism: "Sir, thus it is. This is the proportion. Let me see; forty times forty is sixteen hundred. As three to sixteen hundred, so is the proportion of an Englishman to a Frenchman."

Johnson's achievement in compiling the *Dictionary* becomes even greater when it is realized that he was writing some of his best essays and poems during the same period, for although the booksellers who published the *Dictionary* paid him what was then the large sum of £1575, it was not enough to enable him to support his household, buy materials, and pay the wages of the six amanuenses whom he employed year by year until the task was accomplished. He therefore had to exert himself to earn more money by writing. Thus, in 1749, his early tragedy *Irene* (pronounced *I-re-nĕ*) was produced at long last by his old friend Garrick, by then not only a successful actor but also the manager of Drury Lane. The play, deservedly, was not a success, though Johnson made some profit from it. In the same year appeared his finest poem, *The Vanity of Human Wishes*. The *Rambler* (1750–52) and the later *Idler* (1758–60), Johnson's very un-Addisonian imitations of the *Spectator*, found admiring readers and spread his reputation as a moralist throughout the island.

Boswell said of the *Rambler* essays that "in no writings whatever can be found more bark and steel [i.e., quinine and iron] for the mind." Moral strength and health; the importance of applying reason to experience; the testing of a man by what he does, not by what he says or merely "feels";

faith in God: these are the centers to which Johnson's moral writings always return. As such critics as Walter Jackson Bate remind us, what Johnson uniquely offers us is the quality of his understanding of the human condition, based on wide reading but always ultimately referred to his own passionate and often anguished experience. Such understanding had to be fought for again and again.

Johnson is thought of as the great generalizer, but what gives his generalizations strength is that they are rooted in the particulars of his self-knowledge. He had constantly to fight against what he called "filling the mind" with illusions, in order to avoid the call of duty, his own black melancholy, and the realities of life. The portrait (largely a self-portrait) of Sober in *Idler* 31 is revealing: he occupies his idle hours with crafts and hobbies, and has now taken up chemistry—he "sits and counts the drops as they come from his retort, and forgets that, whilst a drop is falling, a moment flies away." So clear a vision is some distance away from the secure ease of the Addisonian essay.

His theme of themes is expressed in the title of his poem, *The Vanity of Human Wishes,* by which Johnson means the dangerous but all-pervasive illusion of what we now call wishful thinking, the feverish intrusion of our desires and hopes which distorts reality and interferes with the possibility of sensibly relying on what we have reason to expect. Almost all of Johnson's major writings—verse satire, moral essay, or the prose fable *Rasselas* (1759)—bear this theme. In *Rasselas* it is called "the hunger of imagination, which preys upon life," the seeing of things as one would like them to be, rather than as they are. The travelers who are the fable's protagonists pursue supposed guarantees of happiness; they reflect our naïve hopefulness, against the accumulation of contrary experience, that such a guarantee exists.

During this time of great activity, in which he produced the bulk of his moral writings, Johnson developed his characteristic style: the rotund periods, proceeding through balanced or parallel words; phrases or clauses moving to carefully controlled rhythms, in language that is characteristically general, often Latinate, and frequently polysyllabic. It is a style which is at the opposite extreme from Swift's simplicity or Addison's neatness. In Johnson's writings this style never becomes obscure or turgid, for even a very complex sentence reveals—as it should—the structure of the thought, and the learned words are always precisely used. "Sesquipedalian" words are not so frequent in Johnson's writings as his reputation for using them would imply. He learned many of them when he was reading early scientists to collect words for the *Dictionary*—such words as *obtund, exuberate, fugacity, frigorific,* which most people have been willing to forget. But he used many of these strange words in conversation as well as in his writings, often with a peculiarly Johnsonian felicity, describing the operations of the mind with a scientific precision.

After Johnson received his pension in 1762, he no longer had to write for a living, and since he held that "no man but a blockhead" ever wrote for any other reason, he produced as little as he decently could during the last twenty years of his life. His edition of Shakespeare, long delayed, was published in 1765, with its fine preface and its fascinating notes, both textual and explicatory. Johnson's praise of Shakespeare and his discussion and destruction of the doctrine of the three unities are printed below. His last important work is the *Lives of the Poets,* which came out in two parts in 1779 and 1781. These biographical and critical prefaces were written at the instigation of a group of booksellers who had joined together to publish a large collection of the English poets and who wished to give their venture the prestige that it would acquire if Johnson took part in it. The poets to be included (except for four insisted on by Johnson) were selected by the booksellers, and their choice was determined by the current fashions. We have, therefore, a collection that begins with Cowley and Milton and ends with Gray and the poetaster Lord Lyttleton, and that omits poets whom we regard as "standard," such as Chaucer, Spenser, Sidney, or the metaphysicals.

In the *Lives of the Poets* and in the earlier *Life of Richard Savage* (1744), Johnson did much to advance the art of biography in England. The public had long been familiar with biography as panegyric or as scandalous memoir, and therefore Johnson's insistence on truth, even about the subject's defects, and on concrete, often minute, details was a new departure, disliked by many readers, as Boswell was to find when he followed his master's principles both in the *Journal of a Tour to the Hebrides* and in the *Life* itself. "The biographical part of literature is what I love most," Johnson said, for he found every biography useful in revealing human nature and the way men live. His insistence on truth in biography (and knowing that Boswell intended to write his life, he insisted that he should write it truthfully) was due to his conviction that the more truthful such a work is the more useful it will be to all of us who are concerned with the business of living. The value of the lives of the poets varies, for Johnson wrote some more casually than he did others. He is at his best as a critic when he draws up a general character of a writer's genius and when he discusses individual works.

Johnson's taste was conservative, and he therefore liked little in contemporary literature. He valued Richardson for his knowledge of the human heart, but he considered Fielding "low" and immoral, and Sterne merely perversely odd and trivial. Though he loved Collins, he regretted his fanciful subjects and "harsh" diction, and he offended many by his strictures on what he considered Gray's affectations. He poked gentle fun at his friend Thomas Warton's revival of antique words and "Ode, and elegy, and sonnet." But if he was conservative, he was no worshiper of authority, and least of all was he prone to follow mere theory. As a critic Johnson is always the empiricist, testing theory, as he tested all notions, by experience. His attitude toward the rules is perfectly expressed in these words from *Rambler* 156: "It ought to be the first endeavor of a writer to distinguish nature from custom; or that which is established because it is right, from that which is right only because it is established; that he may neither violate essential principles by a desire of novelty, nor debar himself from the attainment of beauties within his view, by a needless fear of breaking rules which no literary dictator has authority to enact." And the perfect illustration of this attitude is his treatment of the long-revered principle of the three dramatic unities in the Preface to Shakespeare.

That there were "essential principles" which any writer must follow seemed to him self-evident. He must adhere to universal truth and experience, i.e., to "Nature"; he must please, but he must also instruct; he must not offend against religion or promote immorality; he must avoid cold and slavish imitation of others, and he must not cultivate "singularity," the eccentrically original. In the passages from the *Lives of the Poets* below, some of his principles are illustrated. The well-known and influential discussion of metaphysical poetry, with its brilliant definition of "wit" as "a kind of *discordia concors,*" at once illustrates Johnson's genius for formulating broad philosophical principles and reveals clearly why he equated the general with the natural. The notorious attack on Milton's *Lycidas,* which damaged Johnson's reputation as a critic for over a century, puzzles us until we recall that Johnson himself had his critical singularities, which in this case stood between him and a liking for a very great poem: he was justly contemptuous of 18th-century pastoral poetry, which was always conventional, artificial, and bookish, and which could be produced by mere imitation; and he had a great dislike on religious grounds for the Renaissance habit of mingling pagan and Christian materials in a poem. The praise of Dryden, Pope, and Shakespeare, on the other hand, is admirable because those poets nobly illustrated the literary standards that Johnson respected throughout his career.

The Vanity of Human Wishes[1]

IN IMITATION OF THE TENTH SATIRE OF JUVENAL

Let Observation, with extensive view,
Survey mankind, from China to Peru;
Remark each anxious toil, each eager strife,
And watch the busy scenes of crowded life;
Then say how hope and fear, desire and hate
O'erspread with snares the clouded maze of fate,
Where wavering man, betrayed by venturous pride
To tread the dreary paths without a guide,
As treacherous phantoms in the mist delude,
Shuns fancied ills, or chases airy good;

1. *The Vanity of Human Wishes* is an imitation of Juvenal's *Satire X*. Although it closely follows the order and the ideas of the Latin poem, it remains a very personal work, for Johnson has used the Roman Stoic's satire as a means of expressing his own Christian stoicism and his sense of the tragic in human life. He has tried to reproduce in English verse the qualities he thought especially Juvenalian: stateliness, pointed sentences, declamatory grandeur. The poem is difficult because of the extreme compactness of the style: every verse is forced to convey the greatest possible amount of meaning, and as a result the syntax is occasionally obscure. At first the language may seem too general, the frequent personifications mere abstractions. But although Johnson's poetic theory demanded that the poet should deal in the general rather than the particular (cf. his phrase "the grandeur of generality") he certainly did not intend that the general should become the merely abstract: observe, for example, how he makes abstract nouns concrete, active, and dramatic by using them as subjects of active and dramatic verbs: "Hate *dogs* their flight, and Insult *mocks* their end" (line 78). And when the more usual 18th-century combination of general adjective modifying general noun is used, the adjectives are carefully chosen for foreseen effects, as in lines 113–16 (in the first three lines they are used to create a cumulative effect of regal splendor, and in the last line a witty and intellectual impression of Cardinal Wolsey's pride and power): "At once is lost the pride of *awful* state, / The *golden* canopy, the *glittering* plate, / The *regal* palace, the *luxurious* board, / The *liveried* army, and the *menial* lord." The personified abstractions of Collins and Gray, however, are essentially pictorial, grouped in expressive attitudes as they would be in an allegorical painting. A comparison of their method of personification with Johnson's can be readily made by studying Gray's *Eton* ode, stanzas 5–8, along with lines 135–164 of the *Vanity*.

How rarely Reason guides the stubborn choice,
Rules the bold hand, or prompts the suppliant voice;
How nations sink, by darling schemes oppressed,
When Vengeance listens to the fool's request.
Fate wings with every wish the afflictive dart,
Each gift of nature, and each grace of art;
With fatal heat impetuous courage glows,
With fatal sweetness elocution flows,
Impeachment stops the speaker's powerful breath,
And restless fire precipitates on death.
  But scarce observed, the knowing and the bold
Fall in the general massacre of gold;
Wide-wasting pest! that rages unconfined,
And crowds with crimes the records of mankind;
For gold his sword the hireling ruffian draws,
For gold the hireling judge distorts the laws;
Wealth heaped on wealth, nor truth nor safety buys,
The dangers gather as the treasures rise.
  Let History tell where rival kings command,
And dubious title shakes the madded land,
When statutes glean the refuse of the sword,
How much more safe the vassal than the lord,
Low skulks the hind beneath the rage of power,
And leaves the wealthy traitor[2] in the Tower,
Untouched his cottage, and his slumbers sound,
Though Confiscation's vultures hover round.
  The needy traveler, serene and gay,
Walks the wild heath, and sings his toil away.
Does envy seize thee? crush the upbraiding joy,
Increase his riches and his peace destroy;
New fears in dire vicissitude invade,
The rustling brake[3] alarms, and quivering shade,
Nor light nor darkness bring his pain relief,
One shows the plunder, and one hides the thief.
  Yet still one general cry the skies assails,
And gain and grandeur load the tainted gales;
Few know the toiling statesman's fear or care,
The insidious rival and the gaping heir.
  Once more, Democritus,[4] arise on earth,
With cheerful wisdom and instructive mirth,
See motley life in modern trappings dressed,
And feed with varied fools the eternal jest:
Thou who couldst laugh where Want enchained Caprice,
Toil crushed Conceit, and man was of a piece;
Where Wealth unloved without a mourner died;
And scarce a sycophant was fed by Pride;
Where ne'er was known the form of mock debate,

2. Johnson first wrote "bonny traitor," recalling the Jacobite uprising of 1745 and the execution of four of its Scot leaders. "Hind": peasant.

3. Thicket.

4. A Greek philosopher of the late 5th century B.C., remembered as the "laughing philosopher" because men's follies only moved him to mirth.

Or seen a new-made mayor's unwieldy state;
Where change of favorites made no change of laws,
And senates heard before they judged a cause;
How wouldst thou shake at Britain's modish tribe,
Dart the quick taunt, and edge the piercing gibe?
Attentive truth and nature to descry,
And pierce each scene with philosophic eye,
To thee were solemn toys or empty show
The robes of pleasures and the veils of woe:
All aid the farce, and all thy mirth maintain,
Whose joys are causeless, or whose griefs are vain.
Such was the scorn that filled the sage's mind,
Renewed at every glance on human kind;
How just that scorn ere yet thy voice declare,
Search every state, and canvass every prayer.
Unnumbered suppliants crowd Preferment's gate,
Athirst for wealth, and burning to be great;
Delusive Fortune hears the incessant call,
They mount, they shine, evaporate, and fall.
On every stage the foes of peace attend,
Hate dogs their flight, and Insult mocks their end.
Love ends with hope, the sinking statesman's door
Pours in the morning worshiper no more;[5]
For growing names the weekly scribbler lies,
To growing wealth the dedicator flies;
From every room descends the painted face,
That hung the bright palladium[6] of the place;
And smoked in kitchens, or in auctions sold,
To better features yields the frame of gold;
For now no more we trace in every line
Heroic worth, benevolence divine:
The form distorted justifies the fall,
And Detestation rids the indignant wall.
But will not Britain hear the last appeal,
Sign her foes' doom, or guard her favorites' zeal?
Through Freedom's sons no more remonstrance rings,
Degrading nobles and controlling kings;
Our supple tribes repress their patriot throats,
And ask no questions but the price of votes,
With weekly libels and septennial ale.[7]
Their wish is full to riot and to rail.
In full-blown dignity, see Wolsey[8] stand,
Law in his voice, and fortune in his hand:
To him the church, the realm, their powers consign,

5. Statesmen gave interviews and received friends and petitioners at levees, or morning receptions.

6. An image of Pallas Athena, which fell from heaven and was preserved at Troy. Not until it was stolen by Diomedes could the city fall to the Greeks.

7. Ministers and even the king freely bought support by bribing members of Parliament, who in turn won elections by buying votes. "Weekly libels": politically motivated lampoons published in the weekly newspapers; "septennial ale": the ale given away by candidates at parliamentary elections, held at least every seven years.

8. Thomas Cardinal Wolsey (ca. 1475–1530), Lord Chancellor and favorite of Henry VIII. Shakespeare dramatized his fall in *Henry VIII*.

Through him the rays of regal bounty shine;
Turned by his nod the stream of honor flows,
His smile alone security bestows:
Still to new heights his restless wishes tower,
Claim leads to claim, and power advances power;
Till conquest unresisted ceased to please,
And rights submitted, left him none to seize.
At length his sovereign frowns—the train of state
Mark the keen glance, and watch the sign to hate.
Where'er he turns, he meets a stranger's eye,
His suppliants scorn him, and his followers fly;
At once is lost the pride of awful state,
The golden canopy, the glittering plate,
The regal palace, the luxurious board,
The liveried army, and the menial lord.
With age, with cares, with maladies oppressed,
He seeks the refuge of monastic rest.
Grief aids disease, remembered folly stings,
And his last sighs reproach the faith of kings.
  Speak thou, whose thoughts at humble peace repine,
Shall Wolsey's wealth, with Wolsey's end be thine?
Or liv'st thou now, with safer pride content,
The wisest justice on the banks of Trent?
For why did Wolsey, near the steeps of fate,
On weak foundations raise the enormous weight?
Why but to sink beneath misfortune's blow,
With louder ruin to the gulfs below?
  What gave great Villiers[9] to the assassin's knife,
And fixed disease on Harley's closing life?
What murdered Wentworth, and what exiled Hyde,
By kings protected and to kings allied?
What but their wish indulged in courts to shine,
And power too great to keep or to resign?
  When first the college rolls receive his name,
The young enthusiast quits his ease for fame;
Resistless burns the fever of renown
Caught from the strong contagion of the gown:
O'er Bodley's dome his future labors spread,
And Bacon's mansion trembles o'er his head.[1]
Are these thy views? proceed, illustrious youth,
And Virtue guard thee to the throne of Truth!
Yet should thy soul indulge the generous heat,

9. George Villiers, 1st Duke of Buckingham, favorite of James I and Charles I, was assassinated in 1628. Mentioned in the following lines are: Robert Harley, Earl of Oxford, Chancellor of the Exchequer and later Lord Treasurer under Queen Anne (1710–14), impeached and imprisoned by the Whigs in 1715; Thomas Wentworth, Earl of Strafford, intimate and adviser of Charles I, impeached by the Long Parliament and executed 1641; Edward Hyde, Earl of Clarendon ("to kings allied" because his daughter married James, Duke of York), Lord Chancellor under Charles II; impeached in 1667, he fled to the Continent.

1. "Bodley's dome" is the Bodleian Library, Oxford. Roger Bacon (ca. 1214–94), scientist and philosopher, taught at Oxford, where his study, according to tradition, would collapse when a man greater than he should appear at Oxford.

Till captive Science yields her last retreat;
Should Reason guide thee with her brightest ray,
And pour on misty Doubt resistless day;
Should no false kindness lure to loose delight,
Nor praise relax, nor difficulty fright;
Should tempting Novelty thy cell refrain,
And Sloth effuse her opiate fumes in vain;
Should Beauty blunt on fops her fatal dart,
Nor claim the triumph of a lettered heart;
Should no disease thy torpid veins invade,
Nor Melancholy's phantoms haunt thy shade;
Yet hope not life from grief or danger free,
Nor think the doom of man reversed for thee:
Deign on the passing world to turn thine eyes,
And pause a while from letters, to be wise;
There mark what ills the scholar's life assail,
Toil, envy, want, the patron,[2] and the jail.
See nations slowly wise, and meanly just,
To buried merit raise the tardy bust.
If dreams yet flatter, once again attend,
Hear Lydiat's life, and Galileo's end.[3]
  Nor deem, when Learning her last prize bestows,
The glittering eminence exempt from foes;
See when the vulgar 'scapes, despised or awed,
Rebellion's vengeful talons seize on Laud.[4]
From meaner minds though smaller fines content,
The plundered palace, or sequestered rent;[5]
Marked out by dangerous parts he meets the shock,
And fatal Learning leads him to the block:
Around his tomb let Art and Genius weep,
But hear his death, ye blockheads, hear and sleep.
  The festal blazes, the triumphal show,
The ravished standard, and the captive foe,
The senate's thanks, the gazette's pompous tale,
With force resistless o'er the brave prevail.
Such bribes the rapid Greek[6] o'er Asia whirled,
For such the steady Romans shook the world;
For such in distant lands the Britons shine,
And stain with blood the Danube or the Rhine;
This power has praise that virtue scarce can warm,
Till fame supplies the universal charm.
Yet Reason frowns on War's unequal game,
Where wasted nations raise a single name,
And mortgaged states their grandsires' wreaths regret

2. In the first edition, "garret." For the reason of the change see Boswell's *Life of Johnson*.

3. Thomas Lydiat (1572–1646), Oxford scholar, died impoverished because of his Royalist sympathies. Galileo (1564–1642), the famous astronomer, was imprisoned as a heretic by the Inquisition in 1633; he died blind.

4. Appointed Archbishop of Canterbury by Charles I, William Laud followed rigorously high-church policies and was executed by order of the Long Parliament in 1645.

5. During the Commonwealth, the estates of many Royalists were pillaged and their incomes confiscated ("sequestered") by the state.

6. Alexander the Great.

From age to age in everlasting debt;
Wreaths which at last the dear-bought right convey
To rust on medals, or on stones decay.
On what foundation stands the warrior's pride,
How just his hopes, let Swedish Charles[7] decide;
A frame of adamant, a soul of fire,
No dangers fright him, and no labors tire;
O'er love, o'er fear, extends his wide domain,
Unconquered lord of pleasure and of pain;
No joys to him pacific scepters yield,
War sounds the trump, he rushes to the field;
Behold surrounding kings their powers combine,
And one capitulate, and one resign;[8]
Peace courts his hand, but spreads her charms in vain;
"Think nothing gained," he cries, "till naught remain,
On Moscow's walls till Gothic standards fly,
And all be mine beneath the polar sky."
The march begins in military state,
And nations on his eye suspended wait;
Stern Famine guards the solitary coast,
And Winter barricades the realms of Frost;
He comes, nor want nor cold his course delay—
Hide, blushing Glory, hide Pultowa's day:
The vanquished hero leaves his broken bands,
And shows his miseries in distant lands;
Condemned a needy supplicant to wait,
While ladies interpose, and slaves debate.
But did not Chance at length her error mend?
Did no subverted empire mark his end?
Did rival monarchs give the fatal wound?
Or hostile millions press him to the ground?
His fall was destined to a barren strand,
A petty fortress, and a dubious hand;
He left the name at which the world grew pale,
To point a moral, or adorn a tale.
All times their scenes of pompous woes afford,
From Persia's tyrant to Bavaria's lord.[9]
In gay hostility, and barbarous pride,
With half mankind embattled at his side,
Great Xerxes comes to seize the certain prey,
And starves exhausted regions in his way;
Attendant Flattery counts his myriads o'er,
Till counted myriads soothe his pride no more;

7. Charles XII of Sweden (1682–1718). Defeated by the Russians at Pultowa (1709), he escaped to Turkey and tried to form an alliance against Russia with the sultan. Returning to Sweden, he attacked Norway and was killed in the attack on Fredrikshald.

8. Frederick IV of Denmark capitulated to Charles in 1700; Augustus II of Poland resigned his throne to Charles in 1704.

9. Xerxes ("Persia's tyrant") invaded Greece and was totally defeated in the sea battle off Salamis, 480 B.C.; the Elector Charles Albert ("Bavaria's Lord") caused the War of the Austrian Succession (1740–48) when he contested the crown of the Empire with Maria Theresa ("Fair Austria" in line 245).

Fresh praise is tried till madness fires his mind,
The waves he lashes, and enchains the wind;
New powers are claimed, new powers are still bestowed,
Till rude resistance lops the spreading god;
The daring Greeks deride the martial show,
And heap their valleys with the gaudy foe;
The insulted sea with humbler thought he gains,
A single skiff to speed his flight remains;
The encumbered oar scarce leaves the dreaded coast
Through purple billows and a floating host.
  The bold Bavarian, in a luckless hour,
Tries the dread summits of Caesarean power,
With unexpected legions bursts away,
And sees defenseless realms receive his sway;
Short sway! fair Austria spreads her mournful charms,
The queen, the beauty, sets the world in arms;
From hill to hill the beacon's rousing blaze
Spreads wide the hope of plunder and of praise;
The fierce Croatian, and the wild Hussar,[1]
With all the sons of ravage crowd the war;
The baffled prince, in honor's flattering bloom
Of hasty greatness finds the fatal doom;
His foes' derision, and his subjects' blame,
And steals to death from anguish and from shame.
  Enlarge my life with multitude of days!
In health, in sickness, thus the suppliant prays;
Hides from himself his state, and shuns to know,
That life protracted is protracted woe.
Time hovers o'er, impatient to destroy,
And shuts up all the passages of joy;
In vain their gifts the bounteous seasons pour,
The fruit autumnal, and the vernal flower;
With listless eyes the dotard views the store,
He views, and wonders that they please no more;
Now pall the tasteless meats, and joyless wines,
And Luxury with sighs her slave resigns.
Approach, ye minstrels, try the soothing strain,
Diffuse the tuneful lenitives[2] of pain:
No sounds, alas! would touch the impervious ear,
Though dancing mountains witnessed Orpheus[2a] near;
Nor lute nor lyre his feeble powers attend,
Nor sweeter music of a virtuous friend,
But everlasting dictates crowd his tongue,
Perversely grave, or positively wrong.
The still returning tale, and lingering jest,
Perplex the fawning niece and pampered guest,
While growing hopes scarce awe the gathering sneer,
And scarce a legacy can bribe to hear;

1. Hungarian light cavalry.
2. Medicines that relieve pain.
2a. A legendary poet who played on the lyre so beautifully that wild beasts were spellbound.

The watchful guests still hint the last offense;
The daughter's petulance, the son's expense,
Improve his heady rage with treacherous skill,
And mold his passions till they make his will.
   Unnumbered maladies his joints invade,
Lay siege to life and press the dire blockade;
But unextinguished avarice still remains,
And dreaded losses aggravate his pains;
He turns, with anxious heart and crippled hands,
His bonds of debt, and mortgages of lands;
Or views his coffers with suspicious eyes,
Unlocks his gold, and counts it till he dies.
But grant, the virtues of a temperate prime
Bless with an age exempt from scorn or crime;
An age that melts with unperceived decay,
And glides in modest innocence away;
Whose peaceful day Benevolence endears,
Whose night congratulating Conscience cheers;
The general favorite as the general friend:
Such age there is, and who shall wish its end?
   Yet even on this her load Misfortune flings,
To press the weary minutes' flagging wings;
New sorrow rises as the day returns,
A sister sickens, or a daughter mourns.
Now kindred Merit fills the sable bier,
Now lacerated Friendship claims a tear;
Year chases year, decay pursues decay,
Still drops some joy from withering life away;
New forms arise, and different views engage,
Superfluous lags the veteran[3] on the stage,
Till pitying Nature signs the last release,
And bids afflicted Worth retire to peace.
   But few there are whom hours like these await,
Who set unclouded in the gulfs of Fate.
From Lydia's monarch[4] should the search descend,
By Solon cautioned to regard his end,
In life's last scene what prodigies surprise,
Fears of the brave, and follies of the wise!
From Marlborough's eyes the streams of dotage flow,
And Swift expires a driveler and a show.[5]
   The teeming mother, anxious for her race,
Begs for each birth the fortune of a face:
Yet Vane could tell what ills from beauty spring;[6]

3. A veteran of life, not of war.

4. Croesus, the wealthy and fortunate king, was warned by Solon not to count himself happy till he ceased to live. He lost his crown to Cyrus the Great of Persia.

5. John Churchill, Duke of Marlborough, England's brilliant general during most of the War of the Spanish Succession (1702–13); Jonathan Swift, who passed the last four years of his life in utter senility.

6. Anne Vane, mistress of Frederick, Prince of Wales (son of George II). Catherine Sedley, mistress of James II.

And Sedley cursed the form that pleased a king.
Ye nymphs of rosy lips and radiant eyes,
Whom Pleasure keeps too busy to be wise,
Whom Joys with soft varieties invite,
By day the frolic, and the dance by night;
Who frown with vanity, who smile with art,
And ask the latest fashion of the heart;
What care, what rules your heedless charms shall save,
Each nymph your rival, and each youth your slave?
Against your fame with Fondness Hate combines,
The rival batters, and the lover mines.
With distant voice neglected Virtue calls,
Less heard and less, the faint remonstrance falls;
Tired with contempt, she quits the slippery reign,
And Pride and Prudence take her seat in vain.
In crowd at once, where none the pass defend,
The harmless freedom, and the private friend.
The guardians yield, by force superior plied:
To Interest, Prudence; and to Flattery, Pride.
Now Beauty falls betrayed, despised, distressed,
And hissing Infamy proclaims the rest.
   Where then shall Hope and Fear their objects find?
Must dull Suspense corrupt the stagnant mind?
Must helpless man, in ignorance sedate,
Roll darkling down the torrent of his fate?
Must no dislike alarm, no wishes rise,
No cries invoke the mercies of the skies?
Inquirer, cease; petitions yet remain,
Which Heaven may hear, nor deem religion vain.
Still raise for good the supplicating voice,
But leave to Heaven the measure and the choice.
Safe in His power, whose eyes discern afar
The secret ambush of a specious prayer.
Implore His aid, in His decisions rest,
Secure, whate'er He gives, He gives the best.
Yet when the sense of sacred presence fires,
And strong devotion to the skies aspires,
Pour forth thy fervors for a healthful mind,
Obedient passions, and a will resigned;
For love, which scarce collective man can fill;[7]
For patience sovereign o'er transmuted ill;
For faith, that panting for a happier seat,
Counts death kind Nature's signal of retreat:
These goods for man the laws of Heaven ordain,
These goods He grants, who grants the power to gain;
With these celestial Wisdom calms the mind,
And makes the happiness she does not find.

1749

7. Which mankind as a whole can hardly overtask.

Prologue Spoken by Mr. Garrick[1]

AT THE OPENING OF THE THEATRE ROYAL, DRURY LANE, 1747

When Learning's triumph o'er her barbarous foes
First reared the stage, immortal Shakespeare rose;
Each change of many-colored life he drew,
Exhausted worlds, and then imagined new:
Existence saw him spurn her bounded reign,
And panting Time toiled after him in vain.
His powerful strokes presiding Truth impressed,
And unresisted Passion stormed the breast.
Then Jonson came, instructed from the school
To please in method and invent by rule;
His studious patience and laborious art
By regular approach essayed the heart;
Cold Approbation gave the lingering bays,
For those who durst not censure, scarce could praise.[2]
A mortal born, he met the general doom,
But left, like Egypt's kings, a lasting tomb.
The wits of Charles[3] found easier ways to fame,
Nor wished for Jonson's art, or Shakespeare's flame;
Themselves they studied; as they felt, they writ;
Intrigue was plot, obscenity was wit.
Vice always found a sympathetic friend;
They pleased their age, and did not aim to mend.
Yet bards like these aspired to lasting praise,
And proudly hoped to pimp in future days.
Their cause was general, their supports were strong,
Their slaves were willing, and their reign was long:
Till Shame regained the post that Sense betrayed,
And Virtue called Oblivion to her aid.
Then, crushed by rules,[4] and weakened as refined,
For years the power of Tragedy declined;
From bard to bard the frigid caution crept,
Till Declamation roared while Passion slept;
Yet still did Virtue deign the stage to tread;
Philosophy remained though Nature fled;
But forced at length her ancient reign to quit,
She saw great Faustus[5] lay the ghost of Wit;
Exulting Folly hailed the joyous day,
And Pantomime and Song confirmed her sway.
But who the coming changes can presage,
And mark the future periods of the stage?
Perhaps if skill could distant times explore,

1. David Garrick, the famous actor, had become joint patentee and manager of Drury Lane Theatre. Boswell says that this Prologue is unrivaled "for just and manly dramatic criticism."

2. Cf. Dryden's contrast of Shakespeare and Ben Jonson in his *Essay of Dramatic Poesy.*

3. The comic poets of the Restoration period.

4. Cf. Johnson's remarks on the dramatic unities in his preface to Shakespeare.

5. Dr. Faustus at that time was a popular subject for both farce and pantomime.

New Behns,[6] new Durfeys, yet remain in store;
Perhaps where Lear has raved, and Hamlet died,
On flying cars new sorcerers may ride;[7]
Perhaps (for who can guess the effects of chance?)
Here Hunt may box, or Mahomet may dance.[8]
  Hard is his lot that, here by fortune placed,
Must watch the wild vicissitudes of taste;
With every meteor of caprice must play,
And chase the new-blown bubbles of the day.
Ah! let not censure term our fate our choice,
The stage but echoes back the public voice;
The drama's laws, the drama's patrons give,
For we that live to please, must please to live.
  Then prompt no more the follies you decry,
As tyrants doom their tools of guilt to die;
'Tis yours this night to bid the reign commence
Of rescued Nature and reviving Sense;
To chase the charms of Sound, the pomp of Show,
For useful Mirth and salutary Woe;
Bid scenic Virtue form the rising age,
And Truth diffuse her radiance from the stage.

1747

On the Death of Dr. Robert Levet[1]

Condemned to Hope's delusive mine,
  As on we toil from day to day,
By sudden blasts, or slow decline,
  Our social comforts drop away.

Well tried through many a varying year,
  See Levet to the grave descend;
Officious,[2] innocent, sincere,
  Of every friendless name the friend.

Yet still he fills Affection's eye,
  Obscurely wise, and coarsely kind;
Nor, lettered Arrogance, deny
  Thy praise to merit unrefined.

When fainting Nature called for aid,
  And hovering Death prepared the blow,

6. Aphra Behn (1640–89), first Englishwoman to earn her living by writing. Thomas Durfey (1653–1723), satirist and writer of songs and plays.

7. It was a common complaint that the use of increasingly elaborate stage machinery was subordinating drama to mere spectacle.

8. Edward Hunt, a popular pugilist; Mahomet, a tightrope dancer.

1. An unlicensed physician, who lived in Johnson's house for many years and who died in 1782. His practice was among the very poor. Boswell wrote: "He was of a strange grotesque appearance, stiff and formal in his manner, and seldom said a word while any company was present."

2. "Kind, doing good offices" (Johnson's *Dictionary*).

His vigorous remedy displayed
The power of art without the show.

In Misery's darkest cavern known,
His useful care was ever nigh,
Where hopeless Anguish poured his groan,
And lonely Want retired to die.

No summons mocked by chill delay,
No petty gain disdained by pride,
The modest wants of every day
The toil of every day supplied.

His virtues walked their narrow round,
Nor made a pause, nor left a void;
And sure the Eternal Master found
The single talent well employed.[3]

The busy day, the peaceful night,
Unfelt, uncounted, glided by;
His frame was firm, his powers were bright,
Though now his eightieth year was nigh.

Then with no throbbing fiery pain,
No cold gradations of decay,
Death broke at once the vital chain,
And freed his soul the nearest way.

1783

A Short Song of Congratulation

Long-expected one and twenty
Lingering year at last is flown,
Pomp and Pleasure, Pride and Plenty,
Great Sir John,[1] are all your own.

Loosened from the minor's tether,
Free to mortgage or to sell,
Wild as wind, and light as feather
Bid the slaves of thrift farewell.

Call the Bettys, Kates, and Jennys
Every name that laughs at Care,
Lavish of your grandsire's guineas,
Show the spirit of an heir.

All that prey on vice and folly
Joy to see their quarry fly,
Here the gamester light and jolly
There the lender grave and sly.

3. In the parable of the talents (Matthew xxv.14–30), Jesus suggests that salvation will be granted to those who make good use of their abilities, however small.

1. Sir John Lade, nephew of Johnson's friend Henry Thrale. He came into his property in 1780, and, as Johnson foretold, he had squandered it all by his death.

Wealth, Sir John, was made to wander,
Let it wander as it will;
See the jockey, see the pander,
Bid them come, and take their fill.

When the bonny blade carouses,
Pockets full, and spirits high,
What are acres? What are houses?
Only dirt, or wet or dry.

If the guardian or the mother
Tell the woes of willful waste,
Scorn their counsel and their pother,
You can hang or drown at last.

1780 1794

Translation of Horace, *Odes*, Book IV.vii[1]

The snow dissolved no more is seen,
The fields, and woods, behold, are green,
The changing year renews the plain,
The rivers know their banks again,
The spritely nymph and naked grace[2]
The mazy dance together trace.
The changing year's successive plan
Proclaims mortality to man.
Rough winter's blasts to spring give way,
Spring yields to summer's sovereign ray,
Then summer sinks in autumn's reign,
And winter chills the world again.
Her losses soon the moon supplies,
But wretched man, when once he lies
Where Priam[3] and his sons are laid,
Is naught but ashes and a shade.
Who knows if Jove who counts our score
Will toss us in a morning more?
What with your friend you nobly share
At least you rescue from your heir.
Not you, Torquatus, boast of Rome,
When Minos once has fixed your doom,[4]
Or eloquence, or splendid birth,
Or virtue shall replace on earth.
Hippolytus[5] unjustly slain

1. Johnson composed this translation the month before his death.
2. One of the Three Graces, emblematic of beauty.
3. Last king of Troy, slain with his sons at the end of the Trojan War.
4. Sentence. L. Manlius Torquatus, a friend of Horace and an advocate, is represented as pleading his case before Minos, judge of the dead.
5. Phaedra, wife of Theseus, falsely accused his chaste son Hippolytus of rape; Theseus brought about the death of his son, and even Diana, goddess of chastity, could not restore him.

Diana calls to life in vain,
Nor can the might of Theseus rend
The chains of hell that hold his friend.[6]

1784

Rambler No. 5[1]

[*On Spring*]

TUESDAY, *April* 3, 1750

Et nunc omnis ager, nunc omnis parturit arbos,
Nunc frondent silvae, nunc formosissimus annus.
VIRGIL, *Eclogues* III. v. 56

Now ev'ry field, now ev'rv tree is green;
Now genial nature's fairest face is seen.
ELPHINSTON

Every man is sufficiently discontented with some circumstances of his present state, to suffer his imagination to range more or less in quest of future happiness, and to fix upon some point of time, in which, by the removal of the inconvenience which now perplexes him, or acquisition of the advantage which he at present wants, he shall find the condition of his life very much improved.

When this time, which is too often expected with great impatience, at last arrives, it generally comes without the blessing for which it was desired; but we solace ourselves with some new prospect, and press forward again with equal eagerness.

It is lucky for a man, in whom this temper prevails, when he turns his hopes upon things wholly out of his own power; since he forbears then to precipitate[2] his affairs, for the sake of the great event that is to complete his felicity, and waits for the blissful hour, with less neglect of the measures necessary to be taken in the mean time.

I have long known a person of this temper, who indulged his dream of happiness with less hurt to himself than such chimerical wishes commonly produce, and adjusted his scheme with such address, that his hopes were in full bloom three parts of the year, and in the other part never wholly blasted. Many, perhaps, would be desirous of learning by what means he procured to himself such a cheap and lasting satisfaction. It was gained by a constant practice of referring the removal of all his

6. Pirithous, held prisoner with Theseus in Hell.

1. The *Rambler*, almost wholly written by Johnson himself, appeared every Tuesday and Saturday from March 20, 1750, to March 14, 1752—years in which Johnson was writing the *Dictionary*. It is a successor of the *Tatler* and the *Spectator*, but it is much more serious in tone than the earlier periodicals. Johnson's reputation as a moralist and a stylist was established by these essays; because of them Boswell first conceived the ambition to seek Johnson's acquaintance.

2. "To hurry blindly or rashly" (Johnson's *Dictionary*).

uneasiness to the coming of the next spring; if his health was impaired, the spring would restore it; if what he wanted was at a high price, it would fall in value in the spring.

The spring, indeed, did often come without any of these effects, but he was always certain that the next would be more propitious; nor was ever convinced that the present spring would fail him before the middle of summer; for he always talked of the spring as coming till it was past, and when it was once past, everyone agreed with him that it was coming.

By long converse with this man, I am, perhaps, brought to feel immoderate pleasure in the contemplation of this delightful season; but I have the satisfaction of finding many, whom it can be no shame to resemble, infected with the same enthusiasm; for there is, I believe, scarce any poet of eminence, who has not left some testimony of his fondness for the flowers, the zephyrs, and the warblers of the spring. Nor has the most luxuriant imagination been able to describe the serenity and happiness of the golden age, otherwise than by giving a perpetual spring, as the highest reward of uncorrupted innocence.

There is, indeed, something inexpressibly pleasing, in the annual renovation of the world, and the new display of the treasures of nature. The cold and darkness of winter, with the naked deformity of every object on which we turn our eyes, make us rejoice at the succeeding season, as well for what we have escaped, as for what we may enjoy; and every budding flower, which a warm situation brings early to our view, is considered by us as a messenger to notify the approach of more joyous days.

The spring affords to a mind, so free from the disturbance of cares or passions as to be vacant[3] to calm amusements, almost every thing that our present state makes us capable of enjoying. The variegated verdure of the fields and woods, the succession of grateful odors, the voice of pleasure pouring out its notes on every side, with the gladness apparently conceived by every animal, from the growth of his food, and the clemency of the weather, throw over the whole earth an air of gaiety, significantly expressed by the smile of nature.

Yet there are men to whom these scenes are able to give no delight, and who hurry away from all the varieties of rural beauty, to lose their hours, and divert their thoughts by cards, or assemblies, a tavern dinner, or the prattle of the day.

It may be laid down as a position which will seldom deceive, that when a man cannot bear his own company there is something wrong. He must fly from himself, either because he feels a tediousness in life from the equipoise of an empty mind, which, having no tendency to one motion more than another but as it is impelled

3. "At leisure" (Johnson's *Dictionary*).

by some external power, must always have recourse to foreign objects; or he must be afraid of the intrusion of some unpleasing ideas, and, perhaps, is struggling to escape from the remembrance of a loss, the fear of a calamity, or some other thought of greater horror.

Those whom sorrow incapacitates to enjoy the pleasures of contemplation, may properly apply to such diversions, provided they are innocent, as lay strong hold on the attention; and those, whom fear of any future affliction chains down to misery, must endeavor to obviate the danger.

My considerations shall, on this occasion, be turned on such as are burthensome to themselves merely because they want subjects for reflection, and to whom the volume of nature is thrown open, without affording them pleasure or instruction, because they never learned to read the characters.

A French author has advanced this seeming paradox, that *very few men know how to take a walk*; and, indeed, it is true, that few know how to take a walk with a prospect of any other pleasure, than the same company would have afforded them at home.

There are animals that borrow their color from the neighboring body, and, consequently, vary their hue as they happen to change their place. In like manner it ought to be the endeavor of every man to derive his reflections from the objects about him; for it is to no purpose that he alters his position, if his attention continues fixed to the same point. The mind should be kept open to the access of every new idea, and so far disengaged from the predominance of particular thoughts, as easily to accommodate itself to occasional entertainment.

A man that has formed this habit of turning every new object to his entertainment, finds in the productions of nature an inexhaustible stock of materials upon which he can employ himself, without any temptations to envy or malevolence; faults, perhaps, seldom totally avoided by those, whose judgment is much exercised upon the works of art. He has always a certain prospect of discovering new reasons for adoring the sovereign author of the universe, and probable hopes of making some discovery of benefit to others, or of profit to himself. There is no doubt but many vegetables and animals have qualities that might be of great use, to the knowledge of which there is not required much force of penetration, or fatigue of study, but only frequent experiments, and close attention. What is said by the chemists of their darling mercury, is, perhaps, true of everybody through the whole creation, that if a thousand lives should be spent upon it, all its properties would not be found out.

Mankind must necessarily be diversified by various tastes, since life affords and requires such multiplicity of employments, and a nation of naturalists is neither to be hoped, or desired; but it is surely not improper to point out a fresh amusement to those who languish in health, and repine in plenty, for want of some source of diversion that may be less easily exhausted, and to inform the multitudes of both sexes, who are burthened with every new day, that there are many shows which they have not seen.

He that enlarges his curiosity after the works of nature, demonstrably multiplies the inlets to happiness; and, therefore, the younger part of my readers, to whom I dedicate this vernal speculation, must excuse me for calling upon them, to make use at once of the spring of the year, and the spring of life; to acquire, while their minds may be yet impressed with new images, a love of innocent pleasures, and an ardor for useful knowledge; and to remember, that a blighted spring makes a barren year, and that the vernal flowers, however beautiful and gay, are only intended by nature as preparatives to autumnal fruits.

Rambler No. 203

[*Futurity*]

Tuesday, February 25, 1752

Cum volet illa dies, quae nil nisi corporis hujus
Jus habet, incerti spatium mihi finiat aevi.
—OVID, *Metamorphoses*, XV. 873–74

Come, soon or late, death's undetermined day,
This mortal being only can decay.
—WELSTED

It seems to be the fate of man to seek all his consolations in futurity. The time present is seldom able to fill desire or imagination with immediate enjoyment, and we are forced to supply its deficiencies by recollection or anticipation.

Everyone has so often detected the fallaciousness of hope, and the inconvenience of teaching himself to expect what a thousand accidents may preclude, that, when time has abated the confidence with which youth rushes out to take possession of the world, we endeavor, or wish, to find entertainment in the review of life, and to repose upon real facts, and certain experience. This is perhaps one reason, among many, why age delights in narratives.

But so full is the world of calamity, that every source of pleasure is polluted, and every retirement of tranquillity disturbed. When time has supplied us with events sufficient to employ our thoughts, it has mingled them with so many disasters, that we shrink from their remembrance, dread their intrusion upon our minds, and fly from them as from enemies that pursue us with torture.

No man past the middle point of life can sit down to feast upon the pleasures of youth without finding the banquet embittered by the cup of sorrow; he may revive lucky accidents, and pleasing extravagancies; many days of harmless frolic, or nights of honest festivity, will perhaps recur; or, if he has been engaged in scenes of action, and acquainted with affairs of difficulty and vicissitudes of fortune, he may enjoy the nobler pleasure of looking back upon distress firmly supported, dangers resolutely encountered, and opposition artfully defeated. Aeneas properly comforts his companions, when, after the horrors of a storm, they have landed on an unknown and desolate country, with the hope that their miseries will be at some distant time recounted with delight.[1] There are few higher gratifications than that of reflection on surmounted evils, when they were not incurred nor protracted by our fault, and neither reproach us with cowardice, nor guilt.

But this felicity is almost always abated by the reflection that they with whom we should be most pleased to share it are now in the grave. A few years make such havoc in human generations, that we soon see ourselves deprived of those with whom we entered the world, and whom the participation of pleasures or fatigues had endeared to our remembrance. The man of enterprise recounts his adventures and expedients, but is forced at the close of the relation to pay a sigh to the names of those that contributed to his success; he that passes his life among the gayer part of mankind, has his remembrance stored with remarks and repartees of wits, whose sprightliness and merriment are now lost in perpetual silence; the trader whose industry has supplied the want of inheritance, repines in solitary plenty at the absence of companions, with whom he had planned out amusements for his latter years; and the scholar, whose merit, after a long series of efforts, raises him from obscurity, looks round in vain from his exaltation for his old friends or enemies, whose applause or mortification would heighten his triumph.

Among Martial's requisites to happiness is, *res non parta labore, sed relicta*, an estate not gained by industry, but left by inheritance. It is necessary to the completion of every good, that it be timely obtained; for whatever comes at the close of life will come too late to give much delight; yet all human happiness has its defects. Of what we do not gain for ourselves we have only a faint and imperfect fruition, because we cannot compare the difference between want and possession, or at least can derive from it no conviction of our own abilities, nor any increase of self-esteem; what we acquire

1. *Aeneid*, I. 203.

by bravery or science, by mental or corporal diligence, comes at last when we cannot communicate, and therefore cannot enjoy it.[2]

Thus every period of life is obliged to borrow its happiness from the time to come. In youth we have nothing past to entertain us, and in age we derive little from retrospect but hopeless sorrow. Yet the future likewise has its limits, which the imagination dreads to approach, but which we see to be not far distant. The loss of our friends and companions impresses hourly upon us the necessity of our own departure; we know that the schemes of man are quickly at an end, that we must soon lie down in the grave with the forgotten multitudes of former ages, and yield our place to others, who, like us, shall be driven a while by hope or fear about the surface of the earth, and then like us be lost in the shades of death.

Beyond this termination of our material existence, we are therefore obliged to extend our hopes; and almost every man indulges his imagination with something, which is not to happen till he has changed his manner of being. Some amuse themselves with entails and settlements, provide for the perpetuation of families and honors, or contrive to obviate the dissipation of the fortunes, which it has been their business to accumulate; others, more refined or exalted, congratulate their own hearts upon the future extent of their reputation, the reverence of distant nations, and the gratitude of unprejudiced posterity.

They whose souls are so chained down to coffers and tenements, that they cannot conceive a state in which they shall look upon them with less solicitude, are seldom attentive or flexible to arguments; but the votaries of fame are capable of reflection, and therefore may be called to reconsider the probability of their expectations.

Whether to be remembered in remote times be worthy of a wise man's wish, has not yet been satisfactorily decided; and, indeed, to be long remembered, can happen to so small a number, that the bulk of mankind has very little interest in the question. There is never room in the world for more than a certain quantity or measure of renown. The necessary business of life, the immediate pleasures or pains of every condition, leave us not leisure beyond a fixed proportion for contemplations which do not forcibly influence our present welfare. When this vacuity is filled, no characters can be admitted into the circulation of fame, but by occupying the place of some that must be thrust into oblivion. The eye of the mind, like that of the body, can only extend its view to new objects, by losing sight of those which are now before it.

2. When Johnson wrote this, his wife Elizabeth ("Tetty") was near death. She died a few weeks later, on the day that the last *Rambler* essay was published. Both the Johnsons thought that the *Rambler* series was the crown of all his work.

Reputation is therefore a meteor which blazes a while and disappears forever; and if we except a few transcendent and invincible names, which no revolutions of opinion or length of time is able to suppress; all those that engage our thoughts, or diversify our conversation, are every moment hasting to obscurity, as new favorites are adopted by fashion.

It is not therefore from this world, that any ray of comfort can proceed, to cheer the gloom of the last hour. But futurity has still its prospects; there is yet happiness in reserve, which, if we transfer our attention to it, will support us in the pains of disease, and the languor of decay. This happiness we may expect with confidence, because it is out of the power of chance, and may be attained by all that sincerely desire and earnestly pursue it. On this therefore every mind ought finally to rest. Hope is the chief blessing of man, and that hope only is rational, of which we are certain that it cannot deceive us.

Idler No. 31[1]

[*On Idleness*]

SATURDAY, *November* 18, 1758

Many moralists have remarked, that Pride has of all human vices the widest dominion, appears in the greatest multiplicity of forms, and lies hid under the greatest variety of disguises; of disguises, which, like the moon's *veil of brightness*, are both *its luster and its shade*, and betray it to others, though they hide it from ourselves.

It is not my intention to degrade Pride from this pre-eminence of mischief, yet I know not whether Idleness may not maintain a very doubtful and obstinate competition.

There are some that profess Idleness in its full dignity, who call themselves the Idle, as Busiris in the play "calls himself the Proud"; [2] who boast that they do nothing, and thank their stars that they have nothing to do; who sleep every night till they can sleep no longer, and rise only that exercise may enable them to sleep again; who prolong the reign of darkness by double curtains, and never see the sun but to "tell him how they hate his beams"; [3] whose whole labor is to vary the postures of indulgence, and whose day differs from their night but as a couch or chair differs from a bed.

1. Johnson wrote and published the *Idler*, a periodical similar to the *Rambler*, from 1758 until 1760.

2. Edward Young, *Busiris* (1719), I.13.

3. *Paradise Lost* IV.37.

These are the true and open votaries of Idleness, for whom she weaves the garlands of poppies, and into whose cup she pours the waters of oblivion; who exist in a state of unruffled stupidity, forgetting and forgotten; who have long ceased to live, and at whose death the survivors can only say, that they have ceased to breathe.

But Idleness predominates in many lives where it is not suspected; for being a vice which terminates in itself, it may be enjoyed without injury to others; and is therefore not watched like Fraud, which endangers property, or like Pride, which naturally seeks its gratifications in another's inferiority. Idleness is a silent and peaceful quality, that neither raises envy by ostentation, nor hatred by opposition; and therefore nobody is busy to censure or detect it.

As Pride sometimes is hid under humility, Idleness is often covered by turbulence and hurry. He that neglects his known duty and real employment, naturally endeavors to crowd his mind with something that may bar out the remembrance of his own folly, and does any thing but what he ought to do with eager diligence, that he may keep himself in his own favor.

Some are always in a state of preparation, occupied in previous measures, forming plans, accumulating materials, and providing for the main affair. These are certainly under the secret power of Idleness. Nothing is to be expected from the workman whose tools are forever to be sought. I was once told by a great master, that no man ever excelled in painting, who was eminently curious about pencils and colors.

There are others to whom Idleness dictates another expedient, by which life may be passed unprofitably away without the tediousness of many vacant hours. The art is, to fill the day with petty business, to have always something in hand which may raise curiosity, but not solicitude, and keep the mind in a state of action, but not of labor.

This art has for many years been practiced by my old friend Sober, with wonderful success. Sober is a man of strong desires and quick imagination, so exactly balanced by the love of ease, that they can seldom stimulate him to any difficult undertaking; they have, however, so much power, that they will not suffer him to lie quite at rest, and though they do not make him sufficiently useful to others, they make him at least weary of himself.

Mr. Sober's chief pleasure is conversation; there is no end of his talk or his attention; to speak or to hear is equally pleasing; for he still fancies that he is teaching or learning something, and is free for the time from his own reproaches.

But there is one time at night when he must go home, that his friends may sleep; and another time in the morning, when all the world agrees to shut out interruption. These are the moments of which poor Sober trembles at the thought. But the misery of these tiresome intervals, he has many means of alleviating. He has persuaded himself that the manual arts are undeservedly overlooked; he has observed in many trades the effects of close thought, and just ratiocination. From speculation he proceeded to practice, and supplied himself with the tools of a carpenter, with which he mended his coalbox very successfully, and which he still continues to employ, as he finds occasion.

He has attempted at other times the crafts of the shoemaker, tinman, plumber, and potter; in all these arts he has failed, and resolves to qualify himself for them by better information. But his daily amusement is chemistry. He has a small furnace, which he employs in distillation, and which has long been the solace of his life. He draws oils and waters, and essences and spirits, which he knows to be of no use; sits and counts the drops as they come from his retort, and forgets that, whilst a drop is falling, a moment flies away.

Poor Sober![4] I have often teased him with reproof, and he has often promised reformation; for no man is so much open to conviction as the Idler, but there is none on whom it operates so little. What will be the effect of this paper I know not; perhaps he will read it and laugh, and light the fire in his furnace; but my hope is that he will quit his trifles, and betake himself to rational and useful diligence.

Idler No. 58

[*Expectations of Pleasure*]

Saturday, May 26, 1759

Pleasure is very seldom found where it is sought. Our brightest blazes of gladness are commonly kindled by unexpected sparks. The flowers which scatter their odors from time to time in the paths of life, grow up without culture from seeds scattered by chance.

Nothing is more hopeless than a scheme of merriment. Wits and humorists are brought together from distant quarters by preconcerted invitations; they come attended by their admirers prepared to laugh and to applaud: they gaze a while on each other, ashamed to be silent, and afraid to speak; every man is discontented with himself, grows angry with those that give him pain, and resolves that he

4. Sober represents aspects of Johnson's own character. He was much given to indolence, and he performed chemical experiments in a small laboratory in his garret.

will contribute nothing to the merriment of such worthless company. Wine inflames the general malignity, and changes sullenness to petulance, till at last none can bear any longer the presence of the rest. They retire to vent their indignation in safer places, where they are heard with attention; their importance is restored, they recover their good humor, and gladden the night with wit and jocularity.

Merriment is always the effect of a sudden impression. The jest which is expected is already destroyed. The most active imagination will be sometimes torpid, under the frigid influence of melancholy, and sometimes occasions will be wanting to tempt the mind, however volatile, to sallies and excursions. Nothing was ever said with uncommon felicity, but by the cooperation of chance; and therefore, wit as well as valor must be content to share its honors with fortune.

All other pleasures are equally uncertain; the general remedy of uneasiness is change of place; almost everyone has some journey of pleasure in his mind, with which he flatters his expectation. He that travels in theory has no inconveniences; he has shade and sunshine at his disposal, and wherever he alights finds tables of plenty and looks of gaiety. These ideas are indulged till the day of departure arrives, the chaise is called, and the progress of happiness begins.

A few miles teach him the fallacies of imagination. The road is dusty, the air is sultry, the horses are sluggish, and the postilion brutal. He longs for the time of dinner that he may eat and rest. The inn is crowded, his orders are neglected, and nothing remains but that he devour in haste what the cook has spoiled, and drive on in quest of better entertainment. He finds at night a more commodious house, but the best is always worse than he expected.

He at last enters his native province, and resolves to feast his mind with the conversation of his old friends, and the recollection of juvenile frolics. He stops at the house of his friend whom he designs to overpower with pleasure by the unexpected interview. He is not known till he tells his name, and revives the memory of himself by a gradual explanation. He is then coldly received, and ceremoniously feasted. He hastes away to another whom his affairs have called to a distant place, and having seen the empty house, goes away disgusted by a disappointment which could not be intended because it could not be foreseen. At the next house he finds every face clouded with misfortune, and is regarded with malevolence as an unreasonable intruder, who comes not to visit but to insult them.[1]

1. Johnson had not been able to bring himself to revisit his own native town, Lichfield, for many years, even though his mother had lived there until her death the previous January. Three years later, when he did return, he found "the streets much narrower and shorter than I thought I had left them, inhabited by a new race of people, to whom I was very little known."

It is seldom that we find either men or places such as we expect them. He that has pictured a prospect upon his fancy, will receive little pleasure from his eyes; he that has anticipated the conversation of a wit, will wonder to what prejudice he owes his reputation. Yet it is necessary to hope, though hope should always be deluded, for hope itself is happiness, and its frustrations, however frequent, are yet less dreadful than its extinction.

From The History of Rasselas, Prince of Abyssinia[1]

Chapter I. Description of a Palace in a Valley

Ye who listen with credulity to the whispers of fancy, and pursue with eagerness the phantoms of hope; who expect that age will perform the promises of youth, and that the deficiencies of the present day will be supplied by the morrow—attend to the history of Rasselas, prince of Abyssinia.

Rasselas was the fourth son of the mighty emperor in whose dominions the Father of Waters[2] begins his course; whose bounty

1. Johnson wrote *Rasselas* in January, 1759, during the evenings of one week, a remarkable instance of his ability to write rapidly and brilliantly under the pressure of necessity. His mother lay dying in Lichfield. Her son, famous for his *Dictionary,* was nonetheless oppressed by poverty and in great need of ready money with which to make her last days comfortable, pay her funeral expenses, and settle her small debts. He was paid £100 for the first edition of *Rasselas,* but not in time to attend her deathbed or her funeral. Because of these circumstances, the tale has often been read as an expression of the gloom of the moment; but acquaintance with Johnson's other writings and his conversation makes it plain that the book expresses his settled view of life and what human beings may reasonably expect from it.

Rasselas is a philosophical fable cast in the popular form of an Oriental tale, a type of fiction that owed its popularity to the vogue of the *Arabian Nights,* first translated into English in the early 18th century. Since the work is a fable, we should not approach it as a novel: psychologically credible characters and a series of intricately involved actions that lead to a necessary resolution and conclusion are not to be found in *Rasselas.* The action, the characters, the majestic prose rhythms, and the melancholy resonance of much of the language serve to articulate the theme, which is very similar to that of *The Vanity of Human Wishes.* Johnson formulated it in a magnificent phrase: the "hunger of imagination which preys incessantly upon life" (Chapter XXXII) and which lures us to "listen with credulity to the whispers of fancy and pursue with eagerness the phantoms of hope" (Chapter I). The tale is a gentle satire on one of the perennial topics of satirists, the folly of all of us who stubbornly cling to our illusions despite the evidence of experience. *Rasselas* is not all darkness and gloom, for Johnson's theme invites comic as well as tragic treatment, and some of the episodes evoke that laughter of the mind which is the effect of high comedy. In its main theme, however—the folly of cherishing the dream of ever attaining unalloyed happiness in a world which can never wholly satisfy our desires, however disinterested—and in many of the sayings of its characters, especially of the sage Imlac, *Rasselas* expresses some of Johnson's own deepest convictions.

2. The Nile.

pours down the streams of plenty, and scatters over half the world the harvests of Egypt.

According to the custom which has descended from age to age among the monarchs of the torrid zone, Rasselas was confined in a private palace, with the other sons and daughters of Abyssinian royalty, till the order of succession should call him to the throne.

The place which the wisdom or policy of antiquity had destined for the residence of the Abyssinian princes was a spacious valley[3] in the kingdom of Amhara, surrounded on every side by mountains, of which the summits overhang the middle part. The only passage by which it could be entered was a cavern that passed under a rock, of which it has long been disputed whether it was the work of nature or of human industry. The outlet of the cavern was concealed by a thick wood, and the mouth which opened into the valley was closed with gates of iron, forged by the artificers of ancient days, so massy that no man could, without the help of engines, open or shut them.

From the mountains on every side rivulets descended that filled all the valley with verdure and fertility, and formed a lake in the middle, inhabited by fish of every species, and frequented by every fowl whom nature has taught to dip the wing in water. This lake discharged its superfluities by a stream, which entered a dark cleft of the mountain on the northern side, and fell with dreadful noise from precipice to precipice till it was heard no more.

The sides of the mountains were covered with trees, the banks of the brooks were diversified with flowers; every blast shook spices from the rocks, and every month dropped fruits upon the ground. All animals that bite the grass, or browse the shrub, whether wild or tame, wandered in this extensive circuit, secured from beasts of prey by the mountains which confined them. On one part were flocks and herds feeding in the pastures, on another all the beasts of chase frisking in the lawns; the sprightly kid was bounding on the rocks, the subtle monkey frolicking in the trees, and the solemn elephant reposing in the shade. All the diversities of the world were brought together, the blessings of nature were collected, and its evils extracted and excluded.

The valley, wide and fruitful, supplied its inhabitants with the necessaries of life, and all delights and superfluities were added at the annual visit which the emperor paid his children, when the iron gate was opened to the sound of music, and during eight days everyone that resided in the valley was required to propose whatever might contribute to make seclusion pleasant, to fill up the

3. Johnson had read of the Happy Valley in the Portuguese Jesuit Father Lobo's book on Abyssinia, which he translated in 1735. The description in this and the immediately following paragraphs illustrates well enough Johnson's preference for the "general" over the "particular" (see Chapter X, below). It owes something to the description of the Garden in *Paradise Lost* IV, and Coleridge's *Kubla Khan* owes something to it.

vacancies of attention, and lessen the tediousness of time. Every desire was immediately granted. All the artificers of pleasure were called to gladden the festivity; the musicians exerted the power of harmony, and the dancers showed their activity before the princes, in hope that they should pass their lives in this blissful captivity, to which those only were admitted whose performance was thought able to add novelty to luxury. Such was the appearance of security and delight which this retirement afforded, that they to whom it was new always desired that it might be perpetual; and as those on whom the iron gate had once closed were never suffered to return, the effect of longer experience could not be known. Thus every year produced new schemes of delight and new competitors for imprisonment.

The palace stood on an eminence, raised about thirty paces above the surface of the lake. It was divided into many squares or courts, built with greater or less magnificence according to the rank of those for whom they were designed. The roofs were turned into arches of massy stone, joined with a cement that grew harder by time, and the building stood from century to century, deriding the solstitial rains and equinoctial hurricanes, without need of reparation.

This house, which was so large as to be fully known to none but some ancient officers, who successively inherited the secrets of the place, was built as if suspicion herself had dictated the plan. To every room there was an open and secret passage; every square had a communication with the rest, either from the upper stories by private galleries, or by subterranean passages from the lower apartments. Many of the columns had unsuspected cavities, in which a long race of monarchs had reposited their treasures. They then closed up the opening with marble, which was never to be removed but in the utmost exigencies of the kingdom, and recorded their accumulations in a book, which was itself concealed in a tower, not entered but by the emperor, attended by the prince who stood next in succession.

Chapter II. The Discontent of Rasselas in the Happy Valley

Here the sons and daughters of Abyssinia lived only to know the soft vicissitudes of pleasure and repose, attended by all that were skillful to delight, and gratified with whatever the senses can enjoy. They wandered in gardens of fragrance, and slept in the fortresses of security. Every art was practiced to make them pleased with their own condition. The sages who instructed them told them of nothing but the miseries of public life, and described all beyond the mountains as regions of calamity, where discord was always raging, and where man preyed upon man.

To heighten their opinion of their own felicity, they were daily entertained with songs, the subject of which was the *happy valley*.

Their appetites were excited by frequent enumerations of different enjoyments, and revelry and merriment was the business of every hour, from the dawn of morning to the close of even.

These methods were generally successful; few of the princes had ever wished to enlarge their bounds, but passed their lives in full conviction that they had all within their reach that art or nature could bestow, and pitied those whom fate had excluded from this seat of tranquility, as the sport of chance and the slaves of misery.

Thus they rose in the morning and lay down at night, pleased with each other and with themselves; all but Rasselas, who, in the twenty-sixth year of his age, began to withdraw himself from their pastimes and assemblies, and to delight in solitary walks and silent meditation. He often sat before tables covered with luxury, and forgot to taste the dainties that were placed before him; he rose abruptly in the midst of the song, and hastily retired beyond the sound of music. His attendants observed the change, and endeavored to renew his love of pleasure. He neglected their officiousness, repulsed their invitations, and spent day after day on the banks of rivulets sheltered with trees, where he sometimes listened to the birds in the branches, sometimes observed the fish playing in the stream, and anon cast his eyes upon the pastures and mountains filled with animals, of which some were biting the herbage, and some sleeping among the bushes.

This singularity of his humor made him much observed. One of the sages, in whose conversation he had formerly delighted, followed him secretly, in hope of discovering the cause of his disquiet. Rasselas, who knew not that anyone was near him, having for some time fixed his eyes upon the goats that were browsing among the rocks, began to compare their condition with his own.

"What," said he, "makes the difference between man and all the rest of the animal creation? Every beast that strays beside me has the same corporal necessities with myself; he is hungry, and crops the grass, he is thirsty, and drinks the stream, his thirst and hunger are appeased, he is satisfied, and sleeps; he rises again, and he is hungry, he is again fed, and is at rest. I am hungry and thirsty like him, but when thirst and hunger cease, I am not at rest; I am, like him, pained with want, but am not, like him, satisfied with fullness. The intermediate hours are tedious and gloomy; I long again to be hungry that I may again quicken my attention. The birds peck the berries or the corn, and fly away to the groves, where they sit in seeming happiness on the branches, and waste their lives in tuning one unvaried series of sounds. I likewise can call the lutanist and the singer, but the sounds that pleased me yesterday weary me today, and will grow yet more wearisome tomorrow. I can discover within me no power of perception which is not glutted with its proper pleasure, yet I do not feel myself delighted. Man has surely some latent sense for which this place affords no gratification, or he has some desires distinct from sense, which must be satisfied before he can be happy."

After this he lifted up his head, and seeing the moon rising, walked towards the palace. As he passed through the fields, and saw the animals around him, "Ye," said he, "are happy, and need not envy me that walk thus among you, burthened with myself; nor do I, ye gentle beings, envy your felicity, for it is not the felicity of man. I have many distresses from which ye are free; I fear pain when I do not feel it; I sometimes shrink at evils recollected, and sometimes start at evils anticipated. Surely the equity of Providence has balanced peculiar sufferings with peculiar enjoyments."

With observations like these the prince amused himself as he returned, uttering them with a plaintive voice, yet with a look that discovered him to feel some complacence in his own perspicacity, and to receive some solace of the miseries of life from consciousness of the delicacy with which he felt, and the eloquence with which he bewailed them. He mingled cheerfully in the diversions of the evening, and all rejoiced to find that his heart was lightened.

Chapter III. The Wants of Him That Wants Nothing

On the next day his old instructor, imagining that he had now made himself acquainted with his disease of mind, was in the hope of curing it by counsel, and officiously sought an opportunity of conference, which the prince, having long considered him as one whose intellects were exhausted, was not very willing to afford. "Why," said he, "does this man thus intrude upon me; shall I be never suffered to forget those lectures which pleased only while they were new, and to become new again must be forgotten?" He then walked into the wood, and composed himself to his usual meditations; when, before his thoughts had taken any settled form, he perceived his pursuer at his side, and was at first prompted by his impatience to go hastily away; but, being unwilling to offend a man whom he had once reverenced and still loved, he invited him to sit down with him on the bank.

The old man, thus encouraged, began to lament the change which had been lately observed in the prince, and to inquire why he so often retired from the pleasures of the palace, to loneliness and silence. "I fly from pleasure," said the prince, "because pleasure has ceased to please; I am lonely because I am miserable, and am unwilling to cloud with my presence the happiness of others." "You, sir," said the sage, "are the first who has complained of misery in the *happy valley*. I hope to convince you that your complaints have no real cause. You are here in full possession of all that the emperor of Abyssinia can bestow; here is neither labor to be endured nor danger to be dreaded, yet here is all that labor or danger can procure or purchase. Look round and tell me which of your wants is without supply; if you want nothing, how are you unhappy?"

"That I want nothing," said the prince, "or that I know not what I want, is the cause of my complaint; if I had any known want, I should have a certain wish; that wish would excite endeavor, and I should not then repine to see the sun move so slowly towards the western mountain, or lament when the day breaks, and sleep will no longer hide me from myself. When I see the kids and the lambs chasing one another, I fancy that I should be happy if I had something to pursue. But, possessing all that I can want, I find one day and one hour exactly like another, except that the latter is still more tedious than the former. Let your experience inform me how the day may now seem as short as in my childhood, while nature was yet fresh and every moment showed me what I never had observed before. I have already enjoyed too much; give me something to desire."

The old man was surprised at this new species of affliction and knew not what to reply, yet was unwilling to be silent. "Sir," said he, "if you had seen the miseries of the world you would know how to value your present state." "Now," said the prince, "you have given me something to desire. I shall long to see the miseries of the world, since the sight of them is necessary to happiness."[4]

Chapter X. Imlac's History Continued. A Dissertation upon Poetry

"Wherever I went, I found that poetry was considered as the highest learning, and regarded with a veneration somewhat approaching to that which man would pay to the angelic nature. And yet it fills me with wonder that, in almost all countries, the most ancient poets are considered as the best: whether it be that every other kind of knowledge is an acquisition gradually attained, and poetry is a gift conferred at once; or that the first poetry of every nation surprised them as a novelty, and retained the credit by consent which it received by accident at first; or whether, as the province of poetry is to describe nature and passion, which are always the same, the first writers took possession of the most striking objects for description and the most probable occurrences for fiction, and left nothing to those that followed them, but transcription of the same events, and new combinations of the same images—whatever be the reason, it is commonly observed that the early writers are in possession of nature, and their followers of art; that the first excel in strength and invention, and the latter in elegance and refinement.

4. In the chapters here omitted Rasselas, meditating escape, comes to know Imlac, a poet and "man of learning" who has experienced life in all its phases, and who, finally despairing of happiness, has willingly retired to the Happy Valley. Imlac's account of his experiences whets the prince's desire to see the worrd and make a "choice of life."

"I was desirous to add my name to this illustrious fraternity. I read all the poets of Persia and Arabia, and was able to repeat by memory the volumes that are suspended in the mosque of Mecca. But I soon found that no man was ever great by imitation. My desire of excellence impelled me to transfer my attention to nature and to life. Nature was to be my subject, and men to be my auditors: I could never describe what I had not seen; I could not hope to move those with delight or terror, whose interests and opinions I did not understand.

"Being now resolved to be a poet, I saw everything with a new purpose; my sphere of attention was suddenly magnified; no kind of knowledge was to be overlooked. I ranged mountains and deserts for images and resemblances, and pictured upon my mind every tree of the forest and flower of the valley. I observed with equal care the crags of the rock and the pinnacles of the palace. Sometimes I wandered along the mazes of the rivulet, and sometimes watched the changes of the summer clouds. To a poet nothing can be useless. Whatever is beautiful, and whatever is dreadful, must be familiar to his imagination; he must be conversant with all that is awfully vast or elegantly little. The plants of the garden, the animals of the wood, the minerals of the earth, and meteors of the sky, must all concur to store his mind with inexhaustible variety: for every idea[5] is useful for the enforcement or decoration of moral or religious truth; and he who knows most will have most power of diversifying his scenes, and of gratifying his reader with remote allusions and unexpected instruction.

"All the appearances of nature I was therefore careful to study, and every country which I have surveyed has contributed something to my poetical powers."

"In so wide a survey," said the prince, "you must surely have left much unobserved. I have lived till now within the circuit of these mountains, and yet cannot walk abroad without the sight of something which I have never beheld before, or never heeded."

"The business of a poet," said Imlac, "is to examine, not the individual, but the species; to remark general properties and large appearances; he does not number the streaks of the tulip, or describe the different shades in the verdure of the forest. He is to exhibit in his portraits of nature such prominent and striking features as recall the original to every mind, and must neglect the minuter discriminations, which one may have remarked and another have neglected, for those characteristics which are alike obvious to vigilance and carelessness.

"But the knowledge of nature is only half the task of a poet; he must be acquainted likewise with all the modes of life. His character requires that he estimate the happiness and misery of every condition; observe the power of all the passions in all their com-

5. Mental image.

binations, and trace the changes of the human mind, as they are modified by various institutions and accidental influences of climate or custom, from the sprightliness of infancy to the despondence of decrepitude. He must divest himself of the prejudices of his age or country; he must consider right and wrong in their abstracted and invariable state; he must disregard present laws and opinions, and rise to general and transcendental[6] truths, which will always be the same. He must, therefore, content himself with the slow progress of his name, contemn the applause of his own time, and commit his claims to the justice of posterity. He must write as the interpreter of nature and the legislator of mankind, and consider himself as presiding over the thoughts and manner of future generations, as a being superior to time and place.

"His labor is not yet at an end; he must know many languages and many sciences; and, that his style may be worthy of his thoughts, must by incessant practice familiarize to himself every delicacy of speech and grace of harmony."

Chapter XI. Imlac's Narrative Continued. A Hint on Pilgrimage

Imlac now felt the enthusiastic fit, and was proceeding to aggrandize his own profession, when the prince cried out: "Enough! thou hast convinced me that no human being can ever be a poet. Proceed with thy narration."

"To be a poet," said Imlac, "is indeed very difficult." "So difficult," returned the prince, "that I will at present hear no more of his labors. Tell me whither you went when you had seen Persia."

"From Persia," said the poet, "I traveled through Syria, and for three years resided in Palestine, where I conversed with great numbers of the northern and western nations of Europe, the nations which are now in possession of all power and all knowledge, whose armies are irresistible, and whose fleets command the remotest parts of the globe. When I compared these men with the natives of our own kingdom, and those that surround us, they appeared almost another order of beings. In their countries it is difficult to wish for anything that may not be obtained; a thousand arts, of which we never heard, are continually laboring for their convenience and pleasure; and whatever their own climate has denied them is supplied by their commerce."

"By what means," said the prince, "are the Europeans thus powerful, or why, since they can so easily visit Asia and Africa for trade or conquest, cannot the Asiatics and Africans invade their coasts, plant colonies in their ports, and give laws to their natural princes? The same wind that carries them back would bring us thither."

"They are more powerful, sir, than we," answered Imlac, "be-

6. "General; pervading many particulars" (Johnson's *Dictionary*).

cause they are wiser; knowledge will always predominate over ignorance, as man governs the other animals. But why their knowledge is more than ours, I know not what reason can be given, but the unsearchable will of the Supreme Being."

"When," said the prince with a sigh, "shall I be able to visit Palestine, and mingle with this mighty confluence of nations? Till that happy moment shall arrive, let me fill up the time with such representations as thou canst give me. I am not ignorant of the motive that assembles such numbers in that place, and cannot but consider it as the center of wisdom and piety, to which the best and wisest men of every land must be continually resorting."

"There are some nations," said Imlac, "that send few visitants to Palestine; for many numerous and learned sects in Europe concur to censure pilgrimage as superstitious, or deride it as ridiculous."

"You know," said the prince, "how little my life has made me acquainted with diversity of opinions. It will be too long to hear the arguments on both sides; you, that have considered them, tell me the result."

"Pilgrimage," said Imlac, "like many other acts of piety, may be reasonable or superstitious, according to the principles upon which it is performed. Long journeys in search of truth are not commanded. Truth, such as is necessary to the regulation of life, is always found where it is honestly sought. Change of place is no natural cause of the increase of piety, for it inevitably produces dissipation of mind. Yet, since men go every day to view the fields where great actions have been performed, and return with stronger impressions of the event, curiosity of the same kind may naturally dispose us to view that country whence our religion had its beginning; and I believe no man surveys those awful scenes without some confirmation of holy resolutions. That the Supreme Being may be more easily propitiated in one place than in another is the dream of idle superstition, but that some places may operate upon our own minds in an uncommon manner is an opinion which hourly experience will justify. He who supposes that his vices may be more successfully combated in Palestine, will, perhaps, find himself mistaken, yet he may go thither without folly; he who thinks they will be more freely pardoned, dishonors at once his reason and religion."

"These," said the prince, "are European distinctions. I will consider them another time. What have you found to be the effect of knowledge? Are those nations happier than we?"

"There is so much infelicity," said the poet, "in the world that scarce any man has leisure from his own distresses to estimate the comparative happiness of others. Knowledge is certainly one of the means of pleasure, as is confessed by the natural desire which every mind feels of increasing its ideas. Ignorance is mere privation, by which nothing can be produced; it is a vacuity in which the soul sits motionless and torpid for want of attraction; and, without knowing why, we always rejoice when we learn, and grieve when we forget. I am therefore inclined to conclude that if nothing counteracts the natural consequence of learning, we grow more happy as our minds take a wider range.

"In enumerating the particular comforts of life, we shall find many advantages on the side of the Europeans. They cure wounds and diseases with which we languish and perish. We suffer inclemencies of weather which they can obviate. They have engines for the despatch of many laborious works, which we must perform by manual industry. There is such communication between distant places that one friend can hardly be said to be absent from another. Their policy removes all public inconveniences; they have roads cut through their mountains, and bridges laid upon their rivers. And, if we descend to the privacies of life, their habitations are more commodious, and their possessions are more secure."

"They are surely happy," said the prince, "who have all these conveniencies, of which I envy none so much as the facility with which separated friends interchange their thoughts."

"The Europeans," answered Imlac, "are less unhappy than we, but they are not happy. Human life is everywhere a state in which much is to be endured, and little to be enjoyed."[7]

Chapter XVI. They Enter Cairo, and Find Every Man Happy

As they approached the city, which filled the strangers with astonishment, "This," said Imlac to the prince, "is the place where travelers and merchants assemble from all the corners of the earth. You will here find men of every character and every occupation. Commerce is here honorable. I will act as a merchant, and you shall live as strangers, who have no other end of travel than curiosity. It will soon be observed that we are rich; our reputation will procure us access to all whom we shall desire to know; you will see all the conditions of humanity, and enable yourself at leisure to make your *choice of life*."

They now entered the town, stunned by the noise, and offended by the crowds. Instruction had not yet so prevailed over habit, but that they wondered to see themselves pass undistinguished along the street, and met by the lowest of the people without reverence or notice. The princess could not at first bear the thought of being leveled with the vulgar, and for some days continued in her chamber, where she was served by her favorite, Pekuah, as in the palace of the valley.

7. In the omitted chapters Rasselas and Imlac tunnel through the mountain, starting from a cavern earlier discovered by Rasselas. Laden with wealth and guided by Imlac, Rasselas, his sister Nekayah, and her maid Pekuah escape from the Happy Valley and make their way to Cairo.

Imlac, who understood traffic,[8] sold part of the jewels the next day, and hired a house, which he adorned with such magnificence that he was immediately considered as a merchant of great wealth. His politeness attracted many acquaintance, and his generosity made him courted by many dependents. His table was crowded by men of every nation, who all admired his knowledge, and solicited his favor. His companions, not being able to mix in the conversation, could make no discovery of their ignorance or surprise, and were gradually initiated in the world as they gained knowledge of the language.

The prince had, by frequent lectures, been taught the use and nature of money; but the ladies could not for a long time comprehend what the merchants did with small pieces of gold and silver, or why things of so little use should be received as equivalent to the necessaries of life.

They studied the language two years, while Imlac was preparing to set before them the various ranks and conditions of mankind. He grew acquainted with all who had anything uncommon in their fortune or conduct. He frequented the voluptuous and the frugal, the idle and the busy, the merchants and the men of learning.

The prince being now able to converse with fluency, and having learned the caution necessary to be observed in his intercourse with strangers, began to accompany Imlac to places of resort, and to enter into all assemblies, that he might make his *choice of life*.

For some time he thought choice needless, because all appeared to him equally happy. Wherever he went he met gaiety and kindness, and heard the song of joy or the laugh of carelessness. He began to believe that the world overflowed with universal plenty, and that nothing was withheld either from want or merit; that every hand showered liberality, and every heart melted with benevolence: "And who then," says he, "will be suffered to be wretched?"

Imlac permitted the pleasing delusion, and was unwilling to crush the hope of inexperience, till one day, having sat awhile silent, "I know not," said the prince, "what can be the reason that I am more unhappy than any of our friends. I see them perpetually and unalterably cheerful, but feel my own mind restless and uneasy. I am unsatisfied with those pleasures which I seem most to court; I live in the crowds of jollity, not so much to enjoy company as to shun myself, and am only loud and merry to conceal my sadness."

"Every man," said Imlac, "may, by examining his own mind, guess what passes in the minds of others; when you feel that your own gaiety is counterfeit, it may justly lead you to suspect that of your companions not to be sincere. Envy is commonly reciprocal. We are long before we are convinced that happiness is never to be found, and each believes it possessed by others, to keep alive the

8. Commerce.

hope of obtaining it for himself. In the assembly where you passed the last night, there appeared such sprightliness of air, and volatility of fancy, as might have suited beings of an higher order, formed to inhabit serener regions, inaccessible to care or sorrow; yet, believe me, prince, there was not one who did not dread the moment when solitude should deliver him to the tyranny of reflection."

"This," said the prince, "may be true of others, since it is true of me; yet, whatever be the general infelicity of man, one condition is more happy than another, and wisdom surely directs us to take the least evil in the *choice of life*."

"The causes of good and evil," answered Imlac, "are so various and uncertain, so often entangled with each other, so diversified by various relations, and so much subject to accidents which cannot be foreseen, that he who would fix his condition upon incontestable reasons of preference must live and die inquiring and deliberating."

"But, surely," said Rasselas, "the wise men, to whom we listen with reverence and wonder, chose that mode of life for themselves which they thought most likely to make them happy."

"Very few," said the poet, "live by choice. Every man is placed in his present condition by causes which acted without his foresight, and with which he did not always willingly co-operate; and therefore you will rarely meet one who does not think the lot of his neighbor better than his own."

"I am pleased to think," said the prince, "that my birth has given me at least one advantage over others, by enabling me to determine for myself. I have here the world before me. I will review it at leisure; surely happiness is somewhere to be found."[9]

Chapter XVIII. The Prince Finds a Wise and Happy Man

As he was one day walking in the street, he saw a spacious building which all were, by the open doors, invited to enter: he followed the stream of people, and found it a hall or school of declamation, in which professors read lectures to their auditory. He fixed his eye upon a sage raised above the rest, who discoursed with great energy on the government of the passions. His look was venerable, his action graceful, his pronunciation clear, and his diction elegant. He showed with great strength of sentiment and variety of illustration that human nature is degraded and debased, when the lower faculties predominate over the higher; that when fancy, the parent of passion, usurps the dominion of the mind, nothing ensues but the natural effect of unlawful government, perturbation, and confusion; that she betrays the fortresses of the intellect to rebels, and excites her children to sedition against reason, their lawful sovereign. He compared reason to the sun, of which the light is constant, uniform and lasting; and fancy to a meteor, of bright but transitory luster,

9. In Chapter XVII, here omitted, Rasselas fails to find happiness among the gay and dissipated young men of Cairo.

irregular in its motion, and delusive in its direction.

He then communicated the various precepts given from time to time for the conquest of passion, and displayed the happiness of those who had obtained the important victory, after which man is no longer the slave of fear, nor the fool of hope; is no more emaciated by envy, inflamed by anger, emasculated by tenderness, or depressed by grief; but walks on calmly through the tumults or the privacies of life, as the sun pursues alike his course through the calm or the stormy sky.

He enumerated many examples of heroes immovable by pain or pleasure, who looked with indifference on those modes or accidents to which the vulgar give the names of good and evil. He exhorted his hearers to lay aside their prejudices, and arm themselves against the shafts of malice or misfortune, by invulnerable patience; concluding that this state only was happiness, and that his happiness was in everyone's power.

Rasselas listened to him with the veneration due to the instructions of a superior being, and, waiting for him at the door, humbly implored the liberty of visiting so great a master of true wisdom. The lecturer hesitated a moment, when Rasselas put a purse of gold into his hand, which he received with a mixture of joy and wonder.

"I have found," said the prince at his return to Imlac, "a man who can teach all that is necessary to be known; who, from the unshaken throne of rational fortitude, looks down on the scenes of life changing beneath him. He speaks, and attention watches his lips. He reasons, and conviction closes his periods. This man shall be my future guide; I will learn his doctrines, and imitate his life."

"Be not too hasty," said Imlac, "to trust or to admire the teachers of morality: they discourse like angels, but they live like men."

Rasselas, who could not conceive how any man could reason so forcibly without feeling the cogency of his own arguments, paid his visit in a few days, and was denied admission. He had now learned the power of money, and made his way by a piece of gold to the inner apartment, where he found the philosopher in a room half darkened, with his eyes misty and his face pale. "Sir," said he, "you are come at a time when all human friendship is useless; what I suffer cannot be remedied, what I have lost cannot be supplied. My daughter, my only daughter, from whose tenderness I expected all the comforts of my age, died last night of a fever. My views, my purposes, my hopes are at an end; I am now a lonely being, disunited from society."

"Sir," said the prince, "mortality is an event by which a wise man can never be surprised; we know that death is always near, and it should therefore always be expected." "Young man," answered the philosopher, "you speak like one that has never felt the pangs of separation." "Have you then forgot the precepts," said Rasselas, "which you so powerfully enforced? Has wisdom no strength to arm the heart against calamity? Consider that external things are naturally variable, but truth and reason are always the same." "What comfort," said the mourner, "can truth and reason afford me? Of what effect are they now, but to tell me that my daughter will not be restored?"

The prince, whose humanity would not suffer him to insult misery with reproof, went away, convinced of the emptiness of rhetorical sound, and the inefficacy of polished periods and studied sentences.

Chapter XIX. A Glimpse of Pastoral Life

He was still eager upon the same inquiry; and having heard of a hermit that lived near the lowest cataract of the Nile, and filled the whole country with the fame of his sanctity, resolved to visit his retreat, and inquire whether that felicity which public life could not afford was to be found in solitude; and whether a man whose age and virtue made him venerable could teach any peculiar art of shunning evils, or enduring them.

Imlac and the princess agreed to accompany him, and, after the necessary preparations, they began their journey. Their way lay through fields, where shepherds tended their flocks and the lambs were playing upon the pasture. "This," said the poet, "is the life which has been often celebrated for its innocence and quiet; let us pass the heat of the day among the shepherds' tents, and know whether all our searches are not to terminate in pastoral simplicity."

The proposal pleased them, and they induced the shepherds, by small presents and familiar questions, to tell their opinion of their own state. They were so rude and ignorant, so little able to compare the good with the evil of the occupation, and so indistinct in their narratives and descriptions, that very little could be learned from them. But it was evident that their hearts were cankered with discontent; that they considered themselves as condemned to labor for the luxury of the rich, and looked up with stupid malevolence toward those that were placed above them.

The princess pronounced with vehemence that she would never suffer these envious savages to be her companions, and that she should not soon be desirous of seeing any more specimens of rustic happiness; but could not believe that all the accounts of primeval pleasures were fabulous, and was yet in doubt whether life had anything that could be justly preferred to the placid gratifications of fields and woods. She hoped that the time would come, when, with a few virtuous and elegant companions, she could gather flowers planted by her own hand, fondle the lambs of her own ewe, and listen without care, among brooks and breezes, to one of her maidens reading in the shade.[1]

Chapter XXII. The Happiness of a Life Led According to Nature

Rasselas went often to an assembly of learned men, who met at stated times to unbend their minds and compare their opinions. Their manners were somewhat coarse, but their conversation was instructive, and their disputations acute, though sometimes too violent, and often continued till neither controvertist remembered upon what question they began. Some faults were almost general among them; everyone was desirous to dictate to the rest, and everyone was pleased to hear the genius or knowledge of another depreciated.

In this assembly Rasselas was relating his interview with the hermit, and the wonder with which he heard him censure a course of life which he had so deliberately chosen, and so laudably followed. The sentiments of the hearers were various. Some were of opinion that the folly of his choice had been justly punished by condemnation to perpetual perseverance. One of the youngest among them, with great vehemence, pronounced him an hypocrite. Some talked of the right of society to the labor of individuals, and considered retirement as a desertion of duty. Others readily allowed that there was a time when the claims of the public were satisfied, and when a man might properly sequester himself, to review his life and purify his heart.

One, who appeared more affected with the narrative than the rest, thought it likely that the hermit would in a few years go back to his retreat, and perhaps, if shame did not restrain, or death intercept him, return once more from his retreat into the world. "For the hope of happiness," said he, "is so strongly impressed that the longest experience is not able to efface it. Of the present state, whatever it be, we feel and are forced to confess the misery; yet when the same state is again at a distance, imagination paints it as desirable. But the time will surely come when desire will be no longer our torment, and no man shall be wretched but by his own fault."

"This," said a philosopher who had heard him with tokens of great impatience, "is the present condition of a wise man. The time is already come when none are wretched but by their own fault. Nothing is more idle than to inquire after happiness, which nature has kindly placed within our reach. The way to be happy is to live according to nature, in obedience to that universal and

1. In the omitted chapters the travelers discover the unease and danger of being wealthy, and then find the hermit, who, far from being piously content, is on the point of abandoning his hermitage and returning to society.

unalterable law with which every heart is originally impressed; which is not written on it by precept, but engraven by destiny, not instilled by education, but infused at our nativity. He that lives according to nature will suffer nothing from the delusions of hope, or importunities of desire; he will receive and reject with equability of temper, and act or suffer as the reason of things shall alternately prescribe. Other men may amuse themselves with subtle definitions, or intricate ratiocination. Let them learn to be wise by easier means; let them observe the hind of the forest, and the linnet of the grove; let them consider the life of animals, whose motions are regulated by instinct; they obey their guide, and are happy. Let us therefore, at length, cease to dispute, and learn to live; throw away the encumbrance of precepts, which they who utter them with so much pride and pomp do not understand, and carry with us this simple and intelligible maxim, that deviation from nature is deviation from happiness."

When he had spoken, he looked round him with a placid air, and enjoyed the consciousness of his own beneficence. "Sir," said the prince with great modesty, "as I, like all the rest of mankind, am desirous of felicity, my closest attention has been fixed upon your discourse. I doubt not the truth of a position which a man so learned has so confidently advanced. Let me only know what it is to live according to nature."

"When I find young men so humble and so docile," said the philosopher, "I can deny them no information which my studies have enabled me to afford. To live according to nature, is to act always with due regard to the fitness arising from the relations and qualities of causes and effects; to concur with the great and unchangeable scheme of universal felicity; to co-operate with the general disposition and tendency of the present system of things."

The prince soon found that this was one of the sages whom he should understand less as he heard him longer. He therefore bowed and was silent; and the philosopher, supposing him satisfied, and the rest vanquished, rose up and departed with the air of a man that had co-operated with the present system.[2]

From *Chapter XXVI. The Princess Continues Her Remarks upon Private Life*

Nekayah, perceiving her brother's attention fixed, proceeded in her narrative.

"In families where there is or is not poverty, there is commonly discord. If a kingdom be, as Imlac tells us, a great family, a family likewise is a little kingdom, torn with factions and exposed to revolutions. An unpracticed observer expects the love of parents and

2. In the omitted chapters Rasselas resolves to observe the happiness of men of high position, leaving the study of domestic life to his sister; they report their findings to each other.

children to be constant and equal; but this kindness seldom continues beyond the years of infancy: in a short time the children become rivals to their parents. Benefits are allayed[3] by reproaches, and gratitude debased by envy.

"Parents and children seldom act in concert; each child endeavors to appropriate the esteem or fondness of the parents, and the parents, with yet less temptation, betray each other to their children. Thus, some place their confidence in the father, and some in the mother, and by degrees the house is filled with artifices and feuds.

"The opinions of children and parents, of the young and the old, are naturally opposite, by the contrary effects of hope and despondence, of expectation and experience, without crime or folly on either side. The colors of life in youth and age appear different, as the face of nature in spring and winter. And how can children credit the assertions of parents, which their own eyes show them to be false?

"Few parents act in such a manner as much to enforce their maxims by the credit of their lives. The old man trusts wholly to slow contrivance and gradual progression; the youth expects to force his way by genius, vigor, and precipitance. The old man pays regard to riches, and the youth reverences virtue. The old man deifies prudence; the youth commits himself to magnanimity and chance. The young man, who intends no ill, believes that none is intended, and therefore acts with openness and candor; but his father, having suffered the injuries of fraud, is impelled to suspect, and too often allured to practice it. Age looks with anger on the temerity of youth, and youth with contempt on the scrupulosity[4] of age. Thus parents and children, for the greatest part, live on to love less and less; and, if those whom nature has thus closely united are the torments of each other, where shall we look for tenderness and consolation?"

"Surely," said the prince, "you must have been unfortunate in your choice of acquaintance: I am unwilling to believe that the most tender of all relations is thus impeded in its effects by natural necessity."

"Domestic discord," answered she, "is not inevitably and fatally necessary, but yet is not easily avoided. We seldom see that a whole family is virtuous; the good and evil cannot well agree, and the evil can yet less agree with one another. Even the virtuous fall sometimes to variance, when their virtues are of different kinds, and tending to extremes. In general, those parents have most reverence who most deserve it; for he that lives well cannot be despised.

"Many other evils infest private life. Some are the slaves of servants whom they have trusted with their affairs. Some are kept in continual anxiety to the caprice of rich relations, whom they cannot

3. To allay is "to join anything to another, so as to abate its predominant qualities" (Johnson's *Dictionary*).

4. "Fear of acting in any manner" (Johnson's *Dictionary*).

please, and dare not offend. Some husbands are imperious, and some wives perverse; and, as it is always more easy to do evil than good, though the wisdom or virtue of one can very rarely make many happy, the folly or vice of one may often make many miserable."

"If such be the general effect of marriage," said the prince, "I shall for the future think it dangerous to connect my interest with that of another, lest I should be unhappy by my partner's fault."

"I have met," said the princess, "with many who live single for that reason; but I never found that their prudence ought to raise envy. They dream away their time without friendship, without fondness, and are driven to rid themselves of the day, for which they have no use, by childish amusements, or vicious delights. They act as beings under the constant sense of some known inferiority that fills their minds with rancor, and their tongues with censure. They are peevish at home, and malevolent abroad; and, as the outlaws of human nature, make it their business and their pleasure to disturb that society which debars them from its privileges. To live without feeling or exciting sympathy, to be fortunate without adding to the felicity of others, or afflicted without tasting the balm of pity, is a state more gloomy than solitude; it is not retreat but exclusion from mankind. Marriage has many pains, but celibacy has no pleasures."[5] * * *

Chapter XXIX. The Debate on Marriage Continued

"The good of the whole," says Rasselas, "is the same with the good of all its parts. If marriage be best for mankind it must be evidently best for individuals, or a permanent and necessary duty must be the cause of evil, and some must be inevitably sacrificed to the convenience of others. In the estimate which you have made of the two states, it appears that the incommodities of a single life are, in a great measure, necessary and certain, but those of the conjugal state accidental and avoidable.

"I cannot forbear to flatter myself that prudence and benevolence will make marriage happy. The general folly of mankind is the cause of general complaint. What can be expected but disappointment and repentance from a choice made in the immaturity of youth, in the ardor of desire, without judgment, without foresight, without inquiry after conformity of opinions, similarity of manners, rectitude of judgment, or purity of sentiment.

"Such is the common process of marriage. A youth and maiden meeting by chance, or brought together by artifice, exchange glances, reciprocate civilities, go home, and dream of one another. Having little to divert attention, or diversify thought, they find

5. In the omitted chapters Rasselas reports that even the highest stations afford no happiness, and the conversation continues.

themselves uneasy when they are apart, and therefore conclude that they shall be happy together. They marry, and discover what nothing but voluntary blindness had before concealed; they wear out life in altercations, and charge nature with cruelty.

"From those early marriages proceeds likewise the rivalry of parents and children: the son is eager to enjoy the world before the father is willing to forsake it, and there is hardly room at once for two generations. The daughter begins to bloom before the mother can be content to fade, and neither can forbear to wish for the absence of the other.

"Surely all these evils may be avoided by that deliberation and delay which prudence prescribes to irrevocable choice. In the variety and jollity of youthful pleasures life may be well enough supported without the help of a partner. Longer time will increase experience, and wider views will allow better opportunities of inquiry and selection: one advantage, as least, will be certain; the parents will be visibly older than their children."

"What reason cannot collect," said Nekayah, "and what experiment has not yet taught, can be known only from the report of others. I have been told that late marriages are not eminently happy. This is a question too important to be neglected, and I have often proposed it to those, whose accuracy of remark, and comprehensiveness of knowledge, made their suffrages worthy of regard. They have generally determined that it is dangerous for a man and woman to suspend their fate upon each other, at a time when opinions are fixed, and habits are established; when friendships have been contracted on both sides, when life has been planned into method, and the mind has long enjoyed the contemplation of its own prospects.

"It is scarcely possible that two traveling through the world under the conduct of chance should have been both directed to the same path, and it will not often happen that either will quit the track which custom has made pleasing. When the desultory levity of youth has settled into regularity, it is soon succeeded by pride ashamed to yield, or obstinacy delighting to contend. And even though mutual esteem produces mutual desire to please, time itself, as it modifies unchangeably the external mien, determines likewise the direction of the passions, and gives an inflexible rigidity to the manners. Long customs are not easily broken: he that attempts to change the course of his own life very often labors in vain; and how shall we do that for others which we are seldom able to do for ourselves?"

"But surely," interposed the prince, "you suppose the chief motive of choice forgotten or neglected. Whenever I shall seek a wife, it shall be my first question, whether she be willing to be led by reason?"

"Thus it is," said Nekayah, "that philosophers are deceived. There are a thousand familiar disputes which reason never can decide; questions that elude investigation, and make logic ridiculous; cases where something must be done, and where little can be said. Consider the state of mankind, and inquire how few can be supposed to act upon any occasions, whether small or great, with all the reasons of action present to their minds. Wretched would be the pair above all names of wretchedness, who should be doomed to adjust by reason every morning all the minute detail of a domestic day.

"Those who marry at an advanced age will probably escape the encroachments of their children; but, in diminution of this advantage, they will be likely to leave them, ignorant and helpless, to a guardian's mercy: or, if that should not happen, they must at least go out of the world before they see those whom they love best either wise or great.

"From their children, if they have less to fear, they have less also to hope, and they lose, without equivalent, the joys of early love, and the convenience of uniting with manners pliant and minds susceptible of new impressions, which might wear away their dissimilitudes by long cohabitation, as soft bodies, by continual attrition, conform their surfaces to each other.

"I believe it will be found that those who marry late are best pleased with their children, and those who marry early with their partners."

"The union of these two affections," said Rasselas, "would produce all that could be wished. Perhaps there is a time when marriage might unite them, a time neither too early for the father, nor too late for the husband."

"Every hour," answered the princess, "confirms my prejudice in favor of the position so often uttered by the mouth of Imlac, 'That nature sets her gifts on the right hand and on the left.' Those conditions, which flatter hope and attract desire, are so constituted that, as we approach one, we recede from another. There are goods so opposed that we cannot seize both, but, by too much prudence, may pass between them at too great a distance to reach either. This is often the fate of long consideration; he does nothing who endeavors to do more than is allowed to humanity. Flatter not yourself with contrarieties of pleasure. Of the blessings set before you make your choice, and be content. No man can taste the fruits of autumn, while he is delighting his scent with the flowers of the spring: no man can, at the same time, fill his cup from the source and from the mouth of the Nile."[6]

6. In Chapter XXX, here omitted, Imlac proposes a visit to the Pyramids.

Chapter XXXI. They Visit the Pyramids

The resolution being thus taken, they set out the next day. They laid tents upon their camels, being resolved to stay among the pyramids till their curiosity was fully satisfied. They traveled gently, turned aside to everything remarkable, stopped from time to time and conversed with the inhabitants, and observed the various appearances of towns ruined and inhabited, of wild and cultivated nature.

When they came to the great pyramid, they were astonished at the extent of the base, and the height of the top. Imlac explained to them the principles upon which the pyramidal form was chosen for a fabric intended to coextend its duration with that of the world; he showed that its gradual diminution gave it such stability as defeated all the common attacks of the elements, and could scarcely be overthrown by earthquakes themselves, the least resistible of natural violence. A concussion that should shatter the pyramid would threaten the dissolution of the continent.

They measured all its dimensions, and pitched their tents at its foot. Next day they prepared to enter its interior apartments, and having hired the common guides, climbed up to the first passage, when the favorite of the princess, looking into the cavity, stepped back and trembled. "Pekuah," said the princess, "of what art thou afraid?" "Of the narrow entrance," answered the lady, "and of the dreadful gloom. I dare not enter a place which must surely be inhabited by unquiet souls. The original possessors of these dreadful vaults will start up before us, and perhaps shut us in forever." She spoke, and threw her arms round the neck of her mistress.

"If all your fear be of apparitions," said the prince, "I will promise you safety. There is no danger from the dead; he that is once buried will be seen no more."

"That the dead are seen no more," said Imlac, "I will not undertake to maintain, against the concurrent and unvaried testimony of all ages, and of all nations. There is no people, rude or learned, among whom apparitions of the dead are not related and believed. This opinion, which perhaps prevails as far as human nature is diffused, could become universal only by its truth; those that never heard of one another would not have agreed in a tale which nothing but experience can make credible. That it is doubted by single cavilers can very little weaken the general evidence; and some who deny it with their tongues confess it by their fears.

"Yet I do not mean to add new terrors to those which have already seized upon Pekuah. There can be no reason why specters should haunt the pyramid more than other places, or why they should have power or will to hurt innocence and purity. Our entrance is no violation of their privileges; we can take nothing from them, how then can we offend them?"

"My dear Pekuah," said the princess, "I will always go before you, and Imlac shall follow you. Remember that you are the companion of the princess of Abyssinia."

"If the princess is pleased that her servant should die," returned the lady, "let her command some death less dreadful than enclosure in this horrid cavern. You know I dare not disobey you; I must go if you command me, but if I once enter, I never shall come back."

The princess saw that her fear was too strong for expostulation or reproof, and, embracing her, told her that she should stay in the tent till their return. Pekuah was yet not satisfied, but entreated the princess not to pursue so dreadful a purpose as that of entering the recesses of the pyramid. "Though I cannot teach courage," said Nekayah, "I must not learn cowardice, nor leave at last undone what I came hither only to do."

Chapter XXXII. They Enter the Pyramid

Pekuah descended to the tents, and the rest entered the pyramid. They passed through the galleries, surveyed the vaults of marble, and examined the chest in which the body of the founder is supposed to have been reposited. They then sat down in one of the most spacious chambers to rest a while before they attempted to return.

"We have now," said Imlac, "gratified our minds with an exact view of the greatest work of man, except the wall of China.

"Of the wall it is very easy to assign the motive. It secured a wealthy and timorous nation from the incursions of barbarians, whose unskillfulness in arts made it easier for them to supply their wants by rapine than by industry, and who from time to time poured in upon the habitations of peaceful commerce, as vultures descend upon domestic fowl. Their celerity and fierceness made the wall necessary, and their ignorance made it efficacious.

"But for the pyramids, no reason has ever been given adequate to the cost and labor of the work. The narrowness of the chambers proves that it could afford no retreat from enemies, and treasures might have been reposited at far less expense with equal security. It seems to have been erected only in compliance with that hunger of imagination which preys incessantly upon life, and must be always appeased by some employment. Those who have already all that they can enjoy must enlarge their desires. He that has built for use till use is supplied, must begin to build for vanity, and extend his plan to the utmost power of human performance, that he may not be soon reduced to form another wish.

"I consider this mighty structure as a monument of the insufficiency of human enjoyments. A king, whose power is unlimited, and whose treasures surmount all real and imaginary wants, is compelled to solace, by the erection of a pyramid, the satiety of dominion and tastelessness of pleasures, and to amuse the tediousness of declining life by seeing thousands laboring without end, and one stone, for no purpose, laid upon another. Whoever thou art, that, not content with a moderate condition, imaginest happiness in royal magnificence, and dreamest that command or riches can feed the appetite of novelty with perpetual gratifications, survey the pyramids, and confess thy folly!"[7]

Chapter XLIV. The Dangerous Prevalence[8] of Imagination

"Disorders of intellect," answered Imlac, "happen much more often than superficial observers will easily believe. Perhaps, if we speak with rigorous exactness, no human mind is in its right state. There is no man whose imagination does not sometimes predominate over his reason, who can regulate his attention wholly by his will, and whose ideas will come and go at his command. No man will be found in whose mind airy notions do not sometimes tyrannize, and force him to hope or fear beyond the limits of sober probability. All power of fancy over reason is a degree of insanity; but while this power is such as we can control and repress, it is not visible to others, nor considered as any depravation of the mental faculties; it is not pronounced madness but when it comes ungovernable, and apparently influences speech or action.

"To indulge the power of fiction, and send imagination out upon the wing, is often the sport of those who delight too much in silent speculation. When we are alone we are not always busy; the labor of excogitation is too violent to last long; the ardor of inquiry will sometimes give way to idleness or satiety. He who has nothing external that can divert him must find pleasure in his own thoughts, and must conceive himself what he is not; for who is pleased with what he is? He then expatiates in boundless futurity, and culls from all imaginable conditions that which for the present moment he should most desire, amuses his desires with impossible enjoyments, and confers upon his pride unattainable dominion. The mind dances from scene to scene, unites all pleasures in all combinations, and riots in delights which nature and fortune, with all their bounty, cannot bestow.

"In time, some particular train of ideas fixes the attention; all other intellectual gratifications are rejected; the mind, in weariness

7. Chapters XXXIII-XLIII are here omitted. While the travelers are in the Pyramid, Pekuah is abducted by an Arab chieftain, from whom she is eventually ransomed. The travelers return to Cairo, and Imlac makes the acquaintance of an astronomer, who proves to be mad, having yielded to the delusion that he has learned to control the weather. Chapter XLIII concludes: "Rasselas * * * inquired of Imlac whether he thought such maladies of the mind frequent, and how they were contracted."

8. Predominance.

or leisure, recurs constantly to the favorite conception, and feasts on the luscious falsehood, whenever she is offended with the bitterness of truth. By degrees the reign of fancy is confirmed; she grows first imperious, and in time despotic. Then fictions begin to operate as realities, false opinions fasten upon the mind, and life passes in dreams of rapture or of anguish.

"This, sir, is one of the dangers of solitude, which the hermit has confessed not always to promote goodness, and the astronomer's misery has proved to be not always propitious to wisdom."

"I will no more," said the favorite, "imagine myself the queen of Abyssinia. I have often spent the hours which the princess gave to my own disposal, in adjusting ceremonies and regulating the court; I have repressed the pride of the powerful, and granted the petitions of the poor; I have built new palaces in more happy situations, planted groves upon the tops of mountains, and have exulted in the beneficence of royalty, till, when the princess entered, I had almost forgotten to bow down before her."

"And I," said the princess, "will not allow myself any more to play the shepherdess in my waking dreams. I have often soothed my thoughts with the quiet and innocence of pastoral employments, till I have in my chamber heard the winds whistle, and the sheep bleat; sometimes freed the lamb entangled in the thicket, and sometimes with my crook encountered the wolf. I have a dress like that of the village maids, which I put on to help my imagination, and a pipe on which I play softly, and suppose myself followed by my flocks."

"I will confess," said the prince, "an indulgence of fantastic delight more dangerous than yours. I have frequently endeavored to image the possibility of a perfect government, by which all wrong should be restrained, all vice reformed, and all the subjects preserved in tranquility and innocence. This thought produced innumerable schemes of reformation, and dictated many useful regulations and salutary edicts. This has been the sport, and sometimes the labor, of my solitude; and I start, when I think with how little anguish I once supposed the death of my father and my brothers."

"Such," says Imlac, "are the effects of visionary schemes; when we first form them, we know them to be absurd, but familiarize them by degrees, and in time lose sight of their folly."

Chapter XLV. They Discourse with an Old Man

The evening was now far past, and they rose to return home. As they walked along the bank of the Nile, delighted with the beams of the moon quivering on the water, they saw at a small distance an old man, whom the prince had often heard in the assembly of the sages. "Yonder," said he, "is one whose years have calmed his passions, but not clouded his reason. Let us close the disquisitions of the night by inquiring what are his sentiments of his own state, that we may know whether youth alone is to struggle with vexation, and whether any better hope remains for the latter part of life."

Here the sage approached and saluted them. They invited him to join their walk, and prattled a while, as acquaintance that had unexpectedly met one another. The old man was cheerful and talkative, and the way seemed short in his company. He was pleased to find himself not disregarded, accompanied them to their house, and, at the prince's request, entered with them. They placed him in the seat of honor, and set wine and conserves before him.

"Sir," said the princess, "an evening walk must give to a man of learning like you pleasures which ignorance and youth can hardly conceive. You know the qualities and the causes of all that you behold, the laws by which the river flows, the periods in which the planets perform their revolutions. Everything must supply you with contemplation, and renew the consciousness of your own dignity."

"Lady," answered he, "let the gay and the vigorous expect pleasure in their excursions; it is enough that age can obtain ease. To me the world has lost its novelty; I look round, and see what I remember to have seen in happier days. I rest against a tree, and consider that in the same shade I once disputed upon the annual overflow of the Nile with a friend who is now silent in the grave. I cast my eyes upward, fix them on the changing moon, and think with pain on the vicissitudes of life. I have ceased to take much delight in physical truth; for what have I to do with those things which I am soon to leave?"

"You may at least recreate yourself," said Imlac, "with the recollection of an honorable and useful life, and enjoy the praise which all agree to give you."

"Praise," said the sage with a sigh, "is to an old man an empty sound. I have neither mother to be delighted with the reputation of her son, nor wife to partake the honors of her husband. I have outlived my friends and my rivals. Nothing is now of much importance; for I cannot extend my interest beyond myself. Youth is delighted with applause, because it is considered as the earnest of some future good, and because the prospect of life is far extended; but to me, who am now declining to decrepitude, there is little to be feared from the malevolence of men, and yet less to be hoped from their affection or esteem. Something they may yet take away, but they can give me nothing. Riches would now be useless, and high employment would be pain. My retrospect of life recalls to my view many opportunities of good neglected, much time squandered upon trifles, and more lost in idleness and vacancy. I leave many great designs unattempted, and many great attempts unfinished. My mind is burthened with no heavy crime, and therefore I compose myself to tranquility; endeavor to abstract my thoughts from hopes and cares which, though reason knows them to be vain, still try to keep their old possession of the heart; expect,[9] with serene humility, that hour which nature cannot long delay; and hope to possess, in a better state, that happiness which here I could not find, and that virtue which here I have not attained."

He arose and went away, leaving his audience not much elated with the hope of long life. The prince consoled himself with remarking that it was not reasonable to be disappointed by this account; for age had never been considered as the season of felicity, and if it was possible to be easy in decline and weakness, it was likely that the days of vigor and alacrity might be happy; that the noon of life might be bright, if the evening could be calm.

The princess suspected that age was querulous and malignant, and delighted to repress the expectations of those who had newly entered the world. She had seen the possessors of estates look with envy on their heirs, and known many who enjoy pleasure no longer than they can confine it to themselves.

Pekuah conjectured that the man was older than he appeared, and was willing to impute his complaints to delirious dejection; or else supposed that he had been unfortunate, and was therefore discontented. "For nothing," said she, "is more common than to call our own condition the condition of life."

Imlac, who had no desire to see them depressed, smiled at the comforts which they could so readily procure to themselves, and remembered that, at the same age, he was equally confident of unmingled prosperity, and equally fertile of consolatory expedients. He forebore to force upon them unwelcome knowledge, which time itself would too soon impress. The princess and her lady retired; the madness of the astronomer hung upon their minds, and they desired Imlac to enter upon his office, and delay next morning the rising of the sun.[1]

Chapter XLIX. The Conclusion, in Which Nothing Is Concluded

It was now the time of the inundation of the Nile: a few days after their visit to the catacombs, the river began to rise.

They were confined to their house. The whole region being under water gave them no invitation to any excursions, and being well supplied with materials for talk, they diverted themselves with comparisons of the different forms of life which they had observed, and with various schemes of happiness which each of them had formed.

9. Await.

1. Chapters XLVI-XLVIII are here omitted. The travelers converse with the astronomer and learn that he too regrets his choice of life. A discourse on the nature of the soul (in the penultimate chapter) raises the hope of happiness in a future state.

Pekuah was never so much charmed with any place as the convent of St. Anthony, where the Arab restored her to the princess, and wished only to fill it with pious maidens, and to be made prioress of the order; she was weary of expectation and disgust,[2] and would gladly be fixed in some unvariable state.

The princess thought that, of all sublunary things, knowledge was the best: she desired first to learn all sciences, and then purposed to found a college of learned women, in which she would preside, that, by conversing with the old and educating the young, she might divide her time between the acquisition and communication of wisdom, and raise up for the next age models of prudence, and patterns of piety.

The prince desired a little kingdom, in which he might administer justice in his own person, and see all the parts of government with his own eyes; but he could never fix the limits of his dominion, and was always adding to the number of his subjects.

Imlac and the astronomer were contented to be driven along the stream of life, without directing their course to any particular port.

Of these wishes that they had formed, they well knew that none could be obtained. They deliberated a while what was to be done, and resolved, when the inundation should cease, to return to Abyssinia.[3]

1759

[A Brief to Free a Slave][1]

It must be agreed that in most ages many countries have had part of their inhabitants in a state of slavery; yet it may be doubted whether slavery can ever be supposed the natural condition of man. It is impossible not to conceive that men in their original state were equal; and very difficult to imagine how one would be subjected to another but by violent compulsion. An individual may, indeed, forfeit his liberty by a crime; but he cannot by that crime forfeit the

2. Aversion.

3. Probably not, as is often suggested, to the Happy Valley (in Chapter I we were told that none who leave the valley can ever return). Presumably the travelers return, with whatever wisdom they have gained, but also with their cherished illusions, to share the common destiny of mankind. But Johnson, hurrying to his conclusion, may have left the place to which they returned vague.

1. Johnson detested slavery and the owners of slaves. Once, "in company with some very grave men at Oxford, his toast was, 'Here's to the next insurrection of the Negroes in the West Indies' "; and in his pamphlet *Taxation No Tyranny* (1775) he put the American rebels down with a devastating question: "how is it that we hear the loudest yelps for liberty among the drivers of Negroes?" Though slavery had been abolished in England in 1772, serfdom still existed in Scotland; and the British remained heavily involved in the slave trade. In 1777 a Negro slave, Joseph Knight, sued for freedom from the Scottish master he had escaped. On his behalf Johnson dictated this argument to Boswell.

liberty of his children. What is true of a criminal seems true likewise of a captive. A man may accept life from a conquering enemy on condition of perpetual servitude; but it is very doubtful whether he can entail[2] that servitude on his descendants; for no man can stipulate without commission for another. The condition which he himself accepts, his son or grandson perhaps would have rejected. If we should admit, what perhaps may with more reason be denied, that there are certain relations between man and man which may make slavery necessary and just,[3] yet it can never be proved that he who is now suing for his freedom ever stood in any of those relations. He is certainly subject by no law, but that of violence, to his present master,[4] who pretends no claim to his obedience, but that he bought him from a merchant of slaves, whose right to sell him never was examined. It is said that, according to the constitutions of Jamaica, he was legally enslaved; these constitutions are merely positive;[5] and apparently injurious to the rights of mankind, because whoever is exposed to sale is condemned to slavery without appeal; by whatever fraud or violence he might have been originally brought into the merchant's power. In our own time princes have been sold, by wretches to whose care they were entrusted, that they might have an European education; but when once they were brought to a market in the plantations, little would avail either their dignity or their wrongs. The laws of Jamaica afford a Negro no redress. His color is considered as a sufficient testimony against him. It is to be lamented that moral right should ever give way to political convenience. But if temptations of interest are sometimes too strong for human virtue, let us at least retain a virtue where there is no temptation to quit it. In the present case there is apparent right on one side, and no convenience on the other. Inhabitants of this island can neither gain riches nor power by taking away the liberty of any part of the human species. The sum of the argument is this: —No man is by nature the property of another: The defendant is, therefore, by nature free: The rights of nature must be some way forfeited before they can be justly taken away: That the defendant has by any act forfeited the rights of nature we require to be proved; and if no proof of such forfeiture can be given, we doubt not but the justice of the court will declare him free.[6]

1777 1792

2. Settle unalterably.
3. Boswell, who strongly disagreed with Johnson's "prejudice" against slavery, argued that "To abolish a *status*, which in all ages GOD has sanctioned, and man has continued, would not only be *robbery* to an innumerable class of our fellow subjects; but it would be extreme cruelty to the African savages."
4. Knight had been kidnapped as a child.
5. Arbitrarily instituted (opposed to *natural* laws).
6. Knight was set free by the Scottish court. The British slave trade was not abolished until 1807.

Rambler No. 4

[*On Fiction*]

Saturday, March 31, 1750

Simul et jucunda et idonea dicere vitae.
—HORACE, *Art of Poetry*, 334
And join both profit and delight in one.
—CREECH

The works of fiction with which the present generation seems more particularly delighted are such as exhibit life in its true state, diversified only by accidents that daily happen in the world, and influenced by passions and qualities which are really to be found in conversing with mankind.

This kind of writing may be termed, not improperly, the comedy of romance, and is to be conducted nearly by the rules of comic poetry. Its province is to bring about natural events by easy means, and to keep up curiosity without the help of wonder: it is therefore precluded from the machines[1] and expedients of the heroic romance, and can neither employ giants to snatch away a lady from the nuptial rites, nor knights to bring her back from captivity; it can neither bewilder its personages in deserts, nor lodge them in imaginary castles.

I remember a remark made by Scaliger upon Pontanus,[2] that all his writings are filled with the same images; and that if you take from him his lilies and his roses, his satyrs and his dryads, he will have nothing left that can be called poetry. In like manner, almost all the fictions of the last age will vanish if you deprive them of a hermit and a wood, a battle and a shipwreck.

Why this wild strain of imagination found reception so long in polite and learned ages, it is not easy to conceive; but we cannot wonder that while readers could be procured, the authors were willing to continue it; for when a man had by practice gained some fluency of language, he had no further care than to retire to his closet, let loose his invention, and heat his mind with incredibilities; a book was thus produced without fear of criticism, without the toil of study, without knowledge of nature, or acquaintance with life.

The task of our present writers is very different; it requires, together with that learning which is to be gained from books, that experience which can never be attained by solitary diligence, but must arise from general converse and accurate observation of the

1. The technical term in neoclassical critical theory for the supernatural agents who intervene in human affairs in epic and tragedy.

2. Julius Caesar Scaliger (1484–1558) criticized the Latin poems of the Italian poet Jovianus Pontanus (1426–1503).

living world. Their performances have, as Horace expresses it, *plus oneris quanto veniae minus,*[3] little indulgence, and therefore more difficulty. They are engaged in portraits of which everyone knows the original, and can detect any deviation from exactness of resemblance. Other writings are safe, except from the malice of learning, but these are in danger from every common reader; as the slipper ill executed was censured by a shoemaker who happened to stop in his way at the Venus of Appeles.[4]

But the fear of not being approved as just copiers of human manners is not the most important concern that an author of this sort ought to have before him. These books are written chiefly to the young, the ignorant, and the idle, to whom they serve as lectures of conduct, and introductions into life. They are the entertainment of minds unfurnished with ideas, and therefore easily susceptible of impressions; not fixed by principles, and therefore easily following the current of fancy; not informed by experience, and consequently open to every false suggestion and partial account.

That the highest degree of reverence should be paid to youth, and that nothing indecent should be suffered to approach their eyes or ears, are precepts extorted by sense and virtue from an ancient writer by no means eminent for chastity of thought.[5] The same kind, though not the same degree, of caution, is required in everything which is laid before them, to secure them from unjust prejudices, perverse opinions, and incongruous combinations of images.

In the romances formerly written, every transaction and sentiment was so remote from all that passes among men that the reader was in very little danger of making any applications to himself; the virtues and crimes were equally beyond his sphere of activity; and he amused himself with heroes and with traitors, deliverers and persecutors, as with beings of another species, whose actions were regulated upon motives of their own, and who had neither faults nor excellencies in common with himself.

But when an adventurer is leveled with the rest of the world, and acts in such scenes of the universal drama as may be the lot of any other man, young spectators fix their eyes upon him with closer attention, and hope, by observing his behavior and success, to regulate their own practices when they shall be engaged in the like part.

For this reason these familiar histories may perhaps be made of greater use than the solemnities of professed morality, and convey the knowledge of vice and virtue with more efficacy than axioms

3. *Epistles* II.i.170.
4. According to Pliny the Younger (*Naturalis Historia* XXXV.85), the Greek painter Apelles of Kos (4th century B.C.) corrected the drawing of a sandal after hearing a shoemaker criticize it as faulty, but when the flattered artisan dared to find fault with the drawing of a leg, the artist bade him "stick to his last."
5. Juvenal, *Satires XIV*.1–58.

and definitions. But if the power of example is so great as to take possession of the memory by a kind of violence, and produce effects almost without the intervention of the will, care ought to be taken that when the choice is unrestrained, the best examples only should be exhibited; and that which is likely to operate so strongly should not be mischievous or uncertain in its effects.

The chief advantage which these fictions have over real life is that their authors are at liberty, though not to invent, yet to select objects, and to cull from the mass of mankind those individuals upon which the attention ought most to be employed; as a diamond, though it cannot be made, may be polished by art, and placed in such situation as to display that luster which before was buried among common stones.

It is justly considered as the greatest excellency of art to imitate nature; but it is necessary to distinguish those parts of nature which are most proper for imitation: greater care is still required in representing life, which is so often discolored by passion or deformed by wickedness. If the world be promiscuously described, I cannot see of what use it can be to read the account; or why it may not be as safe to turn the eye immediately upon mankind as upon a mirror which shows all that presents itself without discrimination.

It is therefore not a sufficient vindication of a character that it is drawn as it appears; for many characters ought never to be drawn: nor of a narrative that the train of events is agreeable to observation and experience; for that observation which is called knowledge of the world will be found much more frequently to make men cunning than good. The purpose of these writings is surely not only to show mankind, but to provide that they may be seen hereafter with less hazard; to teach the means of avoiding the snares which are laid by Treachery for Innocence, without infusing any wish for that superiority with which the betrayer flatters his vanity; to give the power of counteracting fraud without the temptation to practice it; to initiate youth by mock encounters in the art of necessary defense, and to increase prudence without impairing virtue.

Many writers, for the sake of following nature, so mingle good and bad qualities in their principal personages that they are both equally conspicuous; and as we accompany them through their adventures with delight, and are led by degrees to interest ourselves in their favor, we lose the abhorrence of their faults because they do not hinder our pleasure, or perhaps regard them with some kindness for being united with so much merit.

There have been men indeed splendidly wicked, whose endowments threw a brightness on their crimes, and whom scarce any villainy made perfectly detestable because they never could be wholly divested of their excellencies; but such have been in all ages the great corrupters of the world, and their resemblance ought no more to be preserved than the art of murdering without pain.

Some have advanced, without due attention to the consequence of this notion, that certain virtues have their correspondent faults, and therefore that to exhibit either apart is to deviate from probability. Thus men are observed by Swift to be "grateful in the same degree as they are resentful." This principle, with others of the same kind, supposes man to act from a brute impulse, and pursue a certain degree of inclination without any choice of the object; for, otherwise, though it should be allowed that gratitude and resentment arise from the same constitution of the passions, it follows not that they will be equally indulged when reason is consulted; yet, unless that consequence be admitted, this sagacious maxim becomes an empty sound, without any relation to practice or to life.

Nor is it evident that even the first motions to these effects are always in the same proportion. For pride, which produces quickness of resentment, will obstruct gratitude by unwillingness to admit that inferiority which obligation implies; and it is very unlikely that he who cannot think he receives a favor will acknowledge or repay it.

It is of the utmost importance to mankind that positions of this tendency should be laid open and confuted; for while men consider good and evil as springing from the same root, they will spare the one for the sake of the other, and in judging, if not of others at least of themselves, will be apt to estimate their virtues by their vices. To this fatal error all those will contribute who confound the colors of right and wrong, and, instead of helping to settle their boundaries, mix them with so much art that no common mind is able to disunite them.

In narratives where historical veracity has no place, I cannot discover why there should not be exhibited the most perfect idea of virtue; of virtue not angelical, nor above probability (for what we cannot credit, we shall never imitate), but the highest and purest that humanity can reach, which, exercised in such trials as the various revolutions of things shall bring upon it, may, by conquering some calamities and enduring others, teach us what we may hope, and what we can perform. Vice (for vice is necessary to be shown) should always disgust; nor should the graces of gaiety, nor the dignity of courage, be so united with it as to reconcile it to the mind. Wherever it appears, it should raise hatred by the malignity of its practices, and contempt by the meanness of its stratagems: for while it is supported by either parts or spirit, it will be seldom heartily abhorred. The Roman tyrant was content to be hated if he was but feared;[6] and there are thousands of the readers of romances willing to be thought wicked if they may be allowed to be wits. It is therefore to be steadily inculcated that virtue is the highest proof of understanding, and the only solid basis of greatness; and that vice is the natural consequence of narrow thoughts; that it begins in mistake, and ends in ignominy.

Rambler No. 60

[*Biography*]

Saturday, October 13, 1750

—Quid sit pulchrum, quid turpe, quid utile, quid non,
Plenius ac melius Chrysippo et Crantore dicit.
—HORACE, *Epistles*, I.ii. 3–4

Whose works the beautiful and base contain,
Of vice and virtue more instructive rules,
Than all the sober sages of the schools.
—FRANCIS

All joy or sorrow for the happiness or calamities of others is produced by an act of the imagination, that realizes the event, however fictitious, or approximates it, however remote, by placing us, for a time, in the condition of him whose fortune we contemplate; so that we feel, while the deception lasts, whatever motions would be excited by the same good or evil happening to ourselves.

Our passions are therefore more strongly moved, in proportion as we can more readily adopt the pains or pleasure proposed to our minds, by recognizing them as once our own, or considering them as naturally incident to our state of life. It is not easy for the most artful writer to give us an interest in happiness or misery, which we think ourselves never likely to feel, and with which we have never yet been made acquainted. Histories of the downfall of kingdoms, and revolutions of empires, are read with great tranquility; the imperial tragedy pleases common auditors only by its pomp of ornament, and grandeur of ideas; and the man whose faculties have been engrossed by business, and whose heart never fluttered but at the rise or fall of stocks, wonders how the attention can be seized, or the affections agitated, by a tale of love.

Those parallel circumstances, and kindred images to which we readily conform our minds, are, above all other writings, to be found in narratives of the lives of particular persons; and therefore no species of writing seems more worthy of cultivation than biography, since none can be more delightful or more useful, none can more certainly enchain the heart by irresistible interest, or more widely diffuse instruction to every diversity of condition.

6. The Emperor Tiberius. See Suetonius' *Lives of the Caesars.*

The general and rapid narratives of history, which involve a thousand fortunes in the business of a day, and complicate innumerable incidents in one great transaction, afford few lessons applicable to private life, which derives its comforts and its wretchedness from the right or wrong management of things, which nothing but their frequency makes considerable, *Parva si non fiunt quotidie*, says Pliny,[1] and which can have no place in those relations which never descend below the consultation of senates, the motions of armies, and the schemes of conspirators.

I have often thought that there has rarely passed a life of which a judicious and faithful narrative would not be useful. For, not only every man has in the mighty mass of the world great numbers in the same condition with himself, to whom his mistakes and miscarriages, escapes and expedients, would be of immediate and apparent use; but there is such an uniformity in the state of man, considered apart from adventitious and separable decorations and disguises, that there is scarce any possibility of good or ill, but is common to humankind. A great part of the time of those who are placed at the greatest distance by fortune, or by temper, must unavoidably pass in the same manner; and though, when the claims of nature are satisfied, caprice, and vanity, and accident, begin to produce discriminations and peculiarities, yet the eye is not very heedful or quick, which cannot discover the same causes still[2] terminating their influence in the same effects, though sometimes accelerated, sometimes retarded, or perplexed by multiplied combinations. We are all prompted by the same motives, all deceived by the same fallacies, all animated by hope, obstructed by danger, entangled by desire, and seduced by pleasure.

It is frequently objected to relations of particular lives, that they are not distinguished by any striking or wonderful vicissitudes. The scholar who passed his life among his books, the merchant who conducted only his own affairs, the priest whose sphere of action was not extended beyond that of his duty, are considered as no proper objects of public regard, however they might have excelled in their several stations, whatever might have been their learning, integrity, and piety. But this notion arises from false measures of excellence and dignity, and must be eradicated by considering, that in the esteem of uncorrupted reason, what is of most use is of most value.

It is, indeed, not improper to take honest advantages of prejudice, and to gain attention by a celebrated name; but the business of the biographer is often to pass slightly over those performances and incidents, which produce vulgar greatness, to lead the thoughts into domestic privacies, and display the minute details of daily life,

1. Pliny the Younger, *Epistles*, III, i. Johnson translates the phrase in the preceding clause.

2. Always.

where exterior appendages are cast aside, and men excel each other only by prudence and by virtue. The account of Thuanus[3] is, with great propriety, said by its author to have been written, that it might lay open to posterity the private and familiar character of that man, *cujus ingenium et candorem ex ipsius scriptis sunt olim semper mirat uri*, whose candor and genius will to the end of time be by his writings preserved in admiration.

There are many invisible circumstances which, whether we read as inquirers after natural or moral knowledge, whether we intend to enlarge our science, or increase our virtue, are more important than public occurrences. Thus Sallust, the great master of nature, has not forgot, in his account of Catiline,[4] to remark that *his walk was now quick, and again slow*, as an indication of a mind revolving something with violent commotion. Thus the story of Melancthon[5] affords a striking lecture on the value of time, by informing us that when he made an appointment, he expected not only the hour, but the minute to be fixed, that the day might not run out in the idleness of suspense; and all the plans and enterprises of De Witt are now of less importance to the world, than that part of his personal character, which represents him as careful of his health, and negligent of his life.[6]

But biography has often been allotted to writers who seem very little acquainted with the nature of their task, or very negligent about the performance. They rarely afford any other account than might be collected from public papers, but imagine themselves writing a life when they exhibit a chronological series of actions or preferments; and so little regard the manners or behavior of their heroes, that more knowledge may be gained of a man's real character, by a short conversation with one of his servants, than from a formal and studied narrative, begun with his pedigree, and ended with his funeral.

If now and then they condescend to inform the world of particular facts, they are not always so happy as to select the most important. I know not well what advantage posterity can receive from the only circumstance by which Tickell has distinguished Addison from the rest of mankind, the irregularity of his pulse:[7] nor can I think myself overpaid for the time spent in reading the life of Malherbe, by being enabled to relate, after the learned biographer,[8] that Mal-

3. Jacques-Auguste de Thou (1553–1617), an important French historian, of whom Nicholas Rigault wrote a brief biography, a sentence of which Johnson quotes and translates below.
4. Sallust, a Roman historian of the first century B.C., wrote an account of Catiline's conspiracy against the Roman state.
5. Camerarius wrote a life of Melancthon, a German theologian of the 16th century.
6. Sir William Temple, characterizing the Dutch statesman John De Witt.
7. From Thomas Tickell's preface to Addison's *Works* (1721).
8. The life of the French poet François de Malherbe (1555–1628) was written by Honorat de Racan.

herbe had two predominant opinions; one, that the looseness of a single woman might destroy all her boast of ancient descent; the other, that the French beggars made use very improperly and barbarously of the phrase *noble gentleman,* because either word included the sense of both.

There are, indeed, some natural reasons why these narratives are often written by such as were not likely to give much instruction or delight, and why most accounts of particular persons are barren and useless. If a life be delayed till interest and envy are at an end, we may hope for impartiality, but must expect little intelligence; for the incidents which give excellence to biography are of a volatile and evanescent kind, such as soon escape the memory, and are rarely transmitted by tradition. We know how few can portray a living acquaintance, except by his most prominent and observable particularities, and the grosser features of his mind; and it may be easily imagined how much of this little knowledge may be lost in imparting it, and how soon a succession of copies will lose all resemblance of the original.

If the biographer writes from personal knowledge, and makes haste to gratify the public curiosity, there is danger lest his interest, his fear, his gratitude, or his tenderness, overpower his fidelity, and tempt him to conceal, if not to invent. There are many who think it an act of piety to hide the faults or failings of their friends, even when they can no longer suffer by their detection; we therefore see whole ranks of characters adorned with uniform panegyric, and not to be known from one another, but by extrinsic and casual circumstances. "Let me remember," says Hale, "when I find myself inclined to pity a criminal, that there is likewise a pity due to the country."[9] If we owe regard to the memory of the dead, there is yet more respect to be paid to knowledge, to virtue, and to truth.

9. From Gilbert Burnet's *Life and Death of Sir Matthew Hale* (1682).

A Dictionary of the English Language

Before Johnson no standard dictionary of the English language existed. The want had troubled speakers of English for some time, both because Italian and French academies had produced major dictionaries of their own tongues, and because, in the absence of any authority, English seemed likely to change utterly from one generation to another. Many 18th-century authors feared that their own language would soon become obsolete: as Pope wrote in *An Essay on Criticism,*

> Our sons their fathers' failing language see,
> And such as Chaucer is shall Dryden be.

A dictionary could help retard such change; and commercially it would be a book that everyone would need to buy. In 1746 a group of London publishers commissioned Johnson, still an unknown author, to undertake the project. He hoped to finish it in three years; it took him nine. But the quantity and quality of work he accomplished, aided only by six part-time assistants, made him famous as "Dictionary Johnson." The *Dictionary* remained a standard reference book for 100 years.

Johnson's achievement is notable in three respects: its size (40,000 words); the wealth of illustrative quotations; and the excellence of the definitions. No earlier English dictionary rivaled the scope of Johnson's two large folio volumes. About 114,000 quotations, gathered from the best English writers from Sidney to the 18th century, exemplify the usage of words as well as their meanings. Above all it was the definitions, however, which established the authority of Johnson's *Dictionary*. A small selection is only too likely to concentrate on a few amusing or notorious definitions; but the great majority are full, clear, and totally free from eccentricity. Indeed, many of them are still repeated in modern dictionaries. Language, Johnson knew, cannot be fixed once and for all; many of the words he defines have radically changed meaning since the 18th century. Yet Johnson did more than any man of his time to preserve the ideal of a standard English.

From A Dictionary of the English Language

From *Preface*

* * *

A large work is difficult because it is large, even though all its parts might singly be performed with facility; where there are many things to be done, each must be allowed its share of time and labor, in the proportion only which it bears to the whole; nor can it be expected that the stones which form the dome of a temple should be squared and polished like the diamond of a ring.

Of the event of this work, for which, having labored it with so much application, I cannot but have some degree of parental fondness, it is natural to form conjectures. Those who have been persuaded to think well of my design will require that it should fix our language, and put a stop to those alterations which time and chance have hitherto been suffered to make in it without opposition. With this consequence I will confess that I flattered myself for a while;[1] but now begin to fear that I have indulged expectation which neither reason nor experience can justify. When we see men grow old and die at a certain time one after another, from century to century, we laugh at the elixir that promises to prolong life to a thousand years; and with equal justice may the lexicographer be derided, who being able to produce no example of a nation that has preserved their words and phrases from mutability, shall imagine that

1. Johnson's *Plan* (1747) had called for "a dictionary by which the pronunciation of our language may be fixed, and its attainment facilitated; by which its purity may be preserved, its use ascertained, and its duration lengthened."

his dictionary can embalm his language and secure it from corruption and decay, that it is in his power to change sublunary nature, or clear the world at once from folly, vanity, and affectation.

With this hope, however, academies have been instituted, to guard the avenues of their languages, to retain fugitives, and repulse intruders; but their vigilance and activity have hitherto been vain; sounds are too volatile and subtle for legal restraints; to enchain syllables, and to lash the wind, are equally the undertakings of pride, unwilling to measure its desires by its strength. The French language has visibly changed under the inspection of the academy;[2] the style of Amelot's translation of father Paul is observed by Le Courayer to be *un peu passé*;[3] and no Italian will maintain that the diction of any modern writer is not perceptibly different from that of Boccace, Machiavel, or Caro.[4]

Total and sudden transformations of a language seldom happen; conquests and migrations are now very rare: but there are other causes of change, which, though slow in their operation, and invisible in their progress, are perhaps as much superior to human resistance as the revolutions of the sky, or intumescence[5] of the tide. Commerce, however necessary, however lucrative, as it depraves the manners, corrupts the language; they that have frequent intercourse with strangers, to whom they endeavor to accommodate themselves, must in time learn a mingled dialect, like the jargon which serves the traffickers[6] on the Mediterranean and Indian coasts. This will not always be confined to the exchange, the warehouse, or the port, but will be communicated by degrees to other ranks of the people, and be at last incorporated with the current speech.

There are likewise internal causes equally forcible. The language most likely to continue long without alteration would be that of a nation raised a little, and but a little, above barbarity, secluded from strangers, and totally employed in procuring the conveniencies of life; either without books, or, like some of the Mahometan countries, with very few: men thus busied and unlearned, having only such words as common use requires, would perhaps long continue to express the same notions by the same signs. But no such constancy can be expected in a people polished by arts, and classed by subordination, where one part of the community is sustained and accommodated by the labor of the other. Those who have much leisure to

2. The French academy, founded to purify the French language, had produced a dictionary in 1694; but revisions were necessary within a few years.

3. "A bit old-fashioned." Le Courayer's translation (1736) of Father Paolo Sarpi's *History of the Council of Trent* superseded Amelot's (1683).

4. Like Boccaccio (1313–75) and Machiavelli (1469–1527), Annibale Caro (1507–66) was a classic Italian stylist whose work had preceded the dictionary published in 1612 by the Italian academy.

5. Swelling.

6. Traders.

think, will always be enlarging the stock of ideas, and every increase of knowledge, whether real or fancied, will produce new words, or combinations of words. When the mind is unchained from necessity, it will range after convenience; when it is left at large in the fields of speculation, it will shift opinions; as any custom is disused, the words that expressed it must perish with it; as any opinion grows popular, it will innovate speech in the same proportion as it alters practice.

As by the cultivation of various sciences, a language is amplified, it will be more furnished with words deflected from their original sense; the geometrician will talk of a courtier's zenith, or the eccentric virtue of a wild hero, and the physician of sanguine expectations and phlegmatic delays.[7] Copiousness of speech will give opportunities to capricious choice, by which some words will be preferred, and others degraded; vicissitudes of fashion will enforce the use of new, or extend the signification of known terms. The tropes[8] of poetry will make hourly encroachments, and the metaphorical will become the current sense: pronunciation will be varied by levity or ignorance, and the pen must at length comply with the tongue; illiterate writers will at one time or other, by public infatuation, rise into renown, who, not knowing the original import of words, will use them with colloquial licentiousness, confound distinction, and forget propriety. As politeness increases, some expressions will be considered as too gross and vulgar for the delicate, others as too formal and ceremonious for the gay and airy; new phrases are therefore adopted, which must, for the same reasons, be in time dismissed. Swift, in his petty treatise on the English language,[9] allows that new words must sometimes be introduced, but proposes that none should be suffered to become obsolete. But what makes a word obsolete, more than general agreement to forbear it? and how shall it be continued, when it conveys an offensive idea, or recalled again in the mouths of mankind, when it has once by disuse become unfamiliar, and by unfamiliarity unpleasing.

There is another cause of alteration more prevalent than any other, which yet in the present state of the world cannot be obviated. A mixture of two languages will produce a third distinct from both, and they will always be mixed, where the chief part of education, and the most conspicuous accomplishment, is skill in ancient or in foreign tongues. He that has long cultivated another

7. "Zenith" (the point of the sky directly overhead) and "eccentric" (deviating from the center) were originally astronomical and geometrical terms; "sanguine" and "phlegmatic" once referred only to the physiological predominance of blood or phlegm.

8. "A change of a word from its original signification" (Johnson's *Dictionary*).

9. *A Proposal for Correcting, Improving, and Ascertaining the English Tongue* (1712). "Petty": little.

language, will find its words and combinations crowd upon his memory; and haste and negligence, refinement and affectation, will obtrude borrowed terms and exotic expressions.

The great pest of speech is frequency of translation. No book was every turned from one language into another, without imparting something of its native idiom; this is the most mischievous and comprehensive innovation; single words may enter by thousands, and the fabric of the tongue continue the same, but new phraseology changes much at once; it alters not the single stones of the building, but the order[1] of the columns. If an academy should be established for the cultivation of our style, which I, who can never wish to see dependence multiplied, hope the spirit of English liberty will hinder or destroy, let them, instead of compiling grammars and dictionaries, endeavor with all their influence to stop the license of translators, whose idleness and ignorance, if it be suffered to proceed, will reduce us to babble a dialect of France.

If the changes that we fear be thus irresistible, what remains but to acquiesce with silence, as in the other insurmountable distresses of humanity? It remains that we retard what we cannot repel, that we palliate what we cannot cure. Life may be lengthened by care, though death cannot be ultimately defeated: tongues, like governments, have a natural tendency to degeneration; we have long preserved our constitution, let us make some struggles for our language.

In hope of giving longevity to that which its own nature forbids to be immortal, I have devoted this book, the labor of years, to the honor of my country, that we may no longer yield the palm of philology without a contest to the nations of the continent. The chief glory of every people arises from its authors: whether I shall add anything by my own writings to the reputation of English literature, must be left to time. Much of my life has been lost under the pressures of disease; much has been trifled away; and much has always been spent in provision for the day that was passing over me; but I shall not think my employment useless or ignoble, if by my assistance foreign nations, and distant ages, gain access to the propagators of knowledge, and understand the teachers of truth; if my labors afford light to the repositories of science, and add celebrity to Bacon, to Hooker, to Milton, and to Boyle.[2]

When I am animated by this wish, I look with pleasure on my book, however defective, and deliver it to the world with the spirit of a man that has endeavored well. That it will immediately become popular I have not promised to myself: a few wild blunders

1. Architectural mode (Doric, etc.), which determines the style and proportions of columns.

2. Richard Hooker wrote *The Laws of Ecclesiastical Polity* (1594–97), a famous defense of the Church of England. Robert Boyle (1627–91) was a leading physicist and chemist. "Science": knowledge.

and risible absurdities, from which no work of such multiplicity was ever free, may for a time furnish folly with laughter, and harden ignorance in contempt; but useful diligence will at last prevail, and there never can be wanting some who distinguish desert;[3] who will consider that no dictionary of a living tongue ever can be perfect, since while it is hastening to publication, some words are budding, and some falling away; that a whole life cannot be spent upon syntax and etymology, and that even a whole life would not be sufficient; that he, whose design includes whatever language can express, must often speak of what he does not understand; that a writer will sometimes be hurried by eagerness to the end, and sometimes faint with weariness under a task, which Scaliger compares to the labors of the anvil and the mine;[4] that what is obvious is not always known, and what is known is not always present; that sudden fits of inadvertency will surprise vigilance, slight avocations[5] will seduce attention, and casual eclipses of the mind will darken learning; and that the writer shall often in vain trace his memory at the moment of need, for that which yesterday he knew with intuitive readiness, and which will come uncalled into his thoughts tomorrow.

In this work, when it shall be found that much is omitted, let it not be forgotten that much likewise is performed; and though no book was ever spared out of tenderness to the author, and the world is little solicitous to know whence proceeded the faults of that which it condemns; yet it may gratify curiosity to inform it, that the *English Dictionary* was written with little assistance of the learned, and without any patronage of the great;[6] not in the soft obscurities of retirement, or under the shelter of academic bowers, but amidst inconvenience and distraction, in sickness and in sorrow: and it may repress the triumph of malignant criticism to observe, that if our language is not here fully displayed, I have only failed in an attempt which no human powers have hitherto completed. If the lexicons of ancient tongues, now immutably fixed, and comprised in a few volumes, be yet, after the toil of successive ages, inadequate and delusive; if the aggregated knowledge and cooperating diligence of the Italian academicians did not secure them from the censure of Beni;[7] if the embodied critics of France, when fifty years had been spent upon their work, were obliged to change its economy,[8] and give their second edition another form, I may surely

3. Merit.
4. Joseph Justus Scaliger (1540–1609), a great scholar and lexicographer, wrote Latin verses suggesting that criminals should be condemned to lexicography.
5. Whatever calls one aside.
6. See Johnson's letter to Lord Chesterfield below, in Boswell's *Life of Johnson*.
7. Paolo Beni's *L'Anticrusca* (1612) violently attacked the first edition of the *Vocabolario* (the Italian dictionary).
8. Organization.

be contented without the praise of perfection, which, if I could obtain, in this gloom of solitude, what would it avail me? I have protracted my work till most of those whom I wished to please have sunk into the grave,[9] and success and miscarriage are empty sounds: I therefore dismiss it with frigid tranquility, having little to fear or hope from censure or from praise.

[*Some Definitions: A Small Anthology*][1]

ANTHO'LOGY. *n.*

1. A collection of flowers.

To CANT. *v.*

To talk in the jargon of particular professions, or in any kind of formal affected language, or with a peculiar and studied tone of voice.

> Men *cant* endlessly about *materia forma;* and hunt chimeras by rules of art, or dress up ignorance in words of bulk or sound, which may stop up the mouth of inquiry.—*Glanville's Scepsis Scientifica.*

ENTHU'SIASM. *n.*

1. A vain belief of private revelation; a vain confidence of divine favor or communication.

> *Enthusiasm* is founded neither on reason nor divine revelation, but rises from the conceits of a warmed or overweening brain.—*Locke.*

GE'NIUS. *n.*

1. The protecting or ruling power of men, places, or things.

> And as I awake, sweet music breathe,
> Sent by some spirit to mortals good,
> Or th' unseen *genius* of the wood.—*Milton.*

2. A man endowed with superior faculties.
3. Mental power or faculties.
4. Disposition of nature by which anyone is qualified for some peculiar employment.
5. Nature; disposition.

IMA'GINATION. *n.*

1. Fancy; the power of forming ideal pictures; the power of representing things absent to one's self or others.
2. Conception; image in the mind; idea.
3. Contrivance; scheme.

LEXICO'GRAPHER. *n.*

A writer of dictionaries; a harmless drudge, that busies himself in tracing the original, and detailing the signification of words.

9. Johnson's wife had died three years earlier.

1. Johnson's definitions include etymologies and illustrative quotations, some of which are omitted in this selection.

MELANCHO'LY. *n.*
1. A disease, supposed to proceed from a redundance of black bile.
2. A kind of madness, in which the mind is always fixed on one object.
3. A gloomy, pensive, discontented temper.

NA'TURE. *n.*
1. An imaginary being supposed to preside over the material and animal world.

> Thou, *nature*, art my goddess; to thy law
> My services are bound.—*Shakespeare.*

2. The native state or properties of anything, by which it is discriminated from others.
3. The constitution of an animated body.
4. Disposition of mind; temper.
5. The regular course of things.
6. The compass of natural existence.
7. Natural affection, or reverence; native sensations.
8. The state or operation of the material world.
9. Sort; species.
10. Sentiments or images adapted to nature, or comformable to truth and reality.
11. Physics; the science which teaches the qualities of things.

> *Nature* and *nature's* laws lay hid in night,
> God said, Let Newton be, and all was light.—*Pope.*

NE'TWORK. *n.*
Anything reticulated or decussated, at equal distances, with interstices between the intersections.

OATS. *n.*
A grain, which in England is generally given to horses, but in Scotland supports the people.

PA'STERN. *n.*
1. The knee of an horse.[2]

PA'TRON. *n.*
1. One who countenances, supports, or protects. Commonly a wretch who supports with insolence, and is paid with flattery.

PE'NSION. *n.*
An allowance made to anyone without an equivalent. In England it is generally understood to mean pay given to a state hireling for treason to his country.[3]

SA'TIRE. *n.*
A poem in which wickedness or folly is censured. Proper *satire* is

2. "A lady once asked him how he came to define *Pastern* the *knee* of a horse: instead of making an elaborate defense, as she expected, he at once answered, 'Ignorance, Madam, pure ignorance'" (Boswell).
3. In 1762 Johnson was awarded a pension, but he did not revise the definition in later editions.

distinguished, by the generality of the reflections, from a *lampoon*, which is aimed against a particular person; but they are too frequently confounded.

TO'RY. *n.*

One who adheres to the ancient constitution of the state, and the apostolical hierarchy of the church of England, opposed to a whig.

The knight is more a *tory* in the country than the town, because it more advances his interest.—*Addison.*

WHIG. *n.*

2. The name of a faction.

Whoever has a true value for church and state, should avoid the extremes of *whig* for the sake of the former, and the extremes of tory on the account of the latter.—*Swift.*

WIT. *n.*

1. The powers of the mind; the mental faculties; the intellects. This is the original signification.
2. Imagination; quickness of fancy.
3. Sentiments produced by quickness of fancy.
4. A man of fancy.
5. A man of genius.
6. Sense; judgment.
7. In the plural. Sound mind; intellect not crazed.
8. Contrivance; strategem; power of expedients.

1755

From The Preface to Shakespeare[1]

[*Shakespeare's Excellence. General Nature*]

That praises are without reason lavished on the dead, and that the honors due only to excellence are paid to antiquity, is a complaint likely to be always continued by those who, being able to add nothing to truth, hope for eminence from the heresies of paradox;

1. This, the finest piece of Shakespeare criticism in the 18th century, is the culmination of a critical tradition that began with Nicholas Rowe's edition of the plays in 1709 (indeed with Dryden's critical remarks on Shakespeare) and that was continued by subsequent editors, notably Pope, Lewis Theobald, and William Warburton. Johnson's topics are in the main the conventional ones of 18th-century Shakespeare criticism: Shakespeare as the poet of nature, not of learning; as the creator of memorable characters; as a poet who supremely expresses and evokes the passions. Johnson follows his tradition in weighing Shakespeare's poetic virtues against his faults and finding that the virtues outweigh the faults. No one has praised Shakespeare more nobly and generously. The *Preface* is most original when Johnson attacks and dismisses the long-standing reverence in critical theory for the unities of time and place. By appealing to the experience of the playgoer, he demonstrates that, thanks to the imagination of the spectator, the playwright need not contain his action within a period of twenty-four hours or restrict it to one place throughout the drama.

Johnson's edition of Shakespeare also contained footnotes and brief introductions to each of the plays. We reprint here the introductory headnotes to the two *Henry IV* plays and to *King Lear*.

or those who, being forced by disappointment upon consolatory expedients, are willing to hope from posterity what the present age refuses, and flatter themselves that the regard which is yet denied by envy will be at last bestowed by time.

Antiquity, like every other quality that attracts the notice of mankind, has undoubtedly votaries that reverence it not from reason but from prejudice. Some seem to admire indiscriminately whatever has been long preserved, without considering that time has sometimes cooperated with chance; all perhaps are more willing to honor past than present excellence; and the mind contemplates genius through the shades of age, as the eye surveys the sun through artificial opacity. The great contention of criticism is to find the faults of the moderns and the beauties of the ancients. While an author is yet living we estimate his powers by his worst performance; and when he is dead we rate them by his best.

To works, however, of which the excellence is not absolute and definite, but gradual and comparative; to works not raised upon principles demonstrative and scientific, but appealing wholly to observation and experience, no other test can be applied than length of duration and continuance of esteem. What mankind have long possessed they have often examined and compared; and if they persist to value the possession, it is because frequent comparisons have confirmed opinion in its favor. As among the works of nature no man can properly call a river deep or a mountain high, without the knowledge of many mountains and many rivers; so in the productions of genius, nothing can be styled excellent till it has been compared with other works of the same kind. Demonstration[2] immediately displays its power and has nothing to hope or fear from the flux of years; but works tentative and experimental must be estimated by their proportion to the general and collective ability of man, as it is discovered in a long succession of endeavors. Of the first building that was raised, it might be with certainty determined that it was round or square, but whether it was spacious or lofty must have been referred to time. The Pythagorean scale of numbers[3] was at once discovered to be perfect; but the poems of Homer we yet know not to transcend the common limits of human intelligence, but by remarking that nation after nation, and century after century, has been able to do little more than transpose his incidents, new name his characters, and paraphrase his sentiments.

The reverence due to writings that have long subsisted arises, therefore, not from any credulous confidence in the superior wisdom of past ages, or gloomy persuasion of the degeneracy of

2. "The highest degree of deducible or argumental evidence" (Johnson's *Dictionary*).

3. Pythagoras discovered the ratios that determine the principal intervals of the musical scale.

mankind, but is the consequence of acknowledged and indubitable positions, that what has been longest known has been most considered, and what is most considered is best understood.

The poet of whose works I have undertaken the revision may now begin to assume the dignity of an ancient and claim the privilege of established fame and prescriptive veneration. He has long outlived his century, the term commonly fixed as the test of literary merit.[4] Whatever advantages he might once derive from personal allusions, local customs, or temporary opinions, have for many years been lost; and every topic of merriment or motive of sorrow which the modes of artificial life afforded him now only obscure the scenes which they once illuminated. The effects of favor and competition are at an end; the tradition of his friendships and his enmities has perished; his works support no opinion with arguments nor supply any faction with invectives; they can neither indulge vanity nor gratify malignity; but are read without any other reason than the desire of pleasure, and are therefore praised only as pleasure is obtained; yet, thus unassisted by interest or passion, they have passed through variations of taste and changes of manners, and, as they devolved from one generation to another, have received new honors at every transmission.

But because human judgment, though it be gradually gaining upon certainty, never becomes infallible, and approbation, though long continued, may yet be only the approbation of prejudice or fashion, it is proper to inquire by what peculiarities of excellence Shakespeare has gained and kept the favor of his countrymen.

Nothing can please many, and please long, but just representations of general nature. Particular manners can be known to few, and therefore few only can judge how nearly they are copied. The irregular combinations of fanciful invention may delight awhile by that novelty of which the common satiety of life sends us all in quest; but the pleasures of sudden wonder are soon exhausted, and the mind can only repose on the stability of truth.

Shakespeare is, above all writers, at least above all modern writers, the poet of nature, the poet that holds up to his readers a faithful mirror of manners and of life. His characters are not modified by the customs of particular places, unpracticed by the rest of the world; by the peculiarities of studies or professions, which can operate but upon small numbers; or by the accidents of transient fashions or temporary opinions: they are the genuine progeny of common humanity, such as the world will always supply and observation will always find. His persons act and speak by the influence of those general passions and principles by which all minds are agitated and the whole system of life is continued in motion. In the

4. Horace, *Epistles* II.1.39.

writings of other poets a character is too often an individual: in those of Shakespeare it is commonly a species.

It is from this wide extension of design that so much instruction is derived. It is this which fills the plays of Shakespeare with practical axioms and domestic wisdom. It was said of Euripides[5] that every verse was a precept; and it may be said of Shakespeare that from his works may be collected a system of civil and economical prudence. Yet his real power is not shown in the splendor of particular passages, but by the progress of his fable and the tenor of his dialogue; and he that tries to recommend him by select quotations will succeed like the pedant in Hierocles[6] who, when he offered his house to sale, carried a brick in his pocket as a specimen.

It will not easily be imagined how much Shakespeare excels in accommodating his sentiments to real life but by comparing him with other authors. It was observed of the ancient schools of declamation that the more diligently they were frequented, the more was the student disqualified for the world, because he found nothing there which he should ever meet in any other place. The same remark may be applied to every stage but that of Shakespeare. The theater, when it is under any other direction, is peopled by such characters as were never seen, conversing in a language which was never heard, upon topics which will never arise in the commerce of mankind. But the dialogue of this author is often so evidently determined by the incident which produces it, and is pursued with so much ease and simplicity, that it seems scarcely to claim the merit of fiction, but to have been gleaned by diligent selection out of common conversation and common occurrences.

Upon every other stage the universal agent is love, by whose power all good and evil is distributed and every action quickened or retarded. To bring a lover, a lady, and a rival into the fable; to entangle them in contradictory obligations, perplex them with oppositions of interest, and harass them with violence of desires inconsistent with each other; to make them meet in rapture, and part in agony; to fill their mouths with hyperbolical joy and outrageous sorrow; to distress them as nothing human ever was distressed; to deliver them as nothing human ever was delivered, is the business of a modern dramatist. For this, probability is violated, life is misrepresented, and language is depraved. But love is only one of many passions; and as it has no great influence upon the sum of life, it has little operation in the dramas of a poet who caught his ideas from the living world and exhibited only what he saw before him. He knew that any other passion, as it was regular or exorbitant, was a cause of happiness or calamity.

5. The Greek tragic poet (ca. 480–406 B.C.). The observation is Cicero's.

6. Hierocles of Alexandria, a Greek philosopher of the 5th century A.D.

Characters thus ample and general were not easily discriminated and preserved; yet perhaps no poet ever kept his personages more distinct from each other. I will not say with Pope that every speech may be assigned to the proper speaker,[7] because many speeches there are which have nothing characteristical; but perhaps though some may be equally adapted to every person, it will be difficult to find that any can be properly transferred from the present possessor to another claimant. The choice is right when there is reason for choice.

Other dramatists can only gain attention by hyperbolical or aggravated characters, by fabulous and unexampled excellence or depravity, as the writers of barbarous romances invigorated the reader by a giant and a dwarf; and he that should form his expectations of human affairs from the play or from the tale would be equally deceived. Shakespeare has no heroes; his scenes are occupied only by men, who act and speak as the reader thinks that he should himself have spoken or acted on the same occasion; even where the agency is supernatural, the dialogue is level with life. Other writers disguise the most natural passions and most frequent incidents so that he who contemplates them in the book will not know them in the world: Shakespeare approximates[8] the remote, and familiarizes the wonderful; the event which he represents will not happen, but, if it were possible, its effects would probably be such as he has assigned; and it may be said that he has not only shown human nature as it acts in real exigencies, but as it would be found in trials to which it cannot be exposed.

This therefore is the praise of Shakespeare, that his drama is the mirror of life; that he who has mazed his imagination in following the phantoms which other writers raise up before him, may here be cured of his delirious ecstasies by reading human sentiments in human language, by scenes from which a hermit may estimate the transactions of the world, and a confessor predict the progress of the passions.

[*Shakespeare's Faults. The Three Dramatic Unities*]

Shakespeare with his excellencies has likewise faults, and faults sufficient to obscure and overwhelm any other merit. I shall show them in the proportion in which they appear to me, without envious malignity or superstitious veneration. No question can be more innocently discussed than a dead poet's pretensions to renown; and little regard is due to that bigotry which sets candor[1] higher than truth.

His first defect is that to which may be imputed most of the evil

7. In the preface to his edition of Shakespeare's plays (1725).

8. Brings near.

1. Kindness.

in books or in men. He sacrifices virtue to convenience, and is so much more careful to please than to instruct that he seems to write without any moral purpose. From his writings indeed a system of social duty may be selected, for he that thinks reasonably must think morally, but his precepts and axioms drop casually from him; he makes no just distribution of good or evil, nor is always careful to show in the virtuous a disapprobation of the wicked; he carries his persons indifferently through right and wrong, and at the close dismisses them without further care, and leaves their examples to operate by chance. This fault the barbarity of his age cannot extenuate; for it is always a writer's duty to make the world better, and justice is a virtue independent on time or place.

The plots are often so loosely formed that a very slight consideration may improve them, and so carelessly pursued that he seems not always fully to comprehend his own design. He omits opportunities of instructing or delighting which the train of his story seems to force upon him, and apparently rejects those exhibitions which would be more affecting for the sake of those which are more easy.

It may be observed that in many of his plays the latter part is evidently neglected. When he found himself near the end of his work, and in view of his reward, he shortened the labor to snatch the profit. He therefore remits his efforts where he should most vigorously exert them, and his catastrophe is improbably produced or imperfectly represented.

He had no regard to distinction of time or place, but gives to one age or nation, without scruple, the customs, institutions, and opinions of another, at the expense not only of likelihood but of possibility. These faults Pope has endeavored, with more zeal than judgment, to transfer to his imagined interpolators. We need not wonder to find Hector quoting Aristotle, when we see the loves of Theseus and Hippolyta combined with the Gothic mythology of fairies.[2] Shakespeare, indeed, was not the only violator of chronology, for in the same age Sidney, who wanted not the advantages of learning, has, in his *Arcadia,* confounded the pastoral with the feudal times, the days of innocence, quiet, and security with those of turbulence, violence, and adventure.

In his comic scenes he is seldom very successful when he engages his characters in reciprocations of smartness and contests of sarcasm; their jests are commonly gross, and their pleasantry licentious; neither his gentlemen nor his ladies have much delicacy, nor are sufficiently distinguished from his clowns by any appearance of refined manners. Whether he represented the real conversation of

2. In *Troilus and Cressida,* II.2.166, and in *Midsummer Night's Dream,* respectively.

his time is not easy to determine: the reign of Elizabeth is commonly supposed to have been a time of stateliness, formality, and reserve; yet perhaps the relaxations of that severity were not very elegant. There must, however, have been always some modes of gaiety preferable to others, and a writer ought to choose the best.

In tragedy his performance seems constantly to be worse as his labor is more. The effusions of passion, which exigence forces out, are for the most part striking and energetic; but whenever he solicits his invention, or strains his faculties, the offspring of his throes is tumor,[3] meanness, tediousness, and obscurity.

In narration he affects a disproportionate pomp of diction and a wearisome train of circumlocution, and tells the incident imperfectly in many words which might have been more plainly delivered in few. Narration in dramatic poetry is naturally tedious, as it is unanimated and inactive, and obstructs the progress of the action; it should therefore always be rapid and enlivened by frequent interruption. Shakespeare found it an encumbrance, and instead of lightening it by brevity, endeavored to recommend it by dignity and splendor.

His declamations or set speeches are commonly cold and weak, for his power was the power of nature; when he endeavored, like other tragic writers, to catch opportunities of amplification and, instead of inquiring what the occasion demanded, to show how much his stores of knowledge could supply, he seldom escapes without the pity or resentment of his reader.

It is incident to him to be now and then entangled with an unwieldy sentiment which he cannot well express, and will not reject; he struggles with it awhile, and, if it continues stubborn, comprises it in words such as occur, and leaves it to be disentangled and evolved by those who have more leisure to bestow upon it.

Not that always where the language is intricate the thought is subtle, or the image always great where the line is bulky; the equality of words to things is very often neglected, and trivial sentiments and vulgar[4] ideas disappoint the attention, to which they are recommended by sonorous epithets and swelling figures.

But the admirers of this great poet have most reason to complain when he approaches nearest to his highest excellence, and seems fully resolved to sink them in dejection and mollify them with tender emotions by the fall of greatness, the danger of innocence, or the crosses of love. What he does best, he soon ceases to do. He is not long soft and pathetic without some idle conceit or contemptible equivocation. He no sooner begins to move than he counteracts himself; and terror and pity, as they are rising in the mind, are

3. Inflated grandeur, false magnificence.
4. "Mean; low; being of the common rate" (Johnson's *Dictionary*).

checked and blasted by sudden frigidity.

A quibble[1] is to Shakespeare what luminous vapors are to the traveler: he follows it at all adventures; it is sure to lead him out of his way, and sure to engulf him in the mire. It has some malignant power over his mind, and its fascinations are irresistible. Whatever be the dignity or profundity of his disquisitions, whether he be enlarging knowledge or exalting affection, whether he be amusing[2] attention with incidents, or enchaining it in suspense, let but a quibble spring up before him, and he leaves his work unfinished. A quibble is the golden apple for which he will always turn aside from his career[3] or stoop from his elevation. A quibble, poor and barren as it is, gave him such delight that he was content to purchase it by the sacrifice of reason, propriety, and truth. A quibble was to him the fatal Cleopatra for which he lost the world, and was content to lose it.

It will be thought strange that in enumerating the defects of this writer, I have not yet mentioned his neglect of the unities; his violation of those laws which have been instituted and established by the joint authority of poets and critics.

For his other deviations from the art of writing, I resign him to critical justice without making any other demand in his favor than that which must be indulged to all human excellence: that his virtues be rated with his failings. But from the censure which this irregularity may bring upon him I shall, with due reverence to that learning which I must oppose, adventure to try how I can defend him.

His histories, being neither tragedies nor comedies, are not subject to any of their laws; nothing more is necessary to all the praise which they expect than that the changes of action be so prepared as to be understood; that the incidents be various and affecting, and the characters consistent, natural, and distinct. No other unity is intended, and therefore none is to be sought.

In his other works he has well enough preserved the unity of action. He has not, indeed, an intrigue regularly perplexed and regularly unraveled: he does not endeavor to hide his design only to discover it, for this is seldom the order of real events, and Shakespeare is the poet of nature: but his plan has commonly what Aristotle requires,[4] a beginning, a middle, and an end; one event is concatenated with another, and the conclusion follows by easy consequence. There are, perhaps, some incidents that might be spared,

1. Pun.
2. "To entertain with tranquility; to fill with thoughts that engage the mind, without distracting it" (Johnson's *Dictionary*).
3. In Greek legend Atalanta refused to marry any man who could not defeat her in a foot race. Hippomenes won her by dropping, as he ran, three of the golden apples of the Hesperides, which she paused to pick up.
4. *Poetics* VII.

as in other poets there is much talk that only fills up time upon the stage; but the general system makes gradual advances, and the end of the play is the end of expectation.

To the unities of time and place he has shown no regard; and perhaps a nearer view of the principles on which they stand will diminish their value and withdraw from them the veneration which, from the time of Corneille,[5] they have very generally received, by discovering that they have given more trouble to the poet than pleasure to the auditor.

The necessity of observing the unities of time and place arises from the supposed necessity of making the drama credible. The critics hold it impossible that an action of months or years can be possibly believed to pass in three hours; or that the spectator can suppose himself to sit in the theater while ambassadors go and return between distant kings, while armies are levied and towns besieged, while an exile wanders and returns, or till he whom they saw courting his mistress shall lament the untimely fall of his son. The mind revolts from evident falsehood, and fiction loses its force when it departs from the resemblance of reality.

From the narrow limitation of time necessarily arises the contraction of place. The spectator who knows that he saw the first act at Alexandria cannot suppose that he sees the next at Rome, at a distance to which not the dragons of Medea could, in so short a time, have transported him; he knows with certainty that he has not changed his place; and he knows that place cannot change itself, that what was a house cannot become a plain, that what was Thebes can never be Persepolis.

Such is the triumphant language with which a critic exults over the misery of an irregular poet, and exults commonly without resistance or reply. It is time, therefore, to tell him by the authority of Shakespeare that he assumes, as an unquestionable principle, a position which, while his breath is forming it into words, his understanding pronounces to be false. It is false that any representation is mistaken for reality; that any dramatic fable in its materiality was ever credible or, for a single moment, was ever credited.

The objection arising from the impossibility of passing the first hour at Alexandria and the next at Rome supposes that when the play opens the spectator really imagines himself at Alexandria, and believes that his walk to the theater has been a voyage to Egypt, and that he lives in the days of Antony and Cleopatra. Surely he that imagines this may imagine more. He that can take the stage at one time for the palace of the Ptolemies may take it in half an hour for the promontory of Actium. Delusion, if delusion be ad-

5. Pierre Corneille (1606–84), the French playwright, discussed the unities in his *Discours des trois unités* (1660).

mitted, has no certain limitation; if the spectator can be once persuaded that his old acquaintances are Alexander and Caesar, that a room illuminated with candles is the plain of Pharsalia or the bank of Granicus, he is in a state of elevation above the reach of reason or of truth, and from the heights of empyrean poetry may despise the circumscriptions of terrestrial nature. There is no reason why a mind thus wandering in ecstasy should count the clock, or why an hour should not be a century in that calenture[6] of the brain that can make the stage a field.

The truth is that the spectators are always in their senses, and know, from the first act to the last, that the stage is only a stage, and that the players are only players. They came to hear a certain number of lines recited with just gesture and elegant modulation. The lines relate to some action, and an action must be in some place; but the different actions that complete a story may be in places very remote from each other; and where is the absurdity of allowing that space to represent first Athens, and then Sicily, which was always known to be neither Sicily nor Athens but a modern theater?

By supposition, as place is introduced, time may be extended; the time required by the fable elapses, for the most part, between the acts; for, of so much of the action as is represented, the real and poetical duration is the same. If, in the first act, preparations for war against Mithridates are represented to be made in Rome, the event of the war may, without absurdity, be represented, in the catastrophe, as happening in Pontus; we know that there is neither war nor preparation for war; we know that we are neither in Rome nor Pontus, that neither Mithridates nor Lucullus are before us. The drama exhibits successive imitations of successive actions; and why may not the second imitation represent an action that happened years after the first, if it be so connected with it that nothing but time can be supposed to intervene? Time is, of all modes of existence, most obsequious[7] to the imagination; a lapse of years is as easily conceived as a passage of hours. In contemplation we easily contract the time of real actions, and therefore willingly permit it to be contracted when we only see their imitation.

It will be asked how the drama moves if it is not credited. It is credited with all the credit due to a drama. It is credited, whenever it moves, as a just picture of a real original; as representing to the auditor what he would himself feel if he were to do or suffer what is there feigned to be suffered or to be done. The reflection that strikes the heart is not that the evils before us are real evils, but that they are evils to which we ourselves may be exposed. If there

6. A delirium produced by tropical heat, which causes sailors to leap into the sea under the delusion that it is a green field.

7. "Obedient; compliant" (Johnson's *Dictionary*).

be any fallacy, it is not that we fancy the players, but that we fancy ourselves, unhappy for a moment; but we rather lament the possibility than suppose the presence of misery, as a mother weeps over her babe when she remembers that death may take it from her. The delight of tragedy proceeds from our consciousness of fiction; if we thought murders and treasons real, they would please no more.

Imitations produce pain or pleasure, not because they are mistaken for realities, but because they bring realities to mind. When the imagination is recreated by a painted landscape, the trees are not supposed capable to give us shade or the fountains coolness; but we consider how we should be pleased with such fountains playing beside us and such woods waving over us. We are agitated in reading the history of *Henry the Fifth;* yet no man takes his book for the field of Agincourt. A dramatic exhibition is a book recited with concomitants that increase or diminish its effect. Familiar comedy is often more powerful on the theater than in the page; imperial tragedy is always less. The humor of Petruchio may be heightened by grimace; but what voice or what gesture can hope to add dignity or force to the soliloquy of Cato?[8]

A play read affects the mind like a play acted. It is therefore evident that the action is not supposed to be real; and it follows that between the acts a longer or shorter time may be allowed to pass, and that no more account of space or duration is to be taken by the auditor of a drama than by the reader of a narrative, before whom may pass in an hour the life of a hero or the revolutions of an empire.

Whether Shakespeare knew the unities and rejected them by design or deviated from them by happy ignorance, it is, I think, impossible to decide and useless to inquire. We may reasonably suppose that, when he rose to notice, he did not want[9] the counsels and admonitions of scholars and critics, and that he at last deliberately persisted in a practice which he might have begun by chance. As nothing is essential to the fable but unity of action, and as the unities of time and place arise evidently from false assumptions, and, by circumscribing the extent of the drama, lessen its variety, I cannot think it much to be lamented that they were not known by him, or not observed: nor, if such another poet could arise, should I very vehemently reproach him that his first act passed at Venice and his next in Cyprus.[1] Such violations of rules merely positive become the comprehensive genius of Shakespeare, and such censures are suitable to the minute and slender criticism of Voltaire.

8. Petruchio is the hero of Shakespeare's comedy *The Taming of the Shrew*. In Addison's tragedy *Cato* (V.i), the hero soliloquizes on immortality shortly before committing suicide.

9. Lack.

1. As is the case in *Othello*.

Non usque adeo permiscuit imis
Longus summa dies, ut non, si voce Metelli
Serventur leges, malint a Caesare tolli.[2]

Yet when I speak thus slightly of dramatic rules, I cannot but recollect how much wit and learning may be produced against me; before such authorities I am afraid to stand: not that I think the present question one of those that are to be decided by mere authority, but because it is to be suspected that these precepts have not been so easily received but for better reasons than I have yet been able to find. The result of my inquiries, in which it would be ludicrous to boast of impartiality, is that the unities of time and place are not essential to a just drama, that though they may sometimes conduce to pleasure, they are always to be sacrificed to the nobler beauties of variety and instruction; and that a play written with nice observation of critical rules is to be contemplated as an elaborate curiosity, as the product of superfluous and ostentatious art, by which is shown rather what is possible than what is necessary.

He that without diminution of any other excellence shall preserve all the unities unbroken deserves the like applause with the architect who shall display all the orders of architecture in a citadel without any deduction for its strength; but the principal beauty of a citadel is to exclude the enemy, and the greatest graces of a play are to copy nature and instruct life. * * *

[*Henry IV*]

None of Shakespeare's plays are more read than the first and second parts of *Henry the fourth*. Perhaps no author has ever in two plays afforded so much delight. The great events are interesting, for the fate of kingdoms depends upon them; the slighter occurrences are diverting, and, except one or two, sufficiently probable; the incidents are multiplied with wonderful fertility of invention, and the characters diversified with the utmost nicety of discernment, and the profoundest skill in the nature of man.

The prince, who is the hero both of the comic and tragic part, is a young man of great abilities and violent passions, whose sentiments are right, though his actions are wrong; whose virtues are obscured by negligence, and whose understanding is dissipated by levity. In his idle hours he is rather loose than wicked, and when the occasion forces out his latent qualities, he is great without effort, and brave without tumult. The trifler is roused into a hero, and the hero again reposes in the trifler. This character is great, original, and just.[3]

Percy is a rugged soldier, choleric, and quarrelsome, and has only the soldier's virtues, generosity and courage.

2. Lucan, *Pharsalia* III.138–40: "The course of time has not wrought such confusion that the laws would not rather be trampled on by Caesar than saved by Metellus."

3. Exact.

But Falstaff, unimitated, unimitable Falstaff, how shall I describe thee? Thou compound of sense and vice; of sense which may be admired but not esteemed, of vice which may be despised, but hardly detested. Falstaff is a character loaded with faults, and with those faults which naturally produce contempt. He is a thief, and a glutton, a coward, and a boaster, always ready to cheat the weak, and prey upon the poor; to terrify the timorous and insult the defenseless. At once obsequious and malignant, he satirizes in their absence those whom he lives by flattering. He is familiar with the prince only as an agent of vice, but of this familiarity he is so proud as not only to be supercilious and haughty with common men, but to think his interest of importance to the duke of Lancaster. Yet the man thus corrupt, thus despicable, makes himself necessary to the prince that despises him, by the most pleasing of all qualities, perpetual gaiety, by an unfailing power of exciting laughter, which is the more freely indulged, as his wit is not of the splendid or ambitious kind, but consists in easy escapes and sallies of levity, which make sport but raise no envy. It must be observed that he is stained with no enormous or sanguinary crimes, so that his licentiousness is not so offensive but that it may be borne for his mirth.

The moral to be drawn from this representation is that no man is more dangerous than he that with a will to corrupt, hath the power to please; and that neither wit nor honesty ought to think themselves safe with such a companion when they see Henry seduced by Falstaff.

[*King Lear*]

The tragedy of *Lear* is deservedly celebrated among the dramas of Shakespeare. There is perhaps no play which keeps the attention so strongly fixed; which so much agitates our passions and interests our curiosity. The artful involutions[1] of distinct interests, the striking opposition of contrary characters, the sudden changes of fortune, and the quick succession of events, fill the mind with a perpetual tumult of indignation, pity, and hope. There is no scene which does not contribute to the aggravation of the distress or conduct of the action, and scarce a line which does not conduce to the progress of the scene. So powerful is the current of the poet's imagination, that the mind, which once ventures within it, is hurried irresistibly along.

On the seeming improbability of Lear's conduct it may be observed, that he is represented according to histories at that time vulgarly[2] received as true. And perhaps if we turn our thoughts upon the barbarity and ignorance of the age to which this story is referred, it will appear not so unlikely as while we estimate Lear's

1. Entanglements.
2. Popularly.

manners by our own. Such preference of one daughter to another, or resignation of dominion on such conditions, would be yet credible, if told of a petty prince of Guinea or Madagascar. Shakespeare, indeed, by the mention of his Earls and Dukes, has given us the idea of times more civilized, and of life regulated by softer manners; and the truth is, that though he so nicely discriminates, and so minutely describes the characters of men, he commonly neglects and confounds the characters of ages, by mingling customs ancient and modern, English and foreign.

My learned friend Mr. Warton, who has in the *Adventurer* very minutely criticized this play,[3] remarks, that the instances of cruelty are too savage and shocking, and that the intervention of Edmund destroys the simplicity of the story. These objections may, I think, be answered, by repeating that the cruelty of the daughters is an historical fact, to which the poet has added little, having only drawn it into a series by dialogue and action. But I am not able to apologize with equal plausibility for the extrusion of Gloucester's eyes, which seems an act too horrid to be endured in dramatic exhibition, and such as must always compel the mind to relieve its distress by incredulity. Yet let it be remembered that our author well knew what would please the audience for which he wrote.

The injury done by Edmund to the simplicity of the action is abundantly recompensed by the addition of variety, by the art with which he is made to co-operate with the chief design, and the opportunity which he gives the poet of combining perfidy with perfidy, and connecting the wicked son with the wicked daughters, to impress this important moral, that villainy is never at a stop, that crimes lead to crimes, and at last terminate in ruin.

But though this moral be incidentally enforced, Shakespeare has suffered the virtue of Cordelia to perish in a just cause, contrary to the natural ideas of justice, to the hope of the reader, and, what is yet more strange, to the faith of chronicles. Yet this conduct is justified by the Spectator, who blames Tate for giving Cordelia success and happiness in his alteration, and declares that in his opinion, the tragedy "has lost half its beauty."[4] Dennis has remarked, whether justly or not, that to secure the favorable reception of *Cato*, "the town was poisoned with much false and abominable criticism,"[5] and that endeavors had been used to discredit and decry poetical justice. A play in which the wicked prosper, and the virtuous miscarry, may doubtless be good, because it is a just representation of the common events of human life: but since all reasonable beings

3. Joseph Warton (1722–1800) contributed several papers to Johnson's periodical *The Adventurer*; numbers 113, 116, and 122 discuss *King Lear*.

4. Addison, *Spectator* 40. During the 18th century, *King Lear* was regularly performed with a happy ending, in the adaptation by Nahum Tate.

5. John Dennis, "Remarks upon *Cato, a Tragedy*" (1713). Dennis implies that Addison excuses the want of poetic justice in *Lear* in order to justify the absence of poetic justice in his own play, *Cato*.

naturally love justice, I cannot easily be persuaded that the observation of justice makes a play worse; or that if other excellencies are equal, the audience will not always rise better pleased from the final triumph of persecuted virtue.

In the present case the public has decided. Cordelia, from the time of Tate, has always retired with victory and felicity. And, if my sensations could add anything to the general suffrage, I might relate, that I was many years ago so shocked by Cordelia's death, that I know not whether I ever endured to read again the last scenes of the play till I undertook to revise them as an editor.

1765

From LIVES OF THE POETS

From Cowley[1]

[*Metaphysical Wit*]

Wit, like all other things subject by their nature to the choice of man, has its changes and fashions, and at different times takes different forms. About the beginning of the seventeenth century appeared a race of writers that may be termed the metaphysical poets,[2] of whom in a criticism on the works of Cowley it is not improper to give some account.

The metaphysical poets were men of learning, and to show their learning was their whole endeavor; but, unluckily resolving to show it in rhyme, instead of writing poetry they only wrote verses, and very often such verses as stood the trial of the finger better than of the ear; for the modulation was so imperfect that they were only found to be verses by counting the syllables.

If the father of criticism[3] has rightly denominated poetry τέχνη μιμητικὴ, *an imitative art*, these writers will without great wrong lose their right to the name of poets, for they cannot be said to have imitated anything: they neither copied nature nor life; neither painted the forms of matter nor represented the operations of intellect.

Those however who deny them to be poets allow them to be wits. Dryden confesses of himself and his contemporaries that they fall below Donne in it, but maintains that they surpass him in poetry.[4]

1. Abraham Cowley (1618–67) was much admired during the middle of the 17th century. His reputation began to decline before 1700, but he was remembered as a writer of false wit, especially in his love poems *The Mistress*.

2. Presumably Johnson took this now common designation from a hint in Dryden's *Discourse Concerning the Original and Progress of Satire*, 1693. Dryden condemned Donne because "he affects the metaphysics * * * and perplexes the minds of the fair sex with nice speculations of philosophy, when he should engage their hearts, and entertain them with the softnesses of love" (*Essays*, ed. W. P. Ker, II.19).

3. Aristotle in his *Poetics*.

4. *Discourse * * * of Satire* (Ker II.102).

If wit be well described by Pope as being "that which has been often thought, but was never before so well expressed,"[5] they certainly never attained nor ever sought it, for they endeavored to be singular in their thoughts, and were careless of their diction. But Pope's account of wit is undoubtedly erroneous; he depresses it below its natural dignity, and reduces it from strength of thought to happiness of language.

If by a more noble and more adequate conception that be considered as wit which is at once natural and new, that which though not obvious is, upon its first production, acknowledged to be just; if it be that which he that never found it, wonders how he missed; to wit of this kind the metaphysical poets have seldom risen. Their thoughts are often new, but seldom natural; they are not obvious, but neither are they just;[6] and the reader, far from wondering that he missed them, wonders more frequently by what perverseness of industry they were ever found.

But wit, abstracted from its effects upon the hearer, may be more rigorously and philosophically considered as a kind of *discordia concors*;[7] a combination of dissimilar images, or discovery of occult resemblances in things apparently unlike. Of wit, thus defined, they have more than enough. The most heterogeneous ideas are yoked by violence together; nature and art are ransacked for illustrations, comparisons, and allusions; their learning instructs, and their subtlety surprises; but the reader commonly thinks his improvement dearly bought, and, though he sometimes admires, is seldom pleased.

From this account of their compositions it will be readily inferred that they were not successful in representing or moving the affections. As they were wholly employed on something unexpected and surprising, they had no regard to that uniformity of sentiment which enables us to conceive and to excite the pains and the pleasure of other minds: they never inquired what on any occasion they should have said or done, but wrote rather as beholders than partakers of human nature; as beings looking upon good and evil, impassive and at leisure; as Epicurean deities making remarks on the actions of men and the vicissitudes of life, without interest and without emotion. Their courtship was void of fondness and their lamentation of sorrow. Their wish was only to say what they hoped had been never said before.

Nor was the sublime more within their reach than the pathetic; for they never attempted that comprehension and expanse of thought which at once fills the whole mind, and of which the first effect is sudden astonishment, and the second rational admiration.

5. *Essay on Criticism*, lines 297–98.
6. Exact, proper.
7. Literally, "a harmonious discord." Johnson is himself being witty in using this phrase, a familiar philosophical concept denoting the general harmony of God's creation despite its manifold and often contradictory particulars.

Sublimity is produced by aggregation, and littleness by dispersion. Great thoughts are always general, and consist in positions not limited by exceptions, and in descriptions not descending to minuteness. It is with great propriety that subtlety, which in its original import means exility[8] of particles, is taken in its metaphorical meaning for nicety of distinction. Those writers who lay on the watch for novelty could have little hope of greatness; for great things cannot have escaped former observation. Their attempts were always analytic: they broke every image into fragments, and could no more represent by their slender conceits and labored particularities the prospects of nature or the scenes of life, than he who dissects a sunbeam with a prism can exhibit the wide effulgence of a summer noon.

What they wanted however of the sublime they endeavored to supply by hyperbole;[9] their amplification had no limits: they left not only reason but fancy behind them, and produced combinations of confused magnificence that not only could not be credited, but could not be imagined.

Yet great labor directed by great abilities is never wholly lost: if they frequently threw away their wit upon false conceits, they likewise sometimes struck out unexpected truth: if their conceits were farfetched, they were often worth the carriage.[10] To write on their plan it was at least necessary to read and think. No man could be born a metaphysical poet, nor assume the dignity of a writer by descriptions copied from descriptions, by imitations borrowed from imitations, by traditional imagery and hereditary similes, by readiness of rhyme and volubility of syllables.

1779

From Milton[1]

[*Lycidas*]

One of the poems on which much praise has been bestowed is *Lycidas;* of which the diction is harsh,[2] the rhymes uncertain, and the numbers unpleasing. What beauty there is, we must therefore seek in the sentiments and images. It is not to be considered as

8. Thinness.

9. An image heightened beyond reality (see Johnson's *Dictionary*).

10. In the *Life of Addison,* Johnson wrote: "A simile may be compared to lines converging at a point, and is more excellent as the lines approach from greater distance * * * "

1. Johnson's treatment of Milton as man and poet gave great offense to many ardent Miltonians in his own day and damaged his reputation as a critic in the following century. He did not admire Milton's character, and he detested his politics and religion. But no one has praised *Paradise Lost* more handsomely. Especially offensive in the 19th century was his attack on *Lycidas*. Johnson disliked modern pastorals, recognizing that the tradition had been worn threadbare. His views on the genre may be read in *Ramblers* 36 and 37.

2. This notorious word does not mean "unmelodious," but "strained, forced, affected, or labored."

the effusion of real passion; for passion runs not after remote allusions and obscure opinions. Passion plucks no berries from the myrtle and ivy, nor calls upon Arethuse and Mincius, nor tells of "rough satyrs and fauns with cloven heel." Where there is leisure for fiction there is little grief.

In this poem there is no nature, for there is no truth; there is no art, for there is nothing new. Its form is that of a pastoral, easy, vulgar, and therefore disgusting:[3] whatever images it can supply are long ago exhausted; and its inherent improbability always forces dissatisfaction on the mind. When Cowley tells of Hervey that they studied together, it is easy to suppose how much he must miss the companion of his labors and the partner of his discoveries;[4] but what image of tenderness can be excited by these lines!

> We drove afield, and both together heard
> What time the grayfly winds her sultry horn,
> Battening our flocks with the fresh dews of night.

We know that they never drove afield, and that they had no flocks to batten; and though it be allowed that the representation may be allegorical, the true meaning is so uncertain and remote that it is never sought because it cannot be known when it is found.

Among the flocks and copses and flowers appear the heathen deities, Jove and Phoebus, Neptune and Aeolus, with a long train of mythological imagery, such as a college easily supplies. Nothing can less display knowledge or less exercise invention than to tell how a shepherd has lost his companion and must now feed his flocks alone, without any judge of his skill in piping; and how one god asks another god what is become of Lycidas, and how neither god can tell. He who thus grieves will excite no sympathy; he who thus praises will confer no honor.

This poem has yet a grosser fault. With these trifling fictions are mingled the most awful and sacred truths, such as ought never to be polluted with such irreverent combinations. The shepherd likewise is now a feeder of sheep, and afterwards an ecclesiastical pastor, a superintendent of a Christian flock. Such equivocations are always unskillful; but here they are indecent,[5] and at least approach to impiety, of which, however, I believe the writer not to have been conscious.

Such is the power of reputation justly acquired that its blaze drives away the eye from nice examination. Surely no man could have fancied that he read *Lycidas* with pleasure had he not known its author.

3. I.e., displeasing ("disgusting") because its stale conventionality made it "vulgar" by putting it within the reach of the many.

4. Cowley's *On the Death of Mr. William Hervey* (1656).

5. Unbecoming, lacking in decorum.

[*L'Allegro. Il Penseroso*]

Of the two pieces, *L'Allegro* and *Il Penseroso*, I believe opinion is uniform; every man that reads them, reads them with pleasure. The author's design is not, what Theobald [1] has remarked, merely to show how objects derived their colors from the mind, by representing the operation of the same things upon the gay and the melancholy temper, or upon the same man as he is differently disposed; but rather how, among the successive variety of appearances, every disposition of mind takes hold on those by which it may be gratified.

The *cheerful* man hears the lark in the morning; the *pensive* man hears the nightingale in the evening. The *cheerful* man sees the cock strut, and hears the horn and hounds echo in the wood; then walks "not unseen" to observe the glory of the rising sun or listen to the singing milkmaid, and view the labors of the plowman and the mower; then casts his eyes about him over scenes of smiling plenty, and looks up to the distant tower, the residence of some fair inhabitant: thus he pursues rural gaiety through a day of labor or of play, and delights himself at night with the fanciful narratives of superstitious ignorance.

The *pensive* man at one time walks "unseen" to muse at midnight, and at another hears the sullen curfew. If the weather drives him home he sits in a room lighted only by "glowing embers"; or by a lonely lamp outwatches the North Star to discover the habitation of separate souls, and varies the shades of meditation by contemplating the magnificent or pathetic scenes of tragic and epic poetry. When the morning comes, a morning gloomy with rain and wind, he walks into the dark trackless woods, falls asleep by some murmuring water, and with melancholy enthusiasm expects some dream of prognostication or some music played by aerial performers.

Both Mirth and Melancholy are solitary, silent inhabitants of the breast that neither receive nor transmit communication: no mention is therefore made of a philosophical friend or a pleasant companion. The seriousness does not arise from any participation of calamity, nor the gaiety from the pleasures of the bottle.

The man of *cheerfulness* having exhausted the country tries what "towered cities" will afford, and mingles with scenes of splendor, gay assemblies, and nuptial festivities; but he mingles a mere spectator as, when the learned comedies of Jonson or the wild dramas of Shakespeare are exhibited, he attends the theater.

The *pensive* man never loses himself in crowds, but walks the cloister or frequents the cathedral. Milton probably had not yet forsaken the Church.

1. Lewis Theobald (1688–1744), the editor of Shakespeare and the enemy of Pope.

Both his characters delight in music; but he seems to think that cheerful notes would have obtained from Pluto a complete dismission of Eurydice, of whom solemn sounds only procured a conditional release.

For the old age of Cheerfulness he makes no provision; but Melancholy he conducts with great dignity to the close of life. His Cheerfulness is without levity, and his Pensiveness without asperity.

Through these two poems the images are properly selected and nicely distinguished, but the colors of the diction seem not sufficiently discriminated. I know not whether the characters are kept sufficiently apart. No mirth can, indeed, be found in his melancholy; but I am afraid that I always meet some melancholy in his mirth. They are two noble efforts of imagination.

[*Paradise Lost*]

Those little pieces may be dispatched without much anxiety; a greater work calls for greater care. I am now to examine *Paradise Lost*, a poem which, considered with respect to design, may claim the first place, and with respect to performance the second, among the productions of the human mind.

By the general consent of critics the first praise of genius is due to the writer of an epic poem, as it requires an assemblage of all the powers which are singly sufficient for other compositions. Poetry is the art of uniting pleasure with truth, by calling imagination to the help of reason. Epic poetry undertakes to teach the most important truths by the most pleasing precepts, and therefore relates some great event in the most affecting manner. History must supply the writer with the rudiments of narration, which he must improve and exalt by a nobler art, must animate by dramatic energy, and diversify by retrospection and anticipation; morality must teach him the exact bounds and different shades of vice and virtue; from policy and the practice of life he has to learn the discriminations of character and the tendency of the passions, either single or combined; and physiology must supply him with illustrations and images. To put these materials to poetical use is required an imagination capable of painting nature and realizing fiction. Nor is he yet a poet till he has attained the whole extension of his language, distinguished all the delicacies of phrase, and all the colors of words, and learned to adjust their different sounds to all the varieties of metrical modulation.

Bossu is of opinion that the poet's first work is to find a *moral*, which his fable is afterwards to illustrate and establish.[1] This seems to have been the process only of Milton: the moral of other poems is incidental and consequent; in Milton's only it is essential and intrinsic. His purpose was the most useful and the most arduous: "to vindicate the ways of God to man"; to show the reasonableness

1. Père le Bossu wrote a treatise on the epic poem, *Traité du Poëme Épique*, 1675, much admired during the late 17th and early 18th centuries.

of religion, and the necessity of obedience to the Divine Law.

To convey this moral there must be a *fable*, a narration artfully constructed, so as to excite curiosity and surprise expectation. In this part of his work Milton must be confessed to have equaled every other poet. He has involved in his account of the Fall of Man the events which preceded, and those that were to follow it: he has interwoven the whole system of theology with such propriety that every part appears to be necessary, and scarcely any recital is wished shorter for the sake of quickening the progress of the main action.

The subject of an epic poem is naturally an event of great importance. That of Milton is not the destruction of a city, the conduct of a colony, or the foundation of an empire. His subject is the fate of worlds, the revolutions of heaven and of earth; rebellion against the Supreme King raised by the highest order of created beings; the overthrow of their host and the punishment of their crime; the creation of a new race of reasonable creatures; their original happiness and innocence, their forfeiture of immortality, and their restoration to hope and peace.

Great events can be hastened or retarded only by persons of elevated dignity. Before the greatness displayed in Milton's poem all other greatness shrinks away. The weakest of his agents are the highest and noblest of human beings, the original parents of mankind; with whose actions the elements consented; on whose rectitude or deviation of will depended the state of terrestrial nature and the condition of all the future inhabitants of the globe.

Of the other agents in the poem, the chief are such as it is irreverence to name on slight occasions. The rest were lower powers;

> of which the least could wield
> Those elements, and arm him with the force
> Of all their regions; [2]

powers which only the control of Omnipotence restrains from laying creation waste, and filling the vast expanse of space with ruin and confusion. To display the motives and actions of beings thus superior, so far as human reason can examine them or human imagination represent them, is the task which this mighty poet has undertaken and performed.

In the examination of epic poems much speculation is commonly employed upon the *characters*. The characters in the *Paradise Lost* which admit of examination are those of angels and of man; of angels good and evil, of man in his innocent and sinful state.

Among the angels the virtue of Raphael is mild and placid, of easy condescension and free communication; that of Michael is regal and lofty, and, as may seem, attentive to the dignity of his own nature. Abdiel and Gabriel appear occasionally, and act as every

2. ***Paradise Lost*** VI.221.

incident requires; the solitary fidelity of Abdiel is very amiably painted.[3]

Of the evil angels the characters are more diversified. To Satan, as Addison observes, such sentiments are given as suit "the most exalted and most depraved being."[4] Milton has been censured by Clarke for the impiety which sometimes breaks from Satan's mouth. For there are thoughts, as he justly remarks, which no observation of character can justify, because no good man would willingly permit them to pass, however transiently, through his own mind.[5] To make Satan speak as a rebel, without any such expressions as might taint the reader's imagination, was indeed one of the great difficulties in Milton's undertaking, and I cannot but think that he has extricated himself with great happiness. There is in Satan's speeches little that can give pain to a pious ear. The language of rebellion cannot be the same with that of obedience. The malignity of Satan foams in haughtiness and obstinacy; but his expressions are commonly general, and no otherwise offensive than as they are wicked.

The other chiefs of the celestial rebellion are very judiciously discriminated in the first and second books; and the ferocious character of Moloch appears, both in the battle and the council, with exact consistency.

To Adam and to Eve are given during their innocence such sentiments as innocence can generate and utter. Their love is pure benevolence and mutual veneration; their repasts are without luxury and their diligence without toil. Their addresses to their Maker have little more than the voice of admiration and gratitude. Fruition left them nothing to ask, and Innocence left them nothing to fear.

But with guilt enter distrust and discord, mutual accusation, and stubborn self-defense; they regard each other with alienated minds, and dread their Creator as the avenger of their transgression. At last they seek shelter in his mercy, soften to repentance, and melt in supplication. Both before and after the Fall the superiority of Adam is diligently sustained.

Of the *probable* and the *marvelous*,[6] two parts of a vulgar epic poem which immerge the critic in deep consideration, the *Paradise Lost* requires little to be said. It contains the history of a miracle, of Creation and Redemption; it displays the power and the mercy of the Supreme Being: the probable therefore is marvelous, and the marvelous is probable. The substance of the narrative is truth; and as truth allows no choice, it is, like necessity, superior to rule. To the accidental or adventitious parts, as to every thing human, some slight exceptions may be made. But the main fabric is immovably supported.

3. *Paradise Lost* V.803 ff.
4. *Spectator* 303.
5. John Clarke, *Essay upon Study*, 1731.
6. Actions in an epic poem which are wonderful because they exceed the probable.

It is justly remarked by Addison [7] that this poem has, by the nature of its subject, the advantage above all others, that it is universally and perpetually interesting. All mankind will, through all ages, bear the same relation to Adam and to Eve, and must partake of that good and evil which extend to themselves.

Of the *machinery*, so called from θεὸς ἀπὸ μηχανῆς [8] by which is meant the occasional interposition of supernatural power, another fertile topic of critical remarks, here is no room to speak, because every thing is done under the immediate and visible direction of Heaven; but the rule is so far observed that no part of the action could have been accomplished by any other means.

Of *episodes* [9] I think there are only two, contained in Raphael's relation of the war in heaven and Michael's prophetic account of the changes to happen in this world. Both are closely connected with the great action; one was necessary to Adam as a warning, the other as a consolation.

To the completeness or *integrity* of the design nothing can be objected; it has distinctly and clearly what Aristotle requires, a beginning, a middle, and an end. There is perhaps no poem of the same length from which so little can be taken without apparent mutilation. Here are no funeral games, nor is there any long description of a shield. The short digressions at the beginning of the third, seventh, and ninth books might doubtless be spared; but superfluities so beautiful who would take away? or who does not wish that the author of the *Iliad* had gratified succeeding ages with a little knowledge of himself? Perhaps no passages are more frequently or more attentively read than those extrinsic paragraphs; and since the end of poetry is pleasure, that cannot be unpoetical with which all are pleased.

The questions, whether the action of the poem be strictly *one*,[1] whether the poem can be properly termed *heroic*, and who is the hero, are raised by such readers as draw their principles of judgment rather from books than from reason. Milton, though he entitled *Paradise Lost* only a "poem," yet calls it himself "heroic song." [2] Dryden, petulantly and indecently, denies the heroism of Adam because he was overcome; but there is no reason why the hero should not be unfortunate except established practice, since success and virtue do not go necessarily together. Cato is the hero of Lucan, but Lucan's authority will not be suffered by Quintilian to decide. However, if success be necessary, Adam's deceiver was at last crushed; Adam was restored to his Maker's favor, and therefore may securely resume his human rank.

After the scheme and fabric of the poem must be considered its

7. *Spectator* 273.
8. Aristotle, *Poetics* XV.10. "Deus ex machina," the intervention of supernatural powers into the affairs of men.
9. Incidental but related narratives within an epic poem. Johnson is citing *Paradise Lost* V.577 ff. and XI.334 ff.
1. I.e., a single action dealing with a single character.
2. *Paradise Lost* IX.25.

component parts, the sentiments, and the diction.

The *sentiments*, as expressive of manners or appropriated to characters, are for the greater part unexceptionably just. Splendid passages containing lessons of morality or precepts of prudence occur seldom. Such is the original formation of this poem that as it admits no human manners till the Fall, it can give little assistance to human conduct. Its end is to raise the thoughts above sublunary cares or pleasures. Yet the praise of that fortitude, with which Abdiel maintained his singularity of virtue against the scorn of multitudes, may be accommodated to all times; and Raphael's reproof of Adam's curiosity after the planetary motions, with the answer returned by Adam, may be confidently opposed to any rule of life which any poet has delivered.[3]

The thoughts which are occasionally called forth in the progress are such as could only be produced by an imagination in the highest degree fervid and active, to which materials were supplied by incessant study and unlimited curiosity. The heat of Milton's mind might be said to sublimate his learning, to throw off into his work the spirit of science, unmingled with its grosser parts.

He had considered creation in its whole extent, and his descriptions are therefore learned. He had accustomed his imagination to unrestrained indulgence, and his conceptions therefore were extensive. The characteristic quality of his poem is sublimity. He sometimes descends to the elegant, but his element is the great. He can occasionally invest himself with grace; but his natural port is gigantic loftiness. He can please when pleasure is required; but it is his peculiar power to astonish.

He seems to have been well acquainted with his own genius, and to know what it was that Nature had bestowed upon him more bountifully than upon others; the power of displaying the vast, illuminating the splendid, enforcing the awful, darkening the gloomy, and aggravating the dreadful: he therefore chose a subject on which too much could not be said, on which he might tire his fancy without the censure of extravagance.

* * *

The defects and faults of *Paradise Lost*, for faults and defects every work of man must have, it is the business of impartial criticism to discover. As in displaying the excellence of Milton I have not made long quotations, because of selecting beauties there had been no end, I shall in the same general manner mention that which seems to deserve censure; for what Englishman can take delight in transcribing passages, which, if they lessen the reputation of Milton, diminish in some degree the honor of our country?

* * *

The plan of *Paradise Lost* has this inconvenience, that it comprises neither human actions nor human manners. The man and

3. *Paradise Lost* VIII.65 ff.

woman who act and suffer are in a state which no other man or woman can ever know. The reader finds no transaction in which he can be engaged, beholds no condition in which he can by any effort of imagination place himself; he has, therefore, little natural curiosity or sympathy.

We all, indeed, feel the effects of Adam's disobedience; we all sin like Adam, and like him must all bewail our offenses; we have restless and insidious enemies in the fallen angels, and in the blessed spirits we have guardians and friends; in the Redemption of mankind we hope to be included: in the description of heaven and hell we are surely interested, as we are all to reside hereafter either in the regions of horror or of bliss.

But these truths are too important to be new: they have been taught to our infancy; they have mingled with our solitary thoughts and familiar conversation, and are habitually interwoven with the whole texture of life. Being therefore not new they raise no unaccustomed emotion in the mind: what we knew before, we cannot learn; what is not unexpected, cannot surprise.

Of the ideas suggested by these awful scenes, from some we recede with reverence, except when stated hours require their association; and from others we shrink with horror, or admit them only as salutary inflictions, as counterpoises to our interests and passions. Such images rather obstruct the career of fancy than incite it.

Pleasure and terror are indeed the genuine sources of poetry; but poetical pleasure must be such as human imagination can at least conceive, and poetical terror such as human strength and fortitude may combat. The good and evil of Eternity are too ponderous for the wings of wit; the mind sinks under them in passive helplessness, content with calm belief and humble adoration.

Known truths however may take a different appearance, and be conveyed to the mind by a new train of intermediate images. This Milton has undertaken, and performed with pregnancy and vigor of mind peculiar to himself. Whoever considers the few radical positions which the Scriptures afforded him will wonder by what energetic operation he expanded them to such extent and ramified them to so much variety, restrained as he was by religious reverence from licentiousness of fiction.

Here is a full display of the united force of study and genius; of a great accumulation of materials, with judgment to digest and fancy to combine them: Milton was able to select from nature or from story, from ancient fable or from modern science, whatever could illustrate or adorn his thoughts. An accumulation of knowledge impregnated his mind, fermented by study and exalted by imagination.

* * *

But original deficience cannot be supplied. The want of human interest is always felt. *Paradise Lost* is one of the books which the reader admires and lays down, and forgets to take up again. None ever wished it longer than it is. Its perusal is a duty rather than a pleasure. We read Milton for instruction, retire harassed and overburdened, and look elsewhere for recreation; we desert our master, and seek for companions.

* * *

Dryden remarks that Milton has some flats among his elevations.[4] This is only to say that all the parts are not equal. In every work one part must be for the sake of others; a palace must have passages, a poem must have transitions. It is no more to be required that wit should always be blazing than that the sun should always stand at noon. In a great work there is a vicissitude [5] of luminous and opaque parts, as there is in the world a succession of day and night. Milton, when he has expatiated in the sky, may be allowed sometimes to revisit earth; for what other author ever soared so high or sustained his flight so long?

* * *

The highest praise of genius is original invention. Milton cannot be said to have contrived the structure of an epic poem, and therefore owes reverence to that vigor and amplitude of mind to which all generations must be indebted for the art of poetical narration, for the texture of the fable, the variation of incidents, the interposition of dialogue, and all the stratagems that surprise and enchain attention. But of all the borrowers from Homer Milton is perhaps the least indebted. He was naturally a thinker for himself, confident of his own abilities and disdainful of help or hindrance; he did not refuse admission to the thoughts or images of his predecessors, but he did not seek them. From his contemporaries he neither courted nor received support; there is in his writings nothing by which the pride of other authors might be gratified or favor gained, no exchange of praise or solicitation of support. His great works were performed under discountenance and in blindness, but difficulties vanished at his touch; he was born for whatever is arduous; and his work is not the greatest of heroic poems, only because it is not the first.

1779

From Pope

[*Pope's Intellectual Character. Pope and Dryden Compared*]

Of his intellectual character, the constituent and fundamental principle was good sense, a prompt and intuitive perception of consonance and propriety. He saw immediately, of his own conceptions, what was to be chosen, and what to be rejected; and, in

4. Preface to *Sylvae;* see Essays (ed. W. P. Ker), I.268.
5. Change.

the works of others, what was to be shunned, and what was to be copied.

But good sense alone is a sedate and quiescent quality, which manages its possessions well, but does not increase them; it collects few materials for its own operations, and preserves safety, but never gains supremacy. Pope had likewise genius; a mind active, ambitious, and adventurous, always investigating, always aspiring; in its widest searches still longing to go forward, in its highest flights still wishing to be higher; always imagining something greater than it knows, always endeavoring more than it can do.

To assist these powers, he is said to have had great strength and exactness of memory. That which he had heard or read was not easily lost; and he had before him not only what his own meditation suggested, but what he had found in other writers that might be accommodated to his present purpose.

These benefits of nature he improved by incessant and unwearied diligence; he had recourse to every source of intelligence, and lost no opportunity of information; he consulted the living as well as the dead; he read his compositions to his friends, and was never content with mediocrity when excellence could be attained. He considered poetry as the business of his life, and however he might seem to lament his occupation, he followed it with constancy: to make verses was his first labor, and to mend them was his last.

From his attention to poetry he was never diverted. If conversation offered anything that could be improved, he committed it to paper; if a thought, or perhaps an expression more happy than was common, rose to his mind, he was careful to write it; an independent distich was preserved for an opportunity of insertion, and some little fragments have been found containing lines, or parts of lines, to be wrought upon at some other time.

He was one of those few whose labor is their pleasure; he was never elevated to negligence, nor wearied to impatience; he never passed a fault unamended by indifference, nor quitted it by despair. He labored his works first to gain reputation, and afterwards to keep it.

Of composition there are different methods. Some employ at once memory and invention, and, with little intermediate use of the pen, form and polish large masses by continued meditation, and write their productions only when, in their own opinion, they have completed them. It is related of Virgil[1] that his custom was to pour out a great number of verses in the morning, and pass the day in retrenching exuberances and correcting inaccuracies. The method of Pope, as may be collected from his translation, was to write his first thoughts in his first words, and gradually to amplify, decorate, rectify, and refine them.

1. By Suetonius in his brief life of the poet.

With such faculties and such dispositions, he excelled every other writer in *poetical prudence;* he wrote in such a manner as might expose him to few hazards. He used almost always the same fabric of verse; and, indeed, by those few essays which he made of any other, he did not enlarge his reputation. Of this uniformity the certain consequence was readiness and dexterity. By perpetual practice, language had in his mind a systematical arrangement; having always the same use for words, he had words so selected and combined as to be ready at his call. This increase of facility he confessed himself to have perceived in the progress of his translation.

But what was yet of more importance, his effusions were always voluntary, and his subjects chosen by himself. His independence secured him from drudging at a task, and laboring upon a barren topic: he never exchanged praise for money, nor opened a shop of condolence or congratulation. His poems, therefore, were scarce ever temporary. He suffered coronations and royal marriages to pass without a song, and derived no opportunities from recent events, nor any popularity from the accidental disposition of his readers. He was never reduced to the necessity of soliciting the sun to shine upon a birthday, of calling the Graces and Virtues to a wedding, or of saying what multitudes have said before him. When he could produce nothing new, he was at liberty to be silent.

His publications were for the same reason never hasty. He is said to have sent nothing to the press till it had lain two years under his inspection: it is at least certain that he ventured nothing without nice examination. He suffered the tumult of imagination to subside, and the novelties of invention to grow familiar. He knew that the mind is always enamored of its own productions, and did not trust his first fondness. He consulted his friends, and listened with great willingness to criticism; and, what was of more importance, he consulted himself, and let nothing pass against his own judgment.

He professed to have learned his poetry from Dryden, whom, whenever an opportunity was presented, he praised through his whole life with unvaried liberality; and perhaps his character may receive some illustration, if he be compared with his master.

Integrity of understanding and nicety of discernment were not allotted in a less proportion to Dryden than to Pope. The rectitude of Dryden's mind was sufficiently shown by the dismission of his poetical prejudices, and the rejection of unnatural thoughts and rugged numbers. But Dryden never desired to apply all the judgment that he had. He wrote, and professed to write, merely for the people; and when he pleased others, he contented himself. He spent no time in struggles to rouse latent powers; he never attempted to make that better which was already good, nor often to mend what he must have known to be faulty. He wrote, as he tells us, with very little consideration; when occasion or necessity called upon him, he poured out what the present moment happened to supply, and, when once it had passed the press, ejected it from his mind; for when he had no pecuniary interest, he had no further solicitude.

Pope was not content to satisfy; he desired to excel, and therefore always endeavored to do his best: he did not court the candor, but dared the judgment of his reader, and, expecting no indulgence from others, he showed none to himself. He examined lines and words with minute and punctilious observation, and retouched every part with indefatigable diligence, till he had left nothing to be forgiven.

For this reason he kept his pieces very long in his hands, while he considered and reconsidered them. The only poems which can be supposed to have been written with such regard to the times as might hasten their publication were the two satires of *Thirty-Eight*; of which Dodsley[2] told me that they were brought to him by the author, that they might be fairly copied. "Almost every line," he said, "was then written twice over; I gave him a clean transcript, which he sent some time afterwards to me for the press, with almost every line written twice over a second time."

His declaration, that his care for his works ceased at their publication, was not strictly true. His parental attention never abandoned them; what he found amiss in the first edition, he silently corrected in those that followed. He appears to have revised the *Iliad*, and freed it from some of its imperfections; and the *Essay on Criticism* received many improvements after its first appearance. It will seldom be found that he altered without adding clearness, elegance, or vigor. Pope had perhaps the judgment of Dryden; but Dryden certainly wanted the diligence of Pope.

In acquired knowledge, the superiority must be allowed to Dryden, whose education was more scholastic, and who before he became an author had been allowed more time for study, with better means of information. His mind has a larger range, and he collects his images and illustrations from a more extensive circumference of science. Dryden knew more of man in his general nature, and Pope in his local manners. The notions of Dryden were formed by comprehensive speculation, and those of Pope by minute attention. There is more dignity in the knowledge of Dryden, and more certainty in that of Pope.

Poetry was not the sole praise of either; for both excelled likewise in prose; but Pope did not borrow his prose from his predecessor. The style of Dryden is capricious and varied, that of Pope is cautious and uniform; Dryden obeys the motions of his own mind,

2. Robert Dodsley, the publisher.

is sometimes vehement and rapid; Pope is always smooth, uniform, and gentle. Dryden's page is a natural field, rising into inequalities, and diversified by the varied exuberance of abundant vegetation; Pope's is a velvet lawn, shaven by the scythe, and leveled by the roller.

Of genius, that power which constitutes a poet; that quality without which judgment is cold and knowledge is inert; that energy which collects, combines, amplifies, and animates; the superiority must, with some hesitation, be allowed to Dryden. It is not to be inferred that of this poetical vigor Pope had only a little, because Dryden had more; for every other writer since Milton must give place to Pope; and even of Dryden it must be said that if he has brighter paragraphs, he has not better poems. Dryden's performances were always hasty, either excited by some external occasion, or extorted by domestic necessity; he composed without consideration, and published without correction. What his mind could supply at call, or gather in one excursion, was all that he sought, and all that he gave. The dilatory caution of Pope enabled him to condense his sentiments, to multiply his images, and to accumulate all that study might produce, or chance might supply. If the flights of Dryden therefore are higher, Pope continues longer on the wing. If of Dryden's fire the blaze is brighter, of Pope's the heat is more regular and constant. Dryden often surpasses expectation, and Pope never falls below it. Dryden is read with frequent astonishment, and Pope with perpetual delight.

This parallel will, I hope, when it is well considered, be found just; and if the reader should suspect me, as I suspect myself, of some partial fondness for the memory of Dryden, let him not too hastily condemn me; for meditation and inquiry may, perhaps, show him the reasonableness of my determination.

1781

JAMES BOSWELL
(1740–1795)

1763: Meets Samuel Johnson.
1768: Account of Corsica.
1773: Tour of the Highlands and the Hebrides with Johnson.
1791: *Life of Samuel Johnson.*

The discovery within the last half-century of a vast number of James Boswell's personal papers (formerly believed to have been destroyed by his literary executors) has made it possible to know the author of the *Life of Samuel Johnson* better, perhaps, than we can know any other person, dead or living. His published letters and journals (only a portion of those that exist) have made modern readers aware of the serious and absurd, the charming and repellent sides of his character. The journals are the work of a complicated man of genius, who perfected his art as a biographer through his almost lifelong habit of observing himself and recording with unique honesty and completeness his responses to widely varied experience. By the time he met Johnson, when he was only 23, he had already trained himself to listen, to observe, and to remember until he found time to set it all down in writing. Only very rarely, it seems, did he ever take notes of conversations while they were in progress, an action which would quickly have put an end to social discourse. His unusual memory, his instinctive sense of the characteristic, and his disciplined art enabled him in privacy to re-create and vividly preserve the many "scenes" which distinguish his journals as they do the *Life*.

Boswell was the elder son of Alexander Boswell of Auchinleck (pronounced *Aff-léck*) in Ayreshire, a judge who, by virtue of his high office, bore the courtesy title of Lord Auchinleck. As a member of an ancient family and heir to its large estate, Boswell was in the technical sense of the term a gentleman, with entrée into the best circles of Edinburgh and London—not, as he is sometimes represented, a climber who had to toady to his betters. By temperament he was unstable, prone to melancholy, given to romantic excesses of feeling, and thoroughly sensual. The combination of instability and sensuality led him early into the habitual dissipation that ultimately affected his health and shortened his life. After attending the Universities of Edinburgh and Glasgow, and studying law in Utrecht in Holland, he made the grand tour of Germany, Italy, and France, passing through Switzerland where he met and succeeded in captivating the two foremost French men of letters, Rousseau and Voltaire. He visited the beleaguered hero of Corsica, General Pasquale de Paoli, who was leading his people in their revolt against Genoa, and who seemed to European liberals to embody all the civic and military virtues of Republican Rome. Upon returning to England he wrote his first important work, *An Account of Corsica* (1768), which included the journal of his visit to Paoli. It was promptly translated into Dutch, German, French, and Italian, and its young author found himself with a modest European reputation.

By 1769, Boswell was established in what was to prove a successful law practice in Edinburgh and had married his cousin, Margaret Montgomerie. Whenever possible he made a jaunt to London in the spring, where he mingled dissipation with the soberer pleasures of intellectual life, especially in Johnson's circle. In 1773 Johnson, then 64, joined Boswell in a tour of the Highlands and the Hebrides. Boswell delighted in placing his elderly friend in situations which would bring out his essential character, and he was therefore very much pleased to bring Dr. Johnson to Scotland and into the primitive Highlands and the Hebrides, and to watch and record his responses to incidents and people along the way. Almost every aspect of the adventure should have made it impossible, or a least unpleasant. Johnson, far from young and after years of sedentary city living, found himself astride a horse in wild country or in open boats in autumn weather. As a devout Anglican, he was an outspoken enemy of the Presbyterian Church, the national church of Scotland. As a lover of London, he cared little or nothing for scenery and rural life, and even less for such primitive people as the Highlanders were at that time. Moreover, for many years he had half-jestingly, half-seriously, made the Scots as a nation the butt of his satiric wit. But such were Boswell's social tact and Johnson's vigor and curiosity that the tour was a great success. "There have been many people," wrote Boswell of himself, "who built castles in the air, but I believe I am the first that ever attempted to move into them." The trip to the Hebrides is a fine example of this eminently Boswellian trait. Johnson's sober and unflattering account of the trip in his *Journey to the Western Isles of Scotland* (1775) gave some offense to Scottish national pride. Boswell's *Journal of a Tour to the Hebrides* (1785), a preliminary study for the *Life*, is a lively and entertaining diary, kept throughout the journey and approved, at least in part, by Johnson himself.

In 1788, four years after Johnson's death, Boswell abandoned his Scotch practice, removed with his family to London, was admitted to the English bar (but never actually practiced), and, amidst domestic difficulties not made less perplexing by his own frailties, began the *Life*. Fortunately he had the help and encouragement of the distinguished literary scholar Edmond Malone, without whose guidance he might never have finished his task.

The *Life* is the work of an impressive literary artist who was dominated by a Johnsonian regard for accuracy and truth. A lesser craftsman might have been overwhelmed by the very abundance of material that Boswell had to deal with: his own journals, all of Johnson's letters that he could find, his voluminous writings, and every scrap of information that his friends would furnish—all of which had to be collected, verified, and somehow reduced to unity. The *Life* is a record not of Johnson alone but of literary England during the last half of the century. Its pages are populated by men as eminent in their way as was Johnson, most of whom Boswell knew, all of whom are interesting to the reader. But Boswell wrote with his eye on the object, and that object was Samuel Johnson, to whom every detail in the book is relevant, toward whom such eminent persons as Sir Joshua Reynolds, Edmund Burke, Oliver Goldsmith, Lord Chesterfield—even the king himself—always face. Boswell's sense of unity and of proportion is perfect. Although his book is dense with details, they never impede the flow of the narrative.The movement is always forward, individual episodes are designed to reveal the great protagonist in a variety of aspects, and the world that Boswell created and populated is sustained both by the animation of his own imagination and by the vitality of his hero.

Boswell's gift is not only narrative: it is also dramatic. He himself was a good deal of an actor and a superb mimic, with a flair for detecting the characteristic gesture, word, tone, or trait. In reading the journals and the *Life* one often feels that their author is a gifted theatrical improviser, creating dramatic "scenes" (the word is a favorite of his) with living people, and playing simultaneously and with incredible sureness the several roles of contriver of the dialogue, director of the plot, actor in the scene, and applauding audience—for Boswell never failed to watch and applaud or condemn his own curious conduct. The quintessence of Boswell as both a social genius and a literary artist (the two complemented each other) is to be found in his description of his visit to Voltaire: "I placed myself by him. I touched the keys in unison with his imagination. I wish you had heard the music." Boswell's art, as an interviewer, a conversationalist, and a biographer is, like all great art, the product of a deep and humane interpretative imagination. The scene with Voltaire, like all the famous scenes in the *Life*, is contrived with such apparent ease and by seemingly such simple means, that the genius responsible for them may go undetected by the casual reader.

Although the Johnson who has become a part of our heritage is largely Boswell's Johnson, there was much in his life about which Boswell had no first-hand knowledge, and there were aspects of his nature which he did not have much opportunity to observe. When Boswell met him, Johnson was 54, a widower, already established as "Dictionary" Johnson and the author of the *Rambler*, pensioned by the Crown and consequently no longer compelled to earn his living. Boswell knew nothing at first hand of Johnson's boyhood and youth in Lichfield, of his brief stay at Oxford, of his marriage, and of the long, difficult, and heroic years (more than a quarter of a century), during which Johnson made his way up from obscurity to eminence through difficulties that it is painful to imagine. Boswell knew him as the sage, the moralist, the scholar, the critic, and as a man moving in a largely male society in tavern, coffeehouse, and club. The chief glory of the *Life* is the conversation, always dominated by Johnson but not at all a monologue. It is the talk of a man, or rather of men, who have experienced broadly, read widely, observed and reflected on their observations, whose ideas are constantly brought to the test of experience, and whose experience is habitually transmuted into ideas. The book is as large as life and as human as its central character.

From Boswell on the Grand Tour

[*Boswell Interviews Voltaire*[1]]

And whence do I now write to you, my friend?[2] From the château of Monsieur de Voltaire. I had a letter for him from a Swiss colonel at The Hague. I came hither Monday and was presented to him. He received me with dignity and that air of a man who has been much in the world which a Frenchman acquires in perfection. I saw him for about half an hour before dinner. He was not in spirits. Yet he gave me some brilliant sallies. He did not dine with us, and I was obliged to post away immediately after dinner, because the gates of Geneva shut before five and Ferney is a good hour from town. I was by no means satisfied to have been so little time with the monarch of French literature. A happy scheme sprung up in my adventurous mind. Madame Denis, the niece of Monsieur de

1. Voltaire was the name assumed by François Marie Arouet (1694–1778), the most famous French writer of his generation. Playwright, poet, satirist, philosopher, enemy of the church, and irrepressible ironist, after a stormy career he was living in splendor at his chateau at Ferney near the border of Switzerland and France, just outside Geneva. His housekeeper and mistress was his niece Marie-Louise Denis. He and Jean-Jacques Rousseau, whom Boswell had just visited and whose avowed disciple he had become, were deadly enemies.

2. This passage is taken from a letter, dated 28 December, 1764, written to Boswell's closest friend, a young clergyman named William Temple.

Voltaire, had been extremely good to me. She is fond of our language. I wrote her a letter in English begging her interest to obtain for me the privilege of lodging a night under the roof of Monsieur de Voltaire, who, in opposition to our sun, rises in the evening. I was in the finest humor and my letter was full of wit. I told her, "I am a hardy and a vigorous Scot. You may mount me to the highest and coldest garret. I shall not even refuse to sleep upon two chairs in the bedchamber of your maid. I saw her pass through the room where we sat before dinner." I sent my letter on Tuesday by an express. It was shown to Monsieur de Voltaire, who with his own hand wrote this answer in the character of Madame Denis: "You will do us much honor and pleasure. We have few beds. But you will (*shall*) not sleep on two chairs. My uncle, though very sick, hath guessed at your merit. I know it better; for I have seen you longer." * * *

I returned yesterday to this enchanted castle. The magician appeared a very little before dinner. But in the evening he came into the drawing room in great spirits. I placed myself by him. I touched the keys in unison with his imagination. I wish you had heard the music. He was all brilliance. He gave me continued flashes of wit. I got him to speak English, which he does in a degree that made me now and then start up and cry. "Upon my soul this is astonishing!" When he talked our language he was animated with the soul of a Briton. He had bold flights. He had humor. He had an extravagance; he had a forcible oddity of style that the most comical of our *dramatis personae* could not have exceeded. He swore bloodily, as was the fashion when he was in England.[3] He hummed a ballad; he repeated nonsense. Then he talked of our Constitution with a noble enthusiasm. I was proud to hear this from the mouth of an illustrious Frenchman. At last we came upon religion. Then did he rage. The company went to supper. Monsieur de Voltaire and I remained in the drawing room with a great Bible before us; and if ever two mortal men disputed with vehemence, we did. Yes, upon that occasion he was one individual and I another. For a certain portion of time there was a fair opposition between Voltaire and Boswell. The daring bursts of his ridicule confounded my understanding. He stood like an orator of ancient Rome. Tully[4] was never more agitated than he was. He went too far. His aged frame trembled beneath him. He cried, "Oh, I am very sick; my head turns round," and he let himself gently fall upon an easy chair. He recovered. I resumed our conversation, but changed the tone. I talked to him serious and earnest. I demanded of him an honest confession of

3. In 1726, in order to avoid imprisonment because of a quarrel with a nobleman, Voltaire had gone into exile in England, where he remained for three years, meeting many distinguished English writers and statesmen and learning to admire the British Constitution and the English principle of religious toleration. His *Lettres philosophiques sur les Anglais* (1734) expressed his admiration of English institutions and is an indirect criticism of France.

4. Marcus Tullius Cicero.

his real sentiments. He gave it me with candor and with a mild eloquence which touched my heart. I did not believe him capable of thinking in the manner that he declared to me was "from the bottom of his heart." He expressed his veneration—his love—of the Supreme Being, and his entire resignation to the will of Him who is All-wise. He expressed his desire to resemble the Author of Goodness by being good himself. His sentiments go no farther. He does not inflame his mind with grand hopes of the immortality of the soul. He says, it may be, but he knows nothing of it. And his mind is in perfect tranquility. I was moved; I was sorry. I doubted his sincerity. I called to him with emotion, "Are you sincere? are you really sincere?" He answered "Before God, I am." Then with the fire of him whose tragedies have so often shone on the theater of Paris, he said, "I suffer much. But I suffer with patience and resignation; not as a Christian—but as a man."

Temple, was not this an interesting scene? Would a journey from Scotland to Ferney have been too much to obtain such a remarkable interview? * * *

1764 1928

From The Life of Samuel Johnson, LL.D.

[*Plan of the* Life]

* * * Had Dr. Johnson written his own life, in conformity with the opinion which he has given, that every man's life may be best written by himself;[1] had he employed in the preservation of his own history, that clearness of narration and elegance of language in which he has embalmed so many eminent persons, the world would probably have had the most perfect example of biography that was ever exhibited. But although he at different times, in a desultory manner, committed to writing many particulars of the progress of his mind and fortunes, he never had persevering diligence enough to form them into a regular composition. Of these memorials a few have been preserved; but the greater part was consigned by him to the flames, a few days before his death.

As I had the honor and happiness of enjoying his friendship for upwards of twenty years; as I had the scheme of writing his life constantly in view; as he was well apprised of this circumstance, and from time to time obligingly satisfied my inquiries, by communicating to me the incidents of his early years; as I acquired a facility in recollecting, and was very assiduous in recording, his conversation, of which the extraordinary vigor and vivacity constituted one of the first features of his character; and as I have spared no pains in obtaining materials concerning him, from every quarter where I could discover that they were to be found, and have been favored

1. *Idler* 84.

with the most liberal communications by his friends; I flatter myself that few biographers have entered upon such a work as this with more advantages; independent of literary abilities, in which I am not vain enough to compare myself with some great names who have gone before me in this kind of writing. * * *

Instead of melting down my materials into one mass, and constantly speaking in my own person, by which I might have appeared to have more merit in the execution of the work, I have resolved to adopt and enlarge upon the excellent plan of Mr. Mason, in his *Memoirs of Gray*.[2] Wherever narrative is necessary to explain, connect, and supply, I furnish it to the best of my abilities; but in the chronological series of Johnson's life, which I trace as distinctly as I can, year by year, I produce, wherever it is in my power, his own minutes, letters, or conversation, being convinced that this mode is more lively, and will make my readers better acquainted with him than even most of those were who actually knew him, but could know him only partially; whereas there is here an accumulation of intelligence from various points, by which his character is more fully understood and illustrated.

Indeed I cannot conceive a more perfect mode of writing any man's life than not only relating all the most important events of it in their order, but interweaving what he privately wrote, and said, and thought; by which mankind are enabled as it were to see him live, and to "live o'er each scene"[3] with him, as he actually advanced through the several stages of his life. Had his other friends been as diligent and ardent as I was, he might have been almost entirely preserved. As it is, I will venture to say that he will be seen in this work more completely than any man who has ever yet lived.

And he will be seen as he really was; for I profess to write, not his panegyric, which must be all praise, but his Life; which, great and good as he was, must not be supposed to be entirely perfect. To be as he was, is indeed subject of panegyric enough to any man in this state of being; but in every picture there should be shade as well as light, and when I delineate him without reserve, I do what he himself recommended, both by his precept and his example. * * *

I am fully aware of the objections which may be made to the minuteness on some occasions of my detail of Johnson's conversation, and how happily it is adapted for the petty exercise of ridicule, by men of superficial understanding and ludicrous fancy; but I remain firm and confident in my opinion, that minute particulars are frequently characteristic, and always amusing, when they relate to a distinguished man. I am therefore exceedingly unwilling that

2. William Mason, poet and dramatist, published his life of Thomas Gray in 1774.

3. Pope's Prologue to Addison's *Cato*, line 4.

anything, however slight, which my illustrious friend thought it worth his while to express, with any degree of point, should perish. * * *

Of one thing I am certain, that considering how highly the small portion which we have of the table-talk and other anecdotes of our celebrated writers is valued, and how earnestly it is regretted that we have not more, I am justified in preserving rather too many of Johnson's sayings, than too few; especially as from the diversity of dispositions it cannot be known with certainty beforehand, whether what may seem trifling to some, and perhaps to the collector himself, may not be most agreeable to many; and the greater number that an author can please in any degree, the more pleasure does there arise to a benevolent mind. * * *

[*Johnson's Early Years. Marriage and London*]

[1709] Samuel Johnson was born at Lichfield, in Staffordshire, on the 18th of September, N.S.,[4] 1709; and his initiation into the Christian Church was not delayed; for his baptism is recorded, in the register of St. Mary's parish in that city, to have been performed on the day of his birth. His father is there styled *Gentleman*, a circumstance of which an ignorant panegyrist has praised him for not being proud; when the truth is, that the appellation of Gentleman, though now lost in the indiscriminate assumption of *Esquire*, was commonly taken by those who could not boast of gentility. His father was Michael Johnson, a native of Derbyshire, of obscure extraction, who settled in Lichfield as a bookseller and stationer. His mother was Sarah Ford, descended of an ancient race of substantial yeomanry in Warwickshire. They were well advanced in years when they married, and never had more than two children, both sons; Samuel, their first-born, who lived to be the illustrious character whose various excellence I am to endeavor to record, and Nathanael, who died in his twenty-fifth year.

Mr. Michael Johnson was a man of a large and robust body, and of a strong and active mind; yet, as in the most solid rocks veins of unsound substance are often discovered, there was in him a mixture of that disease, the nature of which eludes the most minute inquiry, though the effects are well known to be a weariness of life, an unconcern about those things which agitate the greater part of mankind, and a general sensation of gloomy wretchedness. From him then his son inherited, with some other qualities, "a vile melancholy," which in his too strong expression of any disturbance of the mind, "made him mad all his life, at least not sober." Michael

4. New Style. In 1752 Great Britain adopted the Gregorian Calendar, introduced in 1582 by Pope Gregory XIII, to correct the accumulated inaccuracies of Julius Caesar's calendar, which had been in use since 46 B.C. By 1752 the error amounted to eleven days. Dates before September 2, 1752, must therefore be corrected by adding eleven days or by using the Julian date, followed by "O.S." (Old Style).

was, however, forced by the narrowness of his circumstances to be very diligent in business, not only in his shop, but by occasionally resorting to several towns in the neighborhood, some of which were at a considerable distance from Lichfield. At that time booksellers' shops in the provincial towns of England were very rare, so that there was not one even in Birmingham, in which town old Mr. Johnson used to open a shop every market day. He was a pretty good Latin scholar, and a citizen so creditable as to be made one of the magistrates of Lichfield; and, being a man of good sense, and skill in his trade, he acquired a reasonable share of wealth, of which however he afterwards lost the greatest part, by engaging unsuccessfully in a manufacture of parchment. He was a zealous high-church man and royalist, and retained his attachment to the unfortunate house of Stuart, though he reconciled himself, by casuistical arguments of expediency and necessity, to take the oaths imposed by the prevailing power. * * *

Johnson's mother was a woman of distinguished understanding. I asked his old schoolfellow, Mr. Hector,[5] surgeon of Birmingham, if she was not vain of her son. He said, "She had too much good sense to be vain, but she knew her son's value." Her piety was not inferior to her understanding; and to her must be ascribed those early impressions of religion upon the mind of her son, from which the world afterwards derived so much benefit. He told me that he remembered distinctly having had the first notice of Heaven, "a place to which good people went," and hell, "a place to which bad people went," communicated to him by her, when a little child in bed with her; and that it might be the better fixed in his memory, she sent him to repeat it to Thomas Jackson, their manservant; he not being in the way, this was not done; but there was no occasion for any artificial aid for its preservation. * * *

[1728] That a man in Mr. Michael Johnson's circumstances should think of sending his son to the expensive University of Oxford, at his own charge, seems very improbable. The subject was too delicate to question Johnson upon. But I have been assured by Dr. Taylor[6] that the scheme never would have taken place had not a gentleman of Shropshire, one of his schoolfellows, spontaneously undertaken to support him at Oxford, in the character of his companion; though, in fact, he never received any assistance whatever from that gentleman.

He, however, went to Oxford, and was entered a Commoner of Pembroke College on the 31st of October, 1728, being then in his nineteenth year.

The Reverend Dr. Adams,[7] who afterwards presided over Pembroke College with universal esteem, told me he was present, and

5. Edmund Hector, a lifelong friend of Johnson's.

6. A well-to-do clergyman, who had been Johnson's school fellow in Lichfield.

7. The Rev William Adams, D.D., elected Master of Pembroke in 1775.

gave me some account of what passed on the night of Johnson's arrival at Oxford. On that evening, his father, who had anxiously accompanied him, found means to have him introduced to Mr. Jorden, who was to be his tutor. * * *

His father seemed very full of the merits of his son, and told the company he was a good scholar, and a poet, and wrote Latin verses. His figure and manner appeared strange to them; but he behaved modestly and sat silent, till upon something which occurred in the course of conversation, he suddenly struck in and quoted Macrobius; and thus he gave the first impression of that more extensive reading in which he had indulged himself.

His tutor, Mr. Jorden, fellow of Pembroke, was not, it seems, a man of such abilities as we should conceive requisite for the instructor of Samuel Johnson, who gave me the following account of him. "He was a very worthy man, but a heavy man, and I did not profit much by his instructions. Indeed, I did not attend him much. The first day after I came to college I waited upon him, and then stayed away four. On the sixth, Mr. Jorden asked me why I had not attended. I answered I had been sliding in Christ Church meadow. And this I said with as much *nonchalance* as I am now talking to you. I had no notion that I was wrong or irreverent to my tutor." BOSWELL: "That, Sir, was great fortitude of mind." JOHNSON: "No, Sir; stark insensibility." * * *

[1729] The "morbid melancholy," which was lurking in his constitution, and to which we may ascribe those particularities and that aversion to regular life, which, at a very early period, marked his character, gathered such strength in his twentieth year as to afflict him in a dreadful manner. While he was at Lichfield, in the college vacation of the year 1729, he felt himself overwhelmed with an horrible hypochondria, with perpetual irritation, fretfulness, and impatience; and with a dejection, gloom, and despair, which made existence misery. From this dismal malady he never afterwards was perfectly relieved; and all his labors, and all his enjoyments, were but temporary interruptions of its baleful influence. He told Mr. Paradise[8] that he was sometimes so languid and inefficient that he could not distinguish the hour upon the town-clock. * * *

To Johnson, whose supreme enjoyment was the exercise of his reason, the disturbance or obscuration of that faculty was the evil most to be dreaded. Insanity, therefore, was the object of his most dismal apprehension; and he fancied himself seized by it, or approaching to it, at the very time when he was giving proofs of a more than ordinary soundness and vigor of judgment. That his own diseased imagination should have so far deceived him, is strange; but it is stranger still that some of his friends should have given credit to his groundless opinion, when they had such undoubted

8. John Paradise, a member of the Essex Head Club, which Johnson founded in 1783.

proofs that it was totally fallacious; though it is by no means surprising that those who wish to depreciate him should, since his death, have laid hold of this circumstance, and insisted upon it with very unfair aggravation. * * *

Dr. Adams told me that Johnson, while he was at Pembroke College, "was caressed and loved by all about him, was a gay and frolicsome fellow, and passed there the happiest part of his life." But this is a striking proof of the fallacy of appearances, and how little any of us know of the real internal state even of those whom we see most frequently; for the truth is, that he was then depressed by poverty, and irritated by disease. When I mentioned to him this account as given me by Dr. Adams, he said, "Ah, Sir, I was mad and violent. It was bitterness which they mistook for frolic. I was miserably poor, and I thought to fight my way by my literature and my wit; so I disregarded all power and all authority." * * *

[*1734*] In a man whom religious education has secured from licentious indulgences, the passion of love, when once it has seized him, is exceedingly strong; being unimpaired by dissipation, and totally concentrated in one object. This was experienced by Johnson, when he became the fervent admirer of Mrs. Porter, after her first husband's death. Miss Porter told me that when he was first introduced to her mother, his appearance was very forbidding: he was then lean and lank, so that his immense structure of bones was hideously striking to the eye, and the scars of the scrofula were deeply visible. He also wore his hair,[9] which was straight and stiff, and separated behind: and he often had, seemingly, convulsive starts and odd gesticulations, which tended to excite at once surprise and ridicule. Mrs. Porter was so much engaged by his conversation that she overlooked all these external disadvantages, and said to her daughter, "This is the most sensible man that I ever saw in my life."

[*1735*] Though Mrs. Porter was double the age of Johnson, and her person and manner, as described to me by the late Mr. Garrick,[1] were by no means pleasing to others, she must have had a superiority of understanding and talents, as she certainly inspired him with a more than ordinary passion; and she having signified her willingness to accept of his hand, he went to Lichfield to ask his mother's consent to the marriage, which he could not but be conscious was a very imprudent scheme, both on account of their disparity of years and her want of fortune. But Mrs. Johnson knew too well the ardor of her son's temper, and was too tender a parent to oppose his inclinations.

I know not for what reason the marriage ceremony was not performed at Birmingham; but a resolution was taken that it should be at Derby, for which place the bride and bridegroom set out on horseback, I suppose in very good humor. But though Mr. Topham

9. I.e., he wore no wig.

1. David Garrick (1717–79), the most famous actor of his day. In 1736 he was one of Johnson's three pupils in an unsuccessful school at Edial.

Beauclerk[2] used archly to mention Johnson's having told him, with much gravity, "Sir, it was a love marriage on both sides," I have had from my illustrious friend the following curious account of their journey to church upon the nuptial morn:

9th July: "Sir, she had read the old romances, and had got into her head the fantastical notion that a woman of spirit should use her lover like a dog. So, Sir, at first she told me that I rode too fast, and she could not keep up with me; and, when I rode a little slower, she passed me, and complained that I lagged behind. I was not to be made the slave of caprice; and I resolved to begin as I meant to end. I therefore pushed on briskly, till I was fairly out of her sight. The road lay between two hedges, so I was sure she could not miss it; and I contrived that she should soon come up with me. When she did, I observed her to be in tears." * * *

[1737] Johnson now thought of trying his fortune in London, the great field of genius and exertion, where talents of every kind have the fullest scope and the highest encouragement. It is a memorable circumstance that his pupil David Garrick went thither at the same time, with intention to complete his education, and follow the profession of the law, from which he was soon diverted by his decided preference for the stage.[3] * * *

[1744] * * * He produced one work this year, fully sufficient to maintain the high reputation which he had acquired. This was *The Life of Richard Savage*;[4] a man of whom it is difficult to speak impartially without wondering that he was for some time the intimate companion of Johnson; for his character was marked by profligacy, insolence, and ingratitude: yet, as he undoubtedly had a warm and vigorous, though unregulated mind, had seen life in all its varieties, and been much in the company of the statesmen and wits of his time, he could communicate to Johnson an abundant supply of such materials as his philosophical curiosity most eagerly desired; and as Savage's misfortunes and misconduct had reduced him to the lowest state of wretchedness as a writer for bread, his visits to St. John's Gate[5] naturally brought Johnson and him together.

It is melancholy to reflect that Johnson and Savage were some-

2. Topham Beauclerk, a descendant of Charles II and the actress Nell Gwynn. He was brilliant and dissolute.

3. Johnson had hoped to complete his tragedy *Irene* and to get it produced, but this was not accomplished until Garrick staged it in 1749. Meanwhile Johnson struggled against poverty, at first as a writer and translator for Edward Cave's *Gentleman's Magazine*. He gradually won recognition, but was never financially secure until he was pensioned in 1762. Garrick succeeded in the theater much more rapidly than did Johnson in literature.

4. Richard Savage, poet, courted and gained notoriety by claiming to be the illegitimate son of Earl Rivers and the Countess of Macclesfield, whose husband had divorced her because of her unfaithfulness with Rivers. Savage publicized his claim and persecuted his alleged mother. Johnson and many others believed Savage's story and resented what they considered the lady's inhumanity. Savage was a gifted man, but he lived in poverty as a hack writer, though he was long assisted by Pope and others. He died in a debtor's prison in Bristol in 1743.

5. Where Cave published the *Gentleman's Magazine*.

times in such extreme indigence that they could not pay for a lodging; so that they have wandered together whole nights in the streets. Yet in these almost incredible scenes of distress, we may suppose that Savage mentioned many of the anecdotes with which Johnson afterwards enriched the life of his unhappy companion, and those of other poets.

He told Sir Joshua Reynolds that one night in particular, when Savage and he walked round St. James's Square for want of a lodging, they were not at all depressed by their situation; but in high spirits and brimful of patriotism, traversed the square for several hours, inveighed against the minister, and "resolved they would *stand by their country*." * * *

[1752] That there should be a suspension of his literary labors during a part of the year 1752[6] will not seem strange when it is considered that soon after closing his *Rambler*, he suffered a loss which, there can be no doubt, affected him with the deepest distress. For on the 17th of March, O.S., his wife died. * * *

The following very solemn and affecting prayer was found, after Dr. Johnson's decease, by his servant, Mr. Francis Barber, who delivered it to my worthy friend the Reverend Mr. Strahan, Vicar of Islington, who at my earnest request has obligingly favored me with a copy of it, which he and I compared with the original:

"April 26, 1752, being after 12 at night of the 25th.

"O Lord! Governor of heaven and earth, in whose hands are embodied and departed spirits, if thou hast ordained the souls of the dead to minister to the living, and appointed my departed wife to have care of me, grant that I may enjoy the good effects of her attention and ministration, whether exercised by appearance, impulses, dreams or in any other manner agreeable to thy government. Forgive my presumption, enlighten my ignorance, and however meaner agents are employed, grant me the blessed influences of thy holy Spirit, through Jesus Christ our Lord. Amen." * * *

One night when Beauclerk and Langton[7] had supped at a tavern in London, and sat till about three in the morning, it came into their heads to go and knock up Johnson, and see if they could prevail on him to join them in a ramble. They rapped violently at the door of his chambers in the Temple,[8] till at last he appeared in his shirt, with his little black wig on the top of his head, instead of a nightcap, and a poker in his hand, imagining, probably, that some ruffians were coming to attack him. When he discovered who they were, and was told their errand, he smiled, and with great good

6. Johnson's important works written before the publication of the *Dictionary* are the poems *London* (1738) and *The Vanity of Human Wishes* (1749), the *Life of Savage* (1744), and the essays which made up his periodical *The Rambler* (1750–52).

7. Bennet Langton. As a boy he so much admired the *Rambler* that he sought Johnson's acquaintance. They became lifelong friends.

8. Since Johnson lived in Inner Temple Lane between 1760 and 1765, the "frisk" could not have taken place in the year of his wife's death, where Boswell, for his own convenience, placed it.

humor agreed to their proposal: "What, is it you, you dogs! I'll have a frisk with you." He was soon dressed, and they sallied forth together into Covent Garden, where the greengrocers and fruiterers were beginning to arrange their hampers, just come in from the country. Johnson made some attempts to help them; but the honest gardeners stared so at his figure and manner and odd interference, that he soon saw his services were not relished. They then repaired to one of the neighboring taverns, and made a bowl of that liquor called *Bishop*,[9] which Johnson had always liked; while in joyous contempt of sleep, from which he had been roused, he repeated the festive lines,

Short, O short then be thy reign,
And give us to the world again![1]

They did not stay long, but walked down to the Thames, took a boat, and rowed to Billingsgate. Beauclerk and Johnson were so well pleased with their amusement that they resolved to persevere in dissipation for the rest of the day: but Langton deserted them, being engaged to breakfast with some young ladies. Johnson scolded him for "leaving his social friends, to go and sit with a set of wretched *un-idea'd* girls." Garrick being told of this ramble, said to him smartly, "I heard of your frolic t'other night. You'll be in the *Chronicle*." Upon which Johnson afterwards observed, "*He* durst not do such a thing. His *wife* would not *let* him!" * * *

[*The Letter to Chesterfield*]

[1754] Lord Chesterfield,[2] to whom Johnson had paid the high compliment of addressing to his Lordship the *Plan* of his *Dictionary*, had behaved to him in such a manner as to excite his contempt and indignation. The world has been for many years amused with a story confidently told, and as confidently repeated with additional circumstances, that a sudden disgust was taken by Johnson upon occasion of his having been one day kept long in waiting in his Lordship's antechamber, for which the reason assigned was that he had company with him; and that at last, when the door opened, out walked Colley Cibber;[3] and that Johnson was so violently provoked when he found for whom he had been so long excluded, that he went away in a passion, and never would return. I remember having mentioned this story to George Lord Lyttelton, who told me he was very intimate with Lord Chesterfield; and holding it as a well-known truth, defended Lord Chesterfield, by saying, that Cibber, who had been introduced familiarly by the back stairs, had

9. A drink made of wine, sugar, and either lemon or orange.

1. Misquoted from Lansdowne's *Drinking Song to Sleep.*

2. Philip Dormer Stanhope, Earl of Chesterfield (1694–1773), statesman, wit, man of fashion. His *Letters*, written for the guidance of his natural son, are famous for their worldly good sense and for their expression of the ideal of an 18th-century gentleman.

3. Colley Cibber (1671–1757), playwright, comic actor, and (after 1730) poet laureate. A fine actor but a very bad poet, Cibber was a constant object of ridicule by the wits of the town. Pope made him King of the Dunces in the *Dunciad* of 1743.

probably not been there above ten minutes. It may seem strange even to entertain a doubt concerning a story so long and so widely current, and thus implicitly adopted, if not sanctioned, by the authority which I have mentioned; but Johnson himself assured me that there was not the least foundation for it. He told me that there never was any particular incident which produced a quarrel between Lord Chesterfield and him; but that his Lordship's continued neglect was the reason why he resolved to have no connection with him. When the *Dictionary* was upon the eve of publication, Lord Chesterfield, who, it is said, had flattered himself with expectations that Johnson would dedicate the work to him, attempted, in a courtly manner, to soothe, and insinuate himself with the sage, conscious, as it should seem, of the cold indifference with which he had treated its learned author; and further attempted to conciliate him, by writing two papers in *The World*, in recommendation of the work; and it must be confessed that they contain some studied compliments, so finely turned, that if there had been no previous offense, it is probable that Johnson would have been highly delighted. Praise, in general, was pleasing to him; but by praise from a man of rank and elegant accomplishments, he was peculiarly gratified. * * *

This courtly device failed of its effect. Johnson, who thought that "all was false and hollow,"[4] despised the honeyed words, and was even indignant that Lord Chesterfield should, for a moment, imagine that he could be dupe of such an artifice. His expression to me concerning Lord Chesterfield, upon this occasion, was, "Sir, after making great professions, he had, for many years, taken no notice of me; but when my *Dictionary* was coming out, he fell a-scribbling in *The World* about it. Upon which, I wrote him a letter expressed in civil terms, but such as might show him that I did not mind what he said or wrote, and that I had done with him."

This is that celebrated letter of which so much has been said, and about which curiosity has been so long excited, without being gratified. I for many years solicited Johnson to favor me with a copy of it, that so excellent a composition might not be lost to posterity. He delayed from time to time to give it me; till at last in 1781, when we were on a visit at Mr. Dilly's,[5] at Southill in Bedfordshire, he was pleased to dictate it to me from memory. He afterwards found among his papers a copy of it, which he had dictated to Mr. Baretti,[6] with its title and corrections, in his own handwriting. This he gave to Mr. Langton; adding that if it were to come into print, he wished it to be from that copy. By Mr. Langton's kindness, I am enabled to enrich my work with a perfect transcript of what the world has so eagerly desired to see.

4. *Paradise Lost* II.112.

5. Southill was the country home of Charles and Edward Dilly, publishers. The firm published all of Boswell's serious works and shared in the publication of Johnson's *Lives of the Poets* (1779–81).

6. Giuseppe Baretti, an Italian writer and lexicographer whom Johnson introduced into his circle.

TO THE RIGHT HONORABLE THE EARL OF CHESTERFIELD
February 7, 1755.

MY LORD,

I have been lately informed, by the proprietor of *The World*, that two papers, in which my Dictionary is recommended to the public, were written by your Lordship. To be so distinguished, is an honor, which, being very little accustomed to favors from the great, I know not well how to receive, or in what terms to acknowledge.

When, upon some slight encouragement, I first visited your Lordship, I was overpowered, like the rest of mankind, by the enchantment of your address; and could not forbear to wish that I might boast myself *Le vainqueur du vainqueur de la terre*[7]—that I might obtain that regard for which I saw the world contending; but I found my attendance so little encouraged that neither pride nor modesty would suffer me to continue it. When I had once addressed your Lordship in public, I had exhausted all the art of pleasing which a retired and uncourtly scholar can possess. I had done all that I could; and no man is well pleased to have his all neglected, be it ever so little.

Seven years, my Lord, have now passed since I waited in your outward rooms, or was repulsed from your door; during which time I have been pushing on my work through difficulties of which it is useless to complain, and have brought it, at last, to the verge of publication, without one act of assistance, one word of encouragement, or one smile of favor. Such treatment I did not expect, for I never had a patron before.

The shepherd in Virgil grew at last acquainted with Love, and found him a native of the rocks.[8]

Is not a patron, my Lord, one who looks with unconcern on a man struggling for life in the water, and, when he has reached ground, encumbers him with help? The notice which you have been pleased to take of my labors, had it been early, had been kind; but it has been delayed till I am indifferent, and cannot enjoy it; till I am solitary, and cannot impart it; till I am known, and do not want it. I hope it is no very cynical asperity not to confess obligations where no benefit has been received, or to be unwilling that the public should consider me as owing that to a patron which Providence has enabled me to do for myself.

Having carried on my work thus far with so little obligation to any favorer of learning, I shall not be disappointed though I should conclude it, if less be possible, with less; for I have been long wakened from that dream of hope in which I once boasted myself with so much exultation, my Lord, your Lordship's most humble, most obedient servant,

SAM. JOHNSON.

"While this was the talk of the town," says Dr. Adams, in a letter to me, "I happened to visit Dr. Warburton,[9] who finding that

7. "The conqueror of the conqueror of the earth." From the first line of Scudéry's epic *Alaric* (1654).

8. *Eclogues* VIII.44.

9. William Warburton, Bishop of Gloucester, friend and literary executor of Pope, editor of Pope and Shakespeare, theological controversialist.

I was acquainted with Johnson, desired me earnestly to carry his compliments to him, and to tell him that he honored him for his manly behavior in rejecting these condescensions of Lord Chesterfield, and for resenting the treatment he had received from him, with a proper spirit. Johnson was visibly pleased with this compliment, for he had always a high opinion of Warburton. Indeed, the force of mind which appeared in this letter was congenial with that which Warburton himself amply possessed."

There is a curious minute circumstance which struck me, in comparing the various editions of Johnson's imitations of Juvenal. In the tenth satire, one of the couplets upon the vanity of wishes even for literary distinction stood thus:

> Yet think what ills the scholar's life assail,
> Pride, envy, want, the *garret*, and the jail.

But after experiencing the uneasiness which Lord Chesterfield's fallacious patronage made him feel, he dismissed the word *garret* from the sad group, and in all the subsequent editions the line stands

> Pride, envy, want, the *patron*, and the jail.

[1762] The accession of George the Third to the throne of these kingdoms[1] opened a new and brighter prospect to men of literary merit, who had been honored with no mark of royal favor in the preceding reign. His present Majesty's education in this country, as well as his taste and beneficence, prompted him to be the patron of science and the arts; and early this year Johnson, having been represented to him as a very learned and good man, without any certain provision, his Majesty was pleased to grant him a pension of three hundred pounds a year. The Earl of Bute,[2] who was then Prime Minister, had the honor to announce this instance of his Sovereign's bounty, concerning which many and various stories, all equally erroneous, have been propagated: maliciously representing it as a political bribe to Johnson, to desert his avowed principles, and become the tool of a government which he held to be founded in usurpation. I have taken care to have it in my power to refute them from the most authentic information. Lord Bute told me that Mr. Wedderburne, now Lord Loughborough, was the person who first mentioned this subject to him. Lord Loughborough told me that the pension was granted to Johnson solely as the reward of his literary merit, without any stipulation whatever, or even tacit understanding that he should write for administration. His Lordship added that he was confident the political tracts which Johnson afterwards did write, as they were entirely consonant with his

1. In 1760.
2. An intimate friend of George III's mother, he early gained an ascendancy over the young prince and was largely responsible for the king's autocratic views. He was hated in England both as a favorite and as a Scot.

own opinions, would have been written by him though no pension had been granted to him.[3] * * *

[A *Memorable Year: Boswell Meets Johnson*]

[1763] This is to me a memorable year; for in it I had the happiness to obtain the acquaintance of that extraordinary man whose memoirs I am now writing; an acquaintance which I shall ever esteem as one of the most fortunate circumstances in my life. * * *

Mr. Thomas Davies the actor, who then kept a bookseller's shop in Russel Street, Covent Garden, told me that Johnson was very much his friend, and came frequently to his house, where he more than once invited me to meet him; but by some unlucky accident or other he was prevented from coming to us. * * *

At last, on Monday the 16th of May, when I was sitting in Mr. Davies's back parlor, after having drunk tea with him and Mrs. Davies, Johnson unexpectedly came into the shop; and Mr. Davies having perceived him through the glass door in the room in which we were sitting, advancing towards us—he announced his awful approach to me, somewhat in the manner of an actor in the part of Horatio, when he addresses Hamlet on the appearance of his father's ghost, "Look, my Lord, it comes." I found that I had a very perfect idea of Johnson's figure, from the portrait of him painted by Sir Joshua Reynolds soon after he had published his *Dictionary*, in the attitude of sitting in his easy chair in deep meditation, which was the first picture his friend did for him, which Sir Joshua very kindly presented to me, and from which an engraving has been made for this work. Mr. Davies mentioned my name, and respectfully introduced me to him. I was much agitated; and recollecting his prejudice against the Scotch, of which I had heard much, I said to Davies, "Don't tell where I come from."—"From Scotland," cried Davies roguishly. "Mr. Johnson," said I, "I do indeed come from Scotland, but I cannot help it." I am willing to flatter myself that I meant this as light pleasantry to soothe and conciliate him, and not as an humiliating abasement at the expense of my country. But however that might be, this speech was somewhat unlucky; for with that quickness of wit for which he was so remarkable, he seized the expression "come from Scotland," which I used in the sense of being of that country; and, as if I had said that I had come away from it, or left it, retorted, "That, Sir, I find, is what a very great many of your countrymen cannot help." This stroke stunned me a good deal; and when we had sat down, I felt myself not a little embarrassed, and apprehensive of what might come next. He then addressed himself to Davies: "What do

3. Johnson's few political pamphlets in the 1770's invariably supported the policies of the Crown. The best-known is his answer to the American colonies, *Taxation No Tyranny* (1775). His dislike of the Americans was in large part due to the fact they owned slaves.

you think of Garrick? He has refused me an order for the play for Miss Williams,[4] because he knows the house will be full, and that an order would be worth three shillings." Eager to take any opening to get into conversation with him, I ventured to say, "O Sir, I cannot think Mr. Garrick would grudge such a trifle to you." "Sir," said he, with a stern look, "I have known David Garrick longer than you have done: and I know no right you have to talk to me on the subject." Perhaps I deserved this check; for it was rather presumptuous in me, an entire stranger, to express any doubt of the justice of his animadversion upon his old acquaintance and pupil. I now felt myself much mortified, and began to think that the hope which I had long indulged of obtaining his acquaintance was blasted. And, in truth, had not my ardor been uncommonly strong, and my resolution uncommonly persevering, so rough a reception might have deterred me forever from making any further attempts. Fortunately, however, I remained upon the field not wholly discomfited. * * *

I was highly pleased with the extraordinary vigor of his conversation, and regretted that I was drawn away from it by an engagement at another place. I had, for a part of the evening, been left alone with him, and had ventured to make an observation now and then, which he received very civilly; so that I was satisfied that though there was a roughness in his manner, there was no ill nature in his disposition. Davies followed me to the door, and when I complained to him a little of the hard blows which the great man had given me, he kindly took upon him to console me by saying, "Don't be uneasy. I can see he likes you very well."

A few days afterwards I called on Davies, and asked him if he thought I might take the liberty of waiting on Mr. Johnson at his chambers in the Temple. He said I certainly might, and that Mr. Johnson would take it as a compliment. So upon Tuesday the 24th of May, after having been enlivened by the witty sallies of Messieurs Thornton, Wilkes, Churchill, and Lloyd,[5] with whom I had passed the morning, I boldly repaired to Johnson. His chambers were on the first floor of No. 1, Inner Temple Lane, and I entered them with an impression given me by the Reverend Dr. Blair,[6] of Edinburgh, who had been introduced to him not long before, and described his having "found the giant in his den"; an expression, which, when I came to be pretty well acquainted with Johnson, I repeated to him, and he was diverted at this picturesque account

4. Mrs. Anna Williams (1706–83), a blind poet and friend of Mrs. Johnson. She continued to live in Johnson's house after his wife's death, and habitually sat up to make tea for him whenever he came home.

5. Bonnell Thornton, journalist; Charles Churchill, satirist; Robert Lloyd, poet and essayist. For Wilkes see a later episode. The four were bound together by a common love of wit and dissipation. Boswell enjoyed their company in 1763.

6. The Rev. Hugh Blair (1718–1800), Scottish divine and Professor of Rhetoric and Belles Lettres at the University of Edinburgh.

of himself. Dr. Blair had been presented to him by Dr. James Fordyce.[7] At this time the controversy concerning the pieces published by Mr. James Macpherson, as translations of *Ossian,* was at its height.[8] Johnson had all along denied their authenticity; and, what was still more provoking to their admirers, maintained that they had no merit. The subject having been introduced by Dr. Fordyce, Dr. Blair, relying on the internal evidence of their antiquity, asked Dr. Johnson whether he thought any man of a modern age could have written such poems? Johnson replied, "Yes, Sir, many men, many women, and many children." Johnson, at this time, did not know that Dr. Blair had just published a dissertation, not only defending their authenticity, but seriously ranking them with the poems of Homer and Virgil; and when he was afterwards informed of this circumstance, he expressed some displeasure at Dr. Fordyce's having suggested the topic, and said, "I am not sorry that they got thus much for their pains. Sir, it was like leading one to talk of a book when the author is concealed behind the door."

He received me very courteously; but, it must be confessed that his apartment, and furniture, and morning dress, were sufficiently uncouth. His brown suit of clothes looked very rusty; he had on a little old shriveled unpowdered wig, which was too small for his head; his shirt neck and knees of his breeches were loose; his black worsted stockings ill drawn up; and he had a pair of unbuckled shoes by way of slippers. But all these slovenly particularities were forgotten the moment that he began to talk. Some gentlemen, whom I do not recollect, were sitting with him; and when they went away, I also rose; but he said to me, "Nay, don't go." "Sir," said I, "I am afraid that I intrude upon you. It is benevolent to allow me to sit and hear you." He seemed pleased with this compliment, which I sincerely paid him, and answered, "Sir, I am obliged to any man who visits me." I have preserved the following short minute of what passed this day:

"Madness frequently discovers itself merely by unnecessary deviation from the usual modes of the world. My poor friend Smart showed the disturbance of his mind by falling upon his knees, and saying his prayers in the street, or in any other unusual place. Now although, rationally speaking, it is greater madness not to pray at all than to pray as Smart did, I am afraid there are so many who do not pray, that their understanding is not called in question."

Concerning this unfortunate poet, Christopher Smart, who was confined in a madhouse, he had, at another time, the following

7. A Scottish preacher.

8. Macpherson had imposed on most of his contemporaries, Scottish and English, by convincing them of the genuineness of prose poems which he had concocted but which he claimed to have translated from the original Gaelic of Ossian, a blind epic poet of the 3rd century. The vogue of the poems both in Europe and in America was enormous.

conversation with Dr. Burney:[9] BURNEY. "How does poor Smart do, Sir; is he likely to recover?" JOHNSON. "It seems as if his mind had ceased to struggle with the disease; for he grows fat upon it." BURNEY. "Perhaps, Sir, that may be from want of exercise." JOHNSON. "No, Sir; he has partly as much exercise as he used to have, for he digs in the garden. Indeed, before his confinement, he used for exercise to walk to the ale house; but he was *carried* back again. I did not think he ought to be shut up. His infirmities were not noxious to society. He insisted on people praying with him; and I'd as lief pray with Kit Smart as anyone else. Another charge was that he did not love clean linen; and I have no passion for it." —Johnson continued. "Mankind have a great aversion to intellectual labor; but even supposing knowledge to be easily attainable, more people would be content to be ignorant than would take even a little trouble to acquire it."

Talking of Garrick, he said, "He is the first man in the world for sprightly conversation."

When I rose a second time he again pressed me to stay, which I did. * * *

[*Goldsmith. Sundry Opinions. Johnson Meets His King*]

As Dr. Oliver Goldsmith will frequently appear in this narrative, I shall endeavor to make my readers in some degree acquainted with his singular character. He was a native of Ireland, and a contemporary with Mr. Burke[1] at Trinity College, Dublin, but did not then give much promise of future celebrity. He, however, observed to Mr. Malone,[2] that "though he made no great figure in mathematics, which was a study in much repute there, he could turn an ode of Horace into English better than any of them." He afterwards studied physic at Edinburgh, and upon the Continent; and I have been informed, was enabled to pursue his travels on foot, partly by demanding at universities to enter the lists as a disputant, by which, according to the custom of many of them, he was entitled to the premium of a crown, when luckily for him his challenge was not accepted; so that, as I once observed to Dr. Johnson, he *disputed* his passage through Europe. He then came to England, and was employed successively in the capacities of an usher[3] to an academy, a corrector of the press, a reviewer, and a writer for a newspaper. He had sagacity enough to cultivate assiduously the acquaintance of Johnson, and his faculties were gradually enlarged by the contemplation of such a model. To me and many others it

9. Dr. Charles Burney (1726–1814), historian of music and father of the novelist and diarist Fanny Burney, whom Johnson knew and loved in his old age.

1. Edmund Burke (1729–97), statesman, orator, and political philosopher.

2. Edmond Malone (1741–1812), distinguished editor and literary scholar. He helped Boswell in the writing and publication of the *Life*.

3. An assistant teacher; then a disagreeable and ill-paid job.

appeared that he studiously copied the manner of Johnson, though, indeed, upon a smaller scale.

At this time I think he had published nothing with his name, though it was pretty generally known that *one Dr. Goldsmith* was the author of *An Enquiry into the Present State of Polite Learning in Europe,* and of *The Citizen of the World,* a series of letters supposed to be written from London by a Chinese. No man had the art of displaying, with more advantage as a writer, whatever literary acquisitions he made. "*Nihil quod tetigit non ornavit.*"[4] His mind resembled a fertile, but thin soil. There was a quick, but not a strong vegetation, of whatever chanced to be thrown upon it. No deep root could be struck. The oak of the forest did not grow there; but the elegant shrubbery and the fragrant parterre[5] appeared in gay succession. It has been generally circulated and believed that he was a mere fool in conversation; but, in truth, this has been greatly exaggerated. He had, no doubt, a more than common share of that hurry of ideas which we often find in his countrymen, and which sometimes produces a laughable confusion in expressing them. He was very much what the French call *un étourdi,*[6] and from vanity and an eager desire of being conspicuous wherever he was, he frequently talked carelessly without knowledge of the subject, or even without thought. His person was short, his countenance coarse and vulgar, his deportment that of a scholar awkwardly affecting the easy gentleman. Those who were in any way distinguished, excited envy in him to so ridiculous an excess that the instances of it are hardly credible. When accompanying two beautiful young ladies with their mother on a tour in France, he was seriously angry that more attention was paid to them than to him; and once at the exhibition of the *Fantoccini* in London, when those who sat next him observed with what dexterity a puppet was made to toss a pike, he could not bear that it should have such praise, and exclaimed with some warmth, "Pshaw! I can do it better myself."[7] * * *

I had as my guests this evening at the Mitre Tavern, Dr. Johnson, Dr. Goldsmith, Mr. Thomas Davies, Mr. Eccles, an Irish gentleman, for whose agreeable company I was obliged to Mr. Davies, and the Reverend Mr. John Ogilvie,[8] who was desirous of being in company with my illustrious friend, while I, in my turn, was proud to have the honor of showing one of my countrymen upon what easy terms Johnson permitted me to live with him. * * *

Mr. Ogilvie was unlucky enough to choose for the topic of his

4. "He touched nothing that he did not adorn." From Johnson's epitaph for Goldsmith's monument in Westminster Abbey.
5. A flower garden with beds laid out in patterns.
6. One who acts without thought.
7. It is difficult to believe that Boswell did not recognize that Goldsmith was joking. Indeed, his entire characterization of Goldsmith is not without malice and distortion.
8. An eminent Scottish divine.

conversation the praises of his native country. He began with saying that there was very rich land round Edinburgh. Goldsmith, who had studied physic there, contradicted this, very untruly, with a sneering laugh. Disconcerted a little by this, Mr. Ogilvie then took new ground, where, I suppose, he thought himself perfectly safe; for he observed that Scotland had a great many noble wild prospects. JOHNSON. "I believe, Sir, you have a great many. Norway, too, has noble wild prospects; and Lapland is remarkable for prodigious noble wild prospects. But, Sir, let me tell you, the noblest prospect which a Scotchman ever sees, is the highroad that leads him to England!" This unexpected and pointed sally produced a roar of applause. After all, however, those who admire the rude grandeur of nature cannot deny it to Caledonia. * * *

At night Mr. Johnson and I supped in a private room at the Turk's Head Coffeehouse, in the Strand. "I encourage this house," said he, "for the mistress of it is a good civil woman, and has not much business.

"Sir, I love the acquaintance of young people; because, in the first place, I don't like to think myself growing old. In the next place, young acquaintances must last longest, if they do last; and then, Sir, young men have more virtue than old men: they have more generous sentiments in every respect. I love the young dogs of this age: they have more wit and humor and knowledge of life than we had; but then the dogs are not so good scholars. Sir, in my early years I read very hard. It is a sad reflection, but a true one, that I knew almost as much at eighteen as I do now. My judgment, to be sure, was not so good; but I had all the facts. I remember very well, when I was at Oxford, an old gentleman said to me, 'Young man, ply your book diligently now, and acquire a stock of knowledge; for when years come upon you, you will find that poring upon books will be but an irksome task.' " * * *

He again insisted on the duty of maintaining subordination of rank. "Sir, I would no more deprive a nobleman of his respect than of his money. I consider myself as acting a part in the great system of society, and I do to others as I would have them to do to me. I would behave to a nobleman as I should expect he would behave to me, were I a nobleman and he Sam. Johnson. Sir, there is one Mrs. Macaulay[9] in this town, a great republican. One day when I was at her house, I put on a very grave countenance, and said to her, 'Madam, I am now become a convert to your way of thinking. I am convinced that all mankind are upon an equal footing; and to give you an unquestionable proof, Madam, that I am in earnest, here is a very sensible, civil, well-behaved fellow citizen, your footman; I desire that he may be allowed to sit down and dine with us.' I thus, Sir, showed her the absurdity of the leveling doctrine.

9. Mrs. Catharine Macaulay, at this time much in the public eye as a female historian and a propounder of libertarian and egalitarian ideas.

She has never liked me since. Sir, your levelers wish to level *down* as far as themselves; but they cannot bear leveling *up* to themselves. They would all have some people under them; why not then have some people above them?" * * *

At supper this night he talked of good eating with uncommon satisfaction. "Some people," said he, "have a foolish way of not minding, or pretending not to mind, what they eat. For my part, I mind my belly very studiously, and very carefully; for I look upon it that he who does not mind his belly will hardly mind anything else." He now appeared to me *Jean Bull philosophe*,[1] and he was, for the moment, not only serious but vehement. Yet I have heard him, upon other occasions, talk with great contempt of people who were anxious to gratify their palates; and the 206th number of his *Rambler* is a masterly essay against gulosity.[2] His practice, indeed, I must acknowledge, may be considered as casting the balance of his different opinions upon this subject; for I never knew any man who relished good eating more than he did. When at table, he was totally absorbed in the business of the moment; his looks seemed riveted to his plate; nor would he, unless when in very high company, say one word, or even pay the least attention to what was said by others, till he had satisfied his appetite, which was so fierce, and indulged with such intenseness, that while in the act of eating, the veins of his forehead swelled, and generally a strong perspiration was visible. To those whose sensations were delicate, this could not but be disgusting; and it was doubtless not very suitable to the character of a philosopher, who should be distinguished by self-command. But it must be owned that Johnson, though he could be rigidly *abstemious*, was not a *temperate* man either in eating or drinking. He could refrain, but he could not use moderately. He told me that he had fasted two days without inconvenience, and that he had never been hungry but once. They who beheld with wonder how much he eat upon all occasions when his dinner was to his taste, could not easily conceive what he must have meant by hunger; and not only was he remarkable for the extraordinary quantity which he eat, but he was, or affected to be, a man of very nice discernment in the science of cookery. * * *

[1767] In February, 1767, there happened one of the most remarkable incidents of Johnson's life, which gratified his monarchical enthusiasm, and which he loved to relate with all its circumstances, when requested by his friends. This was his being honored by a private conversation with his Majesty, in the library at the Queen's house. He had frequently visited those splendid rooms and noble collection of books, which he used to say was more numerous and curious than he supposed any person could have made in the time which the King had employed. Mr. Barnard,

1. I.e., John Bull (the typical hard-headed Englishman) in the role of philosopher.
2. Greediness.

the librarian, took care that he should have every accommodation that could contribute to his ease and convenience, while indulging his literary taste in that place; so that he had here a very agreeable resource at leisure hours.

His Majesty having been informed of his occasional visits, was pleased to signify a desire that he should be told when Dr. Johnson came next to the library. Accordingly, the next time that Johnson did come, as soon as he was fairly engaged with a book, on which, while he sat by the fire, he seemed quite intent, Mr Barnard stole round to the apartment where the King was, and, in obedience to his Majesty's commands, mentioned that Dr. Johnson was then in the library. His Majesty said he was at leisure, and would go to him; upon which Mr. Barnard took one of the candles that stood on the King's table, and lighted his Majesty through a suite of rooms, till they came to a private door into the library, of which his Majesty had the key. Being entered, Mr. Barnard stepped forward hastily to Dr. Johnson, who was still in a profound study, and whispered him, "Sir, here is the King." Johnson started up, and stood still. His Majesty approached him, and at once was courteously easy.

His Majesty began by observing that he understood he came sometimes to the library; and then mentioning his having heard that the Doctor had been lately at Oxford, asked him if he was not fond of going thither. To which Johnson answered that he was indeed fond of going to Oxford sometimes, but was likewise glad to come back again. The King then asked him what they were doing at Oxford. Johnson answered, he could not much commend their diligence, but that in some respects they were mended, for they had put their press under better regulations, and were at that time printing Polybius. He was then asked whether there were better libraries at Oxford or Cambridge. He answered, he believed the Bodleian was larger than any they had at Cambridge; at the same time adding, "I hope, whether we have more books or not than they have at Cambridge, we shall make as good use of them as they do." Being asked whether All Souls or Christ Church library was the largest, he answered, "All Souls library is the largest we have, except the Bodleian." "Aye," said the King, "that is the public library."

His Majesty inquired if he was then writing anything. He answered, he was not, for he had pretty well told the world what he knew, and must now read to acquire more knowledge. The King, as it should seem with a view to urge him to rely on his own stores as an original writer, and to continue his labors, then said "I do not think you borrow much from anybody." Johnson said he thought he had already done his part as a writer. "I should have thought so too," said the King, "if you had not written so well."—

Johnson observed to me, upon this, that "No man could have paid a handsomer compliment; and it was fit for a king to pay. It was decisive." When asked by another friend, at Sir Joshua Reynolds's, whether he made any reply to this high compliment, he answered, "No, Sir. When the King had said it, it was to be so. It was not for me to bandy civilities with my sovereign." Perhaps no man who had spent his whole life in courts could have shown a more nice and dignified sense of true politeness than Johnson did in this instance. * * *

[*Fear of Death*]

[1769] When we were alone, I introduced the subject of death, and endeavored to maintain that the fear of it might be got over. I told him that David Hume said to me, he was no more uneasy to think he should *not be* after this life, than that he *had not been* before he began to exist. JOHNSON. "Sir, if he really thinks so, his perceptions are disturbed; he is mad: if he does not think so, he lies. He may tell you, he holds his finger in the flame of a candle, without feeling pain; would you believe him? When he dies, he at least gives up all he has." BOSWELL. "Foote,[3] Sir, told me, that when he was very ill he was not afraid to die." JOHNSON. "It is not true, Sir. Hold a pistol to Foote's breast, or to Hume's breast, and threaten to kill them, and you'll see how they behave." BOSWELL. "But may we not fortify our minds for the approach of death?" Here I am sensible I was in the wrong, to bring before his view what he ever looked upon with horror; for although when in a celestial frame, in his *Vanity of Human Wishes*, he has supposed death to be "kind Nature's signal for retreat," from this state of being to "a happier seat," his thoughts upon this awful change were in general full of dismal apprehensions. His mind resembled the vast amphitheater, the Colosseum at Rome. In the center stood his judgment, which, like a mighty gladiator, combated those apprehensions that, like the wild beasts of the arena, were all around in cells, ready to be let out upon him. After a conflict, he drives them back into their dens; but not killing them, they were still assailing him. To my question, whether we might not fortify our minds for the approach of death, he answered, in a passion, "No, Sir, let it alone. It matters not how a man dies, but how he lives. The act of dying is not of importance, it lasts so short a time." He added (with an earnest look), "A man knows it must be so, and submits. It will do him no good to whine."

I attempted to continue the conversation. He was so provoked that he said, "Give us no more of this"; and was thrown into such a state of agitation that he expressed himself in a way that alarmed

3. Samuel Foote, actor and dramatist, famous for his wit and his skill in mimicry.

and distressed me; showed an impatience that I should leave him, and when I was going away, called to me sternly, "Don't let us meet tomorrow." * * *

[*Ossian. "Talking for Victory"*]

MR. BOSWELL TO DR. JOHNSON

Edinburgh, Feb. 2, 1775.

* * * As to Macpherson, I am anxious to have from yourself a full and pointed account of what has passed between you and him. It is confidently told here that before your book[4] came out he sent to you, to let you know that he understood you meant to deny the authenticity of Ossian's poems; that the originals were in his possession; that you might have inspection of them, and might take the evidence of people skilled in the Erse language; and that he hoped, after this fair offer, you would not be so uncandid as to assert that he had refused reasonable proof. That you paid no regard to his message, but published your strong attack upon him; and then he wrote a letter to you, in such terms as he thought suited to one who had not acted as a man of veracity. * * *

What words were used by Mr. Macpherson in his letter to the venerable sage, I have never heard; but they are generally said to have been of a nature very different from the language of literary contest. Dr. Johnson's answer appeared in the newspapers of the day, and has since been frequently republished; but not with perfect accuracy. I give it as dictated to me by himself, written down in his presence, and authenticated by a note in his own handwriting, "*This, I think, is a true copy.*"

MR. JAMES MACPHERSON,

I received your foolish and impudent letter. Any violence offered me I shall do my best to repel; and what I cannot do for myself, the law shall do for me. I hope I shall never be deterred from detecting what I think a cheat, by the menaces of a ruffian.

What would you have me retract? I thought your book an imposture; I think it an imposture still. For this opinion I have given my reasons to the public, which I here dare you to refute. Your rage I defy. Your abilities, since your Homer, are not so formidable; and what I hear of your morals inclines me to pay regard not to what you shall say, but to what you shall prove. You may print this if you will.

SAM. JOHNSON.

Mr. Macpherson little knew the character of Dr. Johnson if he supposed that he could be easily intimidated; for no man was ever more remarkable for personal courage. He had, indeed, an awful dread of death, or rather, "of something after death"; and what rational man, who seriously thinks of quitting all that he has ever

4. Johnson's *Journey to the Western Islands* (1775), in which he had publicly expressed his views on the Ossianic poems.

known, and going into a new and unknown state of being, can be without that dread? But his fear was from reflection; his courage natural. His fear, in that one instance, was the result of philosophical and religious consideration. He feared death, but he feared nothing else, not even what might occasion death. Many instances of his resolution may be mentioned. One day, at Mr. Beauclerk's house in the country, when two large dogs were fighting, he went up to them, and beat them till they separated; and at another time, when told of the danger there was that a gun might burst if charged with many balls, he put in six or seven, and fired it off against a wall. Mr. Langton told me that when they were swimming together near Oxford, he cautioned Dr. Johnson against a pool which was reckoned particularly dangerous; upon which Johnson directly swam into it. He told me himself that one night he was attacked in the street by four men, to whom he would not yield, but kept them all at bay, till the watch came up, and carried both him and them to the roundhouse. In the playhouse at Lichfield, as Mr. Garrick informed me, Johnson having for a moment quitted a chair which was placed for him between the side-scenes, a gentleman took possession of it, and when Johnson on his return civilly demanded his seat, rudely refused to give it up; upon which Johnson laid hold of it, and tossed him and the chair into the pit. Foote, who so successfully revived the old comedy, by exhibiting living characters, had resolved to imitate Johnson on the stage, expecting great profits from his ridicule of so celebrated a man. Johnson being informed of his intention, and being at dinner at Mr. Thomas Davies's the bookseller, from whom I had the story, he asked Mr. Davies what was the common price of an oak stick; and being answered sixpence, "Why then, Sir," said he, "give me leave to send your servant to purchase me a shilling one. I'll have a double quantity; for I am told Foote means to *take me off*, as he calls it, and I am determined the fellow shall not do it with impunity." Davies took care to acquaint Foote of this, which effectually checked the wantonness of the mimic. Mr. Macpherson's menaces made Johnson provide himself with the same implement of defense; and had he been attacked, I have no doubt that, old as he was, he would have made his corporal prowess be felt as much as his intellectual. * * *

[1776] I mentioned a new gaming club, of which Mr. Beauclerk had given me an account, where the members played to a desperate extent. JOHNSON. "Depend upon it, Sir, this is mere talk. *Who* is ruined by gaming? You will not find six instances in an age. There is a strange rout made about deep play: whereas you have many more people ruined by adventurous trade, and yet we do not hear such an outcry against it." THRALE.[5] "There may be few people

5. Johnson met Henry Thrale, the wealthy brewer, and his charming wife Hester in 1765. Thereafter he was domesticated as much as he wished to be

absolutely ruined by deep play; but very many are much hurt in their circumstances by it." Johnson. "Yes, Sir, and so are very many by other kinds of expense." I had heard him talk once before in the same manner; and at Oxford he said, he wished he had learnt to play at cards. The truth, however, is that he loved to display his ingenuity in argument; and therefore would sometimes in conversation maintain opinions which he was sensible were wrong, but in supporting which, his reasoning and wit would be most conspicuous. He would begin thus: "Why, Sir, as to the good or evil of card playing——" "Now, said Garrick, "he is thinking which side he shall take." He appeared to have a pleasure in contradiction, especially when any opinion whatever was delivered with an air of confidence; so that there was hardly any topic, if not one of the great truths of religion and morality, that he might not have been incited to argue, either for or against. Lord Elibank[6] had the highest admiration of his powers. He once observed to me, "Whatever opinion Johnson maintains, I will not say that he convinces me; but he never fails to show me that he has good reasons for it." I have heard Johnson pay his Lordship this high compliment: "I never was in Lord Elibank's company without learning something." * * *

[*Dinner with Wilkes*]

My worthy booksellers and friends, Messieurs Dilly in the Poultry, at whose hospitable and well-covered table I have seen a greater number of literary men than at any other, except that of Sir Joshua Reynolds, had invited me to meet Mr. Wilkes[7] and some more gentlemen on Wednesday, May 15. "Pray," said I, "let us have Dr. Johnson."—"What, with Mr. Wilkes? not for the world," said Mr. Edward Dilly, "Dr. Johnson would never forgive me."—"Come," said I, "if you'll let me negotiate for you, I will be answerable that all shall go well." Dilly. "Nay, if you will take it upon you, I am sure I shall be very happy to see them both here."

Notwithstanding the high veneration which I entertained for Dr. Johnson, I was sensible that he was sometimes a little actuated by the spirit of contradiction, and by means of that I hoped I

at their house at Streatham near London. There he enjoyed the good things of life, as well as the companionship of Mrs. Thrale and her children. Thrale died in 1781. His widow's marriage to Gabriel Piozzi, an Italian musician, in 1784, caused Johnson to quarrel with her and darkened the last months of his life.

6. Prominent in Scottish literary circles. Johnson, who admired him, had visited him on his tour of Scotland with Boswell in 1773.

7. John Wilkes (1727–97) was obnoxious to the Christian and Tory Johnson in every way. He was profane and dissolute, and his personal life was a public scandal; for over a decade he had been notorious as a courageous, resourceful, and finally victorious opponent of the arbitrary and tyrannical policies of the king and his ministers, and had been the envenomed critic of Lord Bute, to whom Johnson owed his pension. When Johnson met him he had totally defeated his enemies, had served as Lord Mayor, and was again a Member of Parliament, a post from which he had been expelled and driven into exile as an outlaw in 1764. Boswell had found Wilkes a gay and congenial companion in Italy in 1764.

should gain my point. I was persuaded that if I had come upon him with a direct proposal, "Sir, will you dine in company with Jack Wilkes?" he would have flown into a passion, and would probably have answered, "Dine with Jack Wilkes, Sir! I'd as soon dine with Jack Ketch."[8] I therefore, while we were sitting quietly by ourselves at his house in an evening, took occasion to open my plan thus: "Mr. Dilly, Sir, sends his respectful compliments to you, and would be happy if you would do him the honor to dine with him on Wednesday next along with me, as I must soon go to Scotland." JOHNSON. "Sir, I am obliged to Mr. Dilly. I will wait upon him—" BOSWELL. "Provided, Sir, I suppose, that the company which he is to have, is agreeable to you." JOHNSON. "What do you mean, Sir? What do you take me for? Do you think I am so ignorant of the world as to imagine that I am to prescribe to a gentleman what company he is to have at his table?" BOSWELL. "I beg your pardon, Sir, for wishing to prevent you from meeting people whom you might not like. Perhaps he may have some of what he calls his patriotic[9] friends with him." JOHNSON. "Well, Sir, and what then? What care *I* for his *patriotic friends?* Poh!" BOSWELL. "I should not be surprised to find Jack Wilkes there." JOHNSON. "And if Jack Wilkes *should* be there, what is that to *me,* Sir? My dear friend, let us have no more of this. I am sorry to be angry with you; but really it is treating me strangely to talk to me as if I could not meet any company whatever, occasionally." BOSWELL. "Pray forgive me, Sir: I meant well. But you shall meet whoever comes, for me." Thus I secured him, and told Dilly that he would find him very well pleased to be one of his guests on the day appointed.

Upon the much-expected Wednesday, I called on him about half an hour before dinner, as I often did when we were to dine out together, to see that he was ready in time, and to accompany him. I found him buffeting his books, as upon a former occasion, covered with dust, and making no preparation for going abroad. "How is this, Sir?" said I. "Don't you recollect that you are to dine at Mr. Dilly's?" JOHNSON. "Sir, I did not think of going to Dilly's: it went out of my head. I have ordered dinner at home with Mrs. Williams." BOSWELL. "But, my dear Sir, you know you were engaged to Mr. Dilly, and I told him so. He will expect you, and will be much disappointed if you don't come." JOHNSON. "You must talk to Mrs. Williams about this."

Here was a sad dilemma. I feared that what I was so confident I had secured would yet be frustrated. He had accustomed himself

8. After the public hangman, Jack Ketch, died in 1686, his name became the common designation of all those who filled that office.

9. In Tory circles the word had come to be used ironically of those who opposed the government. The "patriots" considered themselves the defenders of the ancient liberties of the English. They included the partisans of both Wilkes and of the American colonists.

to show Mrs. Williams such a degree of humane attention as frequently imposed some restraint upon him; and I knew that if she should be obstinate, he would not stir. I hastened downstairs to the blind lady's room, and told her I was in great uneasiness, for Dr. Johnson had engaged to me to dine this day at Mr. Dilly's, but that he had told me he had forgotten his engagement, and had ordered dinner at home. "Yes, Sir," said she, pretty peevishly, "Dr. Johnson is to dine at home."—"Madam," said I, "his respect for you is such that I know he will not leave you unless you absolutely desire it. But as you have so much of his company, I hope you will be good enough to forego it for a day; as Mr. Dilly is a very worthy man, has frequently had agreeable parties at his house for Dr. Johnson, and will be vexed if the Doctor neglects him today. And then, Madam, be pleased to consider my situation; I carried the message, and I assured Mr. Dilly that Dr. Johnson was to come, and no doubt he has made a dinner, and invited a company, and boasted of the honor he expected to have. I shall be quite disgraced if the Doctor is not there." She gradually softened to my solicitations, which were certainly as earnest as most entreaties to ladies upon any occasion, and was graciously pleased to empower me to tell Dr. Johnson that all things considered, she thought he should certainly go. I flew back to him, still in dust, and careless of what should be the event, "indifferent in his choice to go or stay";[1] but as soon as I had announced to him Mrs. Williams' consent, he roared, "Frank, a clean shirt," and was very soon dressed. When I had him fairly seated in a hackney coach with me, I exulted as much as a fortune hunter who has got an heiress into a post chaise with him to set out for Gretna Green.[2]

When we entered Mr. Dilly's drawing room, he found himself in the midst of a company he did not know. I kept myself snug and silent, watching how he would conduct himself. I observed him whispering to Mr. Dilly, "Who is that gentleman, Sir?"—"Mr. Arthur Lee."—JOHNSON. "Too, too, too" (under his breath), which was one of his habitual mutterings. Mr. Arthur Lee could not but be very obnoxious to Johnson, for he was not only a *patriot* but an *American*.[3] He was afterwards minister from the United States at the court of Madrid. "And who is the gentleman in lace?"—"Mr. Wilkes, Sir." This information confounded him still more; he had some difficulty to restrain himself, and taking up a book, sat down upon a window seat and read, or at least kept his eye upon it intently for some time, till he composed himself. His feel-

1. Addison's *Cato* V.i.40. Boswell cleverly adapts to his own purpose Cato's words, "Indifferent in his choice to sleep or die."

2. A village just across the Scottish border where runaway couples were married by the local innkeeper or the blacksmith.

3. Johnson was extremely hostile to the rebelling American colonists. On one occasion he said: "I am willing to love all mankind, except an American." Lee had been educated in England and Scotland, and had recently been admitted to the English bar. He had been a loyal supporter of Wilkes.

ings, I dare say, were awkward enough. But he no doubt recollected his having rated me for supposing that he could be at all disconcerted by any company, and he, therefore, resolutely set himself to behave quite as an easy man of the world, who could adapt himself at once to the disposition and manners of those whom he might chance to meet.

The cheering sound of "Dinner is upon the table," dissolved his reverie, and we *all* sat down without any symptom of ill humor. There were present, beside Mr. Wilkes, and Mr. Arthur Lee, who was an old companion of mine when he studied physic at Edinburgh, Mr. (now Sir John) Miller, Dr. Lettsom, and Mr. Slater the druggist. Mr. Wilkes placed himself next to Dr. Johnson, and behaved to him with so much attention and politeness that he gained upon him insensibly. No man eat more heartily than Johnson, or loved better what was nice and delicate. Mr. Wilkes was very assiduous in helping him to some fine veal. "Pray give me leave, Sir—It is better here—A little of the brown—Some fat, Sir—A little of the stuffing—Some gravy—Let me have the pleasure of giving you some butter—Allow me to recommend a squeeze of this orange—or the lemon, perhaps, may have more zest."—"Sir, Sir, I am obliged to you, Sir," cried Johnson, bowing, and turning his head to him with a look for some time of "surly virtue," but, in a short while, of complacency.

Foote being mentioned, Johnson said, "He is not a good mimic." One of the company added, "A merry Andrew, a buffoon." JOHNSON. "But he has wit too, and is not deficient in ideas, or in fertility and variety of imagery, and not empty of reading; he has knowledge enough to fill up his part. One species of wit he has in an eminent degree, that of escape. You drive him into a corner with both hands; but he's gone, Sir, when you think you have got him—like an animal that jumps over your head. Then he has a great range for wit; he never lets truth stand between him and a jest, and he is sometimes mighty coarse. Garrick is under many restraints from which Foote is free." WILKES. "Garrick's wit is more like Lord Chesterfield's." JOHNSON. "The first time I was in company with Foote was at Fitzherbert's. Having no good opinion of the fellow, I was resolved not to be pleased; and it is very difficult to please a man against his will. I went on eating my dinner pretty sullenly, affecting not to mind him. But the dog was so very comical, that I was obliged to lay down my knife and fork, throw myself back upon my chair, and fairly laugh it out. No, Sir, he was irresistible. He upon one occasion experienced, in an extraordinary degree, the efficacy of his powers of entertaining. Amongst the many and various modes which he tried of getting money, he became a partner with a small-beer[4] brewer, and he was to have a share of

4. Weak beer, served in the servants' hall.

the profits for procuring customers amongst his numerous acquaintance. Fitzherbert was one who took his small beer; but it was so bad that the servants resolved not to drink it. They were at some loss how to notify their resolution, being afraid of offending their master, who they knew liked Foote much as a companion. At last they fixed upon a little black boy, who was rather a favorite, to be their deputy, and deliver their remonstrance; and having invested him with the whole authority of the kitchen, he was to inform Mr. Fitzherbert, in all their names, upon a certain day, that they would drink Foote's small beer no longer. On that day Foote happened to dine at Fitzherbert's, and this boy served at table; he was so delighted with Foote's stories, and merriment, and grimace, that when he went downstairs, he told them, 'This is the finest man I have ever seen. I will not deliver your message. I will drink his small beer.' "

Somebody observed that Garrick could not have done this. WILKES. "Garrick would have made the small beer still smaller. He is now leaving the stage; but he will play *Scrub*[5] all his life." I knew that Johnson would let nobody attack Garrick but himself, as Garrick once said to me, and I had heard him praise his liberality; so to bring out his commendation of his celebrated pupil, I said, loudly, "I have heard Garrick is liberal." JOHNSON. "Yes, Sir, I know that Garrick has given away more money than any man in England that I am acquainted with, and that not from ostentatious views. Garrick was very poor when he began life; so when he came to have money, he probably was very unskillful in giving away, and saved when he should not. But Garrick began to be liberal as soon as he could; and I am of opinion, the reputation of avarice which he has had, has been very lucky for him, and prevented his having many enemies. You despise a man for avarice, but do not hate him. Garrick might have been much better attacked for living with more splendor than is suitable to a player: if they had had the wit to have assaulted him in that quarter, they might have galled him more. But they have kept clamoring about his avarice, which has rescued him from much obloquy and envy."

Talking of the great difficulty of obtaining authentic information for biography, Johnson told us, "When I was a young fellow I wanted to write the *Life of Dryden*, and in order to get materials, I applied to the only two persons then alive who had seen him; these were old Swinney,[6] and old Cibber. Swinney's information was no more than this, that at Will's Coffeehouse Dryden had a particular chair for himself, which was set by the fire in winter, and was then called his winter chair; and that it was carried out for him to the balcony in summer, and was then called his summer

5. The servant of Squire Sullen in George Farquhar's *Beaux' Stratagem:* a favorite role of Garrick's.

6. Owen Mac Swinney, a playwright.

chair. Cibber could tell no more but that he remembered him a decent old man, arbiter of critical disputes at Will's. You are to consider that Cibber was then at a great distance from Dryden, had perhaps one leg only in the room, and durst not draw in the other." BOSWELL. "Yet Cibber was a man of observation?" JOHNSON. "I think not." BOSWELL. "You will allow his *Apology* to be well done." JOHNSON. "Very well done, to be sure, Sir. That book is a striking proof of the justice of Pope's remark:

> Each might his several province well command,
> Would all but stoop to what they understand."[7]

BOSWELL. "And his plays are good." JOHNSON. "Yes; but that was his trade; *l'esprit du corps:* he had been all his life among players and play writers. I wondered that he had so little to say in conversation, for he had kept the best company, and learnt all that can be got by the ear. He abused Pindar to me, and then showed me an ode of his own, with an absurd couplet, making a linnet soar on an eagle's wing. I told him that when the ancients made a simile, they always made it like something real."

Mr. Wilkes remarked that "among all the bold flights of Shakespeare's imagination, the boldest was making Birnam Wood march to Dunsinane;[8] creating a wood where there never was a shrub; a wood in Scotland! ha! ha! ha!" And he also observed, that "the clannish slavery of the Highlands of Scotland was the single exception to Milton's remark of 'The mountain nymph, sweet Liberty,'[9] being worshiped in all hilly countries."—"When I was at Inverary," said he, "on a visit to my old friend, Archibald, Duke of Argyle, his dependents congratulated me on being such a favorite of his Grace. I said, 'It is then, gentlemen, truly lucky for me; for if I had displeased the Duke, and he had wished it, there is not a Campbell among you but would have been ready to bring John Wilkes's head to him in a charger. It would have been only

> Off with his head! So much for Aylesbury.'[1]

I was then member for Aylesbury." * * *

Mr. Arthur Lee mentioned some Scotch who had taken possession of a barren part of America, and wondered why they should choose it. JOHNSON. "Why, Sir, all barrenness is comparative. The *Scotch* would not know it to be barren." BOSWELL. "Come, come, he is flattering the English. You have now been in Scotland, Sir, and say if you did not see meat and drink enough there." JOHNSON. "Why yes, Sir; meat and drink enough to give the inhabitants sufficient strength to run away from home." All these quick and lively sallies were said sportively, quite in jest, and with a smile, which

7. *Essay on Criticism* I.66–67.
8. *Macbeth* V.v.30–52.
9. *L'Allegro*, line 36.
1. "Off with his head! So much for Buckingham." A line in Cibber's version of Shakespeare's *Richard III.*

showed that he meant only wit. Upon this topic he and Mr. Wilkes could perfectly assimilate; here was a bond of union between them, and I was conscious that as both of them had visited Caledonia, both were fully satisfied of the strange narrow ignorance of those who imagine that it is a land of famine. But they amused themselves with persevering in the old jokes. When I claimed a superiority for Scotland over England in one respect, that no man can be arrested there for a debt merely because another swears it against him; but there must first be the judgment of a court of law ascertaining its justice; and that a seizure of the person, before judgment is obtained, can take place only if his creditor should swear that he is about to fly from the country, or, as it is technically expressed, is *in meditatione fugae:* WILKES. "That, I should think, may be safely sworn of all the Scotch nation." JOHNSON (to Mr. Wilkes). "You must know, Sir, I lately took my friend Boswell and showed him genuine civilized life in an English provincial town. I turned him loose at Lichfield, my native city, that he might see for once real civility: for you know he lives among savages in Scotland, and among rakes in London." WILKES. "Except when he is with grave, sober, decent people like you and me." JOHNSON (smiling). "And we ashamed of him."

They were quite frank and easy. Johnson told the story of his asking Mrs. Macaulay to allow her footman to sit down with them, to prove the ridiculousness of the argument for the equality of mankind; and he said to me afterwards, with a nod of satisfaction, "You saw Mr. Wilkes acquiesced." * * *

This record, though by no means so perfect as I could wish, will serve to give a notion of a very curious interview, which was not only pleasing at the time, but had the agreeable and benignant effect of reconciling any animosity and sweetening any acidity, which in the various bustle of political contest, had been produced in the minds of two men, who, though widely different, had so many things in common—classical learning, modern literature, wit, and humor, and ready repartee—that it would have been much to be regretted if they had been forever at a distance from each other.

Mr. Burke gave me much credit for this successful "negotiation"; and pleasantly said that there was nothing to equal it in the whole history of the *Corps Diplomatique*. * * *

[*Dread of Solitude*]

[1777] I talked to him of misery being "the doom of man" in this life, as displayed in his *Vanity of Human Wishes*. Yet I observed that things were done upon the supposition of happiness; grand houses were built, fine gardens were made, splendid places of public amusement were contrived, and crowded with company. JOHNSON. "Alas, Sir, these are all only struggles for happiness. When

I first entered Ranelagh,[2] it gave an expansion and gay sensation to my mind, such as I never experienced anywhere else. But, as Xerxes wept when he viewed his immense army, and considered that not one of that great multitude would be alive a hundred years afterwards, so it went to my heart to consider that there was not one in all that brilliant circle that was not afraid to go home and think; but that the thoughts of each individual there, would be distressing when alone." * * *

["*A Bottom of Good Sense.*" *Bet Flint.* "*Clear Your Mind of Cant*"]

[1781] Talking of a very respectable author, he told us a curious circumstance in his life, which was that he had married a printer's devil.[3] REYNOLDS. "A printer's devil, Sir! Why, I thought a printer's devil was a creature with a black face and in rags." JOHNSON. "Yes, Sir. But I suppose, he had her face washed, and put clean clothes on her." Then looking very serious, and very earnest: "And she did not disgrace him; the woman had a bottom of good sense." The word *bottom* thus introduced was so ludicrous when contrasted with his gravity, that most of us could not forbear tittering and laughing; though I recollect that the Bishop of Killaloe kept his countenance with perfect steadiness, while Miss Hannah More[4] slyly hid her face behind a lady's back who sat on the same settee with her. His pride could not bear that any expression of his should excite ridicule, when he did not intend it; he therefore resolved to assume and exercise despotic power, glanced sternly around, and called out in a strong tone, "Where's the merriment?" Then collecting himself, and looking awful, to make us feel how he could impose restraint, and as it were searching his mind for a still more ludicrous word, he slowly pronounced, "I say the *woman* was *fundamentally* sensible"; as if he had said, "hear this now, and laugh if you dare." We all sat composed as at a funeral. * * *

He gave us an entertaining account of Bet Flint, a woman of the town, who, with some eccentric talents and much effrontery, forced herself upon his acquaintance. "Bet," said he, "wrote her own Life in verse, which she brought to me, wishing that I would furnish her with a Preface to it" (laughing). "I used to say of her that she was generally slut and drunkard; occasionally, whore and thief. She had, however, genteel lodgings, a spinnet on which she played, and a boy that walked before her chair. Poor Bet was taken up on a charge of stealing a counterpane, and tried at the Old Bailey. Chief Justice ———, who loved a wench, summed up favorably, and she was acquitted. After which Bet said, with a gay and

2. Pleasure gardens in Chelsea, where concerts were held, fireworks displayed, food and drink sold.

3. Apprentice in a print shop.

4. Hannah More (1745–1833), bluestocking and religious writer, one of the promoters of the Sunday School movement.

satisfied air, 'Now that the counterpane is *my own,* I shall make a petticoat of it.' " * * *

[1783] I have no minute of any interview with Johnson till Thursday, May 15, when I find what follows: BOSWELL. "I wish much to be in Parliament, Sir." JOHNSON. "Why, Sir, unless you come resolved to support any administration, you would be the worse for being in Parliament, because you would be obliged to live more expensively." BOSWELL. "Perhaps, Sir, I should be the less happy for being in Parliament. I never would sell my vote, and I should be vexed if things went wrong." JOHNSON. "That's cant,[5] Sir. It would not vex you more in the house than in the gallery: public affairs vex no man." BOSWELL. "Have not they vexed yourself a little, Sir? Have not you been vexed by all the turbulence of this reign, and by that absurd vote of the House of Commons, 'That the influence of the Crown has increased, is increasing, and ought to be diminished?' " JOHNSON. "Sir, I have never slept an hour less, nor eat an ounce less meat. I would have knocked the factious dogs on the head, to be sure; but I was not *vexed.*" BOSWELL. "I declare, Sir, upon my honor, I did imagine I was vexed, and took a pride in it; but it *was,* perhaps, cant; for I own I neither ate less, nor slept less." JOHNSON. "My dear friend, clear your *mind* of cant. You may *talk* as other people do: you may say to a man, 'Sir, I am your most humble servant.' You are *not* his most humble servant. You may say, 'These are bad times; it is a melancholy thing to be reserved to such times.' You don't mind the times. You tell a man, 'I am sorry you had such bad weather the last day of your journey, and were so much wet.' You don't care sixpence whether he is wet or dry. You may *talk* in this manner; it is a mode of talking in society: but don't *think* foolishly." * * *

[*Johnson Prepares for Death*]

My anxious apprehensions at parting with him this year proved to be but too well founded; for not long afterwards he had a dreadful stroke of the palsy, of which there are very full and accurate accounts in letters written by himself, to show with what composure of mind, and resignation to the Divine Will, his steady piety enabled him to behave. * * *

Two days after he wrote thus to Mrs. Thrale:

"On Monday, the 16th, I sat for my picture, and walked a considerable way with little inconvenience. In the afternoon and evening I felt myself light and easy, and began to plan schemes of life. Thus I went to bed, and in a short time waked and sat up, as has been long my custom, when I felt a confusion and indistinctness in my head, which lasted, I suppose, about half a minute. I was alarmed,

5. "A whining pretension to goodness in formal and affected terms" (Johnson's *Dictionary*).

and prayed God that however he might afflict my body, he would spare my understanding. This prayer, that I might try the integrity of my faculties, I made in Latin verse. The lines were not very good, but I knew them not to be very good: I made them easily, and concluded myself to be unimpaired in my faculties.

"Soon after I perceived that I had suffered a paralytic stroke, and that my speech was taken from me. I had no pain, and so little dejection in this dreadful state, that I wondered at my own apathy, and considered that perhaps death itself, when it should come, would excite less horror than seems now to attend it.

"In order to rouse the vocal organs, I took two drams. Wine has been celebrated for the production of eloquence. I put myself into violent motion, and I think repeated it; but all was vain. I then went to bed and strange as it may seem, I think slept. When I saw light, it was time to contrive what I should do. Though God stopped my speech, he left me my hand; I enjoyed a mercy which was not granted to my dear friend Lawrence,[6] who now perhaps overlooks me as I am writing, and rejoices that I have what he wanted. My first note was necessarily to my servant, who came in talking, and could not immediately comprehend why he should read what I put into his hands.

"I then wrote a card to Mr. Allen,[7] that I might have a discreet friend at hand, to act as occasion should require. In penning this note, I had some difficulty; my hand, I knew not how nor why, made wrong letters. I then wrote to Dr. Taylor to come to me, and bring Dr. Heberden; and I sent to Dr. Brocklesby, who is my neighbor.[8] My physicians are very friendly, and give me great hopes; but you may imagine my situation. I have so far recovered my vocal powers as to repeat the Lord's Prayer with no very imperfect articulation. My memory, I hope, yet remains as it was; but such an attack produces solicitude for the safety of every faculty." * * *

[1784] To Mr. Henry White, a young clergyman, with whom he now formed an intimacy, so as to talk to him with great freedom, he mentioned that he could not in general accuse himself of having been an undutiful son. "Once, indeed," said he, "I was disobedient; I refused to attend my father to Uttoxeter market. Pride was the source of that refusal, and the remembrance of it was painful. A few years ago, I desired to atone for this fault; I went to Uttoxeter in very bad weather, and stood for a considerable time bareheaded in the rain, on the spot where my father's stall used to stand. In contrition I stood, and I hope the penance was expiatory."

"I told him," says Miss Seward,[9] "in one of my latest visits to him, of a wonderful learned pig, which I had seen at Nottingham; and which did all that we have observed exhibited by dogs

6. Dr. Thomas Lawrence, president of the Royal College of Physicians and Johnson's own doctor, had died paralyzed shortly before this was written.
7. Edmund Allen, a printer, Johnson's landlord and neighbor.
8. These two physicians attended Johnson on his deathbed.
9. Anna Seward, "the Swan of Lichfield," a poet.

and horses. The subject amused him. 'Then,' said he, 'the pigs are a race unjustly calumniated. *Pig* has, it seems, not been wanting to *man*, but *man* to *pig*. We do not allow *time* for his education, we kill him at a year old.' Mr. Henry White, who was present, observed that if this instance had happened in or before Pope's time, he would not have been justified in instancing the swine as the lowest degree of groveling instinct.[1] Dr. Johnson seemed pleased with the observation, while the person who made it proceeded to remark that great torture must have been employed, ere the indocility of the animal could have been subdued. 'Certainly,' said the Doctor; 'but,' turning to me, 'how old is your pig?' I told him, three years old. 'Then,' said he, 'the pig has no cause to complain; he would have been killed the first year if he had not been *educated*, and protracted existence is a good recompense for very considerable degrees of torture.' "

[*Johnson Faces Death*]

As Johnson had now very faint hopes of recovery, and as Mrs. Thrale was no longer devoted to him, it might have been supposed that he would naturally have chosen to remain in the comfortable house of his beloved wife's daughter,[2] and end his life where he began it. But there was in him an animated and lofty spirit, and however complicated diseases might depress ordinary mortals, all who saw him, beheld and acknowledged the *invictum animum Catonis*.[3] Such was his intellectual ardor even at this time that he said to one friend, "Sir, I look upon every day to be lost, in which I do not make a new acquaintance"; and to another, when talking of his illness, "I will be conquered; I will not capitulate." And such was his love of London, so high a relish had he of its magnificent extent, and variety of intellectual entertainment, that he languished when absent from it, his mind having become quite luxurious from the long habit of enjoying the metropolis; and, therefore, although at Lichfield, surrounded with friends, who loved and revered him, and for whom he had a very sincere affection, he still found that such conversation as London affords, could be found nowhere else. These feelings, joined, probably, to some flattering hopes of aid from the eminent physicians and surgeons in London, who kindly and generously attended him without accepting fees, made him resolve to return to the capital. * * * Death had always been to him an object of terror; so that, though by no means happy, he still clung to life with an eagerness at which many have wondered. At any time when he was ill, he was very much pleased to be told that he looked better. An ingenious mem-

1. *Essay on Man* I.221.
2. Lucy Porter.
3. "The unconquered soul of Cato." An adaptation of a phrase in Horace's *Odes* II.i.24.

ber of the Eumelian Club[4] informs me that upon one occasion when he said to him that he saw health returning to his cheek, Johnson seized him by the hand and exclaimed, "Sir, you are one of the kindest friends I ever had." * * *

Dr. Heberden, Dr. Brocklesby, Dr. Warren, and Dr. Butter, physicians, generously attended him, without accepting any fees, as did Mr. Cruikshank, surgeon; and all that could be done from professional skill and ability was tried, to prolong a life so truly valuable. He himself, indeed, having, on account of his very bad constitution, been perpetually applying himself to medical inquiries, united his own efforts with those of the gentlemen who attended him; and imagining that the dropsical collection of water which oppressed him might be drawn off by making incisions in his body, he, with his usual resolute defiance of pain, cut deep, when he thought that his surgeon had done it too tenderly.

About eight or ten days before his death, when Dr. Brocklesby paid him his morning visit, he seemed very low and desponding, and said, "I have been as a dying man all night." He then emphatically broke out in the words of Shakespeare:

"Canst thou not minister to a mind diseased;
Pluck from the memory a rooted sorrow,
Raze out the written troubles of the brain,
And with some sweet oblivious antidote
Cleanse the stuffed bosom of that perilous stuff
Which weighs upon the heart?"

To which Dr. Brocklesby readily answered, from the same great poet:

"Therein the patient
Must minister to himself."[5]

Johnson expressed himself much satisfied with the application. * * *

Amidst the melancholy clouds which hung over the dying Johnson, his characteristical manner showed itself on different occasions.

When Dr. Warren, in the usual style, hoped that he was better; his answer was, "No, Sir; you cannot conceive with what acceleration I advance towards death."

A man whom he had never seen before was employed one night to sit up with him. Being asked next morning how he liked his attendant, his answer was, "Not at all, Sir: the fellow's an idiot; he is as awkward as a turnspit[6] when first put into the wheel, and as sleepy as a dormouse."

Mr. Windham[7] having placed a pillow conveniently to support

4. A club to which Boswell and Reynolds belonged.

5. *Macbeth* V.iii.40–46.

6. A dog kept to turn the roasting-spit by running within a tread-wheel connected to it (*NED*).

7. William Windham, one of Johnson's younger friends, later a Member of Parliament.

him, he thanked him for his kindness, and said, "That will do—all that a pillow can do." * * *

Johnson, with that native fortitude, which, amidst all his bodily distress and mental sufferings, never forsook him, asked Dr. Brocklesby, as a man in whom he had confidence, to tell him plainly whether he could recover. "Give me," said he, "a direct answer." The Doctor having first asked him if he could bear the whole truth, which way soever it might lead, and being answered that he could, declared that, in his opinion, he could not recover without a miracle. "Then," said Johnson, "I will take no more physic, not even my opiates; for I have prayed that I may render up my soul to God unclouded." In this resolution he persevered, and, at the same time, used only the weakest kinds of sustenance. Being pressed by Mr. Windham to take somewhat more generous nourishment, lest too low a diet should have the very effect which he dreaded, by debilitating his mind, he said, "I will take anything but inebriating sustenance."

The Reverend Mr. Strahan,[8] who was the son of his friend, and had been always one of his great favorites, had, during his last illness, the satisfaction of contributing to soothe and comfort him. That gentleman's house, at Islington, of which he is Vicar, afforded Johnson, occasionally and easily, an agreeable change of place and fresh air; and he attended also upon him in town in the discharge of the sacred offices of his profession.

Mr. Strahan has given me the agreeable assurance that, after being in much agitation, Johnson became quite composed, and continued so till his death.

Dr. Brocklesby, who will not be suspected of fanaticism, obliged me with the following account:

"For some time before his death, all his fears were calmed and absorbed by the prevalence of his faith, and his trust in the merits and *propitiation* of Jesus Christ." * * *

Johnson having thus in his mind the true Christian scheme, at once rational and consolatory, uniting justice and mercy in the Divinity, with the improvement of human nature, previous to his receiving the Holy Sacrament in his apartment, composed and fervently uttered this prayer:

"Almighty and most merciful Father, I am now as to human eyes, it seems, about to commemorate, for the last time, the death of thy Son Jesus Christ, our Saviour and Redeemer. Grant, O Lord, that my whole hope and confidence may be in his merits, and thy mercy; enforce and accept my imperfect repentance; make this commemoration available to the confirmation of my faith, the establishment

8. The Rev. George Strahan (pronounced *Strawn*), who later published Johnson's *Prayers and Meditations*.

of my hope, and the enlargement of my charity; and make the death of thy Son Jesus Christ effectual to my redemption. Have mercy upon me, and pardon the multitude of my offenses. Bless my friends; have mercy upon all men. Support me, by thy Holy Spirit, in the days of weakness, and at the hour of death; and receive me, at my death, to everlasting happiness, for the sake of Jesus Christ. Amen."

Having * * * made his will on the 8th and 9th of December, and settled all his worldly affairs, he languished till Monday, the 13th of that month, when he expired, about seven o'clock in the evening, with so little apparent pain that his attendants hardly perceived when his dissolution took place. * * *

1791

EDMUND BURKE

(1729–1797)

1757:	*Enquiry into the Sublime and Beautiful*
1766:	Elected to Parliament.
1774–77:	Speeches on America.
1782–83:	Serves as Paymaster General.
1786:	Moves for the impeachment of Warren Hastings.
1790:	*Reflections on the Revolution in France*

Burke was born and educated in Dublin, the son of an Anglican father and Catholic mother, and came to London in 1750 to study law at the Middle Temple and make his fortune. But he was never admitted to the bar; instead he gained a reputation as a philosopher and a man of letters. *A Philosophical Enquiry into the Origin of our Ideas of the Sublime and Beautiful* (1757) is an important attempt to explain aesthetic ideas in terms of natural human responses; the sublime, for instance, is that which arouses feelings of terror in the mind and body. When Burke became a founding member of Johnson's famous Club in 1764, he was known as "the first man everywhere," a man who could succeed at any work he chose. Yet already he had begun to devote himself to politics, as secretary to William Hamilton in Ireland, and in 1765 he took a post as secretary to the premier, the Marquis of Rockingham. Shortly afterward he entered Parliament as a "Rockingham Whig," a liberal faction unpopular with the King. Here, for the next twenty-nine years, he served in the opposition—a perpetual opposition interrupted only for eight months, in 1782–83, when he was appointed Paymaster General. Aside from this interlude, Burke spent his talents in a career of politics without power, as a voice of protest and conscience directed not only against the Tory government but against his fellow Whigs.

What is unique about Burke's career, however, is not so much his combination of talents—the philosopher, the literary man, the politician—as his full use of them upon the great issues of his time. The events he witnessed have helped to shape our world: American independence and the birth of the United States, the French Revolution, the founding of Britain's vast colonial empire in the East. No one defined the meaning of these events more profoundly than Burke, or spoke more eloquently about them; the history of the man is a history of his age. But Burke also stands *against* his age; for most of the time he espoused the losing side. In his great speeches on *American Taxation* (1774) and *Conciliation with the Colonies* (1775), as well as his *Letter to the Sheriffs of Bristol* (1777), he spoke for understanding and reconciliation between Britain and America, but could not persuade others to avert the war. In tracts on the Irish question and Catholicism, he argued against the persecution of Irish Catholics that has poisoned relations between England and Ireland to the present day, but he encountered such prejudice that the voters of Bristol cast him out (in 1781 he was re-elected to Parliament from Malton). In a series of speeches on India, most notably the four-day speech opening the trial of Warren Hastings (1788), he pleaded for justice and responsibility in the administration of Britain's colonies, but after a trial of seven years Hastings was acquitted. Most bitter of all was Burke's resistance to the French Revolution, in a stream of impassioned works that includes *Reflections on the Revolution in France* (1790), *An Appeal from the New to the Old Whigs* (1791), *Thoughts on French Affairs* (1791), *Letter to a Noble Lord* (1795), and *Letters on a Regicide Peace* (1796). Despite his hatred of the revolutionaries, Burke sensed that the tide of history was running against him; and when he died, he arranged to keep his burial place secret, lest his corpse be desecrated. "I believe, in any body of men in England, I should have been in the Minority," he once said. "I have always been in the Minority." Yet many later generations have taken his side.

As a political thinker, Burke suggests that every statesman must be partly a visionary, partly a practical man of affairs. Tireless in research, he probably knew more about America and India than did any other man in England. But at the same time, like a poet, he tries to project his imagination beyond the particulars of things as they are, to envision the world as it once was, or as it might be. Thus he is known as a "conservative," who sees the essential continuity between the past and present, and as a "reformer," who preserves institutions by adapting them to meet changing circumstances. Yet such principles are never merely abstract for Burke; they are founded on a sense of history and a respect for concrete reality. Again and again he describes nations as living organisms, like an old oak tree or a family, that grow according to their own nature, not according to a program or theory. A wise statesman will accommodate himself to this nature. He will not, like the "metaphysicians" who inspired the French Revolution, destroy life in the hope of remaking men to his abstract ideal. But, of course, to understand things as they are does not mean to acquiesce in the *status quo*. It requires an active and penetrating intelligence, an intelligence that can confront complexity without oversimplification, and eternal change without despair. Such, for Burke, is the art of politics.

None of Burke's writings illustrates his grasp of fact and his imaginative scope better than his *Speech on Conciliation with the Colonies*. He had studied America in depth—his early *Account of European Settlements in America* (1757) is a standard authority—and his arguments draw on a full sense of the land itself, "Such as she was, such as she would become." The issue, he keeps insisting, is not some mythical America, an idea in the minds of Englishmen, but a country already existing, inhabited by real people with real interests. No solution will work unless it takes account of those realities. American strength, American liberty cannot be blotted out with the stroke of a pen; rather, they can be used to keep England strong and free. In the light of history, Burke's vision of America and his warning against war seem prophetic. Even more impressive than his specific analysis, however, is the example his speech provides of a political mind in action: a mind at once practical, generous, and creative.

From Speech on Conciliation with the Colonies[1]

The proposition is peace. Not peace through the medium of war; not peace to be hunted through the labyrinth of intricate and endless negotiations; not peace to arise out of universal discord, fomented from principle, in all parts of the empire; not peace to depend on the juridical determination of perplexing questions, or the precise marking the shadowy boundaries of a complex government. It is simple peace, sought in its natural course and in its ordinary haunts. It is peace sought in the spirit of peace, and laid in principles purely pacific. I propose, by removing the ground of the difference, and by restoring the *former unsuspecting confidence of the colonies in the mother country*,[2] to give permanent satisfaction to your people—and (far from a scheme of ruling by discord) to reconcile them to each other in the same act and by the bond of the very same interest which reconciles them to British government. * * * I mean to give peace. Peace implies reconciliation; and where there has been a material dispute, reconciliation does in a manner always imply concession on the one part or on the other. In this state of things I make no difficulty in affirming that the proposal ought to originate from us. Great and acknowledged force is not impaired, either in effect or in opinion, by an unwillingness to exert itself. The superior power may offer peace with honor and

1. By the spring of 1775, American resentment of taxation and restraints on trade threatened to erupt into war. In Britain the ruling party of Lord North tried to mollify the colonies without compromising its right to tax them or govern them individually. Burke was convinced, both from his own knowledge of America and from conversation with Benjamin Franklin, that such policies would fail. Moreover, he represented two constituencies which opposed them: the colony of New York, which he served as agent, and the voters of Bristol, a commercial city suffering from the drop in colonial trade. On March 22, 1775, Burke rose in Parliament to present a series of his own resolutions, intended to grant the Americans their right to representation, and thus to enlist them more strongly in the British empire. He spoke for three hours, and even political enemies found him "very reasonable, and very eloquent." The speech immediately became famous; two months later it was published.

2. A quotation from the American Congress at Philadelphia, 1774.

with safety. Such an offer from such a power will be attributed to magnanimity. But the concessions of the weak are the concessions of fear. When such a one is disarmed, he is wholly at the mercy of his superior; and he loses forever that time and those chances which, as they happen to all men, are the strength and resources of all inferior power.

The capital leading questions on which you must this day decide are these two: First, whether you ought to concede; and secondly, what your concession ought to be. On the first of these questions we have gained (as I have just taken the liberty of observing to you) some ground. But I am sensible that a good deal more is still to be done. Indeed, Sir, to enable us to determine both on the one and the other of these great questions with a firm and precise judgment, I think it may be necessary to consider distinctly the true nature and the peculiar circumstances of the object which we have before us: because, after all our struggle, whether we will or not, we must govern America according to that nature and to those circumstances, and not according to our own imaginations, not according to abstract ideas of right, by no means according to mere general theories of government, the resort to which appears to me, in our present situation, no better than arrant trifling. I shall therefore endeavor, with your leave, to lay before you some of the most material of these circumstances in as full and as clear a manner as I am able to state them.

The first thing that we have to consider with regard to the nature of the object is the number of people in the colonies. I have taken for some years a good deal of pains on that point. I can by no calculation justify myself in placing the number below two millions of inhabitants of our own European blood and color—besides at least 500,000 others, who form no inconsiderable part of the strength and opulence of the whole.[3] This, Sir, is, I believe, about the true number. There is no occasion to exaggerate, where plain truth is of so much weight and importance. But whether I put the present numbers too high or too low is a matter of little moment. Such is the strength with which population shoots in that part of the world, that, state the numbers as high as we will, whilst the dispute continues, the exaggeration ends. Whilst we are discussing any given magnitude, they are grown to it. Whilst we spend our time in deliberating on the mode of governing two millions, we shall find we have millions more to manage. Your children do not grow faster from infancy to manhood than they spread from families to communities, and from villages to nations.

I put this consideration of the present and the growing numbers in the front of our deliberation, because, Sir, this consideration will

3. Burke's calculations are correct. Between 1750 and 1775 the population of the colonies had doubled.

make it evident to a blunter discernment than yours, that no partial, narrow, contracted, pinched, occasional system will be at all suitable to such an object. It will show you that it is not to be considered as one of those *minima*[4] which are out of the eye and consideration of the law—not a paltry excrescence of the state—not a mean dependant, who may be neglected with little damage and provoked with little danger. It will prove that some degree of care and caution is required in the handling such an object; it will show that you ought not, in reason, to trifle with so large a mass of the interests and feelings of the human race. You could at no time do so without guilt; and be assured you will not be able to do it long with impunity.

But the population of this country, the great and growing population, though a very important consideration, will lose much of its weight, if not combined with other circumstances. The commerce of your colonies is out of all proportion beyond the numbers of the people. * * *

* * * At the beginning of the century some of these colonies imported corn[5] from the mother country. For some time past the Old World has been fed from the New. The scarcity which you have felt would have been a desolating famine, if this child of your old age, with a true filial piety, with a Roman charity,[6] had not put the full breast of its youthful exuberance to the mouth of its exhausted parent.

As to the wealth which the colonies have drawn from the sea by their fisheries, you had all that matter fully opened at your bar.[7] You surely thought those acquisitions of value, for they seemed even to excite your envy; and yet the spirit by which that enterprising employment has been exercised ought rather, in my opinion, to have raised your esteem and admiration. And pray, Sir, what in the world is equal to it? Pass by the other parts, and look at the manner in which the people of New England have of late carried on the whale-fishery. Whilst we follow them among the tumbling mountains of ice, and behold them penetrating into the deepest frozen recesses of Hudson's Bay and Davis's Straits, whilst we are looking for them beneath the arctic circle, we hear that they have pierced into the opposite region of polar cold, that they are at the antipodes, and engaged under the frozen serpent of the South.[8] Falkland Island, which seemed too remote and romantic an object

4. Matters too small for legal consideration.
5. Grain.
6. The ancient story of Xanthippe, who fed her father Cimon from her own breast, was conventionally called the Roman Charity.
7. Before Parliament. A rail, or bar, separated the part of the House where Members met from the part non-members could visit.
8. The Hydrus, a constellation visible from Antarctica.

for the grasp of national ambition,[9] is but a stage and resting-place in the progress of their victorious industry. Nor is the equinoctial heat more discouraging to them than the accumulated winter of both the poles. We know, that, whilst some of them draw the line and strike the harpoon on the coast of Africa, others run the longitude,[1] and pursue their gigantic game along the coast of Brazil. No sea but what is vexed by their fisheries. No climate that is not witness to their toils. Neither the perseverance of Holland, nor the activity of France, nor the dexterous and firm sagacity of English enterprise, ever carried this most perilous mode of hardy industry to the extent to which it has been pushed by this recent people—a people who are still, as it were, but in the gristle, and not yet hardened into the bone of manhood. When I contemplate these things—when I know that the colonies in general owe little or nothing to any care of ours, and that they are not squeezed into this happy form by the constraints of watchful and suspicious government, but that, through a wise and salutary neglect, a generous nature has been suffered to take her own way to perfection—when I reflect upon these effects, when I see how profitable they have been to us, I feel all the pride of power sink, and all presumption in the wisdom of human contrivances melt and die away within me—my rigor relents—I pardon something to the spirit of liberty.

I am sensible, Sir, that all which I have asserted in my detail is admitted in the gross, but that quite a different conclusion is drawn from it. America, gentlemen say, is a noble object—it is an object well worth fighting for. Certainly it is, if fighting a people be the best way of gaining them. Gentlemen in this respect will be led to their choice of means by their complexions[2] and their habits. Those who understand the military art will of course have some predilection for it. Those who wield the thunder of the state may have more confidence in the efficacy of arms. But I confess, possibly for want of this knowledge, my opinion is much more in favor of prudent management than of force—considering force not as an odious, but a feeble instrument, for preserving a people so numerous, so active, so growing, so spirited as this, in a profitable and subordinate connection with us.

First, Sir, permit me to observe, that the use of force alone is but *temporary*. It may subdue for a moment; but it does not remove the necessity of subduing again: and a nation is not governed which is perpetually to be conquered.

My next objection is its *uncertainty*. Terror is not always the effect of force, and an armament is not a victory. If you do not suc-

9. In 1771, war with Spain had been narrowly averted over the issue of England's right to the Falkland Islands (off the coast of Argentina).

1. Sail south.

2. Temperaments or modes of life.

ceed, you are without resource: for, conciliation failing, force remains; but, force failing, no further hope of reconciliation is left. Power and authority are sometimes bought by kindness; but they can never be begged as alms by an impoverished and defeated violence.

A further objection to force is, that you *impair the object* by your very endeavors to preserve it. The thing you fought for is not the thing which you recover, but depreciated, sunk, wasted, and consumed in the contest. Nothing less will content me than *whole America*. I do not choose to consume its strength along with our own; because in all parts it is the British strength that I consume. I do not choose to be caught by a foreign enemy at the end of this exhausting conflict, and still less in the midst of it. I may escape, but I can make no insurance against such an event. Let me add, that I do not choose wholly to break the American spirit; because it is the spirit that has made the country.

Lastly, we have no sort of *experience* in favor of force as an instrument in the rule of our colonies. Their growth and their utility has been owing to methods altogether different. Our ancient indulgence has been said to be pursued to a fault. It may be so; but we know, if feeling is evidence, that our fault was more tolerable than our attempt to mend it, and our sin far more salutary than our penitence.

These, Sir, are my reasons for not entertaining that high opinion of untried force by which many gentlemen, for whose sentiments in other particulars I have great respect, seem to be so greatly captivated. But there is still behind a third consideration concerning this object, which serves to determine my opinion on the sort of policy which ought to be pursued in the management of America, even more than its population and its commerce: I mean its *temper and character*.

In this character of the Americans a love of freedom is the predominating feature which marks and distinguishes the whole: and as an ardent is always a jealous affection, your colonies become suspicious, restive, and untractable, whenever they see the least attempt to wrest from them by force, or shuffle from them by chicane, what they think the only advantage worth living for. This fierce spirit of liberty is stronger in the English colonies, probably, than in any other people of the earth, and this from a great variety of powerful causes; which, to understand the true temper of their minds, and the direction which this spirit takes, it will not be amiss to lay open somewhat more largely.

First, the people of the colonies are descendants of Englishmen. England, Sir, is a nation which still, I hope, respects, and formerly adored, her freedom. The colonists emigrated from you when this part of your character was most predominant; and they took this bias and direction the moment they parted from your hands. They are therefore not only devoted to liberty, but to liberty according to English ideas and on English principles. Abstract liberty, like other mere abstractions, is not to be found. Liberty inheres in some sensible object;[3] and every nation has formed to itself some favorite point, which by way of eminence becomes the criterion of their happiness. It happened, you know, Sir, that the great contests for freedom in this country were from the earliest times chiefly upon the question of taxing. Most of the contests in the ancient commonwealths turned primarily on the right of election of magistrates, or on the balance among the several orders of the state. The question of money was not with them so immediate. But in England it was otherwise. On this point of taxes the ablest pens and most eloquent tongues have been exercised, the greatest spirits have acted and suffered. In order to give the fullest satisfaction concerning the importance of this point, it was not only necessary for those who in argument defended the excellence of the English Constitution to insist on this privilege of granting money as a dry point of fact, and to prove that the right had been acknowledged in ancient parchments and blind usages to reside in a certain body called a House of Commons: they went much further: they attempted to prove, and they succeeded, that in theory it ought to be so, from the particular nature of a House of Commons, as an immediate representative of the people, whether the old records had delivered this oracle or not. They took infinite pains to inculcate, as a fundamental principle, that in all monarchies the people must in effect themselves, mediately or immediately, possess the power of granting their own money, or no shadow of liberty could subsist. The colonies draw from you, as with their life-blood, these ideas and principles. Their love of liberty, as with you, fixed and attached on this specific point of taxing. Liberty might be safe or might be endangered in twenty other particulars without their being much pleased or alarmed. Here they felt its pulse; and as they found that beat, they thought themselves sick or sound. I do not say whether they were right or wrong in applying your general arguments to their own case. It is not easy, indeed, to make a monopoly of theorems and corollaries. The fact is, that they did thus apply those general arguments; and your mode of governing them, whether through lenity or indolence, through wisdom or mistake, confirmed them in the imagination, that they, as well as you, had an interest in these common principles.

They were further confirmed in this pleasing error by the form of their provincial legislative assemblies. Their governments are popular[4] in an high degree: some are merely[5] popular; in all, the popular representative is the most weighty; and this share of the

3. Object perceived by the senses.
4. Elected by the people. In 18th-century England the masses could not vote.
5. Entirely.

people in their ordinary government never fails to inspire them with lofty sentiments, and with a strong aversion from whatever tends to deprive them of their chief importance.

If anything were wanting to this necessary operation of the form of government, religion would have given it a complete effect. Religion, always a principle of energy, in this new people is no way worn out or impaired; and their mode of professing it is also one main cause of this free spirit. The people are Protestants, and of that kind which is the most adverse to all implicit submission of mind and opinion. This is a persuasion not only favorable to liberty, but built upon it. I do not think, Sir, that the reason of this averseness in the dissenting churches from all that looks like absolute government is so much to be sought in their religious tenets as in their history. Every one knows that the Roman Catholic religion is at least coeval with most of the governments where it prevails, that it has generally gone hand in hand with them, and received a great favor and every kind of support from authority. The Church of England, too, was formed from her cradle under the nursing care of regular government. But the dissenting interests have sprung up in direct opposition to all the ordinary powers of the world, and could justify that opposition only on a strong claim to natural liberty. Their very existence depended on the powerful and unremitted assertion of that claim. All Protestantism, even the most cold and passive, is a sort of dissent. But the religion most prevalent in our northern colonies is a refinement on the principle of resistance: it is the dissidence of dissent, and the protestantism of the Protestant religion. This religion, under a variety of denominations agreeing in nothing but in the communion of the spirit of liberty, is predominant in most of the northern provinces, where the Church of England, notwithstanding its legal rights, is in reality no more than a sort of private sect, not composing, most probably, the tenth of the people. The colonists left England when this spirit was high, and in the emigrants was the highest of all; and even that stream of foreigners which has been constantly flowing into these colonies has, for the greatest part, been composed of dissenters from the establishments of their several countries, and have brought with them a temper and character far from alien to that of the people with whom they mixed.

Sir, I can perceive, by their manner, that some gentlemen object to the latitude of this description, because in the southern colonies the Church of England forms a large body, and has a regular establishment. It is certainly true. There is, however, a circumstance attending these colonies, which, in my opinion, fully counterbalances this difference, and makes the spirit of liberty still more high and haughty than in those to the northward. It is, that in Virginia and the Carolinas they have a vast multitude of slaves. Where this is the case in any part of the world, those who are free are by far the most proud and jealous of their freedom. Freedom is to them not only an enjoyment, but a kind of rank and privilege. Not seeing there, that freedom, as in countries where it is a common blessing, and as broad and general as the air, may be united with much abject toil, with great misery, with all the exterior of servitude, liberty looks, amongst them, like something that is more noble and liberal. I do not mean, Sir, to commend the superior morality of this sentiment, which has at least as much pride as virtue in it,[6] but I cannot alter the nature of man. The fact is so; and these people of the southern colonies are much more strongly, and with an higher and more stubborn spirit, attached to liberty, than those to the northward. Such were all the ancient commonwealths; such were our Gothic ancestors; such in our days were the Poles;[7] and such will be all masters of slaves, who are not slaves themselves. In such a people, the haughtiness of domination combines with the spirit of freedom, fortifies it, and renders it invincible.

Permit me, Sir, to add another circumstance in our colonies, which contributes no mean part towards the growth and effect of this untractable spirit: I mean their education. In no country, perhaps, in the world is the law so general a study. * * * This study renders men acute, inquisitive, dexterous, prompt in attack, ready in defense, full of resources. In other countries, the people, more simple, and of a less mercurial cast, judge of an ill principle in government only by an actual grievance; here they anticipate the evil, and judge the pressure of the grievance by the badness of the principle. They augur misgovernment at a distance, and snuff the approach of tyranny in every tainted breeze.

The last cause of this disobedient spirit in the colonies is hardly less powerful than the rest, as it is not merely moral, but laid deep in the natural constitution of things. Three thousand miles of ocean lie between you and them. No contrivance can prevent the effect of this distance in weakening government. Seas roll, and months pass, between the order and the execution; and the want of a speedy explanation of a single point is enough to defeat an whole system. You have, indeed, winged ministers of vengeance, who carry your bolts in their pounces[8] to the remotest verge of the sea: but there a power steps in, that limits the arrogance of raging passions and furious elements, and says, "So far shalt thou go, and no farther."[9] Who are you, that should fret and rage, and bite the chains of Nature? Nothing worse happens to you than does to all nations

6. Burke himself passionately opposed slavery. In 1765 he had argued against American representation in Parliament on the ground that slave-owners had no right to make laws for free men.

7. Slavery was abolished in Poland in 1772.

8. 1) Talons; 2) gunpowder. Burke compares the ships of the British navy to Milton's avenging angels. Cf. Blake's *America*.

9. A reference to King Canute, who could not command the sea.

who have extensive empire; and it happens in all the forms into which empire can be thrown. In large bodies, the circulation of power must be less vigorous at the extremities. Nature has said it. The Turk cannot govern Egypt, and Arabia, and Kurdistan, as he governs Thrace; nor has he the same dominion in Crimea and Algiers which he has at Brusa and Smyrna. Despotism itself is obliged to truck and huckster. The Sultan gets such obedience as he can. He governs with a loose rein, that he may govern at all; and the whole of the force and vigor of his authority in his center is derived from a prudent relaxation in all his borders. Spain, in her provinces, is perhaps not so well obeyed as you are in yours. She complies, too; she submits; she watches times. This is the immutable condition, the eternal law, of extensive and detached empire.

Then, Sir, from these six capital sources, of descent, of form of government, of religion in the northern provinces, of manners in the southern, of education, of the remoteness of situation from the first mover of government—from all these causes a fierce spirit of liberty has grown up. It has grown with the growth of the people in your colonies, and increased with the increase of their wealth: a spirit, that, unhappily meeting with an exercise of power in England, which, however lawful, is not reconcilable to any ideas of liberty, much less with theirs, has kindled this flame that is ready to consume us.

I do not mean to commend either the spirit in this excess, or the moral causes which produce it. Perhaps a more smooth and accommodating spirit of freedom in them would be more acceptable to us. Perhaps ideas of liberty might be desired more reconcilable with an arbitrary and boundless authority. Perhaps we might wish the colonists to be persuaded that their liberty is more secure when held in trust for them by us (as their guardians during a perpetual minority) than with any part of it in their own hands. But the question is not, whether their spirit deserves praise or blame—what, in the name of God, shall we do with it? You have before you the object, such as it is—with all its glories, with all its imperfections on its head. You see the magnitude, the importance, the temper, the habits, the disorders. By all these considerations we are strongly urged to determine something concerning it. We are called upon to fix some rule and line for our future conduct, which may give a little stability to our politics, and prevent the return of such unhappy deliberations as the present. Every such return will bring the matter before us in a still more untractable form. For what astonishing and incredible things have we not seen already! What monsters have not been generated from this unnatural contention! Whilst every principle of authority and resistance has been pushed, upon both sides, as far as it would go, there is nothing so solid and certain, either in reasoning or in practice, that has not been shaken.

Until very lately, all authority in America seemed to be nothing but an emanation from yours. Even the popular part of the colony constitution derived all its activity, and its first vital movement, from the pleasure of the crown. We thought, Sir, that the utmost which the discontented colonists could do was to disturb authority; we never dreamt they could of themselves supply it, knowing in general what an operose business it is to establish a government absolutely new. But having, for our purposes in this contention, resolved that none but an obedient assembly should sit, the humors[1] of the people there, finding all passage through the legal channel stopped, with great violence broke out another way. Some provinces have tried their experiment, as we have tried ours; and theirs has succeeded. They have formed a government sufficient for its purposes, without the bustle of a revolution, or the troublesome formality of an election. Evident necessity and tacit consent have done the business in an instant. So well they have done it, that Lord Dunmore (the account is among the fragments on your table) tells you that the new institution is infinitely better obeyed than the ancient government ever was in its most fortunate periods. Obedience is what makes government, and not the names by which it is called: not the name of Governor, as formerly, or Committee, as at present. This new government has originated directly from the people, and was not transmitted through any of the ordinary artificial media[2] of a positive constitution. It was not a manufacture ready formed, and transmitted to them in that condition from England. The evil arising from hence is this: that the colonists having once found the possibility of enjoying the advantages of order in the midst of a struggle for liberty, such struggles will not henceforward seem so terrible to the settled and sober part of mankind as they had appeared before the trial.

Pursuing the same plan of punishing by the denial of the exercise of government to still greater lengths, we wholly abrogated the ancient government of Massachusetts. We were confident that the first feeling, if not the very prospect of anarchy, would instantly enforce a complete submission. The experiment was tried. A new, strange, unexpected face of things appeared. Anarchy is found tolerable. A vast province has now subsisted, and subsisted in a considerable degree of health and vigor, for near a twelvemonth, without governor, without public council, without judges, without executive magistrates. How long it will continue in this state, or what may arise out of this unheard-of situation, how can the wisest of us conjecture? Our late experience has taught us that many of those fundamental principles formerly believed infallible are either not of the importance they were imagined to be, or that we have not at all adverted to some other far more important and far more powerful

1. Dispositions.

2. Means.

principles which entirely overrule those we had considered as omnipotent. I am much against any further experiments which tend to put to the proof any more of these allowed opinions which contribute so much to the public tranquillity. In effect, we suffer as much at home by this loosening of all ties, and this concussion[3] of all established opinions, as we do abroad. For, in order to prove that the Americans have no right to their liberties, we are every day endeavoring to subvert the maxims which preserve the whole spirit of our own. To prove that the Americans ought not to be free, we are obliged to depreciate the value of freedom itself; and we never seem to gain a paltry advantage over them in debate, without attacking some of those principles, or deriding some of those feelings, for which our ancestors have shed their blood.

* * *

Sir, I think you must perceive that I am resolved this day to have nothing at all to do with the question of the right of taxation. Some gentlemen startle,[4]—but it is true: I put it totally out of the question. It is less than nothing in my consideration. I do not indeed wonder, nor will you, Sir, that gentlemen of profound learning are fond of displaying it on this profound subject. But my consideration is narrow, confined, and wholly limited to the policy of the question. I do not examine whether the giving away a man's money be a power excepted and reserved out of the general trust of government, and how far all mankind, in all forms of polity, are entitled to an exercise of that right by the charter of Nature,—or whether, on the contrary, a right of taxation is necessarily involved in the general principle of legislation, and inseparable from the ordinary supreme power. These are deep questions, where great names militate against each other, where reason is perplexed, and an appeal to authorities only thickens the confusion: for high and reverend authorities lift up their heads on both sides, and there is no sure footing in the middle. This point is the *great Serbonian bog, betwixt Damiata and Mount Casius old, where armies whole have sunk.*[5] I do not intend to be overwhelmed in that bog, though in such respectable company. The question with me is, not whether you have a right to render your people miserable, but whether it is not your interest to make them happy. It is not what a lawyer tells me I *may* do, but what humanity, reason, and justice tell me I ought to do. Is a politic act the worse for being a generous one? Is no concession proper, but that which is made from your want of right to keep what you grant? Or does it lessen the grace or dignity of relaxing in the exercise of an odious claim, because you have your evidence-room full of titles, and your magazines stuffed with arms

3. Violent shaking.
4. Are startled.
5. *Paradise Lost* II. 592–94.

to enforce them? What signify all those titles and all those arms? Of what avail are they, when the reason of the thing tells me that the assertion of my title is the loss of my suit, and that I could do nothing but wound myself by the use of my own weapons?

Such is steadfastly my opinion of the absolute necessity of keeping up the concord of this empire by a unity of spirit, though in a diversity of operations, that, if I were sure the colonists had, at their leaving this country, sealed a regular compact of servitude, that they had solemnly abjured all the rights of citizens, that they had made a vow to renounce all ideas of liberty for them and their posterity to all generations, yet I should hold myself obliged to conform to the temper I found universally prevalent in my own day, and to govern two million of men, impatient of servitude, on the principles of freedom. I am not determining a point of law; I am restoring tranquillity; and the general character and situation of a people must determine what sort of government is fitted for them. That point nothing else can or ought to determine.

My idea, therefore, without considering whether we yield as matter of right or grant as matter of favor, is, *to admit the people of our colonies into an interest in the Constitution,* and, by recording that admission in the journals of Parliament, to give them as strong an assurance as the nature of the thing will admit that we mean forever to adhere to that solemn declaration of systematic indulgence.

* * *

I do not know that the colonies have, in any general way, or in any cool hour, gone much beyond the demand of immunity in relation to taxes. It is not fair to judge of the temper or dispositions of any man or any set of men, when they are composed and at rest, from their conduct or their expressions in a state of disturbance and irritation. It is, besides, a very great mistake to imagine that mankind follow up practically any speculative principle, either of government or of freedom, as far as it will go in argument and logical illation. We Englishmen stop very short of the principles upon which we support any given part of our Constitution, or even the whole of it together. I could easily, if I had not already tired you, give you very striking and convincing instances of it. This is nothing but what is natural and proper. All government, indeed every human benefit and enjoyment, every virtue and every prudent act, is founded on compromise and barter. We balance inconveniences; we give and take; we remit some rights, that we may enjoy others; and we choose rather to be happy citizens than subtle disputants. As we must give away some natural liberty, to enjoy civil advantages, so we must sacrifice some civil liberties, for the advantages to be derived from the communion and fellowship of a great empire. But, in all fair dealings, the thing bought must bear some proportion to the purchase paid.[6] None will barter away the immediate jewel of his soul. Though a great house is apt to make slaves haughty, yet it is purchasing a part of the artificial importance of a great empire too dear, to pay for it all essential rights, and all the intrinsic dignity of human nature. None of us who would not risk his life rather than fall under a government purely arbitrary. But although there are some amongst us who think our Constitution wants many improvements to make it a complete system of liberty, perhaps none who are of that opinion would think it right to aim at such improvement by disturbing his country and risking everything that is dear to him. In every arduous enterprise, we consider what we are to lose, as well as what we are to gain; and the more and better stake of liberty every people possess, the less they will hazard in a vain attempt to make it more. These are *the cords of man*. Man acts from adequate motives relative to his interest, and not on metaphysical speculations. Aristotle, the great master of reasoning, cautions us, and with great weight and propriety, against this species of delusive geometrical accuracy in moral arguments, as the most fallacious of all sophistry.[7]

The Americans will have no interest contrary to the grandeur and glory of England, when they are not oppressed by the weight of it; and they will rather be inclined to respect the acts of a superintending legislature, when they see them from the acts of that power which is itself the security, not the rival, of their secondary importance. In this assurance my mind most perfectly acquiesces, and I confess I feel not the least alarm from the discontents which are to arise from putting people at their ease; nor do I apprehend the destruction of this empire from giving, by an act of free grace and indulgence, to two millions of my fellow-citizens some share of those rights upon which I have always been taught to value myself.

* * * My hold of the colonies is in the close affection which grows from common names, from kindred blood, from similar privileges, and equal protection. These are ties which, though light as air, are as strong as links of iron. Let the colonies always keep the idea of their civil rights associated with your government,—they will cling and grapple to you, and no force under heaven will be of power to tear them from their allegiance. But let it be once understood that your government may be one thing and their privileges another, that these two things may exist without any mutual relation—the cement is gone, the cohesion is loosened, and everything hastens to decay and dissolution. As long as you have the wisdom to keep the sovereign authority of this country as the sanctuary of liberty, the sacred temple consecrated to our common faith, wherever the chosen race and sons of England worship freedom, they will

6. The money paid for purchase.

7. See the *Ethics*, Book I.

turn their faces towards you. The more they multiply, the more friends you will have; the more ardently they love liberty, the more perfect will be their obedience. Slavery they can have anywhere. It is a weed that grows in every soil. They may have it from Spain, they may have it from Prussia. But, until you become lost to all feeling of your true interest and your natural dignity, freedom they can have from none but you. This is the commodity of price, of which you have the monopoly. This is the true Act of Navigation, which binds to you the commerce of the colonies, and through them secures to you the wealth of the world. Deny them this participation of freedom, and you break that sole bond which originally made, and must still preserve, the unity of the empire. Do not entertain so weak an imagination as that your registers and your bonds, your affidavits and your sufferances, your cockets[8] and your clearances, are what form the great securities of your commerce. Do not dream that your letters of office, and your instructions, and your suspending clauses are the things that hold together the great contexture of this mysterious whole. These things do not make your government. Dead instruments, passive tools as they are, it is the spirit of the English communion that gives all their life and efficacy to them. It is the spirit of the English Constitution, which, infused through the mighty mass, pervades, feeds, unites, invigorates, vivifies every part of the empire, even down to the minutest member.

Is it not the same virtue which does everything for us here in England? Do you imagine, then, that it is the Land-Tax Act which raises your revenue? that it is the annual vote in the Committee of Supply which gives you your army? or that it is the Mutiny Bill which inspires it with bravery and discipline? No! surely, no! It is the love of the people; it is their attachment to their government, from the sense of the deep stake they have in such a glorious institution, which gives you your army and your navy, and infuses into both that liberal obedience without which your army would be a base rabble and your navy nothing but rotten timber.

All this, I know well enough, will sound wild and chimerical to the profane herd of those vulgar and mechanical politicians who have no place among us: a sort of people who think that nothing exists but what is gross and material—and who, therefore, far from being qualified to be directors of the great movement of empire, are not fit to turn a wheel in the machine. But to men truly initiated and rightly taught, these ruling and master principles, which in the opinion of such men as I have mentioned have no substantial existence, are in truth everything, and all in all. Magnanimity in politics is not seldom the truest wisdom; and a great empire and little minds go ill together. If we are conscious of our situation, and glow

8. A custom-house seal or sealed document. All the nouns of this clause are drawn from bureaucratic routine.

with zeal to fill our place as becomes our station and ourselves, we ought to auspicate all our public proceedings on America with the old warning of the Church, *Sursum corda!*[9] We ought to elevate our minds to the greatness of that trust to which the order of Providence has called us. By adverting to the dignity of this high calling our ancestors have turned a savage wilderness into a glorious empire, and have made the most extensive and the only honorable conquests, not by destroying, but by promoting the wealth, the number, the happiness of the human race. Let us get an American revenue as we have got an American empire. English privileges have made it all that it is; English privileges alone will make it all it can be.[1]

1775

9. Lift up your hearts.

1. Burke's resolutions were defeated by a vote of 270 to 78. A month later fighting broke out at Concord and Lexington.

The Poetry of Sensibility

JAMES THOMSON

(1700–1748)

Perhaps it is significant that Thomson, the first and most popular nature poet of the century, did not see London until he was 25 years old. He grew up in the picturesque border country of Roxboroughshire in Scotland and came to London in 1725, bringing with him, in addition to a memory well stored with images of the external world, the earliest version of his descriptive poem *Winter* in 405 lines of blank verse. Published in 1726, it soon became popular. Thomson went on to publish *Summer* (1727), *Spring* (1728), and *Autumn* in the first collected edition of *The Seasons* (1730), to which he added the *Hymn to the Seasons*. During the next sixteen years, because of constant revisions and additions, the poem grew in length to 5,541 lines. The continued popularity of *The Seasons* is easily demonstrated: between 1730 and 1800 it was printed fifty times; and it continued in favor with readers well into the Romantic period.

Thomson is sometimes said to have been a premature "Romantic," but this is hardly the case, for if he was, then so were all his numerous readers in the second quarter of the century. The success that *Winter* enjoyed shows plainly that the poem was not ahead of its time. It should not be hard to believe that 18th-century readers had as catholic tastes as modern readers have: readers who liked *Winter*, also, in that very year (1726), liked Pope's *Odyssey* and Swift's *Gulliver's Travels*. Thomson's blank verse pleased those who were pleased by Pope's couplets; Swift's simple colloquial language charmed those who were also charmed by Thomson's Latinized diction and not infrequent Miltonic tricks of style. The readers who thrilled to the heroic world of Homer and admired the wit of Swift could also enjoy Thomson's poetry of sentiment and visual imagery. In short, it is plain that when in the Preface to the second edition of *Winter* (1726), Thomson called for a poetry dealing with subjects "such as are fair, useful, and magnificent, [executed] so as at once to please, instruct, surprise, and astonish," he spoke not so much *to* as *for* the common reader.

The Seasons set the fashion for the poetry of natural description. Generations of readers learned to look at the external world through Thomson's eyes and with the emotions which he had taught them to feel. The *eye* dominates the literature of external nature during the 18th century as the *imagination* was to do in the poetry of Wordsworth. And Thomson amazed his readers by his capacity to see: the general effects of light and cloud and foliage or the particular image of a leaf tossed in the gale or the slender feet of a robin or the delicate film of ice at the edge of a brook. As the poem grew, it became an *omnium gatherum* of contemporary ideas and interests: natural history; ideas about the nature of man and society, primitive and civilized; the conception of created nature as a source of religious experience, as an object of religious veneration, as a continuing revelation of the Deity himself.

From The Seasons

From *Autumn*

[EVENING AND NIGHT][1]

The western sun withdraws the shortened day;
And humid evening, gliding o'er the sky,
In her chill progress, to the ground condensed
The vapors throws. Where creeping waters ooze,
Where marshes stagnate, and where rivers wind,
Cluster the rolling fogs, and swim along
The dusky-mantled lawn. Meanwhile the moon,
Full-orbed and breaking through the scattered clouds,
Shows her broad visage in the crimsoned east.
Turned to the sun direct, her spotted disk
(Where mountains rise, umbrageous dales descend,
And caverns deep, as optic tube[2] descries)
A smaller earth, gives all his blaze again,
Void of its flame, and sheds a softer day.
Now through the passing cloud she seems to stoop,
Now up the pure cerulean rides sublime.
Wide the pale deluge[3] floats, and streaming mild
O'er the skied[4] mountain to the shadowy vale,
While rocks and floods reflect the quivering gleam,
The whole air whitens with a boundless tide
Of silver radiance trembling round the world.
  But when, half blotted from the sky, her light
Fainting, permits the starry fires to burn
With keener luster through the depth of heaven;
Or quite extinct her deadened orb appears,
And scarce appears, of sickly beamless white;
Oft in this season, silent from the north
A blaze of meteors[5] shoots—ensweeping first
The lower skies, they all at once converge
High to the crown[6] of heaven, and, all at once

1. This passage, like many in *The Seasons*, went through extensive revisions. The opening lines on the harvest moon shining through fog (1082–1102) originally belonged to *Winter*; the descriptions of the aurora borealis (1108–37) and wildfire (1150–64) first appeared in *Summer*. Scientific and visionary, divine and human perspectives are contrasted; and join together in an intricate harmony.

2. Telescope. Observation of the moon had revealed shadows ("umbrageous dales"), hence an irregular surface.

3. I.e., the moonlight.

4. I.e., seeming to touch the sky.

5. Not meteors as we think of them, but the aurora borealis or Northern Lights (multicolored, streaming pulses of light in the upper atmosphere).

6. The corona or central ring of the aurora.

Relapsing quick, as quickly reascend,
And mix and thwart,[7] extinguish and renew,
All ether coursing[8] in a maze of light.
From look to look, contagious through the crowd,
The panic runs, and into wondrous shapes
The appearance throws—armies in meet[9] array,
Thronged with aerial spears and steeds of fire;
Till, the long lines of full-extended war
In bleeding fight commixed, the sanguine flood
Rolls a broad slaughter o'er the plains of heaven.
As thus they scan the visionary scene,
On all sides swells the superstitious din,
Incontinent; and busy frenzy talks
Of blood and battle; cities overturned,
And late at night in swallowing earthquake sunk,
Or hideous wrapped in fierce ascending flame;
Of sallow famine, inundation, storm;
Of pestilence, and every great distress;
Empires subversed,[1] when ruling fate has struck
The unalterable hour; even nature's self
Is deemed to totter on the brink of time.
Not so the man of philosophic eye
And inspect sage:[2] the waving brightness he
Curious surveys, inquisitive to know
The causes and materials, yet unfixed,[3]
Of this appearance beautiful and new.

Now black and deep the night begins to fall,
A shade immense! Sunk in the quenching gloom,
Magnificent and vast, are heaven and earth.
Order confounded lies, all beauty void,
Distinction lost, and gay variety
One universal blot—such the fair power
Of light to kindle and create the whole.
Drear is the state of the benighted wretch
Who then bewildered wanders through the dark
Full of pale fancies and chimeras[4] huge;
Nor visited by one directive ray
From cottage streaming or from airy hall.
Perhaps, impatient as he stumbles on,
Struck from the root of slimy rushes, blue
The wildfire[5] scatters round, or, gathered, trails
A length of flame deceitful o'er the moss;
Whither decoyed by the fantastic blaze,

7. Cross.
8. Running through all the upper sky.
9. Fitting. The aurora had often been associated with cosmic battles, both in literature and popular superstition.
1. Overthrown.
2. Wise examination.
3. Unexplained by science.
4. Imaginary monsters.
5. Will-o'-the-wisp or *ignis fatuus*, a flitting phosphorescent light thought to kindle from the gas of decaying swamp grasses ("slimy rushes").

Now lost and now renewed, he sinks absorbed,
Rider and horse, amid the miry gulf—
While still, from day to day, his pining wife
And plantive children his return await,
In wild conjecture lost. At other times,
Sent by the better genius of the night,
Innoxious,[6] gleaming on the horse's mane,
The meteor sits, and shows the narrow path
That winding leads through pits of death, or else
Instructs him how to take the dangerous ford.

The lengthened night elapsed, the morning shines
Serene, in all her dewy beauty bright,
Unfolding fair the last autumnal day.
And now the mounting sun dispels the fog;
The rigid hoarfrost melts before his beam;
And, hung on every spray, on every blade
Of grass, the myriad dewdrops twinkle round.

1730

An Ode on Aeolus's Harp[1]

Ethereal race, inhabitants of air,[2]
Who hymn your God amid the secret grove,
Ye unseen beings, to my harp repair,
And raise majestic strains, or melt in love.

Those tender notes, how kindly they upbraid!
With what soft woe they thrill the lover's heart!
Sure from the hand of some unhappy maid
Who died of love these sweet complainings part.

But hark! that strain was of a graver tone,
On the deep strings his hand some hermit throws;
Or he, the sacred Bard,[3] who sat alone
In the drear waste and wept his people's woes.

Such was the song which Zion's children sung
When by Euphrates' stream they made their plaint;
And to such sadly solemn notes are strung
Angelic harps to soothe a dying saint.

6. Harmless. "The meteor" is the *ignis lambens* or St. Elmo's Fire, a halo of light that shines on the tips of certain objects during electrical storms.

1. The Aeolian Harp, or Harp of the Wind God, a stringed instrument that plays chords when touched by a current of air, was popularized by Thomson's friend James Oswald, the "Scotch Orpheus." Thomson described its effects in *The Castle of Indolence*, and the spontaneous, naturally inspired music of the harp later became a favorite Romantic theme (see Coleridge's *The Eolian Harp* and *Dejection: An Ode*).

2. The winds, whose god is Aeolus.

3. The prophet Jeremiah is supposed to have written the book of Lamentations, in which the Jewish people ("Zion's children") mourn their captivity in Babylon ("by Euphrates' stream").

Methinks I hear the full celestial choir,
  Through Heaven's high dome their awful anthem raise;
Now chanting clear, and now they all conspire
  To swell the lofty hymn from praise to praise.

Let me, ye wandering spirits of the wind,
  Who, as wild fancy prompts you, touch the string,
Smit with your theme, be in your chorus joined,
  For till you cease my muse forgets to sing.

1748

THOMAS GRAY

(1716–1771)

The man who wrote the English poem best known and most loved by unsophisticated readers was oddly enough a scholarly recluse who lived the quiet life of a university professor in the stagnant atmosphere of mid-18th-century Cambridge, where toward the end of his life he held the Professorship of Modern History without feeling called upon to give a single lecture. He was educated at Eton College, where he made his first intimate friends—Richard West, Thomas Ashton, and Horace Walpole, the son of the Prime Minister. After a little over four years at Cambridge he left without a degree in order to make the grand tour of France and Italy as the guest of his friend Walpole. Their different interests caused a quarrel, and after two years of traveling Gray returned to England alone. Fortunately, a few years later the quarrel was made up, and Walpole, who was Gray's ardent admirer, was able to play an important role in making his friend's poems public. The death of West in 1742 was a depressing event for Gray, who, still alienated from Walpole, felt keenly the loss of this gifted and congenial friend. The Eton *Ode* and possibly some of the stanzas of the *Elegy Written in a Country Churchyard* are associated with this melancholy event.

After 1742 Gray returned to Cambridge, pursuing his studies and indulging his tastes. He was learned in the classics and modern literatures as well as history, and his curiosity led him to explore the then little-known fields of pre-Elizabethan poetry and old Welsh and Norse literature. He was a connoisseur of painting and music, a careful and scientific observer of nature, and an enthusiastic admirer of wild and picturesque landscape. He seldom left Cambridge except to read in the newly opened British Museum or to go in the summer to the Lake District or to Scotland in search of the sublime and beautiful in nature. He wrote little, for he worked slowly and carefully, fastidiously seeking perfection of form and phrase. His early poetry is a carefully impersonal expression of his own somewhat melancholy temperament: the solitary, brooding speaker of the Eton *Ode* and the *Elegy* is a dramatic projection of Gray and of his personal dilemma: though colored by his own feeling, the poems are not confessions, but public reflections on death, the sorrows of life, and the mysteries of human destiny. The later poems—the two grandiloquent Pindaric odes, *The Progress of Poesy* and *The Bard* (1757), and the translations from Welsh and Norse poetry—are accomplished literary exercises. The living Gray is to be sought in his correspondence, where his genial humor, shy affection, and wide intellectual interests are revealed in some of the most delightful letters of the age that made letter writing an art.

Though Gray never knew Collins and had no association with the Wartons in the 1740's, he shared their interests and many of their tastes. The melancholy of Collins' *Ode to Evening* is that of the opening stanzas of the *Elegy*, and in both poems mood and landscape mutually sustain each other. Like Collins Gray wrote both greater and lesser odes (see title note to Dryden's *Ode to * * * Mistress Anne Killigrew*, above), creating a body of lyric poetry entirely characteristic of the midcentury. Without laying aside his veneration for Dryden, whom he considered his master in versification, he could share his contemporaries' enthusiasm for Spenser and Milton—especially the Milton of the minor poems, whom he often echoes. His evocation of the image of the bard, in the second of the Pindaric odes, is very much in the manner of the period. Gray wrote often in a highly artificial diction and a distorted word order (see the first four stanzas of the Eton *Ode*, for example), for he held that "the language of the age is never the language of poetry," a heresy that earned him the harsh criticism of Wordsworth in his Preface to *Lyrical Ballads*.

The *Elegy* stands alone in Gray's work: it is his one poem that belongs to mankind and that is known in many translations. It speaks to our common humanity through an art so subtle that one can know the poem for many years before becoming aware of its scores of echoes from other poems, its author's sure control of language, imagery, cadence, and his subtle modulation of style and tone. If to express the universal is to be classic, then the *Elegy* is one of our true classics. Dr. Johnson, no friend of Gray's poetry in general, long ago said the final word on this aspect of the poem:

> The Churchyard abounds with images which find a mirror in every mind, and with sentiments to which every bosom returns an echo. The four stanzas beginning "Yet even these bones" are to me original: I have never seen the notions in any other place; yet he that reads them here, persuades himself that he has always felt them. Had Gray written often thus, it had been in vain to blame, and useless to praise him.

Ode on a Distant Prospect of Eton College

Ἄνθρωπος· ἱκανὴ πρόφασις εἰς τὸ δυστυχεῖν.[1]
MENANDER

Ye distant spires, ye antique towers,
  That crown the watery glade,
Where grateful Science[2] still adores
  Her Henry's holy shade;[3]
And ye, that from the stately brow

1. "I am a man: sufficient reason for being miserable."
2. Learning.
3. Henry VI founded Eton in 1440.

Of Windsor's heights the expanse below
  Of grove, of lawn, of mead survey,
Whose turf, whose shade, whose flowers among
Wanders the hoary Thames along
  His silver-winding way.

Ah happy hills, ah pleasing shade,
  Ah fields beloved in vain,
Where once my careless childhood strayed,
  A stranger yet to pain!
I feel the gales, that from ye blow,
A momentary bliss bestow,
  As waving fresh their gladsome wing,
My weary soul they seem to soothe,
And, redolent of joy and youth,
  To breathe a second spring.

Say, Father Thames, for thou hast seen
  Full many a sprightly race
Disporting on thy margent green
  The paths of pleasure trace,
Who foremost now delight to cleave
With pliant arm thy glassy wave?
  The captive linnet which enthrall?[4]
What idle progeny succeed[5]
To chase the rolling circle's speed,
  Or urge the flying ball?

While some on earnest business bent
  Their murmuring labors ply
'Gainst graver hours, that bring constraint
  To sweeten liberty:
Some bold adventurers disdain
The limits of their little reign,
  And unknown regions dare descry:
Still as they run they look behind,
They hear a voice in every wind,
  And snatch a fearful joy.

Gay hope is theirs by fancy fed,
  Less pleasing when possessed;
The tear forgot as soon as shed,
  The sunshine of the breast:
Theirs buxom health of rosy hue,
Wild wit, invention ever new,
  And lively cheer of vigor born;
The thoughtless day, the easy night,

4. Make prisoner.
5. I.e., follow in succession Gray's generation; "rolling circle": a hoop.

The spirits pure, the slumbers light,
  That fly the approach of morn.'

Alas, regardless of their doom,
  The little victims play!
No sense have they of ills to come,
  Nor care beyond today.
Yet see how all around 'em wait
The ministers of human fate,
  And black Misfortune's baleful train!
Ah, show them where in ambush stand
To seize their prey the murderous band!
  Ah, tell them they are men!

These shall the fury Passions tear,
  The vultures of the mind,
Disdainful Anger, pallid Fear,
  And Shame that skulks behind;
Or pining Love shall waste their youth,
Or Jealousy with rankling tooth,
  That inly gnaws the secret heart,
And Envy wan, and faded Care,
Grim-visaged comfortless Despair,
  And Sorrow's piercing dart.

Ambition this shall tempt to rise,
  Then whirl the wretch from high,
To bitter Scorn a sacrifice,
  And grinning Infamy.
The stings of Falsehood those shall try,
And hard Unkindness' altered eye,
  That mocks the tear it forced to flow;
And keen Remorse with blood defiled,
And moody Madness laughing wild
  Amid severest woe.

Lo, in the vale of years beneath
  A grisly troop are seen,
The painful family of Death,
  More hideous than their queen:
This racks the joints, this fires the veins,
That every laboring sinew strains,
  Those in the deeper vitals rage:
Lo, Poverty, to fill the band,
That numbs the soul with icy hand,
  And slow-consuming Age.

To each his sufferings: all are men,
  Condemned alike to groan;
The tender for another's pain,
  The unfeeling for his own.

Yet ah! why should they know their fate?
Since sorrow never comes too late,
  And happiness too swiftly flies.
Thought would destroy their paradise.
No more; where ignorance is bliss,
  'Tis folly to be wise.

1742 1747

Ode On the Death of a Favorite Cat[1]

DROWNED IN A TUB OF GOLDFISHES

'Twas on a lofty vase's side,
Where China's gayest art had dyed
  The azure flowers that blow;[2]
Demurest of the tabby kind,
The pensive Selima reclined,
  Gazed on the lake below.

Her conscious tail her joy declared;
The fair round face, the snowy beard,
  The velvet of her paws,
Her coat, that with the tortoise vies,
Her ears of jet, and emerald eyes,
  She saw; and purred applause.

Still had she gazed; but 'midst the tide
Two angel forms were seen to glide,
  The genii of the stream:
Their scaly armor's Tyrian[3] hue
Through richest purple to the view
  Betrayed a golden gleam.

The hapless nymph with wonder saw:
A whisker first and then a claw,
  With many an ardent wish,
She stretched in vain to reach the prize.
What female heart can gold despise?
  What cat's averse to fish?

Presumptuous maid! with looks intent
Again she stretched, again she bent,
  Nor knew the gulf between.
(Malignant Fate sat by and smiled)
The slippery verge her feet beguiled,
  She tumbled headlong in.

1. Selima, one of Horace Walpole's cats, had recently drowned in a china cistern. Gray wrote this memorial at Walpole's request.
2. Bloom.
3. Purple.

Eight times emerging from the flood
She mewed to every watery god,
  Some speedy aid to send.
No dolphin came, no nereid[4] stirred:
Nor cruel Tom, nor Susan heard.
  A favorite has no friend!

From hence, ye beauties, undeceived,
Know, one false step is ne'er retrieved,
  And be with caution bold.
Not all that tempts your wandering eyes
And heedless hearts is lawful prize;
  Nor all that glisters gold.

1747 1748

Hymn to Adversity

Ζῆνα . . .
τὸν φρονεῖν βροτοὺς ὁδώ—
σαντα, τῶ πάθει μάθος
θεντα κυρίως ἔχειν.
AESCHYLUS, *Agamemnon* 174–78[1]

Daughter of Jove, relentless power,
Thou tamer of the human breast,
Whose iron scourge and torturing hour
The bad affright, afflict the best!
Bound in thy adamantine chain,
The proud are taught to taste of pain,
And purple tyrants vainly groan
With pangs unfelt before, unpitied and alone.

When first thy sire to send on earth
Virtue, his darling child, designed,
To thee he gave the heavenly birth,
And bade to form her infant mind.
Stern rugged nurse! thy rigid lore
With patience many a year she bore:
What sorrow was, thou bad'st her know,
And from her own she learned to melt at others' woe.

Scared at thy frown terrific, fly
Self-pleasing Folly's idle brood,
Wild Laughter, Noise, and thoughtless Joy,
And leave us leisure to be good.
Light they disperse, and with them go
The summer friend, the flattering foe;
By vain Prosperity received,
To her they vow their truth, and are again believed.

4. Sea nymph. "Tom" and "Susan" are servants' names.

1. "Zeus, who leads mortals to understanding, who has established as a fixed ordinance that wisdom comes by suffering."

Wisdom, in sable garb arrayed,
Immersed in rapturous thought profound,
And Melancholy, silent maid
With leaden eye, that loves the ground,
Still on thy solemn steps attend:
Warm Charity, the general friend,
With Justice, to herself severe,
And Pity, dropping soft the sadly-pleasing tear.

Oh, gently on thy suppliant's head,
Dread Goddess, lay thy chastening hand!
Not in thy Gorgon[2] terrors clad,
Nor circled with the vengeful band
(As by the impious thou art seen)
With thundering voice, and threatening mien,
With screaming Horror's funeral cry,
Despair, and fell Disease, and ghastly Poverty.

Thy form benign, O Goddess, wear,
Thy milder influence impart,
Thy philosophic train be there
To soften, not to wound, my heart,
The generous spark extinct revive,
Teach me to love and to forgive,
Exact my own defects to scan,
What others are, to feel, and know myself a man.

1742 1753

Elegy Written in a Country Churchyard

The curfew tolls the knell of parting day,
  The lowing herd wind slowly o'er the lea,
The plowman homeward plods his weary way,
  And leaves the world to darkness and to me.

Now fades the glimmering landscape on the sight,
  And all the air a solemn stillness holds,
Save where the beetle wheels his droning flight,
  And drowsy tinklings lull the distant folds;

Save that from yonder ivy-mantled tower
  The moping owl does to the moon complain
Of such, as wandering near her secret bower,
  Molest her ancient solitary reign.

Beneath those rugged elms, that yew tree's shade,
  Where heaves the turf in many a moldering heap,

2. The Gorgons were monsters with snaky locks, one glance of whose eyes turned men to stones; the "vengeful band": the Furies.

Each in his narrow cell forever laid,
The rude[1] forefathers of the hamlet sleep.

The breezy call of incense-breathing Morn,
The swallow twittering from the straw-built shed,
The cock's shrill clarion, or the echoing horn,[2]
No more shall rouse them from their lowly bed.

For them no more the blazing hearth shall burn,
Or busy housewife ply her evening care;
No children run to lisp their sire's return,
Or climb his knees the envied kiss to share.

Oft did the harvest to their sickle yield,
Their furrow oft the stubborn glebe[3] has broke;
How jocund did they drive their team afield!
How bowed the woods beneath their sturdy stroke!

Let not Ambition mock their useful toil,
Their homely joys, and destiny obscure;
Nor Grandeur hear with a disdainful smile
The short and simple annals of the poor.

The boast of heraldry,[4] the pomp of power,
And all that beauty, all that wealth e'er gave,
Awaits alike the inevitable hour.
The paths of glory lead but to the grave.

Nor you, ye proud, impute to these the fault,
If Memory o'er their tomb no trophies[5] raise,
Where through the long-drawn aisle and fretted[6] vault
The pealing anthem swells the note of praise.

Can storied urn[7] or animated bust
Back to its mansion call the fleeting breath?
Can Honor's voice provoke[8] the silent dust,
Or Flattery soothe the dull cold ear of Death?

Perhaps in this neglected spot is laid
Some heart once pregnant with celestial fire;
Hands that the rod of empire might have swayed,
Or waked to ecstasy the living lyre.

But Knowledge to their eyes her ample page
Rich with the spoils of time did ne'er unroll;
Chill Penury repressed their noble rage,
And froze the genial current of the soul.

Full many a gem of purest ray serene,
The dark unfathomed caves of ocean bear:

1. Untaught.
2. The hunter's horn.
3. Soil, turf.
4. Noble birth.
5. An ornamental or symbolic group of figures depicting the achievements of the dead man.
6. Decorated with intersecting lines in relief.
7. A funeral urn with an epitaph inscribed on it; "animated": lifelike.
8. Call forth.

Full many a flower is born to blush unseen,
  And waste its sweetness on the desert air.

Some village Hampden,[9] that with dauntless breast
  The little tyrant of his fields withstood;
Some mute inglorious Milton here may rest,
  Some Cromwell guiltless of his country's blood.

The applause of listening senates to command,
  The threats of pain and ruin to despise,
To scatter plenty o'er a smiling land,
  And read their history in a nation's eyes,

Their lot forbade: nor circumscribed alone
  Their growing virtues, but their crimes confined;
Forbade to wade through slaughter to a throne,
  And shut the gates of mercy on mankind,

The struggling pangs of conscious truth to hide,
  To quench the blushes of ingenuous shame,
Or heap the shrine of Luxury and Pride
  With incense kindled at the Muse's flame.

Far from the madding crowd's ignoble strife,
  Their sober wishes never learned to stray;
Along the cool sequestered vale of life
  They kept the noiseless tenor of their way.

Yet even these bones from insult to protect
  Some frail memorial still erected nigh,
With uncouth rhymes and shapeless sculpture decked,[1]
  Implores the passing tribute of a sigh.

Their name, their years, spelt by the unlettered Muse,
  The place of fame and elegy supply:
And many a holy text around she strews,
  That teach the rustic moralist to die.

For who to dumb Forgetfulness a prey,
  This pleasing anxious being e'er resigned,
Left the warm precincts of the cheerful day,
  Nor cast one longing lingering look behind?

On some fond breast the parting soul relies,
  Some pious drops the closing eye requires;
Even from the tomb the voice of Nature cries,
  Even in our ashes live their wonted fires.

For thee, who mindful of the unhonored dead
  Dost in these lines their artless tale relate;
If chance, by lonely contemplation led,
  Some kindred spirit shall inquire thy fate,

9. John Hampden (1594–1643), who, both as a private citizen and as a Member of Parliament, zealously defended the rights of the people against the autocratic policies of Charles I. A gallant soldier, he was mortally wounded in a skirmish near Oxford.

1. Cf. "the storied urn or animated bust" dedicated inside the church to "the proud" (line 41).

Haply some hoary-headed swain may say,
"Oft have we seen him at the peep of dawn
Brushing with hasty steps the dews away
To meet the sun upon the upland lawn.

"There at the foot of yonder nodding beech
That wreathes its old fantastic roots so high,
His listless length at noontide would he stretch,
And pore upon the brook that babbles by.

"Hard by yon wood, now smiling as in scorn,
Muttering his wayward fancies he would rove,
Now drooping, woeful wan, like one forlorn,
Or crazed with care, or crossed in hopeless love.

"One morn I missed him on the customed hill,
Along the heath and near his favorite tree;
Another came; nor yet beside the rill,
Nor up the lawn, nor at the wood was he;

"The next with dirges due in sad array
Slow through the churchway path we saw him borne.
Approach and read (for thou canst read) the lay,
Graved on the stone beneath yon aged thorn."

THE EPITAPH

Here rests his head upon the lap of Earth
A youth to Fortune and to Fame unknown.
Fair Science[2] *frowned not on his humble birth,*
And Melancholy marked him for her own.

Large was his bounty, and his soul sincere,
Heaven did a recompense as largely send:
He gave to Misery all he had, a tear,
He gained from Heaven ('twas all he wished) a friend.

No farther seek his merits to disclose,
Or draw his frailties from their dread abode
(There they alike in trembling hope repose),
The bosom of his Father and his God.

ca. 1742–50 1751

2. Learning.

WILLIAM COLLINS

(1721–1759)

William Collins was born at Chichester and was educated at Winchester and Oxford. Coming up to London from the university, he tried to establish himself as an author, but he was given rather to planning than to writing books. He came to know Dr. Johnson, who recorded in the *Lives of the Poets* that he had once "delighted to converse with him." In 1746 Collins published his *Odes on Several Descriptive and Allegorical Subjects,* his part in an undertaking, with his friend Joseph Warton, to create a "new," more lyrical and imaginative poetry than the generation of Dryden and Pope had done. Collins' *Odes,* as their title suggests, are addressed to personified abstractions (Fear, Pity, the Passions) which are rendered vividly and pictorially, in expressive attitudes and allegorical groups. The volume was not much liked; Gray, however, commented favorably on it in private; and the enterprising publisher Robert Dodsley included three of the simpler odes in the first volume of his *Miscellany* (1748). The more ambitious odes were thought to be obscure and too "visionary." In form they represent a new version of the "great" or Cowleian ode (see title note to Dryden's *Anne Killigrew,* above), for Collins gave them at least an approximate regularity of structure, since in several of them strophe and antistrophe are more or less symmetrical. Curiously, however, he departed from the normal Pindaric order of parts by placing epodes between strophes and antistrophes.

Inheriting some money, the poet traveled for a while, but fits of depression gradually deepened into total debility. He spent his last years in Chichester, forgotten by all but a small circle of loyal friends. As the century progressed he gained in reputation, although the tendency to find signs of incipient madness in his vividly realized imaginary figures is regrettable. The Romantics admired his poems and felt akin to him as they did to Thomas Chatterton and Robert Burns. The *Ode to Evening,* which combines a chaste and cool classicism with a delicate feeling for landscape and mood, is one of the delightful poems of the century.

Ode Written in the Beginning of the Year 1746

How sleep the brave[1] who sink to rest
By all their country's wishes blest!
When Spring, with dewy fingers cold,
Returns to deck their hallowed mold,
She there shall dress a sweeter sod
Than Fancy's feet have ever trod.

By fairy hands their knell is rung,
By forms unseen their dirge is sung;
There Honor comes, a pilgrim gray,
To bless the turf that wraps their clay,
And Freedom shall awhile repair,
To dwell a weeping hermit there!

1746

1. Collins is presumably thinking of those who lost their lives defending England in 1745, when the Scotch Jacobites, led by Bonnie Prince Charlie, penetrated to within 127 miles of London.

Ode on the Poetical Character[1]

STROPHE

As once, if not with light regard,
I read aright that gifted bard
(Him whose school above the rest
His loveliest Elfin Queen has blest),[2]
One, only one, unrivaled fair,
Might hope the magic girdle wear,
At solemn tourney hung on high,
The wish of each love-darting eye;[3]
Lo! to each other nymph in turn applied,
  As if, in air unseen, some hovering hand,
Some chaste and angel-friend to virgin-fame,
  With whispered spell had burst the starting band,
It left unblest her loathed dishonored side;
  Happier, hopeless fair, if never
  Her baffled hand with vain endeavor
Had touched that fatal zone to her denied!
Young Fancy thus, to me divinest name,
  To whom, prepared and bathed in Heaven
  The cest of amplest power is given:
  To few the godlike gift assigns,
  To gird their blest, prophetic loins,
And gaze her visions wild, and feel unmixed her flame!

EPODE

The band, as fairy legends say,
Was wove on that creating day,
When He,[4] who called with thought to birth
Yon tented sky, this laughing earth,

1. This ode, long held in comparative disregard, has more recently been elevated in critical estimation, for it is now seen as an early, dramatic engagement with one of the central concerns of the Romantic Age—the origin and role of the creative imagination and, indeed, of the poet himself. "It is an allegory," A. S. P. Woodhouse tells us, "whose subject is the *creative imagination* and the poet's passionate desire for its power."

In the strophe an analogy is drawn between the *cestus* or girdle of Venus, which only the chaste can wear, and the cest of Fancy, or the creative imagination. In the epode the act of the creation of the world is presented as an act of the divine imagination.

What is especially new, such critics as Harold Bloom and Northrop Frye suggest, is Collins' implication, in the epode, that "a poet is born from the quasi-sexual union of God and imagination," or Fancy (lines 30–40). Such a reading animates the personifications in a way that we do not encounter again until the work of William Blake. The poet's creative act is divine, analogous to the creation of the world, and he is born of the divine act.

In the antistrophe, Milton is regarded as the type of poet true enough to wear the girdle of Fancy. Collins pictures himself pursuing the "guiding steps" (line 71) of Milton, as of Spenser (in the strophe)—both poet-prophets. He retreats from the elegant school of Waller (and, by implication, that of Pope, as well)—"In vain" (line 72), however, for he lives in an age of sensibility.

2. Edmund Spenser.

3. *Faerie Queene* IV.v tells of the contest of many beautiful ladies for the girdle of Venus.

4. God, on the day of creation.

And dressed with springs, and forests tall,
And poured the main engirting all,
Long by the loved Enthusiast[5] wooed,
Himself in some diviner mood,
Retiring, sate with her alone,
And placed her on his sapphire throne;
The whiles, the vaulted shrine around,
Seraphic wires were heard to sound,
Now sublimest triumph swelling,
Now on love and mercy dwelling;
And she, from out the veiling cloud,
Breathed her magic notes aloud:
And thou, thou rich-haired Youth of Morn,[6]
And all thy subject life was born!
The dangerous Passions kept aloof,
Far from the sainted growing woof:
But near it sate ecstatic Wonder,
Listening the deep applauding thunder:
And Truth, in sunny vest arrayed,
By whose the tarsel's[7] eyes were made;
All the shadowy tribes of Mind,
In braided dance their murmurs joined,
And all the bright uncounted Powers
Who feed on Heaven's ambrosial flowers.
Where is the bard, whose soul can now
Its high presuming hopes avow?
Where he who thinks, with rapture blind,
This hallow'd work[8] for him designed?

ANTISTROPHE

High on some cliff, to Heaven up-piled,
Of rude access, of prospect wild,
Where, tangled round the jealous steep,
Strange shades o'erbrow the valleys deep,
And holy Genii guard the rock,
Its glooms embrown, its springs unlock,
While on its rich ambitious head,
An Eden, like his[9] own, lies spread:
I view that oak, the fancied glades among,
By which as Milton lay, his evening ear,
From many a cloud that dropped ethereal dew,
Nigh sphered in Heaven its native strains could hear:
On which that ancient trump he reached was hung;
  Thither oft, his glory greeting,
  From Waller's[1] myrtle shades retreating,
With many a vow from Hope's aspiring tongue,
My trembling feet his guiding steps pursue;
  In vain—such bliss to one alone,[2]

5. I.e., Fancy.
6. Apollo, god of the sun and of poetry, associated with the poet himself.
7. The falcon's.
8. The girdle of Fancy.
9. Milton's.
1. Edmund Waller (1606–87). The myrtle is the symbol of love poetry, Waller's poetry is thought of as trivial compared to Milton's grandeur.
2. Milton.

Of all the sons of soul was known,
And Heaven, and Fancy, kindred powers,
Have now o'erturned the inspiring bowers,
Or curtained close such scene from every future view.

1746

Ode to Evening[1]

If aught of oaten stop, or pastoral song,
May hope, chaste Eve, to soothe thy modest ear,
Like thy own solemn springs,
Thy springs and dying gales,
O nymph reserved, while now the bright-haired sun
Sits in yon western tent, whose cloudy skirts,
With brede[2] ethereal wove,
O'erhang his wavy bed:
Now air is hushed, save where the weak-eyed bat,
With short shrill shrieks flits by on leathern wing,
Or where the beetle winds
His small but sullen horn,
As oft he rises 'midst the twilight path,
Against the pilgrim borne in heedless hum:
Now teach me, maid composed,
To breathe some softened strain,
Whose numbers, stealing through thy darkening vale,
May not unseemly with its stillness suit,
As, musing slow, I hail
Thy genial loved return!
For when thy folding-star[3] arising shows
His paly circlet, at his warning lamp
The fragrant Hours, and elves
Who slept in flowers the day,
And many a nymph who wreaths her brows with sedge,
And sheds the freshening dew, and, lovelier still,
The pensive Pleasures sweet,
Prepare thy shadowy car.
Then lead, calm vot'ress, where some sheety lake
Cheers the lone heath, or some time-hallowed pile
Or upland fallows gray
Reflect its last cool gleam.
But when chill blustering winds, or driving rain,
Forbid my willing feet, be mine the hut
That from the mountain's side
Views wilds, and swelling floods,

1. Collins borrowed the metrical structure and the rhymeless lines of this ode from Milton's translation of Horace, *Odes* I.5 (1673). The text printed here is based on the revised version, published in Dodsley's *Miscellany* (1748).
2. Embroidery.
3. The evening star, which signals the hour for herding the sheep into the sheepfold.

And hamlets brown, and dim-discovered spires,
And hears their simple bell, and marks o'er all
  Thy dewy fingers draw
  The gradual dusky veil.
While Spring shall pour his showers, as oft he wont,
And bathe thy breathing tresses, meekest Eve;
  While Summer loves to sport
  Beneath thy lingering light;
While sallow Autumn fills thy lap with leaves;
Or Winter, yelling through the troublous air,
  Affrights thy shrinking train,
  And rudely rends thy robes;
So long, sure-found beneath the sylvan shed,
Shall Fancy, Friendship, Science, rose-lipped Health,
  Thy gentlest influence own,
  And hymn thy favorite name!

1746, 1748

Ode on the Death of Mr. Thomson[1]

1

In yonder grave a Druid[2] lies
  Where slowly winds the stealing wave!
The year's best sweets shall duteous rise
  To deck its poet's sylvan grave![3]

2

In yon deep bed of whispering reeds
  His airy harp[4] shall now be laid,
That he, whose heart in sorrow bleeds,
  May love through life the soothing shade.

3

Then maids and youths shall linger here,
  And while its sounds at distance swell,
Shall sadly seem in pity's ear
  To hear the woodland pilgrim's knell.

4

Remembrance oft shall haunt the shore
  When Thames in summer wreaths is dressed,
And oft suspend the dashing oar
  To bid his gentle spirit rest!

1. James Thomson died in 1748 and was buried in the parish church of Richmond, a village on the Thames near London. Collins memorializes the poet, who was his friend, both by imagining a visit to his grave and by filling his own verses with reminiscences of Thomson's poetry.
2. I.e., Thomson himself. The Druids, an order of priests in ancient Britain, had been idealized by Thomson as poet-philosophers of nature. Druidic circles like Stonehenge remain standing in England; and Collins's *Ode* itself might be said to have a circular form (the same beginning and ending).
3. The year pays tribute to Thomson because he wrote *The Seasons*.
4. See Thomson's *Ode on Aeolus's Harp*, above.

5

And oft as ease and health retire
  To breezy lawn or forest deep,
The friend shall view yon whitening spire,[5]
  And mid the varied landscape weep.

6

But thou, who own'st that earthy bed,
  Ah! what will every dirge avail?
Or tears, which love and pity shed
  That mourn beneath the gliding sail!

7

Yet lives there one, whose heedless eye
  Shall scorn thy pale shrine glimmering near?
With him, sweet bard, may fancy die,
  And joy desert the blooming year.

8

But thou, lorn stream, whose sullen tide
  No sedge-crowned sisters[6] now attend,
Now waft me from the green hill's side,
  Whose cold turf hides the buried friend!

9

And see, the fairy valleys fade,
  Dun night has veiled the solemn view!
—Yet once again, dear parted shade,
  Meek nature's child, again adieu!

10

The genial meads,[7] assigned to bless
  Thy life, shall mourn thy early doom,
Their hinds[8] and shepherd girls shall dress
  With simple hands thy rural tomb.

11

Long, long, thy stone and pointed[9] clay
  Shall melt the musing Briton's eyes,
"O! vales and wild woods," shall he say,
  "In yonder grave your Druid lies!"

1749

5. Richmond Church, seen from the water.
6. Naiads or river nymphs, supposed to have deserted the Thames since Thomson's death.
7. Fostering meadows.
8. Peasants.
9. I.e., pointed out to visitors.

CHRISTOPHER SMART

(1722–1771)

In 1756 Christopher Smart, who had won prizes at Pembroke College, Cambridge, as a scholar and poet, and was known in London as a wit and *bon vivant,* was seized by religious mania: "a preternatural excitement to prayer," according to Mrs. Thrale, "which he held it as a duty not to control or repress." If Smart had been content to pray in private, his life might have ended as happily as it began; but unfortunately for him, he insisted on kneeling down in the streets, in parks, in assembly rooms. He became a public nuisance, and the public took its revenge. For most of the next seven years Smart was confined, first in St. Luke's hospital, then in a private madhouse. Here, severed from his wife, his children, and his friends, he began to write a bold new sort of poetry: vivid, concise, abrupt, syntactically daring. Few of his contemporaries noticed it. After Smart's release from the madhouse (1763) he fell into debt—he had always been profligate—and his *Translation of the Psalms of David* (1765) *and Hymns for the Amusement of Children* (1770) were almost completely ignored. He died, forgotten, in a debtor's prison. But in the 19th century his reputation revived, and since the publication of *Jubilate Agno* in 1939 his poems have become newly famous.

The work of Smart's great period (1759–1765) resembles nothing else in English. Its sources lie partly in the classics, especially Horace (whom Smart translated both in verse and prose), but far more in the Old Testament. Above all, the spirit that informs the poetry is praise and celebration, an intense vision of the divine presence shining through ordinary life. Smart believed that the world had been called into being solely to pay homage to its Maker; the function of man, and the poet most of all, was to be "minister of praise at large," to provide a voice of prayer for the whole creation. Thus the hero of his masterpiece, *A Song to David* (1763), is not only King but Psalmist of Israel, the inspired man and poet, possessed by the spirit of the Lord, who orders and blesses everything that exists. Such poets, like the first Creator, strive to construct a microcosm in which every element—word, image, and number—fits into one grand design. The stanzas of *A Song to David* are organized in groups of three and seven (divine numbers), and separate stanzas are devoted to each of David's twelve virtues, the seven days of creation, the ten commandments, the four seasons, the five senses, and finally, in a mighty climax, the five degrees in which David excelled. To critics who accused the poem of incoherence, Smart properly replied that its chief fault, if any, was "the *exact* REGULARITY and METHOD with which it is conducted." At its best, however, the poem transports its reader into that state of adoration "Where ask is have, where seek is find, / Where knock is open wide," a state of true prayer that acknowledges no division between desire and its fulfillment or God and his worshipper.

From Jubilate Agno[1]

[*My Cat Jeoffry*]

For I will consider my Cat Jeoffry.
For he is the servant of the Living God duly and daily serving him.
For at the first glance of the glory of God in the East[2] he worships in his way.
For is this done by wreathing his body seven times round with elegant quickness.
For then he leaps up to catch the musk, wch is the blessing of God upon his prayer.
For he rolls upon prank[3] to work it in.
For having done duty and received blessing he begins to consider himself.
For this he performs in ten degrees.
For first he looks upon his fore-paws to see if they are clean.
For secondly he kicks up behind to clear away there.
For thirdly he works it upon stretch with the fore-paws extended.
For fourthly he sharpens his paws by wood.
For fifthly he washes himself.
For Sixthly he rolls upon wash.
For Seventhly he fleas himself, that he may not be interrupted upon the beat.
For Eighthly he rubs himself against a post.
For Ninthly he looks up for his instructions.
For Tenthly he goes in quest of food.
For having consider'd God and himself he will consider his neighbor.
For if he meets another cat he will kiss her in kindness.
For when he takes his prey he plays with it to give it a chance.
For one mouse in seven escapes by his dallying.
For when his day's work is done his business more properly begins.
For he keeps the Lord's watch in the night against the adversary.
For he counteracts the powers of darkness by his electrical skin & glaring eyes.
For he counteracts the Devil, who is death, by brisking about the life.

1. *Jubilate Agno* (*Rejoice in the Lamb*), written a few lines at a time during Smart's confinement in a madhouse from 1759 to 1763, is (1) a record of his daily life and thoughts; (2) the notebook of a scholar, crammed with puns and obscure learning, which sets out elaborate correspondences between the world of the Bible and modern England; (3) a personal Testament or book of worship, antiphonally arranged in lines beginning alternately with *Let* and *For*, which seeks to join the material and spiritual universes in one unending prayer. It has also come to be recognized, since first published in 1939 by W. F. Stead, as a poem—a poem unique in English for its ecstatic sense of the presence of the Divine Spirit. The most famous passage describes Smart's cat Jeoffry, his only companion during the years of confinement: "For I am possessed of a cat, surpassing in beauty, from whom I take occasion to bless Almighty God." At once a real cat, lovingly observed in all its frisks, and visible evidence of the providential plan, Jeoffry celebrates the Maker, as all things do, in his very being.
2. The sunrise.
3. Prankishly.

For in his morning orisons he loves the sun and the sun loves him.
For he is of the tribe of Tiger.
For the Cherub Cat is a term of the Angel Tiger.[4]
For he has the subtlety and hissing of a serpent, which in goodness he suppresses.
For he will not do destruction if he is well-fed, neither will he spit without provocation.
For he purrs in thankfulness, when God tells him he's a good Cat.
For he is an instrument for the children to learn benevolence upon.
For every house is incomplete without him & a blessing is lacking in the spirit.
For the Lord commanded Moses concerning the cats at the departure of the Children of Israel from Egypt.[5]
For every family had one cat at least in the bag.
For the English Cats are the best in Europe.
For he is the cleanest in the use of his fore-paws of any quadrupede.
For the dexterity of his defence is an instance of the love of God to him exceedingly.
For he is the quickest to his mark of any creature.
For he is tenacious of his point.
For he is a mixture of gravity and waggery.
For he knows that God is his Saviour.
For there is nothing sweeter than his peace when at rest.
For there is nothing brisker than his life when in motion.
For he is of the Lord's poor and so indeed is he called by benevolence perpetually—Poor Jeoffry! poor Jeoffry! the rat has bit thy throat.
For I bless the name of the Lord Jesus that Jeoffry is better.
For the divine spirit comes about his body to sustain it in complete cat.
For his tongue is exceeding pure so that it has in purity what it wants in music.
For he is docile and can learn certain things.
For he can set up with gravity which is patience upon approbation.
For he can fetch and carry, which is patience in employment.
For he can jump over a stick which is patience upon proof positive.
For he can spraggle upon waggle[6] at the word of command.
For he can jump from an eminence into his master's bosom.
For he can catch the cork and toss it again.
For he is hated by the hypocrite and miser.
For the former is afraid of detection.
For the latter refuses the charge.
For he camels his back to bear the first notion of business.
For he is good to think on, if a man would express himself neatly.
For he made a great figure in Egypt for his signal services.
For he killed the Icneumon-rat very pernicious by land.[7]

4. As a cherub is a small angel, so a cat is a small tiger.
5. No cats are mentioned in the Bible.
6. He can sprawl when his master waggles a finger or stick.
7. The Ichneumon, which resembles a weasel, was venerated and domesticated by the ancient Egyptians.

For his ears are so acute that they sting again.
For from this proceeds the passing quickness of his attention.
For by stroking of him I have found out electricity.
For I perceived God's light about him both wax and fire.
For the Electrical fire is the spiritual substance, which God sends from heaven to sustain the bodies both of man and beast.
For God has blessed him in the variety of his movements.
For, though he cannot fly, he is an excellent clamberer.
For his motions upon the face of the earth are more than any other quadrupede.
For he can tread to all the measures upon the music.
For he can swim for life.
For he can creep.

1759–63 1939

A Song to David[1]

David the son of Jesse said, and the man who was raised up on high, the anointed of the God of Jacob, and the sweet psalmist of Israel, said, "The Spirit of the Lord spake by me, and His Word was in my tongue."

—II SAMUEL xxiii.1,2

I

O Thou, that sit'st upon a throne,
With harp of high majestic tone, *[Invocation]*
To praise the King of kings;
And voice of heaven-ascending swell,
Which, while its deeper notes excel,
Clear, as a clarion, rings:

II

To bless each valley, grove and coast,
And charm the cherubs to the post
Of gratitude in throngs;
To keep the days on Zion's mount,
And send the year to his account,
With dances and with songs:

III

O Servant of God's holiest charge,
The minister of praise at large,
Which thou may'st now receive;
From thy blessed mansion hail and hear,
From topmost eminence appear
To this the wreath I weave.[1a]

1. For the first edition of the poem, Smart supplied a summary of the argument, here reprinted as a running series of marginal glosses.

1a. David, a king among men, and now an angel in heaven, serves the King of kings by praising him with music, which keeps the world below in tune; Smart, in turn, sings the praises of David, the poet's intermediary with God.

IV

Great, valiant, pious, good, and clean,
Sublime, contemplative, serene,
Strong, constant, pleasant, wise!
Bright effluence of exceeding grace;
Best man!—the swiftness and the race,
The peril, and the prize!

[The excellence and luster of David's character in twelve points of view;]

V

Great—from the luster of his crown,
From Samuel's horn[2] and God's renown,
Which is the people's voice;
For all the host from rear to van,
Applauded and embraced the man—
The man of God's own choice.

[proved from the history of his life]

VI

Valiant—the word, and up he rose—
The fight—he triumphed o'er the foes,
Whom God's just laws abhor;
And armed in gallant faith he took
Against the boaster,[3] from the brook,
The weapons of the war.

VII

Pious—magnificent and grand;
'Twas he the famous temple planned:
(The seraph in his soul)[4]
Foremost to give the Lord his dues,
Foremost to bless the welcome news,
And foremost to condole.

VIII

Good—from Jehudah's genuine vein,
From God's best nature good in grain,[5]
His aspect and his heart;
To pity, to forgive, to save,
Witness En-gedi's conscious cave,
And Shimei's blunted dart.[6]

IX

Clean—if perpetual prayer be pure,
And love, which could itself inure
To fasting and to fear—
Clean in his gestures, hands, and feet,
To smite the lyre, the dance complete,
To play the sword and spear.

2. "Then Samuel took the horn of oil, and anointed him in the midst of his brethren: and the spirit of the Lord came upon David from that day forward" (I Samuel xvi.13).
3. Goliath, whom David slew with a stone from the brook.
4. According to I Chronicles xxviii, David's plan for the Temple in Jerusalem was directly inspired by the Lord's "seraph" within him.
5. In background and substance; Judah, David's tribe, was the tribe of kings.
6. In a cave in En-gedi, David spared Saul, who had wanted to kill him (I Samuel xxiv); though Shimei threw stones and curses at him, David later refused to take his life (II Samuel xvi, xix).

X

Sublime—invention ever young,
Of vast conception, towering tongue
To God the eternal theme;
Notes from yon exaltations caught,
Unrivaled royalty of thought,
O'er meaner strains supreme.

XI

Contemplative—on God to fix
His musings, and above the six
The sabbath-day he blessed;
'Twas then his thoughts self-conquest pruned,
And heavenly melancholy tuned,
To bless and bear the rest.

XII

Serene—to sow the seeds of peace,
Remembering, when he watched the fleece,
How sweetly Kidron purled[7]—
To further knowledge, silence vice,
And plant perpetual paradise
When God had calmed the world.

XIII

Strong—in the Lord, who could defy
Satan, and all his powers that lie
In sempiternal night;
And hell, and horror, and despair
Were as the lion and the bear[8]
To his undaunted might.

XIV

Constant—in love to God The Truth,
Age, manhood, infancy, and youth—
To Jonathan his friend
Constant, beyond the verge of death;
And Ziba, and Mephibosheth,
His endless fame attend.[9]

XV

Pleasant—and various as the year;
Man, soul, and angel, without peer,
Priest, champion, sage and boy;
In armor, or in ephod[1] clad,
His pomp, his piety was glad;
Majestic was his joy.

XVI

Wise—in recovery from his fall,
Whence rose his eminence o'er all,

7. As a young man, David kept his father's sheep near Kidron, a brook that borders the district of Jerusalem; later, fleeing his own son Absalom, he crossed Kidron into the wilderness.

8. As a shepherd, David slew a lion and a bear with the help of the Lord, as later he slew Goliath (I Samuel xvii).

9. Jonathan's son Mephibosheth was restored to Saul's land by David, and was attended by Saul's servant Ziba.

1. Vestment of a Hebrew priest.

Of all the most reviled;
The light of Israel in his ways,
Wise are his precepts, prayer and praise,
And counsel to his child.[2]

XVII

[He consecrates his genius for consolation and edification]

His muse, bright angel of his verse,
Gives balm for all the thorns that pierce,
For all the pangs that rage;
Blessed light, still gaining on the gloom,
The more than Michal of his bloom,
The Abishag of his age.[3]

XVIII

[The subjects he made choice of—the Supreme Being;]

He sung of God—the mighty source
Of all things—the stupendous force
On which all strength depends;
From whose right arm, beneath whose eyes,
All period, power, and enterprise
Commences, reigns, and ends.

XIX

[angels;]

Angels—their ministry and meed,
Which to and fro with blessings speed,
Or with their citterns[4] wait;
Where Michael with his millions[5] bows,
Where dwells the seraph and his spouse,
The cherub and her mate.

XX

[men of renown;]

Of man—the semblance and effect
Of God and Love—the Saint elect
For infinite applause—
To rule the land, and briny broad,
To be laborious in his laud,
And heroes in his cause.

XXI

[the works of nature in all directions, either particularly or collectively considered]

The world—the clustering spheres he made,
The glorious light, the soothing shade,
Dale, champaign, grove, and hill;
The multitudinous abyss,
Where secrecy remains in bliss,
And wisdom hides her skill.

XXII

Trees, plants, and flowers—of virtuous[6] root;
Gem yielding blossom, yielding fruit,
Choice gums and precious balm;

2. The Proverbs and Psalms were supposed to be intended by David for his son Solomon.
3. More than Michal, his first wife, or Abishag, who ministered to him in old age, David's consolation is his muse, which gives balm for his sorrow as the Holy Spirit for Christ's.
4. Zither or lute.
5. God's legions, commanded by the archangel Michael.
6. Potent, medicinal; "Gem": bud.

Bless ye the nosegay in the vale,
And with the sweeteners of the gale
Enrich the thankful psalm.

XXIII

Of fowl—e'en every beak and wing
Which cheer the winter, hail the spring,
That live in peace or prey;
They that make music, or that mock,
The quail, the brave domestic cock,
The raven, swan, and jay.

XXIV

Of fishes—every size and shape,
Which nature frames of light escape,
Devouring man to shun:
The shells are in the wealthy deep,
The shoals[7] upon the surface leap,
And love the glancing sun.

XXV

Of beasts—the beaver plods his task;
While the sleek tigers roll and bask,
Nor yet the shades arouse;
Her cave the mining coney[8] scoops;
Where o'er the mead the mountain stoops,
The kids exult and browse.

XXVI

Of gems—their virtue and their price,
Which hid in earth from man's device,
Their darts of luster sheathe;
The jasper of the master's stamp,[9]
The topaz blazing like a lamp
Among the mines beneath.

XXVII

[He obtains power over infernal spirits,]

Blessed was the tenderness he felt
When to his graceful harp he knelt,
And did for audience call;
When Satan with his hand he quelled,
And in serene suspense he held
The frantic throes of Saul.[1]

XXVIII

[and the malignity of his enemies;]

His furious foes no more maligned
As he such melody divined,
And sense and soul detained;
Now striking strong, now soothing soft,
He sent the godly sounds aloft,
Or in delight refrained.

7. Schools of fish.
8. Rabbit.
9. Jasper is used to make seals or signets of authority; hid in earth, it signifies no authority but God's.
1. When Saul was oppressed by an evil spirit, David cured him by playing on the harp (I Samuel xvi).

XXIX

When up to heaven his thoughts he piled, *[wins the heart of Michal]*
From fervent lips fair Michal smiled,
As blush to blush she stood;
And chose herself the queen, and gave
Her utmost from her heart, "so brave,
And plays his hymns so good."[2]

XXX

The pillars of the Lord are seven, *[Shows that the pillars of knowledge are the monuments of God's works in the first week]*
Which stand from earth to topmost heaven;
His wisdom drew the plan;
His Word accomplished the design,
From brightest gem to deepest mine,
From CHRIST enthroned to man.[3]

XXXI

Alpha, the cause of causes, first
In station, fountain, whence the burst
Of light, and blaze of day;
Whence bold attempt, and brave advance,
Have motion, life, and ordinance,
And heaven itself its stay.[4]

XXXII

Gamma supports the glorious arch
On which angelic legions march,
And is with sapphires paved;
Thence the fleet clouds are sent adrift,
And thence the painted folds, that lift
The crimson veil, are waved.[5]

XXXIII

Eta with living sculpture breathes,
With verdant carvings, flowery wreathes
Of never-wasting bloom:
In strong relief his goodly base
All instruments of labor grace,
The trowel, spade, and loom.

XXXIV

Next Theta stands to the Supreme—
Who formed, in number, sign,[6] and scheme,
The illustrious lights that are;
And one addressed[7] his saffron robe,

2. Though intended by her father Saul to be a "snare" to David, Michal fell in love with him, as her speech (invented by Smart) indicates.
3. The seven pillars of the house of wisdom, referred to in Proverbs, are associated by the Masons with the building of the first Temple, erected by Solomon in Jerusalem according to divine order. Smart believed that both Proverbs and the Temple had been planned by David. In the following seven stanzas, each pillar is conflated with one of the days of Creation and with a Greek letter that represents one of the names of God. The implicit suggestion is that David, the greatest of poets and leaders, resembles the Creator, who called the universe into being with a Word.
4. Support. On the first day God called forth light.
5. The firmament, created on the second day, is compared to the oracle of the Temple, which holds the ark of the covenant.
6. Constellation.
7. Put on. The sun, with the moon and stars, was created on the fourth day.

And one, clad in a silver globe,
Held rule with every star.

XXXV

Iota's tuned to choral hymns
Of those that fly, while he that swims
In thankful safety lurks;
And foot, and chapitre,[8] and niche,
The various histories enrich
Of God's recorded works.

XXXVI

Sigma presents the social droves,
With him that solitary roves,
And man of all the chief;
Fair on whose face, and stately frame,
Did God impress his hallowed name,
For ocular belief.

XXXVII

OMEGA! GREATEST and the BEST,
Stands sacred to the day of rest,
For gratitude and thought;
Which blessed the world upon his pole,
And gave the universe his goal,
And closed the infernal draught.[9]

XXXVIII

O DAVID, scholar of the Lord!
Such is thy science, whence reward
And infinite degree;[1]
O strength, O sweetness, lasting ripe!
God's harp thy symbol, and thy type[2]
The lion and the bee!

XXXIX

There is but one who ne'er rebelled, *[An exercise upon*
But One by passion unimpelled, *the decalogue]*
By pleasure unenticed;
He from himself his semblance sent,
Grand object of his own content,
And saw the God in CHRIST.

XL

"Tell them, I am," JEHOVA said
To Moses; while earth heard in dread,
And smitten to the heart,

8. Capital of a pillar. The abundance of fish and fowl, created on the fifth day, is compared to the rich decorations of the Temple (I Kings vii).

9. The completed structure of the house of God (the world) shuts out the currents of Hell.

1. Elevation, rank.

2. Emblem. Theologically, a type is something in the Old Testament that prefigures some Christian truth. The lion and the bee, emblemizing the union of strength with sweetness (Judges xiv), prefigure David; and David himself prefigures Christ, though, as the next stanza explains, no man can equal Him, since God is His own type. Stanzas xxxviii and xlix frame a ten-string "harp," the center of the poem, in which each of the ten commandments is interpreted according to the new Law of Christ's teachings.

At once above, beneath, around,
All Nature, without voice or sound,
Replied, "O Lord, THOU ART."

XLI

Thou art—to give and to confirm,
For each his talent and his term;
All flesh thy bounties share:
Thou shalt not call thy brother fool;
The porches[3] of the Christian school
Are meekness, peace, and prayer.

XLII

Open, and naked of offense,
Man's made of mercy, soul, and sense;
God armed the snail and wilk;[4]
Be good to him that pulls thy plough;
Due food and care, due rest, allow
For her that yields thee milk.

XLIII

Rise up before the hoary head,
And God's benign commandment dread,
Which says thou shalt not die;
"Not as I will, but as thou wilt,"[5]
Prayed He whose conscience knew no guilt;
With whose blessed pattern vie.

XLIV

Use all thy passions!—love is thine,
And joy, and jealousy[6] divine,
Thine hope's eternal fort,
And care thy leisure to disturb,
With fear concupiscence to curb,
And rapture to transport.

XLV

Act simply, as occasion asks;
Put mellow wine in seasoned casks;
Till not with ass and bull:
Remember thy baptismal bond;
Keep from commixtures foul and fond,
Nor work thy flax with wool.

XLVI

Distribute: pay the Lord his tithe,
And make the widow's heart-strings blithe;
Resort with those that weep:
As you from all and each expect,
For all and each thy love direct,
And render as you reap.

3. Porticos where ancient philosophers debated.
4. Shellfish (the whelk).
5. Matthew xxvi.39. Christ exemplifies the fifth commandment by submitting to his Father's will.
6. Devotion.

XLVII

The slander and its bearer spurn,
And propagating praise sojourn
To make thy welcome last;
Turn from old Adam to the New;[7]
By hope futurity pursue;
Look upwards to the past.

XLVIII

Control thine eye, salute success,
Honor the wiser, happier bless,
And for thy neighbor feel;
Grutch not of mammon and his leaven,[8]
Work emulation up to heaven
By knowledge and by zeal.

XLIX

O David, highest in the list
Of worthies, on God's ways insist,
The genuine word repeat.[9]
Vain are the documents of men,
And vain the flourish of the pen
That keeps the fool's conceit.

L

[The transcendent virtue of praise and adoration]

Praise above all—for praise prevails;
Heap up the measure, load the scales,
And good to goodness add:
The generous soul her Saviour aids,
But peevish obloquy degrades;
The Lord is great and glad.

LI

For Adoration all the ranks
Of angels yield eternal thanks,
And David in the midst;
With God's good poor, which, last and least
In man's esteem, thou to thy feast,
O blessed bride-groom, bidst.

LII

[An exercise upon the seasons, and the right use of them]

For Adoration seasons change,
And order, truth, and beauty range,
Adjust, attract, and fill:
The grass the polyanthus checks;[1]
And polished porphyry reflects,
By the descending rill.

LIII

Rich almonds color to the prime
For Adoration; tendrils climb,

7. Christ. As elsewhere in this section, Smart interprets the commandment positively, less as a warning against bearing false witness than as encouragement to bear witness to truth.

8. Do not begrudge the wealthy man his rise.

9. "Psalm 119" [Smart's note].

1. Checkers.

And fruit-trees pledge their gems;
And Ivis[2] with her gorgeous vest
Builds for her eggs her cunning nest,
And bell-flowers bow their stems.

LIV

With vinous syrup cedars spout;
From rocks pure honey gushing out,
For ADORATION springs:
All scenes of painting crowd the map
Of nature; to the mermaid's pap
The scaléd infant clings.

LV

The spotted ounce and playsome cubs
Run rustling 'mongst the flowering shrubs,
And lizards feed[3] the moss;
For ADORATION beasts embark,[4]
While waves upholding halcyon's ark
No longer roar and toss.

LVI

While Israel sits beneath his fig,[5]
With coral root and amber sprig
The weaned adventurer sports;
Where to the palm the jasmin cleaves,
For ADORATION 'mong the leaves
The gale his peace reports.

LVII

Increasing days their reign exalt,
Nor in the pink and mottled vault
The opposing spirits tilt;[6]
And, by the coasting reader spied,
The silverlings and crusions[7] glide
For ADORATION gilt.

LVIII

For ADORATION ripening canes
And cocoa's purest milk detains
The western pilgrim's staff;
Where rain in clasping boughs inclosed,
And vines with oranges disposed,
Embower the social laugh.

LIX

Now labor his reward receives,
For ADORATION counts his sheaves

2. "Humming-bird" [Smart's note].
3. Eat; "ounce": lynx.
4. "There is a large quadruped that preys upon fish, and provides himself with a piece of timber for that purpose, with which he is very handy" [Smart's note]; "Halcyon's ark": the kingfisher's nest was supposed to calm the sea by floating on it.
5. According to Micah iv.4, "they shall sit every man under his vine and his fig tree; and none shall make them afraid"; "weaned adventurer": a child. As spring turns into summer, so mankind shall mature into peace.
6. Clouds clash together.
7. Tarpon and carp; "coasting": floating in a boat.

To peace, her bounteous prince;
The nectarine his strong tint imbibes,
And apples of ten thousand tribes,
And quick[8] peculiar quince.

LX

The wealthy crops of whitening rice,
'Mongst thyine[9] woods and groves of spice,
For ADORATION grow;
And, marshalled in the fencèd land,
The peaches and pomegranates stand,
Where wild carnations blow.

LXI

The laurels with the winter strive;
The crocus burnishes alive
Upon the snow-clad earth:
For ADORATION myrtles stay
To keep the garden from dismay,
And bless the sight from dearth.

LXII

The pheasant shows his pompous neck;
And ermine, jealous of a speck[1]
With fear eludes offense:
The sable, with his glossy pride,
For ADORATION is descried,
Where frosts the wave condense.

LXIII

The cheerful holly, pensive yew,
And holy thorn,[2] their trim renew;
The squirrel hoards his nuts:
All creatures batten o'er their stores,
And careful nature all her doors
For ADORATION shuts.

LXIV

For ADORATION, DAVID's psalms
Lift up the heart to deeds of alms;
And he, who kneels and chants,
Prevails his passions to control,
Finds meat and medicine to the soul,
Which for translation[3] pants.

LXV

[An exercise upon the senses, and how to subdue them]

For ADORATION, beyond match,
The scholar[4] bulfinch aims to catch
The soft flute's ivory touch;
And careless on the hazel spray,
The daring redbreast keeps at bay
The damsel's greedy clutch.

8. Pungent.
9. Sweet.
1. Suspicious of distant things.
2. Hawthorn.
3. Transference to heaven.
4. Imitative (the bullfinch can learn a tune).

LXVI

For Adoration, in the skies,
The Lord's philosopher espies
    The Dog, the Ram, and Rose;
The planets' ring, Orion's sword;
Nor is his greatness less adored
    In the vile worm that glows.

LXVII

For Adoration on the strings[5]
The western breezes work their wings,
    The captive ear to sooth—
Hark! 'tis a voice—how still, and small—[6]
That makes the cataracts to fall,
    Or bids the sea be smooth.

LXVIII

For Adoration, incense comes
From bezoar,[7] and Arabian gums;
    And from the civet's fur.
But as for prayer, or ere it faints,
Far better is the breath of saints
    Than galbanum and myrrh.[8]

LXIX

For Adoration from the down
Of damasins[9] to the anana's crown,
    God sends to tempt the taste;
And while the luscious zest invites
The sense, that in the scene delights,
    Commands desire be chaste.

LXX

For Adoration, all the paths
Of grace are open, all the baths
    Of purity refresh;
And all the rays of glory beam
To deck the man of God's esteem,
    Who triumphs o'er the flesh.

LXXI

For Adoration, in the dome
Of Christ the sparrows find an home,
    And on his olives perch:
The swallow also dwells with thee,
O man of God's humility,
    Within his Saviour Church.

LXXII

Sweet is the dew that falls betimes,
And drops upon the leafy limes;

[An amplification in five degrees,]

5. "Aeolian harp" [Smart's note], played by the wind.
6. In I Kings xix.11–12, the Lord does not speak in the wind but in "a still small voice."
7. A medicinal lump that forms in the stomachs of some animals; "civet": civet cat.
8. Gum resins used in incense.
9. Damson plums; "anana's crown": pineapple's tuft.

Sweet Hermon's fragrant air:[1]
Sweet is the lily's silver bell,
And sweet the wakeful tapers smell
That watch for early prayer.

LXXIII

Sweet the young nurse with love intense,
Which smiles o'er sleeping innocence;
Sweet when the lost arrive:
Sweet the musician's ardor beats,
While his vague mind's in quest of sweets,
The choicest flowers to hive.

LXXIV

Sweeter in all the strains of love,
The language of thy turtle dove,
Paired to thy swelling chord;
Sweeter with every grace endued,
The glory of thy gratitude,
Respired unto the Lord.

LXXV

Strong is the horse upon his speed;
Strong in pursuit the rapid glede,[2]
Which makes at once his game:
Strong the tall ostrich on the ground;
Strong through the turbulent profound
Shoots xiphias[3] to his aim.

LXXVI

Strong is the lion—like a coal
His eyeball—like a bastion's mole[4]
His chest against the foes:
Strong the gier-eagle[5] on his sail,
Strong against tide, the enormous whale
Emerges, as he goes.

LXXVII

But stronger still, in earth and air,
And in the sea, the man of prayer;
And far beneath the tide;
And in the seat to faith assigned,
Where ask is have, where seek is find,
Where knock is open wide.

LXXVIII

Beauteous the fleet before the gale;
Beauteous the multitudes in mail,
Ranked arms and crested heads:
Beauteous the garden's umbrage mild,
Walk, water, meditated wild,[6]
And all the bloomy beds.

1. The dew of Hermon, a mountain in Syria, is associated with Zion's dew in Psalm 133.
2. Hawk.
3. "The sword-fish" [Smart's note].
4. Fortified wall.
5. Vulture.
6. Artificial wild place within a garden or park.

LXXIX

Beauteous the moon full on the lawn;
And beauteous, when the veil's withdrawn,
The virgin to her spouse:
Beauteous the temple decked and filled,
When to the heaven of heavens they build
Their heart-directed vows.

LXXX

Beauteous, yea beauteous more than these,
The shepherd king upon his knees,
For his momentous trust;
With wish of infinite conceit,[7]
For man, beast, mute, the small and great,
And prostrate dust to dust.

LXXXI

Precious the bounteous widow's mite;
And precious, for extreme delight,
The largess from the churl:[8]
Precious the ruby's blushing blaze,
And alba's[9] blest imperial rays,
And pure cerulean pearl.

LXXXII

Precious the penitential tear;
And precious is the sigh sincere,
Acceptable to God:
And precious are the winning flowers,
In gladsome Israel's feast of bowers,[1]
Bound on the hallowed sod.

LXXXIII

More precious that diviner part
Of David, even the Lord's own heart,
Great, beautiful, and new:
In all things where it was intent,
In all extremes, in each event,
Proof[2]—answering true to true.

LXXXIV

Glorious the sun in mid career;
Glorious the assembled fires appear;
Glorious the comet's train:
Glorious the trumpet and alarm;
Glorious the almighty stretched-out arm;
Glorious the enraptured main:

LXXXV

Glorious the northern lights astream;
Glorious the song, when God's the theme;

7. Conception; "mute": fish.
8. "Samuel 25:18" [Smart's note]. Against the will of Nabal, a churlish rich man, his wife Abigail gave largess to David.
9. "Revelation 2:17" [Smart's note]; a white stone, given to the church triumphant.
1. The Feast of Tabernacles, or Succoth, ordained five days after the day of atonement, in thanksgiving for deliverance from Egypt.
2. Meeting the test.

Glorious the thunder's roar:
Glorious hosanna from the den;
Glorious the catholic amen;
Glorious the martyr's gore:

LXXXVI

Glorious—more glorious is the crown
Of Him, that brought salvation down
By meekness, called thy Son;
Thou that stupendous truth believed,
And now the matchless deed's achieved,
DETERMINED, DARED, and DONE.

[which is wrought up
to this conclusion, That
the best poet which
ever lived was thought
worthy of the highest
honor which possibly can
be conceived, as
*the Saviour of the
World was ascribed
to his house, and
called his son in the
body.*]

1763

OLIVER GOLDSMITH
(ca. 1730–1774)

It is difficult to distinguish fact from fiction in the accounts that we have of Goldsmith's first thirty years. Unlike the works of most 18th-century authors, his writings contain much that is personal, but it is of little use to biographers, for it has been heightened and romanticized until it belongs at least as much to fiction as to autobiography. The Goldsmith legend, which has served as the poet's biography, is to some degree the creation of Goldmith himself.

He was born in Ireland, the son of an Anglican clergyman whose geniality he inherited and whose improvidence he imitated. He was early disfigured by smallpox and grew up ugly of face, ungraceful of figure, and in his early years apparently stupid and certainly idle. Nonetheless, he was sent to Trinity College, Dublin, as a sizar—i.e., a student who did menial jobs for well-to-do undergraduates—and there he took his A.B. in 1749. After several false starts in choosing a career, he was sent by a generous uncle to study medicine at the University of Edinburgh. Instead of taking a degree, he wandered for a while on the Continent, visiting Holland, France, Italy, and Switzerland. A much romanticized account of this journey can be read in the story of George Primrose in Goldsmith's novel, *The Vicar of Wakefield* (1766). He returned to England in 1756 with a mysteriously acquired M.D. and tried in vain to support himself as a physician among the poor in the Borough of Southwark. After serving for a while as an usher in a school, he drifted into the profession of hack writer for Ralph Griffiths, the proprietor of the *Monthly Review*, and later worked for and with the benevolent publisher Edward Newbery. He first attracted attention by a short book, *An Inquiry into the Present State of Polite Learning in Europe* (1759), in which he traced what he considered to be the decline of the fine arts in mid-18th-century Europe to the lack of enlightened patronage and to the malign influence of criticism and scholarship. From then until his death he earned by his writings very large sums indeed, but his habitual extravagance and generosity kept him always in debt, no matter how ample his income. When he was in funds he lived richly; when he was without money, he borrowed. He died owing the then prodigious sum (for a man whose only source of income was writing) of £2,000.

The variety and excellence of Goldsmith's work is astonishing. His easy and pleasant prose style, his abundant humor, his shrewd observations of character and scene have made his essays constantly popular. His great gift for the comedy of character and situation enabled him to achieve in his two plays, *The Good-Natured Man* (1768) and *She Stoops to Conquer* (1773), a sort of pure and mirthful comedy—uncomplicated by ethical or social criticism and unspoiled by the fashionable sentimentality of the moment—that is unique in the century. His two important poems, *The Traveler, or A Prospect of Society* (1764) and *The Deserted Village*, are distinguished for the purity and harmony of their language The couplets of *The Deserted Village* lack the rhetoric and formality of Pope's or Johnson's couplets and become almost lyrical in sound and movement.

Goldsmith was an intimate of the circle of brilliant men of whom Johnson was the center. Boswell's description of him in famous scenes in the *Life* is certainly ill-natured and unfair. He was not the inspired idiot, the blundering Irishman with a dash of genius, that Boswell and other members of the group insisted he was. His sly humor, often directed against himself, seems not to have been understood by most of his friends, who took pains to repeat solemnly as examples of Irish "bulls" (verbal blunders) what Goldsmith certainly meant in jest. He was not a profound thinker and his learning was not extensive; but even such hack-work compilations as the *History of Rome*, the *History of Greece*, and the *History of Animated Nature*, which he put together carelessly and rapidly, were ensured a certain life by the charm of his manner and style.

The Deserted Village[1]

Sweet Auburn! loveliest village of the plain,
Where health and plenty cheered the laboring swain,
Where smiling spring its earliest visit paid,

1. *The Deserted Village* is an idealization of English rural life, mingled with poignant memories of the poet's own youth in Lissoy, Ireland. Goldsmith was seriously concerned about the effects of the agricultural revolution then in progress which was being hastened by Enclosure Acts. Either for the sake of more profitable farming or to create vast private parks and landscape gardens, arable land was being taken out of the hands of small proprietors (i.e., "enclosed"), thus displacing yeoman farmers who, like their ancestors, had lived for generations in small villages, grazing their cattle on common land and raising food on small holdings. The only alternative available to many such people was to seek employment in the city or to migrate to America. Goldsmith certainly exaggerates the effects of the enclosures, nor are his diatribes against the debilitating influence of luxury borne out by history; Waterloo and the glories of the 19th century lay ahead for England. In the poem Goldsmith opposes "luxury" (the increase of wealth, the growth of cities, the costly country estates of great noblemen and wealthy merchants) to "rural virtue" (the old agrarian economy which supported a sturdy population of independent peas-

And parting summer's lingering blooms delayed:
Dear lovely bowers of innocence and ease,
Seats of my youth, when every sport could please,
How often have I loitered o'er thy green,
Where humble happiness endeared each scene;
How often have I paused on every charm,
The sheltered cot, the cultivated farm,
The never-failing brook, the busy mill,
The decent church that topped the neighboring hill,
The hawthorn bush, with seats beneath the shade,
For talking age and whispering lovers made;
How often have I blessed the coming day,
When toil remitting lent its turn to play,
And all the village train, from labor free,
Led up their sports beneath the spreading tree,
While many a pastime circled in the shade,
The young contending as the old surveyed;
And many a gambol frolicked o'er the ground,
And sleights of art and feats of strength went round;
And still as each repeated pleasure tired,
Succeeding sports the mirthful band inspired;
The dancing pair that simply sought renown,
By holding out to tire each other down;
The swain mistrustless of his smutted face,
While secret laughter tittered round the place;
The bashful virgin's sidelong looks of love,
The matron's glance that would those looks reprove:
These were thy charms, sweet village! sports like these,
With sweet succession, taught even toil to please;
These round thy bowers their cheerful influence shed,
These were thy charms—But all these charms are fled.
  Sweet smiling village, loveliest of the lawn,
Thy sports are fled, and all thy charms withdrawn;
Amidst thy bowers the tyrant's hand is seen,
And desolation saddens all thy green:
One only master grasps the whole domain,
And half a tillage stints thy smiling plain;
No more thy glassy brook reflects the day,
But choked with sedges, works its weedy way;
Along thy glades, a solitary guest,
The hollow-sounding bittern guards its nest;
Amidst thy desert walks the lapwing flies,
And tires their echoes with unvaried cries.
Sunk are thy bowers, in shapeless ruin all,
And the long grass o'ertops the moldering wall,
And, trembling, shrinking from the spoiler's hand,
Far, far away thy children leave the land.
  Ill fares the land, to hastening ills a prey,

---

ants). His poem is thus at once a nostalgic lament for a doomed way of life and a denunciation of what he regarded as the corrupting, destructive force of new wealth.

Where wealth accumulates, and men decay;
Princes and lords may flourish, or may fade;
A breath can make them, as a breath has made;
But a bold peasantry, their country's pride,
When once destroyed, can never be supplied.
A time there was, ere England's griefs began,
When every rood of ground maintained its man;
For him light labor spread her wholesome store,
Just gave what life required, but gave no more:
His best companions, innocence and health;
And his best riches, ignorance of wealth.
But times are altered; Trade's unfeeling train
Usurp the land and dispossess the swain;
Along the lawn, where scattered hamlets rose,
Unwieldy wealth, and cumbrous pomp repose;
And every want to opulence allied,
And every pang that folly pays to pride.
These gentle hours that plenty bade to bloom,
Those calm desires that asked but little room,
Those healthful sports that graced the peaceful scene,
Lived in each look, and brightened all the green;
These far departing seek a kinder shore,
And rural mirth and manners are no more.
Sweet Auburn! parent of the blissful hour,
Thy glades forlorn confess the tyrant's power.
Here, as I take my solitary rounds,
Amidst thy tangling walks, and ruined grounds,
And, many a year elapsed, return to view
Where once the cottage stood, the hawthorn grew,
Remembrance wakes with all her busy train,
Swells at my breast, and turns the past to pain.
In all my wanderings round this world of care,
In all my griefs—and God has given my share—
I still had hopes my latest hours to crown,
Amidst these humble bowers to lay me down;
To husband out life's taper at the close,
And keep the flame from wasting by repose.
I still had hopes, for pride attends us still,
Amidst the swains to show my book-learned skill,
Around my fire an evening group to draw,
And tell of all I felt, and all I saw;
And, as an hare whom hounds and horns pursue,
Pants to the place from whence at first she flew,
I still had hopes, my long vexations past,
Here to return—and die at home at last.
O blest retirement, friend to life's decline,
Retreats from care that never must be mine,
How happy he who crowns in shades like these,
A youth of labor with an age of ease;
Who quits a world where strong temptations try,
And, since 'tis hard to combat, learns to fly!

For him no wretches, born to work and weep,
Explore the mine, or tempt the dangerous deep;
No surly porter stands in guilty state
To spurn imploring famine from the gate;
But on he moves to meet his latter end,
Angels around befriending virtue's friend;
Bends to the grave with unperceived decay,
While Resignation gently slopes the way;
And, all his prospects brightening to the last,
His Heaven commences ere the world be passed!
  Sweet was the sound when oft at evening's close,
Up yonder hill the village murmur rose;
There, as I passed with careless steps and slow,
The mingling notes came softened from below;
The swain responsive as the milkmaid sung,
The sober herd that lowed to meet their young,
The noisy geese that gabbled o'er the pool,
The playful children just let loose from school;
The watchdog's voice that bayed the whispering wind,
And the loud laugh that spoke the vacant[2] mind;
These all in sweet confusion sought the shade,
And filled each pause the nightingale had made.
But now the sounds of population fail,
No cheerful murmurs fluctuate in the gale,
No busy steps the grass-grown footway tread,
For all the bloomy flush of life is fled.
All but yon widowed, solitary thing
That feebly bends beside the plashy spring;
She, wretched matron, forced, in age, for bread,
To strip the brook with mantling cresses spread,
To pick her wintry faggot from the thorn,
To seek her nightly shed, and weep till morn;
She only left of all the harmless train,
The sad historian of the pensive plain.
  Near yonder copse, where once the garden smiled,
And still where many a garden flower grows wild,
There, where a few torn shrubs the place disclose,
The village preacher's modest mansion rose.
A man he was, to all the country dear,
And passing rich with forty pounds a year;
Remote from towns he ran his godly race,
Nor e'er had changed, nor wished to change his place;
Unpracticed he to fawn, or seek for power,
By doctrines fashioned to the varying hour;
Far other aims his heart had learned to prize,
More skilled to raise the wretched than to rise.
His house was known to all the vagrant train,
He chid their wanderings, but relieved their pain;
The long-remembered beggar was his guest,

2. Idle.

Whose beard descending swept his aged breast;
The ruined spendthrift, now no longer proud,
Claimed kindred there, and had his claims allowed;
The broken soldier, kindly bade to stay,
Sate by his fire, and talked the night away;
Wept o'er his wounds, or tales of sorrow done,
Shouldered his crutch, and showed how fields were won.
Pleased with his guests, the good man learned to glow,
And quite forgot their vices in their woe;
Careless their merits, or their faults to scan,
His pity gave ere charity began.
Thus to relieve the wretched was his pride,
And even his failings leaned to Virtue's side;
But in his duty prompt at every call,
He watched and wept, he prayed and felt, for all.
And, as a bird each fond endearment tries,
To tempt its new-fledged offspring to the skies,
He tried each art, reproved each dull delay,
Allured to brighter worlds, and led the way.
Beside the bed where parting life was laid,
And sorrow, guilt, and pain, by turns dismayed,
The reverend champion stood. At his control,
Despair and anguish fled the struggling soul;
Comfort came down the trembling wretch to raise,
And his last faltering accents whispered praise.
At church, with meek and unaffected grace,
His looks adorned the venerable place;
Truth from his lips prevailed with double sway,
And fools, who came to scoff, remained to pray.
The service past, around the pious man,
With steady zeal each honest rustic ran;
Even children followed with endearing wile,
And plucked his gown, to share the good man's smile.
His ready smile a parent's warmth expressed,
Their welfare pleased him, and their cares distressed;
To them his heart, his love, his griefs were given,
But all his serious thoughts had rest in Heaven.
As some tall cliff that lifts its awful form,
Swells from the vale, and midway leaves the storm,
Though round its breast the rolling clouds are spread,
Eternal sunshine settles on its head.
Beside yon straggling fence that skirts the way,
With blossomed furze unprofitably gay,
There, in his noisy mansion, skilled to rule,
The village master taught his little school;
A man severe he was, and stern to view,
I knew him well, and every truant knew;
Well had the boding tremblers learned to trace
The day's disasters in his morning face;
Full well they laughed with counterfeited glee,
At all his jokes, for many a joke had he;

Full well the busy whisper circling round,
Conveyed the dismal tidings when he frowned;
Yet he was kind, or if severe in aught,
The love he bore to learning was in fault;[3]
The village all declared how much he knew;
'Twas certain he could write, and cipher too;
Lands he could measure, terms[4] and tides presage,
And even the story ran that he could gauge.[5]
In arguing too, the parson owned his skill,
For even though vanquished, he could argue still;
While words of learned length, and thundering sound,
Amazed the gazing rustics ranged around;
And still they gazed, and still the wonder grew,
That one small head could carry all he knew.
  But past is all his fame. The very spot
Where many a time he triumphed, is forgot.
Near yonder thorn, that lifts its head on high,
Where once the signpost caught the passing eye,
Low lies that house where nut-brown draughts inspired,
Where graybeard Mirth and smiling Toil retired,
Where village statesmen talked with looks profound,
And news much older than their ale went round.
Imagination fondly stoops to trace
The parlor splendors of that festive place:
The whitewashed wall, the nicely sanded floor,
The varnished clock that clicked behind the door;
The chest contrived a double debt to pay,
A bed by night, a chest of drawers by day;
The pictures placed for ornament and use,
The twelve good rules,[6] the royal game of goose;
The hearth, except when winter chilled the day,
With aspen boughs, and flowers, and fennel gay,
While broken teacups, wisely kept for show,
Ranged o'er the chimney, glistened in a row.
  Vain transitory splendors! Could not all
Reprieve the tottering mansion from its fall!
Obscure it sinks, nor shall it more impart
An hour's importance to the poor man's heart;
Thither no more the peasant shall repair
To sweet oblivion of his daily care;
No more the farmer's news, the barber's tale,
No more the woodman's ballad shall prevail;
No more the smith his dusky brow shall clear,
Relax his ponderous strength, and lean to hear;

3. Since the *l* was silent, "fault" and "aught" rhymed perfectly.
4. Dates on which rent, wages, etc., were due and tenancy began or ended; "tides": feasts and seasons in the church year.
5. Measure the content of casks and other vessels.
6. "The twelve good rules" of conduct, attributed to Charles I, were printed in a broadside that was often seen on the walls of taverns; "goose" was a game in which counters were moved on a board according to the throw of the dice.

The host himself no longer shall be found
Careful to see the mantling bliss[7] go round;
Nor the coy maid, half willing to be pressed,
Shall kiss the cup to pass it to the rest.
Yes! let the rich deride, the proud disdain,
These simple blessings of the lowly train,
To me more dear, congenial to my heart,
One native charm, than all the gloss of art;
Spontaneous joys, where nature has its play,
The soul adopts, and owns their first-born sway;
Lightly they frolic o'er the vacant mind,
Unenvied, unmolested, unconfined.
But the long pomp, the midnight masquerade,
With all the freaks of wanton wealth arrayed,
In these, ere triflers half their wish obtain,
The toiling pleasure sickens into pain;
And, even while fashion's brightest arts decoy,
The heart distrusting asks if this be joy.
Ye friends to truth, ye statesmen, who survey
The rich man's joys increase, the poor's decay,
'Tis yours to judge how wide the limits stand
Between a splendid and an happy land.
Proud swells the tide with loads of freighted ore,
And shouting Folly hails them from her shore;
Hoards, even beyond the miser's wish abound,
And rich men flock from all the world around.
Yet count our gains. This wealth is but a name
That leaves our useful products still the same.
Not so the loss. The man of wealth and pride,
Takes up a space that many poor supplied;
Space for his lake, his park's extended bounds,
Space for his horses, equipage, and hounds;
The robe that wraps his limbs in silken sloth
Has robbed the neighboring fields of half their growth;
His seat, where solitary sports are seen,
Indignant spurns the cottage from the green;
Around the world each needful product flies,
For all the luxuries the world supplies.
While thus the land adorned for pleasure, all
In barren splendor feebly waits the fall.
As some fair female unadorned and plain,
Secure to please while youth confirms her reign,
Slights every borrowed charm that dress supplies,
Nor shares with art the triumph of her eyes:
But when those charms are past, for charms are frail,
When time advances, and when lovers fail,
She then shines forth, solicitous to bless,
In all the glaring impotence of dress.
Thus fares the land, by luxury betrayed;
In nature's simplest charms at first arrayed;

7. Foaming bliss, i.e., foaming ale.

But verging to decline, its splendors rise,
Its vistas strike, its palaces surprise;
While scourged by famine from the smiling land,
The mournful peasant leads his humble band;
And while he sinks without one arm to save,
The country blooms—a garden, and a grave.
Where then, ah where, shall Poverty reside,
To 'scape the pressure of contiguous Pride?
If to some common's fenceless limits strayed,
He drives his flock to pick the scanty blade,
Those fenceless fields the sons of wealth divide,
And even the bare-worn common is denied.
If to the city sped—What waits him there?
To see profusion that he must not share;
To see ten thousand baneful arts combined
To pamper luxury, and thin mankind;
To see those joys the sons of pleasure know,
Extorted from his fellow creature's woe.
Here, while the courtier glitters in brocade,
There the pale artist[8] plies the sickly trade;
Here, while the proud their long-drawn pomps display,
There the black gibbet glooms beside the way.
The dome where Pleasure holds her midnight reign,
Here, richly decked, admits the gorgeous train;
Tumultuous grandeur crowds the blazing square,
The rattling chariots clash, the torches glare.
Sure scenes like these no troubles e'er annoy!
Sure these denote one universal joy!
Are these thy serious thoughts?—Ah, turn thine eyes
Where the poor houseless shivering female lies.
She once, perhaps, in village plenty blest,
Has wept at tales of innocence distressed;
Her modest looks the cottage might adorn,
Sweet as the primrose peeps beneath the thorn;
Now lost to all; her friends, her virtue fled,
Near her betrayer's door she lays her head,
And pinched with cold, and shrinking from the shower,
With heavy heart deplores that luckless hour,
When idly first, ambitious of the town,
She left her wheel and robes of country brown.
Do thine, sweet Auburn, thine, the loveliest train,
Do thy fair tribes participate her pain?
Even now, perhaps, by cold and hunger led,
At proud men's doors they ask a little bread!
Ah, no. To distant climes, a dreary scene,
Where half the convex world intrudes between,
Through torrid tracts with fainting steps they go,
Where wild Altama[9] murmurs to their woe.
Far different there from all that charmed before,
The various terrors of that horrid shore;

8. Artisan.

9. The Altamaha River in Georgia.

Those blazing suns that dart a downward ray,
And fiercely shed intolerable day;
Those matted woods where birds forget to sing,
But silent bats in drowsy clusters cling,
Those poisonous fields with rank luxuriance crowned,
Where the dark scorpion gathers death around;
Where at each step the stranger fears to wake
The rattling terrors of the vengeful snake;
Where crouching tigers wait their hapless prey,[1]
And savage men, more murderous still than they;
While oft in whirls the mad tornado flies,
Mingling the ravaged landscape with the skies.
Far different these from every former scene,
The cooling brook, the grassy vested green,
The breezy covert of the warbling grove,
That only sheltered thefts of harmless love.
  Good Heaven! what sorrows gloomed that parting day,
That called them from their native walks away;
When the poor exiles, every pleasure past,
Hung round their bowers, and fondly looked their last,
And took a long farewell, and wished in vain
For seats like these beyond the western main;
And shuddering still to face the distant deep,
Returned and wept, and still returned to weep.
The good old sire, the first prepared to go
To new-found worlds, and wept for other's woe.
But for himself, in conscious virtue brave,
He only wished for worlds beyond the grave.
His lovely daughter, lovelier in her tears,
The fond companion of his helpless years,
Silent went next, neglectful of her charms,
And left a lover's for a father's arms.
With louder plaints the mother spoke her woes,
And blessed the cot where every pleasure rose;
And kissed her thoughtless babes with many a tear,
And clasped them close in sorrow doubly dear;
Whilst her fond husband strove to lend relief
In all the silent manliness of grief.
  O luxury! Thou cursed by Heaven's decree,
How ill exchanged are things like these for thee!
How do thy potions, with insidious joy,
Diffuse their pleasures only to destroy!
Kingdoms, by thee, to sickly greatness grown,
Boast of a florid vigor not their own.
At every draught more large and large they grow,
A bloated mass of rank unwieldy woe;
Till sapped their strength, and every part unsound,
Down, down they sink, and spread a ruin round.
  Even now the devastation is begun,
And half the business of destruction done;

1. Not the Asiatic tiger, but the puma.

Even now, methinks, as pondering here I stand,
I see the rural Virtues leave the land.
Down where yon anchoring vessel spreads the sail,
That idly waiting flaps with every gale,
Downward they move, a melancholy band,
Pass from the shore, and darken all the strand.
Contented Toil, and hospitable Care,
And kind connubial Tenderness are there;
And Piety, with wishes placed above,
And steady Loyalty, and faithful Love:
And thou, sweet Poetry, thou loveliest maid,
Still first to fly where sensual joys invade;
Unfit in these degenerate times of shame,
To catch the heart, or strike for honest fame;
Dear charming Nymph, neglected and decried,
My shame in crowds, my solitary pride;
Thou source of all my bliss, and all my woe,
That found'st me poor at first, and keep'st me so;
Thou guide by which the nobler arts excel,
Thou nurse of every virtue, fare thee well.
Farewell, and O! where'er thy voice be tried
On Torno's cliffs, or Pambamarca's side,[2]
Whether where equinoctial fervors glow,
Or winter wraps the polar world in snow,
Still let thy voice, prevailing over time,
Redress the rigors of the inclement clime;
Aid slighted truth, with thy persuasive strain
Teach erring man to spurn the rage of gain;
Teach him that states of native strength possessed,
Though very poor, may still be very blest;
That Trade's proud empire hastes to swift decay,
As ocean sweeps the labored mole[3] away;
While self-dependent power can time defy,
As rocks resist the billows and the sky.[4]

1770

2. The river Torne in Sweden falls into the Gulf of Bothnia; Pambamarca is a mountain in Ecuador.

3. The laboriously built breakwater.

4. Johnson composed the last four lines of the poem.

GEORGE CRABBE
(1754–1832)

Crabbe belongs to the early 19th rather than to the 18th century, but his first successful poem is very much a part of the literature of our period. Born to poverty in a small, decayed Suffolk seaport, Aldeburgh, he was apprenticed to a surgeon, but found it impossible to earn a living by practicing in his native village. In 1780 he went to London, and succeeded

neither in finding a patron nor in securing literary employment, until, reduced to desperate straits, he sent an appeal to Edmund Burke, who recognized his merit and gave him timely help. Through Burke's influence *The Library* was published; Dr. Johnson agreed to correct *The Village;* and Crabbe was ordained a minister in the Anglican Church. His appointment as chaplain to the Duke of Rutland enabled him to marry the woman to whom he had long been engaged.

After 1785 he published nothing until 1807, when *The Parish Register* appeared. It was followed by *The Borough* (1810), *Tales* (1812), and *Tales of the Hall* (1819). In these poems, which won the admiration of Wordsworth, Scott, and Byron, Crabbe continued the vein of realism which had distinguished *The Village,* and developed his great gift for narrative and characterization. He was well aware of the difference between his poetry, written in rather prosaic language and heroic couplets, abounding in realistic details and concerned with ordinary people, and that of his two great Romantic contemporaries, Sir Walter Scott and Lord Byron. Scott's medieval and Byron's Oriental tales possessed the charm of the remote and exotic. Crabbe described his own poetry as "poetry without an atmosphere." It is, however, almost always interesting and often dramatic and moving.

The Village was widely read and admired despite the fact that it is not free from faults that Crabbe never overcame: slipshod rhymes, and sometimes flat and often stilted language. But its unrelieved realism and its gloomy darkness of tone set it sharply apart from conventional poems on rural life during the century. Indeed it is an angry, a scornful reply to the sentimental cult of rural simplicity, innocence, and happiness. It glances at the unrealities of the pastoral convention and, somewhat more systematically, it answers Goldsmith's charming idealization of villagers and their life in *The Deserted Village.* Crabbe knew the degrading effect of hopeless poverty, he had observed rural vice, he knew the gulf that sometimes separated the landed gentry from their laboring tenants. Out of recollections of Aldeburgh and the neighboring seacoast he fashioned a setting for his poem in which the penury of a niggardly nature seems the only proper background for the penury of the men who inhabit it. The accuracy and vividness of the details created a poetry of the ugly which is at variance with the long tradition of natural description from Thomson to Cowper.

From The Village

Book I

The village life, and every care that reigns
O'er youthful peasants and declining swains;
What labor yields, and what, that labor past,
Age, in its hour of languor, finds at last;
What form the real picture of the poor,
Demand a song—the Muse can give no more.
Fled are those times when, in harmonious strains,

The rustic poet praised his native plains.
No shepherds now, in smooth altérnate verse,
Their country's beauty or their nymphs' rehearse;
Yet still for these we frame the tender strain,
Still in our lays fond Corydons[1] complain,
And shepherds' boys their amorous pains reveal,
The only pains, alas! they never feel.
On Mincio's[2] banks, in Caesar's bounteous reign,
If Tityrus found the Golden Age again,
Must sleepy bards the flattering dream prolong,
Mechanic echoes of the Mantuan song?
From Truth and Nature shall we widely stray,
Where Virgil, not where Fancy, leads the way?
Yes, thus the Muses sing of happy swains,
Because the Muses never knew their pains.
They boast their peasants' pipes; but peasants now
Resign their pipes and plod behind the plow;
And few, amid the rural tribe, have time
To number syllables, and play with rhyme;
Save honest Duck,[3] what son of verse could share
The poet's rapture, and the peasant's care?
Or the great labors of the field degrade,
With the new peril of a poorer trade?
From this chief cause these idle praises spring,
That themes so easy few forbear to sing;
For no deep thought the trifling subjects ask:
To sing of shepherds is an easy task.
The happy youth assumes the common strain,
A nymph his mistress, and himself a swain;
With no sad scenes he clouds his tuneful prayer,
But all, to look like her, is painted fair.
I grant indeed that fields and flocks have charms
For him that grazes or for him that farms;
But when amid such pleasing scenes I trace
The poor laborious natives of the place,
And see the midday sun, with fervid ray,
On their bare heads and dewy temples play;
While some, with feebler heads and fainter hearts,
Deplore their fortune, yet sustain their parts:
Then shall I dare these real ills to hide
In tinsel trappings of poetic pride?
No; cast by Fortune on a frowning coast,
Which neither groves nor happy valleys boast;
Where other cares than those the Muse relates,
And other shepherds dwell with other mates;
By such examples taught, I paint the cot,

1. "Corydon" is a stock name for a shepherd in pastorals, used by both Theocritus and Virgil.

2. Virgil was born near Mantua, in Italy, not far from the river Mincius. Tityrus is one of the speakers in Virgil's *Eclogues* I.

3. Stephen Duck (1705–56), the "Thresher Poet," was a self-educated agricultural laborer whose verses attracted attention and finally won him the patronage of Queen Caroline.

As Truth will paint it, and as bards will not:
Nor you, ye poor, of lettered scorn complain,
To you the smoothest song is smooth in vain;
O'ercome by labor, and bowed down by time,
Feel you the barren flattery of a rhyme?
Can poets soothe you, when you pine for bread,
By winding myrtles round your ruined shed?
Can their light tales your weighty griefs o'erpower,
Or glad with airy mirth the toilsome hour?
 Lo! where the heath, with withering brake grown o'er,
Lends the light turf that warms the neighboring poor;
From thence a length of burning sand appears,
Where the thin harvest waves its withered ears;
Rank weeds, that every art and care defy,
Reign o'er the land, and rob the blighted rye:
There thistles stretch theii prickly arms afar,
And to the ragged infant threaten war;
There poppies, nodding, mock the hope of toil;
There the blue bugloss paints the sterile soil;
Hardy and high, above the slender sheaf,
The slimy mallow waves her silky leaf;
O'er the young shoot the charlock throws a shade,
And clasping tares cling round the sickly blade;
With mingled tints the rocky coasts abound,
And a sad splendor vainly shines around.
So looks the nymph whom wretched arts adorn,
Betrayed by man, then left for man to scorn;
Whose cheek in vain assumes the mimic rose,
While her sad eyes the troubled breast disclose;
Whose outward splendor is but folly's dress,
Exposing most, when most it gilds distress.
 Here joyless roam a wild amphibious race,
With sullen woe displayed in every face;
Who far from civil arts and social fly,
And scowl at strangers with suspicious eye.
 Here too the lawless merchant of the main
Draws from his plow the intoxicated swain;
Want only claimed the labor of the day,
But vice now steals his nightly rest away.
 Where are the swains, who, daily labor done,
With rural games played down the setting sun;
 Who struck with matchless force the bounding ball,
Or made the ponderous qùoit obliquely fall;
While some huge Ajax, terrible and strong,
Engaged some artful stripling of the throng,
And fell beneath him, foiled, while far around
Hoarse triumph rose, and rocks returned the sound?
Where now are these?—Beneath yon cliff they stand,
To show the freighted pinnace where to land;[4]

4. Crabbe refers to smuggling.

To load the ready steed with guilty haste;
To fly in terror o'er the pathless waste;
Or, when detected in their straggling course,
To foil their foes by cunning or by force;
Or, yielding part (which equal knaves demand),
To gain a lawless passport through the land.
Here, wandering long amid these frowning fields,
I sought the simple life that Nature yields;
Rapine and Wrong and Fear usurped her place,
And a bold, artful, surly, savage race;
Who, only skilled to take the finny tribe,
The yearly dinner, or septennial bribe,[5]
Wait on the shore, and, as the waves run high,
On the tossed vessel bend their eager eye,
Which to their coast directs its venturous way;
Theirs, or the ocean's, miserable prey.
As on their neighboring beach yon swallows stand,
And wait for favoring winds to leave the land,
While still for flight the ready wing is spread:
So waited I the favoring hour, and fled;
Fled from these shores where guilt and famine reign,
And cried, "Ah! hapless they who still remain;
Who still remain to hear the ocean roar,
Whose greedy waves devour the lessening shore;
Till some fierce tide, with more imperious sway,
Sweeps the low hut and all it holds away;
When the sad tenant weeps from door to door,
And begs a poor protection from the poor!"
But these are scenes where Nature's niggard hand
Gave a spare portion to the famished land;
Hers is the fault, if here mankind complain
Of fruitless toil and labor spent in vain.
But yet in other scenes, more fair in view,
Where Plenty smiles—alas! she smiles for few—
And those who taste not, yet behold her store,
Are as the slaves that dig the golden ore,
The wealth around them makes them doubly poor.
Or will you deem them amply paid in health,
Labor's fair child, that languishes with wealth?
Go, then! and see them rising with the sun,
Through a long course of daily toil to run;
See them beneath the dog star's raging heat,
When the knees tremble and the temples beat;
Behold them, leaning on their scythes, look o'er
The labor past, and toils to come explore;
See them alternate suns and showers engage,
And hoard up aches and anguish for their age;
Through fens and marshy moors their steps pursue,
When their warm pores imbibe the evening dew;

5. Paid to electors by candidates for election to Parliament. Since Parliaments must be elected at least every seven years, the bribes are "septennial."

Then own that labor may as fatal be
To these thy slaves, as thine excess to thee.
Amid this tribe too oft a manly pride
Strives in strong toil the fainting heart to hide;
There may you see the youth of slender frame
Contend, with weakness, weariness, and shame;
Yet, urged along, and proudly loath to yield,
He strives to join his fellows of the field;
Till long-contending nature droops at last,
Declining health rejects his poor repast,
His cheerless spouse the coming danger sees,
And mutual murmurs urge the slow disease.
Yet grant them health, 'tis not for us to tell,
Though the head droops not, that the heart is well;
Or will you praise that homely, healthy fare,
Plenteous and plain, that happy peasants share?
Oh! trifle not with wants you cannot feel,
Nor mock the misery of a stinted meal,
Homely, not wholesome; plain, not plenteous; such
As you who praise would never deign to touch.
Ye gentle souls, whom dream of rural ease,
Whom the smooth stream and smoother sonnet please;
Go! if the peaceful cot your praises share,
Go, look within, and ask if peace be there:
If peace be his—that drooping weary sire,
Or theirs, that offspring round their feeble fire;
Or hers, that matron pale, whose trembling hand
Turns on the wretched hearth the expiring brand!
Nor yet can Time itself obtain for these
Life's latest comforts, due respect and ease:
For yonder see that hoary swain, whose age
Can with no cares except his own engage;
Who, propped on that rude staff, looks up to see
The bare arms broken from the withering tree,
On which, a boy, he climbed the loftiest bough,
Then his first joy, but his sad emblem now.
He once was chief in all the rustic trade;
His steady hand the straightest furrow made;
Full many a prize he won, and still is proud
To find the triumphs of his youth allowed.
A transient pleasure sparkles in his eyes;
He hears and smiles, then thinks again and sighs;
For now he journeys to his grave in pain;
The rich disdain him, nay, the poor disdain;
Altérnate masters now their slave command,
Urge the weak efforts of his feeble hand;
And, when his age attempts its task in vain,
With ruthless taunts, of lazy poor complain.
Oft may you see him, when he tends the sheep,
His winter charge, beneath the hillock weep;

Oft hear him murmur to the winds that blow
O'er his white locks and bury them in snow,
When, roused by rage and muttering in the morn
He mends the broken hedge with icy thorn:
"Why do I live, when I desire to be
At once from life and life's long labor free?
Like leaves in spring, the young are blown away,
Without the sorrows of a slow decay;
I, like yon withered leaf, remain behind,
Nipped by the frost, and shivering in the wind;
There it abides till younger buds come on,
As I, now all my fellow swains are gone;
Then, from the rising generation thrust,
It falls, like me, unnoticed to the dust.
"These fruitful fields, these numerous flocks I see,
Are others' gain, but killing cares to me:
To me the children of my youth are lords,
Cool in their looks, but hasty in their words:
Wants of their own demand their care; and who
Feels his own want and succors others too?
A lonely, wretched man, in pain I go,
None need my help, and none relieve my woe;
Then let my bones beneath the turf be laid,
And men forget the wretch they would not aid!"
Thus groan the old, till, by disease oppressed,
They taste a final woe, and then they rest.
Theirs is yon house that holds the parish poor,
Whose walls of mud scarce bear the broken door;
There, where the putrid vapors, flagging, play,
And the dull wheel hums doleful through the day—
There children dwell, who know no parents' care;
Parents, who know no children's love, dwell there!
Heartbroken matrons on their joyless bed,
Forsaken wives, and mothers never wed;
Dejected widows with unheeded tears,
And crippled age with more than childhood fears;
The lame, the blind, and, far the happiest they!
The moping idiot and the madman gay.
Here too the sick their final doom receive,
Here brought, amid the scenes of grief, to grieve,
Where the loud groans from some sad chamber flow,
Mixed with the clamors of the crowd below;
Here, sorrowing, they each kindred sorrow scan,
And the cold charities of man to man:
Whose laws indeed for ruined age provide,
And strong compulsion plucks the scrap from pride;
But still that scrap is bought with many a sigh,
And pride embitters what it can't deny.
Say ye, oppressed by some fantastic woes,
Some jarring nerve that baffles your repose;

Who press the downy couch, while slaves advance
With timid eye to read the distant glance;
Who with sad prayers the weary doctor tease,
To name the nameless ever-new disease;
Who with mock patience dire complaints endure,
Which real pain, and that alone, can cure—
How would ye bear in real pain to lie,
Despised, neglected, left alone to die?
How would ye bear to draw your latest breath,
Where all that's wretched paves the way for death?
  Such is that room which one rude beam divides,
And naked rafters form the sloping sides;
Where the vile bands that bind the thatch are seen,
And lath and mud are all that lie between,
Save one dull pane, that, coarsely patched, gives way
To the rude tempest, yet excludes the day.
Here, on a matted flock, with dust o'erspread,
The drooping wretch reclines his languid head;
For him no hand the cordial cup applies,
Or wipes the tear that stagnates in his eyes;
No friends with soft discourse his pain beguile,
Or promise hope till sickness wears a smile.
  But soon a loud and hasty summons calls,
Shakes the thin roof, and echoes round the walls.
Anon, a figure enters, quaintly neat,
All pride and business, bustle and conceit;
With looks unaltered by these scenes of woe,
With speed that, entering, speaks his haste to go,
He bids the gazing throng around him fly,
And carries fate and physic in his eye:
A potent quack, long versed in human ills,
Who first insults the victim whom he kills;
Whose murderous hand a drowsy Bench protect,[6]
And whose most tender mercy is neglect.
  Paid by the parish for attendance here,
He wears contempt upon his sapient sneer;
In haste he seeks the bed where Misery lies,
Impatience marked in his averted eyes;
And, some habitual queries hurried o'er,
Without reply, he rushes on the door.
His drooping patient, long inured to pain,
And long unheeded, knows remonstrance vain;
He ceases now the feeble help to crave
Of man; and silent sinks into the grave.
  But ere his death some pious doubts arise,
Some simple fears, which "bold bad" men despise:
Fain would he ask the parish priest to prove

6. Crabbe, who had practiced medicine among the poor of Aldeborough, well knew the indifference of the local magistrates ("the drowsy Bench") to the incompetence and callousness of the physician hired by the parish to attend its paupers.

His title certain to the joys above;
For this he sends the murmuring nurse, who calls
The holy stranger to these dismal walls;
And doth not he, the pious man, appear,
He, "passing rich with forty pounds a year"?[7]
Ah! no; a shepherd of a different stock:
And far unlike him, feeds this little flock:
A jovial youth, who thinks his Sunday's task
As much as God or man can fairly ask;
The rest he gives to loves and labors light,
To fields the morning, and to feasts the night;
None better skilled the noisy pack to guide,
To urge their chase, to cheer them or to chide;
A sportsman keen, he shoots through half the day,
And, skilled at whist, devotes the night to play.
Then, while such honors bloom around his head,
Shall he sit sadly by the sick man's bed,
To raise the hope he feels not, or with zeal
To combat fears that e'en the pious feel?
  Now once again the gloomy scene explore,
Less gloomy now; the bitter hour is o'er,
The man of many sorrows sighs no more.—
Up yonder hill, behold how sadly slow
The bier moves winding from the vale below;
There lie the happy dead, from trouble free,
And the glad parish pays the frugal fee.
No more, O Death! thy victim starts to hear
Churchwarden stern, or kingly overseer;
No more the farmer claims his humble bow,
Thou art his lord, the best of tyrants thou!
  Now to the church behold the mourners come,
Sedately torpid and devoutly dumb;
The village children now their games suspend,
To see the bier that bears their ancient friend:
For he was one in all their idle sport,
And like a monarch ruled their little court;
The pliant bow he formed, the flying ball,
The bat, the wicket, were his labors all;
Him now they follow to his grave, and stand
Silent and sad, and gazing, hand in hand;
While bending low, their eager eyes explore
The mingled relics of the parish poor.
The bell tolls late, the moping owl flies round,
Fear marks the flight and magnifies the sound;
The busy priest, detained by weightier care,
Defers his duty till the day of prayer;
And, waiting long, the crowd retire distressed,
To think a poor man's bones should lie unblessed.

1780–83 1783

7. Cf. Goldsmith's *Deserted Village*, line 142.

From The Borough[1]

Letter XXII, The Poor of The Borough: Peter Grimes

Old Peter Grimes made fishing his employ,
His wife he cabined with him and his boy,
And seemed that life laborious to enjoy;
To town came quiet Peter with his fish,
And had of all a civil word and wish.
He left his trade upon the sabbath day,
And took young Peter in his hand to pray;
But soon the stubborn boy from care broke loose,
At first refused, then added his abuse;
His father's love, he scorned, his power defied,
But being drunk, wept sorely when he died.
Yes! then he wept, and to his mind there came
Much of his conduct, and he felt the shame—
How he had oft the good old man reviled,
And never paid the duty of a child;
How, when the father in his Bible read,
He in contempt and anger left the shed;
"It is the word of life," the parent cried;
—"This is the life itself," the boy replied;
And while old Peter in amazement stood,
Gave the hot spirit to his boiling blood;
How he, with oath and furious speech, began
To prove his freedom and assert the man;
And when the parent checked his impious rage,
How he had cursed the tyranny of age—
Nay, once had dealt the sacrilegious blow
On his bare head, and laid his parent low;
The father groaned—"If thou art old," said he,
"And hast a son—thou wilt remember me.
Thy mother left me in a happy time,
Thou kill'dst not her—Heaven spares the double crime."
On an inn-settle,[2] in his maudlin grief,
This he revolved, and drank for his relief.
Now lived the youth in freedom, but debarred
From constant pleasure, and he thought it hard;
Hard that he could not every wish obey,
But must awhile relinquish ale and play;
Hard! that he could not to his cards attend,
But must acquire the money he would spend.
With greedy eye he looked on all he saw,
He knew not justice, and he laughed at law;

1. *The Borough* (1810) consists of 24 verse letters which aim to describe a whole community — Aldeburgh (pronounced *Ald-borough*), the Suffolk fishing village that Crabbe knew so well. In the "Peter Grimes" story (based probably on actual cases of maltreatment of apprentices), the hard landscape, the clear and chilling verse, and the cruel haunted character of Grimes himself join in a single image of harsh reality.

2. Bench in a tavern; "revolved": pondered.

On all he marked he stretched his ready hand;
He fished by water, and he filched by land.
Oft in the night has Peter dropped his oar,
Fled from his boat and sought for prey on shore;
Oft up the hedgerow glided, on his back
Bearing the orchard's produce in a sack,
Or farmyard load, tugged fiercely from the stack;
And as these wrongs to greater numbers rose,
The more he looked on all men as his foes.
  He built a mud-walled hovel, where he kept
His various wealth, and there he ofttimes slept;
But no success could please his cruel soul,
He wished for one to trouble and control;
He wanted some obedient boy to stand
And bear the blow of his outrageous hand,
And hoped to find in some propitious hour
A feeling creature subject to his power.
  Peter had heard there were in London then—
Still have they being!—workhouse-clearing men,
Who, undisturbed by feelings just or kind,
Would parish-boys to needy tradesmen bind;
They in their want a trifling sum would take,
And toiling slaves of piteous orphans make.[3]
  Such Peter sought, and when a lad was found,
The sum was dealt him, and the slave was bound.
Some few in town observed in Peter's trap[4]
A boy, with jacket blue and woolen cap;
But none inquired how Peter used the rope,
Or what the bruise, that made the stripling stoop;
None could the ridges on his back behold,
None sought him shivering in the winter's cold;
None put the question—"Peter, dost thou give
The boy his food?—What, man! the lad must live!
Consider, Peter, let the child have bread,
He'll serve thee better if he's stroked and fed."
None reasoned thus—and some, on hearing cries,
Said calmly, "Grimes is at his exercise."
  Pinned, beaten, cold, pinched, threatened, and abused—
His efforts punished and his food refused—
Awake tormented—soon aroused from sleep—
Struck if he wept, and yet compelled to weep,
The trembling boy dropped down and strove to pray,
Received a blow, and trembling turned away,
Or sobbed and hid his piteous face; while he,
The savage master, grinned in horrid glee;

3. At this time, the poor were confined, at the expense of the local church parish, to "workhouses," where they were put to compulsory labor. It was a common practice for "workhouse-clearing men" to remove young people from the workhouses and "bind them over" (i.e., sell them practically as slaves) to tradesmen.

4. I.e., two-wheeled carriage.

He'd now the power he ever loved to show,
A feeling being subject to his blow.
Thus lived the lad, in hunger, peril, pain,
His tears despised, his supplications vain;
Compelled by fear to lie, by need to steal,
His bed uneasy and unblessed his meal,
For three sad years the boy his tortures bore,
And then his pains and trials were no more.
"How died he, Peter?" when the people said,
He growled—"I found him lifeless in his bed,"
Then tried for softer tone, and sighed, "Poor Sam is dead."
Yet murmurs were there, and some questions asked—
How he was fed, how punished, and how tasked?
Much they suspected, but they little proved,
And Peter passed untroubled and unmoved.
Another boy with equal ease was found,
The money granted, and the victim bound.
And what his fate?—One night it chanced he fell
From the boat's mast and perished in her well,
Where fish were living kept, and where the boy
(So reasoned men) could not himself destroy.
"Yes, so it was," said Peter, "in his play
(For he was idle both by night and day),
He climbed the mainmast and then fell below"—
Then showed his corpse and pointed to the blow.
What said the jury?—They were long in doubt,
But sturdy Peter faced the matter out;
So they dismissed him, saying at the time,
"Keep fast your hatchway when you've boys who climb."
This hit the conscience, and he colored more
Than for the closest questions put before.
Thus all his fears the verdict set aside,
And at the slave-shop Peter still applied.
Then came a boy of manners soft and mild—
Our seamen's wives with grief beheld the child;
All thought (the poor themselves) that he was one
Of gentle blood, some noble sinner's son,
Who had, belike, deceived some humble maid,
Whom he had first seduced and then betrayed.
However this, he seemed a gracious lad,
In grief submissive and with patience sad.
Passive he labored, till his slender frame
Bent with his loads, and he at length was lame;
Strange that a frame so weak could bear so long
The grossest insult and the foulest wrong!
But there were causes: in the town they gave
Fire, food, and comfort to the gentle slave,
And though stern Peter, with a cruel hand
And knotted rope, enforced the rude command,
Yet he considered what he'd lately felt,

And his vile blows with selfish pity dealt.
  One day such drafts[5] the cruel fisher made,
He could not vend them in his borough trade,
But sailed for London mart; the boy was ill,
But ever humbled to his master's will;
And on the river, where they smoothly sailed,
He strove with terror and awhile prevailed;
But new to danger on the angry sea,
He clung affrightened to his master's knee.
The boat grew leaky and the wind was strong,
Rough was the passage and the time was long;
His liquor failed, and Peter's wrath arose—
No more is known—the rest we must suppose,
Or learn of Peter; Peter says, he "spied
The stripling's danger and for harbor tried;
Meantime the fish, and then the apprentice died."
  The pitying women raised a clamor round,
And weeping said, "Thou hast thy 'prentice drowned."
  Now the stern man was summoned to the hall,
To tell his tale before the burghers all;
He gave the account, professed the lad he loved,
And kept his brazen features all unmoved.
  The mayor himself with tone severe replied,
"Henceforth with thee shall never boy abide;
Hire thee a freeman,[6] whom thou durst not beat,
But who, in thy despite, will sleep and eat;
Free thou art now!—Again shouldst thou appear,
Thou'lt find thy sentence, like thy soul, severe."
  Alas! for Peter, not a helping hand,
So was he hated, could he now command.
Alone he rowed his boat, alone he cast
His nets beside, or made his anchor fast;
To hold a rope or hear a curse was none—
He toiled and railed, he groaned and swore alone.
  Thus by himself compelled to live each day,
To wait for certain hours the tide's delay;
At the same times the same dull views to see,
The bounding marsh-bank and the blighted tree;
The water only, when the tides were high,
When low, the mud half-covered and half-dry;
The sunburnt tar that blisters on the planks,
And bank-side stakes in their uneven ranks,
Heaps of entangled weeds that slowly float,
As the tide rolls by the impeded boat.
  When tides were neap[7] and, in the sultry day,
Through the tall bounding mudbanks made their way,
Which on each side rose swelling, and below
The dark warm flood ran silently and slow;

5. Catches of fish.
6. Paid laborer.
7. Low.

There anchoring, Peter chose from man to hide,
There hang his head, and view the lazy tide
In its hot slimy channel slowly glide;
Where the small eels that left the deeper way
For the warm shore within the shallows play;
Where gaping mussels, left upon the mud,
Slope their slow passage to the fallen flood.
Here dull and hopeless he'd lie down and trace
How sidelong crabs had scrawled their crooked race,
Or sadly listen to the tuneless cry
Of fishing gull or clanging goldeneye;[8]
What time the seabirds to the marsh would come,
And the loud bittern, from the bulrush home,
Gave from the salt-ditch side the bellowing boom.
He nursed the feelings these dull scenes produce,
And loved to stop beside the opening sluice;
Where the small stream, confined in narrow bound,
Ran with a dull, unvaried, saddening sound;
Where all, presented to the eye or ear,
Oppressed the soul with misery, grief, and fear.
  Besides these objects, there were places three,
Which Peter seemed with certain dread to see;
When he drew near them he would turn from each,
And loudly whistle till he passed the reach.[9]
  A change of scene to him brought no relief;
In town, 'twas plain, men took him for a thief.
The sailors' wives would stop him in the street,
And say, "Now, Peter, thou'st no boy to beat!"
Infants at play, when they perceived him, ran,
Warning each other—"That's the wicked man!"
He growled an oath, and in an angry tone
Cursed the whole place and wished to be alone.
  Alone he was, the same dull scenes in view,
And still more gloomy in his sight they grew;
Though man he hated, yet employed alone
At bootless labor, he would swear and groan,
Cursing the shoals[1] that glided by the spot,
And gulls that caught them when his arts could not.
  Cold nervous tremblings shook his sturdy frame,
And strange disease—he couldn't say the name;
Wild were his dreams, and oft he rose in fright,
Waked by his view of horrors in the night—
Horrors that would the sternest minds amaze,
Horrors that demons might be proud to raise;
And though he felt forsaken, grieved at heart
To think he lived from all mankind apart,
Yet, if a man approached, in terrors he would start.
  A winter passed since Peter saw the town,
And summer lodgers were again come down.

8. A species of wild duck.
9. The main part of the river.
1. Schools of fish.

These, idly curious, with their glasses spied
The ships in bay, as anchored for the tide—
The river's craft—the bustle of the quay—
And seaport views, which landmen love to see.
One, up the river, had a man and boat
Seen day by day, now anchored, now afloat;
Fisher he seemed; yet used no net nor hook,
Of seafowl swimming by no heed he took,
But on the gliding waves still fixed his lazy look.
At certain stations he would view the stream,
As if he stood bewildered in a dream,
Or that[2] some power had chained him for a time,
To feel a curse or meditate on crime.
This known, some curious, some in pity went,
And others questioned—"Wretch, dost thou repent?"
He heard, he trembled, and in fear resigned
His boat; new terror filled his restless mind;
Furious he grew, and up on the country ran,
And there they seized him—a distempered man.
Him we received, and to a parish-bed,[3]
Followed and cursed, the groaning man was led.
Here when they saw him whom they used to shun,
A lost, lone man, so harassed and undone,
Our gentle females, ever prompt to feel,
Perceived compassion on their anger steal;
His crimes they could not from their memories blot,
But they were grieved, and trembled at his lot.
A priest too came, to whom his words are told;
And all the signs they shuddered to behold.
"Look! look!" they cried, "his limbs with horror shake,
And as he grinds his teeth, what noise they make!
How glare his angry eyes, and yet he's not awake.
See! what cold drops upon his forehead stand,
And how he clenches that broad bony hand."
The priest, attending, found he spoke at times
As one alluding to his fears and crimes:
"It was the fall," he muttered; "I can show
The manner how—I never struck a blow"—
And then aloud—"Unhand me, free my chain!
On oath, he fell—it struck him to the brain—
Why ask my father?—that old man will swear
Against my life; besides, he wasn't there—
What, all agreed?—Am I to die today?—
My Lord, in mercy, give me time to pray."
Then, as they watched him, calmer he became,
And grew so weak he couldn't move his frame,
But murmuring spake—while they could see and hear
The start of terror and the groan of fear;
See the large dew-beads on his forehead rise,

2. I.e., or as if.

3. Bed in a charity hospital.

And the cold death-drop glaze his sunken eyes;
Nor yet he died, but with unwonted force
Seemed with some fancied being to discourse.
He knew not us, or with accustomed art
He hid the knowledge, yet exposed his heart;
'Twas part confession and the rest defense,
A madman's tale, with gleams of waking sense.
"I'll tell you all," he said, "the very day
When the old man first placed them in my way,
My father's spirit—he who always tried
To give me trouble, when he lived and died—
When he was gone, he could not be content
To see my days in painful labor spent,
But would appoint his meetings, and he made
Me watch at these, and so neglect my trade.
" 'Twas one hot noon, all silent, still, serene,
No living being had I lately seen;
I paddled up and down and dipped my net,
But (such his pleasure) I could nothing get—
A father's pleasure, when his toil was done,
To plague and torture thus an only son!
And so I sat and looked upon the stream,
How it ran on and felt as in a dream,
But dream it was not; no!—I fixed my eyes
On the midstream and saw the spirits rise;
I saw my father on the water stand,
And hold a thin pale boy in either hand;
And there they glided ghastly on the top
Of the salt flood, and never touched a drop;
I would have struck them, but they knew the intent,
And smiled upon the oar, and down they went.
"Now, from that day, whenever I began
To dip my net, there stood the hard old man—
He and those boys. I humbled me and prayed
They would be gone—they heeded not, but stayed;
Nor could I turn, nor would the boat go by,
But gazing on the spirits, there was I;
They bade me leap to death, but I was loath to die.
And every day, as sure as day arose,
Would these three spirits meet me ere the close;
To hear and mark them daily was my doom,
And 'Come,' they said, with weak, sad voices, 'come.'
To row away with all my strength I tried,
But there were they, hard by me in the tide,
The three unbodied forms—and 'Come,' still 'come,' they cried.
"Fathers should pity—but this old man shook
His hoary locks, and froze me by a look.
Thrice, when I struck them, through the water came
A hollow groan, that weakened all my frame.

'Father!' said I, 'have mercy!'—He replied,
I know not what—the angry spirit lied—
'Didst thou not draw thy knife?' said he—'Twas true,
But I had pity and my arm withdrew:
He cried for mercy which I kindly gave,
But he has no compassion in his grave.
"There were three places, where they ever rose—
The whole long river has not such as those—
Places accursed, where, if a man remain,
He'll see the things which strike him to the brain;
And there they made me on my paddle lean,
And look at them for hours—accurséd scene!
When they would glide to that smooth eddy-space,
Then bid me leap and join them in the place;
And at my groans each little villain sprite
Enjoyed my pains and vanished in delight.
"In one fierce summer day, when my poor brain
Was burning hot and cruel was my pain,
Then came this father-foe, and there he stood
With his two boys again upon the flood;
There was more mischief in their eyes, more glee
In their pale faces when they glared at me.
Still did they force me on the oar to rest,
And when they saw me fainting and oppressed,
He, with his hand, the old man, scooped the flood,
And there came flame about him mixed with blood;
He bade me stoop and look upon the place,
Then flung the hot-red liquor in my face;
Burning it blazed, and then I roared for pain,
I thought the demons would have turned my brain.
"Still there they stood, and forced me to behold
A place of horrors—they cannot be told—
Where the flood opened, there I heard the shriek
Of tortured guilt—no earthly tongue can speak:
'All days alike! forever!' did they say,
'And unremitted torments every day!'—
Yes, so they said."—But here he ceased and gazed
On all around, affrightened and amazed;
And still he tried to speak, and looked in dread
Of frightened females gathering round his bed;
Then dropped exhausted and appeared at rest,
Till the strong foe the vital powers possessed;
Then with an inward, broken voice he cried,
"Again they come," and muttered as he died.

1810

WILLIAM COWPER
(1731–1800)

There are no saner poems in the language than Cowper's, yet they were written by a man who was periodically insane and who, for forty years, lived with the possibility of madness in full view. One form that his madness took was a conviction that he was damned for having committed the unforgivable sin, the "sin against the Holy Ghost." When he recovered from his first attack, in which he had attempted suicide, he was persuaded by his physician that this conviction was a delusion, and he embraced the doctor's own hopeful Evangelical creed. Relieved of his guilts, he felt inwardly assured of salvation and of the healing and sustaining power of divine grace freely extended to him.

From then on, a refugee from life, he found shelter first, in 1765, in the pious family of the Evangelical clergyman, Morley Unwin, and after Unwin's death, with Mrs. Unwin, who gave him exactly the sort of loving shelter that he needed. They were never separated until her death in 1796, by which time Cowper had experienced his final attack of madness. The removal of Mary Unwin and Cowper from Huntington to Olney (pronounced *Own-y*) in 1765 brought the couple under the influence of the strenuous and fervent Evangelical clergyman John Newton. With him Cowper wrote the famous *Olney Hymns,* still familiar to Methodists and other Nonconformists. But here a second attack of madness, in 1773, not only frustrated his planned marriage to Mary, but left him for the rest of his life with the assurance that he had been cast out by God and was inevitably damned. He never again attended divine service, and the main purpose of his life thereafter was to divert his mind by every possible innocent device from the numb despair that was his lot in life. He gardened, he kept pets, he walked, he wrote letters (some of the best of the century), he conversed, he read—and he wrote poetry. When it was published, it brought him a measure of fame that his modest nature could never have hoped for.

Despair could suppress neither his humor and gentle wit nor the religious side of his nature, which finds expression in the poems of the next decade—not only in their ethical point of view, but in the tone of gentle, if wistful, piety that pervades them. The first volume, *Poems* (didactic and gently satiric verse in heroic couplets), won the praise of Johnson and the approval of the public. But his major work is *The Task,* undertaken at the bidding—hence the title—of the lively and charming Lady Austen, who, when he complained that he had no subject, directed him to write about the sofa in his parlor. It began with a mock-heroic account of the development of the sofa from a simple stool, but it grew into a long meditative poem of over five thousand lines in delicately modulated blank verse. The poet describes in his murmuring voice his small world of country, village, garden, and parlor, and from time to time he glances toward the great world to condemn cities and worldliness, war and slavery, luxury and corruption. The tone is muted, the sensibility delicate, the language on the whole pure and simple. The truthfulness of Cowper's description of landscape and of the human figures that animate it, his moralizing, his generous spirit of humanitarianism, all appealed to the Englishmen of the late 18th century. His religious piety, domestic sentiment, and humanitarianism made his poems especially acceptable to Methodists and their Anglican counterparts, the Evangelicals, who between them were transforming the religious life of England and establishing the values and manners which came to characterize the Victorian age. No poet of the century expressed more completely the interests and taste of the new enlightened and religious middle class.

Many of Cowper's themes are identical with Wordsworth's. No doubt a taste for Cowper's poetry made it easier for some people to accept Wordsworth when he appeared. But the similarity is superficial and deceptive. Cowper may seem a Wordsworth who never beheld the visionary gleam—but such a Wordsworth is inconceivable. We may agree today that Cowper was too highly valued by his contemporaries, but it is agreeable to take up his poems from time to time, and to allow his gentle talk to re-create for us the serenity and simplicity of life in an English village just before the French Revolution announced a new era.

From The Task

From *Book I*

[A LANDSCAPE DESCRIBED. RURAL SOUNDS]

Thou[1] knowest my praise of nature most sincere,
And that my raptures are not conjured up
To serve occasions of poetic pomp,
But genuine, and art partner of them all.
How oft upon yon eminence our pace
Has slackened to a pause, and we have borne
The ruffling wind, scarce conscious that it blew,
While admiration, feeding at the eye,
And still unsated, dwelt upon the scene.
Thence with what pleasure have we just discerned
The distant plow slow moving, and beside
His laboring team, that swerved not from the track,
The sturdy swain diminished to a boy!
Here Ouse,[2] slow winding through a level plain
Of spacious meads with cattle sprinkled o'er,
Conducts the eye along its sinuous course
Delighted. There, fast rooted in their bank,
Stand, never overlooked, our favorite elms,
That screen the herdsman's solitary hut;

1. Mary Unwin.
2. The village of Olney, where Cowper and Mary Unwin were living, is situated on the river Ouse.

While far beyond, and overthwart the stream
That, as with molten glass, inlays the vale,
The sloping land recedes into the clouds;
Displaying on its varied side the grace
Of hedgerow beauties numberless, square tower,
Tall spire, from which the sound of cheerful bells
Just undulates upon the listening ear,
Groves, heaths, and smoking villages, remote.
Scenes must be beautiful, which, daily viewed,
Please daily, and whose novelty survives
Long knowledge and the scrutiny of years—
Praise justly due to those that I describe.
  Nor rural sights alone, but rural sounds,
Exhilarate the spirit, and restore
The tone of languid Nature. Mighty winds,
That sweep the skirt of some far-spreading wood
Of ancient growth, make music not unlike
The dash of ocean on his winding shore,
And lull the spirit while they fill the mind;
Unnumbered branches waving in the blast,
And all their leaves fast fluttering, all at once.
Nor less composure waits upon the roar
Of distant floods, or on the softer voice
Of neighboring fountain, or of rills that slip
Through the cleft rock, and, chiming as they fall
Upon loose pebbles, lose themselves at length
In matted grass, that with a livelier green
Betrays the secret of their silent course.
Nature inanimate employs sweet sounds,
But animated nature sweeter still,
To soothe and satisfy the human ear.
Ten thousand warblers cheer the day, and one
The livelong night: nor these alone, whose notes
Nice-fingered art must emulate in vain,
But cawing rooks, and kites that swim sublime
In still repeated circles, screaming loud,
The jay, the pie, and even the boding owl
That hails the rising moon, have charms for me.
Sounds inharmonious in themselves and harsh,
Yet heard in scenes where peace forever reigns,
And only there, please highly for their sake.

[CRAZY KATE. GYPSIES]

  There often wanders one, whom better days
Saw better clad, in cloak of satin trimmed
With lace, and hat with splendid ribband bound.
A servingmaid was she, and fell in love

With one who left her, went to sea, and died.
Her fancy followed him through foaming waves
To distant shores; and she would sit and weep
At what a sailor suffers; fancy, too,
Delusive most where warmest wishes are,
Would oft anticipate his glad return,
And dream of transports she was not to know.
She heard the doleful tidings of his death—
And never smiled again! And now she roams
The dreary waste; there spends the livelong day,
And there, unless when charity forbids,
The livelong night. A tattered apron hides,
Worn as a cloak, and hardly hides, a gown
More tattered still; and both but ill conceal
A bosom heaved with never-ceasing sighs.
She begs an idle pin of all she meets,
And hoards them in her sleeve; but needful food,
Though pressed with hunger oft, or comelier clothes,
Though pinched with cold, asks never.—Kate is crazed!
  I see a column of slow rising smoke
O'ertop the lofty wood that skirts the wild.
A vagabond and useless tribe there eat
Their miserable meal. A kettle, slung
Between two poles upon a stick transverse,
Receives the morsel—flesh obscene of dog,
Or vermin,[3] or, at best, of cock purloined
From his accustomed perch. Hard faring race!
They pick their fuel out of every hedge,
Which, kindled with dry leaves, just saves unquenched
The spark of life. The sportive wind blows wide
Their fluttering rags, and shows a tawny skin,
The vellum of the pedigree they claim.
Great skill have they in palmistry, and more
To conjure clean away the gold they touch,
Conveying worthless dross into its place;
Loud when they beg, dumb only when they steal.
Strange! that a creature rational, and cast
In human mold, should brutalize by choice
His nature; and, though capable of arts
By which the world might profit, and himself,
Self-banished from society, prefer
Such squalid sloth to honorable toil!
Yet even these, though, feigning sickness oft,
They swathe the forehead, drag the limping limb,
And vex their flesh with artificial sores,
Can change their whine into a mirthful note
When safe occasion offers; and, with dance,

3. Any small, noxious animal, such as a rat or weasel.

And music of the bladder and the bag,
Beguile their woes, and make the woods resound.
Such health and gaiety of heart enjoy
The houseless rovers of the sylvan world;
And, breathing wholesome air, and wandering much,
Need other physic none to heal the effects
Of loathsome diet, penury, and cold.

From *Book III*

[THE STRICKEN DEER]

I was a stricken deer, that left the herd
Long since; with many an arrow deep infixed
My panting side was charged, when I withdrew
To seek a tranquil death in distant shades.
There was I found by one who had himself
Been hurt by the archers. In his side he bore,
And in his hands and feet, the cruel scars.
With gentle force soliciting[4] the darts,
He drew them forth, and healed, and bade me live.
Since then, with few associates, in remote
And silent woods I wander, far from those
My former partners of the peopled scene;
With few associates, and not wishing more.
Here much I ruminate, as much I may,
With other views of men and manners now
Than once, and others of a life to come.
I see that all are wanderers, gone astray
Each in his own delusions; they are lost
In chase of fancied happiness, still wooed
And never won. Dream after dream ensues;
And still they dream that they shall still succeed.
And still are disappointed. Rings the world
With the vain stir. I sum up half mankind
And add two-thirds of the remaining half,
And find the total of their hopes and fears
Dreams, empty dreams.

From Book IV

[THE WINTER EVENING: A BROWN STUDY]

Come evening once again, season of peace,
Return sweet evening, and continue long!
Methinks I see thee in the streaky west,
With matron-step slow-moving, while the night
Treads on thy sweeping train; one hand employed

4. "To endeavor to draw out by the use of gentle force" (*NED*).

5. The post-horn, announcing the arrival of the mail coach.

In letting fall the curtain of repose
On bird and beast, the other charged for man
With sweet oblivion of the cares of day;
Not sumptuously adorned, nor needing aid
Like homely featured night, of clustering gems;
A star or two just twinkling on thy brow
Suffices thee; save that the moon is thine
No less than hers, not worn indeed on high
With ostentatious pageantry, but set
With modest grandeur in thy purple zone,[5]
Resplendent less, but of an ampler round.[6]
Come then and thou shalt find thy votary calm,
Or make me so. Composure is thy gift.
And whether I devote thy gentle hours
To books, to music, or the poet's toil,
To weaving nets for bird-alluring fruit;
Or twining silken threads round ivory reels
When they command whom man was born to please;[7]
I slight thee not, but make thee welcome still.
Just when our drawing rooms begin to blaze
With lights by clear reflection multiplied
From many a mirror, in which he of Gath,
Goliah,[8] might have seen his giant bulk
Whole without stooping, towering crest and all,
My pleasures too begin. But me perhaps
The glowing hearth may satisfy awhile
With faint illumination that uplifts
The shadow to the ceiling, there by fits
Dancing uncouthly to the quivering flame.
Not undelightful is an hour to me
So spent in parlor twilight; such a gloom
Suits well the thoughtful or unthinking mind,
The mind contemplative, with some new theme
Pregnant, or indisposed alike to all.
Laugh ye, who boast your more mercurial powers
That never feel a stupor, know no pause,
Nor need one. I am conscious,[1] and confess,
Fearless, a soul that does not always think.
Me oft has fancy ludicrous and wild
Soothed with a waking dream of houses, towers,
Trees, churches, and strange visages expressed
In the red cinders, while with poring eye
I gazed, myself creating what I saw.

5. Encircling band. Evening is seen both as a personified goddess, whose "zone" is her royal belt, and as a natural phenomenon, where the "zone" is a stripe of color in the sky.
6. The moon looks larger at evening, when just over the horizon, than at night, when it is higher and brighter.
7. I.e., women.
8. Goliath, the giant of Gath slain by David (I Samuel xvii.19–51).
1. Conscious of.

Nor less amused have I quiescent watched
The sooty films that play upon the bars,[2]
Pendulous and foreboding, in the view
Of superstition prophesying still,
Though still deceived, some stranger's near approach.[3]
'Tis thus the understanding takes repose
In indolent vacuity of thought,
And sleeps and is refreshed. Meanwhile the face
Conceals the mood lethargic with a mask
Of deep deliberation, as[4] the man
Were tasked to his full strength, absorbed and lost.
Thus oft reclined at ease, I lose an hour
At evening, till at length the freezing blast
That sweeps the bolted shutter, summons home
The recollected powers, and snapping short
The glassy threads with which the fancy weaves
Her brittle toys, restores me to myself.
How calm is my recess, and how the frost,
Raging abroad, and the rough wind, endear
The silence and the warmth enjoyed within.
I saw the woods and fields at close of day,
A variegated show; the meadows green,
Though faded; and the lands where lately waved
The golden harvest, of a mellow brown,
Upturned so lately by the forceful share.[5]
I saw far off the weedy fallows[6] smile
With verdure not unprofitable, grazed
By flocks fast feeding and selecting each
His favorite herb; while all the leafless groves
That skirt the horizon wore a sable hue,
Scarce noticed in the kindred dusk of eve.
Tomorrow brings a change, a total change!
Which even now, though silently performed
And slowly, and by most unfelt, the face
Of universal nature undergoes.
Fast falls a fleecy shower. The downy flakes,
Descending and with never-ceasing lapse,[7]
Softly alighting upon all below,
Assimilate all objects. Earth receives
Gladly the thickening mantle, and the green
And tender blade that feared the chilling blast,
Escapes unhurt beneath so warm a veil.

1785

2. The grate of a fireplace.
3. The piece of soot that often flaps on the bars of a grate was called a "stranger," and supposed to portend an unexpected visitor. Lines 272–310 may be compared with Coleridge's *Frost at Midnight*.
4. As if.
5. Plowshare.
6. Plowed but unseeded land.
7. Gentle downward glide.

The Castaway

Obscurest night involved the sky,
  The Atlantic billows roared,
When such a destined wretch as I,
  Washed headlong from on board,
Of friends, of hope, of all bereft,
His floating home forever left.

No braver chief[1] could Albion boast
  Than he with whom he went,
Nor ever ship left Albion's coast,
  With warmer wishes sent.
He loved them both, but both in vain,
Nor him beheld, nor her again.

Not long beneath the whelming brine,
  Expert to swim, he lay;
Nor soon he felt his strength decline,
  Or courage die away;
But waged with death a lasting strife,
Supported by despair of life.

He shouted; nor his friends had failed
  To check the vessel's course,
But so the furious blast prevailed,
  That, pitiless perforce,
They left their outcast mate behind,
And scudded still before the wind.

Some succor yet they could afford;
  And, such as storms allow,
The cask, the coop, the floated cord,
  Delayed not to bestow.
But he (they knew) nor ship, nor shore,
Whate'er they gave, should visit more.

Nor, cruel as it seemed, could he
  Their haste himself condemn,
Aware that flight, in such a sea,
  Alone could rescue them;
Yet bitter felt it still to die
Deserted, and his friends so nigh.

He long survives, who lives an hour
  In ocean, self-upheld;

1. George, Lord Anson (1697–1762), in whose *Voyage* (1748), Cowper, years before writing this poem, had read the story of the sailor washed overboard in a storm.

And so long he, with unspent power,
His destiny repelled;
And ever, as the minutes flew,
Entreated help, or cried, "Adieu!"

At length, his transient respite past,
His comrades, who before
Had heard his voice in every blast,
Could catch the sound no more.
For then, by toil subdued, he drank
The stifling wave, and then he sank.

No poet wept him; but the page
Of narrative sincere,
That tells his name, his worth, his age,
Is wet with Anson's tear.
And tears by bards or heroes shed
Alike immortalize the dead.

I therefore purpose not, or dream,
Descanting on his fate,
To give the melancholy theme
A more enduring date:
But misery still delights to trace
Its semblance in another's case.

No voice divine the storm allayed,
No light propitious shone,
When, snatched from all effectual aid,
We perished, each alone;
But I beneath a rougher sea,
And whelmed in deeper gulfs than he.

1799 1803

Poems in Process

Poets in all ages have claimed that their poems were not willed but were inspired, whether by a muse, by divine visitation, or by sudden emergence from the poet's unconscious mind. But as the poet Richard Aldington has remarked, "genius is not enough; one must also work." The working manuscripts of the greatest poets show that, however involuntary the origin of a poem, vision was usually followed by laborious revision before the work achieved the seeming inevitability of its final form.

Milton is the first major English poet for whom we possess drafts of poems indubitably written in his own hand; the excerpt from his manuscript of *Lycidas* shows him altering and expanding his initial efforts. It is no surprise to find Pope, one of the most meticulous of craftsmen, working and reworking his drafts, and radically enlarging *The Rape of the Lock* even after the success which attended its first printed version. But the recently discovered manuscript of Samuel Johnson's greatest poem, *The Vanity of Human Wishes,* is a surprise, for it shows that this neoclassic writer who, in his critical theory, regarded poetry as primarily an art of achieving preconceived ends by tested means, in fact composed with even greater speed and assurance than the Romantic Byron, who liked to represent himself to his readers as dashing off his verses with casual and unreflecting ease. In the manuscript of Gray's *Elegy Written in a Country Churchyard* we find that the poet, by late afterthought, converted a relatively simple elegiac meditation into a longer and much more complex apologia for his chosen way of life. In all these selections we look on as each poet, no matter how rapidly he achieves a result he is willing to let stand, carries on his inevitably tentative efforts to meet the multiple requirements of meaning, syntax, meter, sound pattern, and the constraints imposed by his chosen stanza. And because these are all very good poets, the seeming conflict between the necessities of significance and form results not in the distortion but in the perfection of the poetic statement.

Our transcriptions from the poets' drafts attempt to reproduce, as accurately as the change from script to print will allow, the appearance of the original manuscript page. A poet's first attempt at a line or phrase is reproduced in larger type, his revisions in smaller type. The line numbers which are used to identify an excerpt are those of the final form of the complete poem, as reprinted in the text of this anthology. Within the transcriptions themselves, whether of a manuscript or an early printed version of a poem, the only line numbers are those which occur in the original.

SELECTED BIBLIOGRAPHY

Autograph Poetry in the English Language, 2 vols., 1973, compiled by P. J. Croft, reproduces and transcribes one or more pages of manuscript in the poet's own hand, from the 14th century to the present time; Volume I includes many of the poets represented in this volume of *The Norton Anthology of English Literature*, from John Skelton to George Crabbe. Books which discuss the process of poetic composition and revision, with examples from manuscripts and printed versions, are: Charles D. Abbott, ed., *Poets at Work*, 1948; Phyllis Bartlett, *Poems in Process*, 1951; A. F. Scott, *The Poet's Craft*, 1957. In *Word for Word: A Study of Authors' Alterations*, 1965, Wallace Hildick analyzes the composition of prose fiction, as well as poems. George Sherburn has a revealing study of "Pope at Work" in *Essays on the Eighteenth Century Presented to David Nichol Smith*, 1945.

JOHN MILTON

From Lycidas[1]

[*Lines 1–14*][2]

yet once more O ye laurells and once more
ye myrtl's browne wth Ivie never sere
I come to pluck yor berries harsh and crude
~~before the mellowing yeare~~ and wth forc't fingers rude
~~and crop yor young~~ shatter yor leaves before ye mellowing yeare
bitter constraint, and sad occasion deare
compells me to disturbe yor season due
for ~~young~~ Lycidas is dead, dead ere his prime
young Lycidas and hath not left his peere
who would ^not^ sing for Lycidas he well knew
himselfe to sing & build the loftie rime
he must not flote upon his watrie beare
unwept, and welter to the parching wind
without the meed of some melodious teare

[*Lines 56–63*]

ay mee I fondly dreame
~~had yee~~ bin there, ~~for~~ what could that have don?
~~what could the golden hayrd Calliope~~
for her inchaunting son
~~when shee beheld (the gods farre sighted bee)~~
~~his goarie scalpe rowle downe the Thracian lee~~

* whome universal nature might lament
~~and heaven and hel deplore~~
~~when his divine head downe~~
the streame was sent
downe the Swift Hebrus to Lesbian shore.

1. Transcribed from a manuscript of 50 pages in the library of Trinity College, Cambridge. Among the poems written in Milton's own hand are *Lycidas, Comus,* seven sonnets, and several other short poems. The manuscript has been photographically reproduced. with printed transcriptions, by W. Aldis Wright, *Facsimile of the Manuscript of Milton's Minor Poems* (Cambridge, England, 1899).
2. This draft is written on a separate page of the manuscript, which also contains drafts of the passages, "What could the muse her selfe" and "Bring the rathe primrose," transcribed below.

[THE THIRD AND FOLLOWING LINES ARE REWRITTEN ON A SEPARATE PAGE]

* what could the muse her selfe that Orpheus bore
the muse her selfe for her inchanting son
~~for her inchanting son~~

whome universal nature ~~might~~ [did] lament
when by the rout that made the hideous roare
goarie his ~~divine~~ [gorie] visage down the streame was sent
downe the swift Hebrus to ye Lesbian shoare.

[*Lines* 132–53]

Returne Alpheus the dred voice is past
that shrunk thy streams, returne Sicilian Muse
and call the vales and bid them hither cast
thire bells, and flowrets of a thousand hues
yee vallies low where the mild wispers use
of shades, and wanton winds, and g~~o~~[u]shing brooks * sparely
on whose fresh lap the swart starre *sparely looks ~~faintly~~
* ~~bring~~ hither all yor quaint enamel'd eyes * throw
that on the greene terfe suck the honied showrs
and purple all the gound wth vernal flowrs —— Bring the rathe &c.[3]
to strew the laureat herse where Lycid' lies
for so to interpose a little ease
let our ~~sad~~ [* fraile] thoughts dally wth false surmise * fraile

[LINES 142–50 ARE DRAFTED ON A SEPARATE PAGE, AS FOLLOWS]

Bring the rathe primrose that unwedded dies
~~collu~~ colouring the pale cheeke of uninjoyd love
and that sad floure that strove
to write his owne woes on the vermeil graine
next adde Narcissus y^t still weeps in vaine
the woodbine and ye pancie freak't wth jet
the glowing violet
the cowslip wan that hangs his pensive head
and every bud that sorrows liverie weares

let Daffadillies fill thire cups [with] teares
bid Amaranthus all his beautie shed
to strew the laureat herse &c.

Bring the rathe primrose that forsaken dies
the tufted crowtoe and pale Gessamin

3. I.e., Milton plans to insert here the passage that follows.

ye
the white pinke, and ^ pansie freakt wth jet
the glowing violet
the well-attired woodbine
the muske rose and ~~the garish columbine~~
wth cowslips wan that hang the pensive head
* weare * weares
and every flower that sad escutcheon ^ ~~beares~~ imbroidrie ~~beares~~
&
2 ^ ~~let~~ daffadillies fill thire cups wth teares
1 bid Amaranthus all his beauties shed
to strew &c.

ALEXANDER POPE

From The Rape of the Lock[1]

[*1712 Version: Canto I, Lines 1–24*]

WHAT dire Offence from Am'rous Causes springs,
What mighty Quarrels rise from Trivial Things,
I sing—This Verse to *C—l*, Muse! is due;
This, ev'n *Belinda* may vouchsafe to view:
Slight is the Subject, but not so the Praise,
If she inspire, and He approve my Lays.
Say what strange Motive, Goddess! cou'd compel
A well-bred *Lord* t'assault a gentle *Belle?*
Oh say what stranger Cause, yet unexplor'd,
Cou'd make a gentle *Belle* reject a *Lord?*
And dwells such Rage in *softest Bosoms* then?
And lodge such daring Souls in *Little Men*?
Sol thro' white Curtains did his Beams display,
And op'd those Eyes which brighter shine than they;
Shock just had giv'n himself the rowzing Shake,
And Nymphs prepar'd their *Chocolate* to take;
Thrice the wrought Slipper knock'd against the Ground,
And striking Watches the tenth Hour resound.
Belinda rose, and 'midst attending Dames
Launch'd on the Bosom of the silver *Thames:*
A Train of well-drest Youths around her shone,
And ev'ry Eye was fix'd on her alone;
On her white Breast a sparkling *Cross* she wore,
Which *Jews* might kiss, and Infidels adore.

[*Revised Version: Canto I, Lines 1–22*]

WHAT dire Offence from am'rous Causes springs,
What mighty Contests rise from trivial Things,
I sing—This Verse to *Caryll*, Muse! is due;

1. The first version of *The Rape of the Lock*, published 1712, consisted of two cantos and a total of 334 lines. Two years later, in 1714, Pope published an enlarged version of five cantos and 794 lines, in which he added the supernatural "machinery" of the Sylphs and Gnomes as well as a number of mock-epic episodes. The excerpts reprinted here show how Pope revised and expanded passages which he retained from the first version of the poem. The revised version includes changes that Pope added in later editions of the enlarged text of 1714.

This, ev'n *Belinda* may vouchsafe to view:
Slight is the Subject, but not so the Praise,
If She inspire, and He approve my Lays.
  Say what strange Motive, Goddess! cou'd compel
A well-bred *Lord* t'assault a gentle *Belle*?
Oh say what stranger Cause, yet unexplor'd,
Cou'd make a gentle *Belle* reject a *Lord*?
In Tasks so bold, can Little Men engage,
And in soft Bosoms dwells such mighty Rage?
  Sol thro' white Curtains shot a tim'rous Ray,
And op'd those Eyes that must eclipse the Day;
Now Lapdogs give themselves the rowzing Shake,
And sleepless Lovers, just at Twelve, awake:
Thrice rung the Bell, the Slipper knock'd the Ground,
And the press'd Watch return'd a silver Sound.
Belinda still her downy Pillow prest,
Her Guardian *Sylph* prolong'd the balmy Rest.
'Twas he had summon'd to her silent Bed
The Morning-Dream that hover'd o'er her Head.

[*Revised Version: Canto II, Lines 1–8*]

NOT with more Glories, in th' Etherial Plain,
The Sun first rises o'er the purpled Main,
Than issuing forth, the Rival of his Beams
Launch'd on the Bosom of the Silver *Thames*.
Fair Nymphs, and well-drest Youths around her shone,
But ev'ry Eye was fix'd on her alone.
On her white Breast a sparkling *Cross* she wore,
Which *Jews* might kiss, and Infidels adore.

From An Essay on Man[2]

[*From the First Manuscript*]

1. Learn ~~then thyself~~ **we ourselves**, not God presume to scan,
~~And~~ **But** know, the Study of Mankind is Man.
Plac'd on this Isthmus of a Middle State,
A Being darkly wise, & rudely great.
With too much knowledge for the Sceptic side,
And too much Weakness for a Stoic's Pride,
He hangs between, uncertain where to rest;
Whether to deem himself a God or Beast;
Whether his Mind or Body to prefer,
Born but to die, & reas'ning but to err;
Alike in Ignorance, (~~that~~ **his** Reason such)

2. Two of Pope's holograph manuscripts of *An Essay on Man* have survived. The earlier one is at the Pierpont Morgan Library in New York. The second one, at the Houghton Library, Harvard, was evidently intended as a fair copy for printing; but Pope, who was an inveterate reviser, introduced some last-minute improvements. The passage transcribed here from each of these manuscripts is Pope's famed description of man's "middle state" in the great chain of being; in the published version, it opens Epistle II, lines 1–18.

Who / ~~who thinks~~
Whether he thinks too little or too much:
Chaos of Thought & Passion, all confus'd,
Still by himself abus'd & dis-abus'd:
Created half to rise, & half to fall;
Great Lord of all things, yet a prey to all;
Sole Judge of Truth, in endless Error hurl'd;
The Glory, Jest, and Riddle of the World.

[*From the Second Manuscript*][3]

~~Incipit I~~ ~~Incipit III~~ Know
~~Learn~~ we ourselves, not God presume to scan,
The only Science Convinc'd,
~~But know~~, the Study of Mankind is Man;
[Plac'd on this Isthmus of a Middle State,
A Being darkly wise, and rudely great;
With too much Knowledge for the Sceptic side,
With
~~And~~ too much Weakness for a Stoic's Pride,
in doubt to act or
He hangs between, ~~uncertain where to~~ rest,
Part of
Whether to deem himself a ^ God or Beast;
In doubt
Whether his Mind, or Body to prefer.
~~This born~~ ~~that~~
Born but to die, and reas'ning but to err;
Alike in Ignorance, his Reason such,
Whether he thinks or too much.
~~Who thinks~~ too little, ~~or who thinks too much:~~
Chaos of Thought and Passion, all confus'd,
Still by himself abus'd and dis-abus'd:
Created half to rise, and half to fall;
Great Lord of all things, yet a prey to all;
Sole Judge of Truth, in endless error hurl'd;
The Glory, Jest, and Riddle of the World!

3. In this version of the manuscript, Pope inserted some marginal glosses. In the right-hand margin (next to the line beginning "Learn we ourselves * * * "), he wrote: "Of Man, as an Individual," while next to the line beginning "Plac'd on this Isthmus * * * ," he wrote "His Middle Nature." And in the left-hand margin, a little below the line beginning "With too much knowledge * * * ," he wrote "His Powers, and Imperfections."

SAMUEL JOHNSON

Johnson told Boswell in 1766 that when composing verses "I have generally had them in my mind, perhaps fifty at a time, walking up and down in my room; and then I have written them down, and often, from laziness, have written only half lines. * * * I remember I wrote a hundred lines of *The Vanity of Human Wishes* in a day." When the first manuscript draft of this poem turned up in the 1940's among Boswell's papers at Malahide Castle, it supported Johnson's account, for it had been written and corrected in haste, with only sparse punctuation; while the second half of each line had been filled out, obviously from memory, at some time after the writing of the first half, in a darker ink. In the transcriptions from this manuscript (which is in the collection of Mary Hyde, Somerville, New Jersey), the half-lines and emendations that Johnson added to his initial draft are printed in boldface type.

The draft was written on the right-hand pages of a small homemade pocket book; some words in the added half-line, impinging on the right margin of the page, had to be completed above or below the line. The two added lines, "See Nations slowly wise * * * the tardy Bust," were written on the blank left-hand page, at the place where they were to be inserted. The numeration of every tenth line was added by Johnson in the manuscript, and incorporates these two additional lines.

Johnson published the poem in 1749 and revised it for a second publication in 1755, when it achieved the final form printed in the selections from Johnson, above. It was in 1755 that Johnson introduced his most famous emendation when, after his disillusionment with Lord Chesterfield as literary patron, he substituted in line 162 the word "patron" for "garret": "Toil, envy, want, the patron, and the jail."

From The Vanity of Human Wishes

[*Lines 135–64*]

e
When first the College Rolls **receive his nam**
The young Enthusiast **quits his ease for fame**
Quick fires his breast
~~Each act betrays~~ **the fever of renown**
Caught from **the strong Contagion of the Gown**
On Isis banks he waves, **from noise withdrawn**
In sober state **th' imaginary Lawn**
O'er Bodley's Dome **his future Labours spread**
And Bacon's Mansion **trembles o'er his head.**
Are these thy views, **proceed illustrious Youth**
And Virtue guard **thee to the throne of Trut** **h**
Yet should thy ~~fate~~ **Soul indulge the gen'rous**
Heat
Till Captive Science **yields her last Retreat**
Should Reason **guide thee with her brightest Ray**
And pour on misty Doubt **resistless day**
Should no false kindness **lure to loose delight**
Nor Praise relax, nor **difficulty fright**
Should tempting Novelty **thy cell refrain**
vain
And Sloth's bland opiates **shed their fumes in**
sShould Beuty blunt **on fops her fatal dart**
Nor claim the **triumph of a letter'd heart**
~~S Nor~~ Should no Disease **thy torpid veins invade**
Nor Melancholys Spectres **haunt thy Shade**

hope
Yet ~~dream~~ not Life **from Grief or Danger free,**
Nor think the doom of **Man revers'd for thee**
Deign passing **to**
~~Turn~~ on the‸world ~~awhile~~ **turn thine eyes**
And pause **awhile from Learning to be wise**
There mark what **ill the Scholar's life assail**
the
Toil envy Want ~~a~~ **Garret and the Jayl**
Dreams
If ~~Hope~~ yet flatter **once again attend**
Hear Lydiats life **and Galileo's End.**

See Nations slowly wise, and meanly just,
To buried merit raise the tardy Bust.

THOMAS GRAY

There are three manuscript versions of the *Elegy* in Gray's handwriting; the one reproduced here in part is the earliest of these, preserved at Eton College, England; Gray entitled it "Stanzas wrote in a Country Church-Yard."

It is evident that Gray originally intended to conclude his poem at the end of the fifth stanza transcribed below. At some later time he bracketed off the last four stanzas, introduced a transitional stanza which incorporated the last two lines of the original conclusion, and then went on to write a new and much enlarged conclusion to the poem, which includes the closing "Epitaph." A comparison with the final version of the *Elegy*, above, will show that the author deleted some of these added stanzas, and also made a number of verbal changes, in his published texts of the poem.

From Elegy Written in a Country Churchyard

[*Lines 69–128*]

The struggleing~~s~~ Pangs of conscious Truth to hide,
To quench the Blushes of ingenuous Shame,
crown
And at the Shrine of Luxury & Pride
With **by**
~~Burn~~ Incense hallowd in the Muse's Flame.
kindled at

The thoughtless World to Majesty may bow
Exalt the brave, & idolize Success
But more to Innocence their Safety owe
Than Power & Genius e'er conspired to bless

And thou, who mindful of the unhonour'd Dead
eir
Dost in these notes th~~y~~ artless Tale relate

By Night & lonely Contemplation led
To linger in the gloomy Walks of Fate

Hark how the sacred Calm, that broods around
Bids ev'ry fierce tumultuous Passion cease
In still small Accents whisp'ring from the Ground
A grateful Earnest of eternal Peace

No more with Reason & thyself at Strife
Give anxious Cares & endless Wishes room
But thro' the cool sequester'd Vale of Life
Pursue the silent Tenour of thy Doom.

Far from the madding Crowd's ignoble Strife;
Their sober Wishes never knew to stray:
Along the cool sequester'd Vale of Life
noiseless
They kept the silent Tenour of their Way.

Yet even these Bones from Insult to protect
Some frail Memorial still erected nigh
With
~~In~~ uncouth Rhime, & shapeless Sculpture deckt
Implores the passing Tribute of a Sigh.

Their Name, their Years, spelt by th' unletter'd Muse
The Place of Fame, & Epitaph supply,
And many a holy Text around she strews
That teach the rustic Moralist to die.

For who to dumb Forgetfulness a Prey
This pleasing anxious Being e'er resign'd;
Left the warm Precincts of the chearful Day,
Nor cast one longing lingring Look behind?

On some fond Breast the parting Soul relies,
Some pious Drops the closing Eye requires:
Even from the Tomb the Voice of Nature cries,
And buried Ashes glow with social Fires
For Thee, who mindful &c: as above.[1]

If chance that e'er some pensive Spirit more,
By sympathetic Musings here delay'd,
With vain, tho' kind, Enquiry shall explore
Thy once-loved Haunt, this long-deserted Shade.

Haply some hoary-headed Swain shall say,[2]

1. I.e., Gray indicates that the second bracketed stanza, above, is to be inserted here, except that the opening "And thou" is to be altered to "For Thee."
2. At this point in the manuscript Gray ceases to leave a space between the stanzas. The first edition of 1751, at Gray's request, was printed without any intervals between the stanzas; the intervals were, however, introduced in later editions printed during Gray's lifetime.

Oft have we seen him at the Peep of Dawn
With hasty Footsteps brush the Dews away
On the high Brow of yonder hanging Lawn
Him have we seen the Green-wood Side along,
While o'er the Heath we hied, our Labours done,
Oft as the Woodlark piped her farewell Song
With whistful Eyes pursue the setting Sun.

spreading nodding
Oft at the Foot of yonder hoary Beech
That wreathes its old fantastic Roots so high
His listless Length at Noontide would he stretch,
And pore upon the Brook that babbles by.
With Gestures quaint now smileing as in Scorn,
wayward fancies ~~loved~~ would he
Mutt'ring his fond Conceits he ~~wont to~~ rove:
drooping,
Now woeful wan, ~~he droop'd,~~ as one forlorn
Or crazed with Care, or cross'd in hopeless Love.
One Morn we miss'd him on th' accustom'd Hill,
Along the near
By the Heath-~~side~~, & at his fav'rite Tree.
Another came, nor yet beside the Rill,
by
Nor up the Lawn, nor at the Wood was he.
~~There scatter'd oft, the earliest~~
The next with Dirges meet in sad Array
by
Slow thro the Church-way Path we saw him born
Approach & read, for thou can'st read the Lay
Graved carved yon
Wrote on the Stone beneath that ancient Thorn
Year
There scatter'd oft the earliest of y^{e} ~~Spring~~
showers of
By Hands unseen are frequent Vi'lets found
Redbreast
The Robin loves to build & warble there,
And little Footsteps lightly print the Ground.

Here rests his Head upon the Lap of Earth[3]
A Youth to Fortune & to Fame unknown
Fair Science frown'd not on his humble Birth
And Melancholy mark'd him for her own

Large was his Bounty & his Heart sincere;
Heaven did a Recompence as largely send.
He gave to Mis'ry all he had, a Tear.
He gain'd from Heav'n, 'twas all he wish'd, a Friend

3. These last three stanzas (which Gray in the first edition of 1751 labeled "The Epitaph") are written in the right-hand margin, with the page turned crosswise.

No farther seek his Merits to disclose,
think
Nor seek to draw them from their dread Abode
(His Frailties there in trembling Hope repose)
The Bosom of his Father & his God.

Selected Bibliographies

The Selected Bibliographies incorporate a list of Suggested General Readings on English literature, followed by bibliographies for each of the periods in this volume. For ease of reference, the authors within each period are arranged in alphabetical order. In the one instance where there are also general readings for a group of authors ("Prose of The Seventeenth Century"), the title of the group, with its entries, appears in its alphabetical place; those entries are followed by the names of all the authors in that group, while the bibliographical listing for each of those authors will also be found in its proper alphabetical place. Other cross-references have also been provided as needed.

SUGGESTED GENERAL READINGS

Histories of England and of English Literature

George Macaulay Trevelyan's *History of England*, rev., 1945, is an excellent survey in one volume; for detailed studies of single periods, see *The Oxford History of England*, 15 vols., 1934 ff., by a variety of historians. For single books in the comprehensive 12-volume *Oxford History of English Literature*, edited by F. P. Wilson and Bonamy Dobrée, 1945 ff., see the listings below. *A Guide to English Literature*, ed. Boris Ford, 1954–61, is available in 6 paperback volumes. Useful one-volume histories are Albert C. Baugh and others, *A Literary History of England*, rev., 1967; Hardin Craig and others, *A History of English Literature*, 1950; and (less densely factual, and more a running literary appreciation) David Daiches, *A Critical History of English Literature*, 2 vols., 1961. *Annals of English Literature, 1475–1950*, ed. J. C. Ghosh and others, rev. 1961, lists important publications year by year, together with the significant literary events in each year. Ellen Moers, *Literary Women*, 1976, is a history of the circumstances, inter-influences, and distinctive features of literature written by women.

Drama

Allardyce Nicoll, *British Drama*, rev., 1962, and *A History of English Drama, 1660–1900*, 6 vols., rev., 1952–59.

The Novel

The most detailed, although somewhat pedestrian, history is Ernest A. Baker's *History of the English Novel*, 10 vols., 1924–39. Among the short histories are Walter A. Raleigh, *The English Novel*, rev., 1911, which stops at Walter Scott; and, more up-to-date, Arnold Kettle, *An Introduction to the English Novel*, 2 vols., 1951–53; Walter Allen, *The English Novel*, 1954; Ian Watt, *The Rise of the Novel*, 1957; and Lionel Stevenson, *The English Novel*, 1960.

Poetry

W. J. Courthope, *A History of English Poetry*, 6 vols., 1895–1910, and H. J. C. Grierson and J. C. Smith, *A Critical History of English Poetry*, rev., 1947. In addition, Douglas Bush's two books, *Mythology and the Renaissance Tradition in English Poetry*, 1932, 1957, and *Mythology and the Romantic Tradition in English Poetry*, 1937, 1957, constitute an excellent running account, from their special perspective, of English poetry from the 16th century through T. S. Eliot. Another book which ranges widely in English poetry from the Middle Ages through the 18th century is E. M. W. Tillyard, *The English Epic and Its Background*, 1954.

Literary Criticism

George Saintsbury, *A History of English Criticism*, 1911, is still referred to. More recent histories of English criticism are M. H. Abrams, *The Mirror and the Lamp: Romantic Theory and the Critical Tradition*, 1953; W. K. Wimsatt, Jr. and Cleanth Brooks, *Literary Criticism: A Short History*, 1957; George Watson, *The Literary Critics*, 1962; and René Wellek, *A History of Modern Criticism: 1750–1950*, 1955, of which four of the projected five volumes have been published. René Wellek and Austin Warren, *Theory of Literature*, rev. 1970, is a useful introduction to the variety of scholarly and critical approaches to the study of literature.

Reference Works

The New Cambridge Bibliography of English Literature, ed. George Watson and I. R. Willison, 1969–77, lists all the books of the major and many minor British authors, together with a large selection from biographical, scholarly, and critical works written about these authors. Literary biographies and critical books published since that time can be found in the "Annual Bibliography" *PMLA*; for separate periods, see listings below. F. W. Bateson, ed., *A Guide to English Literature*, rev., 1968, is a selected list of editions, and of scholarly and critical treatments, of all important English writers; for poetry only see A. E. Dyson, ed., *English Poetry: Select Bibliographical Guides*, 1971. *Poetry Explication*, rev. by Joseph M. Kuntz, 1962, lists close analyses of English poems, old and recent, and I. F. Bell and Donald Baird, *The English Novel, 1578–1956*, 1958, provides a useful list of 20th-century criticisms of fiction. Further bibliographical aids are described in Richard D. Altick and Andrew Wright, *Selective Bibliography for the Study of English and American Literature*, 1971, and Arthur G. Kennedy, *A Concise Biblography for Students of English*, rev., 1972.

For compact biographies of English authors, see the multi-volumed *Dictionary of National Biography*, edited by Leslie Stephen and Sidney Lee in 1885–1900, with supplements that carry the work to persons who died up to 1960; condensed biographies will be found in the *Concise Dictionary of National Biography*, Part I (1953) and Part II (1961). Handy reference books on authors, works, and various literary terms and allusions are *The Oxford Companion to English Literature*, edited by Paul Harvey, rev., 1970; *The Reader's Companion to World Literature*, edited by Calvin S. Brown, 1956; *The Oxford Companion to the Theater*, edited by Phyllis Hartnoll, rev., 1967; *Dictionary of World Literature*, edited by Joseph T. Shipley, rev., 1953; and *Encyclopedia of Poetry and Poetics*, edited by Alex Preminger and others, 1965. Low-priced handbooks which define and illustrate literary concepts and terms are: M. H. Abrams, *A Glossary of Literary Terms*, rev., 1971; W. F. Thrall and Addison Hibbard, *A Handbook to Literature*, revised by G. Hugh Holman, 1960; and Lee T. Lemon, *A Glossary for the Study of English*, 1971. A useful and concise reference book is G. M. Kirkwood, *A Short Guide to Classical Mythology*, 1959.

Albert C. Baugh, *A History of the English Language*, rev., 1957, will be found helpful, as will various treatments of English meters and stanza forms, such as: R. M. Alden, *English Verse*, 1903; Karl Shapiro and Robert Beum, *A Prosody Handbook*, 1965; Paul Fussell, Jr., *Poetic Meter and Poetic Form*, 1966; and *The Structure of Verse: Modern Essays in Prosody*, ed. Harvey Gross, 1966.

Intellectual History and Criticism

Students interested in intellectual history as a background for reading English literature will profit from Arthur T. Lovejoy, *The Great Chain of Bering*, 1936, and *Essays in the History of Ideas*, 1948; Marjorie Nicolson, *The Breaking of the Circle*, 1950, *Science and Imagination*, 1956, and *Mountain Gloom and Mountain Glory*, 1959; John Herman Randall, Jr., *The Making of the Modern Mind*, rev., 1940; Basil Willey, *The Seventeenth Century Background*, 1934, *The Eighteenth Century Background*, 1940, and *Nineteenth Century Studies*, 1949; and M. H. Abrams, *Natural Supernaturalism: Tradition and Revolution in Romantic Literature*, 1971. In addition, the following is a selection from those books in literary history and criticism which have been notably influential in shaping modern approaches to English literature and literary forms; Erich Auerbach, *Mimesis: The Representation of Reality in Western Literature*, 1953; Maud Bodkin, *Archetypal Patterns in Poetry*, 1934; Cleanth Brooks, *The Well Wrought Urn*, 1947; Ronald Crane, *The Languages of Criticism and the Structure of Poetry*, 1953, *The Idea of the Humanities*, 2 vols., 1967, and, as editor, *Critics and Criticism, Ancient and Modern*, 1952; T. S. Eliot, *Selected Essays*, 3rd edition, 1951, and *On Po-*

etry and Poets, 1957; William Empson, *Seven Types of Ambiguity,* 3rd edition, 1953; William K. Wimsatt, *The Verbal Icon,* 1954; Francis Fergusson, *The Idea of a Theater,* 1949; Northrop Frye, *Anatomy of Criticism,* 1957; Henry James, *The Art of the Novel: Critical Prefaces,* 1934; F. R. Leavis, *Revaluation,* 1936, and *The Great Tradition* (i.e., in the novel), 1948; C. S. Lewis, *The Allegory of Love,* rev., 1938; John Livingston Lowes, *The Road to Xanadu,* rev., 1930; Percy Lubbock, *The Craft of Fiction,* 1926; I. A. Richards, *Principles of Literary Criticism,* 5th edition, 1934, and *Practical Criticism,* 1930; Caroline Spurgeon, *Shakespeare's Imagery,* 1935; Lionel Trilling, *The Liberal Imagination,* 1950, and *The Opposing Self,* 1955; Edmund Wilson, *Axel's Castle: A Study in the Imaginative Literature of 1870–1930,* 1936, and *The Wound and the Bow,* 1941; Wayne C. Booth, *The Rhetoric of Fiction,* 1961, and *A Rhetoric of Irony,* 1974; W. J. Bate, *The Burden of the Past and the English Past,* 1970; and Harold Bloom, *The Anxiety of Influence,* 1973. A convenient introduction to recent structuralist approaches to literary study is Jonathan Culler's *Structuralist Poetics,* 1975.

THE MIDDLE AGES

The Old English Period

The reader who wishes to acquire historical background for the literature of the period will profit greatly from Dorothy Whitelock's concise study, *The Beginnings of English Society,* 1952. The most detailed history is F. M. Stenton's authoritative *Anglo-Saxon England,* 3rd ed., 1971. Also highly informative are P. Hunter Blair's *An Introduction to Anglo-Saxon England,* 1956, and *Roman Britain and Early England, 55 B.C.—A.D. 871,* 1963. The classic study of the culture of the primitive Germanic peoples is H. M. Chadwick's *The Heroic Age,* 1912. For those who wish to sample basic historical documents of the period, there are available the translations by G. N. Garmonsway of *The Anglo-Saxon Chronicle,* 1953, and by L. Sherley-Price of Bede's *Ecclesiastical History,* published under the title *A History of the English Church and People,* 1955.

All the surviving poetry in Old English is contained in the six volumes edited by G. P. Krapp and E. V. K. Dobbie, *The Anglo-Saxon Poetic Records,* 1931–53, but the absence of glossaries makes this edition difficult for nonspecialists. Excellent texts of the shorter poems translated in this anthology are contained in J. C. Pope's *Seven Old English Poems,* 1966. The standard text of *Beowulf and the Fight of Finnsburg* is F. Klaeber's 3rd edition, 1950; C. L. Wrenn's edition, *Beowulf, with the Finnsburg Fragment,* rev., 1958, is very useful. Modern English translations of many of the Old English poems have been published by C. W. Kennedy under various titles. The present editor's translation is the text included in *Beowulf,* A Norton Critical Edition, edited by Joseph F. Tuso, 1975.

Good critical discussion of Old English literature will be found in Volume I of the *Cambridge History of English Literature*; in Kemp Malone's section of *A Literary History of England,* edited by A. C. Baugh, rev., 1967; in S. B. Greenfield's *A Critical History of Old English Literature,* 1965; and in C. L. Wrenn, *A Study of Old English Literature,* 1966. Important critical articles have been collected by J. B. Bessinger and S. J. Kahrl, *Essential Articles for the Study of Old English Poetry,* 1968. The best critical essay on *Beowulf* remains J. R. R. Tolkien's Gollancz lecture, *Beowulf, the Monsters, and the Critics,* 1937. The most exhaustive scholarly discussion is R. W. Chambers's *Beowulf: An Introduction to the Study of the Poem,* 3rd ed., with a supplement by C. L. Wrenn, 1959. W. W. Lawrence's *Beowulf and the Epic Tradition,* 1928, is still of value. Recent works by Dorothy Whitelock, *The Audience of Beowulf,* 1958; A. C. Brodeur, *The Art of Beowulf,* 1959; Kenneth Sisam, *The Structure of Beowulf,* 1965; and E. B. Irving, *A Reading of Beowulf,* 1968, and *Introduction to Beowulf,* 1969, mingle fine general criticism with some highly specialized discussion. Donald K. Fry has made a useful collection of essays on *Beowulf,* including Tolkien's lecture, in *The Beowulf Poet,* 1968.

The Middle English Period

Good and fairly compact accounts of the history of England between the Norman Conquest and the end of the Middle Ages are contained in the two volumes by Christopher Brooke, *From Alfred to Henry III, 871–1272,* 1961, and George Holmes, *The Later Middle Ages, 1272–1485,* 1962; see also May McKisack, *The Fourteenth Century, 1307–99,* 1959, and D. M. Stenton, *English Society in the Early Middle Ages (1066–1307),* 1951, and

A. R. Myers, *England in the Late Middle Ages*, 1952. Interesting illustrations of life in the Middle Ages, especially in the later centuries, will be found in three books by G. G. Coulton: *Chaucer and His England*, 1908, *The Medieval Scene*, 1930, *Medieval Panorama*, 1938; in Eileen Power's *Medieval People*, 1924; in Edith Rickert's *Chaucer's World*, 1948; in Volume I of G. M. Trevelyan's *Illustrated English Social History, Chaucer's England and the Early Tudors*, 1949; and in R. S. Loomis's *A Mirror of Chaucer's World*, 1965. The spirit of the 15th and late 14th century is brilliantly discussed by J. Huizinga, *The Waning of the Middle Ages*, 1924, 1954.

For general discussions of Middle English literature including Chaucer, see Volume II of the *Cambridge History of English Literature* and A. C. Baugh's section of *A Literary History of England*, edited by Baugh, 1948. W. P. Ker's *English Literature: Medieval*, 1912, is still provocative. D. M. Zesmer's *Guide to English Literature from Beowulf through Chaucer and Medieval Drama*, 1961, is a most useful survey; C. S. Lewis, *The Discarded Image*, 1964, is very popular; W. L. Renwick and H. Orton, *The Beginnings of English Literature to Skelton*, 3rd edition, 1966, is a good survey with bibliographical notes; also useful is H. S. Bennett, *Chaucer and the Fifteenth Century*, 1974. Edward Vasta's collection of essays by various scholars, *Middle English Survey: Critical Essays*, 1965, will offer stimulation to students of *Piers Plowman, Sir Gawain and the Green Knight*, the drama, and the ballads. J. A. Burrow, *Ricardian Poetry: Chaucer, Gower, Langland and the Gawain Poet*, 1971, is extremely interesting on the authors in his title and their period. Chapters 6–10 of Erich Auerbach's *Mimesis: The Representation of Reality in Western Literature*, translated by W. R. Trask, 1953, while dealing with none of the works included in this anthology, shed much light on the spirit of medieval literature. For the Middle English language, see Helge Kökeritz's *A Guide to Chaucer's Pronunciation*, 1954; Samuel Moore's *Historical Outlines of English Sounds and Inflections*, revised by A. H. Marckwardt, 1951; and John W. Clark's *Early English*, 1957.

For general discussion of non-Chaucerian Middle English literature, see R. M. Wilson, *Early Middle English Literature*, 1939, and E. K. Chambers, *English Literature at the Close of the Middle Ages*, 1954, which between them thoroughly cover the beginning and the end of the period. The only recent work attempting to survey the whole non-Chaucerian field is John Spiers's erratic but stimulating *Medieval English Poetry: The Non-Chaucerian Tradition*, 1957. George Kane's *Middle English Literature*, 1951, has good chapters on the romances, the religious lyrics, and *Piers Plowman*, and A. L. Kellogg, *Chaucer, Langland, Arthur*, 1972, treats his selected topics provocatively. A. C. Spearing's *Medieval Dream-Poetry*, 1976, is a fine treatment of the genre. A broad sampling of non-Chaucerian literature in translation is offered by *Medieval English Verse*, edited by R. S. Loomis and R. Willard, 1948.

The standard bibliography is J. E. Wells, *A Manual of the Writings in Middle English, 1050–1400*, 1916; nine supplements extend coverage through 1945. Two volumes of a revised edition of Wells edited by J. B. Severs have appeared, and three volumes in the same series edited by A. E. Hartung; further volumes are approaching publication.

Geoffrey Chaucer

The standard edition of Chaucer's writing is F. N. Robinson's *The Complete Works of Chaucer*, 2nd ed., 1957. The present editor's anthology of Chaucer's poetry, 2nd ed., 1975, from which are taken the selections printed here, is helpful to the nonspecialist, as are A. C. Baugh's *Chaucer's Major Poetry*, 1963, and John H. Fisher's *The Complete Poetry and Prose of Geoffrey Chaucer*, 1977. Vivid presentations of Chaucer in the background of 14th-century England are found in Marchette Chute's *Geoffrey Chaucer of England*, 1946, and D. S. Brewer's *Chaucer and His Time*, 1963. John Gardner's *The Life and Times of Chaucer*, 1977, is a fictionalized biography, fairly lively but unsubstantial. The raw material for Chaucer's biography is contained in *Chaucer Life-Records*, edited by M. M. Crow and C. C. Olson, 1966. For succinct accounts of the sources and literary background of Chaucer's works see R. D. French's *A Chaucer Handbook*, 2nd ed., 1947; reproductions of many of the known sources of the *Canterbury Tales* are contained in the scholarly compendium *Sources and Analogues of Chaucer's Canterbury Tales*, edited by W. F. Bryan and Germaine Dempster, 1941, 1958. Muriel Bowden, *A Commentary on the General Prologue to the Canterbury Tales*, 1948, provides a wealth of background information on the individual Canterbury pilgrims; see also J. M. Manly's *Some New Light on Chaucer*, 1926, and Jill Mann's *Chaucer and Medieval Estates Satire*, 1973.

Various aspects of Chaucer's work are treated by a number of scholars in *Chaucer and Chaucerians*, edited by D. S. Brewer, 1966; *Geoffrey Chaucer (Writers and Their Background)*, also edited by Brewer, 1974; *Companion to Chaucer Studies*, edited by Beryl Rowland, 1968; and *Chaucer's Mind and Art*, edited by A. C. Cawley, 1969. For literary criticism, the following contain stimulating discussions: H. S. Bennett, *Chaucer and the Fifteenth Century*, 1947; D. S. Brewer, *Chaucer*, 3rd ed., 1973; B. H. Bronson, *In Search of Chaucer*, 1960; Robert B. Burlin, *Chaucerian Fiction*, 1977; G. K. Chesterton, *Chaucer*, 1932; Nevill Coghill, *The Poet Chaucer*, 1949, and *Geoffrey Chaucer*, 1956; H. S. Corsa, *Chaucer, Poet of Mirth and Morality*, 1964; W. C. Curry, *Chaucer and the Medieval Sciences*, rev., 1960; Alfred David, *The Strumpet Muse*, 1976; Germaine Dempster, *Dramatic Irony in Chaucer*, 1932; E. T. Donaldson, *Speaking of Chaucer*, 1970; Peter Elbow, *Oppositions in Chaucer*, 1975; D. R. Howard, *The Idea of the Canterbury Tales*, 1976; Maurice Hussey, A. C. Spearing, and James Winny, *An Introduction to Chaucer*, 1965; S. S. Hussey, *Chaucer: An Introduction*, 1971; P. M. Kean, *Chaucer and the Making of English Poetry*, 2 vols., 1972; G. L. Kittredge, *Chaucer and His Poetry*, 1915; W. W. Lawrence, *Chaucer and the Canterbury Tales*, 1950; John Lawlor, *Chaucer*, 1968; J. L. Lowes, *Geoffrey Chaucer and the Development of His Genius*, 1934; R. M. Lumiansky, *Of Sondry Folk*, 1955; Kemp Malone, *Chapters on Chaucer*, 1951; Charles Muscatine, *Chaucer and the French Tradition*, 1957; H. R. Patch, *On Rereading Chaucer*, 1939; R. O. Payne, *The Key of Remembrance*, 1963; Raymond Preston, *Chaucer*, 1952; R. K. Root, *The Poetry of Chaucer*, 2nd ed., 1972; T. W. Ross, *Chaucer's Bawdy*, 1972; P. G. Ruggiers, *The Art of the Canterbury Tales*, 1965; John Speirs, *Chaucer the Maker*, 1951; and J. S. P. Tatlock, *The Mind and Art of Chaucer*, 1950. D. W. Robertson's *A Preface to Chaucer*, 1962, is a most learned, stimulating, doctrinaire, and controversial introduction to the reading of Chaucer. The following are collections of critical essays by various writers: *Discussions of the Canterbury Tales*, edited by C. J. Owen, 1961; *Chaucer Criticism: The Canterbury Tales*, edited by R. J. Schoeck and J. Taylor, 1960; *Chaucer: Modern Essays in Criticism*, edited by E. C. Wagenknecht, 1959; and *Geoffrey Chaucer: A Critical Anthology*, 1969, edited by J. A. Burrow. See also the prefatory remarks on Chaucer's poems in Robinson's edition and the present editor's commentary in his anthology.

The standard bibliographies are E. P. Hammond, *Chaucer: A Bibliographical Manual*, 1908; D. D. Griffith, *Bibliography of Chaucer*, 1955; W. R. Crawford, *Bibliography of Chaucer 1954–63*, 1967; L. Y. Baird, *A Bibliography of Chaucer 1964–1973*, 1977; and A. C. Baugh, *Chaucer*, 1968. See also Caroline Spurgeon's *Five Hundred Years of Chaucer Criticism and Allusion, 1357–1900*, 1925.

Everyman

See entries under **The Second Shepherds' Play.**

Sir Thomas Malory

The Winchester manuscript of Malory's *Morte Darthur*, with full commentary and valuable discussion, is given in Eugène Vinaver's *The Works of Sir Thomas Malory*, 3 vols., 2nd ed., 1967; the one-volume edition, 2nd ed., Oxford, 1970, contains the text only. The Caxton version is most readily available in *Le Morte D'Arthur*, edited by E. Rhys, 1906. Vinaver's *Malory*, 1929, surveys Malory's life and career. A number of critical problems in Malory's work, especially its unity, are discussed in two collections of essays by various scholars: *Essays on Malory*, edited by J. A. W. Bennett, 1963, and *Malory's Originality*, edited by R. M. Lumianski, 1964. Two excellent recent studies of the work are those by L. D. Benson, *Malory's Morte Darthur*, 1976, and Mark Lambert, *Malory: Style and Vision in Le Morte Darthur*, 1975. In *The Ill-Framed Knight*, 1966, William Matthews challenges the traditional identification of the author of the *Morte Darthur* with that knight-prisoner, the details of whose stormy career have been unearthed by scholars interested in the book.

A most valuable summary of the Arthurian literary background is R. S. Loomis's *The Development of Arthurian Romance*, 1963.

Middle English Lyrics

The best selections of Middle English lyrics are *Early English Lyrics*, edited by E. K. Chambers and F. Sidgwick, 1921; *Medieval English Lyrics: A Critical Anthology*, edited by R. T. Davies, 1963; *Middle English Lyrics*, A Norton Critical Edition, edited by M. S. Luria and R. L. Hoffman, 1974; *The Oxford Book of Medieval English Verse*, edited by Celia and Kenneth Sisam, 1970; *English Lyrics before 1500*, edited by Theodore Silverstein, 1971; modernized and semi-modernized selections appear in M. R. Adamson's *A Treasury of Middle English Verse*, 1930, and in R. D. Stevick's *One Hundred Middle English Poems*, 1964. For criticism see A. K. Moore, *The Secular Lyric in Middle English*, 1951, and Kane's chapter in *Middle English Literature*.

Pearl

The standard edition of *Pearl* is that by E. V. Gordon, 1953. Recent critical studies are those of Ian Bishop, *Pearl in Its Setting*, 1968, and P. M. Kean, *The Pearl: An Interpretation*, 1967. Essays by various hands have been collected by R. J. Blanch, *Sir Gawain and Pearl*, 1966, and by John Conley, *The Middle English Pearl: Critical Essays*, 1970. The essay by René Wellek is especially recommended.

Piers Plowman

The most handy edition of *Piers Plowman* is W. W. Skeat's *The Vision of William Concerning Piers the Plowman* * * *, 2 vols., 1886, which gives all three versions. The most scholarly edition of the A text is that edited by George Kane, 1960, and of the B text that by Kane and E. T. Donaldson, 1975. J. A. W. Bennett's edition of the first eight passus of the B text, 1972, is very useful, as is Elizabeth Salter and D. A. Pearsall's selections from C, 1967. There are modern translations by H. W. Wells, *The Vision of Piers Plowman*, 1935; by Nevill Coghill (selections only), *Visions from Piers Plowman*, 1949; and by Margaret Williams, *Piers the Plowman*, 1972. A literal prose translation is J. F. Goodridge's *Langland: Piers the Ploughman*, rev., 1966. The best general account of the poem is in Chapters IV–V of R. W. Chambers's *Man's Unconquerable Mind*, 1939; see also Kane's chapter in *Middle English Literature*. Recent studies by Elizabeth Salter, *Piers Plowman: An Introduction*, 1962, and John Lawlor, *Piers Plowman: An Essay in Criticism*, 1962, are most useful to the beginner, as are chapters on the poem in the works by Howard and Spearing mentioned below under **Sir Gawain and the Green Knight.** Collections of critical essays have been made by Edward Vasta, *Interpretations of Piers Plowman*, 1968; R. J. Blanch, *Style and Symbolism in Piers Plowman*, 1969; and S. S. Hussey, *Piers Plowman: Critical Approaches*, 1969.

Popular Ballads

The great ballad collection is that of F. J. Child, *The English and Scottish Popular Ballads*, 1882, more available in the somewhat abridged edition by H. C. Sargent and G. L. Kittredge, 1904. Selections will be found in *The Faber Book of Ballads*, edited by M. J. C. Hodgart, 1965, and *The Oxford Book of Ballads*, edited by James Kinsley, 1969. For general discussion, see F. B. Gummere, *The Popular Ballads*, 1907; G. H. Gerould, *The Ballad of Tradition*, 1932; W. J. Entwistle. *European Balladry*, 1939; and M. J. C. Hodgart, *The Ballads*, 1950.

The Second Shepherds' Play; Everyman

The classic work on the medieval drama is E. K. Chambers's *The Medieval Stage*, 1905. More recent are Hardin Craig's exhaustive *English Religious Drama of the Middle Ages*, 1955, and O. B. Hardison's fine study, *Christian Rite and Christian Drama in the Middle Ages*, 1965. For a good discussion of the Middle English mystery cycle, see V. A. Kolve's *The Play Called Corpus Christi*, 1966. Good selections of Middle English plays are presented by J. Q. Adams, *Chief Pre-Shakespearean Dramas*, 1924, and by A. C. Cawley, *Everyman and Medieval Miracle Plays*, 1960. Cawley's *The Wakefield Pageants in the Towneley Cycle*, 1958, has a discussion of the work of the "Wakefield Masters" whose hand is seen in the *Second Shepherds' Play*.

Sir Gawain and the Green Knight

The standard Middle English text of the poem is that of J. R. R. Tolkien and E. V. Gordon, 1925 (revised by Norman Davis, 1967). Perhaps easier to use are the editions by R. A. Waldron, 1970, and J. A. Burrow, 1972. Good discussion of various aspects of the poem appear in Marie Borroff's *Sir Gawain and the Green Knight: A Stylistic and Metrical Study*, 1962; L. D. Benson, *Art and Tradition in Sir Gawain and the Green Knight*, 1965 (especially good on the sources); and J. A. Burrow, *A Reading of Sir Gawain and the Green Knight*, 1965. Interesting chapters on the poem are contributed by A. C. Spearing in *Criticism and Medieval Poetry*, 2nd ed., 1972, and *The Gawain Poet*, 1971, and D. R. Howard in *The Three Temptations: Medieval Man in Search of the World*, 1966. There are three collections of critical essays on the poet: R. J. Blanch's *Sir Gawain and Pearl*, 1966; Denton Fox's *Twentieth-Century Interpretations of Sir Gawain and the Green Knight*, 1968; and D. R. Howard and C. K. Zacher's *Critical Studies of Sir Gawain and the Green Knight*.

THE SIXTEENTH CENTURY

General books on the political, social and economic history of the period are: Joel Hurstfield, *The Elizabethan Nation*, 1964; A. H. Dodd, *Life in Elizabethan England*, 1962; J. B. Black, *The Reign of Elizabeth, 1558–1603*, 2nd ed., 1959; G. R. Elton, *England Under the Tudors*, 1955; A. L. Rowse, *The England of Elizabeth*, 1950; J. E. Neale, *Queen Elizabeth I*, 1934; R. H. Tawney, *Religion and the Rise of Capitalism*, 1926; R. H. Tawney and E. Power, *Tudor Economic Documents*, 1924; W. H. Dunham and S. Pargellis, eds., *Complaint and Reform in England*, 1938; J. W. Allen, *A History of Political Thought in the Sixteenth Century*, 3rd ed., 1957; G. Morris, *Political Thought in England: Tyndale to Hooker*, 1953; G. N. Clark, *The Wealth of England, 1496–1760*, 1946; R. H. Tawney, *The Agrarian Problem in the Sixteenth Century*, 1967; J. H. Hexter, *Reappraisals in History*, 1961; A. Simpson, *The Wealth of the Gentry*, 1961; L. Stone, *The Crisis of the Aristocracy, 1558–1641*, 1965; and L. Stone, *Family and Fortune*, 1973.

Discussions of church history include W. H. Frere, *The English Church in the Reigns of Elizabeth and James I*, 1911; A. O. Meyer, *England and the Catholic Church under Queen Elizabeth*, 1916; P. Collinson, *The Elizabethan Puritan Movement*, 1967; and W. Haller, *The Rise of Puritanism*, 1938.

Military, naval, and exploration history are covered in E. G. R. Taylor, *Tudor Geography, 1485–1583* and *Late Tudor and Early Stuart Geography*, 1930 and 1934; J. A. Williamson, *The Age of Drake*, 4th ed., 1960; and G. Mattingly, *The Armada*, 1959.

Intellectual history is covered in E. M. W. Tillyard, *The Elizabethan World Picture*, 1943, 1956; Theodore Spencer, *Shakespeare and the Nature of Man*, 1942; F. R. Johnson, *Astronomical Thought in Renaissance England*, 1937; P. Kocher, *Science and Religion in Elizabethan England*, 1953; Keith Thomas, *Religion and the Decline of Magic*, 1971; and A. R. Hall, *The Scientific Revolution, 1500–1800*, rev., 1966.

Books on the arts and culture include: E. Mercer, *English Art, 1553–1625*, 1962; J. Buxton, *Elizabethan Taste*, 1963; E. Auerbach, *Tudor Artists*, 1954; John Stevens, *Music and Poetry in the Early Tudor Court*, 1961; Bruce Pattison, *Music and Poetry of the English Renaissance*, 1948; W. L. Woodfill, *Musicians in English Society from Elizabeth to Charles I*, 1953; E. H. Fellowes, *The English Madrigal Composers*, 1921; M. C. Boyd, *Elizabethan Music and Music Criticism*, 1940; G. L. Finney, *Musical Backgrounds for English Literature*, 1962; R. Bloomfield, *History of Renaissance Architecture in England*, 1897; J. A. Gotch and W. T. Brown, *Architecture of the Renaissance in England*, 1891–94; T. Garner and A. Stratton, *The Domestic Architecture of England During the Tudor Period*, 1911, 1929; R. Bloomfield, *The Formal Garden in England*, 1901; H. C. Baker and W. G. Constable, *English Painting of the Sixteenth and Seventeenth Centuries*, 1930; and S. Colvin, *Early Engraving and Engravers in England, 1545–1695*, 1905.

The stage and drama are treated in E. K. Chambers, *The Elizabethan Stage*, 4 vols., 1923; F. P. Wilson, *English Drama 1485–1585*, 1969; D. M. Bevington, *From "Mankind" to Marlowe*, 1962; Richard Levin, *The Multiple Plot in English Renaissance Drama*, 1971; A. C. Dessen, *Elizabethan Drama and the Viewer's Eye*, 1977; and C. Walter Hodges, *The Globe Restored*, 1953, 1968, 1973.

The new professions of writing, printing, and publishing are discussed in H. S. Bennett, *English Books and Readers, 1475–1557*, 1952, and *English Books and Readers, 1558–1603*, 1965; E. H. Miller, *The Professional Writer in Elizabethan England*, 1959; R. B. McKerrow, *An Introduction to Bibliography for Literary Students*, 1928; A. W. Pollard, *Shakespeare's Fight with the Pirates*, 1917; and F. P. Wilson, *Shakespeare and the New Bibliography*, 1970.

Anthologies of Elizabethan literary criticism are G. Gregory Smith, *Elizabethan Critical Essays*, 2 vols., 1904, 1937, 1950; and O. B. Hardison, Jr., *English Literary Criticism: The Renaissance*, 1963.

Historical and critical treatments of the various literary genres are Douglas L. Peterson, *The English Lyric from Wyatt to Donne*, 1966; Helen Morris, *Elizabethan Literature*, 1958; Maurice Evans, *English Poetry in the Sixteenth Century*, 1955; Louis B. Wright, *Middle-Class Culture in Elizabethan England*, 1935; Douglas Bush, *Mythology and the Renaissance Tradition in English Poetry*, 1932; Hallett Smith, *Elizabethan Poetry*, 1952; E. A. Baker, *History of the English Novel*, Vol. II, 1929; Walter R. Davis, *Idea and Act in Elizabethan Fiction*, 1969; C. S. Lewis, *English Literature in the Sixteenth Century, Excluding Drama*, 1954; and Alvin Kernan, *The Cankered Muse: Satire of the English Renaissance*, 1959.

Anonymous Lyrics

Thomas Clayton, " 'Sir Henry Lee's Farewell to the Court': the Texts and Authorship of 'His golden locks Time hath to silver turned,' " *English Literary Renaissance* 4 (1974), 268–75. Stephen W. May, "The Authorship of 'My Mind to me a kingdom is,' " *Review of English Studies* n.s. 26 (1975), 385–94.

Thomas Campion

Campion's English works, with a selection from his Latin poetry, edited by Walter R. Davis, 1967; Edward Lowbury, Timothy Salter, and Alison Young, *Thomas Campion, Poet, Composer, Physician*, 1970.

Samuel Daniel

A. C. Sprague has edited *Poems and A Defense of Rhyme*, 1930. Recent studies are Joan Rees, *Samuel Daniel, A Critical and Biographical Study*, 1964; and Cecil Seronsy, *Samuel Daniel*, 1967.

Michael Drayton

The standard edition is by J. W. Hebel, 5 vols., 1931–41. A handy selection is edited by John Buxton, 1953. B. H. Newdigate, *Michael Drayton and his Circle*, 1941, is a biography. A recent work is R. F. Hardin, *Michael Drayton and the Passing of Elizabethan England*, 1973

John Foxe

An indispensable work for the understanding of John Foxe is William Haller, *The Elect Nation: The Meaning and Relevance of Foxe's Book of Martyrs*, 1963. See also J. F. Mozley, *John Foxe and His Book*, 1940.

Thomas Hariot

Rukeyser, Muriel, *The Traces of Thomas Hariot*, 1971; *Thomas Hariot, Renaissance Scientist*, edited by J. W. Shirley, 1974.

Sir Thomas Hoby

The Book of the Courtier, with an introduction by Walter Raleigh, Tudor Translations, 1900; Castiglione's original, *Il Cortegiano*, was edited by V. Cian in 1929. A good account of Castiglione is given in Ralph Roeder, *The Man of the Renaissance*, 1933. Hoby's curious diary, *A Booke of the Travaile and Lief of Me*, is edited by E. Powell as *Camden Miscellany X*, 1902. The qualities of Hoby's prose are discussed in F. O. Matthiessen, *Translation, An Elizabethan Art*, 1931.

Richard Hooker

Hooker's *Works* are now coming out in a Folger Library Edition, 1977–. The first two volumes, which include the *Laws*, are edited by G. Edelen and W. Speed Hill. Izaak Walton wrote the first biography of Hooker; he is corrected in many details by C. J. Sisson, *The Judicious Marriage of Mr. Hooker*, 1940. Studies of his thought are Peter Munz, *The Place of Hooker in the History of Thought*, 1952; and F. J. Shirley, *Richard Hooker and Contemporary Political Ideas*, 1949.

Christopher Marlowe

The most recent edition of the *Complete Works* is edited by Fredson Bowers, 1973. The older edition, in six volumes, under the general editorship of R. H. Case, is modernized but fully annotated. Separate editions of *Dr. Faustus* are by J. D. Jump, 1962; and Roma Gill, 1965. The reconstructed text, from the two versions, was made by Sir W. W. Greg in 1950. J. D. Jump has edited a volume of critical essays, *Marlowe: Dr. Faustus, A Casebook*, 1969. An important recent article is Nicholas Kiessling, "*Dr. Faustus* and the Sin of Bestiality," *Studies in English Literature* XV (1975), 205–11. A facsimile of the first edition of *Hero and Leander, 1598* has an important introduction and textual commentary by L. L. Martz, 1972.

Valuable critical studies are Harry Levin, *The Overreacher*, 1952; F. P. Wilson, *Marlowe and the Early Shakespeare*, 1953; Douglas Cole, *Suffering and Evil in the Plays of Christopher Marlowe*, 1962; and J. B. Steane, *Marlowe: A Critical Study*, 1964.

The circumstances of Marlowe's death are told by their discoverer, Leslie Hotson, in *The Death of Christopher Marlowe*, 1925, and Marlowe's involvement in another fatal quarrel is the subject of Mark Eccles, *Christopher Marlowe in London*, 1934.

Sir Thomas More

The great edition of the complete works is now in progress from the Yale University Press. Vol. 4, *Utopia*, is edited by E. L. Surtz and J. H. Hexter. Robert M. Adams has edited *Utopia*, A Norton Critical Edition, 1976, which includes in full the translation used in this anthology. Significant commentaries are R. A. Ames, *Citizen Thomas More and his Utopia*, 1949; J. H. Hexter, *More's Utopia, the Biography of an Idea*, 1952; E. L. Surtz, *The Praise of Pleasure: Philosophy, Education, and Communism in More's Utopia*, 1957; and Robbin S. Johnson, *More's Utopia: Ideal and Illusion*, 1969. The standard modern life is by R. W. Chambers, 1935.

Thomas Nashe

The standard edition, in 5 volumes, is edited by R. W. McKerrow, rev. by F. P. Wilson, 1958. *Selected Writings*, edited by Stanley Wells, 1965. G. R. Hubbard, *Thomas Nashe, A Critical Introduction*, 1962.

Sir Walter Ralegh

The standard edition of the poems is by A. M. C. Latham, rev., 1950; she also edited the Muses' Library edition, 1951, 1962. Of interest to students of the poetry is W. F. Oakeshott, *The Queen and the Poet*, 1960. A recent excellent book is S. J. Greenblatt, *Sir Walter Ralegh*, 1973.

William Shakespeare

On *1 Henry IV*, see the Norton Critical Edition, edited by James L. Sanderson, rev., 1969; *Henry IV Parts I and II: a Casebook*, edited by G. K. Hunter, 1970; John Dover Wilson, *The Fortunes of Falstaff*, 1944; F. P. Wilson, *Marlowe and the Early Shakespeare*, 1953. Major editions are the *Variorum*, edited by S. B. Hemingway, 1936, with a supplement in *Shakespeare Quarterly* VII, 3, 1956, by G. B. Evans; and the New Arden *1 Henry IV*, edited by A. R. Humphries, 1960.

On *King Lear* see *Shakespeare, King Lear: a Casebook*, edited by Frank Kermode, 1969; Maynard Mack, *King Lear in Our Time*, 1965; W. R. Elton, *King Lear and the Gods*, 1966; Paul A. Jorgensen, *Lear's Self-Discovery*, 1967; S. L. Goldberg, *An Essay on King Lear*, 1974; *Some Facets of King Lear*, ed. R. L. Colie and F. T. Flahiff, 1974. The New Arden *King Lear* is edited by Kenneth Muir, 1952, rev., 1959.

The latest edition of the sonnets, including a facsimile of the first edition, with a modernized text on facing pages and an elaborate commentary, is by Stephen Booth, 1977. This is a successor to his *An Essay on Shakespeare's Sonnets*, 1969. An edition with the annotation on pages facing the modernized text of the sonnets is by W. G. Ingram and T. Redpath, 1965. Among many paperback editions is the Signet Classic, edited by William Burto, with an introduction by W. H. Auden and three critical essays, 1964. Collections of critical essays are *The Sonnets: A Casebook*, edited by Peter Jones, 1977, and Barbara Herrnstein, *Discussions of Shakespeare's Sonnets*, 1964. An exhaustive treatment of the many commentaries and attempts to solve the problems of the sonnets is in Hyder Rollins's *Variorum* edition, 2 vols., 1944. Among recent critical treatments worth attention are *New Essays on Shakespeare's Sonnets*, edited by Hilton Landry, 1976; Giorgio Melchiori, *Shakespeare's Dramatic Meditations*, 1976; and Cyrus Hoy, "Shakespeare and the Revenge of Art," *Rice University Studies* 60 (1974), 71–94.

The poems have been edited by Hyder E. Rollins in the *New Variorum*, edition, 1938. More manageable are the recent editions by F. T. Prince, 1960, and J. C. Maxwell, 1966. William H. Matchett has published *The Phoenix and the Turtle*, 1965; and *Shakespeare Survey 15*, 1962, is largely devoted to Shakespeare's songs, sonnets, and other poems. G. Wilson Knight's *The Mutual Flame*, 1955, discusses the sonnets and *The Phoenix and the Turtle*.

The standard scholarly authority on the life and works is E. K. Chambers, *William Shakespeare, A Study of Facts and Problems*, 1930. More recent essential works dealing with Shakespeare's life are S. Schoenbaum, *William Shakespeare, A Compact Documentary Life*, 1977; and G. E. Bentley, *Shakespeare: A Biographical Handbook*, 1961. Many fields of Shakespeare study are treated by various authorities in *A New Companion to Shakespeare Studies*, edited by Kenneth Muir and S. Schoenbaum, 1971.

Sir Philip Sidney

The definitive edition of Sidney's poetry is by William Ringler, 1962. *The Old Arcadia* is edited by Jean Robertson, 1973, and the *Miscellaneous Prose* edited by K. Duncan-Jones and J. VanDorsten, 1973. The complete works are available in the edition of A. Feuillerat, 1912–26. Critical studies are listed in Mary A. Washington, *Sir Philip Sidney: An Annotated Bibliography of Modern Criticism 1941–1970*, 1972, and William L. Godshalk, "Recent Studies in Sidney," *English Literary Renaissance* 2 (1972), 148–64. The same volume contains R. A. Lanham, "Astrophel and Stella: Pure and Impure Persuasion," pp. 100–15; and O. B. Hardison, Jr., "The Two Voices of Sidney's *Apology for Poetry*," pp. 83–99. A recent important essay is E. S. Donno, "Old Mouse-eaten Records: History in Sidney's *Apology*," *Studies in Philology* 72 (1975), 275–98. Of biographical value are Mona Wilson, *Sir Philip Sidney*, 1931, and James M. Osborn, *Young Philip Sidney*, 1972.

John Skelton

Complete Poems, edited by Philip Henderson, rev., 1948; *Poems of Skelton*, edited by R. S. Kinsman, 1969.

Maurice Pollst, *John Skelton, Poet of Tudor England*, 1971; Stanley Fish, *Skelton's Poetry*, 1961; and Arthur R. Heiserman, *Skelton and Satire*, 1961.

Robert Southwell

The *Poems* of Father Southwell have been edited by James H. McDonald and Nancy Pollard Brown, 1967. Two earlier studies are Christopher Devlin, S.J., *The Life of Robert Southwell, Poet and Martyr*, 1956; and Pierre Janelle, *Robert Southwell the Writer*, 1935.

Edmund Spenser

The most useful selection of Spenser's poetry and criticism of it is *Edmund Spenser's Poetry*, A Norton Critical Edition, edited by Hugh Maclean, 1968, 1979. Guidance to recent work is provided in Waldo F. McNeir and Foster Provost, *Edmund Spenser: An Annotated Bibliography*, 1975. Also valuable is a collection of essays by various authorities, *Contemporary Thought on Edmund Spenser*, edited by R. C. Frushell and B. J. Vondersmith, 1975. The *Epithalamion* has been separately edited by Robert Beum, 1968. Recent important works are Isabel MacCaffrey, *Spenser's Allegory: The Anatomy of Imagination*, 1975; A. Bartlett Giamatti, *Play of Double Senses: Spenser's Faerie Queene*, 1975; and Mark Rose, *Spenser's Art: A Companion to Book I of The Faerie Queene*, 1975. Still standard are William Nelson, *The Poetry of Edmund Spenser*, 1963; Paul J. Alpers, *The Poetry of The Faerie Queene*, 1967; Kathleen Williams, *Spenser's World of Glass*, 1966; and John B. Bender, *Spenser and Literary Pictorialism*, 1972. Older scholarship is summarized in *The Works of Edmund Spenser: A Variorum Edition*, edited by Edwin Greenlaw and others, 10 vols., 1932–49.

Henry Howard, Earl of Surrey

The most recent, though incomplete, edition of Surrey's poems is by Emrys Jones, 1964; an older one is by F. M. Padelford, rev., 1928. *Tottel's Miscellany* is edited by Hyder E. Rollins, rev., 1965. There is a biography by E. Casaday, 1938. Burton Fishman surveys recent studies in *English Literary Renaissance* I (1971), 188–91.

Sir Thomas Wyatt

The most dependable edition of Wyatt is Richard C. Harrier, *The Canon of Sir Thomas Wyatt's Poetry*, 1975. A modernized and annotated edition is by J. Daalder, 1975. The *Collected Poems*, edited by Kenneth Muir and Patricia Thomson, 1969, is sharply criticized in a book-length review by H. A. Mason, *Editing Wyatt*, 1972. *Tottel's Miscellany* is edited by Hyder E. Rollins, rev., 1965. Recent biographical and critical works are Kenneth Muir, *Life and Letters of Sir Thomas Wyatt*, 1963; Patricia Thomson, *Sir Thomas Wyatt and his Background*, 1965; Raymond Southall, *The Courtly Maker*, 1964; Burton Fishman, "Recent Studies in Wyatt and Surrey," *English Literary Renaissance* I (1971), 178–88. Earlier studies are Hallett Smith, "The Art of Sir Thomas Wyatt" *Huntington Library Quarterly* IX (1946), 323–55; E. K. Chambers, *Sir Thomas Wyatt and Some Collected Studies*, 1933; and E. M. W. Tillyard, *The Poetry of Sir Thomas Wyatt*, 1929.

THE SEVENTEENTH CENTURY

Two standard general histories of England during the 17th century are Godfrey Davies, *The Early Stuarts*, 2nd ed., 1959, and G. M. Trevelyan, *England Under the Stuarts*, London, 1949. Clarendon's *History*, dealing with the Civil War and Protectorate, is a fascinating contemporary document, and Samuel Rawson Gardiner's *History of England from 1603 to 1656*, 10 vols., rev., 1894–96, is rich in facts. Over the past decade or so, a prodigious series of books by Christopher Hill, the Master of Balliol (books fundamentally Marxist in their approach), have done much to transfigure our understanding of the 17th-century revolution, seen under its political, economic, and social aspects. One of these, *The Century of Revolution, 1603–1714*, 1966, forms part of the Norton Library History of England. For a less tendentious and in many respects less insightful view the two volumes of C. V. Wedgewood, *The Great Rebellion*, may be consulted: they are *The King's Peace*, 1955, and *The King's War*, 1958. Carl J. Friedrich, *The Age of the Baroque*, 1952, is European in its purview, and cultural as well as political in emphasis.

On the intellectual background of the age, one would do well to consult E. M. W. Tillyard's fascinating little study *The Elizabethan World Picture*, 1943. 1956. modifying its perhaps excessive simplicities by reference to C. S. Lewis's brilliantly forensic *The Discarded Image*, 1964, and to the collection of original documents reproduced in James Winny's *The Frame of Order*, 1957. Sir Herbert J. C.

Grierson's *Cross Currents in English Literature of the 17th Century*, 1929, and Sir Basil Willey's *The Seventeenth Century Background*, 1934, should be supplemented by more recent studies, like John R. Mulder's *The Temple of the Mind*, 1969, and Frances Yates's extraordinary and sometimes questioned series of books on *Giordano Bruno*, 1964, *The Art of Memory*, 1966, and *The Theater of the World*, 1968. Among collections of essays, which are many, one might specify those of Joseph Mazzeo, *Renaissance and 17th-century Studies*, 1964, and of Rosemond Tuve, *Essays in Spenser, Herbert, Milton*, 1970, as particularly likely to stimulate thought.

General literary histories of the age include Douglas Bush, *English Literature in the Earlier Seventeenth Century*, 1945, and a shorter, less bibliographical introduction, C. V. Wedgwood's *Seventeenth Century English Literature*, 1950.

Special studies of social and economic problems in relation to the intellectual life of the day are Max Weber's *The Protestant Ethic and the Spirit of Capitalism*, translated by Talcott Parsons, 1948, 1958, and R. H. Tawney, *Religion and the Rise of Capitalism*, 1937; also, the various criticisms to which this theory has been subjected by H. R. Trevor-Roper and others should not be overlooked. They are mostly to be found in the *Economic History Review*. In a 1967 volume, Lawrence Stone documents *The Crisis of the Aristocracy* from the accession of Elizabeth to the outbreak of the Civil Wars. A. S. P. Woodhouse, in *Puritanism and Liberty*, 1950, studies the crucial debates in Cromwell's army during the period 1647–49; it is a detailed study, but the themes considered have very wide implications. L. C. Knight's *Drama and Society in the Age of Jonson*, 1937, is another close study with general import; and Ricardo Quinones's *The Renaissance Discovery of Time*, 1972, though it starts far outside the 17th century, ends by focusing its findings on John Milton. Perry Miller's *New England Mind: the 17th Century*, 1939 and 1954, though primarily concerned with the new world, is a useful introduction to the Puritan outlook; and William Haller's *The Rise of Puritanism*, 1938, is a classic account of the Puritans viewed through their propaganda; it has particular bearing on Milton.

The growth of science in the 17th century may be studied, not only in Lynn Thorndike's monumental six-volume *History of Magic and Experimental Science*, 1923–1941, but less spaciously in Abraham Wolf's *History of Science, Technology, and Philosophy in the 16th and 17th Centuries*, 2nd ed., prep. by D. McKie, 1950; its impact on the daily thought of men is traced by E. A. Burtt, *Metaphysical Foundations of Modern Science*, rev., 1950. A. O. Lovejoy's *The Great Chain of Being: A Study of the History of an Idea*, 1936, is a classic reconstruction of an important Renaissance idea, and an account of how it decayed in the 17th century and after.

The literary criticism of the age is best studied in the documents collected by G. Gregory Smith, *Elizabethan Critical Essays*, 1904, and by J. E. Spingarn, *Critical Essays of the 17th Century*, 1908–9. Donald L. Clark, in *Rhetoric and Poetry in the Renaissance*, 1922; Rosemond Tuve, in *Elizabethan and Metaphysical Imagery*, 1947; and Ruth Wallerstein, in *Studies in 17th Century Poetic*, 1950, have probed into the relation between critical theory and poetic practice. Finally, Wylie Sypher, *Four Stages of Renaissance Style*, 1955, offers some very interesting and provocative analogies between poetic styles and styles in the graphic arts during the 17th century. Other books in this area, where classifications are indefinite and terminologies luxuriant include Odette de Mourgues, *Metaphysical, Baroque, and Précieux Poetry*, 1953, and Frank Warnke, *Versions of Baroque*, 1972. Also useful to a student of the backgrounds for a metaphysical style is Warnke's *European Metaphysical Poetry*, 1961.

In addition to the references given below for individual poets, the following titles may prove useful for the student of 17th-century poetry: George Saintsbury edited, in three volumes, the texts of the *Minor Poets of the Caroline Period*, 1905–21, and Norman Ault collected some interesting lyrics of the age, *Seventeenth-Century Lyrics*, 1928. Edward Dowden's *Puritan and Anglican*, 1900, and Edmund Gosse's *The Jacobean Poets*, 1894, are older studies which retain a good deal of vitality. They may be supplemented by more recent collections of essays, such as L. C. Knight's *Explorations*, 1946, and, in a more limited context, George Williamson's *Six Metaphysical Poets*, 1967. F. R. Leavis in the first section of *Revaluation*, 1936, strongly followed Eliot's lead in asserting the importance of "the line of wit" for modern readers. A spate of books on the metaphysical poets appeared during the 1930's, of which the best are Joan Bennett's *Five* (originally *Four*) *Metaphysical Poets*, 1934, 1953, 1967 (her poets are Donne, Herbert, Crashaw, Vaughan and Marvell); Helen C. White's *The Metaphysical Poets*,

1936; and J. B. Leishman's book, of the same title, 1934. Louis L. Martz, in *The Poetry of Meditation*, discusses a traditional mode of thought as it influenced the metaphysicals; the same line of investigation is continued in *The Paradise Within*, 1964. Earl Miner's *The Metaphysical Mode from Donne to Cowley*, 1969, is complemented by the same author's *The Cavalier Mode from Jonson to Cotton*, 1971. Mario Praz has made important critical points in his *Studies in 17th-Century Imagery*, 1939, as have Marjorie Nicolson in *The Breaking of the Circle*, 1960; C. V. Wedgwood in *Poetry and Politics Under the Stuarts*, 1960; Harry Levin in *The Myth of the Golden Age in the Renaissance*, 1969; and Rosalie Colie in *Paradoxia Epidemica*, 1966, a study in Renaissance applications of the paradox. Of particular interest to students of classic myth in 17th-century poetry is Douglas Bush's erudite *Mythology and the Renaissance Tradition in English Poetry*, 1932, 1963. Until 1969 *Studies in Philology* published an annual bibliography of Renaissance and 17th-century studies; after that date, the appropriate section of the MLA bibliography should be consulted.

Francis Bacon

The big edition of Bacon is *The Works*, 15 vols., edited by Spedding, Ellis, and Heath, 1860–64. Among the biographical introductions may be recommended that done for the English Men of Letters series by R. W. Church, 1884, and two more recent ones, *Francis Bacon: A Biography*, by Mary Sturt, 1932, and *Bacon*, by Charles Williams, 1933. Christopher Hill's *Intellectual Origins of the English Revolution*, 1965, demonstrates most tellingly the existence of a popular scientific tradition, in the vernacular, which lent body and popular support to Bacon's magisterial scientific dicta. An old-fashioned but still interesting book is *Francis Bacon of Verulam* by Kuno Fischer, translated from the German and published in 1857. Two specialized studies of particular interest are F. H. Anderson's *The Philosophy of Francis Bacon*, 1948, and Brian Vickers, *Francis Bacon and Renaissance Prose*, 1968.

Especially in the late 19th century, an immense amount of nonsense was written setting forth alleged cryptographic evidence for Bacon's authorship of Shakespeare's plays, Spenser's poetry, and various other literary works real or imaginary. William F. and Elizabeth S. Friedman, in *The Shakespearean Ciphers Examined*, 1957, subject all these theories to scrupulous technical examination and dismiss them all as worthless. It would be pleasant if this closed the matter, but that is doubtless too much to hope.

See also entries under **Prose of the Seventeenth Century.**

Francis Beaumont

See entries under **Seventeenth-Century Lyrics.**

Sir Thomas Browne

The standard complete edition of Browne is *The Works of Sir Thomas Browne*, edited in 6 volumes by Geoffrey L. Keynes, 1928–31. Recent studies are those of Joan Bennett, *Sir Thomas Browne*, 1962; F. L. Huntley, 1962 (same title); and Leonard Nathanson, *The Strategy of Truth*, 1967. There is a classic account of the backgrounds of skepticism and fideism in Louis Bredvold, *The Intellectual Milieu of John Dryden*, 1934; this makes frequent reference to Browne.

See also entries under **Prose of the Seventeenth Century.**

Robert Burton

The handiest edition of *The Anatomy* for a modern reader is that of Floyd Dell and P. Jordan-Smith, 1927, in which the Latin quotations and tags are translated. Bergen Evans has written, with professional assistance, an interesting study in *The Psychiatry of Robert Burton*, 1944, and W. R. Mueller an analysis of Burton's background called *The Anatomy of Robert Burton's England*, 1952.

See also entries under **Prose of the Seventeenth Century.**

Thomas Carew

See entries under **Seventeenth-Century Lyrics.**

Abraham Cowley

See entries under **Seventeenth-Century Lyrics.**

Richard Crashaw

The standard edition is that prepared by L. C. Martin, 1927, 2nd ed., 1957. A good selection of Crashaw's verse will be found in *George Herbert and the Seventeenth-Century Religious Poets*, A Norton Critical Edition, edited by Mario A. Di Cesare, 1978. Two interesting books are those of Ruth Wallerstein, *Richard Crashaw: A Study in Style and Poetic Development*, 1935, and of Austin Warren, *Richard Crashaw: A Study in Baroque Sensibility*, 1939, 1957. Influential ideas about Crashaw are found in William Empson, *Seven Types of Ambiguity*, 1935, 1947, 1953; in Wylie

Sypher, *Four Stages of Renaissance Style*, 1955; and in Mario Praz, *The Flaming Heart*, 1958. Also to be consulted are George W. Williams, *Image and Symbol in the Sacred Poetry of Richard Crashaw*, 1963, and Robert Peterson, *The Art of Ecstasy: Teresa, Bernini, and Crashaw*, 1970.

John Donne

For nearly fifty years the standard edition of Donne's poems was that in two volumes edited by Sir Herbert J. C. Grierson, 1912. In 1952 Dame Helen Gardner re-edited the *Divine Poems* and in 1965 a volume of *Elegies and the Songs and Sonnets.* In this same series, W. Milgate added the *Satires, Epigrams, and Verse Letters*, 1967. These new editions alter the text of some poems in some particulars on the basis of new manuscript evidence and offer to redate many of them. It is by no means clear that the text is always improved by the new readings or that the new dating will hold up; William Empson has been a particularly vigorous and outspoken critic. One can only say that many questions remain open. Under the editorship of G. R. Potter and Evelyn Simpson, a new edition of Donne's *Sermons* has been issued in ten volumes, 1953–59. A *Complete Poetry and Selected Prose*, edited by John Hayward, 1929, is one of several handy, handsome popular editions—among which we also note *John Donne's Poetry*, edited by A. L. Clements for the Norton Critical Editions, 1966.

For many years after its publication in 1899, Sir Edmund Gosse's *Life and Letters of John Donne* was the best biography available, though recognized as inadequate in many ways. R. C. Bald's *John Donne, a life*, 1970, though the author most regrettably did not live to give it the finishing touches, adds immensely to our detailed knowledge of Donne's career. Izaak Walton's contemporary "biography" is charming and artistic.

T. S. Eliot's several essays on Donne and the metaphysical poets generally have been most influential; some are to be found in his *Selected Essays*, 1932, others must be sought through his bibliography (by Donald Gallup). Collections of critical essays by several hands have been assembled by Helen Gardner and Frank Kermode (both 1962). Hardly any of Donne's poems have not been the subject of several articles at least; but Cleanth Brooks's *The Well Wrought Urn*, 1947, contains in its discussion of *The Canonization* one of the most influential poetic explications of modern criticism.

Pierre Legouis's *Donne the Craftsman*, 1928, was an interesting early study; more recently, Clay Hunt, 1954, Arnold Stein, 1962, and Wilbur Sanders, 1971, have offered close scrutinies of the poetry. Many specialized studies in different aspects of Donne's thought and technique have appeared, for instance: Mary Ramsay's *Les doctrines mediévales chez Donne*, rev., 1924; Marjorie Nicolson's *The Breaking of the Circle*, 1960 (on Donne and science); and D. L. Guss's *John Donne, Petrarchist*, 1966. Two major studies which dedicate long sections to the poetry of Donne are Rosemond Tuve's influential *Elizabethan and Metaphysical Imagery*, 1947, and Robert Ellrodt's three-volume *L'inspiration personnelle et l'esprit du temps chez les poètes métaphysiques anglais*, 1960. Leonard Unger, in *Donne's Poetry and Modern Criticism*, 1950, undertook to survey a troubled field, which has since become even more troubled and less surveyable. The standard bibliography of Donne, first published by Geoffrey Keynes in 1914, was revised in 1932 and again in 1958.

John Fletcher

See entries under **Seventeenth-Century Lyrics.**

George Herbert

The standard edition of *The Temple* is that edited by F. E. Hutchinson, 1941. A good selection of Herbert's poems will be found in *George Herbert and the Seventeenth-Century Religious Poets*, A Norton Critical Edition, edited by Mario A. Di Cesare, 1978. Margaret Bottrall has written an introductory appreciation, *George Herbert*, 1954, and Rosemond Tuve's *A Reading of George Herbert*, 1952, is, like all her work, erudite and acute. As part of the same revival of interest in Herbert appeared J. H. Summers, *George Herbert, His Religion and His Art*, 1954. Recent studies are those of Arnold Stein, *George Herbert's Lyrics*, 1968, and Helen Vendler, *The Poetry of George Herbert*, 1975. A new *Life of George Herbert*, much fuller than any previous one, is that of Amy M. Charles, 1977.

Robert Herrick

The standard edition is the *Poetical Works*, edited by L. C. Martin, Oxford English Texts, 1956. J. Max Patrick has also produced an edition of the *Complete Poetry*, 1963, and a good selection will be found in *Ben Jonson and the Cavalier Poets*, A Norton Critical Edition, edited by Hugh Maclean, 1974. Various studies have been made of classical influences on Herrick, including those of P. Aiken, 1932; K. McEuen, 1939; and G. W. Regenos, *Philological Quarterly* XXVI (1947), 268–84. F. W. Moorman produced a full-length study, *Robert Herrick*, 1910; and Marchette Chute, joining Herrick with George Herbert, has described their lives, *Two Gentle Men*, 1959. There is an interesting novel about Herrick by Rose Macaulay, *The Shadow Flies*, 1932.

Thomas Hobbes

The standard edition of Hobbes is that edited by Sir William Molesworth: *The English Works* in 11 volumes, the *Opera Philosophica* in five, 1839–45. G. C. Robertson in *Hobbes*, 1886, provides a good general introduction, and for the student of literature there is a useful study of the philosopher's literary theory, by C. D. Thorpe, *The Aesthetic Theory of Thomas Hobbes*, 1940. The most recent edition of *Leviathan* has a very perceptive introduction by Michael Oakeshott, 1946. S. I. Mintz, *The Hunting of Leviathan*, 1958, describes the interesting 17th-century reactions to Hobbes's thought.

See also entries under **Prose of the Seventeenth Century.**

Ben Jonson

The standard edition of Jonson's works is that of C. H. Herford and Percy and Evelyn Simpson, published by the Clarendon Press in eleven volumes, 1925–52. This edition is meticulous in reproducing the old spellings, and typographically it is very elegant; but to find one's way around in it takes some practice. Of earlier editions, the handiest and most correct (though the text has been modernized) is that of W. Gifford, 9 vols., 1875. The Yale edition of Ben Jonson provides a good modernized and annotated version of the major plays (one play to a volume). Handy editions of the verse are those of W. B. Hunter, *The Complete Poetry of Ben Jonson*, 1963, and Ian Donaldson for the Oxford Standard Authors, 1975; Stephen Orgel has edited the *Complete Masques*, 1969. Two useful selected editions of Jonson's work are in the Norton Critical Editions series: *Ben Jonson and the Cavalier Poets*, selected and edited by Hugh Maclean, 1974, and *Ben Jonson's Plays and Masques*, selected and edited by Robert M. Adams, 1979.

Because Jonson's work falls into several different categories, general introductory accounts of the whole man are few. G. Gregory Smith did a biography for the English Men of Letters series, 1919, and a more recent popular introduction, graceful, dexterous, and perceptive, is that of J. B. Bamborough, *Ben Jonson*, 1970. A. C. Swinburne wrote a characteristically acute and enthusiastic *Study of Ben Jonson*, 1889, and Maurice Castelain a weighty *Ben Jonson, l'homme et l'oeuvre*, 1907; both these books, though long out of date, retain the power to instruct and interest. Useful recent studies of the plays are those of E. B. Partridge, *The Broken Circle*, 1958; G. B. Jackson, *Vision and Judgment in Ben Jonson's Dramas*, 1968; and *The World Upside Down* by Ian Donaldson, 1970.

Special studies of the masques generally, and of Jonson's masques in particular, have been written by Enid Welsford, *The Court Masque*, 1927; Allardyce Nicoll, *Stuart Masques and the Renaissance Stage*, 1937; and Stephen Orgel, *The Jonsonian Masque*, 1965. Angus Fletcher's *The Transcendental Masque*, 1971, though mainly about Milton's *Comus*, contains many brilliant speculative insights about masques in general, and an extended discussion of the issues involved in Jonson's quarrel with Inigo Jones. Wesley Trimpi has written a good account of *Ben Jonson's Poems*, 1962; and C. F. Wheeler has studied *Classical Mythology in the Plays, Masques, and Poems of Ben Jonson*, 1938. There are of course many studies of Jonson as a dramatist, the comedies and satires having received particular attention. Jonas Barish has edited *Ben Jonson*, 1963, a collection of critcial essays. In 1938 S. A. Tannenbaum published a *Concise Bibliography* of Jonson, and in 1947 added a Supplement to it.

John Locke

A good course in the history of English philosophy is the best preparation for coming to terms with Locke. Short of that, M. W. Cranston has written an account of the man in *John Locke a Biography*; and of the hundreds of specialized studies of his thought one might begin with a veteran, J. W. Gough, *John Locke's Political Philosophy*, 1900, and a relative newcomer, J. W. Yolton, *John Locke and the Way of Ideas*, 1956.

See also entries under **Prose of the Seventeenth Century.**

Richard Lovelace

See entries under **Seventeenth-Century Lyrics.**

Andrew Marvell

The tercentenary of Marvell's birth, in 1921, produced a volume of essays in tribute to a then-neglected author, among them a highly influential piece by T. S. Eliot. Since then the volume of critical commentary has risen to a crescendo. The standard edition is now the *Poems and Letters*, edited by H. M. Margoliouth, 1927, 1952. Pierre Legouis's *André Marvell, poète, puritain, patriote*, 1928, was translated and abridged in 1968. Another good introduction is that of M. C. Bradbrook and Lloyd Thomas, *Andrew Marvell*, 1940. Ruth Wallerstein's *Studies in 17th Century Poetic*, 1950, are knotty and hard to read, but they illuminate the medieval backgrounds of Marvell's thought. H. E. Toliver, *Marvell's Ironic Vision*, 1965, and J. B. Leishman, *The Art of Marvell's Poetry*, 1966, were but the precursors of a flood of recent books on Marvell. John Wallace, in *Destiny His Choice*, 1968, carefully studies Marvell's intricate political attitudes; Patrick Cullen, in *Spenser, Marvell, and Renaissance Pastoral*, and Donald Friedman, in *Marvell's Pastoral Art*, both 1970, concentrated on Marvell's pastoral poetry. Two general studies appearing in the same year deal with his poetic art as a whole: Rosalie Colie, *My Echoing Song*, and Anne Berthoff, *The Resolved Soul*. In 1968 George de F. Lord edited a collection of critical essays on Marvell, and in 1969, two others appeared, one edited by John Carey, the other by Michael Wilding. In the lustrum 1965–1970, over 2,500 pages of critical commentary were devoted to illuminating Marvell's modest corpus of poetry.

John Milton

Despite occasional textual eccentricities, the opulent Columbia Milton, a complete edition of poetry and prose, 18 vols., 1931–38, is widely accepted as standard; controversy continues over details, however, and anyone interested may consult Harris Fletcher's 4-volume facsimile edition of the *Poetical Works*, 1943–48, Helen Darbishire's radical re-editing of the poetry, 1952–55, and the currently appearing Yale edition of the *Prose Works*, for a spectrum of editorial procedures and principles. Of the annotated editions of *Paradise Lost*, A W. Verity's text, 1910, is probably still the least cumbersome and the most sensible. But it is long out of print, and for most purposes the student will want to use M. Y. Hughes, ed., *Complete Poems and Major Prose*, 1957, or John Carey and Alastair Fowler, eds., *Poems*, 1968. The notes of both editions are weighty, penetrating, and perhaps a bit depressing for the beginner; used with discretion, they may help but not overwhelm. An edition of *Paradise Lost* with deliberately modest annotation has been done by Scott Elledge for the Norton Critical Editions, 1975.

The old grand-scale biography of David Masson in eight volumes, 1881–96, has been replaced by that of W. R. Parker in two volumes, 1968. Sir Walter Raleigh's *Milton*, 1900, is still relevant, though much disputed. Harris Fletcher's *Intellectual Development of John Milton* (two vols., 1956 and 1961) has so far covered 24 years of Milton's development (to 1632). While it takes no account at all of Milton the rebel (in fact, denies his existence), C. S. Lewis's *Preface to Paradise Lost*, 1942, rev., 1960, is bright, persuasive, and enormously useful as a first approach. It may be corrected by A. J. A. Waldock's *Paradise Lost and Its Critics*, 1947; B. Rajan's *Paradise Lost and the 17-Century Reader*, 1947; Joseph Summers, *The Muse's Method*, 1962; Anne Ferry, *Milton's Epic Voice*, 1963, and Helen Gardner, *A Reading of Paradise Lost*, 1965. E. M. W. Tillyard's handbook, *Milton*, 1930, 1949, is in some ways more acute in setting forth the outstanding problems than J. H. Hanford's *Milton Handbook*, which with the help of J. G. Taaffe went into its 5th edition in 1970. David Daiches, under the short, sufficient title of *Milton*, 1961, offers a general introductory survey of the poet's accomplishment; and the beginning student is likely to profit as well by Marjorie H. Nicolson's *John Milton, a Reader's Guide to his Poetry*, 1963, or by Dame Helen Gardner's *Reading of Paradise Lost*. Collections of critical essays have been edited by A. E. Barker, 1965, and Louis L. Martz, 1966; the latter has also done an informative thematic study of *The Paradise Within*, 1964, which includes discussions of Vaughan and Traherne as well as of Milton. Also to be recommended are I. G. MacCaffrey, *Paradise Lost as "Myth,"* 1959; William Empson's provocative *Milton's God*, rev., 1965; and Northrop Frye's characteristically stimulating *Return of Eden*, 1965.

As might have been anticipated, the 300th anniversary of the publication of *Paradise Lost* (1967) brought forth many books on the epic, including Stanley Fish's calisthenic *Surprised by Sin*, Wayne Shumaker's *Unpremeditated Verse*, John Steadman's *Milton and the Renaissance Hero*, and collections of essays edited by A. P. Fiore, *The Upright Heart and Pure*, and R. D. Emma and J. T. Shawcross, *Language and Style in Milton*. Among more recent studies still one should mention W.G.Madsen, *From Shadowy Types to Truth*, 1968, B. Rajan, *The Lofty Rhyme*, 1970, and J. R. Knott, *Milton's Pastoral Vision*, 1971. In

1970 appeared the first volume of a *Variorum Commentary*, edited by M. Y. Hughes.

Specialized studies are beyond enumeration; only a scattering of the most useful can be named here. Robert Bridges has written the best account of *Milton's Prosody*, 2nd ed., 1921; Maurice Kelley has shown the intimate relation of Milton's theology, as expressed in the treatise *On Christion Doctrine* with his views in *Paradise Lost*, in *This Great Argument*, 1941; Malcolm M. Ross, *Poetry and Dogma*, 1954, suggests some of the theological complexities behind Milton's problems with incarnation; F. T. Prince has traced *The Italian Element in Milton's Verse*, 1954; Theodore Banks has studied *Milton's Imagery*, 1950; and Christopher Ricks has written persuasively on Milton's *Grand Style*, 1963. Characteristically incisive is Rosemond Tuve's *Images and Themes in Five Poems by Milton*, 1957. There are several collections of studies bearing on *Lycidas*, including those of C. A. Patrides, 1961, and Scott Elledge, 1966. Douglas Bush, in a series of lectures published as *Paradise Lost in Our Time*, 1945, defended Milton against his New Critical enemies, and sometimes against his friends. D. H. Stevens did the basic bibliography, a *Reference Guide to Milton from 1800 to the Present Day*, 1930; it was supplemented by Harris Fletcher in *Contributions to a Milton Bibliography*, 1931, and by Calvin Huckabay, *Milton Bibliography 1929–1968*, 1969. But the bibliographers seem to have been falling far behind the current terrifying spate of books and articles on Milton.

Sir Isaac Newton

Though Newton was famous throughout most of his life, and has never ceased to be the subject of active intellectual and biographical interest, new investigations and assessments of his work continue to appear. For the two hundredth anniversary of his death the History of Science Society published a volume, in 1928, containing a wide spectrum of papers on his work and its influence. Two biographies are those of L. T. More, 1934, and F. E. Manuel, 1968. Two books by Marjorie Nicolson are useful in showing Newton's relation to the literary and imaginative life of his time: *Newton Demands the Muse*, 1946, and *The Breaking of the Circle*, 1960.

See also entries under **Prose of the Seventeenth Century.**

Samuel Pepys

J. R. Tanner, in a series of lectures reprinted as *Samuel Pepys and the Royal Navy*, 1920, was one of the first to call attention to the serious work of Pepys's life. *Samuel Pepys* by Arthur Bryant appeared in three volumes: *The Man in the Making, The Years of Peril*, and *The Saviour of the Navy*, 1933, 1935, and 1938.

See also entries under **Prose of the Seventeenth Century.**

Prose of the Seventeenth Century

Several recent histories and collections have started to fill out our picture of the development of 17th-century prose. Used in combination with Stanley Fish's anthology of essays, *17th-Century Prose*, 1970, Robert Adolph's *The Rise of Modern Prose Style*, 1968, provides access to a still-much-controverted area. The basic work in the field was that done by Morris Croll in a series of articles on Ciceronian and anti-Ciceronian styles in the 16th and 17th centuries: these were collected posthumously in a volume titled *Style, Rhetoric, and Rhythm*, 1966. R. F. Jones, in *Ancients and Moderns*, 1946, 1961, urged the importance of the new science and the Royal Society, thus making the turning point to modern prose somewhat later than Croll had placed it. Most discussion since has taken place within that framework. George Williamson's *The Senecan Amble*, 1951, deals with an influential variety of jog trot. Other specialized studies are those of W. F. Mitchell, *English Pulpit Oratory*, 1932; Joan Webber, *The Eloquent "I,"* 1968; and Stanley Fish, *Self-Consuming Artifacts*, 1972. D. J. Milburn, *The Age of Wit*, 1966, concerns himself with the century 1650–1750, but is useful for students of the earlier period as well. In a similar series of articles, R. F. Jones discussed the influence of the Royal Society on prose style in the later 17th century; these are collected in R. F. Jones, *The Seventeenth Century*, 1951. William Haller's account of Puritan propaganda techniques in the early century is balanced by an account of late-century developments in G. R. Cragg, *From Puritanism to the Age of Reason*, 1950. And the greatest book written in the 17th, or any other century, is discussed by David Daiches, *The King James Version of the English Bible*, 1941; by C. C. Butterworth, *The Literary Lineage of the King James Bible*, 1941; and by a host of others.

See also entries under **Francis Bacon, Sir Thomas Browne, Robert Burton, Thomas Hobbes, John Locke, Sir Isaac Newton, Samuel Pepys, Thomas Sprat,** and **Izaak Walton.**

Seventeenth-Century Lyrics

A new and more accurate edition of the *Dramatic Works* of Beaumont and Fletcher is in process; five volumes are projected of which three are so far published; the editors are Fredson Bowers, A. Glover, and A. R. Waller. Recent critical studies have not been numerous: we may mention those of W. W. Appleton, *Beaumont and Fletcher*, 1956; Eugene M. Waith, *The Pattern of Tragedy in Beaumont and Fletcher*, 1952; and L. B. Wallis, *Fletcher, Beaumont, and Company*, 1947. Nancy C. Pearse has written an account of *John Fletcher's Chastity Plays*, 1973, describing them as "mirrors of modesty." Over the past hundred years a good deal of quite specialized and increasingly technical work has been done to separate out the contributions of various hands to the different plays first collected in 1647, long after both the authors were dead, as the plays of Beaumont and Fletcher.

Geoffrey Walton in *Metaphysical to Augustan*, 1955, and Jerome Mazzaro in *Transformations in the English Renaissance Lyric*, 1970, provide perspective on the transitions of lyric style. Lowry Nelson, Jr., in *Baroque Lyric Poetry*, 1961, focuses chiefly on Milton but puts him in a Continental context.

The always admirable series of Oxford English Texts includes the poems of Carew, edited by Rhodes Dunlap, 1949; of Lovelace, edited by C. H. Wilkinson, 1930; and of Suckling in two volumes, the plays edited by L. A. Beaurline, the nondramatic works edited by Thomas Clayton, 1971. There has been no edition of Waller since that of G. Thorn-Drury, originally 1893, variously reprinted since. Important work has been done recently on Carew's masque *Coelum Britannicum* by Stephen Orgel and Roy C. Strong in the course of their giant joint study of the work of Inigo Jones, 1973. Waller's contribution to English versification has been described by A. W. Allison, *Towards an Augustan Poetic*, 1962. E. I. Selig has written one slight study of Thomas Carew's poetry, 1958; and W. L. Chernaik another of Waller's, 1968.

After its discovery and first publication by Bertram Dobell in 1903, Traherne's poetry was extended in 1910 by the publication of a second volume, under the editorship of H. I. Bell. The entire corpus has been edited for Oxford English Texts in two volumes by H. M. Margoliouth, 1958. Gladys I. Wade, in *Thomas Traherne*, 1944, includes a selected bibliography of criticism. Recent studies are those of K. W. Salter, 1964; A. L. Clements, 1969; and S. N. Stewart, 1970.

Cowley's *English Writings* were edited in two volumes by A. R. Waller, 1905–6, and his biography written by A. H. Nethercot, *The Muse's Hannibal*, 1931; Robert Hinman did a critical study, *Cowley's World of Order*, 1960.

Selections from, and critical commentary on, many of these poets may be found in two Norton Critical Editions: *Ben Jonson and the Cavalier Poets*, edited by Hugh Maclean, 1974, and *George Herbert and the Seventeenth-Century Religious Poets*, edited by Mario A. Di Cesare, 1978.

Thomas Sprat and the Royal Society

The Royal Society has never lacked for eloquent historians; after Sprat, who wrote when the Society was less than 10 years old, Thomas Birch composed in 1756 a four-volume history. More recently, Dorothy Stimson has written of the Society's beginnings in *Scientists and Amateurs*, 1948; Sir H. Hartley studied in 1960 the origins and founders of the Society; and in 1967 Margery Purver wrote on its concept and creation.

See also entries under **Prose of the Seventeenth Century.**

Sir John Suckling

See entries under **Seventeenth-Century Lyrics.**

Thomas Traherne

See entries under **Seventeenth-Century Lyrics.**

Henry Vaughan

The Works of Henry Vaughan were edited by L. C. Martin, 1914, 1957; selections of his work may be found in two Norton Critical Editions: *Ben Jonson and the Cavalier Poets*, edited by Hugh Maclean, 1974, and *George Herbert and the Seventeenth-Century Religious Poets*, edited by Mario A. Di Cesare, 1978. F. E. Hutchinson wrote the standard life, *Henry Vaughan, a Life and an Interpretation*, 1947. Elizabeth Holmes opened up the interesting topic of *Henry Vaughan and the Hermetic Philosophy*, 1932, and there have been a number of studies in this area since; for instance, E. C. Pettet, *Of Paradise and Light*, 1960, and R. A. Durr, *On the Mystical Poetry of Henry Vaughan*, 1962. Louis Martz's *The Paradise Within*, 1964, gives much careful attention to Vaughan.

Edmund Waller

See entries under **Seventeenth-Century Lyrics.**

Izaak Walton

A major study of Walton the biographer is David Novarr's *The Making of Walton's Lives*, 1958. Editions of *The Complete Angler* are too numerous to describe; for many years, the book has been one of the classics for the fine-binding trade. A life of Walton by Nicolas for the 1836 edition of the *Angler* is said to be particularly meritorious, but no full-length independent biography has yet been published. Under the elegant title of *Every Man a Phoenix*, 1958, Margaret Bottrall has studied 17th-century autobiography.

See also entries under **Prose of the Seventeenth Century.**

John Webster

The reputation of Webster, and particularly of *The Duchess of Malfi*, became a subject of active dispute in the late 19th century, with Swinburne taking a very high position, William Archer a relatively low one. These essays with many others have been reprinted by G. K. and S. K. Hunter, eds., *John Webster, a Critical Anthology*, 1969. Other studies directly and indirectly related to Webster are those of Rupert Brooke, *John Webster and the Elizabethan Drama*, 1917; Fredson Bowers, *Elizabethan Revenge Tragedy*, 1940; Robert Dent, *John Webster's Borrowings*, 1960; and Gunnar Boklund, *The Duchess of Malfi: Sources, Themes, Characters*, 1962. Frank L. Lucas edited the *Complete Works of John Webster*, 1927. Samuel Tannenbaum's *John Webster, a Concise Bibliography*, 1962, updates an earlier bibliography by the same author.

THE RESTORATION AND THE EIGHTEENTH CENTURY

The relevant chapters of George M. Trevelyan's *History of England*, 1926, offer a readable narrative of English history during the 18th century; J. H. Plumb, *England in the Eighteenth Century*, 1950, describes the structure of society. A fuller account is provided by the *Oxford History of England*, in three volumes: Sir George Clark, *The Later Stuarts, 1660–1714*, 1956; Basil Williams and C. H. Stuart, *The Whig Supremacy, 1714–60*, 1962; J. Steven Watson, *The Reign of George III, 1760–1815*, 1960. Studies in the social life of the period abound—among them A. S. Turberville's *English Men and Manners in the Eighteenth Century*, 1926, and as editor, *Johnson's England: An Account of the Life and Manners of His Age*, 2 vols., 1933; M. Dorothy George's *London Life in the Eighteenth Century*, 1925, largely a study of urban poverty; Dorothy Marshall's *English People in the Eighteenth Century*, 1956; George Rudé's *Hanoverian London, 1714–1808*, 1971; and essays on crime and society by E. P. Thompson and others, *Albion's Fatal Tree*, 1976. Three useful guides for the literary student are A. R. Humphreys's *The Augustan World: Society, Thought, and Letters in Eighteenth-Century England*, 1954; Donald Green's *The Age of Exuberance: Backgrounds to Eighteenth-Century English Literature*, 1970; and Pat Rogers's *The Augustan Vision*, 1974.

Helpful books dealing with the intellectual background of the period are Arthur O. Lovejoy's *The Great Chain of Being*, 1942, and *Essays in the History of Ideas*, 1948; Sir Leslie Stephen's *History of English Thought in the Eighteenth Century*, 2 vols., 1876; Basil Willey's *The Eighteenth Century Background*, 1940, a study of the idea of nature; J. W. Johnson's *The Formation of Neo-Classical Thought*, 1967; and John Redwood's *Reason, Ridicule and Religion*, 1976. Paul Hazard's *The European Mind, 1680–1715*, 1953, and *European Thought in the Eighteenth Century*, 1954, are translations from the French by J. L. May, rapid, readable surveys of intellectual movements on the Continent as well as in England. Peter Gay's *The Enlightenment: An Interpretation*, 2 vols., 1969, forcefully defends the philosophers of the "age of reason." Marjorie H. Nicolson's *Newton Demands the Muse: Newton's "Opticks" and the Eighteenth-Century Poets*, 1946, and her many articles, some of which have been republished in *Science and the Imagination*, 1956, are valuable studies of the relation between science and literature in the period may be supplemented by William P. Jones, *The Rhetoric of Science*, 1966. Max Byrd's *Visits to Bedlam*, 1974, and Michael DePorte's *Nightmares and Hobbyhorses*, 1974, both study relations between ideas of madness and literature. Martin Price's *To the Palace of Wisdom: Studies in Order and Energy from Dryden to Blake*, 1964, Paul Fussell's *The Rhetorical World of Augustan Humanism*, 1965, and W. J. Bate's *The Burden of the Past and the English Poet*, 1970, are all thoughtful and stimulating studies that relate ideas to literary art.

Two volumes of the *Oxford History of English Literature* deal with our period in some detail: James Sutherland's *English Literature of the Late Seventeenth Century*, 1969, and Bonamy Dobrée's *English Literature in the Early Eighteenth Century, 1700–1740*, 1959. Briefer surveys of the literature of the age include George Sherburn's "The Restoration and Eighteenth Century" (the standard work), in A. C. Baugh, ed., *A Literary History of England*, rev. 1967; and Roger Lonsdale, ed., *Dryden to Johnson*, 1971, Vol. 4 of the Sphere History of Literature. Oliver Elton's *A Survey of English Literature 1730–1800*, 2 vols., 1928, is much more detailed.

Among books that deal with a single literary mode, James Sutherland's *A Preface to Eighteenth-Century Poetry*, 1948, skillfully introduces a body of poetry that sometimes seems alien to modern readers; it may be supplemented by Ian Jack's *Augustan Satire: Intention and Idiom in English Poetry 1660–1750*, 1952; Rachel Trickett's *The Honest Muse: A Study in Augustan Verse*, 1967; Patricia Spacks's *The Poetry of Vision*, 1967; P. W. K. Stone, *The Art of Poetry, 1750–1820*, 1967; David Morris's *The Religious Sublime*, 1972; and Earl Miner's *The Restoration Mode from Milton to Dryden*, 1974. Allaryce Nicoll's *A History of Restoration Drama 1660–1700*, *A History of Early Eighteenth-Century Drama, 1700–1750*, and *A History of Late Eighteenth-Century Drama, 1750–1800*, rev. 1952, are standard sources of information, supplemented by *The London Stage, 1660–1800*, 11 vols., 1960–68, whose critical introductions are separately available in five paperback books; and by *The Revels History of Drama in English*, Vol. V, *1660–1750*, 1976, and Vol. VI, *1750–1880*, 1975. Five of the most important plays of the period, together with critical commentary and background material on theaters, staging, and audience, will be found in a Norton Critical Edition edited by Scott McMillin *Restoration and Eighteenth-Century Comedy*, 1973. Two collections, Earl Miner, ed., *Restoration Dramatists*, 1966, and John Loftis, ed., *Restoration Drama, Modern Essays in Criticism*, 1966, provide studies by various writers; and Loftis has also analyzed *Comedy and Society from Congreve to Fielding*, 1959. Walter Graham has surveyed *English Literary Periodicals*, 1930; and Donald A. Stauffer, *English Biography before 1700*, 1930, and *The Art of Biography in Eighteenth-Century England*, 2 vols., 1941. John N. Morris, *Versions of the Self: Studies in English Autobiography from John Bunyan to John Stuart Mill*, 1966, and Howard Anderson, Philip B. Daghlian, and Irvin Ehrenpreis, eds., *The Familiar Letter in the Eighteenth Century*, 1966, provide introductions to two influential but neglected genres. Patricia Spacks's *Imagining a Self*, 1976, discusses conceptions of personal identity in many 18th-century autobiographies and novels. The novel is treated in detail in E. A. Baker's *The History of the English Novel*, Vol. III (1930), Vol. IV (1939), Vol. V (1934). This work should be supplemented by two excellent modern studies. Ian Watt's *The Rise of the Novel: Studies in Defoe, Richardson and Fielding*, 1957, and Alan D. McKillop's *The Early Masters of English Fiction*, 1956, which deals with Defoe, Richardson, Fielding, Smollett, and Sterne. Sheridan Baker, "The Idea of Romance in the Eighteenth-Century Novel," *Papers of the Michigan Academy of Science, Arts, and Letters*, XLIX, discusses an important aspect of the background of the novel, as do Ronald Paulson, *Satire and the Novel in Eighteenth Century England*, 1967, and R. F. Brissenden, *Virtue in Distress: Studies in the Novel of Sentiment from Richardson to Sade*, 1974.

Studies of critical movements in this period are numerous and tend to be rather specialized. The two standard collections of neoclassical criticism are Joel E. Spingarn's *Critical Essays of the Seventeenth Century*, Vols. II and III, 1908 (the preface is not yet outdated), and Scott Elledge's *Eighteenth-Century Critical Essays*, 2 vols., 1961. The best statement of the critical canons of the age is Ronald S. Crane's "Neo-Classical Criticism," in J. T. Shipley, ed., *A Dictionary of World Literature*, 1943. The student may also consult Francis Gallaway's *Reason, Rule, and Revolt in English Classicism*, 1940; René Wellek, *A History of Modern Criticism 1750–1950*, 1955, Vol. I; and William K. Wimsatt, Jr., and Cleanth Brooks, *Literary Criticism: A Short History*, 1957. M. H. Abrams, *The Mirror and the Lamp*, 1953, though primarily concerned with romantic theory, has much to say that is valuable about the 18th century.

Studies that discuss the treatment of external nature in the literature of the period (a theme as important for the 18th as it was for the 19th century) include Samuel Holt Monk's *The Sublime: A Study of Critical Theories in Eighteenth-Century England*, 1935, John Arthos's *The Language of Natural Description in Eighteenth-Century Poetry*, 1949, and John Dixon Hunt's *The Figure in the Landscape: Poetry, Painting and Gardening During the Eighteenth Century*, 1977. Martin Battestin compares ideas of religious and artistic order in *The Providence of Wit*, 1974. B. Sprague Allen's *Tides of English Taste 1619–1800*, 2 vols., 1937, on architecture, gardening, and decoration, and Sir Kenneth Clark's *The Gothic Revival*, 2nd ed., 1950, on architecture, are not irrelevant to literature. Jean Hagstrum has studied *The Sister Arts*, 1958, and Lawrence Lipking, *The Ordering of the Arts in Eighteenth-Century England*, 1970. In addition, many of the best essays on 18th-century topics have appeared in collections dedicated to a single scholar: for instance, for Frederick A. Pottle, *From Sensibility to Romanticism*, edited by F. W. Hilles and Harold Bloom, 1965; and for Samuel H. Monk, *Studies in Criticism and Aesthetics, 1660–1800*, edited by Howard Anderson and John S. Shea, 1967. James L. Clifford has collected a number of essays of various writers on the period in *Eighteenth-Century English Literature: Modern Essays in Criticism*, 1959. *Studies in English Literature* devotes its summer issue to the Restoration and Eighteenth Century and includes an article reviewing important work on the period published in the preceding year; *Philological Quarterly* compiles a fuller annual review.

Finally, for further and elaborate bibliographies of 18th-century studies, the student may be referred to the bibliography of English literature, 1600–1800, that has appeared annually since 1926 in *Philological Quarterly*, and, since 1976, in *Eighteenth-Century Studies*.

Joseph Addison and Sir Richard Steele

There is no scholarly edition of the collected works; the Bohn edition of Addison, 6 vols., 1854–56, rev. and enl., 1869–73, is available in libraries. *Letters* were edited by Walter Graham, 1941. *The Spectator* in five volumes was published by Donald F. Bond, 1965. This is the definitive edition. The authoritative biography of Addison is by Peter Smithers, 1968. Edward and Lillian Bloom survey Addison's ideas of society in *Joseph Addison's Sociable Animal*, 1971. Of lives of Steele, George A. Aitken's, 2 vols., 1889; Willard Connely's, 1934; and Calhoun Winton's *Captain Steele: The Early Career of Richard Steele*, 1964, and *Sir Richard Steele, M.P.: The Later Career*, 1970, are the best. Rae Blanchard has edited Steel's *Correspondence*, 1941; *Tracts and Pamphlets*, 1944; *Occasional Verse*, 1952; and also other lesser works. The *Plays* have been edited by Shirley Kenny, 1971. Walter Graham's *English Literary Periodicals*, 1930, may be consulted on both the *Tatler* and the *Spectator*. *The Tatler*, ed. G. A. Aitken, 4 vols., 1898–1899, is the best modern edition of that work. Richmond P. Bond has analyzed *The Tatler: The Making of a Literary Journal*, 1971.

James Boswell

A vast amount has been written about Boswell, much now outmoded by the discovery within the last half century of Boswell's private papers. Most of this outdated material is now simply ill informed, prejudiced, and worthless. Frederick A. Pottle's *James Boswell, The Earlier Years, 1740–1769*, 1966, makes good use of the private papers. C. B. Tinker's lively and percipient *Young Boswell*, 1922, is useful, as is Mary Hyde's *The Impossible Friendship: Boswell and Mrs. Thrale*, 1972. Pottle's *The Literary Career of James Boswell*, 1929 was the first attempt to establish the canon of Boswell's writings. The *Letters*, edited by C. B. Tinker, 2 vols., 1924, will have to be supplemented by the recently recovered correspondence, of which three volumes have been published: Ralph S. Walker, ed. *The Correspondence of James Boswell and John Johnston of Grange*, 1966; Marshall Waingrow, ed., *The Correspondence and Other Papers of James Boswell Relating to the Making of the Life of Johnson*, 1969; and Charles Fifer, ed., *The Correspondence of James Boswell with Certain Members of the Club*, 1976. *The Private Papers of James Boswell from Malahide Castle*, edited by Geoffrey Scott and F. A. Pottle, 18 vols., 1928–34, made available the first of Boswell's papers to be discovered. Volumes of the trade edition of the *Journals*, under the general editorship of F. A. Pottle, appear regularly. The *Journal of a Tour to the Hebrides* has been edited, as first published, by R. W. Chapman, 1924; and, as originally written, by Frederick A. Pottle, 1936. The introductory material and illustrative notes in these volumes and the Malahide papers are of great value.

A wise and sympathetic brief study of Boswell is B. H. Bronson's "Boswell's Boswell," in *Johnson and Boswell*, 1944. *Johnson, Boswell, and Their Circle: Essays Presented to L. F. Powell*, 1965, is a valuable collection. The best edition of the *Life* is L. F. Powell's revised and enlarged edition of the earlier edition by G. B. Hill, 6 vols., 1934–50. A helpful guide through the *Life* is J. L. Smith-Dampier's *Who's Who in Boswell?*, 1935. Mention should perhaps be made of Thomas Babington Macaulay's brilliantly paradoxical, highly prejudiced account of Boswell in his review in 1831 of Croker's edition of the *Life of Johnson*. It blackened

Boswell's reputation for nearly a century and its influence is still alive. It is easily available in any of the numerous printings of Macaulay's *Critical and Historical Essays.*

John Bunyan

Bunyan was a prolific writer: Part II of *The Pilgrim's Progress,* dealing with the journey of Christian's wife and children, appeared in 1684; *The Life and Death of Mr. Badman* in 1680; *The Holy War* in 1682. But these major works form only a small part of all his writings.

The standard life is John Brown's *John Bunyan: His Life, Times, and Work,* 1885, revised by Frank M. Harrison, 1928. The critical edition of *The Pilgrim's Progress* is by J. B. Wharey, 1928, revised by Roger Sharrock, 1960; Sharrock has also edited *Grace Abounding to the Chief of Sinners,* 1962. Among interesting modern studies are George B. Harrison, *John Bunyan: A Study in Personality,* 1928; William Y. Tindall, *John Bunyan, Mechanick, Preacher,* 1934; Henri A. Talon, *John Bunyan, The Man and His Work,* 1951, a translation from the French; U. Milo Kaufmann, *The Pilgrim's Progress and Traditions in Puritan Meditation,* 1966; and Monica Furlong, *Puritan's Progress,* 1975.

Edmund Burke

There is no definitive edition of Burke; E. J. Payne's *Select Works,* 3 vols., 1874–78, has useful notes. *The Sublime and Beautiful* is edited by J. T. Boulton, 1958; the *Correspondence* is complete in 10 vols., edited by Thomas Copeland and others, 1958–1977. For biography, see the life of Philip Magnus, 1939, and the essays by T. W. Copeland, *Our Eminent Friend Edmund Burke,* 1949. Most studies of Burke, like Charles Parkins's *The Moral Basis of Burke's Political Thought,* 1956, and Frank O'Gorman's *Edmund Burke: His Political Philosophy,* 1973, concentrate on his politics; for the literary student, D. C. Bryant's *Edmund Burke and His Literary Friends,* 1939, and Gerald W. Chapman's *Edmund Burke: The Practical Imagination,* 1967, are especially useful.

Samuel Butler

Materials for a full-length biography of Butler do not exist. Of editions of *Hudibras,* Zachary Grey's, 2 vols., 1744, is still useful for its illustrative notes. The best modern edition is John Wilders's, 1967. *Characters,* edited by Charles W. Daves, 1970, is invaluable for studying Butler's opinions; René Lamar has edited *Satires and Miscellaneous Poetry and Prose,* 1928. E. A. Richards's *Hudibras in the Burlesque Tradition,* 1937, is useful. An excellent essay on Butler is included in Ian Jack's *Augustan Satire 1660–1750,* 1952.

William Collins

Lonsdale's edition (see **Gray** below) incorporates an interesting recent discovery, a group of Collins's hitherto unpublished verse, edited by J. S. Cunningham in *Drafts & Fragments of Verse,* 1956. E. G. Ainsworth's *Poor Collins,* 1937, is the most detailed biographical and critical study of the poet. A valuable general work, important for understanding Collins and other 18th-century poets, is Chester F. Chapin's *Personification in Eighteenth-Century English Poetry,* 1955. Geoffrey Hartman includes interesting essays on Collins and Smart in *Beyond Formalism,* 1970, and *The Fate of Reading,* 1975. Frederick W. Hilles and Harold Bloom, eds., *From Sensibility to Romanticism,* 1965, includes an important essay on Collins by A. S. P. Woodhouse.

William Congreve

Congreve's *Complete Works* have been edited by Montague Summers, 4 vols., 1923; and the *Plays* by Herbert Davis in 1967. The best biography is John C. Hodges's *William Congreve the Man,* 1941. Kathleen Lynch's *A Congreve Gallery,* 1951, contains studies of some members of Congreve's circle, including one of Henrietta, Duchess of Marlborough. Maximilian Novak's *William Congreve,* 1971, and Harold Love's *Congreve,* 1975, are both good critical introductions. Criticism of Congreve is abundant in books on Restoration drama. See, for example, Thomas H. Fujimura's *The Restoration Comedy of Wit,* 1952; Dale Underwood's *Etherege and the Seventeenth-Century Comedy,* 1957; Norman N. Holland's *The First Modern Comedies,* 1959; Ian Donaldson's *The World Upside Down: Comedy from Jonson to Fielding,* 1970; Harriet Hawkins's *Likenesses of Truth in Elizabethan and Restoration Drama,* 1972; and Robert Hume's *The Development of English Drama in the Late Seventeenth Century,* 1976.

William Cowper

The poems have been reprinted many times. A convenient modern edition in one volume is H. S. Milford's, 4th ed., 1934. Thomas Wright has edited the *Correspondence,* 4 vols., 1904, and *Unpublished and Uncollected Letters,* 1925. Many letters remain unpublished; better editions of both the letters and the poems are now in preparation. Maurice J. Quinlan's *William Cowper*, 1953, is the most recent scholarly biography. See also his useful edition of Cowper's *Memoir* (first published 1816), in *Proceedings of the American Philosophical Society* XCVII (1953), 359–82. Charles Ryskamp's *William Cowper*, 1959, concentrates on the poet's early life. Useful critical studies include Norman Nicholson's *William Cowper*, 1951, and Morris Golden's *In Search of Stability: The Poetry of William Cowper*, 1960.

George Crabbe

Crabbe's biography was written by his son, George, in 1834. It has been re-edited by E. M. Forster, 1932, and by Edmund Blunden, 1947. The *Poetical Works*, well edited by A. J. and R. M. Carlyle, were published in 1914. *New Poems*, edited by Arthur Pollard, 1960, contains hitherto unpublished poems. Howard Mills has edited *George Crabbe: Tales (1812) and Other Selected Poems*, 1967. Lilian Haddakin's *Poetry of Crabbe*, 1955; Oliver Sigworth's *Nature's Sternest Painter*, 1965; and Peter New's *George Crabbe's Poetry*, 1976, are essays in criticism.

Daniel Defoe

The best biography of Defoe is James Sutherland's *Defoe*, 1937, rev., 1950; Sutherland has also written a fine critical study, *Daniel Defoe*, 1971. The *Letters* were edited by George H. Healey, 1955. Ian Watt's *The Rise of the Novel*, 1957, contains an interesting study of Defoe's novels in relation to social and economic history. Recent full-length studies include John R. Moore's *Daniel Defoe: Citizen of the Modern World*, 1958; Maximilian E. Novak, *Economics and the Fiction of Daniel Defoe*, 1962, and *Defoe and the Nature of Man*, 1963; G. A. Starr, *Defoe and Spiritual Autobiography*, 1965, and *Defoe and Casuistry*, 1971; and Peter Earle, *The World of Defoe*, 1976. J. R. Moore has also provided a useful *Checklist of the Writings of Daniel Defoe*, 1960.

Two of Defoe's novels are in the Norton Critical Editions series: *Moll Flanders*, edited by Edward Kelly, 1974, and *Robinson Crusoe*, edited by Michael Shinagel, 1975.

John Dryden

Charles E. Ward's *Life of John Dryden*, 1961, the standard biography, may be supplemented by the excellent sketch in George R. Noyes's edition of the *Poetical Works*, 2nd ed., 1950. Until recently, the only edition of the *Works* has been the unsatisfactory one in 18 volumes by Sir Walter Scott and George Saintsbury, 1882–93. A new edition of the *Works*, begun under the general editorship of the late Edward N. Hooker and carried on under the late H. T. Swedenberg, has been appearing at intervals since 1956. The poems have been edited by James Kinsley, 4 vols., 1958. W. P. Ker, 1900, 1926, and George Watson, 2 vols., 1962, have edited the *Essays*.

Mark Van Doren's *John Dryden: A Study of His Poetry*, 1920, remains valuable for its fresh critical responses, as do T. S. Eliot's brief studies, *Homage to John Dryden*, 1924, and *John Dryden the Poet, the Dramatist, the Critic*, 1932. Important modern criticism includes Arthur Hoffman's *John Dryden's Imagery*, 1962, Alan Roper's *Dryden's Poetic Kingdoms*, 1965, and Earl Miner's *Dryden's Poetry*, 1967. Louis Bredvold's *The Intellectual Milieu of John Dryden*, 1934, an influential study of Dryden's philosophical, political, and religious ideas, has been superseded, especially with regard to religion, by Philip Harth's fine *Contexts of Dryden's Thought*, 1968. Robert Hume analyzes *Dryden's Criticism*, 1970; Edward Pechter, *Dryden's Classical Theory of Literature*, 1975; and John C. Aden, in *The Critical Opinions of John Dryden, A Dictionary*, 1963, brings together Dryden's critical ideas under convenient headings.

John Gay

The standard life is W. H. Irving's *John Gay: Favorite of the Wits*, 1940. G. C. Farber has edited the *Poetical Works*, 1926, and C. F. Burgess the *Letters*, 1966. Critical studies include Sven Armens, *John Gay, Social Critic*, 1954; Patricia Spacks, *John Gay*, 1965; and Adina Forsgren, *Gay: Poet "of a Lower Order,"* 2 vols., 1964, 1971.

Oliver Goldsmith

The Collected Works of Goldsmith was published by Arthur Friedman in 1966. The standard biography of Goldsmith is Ralph M. Wardle's *Oliver Goldsmith*, 1957. Sir James Prior's *Life of Oliver Goldsmith*, 2 vols., 1837, is the important biography of the last century. Kathleen C. Balderston has edited the *Collected Letters*, 1928; Austin Dobson edited the *Plays*, 1901. An important addition to the canon of Goldsmith's works was made by Ronald S. Crane in his edition of *New Essays*, 1927. The notes in Lonsdale's edition of the *Poems* (see **Gray** below) are valuable; Ricardo Quintana's *Oliver Goldsmith*, 1967, is a useful critical survey.

Thomas Gray

The poems of Gray, Collins, and Goldsmith have been edited, with authoritative notes, by Roger Lonsdale, 1969. The standard edition of Gray's *Works* is that of Edmund Gosse, 4 vols., rev., 1902–6; of the *Correspondence*, that of Paget Toynbee and Leonard Whibley, 3 vols., 1935; of the poems that of H. W. Starr and J. R. Hendrickson, 1966. R. W. Ketton-Cremer's *Thomas Gray*, 1955, is the most recent and the best biography. The best extended critical study is unfortunately in French: Roger Martin's *Essai sur Gray*, 1934. A more specialized study is William P. Jones's *Thomas Gray, Scholar*, 1937. James Downey and Ben Jones have edited a collection of essays on Gray, *Fearful Joy*, 1974. Frederick W. Hilles and Harold Bloom, eds., *From Sensibility to Romanticism*, 1965, contains studies of the *Elegy* by F. Brady, B. H. Bronson, and I. Jack.

Samuel Johnson

Others among Johnson's friends besides Boswell wrote of him: notably, Mrs. Hester Lynch Thrale Piozzi, whose *Anecdotes* appeared in 1786 and have been edited, along with William Shaw's *Anecdotes*, by Arthur Sherbo, 1974; Sir John Hawkins, whose *Life* was published in 1787 and reissued in 1961, edited and abridged by Bertram H. Davis; and Fanny Burney (Mme D'Arblay), from whose diary the Johnsonian passages are found most conveniently in C. B. Tinker's *Dr. Johnson and Fanny Burney*, 1911. James L. Clifford's *Young Sam Johnson*, 1955, is a thorough study of Johnson's early life and a necessary supplement to Boswell's rather sketchy account of Johnson's life before their meeting in 1763. There are fine modern biographies by John Wain, 1975, and W. J. Bate, 1977. The poems were admirably edited by David Nichol Smith and E. L. McAdam, 2nd ed. rev. by J. D. Fleeman, 1974. The best collected edition of Johnson's *Works* appeared as long ago as 1825. A new Yale edition, which has been coming out irregularly since 1958, will eventually become standard. G. B. Hill's edition of *Johnsonian Miscellanies*, 2 vols., 1897, and *The Lives of the Poets*, 3 vols., 1905, both with superb notes, have recently been reprinted. R. W. Chapman's edition of the letters, 3 vols., 1952, is authoritative. There is a valuable survey and bibliography of critical studies, rev., 1970, by J. L. Clifford and D. J. Greene.

Some interesting modern studies of Johnson are J. W. Krutch's *Samuel Johnson*, 1944; B. H. Bronson's "Johnson Agonistes," 1944 (reissued in *Johnson Agonistes and Other Essays*, 1965); W. J. Bate's *The Achievement of Samuel Johnson*, 1955; W. K. Wimsatt, Jr., *The Prose Style of Samuel Johnson*, 1941; Donald J. Greene's *The Politics of Samuel Johnson*, 1960; Arieh Sachs's *Passionate Intelligence: Imagination and Reason in the Work of Samuel Johnson*, 1967; and Paul Fussell's *Samuel Johnson and the Life of Writing*, 1971. *Johnson, Boswell, and Their Circle*, 1965, and Donald J. Greene, ed., *Samuel Johnson, A Collection of Critical Essays*, 1965, bring together short studies by various hands. Aspects of Johnson's criticism are treated in Joseph E. Brown's *The Critical Opinions of Samuel Johnson*, 1926; Jean Hagstrum's *Samuel Johnson's Literary Criticism*, 1952; Leopold Damrosch, Jr., *The Uses of Johnson's Criticism*, 1976; and William Edinger's *Samuel Johnson and Poetic Style*, 1977. E. L. McAdam's *Johnson and Boswell: A Survey of their Writings*, 1969, and D. J. Greene's *Samuel Johnson*, 1970, are brief useful guides.

Lady Mary Wortley Montagu

The standard modern biography is Robert Halsband's *The Life of Lady Mary Wortley Montagu*, 1956. Halsband has also edited *The Complete Letters*, 3 vols., 1965–67; *Selected Letters*, 1970; and, with Isobel Grundy, *Essays and Poems and Simplicity, a Comedy*, 1977.

Alexander Pope

There is no reliable complete edition of all of Pope's works. Defective though it is in many respects, the Victorian edition in 10 volumes by Elwin and Courthope, 1871–89, must still be consulted, though with caution. The excellent Twickenham Edition of the poems, a co-operative undertaking by several scholars (the general editor is John Butt), is now complete in 11 volumes, with valuable introductory and critical materials and notes. A convenient selection in a single volume, with selected notes, omits the translations of Homer. Only one volume of Norman Ault's edition of *The Prose Works*, 1936, was published before the editor's death.

No sound biography of Pope exists. George Sherburn's *Early Career of Alexander Pope*, 1934, is authoritative, but unfortunately it does not study the poet's life beyond about 1726. It is an essential book, for it corrects many misinterpretations and distortions of Pope's character and motives that mar earlier biographies. Maynard Mack's elegant study, *The Garden and the City: Retirement and*

Politics in the Later Poetry of Pope, 1731–1743, 1969, is the first installment of a biography that should set new standards. Howard Erskine-Hill has described *The Social Milieu of Alexander Pope*, 1975. Ault's *New Light on Pope*, 1949, makes important miscellaneous contributions to Pope's biography. Sherburn's edition of the *Correspondence*, 1956, 5 vols., is standard, though soon to be superseded by a new edition under the direction of Mack. R. H. Griffith, *Alexander Pope: A Bibliography*, 1962, is a 2-volume listing of Pope's writings.

The best detailed critical study of the poems is Geoffrey Tillotson's *On the Poetry of Pope*, 2nd ed., 1950; and the same author's *Pope and Human Nature*, 1958, throws light on a difficult subject. Austen Warren's *Alexander Pope as Critic and Humanist*, 1929, though somewhat dated, is still useful. Much information is gathered up in Robert W. Rogers's *The Major Satires of Alexander Pope*, 1955. Reuben A. Brower's *Alexander Pope: The Poetry of Allusion*, 1959, is an enlightening study of Pope's lifelong habit of felicitous quotation from and adaptation of phrases, images, and ideas from earlier European poets, especially, though not exclusively, from the poets of classical antiquity. Aubrey Williams incisively analyzes *Pope's Dunciad*, 1955, and may be supplemented by John F. Sitter's *The Poetry of Pope's Dunciad*, 1971. Maynard Mack, ed., *Essential Articles for the Study of Alexander Pope*, 1964, conveniently brings together a number of short studies.

Matthew Prior

The complete critical edition of Prior is *Literary Works*, edited by H. B. Wright and M. K. Spears, 2 vols., 1971. The older and less complete edition in 2 volumes by A. R. Waller, 1905, 1907, is useful. The best biography is Charles K. Eves's *Matthew Prior, Poet and Diplomatist*, 1939.

John Wilmot, Earl of Rochester

David M. Vieth's fine edition of Rochester's *Complete Poems*, 1968, supersedes the useful earlier edition by Vivian de Sola Pinto, 1964. Pinto's biography, *Enthusiast in Wit*, 1962, may be supplemented by John Harold Wilson's edition of *The Rochester-Savile Letters, 1671–1680*, 1941, and by John Adlard's gathering of source materials, *The Debt to Pleasure*, 1974. The best critical study of Rochester's poems is Dustin Griffin's *Satires Against Man*, 1973.

Christopher Smart

Norman Callan edited Smart's *Collected Poems*, 2 vols., 1949; and there is a good selection by R. E. Brittain, 1950. *Jubilate Agno was* first edited, as *Rejoice in the Lamb*, by W. F. Stead, 1939; W. H. Bond's edition, 1954, is better. On the life, Christopher Devlin's *Poor Kit Smart*, 1961, should be supplemented by Arthur Sherbo's *Christopher Smart, Scholar of the University*, 1967; Moira Dearnley surveys *The Poetry of Christopher Smart*, 1968. Geoffrey Hartman includes interesting essays on Smart and Collins in *Beyond Formalism*, 1970, and *The Fate of Reading*, 1975.

Sir Richard Steele

See entries under **Joseph Addison and Sir Richard Steele.**

Jonathan Swift

Biographers have found it difficult to write of Swift without advancing some special and private thesis about his character and personal life. Louis A. Landa's *Swift and the Church of Ireland*, 1954, is reliable, and Irvin Ehrenpreis's *The Personality of Jonathan Swift*, 1958, is full of good things as well as of a certain amount of ingenious and not wholly convincing theorizing. Ehrenpreis has so far published two excellent volumes of a three-volume biography: *Mr. Swift and His Contemporaries*, 1962, and *Dr. Swift*, 1967.

The standard edition of the poems is by Sir Harold Williams, 3 vols., 1937, rev., 1958. Joseph Horrell's edition of the *Collected Poems*, 2 vols., The Muses' Library, 1958, is less expensive than Williams's and almost, but not entirely, relies on the canon and text established by Williams in his edition. Herbert Davis's edition of the prose works in 16 volumes, published over a period of years, is now complete. Swift's *Correspondence* has been edited by Sir Harold Williams, 5 vols., 1963–65. Distinguished editions of other works are Herbert Davis's *The Drapier's Letters*, 1935; Harold Williams' *Journal to Stella*, 1948; A C. Guthkelch and D. Nichol Smith, *A Tale of a Tub*, 2nd ed., 1958; and Frank H. Ellis, *A Discourse of the Contests and Dissentions Between the Nobles and the Commons in Athens and Rome*, 1967. For the Norton Critical Editions series, Robert A. Greenberg has edited *Gulliver's Travels*, rev., 1971, and *The Writings of Jonathan Swift*. Useful bibliographies have been provided by Arthur H. Scouten in his edition of H. Teerink's *A Bibliography of the Writings of Jonathan Swift*, 1963; Louis A. Landa and James E. Tobin, *Jonathan Swift: A List of Critical Studies Published from 1895 to 1945*, 1945; and James J. Stathis, *A Bibliography of Swift Studies, 1945–65*, 1967.

Critical studies long and short abound. The student should find especially helpful Ricardo Quintana's *The Mind and Art of Jonathan Swift*, 1936, and *Swift: an Introduction*, 1955; and Kathleen Williams's *Jonathan Swift and the Age of Compromise*, 1958. Arthur E. Case's *Four Essays on Gulliver's Travels*, 1945; Maurice Johnson's *The Sin of Wit: Jonathan Swift as a Poet*, 1950; C. J. Rawson's *Gulliver and the Gentle Reader*, 1973; and Nora Jaffe's *The Poet Swift*, 1977, are useful special studies. Most of Herbert Davis's excellent critical pieces on Swift have been brought together in *Jonathan Swift, Essays on his Satire and Other Studies*, 1964; in recent years there have appeared a number of paperbound collections of important essays, particularly those on *Gulliver's Travels*. Milton Voight has summarized the movements in Swift studies in *Swift and the Twentieth Century*, 1964.

James Thomson

The most recent biographical study of Thomson is Douglas Grant's *James Thomson, Poet of "The Seasons,"* 1951. A. D. McKillop has edited *James Thomson, Letters and Documents*, 1958, which contains much about Thomson's friends and the interests of his literary circle, and *James Thomson: The Castle of Indolence and Other Poems*, 1961. There are good notes in James Sambrook's edition of *The Seasons and The Castle of Indolence*, 1972. The most valuable study of the content of *The Seasons* is McKillop's *The Background of Thomson's Seasons*, 1942. Ralph Cohen, *The Art of Discrimination: Thomson's The Seasons and the Language of Criticism*, 1964, is a valuable work which uses responses to the poem to illustrate the development of critical theory; and Cohen has added a critical study, *The Unfolding of the Seasons*, 1970. Patricia Meyer Spacks, *The Poetry of Vision: Five Eighteenth-Century Poets*, 1966, contains a chapter on Thomson, as well as others on Collins, Gray, Smart, and Cowper.

Anne Finch, Countess of Winchilsea

Myra Reynolds added a long biographical introduction to her standard edition of the *Poems*, 1903. Reuben Brower's "Lady Winchilsea and the Poetic Tradition of the Seventeenth Century," *Studies in Philology*, XLII (1945), 61–80, and a chapter of John Buxton's *A Tradition of Poetry*, 1967, correct the notion that she was a "romantic."

Poetic Forms and Literary Terminology

RHYTHM AND METER

Verse is generally distinguished from prose as a more compressed and more regularly rhythmic form of statement. This approximate truth underlines the importance of **meter** in poetry, as the means by which rhythm is measured and described.

In the classical languages, meter was established on a **quantitative** basis, by the regular alternation of long and short syllables (that is, syllables classified according to the time taken to pronounce them). Outside of a few experiments (and the songs of Thomas Campion), this system has never proved congenial to English, which distinguishes, instead, between **stressed** and **unstressed,** or accented and unaccented syllables. Two varieties of accented stress may be distinguished. On the one hand, there is the natural stress pattern of words themselves; *sýllable* is accented on the first syllable, *deplórable* on the second, and so on. Then there is the sort of stress which indicates rhetorical emphasis. If the sentence "You went to Greece?" is given a pronounced accent on the last word, it implies "Greece (of all places)?" If the accent falls on the first word, it implies "you (of all people)?" The meter of poetry—that is, its rhythm—is ordinarily built up out of a regular recurrence of accents, whether established as **word accents** or **rhetorical accents;** once started in the reader's mind, it has (like all rhythm) a persistent effect of its own.

The unit which is repeated to give steady rhythm to a poem is called a **poetic foot;** in English it usually consists of accented and unaccented syllables in one of five fairly simple patterns:

The **iambic foot** (or **iamb**) consists of an unstressed followed by a stressed syllable, as in *uníte, repeát,* or *insíst.* Most English verse falls naturally into the iambic pattern.

The **trochaic foot** (**trochee**) inverts this order; it is a stressed followed by an unstressed syllable—for example, *únit, réaper,* or *ínstant.*

The **anapestic foot** (**anapest**) consists of two unstressed syllables followed by a stressed syllable, as in *intercéde, disarránge,* or *Cameróon.*

The **dactylic foot** (**dactyl**) consists of a stressed syllable followed by two unstressed syllables, as in *Wáshington, Écuador,* or *ápplejack.*

The **spondaic foot** (**spondee**) consists of two successive stressed syllables, as in *heartbreak, headline,* or *Kashmir.*

In all the examples above, word accent and the quality of the metrical foot coincide exactly. But the metrical foot may well consist of several words, or, on the other hand, one word may well consist of several metrical feet. *Phótolithógraphy* consists of two excellent dactyls in a single word; *dárk and with spóts on it*, though it consists of six words rather than one, is also two dactyls—not quite such good ones. When we read a piece of poetry with the intention of discovering its underlying metrical pattern, we are said to **scan** it—that is, we go through it line by line, indicating by conventional signs which are the accented and which the unaccented syllables within the feet (the ictus ′ generally designates accented, the mora ˘ unaccented syllables). We also count the number of feet in each line, or, more properly, **verse**—since a single poetic line is generally called a "verse." Verse lengths are conventionally described in terms derived from the Greek:

Monometer: one foot (of rare occurrence)
Dimeter: two feet (also rare)
Trimeter: three feet
Tetrameter: four feet
Pentameter: five feet
Hexameter: six feet (six iambic feet make an **Alexandrine**)
Heptameter: seven feet (also rare)

Doctor Johnson's little parody of simpleminded poets would thus be scanned this way:

Ĭ pút my̆ hát ŭpón my̆ héad
Ănd wálked ĭntó thĕ Stránd,
Ănd thére Ĭ mét ănóthĕr mán
Whŏse hát wăs ín hĭs hánd.

The poem is iambic in rhythm, alternating tetrameter and trimeter in verse length. The fact that it scans so nicely is, however, no proof that it is good poetry. Quite the contrary. Many of poetry's most subtle effects are achieved by establishing an underlying rhythm and then varying it by means of a whole series of devices, some dramatic and expressive, others designed simply to lend variety and interest to the verse. A well-known sonnet of Shakespeare's (116) begins,

Let me not to the marriage of true minds
Admit impediments. Love is not love
Which alters when it alteration finds,
Or bends with the remover to remove.

It is perfectly possible, if one crushes all one's sensitivities, to read the first line of this poem as mechanical iambic pentameter:

Lĕt mé nŏt tó thĕ márriăge óf trŭe mínds.

But of course nobody ever reads it that way, except to make a point; read with normal English accent and some sense of what it is saying, the line would probably form a pattern something like this:

Lét mĕ nŏt tŏ thĕ márriăge ŏf trúe mínds,

which is neither pentameter nor in any way iambic. The second line is a little more iambic, but, read for expression, falls just as far short of pentameter:

> Ădmit ĭmpédĭmĕnts. Lóve ĭs nŏt lóve.

Only in the third and fourth lines of the sonnet do we get verses which read as well as scan like five iambic feet.

The fact is that perfectly regular metrical verse is easy to write and dull to read. Among the devices in common use for varying too regular a pattern are, for instance, the insertion of a trochaic foot among iambics, especially at the opening of a line, where the soft first syllable of the iambic foot often needs stiffening (see line 1 above); the more or less free addition of extra unaccented syllables; and the use of **caesura,** or strong grammatical pause within a line (conventionally indicated, in scanning, by the sign ||). The second line of the sonnet above is a good example of caesura:

> Admit impediments. || Love is not love.

The strength of the caesura, and its placing in the line, may be varied to produce striking variations of effect. More broadly, the whole relation between the poem's sound- and rhythm-patterns and its pattern as a sequence of assertions (phrases, clauses, sentences) may be manipulated by the poet. Sometimes his statements fit neatly within the lines, so that each line ends with a strong mark of punctuation; they are then known as **end-stopped lines.** Sometimes the sense flows over the ends of the lines, creating **run-on lines**; this process is also known, from the French, as **enjambment** (literally, "straddling").

End-stopped lines (Marlowe, *Hero and Leander,* lines 45–48):

> So lovely fair was Hero, Venus' nun,
> As Nature wept, thinking she was undone,
> Because she took more from her than she left
> And of such wondrous beauty her bereft.

Run-on lines (Keats, *Endymion* I.89–93):

> Full in the middle of this pleasantness
> There stood a marble altar, with a tress
> Of flowers budded newly; and the dew
> Had taken fairy fantasies to strew
> Daisies upon the sacred sward, * * *

Following the example of such poets as Blake, Rimbaud, and Whitman, many poets of the 20th century have undertaken to write what is called **free verse**—that is, verse which has neither a fixed metrical foot, nor (consequently) a fixed number of feet in its lines, but which depends for its rhythm on a pattern of cadences, or the rise and fall of the voice in utterance. All freedom in art is of course relative; free verse, with its special aptitude for metrical variety and nervous, colloquial phrasing—its total responsiveness, in other words, to its subject matter—has so successfully established itself that it is now widely recognized as a new and rather demanding form of artistic discipline.

SENSE AND SOUND

The very words of which poetic lines—whether free or traditional—are composed cause them to have different sounds and produce different effects. Polysyllables, being pronounced fast, often cause a line to move swiftly; monosyllables, especially when heavy and requiring distinct accents, may cause it to move heavily, as in Milton's famous line (*Paradise Lost* II.621):

Rocks, caves, lakes, fens, bogs, dens, and shades of death.

Poetic assertions are often dramatized and reinforced by means of **alliteration**—that is, the use of several nearby words or stressed syllables beginning with the same consonant. When Shakespeare writes (*Sonnet* 64),

Ruin hath taught me thus to ruminate
That Time will come and take my love away,

the rich, round, vague echoes of the first line contrast most effectively with the sharp anxiety and directness of the alliterative *t*'s in the second. When Dryden starts *Absalom and Achitophel* with that wicked couplet,

In pious times, ere priestcraft did begin,
Before polygamy was made a sin,

the satiric undercutting is strongly reinforced by the triple alliteration which links "*p*ious" with "*p*riestcraft" and "*p*olygamy."

Assonance, or repetition of the same or similar vowel sounds within a passage (usually in accented syllables), also serves to enrich it, as in two lines from Keats's *Ode on Melancholy:*

For shade to shade will come too drowsily,
And drown the wakeful anguish of the soul.

It is clear that the round, hollow tones of "dr*ow*sily," repeated in "dr*ow*n" and darkening to the full *o*-sound of "soul," have much to do with the effect of the passage. A related device is **consonance,** or the repetition of a pattern of consonants with changes in the intervening vowels—for example: *linger, longer, languor; rider, reader, raider, ruder.*

Direct verbal imitation of natural sounds (known as **onomatopoeia**) has has been much attempted, from Virgil's galloping horse—

Quadrupedante putrem sonitu quatit ungula campum—

to Tennyson's account, in *The Princess,* of

The moan of doves in immemorial elms,
And murmuring of innumerable bees.

Often ingeniously exploited as a side effect, onomatopoeia is essentially a trick, with about the same value in poetry as it has in music.

RHYME AND STANZA

Rhyme consists of a repetition of accented sounds in words, usually those falling at the end of verse lines. If the rhyme sound is the very last syllable of the line (*rebound, sound*), the rhyme is called **masculine;** if the accented syllable is followed by an unaccented syllable (*hounding, bounding*), the rhyme is called **feminine.** Rhymes amounting to three or more syllables, like forced rhymes, generally have a comic effect in English, and have been freely used for this purpose, e.g., by Ogden Nash (*opportunity, impunity; failure, azalea*). Rhymes occurring within a single line are called **internal**; for instance, the Mother-Goose rhyme, "Mary, Mary, quite contrary," or Coleridge's *Ancient Mariner* ("We were the first that ever burst / Into that silent sea"). **Eye rhymes** are words used as rhymes which look alike but actually sound different (for example, *alone, done; remove, love*); **off rhymes** (sometimes called **partial, imperfect,** or **slant rhymes**) are occasionally the result of pressing exigencies or lack of skill, but are also, at times, used deliberately by modern poets for special effects. For instance, a sonnet by Dylan Thomas contains such "rhymes" as *knees, toes; Eve, grave; van, bone*; and *winter, ladder* (*Holy Sonnet* 3). Pairings like the last two are sometimes loosely described as consonance, rather than rhyme.

Blank verse is unrhymed iambic pentameter; until the recent advent of free verse, it was the only unrhymed measure to achieve general popularity in English. First used by the Earl of Surrey, blank verse was during the 16th century largely dramatic in character. *Paradise Lost* was one of the first nondramatic poems in English to use blank verse. But Milton's authority and his success were so great that during the 18th and 19th centuries blank verse came to be used for a great variety of discursive, descriptive, and philosophical poems—besides remaining the standard metrical form for epics. Thomson's *Seasons*, Cowper's *Task*, Wordsworth's *Prelude*, and Tennyson's *Idylls of the King* were all written in blank verse.

A **stanza** is a recurring unit of a poem, consisting of a number of verses. Certain poetic forms (as a notable example, Pindaric odes) have stanzas comprising a variable number of verses, of varying lengths. Others are more regular, hence easier to describe.

The simplest form of stanza is the **couplet**; it is simply two lines rhyming together. When a single couplet is considered in isolation, it is sometimes called a **distich**; when it includes a complete unified thought, ending with a terminal mark of punctuation, it is called a **closed couplet.** The iambic pentameter couplet seems to work best when it is strict and regular, but to regularize it was a work of considerable time and practice. Even as skillful a versifier as Ben Jonson, though he writes iambic pentameter couplets in a poem like *To Penshurst*, has not yet mastered what we call the **heroic couplet.** This is a strictly iambic pentameter couplet, strongly end-stopped, and with the couplets prevailingly closed. Heroic couplets generally are varied by means of a decided caesura, and limited to precisely ten syllables per line. The heroic couplet is the principal form of English neoclassical style. A model of its swift, keen, yet weighty wit is the opening of Dryden's *Absalom and Achitophel*. Occasionally, as in this poem, heroic couplets are varied by the introduction of a third rhyme, to make a **tercet** (usually enclosed by a marginal brace); and a striking terminal effect is sometimes achieved by the introduction of an Alexandrine (a line of iambic hexameter) as the third line of the tercet.

Another customary and challenging form of couplet is the **tetrameter,** or **four-beat couplet.** The more closely rhymes recur, the harder couplets are to manage; in addition, a four-beat line is hard to divide by caesura without splitting it into two tick-tock dimeters. For this reason, tetrameter couplets have posed a perpetual challenge to poets, and still provide an admirable finger-exercise for aspiring versifiers. A model of tetrameter couplets managed with marvelous variety, complexity, and expressiveness is Marvell's *To His Coy Mistress:*

> Thou by the Indian Ganges' side
> Shouldst rubies find; I by the tide
> Of Humber would complain. I would
> Love you ten years before the flood,
> And you should, if you please, refuse
> Till the conversion of the Jews.

English has not done much with rhymes grouped in threes, but has borrowed from Italian the form known as ***terza rima,*** in which Dante composed his *Divine Comedy*. This form consists of linked groups of three rhymes according to the following pattern: *aba bcb cdc ded,* etc. Shelley's *Ode to the West Wind* is composed in stanzas of *terza rima,* the poem as a whole ending with a couplet.

Quatrains are stanzas of four lines; the lines usually rhyme alternately, *abab,* or in the second and fourth lines, *abcb*. When they alternate tetrameter and trimeter lines, as in Johnson's little poem about men in hats (above), or as in *Sir Patrick Spens,* they are called **ballad stanza.** Dryden's *Annus Mirabilis* and Gray's *Elegy Written in a Country Churchyard* are in heroic quatrains; these rhyme alternately, and employ five-stress iambic verse throughout. Tennyson used for *In Memoriam* a tetrameter quatrain rhymed *abba,* and FitzGerald translated *The Rubáiyát of Omar Khayyám* into a pentameter rhymed *aaba;* but these forms have not been very generally adopted.

Chaucer's *Troilus and Criseyde* is an early example in English of **rime royal,** a seven-line iambic pentameter stanza consisting essentially of a quatrain dovetailed onto two couplets, according to the rhyme scheme *ababbcc* (the fourth line serves both as the final line of the quatrain and the first line of the first couplet). Closely akin to rime royal, but differentiated by an extra *a*-rhyme between the two *b*-rhymes, is **ottava rima,** that is, an eight-line stanza rhyming *abababcc*. As its name suggests, ottava rima is of Italian origin; it was first used in English by Wyatt. Its final couplet, being less prepared for than in rime royal, and usually set off as a separate verbal unit, has a special witty snap to it, for which Byron found good use in *Don Juan*.

The longest and most intricate stanza generally used for narrative purposes in English is that devised by Edmund Spenser for *The Faerie Queene*. The **Spenserian stanza** has nine lines rhyming *ababbcbcc;* the first eight lines are pentameter, the last line an Alexandrine. Slow-moving, intricate of pattern, and demanding in its rhyme scheme (the *b*-sound recurs four times, the *c*-sound three), the Spenserian stanza has nonetheless appealed widely to poets seeking a rich and complicated metrical form. Keats's *Eve of St. Agnes* and Shelley's *Adonais* are brilliantly successful 19th-century examples of its use.

The **sonnet,** originally a stanza of Italian origin which has developed into an independent lyric form, is usually defined as fourteen lines of iambic pentameter. None of the elements in this definition is absolute. The first sonnet of Sidney's *Astrophel and Stella* is in hexameters, and Milton has one sonnet of twenty lines (*On the New Forcers of Conscience*), while Meredith wrote a whole series of sixteen-line sonnets (*Modern Love*). Most sonnets, however, conform to the definition. Sonnets generally follow one of two conventional rhyme schemes. The **Petrarchan** or **Italian sonnet** is divided into sections of eight lines (**octave**) and six lines (**sestet**), rhyming *abba abba* and *cdecde*. (There are many variations of the rhyme scheme in the sestet; that described is the most frequent.) Under this arrangement, the poet tends to use his octave to state the problem and his sestet to resolve it. The **English** or **Shakespearean** sonnet takes the form of three quatrains and a final couplet, rhyming *abab cdcd efef gg*. The couplet is ideally suited for producing a summary statement or witty twist after the problem has been turned about in the three quatrains. Both these forms represent ideal models, not absolute prescriptions. Many sonnets approximate these patterns without following them precisely; indeed, the term "sonnet" was slow in acquiring any meaning more specific than that of "short lyric poem." Among Donne's *Songs and Sonnets* there is just one sonnet in the more modern sense, *The Token*, and it has eighteen lines.

In the Elizabethan period, the sonnet underwent its most intensive cultivation in connection with themes of courtly love. Perhaps in revulsion, Donne used the sonnet mostly to express religious devotion (*Holy Sonnets, La Corona*), while Milton employed it on satiric, social, or political themes. In Wordsworth, it expanded in the direction of moral reflection and commentary, while G. M. Hopkins loaded it with a rich philosophical and rhetorical complexity which sometimes threatened to swamp the form altogether. But the applications of the sonnet are truly limitless, for it is a form just long and complex enough to provide compressed yet dignified statement of almost any major theme.

In blank verse or irregularly rhymed verse, where stanzaic divisions do not exist or are indistinct, the poetry sometimes falls into **verse paragraphs,** which are in effect divisions of sense like prose paragraphs. This division can be clearly seen in Milton's *Lycidas* or Spenser's *Epithalamion*. In the latter poem, it is reinforced by a **refrain,** which is simply a line repeated at the end of each stanza. Ballads also customarily have refrains; for example, the refrain of *Lord Randall* is

mother, make my bed soon,
For I'm weary wi' hunting, and fain wald lie down.

FIGURATIVE LANGUAGE

The act of bringing words together into rich and vigorous poetic lines is complex and demanding, chiefly because so many variables require control. There is the "thought" of the lines, their verbal texture, their emotional resonance, the developing perspective of the reader—all these to be managed at once. One of the poet's chief resources toward this end is figurative language. Here, as in matters of meter, one may distinguish a great variety of devices, some of which we use in everyday speech without special awareness of their names and natures. When we say someone eats "like a horse" or "like a bird," we are using a **simile,** that is, a comparison marked out by a specific word of likening—"like" or "as." When we omit the word of comparison but imply a likeness—as in the sentence, "That hog has guzzled all the champagne"—we are making use of **metaphor.** The **epic simile,** frequent in epic poetry, is an extended simile in which the thing compared is described as an object in its own right, beyond its point of likeness with the main subject. Milton starts to compare Satan to Leviathan, but concludes his simile with the story of a sailor who moored his ship by mistake, one night, to a whale (*Paradise Lost* I.200–208). Metaphors and similes have been complexly but usefully distinguished according to their special effects; they may be, for instance, violent, comic, degrading, decorative.

When we speak of "forty head of cattle" or ask someone to "lend a hand" with a job, we are using **synecdoche,** a figure which substitutes the part for the whole. When we speak of a statement "coming from the White House," or a man much interested in "the turf," we are using **metonymy,** or the substitution of one term for another with which it is closely associated. **Antithesis** is a device for placing opposing ideas in grammatical parallel, as, for example, in the following passage from Pope's *Rape of the Lock* (V.25–30), where there are more examples of antithesis than there are lines:

> But since, alas! frail beauty must decay,
> Curled or uncurled, since locks will turn to gray;
> Since painted, or not painted, all shall fade,
> And she who scorns a man must die a maid;
> What then remains but well our power to use,
> And keep good humor still whate'er we lose?

Irony is a verbal device which implies an attitude quite different from (and often opposite to) that which is literally expressed. When Job answers his comforters, saying "No doubt but ye are the people, and wisdom shall die with you" (Job xii.2), he is using irony thick to the point of sarcasm. When Eliot writes, in *Whispers of Immortality,* that "Grishkin is nice," the adjective is carefully chosen to let an ironic grimace of distaste appear. And when Donne "proves," in *The Canonization,* that he and his mistress are going to found a new religion of love, he seems to be inviting us to take a subtly ironic attitude toward religion as well as love.

Because it is easy to see through, **hyperbole,** or willful exaggeration, is a favorite device of irony—which is not to say that it may not be "serious" as well. When she hears that a young man is "dying for love" of her, a sensible girl does not accept this statement literally, but it may convey a serious meaning to her nonetheless. The **pun,** or play on words (known to the learned, sometimes, as **paronomasia**), may also be serious or comic in intent; witness, for example, the famous series of puns in Donne's *Hymn to God the Father.* **Oxymoron** is a figure of flat contradiction—for instance, Milton's famous description of hell as containing "darkness visible" (*Paradise Lost* I.63). A **paradox** is a statement which seems absurd but turns out to have rational meaning after all, usually in some unexpected sense; Donne speaks of fear being great courage and high valor (*Satire III,* line 16), and turns out to mean that fear of God is greater courage than any earthly bravery. The **Petrarchan conceit** was an ingenious, complimentary comparison or turn of thought; Wyatt compares the state of a lover to a ship tossed in a storm, and a hundred different sonneteers explored the possibility of describing their ladies' anatomy in conventional Petrarchan conceits—her teeth like pearls, lips like rubies, hair like finespun gold, etc. On the other hand, the **metaphysical conceit** was a more ingenious many-leveled comparison, worked out in some detail and giving a strong sense of the poet's ingenuity in overcoming obstacles—for instance, Donne's comparison of separated lovers to the legs of a compass (*A Valediction: Forbidding Mourning*) or Herbert's comparison of devotion to a pulley (*The Pulley*).

Images are often described as "mental pictures"; it is more accurate to say that they are verbal representations of something capable of being visualized: some readers have such mental pictures, some do not. Images not only convey what things look like, but direct us, by their pattern of associated and involved feelings, in our reactions to what is being represented. Indeed, there may be such a weight of meaning or feeling behind the image that the verbal picture itself becomes transparent and its "meaning" becomes primary. Abstract ideas can get attached to specific images—water, snake, bird, sun, worm, lion, whatever—in a multitude of ways, of which the reader need sometimes only be reminded. Of course the poet can also be arbitrary about it, letting his reader know simply that Red Cross "stands for" Holiness and Archimago "stands for" Hypocrisy. If that's as far as it goes, we have a primitive variety of **allegory.** But the relation between the tenor of the image (its abstract meaning) and the vehicle (the concrete picture) can be much more indefinite and insubstantial. If the poet mentions a peacock, he may or may not intend his reader to think of immortality, because the unfolding of the peacock's tail and the opening of its "eyes" has traditionally suggested the rebirth of the soul after death. If that is the way the image works, then it is a **symbol.** Or again, if the poet mentions a fish, he may well intend the reader to think of Christ. This isn't because of any similarity between the fish and Christ; the identification depends on a mildly esoteric bit of information, that the Greek word for fish, *ichthys,* forms an anagram of the Greek words for "Jesus Christ, Son of God, Savior." When the connection between tenor and vehicle is arbitrary, or involves the elements of a puzzle, the image may be referred to as an **emblem.** In the 16th and 17th centuries, emblems often took the form of puzzling little drawings, the meaning of which was explained in appended verses: for an example see the emblem prefixed to Crashaw's poem *To the Countess of Denbigh* (in Volume 1).

Personification is the attribution of human qualities to an inanimate object (for example, the Sea) or an abstract concept (Freedom); a special variety of it is called (in a **term** of John Ruskin's invention) the **pathetic fallacy.** When we speak of leaves "dancing" or a lake "smiling," we attribute human traits to nonhuman objects. Ruskin thought this was false and therefore "morbid"; modern criticism tends to view the practice as artistically and morally neutral. A more formal and abstract variety of personification is **allegory,** in which a narrative (such as *Pilgrim's Progress*) is constructed by representing general concepts (Faithfulness, Sin, Despair) as persons. A **fable** (like the Nun's Priest's Tale) represents beasts behaving like humans; a **parable** is a brief story, or simply an observation, with strong moral application; and an **exemplum** is a story told to illustrate a point in a sermon. A special series of devices, nearly obsolete today, used to be available to poets who could count on readers trained in the classics. These were the devices of **classical epithet** and **allusion.** In their simplest form, the classic myths used to provide a repertoire of agreeable stage properties, and a convenient shorthand for expressing emotional attitudes. Picturesque creatures like centaurs, satyrs, and sphinxes, heroes and heroines like Hector and Helen, and the whole pantheon of Olympic deities could be used to make ready reference to a great many aspects of human nature. One does not have to explain the problems of a man who is "cleaning the Augean stables"; if he is afflicted with an "Achilles' heel," or is assailing "Hydra-headed difficulties," his state is clear. These epithets, or descriptive phrases, making reference to mythological stories, suggest in a phrase situations which would normally require cumbersome explanations. Conceivably other mythologies might have served the same end in analogous ways. But because they could be taken for granted as the common possession of all educated readers, the classic myths entered into English literature as early as Chaucer, and are only now passing away as a viable system of allusions. In poets like Spenser and Milton, classical allusion becomes a kind of enormously learned game, in which the poet seeks to make his points as indirectly as possible. For instance, Spenser writes in the *Epithalamion*, lines 328–29:

> Lyke as when Jove with fayre Alcmena lay,
> When he begot the great Tirynthian **groome.**

The mere mention of Alcmena in the first line suggests, to the knowing reader, Hercules; Spenser's problem in the second line is to find a way of referring to him which is neither redundant nor heavy-handed. "Tirynthian" reminds us of his long connection with the city of Tiryns, stretching our minds (as it were) across his whole career; and **"groome"** compresses references to a man-child, a servant, and a bridegroom, all of which apply to different aspects of Hercules' history. Thus, far from simply avoiding redundancy, Spenser has enriched the whole texture of his verse, thought, and feeling by his gift for precise classical epithet.

PERIODS

Dividing English literature into manageable, more or less homogeneous periods is bound to be an arbitrary, an inexact, and in the end an inconsistent procedure. But a few handy dates are worth memorizing as a frame on which to hang details. Chaucer died in 1400; he was the literary high point of the English **Middle Ages,** a millennium reaching from 500 to 1500. Though no thousand-year period of existence can be compressed to a phrase, we may say that the Christian church structured and came close to dominating the imaginative life of this period. The first flowering of the English **Renaissance** took place around 1500; it has often been called the **Age of Humanism.** Less a formal philosophy than an attitude of interest in the full potentialities of the human mind, Humanism took on many colorings; most English writers, as **Christian Humanists,** tried to reconcile or combine the values of Greece and Rome with those of Christianity, while granting the former an independent authenticity that the Middle Ages had never conceded. The precise end of the Renaissance, with its tumultuous sense of human potential and delight in verbal invention, is hard to fix; but the death of Dryden in 1700 is a handy date for marking the onset of the **Age of Reason,** also called the **Enlightenment** or the **Neo-Classical Age.** Frequently, this age is expanded to include also the **Restoration** (1660–1700). The new era, emphasizing correctness, sought to discipline the individual consciousness to a generalized definition of rational human nature, one pattern for which was sought in the classics. To this vision of general human nature the age tended to subordinate any particular religious dispensation or creed, any social custom peculiar to a single time or place. The publication of *Lyrical Ballads* in 1798 opens the English **Age of Romanticism,** in which many writers undertook to explore the individual human mind independent of Christian dogma, and also as transcending experience—as an agent with active characteristics and initiatives of its own.

After 1798, the periods of English literature get shorter and less distinct. (From a longer perspective than we can easily assume, the whole era from 1798 to the present may someday be known as the age of Romanticism.) For the last half of the 19th century we have no real name but that of the ruling monarch: it is the **Age of Victorianism.** Some writers have tried to follow through with **Edwardian** for the period 1901–1910, and **Georgian** for the period after 1910. But George V ruled till 1936, and the postwar generation did not at all think of themselves as Georgians. Besides, somewhere in here we have to find room to start the **Modern Period,** whatever that is—if only so that we will have space to inaugurate our own time, for which there exist as yet only makeshift titles like the **Post-Modern Age.** Concerning all these periods, it is idle to dispute exact boundaries and precise characteristics. They don't have or need any, for the simple reason that their only function is to help the memory make a few gross distinctions and groupings within an otherwise uncontrollable sea of particulars.

SCHOOLS

Within the broad periods it is customary to group in **schools** writers who show common stylistic traits or thematic concerns. Whether they considered themselves a group doesn't much matter. None of the **Romantic poets** knew they were being romantic, although Hazlitt, Shelley, and other writers of the time recognized shared features that they called "the spirit of the age." The followers of Spenser are known as **Spenserians;** they knew they liked Spenser, but didn't realize that made them a group. **Cavalier** poets are set decisively apart from **metaphysical** poets, though pretty surely none of the two dozen men involved knew that was what they were. And so with the **Gothic novelists,** and the so-called **Graveyard School** at the end of the 18th century, so with the modern surrealists. These schools are generally grouped, defined, and named by scholars and critics after the event. Use of a common form or subject matter constitutes a more superficial similarity than use of a common style, common techniques, or common philosophical backgrounds. But literary history, being nothing if not pragmatic, makes use of all sorts of common denominators.

Intellectual affinities have led some writers to be classified under the names of the philosophical schools of Greece and Rome. These are chiefly the **Epicureans,** who specify that the aim of life and the source of value is pleasure; the **Stoics,** who emphasize the avoidance of pain and the dignified endurance of what cannot be avoided; and the **Skeptics,** who doubt that anything can be known for sure. These categories are useful as capsule descriptions, but they aren't very tidy, as they overlap one another and cut across other categories. Dryden is an author strongly tinged with **skepticism,** but many of his poems suggest an unabashed **epicureanism.** *The Vanity of Human Wishes,* by Doctor Johnson, is the classic poem in English of **stoic** philosophy, but it also expresses a particularly strong coloring of **Christian humanism.**

Plato and **Aristotle,** as they summarized contrasting attitudes toward existence, are often used to define the outlook of writers. Both were prolific writers of enormous range and complexity, but in literary contexts their names most often define attitudes toward reality. Aristotle tended to find reality, not exclusively but primarily, in concrete and particular substances, which he brilliantly categorized and generalized. Plato tended to place reality in abstract ideal forms, of which the concrete things we experience in daily life are but partial and shadowy manifestations. During the Middle Ages, the Dominican friars (St. Thomas Aquinas was one) were **Aristotelians;** the Franciscans (St. Bonaventura was one) were **Platonists.** During the Renaissance Spenser, and during the Romantic period Shelley, were **Platonists** or **Neo-Platonists.** (A neo-Platonist is a Platonist diluted with other world-views—perhaps Pythagorean mysticism, perhaps Christian theology, perhaps Aristotelian thought itself. In a narrower sense, the term is applied to philosophers writing in the tradition of Plotinus (3rd century A.D.), who held that all things in the world, spiritual and material, "emanate," or flow out, from the "Absolute," or the "One"—the single source of all truth, goodness, and beauty. **Aristotelianism,** as it is more commonsensical, had faded by Spenser's time to the common teaching of the schools, and by Shelley's time to the practical, pragmatic materialism of everyday life.

SECTS

Religious distinctions and denominations are important in British social history, hence deeply woven into the nation's literature. The numerous (over 300) British churches and sects divide along a scale from high to low, depending on the amount of authority they give to the church or the amount of liberty they concede to the individual conscience. At one end of the scale is the **Roman Catholic Church,** asserting papal infallibility, universal jurisdiction, and the supreme importance of hierarchy as guide and intercessor. For political and social reasons, Catholicism struck deep roots in Ireland but was the object of prolonged, bitter hatred on the part of Protestants from the Reformation through the 19th century. The **Established English (Anglican) Episcopal Church** has been the official national church since the 16th century; it enjoys the support (once direct and exclusive, now indirect and peripheral) of the national government. Its creed is defined by Thirty-Nine Articles, but these are intentionally vague, so there are numerous ways of adhering to the Church of England. Roughly and intermittently, the chief classes of Anglicans have been known as **High Church** (with its highest portion calling itself **Anglo-Catholic**); **Broad Church** or **Latitudinarian** (when they get so broad that they admit anyone believing in God, they may be known as **Deists,** or some may leave the church altogether and be known as **Unitarians**); and **Low Church,** whose adherents may stay in the English church and yet come close to shaking hands with **Presbyterians** or **Methodists.** These various groups may be arranged, from the High down to the Low Church, in direct relation to the amount of ritual each prefers and in the degree of authority conceded to the upper clergy—and in inverse relation to the importance ascribed to a saving faith directly infused by God into an individual conscience.

All Protestants who decline to subscribe to the English established church are classed as **Dissenters** or **Nonconformists**; for a time in the 16th and 17th centuries, they were also known as **Puritans.** The **Presbyterians** model their church government on that established by John Calvin in the Swiss city of Geneva. It has no bishops, and therefore is more democratic for the clergy; but it gains energy by associating lay elders with clergymen in matters of social discipline, and tends to be strict with the ungodly. From its first reformation the Scottish Kirk was fixed on the Presbyterian model. During the civil wars of the 17th century, a great many sects sprang up on the left wing of the Presbyterians, most of them touched by Calvinism but some rebelling against it; a few of these still survive. The **Independents** became our modern **Congregationalists**; the **Quakers** are still Quakers, as **Baptists** are still Baptists, though multiply divided. But many of the sects flourished and perished within the space of a few years. Among these now-vanished groups were the Shakers (though a few groups still exist in America), the Seekers, the Ranters, the Anabaptists, the Muggletonians, the Fifth Monarchy Men, the Family of Love, the Sweet Singers of Israel, and many others, forgotten by all except scholars. During the 18th and 19th centuries, new sects arose, supplanting old ones; the **Methodists,** under John and Charles Wesley, became numerous and important, taking root particularly in Wales. (The three "subject" nationalities, Ireland, Scotland, and Wales, thus turned three different ways to avoid the Anglican church.) With the passage of time a small number of Swedenborgians sprang up, followers of the Swedish mystic Emmanuel Swedenborg—to be followed by the Plymouth Brethren, Christian Scientists, Jehovah's Witnesses, and countless other 19th-century groups. All these sects constantly grow, shrink, split, and occasionally disappear as they succeed or fail in attracting new converts.

Within the various churches and sects, independent of them all but amazingly persistent, there has always survived a stream of **esoteric** or **hermetic** thought—a belief in occult powers, and sometimes in magic as well, exemplified by the pseudo-sciences of astrology and alchemy but taking many other forms. From the mythical Egyptian seer Hermes Trismegistus through Paracelsus, Cornelius Agrippa, Giordano Bruno, Jakob Boehme, the society of Rosicrucians, and a hundred other shadowy figures, the line can be traced to William Blake and William Butler Yeats, who both in their different ways brought hermetic protestantism close to its ultimate goal, a mystic church of one single man, poised within his own mind-elaborated cosmos.

TERMS OF ART

The following section groups together various sets of frequently used and closely related literary terms in an effort to discriminate and define them.

Allegory, Symbolism. They are both extended metaphors, distinguished chiefly by the fact that the figures in an **allegory** are more tightly and unequivocally related to their underlying meanings than in a work of symbolism. Though he has other significances as well, Spenser's Red-Cross Knight stands squarely for Holiness. In a work of **symbolism,** the meaning of the individual symbol grows out of its configuration with other symbols—it is an indirect and multiplex, not a one-for-one relation, as in Blake's poem *The Sick Rose*.

Baroque and **Mannerist** are terms imported into literary study from the history of art, and applied by analogy. Michelangelo is a **baroque** artist; he holds great masses in powerful dynamic tension, his style is heavily ornamented and restless. In these respects he is sometimes compared to Milton. El Greco is a **mannerist,** whose gaunt and distorted figures often seem to be laboring under great spiritual stress, whose light seems to be focused in spots against a dark background. He has been compared to Donne. Analogies of this sort are occasionally suggestive, but they must be carefully handled to avoid degenerating into parallels which are forced and nominal rather than substantial.

Burlesque and **Mock Heroic** differ in that the former makes its subject mean and absurd by directly cutting it down, the latter makes it subject ludicrous by inflating it. In Pope's mock-heroic **Dunciad,** the figure of Dulness (Colley Cibber) is given inappropriately heroic dimensions; in Butler's burlesque **Hudibras,** the knightly hero is characterized by low and vulgar attributes, and persistently engages in inappropriately low adventures.

Genre, Decorum. A **genre** is an established literary form, such as a stage comedy, the picaresque novel, the epic, the sonnet. Being of a certain genre predisposes a work to represent certain characters and events and to seek certain effects. Its success in achieving these effects and avoiding incongruous ones can thus be judged; and this is one sort of **decorum** (fittingness), the decorum of genre. Satire was once considered a low, popular form, for which only low, popular speech was decorous (fitting). There are also decorums of character, of occasion, of rhetorical mode, etc.

Gothic and **Classic** distinguish styles and tendencies in art and literature. **Gothic** implies vital, primitive, and deeply energetic work, with the qualities of Northern barbarism. **Classic** implies lucid, rational, and idealized work, as in the Southern sunlit civilizations of Greece and Rome. For the 18th century, the classics, which had proved their universality by maintaining their popularity for so many centuries, were the school of all civilized thinking; "Gothic" was a term connoting barbarity, wild and disorganized details, and a lack of artistic decorum and control. For a man like Ruskin, deeply imbued with the ideal of organic unity, "Gothic" was a term of ultimate approval; partly under his influence, Victorian Gothic (often called the "Gothic Revival") became a widely popular style. Currently, the term "Gothic" refers mainly to the artistic (and primarily architectural) style prevalent in Western Europe from the 12th to about the end of the 15th century.

Humors and **Temperaments** are psychological terms used by Renaissance writers. The four basic humors of every constitution were the **choleric** (bile), the **sanguine** (blood), the **phlegmatic** (phlegm), and the **melancholy** (black bile). A man's **temperament** was determined by the mixture of these humors, the way in which they were "tempered." When a particular humor predominated, it pushed the character in that direction: choler = anger; sanguine = geniality; phlegm = cold torpor; and melancholy = gloomy self-absorption.

Imitation and **Parody** are devices by which a literary work assumes an attitude toward its own predecessor. **Imitation** involves not simply copying, but transposing the different features of the earlier work into modern particulars, while retaining the same pattern and the same approximate tonal level. **Parody** generally lowers the level of its original; it is a device of ridicule, though sometimes of self-ridicule. When Joyce parodies ancient Irish legend (as in the "Cyclops" chapter of *Ulysses*), there is no separating ridicule of the past from contempt for the present.

Irony, Sarcasm, Satire. Irony and **sarcasm** are distinct, though both are ways of saying one thing and meaning another. Sarcasm is broader and more deliberate in its reversal of meanings; irony may be, and in literature generally is, very fine. It often conveys an attitude of detachment. In **dramatic irony,** a character says something which has one meaning for him but quite another for the privileged audience. **Satire** includes all of the many literary ways for diminishing a subject by making it ridiculous.

Myth and **Legend** are stories which incorporate themselves into men's instinctual thinking. **Myths** are narratives which purport to account, in supernatural terms, for why the world is as it is, why men act as they do. Myths often spring up to explain rituals, the original meanings of which have been forgotten; or they may be folk tales based on popular nightmares or fantasies. An ordinary or even inferior tale may take on mythic dimensions—witness Mary Wollstonecraft Shelley's *Frankenstein* or the wooden volumes of Horatio Alger, Jr. A **legend** is any old and popularly repeated story; the word usually implies, in addition, that the story is false. But a proper myth hardly pretends to be historically true—it is a flowering of the mind into narrative. Three great bodies of mythical material are the Celtic, the Norse or Germanic, and the classical fables. A body of associated myths is a **mythology**; a student and collector of myths is a **mythographer.**

Ode, Elegy, Lyric. Lyric poetry gets its name from once having been set to music and chanted to the accompaniment of a lyre; but that's ancient history. Now any short poem directly expressing the poet's thought or feeling will be classed as a lyric; and within this general class, **odes** and **elegies** are two specific varieties. The former implies a dignified occasion and a formal effort to praise or judge its subject. **Pindaric odes,** following the example of the Theban Pindar, are enthusiastic, irregular, and sublime; **Horatian odes,** after the Roman Horace, are cool, judicious, and regular. **Elegies** were originally poems written in elegiac meter, alternating hexameters and pentameters. This limping meter, which has never done as well in English as in the classical tongues, was thought appropriate to the expression of serious, even mournful sentiments. In the narrow sense, then, an elegy is a poem of mourning for the dead. But it can also be any pensive poem on a meditative theme; and a man like Donne, who enjoyed overstepping boundaries, wrote some elegies which are jocose, even bawdy.

Realism and **Naturalism** are both terms used to describe fiction which aims at minute fidelity to actual existence. **Realism** connotes an attempt to give the illusion of ordinary life, in which unexceptional people undergo everyday experiences. **Naturalism** is associated with the example of **Émile** Zola and the thesis that a novel should present a "slice of life," a cross-section of actual existence; the emphasis is usually on man's instinctual nature, especially the sexual and acquisitive instincts. This type flourished during the late 19th and early 20th centuries. Harold Biffen, a character in George Gissing's novel *New Grub Street*, is devoting his life to a work of "absolute realism in the sphere of the ignobly decent"—and this can epitomize realism. A work of naturalism, on the other hand, might be said to devote itself to the ignobly indecent.

Romance, Novel. Medieval romances are narratives of adventure, following a hero through the successive episodes of a quest toward his chosen or appointed goal. Novels are more or less realistic studies of social relationships, more tightly structured than romances, less given to the fabulous, and dealing generally with the middle strata of society. But these distinctions were far from airtight to begin with, and with the years have grown steadily vaguer. Is Kafka's *The Castle* a novel or a romance? It is always called the former, it looks much more like the latter, and it is actually more like an extended parable.

Style in a minimal sense is the way anyone uses language; thus each of us possesses (for better or worse) his own style. In the better sense, of language endowed with point and force, language of special distinction which accomplishes its ends swiftly and clearly, it has been described by Swift as "proper words in proper places"—a definition on which there is no improving.

Wit is one of those words which are too useful ever to be defined. As employed during the 17th and 18th centuries, it may mean general intelligence or the ability to say something funny, wisdom or ability, prudence, fancy, vivacity of speech, quickness of repartee, spiritual insight, and a plethora of other qualities.

A LONDON PLAYHOUSE OF SHAKESPEARE'S TIME

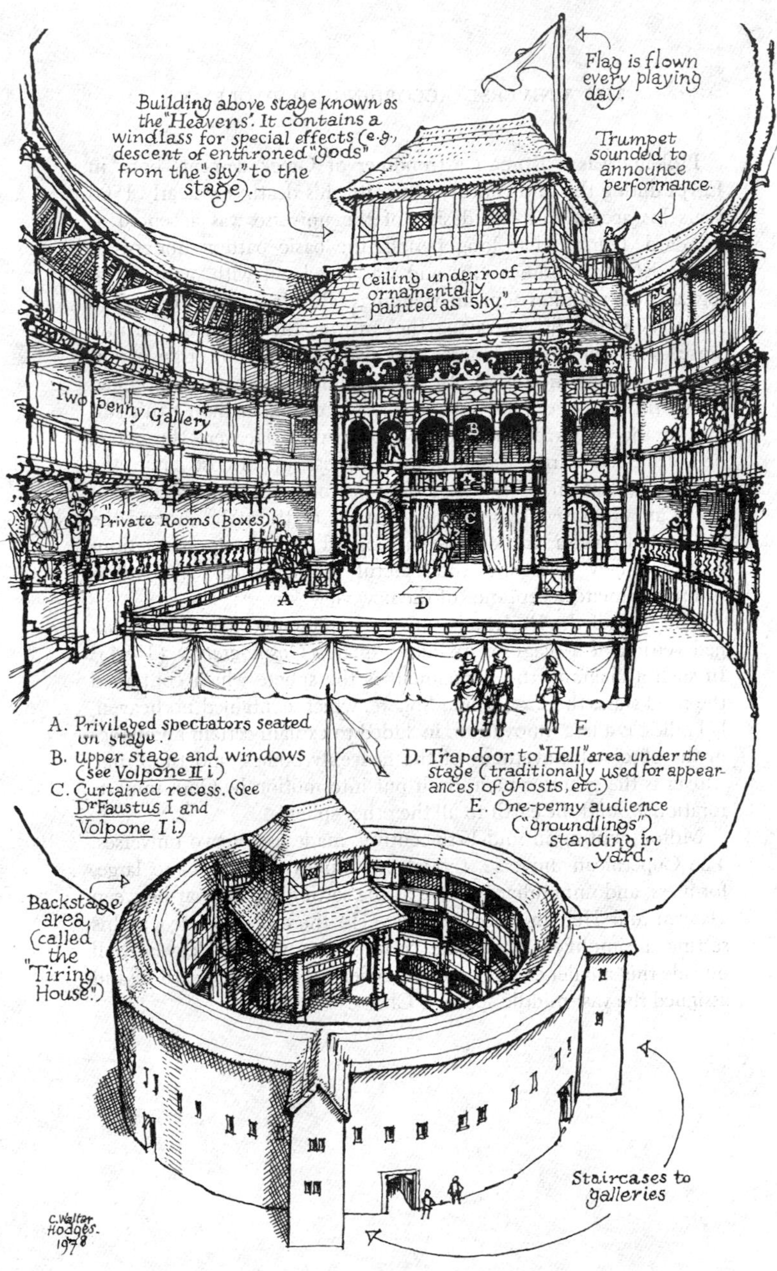

THE UNIVERSE ACCORDING TO PTOLEMY

Ptolemy was a Roman astronomer of Greek descent, born in Egypt during the 2nd century A.D.; after his death, for nearly 1500 years his account of the design of the universe was accepted as standard. During that long period, the basic pattern underwent many detailed modifications and was fitted out with many astrological and pseudo-scientific trappings. But in essence Ptolemy's followers agreed in portraying the earth as the center of the universe, with the sun, planets, and fixed stars set in transparent spheres orbiting around it. In this scheme of things, as modified for Christian usage, Hell was usually placed under the earth's surface at the center of the cosmic globe, while Heaven, the abode of the blessed spirits, was in the outermost, uppermost circle, the empyrean. But in 1543 the Polish astronomer Copernicus proposed an alternative hypothesis—that the earth rotates around the sun, not vice versa; and despite theological opposition, observations with the new telescope and careful mathematical calculations insured ultimate acceptance of the new view.

The map of the Ptolemaic universe represented here is a simplified version of a diagram in Peter Apian's *Cosmography* (1584). In such a diagram, the Firmament is the sphere which contained the fixed stars; the Crystalline Sphere, which contained no heavenly bodies, is a late innovation, included to explain certain anomalies in the observed movement of the heavenly bodies; and the Prime Mover is the sphere which, itself put into motion by God, imparts rotation around the earth to all the other spheres.

Milton, writing in mid-17th-century, made use of two universes. The Copernican universe, though he alludes to it, was too large, formless, and unfamiliar to serve as the setting for the war between Heaven and Hell in *Paradise Lost*. He therefore adopted as his setting a simplified Ptolemaic cosmos, but placed Heaven well outside this smaller earth-centered universe, Hell far beneath it, and assigned the vast middle space to Chaos.

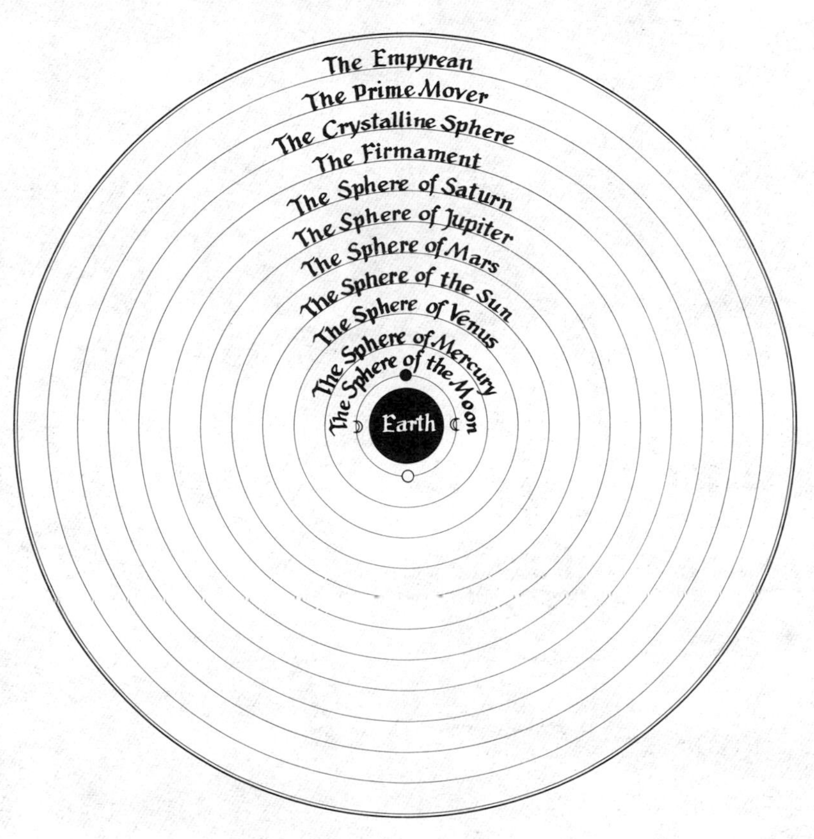

The Empyrean
The Prime Mover
The Crystalline Sphere
The Firmament
The Sphere of Saturn
The Sphere of Jupiter
The Sphere of Mars
The Sphere of the Sun
The Sphere of Venus
The Sphere of Mercury
The Sphere of the Moon
Earth

Index